BUSINESS STATISTICS OF THE UNITED STATES

BUSINESS STATISTICS OF THE UNITED STATES

PATTERNS OF ECONOMIC CHANGE

20TH EDITION
2015

Edited by Susan Ockert

Associate Editor
Mary Meghan Ryan

Lanham, MD

Published in the United States of America
by Bernan Press, a wholly owned subsidiary of
The Rowman & Littlefield Publishing Group, Inc.
4501 Forbes Boulevard, Suite 200
Lanham, Maryland 20706

Bernan Press
800-462-6420
www.rowman.com

ISBN-13: 978-1-59888-794-5
ISSN: 1086-8488

CONTENTS

PREFACE

Business Statistics of the United States: Patterns of Economic Change, 20th Edition, 2015 is a basic desk reference for anyone requiring statistics on the U.S. economy. It contains over 3,000 economic time series portraying the period from World War II to December 2014 in industry, product, and demographic detail. In the case of about 200 key series, the period from 1929 through 1948 is depicted as well.

Additionally, for three important statistical series that have been compiled monthly on a continuous basis, monthly and annual data are included going back to 1919 for industrial production and 1913 for consumer and producer prices. Annual data for money and credit have also been taken back before 1929, including money supply figures back to 1892 and some interest rates back to 1919.

The National Income and Product Accounts (NIPAs) were comprehensively revised in July 2013, changing some measurement concepts, changing base periods for price indexes and real output, and as a result altering all the data back to 1929. *Business Statistics* incorporates fully revised data for over 700 series from this data set and productivity and costs series that are based on the revised NIPAs, all extended and updated through 2013. The important new concepts introduced in the NIPA revision are explained in the Notes and Definitions to Chapters 1, 4, 5, and 6. In all, this edition provides, in one volume, unparalleled, up-to-date background information on the course of the U.S. economy.

The data are predominantly from federal government sources. Of equal importance are the extensive background notes for each chapter, which help users to understand the data, use them appropriately, and, if desired, seek additional information from the source agencies.

Chapters are organized according to subject matter. For most time series, users will find an initial page displaying the latest two years of monthly data, or three years of quarterly data, for the most recent completed years, along with annual averages for the last completed 40, 50, or even 60 years.

For the most important series for which we have long-term historical data, this initial page will be labeled with "A" after the table number, and identified in the title by the additional words "Recent Data". It will be immediately followed by pages labeled with "B" after the table number and identified by the words "Historical Data", which will show all available historical data annually back as far as possible, and monthly or quarterly back to the earliest available postwar year. In some cases, additional tables of historical data will be included.

The Plan of the Book

The history of the U.S. economy is told in major U.S. government sets of statistical data: the national income and product accounts compiled by the Bureau of Economic Analysis (BEA); the data on labor force, employment, hours, earnings, and productivity compiled by the Bureau of Labor Statistics (BLS); the price indexes collected by BLS; and the financial market and industrial production data compiled primarily by the Board of Governors of the Federal Reserve System (FRB). All of these sets exist in annual and either monthly or quarterly form beginning in 1946, 1947, or 1948; many are available, at least annually, as far back as 1929, and a few even farther back; and three are available monthly back to the teens of the 20th century.

In Part A, *Business Statistics* presents the aggregate United States economy in a number of important dimensions. The presentations begin with the national income and product accounts, or NIPAs. The NIPAs comprise a comprehensive, thorough, and internally consistent body of data. They measure the value of the total output of the U.S. economy (the gross domestic product, or GDP) and they allocate that value between its quantity, or "real," and price components. They show how the value of aggregate demand is generated by consumers, business investors, government, and foreign customers; how much of aggregate demand is supplied by imports and how much by domestic production; and how the income generated in domestic production is distributed between labor and capital.

Production estimates covering only the sectors of the economy traditionally labeled "industrial"—manufacturing, mining, and utilities—are shown in Chapter 2, after the presentation of the overall NIPAs in Chapter 1.

Median income—the best measure of the economic well-being of the typical American—income distribution, and poverty statistics from a Census household survey are presented in Chapter 3.

Then, more detail from the NIPAs is presented for the demand components of economic activity. GDP, by its product-side definition, consists of the sum of consumption expenditures, business investment in fixed capital and inventories, government purchases of goods and services, and exports minus imports—as in the elementary economics blackboard identity "GDP = C + I + G + (X − M)." Chapters on each of these components—consumption, investment, government, and foreign trade—are presented in Part A.

Following these chapters, there are a chapter on prices, two chapters on the compensation of labor and capital inputs and the amount and productivity of labor input, one chapter on energy inputs into production and consumption, and one chapter on money, interest, assets, and debt.

At the end of Part A, comparisons of output, prices, and labor markets among major industrial countries are presented, along with statistics on the value of the dollar against other currencies.

While GDP is initially defined and measured by adding up its demand categories and subtracting imports, this output is produced in industries—some in the old-line heavy industries such as manufacturing, mining, and utilities, but an increasing share in the huge and heterogeneous group known as "service-providing" industries. Part A gives a number of measures of activity classified by industry or industrial sector: industrial production, profits, and employment-related data. Further industry information is provided in Part B, including new quarterly indicators of GDP by industry.

Industry data collection is important because demands for goods and services are channeled into demands for labor and capital through the industries responsible for producing the requested goods and services. These data are reported using the North American Industry Classification System (NAICS). This system, introduced in 1997 to replace the older Standard Industrial Classification System (SIC), delineates industries that are better defined in relation to today's demands and more closely related to each other by technology. Notable examples include more detailed data available on service industries, a more rational grouping of the Computer and electronic product manufacturing subsector, and the creation of the Information sector. See the References at the end of this Preface.

NAICS industries are groupings of producing units—not of products as such—and are grouped according to similarity of production processes. This is done in order to collect consistent data on inputs and outputs, which are then used to measure important concepts, such as productivity and input-output parameters. Emphasis on the production process helps to explain a number of ways in which the NAICS differs from the SIC.

- Manufacturing activities at retail locations, such as bakeries, have been classified separately from retail activity and put into the Food manufacturing industry.

- Central administrative offices of companies have a new sector of their own, Management of companies and enterprises (sector 55). For example, the headquarters office of a food-producing corporation is considered part of the new sector instead of part of the Food manufacturing industry.

- Reproduction of packaged software, which was classified as a business service in the SIC, is now classified in sector 334, Computer and electronic product manufacturing, as a manufacturing process.

- Electronic markets and agents and brokers, formerly undifferentiated components of wholesale trade industries, have a sector of their own (425).

- Retail trade in NAICS (sectors 44 and 45) now includes establishments such as office supply stores, computer and software stores, building materials dealers, plumbing supply stores, and electrical supply stores, that display merchandise and use mass-media advertising to sell to individuals as well as to businesses, which were formerly classified in wholesale trade.

In Part B, *Business Statistics* shows GDP, income, employment, hours, and earnings by industry, followed by statistics for key sectors such as petroleum, housing, manufacturing, retail trade, and services.

Notes and definitions. Productive use of economic data requires accurate knowledge about the sources and meaning of the data. The notes and definitions for each chapter, shown immediately after that chapter's tables, contain definitions, descriptions of recent data revisions, and references to sources of additional technical information. They also include information about data availability and revision and release schedules, which helps users to readily access the latest current values if they need to keep up with the data month by month or quarter by quarter.

A Note on the Importance of Economic Statistics

To retrieve money and credit data for earlier years, a previous editor of *Business Statistics* had to consult old printed volumes, where she encountered some inspiring prefatory words in the Federal Reserve Board volume *Banking and Monetary Statistics* (1943). These words were written by the Fed's longtime statistics chief E. A. Goldenweiser, in the stately cadences of an earlier era, about the financial statistics collected in that volume. But they well express the hope and expectation of statisticians and economists that their work can lead to better economic decisions:

"These serried ranks of organized statistics on banking and finance, even though they may inspire awe, should also inspire confidence. They are an augury that credit policy can be based in the future, as in the past, on fact rather than on fancy."

The History of *Business Statistics*

The history of *Business Statistics* began with the publication, many years ago, of the first edition of a volume with the same name by the U.S. Department of Commerce's Bureau of Economic Analysis (BEA). After 27 periodic editions, the last of which appeared in 1992, BEA found it necessary, for budgetary and other reasons, to discontinue both the publication and the maintenance of the database from which the publication was derived.

The individual statistical series gathered together here are all publicly available. However, the task of gathering them from the numerous different sources within the government and assembling them into one coherent database is impractical for most data users. Even when current data are readily available, obtaining the full historical time series is often time-consuming and difficult. Definitions and other documentation can also be inconvenient to find. Believing that a *Business Statistics* compilation was too valuable to be lost to the public, Bernan Press published the first edition of the present publication, edited by Dr. Courtenay M. Slater, in 1995. The first edition received a warm welcome from users of economic data. Dr. Slater, formerly chief economist of the Department of Commerce, continued to develop *Business Statistics* through four subsequent annual editions. The current editor worked with Dr. Slater on the fourth and fifth editions. In subsequent editions, she has continued in the tradition established by Dr. Slater of ensuring high-quality data, while revising and expanding the book's scope to include significant new aspects of the U.S. economy and longer historical background.

Nearly all of the statistical data in this book are from federal government sources and all are available in the public domain. Sources are given in the applicable notes and definitions.

The data in this volume meet the publication standards of the federal statistical agencies from which they were obtained. Every effort has been made to select data that are accurate, meaningful, and useful. All statistical data are subject to error arising from sampling variability, reporting errors, incomplete coverage, imputation, and other causes. The responsibility of the editor and publisher of this volume is limited to reasonable care in the reproduction and presentation of data obtained from established sources.

The 2015 edition has been edited by Susan Ockert, in association with Mary Meghan Ryan.

Susan Ockert has worked as an economist in the military, for the federal government, and at regional and state levels. She earned her Masters of Economics at George Mason University in Fairfax, Virginia as well as her Masters of International Management at the Thunderbird University in Glendale, Arizona. She currently teaches economics at the collegiate level.

References

The NAICS is explained and laid out in *North American Industry Classification System: United States, 2012*, from the Executive Office of the President, Office of Management and Budget. This presents the second five-year updating of the system, which was first introduced in 1997. Changes introduced in these updatings have been minor and have not affected the definitions of the industry divisions presented in *Business Statistics*.

Information on differences between NAICS and SIC can be found in *North American Industry Classification System: United States, 1997*, from the Executive Office of the President, Office of Management and Budget (which contains matches between the 1997 NAICS and the 1987 SIC); and *North American Industry Classification System: United States, 2002* (which contains matches that show the relatively few changes from the 1997 NAICS to the 2002 NAICS).

All three of these volumes are available from Bernan Press. These volumes fully describe the development and application of the new classification system and are the sources for the material presented in this volume. Information is also available on the NAICS Web site at <http://www.census.gov/naics>.

THE U.S. ECONOMY 1929–1948

While there has been much discussion in recent years of the "Great Depression," there is surprisingly little familiarity with the basic statistical record of the period between 1929 and the end of World War II. Reproducing material from Chapter 18 of the 15th edition of *Business Statistics,* we present here an explanation of that period from the NBER business cycle perspective, along with a graphic overview and narration of its economic developments as recorded in the statistics now presented in Part A of this volume.

As NBER perceives it, a downtrend in economic activity began in August 1929 (before the stock market crash) and lasted until March 1933. This 43-month period has been called the "Great Contraction". It was the longest period of economic decline since the 1870s, and more than double the length of the longest recession identified and completed since that time (the one from December 2007 to June 2009, which lasted 18 months). For the rest of the 1930s—excepting a 13-month recession in 1937–1938—the economy is viewed by the NBER as having been in an expansion phase. The NBER chronology does not use the term "depression."

However, the term "Great Depression" is often colloquially used for the entire 1929–1939 period, even though the economy was expanding for most of the period following March 1933. This is because economic activity during that time, though increasing, remained below the likely capacity of the economy, as is indicated in Figures A-2 and A-3 below.

It should also be noted that NBER construes the entire period from June 1938 through February 1945 as a business cycle expansion. The recovery from the 1937–1938 recession merged into a further, continued rise in activity that reflected the outbreak of war in Europe in September 1939, a consequent preparedness effort in the United States, and an increase in demand from abroad for U.S. output. The United States entered the war after being attacked by Japan in December 1941, launching an all-out war production effort at that time.

The February 1945 end of the "wartime expansion" (as NBER terms the period June 1938–February 1945) preceded the end of the war (the European war ended in May 1945 and the Pacific war concluded in August 1945). A brief recession associated with demobilization occurred from February to October 1945, followed by the first postwar expansion, which lasted from October 1945 to November 1948.

In the graphs that follow, summary annual statistics for the years 1929 through 1948 are presented, depicting the economy during two of its most tumultuous decades. This period encompasses the "great contraction," the economic collapse that began in August 1929 and lasted until March 1933; a subsequent period of recovery, which failed to return many important economic indicators to their expected trend levels and was interrupted by a new, though less severe, recession; apprehension of coming war, then the outbreak of war in Europe in September 1939, leading to increased war-related production; United States participation in all-out war, beginning with the Japanese attack on Pearl Harbor on December 7, 1941, and ending in 1945, with supercharged production and employment rates; then, rapid demobilization, and return to a high peacetime rate of economic activity by 1948.

For a first overall view of the economy during these decades, Figure A-1 shows total U.S. employment as calculated by the Bureau of Economic Analysis, including all private and government jobs, both civilian and military. In this graph a trend line is shown connecting the two peacetime high employment levels of 1929 and 1948.

Figure A-1. Employment, 1929–1948 (ratio scale)

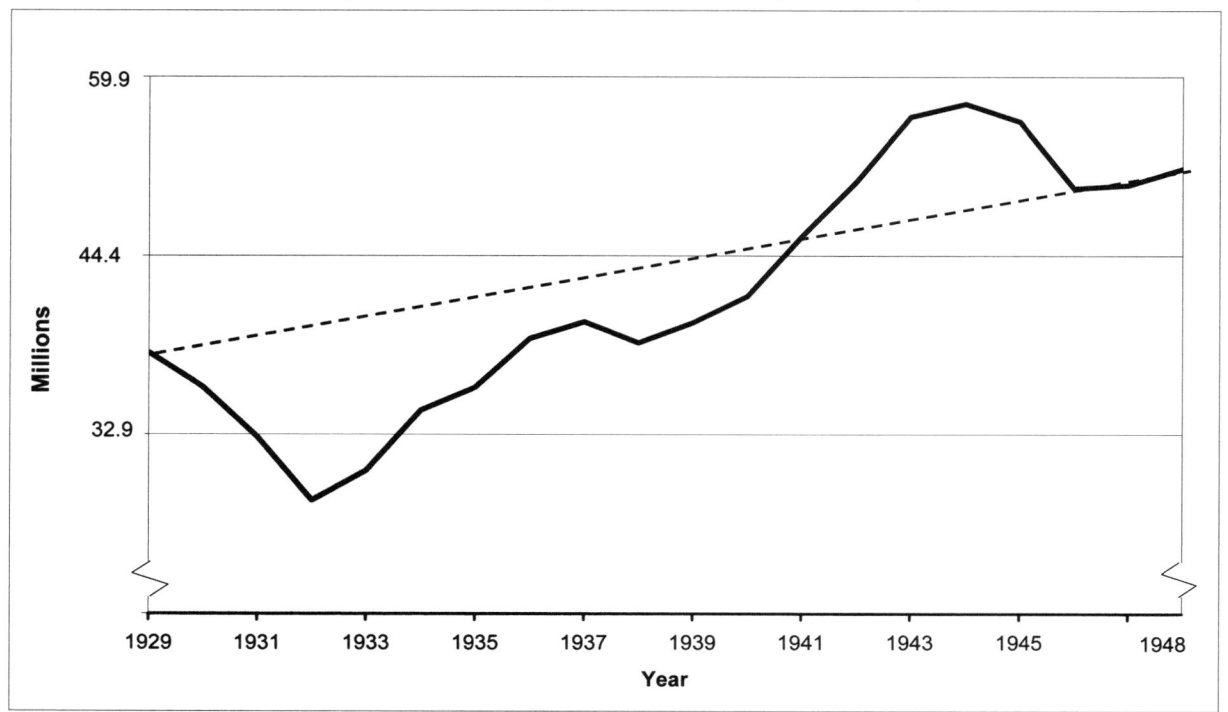

EMPLOYMENT, 1929–1948

GRAPH

- More than one-fifth of all the jobs held in the U.S. economy in 1929 were gone by 1932. In the subsequent recovery, total employment was back at the 1929 level by 1936, but only because of government employment, including over 3 ½ million work relief jobs; private industry employment would not recover to its 1929 level until 1941. (Table 10-21)

- Because the recovery was incomplete and economic activity did not recover to a trend level until after the decade's end, the entire decade of the 1930s is often described as "The Great Depression."

- During the war, men were drafted into the armed forces, practically all of the unemployed were put back to work, and women were drawn into the labor force, resulting in a period of what might be called "super-employment." After the war, employment fell back to a more normal trend level. (Tables 10-1C and 10-21)

Figure A-2. Unemployment Rates, 1929–1948

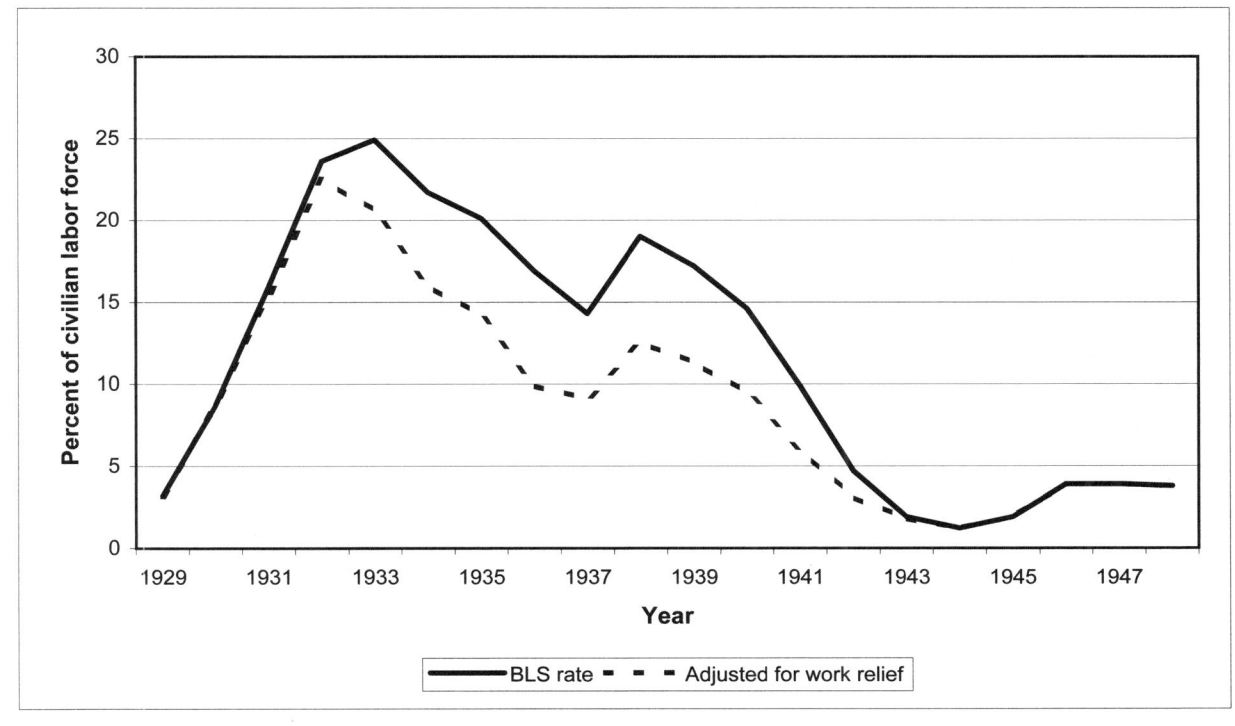

UNEMPLOYMENT RATES, 1929–1948

GRAPH

- The unemployment rates for the prewar period calculated by the Bureau of Labor Statistics, unlike the employment data used in Figure A-1, count people on government work relief programs as unemployed. By this reckoning, unemployment rose from 3.2 percent of the civilian labor force in 1929 to a peak of 24.9 percent in 1933, and got no lower than 14.3 percent for the rest of the 1930s, as shown in Figure A-2. (Table 10-1C)

- State and local governments started hiring people for work relief in 1930. The Federal government's programs began in 1933, and in 1936 and 1938 agencies such as the WPA and the CCC employed over 3 ½ million people. When workers in these programs are counted as employed rather than unemployed, the high point for unemployment was 22.5 percent in 1932, and it was reduced to 9.1 percent in 1937, as shown by the dashed line in Figure A-2. (Tables 10-1C and 10-21; see Notes and Definitions to Chapter 10 for further explanation.)

- By 1943, the economy reached a state of over-full employment, which would have been associated with runaway inflation if not for comprehensive price, wage, and production controls; the years of full wartime production, 1943 through 1945, all saw unemployment rates below 2 percent. After demobilization, the unemployment rate returned to just under 4 percent. (Table 10-1C)

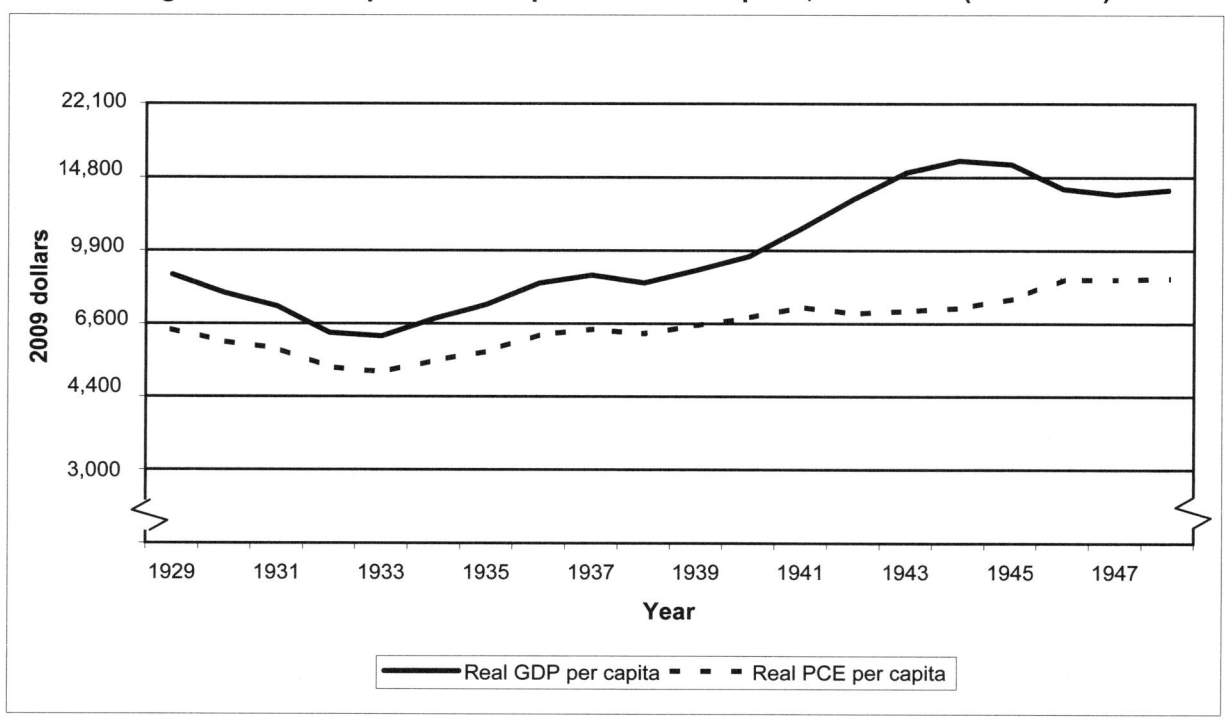

Figure A-3. Per Capita Real Output and Consumption, 1929–1948 (ratio scale)

PER CAPITA REAL OUTPUT AND CONSUMPTION, 1929–1948

GRAPH

- Real GDP declined 26.7 percent from 1929 to 1933—28.9 percent on a per capita basis. Per capita output recovered almost to the 1929 level in 1937 but fell back 4.1 percent in the 1938 recession. Output then nearly doubled from 1939 to the peak war production year, 1944; the per capita annual growth rate was 12.4 percent. Output fell back during the demobilization, but in 1948 was still at a per capita level representing a 5.0 percent per year growth rate since 1939. (Tables 1-3B and 4-1B)

- Per capita personal consumption expenditures fell 20.9 percent from 1929 to 1933. The decline would have been greater if consumers had not dipped into their assets to keep their living standards from declining as steeply as their incomes; the personal saving rate was negative in 1932 and 1933. Real per capita consumption recovered to the 1929 level by 1937. Despite rationing and shortages, real per capita consumption spending declined little during the war years. In 1948, it was 29.3 percent above the 1939 level. (Table 1-3B)

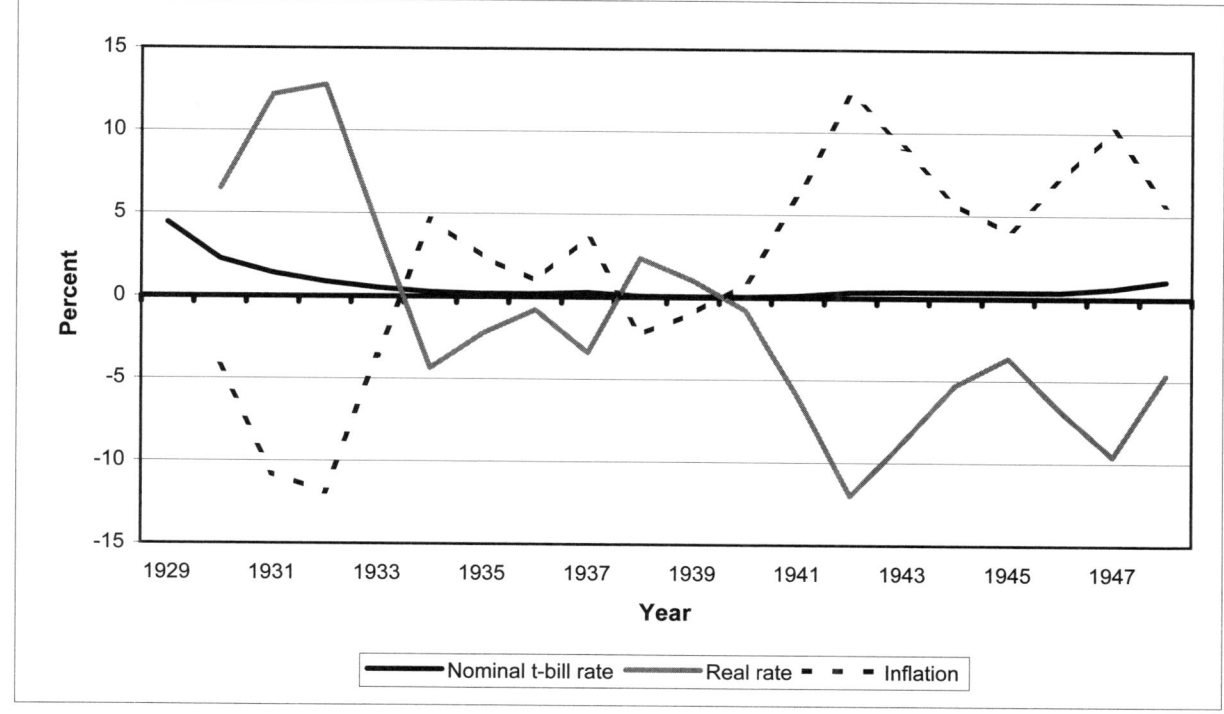

Figure A-4. Inflation and Nominal and Real Interest Rates, 1929–1948

INFLATION AND NOMINAL AND REAL INTEREST RATES, 1929–1948

GRAPH

- Why was the 1929–1933 contraction so deep and long-lasting? By some, blame is placed on U.S. government tax increases and imposition of new trade barriers (the Smoot-Hawley Tariff), which undoubtedly made their contribution. A substantial number of well-regarded economists, however, point primarily to deflation and its interaction with debt. The price index for personal consumption expenditures, whose rate of change is shown in Figure A-4, declined 27.2 percent from 1929 to 1933, for an annual average <u>deflation</u> rate of 7.6 percent. Current and prospective price declines make debt more burdensome and debtors more likely to default, as interest payments remain fixed while incomes and asset values decline. (Table 1-6B)

- Current and prospective price declines also make borrowing prohibitively expensive; a low nominal interest rate becomes high in real terms (since the real rate is the nominal rate <u>minus</u> the inflation rate, and subtraction means changing the sign and adding). A dollar in the hands of a prospective lender will be worth more in terms of purchasing power if he simply holds on to it than if he invests it in some real economic asset or activity whose price will be lower at the end of the year. There is no feasible way for a central bank to lower interest rates below zero in order to reduce real rates in the presence of deflation. As Figure A-4 shows, real rates were high from 1930 through 1933 despite near-zero market nominal rates on Treasury bills. (Tables 12-9B and 1-6B)

Figure A-5. Money and Credit Growth, 1930–1948

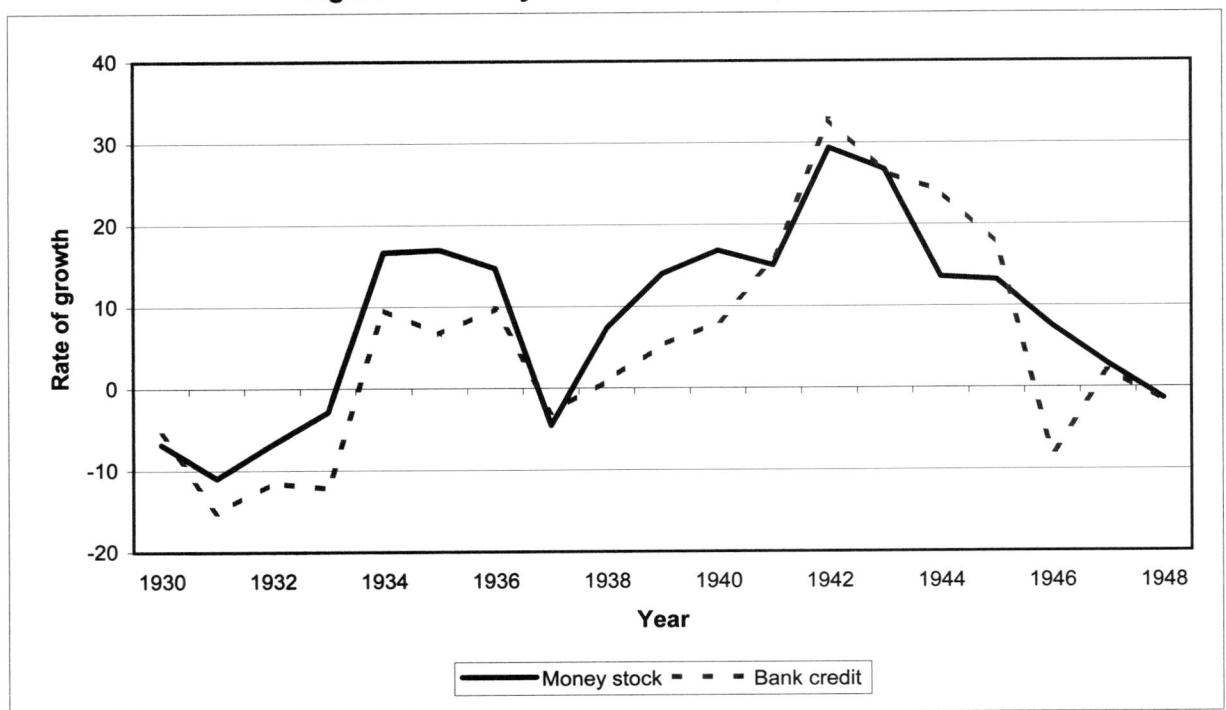

MONEY AND CREDIT GROWTH, 1930–1948

GRAPH

- Deflation was rooted in deep and sustained declines in the dollar volumes of money and credit, as shown in Tables 12-1B and illustrated in Figure A-5. The money stock (currency and demand deposits) declined 27 percent from June 30, 1929, to June 30, 1933. Loans and investments at all commercial banks declined 29 percent over the same period. Commercial paper outstanding plunged 76 percent between December 1929 and December 1932, and bankers' acceptances were down 59 percent.

- Positive money and credit growth after 1933 was reflected in moderate rates of price increase and moderately negative—which means stimulative—real interest rates. As can be seen in Figures A-4 and A-5, there was a monetary component to the 1937–38 recession. There was also a premature federal budget retrenchment at that time (Table 6-14B).

- During the war, monetary policy was pre-empted by wartime needs. Interest rates were held low to facilitate the financing of huge federal deficits (Tables 6-14B and 12-9B).

- Worker incomes increased during the wartime boom as employment, average hours, and hourly wages all rose. But inflation and consumer spending were held down by price and production controls and rationing. Personal saving rates soared when there was little to buy and the government emphasized the sale of "war bonds"; the saving rate reached 26 percent in 1943 and 1944, then fell back to 4.2 percent in 1947, almost equal to its 1929 level. (Tables 1-6B, 4-1B, 8-1C, and 10-9)

GENERAL NOTES

These notes provide general information about the data in Tables 1-1 through 16-14. Specific notes with information about data sources, definitions, methodology, revisions, and sources of additional information follow the tables in each chapter.

Main Divisions of the Book

The tables are presented in two parts:

Part A (Tables 1-1 through 13-2) pertains principally to the U.S. economy as a whole. Generally, each table presents, on its initial page, annual averages as far back as data availability and space permit, and quarterly or monthly values for the most recent year or years. For many important series, this initial page is followed by full annual and quarterly or monthly histories as far back as they are available on a continuous, consistent basis. Some chapters present data for the United States only in aggregate, while others—such as the chapters concerning industrial production and capacity utilization (chapter 2), capital expenditures (chapter 5), profits (chapter 9), and employment, hours, and earnings (chapter 10)—also have detail for industry groups.

Data by industry are classified using the North American Industry Classification System (NAICS), as far back as such data are made available by the source agencies.

Part B focuses on the individual industries that together produce the gross domestic product (GDP).

- Chapter 14 contains data on the value of GDP, quantity production trends, and factor income by NAICS industry group.

- Chapter 15 provides further detail on payroll employment, hours, and earnings classified according to NAICS.

- Chapter 16 presents various data sets for key economic sectors. Some of the tables are based on definitions of products, rather than of producing establishments, and are valid for either classification system. This is the case for Tables 16-1, New Construction; 16-2, Housing Starts and Building Permits, New House Sales, and Prices; and 16-7, Motor Vehicle Sales and Inventories. Tables 16-3 through 16-6 and 16-8, 16-10, and 16-11, which cover manufacturing and retail and wholesale trade, show data classified according to NAICS. Table 16-14 presents data for services industries classified according to NAICS.

Characteristics of the Tables and the Data

The subtitles or column headings for the data tables normally indicate whether the data are *seasonally adjusted, not*

seasonally adjusted, or *at a seasonally adjusted annual rate.* These descriptions refer to the monthly or quarterly data, rather than the annual data; annual data by definition require no seasonal adjustment. Annual values are normally calculated as totals or averages, as appropriate, of unadjusted data. Such annual values are shown in either or both adjusted or unadjusted data columns.

Seasonal adjustment removes from a monthly or quarterly time series the average impact of variations that normally occur at about the same time each year, due to occurrences such as weather, holidays, and tax payment dates.

A simplified example of the process of seasonal adjustment, or deseasonalizing, can indicate its importance in the interpretation of economic time series. Statisticians compare actual monthly data for a number of years with "moving average" trends of the monthly data for the 12 months centered on each month's data. For example, they may find that in November, sales values are usually about 95 percent of the moving average, while in December, usual sales values are 110 percent of the average. Suppose that actual November sales in the current year are $100 and December sales are $105. The seasonally adjusted value for November will be $105 ($100/0.95) while the value for December will be $95 ($105/1.10). Thus, an apparent increase in the unadjusted data turns out to be a decrease when adjusted for the usual seasonal pattern.

The statistical method used to achieve the seasonal adjustment may vary from one data set to another. Many of the data are adjusted by a computer method known as X-12-ARIMA, developed by the Census Bureau. A description of the method is found in "New Capabilities and Methods of the X-12-ARIMA Seasonal Adjustment Program," by David F. Findley, Brian C. Monsell, William R. Bell, Mark C. Otto and Bor-Chung Chen (*Journal of Business and Economic Statistics*, April 1998). This article can be downloaded from the Bureau of the Census Web site at <http://www.census.gov>.

Production and sales data presented at *annual rates*—such as NIPA data in dollars, or motor vehicle data in number of units—show values at their annual equivalents: the values that would be registered if the seasonally adjusted rate of activity measured during a particular month or quarter were maintained for a full year. Specifically, seasonally adjusted monthly values are multiplied by 12 and quarterly values by 4 to yield seasonally adjusted annual rates.

Percent changes at seasonally adjusted annual rates for quarterly time periods are calculated using a compound interest formula, by raising the quarter-to-quarter percent change in a seasonally adjusted series to the fourth power.

Indexes. In many of the most important data sets presented in this volume, aggregate measures of prices and quantities are expressed in the form of indexes. The most basic and familiar form of index, the original Consumer Price Index, begins with a "market basket" of goods and services purchased in a base period, with each product category valued at its dollar prices—the amount spent on that category by the average consumer. The value weight ascribed to each component of the market basket is moved forward by the observed change in the price of the item selected to represent that component. These weighted component prices—which constitute the quantities in the base period repriced in the prices of subsequent periods—are aggregated, divided by the base period aggregate, and multiplied by 100 to provide an index number. An index calculated in this way is known as a *Laspeyres index*. In general, economists believe that Laspeyres price indexes have an upward bias, showing more price increase than they would if account were taken of consumers' ability to change spending patterns and maintain the same level of satisfaction in response to changing relative prices.

A *Paasche index* is one that uses the weights of the current period. Since the weights in the Paasche index change in each period, Paasche indexes only provide acceptable indications of change relative to the base period. Paasche indexes for two periods neither of which is the base period cannot be correctly compared: for example, a Paasche price index for a recent period might increase from the period just preceding even if no prices changed between those two periods, if there was a change in the composition of output toward prices that had previously increased more from the base period. When the national income and product account (NIPA) measures of real output were Laspeyres measures, using the weights of a single base year, the implicit deflators (current-dollar values divided by constant-dollar values) were Paasche indexes. Just as Laspeyres price indexes are upward-biased, Paasche price indexes are downward-biased because they overestimate consumers' ability to maintain the same level of satisfaction by changing spending patterns.

In recent years, government statisticians—with the aid of complex computer programs—have developed measures of real output and prices that minimize bias by using the weights of both periods and updating the weights for each period-to-period comparison. Such measures are described as chained indexes and are used in the NIPAs, the index of industrial production, and an experimental consumer price index. Chained measures are discussed more fully in the notes and definitions for Chapter 1, Chapter 2, and Chapter 8. The "Fisher Ideal" index, the "superlative" index, and the "Tornqvist formula" are all types of chained indexes that use weights for both periods under comparison.

Detail may not sum to totals due to rounding. Since annual data are typically calculated by source agencies as the annual totals or averages of not-seasonally-adjusted data, they therefore will not be precisely equal to the annual totals or averages of monthly seasonally-adjusted data. Also, seasonal adjustment procedures are typically multiplicative rather than additive, which may also prevent seasonally adjusted data from adding or averaging to the annual figure. Percent changes and growth rates may have been calculated using unrounded data and therefore differ from those using the published figures.

The data in this volume are from federal government sources and may be reproduced freely. A list of data sources is shown below.

The tables in this volume incorporate data revisions and corrections released by the source agencies through mid-2014, including the July annual revision of the NIPAs and the resulting August revision of productivity and costs.

Data Sources

The source agencies for the data in this volume are listed below. The specific source or sources for each particular data set are identified at the beginning of the notes and definitions for the relevant data pages.

Board of Governors of the Federal Reserve System
20th Street & Constitution Avenue NW
Washington, DC 20551

Data Inquiries and Publication Sales: Publications Services
Mail Stop 127
Board of Governors of the Federal Reserve System
Washington, DC 20551
Phone: (202) 452-3245

Quarterly Publication: As of 2006, the *Federal Reserve Bulletin* is available free of charge and only on the Federal Reserve Web site.
URL: http://www.federalreserve.gov

Census Bureau
U.S. Department of Commerce
4700 Silver Hill Road
Washington, DC 20233
URL: http://www.census.gov
Ordering Data Products: Call Center: (301) 763-INFO (4636)
E-mail Questions: webmaster@census.gov
E-sales: http://www.census.gov/mp/www/censtore.html

Bureau of Economic Analysis
U.S. Department of Commerce
Washington, DC 20230

Data Inquiries: Public Information Office
Phone: (202) 606-9900
Monthly Publication:
Survey of Current Business
Available online.
URL: http://www.bea.gov

Bureau of Labor Statistics
U.S. Department of Labor
2 Massachusetts Avenue NE
Washington, DC 20212-0001
(202) 691-5200
URL: http://www.bls.gov

Data Inquiries: Blsdata_staff@bls.gov
Monthly Publications available online: *Monthly Labor Review*
Employment and Earnings
Compensation and Working Conditions
Producer Price Indexes
CPI Detailed Report

Employment and Training Administration
U.S. Department of Labor
200 Constitution Avenue NW
Washington, DC 20210
(877) US2-JOBS
URL: http://www.doleta.gov
http://www.itsc.state.md.us

Energy Information Administration
U.S. Department of Energy
1000 Independence Avenue SW
Washington, DC 20585

Data Inquiries and Publications:
National Energy Information Center
Phone: (202) 586-8800
E-mail: infoctr@eia.doe.gov

Monthly Publication: *Monthly Energy Review*, as of 2007
available only on the EIA Web site, free of charge.
URL: http://www.eia.doe.gov

Federal Housing Finance Agency
FHFAinfo@FHFA.gov
(202) 414-6921,6922
(202) 414-6376
URL: http://www.fhfa.gov/hpi

U.S. Department of the Treasury
Office of International Affairs
Treasury International Capital System
URL: http://www.treas.gov/tic

To order government publications
Superintendent of Documents
Government Printing Office
Washington, DC 20402
(202) 512-1800
URL: http://bookstore.gpo.gov

PART A

THE U.S. ECONOMY

CHAPTER 1: NATIONAL INCOME AND PRODUCT

Section 1a: Gross Domestic Product: Values, Quantities, and Prices

Figure 1-1: Output Per Capita, 1950–2014
(2009 dollars, ratio scale)

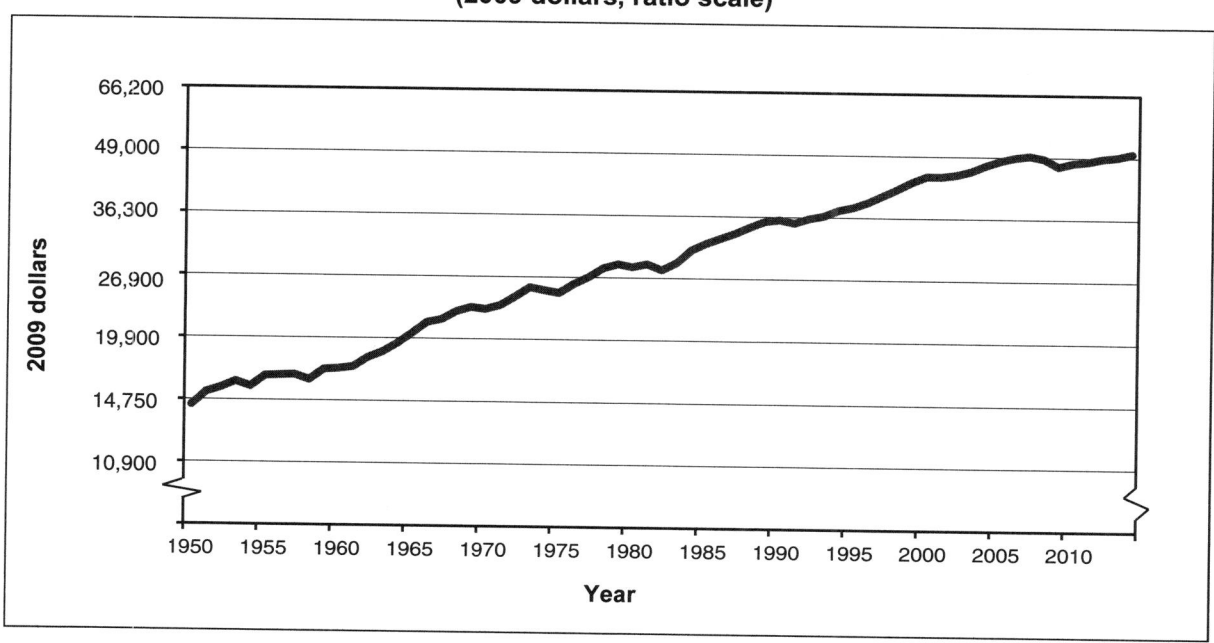

- As presented in the preface, the output approach to GDP consists of four components: consumption, business investment, government taxes and spending and the foreign trade balance (exports – imports). GDP is one of the most comprehensive and closely watched economic statistics in not only the United States but also globally. Both current and real (without inflation) GDP is calculated along with its growth rate. For more details of GDP, see the Notes and Definitions at the end of this chapter.

- Total output of goods and services in the United States (real gross domestic product, or GDP), expressed in constant 2009-value dollars to remove the effect of inflation, rose from $2.18 trillion in 1950 to $15.96 trillion in 2014. This was a more than seven-fold increase in real value over the 64-year period, with an annual average growth rate of 3.2 percent per year. (Table 1-2A)

- Real GDP per capita—the constant-dollar average value of production for each man, woman, and child in the population—rose from $14,398 (2009 dollars) in 1950 to $49,300 in 2007, a growth rate of 2.2 percent per year. Reflecting the recession that began in December 2007, it declined 4.8 percent from 2007 to 2009. Over the five years since then, per capita GDP recovered 6.6 percent and surpassed its 2007 peak. The history of per capita GDP is charted in Figure 1-1, graphed on a "ratio scale," with equal vertical distances signifying equal percent changes. (Table 1-3A)

- Measured in current dollars, the value of GDP has increased even faster, reflecting increases in the average price level in addition to real growth. Current-dollar GDP rose from $300 billion in 1950 to over $17 trillion currently. (Table 1-1A) The price level in 2014 was 7.9 times that in 1950, reflecting an average inflation rate of 3.3 percent per year. (Table 1-6A) Annual changes in the chain-type price index for GDP ranged from inflation of 9 percent or more in 1947, 1974–1975, and 1980–1981 to changes of no more than 1.2 percent in 1949–1950, 1954, 1959, 1961, 1963, 1998, 2009, and 2010. Over the last 14 years, inflation averaged 2.1 percent per year; it was 1.4 percent in 2014. (Tables 1-6A and B)

Table 1-1A. Gross Domestic Product: Recent Data

(Billions of dollars, quarterly data are at seasonally adjusted annual rates.)

NIPA Tables 1.1.5, 1.2.5

Year and quarter	Gross domestic product	Personal consumption expenditures	Gross private domestic investment				Exports and imports of goods and services			Government consumption expenditures and gross investment			Addendum: final sales of domestic product
			Total	Fixed investment		Change in private inventories	Net exports	Exports	Imports	Total	Federal	State and local	
				Nonresidential	Residential								
1950	300.2	192.2	56.5	30.0	20.7	5.8	0.7	12.4	11.6	50.7	29.5	21.3	294.4
1951	347.3	208.5	62.8	34.2	18.7	9.9	2.5	17.1	14.6	73.5	50.0	23.6	337.4
1952	367.7	219.5	57.3	34.9	18.9	3.5	1.2	16.5	15.3	89.8	64.8	25.0	364.2
1953	389.7	233.0	60.4	38.8	19.7	1.9	-0.7	15.3	16.0	97.0	70.3	26.7	387.8
1954	391.1	239.9	58.1	38.6	21.4	-1.9	0.4	15.8	15.4	92.8	63.3	29.5	393.1
1955	426.2	258.7	73.8	43.4	25.4	5.0	0.5	17.7	17.2	93.3	61.0	32.2	421.2
1956	450.1	271.6	77.7	49.7	24.0	4.0	2.4	21.3	18.9	98.5	63.1	35.4	446.2
1957	474.9	286.7	76.5	53.1	22.6	0.8	4.1	24.0	19.9	107.5	68.4	39.1	474.1
1958	482.0	296.0	70.9	48.5	22.8	-0.4	0.5	20.6	20.0	114.5	71.5	43.0	482.4
1959	522.5	317.5	85.7	53.1	28.6	3.9	0.4	22.7	22.3	118.9	73.5	45.3	518.5
1960	543.3	331.6	86.5	56.4	26.9	3.2	4.2	27.0	22.8	121.0	72.8	48.2	540.1
1961	563.3	342.0	86.6	56.6	27.0	3.0	4.9	27.6	22.7	129.8	77.4	52.5	560.3
1962	605.1	363.1	97.0	61.2	29.6	6.1	4.1	29.1	25.0	140.9	85.5	55.4	599.0
1963	638.6	382.5	103.3	64.8	32.9	5.6	4.9	31.1	26.1	147.9	87.8	60.0	633.0
1964	685.8	411.2	112.2	72.2	35.1	4.8	6.9	35.0	28.1	155.5	90.2	65.3	681.0
1965	743.7	443.6	129.6	85.2	35.2	9.2	5.6	37.1	31.5	164.9	93.1	71.7	734.5
1966	815.0	480.6	144.2	97.2	33.4	13.6	3.9	40.9	37.1	186.4	106.5	79.8	801.4
1967	861.7	507.4	142.7	99.2	33.6	9.9	3.6	43.5	39.9	208.1	120.0	88.1	851.9
1968	942.5	557.4	156.9	107.7	40.2	9.1	1.4	47.9	46.6	226.8	127.9	98.8	933.4
1969	1 019.9	604.5	173.6	120.0	44.4	9.2	1.4	51.9	50.5	240.4	131.1	109.3	1 010.7
1970	1 075.9	647.7	170.1	124.6	43.4	2.0	4.0	59.7	55.8	254.2	132.7	121.4	1 073.9
1971	1 167.8	701.0	196.8	130.4	58.2	8.3	0.6	63.0	62.3	269.3	134.4	134.9	1 159.5
1972	1 282.4	769.4	228.1	146.6	72.4	9.1	-3.4	70.8	74.2	288.2	141.5	146.7	1 273.3
1973	1 428.5	851.1	266.9	172.7	78.3	15.9	4.1	95.3	91.2	306.4	145.6	160.8	1 412.7
1974	1 548.8	932.0	274.5	191.1	69.5	14.0	-0.8	126.7	127.5	343.1	158.1	185.0	1 534.8
1975	1 688.9	1 032.8	257.3	196.8	66.7	-6.3	16.0	138.7	122.7	382.9	172.8	210.2	1 695.2
1976	1 877.6	1 150.2	323.2	219.3	86.8	17.1	-1.6	149.5	151.1	405.8	183.8	222.1	1 860.5
1977	2 086.0	1 276.7	396.6	259.1	115.2	22.3	-23.1	159.4	182.4	435.8	198.8	237.0	2 063.6
1978	2 356.6	1 426.2	478.4	314.6	138.0	25.8	-25.4	186.9	212.3	477.4	216.7	260.7	2 330.8
1979	2 632.1	1 589.5	539.7	373.8	147.8	18.0	-22.5	230.1	252.7	525.5	237.7	287.8	2 614.2
1980	2 862.5	1 754.6	530.1	406.9	129.5	-6.3	-13.1	280.8	293.8	590.8	272.4	318.5	2 868.8
1981	3 211.0	1 937.5	631.2	472.9	128.5	29.8	-12.5	305.2	317.8	654.7	311.7	343.0	3 181.1
1982	3 345.0	2 073.9	581.0	485.1	110.8	-14.9	-20.0	283.2	303.2	710.0	345.6	364.4	3 359.9
1983	3 638.1	2 286.5	637.5	482.2	161.1	-5.8	-51.6	277.0	328.6	765.7	380.2	385.6	3 643.9
1984	4 040.7	2 498.2	820.1	564.3	190.4	65.4	-102.7	302.4	405.1	825.2	407.6	417.5	3 975.3
1985	4 346.7	2 722.7	829.6	607.7	200.1	21.8	-114.0	303.2	417.2	908.4	449.3	459.2	4 324.9
1986	4 590.2	2 898.4	849.1	607.8	234.8	6.6	-131.9	321.0	452.9	974.5	478.4	496.1	4 583.6
1987	4 870.2	3 092.1	892.2	615.2	249.8	27.1	-144.8	363.9	508.7	1 030.8	500.2	530.5	4 843.1
1988	5 252.6	3 346.9	937.0	662.3	256.2	18.5	-109.4	444.6	554.0	1 078.2	508.8	569.3	5 234.1
1989	5 657.7	3 592.8	999.7	716.0	256.0	27.7	-86.7	504.3	591.0	1 151.9	531.4	620.5	5 630.0
1990	5 979.6	3 825.6	993.5	739.2	239.7	14.5	-77.9	551.9	629.7	1 238.4	560.0	678.3	5 965.0
1991	6 174.0	3 960.2	944.3	723.6	221.2	-0.4	-28.6	594.9	623.5	1 298.2	580.7	717.4	6 174.4
1992	6 539.3	4 215.7	1 013.0	741.9	254.7	16.3	-34.7	633.1	667.8	1 345.4	586.6	758.8	6 523.0
1993	6 878.7	4 471.0	1 106.8	799.2	286.8	20.8	-65.2	654.8	720.0	1 366.1	578.4	787.7	6 857.9
1994	7 308.8	4 741.0	1 256.5	868.9	323.8	63.8	-92.5	720.9	813.4	1 403.7	572.7	831.1	7 245.0
1995	7 664.1	4 984.2	1 317.5	962.2	324.1	31.2	-89.8	812.8	902.6	1 452.2	575.4	876.8	7 632.9
1996	8 100.2	5 268.1	1 432.1	1 043.2	358.1	30.8	-96.4	867.6	964.0	1 496.4	578.2	918.2	8 069.4
1997	8 608.5	5 560.7	1 595.6	1 149.1	375.6	70.9	-102.0	953.8	1 055.8	1 554.2	582.4	971.8	8 537.6
1998	9 089.2	5 903.0	1 735.3	1 252.8	418.8	63.7	-162.7	953.0	1 115.7	1 613.5	584.1	1 029.4	9 025.4
1999	9 660.6	6 307.0	1 884.2	1 361.6	461.8	60.8	-256.6	992.0	1 248.6	1 726.0	610.4	1 115.6	9 599.8
2000	10 284.8	6 792.4	2 033.8	1 493.8	485.4	54.5	-375.8	1 096.8	1 472.6	1 834.4	632.4	1 202.0	10 230.2
2001	10 621.8	7 103.1	1 928.6	1 453.9	513.0	-38.3	-368.7	1 026.7	1 395.4	1 958.8	669.2	1 289.5	10 660.1
2002	10 977.5	7 384.1	1 925.0	1 348.9	557.6	18.5	-426.5	1 002.5	1 429.0	2 094.9	740.6	1 354.3	10 959.0
2003	11 510.7	7 765.5	2 027.9	1 371.7	636.9	19.3	-503.7	1 040.3	1 543.9	2 220.8	824.8	1 396.0	11 491.4
2004	12 274.9	8 260.0	2 276.7	1 463.1	749.7	63.9	-619.2	1 181.5	1 800.7	2 357.4	892.4	1 465.0	12 211.1
2005	13 093.7	8 794.1	2 527.1	1 611.5	856.1	59.6	-721.2	1 308.9	2 030.1	2 493.7	946.3	1 547.4	13 034.1
2006	13 855.9	9 304.0	2 680.6	1 776.3	837.4	67.0	-770.9	1 476.3	2 247.3	2 642.2	1 002.0	1 640.2	13 788.9
2007	14 477.6	9 750.5	2 643.7	1 920.6	688.7	34.5	-718.5	1 664.6	2 383.2	2 801.9	1 049.8	1 752.2	14 443.2
2008	14 718.6	10 013.6	2 424.8	1 941.0	515.9	-32.0	-723.1	1 841.9	2 565.0	3 003.2	1 155.6	1 847.6	14 750.6
2009	14 418.7	9 847.0	1 878.1	1 633.4	392.2	-147.6	-395.4	1 587.7	1 983.2	3 089.1	1 217.7	1 871.4	14 566.3
2010	14 964.4	10 202.2	2 100.8	1 658.2	381.1	61.5	-512.7	1 852.3	2 365.0	3 174.0	1 303.9	1 870.2	14 902.8
2011	15 517.9	10 689.3	2 239.9	1 812.1	386.0	41.8	-580.0	2 106.4	2 686.4	3 168.7	1 303.5	1 865.3	15 476.2
2012	16 155.3	11 050.6	2 511.7	2 007.7	442.2	61.8	-565.7	2 198.2	2 763.8	3 158.6	1 292.5	1 866.1	16 093.5
2013	16 663.2	11 392.3	2 665.0	2 084.3	508.9	71.8	-508.4	2 263.3	2 771.7	3 114.2	1 230.6	1 883.6	16 591.4
2014	17 348.1	11 865.9	2 860.0	2 233.7	549.2	77.1	-530.0	2 341.9	2 871.9	3 152.1	1 219.9	1 932.3	17 270.9
2012													
1st quarter	15 973.9	10 956.2	2 460.8	1 971.5	423.8	65.4	-614.7	2 169.6	2 784.3	3 171.6	1 300.5	1 871.0	15 908.4
2nd quarter	16 121.9	11 008.3	2 534.8	2 016.2	429.4	89.3	-580.9	2 199.8	2 780.7	3 159.6	1 293.7	1 865.9	16 032.6
3rd quarter	16 227.9	11 073.6	2 529.9	2 011.7	444.1	74.1	-535.2	2 209.4	2 744.5	3 159.6	1 297.0	1 862.6	16 153.9
4th quarter	16 297.3	11 164.3	2 521.3	2 031.2	471.7	18.4	-531.8	2 214.0	2 745.8	3 143.5	1 278.9	1 864.6	16 278.9
2013													
1st quarter	16 440.7	11 271.8	2 578.3	2 052.1	489.6	36.5	-529.2	2 226.6	2 755.8	3 119.8	1 250.4	1 869.4	16 404.2
2nd quarter	16 526.8	11 322.8	2 620.4	2 064.6	507.1	48.7	-527.8	2 237.6	2 765.4	3 111.4	1 234.2	1 877.2	16 478.1
3rd quarter	16 727.5	11 417.7	2 711.5	2 085.9	520.0	105.6	-512.4	2 264.3	2 776.7	3 110.7	1 220.4	1 890.3	16 621.9
4th quarter	16 957.6	11 556.9	2 749.9	2 134.5	519.0	96.4	-464.3	2 324.5	2 788.8	3 115.1	1 217.6	1 897.5	16 861.2
2014													
1st quarter	16 984.3	11 640.3	2 751.1	2 181.9	526.4	42.7	-529.4	2 301.5	2 830.8	3 122.3	1 214.8	1 907.5	16 941.6
2nd quarter	17 270.0	11 813.0	2 841.6	2 211.7	540.9	88.9	-530.9	2 356.2	2 887.0	3 146.3	1 216.9	1 929.4	17 181.0
3rd quarter	17 522.1	11 949.1	2 910.2	2 267.0	554.8	88.3	-514.6	2 360.6	2 875.2	3 177.4	1 233.1	1 944.3	17 433.8
4th quarter	17 615.9	12 061.4	2 937.2	2 274.1	574.6	88.5	-545.2	2 349.5	2 894.6	3 162.5	1 214.7	1 947.8	17 527.4

Table 1-1B. Gross Domestic Product: Historical Data

(Billions of dollars, quarterly data are at seasonally adjusted annual rates.)

NIPA Tables 1.1.5, 1.2.5

Year and quarter	Gross domestic product	Personal consumption expenditures	Gross private domestic investment Total	Fixed investment Nonresidential	Fixed investment Residential	Change in private inventories	Net exports	Exports	Imports	Government Total	Federal	State and local	Addendum: Final sales of domestic product
1929	104.6	77.4	17.2	11.6	4.1	1.5	0.4	5.9	5.6	9.6	1.9	7.7	103.0
1930	92.2	70.1	11.4	9.2	2.5	-0.2	0.3	4.4	4.1	10.3	2.0	8.3	92.4
1931	77.4	60.7	6.5	5.8	1.9	-1.1	0.0	2.9	2.9	10.2	2.0	8.1	78.5
1932	59.5	48.7	1.8	3.3	0.9	-2.4	0.0	2.0	1.9	9.0	2.0	7.0	61.9
1933	57.2	45.9	2.3	3.0	0.7	-1.4	0.1	2.0	1.9	8.9	2.4	6.5	58.6
1934	66.8	51.5	4.3	3.8	1.0	-0.6	0.3	2.6	2.2	10.7	3.4	7.3	67.4
1935	74.3	55.9	7.4	4.8	1.4	1.1	-0.2	2.8	3.0	11.2	3.6	7.6	73.1
1936	84.9	62.2	9.4	6.4	1.8	1.2	-0.1	3.0	3.2	13.4	5.8	7.7	83.7
1937	93.0	66.8	13.0	8.2	2.2	2.6	0.1	4.0	4.0	13.1	5.3	7.9	90.4
1938	87.4	64.3	7.9	6.3	2.2	-0.6	1.0	3.8	2.8	14.2	5.9	8.3	88.0
1939	93.5	67.2	10.2	6.9	3.2	0.2	0.8	4.0	3.1	15.2	6.2	9.0	93.3
1940	102.9	71.3	14.6	8.5	3.6	2.4	1.5	4.9	3.4	15.6	6.8	8.8	100.6
1941	129.4	81.1	19.4	10.8	4.2	4.3	1.0	5.5	4.4	27.9	19.1	8.8	125.0
1942	166.0	89.0	11.8	7.5	2.4	1.9	-0.3	4.4	4.6	65.5	56.7	8.8	164.1
1943	203.1	99.9	7.4	6.6	1.6	-0.7	-2.2	4.0	6.3	98.1	89.5	8.6	203.9
1944	224.6	108.6	9.2	8.6	1.5	-0.9	-2.0	4.9	6.9	108.7	100.1	8.6	225.5
1945	228.2	120.0	12.4	12.1	1.8	-1.5	-0.8	6.8	7.5	96.6	87.3	9.3	229.6
1946	227.8	144.3	33.1	19.2	8.0	6.0	7.2	14.2	7.0	43.2	32.1	11.1	221.8
1947	249.9	162.0	37.1	25.5	12.2	-0.6	10.8	18.7	7.9	40.0	25.8	14.2	250.5
1948	274.8	175.0	50.3	28.9	15.8	5.7	5.5	15.5	10.1	44.0	27.1	16.9	269.1
1949	272.8	178.5	39.1	26.9	14.8	-2.7	5.2	14.5	9.2	50.0	30.5	19.6	275.5
1947													
1st quarter	243.1	156.3	35.9	24.8	10.5	0.5	10.9	18.4	7.5	40.1	26.6	13.4	242.6
2nd quarter	246.3	160.2	34.5	25.2	10.6	-1.2	11.3	19.5	8.2	40.3	26.5	13.8	247.5
3rd quarter	250.1	163.7	34.9	25.4	12.5	-2.9	11.8	19.4	7.7	39.8	25.3	14.5	253.0
4th quarter	260.3	167.8	43.2	26.5	15.3	1.5	9.3	17.6	8.3	40.0	24.8	15.2	258.9
1948													
1st quarter	266.2	170.5	47.2	28.2	15.3	3.6	7.3	16.9	9.6	41.2	25.5	15.7	262.5
2nd quarter	272.9	174.3	50.3	28.0	16.4	5.9	5.2	15.2	10.0	43.1	26.7	16.4	267.0
3rd quarter	279.5	177.2	52.5	29.1	16.3	7.2	4.9	15.4	10.5	44.8	27.5	17.3	272.3
4th quarter	280.7	178.1	51.3	30.2	15.2	6.0	4.5	14.6	10.1	46.8	28.7	18.0	274.7
1949													
1st quarter	275.4	177.0	43.1	28.6	14.2	0.4	6.5	16.1	9.6	48.8	30.2	18.6	275.0
2nd quarter	271.7	178.6	36.2	27.5	13.9	-5.1	6.3	15.6	9.4	50.6	31.3	19.3	276.8
3rd quarter	273.3	177.9	39.5	26.1	14.7	-1.3	5.2	14.1	8.9	50.6	30.5	20.1	274.6
4th quarter	271.0	180.4	37.5	25.6	16.5	-4.7	3.0	12.1	9.1	50.1	29.8	20.3	275.7
1950													
1st quarter	281.2	183.1	46.7	26.4	18.3	2.0	2.2	11.7	9.5	49.2	28.6	20.6	279.2
2nd quarter	290.7	187.0	52.3	28.9	20.6	2.8	1.6	11.9	10.2	49.9	29.0	20.9	287.9
3rd quarter	308.5	200.7	58.6	31.9	22.6	4.2	-0.7	12.3	13.0	50.0	28.4	21.5	304.3
4th quarter	320.3	198.1	68.4	32.9	21.5	14.0	-0.2	13.5	13.7	53.9	31.8	22.1	306.3
1951													
1st quarter	336.4	209.4	64.6	33.1	21.1	10.4	0.2	15.0	14.9	62.3	39.6	22.7	326.0
2nd quarter	344.5	205.1	67.4	34.1	18.5	14.8	1.9	17.1	15.2	70.0	46.6	23.4	329.7
3rd quarter	351.8	207.8	62.0	34.8	17.4	9.7	3.7	18.1	14.3	78.3	54.3	24.0	342.0
4th quarter	356.6	211.7	57.1	34.6	17.7	4.7	4.2	18.2	14.0	83.6	59.3	24.2	351.9
1952													
1st quarter	360.2	213.1	58.1	35.1	18.3	4.7	3.7	18.7	15.0	85.3	60.9	24.3	355.5
2nd quarter	361.4	217.2	53.0	35.8	18.8	-1.5	2.0	16.6	14.6	89.2	64.1	25.1	362.9
3rd quarter	368.1	219.7	57.2	32.9	18.8	5.6	0.0	15.2	15.3	91.2	66.2	25.0	362.5
4th quarter	381.2	227.9	60.7	35.8	19.6	5.3	-1.0	15.3	16.3	93.7	68.1	25.6	376.0
1953													
1st quarter	388.5	231.5	61.7	37.8	20.0	3.9	-0.7	15.1	15.8	96.0	69.7	26.4	384.6
2nd quarter	392.3	233.2	62.1	38.5	20.1	3.6	-1.3	15.2	16.4	98.2	71.9	26.2	388.7
3rd quarter	391.7	233.9	61.4	39.6	19.5	2.3	-0.6	15.8	16.3	96.9	70.0	26.9	389.4
4th quarter	386.5	233.4	56.4	39.2	19.3	-2.0	-0.3	15.2	15.5	97.0	69.5	27.5	388.5
1954													
1st quarter	385.9	235.4	55.7	38.3	19.4	-2.0	-0.4	14.4	14.8	95.1	66.8	28.4	387.9
2nd quarter	386.7	238.2	55.4	38.2	20.7	-3.4	0.3	16.4	16.2	92.8	63.7	29.1	390.1
3rd quarter	391.6	240.6	59.0	38.9	22.2	-2.1	0.6	15.9	15.3	91.4	61.3	30.1	393.7
4th quarter	400.3	245.4	62.1	38.9	23.6	-0.3	1.1	16.6	15.5	91.6	61.2	30.4	400.7
1955													
1st quarter	413.8	251.8	68.7	39.5	25.4	3.8	1.1	17.3	16.2	92.2	60.7	31.5	409.9
2nd quarter	422.2	256.8	72.7	42.1	26.0	4.6	-0.2	16.9	17.1	92.8	60.9	32.0	417.6
3rd quarter	430.9	261.0	74.7	44.8	25.6	4.3	0.7	18.1	17.4	94.4	61.9	32.5	426.6
4th quarter	437.8	265.1	78.9	47.1	24.6	7.2	0.2	18.3	18.1	93.6	60.5	33.1	430.6
1956													
1st quarter	440.5	266.6	78.3	47.8	24.1	6.4	0.4	19.4	18.9	95.2	61.0	34.2	434.1
2nd quarter	446.8	269.3	77.0	49.1	24.4	3.6	1.9	20.9	19.0	98.6	63.5	35.1	443.2
3rd quarter	452.0	272.5	78.3	50.7	24.0	3.6	2.6	21.8	19.3	98.6	62.8	35.8	448.4
4th quarter	461.3	277.9	77.1	51.4	23.5	2.2	4.5	23.1	18.5	101.7	65.2	36.5	459.0
1957													
1st quarter	470.6	282.3	77.7	52.5	23.1	2.2	4.8	24.9	20.1	105.7	67.9	37.8	468.4
2nd quarter	472.8	284.6	77.9	52.6	22.6	2.7	4.1	24.4	20.3	106.2	67.5	38.7	470.2
3rd quarter	480.3	289.2	79.3	54.1	22.5	2.8	4.0	23.8	19.8	107.8	68.4	39.4	477.5
4th quarter	475.7	290.8	71.0	53.2	22.3	-4.5	3.4	23.0	19.6	110.4	70.0	40.4	480.2
1958													
1st quarter	468.4	290.3	66.7	49.4	21.4	-4.0	1.1	20.5	19.5	110.2	68.7	41.5	472.4
2nd quarter	472.8	293.2	65.1	47.8	21.5	-4.2	0.5	20.5	20.1	114.0	71.5	42.5	477.0
3rd quarter	486.7	298.3	72.0	47.4	23.0	1.5	0.9	20.6	19.7	115.5	71.9	43.6	485.1
4th quarter	500.4	302.2	80.0	49.3	25.4	5.2	-0.3	20.6	20.8	118.4	73.9	44.5	495.1

Table 1-1B. Gross Domestic Product: Historical Data—Continued

(Billions of dollars, quarterly data are at seasonally adjusted annual rates.) NIPA Tables 1.1.5, 1.2.5

Year and quarter	Gross domestic product	Personal consumption expenditures	Gross private domestic investment				Exports and imports of goods and services			Government consumption expenditures and gross investment			Addendum: Final sales of domestic product
			Total	Fixed investment		Change in private inventories	Net exports	Exports	Imports	Total	Federal	State and local	
				Nonresidential	Residential								
1959													
1st quarter	511.1	309.9	83.2	50.9	28.3	3.9	0.4	21.8	21.4	117.6	72.3	45.3	507.2
2nd quarter	524.2	315.9	89.4	52.7	29.4	7.3	0.0	22.6	22.5	119.0	73.6	45.4	517.0
3rd quarter	525.2	321.1	83.6	54.4	28.8	0.4	0.6	23.5	22.9	119.9	74.5	45.4	524.8
4th quarter	529.3	323.2	86.5	54.4	28.0	4.1	0.6	23.1	22.5	119.0	73.8	45.2	525.2
1960													
1st quarter	543.3	326.7	96.5	56.3	29.0	11.2	2.7	26.0	23.3	117.4	70.9	46.5	532.1
2nd quarter	542.7	332.6	87.1	57.2	26.7	3.2	4.2	27.6	23.5	118.9	71.0	47.8	539.5
3rd quarter	546.0	332.5	86.4	56.2	25.9	4.3	4.2	27.0	22.9	122.9	74.1	48.8	541.7
4th quarter	541.1	334.5	76.0	55.9	25.9	-5.8	5.8	27.5	21.7	124.9	75.3	49.6	546.9
1961													
1st quarter	545.9	335.0	78.4	55.0	25.9	-2.5	5.8	27.5	21.7	126.8	75.3	51.5	548.5
2nd quarter	557.4	339.9	84.1	56.2	26.1	1.8	5.5	27.4	21.9	127.9	76.2	51.7	555.6
3rd quarter	568.2	342.8	90.9	56.7	27.6	6.7	3.9	27.2	23.3	130.6	78.1	52.5	561.6
4th quarter	581.6	350.1	92.9	58.5	28.5	6.0	4.4	28.3	23.9	134.2	79.9	54.3	575.6
1962													
1st quarter	595.2	355.4	98.1	59.7	29.0	9.4	4.0	28.3	24.3	137.8	83.3	54.5	585.8
2nd quarter	602.6	361.0	96.7	61.4	29.9	5.4	5.8	30.7	24.9	139.1	84.1	55.0	597.1
3rd quarter	609.6	364.9	98.2	62.1	29.9	6.2	3.8	29.0	25.1	142.7	87.0	55.7	603.4
4th quarter	613.1	371.1	95.0	61.8	29.8	3.4	2.8	28.4	25.6	144.2	87.6	56.6	609.8
1963													
1st quarter	622.7	374.7	99.7	62.0	30.8	6.9	3.9	29.1	25.2	144.4	86.2	58.2	615.8
2nd quarter	631.8	378.9	101.6	63.9	32.9	4.8	6.5	32.4	25.9	144.8	85.7	59.1	627.0
3rd quarter	645.0	385.8	104.6	65.7	33.2	5.7	3.9	30.6	26.7	150.6	89.8	60.8	639.2
4th quarter	654.8	390.5	107.2	67.7	34.5	5.1	5.4	32.2	26.8	151.7	89.6	62.1	649.8
1964													
1st quarter	671.1	400.1	110.5	69.1	36.2	5.1	7.3	34.2	27.0	153.3	90.0	63.2	666.0
2nd quarter	680.8	408.1	110.5	71.1	35.0	4.5	7.1	34.8	27.7	155.1	90.1	65.0	676.3
3rd quarter	692.8	417.0	112.6	73.4	34.5	4.7	6.4	34.8	28.4	156.8	90.8	66.0	688.1
4th quarter	698.4	419.6	115.0	75.3	34.6	5.0	6.9	36.2	29.3	156.9	89.9	67.0	693.4
1965													
1st quarter	719.2	430.3	126.5	80.2	34.8	11.5	4.6	33.1	28.5	157.8	89.4	68.4	707.7
2nd quarter	732.4	437.2	127.0	83.4	35.1	8.6	7.5	39.1	31.7	160.6	90.1	70.6	723.8
3rd quarter	750.2	446.4	131.2	86.7	35.3	9.3	4.9	36.9	32.0	167.6	94.4	73.2	740.9
4th quarter	773.1	460.4	133.8	90.6	35.5	7.6	5.5	39.5	33.9	173.5	98.7	74.8	765.5
1966													
1st quarter	797.3	470.8	144.2	94.4	35.9	13.9	4.4	39.4	35.0	177.9	101.2	76.8	783.5
2nd quarter	807.2	475.9	143.5	96.8	34.4	12.3	5.2	41.5	36.2	182.6	104.0	78.6	794.8
3rd quarter	820.8	485.0	143.2	98.3	33.0	11.9	2.2	40.4	38.2	190.4	109.9	80.5	808.9
4th quarter	834.9	490.8	145.9	99.2	30.2	16.5	3.6	42.4	38.8	194.7	111.1	83.5	818.4
1967													
1st quarter	846.0	495.1	142.8	98.0	29.4	15.4	4.6	44.0	39.4	203.6	117.9	85.7	830.6
2nd quarter	851.1	504.2	137.5	98.3	32.9	6.3	4.5	43.5	39.0	204.8	117.9	87.0	844.7
3rd quarter	866.6	511.4	142.8	98.8	34.8	9.3	2.9	42.4	39.5	209.4	120.9	88.5	857.4
4th quarter	883.2	518.9	147.7	101.7	37.5	8.4	2.2	43.9	41.7	214.4	123.1	91.2	874.8
1968													
1st quarter	911.1	536.9	152.3	105.6	38.3	8.4	1.1	45.5	44.4	220.9	126.3	94.5	902.7
2nd quarter	936.3	550.6	158.9	105.3	39.6	14.1	1.9	47.4	45.4	224.8	127.1	97.7	922.2
3rd quarter	952.3	566.7	155.7	107.6	40.4	7.7	1.3	49.5	48.2	228.6	128.5	100.1	944.7
4th quarter	970.1	575.6	160.8	112.2	42.6	6.0	1.1	49.2	48.2	232.7	129.7	103.0	964.1
1969													
1st quarter	995.4	587.8	172.4	116.0	44.9	11.5	0.2	44.0	43.8	235.0	129.6	105.5	983.9
2nd quarter	1 011.4	599.2	172.7	118.4	45.1	9.2	1.2	53.9	52.7	238.2	129.7	108.5	1 002.1
3rd quarter	1 032.0	609.5	177.6	122.4	45.0	10.2	1.0	53.3	52.4	244.0	133.3	110.6	1 021.8
4th quarter	1 040.7	621.5	171.6	123.3	42.5	5.8	3.3	56.5	53.1	244.3	131.9	112.4	1 035.0
1970													
1st quarter	1 053.5	632.6	168.1	123.8	42.5	1.8	3.4	56.9	53.5	249.4	133.5	115.9	1 051.7
2nd quarter	1 070.1	642.5	171.5	125.0	41.4	5.1	5.4	60.6	55.2	250.7	131.7	119.0	1 065.0
3rd quarter	1 088.5	654.5	173.9	126.3	42.6	5.1	3.8	60.3	56.4	256.2	132.3	123.9	1 083.4
4th quarter	1 091.5	661.2	166.8	123.5	47.2	-4.0	3.2	61.1	57.9	260.4	133.5	126.9	1 095.4
1971													
1st quarter	1 137.8	680.2	189.5	126.3	51.0	12.3	4.4	63.1	58.7	263.7	133.3	130.4	1 125.6
2nd quarter	1 159.4	694.3	197.3	129.5	57.0	10.9	-0.2	63.1	63.3	268.0	134.2	133.8	1 148.5
3rd quarter	1 180.3	706.7	202.1	131.2	60.7	10.2	-0.1	65.4	65.5	271.7	135.5	136.2	1 170.1
4th quarter	1 193.6	722.9	198.4	134.7	64.0	-0.3	-1.7	60.3	61.9	274.0	134.7	139.3	1 193.9
1972													
1st quarter	1 233.8	740.1	213.0	140.6	69.2	3.2	-3.5	68.6	72.2	284.3	141.4	142.9	1 230.6
2nd quarter	1 270.1	758.6	226.8	144.0	70.8	12.0	-4.3	67.2	71.4	289.0	144.6	144.4	1 258.1
3rd quarter	1 293.8	777.1	233.1	147.0	72.4	13.7	-2.6	71.5	74.1	286.3	138.5	147.8	1 280.1
4th quarter	1 332.0	801.9	239.7	155.0	77.3	7.5	-3.1	76.1	79.2	293.5	141.7	151.8	1 324.5
1973													
1st quarter	1 380.7	826.5	254.3	162.8	80.9	10.6	-1.4	84.0	85.4	301.3	145.9	155.4	1 370.1
2nd quarter	1 417.6	842.0	268.2	171.3	78.7	18.2	2.5	91.9	89.5	304.9	146.5	158.4	1 399.4
3rd quarter	1 436.8	860.5	264.3	176.6	77.9	9.8	6.4	97.6	91.1	305.6	143.4	162.2	1 427.1
4th quarter	1 479.1	875.6	280.9	180.1	75.7	25.0	9.0	107.6	98.7	313.7	146.5	167.2	1 454.1
1974													
1st quarter	1 494.7	893.8	268.4	183.4	72.4	12.5	6.4	116.7	110.3	326.1	151.9	174.3	1 482.1
2nd quarter	1 534.2	922.3	277.4	188.8	71.2	17.4	-2.7	126.7	129.4	337.3	154.7	182.5	1 516.8
3rd quarter	1 563.4	951.1	271.0	194.5	70.9	5.6	-7.0	126.6	133.6	348.3	159.5	188.8	1 557.8
4th quarter	1 603.0	960.9	281.3	197.6	63.3	20.4	0.0	136.6	136.6	360.8	166.4	194.4	1 582.6

Table 1-1B. Gross Domestic Product: Historical Data—*Continued*

(Billions of dollars, quarterly data are at seasonally adjusted annual rates.)

NIPA Tables 1.1.5, 1.2.5

Year and quarter	Gross domestic product	Personal consumption expenditures	Gross private domestic investment				Exports and imports of goods and services			Government consumption expenditures and gross investment			Addendum: Final sales of domestic product
			Total	Fixed investment		Change in private inventories	Net exports	Exports	Imports	Total	Federal	State and local	
				Nonresidential	Residential								
1975													
1st quarter	1 619.6	987.1	244.3	193.1	61.2	-10.0	16.5	141.4	124.9	371.7	167.6	204.1	1 629.6
2nd quarter	1 656.4	1 015.8	243.3	193.3	64.0	-14.0	21.6	136.8	115.2	375.8	169.0	206.8	1 670.4
3rd quarter	1 713.8	1 049.6	265.2	197.8	68.8	-1.4	12.0	134.1	122.1	387.0	174.9	212.1	1 715.2
4th quarter	1 765.9	1 078.5	276.2	202.9	73.0	0.3	13.8	142.5	128.7	397.3	179.7	217.6	1 765.5
1976													
1st quarter	1 824.5	1 112.3	304.6	209.5	80.4	14.7	4.7	143.6	138.9	402.9	180.5	222.4	1 809.8
2nd quarter	1 856.9	1 132.0	322.3	215.0	84.8	22.4	-0.5	146.6	147.1	403.2	182.0	221.2	1 834.5
3rd quarter	1 890.5	1 161.3	328.3	222.6	84.9	20.8	-4.1	151.8	155.8	404.9	183.6	221.3	1 869.7
4th quarter	1 938.4	1 195.1	337.6	230.2	96.9	10.5	-6.6	156.1	162.7	412.3	189.0	223.3	1 927.9
1977													
1st quarter	1 992.5	1 230.6	360.3	243.3	102.2	14.8	-21.1	155.4	176.4	422.7	192.9	229.8	1 977.7
2nd quarter	2 060.2	1 258.5	389.7	253.7	116.5	19.5	-21.1	161.9	183.0	433.1	197.7	235.3	2 040.7
3rd quarter	2 122.4	1 289.7	414.1	263.3	120.0	30.9	-20.6	162.3	182.9	439.1	200.0	239.1	2 091.5
4th quarter	2 168.7	1 327.9	422.3	275.9	122.2	24.1	-29.6	157.8	187.4	448.1	204.5	243.6	2 144.6
1978													
1st quarter	2 208.7	1 357.8	434.8	282.4	126.9	25.5	-38.7	164.6	203.3	454.8	207.7	247.1	2 183.2
2nd quarter	2 336.6	1 415.3	470.6	309.3	137.0	24.3	-22.6	186.2	208.8	473.3	214.8	258.5	2 312.3
3rd quarter	2 398.9	1 446.2	492.4	325.1	142.3	25.0	-23.8	191.3	215.1	484.0	218.6	265.4	2 373.9
4th quarter	2 482.2	1 485.4	515.8	341.4	145.8	28.5	-16.4	205.4	221.8	497.4	225.8	271.7	2 453.7
1979													
1st quarter	2 531.6	1 521.0	525.8	356.7	145.3	23.9	-18.2	211.7	229.8	502.9	229.1	273.8	2 507.7
2nd quarter	2 595.9	1 561.5	539.3	364.3	147.6	27.4	-22.2	220.9	243.1	517.3	234.9	282.4	2 568.5
3rd quarter	2 670.4	1 616.0	545.6	383.0	150.5	12.1	-23.0	234.3	257.3	531.8	238.8	293.0	2 658.3
4th quarter	2 730.7	1 659.5	547.9	391.3	148.0	8.6	-26.8	253.7	280.5	550.2	248.1	302.1	2 722.2
1980													
1st quarter	2 796.5	1 706.5	554.6	404.5	140.2	9.9	-35.8	268.5	304.3	571.2	259.7	311.6	2 786.6
2nd quarter	2 799.9	1 708.9	519.3	394.7	116.9	7.8	-15.2	277.4	292.6	586.9	271.0	315.9	2 792.2
3rd quarter	2 860.0	1 767.7	495.1	405.7	123.2	-33.9	5.5	284.7	279.2	591.8	272.0	319.8	2 893.9
4th quarter	2 993.5	1 835.4	551.5	422.8	137.8	-9.1	-6.7	292.5	299.2	613.4	286.8	326.6	3 002.6
1981													
1st quarter	3 131.8	1 890.7	619.4	443.0	137.6	38.8	-14.3	305.5	319.7	636.0	296.5	339.4	3 093.0
2nd quarter	3 167.3	1 921.9	609.8	462.9	135.3	11.7	-13.5	308.5	322.0	649.0	309.4	339.6	3 155.5
3rd quarter	3 261.2	1 961.2	652.3	482.1	126.2	44.0	-7.6	302.3	309.9	655.2	312.5	342.7	3 217.2
4th quarter	3 283.5	1 976.1	643.4	503.8	114.8	24.8	-14.8	304.7	319.4	678.8	328.5	350.3	3 258.7
1982													
1st quarter	3 273.8	2 014.4	588.3	500.1	109.7	-21.5	-16.3	293.2	309.5	687.4	332.5	354.9	3 295.3
2nd quarter	3 331.3	2 041.1	593.6	490.1	107.7	-4.2	-4.4	294.7	299.1	701.0	339.5	361.5	3 335.4
3rd quarter	3 367.1	2 089.2	593.0	478.7	108.4	5.8	-29.6	279.6	309.3	714.5	347.6	366.9	3 361.3
4th quarter	3 407.8	2 150.9	549.2	471.5	117.5	-39.8	-29.6	265.3	294.9	737.2	362.9	374.4	3 447.6
1983													
1st quarter	3 480.3	2 190.6	565.5	462.1	138.5	-35.1	-24.5	270.7	295.3	748.8	370.1	378.7	3 515.4
2nd quarter	3 583.8	2 254.5	613.8	466.4	155.0	-7.7	-45.4	272.5	318.0	761.0	378.8	382.2	3 591.5
3rd quarter	3 692.3	2 324.3	652.3	485.4	171.1	-4.2	-65.2	278.2	343.4	780.9	391.7	389.2	3 696.5
4th quarter	3 796.1	2 376.7	718.5	514.7	179.9	23.9	-71.4	286.6	358.0	772.3	380.1	392.2	3 772.2
1984													
1st quarter	3 912.8	2 422.8	790.9	531.5	186.4	73.0	-95.0	293.0	388.0	794.2	391.1	403.0	3 839.8
2nd quarter	4 015.0	2 481.2	818.9	558.3	191.3	69.3	-104.3	302.2	406.5	819.2	406.9	412.2	3 945.7
3rd quarter	4 087.4	2 519.7	838.9	576.6	190.9	71.3	-103.8	305.7	409.6	832.7	409.5	423.2	4 016.0
4th quarter	4 147.6	2 568.9	831.7	590.9	192.9	48.0	-107.8	308.6	416.4	854.7	423.0	431.7	4 099.6
1985													
1st quarter	4 237.0	2 643.9	809.9	599.4	194.2	16.2	-91.3	306.0	397.3	874.5	432.2	442.3	4 220.8
2nd quarter	4 302.3	2 691.2	827.0	609.1	196.3	21.6	-114.4	304.1	418.6	898.5	443.8	454.7	4 280.7
3rd quarter	4 394.6	2 764.7	822.2	604.4	201.4	16.3	-116.9	297.3	414.2	924.6	458.7	465.9	4 378.3
4th quarter	4 453.1	2 790.9	859.5	618.1	208.4	33.1	-133.4	305.4	438.9	936.1	462.4	473.7	4 420.0
1986													
1st quarter	4 516.3	2 834.7	863.5	613.5	219.5	30.4	-126.0	313.4	439.4	944.2	459.7	484.4	4 485.9
2nd quarter	4 555.2	2 863.0	855.2	605.0	234.6	15.7	-128.9	315.1	444.0	965.8	474.5	491.3	4 539.6
3rd quarter	4 619.6	2 929.7	835.8	602.0	240.9	-7.0	-139.0	320.5	459.4	993.0	492.9	500.2	4 626.6
4th quarter	4 669.4	2 966.1	842.1	610.6	244.3	-12.8	-133.6	335.0	468.6	994.8	486.4	508.4	4 682.2
1987													
1st quarter	4 736.2	2 998.3	871.2	596.6	246.7	28.0	-141.2	336.5	477.7	1 008.0	489.6	518.4	4 708.3
2nd quarter	4 821.5	3 068.8	874.6	608.4	249.7	16.5	-147.0	355.4	502.3	1 025.0	499.2	525.9	4 804.9
3rd quarter	4 900.5	3 133.5	876.5	625.5	250.0	1.0	-145.5	371.9	517.3	1 036.0	502.2	533.7	4 899.5
4th quarter	5 022.7	3 167.6	946.5	630.5	252.8	63.1	-145.4	392.1	537.5	1 054.0	509.8	544.2	4 959.6
1988													
1st quarter	5 090.6	3 249.0	908.6	641.5	250.1	17.0	-124.0	418.7	542.7	1 057.0	504.0	553.0	5 073.7
2nd quarter	5 207.7	3 309.0	934.5	659.4	255.5	19.6	-106.6	439.5	546.1	1 070.8	505.4	565.4	5 188.1
3rd quarter	5 299.5	3 378.3	942.0	666.3	257.5	18.2	-99.3	453.6	552.8	1 078.4	505.8	572.6	5 281.3
4th quarter	5 412.7	3 451.3	962.8	681.9	261.7	19.1	-107.7	466.6	574.3	1 106.4	520.0	586.4	5 393.6
1989													
1st quarter	5 527.4	3 506.1	1 005.4	696.3	260.9	48.1	-101.0	485.2	586.2	1 116.9	517.5	599.3	5 479.2
2nd quarter	5 628.4	3 569.5	1 001.0	708.9	255.8	36.3	-88.2	507.2	595.4	1 146.1	531.8	614.3	5 592.2
3rd quarter	5 711.6	3 625.6	996.5	731.2	255.5	9.8	-75.1	509.4	584.4	1 164.6	538.5	626.1	5 701.7
4th quarter	5 763.4	3 670.1	995.9	727.5	251.9	16.6	-82.8	515.4	598.2	1 180.2	537.7	642.5	5 746.9
1990													
1st quarter	5 890.8	3 754.5	1 010.8	740.9	256.0	14.0	-88.5	538.2	626.8	1 214.0	552.6	661.4	5 876.9
2nd quarter	5 974.7	3 800.2	1 014.8	734.2	246.9	33.7	-68.8	545.9	614.8	1 228.6	559.5	669.1	5 941.0
3rd quarter	6 029.5	3 863.4	1 000.7	744.3	234.5	21.9	-75.0	555.1	630.1	1 240.4	558.0	682.4	6 007.6
4th quarter	6 023.3	3 884.4	947.6	737.6	221.3	-11.3	-79.1	568.2	647.3	1 270.4	570.0	700.5	6 034.7

Table 1-1B. Gross Domestic Product: Historical Data—*Continued*

(Billions of dollars, quarterly data are at seasonally adjusted annual rates.)

| Year and quarter | Gross domestic product | Personal consumption expenditures | Gross private domestic investment | | | | Exports and imports of goods and services | | | Government consumption expenditures and gross investment | | | Addendum: Final sales of domestic product |
| | | | Total | Fixed investment | | Change in private inventories | Net exports | Exports | Imports | Total | Federal | State and local | |
				Nonresidential	Residential								
1991													
1st quarter	6 054.9	3 890.2	924.6	729.8	210.3	-15.5	-47.1	573.2	620.3	1 287.2	582.9	704.3	6 070.4
2nd quarter	6 143.6	3 943.7	926.6	726.8	217.8	-18.0	-23.2	590.7	613.9	1 296.6	585.5	711.1	6 161.6
3rd quarter	6 218.4	3 989.6	947.5	720.1	226.5	0.8	-21.1	600.6	621.7	1 302.4	580.9	721.5	6 217.6
4th quarter	6 279.3	4 017.1	978.8	717.6	230.1	31.1	-23.1	615.2	638.3	1 306.5	573.7	732.9	6 248.2
1992													
1st quarter	6 380.8	4 117.7	956.8	714.2	242.4	0.2	-20.5	625.3	645.8	1 326.9	578.6	748.3	6 380.6
2nd quarter	6 492.3	4 173.4	1 013.1	736.7	253.2	23.2	-32.8	626.2	659.0	1 338.7	582.2	756.5	6 469.1
3rd quarter	6 586.5	4 245.4	1 024.2	748.6	255.1	20.5	-38.5	639.4	677.9	1 355.4	592.7	762.8	6 566.0
4th quarter	6 697.6	4 326.2	1 058.0	768.3	268.3	21.3	-47.1	641.4	688.5	1 360.5	593.0	767.5	6 676.2
1993													
1st quarter	6 748.2	4 368.5	1 083.9	776.6	271.4	35.9	-55.7	643.6	699.3	1 351.5	577.0	774.5	6 712.2
2nd quarter	6 829.6	4 437.5	1 094.5	792.4	278.0	24.1	-63.2	653.1	716.3	1 360.9	575.6	785.3	6 805.5
3rd quarter	6 904.2	4 506.0	1 095.9	798.4	290.9	6.6	-68.4	650.9	719.3	1 370.6	578.9	791.7	6 897.6
4th quarter	7 032.8	4 572.0	1 153.0	829.5	306.9	16.6	-73.4	671.6	745.0	1 381.3	582.0	799.3	7 016.2
1994													
1st quarter	7 136.3	4 640.9	1 202.1	841.1	315.6	45.4	-80.6	681.2	761.8	1 373.9	564.4	809.5	7 090.9
2nd quarter	7 269.8	4 702.9	1 265.1	855.7	327.9	81.4	-90.6	707.0	797.6	1 392.4	569.0	823.4	7 188.4
3rd quarter	7 352.3	4 773.1	1 251.6	871.9	326.4	53.2	-96.9	736.9	833.8	1 424.4	584.0	840.5	7 299.0
4th quarter	7 476.7	4 847.2	1 307.2	906.6	325.4	75.1	-101.9	758.6	860.6	1 424.2	573.4	850.8	7 401.5
1995													
1st quarter	7 545.3	4 883.3	1 327.3	944.3	321.8	61.2	-105.3	781.6	886.9	1 440.0	577.6	862.4	7 484.1
2nd quarter	7 604.9	4 955.0	1 303.8	956.6	313.5	33.8	-109.5	798.9	908.3	1 455.6	579.7	875.9	7 571.2
3rd quarter	7 706.5	5 020.5	1 303.2	965.5	326.4	11.3	-74.4	831.4	905.8	1 457.3	576.9	880.4	7 695.2
4th quarter	7 799.5	5 077.9	1 335.6	982.5	334.6	18.4	-69.8	839.4	909.2	1 455.7	567.3	888.5	7 781.1
1996													
1st quarter	7 893.1	5 153.8	1 355.2	1 003.6	344.7	6.9	-88.8	847.9	936.7	1 472.9	577.2	895.8	7 886.3
2nd quarter	8 061.5	5 244.1	1 418.6	1 026.6	361.4	30.5	-93.7	859.0	952.8	1 492.5	582.5	910.0	8 031.0
3rd quarter	8 159.0	5 298.3	1 474.4	1 059.1	364.3	51.1	-114.2	859.6	973.8	1 500.5	576.9	923.6	8 108.0
4th quarter	8 287.1	5 376.1	1 480.0	1 083.5	361.8	34.7	-88.8	903.8	992.6	1 519.8	576.3	943.6	8 252.4
1997													
1st quarter	8 402.1	5 456.7	1 522.0	1 106.8	365.4	49.8	-108.8	918.4	1 027.2	1 532.2	572.1	960.1	8 352.3
2nd quarter	8 551.9	5 495.1	1 589.9	1 129.2	372.3	88.4	-85.2	954.5	1 039.7	1 552.2	585.7	966.5	8 463.6
3rd quarter	8 691.8	5 603.5	1 625.3	1 178.4	379.0	67.9	-96.8	974.1	1 070.9	1 559.8	585.4	974.4	8 623.8
4th quarter	8 788.3	5 687.6	1 645.3	1 181.9	385.8	77.7	-117.0	968.3	1 085.3	1 572.4	586.5	985.9	8 710.7
1998													
1st quarter	8 889.7	5 745.9	1 712.3	1 212.4	394.8	105.1	-135.2	963.0	1 098.2	1 566.7	571.5	995.3	8 784.6
2nd quarter	8 994.7	5 857.8	1 694.8	1 246.1	411.3	37.3	-162.3	947.3	1 109.6	1 604.4	586.6	1 017.8	8 957.4
3rd quarter	9 146.5	5 952.8	1 739.8	1 259.8	427.6	52.4	-174.6	935.3	1 109.9	1 628.6	584.7	1 043.8	9 094.1
4th quarter	9 325.7	6 055.5	1 794.4	1 292.9	441.5	60.0	-178.7	966.3	1 145.0	1 654.3	593.6	1 060.8	9 265.6
1999													
1st quarter	9 447.1	6 129.0	1 850.6	1 319.9	447.4	83.4	-208.5	961.6	1 170.1	1 676.0	594.5	1 081.5	9 363.7
2nd quarter	9 557.0	6 253.0	1 845.8	1 351.4	459.3	35.1	-245.4	972.8	1 218.2	1 703.7	601.1	1 102.6	9 521.9
3rd quarter	9 712.3	6 357.2	1 890.9	1 383.8	466.6	40.5	-276.1	1 002.4	1 278.5	1 740.2	614.6	1 125.6	9 671.8
4th quarter	9 926.1	6 488.9	1 949.4	1 391.4	473.8	84.2	-296.5	1 031.2	1 327.7	1 784.2	631.6	1 152.7	9 841.9
2000													
1st quarter	10 031.0	6 642.7	1 945.9	1 445.5	484.2	16.2	-352.8	1 054.0	1 406.8	1 795.1	618.1	1 177.0	10 014.9
2nd quarter	10 278.3	6 737.3	2 071.8	1 494.7	486.6	90.4	-359.6	1 092.7	1 452.3	1 828.9	639.3	1 189.6	10 187.9
3rd quarter	10 357.4	6 845.1	2 055.8	1 515.5	483.1	57.2	-388.5	1 125.2	1 513.7	1 845.0	636.2	1 208.9	10 300.2
4th quarter	10 472.3	6 944.4	2 061.6	1 519.4	487.8	54.3	-402.4	1 115.4	1 517.8	1 868.7	636.1	1 232.6	10 417.9
2001													
1st quarter	10 508.1	7 020.4	1 967.5	1 501.5	496.7	-30.6	-391.7	1 096.7	1 488.4	1 911.9	652.5	1 259.4	10 538.8
2nd quarter	10 638.4	7 072.1	1 967.0	1 467.6	511.0	-11.6	-359.3	1 054.6	1 413.9	1 958.6	666.4	1 292.3	10 649.9
3rd quarter	10 639.5	7 103.4	1 937.3	1 445.0	522.4	-30.1	-366.7	998.5	1 365.2	1 965.5	674.9	1 290.6	10 669.6
4th quarter	10 701.3	7 216.6	1 842.7	1 401.5	522.1	-80.8	-357.0	957.1	1 314.1	1 999.1	683.3	1 315.8	10 782.1
2002													
1st quarter	10 834.4	7 251.4	1 910.0	1 371.9	538.3	-0.2	-375.3	973.3	1 348.6	2 048.3	714.4	1 333.9	10 834.7
2nd quarter	10 934.8	7 344.5	1 925.6	1 351.6	554.8	19.1	-416.0	1 007.5	1 423.5	2 080.6	733.1	1 347.6	10 915.6
3rd quarter	11 037.1	7 433.1	1 927.9	1 343.7	558.9	25.3	-431.6	1 021.6	1 453.2	2 107.7	746.2	1 361.6	11 011.8
4th quarter	11 103.8	7 507.2	1 936.5	1 328.4	578.3	29.8	-483.0	1 007.6	1 490.6	2 143.1	768.8	1 374.2	11 074.0
2003													
1st quarter	11 230.1	7 593.5	1 960.2	1 327.8	601.4	31.0	-501.6	1 011.5	1 513.1	2 178.0	789.3	1 388.7	11 199.1
2nd quarter	11 370.7	7 684.6	1 970.5	1 359.1	611.9	-0.4	-501.4	1 012.3	1 513.7	2 216.9	831.4	1 385.5	11 371.0
3rd quarter	11 625.1	7 845.5	2 048.3	1 388.5	651.6	8.1	-499.9	1 042.5	1 542.4	2 231.2	830.5	1 400.8	11 617.0
4th quarter	11 816.8	7 938.5	2 132.8	1 411.5	682.9	38.4	-511.7	1 094.8	1 606.5	2 257.3	848.1	1 409.3	11 778.4
2004													
1st quarter	11 988.4	8 076.8	2 155.2	1 400.3	706.0	48.9	-546.6	1 141.3	1 687.9	2 303.1	872.5	1 430.6	11 939.5
2nd quarter	12 181.4	8 186.3	2 259.5	1 440.2	743.1	76.2	-608.0	1 172.3	1 780.3	2 343.6	886.7	1 456.8	12 105.2
3rd quarter	12 367.7	8 312.7	2 311.3	1 485.6	763.4	62.3	-638.0	1 186.0	1 824.0	2 381.8	906.9	1 474.9	12 305.5
4th quarter	12 562.2	8 464.3	2 380.8	1 526.5	786.2	68.0	-684.0	1 226.4	1 910.5	2 401.2	903.3	1 497.9	12 494.1
2005													
1st quarter	12 813.7	8 573.1	2 475.2	1 560.5	815.1	99.5	-676.8	1 268.2	1 945.0	2 442.2	931.2	1 511.0	12 714.2
2nd quarter	12 974.1	8 723.9	2 469.5	1 595.2	843.7	30.6	-689.1	1 300.1	1 989.2	2 469.7	938.2	1 531.5	12 943.5
3rd quarter	13 205.4	8 888.1	2 527.2	1 633.8	875.5	17.9	-731.4	1 310.9	2 042.3	2 521.6	963.1	1 558.4	13 187.5
4th quarter	13 381.6	8 991.3	2 636.5	1 656.4	889.9	90.2	-787.5	1 356.4	2 143.9	2 541.3	952.8	1 588.5	13 291.4
2006													
1st quarter	13 648.9	9 134.3	2 699.7	1 729.4	895.9	74.4	-777.2	1 417.2	2 194.4	2 592.2	995.3	1 596.9	13 574.5
2nd quarter	13 799.8	9 253.7	2 697.0	1 761.0	858.7	77.3	-781.6	1 463.4	2 245.0	2 630.7	998.7	1 631.9	13 722.5
3rd quarter	13 908.5	9 374.3	2 684.4	1 793.6	813.7	77.1	-805.6	1 480.1	2 285.7	2 655.4	1 000.4	1 655.0	13 831.4
4th quarter	14 066.4	9 453.6	2 641.6	1 821.2	781.3	39.1	-719.4	1 544.5	2 263.9	2 690.6	1 013.5	1 677.0	14 027.3

Table 1-1B. Gross Domestic Product: Historical Data—*Continued*

(Billions of dollars, quarterly data are at seasonally adjusted annual rates.)

NIPA Tables 1.1.5, 1.2.5

Year and quarter	Gross domestic product	Personal consump-tion expen-ditures	Gross private domestic investment				Exports and imports of goods and services			Government consumption expenditures and gross investment			Addendum: Final sales of domestic product
			Total	Fixed investment		Change in private inventories	Net exports	Exports	Imports	Total	Federal	State and local	
				Nonresi-dential	Residential								
2007													
1st quarter	14 233.2	9 591.9	2 634.2	1 864.7	749.3	20.2	-728.5	1 580.5	2 308.9	2 735.6	1 018.3	1 717.3	14 213.1
2nd quarter	14 422.3	9 700.9	2 671.9	1 907.5	717.3	47.1	-733.0	1 625.1	2 358.0	2 782.5	1 040.8	1 741.7	14 375.2
3rd quarter	14 569.7	9 799.2	2 658.2	1 937.9	671.7	48.6	-712.1	1 687.5	2 399.6	2 824.3	1 063.9	1 760.5	14 521.0
4th quarter	14 685.3	9 910.0	2 610.6	1 972.3	616.4	21.9	-700.6	1 765.4	2 466.0	2 865.3	1 076.1	1 789.1	14 663.4
2008													
1st quarter	14 668.4	9 974.4	2 527.0	1 981.6	565.5	-20.1	-756.8	1 814.6	2 571.4	2 923.8	1 110.7	1 813.1	14 688.6
2nd quarter	14 813.0	10 095.8	2 493.3	1 978.7	538.4	-23.9	-759.4	1 920.5	2 679.9	2 983.4	1 140.5	1 842.9	14 836.9
3rd quarter	14 843.0	10 124.9	2 435.9	1 947.3	507.4	-18.8	-773.6	1 923.6	2 697.2	3 055.9	1 180.0	1 875.9	14 861.8
4th quarter	14 549.9	9 859.6	2 243.1	1 856.2	452.1	-65.1	-602.4	1 709.1	2 311.6	3 049.7	1 191.2	1 858.5	14 615.1
2009													
1st quarter	14 383.9	9 770.2	1 972.1	1 712.3	405.5	-145.6	-393.9	1 519.5	1 913.4	3 035.4	1 182.2	1 853.1	14 529.5
2nd quarter	14 340.4	9 769.8	1 825.9	1 637.5	376.3	-187.9	-341.7	1 522.7	1 864.5	3 086.5	1 214.6	1 871.9	14 528.3
3rd quarter	14 384.1	9 890.8	1 786.4	1 600.3	392.0	-205.9	-405.6	1 596.4	2 002.0	3 112.5	1 233.2	1 879.3	14 590.1
4th quarter	14 566.5	9 957.1	1 928.0	1 583.6	395.2	-50.8	-440.6	1 712.3	2 152.9	3 122.0	1 240.7	1 881.3	14 617.3
2010													
1st quarter	14 681.1	10 044.5	1 989.5	1 594.4	383.1	12.1	-488.7	1 753.2	2 241.9	3 135.7	1 269.2	1 866.5	14 669.0
2nd quarter	14 888.6	10 137.7	2 092.7	1 641.8	400.8	50.1	-523.2	1 814.0	2 337.3	3 181.5	1 304.6	1 876.9	14 838.5
3rd quarter	15 057.7	10 233.4	2 164.6	1 677.4	365.6	121.5	-535.0	1 869.8	2 404.9	3 194.7	1 321.6	1 873.1	14 936.1
4th quarter	15 230.2	10 393.2	2 156.5	1 719.3	374.7	62.4	-503.7	1 972.2	2 475.9	3 184.2	1 320.1	1 864.2	15 167.8
2011													
1st quarter	15 238.4	10 523.5	2 123.5	1 722.4	374.8	26.3	-562.5	2 033.3	2 595.8	3 153.8	1 298.1	1 855.8	15 212.1
2nd quarter	15 460.9	10 651.4	2 212.7	1 768.5	381.1	63.0	-586.9	2 108.3	2 695.3	3 183.8	1 314.9	1 869.0	15 397.9
3rd quarter	15 587.1	10 754.5	2 228.2	1 854.5	388.6	-14.9	-572.4	2 142.9	2 715.3	3 176.8	1 305.9	1 870.9	15 602.0
4th quarter	15 785.3	10 827.9	2 395.2	1 902.9	399.6	92.6	-598.1	2 141.0	2 739.1	3 160.4	1 294.9	1 865.5	15 692.7
2012													
1st quarter	15 973.9	10 956.2	2 460.8	1 971.5	423.8	65.4	-614.7	2 169.6	2 784.3	3 171.6	1 300.5	1 871.0	15 908.4
2nd quarter	16 121.9	11 008.3	2 534.8	2 016.2	429.4	89.3	-580.9	2 199.8	2 780.7	3 159.6	1 293.7	1 865.9	16 032.6
3rd quarter	16 227.9	11 073.6	2 529.9	2 011.7	444.1	74.1	-535.2	2 209.4	2 744.5	3 159.6	1 297.0	1 862.6	16 153.9
4th quarter	16 297.3	11 164.3	2 521.3	2 031.2	471.7	18.4	-531.8	2 214.0	2 745.8	3 143.5	1 278.9	1 864.6	16 278.9
2013													
1st quarter	16 440.7	11 271.8	2 578.3	2 052.1	489.6	36.5	-529.2	2 226.6	2 755.8	3 119.8	1 250.4	1 869.4	16 404.2
2nd quarter	16 526.8	11 322.8	2 620.4	2 064.6	507.1	48.7	-527.8	2 237.6	2 765.4	3 111.4	1 234.2	1 877.2	16 478.1
3rd quarter	16 727.5	11 417.7	2 711.5	2 085.9	520.0	105.6	-512.4	2 264.3	2 776.7	3 110.7	1 220.4	1 890.3	16 621.9
4th quarter	16 957.6	11 556.9	2 749.9	2 134.5	519.0	96.4	-464.3	2 324.5	2 788.8	3 115.1	1 217.6	1 897.5	16 861.2
2014													
1st quarter	16 984.3	11 640.3	2 751.1	2 181.9	526.4	42.7	-529.4	2 301.5	2 830.8	3 122.3	1 214.8	1 907.5	16 941.6
2nd quarter	17 270.0	11 813.0	2 841.6	2 211.7	540.9	88.9	-530.9	2 356.2	2 887.0	3 146.3	1 216.9	1 929.4	17 181.0
3rd quarter	17 522.1	11 949.1	2 910.2	2 267.0	554.8	88.3	-514.6	2 360.6	2 875.2	3 177.4	1 233.1	1 944.3	17 433.8
4th quarter	17 615.9	12 061.4	2 937.2	2 274.1	574.6	88.5	-545.2	2 349.5	2 894.6	3 162.5	1 214.7	1 947.8	17 527.4

Table 1-2A. Real Gross Domestic Product: Recent Data

(Billions of chained [2009] dollars, quarterly data are at seasonally adjusted annual rates.)   **NIPA Tables 1.1.6, 1.2.6**

Year and quarter	Gross domestic product	Personal consumption expenditures	Gross private domestic investment — Total	Fixed investment — Nonresidential	Fixed investment — Residential	Change in private inventories	Net exports	Exports	Imports	Government — Total	Government — Federal	Government — State and local	Residual	Addendum: final sales of domestic product
1950	2 184.0	1 360.5	293.7	. . .	. . .	. . .	. . .	58.4	70.5	569.6	. . .	. . .	-27.7	2 167.1
1951	2 360.0	1 381.7	294.5	. . .	. . .	. . .	. . .	71.5	73.3	778.9	. . .	. . .	-93.3	2 328.5
1952	2 456.1	1 425.3	270.4	. . .	. . .	. . .	. . .	68.4	79.7	931.7	. . .	. . .	-160.0	2 457.5
1953	2 571.4	1 493.3	285.6	. . .	. . .	. . .	. . .	63.9	87.2	994.8	. . .	. . .	-179.0	2 580.5
1954	2 556.9	1 524.7	274.4	. . .	. . .	. . .	. . .	66.9	82.9	931.1	. . .	. . .	-157.3	2 588.9
1955	2 739.0	1 637.3	337.7	. . .	. . .	. . .	. . .	74.1	92.9	901.0	. . .	. . .	-118.2	2 733.9
1956	2 797.4	1 685.1	336.8	. . .	. . .	. . .	. . .	86.3	100.4	903.2	. . .	. . .	-113.6	2 800.5
1957	2 856.3	1 726.8	324.2	. . .	. . .	. . .	. . .	93.9	104.7	944.8	. . .	. . .	-128.7	2 874.7
1958	2 835.3	1 741.7	300.6	. . .	. . .	. . .	. . .	81.2	109.6	976.7	. . .	. . .	-155.3	2 858.6
1959	3 031.0	1 840.5	358.4	. . .	. . .	. . .	. . .	89.5	121.2	1 000.9	. . .	. . .	-137.1	3 031.9
1960	3 108.7	1 891.0	359.7	. . .	. . .	. . .	. . .	105.1	122.8	1 007.0	. . .	. . .	-131.3	3 114.1
1961	3 188.1	1 929.9	360.9	. . .	. . .	. . .	. . .	105.6	122.0	1 060.6	. . .	. . .	-146.9	3 195.7
1962	3 383.1	2 025.4	403.8	. . .	. . .	. . .	. . .	111.0	135.8	1 129.5	. . .	. . .	-150.8	3 374.4
1963	3 530.4	2 108.8	431.2	. . .	. . .	. . .	. . .	118.9	139.5	1 157.1	. . .	. . .	-146.1	3 525.3
1964	3 734.0	2 234.4	465.2	. . .	. . .	. . .	. . .	132.9	146.9	1 185.9	. . .	. . .	-137.5	3 734.8
1965	3 976.7	2 376.0	529.6	. . .	. . .	. . .	. . .	136.6	162.5	1 224.2	. . .	. . .	-127.2	3 955.2
1966	4 238.9	2 510.6	577.1	. . .	. . .	. . .	. . .	146.0	186.7	1 331.0	. . .	. . .	-139.1	4 196.9
1967	4 355.2	2 585.6	556.9	. . .	. . .	. . .	. . .	149.4	200.3	1 436.4	. . .	. . .	-172.8	4 334.1
1968	4 569.0	2 734.0	590.2	. . .	. . .	. . .	. . .	161.2	230.1	1 485.7	. . .	. . .	-172.0	4 553.4
1969	4 712.5	2 836.2	623.1	. . .	. . .	. . .	. . .	169.0	243.2	1 488.0	. . .	. . .	-160.6	4 697.7
1970	4 722.0	2 903.0	585.2	. . .	. . .	. . .	. . .	187.0	253.6	1 457.7	. . .	. . .	-157.3	4 740.5
1971	4 877.6	3 013.8	645.5	. . .	. . .	. . .	. . .	190.3	267.1	1 431.0	. . .	. . .	-135.9	4 870.6
1972	5 134.3	3 198.7	718.2	. . .	. . .	. . .	. . .	205.1	297.2	1 424.2	. . .	. . .	-114.7	5 126.0
1973	5 424.1	3 357.2	796.8	. . .	. . .	. . .	. . .	243.8	311.0	1 419.6	. . .	. . .	-82.3	5 392.4
1974	5 396.0	3 329.5	744.0	. . .	. . .	. . .	. . .	263.0	303.9	1 451.8	. . .	. . .	-88.4	5 378.4
1975	5 385.4	3 405.1	623.5	. . .	. . .	. . .	. . .	261.4	270.1	1 483.8	. . .	. . .	-118.3	5 434.6
1976	5 675.4	3 595.0	742.5	. . .	. . .	. . .	. . .	272.8	323.0	1 491.6	. . .	. . .	-103.5	5 651.9
1977	5 937.0	3 746.5	848.4	. . .	. . .	. . .	. . .	279.4	358.3	1 509.2	. . .	. . .	-88.2	5 900.9
1978	6 267.2	3 911.2	946.6	. . .	. . .	. . .	. . .	308.8	389.3	1 553.7	. . .	. . .	-63.8	6 225.5
1979	6 466.2	4 004.1	979.8	. . .	. . .	. . .	. . .	339.4	395.8	1 582.6	. . .	. . .	-43.9	6 450.3
1980	6 450.4	3 991.5	881.2	. . .	. . .	. . .	. . .	376.0	369.5	1 612.5	. . .	. . .	-41.3	6 492.1
1981	6 617.7	4 050.8	958.7	. . .	. . .	. . .	. . .	380.6	379.3	1 628.0	. . .	. . .	-21.1	6 587.0
1982	6 491.3	4 108.4	833.7	. . .	. . .	. . .	. . .	351.5	374.5	1 658.0	. . .	. . .	-85.8	6 546.7
1983	6 792.0	4 342.6	911.5	. . .	. . .	. . .	. . .	342.5	421.7	1 721.6	. . .	. . .	-104.5	6 830.6
1984	7 285.0	4 571.6	1 160.3	. . .	. . .	. . .	. . .	370.4	524.4	1 783.2	. . .	. . .	-76.1	7 196.3
1985	7 593.8	4 811.9	1 159.5	. . .	. . .	. . .	. . .	382.8	558.4	1 904.0	. . .	. . .	-106.0	7 581.7
1986	7 860.5	5 014.0	1 161.3	. . .	. . .	. . .	. . .	412.2	606.1	2 007.7	. . .	. . .	-128.6	7 872.6
1987	8 132.6	5 183.6	1 194.4	. . .	. . .	. . .	. . .	457.1	642.0	2 066.9	. . .	. . .	-127.4	8 113.1
1988	8 474.5	5 400.5	1 223.8	. . .	. . .	. . .	. . .	531.2	667.2	2 094.8	. . .	. . .	-108.6	8 466.9
1989	8 786.4	5 558.1	1 273.4	. . .	. . .	. . .	. . .	592.7	696.6	2 155.1	. . .	. . .	-96.3	8 765.5
1990	8 955.0	5 672.6	1 240.6	. . .	. . .	. . .	. . .	645.0	721.5	2 224.3	. . .	. . .	-106.0	8 952.7
1991	8 948.4	5 685.6	1 158.8	. . .	. . .	. . .	. . .	687.6	720.4	2 250.9	. . .	. . .	-114.1	8 968.6
1992	9 266.6	5 896.5	1 243.7	. . .	. . .	. . .	. . .	735.3	771.0	2 262.1	. . .	. . .	-100.0	9 262.5
1993	9 521.0	6 101.4	1 343.1	. . .	. . .	. . .	. . .	759.4	837.6	2 243.3	. . .	. . .	-88.6	9 511.0
1994	9 905.4	6 338.0	1 502.3	. . .	. . .	. . .	. . .	826.5	937.5	2 245.5	. . .	. . .	-69.4	9 837.7
1995	10 174.8	6 527.6	1 550.8	. . .	. . .	. . .	. . .	911.5	1 012.5	2 257.5	. . .	. . .	-60.1	10 151.3
1996	10 561.0	6 755.6	1 686.7	. . .	. . .	. . .	. . .	986.0	1 100.6	2 279.2	. . .	. . .	-45.9	10 536.6
1997	11 034.9	7 009.9	1 879.0	. . .	. . .	. . .	. . .	1 103.5	1 248.8	2 322.0	. . .	. . .	-30.7	10 956.0
1998	11 525.9	7 384.7	2 058.3	. . .	. . .	. . .	. . .	1 129.3	1 394.8	2 370.5	. . .	. . .	-22.1	11 452.3
1999	12 065.9	7 775.9	2 231.4	1 510.1	633.8	75.5	-377.1	1 159.1	1 536.2	2 451.7	815.3	1 643.6	-112.4	11 994.9
2000	12 559.7	8 170.7	2 375.5	1 647.7	637.9	66.2	-477.8	1 258.4	1 736.2	2 498.2	817.7	1 689.1	-83.6	12 494.9
2001	12 682.2	8 382.6	2 231.4	1 608.4	643.7	-46.2	-502.1	1 184.9	1 687.0	2 592.4	849.8	1 751.5	-90.9	12 729.6
2002	12 908.8	8 598.8	2 218.2	1 498.0	682.7	22.5	-584.3	1 164.5	1 748.8	2 705.8	910.8	1 802.4	-70.5	12 888.9
2003	13 271.1	8 867.6	2 308.7	1 526.1	744.5	22.6	-641.9	1 185.0	1 826.9	2 764.3	973.0	1 795.3	-45.5	13 249.0
2004	13 773.5	9 208.2	2 511.3	1 605.4	818.9	71.4	-734.8	1 300.6	2 035.3	2 802.2	1 017.1	1 792.8	-19.6	13 702.2
2005	14 234.2	9 531.8	2 672.6	1 717.4	872.6	64.3	-782.3	1 381.9	2 164.2	2 826.2	1 034.8	1 792.3	-2.2	14 168.8
2006	14 613.8	9 821.7	2 730.0	1 839.6	806.6	71.6	-794.3	1 506.8	2 301.0	2 869.3	1 060.9	1 808.8	-3.8	14 542.3
2007	14 873.7	10 041.6	2 644.1	1 948.4	654.8	35.5	-712.6	1 646.4	2 359.0	2 914.4	1 078.7	1 836.1	-9.7	14 836.2
2008	14 830.4	10 007.2	2 396.0	1 934.4	497.7	-33.7	-557.8	1 740.8	2 298.6	2 994.8	1 152.3	1 842.4	-13.6	14 865.7
2009	14 418.7	9 847.0	1 878.1	1 633.4	392.2	-147.6	-395.4	1 587.7	1 983.2	3 089.1	1 217.7	1 871.4	0.2	14 566.3
2010	14 783.8	10 036.3	2 120.4	1 673.8	382.4	58.2	-458.8	1 776.6	2 235.4	3 091.4	1 270.7	1 820.8	-1.1	14 722.2
2011	15 020.6	10 263.5	2 230.4	1 802.3	384.5	37.6	-459.4	1 898.3	2 357.7	2 997.4	1 236.4	1 761.0	-10.8	14 979.0
2012	15 354.6	10 413.2	2 465.7	1 964.1	436.5	54.7	-447.1	1 963.2	2 410.2	2 941.6	1 213.5	1 728.1	-19.7	15 292.3
2013	15 583.3	10 590.4	2 577.3	2 023.7	478.0	61.4	-417.5	2 018.1	2 435.6	2 854.9	1 144.1	1 710.2	-23.9	15 511.4
2014	15 961.7	10 875.7	2 717.2	2 148.3	486.4	68.0	-442.5	2 086.4	2 528.9	2 838.3	1 116.3	1 720.8	-35.1	15 881.7
2012														
1st quarter	15 291.0	10 379.0	2 429.6	1 938.1	422.5	56.0	-462.7	1 942.6	2 405.3	2 963.7	1 223.9	1 739.8	-15.1	15 225.0
2nd quarter	15 362.4	10 396.6	2 489.1	1 973.7	426.3	76.6	-452.7	1 964.4	2 417.0	2 949.4	1 214.8	1 734.5	-17.4	15 276.9
3rd quarter	15 380.8	10 424.1	2 482.0	1 963.4	437.3	70.6	-446.8	1 974.1	2 420.9	2 940.9	1 216.2	1 724.7	-19.9	15 302.7
4th quarter	15 384.3	10 453.2	2 462.2	1 981.4	459.8	15.5	-426.0	1 971.7	2 397.8	2 912.3	1 199.0	1 713.3	-26.5	15 364.6
2013														
1st quarter	15 457.2	10 518.2	2 505.1	2 000.7	469.9	25.2	-425.9	1 976.6	2 402.6	2 878.8	1 170.1	1 708.5	-26.5	15 424.7
2nd quarter	15 500.2	10 554.3	2 537.2	2 005.7	480.3	39.6	-434.2	2 000.5	2 434.7	2 864.1	1 153.2	1 710.4	-25.9	15 451.9
3rd quarter	15 614.4	10 598.9	2 619.7	2 023.1	486.0	93.6	-428.3	2 021.1	2 449.4	2 848.1	1 136.3	1 711.1	-22.5	15 508.9
4th quarter	15 761.5	10 690.4	2 647.1	2 065.5	475.9	87.2	-381.5	2 074.2	2 455.7	2 828.5	1 116.9	1 710.6	-20.6	15 660.0
2014														
1st quarter	15 724.9	10 724.7	2 630.5	2 106.9	472.6	36.9	-434.0	2 038.7	2 472.7	2 828.4	1 117.8	1 709.6	-27.2	15 675.7
2nd quarter	15 901.5	10 826.3	2 709.5	2 129.8	484.4	77.1	-443.3	2 086.8	2 530.1	2 836.5	1 114.5	1 720.8	-31.5	15 809.7
3rd quarter	16 068.8	10 918.6	2 758.1	2 176.3	488.5	79.9	-429.1	2 096.0	2 525.1	2 849.2	1 124.7	1 723.5	-40.3	15 978.6
4th quarter	16 151.4	11 033.3	2 772.5	2 180.0	500.2	78.2	-463.6	2 123.9	2 587.5	2 839.0	1 108.3	1 729.3	-41.5	16 062.9

Note: Chained (2009) dollar series are calculated as the product of the chain-type quantity index and the 2009 current-dollar value of the corresponding series, divided by 100. Because the formula for the chain-type quantity indexes uses weights from more than one period, the corresponding chained-dollar estimates are usually not additive. The residual column is the difference between the total and the sum of the most detailed components shown in the Bureau of Economic Analysis (BEA) published data.

. . . = Not available.

Table 1-2B. Real Gross Domestic Product: Historical Data

(Billions of chained [2009] dollars, quarterly data are at seasonally adjusted annual rates.)   **NIPA Tables 1.1.6, 1.2.6**

Year and quarter	Gross domestic product	Personal consumption expenditures	Gross private domestic investment Total	Fixed investment Nonresidential	Fixed investment Residential	Change in private inventories	Net exports	Exports	Imports	Govt Total	Federal	State and local	Residual	Addendum: Final sales of domestic product
1929	1 056.6	781.0	123.6	...	...	...	...	40.5	52.7	165.7	...	...	-1.5	1 067.5
1930	966.7	739.1	84.2	...	...	...	...	33.5	45.8	182.5	...	...	-26.8	995.4
1931	904.8	716.1	54.7	...	...	...	...	27.8	40.0	190.1	...	...	-43.9	937.7
1932	788.2	651.9	20.2	...	...	...	...	21.8	33.1	184.2	...	...	-56.8	832.3
1933	778.3	637.6	27.3	...	...	...	...	21.9	34.5	178.0	...	...	-52.0	807.4
1934	862.2	683.1	45.2	...	...	...	...	24.4	35.3	199.7	...	...	-54.9	883.7
1935	939.0	724.6	78.6	...	...	...	...	25.7	46.2	206.0	...	...	-49.7	939.0
1936	1 060.5	798.3	99.3	...	...	...	...	27.0	45.7	239.1	...	...	-57.5	1 062.1
1937	1 114.6	827.8	122.3	...	...	...	...	34.0	51.4	229.4	...	...	-47.5	1 106.3
1938	1 077.7	814.6	84.2	...	...	...	...	33.6	40.0	246.8	...	...	-61.5	1 091.6
1939	1 163.6	860.1	105.6	...	...	...	...	35.5	42.0	268.3	...	...	-63.9	1 171.4
1940	1 266.1	904.7	143.8	...	...	...	...	40.4	43.0	277.9	...	...	-57.7	1 251.6
1941	1 490.3	968.6	176.0	...	...	...	...	41.4	52.9	467.1	...	...	-109.9	1 460.8
1942	1 771.8	945.7	98.0	...	...	...	...	27.3	48.0	1 084.2	...	...	-335.4	1 771.1
1943	2 073.7	972.0	61.1	...	...	...	...	23.0	60.5	1 626.0	...	...	-547.9	2 100.6
1944	2 239.4	999.7	73.0	...	...	...	...	24.8	63.3	1 826.3	...	...	-621.1	2 268.9
1945	2 217.8	1 061.5	93.9	...	...	...	...	34.7	67.3	1 604.5	...	...	-509.5	2 253.7
1946	1 960.9	1 193.6	225.0	...	...	...	...	74.9	55.8	566.8	...	...	-43.6	1 932.7
1947	1 939.4	1 216.4	216.5	...	...	...	...	85.4	53.0	482.5	...	...	-8.4	1 967.7
1948	2 020.0	1 243.9	272.9	...	...	...	...	67.3	61.8	510.6	...	...	-12.9	2 001.2
1949	2 008.9	1 278.5	210.9	...	...	...	...	66.7	59.6	566.1	...	...	-53.7	2 046.9
1947														
1st quarter	1 934.5	1 199.4	222.7	...	...	...	...	91.0	54.7	478.7	...	...	-2.6	1 949.8
2nd quarter ...	1 932.3	1 219.3	205.6	...	...	...	...	89.8	55.7	482.8	...	...	-9.5	1 962.9
3rd quarter ...	1 930.3	1 223.3	199.6	...	...	...	...	85.3	49.4	485.9	...	...	-14.4	1 977.9
4th quarter	1 960.7	1 223.6	238.2	...	...	...	...	75.6	52.1	482.5	...	...	-7.1	1 980.4
1948														
1st quarter ...	1 989.5	1 229.8	262.6	...	...	...	...	72.2	58.8	488.6	...	...	-4.9	1 987.1
2nd quarter ...	2 021.9	1 244.1	278.9	...	...	...	...	65.4	61.1	505.0	...	...	-10.4	1 997.8
3rd quarter ...	2 033.2	1 245.9	281.7	...	...	...	...	67.0	64.3	515.0	...	...	-12.1	2 001.8
4th quarter	2 035.3	1 255.8	268.3	...	...	...	...	64.6	63.2	533.8	...	...	-24.0	2 017.8
1949														
1st quarter	2 007.5	1 257.9	228.0	...	...	...	...	72.3	61.3	548.6	...	...	-38.0	2 025.8
2nd quarter ...	2 000.8	1 277.1	197.7	...	...	...	...	71.7	60.4	572.5	...	...	-57.8	2 051.9
3rd quarter ...	2 022.8	1 280.0	214.1	...	...	...	...	65.7	58.0	577.6	...	...	-56.6	2 051.0
4th quarter	2 004.7	1 298.8	203.6	...	...	...	...	56.9	58.8	565.8	...	...	-61.6	2 058.8
1950														
1st quarter	2 084.6	1 320.4	251.9	...	...	...	...	56.0	60.5	557.1	...	...	-40.3	2 091.8
2nd quarter ...	2 147.6	1 342.1	278.9	...	...	...	...	56.6	63.8	566.6	...	...	-32.8	2 147.7
3rd quarter ...	2 230.4	1 411.0	302.9	...	...	...	...	58.1	78.8	557.3	...	...	-20.1	2 224.0
4th quarter	2 273.4	1 368.4	341.3	...	...	...	...	62.8	78.9	597.2	...	...	-17.4	2 204.9
1951														
1st quarter	2 304.5	1 401.5	306.6	...	...	...	...	66.0	78.9	660.9	...	...	-51.5	2 271.6
2nd quarter ...	2 344.5	1 361.9	313.6	...	...	...	...	72.4	76.3	748.8	...	...	-75.9	2 284.7
3rd quarter ...	2 392.8	1 377.7	290.5	...	...	...	...	74.2	69.8	830.9	...	...	-110.7	2 361.2
4th quarter	2 398.1	1 385.8	267.3	...	...	...	...	73.5	68.0	874.8	...	...	-135.3	2 396.7
1952														
1st quarter	2 423.5	1 388.9	274.3	...	...	...	...	77.4	75.9	900.5	...	...	-141.7	2 417.7
2nd quarter ...	2 428.5	1 416.1	253.6	...	...	...	...	68.9	75.5	930.7	...	...	-165.3	2 458.4
3rd quarter ...	2 446.1	1 423.0	267.2	...	...	...	...	63.5	80.1	940.0	...	...	-167.5	2 436.7
4th quarter	2 526.4	1 473.3	286.5	...	...	...	...	63.9	87.3	955.6	...	...	-165.6	2 517.0
1953														
1st quarter	2 573.4	1 490.8	292.6	...	...	...	...	62.8	85.2	985.5	...	...	-173.1	2 570.9
2nd quarter ...	2 593.5	1 499.8	294.3	...	...	...	...	63.2	89.6	1 005.9	...	...	-180.1	2 591.8
3rd quarter ...	2 578.9	1 496.3	288.1	...	...	...	...	65.8	89.2	995.2	...	...	-177.3	2 586.5
4th quarter	2 539.8	1 486.4	267.3	...	...	...	...	63.6	84.9	992.4	...	...	-185.0	2 572.9
1954														
1st quarter	2 528.0	1 491.8	265.4	...	...	...	...	60.7	80.0	967.3	...	...	-177.2	2 558.3
2nd quarter ...	2 530.7	1 511.3	264.8	...	...	...	...	69.5	87.1	934.3	...	...	-162.1	2 567.9
3rd quarter ...	2 559.4	1 531.8	277.6	...	...	...	...	67.2	81.9	914.3	...	...	-149.6	2 593.7
4th quarter	2 609.3	1 564.0	289.7	...	...	...	...	70.3	82.7	908.6	...	...	-140.6	2 635.7
1955														
1st quarter	2 683.8	1 599.1	318.7	...	...	...	...	73.0	87.5	909.2	...	...	-128.7	2 686.1
2nd quarter ...	2 727.5	1 629.7	337.9	...	...	...	...	71.2	92.5	900.5	...	...	-119.3	2 720.9
3rd quarter ...	2 764.1	1 649.8	343.1	...	...	...	...	75.9	94.1	906.1	...	...	-116.7	2 760.7
4th quarter	2 780.8	1 670.5	351.1	...	...	...	...	76.3	97.5	888.3	...	...	-107.9	2 768.1
1956														
1st quarter	2 770.0	1 673.2	341.1	...	...	...	...	79.9	101.6	888.1	...	...	-110.7	2 763.7
2nd quarter ...	2 792.9	1 678.8	338.4	...	...	...	...	85.3	101.0	905.9	...	...	-114.5	2 795.2
3rd quarter ...	2 790.6	1 682.6	335.4	...	...	...	...	88.1	101.9	898.3	...	...	-111.9	2 797.4
4th quarter	2 836.2	1 705.8	332.2	...	...	...	...	92.1	97.2	920.7	...	...	-117.4	2 845.7
1957														
1st quarter	2 854.5	1 717.5	327.1	...	...	...	...	98.1	105.0	940.7	...	...	-123.9	2 871.3
2nd quarter ...	2 848.2	1 720.5	326.8	...	...	...	...	95.2	105.8	935.7	...	...	-124.2	2 861.4
3rd quarter ...	2 875.9	1 734.1	334.2	...	...	...	...	92.5	103.8	943.5	...	...	-124.6	2 883.4
4th quarter	2 846.4	1 734.9	308.5	...	...	...	...	89.7	104.1	959.3	...	...	-141.9	2 882.6

Note: Chained (2009) dollar series are calculated as the product of the chain-type quantity index and the 2009 current-dollar value of the corresponding series, divided by 100. Because the formula for the chain-type quantity indexes uses weights from more than one period, the corresponding chained-dollar estimates are usually not additive. The residual column is the difference between the total and the sum of the most detailed components shown in the Bureau of Economic Analysis (BEA) published data.

. . . = Not available.

Table 1-2B. Real Gross Domestic Product: Historical Data—*Continued*

(Billions of chained [2009] dollars, quarterly data are at seasonally adjusted annual rates.)   NIPA Tables 1.1.6, 1.2.6

| Year and quarter | Gross domestic product | Personal consump-tion expen-ditures | Gross private domestic investment | | | | Exports and imports of goods and services | | | Government consumption expenditures and gross investment | | | Residual | Adden-dum: Final sales of domestic product |
| | | | Total | Fixed investment | | Change in private inventories | Net exports | Exports | Imports | Total | Federal | State and local | | |
				Nonresi-dential	Residential									
1958														
1st quarter	2 772.7	1 711.1	287.7	. . .	. . .	. . .	. . .	80.8	105.7	950.8	. . .	. . .	-152.0	2 812.0
2nd quarter ...	2 790.9	1 725.1	281.9	. . .	. . .	. . .	. . .	81.2	110.2	974.7	. . .	. . .	-161.8	2 828.0
3rd quarter	2 855.5	1 753.5	303.5	. . .	. . .	. . .	. . .	81.5	108.5	980.6	. . .	. . .	-155.1	2 869.1
4th quarter	2 922.3	1 777.1	329.4	. . .	. . .	. . .	. . .	81.2	114.2	1 000.7	. . .	. . .	-151.9	2 925.1
1959														
1st quarter	2 976.6	1 809.4	347.4	. . .	. . .	. . .	. . .	86.6	117.1	989.4	. . .	. . .	-139.1	2 980.6
2nd quarter ...	3 049.0	1 837.3	374.4	. . .	. . .	. . .	. . .	89.5	122.8	1 001.7	. . .	. . .	-131.1	3 029.9
3rd quarter	3 043.1	1 856.5	350.2	. . .	. . .	. . .	. . .	92.3	124.0	1 010.3	. . .	. . .	-142.2	3 063.3
4th quarter	3 055.1	1 858.6	361.6	. . .	. . .	. . .	. . .	89.8	120.8	1 002.1	. . .	. . .	-136.2	3 053.8
1960														
1st quarter	3 123.2	1 876.3	398.0	. . .	. . .	. . .	. . .	101.1	125.4	985.2	. . .	. . .	-112.0	3 087.7
2nd quarter ...	3 111.3	1 900.1	360.9	. . .	. . .	. . .	. . .	107.5	126.3	995.8	. . .	. . .	-126.7	3 118.6
3rd quarter	3 119.1	1 892.5	360.0	. . .	. . .	. . .	. . .	104.8	122.6	1 020.0	. . .	. . .	-135.6	3 117.2
4th quarter	3 081.3	1 894.9	320.1	. . .	. . .	. . .	. . .	106.9	116.8	1 026.8	. . .	. . .	-150.6	3 132.9
1961														
1st quarter	3 102.3	1 894.4	328.4	. . .	. . .	. . .	. . .	106.2	116.3	1 042.0	. . .	. . .	-152.4	3 138.6
2nd quarter ...	3 159.9	1 922.6	351.4	. . .	. . .	. . .	. . .	104.7	117.7	1 044.4	. . .	. . .	-145.5	3 172.7
3rd quarter	3 212.6	1 932.0	378.7	. . .	. . .	. . .	. . .	104.2	125.5	1 066.4	. . .	. . .	-143.2	3 199.7
4th quarter	3 277.7	1 970.7	385.0	. . .	. . .	. . .	. . .	107.4	128.4	1 089.7	. . .	. . .	-146.7	3 271.9
1962														
1st quarter	3 336.8	1 991.7	405.7	. . .	. . .	. . .	. . .	107.1	132.4	1 110.7	. . .	. . .	-146.0	3 312.7
2nd quarter ...	3 372.7	2 016.1	402.5	. . .	. . .	. . .	. . .	117.4	135.2	1 116.0	. . .	. . .	-144.1	3 367.5
3rd quarter	3 404.8	2 032.5	409.4	. . .	. . .	. . .	. . .	110.8	137.0	1 141.7	. . .	. . .	-152.6	3 394.8
4th quarter	3 418.0	2 061.3	397.4	. . .	. . .	. . .	. . .	108.4	138.6	1 149.6	. . .	. . .	-160.1	3 422.7
1963														
1st quarter	3 456.1	2 075.2	418.3	. . .	. . .	. . .	. . .	111.0	135.4	1 134.1	. . .	. . .	-147.1	3 439.6
2nd quarter ...	3 501.1	2 095.1	425.0	. . .	. . .	. . .	. . .	124.0	138.6	1 135.1	. . .	. . .	-139.5	3 499.1
3rd quarter	3 569.5	2 123.7	438.0	. . .	. . .	. . .	. . .	117.3	142.1	1 185.4	. . .	. . .	-152.8	3 563.8
4th quarter	3 595.0	2 141.4	443.4	. . .	. . .	. . .	. . .	123.2	141.7	1 173.7	. . .	. . .	-145.0	3 598.8
1964														
1st quarter	3 672.7	2 183.6	460.0	. . .	. . .	. . .	. . .	130.8	141.5	1 177.3	. . .	. . .	-137.5	3 674.7
2nd quarter ...	3 716.4	2 222.0	458.3	. . .	. . .	. . .	. . .	133.0	144.7	1 187.9	. . .	. . .	-140.1	3 719.8
3rd quarter	3 766.9	2 262.8	469.0	. . .	. . .	. . .	. . .	131.9	148.6	1 189.4	. . .	. . .	-137.6	3 766.0
4th quarter	3 780.2	2 269.2	473.5	. . .	. . .	. . .	. . .	135.9	152.6	1 189.0	. . .	. . .	-134.8	3 778.7
1965														
1st quarter	3 873.5	2 319.8	518.6	. . .	. . .	. . .	. . .	121.2	147.1	1 187.7	. . .	. . .	-126.7	3 839.9
2nd quarter ...	3 926.4	2 345.5	520.0	. . .	. . .	. . .	. . .	144.0	164.5	1 202.0	. . .	. . .	-120.6	3 909.2
3rd quarter	4 006.2	2 385.9	538.1	. . .	. . .	. . .	. . .	135.7	165.2	1 241.7	. . .	. . .	-130.0	3 983.0
4th quarter	4 100.6	2 452.9	541.6	. . .	. . .	. . .	. . .	145.5	173.2	1 265.4	. . .	. . .	-131.6	4 088.6
1966														
1st quarter	4 201.9	2 489.1	584.9	. . .	. . .	. . .	. . .	143.0	177.7	1 289.0	. . .	. . .	-126.4	4 158.7
2nd quarter ...	4 219.1	2 495.4	576.2	. . .	. . .	. . .	. . .	149.2	182.1	1 313.4	. . .	. . .	-133.0	4 180.5
3rd quarter	4 249.2	2 523.8	572.0	. . .	. . .	. . .	. . .	143.6	192.3	1 349.1	. . .	. . .	-147.0	4 217.1
4th quarter	4 285.6	2 534.2	575.3	. . .	. . .	. . .	. . .	148.3	194.5	1 372.4	. . .	. . .	-150.1	4 231.3
1967														
1st quarter	4 324.9	2 548.9	561.2	. . .	. . .	. . .	. . .	151.2	197.5	1 429.8	. . .	. . .	-168.7	4 276.7
2nd quarter ...	4 328.7	2 583.7	540.9	. . .	. . .	. . .	. . .	149.8	196.0	1 424.2	. . .	. . .	-173.9	4 323.1
3rd quarter	4 366.1	2 596.9	556.8	. . .	. . .	. . .	. . .	146.2	198.5	1 440.2	. . .	. . .	-175.5	4 348.2
4th quarter	4 401.2	2 612.7	568.8	. . .	. . .	. . .	. . .	150.4	209.0	1 451.4	. . .	. . .	-173.1	4 388.3
1968														
1st quarter	4 490.6	2 674.8	580.2	. . .	. . .	. . .	. . .	154.7	221.3	1 477.2	. . .	. . .	-175.0	4 479.0
2nd quarter ...	4 566.4	2 715.6	602.4	. . .	. . .	. . .	. . .	157.8	224.7	1 485.0	. . .	. . .	-169.7	4 524.8
3rd quarter	4 599.3	2 766.6	586.0	. . .	. . .	. . .	. . .	167.1	238.2	1 489.7	. . .	. . .	-171.9	4 590.2
4th quarter	4 619.8	2 779.1	592.3	. . .	. . .	. . .	. . .	165.0	236.2	1 491.0	. . .	. . .	-171.4	4 619.6
1969														
1st quarter	4 691.6	2 810.2	627.2	. . .	. . .	. . .	. . .	145.2	213.9	1 494.7	. . .	. . .	-171.8	4 667.2
2nd quarter ...	4 706.7	2 828.2	623.5	. . .	. . .	. . .	. . .	177.8	256.1	1 490.0	. . .	. . .	-156.7	4 691.2
3rd quarter	4 736.1	2 841.9	636.2	. . .	. . .	. . .	. . .	173.6	252.8	1 493.5	. . .	. . .	-156.3	4 715.4
4th quarter	4 715.5	2 864.6	605.5	. . .	. . .	. . .	. . .	179.5	250.0	1 473.9	. . .	. . .	-158.0	4 717.0
1970														
1st quarter	4 707.1	2 882.3	587.4	. . .	. . .	. . .	. . .	180.9	249.2	1 466.9	. . .	. . .	-161.2	4 728.1
2nd quarter ...	4 715.4	2 895.6	588.7	. . .	. . .	. . .	. . .	188.9	254.1	1 450.2	. . .	. . .	-153.9	4 719.5
3rd quarter	4 757.2	2 921.1	598.3	. . .	. . .	. . .	. . .	188.3	253.5	1 456.5	. . .	. . .	-153.5	4 761.5
4th quarter	4 708.3	2 913.1	566.5	. . .	. . .	. . .	. . .	190.1	257.5	1 457.2	. . .	. . .	-161.1	4 752.8
1971														
1st quarter	4 834.3	2 968.9	632.5	. . .	. . .	. . .	. . .	190.8	254.4	1 436.1	. . .	. . .	-139.6	4 810.3
2nd quarter ...	4 861.9	2 996.1	650.5	. . .	. . .	. . .	. . .	190.4	273.6	1 432.8	. . .	. . .	-134.3	4 843.6
3rd quarter	4 900.0	3 020.0	658.4	. . .	. . .	. . .	. . .	198.3	279.7	1 432.4	. . .	. . .	-129.4	4 885.2
4th quarter	4 914.3	3 070.2	640.6	. . .	. . .	. . .	. . .	181.7	260.7	1 422.6	. . .	. . .	-140.1	4 943.3
1972														
1st quarter	5 002.4	3 110.8	682.9	. . .	. . .	. . .	. . .	201.4	298.8	1 429.3	. . .	. . .	-123.2	5 012.9
2nd quarter ...	5 118.3	3 170.2	721.6	. . .	. . .	. . .	. . .	195.5	288.2	1 438.0	. . .	. . .	-118.8	5 094.5
3rd quarter	5 165.4	3 219.1	731.9	. . .	. . .	. . .	. . .	207.4	294.2	1 409.3	. . .	. . .	-108.1	5 138.7
4th quarter	5 251.2	3 294.6	736.5	. . .	. . .	. . .	. . .	216.1	307.5	1 420.1	. . .	. . .	-108.6	5 257.8

Note: Chained (2009) dollar series are calculated as the product of the chain-type quantity index and the 2009 current-dollar value of the corresponding series, divided by 100. Because the formula for the chain-type quantity indexes uses weights from more than one period, the corresponding chained-dollar estimates are usually not additive. The residual column is the difference between the total and the sum of the most detailed components shown in the Bureau of Economic Analysis (BEA) published data.

. . . = Not available.

Table 1-2B. Real Gross Domestic Product: Historical Data—*Continued*

(Billions of chained [2009] dollars, quarterly data are at seasonally adjusted annual rates.)

NIPA Tables 1.1.6, 1.2.6

Year and quarter	Gross domestic product	Personal consump-tion expen-ditures	Gross private domestic investment					Exports and imports of goods and services			Government consumption expenditures and gross investment			Residual	Adden-dum: Final sales of domestic product
			Total	Fixed investment		Change in private inventories	Net exports	Exports	Imports	Total	Federal	State and local		
				Nonresi-dential	Residential										
1973															
1st quarter	5 380.5	3 354.8	779.6	. . .	. . .	. . .	. . .	232.0	321.7	1 431.6	. . .	. . .	-95.8	5 368.7
2nd quarter ...	5 441.5	3 353.4	812.9	. . .	. . .	. . .	. . .	243.2	312.4	1 424.5	. . .	. . .	-80.1	5 394.8
3rd quarter ...	5 411.9	3 365.3	783.4	. . .	. . .	. . .	. . .	244.0	303.8	1 406.4	. . .	. . .	-83.4	5 399.9
4th quarter	5 462.4	3 355.5	811.3	. . .	. . .	. . .	. . .	256.0	306.0	1 415.8	. . .	. . .	-70.2	5 406.4
1974															
1st quarter	5 417.0	3 326.2	765.0	. . .	. . .	. . .	. . .	259.2	295.7	1 442.4	. . .	. . .	-80.1	5 401.0
2nd quarter ...	5 431.3	3 337.9	761.9	. . .	. . .	. . .	. . .	271.8	311.3	1 451.6	. . .	. . .	-80.6	5 407.5
3rd quarter ...	5 378.7	3 351.6	722.4	. . .	. . .	. . .	. . .	257.2	305.9	1 453.5	. . .	. . .	-100.1	5 390.8
4th quarter	5 357.2	3 302.5	726.8	. . .	. . .	. . .	. . .	263.9	302.8	1 459.9	. . .	. . .	-93.1	5 314.1
1975															
1st quarter	5 292.4	3 330.1	609.7	. . .	. . .	. . .	. . .	265.8	272.4	1 476.1	. . .	. . .	-116.9	5 352.6
2nd quarter ...	5 333.2	3 385.7	591.6	. . .	. . .	. . .	. . .	258.0	250.6	1 466.2	. . .	. . .	-117.7	5 407.4
3rd quarter ...	5 421.4	3 434.1	637.5	. . .	. . .	. . .	. . .	253.7	271.5	1 489.5	. . .	. . .	-121.9	5 455.7
4th quarter	5 494.4	3 470.5	655.2	. . .	. . .	. . .	. . .	268.0	286.0	1 503.4	. . .	. . .	-116.7	5 522.6
1976															
1st quarter	5 618.5	3 539.9	718.5	. . .	. . .	. . .	. . .	266.2	303.9	1 506.5	. . .	. . .	-108.7	5 599.5
2nd quarter ...	5 661.0	3 572.4	746.9	. . .	. . .	. . .	. . .	268.9	317.1	1 491.4	. . .	. . .	-101.5	5 619.2
3rd quarter ...	5 689.8	3 610.3	749.5	. . .	. . .	. . .	. . .	276.7	330.0	1 483.9	. . .	. . .	-100.6	5 654.8
4th quarter	5 732.5	3 657.5	755.1	. . .	. . .	. . .	. . .	279.5	340.9	1 484.4	. . .	. . .	-103.1	5 734.2
1977															
1st quarter	5 799.2	3 699.3	790.1	. . .	. . .	. . .	. . .	275.0	357.1	1 497.3	. . .	. . .	-105.4	5 788.5
2nd quarter ...	5 913.0	3 719.7	846.8	. . .	. . .	. . .	. . .	282.4	360.3	1 512.0	. . .	. . .	-87.6	5 880.7
3rd quarter ...	6 017.6	3 755.2	889.6	. . .	. . .	. . .	. . .	284.6	355.3	1 515.4	. . .	. . .	-71.9	5 942.6
4th quarter	6 018.2	3 811.8	867.3	. . .	. . .	. . .	. . .	275.5	360.4	1 512.1	. . .	. . .	-88.1	5 991.7
1978															
1st quarter	6 039.2	3 833.8	884.2	. . .	. . .	. . .	. . .	281.9	384.5	1 513.9	. . .	. . .	-90.1	5 999.9
2nd quarter ...	6 274.0	3 915.6	941.6	. . .	. . .	. . .	. . .	311.3	385.8	1 554.1	. . .	. . .	-62.8	6 235.2
3rd quarter ...	6 335.3	3 932.0	969.1	. . .	. . .	. . .	. . .	314.7	390.8	1 566.4	. . .	. . .	-56.1	6 292.4
4th quarter	6 420.3	3 963.5	991.5	. . .	. . .	. . .	. . .	327.2	396.2	1 580.6	. . .	. . .	-46.3	6 374.5
1979															
1st quarter	6 433.0	3 983.6	993.1	. . .	. . .	. . .	. . .	327.5	395.1	1 566.9	. . .	. . .	-43.0	6 396.4
2nd quarter ...	6 440.8	3 981.3	992.2	. . .	. . .	. . .	. . .	328.4	397.2	1 583.0	. . .	. . .	-46.9	6 398.0
3rd quarter ...	6 487.1	4 020.4	975.5	. . .	. . .	. . .	. . .	340.2	391.1	1 585.1	. . .	. . .	-43.0	6 489.4
4th quarter	6 503.9	4 031.2	958.2	. . .	. . .	. . .	. . .	361.6	399.7	1 595.4	. . .	. . .	-42.8	6 517.7
1980															
1st quarter	6 524.9	4 025.0	951.6	. . .	. . .	. . .	. . .	371.7	400.0	1 620.2	. . .	. . .	-43.6	6 530.6
2nd quarter ...	6 392.6	3 934.5	870.7	. . .	. . .	. . .	. . .	378.7	371.0	1 625.9	. . .	. . .	-46.2	6 403.9
3rd quarter ...	6 382.9	3 976.9	813.3	. . .	. . .	. . .	. . .	377.9	344.3	1 601.9	. . .	. . .	-42.8	6 487.1
4th quarter	6 501.2	4 029.6	889.2	. . .	. . .	. . .	. . .	375.6	362.8	1 601.8	. . .	. . .	-32.2	6 546.9
1981															
1st quarter	6 635.7	4 050.8	971.7	. . .	. . .	. . .	. . .	382.7	378.3	1 622.8	. . .	. . .	-14.0	6 581.1
2nd quarter ...	6 587.3	4 050.1	931.3	. . .	. . .	. . .	. . .	384.8	378.9	1 627.9	. . .	. . .	-27.9	6 597.1
3rd quarter ...	6 662.9	4 066.4	983.5	. . .	. . .	. . .	. . .	376.6	374.6	1 621.6	. . .	. . .	-10.6	6 602.2
4th quarter	6 585.1	4 035.9	948.4	. . .	. . .	. . .	. . .	378.4	385.3	1 639.9	. . .	. . .	-32.2	6 567.5
1982															
1st quarter	6 475.0	4 062.6	854.9	. . .	. . .	. . .	. . .	362.0	374.3	1 638.2	. . .	. . .	-68.4	6 544.5
2nd quarter ...	6 510.2	4 077.6	853.8	. . .	. . .	. . .	. . .	364.1	368.2	1 648.9	. . .	. . .	-66.0	6 542.9
3rd quarter ...	6 486.8	4 109.1	845.7	. . .	. . .	. . .	. . .	348.0	385.3	1 659.3	. . .	. . .	-90.0	6 502.1
4th quarter	6 493.1	4 184.1	780.3	. . .	. . .	. . .	. . .	332.1	370.2	1 685.8	. . .	. . .	-119.0	6 597.2
1983															
1st quarter	6 578.2	4 224.8	807.5	. . .	. . .	. . .	. . .	337.4	378.6	1 701.9	. . .	. . .	-114.8	6 671.5
2nd quarter ...	6 728.3	4 308.4	879.1	. . .	. . .	. . .	. . .	338.4	407.7	1 719.1	. . .	. . .	-109.0	6 769.8
3rd quarter ...	6 860.0	4 384.0	934.2	. . .	. . .	. . .	. . .	343.5	439.5	1 747.3	. . .	. . .	-109.5	6 894.7
4th quarter	7 001.5	4 453.1	1 025.1	. . .	. . .	. . .	. . .	350.5	461.1	1 718.0	. . .	. . .	-84.1	6 986.3
1984															
1st quarter	7 140.6	4 490.9	1 124.2	. . .	. . .	. . .	. . .	357.8	498.1	1 738.1	. . .	. . .	-72.3	7 038.8
2nd quarter ...	7 266.0	4 554.9	1 160.7	. . .	. . .	. . .	. . .	366.7	519.0	1 777.1	. . .	. . .	-74.4	7 169.7
3rd quarter ...	7 337.5	4 589.9	1 185.8	. . .	. . .	. . .	. . .	374.8	532.4	1 791.8	. . .	. . .	-72.4	7 236.8
4th quarter	7 396.0	4 650.6	1 170.4	. . .	. . .	. . .	. . .	382.4	548.0	1 826.0	. . .	. . .	-85.4	7 339.8
1985															
1st quarter	7 469.5	4 729.7	1 138.3	. . .	. . .	. . .	. . .	383.4	535.9	1 848.0	. . .	. . .	-94.0	7 466.4
2nd quarter ...	7 537.9	4 774.1	1 157.7	. . .	. . .	. . .	. . .	382.5	562.3	1 891.0	. . .	. . .	-105.1	7 528.6
3rd quarter ...	7 655.2	4 865.8	1 149.8	. . .	. . .	. . .	. . .	377.0	556.8	1 935.4	. . .	. . .	-116.0	7 650.2
4th quarter	7 712.6	4 878.3	1 192.2	. . .	. . .	. . .	. . .	388.3	578.7	1 941.8	. . .	. . .	-109.3	7 681.6
1986															
1st quarter	7 784.1	4 919.6	1 191.9	. . .	. . .	. . .	. . .	400.5	578.1	1 958.0	. . .	. . .	-107.8	7 757.8
2nd quarter ...	7 819.8	4 974.6	1 171.0	. . .	. . .	. . .	. . .	404.8	602.7	1 997.8	. . .	. . .	-125.7	7 820.1
3rd quarter ...	7 898.6	5 064.7	1 139.5	. . .	. . .	. . .	. . .	414.1	619.4	2 043.4	. . .	. . .	-143.7	7 932.3
4th quarter	7 939.5	5 097.1	1 143.0	. . .	. . .	. . .	. . .	429.5	624.2	2 031.5	. . .	. . .	-137.4	7 980.2
1987															
1st quarter	7 995.0	5 097.9	1 173.8	. . .	. . .	. . .	. . .	429.8	620.5	2 044.3	. . .	. . .	-130.3	7 972.0
2nd quarter ...	8 084.7	5 168.6	1 174.4	. . .	. . .	. . .	. . .	447.5	636.0	2 062.9	. . .	. . .	-132.7	8 083.1
3rd quarter ...	8 158.0	5 228.5	1 174.6	. . .	. . .	. . .	. . .	466.9	648.3	2 067.7	. . .	. . .	-131.4	8 181.3
4th quarter	8 292.7	5 239.5	1 254.6	. . .	. . .	. . .	. . .	484.3	663.2	2 092.8	. . .	. . .	-115.3	8 216.0

Note: Chained (2009) dollar series are calculated as the product of the chain-type quantity index and the 2009 current-dollar value of the corresponding series, divided by 100. Because the formula for the chain-type quantity indexes uses weights from more than one period, the corresponding chained-dollar estimates are usually not additive. The residual column is the difference between the total and the sum of the most detailed components shown in the Bureau of Economic Analysis (BEA) published data.

. . . = Not available.

Table 1-2B. Real Gross Domestic Product: Historical Data—*Continued*

(Billions of chained [2009] dollars, quarterly data are at seasonally adjusted annual rates.)

NIPA Tables 1.1.6, 1.2.6

Year and quarter	Gross domestic product	Personal consumption expenditures	Gross private domestic investment Total	Fixed investment Nonresidential	Fixed investment Residential	Change in private inventories	Net exports	Exports	Imports	Total	Federal	State and local	Residual	Addendum: Final sales of domestic product
1988														
1st quarter	8 339.3	5 332.7	1 194.4	. . .	. . .	. . .	. . .	511.2	660.1	2 078.6	. . .	. . .	-117.5	8 338.6
2nd quarter ...	8 449.5	5 371.8	1 222.9	. . .	. . .	. . .	. . .	525.5	652.5	2 086.1	. . .	. . .	-104.3	8 442.3
3rd quarter	8 498.3	5 417.7	1 229.7	. . .	. . .	. . .	. . .	535.9	667.9	2 087.5	. . .	. . .	-104.6	8 489.7
4th quarter	8 610.9	5 479.7	1 248.4	. . .	. . .	. . .	. . .	552.2	688.3	2 126.8	. . .	. . .	-107.9	8 597.0
1989														
1st quarter	8 697.7	5 505.0	1 290.7	. . .	. . .	. . .	. . .	568.7	691.5	2 117.2	. . .	. . .	-92.4	8 645.4
2nd quarter ...	8 766.1	5 530.9	1 278.3	. . .	. . .	. . .	. . .	593.6	694.8	2 151.8	. . .	. . .	-93.7	8 731.3
3rd quarter	8 831.5	5 585.9	1 266.9	. . .	. . .	. . .	. . .	599.7	693.8	2 169.8	. . .	. . .	-97.0	8 837.3
4th quarter	8 850.2	5 610.5	1 257.7	. . .	. . .	. . .	. . .	608.7	706.4	2 181.5	. . .	. . .	-101.8	8 847.7
1990														
1st quarter	8 947.1	5 658.7	1 270.0	. . .	. . .	. . .	. . .	635.2	728.8	2 215.8	. . .	. . .	-103.8	8 947.5
2nd quarter ...	8 981.7	5 676.4	1 270.4	. . .	. . .	. . .	. . .	643.1	727.6	2 221.2	. . .	. . .	-101.8	8 951.7
3rd quarter	8 983.9	5 699.3	1 245.6	. . .	. . .	. . .	. . .	648.0	724.6	2 219.9	. . .	. . .	-104.3	8 971.2
4th quarter	8 907.4	5 656.2	1 176.3	. . .	. . .	. . .	. . .	653.7	705.2	2 240.2	. . .	. . .	-113.8	8 940.1
1991														
1st quarter	8 865.6	5 636.7	1 137.1	. . .	. . .	. . .	. . .	657.7	697.1	2 251.2	. . .	. . .	-120.0	8 905.8
2nd quarter ...	8 934.4	5 684.0	1 137.2	. . .	. . .	. . .	. . .	681.6	709.5	2 259.2	. . .	. . .	-118.1	8 978.7
3rd quarter	8 977.3	5 711.6	1 159.8	. . .	. . .	. . .	. . .	697.8	729.5	2 250.8	. . .	. . .	-113.2	8 996.6
4th quarter	9 016.4	5 710.1	1 201.0	. . .	. . .	. . .	. . .	713.5	745.6	2 242.3	. . .	. . .	-104.9	8 993.4
1992														
1st quarter	9 123.0	5 817.3	1 178.9	. . .	. . .	. . .	. . .	726.4	751.0	2 259.7	. . .	. . .	-108.3	9 141.1
2nd quarter ...	9 223.5	5 857.2	1 245.7	. . .	. . .	. . .	. . .	726.7	763.4	2 256.8	. . .	. . .	-99.5	9 209.5
3rd quarter	9 313.2	5 920.6	1 255.8	. . .	. . .	. . .	. . .	742.1	775.4	2 268.4	. . .	. . .	-98.3	9 304.2
4th quarter	9 406.5	5 991.1	1 294.2	. . .	. . .	. . .	. . .	745.9	794.0	2 263.5	. . .	. . .	-94.2	9 395.1
1993														
1st quarter	9 424.1	6 013.8	1 324.6	. . .	. . .	. . .	. . .	747.6	811.2	2 237.8	. . .	. . .	-88.5	9 388.5
2nd quarter ...	9 480.1	6 067.8	1 332.1	. . .	. . .	. . .	. . .	756.5	827.9	2 240.3	. . .	. . .	-88.7	9 462.3
3rd quarter	9 526.3	6 134.8	1 323.1	. . .	. . .	. . .	. . .	754.5	838.8	2 245.1	. . .	. . .	-92.4	9 542.3
4th quarter	9 653.5	6 189.1	1 392.5	. . .	. . .	. . .	. . .	778.9	872.5	2 250.0	. . .	. . .	-84.5	9 651.0
1994														
1st quarter	9 748.2	6 260.1	1 446.2	. . .	. . .	. . .	. . .	786.5	892.9	2 222.1	. . .	. . .	-73.8	9 703.9
2nd quarter ...	9 881.4	6 308.6	1 517.1	. . .	. . .	. . .	. . .	813.1	926.1	2 235.1	. . .	. . .	-66.4	9 788.3
3rd quarter	9 939.7	6 357.5	1 492.2	. . .	. . .	. . .	. . .	843.5	952.2	2 272.7	. . .	. . .	-74.0	9 888.1
4th quarter	10 052.5	6 425.9	1 553.5	. . .	. . .	. . .	. . .	863.0	979.0	2 252.2	. . .	. . .	-63.1	9 970.6
1995														
1st quarter	10 086.9	6 442.9	1 570.3	. . .	. . .	. . .	. . .	879.6	1 000.4	2 256.8	. . .	. . .	-62.3	10 021.6
2nd quarter ...	10 122.1	6 500.7	1 537.7	. . .	. . .	. . .	. . .	891.9	1 009.9	2 268.6	. . .	. . .	-66.9	10 092.8
3rd quarter	10 208.8	6 560.3	1 528.6	. . .	. . .	. . .	. . .	930.5	1 013.4	2 262.4	. . .	. . .	-59.6	10 213.8
4th quarter	10 281.2	6 606.4	1 566.7	. . .	. . .	. . .	. . .	943.8	1 026.4	2 242.1	. . .	. . .	-51.4	10 277.2
1996														
1st quarter	10 348.7	6 667.7	1 590.6	. . .	. . .	. . .	. . .	955.2	1 059.7	2 246.8	. . .	. . .	-51.9	10 361.5
2nd quarter ...	10 529.4	6 740.1	1 667.7	. . .	. . .	. . .	. . .	970.7	1 083.4	2 282.8	. . .	. . .	-48.5	10 511.9
3rd quarter	10 626.8	6 780.7	1 744.5	. . .	. . .	. . .	. . .	978.6	1 118.6	2 285.2	. . .	. . .	-43.6	10 565.3
4th quarter	10 739.1	6 834.0	1 743.9	. . .	. . .	. . .	. . .	1 039.6	1 140.6	2 301.9	. . .	. . .	-39.7	10 707.5
1997														
1st quarter	10 820.9	6 906.1	1 781.6	. . .	. . .	. . .	. . .	1 059.4	1 189.3	2 301.3	. . .	. . .	-38.2	10 782.4
2nd quarter ...	10 984.2	6 937.4	1 880.0	. . .	. . .	. . .	. . .	1 101.7	1 229.3	2 325.3	. . .	. . .	-30.9	10 874.8
3rd quarter	11 124.0	7 056.1	1 913.6	. . .	. . .	. . .	. . .	1 127.2	1 274.6	2 329.0	. . .	. . .	-27.3	11 047.2
4th quarter	11 210.3	7 139.9	1 940.7	. . .	. . .	. . .	. . .	1 125.7	1 302.1	2 332.5	. . .	. . .	-26.4	11 119.7
1998														
1st quarter	11 321.2	7 213.6	2 027.1	. . .	. . .	. . .	. . .	1 130.9	1 351.0	2 319.0	. . .	. . .	-18.4	11 195.3
2nd quarter ...	11 431.0	7 341.0	2 013.4	. . .	. . .	. . .	. . .	1 118.5	1 381.9	2 366.0	. . .	. . .	-26.0	11 388.3
3rd quarter	11 580.6	7 437.5	2 067.2	. . .	. . .	. . .	. . .	1 113.3	1 400.5	2 387.6	. . .	. . .	-24.5	11 519.6
4th quarter	11 770.7	7 546.8	2 125.5	. . .	. . .	. . .	. . .	1 154.5	1 445.7	2 409.4	. . .	. . .	-19.8	11 706.1
1999														
1st quarter	11 864.7	7 618.7	2 186.1	1 459.0	623.0	97.5	-340.4	1 126.4	1 466.9	2 418.1	801.2	1 624.5	-137.3	11 773.6
2nd quarter ...	11 962.5	7 731.5	2 188.0	1 497.3	632.7	45.3	-371.1	1 137.9	1 509.0	2 431.7	805.2	1 634.0	-112.1	11 921.8
3rd quarter	12 113.1	7 819.3	2 242.8	1 539.3	637.4	51.5	-393.9	1 171.3	1 565.2	2 460.3	819.4	1 648.0	-99.0	12 066.3
4th quarter	12 323.3	7 934.1	2 308.6	1 544.9	642.1	107.5	-402.9	1 200.9	1 603.8	2 496.7	835.6	1 668.1	-101.1	12 218.0
2000														
1st quarter	12 359.1	8 054.9	2 287.8	1 599.9	645.3	23.6	-449.0	1 219.2	1 668.1	2 476.2	804.6	1 680.8	-80.1	12 340.0
2nd quarter ...	12 592.5	8 132.2	2 424.5	1 650.5	641.9	108.7	-464.9	1 254.7	1 719.6	2 506.4	832.8	1 681.2	-83.1	12 483.4
3rd quarter	12 607.7	8 211.3	2 394.1	1 667.9	632.0	68.7	-493.5	1 285.5	1 779.0	2 501.2	818.9	1 691.0	-84.8	12 540.3
4th quarter	12 679.3	8 284.4	2 395.6	1 672.3	632.6	63.9	-503.8	1 274.3	1 778.1	2 509.0	814.6	1 703.6	-87.0	12 615.8
2001														
1st quarter	12 643.3	8 319.4	2 285.3	1 658.8	635.3	-37.9	-494.0	1 254.5	1 748.5	2 546.3	832.3	1 722.9	-83.3	12 681.9
2nd quarter ...	12 710.3	8 340.8	2 277.1	1 621.2	645.2	-12.8	-483.8	1 213.0	1 696.8	2 596.4	848.7	1 756.8	-101.0	12 725.7
3rd quarter	12 670.1	8 371.2	2 236.6	1 600.0	649.2	-36.9	-508.7	1 154.1	1 662.8	2 594.6	855.9	1 747.3	-104.5	12 708.2
4th quarter	12 705.3	8 499.1	2 126.9	1 553.6	645.0	-97.4	-521.8	1 118.0	1 639.8	2 632.4	862.6	1 778.9	-73.4	12 802.6
2002														
1st quarter	12 822.3	8 524.6	2 202.8	1 522.1	666.2	-3.8	-546.0	1 140.9	1 686.9	2 671.3	884.0	1 795.9	-80.0	12 828.1
2nd quarter ...	12 893.0	8 568.1	2 224.9	1 501.9	682.7	26.5	-567.7	1 172.1	1 739.8	2 696.9	904.7	1 799.8	-74.5	12 870.4
3rd quarter	12 955.8	8 628.0	2 224.6	1 493.0	684.7	32.4	-585.1	1 180.5	1 765.6	2 717.8	919.0	1 805.9	-60.5	12 926.0
4th quarter	12 964.0	8 674.4	2 220.7	1 475.1	697.1	35.1	-638.4	1 164.5	1 802.9	2 737.1	935.7	1 807.9	-67.1	12 931.2

Note: Chained (2009) dollar series are calculated as the product of the chain-type quantity index and the 2009 current-dollar value of the corresponding series, divided by 100. Because the formula for the chain-type quantity indexes uses weights from more than one period, the corresponding chained-dollar estimates are usually not additive. The residual column is the difference between the total and the sum of the most detailed components shown in the Bureau of Economic Analysis (BEA) published data.

. . . = Not available.

Table 1-2B. Real Gross Domestic Product: Historical Data—*Continued*

(Billions of chained [2009] dollars, quarterly data are at seasonally adjusted annual rates.)

| Year and quarter | Gross domestic product | Personal consump-tion expen-ditures | Gross private domestic investment | | | | Exports and imports of goods and services | | | Government consumption expenditures and gross investment | | | Residual | Adden-dum: Final sales of domestic product |
| | | | Total | Fixed investment | | Change in private inventories | Net exports | Exports | Imports | Total | Federal | State and local | | |
				Nonresi-dential	Residential									
2003														
1st quarter	13 031.2	8 712.5	2 239.5	1 478.6	709.8	36.3	-620.3	1 157.6	1 777.9	2 728.3	935.9	1 798.5	-63.0	12 995.4
2nd quarter ...	13 152.1	8 809.5	2 251.3	1 514.3	721.0	-0.2	-649.7	1 156.2	1 805.9	2 771.2	982.8	1 791.7	-50.7	13 152.6
3rd quarter	13 372.4	8 939.4	2 330.9	1 544.7	762.3	7.6	-642.1	1 187.0	1 829.1	2 771.2	977.1	1 798.0	-37.3	13 364.6
4th quarter	13 528.7	9 008.8	2 413.1	1 566.8	785.0	46.6	-655.4	1 239.2	1 894.6	2 786.3	996.0	1 793.0	-32.1	13 483.2
2004														
1st quarter	13 606.5	9 096.4	2 414.5	1 549.4	794.2	56.4	-676.1	1 276.6	1 952.7	2 793.9	1 003.0	1 793.3	-28.2	13 551.1
2nd quarter ...	13 706.2	9 155.5	2 500.9	1 583.8	819.5	81.9	-740.0	1 293.1	2 033.0	2 809.9	1 013.0	1 799.0	-22.2	13 624.3
3rd quarter	13 830.8	9 243.0	2 539.4	1 626.9	825.3	71.1	-753.0	1 300.6	2 053.6	2 820.7	1 030.7	1 791.0	-16.3	13 759.6
4th quarter	13 950.4	9 337.8	2 590.6	1 661.4	836.7	76.2	-769.9	1 332.1	2 102.0	2 808.2	1 021.8	1 787.7	-11.0	13 873.9
2005														
1st quarter	14 099.1	9 409.2	2 664.4	1 681.9	856.4	111.3	-774.1	1 352.6	2 126.8	2 814.1	1 027.6	1 787.6	-10.1	13 988.8
2nd quarter ...	14 172.7	9 511.5	2 630.5	1 706.1	872.3	33.0	-773.5	1 377.6	2 151.2	2 818.9	1 029.8	1 790.2	-0.4	14 138.5
3rd quarter	14 291.8	9 585.2	2 657.9	1 737.4	881.9	18.2	-777.7	1 379.2	2 156.9	2 841.0	1 048.6	1 792.9	3.7	14 271.7
4th quarter	14 373.4	9 621.3	2 737.6	1 744.3	879.9	94.8	-803.9	1 418.1	2 222.0	2 830.7	1 033.2	1 798.6	-2.3	14 276.4
2006														
1st quarter	14 546.1	9 729.2	2 773.8	1 808.7	871.7	78.6	-799.0	1 471.0	2 269.9	2 853.5	1 058.9	1 794.9	1.1	14 468.8
2nd quarter ...	14 589.6	9 781.0	2 755.7	1 831.3	827.8	84.4	-799.1	1 498.5	2 297.6	2 864.1	1 057.7	1 806.9	-4.6	14 506.3
3rd quarter	14 602.6	9 838.1	2 727.6	1 853.1	781.6	81.9	-819.7	1 495.5	2 315.2	2 870.4	1 058.0	1 813.0	-6.7	14 520.3
4th quarter	14 716.9	9 938.4	2 663.0	1 865.2	745.2	41.4	-759.3	1 562.1	2 321.4	2 889.1	1 069.0	1 820.6	-5.5	14 673.7
2007														
1st quarter	14 726.0	9 990.7	2 638.5	1 897.2	711.2	19.6	-771.0	1 587.7	2 358.7	2 882.7	1 054.5	1 829.0	-6.7	14 703.3
2nd quarter ...	14 838.7	10 024.6	2 674.7	1 934.4	682.7	49.4	-753.7	1 615.7	2 369.4	2 907.0	1 071.2	1 836.4	-7.1	14 785.5
3rd quarter	14 938.5	10 069.2	2 658.1	1 964.4	639.2	50.2	-703.2	1 665.6	2 368.7	2 928.0	1 091.6	1 836.7	-10.3	14 885.9
4th quarter	14 991.8	10 081.8	2 605.2	1 997.6	586.1	23.0	-622.6	1 716.7	2 339.3	2 939.8	1 097.5	1 842.5	-15.3	14 970.1
2008														
1st quarter	14 889.5	10 061.0	2 517.5	1 998.1	540.0	-20.2	-623.7	1 737.9	2 361.6	2 952.0	1 115.2	1 836.9	-20.1	14 909.4
2nd quarter ...	14 963.4	10 077.9	2 472.6	1 986.6	516.3	-26.4	-550.4	1 790.0	2 340.4	2 975.0	1 135.7	1 839.3	-17.6	14 992.9
3rd quarter	14 891.6	10 005.1	2 403.8	1 933.0	490.9	-20.7	-526.9	1 766.1	2 293.0	3 016.2	1 169.1	1 847.1	-7.2	14 910.7
4th quarter	14 577.0	9 884.7	2 190.0	1 820.1	443.6	-67.4	-530.3	1 669.2	2 199.5	3 035.9	1 189.3	1 846.6	-10.1	14 650.0
2009														
1st quarter	14 375.0	9 850.8	1 937.7	1 688.3	401.0	-144.5	-451.3	1 535.3	1 986.7	3 040.5	1 180.1	1 860.4	-9.8	14 527.4
2nd quarter ...	14 355.6	9 806.4	1 820.5	1 634.0	377.0	-190.1	-366.3	1 539.4	1 905.7	3 096.0	1 218.9	1 877.1	-1.9	14 545.8
3rd quarter	14 402.5	9 865.9	1 804.7	1 613.1	395.4	-206.1	-383.6	1 593.3	1 977.0	3 113.0	1 235.6	1 877.4	4.6	14 605.1
4th quarter	14 541.9	9 864.8	1 949.6	1 598.4	395.7	-49.6	-380.4	1 682.9	2 063.4	3 106.8	1 236.2	1 870.6	6.8	14 586.9
2010														
1st quarter	14 604.8	9 917.7	2 012.9	1 615.0	383.0	9.8	-408.8	1 708.2	2 116.9	3 084.3	1 247.8	1 836.5	4.0	14 591.5
2nd quarter ...	14 745.9	9 998.4	2 116.9	1 659.3	403.5	48.8	-469.7	1 748.1	2 217.8	3 106.2	1 273.4	1 832.8	-1.8	14 694.3
3rd quarter	14 845.5	10 063.1	2 185.7	1 692.8	368.1	116.2	-498.4	1 797.5	2 296.0	3 103.5	1 285.0	1 818.5	-1.8	14 724.5
4th quarter	14 939.0	10 166.1	2 166.1	1 728.1	375.1	58.1	-458.1	1 852.6	2 310.7	3 071.5	1 276.4	1 795.2	-5.0	14 878.3
2011														
1st quarter	14 881.3	10 217.1	2 125.9	1 724.1	374.4	25.1	-466.2	1 862.3	2 328.5	3 012.2	1 241.2	1 771.1	-10.4	14 855.3
2nd quarter ...	14 989.6	10 237.7	2 208.0	1 761.0	379.3	57.5	-455.2	1 890.7	2 345.9	3 009.0	1 246.0	1 763.0	-3.4	14 924.5
3rd quarter	15 021.1	10 282.2	2 214.0	1 840.8	386.8	-13.0	-454.3	1 910.6	2 364.9	2 990.0	1 233.3	1 756.8	-17.0	15 035.1
4th quarter	15 190.3	10 316.8	2 373.7	1 883.1	397.6	80.8	-461.7	1 929.7	2 391.3	2 978.3	1 225.2	1 753.1	-12.0	15 101.0
2012														
1st quarter	15 291.0	10 379.0	2 429.6	1 938.1	422.5	56.0	-462.7	1 942.6	2 405.3	2 963.7	1 223.9	1 739.8	-15.1	15 225.0
2nd quarter ...	15 362.4	10 396.6	2 489.1	1 973.7	426.3	76.6	-452.7	1 964.4	2 417.0	2 949.4	1 214.8	1 734.5	-17.4	15 276.9
3rd quarter	15 380.8	10 424.1	2 482.0	1 963.4	437.3	70.6	-446.8	1 974.1	2 420.9	2 940.9	1 216.2	1 724.7	-19.9	15 302.7
4th quarter	15 384.3	10 453.2	2 462.2	1 981.4	459.8	15.5	-426.0	1 971.7	2 397.8	2 912.3	1 199.0	1 713.3	-26.5	15 364.6
2013														
1st quarter	15 457.2	10 518.2	2 505.1	2 000.7	469.9	25.2	-425.9	1 976.6	2 402.6	2 878.8	1 170.1	1 708.5	-26.5	15 424.7
2nd quarter ...	15 500.2	10 554.3	2 537.2	2 005.7	480.3	39.6	-434.2	2 000.5	2 434.7	2 864.1	1 153.2	1 710.4	-25.9	15 451.9
3rd quarter	15 614.4	10 598.9	2 619.7	2 023.1	486.0	93.6	-428.3	2 021.1	2 449.4	2 848.1	1 136.3	1 711.1	-22.5	15 508.9
4th quarter	15 761.5	10 690.4	2 647.1	2 065.5	475.9	87.2	-381.5	2 074.2	2 455.7	2 828.5	1 116.9	1 710.6	-20.6	15 660.0
2014														
1st quarter	15 724.9	10 724.7	2 630.5	2 106.9	472.6	36.9	-434.0	2 038.7	2 472.7	2 828.4	1 117.8	1 709.6	-27.2	15 675.7
2nd quarter ...	15 901.5	10 826.3	2 709.5	2 129.8	484.4	77.1	-443.3	2 086.8	2 530.1	2 836.5	1 114.5	1 720.8	-31.5	15 809.7
3rd quarter	16 068.8	10 918.6	2 758.1	2 176.3	488.5	79.9	-429.1	2 096.0	2 525.1	2 849.2	1 124.7	1 723.5	-40.3	15 978.6
4th quarter	16 151.4	11 033.3	2 772.5	2 180.0	500.2	78.2	-463.6	2 123.9	2 587.5	2 839.0	1 108.3	1 729.3	-41.5	16 062.9

Note: Chained (2009) dollar series are calculated as the product of the chain-type quantity index and the 2009 current-dollar value of the corresponding series, divided by 100. Because the formula for the chain-type quantity indexes uses weights from more than one period, the corresponding chained-dollar estimates are usually not additive. The residual column is the difference between the total and the sum of the most detailed components shown in the Bureau of Economic Analysis (BEA) published data.

Table 1-3A. U.S. Population and Per Capita Product and Income: Recent Data

(Dollars, except as noted; quarterly data are at seasonally adjusted annual rates.)

NIPA Table 7.1

		Current dollars							Chained (2009) dollars					
	Population (mid-period, thousands)				Personal consumption expenditures						Personal consumption expenditures			
Year and quarter		Gross domestic product	Personal income	Disposable personal income	Total	Durable goods	Nondurable goods	Services	Gross domestic product	Disposable personal income	Total	Durable goods	Nondurable goods	Services
1950	151 684	1 979	1 542	1 417	1 267	214	556	497	14 398	10 033	8 969	446	3 254	5 281
1951	154 287	2 251	1 714	1 539	1 351	206	603	543	15 296	10 197	8 955	402	3 248	5 498
1952	156 954	2 343	1 801	1 597	1 398	199	621	578	15 649	10 371	9 081	387	3 313	5 647
1953	159 565	2 443	1 877	1 669	1 460	217	628	615	16 115	10 697	9 359	425	3 360	5 788
1954	162 391	2 409	1 863	1 678	1 477	208	628	641	15 745	10 661	9 389	416	3 354	5 886
1955	165 275	2 579	1 964	1 765	1 565	247	645	673	16 573	11 172	9 906	496	3 466	6 074
1956	168 221	2 676	2 071	1 854	1 614	239	666	710	16 630	11 502	10 017	469	3 525	6 253
1957	171 274	2 772	2 151	1 924	1 674	245	686	742	16 677	11 589	10 082	465	3 532	6 353
1958	174 141	2 768	2 179	1 958	1 700	227	701	772	16 282	11 519	10 002	422	3 520	6 451
1959	177 130	2 950	2 276	2 038	1 793	253	721	818	17 112	11 811	10 390	464	3 616	6 655
1960	180 760	3 006	2 338	2 083	1 834	252	727	855	17 198	11 877	10 461	464	3 602	6 776
1961	183 742	3 066	2 401	2 143	1 861	241	733	888	17 351	12 097	10 504	441	3 615	6 912
1962	186 590	3 243	2 514	2 238	1 946	265	748	933	18 131	12 482	10 855	484	3 670	7 128
1963	189 300	3 373	2 603	2 315	2 021	286	760	974	18 650	12 766	11 140	521	3 695	7 325
1964	191 927	3 573	2 753	2 482	2 142	310	796	1 037	19 456	13 485	11 642	562	3 816	7 654
1965	194 347	3 827	2 937	2 641	2 282	342	840	1 101	20 462	14 144	12 226	624	3 958	7 978
1966	196 599	4 146	3 157	2 819	2 445	365	905	1 175	21 561	14 726	12 770	668	4 130	8 276
1967	198 752	4 336	3 350	2 983	2 553	372	931	1 250	21 913	15 198	13 009	670	4 173	8 521
1968	200 745	4 695	3 640	3 207	2 777	423	995	1 359	22 760	15 728	13 619	737	4 307	8 882
1969	202 736	5 031	3 947	3 432	2 982	446	1 057	1 479	23 244	16 102	13 990	757	4 382	9 186
1970	205 089	5 246	4 216	3 713	3 158	439	1 116	1 604	23 024	16 643	14 155	729	4 428	9 438
1971	207 692	5 623	4 488	3 998	3 375	493	1 154	1 728	23 485	17 191	14 511	792	4 455	9 642
1972	209 924	6 109	4 876	4 287	3 665	555	1 226	1 885	24 458	17 821	15 237	881	4 586	10 088
1973	211 939	6 740	5 372	4 747	4 016	616	1 350	2 050	25 593	18 725	15 841	964	4 673	10 466
1974	213 898	7 241	5 841	5 135	4 357	609	1 502	2 246	25 227	18 343	15 566	894	4 517	10 571
1975	215 981	7 820	6 329	5 645	4 782	658	1 617	2 507	24 934	18 613	15 766	887	4 512	10 863
1976	218 086	8 609	6 871	6 079	5 274	773	1 732	2 769	26 024	19 002	16 484	988	4 681	11 221
1977	220 289	9 469	7 511	6 613	5 795	871	1 854	3 070	26 951	19 406	17 007	1 065	4 740	11 569
1978	222 629	10 585	8 353	7 322	6 406	958	2 022	3 425	28 151	20 080	17 568	1 109	4 859	11 977
1979	225 106	11 693	9 232	8 037	7 061	1 005	2 273	3 783	28 725	20 248	17 788	1 091	4 930	12 207
1980	227 726	12 570	10 177	8 861	7 705	994	2 518	4 193	28 325	20 158	17 528	993	4 865	12 261
1981	230 008	13 960	11 289	9 785	8 424	1 061	2 719	4 644	28 772	20 458	17 611	993	4 877	12 351
1982	232 218	14 405	11 969	10 442	8 931	1 090	2 783	5 058	27 953	20 685	17 692	982	4 881	12 477
1983	234 333	15 526	12 675	11 170	9 758	1 259	2 897	5 602	28 984	21 214	18 532	1 112	4 994	13 008
1984	236 394	17 093	13 883	12 284	10 568	1 447	3 052	6 068	30 817	22 480	19 339	1 259	5 155	13 393
1985	238 506	18 225	14 743	12 991	11 416	1 595	3 175	6 646	31 839	22 960	20 175	1 373	5 264	13 972
1986	240 683	19 071	15 480	13 661	12 042	1 751	3 217	7 075	32 659	23 632	20 832	1 491	5 402	14 292
1987	242 843	20 055	16 290	14 274	12 733	1 820	3 353	7 559	33 489	23 929	21 346	1 507	5 446	14 801
1988	245 061	21 434	17 450	15 386	13 657	1 939	3 519	8 200	34 581	24 826	22 037	1 578	5 539	15 327
1989	247 387	22 870	18 675	16 380	14 523	1 998	3 757	8 768	35 517	25 340	22 467	1 598	5 635	15 666
1990	250 181	23 901	19 611	17 235	15 291	1 987	3 974	9 331	35 794	25 555	22 674	1 573	5 637	15 957
1991	253 530	24 352	20 011	17 688	15 620	1 882	4 024	9 714	35 295	25 395	22 426	1 469	5 546	16 003
1992	256 922	25 452	21 069	18 684	16 408	1 978	4 107	10 324	36 068	26 133	22 951	1 533	5 579	16 431
1993	260 282	26 428	21 703	19 211	17 178	2 119	4 191	10 868	36 580	26 216	23 441	1 626	5 647	16 718
1994	263 455	27 742	22 536	19 906	17 996	2 305	4 325	11 366	37 598	26 611	24 057	1 735	5 797	17 025
1995	266 588	28 749	23 561	20 753	18 696	2 385	4 426	11 886	38 167	27 180	24 486	1 782	5 870	17 328
1996	269 714	30 033	24 719	21 615	19 532	2 507	4 603	12 422	39 156	27 719	25 047	1 893	5 970	17 629
1997	272 958	31 538	25 941	22 527	20 372	2 621	4 731	13 020	40 427	28 397	25 681	2 023	6 073	17 977
1998	276 154	32 913	27 498	23 759	21 376	2 822	4 814	13 740	41 737	29 723	26 741	2 241	6 226	18 587
1999	279 328	34 585	28 599	24 617	22 579	3 063	5 124	14 393	43 196	30 350	27 838	2 500	6 465	19 087
2000	282 398	36 419	30 585	26 206	24 053	3 232	5 454	15 367	44 475	31 524	28 933	2 685	6 599	19 828
2001	285 225	37 240	31 525	27 179	24 904	3 301	5 553	16 050	44 464	32 075	29 390	2 798	6 647	20 093
2002	287 955	38 122	31 789	28 127	25 643	3 422	5 602	16 619	44 829	32 754	29 862	2 975	6 706	20 275
2003	290 626	39 606	32 657	29 198	26 720	3 501	5 863	17 356	45 664	33 342	30 512	3 157	6 877	20 531
2004	293 262	41 857	34 280	30 697	28 166	3 682	6 208	18 276	46 967	34 221	31 399	3 386	7 037	20 993
2005	295 993	44 237	35 859	31 760	29 711	3 808	6 598	19 304	48 090	34 424	32 203	3 537	7 204	21 465
2006	298 818	46 369	38 130	33 589	31 136	3 869	6 960	20 307	48 905	35 458	32 868	3 653	7 370	21 841
2007	301 696	47 987	39 776	34 826	32 319	3 927	7 216	21 177	49 300	35 866	33 284	3 784	7 422	22 063
2008	304 543	48 330	41 052	36 101	32 881	3 619	7 465	21 796	48 697	36 078	32 860	3 557	7 272	22 028
2009	307 240	46 930	39 366	35 616	32 050	3 331	7 080	21 640	46 930	35 616	32 050	3 331	7 080	21 640
2010	309 808	48 302	40 274	36 274	32 931	3 456	7 399	22 076	47 719	35 684	32 395	3 504	7 177	21 716
2011	312 172	49 710	42 459	37 804	34 242	3 605	7 916	22 721	48 116	36 298	32 878	3 689	7 250	21 948
2012	314 499	51 368	44 245	39 440	35 137	3 790	8 099	23 248	48 822	37 165	33 111	3 931	7 242	21 965
2013	316 839	52 592	44 402	39 123	35 956	3 907	8 203	23 847	49 184	36 369	33 425	4 127	7 322	22 021
2014	319 173	54 353	46 038	40 461	37 177	4 011	8 360	24 806	50 010	37 084	34 075	4 337	7 419	22 385
2012														
1st quarter	313 623	50 933	43 563	38 868	34 934	3 759	8 085	23 091	48 756	36 821	33 094	3 870	7 250	21 995
2nd quarter	314 155	51 318	43 972	39 221	35 041	3 761	8 071	23 209	48 901	37 041	33 094	3 890	7 244	21 983
3rd quarter	314 790	51 552	44 052	39 250	35 178	3 794	8 102	23 282	48 860	36 948	33 114	3 946	7 246	21 950
4th quarter	315 430	51 667	45 388	40 415	35 394	3 845	8 138	23 410	48 772	37 841	33 140	4 016	7 226	21 934
2013														
1st quarter	315 957	52 035	43 966	38 772	35 675	3 910	8 205	23 560	48 922	36 180	33 290	4 094	7 299	21 938
2nd quarter	316 499	52 218	44 313	39 003	35 775	3 904	8 136	23 736	48 974	36 356	33 347	4 110	7 300	21 981
3rd quarter	317 136	52 746	44 575	39 299	36 002	3 902	8 219	23 882	49 236	36 481	33 421	4 135	7 327	22 004
4th quarter	317 765	53 365	44 752	39 415	36 369	3 911	8 251	24 207	49 601	36 460	33 642	4 168	7 360	22 160
2014														
1st quarter	318 288	53 361	45 347	39 893	36 572	3 906	8 268	24 398	49 405	36 755	33 695	4 189	7 356	22 199
2nd quarter	318 833	54 166	45 832	40 331	37 051	4 012	8 382	24 657	49 874	36 962	33 956	4 320	7 405	22 295
3rd quarter	319 470	54 847	46 248	40 638	37 403	4 054	8 427	24 922	50 298	37 134	34 177	4 390	7 435	22 424
4th quarter	320 100	55 033	46 722	40 977	37 680	4 072	8 362	25 246	50 457	37 484	34 468	4 447	7 478	22 619

Table 1-3B. U.S. Population and Per Capita Product and Income: Historical Data

(Dollars, except as noted; quarterly data are at seasonally adjusted annual rates.)   **NIPA Table 7.1**

Year and quarter	Population (mid-period, thou-sands)	Current dollars							Chained (2009) dollars					
		Gross domestic product	Personal income	Dispos-able personal income	Personal consumption expenditures				Gross domestic product	Dispos-able personal income	Personal consumption expenditures			
					Total	Durable goods	Nondur-able goods	Services			Total	Durable goods	Nondur-able goods	Services
1929	121 878	858	700	685	635	81	278	276	8 669	6 917	6 408	263	2 479	3 812
1930	123 188	748	621	608	569	62	248	260	7 847	6 411	6 000	215	2 325	3 693
1931	124 149	623	529	521	489	48	208	233	7 288	6 145	5 768	185	2 282	3 571
1932	124 949	476	402	396	390	32	161	197	6 308	5 306	5 218	140	2 068	3 334
1933	125 690	455	376	369	366	30	159	177	6 192	5 122	5 073	135	2 048	3 191
1934	126 485	528	427	420	407	36	189	182	6 817	5 579	5 401	154	2 201	3 327
1935	127 362	583	478	469	439	43	205	191	7 373	6 080	5 689	185	2 311	3 419
1936	128 181	662	540	530	485	53	228	205	8 273	6 802	6 228	224	2 559	3 607
1937	128 961	721	579	564	518	57	240	221	8 643	6 990	6 419	234	2 606	3 753
1938	129 969	672	532	517	494	47	230	217	8 292	6 556	6 268	193	2 623	3 694
1939	131 028	713	562	551	513	55	235	224	8 881	7 046	6 565	227	2 721	3 807
1940	132 122	779	601	588	540	63	245	232	9 583	7 464	6 847	257	2 813	3 921
1941	133 402	970	734	716	608	77	279	252	11 171	8 558	7 261	294	2 954	4 113
1942	134 860	1 231	940	903	660	57	322	282	13 138	9 598	7 012	185	2 929	4 293
1943	136 739	1 485	1 142	1 020	731	55	357	319	15 166	9 922	7 109	163	2 907	4 572
1944	138 397	1 623	1 226	1 099	785	56	381	348	16 181	10 109	7 223	149	2 933	4 769
1945	139 928	1 631	1 256	1 117	857	65	418	374	15 850	9 885	7 586	164	3 080	4 970
1946	141 389	1 611	1 292	1 170	1 021	121	489	411	13 869	9 679	8 442	292	3 324	5 142
1947	144 126	1 734	1 350	1 213	1 124	151	538	434	13 457	9 109	8 440	336	3 241	5 066
1948	146 631	1 874	1 457	1 326	1 194	167	566	461	13 776	9 425	8 483	352	3 210	5 111
1949	149 188	1 829	1 416	1 304	1 196	178	546	472	13 466	9 340	8 569	374	3 202	5 144
1947														
1st quarter	143 156	1 698	1 328	1 194	1 092	145	523	424	13 513	9 167	8 378	326	3 225	5 057
2nd quarter	143 803	1 713	1 320	1 185	1 114	148	535	431	13 437	9 022	8 479	331	3 266	5 107
3rd quarter	144 462	1 731	1 369	1 232	1 133	151	544	438	13 362	9 211	8 468	334	3 266	5 073
4th quarter	145 135	1 794	1 382	1 239	1 156	162	551	443	13 510	9 036	8 431	354	3 208	5 023
1948														
1st quarter	145 761	1 826	1 418	1 272	1 170	162	559	449	13 649	9 175	8 437	351	3 205	5 055
2nd quarter	146 341	1 865	1 450	1 320	1 191	164	568	458	13 816	9 424	8 501	352	3 223	5 114
3rd quarter	146 973	1 902	1 481	1 356	1 206	172	568	466	13 834	9 537	8 477	356	3 190	5 119
4th quarter	147 659	1 901	1 478	1 353	1 206	169	567	470	13 784	9 546	8 505	350	3 217	5 146
1949														
1st quarter	148 298	1 857	1 431	1 311	1 193	165	558	471	13 537	9 318	8 482	342	3 215	5 157
2nd quarter	148 891	1 825	1 418	1 304	1 199	177	550	472	13 438	9 326	8 578	370	3 211	5 162
3rd quarter	149 529	1 827	1 408	1 299	1 190	183	537	471	13 528	9 346	8 560	386	3 170	5 129
4th quarter	150 211	1 804	1 405	1 299	1 201	189	539	473	13 346	9 356	8 646	399	3 207	5 121
1950														
1st quarter	150 852	1 864	1 501	1 391	1 214	194	540	479	13 819	10 035	8 753	413	3 234	5 162
2nd quarter	151 385	1 921	1 505	1 389	1 235	197	547	491	14 186	9 969	8 866	415	3 260	5 274
3rd quarter	152 039	2 029	1 554	1 429	1 320	246	570	504	14 670	10 051	9 280	511	3 302	5 333
4th quarter	152 724	2 097	1 605	1 457	1 297	218	567	512	14 886	10 067	8 960	446	3 214	5 342
1951														
1st quarter	153 336	2 194	1 659	1 500	1 365	232	600	533	15 029	10 038	9 140	458	3 260	5 466
2nd quarter	153 947	2 237	1 711	1 539	1 332	200	594	539	15 229	10 221	8 846	391	3 200	5 481
3rd quarter	154 655	2 275	1 731	1 552	1 343	195	602	546	15 472	10 290	8 908	382	3 252	5 524
4th quarter	155 389	2 295	1 753	1 562	1 363	196	614	553	15 433	10 223	8 918	379	3 275	5 512
1952														
1st quarter	156 033	2 308	1 759	1 561	1 366	197	607	561	15 532	10 176	8 901	380	3 234	5 557
2nd quarter	156 644	2 307	1 778	1 574	1 387	198	617	572	15 503	10 264	9 040	385	3 297	5 622
3rd quarter	157 324	2 340	1 815	1 610	1 397	187	626	583	15 548	10 425	9 045	361	3 340	5 672
4th quarter	158 043	2 412	1 849	1 640	1 442	213	635	594	15 985	10 601	9 322	421	3 374	5 726
1953														
1st quarter	158 648	2 449	1 870	1 660	1 459	222	634	604	16 221	10 689	9 397	434	3 382	5 763
2nd quarter	159 234	2 463	1 888	1 678	1 465	220	631	613	16 287	10 788	9 419	430	3 385	5 810
3rd quarter	159 963	2 449	1 879	1 671	1 463	216	624	622	16 122	10 688	9 354	425	3 338	5 819
4th quarter	160 713	2 405	1 870	1 665	1 452	210	622	621	15 803	10 602	9 249	411	3 328	5 749
1954														
1st quarter	161 389	2 391	1 862	1 675	1 459	204	627	628	15 664	10 612	9 244	397	3 346	5 778
2nd quarter	162 044	2 386	1 852	1 667	1 470	208	625	637	15 617	10 579	9 326	414	3 323	5 854
3rd quarter	162 792	2 405	1 856	1 672	1 478	204	628	646	15 722	10 642	9 410	414	3 350	5 929
4th quarter	163 585	2 447	1 880	1 694	1 500	214	632	654	15 951	10 794	9 560	438	3 390	5 971
1955														
1st quarter	164 266	2 519	1 911	1 720	1 533	234	636	662	16 338	10 924	9 735	475	3 411	6 016
2nd quarter	164 926	2 560	1 949	1 753	1 557	247	643	667	16 537	11 120	9 881	499	3 460	6 036
3rd quarter	165 674	2 601	1 985	1 784	1 576	256	645	674	16 684	11 273	9 958	512	3 467	6 071
4th quarter	166 481	2 630	2 006	1 801	1 592	249	655	688	16 703	11 350	10 034	497	3 521	6 161
1956														
1st quarter	167 190	2 635	2 031	1 819	1 594	237	661	696	16 568	11 418	10 008	472	3 545	6 194
2nd quarter	167 869	2 661	2 057	1 841	1 604	237	663	704	16 637	11 479	10 001	471	3 522	6 228
3rd quarter	168 654	2 680	2 079	1 860	1 616	235	667	714	16 546	11 484	9 977	460	3 508	6 264
4th quarter	169 497	2 721	2 113	1 890	1 640	245	671	724	16 733	11 601	10 064	473	3 519	6 314
1957														
1st quarter	170 218	2 765	2 131	1 904	1 659	250	678	730	16 770	11 586	10 090	479	3 525	6 312
2nd quarter	170 915	2 766	2 150	1 922	1 665	247	682	737	16 664	11 620	10 067	466	3 524	6 340
3rd quarter	171 684	2 798	2 168	1 940	1 684	244	695	745	16 751	11 631	10 101	461	3 557	6 357
4th quarter	172 463	2 758	2 154	1 929	1 686	240	690	755	16 505	11 509	10 059	453	3 517	6 397

Table 1-3B. U.S. Population and Per Capita Product and Income: Historical Data—*Continued*

(Dollars, except as noted; quarterly data are at seasonally adjusted annual rates.)   **NIPA Table 7.1**

Year and quarter	Population (mid-period, thousands)	Current dollars							Chained (2009) dollars					
		Gross domestic product	Personal income	Disposable personal income	Personal consumption expenditures				Gross domestic product	Disposable personal income	Personal consumption expenditures			
					Total	Durable goods	Nondurable goods	Services			Total	Durable goods	Nondurable goods	Services
1958														
1st quarter	173 116	2 705	2 151	1 931	1 677	228	692	757	16 016	11 379	9 884	421	3 473	6 365
2nd quarter	173 781	2 721	2 157	1 940	1 687	222	697	768	16 060	11 411	9 927	413	3 491	6 433
3rd quarter	174 535	2 788	2 195	1 972	1 709	226	705	779	16 360	11 590	10 047	420	3 539	6 492
4th quarter	175 340	2 854	2 211	1 986	1 724	232	708	784	16 666	11 678	10 135	434	3 571	6 504
1959														
1st quarter	176 045	2 903	2 240	2 009	1 760	248	716	796	16 908	11 730	10 278	455	3 603	6 557
2nd quarter	176 727	2 966	2 279	2 041	1 787	257	719	811	17 253	11 871	10 396	471	3 619	6 629
3rd quarter	177 481	2 959	2 282	2 042	1 809	261	722	826	17 146	11 805	10 460	478	3 618	6 690
4th quarter	178 268	2 969	2 304	2 058	1 813	247	726	839	17 138	11 837	10 426	453	3 624	6 741
1960														
1st quarter	179 694	3 024	2 321	2 069	1 818	253	721	844	17 380	11 883	10 442	464	3 604	6 748
2nd quarter	180 335	3 009	2 341	2 086	1 844	257	732	855	17 253	11 915	10 536	473	3 631	6 798
3rd quarter	181 094	3 015	2 345	2 088	1 836	254	727	856	17 223	11 885	10 450	467	3 594	6 761
4th quarter	181 915	2 974	2 343	2 087	1 839	246	728	865	16 938	11 827	10 417	453	3 580	6 796
1961														
1st quarter	182 634	2 989	2 358	2 103	1 834	231	730	872	16 986	11 895	10 373	426	3 587	6 837
2nd quarter	183 337	3 040	2 383	2 127	1 854	236	732	886	17 236	12 030	10 487	434	3 622	6 911
3rd quarter	184 103	3 086	2 412	2 154	1 862	242	731	889	17 450	12 139	10 494	442	3 609	6 903
4th quarter	184 894	3 146	2 449	2 189	1 894	252	736	905	17 728	12 320	10 659	462	3 643	6 995
1962														
1st quarter	185 553	3 208	2 478	2 211	1 915	257	743	915	17 983	12 394	10 734	470	3 660	7 036
2nd quarter	186 203	3 236	2 508	2 235	1 939	263	745	930	18 113	12 480	10 828	481	3 662	7 116
3rd quarter	186 926	3 261	2 523	2 243	1 952	265	749	938	18 215	12 497	10 873	483	3 676	7 149
4th quarter	187 680	3 267	2 546	2 261	1 978	275	754	949	18 212	12 556	10 983	502	3 682	7 210
1963														
1st quarter	188 299	3 307	2 567	2 279	1 990	279	757	954	18 354	12 622	11 021	510	3 690	7 215
2nd quarter	188 906	3 345	2 584	2 296	2 006	285	756	964	18 534	12 699	11 091	520	3 690	7 271
3rd quarter	189 631	3 401	2 612	2 324	2 035	288	766	981	18 823	12 790	11 199	524	3 710	7 370
4th quarter	190 362	3 440	2 651	2 361	2 051	293	763	995	18 885	12 949	11 249	530	3 691	7 442
1964														
1st quarter	190 954	3 515	2 693	2 412	2 095	304	778	1 013	19 233	13 162	11 435	549	3 742	7 538
2nd quarter	191 560	3 554	2 734	2 474	2 130	310	791	1 029	19 401	13 473	11 599	562	3 802	7 619
3rd quarter	192 256	3 604	2 774	2 506	2 169	319	806	1 044	19 593	13 598	11 770	578	3 862	7 691
4th quarter	192 938	3 620	2 810	2 534	2 175	308	808	1 059	19 593	13 703	11 761	558	3 856	7 769
1965														
1st quarter	193 467	3 718	2 859	2 565	2 224	336	815	1 073	20 021	13 826	11 991	609	3 882	7 836
2nd quarter	193 994	3 775	2 901	2 600	2 254	334	829	1 091	20 240	13 945	12 091	608	3 908	7 934
3rd quarter	194 647	3 854	2 965	2 672	2 293	343	843	1 108	20 582	14 279	12 257	627	3 954	8 016
4th quarter	195 279	3 959	3 024	2 725	2 358	354	873	1 130	20 999	14 520	12 561	651	4 087	8 126
1966														
1st quarter	195 763	4 073	3 081	2 767	2 405	369	889	1 146	21 464	14 628	12 715	680	4 107	8 189
2nd quarter	196 277	4 112	3 123	2 789	2 424	355	903	1 166	21 496	14 627	12 713	651	4 135	8 256
3rd quarter	196 877	4 169	3 181	2 836	2 463	367	913	1 183	21 583	14 760	12 819	671	4 152	8 298
4th quarter	197 481	4 228	3 240	2 883	2 485	368	913	1 204	21 701	14 885	12 833	668	4 127	8 362
1967														
1st quarter	197 967	4 274	3 287	2 927	2 501	359	921	1 220	21 847	15 070	12 876	654	4 164	8 419
2nd quarter	198 455	4 288	3 314	2 957	2 541	375	927	1 238	21 812	15 151	13 019	681	4 184	8 479
3rd quarter	199 012	4 355	3 374	3 003	2 570	375	933	1 261	21 939	15 251	13 049	673	4 169	8 570
4th quarter	199 572	4 425	3 423	3 042	2 600	379	941	1 280	22 053	15 318	13 092	673	4 176	8 617
1968														
1st quarter	199 995	4 556	3 513	3 120	2 684	404	968	1 312	22 454	15 547	13 374	713	4 249	8 732
2nd quarter	200 452	4 671	3 605	3 197	2 747	414	987	1 346	22 781	15 770	13 547	727	4 291	8 848
3rd quarter	200 997	4 738	3 687	3 230	2 820	436	1 009	1 375	22 883	15 766	13 764	758	4 348	8 937
4th quarter	201 538	4 814	3 755	3 279	2 856	436	1 017	1 403	22 923	15 831	13 790	751	4 337	9 011
1969														
1st quarter	201 955	4 929	3 819	3 311	2 911	446	1 034	1 431	23 231	15 830	13 915	764	4 376	9 072
2nd quarter	202 419	4 996	3 905	3 383	2 960	447	1 048	1 465	23 252	15 968	13 972	760	4 376	9 163
3rd quarter	202 986	5 084	4 000	3 487	3 003	446	1 064	1 492	23 332	16 260	14 001	756	4 380	9 210
4th quarter	203 584	5 112	4 064	3 545	3 053	446	1 079	1 527	23 162	16 339	14 071	750	4 396	9 297
1970														
1st quarter	204 086	5 162	4 125	3 612	3 100	439	1 100	1 561	23 064	16 459	14 123	737	4 423	9 374
2nd quarter	204 721	5 227	4 199	3 684	3 139	445	1 107	1 587	23 033	16 601	14 144	743	4 407	9 404
3rd quarter	205 419	5 299	4 255	3 765	3 186	448	1 118	1 620	23 159	16 803	14 220	744	4 423	9 479
4th quarter	206 130	5 295	4 283	3 791	3 208	424	1 138	1 646	22 841	16 703	14 132	692	4 460	9 494
1971														
1st quarter	206 763	5 503	4 367	3 892	3 290	474	1 141	1 675	23 381	16 986	14 359	764	4 464	9 530
2nd quarter	207 362	5 591	4 467	3 982	3 348	487	1 152	1 709	23 447	17 184	14 449	779	4 461	9 598
3rd quarter	208 000	5 675	4 522	4 030	3 397	497	1 156	1 744	23 557	17 222	14 519	797	4 439	9 659
4th quarter	208 642	5 721	4 595	4 089	3 465	514	1 168	1 783	23 554	17 369	14 715	828	4 455	9 780
1972														
1st quarter	209 142	5 899	4 714	4 142	3 539	529	1 181	1 828	23 919	17 407	14 874	845	4 459	9 922
2nd quarter	209 637	6 059	4 787	4 198	3 619	544	1 213	1 862	24 415	17 543	15 122	865	4 569	10 019
3rd quarter	210 181	6 156	4 897	4 305	3 697	559	1 237	1 900	24 576	17 835	15 316	885	4 620	10 128
4th quarter	210 737	6 321	5 104	4 501	3 805	586	1 272	1 947	24 918	18 493	15 634	929	4 695	10 282

Table 1-3B. U.S. Population and Per Capita Product and Income: Historical Data—*Continued*

(Dollars, except as noted; quarterly data are at seasonally adjusted annual rates.)

NIPA Table 7.1

Year and quarter	Population (mid-period, thousands)	Current dollars							Chained (2009) dollars					
		Gross domestic product	Personal income	Disposable personal income	Personal consumption expenditures				Gross domestic product	Disposable personal income	Personal consumption expenditures			
					Total	Durable goods	Nondurable goods	Services			Total	Durable goods	Nondurable goods	Services
1973														
1st quarter	211 192	6 538	5 177	4 578	3 913	624	1 304	1 985	25 477	18 585	15 885	986	4 713	10 392
2nd quarter	211 663	6 697	5 304	4 693	3 978	620	1 329	2 029	25 708	18 691	15 843	972	4 662	10 457
3rd quarter	212 191	6 771	5 420	4 788	4 055	616	1 366	2 072	25 505	18 726	15 860	961	4 673	10 501
4th quarter	212 708	6 954	5 586	4 928	4 116	603	1 399	2 114	25 680	18 885	15 775	936	4 643	10 515
1974														
1st quarter	213 144	7 012	5 651	4 981	4 193	594	1 449	2 150	25 415	18 536	15 605	913	4 571	10 478
2nd quarter	213 602	7 183	5 760	5 063	4 318	611	1 489	2 218	25 427	18 324	15 627	915	4 531	10 559
3rd quarter	214 147	7 301	5 915	5 191	4 441	637	1 530	2 274	25 117	18 295	15 651	918	4 529	10 584
4th quarter	214 700	7 466	6 037	5 303	4 475	592	1 541	2 342	24 952	18 225	15 382	829	4 437	10 663
1975														
1st quarter	215 135	7 528	6 117	5 382	4 588	613	1 563	2 413	24 601	18 158	15 479	845	4 437	10 740
2nd quarter	215 652	7 681	6 249	5 687	4 710	634	1 599	2 478	24 731	18 956	15 700	859	4 524	10 848
3rd quarter	216 289	7 924	6 399	5 693	4 853	679	1 646	2 528	25 065	18 625	15 877	910	4 555	10 869
4th quarter	216 848	8 143	6 548	5 817	4 974	707	1 659	2 608	25 338	18 719	16 004	934	4 532	10 993
1976														
1st quarter	217 314	8 396	6 686	5 938	5 118	751	1 691	2 676	25 854	18 898	16 289	979	4 614	11 098
2nd quarter	217 776	8 527	6 784	6 006	5 198	762	1 713	2 723	25 994	18 956	16 404	981	4 675	11 148
3rd quarter	218 338	8 659	6 933	6 127	5 319	778	1 743	2 798	26 059	19 047	16 536	990	4 699	11 255
4th quarter	218 917	8 855	7 079	6 244	5 459	801	1 780	2 878	26 186	19 109	16 707	1 003	4 735	11 381
1977														
1st quarter	219 427	9 081	7 200	6 340	5 608	838	1 807	2 963	26 429	19 059	16 859	1 037	4 721	11 491
2nd quarter	219 956	9 366	7 403	6 513	5 722	860	1 835	3 026	26 883	19 250	16 911	1 059	4 710	11 507
3rd quarter	220 573	9 622	7 594	6 694	5 847	879	1 858	3 109	27 282	19 490	17 025	1 072	4 720	11 599
4th quarter	221 201	9 804	7 844	6 901	6 003	907	1 915	3 181	27 207	19 810	17 232	1 091	4 807	11 677
1978														
1st quarter	221 719	9 962	8 005	7 049	6 124	894	1 944	3 286	27 238	19 904	17 291	1 060	4 817	11 835
2nd quarter	222 281	10 512	8 251	7 247	6 367	973	2 001	3 393	28 225	20 050	17 616	1 136	4 842	11 982
3rd quarter	222 933	10 760	8 466	7 406	6 487	972	2 044	3 471	28 418	20 135	17 638	1 117	4 865	12 032
4th quarter	223 583	11 102	8 689	7 583	6 644	994	2 099	3 550	28 715	20 235	17 727	1 123	4 913	12 059
1979														
1st quarter	224 152	11 294	8 920	7 788	6 785	996	2 162	3 628	28 699	20 398	17 772	1 107	4 922	12 151
2nd quarter	224 737	11 551	9 077	7 911	6 948	988	2 225	3 735	28 659	20 169	17 715	1 079	4 900	12 195
3rd quarter	225 418	11 846	9 340	8 121	7 169	1 024	2 317	3 827	28 778	20 204	17 836	1 105	4 942	12 207
4th quarter	226 117	12 077	9 589	8 328	7 339	1 013	2 385	3 941	28 763	20 230	17 828	1 074	4 953	12 275
1980														
1st quarter	226 754	12 333	9 838	8 582	7 526	1 023	2 469	4 033	28 775	20 241	17 751	1 054	4 937	12 259
2nd quarter	227 389	12 313	9 925	8 640	7 515	932	2 489	4 095	28 113	19 892	17 303	938	4 856	12 147
3rd quarter	228 070	12 540	10 248	8 923	7 751	988	2 528	4 235	27 987	20 074	17 437	976	4 830	12 246
4th quarter	228 689	13 090	10 692	9 297	8 026	1 033	2 585	4 407	28 428	20 413	17 620	1 003	4 836	12 394
1981														
1st quarter	229 155	13 667	10 927	9 483	8 251	1 074	2 680	4 497	28 957	20 316	17 677	1 030	4 869	12 341
2nd quarter	229 674	13 790	11 109	9 617	8 368	1 049	2 712	4 607	28 681	20 266	17 634	987	4 879	12 391
3rd quarter	230 301	14 161	11 497	9 947	8 516	1 094	2 732	4 690	28 931	20 624	17 657	1 015	4 877	12 346
4th quarter	230 903	14 220	11 619	10 092	8 558	1 026	2 753	4 779	28 519	20 611	17 479	939	4 883	12 325
1982														
1st quarter	231 395	14 148	11 734	10 210	8 705	1 065	2 765	4 875	27 982	20 592	17 557	967	4 881	12 347
2nd quarter	231 906	14 365	11 895	10 344	8 801	1 075	2 754	4 972	28 073	20 665	17 583	969	4 862	12 403
3rd quarter	232 498	14 482	12 042	10 536	8 986	1 084	2 795	5 107	27 900	20 723	17 674	974	4 870	12 490
4th quarter	233 074	14 621	12 204	10 674	9 229	1 134	2 818	5 277	27 859	20 765	17 952	1 016	4 908	12 667
1983														
1st quarter	233 546	14 902	12 339	10 837	9 380	1 151	2 813	5 415	28 167	20 901	18 090	1 024	4 914	12 806
2nd quarter	234 028	15 314	12 528	10 992	9 634	1 237	2 876	5 520	28 750	21 006	18 410	1 096	4 962	12 942
3rd quarter	234 603	15 738	12 749	11 277	9 907	1 289	2 934	5 684	29 241	21 270	18 687	1 136	5 025	13 092
4th quarter	235 153	16 143	13 082	11 570	10 107	1 358	2 962	5 787	29 774	21 678	18 937	1 189	5 074	13 193
1984														
1st quarter	235 605	16 607	13 444	11 911	10 283	1 407	2 998	5 878	30 307	22 078	19 061	1 232	5 077	13 230
2nd quarter	236 082	17 007	13 771	12 202	10 510	1 446	3 060	6 005	30 777	22 400	19 294	1 258	5 178	13 313
3rd quarter	236 657	17 271	14 058	12 435	10 647	1 445	3 062	6 140	31 005	22 652	19 395	1 255	5 169	13 453
4th quarter	237 232	17 483	14 254	12 585	10 829	1 492	3 089	6 248	31 176	22 783	19 604	1 293	5 196	13 575
1985														
1st quarter	237 673	17 827	14 501	12 682	11 124	1 548	3 124	6 452	31 428	22 687	19 900	1 335	5 218	13 795
2nd quarter	238 176	18 064	14 639	13 007	11 299	1 567	3 161	6 572	31 649	23 075	20 044	1 348	5 248	13 898
3rd quarter	238 789	18 404	14 799	13 033	11 578	1 660	3 185	6 733	32 058	22 938	20 377	1 431	5 278	14 054
4th quarter	239 387	18 602	15 032	13 241	11 658	1 603	3 231	6 825	32 218	23 144	20 378	1 378	5 311	14 140
1986														
1st quarter	239 861	18 829	15 252	13 475	11 818	1 633	3 249	6 937	32 453	23 386	20 510	1 403	5 368	14 165
2nd quarter	240 368	18 951	15 396	13 609	11 911	1 694	3 193	7 024	32 533	23 647	20 696	1 450	5 404	14 228
3rd quarter	240 962	19 172	15 565	13 741	12 158	1 850	3 200	7 109	32 779	23 755	21 019	1 570	5 402	14 322
4th quarter	241 539	19 332	15 703	13 815	12 280	1 826	3 225	7 229	32 870	23 741	21 103	1 541	5 433	14 451
1987														
1st quarter	242 009	19 570	15 913	14 051	12 389	1 729	3 295	7 365	33 036	23 890	21 065	1 447	5 430	14 635
2nd quarter	242 520	19 881	16 127	14 017	12 654	1 811	3 349	7 494	33 336	23 609	21 312	1 503	5 460	14 754
3rd quarter	243 120	20 157	16 382	14 370	12 889	1 894	3 376	7 619	33 556	23 978	21 506	1 561	5 451	14 854
4th quarter	243 721	20 608	16 734	14 654	12 997	1 846	3 392	7 758	34 025	24 239	21 498	1 515	5 444	14 961

Table 1-3B. U.S. Population and Per Capita Product and Income: Historical Data—*Continued*

(Dollars, except as noted; quarterly data are at seasonally adjusted annual rates.)

NIPA Table 7.1

| Year and quarter | Population (mid-period, thou-sands) | Current dollars | | | | | | | Chained (2009) dollars | | | | | |
| | | Gross domestic product | Personal income | Dispos-able personal income | Personal consumption expenditures | | | | Gross domestic product | Dispos-able personal income | Personal consumption expenditures | | | |
					Total	Durable goods	Nondur-able goods	Services			Total	Durable goods	Nondur-able goods	Services
1988														
1st quarter	244 208	20 845	17 009	14 953	13 304	1 926	3 433	7 945	34 148	24 543	21 837	1 584	5 492	15 138
2nd quarter	244 716	21 281	17 276	15 242	13 522	1 934	3 488	8 100	34 528	24 744	21 951	1 581	5 524	15 240
3rd quarter	245 354	21 599	17 603	15 538	13 769	1 917	3 549	8 303	34 637	24 917	22 081	1 556	5 547	15 418
4th quarter	245 966	22 006	17 909	15 806	14 031	1 977	3 603	8 452	35 008	25 095	22 278	1 593	5 591	15 512
1989														
1st quarter	246 460	22 427	18 391	16 148	14 226	1 974	3 662	8 590	35 291	25 354	22 336	1 582	5 605	15 585
2nd quarter	247 017	22 786	18 572	16 278	14 450	1 997	3 756	8 697	35 488	25 222	22 391	1 600	5 601	15 614
3rd quarter	247 698	23 059	18 745	16 437	14 637	2 041	3 780	8 816	35 654	25 325	22 551	1 632	5 642	15 680
4th quarter	248 374	23 205	18 988	16 654	14 777	1 980	3 830	8 966	35 633	25 459	22 589	1 578	5 690	15 786
1990														
1st quarter	248 936	23 664	19 335	16 995	15 082	2 070	3 913	9 098	35 941	25 615	22 731	1 641	5 670	15 836
2nd quarter	249 711	23 926	19 578	17 197	15 218	1 996	3 928	9 294	35 968	25 688	22 732	1 581	5 659	15 980
3rd quarter	250 595	24 061	19 756	17 358	15 417	1 970	4 003	9 444	35 850	25 607	22 743	1 560	5 648	16 053
4th quarter	251 482	23 951	19 774	17 385	15 446	1 912	4 051	9 483	35 419	25 315	22 491	1 512	5 571	15 958
1991														
1st quarter	252 258	24 003	19 757	17 454	15 422	1 870	4 020	9 531	35 145	25 290	22 345	1 465	5 557	15 905
2nd quarter	253 063	24 277	19 928	17 612	15 584	1 878	4 038	9 668	35 305	25 384	22 461	1 468	5 572	16 015
3rd quarter	253 965	24 485	20 057	17 733	15 709	1 907	4 034	9 769	35 348	25 386	22 490	1 485	5 561	16 024
4th quarter	254 835	24 641	20 300	17 951	15 763	1 874	4 005	9 884	35 381	25 516	22 407	1 456	5 495	16 069
1992														
1st quarter	255 585	24 965	20 698	18 394	16 111	1 941	4 060	10 109	35 694	25 987	22 761	1 509	5 560	16 286
2nd quarter	256 439	25 317	21 015	18 648	16 274	1 954	4 084	10 237	35 968	26 171	22 840	1 514	5 565	16 360
3rd quarter	257 386	25 590	21 173	18 779	16 494	1 990	4 122	10 382	36 184	26 189	23 003	1 541	5 577	16 475
4th quarter	258 277	25 932	21 385	18 911	16 750	2 025	4 161	10 564	36 420	26 188	23 196	1 566	5 614	16 601
1993														
1st quarter	259 039	26 051	21 455	19 074	16 864	2 038	4 166	10 661	36 381	26 258	23 216	1 577	5 603	16 614
2nd quarter	259 826	26 285	21 655	19 178	17 079	2 109	4 181	10 789	36 486	26 224	23 353	1 623	5 630	16 644
3rd quarter	260 714	26 482	21 736	19 208	17 283	2 135	4 191	10 958	36 539	26 150	23 531	1 635	5 667	16 778
4th quarter	261 547	26 889	21 965	19 383	17 481	2 194	4 226	11 061	36 909	26 238	23 663	1 669	5 688	16 835
1994														
1st quarter	262 250	27 212	22 104	19 535	17 696	2 245	4 259	11 192	37 171	26 351	23 871	1 705	5 749	16 929
2nd quarter	263 020	27 640	22 447	19 794	17 880	2 276	4 289	11 315	37 569	26 552	23 985	1 718	5 777	16 999
3rd quarter	263 870	27 863	22 624	19 989	18 089	2 309	4 357	11 423	37 669	26 624	24 093	1 730	5 808	17 060
4th quarter	264 678	28 248	22 965	20 300	18 314	2 387	4 394	11 532	37 980	26 912	24 278	1 786	5 852	17 109
1995														
1st quarter	265 388	28 431	23 267	20 537	18 401	2 341	4 397	11 663	38 008	27 096	24 277	1 744	5 857	17 185
2nd quarter	266 142	28 575	23 447	20 641	18 618	2 356	4 422	11 840	38 033	27 080	24 426	1 757	5 869	17 311
3rd quarter	267 000	28 863	23 659	20 842	18 803	2 407	4 433	11 963	38 235	27 235	24 571	1 801	5 871	17 385
4th quarter	267 820	29 122	23 866	20 990	18 960	2 435	4 449	12 075	38 389	27 308	24 667	1 826	5 884	17 430
1996														
1st quarter	268 487	29 399	24 243	21 257	19 196	2 458	4 511	12 227	38 544	27 501	24 834	1 842	5 907	17 560
2nd quarter	269 251	29 941	24 659	21 541	19 477	2 512	4 604	12 361	39 106	27 685	25 033	1 895	5 966	17 614
3rd quarter	270 128	30 204	24 857	21 734	19 614	2 515	4 614	12 484	39 340	27 815	25 102	1 902	5 989	17 652
4th quarter	270 991	30 581	25 112	21 926	19 839	2 545	4 680	12 613	39 629	27 871	25 218	1 933	6 018	17 691
1997														
1st quarter	271 709	30 923	25 505	22 185	20 083	2 597	4 715	12 771	39 825	28 077	25 417	1 980	6 039	17 801
2nd quarter	272 487	31 385	25 728	22 365	20 166	2 556	4 690	12 920	40 311	28 236	25 460	1 968	6 025	17 884
3rd quarter	273 391	31 792	26 057	22 615	20 496	2 644	4 747	13 106	40 689	28 477	25 810	2 049	6 101	18 040
4th quarter	274 246	32 045	26 467	22 938	20 739	2 688	4 770	13 281	40 877	28 796	26 035	2 095	6 125	18 179
1998														
1st quarter	274 950	32 332	26 989	23 366	20 898	2 683	4 754	13 461	41 176	29 334	26 236	2 106	6 153	18 347
2nd quarter	275 703	32 625	27 378	23 669	21 247	2 790	4 789	13 668	41 461	29 662	26 626	2 207	6 211	18 536
3rd quarter	276 564	33 072	27 680	23 908	21 524	2 839	4 827	13 858	41 873	29 871	26 893	2 262	6 236	18 703
4th quarter	277 400	33 618	27 941	24 091	21 830	2 975	4 886	13 969	42 432	30 023	27 206	2 389	6 301	18 759
1999														
1st quarter	278 103	33 970	28 184	24 308	22 039	2 948	4 980	14 111	42 663	30 216	27 395	2 388	6 401	18 861
2nd quarter	278 864	34 271	28 359	24 431	22 423	3 065	5 085	14 273	42 897	30 208	27 725	2 495	6 443	18 997
3rd quarter	279 751	34 718	28 652	24 646	22 725	3 114	5 146	14 464	43 299	30 314	27 951	2 547	6 452	19 146
4th quarter	280 592	35 376	29 195	25 081	23 126	3 123	5 283	14 720	43 919	30 668	28 276	2 570	6 564	19 343
2000														
1st quarter	281 304	35 659	30 022	25 724	23 614	3 274	5 303	15 037	43 935	31 192	28 634	2 706	6 490	19 590
2nd quarter	282 002	36 448	30 409	26 046	23 891	3 198	5 443	15 250	44 654	31 438	28 837	2 649	6 603	19 777
3rd quarter	282 769	36 629	30 855	26 442	24 208	3 224	5 507	15 477	44 586	31 719	29 039	2 687	6 628	19 908
4th quarter	283 518	36 937	31 048	26 608	24 494	3 230	5 563	15 700	44 721	31 742	29 220	2 699	6 674	20 034
2001														
1st quarter	284 169	36 978	31 535	26 952	24 705	3 261	5 532	15 911	44 492	31 940	29 276	2 737	6 619	20 092
2nd quarter	284 838	37 349	31 590	26 994	24 829	3 228	5 583	16 018	44 623	31 836	29 282	2 728	6 635	20 095
3rd quarter	285 584	37 255	31 482	27 581	24 873	3 235	5 571	16 067	44 366	32 504	29 313	2 752	6 648	20 077
4th quarter	286 311	37 377	31 492	27 189	25 205	3 478	5 524	16 203	44 376	32 020	29 685	2 974	6 687	20 107
2002														
1st quarter	286 935	37 759	31 567	27 840	25 272	3 398	5 523	16 351	44 687	32 728	29 709	2 931	6 697	20 186
2nd quarter	287 574	38 024	31 783	28 134	25 539	3 407	5 592	16 541	44 834	32 821	29 795	2 953	6 686	20 256
3rd quarter	288 303	38 283	31 820	28 168	25 782	3 481	5 607	16 694	44 938	32 696	29 927	3 032	6 685	20 285
4th quarter	289 007	38 421	31 985	28 363	25 976	3 402	5 687	16 887	44 857	32 773	30 014	2 983	6 756	20 371

Table 1-3B. U.S. Population and Per Capita Product and Income: Historical Data—*Continued*

(Dollars, except as noted; quarterly data are at seasonally adjusted annual rates.)

NIPA Table 7.1

| Year and quarter | Population (mid-period, thousands) | Current dollars | | | | | | | Chained (2009) dollars | | | | | |
| | | Gross domestic product | Personal income | Disposable personal income | Personal consumption expenditures | | | | Gross domestic product | Disposable personal income | Personal consumption expenditures | | | |
					Total	Durable goods	Nondurable goods	Services			Total	Durable goods	Nondurable goods	Services
2003														
1st quarter	289 609	38 777	32 114	28 584	26 220	3 363	5 810	17 047	44 996	32 796	30 084	2 986	6 788	20 405
2nd quarter	290 253	39 175	32 469	28 958	26 475	3 472	5 748	17 255	45 312	33 197	30 351	3 116	6 823	20 473
3rd quarter	290 974	39 952	32 822	29 539	26 963	3 582	5 921	17 460	45 957	33 657	30 722	3 247	6 932	20 575
4th quarter	291 669	40 515	33 220	29 708	27 217	3 586	5 973	17 658	46 384	33 713	30 887	3 280	6 963	20 671
2004														
1st quarter	292 237	41 023	33 560	30 094	27 638	3 635	6 088	17 915	46 560	33 893	31 127	3 328	7 002	20 819
2nd quarter	292 875	41 592	34 047	30 537	27 952	3 659	6 151	18 141	46 799	34 152	31 261	3 354	7 009	20 919
3rd quarter	293 603	42 124	34 436	30 800	28 313	3 693	6 219	18 401	47 107	34 247	31 481	3 411	7 045	21 039
4th quarter	294 334	42 680	35 070	31 353	28 757	3 741	6 370	18 646	47 396	34 589	31 725	3 450	7 091	21 195
2005														
1st quarter	294 957	43 443	35 121	31 145	29 066	3 765	6 428	18 873	47 800	34 183	31 900	3 479	7 167	21 262
2nd quarter	295 588	43 892	35 585	31 533	29 514	3 859	6 485	19 170	47 947	34 380	32 178	3 570	7 183	21 421
3rd quarter	296 340	44 562	36 101	31 961	29 993	3 865	6 682	19 446	48 228	34 469	32 345	3 602	7 181	21 558
4th quarter	297 086	45 043	36 624	32 396	30 265	3 744	6 798	19 723	48 381	34 666	32 386	3 497	7 285	21 616
2006														
1st quarter	297 736	45 842	37 652	33 217	30 679	3 874	6 847	19 958	48 856	35 380	32 677	3 632	7 329	21 712
2nd quarter	298 408	46 245	37 969	33 448	31 010	3 844	6 955	20 212	48 891	35 354	32 777	3 620	7 337	21 820
3rd quarter	299 180	46 489	38 238	33 696	31 333	3 870	7 051	20 412	48 809	35 363	32 884	3 660	7 354	21 864
4th quarter	299 946	46 896	38 657	33 991	31 518	3 888	6 986	20 644	49 065	35 734	33 134	3 699	7 458	21 969
2007														
1st quarter	300 609	47 348	39 322	34 457	31 908	3 903	7 081	20 923	48 987	35 889	33 235	3 733	7 457	22 035
2nd quarter	301 284	47 869	39 659	34 720	32 199	3 933	7 190	21 076	49 251	35 878	33 273	3 778	7 425	22 055
3rd quarter	302 062	48 234	39 884	34 918	32 441	3 940	7 231	21 270	49 455	35 880	33 335	3 810	7 416	22 093
4th quarter	302 829	48 494	40 235	35 209	32 725	3 930	7 359	21 436	49 506	35 819	33 292	3 816	7 392	22 070
2008														
1st quarter	303 494	48 332	40 749	35 688	32 865	3 797	7 427	21 642	49 060	35 998	33 150	3 699	7 335	22 111
2nd quarter	304 160	48 701	41 821	36 742	33 192	3 748	7 624	21 821	49 196	36 677	33 134	3 679	7 370	22 079
3rd quarter	304 902	48 681	41 113	36 175	33 207	3 614	7 702	21 891	48 841	35 747	32 814	3 558	7 255	22 001
4th quarter	305 616	47 609	40 528	35 801	32 261	3 322	7 108	21 832	47 697	35 892	32 344	3 294	7 128	21 924
2009														
1st quarter	306 237	46 970	39 387	35 459	31 904	3 305	6 939	21 661	46 941	35 752	32 167	3 294	7 119	21 756
2nd quarter	306 866	46 732	39 489	35 798	31 837	3 274	6 986	21 577	46 781	35 932	31 957	3 267	7 053	21 636
3rd quarter	307 573	46 767	39 232	35 546	32 158	3 400	7 150	21 608	46 826	35 456	32 076	3 416	7 063	21 597
4th quarter	308 285	47 250	39 356	35 658	32 298	3 343	7 243	21 712	47 170	35 328	31 999	3 346	7 083	21 569
2010														
1st quarter	308 901	47 527	39 608	35 744	32 517	3 367	7 331	21 818	47 280	35 293	32 106	3 383	7 127	21 595
2nd quarter	309 472	48 110	40 111	36 183	32 758	3 440	7 306	22 012	47 649	35 686	32 308	3 478	7 148	21 683
3rd quarter	310 105	48 557	40 450	36 396	33 000	3 467	7 376	22 157	47 872	35 790	32 451	3 527	7 178	21 747
4th quarter	310 752	49 011	40 921	36 768	33 445	3 549	7 580	22 316	48 074	35 965	32 715	3 628	7 255	21 836
2011														
1st quarter	311 289	48 952	42 011	37 432	33 806	3 583	7 770	22 454	47 805	36 342	32 822	3 668	7 276	21 883
2nd quarter	311 832	49 581	42 314	37 686	34 157	3 567	7 939	22 651	48 069	36 222	32 831	3 637	7 265	21 932
3rd quarter	312 472	49 883	42 715	38 009	34 417	3 597	7 966	22 855	48 072	36 340	32 906	3 676	7 232	22 007
4th quarter	313 095	50 417	42 793	38 087	34 583	3 673	7 988	22 923	48 516	36 289	32 951	3 774	7 226	21 967
2012														
1st quarter	313 623	50 933	43 563	38 868	34 934	3 759	8 085	23 091	48 756	36 821	33 094	3 870	7 250	21 995
2nd quarter	314 155	51 318	43 972	39 221	35 041	3 761	8 071	23 209	48 901	37 041	33 094	3 890	7 244	21 983
3rd quarter	314 790	51 552	44 052	39 250	35 178	3 794	8 102	23 282	48 860	36 948	33 114	3 946	7 246	21 950
4th quarter	315 430	51 667	45 388	40 415	35 394	3 845	8 138	23 410	48 772	37 841	33 140	4 016	7 226	21 934
2013														
1st quarter	315 957	52 035	43 966	38 772	35 675	3 910	8 205	23 560	48 922	36 180	33 290	4 094	7 299	21 938
2nd quarter	316 499	52 218	44 313	39 003	35 775	3 904	8 136	23 736	48 974	36 356	33 347	4 110	7 300	21 981
3rd quarter	317 136	52 746	44 575	39 299	36 002	3 902	8 219	23 882	49 236	36 481	33 421	4 135	7 327	22 004
4th quarter	317 765	53 365	44 752	39 415	36 369	3 911	8 251	24 207	49 601	36 460	33 642	4 168	7 360	22 160
2014														
1st quarter	318 288	53 361	45 347	39 893	36 572	3 906	8 268	24 398	49 405	36 755	33 695	4 189	7 356	22 199
2nd quarter	318 833	54 166	45 832	40 331	37 051	4 012	8 382	24 657	49 874	36 962	33 956	4 320	7 405	22 295
3rd quarter	319 470	54 847	46 248	40 638	37 403	4 054	8 427	24 922	50 298	37 134	34 177	4 390	7 435	22 424
4th quarter	320 100	55 033	46 722	40 977	37 680	4 072	8 362	25 246	50 457	37 484	34 468	4 447	7 478	22 619

Table 1-4A. Contributions to Percent Change in Real Gross Domestic Product: Recent Data

(Percent, percentage points.)   NIPA Table 1.1.2

Year and quarter	Percent change at seasonally adjusted annual rate, real GDP	Personal consumption expenditures	Gross private domestic investment				Exports and imports of goods and services			Government consumption expenditures and gross investment		
			Total	Fixed investment		Change in private inventories	Net exports	Exports	Imports	Total	Federal	State and local
				Nonresidential	Residential							
1950	8.7	4.20	5.68	0.91	1.99	2.78	-1.28	-0.65	-0.63	0.11	-0.47	0.58
1951	8.1	1.00	0.05	0.42	-1.11	0.74	0.79	0.96	-0.16	6.22	6.16	0.06
1952	4.1	1.90	-1.44	-0.01	-0.09	-1.34	-0.57	-0.21	-0.36	4.18	4.07	0.11
1953	4.7	2.85	0.87	0.95	0.19	-0.27	-0.68	-0.30	-0.38	1.65	1.32	0.33
1954	-0.6	1.25	-0.61	-0.14	0.42	-0.89	0.39	0.19	0.20	-1.60	-2.20	0.59
1955	7.1	4.50	3.44	1.06	0.88	1.50	-0.04	0.43	-0.47	-0.78	-1.31	0.54
1956	2.1	1.77	-0.05	0.70	-0.47	-0.28	0.36	0.69	-0.33	0.05	-0.20	0.25
1957	2.1	1.49	-0.64	0.20	-0.31	-0.53	0.24	0.41	-0.17	1.01	0.55	0.47
1958	-0.7	0.52	-1.16	-1.04	0.05	-0.17	-0.87	-0.67	-0.19	0.77	0.07	0.69
1959	6.9	3.49	2.82	0.81	1.18	0.83	0.00	0.44	-0.44	0.59	0.29	0.30
1960	2.6	1.67	0.06	0.56	-0.37	-0.13	0.70	0.75	-0.06	0.14	-0.24	0.38
1961	2.6	1.26	0.05	0.08	0.02	-0.05	0.05	0.03	0.03	1.19	0.65	0.54
1962	6.1	3.00	1.82	0.81	0.46	0.55	-0.21	0.25	-0.45	1.50	1.23	0.28
1963	4.4	2.47	1.08	0.59	0.57	-0.07	0.23	0.34	-0.11	0.57	0.03	0.54
1964	5.8	3.56	1.27	1.08	0.31	-0.12	0.35	0.57	-0.22	0.58	-0.05	0.63
1965	6.5	3.79	2.26	1.75	-0.13	0.64	-0.29	0.14	-0.44	0.74	0.10	0.63
1966	6.6	3.37	1.56	1.40	-0.40	0.56	-0.28	0.35	-0.63	1.94	1.34	0.61
1967	2.7	1.76	-0.62	-0.04	-0.11	-0.47	-0.21	0.12	-0.33	1.82	1.32	0.50
1968	4.9	3.38	0.99	0.55	0.53	-0.09	-0.29	0.39	-0.68	0.83	0.22	0.62
1969	3.1	2.21	0.93	0.79	0.14	0.00	-0.03	0.25	-0.28	0.04	-0.33	0.37
1970	0.2	1.39	-1.03	-0.10	-0.22	-0.70	0.33	0.54	-0.21	-0.49	-0.80	0.31
1971	3.3	2.29	1.63	-0.01	1.08	0.56	-0.18	0.10	-0.28	-0.44	-0.80	0.36
1972	5.2	3.67	1.90	0.97	0.87	0.06	-0.19	0.42	-0.61	-0.11	-0.37	0.26
1973	5.6	2.97	1.95	1.50	-0.04	0.48	0.79	1.08	-0.28	-0.07	-0.40	0.32
1974	-0.5	-0.50	-1.24	0.10	-1.08	-0.26	0.73	0.56	0.17	0.49	0.07	0.42
1975	-0.2	1.36	-2.90	-1.13	-0.54	-1.23	0.86	-0.05	0.91	0.49	0.05	0.43
1976	5.4	3.41	2.91	0.66	0.88	1.37	-1.05	0.36	-1.40	0.12	0.02	0.10
1977	4.6	2.59	2.47	1.26	0.97	0.24	-0.70	0.19	-0.89	0.26	0.21	0.04
1978	5.6	2.69	2.21	1.72	0.38	0.12	0.04	0.80	-0.76	0.61	0.24	0.37
1979	3.2	1.44	0.71	1.33	-0.22	-0.40	0.64	0.80	-0.16	0.38	0.21	0.16
1980	-0.2	-0.19	-2.07	0.00	-1.18	-0.89	1.64	0.95	0.69	0.38	0.40	-0.02
1981	2.6	0.91	1.63	0.87	-0.37	1.13	-0.15	0.12	-0.27	0.20	0.43	-0.23
1982	-1.9	0.86	-2.55	-0.53	-0.72	-1.30	-0.59	-0.71	0.12	0.38	0.36	0.01
1983	4.6	3.54	1.60	-0.06	1.38	0.28	-1.32	-0.21	-1.10	0.81	0.67	0.14
1984	7.3	3.32	4.73	2.18	0.65	1.90	-1.54	0.61	-2.15	0.76	0.35	0.41
1985	4.2	3.25	-0.01	0.91	0.11	-1.03	-0.39	0.24	-0.63	1.38	0.80	0.59
1986	3.5	2.63	0.03	-0.24	0.58	-0.31	-0.29	0.53	-0.82	1.14	0.61	0.53
1987	3.5	2.14	0.53	0.01	0.10	0.41	0.17	0.76	-0.59	0.63	0.39	0.24
1988	4.2	2.66	0.45	0.63	-0.05	-0.13	0.81	1.22	-0.41	0.28	-0.13	0.42
1989	3.7	1.86	0.72	0.71	-0.16	0.17	0.51	0.97	-0.46	0.59	0.16	0.43
1990	1.9	1.31	-0.45	0.14	-0.38	-0.21	0.40	0.78	-0.37	0.66	0.20	0.46
1991	-0.1	0.15	-1.09	-0.48	-0.35	-0.25	0.62	0.60	0.01	0.25	0.00	0.25
1992	3.6	2.38	1.11	0.34	0.49	0.28	-0.04	0.66	-0.70	0.11	-0.14	0.24
1993	2.7	2.24	1.23	0.84	0.32	0.07	-0.56	0.31	-0.87	-0.17	-0.31	0.14
1994	4.0	2.52	1.90	0.91	0.38	0.61	-0.40	0.84	-1.24	0.02	-0.30	0.32
1995	2.7	1.94	0.55	1.15	-0.15	-0.44	0.12	1.02	-0.89	0.10	-0.21	0.31
1996	3.8	2.28	1.49	1.13	0.35	0.02	-0.15	0.86	-1.01	0.18	-0.09	0.27
1997	4.5	2.45	2.00	1.37	0.11	0.52	-0.31	1.26	-1.57	0.35	-0.06	0.40
1998	4.5	3.45	1.76	1.42	0.38	-0.04	-1.13	0.25	-1.39	0.38	-0.06	0.44
1999	4.7	3.44	1.60	1.32	0.29	-0.02	-0.97	0.27	-1.24	0.61	0.13	0.49
2000	4.1	3.32	1.25	1.27	0.03	-0.05	-0.82	0.88	-1.70	0.34	0.02	0.32
2001	1.0	1.71	-1.19	-0.34	0.04	-0.89	-0.22	-0.61	0.40	0.67	0.24	0.43
2002	1.8	1.72	-0.11	-0.93	0.29	0.53	-0.64	-0.16	-0.47	0.81	0.46	0.35
2003	2.8	2.10	0.71	0.23	0.47	0.02	-0.42	0.16	-0.59	0.42	0.47	-0.05
2004	3.8	2.59	1.55	0.62	0.56	0.37	-0.66	0.89	-1.55	0.31	0.33	-0.02
2005	3.3	2.36	1.20	0.83	0.41	-0.04	-0.34	0.61	-0.94	0.12	0.13	0.00
2006	2.7	2.04	0.42	0.87	-0.50	0.04	-0.08	0.90	-0.99	0.29	0.18	0.11
2007	1.8	1.50	-0.61	0.76	-1.13	-0.23	0.58	0.99	-0.41	0.30	0.12	0.18
2008	-0.3	-0.23	-1.71	-0.09	-1.12	-0.49	1.11	0.67	0.44	0.54	0.50	0.04
2009	-2.8	-1.08	-3.52	-2.04	-0.73	-0.76	1.19	-1.07	2.26	0.64	0.44	0.20
2010	2.5	1.32	1.66	0.28	-0.07	1.45	-0.46	1.33	-1.79	0.02	0.37	-0.35
2011	1.6	1.55	0.73	0.85	0.01	-0.14	-0.02	0.87	-0.89	-0.65	-0.24	-0.41
2012	2.2	1.01	1.52	1.05	0.33	0.14	0.08	0.46	-0.38	-0.38	-0.15	-0.22
2013	1.5	1.16	0.70	0.38	0.27	0.06	0.20	0.38	-0.18	-0.58	-0.46	-0.12
2014	2.4	1.84	0.87	0.77	0.05	0.05	-0.18	0.46	-0.63	-0.11	-0.18	0.07
2012												
1st quarter	2.7	1.63	1.47	1.37	0.63	-0.53	-0.02	0.37	-0.40	-0.40	-0.03	-0.36
2nd quarter	1.9	0.45	1.53	0.88	0.10	0.56	0.28	0.61	-0.33	-0.39	-0.24	-0.14
3rd quarter	0.5	0.72	-0.18	-0.27	0.27	-0.18	0.16	0.27	-0.10	-0.22	0.04	-0.26
4th quarter	0.1	0.78	-0.51	0.46	0.57	-1.54	0.58	-0.07	0.65	-0.75	-0.45	-0.30
2013												
1st quarter	1.9	1.74	1.05	0.51	0.26	0.28	-0.01	0.12	-0.13	-0.88	-0.75	-0.12
2nd quarter	1.1	0.96	0.78	0.14	0.27	0.38	-0.24	0.64	-0.89	-0.38	-0.43	0.05
3rd quarter	3.0	1.17	2.07	0.44	0.15	1.48	0.16	0.55	-0.39	-0.42	-0.44	0.02
4th quarter	3.8	2.36	0.71	1.05	-0.26	-0.08	1.26	1.42	-0.16	-0.51	-0.49	-0.01
2014												
1st quarter	-0.9	0.85	-0.38	1.00	-0.09	-1.29	-1.39	-0.95	-0.44	0.00	0.02	-0.03
2nd quarter	4.6	2.60	1.99	0.56	0.31	1.12	-0.24	1.28	-1.52	0.21	-0.08	0.29
3rd quarter	4.3	2.34	1.22	1.12	0.11	-0.01	0.39	0.24	0.15	0.33	0.26	0.07
4th quarter	2.1	2.86	0.36	0.09	0.31	-0.03	-0.89	0.71	-1.60	-0.26	-0.41	0.15

Table 1-4B. Contributions to Percent Change in Real Gross Domestic Product: Historical Data

(Percent; percentage points.)

NIPA Table 1.1.2

Year and quarter	Percent change at seasonally adjusted annual rate, real GDP	Personal consump-tion expen-ditures	Gross private domestic investment				Exports and imports of goods and services			Government consumption expenditures and gross investment		
			Total	Fixed investment		Change in private inventories	Net exports	Exports	Imports	Total	Federal	State and local
				Nonresi-dential	Residential							
1929	. . .	. . .	. . .	. . .	. . .	. . .	. . .	. . .	. . .	. . .	. . .	. . .
1930	-8.5	-3.96	-5.18	-1.84	-1.50	-1.84	-0.30	-0.96	0.65	0.94	0.19	0.74
1931	-6.4	-2.37	-4.28	-3.32	-0.40	-0.56	-0.22	-0.77	0.54	0.48	0.08	0.40
1932	-12.9	-7.00	-5.28	-2.78	-1.02	-1.48	-0.19	-0.80	0.61	-0.42	0.05	-0.47
1933	-1.3	-1.79	1.16	-0.44	-0.24	1.84	-0.11	0.02	-0.13	-0.52	0.76	-1.28
1934	10.8	5.71	2.84	1.31	0.38	1.14	0.33	0.41	-0.08	1.91	1.37	0.54
1935	8.9	4.69	4.54	1.41	0.56	2.58	-0.83	0.21	-1.04	0.50	0.14	0.36
1936	12.9	7.68	2.58	2.10	0.47	0.01	0.24	0.19	0.05	2.44	2.43	0.01
1937	5.1	2.72	2.57	1.42	0.17	0.98	0.45	0.93	-0.48	-0.64	-0.65	0.02
1938	-3.3	-1.15	-4.13	-2.13	0.01	-2.01	0.88	-0.05	0.93	1.09	0.60	0.49
1939	8.0	4.11	2.39	0.71	1.03	0.65	0.07	0.24	-0.17	1.41	0.49	0.92
1940	8.8	3.72	3.99	1.60	0.42	1.97	0.52	0.61	-0.08	0.57	0.87	-0.30
1941	17.7	4.90	3.13	1.58	0.21	1.34	-0.64	0.12	-0.76	10.31	10.83	-0.52
1942	18.9	-1.50	-6.45	-3.16	-1.55	-1.74	-1.19	-1.51	0.32	28.03	28.64	-0.61
1943	17.0	1.52	-2.63	-0.72	-0.55	-1.36	-1.16	-0.42	-0.73	19.31	19.75	-0.44
1944	8.0	1.42	0.72	0.88	-0.10	-0.05	0.01	0.15	-0.15	5.84	5.98	-0.14
1945	-1.0	3.01	1.20	1.40	0.10	-0.30	0.66	0.86	-0.19	-5.84	-5.97	0.14
1946	-11.6	6.29	7.36	2.30	2.30	2.76	3.72	3.16	0.56	-28.95	-29.34	0.39
1947	-1.1	1.21	-0.56	1.28	1.02	-2.86	1.05	0.89	0.16	-2.80	-3.46	0.66
1948	4.1	1.47	3.89	0.48	0.96	2.45	-2.13	-1.59	-0.54	0.93	0.57	0.35
1949	-0.5	1.77	-4.15	-0.94	-0.43	-2.79	0.08	-0.05	0.13	1.77	0.85	0.92
1947												
1st quarter	. . .	. . .	. . .	. . .	. . .	. . .	. . .	. . .	. . .	. . .	. . .	. . .
2nd quarter	-0.4	4.30	-4.71	-0.59	-0.88	-3.25	-0.68	-0.42	-0.26	0.65	0.34	0.31
3rd quarter	-0.4	0.93	-1.83	-0.66	2.67	-3.84	-0.16	-1.68	1.52	0.65	0.12	0.52
4th quarter	6.4	0.24	10.67	1.33	3.97	5.37	-4.22	-3.52	-0.70	-0.24	-0.62	0.38
1948												
1st quarter	6.0	1.50	6.26	2.62	-0.31	3.95	-2.98	-1.31	-1.67	1.23	1.23	0.00
2nd quarter	6.7	3.11	4.31	-1.26	1.38	4.18	-3.00	-2.37	-0.63	2.24	1.57	0.67
3rd quarter	2.3	0.37	0.91	0.21	-0.75	1.46	-0.32	0.49	-0.81	1.30	0.88	0.42
4th quarter	0.4	1.83	-3.04	1.00	-1.74	-2.30	-0.60	-0.79	0.20	2.24	1.66	0.57
1949												
1st quarter	-5.4	0.17	-9.95	-2.06	-1.63	-6.26	2.84	2.44	0.40	1.58	0.59	0.99
2nd quarter	-1.3	3.56	-7.86	-1.55	-0.33	-5.98	0.02	-0.16	0.18	2.94	1.48	1.45
3rd quarter	4.5	0.15	4.98	-1.77	1.74	5.00	-1.31	-1.87	0.55	0.66	-0.50	1.16
4th quarter	-3.5	3.27	-2.51	-0.36	2.67	-4.82	-2.86	-2.66	-0.19	-1.44	-2.01	0.57
1950												
1st quarter	16.9	4.04	14.11	1.36	2.88	9.87	-0.56	-0.21	-0.36	-0.66	-1.46	0.80
2nd quarter	12.7	4.01	7.60	3.32	2.62	1.66	-0.49	0.23	-0.72	1.53	1.26	0.27
3rd quarter	16.3	13.39	6.42	3.45	1.60	1.37	-2.77	0.44	-3.21	-0.71	-0.75	0.04
4th quarter	8.0	-7.71	9.62	-0.07	-1.35	11.04	1.25	1.29	-0.04	4.79	4.78	0.02
1951												
1st quarter	5.6	6.32	-8.87	-1.16	-1.40	-6.32	0.80	0.82	-0.02	7.34	7.61	-0.27
2nd quarter	7.1	-6.88	1.66	0.47	-3.37	4.56	2.33	1.78	0.55	10.01	9.55	0.46
3rd quarter	8.5	2.88	-5.57	0.52	-1.36	-4.73	1.96	0.50	1.46	9.23	9.09	0.14
4th quarter	0.9	1.31	-5.40	-0.54	0.18	-5.03	0.15	-0.17	0.32	4.83	4.86	-0.03
1952												
1st quarter	4.3	0.32	1.72	0.54	0.51	0.66	-0.76	1.14	-1.90	3.02	2.91	0.10
2nd quarter	0.8	4.48	-4.71	0.75	0.37	-5.82	-2.22	-2.19	-0.03	3.29	2.71	0.58
3rd quarter	2.9	1.07	3.26	-2.95	-0.21	6.42	-2.41	-1.36	-1.05	1.00	1.72	-0.72
4th quarter	13.8	8.60	4.66	3.34	1.13	0.19	-1.28	0.20	-1.48	1.81	1.15	0.65
1953												
1st quarter	7.7	2.86	1.35	2.06	0.34	-1.05	0.24	-0.18	0.42	3.20	2.62	0.58
2nd quarter	3.2	1.33	0.40	0.41	0.07	-0.08	-0.70	0.15	-0.85	2.13	2.16	-0.03
3rd quarter	-2.2	-0.71	-1.20	0.92	-0.76	-1.36	0.67	0.65	0.03	-0.99	-1.70	0.71
4th quarter	-5.9	-1.76	-4.24	-0.28	-0.16	-3.80	0.24	-0.53	0.77	-0.17	-0.85	0.67
1954												
1st quarter	-1.8	0.65	-0.16	-0.97	0.22	0.58	0.13	-0.73	0.86	-2.45	-3.47	1.01
2nd quarter	0.4	2.97	0.07	-0.27	1.32	-0.98	0.67	2.11	-1.44	-3.28	-3.41	0.12
3rd quarter	4.6	3.19	3.02	1.09	1.32	0.61	0.36	-0.58	0.94	-1.94	-2.79	0.84
4th quarter	8.0	5.10	2.89	0.04	1.43	1.42	0.48	0.70	-0.22	-0.44	-0.60	0.16
1955												
1st quarter	11.9	5.56	6.40	0.77	1.76	3.87	-0.39	0.57	-0.95	0.34	-0.95	1.29
2nd quarter	6.7	4.64	4.05	2.31	0.33	1.41	-1.37	-0.43	-0.94	-0.64	-1.05	0.41
3rd quarter	5.5	2.96	1.06	2.00	-0.55	-0.39	0.70	1.03	-0.33	0.77	0.79	-0.02
4th quarter	2.4	3.07	1.54	1.22	-1.01	1.33	-0.56	0.05	-0.61	-1.62	-1.82	0.20
1956												
1st quarter	-1.5	0.38	-2.11	-0.61	-0.60	-0.90	0.07	0.80	-0.73	0.13	-0.21	0.34
2nd quarter	3.4	0.79	-0.58	0.73	-0.15	-1.17	1.25	1.20	0.05	1.88	1.47	0.41
3rd quarter	-0.3	0.51	-0.61	0.39	-0.43	-0.57	0.42	0.62	-0.20	-0.66	-0.82	0.17
4th quarter	6.7	3.34	-0.54	0.00	-0.33	-0.21	1.63	0.88	0.75	2.27	1.93	0.34
1957												
1st quarter	2.6	1.64	-0.95	0.23	-0.29	-0.90	-0.01	1.31	-1.32	1.93	1.15	0.79
2nd quarter	-0.9	0.41	-0.06	-0.08	-0.47	0.49	-0.80	-0.62	-0.18	-0.43	-0.71	0.28
3rd quarter	4.0	1.93	1.43	0.93	-0.25	0.75	-0.26	-0.55	0.30	0.85	0.38	0.47
4th quarter	-4.0	0.12	-5.17	-0.99	-0.02	-4.16	-0.61	-0.55	-0.06	1.63	0.81	0.82

. . . = Not available.

Table 1-4B. Contributions to Percent Change in Real Gross Domestic Product: Historical Data—*Continued*

(Percent; percentage points.)

NIPA Table 1.1.2

Year and quarter	Percent change at seasonally adjusted annual rate, real GDP	Personal consump-tion expen-ditures	Gross private domestic investment				Exports and imports of goods and services			Government consumption expenditures and gross investment		
			Total	Fixed investment		Change in private inventories	Net exports	Exports	Imports	Total	Federal	State and local
				Nonresi-dential	Residential							
1958												
1st quarter	-10.0	-3.24	-4.12	-2.69	-0.71	-0.72	-2.05	-1.83	-0.22	-0.57	-1.54	0.97
2nd quarter	2.6	2.11	-1.23	-1.53	0.07	0.23	-0.63	0.12	-0.74	2.41	1.89	0.52
3rd quarter	9.6	4.25	4.41	-0.41	1.31	3.50	0.28	0.10	0.18	0.63	-0.16	0.79
4th quarter	9.7	3.49	5.26	1.45	1.96	1.84	-0.97	-0.01	-0.96	1.91	1.25	0.66
1959												
1st quarter	7.7	4.59	3.82	1.18	2.27	0.36	0.52	1.12	-0.59	-1.27	-1.40	0.13
2nd quarter	10.1	3.95	5.37	1.14	0.77	3.46	-0.31	0.61	-0.92	1.08	0.97	0.11
3rd quarter	-0.8	2.61	-4.41	1.07	-0.42	-5.06	0.34	0.56	-0.22	0.69	0.66	0.04
4th quarter	1.6	0.32	2.05	-0.11	-0.62	2.77	-0.03	-0.47	0.44	-0.77	-0.59	-0.17
1960												
1st quarter	9.2	2.37	6.61	1.48	0.67	4.46	1.65	2.23	-0.58	-1.42	-2.02	0.59
2nd quarter	-1.5	3.05	-6.61	0.63	-1.73	-5.51	1.13	1.22	-0.09	0.93	0.09	0.84
3rd quarter	1.0	-0.97	-0.19	-0.72	-0.58	1.11	0.02	-0.51	0.53	2.14	1.61	0.52
4th quarter	-4.8	0.34	-6.92	-0.07	-0.02	-6.83	1.21	0.41	0.80	0.61	0.21	0.40
1961												
1st quarter	2.7	-0.05	1.52	-0.57	0.08	2.02	-0.07	-0.14	0.07	1.35	0.17	1.18
2nd quarter	7.6	3.70	4.17	0.92	0.08	3.18	-0.47	-0.27	-0.19	0.24	0.48	-0.25
3rd quarter	6.8	1.22	4.81	0.40	1.02	3.39	-1.14	-0.10	-1.04	1.94	1.62	0.32
4th quarter	8.3	4.89	1.22	1.22	0.67	-0.67	0.21	0.60	-0.39	2.03	1.02	1.01
1962												
1st quarter	7.4	2.59	3.56	0.79	0.35	2.42	-0.54	-0.05	-0.49	1.80	2.07	-0.27
2nd quarter	4.4	2.95	-0.46	1.07	0.61	-2.14	1.46	1.81	-0.36	0.44	0.19	0.25
3rd quarter	3.9	1.95	1.12	0.50	-0.01	0.64	-1.34	-1.14	-0.21	2.13	1.68	0.45
4th quarter	1.6	3.40	-1.89	-0.16	-0.03	-1.71	-0.61	-0.41	-0.20	0.66	0.28	0.38
1963												
1st quarter	4.5	1.65	3.28	0.10	0.69	2.49	0.83	0.44	0.39	-1.23	-1.92	0.69
2nd quarter	5.3	2.33	1.07	1.24	1.42	-1.60	1.82	2.19	-0.37	0.11	-0.23	0.33
3rd quarter	8.0	3.32	2.11	1.12	0.40	0.58	-1.48	-1.08	-0.41	4.10	3.10	1.00
4th quarter	2.9	1.99	0.83	1.18	0.65	-0.99	1.01	0.95	0.06	-0.95	-1.46	0.51
1964												
1st quarter	8.9	4.77	2.60	0.88	1.30	0.43	1.25	1.22	0.03	0.31	-0.26	0.58
2nd quarter	4.8	4.21	-0.18	0.97	-1.08	-0.06	-0.01	0.34	-0.35	0.82	-0.04	0.85
3rd quarter	5.5	4.44	1.56	1.35	-0.33	0.53	-0.58	-0.15	-0.43	0.13	-0.29	0.41
4th quarter	1.4	0.69	0.59	0.92	-0.35	0.03	0.16	0.60	-0.44	-0.02	-0.43	0.41
1965												
1st quarter	10.2	5.47	6.38	2.81	0.10	3.46	-1.59	-2.22	0.63	-0.02	-0.38	0.36
2nd quarter	5.6	2.70	0.17	1.66	0.17	-1.66	1.62	3.46	-1.85	1.10	0.12	0.98
3rd quarter	8.4	4.19	2.49	1.68	0.10	0.72	-1.27	-1.21	-0.06	2.97	1.87	1.10
4th quarter	9.8	6.79	0.61	1.89	-0.37	-0.91	0.62	1.44	-0.82	1.76	1.17	0.59
1966												
1st quarter	10.2	3.58	5.71	1.96	0.46	3.29	-0.80	-0.36	-0.44	1.75	1.27	0.48
2nd quarter	1.6	0.60	-1.05	0.75	-1.42	-0.38	0.43	0.86	-0.43	1.67	1.38	0.30
3rd quarter	2.9	2.69	-0.51	0.62	-0.56	-0.57	-1.76	-0.78	-0.99	2.47	2.01	0.46
4th quarter	3.5	0.98	0.42	0.01	-1.69	2.11	0.46	0.65	-0.19	1.61	0.60	1.00
1967												
1st quarter	3.7	1.38	-1.72	-0.75	-0.40	-0.58	0.13	0.39	-0.26	3.93	3.44	0.49
2nd quarter	0.3	3.20	-2.45	-0.10	1.60	-3.95	-0.02	-0.19	0.17	-0.38	-0.60	0.23
3rd quarter	3.5	1.22	1.90	-0.08	0.83	1.15	-0.72	-0.49	-0.23	1.09	0.93	0.16
4th quarter	3.2	1.46	1.42	0.92	0.93	-0.43	-0.40	0.56	-0.95	0.78	0.06	0.72
1968												
1st quarter	8.4	5.66	1.43	1.37	0.06	0.00	-0.52	0.58	-1.10	1.80	1.03	0.77
2nd quarter	6.9	3.64	2.62	-0.57	0.42	2.77	0.11	0.41	-0.30	0.56	-0.26	0.82
3rd quarter	2.9	4.42	-1.84	0.60	0.34	-2.79	0.02	1.18	-1.16	0.32	-0.28	0.60
4th quarter	1.8	1.07	0.71	1.21	0.24	-0.74	-0.09	-0.26	0.17	0.10	-0.25	0.35
1969												
1st quarter	6.4	2.67	3.97	1.17	0.60	2.20	-0.55	-2.43	1.88	0.28	-0.12	0.40
2nd quarter	1.3	1.50	-0.40	0.49	-0.17	-0.72	0.48	3.94	-3.46	-0.30	-0.66	0.36
3rd quarter	2.5	1.14	1.41	1.06	-0.14	0.49	-0.24	-0.51	0.27	0.21	0.10	0.11
4th quarter	-1.7	1.88	-3.30	-0.24	-1.20	-1.86	0.94	0.71	0.23	-1.25	-1.17	-0.08
1970												
1st quarter	-0.7	1.46	-1.93	-0.32	0.01	-1.62	0.23	0.16	0.07	-0.47	-0.88	0.41
2nd quarter	0.7	1.11	0.14	-0.31	-1.00	1.45	0.55	0.95	-0.40	-1.10	-1.34	0.24
3rd quarter	3.6	2.15	1.04	0.15	0.88	0.01	-0.01	-0.06	0.05	0.42	-0.60	1.01
4th quarter	-4.0	-0.59	-3.41	-1.62	1.58	-3.37	-0.11	0.21	-0.32	0.06	-0.18	0.24
1971												
1st quarter	11.1	4.79	7.28	0.36	0.92	6.00	0.37	0.11	0.26	-1.30	-1.52	0.22
2nd quarter	2.3	2.24	1.85	0.58	1.73	-0.46	-1.58	-0.04	-1.54	-0.21	-0.55	0.34
3rd quarter	3.2	1.94	0.83	0.22	0.91	-0.29	0.42	0.90	-0.48	-0.03	-0.19	0.16
4th quarter	1.2	3.98	-1.81	0.96	0.79	-3.57	-0.35	-1.86	1.52	-0.65	-1.23	0.59
1972												
1st quarter	7.4	3.21	4.52	1.55	1.40	1.57	-0.80	2.21	-3.01	0.45	0.31	0.13
2nd quarter	9.6	4.62	4.14	0.83	0.43	2.88	0.22	-0.64	0.87	0.60	0.67	-0.07
3rd quarter	3.7	3.67	1.09	0.70	0.10	0.29	0.79	1.26	-0.46	-1.82	-2.18	0.36
4th quarter	6.8	5.63	0.57	2.19	0.80	-2.43	-0.10	0.92	-1.03	0.71	0.08	0.63
1973												
1st quarter	10.2	4.46	4.38	1.96	0.79	1.63	0.58	1.68	-1.10	0.79	0.57	0.22
2nd quarter	4.6	-0.10	3.23	1.74	-1.22	2.72	1.89	1.16	0.73	-0.41	-0.48	0.07
3rd quarter	-2.2	0.84	-2.67	0.73	-0.96	-2.43	0.75	0.06	0.69	-1.09	-1.56	0.47
4th quarter	3.8	-0.69	2.78	0.36	-0.98	3.41	1.12	1.33	-0.21	0.57	0.01	0.56

Table 1-4B. Contributions to Percent Change in Real Gross Domestic Product: Historical Data—*Continued*

(Percent; percentage points.)

NIPA Table 1.1.2

Year and quarter	Percent change at seasonally adjusted annual rate, real GDP	Personal consump-tion expen-ditures	Gross private domestic investment				Exports and imports of goods and services			Government consumption expenditures and gross investment		
			Total	Fixed investment		Change in private inventories	Net exports	Exports	Imports	Total	Federal	State and local
				Nonresi-dential	Residential							
1974												
1st quarter	-3.3	-2.06	-4.15	-0.06	-1.34	-2.76	1.34	0.36	0.98	1.59	1.01	0.58
2nd quarter	1.1	0.87	-0.24	-0.09	-0.78	0.63	-0.14	1.51	-1.65	0.57	-0.02	0.58
3rd quarter	-3.8	1.04	-3.78	-0.48	-0.61	-2.69	-1.22	-1.81	0.59	0.15	0.21	-0.06
4th quarter	-1.6	-3.49	0.29	-1.28	-2.34	3.91	1.19	0.85	0.35	0.42	0.39	0.04
1975												
1st quarter	-4.7	2.06	-11.55	-2.77	-0.88	-7.90	3.69	0.24	3.45	1.06	-0.38	1.44
2nd quarter	3.1	4.11	-1.89	-1.14	0.44	-1.19	1.47	-1.01	2.48	-0.57	-0.21	-0.36
3rd quarter	6.8	3.56	4.52	0.50	1.02	2.99	-2.80	-0.55	-2.25	1.50	0.86	0.63
4th quarter	5.5	2.61	1.78	0.53	0.69	0.56	0.25	1.76	-1.51	0.87	0.21	0.65
1976												
1st quarter	9.3	4.91	6.25	0.96	1.57	3.72	-2.05	-0.22	-1.83	0.23	-0.33	0.56
2nd quarter	3.1	2.23	2.73	0.58	0.43	1.72	-1.02	0.31	-1.33	-0.88	-0.04	-0.84
3rd quarter	2.1	2.59	0.26	1.00	-0.29	-0.45	-0.38	0.91	-1.29	-0.42	-0.10	-0.31
4th quarter	3.0	3.23	0.49	0.91	2.18	-2.61	-0.75	0.33	-1.08	0.06	0.20	-0.14
1977												
1st quarter	4.7	2.90	3.14	1.77	0.61	0.76	-2.08	-0.51	-1.57	0.78	0.34	0.44
2nd quarter	8.1	1.45	5.22	1.40	2.29	1.53	0.55	0.85	-0.30	0.87	0.59	0.28
3rd quarter	7.3	2.37	3.94	1.05	-0.07	2.96	0.75	0.24	0.51	0.20	0.25	-0.05
4th quarter	0.0	3.62	-1.88	1.56	-0.28	-3.17	-1.49	-1.00	-0.49	-0.21	-0.27	0.06
1978												
1st quarter	1.4	1.36	1.69	0.52	0.20	0.97	-1.70	0.66	-2.35	0.05	0.06	-0.01
2nd quarter	16.5	5.44	5.67	4.12	1.13	0.41	3.11	3.18	-0.07	2.26	0.90	1.36
3rd quarter	4.0	1.00	2.48	1.81	0.27	0.40	-0.13	0.34	-0.47	0.63	0.12	0.51
4th quarter	5.5	1.93	2.02	1.74	-0.04	0.32	0.79	1.28	-0.49	0.73	0.31	0.42
1979												
1st quarter	0.8	1.21	0.15	1.21	-0.57	-0.49	0.13	0.03	0.10	-0.69	0.04	-0.73
2nd quarter	0.5	-0.16	-0.07	-0.10	-0.41	0.44	-0.10	0.09	-0.18	0.81	0.41	0.40
3rd quarter	2.9	2.35	-1.39	1.61	-0.28	-2.72	1.84	1.22	0.62	0.11	-0.04	0.14
4th quarter	1.0	0.61	-1.46	0.11	-0.91	-0.66	1.38	2.18	-0.81	0.51	0.03	0.48
1980												
1st quarter	1.3	-0.42	-0.56	0.59	-1.69	0.54	1.04	1.00	0.04	1.24	1.05	0.20
2nd quarter	-7.9	-5.48	-6.68	-2.67	-3.71	-0.30	3.98	0.73	3.25	0.31	0.89	-0.58
3rd quarter	-0.6	2.62	-4.94	0.35	0.51	-5.80	2.96	-0.07	3.03	-1.24	-0.55	-0.70
4th quarter	7.6	3.32	6.53	1.19	1.62	3.73	-2.25	-0.19	-2.06	0.02	0.23	-0.21
1981												
1st quarter	8.5	1.36	6.97	1.18	-0.43	6.22	-0.89	0.82	-1.71	1.09	0.74	0.36
2nd quarter	-2.9	-0.02	-3.31	1.17	-0.55	-3.93	0.18	0.25	-0.07	0.26	1.08	-0.82
3rd quarter	4.7	0.99	4.32	1.39	-1.32	4.24	-0.34	-0.80	0.45	-0.30	-0.18	-0.12
4th quarter	-4.6	-1.80	-2.82	1.44	-1.61	-2.65	-0.90	0.17	-1.08	0.93	0.60	0.33
1982												
1st quarter	-6.5	1.61	-7.59	-1.45	-0.81	-5.33	-0.49	-1.62	1.12	-0.05	0.07	-0.11
2nd quarter	2.2	0.89	-0.06	-1.89	-0.44	2.26	0.81	0.19	0.61	0.56	0.41	0.15
3rd quarter	-1.4	1.88	-0.62	-1.72	-0.02	1.11	-3.22	-1.57	-1.65	0.53	0.53	-0.01
4th quarter	0.4	4.51	-5.37	-1.05	1.01	-5.33	-0.10	-1.52	1.43	1.35	1.03	0.32
1983												
1st quarter	5.3	2.45	2.36	-0.92	2.36	0.92	-0.29	0.50	-0.78	0.82	0.67	0.15
2nd quarter	9.4	5.06	5.96	0.67	1.86	3.43	-2.46	0.11	-2.57	0.89	0.98	-0.08
3rd quarter	8.1	4.50	4.40	2.13	1.70	0.57	-2.25	0.47	-2.72	1.42	1.05	0.37
4th quarter	8.5	4.06	6.94	3.14	0.79	3.01	-1.14	0.63	-1.76	-1.36	-1.39	0.03
1984												
1st quarter	8.2	2.26	7.23	1.71	0.58	4.94	-2.31	0.65	-2.96	1.01	0.47	0.54
2nd quarter	7.2	3.64	2.57	2.52	0.34	-0.29	-0.87	0.76	-1.63	1.87	1.31	0.56
3rd quarter	4.0	1.95	1.69	1.70	-0.22	0.21	-0.36	0.66	-1.02	0.70	0.00	0.71
4th quarter	3.2	3.29	-1.08	1.34	0.02	-2.44	-0.56	0.60	-1.16	1.58	1.16	0.42
1985												
1st quarter	4.0	4.23	-2.14	0.67	0.05	-2.86	0.94	0.07	0.87	1.01	0.48	0.52
2nd quarter	3.7	2.35	1.34	0.83	0.16	0.35	-1.90	-0.08	-1.83	1.93	1.18	0.76
3rd quarter	6.4	4.82	-0.43	-0.62	0.34	-0.15	-0.01	-0.42	0.41	1.98	1.31	0.68
4th quarter	3.0	0.62	2.80	1.00	0.40	1.40	-0.66	0.78	-1.44	0.27	-0.05	0.32
1986												
1st quarter	3.8	2.10	0.04	-0.55	0.76	-0.17	0.92	0.82	0.10	0.70	-0.09	0.78
2nd quarter	1.9	2.77	-1.30	-1.12	1.12	-1.30	-1.33	0.27	-1.60	1.70	1.28	0.42
3rd quarter	4.1	4.55	-1.97	-0.63	0.28	-1.62	-0.45	0.62	-1.07	1.95	1.55	0.40
4th quarter	2.1	1.62	0.24	0.48	0.05	-0.29	0.71	1.03	-0.32	-0.48	-0.63	0.15
1987												
1st quarter	2.8	0.05	1.98	-1.26	-0.04	3.28	0.23	0.03	0.20	0.57	0.35	0.23
2nd quarter	4.6	3.54	0.08	1.00	0.07	-0.99	0.14	1.18	-1.05	0.81	0.71	0.10
3rd quarter	3.7	2.97	0.03	1.39	-0.17	-1.19	0.45	1.28	-0.83	0.23	0.08	0.15
4th quarter	6.8	0.57	4.94	-0.05	0.04	4.95	0.18	1.15	-0.97	1.08	0.49	0.59
1988												
1st quarter	2.3	4.49	-3.62	0.41	-0.36	-3.68	1.94	1.74	0.20	-0.54	-1.00	0.47
2nd quarter	5.4	1.89	1.72	1.14	0.25	0.33	1.44	0.94	0.50	0.34	-0.21	0.55
3rd quarter	2.3	2.17	0.38	0.32	0.01	0.05	-0.31	0.66	-0.97	0.08	-0.12	0.20
4th quarter	5.4	2.93	1.11	0.71	0.13	0.27	-0.21	1.04	-1.25	1.56	1.04	0.53
1989												
1st quarter	4.1	1.18	2.41	0.80	-0.19	1.80	0.85	1.03	-0.17	-0.35	-0.70	0.35
2nd quarter	3.2	1.20	-0.70	0.68	-0.59	-0.79	1.35	1.53	-0.18	1.34	0.86	0.48
3rd quarter	3.0	2.52	-0.64	1.29	-0.08	-1.84	0.44	0.37	0.07	0.70	0.28	0.42
4th quarter	0.9	1.13	-0.53	-0.52	-0.38	0.37	-0.20	0.54	-0.73	0.45	-0.15	0.59

Table 1-4B. Contributions to Percent Change in Real Gross Domestic Product: Historical Data—*Continued*

(Percent; percentage points.)   **NIPA Table 1.1.2**

Year and quarter	Percent change at seasonally adjusted annual rate, real GDP	Personal consump-tion expen-ditures	Gross private domestic investment				Exports and imports of goods and services			Government consumption expenditures and gross investment		
			Total	Fixed investment		Change in private inventories	Net exports	Exports	Imports	Total	Federal	State and local
				Nonresi-dential	Residential							
1990												
1st quarter	4.5	2.21	0.69	0.63	0.16	-0.10	0.25	1.56	-1.31	1.30	0.61	0.69
2nd quarter	1.6	0.80	0.03	-0.66	-0.68	1.38	0.52	0.46	0.07	0.20	0.11	0.09
3rd quarter	0.1	1.02	-1.30	0.32	-0.89	-0.73	0.44	0.28	0.16	-0.05	-0.36	0.31
4th quarter	-3.4	-1.96	-3.64	-0.78	-0.90	-1.96	1.47	0.33	1.13	0.76	0.24	0.52
1991												
1st quarter	-1.9	-0.92	-2.04	-1.00	-0.78	-0.26	0.69	0.24	0.45	0.41	0.34	0.07
2nd quarter	3.1	2.14	0.05	-0.26	0.42	-0.12	0.65	1.38	-0.73	0.30	0.11	0.19
3rd quarter	1.9	1.24	1.21	-0.42	0.48	1.16	-0.21	0.91	-1.12	-0.30	-0.58	0.28
4th quarter	1.8	-0.07	2.15	-0.05	0.29	1.91	-0.02	0.87	-0.89	-0.31	-0.63	0.33
1992												
1st quarter	4.8	4.85	-1.15	-0.19	0.84	-1.80	0.44	0.72	-0.28	0.67	0.07	0.60
2nd quarter	4.5	1.79	3.40	1.44	0.53	1.43	-0.63	0.03	-0.66	-0.08	-0.02	-0.07
3rd quarter	3.9	2.80	0.51	0.69	0.01	-0.19	0.19	0.82	-0.64	0.45	0.43	0.02
4th quarter	4.1	3.08	1.92	1.19	0.60	0.13	-0.77	0.20	-0.97	-0.16	-0.13	-0.03
1993												
1st quarter	0.8	0.97	1.48	0.44	0.01	1.03	-0.79	0.09	-0.88	-0.92	-1.06	0.14
2nd quarter	2.4	2.32	0.38	0.88	0.22	-0.72	-0.40	0.46	-0.85	0.09	-0.28	0.37
3rd quarter	2.0	2.86	-0.41	0.36	0.61	-1.38	-0.66	-0.10	-0.55	0.17	-0.07	0.24
4th quarter	5.4	2.33	3.38	1.65	0.87	0.87	-0.45	1.22	-1.67	0.18	-0.04	0.22
1994												
1st quarter	4.0	2.99	2.58	0.50	0.26	1.82	-0.62	0.38	-1.00	-0.97	-1.15	0.18
2nd quarter	5.6	2.04	3.37	0.70	0.57	2.09	-0.30	1.29	-1.59	0.46	-0.06	0.52
3rd quarter	2.4	2.02	-1.15	0.77	-0.27	-1.65	0.22	1.45	-1.23	1.29	0.76	0.53
4th quarter	4.6	2.83	2.79	1.83	-0.27	1.24	-0.32	0.93	-1.25	-0.68	-0.86	0.18
1995												
1st quarter	1.4	0.71	0.70	1.80	-0.39	-0.70	-0.20	0.78	-0.98	0.16	-0.19	0.36
2nd quarter	1.4	2.33	-1.49	0.47	-0.52	-1.43	0.15	0.58	-0.43	0.41	0.05	0.36
3rd quarter	3.5	2.40	-0.41	0.31	0.61	-1.33	1.66	1.82	-0.15	-0.19	-0.24	0.05
4th quarter	2.9	1.83	1.69	0.97	0.33	0.40	0.01	0.62	-0.61	-0.66	-0.90	0.24
1996												
1st quarter	2.7	2.41	1.07	1.22	0.45	-0.59	-1.01	0.53	-1.54	0.17	0.25	-0.08
2nd quarter	7.2	2.88	3.39	1.36	0.77	1.26	-0.33	0.73	-1.05	1.22	0.56	0.66
3rd quarter	3.7	1.59	3.23	1.59	-0.04	1.68	-1.15	0.36	-1.51	0.08	-0.32	0.39
4th quarter	4.3	2.08	-0.05	1.30	-0.20	-1.14	1.73	2.64	-0.91	0.53	-0.12	0.65
1997												
1st quarter	3.1	2.78	1.47	1.20	0.09	0.18	-1.13	0.85	-1.98	-0.04	-0.46	0.42
2nd quarter	6.2	1.23	3.98	1.11	0.25	2.62	0.20	1.78	-1.57	0.76	0.59	0.17
3rd quarter	5.2	4.44	1.33	2.33	0.17	-1.17	-0.70	1.05	-1.75	0.12	-0.05	0.17
4th quarter	3.1	3.07	1.06	0.33	0.19	0.55	-1.10	-0.05	-1.05	0.11	-0.07	0.18
1998												
1st quarter	4.0	2.67	3.36	1.65	0.37	1.35	-1.62	0.21	-1.83	-0.40	-0.75	0.35
2nd quarter	3.9	4.58	-0.49	1.74	0.62	-2.86	-1.59	-0.47	-1.12	1.45	0.63	0.81
3rd quarter	5.3	3.46	2.04	0.79	0.54	0.71	-0.83	-0.18	-0.65	0.67	-0.15	0.82
4th quarter	6.7	3.88	2.18	1.55	0.44	0.18	-0.01	1.53	-1.54	0.68	0.32	0.37
1999												
1st quarter	3.2	2.49	2.16	1.17	0.07	0.91	-1.69	-0.99	-0.69	0.27	-0.23	0.50
2nd quarter	3.3	3.88	0.05	1.44	0.30	-1.68	-1.00	0.42	-1.42	0.41	0.13	0.27
3rd quarter	5.1	3.02	1.94	1.57	0.15	0.22	-0.69	1.21	-1.90	0.86	0.45	0.40
4th quarter	7.1	3.93	2.33	0.22	0.15	1.97	-0.23	1.06	-1.29	1.09	0.52	0.57
2000												
1st quarter	1.2	4.01	-0.71	2.00	0.10	-2.81	-1.54	0.64	-2.18	-0.59	-0.95	0.36
2nd quarter	7.8	2.62	4.72	1.85	-0.10	2.97	-0.47	1.25	-1.72	0.90	0.88	0.02
3rd quarter	0.5	2.55	-1.01	0.60	-0.29	-1.31	-0.92	1.05	-1.97	-0.15	-0.42	0.27
4th quarter	2.3	2.35	0.06	0.13	0.02	-0.08	-0.34	-0.37	0.02	0.23	-0.13	0.35
2001												
1st quarter	-1.1	1.09	-3.60	-0.51	0.08	-3.17	0.31	-0.65	0.96	1.07	0.53	0.54
2nd quarter	2.1	0.67	-0.24	-1.31	0.29	0.77	0.28	-1.37	1.64	1.43	0.49	0.95
3rd quarter	-1.3	0.96	-1.29	-0.72	0.12	-0.69	-0.88	-1.92	1.05	-0.05	0.21	-0.26
4th quarter	1.1	4.06	-3.54	-1.55	-0.13	-1.86	-0.48	-1.17	0.69	1.07	0.20	0.88
2002												
1st quarter	3.7	0.82	2.50	-1.02	0.64	2.89	-0.69	0.72	-1.42	1.11	0.64	0.47
2nd quarter	2.2	1.37	0.73	-0.66	0.49	0.90	-0.60	0.98	-1.58	0.73	0.62	0.11
3rd quarter	2.0	1.88	0.00	-0.31	0.06	0.25	-0.51	0.26	-0.77	0.59	0.42	0.17
4th quarter	0.3	1.44	-0.14	-0.64	0.37	0.13	-1.60	-0.50	-1.10	0.55	0.50	0.05
2003												
1st quarter	2.1	1.19	0.57	0.04	0.39	0.15	0.57	-0.21	0.78	-0.24	0.02	-0.26
2nd quarter	3.8	3.02	0.37	1.09	0.34	-1.06	-0.86	-0.04	-0.83	1.23	1.42	-0.19
3rd quarter	6.9	4.04	2.51	0.95	1.25	0.31	0.30	0.96	-0.66	0.02	-0.16	0.18
4th quarter	4.8	2.12	2.53	0.69	0.67	1.16	-0.31	1.58	-1.90	0.43	0.56	-0.13
2004												
1st quarter	2.3	2.62	0.07	-0.50	0.27	0.30	-0.58	1.11	-1.70	0.21	0.20	0.01
2nd quarter	3.0	1.76	2.60	1.06	0.75	0.79	-1.84	0.49	-2.33	0.44	0.29	0.15
3rd quarter	3.7	2.59	1.17	1.30	0.17	-0.31	-0.37	0.22	-0.60	0.30	0.51	-0.21
4th quarter	3.5	2.78	1.52	1.03	0.34	0.15	-0.47	0.93	-1.40	-0.33	-0.25	-0.08
2005												
1st quarter	4.3	2.09	2.17	0.60	0.60	0.97	-0.10	0.61	-0.71	0.18	0.17	0.00
2nd quarter	2.1	2.92	-0.99	0.69	0.48	-2.16	0.04	0.73	-0.69	0.14	0.06	0.07
3rd quarter	3.4	2.09	0.81	0.90	0.29	-0.38	-0.10	0.05	-0.14	0.60	0.53	0.07
4th quarter	2.3	1.00	2.32	0.20	-0.06	2.18	-0.73	1.12	-1.85	-0.29	-0.43	0.15

Table 1-4B. Contributions to Percent Change in Real Gross Domestic Product: Historical Data—*Continued*

(Percent; percentage points.)

NIPA Table 1.1.2

Year and quarter	Percent change at seasonally adjusted annual rate, real GDP	Personal consump-tion expen-ditures	Gross private domestic investment				Exports and imports of goods and services			Government consumption expenditures and gross investment		
			Total	Fixed investment		Change in private inventories	Net exports	Exports	Imports	Total	Federal	State and local
				Nonresi-dential	Residential							
2006												
1st quarter	4.9	3.01	1.10	1.84	-0.25	-0.49	0.18	1.52	-1.34	0.61	0.71	-0.11
2nd quarter	1.2	1.41	-0.51	0.63	-1.33	0.19	0.02	0.78	-0.76	0.27	-0.04	0.31
3rd quarter	0.4	1.56	-0.80	0.61	-1.39	-0.02	-0.57	-0.08	-0.48	0.16	0.01	0.16
4th quarter	3.2	2.75	-1.83	0.34	-1.09	-1.07	1.74	1.90	-0.16	0.51	0.30	0.20
2007												
1st quarter	0.2	1.43	-0.71	0.89	-1.01	-0.58	-0.31	0.72	-1.03	-0.16	-0.39	0.23
2nd quarter	3.1	0.93	1.02	1.03	-0.84	0.83	0.48	0.78	-0.30	0.66	0.46	0.20
3rd quarter	2.7	1.21	-0.44	0.81	-1.26	0.01	1.39	1.38	0.01	0.56	0.55	0.01
4th quarter	1.4	0.34	-1.44	0.88	-1.53	-0.79	2.22	1.41	0.81	0.31	0.16	0.15
2008												
1st quarter	-2.7	-0.56	-2.36	0.00	-1.31	-1.05	-0.11	0.57	-0.67	0.32	0.47	-0.15
2nd quarter	2.0	0.48	-1.21	-0.31	-0.67	-0.24	2.11	1.49	0.62	0.62	0.56	0.07
3rd quarter	-1.9	-1.94	-1.86	-1.42	-0.71	0.26	0.77	-0.69	1.46	1.13	0.91	0.22
4th quarter	-8.2	-3.16	-5.74	-3.00	-1.29	-1.45	0.15	-2.68	2.83	0.56	0.56	0.00
2009												
1st quarter	-5.4	-0.86	-7.02	-3.58	-1.17	-2.26	2.30	-3.62	5.92	0.15	-0.24	0.39
2nd quarter	-0.5	-1.19	-3.25	-1.46	-0.66	-1.12	2.34	0.14	2.20	1.56	1.09	0.47
3rd quarter	1.3	1.68	-0.40	-0.54	0.52	-0.38	-0.45	1.53	-1.98	0.48	0.47	0.01
4th quarter	3.9	-0.01	4.05	-0.37	0.01	4.40	0.06	2.53	-2.47	-0.17	0.02	-0.19
2010												
1st quarter	1.7	1.46	1.77	0.46	-0.35	1.66	-0.85	0.71	-1.55	-0.63	0.32	-0.95
2nd quarter	3.9	2.23	2.86	1.21	0.56	1.09	-1.77	1.12	-2.90	0.61	0.71	-0.10
3rd quarter	2.7	1.77	1.86	0.90	-0.94	1.90	-0.83	1.38	-2.20	-0.07	0.32	-0.39
4th quarter	2.5	2.79	-0.51	0.94	0.19	-1.63	1.12	1.53	-0.41	-0.87	-0.23	-0.63
2011												
1st quarter	-1.5	1.38	-1.07	-0.09	-0.02	-0.96	-0.24	0.27	-0.51	-1.60	-0.95	-0.65
2nd quarter	2.9	0.57	2.14	0.97	0.13	1.04	0.31	0.82	-0.51	-0.08	0.14	-0.22
3rd quarter	0.8	1.20	0.15	2.06	0.19	-2.10	0.01	0.57	-0.56	-0.52	-0.35	-0.17
4th quarter	4.6	0.94	4.16	1.08	0.28	2.80	-0.21	0.56	-0.76	-0.31	-0.21	-0.10
2012												
1st quarter	2.7	1.63	1.47	1.37	0.63	-0.53	-0.02	0.37	-0.40	-0.40	-0.03	-0.36
2nd quarter	1.9	0.45	1.53	0.88	0.10	0.56	0.28	0.61	-0.33	-0.39	-0.24	-0.14
3rd quarter	0.5	0.72	-0.18	-0.27	0.27	-0.18	0.16	0.27	-0.10	-0.22	0.04	-0.26
4th quarter	0.1	0.78	-0.51	0.46	0.57	-1.54	0.58	-0.07	0.65	-0.75	-0.45	-0.30
2013												
1st quarter	1.9	1.74	1.05	0.51	0.26	0.28	-0.01	0.12	-0.13	-0.88	-0.75	-0.12
2nd quarter	1.1	0.96	0.78	0.14	0.27	0.38	-0.24	0.64	-0.89	-0.38	-0.43	0.05
3rd quarter	3.0	1.17	2.07	0.44	0.15	1.48	0.16	0.55	-0.39	-0.42	-0.44	0.02
4th quarter	3.8	2.36	0.71	1.05	-0.26	-0.08	1.26	1.42	-0.16	-0.51	-0.49	-0.01
2014												
1st quarter	-0.9	0.85	-0.38	1.00	-0.09	-1.29	-1.39	-0.95	-0.44	0.00	0.02	-0.03
2nd quarter	4.6	2.60	1.99	0.56	0.31	1.12	-0.24	1.28	-1.52	0.21	-0.08	0.29
3rd quarter	4.3	2.34	1.22	1.12	0.11	-0.01	0.39	0.24	0.15	0.33	0.26	0.07
4th quarter	2.1	2.86	0.36	0.09	0.31	-0.03	-0.89	0.71	-1.60	-0.26	-0.41	0.15

Table 1-5A. Chain-Type Quantity Indexes for Gross Domestic Product and Domestic Purchases: Recent Data

(Index numbers, 2009 = 100.)

NIPA Tables 1.1.3, 1.4.3, 2.3.3

Year and quarter	Gross domestic product, total	Personal consumption expenditures		Private fixed investment			Exports and imports of goods and services		Government consumption expenditures and gross investment			Gross domestic purchases
		Total	Excluding food and energy	Total	Nonresidential	Residential	Exports	Imports	Total	Federal	State and local	
1950	15.1	13.8	11.3	13.9	8.3	49.3	3.7	3.6	18.4	21.5	16.0	15.0
1951	16.4	14.0	11.5	13.3	8.7	41.4	4.5	3.7	25.2	35.1	16.1	16.1
1952	17.0	14.5	11.8	13.2	8.7	40.7	4.3	4.0	30.2	45.0	16.4	16.8
1953	17.8	15.2	12.4	14.3	9.5	42.2	4.0	4.4	32.2	48.4	17.2	17.7
1954	17.7	15.5	12.6	14.5	9.4	45.7	4.2	4.2	30.1	42.5	18.7	17.6
1955	19.0	16.6	13.6	16.4	10.4	53.1	4.7	4.7	29.2	39.1	20.0	18.8
1956	19.4	17.1	14.0	16.6	11.1	48.9	5.4	5.1	29.2	38.6	20.7	19.1
1957	19.8	17.5	14.3	16.5	11.3	46.0	5.9	5.3	30.6	40.1	21.9	19.5
1958	19.7	17.7	14.4	15.5	10.3	46.5	5.1	5.5	31.6	40.3	23.7	19.5
1959	21.0	18.7	15.3	17.6	11.1	58.1	5.6	6.1	32.4	41.1	24.5	20.9
1960	21.6	19.2	15.8	17.8	11.7	54.2	6.6	6.2	32.6	40.4	25.6	21.3
1961	22.1	19.6	16.2	17.9	11.8	54.4	6.7	6.2	34.3	42.3	27.1	21.8
1962	23.5	20.6	17.1	19.4	12.7	59.6	7.0	6.8	36.6	46.1	27.9	23.2
1963	24.5	21.4	18.0	20.9	13.5	66.6	7.5	7.0	37.5	46.2	29.6	24.2
1964	25.9	22.7	19.2	22.8	14.9	70.6	8.4	7.4	38.4	46.1	31.6	25.5
1965	27.6	24.1	20.5	25.2	17.4	68.8	8.6	8.2	39.6	46.4	33.7	27.2
1966	29.4	25.5	21.7	26.8	19.6	63.0	9.2	9.4	43.1	51.4	35.8	29.1
1967	30.2	26.3	22.4	26.5	19.5	61.4	9.4	10.1	46.5	56.6	37.5	30.0
1968	31.7	27.8	23.7	28.4	20.4	69.7	10.2	11.6	48.1	57.4	39.8	31.5
1969	32.7	28.8	24.7	30.0	21.8	71.9	10.6	12.3	48.2	56.0	41.2	32.5
1970	32.7	29.5	25.2	29.4	21.7	68.1	11.8	12.8	47.2	52.6	42.4	32.5
1971	33.8	30.6	26.3	31.4	21.6	86.2	12.0	13.5	46.3	49.2	43.7	33.6
1972	35.6	32.5	28.1	35.0	23.5	101.2	12.9	15.0	46.1	47.7	44.7	35.5
1973	37.6	34.1	29.9	38.0	26.6	100.6	15.4	15.7	46.0	46.0	45.9	37.2
1974	37.4	33.8	29.9	35.9	26.9	80.8	16.6	15.3	47.0	46.3	47.6	36.7
1975	37.4	34.6	30.5	32.4	24.4	71.1	16.5	13.6	48.0	46.6	49.3	36.3
1976	39.4	36.5	32.3	35.6	25.8	86.8	17.2	16.3	48.3	46.6	49.7	38.7
1977	41.2	38.0	33.9	40.4	28.6	104.6	17.6	18.1	48.9	47.7	49.9	40.7
1978	43.5	39.7	35.7	45.1	32.6	111.6	19.5	19.6	50.3	48.9	51.6	43.0
1979	44.8	40.7	36.7	47.7	35.8	107.4	21.4	20.0	51.2	50.0	52.3	44.0
1980	44.7	40.5	36.7	44.9	35.8	84.9	23.7	18.6	52.2	52.2	52.2	43.2
1981	45.9	41.1	37.5	46.1	38.0	77.9	24.0	19.1	52.7	54.5	51.2	44.4
1982	45.0	41.7	38.1	43.0	36.6	63.8	22.1	18.9	53.7	56.6	51.2	43.8
1983	47.1	44.1	40.6	46.2	36.5	90.6	21.6	21.3	55.7	60.2	51.9	46.4
1984	50.5	46.4	43.0	53.7	42.6	104.0	23.3	26.4	57.7	62.2	53.9	50.5
1985	52.7	48.9	45.6	56.6	45.4	106.4	24.1	28.2	61.6	67.2	56.9	52.7
1986	54.5	50.9	47.7	57.7	44.6	119.6	26.0	30.6	65.0	71.1	59.8	54.7
1987	56.4	52.6	49.6	58.0	44.6	121.9	28.8	32.4	66.9	73.8	61.1	56.4
1988	58.8	54.8	51.8	59.9	46.9	120.8	33.5	33.6	67.8	72.8	63.4	58.3
1989	60.9	56.4	53.4	61.8	49.5	116.9	37.3	35.1	69.8	74.1	66.0	60.1
1990	62.1	57.6	54.7	61.0	50.1	107.0	40.6	36.4	72.0	75.6	68.7	61.0
1991	62.1	57.7	54.8	57.8	48.1	97.5	43.3	36.3	72.9	75.6	70.2	60.6
1992	64.3	59.9	57.2	61.0	49.5	110.9	46.3	38.9	73.2	74.5	71.6	62.7
1993	66.0	62.0	59.3	65.7	53.2	120.0	47.8	42.2	72.6	71.9	72.5	64.8
1994	68.7	64.4	61.8	71.0	57.4	130.7	52.1	47.3	72.7	69.4	74.5	67.7
1995	70.6	66.3	63.8	75.4	63.0	126.3	57.4	51.1	73.1	67.6	76.5	69.4
1996	73.2	68.6	66.3	82.1	68.7	136.6	62.1	55.5	73.8	66.8	78.3	72.1
1997	76.5	71.2	69.1	89.1	76.1	139.9	69.5	63.0	75.2	66.2	81.1	75.5
1998	79.9	75.0	73.2	98.2	84.3	152.0	71.1	70.3	76.7	65.7	84.3	79.7
1999	83.7	79.0	77.3	106.9	92.4	161.6	73.0	77.5	79.4	67.0	87.8	84.1
2000	87.1	83.0	81.6	114.3	100.9	162.6	79.3	87.5	80.9	67.2	90.3	88.1
2001	88.0	85.1	83.9	112.6	98.5	164.1	74.6	85.1	83.9	69.8	93.6	89.2
2002	89.5	87.3	86.3	108.7	91.7	174.0	73.3	88.2	87.6	74.8	96.3	91.3
2003	92.0	90.1	89.2	113.0	93.4	189.8	74.6	92.1	89.5	79.9	95.9	94.1
2004	95.5	93.5	92.8	120.6	98.3	208.8	81.9	102.6	90.9	83.5	95.8	98.1
2005	98.7	96.8	96.2	128.9	105.1	222.5	87.0	109.1	91.5	85.0	95.8	101.5
2006	101.4	99.7	99.4	131.4	112.6	205.6	94.9	116.0	92.9	87.1	96.7	104.2
2007	103.2	102.0	101.8	128.8	119.3	166.9	103.7	119.0	94.3	88.6	98.1	105.4
2008	102.9	101.6	101.8	120.1	118.4	126.9	109.6	115.9	96.9	94.6	98.5	104.0
2009	100.0	100.0	100.0	100.0	100.0	100.0	100.0	100.0	100.0	100.0	100.0	100.0
2010	102.5	101.9	102.0	101.5	102.5	97.5	111.9	112.7	100.1	104.4	97.3	102.9
2011	104.2	104.2	104.7	107.9	110.3	98.0	119.6	118.9	97.0	101.5	94.1	104.5
2012	106.5	105.8	106.6	118.5	120.2	111.3	123.6	121.5	95.2	99.7	92.3	106.7
2013	108.1	107.6	108.5	123.5	123.9	121.9	127.1	122.8	92.4	94.0	91.4	108.0
2014	110.7	110.4	111.7	130.0	131.5	124.0	131.4	127.5	91.9	91.7	92.0	110.7
2012												
1st quarter	106.1	105.4	106.4	116.5	118.7	107.7	122.4	121.3	95.9	100.5	93.0	106.4
2nd quarter	106.5	105.6	106.3	118.5	120.8	108.7	123.7	121.9	95.5	99.8	92.7	106.8
3rd quarter	106.7	105.9	106.6	118.5	120.2	111.5	124.3	122.1	95.2	99.9	92.2	106.9
4th quarter	106.7	106.2	107.1	120.5	121.3	117.2	124.2	120.9	94.3	98.5	91.6	106.7
2013												
1st quarter	107.2	106.8	107.6	122.0	122.5	119.8	124.5	121.1	93.2	96.1	91.3	107.2
2nd quarter	107.5	107.2	108.0	122.7	122.8	122.5	126.0	122.8	92.7	94.7	91.4	107.6
3rd quarter	108.3	107.6	108.6	123.9	123.9	123.9	127.3	123.5	92.2	93.3	91.4	108.3
4th quarter	109.3	108.6	109.5	125.4	126.5	121.3	130.6	123.8	91.6	91.7	91.4	109.0
2014												
1st quarter	109.1	108.9	109.8	127.3	129.0	120.5	128.4	124.7	91.6	91.8	91.4	109.1
2nd quarter	110.3	109.9	111.1	129.0	130.4	123.5	131.4	127.6	91.8	91.5	92.0	110.3
3rd quarter	111.4	110.9	112.4	131.5	133.2	124.5	132.0	127.3	92.2	92.4	92.1	111.4
4th quarter	112.0	112.0	113.6	132.3	133.5	127.5	133.8	130.5	91.9	91.0	92.4	112.2

Table 1-5B. Chain-Type Quantity Indexes for Gross Domestic Product and Domestic Purchases: Historical Data

(Index numbers, 2009 = 100.)

NIPA Tables 1.1.3, 1.4.3, 2.3.3

Year and quarter	Gross domestic product, total	Personal consumption expenditures		Private fixed investment			Exports and imports of goods and services		Government consumption expenditures and gross investment			Gross domestic purchases
		Total	Excluding food and energy	Total	Nonresidential	Residential	Exports	Imports	Total	Federal	State and local	
1929	7.3	7.9	6.5	7.6	5.5	20.4	2.6	2.7	5.4	2.1	10.4	7.3
1930	6.7	7.5	6.1	5.9	4.5	12.6	2.1	2.3	5.9	2.4	11.5	6.7
1931	6.3	7.3	5.9	4.2	3.1	10.7	1.8	2.0	6.2	2.4	12.0	6.3
1932	5.5	6.6	5.3	2.6	1.9	6.1	1.4	1.7	6.0	2.5	11.4	5.5
1933	5.4	6.5	5.1	2.3	1.8	5.1	1.4	1.7	5.8	3.0	10.2	5.4
1934	6.0	6.9	5.4	3.0	2.2	6.6	1.5	1.8	6.5	4.0	10.7	6.0
1935	6.5	7.4	5.7	3.7	2.8	9.0	1.6	2.3	6.7	4.1	11.1	6.5
1936	7.4	8.1	6.3	4.9	3.7	11.2	1.7	2.3	7.7	6.2	11.1	7.4
1937	7.7	8.4	6.5	5.7	4.4	12.1	2.1	2.6	7.4	5.6	11.1	7.7
1938	7.5	8.3	6.3	4.6	3.3	12.1	2.1	2.0	8.0	6.1	11.7	7.4
1939	8.1	8.7	6.8	5.4	3.7	17.0	2.2	2.1	8.7	6.6	12.9	8.0
1940	8.8	9.2	7.1	6.5	4.4	19.0	2.5	2.2	9.0	7.5	12.5	8.7
1941	10.3	9.8	7.7	7.4	5.3	20.2	2.6	2.7	15.1	19.8	11.7	10.3
1942	12.3	9.6	7.5	4.4	3.3	10.5	1.7	2.4	35.1	59.1	10.7	12.3
1943	14.4	9.9	8.0	3.5	2.8	6.5	1.5	3.1	52.6	94.1	9.8	14.6
1944	15.5	10.2	8.2	4.2	3.5	5.6	1.6	3.2	59.1	107.2	9.4	15.7
1945	15.4	10.8	8.7	5.5	4.8	6.4	2.2	3.4	51.9	92.7	9.8	15.5
1946	13.6	12.1	9.6	9.8	7.0	25.5	4.7	2.8	18.3	26.0	10.7	13.1
1947	13.5	12.4	9.8	11.6	8.0	32.6	5.4	2.7	15.6	19.5	12.2	12.8
1948	14.0	12.6	10.1	12.7	8.4	39.0	4.2	3.1	16.5	20.7	12.9	13.7
1949	13.9	13.0	10.5	11.7	7.6	36.1	4.2	3.0	18.3	22.4	14.8	13.6
1947												
1st quarter	13.4	12.2	0.0	11.5	8.1	30.0	5.7	2.8	15.5	19.6	11.9	12.8
2nd quarter	13.4	12.4	0.0	11.2	8.0	28.5	5.7	2.8	15.6	19.7	12.0	12.8
3rd quarter	13.4	12.4	0.0	11.5	7.8	32.9	5.4	2.5	15.7	19.7	12.3	12.7
4th quarter	13.6	12.4	0.0	12.5	8.1	39.2	4.8	2.6	15.6	19.3	12.5	13.1
1948												
1st quarter	13.8	12.5	0.0	12.9	8.5	38.7	4.5	3.0	15.8	19.7	12.5	13.4
2nd quarter	14.0	12.6	0.0	12.8	8.2	40.9	4.1	3.1	16.3	20.4	12.8	13.7
3rd quarter	14.1	12.7	0.0	12.7	8.3	39.6	4.2	3.2	16.7	20.8	13.0	13.8
4th quarter	14.1	12.8	0.0	12.6	8.5	36.7	4.1	3.2	17.3	21.8	13.3	13.8
1949												
1st quarter	13.9	12.8	0.0	11.9	8.1	34.0	4.6	3.1	17.8	22.2	13.9	13.5
2nd quarter	13.9	13.0	0.0	11.5	7.8	33.4	4.5	3.0	18.5	23.0	14.6	13.5
3rd quarter	14.0	13.0	0.0	11.5	7.4	36.3	4.1	2.9	18.7	22.7	15.2	13.7
4th quarter	13.9	13.2	0.0	11.9	7.3	40.7	3.6	3.0	18.3	21.7	15.5	13.7
1950												
1st quarter	14.5	13.4	0.0	12.6	7.5	45.3	3.5	3.1	18.0	20.8	15.9	14.2
2nd quarter	14.9	13.6	0.0	13.7	8.2	49.6	3.6	3.2	18.3	21.3	16.0	14.7
3rd quarter	15.5	14.3	0.0	14.7	8.8	52.3	3.7	4.0	18.0	20.6	16.0	15.4
4th quarter	15.8	13.9	0.0	14.4	8.8	49.9	4.0	4.0	19.3	23.2	16.1	15.6
1951												
1st quarter	16.0	14.2	0.0	13.9	8.6	47.3	4.2	4.0	21.4	27.6	15.9	15.8
2nd quarter	16.3	13.8	0.0	13.3	8.7	41.0	4.6	3.8	24.2	33.1	16.2	16.0
3rd quarter	16.6	14.0	0.0	13.1	8.8	38.4	4.7	3.5	26.9	38.4	16.2	16.2
4th quarter	16.6	14.1	0.0	13.0	8.6	38.8	4.6	3.4	28.3	41.4	16.2	16.3
1952												
1st quarter	16.8	14.1	0.0	13.2	8.7	39.8	4.9	3.8	29.2	43.0	16.3	16.5
2nd quarter	16.8	14.4	0.0	13.4	8.9	40.5	4.3	3.8	30.1	44.7	16.6	16.6
3rd quarter	17.0	14.5	0.0	12.7	8.2	40.1	4.0	4.0	30.4	45.8	16.2	16.8
4th quarter	17.5	15.0	0.0	13.7	8.9	42.3	4.0	4.4	30.9	46.5	16.5	17.4
1953												
1st quarter	17.8	15.1	0.0	14.2	9.4	43.0	4.0	4.3	31.9	48.1	16.9	17.7
2nd quarter	18.0	15.2	0.0	14.3	9.5	43.1	4.0	4.5	32.6	49.5	16.9	17.9
3rd quarter	17.9	15.2	0.0	14.3	9.7	41.5	4.1	4.5	32.2	48.3	17.3	17.8
4th quarter	17.6	15.1	0.0	14.2	9.6	41.2	4.0	4.3	32.1	47.7	17.7	17.5
1954												
1st quarter	17.5	15.2	0.0	14.0	9.4	41.6	3.8	4.0	31.3	45.3	18.4	17.4
2nd quarter	17.6	15.3	0.0	14.2	9.3	44.3	4.4	4.4	30.2	43.0	18.4	17.4
3rd quarter	17.8	15.6	0.0	14.8	9.5	47.0	4.2	4.1	29.6	41.1	18.9	17.6
4th quarter	18.1	15.9	0.0	15.1	9.5	50.0	4.4	4.2	29.4	40.7	19.0	17.9
1955												
1st quarter	18.6	16.2	0.0	15.7	9.7	53.6	4.6	4.4	29.4	39.9	19.8	18.4
2nd quarter	18.9	16.6	0.0	16.3	10.2	54.4	4.5	4.7	29.2	39.1	20.1	18.8
3rd quarter	19.2	16.8	0.0	16.7	10.7	53.2	4.8	4.7	29.3	39.5	20.0	19.0
4th quarter	19.3	17.0	0.0	16.8	11.0	51.0	4.8	4.9	28.8	38.1	20.2	19.1

Table 1-5B. Chain-Type Quantity Indexes for Gross Domestic Product and Domestic Purchases: Historical Data—*Continued*

(Index numbers, 2009 = 100.)

NIPA Tables 1.1.3, 1.4.3, 2.3.3

Year and quarter	Gross domestic product, total	Personal consumption expenditures		Private fixed investment			Exports and imports of goods and services		Government consumption expenditures and gross investment			Gross domestic purchases
		Total	Excluding food and energy	Total	Nonresi-dential	Residential	Exports	Imports	Total	Federal	State and local	
1956												
1st quarter	19.2	17.0	0.0	16.5	10.9	49.7	5.0	5.1	28.7	37.9	20.4	19.0
2nd quarter	19.4	17.0	0.0	16.7	11.1	49.5	5.4	5.1	29.3	38.8	20.6	19.1
3rd quarter	19.4	17.1	0.0	16.7	11.2	48.5	5.5	5.1	29.1	38.2	20.7	19.1
4th quarter	19.7	17.3	0.0	16.6	11.2	47.8	5.8	4.9	29.8	39.5	20.9	19.3
1957												
1st quarter	19.8	17.4	0.0	16.6	11.3	47.1	6.2	5.3	30.5	40.3	21.5	19.5
2nd quarter	19.8	17.5	0.0	16.4	11.3	46.0	6.0	5.3	30.3	39.8	21.6	19.4
3rd quarter	19.9	17.6	0.0	16.6	11.5	45.4	5.8	5.2	30.5	39.9	21.9	19.7
4th quarter	19.7	17.6	0.0	16.3	11.2	45.4	5.7	5.3	31.1	40.4	22.5	19.5
1958												
1st quarter	19.2	17.4	0.0	15.4	10.5	43.6	5.1	5.3	30.8	39.2	23.1	19.1
2nd quarter	19.4	17.5	0.0	15.0	10.1	43.7	5.1	5.6	31.6	40.5	23.5	19.2
3rd quarter	19.8	17.8	0.0	15.3	10.0	46.9	5.1	5.5	31.7	40.3	24.0	19.7
4th quarter	20.3	18.0	0.0	16.2	10.4	51.8	5.1	5.8	32.4	41.2	24.4	20.2
1959												
1st quarter	20.6	18.4	15.0	17.1	10.7	57.6	5.5	5.9	32.0	40.4	24.5	20.5
2nd quarter	21.1	18.7	15.3	17.6	11.0	59.6	5.6	6.2	32.4	41.1	24.6	21.0
3rd quarter	21.1	18.9	15.5	17.8	11.3	58.5	5.8	6.3	32.7	41.7	24.6	21.0
4th quarter	21.2	18.9	15.5	17.6	11.3	56.8	5.7	6.1	32.4	41.2	24.5	21.0
1960												
1st quarter	21.7	19.1	15.7	18.2	11.7	58.6	6.4	6.3	31.9	39.7	24.9	21.4
2nd quarter	21.6	19.3	15.9	17.9	11.8	53.8	6.8	6.4	32.2	39.8	25.5	21.3
3rd quarter	21.6	19.2	15.8	17.5	11.6	52.2	6.6	6.2	33.0	41.0	25.9	21.3
4th quarter	21.4	19.2	15.8	17.5	11.6	52.1	6.7	5.9	33.2	41.1	26.2	21.0
1961												
1st quarter	21.5	19.2	15.8	17.3	11.4	52.3	6.7	5.9	33.7	41.3	27.0	21.2
2nd quarter	21.9	19.5	16.0	17.6	11.7	52.6	6.6	5.9	33.8	41.6	26.8	21.6
3rd quarter	22.3	19.6	16.2	18.0	11.8	55.4	6.6	6.3	34.5	42.8	27.0	22.0
4th quarter	22.7	20.0	16.6	18.6	12.2	57.3	6.8	6.5	35.3	43.6	27.8	22.5
1962												
1st quarter	23.1	20.2	16.8	18.9	12.4	58.3	6.7	6.7	36.0	45.3	27.6	22.9
2nd quarter	23.4	20.5	17.1	19.5	12.8	60.1	7.4	6.8	36.1	45.4	27.7	23.1
3rd quarter	23.6	20.6	17.2	19.6	12.9	60.1	7.0	6.9	37.0	46.8	28.1	23.4
4th quarter	23.7	20.9	17.5	19.6	12.9	60.0	6.8	7.0	37.2	47.0	28.4	23.5
1963												
1st quarter	24.0	21.1	17.6	19.8	12.9	62.1	7.0	6.8	36.7	45.4	28.9	23.7
2nd quarter	24.3	21.3	17.9	20.7	13.3	66.5	7.8	7.0	36.7	45.2	29.2	23.9
3rd quarter	24.8	21.6	18.1	21.2	13.7	67.8	7.4	7.2	38.4	47.8	29.9	24.5
4th quarter	24.9	21.7	18.3	21.9	14.1	69.9	7.8	7.1	38.0	46.5	30.3	24.6
1964												
1st quarter	25.5	22.2	18.7	22.6	14.4	74.2	8.2	7.1	38.1	46.3	30.8	25.0
2nd quarter	25.8	22.6	19.1	22.6	14.7	70.5	8.4	7.3	38.5	46.3	31.5	25.3
3rd quarter	26.1	23.0	19.4	22.9	15.2	69.4	8.3	7.5	38.5	46.0	31.8	25.7
4th quarter	26.2	23.0	19.5	23.1	15.5	68.2	8.6	7.7	38.5	45.6	32.2	25.8
1965												
1st quarter	26.9	23.6	20.0	24.2	16.5	68.5	7.6	7.4	38.4	45.2	32.4	26.6
2nd quarter	27.2	23.8	20.2	24.9	17.1	69.1	9.1	8.3	38.9	45.3	33.3	26.8
3rd quarter	27.8	24.2	20.6	25.5	17.7	69.4	8.5	8.3	40.2	47.0	34.2	27.5
4th quarter	28.4	24.9	21.1	26.1	18.4	68.1	9.2	8.7	41.0	48.1	34.7	28.1
1966												
1st quarter	29.1	25.3	21.5	27.1	19.2	69.8	9.0	9.0	41.7	49.2	35.1	28.8
2nd quarter	29.3	25.3	21.5	26.9	19.5	64.4	9.4	9.2	42.5	50.6	35.4	28.9
3rd quarter	29.5	25.6	21.8	26.9	19.8	62.2	9.0	9.7	43.7	52.5	35.8	29.3
4th quarter	29.7	25.7	22.0	26.2	19.8	55.7	9.3	9.8	44.4	53.1	36.7	29.5
1967												
1st quarter	30.0	25.9	22.0	25.7	19.4	54.2	9.5	10.0	46.3	56.5	37.1	29.7
2nd quarter	30.0	26.2	22.4	26.3	19.4	60.4	9.4	9.9	46.1	55.9	37.4	29.8
3rd quarter	30.3	26.4	22.5	26.6	19.4	63.6	9.2	10.0	46.6	56.9	37.5	30.1
4th quarter	30.5	26.5	22.6	27.4	19.8	67.3	9.5	10.5	47.0	56.9	38.2	30.4
1968												
1st quarter	31.1	27.2	23.2	28.0	20.3	67.5	9.7	11.2	47.8	57.9	38.9	31.0
2nd quarter	31.7	27.6	23.6	28.0	20.1	69.1	9.9	11.3	48.1	57.6	39.6	31.5
3rd quarter	31.9	28.1	24.0	28.4	20.4	70.5	10.5	12.0	48.2	57.3	40.2	31.8
4th quarter	32.0	28.2	24.2	29.1	20.9	71.5	10.4	11.9	48.3	57.0	40.5	31.9

Table 1-5B. Chain-Type Quantity Indexes for Gross Domestic Product and Domestic Purchases: Historical Data—*Continued*

(Index numbers, 2009 = 100.)

NIPA Tables 1.1.3, 1.4.3, 2.3.3

Year and quarter	Gross domestic product											Gross domestic purchases
	Gross domestic product, total	Personal consumption expenditures		Private fixed investment			Exports and imports of goods and services		Government consumption expenditures and gross investment			
		Total	Excluding food and energy	Total	Nonresidential	Residential	Exports	Imports	Total	Federal	State and local	
1969												
1st quarter	32.5	28.5	24.4	29.9	21.5	73.9	9.1	10.8	48.4	56.8	40.9	32.4
2nd quarter	32.6	28.7	24.6	30.0	21.7	73.2	11.2	12.9	48.2	56.1	41.2	32.5
3rd quarter	32.8	28.9	24.7	30.5	22.2	72.6	10.9	12.7	48.3	56.2	41.3	32.7
4th quarter	32.7	29.1	24.9	29.8	22.1	67.7	11.3	12.6	47.7	55.0	41.3	32.5
1970												
1st quarter	32.6	29.3	25.0	29.6	21.9	67.7	11.4	12.6	47.5	54.0	41.7	32.4
2nd quarter	32.7	29.4	25.2	29.0	21.8	63.5	11.9	12.8	46.9	52.6	41.9	32.4
3rd quarter	33.0	29.7	25.4	29.5	21.8	67.2	11.9	12.8	47.1	52.0	42.8	32.7
4th quarter	32.7	29.6	25.2	29.5	21.1	74.0	12.0	13.0	47.2	51.8	43.1	32.4
1971												
1st quarter	33.5	30.2	25.8	30.1	21.3	77.8	12.0	12.8	46.5	50.1	43.2	33.3
2nd quarter	33.7	30.4	26.1	31.3	21.6	85.3	12.0	13.8	46.4	49.5	43.6	33.6
3rd quarter	34.0	30.7	26.4	31.8	21.7	89.2	12.5	14.1	46.4	49.3	43.7	33.8
4th quarter	34.1	31.2	26.9	32.6	22.1	92.7	11.4	13.1	46.1	48.0	44.3	33.9
1972												
1st quarter	34.7	31.6	27.4	34.0	22.8	98.7	12.7	15.1	46.3	48.4	44.4	34.6
2nd quarter	35.5	32.2	27.8	34.6	23.2	100.6	12.3	14.5	46.5	49.0	44.3	35.4
3rd quarter	35.8	32.7	28.3	35.0	23.5	101.0	13.1	14.8	45.6	46.7	44.7	35.6
4th quarter	36.4	33.5	29.0	36.5	24.6	104.6	13.6	15.5	46.0	46.7	45.3	36.2
1973												
1st quarter	37.3	34.1	29.8	38.0	25.7	108.1	14.6	16.2	46.3	47.3	45.5	37.1
2nd quarter	37.7	34.1	29.9	38.2	26.6	102.5	15.3	15.8	46.1	46.7	45.6	37.3
3rd quarter	37.5	34.2	30.0	38.1	27.0	98.1	15.4	15.3	45.5	45.0	46.0	37.1
4th quarter	37.9	34.1	30.0	37.8	27.2	93.6	16.1	15.4	45.8	45.0	46.6	37.3
1974												
1st quarter	37.6	33.8	29.9	37.1	27.2	87.5	16.3	14.9	46.7	46.1	47.2	36.8
2nd quarter	37.7	33.9	30.0	36.6	27.2	84.0	17.1	15.7	47.0	46.1	47.8	36.9
3rd quarter	37.3	34.0	30.0	36.0	26.9	81.2	16.2	15.4	47.1	46.3	47.7	36.7
4th quarter	37.2	33.5	29.5	34.1	26.2	70.6	16.6	15.3	47.3	46.7	47.7	36.4
1975												
1st quarter	36.7	33.8	29.8	32.1	24.7	66.6	16.7	13.7	47.8	46.2	49.1	35.7
2nd quarter	37.0	34.4	30.2	31.8	24.1	68.5	16.3	12.6	47.5	46.0	48.8	35.8
3rd quarter	37.6	34.9	30.8	32.5	24.3	73.0	16.0	13.7	48.2	46.9	49.4	36.7
4th quarter	38.1	35.2	31.3	33.2	24.6	76.2	16.9	14.4	48.7	47.1	50.0	37.2
1976												
1st quarter	39.0	35.9	31.9	34.5	25.2	83.4	16.8	15.3	48.8	46.7	50.6	38.2
2nd quarter	39.3	36.3	32.1	35.1	25.5	85.4	16.9	16.0	48.3	46.7	49.7	38.6
3rd quarter	39.5	36.7	32.4	35.5	26.1	84.1	17.4	16.6	48.0	46.5	49.4	38.8
4th quarter	39.8	37.1	32.8	37.2	26.6	94.3	17.6	17.2	48.1	46.7	49.2	39.2
1977												
1st quarter	40.2	37.6	33.3	38.5	27.5	97.1	17.3	18.0	48.5	47.1	49.7	39.8
2nd quarter	41.0	37.8	33.6	40.5	28.3	107.7	17.8	18.2	48.9	47.8	50.0	40.6
3rd quarter	41.7	38.1	34.0	41.0	28.9	107.4	17.9	17.9	49.1	48.1	49.9	41.2
4th quarter	41.7	38.7	34.5	41.7	29.7	106.2	17.3	18.2	49.0	47.7	50.0	41.4
1978												
1st quarter	41.9	38.9	34.7	42.1	30.0	107.1	17.8	19.4	49.0	47.8	50.0	41.7
2nd quarter	43.5	39.8	35.8	44.9	32.3	112.3	19.6	19.5	50.3	48.9	51.5	43.0
3rd quarter	43.9	39.9	36.0	46.2	33.4	113.6	19.8	19.7	50.7	49.1	52.1	43.4
4th quarter	44.5	40.3	36.3	47.2	34.5	113.4	20.6	20.0	51.2	49.5	52.6	43.9
1979												
1st quarter	44.6	40.5	36.4	47.6	35.3	110.6	20.6	19.9	50.7	49.6	51.7	43.9
2nd quarter	44.7	40.4	36.5	47.3	35.3	108.6	20.7	20.0	51.2	50.2	52.2	44.0
3rd quarter	45.0	40.8	37.0	48.1	36.3	107.3	21.4	19.7	51.3	50.1	52.4	44.1
4th quarter	45.1	40.9	37.1	47.7	36.4	103.0	22.8	20.2	51.6	50.1	53.0	44.1
1980												
1st quarter	45.3	40.9	37.0	47.1	36.8	95.1	23.4	20.2	52.4	51.6	53.2	44.1
2nd quarter	44.3	40.0	36.0	43.2	35.1	77.5	23.9	18.7	52.6	52.8	52.5	42.8
3rd quarter	44.3	40.4	36.6	43.7	35.3	79.8	23.8	17.4	51.9	52.0	51.7	42.5
4th quarter	45.1	40.9	37.3	45.4	36.1	87.3	23.7	18.3	51.9	52.3	51.5	43.5
1981												
1st quarter	46.0	41.1	37.6	45.8	36.8	85.2	24.1	19.1	52.5	53.3	51.9	44.5
2nd quarter	45.7	41.1	37.5	46.2	37.6	82.4	24.2	19.1	52.7	54.8	50.9	44.2
3rd quarter	46.2	41.3	37.7	46.2	38.4	76.0	23.7	18.9	52.5	54.6	50.7	44.7
4th quarter	45.7	41.0	37.3	46.0	39.3	68.1	23.8	19.4	53.1	55.4	51.1	44.3

Table 1-5B. Chain-Type Quantity Indexes for Gross Domestic Product and Domestic Purchases: Historical Data—*Continued*

(Index numbers, 2009 = 100.)

NIPA Tables 1.1.3, 1.4.3, 2.3.3

Year and quarter	Gross domestic product											Gross domestic purchases
	Gross domestic product, total	Personal consumption expenditures		Private fixed investment			Exports and imports of goods and services		Government consumption expenditures and gross investment			
		Total	Excluding food and energy	Total	Nonresidential	Residential	Exports	Imports	Total	Federal	State and local	
1982												
1st quarter	44.9	41.3	37.5	44.6	38.3	64.2	22.8	18.9	53.0	55.4	51.0	43.6
2nd quarter	45.2	41.4	37.7	43.1	37.0	62.1	22.9	18.6	53.4	56.0	51.2	43.7
3rd quarter	45.0	41.7	38.1	42.1	36.0	62.0	21.9	19.4	53.7	56.7	51.2	43.9
4th quarter	45.0	42.5	38.9	42.1	35.3	67.0	20.9	18.7	54.6	58.1	51.6	44.0
1983												
1st quarter	45.6	42.9	39.4	43.1	34.8	78.5	21.3	19.1	55.1	59.0	51.7	44.6
2nd quarter	46.7	43.8	40.2	44.7	35.3	87.6	21.3	20.6	55.7	60.4	51.6	45.9
3rd quarter	47.6	44.5	40.9	47.2	36.8	96.2	21.6	22.2	56.6	61.8	52.1	47.0
4th quarter	48.6	45.2	41.7	49.9	39.0	100.2	22.1	23.2	55.6	59.7	52.1	48.1
1984												
1st quarter	49.5	45.6	42.3	51.4	40.3	103.2	22.5	25.1	56.3	60.4	52.8	49.4
2nd quarter	50.4	46.3	42.8	53.4	42.1	105.0	23.1	26.2	57.5	62.3	53.5	50.3
3rd quarter	50.9	46.6	43.2	54.5	43.4	103.8	23.6	26.8	58.0	62.3	54.4	50.8
4th quarter	51.3	47.2	43.9	55.5	44.4	103.9	24.1	27.6	59.1	64.0	54.9	51.3
1985												
1st quarter	51.8	48.0	44.7	56.0	44.9	104.1	24.1	27.0	59.8	64.8	55.6	51.7
2nd quarter	52.3	48.5	45.2	56.7	45.6	105.0	24.1	28.4	61.2	66.6	56.6	52.4
3rd quarter	53.1	49.4	46.2	56.4	45.1	107.0	23.7	28.1	62.7	68.7	57.5	53.2
4th quarter	53.5	49.5	46.2	57.5	45.9	109.3	24.5	29.2	62.9	68.6	58.0	53.7
1986												
1st quarter	54.0	50.0	46.7	57.7	45.4	113.8	25.2	29.2	63.4	68.5	59.0	54.0
2nd quarter	54.2	50.5	47.2	57.7	44.5	120.3	25.5	30.4	64.7	70.7	59.6	54.4
3rd quarter	54.8	51.4	48.3	57.4	44.0	121.9	26.1	31.2	66.1	73.3	60.2	55.0
4th quarter	55.1	51.8	48.6	57.9	44.4	122.3	27.1	31.5	65.8	72.1	60.4	55.2
1987												
1st quarter	55.4	51.8	48.7	56.9	43.4	122.1	27.1	31.3	66.2	72.7	60.7	55.6
2nd quarter	56.1	52.5	49.4	57.8	44.3	122.5	28.2	32.1	66.8	73.9	60.8	56.1
3rd quarter	56.6	53.1	50.1	58.8	45.5	121.5	29.4	32.7	66.9	74.0	61.0	56.6
4th quarter	57.5	53.2	50.2	58.7	45.4	121.7	30.5	33.4	67.7	74.7	61.8	57.5
1988												
1st quarter	57.8	54.2	51.1	58.8	45.8	119.5	32.2	33.3	67.3	72.9	62.5	57.5
2nd quarter	58.6	54.6	51.4	59.9	46.8	121.0	33.1	32.9	67.5	72.4	63.3	58.0
3rd quarter	58.9	55.0	51.9	60.2	47.1	121.1	33.8	33.7	67.6	72.1	63.6	58.4
4th quarter	59.7	55.6	52.6	60.9	47.8	121.8	34.8	34.7	68.8	74.0	64.4	59.2
1989												
1st quarter	60.3	55.9	52.8	61.4	48.5	120.7	35.8	34.9	68.5	72.6	64.9	59.7
2nd quarter	60.8	56.2	53.2	61.5	49.2	116.9	37.4	35.0	69.7	74.3	65.6	59.9
3rd quarter	61.3	56.7	53.8	62.6	50.4	116.3	37.8	35.0	70.2	74.8	66.2	60.3
4th quarter	61.4	57.0	53.8	61.8	49.9	113.9	38.3	35.6	70.6	74.5	67.1	60.5
1990												
1st quarter	62.1	57.5	54.6	62.5	50.6	114.9	40.0	36.7	71.7	75.7	68.1	61.1
2nd quarter	62.3	57.6	54.7	61.3	49.9	110.3	40.5	36.7	71.9	75.9	68.3	61.2
3rd quarter	62.3	57.9	54.9	60.8	50.3	104.4	40.8	36.5	71.9	75.2	68.7	61.2
4th quarter	61.8	57.4	54.5	59.2	49.5	98.4	41.2	35.6	72.5	75.7	69.5	60.5
1991												
1st quarter	61.5	57.2	54.3	57.6	48.5	93.2	41.4	35.2	72.9	76.4	69.6	60.1
2nd quarter	62.0	57.7	54.7	57.8	48.2	96.1	42.9	35.8	73.1	76.6	69.9	60.4
3rd quarter	62.3	58.0	55.0	57.8	47.8	99.3	43.9	36.8	72.9	75.4	70.3	60.8
4th quarter	62.5	58.0	55.1	58.1	47.8	101.3	44.9	37.6	72.6	74.1	70.8	61.0
1992												
1st quarter	63.3	59.1	56.3	58.7	47.6	107.1	45.7	37.9	73.2	74.2	71.7	61.7
2nd quarter	64.0	59.5	56.7	60.7	49.2	110.7	45.8	38.5	73.1	74.2	71.6	62.5
3rd quarter	64.6	60.1	57.4	61.4	49.9	110.8	46.7	39.1	73.4	75.0	71.6	63.0
4th quarter	65.2	60.8	58.1	63.2	51.2	115.0	47.0	40.0	73.3	74.7	71.6	63.8
1993												
1st quarter	65.4	61.1	58.4	63.6	51.8	115.1	47.1	40.9	72.4	72.5	71.8	64.0
2nd quarter	65.7	61.6	59.0	64.8	52.8	116.6	47.6	41.7	72.5	71.9	72.4	64.5
3rd quarter	66.1	62.3	59.6	65.8	53.2	121.0	47.5	42.3	72.7	71.7	72.8	64.9
4th quarter	67.0	62.9	60.2	68.4	55.1	127.2	49.1	44.0	72.8	71.6	73.1	65.8
1994												
1st quarter	67.6	63.6	60.9	69.3	55.7	129.1	49.5	45.0	71.9	69.1	73.4	66.6
2nd quarter	68.5	64.1	61.4	70.7	56.6	133.3	51.2	46.7	72.4	69.0	74.2	67.5
3rd quarter	68.9	64.6	62.0	71.2	57.5	131.3	53.1	48.0	73.6	70.7	75.1	67.9
4th quarter	69.7	65.3	62.8	73.0	59.8	129.3	54.4	49.4	72.9	68.7	75.4	68.7
1995												
1st quarter	70.0	65.4	62.9	74.5	62.0	126.4	55.4	50.4	73.1	68.3	76.0	69.0
2nd quarter	70.2	66.0	63.5	74.5	62.6	122.5	56.2	50.9	73.4	68.4	76.6	69.2
3rd quarter	70.8	66.6	64.2	75.5	63.0	127.0	58.6	51.1	73.2	67.8	76.6	69.5
4th quarter	71.3	67.1	64.7	77.0	64.3	129.5	59.4	51.8	72.6	65.8	77.0	70.0

Table 1-5B. Chain-Type Quantity Indexes for Gross Domestic Product and Domestic Purchases: Historical Data—*Continued*

(Index numbers, 2009 = 100.)

NIPA Tables 1.1.3, 1.4.3, 2.3.3

Year and quarter	Gross domestic product	Personal consumption expenditures		Private fixed investment			Exports and imports of goods and services		Government consumption expenditures and gross investment			Gross domestic purchases
	Gross domestic product, total	Total	Excluding food and energy	Total	Nonresidential	Residential	Exports	Imports	Total	Federal	State and local	
1996												
1st quarter	71.8	67.7	65.3	79.0	65.9	132.8	60.2	53.4	72.7	66.3	76.9	70.6
2nd quarter	73.0	68.4	66.1	81.4	67.6	138.6	61.1	54.6	73.9	67.5	78.0	71.9
3rd quarter	73.7	68.9	66.6	83.3	69.8	138.3	61.6	56.4	74.0	66.8	78.7	72.7
4th quarter	74.5	69.4	67.2	84.6	71.5	136.8	65.5	57.5	74.5	66.4	79.9	73.2
1997												
1st quarter	75.0	70.1	68.0	86.1	73.1	137.5	66.7	60.0	74.5	65.3	80.7	74.0
2nd quarter	76.2	70.5	68.3	87.8	74.7	139.4	69.4	62.0	75.3	66.7	81.0	75.1
3rd quarter	77.2	71.7	69.6	90.9	78.0	140.7	71.0	64.3	75.4	66.5	81.3	76.1
4th quarter	77.7	72.5	70.5	91.6	78.5	142.2	70.9	65.7	75.5	66.4	81.6	76.9
1998												
1st quarter	78.5	73.3	71.4	94.3	81.0	145.2	71.2	68.1	75.1	64.5	82.2	78.0
2nd quarter	79.3	74.6	72.6	97.4	83.7	150.2	70.4	69.7	76.6	66.1	83.7	79.0
3rd quarter	80.3	75.5	73.7	99.3	85.0	154.6	70.1	70.6	77.3	65.7	85.2	80.2
4th quarter	81.6	76.6	75.0	102.0	87.4	158.2	72.7	72.9	78.0	66.4	85.9	81.5
1999												
1st quarter	82.3	77.4	75.6	103.7	89.3	158.8	70.9	74.0	78.3	65.8	86.8	82.5
2nd quarter	83.0	78.5	76.8	106.2	91.7	161.3	71.7	76.1	78.7	66.1	87.3	83.4
3rd quarter	84.0	79.4	77.7	108.6	94.2	162.5	73.8	78.9	79.6	67.3	88.1	84.6
4th quarter	85.5	80.6	79.0	109.1	94.6	163.7	75.6	80.9	80.8	68.6	89.1	86.0
2000												
1st quarter	85.7	81.8	80.5	112.2	97.9	164.5	76.8	84.1	80.2	66.1	89.8	86.6
2nd quarter	87.3	82.6	81.1	114.7	101.0	163.7	79.0	86.7	81.1	68.4	89.8	88.3
3rd quarter	87.4	83.4	82.0	115.1	102.1	161.1	81.0	89.7	81.0	67.3	90.4	88.6
4th quarter	87.9	84.1	82.7	115.4	102.4	161.3	80.3	89.7	81.2	66.9	91.0	89.1
2001												
1st quarter	87.7	84.5	83.1	114.8	101.6	162.0	79.0	88.2	82.4	68.4	92.1	88.8
2nd quarter	88.2	84.7	83.5	113.3	99.2	164.5	76.4	85.6	84.1	69.7	93.9	89.2
3rd quarter	87.9	85.0	83.8	112.4	98.0	165.5	72.7	83.8	84.0	70.3	93.4	89.1
4th quarter	88.1	86.3	85.3	109.8	95.1	164.4	70.4	82.7	85.2	70.8	95.1	89.5
2002												
1st quarter	88.9	86.6	85.6	109.1	93.2	169.8	71.9	85.1	86.5	72.6	96.0	90.4
2nd quarter	89.4	87.0	86.0	108.9	91.9	174.1	73.8	87.7	87.3	74.3	96.2	91.0
3rd quarter	89.9	87.6	86.6	108.5	91.4	174.6	74.3	89.0	88.0	75.5	96.5	91.6
4th quarter	89.9	88.1	87.0	108.2	90.3	177.7	73.3	90.9	88.6	76.8	96.6	92.0
2003												
1st quarter	90.4	88.5	87.4	108.9	90.5	181.0	72.9	89.6	88.3	76.9	96.1	92.3
2nd quarter	91.2	89.5	88.6	111.3	92.7	183.8	72.8	91.1	89.7	80.7	95.7	93.3
3rd quarter	92.7	90.8	89.9	114.8	94.6	194.4	74.8	92.2	89.7	80.2	96.1	94.8
4th quarter	93.8	91.5	90.7	117.0	95.9	200.1	78.1	95.5	90.2	81.8	95.8	95.9
2004												
1st quarter	94.4	92.4	91.6	116.6	94.9	202.5	80.4	98.5	90.4	82.4	95.8	96.6
2nd quarter	95.1	93.0	92.3	119.6	97.0	208.9	81.4	102.5	91.0	83.2	96.1	97.7
3rd quarter	95.9	93.9	93.3	122.0	99.6	210.4	81.9	103.6	91.3	84.6	95.7	98.6
4th quarter	96.8	94.8	94.2	124.3	101.7	213.3	83.9	106.0	90.9	83.9	95.5	99.5
2005												
1st quarter	97.8	95.6	94.9	126.3	103.0	218.3	85.2	107.2	91.1	84.4	95.5	100.6
2nd quarter	98.3	96.6	96.1	128.3	104.4	222.4	86.8	108.5	91.3	84.6	95.7	101.0
3rd quarter	99.1	97.3	96.8	130.3	106.4	224.8	86.9	108.8	92.0	86.1	95.8	101.9
4th quarter	99.7	97.7	97.2	130.6	106.8	224.3	89.3	112.0	91.6	84.8	96.1	102.6
2006												
1st quarter	100.9	98.8	98.6	133.3	110.7	222.2	92.6	114.5	92.4	87.0	95.9	103.7
2nd quarter	101.2	99.3	99.0	132.1	112.1	211.1	94.4	115.9	92.7	86.9	96.6	104.0
3rd quarter	101.3	99.9	99.5	130.8	113.4	199.3	94.2	116.7	92.9	86.9	96.9	104.3
4th quarter	102.1	100.9	100.6	129.5	114.2	190.0	98.4	117.1	93.5	87.8	97.3	104.6
2007												
1st quarter	102.1	101.5	101.1	129.3	116.1	181.3	100.0	118.9	93.3	86.6	97.7	104.8
2nd quarter	102.9	101.8	101.6	129.6	118.4	174.0	101.8	119.5	94.1	88.0	98.1	105.4
3rd quarter	103.6	102.3	102.1	128.8	120.3	163.0	104.9	119.4	94.8	89.6	98.1	105.7
4th quarter	104.0	102.4	102.4	127.7	122.3	149.4	108.1	118.0	95.2	90.1	98.5	105.5
2008												
1st quarter	103.3	102.2	102.2	125.3	122.3	137.7	109.5	119.1	95.6	91.6	98.2	104.9
2nd quarter	103.8	102.3	102.4	123.6	121.6	131.6	112.7	118.0	96.3	93.3	98.3	104.8
3rd quarter	103.3	101.6	102.0	119.7	118.3	125.2	111.2	115.6	97.6	96.0	98.7	104.1
4th quarter	101.1	100.4	100.6	111.8	111.4	113.1	105.1	110.9	98.3	97.7	98.7	102.0
2009												
1st quarter	99.7	100.0	100.1	103.1	103.4	102.2	96.7	100.2	98.4	96.9	99.4	100.1
2nd quarter	99.6	99.6	99.6	99.3	100.0	96.1	97.0	96.1	100.2	100.1	100.3	99.4
3rd quarter	99.9	100.2	100.2	99.1	98.8	100.8	100.4	99.7	100.8	101.5	100.3	99.8
4th quarter	100.9	100.2	100.1	98.4	97.9	100.9	106.0	104.0	100.6	101.5	100.0	100.7

Table 1-5B. Chain-Type Quantity Indexes for Gross Domestic Product and Domestic Purchases: Historical Data—*Continued*

(Index numbers, 2009 = 100.)

NIPA Tables 1.1.3, 1.4.3, 2.3.3

Year and quarter	Gross domestic product, total	Personal consumption expenditures		Private fixed investment			Exports and imports of goods and services		Government consumption expenditures and gross investment			Gross domestic purchases
		Total	Excluding food and energy	Total	Nonresi-dential	Residential	Exports	Imports	Total	Federal	State and local	
2010												
1st quarter	101.3	100.7	100.6	98.6	98.9	97.6	107.6	106.7	99.8	102.5	98.1	101.3
2nd quarter	102.3	101.5	101.6	101.8	101.6	102.9	110.1	111.8	100.6	104.6	97.9	102.7
3rd quarter	103.0	102.2	102.3	101.7	103.6	93.8	113.2	115.8	100.5	105.5	97.2	103.6
4th quarter	103.6	103.2	103.3	103.8	105.8	95.6	116.7	116.5	99.4	104.8	95.9	104.0
2011												
1st quarter	103.2	103.8	104.0	103.6	105.6	95.4	117.3	117.4	97.5	101.9	94.6	103.6
2nd quarter	104.0	104.0	104.4	105.7	107.8	96.7	119.1	118.3	97.4	102.3	94.2	104.3
3rd quarter	104.2	104.4	104.9	110.0	112.7	98.6	120.3	119.2	96.8	101.3	93.9	104.5
4th quarter	105.4	104.8	105.5	112.6	115.3	101.4	121.5	120.6	96.4	100.6	93.7	105.7
2012												
1st quarter	106.1	105.4	106.4	116.5	118.7	107.7	122.4	121.3	95.9	100.5	93.0	106.4
2nd quarter	106.5	105.6	106.3	118.5	120.8	108.7	123.7	121.9	95.5	99.8	92.7	106.8
3rd quarter	106.7	105.9	106.6	118.5	120.2	111.5	124.3	122.1	95.2	99.9	92.2	106.9
4th quarter	106.7	106.2	107.1	120.5	121.3	117.2	124.2	120.9	94.3	98.5	91.6	106.7
2013												
1st quarter	107.2	106.8	107.6	122.0	122.5	119.8	124.5	121.1	93.2	96.1	91.3	107.2
2nd quarter	107.5	107.2	108.0	122.7	122.8	122.5	126.0	122.8	92.7	94.7	91.4	107.6
3rd quarter	108.3	107.6	108.6	123.9	123.9	123.9	127.3	123.5	92.2	93.3	91.4	108.3
4th quarter	109.3	108.6	109.5	125.4	126.5	121.3	130.6	123.8	91.6	91.7	91.4	109.0
2014												
1st quarter	109.1	108.9	109.8	127.3	129.0	120.5	128.4	124.7	91.6	91.8	91.4	109.1
2nd quarter	110.3	109.9	111.1	129.0	130.4	123.5	131.4	127.6	91.8	91.5	92.0	110.3
3rd quarter	111.4	110.9	112.4	131.5	133.2	124.5	132.0	127.3	92.2	92.4	92.1	111.4
4th quarter	112.0	112.0	113.6	132.3	133.5	127.5	133.8	130.5	91.9	91.0	92.4	112.2

Table 1-6A. Chain-Type Price Indexes for Gross Domestic Product and Domestic Purchases: Recent Data

(Index numbers, 2009 = 100.)

NIPA Tables 1.1.4, 1.6.4, 2.3.4

Year and quarter	Gross domestic product, total	Personal consumption expenditures		Private fixed investment			Exports and imports of goods and services		Government consumption expenditures and gross investment			Gross domestic purchases
		Total	Excluding food and energy	Total	Nonresidential	Residential	Exports	Imports	Total	Federal	State and local	
1950	13.7	14.1	14.3	18.2	22.2	10.7	21.6	16.6	8.9	11.3	7.1	13.5
1951	14.7	15.1	15.2	19.7	24.3	11.5	24.4	20.1	9.4	11.7	7.8	14.4
1952	15.0	15.4	15.5	20.2	24.8	11.8	24.6	19.4	9.6	11.8	8.1	14.7
1953	15.2	15.6	15.8	20.3	25.1	11.9	24.5	18.5	9.8	11.9	8.3	14.9
1954	15.3	15.7	16.0	20.5	25.3	12.0	24.2	18.8	10.0	12.2	8.4	15.1
1955	15.6	15.8	16.1	20.8	25.7	12.2	24.4	18.7	10.4	12.8	8.6	15.3
1956	16.1	16.1	16.5	22.0	27.6	12.5	25.2	19.0	10.9	13.4	9.2	15.8
1957	16.7	16.6	17.0	22.8	28.9	12.5	26.2	19.2	11.4	14.0	9.5	16.3
1958	17.1	17.0	17.4	22.9	29.1	12.5	25.9	18.4	11.7	14.6	9.7	16.7
1959	17.3	17.3	17.8	23.1	29.5	12.6	25.9	18.6	11.9	14.7	9.9	16.9
1960	17.5	17.5	18.1	23.3	29.7	12.6	26.3	18.8	12.0	14.8	10.1	17.1
1961	17.7	17.7	18.3	23.2	29.6	12.7	26.7	18.8	12.2	15.0	10.3	17.3
1962	17.9	17.9	18.6	23.2	29.6	12.7	26.8	18.6	12.5	15.2	10.6	17.5
1963	18.1	18.1	18.8	23.2	29.6	12.6	26.7	18.9	12.8	15.6	10.8	17.7
1964	18.4	18.4	19.1	23.3	29.8	12.7	26.9	19.3	13.1	16.1	11.1	18.0
1965	18.7	18.7	19.3	23.7	30.2	13.0	27.8	19.6	13.5	16.5	11.4	18.3
1966	19.3	19.2	19.8	24.2	30.6	13.5	28.6	20.0	14.0	17.0	11.9	18.8
1967	19.8	19.6	20.4	24.9	31.4	14.0	29.7	20.1	14.5	17.4	12.5	19.3
1968	20.7	20.4	21.2	25.9	32.5	14.7	30.4	20.4	15.3	18.3	13.3	20.2
1969	21.7	21.3	22.2	27.2	33.9	15.7	31.4	21.0	16.2	19.2	14.2	21.1
1970	22.8	22.3	23.3	28.3	35.5	16.2	32.6	22.2	17.4	20.7	15.3	22.3
1971	24.0	23.3	24.4	29.8	37.1	17.2	33.8	23.6	18.8	22.4	16.5	23.5
1972	25.0	24.1	25.2	31.0	38.4	18.2	35.3	25.2	20.2	24.4	17.6	24.5
1973	26.4	25.4	26.1	32.8	40.0	19.9	39.9	29.6	21.6	26.0	18.7	25.9
1974	28.8	28.0	28.2	36.0	43.8	21.9	49.2	42.3	23.6	28.0	20.8	28.5
1975	31.4	30.3	30.6	40.4	49.6	23.9	54.2	45.9	25.8	30.5	22.8	31.1
1976	33.2	32.0	32.4	42.7	52.3	25.5	56.0	47.3	27.2	32.4	23.9	32.8
1977	35.2	34.1	34.5	46.0	55.8	28.1	58.3	51.4	28.9	34.3	25.4	35.0
1978	37.7	36.5	36.8	49.8	59.5	31.5	61.8	55.0	30.7	36.4	27.0	37.5
1979	40.8	39.7	39.5	54.3	64.3	35.1	69.3	64.5	33.2	39.0	29.4	40.7
1980	44.5	44.0	43.1	59.4	70.0	38.9	76.3	80.3	36.6	42.9	32.6	45.0
1981	48.7	47.9	46.9	64.8	76.7	42.0	82.0	84.6	40.2	46.9	35.8	49.1
1982	51.6	50.6	49.9	68.5	81.0	44.3	82.3	81.8	42.8	50.2	38.0	51.9
1983	53.7	52.7	52.5	68.7	80.9	45.3	82.7	78.7	44.5	51.8	39.7	53.7
1984	55.6	54.7	54.6	69.4	81.2	46.7	83.4	78.0	46.3	53.8	41.4	55.5
1985	57.3	56.7	56.9	70.4	82.0	48.0	81.0	75.5	47.7	54.9	43.1	57.2
1986	58.5	57.9	58.9	72.1	83.4	50.1	79.6	75.5	48.5	55.2	44.3	58.3
1987	59.9	59.7	60.7	73.6	84.4	52.2	81.4	80.0	49.9	55.7	46.4	60.0
1988	62.0	62.0	63.3	75.6	86.5	54.1	85.6	83.8	51.5	57.4	48.0	62.1
1989	64.4	64.6	65.9	77.6	88.5	55.8	87.0	85.7	53.5	58.9	50.3	64.5
1990	66.8	67.4	68.5	79.3	90.4	57.1	87.5	88.1	55.7	60.8	52.8	67.0
1991	69.1	69.7	70.9	80.7	92.1	57.8	88.4	87.4	57.7	63.1	54.6	69.1
1992	70.6	71.5	73.0	80.7	91.8	58.6	88.0	87.5	59.5	64.6	56.6	70.7
1993	72.3	73.3	75.0	81.6	92.0	60.9	88.1	86.8	60.9	66.0	58.0	72.3
1994	73.9	74.8	76.7	82.9	92.7	63.2	89.2	87.6	62.5	67.8	59.6	73.8
1995	75.4	76.4	78.3	84.2	93.6	65.4	91.2	90.0	64.3	69.9	61.2	75.4
1996	76.8	78.0	79.8	84.3	93.0	66.8	89.9	88.5	65.7	71.1	62.6	76.7
1997	78.1	79.3	81.2	84.4	92.5	68.4	88.3	85.4	66.9	72.2	64.0	77.9
1998	78.9	79.9	82.2	84.0	91.0	70.2	86.3	80.8	68.1	73.1	65.3	78.4
1999	80.1	81.1	83.3	84.2	90.2	72.9	85.6	81.3	70.4	74.9	67.9	79.6
2000	81.9	83.1	84.7	85.5	90.7	76.1	87.2	84.8	73.4	77.3	71.2	81.6
2001	83.8	84.7	86.3	86.3	90.4	79.7	86.6	82.7	75.6	78.7	73.6	83.2
2002	85.0	85.9	87.8	86.6	90.0	81.7	86.1	81.7	77.4	81.3	75.1	84.4
2003	86.7	87.6	89.0	87.7	89.9	85.5	87.8	84.5	80.3	84.8	77.8	86.2
2004	89.1	89.7	90.8	90.5	91.1	91.5	90.8	88.5	83.9	87.7	81.7	88.7
2005	92.0	92.3	92.7	94.5	93.8	98.1	94.7	93.8	88.2	91.4	86.3	91.9
2006	94.8	94.7	94.8	98.2	96.6	103.8	98.0	97.7	92.1	94.4	90.7	94.8
2007	97.3	97.1	96.8	100.0	98.6	105.2	101.1	101.0	96.1	97.3	95.4	97.4
2008	99.2	100.1	98.8	101.0	100.3	103.6	105.8	111.6	100.3	100.3	100.3	100.2
2009	100.0	100.0	100.0	100.0	100.0	100.0	100.0	100.0	100.0	100.0	100.0	100.2
2010	101.2	101.7	101.3	99.2	99.1	99.6	104.3	105.8	102.7	102.6	102.7	101.5
2011	103.3	104.1	102.8	100.5	100.5	100.4	111.0	113.9	105.7	105.4	105.9	104.0
2012	105.2	106.1	104.7	102.1	102.2	101.3	112.0	114.7	107.4	106.5	108.0	105.8
2013	106.9	107.6	106.4	103.7	103.0	106.5	112.1	113.8	109.1	107.6	110.1	107.3
2014	108.7	109.1	108.0	105.7	104.0	112.9	112.3	113.6	111.1	109.3	112.3	109.0
2012												
1st quarter	104.5	105.6	104.1	101.5	101.7	100.3	111.7	115.8	107.0	106.3	107.5	105.3
2nd quarter	104.9	105.9	104.6	101.9	102.2	100.7	112.0	115.0	107.1	106.5	107.6	105.6
3rd quarter	105.5	106.2	104.9	102.3	102.5	101.6	111.9	113.4	107.4	106.6	108.0	105.9
4th quarter	105.9	106.8	105.4	102.5	102.5	102.6	112.3	114.5	107.9	106.7	108.8	106.4
2013												
1st quarter	106.3	107.2	105.8	102.9	102.6	104.2	112.6	114.7	108.4	106.9	109.4	106.8
2nd quarter	106.6	107.3	106.1	103.4	102.9	105.6	111.9	113.6	108.6	107.0	109.8	107.0
3rd quarter	107.2	107.7	106.5	103.8	103.1	107.0	112.0	113.4	109.2	107.4	110.5	107.5
4th quarter	107.6	108.1	107.0	104.4	103.3	109.1	112.1	113.6	110.1	109.0	110.9	108.0
2014												
1st quarter	108.0	108.5	107.3	105.1	103.6	111.4	112.9	114.5	110.4	108.7	111.6	108.4
2nd quarter	108.6	109.1	107.9	105.3	103.8	111.7	112.9	114.1	110.9	109.2	112.1	108.9
3rd quarter	109.0	109.4	108.2	106.0	104.2	113.6	112.6	113.8	110.9	109.2	112.1	108.9
4th quarter	109.1	109.3	108.5	106.3	104.3	114.9	110.6	111.9	111.4	109.6	112.8	109.3

Table 1-6B. Chain-Type Price Indexes for Gross Domestic Product and Domestic Purchases: Historical Data

(Index numbers, 2009 = 100.)   NIPA Tables 1.1.4, 1.6.4, 2.3.4

Year and quarter	Gross domestic product, total	Personal consumption expenditures		Private fixed investment			Exports and imports of goods and services		Government consumption expenditures and gross investment			Gross domestic purchases
		Total	Excluding food and energy	Total	Nonresidential	Residential	Exports	Imports	Total	Federal	State and local	
1929	9.9	9.9	10.1	10.3	13.2	5.1	15.0	10.7	5.8	7.3	4.0	9.7
1930	9.5	9.5	9.7	9.9	12.5	5.0	13.6	9.1	5.6	6.9	3.9	9.3
1931	8.6	8.5	8.9	9.1	11.7	4.6	10.7	7.3	5.4	6.9	3.6	8.4
1932	7.6	7.5	7.9	8.1	10.6	3.7	9.3	5.9	4.9	6.6	3.3	7.4
1933	7.4	7.2	7.5	7.9	10.3	3.7	9.3	5.6	5.0	6.6	3.4	7.2
1934	7.8	7.5	7.7	8.3	10.7	4.1	10.7	6.4	5.4	7.0	3.6	7.5
1935	7.9	7.7	7.8	8.3	10.8	4.0	11.0	6.5	5.4	7.1	3.7	7.7
1936	8.0	7.8	7.9	8.4	10.8	4.2	11.4	7.0	5.6	7.7	3.7	7.8
1937	8.3	8.1	8.2	9.1	11.6	4.6	12.1	7.8	5.7	7.8	3.8	8.1
1938	8.2	7.9	8.2	9.2	11.7	4.8	11.6	7.2	5.8	7.9	3.8	7.9
1939	8.0	7.8	8.1	9.2	11.6	4.8	11.4	7.5	5.7	7.8	3.7	7.8
1940	8.1	7.9	8.2	9.4	11.9	4.9	12.4	8.0	5.6	7.5	3.8	7.9
1941	8.7	8.4	8.6	10.1	12.6	5.4	13.5	8.5	6.0	7.9	4.0	8.4
1942	9.4	9.4	9.6	11.1	14.0	5.8	16.4	9.7	6.0	7.9	4.4	9.1
1943	9.8	10.3	10.3	11.7	14.6	6.3	17.9	10.5	6.0	7.8	4.7	9.5
1944	10.1	10.9	11.1	12.1	15.0	6.9	20.1	11.0	6.0	7.7	4.9	9.7
1945	10.3	11.3	11.6	12.5	15.4	7.3	20.0	11.3	6.0	7.7	5.1	10.0
1946	11.6	12.1	12.3	13.7	17.0	8.0	19.3	12.6	7.6	10.1	5.6	11.3
1947	12.9	13.3	13.3	16.1	19.7	9.5	22.4	15.1	8.3	10.9	6.2	12.6
1948	13.6	14.1	14.1	17.4	21.3	10.3	23.6	16.4	8.6	10.8	7.0	13.3
1949	13.6	14.0	14.1	17.8	21.8	10.5	22.2	15.7	8.8	11.2	7.1	13.3
1947												
1st quarter	12.6	13.0	. . .	15.4	18.9	9.0	20.6	13.9	8.4	11.2	6.1	12.3
2nd quarter	12.8	13.1	. . .	15.9	19.4	9.5	22.1	14.8	8.4	11.0	6.2	12.5
3rd quarter	13.0	13.4	. . .	16.3	20.0	9.7	23.2	15.6	8.2	10.6	6.3	12.6
4th quarter	13.2	13.7	. . .	16.7	20.3	9.9	23.8	16.2	8.3	10.6	6.5	12.9
1948												
1st quarter	13.4	13.9	. . .	16.8	20.4	10.1	23.9	16.5	8.4	10.7	6.7	13.1
2nd quarter	13.6	14.0	. . .	17.2	21.0	10.2	23.8	16.6	8.5	10.7	6.9	13.2
3rd quarter	13.8	14.2	. . .	17.7	21.7	10.5	23.5	16.4	8.7	10.8	7.1	13.5
4th quarter	13.8	14.2	. . .	17.9	22.0	10.5	23.2	16.2	8.8	10.9	7.2	13.5
1949												
1st quarter	13.7	14.1	. . .	17.9	21.9	10.6	22.8	15.8	8.9	11.2	7.2	13.4
2nd quarter	13.7	14.0	. . .	17.9	21.8	10.6	22.3	15.6	8.8	11.2	7.0	13.3
3rd quarter	13.5	13.9	. . .	17.7	21.7	10.3	22.0	15.6	8.8	11.0	7.0	13.2
4th quarter	13.6	13.9	. . .	17.6	21.6	10.4	21.7	15.6	8.9	11.3	7.0	13.3
1950												
1st quarter	13.5	13.9	. . .	17.6	21.6	10.3	21.4	15.9	8.8	11.3	6.9	13.2
2nd quarter	13.6	13.9	. . .	17.9	21.9	10.6	21.4	16.3	8.8	11.2	7.0	13.3
3rd quarter	13.8	14.2	. . .	18.4	22.3	11.0	21.6	16.8	9.0	11.3	7.2	13.6
4th quarter	14.1	14.5	. . .	18.7	23.1	11.0	22.0	17.6	9.0	11.3	7.4	13.8
1951												
1st quarter	14.5	14.9	. . .	19.4	23.8	11.3	23.3	19.0	9.4	11.8	7.6	14.3
2nd quarter	14.6	15.1	. . .	19.6	24.2	11.5	24.2	20.0	9.4	11.6	7.7	14.4
3rd quarter	14.7	15.1	. . .	19.8	24.4	11.5	24.9	20.6	9.4	11.6	7.9	14.4
4th quarter	14.9	15.3	. . .	20.0	24.7	11.6	25.3	20.7	9.6	11.8	8.0	14.6
1952												
1st quarter	14.9	15.4	. . .	20.1	24.8	11.7	24.7	19.9	9.5	11.6	8.0	14.6
2nd quarter	14.9	15.4	. . .	20.2	24.9	11.8	24.6	19.5	9.6	11.8	8.1	14.7
3rd quarter	15.1	15.5	. . .	20.2	24.8	11.9	24.5	19.2	9.7	11.9	8.3	14.8
4th quarter	15.1	15.5	. . .	20.2	24.8	11.8	24.5	18.9	9.8	12.1	8.3	14.8
1953												
1st quarter	15.1	15.5	. . .	20.2	24.8	11.9	24.6	18.7	9.7	11.9	8.3	14.8
2nd quarter	15.2	15.6	. . .	20.3	25.0	11.9	24.6	18.5	9.8	11.9	8.3	14.9
3rd quarter	15.2	15.6	. . .	20.5	25.2	12.0	24.5	18.5	9.7	11.9	8.3	14.9
4th quarter	15.3	15.7	. . .	20.4	25.2	11.9	24.4	18.5	9.8	12.0	8.3	15.0
1954												
1st quarter	15.3	15.8	. . .	20.4	25.3	11.9	24.3	18.7	9.8	12.1	8.3	15.0
2nd quarter	15.4	15.8	. . .	20.5	25.4	11.9	24.2	18.8	9.9	12.2	8.4	15.1
3rd quarter	15.3	15.7	. . .	20.5	25.2	12.0	24.1	18.9	10.0	12.2	8.5	15.1
4th quarter	15.4	15.7	. . .	20.5	25.3	12.0	24.1	18.9	10.1	12.4	8.5	15.1
1955												
1st quarter	15.4	15.8	. . .	20.6	25.2	12.1	24.2	18.7	10.1	12.5	8.5	15.1
2nd quarter	15.5	15.8	. . .	20.7	25.4	12.2	24.3	18.7	10.3	12.8	8.5	15.2
3rd quarter	15.6	15.8	. . .	20.9	25.8	12.3	24.4	18.7	10.4	12.9	8.7	15.3
4th quarter	15.7	15.9	. . .	21.2	26.3	12.3	24.6	18.8	10.5	13.0	8.8	15.4
1956												
1st quarter	15.9	15.9	. . .	21.6	27.0	12.4	24.8	18.8	10.7	13.2	9.0	15.6
2nd quarter	16.0	16.1	. . .	21.9	27.2	12.6	25.0	19.0	10.9	13.4	9.1	15.7
3rd quarter	16.2	16.2	. . .	22.2	27.9	12.6	25.3	19.1	11.0	13.5	9.2	15.9
4th quarter	16.3	16.3	. . .	22.4	28.2	12.5	25.6	19.3	11.1	13.6	9.3	16.0
1957												
1st quarter	16.5	16.5	. . .	22.6	28.7	12.5	26.0	19.3	11.2	13.9	9.4	16.1
2nd quarter	16.6	16.6	. . .	22.7	28.8	12.5	26.2	19.3	11.4	14.0	9.6	16.3
3rd quarter	16.7	16.7	. . .	22.9	29.0	12.6	26.2	19.2	11.4	14.1	9.6	16.4
4th quarter	16.8	16.8	. . .	23.0	29.2	12.6	26.2	19.0	11.5	14.2	9.6	16.5

. . . = Not available.

Table 1-6B. Chain-Type Price Indexes for Gross Domestic Product and Domestic Purchases: Historical Data—*Continued*

(Index numbers, 2009 = 100.)

| Year and quarter | Gross domestic product, total | Personal consumption expenditures | | Private fixed investment | | | Exports and imports of goods and services | | Government consumption expenditures and gross investment | | | Gross domestic purchases |
		Total	Excluding food and energy	Total	Nonresidential	Residential	Exports	Imports	Total	Federal	State and local	
1958												
1st quarter	17.0	17.0	. . .	22.8	29.0	12.5	26.0	18.6	11.6	14.4	9.6	16.6
2nd quarter	17.0	17.0	. . .	22.9	29.1	12.5	25.9	18.4	11.7	14.5	9.7	16.7
3rd quarter	17.1	17.0	. . .	22.9	29.2	12.5	25.8	18.4	11.8	14.6	9.7	16.7
4th quarter	17.1	17.0	. . .	23.0	29.3	12.5	25.9	18.4	11.8	14.7	9.8	16.7
1959												
1st quarter	17.2	17.1	17.6	23.0	29.3	12.5	25.7	18.4	11.9	14.7	9.9	16.8
2nd quarter	17.2	17.2	17.7	23.1	29.5	12.6	25.8	18.5	11.9	14.7	9.9	16.9
3rd quarter	17.3	17.3	17.8	23.2	29.6	12.6	26.0	18.6	11.9	14.7	9.9	16.9
4th quarter	17.4	17.4	17.9	23.2	29.7	12.6	26.3	18.8	11.9	14.7	9.9	17.0
1960												
1st quarter	17.4	17.4	18.0	23.2	29.7	12.6	26.3	18.8	11.9	14.7	10.0	17.0
2nd quarter	17.5	17.5	18.0	23.3	29.7	12.6	26.3	18.7	11.9	14.7	10.0	17.1
3rd quarter	17.6	17.6	18.1	23.3	29.7	12.6	26.4	18.8	12.1	14.9	10.1	17.2
4th quarter	17.6	17.7	18.2	23.2	29.7	12.7	26.3	18.8	12.2	15.0	10.1	17.2
1961												
1st quarter	17.7	17.7	18.2	23.2	29.6	12.6	26.4	18.8	12.2	15.0	10.2	17.3
2nd quarter	17.7	17.7	18.3	23.2	29.6	12.7	26.8	18.8	12.2	15.0	10.3	17.3
3rd quarter	17.7	17.8	18.4	23.2	29.6	12.7	26.7	18.8	12.2	15.0	10.4	17.3
4th quarter	17.8	17.8	18.4	23.2	29.6	12.7	26.9	18.8	12.3	15.0	10.4	17.4
1962												
1st quarter	17.9	17.9	18.5	23.2	29.6	12.7	27.0	18.5	12.4	15.1	10.6	17.4
2nd quarter	17.9	17.9	18.5	23.2	29.6	12.7	26.7	18.6	12.5	15.2	10.6	17.5
3rd quarter	18.0	18.0	18.6	23.2	29.6	12.7	26.7	18.5	12.5	15.3	10.6	17.5
4th quarter	18.0	18.0	18.6	23.2	29.6	12.7	26.7	18.6	12.5	15.3	10.7	17.6
1963												
1st quarter	18.1	18.1	18.7	23.2	29.6	12.7	26.8	18.8	12.7	15.6	10.8	17.7
2nd quarter	18.1	18.1	18.8	23.2	29.6	12.6	26.7	18.9	12.8	15.6	10.8	17.7
3rd quarter	18.1	18.2	18.8	23.1	29.6	12.5	26.7	19.0	12.7	15.4	10.9	17.7
4th quarter	18.2	18.2	18.9	23.2	29.7	12.6	26.7	19.1	12.9	15.8	10.9	17.8
1964												
1st quarter	18.3	18.3	19.0	23.1	29.7	12.4	26.8	19.2	13.0	16.0	11.0	17.9
2nd quarter	18.4	18.4	19.1	23.3	29.8	12.6	26.8	19.3	13.1	16.0	11.0	18.0
3rd quarter	18.4	18.4	19.1	23.3	29.8	12.7	27.0	19.3	13.2	16.2	11.1	18.0
4th quarter	18.5	18.5	19.2	23.6	30.0	13.0	27.3	19.4	13.2	16.2	11.1	18.1
1965												
1st quarter	18.6	18.6	19.2	23.6	30.0	12.9	27.9	19.5	13.3	16.2	11.3	18.2
2nd quarter	18.7	18.7	19.3	23.6	30.1	13.0	27.8	19.5	13.4	16.3	11.3	18.3
3rd quarter	18.8	18.7	19.4	23.7	30.2	12.9	27.8	19.6	13.5	16.5	11.4	18.4
4th quarter	18.9	18.8	19.4	24.0	30.3	13.3	27.7	19.8	13.7	16.9	11.5	18.5
1966												
1st quarter	19.0	18.9	19.5	23.9	30.3	13.1	28.2	19.9	13.8	16.9	11.7	18.6
2nd quarter	19.2	19.1	19.7	24.2	30.6	13.6	28.4	20.1	13.9	16.9	11.9	18.8
3rd quarter	19.4	19.2	19.8	24.2	30.7	13.5	28.7	20.0	14.1	17.2	12.0	18.9
4th quarter	19.5	19.4	20.0	24.5	30.9	13.8	29.2	20.2	14.2	17.2	12.2	19.1
1967												
1st quarter	19.6	19.4	20.1	24.6	31.1	13.8	29.7	20.2	14.2	17.1	12.3	19.1
2nd quarter	19.7	19.5	20.3	24.7	31.2	13.9	29.7	20.1	14.4	17.3	12.4	19.2
3rd quarter	19.9	19.7	20.4	24.9	31.4	14.0	29.7	20.1	14.5	17.5	12.6	19.4
4th quarter	20.1	19.9	20.6	25.2	31.7	14.2	29.8	20.1	14.8	17.8	12.8	19.6
1968												
1st quarter	20.3	20.1	20.9	25.5	32.0	14.5	30.0	20.3	15.0	17.9	13.0	19.8
2nd quarter	20.6	20.3	21.1	25.7	32.3	14.6	30.7	20.4	15.1	18.1	13.2	20.0
3rd quarter	20.8	20.5	21.4	25.9	32.6	14.6	30.3	20.5	15.4	18.4	13.3	20.2
4th quarter	21.0	20.7	21.6	26.4	33.1	15.2	30.5	20.6	15.6	18.7	13.6	20.5
1969												
1st quarter	21.3	20.9	21.8	26.7	33.3	15.5	31.0	20.7	15.7	18.7	13.8	20.7
2nd quarter	21.5	21.2	22.1	27.0	33.6	15.7	31.0	20.8	16.0	19.0	14.1	21.0
3rd quarter	21.8	21.5	22.4	27.3	34.0	15.8	31.4	20.9	16.3	19.5	14.3	21.3
4th quarter	22.1	21.7	22.6	27.6	34.4	16.0	32.2	21.5	16.6	19.7	14.6	21.6
1970												
1st quarter	22.4	22.0	22.9	27.8	34.8	16.0	32.2	21.7	17.0	20.3	14.9	21.9
2nd quarter	22.7	22.2	23.1	28.4	35.4	16.6	32.8	21.9	17.3	20.6	15.2	22.2
3rd quarter	22.9	22.4	23.4	28.4	35.6	16.1	32.7	22.5	17.6	20.9	15.5	22.4
4th quarter	23.2	22.7	23.7	28.7	36.1	16.3	32.8	22.7	17.9	21.2	15.8	22.7
1971												
1st quarter	23.6	22.9	24.0	29.2	36.6	16.7	33.8	23.3	18.4	21.8	16.1	23.0
2nd quarter	23.9	23.2	24.3	29.6	37.0	17.1	33.9	23.4	18.7	22.2	16.4	23.3
3rd quarter	24.1	23.4	24.5	30.0	37.3	17.4	33.7	23.6	19.0	22.6	16.7	23.6
4th quarter	24.3	23.6	24.7	30.2	37.6	17.6	33.9	24.0	19.3	23.0	16.8	23.8
1972												
1st quarter	24.7	23.8	24.9	30.6	38.0	17.9	34.8	24.4	19.9	24.0	17.2	24.2
2nd quarter	24.9	24.0	25.1	30.8	38.3	18.0	35.1	25.0	20.1	24.2	17.4	24.4
3rd quarter	25.1	24.2	25.3	31.1	38.5	18.3	35.2	25.4	20.3	24.4	17.7	24.6
4th quarter	25.4	24.4	25.4	31.6	38.8	18.8	36.0	26.0	20.7	24.9	17.9	24.9

. . . = Not available.

Table 1-6B. Chain-Type Price Indexes for Gross Domestic Product and Domestic Purchases: Historical Data—*Continued*

(Index numbers, 2009 = 100.)

NIPA Tables 1.1.4, 1.6.4, 2.3.4

Year and quarter	Gross domestic product, total	Personal consumption expenditures		Private fixed investment			Exports and imports of goods and services		Government consumption expenditures and gross investment			Gross domestic purchases
		Total	Excluding food and energy	Total	Nonresidential	Residential	Exports	Imports	Total	Federal	State and local	
1973												
1st quarter	25.7	24.7	25.6	31.9	39.1	19.1	37.1	26.8	21.0	25.3	18.3	25.2
2nd quarter	26.1	25.1	25.9	32.4	39.7	19.6	38.7	28.9	21.4	25.7	18.6	25.7
3rd quarter	26.6	25.6	26.3	33.1	40.3	20.2	41.0	30.2	21.7	26.2	18.8	26.1
4th quarter	27.1	26.1	26.7	33.6	40.8	20.6	43.0	32.5	22.2	26.7	19.2	26.6
1974												
1st quarter	27.6	26.9	27.1	34.2	41.5	21.0	46.0	37.7	22.6	27.0	19.7	27.3
2nd quarter	28.3	27.6	27.8	35.2	42.8	21.5	47.6	42.0	23.2	27.6	20.4	28.1
3rd quarter	29.1	28.4	28.6	36.6	44.5	22.2	50.3	44.2	24.0	28.3	21.1	28.9
4th quarter	30.0	29.1	29.3	38.0	46.5	22.8	52.9	45.6	24.7	29.3	21.8	29.8
1975												
1st quarter	30.7	29.7	29.9	39.3	48.2	23.4	54.3	46.3	25.2	29.8	22.2	30.4
2nd quarter	31.1	30.0	30.3	40.2	49.4	23.8	54.2	46.4	25.6	30.2	22.7	30.8
3rd quarter	31.7	30.6	30.8	40.7	50.1	24.0	54.0	45.4	26.0	30.6	23.0	31.4
4th quarter	32.2	31.1	31.3	41.3	50.8	24.5	54.4	45.4	26.4	31.3	23.2	31.9
1976												
1st quarter	32.6	31.4	31.8	41.7	51.3	24.6	55.1	46.2	26.7	31.7	23.5	32.2
2nd quarter	32.9	31.7	32.1	42.4	52.0	25.3	55.8	46.9	27.0	32.0	23.8	32.5
3rd quarter	33.3	32.2	32.6	43.0	52.7	25.7	56.1	47.7	27.3	32.4	24.0	33.0
4th quarter	33.9	32.7	33.1	43.7	53.4	26.2	57.1	48.2	27.8	33.2	24.2	33.5
1977												
1st quarter	34.4	33.3	33.7	44.6	54.5	26.9	57.7	49.9	28.2	33.7	24.7	34.1
2nd quarter	35.0	33.9	34.2	45.4	55.3	27.6	58.6	51.3	28.6	34.0	25.2	34.7
3rd quarter	35.4	34.4	34.8	46.4	56.3	28.5	58.3	52.0	29.0	34.2	25.6	35.2
4th quarter	36.0	34.9	35.3	47.4	57.2	29.4	58.6	52.5	29.6	35.2	26.0	35.8
1978												
1st quarter	36.6	35.4	35.9	48.3	58.1	30.2	59.7	53.4	30.0	35.7	26.4	36.4
2nd quarter	37.3	36.2	36.5	49.3	59.0	31.1	61.2	54.7	30.5	36.0	26.8	37.1
3rd quarter	38.0	36.8	37.1	50.3	60.0	32.0	62.2	55.6	30.9	36.6	27.2	37.8
4th quarter	38.8	37.5	37.8	51.3	61.0	32.8	64.3	56.6	31.5	37.4	27.6	38.5
1979												
1st quarter	39.5	38.2	38.3	52.4	62.3	33.5	66.1	58.8	32.1	37.9	28.3	39.2
2nd quarter	40.4	39.2	39.1	53.7	63.7	34.6	68.8	61.8	32.7	38.5	28.9	40.2
3rd quarter	41.2	40.2	39.8	55.0	65.0	35.7	70.4	66.4	33.6	39.1	29.9	41.2
4th quarter	42.0	41.2	40.7	56.1	66.3	36.6	71.7	70.8	34.5	40.6	30.5	42.2
1980												
1st quarter	43.0	42.4	41.7	57.4	67.7	37.6	73.9	76.7	35.3	41.3	31.3	43.4
2nd quarter	43.9	43.5	42.6	58.7	69.3	38.4	74.9	79.5	36.1	42.2	32.1	44.4
3rd quarter	44.9	44.5	43.5	60.0	70.8	39.3	77.0	81.7	36.9	42.9	33.0	45.4
4th quarter	46.2	45.6	44.6	61.3	72.2	40.2	79.6	83.2	38.3	45.0	33.9	46.6
1981												
1st quarter	47.4	46.7	45.6	62.9	74.2	41.1	81.6	85.3	39.2	45.7	35.0	47.8
2nd quarter	48.2	47.5	46.4	64.3	76.0	41.8	81.9	85.8	39.9	46.3	35.7	48.7
3rd quarter	49.1	48.3	47.3	65.4	77.4	42.3	82.1	83.6	40.4	47.1	36.1	49.5
4th quarter	50.0	49.0	48.1	66.7	79.1	42.9	82.3	83.8	41.4	48.7	36.6	50.3
1982												
1st quarter	50.7	49.7	48.8	67.5	80.0	43.6	82.8	83.5	42.0	49.3	37.2	51.0
2nd quarter	51.3	50.1	49.5	68.4	81.0	44.2	82.8	82.0	42.5	49.8	37.7	51.5
3rd quarter	52.0	50.9	50.3	68.8	81.5	44.6	82.2	81.1	43.1	50.4	38.3	52.2
4th quarter	52.6	51.5	51.0	69.0	81.7	44.8	81.7	80.4	43.7	51.3	38.8	52.8
1983												
1st quarter	53.0	51.9	51.7	68.8	81.2	45.0	82.0	78.7	44.0	51.5	39.1	53.1
2nd quarter	53.4	52.4	52.1	68.6	80.9	45.1	82.3	78.7	44.3	51.5	39.5	53.4
3rd quarter	53.9	53.1	52.9	68.6	80.8	45.4	82.8	78.9	44.7	52.0	39.9	54.0
4th quarter	54.3	53.5	53.3	68.8	80.7	45.8	83.6	78.4	45.0	52.3	40.2	54.3
1984												
1st quarter	54.9	54.0	53.8	68.9	80.8	46.1	83.7	78.6	45.7	53.2	40.8	54.9
2nd quarter	55.4	54.6	54.4	69.3	81.1	46.4	84.2	79.1	46.1	53.6	41.2	55.3
3rd quarter	55.8	55.0	55.0	69.6	81.3	46.9	83.4	77.7	46.5	54.0	41.6	55.7
4th quarter	56.2	55.3	55.4	69.8	81.4	47.3	82.5	76.7	46.8	54.3	42.0	56.0
1985												
1st quarter	56.8	56.0	56.1	70.0	81.6	47.5	81.6	74.9	47.3	54.8	42.5	56.6
2nd quarter	57.2	56.5	56.6	70.2	81.8	47.7	81.3	75.2	47.5	54.7	42.9	56.9
3rd quarter	57.5	56.9	57.2	70.5	82.1	48.0	80.6	75.1	47.8	54.8	43.3	57.3
4th quarter	57.8	57.3	57.6	70.9	82.5	48.6	80.4	76.6	48.2	55.3	43.7	57.7
1986												
1st quarter	58.1	57.7	58.2	71.3	82.7	49.2	80.0	76.7	48.2	55.1	43.9	58.0
2nd quarter	58.3	57.6	58.6	71.8	83.2	49.7	79.6	74.4	48.3	55.2	44.1	58.1
3rd quarter	58.6	57.9	59.0	72.4	83.7	50.4	79.1	74.9	48.6	55.3	44.4	58.4
4th quarter	59.0	58.3	59.5	72.9	84.1	50.9	79.7	75.8	49.0	55.4	45.0	58.8
1987												
1st quarter	59.3	58.8	59.9	73.2	84.2	51.5	80.0	77.8	49.3	55.3	45.7	59.3
2nd quarter	59.7	59.4	60.4	73.3	84.2	52.0	81.2	79.8	49.7	55.5	46.2	59.7
3rd quarter	60.1	59.9	61.0	73.6	84.2	52.5	81.5	80.6	50.1	55.8	46.7	60.2
4th quarter	60.6	60.5	61.6	74.3	85.0	53.0	82.8	81.9	50.4	56.0	47.0	60.7

Table 1-6B. Chain-Type Price Indexes for Gross Domestic Product and Domestic Purchases: Historical Data—*Continued*

(Index numbers, 2009 = 100.)

NIPA Tables 1.1.4, 1.6.4, 2.3.4

Year and quarter	Gross domestic product, total	Personal consumption expenditures		Private fixed investment			Exports and imports of goods and services		Government consumption expenditures and gross investment			Gross domestic purchases
		Total	Excluding food and energy	Total	Nonresidential	Residential	Exports	Imports	Total	Federal	State and local	
1988												
1st quarter	61.1	60.9	62.2	74.9	85.8	53.4	83.8	83.0	50.9	56.8	47.3	61.2
2nd quarter	61.7	61.6	62.9	75.4	86.2	53.9	85.5	84.5	51.3	57.3	47.7	61.8
3rd quarter	62.4	62.4	63.7	75.8	86.6	54.2	86.5	83.6	51.7	57.6	48.1	62.4
4th quarter	63.0	63.0	64.4	76.5	87.4	54.8	86.4	84.3	52.0	57.7	48.7	63.0
1989												
1st quarter	63.6	63.7	65.0	76.9	87.9	55.1	87.2	85.6	52.8	58.5	49.4	63.7
2nd quarter	64.3	64.5	65.6	77.4	88.3	55.8	87.3	86.5	53.3	58.8	50.0	64.4
3rd quarter	64.7	64.9	66.1	77.8	88.8	56.0	86.8	85.1	53.7	59.1	50.5	64.8
4th quarter	65.2	65.4	66.7	78.2	89.2	56.4	86.5	85.5	54.1	59.3	51.2	65.2
1990												
1st quarter	65.9	66.4	67.5	78.7	89.7	56.8	86.6	86.8	54.8	60.0	51.9	66.1
2nd quarter	66.6	66.9	68.2	79.0	90.0	57.0	86.8	85.3	55.3	60.5	52.4	66.6
3rd quarter	67.2	67.8	68.9	79.5	90.7	57.3	87.6	87.8	55.9	60.9	53.0	67.3
4th quarter	67.7	68.7	69.4	79.9	91.3	57.3	88.9	92.6	56.7	61.8	53.8	68.1
1991												
1st quarter	68.4	69.0	70.0	80.6	92.2	57.5	89.1	89.8	57.2	62.7	54.0	68.6
2nd quarter	68.8	69.4	70.6	80.7	92.2	57.8	88.6	87.3	57.4	62.8	54.3	68.9
3rd quarter	69.3	69.9	71.2	80.8	92.2	58.1	88.0	86.0	57.9	63.3	54.8	69.3
4th quarter	69.7	70.4	71.7	80.5	91.9	57.9	88.1	86.4	58.3	63.6	55.3	69.7
1992												
1st quarter	70.0	70.8	72.3	80.4	91.8	57.7	88.0	86.8	58.7	64.0	55.8	70.1
2nd quarter	70.5	71.3	72.8	80.6	91.7	58.3	88.1	87.2	59.3	64.5	56.4	70.5
3rd quarter	70.8	71.7	73.2	80.7	91.8	58.7	88.1	88.3	59.8	64.9	56.9	70.9
4th quarter	71.3	72.2	73.8	81.0	91.8	59.5	87.9	87.6	60.1	65.2	57.3	71.4
1993												
1st quarter	71.7	72.6	74.3	81.3	91.9	60.1	88.0	87.1	60.4	65.4	57.6	71.8
2nd quarter	72.1	73.1	74.8	81.6	91.9	60.8	88.2	87.4	60.7	65.8	58.0	72.2
3rd quarter	72.5	73.5	75.3	81.7	91.9	61.3	88.2	86.6	61.0	66.3	58.1	72.5
4th quarter	72.9	73.9	75.6	82.0	92.2	61.5	88.1	86.2	61.4	66.7	58.4	72.9
1994												
1st quarter	73.3	74.1	76.0	82.4	92.4	62.3	88.5	86.2	61.8	67.0	58.9	73.2
2nd quarter	73.7	74.6	76.5	82.7	92.6	62.7	88.9	87.0	62.3	67.7	59.3	73.6
3rd quarter	74.0	75.1	76.9	83.0	92.8	63.4	89.3	88.5	62.7	67.9	59.8	74.1
4th quarter	74.4	75.4	77.3	83.4	92.9	64.2	89.9	88.8	63.2	68.5	60.3	74.5
1995												
1st quarter	74.9	75.8	77.7	83.9	93.3	64.9	90.8	89.5	63.8	69.5	60.7	74.9
2nd quarter	75.2	76.2	78.2	84.2	93.6	65.3	91.6	90.8	64.2	69.6	61.1	75.3
3rd quarter	75.5	76.5	78.5	84.5	93.8	65.5	91.3	90.3	64.4	69.9	61.4	75.6
4th quarter	75.9	76.9	78.9	84.4	93.6	65.9	90.9	89.4	64.9	70.8	61.6	75.9
1996												
1st quarter	76.3	77.3	79.2	84.3	93.3	66.2	90.7	89.3	65.5	71.5	62.2	76.3
2nd quarter	76.6	77.8	79.6	84.2	92.9	66.5	90.4	88.8	65.4	70.8	62.3	76.5
3rd quarter	76.9	78.1	80.0	84.4	92.9	67.2	89.8	87.9	65.7	71.0	62.7	76.9
4th quarter	77.3	78.7	80.4	84.3	92.7	67.5	88.8	87.9	66.1	71.2	63.2	77.3
1997												
1st quarter	77.6	79.0	80.7	84.4	92.6	67.8	88.6	87.2	66.6	71.9	63.6	77.6
2nd quarter	78.0	79.2	81.1	84.4	92.6	68.1	88.5	85.4	66.8	72.1	63.8	77.7
3rd quarter	78.2	79.4	81.3	84.5	92.5	68.7	88.3	84.8	67.0	72.2	64.1	77.9
4th quarter	78.5	79.7	81.6	84.5	92.1	69.2	87.9	84.1	67.4	72.6	64.6	78.2
1998												
1st quarter	78.6	79.7	81.8	84.1	91.6	69.4	87.0	82.1	67.6	72.8	64.7	78.1
2nd quarter	78.8	79.8	82.1	84.0	91.1	69.8	86.6	81.1	67.8	72.9	65.0	78.2
3rd quarter	79.1	80.0	82.3	83.9	90.8	70.5	85.9	80.0	68.2	73.1	65.5	78.4
4th quarter	79.3	80.2	82.6	84.0	90.5	71.2	85.6	80.0	68.7	73.4	66.0	78.7
1999												
1st quarter	79.6	80.5	82.9	84.1	90.5	71.8	85.4	79.8	69.3	74.2	66.6	78.9
2nd quarter	79.9	80.9	83.1	84.2	90.3	72.6	85.5	80.8	70.1	74.7	67.5	79.4
3rd quarter	80.2	81.3	83.4	84.1	89.9	73.2	85.6	81.7	70.7	75.0	68.3	79.8
4th quarter	80.6	81.8	83.8	84.4	90.1	73.8	85.9	82.8	71.5	75.6	69.1	80.2
2000												
1st quarter	81.2	82.5	84.2	84.9	90.4	75.0	86.5	84.4	72.5	76.8	70.0	81.0
2nd quarter	81.6	82.9	84.5	85.3	90.6	75.8	87.1	84.5	73.0	76.8	70.8	81.4
3rd quarter	82.2	83.4	84.9	85.7	90.9	76.4	87.5	85.1	73.8	77.7	71.5	81.9
4th quarter	82.6	83.8	85.3	85.9	90.9	77.1	87.5	85.4	74.5	78.1	72.4	82.4
2001												
1st quarter	83.1	84.4	85.8	85.9	90.5	78.2	87.4	85.2	75.1	78.4	73.1	82.8
2nd quarter	83.7	84.8	86.1	86.2	90.5	79.2	87.0	83.4	75.4	78.5	73.6	83.2
3rd quarter	84.0	84.9	86.4	86.4	90.3	80.5	86.6	82.2	75.8	78.9	73.9	83.4
4th quarter	84.2	84.9	86.8	86.5	90.2	80.9	85.6	80.2	75.9	79.2	74.0	83.4
2002												
1st quarter	84.5	85.1	87.1	86.4	90.1	80.8	85.3	80.0	76.7	80.8	74.3	83.7
2nd quarter	84.8	85.7	87.6	86.5	90.0	81.3	86.0	81.8	77.2	81.0	74.9	84.2
3rd quarter	85.2	86.2	88.0	86.6	90.0	81.6	86.5	82.3	77.6	81.2	75.4	84.6
4th quarter	85.6	86.6	88.3	87.0	90.1	83.0	86.5	82.7	78.3	82.2	76.0	85.0

Table 1-6B. Chain-Type Price Indexes for Gross Domestic Product and Domestic Purchases: Historical Data—Continued

(Index numbers, 2009 = 100.)

NIPA Tables 1.1.4, 1.6.4, 2.3.4

Year and quarter	Gross domestic product											Gross domestic purchases
	Gross domestic product, total	Personal consumption expenditures		Private fixed investment			Exports and imports of goods and services		Government consumption expenditures and gross investment			
		Total	Excluding food and energy	Total	Nonresidential	Residential	Exports	Imports	Total	Federal	State and local	
2003												
1st quarter	86.2	87.2	88.5	87.4	89.8	84.8	87.4	85.1	79.8	84.3	77.2	85.8
2nd quarter	86.5	87.2	88.9	87.4	89.7	84.9	87.6	83.8	80.0	84.6	77.3	85.9
3rd quarter	86.9	87.8	89.2	87.7	89.9	85.5	87.8	84.3	80.5	85.0	77.9	86.4
4th quarter	87.4	88.1	89.5	88.4	90.1	87.0	88.4	84.8	81.0	85.1	78.6	86.8
2004												
1st quarter	88.1	88.8	90.0	89.2	90.4	88.9	89.4	86.5	82.4	87.0	79.8	87.6
2nd quarter	88.9	89.4	90.6	90.1	90.9	90.7	90.7	87.6	83.4	87.5	81.0	88.4
3rd quarter	89.4	89.9	91.0	91.0	91.3	92.5	91.2	88.9	84.4	88.0	82.3	89.1
4th quarter	90.1	90.7	91.4	91.9	91.9	94.0	92.1	90.9	85.5	88.4	83.8	89.9
2005												
1st quarter	90.9	91.1	92.0	92.9	92.8	95.2	93.8	91.5	86.8	90.6	84.5	90.6
2nd quarter	91.5	91.7	92.5	93.9	93.5	96.8	94.4	92.5	87.6	91.1	85.6	91.3
3rd quarter	92.4	92.7	92.9	95.1	94.0	99.3	95.1	94.7	88.8	91.8	86.9	92.3
4th quarter	93.1	93.5	93.5	96.3	95.0	101.1	95.7	96.5	89.8	92.2	88.3	93.2
2006												
1st quarter	93.8	93.9	94.0	97.2	95.6	102.7	96.4	96.7	90.8	94.0	89.0	93.9
2nd quarter	94.6	94.6	94.6	97.9	96.2	103.7	97.7	97.7	91.9	94.4	90.3	94.6
3rd quarter	95.3	95.3	95.1	98.4	96.8	104.1	99.0	98.7	92.5	94.6	91.3	95.3
4th quarter	95.6	95.1	95.5	99.2	97.7	104.8	98.9	97.5	93.1	94.8	92.1	95.4
2007												
1st quarter	96.7	96.0	96.2	99.8	98.3	105.3	99.6	97.9	94.9	96.6	93.9	96.4
2nd quarter	97.2	96.8	96.5	100.0	98.6	105.1	100.6	99.5	95.7	97.2	94.8	97.1
3rd quarter	97.5	97.3	97.0	100.0	98.6	105.1	101.4	101.3	96.5	97.5	95.9	97.6
4th quarter	97.9	98.3	97.6	100.1	98.7	105.2	102.9	105.4	97.5	98.1	97.1	98.4
2008												
1st quarter	98.5	99.1	98.2	100.3	99.1	104.8	104.5	108.9	99.1	99.6	98.7	99.3
2nd quarter	98.9	100.2	98.7	100.5	99.6	104.4	107.3	114.6	100.3	100.4	100.2	100.2
3rd quarter	99.6	101.2	99.1	101.2	100.7	103.4	109.0	117.7	101.3	100.9	101.6	101.2
4th quarter	99.8	99.7	99.2	101.9	102.0	102.0	102.4	105.2	100.5	100.2	100.6	100.3
2009												
1st quarter	100.0	99.2	99.4	101.4	101.4	101.2	99.0	96.4	99.8	100.2	99.6	99.6
2nd quarter	99.9	99.6	99.9	100.2	100.2	99.8	99.0	97.9	99.7	99.7	99.7	99.7
3rd quarter	99.9	100.3	100.1	99.2	99.2	99.1	100.2	101.3	100.0	99.8	100.1	100.0
4th quarter	100.2	100.9	100.7	99.3	99.1	99.9	101.8	104.4	100.5	100.4	100.6	100.6
2010												
1st quarter	100.5	101.3	100.9	99.0	98.7	100.0	102.7	105.9	101.7	101.7	101.6	101.0
2nd quarter	101.0	101.4	101.2	99.0	99.0	99.3	103.8	105.4	102.4	102.5	102.4	101.3
3rd quarter	101.4	101.7	101.4	99.1	99.1	99.3	104.1	104.7	102.9	102.9	103.0	101.6
4th quarter	102.0	102.2	101.6	99.6	99.5	99.9	106.5	107.1	103.7	103.4	103.8	102.2
2011												
1st quarter	102.4	103.0	102.0	100.0	99.9	100.1	109.2	111.5	104.7	104.6	104.8	102.9
2nd quarter	103.2	104.0	102.6	100.5	100.4	100.5	111.5	114.9	105.8	105.5	106.0	103.9
3rd quarter	103.8	104.6	103.1	100.7	100.8	100.5	112.2	114.8	106.2	105.9	106.5	104.4
4th quarter	103.9	105.0	103.5	101.0	101.1	100.5	111.0	114.6	106.1	105.7	106.4	104.6
2012												
1st quarter	104.5	105.6	104.1	101.5	101.7	100.3	111.7	115.8	107.0	106.3	107.5	105.3
2nd quarter	104.9	105.9	104.6	101.9	102.2	100.7	112.0	115.0	107.1	106.5	107.6	105.6
3rd quarter	105.5	106.2	104.9	102.3	102.5	101.6	111.9	113.4	107.4	106.6	108.0	105.9
4th quarter	105.9	106.8	105.4	102.5	102.5	102.6	112.3	114.5	107.9	106.7	108.8	106.4
2013												
1st quarter	106.3	107.2	105.8	102.9	102.6	104.2	112.6	114.7	108.4	106.9	109.4	106.8
2nd quarter	106.6	107.3	106.1	103.4	102.9	105.6	111.9	113.6	108.6	107.0	109.8	107.0
3rd quarter	107.2	107.7	106.5	103.8	103.1	107.0	112.0	113.4	109.2	107.4	110.5	107.5
4th quarter	107.6	108.1	107.0	104.4	103.3	109.1	112.1	113.6	110.1	109.0	110.9	108.0
2014												
1st quarter	108.0	108.5	107.3	105.1	103.6	111.4	112.9	114.5	110.4	108.7	111.6	108.4
2nd quarter	108.6	109.1	107.9	105.3	103.8	111.7	112.9	114.1	110.9	109.2	112.1	108.9
3rd quarter	109.0	109.4	108.2	106.0	104.2	113.6	112.6	113.8	111.5	109.6	112.8	109.3
4th quarter	109.1	109.3	108.5	106.3	104.3	114.9	110.6	111.9	111.4	109.6	112.6	109.3

Table 1-7. Final Sales

(Quarterly dollar data are at seasonally adjusted annual rates.)

NIPA Tables 1.4.4, 1.4.5, 1.4.6

Year and quarter	Final sales of domestic product			Final sales to domestic purchasers		
	Billions of dollars	Billions of chained (2009) dollars	Chain-type price index, 2009 = 100	Billions of dollars	Billions of chained (2009) dollars	Chain-type price index, 2009 = 100
1950	294.4	2 167.1	13.6	293.7	2 201.6	13.4
1951	337.4	2 328.5	14.5	334.9	2 348.0	14.3
1952	364.2	2 457.5	14.9	363.1	2 493.0	14.6
1953	387.8	2 580.5	15.1	388.5	2 635.5	14.8
1954	393.1	2 588.9	15.2	392.7	2 633.7	14.9
1955	421.2	2 733.9	15.4	420.7	2 782.4	15.1
1956	446.2	2 800.5	16.0	443.8	2 840.1	15.7
1957	474.1	2 874.7	16.5	470.0	2 908.9	16.2
1958	482.4	2 858.6	16.9	481.9	2 917.9	16.5
1959	518.5	3 031.9	17.1	518.1	3 095.0	16.8
1960	540.1	3 114.1	17.4	535.8	3 157.2	17.0
1961	560.3	3 195.7	17.6	555.4	3 238.9	17.2
1962	599.0	3 374.4	17.8	594.9	3 428.4	17.4
1963	633.0	3 525.3	18.0	628.0	3 574.7	17.6
1964	681.0	3 734.8	18.3	674.1	3 775.9	17.9
1965	734.5	3 955.2	18.6	728.9	4 012.3	18.2
1966	801.4	4 196.9	19.1	797.5	4 271.0	18.7
1967	851.9	4 334.1	19.7	848.3	4 420.6	19.2
1968	933.4	4 553.4	20.5	932.1	4 658.1	20.0
1969	1 010.7	4 697.7	21.6	1 009.3	4 807.5	21.0
1970	1 073.9	4 740.5	22.7	1 069.9	4 835.5	22.2
1971	1 159.5	4 870.6	23.9	1 158.9	4 977.5	23.3
1972	1 273.3	5 126.0	24.9	1 276.7	5 247.9	24.4
1973	1 412.7	5 392.4	26.3	1 408.6	5 477.7	25.7
1974	1 534.8	5 378.4	28.6	1 535.6	5 423.1	28.4
1975	1 695.2	5 434.6	31.3	1 679.2	5 432.8	31.0
1976	1 860.5	5 651.9	33.0	1 862.1	5 709.5	32.7
1977	2 063.6	5 900.9	35.0	2 086.7	6 000.6	34.8
1978	2 330.8	6 225.5	37.5	2 356.1	6 324.3	37.3
1979	2 614.2	6 450.3	40.6	2 636.7	6 509.1	40.6
1980	2 868.8	6 492.1	44.3	2 881.9	6 444.9	44.8
1981	3 181.1	6 587.0	48.4	3 193.7	6 548.1	48.9
1982	3 359.9	6 546.7	51.4	3 379.9	6 547.0	51.7
1983	3 643.9	6 830.6	53.4	3 695.5	6 915.2	53.5
1984	3 975.3	7 196.3	55.3	4 078.0	7 385.6	55.3
1985	4 324.9	7 581.7	57.2	4 438.9	7 799.9	57.0
1986	4 583.6	7 872.6	58.3	4 715.5	8 113.3	58.2
1987	4 843.1	8 113.1	59.8	4 987.8	8 340.6	59.8
1988	5 234.1	8 466.9	61.9	5 343.5	8 627.9	61.9
1989	5 630.0	8 765.5	64.3	5 716.7	8 882.8	64.4
1990	5 965.0	8 952.7	66.7	6 042.9	9 034.1	66.9
1991	6 174.4	8 968.6	68.9	6 203.1	8 994.5	69.0
1992	6 523.0	9 262.5	70.5	6 557.7	9 291.5	70.6
1993	6 857.9	9 511.0	72.2	6 923.1	9 591.2	72.2
1994	7 245.0	9 837.7	73.7	7 337.5	9 956.0	73.7
1995	7 632.9	10 151.3	75.3	7 722.6	10 257.3	75.3
1996	8 069.4	10 536.6	76.7	8 165.8	10 657.7	76.6
1997	8 537.6	10 956.0	78.0	8 639.5	11 110.3	77.8
1998	9 025.4	11 452.3	78.9	9 188.2	11 734.2	78.3
1999	9 599.8	11 994.9	80.0	9 856.4	12 391.9	79.5
2000	10 230.2	12 494.9	81.9	10 606.0	12 994.0	81.6
2001	10 660.1	12 729.6	83.7	11 028.8	13 257.3	83.2
2002	10 959.0	12 888.9	85.0	11 385.5	13 499.6	84.3
2003	11 491.4	13 249.0	86.7	11 995.0	13 917.4	86.2
2004	12 211.1	13 702.2	89.1	12 830.2	14 461.3	88.7
2005	13 034.1	14 168.8	92.0	13 755.3	14 975.8	91.9
2006	13 788.9	14 542.3	94.8	14 559.9	15 361.0	94.8
2007	14 443.2	14 836.2	97.4	15 161.7	15 570.2	97.4
2008	14 750.6	14 865.7	99.2	15 473.6	15 435.8	100.2
2009	14 566.3	14 566.3	100.0	14 961.7	14 961.7	100.0
2010	14 902.8	14 722.2	101.2	15 415.5	15 183.6	101.5
2011	15 476.2	14 979.0	103.3	16 056.2	15 442.5	104.0
2012	16 093.5	15 292.3	105.2	16 659.1	15 742.4	105.8
2013	16 591.4	15 511.4	107.0	17 099.8	15 929.8	107.3
2014	17 270.9	15 881.7	108.7	17 800.9	16 326.3	109.0
2012						
1st quarter	15 908.4	15 225.0	104.5	16 523.2	15 691.9	105.3
2nd quarter	16 032.6	15 276.9	104.9	16 613.5	15 733.1	105.6
3rd quarter	16 153.9	15 302.7	105.6	16 689.1	15 752.5	105.9
4th quarter	16 278.9	15 364.6	106.0	16 810.8	15 791.9	106.5
2013						
1st quarter	16 404.2	15 424.7	106.4	16 933.4	15 851.6	106.8
2nd quarter	16 478.1	15 451.9	106.6	17 005.9	15 887.9	107.0
3rd quarter	16 621.9	15 508.9	107.2	17 134.3	15 938.8	107.5
4th quarter	16 861.2	15 660.0	107.7	17 325.5	16 041.0	108.0
2014						
1st quarter	16 941.6	15 675.7	108.1	17 470.9	16 111.4	108.4
2nd quarter	17 181.0	15 809.7	108.7	17 711.9	16 255.4	109.0
3rd quarter	17 433.8	15 978.6	109.1	17 948.3	16 409.2	109.4
4th quarter	17 527.4	16 062.9	109.1	18 072.6	16 529.2	109.3

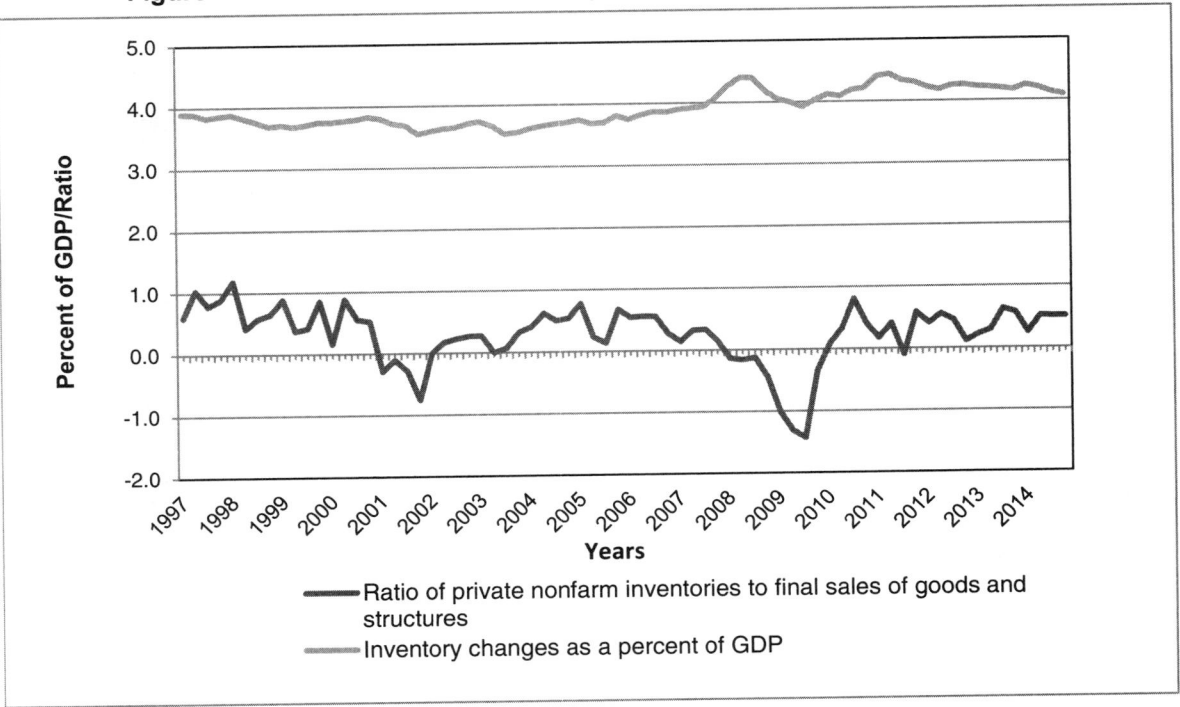

Figure 1-2: Private Nonfarm Inventory-Sales Ratios, Quarterly 1997–2014

- The change in inventories is part of business investment component that, although small, can be volatile and even negative, reflecting the fact that production is frequently more variable than sales. When inventory change is positive, the economy is producing more than is sold. This is the normal condition, as inventories grow to accommodate a growing level of sales. When inventory change is negative, production is below the rate of sales—which could be because sales rose faster than anticipated, causing involuntary inventory reduction, or on the other hand because production was deliberately cut back in order to get rid of unwanted stocks. Furthermore, it is the change in inventory change—the change in an already volatile number—that drives the GDP's growth rate.

- In 2009, following a rapid and unwanted rise in inventories, stocks were reduced at a record rate of $148 billion (2009 dollars), contributing 0.76 percentage points to the 2.8 percent decline in GDP. In 2010, the resumption of inventory-building contributed 1.45 percentage points, more than half of the 2.5 percent GDP increase. This was the largest positive contribution from inventories since 1984. (Tables 1-2A, 1-8A and 1-4A)

- Inventory-sales ratios, such as the version shown in Figure 1-2, show stocks in recent periods to be fluctuating around 2008's historical low. Of note, 2014's ratio was 2.32, three percentage points below the 2008 amount. Inventory investment has been moderate and variable during the recovery. (Tables 1-8A and B)

Table 1-8A. Inventory Change and Inventory-Sales Ratios: Recent Data

(Quarterly dollar data are at seasonally adjusted annual rates.)

NIPA Tables 5.7.5B, 5.7.6B, 5.8.5B, 5.8.6B

Year and quarter	Change in private inventories				Ratio, inventories at end of quarter to monthly rate of sales during the quarter					
	Billions of current dollars		Billions of chained dollars [1]		Total private inventories to final sales of domestic business		Nonfarm inventories to final sales of domestic business		Nonfarm inventories to final sales of goods and structures	
	Farm	Nonfarm	Farm	Nonfarm	Current dollars	Chained dollars[1]	Current dollars	Chained dollars[1]	Current dollars	Chained dollars[1]
OLD BASIS										
1955	-0.6	5.6	-1.9	18.7	4.43	3.44	2.95	2.29	3.87	3.94
1956	-1.0	4.9	-3.2	15.6	4.47	3.45	3.03	2.35	4.00	4.07
1957	0.1	0.7	0.4	2.4	4.46	3.48	3.01	2.37	4.01	4.14
1958	2.0	-2.3	5.8	-7.7	4.50	3.44	2.90	2.30	3.88	4.00
1959	-1.6	5.5	-4.7	19.9	4.26	3.37	2.90	2.32	3.94	4.08
1960	0.6	2.7	1.7	9.9	4.22	3.37	2.89	2.34	3.93	4.10
1961	0.9	2.1	2.5	7.8	4.12	3.30	2.81	2.29	3.84	4.03
1962	0.6	5.5	1.7	20.4	4.14	3.32	2.82	2.34	3.87	4.11
1963	0.5	5.1	1.4	19.0	3.95	3.25	2.78	2.32	3.81	4.07
1964	-1.2	6.0	-3.8	21.8	3.79	3.17	2.75	2.31	3.79	4.07
1965	0.8	8.4	2.5	30.5	3.77	3.09	2.72	2.29	3.71	3.99
1966	-0.5	14.1	-1.4	50.2	3.92	3.26	2.92	2.50	4.01	4.38
1967	0.9	9.0	2.5	31.5	3.90	3.35	2.99	2.59	4.14	4.57
1968	1.4	7.7	4.1	26.5	3.79	3.33	2.90	2.58	4.03	4.56
1969	0.0	9.2	0.0	30.9	3.88	3.40	2.98	2.68	4.18	4.76
1970	-0.8	2.8	-2.4	8.6	3.81	3.39	2.96	2.68	4.23	4.83
1971	1.7	6.6	4.1	20.6	3.76	3.33	2.88	2.64	4.12	4.75
1972	0.3	8.8	0.4	26.7	3.74	3.18	2.77	2.55	3.94	4.53
1973	1.5	14.4	1.8	40.5	4.20	3.22	2.98	2.62	4.22	4.67
1974	-2.8	16.8	-4.4	39.0	4.52	3.46	3.54	2.88	5.11	5.26
1975	3.4	-9.6	5.8	-21.4	4.04	3.26	3.16	2.66	4.59	4.88
1976	-0.8	18.0	-1.6	37.6	3.95	3.23	3.19	2.68	4.68	4.92
1977	4.5	17.8	7.2	35.7	3.89	3.22	3.16	2.67	4.63	4.87
1978	1.4	24.4	2.1	44.9	3.98	3.14	3.15	2.63	4.54	4.73
1979	3.6	14.4	4.2	23.8	4.19	3.16	3.34	2.64	4.85	4.75
1980	-6.1	-0.2	-7.2	-0.4	4.24	3.13	3.44	2.65	5.08	4.82
1981	8.8	21.0	10.1	28.2	4.17	3.28	3.49	2.75	5.20	5.03
1982	5.8	-20.7	7.5	-27.4	3.97	3.23	3.30	2.68	5.10	4.99
1983	-15.4	9.6	-17.4	10.7	3.69	2.98	3.08	2.52	4.77	4.64
1984	5.7	59.7	6.3	72.3	3.72	3.05	3.16	2.60	4.89	4.72
1985	5.8	16.1	7.0	18.4	3.51	2.98	3.01	2.53	4.74	4.65
1986	-1.5	8.0	-2.3	10.4	3.25	2.90	2.82	2.47	4.49	4.53
1987	-6.4	33.6	-9.1	41.1	3.33	2.90	2.90	2.50	4.65	4.62
1988	-11.9	30.4	-13.1	35.4	3.29	2.81	2.86	2.47	4.63	4.55
1989	0.0	27.7	0.0	30.8	3.23	2.80	2.83	2.47	4.63	4.56
1990	2.4	12.2	2.5	14.0	3.22	2.83	2.82	2.49	4.71	4.66
1991	-1.3	0.9	-1.8	0.4	3.06	2.83	2.70	2.50	4.62	4.74
1992	6.3	10.1	7.1	11.0	2.92	2.73	2.56	2.39	4.41	4.53
1993	-6.2	27.0	-7.5	29.8	2.85	2.68	2.51	2.38	4.33	4.47
1994	12.0	51.8	13.7	55.9	2.89	2.72	2.56	2.40	4.39	4.47
1995	-11.1	42.2	-13.0	44.3	2.88	2.69	2.58	2.40	4.45	4.46
1996	8.6	22.1	8.3	23.2	2.76	2.62	2.47	2.33	4.24	4.28
1997	3.3	67.7	3.7	73.6	2.70	2.65	2.42	2.37	4.17	4.32
NEW BASIS										
1997	3.3	67.7	4.1	80.5	2.60	2.63	2.33	2.35	3.86	4.16
1998	1.3	62.5	1.9	76.4	2.46	2.60	2.24	2.32	3.69	4.07
1999	-2.7	63.5	-4.2	77.7	2.48	2.59	2.27	2.33	3.75	4.08
2000	-1.4	55.9	-2.0	67.1	2.50	2.59	2.28	2.34	3.83	4.12
2001	0.0	-38.3	0.1	-45.8	2.32	2.51	2.12	2.26	3.55	3.97
2002	-2.5	21.0	-3.5	25.5	2.37	2.53	2.16	2.29	3.71	4.09
2003	0.1	19.2	0.1	22.4	2.31	2.43	2.09	2.20	3.56	3.86
2004	8.8	55.1	9.0	62.4	2.38	2.44	2.16	2.21	3.71	3.89
2005	0.2	59.4	0.3	63.9	2.42	2.44	2.21	2.21	3.81	3.89
2006	-3.6	70.5	-4.2	75.4	2.43	2.44	2.23	2.23	3.86	3.93
2007	-0.7	35.2	-0.9	36.5	2.53	2.43	2.30	2.22	4.07	3.93
2008	1.6	-33.6	1.1	-35.0	2.52	2.49	2.29	2.27	4.18	4.13
2009	-1.6	-146.0	-1.6	-146.0	2.40	2.35	2.19	2.13	4.03	3.89
2010	-7.3	68.9	-7.0	65.9	2.53	2.35	2.28	2.14	4.22	3.92
2011	2.1	39.7	1.4	36.6	2.62	2.33	2.33	2.13	4.31	3.86
2012	-19.5	81.3	-12.6	72.7	2.60	2.33	2.34	2.16	4.26	3.86
2013	11.3	60.5	6.7	54.3	2.53	2.32	2.29	2.15	4.17	3.81
2014	5.9	71.2	3.7	65.0	2.48	2.32	2.23	2.14	4.09	3.81
2012										
1st quarter	-8.6	74.0	-6.6	65.8	2.59	2.32	2.31	2.12	4.23	3.83
2nd quarter	-15.3	104.6	-10.3	92.0	2.56	2.33	2.29	2.14	4.18	3.84
3rd quarter	-31.5	105.5	-19.0	97.7	2.60	2.34	2.33	2.16	4.25	3.88
4th quarter	-22.6	41.0	-14.5	35.3	2.60	2.33	2.34	2.16	4.26	3.86
2013										
1st quarter	7.9	28.6	1.8	23.5	2.58	2.32	2.32	2.15	4.23	3.83
2nd quarter	10.4	38.3	5.8	32.9	2.56	2.32	2.31	2.15	4.22	3.83
3rd quarter	14.8	90.7	9.3	84.0	2.55	2.33	2.30	2.16	4.20	3.84
4th quarter	11.9	84.5	9.9	76.6	2.53	2.32	2.29	2.15	4.17	3.81
2014										
1st quarter	2.7	40.0	1.3	36.2	2.58	2.33	2.32	2.16	4.25	3.84
2nd quarter	7.7	81.3	3.6	74.5	2.56	2.33	2.30	2.15	4.21	3.82
3rd quarter	8.0	80.3	5.8	74.5	2.52	2.32	2.27	2.14	4.13	3.79
4th quarter	5.4	83.1	4.2	74.9	2.48	2.32	2.23	2.14	4.09	3.81

[1]Before 1997, 2005 dollars; 1997 forward, 2009 dollars.

Table 1-8B. Inventory Change and Inventory-Sales Ratios: Historical Data

(Quarterly dollar data are at seasonally adjusted annual rates.)

NIPA Tables 5.7.5B, 5.7.6B, 5.8.5B, 5.8.6B

| Year and quarter | Change in private inventories | | | | Ratio, inventories at end of quarter to monthly rate of sales during the quarter | | | | | |
| | Billions of current dollars | | Billions of chained dollars [1] | | Total private inventories to final sales of domestic business | | Nonfarm inventories to final sales of domestic business | | Nonfarm inventories to final sales of goods and structures | |
	Farm	Nonfarm	Farm	Nonfarm	Current dollars	Chained dollars[1]	Current dollars	Chained dollars[1]	Current dollars	Chained dollars[1]
OLD BASIS										
1929	-0.1	1.7	-0.6	10.6	. . .	. . .	. . .	. . .	. . .	. . .
1930	-0.3	0.0	-1.7	-2.4	. . .	. . .	. . .	. . .	. . .	. . .
1931	0.5	-1.6	3.1	-13.4	. . .	. . .	. . .	. . .	. . .	. . .
1932	0.1	-2.5	0.8	-21.2	. . .	. . .	. . .	. . .	. . .	. . .
1933	-0.1	-1.3	-1.1	-9.4	. . .	. . .	. . .	. . .	. . .	. . .
1934	-0.8	0.2	-5.7	1.0	. . .	. . .	. . .	. . .	. . .	. . .
1935	0.7	0.4	4.0	2.5	. . .	. . .	. . .	. . .	. . .	. . .
1936	-0.9	2.0	-5.4	15.5	. . .	. . .	. . .	. . .	. . .	. . .
1937	0.9	1.7	4.1	7.9	. . .	. . .	. . .	. . .	. . .	. . .
1938	0.4	-1.0	2.8	-6.0	. . .	. . .	. . .	. . .	. . .	. . .
1939	-0.1	0.3	-1.1	2.7	. . .	. . .	. . .	. . .	. . .	. . .
1940	0.5	1.9	2.8	12.4	. . .	. . .	. . .	. . .	. . .	. . .
1941	0.4	3.9	1.9	24.3	. . .	. . .	. . .	. . .	. . .	. . .
1942	1.3	0.6	5.6	3.0	. . .	. . .	. . .	. . .	. . .	. . .
1943	-0.2	-0.5	-1.1	-2.3	. . .	. . .	. . .	. . .	. . .	. . .
1944	-0.3	-0.6	-1.5	-2.5	. . .	. . .	. . .	. . .	. . .	. . .
1945	-0.9	-0.6	-3.3	-3.8	. . .	. . .	. . .	. . .	. . .	. . .
1946	-0.2	6.2	-1.0	31.8	. . .	. . .	. . .	. . .	. . .	. . .
1947	-1.8	1.2	-4.5	4.4	. . .	. . .	. . .	. . .	. . .	. . .
1948	2.7	3.0	6.1	12.4	. . .	. . .	. . .	. . .	. . .	. . .
1949	-0.6	-2.1	-1.9	-8.6	. . .	. . .	. . .	. . .	. . .	. . .
1950	-0.1	5.9	-0.3	22.8	5.81	3.67	3.04	2.30	3.94	3.97
1951	1.0	8.9	2.1	28.4	5.85	3.76	3.15	2.46	4.07	4.24
1952	1.4	2.1	3.1	7.4	5.24	3.74	3.06	2.45	3.98	4.23
1953	0.7	1.2	2.0	4.5	5.04	3.74	3.08	2.45	4.04	4.22
1954	0.2	-2.1	0.5	-7.5	4.74	3.52	2.88	2.28	3.81	3.94
1947										
1st quarter	-1.1	1.6	-0.4	6.6	5.93	3.88	2.82	2.27	3.71	3.99
2nd quarter	-2.7	1.5	-4.5	4.2	5.89	3.84	2.82	2.27	3.69	4.00
3rd quarter	-2.5	-0.4	-6.8	-3.7	6.02	3.76	2.76	2.23	3.61	3.93
4th quarter	-0.8	2.3	-6.3	10.5	6.30	3.74	2.81	2.25	3.65	3.93
1948										
1st quarter	1.3	2.4	1.6	11.7	6.00	3.76	2.87	2.27	3.71	3.96
2nd quarter	2.8	3.0	7.7	11.9	6.02	3.81	2.89	2.30	3.76	4.03
3rd quarter	3.4	3.7	8.3	15.0	5.88	3.88	2.97	2.34	3.85	4.10
4th quarter	3.1	2.9	6.6	11.1	5.74	3.91	3.00	2.36	3.90	4.13
1949										
1st quarter	-0.2	0.6	-1.2	-0.4	5.66	3.90	2.97	2.36	3.88	4.14
2nd quarter	-1.2	-4.0	-3.0	-15.1	5.38	3.82	2.83	2.30	3.70	4.02
3rd quarter	-0.9	-0.4	-2.3	-0.6	5.39	3.81	2.82	2.29	3.69	4.00
4th quarter	-0.2	-4.5	-0.9	-18.4	5.23	3.73	2.77	2.23	3.61	3.87
1950										
1st quarter	-0.1	2.2	-1.0	9.7	5.26	3.69	2.76	2.22	3.61	3.84
2nd quarter	-1.3	4.2	-2.5	16.2	5.27	3.62	2.75	2.20	3.57	3.79
3rd quarter	0.5	3.7	0.6	15.2	5.21	3.47	2.72	2.12	3.50	3.63
4th quarter	0.7	13.4	1.5	50.2	5.81	3.67	3.04	2.30	3.94	3.97
1951										
1st quarter	1.2	9.2	2.6	29.0	5.94	3.68	3.12	2.33	4.01	4.01
2nd quarter	0.9	13.8	2.5	44.3	5.99	3.81	3.25	2.45	4.23	4.28
3rd quarter	0.8	9.0	1.6	29.3	5.89	3.79	3.20	2.47	4.16	4.29
4th quarter	1.1	3.6	1.7	11.0	5.85	3.76	3.15	2.46	4.07	4.24
1952										
1st quarter	1.0	3.8	2.7	12.8	5.77	3.79	3.16	2.49	4.11	4.31
2nd quarter	1.9	-3.4	3.6	-10.5	5.63	3.75	3.08	2.44	4.01	4.24
3rd quarter	2.2	3.4	4.5	11.2	5.63	3.85	3.15	2.51	4.13	4.38
4th quarter	0.5	4.8	1.5	16.2	5.24	3.74	3.06	2.45	3.98	4.23
1953										
1st quarter	0.8	3.1	2.5	10.6	5.06	3.69	3.02	2.42	3.93	4.17
2nd quarter	-0.7	4.3	-0.2	14.1	5.00	3.69	3.06	2.43	3.99	4.20
3rd quarter	0.7	1.6	1.8	5.8	4.99	3.72	3.09	2.45	4.05	4.23
4th quarter	2.1	-4.1	3.8	-12.3	5.04	3.74	3.08	2.45	4.04	4.22
1954										
1st quarter	0.8	-2.8	2.1	-9.2	5.02	3.72	3.04	2.42	4.01	4.20
2nd quarter	-0.2	-3.2	0.5	-10.8	4.91	3.66	2.98	2.38	3.93	4.11
3rd quarter	0.7	-2.8	0.8	-9.1	4.85	3.59	2.93	2.32	3.89	4.04
4th quarter	-0.5	0.2	-1.5	-0.9	4.74	3.52	2.88	2.28	3.81	3.94
1955										
1st quarter	-0.1	3.9	-1.7	14.0	4.68	3.46	2.86	2.25	3.77	3.88
2nd quarter	-1.1	5.7	-2.1	20.0	4.57	3.44	2.87	2.26	3.73	3.83
3rd quarter	-1.3	5.6	-2.0	17.9	4.47	3.42	2.89	2.26	3.77	3.85
4th quarter	0.3	6.9	-1.6	22.7	4.43	3.44	2.95	2.29	3.87	3.94
1956										
1st quarter	0.0	6.4	-2.9	20.8	4.50	3.48	3.00	2.33	3.96	4.02
2nd quarter	-1.5	5.0	-3.4	16.2	4.57	3.48	3.03	2.35	3.99	4.04
3rd quarter	-0.8	4.3	-3.2	13.2	4.50	3.48	3.02	2.36	3.98	4.07
4th quarter	-1.6	3.9	-3.3	12.1	4.47	3.45	3.03	2.35	4.00	4.07

[1]Before 1997, 2005 dollars; 1997 forward, 2009 dollars.
. . . = Not available.

Table 1-8B. Inventory Change and Inventory-Sales Ratios: Historical Data—*Continued*

(Quarterly dollar data are at seasonally adjusted annual rates.)

NIPA Tables 5.7.5B, 5.7.6B, 5.8.5B, 5.8.6B

Year and quarter	Change in private inventories				Ratio, inventories at end of quarter to monthly rate of sales during the quarter					
	Billions of current dollars		Billions of chained dollars [1]		Total private inventories to final sales of domestic business		Nonfarm inventories to final sales of domestic business		Nonfarm inventories to final sales of goods and structures	
	Farm	Nonfarm	Farm	Nonfarm	Current dollars	Chained dollars[1]	Current dollars	Chained dollars[1]	Current dollars	Chained dollars[1]
1957										
1st quarter	0.3	1.9	-0.9	5.7	4.44	3.44	3.02	2.35	3.97	4.05
2nd quarter	0.7	2.0	-0.2	6.8	4.48	3.48	3.04	2.38	4.00	4.11
3rd quarter	0.5	2.3	1.8	7.5	4.46	3.47	3.03	2.38	3.99	4.10
4th quarter	-1.0	-3.5	1.1	-10.2	4.46	3.48	3.01	2.37	4.01	4.14
1958										
1st quarter	2.2	-6.3	7.6	-20.4	4.67	3.56	3.04	2.41	4.06	4.20
2nd quarter	1.6	-5.8	6.9	-18.6	4.65	3.56	3.00	2.38	4.00	4.17
3rd quarter	2.2	-0.7	6.2	-2.5	4.58	3.48	2.92	2.32	3.92	4.07
4th quarter	1.8	3.4	2.5	10.6	4.50	3.44	2.90	2.30	3.88	4.00
1959										
1st quarter	-0.3	4.2	-3.5	14.9	4.37	3.35	2.83	2.25	3.79	3.93
2nd quarter	-1.9	9.2	-5.3	33.8	4.33	3.34	2.86	2.27	3.85	3.98
3rd quarter	-2.3	2.6	-5.4	9.6	4.25	3.31	2.84	2.27	3.82	3.96
4th quarter	-1.8	5.9	-4.6	21.1	4.26	3.37	2.90	2.32	3.94	4.08
1960										
1st quarter	0.6	10.6	0.4	39.0	4.29	3.37	2.93	2.35	3.96	4.10
2nd quarter	0.9	2.4	1.9	9.0	4.21	3.36	2.91	2.34	3.95	4.11
3rd quarter	1.0	3.3	3.1	12.1	4.27	3.41	2.95	2.38	3.99	4.15
4th quarter	-0.2	-5.6	1.5	-20.2	4.22	3.37	2.89	2.34	3.93	4.10
1961										
1st quarter	0.6	-3.1	2.5	-11.3	4.19	3.35	2.86	2.32	3.90	4.07
2nd quarter	0.6	1.2	2.2	4.7	4.12	3.33	2.83	2.30	3.89	4.07
3rd quarter	0.9	5.7	2.6	21.0	4.17	3.35	2.85	2.32	3.89	4.08
4th quarter	1.4	4.6	2.8	16.8	4.12	3.30	2.81	2.29	3.84	4.03
1962										
1st quarter	1.5	7.9	2.5	29.0	4.15	3.32	2.82	2.32	3.85	4.07
2nd quarter	0.2	5.2	0.8	19.2	4.09	3.29	2.80	2.31	3.84	4.06
3rd quarter	0.2	5.9	1.4	22.0	4.17	3.32	2.83	2.33	3.87	4.09
4th quarter	0.4	3.0	2.2	11.3	4.14	3.32	2.82	2.34	3.87	4.11
1963										
1st quarter	1.9	4.9	7.5	18.2	4.12	3.34	2.83	2.35	3.87	4.12
2nd quarter	0.1	4.8	0.7	17.4	4.04	3.29	2.79	2.32	3.83	4.08
3rd quarter	-0.6	6.4	-1.7	23.6	4.00	3.27	2.79	2.33	3.81	4.07
4th quarter	0.6	4.5	-0.8	16.7	3.95	3.25	2.78	2.32	3.81	4.07
1964										
1st quarter	-0.6	5.8	-3.9	21.1	3.85	3.19	2.74	2.29	3.75	4.01
2nd quarter	-1.2	5.7	-4.3	20.7	3.79	3.17	2.73	2.29	3.75	4.02
3rd quarter	-1.8	6.5	-4.2	23.8	3.78	3.15	2.73	2.29	3.74	4.00
4th quarter	-1.1	6.1	-3.1	21.7	3.79	3.17	2.75	2.31	3.79	4.07
1965										
1st quarter	0.3	11.2	0.9	40.8	3.81	3.17	2.76	2.33	3.79	4.08
2nd quarter	1.1	7.4	2.9	26.9	3.82	3.15	2.75	2.32	3.79	4.08
3rd quarter	0.8	8.5	3.1	30.5	3.78	3.14	2.76	2.32	3.78	4.06
4th quarter	1.0	6.6	3.2	23.7	3.77	3.09	2.72	2.29	3.71	3.99
1966										
1st quarter	0.6	13.2	1.1	46.8	3.80	3.09	2.73	2.31	3.71	4.00
2nd quarter	-1.7	14.0	-2.7	50.2	3.86	3.16	2.80	2.38	3.83	4.16
3rd quarter	-0.6	12.4	-1.7	43.7	3.91	3.19	2.84	2.42	3.88	4.22
4th quarter	-0.4	16.9	-2.3	59.9	3.92	3.26	2.92	2.50	4.01	4.38
1967										
1st quarter	1.7	13.7	3.4	48.6	3.94	3.32	2.98	2.55	4.11	4.50
2nd quarter	2.1	4.2	7.6	14.7	3.92	3.31	2.95	2.54	4.07	4.46
3rd quarter	0.5	8.7	1.4	29.7	3.92	3.34	2.97	2.57	4.10	4.52
4th quarter	-0.9	9.3	-2.2	33.1	3.90	3.35	2.99	2.59	4.14	4.57
1968										
1st quarter	3.0	5.4	7.3	19.1	3.87	3.32	2.94	2.57	4.08	4.51
2nd quarter	4.3	9.8	13.4	33.9	3.87	3.34	2.93	2.58	4.07	4.55
3rd quarter	0.2	7.5	1.2	25.1	3.81	3.32	2.90	2.56	4.03	4.51
4th quarter	-2.0	8.0	-5.5	27.8	3.79	3.33	2.90	2.58	4.03	4.56
1969										
1st quarter	1.8	9.7	3.9	33.0	3.79	3.32	2.90	2.59	4.02	4.54
2nd quarter	1.4	7.8	4.4	26.6	3.83	3.35	2.91	2.61	4.06	4.61
3rd quarter	-1.2	11.4	-2.5	38.6	3.83	3.38	2.94	2.64	4.10	4.67
4th quarter	-1.9	7.7	-5.8	25.5	3.88	3.40	2.98	2.68	4.18	4.76
1970										
1st quarter	1.6	0.2	3.4	0.0	3.86	3.38	2.96	2.66	4.18	4.74
2nd quarter	0.4	4.7	1.9	14.9	3.85	3.40	2.96	2.68	4.20	4.80
3rd quarter	-1.8	6.9	-4.4	21.9	3.84	3.39	2.97	2.67	4.22	4.79
4th quarter	-3.5	-0.5	-10.3	-2.2	3.81	3.39	2.96	2.68	4.23	4.83
1971										
1st quarter	2.5	9.7	6.6	31.3	3.83	3.38	2.95	2.68	4.21	4.81
2nd quarter	4.2	6.7	10.7	20.6	3.81	3.39	2.94	2.68	4.20	4.81
3rd quarter	2.3	7.9	5.8	25.2	3.80	3.38	2.93	2.68	4.18	4.80
4th quarter	-2.3	2.0	-6.8	5.4	3.76	3.33	2.88	2.64	4.12	4.75

[1] Before 1997, 2005 dollars; 1997 forward, 2009 dollars.

Table 1-8B. Inventory Change and Inventory-Sales Ratios: Historical Data—Continued

(Quarterly dollar data are at seasonally adjusted annual rates.) **NIPA Tables 5.7.5B, 5.7.6B, 5.8.5B, 5.8.6B**

Year and quarter	Change in private inventories				Ratio, inventories at end of quarter to monthly rate of sales during the quarter					
	Billions of current dollars		Billions of chained dollars [1]		Total private inventories to final sales of domestic business		Nonfarm inventories to final sales of domestic business		Nonfarm inventories to final sales of goods and structures	
	Farm	Nonfarm	Farm	Nonfarm	Current dollars	Chained dollars[1]	Current dollars	Chained dollars[1]	Current dollars	Chained dollars[1]
1972										
1st quarter	-0.5	3.7	0.1	11.1	3.72	3.30	2.84	2.62	4.06	4.69
2nd quarter	2.0	10.0	6.8	30.6	3.75	3.27	2.83	2.60	4.03	4.64
3rd quarter	1.0	12.7	1.9	38.5	3.77	3.26	2.83	2.60	4.05	4.66
4th quarter	-1.4	8.9	-7.1	26.5	3.74	3.18	2.77	2.55	3.94	4.53
1973										
1st quarter	-4.2	14.8	-10.7	42.9	3.86	3.11	2.79	2.52	3.92	4.45
2nd quarter	5.0	13.2	12.0	38.3	4.03	3.15	2.86	2.54	4.02	4.51
3rd quarter	2.6	7.2	3.5	20.0	4.11	3.16	2.87	2.56	4.05	4.55
4th quarter	2.8	22.2	2.3	60.9	4.20	3.22	2.98	2.62	4.22	4.67
1974										
1st quarter	-3.3	15.9	-5.2	39.7	4.26	3.27	3.13	2.68	4.42	4.76
2nd quarter	1.0	16.4	0.9	39.6	4.29	3.31	3.28	2.72	4.67	4.86
3rd quarter	-0.1	5.7	1.7	11.7	4.45	3.34	3.40	2.75	4.84	4.93
4th quarter	-8.7	29.2	-15.0	64.9	4.52	3.46	3.54	2.88	5.11	5.26
1975										
1st quarter	7.1	-17.1	16.4	-38.3	4.32	3.42	3.41	2.82	4.94	5.16
2nd quarter	3.1	-17.1	5.4	-38.6	4.26	3.35	3.30	2.75	4.81	5.06
3rd quarter	0.8	-2.2	-1.0	-5.0	4.18	3.31	3.24	2.71	4.69	4.95
4th quarter	2.5	-2.1	2.3	-3.7	4.04	3.26	3.16	2.66	4.59	4.88
1976										
1st quarter	-0.5	15.2	0.1	33.2	4.00	3.22	3.14	2.64	4.56	4.83
2nd quarter	-1.8	24.3	-1.9	51.8	4.07	3.26	3.21	2.69	4.67	4.91
3rd quarter	2.0	18.8	5.4	38.9	4.04	3.28	3.23	2.70	4.74	4.96
4th quarter	-3.0	13.6	-9.8	26.5	3.95	3.23	3.19	2.68	4.68	4.92
1977										
1st quarter	-1.3	16.1	-7.0	33.0	3.96	3.22	3.21	2.68	4.72	4.92
2nd quarter	5.3	14.2	11.3	27.8	3.88	3.19	3.16	2.65	4.62	4.84
3rd quarter	4.4	26.5	16.3	53.8	3.86	3.22	3.16	2.67	4.63	4.88
4th quarter	9.8	14.4	8.4	28.1	3.89	3.22	3.16	2.67	4.63	4.87
1978										
1st quarter	-0.6	26.1	-3.6	48.9	4.02	3.26	3.21	2.72	4.78	5.00
2nd quarter	0.4	23.9	0.2	44.2	3.92	3.14	3.12	2.62	4.55	4.75
3rd quarter	7.2	17.8	11.1	32.3	3.95	3.15	3.13	2.62	4.54	4.74
4th quarter	-1.5	30.0	0.5	54.1	3.98	3.14	3.15	2.63	4.54	4.73
1979										
1st quarter	4.2	19.6	6.6	33.0	4.15	3.17	3.22	2.65	4.66	4.78
2nd quarter	3.1	24.3	5.3	40.4	4.19	3.21	3.29	2.69	4.78	4.87
3rd quarter	6.6	5.5	7.0	8.2	4.16	3.16	3.28	2.64	4.74	4.73
4th quarter	0.3	8.3	-1.9	13.4	4.19	3.16	3.34	2.64	4.85	4.75
1980										
1st quarter	-0.6	10.5	-2.6	17.4	4.25	3.17	3.45	2.66	5.02	4.78
2nd quarter	-5.2	13.0	-5.9	19.3	4.40	3.28	3.57	2.76	5.26	5.02
3rd quarter	-12.5	-21.4	-14.2	-32.6	4.34	3.18	3.50	2.68	5.15	4.88
4th quarter	-6.1	-3.0	-6.0	-5.8	4.24	3.13	3.44	2.65	5.08	4.82
1981										
1st quarter	6.8	31.9	10.3	44.6	4.26	3.17	3.48	2.67	5.13	4.84
2nd quarter	9.9	1.8	10.9	1.7	4.24	3.18	3.47	2.67	5.15	4.87
3rd quarter	11.8	32.1	14.5	42.6	4.20	3.22	3.48	2.71	5.16	4.93
4th quarter	6.5	18.3	4.5	23.8	4.17	3.28	3.49	2.75	5.20	5.03
1982										
1st quarter	5.1	-26.5	6.7	-34.3	4.19	3.28	3.46	2.74	5.20	5.03
2nd quarter	4.3	-8.5	6.4	-12.2	4.15	3.28	3.42	2.74	5.17	5.04
3rd quarter	9.0	-3.2	12.0	-5.5	4.12	3.33	3.43	2.77	5.26	5.15
4th quarter	4.6	-44.4	4.9	-57.5	3.97	3.23	3.30	2.68	5.10	4.99
1983										
1st quarter	-7.3	-27.8	-10.4	-37.3	3.89	3.15	3.19	2.62	4.98	4.89
2nd quarter	-13.0	5.3	-12.6	6.5	3.81	3.09	3.14	2.58	4.89	4.80
3rd quarter	-32.4	28.2	-37.7	34.3	3.73	3.03	3.12	2.55	4.86	4.73
4th quarter	-8.8	32.7	-9.0	39.4	3.69	2.98	3.08	2.52	4.77	4.64
1984										
1st quarter	5.5	67.5	7.4	81.9	3.78	3.02	3.15	2.56	4.87	4.71
2nd quarter	5.6	63.7	6.4	77.2	3.76	3.03	3.16	2.57	4.88	4.69
3rd quarter	6.8	64.5	8.1	78.9	3.75	3.06	3.18	2.60	4.93	4.75
4th quarter	5.0	43.0	3.3	51.0	3.72	3.05	3.16	2.60	4.89	4.72
1985										
1st quarter	7.9	8.3	8.4	8.8	3.60	3.00	3.06	2.55	4.77	4.65
2nd quarter	4.2	17.4	4.8	20.3	3.55	2.99	3.04	2.55	4.76	4.66
3rd quarter	6.6	9.7	9.1	12.0	3.47	2.96	2.98	2.51	4.67	4.60
4th quarter	4.3	28.8	5.9	32.7	3.51	2.98	3.01	2.53	4.74	4.65
1986										
1st quarter	2.5	27.8	1.7	33.3	3.42	2.97	2.94	2.52	4.65	4.63
2nd quarter	-3.5	19.1	-5.9	22.3	3.37	2.97	2.92	2.53	4.63	4.65
3rd quarter	-3.1	-3.9	-4.3	-5.5	3.29	2.92	2.85	2.49	4.52	4.55
4th quarter	-1.8	-11.0	-0.6	-8.5	3.25	2.90	2.82	2.47	4.49	4.53

[1]Before 1997, 2005 dollars; 1997 forward, 2009 dollars.

Table 1-8B. Inventory Change and Inventory-Sales Ratios: Historical Data—*Continued*

(Quarterly dollar data are at seasonally adjusted annual rates.)

NIPA Tables 5.7.5B, 5.7.6B, 5.8.5B, 5.8.6B

Year and quarter	Change in private inventories				Ratio, inventories at end of quarter to monthly rate of sales during the quarter					
	Billions of current dollars		Billions of chained dollars [1]		Total private inventories to final sales of domestic business		Nonfarm inventories to final sales of domestic business		Nonfarm inventories to final sales of goods and structures	
	Farm	Nonfarm	Farm	Nonfarm	Current dollars	Chained dollars[1]	Current dollars	Chained dollars[1]	Current dollars	Chained dollars[1]
1987										
1st quarter	-7.7	35.6	-9.7	44.5	3.31	2.94	2.86	2.51	4.62	4.66
2nd quarter	-10.7	27.2	-14.5	33.1	3.30	2.90	2.86	2.49	4.60	4.60
3rd quarter	-4.0	5.0	-5.2	4.1	3.25	2.85	2.82	2.45	4.52	4.51
4th quarter	-3.3	66.4	-7.0	82.5	3.33	2.90	2.90	2.50	4.65	4.62
1988										
1st quarter	-4.4	21.4	-7.6	25.1	3.30	2.86	2.86	2.47	4.61	4.56
2nd quarter	-12.2	31.9	-15.2	38.0	3.29	2.83	2.85	2.46	4.60	4.52
3rd quarter	-11.2	29.4	-11.4	32.6	3.30	2.83	2.85	2.47	4.63	4.57
4th quarter	-19.7	38.8	-18.3	45.9	3.29	2.81	2.86	2.47	4.63	4.55
1989										
1st quarter	7.2	41.0	7.8	46.6	3.32	2.83	2.89	2.48	4.70	4.58
2nd quarter	2.9	33.2	3.6	37.6	3.28	2.83	2.87	2.48	4.65	4.56
3rd quarter	-5.5	15.5	-5.8	16.9	3.21	2.79	2.82	2.45	4.55	4.49
4th quarter	-4.6	21.2	-5.6	22.3	3.23	2.80	2.83	2.47	4.63	4.56
1990										
1st quarter	1.8	12.1	1.7	13.3	3.18	2.78	2.78	2.45	4.53	4.50
2nd quarter	-1.5	35.3	-2.6	39.9	3.17	2.81	2.78	2.47	4.58	4.60
3rd quarter	4.0	17.9	4.4	20.3	3.20	2.82	2.82	2.48	4.67	4.63
4th quarter	5.2	-16.6	6.7	-17.7	3.22	2.83	2.82	2.49	4.71	4.66
1991										
1st quarter	0.0	-15.6	0.7	-18.1	3.18	2.85	2.78	2.51	4.65	4.71
2nd quarter	-0.7	-17.3	-0.5	-20.6	3.08	2.81	2.70	2.47	4.55	4.66
3rd quarter	-10.9	11.7	-13.8	13.1	3.04	2.81	2.69	2.48	4.54	4.67
4th quarter	6.4	24.7	6.1	27.1	3.06	2.83	2.70	2.50	4.62	4.74
1992										
1st quarter	8.0	-7.8	10.5	-7.5	3.00	2.78	2.63	2.44	4.52	4.64
2nd quarter	9.4	13.8	10.9	13.2	2.99	2.77	2.62	2.43	4.50	4.61
3rd quarter	5.1	15.4	4.7	16.6	2.96	2.75	2.60	2.41	4.47	4.57
4th quarter	2.5	18.9	2.4	21.6	2.92	2.73	2.56	2.39	4.41	4.53
1993										
1st quarter	-5.6	41.6	-6.2	46.5	2.95	2.75	2.58	2.42	4.47	4.60
2nd quarter	-4.9	29.0	-5.3	32.3	2.92	2.74	2.57	2.41	4.44	4.56
3rd quarter	-12.5	19.1	-14.2	20.6	2.89	2.72	2.54	2.40	4.42	4.55
4th quarter	-1.7	18.3	-4.1	19.9	2.85	2.68	2.51	2.38	4.33	4.47
1994										
1st quarter	16.5	28.8	19.4	31.1	2.87	2.69	2.51	2.38	4.33	4.48
2nd quarter	17.1	64.3	21.0	70.0	2.86	2.71	2.53	2.39	4.37	4.49
3rd quarter	10.7	42.5	10.6	46.1	2.86	2.71	2.53	2.39	4.36	4.48
4th quarter	3.7	71.5	3.7	76.3	2.89	2.72	2.56	2.40	4.39	4.47
1995										
1st quarter	-5.8	67.0	-5.9	71.2	2.93	2.75	2.62	2.43	4.49	4.52
2nd quarter	-13.7	47.4	-13.6	50.1	2.94	2.75	2.64	2.44	4.55	4.55
3rd quarter	-20.4	31.7	-26.4	32.8	2.90	2.71	2.60	2.41	4.49	4.50
4th quarter	-4.4	22.8	-6.2	22.9	2.88	2.69	2.58	2.40	4.45	4.46
1996										
1st quarter	1.1	5.8	-2.9	6.2	2.84	2.66	2.55	2.38	4.39	4.42
2nd quarter	11.8	18.6	7.4	19.8	2.81	2.63	2.51	2.35	4.30	4.35
3rd quarter	17.1	34.0	27.4	35.0	2.81	2.65	2.50	2.35	4.29	4.34
4th quarter	4.5	30.2	1.3	31.7	2.76	2.62	2.47	2.33	4.24	4.28
1997										
1st quarter	-0.5	50.3	-10.8	53.3	2.74	2.62	2.45	2.33	4.21	4.28
2nd quarter	0.8	87.6	8.2	95.7	2.73	2.65	2.44	2.36	4.21	4.33
3rd quarter	8.3	59.6	10.1	65.5	2.69	2.63	2.41	2.34	4.14	4.27
4th quarter	4.7	73.1	7.2	79.8	2.70	2.65	2.42	2.37	4.17	4.32
NEW BASIS										
1997										
1st quarter	-0.6	50.3	-9.0	59.3	2.64	2.60	2.36	2.31	3.90	4.12
2nd quarter	0.8	87.6	8.7	104.2	2.63	2.63	2.35	2.34	3.89	4.16
3rd quarter	8.3	59.6	10.0	71.1	2.59	2.61	2.32	2.32	3.83	4.11
4th quarter	4.6	73.1	6.6	87.3	2.60	2.63	2.33	2.35	3.86	4.16
1998										
1st quarter	5.6	99.5	6.2	121.1	2.59	2.66	2.33	2.38	3.88	4.21
2nd quarter	-4.9	42.2	-2.6	51.4	2.54	2.63	2.30	2.35	3.82	4.16
3rd quarter	0.5	51.9	3.0	63.9	2.50	2.63	2.27	2.35	3.76	4.14
4th quarter	3.8	56.2	0.9	69.1	2.46	2.60	2.24	2.32	3.69	4.07
1999										
1st quarter	4.1	79.3	-1.9	97.5	2.47	2.62	2.25	2.35	3.71	4.12
2nd quarter	-0.2	35.3	1.1	43.6	2.45	2.60	2.23	2.33	3.68	4.07
3rd quarter	-9.1	49.6	-12.0	60.6	2.46	2.58	2.24	2.32	3.71	4.06
4th quarter	-5.7	90.0	-3.9	109.1	2.48	2.59	2.27	2.33	3.75	4.08
2000										
1st quarter	-17.7	33.9	-20.5	41.0	2.47	2.56	2.26	2.31	3.75	4.05
2nd quarter	5.9	84.5	6.9	101.4	2.47	2.57	2.26	2.32	3.77	4.08
3rd quarter	-1.1	58.4	-2.3	69.7	2.47	2.58	2.27	2.34	3.79	4.10
4th quarter	7.3	47.0	7.9	56.3	2.50	2.59	2.28	2.34	3.83	4.12

[1]Before 1997, 2005 dollars; 1997 forward, 2009 dollars.

Table 1-8B. Inventory Change and Inventory-Sales Ratios: Historical Data—*Continued*

(Quarterly dollar data are at seasonally adjusted annual rates.)   NIPA Tables 5.7.5B, 5.7.6B, 5.8.5B, 5.8.6B

Year and quarter	Change in private inventories				Ratio, inventories at end of quarter to monthly rate of sales during the quarter					
	Billions of current dollars		Billions of chained dollars [1]		Total private inventories to final sales of domestic business		Nonfarm inventories to final sales of domestic business		Nonfarm inventories to final sales of goods and structures	
	Farm	Nonfarm	Farm	Nonfarm	Current dollars	Chained dollars [1]	Current dollars	Chained dollars [1]	Current dollars	Chained dollars [1]
2001										
1st quarter	5.6	-36.2	6.7	-43.5	2.48	2.57	2.25	2.32	3.80	4.09
2nd quarter	-3.0	-8.6	-3.3	-9.7	2.43	2.56	2.22	2.31	3.72	4.07
3rd quarter	1.8	-31.9	1.7	-38.0	2.40	2.56	2.19	2.31	3.69	4.07
4th quarter	-4.3	-76.6	-4.6	-92.2	2.32	2.51	2.12	2.26	3.55	3.97
2002										
1st quarter	4.1	-4.3	2.7	-6.1	2.33	2.51	2.12	2.26	3.59	3.99
2nd quarter	-10.3	29.5	-10.9	35.8	2.33	2.51	2.13	2.27	3.63	4.03
3rd quarter	-2.9	28.2	-3.7	35.5	2.34	2.51	2.14	2.27	3.65	4.04
4th quarter	-0.8	30.6	-2.0	36.8	2.37	2.53	2.16	2.29	3.71	4.09
2003										
1st quarter	2.8	28.2	3.3	33.0	2.39	2.53	2.17	2.28	3.74	4.07
2nd quarter	-1.4	1.0	-1.0	0.7	2.34	2.49	2.13	2.26	3.67	4.00
3rd quarter	0.9	7.3	0.2	7.4	2.30	2.44	2.08	2.21	3.54	3.87
4th quarter	-2.1	40.5	-1.9	48.6	2.31	2.43	2.09	2.20	3.56	3.86
2004										
1st quarter	4.4	44.4	5.7	50.7	2.34	2.43	2.11	2.20	3.62	3.89
2nd quarter	18.4	57.8	15.7	65.9	2.37	2.45	2.13	2.21	3.66	3.90
3rd quarter	7.7	54.6	8.4	62.8	2.38	2.44	2.15	2.21	3.69	3.89
4th quarter	4.7	63.4	6.0	70.3	2.38	2.44	2.16	2.21	3.71	3.89
2005										
1st quarter	-6.7	106.2	-5.0	115.8	2.40	2.45	2.18	2.22	3.75	3.91
2nd quarter	0.9	29.7	0.8	32.1	2.36	2.43	2.15	2.20	3.69	3.85
3rd quarter	4.3	13.6	3.3	14.9	2.37	2.41	2.16	2.19	3.70	3.82
4th quarter	2.3	87.9	1.9	92.6	2.42	2.44	2.21	2.21	3.81	3.89
2006										
1st quarter	3.7	70.7	1.7	76.9	2.39	2.42	2.19	2.20	3.75	3.83
2nd quarter	-8.1	85.4	-7.3	90.8	2.42	2.44	2.22	2.22	3.82	3.89
3rd quarter	-6.3	83.4	-6.3	87.7	2.45	2.47	2.24	2.25	3.87	3.96
4th quarter	-3.6	42.7	-4.7	46.2	2.43	2.44	2.23	2.23	3.86	3.93
2007										
1st quarter	5.3	14.9	3.2	16.4	2.45	2.44	2.23	2.23	3.90	3.94
2nd quarter	-5.0	52.0	-3.8	53.2	2.46	2.44	2.24	2.23	3.92	3.94
3rd quarter	-2.3	51.0	-2.0	52.3	2.47	2.44	2.25	2.23	3.94	3.95
4th quarter	-0.8	22.8	-1.1	24.1	2.53	2.43	2.30	2.22	4.07	3.93
2008										
1st quarter	-6.9	-13.3	-4.9	-15.0	2.63	2.44	2.40	2.23	4.27	3.98
2nd quarter	3.9	-27.8	2.2	-28.8	2.72	2.42	2.47	2.21	4.41	3.92
3rd quarter	6.6	-25.4	4.6	-25.7	2.70	2.44	2.45	2.23	4.40	3.97
4th quarter	2.8	-67.9	2.7	-70.4	2.52	2.49	2.29	2.27	4.18	4.13
2009										
1st quarter	-0.3	-145.3	-0.7	-144.2	2.45	2.48	2.22	2.26	4.05	4.13
2nd quarter	-1.0	-186.9	-1.0	-189.3	2.42	2.43	2.20	2.21	4.00	4.04
3rd quarter	-5.0	-200.9	-4.2	-201.6	2.37	2.36	2.15	2.14	3.92	3.89
4th quarter	0.0	-50.8	-0.5	-48.8	2.40	2.35	2.19	2.13	4.03	3.89
2010										
1st quarter	-1.3	13.3	-3.0	12.9	2.45	2.35	2.23	2.13	4.12	3.90
2nd quarter	-5.9	56.1	-5.8	54.6	2.43	2.34	2.21	2.13	4.09	3.89
3rd quarter	-11.6	133.2	-9.9	126.8	2.49	2.37	2.25	2.16	4.19	3.97
4th quarter	-10.5	72.8	-9.5	69.1	2.53	2.35	2.28	2.14	4.22	3.92
2011										
1st quarter	0.5	25.7	0.2	25.2	2.64	2.35	2.37	2.15	4.41	3.95
2nd quarter	-1.3	64.3	-0.2	58.9	2.66	2.35	2.39	2.15	4.44	3.95
3rd quarter	3.8	-18.7	2.1	-15.9	2.62	2.32	2.34	2.12	4.34	3.88
4th quarter	5.3	87.4	3.4	78.3	2.62	2.33	2.33	2.13	4.31	3.86
2012										
1st quarter	-8.6	74.0	-6.6	65.8	2.59	2.32	2.31	2.12	4.23	3.83
2nd quarter	-15.3	104.6	-10.3	92.0	2.56	2.33	2.29	2.14	4.18	3.84
3rd quarter	-31.5	105.5	-19.0	97.7	2.60	2.34	2.33	2.16	4.25	3.88
4th quarter	-22.6	41.0	-14.5	35.3	2.60	2.33	2.34	2.16	4.26	3.86
2013										
1st quarter	7.9	28.6	1.8	23.5	2.58	2.32	2.32	2.15	4.23	3.83
2nd quarter	10.4	38.3	5.8	32.9	2.56	2.32	2.31	2.15	4.22	3.83
3rd quarter	14.8	90.7	9.3	84.0	2.55	2.33	2.30	2.16	4.20	3.84
4th quarter	11.9	84.5	9.9	76.6	2.53	2.32	2.29	2.15	4.17	3.81
2014										
1st quarter	2.7	40.0	1.3	36.2	2.58	2.33	2.32	2.16	4.25	3.84
2nd quarter	7.7	81.3	3.6	74.5	2.56	2.33	2.30	2.15	4.21	3.82
3rd quarter	8.0	80.3	5.8	74.5	2.52	2.32	2.27	2.14	4.13	3.79
4th quarter	5.4	83.1	4.2	74.9	2.48	2.32	2.23	2.14	4.09	3.81

[1]Before 1997, 2005 dollars; 1997 forward, 2009 dollars.

Figure 1-3: Shares of Aggregate Final Demand, 1950–2014
(percent of total)

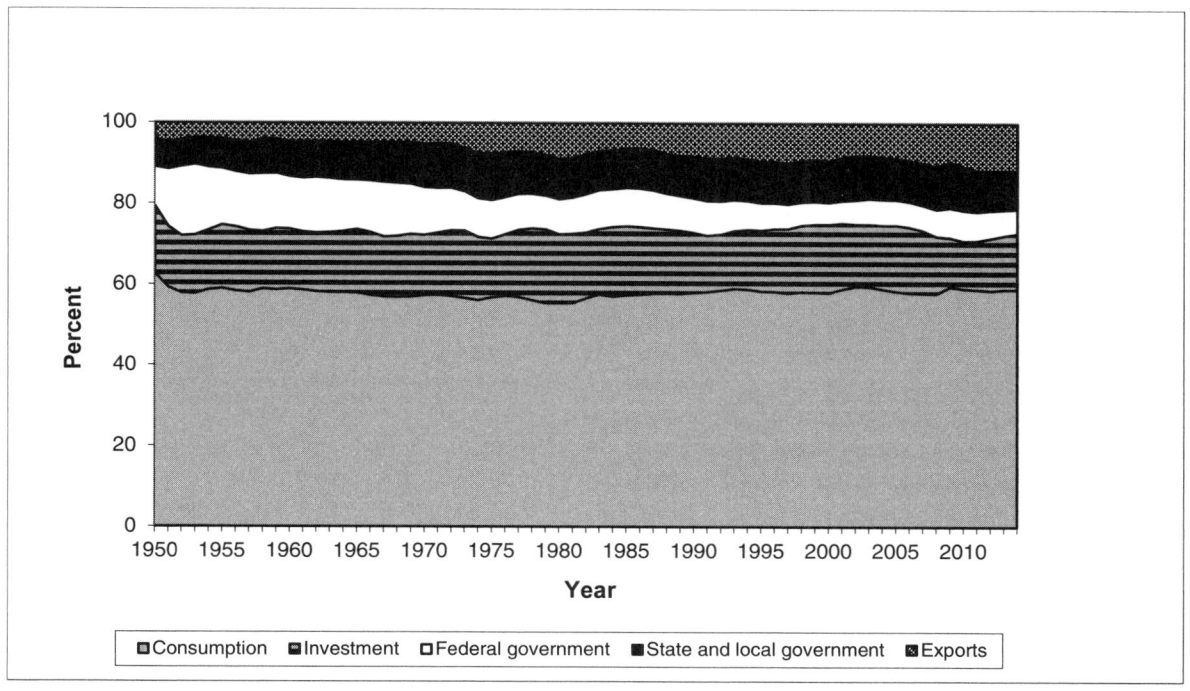

- People often want to know how various sources of demand, especially consumption spending, affect GDP. Often, it is said that consumption "accounts for" about 70 percent, or sometimes two-thirds, of GDP. That is based on a NIPA table showing the components of GDP as a percent of total GDP. In such a calculation, personal consumption expenditures (PCE) amounted to 68.4 percent of total GDP in 2014, up from a range of 60 to 65 percent earlier in the postwar period. (Table 1-1A)

- Is "amounted to" the same as "accounted for"? No, because the value of PCE includes imported goods and services—coffee, cocoa, and bananas; crude oil from the Middle East, transformed into gasoline; clothing, cars, and toys manufactured overseas—even the money that U.S. consumers spend when they travel. These imports included in PCE don't account for demand for U.S. GDP, which excludes imports; instead, they account for demand for GDP in China and other countries that export to us.

- It is not possible with NIPA data to precisely estimate and subtract out the import content of PCE, and so there is no way to precisely estimate PCE's contribution to GDP. What we can do is calculate PCE and the other sources of aggregate final demand for U.S. output as shares of total final demand; this is shown in Table 1-10 and Figure 1-3. These shares also approximate their contributions to GDP (excluding inventory change) if each final demand source has, in aggregate, about the same percentage import content as total GDP.

- Consumption spending has remained under 60 percent of final demand ever since 1951. (It was greater in 1946 through 1950, as consumers made up for wartime deprivations.) It was near 59 percent in each of the past five years; it has been less in years when investment shares were high. The share of exports has nearly tripled, while the federal government direct spending share remains at less than half of its Korean War highs. (This measure of federal spending does not include government financing of medical care and other consumption spending through transfer payment programs such as Social Security and Medicare.) State and local governments increased their share through the early 1970s. Nonresidential and residential investment displays the most cyclical variation in their shares. (Table 1-10)

- The share of imports in the total supply of goods and services in the U.S. market rose from around 4 percent in the 1950s to more than 14 percent in recent years. Only in 2009, the year of maximum inventory liquidation, did the import share temporarily dip back to 12.1 percent. (Table 1-9)

Table 1-9. Shares of Aggregate Supply

(Billions of dollars, quarterly dollar data are at seasonally adjusted rates, percents.)   **NIPA Table 1.1.5**

Year and quarter	Aggregate supply (billions of dollars)			Shares of aggregate supply (percent)	
	Total	GDP	Imports	Domestic production (GDP)	Imports
1950	311.8	300.2	11.6	96.3	3.7
1951	361.9	347.3	14.6	96.0	4.0
1952	383.0	367.7	15.3	96.0	4.0
1953	405.7	389.7	16.0	96.1	3.9
1954	406.5	391.1	15.4	96.2	3.8
1955	443.4	426.2	17.2	96.1	3.9
1956	469.0	450.1	18.9	96.0	4.0
1957	494.8	474.9	19.9	96.0	4.0
1958	502.0	482.0	20.0	96.0	4.0
1959	544.8	522.5	22.3	95.9	4.1
1960	566.1	543.3	22.8	96.0	4.0
1961	586.0	563.3	22.7	96.1	3.9
1962	630.1	605.1	25.0	96.0	4.0
1963	664.7	638.6	26.1	96.1	3.9
1964	713.9	685.8	28.1	96.1	3.9
1965	775.2	743.7	31.5	95.9	4.1
1966	852.1	815.0	37.1	95.6	4.4
1967	901.6	861.7	39.9	95.6	4.4
1968	989.1	942.5	46.6	95.3	4.7
1969	1 070.4	1 019.9	50.5	95.3	4.7
1970	1 131.7	1 075.9	55.8	95.1	4.9
1971	1 230.1	1 167.8	62.3	94.9	5.1
1972	1 356.6	1 282.4	74.2	94.5	5.5
1973	1 519.7	1 428.5	91.2	94.0	6.0
1974	1 676.3	1 548.8	127.5	92.4	7.6
1975	1 811.6	1 688.9	122.7	93.2	6.8
1976	2 028.7	1 877.6	151.1	92.6	7.4
1977	2 268.4	2 086.0	182.4	92.0	8.0
1978	2 568.9	2 356.6	212.3	91.7	8.3
1979	2 884.8	2 632.1	252.7	91.2	8.8
1980	3 156.3	2 862.5	293.8	90.7	9.3
1981	3 528.8	3 211.0	317.8	91.0	9.0
1982	3 648.2	3 345.0	303.2	91.7	8.3
1983	3 966.7	3 638.1	328.6	91.7	8.3
1984	4 445.8	4 040.7	405.1	90.9	9.1
1985	4 763.9	4 346.7	417.2	91.2	8.8
1986	5 043.1	4 590.2	452.9	91.0	9.0
1987	5 378.9	4 870.2	508.7	90.5	9.5
1988	5 806.6	5 252.6	554.0	90.5	9.5
1989	6 248.7	5 657.7	591.0	90.5	9.5
1990	6 609.3	5 979.6	629.7	90.5	9.5
1991	6 797.5	6 174.0	623.5	90.8	9.2
1992	7 207.1	6 539.3	667.8	90.7	9.3
1993	7 598.7	6 878.7	720.0	90.5	9.5
1994	8 122.2	7 308.8	813.4	90.0	10.0
1995	8 566.7	7 664.1	902.6	89.5	10.5
1996	9 064.2	8 100.2	964.0	89.4	10.6
1997	9 664.3	8 608.5	1 055.8	89.1	10.9
1998	10 204.9	9 089.2	1 115.7	89.1	10.9
1999	10 909.2	9 660.6	1 248.6	88.6	11.4
2000	11 757.4	10 284.8	1 472.6	87.5	12.5
2001	12 017.2	10 621.8	1 395.4	88.4	11.6
2002	12 406.5	10 977.5	1 429.0	88.5	11.5
2003	13 054.6	11 510.7	1 543.9	88.2	11.8
2004	14 075.6	12 274.9	1 800.7	87.2	12.8
2005	15 123.8	13 093.7	2 030.1	86.6	13.4
2006	16 103.2	13 855.9	2 247.3	86.0	14.0
2007	16 860.8	14 477.6	2 383.2	85.9	14.1
2008	17 283.6	14 718.6	2 565.0	85.2	14.8
2009	16 401.9	14 418.7	1 983.2	87.9	12.1
2010	17 329.4	14 964.4	2 365.0	86.4	13.6
2011	18 204.3	15 517.9	2 686.4	85.2	14.8
2012	18 919.1	16 155.3	2 763.8	85.4	14.6
2013	19 434.9	16 663.2	2 771.7	85.7	14.3
2014	20 220.0	17 348.1	2 871.9	85.8	14.2
2012					
1st quarter	18 758.2	15 973.9	2 784.3	85.2	14.8
2nd quarter	18 902.6	16 121.9	2 780.7	85.3	14.7
3rd quarter	18 972.4	16 227.9	2 744.5	85.5	14.5
4th quarter	19 043.1	16 297.3	2 745.8	85.6	14.4
2013					
1st quarter	19 196.5	16 440.7	2 755.8	85.6	14.4
2nd quarter	19 292.2	16 526.8	2 765.4	85.7	14.3
3rd quarter	19 504.2	16 727.5	2 776.7	85.8	14.2
4th quarter	19 746.4	16 957.6	2 788.8	85.9	14.1
2014					
1st quarter	19 815.1	16 984.3	2 830.8	85.7	14.3
2nd quarter	20 157.0	17 270.0	2 887.0	85.7	14.3
3rd quarter	20 397.3	17 522.1	2 875.2	85.9	14.1
4th quarter	20 510.5	17 615.9	2 894.6	85.9	14.1

Table 1-10. Shares of Aggregate Final Demand

(Billions of dollars, quarterly dollar data are at seasonally adjusted rates, percents.)

NIPA Table 1.1.5

Year and quarter	Aggregate final demand (billions of dollars)							Shares of aggregate final demand (percent)					
	Total	Consumption (PCE)	Nonresidential fixed investment	Residential investment	Exports	Government consumption and gross investment		PCE	Nonresidential investment	Residential investment	Exports	Federal government	State and local government
						Federal	State and local						
1950	306.1	192.2	30.0	20.7	12.4	29.5	21.3	62.8	9.8	6.8	4.1	9.6	7.0
1951	352.1	208.5	34.2	18.7	17.1	50.0	23.6	59.2	9.7	5.3	4.9	14.2	6.7
1952	379.6	219.5	34.9	18.9	16.5	64.8	25.0	57.8	9.2	5.0	4.3	17.1	6.6
1953	403.8	233.0	38.8	19.7	15.3	70.3	26.7	57.7	9.6	4.9	3.8	17.4	6.6
1954	408.5	239.9	38.6	21.4	15.8	63.3	29.5	58.7	9.4	5.2	3.9	15.5	7.2
1955	438.4	258.7	43.4	25.4	17.7	61.0	32.2	59.0	9.9	5.8	4.0	13.9	7.3
1956	465.1	271.6	49.7	24.0	21.3	63.1	35.4	58.4	10.7	5.2	4.6	13.6	7.6
1957	493.9	286.7	53.1	22.6	24.0	68.4	39.1	58.0	10.8	4.6	4.9	13.8	7.9
1958	502.4	296.0	48.5	22.8	20.6	71.5	43.0	58.9	9.7	4.5	4.1	14.2	8.6
1959	540.7	317.5	53.1	28.6	22.7	73.5	45.3	58.7	9.8	5.3	4.2	13.6	8.4
1960	562.9	331.6	56.4	26.9	27.0	72.8	48.2	58.9	10.0	4.8	4.8	12.9	8.6
1961	583.1	342.0	56.6	27.0	27.6	77.4	52.5	58.7	9.7	4.6	4.7	13.3	9.0
1962	623.9	363.1	61.2	29.6	29.1	85.5	55.4	58.2	9.8	4.7	4.7	13.7	8.9
1963	659.1	382.5	64.8	32.9	31.1	87.8	60.0	58.0	9.8	5.0	4.7	13.3	9.1
1964	709.0	411.2	72.2	35.1	35.0	90.2	65.3	58.0	10.2	5.0	4.9	12.7	9.2
1965	765.9	443.6	85.2	35.2	37.1	93.1	71.7	57.9	11.1	4.6	4.8	12.2	9.4
1966	838.4	480.6	97.2	33.4	40.9	106.5	79.8	57.3	11.6	4.0	4.9	12.7	9.5
1967	891.8	507.4	99.2	33.6	43.5	120.0	88.1	56.9	11.1	3.8	4.9	13.5	9.9
1968	979.9	557.4	107.7	40.2	47.9	127.9	98.8	56.9	11.0	4.1	4.9	13.1	10.1
1969	1 061.2	604.5	120.0	44.4	51.9	131.1	109.3	57.0	11.3	4.2	4.9	12.4	10.3
1970	1 129.5	647.7	124.6	43.4	59.7	132.7	121.4	57.3	11.0	3.8	5.3	11.7	10.7
1971	1 221.9	701.0	130.4	58.2	63.0	134.4	134.9	57.4	10.7	4.8	5.2	11.0	11.0
1972	1 347.4	769.4	146.6	72.4	70.8	141.5	146.7	57.1	10.9	5.4	5.3	10.5	10.9
1973	1 503.8	851.1	172.7	78.3	95.3	145.6	160.8	56.6	11.5	5.2	6.3	9.7	10.7
1974	1 662.4	932.0	191.1	69.5	126.7	158.1	185.0	56.1	11.5	4.2	7.6	9.5	11.1
1975	1 818.0	1 032.8	196.8	66.7	138.7	172.8	210.2	56.8	10.8	3.7	7.6	9.5	11.6
1976	2 011.7	1 150.2	219.3	86.8	149.5	183.8	222.1	57.2	10.9	4.3	7.4	9.1	11.0
1977	2 246.2	1 276.7	259.1	115.2	159.4	198.8	237.0	56.8	11.5	5.1	7.1	8.9	10.6
1978	2 543.1	1 426.2	314.6	138.0	186.9	216.7	260.7	56.1	12.4	5.4	7.3	8.5	10.3
1979	2 866.7	1 589.5	373.8	147.8	230.1	237.7	287.8	55.4	13.0	5.2	8.0	8.3	10.0
1980	3 162.7	1 754.6	406.9	129.5	280.8	272.4	318.5	55.5	12.9	4.1	8.9	8.6	10.1
1981	3 498.8	1 937.5	472.9	128.5	305.2	311.7	343.0	55.4	13.5	3.7	8.7	8.9	9.8
1982	3 663.0	2 073.9	485.1	110.8	283.2	345.6	364.4	56.6	13.2	3.0	7.7	9.4	9.9
1983	3 972.6	2 286.5	482.2	161.1	277.0	380.2	385.6	57.6	12.1	4.1	7.0	9.6	9.7
1984	4 380.4	2 498.2	564.3	190.4	302.4	407.6	417.5	57.0	12.9	4.3	6.9	9.3	9.5
1985	4 742.2	2 722.7	607.7	200.1	303.2	449.3	459.2	57.4	12.8	4.2	6.4	9.5	9.7
1986	5 036.5	2 898.4	607.8	234.8	321.0	478.4	496.1	57.5	12.1	4.7	6.4	9.5	9.9
1987	5 351.7	3 092.1	615.2	249.8	363.9	500.2	530.5	57.8	11.5	4.7	6.8	9.3	9.9
1988	5 788.1	3 346.9	662.3	256.2	444.6	508.8	569.3	57.8	11.4	4.4	7.7	8.8	9.8
1989	6 221.0	3 592.8	716.0	256.0	504.3	531.4	620.5	57.8	11.5	4.1	8.1	8.5	10.0
1990	6 594.7	3 825.6	739.2	239.7	551.9	560.0	678.3	58.0	11.2	3.6	8.4	8.5	10.3
1991	6 798.0	3 960.2	723.6	221.2	594.9	580.7	717.4	58.3	10.6	3.3	8.8	8.5	10.6
1992	7 190.8	4 215.7	741.9	254.7	633.1	586.6	758.8	58.6	10.3	3.5	8.8	8.2	10.6
1993	7 577.9	4 471.0	799.2	286.8	654.8	578.4	787.7	59.0	10.5	3.8	8.6	7.6	10.4
1994	8 058.4	4 741.0	868.9	323.8	720.9	572.7	831.1	58.8	10.8	4.0	8.9	7.1	10.3
1995	8 535.5	4 984.2	962.2	324.1	812.8	575.4	876.8	58.4	11.3	3.8	9.5	6.7	10.3
1996	9 033.4	5 268.1	1 043.2	358.1	867.6	578.2	918.2	58.3	11.5	4.0	9.6	6.4	10.2
1997	9 593.4	5 560.7	1 149.1	375.6	953.8	582.4	971.8	58.0	12.0	3.9	9.9	6.1	10.1
1998	10 141.1	5 903.0	1 252.8	418.8	953.0	584.1	1 029.4	58.2	12.4	4.1	9.4	5.8	10.2
1999	10 848.4	6 307.0	1 361.6	461.8	992.0	610.4	1 115.6	58.1	12.6	4.3	9.1	5.6	10.3
2000	11 702.8	6 792.4	1 493.8	485.4	1 096.8	632.4	1 202.0	58.0	12.8	4.1	9.4	5.4	10.3
2001	12 055.4	7 103.1	1 453.9	513.0	1 026.7	669.2	1 289.5	58.9	12.1	4.3	8.5	5.6	10.7
2002	12 388.0	7 384.1	1 348.9	557.6	1 002.5	740.6	1 354.3	59.6	10.9	4.5	8.1	6.0	10.9
2003	13 035.2	7 765.5	1 371.7	636.9	1 040.3	824.8	1 396.0	59.6	10.5	4.9	8.0	6.3	10.7
2004	14 011.7	8 260.0	1 463.1	749.7	1 181.5	892.4	1 465.0	59.0	10.4	5.4	8.4	6.4	10.5
2005	15 064.3	8 794.1	1 611.5	856.1	1 308.9	946.3	1 547.4	58.4	10.7	5.7	8.7	6.3	10.3
2006	16 036.2	9 304.0	1 776.3	837.4	1 476.3	1 002.0	1 640.2	58.0	11.1	5.2	9.2	6.2	10.2
2007	16 826.4	9 750.5	1 920.6	688.7	1 664.6	1 049.8	1 752.2	57.9	11.4	4.1	9.9	6.2	10.4
2008	17 315.6	10 013.6	1 941.0	515.9	1 841.9	1 155.6	1 847.6	57.8	11.2	3.0	10.6	6.7	10.7
2009	16 549.4	9 847.0	1 633.4	392.2	1 587.7	1 217.7	1 871.4	59.5	9.9	2.4	9.6	7.4	11.3
2010	17 267.9	10 202.2	1 658.2	381.1	1 852.3	1 303.9	1 870.2	59.1	9.6	2.2	10.7	7.6	10.8
2011	18 162.6	10 689.3	1 812.1	386.0	2 106.4	1 303.5	1 865.3	58.9	10.0	2.1	11.6	7.2	10.3
2012	18 857.3	11 050.6	2 007.7	442.2	2 198.2	1 292.5	1 866.1	58.6	10.6	2.3	11.7	6.9	9.9
2013	19 363.0	11 392.3	2 084.3	508.9	2 263.3	1 230.6	1 883.6	58.8	10.8	2.6	11.7	6.4	9.7
2014	20 142.9	11 865.9	2 233.7	549.2	2 341.9	1 219.9	1 932.3	58.9	11.1	2.7	11.6	6.1	9.6
2012													
1st quarter	18 692.6	10 956.2	1 971.5	423.8	2 169.6	1 300.5	1 871.0	58.6	10.5	2.3	11.6	7.0	10.0
2nd quarter	18 813.3	11 008.3	2 016.2	429.4	2 199.8	1 293.7	1 865.9	58.5	10.7	2.3	11.7	6.9	9.9
3rd quarter	18 898.4	11 073.6	2 011.7	444.1	2 209.4	1 297.0	1 862.6	58.6	10.6	2.3	11.7	6.9	9.9
4th quarter	19 024.7	11 164.3	2 031.2	471.7	2 214.0	1 278.9	1 864.6	58.7	10.7	2.5	11.6	6.7	9.8
2013													
1st quarter	19 159.9	11 271.8	2 052.1	489.6	2 226.6	1 250.4	1 869.4	58.8	10.7	2.6	11.6	6.5	9.8
2nd quarter	19 243.5	11 322.8	2 064.6	507.1	2 237.6	1 234.2	1 877.2	58.8	10.7	2.6	11.6	6.4	9.8
3rd quarter	19 398.6	11 417.7	2 085.9	520.0	2 264.3	1 220.4	1 890.3	58.9	10.8	2.7	11.7	6.3	9.7
4th quarter	19 650.0	11 556.9	2 134.5	519.0	2 324.5	1 217.6	1 897.5	58.8	10.9	2.6	11.8	6.2	9.7
2014													
1st quarter	19 772.4	11 640.3	2 181.9	526.4	2 301.5	1 214.8	1 907.5	58.9	11.0	2.7	11.6	6.1	9.6
2nd quarter	20 068.1	11 813.0	2 211.7	540.9	2 356.2	1 216.9	1 929.4	58.9	11.0	2.7	11.7	6.1	9.6
3rd quarter	20 308.9	11 949.1	2 267.0	554.8	2 360.6	1 233.1	1 944.3	58.8	11.2	2.7	11.6	6.1	9.6
4th quarter	20 422.1	12 061.4	2 274.1	574.6	2 349.5	1 214.7	1 947.8	59.1	11.1	2.8	11.5	5.9	9.5

Section 1b: Income and Value Added

Figure 1-4: Shares of Income, 1959–2014

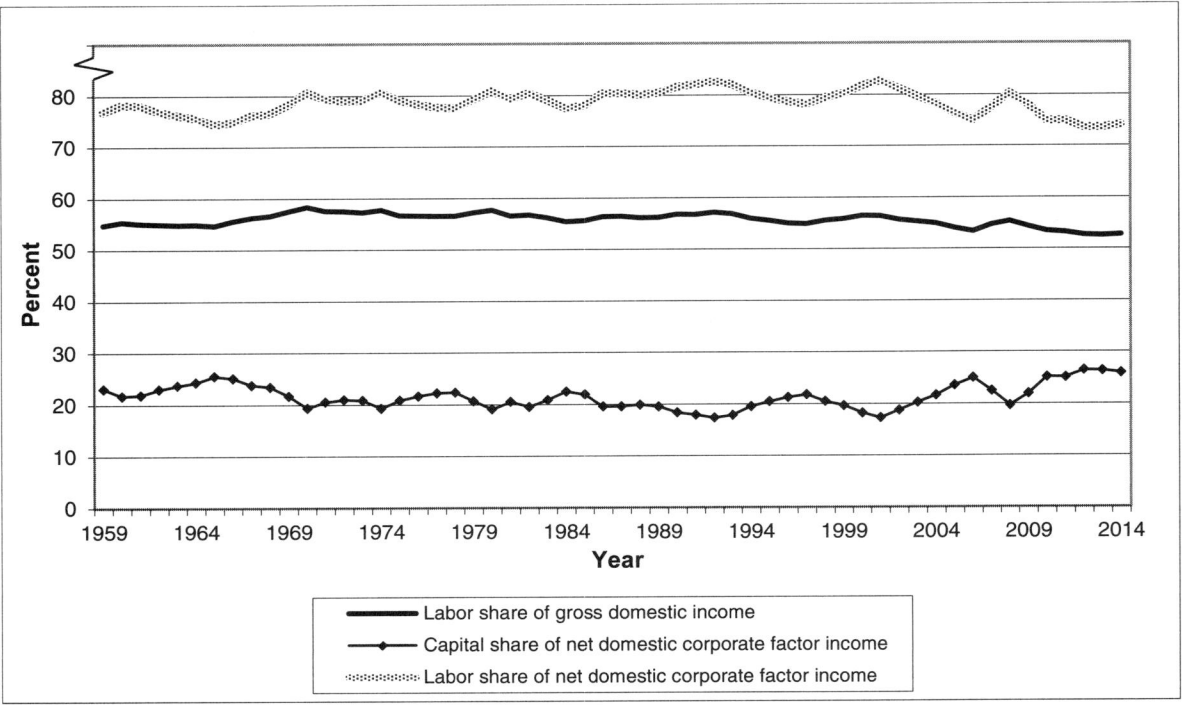

Legend:
— Labor share of gross domestic income
—♦— Capital share of net domestic corporate factor income
········· Labor share of net domestic corporate factor income

- Recent years have seen a decline in the share of national income paid to workers—not just the share paid out as worker wages, but in total compensation, including all health and other benefits. One indicator of this can be seen in a later chapter, in Tables 9-3A and B, where Bureau of Labor Statistics calculations (based on BEA data) document a declining labor share in the value of output of private nonfarm business. In the tables in Section 1b immediately following this page, BEA compilations show the composition of domestic income, national income, and corporate value added. Table 1-16 shows income share percentages calculated by the editors based on these data. Labor shares rise temporarily in recession years (when the "pie" is smaller) but aside from that effect they have declined over much of the period, and the decline has accelerated in recent years.

- Employee compensation has fallen since the early 1970s to a record low of 52.5 percent in 2013, as shown in the middle line in Figure 1-4. One factor in this decline has been a rising share of output required to replace used-up capital ("consumption of fixed capital"), reflecting increased use of capital per unit of production. In addition, the "net operating surplus," which is largely profits, interest, and proprietor's income, reached a new peak in 2013. In 2014, employee compensation increased slightly to 52.7 percent of gross domestic income. (Tables 1-12 and 1-16)

- Narrowing the focus to the corporate business sector, net income shares become clearer. (Proprietor's, i.e. unincorporated business; income includes a labor compensation component of uncertain size.) Total net factor income (that is, net of capital consumption) can be completely attributed to either labor or capital. These shares are also charted in Figure 1-4. Between 1959 and 2004, the shares vary cyclically but seem stable over time, averaging 79 percent for labor and 21 percent for capital. Since then, they have broken out of that range. The capital share did dip in 2008 to 19.7, to a level higher than in any previous recession, and it reached a new high of 26.4 percent in 2012, with a corresponding new low of 73.6 percent for workers. (Tables 1-14 and 1-16) By 2014, capital shares fell 1.5 percent.

Table 1-11. Relation of Gross Domestic Product, Gross and Net National Product, National Income, and Personal Income

(Billions of dollars, quarterly data are at seasonally adjusted annual rates.) **NIPA Table 1.7.5**

Year and quarter	Gross domestic product	Plus: Income receipts from the rest of the world	Less: Income payments to the rest of the world	Equals: Gross national product	Less: Consumption of fixed capital									Equals: Net national product
					Total	Private					Government			
						Total	Domestic business			House-holds and institutions	Total	General govern-ment	Govern-ment enter-prises	
							Total	Capital consump-tion allow-ances	Less: Capital consump-tion ad-justment					
1955	426.2	3.5	1.1	428.6	48.9	35.0	28.9	28.3	-0.6	6.1	13.9	13.1	0.8	379.7
1956	450.1	3.9	1.1	452.9	54.1	38.8	32.2	30.8	-1.3	6.6	15.3	14.5	0.9	398.8
1957	474.9	4.3	1.2	477.9	58.9	42.3	35.2	33.5	-1.7	7.1	16.7	15.7	0.9	419.0
1958	482.0	3.9	1.2	484.7	62.4	44.9	37.5	35.3	-2.3	7.4	17.5	16.5	1.0	422.2
1959	522.5	4.3	1.5	525.2	65.4	46.8	39.0	37.5	-1.5	7.8	18.6	17.6	1.0	459.8
1960	543.3	4.9	1.8	546.4	67.9	48.2	40.0	39.7	-0.3	8.2	19.7	18.6	1.1	478.5
1961	563.3	5.3	1.8	566.8	70.6	49.8	41.3	41.7	0.4	8.5	20.8	19.7	1.2	496.2
1962	605.1	5.9	1.8	609.2	74.1	51.8	42.9	46.6	3.6	8.8	22.3	21.1	1.2	535.1
1963	638.6	6.5	2.1	643.1	78.0	54.2	44.9	49.9	5.0	9.3	23.8	22.5	1.3	565.1
1964	685.8	7.2	2.3	690.7	82.4	57.3	47.4	53.2	5.8	9.9	25.1	23.7	1.4	608.3
1965	743.7	7.9	2.6	749.0	88.0	61.6	50.9	57.0	6.1	10.7	26.4	24.9	1.5	661.0
1966	815.0	8.1	3.0	820.1	95.3	67.2	55.6	61.9	6.2	11.5	28.1	26.5	1.6	724.8
1967	861.7	8.7	3.3	867.1	103.5	73.3	60.9	66.9	6.0	12.4	30.2	28.4	1.8	763.6
1968	942.5	10.1	4.0	948.6	113.3	80.6	67.0	72.5	5.6	13.6	32.7	30.8	2.0	835.2
1969	1 019.9	11.8	5.7	1 026.0	124.9	89.4	74.2	79.7	5.5	15.2	35.4	33.2	2.2	901.1
1970	1 075.9	12.8	6.4	1 082.3	136.8	98.3	81.8	85.9	4.1	16.5	38.5	36.1	2.5	945.5
1971	1 167.8	14.0	6.4	1 175.4	148.9	107.6	89.4	92.3	2.9	18.2	41.2	38.4	2.8	1 026.5
1972	1 282.4	16.3	7.7	1 291.0	160.9	117.5	97.2	102.3	5.2	20.3	43.4	40.3	3.1	1 130.1
1973	1 428.5	23.5	10.9	1 441.2	178.1	131.5	108.2	111.9	3.7	23.3	46.6	43.1	3.5	1 263.1
1974	1 548.8	29.8	14.3	1 564.3	206.2	153.2	126.1	123.9	-2.2	27.0	53.0	48.7	4.3	1 358.2
1975	1 688.9	28.0	15.0	1 701.9	237.5	178.8	147.9	135.9	-12.0	30.9	58.7	53.7	5.1	1 464.4
1976	1 877.6	32.4	15.5	1 894.4	259.2	196.5	162.2	147.4	-14.8	34.3	62.7	57.2	5.5	1 635.2
1977	2 086.0	37.2	16.9	2 106.2	288.3	221.1	181.5	167.0	-14.5	39.6	67.2	61.2	6.0	1 817.9
1978	2 356.6	46.3	24.7	2 378.2	325.1	252.1	205.5	189.4	-16.2	46.6	72.9	66.3	6.7	2 053.1
1979	2 632.1	68.3	36.4	2 664.1	371.1	290.7	236.4	216.1	-20.2	54.4	80.4	72.8	7.6	2 292.9
1980	2 862.5	79.1	44.9	2 896.7	426.0	335.0	272.8	245.8	-26.9	62.2	91.0	82.3	8.8	2 470.7
1981	3 211.0	92.0	59.1	3 243.9	485.0	381.9	313.5	301.2	-12.3	68.5	103.1	93.1	10.0	2 758.8
1982	3 345.0	101.0	64.5	3 381.5	534.3	420.4	347.5	343.1	-4.4	72.9	113.9	103.1	10.9	2 847.2
1983	3 638.1	101.9	64.8	3 675.2	560.5	438.8	362.8	385.6	22.8	76.0	121.8	110.3	11.5	3 114.7
1984	4 040.7	121.9	85.6	4 077.0	594.3	463.5	382.7	435.6	52.9	80.9	130.8	118.7	12.2	3 482.6
1985	4 346.7	112.7	87.3	4 372.1	636.7	496.4	410.3	493.5	83.2	86.2	140.2	127.3	12.9	3 735.4
1986	4 590.2	111.3	94.4	4 607.1	682.2	531.6	438.1	512.0	73.9	93.4	150.6	136.8	13.8	3 924.9
1987	4 870.2	123.3	105.8	4 887.7	728.0	566.3	464.5	533.1	68.6	101.8	161.6	147.0	14.6	4 159.8
1988	5 252.6	152.1	129.5	5 275.3	782.4	608.3	498.4	563.7	65.3	109.9	174.1	158.5	15.6	4 492.9
1989	5 657.7	177.7	152.9	5 682.5	836.1	650.1	531.8	589.5	57.7	118.2	186.0	169.3	16.7	4 846.4
1990	5 979.6	188.9	154.2	6 014.3	886.8	689.0	563.9	596.0	32.1	125.1	197.8	180.0	17.9	5 127.5
1991	6 174.0	168.4	136.8	6 205.6	931.1	722.4	591.8	611.6	19.8	130.6	208.8	189.9	18.8	5 274.5
1992	6 539.3	152.1	121.0	6 570.4	959.7	744.2	607.9	628.4	20.5	136.3	215.6	195.8	19.8	5 610.7
1993	6 878.7	155.6	123.6	6 910.7	1 003.6	780.0	634.2	658.9	24.7	145.7	223.6	202.5	21.1	5 907.1
1994	7 308.8	184.5	160.7	7 332.6	1 055.6	824.3	669.0	701.6	32.6	155.3	231.2	208.9	22.4	6 277.0
1995	7 664.1	229.8	201.1	7 692.8	1 122.8	882.6	717.8	753.9	36.2	164.8	240.2	216.6	23.6	6 570.0
1996	8 100.2	246.4	214.6	8 132.0	1 176.0	931.0	758.4	808.3	50.0	172.7	245.0	220.4	24.6	6 956.0
1997	8 608.5	280.1	256.0	8 632.6	1 240.0	990.1	807.9	877.0	69.1	182.1	249.9	224.6	25.3	7 392.7
1998	9 089.2	286.8	268.5	9 107.4	1 310.3	1 054.9	860.4	941.4	81.0	194.5	255.3	228.9	26.4	7 797.1
1999	9 660.6	321.4	294.3	9 687.8	1 400.9	1 135.9	925.0	1 023.8	98.9	210.9	264.9	236.9	28.0	8 286.9
2000	10 284.8	382.7	345.7	10 321.8	1 514.2	1 236.6	1 006.5	1 096.1	89.5	230.1	277.7	247.7	30.0	8 807.5
2001	10 621.8	325.3	273.5	10 673.6	1 604.0	1 317.7	1 067.5	1 180.1	112.6	250.2	286.3	254.9	31.4	9 069.6
2002	10 977.5	315.8	267.2	11 026.1	1 662.1	1 368.0	1 101.4	1 284.9	183.5	266.6	294.1	261.2	32.9	9 364.0
2003	11 510.7	356.1	289.0	11 577.8	1 727.2	1 422.4	1 131.6	1 305.4	173.9	290.8	304.9	270.3	34.6	9 850.6
2004	12 274.9	451.4	362.3	12 364.1	1 831.7	1 509.3	1 185.9	1 335.4	149.4	323.4	322.4	284.9	37.5	10 532.4
2005	13 093.7	575.8	483.2	13 186.3	1 982.0	1 635.3	1 273.2	1 174.2	-99.0	362.1	346.7	305.6	41.0	11 204.3
2006	13 855.9	724.2	656.6	13 923.5	2 136.0	1 765.0	1 368.8	1 250.0	-118.8	396.2	371.0	326.6	44.4	11 787.5
2007	14 477.6	875.7	750.1	14 603.2	2 264.4	1 865.0	1 451.2	1 330.0	-121.2	413.7	399.4	351.4	48.0	12 338.9
2008	14 718.6	856.9	684.9	14 890.6	2 363.4	1 936.9	1 522.3	1 584.7	62.4	414.6	426.5	375.5	51.0	12 527.2
2009	14 418.7	648.9	497.8	14 569.8	2 368.4	1 925.7	1 522.4	1 558.6	36.2	403.3	442.7	390.3	52.5	12 201.4
2010	14 964.4	720.0	514.1	15 170.3	2 381.6	1 923.5	1 523.0	1 599.9	76.9	400.5	458.1	403.8	54.3	12 788.8
2011	15 517.9	792.6	546.0	15 764.6	2 450.6	1 971.1	1 572.8	1 823.4	250.6	398.2	479.6	422.1	57.5	13 313.9
2012	16 155.3	801.5	563.9	16 392.8	2 534.2	2 038.0	1 633.4	1 652.2	18.8	404.6	496.2	436.1	60.1	13 858.6
2013	16 663.2	826.2	575.8	16 913.5	2 632.8	2 126.6	1 699.4	1 735.0	35.6	427.2	506.2	444.2	62.1	14 280.7
2014	17 348.1	854.3	591.2	17 611.2	2 746.7	2 229.9	1 775.2	1 815.6	40.4	454.8	516.8	452.6	64.2	14 864.5
2012														
1st quarter	15 973.9	809.7	558.5	16 225.1	2 501.2	2 010.2	1 610.9	1 613.8	2.9	399.4	491.0	431.8	59.3	13 723.8
2nd quarter	16 121.9	786.5	555.0	16 353.3	2 524.4	2 029.1	1 627.2	1 638.0	10.8	401.9	495.3	435.4	59.9	13 828.9
3rd quarter	16 227.9	804.9	567.8	16 465.0	2 546.5	2 047.9	1 641.6	1 664.2	22.6	406.3	498.6	438.2	60.4	13 918.5
4th quarter	16 297.3	805.0	574.4	16 528.0	2 564.7	2 064.7	1 653.9	1 692.9	39.1	410.8	500.0	439.2	60.9	13 963.3
2013														
1st quarter	16 440.7	805.2	584.1	16 661.7	2 589.7	2 087.6	1 670.4	1 696.8	26.4	417.2	502.1	440.8	61.3	14 072.1
2nd quarter	16 526.8	825.8	578.6	16 774.0	2 618.3	2 113.4	1 690.2	1 725.2	34.9	423.1	505.0	443.1	61.9	14 155.7
3rd quarter	16 727.5	833.2	569.3	16 991.4	2 645.7	2 138.4	1 708.3	1 748.9	40.5	430.1	507.3	445.0	62.3	14 345.7
4th quarter	16 957.6	840.5	571.2	17 226.9	2 677.6	2 167.1	1 728.7	1 769.2	40.5	438.4	510.5	447.7	62.8	14 549.3
2014														
1st quarter	16 984.3	840.0	581.2	17 243.1	2 708.3	2 195.2	1 747.2	1 787.6	40.4	448.0	513.1	449.8	63.3	14 534.8
2nd quarter	17 270.0	850.4	593.3	17 527.0	2 732.8	2 217.3	1 766.4	1 804.9	38.5	450.9	515.5	451.6	63.9	14 794.3
3rd quarter	17 522.1	869.7	597.8	17 794.0	2 761.5	2 243.1	1 785.7	1 824.5	38.8	457.4	518.4	453.8	64.5	15 032.5
4th quarter	17 615.9	857.0	592.3	17 880.6	2 784.2	2 264.0	1 801.3	1 845.3	44.0	462.8	520.2	455.2	65.0	15 096.3

Table 1-11. Relation of Gross Domestic Product, Gross and Net National Product, National Income, and Personal Income—Continued

(Billions of dollars, quarterly data are at seasonally adjusted annual rates.)

NIPA Table 1.7.5

Year and quarter	Net national product	Less: Statistical discrepancy	Equals: National income	Less: Corporate profits with IVA and CCAdj	Less: Taxes on production and imports less subsidies	Less: Contributions for government social insurance, domestic	Less: Net interest and miscellaneous payments on assets	Less: Business current transfer payments, net	Less: Current surplus of government enterprises	Plus: Personal income receipts on assets	Plus: Personal current transfer receipts	Equals: Personal income	Addendum: Gross national income
1955	379.7	2.1	377.6	50.2	31.3	9.1	6.3	1.3	. . .	29.4	15.7	324.6	426.5
1956	398.8	-2.1	400.9	49.6	33.5	10.0	6.9	1.7	. . .	32.4	16.8	348.4	455.0
1957	419.0	-0.4	419.4	49.1	35.5	11.4	8.1	1.8	. . .	35.6	19.5	368.5	478.3
1958	422.2	0.6	421.6	43.9	36.4	11.4	9.6	1.7	. . .	37.3	23.5	379.5	484.1
1959	459.8	0.1	459.6	55.5	40.0	13.8	9.7	1.7	0.5	40.6	24.2	403.2	525.1
1960	478.5	-1.4	479.9	54.7	43.4	16.4	10.7	1.7	0.5	44.3	25.7	422.5	547.8
1961	496.2	-1.0	497.2	55.9	45.0	17.0	12.6	1.9	0.3	47.2	29.5	441.1	567.8
1962	535.1	-0.1	535.2	64.0	48.1	19.1	14.3	2.1	0.4	51.6	30.4	469.1	609.3
1963	565.1	-1.5	566.6	70.5	51.2	21.7	15.3	2.5	0.8	56.0	32.2	492.8	644.6
1964	608.3	0.0	608.3	77.7	54.5	22.4	17.5	3.0	0.8	62.5	33.5	528.4	690.7
1965	661.0	0.8	660.3	89.3	57.7	23.4	19.8	3.5	0.7	68.7	36.2	570.8	748.2
1966	724.8	5.1	719.7	96.1	59.3	31.3	22.5	3.4	0.3	74.2	39.6	620.6	815.0
1967	763.6	3.4	760.2	93.9	64.1	34.9	25.7	3.6	0.2	79.8	48.0	665.7	863.7
1968	835.2	3.2	832.1	101.7	72.2	38.7	27.6	4.2	0.3	87.3	56.1	730.7	945.4
1969	901.1	1.6	899.5	98.4	79.3	44.1	33.6	4.8	0.0	98.7	62.3	800.3	1 024.4
1970	945.5	5.3	940.1	86.2	86.6	46.4	40.5	4.4	-1.2	112.7	74.7	864.6	1 076.9
1971	1 026.5	9.5	1 017.0	100.6	95.8	51.2	45.2	4.2	-1.7	122.3	88.1	932.1	1 165.9
1972	1 130.1	7.1	1 123.0	117.2	101.3	59.2	49.3	4.8	-1.2	133.3	97.9	1 023.6	1 283.9
1973	1 263.1	6.1	1 257.0	133.4	112.0	75.5	57.2	5.7	-2.2	150.6	112.6	1 138.5	1 435.1
1974	1 358.2	7.4	1 350.8	125.7	121.6	85.2	73.5	6.8	-2.7	175.4	133.3	1 249.3	1 556.9
1975	1 464.4	13.2	1 451.1	138.9	130.8	89.3	85.9	9.0	-4.4	195.3	170.0	1 366.9	1 688.7
1976	1 635.2	20.5	1 614.8	174.3	141.3	101.3	89.9	9.1	-2.7	212.6	184.3	1 498.5	1 874.0
1977	1 817.9	19.3	1 798.7	205.8	152.6	113.1	105.9	8.1	-3.3	243.4	194.6	1 654.6	2 087.0
1978	2 053.1	23.2	2 029.9	238.6	162.0	131.3	118.8	10.4	-2.8	278.0	209.9	1 859.7	2 355.0
1979	2 292.9	44.8	2 248.2	249.0	171.6	152.7	141.0	12.8	-3.2	318.3	235.6	2 078.2	2 619.3
1980	2 470.7	43.9	2 426.8	223.6	190.5	166.2	186.2	14.0	-5.1	386.0	280.1	2 317.5	2 852.8
1981	2 758.8	36.7	2 722.1	247.5	224.2	195.7	238.4	16.9	-5.2	472.9	319.0	2 596.5	3 207.2
1982	2 847.2	6.8	2 840.4	229.9	225.9	208.9	277.5	19.3	-3.8	541.3	355.5	2 779.5	3 374.7
1983	3 114.7	54.2	3 060.5	279.8	242.0	226.0	291.8	21.7	-2.3	584.3	384.3	2 970.3	3 621.1
1984	3 482.6	38.7	3 444.0	337.9	268.7	257.5	336.1	29.2	-1.4	665.1	400.6	3 281.8	4 038.3
1985	3 735.4	51.3	3 684.2	354.5	286.8	281.4	348.0	34.1	1.3	712.8	425.4	3 516.3	4 320.8
1986	3 924.9	76.7	3 848.2	324.4	298.5	303.4	365.2	36.0	2.0	755.3	451.6	3 725.7	4 530.4
1987	4 159.8	40.6	4 119.2	366.0	317.3	323.1	369.5	33.3	2.2	779.9	468.1	3 955.9	4 847.2
1988	4 492.9	-0.5	4 493.4	414.9	345.0	361.5	394.7	32.8	5.0	839.4	497.5	4 276.3	5 275.8
1989	4 846.4	64.2	4 782.2	414.2	371.4	385.2	442.7	38.3	6.7	951.9	544.2	4 619.9	5 618.3
1990	5 127.5	91.4	5 036.1	417.2	398.0	410.1	450.1	39.2	3.2	991.2	596.9	4 906.4	5 922.9
1991	5 274.5	88.4	5 186.1	451.3	429.6	430.2	408.5	38.9	7.8	985.5	668.1	5 073.4	6 117.3
1992	5 610.1	110.9	5 499.7	475.3	453.3	455.0	383.7	39.7	9.9	982.1	748.0	5 413.0	6 459.5
1993	5 907.1	152.3	5 754.8	522.0	466.4	477.4	371.4	39.4	10.8	988.6	793.0	5 649.0	6 758.4
1994	6 277.0	136.8	6 140.2	621.9	512.7	508.2	365.9	40.7	11.8	1 029.4	829.0	5 937.3	7 195.8
1995	6 570.0	90.6	6 479.5	703.0	523.1	532.8	376.5	45.0	15.6	1 114.0	883.5	6 281.0	7 602.3
1996	6 956.0	56.6	6 899.4	786.1	545.5	555.1	381.9	52.6	16.9	1 176.5	929.2	6 667.0	8 075.4
1997	7 392.7	12.3	7 380.4	865.8	577.8	587.2	414.7	50.1	17.5	1 258.5	954.9	7 080.7	8 620.3
1998	7 797.1	-60.1	7 857.3	804.1	603.1	624.7	477.8	64.1	16.3	1 342.5	983.9	7 593.7	9 167.6
1999	8 286.9	-37.5	8 324.4	830.2	628.4	661.3	488.0	67.8	16.2	1 329.7	1 026.2	7 988.4	9 725.3
2000	8 807.5	-99.5	8 907.0	781.2	662.7	705.8	565.0	85.3	10.7	1 453.5	1 087.3	8 637.1	10 421.3
2001	9 069.6	-115.0	9 184.6	754.0	669.0	733.2	566.4	99.1	5.2	1 441.3	1 192.6	8 991.6	10 788.6
2002	9 364.0	-72.8	9 436.8	907.2	721.2	751.5	490.5	80.7	7.0	1 390.4	1 284.7	9 153.9	11 098.9
2003	9 850.6	-13.6	9 864.2	1 056.4	758.9	779.3	466.2	76.3	3.9	1 420.5	1 347.3	9 491.1	11 591.4
2004	10 532.4	-8.6	10 540.9	1 283.3	817.6	829.2	403.5	81.4	-1.8	1 503.7	1 421.3	10 052.9	12 372.6
2005	11 204.3	-35.5	11 239.8	1 477.7	873.6	873.3	496.8	93.9	-6.4	1 666.5	1 516.7	10 614.0	13 221.8
2006	11 787.5	-217.3	12 004.8	1 646.5	940.5	922.6	580.9	82.6	-9.3	1 938.4	1 614.6	11 393.9	14 140.8
2007	12 338.9	17.5	12 321.4	1 529.0	980.0	961.4	663.4	98.6	-16.4	2 166.6	1 728.1	12 000.2	14 585.7
2008	12 527.2	99.4	12 427.8	1 285.1	989.4	988.2	693.4	114.4	-21.2	2 167.1	1 956.6	12 502.2	14 791.2
2009	12 201.4	75.3	12 126.1	1 397.0	967.8	964.4	563.4	124.9	-20.6	1 818.0	2 147.5	12 094.8	14 494.5
2010	12 788.8	49.2	12 739.5	1 746.4	1 001.2	984.1	489.4	128.5	-22.9	1 739.6	2 324.7	12 477.1	15 121.1
2011	13 313.9	-38.3	13 352.3	1 816.6	1 042.6	917.8	488.1	131.5	-24.5	1 913.9	2 360.5	13 254.5	15 802.9
2012	13 858.6	-203.3	14 061.9	1 998.2	1 074.0	951.6	527.7	104.7	-19.3	2 123.8	2 366.3	13 915.1	16 596.1
2013	14 280.7	-177.6	14 458.3	2 037.4	1 118.6	1 106.8	513.5	119.4	-18.8	2 060.4	2 426.6	14 068.4	17 091.2
2014	14 864.5	-212.0	15 076.5	2 072.9	1 155.8	1 159.0	532.3	127.3	-18.3	2 117.5	2 529.2	14 694.2	17 823.2
2012													
1st quarter	13 723.8	-218.7	13 942.5	2 016.0	1 070.7	941.6	525.0	117.6	-21.3	2 026.0	2 343.4	13 662.4	16 443.8
2nd quarter	13 828.9	-168.3	13 997.2	1 993.6	1 071.3	944.9	530.7	107.9	-19.4	2 081.4	2 364.4	13 814.1	16 521.6
3rd quarter	13 918.5	-143.8	14 062.3	1 999.0	1 070.6	948.0	553.1	97.2	-18.2	2 086.0	2 368.5	13 867.1	16 608.8
4th quarter	13 963.3	-282.2	14 245.5	1 984.0	1 083.5	971.8	502.2	96.0	-18.3	2 301.6	2 389.1	14 316.9	16 810.2
2013													
1st quarter	14 072.1	-185.5	14 257.6	1 997.3	1 109.4	1 088.5	526.1	108.9	-17.7	2 040.3	2 406.0	13 891.3	16 847.3
2nd quarter	14 155.7	-260.3	14 416.0	2 045.4	1 111.6	1 105.0	505.2	115.9	-18.7	2 057.7	2 415.9	14 025.2	17 034.4
3rd quarter	14 345.7	-155.1	14 500.8	2 042.1	1 123.7	1 111.8	504.6	116.2	-18.8	2 076.9	2 438.3	14 136.3	17 146.5
4th quarter	14 549.3	-109.6	14 658.9	2 064.7	1 129.8	1 122.0	518.3	136.5	-19.9	2 066.8	2 446.4	14 220.7	17 336.5
2014													
1st quarter	14 534.8	-175.3	14 710.1	1 924.7	1 137.9	1 144.5	555.6	110.0	-17.6	2 102.7	2 476.0	14 433.5	17 418.4
2nd quarter	14 794.3	-187.0	14 981.3	2 070.5	1 152.3	1 151.2	535.9	112.0	-18.4	2 121.8	2 513.1	14 612.8	17 714.0
3rd quarter	15 032.5	-224.0	15 256.5	2 161.0	1 163.5	1 162.9	515.8	168.5	-18.4	2 115.0	2 556.5	14 774.8	18 018.0
4th quarter	15 096.3	-261.8	15 358.2	2 135.5	1 169.5	1 177.2	521.9	118.7	-18.6	2 130.6	2 571.0	14 955.7	18 142.4

. . . = Not available.

Table 1-12. Gross Domestic Income by Type of Income

(Billions of dollars, quarterly data are at seasonally adjusted annual rates.)

NIPA Tables 1.1.5, 1.10

Year and quarter	Gross domestic income	Compensation of employees			Taxes on production and imports	Less: Subsidies	Net operating surplus	Private enterprises				
		Total	Wages and salaries	Supplements to wages and salaries			Total	Total	Net interest and miscellaneous payments, domestic industries	Business current transfer payments, net	Proprietors' income with IVA and CCAdj	Rental income of persons with CCAdj
1955	424.1	231.0	212.2	18.7	31.5	0.2	. . .	112.9	6.1	1.3	44.3	13.4
1956	452.2	249.7	229.1	20.6	34.2	0.7	. . .	114.9	6.9	1.7	45.8	13.7
1957	475.2	263.1	240.0	23.0	36.6	1.1	. . .	117.8	8.1	1.8	47.8	14.1
1958	481.4	265.2	241.4	23.8	37.7	1.4	. . .	117.5	9.5	1.7	50.2	14.8
1959	522.3	286.4	259.9	26.5	41.1	1.1	130.5	129.9	9.6	1.7	50.3	15.6
1960	544.6	302.0	273.0	29.0	44.5	1.1	131.3	130.9	10.5	1.7	50.6	16.5
1961	564.3	311.2	280.7	30.6	47.0	2.0	137.5	137.2	12.2	1.9	53.2	17.2
1962	605.2	333.0	299.5	33.6	50.4	2.3	150.0	149.6	13.9	2.1	55.2	18.0
1963	640.1	351.2	314.9	36.3	53.4	2.2	159.7	158.9	14.8	2.5	56.4	18.7
1964	685.8	376.9	337.8	39.0	57.3	2.7	172.0	171.2	17.0	3.0	59.1	18.8
1965	743.0	406.3	363.8	42.6	60.7	3.0	190.9	190.2	19.2	3.5	63.7	19.3
1966	809.9	450.3	400.3	50.0	63.2	3.9	205.1	204.8	22.0	3.4	67.9	19.9
1967	858.3	482.9	429.0	53.9	67.9	3.8	207.8	207.6	25.1	3.6	69.5	20.3
1968	939.3	532.1	472.0	60.1	76.4	4.2	221.7	221.4	27.1	4.2	73.8	20.1
1969	1 018.3	586.0	518.3	67.7	83.9	4.5	228.1	228.1	34.1	4.8	77.0	20.4
1970	1 070.5	625.1	551.5	73.6	91.4	4.8	222.0	223.2	41.2	4.4	77.8	20.7
1971	1 158.3	667.0	584.5	82.5	100.5	4.7	246.6	248.3	45.5	4.2	83.9	21.9
1972	1 275.3	733.6	638.8	94.9	107.9	6.6	279.5	280.6	50.3	4.8	95.1	22.8
1973	1 422.4	815.1	708.8	106.3	117.2	5.2	317.3	319.5	59.5	5.7	112.5	23.3
1974	1 541.4	890.3	772.3	118.0	124.9	3.3	323.3	326.0	75.4	6.8	112.2	23.3
1975	1 675.7	950.2	814.9	135.3	135.3	4.5	357.1	361.5	87.5	9.0	118.2	22.5
1976	1 857.1	1 051.3	899.8	151.5	146.4	5.1	405.4	408.1	89.6	9.1	131.0	20.6
1977	2 066.7	1 169.0	994.2	174.8	159.7	7.1	456.8	460.1	104.6	8.1	144.5	16.2
1978	2 333.4	1 320.3	1 120.7	199.7	170.9	8.9	526.1	528.9	120.0	10.4	166.0	16.9
1979	2 587.4	1 481.1	1 253.4	227.7	180.1	8.5	563.6	566.8	143.6	12.8	179.4	16.6
1980	2 818.6	1 626.3	1 373.5	252.8	200.3	9.8	575.7	580.8	187.4	14.0	171.6	19.7
1981	3 174.2	1 795.4	1 511.5	283.9	235.6	11.5	669.6	674.8	235.0	16.9	179.7	25.4
1982	3 338.2	1 894.5	1 587.7	306.8	240.9	15.0	683.5	687.3	273.4	19.3	171.2	26.1
1983	3 584.0	2 014.1	1 677.7	336.4	263.3	21.3	767.4	769.7	289.6	21.7	186.3	27.5
1984	4 002.0	2 217.6	1 845.1	372.5	289.8	21.1	921.4	922.8	336.2	29.2	228.2	27.9
1985	4 295.5	2 389.2	1 982.8	406.4	308.1	21.4	982.9	981.6	360.6	34.1	241.1	29.5
1986	4 513.4	2 545.6	2 104.1	441.5	323.4	24.9	987.1	985.2	385.9	36.0	256.5	21.9
1987	4 829.7	2 725.7	2 257.6	468.0	347.5	30.3	1 058.8	1 056.6	398.7	33.3	286.5	20.2
1988	5 253.1	2 950.9	2 440.6	510.3	374.5	29.5	1 174.8	1 169.8	428.2	32.8	325.8	25.1
1989	5 593.5	3 143.9	2 584.3	559.5	398.9	27.4	1 242.1	1 235.4	483.7	38.3	341.9	24.4
1990	5 888.2	3 345.0	2 743.5	601.5	425.0	27.0	1 258.4	1 255.2	489.1	39.2	354.4	31.4
1991	6 085.7	3 454.7	2 817.2	637.5	457.1	27.5	1 270.2	1 262.3	450.6	38.9	356.0	42.0
1992	6 428.4	3 674.1	2 968.5	705.6	483.4	30.1	1 341.3	1 331.4	422.8	39.7	402.4	64.3
1993	6 726.4	3 824.0	3 082.7	741.3	503.1	36.7	1 432.4	1 421.6	413.0	39.4	430.5	93.6
1994	7 171.9	4 014.1	3 240.6	773.5	545.2	32.5	1 589.5	1 577.7	416.0	40.7	459.5	117.5
1995	7 573.5	4 206.7	3 422.1	784.6	557.9	34.8	1 720.9	1 705.3	436.6	45.0	484.5	129.2
1996	8 043.6	4 426.2	3 620.6	805.6	580.8	35.2	1 895.9	1 879.0	447.9	52.6	547.4	147.0
1997	8 596.2	4 719.1	3 881.2	837.8	611.6	33.8	2 059.4	2 041.9	493.7	50.1	587.9	152.0
1998	9 149.3	5 082.4	4 186.2	896.2	639.5	36.4	2 153.6	2 137.3	557.8	64.1	644.2	169.9
1999	9 698.1	5 417.5	4 465.2	952.3	673.6	45.2	2 251.4	2 235.2	575.7	67.8	700.4	183.1
2000	10 384.3	5 863.1	4 832.4	1 030.7	708.6	45.8	2 344.2	2 333.4	667.6	85.3	757.8	187.7
2001	10 736.8	6 053.8	4 961.6	1 092.1	727.7	58.7	2 410.1	2 404.9	677.8	99.1	836.8	207.5
2002	11 050.3	6 149.7	5 004.2	1 145.5	762.6	41.4	2 517.3	2 510.3	592.9	80.7	871.0	217.3
2003	11 524.3	6 372.7	5 146.1	1 226.6	808.0	49.1	2 665.4	2 661.5	557.4	76.3	900.1	238.0
2004	12 283.5	6 748.8	5 431.2	1 317.6	863.9	46.4	2 885.5	2 887.3	510.1	81.4	962.1	255.4
2005	13 129.2	7 097.9	5 703.1	1 394.8	934.5	60.9	3 175.7	3 182.1	632.2	93.6	979.0	238.4
2006	14 073.2	7 513.7	6 068.8	1 444.9	991.9	51.5	3 483.0	3 492.3	758.1	82.6	1 053.7	207.5
2007	14 460.1	7 908.8	6 405.7	1 503.1	1 034.6	54.6	3 307.0	3 323.5	880.7	98.6	979.2	189.4
2008	14 619.2	8 090.0	6 543.6	1 546.4	1 041.9	52.6	3 176.5	3 197.7	916.4	114.4	1 026.5	262.1
2009	14 343.4	7 795.7	6 260.1	1 535.6	1 026.1	58.3	3 211.6	3 232.2	760.9	124.9	973.0	333.7
2010	14 915.2	7 969.5	6 385.6	1 583.9	1 057.1	55.9	3 562.8	3 585.7	670.6	128.5	1 032.7	402.8
2011	15 556.3	8 277.1	6 641.2	1 635.9	1 102.6	60.1	3 785.9	3 810.5	655.2	131.5	1 143.7	485.3
2012	16 358.5	8 618.5	6 938.9	1 679.6	1 132.1	58.0	4 131.7	4 151.0	691.9	104.7	1 241.4	525.3
2013	16 840.8	8 848.7	7 123.5	1 725.3	1 178.0	59.4	4 240.6	4 259.4	668.9	119.4	1 285.1	563.4
2014	17 560.1	9 258.4	7 487.2	1 771.2	1 213.7	57.9	4 399.2	4 417.5	678.0	127.3	1 346.7	610.8
2012												
1st quarter	16 192.6	8 512.4	6 849.5	1 662.9	1 129.1	58.4	4 108.3	4 129.5	686.6	117.6	1 213.6	517.0
2nd quarter	16 290.2	8 559.1	6 887.6	1 671.5	1 129.3	58.1	4 135.4	4 154.8	694.4	107.9	1 240.2	523.0
3rd quarter	16 371.8	8 596.5	6 915.8	1 680.8	1 126.8	56.3	4 158.2	4 176.4	718.3	97.2	1 245.8	527.3
4th quarter	16 579.5	8 806.2	7 102.8	1 703.4	1 142.9	59.4	4 125.1	4 143.4	668.0	96.0	1 266.0	534.0
2013												
1st quarter	16 626.2	8 705.5	7 000.2	1 705.3	1 168.6	59.2	4 221.6	4 239.3	687.7	108.9	1 288.9	547.9
2nd quarter	16 787.2	8 829.7	7 107.8	1 721.9	1 171.3	59.7	4 227.6	4 246.3	660.2	115.9	1 279.7	556.5
3rd quarter	16 882.6	8 884.9	7 153.1	1 731.8	1 183.2	59.5	4 228.3	4 247.1	658.0	116.2	1 287.5	569.7
4th quarter	17 067.2	8 974.9	7 232.8	1 742.1	1 188.9	59.0	4 284.9	4 304.8	669.8	136.5	1 284.3	579.4
2014												
1st quarter	17 159.6	9 112.6	7 358.9	1 753.7	1 196.1	58.1	4 200.7	4 218.3	702.3	110.0	1 304.8	591.0
2nd quarter	17 457.0	9 186.8	7 424.0	1 762.7	1 210.2	57.9	4 385.1	4 403.6	678.0	112.0	1 346.3	605.5
3rd quarter	17 746.1	9 299.4	7 523.4	1 776.0	1 221.7	58.2	4 521.7	4 540.1	661.5	168.5	1 357.8	618.4
4th quarter	17 877.8	9 434.7	7 642.4	1 792.3	1 227.0	57.5	4 489.4	4 508.0	670.1	118.7	1 377.9	628.4

. . . = Not available.

Table 1-12. Gross Domestic Income by Type of Income—*Continued*

(Billions of dollars, quarterly data are at seasonally adjusted annual rates.)

NIPA Tables 1.1.5, 1.10

Year and quarter	Net operating surplus—*Continued*					Current surplus of government enterprises	Consumption of fixed capital			Statistical discrepancy	Gross domestic product
	Private enterprises—*Continued*										
	Corporate profits with IVA and CCAdj, domestic industries						Total	Private	Government		
	Total	Taxes on corporate income	Profits after tax								
			Total	Net dividends	Undistributed corporate profits						
1955	47.8	22.0	25.8	8.9	16.9	. . .	48.9	35.0	13.9	2.1	426.2
1956	46.8	22.0	24.8	9.5	15.4	. . .	54.1	38.8	15.3	-2.1	450.1
1957	46.0	21.4	24.6	9.9	14.8	. . .	58.9	42.3	16.7	-0.4	474.9
1958	41.3	19.0	22.4	9.8	12.5	. . .	62.4	44.9	17.5	0.6	482.0
1959	52.8	23.7	29.1	10.7	18.4	0.5	65.4	46.8	18.6	0.1	522.5
1960	51.5	22.8	28.8	11.4	17.4	0.5	67.9	48.2	19.7	-1.4	543.3
1961	52.6	22.9	29.7	11.5	18.2	0.3	70.6	49.8	20.8	-1.0	563.3
1962	60.3	24.1	36.2	12.4	23.8	0.4	74.1	51.8	22.3	-0.1	605.1
1963	66.4	26.4	40.1	13.6	26.5	0.8	78.0	54.2	23.8	-1.5	638.6
1964	73.2	28.2	45.1	15.0	30.1	0.8	82.4	57.3	25.1	0.0	685.8
1965	84.6	31.1	53.5	16.9	36.6	0.7	88.0	61.6	26.4	0.8	743.7
1966	91.6	33.9	57.7	17.8	39.9	0.3	95.3	67.2	28.1	5.1	815.0
1967	89.1	32.9	56.2	18.3	37.9	0.2	103.5	73.3	30.2	3.4	861.7
1968	96.1	39.6	56.5	20.2	36.3	0.3	113.3	80.6	32.7	3.2	942.5
1969	91.8	40.0	51.8	20.4	31.4	0.0	124.9	89.4	35.4	1.6	1 019.9
1970	79.1	34.8	44.4	20.4	24.0	-1.2	136.8	98.3	38.5	5.3	1 075.9
1971	92.8	38.2	54.6	20.3	34.3	-1.7	148.9	107.6	41.2	9.5	1 167.8
1972	107.7	42.3	65.3	21.9	43.4	-1.2	160.9	117.5	43.4	7.1	1 282.4
1973	118.5	50.0	68.5	23.1	45.4	-2.2	178.1	131.5	46.6	6.1	1 428.5
1974	108.2	52.8	55.5	23.5	32.0	-2.7	206.2	153.2	53.0	7.4	1 548.8
1975	124.2	51.6	72.6	26.4	46.2	-4.4	237.5	178.8	58.7	13.2	1 688.9
1976	157.8	65.3	92.5	30.1	62.4	-2.7	259.2	196.5	62.7	20.5	1 877.6
1977	186.7	74.4	112.2	33.7	78.5	-3.3	288.3	221.1	67.2	19.3	2 086.0
1978	215.7	84.9	130.8	39.6	91.2	-2.8	325.1	252.1	72.9	23.2	2 356.6
1979	214.4	90.0	124.4	41.5	82.9	-3.2	371.1	290.7	80.4	44.8	2 632.1
1980	188.1	87.2	100.9	47.3	53.6	-5.1	426.0	335.0	91.0	43.9	2 862.5
1981	217.8	84.3	133.5	58.3	75.2	-5.2	485.0	381.9	103.1	36.7	3 211.0
1982	197.3	66.5	130.8	61.3	69.4	-3.8	534.3	420.4	113.9	6.8	3 345.0
1983	244.7	80.6	164.1	71.3	92.7	-2.3	560.5	438.8	121.8	54.2	3 638.1
1984	301.3	97.5	203.8	78.5	125.3	-1.4	594.3	463.5	130.8	38.7	4 040.7
1985	316.4	99.4	217.0	85.7	131.3	1.3	636.7	496.4	140.2	51.3	4 346.7
1986	284.9	109.7	175.2	88.3	86.9	2.0	682.2	531.6	150.6	76.7	4 590.2
1987	318.0	130.4	187.5	95.6	91.9	2.2	728.0	566.3	161.6	40.6	4 870.2
1988	357.9	141.6	216.3	98.0	118.2	5.0	782.4	608.3	174.1	-0.5	5 252.6
1989	347.1	146.1	201.0	126.4	74.7	6.7	836.1	650.1	186.0	64.2	5 657.7
1990	341.1	145.4	195.6	144.1	51.6	3.2	886.8	689.0	197.8	91.4	5 979.6
1991	374.9	138.6	236.3	156.2	80.1	7.8	931.1	722.4	208.8	88.4	6 174.0
1992	402.2	148.7	253.5	161.5	92.0	9.9	959.7	744.2	215.6	110.9	6 539.3
1993	445.1	171.0	274.0	184.7	89.3	10.8	1 003.6	780.0	223.6	152.3	6 878.7
1994	543.9	193.1	350.8	197.8	153.0	11.8	1 055.6	824.3	231.2	136.8	7 308.8
1995	610.1	217.8	392.2	226.2	166.1	15.6	1 122.8	882.6	240.2	90.6	7 664.1
1996	684.1	231.5	452.6	263.1	189.5	16.9	1 176.0	931.0	245.0	56.6	8 100.2
1997	758.2	245.4	512.8	292.2	220.6	17.5	1 240.0	990.1	249.9	12.3	8 608.5
1998	701.3	248.4	453.0	314.8	138.2	16.3	1 310.3	1 054.9	255.3	-60.1	9 089.2
1999	708.2	258.8	449.4	306.4	143.1	16.2	1 400.9	1 135.9	264.9	-37.5	9 660.6
2000	635.0	265.1	369.9	355.4	14.5	10.7	1 514.2	1 236.6	277.7	-99.5	10 284.8
2001	583.6	203.3	380.3	329.9	50.4	5.2	1 604.0	1 317.7	286.3	-115.0	10 621.8
2002	748.4	192.3	556.1	352.3	203.8	7.0	1 662.1	1 368.0	294.1	-72.8	10 977.5
2003	889.7	243.8	646.0	401.9	244.1	3.9	1 727.2	1 422.4	304.9	-13.6	11 510.7
2004	1 078.3	306.1	772.2	501.8	270.4	-1.8	1 831.7	1 509.3	322.4	-8.6	12 274.9
2005	1 238.7	412.4	826.3	319.7	506.6	-6.4	1 982.0	1 635.3	346.7	-35.5	13 093.7
2006	1 390.3	473.4	917.0	648.1	268.9	-9.3	2 136.0	1 765.0	371.0	-217.3	13 855.9
2007	1 175.6	445.5	730.1	678.5	51.6	-16.4	2 264.4	1 865.0	399.4	17.5	14 477.6
2008	878.4	309.1	569.3	628.1	-58.8	-21.2	2 363.4	1 936.9	426.5	99.4	14 718.6
2009	1 039.8	269.4	770.3	456.5	313.8	-20.6	2 368.4	1 925.7	442.7	75.3	14 418.7
2010	1 351.2	370.6	980.7	442.5	538.1	-22.9	2 381.6	1 923.5	458.1	49.2	14 964.4
2011	1 394.7	379.1	1 015.6	548.8	466.9	-24.5	2 450.6	1 971.1	479.6	-38.3	15 517.9
2012	1 587.8	447.6	1 140.2	680.1	460.1	-19.3	2 534.2	2 038.0	496.2	-203.3	16 155.3
2013	1 622.6	468.9	1 153.7	777.7	376.0	-18.8	2 632.8	2 126.6	506.2	-177.6	16 663.2
2014	1 654.7	513.9	1 140.9	724.4	416.5	-18.3	2 746.7	2 229.9	516.8	-212.0	17 348.1
2012											
1st quarter	1 594.7	442.7	1 152.1	608.7	543.3	-21.3	2 501.2	2 010.2	491.0	-218.7	15 973.9
2nd quarter	1 589.4	449.9	1 139.4	615.2	524.3	-19.4	2 524.4	2 029.1	495.3	-168.3	16 121.9
3rd quarter	1 587.9	451.0	1 136.9	638.0	499.0	-18.2	2 546.5	2 047.9	498.6	-143.8	16 227.9
4th quarter	1 579.3	446.9	1 132.4	858.5	273.9	-18.3	2 564.7	2 064.7	500.0	-282.2	16 297.3
2013											
1st quarter	1 605.9	454.9	1 151.0	680.9	470.1	-17.7	2 589.7	2 087.6	502.1	-185.5	16 440.7
2nd quarter	1 634.0	461.3	1 172.8	887.0	285.8	-18.7	2 618.3	2 113.4	505.0	-260.3	16 526.8
3rd quarter	1 615.7	475.6	1 140.1	765.4	374.6	-18.8	2 645.7	2 138.4	507.3	-155.1	16 727.5
4th quarter	1 634.8	483.8	1 151.0	777.5	373.5	-19.9	2 677.6	2 167.1	510.5	-109.6	16 957.6
2014											
1st quarter	1 510.3	497.3	1 013.0	728.1	284.8	-17.6	2 708.3	2 195.2	513.1	-175.3	16 984.3
2nd quarter	1 661.9	527.4	1 134.4	728.7	405.7	-18.4	2 732.8	2 217.3	515.5	-187.0	17 270.0
3rd quarter	1 733.9	518.4	1 215.6	706.8	508.8	-18.4	2 761.5	2 243.1	518.4	-224.0	17 522.1
4th quarter	1 712.8	512.3	1 200.5	734.0	466.5	-18.6	2 784.2	2 264.0	520.2	-261.8	17 615.9

. . . = Not available.

Table 1-13A. National Income by Type of Income: Recent Data

(Billions of dollars, quarterly data are at seasonally adjusted annual rates.)

NIPA Tables 1.7.5, 1.12

Year and quarter	National income, total	Compensation of employees							Proprietors' income with IVA and CCAdj			Rental income of persons with CCAdj
		Total	Wages and salaries			Supplements to wages and salaries			Total	Farm	Nonfarm	
			Total	Government	Other	Total	Employer contributions for:					
							Employee pension and insurance funds	Government social insurance				
1955	377.6	230.9	212.2	36.6	175.6	18.7	13.6	5.2	44.3	10.7	33.6	13.4
1956	400.9	249.6	229.0	38.8	190.2	20.6	14.9	5.7	45.8	10.6	35.2	13.7
1957	419.4	263.0	240.0	41.0	198.9	23.0	16.7	6.4	47.8	10.6	37.2	14.1
1958	421.6	265.1	241.3	44.1	197.2	23.8	17.5	6.3	50.2	12.4	37.7	14.8
1959	459.6	286.3	259.8	46.1	213.8	26.5	18.6	7.9	50.3	10.0	40.3	15.6
1960	479.9	301.9	272.9	49.2	223.7	29.0	19.7	9.3	50.6	10.6	39.9	16.5
1961	497.2	311.1	280.5	52.5	228.0	30.6	21.0	9.6	53.2	11.2	42.0	17.2
1962	535.2	332.9	299.4	56.3	243.0	33.6	22.4	11.2	55.2	11.2	44.0	18.0
1963	566.6	351.2	314.9	60.0	254.8	36.3	23.9	12.4	56.4	11.0	45.4	18.7
1964	608.3	376.8	337.8	64.9	272.9	39.0	26.4	12.6	59.1	9.8	49.4	18.8
1965	660.3	406.3	363.8	69.9	293.8	42.6	29.5	13.1	63.7	12.0	51.6	19.3
1966	719.7	450.3	400.3	78.4	321.9	50.0	33.1	16.8	67.9	13.0	54.9	19.9
1967	760.2	482.9	429.0	86.5	342.5	53.9	35.9	18.0	69.5	11.6	57.8	20.3
1968	832.1	532.1	472.0	96.7	375.3	60.1	40.2	20.0	73.8	11.7	62.2	20.1
1969	899.5	586.0	518.3	105.6	412.7	67.7	44.9	22.8	77.0	12.8	64.2	20.4
1970	940.1	625.1	551.6	117.2	434.3	73.6	49.7	23.8	77.8	12.9	64.9	20.7
1971	1 017.0	667.0	584.5	126.8	457.8	82.5	56.0	26.4	83.9	13.4	70.5	21.9
1972	1 123.0	733.6	638.8	137.9	500.9	94.9	63.7	31.2	95.1	17.0	78.1	22.8
1973	1 257.0	815.0	708.8	148.8	560.0	106.3	66.5	39.8	112.5	29.1	83.4	23.3
1974	1 350.8	890.3	772.3	160.5	611.8	118.0	73.3	44.7	112.2	23.5	88.7	23.3
1975	1 451.1	950.2	814.8	176.2	638.6	135.3	88.6	46.7	118.2	22.0	96.2	22.5
1976	1 614.8	1 051.2	899.7	188.9	710.8	151.5	97.1	54.4	131.0	17.2	113.8	20.6
1977	1 798.7	1 169.0	994.2	202.6	791.6	174.8	113.7	61.1	144.5	16.0	128.5	16.2
1978	2 029.9	1 320.2	1 120.6	220.0	900.6	199.7	128.1	71.5	166.0	19.9	146.1	16.9
1979	2 248.2	1 481.0	1 253.3	237.1	1 016.2	227.7	145.1	82.6	179.4	22.2	157.3	16.6
1980	2 426.8	1 626.2	1 373.4	261.5	1 112.0	252.8	163.9	88.9	171.6	11.7	159.9	19.7
1981	2 722.1	1 795.3	1 511.4	285.8	1 225.5	283.9	180.3	103.6	179.7	19.0	160.7	25.4
1982	2 840.4	1 894.3	1 587.5	307.5	1 280.0	306.8	197.0	109.8	171.2	13.3	157.9	26.1
1983	3 060.5	2 013.9	1 677.5	324.8	1 352.7	336.4	216.5	119.9	186.3	6.2	180.1	27.5
1984	3 444.0	2 217.4	1 844.9	348.1	1 496.8	372.5	233.5	139.0	228.2	20.9	207.3	27.9
1985	3 684.2	2 389.0	1 982.6	373.9	1 608.7	406.4	258.7	147.7	241.1	21.0	220.1	29.5
1986	3 848.2	2 543.8	2 102.3	397.2	1 705.1	441.5	283.6	157.9	256.5	22.8	233.7	21.9
1987	4 119.2	2 724.3	2 256.3	423.1	1 833.2	468.0	301.8	166.3	286.5	28.9	257.6	20.2
1988	4 493.4	2 950.0	2 439.8	452.0	1 987.7	510.3	325.6	184.6	325.8	26.8	299.1	25.1
1989	4 782.2	3 142.6	2 583.1	481.1	2 101.9	559.5	365.8	193.7	341.9	33.0	308.9	24.4
1990	5 036.1	3 342.7	2 741.2	519.0	2 222.2	601.5	395.0	206.5	354.4	32.2	322.3	31.4
1991	5 186.1	3 452.0	2 814.5	548.8	2 265.7	637.5	422.4	215.1	356.0	26.8	329.2	42.0
1992	5 499.7	3 671.1	2 965.5	572.0	2 393.5	705.6	477.2	228.4	402.4	34.8	367.6	64.3
1993	5 754.8	3 820.7	3 079.3	589.0	2 490.3	741.3	501.7	239.7	430.5	31.4	399.2	93.6
1994	6 140.2	4 010.1	3 236.6	609.5	2 627.1	773.5	519.4	254.1	459.5	34.7	424.8	117.5
1995	6 479.5	4 202.6	3 418.0	629.0	2 789.0	784.6	520.5	264.1	484.5	22.0	462.4	129.2
1996	6 899.4	4 422.1	3 616.5	648.1	2 968.4	805.6	530.8	274.8	547.4	37.3	510.1	147.0
1997	7 380.4	4 714.7	3 876.8	671.9	3 205.0	837.8	548.3	289.6	587.9	32.4	555.5	152.0
1998	7 857.3	5 077.8	4 181.6	701.3	3 480.3	896.2	589.0	307.2	644.2	28.4	615.7	169.9
1999	8 324.4	5 410.3	4 458.0	733.8	3 724.2	952.3	629.0	323.3	700.4	28.1	672.3	183.1
2000	8 907.0	5 856.6	4 825.9	779.8	4 046.1	1 030.7	685.5	345.2	757.8	31.5	726.3	187.7
2001	9 184.6	6 046.5	4 954.4	822.0	4 132.4	1 092.1	734.1	358.0	836.8	32.1	804.7	207.5
2002	9 436.8	6 141.9	4 996.4	873.2	4 123.3	1 145.5	779.5	366.0	871.0	19.9	851.1	217.3
2003	9 864.2	6 364.5	5 137.8	913.3	4 224.5	1 226.6	844.1	382.5	900.1	38.0	862.0	238.0
2004	10 540.9	6 739.5	5 421.9	952.7	4 469.3	1 317.6	908.9	408.7	962.1	50.4	911.6	255.4
2005	11 239.8	7 086.8	5 692.0	991.5	4 700.4	1 394.8	966.8	428.1	979.0	46.4	932.6	238.4
2006	12 004.8	7 502.3	6 057.4	1 035.0	5 022.4	1 444.9	997.6	447.4	1 053.7	36.0	1 017.7	207.5
2007	12 321.4	7 898.3	6 395.2	1 088.8	5 306.3	1 503.1	1 041.4	461.7	979.2	38.1	941.1	189.4
2008	12 427.8	8 078.3	6 531.9	1 144.1	5 387.8	1 546.4	1 075.1	471.3	1 026.5	47.0	979.5	262.1
2009	12 126.1	7 787.0	6 251.4	1 175.1	5 076.3	1 535.6	1 077.5	458.1	973.0	35.5	937.5	333.7
2010	12 739.5	7 961.4	6 377.5	1 191.1	5 186.4	1 583.9	1 114.6	469.4	1 032.7	46.0	986.7	402.8
2011	13 352.3	8 269.0	6 633.2	1 194.8	5 438.4	1 635.9	1 142.0	493.9	1 143.7	75.5	1 068.1	485.3
2012	14 061.9	8 609.9	6 930.3	1 198.2	5 732.0	1 679.6	1 165.3	514.3	1 241.4	61.6	1 179.8	525.3
2013	14 458.3	8 839.7	7 114.4	1 207.6	5 906.8	1 725.3	1 197.8	527.5	1 285.1	88.8	1 196.3	563.4
2014	15 076.5	9 248.9	7 477.8	1 237.2	6 240.5	1 771.2	1 224.0	547.2	1 346.7	78.1	1 268.6	610.8
2012												
1st quarter	13 942.5	8 504.0	6 841.1	1 200.0	5 641.1	1 662.9	1 153.6	509.3	1 213.6	62.4	1 151.1	517.0
2nd quarter	13 997.2	8 550.0	6 878.5	1 196.1	5 682.4	1 671.5	1 160.7	510.8	1 240.2	59.5	1 180.7	523.0
3rd quarter	14 062.3	8 587.6	6 906.8	1 196.2	5 710.7	1 680.8	1 168.9	511.9	1 245.8	59.4	1 186.3	527.3
4th quarter	14 245.5	8 798.0	7 094.6	1 200.7	5 893.9	1 703.4	1 178.0	525.4	1 266.0	64.9	1 201.1	534.0
2013												
1st quarter	14 257.6	8 696.7	6 991.4	1 203.3	5 788.1	1 705.3	1 186.2	519.1	1 288.9	93.9	1 195.0	547.9
2nd quarter	14 416.0	8 820.4	7 098.5	1 205.0	5 893.5	1 721.9	1 194.9	527.0	1 279.7	90.2	1 189.5	556.5
3rd quarter	14 500.8	8 875.7	7 143.9	1 205.1	5 938.8	1 731.8	1 202.1	529.6	1 287.5	93.9	1 193.6	569.7
4th quarter	14 658.9	8 965.9	7 223.8	1 217.2	6 006.6	1 742.1	1 208.0	534.1	1 284.3	77.1	1 207.2	579.4
2014												
1st quarter	14 710.1	9 103.7	7 350.0	1 223.4	6 126.6	1 753.7	1 213.1	540.5	1 304.8	71.7	1 233.0	591.0
2nd quarter	14 981.3	9 177.3	7 414.5	1 234.2	6 180.3	1 762.7	1 219.4	543.3	1 346.3	88.8	1 257.5	605.5
3rd quarter	15 256.5	9 289.9	7 513.9	1 243.2	6 270.7	1 776.0	1 227.1	548.9	1 357.8	77.2	1 280.6	618.4
4th quarter	15 358.2	9 424.9	7 632.6	1 248.2	6 384.4	1 792.3	1 236.3	556.0	1 377.9	74.8	1 303.0	628.4

Table 1-13A. National Income by Type of Income: Recent Data—*Continued*

(Billions of dollars, quarterly data are at seasonally adjusted annual rates.)   **NIPA Tables 1.7.5, 1.12**

| Year and quarter | Corporate profits with IVA and CCAdj | | | | | Net interest and miscellaneous payments | Taxes on production and imports | Less: Subsidies | Business current transfer payments, net | | | Current surplus of government enterprises | Addendum: Net national factor income |
| | Total | Taxes on corporate income | Profits after tax | | | | | | | | | | |
			Total	Net dividends	Undistributed corporate profits				Total [1]	To persons	To government		
1955	50.2	22.0	28.1	10.5	17.6	6.3	31.5	0.2	1.3	0.9	0.4	. . .	345.1
1956	49.6	22.0	27.7	11.3	16.4	6.9	34.2	0.7	1.7	1.2	0.4	. . .	365.7
1957	49.1	21.4	27.7	11.7	16.0	8.1	36.6	1.1	1.8	1.4	0.4	. . .	382.1
1958	43.9	19.0	24.9	11.6	13.3	9.6	37.7	1.4	1.7	1.2	0.5	. . .	383.6
1959	55.5	23.7	31.8	12.6	19.2	9.7	41.1	1.1	1.7	1.3	0.3	0.5	417.4
1960	54.7	22.8	31.9	13.4	18.5	10.7	44.5	1.1	1.7	1.3	0.4	0.5	434.3
1961	55.9	22.9	33.1	13.9	19.2	12.6	47.0	2.0	1.9	1.4	0.5	0.3	450.0
1962	64.0	24.1	39.9	15.0	24.9	14.3	50.4	2.3	2.1	1.5	0.6	0.4	484.6
1963	70.5	26.4	44.1	16.2	27.9	15.3	53.4	2.2	2.5	1.9	0.7	0.8	512.1
1964	77.7	28.2	49.6	18.2	31.4	17.5	57.3	2.7	3.0	2.2	0.8	0.8	550.0
1965	89.3	31.1	58.2	20.2	38.0	19.8	60.7	3.0	3.5	2.3	1.2	0.7	598.4
1966	96.1	33.9	62.2	20.7	41.6	22.5	63.2	3.9	3.4	2.1	1.3	0.3	656.8
1967	93.9	32.9	61.0	21.5	39.5	25.7	67.9	3.8	3.6	2.3	1.4	0.2	692.3
1968	101.7	39.6	62.1	23.5	38.6	27.6	76.4	4.2	4.2	2.8	1.4	0.3	755.3
1969	98.4	40.0	58.4	24.2	34.2	33.6	83.9	4.5	4.8	3.3	1.5	0.0	815.4
1970	86.2	34.8	51.5	24.3	27.2	40.5	91.4	4.8	4.4	2.9	1.4	-1.2	850.4
1971	100.6	38.2	62.5	25.0	37.5	45.2	100.5	4.7	4.2	2.7	1.5	-1.7	918.7
1972	117.2	42.3	74.9	26.8	48.0	49.3	107.9	6.6	4.8	3.1	1.7	-1.2	1 018.1
1973	133.4	50.0	83.4	29.9	53.5	57.2	117.2	5.2	5.7	3.9	1.8	-2.2	1 141.5
1974	125.7	52.8	72.9	33.2	39.7	73.5	124.9	3.3	6.8	4.7	2.1	-2.7	1 225.1
1975	138.9	51.6	87.2	33.0	54.3	85.9	135.3	4.5	9.0	6.8	2.2	-4.4	1 315.7
1976	174.3	65.3	109.1	39.0	70.0	89.9	146.4	5.1	9.1	6.7	2.4	-2.7	1 467.1
1977	205.8	74.4	131.3	44.8	86.6	105.9	159.7	7.1	8.1	5.1	3.0	-3.3	1 641.3
1978	238.6	84.9	153.7	50.8	102.9	118.8	170.9	8.9	10.4	6.5	3.9	-2.8	1 860.5
1979	249.0	90.0	159.0	57.5	101.4	141.0	180.1	8.5	12.8	8.2	4.5	-3.2	2 067.0
1980	223.6	87.2	136.4	64.1	72.3	186.2	200.3	9.8	14.0	8.6	5.4	-5.1	2 227.3
1981	247.5	84.3	163.2	73.8	89.4	238.4	235.6	11.5	16.9	11.2	5.7	-5.2	2 486.2
1982	229.9	66.5	163.4	77.7	85.6	277.5	240.9	15.0	19.3	12.4	6.9	-3.8	2 599.0
1983	279.8	80.6	199.1	83.5	115.7	291.8	263.3	21.3	21.7	13.8	7.9	-2.3	2 799.2
1984	337.9	97.5	240.4	90.8	149.5	336.1	289.8	21.1	29.2	19.7	9.4	-1.4	3 147.5
1985	354.5	99.4	255.1	97.5	157.5	348.0	308.1	21.4	34.1	22.3	11.8	1.3	3 362.0
1986	324.4	109.7	214.7	106.2	108.5	365.2	323.4	24.9	36.0	22.9	13.0	2.0	3 511.8
1987	366.0	130.4	235.5	112.3	123.2	369.5	347.5	30.3	33.3	20.2	13.1	2.2	3 766.5
1988	414.9	141.6	273.2	129.9	143.3	394.7	374.5	29.5	32.8	20.6	12.2	5.0	4 110.6
1989	414.2	146.1	268.2	158.0	110.2	442.7	398.9	27.4	38.3	23.2	15.1	6.7	4 365.8
1990	417.2	145.4	271.7	169.1	102.7	450.1	425.0	27.0	39.2	22.2	17.0	3.2	4 595.7
1991	451.3	138.6	312.7	180.5	132.2	408.5	457.1	27.5	38.9	17.6	21.3	7.8	4 709.8
1992	475.3	148.7	326.6	189.5	137.1	383.7	483.4	30.1	39.7	16.3	23.6	9.9	4 996.8
1993	522.0	171.0	351.0	205.3	145.6	371.4	503.1	36.7	39.4	14.1	25.6	10.8	5 238.2
1994	621.9	193.1	428.8	236.0	192.8	365.9	545.2	32.5	40.7	13.3	27.9	11.8	5 575.0
1995	703.0	217.8	485.2	259.0	226.2	376.5	557.9	34.8	45.0	18.7	24.9	15.6	5 895.8
1996	786.1	231.5	554.6	303.5	251.1	381.9	580.8	35.2	52.6	22.9	30.7	16.9	6 284.3
1997	865.8	245.4	620.3	339.5	280.9	414.7	611.6	33.8	50.1	19.4	29.8	17.5	6 735.1
1998	804.1	248.4	555.7	357.1	198.7	477.8	639.5	36.4	64.1	26.0	34.3	16.3	7 173.8
1999	830.2	258.8	571.4	347.9	223.5	488.0	673.6	45.2	67.8	34.0	36.5	16.2	7 612.0
2000	781.2	265.1	516.1	384.7	131.4	565.0	708.6	45.8	85.3	42.4	41.9	10.7	8 148.3
2001	754.0	203.3	550.7	370.6	180.2	566.4	727.7	58.7	99.1	46.8	43.9	5.2	8 411.4
2002	907.2	192.3	714.8	400.2	314.7	490.5	762.6	41.4	80.7	34.2	46.2	7.0	8 628.0
2003	1 056.4	243.8	812.6	434.0	378.6	466.2	808.0	49.1	76.3	26.3	48.3	3.9	9 025.1
2004	1 283.3	306.1	977.3	564.1	413.2	403.5	863.9	46.4	81.4	16.8	52.4	-1.8	9 643.8
2005	1 477.7	412.4	1 065.3	580.5	484.8	496.8	934.5	60.9	93.9	25.7	53.4	-6.4	10 278.7
2006	1 646.5	473.4	1 173.1	726.0	447.1	580.9	991.9	51.5	82.6	21.5	58.3	-9.3	10 991.0
2007	1 529.0	445.5	1 083.5	818.9	264.6	663.4	1 034.6	54.6	98.6	30.6	62.0	-16.4	11 259.3
2008	1 285.1	309.1	976.0	808.6	167.3	693.4	1 041.9	52.6	114.4	36.6	70.6	-21.2	11 345.3
2009	1 397.0	269.4	1 127.5	574.6	552.9	563.4	1 026.1	58.3	124.9	38.7	88.5	-20.6	11 054.0
2010	1 746.4	370.6	1 375.9	564.0	811.9	489.4	1 057.1	55.9	128.5	43.0	87.2	-22.9	11 632.7
2011	1 816.6	379.1	1 437.5	703.7	733.9	488.1	1 102.6	60.1	131.5	50.2	89.2	-24.5	12 202.7
2012	1 998.2	447.6	1 550.5	859.4	691.2	527.7	1 132.1	58.0	104.7	42.7	72.6	-19.3	12 902.5
2013	2 037.4	468.9	1 568.5	924.0	644.5	513.5	1 178.0	59.4	119.4	41.2	91.9	-18.8	13 239.1
2014	2 072.9	513.9	1 559.1	860.0	699.0	532.3	1 213.7	57.9	127.3	42.0	94.8	-18.3	13 811.7
2012													
1st quarter	2 016.0	442.7	1 573.3	779.7	793.6	525.0	1 129.1	58.4	117.6	45.7	80.5	-21.3	12 775.5
2nd quarter	1 993.6	449.9	1 543.7	811.0	732.7	530.7	1 129.3	58.1	107.9	43.1	73.5	-19.4	12 837.5
3rd quarter	1 999.0	451.0	1 548.1	820.8	727.3	553.1	1 126.8	56.3	97.2	41.4	66.6	-18.2	12 912.8
4th quarter	1 984.0	446.9	1 537.1	1 026.1	511.0	502.2	1 142.9	59.4	96.0	40.7	69.6	-18.3	13 084.2
2013													
1st quarter	1 997.3	454.9	1 542.4	814.2	728.3	526.1	1 168.6	59.2	108.9	40.8	86.4	-17.7	13 056.9
2nd quarter	2 045.4	461.3	1 584.1	1 065.2	519.0	505.2	1 171.3	59.7	115.9	41.0	88.8	-18.7	13 207.2
3rd quarter	2 042.1	475.6	1 566.5	870.1	696.5	504.6	1 183.2	59.5	116.2	41.3	84.9	-18.8	13 279.7
4th quarter	2 064.7	483.8	1 580.9	946.7	634.2	518.3	1 188.9	59.0	136.5	41.5	107.6	-19.9	13 412.5
2014													
1st quarter	1 924.7	497.3	1 427.4	857.3	570.2	555.6	1 196.1	58.1	110.0	41.8	82.2	-17.6	13 479.7
2nd quarter	2 070.5	527.4	1 543.1	857.1	686.0	535.9	1 210.2	57.9	112.0	42.0	79.5	-18.4	13 735.4
3rd quarter	2 161.0	518.4	1 642.7	853.6	789.1	515.8	1 221.7	58.2	168.5	42.1	133.1	-18.4	13 943.0
4th quarter	2 135.5	512.3	1 623.2	872.2	751.0	521.9	1 227.0	57.5	118.7	42.1	84.3	-18.6	14 088.6

[1] Includes net transfer payments to the rest of the world, not shown separately.
. . . = Not available.

Table 1-13B. National Income by Type of Income: Historical Data

(Billions of dollars, quarterly data are at seasonally adjusted annual rates.)

NIPA Tables 1.7.5, 1.12

Year and quarter	National income, total	Compensation of employees							Proprietors' income with IVA and CCAdj			Rental income of persons with CCAdj
		Total	Wages and salaries			Supplements to wages and salaries			Total	Farm	Nonfarm	
			Total	Government	Other	Total	Employer contributions for:					
							Employee pension and insurance funds	Government social insurance				
1929	94.2	51.4	50.5	5.0	45.5	1.0	1.0	0.0	14.0	5.7	8.4	6.1
1930	83.1	47.2	46.2	5.2	41.0	1.0	1.0	0.0	10.9	3.9	7.0	5.4
1931	67.7	40.1	39.2	5.3	33.9	1.0	1.0	0.0	8.3	3.0	5.3	4.4
1932	51.3	31.4	30.5	5.0	25.5	0.9	0.9	0.0	5.0	1.8	3.3	3.6
1933	49.0	29.8	29.0	5.2	23.9	0.8	0.8	0.0	5.3	2.2	3.0	2.9
1934	58.3	34.6	33.7	6.1	27.6	0.9	0.8	0.0	7.0	2.6	4.4	2.5
1935	66.4	37.7	36.7	6.5	30.2	1.0	1.0	0.0	10.1	4.9	5.2	2.6
1936	75.2	43.3	42.0	7.9	34.1	1.4	1.1	0.2	10.4	3.9	6.4	2.7
1937	83.7	48.4	46.1	7.5	38.6	2.2	1.2	1.0	12.5	5.6	6.9	3.0
1938	77.1	45.5	43.0	8.3	34.8	2.5	1.3	1.2	10.6	4.0	6.6	3.5
1939	82.5	48.6	46.0	8.2	37.7	2.6	1.3	1.3	11.1	4.0	7.1	3.7
1940	91.6	52.8	49.9	8.5	41.4	2.9	1.6	1.4	12.2	4.1	8.2	3.8
1941	117.4	66.2	62.1	10.2	51.9	4.2	2.4	1.7	16.7	6.0	10.6	4.4
1942	152.4	88.1	82.1	16.0	66.1	6.0	4.0	2.0	23.3	9.7	13.7	5.5
1943	187.3	112.8	105.8	26.6	79.2	7.0	4.7	2.3	28.2	11.5	16.7	6.0
1944	201.0	124.4	116.7	33.0	83.8	7.7	5.1	2.5	29.3	11.4	17.9	6.3
1945	201.4	126.4	117.5	34.9	82.6	8.9	5.4	3.5	30.8	11.8	19.0	6.6
1946	201.5	122.6	112.0	20.7	91.3	10.6	5.5	5.1	35.7	14.2	21.5	6.9
1947	219.0	132.5	123.1	17.5	105.6	9.4	5.5	3.9	34.6	14.3	20.2	6.9
1948	245.1	144.5	135.6	19.0	116.5	8.9	5.9	3.0	39.3	16.7	22.6	7.5
1949	240.0	144.5	134.7	20.8	113.9	9.8	6.4	3.3	34.7	12.0	22.7	7.8
1947												
1st quarter	213.6	129.1	118.9	17.1	101.7	10.3	5.6	4.7	36.2	16.0	20.2	6.7
2nd quarter	215.9	130.9	121.3	17.3	103.9	9.7	5.4	4.3	33.3	12.4	20.9	6.8
3rd quarter	219.3	132.9	124.0	17.6	106.4	8.9	5.4	3.5	33.9	14.1	19.8	7.0
4th quarter	227.2	137.0	128.3	18.0	110.3	8.7	5.5	3.2	35.0	14.9	20.0	7.2
1948												
1st quarter	236.1	140.6	131.7	18.3	113.4	8.9	5.7	3.2	36.4	14.5	21.9	7.3
2nd quarter	244.3	142.2	133.4	18.6	114.7	8.9	5.9	3.0	40.2	18.0	22.3	7.5
3rd quarter	249.1	147.0	138.1	19.3	118.8	8.9	6.0	2.9	40.6	17.9	22.7	7.5
4th quarter	251.0	148.1	139.1	19.9	119.2	9.0	6.1	2.9	39.9	16.4	23.5	7.6
1949												
1st quarter	243.6	146.4	136.7	20.4	116.4	9.7	6.2	3.5	35.4	12.7	22.7	7.5
2nd quarter	240.1	144.9	135.0	20.7	114.3	9.9	6.3	3.5	34.9	12.1	22.8	7.7
3rd quarter	240.2	143.8	134.0	21.1	112.9	9.8	6.5	3.3	34.2	11.6	22.6	7.9
4th quarter	236.3	143.0	133.2	21.2	112.0	9.8	6.7	3.0	34.2	11.5	22.7	8.1
1950												
1st quarter	246.7	147.2	136.9	21.2	115.6	10.3	7.1	3.3	36.2	12.2	24.0	8.5
2nd quarter	258.8	153.8	143.0	21.8	121.2	10.8	7.5	3.3	36.8	12.2	24.6	8.7
3rd quarter	275.9	162.5	151.0	23.0	128.1	11.5	8.1	3.4	38.5	13.1	25.4	8.8
4th quarter	286.4	170.3	158.1	24.5	133.5	12.3	8.7	3.6	38.5	13.9	24.6	9.1
1951												
1st quarter	298.2	178.8	165.3	26.7	138.6	13.5	9.4	4.0	40.9	15.0	25.9	9.3
2nd quarter	305.6	185.1	171.0	28.5	142.5	14.1	10.0	4.1	42.5	15.4	27.1	9.6
3rd quarter	310.9	188.1	173.5	30.2	143.3	14.6	10.5	4.1	43.2	15.1	28.1	9.9
4th quarter	317.4	191.7	176.6	31.5	145.1	15.1	11.0	4.1	43.7	15.7	28.0	10.1
1952												
1st quarter	318.9	196.4	181.0	32.4	148.6	15.3	11.2	4.1	41.7	13.7	28.0	10.4
2nd quarter	320.9	197.7	182.1	33.1	149.0	15.6	11.5	4.1	43.0	14.5	28.4	10.7
3rd quarter	327.4	201.8	186.0	33.8	152.2	15.8	11.7	4.1	44.7	16.0	28.8	10.9
4th quarter	338.9	209.6	193.5	34.2	159.3	16.1	11.9	4.2	42.8	13.0	29.7	11.3
1953												
1st quarter	345.0	213.4	197.1	34.3	162.7	16.3	12.1	4.2	43.0	13.0	29.9	11.6
2nd quarter	347.8	216.5	200.0	34.4	165.7	16.5	12.3	4.2	42.3	12.4	29.9	11.9
3rd quarter	346.2	216.8	200.1	34.3	165.9	16.7	12.4	4.3	41.2	11.7	29.5	12.2
4th quarter	338.6	215.4	198.7	34.4	164.3	16.7	12.5	4.2	41.6	11.5	30.0	12.5
1954												
1st quarter	340.2	213.4	196.4	34.4	162.0	17.0	12.4	4.6	42.7	12.9	29.8	12.8
2nd quarter	340.5	213.0	196.0	34.7	161.2	17.0	12.4	4.6	42.1	11.7	30.4	13.0
3rd quarter	343.9	213.5	196.3	35.1	161.2	17.2	12.6	4.6	42.2	11.8	30.5	13.1
4th quarter	352.9	217.8	200.4	35.4	165.0	17.5	12.8	4.6	42.0	10.7	31.3	13.3
1955												
1st quarter	365.3	222.2	204.1	35.5	168.6	18.2	13.1	5.0	43.7	10.9	32.7	13.3
2nd quarter	374.7	228.4	209.9	36.2	173.6	18.6	13.4	5.1	44.3	11.3	33.0	13.4
3rd quarter	382.1	234.2	215.2	37.4	177.8	19.0	13.7	5.2	44.6	10.7	33.9	13.4
4th quarter	388.4	238.7	219.5	37.3	182.2	19.3	14.0	5.3	44.5	10.0	34.5	13.5
1956												
1st quarter	392.1	243.2	223.3	37.8	185.4	19.9	14.3	5.6	44.9	10.2	34.7	13.6
2nd quarter	397.9	247.9	227.5	38.5	189.0	20.4	14.7	5.7	45.3	10.4	34.9	13.6
3rd quarter	402.7	250.8	230.0	39.2	190.8	20.8	15.2	5.7	46.4	10.9	35.5	13.7
4th quarter	410.9	256.7	235.4	39.7	195.7	21.4	15.6	5.8	46.8	10.9	35.8	13.8
1957												
1st quarter	417.6	260.6	238.3	40.2	198.0	22.4	16.0	6.4	46.9	9.9	37.0	13.9
2nd quarter	419.7	262.5	239.6	40.7	198.9	22.8	16.4	6.4	47.7	10.5	37.2	14.0
3rd quarter	423.4	265.1	241.8	41.5	200.3	23.3	16.9	6.4	48.8	11.0	37.8	14.1
4th quarter	416.9	263.7	240.1	41.6	198.5	23.6	17.3	6.3	47.7	10.7	37.0	14.3

Table 1-13B. National Income by Type of Income: Historical Data—*Continued*

(Billions of dollars, quarterly data are at seasonally adjusted annual rates.)

NIPA Tables 1.7.5, 1.12

| Year and quarter | Corporate profits with IVA and CCAdj | | | | | Net interest and miscel-laneous payments | Taxes on production and imports | Less: Subsidies | Business current transfer payments, net | | | Current surplus of govern-ment enterprises | Addendum: Net national factor income |
| | Total | Taxes on corporate income | Profits after tax | | | | | | Total [1] | To persons | To govern-ment | | |
			Total	Net dividends	Undis-tributed corporate profits								
1929	10.8	1.4	9.5	5.8	3.7	4.6	6.8	0.0	0.5	0.4	0.1	0.0	86.9
1930	7.5	0.8	6.7	5.5	1.2	4.8	7.0	0.1	0.5	0.4	0.1	0.0	75.8
1931	3.0	0.5	2.5	4.1	-1.6	4.8	6.7	0.1	0.5	0.4	0.1	0.0	60.6
1932	-0.2	0.4	-0.6	2.5	-3.1	4.5	6.6	0.1	0.6	0.5	0.1	0.0	44.3
1933	-0.2	0.5	-0.7	2.0	-2.7	4.0	6.9	0.2	0.5	0.4	0.1	0.0	41.7
1934	2.5	0.7	1.8	2.6	-0.8	4.0	7.6	0.5	0.5	0.4	0.1	0.0	50.7
1935	4.0	1.0	3.1	2.8	0.2	4.1	8.0	0.6	0.5	0.4	0.1	0.0	58.5
1936	6.2	1.4	4.8	4.5	0.3	3.8	8.5	0.3	0.5	0.4	0.1	0.0	66.4
1937	7.1	1.5	5.6	4.7	0.9	3.7	8.9	0.3	0.5	0.4	0.1	0.0	74.6
1938	5.0	1.0	4.0	3.2	0.8	3.6	8.9	0.5	0.4	0.3	0.2	0.0	68.2
1939	6.6	1.4	5.2	3.8	1.4	3.6	9.1	0.8	0.4	0.3	0.2	0.0	73.7
1940	9.9	2.8	7.0	4.0	3.0	3.3	9.8	0.8	0.5	0.3	0.2	0.0	82.1
1941	15.7	7.6	8.1	4.4	3.7	3.3	11.1	0.5	0.5	0.4	0.2	0.0	106.3
1942	20.8	11.4	9.4	4.3	5.1	3.2	11.5	0.5	0.5	0.3	0.2	0.0	140.9
1943	24.9	14.1	10.8	4.4	6.4	2.9	12.4	0.6	0.6	0.4	0.3	0.0	174.8
1944	25.0	12.9	12.0	4.6	7.4	2.4	13.7	1.0	0.8	0.4	0.4	0.0	187.5
1945	20.5	10.7	9.8	4.6	5.2	2.3	15.1	1.1	0.9	0.5	0.4	0.0	186.6
1946	18.2	9.1	9.1	5.6	3.6	1.9	16.8	1.4	0.7	0.4	0.3	0.0	185.3
1947	24.2	11.3	12.9	6.3	6.6	2.5	18.1	0.4	0.7	0.4	0.3	0.0	200.6
1948	31.4	12.4	19.0	7.0	11.9	2.6	19.7	0.5	0.7	0.4	0.3	0.0	225.2
1949	29.1	10.2	18.9	7.2	11.6	2.9	20.9	0.5	0.7	0.4	0.3	0.0	219.0
1947													
1st quarter	21.5	11.6	9.9	6.0	3.9	2.3	17.7	0.5	0.7	0.4	0.3	...	195.7
2nd quarter	24.5	10.9	13.5	6.3	7.2	2.4	17.7	0.4	0.7	0.4	0.3	...	197.9
3rd quarter	24.6	10.8	13.8	6.5	7.3	2.6	18.0	0.4	0.7	0.4	0.3	...	200.9
4th quarter	26.1	11.8	14.3	6.4	7.9	2.6	19.0	0.3	0.7	0.4	0.3	...	207.8
1948													
1st quarter	30.0	12.1	17.8	7.0	10.8	2.5	19.0	0.4	0.7	0.4	0.4	...	216.8
2nd quarter	31.8	12.8	19.0	6.7	12.3	2.6	19.7	0.3	0.7	0.4	0.3	...	224.3
3rd quarter	31.2	12.6	18.6	7.1	11.5	2.7	20.0	0.6	0.7	0.4	0.3	...	229.0
4th quarter	32.7	12.2	20.5	7.4	13.2	2.7	20.3	0.9	0.7	0.4	0.3	...	230.9
1949													
1st quarter	31.0	11.0	20.0	7.2	12.7	2.8	20.4	0.6	0.7	0.3	0.3	...	223.2
2nd quarter	28.7	9.7	18.9	7.2	11.7	2.9	20.8	0.4	0.7	0.3	0.3	...	219.0
3rd quarter	29.9	10.1	19.8	7.1	12.7	2.9	21.3	0.5	0.7	0.4	0.3	...	218.8
4th quarter	26.6	9.9	16.7	7.4	9.3	3.0	21.2	0.5	0.7	0.4	0.3	...	214.9
1950													
1st quarter	30.1	13.6	16.4	8.3	8.1	3.1	21.6	0.7	0.7	0.4	0.3	...	225.1
2nd quarter	33.9	16.3	17.6	8.4	9.2	3.2	22.5	0.8	0.8	0.5	0.3	...	236.4
3rd quarter	38.4	19.9	18.5	9.2	9.4	3.2	24.4	0.8	0.9	0.6	0.3	...	251.4
4th quarter	41.8	21.8	20.0	9.5	10.5	3.3	23.4	1.1	0.9	0.7	0.3	...	263.2
1951													
1st quarter	40.7	26.3	14.4	8.4	6.1	3.4	25.1	1.2	1.1	0.8	0.3	...	273.2
2nd quarter	40.6	22.3	18.3	8.6	9.7	3.7	24.1	1.1	1.2	0.9	0.3	...	281.5
3rd quarter	41.1	20.1	21.0	8.6	12.4	3.8	24.5	0.9	1.2	0.9	0.3	...	286.1
4th quarter	42.4	21.5	20.8	8.7	12.2	3.9	25.3	1.0	1.2	0.9	0.3	...	291.8
1952													
1st quarter	40.0	19.8	20.2	8.2	12.1	3.9	26.1	0.8	1.2	0.9	0.3	...	292.4
2nd quarter	38.1	18.7	19.5	8.7	10.8	4.1	26.9	0.8	1.2	0.9	0.3	...	293.5
3rd quarter	38.1	18.6	19.5	8.6	10.9	4.2	27.3	0.8	1.2	0.9	0.3	...	299.7
4th quarter	42.4	20.5	21.9	8.8	13.1	4.3	28.1	0.7	1.2	0.9	0.3	...	310.3
1953													
1st quarter	43.3	21.6	21.7	8.4	13.3	4.5	28.7	0.7	1.2	0.9	0.3	...	315.8
2nd quarter	42.5	21.7	20.8	9.2	11.6	4.7	29.2	0.4	1.2	0.9	0.3	...	317.9
3rd quarter	41.3	21.2	20.1	9.0	11.0	4.9	29.3	0.7	1.2	0.8	0.3	...	316.4
4th quarter	34.0	16.6	17.4	8.9	8.5	5.1	29.2	0.2	1.1	0.8	0.3	...	308.5
1954													
1st quarter	36.5	16.4	20.1	9.4	10.7	5.3	28.7	0.1	1.0	0.6	0.3	...	310.7
2nd quarter	37.8	16.9	20.9	8.9	12.1	5.6	28.8	0.7	0.9	0.5	0.3	...	311.5
3rd quarter	39.9	17.9	22.0	9.3	12.7	5.8	28.7	0.3	0.9	0.5	0.4	...	314.6
4th quarter	43.6	19.3	24.3	9.5	14.8	6.0	29.3	0.2	0.9	0.6	0.4	...	322.7
1955													
1st quarter	48.8	21.3	27.5	10.0	17.4	6.2	30.2	0.3	1.1	0.7	0.4	...	334.2
2nd quarter	50.1	21.6	28.5	10.2	18.3	6.3	31.2	0.3	1.2	0.9	0.4	...	342.5
3rd quarter	50.2	22.2	28.0	10.8	17.2	6.3	31.9	0.0	1.4	1.0	0.4	...	348.8
4th quarter	51.6	23.1	28.5	10.9	17.6	6.4	32.5	0.2	1.5	1.1	0.4	...	354.7
1956													
1st quarter	49.4	22.0	27.4	11.2	16.2	6.7	33.0	0.3	1.6	1.2	0.4	...	357.7
2nd quarter	49.6	22.5	27.2	11.2	16.0	6.8	33.6	0.5	1.6	1.2	0.4	...	363.2
3rd quarter	49.3	21.1	28.2	11.2	17.0	7.1	34.6	0.9	1.7	1.3	0.4	...	367.3
4th quarter	50.2	22.3	27.9	11.6	16.3	7.1	35.7	1.2	1.7	1.3	0.4	...	374.6
1957													
1st quarter	51.7	22.8	28.8	11.6	17.2	7.8	36.1	1.3	1.8	1.4	0.4	...	380.9
2nd quarter	50.3	21.9	28.4	11.8	16.6	8.0	36.6	1.2	1.8	1.4	0.4	...	382.5
3rd quarter	49.3	21.4	27.9	11.9	16.0	8.3	37.0	1.1	1.8	1.4	0.4	...	385.6
4th quarter	45.3	19.6	25.7	11.7	14.0	8.3	36.7	1.0	1.8	1.4	0.4	...	379.3

[1] Includes net transfer payments to the rest of the world, not shown separately.
. . . = Not available.

Table 1-13B. National Income by Type of Income: Historical Data—*Continued*

(Billions of dollars, quarterly data are at seasonally adjusted annual rates.)

NIPA Tables 1.7.5, 1.12

Year and quarter	National income, total	Compensation of employees							Proprietors' income with IVA and CCAdj			Rental income of persons with CCAdj
		Total	Wages and salaries			Supplements to wages and salaries			Total	Farm	Nonfarm	
			Total	Government	Other	Total	Employer contributions for:					
							Employee pension and insurance funds	Government social insurance				
1958												
1st quarter	411.1	260.2	236.7	42.0	194.7	23.5	17.2	6.3	50.3	13.3	36.9	14.6
2nd quarter	413.0	259.9	236.3	43.1	193.2	23.6	17.3	6.3	50.3	13.0	37.3	14.8
3rd quarter	425.3	267.7	243.8	46.1	197.7	23.8	17.5	6.4	50.1	12.1	38.0	14.9
4th quarter	437.1	272.7	248.4	45.3	203.2	24.3	17.8	6.4	49.9	11.2	38.7	15.0
1959												
1st quarter	449.2	280.2	254.0	45.5	208.6	26.2	18.5	7.8	50.1	10.9	39.2	15.0
2nd quarter	463.2	286.9	260.6	45.8	214.7	26.4	18.5	7.9	50.3	9.9	40.5	15.4
3rd quarter	460.5	287.4	260.9	46.2	214.7	26.5	18.6	7.9	50.4	9.4	41.0	15.8
4th quarter	465.7	290.7	263.9	46.7	217.2	26.8	18.9	7.9	50.6	10.1	40.5	16.0
1960												
1st quarter	479.1	299.3	270.7	47.7	223.0	28.5	19.3	9.3	49.7	9.6	40.1	16.2
2nd quarter	479.8	302.3	273.4	48.6	224.8	28.9	19.6	9.3	50.7	10.6	40.1	16.4
3rd quarter	481.2	303.2	274.0	49.9	224.1	29.2	19.9	9.3	50.9	11.0	39.9	16.5
4th quarter	479.4	302.7	273.3	50.5	222.8	29.4	20.2	9.2	51.0	11.3	39.7	16.7
1961												
1st quarter	481.4	303.7	273.8	51.1	222.7	30.0	20.5	9.5	52.3	11.5	40.8	16.9
2nd quarter	491.1	308.0	277.6	51.8	225.8	30.3	20.8	9.6	52.6	10.9	41.8	17.1
3rd quarter	500.9	313.0	282.3	52.8	229.5	30.8	21.1	9.6	53.3	11.0	42.3	17.3
4th quarter	515.5	319.7	288.4	54.2	234.2	31.2	21.5	9.8	54.5	11.5	43.0	17.5
1962												
1st quarter	524.6	326.2	293.3	55.3	238.0	32.9	21.9	11.0	55.3	11.9	43.5	17.7
2nd quarter	531.8	332.1	298.7	56.0	242.8	33.4	22.2	11.2	55.0	11.1	43.9	18.0
3rd quarter	538.2	334.9	301.2	56.5	244.7	33.8	22.5	11.2	54.9	10.7	44.2	18.2
4th quarter	546.2	338.4	304.2	57.6	246.6	34.1	22.9	11.3	55.8	11.3	44.5	18.3
1963												
1st quarter	553.0	343.4	308.0	58.6	249.3	35.4	23.2	12.2	56.0	11.4	44.6	18.5
2nd quarter	562.1	348.3	312.4	59.4	253.0	36.0	23.6	12.3	55.8	10.8	45.0	18.7
3rd quarter	570.6	353.4	316.8	60.2	256.7	36.6	24.1	12.5	56.2	10.7	45.5	18.8
4th quarter	580.6	359.6	322.2	61.9	260.3	37.3	24.7	12.6	57.6	11.1	46.5	18.8
1964												
1st quarter	593.0	366.0	328.2	63.1	265.1	37.8	25.3	12.4	57.9	9.9	48.0	18.8
2nd quarter	603.1	373.5	334.8	64.2	270.7	38.6	26.1	12.6	58.8	9.5	49.3	18.8
3rd quarter	614.5	380.9	341.4	65.7	275.7	39.5	26.7	12.7	59.3	9.3	50.0	18.9
4th quarter	622.7	387.0	346.7	66.8	279.9	40.3	27.5	12.8	60.5	10.4	50.1	18.8
1965												
1st quarter	641.3	393.8	352.8	67.5	285.4	41.0	28.2	12.8	61.9	11.4	50.5	19.1
2nd quarter	652.6	400.8	358.9	68.5	290.3	42.0	29.0	13.0	63.2	12.0	51.2	19.3
3rd quarter	663.8	409.3	366.2	70.5	295.7	43.1	29.9	13.2	64.0	12.2	51.8	19.5
4th quarter	683.2	421.4	377.1	73.2	304.0	44.3	30.9	13.4	65.6	12.5	53.0	19.5
1966												
1st quarter	703.5	434.1	385.8	74.9	310.8	48.3	31.9	16.5	69.2	14.9	54.4	19.8
2nd quarter	713.4	445.4	395.9	76.9	319.0	49.5	32.8	16.7	67.2	12.7	54.5	19.8
3rd quarter	724.7	456.7	406.1	79.8	326.3	50.6	33.6	17.0	67.2	12.3	54.9	20.0
4th quarter	737.2	464.9	413.5	82.0	331.5	51.4	34.3	17.2	68.1	12.2	55.9	20.0
1967												
1st quarter	743.5	471.1	418.8	83.5	335.4	52.3	34.7	17.6	68.9	11.9	57.0	20.3
2nd quarter	750.2	476.8	423.6	85.0	338.6	53.2	35.4	17.8	68.5	11.1	57.4	20.4
3rd quarter	765.6	486.4	432.0	87.1	344.9	54.4	36.3	18.2	70.5	12.0	58.6	20.4
4th quarter	781.5	497.4	441.6	90.4	351.2	55.8	37.3	18.6	70.0	11.5	58.4	20.3
1968												
1st quarter	802.5	512.2	454.2	92.8	361.5	57.9	38.5	19.4	71.7	11.6	60.1	20.1
2nd quarter	823.7	525.3	465.9	95.2	370.7	59.4	39.6	19.8	73.2	11.2	61.9	20.1
3rd quarter	842.8	539.2	478.3	98.7	379.6	60.9	40.7	20.1	75.0	11.8	63.2	20.2
4th quarter	859.3	551.7	489.4	100.1	389.4	62.3	41.9	20.5	75.5	12.0	63.5	20.0
1969												
1st quarter	875.7	564.2	499.1	101.3	397.8	65.2	43.1	22.1	75.6	11.6	64.1	20.2
2nd quarter	892.1	578.2	511.4	103.1	408.3	66.9	44.3	22.5	77.1	12.5	64.6	20.3
3rd quarter	910.8	595.0	526.4	108.2	418.3	68.6	45.6	23.0	78.0	13.1	64.8	20.5
4th quarter	919.4	606.6	536.5	109.8	426.6	70.1	46.7	23.4	77.3	14.1	63.2	20.5
1970												
1st quarter	923.9	616.7	545.1	114.4	430.7	71.6	47.9	23.7	77.1	13.5	63.5	20.5
2nd quarter	935.8	622.0	549.1	116.5	432.6	72.9	49.1	23.9	76.7	12.4	64.3	20.3
3rd quarter	950.3	630.0	555.7	118.3	437.4	74.3	50.3	23.9	78.5	13.2	65.3	20.9
4th quarter	950.6	631.8	556.4	119.7	436.6	75.5	51.6	23.9	78.9	12.5	66.4	21.2
1971												
1st quarter	987.4	649.9	570.5	123.9	446.6	79.4	53.3	26.1	80.3	13.1	67.2	21.2
2nd quarter	1 007.3	661.8	580.4	125.6	454.8	81.4	55.0	26.4	82.8	13.3	69.6	21.8
3rd quarter	1 025.5	672.2	588.8	128.0	460.8	83.4	56.9	26.5	84.6	13.0	71.6	22.2
4th quarter	1 047.9	684.2	598.4	129.6	468.8	85.8	59.0	26.8	87.9	14.2	73.6	22.6
1972												
1st quarter	1 081.2	710.6	618.5	134.2	484.3	92.1	61.5	30.6	87.9	13.1	74.8	23.2
2nd quarter	1 101.7	724.7	630.4	135.7	494.7	94.4	63.3	31.0	91.3	15.4	75.9	20.3
3rd quarter	1 131.4	738.1	642.3	138.4	503.9	95.8	64.6	31.2	95.5	17.2	78.4	24.0
4th quarter	1 177.6	761.2	664.0	143.3	520.7	97.2	65.4	31.8	105.6	22.4	83.3	23.9

Table 1-13B. National Income by Type of Income: Historical Data—*Continued*

(Billions of dollars, quarterly data are at seasonally adjusted annual rates.)

NIPA Tables 1.7.5, 1.12

| Year and quarter | Corporate profits with IVA and CCAdj | | | | | Net interest and miscellaneous payments | Taxes on production and imports | Less: Subsidies | Business current transfer payments, net | | | Current surplus of government enterprises | Addendum: Net national factor income |
| | Total | Taxes on corporate income | Profits after tax | | | | | | Total ¹ | To persons | To government | | |
			Total	Net dividends	Undistributed corporate profits								
1958													
1st quarter	39.5	16.9	22.5	11.6	11.0	9.1	36.8	1.1	1.8	1.3	0.5	. . .	373.6
2nd quarter	40.6	17.2	23.4	11.7	11.7	9.6	37.3	1.3	1.7	1.3	0.5	. . .	375.2
3rd quarter	44.8	19.4	25.4	11.7	13.7	9.9	37.8	1.5	1.7	1.2	0.5	. . .	387.3
4th quarter	50.6	22.3	28.3	11.4	16.9	10.0	38.9	1.6	1.6	1.2	0.4	. . .	398.2
1959													
1st quarter	54.3	23.5	30.8	12.1	18.7	8.9	39.8	1.1	1.6	1.3	0.3	0.5	408.4
2nd quarter	59.1	25.7	33.3	12.5	20.9	9.9	40.3	0.9	1.7	1.3	0.3	0.5	421.6
3rd quarter	54.2	23.1	31.1	12.8	18.3	9.9	41.7	1.1	1.7	1.3	0.3	0.5	417.6
4th quarter	54.5	22.6	32.0	13.0	19.0	10.2	42.4	1.1	1.7	1.4	0.3	0.6	422.1
1960													
1st quarter	58.6	25.1	33.5	13.2	20.3	10.3	43.7	1.0	1.7	1.3	0.4	0.5	434.1
2nd quarter	54.8	23.1	31.7	13.2	18.5	10.3	44.3	1.3	1.7	1.3	0.4	0.6	434.4
3rd quarter	53.8	22.0	31.8	13.5	18.2	10.9	44.9	1.0	1.7	1.3	0.4	0.4	435.2
4th quarter	51.5	20.9	30.6	13.5	17.1	11.3	45.3	1.2	1.8	1.3	0.5	0.4	433.2
1961													
1st quarter	50.2	20.7	29.6	13.6	16.0	11.8	45.8	1.6	1.9	1.3	0.5	0.3	435.0
2nd quarter	54.5	22.1	32.4	13.6	18.7	12.3	46.5	2.0	1.9	1.3	0.5	0.3	444.5
3rd quarter	57.2	23.4	33.9	13.9	19.9	12.7	47.3	2.2	1.9	1.4	0.5	0.3	453.6
4th quarter	61.8	25.4	36.4	14.5	21.9	13.5	48.4	2.3	2.0	1.4	0.6	0.5	466.9
1962													
1st quarter	62.6	23.9	38.6	14.6	24.1	13.3	49.4	2.3	2.0	1.5	0.6	0.4	475.1
2nd quarter	62.5	23.7	38.9	15.0	23.9	14.3	49.9	2.4	2.1	1.5	0.6	0.3	481.8
3rd quarter	64.2	24.4	39.9	15.2	24.7	14.7	50.9	2.2	2.1	1.6	0.6	0.4	486.9
4th quarter	66.9	24.5	42.4	15.4	27.0	15.1	51.3	2.2	2.2	1.6	0.6	0.4	494.5
1963													
1st quarter	67.2	24.6	42.6	15.8	26.9	14.8	52.0	2.0	2.4	1.8	0.6	0.7	499.9
2nd quarter	70.2	26.3	44.0	16.1	27.9	15.0	52.9	2.2	2.5	1.8	0.7	0.8	508.0
3rd quarter	71.7	27.0	44.7	16.3	28.3	15.5	53.9	2.3	2.5	1.9	0.7	0.8	515.6
4th quarter	73.0	27.7	45.3	16.8	28.5	15.9	54.7	2.4	2.6	2.0	0.7	0.9	524.9
1964													
1st quarter	77.1	27.9	49.1	17.5	31.7	16.7	55.7	2.7	2.7	2.1	0.6	0.9	536.5
2nd quarter	77.3	28.0	49.4	18.0	31.3	17.3	56.7	2.9	2.8	2.2	0.6	0.8	545.6
3rd quarter	78.4	28.6	49.9	18.4	31.4	18.0	57.9	2.6	3.2	2.2	1.0	0.6	555.5
4th quarter	78.0	28.2	49.9	18.9	31.0	18.2	58.8	2.7	3.3	2.3	1.0	0.8	562.5
1965													
1st quarter	85.8	29.6	56.3	19.2	37.1	19.1	60.2	2.9	3.5	2.3	1.2	0.7	579.8
2nd quarter	88.0	30.5	57.5	19.9	37.7	19.6	60.3	3.0	3.5	2.3	1.2	0.8	590.9
3rd quarter	89.3	31.1	58.2	20.5	37.6	20.1	60.5	3.0	3.5	2.2	1.2	0.7	602.2
4th quarter	94.0	33.1	60.9	21.2	39.7	20.1	61.8	3.1	3.4	2.2	1.3	0.5	620.6
1966													
1st quarter	97.4	34.2	63.2	21.3	41.9	21.3	61.4	3.6	3.4	2.2	1.3	0.5	641.8
2nd quarter	96.4	34.2	62.2	20.9	41.3	22.0	62.8	3.9	3.4	2.1	1.3	0.3	650.7
3rd quarter	94.8	33.9	61.0	20.5	40.4	22.8	63.7	4.1	3.4	2.1	1.3	0.1	661.6
4th quarter	95.9	33.3	62.6	20.0	42.6	23.9	64.9	4.2	3.4	2.1	1.3	0.2	672.9
1967													
1st quarter	93.3	32.5	60.8	21.1	39.8	24.7	65.6	4.0	3.5	2.2	1.3	0.1	678.3
2nd quarter	92.2	32.2	60.0	21.7	38.3	25.6	66.8	3.9	3.6	2.2	1.4	0.2	683.4
3rd quarter	93.2	32.5	60.7	22.1	38.7	26.0	68.7	3.7	3.7	2.3	1.4	0.3	696.6
4th quarter	96.7	34.4	62.3	21.2	41.1	26.4	70.6	3.7	3.8	2.4	1.4	0.0	710.8
1968													
1st quarter	98.1	38.7	59.4	22.6	36.8	26.8	73.4	4.0	3.9	2.5	1.4	0.3	728.9
2nd quarter	102.1	39.5	62.6	23.4	39.2	27.3	75.4	4.2	4.1	2.7	1.4	0.3	748.0
3rd quarter	102.6	39.7	63.0	24.0	39.0	27.7	77.7	4.2	4.3	2.9	1.4	0.3	764.7
4th quarter	104.1	40.6	63.5	24.2	39.3	28.4	79.1	4.2	4.4	3.0	1.4	0.2	779.8
1969													
1st quarter	103.5	41.5	62.0	24.0	38.1	31.2	80.6	4.3	4.7	3.3	1.5	0.0	794.7
2nd quarter	100.3	40.4	59.9	24.1	35.8	32.9	82.9	4.5	4.8	3.4	1.5	0.0	808.9
3rd quarter	97.4	39.1	58.3	24.3	34.0	34.6	85.2	4.7	4.8	3.4	1.5	0.0	825.5
4th quarter	92.4	38.9	53.6	24.6	29.0	35.7	86.7	4.7	4.8	3.3	1.5	0.0	832.5
1970													
1st quarter	84.7	34.5	50.2	24.5	25.7	37.4	88.5	4.7	4.6	3.1	1.5	-0.7	836.3
2nd quarter	88.5	34.7	53.8	24.3	29.6	39.5	90.5	4.8	4.5	3.0	1.5	-1.3	846.9
3rd quarter	88.4	35.7	52.7	24.2	28.4	41.8	92.5	4.7	4.2	2.8	1.4	-1.3	859.5
4th quarter	83.5	34.2	49.3	24.2	25.1	43.2	94.1	4.8	4.1	2.8	1.4	-1.5	858.7
1971													
1st quarter	96.6	37.8	58.8	25.0	33.8	44.3	97.7	4.8	4.1	2.7	1.5	-1.9	892.3
2nd quarter	98.7	38.6	60.2	25.0	35.2	45.3	98.9	4.8	4.1	2.7	1.4	-1.4	910.5
3rd quarter	101.4	37.9	63.5	25.2	38.4	45.5	101.7	4.5	4.2	2.7	1.5	-1.8	925.9
4th quarter	105.8	38.4	67.4	24.9	42.5	45.8	103.7	4.6	4.2	2.8	1.5	-1.7	946.3
1972													
1st quarter	111.5	40.4	71.2	26.1	45.0	46.6	104.6	6.1	4.5	2.9	1.6	-1.6	979.8
2nd quarter	113.4	40.7	72.8	26.4	46.3	47.9	106.8	6.2	4.7	3.0	1.7	-1.3	997.6
3rd quarter	118.2	42.0	76.2	27.1	49.1	50.2	108.9	7.2	4.9	3.2	1.7	-1.1	1 026.0
4th quarter	125.7	46.4	79.4	27.7	51.7	52.4	111.5	7.1	5.0	3.3	1.7	-0.7	1 068.8

¹Includes net transfer payments to the rest of the world, not shown separately.
. . . = Not available.

Table 1-13B. National Income by Type of Income: Historical Data—*Continued*

(Billions of dollars, quarterly data are at seasonally adjusted annual rates.)

NIPA Tables 1.7.5, 1.12

Year and quarter	National income, total	Compensation of employees Total	Wages and salaries Total	Government	Other	Supplements to wages and salaries Total	Employee pension and insurance funds	Government social insurance	Proprietors' income with IVA and CCAdj Total	Farm	Nonfarm	Rental income of persons with CCAdj
1973												
1st quarter	1 214.7	787.8	683.4	145.0	538.3	104.4	65.7	38.7	104.1	21.8	82.4	23.6
2nd quarter	1 239.4	805.6	700.2	147.2	553.0	105.4	66.0	39.3	109.9	27.6	82.4	23.5
3rd quarter	1 267.8	822.8	716.2	149.6	566.6	106.6	66.6	39.9	113.8	29.5	84.3	22.5
4th quarter	1 306.0	844.1	735.3	153.4	582.0	108.7	67.6	41.1	122.2	37.5	84.7	23.4
1974												
1st quarter	1 318.2	860.9	748.2	155.6	592.5	112.7	69.1	43.6	115.7	28.6	87.1	23.7
2nd quarter	1 338.9	881.1	765.3	158.2	607.1	115.8	71.3	44.5	108.6	20.1	88.5	23.1
3rd quarter	1 364.9	902.8	783.1	161.3	621.8	119.7	74.4	45.3	111.0	21.5	89.5	23.4
4th quarter	1 381.1	916.5	792.5	166.9	625.6	124.0	78.6	45.4	113.5	23.7	89.8	23.2
1975												
1st quarter	1 388.0	921.2	791.9	170.5	621.4	129.3	83.5	45.7	112.7	19.7	93.0	22.9
2nd quarter	1 418.8	934.1	800.4	174.5	625.9	133.8	87.8	46.0	114.3	20.1	94.2	22.6
3rd quarter	1 477.0	959.0	821.3	177.8	643.5	137.7	90.7	47.0	120.7	23.8	96.9	22.5
4th quarter	1 520.8	986.4	845.8	182.2	663.6	140.6	92.4	48.2	125.2	24.3	100.8	22.1
1976												
1st quarter	1 571.3	1 017.6	871.2	184.8	686.4	146.4	93.3	53.1	126.4	19.4	107.0	21.9
2nd quarter	1 596.9	1 038.4	889.4	187.3	702.1	149.0	95.1	53.9	128.6	17.0	111.6	20.8
3rd quarter	1 628.9	1 061.2	908.5	189.5	719.0	152.8	97.9	54.9	132.7	16.1	116.6	20.3
4th quarter	1 661.9	1 087.7	929.9	194.1	735.8	157.7	102.1	55.7	136.2	16.3	119.9	19.4
1977												
1st quarter	1 705.6	1 116.3	950.0	196.7	753.3	166.2	107.2	59.1	138.6	16.0	122.6	17.1
2nd quarter	1 776.0	1 153.4	980.9	199.7	781.2	172.5	111.9	60.6	140.5	14.1	126.4	16.6
3rd quarter	1 832.8	1 185.3	1 007.5	203.7	803.8	177.8	116.1	61.7	142.4	11.8	130.6	15.8
4th quarter	1 880.3	1 221.0	1 038.2	210.3	827.9	182.8	119.8	63.0	156.5	22.0	134.5	15.3
1978												
1st quarter	1 920.3	1 255.8	1 064.2	214.0	850.3	191.6	122.8	68.8	158.5	18.5	140.0	16.5
2nd quarter	2 014.3	1 302.9	1 106.0	217.2	888.8	197.0	126.0	71.0	166.1	20.9	145.2	16.2
3rd quarter	2 060.3	1 339.2	1 137.1	221.5	915.6	202.0	129.8	72.3	168.3	20.8	147.6	17.4
4th quarter	2 124.8	1 383.0	1 175.0	227.4	947.6	208.0	133.9	74.1	170.9	19.5	151.4	17.6
1979												
1st quarter	2 181.1	1 427.3	1 208.4	231.1	977.2	219.0	138.5	80.5	180.1	23.8	156.3	17.8
2nd quarter	2 219.6	1 458.3	1 234.0	233.1	1 000.9	224.2	142.6	81.6	179.2	21.8	157.3	15.6
3rd quarter	2 270.7	1 498.8	1 268.2	238.2	1 030.0	230.6	147.3	83.3	180.7	22.3	158.5	15.4
4th quarter	2 321.2	1 539.7	1 302.7	246.1	1 056.6	237.0	152.1	84.9	177.8	20.8	157.0	17.6
1980												
1st quarter	2 366.6	1 579.2	1 334.9	251.3	1 083.6	244.4	157.0	87.3	167.6	13.3	154.3	20.0
2nd quarter	2 358.0	1 600.5	1 351.0	257.7	1 093.3	249.5	161.7	87.7	160.3	3.1	157.2	14.1
3rd quarter	2 425.7	1 631.2	1 376.1	263.0	1 113.1	255.1	166.2	89.0	173.4	11.7	161.7	17.0
4th quarter	2 556.8	1 694.0	1 431.7	273.8	1 157.9	262.3	170.5	91.7	185.0	18.7	166.3	27.8
1981												
1st quarter	2 642.6	1 745.2	1 469.1	278.7	1 190.3	276.2	174.5	101.7	188.2	17.6	170.6	26.2
2nd quarter	2 684.2	1 777.5	1 496.2	282.1	1 214.1	281.3	178.3	102.9	176.4	18.2	158.2	24.4
3rd quarter	2 773.6	1 815.4	1 528.7	286.8	1 241.9	286.7	182.1	104.5	182.3	23.3	158.9	24.1
4th quarter	2 788.1	1 843.0	1 551.5	295.7	1 255.8	291.5	186.2	105.3	171.8	17.0	154.9	27.0
1982												
1st quarter	2 791.9	1 866.4	1 567.2	300.4	1 266.8	299.2	190.2	109.0	165.2	14.4	150.8	27.6
2nd quarter	2 838.1	1 885.1	1 580.9	304.6	1 276.3	304.1	194.5	109.6	169.4	12.8	156.6	24.0
3rd quarter	2 858.0	1 905.3	1 596.1	309.2	1 286.9	309.3	199.1	110.1	170.7	11.9	158.8	25.9
4th quarter	2 873.7	1 920.4	1 605.9	316.0	1 289.9	314.6	204.3	110.3	179.5	14.2	165.3	27.0
1983												
1st quarter	2 934.4	1 949.9	1 623.1	319.3	1 303.7	326.9	209.8	117.1	183.3	12.9	170.4	27.4
2nd quarter	3 014.3	1 988.6	1 655.1	323.0	1 332.1	333.5	214.7	118.7	182.6	7.9	174.8	27.4
3rd quarter	3 094.5	2 031.2	1 691.8	327.1	1 364.7	339.5	219.0	120.5	183.8	0.2	183.6	27.4
4th quarter	3 198.8	2 085.9	1 740.1	329.7	1 410.4	345.8	222.6	123.2	195.3	3.8	191.5	27.7
1984												
1st quarter	3 331.3	2 147.1	1 785.2	339.0	1 446.2	361.9	226.3	135.6	221.9	19.5	202.4	26.9
2nd quarter	3 418.3	2 196.8	1 828.2	344.8	1 483.4	368.6	230.4	138.2	231.8	21.3	210.5	25.2
3rd quarter	3 484.7	2 242.6	1 866.7	351.6	1 515.2	375.9	235.6	140.3	232.4	20.4	211.9	27.6
4th quarter	3 541.8	2 283.1	1 899.5	357.2	1 542.4	383.5	241.5	142.0	226.9	22.5	204.4	31.9
1985												
1st quarter	3 607.4	2 327.0	1 933.8	365.6	1 568.2	393.3	248.6	144.7	240.7	22.8	217.8	30.2
2nd quarter	3 655.4	2 365.0	1 963.2	370.0	1 593.2	401.8	255.3	146.4	238.5	20.4	218.0	29.2
3rd quarter	3 716.2	2 406.7	1 996.1	376.8	1 619.3	410.6	262.1	148.5	240.7	19.3	221.5	30.3
4th quarter	3 757.7	2 457.1	2 037.1	383.0	1 654.0	420.0	268.7	151.4	244.3	21.4	223.0	28.4
1986												
1st quarter	3 809.1	2 493.3	2 063.5	387.9	1 675.6	429.8	274.7	155.0	245.6	18.3	227.4	24.8
2nd quarter	3 820.4	2 519.1	2 081.8	393.6	1 688.3	437.2	280.8	156.4	251.6	19.6	232.0	24.2
3rd quarter	3 859.9	2 557.1	2 111.7	399.7	1 712.0	445.3	286.6	158.7	264.4	26.6	237.8	20.5
4th quarter	3 903.4	2 605.9	2 152.2	407.6	1 744.6	453.7	292.4	161.3	264.2	26.6	237.6	18.1
1987												
1st quarter	3 975.2	2 651.0	2 193.7	414.6	1 779.1	457.3	294.4	162.9	275.4	27.3	248.2	18.8
2nd quarter	4 073.4	2 694.2	2 230.1	420.1	1 810.0	464.2	299.4	164.7	282.3	29.0	253.3	17.4
3rd quarter	4 167.3	2 741.8	2 270.6	424.9	1 845.7	471.2	304.2	167.0	289.5	28.8	260.7	21.0
4th quarter	4 260.9	2 810.3	2 330.7	432.8	1 897.8	479.6	309.2	170.4	298.6	30.4	268.2	23.7

Table 1-13B. National Income by Type of Income: Historical Data—*Continued*

(Billions of dollars, quarterly data are at seasonally adjusted annual rates.)   **NIPA Tables 1.7.5, 1.12**

| Year and quarter | Corporate profits with IVA and CCAdj | | | | | Net interest and miscel-laneous payments | Taxes on production and imports | Less: Subsidies | Business current transfer payments, net | | | Current surplus of govern-ment enterprises | Addendum: Net national factor income |
| | Total | Taxes on corporate income | Profits after tax | | | | | | | | | | |
			Total	Net dividends	Undis-tributed corporate profits				Total [1]	To persons	To govern-ment		
1973													
1st quarter	133.5	49.7	83.8	28.4	55.4	53.0	114.6	5.9	5.6	3.6	1.9	-1.6	1 102.1
2nd quarter	131.3	50.2	81.0	29.3	51.7	54.8	116.2	5.7	5.9	3.9	2.0	-2.0	1 125.0
3rd quarter	133.0	48.6	84.4	30.4	54.0	58.9	118.4	4.7	5.6	4.1	1.6	-2.4	1 150.9
4th quarter	135.8	51.4	84.4	31.5	52.9	62.3	119.7	4.6	5.8	4.2	1.6	-2.8	1 187.8
1974													
1st quarter	130.3	49.7	80.6	32.5	48.0	66.8	120.8	3.6	6.3	4.3	2.0	-2.7	1 197.3
2nd quarter	128.9	52.2	76.8	33.3	43.5	71.6	124.1	2.9	6.6	4.5	2.1	-2.1	1 213.3
3rd quarter	124.3	57.3	67.0	33.6	33.4	75.2	127.1	3.2	7.0	4.9	2.1	-2.7	1 236.8
4th quarter	119.3	51.9	67.4	33.5	33.9	80.4	127.7	3.6	7.3	5.2	2.1	-3.2	1 252.9
1975													
1st quarter	117.8	43.8	74.0	32.9	41.0	84.4	128.8	4.2	8.4	6.1	2.2	-4.0	1 259.0
2nd quarter	128.9	46.8	82.2	32.7	49.5	85.1	133.0	4.3	9.1	6.9	2.2	-4.2	1 285.1
3rd quarter	149.8	57.2	92.6	32.9	59.7	86.7	138.2	4.6	9.3	7.1	2.2	-4.6	1 338.7
4th quarter	159.0	58.8	100.2	33.4	66.8	87.3	141.1	4.9	9.4	7.2	2.2	-4.7	1 380.0
1976													
1st quarter	175.1	66.6	108.5	36.2	72.3	86.8	141.7	5.1	9.5	7.0	2.5	-2.7	1 427.9
2nd quarter	173.2	65.2	108.0	38.1	69.9	89.3	144.9	4.8	9.4	7.0	2.4	-2.7	1 450.3
3rd quarter	174.7	64.9	109.9	39.9	69.9	90.9	147.7	5.1	9.1	6.7	2.4	-2.6	1 479.9
4th quarter	174.3	64.5	109.9	41.9	68.0	92.6	151.3	5.5	8.6	6.1	2.5	-2.7	1 510.2
1977													
1st quarter	184.1	68.8	115.3	42.7	72.6	95.2	154.8	5.8	8.2	5.5	2.7	-3.0	1 551.4
2nd quarter	204.9	74.4	130.5	43.9	86.6	103.6	158.0	5.9	7.8	5.0	2.8	-3.1	1 619.0
3rd quarter	219.6	76.7	142.9	45.6	97.3	110.1	161.5	6.4	8.0	4.9	3.2	-3.6	1 673.3
4th quarter	214.5	77.8	136.6	46.8	89.8	114.5	164.3	10.3	8.3	5.0	3.3	-3.7	1 721.7
1978													
1st quarter	209.9	72.5	137.4	48.3	89.2	115.7	166.9	8.7	9.4	5.6	3.7	-3.6	1 756.4
2nd quarter	239.7	86.6	153.1	49.5	103.7	117.8	173.1	8.4	10.0	6.2	3.9	-3.2	1 842.8
3rd quarter	246.2	87.4	158.8	51.8	107.0	118.9	169.7	8.3	10.7	6.7	4.0	-1.9	1 890.0
4th quarter	258.4	92.9	165.5	53.7	111.8	122.7	173.9	10.4	11.4	7.3	4.1	-2.7	1 952.6
1979													
1st quarter	249.7	90.1	159.6	55.4	104.2	128.7	176.4	8.4	12.3	7.9	4.4	-2.8	2 003.6
2nd quarter	252.1	90.9	161.2	56.9	104.3	134.9	178.5	8.8	12.7	8.2	4.5	-2.9	2 040.1
3rd quarter	250.1	90.6	159.5	58.0	101.4	143.2	180.9	8.1	13.0	8.4	4.6	-3.1	2 088.1
4th quarter	244.0	88.4	155.6	59.7	95.9	157.3	184.6	8.9	13.1	8.5	4.6	-4.0	2 136.4
1980													
1st quarter	237.5	97.0	140.5	61.8	78.7	173.0	189.5	9.2	13.2	8.2	5.0	-4.1	2 177.2
2nd quarter	207.0	77.2	129.8	64.3	65.5	180.1	196.9	9.6	13.4	8.3	5.1	-4.8	2 162.1
3rd quarter	214.6	83.2	131.5	64.7	66.8	186.6	204.3	10.1	13.7	8.7	5.0	-5.1	2 222.8
4th quarter	235.1	91.4	143.8	65.6	78.2	205.0	210.6	10.3	15.7	9.3	6.4	-6.2	2 347.0
1981													
1st quarter	244.4	91.1	153.2	68.7	84.5	208.6	230.8	10.6	16.4	10.4	6.1	-6.6	2 412.5
2nd quarter	240.8	82.6	158.2	72.7	85.5	228.4	235.5	10.7	16.6	11.0	5.6	-4.6	2 447.5
3rd quarter	257.8	86.2	171.7	75.9	95.8	255.6	237.5	11.1	17.1	11.5	5.6	-5.1	2 535.2
4th quarter	246.9	77.4	169.5	77.7	91.8	260.9	238.8	13.5	17.5	11.9	5.7	-4.4	2 549.6
1982													
1st quarter	221.8	65.7	156.1	77.7	78.4	272.7	237.4	14.0	18.6	12.0	6.6	-3.8	2 553.7
2nd quarter	236.2	68.4	167.8	76.5	91.2	283.2	238.3	13.6	19.2	12.3	6.9	-3.7	2 598.0
3rd quarter	233.7	68.6	165.1	77.1	87.9	278.0	241.8	13.0	19.5	12.5	7.0	-3.9	2 613.6
4th quarter	227.7	63.2	164.5	79.5	85.0	276.1	246.3	19.4	20.0	12.7	7.2	-3.8	2 630.6
1983													
1st quarter	244.6	64.2	180.4	81.0	99.4	281.1	250.7	19.9	20.3	12.8	7.5	-3.0	2 686.3
2nd quarter	274.7	79.2	195.5	82.1	113.4	282.9	261.2	21.6	20.9	13.2	7.7	-2.5	2 756.2
3rd quarter	291.2	88.3	203.0	84.3	118.6	295.8	267.5	22.2	21.9	14.0	7.9	-2.1	2 829.5
4th quarter	308.6	90.9	217.6	86.4	131.3	307.2	273.7	21.5	23.6	15.3	8.4	-1.6	2 924.6
1984													
1st quarter	336.6	103.9	232.7	88.6	144.1	313.8	281.6	21.2	26.7	17.6	9.1	-2.1	3 046.4
2nd quarter	338.2	102.9	235.3	90.9	144.5	332.6	287.7	21.0	28.6	19.2	9.4	-1.6	3 124.5
3rd quarter	333.6	91.1	242.5	91.1	151.5	348.3	292.2	20.9	30.1	20.6	9.6	-1.3	3 184.5
4th quarter	343.1	92.3	250.8	92.7	158.1	349.7	297.5	21.2	31.2	21.5	9.7	-0.5	3 234.7
1985													
1st quarter	347.9	98.7	249.2	95.4	153.8	349.3	301.0	21.1	32.2	21.9	10.3	0.2	3 295.1
2nd quarter	351.5	97.0	254.6	97.0	157.6	346.9	305.7	21.0	38.1	22.1	16.0	1.5	3 331.0
3rd quarter	368.9	102.3	266.6	98.3	168.3	344.5	311.9	21.3	32.8	22.3	10.5	1.8	3 391.1
4th quarter	349.7	99.7	250.0	99.5	150.5	351.5	313.9	22.0	33.1	22.6	10.5	1.6	3 431.0
1986													
1st quarter	340.7	106.6	234.1	103.2	130.9	366.4	317.5	23.1	42.1	23.3	18.7	1.9	3 470.8
2nd quarter	326.6	106.3	220.2	106.4	113.9	367.2	319.5	24.2	34.5	23.5	11.1	2.0	3 488.7
3rd quarter	315.6	107.3	208.2	107.5	100.8	366.4	326.2	25.5	33.2	23.0	10.2	2.0	3 524.0
4th quarter	314.7	118.5	196.2	107.6	88.6	360.8	330.4	26.8	34.0	22.0	12.0	2.1	3 563.8
1987													
1st quarter	325.9	118.7	207.1	108.8	98.3	359.9	336.0	28.3	34.0	21.3	12.7	2.5	3 630.9
2nd quarter	362.9	132.8	230.1	109.8	120.2	366.1	344.4	30.4	34.4	20.6	13.8	2.2	3 722.9
3rd quarter	386.4	137.9	248.5	113.3	135.2	373.1	352.4	31.3	32.5	19.7	12.8	2.0	3 811.7
4th quarter	388.8	132.4	256.4	117.2	139.2	378.9	357.4	31.1	32.3	19.3	13.0	2.0	3 900.3

[1]Includes net transfer payments to the rest of the world, not shown separately.

Table 1-13B. National Income by Type of Income: Historical Data—*Continued*

(Billions of dollars, quarterly data are at seasonally adjusted annual rates.)

NIPA Tables 1.7.5, 1.12

Year and quarter	National income, total	Compensation of employees							Proprietors' income with IVA and CCAdj			Rental income of persons with CCAdj
		Total	Wages and salaries			Supplements to wages and salaries			Total	Farm	Nonfarm	
			Total	Government	Other	Total	Employer contributions for:					
							Employee pension and insurance funds	Government social insurance				
1988												
1st quarter	4 351.7	2 861.0	2 367.3	442.8	1 924.4	493.8	314.1	179.6	319.3	33.3	286.0	23.0
2nd quarter	4 444.5	2 926.1	2 422.1	449.0	1 973.0	504.0	320.6	183.4	322.8	27.4	295.3	22.6
3rd quarter	4 536.1	2 978.0	2 463.0	454.7	2 008.3	514.9	328.7	186.2	334.0	28.8	305.2	23.9
4th quarter	4 641.2	3 035.1	2 506.8	461.6	2 045.2	528.3	339.0	189.3	327.3	17.7	309.7	30.9
1989												
1st quarter	4 723.2	3 084.0	2 542.2	470.8	2 071.3	541.8	351.0	190.9	348.7	36.7	312.0	26.8
2nd quarter	4 755.2	3 117.5	2 563.4	476.8	2 086.6	554.1	361.7	192.4	340.3	32.6	307.7	24.7
3rd quarter	4 806.5	3 157.6	2 592.0	484.9	2 107.1	565.6	371.3	194.3	338.0	30.3	307.7	22.7
4th quarter	4 843.8	3 211.2	2 634.6	491.9	2 142.7	576.6	379.4	197.2	340.7	32.5	308.2	23.4
1990												
1st quarter	4 952.2	3 278.8	2 686.8	505.9	2 180.9	592.0	389.0	203.0	346.7	34.5	312.2	25.9
2nd quarter	5 034.8	3 334.8	2 735.9	515.8	2 220.1	598.9	392.6	206.2	352.3	32.7	319.6	30.2
3rd quarter	5 064.7	3 373.9	2 768.7	523.2	2 245.5	605.2	396.9	208.3	360.3	31.8	328.5	34.8
4th quarter	5 092.6	3 383.2	2 773.4	531.3	2 242.1	609.8	401.6	208.2	358.4	29.7	328.8	34.6
1991												
1st quarter	5 120.9	3 395.1	2 776.0	543.9	2 232.1	619.1	407.1	212.0	349.1	26.2	322.9	36.2
2nd quarter	5 156.4	3 430.2	2 801.2	547.1	2 254.1	629.0	415.2	213.8	354.8	27.8	326.9	38.6
3rd quarter	5 204.7	3 469.2	2 826.5	550.0	2 276.5	642.7	426.3	216.4	355.5	24.5	331.0	43.0
4th quarter	5 262.5	3 513.5	2 854.2	554.0	2 300.2	659.3	441.0	218.3	364.5	28.6	335.9	50.2
1992												
1st quarter	5 392.4	3 597.6	2 913.5	564.8	2 348.7	684.2	459.1	225.1	380.8	32.9	347.9	53.9
2nd quarter	5 476.6	3 654.4	2 952.8	570.6	2 382.2	701.6	473.8	227.8	397.4	35.4	362.0	61.1
3rd quarter	5 516.2	3 690.7	2 976.1	574.7	2 401.4	714.6	484.6	230.0	410.1	36.7	373.4	68.0
4th quarter	5 613.8	3 741.9	3 019.9	577.9	2 442.0	722.0	491.3	230.7	421.2	34.0	387.1	74.3
1993												
1st quarter	5 619.9	3 747.9	3 018.5	585.4	2 433.1	729.4	494.7	234.7	421.3	28.6	392.8	83.2
2nd quarter	5 722.7	3 803.3	3 065.5	585.7	2 479.8	737.8	498.9	238.9	432.0	34.9	397.1	91.9
3rd quarter	5 768.5	3 838.0	3 093.3	591.5	2 501.9	744.7	503.7	241.0	426.0	26.1	399.9	96.3
4th quarter	5 908.1	3 893.5	3 140.1	593.5	2 546.5	753.4	509.3	244.1	442.6	35.8	406.8	103.2
1994												
1st quarter	5 974.2	3 917.2	3 152.8	601.2	2 551.6	764.4	515.0	249.4	452.9	41.8	411.2	112.7
2nd quarter	6 101.4	3 997.2	3 224.6	608.4	2 616.2	772.6	519.2	253.3	456.9	36.7	420.3	117.4
3rd quarter	6 190.2	4 035.1	3 258.0	611.8	2 646.2	777.0	521.8	255.3	459.7	32.1	427.5	120.7
4th quarter	6 295.2	4 091.0	3 310.9	616.5	2 694.4	780.1	521.6	258.6	468.5	28.0	440.4	119.0
1995												
1st quarter	6 362.0	4 141.3	3 360.6	624.9	2 735.7	780.8	519.9	260.8	470.5	20.3	450.2	122.2
2nd quarter	6 424.1	4 177.6	3 395.3	627.6	2 767.7	782.3	519.5	262.9	475.2	18.4	456.8	126.1
3rd quarter	6 523.3	4 223.7	3 438.2	630.2	2 808.0	785.4	520.1	265.3	487.8	21.4	466.4	130.2
4th quarter	6 608.4	4 268.0	3 478.0	633.4	2 844.6	790.0	522.5	267.5	504.4	28.0	476.3	138.3
1996												
1st quarter	6 729.8	4 321.4	3 525.9	641.5	2 884.4	795.5	525.9	269.6	526.8	36.9	489.9	143.9
2nd quarter	6 857.6	4 393.5	3 590.6	646.3	2 944.3	802.8	529.4	273.4	551.0	44.2	506.9	146.0
3rd quarter	6 938.5	4 455.7	3 646.7	650.1	2 996.5	809.0	532.5	276.5	551.1	33.5	517.6	148.0
4th quarter	7 071.6	4 517.9	3 702.7	654.5	3 048.2	815.2	535.5	279.7	560.6	34.7	525.8	149.9
1997												
1st quarter	7 192.4	4 599.5	3 777.3	663.2	3 114.1	822.2	538.4	283.8	579.4	37.8	541.6	149.0
2nd quarter	7 304.3	4 665.8	3 835.5	667.8	3 167.7	830.2	543.2	287.1	579.0	28.1	550.9	149.9
3rd quarter	7 453.0	4 745.4	3 903.7	674.8	3 228.9	841.7	550.7	291.0	592.5	32.4	560.0	152.6
4th quarter	7 571.8	4 848.1	3 990.9	681.6	3 309.2	857.2	560.8	296.5	600.6	31.2	569.4	156.8
1998												
1st quarter	7 673.1	4 950.4	4 076.3	691.2	3 385.1	874.1	573.0	301.1	621.4	27.9	593.5	161.5
2nd quarter	7 799.0	5 035.9	4 146.2	698.1	3 448.1	889.7	584.5	305.2	633.7	26.4	607.2	167.2
3rd quarter	7 930.2	5 120.9	4 216.8	705.0	3 511.8	904.1	594.7	309.3	649.0	26.6	622.5	172.6
4th quarter	8 026.8	5 204.2	4 287.1	710.9	3 576.2	917.0	603.7	313.3	672.7	32.9	639.7	178.1
1999												
1st quarter	8 178.6	5 298.8	4 368.9	721.3	3 647.6	929.9	610.7	319.3	686.0	33.6	652.3	180.8
2nd quarter	8 250.1	5 352.5	4 410.7	728.1	3 682.7	941.7	620.7	321.0	694.1	28.1	665.9	184.1
3rd quarter	8 343.6	5 429.7	4 472.0	737.6	3 734.5	957.7	634.0	323.6	703.8	26.2	677.6	183.9
4th quarter	8 525.4	5 560.2	4 580.3	748.1	3 832.3	979.9	650.4	329.4	717.9	24.5	693.4	183.6
2000												
1st quarter	8 766.2	5 759.9	4 752.9	765.9	3 987.1	1 006.9	665.8	341.2	724.9	27.0	697.8	184.2
2nd quarter	8 856.3	5 800.8	4 780.1	778.6	4 001.4	1 020.7	679.1	341.6	755.2	33.4	721.9	184.3
3rd quarter	8 976.8	5 914.0	4 872.6	784.2	4 088.4	1 041.4	693.5	347.9	764.7	31.8	732.8	186.9
4th quarter	9 028.7	5 951.7	4 897.8	790.4	4 107.4	1 053.8	703.7	350.2	786.3	33.7	752.6	195.4
2001												
1st quarter	9 171.5	6 059.4	4 982.8	804.5	4 178.2	1 076.7	717.4	359.3	816.2	34.0	782.1	201.7
2nd quarter	9 208.8	6 050.2	4 963.8	815.5	4 148.3	1 086.3	727.9	358.4	835.0	32.5	802.5	207.5
3rd quarter	9 165.5	6 033.7	4 936.6	828.6	4 108.0	1 097.1	740.1	357.0	851.5	32.6	819.0	210.1
4th quarter	9 192.7	6 042.9	4 934.6	839.4	4 095.2	1 108.3	751.1	357.2	844.4	29.2	815.2	210.8
2002												
1st quarter	9 317.6	6 074.8	4 952.5	861.6	4 090.9	1 122.3	759.7	362.6	861.1	17.9	843.3	215.2
2nd quarter	9 394.5	6 137.7	5 000.7	870.4	4 130.3	1 137.0	770.7	366.3	864.8	12.8	852.0	217.4
3rd quarter	9 455.5	6 161.4	5 010.9	877.8	4 133.1	1 150.6	783.4	367.1	873.9	21.3	852.6	216.8
4th quarter	9 579.7	6 193.7	5 021.5	882.7	4 138.8	1 172.1	804.0	368.1	884.3	27.7	856.6	219.8

Table 1-13B. National Income by Type of Income: Historical Data—*Continued*

(Billions of dollars, quarterly data are at seasonally adjusted annual rates.)

NIPA Tables 1.7.5, 1.12

| Year and quarter | Corporate profits with IVA and CCAdj | | | | | Net interest and miscellaneous payments | Taxes on production and imports | Less: Subsidies | Business current transfer payments, net | | | Current surplus of government enterprises | Addendum: Net national factor income |
| | Total | Taxes on corporate income | Profits after tax | | | | | | Total 1 | To persons | To government | | |
			Total	Net dividends	Undistributed corporate profits								
1988													
1st quarter	394.5	129.3	265.2	121.7	143.4	386.3	365.1	30.4	31.1	19.6	11.5	1.7	3 984.1
2nd quarter	409.1	136.6	272.4	126.4	146.0	383.6	372.6	29.8	31.7	20.1	11.6	5.9	4 064.2
3rd quarter	415.7	146.7	269.1	132.8	136.3	396.9	377.6	29.2	33.2	20.8	12.4	6.0	4 148.5
4th quarter	440.2	153.9	286.3	138.7	147.6	412.1	382.5	28.6	35.1	21.9	13.2	6.5	4 245.7
1989													
1st quarter	423.9	158.4	265.5	148.0	117.5	432.9	391.1	28.0	37.2	23.3	14.0	6.5	4 316.3
2nd quarter	415.9	145.0	270.8	155.7	115.1	442.5	397.4	27.4	37.7	23.1	14.5	6.7	4 340.9
3rd quarter	416.5	140.4	276.1	161.1	115.0	449.2	403.8	27.1	39.1	23.2	15.9	6.6	4 384.0
4th quarter	400.7	140.5	260.3	167.1	93.1	446.0	403.2	27.3	39.0	23.1	16.0	6.8	4 422.1
1990													
1st quarter	413.5	139.3	274.2	170.2	104.0	451.0	419.4	27.1	39.4	23.3	16.1	4.6	4 516.0
2nd quarter	433.4	144.9	288.5	169.9	118.6	449.3	419.5	26.9	39.0	22.9	16.0	3.3	4 600.0
3rd quarter	407.1	149.8	257.3	170.0	87.3	447.0	426.9	26.9	38.9	21.9	17.0	2.8	4 623.1
4th quarter	414.6	147.7	266.9	166.2	100.8	452.9	434.2	27.0	39.5	20.7	18.8	2.2	4 643.7
1991													
1st quarter	454.0	141.6	312.3	175.2	137.1	424.2	444.3	27.1	39.8	19.2	20.6	5.5	4 658.5
2nd quarter	451.5	136.8	314.7	180.2	134.6	410.3	451.6	27.2	38.7	17.9	20.7	8.0	4 685.3
3rd quarter	449.4	137.4	311.9	183.1	128.8	407.3	461.2	27.5	38.5	17.0	21.5	8.2	4 724.3
4th quarter	450.5	138.5	312.0	183.6	128.4	392.3	471.3	28.1	38.7	16.4	22.2	9.6	4 771.0
1992													
1st quarter	476.5	148.2	328.3	185.2	143.2	387.8	476.2	28.6	38.6	16.5	22.4	9.4	4 896.7
2nd quarter	477.8	149.8	328.1	188.2	139.9	385.6	481.1	29.2	38.4	16.5	22.0	10.2	4 976.2
3rd quarter	463.2	144.0	319.2	191.0	128.2	379.1	485.9	30.4	38.9	16.3	22.7	10.7	5 011.1
4th quarter	483.5	152.8	330.7	193.7	137.0	382.4	490.3	32.2	43.0	15.9	27.1	9.4	5 103.3
1993													
1st quarter	481.3	158.1	323.1	196.6	126.6	382.5	489.8	35.5	40.2	15.1	25.1	9.1	5 116.2
2nd quarter	509.4	170.1	339.3	201.1	138.2	375.1	497.9	37.6	39.3	14.4	25.1	11.3	5 211.7
3rd quarter	523.6	162.1	361.5	207.6	153.9	367.5	505.0	37.7	38.7	13.7	25.4	11.1	5 251.4
4th quarter	573.7	193.8	379.9	216.0	163.9	360.4	519.8	36.0	39.3	13.1	26.9	11.6	5 373.4
1994													
1st quarter	581.6	174.5	407.0	225.6	181.4	358.5	531.9	33.6	40.7	12.8	28.7	12.2	5 422.9
2nd quarter	604.5	183.6	420.9	233.8	187.1	361.8	544.2	32.4	39.7	12.8	27.7	12.1	5 537.8
3rd quarter	638.5	201.1	437.4	240.0	197.4	364.9	550.2	31.9	41.3	13.2	28.4	11.7	5 619.0
4th quarter	663.1	213.3	449.8	244.5	205.3	378.6	554.7	32.2	41.2	14.2	26.8	11.3	5 720.2
1995													
1st quarter	664.7	217.6	447.1	247.8	199.3	383.1	554.9	34.0	43.6	16.0	25.9	15.7	5 781.8
2nd quarter	689.2	214.8	474.5	253.2	221.2	376.6	553.7	34.6	44.9	17.8	25.1	15.4	5 844.7
3rd quarter	723.2	221.7	501.5	261.8	239.7	373.1	559.2	35.1	45.8	19.6	24.6	15.6	5 937.9
4th quarter	735.0	217.3	517.7	273.0	244.6	373.1	563.9	35.5	45.5	21.4	23.9	15.8	6 018.8
1996													
1st quarter	768.9	221.6	547.4	286.3	261.1	370.3	570.8	35.5	46.8	22.8	24.7	16.5	6 131.3
2nd quarter	781.4	233.4	548.0	298.8	249.3	378.5	577.7	35.4	48.2	23.5	25.8	16.7	6 250.4
3rd quarter	786.6	233.8	552.8	309.8	243.0	384.7	581.6	35.2	48.9	23.2	26.8	17.2	6 326.0
4th quarter	807.3	237.1	570.2	319.3	250.9	394.0	592.9	34.8	66.7	21.9	45.5	17.3	6 429.6
1997													
1st quarter	835.3	238.2	597.0	327.7	269.4	403.8	595.6	34.4	46.9	19.7	27.8	17.4	6 566.9
2nd quarter	857.7	242.9	614.8	335.7	279.0	409.9	610.3	33.6	47.4	18.7	28.5	18.1	6 662.2
3rd quarter	892.6	255.1	637.5	343.5	294.0	416.0	616.6	33.4	53.5	19.0	33.4	17.3	6 799.0
4th quarter	877.5	245.5	632.0	350.9	281.1	429.1	624.0	33.8	52.5	20.4	29.6	17.1	6 912.0
1998													
1st quarter	808.5	248.5	560.0	357.1	202.8	460.7	629.1	33.8	58.9	22.8	31.1	16.4	7 002.5
2nd quarter	805.2	245.5	559.7	359.9	199.8	479.6	635.5	35.0	60.4	25.1	30.4	16.7	7 121.4
3rd quarter	813.2	252.2	561.0	358.5	202.6	489.0	643.0	36.8	62.6	27.1	31.8	16.6	7 244.8
4th quarter	789.6	247.2	542.3	352.8	189.5	482.1	650.3	39.9	74.3	28.9	43.9	15.4	7 326.6
1999													
1st quarter	842.2	256.2	586.0	344.5	241.4	473.2	657.5	42.4	65.2	31.2	35.6	17.3	7 481.0
2nd quarter	835.6	254.1	581.5	341.8	239.7	478.7	667.1	45.0	66.4	32.8	36.2	16.7	7 545.0
3rd quarter	819.2	259.2	560.0	346.6	213.5	490.3	679.0	46.4	67.9	34.8	36.2	16.2	7 627.0
4th quarter	823.9	265.7	558.3	358.7	199.6	509.6	690.8	46.9	71.8	37.1	37.8	14.5	7 795.2
2000													
1st quarter	803.3	274.3	529.0	375.7	153.2	547.1	698.6	45.1	79.1	39.8	41.0	14.2	8 019.4
2nd quarter	792.8	273.1	519.6	386.9	132.8	565.3	707.3	45.5	83.3	41.5	41.8	12.8	8 098.4
3rd quarter	775.8	254.7	521.1	390.2	130.9	573.3	711.3	45.8	87.2	43.3	42.0	9.4	8 214.8
4th quarter	753.0	258.3	494.7	386.0	108.8	574.1	717.1	47.0	91.7	45.2	42.8	6.5	8 260.4
2001													
1st quarter	743.6	224.5	519.1	374.2	144.9	577.4	724.1	55.2	98.5	47.9	42.8	5.8	8 398.4
2nd quarter	774.0	216.6	557.4	368.3	189.1	575.5	724.1	62.0	100.5	48.3	43.2	4.0	8 442.3
3rd quarter	742.3	195.0	547.3	367.1	180.2	564.8	725.4	71.2	100.1	47.0	44.2	8.8	8 402.4
4th quarter	756.2	177.0	579.2	372.7	206.5	548.0	737.2	46.4	97.5	43.9	45.2	2.2	8 402.4
2002													
1st quarter	850.7	179.3	671.5	386.8	284.6	521.3	745.0	42.6	87.8	39.1	46.6	4.3	8 523.2
2nd quarter	881.0	186.0	695.1	398.8	296.2	490.5	756.6	39.8	81.4	35.2	45.9	4.8	8 591.5
3rd quarter	910.1	193.7	716.4	403.7	312.7	475.5	771.8	41.4	77.5	32.3	45.9	9.8	8 637.7
4th quarter	986.8	210.4	776.4	411.4	365.0	474.8	777.0	41.7	76.0	30.2	46.6	9.1	8 759.4

1Includes net transfer payments to the rest of the world, not shown separately.

Table 1-13B. National Income by Type of Income: Historical Data—*Continued*

(Billions of dollars, quarterly data are at seasonally adjusted annual rates.)

NIPA Tables 1.7.5, 1.12

Year and quarter	National income, total	Compensation of employees							Proprietors' income with IVA and CCAdj			Rental income of persons with CCAdj
		Total	Wages and salaries			Supplements to wages and salaries			Total	Farm	Nonfarm	
			Total	Government	Other	Total	Employer contributions for:					
							Employee pension and insurance funds	Government social insurance				
2003												
1st quarter	9 637.2	6 226.6	5 030.9	904.8	4 126.1	1 195.6	821.2	374.4	880.2	31.1	849.1	226.8
2nd quarter	9 778.1	6 318.7	5 102.0	912.4	4 189.6	1 216.7	836.8	379.9	894.1	38.9	855.3	234.0
3rd quarter	9 933.0	6 403.8	5 166.9	915.6	4 251.3	1 237.0	852.1	384.9	907.2	39.8	867.4	239.9
4th quarter	10 108.5	6 508.7	5 251.6	920.4	4 331.2	1 257.1	866.2	390.9	918.7	42.4	876.3	251.3
2004												
1st quarter	10 292.3	6 565.7	5 281.3	941.8	4 339.5	1 284.4	885.0	399.4	947.2	55.3	891.9	254.6
2nd quarter	10 466.5	6 690.3	5 383.6	950.6	4 433.0	1 306.6	900.4	406.2	961.9	53.0	908.9	258.7
3rd quarter	10 659.3	6 823.3	5 492.1	955.7	4 536.5	1 331.2	917.6	413.6	962.1	44.9	917.2	254.6
4th quarter	10 745.7	6 878.9	5 530.6	962.6	4 568.1	1 348.2	932.6	415.6	977.1	48.7	928.4	253.8
2005												
1st quarter	10 981.6	6 952.6	5 579.9	982.5	4 597.4	1 372.7	950.8	421.9	953.3	45.4	907.9	246.1
2nd quarter	11 118.5	7 027.4	5 639.7	987.6	4 652.0	1 387.7	962.6	425.0	960.5	49.0	911.6	242.9
3rd quarter	11 324.4	7 142.2	5 737.3	994.5	4 742.8	1 405.0	974.2	430.8	991.7	48.4	943.3	231.6
4th quarter	11 534.7	7 225.0	5 811.0	1 001.4	4 809.5	1 414.1	979.5	434.5	1 010.3	42.7	967.7	233.1
2006												
1st quarter	11 864.2	7 406.9	5 976.1	1 018.9	4 957.3	1 430.7	986.2	444.6	1 058.7	36.9	1 021.8	223.2
2nd quarter	11 955.0	7 453.0	6 015.2	1 028.1	4 987.1	1 437.7	992.1	445.6	1 062.2	35.9	1 026.3	211.9
3rd quarter	12 061.5	7 508.5	6 060.9	1 040.8	5 020.1	1 447.7	1 000.9	446.7	1 051.1	35.0	1 016.1	204.3
4th quarter	12 138.2	7 641.0	6 177.4	1 052.1	5 125.3	1 463.6	1 011.1	452.5	1 042.7	36.1	1 006.7	190.7
2007												
1st quarter	12 225.8	7 832.1	6 347.9	1 076.2	5 271.8	1 484.2	1 023.5	460.7	992.3	39.2	953.2	177.9
2nd quarter	12 322.8	7 866.8	6 370.9	1 082.5	5 288.5	1 495.9	1 035.8	460.1	972.8	34.3	938.5	189.6
3rd quarter	12 328.1	7 902.1	6 393.9	1 092.4	5 301.5	1 508.2	1 047.7	460.5	966.0	35.2	930.9	192.9
4th quarter	12 408.8	7 992.0	6 467.9	1 104.4	5 363.6	1 524.1	1 058.7	465.4	985.5	43.8	941.8	197.2
2008												
1st quarter	12 474.5	8 077.9	6 539.0	1 127.6	5 411.4	1 538.9	1 068.0	470.9	1 017.7	55.6	962.2	225.3
2nd quarter	12 514.9	8 077.3	6 531.6	1 137.9	5 393.7	1 545.7	1 074.9	470.8	1 045.9	50.0	995.9	250.0
3rd quarter	12 541.2	8 094.9	6 543.9	1 151.0	5 392.9	1 551.0	1 078.6	472.4	1 040.9	42.8	998.1	273.4
4th quarter	12 180.7	8 062.8	6 512.9	1 160.0	5 353.0	1 549.9	1 078.8	471.1	1 001.3	39.6	961.7	299.8
2009												
1st quarter	12 009.4	7 762.4	6 230.6	1 166.9	5 063.7	1 531.8	1 075.3	456.5	944.2	30.2	914.0	310.8
2nd quarter	12 002.0	7 790.5	6 256.3	1 176.0	5 080.3	1 534.2	1 074.9	459.3	944.6	31.9	912.8	325.0
3rd quarter	12 134.2	7 774.0	6 238.9	1 177.7	5 061.3	1 535.0	1 077.4	457.7	976.9	35.7	941.2	344.4
4th quarter	12 358.8	7 821.0	6 279.8	1 180.0	5 099.7	1 541.3	1 082.3	458.9	1 026.3	44.1	982.2	354.6
2010												
1st quarter	12 457.0	7 801.7	6 239.6	1 187.4	5 052.1	1 562.1	1 097.6	464.4	1 017.6	39.2	978.5	380.5
2nd quarter	12 620.8	7 947.1	6 365.5	1 196.8	5 168.7	1 581.6	1 111.8	469.8	1 024.7	43.2	981.5	397.3
3rd quarter	12 868.8	8 019.1	6 426.4	1 190.3	5 236.1	1 592.8	1 121.6	471.2	1 029.2	48.4	980.8	408.3
4th quarter	13 011.5	8 077.9	6 478.6	1 189.8	5 288.8	1 599.3	1 127.3	472.0	1 059.3	53.2	1 006.0	425.0
2011												
1st quarter	13 091.2	8 209.7	6 583.6	1 191.7	5 392.0	1 626.1	1 133.8	492.3	1 103.2	75.6	1 027.6	460.1
2nd quarter	13 255.9	8 248.9	6 615.5	1 198.8	5 416.8	1 633.4	1 140.2	493.2	1 125.2	72.3	1 052.9	478.0
3rd quarter	13 454.8	8 332.0	6 689.6	1 198.4	5 491.2	1 642.4	1 145.1	497.3	1 161.8	77.9	1 083.8	491.6
4th quarter	13 607.2	8 285.4	6 643.9	1 190.2	5 453.6	1 641.6	1 148.8	492.7	1 184.5	76.4	1 108.1	511.6
2012												
1st quarter	13 942.5	8 504.0	6 841.1	1 200.0	5 641.1	1 662.9	1 153.6	509.3	1 213.6	62.4	1 151.1	517.0
2nd quarter	13 997.2	8 550.0	6 878.5	1 196.1	5 682.4	1 671.5	1 160.7	510.8	1 240.2	59.5	1 180.7	523.0
3rd quarter	14 062.3	8 587.6	6 906.8	1 196.2	5 710.7	1 680.8	1 168.9	511.9	1 245.8	59.4	1 186.3	527.3
4th quarter	14 245.5	8 798.0	7 094.6	1 200.7	5 893.9	1 703.4	1 178.0	525.4	1 266.0	64.9	1 201.1	534.0
2013												
1st quarter	14 257.6	8 696.7	6 991.4	1 203.3	5 788.1	1 705.3	1 186.2	519.1	1 288.9	93.9	1 195.0	547.9
2nd quarter	14 416.0	8 820.4	7 098.5	1 205.0	5 893.5	1 721.9	1 194.9	527.0	1 279.7	90.2	1 189.5	556.5
3rd quarter	14 500.8	8 875.7	7 143.9	1 205.1	5 938.8	1 731.8	1 202.1	529.6	1 287.5	93.9	1 193.6	569.7
4th quarter	14 658.9	8 965.9	7 223.8	1 217.2	6 006.6	1 742.1	1 208.0	534.1	1 284.3	77.1	1 207.2	579.4
2014												
1st quarter	14 710.1	9 103.7	7 350.0	1 223.4	6 126.6	1 753.7	1 213.1	540.5	1 304.8	71.7	1 233.0	591.0
2nd quarter	14 981.3	9 177.3	7 414.5	1 234.2	6 180.3	1 762.7	1 219.4	543.3	1 346.3	88.8	1 257.5	605.5
3rd quarter	15 256.5	9 289.9	7 513.9	1 243.2	6 270.7	1 776.0	1 227.1	548.9	1 357.8	77.2	1 280.6	618.4
4th quarter	15 358.2	9 424.9	7 632.6	1 248.2	6 384.4	1 792.3	1 236.3	556.0	1 377.9	74.8	1 303.0	628.4

Table 1-13B. National Income by Type of Income: Historical Data—*Continued*

(Billions of dollars, quarterly data are at seasonally adjusted annual rates.)   **NIPA Tables 1.7.5, 1.12**

| Year and quarter | Corporate profits with IVA and CCAdj | | | | | Net interest and miscel-laneous payments | Taxes on production and imports | Less: Subsidies | Business current transfer payments, net | | | Current surplus of govern-ment enterprises | Addendum: Net national factor income |
| | Total | Taxes on corporate income | Profits after tax | | | | | | Total [1] | To persons | To govern-ment | | |
			Total	Net dividends	Undis-tributed corporate profits								
2003													
1st quarter	988.2	231.5	756.6	411.5	345.2	488.0	788.6	45.0	77.7	29.6	47.2	6.1	8 809.8
2nd quarter	1 028.9	227.0	801.9	412.8	389.1	477.9	800.7	57.1	76.4	28.0	47.6	4.5	8 953.6
3rd quarter	1 076.4	247.2	829.1	436.4	392.8	458.9	814.8	47.0	75.9	25.5	48.6	3.0	9 086.2
4th quarter	1 132.1	269.3	862.8	475.3	387.5	439.9	828.0	47.2	75.0	22.0	49.7	2.0	9 250.8
2004													
1st quarter	1 238.7	277.6	961.1	515.5	445.6	409.6	843.4	44.7	77.8	17.5	51.5	0.1	9 415.7
2nd quarter	1 266.8	298.2	968.6	543.1	425.5	398.5	855.5	43.7	79.5	15.4	52.5	-0.9	9 576.2
3rd quarter	1 325.7	320.4	1 005.3	549.0	456.2	394.4	868.6	45.1	78.5	15.7	53.0	-2.7	9 760.0
4th quarter	1 302.2	328.1	974.1	648.7	325.4	411.5	888.4	52.0	89.6	18.4	52.5	-3.7	9 823.4
2005													
1st quarter	1 427.8	405.1	1 022.7	556.6	466.0	460.4	908.4	56.5	94.5	23.5	52.2	-4.9	10 040.2
2nd quarter	1 446.0	395.6	1 050.4	571.4	478.9	481.3	929.5	60.7	97.4	26.4	53.1	-5.7	10 158.1
3rd quarter	1 474.3	403.1	1 071.2	576.8	494.4	516.5	944.7	62.1	93.0	27.2	53.4	-7.3	10 356.2
4th quarter	1 562.9	445.7	1 117.2	617.3	499.9	528.9	955.6	64.3	90.7	25.8	54.9	-7.6	10 560.3
2006													
1st quarter	1 627.4	460.7	1 166.7	687.4	479.3	553.1	975.7	55.7	80.8	22.2	56.7	-5.9	10 869.4
2nd quarter	1 649.2	475.2	1 174.0	718.3	455.7	571.1	988.3	51.5	79.1	20.5	57.7	-8.1	10 947.3
3rd quarter	1 693.5	496.7	1 196.8	734.9	461.9	583.5	996.9	49.9	84.0	20.6	58.8	-10.4	11 040.9
4th quarter	1 615.9	460.8	1 155.0	763.4	391.6	616.1	1 007.0	48.7	86.4	22.6	59.9	-12.8	11 106.3
2007													
1st quarter	1 530.9	474.2	1 056.8	781.9	274.8	634.2	1 022.0	49.5	101.5	26.5	60.9	-15.7	11 167.5
2nd quarter	1 596.9	468.1	1 128.8	822.6	306.2	639.9	1 032.0	58.2	98.8	29.7	60.9	-15.7	11 266.0
3rd quarter	1 518.1	431.1	1 087.1	833.6	253.5	682.1	1 038.8	55.9	99.6	32.2	61.6	-15.6	11 261.2
4th quarter	1 470.0	408.8	1 061.2	837.6	223.7	697.6	1 045.5	54.7	94.3	34.1	64.5	-18.8	11 342.4
2008													
1st quarter	1 383.4	355.3	1 028.1	867.8	160.3	691.7	1 038.1	51.9	112.3	35.3	67.1	-20.2	11 396.1
2nd quarter	1 367.6	344.1	1 023.5	829.8	193.7	689.2	1 047.9	51.6	109.8	36.3	67.2	-21.2	11 430.0
3rd quarter	1 371.3	312.6	1 058.7	800.2	258.6	676.8	1 049.2	52.1	108.1	37.1	66.0	-21.5	11 457.4
4th quarter	1 017.9	224.4	793.5	736.7	56.8	715.9	1 032.4	54.7	127.3	37.8	82.0	-21.9	11 097.7
2009													
1st quarter	1 259.0	215.0	1 044.0	681.3	362.7	671.1	1 014.1	55.2	125.0	37.9	85.8	-21.8	10 947.3
2nd quarter	1 301.0	240.4	1 060.6	585.2	475.4	562.0	1 019.4	55.4	135.2	38.3	100.3	-20.4	10 923.2
3rd quarter	1 463.3	285.0	1 178.3	526.7	651.6	514.4	1 030.1	67.1	117.7	38.9	82.9	-19.5	11 072.9
4th quarter	1 564.7	337.4	1 227.3	505.4	721.9	506.1	1 041.0	55.7	121.5	39.7	84.9	-20.7	11 272.7
2010													
1st quarter	1 658.5	344.8	1 313.7	521.8	791.8	503.3	1 042.2	54.9	129.3	40.6	85.4	-21.2	11 361.5
2nd quarter	1 666.4	351.7	1 314.8	542.8	772.0	482.7	1 054.2	55.5	126.5	41.9	84.5	-22.6	11 518.2
3rd quarter	1 814.0	387.5	1 426.6	576.0	850.5	483.6	1 063.1	56.2	131.1	43.3	89.2	-23.5	11 754.3
4th quarter	1 846.7	398.3	1 448.4	615.2	833.3	488.0	1 069.0	56.9	127.0	46.1	89.7	-24.3	11 896.8
2011													
1st quarter	1 677.4	397.5	1 279.9	658.0	621.9	493.5	1 087.6	58.6	142.6	49.4	91.8	-24.5	11 943.9
2nd quarter	1 790.0	383.4	1 406.6	681.8	724.8	465.6	1 104.2	59.9	127.9	51.1	89.6	-24.1	12 107.8
3rd quarter	1 826.6	351.0	1 475.6	719.1	756.6	493.4	1 104.0	61.0	131.0	51.1	90.0	-24.6	12 305.4
4th quarter	1 972.5	384.5	1 588.0	755.9	832.1	499.6	1 114.6	60.8	124.6	49.4	85.5	-24.9	12 453.6
2012													
1st quarter	2 016.0	442.7	1 573.3	779.7	793.6	525.0	1 129.1	58.4	117.6	45.7	80.5	-21.3	12 775.5
2nd quarter	1 993.6	449.9	1 543.7	811.0	732.7	530.7	1 129.3	58.1	107.9	43.1	73.5	-19.4	12 837.5
3rd quarter	1 999.0	451.0	1 548.1	820.8	727.3	553.1	1 126.8	56.3	97.2	41.4	66.6	-18.2	12 912.8
4th quarter	1 984.0	446.9	1 537.1	1 026.1	511.0	502.2	1 142.9	59.4	96.0	40.7	69.6	-18.3	13 084.2
2013													
1st quarter	1 997.3	454.9	1 542.4	814.2	728.3	526.1	1 168.6	59.2	108.9	40.8	86.4	-17.7	13 056.9
2nd quarter	2 045.4	461.3	1 584.1	1 065.2	519.0	505.2	1 171.3	59.7	115.9	41.0	88.8	-18.7	13 207.2
3rd quarter	2 042.1	475.6	1 566.5	870.1	696.5	504.6	1 183.2	59.5	116.2	41.3	84.9	-18.8	13 279.7
4th quarter	2 064.7	483.8	1 580.9	946.7	634.2	518.3	1 188.9	59.0	136.5	41.5	107.6	-19.9	13 412.5
2014													
1st quarter	1 924.7	497.3	1 427.4	857.3	570.2	555.6	1 196.1	58.1	110.0	41.8	82.2	-17.6	13 479.7
2nd quarter	2 070.5	527.4	1 543.1	857.1	686.0	535.9	1 210.2	57.9	112.0	42.0	79.5	-18.4	13 735.4
3rd quarter	2 161.0	518.4	1 642.7	853.6	789.1	515.8	1 221.7	58.2	168.5	42.1	133.1	-18.4	13 943.0
4th quarter	2 135.5	512.3	1 623.2	872.2	751.0	521.9	1 227.0	57.5	118.7	42.1	84.3	-18.6	14 088.6

[1] Includes net transfer payments to the rest of the world, not shown separately.

Table 1-14. Gross and Net Value Added of Domestic Corporate Business

(Billions of dollars, quarterly data are at seasonally adjusted annual rates.)

NIPA Table 1.14

Year and quarter	Gross value added of corporate business, total	Consumption of fixed capital	Net value added			Net operating surplus			Corporate profits with IVA and CCAdj		Profits after tax			Gross value added of financial corporate business
			Total	Compensation of employees	Taxes on production and imports less subsidies	Total	Net interest and miscellaneous payments	Business current transfer payments	Total	Taxes on corporate income	Total	Net dividends	Undistributed	
1950	162.2	13.3	148.9	98.7	14.8	35.4	-0.1	0.7	34.8	17.9	16.9	7.9	9.0	7.3
1951	185.8	15.1	170.7	114.6	15.9	40.3	-0.2	1.0	39.5	22.6	16.9	7.4	9.5	8.2
1952	195.1	16.1	179.0	123.0	17.3	38.6	-0.2	1.0	37.8	19.4	18.4	7.5	10.9	9.2
1953	209.3	17.3	192.0	134.0	18.5	39.5	0.0	1.0	38.5	20.3	18.2	7.8	10.5	10.2
1954	206.9	18.3	188.6	132.2	17.9	38.5	0.2	0.7	37.5	17.6	19.9	7.9	12.0	10.8
1955	233.1	19.6	213.6	144.6	19.8	49.1	0.2	1.1	47.8	22.0	25.8	8.9	16.9	11.8
1956	250.2	22.1	228.1	158.2	21.5	48.4	0.1	1.4	46.8	22.0	24.8	9.5	15.4	12.9
1957	261.8	24.6	237.2	166.5	22.8	47.9	0.3	1.6	46.0	21.4	24.6	9.9	14.8	13.8
1958	256.9	26.4	230.5	164.0	23.1	43.4	0.7	1.4	41.3	19.0	22.4	9.8	12.5	14.7
1959	287.5	27.6	259.9	180.3	25.6	54.1	-0.1	1.4	52.8	23.7	29.1	10.7	18.4	15.9
1960	300.0	28.5	271.5	190.7	27.8	52.9	-0.1	1.5	51.5	22.8	28.8	11.4	17.4	17.5
1961	308.8	29.5	279.3	195.6	28.9	54.8	0.5	1.7	52.6	22.9	29.7	11.5	18.2	18.4
1962	336.0	30.8	305.2	211.0	31.2	63.0	0.9	1.9	60.3	24.1	36.2	12.4	23.8	19.3
1963	357.5	32.4	325.0	222.7	33.2	69.2	0.5	2.3	66.4	26.4	40.1	13.6	26.5	19.6
1964	386.1	34.4	351.7	239.2	35.6	76.9	0.9	2.7	73.2	28.2	45.1	15.0	30.1	21.6
1965	423.9	37.1	386.7	259.9	37.8	89.1	1.3	3.1	84.6	31.1	53.5	16.9	36.6	23.2
1966	465.2	40.9	424.3	288.5	38.9	96.9	2.4	2.9	91.6	33.9	57.7	17.8	39.9	25.1
1967	491.3	45.1	446.2	308.4	41.4	96.4	4.2	3.1	89.1	32.9	56.2	18.3	37.9	28.1
1968	542.2	50.0	492.2	340.2	47.8	104.2	4.4	3.7	96.1	39.6	56.5	20.2	36.3	31.3
1969	590.8	55.7	535.1	377.5	52.9	104.7	8.6	4.3	91.8	40.0	51.8	20.4	31.4	36.2
1970	612.3	61.8	550.5	398.0	57.0	95.5	12.6	3.7	79.1	34.8	44.4	20.4	24.0	39.4
1971	661.1	67.6	593.5	421.7	62.8	109.0	12.8	3.4	92.8	38.2	54.6	20.3	34.3	43.1
1972	733.2	73.4	659.7	468.2	67.3	124.3	12.7	3.9	107.7	42.3	65.3	21.9	43.4	47.2
1973	820.5	82.0	738.5	526.1	74.1	138.4	15.1	4.8	118.5	50.0	68.5	23.1	45.4	51.7
1974	889.9	96.0	793.9	577.3	78.6	138.0	23.4	6.3	108.2	52.8	55.5	23.5	32.0	59.9
1975	966.0	113.5	852.4	607.8	84.5	160.1	27.7	8.2	124.2	51.6	72.6	26.4	46.2	67.6
1976	1 087.8	125.0	962.7	682.8	91.4	188.5	23.2	7.6	157.8	65.3	92.5	30.1	62.4	73.0
1977	1 233.0	140.5	1 092.5	771.7	100.0	220.8	28.1	6.0	186.7	74.4	112.2	33.7	78.5	85.5
1978	1 407.5	159.3	1 248.3	884.7	108.7	254.9	31.3	7.9	215.7	84.9	130.8	39.6	91.2	103.4
1979	1 565.0	183.4	1 381.7	1 004.4	115.0	262.2	37.0	10.8	214.4	90.0	124.4	41.5	82.9	114.6
1980	1 702.7	212.1	1 490.7	1 102.0	128.6	260.1	59.9	12.0	188.1	87.2	100.9	47.3	53.6	128.5
1981	1 935.2	244.9	1 690.3	1 220.6	154.4	315.3	83.3	14.3	217.8	84.3	133.5	58.3	75.2	146.8
1982	2 018.8	272.5	1 746.2	1 275.1	161.3	309.8	95.9	16.6	197.3	66.5	130.8	61.3	69.4	164.5
1983	2 172.9	285.9	1 887.1	1 353.0	177.4	356.6	92.4	19.5	244.7	80.6	164.1	71.3	92.7	187.4
1984	2 435.3	303.2	2 132.1	1 501.1	195.6	435.4	107.2	26.9	301.3	97.5	203.8	78.5	125.3	209.7
1985	2 605.8	326.9	2 279.0	1 615.9	209.0	454.0	106.7	30.9	316.4	99.4	217.0	85.7	131.3	236.3
1986	2 712.5	349.9	2 362.6	1 723.4	219.6	419.6	105.4	29.3	284.9	109.7	175.2	88.3	86.9	247.1
1987	2 902.9	371.3	2 531.6	1 847.6	233.4	450.6	107.7	24.9	318.0	130.4	187.5	95.6	91.9	260.4
1988	3 151.3	399.4	2 751.9	2 002.3	252.0	497.6	113.3	26.4	357.9	141.6	216.3	98.0	118.2	276.8
1989	3 329.0	427.2	2 901.8	2 119.3	267.5	514.9	134.2	33.6	347.1	146.1	201.0	126.4	74.7	308.2
1990	3 477.3	455.3	3 022.0	2 234.9	284.5	502.6	127.6	34.0	341.1	145.4	195.6	144.1	51.6	316.0
1991	3 564.1	480.9	3 083.2	2 277.8	307.9	497.5	89.0	33.7	374.9	138.6	236.3	156.2	80.1	332.3
1992	3 750.6	496.2	3 254.3	2 420.5	325.9	507.9	71.8	34.0	402.2	148.7	253.5	161.5	92.0	373.4
1993	3 926.9	519.8	3 407.1	2 515.7	343.8	547.6	70.8	31.8	445.1	171.0	274.0	184.7	89.3	391.6
1994	4 219.3	550.4	3 668.9	2 649.0	376.1	643.8	67.6	32.2	543.9	193.1	350.8	197.8	153.0	402.8
1995	4 483.9	593.6	3 890.3	2 787.9	384.8	717.6	70.7	36.9	610.1	217.8	392.2	226.2	166.1	442.5
1996	4 780.2	629.8	4 150.4	2 953.7	398.4	798.3	70.4	43.7	684.1	231.5	452.6	263.1	189.5	484.0
1997	5 153.6	674.0	4 479.6	3 176.6	416.9	886.1	93.5	34.4	758.2	245.4	512.8	292.2	220.6	545.2
1998	5 485.8	719.3	4 766.5	3 447.5	430.8	888.3	134.1	52.8	701.3	248.4	453.0	314.8	138.2	612.1
1999	5 815.5	774.6	5 040.9	3 684.3	454.0	902.6	140.5	53.9	708.2	258.8	449.4	306.4	143.1	645.6
2000	6 227.3	844.5	5 382.8	4 008.9	479.8	894.1	186.6	72.4	635.0	265.1	369.9	355.4	14.5	714.3
2001	6 226.0	894.9	5 331.1	4 015.6	476.3	839.2	170.4	85.1	583.6	203.3	380.3	329.9	50.4	754.8
2002	6 318.8	920.5	5 398.3	3 973.9	506.3	918.1	107.7	61.9	748.4	192.3	556.1	352.3	203.8	779.9
2003	6 544.3	941.5	5 602.8	4 042.0	532.6	1 028.1	87.3	51.0	889.7	243.8	646.0	401.9	244.1	819.8
2004	6 967.7	982.7	5 985.0	4 241.5	571.5	1 172.0	39.2	54.5	1 078.3	306.1	772.2	501.8	270.4	859.8
2005	7 484.0	1 051.6	6 432.4	4 444.5	616.5	1 371.4	72.9	59.8	1 238.7	412.4	826.3	319.7	506.6	951.9
2006	8 026.3	1 128.6	6 897.7	4 683.2	655.8	1 558.7	120.1	48.2	1 390.3	473.4	917.0	648.1	268.9	1 038.3
2007	8 189.1	1 197.5	6 991.6	4 893.0	681.2	1 417.4	172.9	68.9	1 175.6	445.5	730.1	678.5	51.6	985.2
2008	8 092.4	1 259.2	6 833.2	4 939.7	685.0	1 208.5	234.5	95.7	878.4	309.1	569.3	628.1	-58.8	835.7
2009	7 823.9	1 260.6	6 563.3	4 610.0	659.3	1 294.1	157.5	96.7	1 039.8	269.4	770.3	456.5	313.8	964.1
2010	8 235.5	1 262.5	6 973.0	4 706.9	685.9	1 580.2	129.1	99.8	1 351.2	370.6	980.7	442.5	538.1	996.7
2011	8 611.8	1 298.8	7 313.0	4 937.9	721.9	1 653.2	149.1	109.3	1 394.7	379.1	1 015.6	548.8	466.9	1 019.5
2012	9 148.8	1 351.0	7 797.8	5 191.8	742.0	1 863.9	209.3	66.8	1 587.8	447.6	1 140.2	680.1	460.1	1 136.9
2013	9 454.0	1 405.0	8 048.9	5 355.2	778.7	1 915.0	216.3	76.2	1 622.6	468.9	1 153.7	777.7	376.0	1 137.1
2014	9 890.4	1 467.3	8 423.1	5 640.8	808.6	1 973.7	226.3	92.7	1 654.7	513.9	1 140.9	724.4	416.5	1 249.5
2012														
1st quarter	9 047.5	1 331.4	7 716.1	5 109.4	740.1	1 866.6	187.3	84.6	1 594.7	442.7	1 152.1	608.7	543.3	1 119.6
2nd quarter	9 100.8	1 346.1	7 754.7	5 147.3	739.6	1 867.8	207.5	70.9	1 589.4	449.9	1 139.4	615.2	524.3	1 110.4
3rd quarter	9 135.3	1 358.3	7 776.9	5 172.8	739.2	1 864.9	219.3	57.8	1 587.9	451.0	1 136.9	638.0	499.0	1 152.5
4th quarter	9 311.6	1 368.2	7 943.5	5 337.9	749.3	1 856.3	223.2	53.8	1 579.3	446.9	1 132.4	858.5	273.9	1 165.2
2013														
1st quarter	9 289.7	1 381.4	7 908.3	5 247.6	772.3	1 888.4	217.3	65.3	1 605.9	454.9	1 151.0	680.9	470.1	1 080.7
2nd quarter	9 436.1	1 397.6	8 038.6	5 343.4	774.2	1 921.0	214.9	72.1	1 634.0	461.3	1 172.8	887.0	285.8	1 115.8
3rd quarter	9 484.1	1 412.2	8 071.9	5 384.2	782.3	1 905.3	215.4	74.3	1 615.7	475.6	1 140.1	765.4	374.6	1 149.0
4th quarter	9 605.9	1 428.9	8 177.0	5 445.5	786.1	1 945.4	217.5	93.1	1 634.8	483.8	1 151.0	777.5	373.5	1 203.1
2014														
1st quarter	9 584.5	1 443.3	8 141.2	5 537.5	796.8	1 807.0	221.9	74.8	1 510.3	497.3	1 013.0	728.1	284.8	1 137.9
2nd quarter	9 819.9	1 460.3	8 359.7	5 586.5	806.2	1 966.9	225.7	79.3	1 661.9	527.4	1 134.4	728.7	405.7	1 234.9
3rd quarter	10 050.7	1 476.4	8 574.4	5 668.1	813.9	2 092.3	228.6	129.8	1 733.9	518.4	1 215.6	706.8	508.8	1 320.8
4th quarter	10 106.5	1 489.4	8 617.1	5 771.0	817.5	2 028.7	229.1	86.8	1 712.8	512.3	1 200.5	734.0	466.5	1 304.2

Table 1-15. Gross Value Added of Nonfinancial Domestic Corporate Business in Current and Chained Dollars

(Billions of dollars, quarterly data are at seasonally adjusted annual rates.)   **NIPA Table 1.14**

Year and quarter	Current-dollar gross value added													Gross value added in billions of chained (2009) dollars
	Total	Consumption of fixed capital	Net value added											
			Total	Compensation of employees	Taxes on production and imports less subsidies	Net operating surplus								
						Total	Net interest and miscellaneous payments	Business current transfer payments	Corporate profits with IVA and CCAdj					
									Total	Taxes on corporate income	Profits after tax			
											Total	Net dividends	Undistributed	
1955	221.4	18.9	202.5	137.9	19.2	45.4	1.7	1.0	42.7	20.1	22.6	8.4	14.2	1 044.8
1956	237.2	21.4	215.9	150.8	20.8	44.3	1.8	1.0	41.4	19.9	21.5	9.0	12.5	1 080.9
1957	247.9	23.8	224.2	158.4	22.0	43.7	2.3	1.1	40.3	19.0	21.4	9.2	12.1	1 095.4
1958	242.2	25.5	216.8	155.2	22.3	39.2	2.8	1.2	35.2	16.1	19.2	9.1	10.0	1 054.0
1959	271.6	26.7	245.0	170.8	24.4	49.8	3.0	1.3	45.5	20.7	24.8	9.8	15.0	1 172.5
1960	282.5	27.6	254.9	180.4	26.6	47.9	3.3	1.3	43.3	19.1	24.2	10.5	13.7	1 212.1
1961	290.4	28.6	261.9	184.5	27.6	49.7	3.8	1.4	44.5	19.4	25.1	10.6	14.5	1 241.0
1962	316.8	29.8	287.0	199.3	29.9	57.8	4.5	1.6	51.8	20.6	31.2	11.6	19.6	1 346.1
1963	337.8	31.3	306.5	210.1	31.7	64.7	4.8	1.6	58.3	22.8	35.5	12.4	23.1	1 429.1
1964	364.5	33.3	331.3	225.7	33.9	71.7	5.3	1.9	64.6	23.9	40.7	14.0	26.7	1 529.4
1965	400.7	35.8	364.9	245.4	36.0	83.5	6.0	2.1	75.4	27.1	48.3	16.2	32.1	1 658.0
1966	440.1	39.4	400.7	272.9	37.0	90.9	7.2	2.6	81.1	29.5	51.6	16.8	34.8	1 780.6
1967	463.2	43.5	419.7	291.1	39.3	89.3	8.6	2.7	78.1	27.8	50.2	17.3	33.0	1 831.6
1968	510.9	48.1	462.8	320.9	45.5	96.4	10.1	2.9	83.4	33.5	49.8	19.0	30.8	1 950.4
1969	554.6	53.5	501.1	356.1	50.2	94.9	13.5	3.0	78.3	33.3	45.0	19.0	25.9	2 028.4
1970	572.8	59.3	513.6	374.5	54.2	84.8	17.8	3.2	63.9	27.3	36.6	18.3	18.3	2 010.8
1971	618.0	64.7	553.3	396.2	59.5	97.6	18.8	3.6	75.2	30.0	45.2	18.1	27.0	2 090.0
1972	685.9	70.2	615.8	439.9	63.7	112.2	20.0	3.9	88.3	33.8	54.5	19.7	34.8	2 248.4
1973	768.8	78.2	690.7	495.1	70.1	125.5	23.7	4.5	97.2	40.4	56.8	20.8	36.1	2 385.0
1974	830.1	91.4	738.7	542.9	74.4	121.3	30.2	3.7	87.4	42.8	44.6	21.5	23.0	2 348.8
1975	898.3	107.7	790.6	569.0	80.2	141.4	32.4	4.7	104.3	41.9	62.4	24.6	37.8	2 315.5
1976	1 014.8	118.3	896.5	640.0	86.7	169.8	30.1	6.7	133.0	53.5	79.6	27.8	51.8	2 505.0
1977	1 147.5	132.6	1 015.0	723.3	94.6	197.0	33.2	8.7	155.1	60.6	94.6	30.9	63.6	2 689.5
1978	1 304.1	150.2	1 154.0	829.5	102.7	221.7	36.8	9.2	175.8	67.6	108.2	35.9	72.3	2 864.2
1979	1 450.4	172.4	1 278.0	942.4	108.8	226.8	43.8	9.0	174.0	70.6	103.4	37.6	65.8	2 956.0
1980	1 574.2	198.9	1 375.4	1 030.7	121.5	223.1	57.8	9.6	155.7	68.2	87.5	44.7	42.8	2 927.1
1981	1 788.4	229.1	1 559.3	1 139.9	146.7	272.8	72.2	10.7	189.9	66.0	123.9	52.5	71.4	3 045.9
1982	1 854.3	253.9	1 600.4	1 183.3	152.9	264.2	82.8	8.1	173.3	48.8	124.5	54.1	70.5	2 979.4
1983	1 985.5	264.6	1 720.9	1 250.1	168.0	302.8	82.3	10.0	210.5	61.7	148.8	63.2	85.6	3 125.2
1984	2 225.5	279.0	1 946.6	1 388.2	185.0	373.4	93.5	10.9	268.9	75.9	193.0	67.2	125.8	3 403.6
1985	2 369.5	299.0	2 070.6	1 490.1	196.6	383.9	97.5	15.4	271.1	71.1	200.0	72.0	128.0	3 561.3
1986	2 465.3	317.9	2 147.5	1 578.2	204.6	364.7	107.6	26.9	230.2	76.2	154.0	72.9	81.1	3 654.2
1987	2 642.5	334.7	2 307.8	1 685.5	216.8	405.5	116.5	29.7	259.4	94.2	165.1	76.3	88.9	3 848.0
1988	2 874.5	357.7	2 516.8	1 825.3	233.8	457.7	136.2	27.0	294.5	104.0	190.5	82.2	108.4	4 084.4
1989	3 020.8	380.1	2 640.7	1 934.8	248.2	457.8	160.1	23.5	274.1	101.2	172.9	105.4	67.6	4 162.0
1990	3 161.2	403.0	2 758.3	2 037.5	263.5	457.2	170.2	24.9	262.1	98.5	163.7	118.3	45.4	4 222.2
1991	3 231.8	424.5	2 807.3	2 071.1	285.7	450.5	157.2	26.1	267.2	88.6	178.6	125.5	53.1	4 200.4
1992	3 377.1	437.8	2 939.4	2 188.7	302.5	448.2	132.0	30.7	285.6	94.4	191.1	134.3	56.9	4 328.5
1993	3 535.3	457.9	3 077.3	2 271.0	319.3	487.0	117.9	29.5	339.6	108.0	231.6	149.2	82.4	4 435.2
1994	3 816.5	484.8	3 331.8	2 398.7	350.7	582.3	116.9	34.7	430.8	132.4	298.4	158.0	140.4	4 708.1
1995	4 041.4	523.7	3 517.7	2 524.6	358.7	634.4	126.3	30.2	477.9	140.3	337.6	178.0	159.6	4 935.4
1996	4 296.1	557.4	3 738.8	2 667.7	371.7	699.4	119.7	37.3	542.3	152.9	389.4	197.6	191.8	5 224.7
1997	4 608.4	598.4	4 010.0	2 862.6	388.9	758.6	127.0	38.5	593.1	161.4	431.7	215.9	215.8	5 573.4
1998	4 873.7	638.2	4 235.5	3 093.8	402.9	738.7	146.8	34.1	557.8	158.7	399.2	241.0	158.1	5 889.8
1999	5 169.9	683.4	4 486.5	3 310.0	424.6	751.9	159.9	45.6	546.4	171.4	375.0	224.7	150.4	6 210.3
2000	5 513.0	741.9	4 771.1	3 597.3	449.9	723.9	198.4	45.5	480.1	170.2	309.9	251.3	58.6	6 550.6
2001	5 471.2	785.3	4 685.9	3 584.6	445.0	656.3	219.1	55.3	382.0	111.2	270.7	245.4	25.3	6 411.5
2002	5 538.9	804.7	4 734.2	3 542.0	472.9	719.3	198.6	52.3	468.4	97.1	371.3	254.8	116.5	6 466.3
2003	5 724.4	818.0	4 906.5	3 595.7	495.8	815.0	169.8	61.8	583.4	132.9	450.5	293.4	157.2	6 606.8
2004	6 107.9	850.2	5 257.7	3 762.8	530.9	964.1	159.9	62.0	742.2	187.0	555.2	364.5	190.7	6 904.1
2005	6 532.1	909.9	5 622.2	3 930.3	573.2	1 118.7	173.6	74.2	870.9	271.9	599.1	170.8	428.3	7 131.7
2006	6 988.0	979.4	6 008.7	4 129.3	610.1	1 269.3	183.9	70.4	1 015.0	307.7	707.3	471.1	236.2	7 406.3
2007	7 203.9	1 040.3	6 163.6	4 305.3	632.5	1 225.8	249.0	62.2	914.6	293.8	620.8	484.6	136.2	7 480.5
2008	7 256.8	1 093.9	6 162.8	4 358.0	632.7	1 172.2	307.5	50.3	814.3	227.4	586.9	474.2	112.7	7 383.9
2009	6 859.8	1 092.0	5 767.8	4 088.4	605.9	1 073.5	283.7	71.8	718.1	177.8	540.2	351.4	188.9	6 859.8
2010	7 238.7	1 094.6	6 144.2	4 158.7	633.0	1 352.5	286.2	83.3	983.0	220.6	762.4	375.5	387.0	7 240.0
2011	7 592.3	1 139.2	6 453.1	4 363.4	670.6	1 419.1	289.7	90.4	1 039.0	228.8	810.2	441.0	369.2	7 421.5
2012	8 011.9	1 186.2	6 825.7	4 593.3	690.4	1 542.0	298.5	93.9	1 149.7	266.7	883.0	517.9	365.0	7 720.9
2013	8 316.8	1 232.2	7 084.6	4 747.4	724.9	1 612.3	280.4	95.1	1 236.8	284.6	952.2	525.2	427.0	7 954.8
2014	8 641.0	1 285.7	7 355.2	4 995.8	745.2	1 614.3	258.1	85.1	1 271.1	316.2	954.9	573.8	381.1	8 207.3
2012														
1st quarter	7 927.8	1 170.3	6 757.5	4 539.1	688.2	1 530.2	297.7	97.4	1 135.1	265.8	869.3	463.0	406.3	7 707.8
2nd quarter	7 990.4	1 182.0	6 808.4	4 564.1	688.7	1 555.7	300.0	93.8	1 161.9	260.9	901.0	466.1	434.9	7 724.7
3rd quarter	7 982.8	1 192.1	6 790.7	4 580.8	687.7	1 522.2	299.5	89.0	1 133.7	259.8	874.0	493.2	380.7	7 652.4
4th quarter	8 146.5	1 200.4	6 946.1	4 689.2	696.9	1 560.0	296.7	95.4	1 167.9	280.3	887.6	649.4	238.2	7 798.9
2013														
1st quarter	8 209.1	1 212.2	6 996.8	4 676.8	718.9	1 601.1	289.6	94.8	1 216.7	289.4	927.3	529.0	398.3	7 852.2
2nd quarter	8 320.3	1 226.2	7 094.1	4 739.7	720.6	1 633.8	283.5	95.0	1 255.2	284.4	970.9	505.9	465.0	7 966.7
3rd quarter	8 335.1	1 238.4	7 096.7	4 766.5	728.1	1 602.0	277.7	91.5	1 232.8	281.1	951.6	589.6	362.1	7 977.7
4th quarter	8 402.8	1 252.0	7 150.8	4 806.7	731.7	1 612.4	270.9	99.0	1 242.6	283.6	959.0	476.4	482.6	8 022.6
2014														
1st quarter	8 446.6	1 266.5	7 180.1	4 928.2	734.2	1 517.7	263.8	85.6	1 168.3	303.4	864.8	588.9	275.9	8 027.0
2nd quarter	8 585.1	1 279.8	7 305.3	4 960.3	743.0	1 602.0	258.9	83.2	1 259.8	315.5	944.3	585.8	358.5	8 148.2
3rd quarter	8 729.9	1 292.8	7 437.1	5 013.7	750.1	1 673.4	256.0	89.9	1 327.5	321.8	1 005.7	542.7	463.0	8 252.3
4th quarter	8 802.3	1 303.8	7 498.5	5 080.9	753.4	1 664.2	253.6	81.7	1 329.0	324.2	1 004.8	577.9	426.9	8 401.6

Table 1-16. Shares of Income

(Billions of dollars, percent, quarterly data are at seasonally adjusted annual rates.)

NIPA Tables 1.10, 1.14

Year and quarter	Gross domestic income, total economy									Net factor income, domestic corporate business				
	Billions of dollars					Percent of total				Billions of dollars			Percent of total	
	Total	Compensation of employees	Taxes on production and imports less subsidies	Net operating surplus	Consumption of fixed capital	Compensation of employees	Taxes on production and imports less subsidies	Net operating surplus	Consumption of fixed capital	Total	Compensation of employees	Net operating surplus	Compensation	Net operating surplus
1959	522.3	286.4	40.0	130.5	65.4	54.8	7.7	25.0	12.5	234.4	180.3	54.1	76.9	23.1
1960	544.6	302.0	43.4	131.3	67.9	55.5	8.0	24.1	12.5	243.6	190.7	52.9	78.3	21.7
1961	564.3	311.2	45.0	137.5	70.6	55.1	8.0	24.4	12.5	250.4	195.6	54.8	78.1	21.9
1962	605.2	333.0	48.1	150.0	74.1	55.0	7.9	24.8	12.2	274.0	211.0	63.0	77.0	23.0
1963	640.1	351.2	51.2	159.7	78.0	54.9	8.0	24.9	12.2	291.9	222.7	69.2	76.3	23.7
1964	685.8	376.9	54.6	172.0	82.4	55.0	8.0	25.1	12.0	316.1	239.2	76.9	75.7	24.3
1965	743.0	406.3	57.7	190.9	88.0	54.7	7.8	25.7	11.8	349.0	259.9	89.1	74.5	25.5
1966	809.9	450.3	59.3	205.1	95.3	55.6	7.3	25.3	11.8	385.4	288.5	96.9	74.9	25.1
1967	858.3	482.9	64.1	207.8	103.5	56.3	7.5	24.2	12.1	404.8	308.4	96.4	76.2	23.8
1968	939.3	532.1	72.2	221.7	113.3	56.6	7.7	23.6	12.1	444.4	340.2	104.2	76.6	23.4
1969	1 018.3	586.0	79.4	228.1	124.9	57.5	7.8	22.4	12.3	482.2	377.5	104.7	78.3	21.7
1970	1 070.5	625.1	86.6	222.0	136.8	58.4	8.1	20.7	12.8	493.5	398.0	95.5	80.6	19.4
1971	1 158.3	667.0	95.8	246.6	148.9	57.6	8.3	21.3	12.9	530.7	421.7	109.0	79.5	20.5
1972	1 275.3	733.6	101.3	279.5	160.9	57.5	7.9	21.9	12.6	592.5	468.2	124.3	79.0	21.0
1973	1 422.4	815.1	112.0	317.3	178.1	57.3	7.9	22.3	12.5	664.5	526.1	138.4	79.2	20.8
1974	1 541.4	890.3	121.6	323.3	206.2	57.8	7.9	21.0	13.4	715.3	577.3	138.0	80.7	19.3
1975	1 675.7	950.2	130.8	357.1	237.5	56.7	7.8	21.3	14.2	767.9	607.8	160.1	79.2	20.8
1976	1 857.1	1 051.3	141.3	405.4	259.2	56.6	7.6	21.8	14.0	871.3	682.8	188.5	78.4	21.6
1977	2 066.7	1 169.0	152.6	456.8	288.3	56.6	7.4	22.1	13.9	992.5	771.7	220.8	77.8	22.2
1978	2 333.4	1 320.3	162.0	526.1	325.1	56.6	6.9	22.5	13.9	1 139.6	884.7	254.9	77.6	22.4
1979	2 587.4	1 481.1	171.6	563.6	371.1	57.2	6.6	21.8	14.3	1 266.6	1 004.4	262.2	79.3	20.7
1980	2 818.6	1 626.3	190.5	575.7	426.0	57.7	6.8	20.4	15.1	1 362.1	1 102.0	260.1	80.9	19.1
1981	3 174.2	1 795.4	224.1	669.6	485.0	56.6	7.1	21.1	15.3	1 535.9	1 220.6	315.3	79.5	20.5
1982	3 338.2	1 894.5	225.9	683.5	534.3	56.8	6.8	20.5	16.0	1 584.9	1 275.1	309.8	80.5	19.5
1983	3 584.0	2 014.1	242.0	767.4	560.5	56.2	6.8	21.4	15.6	1 709.6	1 353.0	356.6	79.1	20.9
1984	4 002.0	2 217.6	268.7	921.4	594.3	55.4	6.7	23.0	14.9	1 936.5	1 501.1	435.4	77.5	22.5
1985	4 295.5	2 389.2	286.7	982.9	636.7	55.6	6.7	22.9	14.8	2 069.9	1 615.9	454.0	78.1	21.9
1986	4 513.4	2 545.6	298.5	987.1	682.2	56.4	6.6	21.9	15.1	2 143.0	1 723.4	419.6	80.4	19.6
1987	4 829.7	2 725.7	317.2	1 058.8	728.0	56.4	6.6	21.9	15.1	2 298.2	1 847.6	450.6	80.4	19.6
1988	5 253.1	2 950.9	345.0	1 174.8	782.4	56.2	6.6	22.4	14.9	2 499.9	2 002.3	497.6	80.1	19.9
1989	5 593.5	3 143.9	371.5	1 242.1	836.1	56.2	6.6	22.2	14.9	2 634.2	2 119.3	514.9	80.5	19.5
1990	5 888.2	3 345.0	398.0	1 258.4	886.8	56.8	6.8	21.4	15.1	2 737.5	2 234.9	502.6	81.6	18.4
1991	6 085.7	3 454.7	429.6	1 270.2	931.1	56.8	7.1	20.9	15.3	2 775.3	2 277.8	497.5	82.1	17.9
1992	6 428.4	3 674.1	453.3	1 341.3	959.7	57.2	7.1	20.9	14.9	2 928.4	2 420.5	507.9	82.7	17.3
1993	6 726.4	3 824.0	466.4	1 432.4	1 003.6	56.9	6.9	21.3	14.9	3 063.3	2 515.7	547.6	82.1	17.9
1994	7 171.9	4 014.1	512.7	1 589.5	1 055.6	56.0	7.1	22.2	14.7	3 292.8	2 649.0	643.8	80.4	19.6
1995	7 573.5	4 206.7	523.1	1 720.9	1 122.8	55.5	6.9	22.7	14.8	3 505.5	2 787.9	717.6	79.5	20.5
1996	8 043.6	4 426.2	545.6	1 895.9	1 176.0	55.0	6.8	23.6	14.6	3 752.0	2 953.7	798.3	78.7	21.3
1997	8 596.2	4 719.1	577.8	2 059.4	1 240.0	54.9	6.7	24.0	14.4	4 062.7	3 176.6	886.1	78.2	21.8
1998	9 149.3	5 082.4	603.1	2 153.6	1 310.3	55.5	6.6	23.5	14.3	4 335.8	3 447.5	888.3	79.5	20.5
1999	9 698.1	5 417.5	628.4	2 251.4	1 400.9	55.9	6.5	23.2	14.4	4 586.9	3 684.3	902.6	80.3	19.7
2000	10 384.3	5 863.4	662.8	2 344.2	1 514.2	56.5	6.4	22.6	14.6	4 903.0	4 008.9	894.1	81.8	18.2
2001	10 736.8	6 053.8	669.0	2 410.1	1 604.0	56.4	6.2	22.4	14.9	4 854.8	4 015.6	839.2	82.7	17.3
2002	11 050.3	6 149.7	721.2	2 517.3	1 662.1	55.7	6.5	22.8	15.0	4 892.0	3 973.9	918.1	81.2	18.8
2003	11 524.3	6 372.7	758.9	2 665.4	1 727.2	55.3	6.6	23.1	15.0	5 070.1	4 042.0	1 028.1	79.7	20.3
2004	12 283.5	6 748.8	817.5	2 885.5	1 831.7	54.9	6.7	23.5	14.9	5 413.5	4 241.5	1 172.0	78.4	21.6
2005	13 129.2	7 097.9	873.6	3 175.7	1 982.0	54.1	6.7	24.2	15.1	5 815.9	4 444.5	1 371.4	76.4	23.6
2006	14 073.2	7 513.7	940.4	3 483.0	2 136.0	53.4	6.7	24.7	15.2	6 241.9	4 683.2	1 558.7	75.0	25.0
2007	14 460.1	7 908.8	980.0	3 307.0	2 264.4	54.7	6.8	22.9	15.7	6 310.4	4 893.0	1 417.4	77.5	22.5
2008	14 619.2	8 090.0	989.3	3 176.5	2 363.4	55.3	6.8	21.7	16.2	6 148.2	4 939.7	1 208.5	80.3	19.7
2009	14 343.4	7 795.7	967.8	3 211.6	2 368.4	54.4	6.7	22.4	16.5	5 904.1	4 610.0	1 294.1	78.1	21.9
2010	14 915.2	7 969.5	1 001.2	3 562.8	2 381.6	53.4	6.7	23.9	16.0	6 287.1	4 706.9	1 580.2	74.9	25.1
2011	15 556.3	8 277.1	1 042.5	3 785.9	2 450.6	53.2	6.7	24.3	15.8	6 591.1	4 937.9	1 653.2	74.9	25.1
2012	16 358.5	8 618.5	1 074.1	4 131.7	2 534.2	52.7	6.6	25.3	15.5	7 055.7	5 191.8	1 863.9	73.6	26.4
2013	16 840.8	8 848.7	1 118.6	4 240.6	2 632.8	52.5	6.6	25.2	15.6	7 270.2	5 355.2	1 915.0	73.7	26.3
2014	17 560.1	9 258.4	1 155.8	4 399.2	2 746.7	52.7	6.6	25.1	15.6	7 614.5	5 640.8	1 973.7	74.1	25.9
2012														
1st quarter	16 192.6	8 512.4	1 070.7	4 108.3	2 501.2	52.6	6.6	25.4	15.4	6 976.0	5 109.4	1 866.6	73.2	26.8
2nd quarter	16 290.2	8 559.1	1 071.2	4 135.4	2 524.4	52.5	6.6	25.4	15.5	7 015.1	5 147.3	1 867.8	73.4	26.6
3rd quarter	16 371.8	8 596.5	1 070.5	4 158.2	2 546.5	52.5	6.5	25.4	15.6	7 037.7	5 172.8	1 864.9	73.5	26.5
4th quarter	16 579.5	8 806.2	1 083.5	4 125.1	2 564.7	53.1	6.5	24.9	15.5	7 194.2	5 337.9	1 856.3	74.2	25.8
2013														
1st quarter	16 626.2	8 705.5	1 109.4	4 221.6	2 589.7	52.4	6.7	25.4	15.6	7 136.0	5 247.6	1 888.4	73.5	26.5
2nd quarter	16 787.2	8 829.7	1 111.6	4 227.6	2 618.3	52.6	6.6	25.2	15.6	7 264.4	5 343.4	1 921.0	73.6	26.4
3rd quarter	16 882.6	8 884.9	1 123.7	4 228.3	2 645.7	52.6	6.7	25.0	15.7	7 289.6	5 384.3	1 905.3	73.9	26.1
4th quarter	17 067.2	8 974.9	1 129.9	4 284.9	2 677.6	52.6	6.6	25.1	15.7	7 390.9	5 445.5	1 945.4	73.7	26.3
2014														
1st quarter	17 159.6	9 112.6	1 138.0	4 200.7	2 708.3	53.1	6.6	24.5	15.8	7 344.5	5 537.5	1 807.0	75.4	24.6
2nd quarter	17 457.0	9 186.8	1 152.3	4 385.1	2 732.8	52.6	6.6	25.1	15.7	7 553.4	5 586.5	1 966.9	74.0	26.0
3rd quarter	17 746.1	9 299.4	1 163.5	4 521.7	2 761.5	52.4	6.6	25.5	15.6	7 760.4	5 668.1	2 092.3	73.0	27.0
4th quarter	17 877.8	9 434.7	1 169.5	4 489.4	2 784.2	52.8	6.5	25.1	15.6	7 799.7	5 771.0	2 028.7	74.0	26.0

Table 1-17. Rates of Return and Related Data for Domestic Nonfinancial Corporations

Year	Rates of return (percent)					Shares of net value added (percent)					Tax liability as a percent of produced assets	Q1 ratio	Q2 ratio
	Net operating surplus		Corporate profits		Net interest	Net operating surplus		Corporate profits		Net interest			
	Before tax	After tax	Before tax	After tax		Before tax	After tax	Before tax	After tax				
1960	9.6	5.7	8.7	4.7	0.7	18.4	10.9	16.6	9.1	1.3	3.9	0.75	0.91
1961	9.7	5.8	8.7	4.8	0.7	18.6	11.1	16.6	9.1	1.4	3.9	0.86	1.01
1962	11.1	7.1	9.9	5.9	0.9	19.9	12.7	17.8	10.6	1.5	4.0	0.80	0.96
1963	11.9	7.6	10.6	6.4	0.9	20.7	13.2	18.6	11.1	1.5	4.3	0.85	1.01
1964	12.7	8.3	11.4	7.1	0.9	21.3	14.0	19.1	11.9	1.6	4.3	0.95	1.11
1965	13.8	9.2	12.4	7.8	1.0	22.4	15.0	20.2	12.7	1.6	4.6	1.02	1.18
1966	13.7	9.1	12.2	7.6	1.1	22.0	14.6	19.6	12.2	1.8	4.6	0.82	0.98
1967	12.4	8.4	10.8	6.8	1.2	20.7	14.1	18.0	11.4	2.0	4.0	0.97	1.14
1968	12.2	7.8	10.6	6.1	1.3	20.2	12.9	17.4	10.1	2.1	4.4	1.06	1.22
1969	10.9	6.9	9.0	5.0	1.5	18.2	11.5	15.0	8.4	2.6	4.0	0.80	0.97
1970	8.9	5.9	6.7	3.7	1.8	15.8	10.5	11.9	6.6	3.2	3.0	0.73	0.90
1971	9.4	6.4	7.3	4.3	1.8	16.9	11.5	13.1	7.6	3.2	3.0	0.79	0.96
1972	9.8	6.7	7.7	4.6	1.7	17.2	11.7	13.5	8.0	3.0	3.1	0.91	1.08
1973	9.7	6.3	7.5	4.1	1.8	16.8	11.0	13.0	7.1	3.2	3.4	0.64	0.81
1974	7.7	4.7	5.4	2.4	1.9	14.8	9.0	10.5	4.7	3.7	3.0	0.37	0.52
1975	8.1	5.5	6.1	3.5	1.7	16.9	11.6	12.6	7.3	3.6	2.6	0.44	0.58
1976	8.6	5.6	6.8	3.8	1.4	17.3	11.3	13.6	7.6	2.9	3.0	0.49	0.64
1977	9.0	5.9	7.1	4.1	1.4	17.7	11.7	14.0	8.0	2.8	3.0	0.39	0.53
1978	8.8	5.8	6.9	3.9	1.5	17.2	11.3	13.5	7.6	2.9	3.0	0.36	0.50
1979	7.8	5.0	5.8	3.0	1.6	15.8	10.2	11.7	6.2	3.3	2.7	0.38	0.50
1980	6.7	4.4	4.5	2.2	1.8	14.4	9.5	9.7	4.8	4.0	2.3	0.43	0.55
1981	7.4	5.4	5.0	3.0	2.0	15.9	11.6	10.8	6.5	4.3	2.0	0.35	0.46
1982	6.6	5.2	4.2	2.9	2.1	14.9	11.9	9.5	6.5	4.9	1.4	0.36	0.47
1983	7.5	5.8	5.2	3.5	2.1	16.4	12.8	11.3	7.7	4.5	1.7	0.41	0.52
1984	8.8	6.9	6.3	4.4	2.2	17.9	13.9	12.8	8.9	4.4	1.9	0.37	0.49
1985	8.6	6.9	6.0	4.3	2.2	17.2	13.8	12.0	8.5	4.5	1.7	0.43	0.57
1986	8.1	6.3	5.2	3.4	2.2	16.2	12.6	10.4	6.8	4.5	1.8	0.49	0.64
1987	8.7	6.6	5.9	3.7	2.2	16.9	12.7	11.3	7.2	4.2	2.1	0.48	0.64
1988	9.4	7.2	6.5	4.3	2.3	17.8	13.6	12.3	8.1	4.4	2.2	0.50	0.68
1989	9.0	7.0	5.7	3.7	2.9	17.2	13.3	10.8	7.0	5.4	2.0	0.58	0.76
1990	8.5	6.7	5.3	3.4	2.8	16.4	12.8	10.1	6.5	5.4	1.9	0.52	0.70
1991	7.9	6.2	4.9	3.2	2.5	15.4	12.2	9.5	6.3	4.9	1.6	0.68	0.87
1992	7.7	6.0	5.3	3.5	2.0	14.8	11.5	10.0	6.8	3.9	1.7	0.73	0.92
1993	8.2	6.4	5.9	4.0	1.8	15.5	12.0	11.2	7.6	3.4	1.9	0.78	0.99
1994	9.1	6.9	6.9	4.7	1.7	16.7	12.6	12.7	8.6	3.1	2.2	0.73	0.95
1995	9.4	7.2	7.1	4.9	1.8	17.3	13.2	13.1	9.0	3.3	2.2	0.92	1.14
1996	10.0	7.8	7.8	5.5	1.7	18.3	14.2	14.2	10.1	3.1	2.3	0.93	1.15
1997	10.4	8.1	8.1	5.8	1.8	18.7	14.6	14.6	10.5	3.2	2.3	1.13	1.36
BASED ON COMPREHENSIVE NIPA REVISION													
1998	9.1	7.2	...	...	...	17.4	13.7	...	...	...	...	1.35	1.59
1999	8.8	6.8	...	...	...	16.8	12.9	...	...	...	...	1.70	1.94
2000	8.0	6.1	...	...	...	15.2	11.6	...	...	...	...	1.37	1.62
2001	6.9	5.7	...	...	...	14.0	11.6	...	...	...	...	1.14	1.41
2002	7.3	6.3	...	...	...	15.2	13.1	...	...	...	...	0.83	1.10
2003	8.0	6.7	...	...	...	16.6	13.9	...	...	...	...	1.07	1.33
2004	9.0	7.2	...	...	...	18.3	14.8	...	...	...	...	1.12	1.37
2005	9.6	7.2	...	...	...	19.9	15.1	...	...	...	...	1.08	1.31
2006	10.0	7.6	...	...	...	21.1	16.0	...	...	...	...	1.15	1.37
2007	9.1	6.9	...	...	...	19.9	15.1	...	...	...	...	1.16	1.37
2008	8.2	6.6	...	...	...	19.0	15.3	...	...	...	...	0.70	0.91
2009	7.5	6.2	...	...	...	18.6	15.5	...	...	...	...	0.87	1.09
2010	9.4	7.9	...	...	...	22.0	18.4	...	...	...	...	1.00	1.24
2011	9.5	8.0	...	...	...	22.0	18.4	...	...	...	...	0.96	1.20
2012	10.1	8.3	...	...	...	22.8	18.8	...	...	...	...	1.03	1.28
2013	9.9	7.9	...	...	...	22.6	17.9	...	...	...	...	1.29	1.55
2014	9.6	7.3	...	...	...	22.0	16.7	...	...	...	...	1.34	1.61

Note: See notes and definitions for explanation.
. . . = Not available.

NOTES AND DEFINITIONS, CHAPTER 1

Tables 1-1 through 1-17
National Income and Product

SOURCE: U.S. DEPARTMENT OF COMMERCE, BUREAU OF ECONOMIC ANALYSIS (BEA)

The Bureau of Economic Analysis (BEA) within the U.S. Department of Commerce, collects and produces data on how the U.S. economy is functioning. The National Income and Product Accounts (NIPA) are a set of economic accounts that provide information on the value and composition of output produced in the United States during a given period and on the types and uses of the income generated by that production. Featured in the NIPAs is gross domestic product (GDP), which measures the value of the goods and services produced by the U.S. economy in a given time period. GDP is one of the most comprehensive and closely watched economic statistics.

These tables, and others in the chapters that follow, incorporate the results of the 2015 updating of the National Income and Product Accounts (NIPAs) of the United States. Less comprehensive than the 2013 revision, revisions were generally limited to the first quarter of 2012 to the first quarter of 2015.

The 2013 comprehensive benchmark revision, first incorporated in the 18th edition of *Business Statistics*, altered concepts and numbers all the way back to 1929. BEA adopted an expansion of the basic concept of production embodied in the accounts and changed the method of accounting for an important category of pension plans. Also, the constant-dollar or "real" estimates were restated to 2009 dollars, so that the levels shown are different even if the indicated rates of change are the same.

Fixed investment, one of the basic building blocks of the estimation of gross domestic product, was expanded in this revision by recognizing expenditures for research and development by business, government, and nonprofit institutions serving households (NPISHs) as investment.

The workers and capital that produce this R&D have always been reported in the labor and capital tabulations, but were treated as if they were costs of producing this year's output only. In the national income accounting as in conventional business accounting, the full costs of the R&D were subtracted from current-year business receipts in calculating business profit.

Now, in the NIPAs, the estimated value of the research over the whole life of the product—for example, from the estimated future sales of a new drug—is added to the value produced this year. However, this R&D will lose value over time and, as with a piece of machinery, its use and obsolescence, called consumption of fixed capital (CFC), is estimated and charged against GDP in each year that this capital is in use. For that reason, this change adds more to gross national product than to net national product and income.

The basic concept of the NIPAs requires equivalence (except for measurement error) between the value of output and the income and other charges against that value. The higher values of production are balanced on the income side of the accounts by the higher capital consumption allowances and by addition, to profits and other operating surplus (nonlabor income) components, of the net R&D investment—the difference between gross investment value and current year's CFC. (This does not change the tax accounting treatment. The firm still gets to charge off the entire expenditure in the year it is made, which is the most favorable treatment possible.)

Similarly, BEA is now capitalizing private spending for certain entertainment, literary, and other artistic originals as fixed investment. This includes movies, books, music, and long-lived TV programs such as situation comedies and drama (but not news, sports, games, or reality shows).

In a third expansion of the GDP investment definition, all ownership transfer costs for residential and nonresidential structures are capitalized (instead of only broker's commissions as in the previous treatment).

The other important conceptual change introduced in this revision was the adoption of accrual instead of cash accounting for defined benefit pension plans. This does not increase income and saving (or dis-saving) overall, but relocates it. Pension benefits are credited to the labor income and saving of employees when earned instead of when paid—matched by an equal and opposite change in the surplus or deficit of the employing government or business.

All the quarterly NIPA data published here, including indexes of quantity and price, are seasonally adjusted; this is not specifically noted on each table. All of the quarterly level values in current and constant dollars are also expressed at annual rates, which means that seasonally adjusted quarterly levels have been multiplied by 4 so that their scale will be comparable with the annual values shown, and this is noted on the pertinent *Business Statistics* tables. Where quarterly percent changes are shown, they are expressed as seasonally adjusted annual rates, which means that the quarter-to-quarter change in the level of GDP is calculated and then raised to the 4th power in order to express what that rate of change would be if continued over an entire year; this is noted in the column headings. For further information on these concepts see "General Notes" at the front of this volume.

Each table is notated, just above the table at the right-hand side, with the numbers of the NIPA tables from which the data are drawn.

All data and references are available on the BEA website, <http://www.bea.gov>.

Definitions and notes on the data: Basic concepts of total output and income (Tables 1-1, 1-11, 1-12, and 1-13)

The NIPAs depict the U.S. economy in several different dimensions. The basic concept, and the measure that is now most frequently cited, is gross domestic product (GDP), which is the market value of all goods and services produced by labor and property located in the United States.

In principle, GDP can be measured by summing the values created by each industry in the economy. However, it can also, and more readily, be measured by summing all the final demands for the economy's output. This final-demand approach also has the advantage of depicting the origins of demand for economic production, whether from consumers, businesses, or government.

Since production for the market necessarily generates incomes equal to its value, there is also an income total that corresponds to the production value total. This income can be measured and its distribution among labor, capital, and other income recipients can be depicted.

The relationships of several of these major concepts are illustrated in Table 1-11. The definitions of these concepts are as follows:

Gross domestic product (GDP), the featured measure of the value of U.S. output, is the market value of the goods and services produced by labor and property located in the United States. Market values represent output valued at the prices paid by the final customer, and therefore include taxes on production and imports, such as sales taxes, customs duties, and taxes on property.

The term "gross" in gross domestic product and gross national product is used to indicate that capital consumption allowances (economic depreciation) have not been deducted.

GDP is primarily measured by summing the values of all of the final demands in the economy, net of the demands met by imports; this is shown in Table 1-1. Specifically, GDP is the sum of personal consumption expenditures (PCE), gross private domestic investment (including change in private inventories and before deduction of charges for consumption of fixed capital), net exports of goods and services, and government consumption expenditures and gross investment. GDP measured in this way excludes duplication involving "intermediate" purchases of goods and services (goods and services purchased by industries and used in production), the value of which is already included in the value of the final products. Production of any intermediate goods that are not used in further production in the current period is captured in the measurement of inventory change.

In concept, GDP is equal to the sum of the economic value added by (also referred to as "gross product originating in") all

industries in the United States. This, in turn, also makes it the conceptual equivalent of *gross domestic income (GDI)*, a new concept introduced in the 2003 revision. GDI is the sum of the incomes earned in each domestic industry, plus the taxes on production and imports and less the subsidies that account for the difference between output value and factor input value. This derivation is shown in Table 1-12. Since the incomes and taxes can be measured directly, they can be summed to a total that is equivalent to GDP in concept but differs due to imperfections in measurement. The difference between the two is known as the *statistical discrepancy*. It is defined as GDP minus GDI, and is shown in Tables 1-11 and 1-12.

Gross national product (GNP) refers to all goods and services produced by labor and property supplied by U.S. residents—whether located in the United States or abroad—expressed at market prices. It is equal to GDP, plus *income receipts from the rest of the world*, less *income payments to the rest of the world*. *Domestic* production and income refer to the <u>location</u> of the factors of production, with only factors located in the United States included; *national* production and income refer to the <u>ownership</u> of the factors of production, with only factors owned by United States residents included.

Before the comprehensive NIPA revisions that were made in 1991, GNP was the commonly used measure of U.S. production. However, GDP is clearly preferable to GNP when used in conjunction with indicators such as employment, hours worked, and capital utilized—for example, in the calculation of labor and capital productivity—because it is confined to production taking place within the borders of the United States. It is also the measure used by almost all other countries, thus facilitating international comparisons such as those shown in Chapter 13.

The income-side aggregate corresponding to GNP is *gross national income (GNI)*, shown as an addendum to Table 1-11. It consists of gross domestic income plus income receipts from the rest of the world, less income payments to the rest of the world. It is used as the denominator for a national saving-income ratio, presented in Chapter 5. National income is the preferred measure for calculating and comparing saving, since it is the income aggregate from which that saving arises. As with GDP and gross domestic income, the statistical discrepancy indicates the difference between the product-side and income-side measurement of the same concept.

Net national product is the market value, net of depreciation, of goods and services attributable to the labor and property supplied by U.S. residents. It is equal to GNP minus the *consumption of fixed capital (CFC)*. CFC relates only to fixed capital located in the United States. (Investment in that capital is measured by private fixed investment and government gross investment.) As of the 2009 comprehensive revision, CFC represents only the normal using-up of capital in the process of production, and no longer includes extraordinary disaster losses such as those caused by Hurricane Katrina and the 9/11 attacks. These losses are still estimated and used to write down the estimates of the capital stock, but they no longer have negative effects on our calculation of current income from production.

National income has been redefined and now includes all net incomes (net of the consumption of fixed capital) earned by U.S. residents, and also includes not only "factor incomes"—net incomes received by labor and capital as a result of their participation in the production process, but also "nonfactor charges"—taxes on production and imports, business transfer payments, and the current surplus of government enterprises, less subsidies. This change has been made to conform with the international guidelines for national accounts, *System of National Accounts (SNA) 1993.* According to *SNA 1993,* these charges cannot be eliminated from the input and output prices.

Since national income now includes the nonfactor charges, it is conceptually equivalent to *net national product* and differs only by the amount of the statistical discrepancy.

The concept formerly known as "national income," which excludes the nonfactor charges, is still included in the accounts as an addendum item, now called "net national factor income." It is shown in Table 1-13. *Net national factor income* consists of compensation of employees, proprietors' income with inventory valuation and capital consumption adjustments (IVA and CCadj, respectively), rental income of persons with capital consumption adjustment, corporate profits with inventory valuation and capital consumption adjustments, and net interest.

By definition, national income and its components exclude all income from capital gains (increases in the value of owned assets). Such increases have no counterpart on the production side of the accounts. This exclusion is partly accomplished by means of the inventory valuation and capital consumption adjustments, which will be described in the definitions of the components of product and income.

Definitions and notes on the data: Imputation

The term *imputation* will appear from time to time in the definitions of product and income components. Imputed values are values estimated by BEA statisticians for certain important product and income components that are not explicitly valued in the source data, usually because a market transaction in money terms is not involved. Imputed values appear on both the product and income side of the accounts; they add equal amounts to income and spending, so that no imputed saving is created.

One important example is the imputed rent on owner-occupied housing. The building of such housing is counted as investment, yet in the monetary accounts of the household sector, there is no income from that investment nor any rental paid for it. In the NIPAs, the rent that each such dwelling would earn if rented is estimated and added to both national and personal income

(as part of rental income receipts) and to personal consumption expenditures (as part of expenditures on housing services).

Another important example is imputed interest. For example, many individuals keep monetary balances in a bank or other financial institution, receiving either no interest or below-market interest, but receiving the institution's services, such as clearing checks and otherwise facilitating payments, with little or no charge. In this case, where is the product generated by the institution's workers and capital? In the NIPAs, the depositor is imputed a market-rate-based interest return on his or her balance, which is then imputed as a service charge received by the institution, and therefore included in the value of the institution's output.

Definitions and notes on the data: Components of product (Tables 1-1 through 1-6)

Personal consumption expenditures (PCE) are goods and services purchased by persons residing in the United States. PCE consists mainly of purchases of new goods and services by individuals from businesses. It includes purchases that are financed by insurance, such as government-provided and private medical insurance. In addition, PCE includes purchases of new goods and services by nonprofit institutions, net purchases of used goods ("net" here indicates purchases of used goods from business less sales of used goods to business) by individuals and nonprofit institutions, and purchases abroad of goods and services by U.S. residents traveling or working in foreign countries. PCE also includes purchases for certain goods and services provided by government agencies. (See the notes and definitions for Chapter 4 for additional information.) In the 2009 revision, new detail was provided on the allocation of PCE between the household and nonprofit sectors.

Gross private domestic investment consists of gross private fixed investment and change in private inventories.

Private fixed investment consists of both nonresidential and residential fixed investment. The term "residential" refers to the construction and equipping of living quarters for permanent occupancy. Hotels and motels are included in *nonresidential fixed investment*, as described subsequently in this section.

Private fixed investment consists of purchases of fixed assets, which are commodities that will be used in a production process for more than one year, including replacements and additions to the capital stock, and now also including research and development and other intellectual property. It is measured "gross," before a deduction for consumption of existing fixed capital. It covers all investment by private businesses and non-profit institutions in the United States, regardless of whether the investment is owned by U.S. residents. The residential component includes investment in owner-occupied housing; the homeowner is treated equivalently to a business in these investment accounts. (However, when GDP by sector is calculated, owner-occupied housing is no longer included in the business sector. It is allocated to the households and institutions sector.) Private fixed investment does not include purchases of the same types of equipment and structures by government agencies, which are included in government gross investment, nor does it include investment by U.S. residents in other countries.

Nonresidential fixed investment is the total of nonresidential structures, nonresidential equipment, and intellectual property.

Nonresidential structures consists of new construction, brokers' commissions and other ownership transfer costs on sales of structures, and net purchases of used structures by private business and by nonprofit institutions from government agencies (that is, purchases of used structures from government minus sales of used structures to government). New construction also includes hotels and motels and mining exploration, shafts, and wells.

Nonresidential equipment consists of private business purchases on capital account of new machinery, equipment, and vehicles; dealers' margins on sales of used equipment; and net purchases of used equipment from government agencies, persons, and the rest of the world (that is, purchases of such equipment minus sales of such equipment). It does not include the estimated personal-use portion of equipment purchased for both business and personal use, which is allocated to PCE.

Intellectual property consists of purchases and in-house production of software; research and development; and private expenditures for specified entertainment, literary, and artistic originals. (See above for further description.)

Residential private fixed investment consists of both residential structures and residential producers' durable equipment (including such equipment as appliances owned by landlords and rented to tenants). Investment in structures consists of new units, improvements to existing units, purchases of manufactured homes, brokers' commissions and other ownership transfer costs on the sale of residential property, and net purchases of used residential structures from government agencies (that is, purchases of such structures from government minus sales of such structures to government). As noted above, it includes investment in owner-occupied housing.

Change in private inventories is the change in the physical volume of inventories held by businesses, with that change being valued at the average price of the period. It differs from the change in the book value of inventories reported by most businesses; an *inventory valuation adjustment (IVA)* converts book value change using historical cost valuations to the change in physical volume, valued at average replacement cost.

Net exports of goods and services is *exports of goods and services* less *imports of goods and services*. It does not include income payments or receipts or transfer payments to and from the rest of the world.

Government consumption expenditures is the estimated value of the services produced by governments (federal, state, and local) for current consumption. Since these are generally not sold, there is no market valuation and they are priced at the cost of inputs. The input costs consist of the compensation of general government employees; the estimated consumption of general government fixed capital including software and R&D (CFC, or economic depreciation); and the cost of goods and services purchased by government less the value of sales to other sectors. The value of investment in equipment and structures produced by government workers and capital is also subtracted, and is instead included in government investment. Government sales to other sectors consist primarily of receipts of tuition payments for higher education and receipts of charges for medical care.

This definition of government consumption expenditures differs in concept—but not in the amount contributed to GDP—from the treatment in existence before the 2003 revision of the NIPAs. In the current definition, goods and services purchased by government are considered to be intermediate output. In the previous definition, they were considered to be final sales. Since their value is added to the other components to yield total government consumption expenditures, the dollar total contributed to GDP is the same. The only practical difference is that the goods purchased disappear from the goods account and appear in the services account instead. In the industry sector accounts, the value added by government is also unchanged. It continues to be measured as the sum of compensation and CFC, or equivalently as gross government output less the value of goods and services purchased.

Gross government investment consists of general government and government enterprise expenditures for fixed assets (structures, equipment, software, and R&D). Government inventory investment is included in government consumption expenditures.

Definitions and notes on the data: Real values, quantity and price indexes (Tables 1-2 through 1-7)

Real, or chained (2009) dollar, estimates are estimates from which the effect of price change has been removed. Prior to the 1996 comprehensive revision, constant-dollar measures were obtained by combining real output measures for different goods and services using the relative prices of a single year as weights for the entire time span of the series. In the recent environment of rapid technological change, which has caused the prices of computers and electronic components to decline rapidly relative to other prices, this method distorts the measurement of economic growth and causes excessive revisions of growth rates at each benchmark revision. The current, chained-dollar measure changes the relative price weights each year, as relative prices shift over time. As a result, recent changes in relative prices do not change historical growth rates.

Chained-dollar estimates, although expressed for continuity's sake as if they had occurred according to the prices of a single year (currently 2009), are usually not additive. This means that because of the changes in price weights each year, the chained (2009) dollar components in any given table for any year other than 2009 usually do not add to the chained (2009) dollar total. The amount of the difference for the major components of GDP is called the *residual* and is shown in Table 1-2. It is specific to each individual BEA tabulation, corresponding to the sum of the lowest level of aggregation on that tabulation. In time periods close to the base year, residuals are usually quite small; over longer periods, the differences become much larger. For this reason, BEA no longer publishes chained-dollar estimates prior to 1999, except for selected aggregate series. For the more detailed components of GDP, historical trends and fluctuations in real volumes are represented by *chain-type quantity indexes,* which are presented in Tables 1-5, 4-3, 5-4, 5-6, 6-6, 6-7, 6-11, 6-16, 7-2, 7-5, and 14-2.

Chain-weighting leads to complexity in estimating the contribution of economic sectors to an overall change in output: it becomes difficult, for someone without access to the complicated statistical methods that BEA uses, to find the correct answers to questions such as "How much are government spending cuts contributing to the drag on GDP growth?" Because of this, BEA is now calculating and publishing estimates of the arithmetic contribution of each major component to the total change in real GDP. *Business Statistics* reproduces these calculations in Table 1-4. (As will be explained later, users of these calculations should, however, bear in mind that imports are treated as a negative contribution to GDP instead of being subtracted from the demand components that give rise to them.) For further information, see J. Steven Landefeld, Brent R. Moulton, and Cindy M. Vojtech, "Chained-Dollar Indexes: Issues, Tips on Their Use, and Upcoming Changes," *Survey of Current Business* (November 2003); and J. Steven Landefeld and Robert P. Parker, "BEA's Chain Indexes, Time Series, and Measures of Long-Term Economic Growth," *Survey of Current Business* (May 1997).

GDP price indexes measure price changes between any two adjacent years (or quarters) for a fixed "market basket" of goods and services consisting of the average quantities purchased in those two years (or quarters). The annual measures are chained together to form an index with prices in 2009 set to equal 100. Using average quantities as weights while changing weights each period eliminates the substitution bias that arises in more conventional indexes, in which weights are taken from a single base period that usually takes place early in the period under measurement. Generally, using a single, early base period leads to an overstatement of price increase. The CPI-U and the CPI-W are examples of such conventional indexes, technically known as "Laspeyres" indexes. See the "General Notes" at the beginning of this volume and the notes and definitions for Chapter 8 for further explanation.

The chain-type formula guarantees that a GDP price index change will differ only trivially from the change in the implicit deflator (ratio of current-dollar to real value, expressed as a percent). Therefore, *Business Statistics* is no longer publishing a separate table of implicit deflators.

Definitions and notes on the data: BEA aggregates of sales and purchases (Tables 1-1 and 1-5 through 1-7)

Final sales of domestic product is GDP minus change in private inventories. It is the sum of personal consumption expenditures, gross private domestic fixed investment, government consumption expenditures and gross investment, and net exports of goods and services.

Gross domestic purchases is the market value of goods and services purchased by U.S. residents, regardless of where those goods and services were produced. It is GDP minus net exports (that is, minus exports plus imports) of goods and services; equivalently, it is the sum of personal consumption expenditures, gross private domestic investment, and government consumption expenditures and gross investment. The price index for gross domestic purchases is therefore a measure of price change for goods and services purchased by (rather than produced by) U.S. residents.

Final sales to domestic purchasers is gross domestic purchases minus change in private inventories.

Definitions and notes on the data: U.S. Population and per capita product and income estimates (Table 1-3)

In Table 1-3, annual and quarterly measures of product, income, and consumption spending are expressed in per capita terms— the aggregate dollar amount divided by the U.S. population. Population data from 1991 forward reflect the results of the 2010 Censuses.

Definitions and notes on the data: Inventory-sales ratios (Table 1-8)

Inventories to sales ratios. The ratios shown in Table 1-8 are based on the inventory estimates underlying the measurement of inventory change in the NIPAs. They include data and estimates for not only the inventories held in manufacturing and trade (which are shown in Chapter 16), but also stocks held by all other businesses in the U.S. economy.

For the current-dollar ratios, inventories at the end of each quarter are valued in the prices that prevailed at the end of that quarter.

For the constant-dollar ratios, they are valued in chained (2009) dollars. In both cases, the inventory-sales ratio is the value of the inventories at the end of the quarter divided by quarterly total sales at monthly rates (quarterly totals divided by 3). In other words, they represent how many months' supply businesses had on hand at the end of the period. This makes them comparable in concept and order of magnitude to the ratios shown in Chapter 16. Annual ratios are those for the fourth quarter.

Inventory data consistent with the 2013 revision are only available from 1997 to date. Tables 1-8A and B show the old estimates for earlier years with an overlap period.

Definitions and notes on the data: Shares of aggregate supply and demand (Tables 1-9 and 1-10)

These tables, developed by the previous editor of *Business Statistics*, are not official NIPA calculations. They are components of current-dollar GDP rearranged in order to highlight relationships that are not always apparent in the official presentation of the NIPAs.

Aggregate supply combines domestic production (GDP) and imports, the two sources that, between them, supply the goods and services demanded by consumers, businesses, and governments in the U.S. economy. In this table the user can observe the growing share of imports that satisfy demands in the U.S. marketplace.

Aggregate final demand is the sum of all final (that is, excluding inventory change) demands for goods and services in the U.S. market—consumption spending, fixed investment, exports, and government consumption and investment. It is different from *final sales of domestic product* (Tables 1-1 and 1-7) because imports are not subtracted; in this table, imports are considered a source of supply, not a negative element of demand. It is different from *gross domestic purchases* (Tables 1-5 and 1-6) because it includes exports, since they are a source of demand for U.S. output, but excludes inventory change. It is like *final sales to domestic purchasers* (Table 1-7) in excluding inventory change, but different because it also includes exports.

Table 1-10 provides alternative data on the question of the relative importance of consumption spending and other final demands to the U.S. economy. NIPA statistics on PCE as a percent of GDP are frequently cited, but there is a problem with this, since PCE includes the value of imports while GDP does not.

Definitions and notes on the data: Components of income (Tables 1-11, 1-12 and 1-13)

There are now two different presentations of aggregate income for the United States: *gross domestic income* (Table 1-12) and *national income* (Table 1-13). As noted above, domestic income refers to income generated from production within the United States, while national income refers to income received by residents of the United States. This means that some of the income components differ between the two tables. Domestic income payments include payments to the rest of the world from domestic industries. National income payments exclude payments to the rest of the world but include payments received by U.S. residents from the rest of the world. These differences are seen in employee compensation, interest, and corporate profits. Taxes on production and imports, taxes on corporate income, business transfer payments, subsidies, proprietors' income, rental income, and the current surplus of government enterprises are the same in both accounts.

All income entries are now calculated on an accrual basis, associating the income with the period in which it was earned rather than when it was paid.

A third important income aggregate is *personal income*. The derivation of this well-known statistic from national income is shown in Table 1-11. See Chapter 4 and its notes and definitions for data and more information.

Compensation of employees is the income accruing to employees as remuneration for their work. It is the sum of wage and salary accruals and supplements to wages and salaries. In the domestic income account, it refers to all payments generated by domestic production, including those to workers residing in the "rest of the world." In the national and personal income accounts, there is a slightly different "compensation of employees," including that received by U.S. residents from the rest of the world but excluding that paid from the domestic production account to workers residing elsewhere.

Wages and salaries consists of the monetary remuneration of employees, including the compensation of corporate officers; corporate directors' fees paid to directors who are also employees of the corporation; commissions, tips, and bonuses; voluntary employee contributions to certain deferred compensation plans, such as 401(k) plans; and receipts-in-kind that represent income. As of the 2003 revision, it also includes judicial fees to jurors and witnesses, compensation of prison inmates, and marriage fees to justices of the peace, all of which were formerly included in "other labor income."

In concept, wages and salaries include the value of the exercise by employees of "nonqualified stock options," in which an employee is allowed to buy stock for less than its current market price. (Actual measurement of these values involves a number of problems, particularly in the short run. Such stock options are not included in the monthly wage data from the Bureau of Labor Statistics, which are the main source for current extrapolations of wages and salaries, and are not consistently reported in corporate financial statements. They are, however, generally included in the unemployment insurance wage data that are used to correct the preliminary wage and salary estimates.)

Another form of stock option, the "incentive stock option," leads to a capital gain only and is thus not included in the definition of wages and salaries.

Supplements to wages and salaries consists of *employer contributions for employee pension and insurance funds* and *employer contributions for government social insurance.*

Employer contributions for employee pension and insurance funds consists of employer payments (including payments-in-kind) to private pension and profit-sharing plans, private group health and life insurance plans, privately administered workers' compensation plans, government employee retirement plans, and supplemental unemployment benefit plans. They are now measured in the period in which the employee earns the obligation rather than when the employer makes the cash payment into the fund. This includes the major part of what was once called "other labor income." The remainder of "other labor income" has been reclassified as wages and salaries, as noted above.

Employer contributions for government social insurance consists of employer payments under the following federal, state, and local government programs: old-age, survivors, and disability insurance (Social Security); hospital insurance (Medicare); unemployment insurance; railroad retirement; pension benefit guaranty; veterans' life insurance; publicly administered workers' compensation; military medical insurance; and temporary disability insurance.

Taxes on production and imports is included in the gross domestic income account to make it comparable in concept to gross domestic product. It consists of federal excise taxes and customs duties and of state and local sales taxes, property taxes (including residential real estate taxes), motor vehicle license taxes, severance taxes, special assessments, and other taxes. It is equal to the former "indirect business taxes and nontax liabilities" less most of the nontax liabilities, which have now been reclassified as "business transfer payments."

Subsidies (payments by government to business other than purchases of goods and services) are now presented separately from the current surplus of government enterprises, which is presented as a component of net operating surplus. However, for data representing the years before 1959, subsidies continue to be presented as net of the current surplus of government enterprises, since detailed data to separate the series for this period are not available.

Net operating surplus is a new aggregate introduced in the 2003 NIPA revision—a grouping of the business income components of the gross domestic income account. It represents the net income accruing to business capital. It is equal to gross domestic income minus compensation of employees, taxes on production and imports less subsidies (that is, the taxes are taken out of income and the subsidies are put in), and consumption of fixed capital (CFC). Net operating surplus consists of the surplus for private enterprises and the current surplus of government enterprises. The net operating surplus of private enterprises comprises net interest and miscellaneous payments, business current transfer payments, proprietors' income, rental income of persons, and corporate profits.

Net interest and miscellaneous payments, domestic industries consists of interest paid by domestic private enterprises and of rents and royalties paid by private enterprises to government, less interest received by domestic private enterprises. Interest received does not include interest received by noninsured pension plans, which are recorded as being directly received by persons in personal income. Both interest categories include monetary and imputed interest. In the *national* account, interest paid to the rest of the world is subtracted from the interest paid by domestic industries and interest received from the rest of the world is added. Interest payments on mortgage and home improvement loans and on home equity loans are included as net interest in the private enterprises account.

It should be noted that net interest does not include interest paid by federal, state, or local governments. In fact, government interest does not enter into the national and domestic income accounts, though it does appear as a component of personal income. The NIPAs draw a distinction between interest paid by government and that paid by business.

The reasoning behind this distinction is that interest paid by <u>business</u> is one of the income counterparts of the production side of the account. The value of business production (as measured by its output of goods and services) includes the value added by business capital, and interest paid by business to its lenders is part of the total return to business capital.

However, there is no product flow in the accounts that is a counterpart to the payment of interest by <u>government</u>. The output of government does not have a market value. For purposes of GDP measurement, BEA estimates the government contribution to GDP as the sum of government's compensation of employees, purchases of goods and services, and consumption of government fixed capital. (See above, and also the notes and definitions to Chapter 6.) This implies an estimate (described as "conservative" by BEA) that the <u>net</u> return to government capital is zero—that is, that the gross return is just sufficient to pay down the depreciation. Consequently, this assumption generates no income, imputed or actual, that might correspond to the government's interest payment.

Supporting the distinction between business and government interest payments, it may be noted that most federal government debt was not incurred to finance investment, but rather to finance wars, to avoid tax increases and spending cuts during recessions, or to stimulate the economy. Furthermore, some of the largest and most productive government investments—highways—are typically financed by taxes on a pay-as-you-go basis and not by borrowing.

Business current transfer payments, net consists of payments to persons, government, and the rest of the world by private business for which no current services are performed. Net insurance settlements—actual insured losses (or claims payable) less a normal level of losses—are treated as transfer payments. Payments to government consist of federal deposit insurance premiums, fines, regulatory and inspection fees, tobacco settlements, and other miscellaneous payments previously classified as "nontaxes." Taxes paid by domestic corporations to foreign governments, formerly classified as transfer payments, are now counted as taxes on corporate income.

In the NIPAs, capital income other than interest—corporate profits, proprietors' income, and rental income—is converted from the basis usually shown in the books of business, and reported to the Internal Revenue Service, to a basis that more closely represents income from current production. In the business accounts that provide the source data, depreciation of structures and equipment typically reflects a historical cost basis and a possibly arbitrary service life allowed by law to be used for tax purposes. BEA adjusts these values to reflect the average actual life of the capital goods and the cost of replacing them in the current period's prices. This conversion is done for all three forms of capital income. In addition, corporate and proprietors' incomes also require an adjustment for inventory valuation to exclude any profits or losses that might appear in the books, should the cost of inventory acquisition not be valued in the current period's prices. These two adjustments are called the *capital consumption adjustment (CCAdj)* and the *inventory valuation adjustment (IVA)*. They are described in more detail below.

Proprietors' income with inventory valuation and capital consumption adjustments is the current-production income (including income-in-kind) of sole proprietorships and partnerships and of tax-exempt cooperatives. The imputed net rental income of owner-occupants of farm dwellings is included, but the imputed net rental income of owner-occupants of nonfarm dwellings is included in rental income of persons. Fees paid to outside directors of corporations are included. Proprietors' income excludes dividends and monetary interest received by nonfinancial business and rental incomes received by persons not primarily engaged in the real estate business; these incomes are included in dividends, net interest, and rental income of persons, respectively.

Rental income of persons with capital consumption adjustment is the net current-production income of persons from the rental of real property (except for the income of persons primarily engaged in the real estate business), the imputed net rental income of owner-occupants of nonfarm dwellings, and the royalties received by persons from patents, copyrights, and rights to natural resources. Consistent with the classification of investment in owner-occupied housing as business investment, the homeowner is considered to be paying himself or herself the rental value of the house (classified as PCE for services) and receiving as net income the amount of the rental that remains after paying interest and other costs.

Corporate profits with inventory valuation and capital consumption adjustments, often referred to as "economic profits," is the current-production income, net of economic depreciation, of organizations treated as corporations in the NIPAs. These organizations consist of all entities required to file federal corporate tax returns, including mutual financial institutions and cooperatives subject to federal income tax; private noninsured pension funds; nonprofit institutions that primarily serve business; Federal Reserve Banks, which accrue income stemming from the conduct of monetary policy; and federally sponsored credit agencies. This income is measured as receipts less expenses as defined in federal tax law, except for the following differences: receipts exclude capital gains and dividends received; expenses exclude depletion and capital losses and losses resulting from bad debts; inventory withdrawals are valued at replacement cost; and depreciation is on a consistent accounting basis and is valued at replacement cost.

Since *national* income is defined as the income of U.S. residents, its profits component includes income earned abroad by U.S. corporations and excludes income earned by the rest of the world within the United States.

Taxes on corporate income consists of taxes on corporate income paid to government and to the rest of the world.

Taxes on corporate income paid to government is the sum of federal, state, and local income taxes on all income subject to taxes. This income includes capital gains and other income excluded from profits before tax. These taxes are measured on an accrual basis, net of applicable tax credits.

Taxes on corporate income paid to the rest of the world consists of nonresident taxes, which are those paid by domestic corporations to foreign governments. These taxes were formerly classified as "business transfer payments to the rest of the world."

Profits after tax is total corporate profits with IVA and CCAdj less taxes on corporate income. It consists of dividends and undistributed corporate profits.

Dividends is payments in cash or other assets, excluding those made using corporations' own stock, that are made by corporations to stockholders. In the domestic account, these are payments by domestic industries to stockholders in the United States and abroad; in the national account, these are dividends received by U.S. residents from domestic and foreign industries. The payments are measured net of dividends received by U.S. corporations. Dividends paid to state and local government social insurance funds and general government are included.

Undistributed profits is corporate profits after tax with IVA and CCAdj less dividends.

The *inventory valuation adjustment (IVA)* is the difference between the cost of inventory withdrawals valued at replacement cost and the cost as valued in the source data used to determine profits before tax, which in many cases charge inventories at acquisition cost. It is calculated separately for corporate profits and for nonfarm proprietors' income. Its behavior is determined by price changes, especially for materials. When prices are rising, which has been typical of much of the postwar period, the business-reported value of inventory change will include a capital gains component, which needs to be removed from reported inventory change on the product side in order to correctly measure the change in the volume of inventories, and from reported profits on the income side of the accounts in order to remove the capital gains element. At such times, the IVA will be a negative figure, which is added to reported profits to yield economic profits. Occasionally, falling prices—especially for petroleum and products—will result in a positive IVA. No adjustment is needed for farm proprietors' income, as farm inventories are measured on a current-market-cost basis.

Consumption of fixed capital (CFC) is a charge for the using-up of private and government fixed capital located in the United States. It is not based on the depreciation schedules allowed in tax law, but instead on studies of prices of used equipment and structures in resale markets and other service life information.

For general government and for nonprofit institutions that primarily serve individuals, CFC on their capital assets is recorded in government consumption expenditures and in personal consumption expenditures, respectively. It is considered to be the value of the current services of the fixed capital assets owned and used by these entities.

Private capital consumption allowances consists of tax-return-based depreciation charges for corporations and nonfarm proprietorships; BEA estimates for R&D and other intellectual property; and historical cost depreciation (calculated by BEA using a geometric pattern of price declines) for farm proprietorships, rental income of persons, and nonprofit institutions.

The *private capital consumption adjustment (CCAdj)* is the difference between private capital consumption allowances and private consumption of fixed capital. The CCAdj has two parts:

- The first component of CCAdj converts tax-return-based depreciation to consistent historical cost accounting based on actual service lives of capital. In the postwar period, this has usually been a large positive number, that is, a net addition to profits and subtraction from reported depreciation. This is the case because U.S. tax law typically allows depreciation periods shorter than actual service lives. Tax depreciation was accelerated even further for 2001 through 2004. This component is a reallocation of gross business saving from depreciation to profits; gross saving is unchanged, with exactly offsetting changes in capital consumption and net saving.

- The second component is analogous to the IVA: it converts reported business capital consumption allowances from the historical cost basis to a replacement cost basis. It is determined by the price behavior of capital goods. These prices

have had an upward drift in the postwar period, which has been much more stable than the changes in materials prices. Hence, this component is consistently negative (serving to reduce economic profits relative to the reported data) but less volatile than the IVA.

In 1982 through 2004, positive values for the first component outweighed negative values for the second, resulting in a net positive CCAdj, an addition to profits. However, when the accelerated depreciation expired in 2005, there was a sharp decline in the consistent-accounting adjustment and it was outweighed by the price adjustment. This led to negative CCAdjs in 2005 through 2007, reducing profits from the reported numbers.

Definitions and notes on the data: Gross value added of domestic corporate business (Tables 1-14 and 1-15)

Gross value added is the term now used for what was formerly called "gross domestic product originating." It represents the share of the GDP that is produced in the specified sector or industry. Tables 1-14 and 1-15 show the current-dollar value of gross value added for all domestic corporate business and its financial and nonfinancial components. For the total and for nonfinancial corporations, consumption of fixed capital and net value added are shown, as is the allocation of net value added among employee compensation, taxes and transfer payments, and capital income. Constant-dollar values are also shown for nonfinancial corporations.

The data for nonfinancial corporations are often considered to be somewhat sturdier than data for the other sectors of the economy, since they exclude sectors whose outputs are difficult to evaluate—households, institutions, general government, and financial business—as well as excluding all noncorporate business, in which the separate contributions of labor and capital are not readily measured.

Data availability and revisions

Annual data are available beginning with 1929. Quarterly data begin with 1946 for current-dollar values and 1947 for quantity and price measures such as real GDP and the GDP price index. Not all data are available for all time periods.

New data are normally released toward the end of each month. The "advance" estimate of GDP for each calendar quarter is released at the end of the month after the quarter's end. The "second" estimate, including more complete product data and the first estimates of corporate profits, is released at the end of the second month after the quarter's end, and a "third" estimate including still more complete data at the end of the third month. Wage and salary and related income-side components may be revised for previous quarters as well.

At the end of each July, there is an "annual" revision, incorporating more complete data and other improvements, affecting at least the previous 3 years. Every five years, there is a "comprehensive" revision, such as the 2013 revision incorporated in this volume, corresponding with updated statistics from the quinquennial benchmark input-output accounts and incorporating a revision of the base year for constant-price and index numbers.

The most recent data are published each month in the Survey of Current Business. Current and historical data may be obtained from the BEA Web site at <http://www.bea.gov> and the STAT-USA subscription Web site at <http://www.stat-usa.gov>.

References

The 2015 annual revision of the NIPAs is presented and described in a July 30, 2015 release on the BEA Web site, and will be described in more detail in the August 2015 *Survey of Current Business*. The 2013 changes in definitions and presentations are described in "Preview of the 2013 Comprehensive Revision of the National Income and Product Accounts," *Survey of Current Business (SCB),* March 2013, and a subsequent article in the September 2013 *SCB*. Earlier revisions are described in annual *SCB* articles in September or August issues.

Other documentation available on the BEA Web site at <http://www.bea.gov> includes the following: "NIPA Handbook: Concepts and Methods of the U.S. National Income and Product Accounts, October 2009"; separate chapters from the Handbook on Personal Consumption Expenditures, Private Fixed Investment, and Change in Private Inventories; "Measuring the Economy: A Primer on GDP and the National Income and Product Accounts"; "An Introduction to the National Income and Product Accounts"; and "Taking the Pulse of the Economy: Measuring GDP," *Journal of Economic Perspectives*, Spring 2008.

The treatment of employee stock options is discussed in Carol Moylan, "Treatment of Employee Stock Options in the U.S. National Economic Accounts," available on the BEA Web site at <http://www.bea.gov>.

The data for 1929 through 1946 published here have been calculated after the fact and differ from the national income data that were currently available during the 1930s and 1940s. For an article on what was available at that time and the history of the NIPAs during that period, see Rosemary D. Marcuss and Richard E. Kane, "U.S. National Income and Product Statistics: Born of the Great Depression and World War II," *Survey of Current Business,* February 2007, pp. 32-46.

Definitions and notes on the data: Rates of return and related data for domestic nonfinancial corporations (Table 1-17)

Table 1-17 shows various measures of the return to capital in domestic nonfinancial corporate business. The measure of

capital is the value of produced assets, which is the current-cost value of the net stock of equipment and software and structures and the replacement-cost value of inventories. The basic measure of the total return to capital is the net operating surplus, which is the sum of corporate profits, net interest paid, and net business transfer payments. Table 1-15 displays the same concept. In both cases, corporate profits are adjusted to an economic profits basis by including the inventory valuation and capital consumption adjustments.

Rates of return are total net operating surplus and its major components, before and after corporate taxes, as a percent of the value of produced assets. (For the earlier years, based on unrevised concepts and data, *tax liability* is also shown as a percent of produced assets.)

Shares of net value added are total net operating surplus and (for earlier years) its major components, before and after corporate taxes, as a percent of net value added in nonfinancial domestic corporate business. Net value added, shown in Table 1-15, is the value of the industry's output after deducting the consumption of fixed capital, and is the sum of compensation of employees, the net operating surplus, and taxes on production and imports less subsidies.

A *Q ratio* (often known as "Tobin's Q" for the economist James Tobin, who originally proposed it) is the ratio of the valuation of assets in financial markets to the current-cost value of produced assets. A value of Q above 1 indicates that ownership claims to existing assets are more expensive than the cost of purchasing new assets. A high value of Q is therefore more conducive to new investment. Table 1-17 shows the BEA calculation of two variations of the Q ratio. *Q1* is the market value of outstanding equity divided by the net stock of produced assets valued at current, or replacement, cost. *Q2* is the market value of outstanding equity plus book value of outstanding corporate bonds divided by the net stock of produced assets valued at current cost. According to BEA, "The inclusion of bonds makes Q2 a more complete measure of invested capital, but including them at historical cost is clearly inconsistent with the underlying rationale for Q, which is to provide a comparison of market valuation with replacement cost."

The rate of return data do not follow the general NIPA publication and revision schedule. They were initially presented and described in "Note on the Returns for Domestic Nonfinancial Corporations in 1960–2005," *Survey of Current Business* (May 2006), pp. 6–10, and updated in *SCB* articles in subsequent years; data for 1960 through 1997 on that basis, but not reflecting the comprehensive revision, are shown in Table 1-17. The data shown from 1997 forward through 2013 were revised and updated most recently in "Returns for Domestic Nonfinancial Business," *Survey of Current Business* (June 2014), pp. 1-6, reflecting the 2013 comprehensive revision of the NIPAs and the 2014 comprehensive revision of the industry economic accounts.

CHAPTER 2: INDUSTRIAL PRODUCTION AND CAPACITY UTILIZATION

Figure 2-1: Capacity Utilization: Total Manufacturing and High-Tech Industries, 1948–2014

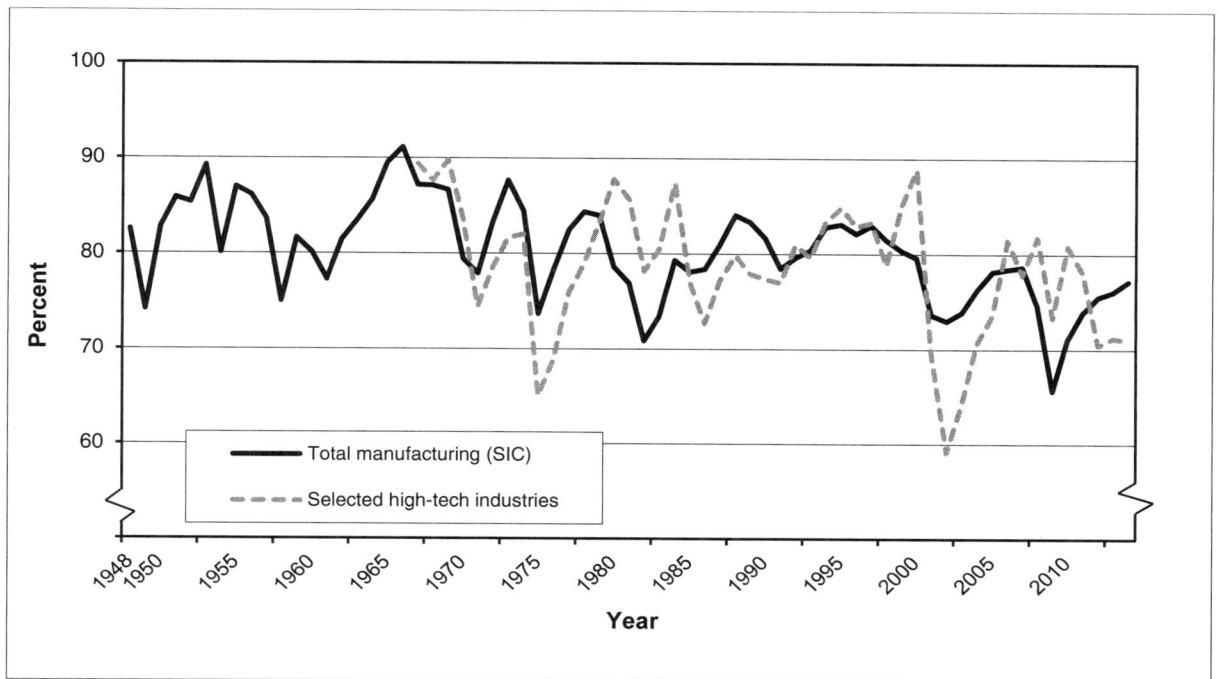

- Manufacturing capacity utilization is a key statistic for the U.S. economy, despite being limited to a sector that by some measures has diminished in importance. The Federal Reserve also provides measures of capacity utilization for "total industry"—manufacturing, mining, and utilities. However, mining and utilities are less significant in the context of business cycle analysis, and much of the variation in capacity use by utilities is a result of transitory weather variations, not economic factors. Manufacturing utilization is an important indicator of inflationary pressure and also measures an important element in the demand for new capital goods. See Notes and Definitions at the end of the chapter.

- Industrial production peaked at 100.8 percent of its 2007 average in November and December 2007 and then fell to a low of 83.8 percent in June 2009, a decline of 17 percent. Industrial production continued to rise in 2013 and 2014. In November 2014, industrial production reached an historical high of 106.3. (Table 2-4A)

- Manufacturing capacity utilization reached a high point of 79.1 percent in April 2007—lower than in previous periods of high activity—and then drifted down slightly for the rest of 2007, as capacity growth exceeded the increase in output. Then output plunged in 2008 and early 2009, and utilization collapsed to 69.0 percent in May and June 2009, by far the lowest in the entire postwar period. By December 2014, utilization had recovered to 78.0 percent, slightly below its longer-term average of 78.7. (Table 2-4A)

- Capacity utilization in the high-tech industries (computers and office equipment, communications equipment, and semiconductors and related electronic components) has been somewhat more volatile than in the rest of industry, as seen in Figure 2-1. (Tables 2-3 and 2-4A)

Table 2-1. Industrial Production Indexes by Market Groups

(Seasonally adjusted, 2007 = 100.)

Year and month	Total industrial production	Final products and nonindustrial supplies							
			Consumer goods						
		Total	Total	Durable consumer goods					Nondurable consumer goods
				Total	Automotive products	Home electronics	Appliances, furniture, and carpeting	Miscellaneous durable goods	Total
1968	37.0	36.3	45.3	33.1	33.8	0.9	49.0	48.1	51.0
1969	38.7	37.6	47.0	34.5	34.0	0.9	51.7	52.0	52.8
1970	37.4	36.4	46.4	31.8	28.6	0.8	51.1	50.2	53.7
1971	37.9	37.0	49.1	36.0	36.4	0.9	54.0	52.9	55.2
1972	41.6	40.4	53.1	40.3	39.3	1.1	63.4	59.5	58.7
1973	45.0	43.4	55.5	43.4	42.6	1.2	68.5	62.2	60.5
1974	44.8	43.3	53.9	39.5	36.9	1.1	62.4	59.9	60.6
1975	40.9	40.3	51.7	35.8	35.5	1.0	53.5	53.1	59.5
1976	44.1	43.1	55.9	40.4	40.4	1.2	60.4	59.2	63.3
1977	47.4	46.7	59.4	45.4	45.7	1.4	67.7	65.5	65.6
1978	50.0	49.5	61.3	46.5	45.4	1.5	71.3	67.8	67.9
1979	51.5	51.1	60.4	44.8	40.8	1.5	71.5	68.4	67.5
1980	50.2	50.4	58.1	39.0	31.5	1.6	66.6	62.7	67.6
1981	50.9	51.5	58.6	39.6	32.4	1.7	65.7	63.6	67.9
1982	48.3	50.2	58.4	37.3	31.5	1.5	59.5	60.2	69.1
1983	49.6	51.6	60.5	41.4	36.6	2.1	65.6	62.0	69.9
1984	54.0	55.9	63.3	46.4	40.9	2.7	73.1	68.5	71.3
1985	54.7	57.3	63.9	46.4	40.8	2.8	72.7	68.6	72.2
1986	55.2	58.5	66.1	49.3	43.9	3.5	76.2	70.8	73.9
1987	58.1	61.4	68.9	52.3	47.0	3.5	80.3	75.3	76.6
1988	61.1	64.4	71.5	54.8	49.2	4.4	81.7	78.6	79.1
1989	61.6	65.0	71.8	56.1	50.8	4.9	82.5	79.1	78.9
1990	62.2	65.8	72.1	54.5	47.8	5.4	80.4	78.4	80.2
1991	61.3	64.8	72.1	52.1	44.9	6.3	74.9	75.6	81.4
1992	63.0	66.4	74.2	57.1	52.1	7.2	79.3	78.0	82.0
1993	65.1	68.5	76.5	61.7	57.2	9.1	83.7	81.5	83.2
1994	68.5	71.5	79.7	67.2	62.8	11.8	89.6	86.0	85.2
1995	71.8	74.4	82.0	69.9	64.7	17.2	89.2	88.5	87.3
1996	74.9	77.3	83.5	72.1	65.8	20.7	90.2	91.5	88.5
1997	80.4	82.4	86.5	77.0	70.9	28.8	94.1	93.6	90.5
1998	85.0	87.0	89.5	82.6	76.2	37.3	100.3	96.8	92.5
1999	88.7	89.7	91.5	89.0	84.6	47.4	103.6	99.0	92.5
2000	92.2	92.5	93.2	91.6	86.1	54.0	106.6	101.8	93.9
2001	89.1	90.1	92.2	87.3	82.8	55.0	101.9	94.4	94.1
2002	89.3	89.7	94.0	92.5	90.9	55.7	104.4	96.8	94.6
2003	90.4	90.8	95.3	95.3	95.7	60.9	104.4	96.8	95.2
2004	92.5	92.6	96.4	97.0	95.7	69.9	107.6	98.7	96.1
2005	95.5	96.2	99.0	97.9	94.2	78.6	109.7	101.7	99.3
2006	97.6	98.4	99.5	98.3	93.0	94.2	106.5	103.3	99.9
2007	100.0	100.0	100.0	100.0	100.0	100.0	100.0	100.0	100.0
2008	96.6	95.8	95.1	88.8	84.8	109.6	87.4	92.5	97.2
2009	85.7	85.0	88.6	74.0	73.1	93.9	66.2	76.3	93.4
2010	90.6	87.7	89.6	79.4	83.3	59.9	65.6	81.5	92.9
2011	93.6	89.7	90.9	83.3	90.0	60.8	65.2	83.7	93.4
2012	97.1	92.5	92.5	90.0	100.8	59.5	67.9	87.5	93.5
2013	99.9	94.8	94.7	96.9	109.5	60.6	71.1	94.3	94.5
2014	104.1	98.0	97.4	102.7	118.4	63.2	76.2	96.5	96.3
2013									
January	98.4	93.4	93.5	93.3	103.6	57.2	69.9	92.6	94.0
February	99.0	94.2	94.3	94.8	106.0	59.9	69.2	93.8	94.5
March	99.5	94.8	94.9	95.7	108.2	60.8	69.4	93.4	95.0
April	99.3	94.5	94.6	95.6	107.9	60.9	69.8	93.2	94.7
May	99.4	94.3	94.2	95.8	108.5	60.2	70.3	92.8	94.1
June	99.6	94.6	94.4	96.8	109.9	61.6	70.4	93.8	94.1
July	99.4	94.0	93.7	95.7	106.6	60.5	71.0	94.8	93.4
August	100.0	94.6	94.1	97.5	110.3	61.1	71.8	94.6	93.5
September	100.7	95.4	94.9	98.1	111.8	60.1	71.2	94.7	94.4
October	100.8	95.8	95.4	98.6	111.8	61.1	72.7	95.4	94.9
November	101.4	96.0	95.8	100.3	114.5	61.9	73.2	96.4	94.9
December	101.6	96.4	96.6	100.4	115.0	61.8	74.1	95.5	96.0
2014									
January	101.3	95.8	95.8	97.2	108.4	60.2	73.1	95.7	95.7
February	102.3	97.2	97.3	99.9	115.1	60.9	70.8	95.6	96.9
March	103.1	97.8	97.9	100.7	115.9	60.5	73.0	96.0	97.6
April	103.2	97.5	97.4	100.7	115.2	61.7	74.7	95.9	96.8
May	103.7	97.6	97.1	102.2	117.9	63.2	75.6	96.1	96.0
June	104.1	97.5	96.8	102.9	118.6	64.5	76.3	96.6	95.5
July	104.5	98.2	97.5	107.5	127.7	62.9	78.8	96.8	95.1
August	104.5	97.8	96.5	103.6	120.5	64.7	76.8	95.8	94.9
September	105.2	98.4	97.4	103.3	118.6	63.6	78.3	96.8	96.2
October	105.1	98.6	97.1	103.1	117.5	64.2	79.1	97.3	95.8
November	106.3	100.1	99.2	106.9	125.0	65.5	78.5	98.5	97.5
December	106.2	99.5	98.7	106.4	123.7	66.0	80.3	97.7	97.0

Table 2-1. Industrial Production Indexes by Market Groups—Continued

(Seasonally adjusted, 2007 = 100.)

Year and month	Nondurable non-energy consumer goods — Total	Foods and tobacco	Clothing	Chemical products	Paper products	Consumer energy products	Business equipment — Total	Transit	Information processing	Industrial and other	Defense and space equipment	Construction supplies	Business supplies
1968	53.1	55.9	329.5	22.9	57.9	42.1	16.5	61.7	1.1	46.1	66.3	48.1	32.7
1969	54.6	57.4	334.4	24.0	60.0	45.0	17.6	60.8	1.2	49.1	63.2	50.2	34.8
1970	55.2	58.2	324.7	26.1	57.8	47.6	17.0	53.3	1.3	47.4	53.5	48.4	34.9
1971	56.6	60.0	322.8	27.6	59.0	49.9	16.2	51.6	1.2	45.3	48.1	49.9	36.0
1972	60.3	63.4	351.3	30.2	59.5	52.6	18.4	56.3	1.4	51.5	46.8	56.7	39.6
1973	62.3	65.1	358.1	32.4	61.5	53.6	21.3	67.2	1.6	58.6	51.2	61.5	42.1
1974	62.0	65.4	335.7	34.2	60.6	55.0	22.5	65.5	1.9	61.1	52.9	60.0	41.9
1975	60.4	64.3	326.1	33.0	57.1	56.2	20.1	57.6	1.9	53.5	53.4	50.8	38.7
1976	64.3	68.5	343.5	35.9	59.4	59.1	21.4	59.6	2.2	55.7	51.8	54.7	41.2
1977	66.6	69.9	360.4	37.4	64.9	61.4	24.8	70.8	2.9	60.7	46.4	59.6	44.7
1978	69.2	72.5	369.0	39.7	68.1	62.6	27.9	82.0	3.7	65.0	47.3	63.0	47.1
1979	68.3	72.0	348.7	39.8	68.9	64.2	31.5	95.8	4.6	69.0	50.6	64.6	48.7
1980	69.1	73.1	355.0	39.6	69.7	61.8	32.2	90.3	5.8	66.7	60.1	59.8	47.6
1981	69.7	73.5	354.8	40.2	71.5	61.4	33.2	84.5	6.9	66.5	65.1	58.8	48.8
1982	71.0	75.9	353.8	40.3	73.3	61.8	30.4	64.7	7.9	57.6	77.9	53.4	48.2
1983	71.9	76.0	363.9	40.8	76.4	62.3	30.6	63.8	9.1	53.4	78.3	57.2	50.5
1984	73.2	76.9	365.5	41.7	80.3	64.2	35.1	65.8	11.1	60.9	89.8	62.2	54.9
1985	74.3	79.2	350.1	42.2	84.4	64.2	36.4	68.0	12.0	61.6	100.5	63.7	56.3
1986	76.2	80.5	349.9	45.4	85.6	65.5	35.9	62.3	12.1	61.3	106.7	65.9	58.1
1987	78.9	82.4	353.1	49.0	90.5	67.9	38.3	63.2	13.8	63.5	109.0	70.1	61.6
1988	81.2	84.7	347.9	51.9	93.0	71.4	42.3	70.5	15.6	69.0	109.9	71.7	63.9
1989	80.8	84.1	332.1	53.0	93.3	71.9	43.7	74.2	16.0	71.3	110.1	71.4	64.8
1990	82.6	86.5	325.7	54.9	95.1	71.4	45.3	79.4	17.3	70.8	106.1	70.9	66.3
1991	83.5	86.9	324.8	56.9	95.6	73.6	44.6	82.5	17.4	67.1	98.3	67.0	65.4
1992	84.5	88.1	332.1	56.7	96.8	72.6	46.4	80.6	19.6	68.2	91.1	69.8	66.9
1993	85.2	87.4	338.7	58.3	99.0	75.8	48.6	75.5	21.4	72.8	86.0	72.8	69.0
1994	87.5	90.9	344.9	59.5	98.0	76.7	51.8	73.1	24.1	77.7	80.7	78.1	71.8
1995	89.6	93.3	343.5	62.1	98.6	78.8	56.5	71.2	29.1	82.6	77.8	79.8	74.8
1996	90.2	93.0	334.5	65.1	98.3	82.3	62.1	75.4	35.5	85.5	75.7	83.4	77.7
1997	93.0	94.4	333.4	68.8	107.0	81.6	71.2	88.8	44.9	90.7	74.6	87.4	83.2
1998	95.4	96.8	313.5	72.2	112.0	81.7	79.1	104.2	53.3	93.5	77.7	92.1	87.9
1999	94.7	94.9	301.8	73.5	114.2	84.5	83.5	102.0	64.8	91.4	75.4	94.4	91.6
2000	96.0	96.4	289.4	76.2	113.8	86.3	89.7	90.3	78.4	96.8	67.0	96.5	95.3
2001	96.1	96.4	250.5	80.5	110.6	87.3	84.1	87.0	76.0	87.5	73.6	92.1	91.7
2002	95.8	94.6	192.9	87.1	109.0	91.1	78.5	80.0	66.2	86.1	74.4	92.2	91.9
2003	96.5	95.8	181.5	89.2	105.0	91.6	78.3	75.4	68.8	85.7	79.1	92.0	93.4
2004	97.3	97.1	150.8	91.4	105.6	92.9	82.1	79.6	74.4	88.0	77.2	94.2	95.1
2005	100.5	100.4	141.9	96.3	104.6	96.1	87.7	87.1	80.0	92.8	84.9	98.7	98.2
2006	101.4	100.5	132.1	99.6	104.5	95.8	95.8	101.1	91.1	96.4	84.1	101.1	99.2
2007	100.0	100.0	100.0	100.0	100.0	100.0	100.0	100.0	100.0	100.0	100.0	100.0	100.0
2008	96.4	96.5	88.4	96.4	95.4	99.7	97.7	92.6	101.1	98.0	106.9	90.7	96.0
2009	91.5	95.0	60.7	88.6	86.2	99.8	80.1	71.5	89.9	78.5	102.4	69.9	86.0
2010	90.2	95.3	62.3	84.7	83.3	102.0	86.7	84.3	91.1	84.9	110.5	72.5	88.0
2011	90.8	95.8	60.5	86.5	81.4	102.4	91.5	86.1	91.0	93.2	106.7	74.7	88.9
2012	91.7	99.1	58.8	84.2	78.9	100.0	98.3	99.9	96.2	97.8	111.8	78.1	90.5
2013	91.7	100.1	60.2	83.2	75.6	104.0	101.9	106.0	99.9	100.2	114.4	81.4	92.4
2014	93.2	101.7	61.9	85.3	73.4	107.0	107.0	111.5	102.1	106.3	116.5	84.9	94.7
2013													
January	91.9	100.1	59.9	83.8	76.7	101.3	98.8	102.1	98.7	96.7	114.1	80.2	91.4
February	92.2	101.6	60.2	82.5	76.7	102.2	100.6	103.5	98.7	99.4	113.8	81.7	91.5
March	91.8	100.7	59.2	82.9	75.5	106.0	101.9	105.4	98.4	101.0	113.7	81.0	91.8
April	91.4	99.7	57.9	83.6	75.2	106.0	101.5	106.6	98.6	99.8	113.5	80.7	91.8
May	91.3	99.4	59.3	83.7	75.4	103.7	101.6	106.1	99.3	99.8	113.5	80.4	92.0
June	92.0	100.4	59.6	84.0	74.8	101.6	102.2	107.0	98.8	100.7	114.0	80.8	92.0
July	91.1	99.0	59.5	83.7	75.2	101.5	101.0	104.2	99.1	99.7	113.1	81.1	92.0
August	91.4	99.6	60.5	83.0	76.3	100.7	102.3	106.2	100.4	100.6	115.0	81.3	92.4
September	91.5	99.7	61.5	82.9	76.6	104.1	103.4	108.1	101.6	101.4	116.1	82.0	93.0
October	91.5	100.0	61.7	82.7	75.6	106.4	103.4	107.3	101.8	101.7	115.7	82.7	93.2
November	91.4	99.9	60.9	82.9	74.7	107.0	103.2	107.6	101.3	101.4	115.3	83.0	93.4
December	92.4	101.2	62.0	83.5	74.7	108.2	102.6	107.4	101.4	100.4	115.6	82.6	93.8
2014													
January	91.3	100.0	61.4	82.5	74.9	110.7	102.4	104.1	101.1	101.5	114.4	82.3	93.9
February	92.0	101.2	60.9	82.8	74.1	113.6	104.9	107.6	100.6	104.7	114.8	83.0	94.3
March	93.1	102.3	62.4	84.6	72.3	112.9	105.8	109.1	101.7	105.3	115.7	83.6	94.2
April	93.5	103.0	62.2	84.6	72.8	108.3	106.3	110.6	101.0	105.8	116.1	82.9	94.0
May	92.8	101.7	61.7	84.1	74.1	107.1	107.2	111.9	101.1	106.8	116.1	84.0	94.3
June	93.3	101.5	61.2	85.6	75.3	103.2	106.9	112.9	101.0	105.9	116.6	84.4	94.2
July	93.1	100.8	62.2	86.0	74.9	102.0	108.2	117.1	101.0	106.6	117.1	85.6	94.1
August	93.1	100.8	60.2	86.5	73.7	101.3	108.0	113.4	101.9	107.3	117.1	85.9	94.5
September	93.6	102.0	61.8	86.6	71.8	105.1	107.6	113.6	102.6	106.3	117.8	86.1	95.4
October	93.2	101.5	61.8	86.0	71.9	105.0	108.8	112.3	103.9	108.5	117.4	86.7	95.8
November	94.3	103.0	62.7	87.0	71.6	108.5	110.4	114.5	104.0	110.4	117.6	86.7	96.7
December	94.6	103.3	64.6	87.3	70.8	105.4	109.0	113.5	104.7	108.0	117.8	87.8	95.9

Table 2-1. Industrial Production Indexes by Market Groups—*Continued*

(Seasonally adjusted, 2007 = 100.)

Year and month	Materials Total	Non-energy materials Total	Durable Total	Consumer parts	Equipment parts	Other	Nondurable Total	Textile	Paper	Chemicals	Energy materials
1968	36.9	29.3	21.8	56.1	4.5	56.9	49.3	114.5	52.8	33.1	70.6
1969	39.1	31.2	22.9	56.5	4.8	60.6	53.4	117.6	57.3	36.8	74.2
1970	37.8	29.3	20.8	47.4	4.4	56.6	53.7	113.3	56.8	37.6	77.8
1971	38.3	29.9	20.9	52.5	4.4	54.5	56.0	118.6	59.4	39.9	78.5
1972	42.2	33.5	23.6	58.4	5.1	61.6	61.7	124.9	63.3	46.4	81.5
1973	46.0	37.1	27.0	67.8	6.0	68.3	64.8	121.6	68.3	51.2	83.5
1974	45.9	37.0	26.7	60.0	6.3	68.1	65.7	113.7	71.7	52.6	83.1
1975	40.8	31.7	22.3	48.4	5.4	56.9	58.8	111.3	62.4	44.1	82.4
1976	44.4	35.3	24.9	61.8	5.8	61.1	65.2	123.9	68.6	50.5	84.2
1977	47.5	38.3	27.1	67.6	6.6	64.7	69.9	132.0	71.7	56.1	86.9
1978	49.9	40.7	29.3	71.5	7.4	69.0	72.5	130.6	75.2	59.6	87.9
1979	51.2	41.9	30.3	67.6	8.2	70.7	73.9	129.4	78.2	62.0	90.3
1980	49.3	39.4	28.0	52.1	8.4	65.5	71.5	126.5	78.8	57.4	91.0
1981	49.6	39.5	28.1	49.6	8.6	65.6	72.0	123.7	80.3	57.9	91.9
1982	45.8	35.6	24.5	42.1	7.9	55.4	68.3	113.1	81.0	51.9	88.0
1983	47.0	38.0	26.1	51.2	8.0	57.9	73.1	126.7	86.1	57.4	85.2
1984	51.5	42.4	30.3	60.9	9.7	64.1	76.3	126.3	91.5	61.0	90.6
1985	51.4	42.4	30.5	63.4	9.6	63.7	75.7	119.4	91.0	59.9	90.0
1986	51.3	43.2	30.9	62.8	9.8	64.9	78.1	124.3	94.9	62.8	86.5
1987	54.0	46.1	33.0	64.4	10.8	69.4	82.7	139.2	99.5	68.3	88.6
1988	57.1	49.0	35.7	69.7	11.7	74.4	85.8	137.8	102.8	72.4	91.6
1989	57.5	49.3	35.9	66.2	12.1	74.7	86.5	140.7	102.8	73.4	92.5
1990	57.8	49.4	35.9	61.6	12.5	75.0	86.8	133.6	103.1	74.2	94.4
1991	57.0	48.4	34.9	58.2	12.5	71.8	85.8	133.5	100.9	73.1	94.5
1992	58.8	50.7	37.2	65.4	13.2	75.6	87.9	141.2	103.4	74.9	93.6
1993	60.8	53.0	39.6	74.0	14.1	78.5	88.9	146.9	103.4	75.4	93.8
1994	64.7	57.2	44.1	85.4	16.0	84.4	91.6	155.8	107.3	77.7	95.3
1995	68.4	61.2	48.7	88.7	19.5	87.5	92.5	153.2	110.1	78.3	96.8
1996	71.9	65.0	53.8	91.0	24.0	90.1	91.6	148.9	106.6	78.7	98.3
1997	77.7	71.8	61.3	98.0	30.4	94.7	95.9	155.5	107.7	84.4	98.2
1998	82.3	77.2	68.0	101.3	37.5	97.2	97.2	154.1	108.8	84.6	98.4
1999	87.3	83.2	75.7	111.5	45.9	98.8	98.4	151.0	110.4	87.0	97.9
2000	91.8	88.3	83.1	111.5	57.2	99.7	97.8	144.5	108.6	87.2	99.6
2001	87.7	83.4	78.8	98.6	57.0	92.9	91.4	127.8	103.0	80.8	98.3
2002	88.6	84.7	80.0	103.5	57.7	92.9	93.1	129.6	103.3	83.6	97.9
2003	89.8	86.2	82.7	102.4	64.3	92.1	92.3	122.9	99.9	84.1	97.9
2004	92.4	89.8	87.2	102.5	71.1	95.8	94.1	117.5	101.1	88.5	97.9
2005	94.6	93.4	92.2	103.6	80.4	97.9	95.2	120.4	100.7	89.3	96.8
2006	96.5	95.7	95.7	100.8	88.0	100.1	95.6	109.3	99.9	91.2	98.0
2007	100.0	100.0	100.0	100.0	100.0	100.0	100.0	100.0	100.0	100.0	100.0
2008	97.6	95.6	97.4	84.3	106.6	95.3	92.7	86.9	95.5	89.1	100.8
2009	86.6	79.7	76.7	56.4	89.6	74.6	84.0	71.4	83.8	79.4	98.4
2010	94.2	89.0	89.4	74.4	105.9	82.9	88.4	79.4	85.3	87.3	102.5
2011	98.6	93.7	98.0	81.3	122.2	87.3	87.7	78.1	85.2	86.2	106.3
2012	103.1	98.1	104.9	89.2	135.0	90.6	88.6	78.7	83.2	87.9	110.9
2013	106.4	100.8	108.9	94.1	140.5	93.3	88.9	77.3	82.8	90.5	115.3
2014	111.8	104.5	115.0	100.6	149.2	97.7	90.4	78.8	81.2	91.7	123.6
2013											
January	104.8	100.1	107.4	94.1	137.4	92.4	90.0	77.8	82.9	90.1	112.0
February	105.1	100.2	107.8	93.6	138.3	92.8	89.9	77.5	83.2	90.5	112.7
March	105.5	100.1	107.6	92.6	137.9	92.9	89.8	78.1	82.9	90.0	114.1
April	105.4	99.9	107.7	92.5	139.0	92.5	89.3	76.4	82.6	89.6	114.1
May	105.9	100.5	107.9	93.1	139.8	92.3	90.3	76.1	83.5	91.2	114.4
June	106.0	100.6	108.1	92.6	140.3	92.5	90.2	77.4	83.4	91.1	114.6
July	106.3	100.5	108.1	91.5	140.2	92.9	90.1	76.6	83.2	90.7	115.6
August	106.9	101.3	109.3	94.5	142.2	93.2	90.2	77.2	83.3	91.2	115.8
September	107.4	101.2	109.8	95.1	142.4	93.7	89.4	77.1	81.9	90.3	117.6
October	107.3	101.6	110.5	95.4	143.0	94.5	89.5	77.7	82.7	90.0	116.3
November	108.2	102.0	111.4	97.3	143.6	95.3	89.3	78.5	81.6	89.8	118.1
December	108.1	102.1	110.8	97.1	142.3	95.0	90.3	77.6	82.2	91.2	117.8
2014											
January	108.3	101.1	110.0	94.9	142.6	94.0	89.1	76.3	81.7	89.8	119.8
February	108.7	102.5	112.1	96.9	145.8	95.6	89.4	73.3	80.3	90.3	118.9
March	109.9	103.1	112.9	97.8	146.5	96.2	89.8	78.8	80.6	90.6	121.0
April	110.4	103.4	113.3	97.8	146.6	96.9	90.0	78.9	82.2	90.5	121.8
May	111.3	104.1	114.8	99.6	149.3	97.7	89.7	76.4	81.0	90.6	123.1
June	112.4	104.9	116.1	100.9	149.5	99.6	89.8	77.7	81.5	90.8	124.6
July	112.4	105.5	116.9	105.3	149.7	99.5	90.1	79.5	80.7	91.7	123.7
August	112.9	105.4	116.4	102.1	150.5	99.2	90.7	78.9	81.1	92.5	124.9
September	113.7	105.7	116.7	102.3	152.2	98.8	90.9	80.2	81.2	92.8	126.8
October	113.5	105.8	116.7	103.3	152.9	98.2	91.1	80.8	80.7	93.0	126.0
November	114.1	106.7	117.6	105.3	154.4	98.5	91.9	82.5	81.2	93.7	126.2
December	114.7	106.9	118.0	104.7	152.6	100.2	91.9	82.9	81.8	93.9	127.3

Table 2-1. Industrial Production Indexes by Market Groups—*Continued*

(Seasonally adjusted, 2007 = 100.)

Year and month	Special aggregates											Total non-energy, excluding high-tech
	Energy						Non-energy					
									Selected high-tech			
	Total	Consumer energy products	Commercial energy products	Oil and gas well drilling	Converted fuels	Primary energy	Total	Total	Computers and peripheral equipment	Communications equipment	Semiconductors and related components	
1968	57.3	42.1	29.0	. . .	55.7	82.7	33.3	0.1	. . .	. . .	. . .	51.3
1969	60.4	45.0	30.5	. . .	59.6	85.6	34.8	0.1	. . .	. . .	. . .	53.4
1970	63.3	47.6	32.8	. . .	62.7	89.7	33.3	0.1	. . .	. . .	. . .	50.9
1971	64.5	49.9	34.5	. . .	64.4	89.0	33.8	0.1	. . .	. . .	. . .	51.8
1972	67.4	52.6	36.4	57.1	68.4	90.4	37.3	0.1	0.0	3.3	0.1	57.0
1973	69.2	53.6	38.4	53.7	71.1	91.5	40.7	0.2	0.1	3.6	0.1	61.9
1974	69.5	55.0	38.4	62.4	70.1	91.9	40.5	0.2	0.1	3.9	0.1	61.2
1975	69.7	56.2	39.8	70.4	67.6	92.7	36.2	0.2	0.1	3.8	0.1	54.6
1976	72.0	59.1	41.9	79.3	71.3	92.7	39.4	0.3	0.1	4.0	0.1	59.1
1977	74.8	61.4	43.3	100.7	74.0	95.4	42.7	0.3	0.2	4.8	0.2	63.6
1978	76.1	62.6	44.6	112.2	73.4	97.7	45.5	0.4	0.3	5.3	0.2	67.1
1979	78.3	64.2	46.7	119.6	76.1	99.9	46.8	0.5	0.4	6.3	0.2	68.4
1980	78.6	61.8	45.9	141.5	74.6	102.0	45.3	0.7	0.6	7.6	0.3	65.2
1981	79.8	61.4	47.1	170.0	73.6	104.0	45.8	0.8	0.8	8.1	0.3	65.3
1982	76.9	61.8	47.7	149.6	67.7	101.0	43.2	0.9	1.0	8.6	0.3	60.9
1983	74.7	62.3	48.7	115.9	67.6	96.6	45.3	1.1	1.4	9.1	0.4	63.1
1984	79.0	64.2	51.3	126.2	71.8	102.8	49.8	1.5	2.0	9.7	0.5	68.6
1985	78.8	64.2	53.2	115.6	71.5	102.1	50.7	1.5	2.4	9.4	0.5	69.6
1986	76.1	65.5	54.7	56.3	68.9	97.9	51.8	1.6	2.5	8.9	0.6	71.2
1987	78.3	67.9	57.6	54.3	72.4	98.7	54.8	1.9	3.3	10.0	0.7	74.5
1988	81.4	71.4	59.5	65.2	75.8	101.4	57.8	2.3	4.0	11.9	0.8	77.8
1989	82.2	71.9	61.7	56.8	78.6	100.7	58.3	2.4	4.2	12.3	0.9	78.2
1990	83.6	71.4	63.5	60.1	79.2	103.4	58.7	2.7	4.5	14.6	1.0	78.2
1991	84.0	73.6	64.4	46.8	79.3	103.5	57.6	2.9	4.7	15.2	1.1	76.2
1992	82.9	72.6	64.0	32.7	80.8	101.0	59.7	3.5	5.9	17.4	1.3	78.2
1993	84.4	75.8	65.9	45.5	82.3	100.1	61.9	4.1	7.3	20.0	1.5	80.3
1994	86.1	76.7	68.5	54.0	83.6	101.8	65.5	5.3	9.1	24.0	2.0	83.8
1995	87.8	78.8	70.9	52.6	84.8	103.4	69.0	7.4	12.6	29.4	3.0	86.0
1996	90.0	82.3	73.2	56.4	86.3	104.8	72.3	10.6	17.9	36.9	4.6	87.3
1997	90.5	81.6	76.2	64.7	87.6	103.8	78.5	15.6	25.4	50.4	7.2	91.6
1998	90.7	81.7	77.5	60.5	88.7	103.4	83.8	21.8	34.9	59.8	10.9	94.9
1999	91.3	84.5	80.5	47.4	90.3	101.4	87.9	31.3	45.9	76.3	17.3	96.1
2000	93.6	86.3	83.7	67.2	92.4	102.7	91.6	43.8	53.5	102.9	26.7	96.8
2001	93.6	87.3	85.1	81.4	89.2	102.4	87.9	44.8	54.1	95.5	28.9	92.1
2002	94.0	91.1	86.9	58.7	91.2	100.7	88.0	44.5	53.3	71.4	33.5	92.3
2003	95.0	91.6	91.2	68.2	91.8	100.4	89.1	53.4	57.8	73.8	44.9	92.3
2004	95.7	92.9	94.1	74.5	94.0	99.3	91.6	60.6	58.4	81.9	54.0	94.2
2005	96.3	96.1	96.7	83.7	95.3	97.3	95.2	71.1	69.6	80.8	67.5	97.1
2006	97.4	95.8	97.3	96.6	95.2	98.9	97.6	84.9	86.5	98.0	78.7	98.5
2007	100.0	100.0	100.0	100.0	100.0	100.0	100.0	100.0	100.0	100.0	100.0	100.0
2008	100.7	99.7	100.2	104.4	98.2	101.7	95.2	115.5	118.9	96.0	123.4	94.1
2009	97.7	99.8	98.5	61.4	93.0	100.1	81.8	103.0	104.1	81.2	113.3	80.6
2010	101.5	102.0	99.9	82.3	98.9	103.5	86.9	127.6	85.0	81.5	172.0	84.9
2011	104.7	102.4	100.8	99.2	98.2	108.9	89.9	146.4	68.8	88.7	213.6	87.3
2012	107.2	100.0	100.9	103.9	98.7	114.9	93.8	164.7	63.8	90.5	252.5	90.7
2013	110.9	104.0	103.2	97.2	97.2	121.2	96.3	180.5	69.9	90.4	282.3	92.8
2014	117.5	107.0	105.6	102.4	99.2	131.6	99.6	191.3	70.7	90.1	305.0	95.9
2013												
January	108.1	101.3	101.9	96.5	95.3	117.5	95.2	175.3	65.3	89.6	274.5	91.8
February	108.8	102.2	102.1	97.1	97.9	117.6	95.8	174.3	66.0	89.4	272.2	92.5
March	110.6	106.0	102.9	97.0	102.3	117.9	95.8	175.2	66.4	89.4	273.8	92.5
April	110.6	106.0	103.1	96.4	97.6	119.6	95.6	178.3	66.9	89.5	280.1	92.2
May	110.2	103.7	102.6	96.3	96.2	120.5	95.8	180.9	67.9	89.6	284.9	92.4
June	109.8	101.6	101.5	96.8	95.1	121.0	96.2	180.4	68.9	89.7	283.2	92.8
July	110.5	101.5	102.2	97.3	94.2	122.7	95.8	182.2	71.4	89.8	285.4	92.3
August	110.5	100.7	102.3	98.1	94.3	122.9	96.5	183.9	73.0	90.1	288.0	93.0
September	112.6	104.1	104.1	98.4	97.2	124.3	96.8	183.1	74.0	90.8	285.3	93.3
October	112.2	106.4	104.3	97.2	97.2	122.6	97.0	184.2	73.0	91.5	287.8	93.5
November	113.7	107.0	105.9	97.5	99.0	124.5	97.3	184.5	73.5	92.2	287.6	93.7
December	113.8	108.2	106.0	98.1	99.6	123.8	97.5	183.2	72.2	93.2	285.0	94.0
2014												
January	115.9	110.7	108.4	97.9	102.7	125.5	96.5	182.9	68.0	90.3	288.7	93.0
February	115.7	113.6	107.1	97.7	101.3	124.7	97.8	185.6	69.3	88.6	294.6	94.3
March	116.8	112.9	105.3	99.6	102.8	127.0	98.6	186.9	70.2	87.5	297.6	95.0
April	116.3	108.3	104.4	100.9	98.0	129.6	98.8	189.7	67.4	89.2	304.1	95.2
May	116.9	107.1	104.2	101.9	98.7	131.1	99.3	194.1	68.7	90.4	311.7	95.5
June	117.1	103.2	103.0	102.3	98.3	133.2	99.8	194.4	70.8	90.8	311.0	96.1
July	116.3	102.0	103.0	102.8	95.0	133.0	100.6	193.5	70.2	90.5	309.5	96.9
August	117.1	101.3	103.6	104.6	97.4	133.9	100.3	192.8	73.0	88.0	308.1	96.6
September	119.4	105.1	106.9	106.6	99.5	135.7	100.4	193.9	72.0	88.6	310.6	96.7
October	118.8	105.0	106.5	105.8	99.8	134.5	100.6	195.7	72.1	91.9	312.3	96.8
November	119.9	108.5	108.7	105.3	101.1	134.4	101.8	195.8	73.8	93.1	310.6	98.0
December	119.7	105.4	106.2	103.3	97.3	137.0	101.8	194.7	71.3	93.0	309.9	98.0

. . . = Not available.

Table 2-2. Industrial Production Indexes by NAICS Industry Groups

(Seasonally adjusted, 2007 = 100.)

Year and month	Total industrial production	Manu-facturing (SIC)	Manufacturing (NAICS)											
			Total	Durable goods manufacturing									
				Total	Wood products	Nonmetallic mineral products	Primary metals	Fabricated metal products	Machinery	Computer and electronic products	Electrical equipment, appliances, and components	Motor vehicles and parts	Aerospace and miscel-laneous transport equipment
1968	37.0	33.4	. . .	. . .	. . .	. . .	. . .	. . .	. . .	. . .	. . .	. . .	. . .
1969	38.7	34.9	. . .	. . .	. . .	. . .	. . .	. . .	. . .	. . .	. . .	. . .	. . .
1970	37.4	33.4	. . .	. . .	. . .	. . .	. . .	. . .	. . .	. . .	. . .	. . .	. . .
1971	37.9	33.9	. . .	. . .	. . .	. . .	. . .	. . .	. . .	. . .	. . .	. . .	. . .
1972	41.6	37.4	36.0	25.5	70.7	67.7	110.2	60.3	56.4	0.7	67.9	43.3	55.5
1973	45.0	40.8	39.3	28.6	68.4	72.6	128.2	66.6	65.2	0.9	76.4	49.5	63.3
1974	44.8	40.7	39.2	28.4	62.2	71.8	131.4	65.4	68.3	1.0	74.6	42.5	64.3
1975	40.9	36.4	35.0	24.7	57.7	64.3	101.9	56.5	59.5	0.9	59.9	37.1	61.1
1976	44.1	39.7	38.3	27.0	64.9	67.9	108.2	60.6	62.1	1.1	67.6	47.3	57.2
1977	47.4	43.1	41.6	29.7	70.0	72.3	109.3	65.7	67.8	1.3	74.5	53.8	57.6
1978	50.0	45.7	44.1	32.0	70.9	77.0	116.2	68.9	73.1	1.7	79.1	56.1	63.6
1979	51.5	47.1	45.5	33.6	68.6	76.9	118.9	72.0	77.1	2.0	82.3	51.4	74.0
1980	50.2	45.5	43.8	32.1	63.5	69.4	104.4	67.9	73.4	2.5	77.4	37.9	79.6
1981	50.9	46.0	44.2	32.5	62.1	66.4	104.5	67.4	72.7	2.9	76.4	36.9	75.8
1982	48.3	43.5	41.7	29.7	55.7	58.8	73.9	60.4	60.8	3.2	68.9	33.3	70.9
1983	49.6	45.6	43.8	31.2	64.6	63.3	75.7	60.8	54.9	3.7	71.2	42.5	67.8
1984	54.0	50.0	48.1	35.6	69.1	68.3	83.1	66.2	64.0	4.6	80.2	50.9	72.3
1985	54.7	50.8	48.9	36.4	70.0	69.6	76.7	67.2	64.2	4.9	78.9	52.9	77.3
1986	55.2	52.0	50.0	37.0	76.0	72.5	74.9	66.7	63.2	5.1	80.4	52.8	81.3
1987	58.1	54.9	52.8	39.2	82.9	76.5	80.7	68.0	64.5	5.8	81.5	54.7	84.3
1988	61.1	57.8	55.8	42.1	82.8	78.0	90.3	71.4	71.0	6.4	85.5	58.5	88.7
1989	61.6	58.3	56.3	42.6	81.6	77.4	88.2	70.9	73.7	6.6	84.2	57.9	94.0
1990	62.2	58.8	56.8	42.7	80.7	76.2	87.1	70.0	71.9	7.2	82.0	54.4	94.4
1991	61.3	57.6	55.7	41.4	75.5	70.2	81.8	66.8	67.5	7.5	77.8	52.0	91.1
1992	63.0	59.7	57.9	43.5	79.6	73.2	83.8	68.9	67.3	8.4	82.4	59.2	84.2
1993	65.1	61.8	60.0	45.9	80.5	74.8	87.9	71.5	72.3	9.3	87.6	65.4	78.5
1994	68.5	65.4	63.8	49.8	85.3	79.0	94.6	77.7	79.2	10.9	94.0	75.1	70.5
1995	71.8	68.8	67.3	54.0	87.3	81.3	95.6	82.5	84.8	14.0	96.2	77.3	67.0
1996	74.9	72.2	70.7	58.9	90.2	86.6	97.9	85.5	87.7	18.2	99.1	77.9	69.6
1997	80.4	78.2	76.7	65.9	92.8	89.4	102.0	89.4	92.6	24.4	102.8	84.0	77.7
1998	85.0	83.4	81.8	72.9	97.0	94.0	103.8	92.3	95.0	31.3	106.6	88.4	90.0
1999	88.7	87.6	86.0	78.9	100.6	94.9	103.7	92.9	93.0	41.0	108.4	98.1	86.6
2000	92.2	91.3	89.8	84.8	99.3	94.9	100.3	96.6	97.7	53.6	113.9	97.4	76.0
2001	89.1	87.5	86.3	80.9	93.1	91.4	91.3	89.6	86.4	54.4	102.5	88.8	80.8
2002	89.3	87.8	86.7	80.8	96.6	91.6	91.3	87.6	83.3	53.0	94.5	97.6	76.5
2003	90.4	88.9	88.0	82.9	96.6	92.4	89.8	86.6	82.8	60.3	92.1	101.1	73.1
2004	92.5	91.4	90.6	86.2	99.2	95.3	97.7	86.9	86.3	68.3	93.7	101.7	72.0
2005	95.5	95.0	94.4	91.2	105.9	99.4	95.2	90.9	91.6	77.0	95.3	102.3	80.2
2006	97.6	97.4	97.0	95.4	106.9	101.1	98.0	95.9	95.9	87.4	96.0	100.8	85.2
2007	100.0	100.0	100.0	100.0	100.0	100.0	100.0	100.0	100.0	100.0	100.0	100.0	100.0
2008	96.6	95.3	95.4	96.6	85.4	88.4	100.0	96.4	97.3	108.1	96.3	80.0	101.9
2009	85.7	82.4	82.4	78.6	65.3	66.6	74.0	74.2	75.7	97.0	75.6	58.6	92.8
2010	90.6	87.3	87.9	87.2	67.6	68.6	91.1	79.0	84.6	111.3	78.6	77.8	94.0
2011	93.6	90.3	91.1	93.2	68.4	70.2	97.4	85.3	95.6	122.0	83.4	84.8	94.3
2012	97.1	94.0	95.1	100.0	71.6	71.4	99.6	91.4	101.1	135.0	86.0	97.4	102.2
2013	99.9	96.5	97.9	104.4	78.1	74.0	100.8	94.7	102.9	144.4	88.4	105.0	105.4
2014	104.1	99.8	101.5	109.8	81.4	78.2	105.3	98.5	110.0	150.8	91.4	113.2	109.7
2013													
January	98.4	95.4	96.6	102.1	76.1	72.8	100.2	93.1	99.6	141.6	87.4	100.4	104.0
February	99.0	95.9	97.3	103.2	77.7	73.8	99.9	94.7	101.9	141.5	88.6	102.0	104.6
March	99.5	96.0	97.4	103.5	77.0	73.8	99.0	94.1	103.1	141.6	87.8	103.8	104.9
April	99.3	95.8	97.2	103.4	75.9	72.4	99.7	93.8	101.8	143.0	87.6	103.6	105.5
May	99.4	96.1	97.4	103.7	76.4	73.8	99.9	93.5	101.7	144.5	87.8	104.0	105.4
June	99.6	96.4	97.8	104.0	76.9	74.0	98.7	93.8	102.7	143.9	88.3	105.3	105.6
July	99.4	96.0	97.3	103.5	77.0	74.0	100.9	94.1	101.6	144.3	88.3	101.8	104.3
August	100.0	96.7	98.0	104.9	78.5	74.3	100.7	94.6	103.5	146.1	88.9	105.7	105.6
September	100.7	96.9	98.3	105.5	79.4	74.5	100.8	94.9	104.6	146.3	88.3	107.5	106.1
October	100.8	97.3	98.7	106.1	80.8	74.6	103.6	95.6	105.3	147.0	89.1	106.6	106.3
November	101.4	97.6	99.1	106.8	81.4	75.3	103.2	97.1	105.6	146.5	89.6	109.6	106.0
December	101.6	97.7	99.3	106.2	80.2	74.2	102.5	96.6	102.9	146.0	89.8	109.7	106.1
2014													
January	101.3	96.8	98.2	105.2	78.0	75.5	100.1	96.1	105.3	146.7	89.3	103.2	104.0
February	102.3	98.0	99.5	107.3	78.1	75.0	103.1	97.1	108.5	147.4	90.1	110.1	104.6
March	103.1	98.8	100.4	108.1	79.3	76.0	102.5	97.4	108.8	149.0	90.8	110.5	104.9
April	103.2	99.1	100.8	108.4	80.3	76.5	104.4	97.7	108.1	149.7	90.0	110.7	105.5
May	103.7	99.5	101.1	109.7	80.7	77.4	105.6	98.3	109.6	151.3	91.2	113.3	105.4
June	104.1	99.9	101.6	110.3	80.9	78.3	108.7	99.6	108.7	151.1	91.9	113.3	105.6
July	104.5	100.8	102.5	111.9	82.8	79.7	109.2	99.9	109.5	150.5	91.7	123.9	104.3
August	104.5	100.4	102.2	110.9	83.1	79.8	108.3	98.5	111.0	151.3	92.5	115.0	105.6
September	105.2	100.6	102.5	111.1	82.2	80.3	107.0	99.6	110.4	152.3	92.5	112.9	106.1
October	105.1	100.8	102.7	111.5	83.4	79.9	105.7	99.7	113.8	153.6	92.2	112.3	106.3
November	106.3	102.0	103.9	112.8	83.1	79.9	104.3	99.9	116.1	153.5	92.8	119.1	106.0
December	106.2	101.9	103.9	112.5	84.2	81.0	106.8	100.1	112.2	154.1	92.2	117.6	106.1

. . . = Not available.

Table 2-2. Industrial Production Indexes by NAICS Industry Groups—*Continued*

(Seasonally adjusted, 2007 = 100.)

| Year and month | Durable goods manufacturing—*Continued* | | Manufacturing (NAICS)—*Continued* Nondurable goods manufacturing | | | | | | | | | Other manu-facturing (non-NAICS) |
	Furniture and related products	Miscel-laneous manu-facturing	Total	Food, beverage, and tobacco products	Textile and product mills	Apparel and leather	Paper	Printing and support	Petroleum and coal products	Chemicals	Plastics and rubber products	
1968	...	...	...	...	...	...	...	...	...	...	...	...
1969	...	...	...	...	...	...	...	...	...	...	...	...
1970	...	...	...	...	...	...	...	...	...	...	...	...
1971	...	...	...	...	...	...	...	...	...	...	...	...
1972	55.7	37.6	57.2	62.0	112.9	292.8	68.1	49.4	65.5	41.1	34.7	75.3
1973	58.4	38.8	59.9	62.8	111.9	297.7	73.7	52.0	64.4	45.0	39.2	77.7
1974	53.8	37.9	60.1	63.6	103.0	280.0	76.9	50.4	69.5	46.8	37.8	78.2
1975	46.0	35.4	55.7	62.5	99.6	272.7	66.5	47.1	68.5	41.1	31.9	74.4
1976	51.2	38.5	60.8	66.8	110.8	286.9	73.4	50.5	75.9	46.0	35.2	76.7
1977	58.6	41.9	64.9	68.3	120.9	300.8	76.6	54.7	81.2	50.1	41.6	84.1
1978	63.1	42.8	67.3	70.7	120.6	307.5	80.1	57.9	82.1	52.6	43.5	87.0
1979	62.7	43.1	67.7	70.4	120.2	288.8	81.3	59.6	87.7	53.8	42.9	88.8
1980	60.5	40.8	65.7	71.5	115.4	294.5	81.1	60.1	77.7	50.9	38.4	91.9
1981	60.0	42.3	66.3	72.3	113.0	294.2	82.2	61.6	74.1	51.7	40.6	94.1
1982	56.6	42.8	65.3	74.4	105.0	292.5	80.8	66.2	70.8	48.4	40.0	95.2
1983	62.0	42.8	68.4	74.5	118.0	300.7	86.0	71.2	72.0	51.7	43.5	97.8
1984	69.5	46.3	71.5	75.5	120.9	300.7	90.4	77.5	73.5	54.8	50.2	102.3
1985	70.1	46.9	71.9	78.0	116.5	287.7	88.6	80.6	72.5	54.4	52.2	106.3
1986	73.2	48.0	74.0	79.0	121.1	286.6	92.3	84.7	72.1	56.8	54.4	108.4
1987	78.4	51.7	78.0	80.6	133.2	289.8	95.3	91.0	75.5	61.2	60.2	114.7
1988	77.6	56.5	80.6	82.8	131.9	284.9	99.1	93.9	77.8	64.8	62.9	114.2
1989	77.2	57.3	81.1	82.4	134.0	272.5	100.2	94.2	77.0	66.0	65.0	112.6
1990	75.6	60.1	82.4	84.7	128.5	266.5	100.1	97.8	77.1	67.5	66.8	111.2
1991	69.9	61.3	82.1	85.3	126.6	265.0	100.3	94.7	76.0	67.3	66.1	106.7
1992	75.5	63.9	84.2	86.4	133.4	272.4	102.8	99.9	75.7	68.3	71.1	104.5
1993	78.6	67.5	85.4	86.2	138.5	278.1	104.0	100.2	76.2	69.1	76.2	105.3
1994	81.3	68.0	88.4	89.1	145.9	281.5	108.5	101.3	78.3	70.9	82.5	104.4
1995	82.7	70.6	89.9	91.6	144.4	279.7	110.1	102.8	79.7	72.1	84.6	104.4
1996	83.4	74.1	90.2	90.9	141.0	273.3	106.6	103.5	81.6	73.6	87.4	103.4
1997	92.1	76.1	93.5	92.8	148.5	272.9	108.9	105.6	84.3	78.0	92.8	112.1
1998	98.6	80.5	94.9	95.6	147.3	257.1	109.8	106.8	82.7	79.2	96.1	118.8
1999	101.9	82.2	95.5	93.9	147.3	245.8	110.6	106.8	86.0	80.8	101.2	122.2
2000	103.6	86.8	95.9	95.3	144.2	235.2	107.7	107.8	85.2	81.9	102.3	121.9
2001	97.1	85.8	93.1	95.0	129.0	201.0	101.6	104.2	84.7	80.5	96.4	114.0
2002	100.8	90.6	94.2	94.1	129.3	158.8	102.9	102.1	89.3	85.1	99.8	110.1
2003	99.1	93.4	94.4	95.9	124.2	147.5	100.4	98.1	87.9	86.5	99.9	106.9
2004	101.8	93.4	95.9	96.3	122.7	129.3	101.2	98.5	93.1	90.0	101.1	107.8
2005	105.5	99.5	98.3	99.8	124.5	126.1	100.7	98.6	95.6	92.9	102.2	107.4
2006	103.9	102.6	98.8	99.9	113.0	123.1	99.6	97.8	97.3	95.2	102.8	106.1
2007	100.0	100.0	100.0	100.0	100.0	100.0	100.0	100.0	100.0	100.0	100.0	100.0
2008	90.3	101.6	94.1	97.2	87.9	80.6	95.8	93.8	95.6	92.5	90.6	93.5
2009	65.5	94.2	86.9	96.5	69.7	59.4	85.4	78.8	94.3	83.5	75.8	80.7
2010	64.7	97.5	88.7	96.7	74.4	60.0	87.2	78.8	93.5	86.3	82.6	76.4
2011	66.5	98.4	88.9	96.8	74.0	58.9	87.3	78.0	94.7	86.3	84.0	74.3
2012	68.4	102.8	90.0	100.2	74.5	57.6	85.4	76.1	95.4	86.4	86.9	72.8
2013	70.6	109.8	91.2	101.4	73.4	59.1	85.0	75.7	96.2	87.5	90.9	68.9
2014	75.6	114.8	93.1	103.2	74.5	60.2	82.8	77.4	98.4	89.4	97.2	65.8
2013												
January	67.9	107.6	91.0	101.5	73.8	58.8	85.2	75.3	96.2	87.3	89.5	69.7
February	69.4	108.3	91.2	102.4	73.4	59.2	85.6	75.0	96.8	86.9	89.1	69.3
March	70.3	108.6	91.1	101.8	73.8	58.1	85.2	75.6	96.7	87.1	90.2	68.6
April	70.9	107.9	90.8	100.9	72.6	56.8	85.1	75.4	95.7	87.4	90.2	68.6
May	70.5	108.3	91.1	100.6	72.4	58.4	86.2	75.6	95.6	87.9	90.7	68.7
June	71.6	109.6	91.3	101.6	73.3	58.7	85.4	75.5	95.3	88.0	91.0	68.4
July	70.0	109.7	91.0	100.6	72.8	58.8	85.6	75.2	95.9	87.7	91.2	69.1
August	70.7	109.8	91.1	100.9	73.3	59.5	85.5	75.3	95.8	87.6	90.8	69.6
September	70.5	110.8	90.9	100.9	73.3	60.4	84.1	74.5	96.8	87.2	90.5	70.6
October	70.7	111.5	91.2	101.3	73.5	60.4	84.6	76.0	96.6	87.3	91.9	68.9
November	72.0	112.4	91.2	101.3	74.3	59.5	83.5	76.2	96.6	87.3	92.2	67.8
December	72.9	112.9	92.2	102.7	74.0	60.6	83.5	78.3	96.8	88.5	92.5	67.7
2014												
January	72.0	110.5	91.1	101.3	72.5	59.9	83.4	76.8	96.2	87.1	92.2	67.4
February	71.3	111.9	91.7	102.7	70.4	59.2	81.8	76.9	96.8	87.6	93.3	67.5
March	74.2	113.3	92.7	103.6	73.6	60.8	81.8	77.7	96.7	88.4	95.1	66.7
April	74.6	113.4	93.0	104.1	74.0	60.7	84.3	76.6	95.7	88.3	94.4	66.9
May	74.7	114.9	92.5	103.1	73.1	60.2	82.7	76.8	95.6	88.1	96.7	67.1
June	75.4	115.3	92.7	102.8	73.9	59.7	82.8	77.5	95.3	88.9	98.5	67.4
July	76.3	115.2	93.0	102.1	75.4	60.7	82.4	77.7	95.9	89.5	97.7	66.5
August	75.8	114.4	93.4	102.3	75.1	58.5	82.8	77.4	95.8	90.2	98.5	65.5
September	77.4	116.2	93.8	103.3	75.3	60.0	82.8	77.3	96.8	90.5	99.0	64.2
October	77.6	116.7	93.7	103.1	76.2	60.0	82.5	77.6	96.6	90.8	99.2	63.8
November	78.3	118.6	94.9	104.8	77.5	60.8	83.2	78.1	96.6	91.3	101.5	63.4
December	79.8	117.9	95.2	105.0	77.3	62.7	83.6	78.7	96.8	91.8	100.9	62.5

. . . = Not available.

Table 2-2. Industrial Production Indexes by NAICS Industry Groups—*Continued*

(Seasonally adjusted, 2007 = 100.)

Year and month	Mining	Utilities			Selected high-tech industries	Excluding selected high-tech industries	Stage-of-process groups		
		Total	Electric	Natural gas			Crude	Primary and semi-finished	Finished
1968	. . .	. . .	. . .	. . .	0.1	52.7	. . .	. . .	. . .
1969	. . .	. . .	. . .	. . .	0.1	55.0	. . .	. . .	. . .
1970	. . .	. . .	. . .	. . .	0.1	53.1	. . .	. . .	. . .
1971	. . .	. . .	. . .	. . .	0.1	54.1	. . .	. . .	. . .
1972	106.2	46.4	37.0	112.2	0.1	59.1	. . .	. . .	. . .
1973	106.8	49.1	40.3	107.7	0.2	63.6	. . .	. . .	. . .
1974	105.3	48.9	40.5	104.1	0.2	63.0	. . .	. . .	. . .
1975	102.8	49.8	42.3	97.4	0.2	57.4	. . .	. . .	. . .
1976	103.5	52.1	45.0	96.3	0.3	61.6	. . .	. . .	. . .
1977	105.9	54.2	47.9	93.0	0.3	65.9	. . .	. . .	. . .
1978	109.2	55.6	49.4	93.8	0.4	69.0	. . .	. . .	. . .
1979	112.5	56.8	50.5	96.3	0.5	70.5	. . .	. . .	. . .
1980	114.5	57.3	51.3	94.2	0.7	67.9	. . .	. . .	. . .
1981	117.5	58.1	52.7	92.1	0.8	68.3	. . .	. . .	. . .
1982	111.7	56.2	51.4	86.5	0.9	64.3	. . .	. . .	. . .
1983	105.8	56.7	52.9	81.0	1.1	65.5	. . .	. . .	. . .
1984	112.6	60.0	55.9	86.0	1.5	70.6	. . .	. . .	. . .
1985	110.4	61.3	58.0	82.5	1.5	71.3	. . .	. . .	. . .
1986	102.4	61.8	61.8	78.4	1.6	72.0	95.1	50.5	53.5
1987	103.4	64.7	64.7	82.0	1.9	75.1	98.2	53.4	56.1
1988	106.0	68.4	68.4	87.0	2.3	78.4	101.5	56.2	59.3
1989	104.8	70.6	70.6	90.2	2.4	78.9	101.6	56.6	60.1
1990	106.3	71.9	71.9	87.1	2.7	79.1	103.1	56.7	61.2
1991	104.0	73.7	73.7	89.5	2.9	77.5	100.4	55.7	60.6
1992	101.7	73.6	73.6	92.0	3.5	79.0	99.6	58.0	62.1
1993	101.7	76.2	76.2	95.5	4.1	81.0	98.4	60.7	63.8
1994	104.0	77.7	77.7	96.1	5.3	84.2	100.5	64.9	66.4
1995	103.9	80.5	80.5	98.6	7.4	86.3	100.9	68.5	69.6
1996	105.6	82.8	82.8	103.3	10.6	87.7	100.6	72.4	72.4
1997	107.6	82.8	82.8	101.3	15.6	91.4	103.3	78.0	78.1
1998	105.6	84.9	84.9	94.7	21.8	94.2	101.3	83.0	83.5
1999	100.1	87.4	87.4	97.4	31.3	95.3	99.4	88.5	85.9
2000	102.8	89.9	89.9	100.3	43.8	96.3	99.6	92.9	89.0
2001	103.2	89.5	89.5	98.9	44.8	92.5	96.9	88.8	86.9
2002	98.4	92.3	92.3	101.8	44.5	92.7	95.2	90.2	86.0
2003	98.5	94.1	94.1	102.7	53.4	92.9	95.3	91.2	87.5
2004	98.2	95.3	95.3	100.5	60.6	94.5	96.6	93.5	89.6
2005	97.0	97.3	97.3	98.9	71.1	96.9	95.7	96.6	94.0
2006	99.2	96.7	96.7	93.0	84.9	98.2	97.7	97.8	97.2
2007	100.0	100.0	100.0	100.0	100.0	100.0	100.0	100.0	100.0
2008	101.2	99.9	99.9	102.3	115.5	95.8	98.9	96.0	96.3
2009	95.7	97.5	97.5	100.4	103.0	85.0	92.5	82.3	86.6
2010	100.7	101.0	101.0	102.2	127.6	89.2	98.8	88.8	88.9
2011	106.8	100.8	100.8	102.4	146.4	91.8	102.9	91.9	91.2
2012	113.5	98.7	98.7	96.9	164.7	95.0	107.7	94.5	95.4
2013	118.9	100.7	100.7	107.9	180.5	97.5	111.8	97.0	97.9
2014	129.6	102.0	102.0	111.1	191.3	101.4	119.2	100.2	101.6
2013									
January	115.0	99.0	98.5	101.7	175.3	96.1	108.9	95.9	96.5
February	115.8	99.8	99.1	104.4	174.3	96.7	109.5	96.5	97.3
March	116.1	103.5	102.0	113.5	175.2	97.1	109.7	97.0	97.7
April	117.0	102.2	100.8	112.0	178.3	96.9	110.1	96.7	97.4
May	117.7	100.2	99.4	105.7	180.9	97.0	111.3	96.4	97.5
June	118.7	98.5	97.8	103.3	180.4	97.2	111.8	96.0	98.2
July	120.2	97.9	96.9	104.8	182.2	97.0	112.8	96.1	97.2
August	120.6	97.6	96.6	104.2	183.9	97.5	113.3	96.5	98.0
September	122.6	100.3	99.5	105.0	183.1	98.2	114.2	97.4	98.5
October	120.2	101.8	100.8	108.0	184.2	98.3	112.6	98.1	98.6
November	121.3	103.7	102.0	116.0	184.5	98.9	113.4	98.9	98.8
December	121.6	103.8	102.0	116.6	183.2	99.1	113.7	98.8	99.3
2014									
January	122.9	107.3	105.3	120.7	182.9	98.8	114.3	99.1	98.0
February	123.0	107.0	105.4	118.1	185.6	99.7	114.5	99.7	99.7
March	125.1	106.5	104.3	121.8	186.9	100.6	115.9	100.1	100.8
April	127.7	101.0	99.9	108.4	189.7	100.6	118.0	99.2	101.1
May	129.0	101.3	100.1	109.1	194.1	101.0	118.7	99.8	101.3
June	131.1	99.3	98.7	103.4	194.4	101.4	120.1	100.1	101.4
July	131.3	96.3	95.1	104.4	193.5	101.8	120.4	99.8	102.5
August	132.5	97.0	96.2	102.5	192.8	101.8	121.4	99.9	101.9
September	133.8	101.2	100.2	107.6	193.9	102.5	122.4	100.9	102.2
October	132.3	101.6	101.1	105.2	195.7	102.5	121.4	101.0	102.4
November	131.5	105.3	103.2	119.5	195.8	103.6	120.9	102.3	104.3
December	135.0	100.0	99.6	101.8	194.7	103.6	123.3	101.4	103.9

. . . = Not available.

Table 2-3. Capacity Utilization by NAICS Industry Groups

(Output as a percent of capacity, seasonally adjusted.)

Year and month	Total industry	Total manufacturing (SIC)	Manufacturing (NAICS) Total	Durable goods manufacturing Total	Wood products	Nonmetallic mineral products	Primary metals	Fabricated metal products	Machinery	Computer and electronic products	Electrical equipment, appliances, and components	Motor vehicles and parts	Aerospace and miscellaneous transportation equipment
1968	87.3	87.1	...	87.3	...	78.4	84.8	87.2	85.1	...	...	90.1	90.2
1969	87.4	86.6	...	87.1	...	79.7	88.4	86.1	86.7	...	...	86.7	86.2
1970	81.2	79.4	...	77.8	...	73.9	79.5	78.4	79.7	...	...	66.4	75.2
1971	79.6	77.9	...	75.5	...	75.6	73.1	78.3	73.8	...	...	79.1	66.8
1972	84.7	83.4	83.3	82.1	92.3	79.6	82.9	85.0	83.2	80.7	89.8	84.3	65.6
1973	88.3	87.7	87.8	88.6	87.8	84.1	94.6	90.9	92.5	85.2	97.7	91.8	73.5
1974	85.1	84.4	84.5	84.7	77.9	81.7	96.5	86.1	91.9	83.2	91.6	76.7	74.3
1975	75.8	73.7	73.6	71.8	70.2	73.0	75.2	72.3	77.6	68.7	70.7	66.1	70.8
1976	79.8	78.3	78.4	76.5	79.5	77.6	78.6	75.9	79.9	72.0	78.7	81.8	66.2
1977	83.4	82.5	82.4	81.2	86.2	82.5	79.2	80.0	85.5	77.8	85.4	90.0	66.2
1978	85.1	84.4	84.3	83.8	84.8	86.5	84.2	80.6	88.6	80.4	87.7	90.7	72.4
1979	85.0	84.0	84.0	84.1	80.0	84.4	86.1	81.6	90.1	83.7	88.9	80.9	81.8
1980	80.8	78.7	78.4	77.5	72.4	75.1	75.9	75.0	83.5	86.9	81.8	59.8	84.4
1981	79.6	76.9	76.6	75.1	70.6	72.5	77.8	72.7	80.5	84.5	79.0	57.2	76.9
1982	73.6	70.9	70.3	66.5	63.7	65.0	56.9	64.6	66.6	80.9	69.8	50.7	69.8
1983	74.9	73.4	72.9	68.7	75.2	70.6	59.5	66.6	60.5	81.9	73.0	67.2	66.4
1984	80.4	79.3	78.9	76.9	81.0	75.7	69.0	73.7	70.9	87.4	82.5	81.6	69.8
1985	79.2	78.1	77.6	75.7	79.6	76.0	67.3	74.2	70.6	80.2	79.2	83.4	72.4
1986	78.6	78.4	78.0	75.4	83.6	78.4	69.5	73.9	70.1	77.4	80.2	79.1	73.9
1987	81.2	81.0	80.6	77.6	85.6	80.7	78.3	75.5	72.0	79.8	82.4	78.1	75.4
1988	84.3	84.1	83.8	82.1	84.1	81.7	88.9	80.3	80.4	81.4	87.2	83.1	79.8
1989	83.8	83.3	83.2	81.9	82.2	80.8	86.5	79.9	84.2	78.8	86.2	81.4	85.3
1990	82.5	81.7	81.6	79.5	80.4	79.1	85.3	77.8	81.8	78.7	83.9	72.4	84.9
1991	79.8	78.5	78.4	75.3	76.3	73.1	79.7	74.1	76.6	77.6	79.0	64.3	83.3
1992	80.6	79.6	79.6	77.2	78.8	76.9	81.2	76.2	75.4	79.3	82.1	72.7	78.0
1993	81.4	80.4	80.3	78.5	78.9	78.8	85.4	77.0	78.8	77.6	86.4	79.0	73.6
1994	83.6	82.8	82.9	81.6	82.8	81.6	90.8	81.3	83.5	80.4	91.6	86.3	67.7
1995	83.9	83.1	83.1	82.1	80.8	81.8	88.9	83.1	85.5	83.0	91.2	83.5	65.2
1996	83.4	82.1	82.2	81.5	81.1	85.2	88.7	82.5	84.6	81.3	90.0	80.4	67.7
1997	84.1	83.0	82.8	82.1	81.0	84.3	89.8	81.5	84.8	81.4	88.6	81.5	73.4
1998	82.7	81.5	81.2	80.4	81.1	84.5	86.3	79.7	81.6	81.4	86.3	78.7	81.4
1999	81.7	80.4	80.0	79.9	81.5	82.2	84.2	77.5	76.1	81.0	84.0	83.3	75.5
2000	81.4	79.6	79.2	79.4	78.4	79.2	82.0	78.6	77.2	84.2	86.7	81.4	65.3
2001	76.0	73.6	73.2	71.3	72.6	74.4	73.7	72.5	68.0	69.6	77.5	72.6	69.7
2002	74.9	73.0	72.5	70.0	75.0	74.3	75.5	71.5	67.0	61.1	73.7	78.6	66.3
2003	75.9	73.9	73.5	71.0	76.2	74.3	73.8	72.9	68.6	64.5	74.8	78.3	63.6
2004	78.0	76.2	75.9	73.8	79.2	74.5	81.5	75.1	72.5	71.0	77.4	77.0	63.1
2005	79.9	78.2	78.0	76.1	80.9	75.1	79.1	78.8	76.2	72.7	81.1	77.4	69.8
2006	80.2	78.4	78.4	77.3	78.1	73.4	78.9	83.6	79.2	77.0	83.2	72.3	73.1
2007	80.5	78.7	78.8	78.3	73.0	68.3	80.3	86.1	82.5	76.5	87.8	71.9	85.0
2008	77.6	74.6	74.5	74.7	65.1	58.9	77.1	81.3	80.1	78.0	85.4	58.6	84.1
2009	68.7	65.6	65.4	61.3	52.3	45.5	54.9	64.3	62.8	71.1	68.2	43.9	73.8
2010	73.8	71.1	71.3	68.6	56.2	49.2	69.2	71.5	70.8	77.5	73.4	59.0	73.2
2011	76.3	73.9	74.3	72.4	59.3	52.6	74.0	78.2	78.5	76.7	79.5	64.1	71.0
2012	77.3	75.5	76.0	74.9	63.9	55.4	75.4	81.2	80.1	73.6	81.9	71.9	75.0
2013	77.9	76.1	76.7	75.7	70.4	58.9	76.0	80.5	78.5	73.5	82.9	75.9	75.6
2014	79.1	77.2	77.9	77.3	71.3	63.3	78.7	80.8	81.3	72.2	84.3	81.0	77.2
2013													
January	77.4	75.8	76.4	75.1	68.6	57.3	75.9	80.6	77.4	73.7	82.5	73.0	75.5
February	77.8	76.1	76.8	75.7	70.0	58.3	75.6	81.6	78.9	73.3	83.5	74.0	75.8
March	78.0	76.1	76.7	75.7	69.4	58.4	74.9	80.9	79.6	73.1	82.7	75.2	75.8
April	77.8	75.8	76.5	75.5	68.6	57.4	75.4	80.3	78.4	73.6	82.4	75.0	75.9
May	77.8	75.9	76.6	75.5	69.0	58.7	75.5	79.8	78.0	74.1	82.4	75.3	76.1
June	77.8	76.1	76.7	75.6	69.5	58.9	74.5	79.8	78.5	73.5	82.8	76.1	75.8
July	77.5	75.6	76.2	75.0	69.6	59.0	76.0	79.8	77.5	73.5	82.8	73.5	74.8
August	77.8	76.1	76.7	75.8	70.9	59.3	75.8	80.0	78.7	74.0	83.2	76.3	75.5
September	78.3	76.2	76.7	76.0	71.6	59.6	75.8	80.0	79.3	73.8	82.5	77.5	75.7
October	78.2	76.3	76.9	76.3	72.8	59.8	77.8	80.4	79.6	73.8	83.2	76.8	75.8
November	78.5	76.4	77.1	76.6	73.2	60.5	77.5	81.4	79.5	73.2	83.5	78.8	75.4
December	78.5	76.4	77.1	75.9	72.0	59.6	76.9	80.7	77.3	72.5	83.5	78.8	75.3
2014													
January	78.1	75.5	76.1	75.0	69.8	60.7	75.0	80.0	78.9	72.5	83.0	74.1	74.5
February	78.6	76.4	77.0	76.3	69.7	60.4	77.2	80.7	81.1	72.5	83.6	79.0	75.2
March	79.1	76.8	77.6	76.7	70.6	61.3	76.7	80.6	81.0	72.9	84.2	79.2	76.2
April	79.0	77.0	77.7	76.7	71.2	61.8	78.1	80.6	80.3	72.8	83.3	79.3	76.3
May	79.1	77.1	77.8	77.4	71.2	62.5	78.9	80.9	81.2	73.1	84.3	81.0	77.3
June	79.2	77.3	78.0	77.6	71.2	63.3	81.2	81.7	80.3	72.5	84.7	80.9	77.9
July	79.3	77.8	78.5	78.6	72.5	64.5	81.5	81.7	80.7	71.8	84.4	88.4	78.0
August	79.1	77.4	78.2	77.6	72.4	64.6	80.8	80.3	81.6	71.7	85.0	81.9	78.1
September	79.4	77.4	78.2	77.5	71.3	65.0	79.8	80.9	81.0	71.7	85.0	80.4	78.6
October	79.2	77.4	78.2	77.7	72.1	64.8	78.7	80.7	83.2	71.9	84.5	79.9	78.3
November	79.8	78.1	79.0	78.3	71.5	64.8	77.6	80.6	84.7	71.4	84.9	84.6	78.3
December	79.5	78.0	78.9	77.9	72.1	65.8	79.5	80.6	81.6	71.2	84.2	83.4	78.3

. . . = Not available.

Table 2-3. Capacity Utilization by NAICS Industry Groups—*Continued*

(Output as a percent of capacity, seasonally adjusted.)

Year and month	Durable goods manufacturing —Continued		Manufacturing (NAICS)—*Continued* Nondurable goods manufacturing									Other manufacturing (non-NAICS)
	Furniture and related products	Miscellaneous manufacturing	Total	Food, beverage, and tobacco products	Textile and product mills	Apparel and leather	Paper	Printing and support	Petroleum and coal products	Chemicals	Plastics and rubber products	
1968	91.3	. . .	86.5	84.8	. . .	. . .	89.3	. . .	95.7	80.1	91.1	. . .
1969	92.4	. . .	86.1	85.0	. . .	. . .	91.1	. . .	96.0	79.1	90.3	. . .
1970	83.5	. . .	82.1	84.0	. . .	. . .	86.2	. . .	96.0	76.1	79.2	. . .
1971	84.2	. . .	81.7	83.9	. . .	. . .	86.9	. . .	94.7	75.3	79.8	. . .
1972	93.5	80.4	85.2	85.1	88.9	81.6	91.4	92.3	93.1	80.0	88.5	85.7
1973	94.5	79.5	86.6	84.8	86.3	82.1	94.9	94.0	90.4	83.7	92.5	84.7
1974	83.5	74.6	84.2	83.8	76.3	76.3	94.9	88.0	92.6	84.1	84.2	82.7
1975	69.5	67.7	76.1	80.2	72.5	74.5	80.5	79.6	83.7	71.8	70.1	77.3
1976	76.4	72.3	81.1	83.2	81.4	78.1	87.6	82.3	86.0	77.8	77.3	77.6
1977	84.6	77.6	84.3	82.9	88.6	81.7	90.1	86.0	87.7	81.3	88.4	83.2
1978	86.1	78.7	85.2	83.5	87.7	83.9	92.2	87.4	86.4	82.5	88.7	85.0
1979	80.7	78.4	83.8	81.1	87.2	79.0	90.7	86.0	88.6	82.9	83.7	85.6
1980	74.9	73.2	79.6	80.8	83.3	79.9	88.2	83.7	76.2	76.6	74.2	86.8
1981	71.8	75.7	78.8	80.4	80.6	78.7	86.8	81.2	72.8	75.9	77.6	87.5
1982	66.4	73.7	76.3	81.3	74.4	77.8	83.8	82.4	71.2	69.2	74.5	87.3
1983	72.2	70.8	79.4	80.8	84.0	81.1	88.8	84.3	74.4	72.8	81.6	87.9
1984	79.1	76.0	82.1	81.3	85.8	81.3	91.2	87.1	78.5	75.9	91.3	89.4
1985	77.2	74.0	80.4	82.6	81.5	78.0	87.9	84.8	80.1	73.4	87.0	90.4
1986	79.0	74.0	81.8	82.8	84.2	79.9	90.2	85.6	81.9	75.9	85.3	88.8
1987	82.8	77.2	84.8	83.8	91.4	82.3	90.2	89.3	82.3	80.9	89.5	90.6
1988	80.4	81.8	86.2	85.4	88.8	82.4	91.3	90.4	83.2	84.3	89.0	88.6
1989	78.9	79.8	85.0	83.8	88.6	80.6	90.4	89.1	84.2	83.3	87.0	85.4
1990	75.9	79.7	84.2	84.0	83.6	79.3	89.3	89.0	84.7	82.9	83.7	83.7
1991	70.5	78.3	82.3	83.0	81.7	80.6	87.7	84.1	82.7	81.1	78.5	80.7
1992	76.5	76.9	82.7	82.4	85.5	82.9	88.4	86.1	85.3	79.9	81.8	80.0
1993	79.0	77.0	82.7	80.9	87.8	84.0	89.0	84.4	89.0	79.3	86.4	81.2
1994	80.4	76.8	84.5	83.3	90.1	85.1	90.7	83.6	88.9	80.5	91.3	81.4
1995	79.8	79.2	84.5	84.4	86.2	84.9	89.4	82.9	89.5	80.7	89.6	82.2
1996	78.5	80.4	83.2	82.5	82.4	83.6	85.4	82.7	91.7	80.6	88.5	80.6
1997	82.7	78.6	83.9	82.5	84.5	83.6	87.4	81.0	95.2	81.6	89.3	85.6
1998	82.3	78.8	82.3	82.9	82.1	77.4	87.3	79.5	92.7	78.9	88.0	86.8
1999	80.0	76.2	80.3	78.7	81.8	76.5	86.7	77.9	90.4	77.3	86.7	87.1
2000	76.7	75.7	79.0	77.6	79.6	79.3	84.4	77.2	89.0	76.4	82.7	87.2
2001	69.9	71.9	75.7	76.4	71.7	74.2	80.1	74.9	88.1	72.1	76.9	82.6
2002	71.8	73.1	76.0	75.6	73.7	67.1	82.1	75.3	88.6	73.6	79.0	81.4
2003	70.6	74.4	76.8	77.5	72.8	69.9	81.9	74.3	89.7	73.7	79.5	81.5
2004	75.8	74.6	78.6	77.6	74.8	70.6	83.2	75.4	92.8	76.2	83.5	82.7
2005	79.2	77.3	80.2	79.4	78.2	75.7	83.6	76.0	92.0	76.7	84.4	82.0
2006	78.4	76.8	79.6	79.0	75.0	75.0	83.5	74.9	89.4	77.0	82.3	79.9
2007	75.1	73.1	79.3	78.7	71.9	76.2	83.6	76.1	87.6	77.9	79.0	76.4
2008	71.3	74.0	74.2	76.2	67.2	75.8	81.8	70.7	81.7	71.3	70.7	77.4
2009	58.4	69.7	70.3	75.7	56.2	60.1	76.5	61.4	78.3	67.7	61.1	70.0
2010	61.7	74.1	74.5	76.3	63.2	64.7	81.5	65.1	80.4	73.7	70.1	66.6
2011	65.5	75.7	76.5	77.5	65.4	66.7	82.4	66.8	83.9	75.6	72.3	65.1
2012	69.4	77.0	77.4	80.2	68.2	68.1	81.9	67.6	82.9	75.3	74.0	64.2
2013	72.6	76.4	77.8	80.2	69.2	72.7	83.1	69.2	82.8	75.4	76.1	61.7
2014	77.4	75.2	78.7	80.3	71.7	76.3	82.6	72.0	84.4	76.1	78.5	59.4
2013												
January	69.7	77.9	77.9	80.8	68.8	71.1	82.9	68.1	82.9	75.6	75.5	62.1
February	71.3	77.8	78.1	81.4	68.7	71.8	83.4	68.0	83.4	75.2	75.1	61.8
March	72.3	77.5	78.0	80.8	69.1	70.7	83.1	68.7	83.3	75.3	75.9	61.2
April	72.9	76.5	77.7	80.0	68.2	69.3	83.1	68.6	82.4	75.5	75.8	61.1
May	72.6	76.2	77.8	79.8	68.2	71.6	84.3	69.0	82.3	75.9	76.2	61.4
June	73.8	76.5	78.0	80.5	69.1	72.2	83.5	69.0	82.0	75.9	76.3	61.2
July	72.1	76.0	77.7	79.6	68.8	72.5	83.8	68.9	82.5	75.5	76.4	61.9
August	72.8	75.6	77.7	79.7	69.4	73.5	83.8	69.1	82.4	75.4	75.9	62.4
September	72.5	75.8	77.5	79.6	69.5	74.9	82.5	68.4	83.3	74.9	76.3	63.4
October	72.7	75.7	77.7	79.8	69.8	75.0	83.1	69.9	83.1	75.0	76.5	61.9
November	74.1	75.8	77.6	79.8	70.7	74.1	82.1	70.2	83.1	74.9	76.5	60.9
December	74.8	75.7	78.4	80.7	70.5	75.7	82.1	72.2	83.2	75.8	76.5	60.9
2014												
January	73.9	73.8	77.4	79.5	69.2	74.9	82.2	71.0	83.2	74.6	76.0	60.7
February	73.2	74.3	77.8	80.5	67.3	74.3	80.8	71.1	84.0	74.9	76.7	60.8
March	76.1	74.9	78.6	81.1	70.5	76.4	80.9	71.9	84.9	75.5	77.9	60.1
April	76.4	74.7	78.8	81.4	70.9	76.5	83.6	71.1	85.8	75.4	77.0	60.4
May	76.5	75.5	78.2	80.5	70.1	76.0	82.2	71.3	84.1	75.1	78.6	60.6
June	77.2	75.5	78.4	80.1	71.0	75.5	82.5	72.0	82.9	75.7	79.7	60.9
July	78.1	75.2	78.5	79.4	72.6	76.9	82.2	72.4	84.7	76.2	78.8	60.2
August	77.5	74.5	78.7	79.5	72.4	74.3	82.8	72.1	85.0	76.6	79.1	59.3
September	79.0	75.4	79.0	80.1	72.7	76.2	83.0	72.1	84.6	76.8	79.1	58.1
October	79.2	75.5	78.8	79.8	73.6	76.4	83.0	72.5	83.2	76.9	79.0	57.8
November	79.9	76.5	79.7	81.0	74.9	77.5	83.9	73.1	84.6	77.3	80.4	57.5
December	81.3	75.9	79.9	81.0	74.8	80.1	84.5	73.8	85.5	77.7	79.7	56.8

. . . = Not available.

Table 2-3. Capacity Utilization by NAICS Industry Groups—*Continued*

(Output as a percent of capacity, seasonally adjusted.)

Year and month	Mining	Utilities	Selected high-tech industries				Measures excluding selected high-tech industries		Stage-of-process groups		
			Total	Computers and peripheral equipment	Communications equipment	Semiconductors and related electronic components	Total industry	Manufacturing	Crude	Primary and semi-finished	Finished
1968	83.6	95.1	87.7	. . .	. . .	. . .	87.2	87.0	83.4	86.8	87.1
1969	86.7	96.8	89.8	. . .	. . .	. . .	87.1	86.4	85.6	88.1	85.6
1970	89.2	96.3	83.5	. . .	. . .	. . .	81.0	79.2	85.1	81.5	78.1
1971	87.8	94.7	74.4	. . .	. . .	. . .	80.0	78.3	84.2	81.6	75.6
1972	90.7	95.3	78.6	81.6	73.2	84.6	84.9	83.6	88.4	88.2	79.6
1973	91.5	93.3	81.6	82.0	75.1	91.2	88.5	87.9	90.0	92.1	83.2
1974	91.0	86.9	82.0	88.3	73.3	87.6	85.2	84.5	90.9	87.3	80.3
1975	89.3	85.1	65.0	69.0	62.1	64.8	76.2	74.1	83.8	75.3	73.7
1976	89.4	85.5	68.8	76.8	62.0	69.7	80.2	78.8	86.9	80.1	76.8
1977	89.5	86.6	75.9	77.8	72.4	78.2	83.7	82.8	89.1	84.5	79.9
1978	89.7	86.9	79.0	77.8	77.4	82.1	85.3	84.6	88.7	86.2	82.2
1979	91.3	87.0	83.2	78.3	85.6	87.1	85.1	84.0	89.9	85.9	81.8
1980	91.4	85.5	87.8	86.9	91.7	85.1	80.5	78.2	89.4	78.8	79.4
1981	90.9	84.4	85.7	85.3	89.2	83.2	79.3	76.4	89.3	77.2	77.5
1982	84.2	80.2	78.2	70.3	87.1	81.4	73.4	70.4	82.4	70.6	73.0
1983	79.9	79.6	80.5	75.8	85.8	81.5	74.6	73.0	79.9	74.5	73.0
1984	85.9	82.2	87.4	85.4	85.3	90.9	80.1	78.8	85.7	81.2	77.2
1985	84.4	81.9	77.1	76.3	78.5	76.8	79.4	78.2	83.8	79.9	76.6
1986	77.6	81.1	72.7	72.8	75.1	70.9	79.0	78.8	79.1	79.8	77.1
1987	80.3	83.6	77.2	73.8	79.4	79.4	81.4	81.3	82.8	82.9	78.7
1988	84.3	86.7	79.9	76.2	84.0	81.0	84.6	84.4	86.3	85.9	81.8
1989	85.0	86.9	77.9	74.9	79.9	79.4	84.2	83.7	86.7	84.8	81.8
1990	86.6	86.5	77.4	71.4	82.1	80.2	82.8	82.0	87.7	82.7	80.7
1991	84.9	87.9	77.0	73.6	78.4	78.7	80.0	78.6	85.2	79.9	78.3
1992	84.6	86.3	81.0	78.3	79.5	83.3	80.6	79.5	85.5	81.5	78.2
1993	85.4	88.3	79.6	79.8	81.4	78.4	81.6	80.4	85.6	83.2	78.3
1994	86.9	88.4	83.4	75.7	83.0	87.3	83.6	82.8	87.9	86.4	79.2
1995	87.6	89.4	84.9	80.5	79.2	89.4	83.8	82.9	88.7	86.3	79.8
1996	90.3	90.9	82.9	86.0	76.7	84.4	83.4	82.1	89.1	85.5	79.3
1997	91.5	90.4	83.3	81.6	80.2	85.5	84.1	82.9	90.6	86.0	80.2
1998	89.0	92.7	78.8	78.0	84.6	76.4	83.0	81.7	87.1	84.1	80.0
1999	85.8	94.2	85.1	83.1	88.6	84.0	81.3	79.9	86.0	84.2	77.8
2000	90.6	93.9	88.9	80.5	90.9	91.3	80.7	78.7	88.6	84.0	76.6
2001	90.2	89.6	69.5	70.9	69.6	69.0	76.5	74.1	85.6	77.3	72.3
2002	86.2	87.6	59.1	68.8	45.5	63.6	76.1	74.2	83.1	77.3	70.5
2003	88.0	85.8	64.2	73.4	46.1	72.2	76.7	74.7	84.9	78.1	71.4
2004	88.4	84.5	70.6	77.8	52.9	78.5	78.4	76.7	86.6	80.0	73.2
2005	88.7	84.9	73.6	75.8	55.2	83.2	80.3	78.5	86.7	81.7	75.3
2006	90.3	83.0	81.4	77.6	75.0	87.1	80.1	78.3	88.2	81.1	76.0
2007	89.5	85.5	77.8	76.4	76.2	78.3	80.7	78.7	88.7	80.8	77.1
2008	89.8	84.0	81.7	78.6	85.9	81.8	77.4	74.2	87.0	76.8	74.1
2009	80.7	80.7	73.3	90.9	80.8	65.2	68.5	65.3	78.2	66.0	68.5
2010	84.5	82.9	80.8	87.2	80.2	78.0	73.6	70.6	83.9	71.9	72.2
2011	86.3	81.4	78.1	79.5	79.3	77.6	76.2	73.7	85.0	74.4	74.5
2012	86.8	78.4	70.4	71.5	75.8	69.0	77.5	75.8	85.3	75.0	76.3
2013	87.5	79.6	71.2	69.3	77.2	70.4	78.2	76.3	86.0	76.2	76.3
2014	89.0	79.9	70.9	66.8	75.2	70.7	79.5	77.6	86.9	77.6	77.1
2013											
January	86.1	78.4	70.5	69.3	76.8	69.3	77.7	76.1	85.0	75.5	76.1
February	86.5	79.0	69.8	69.3	76.7	68.5	78.1	76.5	85.3	75.9	76.6
March	86.4	81.9	69.9	68.7	76.8	68.7	78.3	76.4	85.2	76.3	76.7
April	86.8	80.8	70.9	68.4	76.9	70.2	78.0	76.1	85.3	76.1	76.3
May	87.1	79.3	71.8	68.5	76.9	71.3	78.0	76.1	86.1	75.8	76.2
June	87.6	77.9	71.4	68.6	76.9	70.8	78.0	76.3	86.3	75.5	76.6
July	88.4	77.4	71.9	70.2	76.8	71.3	77.8	75.8	86.8	75.5	75.6
August	88.4	77.1	72.4	70.9	76.9	71.8	78.1	76.3	86.9	75.8	76.0
September	89.5	79.2	71.8	71.1	77.3	70.9	78.5	76.4	87.4	76.4	76.2
October	87.4	80.3	71.9	69.6	77.8	71.3	78.4	76.5	85.9	76.9	76.1
November	87.8	81.8	71.7	69.5	78.1	70.9	78.7	76.6	86.2	77.4	76.1
December	87.6	81.8	70.8	67.8	78.8	69.8	78.8	76.7	86.1	77.2	76.2
2014											
January	87.9	84.5	70.3	63.8	76.2	70.3	78.4	75.8	86.0	77.4	75.1
February	87.5	84.2	71.0	64.8	74.5	71.3	78.9	76.7	85.8	77.7	76.3
March	88.3	83.7	71.1	65.6	73.4	71.4	79.4	77.2	86.4	77.9	77.0
April	89.6	79.4	71.6	63.0	74.7	72.3	79.3	77.3	87.4	77.1	77.0
May	89.8	79.5	72.7	64.4	75.6	73.4	79.4	77.4	87.4	77.4	77.1
June	90.5	77.9	72.3	66.6	75.8	72.4	79.5	77.6	87.9	77.5	77.0
July	90.0	75.5	71.4	66.3	75.4	71.3	79.6	78.2	87.6	77.2	77.7
August	90.0	76.0	70.6	69.3	73.3	70.2	79.4	77.8	87.7	77.1	77.1
September	90.2	79.1	70.4	68.7	73.6	70.0	79.8	77.8	87.8	77.8	77.1
October	88.4	79.4	70.5	69.0	76.2	69.6	79.5	77.8	86.6	77.7	77.2
November	87.2	82.2	70.0	70.9	77.2	68.5	80.2	77.8	86.6	77.7	78.4
December	88.8	78.0	69.1	68.8	76.9	67.7	80.0	78.5	86.7	77.7	78.0

. . . = Not available.

Table 2-4A. Industrial Production and Capacity Utilization, Historical Data, 1947–2014

(Seasonally adjusted.)

Year and month	Production indexes, 2007 = 100									Capacity utilization (output as percent of capacity)	
	Total industry	Manufac-turing (SIC)	Market groups								Total industry	Manufac-turing (SIC)
			Consumer goods			Business equipment	Defense and space equipment	Construction supplies	Business supplies	Materials		
			Total	Durable	Nondurable							
1947	13.8	12.5	18.1	12.0	21.3	6.0	6.8	21.3	11.7	13.7	. . .	. . .
1948	14.4	13.0	18.7	12.5	21.9	6.3	8.0	22.8	12.1	14.3	. . .	82.5
1949	13.6	12.3	18.6	11.9	22.1	5.5	8.3	20.9	12.0	13.1	. . .	74.2
1950	15.7	14.3	21.2	15.8	23.9	5.9	9.8	25.2	13.4	15.6	. . .	82.8
1951	17.1	15.4	21.0	13.8	24.8	7.2	24.1	26.2	14.2	17.3	. . .	85.8
1952	17.7	16.1	21.5	13.3	25.8	8.1	33.9	26.0	14.1	17.6	. . .	85.4
1953	19.2	17.5	22.8	15.6	26.5	8.5	40.6	27.9	15.0	19.5	. . .	89.3
1954	18.2	16.4	22.6	14.5	26.8	7.4	35.7	27.5	15.2	18.0	. . .	80.1
1955	20.5	18.5	25.3	17.8	28.9	8.1	32.7	31.6	17.1	21.3	. . .	87.0
1956	21.4	19.2	26.2	17.3	30.8	9.3	32.0	32.5	18.1	21.8	. . .	86.1
1957	21.7	19.4	26.8	17.2	31.7	9.7	33.4	32.1	18.3	21.8	. . .	83.6
1958	20.3	18.1	26.6	15.3	32.7	8.2	33.5	31.0	18.1	19.7	. . .	75.0
1959	22.7	20.4	29.2	18.1	34.9	9.2	35.4	34.7	19.7	22.7	. . .	81.6
1960	23.2	20.8	30.3	19.1	36.0	9.5	36.3	33.9	20.4	23.0	. . .	80.1
1961	23.4	20.8	30.9	18.9	37.2	9.2	36.9	34.2	21.1	23.0	. . .	77.3
1962	25.3	22.7	33.0	21.3	39.0	10.0	42.7	36.3	22.4	25.1	. . .	81.4
1963	26.8	24.1	34.8	23.2	40.7	10.5	46.1	38.0	23.8	26.7	. . .	83.5
1964	28.6	25.7	36.8	24.9	42.7	11.7	44.6	40.3	25.5	28.8	. . .	85.6
1965	31.5	28.5	39.7	29.2	44.6	13.4	49.4	42.7	27.2	32.1	. . .	89.5
1966	34.3	31.1	41.7	30.9	46.7	15.5	58.0	44.5	29.3	35.0	. . .	91.1
1967	35.0	31.7	42.7	29.7	49.1	15.8	66.2	45.7	30.8	34.7	87.0	87.2
1968	37.0	33.4	45.3	33.1	51.0	16.5	66.3	48.1	32.7	36.9	87.3	87.1
1969	38.7	34.9	47.0	34.5	52.8	17.6	63.2	50.2	34.8	39.1	87.4	86.6
1970	37.4	33.4	46.4	31.8	53.7	17.0	53.5	48.4	34.9	37.8	81.2	79.4
1971	37.9	33.9	49.1	36.0	55.2	16.2	48.1	49.9	36.0	38.3	79.6	77.9
1972	41.6	37.4	53.1	40.3	58.7	18.4	46.8	56.7	39.6	42.2	84.7	83.4
1973	45.0	40.8	55.5	43.4	60.5	21.3	51.2	61.5	42.1	46.0	88.3	87.7
1974	44.8	40.7	53.9	39.5	60.6	22.5	52.9	60.0	41.9	45.9	85.1	84.4
1975	40.9	36.4	51.7	35.8	59.5	20.1	53.4	50.8	38.7	40.8	75.8	73.7
1976	44.1	39.7	55.9	40.4	63.3	21.4	51.8	54.7	41.2	44.4	79.8	78.3
1977	47.4	43.1	59.4	45.4	65.6	24.8	46.4	59.6	44.7	47.5	83.4	82.5
1978	50.0	45.7	61.3	46.5	67.9	27.9	47.3	63.0	47.1	49.9	85.1	84.4
1979	51.5	47.1	60.4	44.8	67.5	31.5	50.6	64.6	48.7	51.2	85.0	84.0
1980	50.2	45.5	58.1	39.0	67.6	32.2	60.1	59.8	47.6	49.3	80.8	78.7
1981	50.9	46.0	58.6	39.6	67.9	33.2	65.1	58.8	48.8	49.6	79.6	76.9
1982	48.3	43.5	58.4	37.3	69.1	30.4	77.9	53.4	48.2	45.8	73.6	70.9
1983	49.6	45.6	60.5	41.4	69.9	30.6	78.3	57.2	50.5	47.0	74.9	73.4
1984	54.0	50.0	63.3	46.4	71.3	35.1	89.8	62.2	54.9	51.5	80.4	79.3
1985	54.7	50.8	63.9	46.4	72.2	36.4	100.5	63.7	56.3	51.4	79.2	78.1
1986	55.2	52.0	66.1	49.3	73.9	35.9	106.7	65.9	58.1	51.3	78.6	78.4
1987	58.1	54.9	68.9	52.3	76.6	38.3	109.0	70.1	61.6	54.0	81.2	81.0
1988	61.1	57.8	71.5	54.8	79.1	42.3	109.9	71.7	63.9	57.1	84.3	84.1
1989	61.6	58.3	71.8	56.1	78.9	43.7	110.1	71.4	64.8	57.5	83.8	83.3
1990	62.2	58.8	72.1	54.5	80.2	45.3	106.1	70.9	66.3	57.8	82.5	81.7
1991	61.3	57.6	72.1	52.1	81.4	44.6	98.3	67.0	65.4	57.0	79.8	78.5
1992	63.0	59.7	74.2	57.1	82.0	46.4	91.1	69.8	66.9	58.8	80.6	79.6
1993	65.1	61.8	76.5	61.7	83.2	48.6	86.0	72.8	69.0	60.8	81.4	80.4
1994	68.5	65.4	79.7	67.2	85.2	51.8	80.7	78.1	71.8	64.7	83.6	82.8
1995	71.8	68.8	82.0	69.9	87.3	56.5	77.8	79.8	74.8	68.4	83.9	83.1
1996	74.9	72.2	83.5	72.1	88.5	62.1	75.7	83.4	77.7	71.9	83.4	82.1
1997	80.4	78.2	86.5	77.0	90.5	71.2	74.6	87.4	83.2	77.7	84.1	83.0
1998	85.0	83.4	89.5	82.6	92.5	79.1	77.7	92.1	87.9	82.3	82.7	81.5
1999	88.7	87.6	91.5	89.0	92.5	83.5	75.4	94.4	91.6	87.3	81.7	80.4
2000	92.2	91.3	93.2	91.6	93.9	89.7	67.0	96.5	95.3	91.8	81.4	79.6
2001	89.1	87.5	92.2	87.3	94.1	84.1	73.6	92.1	91.7	87.7	76.0	73.6
2002	89.3	87.8	94.0	92.5	94.6	78.5	74.4	92.2	91.9	88.6	74.9	73.0
2003	90.4	88.9	95.3	95.3	95.2	78.3	79.1	92.0	93.4	89.8	75.9	73.9
2004	92.5	91.4	96.4	97.0	96.1	82.1	77.2	94.2	95.1	92.4	78.0	76.2
2005	95.5	95.0	99.0	97.9	99.3	87.7	84.9	98.7	98.2	94.6	79.9	78.2
2006	97.6	97.4	99.5	98.3	99.9	95.8	84.1	101.1	99.2	96.5	80.2	78.4
2007	100.0	100.0	100.0	100.0	100.0	100.0	100.0	100.0	100.0	100.0	80.5	78.7
2008	96.6	95.3	95.1	88.8	97.2	97.7	106.9	90.7	96.0	97.6	77.6	74.6
2009	85.7	82.4	88.6	74.0	93.4	80.1	102.4	69.9	86.0	86.6	68.7	65.6
2010	90.6	87.3	89.6	79.4	92.9	86.7	110.5	72.5	88.0	94.2	73.8	71.1
2011	93.6	90.3	90.9	83.3	93.4	91.5	106.7	74.7	88.9	98.6	76.3	73.9
2012	97.1	94.0	92.5	90.0	93.5	98.3	111.8	78.1	90.5	103.1	77.3	75.5
2013	99.9	96.5	94.7	96.9	94.5	101.9	114.4	81.4	92.4	106.4	77.9	76.1
2014	104.1	99.8	97.4	102.7	96.3	107.0	116.5	84.9	94.7	111.8	79.1	77.2
1948												
January	14.3	12.9	18.7	12.6	21.8	6.3	7.1	22.9	12.0	14.0	. . .	. . .
February	14.3	12.9	18.8	12.4	22.0	6.3	7.4	22.7	12.1	14.1	. . .	. . .
March	14.2	12.9	18.5	12.5	21.7	6.3	7.6	22.8	12.1	13.9	. . .	. . .
April	14.2	12.9	18.7	12.4	22.0	6.3	7.7	22.6	12.0	13.8	. . .	. . .
May	14.4	13.0	18.6	12.1	22.0	6.3	7.6	22.8	12.1	14.5	. . .	. . .
June	14.6	13.1	18.9	12.7	22.2	6.3	7.8	22.6	12.2	14.6	. . .	. . .
July	14.6	13.2	18.9	13.0	21.9	6.4	8.0	23.2	12.1	14.7	. . .	. . .
August	14.6	13.1	18.7	12.8	21.8	6.4	8.2	23.1	12.3	14.5	. . .	. . .
September	14.5	13.0	18.6	12.4	21.8	6.3	8.4	22.8	12.1	14.5	. . .	. . .
October	14.6	13.1	18.8	12.8	21.9	6.2	8.5	23.3	12.2	14.5	. . .	. . .
November	14.4	12.9	18.6	12.3	22.0	6.2	8.7	22.6	12.2	14.4	. . .	. . .
December	14.3	12.8	18.4	11.8	21.8	6.2	8.7	22.4	12.2	14.3	. . .	. . .

. . . = Not available.

Table 2-4A. Industrial Production and Capacity Utilization, Historical Data, 1947–2014—*Continued*

(Seasonally adjusted.)

Year and month	Total industry	Manufac-turing (SIC)	Consumer goods			Business equipment	Defense and space equipment	Construction supplies	Business supplies	Materials	Total industry	Manufac-turing (SIC)
			Total	Durable	Nondurable							
1949												
January	14.1	12.7	18.2	11.5	21.7	6.0	8.6	21.8	12.0	14.1	. . .	77.9
February	14.0	12.5	18.1	11.3	21.8	6.0	8.6	21.3	11.8	14.0	. . .	76.9
March	13.7	12.4	18.3	11.3	22.0	5.8	8.5	21.1	11.9	13.4	. . .	75.9
April	13.6	12.2	18.2	11.3	21.9	5.8	8.4	20.7	11.8	13.2	. . .	74.2
May	13.4	12.1	18.2	11.2	22.0	5.6	8.5	20.5	11.9	12.9	. . .	73.2
June	13.4	12.1	18.4	11.5	22.0	5.5	8.6	20.5	11.9	12.7	. . .	73.1
July	13.4	12.1	18.6	11.9	22.1	5.4	8.5	20.2	11.9	12.6	. . .	73.1
August	13.5	12.3	18.8	12.1	22.3	5.4	8.4	20.4	12.0	12.8	. . .	73.6
September	13.7	12.5	19.1	12.5	22.4	5.3	8.3	21.1	12.1	13.1	. . .	74.8
October	13.2	12.0	19.1	12.7	22.5	5.1	8.0	20.4	12.3	11.7	. . .	71.7
November	13.5	12.1	18.9	12.0	22.4	5.0	8.0	21.1	12.2	12.8	. . .	72.0
December	13.7	12.4	18.7	11.9	22.2	5.0	7.9	22.0	12.3	13.4	. . .	73.6
1950												
January	14.0	12.7	19.4	13.3	22.7	5.1	7.8	21.7	12.4	13.5	. . .	74.9
February	14.0	12.8	19.5	13.2	22.7	5.2	7.8	22.6	12.7	13.3	. . .	75.4
March	14.5	13.0	19.9	13.8	23.0	5.3	7.9	23.1	12.8	14.2	. . .	76.4
April	15.0	13.6	20.4	14.8	23.3	5.4	8.1	24.3	13.0	14.8	. . .	79.2
May	15.3	13.9	20.9	15.5	23.5	5.7	8.4	24.5	13.1	15.2	. . .	81.0
June	15.8	14.3	21.4	16.8	23.7	5.9	8.7	25.4	13.2	15.8	. . .	83.1
July	16.3	14.8	22.1	17.5	24.2	6.1	9.1	26.1	13.5	16.2	. . .	85.5
August	16.8	15.3	22.8	18.1	25.1	6.4	10.1	26.6	13.9	16.7	. . .	88.4
September	16.7	15.2	22.2	17.2	24.7	6.3	11.1	26.6	13.8	16.7	. . .	87.2
October	16.8	15.3	22.1	16.9	24.6	6.4	11.9	26.9	14.0	17.1	. . .	87.5
November	16.8	15.3	22.0	16.5	24.6	6.4	12.8	26.9	14.0	16.9	. . .	87.0
December	17.1	15.5	22.3	16.4	25.3	6.5	13.8	26.9	14.2	17.2	. . .	88.1
1951												
January	17.1	15.6	22.4	16.1	25.7	6.6	15.4	27.2	14.4	17.0	. . .	88.3
February	17.2	15.6	22.4	16.1	25.6	6.7	17.8	26.9	14.2	17.1	. . .	88.3
March	17.3	15.7	22.1	16.0	25.1	6.8	20.2	27.0	14.5	17.5	. . .	88.4
April	17.3	15.7	21.7	15.3	25.0	7.0	22.1	26.9	14.8	17.6	. . .	88.2
May	17.3	15.6	21.3	14.5	24.8	7.1	22.8	26.7	14.6	17.7	. . .	87.4
June	17.2	15.6	21.0	13.8	24.7	7.1	24.0	26.5	14.4	17.8	. . .	86.6
July	16.9	15.3	20.3	12.4	24.5	7.2	25.4	25.9	14.2	17.5	. . .	84.9
August	16.8	15.1	19.9	11.5	24.3	7.3	26.2	25.8	14.1	17.2	. . .	83.6
September	16.9	15.2	20.1	12.0	24.3	7.5	27.1	25.7	14.0	17.3	. . .	83.7
October	16.9	15.1	19.9	11.9	24.2	7.6	28.2	25.5	13.6	17.1	. . .	83.1
November	17.0	15.3	20.3	12.2	24.6	7.7	29.8	25.3	13.7	17.1	. . .	83.6
December	17.1	15.4	20.4	12.3	24.7	7.8	30.5	25.3	13.8	17.1	. . .	83.9
1952												
January	17.3	15.5	20.6	12.3	25.0	8.0	31.0	25.7	13.8	17.5	. . .	84.4
February	17.4	15.6	20.7	12.2	25.3	8.1	31.3	25.9	13.8	17.4	. . .	84.6
March	17.4	15.7	20.8	12.5	25.3	8.2	31.4	25.7	13.9	17.4	. . .	84.7
April	17.3	15.6	20.8	12.4	25.3	8.1	31.8	25.3	13.8	17.1	. . .	83.6
May	17.1	15.5	20.8	12.7	25.1	8.2	32.8	24.9	13.7	16.8	. . .	83.1
June	17.0	15.4	21.4	12.9	26.0	8.2	33.8	24.8	14.0	15.9	. . .	81.9
July	16.7	15.0	21.0	11.6	26.0	7.8	34.0	24.7	14.1	15.5	. . .	79.8
August	17.8	16.1	21.4	12.8	26.1	8.0	34.5	26.4	14.2	17.5	. . .	85.1
September	18.4	16.7	22.0	14.1	26.1	8.2	35.1	26.7	14.4	18.6	. . .	87.7
October	18.6	16.9	22.3	14.6	26.3	8.2	36.3	27.0	14.6	18.5	. . .	88.8
November	19.0	17.3	22.8	15.5	26.6	8.4	37.0	27.5	14.7	19.1	. . .	90.2
December	19.1	17.4	22.8	15.6	26.6	8.4	38.1	27.6	14.7	19.1	. . .	90.5
1953												
January	19.1	17.4	23.0	16.2	26.5	8.5	38.7	28.1	14.5	19.0	. . .	90.5
February	19.2	17.6	23.2	16.3	26.7	8.5	39.5	28.5	14.8	19.5	. . .	91.1
March	19.4	17.7	23.2	16.5	26.6	8.6	40.3	28.6	15.1	19.7	. . .	91.4
April	19.5	17.8	23.1	16.3	26.7	8.6	40.8	28.7	15.1	19.9	. . .	91.5
May	19.6	17.9	23.2	16.4	26.8	8.6	41.5	28.1	15.2	20.3	. . .	91.7
June	19.5	17.8	22.9	15.8	26.7	8.5	41.8	27.9	15.2	20.3	. . .	90.7
July	19.8	17.9	22.9	15.7	26.6	8.6	42.1	28.3	15.3	20.5	. . .	91.0
August	19.6	17.9	22.8	15.6	26.5	8.6	41.8	28.1	15.3	20.0	. . .	90.6
September	19.2	17.5	22.5	14.9	26.4	8.5	41.8	27.6	15.2	19.5	. . .	88.3
October	19.1	17.3	22.5	14.8	26.5	8.5	41.4	27.7	15.0	18.9	. . .	87.2
November	18.6	16.9	22.1	14.3	26.3	8.2	38.7	27.2	15.0	18.4	. . .	84.7
December	18.2	16.4	21.8	13.8	26.0	8.1	39.0	26.6	14.8	18.0	. . .	82.3
1954												
January	18.0	16.3	21.9	13.6	26.3	7.8	38.2	27.1	14.8	17.8	. . .	81.3
February	18.1	16.2	22.1	13.9	26.5	7.7	38.0	27.2	14.9	17.7	. . .	80.8
March	18.0	16.2	22.2	13.9	26.5	7.6	37.5	27.0	14.9	17.6	. . .	80.2
April	17.9	16.1	22.2	14.0	26.4	7.5	36.8	27.0	15.0	17.5	. . .	79.4
May	18.0	16.2	22.3	14.3	26.4	7.5	36.3	27.3	15.0	17.8	. . .	79.8
June	18.0	16.2	22.4	14.4	26.5	7.4	35.7	26.7	15.1	18.0	. . .	79.9
July	18.1	16.2	22.5	14.2	26.8	7.4	35.6	26.6	14.9	18.1	. . .	79.4
August	18.0	16.1	22.5	14.4	26.8	7.3	34.8	26.5	15.0	18.0	. . .	78.8
September	18.1	16.2	22.8	14.5	27.0	7.2	34.5	27.8	15.5	17.8	. . .	79.2
October	18.3	16.4	22.8	14.7	27.1	7.2	34.1	28.7	15.6	18.2	. . .	79.7
November	18.6	16.7	23.3	15.1	27.6	7.3	33.9	29.0	15.8	18.5	. . .	80.9
December	18.8	16.9	23.7	15.7	27.8	7.4	33.4	29.2	16.0	18.9	. . .	81.8

. . . = Not available.

Table 2-4A. Industrial Production and Capacity Utilization, Historical Data, 1947–2014—*Continued*

(Seasonally adjusted.)

Year and month	Production indexes, 2007 = 100										Capacity utilization (output as percent of capacity)	
	Total industry	Manufac-turing (SIC)	Market groups								Total industry	Manufac-turing (SIC)
			Consumer goods			Business equipment	Defense and space equipment	Construction supplies	Business supplies	Materials		
			Total	Durable	Nondurable							
1955												
January	19.2	17.4	24.3	16.8	27.9	7.4	33.2	29.7	16.2	19.5	. . .	83.5
February	19.5	17.5	24.4	16.9	27.9	7.5	33.2	30.1	16.4	20.0	. . .	84.1
March	19.9	18.0	24.8	17.4	28.4	7.6	33.0	31.1	16.8	20.5	. . .	85.8
April	20.2	18.2	25.0	17.7	28.6	7.9	33.0	31.3	16.7	20.9	. . .	86.7
May	20.5	18.5	25.3	18.1	28.8	8.0	33.0	31.4	17.0	21.3	. . .	87.9
June	20.5	18.6	25.1	17.8	28.7	8.1	32.7	32.0	17.1	21.4	. . .	87.6
July	20.7	18.6	25.2	18.0	28.7	8.1	32.6	32.0	17.1	21.7	. . .	87.7
August	20.7	18.6	25.3	18.0	28.7	8.2	32.4	32.0	17.0	21.6	. . .	87.3
September	20.8	18.7	25.4	18.1	29.0	8.2	32.5	32.2	17.4	21.9	. . .	87.5
October	21.1	19.0	25.9	18.2	29.7	8.6	32.3	32.2	17.5	22.1	. . .	88.4
November	21.2	19.0	26.0	18.0	29.9	8.6	32.3	32.6	17.8	22.0	. . .	88.3
December	21.3	19.3	26.1	17.9	30.2	8.8	32.4	32.8	17.6	22.2	. . .	89.0
1956												
January	21.4	19.2	26.1	17.8	30.3	8.8	32.0	33.3	17.8	22.3	. . .	88.2
February	21.2	19.1	26.1	17.4	30.4	9.0	31.7	33.2	17.8	21.9	. . .	87.4
March	21.2	19.1	26.0	17.5	30.4	9.1	31.0	33.1	18.0	21.8	. . .	87.0
April	21.4	19.3	26.1	17.7	30.4	9.3	31.2	33.0	18.2	21.9	. . .	87.8
May	21.2	19.1	26.0	17.3	30.5	9.3	31.3	32.5	18.0	21.5	. . .	86.3
June	21.0	18.9	25.9	16.9	30.6	9.3	31.3	32.1	18.0	21.2	. . .	85.3
July	20.4	18.2	26.0	16.9	30.7	9.3	31.3	30.5	18.0	19.5	. . .	81.5
August	21.2	19.0	26.1	16.9	30.9	9.4	31.7	32.0	18.1	21.3	. . .	84.9
September	21.7	19.3	26.1	16.7	31.0	9.5	32.0	32.9	18.1	22.5	. . .	86.0
October	21.9	19.5	26.3	16.9	31.2	9.6	32.8	32.6	18.2	22.8	. . .	86.5
November	21.7	19.4	26.2	16.6	31.1	9.7	33.3	32.4	18.2	22.3	. . .	85.8
December	22.0	19.7	26.4	17.3	31.0	9.8	34.1	33.0	18.3	22.7	. . .	86.8
1957												
January	21.9	19.7	26.5	17.4	31.2	10.0	34.2	32.5	18.4	22.3	. . .	86.2
February	22.1	19.9	26.9	17.7	31.5	10.2	34.4	33.5	18.4	22.4	. . .	87.0
March	22.1	19.9	26.9	17.6	31.7	10.1	34.4	32.9	18.3	22.3	. . .	86.4
April	21.8	19.6	26.7	17.1	31.6	9.9	34.5	32.2	18.4	22.0	. . .	85.0
May	21.7	19.5	26.7	17.0	31.7	9.8	33.9	32.1	18.5	21.9	. . .	84.2
June	21.8	19.6	26.8	17.3	31.7	9.8	34.1	32.3	18.3	22.0	. . .	84.6
July	21.9	19.6	26.9	17.1	32.0	9.8	33.8	32.4	18.4	22.2	. . .	84.3
August	21.9	19.6	27.1	17.6	31.9	9.8	33.8	32.1	18.4	22.2	. . .	84.2
September	21.7	19.5	27.1	17.5	32.0	9.7	33.1	31.9	18.4	21.9	. . .	83.2
October	21.4	19.1	26.7	16.9	31.7	9.4	32.3	31.5	18.2	21.6	. . .	81.4
November	20.9	18.7	26.6	16.9	31.6	9.2	31.2	31.1	18.0	20.8	. . .	79.4
December	20.5	18.3	26.4	16.1	31.9	8.9	31.0	30.7	18.0	20.1	. . .	77.5
1958												
January	20.1	17.9	26.1	15.5	31.8	8.7	31.4	30.3	17.9	19.5	. . .	75.7
February	19.7	17.5	25.9	14.9	31.8	8.4	31.6	29.3	17.8	18.9	. . .	73.8
March	19.5	17.3	25.7	14.4	31.8	8.2	32.2	29.1	17.9	18.4	. . .	72.7
April	19.1	17.0	25.4	13.9	31.8	8.1	32.7	28.8	17.7	18.0	. . .	71.3
May	19.3	17.2	25.8	14.4	32.1	7.9	33.1	29.7	17.7	18.2	. . .	71.9
June	19.8	17.8	26.3	14.8	32.6	7.9	34.0	30.9	17.9	18.9	. . .	73.9
July	20.1	17.9	26.7	15.0	33.0	7.9	34.1	30.7	17.9	19.4	. . .	74.3
August	20.5	18.3	26.8	15.3	33.0	8.1	34.4	32.1	18.2	20.0	. . .	75.7
September	20.7	18.5	26.5	14.2	33.2	8.1	34.6	32.2	18.4	20.5	. . .	76.2
October	21.0	18.6	26.7	14.9	33.2	8.2	34.6	32.1	18.7	20.9	. . .	76.4
November	21.6	19.3	28.0	17.5	33.6	8.4	34.9	33.4	18.8	21.5	. . .	79.1
December	21.6	19.3	28.1	17.5	33.6	8.4	34.9	33.0	18.7	21.5	. . .	79.0
1959												
January	21.9	19.6	28.5	17.6	34.1	8.6	35.1	33.6	19.2	21.9	. . .	80.2
February	22.4	20.0	28.7	17.7	34.4	8.7	34.7	34.5	19.4	22.6	. . .	81.4
March	22.7	20.3	28.7	18.0	34.3	8.8	34.9	35.4	19.5	23.2	. . .	82.5
April	23.2	20.7	29.1	18.1	34.8	9.1	35.1	36.4	19.5	23.8	. . .	84.0
May	23.5	21.0	29.3	18.5	34.8	9.3	35.4	36.7	19.5	24.4	. . .	84.9
June	23.5	21.1	29.1	18.7	34.6	9.6	35.5	36.6	19.7	24.2	. . .	84.8
July	23.0	20.7	29.5	19.0	34.9	9.6	35.6	35.1	20.0	22.8	. . .	83.0
August	22.2	19.9	29.5	18.5	35.3	9.5	35.4	32.9	19.9	21.1	. . .	79.5
September	22.2	19.8	29.4	17.9	35.5	9.4	35.6	32.6	20.0	21.1	. . .	79.0
October	22.0	19.6	29.3	18.4	35.0	9.4	35.6	32.7	20.0	20.8	. . .	78.2
November	22.1	19.8	28.7	16.1	35.5	9.2	35.5	33.8	20.0	21.7	. . .	78.5
December	23.5	21.1	29.6	18.1	35.6	9.3	35.8	36.4	20.1	24.0	. . .	83.6
1960												
January	24.1	21.7	30.6	20.1	35.8	9.7	36.1	36.2	20.4	24.7	. . .	85.6
February	23.9	21.5	30.2	19.9	35.4	9.8	36.3	35.8	20.4	24.4	. . .	84.6
March	23.7	21.3	30.2	19.5	35.8	9.8	36.4	34.7	20.4	24.0	. . .	83.2
April	23.5	21.1	30.4	19.4	36.1	9.7	36.2	34.7	20.6	23.4	. . .	82.3
May	23.5	21.0	30.6	19.6	36.3	9.7	36.6	34.3	20.8	23.2	. . .	81.5
June	23.2	20.7	30.4	19.4	36.1	9.6	35.7	33.7	20.5	22.8	. . .	80.2
July	23.1	20.7	30.1	18.7	36.1	9.5	36.6	34.0	20.6	22.8	. . .	79.7
August	23.1	20.6	30.2	18.9	36.1	9.3	36.8	33.2	20.4	22.7	. . .	79.1
September	22.8	20.4	30.1	18.7	36.0	9.3	36.7	32.9	20.3	22.4	. . .	77.9
October	22.8	20.4	30.4	18.9	36.4	9.2	36.3	33.0	20.4	22.3	. . .	77.5
November	22.5	20.0	29.8	18.2	36.0	9.2	36.4	32.6	20.4	21.7	. . .	75.8
December	22.1	19.6	29.6	17.6	36.0	8.9	35.9	32.2	20.0	21.1	. . .	74.3

. . . = Not available.

Table 2-4A. Industrial Production and Capacity Utilization, Historical Data, 1947–2014—*Continued*

(Seasonally adjusted.)

Year and month	Production indexes, 2007 = 100										Capacity utilization (output as percent of capacity)	
	Total industry	Manufac-turing (SIC)	Market groups								Total industry	Manufac-turing (SIC)
			Consumer goods			Business equipment	Defense and space equipment	Construction supplies	Business supplies	Materials		
			Total	Durable	Nondurable							
1961												
January	22.1	19.7	29.4	17.0	36.1	9.0	36.3	31.9	20.3	21.3	. . .	74.1
February	22.1	19.6	29.5	16.9	36.3	8.9	36.0	31.8	20.4	21.1	. . .	73.5
March	22.2	19.7	29.5	16.9	36.3	8.9	35.9	32.6	20.6	21.3	. . .	73.9
April	22.7	20.2	30.2	18.1	36.7	9.0	36.0	33.4	20.7	22.0	. . .	75.4
May	23.0	20.5	30.6	18.7	36.9	9.0	36.0	33.5	20.8	22.6	. . .	76.4
June	23.3	20.8	30.9	19.3	37.1	9.1	36.0	34.2	20.9	23.0	. . .	77.3
July	23.6	21.1	31.2	19.6	37.2	9.1	36.3	34.8	21.2	23.3	. . .	78.1
August	23.8	21.3	31.4	19.7	37.6	9.2	36.4	35.2	21.3	23.7	. . .	79.0
September	23.8	21.2	30.9	18.6	37.4	9.3	37.2	35.5	21.2	23.8	. . .	78.2
October	24.2	21.6	31.7	19.6	38.0	9.3	38.1	35.7	21.5	24.2	. . .	79.6
November	24.6	22.0	32.3	20.5	38.4	9.6	39.0	35.5	21.7	24.5	. . .	80.8
December	24.8	22.3	32.4	20.9	38.4	9.6	39.7	35.7	21.9	24.9	. . .	81.6
1962												
January	24.6	22.0	32.1	20.4	38.2	9.6	40.1	34.1	21.9	24.7	. . .	80.2
February	25.0	22.4	32.3	20.5	38.5	9.7	40.8	36.0	22.1	25.1	. . .	81.4
March	25.1	22.6	32.6	20.8	38.7	9.8	41.4	36.5	22.0	25.1	. . .	81.9
April	25.2	22.6	32.8	21.3	38.7	9.9	41.7	36.0	22.0	25.1	. . .	81.7
May	25.2	22.5	33.0	21.5	39.0	9.9	42.0	36.0	22.4	24.8	. . .	81.3
June	25.1	22.5	32.8	21.1	38.9	10.0	42.4	36.2	22.4	24.7	. . .	80.9
July	25.4	22.7	33.4	21.6	39.4	10.1	43.3	36.1	22.3	24.9	. . .	81.5
August	25.4	22.7	33.0	21.3	39.0	10.2	43.9	36.7	22.5	24.9	. . .	81.4
September	25.5	22.9	33.2	21.5	39.2	10.2	44.0	37.2	22.7	25.2	. . .	81.8
October	25.6	22.9	33.1	21.6	39.1	10.2	44.1	36.5	22.6	25.2	. . .	81.4
November	25.7	23.1	33.3	21.7	39.2	10.2	44.6	36.7	22.8	25.4	. . .	81.8
December	25.7	23.1	33.5	21.8	39.4	10.1	44.7	37.0	22.6	25.2	. . .	81.7
1963												
January	25.9	23.2	33.9	22.0	40.0	10.1	46.8	36.1	22.8	25.3	. . .	81.9
February	26.2	23.4	34.3	22.3	40.4	10.2	46.5	36.2	23.0	25.7	. . .	82.4
March	26.3	23.6	34.4	22.3	40.6	10.2	46.2	36.6	22.8	26.1	. . .	82.6
April	26.6	23.9	34.6	22.5	40.7	10.3	46.2	37.8	23.6	26.3	. . .	83.5
May	26.9	24.1	34.6	22.9	40.6	10.2	46.2	38.7	23.8	26.9	. . .	84.0
June	27.0	24.2	34.8	23.3	40.7	10.3	46.1	38.5	23.7	27.0	. . .	83.9
July	26.9	24.1	34.7	23.2	40.5	10.4	45.7	38.4	23.9	26.8	. . .	83.3
August	26.9	24.2	35.0	23.3	40.9	10.7	45.8	38.5	24.0	26.5	. . .	83.5
September	27.2	24.4	35.1	23.7	40.8	10.7	46.0	38.2	24.2	27.1	. . .	83.8
October	27.4	24.6	35.4	23.7	41.1	10.8	46.0	38.8	24.4	27.2	. . .	84.3
November	27.5	24.6	35.4	24.0	41.1	10.9	45.8	39.2	24.7	27.4	. . .	84.3
December	27.5	24.6	35.6	24.0	41.5	10.9	46.0	38.7	24.5	27.2	. . .	84.0
1964												
January	27.7	24.9	35.9	24.1	41.9	11.2	45.5	38.9	24.8	27.4	. . .	84.5
February	27.9	25.0	35.9	24.2	41.7	11.1	45.1	39.9	24.9	27.9	. . .	84.7
March	27.9	25.0	35.7	24.0	41.6	11.3	45.0	40.0	25.1	27.9	. . .	84.4
April	28.3	25.5	36.6	24.7	42.6	11.5	44.9	40.2	25.4	28.2	. . .	85.6
May	28.5	25.6	36.9	24.8	43.0	11.7	44.1	40.4	25.6	28.4	. . .	85.6
June	28.6	25.6	36.8	25.1	42.7	11.7	43.9	40.1	25.7	28.6	. . .	85.4
July	28.8	25.8	37.3	25.5	43.3	11.9	43.8	40.9	25.7	28.7	. . .	85.9
August	29.0	26.0	37.3	25.7	43.0	11.9	44.0	40.5	25.6	29.3	. . .	86.1
September	29.1	26.1	36.8	25.1	42.7	12.0	44.3	40.2	25.6	29.7	. . .	86.2
October	28.7	25.7	36.1	22.5	43.3	11.9	44.6	40.3	25.6	29.2	. . .	84.6
November	29.5	26.5	37.5	25.5	43.4	12.3	45.1	41.3	25.8	30.1	. . .	86.8
December	29.9	27.0	38.2	27.0	43.7	12.5	45.4	40.7	26.1	30.4	. . .	88.0
1965												
January	30.2	27.3	38.8	27.5	44.3	12.5	45.9	41.0	26.3	30.8	. . .	88.6
February	30.4	27.5	38.9	27.9	44.2	12.7	46.4	42.1	26.4	30.9	. . .	88.7
March	30.8	27.8	39.2	28.6	44.2	12.8	47.2	42.4	26.7	31.4	. . .	89.3
April	30.9	28.0	39.1	28.6	44.1	13.0	47.8	41.8	26.7	31.7	. . .	89.3
May	31.2	28.2	39.4	28.8	44.4	13.1	48.8	42.2	27.0	31.8	. . .	89.4
June	31.4	28.4	39.5	29.0	44.4	13.3	49.4	42.3	27.1	32.2	. . .	89.5
July	31.7	28.8	39.5	29.2	44.3	13.6	50.2	43.5	27.1	32.5	. . .	90.3
August	31.9	28.8	39.5	28.9	44.4	13.6	50.6	43.0	27.4	32.8	. . .	89.9
September	31.9	28.9	40.0	29.5	45.0	13.8	50.7	42.7	27.4	32.5	. . .	89.6
October	32.3	29.1	40.3	29.8	45.1	14.0	51.4	43.3	27.7	32.9	. . .	89.8
November	32.4	29.2	40.5	30.0	45.4	14.3	51.8	43.9	27.9	32.8	. . .	89.6
December	32.8	29.7	40.7	30.6	45.3	14.6	52.4	44.9	28.3	33.1	. . .	90.5
1966												
January	33.1	30.0	40.9	30.7	45.6	14.9	53.5	44.8	28.3	33.6	. . .	90.9
February	33.3	30.2	41.0	30.6	45.8	14.8	54.3	44.4	28.6	33.9	. . .	90.9
March	33.8	30.6	41.3	30.9	46.2	15.1	54.7	45.2	28.9	34.6	. . .	91.6
April	33.8	30.8	41.5	31.4	46.1	15.2	55.9	45.2	28.6	34.5	. . .	91.5
May	34.2	31.0	41.5	30.9	46.4	15.4	56.9	45.5	29.0	34.9	. . .	91.6
June	34.3	31.1	41.6	30.9	46.6	15.6	57.7	44.8	29.4	35.1	. . .	91.5
July	34.5	31.3	41.6	30.4	46.9	15.8	58.5	45.2	29.7	35.2	. . .	91.4
August	34.5	31.3	41.4	29.9	47.0	15.9	59.3	43.9	29.6	35.5	. . .	91.1
September	34.9	31.6	41.6	30.1	47.1	16.1	60.1	43.9	29.8	35.8	. . .	91.2
October	35.1	31.9	42.4	31.6	47.5	16.0	61.0	44.0	29.8	36.0	. . .	91.6
November	34.9	31.6	42.2	30.7	47.7	15.8	62.1	44.0	29.9	35.4	. . .	90.1
December	34.9	31.7	42.1	30.3	47.8	16.0	62.8	43.9	29.9	35.4	. . .	90.0

. . . = Not available.

Table 2-4A. Industrial Production and Capacity Utilization, Historical Data, 1947–2014—Continued

(Seasonally adjusted.)

Year and month	Total industry	Manufac-turing (SIC)	Production indexes, 2007 = 100								Capacity utilization (output as percent of capacity)	
			Market groups								Total industry	Manufac-turing (SIC)
			Consumer goods			Business equipment	Defense and space equipment	Construction supplies	Business supplies	Materials		
			Total	Durable	Nondurable							
1967												
January	35.1	31.8	42.5	29.6	48.9	15.9	63.8	45.1	30.5	35.3	89.4	89.8
February	34.7	31.4	41.9	28.8	48.5	15.9	64.6	44.7	30.3	34.6	88.0	88.4
March	34.5	31.3	42.1	29.0	48.5	15.9	65.3	44.8	30.4	34.0	87.1	87.5
April	34.8	31.5	42.8	29.2	49.5	15.9	65.9	44.6	30.6	34.3	87.5	87.7
May	34.5	31.3	42.0	28.8	48.5	15.9	66.4	45.3	30.1	33.9	86.4	86.6
June	34.5	31.2	42.1	28.5	48.9	15.9	66.2	45.6	30.3	33.9	86.0	86.1
July	34.5	31.1	42.0	28.9	48.5	15.5	66.6	45.8	30.4	33.8	85.4	85.3
August	35.1	31.7	42.4	29.2	49.0	15.8	66.7	46.3	31.2	34.9	86.6	86.5
September	35.1	31.7	42.5	29.1	49.2	15.8	66.9	46.7	31.3	34.6	86.1	86.1
October	35.3	31.9	43.1	29.7	49.7	15.6	67.4	46.4	31.5	35.1	86.4	86.4
November	35.8	32.5	44.0	31.3	50.1	16.0	67.6	46.7	31.6	35.5	87.3	87.5
December	36.2	32.8	44.7	32.6	50.5	16.2	67.5	46.7	31.6	35.9	87.8	88.0
1968												
January	36.2	32.8	44.1	31.6	50.1	16.3	67.3	47.0	31.7	36.1	87.4	87.4
February	36.3	32.9	44.4	32.1	50.2	16.3	68.0	47.5	31.9	36.1	87.4	87.4
March	36.4	33.0	44.6	32.1	50.7	16.4	66.7	47.6	31.9	36.2	87.3	87.2
April	36.5	33.0	44.6	32.1	50.6	16.3	65.4	47.8	32.2	36.5	87.1	86.9
May	36.9	33.4	44.8	32.5	50.7	16.6	66.3	48.0	32.5	37.0	87.7	87.6
June	37.0	33.5	45.1	32.8	50.9	16.5	66.6	48.1	32.7	37.2	87.7	87.4
July	37.0	33.4	45.0	32.5	50.9	16.4	66.7	48.1	32.6	37.2	87.2	86.7
August	37.1	33.5	45.5	33.0	51.5	16.5	66.8	48.3	33.0	37.0	87.1	86.8
September	37.2	33.6	45.7	33.3	51.6	16.7	66.8	47.9	33.1	37.1	87.1	86.5
October	37.3	33.8	46.0	33.7	51.7	16.9	65.0	47.9	33.3	37.2	86.9	86.6
November	37.8	34.3	46.6	34.5	52.2	16.9	65.7	49.0	33.7	37.7	87.7	87.5
December	37.9	34.3	46.3	34.8	51.5	17.0	65.3	49.9	33.9	37.9	87.7	87.1
1969												
January	38.1	34.5	46.6	34.7	52.0	17.3	65.4	50.3	34.0	38.1	87.9	87.3
February	38.4	34.7	46.9	34.7	52.6	17.3	65.0	50.7	33.9	38.5	88.1	87.7
March	38.7	35.0	47.3	34.9	53.0	17.4	65.2	50.9	35.0	38.7	88.5	88.0
April	38.5	34.9	46.6	34.0	52.5	17.6	64.7	50.5	34.5	38.8	87.8	87.3
May	38.4	34.7	46.2	33.5	52.2	17.5	64.6	50.1	34.8	38.7	87.2	86.6
June	38.8	34.9	46.8	34.7	52.3	17.7	63.7	50.4	35.1	39.3	87.7	86.8
July	39.0	35.2	47.6	34.7	53.6	17.9	63.4	49.9	34.9	39.3	87.9	87.1
August	39.1	35.2	47.5	35.0	53.2	17.8	62.5	49.9	35.0	39.7	87.8	86.9
September	39.0	35.2	47.1	34.7	52.9	18.0	62.1	49.9	35.0	39.8	87.4	86.5
October	39.1	35.2	47.1	34.9	52.8	18.0	61.5	50.1	35.1	39.8	87.2	86.2
November	38.7	34.9	46.7	33.4	53.1	17.6	60.4	49.8	34.9	39.6	86.0	85.0
December	38.6	34.7	46.8	33.3	53.3	17.5	59.7	49.5	35.3	39.3	85.5	84.2
1970												
January	37.9	33.9	46.0	31.5	53.2	17.3	58.9	47.9	35.2	38.4	83.7	82.1
February	37.8	33.9	46.5	32.0	53.6	17.4	57.9	47.8	35.0	38.2	83.3	81.9
March	37.8	33.8	46.4	32.3	53.3	17.4	56.6	48.2	35.2	38.1	83.0	81.4
April	37.7	33.7	46.6	32.3	53.6	17.4	55.3	48.7	35.0	37.9	82.5	80.9
May	37.7	33.6	46.9	32.3	54.0	17.4	54.1	48.7	34.9	37.7	82.1	80.5
June	37.5	33.5	47.0	32.9	53.8	17.3	53.2	48.5	34.9	37.6	81.6	80.0
July	37.6	33.6	47.1	33.0	53.9	17.2	52.3	49.1	35.0	37.8	81.6	80.0
August	37.6	33.4	46.3	32.0	53.3	17.2	51.9	48.9	34.7	38.2	81.2	79.2
September	37.3	33.1	46.1	31.1	53.6	16.8	51.4	48.8	34.9	37.9	80.4	78.3
October	36.6	32.4	45.5	29.3	53.9	16.3	50.7	48.3	34.8	36.9	78.5	76.3
November	36.3	32.2	45.2	29.4	53.4	16.2	50.3	47.7	34.9	36.7	77.8	75.6
December	37.2	33.0	47.2	32.8	54.3	16.4	49.7	48.2	34.9	37.6	79.4	77.3
1971												
January	37.4	33.3	47.9	34.1	54.5	16.0	50.1	48.2	35.1	38.1	79.7	77.8
February	37.4	33.3	47.9	34.8	54.0	16.1	48.9	48.6	35.4	37.9	79.4	77.6
March	37.3	33.3	48.0	34.9	54.2	15.9	48.5	48.4	35.1	37.9	79.1	77.2
April	37.5	33.4	48.4	35.1	54.7	15.9	48.5	48.8	35.5	38.2	79.3	77.4
May	37.7	33.7	48.4	35.7	54.4	15.7	49.1	49.1	35.6	38.6	79.5	77.8
June	37.9	33.8	48.8	35.9	54.8	15.8	48.4	49.6	35.4	38.8	79.7	77.8
July	37.8	33.8	49.5	36.6	55.5	15.8	48.0	50.0	36.3	37.9	79.2	77.7
August	37.6	33.4	49.0	36.2	54.9	16.1	48.0	49.2	35.9	37.6	78.6	76.6
September	38.2	34.1	49.4	36.2	55.6	16.5	47.5	51.0	36.5	38.4	79.7	77.9
October	38.5	34.6	50.1	36.8	56.3	16.6	47.2	51.7	36.7	38.5	80.1	78.9
November	38.6	34.7	50.5	37.2	56.7	16.7	46.8	51.9	37.1	38.5	80.2	79.0
December	39.1	35.0	50.8	37.4	57.1	16.8	46.1	52.8	37.3	39.3	80.9	79.5
1972												
January	40.0	35.9	47.9	38.5	57.6	17.3	46.1	54.2	37.9	40.6	82.7	81.4
February	40.4	36.2	47.9	38.6	57.9	17.6	46.2	54.4	38.6	41.0	83.2	81.8
March	40.7	36.5	48.0	38.4	58.2	17.8	46.6	54.8	39.0	41.4	83.7	82.2
April	41.1	36.9	48.4	39.5	58.4	18.1	46.8	55.4	39.0	41.8	84.3	82.9
May	41.1	36.9	48.4	39.2	58.2	18.1	46.4	55.7	39.2	41.9	84.1	82.7
June	41.2	37.1	48.8	39.2	58.2	18.2	46.4	56.2	39.5	42.0	84.1	82.8
July	41.2	37.1	49.5	40.0	58.3	18.2	46.3	57.0	39.5	41.7	83.8	82.6
August	41.7	37.6	49.0	40.4	59.0	18.5	46.3	57.4	40.0	42.3	84.7	83.5
September	42.0	37.9	49.4	40.8	59.2	18.7	46.7	57.9	40.0	42.7	85.1	83.9
October	42.6	38.4	50.1	41.7	59.9	19.1	46.7	58.7	40.7	43.1	86.0	84.9
November	43.1	38.9	50.5	42.7	59.8	19.5	48.0	59.2	40.8	43.8	86.8	85.7
December	43.6	39.4	50.8	43.6	60.0	19.7	48.8	59.0	40.9	44.5	87.5	86.6

Table 2-4A. Industrial Production and Capacity Utilization, Historical Data, 1947–2014—*Continued*

(Seasonally adjusted.)

Year and month	Total industry	Manufac-turing (SIC)	Production indexes, 2007 = 100								Capacity utilization (output as percent of capacity)	
			Market groups								Total industry	Manufac-turing (SIC)
			Consumer goods			Business equipment	Defense and space equipment	Construction supplies	Business supplies	Materials		
			Total	Durable	Nondurable							
1973												
January	43.9	39.7	55.1	43.4	59.9	20.0	49.4	59.7	41.2	44.8	87.8	86.9
February	44.6	40.4	55.8	44.2	60.5	20.5	50.4	60.8	41.7	45.5	88.8	88.1
March	44.6	40.4	55.9	44.3	60.7	20.6	50.2	61.2	41.7	45.4	88.6	88.0
April	44.5	40.4	55.4	43.6	60.2	20.8	50.0	61.0	41.7	45.5	88.1	87.5
May	44.8	40.6	55.7	43.5	60.8	21.0	50.3	61.3	41.9	45.8	88.4	87.8
June	44.8	40.6	55.3	43.4	60.3	21.2	50.8	61.4	42.0	45.8	88.1	87.4
July	45.0	40.8	55.2	43.3	60.1	21.4	51.9	61.9	42.2	46.0	88.2	87.5
August	44.9	40.7	54.7	42.0	60.2	21.5	51.9	62.0	42.2	46.1	87.8	87.0
September	45.3	41.0	55.6	43.4	60.7	21.9	51.9	61.9	42.3	46.3	88.3	87.5
October	45.6	41.4	55.8	43.1	61.2	22.1	53.1	61.8	42.7	46.6	88.6	87.9
November	45.9	41.7	55.9	43.1	61.5	22.3	52.6	62.3	42.7	47.0	88.8	88.3
December	45.8	41.7	54.9	42.2	60.4	22.4	52.3	62.7	42.3	47.2	88.3	88.1
1974												
January	45.4	41.4	54.2	40.1	60.7	22.4	52.1	62.8	42.4	46.8	87.4	87.1
February	45.3	41.2	54.0	39.9	60.5	22.3	52.5	62.1	42.2	46.7	86.9	86.5
March	45.3	41.2	54.1	40.0	60.6	22.5	52.5	62.2	42.2	46.5	86.7	86.2
April	45.2	41.0	53.9	39.7	60.5	22.3	52.4	61.7	42.3	46.5	86.2	85.6
May	45.5	41.3	54.4	39.8	61.2	22.6	52.6	61.9	42.5	46.8	86.6	85.9
June	45.5	41.3	54.6	40.4	61.3	22.7	51.8	61.6	42.7	46.6	86.4	85.8
July	45.5	41.2	54.5	40.2	61.1	22.6	52.4	60.4	42.3	46.8	86.2	85.4
August	45.0	40.9	54.5	40.2	61.1	22.6	53.5	59.7	42.2	45.9	85.2	84.5
September	45.1	41.0	54.0	40.1	60.4	23.1	53.6	59.3	41.9	46.1	85.1	84.4
October	44.9	40.6	54.1	39.6	60.8	23.1	54.4	58.2	41.7	45.8	84.6	83.6
November	43.4	39.4	52.5	37.7	59.5	22.8	54.1	56.3	40.8	43.8	81.6	80.9
December	41.9	37.7	50.9	34.6	59.0	21.8	53.5	53.7	40.0	42.1	78.6	77.1
1975												
January	41.3	36.9	49.7	33.2	58.0	21.4	53.8	53.5	39.4	41.8	77.4	75.5
February	40.4	35.9	49.0	32.2	57.6	20.6	51.1	51.9	38.6	40.8	75.5	73.2
March	39.9	35.4	49.2	32.6	57.5	20.3	51.6	49.9	38.0	40.2	74.6	72.1
April	40.0	35.3	50.2	33.9	58.4	20.1	51.3	49.4	38.2	39.9	74.5	71.9
May	39.9	35.3	50.5	34.7	58.2	19.9	53.7	49.5	38.0	39.7	74.2	71.7
June	40.2	35.7	51.2	35.1	59.2	19.7	54.5	49.2	38.1	40.0	74.6	72.2
July	40.6	36.2	52.5	36.9	60.1	19.8	53.9	50.0	38.5	40.2	75.3	73.2
August	40.9	36.5	52.8	37.4	60.2	19.7	53.5	50.5	38.8	40.8	75.8	73.7
September	41.5	37.1	53.5	38.1	60.9	20.0	55.1	51.0	38.9	41.3	76.6	74.7
October	41.6	37.3	53.6	38.0	61.1	20.0	55.0	51.3	39.1	41.5	76.7	74.9
November	41.7	37.4	53.8	38.0	61.4	20.0	52.8	51.5	39.2	41.7	76.8	75.0
December	42.3	37.9	54.2	38.7	61.7	20.3	54.4	51.6	39.6	42.3	77.6	75.8
1976												
January	42.9	38.4	55.0	39.4	62.5	20.6	54.3	52.9	40.0	43.0	78.6	76.7
February	43.3	38.9	55.2	39.8	62.4	20.7	54.3	53.7	40.2	43.6	79.1	77.6
March	43.3	39.0	55.0	39.8	62.3	20.8	54.3	52.9	40.3	43.8	79.0	77.6
April	43.6	39.3	55.2	39.8	62.5	21.0	53.1	53.6	40.5	44.1	79.4	78.0
May	43.8	39.5	55.7	39.8	63.2	21.2	52.7	54.2	40.7	44.2	79.5	78.2
June	43.8	39.5	55.4	39.6	63.0	21.2	52.0	54.6	40.4	44.3	79.4	78.0
July	44.0	39.8	55.8	39.8	63.4	21.4	50.6	55.8	41.1	44.4	79.7	78.4
August	44.3	40.0	55.9	40.4	63.2	21.8	50.7	55.2	41.2	44.9	80.0	78.7
September	44.5	40.1	55.9	40.2	63.4	21.7	50.3	55.6	42.1	45.0	80.1	78.8
October	44.5	40.1	56.4	40.7	63.8	21.8	50.2	55.6	42.3	44.7	80.0	78.6
November	45.2	40.6	57.3	42.0	64.5	22.5	49.9	55.9	42.5	45.3	80.9	79.4
December	45.6	41.1	57.9	43.0	64.8	22.9	48.9	56.2	42.9	45.8	81.6	80.0
1977												
January	45.4	40.9	57.8	42.8	64.7	22.9	48.3	55.3	42.8	45.4	80.9	79.6
February	46.0	41.7	58.5	43.3	65.5	23.4	48.2	56.5	43.3	46.0	81.9	80.7
March	46.6	42.3	58.5	44.5	64.8	23.8	47.2	57.7	43.6	46.9	82.8	81.7
April	47.0	42.7	58.9	44.9	65.2	24.2	47.5	59.1	44.1	47.3	83.4	82.4
May	47.4	43.1	59.0	45.1	65.1	24.7	47.4	60.0	44.5	47.7	83.8	82.9
June	47.8	43.5	59.4	46.0	65.2	25.2	47.3	60.5	44.9	47.9	84.2	83.3
July	47.9	43.5	59.6	46.0	65.4	25.4	47.2	60.5	45.1	47.9	84.1	83.1
August	47.9	43.7	59.6	46.0	65.5	25.4	46.9	61.0	45.3	47.8	83.9	83.3
September	48.1	43.8	59.8	46.2	65.6	25.6	47.0	60.7	45.5	48.2	84.1	83.2
October	48.2	43.9	60.3	46.2	66.4	25.5	42.8	60.8	45.5	48.4	84.1	83.1
November	48.3	43.9	60.2	46.2	66.4	25.5	42.4	61.0	45.5	48.4	83.9	83.0
December	48.3	44.4	60.8	46.4	67.1	25.8	45.2	61.7	45.9	48.0	83.8	83.6
1978												
January	47.7	43.8	59.3	44.0	66.3	25.3	45.8	60.5	45.8	47.5	82.4	82.1
February	47.9	43.9	60.3	45.1	67.1	25.9	43.4	60.3	45.9	47.4	82.5	82.2
March	48.8	44.7	61.4	46.5	68.1	26.7	47.3	61.5	46.6	48.1	83.9	83.4
April	49.8	45.4	61.8	47.4	68.2	27.3	47.1	62.8	46.7	49.6	85.3	84.4
May	50.0	45.5	61.4	46.6	68.0	27.3	47.3	62.8	46.9	50.1	85.4	84.4
June	50.3	45.9	61.8	46.9	68.4	27.8	47.9	63.3	47.4	50.3	85.7	84.8
July	50.3	45.9	61.5	46.9	67.8	28.0	47.8	63.2	47.3	50.3	85.4	84.5
August	50.5	46.1	61.4	46.7	67.8	28.6	48.3	63.3	47.3	50.4	85.5	84.7
September	50.7	46.3	61.5	46.4	68.2	28.9	48.4	63.6	47.5	50.5	85.6	84.8
October	51.1	46.7	61.4	46.6	68.0	29.5	47.9	64.2	47.7	51.1	86.0	85.2
November	51.4	47.1	61.6	46.7	68.2	30.0	47.6	64.6	47.9	51.5	86.4	85.7
December	51.7	47.5	61.8	46.9	68.4	30.3	48.3	65.7	48.3	51.7	86.7	86.1

Table 2-4A. Industrial Production and Capacity Utilization, Historical Data, 1947–2014—*Continued*

(Seasonally adjusted.)

Year and month	Production indexes, 2007 = 100										Capacity utilization (output as percent of capacity)	
	Total industry	Manufac-turing (SIC)	Market groups								Total industry	Manufac-turing (SIC)
			Consumer goods			Business equipment	Defense and space equipment	Construction supplies	Business supplies	Materials		
			Total	Durable	Nondurable							
1979												
January	51.4	47.1	61.6	47.2	67.9	30.6	48.6	64.0	48.3	51.0	85.9	85.1
February	51.7	47.3	61.2	46.7	67.7	31.0	49.6	64.5	48.8	51.4	86.1	85.2
March	51.8	47.5	61.5	46.6	68.1	31.2	49.2	65.3	49.0	51.5	86.2	85.4
April	51.3	46.7	60.4	44.3	67.8	30.6	48.0	64.2	48.7	51.2	85.0	83.8
May	51.7	47.3	60.7	45.6	67.6	31.4	48.8	64.6	48.9	51.5	85.5	84.6
June	51.7	47.4	60.5	45.0	67.5	31.6	49.2	64.9	48.6	51.5	85.3	84.5
July	51.6	47.4	60.0	44.5	67.1	31.9	50.1	64.9	48.7	51.3	85.0	84.4
August	51.3	46.8	59.3	42.6	67.3	31.5	50.8	64.2	48.9	51.1	84.2	83.1
September	51.3	47.0	59.7	44.1	66.9	32.4	51.2	64.4	48.3	50.8	84.1	83.1
October	51.6	47.1	59.8	43.8	67.3	31.9	52.8	64.8	48.8	51.3	84.4	83.2
November	51.5	47.0	59.7	43.1	67.5	31.9	54.0	64.7	49.0	51.1	84.2	82.8
December	51.6	47.1	59.7	42.9	67.7	32.1	55.1	64.9	49.0	51.1	84.0	82.8
1980												
January	51.8	47.3	59.4	42.1	67.7	32.7	55.8	64.7	48.6	51.4	84.2	82.9
February	51.8	47.3	59.7	41.9	68.3	32.8	58.0	63.7	48.7	51.3	84.1	82.7
March	51.7	46.9	59.3	41.1	68.1	32.6	58.6	63.0	48.6	51.3	83.7	81.9
April	50.6	46.0	58.3	39.4	67.7	32.3	59.2	60.0	47.8	50.0	81.8	80.0
May	49.4	44.6	57.1	36.9	67.3	31.7	59.5	57.6	46.8	48.6	79.7	77.4
June	48.8	43.9	56.8	36.3	67.3	31.4	60.2	56.4	46.3	47.7	78.5	76.1
July	48.5	43.5	56.9	36.2	67.4	31.4	60.7	56.1	46.5	47.0	77.9	75.2
August	48.6	43.8	57.1	36.5	67.5	31.4	60.9	56.8	46.7	47.1	77.9	75.5
September	49.4	44.5	57.6	38.2	67.2	31.9	61.0	58.2	47.3	48.1	79.0	76.5
October	50.0	45.3	58.0	38.9	67.5	32.6	61.9	59.5	47.4	48.7	79.8	77.6
November	50.9	46.2	58.3	39.9	67.3	33.1	62.7	60.7	48.0	49.9	81.0	78.9
December	51.2	46.3	58.3	39.3	67.6	33.2	62.9	60.7	48.5	50.3	81.3	78.9
1981												
January	50.9	46.2	58.3	39.2	67.8	33.3	62.6	60.5	48.6	49.8	80.6	78.4
February	50.7	45.9	58.2	39.0	67.7	32.9	62.5	60.0	48.1	49.6	80.1	77.7
March	50.9	46.0	58.2	39.6	67.3	33.2	62.6	60.2	48.1	49.9	80.3	77.8
April	50.7	46.3	58.3	40.1	67.2	33.6	62.6	60.2	48.4	49.2	79.7	77.9
May	51.0	46.5	58.9	40.7	67.8	33.6	63.1	60.2	49.0	49.5	80.0	78.1
June	51.3	46.3	58.5	40.3	67.4	33.4	63.5	59.2	49.2	50.2	80.2	77.5
July	51.6	46.4	58.9	40.5	67.9	33.4	64.3	59.3	49.4	50.5	80.5	77.4
August	51.6	46.4	58.9	40.3	68.0	33.5	65.2	59.2	49.1	50.5	80.3	77.3
September	51.2	46.2	58.4	39.3	67.7	33.4	66.4	58.7	49.2	50.1	79.6	76.7
October	50.9	45.7	58.7	39.2	68.5	33.3	67.9	57.0	48.8	49.4	78.8	75.8
November	50.3	45.2	58.7	38.5	68.8	32.8	69.6	56.1	48.6	48.5	77.8	74.7
December	49.8	44.4	58.1	36.9	68.9	32.3	71.4	55.1	48.5	47.9	76.7	73.3
1982												
January	48.8	43.4	57.1	35.9	68.0	31.1	70.7	53.3	47.8	47.1	75.1	71.4
February	49.7	44.6	58.6	37.2	69.5	32.1	74.6	55.1	48.8	47.6	76.4	73.2
March	49.4	44.2	58.2	37.0	69.0	31.7	75.8	53.9	48.6	47.3	75.7	72.4
April	48.9	43.9	58.2	37.8	68.6	31.3	76.7	53.6	48.4	46.7	74.9	71.8
May	48.6	43.8	58.3	37.8	68.6	31.1	78.2	53.9	48.1	46.2	74.3	71.6
June	48.5	43.8	58.6	38.0	69.0	30.5	78.5	53.4	48.1	46.0	73.9	71.3
July	48.3	43.7	58.8	38.2	69.1	30.5	79.6	53.3	48.1	45.7	73.5	71.2
August	47.9	43.4	58.6	37.7	69.2	29.8	79.5	53.3	48.1	45.2	72.8	70.5
September	47.8	43.3	58.6	37.2	69.5	29.6	80.5	53.5	48.2	45.0	72.5	70.2
October	47.4	42.8	58.7	36.7	69.9	29.0	80.0	52.7	48.0	44.4	71.8	69.3
November	47.2	42.5	58.5	36.7	69.7	28.8	80.3	52.4	48.0	44.2	71.5	68.8
December	46.8	42.4	57.8	36.6	68.5	29.1	79.7	52.0	47.8	43.9	70.9	68.5
1983												
January	47.7	43.4	59.0	38.2	69.5	29.2	79.3	53.9	48.4	44.9	72.2	70.1
February	47.4	43.3	58.3	38.1	68.4	29.1	77.9	53.6	48.3	44.7	71.7	70.0
March	47.8	43.8	58.5	38.6	68.4	29.4	78.0	54.3	49.1	45.1	72.3	70.7
April	48.4	44.3	59.7	39.5	69.8	29.4	77.3	55.0	49.6	45.7	73.2	71.4
May	48.7	44.8	59.9	40.3	69.7	29.8	77.1	56.0	49.7	46.0	73.7	72.3
June	49.0	45.1	60.1	41.0	69.5	30.0	76.5	57.0	49.9	46.3	74.0	72.8
July	49.8	45.8	60.9	41.9	70.2	30.6	77.4	58.2	50.6	47.1	75.1	73.8
August	50.3	46.1	61.5	42.7	70.6	30.8	77.9	58.4	51.1	47.7	75.9	74.3
September	51.1	47.0	62.3	43.5	71.4	31.7	78.8	59.2	52.0	48.4	77.0	75.7
October	51.5	47.5	61.9	44.0	70.5	32.1	79.7	60.1	52.2	49.1	77.6	76.5
November	51.6	47.7	61.9	44.0	70.5	32.3	80.1	59.9	52.4	49.3	77.8	76.7
December	51.9	47.8	62.0	45.0	70.0	32.7	80.9	60.1	52.5	49.5	78.1	76.8
1984												
January	52.9	48.7	63.3	46.1	71.4	33.4	83.2	60.5	53.5	50.5	79.6	78.1
February	53.2	49.3	63.2	46.2	71.1	33.7	84.9	61.9	53.6	50.8	79.9	78.9
March	53.5	49.5	63.4	46.3	71.4	34.0	85.5	61.5	54.1	51.0	80.1	79.1
April	53.8	49.7	63.6	46.3	71.7	34.3	87.6	61.9	54.1	51.4	80.5	79.4
May	54.1	49.9	63.3	45.8	71.6	34.5	88.5	62.1	54.8	51.8	80.8	79.4
June	54.2	50.1	63.3	45.9	71.4	35.0	89.6	62.5	55.1	51.9	80.9	79.6
July	54.4	50.3	63.3	46.4	71.1	35.4	88.7	62.3	55.3	52.1	81.0	79.8
August	54.5	50.4	62.9	46.7	70.4	35.8	91.7	62.5	55.4	52.0	80.9	79.7
September	54.4	50.3	62.8	46.1	70.6	36.0	93.8	62.8	55.3	51.8	80.6	79.4
October	54.3	50.5	63.3	45.7	71.6	36.2	94.5	62.5	55.6	51.3	80.3	79.4
November	54.5	50.7	63.5	46.4	71.5	36.5	93.8	62.4	55.9	51.5	80.4	79.5
December	54.6	50.9	63.8	46.9	71.7	36.8	95.6	63.1	55.5	51.3	80.3	79.5

Table 2-4A. Industrial Production and Capacity Utilization, Historical Data, 1947–2014—*Continued*

(Seasonally adjusted.)

Year and month	Total industry	Manufac-turing (SIC)	Consumer goods Total	Durable	Nondurable	Business equipment	Defense and space equipment	Construction supplies	Business supplies	Materials	Capacity utilization Total industry	Manufac-turing (SIC)
1985												
January	54.4	50.7	63.4	46.4	71.3	36.6	96.0	61.9	55.6	51.4	79.9	79.0
February	54.7	50.5	63.9	46.0	72.3	36.4	96.9	62.1	56.1	51.6	80.0	78.5
March	54.7	50.9	63.8	46.5	71.9	36.7	98.4	63.7	56.0	51.5	79.9	78.9
April	54.6	50.7	63.4	45.8	71.7	36.4	98.7	63.7	56.3	51.5	79.5	78.3
May	54.7	50.8	63.5	45.8	71.8	36.5	99.2	63.9	56.5	51.5	79.4	78.2
June	54.7	50.9	63.7	45.7	72.3	36.6	100.6	64.4	56.1	51.4	79.3	78.2
July	54.3	50.6	63.4	45.8	71.8	36.3	99.7	64.0	55.7	51.0	78.6	77.5
August	54.6	50.9	63.8	46.3	72.0	36.4	101.4	64.2	56.3	51.1	78.8	77.8
September	54.8	50.9	64.2	46.3	72.6	36.3	102.0	64.2	56.7	51.4	78.9	77.7
October	54.6	50.8	64.1	46.0	72.6	36.2	103.1	64.3	56.2	51.1	78.5	77.4
November	54.8	51.1	64.4	47.1	72.5	36.6	104.4	64.3	56.4	51.1	78.6	77.8
December	55.3	51.3	65.1	47.3	73.5	36.5	105.5	64.0	57.2	51.8	79.3	78.0
1986												
January	55.6	51.9	65.8	48.5	73.9	36.5	106.1	65.5	57.6	51.9	79.6	78.8
February	55.2	51.6	65.2	48.1	73.2	36.1	104.6	64.8	57.1	51.7	79.0	78.2
March	54.9	51.4	65.0	48.2	72.9	36.1	105.6	65.0	56.9	51.2	78.4	78.0
April	54.9	51.6	65.4	48.1	73.5	35.9	105.8	65.6	57.4	51.1	78.4	78.2
May	55.0	51.7	65.8	48.2	74.0	35.8	106.2	66.0	57.8	51.0	78.4	78.3
June	54.8	51.5	65.9	48.8	73.8	35.4	106.6	65.3	58.3	50.8	78.1	77.9
July	55.2	51.9	66.3	49.4	74.2	35.6	107.6	65.8	58.3	51.2	78.5	78.3
August	55.0	52.0	66.2	49.6	73.9	35.7	107.5	66.4	58.3	50.9	78.3	78.4
September	55.1	52.1	66.3	50.0	73.8	35.7	107.2	66.4	58.4	51.0	78.3	78.4
October	55.4	52.3	66.6	50.0	74.2	35.7	107.5	66.4	58.8	51.3	78.6	78.6
November	55.6	52.5	67.0	50.7	74.6	35.7	108.1	66.6	58.9	51.6	78.8	78.8
December	56.1	53.0	67.6	51.6	75.0	36.1	108.2	67.0	59.7	52.0	79.4	79.4
1987												
January	56.0	52.8	67.0	51.3	74.1	36.2	108.6	67.7	59.2	51.9	79.6	78.9
February	56.7	53.6	67.8	52.2	74.9	37.0	109.2	69.0	59.7	52.5	79.0	79.9
March	56.8	53.6	68.0	51.9	75.4	36.9	108.9	68.6	60.1	52.6	78.4	79.8
April	57.1	53.9	67.9	51.6	75.4	37.2	109.0	69.0	60.7	53.1	78.4	80.0
May	57.5	54.3	68.5	51.9	76.1	37.5	108.7	69.5	61.4	53.4	78.4	80.4
June	57.8	54.5	68.6	51.4	76.6	37.9	108.3	69.8	61.7	53.7	78.1	80.5
July	58.2	54.9	69.0	51.3	77.3	38.0	108.0	70.0	62.1	54.1	78.5	80.9
August	58.6	55.2	69.5	51.8	77.7	38.5	109.0	70.5	62.3	54.5	78.3	81.1
September	58.7	55.5	69.1	52.2	76.9	39.1	109.3	70.8	62.5	54.7	78.3	81.4
October	59.6	56.4	70.4	53.9	77.9	40.0	109.0	71.9	63.0	55.5	78.6	82.6
November	60.0	56.8	70.4	53.9	78.0	40.4	109.5	71.9	63.0	56.0	78.8	82.9
December	60.2	57.1	70.5	53.5	78.4	40.8	110.4	72.5	63.1	56.3	79.4	83.3
1988												
January	60.3	57.0	70.9	53.2	79.0	40.9	112.7	71.3	63.4	56.1	83.4	83.1
February	60.5	57.1	71.2	53.2	79.5	41.1	111.1	71.9	63.8	56.3	83.7	83.2
March	60.6	57.3	71.2	53.7	79.2	41.5	110.3	72.2	63.8	56.5	83.8	83.4
April	61.0	57.8	71.6	54.9	79.2	42.0	109.3	71.9	63.8	56.9	84.2	84.0
May	60.9	57.7	71.3	54.9	78.8	42.2	109.2	72.1	63.3	56.9	84.1	83.9
June	61.1	57.8	71.3	55.2	78.7	42.6	108.4	71.6	63.5	57.1	84.3	84.0
July	61.1	57.8	71.3	53.9	79.3	42.3	109.7	71.6	63.8	57.3	84.4	84.0
August	61.4	57.8	71.9	54.4	79.9	42.4	109.4	71.1	64.4	57.5	84.7	84.0
September	61.2	58.0	71.4	55.4	78.6	42.7	109.8	71.4	63.9	57.2	84.4	84.2
October	61.5	58.3	71.9	55.9	79.2	43.1	109.9	71.6	64.2	57.4	84.7	84.6
November	61.6	58.5	72.0	56.5	78.9	43.2	109.7	71.9	64.1	57.6	84.8	84.8
December	61.9	58.7	72.3	57.2	79.1	43.3	110.2	72.1	64.4	57.9	85.1	85.0
1989												
January	62.0	59.2	72.3	58.4	78.4	43.7	110.3	73.3	64.4	58.0	85.2	85.6
February	61.8	58.6	72.4	57.8	78.8	43.6	110.2	71.5	64.6	57.6	84.7	84.6
March	62.0	58.6	72.5	56.9	79.6	43.4	109.4	71.7	65.3	57.8	84.8	84.4
April	62.0	58.7	72.4	57.4	79.1	44.0	111.0	71.7	64.8	57.7	84.7	84.4
May	61.6	58.2	71.6	56.1	78.6	43.4	111.5	71.1	64.5	57.5	84.0	83.5
June	61.6	58.3	71.7	55.4	79.1	44.0	111.2	71.2	64.8	57.3	83.9	83.5
July	61.0	57.7	70.2	53.7	77.7	43.5	111.7	71.2	64.2	57.0	82.9	82.4
August	61.5	58.1	71.3	55.6	78.4	44.1	112.2	71.2	64.5	57.3	83.4	82.8
September	61.4	58.0	71.0	55.6	78.0	44.0	111.6	71.1	64.7	57.1	83.0	82.5
October	61.3	57.9	71.3	54.6	78.9	43.3	107.5	71.3	64.8	57.3	82.8	82.1
November	61.5	58.0	71.5	55.0	79.1	43.6	105.9	71.3	65.1	57.4	82.8	82.1
December	61.9	58.1	72.8	55.6	80.7	44.2	108.3	70.5	65.5	57.3	83.1	81.9
1990												
January	61.5	57.9	71.1	52.5	79.8	43.9	108.8	72.0	66.0	57.1	82.4	81.5
February	62.1	58.8	72.0	55.8	79.4	44.6	108.5	72.4	65.8	57.7	83.0	82.5
March	62.4	59.1	72.5	56.8	79.6	45.3	108.0	72.2	66.2	57.9	83.3	82.7
April	62.3	58.9	72.3	55.6	79.9	45.2	107.2	71.5	66.2	57.9	83.0	82.3
May	62.4	59.0	72.2	56.1	79.5	45.6	106.3	71.1	66.6	58.0	83.0	82.3
June	62.6	59.2	73.0	56.9	80.3	45.7	106.0	71.3	66.4	58.1	83.1	82.3
July	62.6	59.1	72.4	55.3	80.2	45.9	106.7	70.7	66.7	58.1	82.8	82.0
August	62.7	59.2	72.6	55.2	80.5	46.0	105.0	70.7	66.6	58.4	82.9	82.1
September	62.9	59.2	73.3	55.5	81.4	46.1	104.7	70.4	66.7	58.4	82.9	81.9
October	62.4	58.8	72.2	53.7	80.7	45.8	105.0	69.5	66.6	58.1	82.2	81.1
November	61.6	58.1	71.4	50.9	80.9	44.7	103.3	69.6	66.2	57.4	81.0	80.0
December	61.2	57.6	70.9	50.1	80.6	44.4	104.4	69.1	65.8	56.9	80.4	79.3

Table 2-4A. Industrial Production and Capacity Utilization, Historical Data, 1947–2014—*Continued*

(Seasonally adjusted.)

Year and month	Total industry	Manufac-turing (SIC)	Consumer goods Total	Durable	Nondurable	Business equipment	Defense and space equipment	Construction supplies	Business supplies	Materials	Capacity utilization Total industry	Manufac-turing (SIC)
1991												
January	60.9	57.2	71.2	50.1	81.1	44.1	103.2	66.5	65.6	56.5	79.9	78.5
February	60.5	56.9	70.6	49.0	80.7	43.9	102.2	66.3	65.1	56.3	79.3	77.9
March	60.2	56.5	70.6	49.3	80.6	43.9	101.6	65.5	64.3	55.8	78.7	77.3
April	60.3	56.6	70.6	50.3	80.1	43.8	98.8	66.0	64.7	56.1	78.8	77.4
May	60.9	57.0	71.8	51.2	81.5	44.1	96.9	66.1	65.3	56.5	79.5	77.9
June	61.5	57.7	72.9	52.6	82.3	44.8	97.4	67.3	65.7	56.9	80.2	78.6
July	61.5	57.8	72.5	53.4	81.3	44.7	96.5	67.0	65.2	57.3	80.1	78.7
August	61.6	58.0	72.5	52.6	81.7	44.7	97.2	67.8	65.6	57.4	80.1	78.8
September	62.1	58.6	73.6	54.8	82.2	45.3	96.9	68.0	66.0	57.7	80.7	79.6
October	62.0	58.4	73.3	54.5	82.0	44.9	97.1	67.3	65.8	57.8	80.5	79.3
November	61.9	58.3	73.4	54.6	82.1	44.9	96.4	67.9	65.9	57.6	80.3	79.1
December	61.7	58.2	72.5	54.2	80.9	45.0	95.6	67.9	65.8	57.6	79.9	78.9
1992												
January	61.3	57.9	71.7	51.8	81.0	44.0	94.3	68.0	65.7	57.5	79.3	78.2
February	61.8	58.4	72.5	53.9	81.0	45.1	93.7	68.5	65.7	57.8	79.8	78.7
March	62.3	59.0	73.2	55.1	81.5	45.4	93.3	68.9	66.2	58.3	80.3	79.4
April	62.7	59.3	73.8	56.1	82.0	45.9	91.5	69.5	66.7	58.6	80.7	79.6
May	63.0	59.6	74.3	57.8	81.8	46.4	91.2	70.2	66.8	58.7	80.8	79.9
June	63.0	59.8	73.8	57.0	81.5	46.5	91.0	69.8	66.7	58.9	80.6	79.9
July	63.5	60.3	74.8	58.5	82.2	46.9	90.1	70.2	67.2	59.4	81.1	80.4
August	63.2	60.1	74.9	58.0	82.5	46.7	89.9	70.4	67.1	58.7	80.6	79.8
September	63.3	60.1	74.5	57.8	82.0	46.9	89.7	70.3	67.3	59.1	80.6	79.7
October	63.8	60.5	75.5	59.1	83.0	47.2	89.5	70.5	67.6	59.4	81.0	80.0
November	64.1	60.7	75.7	59.6	83.0	47.5	89.5	70.3	67.8	59.8	81.2	80.1
December	64.1	60.6	75.8	60.3	82.8	47.7	89.4	70.5	68.1	59.6	81.1	79.8
1993												
January	64.4	61.3	76.1	61.1	82.9	48.1	88.7	70.8	68.2	60.0	81.3	80.4
February	64.6	61.4	76.2	60.9	83.1	48.0	88.2	71.9	68.5	60.4	81.5	80.4
March	64.6	61.2	76.3	61.2	83.0	48.1	87.1	71.3	69.0	60.2	81.3	80.1
April	64.8	61.6	76.4	61.6	83.0	48.4	87.2	71.6	69.0	60.5	81.4	80.4
May	64.6	61.5	75.8	61.6	82.1	48.5	86.2	72.5	68.7	60.3	81.0	80.2
June	64.7	61.4	75.9	61.0	82.6	48.1	85.6	72.4	68.8	60.6	81.1	80.0
July	64.9	61.6	76.6	60.9	83.7	48.1	86.5	72.8	68.9	60.6	81.2	80.1
August	64.9	61.5	76.5	60.3	83.9	47.8	84.9	73.0	69.1	60.7	81.1	79.8
September	65.2	61.9	76.7	61.5	83.6	48.5	85.3	73.4	69.2	60.9	81.3	80.2
October	65.7	62.4	77.1	63.0	83.4	49.4	84.5	74.1	69.4	61.4	81.8	80.8
November	65.9	62.7	77.2	63.6	83.3	49.7	84.4	74.7	69.4	61.8	82.0	81.0
December	66.3	63.0	77.3	63.8	83.4	50.0	83.6	75.6	69.9	62.2	82.3	81.3
1994												
January	66.5	63.1	77.9	64.8	83.8	50.3	82.8	75.3	70.4	62.3	82.5	81.3
February	66.6	63.2	78.1	64.7	84.0	49.9	81.4	74.7	70.4	62.5	82.3	81.2
March	67.3	64.0	78.7	65.3	84.7	50.4	82.3	76.1	70.9	63.2	83.0	82.0
April	67.6	64.6	78.8	66.1	84.5	50.8	82.5	77.3	71.2	63.7	83.2	82.5
May	68.0	65.0	79.4	66.4	85.1	50.9	81.4	77.9	71.3	64.1	83.4	82.8
June	68.4	65.2	80.0	66.9	85.8	51.2	80.3	78.0	72.0	64.6	83.7	82.7
July	68.6	65.4	79.6	67.1	85.2	51.8	79.8	78.7	71.7	64.9	83.6	82.8
August	68.9	66.0	80.5	68.2	85.9	51.9	78.7	78.7	71.8	65.3	83.8	83.1
September	69.2	66.2	80.1	68.5	85.2	52.4	79.5	79.4	72.2	65.6	83.8	83.2
October	69.8	66.9	80.9	69.4	86.0	53.3	79.3	79.8	72.7	66.1	84.2	83.7
November	70.2	67.4	80.9	69.3	86.1	53.9	80.2	79.9	73.0	66.7	84.4	84.0
December	70.9	68.2	81.5	69.9	86.6	54.4	80.0	80.7	73.5	67.7	85.0	84.6
1995												
January	71.1	68.3	81.4	70.3	86.3	54.7	80.3	80.8	73.7	67.8	84.8	84.4
February	71.0	68.2	81.7	70.0	86.8	54.7	78.9	79.8	73.7	67.7	84.4	83.9
March	71.2	68.4	81.6	69.9	86.8	55.1	79.1	79.7	74.0	67.8	84.3	83.7
April	71.1	68.3	81.3	69.8	86.4	55.2	78.5	79.2	73.9	68.0	83.9	83.3
May	71.3	68.3	81.5	69.2	87.0	55.7	78.5	78.7	74.2	68.1	83.9	83.1
June	71.6	68.7	81.9	69.6	87.4	56.4	79.0	78.9	74.6	68.1	83.9	83.1
July	71.3	68.3	81.5	68.2	87.4	56.3	78.2	78.7	74.6	67.8	83.2	82.3
August	72.2	69.0	82.8	70.4	88.3	57.4	78.0	79.4	75.4	68.6	84.0	82.8
September	72.5	69.6	82.9	71.1	88.0	57.9	77.6	80.7	75.4	68.9	84.0	83.2
October	72.4	69.6	82.2	70.3	87.4	57.7	76.5	80.6	75.6	69.0	83.6	82.7
November	72.6	69.6	82.4	70.3	87.8	57.9	74.8	80.6	75.9	69.2	83.4	82.4
December	72.8	69.9	82.7	70.8	87.9	58.4	75.0	81.1	75.9	69.5	83.4	82.3
1996												
January	72.4	69.3	81.7	68.9	87.4	57.6	74.1	79.8	75.6	69.4	82.5	81.3
February	73.5	70.4	83.1	70.9	88.5	59.2	76.2	80.8	76.5	70.3	83.4	82.1
March	73.4	70.3	82.6	68.6	88.8	59.0	76.4	81.7	76.5	70.3	83.0	81.5
April	74.0	71.0	83.3	71.8	88.4	60.4	76.2	82.0	76.4	70.9	83.3	82.0
May	74.5	71.5	83.4	72.1	88.4	61.2	76.3	82.9	77.2	71.4	83.6	82.2
June	75.2	72.3	84.1	73.6	88.7	62.2	75.8	84.3	77.4	72.0	83.9	82.6
July	75.1	72.5	83.4	74.0	87.5	62.9	76.2	83.7	77.4	72.0	83.3	82.3
August	75.6	73.0	83.3	73.3	87.7	63.5	76.1	84.6	78.2	72.7	83.5	82.4
September	76.0	73.4	84.0	73.4	88.6	63.9	76.1	84.9	78.6	73.0	83.6	82.6
October	76.0	73.4	83.6	72.2	88.6	63.8	75.7	85.0	78.8	73.2	83.2	82.0
November	76.6	74.0	84.5	73.1	89.6	64.7	75.1	85.6	79.4	73.6	83.5	82.2
December	77.1	74.6	84.8	74.3	89.4	66.0	75.2	85.2	79.8	74.1	83.6	82.4

Table 2-4A. Industrial Production and Capacity Utilization, Historical Data, 1947–2014—*Continued*

(Seasonally adjusted.)

Year and month	Production indexes, 2007 = 100										Capacity utilization (output as percent of capacity)	
	Total industry	Manufac-turing (SIC)	Market groups								Total industry	Manufac-turing (SIC)
			Consumer goods			Business equipment	Defense and space equipment	Construction supplies	Business supplies	Materials		
			Total	Durable	Nondurable							
1997												
January	77.2	74.7	84.5	73.7	89.2	66.2	74.1	84.4	80.4	74.3	83.3	82.1
February	78.1	75.7	85.0	75.0	89.3	67.3	74.6	86.0	81.2	75.4	83.9	82.7
March	78.7	76.6	85.6	76.0	89.8	68.5	74.4	87.0	81.5	75.9	84.0	83.1
April	78.8	76.4	84.7	74.0	89.5	68.8	74.4	86.6	81.8	76.3	83.6	82.5
May	79.3	77.1	85.3	74.8	89.9	69.7	74.3	87.2	82.3	76.7	83.7	82.7
June	79.7	77.6	85.4	76.3	89.3	70.7	74.2	87.0	82.6	77.1	83.6	82.7
July	80.1	78.0	85.7	74.9	90.4	70.8	74.7	87.2	83.3	77.8	83.9	82.8
August	81.2	79.3	87.0	78.3	90.7	72.9	74.8	87.7	83.5	78.7	84.2	83.2
September	81.9	79.9	87.7	79.3	91.3	73.3	74.8	88.2	84.5	79.5	84.4	83.3
October	82.5	80.4	88.9	79.6	92.9	74.2	75.0	88.7	85.4	79.5	84.6	83.4
November	83.2	81.3	89.2	81.6	92.4	75.7	74.6	89.0	85.7	80.5	84.8	83.8
December	83.5	81.7	88.7	81.4	91.8	76.1	75.6	90.1	85.9	81.1	84.5	83.5
1998												
January	83.9	82.3	89.1	81.7	92.1	77.1	76.2	90.7	85.9	81.4	84.4	83.5
February	84.0	82.4	88.9	81.6	92.0	77.3	76.6	91.1	86.1	81.4	83.9	83.0
March	84.1	82.3	89.1	81.8	92.2	77.6	76.2	90.5	86.6	81.3	83.4	82.3
April	84.4	82.7	89.6	82.1	92.8	77.8	76.1	90.9	86.9	81.6	83.2	82.1
May	84.9	83.2	90.0	82.7	93.1	78.3	77.0	92.0	87.7	82.2	83.2	81.9
June	84.4	82.6	89.0	78.7	93.4	78.3	77.3	91.8	87.8	81.7	82.2	80.7
July	84.1	82.2	88.1	75.3	93.6	77.7	78.4	92.1	88.3	81.4	81.4	79.9
August	85.9	84.3	90.8	84.8	93.4	80.4	78.7	92.5	88.9	82.8	82.6	81.3
September	85.6	84.0	89.9	84.3	92.3	80.3	78.2	92.2	88.8	82.8	82.0	80.6
October	86.3	84.8	90.4	86.0	92.2	81.3	79.9	93.3	89.1	83.6	82.3	81.0
November	86.2	84.9	89.8	85.8	91.5	81.2	79.7	93.4	89.4	83.7	81.8	80.7
December	86.5	85.4	89.8	86.5	91.1	81.4	79.1	94.5	89.3	84.3	81.8	80.7
1999												
January	86.9	85.6	90.7	86.5	92.5	81.6	78.9	94.0	90.0	84.5	81.8	80.6
February	87.3	86.2	91.0	87.2	92.6	82.2	79.6	94.0	90.1	85.0	81.8	80.8
March	87.5	86.2	90.9	87.0	92.5	82.0	79.3	93.1	90.5	85.5	81.6	80.4
April	87.7	86.5	90.8	88.0	91.9	82.2	78.4	93.3	90.7	86.0	81.5	80.3
May	88.3	87.3	91.7	88.8	92.9	83.4	77.5	93.7	91.2	86.5	81.8	80.7
June	88.1	87.0	90.8	88.3	91.8	83.0	76.3	93.6	91.1	86.8	81.4	80.1
July	88.7	87.4	90.4	88.3	91.3	83.8	75.8	94.3	91.8	88.0	81.6	80.1
August	89.1	88.0	91.6	90.4	92.1	84.2	75.2	94.2	91.8	88.0	81.6	80.2
September	88.9	87.7	91.0	89.4	91.7	84.0	72.8	94.4	91.9	87.9	81.0	79.6
October	90.0	89.0	92.7	92.1	93.0	84.6	72.0	95.5	92.7	89.0	81.8	80.5
November	90.4	89.6	92.6	91.4	93.1	84.6	70.3	96.1	93.2	90.0	81.9	80.6
December	91.2	90.3	93.6	91.4	94.4	85.2	69.2	97.0	93.9	90.7	82.2	80.8
2000												
January	91.1	90.3	92.4	93.1	92.2	86.7	69.3	97.4	94.1	90.8	81.9	80.6
February	91.4	90.5	92.9	92.7	93.1	87.2	67.7	97.6	94.2	91.0	81.9	80.4
March	91.8	91.1	92.7	92.6	92.8	88.2	67.2	97.7	94.9	91.6	81.9	80.6
April	92.5	91.8	93.5	93.7	93.5	89.4	66.1	98.2	95.9	92.0	82.2	80.8
May	92.7	91.7	93.6	93.3	93.8	89.9	65.6	96.6	96.0	92.4	82.1	80.4
June	92.7	91.8	93.7	93.0	94.1	90.0	66.4	96.3	95.8	92.6	81.9	80.2
July	92.6	92.0	93.3	91.3	94.1	90.8	67.9	96.7	95.9	92.2	81.6	80.0
August	92.3	91.3	92.8	91.1	93.5	90.4	66.3	96.0	95.7	92.1	81.0	79.2
September	92.7	91.6	93.6	91.2	94.6	91.2	63.4	96.2	95.6	92.3	81.1	79.2
October	92.3	91.4	92.9	90.7	93.7	91.0	66.5	95.7	95.2	92.1	80.6	78.6
November	92.3	91.1	93.2	88.6	95.0	90.8	68.5	95.5	95.4	91.8	80.3	78.1
December	92.1	90.5	93.7	87.4	96.2	90.1	69.1	94.3	95.1	91.2	79.9	77.4
2001												
January	91.4	89.9	93.0	85.8	95.7	89.9	71.0	94.5	94.8	90.1	79.1	76.6
February	90.8	89.4	92.3	85.6	94.9	89.5	70.6	93.6	93.6	89.7	78.3	75.9
March	90.6	89.1	92.1	87.4	94.0	89.0	72.5	93.7	93.0	89.4	77.9	75.5
April	90.3	88.8	92.6	87.9	94.4	86.9	73.1	93.5	92.5	89.1	77.5	75.1
May	89.6	88.1	92.4	88.5	93.9	85.3	73.4	92.9	91.8	88.4	76.7	74.3
June	89.0	87.5	92.2	87.6	93.9	84.5	74.6	92.2	91.4	87.5	76.0	73.6
July	88.6	87.1	91.8	88.2	93.3	83.6	75.5	92.2	91.3	86.8	75.4	73.1
August	88.4	86.7	92.0	87.3	93.8	82.2	74.4	91.2	91.0	86.9	75.1	72.6
September	88.1	86.5	91.5	86.5	93.5	81.1	75.0	91.2	91.1	86.8	74.7	72.3
October	87.6	85.9	92.0	85.9	94.3	79.5	74.8	90.1	90.4	86.3	74.2	71.7
November	87.2	85.6	91.8	87.2	93.7	79.0	74.0	89.8	89.7	85.7	73.6	71.4
December	87.2	85.9	92.4	89.2	93.6	78.4	73.8	90.6	89.9	85.4	73.5	71.6
2002												
January	87.7	86.3	93.3	89.3	94.9	78.2	73.5	90.3	89.8	86.2	73.9	71.9
February	87.7	86.3	92.7	89.6	93.9	78.0	72.9	90.7	89.9	86.7	73.8	71.8
March	88.4	87.0	93.4	90.3	94.7	78.5	72.9	92.1	90.7	87.4	74.3	72.3
April	88.8	87.2	93.4	91.7	94.1	78.0	72.9	92.0	91.5	88.3	74.6	72.5
May	89.2	87.6	93.7	92.1	94.3	78.4	73.0	92.5	91.9	88.7	74.8	72.8
June	90.0	88.6	94.8	93.1	95.5	79.1	73.8	93.3	92.5	89.6	75.5	73.7
July	89.8	88.3	94.8	94.6	94.9	78.4	73.9	91.9	92.5	89.4	75.3	73.4
August	89.9	88.5	94.2	93.5	94.4	79.0	74.2	92.4	92.4	89.7	75.3	73.5
September	89.9	88.6	94.3	93.6	94.6	78.9	75.6	93.2	92.7	89.6	75.4	73.6
October	89.7	88.3	94.2	92.8	94.7	78.6	76.2	92.8	93.1	89.0	75.2	73.3
November	90.1	88.7	94.9	95.2	94.8	78.7	75.7	92.8	92.8	89.6	75.6	73.7
December	89.7	88.3	94.1	93.5	94.3	78.1	78.7	92.1	92.7	89.4	75.2	73.3

Table 2-4A. Industrial Production and Capacity Utilization, Historical Data, 1947–2014—*Continued*

(Seasonally adjusted.)

Year and month	Production indexes, 2007 = 100										Capacity utilization (output as percent of capacity)	
	Total industry	Manufac-turing (SIC)	Market groups								Total industry	Manufac-turing (SIC)
			Consumer goods			Business equipment	Defense and space equipment	Construction supplies	Business supplies	Materials		
			Total	Durable	Nondurable							
2003												
January	90.3	88.7	94.6	94.8	94.5	78.4	78.7	92.4	94.2	89.9	75.8	73.7
February	90.5	88.8	95.7	93.7	96.5	78.2	79.7	91.7	93.9	90.0	76.0	73.8
March	90.4	88.9	95.7	94.0	96.4	78.3	79.7	91.3	94.0	89.5	75.9	73.9
April	89.7	88.2	94.8	93.0	95.5	77.4	79.0	90.3	92.9	89.0	75.3	73.2
May	89.7	88.2	94.7	93.2	95.2	77.4	79.7	91.5	93.2	89.0	75.4	73.3
June	89.7	88.6	94.7	94.3	94.8	77.6	79.9	91.8	92.5	89.1	75.4	73.6
July	90.3	88.9	95.9	97.4	95.3	77.4	79.3	91.6	93.3	89.4	75.9	73.9
August	90.0	88.5	95.0	94.8	95.0	78.0	79.3	92.0	93.0	89.4	75.7	73.5
September	90.5	89.1	95.7	97.4	95.1	78.6	79.5	91.8	93.1	89.9	76.2	74.1
October	90.6	89.2	95.0	96.4	94.4	78.6	79.4	92.3	93.4	90.5	76.2	74.2
November	91.3	90.1	95.7	97.4	95.0	80.3	78.7	93.5	93.9	90.9	76.8	74.9
December	91.2	89.8	95.8	97.6	95.1	79.8	76.6	93.3	93.6	90.9	76.8	74.8
2004												
January	91.4	89.8	96.3	98.8	95.4	80.0	74.5	93.3	94.1	91.1	77.0	74.8
February	91.9	90.4	96.8	98.6	96.1	81.0	76.0	93.2	94.7	91.5	77.4	75.3
March	91.4	90.2	95.6	97.6	94.9	80.8	76.2	93.3	93.9	91.3	77.1	75.3
April	91.8	90.6	96.2	97.8	95.6	80.8	76.1	93.2	94.4	91.6	77.4	75.6
May	92.5	91.3	96.7	96.9	96.6	81.8	76.7	94.3	95.1	92.4	78.0	76.2
June	91.7	90.6	95.4	94.8	95.6	81.5	75.7	93.6	94.9	91.7	77.4	75.7
July	92.5	91.4	95.6	95.3	95.7	83.2	76.9	94.8	95.4	92.5	78.0	76.4
August	92.5	91.8	96.0	96.1	96.0	82.8	77.5	94.8	95.2	92.4	78.1	76.7
September	92.5	91.8	96.1	95.7	96.3	83.0	78.5	94.0	95.2	92.4	78.1	76.6
October	93.4	92.7	97.0	97.8	96.8	83.8	78.6	95.6	95.7	93.4	78.9	77.4
November	93.6	92.6	96.9	96.6	97.1	83.2	79.4	95.3	96.1	93.9	79.0	77.3
December	94.3	93.2	97.6	97.7	97.6	83.8	80.1	95.2	96.9	94.6	79.5	77.7
2005												
January	94.7	93.9	98.1	97.1	98.4	85.1	80.2	96.3	97.5	94.7	79.8	78.2
February	95.3	94.7	98.4	99.0	98.2	86.1	83.2	97.0	97.4	95.5	80.3	78.7
March	95.2	94.3	98.2	97.6	98.4	85.8	84.9	96.0	97.6	95.5	80.1	78.2
April	95.4	94.6	98.0	96.3	98.5	86.9	86.3	97.7	97.9	95.3	80.1	78.3
May	95.5	94.9	98.7	96.6	99.3	87.7	86.1	97.9	97.9	95.1	80.2	78.4
June	95.9	95.1	99.5	97.2	100.2	87.5	86.9	97.1	98.4	95.4	80.4	78.4
July	95.7	94.9	99.2	95.7	100.3	87.5	86.2	97.9	98.1	95.1	80.1	78.0
August	95.9	95.2	99.6	98.4	99.9	88.0	87.2	98.2	98.2	95.0	80.1	78.1
September	94.0	94.2	99.5	99.5	99.5	85.7	83.7	99.6	98.3	91.2	78.4	77.1
October	95.2	95.6	99.5	100.7	99.2	90.2	84.6	101.5	98.6	92.5	79.3	78.1
November	96.1	96.3	99.3	99.2	99.3	91.4	84.7	102.1	98.9	94.3	79.9	78.6
December	96.7	96.4	100.1	97.8	100.8	90.9	84.6	102.9	99.3	95.1	80.3	78.5
2006												
January	96.8	97.2	99.0	99.3	98.9	92.4	83.0	103.6	99.1	95.7	80.2	79.0
February	96.8	97.0	98.8	98.4	98.9	92.9	83.6	102.8	99.1	95.9	80.2	78.7
March	97.1	96.9	99.5	99.2	99.7	93.6	81.5	102.5	99.5	95.8	80.3	78.5
April	97.4	97.5	99.6	99.2	99.8	95.5	81.9	102.1	99.5	96.1	80.4	78.8
May	97.3	97.0	99.5	98.8	99.8	95.0	81.5	101.1	99.3	96.1	80.2	78.3
June	97.7	97.3	100.0	99.7	100.2	95.6	82.0	100.8	99.4	96.5	80.4	78.5
July	97.7	97.1	99.2	96.1	100.2	96.6	83.5	101.0	99.4	96.8	80.3	78.2
August	98.0	97.6	100.0	98.9	100.4	97.2	83.5	100.2	99.1	97.0	80.4	78.5
September	97.8	97.7	99.5	97.2	100.2	97.2	84.5	99.9	98.9	97.0	80.1	78.4
October	97.8	97.3	99.6	95.9	100.7	97.4	86.1	98.8	99.1	96.8	79.9	78.0
November	97.7	97.4	99.7	97.1	100.5	97.2	87.8	98.5	98.6	96.6	79.7	77.8
December	98.6	98.8	100.0	99.9	100.1	98.5	89.7	101.5	99.2	97.7	80.3	78.8
2007												
January	98.2	98.3	99.7	97.8	100.3	96.2	92.0	99.5	99.2	97.5	79.7	78.2
February	99.2	98.7	101.1	99.0	101.8	97.2	92.8	99.9	100.2	98.4	80.4	78.4
March	99.4	99.5	100.0	99.2	100.3	99.5	91.8	101.0	100.1	98.9	80.4	78.8
April	100.1	100.2	100.7	101.5	100.5	100.5	94.5	100.8	100.7	99.6	80.8	79.2
May	100.1	100.1	100.4	100.9	100.2	100.3	96.7	100.6	100.4	100.0	80.7	78.9
June	100.1	100.4	100.4	102.0	99.9	99.8	100.2	101.0	100.1	99.9	80.6	79.0
July	100.2	100.5	100.4	101.4	100.1	99.6	101.4	100.6	99.5	100.2	80.5	78.9
August	100.3	100.1	100.3	100.9	100.1	99.5	103.2	99.9	99.9	100.5	80.5	78.5
September	100.7	100.6	100.3	99.5	100.5	101.4	105.9	99.9	100.4	100.8	80.8	78.7
October	100.2	100.2	99.1	99.3	99.0	100.9	105.6	98.9	99.8	100.9	80.4	78.3
November	100.8	100.7	99.0	99.3	98.9	102.0	107.7	98.7	100.2	101.8	80.8	78.6
December	100.7	100.8	98.7	99.2	98.5	103.1	108.2	99.1	99.7	101.7	80.8	78.6
2008												
January	100.5	100.4	98.5	96.8	99.1	103.3	108.9	98.9	99.6	101.2	80.7	78.3
February	100.2	99.8	98.2	95.3	99.2	104.0	107.9	97.0	99.6	100.9	80.5	77.8
March	100.0	99.5	97.2	94.2	98.2	103.9	108.2	95.7	99.2	101.1	80.3	77.6
April	99.2	98.5	96.7	92.0	98.2	102.0	107.9	94.2	98.3	100.6	79.8	76.8
May	98.8	98.0	96.3	91.6	97.8	102.3	107.4	93.4	97.6	100.0	79.4	76.5
June	98.6	97.5	96.0	91.9	97.4	101.9	109.1	92.4	96.9	100.0	79.3	76.2
July	98.1	96.4	95.0	88.3	97.1	101.3	107.3	92.2	96.2	99.9	78.9	75.4
August	96.6	95.2	93.7	86.2	96.1	98.2	107.5	90.2	95.4	98.3	77.7	74.6
September	92.5	92.0	93.2	86.0	95.5	90.1	104.9	87.8	94.2	92.1	74.3	72.1
October	93.3	91.4	93.4	83.8	96.5	87.6	105.2	86.5	93.7	94.5	74.9	71.8
November	92.1	89.2	92.6	81.3	96.4	88.9	104.6	82.2	92.1	92.9	73.9	70.2
December	89.5	86.2	90.9	78.1	95.1	89.4	103.6	77.6	89.3	89.4	71.7	67.9

Table 2-4A. Industrial Production and Capacity Utilization, Historical Data, 1947–2014—*Continued*

(Seasonally adjusted.)

Year and month	Production indexes, 2007 = 100										Capacity utilization (output as percent of capacity)	
	Total industry	Manufac-turing (SIC)	Market groups								Total industry	Manufac-turing (SIC)
			Consumer goods			Business equipment	Defense and space equipment	Construction supplies	Business supplies	Materials		
			Total	Durable	Nondurable							
2009												
January	87.5	83.7	89.0	70.3	95.1	84.2	103.3	74.5	88.4	88.0	70.1	66.1
February	86.9	83.5	88.9	71.5	94.7	84.0	102.5	73.2	87.1	87.3	69.5	66.0
March	85.6	82.0	88.7	71.7	94.3	82.0	100.8	70.7	86.1	85.8	68.5	65.0
April	84.9	81.4	88.4	72.1	93.8	80.2	100.1	69.4	85.7	85.2	67.9	64.6
May	84.0	80.5	87.1	69.0	93.2	78.1	100.1	69.1	85.1	84.7	67.2	64.0
June	83.7	80.3	86.8	68.7	92.8	77.2	100.7	69.1	85.1	84.4	66.9	63.9
July	84.6	81.4	88.0	75.6	92.1	77.8	102.3	69.2	84.9	85.3	67.6	64.9
August	85.4	82.1	88.6	76.0	92.7	78.8	103.2	69.6	85.2	86.4	68.3	65.7
September	86.0	82.8	89.4	78.9	92.9	78.9	104.3	69.1	85.4	87.2	68.9	66.3
October	86.3	82.9	89.9	77.5	93.9	79.4	103.6	68.3	86.1	87.4	69.3	66.5
November	86.6	83.8	89.2	78.8	92.6	79.3	103.9	69.4	86.0	88.5	69.7	67.3
December	86.9	83.7	89.1	77.7	92.8	80.9	104.2	67.8	87.3	88.7	70.0	67.4
2010												
January	88.0	84.6	89.9	78.5	93.6	82.1	106.9	69.0	87.4	90.0	71.0	68.2
February	88.2	84.5	89.1	77.0	93.0	81.6	107.5	69.0	87.2	91.1	71.4	68.3
March	88.9	85.6	89.1	77.8	92.9	83.3	110.4	70.3	87.0	92.0	72.1	69.3
April	89.2	86.4	88.2	77.9	91.7	84.5	111.7	72.6	87.4	92.6	72.5	70.0
May	90.6	87.6	90.0	80.5	93.2	86.4	112.0	73.1	88.2	93.9	73.8	71.2
June	90.8	87.6	89.8	79.5	93.1	87.0	111.7	73.2	88.3	94.5	74.1	71.3
July	91.4	88.4	90.3	82.5	92.8	88.7	113.3	73.2	88.4	94.9	74.7	72.0
August	91.7	88.5	90.0	79.9	93.3	88.9	113.7	73.7	88.5	95.5	75.0	72.2
September	91.9	88.5	89.6	79.6	92.9	89.3	111.4	73.7	88.5	96.3	75.3	72.4
October	91.6	88.6	89.7	81.1	92.6	88.9	109.7	74.1	87.7	95.9	75.1	72.5
November	91.8	88.7	89.1	79.2	92.3	89.5	109.2	74.5	88.7	96.3	75.3	72.7
December	92.6	89.1	90.1	78.9	93.7	89.9	108.6	73.6	89.1	97.4	76.0	73.0
2011												
January	92.6	89.3	90.4	80.4	93.7	90.5	108.2	73.3	88.7	97.2	76.0	73.2
February	92.1	89.2	90.1	81.8	92.8	90.8	107.1	72.9	88.4	96.4	75.6	73.3
March	93.0	89.8	90.3	83.1	92.7	90.6	106.2	73.5	89.0	98.1	76.3	73.8
April	92.6	89.3	90.2	80.5	93.3	89.7	105.6	73.5	88.5	97.5	75.8	73.3
May	92.9	89.5	90.5	81.7	93.4	90.4	105.7	74.5	88.8	97.6	76.0	73.4
June	93.1	89.6	90.3	81.3	93.3	90.4	104.7	74.7	88.5	98.3	76.1	73.5
July	93.7	90.3	91.4	83.9	93.9	91.1	105.4	75.6	89.0	98.5	76.4	74.0
August	94.1	90.6	91.7	84.1	94.3	91.9	106.1	75.2	89.4	99.0	76.6	74.2
September	94.2	90.9	91.6	84.4	94.0	92.1	106.1	75.3	89.8	99.2	76.6	74.3
October	94.7	91.4	91.8	86.3	93.8	93.0	107.2	75.4	89.2	100.0	76.8	74.6
November	94.8	91.3	91.3	85.5	93.3	93.5	109.5	75.4	88.6	100.5	76.7	74.4
December	95.2	92.0	91.2	86.6	92.9	94.1	109.1	76.9	89.0	101.0	76.8	74.8
2012												
January	96.0	92.9	91.8	89.1	92.9	95.4	110.2	77.3	89.5	102.0	77.3	75.5
February	96.4	93.5	92.1	88.9	93.4	96.1	111.9	78.4	90.1	102.1	77.4	75.8
March	96.0	93.2	91.1	88.6	92.2	96.7	111.8	78.1	89.6	101.9	76.9	75.4
April	96.8	93.9	92.1	89.8	93.1	97.5	111.0	79.1	90.6	102.6	77.4	75.8
May	97.1	93.7	92.8	89.5	94.2	98.1	110.0	78.4	91.1	102.7	77.4	75.5
June	97.2	94.0	92.5	90.1	93.6	99.3	109.5	77.6	90.9	102.9	77.3	75.6
July	97.7	94.4	93.2	91.4	94.0	99.4	111.7	77.3	90.9	103.7	77.6	75.8
August	97.1	94.0	92.4	89.2	93.6	99.5	112.2	77.5	90.6	102.9	77.0	75.3
September	97.4	94.1	92.7	89.2	94.1	99.1	112.8	77.7	90.5	103.4	77.0	75.3
October	97.3	93.7	92.3	89.8	93.4	98.2	112.3	77.6	90.5	103.7	76.9	74.8
November	98.3	94.9	93.3	91.2	94.3	100.3	114.0	79.0	91.1	104.4	77.5	75.7
December	98.4	95.6	93.1	93.6	93.4	100.7	114.4	79.8	90.9	104.6	77.5	76.1
2013												
January	98.4	95.4	93.5	93.3	94.0	98.8	114.1	80.2	91.4	104.8	77.4	75.8
February	99.0	95.9	94.3	94.8	94.5	100.6	113.8	81.7	91.5	105.1	77.8	76.1
March	99.5	96.0	94.9	95.7	95.0	101.9	113.7	81.0	91.8	105.5	78.0	76.1
April	99.3	95.8	94.6	95.6	94.7	101.5	113.5	80.7	91.8	105.4	77.8	75.8
May	99.4	96.1	94.2	95.8	94.1	101.6	113.5	80.4	92.0	105.9	77.8	75.9
June	99.6	96.4	94.4	96.8	94.1	102.2	114.0	80.8	92.0	106.0	77.8	76.1
July	99.4	96.0	93.7	95.7	93.4	101.0	113.1	81.1	92.0	106.3	77.5	75.6
August	100.0	96.7	94.1	97.5	93.5	102.3	115.0	81.3	92.4	106.9	77.8	76.1
September	100.7	96.9	94.9	98.1	94.4	103.4	116.1	82.0	93.0	107.4	78.3	76.2
October	100.8	97.3	95.4	98.6	94.9	103.4	115.7	82.7	93.2	107.3	78.2	76.3
November	101.4	97.6	95.8	100.3	94.9	103.2	115.3	83.0	93.4	108.2	78.5	76.4
December	101.6	97.7	96.6	100.4	96.0	102.6	115.6	82.6	93.8	108.1	78.5	76.4
2014												
January	101.3	96.8	95.8	97.2	95.7	102.4	114.4	82.3	93.9	108.3	78.1	75.5
February	102.3	98.0	97.3	99.9	96.9	104.9	114.8	83.0	94.3	108.7	78.6	76.4
March	103.1	98.8	97.9	100.7	97.6	105.8	115.7	83.6	94.2	109.9	79.1	76.8
April	103.2	99.1	97.4	100.7	96.8	106.3	116.1	82.9	94.0	110.4	79.0	77.0
May	103.7	99.5	97.1	102.2	96.0	107.2	116.1	84.0	94.3	111.3	79.1	77.1
June	104.1	99.9	96.8	102.9	95.5	106.9	116.6	84.4	94.2	112.4	79.2	77.3
July	104.5	100.8	97.5	107.5	95.1	108.2	117.1	85.6	94.1	112.4	79.3	77.8
August	104.5	100.4	96.5	103.6	94.9	108.0	117.1	85.9	94.5	112.9	79.1	77.4
September	105.2	100.6	97.4	103.3	96.2	107.6	117.8	86.1	95.4	113.7	79.4	77.4
October	105.1	100.8	97.1	103.1	95.8	108.8	117.4	86.7	95.8	113.5	79.2	77.4
November	106.3	102.0	99.2	106.9	97.5	110.4	117.6	86.7	96.7	114.1	79.8	78.1
December	106.2	101.9	98.7	106.4	97.0	109.0	117.8	87.8	95.9	114.7	79.5	78.0

Table 2-4B. Industrial Production: Historical Data, 1919–1947

(Seasonally adjusted, 2007 = 100.)

Year and month	January	February	March	April	May	June	July	August	September	October	November	December	Annual averages
1919													
Industrial production, total ...	4.86	4.64	4.51	4.59	4.62	4.91	5.21	5.29	5.18	5.13	5.05	5.13	4.92
Manufacturing	4.60	4.50	4.33	4.43	4.41	4.72	4.98	5.10	4.91	4.81	4.98	4.89	4.71
1920													
Industrial production, total ..	5.61	5.61	5.50	5.21	5.34	5.40	5.26	5.29	5.10	4.89	4.48	4.21	5.15
Manufacturing	5.39	5.39	5.27	4.96	5.13	5.13	4.93	4.96	4.84	4.57	4.09	3.80	4.86
1921													
Industrial production, total ..	3.97	3.89	3.78	3.78	3.89	3.87	3.84	3.97	4.00	4.24	4.19	4.16	3.96
Manufacturing	3.61	3.61	3.51	3.51	3.63	3.61	3.61	3.76	3.80	3.97	4.02	3.97	3.70
1922													
Industrial production, total ..	4.32	4.51	4.75	4.59	4.83	5.07	5.07	4.97	5.23	5.53	5.77	5.93	5.05
Manufacturing	4.07	4.16	4.36	4.55	4.79	5.01	5.06	4.86	5.01	5.22	5.42	5.58	4.82
1923													
Industrial production, total ..	5.80	5.88	6.07	6.20	6.28	6.23	6.17	6.07	5.93	5.91	5.91	5.77	6.01
Manufacturing	5.49	5.54	5.78	5.85	5.97	5.90	5.80	5.66	5.63	5.54	5.54	5.46	5.64
1924													
Industrial production, total ...	5.91	6.01	5.91	5.72	5.48	5.23	5.15	5.34	5.53	5.66	5.77	5.93	5.63
Manufacturing	5.56	5.68	5.58	5.44	5.18	4.91	4.84	5.01	5.20	5.34	5.46	5.66	5.30
1925													
Industrial production, total ..	6.12	6.12	6.12	6.17	6.15	6.09	6.25	6.15	6.07	6.31	6.44	6.52	6.20
Manufacturing	5.83	5.85	5.87	5.87	5.83	5.80	5.92	5.83	5.85	6.09	6.26	6.40	5.91
1926													
Industrial production, total ..	6.41	6.41	6.50	6.50	6.44	6.52	6.55	6.63	6.74	6.74	6.71	6.68	6.57
Manufacturing	6.26	6.21	6.19	6.19	6.14	6.21	6.21	6.28	6.40	6.36	6.31	6.28	6.25
1927													
Industrial production, total ..	6.66	6.71	6.79	6.63	6.68	6.66	6.58	6.58	6.47	6.33	6.33	6.36	6.57
Manufacturing	6.23	6.28	6.33	6.31	6.33	6.33	6.28	6.23	6.14	6.04	6.02	6.09	6.19
1928													
Industrial production, total ..	6.50	6.55	6.60	6.58	6.66	6.71	6.79	6.92	6.98	7.11	7.25	7.38	6.83
Manufacturing	6.21	6.28	6.31	6.28	6.38	6.45	6.55	6.69	6.72	6.84	6.98	7.10	6.51
1929													
Industrial production, total ..	7.49	7.46	7.49	7.62	7.76	7.81	7.92	7.84	7.78	7.65	7.27	6.95	7.58
Manufacturing	7.15	7.13	7.20	7.29	7.44	7.53	7.61	7.56	7.41	7.34	6.93	6.52	7.23
1930													
Industrial production, total ..	6.95	6.92	6.82	6.76	6.66	6.47	6.17	6.04	5.93	5.77	5.64	5.50	6.30
Manufacturing	6.60	6.55	6.33	6.43	6.31	6.14	5.85	5.63	5.58	5.39	5.25	5.13	5.94
1931													
Industrial production, total ..	5.48	5.50	5.61	5.64	5.56	5.42	5.34	5.15	4.91	4.72	4.67	4.64	5.22
Manufacturing	5.13	5.18	5.27	5.27	5.22	5.03	4.96	4.79	4.57	4.36	4.28	4.26	4.86
1932													
Industrial production, total ..	4.51	4.40	4.35	4.05	3.92	3.78	3.68	3.78	4.03	4.16	4.16	4.08	4.09
Manufacturing	4.21	4.09	3.95	3.71	3.61	3.49	3.37	3.47	3.71	3.80	3.83	3.76	3.74
1933													
Industrial production, total ..	4.00	4.03	3.78	4.05	4.72	5.45	5.96	5.72	5.40	5.13	4.83	4.86	4.82
Manufacturing	3.71	3.61	3.39	3.76	4.41	5.13	5.66	5.32	5.06	4.77	4.45	4.50	4.44
1934													
Industrial production, total ..	5.02	5.26	5.50	5.50	5.61	5.50	5.13	5.07	4.78	4.99	5.05	5.37	5.25
Manufacturing	4.65	4.91	5.10	5.20	5.27	5.15	4.74	4.72	4.45	4.62	4.69	5.03	4.87
1935													
Industrial production, total ..	5.80	5.91	5.88	5.77	5.77	5.85	5.85	6.07	6.23	6.41	6.55	6.63	6.06
Manufacturing	5.49	5.58	5.51	5.46	5.44	5.42	5.58	5.80	5.95	6.11	6.26	6.33	5.72
1936													
Industrial production, total ..	6.52	6.36	6.44	6.84	6.98	7.11	7.25	7.35	7.49	7.60	7.81	8.05	7.15
Manufacturing	6.21	6.02	6.14	6.52	6.69	6.84	6.96	7.08	7.20	7.32	7.51	7.75	6.82
1937													
Industrial production, total ..	8.03	8.13	8.32	8.32	8.35	8.24	8.29	8.24	7.97	7.38	6.66	6.07	7.83
Manufacturing	7.75	7.87	7.92	8.04	8.09	7.94	7.99	7.90	7.61	6.98	6.16	5.51	7.43
1938													
Industrial production, total ..	5.93	5.88	5.88	5.77	5.64	5.69	6.01	6.33	6.52	6.68	6.95	7.03	6.19
Manufacturing	5.42	5.39	5.42	5.25	5.22	5.22	5.54	5.90	6.09	6.28	6.57	6.62	5.72

Table 2-4B. Industrial Production: Historical Data, 1919–1947—*Continued*

(Seasonally adjusted, 2007 = 100.)

Year and month	January	February	March	April	May	June	July	August	September	October	November	December	Annual averages
1939													
Industrial production, total	7.03	7.09	7.11	7.09	7.06	7.22	7.43	7.54	8.00	8.40	8.62	8.62	7.61
Products	7.09	7.11	7.19	7.19	7.25	7.32	7.46	7.54	7.77	7.99	8.14	8.20	7.53
Consumer goods	10.62	10.62	10.79	10.79	10.83	10.93	11.07	11.11	11.28	11.39	11.49	11.53	11.04
Materials	6.72	6.82	6.82	6.61	6.58	6.90	7.20	7.28	8.10	8.88	9.04	9.04	7.51
Manufacturing	6.31	6.36	6.36	6.28	6.28	6.43	6.62	6.81	7.20	7.61	7.75	7.85	6.83
1940													
Industrial production, total	8.51	8.24	8.05	8.21	8.45	8.72	8.83	8.88	9.07	9.21	9.42	9.74	8.78
Products	8.12	8.04	7.96	8.04	8.14	8.33	8.33	8.43	8.67	8.83	8.99	9.31	8.44
Consumer goods	11.49	11.46	11.32	11.39	11.46	11.56	11.53	11.53	11.84	12.05	12.29	12.67	11.73
Materials	8.80	8.32	8.00	8.24	8.61	9.06	9.30	9.38	9.49	9.59	9.78	10.13	9.07
Manufacturing	7.73	7.49	7.32	7.39	7.70	8.04	8.14	8.26	8.43	8.55	8.69	9.00	8.06
1941													
Industrial production, total	9.98	10.28	10.60	10.63	11.11	11.19	11.33	11.46	11.46	11.57	11.62	11.81	11.09
Products	9.60	9.89	10.15	10.37	10.71	10.81	10.89	11.03	11.05	11.16	11.21	11.37	10.70
Consumer goods	12.92	13.30	13.65	13.89	14.31	14.35	14.35	14.38	14.31	14.31	14.35	14.35	14.05
Materials	10.26	10.55	10.93	10.69	11.35	11.51	11.67	11.75	11.75	11.81	11.89	12.13	11.35
Manufacturing	9.17	9.51	9.75	10.01	10.35	10.47	10.59	10.66	10.64	10.74	10.76	10.90	10.29
1942													
Industrial production, total	12.05	12.27	12.40	12.05	12.08	12.11	12.40	12.78	13.07	13.50	13.82	14.15	12.71
Products	11.71	12.00	12.14	11.37	11.40	11.45	11.77	12.11	12.53	12.98	13.41	13.83	12.22
Consumer goods	14.62	14.45	14.45	12.47	12.33	12.12	12.29	12.40	12.43	12.64	12.71	12.99	13.01
Materials	12.15	12.34	12.45	12.77	12.74	12.77	13.01	13.38	13.54	13.91	14.13	14.29	13.11
Manufacturing	11.15	11.41	11.58	11.24	11.29	11.36	11.72	12.11	12.47	12.93	13.29	13.65	12.00
1943													
Industrial production, total	14.28	14.66	14.76	14.95	15.06	14.98	15.43	15.76	16.16	16.40	16.61	16.40	15.44
Products	13.88	14.20	14.36	14.54	14.68	14.83	15.23	15.49	15.92	16.16	16.39	16.05	15.14
Consumer goods	12.60	12.71	12.74	12.88	13.09	13.30	13.51	13.58	13.68	13.58	13.55	13.27	13.22
Materials	14.50	14.87	15.03	15.17	15.14	14.77	15.33	15.62	16.02	16.28	16.42	16.42	15.44
Manufacturing	13.84	14.13	14.25	14.42	14.52	14.56	14.90	15.21	15.62	15.96	16.18	15.91	14.93
1944													
Industrial production, total	16.59	16.72	16.70	16.70	16.59	16.53	16.51	16.72	16.61	16.67	16.53	16.48	16.61
Products	16.26	16.42	16.42	16.47	16.45	16.50	16.63	16.82	16.68	16.71	16.50	16.37	16.52
Consumer goods	13.41	13.48	13.65	13.72	13.82	13.89	13.96	14.28	13.96	14.00	13.96	13.96	13.85
Materials	16.58	16.71	16.63	16.58	16.34	16.10	15.86	16.04	16.02	16.07	16.10	16.18	16.27
Manufacturing	16.15	16.27	16.25	16.22	16.10	16.08	16.08	16.30	16.20	16.25	16.10	16.10	16.16
1945													
Industrial production, total	16.32	16.27	16.16	15.86	15.43	15.08	14.74	13.21	12.02	11.54	11.97	12.02	14.26
Products	16.24	16.05	15.81	15.52	15.10	14.81	14.57	12.98	11.63	11.34	11.50	11.53	13.96
Consumer goods	14.17	14.07	14.03	14.14	14.17	14.28	14.24	13.61	14.28	14.49	14.90	15.08	14.29
Materials	15.99	16.15	16.18	15.94	15.51	15.11	14.55	13.19	12.21	11.54	12.34	12.47	14.29
Manufacturing	15.89	15.82	15.65	15.31	14.83	14.42	14.08	12.37	11.00	10.57	10.86	10.98	13.51
1946													
Industrial production, total	11.35	10.79	11.92	11.70	11.27	11.97	12.37	12.83	13.07	13.31	13.39	13.47	12.28
Products	11.40	11.29	11.56	11.74	11.61	11.74	12.00	12.40	12.74	12.96	13.09	13.22	12.14
Consumer goods	15.74	16.37	16.26	16.44	16.50	16.54	16.92	17.48	17.83	18.04	18.28	18.39	17.08
Materials	10.93	9.62	12.10	11.30	10.45	11.91	12.61	13.09	13.17	13.46	13.43	13.51	12.13
Manufacturing	10.23	9.58	10.78	10.81	10.30	10.88	11.24	11.75	11.99	12.25	12.40	12.45	11.21
1947													
Industrial production, total	13.64	13.72	13.80	13.69	13.74	13.74	13.66	13.74	13.85	13.98	14.17	14.23	13.81
Products	13.35	13.41	13.46	13.46	13.49	13.46	13.43	13.51	13.64	13.83	14.01	14.09	13.60
Consumer goods	18.00	17.93	18.00	17.93	17.79	17.83	17.90	18.04	18.21	18.49	18.77	18.80	18.14
Materials	13.51	13.62	14.07	13.73	13.78	13.65	13.51	13.49	13.67	13.78	14.10	13.94	13.74
Manufacturing	12.40	12.45	12.49	12.52	12.42	12.42	12.35	12.42	12.47	12.64	12.83	12.85	12.52

NOTES AND DEFINITIONS, CHAPTER 2

Tables 2-1 through 2-4

Industrial Production and Capacity Utilization

SOURCE: BOARD OF GOVERNORS OF THE FEDERAL RESERVE SYSTEM

The *industrial production index* measures changes in the physical volume or quantity of output of manufacturing, mining, and electric and gas utilities. *Capacity utilization* is calculated by dividing a seasonally adjusted industrial production index for an industry or group of industries by a related index of productive capacity.

The index of industrial production is one of the oldest continuous statistical series maintained by the Federal government, and one of the few economic indicators for which monthly data are available before the post-World-War-II period. This edition of *Business Statistics* reprints monthly and annual values for total industrial production and its manufacturing component beginning with January 1919.

In 2011 a revision of the entire industrial production data system included rebasing all of the indexes from the previous comparison base, 2002 = 100, to 2007 = 100. This affected the levels of all current and historical production indexes, though not necessarily the changes that they record over time. All the data shown here reflect the 2011 and all subsequent revisions through May 2014.

Around the 15th day of each month, the Federal Reserve issues estimates of industrial production and capacity utilization for the previous month. The production estimates are in the form of index numbers (2007 = 100) that reflect the monthly levels of total output of the nation's factories, mines, and gas and electric utilities expressed as a percent of the monthly average in the 2007 base year. Capacity estimates are expressed as index numbers, 2007 <u>output</u> (not 2007 <u>capacity</u>) = 100, and capacity utilization is measured by the production index as a percent of the capacity index. Since, for each component industry, the bases of those two indexes are the same, this procedure yields production as a percent of capacity. Monthly estimates are subject to revision in subsequent months, as well as to annual and comprehensive revisions in subsequent years.

Definitions and notes on the Data

The index of industrial production measures a large portion of the goods output of the national economy on a monthly basis. This portion, together with construction, has also accounted for the bulk of the variation in output over the course of many historical business cycles. The substantial industrial detail included in the index illuminates structural developments in the economy.

The total industrial production index and the indexes for its major components are constructed from individual industry series (312 series for data from 1997 forward) based on the 2012 North American Industry Classification System (NAICS). See the Preface to this volume for information on NAICS.

The Federal Reserve has been able to provide a longer continuous historical series on the NAICS basis than some other government agencies. In a major research effort, the Fed and the Census Bureau's Center for Economic Studies re-coded data from seven Censuses of Manufactures, beginning in 1963, to establish benchmark NAICS data for output, value added, and capacity utilization. The resulting indexes are shown annually for the last 42 years (47 years for aggregate levels) in Tables 2-1 through 2-3.

The Fed's featured indexes for total industry and total manufacturing are on the Standard Industrial Classification (SIC) basis and do <u>not</u> observe the reclassifications under NAICS of the logging industry to the Agriculture sector and the publishing industry to the Information sector. (The reason cited by the Fed was to avoid "changing the scope or historical continuity of these statistics.") One advantage of the SIC index for capacity utilization is that it is a continuous series back to 1948 (shown in Table 2-4A). On the new NAICS basis, production and capacity utilization are shown back to 1972 in Tables 2-2 and 2-3.

The individual series components of the indexes are grouped in two ways: market groups and industry groups.

Market groups. For analyzing market trends and product flows, the individual series are grouped into two major divisions: *final products and nonindustrial supplies* and *materials. Final products* consists of products purchased by consumers, businesses, or government for final use. *Nonindustrial supplies* are expected to become inputs in nonindustrial sectors: the two major subgroups are *construction supplies* and *business supplies. Materials* comprises industrial output that requires further processing within the industrial sector. This twofold division distinguishes between products that are ready to ship outside the industrial sector and those that will stay within the sector for further processing.

Final products are divided into *consumer goods* and *equipment*, and *equipment* is divided into *business equipment* and *defense and space equipment.* Further subdivisions of each market group are based on type of product and the market destination for the product.

Industry groups are typically groupings by 3-digit NAICS industries and major aggregates of these industries—for example, *durable goods* and *nondurable goods manufacturing, mining,* and *utilities.* Indexes are also calculated for *stage-of-process* industry groups—*crude, primary and semifinished,* and *finished* processing. The stage-of-process grouping was a new feature in the 2002 revision, replacing the two narrower and less well-defined "primary processing manufacturing" and "advanced processing manufacturing" groups that were previously published. *Crude processing* consists of logging, much of mining, and certain basic manufacturing activities in the chemical, paper, and metals industries. *Primary and semifinished processing* represents industries that produce materials and parts used as inputs by other industries. *Finished processing* includes industries that produce goods in their finished form for use by consumers, business investment, or government.

The indexes of industrial production are constructed using data from a variety of sources. Current monthly estimates of production are based on measures of physical output where possible and appropriate. For a few high-tech industries, the estimated value of nominal output is deflated by a corresponding price index. For industries in which such direct measurement is not possible on a monthly basis, output is inferred from production-worker hours, adjusted for trends in worker productivity derived from annual and benchmark revisions. (Between the 1960s and 1997, electric power consumption was used as a monthly output indicator for some industries instead of hours. However, the coverage of the electric power consumption survey deteriorated, and in the 2005 revision, the decision was made to resume the use of hours in those industries, beginning with the data for 1997.)

In annual and benchmark revisions, the individual indexes are revised using data from the quinquennial Censuses of Manufactures and Mineral Industries, the Annual Survey of Manufactures, and the quarterly Survey of Plant Capacity, prepared by the Census Bureau; deflators from the Producer Price Indexes and other sources; the *Minerals Yearbook*, prepared by the Department of the Interior; publications from the Department of Energy; and other sources.

The weights used in compiling the indexes are based on Census value added—the difference between the value of production and the cost of materials and supplies consumed. Census value added differs in some respects from the economic concept of industry value added used in the national income and product accounts (NIPAs). Industry value added as defined in the NIPAs is not available in sufficient detail for the industrial production indexes. See Chapter 14 for data and a description of NIPA value added (equivalently, gross domestic product) by major industry group.

Before 1972, a linked-Laspeyres formula (base period prices) is used to compute the weighted individual indexes. Beginning with 1972, the index uses a version of the Fisher-ideal index formula—a chain-weighting (continually updated average price) system similar to that in the NIPAs. See the "General Notes" article at the front of this book and the notes and definitions for Chapter 1 for more information. Chain-weighting keeps the index from being distorted by the use of obsolete relative prices.

For the purpose of these value-added weights, value added per unit of output is based on data from the Censuses of Manufacturing and Mineral Industries, the Census Bureau's Annual Survey of Manufactures, and revenue and expense data reported by the Department of Energy and the American Gas Association, which are projected into recent years by using changes in relevant Producer Price Indexes.

To separate seasonal movements from cyclical patterns and underlying trends, each component of the index is seasonally adjusted by the Census X-12-ARIMA method.

The index does not cover production on farms, in the construction industry, in transportation, or in various trade and service industries. A number of groups and subgroups include data for individual series not published separately.

Capacity utilization is calculated for the manufacturing, mining, and electric and gas utilities industries. Output is measured by seasonally adjusted indexes of industrial production. The capacity indexes attempt to capture the concept of sustainable maximum output, which is defined as the greatest level of output that a plant can maintain within the framework of a realistic work schedule, taking account of normal downtime and assuming sufficient availability of inputs to operate the machinery and equipment in place. The 89 individual industry capacity indexes are based on a variety of data, including capacity data measured in physical units compiled by government agencies and trade associations, Census Bureau surveys of utilization rates and investment, and estimates of growth of the capital stock.

In the "Explanatory Note" to its monthly release, the Federal Reserve includes the following "Perspective. Over the 1972–2012 period, the average total industry utilization rate is 80.2 percent; for manufacturing, the average factory operating rate has been 78.7 percent. Industrial plants usually operate at capacity utilization rates that are well below 100 percent: none of the broad aggregates has ever reached 100 percent. For total industry and total manufacturing, utilization rates have exceeded 90 percent only in wartime."

Revisions

Revisions normally occur annually. The data shown in this volume incorporate the annual revision released March 28, 2014, and subsequent updates through May 2014. New data incorporated in this revision include new minerals data through 2012 and new capacity data including the Census Quarterly Survey of Plant Capacity through the fourth quarter of 2013.

Data availability

Data are available monthly in Federal Reserve release G.17. Current and historical data and background information are available on the Federal Reserve Web site at <http://www.federalreserve.gov>.

Chain-weighting makes it difficult for the user to analyze in detail the sources of aggregate output change. An "Explanatory Note," included in each month's index release, provides some assistance for the user, including a reference to a an Internet location with the exact contribution of a monthly change in a component index to the monthly change in the total index.

References

The G.17 release each month contains extensive explanatory material, as well as references for further detail.

An earlier detailed description of the industrial production index, together with a history of the index, a glossary of terms, and a bibliography is presented in *Industrial Production—1986 Edition*, available from Publication Services, Mail Stop 127, Board of Governors of the Federal Reserve System, Washington, DC 20551.

CHAPTER 3: INCOME DISTRIBUTION AND POVERTY

Section 3a: Household and Family Income

**Figure 3-1: Median and Mean Household Income, 1967–2013
(2013 dollars)**

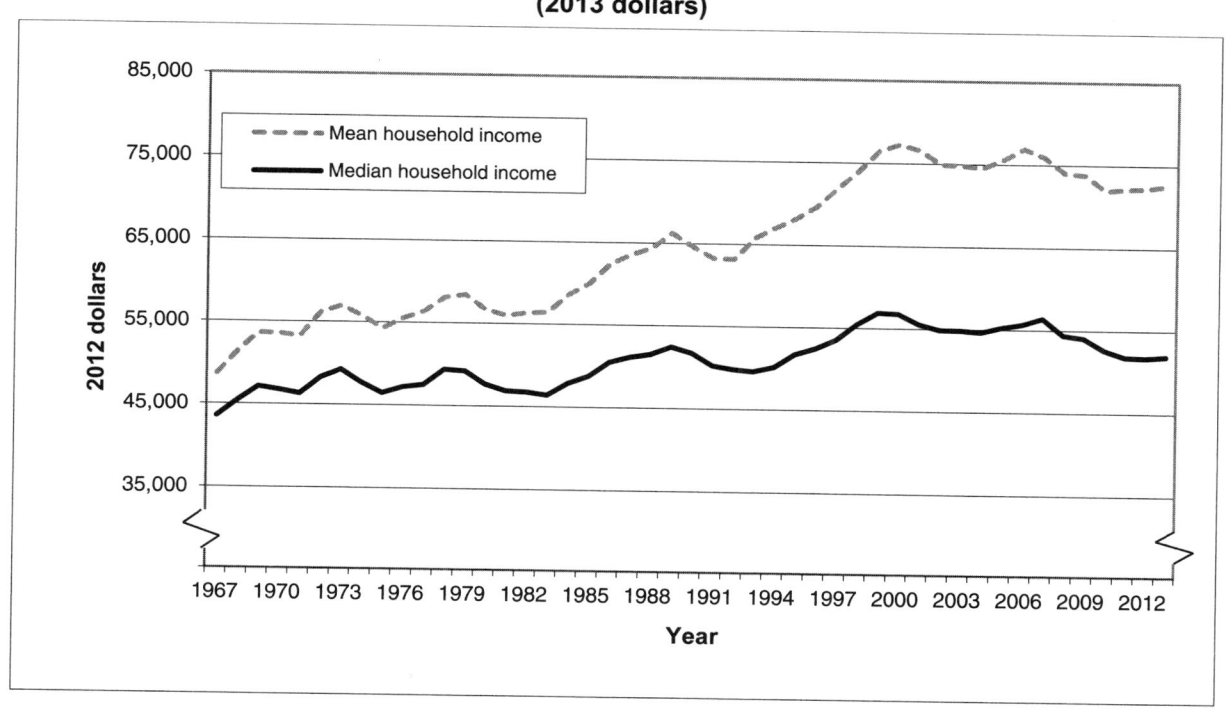

- Measured as cash income before taxes, median household income in 2013 was $51,939, up 0.3 percent from the previous year in constant (2013) dollars. This change was not in itself statistically significant, but it was the first increase since 2007, i.e. before the beginning of the Great Recession. Income was 8.7 percent below the all-time peak in 1999. From 1999 to 2007, real median household income declined 0.8 percent. In contrast, between 1978, before stagflation, and 1999 income <u>rose</u> an average 0.7 percent <u>per year</u>. Median income is the income of the household at the middle of the income distribution. (Table 3-1)

- The Census Bureau also tabulates "mean income," which is the sum of all the reported household incomes divided by the number of households; this is also shown in Figure 3-1 above. Mean income is higher than median income when the distribution of income is skewed upward by very large incomes at the top of the distribution. (Table 3-1)

- Household income inequality, as measured by the "Gini coefficient," declined from .463 to .459 in 2013, indicating a declining income inequality. A new measure of inequality based on "equivalence-adjusted income," which takes account of the size and composition of the household, also remained at a new record; it is slightly lower in level than the raw "Gini" but has increased 27 percent since 1967, compared with 18 percent for the unadjusted measure. (Table 3-4)

- The ratio of women's to men's earnings for year-round, full-time workers increased from about 0.6 in 1980 to 0.778 in 2007, but dropped slightly until 2012. The 2013 rate was .783, up 2.3 percent. Men's median earnings were 4.6 percent below their all-time high in 1973, in real terms, while women's were up 32.0 percent over that time span. Since 2007, men's real earnings are down 1.2 percent and women's down 0.7 percent. (Table 3-1)

Table 3-1. Median and Mean Household Income and Median Earnings

(2013 dollars, except as noted.)

Year	Number of households (thousands)	Average size of household (number of people)	Median household income — All races	White Total	White Not Hispanic	Black	Asian [1]	Hispanic (any race)	Mean household income, all races	Male workers	Female workers	Ratio, female to male
1960	. . .	. . .	. . .	. . .	. . .	. . .	. . .	. . .	. . .	36 950	22 419	0.607
1961	. . .	. . .	. . .	. . .	. . .	. . .	. . .	. . .	. . .	38 128	22 591	0.593
1962	. . .	. . .	. . .	. . .	. . .	. . .	. . .	. . .	. . .	38 825	23 023	0.593
1963	. . .	. . .	. . .	. . .	. . .	. . .	. . .	. . .	. . .	39 801	23 461	0.589
1964	. . .	. . .	. . .	. . .	. . .	. . .	. . .	. . .	. . .	40 730	24 091	0.591
1965	. . .	. . .	. . .	. . .	. . .	. . .	. . .	. . .	. . .	41 311	24 755	0.599
1966	60 813	. . .	43 558	45 424	. . .	26 374	. . .	. . .	48 717	43 115	24 815	0.576
1967	62 214	. . .	45 435	47 307	. . .	27 896	. . .	. . .	51 403	43 796	25 307	0.578
1968	63 401	. . .	47 124	49 180	. . .	29 727	. . .	. . .	53 613	44 972	26 153	0.582
1969	. . .	. . .	. . .	. . .	. . .	. . .	. . .	. . .	. . .	46 214	27 958	0.605
1970	64 778	. . .	46 759	48 702	. . .	29 643	. . .	. . .	53 542	48 001	28 498	0.594
1971	66 676	. . .	46 304	48 433	. . .	28 609	. . .	. . .	53 254	48 207	28 686	0.595
1972	68 251	. . .	48 287	50 658	51 380	29 569	. . .	. . .	56 200	50 802	29 395	0.579
1973	69 859	. . .	49 262	51 629	52 084	30 391	. . .	38 229	56 971	52 421	29 688	0.566
1974	71 163	. . .	47 702	49 888	50 314	29 669	. . .	38 165	55 784	50 540	29 694	0.588
1975	72 867	2.89	46 945	48 579	48 945	29 163	. . .	37 942	54 244	50 225	29 541	0.588
1976	74 142	2.86	47 224	49 469	50 477	29 415	. . .	34 899	55 548	50 087	30 149	0.602
1977	76 030	2.81	47 523	49 974	50 965	29 490	. . .	35 621	56 375	51 213	30 176	0.589
1978	77 330	2.78	49 362	51 315	52 282	30 838	. . .	37 281	58 098	51 544	30 638	0.594
1979	80 776	2.76	49 225	51 611	52 338	30 302	. . .	38 676	58 474	50 878	30 355	0.597
1980	82 368	2.73	47 668	50 290	51 180	28 972	. . .	39 001	56 693	50 096	30 138	0.602
1981	83 527	2.72	46 877	49 528	50 243	27 793	. . .	36 743	56 002	49 791	29 494	0.592
1982	83 918	2.73	46 751	48 944	49 764	27 739	. . .	37 602	56 342	48 851	30 163	0.617
1983	85 407	2.71	46 425	48 685	. . .	27 628	. . .	35 179	56 463	48 639	30 931	0.636
1984	86 789	2.69	47 866	50 497	51 546	28 767	. . .	35 357	58 648	49 581	31 562	0.637
1985	88 458	2.67	48 761	51 424	52 581	30 595	. . .	36 286	60 009	49 952	32 257	0.646
1986	89 479	2.66	50 488	53 079	54 286	30 580	. . .	36 058	62 375	51 216	32 916	0.643
1987	91 124	2.64	51 121	53 861	55 342	30 742	63 214	37 215	63 575	50 895	33 172	0.652
1988	92 830	2.62	51 514	54 458	55 958	31 044	61 054	37 929	64 365	50 437	33 313	0.660
1989	93 347	2.63	52 432	55 153	56 339	32 801	65 485	38 522	66 243	49 575	34 045	0.687
1990	94 312	2.63	51 735	53 960	55 194	32 268	66 433	39 762	64 624	47 821	34 248	0.716
1991	95 669	2.62	50 249	52 656	53 914	31 369	60 796	38 581	63 253	49 073	34 282	0.699
1992	96 426	2.66	49 836	52 395	54 154	30 509	61 492	37 848	63 182	49 122	34 771	0.708
1993	97 107	2.67	49 594	52 323	54 249	31 008	60 875	36 759	65 766	48 270	34 523	0.715
1994	98 990	2.65	50 148	52 889	54 596	32 682	62 921	36 331	67 041	47 956	34 513	0.720
1995	99 627	2.65	51 719	54 284	56 427	33 987	61 642	36 403	68 204	47 803	34 145	0.714
1996	101 016	2.64	52 471	54 939	57 342	34 716	63 979	34 696	69 666	47 521	35 053	0.738
1997	102 528	2.62	53 551	56 397	58 720	36 250	65 481	36 821	71 910	48 730	36 139	0.742
1998	103 874	2.61	55 497	58 390	60 569	36 181	66 560	38 534	74 007	50 444	36 910	0.732
1999	106 434	2.60	56 895	59 172	61 733	39 019	71 244	40 433	76 524	50 876	36 791	0.723
2000	108 209	2.58	56 800	59 406	61 715	40 131	75 423	42 984	77 287	50 391	37 148	0.737
2001	109 297	2.58	55 562	58 574	60 927	38 776	70 571	44 367	76 588	50 361	38 440	0.763
2002	111 278	2.57	54 913	. . .	. . .	. . .	. . .	44 164	74 910	51 055	39 108	0.766
2003	112 000	2.57	54 865	. . .	. . .	. . .	. . .	42 863	74 812	51 509	38 914	0.755
2004	113 343	2.57	54 674	. . .	. . .	. . .	. . .	41 793	74 569	50 311	38 526	0.766
2005	114 384	2.57	55 278	. . .	. . .	. . .	. . .	42 264	75 584	49 383	38 014	0.770
2006	116 011	2.56	55 689	. . .	. . .	. . .	. . .	42 917	76 912	48 826	37 566	0.769
2007	116 783	2.56	56 436	. . .	. . .	. . .	. . .	43 650	75 957	50 684	39 436	0.778
2008	117 181	2.57	54 423	. . .	. . .	. . .	. . .	43 455	74 029	50 165	38 673	0.771
2009	117 538	2.59	54 059	. . .	. . .	. . .	. . .	41 018	73 824	51 181	39 399	0.770
2010	119 927	2.56	52 646	. . .	. . .	. . .	. . .	41 312	72 001	51 231	39 411	0.769
2011	121 084	2.55	51 842	. . .	. . .	. . .	. . .	40 205	72 166	49 924	38 444	0.770
2012	122 459	2.54	51 758	. . .	. . .	. . .	. . .	40 004	72 310	50 116	38 340	0.765
2013	122 952	2.55	51 939	. . .	. . .	. . .	. . .	39 572	72 641	50 033	39 157	0.783
By race												
Race alone												
2002	. . .	. . .	. . .	58 380	60 729	37 584	68 143	. . .	. . .	. . .	. . .	. . .
2003	. . .	. . .	. . .	57 795	60 513	37 547	70 547	. . .	. . .	. . .	. . .	. . .
2004	. . .	. . .	. . .	57 540	60 318	37 114	70 916	. . .	. . .	. . .	. . .	. . .
2005	. . .	. . .	. . .	57 936	60 597	36 821	72 899	. . .	. . .	. . .	. . .	. . .
2006	. . .	. . .	. . .	58 545	60 567	36 935	74 218	. . .	. . .	. . .	. . .	. . .
2007	. . .	. . .	. . .	58 550	61 702	38 104	74 265	. . .	. . .	. . .	. . .	. . .
2008	. . .	. . .	. . .	56 597	60 078	37 021	71 013	. . .	. . .	. . .	. . .	. . .
2009	. . .	. . .	. . .	56 323	59 146	35 387	71 101	. . .	. . .	. . .	. . .	. . .
2010	. . .	. . .	. . .	55 246	58 185	34 321	68 654	. . .	. . .	. . .	. . .	. . .
2011	. . .	. . .	. . .	54 079	57 392	33 380	67 456	. . .	. . .	. . .	. . .	. . .
2012	. . .	. . .	. . .	54 486	57 837	33 805	69 633	. . .	. . .	. . .	. . .	. . .
2013	. . .	. . .	. . .	55 257	58 270	34 598	67 065	. . .	. . .	. . .	. . .	. . .
Race alone or in combination												
2002	. . .	. . .	. . .	. . .	. . .	37 780	67 701	. . .	. . .	. . .	. . .	. . .
2003	. . .	. . .	. . .	. . .	. . .	37 603	69 993	. . .	. . .	. . .	. . .	. . .
2004	. . .	. . .	. . .	. . .	. . .	37 287	70 848	. . .	. . .	. . .	. . .	. . .
2005	. . .	. . .	. . .	. . .	. . .	36 935	72 845	. . .	. . .	. . .	. . .	. . .
2006	. . .	. . .	. . .	. . .	. . .	37 124	73 827	. . .	. . .	. . .	. . .	. . .
2007	. . .	. . .	. . .	. . .	. . .	38 301	74 010	. . .	. . .	. . .	. . .	. . .
2008	. . .	. . .	. . .	. . .	. . .	37 158	70 938	. . .	. . .	. . .	. . .	. . .
2009	. . .	. . .	. . .	. . .	. . .	35 568	70 671	. . .	. . .	. . .	. . .	. . .
2010	. . .	. . .	. . .	. . .	. . .	34 355	67 872	. . .	. . .	. . .	. . .	. . .
2011	. . .	. . .	. . .	. . .	. . .	33 522	67 317	. . .	. . .	. . .	. . .	. . .
2012	. . .	. . .	. . .	. . .	. . .	34 208	69 173	. . .	. . .	. . .	. . .	. . .
2013	. . .	. . .	. . .	. . .	. . .	34 775	67 366	. . .	. . .	. . .	. . .	. . .

[1] For 1987 through 2001, Asian and Pacific Islander.
. . . = Not available.

Table 3-2. Median Income and Poverty Rates by Race and Hispanic Origin Using 3–Year Moving Averages

(Income in 2013 dollars; percent of population.)

Race and Hispanic origin	Median household income, 2013 dollars								
	2003–2005	2004–2006	2005–2007	2006–2008	2007–2009	2008–2010	2009–2011	2010–2012	2002–2004
All Races	54 032	54 152	54 423	55 002	54 721	54 185	52 940	52 092	51 336
White alone or in combination	56 969	56 831	57 081	57 413	56 993	56 248	55 137	54 294	53 651
White alone	57 076	56 930	57 176	57 508	57 068	56 338	55 252	54 425	53 822
Not Hispanic	58 432	58 390	58 407	58 853	58 686	58 228	57 097	56 232	. . .
Black alone or in combination	37 019	36 741	36 584	36 917	36 990	36 479	35 182	33 988	33 541
Black alone	36 880	36 629	36 427	36 752	36 818	36 310	35 067	33 871	33 351
American Indian and Alaskan Native alone or in combination	44 055	43 777	42 554	42 113	42 014	41 470	40 387	38 781	37 757
American Indian and Alaskan Native alone	40 183	39 555	38 371	38 693	37 932	38 002	36 081	34 649	33 801
Asian alone or in combination	68 519	70 208	71 468	72 507	71 881	70 844	68 827	67 637	67 145
Asian alone	68 868	70 430	71 637	72 737	72 118	71 094	69 250	68 081	67 599
Native Hawaiian and Other Pacific Islander alone or in combination	63 381	63 055	62 491	63 784	63 705	61 848	60 728	58 479	56 136
Native Hawaiian and Other Pacific Islander alone	62 776	63 892	62 624	62 321	62 003	61 245	60 802	58 539	55 764
Hispanic (any race)	41 701	41 718	42 329	42 720	42 096	41 328	40 260	39 927	39 355

Race and Hispanic origin	Poverty rates								
	2003–2005	2004–2006	2005–2007	2006–2008	2007–2009	2008–2010	2009–2011	2010–2012	2011–2013
All Races	12.4	12.6	12.4	12.5	12.7	13.4	14.2	14.8	15.0
White alone or in combination	10.6	10.7	10.6	10.5	10.8	11.5	12.3	12.9	13.0
White alone	10.5	10.6	10.5	10.4	10.7	11.3	12.2	12.7	12.8
Not Hispanic	8.3	8.4	8.3	8.2	8.3	8.7	9.3	9.7	9.8
Black alone or in combination	24.3	24.6	24.3	24.4	24.4	25.0	26.0	26.9	27.3
Black alone	24.4	24.7	24.4	24.6	24.5	25.0	26.0	26.9	27.4
American Indian and Alaskan Native alone or in combination	19.2	19.7	19.2	21.2	21.6	21.9	23.7	24.4	26.0
American Indian and Alaskan Native alone	24.3	25.3	24.3	26.6	26.7	26.1	27.8	28.3	30.5
Asian alone or in combination	10.5	10.8	10.5	10.4	10.6	11.4	12.0	12.2	11.9
Asian alone	10.6	10.9	10.6	10.5	10.8	11.5	12.1	12.3	12.0
Native Hawaiian and Other Pacific Islander alone or in combination	. . .	. . .	. . .	. . .	. . .	. . .	. . .	. . .	. . .
Native Hawaiian and Other Pacific Islander alone	. . .	. . .	. . .	. . .	. . .	. . .	. . .	. . .	. . .
Hispanic (any race)	22.1	22.0	22.1	21.3	21.8	23.3	25.0	25.7	25.8

. . . = Not available.

Table 3-3. Median Family Income by Type of Family

(2013 dollars, except as noted.)

Year	All families	Married couples			Male householder [1]	Female householder [1]	4-person families	Average size of family (number of people)
		Total	Wife in paid labor force	Wife not in paid labor force				
1947	27 651	28 362	. . .	. . .	26 784	19 814	30 032	3.64
1948	26 920	27 638	. . .	. . .	27 833	17 434	29 294	3.58
1949	26 573	27 325	32 987	26 154	24 127	17 986	28 890	3.54
1950	28 035	29 108	33 813	28 002	26 312	16 235	31 042	3.54
1951	29 035	30 037	36 253	28 448	27 024	17 379	32 269	3.54
1952	29 905	31 220	37 669	29 305	27 791	17 182	33 618	3.53
1953	32 393	33 378	41 273	31 438	31 408	18 747	. . .	3.59
1954	31 538	32 795	40 386	30 660	30 380	17 362	. . .	3.59
1955	33 587	34 963	42 740	32 887	31 853	18 785	37 395	3.58
1956	35 782	37 227	44 593	34 771	31 193	20 616	39 817	3.60
1957	35 993	37 377	44 509	35 029	33 203	20 026	39 776	3.64
1958	35 882	37 490	43 831	35 148	30 048	19 334	40 100	3.65
1959	37 897	39 611	46 908	37 197	32 272	19 337	42 465	3.67
1960	38 684	40 426	47 495	37 996	33 453	20 430	43 330	3.70
1961	39 083	41 141	48 984	38 108	34 544	20 397	43 866	3.67
1962	40 188	42 260	50 343	38 893	38 535	21 127	45 586	3.68
1963	41 591	43 881	51 841	40 193	38 004	21 371	47 508	3.70
1964	43 133	45 517	53 646	41 617	38 032	22 706	49 168	3.70
1965	44 990	46 982	55 596	42 630	39 759	22 841	50 442	3.69
1966	47 366	49 290	58 144	44 825	40 448	25 217	52 453	3.67
1967	48 376	51 474	60 712	46 412	41 552	26 185	54 846	3.63
1968	50 652	53 656	62 705	48 205	42 959	26 271	57 705	3.60
1969	52 989	56 180	65 325	49 877	46 849	27 087	59 674	3.58
1970	52 825	56 299	65 722	49 811	48 247	27 266	59 785	3.57
1971	52 751	56 367	65 922	49 976	44 735	26 229	59 629	3.53
1972	55 353	59 272	69 202	52 565	51 315	26 601	63 779	3.48
1973	56 475	61 053	71 405	53 508	50 340	27 166	64 249	3.44
1974	54 966	59 316	69 106	52 107	49 666	27 641	63 772	3.42
1975	54 008	58 527	67 857	50 201	51 158	26 943	62 389	3.39
1976	55 682	60 316	69 727	51 858	47 872	26 843	64 456	3.37
1977	56 056	61 683	70 969	52 744	50 835	27 189	65 559	3.33
1978	57 803	63 374	72 447	52 940	52 318	27 974	66 939	3.31
1979	58 573	64 081	74 344	52 948	50 262	29 545	67 320	3.29
1980	56 585	62 286	72 347	51 065	47 154	28 014	65 492	3.27
1981	55 021	61 600	71 878	49 951	48 880	26 935	64 571	3.25
1982	54 312	60 306	70 325	49 366	46 679	26 617	64 014	3.26
1983	54 638	60 653	71 370	48 659	48 559	26 205	64 872	3.24
1984	56 447	63 235	74 032	50 358	49 810	27 340	66 406	3.23
1985	57 261	64 208	75 215	50 698	46 705	28 202	67 671	3.21
1986	59 737	66 524	77 760	52 325	50 619	27 674	70 399	3.19
1987	60 750	68 418	79 936	52 257	49 448	28 802	72 747	3.17
1988	60 910	68 853	80 812	51 504	50 761	29 037	73 890	3.16
1989	62 059	69 920	82 108	52 144	50 511	29 824	73 940	3.17
1990	61 082	68 930	80 820	52 291	50 185	29 255	71 618	3.18
1991	59 945	68 378	80 344	50 164	47 289	27 842	71 816	3.17
1992	59 494	68 143	80 970	49 085	44 859	27 695	71 984	3.19
1993	58 671	68 269	81 285	47 970	42 016	27 690	71 692	3.20
1994	60 279	69 879	82 858	48 457	43 133	28 344	73 070	3.19
1995	61 637	71 428	84 725	49 137	46 076	29 886	75 412	3.20
1996	62 536	73 486	86 310	49 893	46 717	29 436	76 164	3.19
1997	64 495	74 659	87 796	52 136	47 697	30 423	77 204	3.18
1998	66 703	77 326	90 985	53 036	50 924	31 631	80 010	3.18
1999	68 268	78 991	92 939	53 797	52 201	33 220	83 540	3.15
2000	68 626	79 944	93 655	54 084	51 034	34 786	84 774	3.14
2001	67 640	79 387	93 201	53 660	48 144	33 874	83 259	3.15
2002	66 918	79 154	94 273	51 926	48 866	34 214	81 229	3.13
2003	66 723	78 883	95 208	52 084	48 170	33 627	82 445	3.13
2004	66 670	78 466	94 779	52 061	49 775	33 259	81 422	3.13
2005	67 053	78 641	93 973	53 048	49 055	32 508	83 899	3.13
2006	67 481	80 186	95 649	52 865	48 345	33 308	84 820	3.13
2007	68 931	81 552	97 108	53 173	49 835	34 037	85 019	3.15
2008	66 560	78 701	93 716	52 475	47 140	32 597	82 734	3.15
2009	65 257	77 789	93 342	51 748	45 071	32 331	80 807	3.16
2010	64 356	77 182	93 374	52 066	46 161	31 149	79 863	3.14
2011	63 152	76 426	92 197	52 215	44 608	31 340	78 270	3.13
2012	63 145	76 633	93 113	51 620	42 974	31 132	80 856	3.12
2013	63 815	76 339	94 299	51 839	44 475	31 408	80 356	3.14

[1]No spouse present.
. . . = Not available.

Table 3-4. Shares of Aggregate Income Received by Each Fifth and Top 5 Percent of Households

Year	Money income							Equivalence-adjusted income						
	Share of aggregate income (percent)						Gini coefficient	Share of aggregate income (percent)						Gini coefficient
	Lowest fifth	Second fifth	Third fifth	Fourth fifth	Highest fifth	Top 5 percent		Lowest fifth	Second fifth	Third fifth	Fourth fifth	Highest fifth	Top 5 percent	
1967	4.0	10.8	17.3	24.2	43.6	17.2	0.397	5.6	12.0	17.1	23.2	42.1	. . .	0.362
1968	4.2	11.1	17.6	24.5	42.6	16.3	0.386	5.8	12.3	17.4	23.4	41.1	. . .	0.351
1969	4.1	10.9	17.5	24.5	43.0	16.6	0.391	5.8	12.2	17.3	23.4	41.3	. . .	0.353
1970	4.1	10.8	17.4	24.5	43.3	16.6	0.394	5.7	12.1	17.3	23.4	41.5	. . .	0.357
1971	4.1	10.6	17.3	24.5	43.5	16.7	0.396	5.7	12.0	17.2	23.4	41.7	. . .	0.359
1972	4.1	10.4	17.0	24.5	43.9	17.0	0.401	5.6	11.9	17.2	23.4	41.9	. . .	0.362
1973	4.2	10.4	17.0	24.5	43.9	16.9	0.400	5.6	12.0	17.2	23.5	41.7	. . .	0.360
1974	4.3	10.6	17.0	24.6	43.5	16.5	0.395	5.8	12.1	17.3	23.6	41.2	. . .	0.354
1975	4.3	10.4	17.0	24.7	43.6	16.5	0.397	5.6	11.9	17.3	23.6	41.6	. . .	0.359
1976	4.3	10.3	17.0	24.7	43.7	16.6	0.398	5.6	11.8	17.4	23.8	41.5	. . .	0.359
1977	4.2	10.2	16.9	24.7	44.0	16.8	0.402	5.5	11.7	17.3	23.7	41.7	. . .	0.362
1978	4.2	10.2	16.8	24.7	44.1	16.8	0.402	5.4	11.8	17.3	23.7	41.8	. . .	0.363
1979	4.1	10.2	16.8	24.6	44.2	16.9	0.404	5.3	11.7	17.2	23.8	41.9	. . .	0.366
1980	4.2	10.2	16.8	24.7	44.1	16.5	0.403	5.2	11.6	17.3	24.0	41.9	. . .	0.367
1981	4.1	10.1	16.7	24.8	44.3	16.5	0.406	5.0	11.4	17.2	24.0	42.4	. . .	0.373
1982	4.0	10.0	16.5	24.5	45.0	17.0	0.412	4.7	11.1	17.0	23.9	43.2	. . .	0.384
1983	4.0	9.9	16.4	24.6	45.1	17.0	0.414	4.6	11.0	16.9	24.0	43.5	. . .	0.389
1984	4.0	9.9	16.3	24.6	45.2	17.1	0.415	4.6	11.0	16.8	24.0	43.6	. . .	0.389
1985	3.9	9.8	16.2	24.4	45.6	17.6	0.419	4.6	10.9	16.7	23.7	44.1	. . .	0.394
1986	3.8	9.7	16.2	24.3	46.1	18.0	0.425	4.5	10.8	16.6	23.8	44.3	. . .	0.397
1987	3.8	9.6	16.1	24.3	46.2	18.2	0.426	4.4	10.8	16.7	23.8	44.4	. . .	0.399
1988	3.8	9.6	16.0	24.2	46.3	18.3	0.426	4.4	10.7	16.5	23.7	44.7	. . .	0.402
1989	3.8	9.5	15.8	24.0	46.8	18.9	0.431	4.4	10.5	16.3	23.4	45.4	. . .	0.408
1990	3.8	9.6	15.9	24.0	46.6	18.5	0.428	4.4	10.6	16.3	23.5	45.1	. . .	0.406
1991	3.8	9.6	15.9	24.2	46.5	18.1	0.428	4.3	10.6	16.5	23.7	45.0	. . .	0.406
1992	3.8	9.4	15.8	24.2	46.9	18.6	0.433	4.1	10.3	16.3	23.7	45.5	. . .	0.413
1993	3.6	9.0	15.1	23.5	48.9	21.0	0.454	3.9	9.8	15.6	23.0	47.7	. . .	0.436
1994	3.6	8.9	15.0	23.4	49.1	21.2	0.456	4.0	9.8	15.6	22.8	47.8	. . .	0.436
1995	3.7	9.1	15.2	23.3	48.7	21.0	0.450	4.1	9.9	15.6	22.8	47.6	. . .	0.433
1996	3.6	9.0	15.1	23.3	49.0	21.4	0.455	4.0	9.8	15.5	22.7	47.9	. . .	0.437
1997	3.6	8.9	15.0	23.2	49.4	21.7	0.459	4.0	9.8	15.4	22.6	48.3	. . .	0.440
1998	3.6	9.0	15.0	23.2	49.2	21.4	0.456	4.0	9.8	15.4	22.7	48.1	. . .	0.439
1999	3.6	8.9	14.9	23.2	49.4	21.5	0.458	4.0	9.7	15.3	22.6	48.4	. . .	0.441
2000	3.6	8.9	14.8	23.0	49.8	22.1	0.462	4.1	9.8	15.2	22.3	48.6	. . .	0.442
2001	3.5	8.7	14.6	23.0	50.1	22.4	0.466	4.0	9.6	15.2	22.4	48.8	. . .	0.446
2002	3.5	8.8	14.8	23.3	49.7	21.7	0.462	4.0	9.6	15.2	22.7	48.4	. . .	0.443
2003	3.4	8.7	14.8	23.4	49.8	21.4	0.464	3.9	9.5	15.2	22.8	48.6	. . .	0.445
2004	3.4	8.7	14.7	23.2	50.1	21.8	0.466	3.8	9.6	15.2	22.7	48.7	. . .	0.447
2005	3.4	8.6	14.6	23.0	50.4	22.2	0.469	3.8	9.5	15.1	22.6	49.1	. . .	0.450
2006	3.4	8.6	14.5	22.9	50.5	22.3	0.470	3.8	9.4	14.9	22.5	49.3	. . .	0.452
2007	3.4	8.7	14.8	23.4	49.7	21.2	0.463	3.8	9.5	15.3	22.9	48.5	. . .	0.444
2008	3.4	8.6	14.7	23.3	50.0	21.5	0.466	3.7	9.4	15.1	22.8	48.9	21.4	0.450
2009	3.4	8.6	14.6	23.2	50.3	21.7	0.468	3.6	9.3	15.0	22.9	49.4	21.7	0.456
2010	3.3	8.5	14.6	23.4	50.3	21.3	0.470	3.4	9.2	15.0	23.1	49.2	21.0	0.456
2011	3.2	8.4	14.3	23.0	51.1	22.3	0.477	3.4	9.0	14.8	22.8	50.0	22.1	0.463
2012	3.2	8.3	14.4	23.0	51.0	22.3	0.477	3.4	9.0	14.8	22.9	49.9	22.1	0.463
2013	3.2	8.4	14.4	23.0	51.0	22.2	0.476	3.5	9.1	14.9	22.9	49.6	22.3	0.459

. . . = Not available.

Table 3-5. Shares of Aggregate Income Received by Each Fifth and Top 5 Percent of Families

Year	Number of families (thousands)	Share of aggregate income (percent)						Mean family income (2013 dollars)						Gini coefficient
		Lowest fifth	Second fifth	Third fifth	Fourth fifth	Highest fifth	Top 5 percent	Lowest fifth	Second fifth	Third fifth	Fourth fifth	Highest fifth	Top 5 percent	
1947	37 237	5.0	11.9	17.0	23.1	43.0	17.5	. . .	. . .	. . .	. . .	. . .	. . .	0.376
1948	38 624	4.9	12.1	17.3	23.2	42.4	17.1	. . .	. . .	. . .	. . .	. . .	. . .	0.371
1949	39 303	4.5	11.9	17.3	23.5	42.7	16.9	. . .	. . .	. . .	. . .	. . .	. . .	0.378
1950	39 929	4.5	12.0	17.4	23.4	42.7	17.3	. . .	. . .	. . .	. . .	. . .	. . .	0.379
1951	40 578	5.0	12.4	17.6	23.4	41.6	16.8	. . .	. . .	. . .	. . .	. . .	. . .	0.363
1952	40 832	4.9	12.3	17.4	23.4	41.9	17.4	. . .	. . .	. . .	. . .	. . .	. . .	0.368
1953	41 202	4.7	12.5	18.0	23.9	40.9	15.7	. . .	. . .	. . .	. . .	. . .	. . .	0.359
1954	41 951	4.5	12.1	17.7	23.9	41.8	16.3	. . .	. . .	. . .	. . .	. . .	. . .	0.371
1955	42 889	4.8	12.3	17.8	23.7	41.3	16.4	. . .	. . .	. . .	. . .	. . .	. . .	0.363
1956	43 497	5.0	12.5	17.9	23.7	41.0	16.1	. . .	. . .	. . .	. . .	. . .	. . .	0.358
1957	43 696	5.1	12.7	18.1	23.8	40.4	15.6	. . .	. . .	. . .	. . .	. . .	. . .	0.351
1958	44 232	5.0	12.5	18.0	23.9	40.6	15.4	. . .	. . .	. . .	. . .	. . .	. . .	0.354
1959	45 111	4.9	12.3	17.9	23.8	41.1	15.9	. . .	. . .	. . .	. . .	. . .	. . .	0.361
1960	45 539	4.8	12.2	17.8	24.0	41.3	15.9	. . .	. . .	. . .	. . .	. . .	. . .	0.364
1961	46 418	4.7	11.9	17.5	23.8	42.2	16.6	. . .	. . .	. . .	. . .	. . .	. . .	0.374
1962	47 059	5.0	12.1	17.6	24.0	41.3	15.7	. . .	. . .	. . .	. . .	. . .	. . .	0.362
1963	47 540	5.0	12.1	17.7	24.0	41.2	15.8	. . .	. . .	. . .	. . .	. . .	. . .	0.362
1964	47 956	5.1	12.0	17.7	24.0	41.2	15.9	. . .	. . .	. . .	. . .	. . .	. . .	0.361
1965	48 509	5.2	12.2	17.8	23.9	40.9	15.5	. . .	. . .	. . .	. . .	. . .	. . .	0.356
1966	49 214	5.6	12.4	17.8	23.8	40.5	15.6	14 536	32 270	46 173	61 812	105 493	161 986	0.349
1967	50 111	5.4	12.2	17.5	23.5	41.4	16.4	14 762	33 011	47 448	63 635	112 364	177 778	0.358
1968	50 823	5.6	12.4	17.7	23.7	40.5	15.6	15 911	34 703	49 579	66 306	113 300	174 656	0.348
1969	51 586	5.6	12.4	17.7	23.7	40.6	15.6	16 417	36 256	51 881	69 500	119 028	182 819	0.349
1970	52 227	5.4	12.2	17.6	23.8	40.9	15.6	16 169	35 752	51 693	69 730	119 909	182 589	0.353
1971	53 296	5.5	12.0	17.6	23.8	41.1	15.7	16 183	35 227	51 541	69 801	120 224	183 311	0.355
1972	54 373	5.5	11.9	17.5	23.9	41.4	15.9	16 889	36 851	54 129	73 919	128 200	196 538	0.359
1973	55 053	5.5	11.9	17.5	24.0	41.1	15.5	17 331	37 540	55 158	75 380	129 332	195 183	0.356
1974	55 698	5.7	12.0	17.6	24.1	40.6	14.8	17 637	37 231	54 355	74 470	125 482	183 029	0.355
1975	56 245	5.6	11.9	17.7	24.2	40.7	14.9	16 945	35 823	53 265	72 931	122 901	180 288	0.357
1976	56 710	5.6	11.9	17.7	24.2	40.7	14.9	17 355	36 729	54 789	74 859	125 993	184 403	0.358
1977	57 215	5.5	11.7	17.6	24.3	40.9	14.9	17 281	36 940	55 557	76 638	129 109	188 221	0.363
1978	57 804	5.4	11.7	17.6	24.2	41.1	15.1	17 525	38 006	57 069	78 628	133 423	195 518	0.363
1979	59 550	5.4	11.6	17.5	24.1	41.4	15.3	17 679	38 224	57 645	79 363	136 124	201 495	0.365
1980	60 309	5.3	11.6	17.6	24.4	41.1	14.6	17 009	37 026	55 934	77 601	130 656	185 739	0.365
1981	61 019	5.3	11.4	17.5	24.6	41.2	14.4	16 480	35 837	54 812	76 955	129 122	180 426	0.369
1982	61 393	5.0	11.3	17.2	24.4	42.2	15.3	15 546	35 273	53 861	76 407	132 027	188 896	0.380
1983	62 015	4.9	11.2	17.2	24.5	42.4	15.3	15 309	35 223	54 193	77 236	133 920	193 087	0.382
1984	62 706	4.8	11.1	17.1	24.5	42.5	15.4	15 831	36 246	55 922	79 968	138 982	200 943	0.383
1985	63 558	4.8	11.0	16.9	24.3	43.1	16.1	16 013	36 746	56 734	81 323	144 524	215 977	0.389
1986	64 491	4.7	10.9	16.9	24.1	43.4	16.5	16 466	38 019	58 901	84 160	151 586	230 193	0.392
1987	65 204	4.6	10.7	16.8	24.0	43.8	17.2	16 448	38 498	59 780	85 557	156 357	244 768	0.393
1988	65 837	4.6	10.7	16.7	24.0	44.0	17.2	16 590	38 633	60 118	86 338	158 417	247 521	0.395
1989	66 090	4.6	10.6	16.5	23.7	44.6	17.9	16 921	39 366	61 157	87 988	165 673	265 394	0.401
1990	66 322	4.6	10.8	16.6	23.8	44.3	17.4	16 746	39 059	60 154	86 509	160 773	252 260	0.396
1991	67 173	4.5	10.7	16.6	24.1	44.2	17.1	16 003	37 986	58 942	85 487	157 059	243 022	0.397
1992	68 216	4.3	10.5	16.5	24.0	44.7	17.6	15 370	37 073	58 568	85 132	158 421	249 424	0.404
1993	68 506	4.1	9.9	15.7	23.3	47.0	20.3	15 239	36 599	57 998	85 976	173 712	299 822	0.429
1994	69 313	4.2	10.0	15.7	23.3	46.9	20.1	15 913	37 650	59 455	87 886	177 115	303 857	0.426
1995	69 597	4.4	10.1	15.8	23.2	46.5	20.0	16 853	38 829	60 793	88 948	178 703	306 477	0.421
1996	70 241	4.2	10.0	15.8	23.1	46.8	20.3	16 595	39 122	61 884	90 423	183 066	316 733	0.425
1997	70 884	4.2	9.9	15.7	23.0	47.2	20.7	17 198	40 299	63 582	93 234	191 544	335 233	0.429
1998	71 551	4.2	9.9	15.7	23.0	47.3	20.7	17 621	41 474	65 642	96 264	198 136	346 794	0.430
1999	73 206	4.3	9.9	15.6	23.0	47.2	20.3	18 339	42 627	67 284	99 309	203 535	350 932	0.429
2000	73 778	4.3	9.8	15.4	22.7	47.7	21.1	18 829	43 052	67 663	99 721	209 225	370 751	0.433
2001	74 340	4.2	9.7	15.4	22.9	47.7	21.0	18 184	42 106	66 841	99 404	207 046	363 543	0.435
2002	75 616	4.2	9.7	15.5	23.0	47.6	20.8	17 890	41 507	66 201	98 461	203 313	355 821	0.434
2003	76 232	4.1	9.6	15.5	23.2	47.6	20.5	17 317	41 068	66 187	99 516	203 896	351 391	0.436
2004	76 866	4.0	9.6	15.4	23.0	47.9	20.9	17 260	41 083	65 936	98 511	205 022	357 180	0.438
2005	77 418	4.0	9.6	15.3	22.9	48.1	21.1	17 368	41 326	66 131	98 908	207 344	363 000	0.440
2006	78 454	4.0	9.5	15.1	22.9	48.5	21.5	17 696	41 873	66 603	100 663	213 399	377 744	0.444
2007	77 908	4.1	9.7	15.6	23.3	47.3	20.1	17 794	42 417	68 042	101 748	206 560	350 619	0.432
2008	78 874	4.0	9.6	15.5	23.1	47.8	20.5	16 962	40 657	65 672	98 281	203 045	348 640	0.438
2009	78 867	3.9	9.4	15.3	23.2	48.2	20.7	16 367	39 656	64 129	97 373	202 840	347 929	0.443
2010	79 559	3.8	9.5	15.4	23.5	47.8	20.0	15 715	38 871	63 355	96 659	197 055	329 487	0.440
2011	80 529	3.8	9.3	15.1	23.0	48.9	21.3	15 601	38 341	62 307	95 180	202 067	351 728	0.450
2012	80 944	3.8	9.2	15.1	23.0	48.9	21.3	15 534	38 184	62 464	95 474	202 559	352 338	0.451
2013	81 217	3.8	9.3	15.1	23.0	48.8	21.2	16 109	39 514	63 916	97 207	206 687	358 722	0.448

. . . = Not available.

Section 3b: Poverty

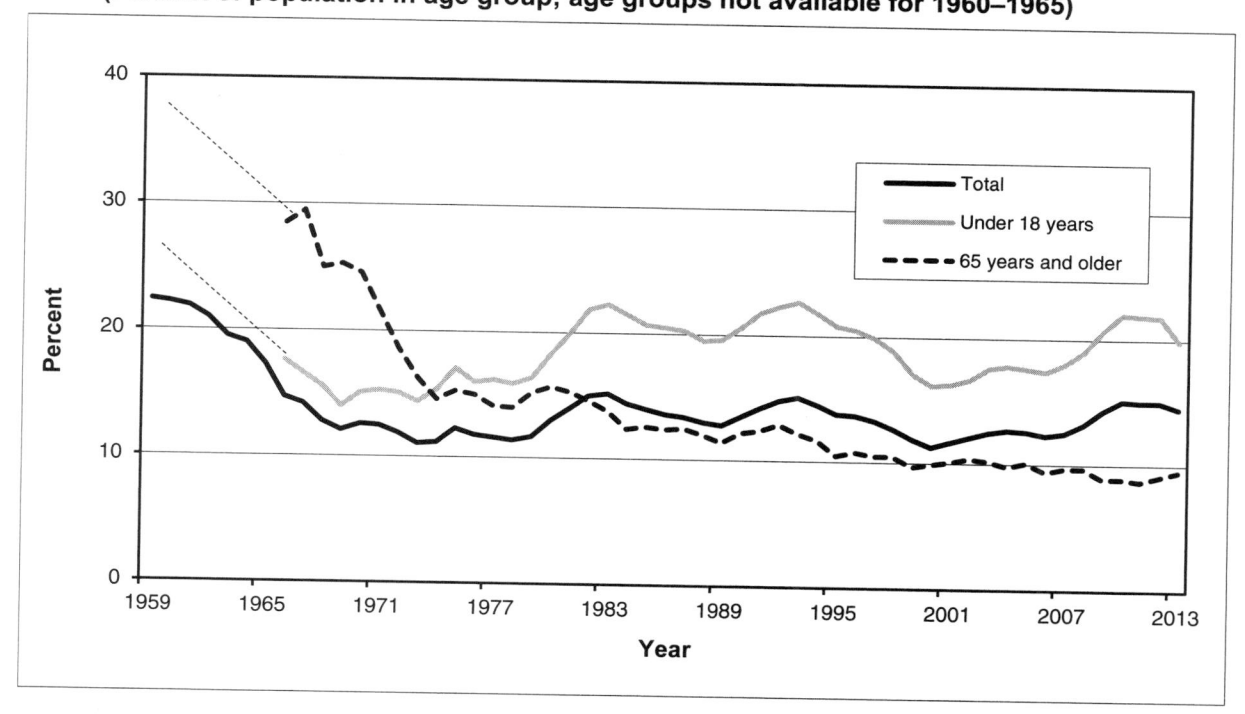

Figure 3-2: Poverty Rates: Total, Children, and Seniors, 1959–2013
(Percent of population in age group; age groups not available for 1960–1965)

- The number of Americans with family money incomes below the official poverty line was 14.5 percent of the population in 2013. (Table 3-7)

- According to the official calculation, 19.9 percent of children under 18 lived in families below the poverty level in 2013, the first decrease in the poverty rate since 2006. Only 9.5 percent of the population 65 years and older were poor, an increase of 0.4%. In 1959, the first poverty rate calculations showed more than one-third of all seniors living in poverty, compared with 17 percent of working-age adults and 27 percent of children. Between 1959 and 1974, ad hoc legislative changes raised Social Security benefits by a cumulative 104 percent—exceeding the 69 percent increase in consumer prices—and since then, each year's benefits have been indexed to the rate of change in the Consumer Price Index, Urban Wage Earners and Clerical Workers (CPI-W). As a result, since the early 1980s, officially-measured senior poverty has been consistently lower than the population average. (Table 3-9)

- The official poverty rate among Hispanics (who may be of any race) was 23.5 percent in 2013 compared with 9.6 percent for non-Hispanic Whites. Poverty among Blacks remained at 27.2 percent and poverty among Asians was 10.5 percent. (Table 3-7)

- For the 'working poor,' the poverty rate remained at 34.4 percent in 2013. For those workers who had full-time jobs, the poverty rate declined from 9.1 percent in 2012 to 8.8 percent in 2013. (Table 3-10)

- However, the official thresholds do not specifically include medical expenses or account for the disproportionate effect of medical price inflation on senior budgets. The new Supplemental Poverty Measure (SPM) does include these effects and is shown in Table 3-13.

- The poverty rate for children, on the other hand, has always been higher than the average even though it includes more complete account of government programs benefiting families with children. (See Table 3-13)

Table 3-6. Weighted Average Poverty Thresholds by Family Size

(Dollars.)

Year	Unrelated individuals			Families of 2 people			Families, all ages								CPI-U, all items (1982–1984 = 100)
	All ages	Under 65 years	65 years and older	All ages	House-holder under 65 years	House-holder 65 years and older	3 people	4 people	5 people	6 people	7 people or more (before 1980)	7 people	8 people	9 people or more	
1959	1 467	1 503	1 397	1 894	1 952	1 761	2 324	2 973	3 506	3 944	4 849	. . .	. . .	. . .	29.2
1960	1 490	1 526	1 418	1 924	1 982	1 788	2 359	3 022	3 560	4 002	4 921	. . .	. . .	. . .	29.6
1961	1 506	1 545	1 433	1 942	2 005	1 808	2 383	3 054	3 597	4 041	4 967	. . .	. . .	. . .	29.9
1962	1 519	1 562	1 451	1 962	2 027	1 828	2 412	3 089	3 639	4 088	5 032	. . .	. . .	. . .	30.3
1963	1 539	1 581	1 470	1 988	2 052	1 850	2 442	3 128	3 685	4 135	5 092	. . .	. . .	. . .	30.6
1964	1 558	1 601	1 488	2 015	2 079	1 875	2 473	3 169	3 732	4 193	5 156	. . .	. . .	. . .	31.0
1965	1 582	1 626	1 512	2 048	2 114	1 906	2 514	3 223	3 797	4 264	5 248	. . .	. . .	. . .	31.5
1966	1 628	1 674	1 556	2 107	2 175	1 961	2 588	3 317	3 908	4 388	5 395	. . .	. . .	. . .	32.5
1967	1 675	1 722	1 600	2 168	2 238	2 017	2 661	3 410	4 019	4 516	5 550	. . .	. . .	. . .	33.4
1968	1 748	1 797	1 667	2 262	2 333	2 102	2 774	3 553	4 188	4 706	5 789	. . .	. . .	. . .	34.8
1969	1 840	1 893	1 757	2 383	2 458	2 215	2 924	3 743	4 415	4 958	6 101	. . .	. . .	. . .	36.7
1970	1 954	2 010	1 861	2 525	2 604	2 348	3 099	3 968	4 680	5 260	6 468	. . .	. . .	. . .	38.8
1971	2 040	2 098	1 940	2 633	2 716	2 448	3 229	4 137	4 880	5 489	6 751	. . .	. . .	. . .	40.5
1972	2 109	2 168	2 005	2 724	2 808	2 530	3 339	4 275	5 044	5 673	6 983	. . .	. . .	. . .	41.8
1973	2 247	2 307	2 130	2 895	2 984	2 688	3 548	4 540	5 358	6 028	7 435	. . .	. . .	. . .	44.4
1974	2 495	2 562	2 364	3 211	3 312	2 982	3 936	5 038	5 950	6 699	8 253	. . .	. . .	. . .	49.3
1975	2 724	2 797	2 581	3 506	3 617	3 257	4 293	5 500	6 499	7 316	9 022	. . .	. . .	. . .	53.8
1976	2 884	2 959	2 730	3 711	3 826	3 445	4 540	5 815	6 876	7 760	9 588	. . .	. . .	. . .	56.9
1977	3 075	3 152	2 906	3 951	4 072	3 666	4 833	6 191	7 320	8 261	10 216	. . .	. . .	. . .	60.6
1978	3 311	3 392	3 127	4 249	4 383	3 944	5 201	6 662	7 880	8 891	11 002	. . .	. . .	. . .	65.2
1979	3 689	3 778	3 479	4 725	4 878	4 390	5 784	7 412	8 775	9 914	12 280	. . .	. . .	. . .	72.6
1980	4 190	4 290	3 949	5 363	5 537	4 983	6 565	8 414	9 966	11 269	13 955	12 761	14 199	16 896	82.4
1981	4 620	4 729	4 359	5 917	6 111	5 498	7 250	9 287	11 007	12 449	. . .	14 110	15 655	18 572	90.9
1982	4 901	5 019	4 626	6 281	6 487	5 836	7 693	9 862	11 684	13 207	. . .	15 036	16 719	19 698	96.5
1983	5 061	5 180	4 775	6 483	6 697	6 023	7 938	10 178	12 049	13 630	. . .	15 500	17 170	20 310	99.6
1984	5 278	5 400	4 979	6 762	6 983	6 282	8 277	10 609	12 566	14 207	. . .	16 096	17 961	21 247	103.9
1985	5 469	5 593	5 156	6 998	7 231	6 503	8 573	10 989	13 007	14 696	. . .	16 656	18 512	22 083	107.6
1986	5 572	5 701	5 255	7 138	7 372	6 630	8 737	11 203	13 259	14 986	. . .	17 049	18 791	22 497	109.6
1987	5 778	5 909	5 447	7 397	7 641	6 872	9 056	11 611	13 737	15 509	. . .	17 649	19 515	23 105	113.6
1988	6 022	6 155	5 674	7 704	7 958	7 157	9 435	12 092	14 304	16 146	. . .	18 232	20 253	24 129	118.3
1989	6 310	6 451	5 947	8 076	8 343	7 501	9 885	12 674	14 990	16 921	. . .	19 162	21 328	25 480	124.0
1990	6 652	6 800	6 268	8 509	8 794	7 905	10 419	13 359	15 792	17 839	. . .	20 241	22 582	26 848	130.7
1991	6 932	7 086	6 532	8 865	9 165	8 241	10 860	13 924	16 456	18 587	. . .	21 058	23 582	27 942	136.2
1992	7 143	7 299	6 729	9 137	9 443	8 487	11 186	14 335	16 952	19 137	. . .	21 594	24 053	28 745	140.3
1993	7 363	7 518	6 930	9 414	9 728	8 740	11 522	14 763	17 449	19 718	. . .	22 383	24 838	29 529	144.5
1994	7 547	7 710	7 108	9 661	9 976	8 967	11 821	15 141	17 900	20 235	. . .	22 923	25 427	30 300	148.2
1995	7 763	7 929	7 309	9 933	10 259	9 219	12 158	15 569	18 408	20 804	. . .	23 552	26 237	31 280	152.4
1996	7 995	8 163	7 525	10 233	10 564	9 491	12 516	16 036	18 952	21 389	. . .	24 268	27 091	31 971	156.9
1997	8 183	8 350	7 698	10 473	10 805	9 712	12 802	16 400	19 380	21 886	. . .	24 802	27 593	32 566	160.5
1998	8 316	8 480	7 818	10 634	10 972	9 862	13 003	16 660	19 680	22 228	. . .	25 257	28 166	33 339	163.0
1999	8 499	8 667	7 990	10 864	11 213	10 075	13 289	17 030	20 128	22 730	. . .	25 918	28 970	34 436	166.6
2000	8 791	8 959	8 259	11 235	11 589	10 418	13 740	17 604	20 815	23 533	. . .	26 750	29 701	35 150	172.2
2001	9 039	9 214	8 494	11 569	11 920	10 715	14 128	18 104	21 405	24 195	. . .	27 517	30 627	36 286	177.1
2002	9 183	9 359	8 628	11 756	12 110	10 885	14 348	18 392	21 744	24 576	. . .	28 001	30 907	37 062	179.9
2003	9 393	9 573	8 825	12 015	12 384	11 133	14 680	18 810	22 245	25 122	. . .	28 544	31 589	37 656	184.0
2004	9 646	9 827	9 060	12 335	12 714	11 430	15 066	19 307	22 830	25 787	. . .	29 233	32 641	39 062	188.9
2005	9 973	10 160	9 367	12 755	13 145	11 815	15 577	19 971	23 613	26 683	. . .	30 249	33 610	40 288	195.3
2006	10 294	10 488	9 669	13 167	13 569	12 201	16 079	20 614	24 382	27 560	. . .	31 205	34 774	41 499	201.6
2007	10 590	10 787	9 944	13 540	13 954	12 550	16 530	21 203	25 080	28 323	. . .	32 233	35 816	42 739	207.3
2008	10 991	11 201	10 326	14 051	14 417	13 014	17 163	22 025	26 049	29 456	. . .	33 529	37 220	44 346	215.3
2009	10 956	11 161	10 289	13 991	14 439	12 982	17 098	21 954	25 991	29 405	. . .	33 372	37 252	44 366	214.5
2010	11 137	11 344	10 458	14 216	14 676	13 194	17 373	22 315	26 442	29 904	. . .	34 019	37 953	45 224	218.1
2011	11 484	11 702	10 788	14 657	15 139	13 609	17 916	23 021	27 251	30 847	. . .	35 085	39 064	46 572	224.9
2012	11 720	11 945	11 011	14 937	15 450	13 892	18 284	23 492	27 827	31 471	. . .	35 743	39 688	47 297	229.6
2013	11 888	12 119	11 173	15 142	15 679	14 095	18 552	23 834	28 265	31 925	. . .	36 384	40 484	48 065	233.0

. . . = Not available.

Table 3-7. Poverty Status of People by Race and Hispanic Origin

(Thousands of people, percent of population.)

Year	Number of people, all races	All races Number	All races Poverty rate (percent)	White Number	White Poverty rate (percent)	White, not Hispanic Number	White, not Hispanic Poverty rate (percent)	Black Number	Black Poverty rate (percent)	Asian[1] Number	Asian[1] Poverty rate (percent)	Hispanic (any race) Number	Hispanic (any race) Poverty rate (percent)
1959	176 557	39 490	22.4	28 484	18.1	...	...	9 927	55.1	...	...	...	...
1960	179 503	39 851	22.2	28 309	17.8	...	...	...	...	...	...	...	...
1961	181 277	39 628	21.9	27 890	17.4	...	...	...	...	...	...	...	...
1962	184 276	38 625	21.0	26 672	16.4	...	...	...	...	...	...	...	...
1963	187 258	36 436	19.5	25 238	15.3	...	...	...	...	...	...	...	...
1964	189 710	36 055	19.0	24 957	14.9	...	...	...	...	...	...	...	...
1965	191 413	33 185	17.3	22 496	13.3	...	...	...	...	...	...	...	...
1966	193 388	28 510	14.7	19 290	11.3	...	...	8 867	41.8	...	...	...	...
1967	195 672	27 769	14.2	18 983	11.0	...	...	8 486	39.3	...	...	...	...
1968	197 628	25 389	12.8	17 395	10.0	...	...	7 616	34.7	...	...	...	...
1969	199 517	24 147	12.1	16 659	9.5	...	...	7 095	32.2	...	...	...	...
1970	202 183	25 420	12.6	17 484	9.9	...	...	7 548	33.5	...	...	...	...
1971	204 554	25 559	12.5	17 780	9.9	...	...	7 396	32.5	...	...	...	...
1972	206 004	24 460	11.9	16 203	9.0	...	...	7 710	33.3	...	...	2 414	22.8
1973	207 621	22 973	11.1	15 142	8.4	12 864	7.5	7 388	31.4	...	...	2 366	21.9
1974	209 362	23 370	11.2	15 736	8.6	13 217	7.7	7 182	30.3	...	...	2 575	23.0
1975	210 864	25 877	12.3	17 770	9.7	14 883	8.6	7 545	31.3	...	...	2 991	26.9
1976	212 303	24 975	11.8	16 713	9.1	14 025	8.1	7 595	31.1	...	...	2 783	24.7
1977	213 867	24 720	11.6	16 416	8.9	13 802	8.0	7 726	31.3	...	...	2 700	22.4
1978	215 656	24 497	11.4	16 259	8.7	13 755	7.9	7 625	30.6	...	...	2 607	21.6
1979	222 903	26 072	11.7	17 214	9.0	14 419	8.1	8 050	31.0	...	...	2 921	21.8
1980	225 027	29 272	13.0	19 699	10.2	16 365	9.1	8 579	32.5	...	...	3 491	25.7
1981	227 157	31 822	14.0	21 553	11.1	17 987	9.9	9 173	34.2	...	...	3 713	26.5
1982	229 412	34 398	15.0	23 517	12.0	19 362	10.6	9 697	35.6	...	...	4 301	29.9
1983	231 700	35 303	15.2	23 984	12.1	19 538	10.8	9 882	35.7	...	...	4 633	28.0
1984	233 816	33 700	14.4	22 955	11.5	18 300	10.0	9 490	33.8	...	...	4 806	28.4
1985	236 594	33 064	14.0	22 860	11.4	17 839	9.7	8 926	31.3	...	...	5 236	29.0
1986	238 554	32 370	13.6	22 183	11.0	17 244	9.4	8 983	31.1	...	...	5 117	27.3
1987	240 982	32 221	13.4	21 195	10.4	16 029	8.7	9 520	32.4	1 021	16.1	5 422	28.0
1988	243 530	31 745	13.0	20 715	10.1	15 565	8.4	9 356	31.3	1 117	17.3	5 357	26.7
1989	245 992	31 528	12.8	20 785	10.0	15 599	8.3	9 302	30.7	939	14.1	5 430	26.2
1990	248 644	33 585	13.5	22 326	10.7	16 622	8.8	9 837	31.9	858	12.2	6 006	28.1
1991	251 192	35 708	14.2	23 747	11.3	17 741	9.4	10 242	32.7	996	13.8	6 339	28.7
1992	256 549	38 014	14.8	25 259	11.9	18 202	9.6	10 827	33.4	985	12.7	7 592	29.6
1993	259 278	39 265	15.1	26 226	12.2	18 882	9.9	10 877	33.1	1 134	15.3	8 126	30.6
1994	261 616	38 059	14.5	25 379	11.7	18 110	9.4	10 196	30.6	974	14.6	8 416	30.7
1995	263 733	36 425	13.8	24 423	11.2	16 267	8.5	9 872	29.3	1 411	14.6	8 574	30.3
1996	266 218	36 529	13.7	24 650	11.2	16 462	8.6	9 694	28.4	1 454	14.5	8 697	29.4
1997	268 480	35 574	13.3	24 396	11.0	16 491	8.6	9 116	26.5	1 468	14.0	8 308	27.1
1998	271 059	34 476	12.7	23 454	10.5	15 799	8.2	9 091	26.1	1 360	12.5	8 070	25.6
1999	276 208	32 791	11.9	22 169	9.8	14 735	7.7	8 441	23.6	1 285	10.7	7 876	22.7
2000	278 944	31 581	11.3	21 645	9.5	14 366	7.4	7 982	22.5	1 258	9.9	7 747	21.5
2001	281 475	32 907	11.7	22 739	9.9	15 271	7.8	8 136	22.7	1 275	10.2	7 997	21.4
2002	285 317	34 570	12.1	...	...	...	...	...	...	...	...	8 555	21.8
2003	287 699	35 861	12.5	...	...	...	...	...	...	...	...	9 051	22.5
2004	290 617	37 040	12.7	...	...	...	...	...	...	...	...	9 122	21.9
2005	293 135	36 950	12.6	...	...	...	...	...	...	...	...	9 368	21.8
2006	296 450	36 460	12.3	...	...	...	...	...	...	...	...	9 243	20.6
2007	298 699	37 276	12.5	...	...	...	...	...	...	...	...	9 890	21.5
2008	301 041	39 829	13.2	...	...	...	...	...	...	...	...	10 987	23.2
2009	303 820	43 569	14.3	...	...	...	...	...	...	...	...	12 350	25.3
2010	306 130	46 343	15.1	...	...	...	...	...	...	...	...	13 522	26.5
2011	308 456	46 247	15.0	...	...	...	...	...	...	...	...	13 244	25.3
2012	310 648	46 496	15.0	...	...	...	...	...	...	...	...	13 616	25.6
2013	312 965	45 318	14.5	...	...	...	...	...	...	...	...	12 744	23.5
By race													
Race alone													
2002	...	...	...	23 466	10.2	15 567	8.0	8 602	24.1	1 161	10.1	...	...
2003	...	...	...	24 272	10.5	15 902	8.2	8 781	24.4	1 401	11.8	...	...
2004	...	...	...	25 327	10.8	16 908	8.7	9 014	24.7	1 201	9.8	...	...
2005	...	...	...	24 872	10.6	16 227	8.3	9 168	24.9	1 402	11.1	...	...
2006	...	...	...	24 416	10.3	16 013	8.2	9 048	24.3	1 353	10.3	...	...
2007	...	...	...	25 120	10.5	16 032	8.2	9 237	24.5	1 349	10.2	...	...
2008	...	...	...	26 990	11.2	17 024	8.6	9 379	24.7	1 576	11.8	...	...
2009	...	...	...	29 830	12.3	18 530	9.4	9 944	25.8	1 746	12.5	...	...
2010	...	...	...	31 083	13.0	19 251	9.9	10 746	27.4	1 899	12.2	...	...
2011	...	...	...	30 849	12.8	19 171	9.8	10 929	27.6	1 973	12.3	...	...
2012	...	...	...	30 816	12.7	18 940	9.7	10 911	27.2	1 921	11.7	...	...
2013	...	...	...	29 936	12.3	18 796	9.6	11 041	27.2	1 785	10.5	...	...
Race alone or in combination													
2010	...	...	...	...	...	...	...	11 597	27.4	2 064	12.0	...	...
2011	...	...	...	...	...	...	...	11 730	27.5	2 189	12.3	...	...
2012	...	...	...	...	...	...	...	11 809	27.1	2 072	11.4	...	...
2013	...	...	...	...	...	...	...	11 959	27.1	1 974	10.4	...	...

[1] For 1987 through 2001, Asian and Pacific Islander.
. . . = Not available.

Table 3-8. Poverty Status of Families by Type of Family

(Thousands of families, percent.)

Year	Married couple families				Families with no spouse present						Unrelated individuals	
	Number of families		Poverty rate (percent)		Male householder			Female householder				
						Poverty rate (percent)			Poverty rate (percent)		Below poverty level	Poverty rate
	Total	Total below poverty level	Total	With children under 18 years	Familes below poverty level	Total	With children under 18 years	Familes below poverty level	Total	With children under 18 years		
1959	39 335	. . .	. . .	. . .	. . .	. . .	. . .	1 916	42.6	59.9	4 928	46.1
1960	39 624	. . .	. . .	. . .	. . .	. . .	. . .	1 955	42.4	56.3	4 926	45.2
1961	40 405	. . .	. . .	. . .	. . .	. . .	. . .	1 954	42.1	56.0	5 119	45.9
1962	40 923	. . .	. . .	. . .	. . .	. . .	. . .	2 034	42.9	59.7	5 002	45.4
1963	41 311	. . .	. . .	. . .	. . .	. . .	. . .	1 972	40.4	55.7	4 938	44.2
1964	41 648	. . .	. . .	. . .	. . .	. . .	. . .	1 822	36.4	49.7	5 143	42.7
1965	42 107	. . .	. . .	. . .	. . .	. . .	. . .	1 916	38.4	52.2	4 827	39.8
1966	42 553	. . .	. . .	. . .	. . .	. . .	. . .	1 721	33.1	47.1	4 701	38.3
1967	43 292	. . .	. . .	. . .	. . .	. . .	. . .	1 774	33.3	44.5	4 998	38.1
1968	43 842	. . .	. . .	. . .	. . .	. . .	. . .	1 755	32.3	44.6	4 694	34.0
1969	44 436	. . .	. . .	. . .	. . .	. . .	. . .	1 827	32.7	44.9	4 972	34.0
1970	44 739	. . .	. . .	. . .	. . .	. . .	. . .	1 952	32.5	43.8	5 090	32.9
1971	45 752	. . .	. . .	. . .	. . .	. . .	. . .	2 100	33.9	44.9	5 154	31.6
1972	46 314	. . .	. . .	. . .	. . .	. . .	. . .	2 158	32.7	44.5	4 883	29.0
1973	46 812	2 482	5.3	. . .	154	10.7	. . .	2 193	32.2	43.2	4 674	25.6
1974	47 069	2 474	5.3	6.0	125	8.9	15.4	2 324	32.1	43.7	4 553	24.1
1975	47 318	2 904	6.1	7.2	116	8.0	11.7	2 430	32.5	44.0	5 088	25.1
1976	47 497	2 606	5.5	6.4	162	10.8	15.4	2 543	33.0	44.1	5 344	24.9
1977	47 385	2 524	5.3	6.3	177	11.1	14.8	2 610	31.7	41.8	5 216	22.6
1978	47 692	2 474	5.2	5.9	152	9.2	14.7	2 654	31.4	42.2	5 435	22.1
1979	49 112	2 640	5.4	6.1	176	10.2	15.5	2 645	30.4	39.6	5 743	21.9
1980	49 294	3 032	6.2	7.7	213	11.0	18.0	2 972	32.7	42.9	6 227	22.9
1981	49 630	3 394	6.8	8.7	205	10.3	14.0	3 252	34.6	44.3	6 490	23.4
1982	49 908	3 789	7.6	9.8	290	14.4	20.6	3 434	36.3	47.8	6 458	23.1
1983	50 081	3 815	7.6	10.1	268	13.2	20.2	3 564	36.0	47.1	6 740	23.1
1984	50 350	3 488	6.9	9.4	292	13.1	18.1	3 498	34.5	45.7	6 609	21.8
1985	50 933	3 438	6.7	8.9	311	12.9	17.1	3 474	34.0	45.4	6 725	21.5
1986	51 537	3 123	6.1	8.0	287	11.4	17.8	3 613	34.6	46.0	6 846	21.6
1987	51 675	3 011	5.8	7.7	340	12.0	16.8	3 654	34.2	45.5	6 857	20.8
1988	52 100	2 897	5.6	7.2	336	11.8	18.0	3 642	33.4	44.7	7 070	20.6
1989	52 317	2 931	5.6	7.3	348	12.1	18.1	3 504	32.2	42.8	6 760	19.2
1990	52 147	2 981	5.7	7.8	349	12.0	18.8	3 768	33.4	44.5	7 446	20.7
1991	52 457	3 158	6.0	8.3	392	13.0	19.6	4 161	35.6	47.1	7 773	21.1
1992	53 090	3 385	6.4	8.6	484	15.8	22.5	4 275	35.4	46.2	8 075	21.9
1993	53 181	3 481	6.5	9.0	488	16.8	22.5	4 424	35.6	46.1	8 388	22.1
1994	53 865	3 272	6.1	8.3	549	17.0	22.6	4 232	34.6	44.0	8 287	21.5
1995	53 570	2 982	5.6	7.5	493	14.0	19.7	4 057	32.4	41.5	8 247	20.9
1996	53 604	3 010	5.6	7.5	531	13.8	20.0	4 167	32.6	41.9	8 452	20.8
1997	54 321	2 821	5.2	7.1	507	13.0	18.7	3 995	31.6	41.0	8 687	20.8
1998	54 778	2 879	5.3	6.9	476	12.0	16.6	3 831	29.9	38.7	8 478	19.9
1999	56 290	2 748	4.9	6.4	485	11.8	16.3	3 559	27.8	35.7	8 400	19.1
2000	56 598	2 637	4.7	6.0	485	11.3	15.3	3 278	25.4	33.0	8 653	19.0
2001	56 755	2 760	4.9	6.1	583	13.1	17.7	3 470	26.4	33.6	9 226	19.9
2002	57 327	3 052	5.3	6.8	564	12.1	16.6	3 613	26.5	33.7	9 618	20.4
2003	57 725	3 115	5.4	7.0	636	13.5	19.1	3 856	28.0	35.5	9 713	20.4
2004	57 983	3 216	5.5	7.0	657	13.4	17.1	3 962	28.3	35.9	9 926	20.4
2005	58 189	2 944	5.1	6.5	669	13.0	17.6	4 044	28.7	36.2	10 425	21.1
2006	58 964	2 910	4.9	6.4	671	13.2	17.9	4 087	28.3	36.5	9 977	20.0
2007	58 395	2 849	4.9	6.7	696	13.6	17.5	4 078	28.3	37.0	10 189	19.7
2008	59 137	3 261	5.5	7.5	723	13.8	17.6	4 163	28.7	37.2	10 710	20.8
2009	58 428	3 409	5.8	8.3	942	16.9	23.7	4 441	29.9	38.5	11 678	22.0
2010	58 667	3 681	6.3	9.0	892	15.8	24.1	4 827	31.7	40.9	12 449	22.9
2011	58 963	3 652	6.2	8.8	950	16.1	21.9	4 894	31.2	40.9	12 416	22.8
2012	59 224	3 705	6.3	8.9	1 023	16.4	22.6	4 793	30.9	40.9	12 558	22.4
2013	59 692	3 476	5.8	7.6	1 008	15.9	20.0	4 646	30.6	39.6	13 181	23.3

. . . = Not available.

Table 3-9. Poverty Status of People by Sex and Age

(Thousands of people, percent of population.)

| Year | Poverty status of people by sex | | | | Poverty status of people by age | | | | | |
| | Males below poverty level | | Females below poverty level | | Children under 18 years below poverty level | | People 18 to 64 years below poverty level | | People 65 years and older below poverty level | |
	Number (thousands)	Poverty rate (percent)	Number (thousands)	Poverty rate (percent)	Number (thousands)	Poverty rate (percent)	Number (thousands)	Poverty rate (percent)	Number (thousands)	Poverty rate (percent)
1959	. . .	. . .	. . .	. . .	17 552	27.3	16 457	17.0	5 481	35.2
1966	12 225	13.0	16 265	16.3	12 389	17.6	11 007	10.5	5 114	28.5
1967	11 813	12.5	15 951	15.8	11 656	16.6	10 725	10.0	5 388	29.5
1968	10 793	11.3	14 578	14.3	10 954	15.6	9 803	9.0	4 632	25.0
1969	10 292	10.6	13 978	13.6	9 691	14.0	9 669	8.7	4 787	25.3
1970	10 879	11.1	14 632	14.0	10 440	15.1	10 187	9.0	4 793	24.6
1971	10 708	10.8	14 841	14.1	10 551	15.3	10 735	9.3	4 273	21.6
1972	10 190	10.2	14 258	13.4	10 284	15.1	10 438	8.8	3 738	18.6
1973	9 642	9.6	13 316	12.5	9 642	14.4	9 977	8.3	3 354	16.3
1974	9 945	9.8	13 429	12.5	10 156	15.4	10 132	8.3	3 085	14.6
1975	10 908	10.7	14 970	13.8	11 104	17.1	11 456	9.2	3 317	15.3
1976	10 373	10.1	14 603	13.4	10 273	16.0	11 389	9.0	3 313	15.0
1977	10 340	10.0	14 381	13.0	10 288	16.2	11 316	8.8	3 177	14.1
1978	10 017	9.6	14 480	13.0	9 931	15.9	11 332	8.7	3 233	14.0
1979	10 861	10.1	15 211	13.2	10 377	16.4	12 014	8.9	3 682	15.2
1980	12 207	11.2	17 065	14.7	11 543	18.3	13 858	10.1	3 871	15.7
1981	13 360	12.1	18 462	15.8	12 505	20.0	15 464	11.1	3 853	15.3
1982	14 842	13.4	19 556	16.5	13 647	21.9	17 000	12.0	3 751	14.6
1983	15 296	13.6	20 006	16.8	13 911	22.3	17 767	12.4	3 625	13.8
1984	14 537	12.8	19 163	15.9	13 420	21.5	16 952	11.7	3 330	12.4
1985	14 140	12.3	18 923	15.6	13 010	20.7	16 598	11.3	3 456	12.6
1986	13 721	11.8	18 649	15.2	12 876	20.5	16 017	10.8	3 477	12.4
1987	13 781	11.8	18 439	14.9	12 843	20.3	15 815	10.6	3 563	12.5
1988	13 599	11.5	18 146	14.5	12 455	19.5	15 809	10.5	3 481	12.0
1989	13 366	11.2	18 162	14.4	12 590	19.6	15 575	10.2	3 363	11.4
1990	14 211	11.7	19 373	15.2	13 431	20.6	16 496	10.7	3 658	12.2
1991	15 082	12.3	20 626	16.0	14 341	21.8	17 586	11.4	3 781	12.4
1992	16 222	12.9	21 792	16.6	15 294	22.3	18 793	11.9	3 928	12.9
1993	16 900	13.3	22 365	16.9	15 727	22.7	19 781	12.4	3 755	12.2
1994	16 316	12.8	21 744	16.3	15 289	21.8	19 107	11.9	3 663	11.7
1995	15 683	12.2	20 742	15.4	14 665	20.8	18 442	11.4	3 318	10.5
1996	15 611	12.0	20 918	15.4	14 463	20.5	18 638	11.4	3 428	10.8
1997	15 187	11.6	20 387	14.9	14 113	19.9	18 085	10.9	3 376	10.5
1998	14 712	11.1	19 764	14.3	13 467	18.9	17 623	10.5	3 386	10.5
1999	14 079	10.4	18 712	13.2	12 280	17.1	17 289	10.1	3 222	9.7
2000	13 536	9.9	18 045	12.6	11 587	16.2	16 671	9.6	3 323	9.9
2001	14 327	10.4	18 580	12.9	11 733	16.3	17 760	10.1	3 414	10.1
2002	15 162	10.9	19 408	13.3	12 133	16.7	18 861	10.6	3 576	10.4
2003	15 783	11.2	20 078	13.7	12 866	17.6	19 443	10.8	3 552	10.2
2004	16 399	11.5	20 641	13.9	13 041	17.8	20 545	11.3	3 453	9.8
2005	15 950	11.1	21 000	14.1	12 896	17.6	20 450	11.1	3 603	10.1
2006	16 000	11.0	20 460	13.6	12 827	17.4	20 239	10.8	3 394	9.4
2007	16 302	11.1	20 973	13.8	13 324	18.0	20 396	10.9	3 556	9.7
2008	17 698	12.0	22 131	14.4	14 068	19.0	22 105	11.7	3 656	9.7
2009	19 475	13.0	24 094	15.6	15 451	20.7	24 684	12.9	3 433	8.9
2010	20 893	14.0	25 451	16.3	16 286	22.0	26 499	13.8	3 558	8.9
2011	20 501	13.6	25 746	16.3	16 134	21.9	26 492	13.7	3 620	8.7
2012	20 656	13.6	25 840	16.3	16 073	21.8	26 497	13.7	3 926	9.1
2013	20 119	13.1	25 188	15.8	14 659	19.9	26 429	13.6	4 231	9.5

. . . = Not available.

Table 3-10. Working-Age Poor People by Work Experience

(Thousands of people, percent of population [poverty rate], percent of total poor people.)

Year	Total number of working-age poor people	Worked		Worked year-round, full-time			Worked less than year-round or full-time			Did not work		
		Number	Percent of total poor	Number	Poverty rate (percent)	Percent of total poor	Number	Poverty rate (percent)	Percent of total poor	Number	Poverty rate (percent)	Percent of total poor
16 Years and Over												
1978	16 914	6 599	39.0	1 309	. . .	7.7	5 290	. . .	31.3	10 315	. . .	61.0
1979	16 803	6 601	39.3	1 394	. . .	8.3	5 207	. . .	31.0	10 202	. . .	60.7
1980	18 892	7 674	40.6	1 644	. . .	8.7	6 030	. . .	31.9	11 218	. . .	59.4
1981	20 571	8 524	41.4	1 881	. . .	9.1	6 643	. . .	32.3	12 047	. . .	58.6
1982	22 100	9 013	40.8	1 999	. . .	9.0	7 014	. . .	31.7	13 087	. . .	59.2
1983	22 741	9 329	41.0	2 064	. . .	9.1	7 265	. . .	31.9	13 412	. . .	59.0
1984	21 541	8 999	41.8	2 076	. . .	9.6	6 923	. . .	32.1	12 542	. . .	58.2
1985	21 243	9 008	42.4	1 972	. . .	9.3	7 036	. . .	33.1	12 235	. . .	57.6
1986	20 688	8 743	42.3	2 007	. . .	9.7	6 736	. . .	32.6	11 945	. . .	57.7
1987	20 546	8 258	40.2	1 821	2.4	8.9	6 436	12.5	31.3	12 288	21.6	59.8
1988	20 323	8 363	41.2	1 929	2.4	9.5	6 434	12.7	31.7	11 960	21.2	58.8
1989	19 952	8 376	42.0	1 908	2.4	9.6	6 468	12.5	32.4	11 576	20.8	58.0
1990	21 242	8 716	41.0	2 076	2.6	9.8	6 639	12.6	31.3	12 526	22.1	59.0
1991	22 530	9 208	40.9	2 103	2.6	9.3	7 105	13.4	31.5	13 322	22.8	59.1
1992	23 951	9 739	40.6	2 211	2.7	9.2	7 529	14.1	31.4	14 212	23.7	59.3
1993	24 832	10 144	40.8	2 408	2.9	9.7	7 737	14.6	31.2	14 688	24.2	59.1
1994	24 108	9 829	40.8	2 520	2.9	10.5	7 309	13.9	30.3	14 279	23.6	59.2
1995	23 077	9 484	41.1	2 418	2.7	10.5	7 066	13.7	30.6	13 593	22.3	58.9
1996	23 472	9 586	40.8	2 263	2.5	9.6	7 322	14.1	31.2	13 886	22.7	59.2
1997	22 753	9 444	41.5	2 345	2.5	10.3	7 098	13.8	31.2	13 309	21.7	58.5
1998	22 256	9 133	41.0	2 804	2.9	12.6	6 330	12.7	28.4	13 123	21.1	59.0
1999	21 762	9 251	42.5	2 559	2.6	11.8	6 692	13.2	30.8	12 511	19.9	57.5
2000	21 080	8 511	40.4	2 439	2.4	11.6	6 072	12.1	28.8	12 569	19.8	59.6
2001	22 245	8 530	38.3	2 567	2.6	11.5	5 964	11.8	26.8	13 715	20.6	61.7
2002	23 601	8 954	37.9	2 635	2.6	11.2	6 318	12.4	26.8	14 647	21.0	62.1
2003	24 266	8 820	36.3	2 636	2.6	10.9	6 183	12.2	25.5	15 446	21.5	63.7
2004	25 256	9 384	37.2	2 891	2.8	11.4	6 493	12.8	25.7	15 872	21.7	62.8
2005	25 381	9 340	36.8	2 894	2.8	11.4	6 446	12.8	25.4	16 041	21.8	63.2
2006	24 896	9 181	36.9	2 906	2.7	11.7	6 275	12.6	25.2	15 715	21.1	63.1
2007	25 297	9 089	35.9	2 768	2.5	10.9	6 320	12.7	25.0	16 208	21.5	64.1
2008	27 216	10 085	37.1	2 754	2.6	10.1	7 331	13.5	26.9	17 131	22.0	62.9
2009	29 625	10 680	36.1	2 641	2.7	8.9	8 039	14.5	27.1	18 945	22.7	63.9
2010	31 731	10 742	33.9	2 640	2.7	8.3	8 102	15.0	25.5	20 989	23.9	66.1
2011	31 630	10 588	33.5	2 770	2.7	8.8	7 818	14.9	24.7	21 042	23.6	66.5
2012	31 933	10 977	34.4	2 904	2.8	9.1	8 073	15.0	25.3	20 956	23.6	65.6
2013	32 011	11 025	34.4	2 812	2.7	8.8	8 213	15.8	26.6	20 986	23.2	65.6

. . . = Not available.

Section 3c: Alternative Measures of Income and Poverty

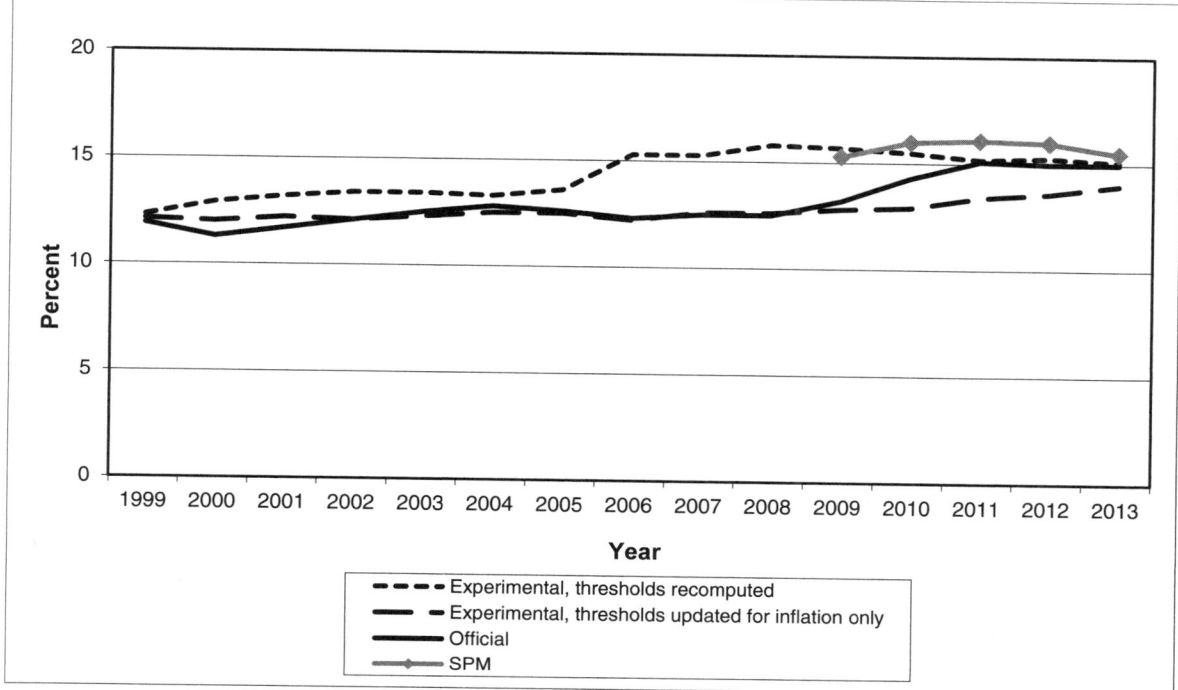

Figure 3-3: Poverty Rates, Official, Experimental, and SPM, 1999–2013

Legend:
- - - - Experimental, thresholds recomputed
- - - Experimental, thresholds updated for inflation only
——— Official
—◆— SPM

- For the years 1999 forward, the Census Bureau has calculated several experimental poverty measures based on recommendations by a special National Academy of Sciences (NAS) panel. And for 2009 through 2012 the Bureau has released a "Supplemental Poverty Measure" (SPM), based on further refinement of these recommendations. In Figure 3-3, two of the experimental measures are shown along with the official rate and the SPM. The SPM and all of the experimental measures use broader and more realistic definitions of both needs and "resources" (income) than the official rate. Also, the SPM and the two experimental measures shown in the graph include adjustment for geographic differences in the cost of living, and adjust for differing health care needs by excluding medical out-of-pocket expenses from the resources of the measurement unit. The thresholds for the experimental measures were initially based on needs estimated for the year 1999; in that year, the two experimental measures shown in Figure 3-3 indicated a poverty rate of 12.1 percent, compared with 11.9 percent in the official rate. (Table 3-12)

- One of those experimental measures updates the thresholds for inflation only, using the CPI-U, as is the case with the official series. This measure tracks the official series fairly closely through 2007. In the recession years, it increases less than the official measure, probably because resources are on an after-tax basis and include food aid and the Employment Tax Credit. (Table 3-12)

- The other experimental measure re-computes the thresholds each year using the percent increase in a 3-year average of <u>median</u> expenditures on necessities instead of the price increase. The poverty rate with this method rises even in a year of economic expansion such as 2000, diverges even more sharply upward in 2007 and 2008, and declines slightly over the next five years. (Table 3-12)

- The SPM is similar to the higher of the experimental rates in 2009. Unlike that rate and like the official and CPI-based experimental rates, it increases in 2010 and remains high through 2013 (16.6). It also changes poverty incidence among demographic and geographic groups. (Tables 3-12 and 3-13)

- Since the SPM includes many adjustments, differences do exist. For example, the poverty rate for persons 65 and older was 14.6 percent in 2013, much closer to the rate of 15.4 percent for working-age adults. The SPM rate for children, on the other hand, has always been higher than the average. In 2013, the percentage was 16.4 compared to 19.9 (Table 3-13)

Table 3-11. Poverty Rates and Income Distribution Coefficients for People, Based on Alternative Definitions of Income

Year	Definition 1, MI: Money income excluding capital gains (current official measure)			Definition 4: Money income before taxes and cash transfers, plus realized capital gains (losses) and health insurance supplements		
	Poverty rate (percent)		Gini coefficient [2]	Poverty rate (percent)		Gini coefficient
	Official threshold	CPI-U-RS threshold [1]		Official threshold	CPI-U-RS threshold [1]	
1979	11.7	10.6	0.403	18.8	17.8	0.460
1980	13.0	11.5	0.401	20.1	19.0	0.462
1981	14.0	12.2	0.404	21.1	19.8	0.466
1982	15.0	13.2	0.409	22.0	20.6	0.475
1983	15.2	13.7	0.412	21.8	20.6	0.478
1984	14.4	12.8	0.413	20.8	19.5	0.477
1985	14.0	12.5	0.418	20.4	19.1	0.486
1986	13.6	12.2	0.423	19.9	18.7	0.505
1987	13.4	12.1	0.424	19.7	18.7	0.488
1988	13.0	11.7	0.425	19.7	18.5	0.489
1989	12.8	11.3	0.429	19.4	18.1	0.492
1990	13.5	11.9	0.426	19.9	18.7	0.487
1991	14.2	12.4	0.425	21.1	19.7	0.490
1992	14.8	13.1	0.430	22.1	20.6	0.497
1993	15.1	13.4	0.448	22.6	21.1	0.514
1994	14.5	12.6	0.450	22.0	20.3	0.515
1995	13.8	11.7	0.444	21.1	19.5	0.509
1996	13.7	11.6	0.447	20.8	19.1	0.511
1997	13.3	11.3	0.448	20.3	18.7	0.513
1998	12.7	10.6	0.446	19.3	17.4	0.509
1999	11.9	9.9	0.445	18.7	16.9	0.508
2000	11.3	9.7	0.447	18.0	16.5	0.506
2001	11.7	9.9	0.450	18.5	16.9	0.510
2002	12.1	10.1	0.448	19.0	17.4	. . .
2003	12.5	10.5	0.450	19.5	17.8	. . .
2004	12.7	10.8	0.450	20.0	18.3	0.503
2005	12.6	10.8	0.450	19.7	18.1	0.501
2006	12.3	10.5	0.447	18.9	17.3	0.495
2007	12.5	11.0	0.443	19.3	18.0	0.492
2008 [4]	13.2	11.7	0.446	20.8	19.6	0.497
2009 [4]	14.3	12.8	0.447	23.0	21.6	0.505

Year	Definition 14, MI - Tx + NC: Income after all taxes and transfers			Definition 15, MI - Tx + NC + HE: Income after all taxes and transfers, plus net imputed return on equity in own home		
	Poverty rate (percent)		Gini coefficient [3]	Poverty rate (percent)		Gini coefficient [3]
	Official threshold	CPI-U-RS threshold [1]		Official threshold	CPI-U-RS threshold [1]	
1979	8.9	7.9	0.359	7.5	6.7	0.352
1980	10.1	8.6	0.354	8.2	7.0	0.347
1981	11.5	9.8	0.358	8.7	7.3	0.350
1982	12.3	10.6	0.366	9.9	8.5	0.359
1983	12.7	11.0	0.374	10.4	9.0	0.368
1984	12.0	10.4	0.378	9.9	8.6	0.372
1985	11.7	10.1	0.385	9.9	8.6	0.381
1986	11.3	9.8	0.409	10.1	8.6	0.404
1987	11.0	9.5	0.382	9.7	8.2	0.380
1988	10.8	9.4	0.385	9.4	8.2	0.384
1989	10.4	8.8	0.389	9.1	7.6	0.387
1990	10.9	9.3	0.382	9.8	8.3	0.381
1991	11.4	9.7	0.380	10.3	8.6	0.379
1992	11.9	10.2	0.385	10.7	9.1	0.381
1993	12.1	10.3	0.398	11.2	9.4	0.395
1994	11.1	9.2	0.400	10.0	8.3	0.395
1995	10.3	8.5	0.394	9.4	7.6	0.388
1996	10.2	8.4	0.398	9.3	7.6	0.392
1997	10.0	8.2	0.403	9.2	7.5	0.397
1998	9.5	7.7	0.405	8.8	7.1	0.399
1999	8.9	7.2	0.408	8.2	6.5	0.402
2000	8.8	7.2	0.410	8.0	6.5	0.402
2001	9.0	7.3	0.412	8.3	6.7	0.407
2002	9.3	7.7	0.394	8.6	7.1	0.388
2003	9.7	7.9	0.394	9.0	7.4	0.390
2004	9.6	7.9	0.404	8.8	7.2	0.398
2005	9.6	8.1	0.402	8.9	7.4	0.398
2006	9.3	7.9	0.405	8.7	7.4	0.400
2007	9.5	8.3	0.403	9.1	7.9	0.399
2008 [4]	9.8	8.4	0.392	9.2	7.9	0.389
2009 [4]	10.1	8.7	0.392	9.7	8.4	0.388

[1] Before 1987, threshold based on CPI-U-X1.
[2] Calculated for comparability by same method as the other coefficients in this table; differs from official calculation in Table 3-4.
[3] Earlier years not comparable with 2002 and subsequent years because of a change in tax estimating model.
[4] 2008 and 2009 data do not include estimates of capital gains (losses).
. . . = Not available.

Table 3-12. Official and Experimental Poverty Rates and Supplemental Poverty Measure

(Percent of population.)

Measurement method	Capital gains included in income								
	1999	2000	2001	2002 (new tax model)	2003	2004	2005	2006	2007
Official measure	11.9	11.3	11.7	12.1	12.5	12.8	12.6	12.3	12.5
Experimental									
MSI-GA-CPI	12.1	12.0	12.2	12.1	12.3	12.5	12.5	12.2	12.6
MIT-GA-CPI	12.7	12.5	12.5	12.6	12.7	13.0	13.0	12.6	13.0
MSI-NGA-CPI	12.2	12.1	12.3	12.3	12.4	12.7	12.6	12.4	12.6
MIT-NGA-CPI	12.8	12.7	12.7	12.8	12.7	13.1	13.0	12.8	12.9
MSI-GA-CE	12.1	12.3	12.9	13.2	13.4	13.4	13.3	13.6	15.3
MIT-GA-CE	12.7	12.8	13.2	13.7	13.9	14.0	14.1	14.1	15.9
MSI-NGA-CE	12.2	12.5	13.0	13.4	13.5	13.4	13.5	13.7	15.1
MIT-NGA-CE	12.8	13.0	13.4	13.9	14.1	14.1	14.2	14.2	16.0
Supplemental poverty measure	. . .	. . .	. . .	. . .	. . .	. . .	. . .	. . .	. . .

Measurement method	Capital gains and losses excluded from income						
	2007	2008	2009	2010	2011	2012	2013
Official measure	12.5	13.2	14.3	15.1	15.0	15.0	14.5
Experimental							
MSI-GA-CPI	12.6	12.8	12.9	13.4	13.6	14.0	13.9
MIT-GA-CPI	13.0	13.2	13.2	13.8	13.9	14.5	14.3
MSI-NGA-CPI	12.6	12.8	12.8	13.5	13.5	14.0	13.8
MIT-NGA-CPI	13.0	13.1	13.3	14.0	13.8	14.4	14.4
MSI-GA-CE	15.3	15.8	15.7	15.5	15.2	15.3	15.1
MIT-GA-CE	15.9	16.9	17.3	17.2	16.9	16.8	16.6
MSI-NGA-CE	15.2	15.7	15.7	15.6	15.0	15.3	15.1
MIT-NGA-CE	16.1	17.1	17.3	17.3	16.9	16.9	16.6
Supplemental poverty measure	. . .	. . .	15.3	16.0	16.1	16.0	15.5

Note: The Census Bureau changed the way it modeled taxes in the experimental measures, effective with the revised 2002 estimates. Consequently, comparisons of 2002 and later data with earlier years may be affected.

MSI means "Medical out-of-pocket expenses subtracted from income."
MIT means "Medical out-of-pocket expenses in the thresholds."
GA means "Geographic adjustment (of poverty thresholds)."
NGA means "No geographic adjustment (of poverty thresholds)."
CPI means "Thresholds were adjusted since 1999 using the Consumer Price Index for All Urban Consumers."
CE means "Thresholds were recomputed since 1999 using data from the Consumer Expenditure Survey."

See notes and definitions for further explanation.
. . . = Not available.

Table 3-13. Number and Percent of People in Poverty Using the Supplemental Poverty Measure, 2011–2012, and Comparison With Official Measures in 2012

(Numbers in thousands; percent of population.)

Characteristic	SPM 2011		SPM 2012, revised		SPM 2013		Official 2013[1]	
	Number	Percent	Number	Percent	Number	Percent	Number	Percent
All People	49 567	16.0	49 730	16.0	48 671	15.5	45 318	14.5
Sex								
Male	23 057	15.3	23 278	15.3	22 839	14.9	20 119	13.1
Female	26 511	16.8	26 452	16.7	25 832	16.2	25 199	15.8
Age								
Under 18 years	13 349	18.0	13 358	18.0	12 177	16.4	14 659	19.9
18 to 64 years	29 971	15.5	29 953	15.5	29 987	15.4	26 429	13.6
65 years and older	6 247	15.1	6 419	14.8	6 507	14.6	4 231	9.5
Type of Unit								
In married-couple unit	18 488	9.9	18 703	10.0	17 855	9.5	12 630	6.7
In female householder unit	18 969	29.9	18 137	28.9	17 959	285.0	17 998	28.6
In male household unit	7 071	21.9	7 766	23.1	7 853	23.1	6 357	18.7
In new SPM unit	5 039	18.7	5 124	18.4	5 004	17.9	8 764	31.4
Race and Hispanic Origin								
White	34 339	14.2	34 002	14.0	33 445	13.7	29 936	12.3
White, not Hispanic	21 406	11.0	20 946	10.7	20 946	10.7	18 796	9.6
Black	10 180	25.6	10 363	25.8	10 056	24.7	11 041	27.2
Asian	2 715	16.9	2 737	16.7	2 800	16.4	1 785	10.5
Hispanic, any race	14 589	27.9	14 819	27.8	14 085	26.0	12 744	23.5
Nativity								
Native born	39 280	14.6	39 538	14.6	38 928	14.3	37 921	13.9
Foreign born	10 288	25.7	10 192	25.4	9 742	23.8	7 797	18.0
Naturalized citizen	3 280	18.3	3 361	18.5	3 356	17.5	2 425	12.7
Not a citizen	7 007	31.8	6 831	31.2	6 387	29.2	4 972	22.8
Tenure								
Owner	19 955	9.7	20 512	9.9	20 504	9.8	16 127	7.7
Owner/ mortgage	11 114	8.1	11 676	8.5	11 267	8.3	7 739	5.7
Owner/no-mortgage/rent-free	9 580	13.0	9 694	13.4	9 970	13.1	9 254	12.2
Renter	28 873	29.3	28 360	28.1	27 434	27.1	28 755	28.4
Residence								
Inside metropolitan statistical areas	43 203	16.5	43 064	16.4	42 452	15.9	37 746	14.2
Inside principal cities	21 681	21.6	21 401	21.1	20 516	20.1	19 530	19.1
Outside principal cities	21 521	13.4	21 664	13.4	21 936	13.4	18 217	11.1
Outside metropolitan statistical areas	6 365	13.4	6 666	13.9	6 220	13.2	7 572	16.1
Region								
Northeast	8 232	15.0	8 570	15.5	7 947	14.3	7 046	12.7
Midwest	8 431	12.8	8 268	12.4	8 351	12.5	8 590	12.8
South	18 372	16.0	18 939	16.3	18 565	15.9	18 870	16.1
West	14 533	20.0	13 953	19.0	13 809	18.7	10 812	14.7
Health Insurance Coverage								
With private insurance	15 000	7.6	15 273	7.7	16 439	8.2	10 440	5.2
With public, no private insurance	19 587	31.1	19 655	30.5	20 032	28.5	23 996	34.1
Not insured	14 981	30.8	14 802	30.9	12 201	29.1	11 313	27.0
Work Experience								
Total, 18 to 64 years	29 971	15.5	29 953	15.5	29 987	15.4	26 429	13.6
All workers	13 585	9.4	14 066	9.6	14 357	9.8	10 736	7.3
Full-time, year-round	4 967	5.1	5 252	5.3	5 479	5.4	2 771	2.7
Less than full-time, year-round	8 618	18.4	8 814	18.7	8 878	19.6	7 965	17.5
Did not work at least 1 week	16 386	33.4	15 887	33.2	15 630	32.2	15 693	32.3
Disability Status								
Total, 18 to 64 years	29 971	15.5	29 953	15.5	29 987	15.4	26 429	13.6
With a disability	4 133	27.6	3 979	26.5	4 126	27.3	4 352	28.6
With no disability	25 746	14.5	25 921	14.6	25 799	14.4	22 023	12.3

[1]Differs from published official rates because these figures include unrelated individuals under 15 years of age as does the SPM.

NOTES AND DEFINITIONS, CHAPTER 3

Tables 3-1 through 3-13
Income Distribution and Poverty

SOURCE: U.S. DEPARTMENT OF COMMERCE, BUREAU OF THE CENSUS

All data in this chapter are derived from the Current Population Survey (CPS), which is also the source of the data on labor force, employment, and unemployment used in Chapter 10. (See the notes and definitions for Tables 10-1 through 10-5.) In March of each year (with some data also collected in February and April), the households in this monthly survey are asked additional questions concerning earnings and other income in the previous year. This additional information, informally known as the "March Supplement," is now formally known as the Current Population Survey Annual Social and Economic Supplement (CPS-ASEC). It was previously called the Annual Demographic Supplement.

The population represented by the income and poverty survey is the civilian noninstitutional population of the United States and members of the armed forces in the United States living off post or with their families on post, but excluding all other members of the armed forces. This is slightly different from the population base for the civilian employment and unemployment data, which excludes those armed forces households. As it is a survey of households, homeless persons are not included.

Definitions: Racial classification and hispanic origin

In 2002 and all earlier years, the CPS required respondents to report identification with only one race group. Since 2003, the CPS has allowed respondents to choose more than one race group. Income data for 2002 were collected in early 2003; thus, in the data for 2002 and all subsequent years, an individual could report identification with more than one race group. In the 2000 census, about 2.6 percent of people reported identification with more than one race.

Therefore, data from 2002 onward that are classified by race are not strictly comparable with race-classified data for 2001 and earlier years. As alternative approaches to dealing with this problem, the Census Bureau has tabulated two different race concepts for each racial category in a number of cases. In the case of Blacks, for example, this means there is one income measure for "Black alone," consisting of persons who report Black and no other race, and one for "Black alone or in combination," which includes all the "Black alone" reporters plus those who report Black in combination with any other race. The tables in this volume show both the "alone" and the "alone or in combination" values where available.

The race classifications now used in the CPS are *White, Black, Asian, American Indian and Alaska Native,* and *Native Hawaiian and Other Pacific Islander.* (Native Hawaiians and other Pacific Islanders were included in the "Asian" category in the data for 1987 through 2001.) The last two of these five racial groups are too small to provide reliable data for a single year, but in new Census Bureau tables available on the website, household income and poverty data for all five groups are presented in 2- and 3-year averages. Table 3-2 displays some of these data.

Hispanic origin is a separate question in the survey—not a racial classification—and Hispanics may be of any race. A subgroup of *White non-Hispanic* is shown in some tables. According to the Census Bureau, data users should exercise caution when interpreting aggregate results for the Hispanic population or for race groups because these populations consist of many distinct groups that differ in socioeconomic characteristics, culture, and recent immigration status." ("Income, Poverty, and Health Insurance Coverage in the United States: 2012," footnote 2, p. 2)

Definitions: General

A *household* consists of all persons who occupy a housing unit. A household includes the related family members and all the unrelated persons, if any (such as lodgers, foster children, wards, or employees), who share the housing unit. A person living alone in a housing unit or a group of unrelated persons sharing a housing unit as partners is also counted as a household. The count of households excludes group quarters.

Earnings includes all income from work, including wages, salaries, armed forces pay, commissions, tips, piece-rate payments, and cash bonuses, before deductions such as taxes, bonds, pensions, and union dues. This category also includes net income from nonfarm self-employment and farm self-employment. Wage and salary supplements that are paid directly by the employer, such as the employer share of Social Security taxes and the cost of employer-provided health insurance, are not included.

Income, in the official definition used in the survey, is money income, including *earnings* from work as defined above; unemployment compensation; workers' compensation; Social Security; Supplemental Security Income; cash public assistance (welfare payments); veterans' payments; survivor benefits; disability benefits; pension or retirement income; interest income; dividends (but not capital gains); rents, royalties, and payments from estates or trusts; educational assistance, such as scholarships or grants; child support; alimony; financial assistance from outside of the household; and other cash income regularly received, such as foster child payments, military family allotments, and foreign government pensions. Receipts not counted as income include capital gains or losses, withdrawals of bank deposits, money borrowed, tax refunds, gifts, and lump-sum inheritances or insurance payments.

A *year-round, full-time worker* is a person who worked 35 or more hours per week and 50 or more weeks during the previous calendar year.

A *family* is a group of two or more persons related by birth, marriage, or adoption who reside together.

Unrelated individuals are persons 15 years old and over who are not living with any relatives. In the official poverty measure, the poverty status of unrelated individuals is determined independently of and is not affected by the incomes of other persons with whom they may share a household.

Median income is the amount of income that divides a ranked income distribution into two equal groups, with half having incomes above the median, and half having incomes below the median. The median income for persons is based on persons 15 years old and over with income. Since median income is updated annually to inflation adjusted current dollars, comparison between editions is not possible.

Mean income is the amount obtained by dividing the total aggregate income of a group by the number of units in that group. In this survey, as in most surveys of incomes, means are higher than medians because of the skewed nature of the income distribution.

Historical income figures are shown in constant *2013 dollars*. All constant-dollar figures are converted from current-dollar values using the *CPI-U-RS* (the Consumer Price Index, All Urban, Research Series), which measures changes in prices for past periods using the methodologies of the current CPI, and is similar in concept and behavior to the deflators used in the NIPAs for consumer income and spending. See Chapter 8 for CPI-U-RS data and the corresponding notes and definitions.

Definitions: Income distribution

Income distribution is portrayed by dividing the total ranked distribution of families or households into *fifths*, also known as *quintiles*, and also by separately tabulating the top 5 percent (which is included in the highest fifth). The households or families are arrayed from those with the lowest income to those with the highest income, then divided into five groups, with each group containing one-fifth of the total number of households. Within each quintile, incomes are summed and calculated as a share of total income for all quintiles, and are averaged to show the average (mean) income within that quintile.

A statistical measure that summarizes the dispersion of income across the entire income distribution is the *Gini coefficient* (also known as Gini ratio, Gini index, or index of income concentration), which can take values ranging from 0 to 1. A Gini value of 1 indicates "perfect" inequality; that is, one household has all the income and the rest have none. A value of 0 indicates "perfect" equality, a situation in which each household has the same income.

There are differences between the Gini coefficients for the official income measure presented in the report's main tables and those presented in Table 3-11. In the latter, the coefficients were recalculated, using a slightly different method, for comparability with the other income definitions.

A new "equivalence-adjusted" measure of household income inequality was introduced recently and is displayed in Table 3-4. For a Census-defined household, a given level of money income can have different implications for that household's well-being, depending on the size of the household and how many children, if any, are in the household. Since there have been substantial changes over past decades in the average size and composition of households, some have questioned the pertinence of standard income distribution tables. In response, the Census Bureau now also reports measures of income inequality for households using "equivalence-adjusted" income.

The equivalence adjustment is based on a three-parameter scale reflecting the size of the household and the facts that children consume less than adults; that as family size increases, expenses do not increase at the same rate; and that the increase in expenses is larger for the first child of a single-parent family than the first child of a two-adult family. The same equivalence concept is used in the poverty thresholds for the NAS-based alternative poverty estimates shown in Tables 3-12 and 3-13 and described later in these Notes.

As can be seen in Table 3-4, the equivalence-adjusted measures generally show somewhat less inequality than the raw money income measures, but they show a greater rise in inequality over the period 1967–2013.

Definitions: Poverty

The *number of people below poverty level,* or the number of poor people, is the number of people with family or individual incomes below a specified level that is intended to measure the cost of a minimum standard of living. These minimum levels vary by size and composition of family and are known as *poverty thresholds*.

The official poverty thresholds are based on a definition developed in 1964 by Mollie Orshansky of the Social Security Administration. She calculated food budgets for families of various sizes and compositions, using an "economy food plan" developed by the U.S. Department of Agriculture (the cheapest of four plans developed). Reflecting a 1955 Department of Agriculture survey that found that families of three or more persons spent about one-third of their after-tax incomes on food,

Orshansky multiplied the costs of the food plan by 3 to arrive at a set of thresholds for poverty income for families of three or larger. For 2-person families, the multiplier was 3.7; for 1-person families, the threshold was 80 percent of the two-person threshold.

These poverty thresholds have been adjusted each year for price increases, using the percent change in the Consumer Price Index for All Urban Consumers (CPI-U).

For more information on the Orshansky thresholds (the description of which has been simplified here), see Gordon Fisher, "The Development of the Orshansky Thresholds and Their Subsequent History as the Official U.S. Poverty Measure" (May 1992), available on the Census Bureau Web site at http://www.census.gov/hhes/poverty/povmeas/papers/orshansky.html.

The *poverty rate* for a demographic group is the number of poor people or poor families in that group expressed as a percentage of the total number of people or families in the group.

Average poverty thresholds. The thresholds used to calculate the official poverty rates vary not only with the size of the family but with the number of children in the family. For example, the threshold for a three-person family in 2011 was $17,595 if there were no children in the family but $18,123 if the family consisted of 1 adult and 2 children. There are 48 different threshold values depending on size of household, number of children, and whether the householder is 65 years old or over (with <u>lower</u> thresholds for the older householders). The full matrix of thresholds is shown in the report referenced below. To give a general sense of the "poverty line," the Census Bureau also publishes the <u>average</u> threshold for each size family, based on the actual mix of family types in that year. These are the values shown in *Business Statistics* in Table 3-6 to represent the history of poverty thresholds. The preliminary <u>average</u> value for 3-person families in 2013, as shown in Table 3-6, was $18,853, a weighted average of the values actually used for the 3 different possible family compositions.

A person with *work experience* (Table 3-10) is one who, during the preceding calendar year and on a part-time or full-time basis, did any work for pay or profit or worked without pay on a family-operated farm or business at any time during the year. A *year-round* worker is one who worked for 50 weeks or more during the preceding calendar year. A person is classified as having worked *full-time* if he or she worked 35 hours or more per week during a majority of the weeks worked. A *year-round, full-time worker* is a person who worked 35 or more hours per week and 50 or more weeks during the previous calendar year.

Toward Better measures of income and poverty

The definition of the official poverty rate is established by the Office of Management of Budget in the Executive Office of the President and has not been substantially changed since 1969.

Criticisms of the current definition are legion. In response to these criticisms, the Census Bureau has published extensive research work illustrating the effects of various ways of modifying income definitions and poverty thresholds. Some of the results of this work are published here in Tables 3-11 through 3-13 and explained in the notes and definitions below.

Improving the income concept

One type of criticism accepted the general concept of the Orshansky threshold but recommended making the income definition more realistic by including some or all of the following: capital gains; taxes and tax credits; noncash food, housing, and health benefits provided by government and employers; and the value of homeownership. There is debate about whether it is appropriate to use income data augmented in this way in conjunction with the official thresholds. The original 1964 thresholds made no allowance for health insurance or other health expenses—in effect, they assumed that the poor would get free medical care, or at least that the poverty calculation was not required to allow for medical needs—and because of the imprecision of Orshansky's multiplier it is not clear to what extent they include housing expenses in a way that is comparable with the inclusion of a homeownership component in income. Nevertheless, the Census Bureau has calculated and published income and poverty figures based on broadened income definitions and either the official thresholds or thresholds that are closely related to the official ones. Some of these calculations are presented in Table 3-11 and described below.

Still accepting the validity of the basic Orshansky threshold concept, some critics have also argued that use of the CPI-U in the official measure to update the thresholds each year has overstated the price increase, and that an inflator such as the CPI-U-RS should be used instead. (See the notes and definitions for Chapter 8.) Use of the CPI-U-RS leads to lower poverty thresholds beginning in the late 1970s, when the CPI began to be distorted by housing and other biases subsequently corrected by new methods; these newer methods were not carried backward to revise the <u>official</u> CPI-U. Table 3-11 also shows poverty rates using the lower CPI-U-RS thresholds. Use of the CPI-U-RS, which does carry current methods back and thereby revises the CPI time series, eliminates a presumed upward bias in the poverty rate <u>relative to the poverty rates estimated before the bias emerged</u>. This is a bias in the behavior of the time series <u>given the concept of the Orshansky threshold</u>, not necessarily a bias in the current <u>level</u> of poverty, since all the other criticisms of the Orshansky thresholds need to be considered when assessing the general adequacy of today's poverty measurements.

Alternative definitions of income with Orshansky-type poverty thresholds—Table 3-11

The Census Bureau has calculated "alternative" income and poverty measures based on a number of different definitions of income. In many cases, these measures require simulation—use of data from sources other than the CPS to estimate elements of family and individual income and expenses. One system of income definition alternatives, shown in Table 3-11, was used for data through 2003 and has been selectively updated through 2009. The updated data for 2009 are shown on the website under the category "Effect of Benefits and Taxes on Income and Poverty: 2009." This system provides poverty rates including and excluding the effects of government tax and transfer programs, demonstrating the effects of these programs in alleviating poverty.

Table 3-11 shows household income distribution and poverty data through 2009 according to this system of alternative income definitions, which was last used in published reports for 2003 data, issued in June 2005.

Definition 1, also known as "MI," is the official Census Bureau definition of money income described above.

Definition 4 is Definition 1 income minus government cash transfers (Social Security, unemployment compensation, workers' compensation, veterans' payments, railroad retirement, Black Lung payments, government education assistance, Supplemental Security Income, and welfare payments), plus realized capital gains and employers' payments for health insurance coverage. Capital gains and health insurance were not collected in the CPS but were simulated using statistical data from the Internal Revenue Service and the National Medical Care Expenditure Survey. Definition 4 is the closest approach in this set of calculations to a measure of the income generated by the workings of the economy before government interventions in the form of taxes and transfer payments.

Definition 14, also known as "MI – Tx + NC," is income after all government income and earnings tax and transfer interventions. It consists of Definition 4 income minus payroll taxes and federal and state income taxes, plus the Earned Income Credit; plus all of the cash transfers listed above as being subtracted from money income to yield Definition 4; plus the "fungible" value of Medicare and Medicaid (see below for definition); plus the value of regular-price school lunches provided by government; and plus the value of noncash transfers, including food stamps (now called the Supplemental Nutrition Assistance Program, or SNAP), rent subsidies, and free and reduced-price school lunches. The tax information is not collected in the CPS but was simulated using statistical data from the Internal Revenue Service, Social Security payroll tax formulas, and a model of each state's income tax regulations.

The "fungible" value approach to medical benefits counts such benefits as income only to the extent that they free up resources that would have been spent on medical care. Therefore, if family income is not sufficient to cover the family's basic food and housing requirements, Medicare and Medicaid are treated as having no income value. Data on average Medicare and Medicaid outlays per enrollee are used in the valuation process. It appears that the inclusion of these estimates of fungible values makes little difference in the overall poverty rate, reducing it by just 0.2 percentage points in 2009.

Food stamp or SNAP values are reported in the March CPS. Estimates of other government subsidy payments use data from the Department of Agriculture (for school lunches) and the 1985 American Housing Survey.

Definition 15 ("MI – Tx + NC + HE") is Definition 14 income plus the net imputed return on equity in owner-occupied housing—the calculated annual benefit of converting one's home equity into an annuity, net of property taxes. This concept can be thought of as measuring the extent to which equity in the home relieves the owner of the need for rental or mortgage payments. Information from the 1987 American Housing Survey is used to assign values of home equity and amounts of property taxes. Since disposable personal income in the national income and product accounts (NIPAs) includes the imputed rent on owner-occupied housing plus most of the cash and in-kind transfers included in Definitions 14 and 15, Definition 15 is the Census Bureau income definition closest to the NIPA concept.

Improving the concepts of income and poverty together

Another type of criticism argues that the official thresholds are also no longer relevant to today's needs, and that the concepts of income (or "resources") and of the threshold level that depicts a minimum adequate standard of living need to be rethought together. These critics cite the availability of more up-to-date and detailed information about consumer spending at various income levels. The Consumer Expenditure Survey (CEX), originally designed to provide the weights for the Consumer Price Index, is now conducted quarterly and provides extensive data on consumer spending patterns. To give just one example of the information available now that was not available to Mollie Orshansky, the CEX indicates that food now accounts for one-sixth, not one-third, of total family expenditures, even among low-income families. (For data from, and notes on, the Consumer Expenditure Survey, see Bernan Press, *Handbook of U.S. Labor Statistics.*)

A special panel of the National Academy of Sciences (NAS) undertook a study that reconsidered both resources and thresholds. The Census Bureau has calculated and published experimental poverty rates for 1999 through 2013, developed following NAS recommendations, which are presented in Table 3-12. Beginning in November 2011 the Bureau has issued "The Research Supplemental Poverty Measure" or SPM for the most recent two years, a further refinement of the NAS recommendations; SPM measures are presented in Tables 3-12 and 3-13.

Experimental measures based on NAS recommendations—Table 3-12

Several alternative poverty rates that redefined both resources and needs were presented in "Alternative Poverty Estimates in the United States: 2003" (see below for complete reference) and have been updated through 2013 on the Census Bureau Web site at www.census.gov, under the general heading "NAS-based Experimental Poverty Estimates."

To derive these estimates, a baseline set of poverty thresholds for the year 1999, based on data from the CEX for the years 1997–1999, was developed as follows:

- A reference family type was selected: a 2-adult, 2-child family.

- The definition of necessities for the purpose of the poverty threshold was expenditures on food, clothing, shelter, and utilities (FCSU), augmented by a multiplier of between 1.15 and 1.25 to include other needs such as household and personal supplies. The definition of food includes food away from home. Expenses on shelter include interest (but not principal repayment) for homeowners and rent for renters.

- The numerical estimates were derived as follows: FCSU expenditures for reference families falling between the 30th and 35th percentile of the distribution of expenditures in the CEX, based on 1997–1999 data but expressed in 1999 dollars, were calculated and expanded by the multiplier percentages. The midpoint of these estimates was then selected as the poverty threshold; it turned out to be 96.725 percent of FCSU expenditures by the median household.

- For health care, three different treatments were developed; these treatments are described below.

- Three-parameter equivalence scale adjustments were used to convert the threshold for the reference family to thresholds for other family sizes and compositions, accounting for the differing needs of adults and children and the economies of scale of living in larger families.

- For some of the experimental measures, thresholds were adjusted geographically to reflect differences in the cost of living (in practice, difference in housing costs) in different areas.

The family incomes to be compared with these poverty thresholds were defined and measured to include the effects of all taxes, tax credits, and in-kind benefits such as food stamps, but not the value of homeownership, and to allow for expenses such as child care that are necessary to hold a job.

The eight experimental measures shown in Table 3-12 are as originally presented in Table B-3 in "Alternative Poverty Estimates in the United States: 2003," and most recently updated in the table "Official and National Academy of Sciences (NAS) Based Poverty Rates: 1999 to 2011" on the Census Bureau Web site. The following abbreviations are used to define the alternative definitions of poverty that are presented in this table.

MSI indicates that in calculating the poverty rate, medical out-of-pocket expenses are subtracted from family income before comparing that income to the family's threshold.

MIT indicates that poverty thresholds were increased to take the family's potential medical out-of-pocket expenses into account, using the CEX and the 1996 Medical Expenditures Panel Survey, with the amounts depending on family size, age, and health insurance coverage.

GA indicates that the thresholds were adjusted for geographic differences in the cost of living. Measures labeled NGA were not.

CPI indicates that the thresholds established for 1999 were updated to succeeding years using the percent change in the CPI-U. In effect, the thresholds for these measures have been held constant in real (inflation-adjusted) terms since 1999, just as the official thresholds have been held constant in real terms—in intention, and in fact except for bias in the price indexes—since 1964.

CE indicates that the thresholds were updated using the percent change in _median_ FCSU expenditures from the latest available 12 quarters of CEX data. This means that if the actual real FCSU spending of middle-income families rises (or falls), the real standard of living represented by the poverty thresholds will rise (or fall) commensurately.

Supplemental Poverty Measure— Tables 3-12 and 3-13

In March of 2010, an Interagency Technical Working Group produced suggestions for a Supplemental Poverty Measure (SPM), which were first implemented in the "Research Supplemental Poverty Measure: 2010" issued by the Census Bureau in November 2011. The SPM goes beyond the experimental measures just described, and takes advantage of new data from questions introduced in the CPS-ASEC in recent years. In the new SPM:

- The measurement unit now covers not just the family but "all related individuals who live at the same address, including any co-resident unrelated children who are cared for by the family (such as foster children) and any co-habitors and their children." This redefinition adds unrelated individuals under the age of 15 to the universe measured by the official rate. The "official" measures shown in Table 3-13 have been adjusted to include these individuals, and are therefore slightly higher than the regular published official rates shown in Tables 3-7 through 3-12.

- The SPM thresholds are calculated separately for three housing status groups: owners with mortgages, owners without mortgages, and renters. For each of these three groups the basic threshold represents the 33rd percentile of expenditures on food, clothing, shelter, and utilities (FCSU), averaged over a five-year period, by consumer units with two children, multiplied by 1.2 to allow for other needs. (Before averaging, the expenditures are converted to their dollar values in the prices of the threshold year using the CPI-U.) The consumer units selected for calculating the threshold include not only two-adult two-child families but also other types with two children, such as single-parent families. But they are adjusted to a four-person basis, using the equivalence scales, before averaging them to determine the basic threshold appropriate to a two-adult two-child household. Then that threshold is used as the basis for calculating thresholds for other size measurement units, again using the three-parameter equivalence scales for family size and composition, and for geographic differences.

- The thresholds are updated each year, using an updated five-year moving average of FCSU at the 33rd percentile, expressed in the prices of the new threshold year. Thus the thresholds are adjusted for inflation, but in addition, the "real" (constant-dollar) purchasing power of the poverty threshold will change (gradually) over time as the real standard of FCSU spending in the 33rd percentile changes. The real value of the threshold will likely change more slowly and gradually than in the "experimental" measures described above, because of using five instead of three years in the average.

- Family resources include cash income, plus in-kind benefits that families can use to meet their FCSU needs (for example, the Supplemental Nutrition Assistance Program [SNAP] formerly known as food stamps), minus income and payroll taxes, plus tax credits, minus childcare and other work-related expenses, minus child support payments to another household, and minus out-of-pocket medical expenses.

The SPM is not intended to replace the official poverty measure and is not to be used in calculations affecting program eligibility and funding distribution. According to the report referenced above, it is "designed to provide information on aggregate levels of economic need at a national level or within large subpopulations or areas…providing further understanding of economic conditions and trends." Census Bureau presentation of the SPM has focused on the different distribution of the poverty population indicated by the new measures, as shown in Table 3-13.

Notes on the data

The following are the principal changes that may affect year-to-year comparability of all income and poverty data from the CPS.

- Beginning in 1952, the estimates are based on 1950 census population controls. Earlier figures were based on 1940 census population controls.

- Beginning in 1962, 1960 census–based sample design and population controls are fully implemented.

- With 1971 and 1972 data, 1970 census–based sample design and population controls were introduced.

- With 1983–1985 data, 1980 census–based sample design was introduced; 1980 population controls were introduced; and these were extended back to 1979 data.

- With 1993 data, there was a major redesign of the CPS, including the introduction of computer-assisted interviewing. The limits used to "code" reported income amounts were changed, resulting in reporting of higher income values for the highest-income families and, consequently, an exaggerated year-to-year increase in income inequality. (It is possible that this jump actually reflects in one year an increase that had emerged more gradually, so that the distribution measures for 1993 and later years may be properly comparable with data for decades earlier even if they should not be directly compared with 1992.) In addition, 1990 census–based population controls were introduced, and these were extended back to the 1992 data.

- With 1995 data, the 1990 census–based sample design was implemented and the sample was reduced by 7,000 households.

- Data for 2001 implemented population controls based on the 2000 census, which were carried back to 2000 and 1999 data as well. Data from 2000 forward also incorporate results from a 28,000-household sample expansion.

- Beginning with the data for 2010 presented here, population controls based on the 2010 census were implemented. (This resulted in some revision of CPS data initially published for 2010.)

For more information on these and other changes that could affect comparability, see "Current Population Survey Technical Paper 63RV: Design and Methodology" (March 2002) and footnotes to CPS historical income tables, both available on the Census Bureau Web site at www.census.gov/hhes/income.

Data availability

Data embodying the official definitions of income and poverty are published annually in late summer or early fall by the Census Bureau, as part of a series with the general title *Current Population Reports: Consumer Income, P60*. Most of the data up to 2012 in this chapter were derived from report P60-245, "Income, Poverty, and Health Insurance Coverage in the United States: 2012" (September 2013), and from the "Historical Income Tables" and "Historical Poverty Tables" on the Census Web site (see below for the address). In 2013, the Census Bureau split the previous report in two. Health insurance coverage is now published separately from income and poverty. The historical tables can be found in the "CPS-ASEC" section under the "Data" category.

The data in Table 3-11 were first published in two reports, both issued in June 2005: P60-228, "Alternative Income Estimates in the United States: 2003," and P60-227, "Alternative Poverty Estimates in the United States: 2003." Updates available on the website are cited in the table description above. Corrections to the 2006 data on the website were obtained from Census Bureau staff.

The NAS-based experimental data used in Table 3-12 are from the Census Bureau Web site, as specified in the description above.

The SPM data in Tables 3-12 and 3-13 are from reports entitled "The Research Supplemental Poverty Measure." Reports for 2012, 2011, and 2010 respectively are numbered P60-247, P60-244, and P60-241, and are available on the Census Web site.

All these reports and related data, including historical tabulations, used in *Business Statistics* are available on the Census Bureau Web site at <http://www.census.gov>, under the general headings of "Income" and "Poverty."

References

Definitions and descriptions of the concepts and data of all series are provided in the source documents listed above and in the references contained therein.

CHAPTER 4: CONSUMER INCOME AND SPENDING

Figure 4-1: Personal Saving Rate, 1955–2014
(Saving as a percent of disposable personal income)

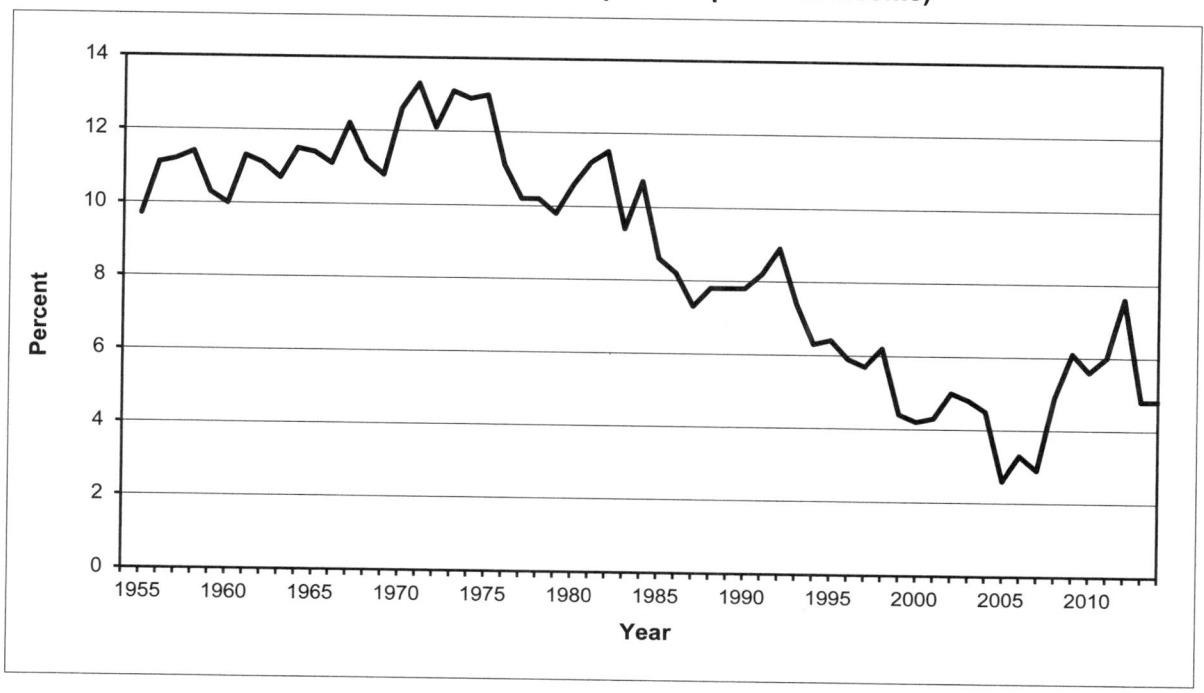

- The personal saving rate—now defined to include saving in individual pension plans as the earned benefits rather than the employer contributions—got as high as 13 percent in the early 1970s. (Benefits from social insurance systems such as Social Security, unlike those in private and government employee retirement plans, do not figure in personal saving; any excess of receipts over payments is counted as government saving.) Since then the personal saving rate entered a downtrend, and hit the lowest rates since the Great Depression in the real estate bubble years 2005 through 2007. Saving as a percent of disposable personal income has increased somewhat since then and averaged 4.8 percent for both 2013 and 2014. (Tables 4-1A and B)

- It should be noted that personal income does not, by definition, include any capital gains. Despite that, taxes on realized capital gains are deducted (along with all other income taxes) from personal income to get after-tax income. Capital gains, both realized and unrealized, can be a source of spending power in addition to current disposable income; during the housing price bubble they were converted into cash by asset sales, refinancing, and home equity loans, all of which were reflected in low saving rates. (Table 12-11)

- Government social benefits were 4.6 percent of personal income in 1955, rising to 14.1 percent in the high-employment year 2007 and increased to 16.9 percent in 2014. In the recession they rose further, to 18.0 percent in 2010, falling back somewhat to 16.7 percent by 2013. It should be understood that this category counts as income all spending financed by government health insurance programs such as Medicare and Medicaid, simultaneously counting that spending as personal consumption expenditures rather than direct government spending in the NIPAs. (Table 4-1A)

Table 4-1A. Personal Income and Its Disposition: Recent Data

(Billions of current dollars, except as noted; quarterly data are at seasonally adjusted annual rates.) **NIPA Table 2.1**

	Personal income											
					Personal income receipts on assets		Personal current transfer receipts					
								Government social benefits to persons				
Year and quarter	Total	Compensation of employees	Proprietors' income with IVA and CCAdj	Rental income of persons with CCAdj	Personal interest income	Personal dividend income	Total	Social Security and Medicare	Government unemployment insurance	Veterans	Medicaid	Other government benefits to persons
1955	324.6	230.9	44.3	13.4	18.9	10.5	14.8	4.9	1.6	4.4	. . .	3.9
1956	348.4	249.6	45.8	13.7	21.2	11.3	15.6	5.7	1.6	4.3	. . .	4.0
1957	368.5	263.0	47.8	14.1	23.8	11.7	18.1	7.3	1.9	4.5	. . .	4.4
1958	379.5	265.1	50.2	14.8	25.8	11.6	22.2	8.5	4.2	4.6	. . .	4.9
1959	403.2	286.3	50.3	15.6	28.0	12.6	22.9	10.2	2.9	4.5	. . .	5.4
1960	422.5	301.9	50.6	16.5	31.0	13.4	24.4	11.1	3.1	4.5	. . .	5.7
1961	441.1	311.1	53.2	17.2	33.2	13.9	28.1	12.6	4.4	4.9	. . .	6.2
1962	469.1	332.9	55.2	18.0	36.6	15.0	28.8	14.3	3.2	4.6	. . .	6.8
1963	492.8	351.2	56.4	18.7	39.8	16.2	30.3	15.2	3.1	4.8	. . .	7.3
1964	528.4	376.8	59.1	18.8	44.3	18.2	31.3	16.0	2.8	4.6	. . .	7.9
1965	570.8	406.3	63.7	19.3	48.5	20.2	33.9	18.1	2.4	4.8	. . .	8.6
1966	620.6	450.3	67.9	19.9	53.5	20.7	37.5	19.8	1.9	4.8	1.9	8.1
1967	665.7	482.9	69.5	20.3	58.3	21.5	45.8	21.1	2.2	5.5	2.7	9.4
1968	730.7	532.1	73.8	20.1	63.8	23.5	53.3	24.6	2.2	5.9	4.0	10.8
1969	800.3	586.0	77.0	20.4	74.4	24.2	59.0	26.4	2.3	6.6	4.6	12.4
1970	864.6	625.1	77.8	20.7	88.3	24.3	71.7	31.4	4.2	7.5	5.5	16.0
1971	932.1	667.0	83.9	21.9	97.3	25.0	85.4	36.6	6.2	8.4	6.7	19.4
1972	1 023.6	733.6	95.1	22.8	106.5	26.8	94.8	40.9	6.0	9.4	8.2	21.4
1973	1 138.5	815.0	112.5	23.3	120.8	29.9	108.6	50.7	4.6	10.2	9.6	23.3
1974	1 249.3	890.3	112.2	23.3	142.2	33.2	128.6	57.6	7.0	11.6	11.2	28.4
1975	1 366.9	950.2	118.2	22.5	162.4	32.9	163.1	65.9	18.1	14.0	13.9	35.7
1976	1 498.5	1 051.2	131.0	20.6	173.6	39.0	177.6	74.5	16.4	13.8	15.5	38.7
1977	1 654.6	1 169.0	144.5	16.2	198.7	44.7	189.5	83.2	13.1	13.3	16.7	40.9
1978	1 859.7	1 320.2	166.0	16.9	227.3	50.7	203.4	91.4	9.4	13.6	18.6	44.9
1979	2 078.2	1 481.0	179.4	16.6	260.9	57.4	227.3	102.6	9.7	14.2	21.1	49.9
1980	2 317.5	1 626.2	171.6	19.7	322.0	64.0	271.5	118.6	16.1	14.7	23.9	62.1
1981	2 596.5	1 795.3	179.7	25.4	399.2	73.6	307.8	138.6	15.9	15.8	27.7	66.3
1982	2 779.5	1 894.3	171.2	26.1	463.7	77.6	343.1	153.7	25.2	16.3	30.2	66.8
1983	2 970.3	2 013.9	186.3	27.5	501.0	83.3	370.5	164.4	26.4	16.4	33.9	71.5
1984	3 281.8	2 217.4	228.2	27.9	574.4	90.6	380.9	173.0	16.0	16.3	36.6	74.3
1985	3 516.3	2 389.0	241.1	29.5	615.4	97.4	403.1	183.3	15.9	16.6	39.7	78.0
1986	3 725.7	2 543.8	256.5	21.9	649.3	106.0	428.6	193.6	16.5	16.6	43.6	83.0
1987	3 955.9	2 724.3	286.5	20.2	667.7	112.2	447.9	201.0	14.6	16.5	47.8	86.4
1988	4 276.3	2 950.0	325.8	25.1	709.6	129.7	476.9	213.9	13.3	16.7	53.0	93.6
1989	4 619.9	3 142.6	341.9	24.4	794.2	157.8	521.1	227.4	14.4	17.2	60.8	103.1
1990	4 906.4	3 342.7	354.4	31.4	822.4	168.8	574.7	244.1	18.2	17.7	73.1	113.9
1991	5 073.4	3 452.0	356.0	42.0	805.3	180.2	650.5	264.2	26.8	18.1	96.9	127.0
1992	5 413.0	3 671.1	402.4	64.3	793.1	189.1	731.8	281.8	39.6	18.6	116.2	142.9
1993	5 649.0	3 820.7	430.5	93.6	783.9	204.7	778.9	297.9	34.8	19.3	130.1	150.0
1994	5 937.3	4 010.1	459.5	117.5	794.2	235.2	815.7	312.2	23.9	19.7	139.4	156.1
1995	6 281.0	4 202.6	484.5	129.2	856.0	258.0	864.7	327.7	21.7	20.5	149.6	164.0
1996	6 667.0	4 422.1	547.4	147.0	874.3	302.2	906.3	342.0	22.3	21.4	158.2	167.6
1997	7 080.7	4 714.7	587.9	152.0	920.5	337.9	935.4	356.6	20.1	22.3	163.1	166.4
1998	7 593.7	5 077.8	644.2	169.9	987.1	355.4	957.9	369.2	19.7	23.3	170.2	170.0
1999	7 988.4	5 410.3	700.4	183.1	983.3	346.4	992.2	379.9	20.5	24.1	184.6	174.1
2000	8 637.1	5 856.6	757.8	187.7	1 070.2	383.3	1 044.9	401.4	20.7	25.0	199.5	179.1
2001	8 991.6	6 046.5	836.8	207.5	1 072.2	369.2	1 145.8	425.1	31.9	26.6	227.3	192.4
2002	9 153.9	6 141.9	871.0	217.3	991.8	398.6	1 250.5	446.9	53.5	29.5	250.0	211.4
2003	9 491.1	6 364.5	900.1	238.0	988.2	432.3	1 321.1	463.5	53.2	31.8	264.5	231.3
2004	10 052.9	6 739.5	962.1	255.4	941.7	562.1	1 404.6	485.5	36.4	34.0	289.8	254.4
2005	10 614.0	7 086.8	979.0	238.4	1 088.1	578.3	1 491.0	512.7	31.8	36.4	304.4	273.6
2006	11 393.9	7 502.3	1 053.7	207.5	1 214.7	723.7	1 593.1	544.1	30.4	38.9	299.1	281.5
2007	12 000.2	7 898.3	979.2	189.4	1 350.1	816.5	1 697.5	575.7	32.7	41.7	324.2	294.2
2008	12 502.2	8 078.3	1 026.5	262.1	1 361.6	805.4	1 920.0	605.5	51.1	45.0	338.3	417.0
2009	12 094.8	7 787.0	973.0	333.7	1 264.3	553.7	2 108.8	664.5	131.2	51.5	369.2	397.8
2010	12 477.1	7 961.4	1 032.7	402.8	1 195.0	544.6	2 281.7	690.2	138.9	58.0	396.6	484.3
2011	13 254.5	8 269.0	1 143.7	485.3	1 231.6	682.2	2 310.2	713.3	107.2	63.3	405.7	484.9
2012	13 915.1	8 609.9	1 241.4	525.3	1 288.8	834.9	2 323.6	762.1	83.8	70.1	417.3	434.0
2013	14 068.4	8 839.7	1 285.1	563.4	1 271.3	789.0	2 385.5	799.0	62.3	79.1	439.7	430.8
2014	14 694.2	9 248.9	1 346.7	610.8	1 302.0	815.5	2 487.2	834.6	35.8	83.7	487.4	447.9
2012												
1st quarter	13 662.4	8 504.0	1 213.6	517.0	1 270.3	755.7	2 297.7	753.2	96.0	67.2	400.4	433.2
2nd quarter	13 814.1	8 550.0	1 240.2	523.0	1 295.0	786.4	2 321.3	759.4	86.0	69.0	421.1	432.6
3rd quarter	13 867.1	8 587.6	1 245.8	527.3	1 289.8	796.2	2 327.1	765.1	78.2	71.3	419.0	434.3
4th quarter	14 316.9	8 798.0	1 266.0	534.0	1 300.2	1 001.5	2 348.4	770.8	75.0	72.9	428.6	435.6
2013												
1st quarter	13 891.3	8 696.7	1 288.9	547.9	1 271.3	768.9	2 365.2	789.8	69.0	76.2	426.1	432.3
2nd quarter	14 025.2	8 820.4	1 279.7	556.5	1 262.9	794.8	2 374.9	795.1	64.4	79.1	435.9	432.0
3rd quarter	14 136.3	8 875.7	1 287.5	569.7	1 270.1	806.8	2 397.0	802.5	59.3	80.1	448.4	431.2
4th quarter	14 220.7	8 965.9	1 284.3	579.4	1 281.1	785.7	2 404.8	808.8	56.6	80.8	448.6	427.5
2014												
1st quarter	14 433.5	9 103.7	1 304.8	591.0	1 320.2	782.5	2 434.2	824.5	39.7	82.0	463.0	435.5
2nd quarter	14 612.8	9 177.3	1 346.3	605.5	1 310.0	811.9	2 471.1	833.2	36.0	82.3	473.6	450.5
3rd quarter	14 774.8	9 289.9	1 357.8	618.4	1 288.1	826.8	2 514.4	837.2	34.6	83.8	505.9	452.2
4th quarter	14 955.7	9 424.9	1 377.9	628.4	1 289.8	840.8	2 528.9	843.8	32.9	86.7	507.1	453.3

. . . = Not available.

Table 4-1A. Personal Income and Its Disposition: Recent Data—*Continued*

(Billions of current dollars, except as noted; quarterly data are at seasonally adjusted annual rates.)

NIPA Table 2.1

Year and quarter	Personal income—Continued		Less: Personal current taxes	Equals: Disposable personal income	Less: Personal outlays						Equals: Personal saving		Billions of chained (2009) dollars	
	Personal current transfer receipts—Continued From business, net	Less: Contributions for government social insurance, domestic			Total	Personal consumption expenditures	Personal interest payments	Personal current transfer payments			Billions of dollars	Percent of disposable personal income	Percent income excluding current transfers	Disposable personal income
								Total	To government	To the rest of the world, net				
1955	0.9	9.1	32.9	291.7	263.5	258.7	4.0	0.9	0.4	0.4	28.2	9.7	1 955.2	1 846.5
1956	1.2	10.0	36.6	311.8	277.1	271.6	4.6	1.0	0.5	0.5	34.7	11.1	2 057.5	1 934.8
1957	1.4	11.4	38.9	329.6	292.7	286.7	4.9	1.1	0.6	0.5	36.9	11.2	2 101.5	1 984.9
1958	1.2	11.4	38.5	340.9	302.0	296.0	5.0	1.0	0.6	0.4	38.9	11.4	2 094.7	2 005.9
1959	1.3	13.8	42.3	360.9	323.8	317.5	5.5	0.8	0.3	0.5	37.1	10.3	2 196.7	2 092.1
1960	1.3	16.4	46.1	376.5	338.6	331.6	6.2	0.8	0.3	0.5	37.8	10.0	2 262.9	2 146.9
1961	1.4	17.0	47.3	393.8	349.5	342.0	6.5	1.0	0.5	0.5	44.4	11.3	2 323.1	2 222.7
1962	1.5	19.1	51.6	417.5	371.2	363.1	7.0	1.1	0.5	0.6	46.4	11.1	2 447.0	2 328.9
1963	1.9	21.7	54.6	438.3	391.6	382.5	7.9	1.2	0.5	0.7	46.7	10.7	2 539.7	2 416.5
1964	2.2	22.4	52.1	476.3	421.4	411.2	8.9	1.3	0.6	0.7	54.8	11.5	2 689.0	2 588.1
1965	2.3	23.4	57.7	513.2	454.9	443.6	9.9	1.4	0.6	0.8	58.3	11.4	2 863.9	2 748.9
1966	2.1	31.3	66.4	554.2	492.8	480.6	10.7	1.6	0.8	0.8	61.4	11.1	3 034.8	2 895.0
1967	2.3	34.9	73.0	592.8	520.6	507.4	11.1	2.0	1.0	1.0	72.2	12.2	3 147.7	3 020.6
1968	2.8	38.7	87.0	643.8	571.7	557.4	12.2	2.0	1.0	1.0	72.1	11.2	3 308.9	3 157.4
1969	3.3	44.1	104.5	695.8	620.7	604.5	14.0	2.2	1.1	1.1	75.0	10.8	3 462.5	3 264.4
1970	2.9	46.4	103.1	761.5	665.5	647.7	15.2	2.6	1.3	1.3	96.1	12.6	3 540.6	3 413.2
1971	2.7	51.2	101.7	830.4	720.3	701.0	16.6	2.8	1.5	1.4	110.1	13.3	3 628.8	3 570.4
1972	3.1	59.2	123.6	899.9	790.7	769.4	18.1	3.2	1.8	1.4	109.2	12.1	3 848.1	3 741.2
1973	3.9	75.5	132.4	1 006.1	874.3	851.1	19.8	3.4	1.8	1.6	131.8	13.1	4 046.8	3 968.6
1974	4.7	85.2	151.0	1 098.3	956.6	932.0	21.2	3.4	2.1	1.4	141.7	12.9	3 987.0	3 923.6
1975	6.8	89.3	147.6	1 219.3	1 060.3	1 032.8	23.7	3.8	2.5	1.3	159.0	13.0	3 946.3	4 020.0
1976	6.7	101.3	172.7	1 325.8	1 178.5	1 150.2	23.9	4.4	3.0	1.4	147.3	11.1	4 107.5	4 144.0
1977	5.1	113.1	197.9	1 456.7	1 308.5	1 276.7	27.0	4.8	3.5	1.4	148.2	10.2	4 284.5	4 274.8
1978	6.5	131.3	229.6	1 630.1	1 463.5	1 426.2	31.9	5.4	3.9	1.6	166.6	10.2	4 524.7	4 470.5
1979	8.2	152.7	268.9	1 809.3	1 631.7	1 589.5	36.2	6.0	4.3	1.7	177.5	9.8	4 641.9	4 557.8
1980	8.6	166.2	299.5	2 018.0	1 804.8	1 754.6	43.2	6.9	5.0	2.0	213.2	10.6	4 634.6	4 590.5
1981	11.2	195.7	345.8	2 250.7	1 998.3	1 937.5	49.2	11.5	6.0	5.6	252.5	11.2	4 761.6	4 705.6
1982	12.4	208.9	354.7	2 424.7	2 147.0	2 073.9	59.3	13.8	7.1	6.7	277.7	11.5	4 801.9	4 803.3
1983	13.8	226.0	352.9	2 617.4	2 370.4	2 286.5	68.8	15.1	8.1	7.0	247.0	9.4	4 911.4	4 971.0
1984	19.7	257.5	377.9	2 903.9	2 591.8	2 498.2	76.6	17.1	9.2	7.9	312.1	10.7	5 272.5	5 314.0
1985	22.3	281.4	417.8	3 098.5	2 833.4	2 722.7	92.0	18.8	10.4	8.3	265.1	8.6	5 462.8	5 476.2
1986	22.9	303.4	437.8	3 287.9	3 018.5	2 898.4	99.0	21.1	12.0	9.1	269.4	8.2	5 664.0	5 687.8
1987	20.2	323.1	489.6	3 466.3	3 214.2	3 092.1	98.9	23.2	13.2	10.0	252.1	7.3	5 847.0	5 811.0
1988	20.6	361.5	505.9	3 770.4	3 475.7	3 346.9	103.1	25.6	14.8	10.8	294.8	7.8	6 097.5	6 083.9
1989	23.2	385.2	567.7	4 052.1	3 735.6	3 592.8	114.8	28.0	16.5	11.6	316.5	7.8	6 305.0	6 268.7
1990	22.2	410.1	594.7	4 311.8	3 976.3	3 825.6	120.1	30.6	18.4	12.2	335.4	7.8	6 390.2	6 393.5
1991	17.6	430.2	588.9	4 484.5	4 118.6	3 960.2	121.8	36.7	22.6	14.1	365.9	8.2	6 324.7	6 438.4
1992	16.3	455.0	612.8	4 800.2	4 374.2	4 215.7	118.1	40.5	26.0	14.5	426.0	8.9	6 525.0	6 714.2
1993	14.1	477.4	648.8	5 000.2	4 632.6	4 471.0	116.0	45.6	28.6	17.1	367.6	7.4	6 626.7	6 823.6
1994	13.3	508.2	693.1	5 244.2	4 912.8	4 741.0	122.0	49.8	30.9	18.9	331.4	6.3	6 829.0	7 010.7
1995	18.7	532.8	748.4	5 532.6	5 179.6	4 984.2	142.6	52.9	32.6	20.3	352.9	6.4	7 068.9	7 245.8
1996	22.9	555.1	837.1	5 829.9	5 484.7	5 268.1	159.1	57.6	34.9	22.6	345.2	5.9	7 358.0	7 476.1
1997	19.4	587.2	931.8	6 148.8	5 796.7	5 560.7	172.1	63.9	38.2	25.7	352.2	5.7	7 722.2	7 751.3
1998	26.0	624.7	1 032.4	6 561.3	6 156.0	5 903.0	183.4	69.5	39.9	29.7	405.3	6.2	8 268.8	8 208.1
1999	34.0	661.3	1 112.1	6 876.3	6 573.0	6 307.0	190.2	75.8	44.1	31.8	303.3	4.4	8 583.7	8 477.7
2000	42.4	705.8	1 236.6	7 400.5	7 092.8	6 792.4	217.5	82.9	48.8	34.1	307.7	4.2	9 081.8	8 902.2
2001	46.8	733.2	1 239.3	7 752.3	7 417.1	7 103.1	223.2	90.8	52.9	37.9	335.2	4.3	9 203.9	9 148.7
2002	34.2	751.5	1 054.7	8 099.2	7 693.9	7 384.1	213.0	96.9	56.4	40.5	405.3	5.0	9 163.7	9 431.6
2003	26.3	779.3	1 005.3	8 485.8	8 076.2	7 765.5	209.8	100.8	60.5	40.3	409.6	4.8	9 299.5	9 690.1
2004	16.8	829.2	1 050.6	9 002.3	8 592.9	8 260.0	221.8	111.1	66.9	44.2	409.4	4.5	9 622.4	10 035.7
2005	25.7	873.3	1 213.2	9 400.8	9 157.7	8 794.1	248.8	114.8	71.6	43.2	243.1	2.6	9 860.4	10 189.4
2006	21.5	922.6	1 357.1	10 036.9	9 705.5	9 304.0	275.1	126.4	76.6	49.7	331.4	3.3	10 323.5	10 595.4
2007	30.6	961.4	1 493.2	10 507.0	10 197.2	9 750.5	305.9	140.8	81.0	59.8	309.8	2.9	10 578.7	10 820.6
2008	36.6	988.2	1 507.8	10 994.4	10 457.7	10 013.6	289.6	154.4	82.8	71.7	536.7	4.9	10 538.8	10 987.3
2009	38.7	964.4	1 152.3	10 942.5	10 275.1	9 847.0	273.9	154.2	83.5	70.7	667.4	6.1	9 947.3	10 942.5
2010	43.0	984.1	1 239.3	11 237.9	10 607.9	10 202.2	250.8	154.9	83.9	71.0	630.0	5.6	9 987.3	11 055.1
2011	50.2	917.8	1 453.2	11 801.4	11 091.2	10 689.3	241.4	160.5	85.5	75.1	710.1	6.0	10 460.1	11 331.2
2012	42.7	951.6	1 511.4	12 403.7	11 457.0	11 050.6	240.6	165.8	91.1	74.7	946.7	7.6	10 882.7	11 688.3
2013	41.2	1 106.8	1 672.8	12 395.6	11 805.7	11 392.3	244.2	169.3	92.6	76.6	589.9	4.8	10 822.3	11 523.1
2014	42.0	1 159.0	1 780.2	12 913.9	12 293.7	11 865.9	254.2	173.6	95.3	78.3	620.2	4.8	11 149.8	11 836.3
2012														
1st quarter	45.7	941.6	1 472.4	12 190.0	11 362.0	10 956.2	240.8	165.0	89.0	76.0	828.0	6.8	10 722.7	11 547.8
2nd quarter	43.1	944.9	1 492.8	12 321.3	11 415.6	11 008.3	240.1	167.1	90.9	76.3	905.7	7.4	10 813.5	11 636.7
3rd quarter	41.4	948.0	1 511.7	12 355.4	11 476.9	11 073.6	240.9	162.4	92.0	70.4	878.5	7.1	10 824.2	11 630.8
4th quarter	40.7	971.8	1 568.7	12 748.1	11 573.6	11 164.3	240.8	168.5	92.4	76.1	1 174.6	9.2	11 168.1	11 936.1
2013														
1st quarter	40.8	1 088.5	1 641.1	12 250.3	11 683.3	11 271.8	240.6	170.8	92.2	78.6	567.0	4.6	10 717.4	11 431.2
2nd quarter	41.0	1 105.0	1 680.8	12 344.4	11 734.7	11 322.8	242.5	169.4	92.3	77.2	609.7	4.9	10 821.3	11 506.5
3rd quarter	41.3	1 111.8	1 673.2	12 463.1	11 830.4	11 417.7	245.8	167.0	92.7	74.3	632.7	5.1	10 859.1	11 569.3
4th quarter	41.5	1 122.0	1 696.0	12 524.7	11 974.4	11 556.9	247.7	169.8	93.4	76.4	550.3	4.4	10 891.6	11 585.6
2014														
1st quarter	41.8	1 144.5	1 736.0	12 697.5	12 060.3	11 640.3	249.0	170.9	94.4	76.5	637.2	5.0	11 017.0	11 698.8
2nd quarter	42.0	1 151.2	1 754.1	12 858.7	12 235.2	11 813.0	250.5	171.7	95.2	76.5	623.5	4.8	11 089.0	11 784.7
3rd quarter	42.1	1 162.9	1 792.0	12 982.7	12 377.0	11 949.1	254.3	173.6	95.7	77.9	605.7	4.7	11 164.6	11 863.1
4th quarter	42.1	1 177.2	1 838.8	13 116.8	12 502.5	12 061.4	263.1	178.0	95.9	82.2	614.3	4.7	11 329.0	11 998.7

Table 4-1B. Personal Income and Its Disposition: Historical

(Billions of current dollars, except as noted; quarterly data are at seasonally adjusted annual rates.)   **NIPA Table 2.1**

| Year and quarter | Personal income | | | | | | | Less: Personal current taxes | Equals: Disposable personal income | Less: Personal outlays | Equals: Personal saving | | Billions of chained (2009) dollars | |
	Total	Compensation of employees	Proprietors' income with IVA and CCAdj	Rental income of persons with CCAdj	Personal income receipts on assets	Personal current transfer receipts	Less: Contributions for government social insurance, domestic				Billions of dollars	Percent of disposable personal income	Personal income excluding current transfers	Disposable personal income
1929	85.3	51.4	14.0	6.1	12.6	1.2	0.1	1.7	83.5	79.6	3.9	4.7	848.4	843.0
1930	76.5	47.2	10.9	5.4	11.9	1.2	0.1	1.6	74.9	71.6	3.3	4.4	793.4	789.7
1931	65.6	40.1	8.3	4.4	10.5	2.3	0.1	1.0	64.6	61.8	2.8	4.3	747.0	762.9
1932	50.3	31.4	5.0	3.6	8.6	1.7	0.1	0.7	49.5	49.7	-0.1	-0.2	649.3	663.0
1933	47.2	29.8	5.3	2.9	7.6	1.7	0.1	0.8	46.4	46.8	-0.4	-0.8	631.6	643.8
1934	54.1	34.6	7.0	2.5	8.3	1.8	0.1	0.9	53.2	52.3	0.9	1.7	694.4	705.7
1935	60.8	37.7	10.1	2.6	8.5	2.0	0.1	1.1	59.8	56.8	3.0	5.1	762.5	774.3
1936	69.2	43.3	10.4	2.7	10.0	3.1	0.3	1.3	67.9	63.1	4.8	7.0	848.9	871.9
1937	74.7	48.4	12.5	3.0	10.4	2.0	1.5	1.9	72.8	67.9	4.9	6.7	900.7	901.4
1938	69.1	45.5	10.6	3.5	8.8	2.4	1.6	1.9	67.2	65.3	2.0	2.9	845.2	852.0
1939	73.6	48.6	11.1	3.7	9.4	2.5	1.8	1.5	72.1	68.2	3.9	5.4	910.0	923.2
1940	79.4	52.8	12.2	3.8	9.7	2.7	1.9	1.7	77.7	72.4	5.3	6.8	973.6	986.2
1941	97.9	66.2	16.7	4.4	10.2	2.7	2.3	2.3	95.6	82.3	13.3	13.9	1 137.6	1 141.7
1942	126.7	88.1	23.3	5.5	10.0	2.7	2.9	4.9	121.8	90.0	31.9	26.2	1 318.0	1 294.4
1943	156.2	112.8	28.2	6.0	10.4	2.5	3.8	16.7	139.4	100.8	38.6	27.7	1 495.3	1 356.7
1944	169.7	124.4	29.3	6.3	10.9	3.1	4.3	17.7	152.0	109.7	42.4	27.9	1 533.0	1 399.0
1945	175.8	126.4	30.8	6.6	11.7	5.6	5.3	19.4	156.3	121.2	35.2	22.5	1 505.2	1 383.1
1946	182.7	122.6	35.7	6.9	13.6	10.6	6.6	17.2	165.5	145.9	19.6	11.8	1 423.6	1 368.6
1947	194.6	132.5	34.6	6.9	15.4	10.8	5.6	19.8	174.8	163.8	11.0	6.3	1 380.3	1 312.9
1948	213.7	144.5	39.3	7.5	16.8	10.3	4.6	19.2	194.5	177.2	17.2	8.9	1 445.7	1 382.1
1949	211.2	144.5	34.7	7.8	17.9	11.2	4.9	16.7	194.5	180.9	13.6	7.0	1 432.9	1 393.3
1950	233.9	158.5	37.5	8.8	20.7	14.0	5.5	18.9	215.0	195.0	20.0	9.3	1 556.8	1 521.9
1951	264.5	185.9	42.6	9.7	21.4	11.4	6.6	27.1	237.4	211.5	25.9	10.9	1 677.0	1 573.3
1952	282.7	201.3	43.0	10.8	22.5	11.9	6.9	32.0	250.7	222.8	27.8	11.1	1 758.5	1 627.8
1953	299.6	215.5	42.0	12.0	24.6	12.5	7.1	33.2	266.3	237.1	29.2	11.0	1 839.7	1 706.9
1954	302.6	214.4	42.3	13.1	26.6	14.3	8.1	30.2	272.4	244.2	28.2	10.3	1 832.0	1 731.3
1950														
1st quarter	226.5	147.2	36.2	8.5	19.7	20.2	5.3	16.6	209.9	185.7	24.2	11.5	1 487.9	1 513.7
2nd quarter ...	227.8	153.8	36.8	8.7	20.1	13.8	5.3	17.6	210.2	189.7	20.6	9.8	1 536.5	1 509.2
3rd quarter ...	236.2	162.5	38.5	8.8	21.1	10.8	5.5	18.9	217.3	203.5	13.8	6.3	1 585.1	1 528.1
4th quarter	245.1	170.3	38.5	9.1	21.8	11.1	5.8	22.5	222.6	201.0	21.5	9.7	1 616.5	1 537.5
1951														
1st quarter	254.4	178.8	40.9	9.3	20.9	11.1	6.6	24.4	229.9	212.3	17.6	7.7	1 628.5	1 539.3
2nd quarter ...	263.3	185.1	42.5	9.6	21.4	11.4	6.7	26.4	237.0	208.0	28.9	12.2	1 672.9	1 573.5
3rd quarter ...	267.8	188.1	43.2	9.9	21.6	11.6	6.6	27.8	240.0	210.7	29.3	12.2	1 698.9	1 591.4
4th quarter	272.3	191.7	43.7	10.1	21.9	11.6	6.7	29.6	242.7	214.7	28.0	11.5	1 706.9	1 588.5
1952														
1st quarter	274.5	196.4	41.7	10.4	21.6	11.4	6.9	30.9	243.6	216.2	27.4	11.3	1 714.7	1 587.7
2nd quarter ...	278.4	197.7	43.0	10.7	22.4	11.5	6.8	31.8	246.6	220.4	26.2	10.6	1 740.0	1 607.8
3rd quarter ...	285.5	201.8	44.7	10.9	22.7	12.3	6.9	32.3	253.2	223.1	30.1	11.9	1 769.7	1 640.2
4th quarter	292.2	209.6	42.8	11.3	23.3	12.3	7.1	33.1	259.1	231.5	27.6	10.7	1 809.3	1 675.4
1953														
1st quarter	296.7	213.4	43.0	11.6	23.5	12.4	7.1	33.4	263.3	235.3	28.0	10.6	1 831.4	1 695.8
2nd quarter ...	300.6	216.5	42.3	11.9	24.7	12.3	7.1	33.4	267.1	237.3	29.9	11.2	1 853.7	1 717.9
3rd quarter ...	300.5	216.8	41.2	12.2	25.0	12.5	7.2	33.2	267.3	238.1	29.2	10.9	1 841.9	1 709.7
4th quarter	300.5	215.4	41.6	12.5	25.2	12.9	7.1	32.9	267.6	237.7	29.9	11.2	1 831.6	1 704.0
1954														
1st quarter	300.5	213.4	42.7	12.8	26.2	13.5	8.1	30.2	270.3	239.7	30.6	11.3	1 818.5	1 712.7
2nd quarter ...	300.2	213.0	42.1	13.0	26.0	14.1	8.0	30.0	270.2	242.4	27.8	10.3	1 815.0	1 714.3
3rd quarter ...	302.2	213.5	42.2	13.1	26.8	14.5	8.1	30.0	272.2	245.1	27.0	9.9	1 831.3	1 732.5
4th quarter	307.6	217.8	42.0	13.3	27.4	15.2	8.1	30.5	277.1	249.8	27.3	9.9	1 863.1	1 765.7
1955														
1st quarter	313.9	222.2	43.7	13.3	28.3	15.3	8.9	31.4	282.5	256.3	26.3	9.3	1 896.9	1 794.5
2nd quarter ...	321.5	228.4	44.3	13.4	28.8	15.6	9.0	32.4	289.1	261.6	27.5	9.5	1 940.7	1 834.0
3rd quarter ...	328.9	234.2	44.6	13.4	29.9	15.9	9.2	33.4	295.5	266.0	29.5	10.0	1 978.3	1 867.7
4th quarter	334.0	238.7	44.5	13.5	30.6	16.0	9.3	34.2	299.8	270.2	29.6	9.9	2 004.6	1 889.5
1956														
1st quarter	339.5	243.2	44.9	13.6	31.4	16.3	9.9	35.4	304.1	272.0	32.1	10.6	2 028.4	1 909.0
2nd quarter ...	345.3	247.9	45.3	13.6	32.0	16.6	10.0	36.2	309.1	274.8	34.3	11.1	2 049.7	1 927.1
3rd quarter ...	350.6	250.8	46.4	13.7	32.7	17.1	10.0	36.9	313.7	278.1	35.6	11.3	2 059.4	1 936.9
4th quarter	358.2	256.7	46.8	13.8	33.7	17.3	10.1	37.9	320.3	283.6	36.8	11.5	2 092.3	1 966.3
1957														
1st quarter	362.8	260.6	46.9	13.9	34.5	18.2	11.4	38.6	324.2	288.2	36.0	11.1	2 096.0	1 972.1
2nd quarter ...	367.5	262.5	47.7	14.0	35.4	19.4	11.4	39.0	328.5	290.5	38.0	11.6	2 104.0	1 986.0
3rd quarter ...	372.2	265.1	48.8	14.1	36.0	19.6	11.5	39.2	333.0	295.2	37.8	11.4	2 114.1	1 996.8
4th quarter	371.5	263.7	47.7	14.3	36.3	20.8	11.3	38.8	332.7	296.8	35.9	10.8	2 092.1	1 984.9
1958														
1st quarter	372.4	260.2	50.3	14.6	36.6	22.1	11.3	38.2	334.2	296.4	37.8	11.3	2 064.5	1 969.8
2nd quarter ...	374.8	259.9	50.3	14.8	37.2	23.9	11.3	37.7	337.1	299.2	37.8	11.2	2 064.1	1 983.0
3rd quarter ...	383.1	267.7	50.1	14.9	37.6	24.2	11.4	38.9	344.1	304.2	39.9	11.6	2 109.7	2 022.9
4th quarter	387.6	272.7	49.9	15.0	37.9	23.7	11.5	39.4	348.2	308.2	40.0	11.5	2 140.0	2 047.6

Table 4-1B. Personal Income and Its Disposition: Historical—*Continued*

(Billions of current dollars, except as noted; quarterly data are at seasonally adjusted annual rates.)

NIPA Table 2.1

Year and quarter	Personal income							Less: Personal current taxes	Equals: Disposable personal income	Less: Personal outlays	Equals: Personal saving		Billions of chained (2009) dollars	
	Total	Compensation of employees	Proprietors' income with IVA and CCAdj	Rental income of persons with CCAdj	Personal income receipts on assets	Personal current transfer receipts	Less: Contributions for government social insurance, domestic				Billions of dollars	Percent of disposable personal income	Personal income excluding current transfers	Disposable personal income
1959														
1st quarter	394.4	280.2	50.1	15.0	38.8	24.0	13.7	40.8	353.6	315.8	37.8	10.7	2 162.8	2 065.0
2nd quarter ...	402.7	286.9	50.3	15.4	40.0	23.9	13.9	42.0	360.7	322.0	38.7	10.7	2 203.0	2 098.0
3rd quarter	405.0	287.4	50.4	15.8	41.2	24.2	13.9	42.7	362.4	327.4	34.9	9.6	2 202.1	2 095.1
4th quarter	410.7	290.7	50.6	16.0	42.4	24.8	13.9	43.7	366.9	329.8	37.1	10.1	2 218.8	2 110.1
1960														
1st quarter	417.1	299.3	49.7	16.2	43.6	24.6	16.4	45.3	371.8	333.5	38.3	10.3	2 253.9	2 135.2
2nd quarter ...	422.1	302.3	50.7	16.4	43.9	25.3	16.5	46.0	376.1	339.6	36.5	9.7	2 267.2	2 148.6
3rd quarter	424.7	303.2	50.9	16.5	44.6	26.0	16.5	46.5	378.2	339.7	38.5	10.2	2 269.0	2 152.4
4th quarter	426.2	302.7	51.0	16.7	45.1	27.0	16.4	46.4	379.7	341.8	38.0	10.0	2 261.5	2 151.5
1961														
1st quarter	430.7	303.7	52.3	16.9	45.6	28.8	16.7	46.5	384.1	342.4	41.7	10.9	2 272.3	2 172.4
2nd quarter ...	436.9	308.0	52.6	17.1	46.4	29.7	16.9	46.9	390.0	347.4	42.6	10.9	2 303.1	2 205.5
3rd quarter	444.0	313.0	53.3	17.3	47.5	29.9	17.1	47.4	396.6	350.3	46.2	11.7	2 333.6	2 234.8
4th quarter	452.8	319.7	54.5	17.5	49.1	29.4	17.3	48.1	404.7	357.8	46.9	11.6	2 383.4	2 277.9
1962														
1st quarter	459.7	326.2	55.3	17.7	49.4	30.0	18.9	49.4	410.3	363.1	47.2	11.5	2 408.4	2 299.7
2nd quarter ...	467.0	332.1	55.0	18.0	51.1	30.0	19.1	50.9	416.1	369.0	47.2	11.3	2 440.8	2 323.9
3rd quarter	471.7	334.9	54.9	18.2	52.5	30.4	19.2	52.3	419.4	373.1	46.3	11.0	2 458.0	2 336.0
4th quarter	477.9	338.4	55.8	18.3	53.6	31.2	19.3	53.6	424.3	379.5	44.8	10.6	2 481.1	2 356.6
1963														
1st quarter	483.3	343.4	56.0	18.5	54.0	32.6	21.3	54.1	429.2	383.4	45.8	10.7	2 495.6	2 376.8
2nd quarter ...	488.1	348.3	55.8	18.7	55.2	31.7	21.5	54.3	433.8	387.8	46.0	10.6	2 524.0	2 398.9
3rd quarter	495.3	353.4	56.2	18.8	56.6	32.0	21.8	54.6	440.7	395.1	45.5	10.3	2 549.9	2 425.4
4th quarter	504.7	359.6	57.6	18.8	58.2	32.5	22.0	55.2	449.5	400.1	49.4	11.0	2 589.3	2 465.0
1964														
1st quarter	514.3	366.0	57.9	18.8	60.0	33.6	22.0	53.8	460.6	409.9	50.7	11.0	2 623.5	2 513.4
2nd quarter ...	523.7	373.5	58.8	18.8	61.7	33.2	22.3	49.7	474.0	418.2	55.8	11.8	2 670.8	2 580.9
3rd quarter	533.3	380.9	59.3	18.9	63.3	33.5	22.5	51.6	481.7	427.5	54.3	11.3	2 712.3	2 614.2
4th quarter	542.1	387.0	60.5	18.8	64.8	33.7	22.7	53.2	488.8	430.3	58.6	12.0	2 749.2	2 643.9
1965														
1st quarter	553.1	393.8	61.9	19.1	66.1	35.0	22.9	57.0	496.2	441.1	55.1	11.1	2 793.2	2 675.0
2nd quarter ...	562.7	400.8	63.2	19.3	68.0	34.6	23.2	58.4	504.3	448.5	55.8	11.1	2 832.8	2 705.3
3rd quarter	577.1	409.3	64.0	19.5	69.7	38.1	23.6	57.0	520.1	457.9	62.1	11.9	2 880.3	2 779.5
4th quarter	590.4	421.4	65.6	19.5	71.1	36.9	24.0	58.3	532.2	472.0	60.1	11.3	2 949.3	2 835.4
1966														
1st quarter	603.1	434.1	69.2	19.8	72.5	37.8	30.4	61.5	541.6	482.6	59.0	10.9	2 988.7	2 863.5
2nd quarter ...	613.0	445.4	67.2	19.8	73.6	37.9	30.8	65.6	547.5	488.0	59.5	10.9	3 016.1	2 870.9
3rd quarter	626.3	456.7	67.2	20.0	74.7	39.6	31.9	67.9	558.4	497.3	61.1	10.9	3 053.0	2 905.9
4th quarter	639.8	464.9	68.1	20.0	75.8	43.1	32.2	70.6	569.3	503.3	65.9	11.6	3 081.2	2 939.6
1967														
1st quarter	650.6	471.1	68.9	20.3	77.9	46.1	33.6	71.2	579.5	507.9	71.6	12.3	3 112.6	2 983.4
2nd quarter ...	657.7	476.8	68.5	20.4	79.4	47.2	34.6	70.9	586.7	517.6	69.1	11.8	3 128.3	3 006.8
3rd quarter	671.6	486.4	70.5	20.4	80.7	48.7	35.2	73.8	597.7	524.6	73.2	12.2	3 162.7	3 035.1
4th quarter	683.1	497.4	70.0	20.3	81.3	50.0	36.0	75.9	607.2	532.2	75.0	12.4	3 187.2	3 057.1
1968														
1st quarter	702.6	512.2	71.7	20.1	83.9	52.4	37.6	78.6	624.1	550.4	73.7	11.8	3 239.6	3 109.3
2nd quarter ...	722.6	525.3	73.2	20.1	86.5	55.9	38.4	81.7	640.9	564.6	76.4	11.9	3 288.2	3 161.2
3rd quarter	741.0	539.2	75.0	20.2	88.4	57.3	39.1	91.9	649.1	581.2	67.9	10.5	3 337.4	3 168.9
4th quarter	756.7	551.7	75.5	20.0	90.4	58.7	39.7	95.9	660.8	590.5	70.3	10.6	3 369.9	3 190.5
1969														
1st quarter	771.3	564.2	75.6	20.2	93.7	60.4	42.9	102.6	668.7	603.2	65.5	9.8	3 398.6	3 197.0
2nd quarter ...	790.4	578.2	77.1	20.3	96.9	61.5	43.7	105.7	684.8	615.3	69.5	10.1	3 440.4	3 232.2
3rd quarter	812.0	595.0	78.0	20.5	100.2	62.9	44.6	104.1	707.9	626.0	81.9	11.6	3 492.9	3 300.6
4th quarter	827.3	606.6	77.3	20.5	103.9	64.3	45.3	105.6	721.7	638.4	83.2	11.5	3 516.7	3 326.5
1970														
1st quarter	841.8	616.7	77.1	20.5	107.4	66.1	46.0	104.6	737.2	649.9	87.3	11.8	3 534.2	3 359.0
2nd quarter ...	859.6	622.0	76.7	20.3	110.8	76.1	46.3	105.5	754.1	660.2	93.9	12.5	3 531.2	3 398.5
3rd quarter	874.0	630.0	78.5	20.9	115.0	76.3	46.7	100.7	773.4	672.4	101.0	13.1	3 560.2	3 451.7
4th quarter	882.9	631.8	78.9	21.2	117.3	80.1	46.5	101.5	781.4	679.4	102.0	13.1	3 537.3	3 442.9
1971														
1st quarter	903.0	649.9	80.3	21.2	120.0	82.0	50.5	98.3	804.6	698.8	105.8	13.2	3 583.2	3 512.0
2nd quarter ...	926.4	661.8	82.8	21.8	121.4	89.6	51.0	100.7	825.7	713.3	112.4	13.6	3 611.3	3 563.2
3rd quarter	940.5	672.2	84.6	22.2	123.3	89.6	51.3	102.3	838.2	726.3	111.9	13.4	3 636.6	3 582.2
4th quarter	958.7	684.2	87.9	22.6	124.6	91.3	51.9	105.5	853.2	743.0	110.2	12.9	3 684.3	3 624.0
1972														
1st quarter	986.0	710.6	87.9	23.2	128.1	94.3	58.1	119.8	866.2	760.7	105.5	12.2	3 747.5	3 640.6
2nd quarter ...	1 003.5	724.7	91.3	20.3	131.0	94.9	58.8	123.4	880.1	779.8	100.3	11.4	3 796.8	3 677.8
3rd quarter	1 029.2	738.1	95.5	24.0	135.0	96.0	59.5	124.3	904.9	798.7	106.3	11.7	3 865.5	3 748.5
4th quarter	1 075.7	761.2	105.6	23.9	139.0	106.4	60.4	127.1	948.6	823.8	124.8	13.2	3 982.4	3 897.2

Table 4-1B. Personal Income and Its Disposition: Historical—*Continued*

(Billions of current dollars, except as noted; quarterly data are at seasonally adjusted annual rates.)   **NIPA Table 2.1**

| Year and quarter | Personal income | | | | | | | Less: Personal current taxes | Equals: Disposable personal income | Less: Personal outlays | Equals: Personal saving | | Billions of chained (2009) dollars | |
	Total	Compensation of employees	Proprietors' income with IVA and CCAdj	Rental income of persons with CCAdj	Personal income receipts on assets	Personal current transfer receipts	Less: Contributions for government social insurance, domestic				Billions of dollars	Percent of disposable personal income	Personal income excluding current transfers	Disposable personal income
1973														
1st quarter	1 093.3	787.8	104.1	23.6	142.3	109.1	73.6	126.4	966.9	848.6	118.3	12.2	3 995.3	3 924.9
2nd quarter ...	1 122.6	805.6	109.9	23.5	146.9	111.5	74.7	129.2	993.4	864.8	128.7	13.0	4 026.8	3 956.2
3rd quarter	1 150.0	822.8	113.8	22.5	153.8	113.3	76.1	134.1	1 016.0	883.6	132.3	13.0	4 054.7	3 973.4
4th quarter	1 188.2	844.1	122.2	23.4	159.6	116.5	77.6	140.0	1 048.2	900.3	147.9	14.1	4 107.1	4 017.1
1974														
1st quarter ...	1 204.4	860.9	115.7	23.7	165.4	121.9	83.1	142.8	1 061.6	917.4	144.2	13.6	4 028.7	3 950.9
2nd quarter ...	1 230.4	881.1	108.6	23.1	172.4	129.9	84.7	148.9	1 081.5	946.4	135.0	12.5	3 982.8	3 914.0
3rd quarter ...	1 266.6	902.8	111.0	23.4	178.6	137.1	86.4	154.9	1 111.7	976.0	135.7	12.2	3 980.4	3 917.7
4th quarter ...	1 296.0	916.5	113.5	23.2	185.2	144.3	86.6	157.6	1 138.5	986.5	152.0	13.3	3 958.6	3 912.9
1975														
1st quarter	1 315.9	921.2	112.7	22.9	190.8	155.9	87.6	158.0	1 157.9	1 014.0	143.9	12.4	3 913.6	3 906.5
2nd quarter	1 347.5	934.1	114.3	22.6	192.9	171.5	88.0	121.1	1 226.5	1 043.0	183.5	15.0	3 919.6	4 087.8
3rd quarter	1 384.1	959.0	120.7	22.5	196.8	174.8	89.8	152.8	1 231.3	1 077.5	153.8	12.5	3 956.5	4 028.4
4th quarter	1 420.0	986.4	125.2	22.1	200.5	177.6	91.8	158.5	1 261.5	1 106.7	154.8	12.3	3 997.8	4 059.2
1976														
1st quarter ...	1 453.0	1 017.6	126.4	21.9	204.2	181.8	98.9	162.5	1 290.5	1 140.1	150.3	11.7	4 045.5	4 106.9
2nd quarter ...	1 477.4	1 038.4	128.6	20.8	210.0	180.0	100.4	169.3	1 308.1	1 159.9	148.1	11.3	4 094.4	4 128.2
3rd quarter ...	1 513.8	1 061.2	132.7	20.3	215.0	186.7	102.2	176.1	1 337.7	1 189.7	148.0	11.1	4 125.6	4 158.6
4th quarter ...	1 549.6	1 087.7	136.2	19.4	221.3	188.8	103.8	182.7	1 366.9	1 224.1	142.8	10.4	4 164.7	4 183.4
1977														
1st quarter	1 580.0	1 116.3	138.6	17.1	226.3	191.0	109.3	188.8	1 391.2	1 260.9	130.3	9.4	4 175.6	4 182.1
2nd quarter	1 628.3	1 153.4	140.5	16.6	238.5	191.4	112.1	195.7	1 432.6	1 289.9	142.7	10.0	4 246.8	4 234.2
3rd quarter	1 675.0	1 185.3	142.4	15.8	249.3	196.6	114.3	198.6	1 476.5	1 322.0	154.5	10.5	4 304.7	4 299.0
4th quarter	1 735.0	1 221.0	156.5	15.3	259.6	199.3	116.7	208.5	1 526.5	1 361.3	165.2	10.8	4 408.3	4 382.1
1978														
1st quarter	1 774.9	1 255.8	158.5	16.5	266.9	203.3	126.2	212.0	1 562.9	1 392.8	170.1	10.9	4 437.5	4 413.0
2nd quarter ...	1 833.9	1 302.9	166.1	16.2	273.7	205.1	130.1	223.1	1 610.9	1 452.0	158.9	9.9	4 506.3	4 456.6
3rd quarter	1 887.3	1 339.2	168.3	17.4	281.3	213.9	132.8	236.3	1 651.0	1 484.4	166.7	10.1	4 549.7	4 488.8
4th quarter	1 942.7	1 383.0	170.9	17.6	290.1	217.2	136.0	247.2	1 695.5	1 524.9	170.7	10.1	4 604.3	4 524.2
1979														
1st quarter	1 999.4	1 427.3	180.1	17.8	300.2	222.7	148.8	253.6	1 745.7	1 561.2	184.5	10.6	4 653.2	4 572.3
2nd quarter	2 039.9	1 458.3	179.2	15.6	310.3	227.4	150.9	262.0	1 777.9	1 602.9	175.0	9.8	4 621.0	4 532.8
3rd quarter	2 105.4	1 498.8	180.7	15.4	321.7	243.0	154.2	274.8	1 830.5	1 658.8	171.8	9.4	4 633.5	4 554.2
4th quarter	2 168.2	1 539.7	177.8	17.6	341.2	249.1	157.1	285.2	1 883.0	1 704.1	178.9	9.5	4 661.9	4 574.3
1980														
1st quarter	2 230.8	1 579.2	167.6	20.0	367.7	259.4	163.1	284.8	1 946.0	1 756.3	189.7	9.7	4 649.7	4 589.8
2nd quarter ...	2 256.8	1 600.5	160.3	14.1	380.5	264.6	163.2	292.2	1 964.6	1 758.6	206.0	10.5	4 586.7	4 523.1
3rd quarter ...	2 337.2	1 631.2	173.4	17.0	385.6	296.6	166.6	302.2	2 035.0	1 816.9	218.1	10.7	4 591.0	4 578.3
4th quarter ...	2 445.1	1 694.0	185.0	27.8	410.1	300.0	171.8	318.9	2 126.2	1 887.3	239.0	11.2	4 709.6	4 668.1
1981														
1st quarter	2 503.9	1 745.2	188.2	26.2	429.4	306.5	191.6	330.9	2 173.0	1 947.3	225.8	10.4	4 707.9	4 655.6
2nd quarter ...	2 551.4	1 777.5	176.4	24.4	457.4	309.9	194.1	342.7	2 208.8	1 981.0	227.8	10.3	4 723.5	4 654.5
3rd quarter	2 647.8	1 815.4	182.3	24.1	495.2	328.5	197.7	356.9	2 290.9	2 023.5	267.3	11.7	4 808.7	4 749.8
4th quarter	2 682.9	1 843.0	171.8	27.0	509.5	331.1	199.4	352.7	2 330.3	2 041.2	289.0	12.4	4 803.3	4 759.1
1982														
1st quarter	2 715.1	1 866.4	165.2	27.6	526.8	336.3	207.2	352.5	2 362.6	2 083.1	279.5	11.8	4 797.5	4 764.8
2nd quarter ...	2 758.6	1 885.1	169.4	24.0	542.9	345.5	208.4	359.7	2 398.8	2 113.1	285.7	11.9	4 820.7	4 792.3
3rd quarter ...	2 799.8	1 905.3	170.7	25.9	545.5	362.1	209.8	350.1	2 449.6	2 163.8	285.8	11.7	4 794.4	4 818.0
4th quarter	2 844.5	1 920.4	179.5	27.0	549.9	377.9	210.2	356.6	2 487.9	2 228.2	259.7	10.4	4 798.2	4 839.7
1983														
1st quarter	2 881.8	1 949.9	183.3	27.4	560.8	380.7	220.4	350.9	2 530.9	2 270.4	260.6	10.3	4 823.7	4 881.3
2nd quarter ...	2 931.9	1 988.6	182.6	27.4	570.0	386.9	223.6	359.6	2 572.4	2 337.0	235.4	9.2	4 863.6	4 915.9
3rd quarter ...	2 991.1	2 031.2	183.8	27.4	593.3	382.5	227.2	345.4	2 645.6	2 409.7	235.9	8.9	4 920.2	4 990.1
4th quarter	3 076.3	2 085.9	195.3	27.7	613.0	387.0	232.6	355.7	2 720.6	2 464.5	256.1	9.4	5 038.8	5 097.6
1984														
1st quarter	3 167.4	2 147.1	221.9	26.9	628.6	393.9	251.0	361.2	2 806.3	2 512.1	294.2	10.5	5 141.1	5 201.8
2nd quarter ...	3 251.2	2 196.8	231.8	25.2	655.0	398.3	255.8	370.4	2 880.7	2 573.4	307.4	10.7	5 237.2	5 288.3
3rd quarter ...	3 327.0	2 242.6	232.4	27.6	683.3	401.0	259.9	384.1	2 942.9	2 614.9	328.1	11.1	5 330.0	5 360.8
4th quarter	3 381.6	2 283.1	226.9	31.9	693.4	409.4	263.1	395.9	2 985.6	2 666.8	318.8	10.7	5 380.6	5 404.9
1985														
1st quarter	3 446.4	2 327.0	240.7	30.2	703.9	420.0	275.4	432.3	3 014.1	2 749.7	264.4	8.8	5 413.9	5 392.0
2nd quarter ...	3 486.6	2 365.0	238.5	29.2	710.1	422.6	278.8	388.5	3 098.0	2 800.5	297.6	9.6	5 435.3	5 495.8
3rd quarter ...	3 533.8	2 406.7	240.7	30.3	710.9	427.9	282.8	421.5	3 112.2	2 877.2	235.1	7.6	5 466.1	5 477.4
4th quarter	3 598.6	2 457.1	244.3	28.4	726.3	430.9	288.4	428.9	3 169.7	2 906.3	263.4	8.3	5 536.9	5 540.3
1986														
1st quarter	3 658.5	2 493.3	245.6	24.8	749.5	443.2	297.9	426.3	3 232.2	2 952.9	279.3	8.6	5 580.0	5 609.4
2nd quarter ...	3 700.7	2 519.1	251.6	24.2	757.4	449.1	300.7	429.4	3 271.2	2 982.6	288.6	8.8	5 649.7	5 683.9
3rd quarter ...	3 750.6	2 557.1	264.4	20.5	757.6	456.1	305.0	439.5	3 311.2	3 050.2	260.9	7.9	5 695.4	5 724.1
4th quarter	3 793.0	2 605.9	264.2	18.1	756.9	457.8	310.1	456.0	3 336.9	3 088.4	248.6	7.4	5 731.3	5 734.4

Table 4-1B. Personal Income and Its Disposition: Historical—*Continued*

(Billions of current dollars, except as noted; quarterly data are at seasonally adjusted annual rates.)   **NIPA Table 2.1**

| Year and quarter | Personal income | | | | | | | Less: Personal current taxes | Equals: Disposable personal income | Less: Personal outlays | Equals: Personal saving | | Billions of chained (2009) dollars | |
	Total	Compensation of employees	Proprietors' income with IVA and CCAdj	Rental income of persons with CCAdj	Personal income receipts on assets	Personal current transfer receipts	Less: Contributions for government social insurance, domestic				Billions of dollars	Percent of disposable personal income	Personal income excluding current transfers	Disposable personal income
1987														
1st quarter	3 851.1	2 651.0	275.4	18.8	759.2	463.1	316.5	450.7	3 400.4	3 118.8	281.6	8.3	5 760.5	5 781.6
2nd quarter ...	3 911.2	2 694.2	282.3	17.4	769.4	468.1	320.2	511.7	3 399.5	3 189.9	209.6	6.2	5 798.9	5 725.5
3rd quarter	3 982.7	2 741.8	289.5	21.0	785.8	469.2	324.5	489.0	3 493.7	3 256.6	237.1	6.8	5 862.6	5 829.6
4th quarter	4 078.5	2 810.3	298.6	23.7	805.0	472.2	331.2	507.0	3 571.5	3 291.5	280.0	7.8	5 965.1	5 907.5
1988														
1st quarter	4 153.8	2 861.0	319.3	23.0	812.6	489.9	352.1	502.1	3 651.7	3 374.4	277.3	7.6	6 013.6	5 993.7
2nd quarter ...	4 227.8	2 926.1	322.8	22.6	821.9	493.5	359.1	497.8	3 730.0	3 436.5	293.5	7.9	6 062.2	6 055.2
3rd quarter	4 318.9	2 978.0	334.0	23.9	847.9	499.6	364.4	506.7	3 812.3	3 507.9	304.4	8.0	6 124.9	6 113.5
4th quarter	4 404.9	3 035.1	327.3	30.9	875.1	506.8	370.3	517.2	3 887.7	3 583.8	303.8	7.8	6 189.2	6 172.6
1989														
1st quarter	4 532.7	3 084.0	348.7	26.8	921.6	531.4	379.8	552.9	3 979.8	3 644.0	335.8	8.4	6 282.5	6 248.8
2nd quarter ...	4 587.6	3 117.5	340.3	24.7	949.2	538.8	382.8	566.7	4 021.0	3 711.4	309.5	7.7	6 273.6	6 230.4
3rd quarter	4 643.0	3 157.6	338.0	22.7	963.2	547.9	386.4	571.6	4 071.5	3 769.6	301.9	7.4	6 309.4	6 272.8
4th quarter	4 716.1	3 211.2	340.7	23.4	973.9	558.8	391.9	579.8	4 136.3	3 817.5	318.8	7.7	6 355.3	6 323.2
1990														
1st quarter	4 813.2	3 278.8	346.7	25.9	986.4	579.5	404.1	582.5	4 230.7	3 902.7	328.1	7.8	6 381.0	6 376.5
2nd quarter ...	4 888.9	3 334.8	352.3	30.2	989.5	590.5	408.3	594.6	4 294.3	3 949.0	345.3	8.0	6 420.8	6 414.6
3rd quarter	4 950.6	3 373.9	360.3	34.8	995.7	600.0	414.1	600.7	4 349.9	4 015.5	334.5	7.7	6 418.1	6 417.0
4th quarter	4 972.9	3 383.2	358.4	34.6	993.1	617.5	413.9	600.9	4 372.0	4 038.1	333.9	7.6	6 341.9	6 366.2
1991														
1st quarter	4 983.8	3 395.1	349.1	36.2	986.3	641.6	424.5	580.8	4 403.0	4 046.7	356.3	8.1	6 291.5	6 379.7
2nd quarter ...	5 043.0	3 430.2	354.8	38.6	985.7	661.4	427.7	586.0	4 457.0	4 101.8	355.2	8.0	6 315.2	6 423.9
3rd quarter	5 093.7	3 469.2	355.5	43.0	987.8	670.8	432.6	590.2	4 503.4	4 148.7	354.7	7.9	6 331.9	6 447.2
4th quarter	5 173.1	3 513.5	364.5	50.2	982.0	698.8	435.9	598.6	4 574.5	4 177.2	397.3	8.7	6 360.0	6 502.3
1992														
1st quarter	5 290.2	3 597.6	380.8	53.9	979.5	727.0	448.7	588.8	4 701.4	4 274.3	427.1	9.1	6 446.7	6 641.9
2nd quarter ...	5 389.1	3 654.4	397.4	61.1	984.4	745.6	453.7	607.1	4 782.0	4 330.8	451.1	9.4	6 517.0	6 711.4
3rd quarter	5 449.6	3 690.7	410.1	68.0	981.0	757.6	457.8	616.1	4 833.5	4 408.3	425.1	8.8	6 543.4	6 740.7
4th quarter	5 523.3	3 741.9	421.2	74.3	983.7	762.0	459.6	639.1	4 884.2	4 483.5	400.8	8.2	6 593.7	6 763.8
1993														
1st quarter	5 557.6	3 747.9	421.3	83.2	991.0	781.6	467.5	616.8	4 940.9	4 529.3	411.5	8.3	6 574.8	6 801.7
2nd quarter ...	5 626.5	3 803.3	432.0	91.9	988.8	786.0	475.6	643.6	4 982.9	4 598.9	384.0	7.7	6 618.9	6 813.7
3rd quarter	5 666.9	3 838.0	426.0	96.3	986.7	799.9	480.1	659.2	5 007.7	4 667.0	340.6	6.8	6 626.1	6 817.7
4th quarter	5 745.0	3 893.5	442.6	103.2	987.9	804.3	486.6	675.5	5 069.5	4 735.1	334.4	6.6	6 688.1	6 862.5
1994														
1st quarter	5 796.7	3 917.2	452.9	112.7	994.1	818.1	498.4	673.6	5 123.1	4 805.6	317.5	6.2	6 715.7	6 910.6
2nd quarter ...	5 904.1	3 997.2	456.9	117.4	1 016.1	822.9	506.4	697.8	5 206.2	4 872.0	334.3	6.4	6 816.1	6 983.8
3rd quarter	5 969.9	4 035.1	459.7	120.7	1 038.1	826.9	510.6	695.4	5 274.5	4 948.2	326.3	6.2	6 850.2	7 025.3
4th quarter	6 078.4	4 091.0	468.5	119.0	1 069.3	848.0	517.4	705.4	5 373.0	5 025.4	347.6	6.5	6 934.0	7 123.0
1995														
1st quarter	6 174.8	4 141.3	470.5	122.2	1 092.6	874.0	525.7	724.5	5 450.3	5 065.6	384.6	7.1	6 993.7	7 190.9
2nd quarter ...	6 240.2	4 177.6	475.2	126.1	1 108.1	883.5	530.1	746.7	5 493.5	5 147.6	345.9	6.3	7 027.9	7 207.3
3rd quarter	6 317.0	4 223.7	487.8	130.2	1 120.4	890.4	535.3	752.2	5 564.8	5 219.4	345.5	6.2	7 091.1	7 271.7
4th quarter	6 391.8	4 268.0	504.4	138.3	1 135.1	886.0	540.0	770.2	5 621.6	5 286.0	335.6	6.0	7 163.0	7 313.7
1996														
1st quarter	6 508.9	4 321.4	526.8	143.9	1 145.0	916.0	544.2	801.7	5 707.2	5 363.0	344.3	6.0	7 235.8	7 383.7
2nd quarter ...	6 639.4	4 393.5	551.0	146.0	1 164.5	936.4	552.1	839.5	5 799.8	5 458.2	341.7	5.9	7 329.8	7 454.3
3rd quarter	6 714.6	4 455.7	551.1	148.0	1 186.7	931.8	558.7	843.6	5 871.1	5 517.8	353.3	6.0	7 400.8	7 513.7
4th quarter	6 805.2	4 517.9	560.6	149.9	1 209.6	932.6	565.4	863.6	5 941.6	5 600.0	341.7	5.8	7 465.1	7 552.9
1997														
1st quarter	6 929.8	4 599.5	579.4	149.0	1 227.3	950.2	575.5	902.1	6 027.7	5 684.0	343.8	5.7	7 567.8	7 628.7
2nd quarter ...	7 010.5	4 665.8	579.0	149.9	1 248.0	950.0	582.2	916.2	6 094.3	5 728.6	365.7	6.0	7 651.2	7 693.9
3rd quarter	7 123.8	4 745.4	592.5	152.6	1 267.4	956.2	590.2	941.1	6 182.7	5 842.5	340.2	5.5	7 766.5	7 785.5
4th quarter	7 258.6	4 848.1	600.6	156.8	1 291.1	963.1	601.0	967.9	6 290.7	5 931.6	359.2	5.7	7 903.1	7 897.1
1998														
1st quarter	7 420.5	4 950.4	621.4	161.5	1 324.4	974.7	611.8	996.1	6 424.4	5 988.5	435.9	6.8	8 092.2	8 065.3
2nd quarter ...	7 548.1	5 035.9	633.7	167.2	1 350.7	981.1	620.4	1 022.3	6 525.7	6 110.3	415.4	6.4	8 229.7	8 178.0
3rd quarter	7 655.4	5 120.9	649.0	172.6	1 357.3	984.5	629.0	1 043.2	6 612.1	6 209.6	402.6	6.1	8 334.7	8 261.4
4th quarter	7 750.8	5 204.2	672.7	178.1	1 337.8	995.4	637.4	1 068.0	6 682.8	6 315.4	367.4	5.5	8 419.0	8 328.5
1999														
1st quarter	7 838.1	5 298.8	686.0	180.8	1 310.4	1 014.6	652.5	1 078.1	6 760.0	6 385.7	374.4	5.5	8 482.1	8 403.1
2nd quarter ...	7 908.3	5 352.5	694.1	184.1	1 316.2	1 017.8	656.4	1 095.4	6 812.9	6 516.9	296.0	4.3	8 519.8	8 423.9
3rd quarter	8 015.5	5 429.7	703.8	183.9	1 329.3	1 030.9	662.2	1 120.8	6 894.7	6 626.5	268.2	3.9	8 590.9	8 480.3
4th quarter	8 191.7	5 560.2	717.9	183.6	1 362.8	1 041.4	674.1	1 154.2	7 037.6	6 763.0	274.6	3.9	8 743.0	8 605.1
2000														
1st quarter	8 445.3	5 759.9	724.9	184.2	1 417.0	1 056.7	697.5	1 209.0	7 236.3	6 925.8	310.5	4.3	8 959.2	8 774.6
2nd quarter ...	8 575.3	5 800.8	755.2	184.3	1 450.1	1 083.7	698.9	1 230.4	7 344.9	7 030.4	314.5	4.3	9 042.6	8 865.6
3rd quarter	8 724.9	5 914.0	764.7	186.9	1 472.4	1 098.0	711.2	1 247.9	7 477.0	7 154.2	322.7	4.3	9 149.0	8 969.2
4th quarter	8 802.8	5 951.7	786.3	195.4	1 474.5	1 110.8	715.8	1 258.9	7 543.8	7 260.9	282.9	3.8	9 176.3	8 999.5

Table 4-1B. Personal Income and Its Disposition: Historical—*Continued*

(Billions of current dollars, except as noted; quarterly data are at seasonally adjusted annual rates.)   **NIPA Table 2.1**

| Year and quarter | Personal income | | | | | | | Less: Personal current taxes | Equals: Disposable personal income | Less: Personal outlays | Equals: Personal saving | | Billions of chained (2009) dollars | |
	Total	Compensation of employees	Proprietors' income with IVA and CCAdj	Rental income of persons with CCAdj	Personal income receipts on assets	Personal current transfer receipts	Less: Contributions for government social insurance, domestic				Billions of dollars	Percent of disposable personal income	Personal income excluding current transfers	Disposable personal income
2001														
1st quarter	8 961.2	6 059.4	816.2	201.7	1 463.7	1 155.6	735.5	1 302.1	7 659.1	7 336.1	322.9	4.2	9 249.8	9 076.2
2nd quarter ...	8 997.9	6 050.2	835.0	207.5	1 451.9	1 187.4	734.0	1 309.0	7 689.0	7 387.6	301.4	3.9	9 211.6	9 068.2
3rd quarter ...	8 990.7	6 033.7	851.5	210.1	1 434.7	1 192.2	731.5	1 114.0	7 876.7	7 419.5	457.2	5.8	9 190.5	9 282.6
4th quarter	9 016.5	6 042.9	844.4	210.8	1 415.0	1 235.2	731.7	1 232.2	7 784.4	7 525.2	259.2	3.3	9 164.3	9 167.8
2002														
1st quarter	9 057.7	6 074.8	861.1	215.2	1 392.0	1 259.9	745.4	1 069.5	7 988.2	7 557.6	430.6	5.4	9 167.0	9 390.8
2nd quarter ...	9 139.9	6 137.7	864.8	217.4	1 390.4	1 281.7	752.1	1 049.3	8 090.5	7 656.1	434.4	5.4	9 167.4	9 438.4
3rd quarter ...	9 173.9	6 161.4	873.9	216.8	1 383.7	1 291.6	753.5	1 053.1	8 120.8	7 745.8	375.0	4.6	9 149.5	9 426.3
4th quarter	9 243.9	6 193.7	884.3	219.8	1 395.5	1 305.6	755.0	1 046.7	8 197.2	7 816.2	381.0	4.6	9 172.4	9 471.6
2003														
1st quarter	9 300.4	6 226.6	880.2	226.8	1 407.5	1 323.7	764.4	1 022.4	8 278.1	7 895.2	382.9	4.6	9 152.3	9 498.0
2nd quarter ...	9 424.3	6 318.7	894.1	234.0	1 411.3	1 340.4	774.2	1 019.2	8 405.2	7 994.5	410.7	4.9	9 267.2	9 635.5
3rd quarter ...	9 550.3	6 403.8	907.2	239.9	1 421.1	1 361.6	783.4	955.2	8 595.1	8 158.2	436.9	5.1	9 330.3	9 793.4
4th quarter	9 689.4	6 508.7	918.7	251.3	1 442.1	1 363.6	795.0	1 024.6	8 664.8	8 257.0	407.8	4.7	9 448.4	9 833.0
2004														
1st quarter	9 807.4	6 565.7	947.2	254.6	1 451.7	1 398.7	810.4	1 013.0	8 794.5	8 398.6	395.9	4.5	9 470.2	9 904.7
2nd quarter ...	9 971.4	6 690.3	961.9	258.7	1 468.2	1 416.3	823.9	1 027.9	8 943.5	8 513.4	430.2	4.8	9 567.9	10 002.3
3rd quarter ...	10 110.5	6 823.3	962.1	254.6	1 484.6	1 424.6	838.7	1 067.5	9 042.9	8 649.7	393.2	4.3	9 658.0	10 054.9
4th quarter	10 322.3	6 878.9	977.1	253.8	1 610.5	1 445.8	843.7	1 094.0	9 228.2	8 809.8	418.5	4.5	9 792.6	10 180.6
2005														
1st quarter	10 359.1	6 952.6	953.3	246.1	1 577.6	1 489.3	859.8	1 172.5	9 186.6	8 912.4	274.2	3.0	9 734.8	10 082.5
2nd quarter ...	10 518.6	7 027.4	960.5	242.9	1 641.9	1 513.0	867.1	1 197.7	9 320.8	9 092.4	228.4	2.5	9 818.5	10 162.3
3rd quarter ...	10 698.1	7 142.2	991.7	231.6	1 684.2	1 527.5	879.1	1 226.6	9 471.4	9 260.4	211.1	2.2	9 890.0	10 214.4
4th quarter	10 880.5	7 225.0	1 010.3	233.1	1 762.1	1 537.2	887.3	1 256.1	9 624.4	9 365.6	258.8	2.7	9 997.9	10 298.7
2006														
1st quarter	11 210.5	7 406.9	1 058.7	223.2	1 847.6	1 589.4	915.4	1 320.7	9 889.8	9 513.6	376.2	3.8	10 247.7	10 534.0
2nd quarter ...	11 330.2	7 453.0	1 062.2	211.9	1 917.5	1 604.5	918.8	1 349.2	9 981.1	9 648.6	332.5	3.3	10 279.9	10 549.8
3rd quarter ...	11 440.1	7 508.5	1 051.1	204.3	1 969.0	1 629.1	921.9	1 358.9	10 081.2	9 782.0	299.2	3.0	10 296.3	10 579.9
4th quarter	11 595.0	7 641.0	1 042.7	190.7	2 019.5	1 635.4	934.3	1 399.5	10 195.5	9 877.8	317.8	3.1	10 470.3	10 718.4
2007														
1st quarter	11 820.6	7 832.1	992.3	177.9	2 069.2	1 706.7	957.7	1 462.6	10 358.0	10 018.5	339.5	3.3	10 534.4	10 788.7
2nd quarter ...	11 948.5	7 866.8	972.8	189.6	2 168.9	1 708.4	958.0	1 488.0	10 460.5	10 144.7	315.8	3.0	10 581.8	10 809.5
3rd quarter ...	12 047.4	7 902.1	966.0	192.9	2 213.4	1 732.9	959.8	1 500.1	10 547.3	10 258.8	288.6	2.7	10 598.7	10 837.9
4th quarter	12 184.2	7 992.0	985.5	197.2	2 215.1	1 764.4	970.1	1 522.0	10 662.2	10 366.8	295.4	2.8	10 600.5	10 847.0
2008														
1st quarter	12 367.0	8 077.9	1 017.7	225.3	2 228.3	1 804.1	986.5	1 535.8	10 831.2	10 433.1	398.1	3.7	10 654.6	10 925.3
2nd quarter ...	12 720.4	8 077.3	1 045.9	250.0	2 186.4	2 148.0	987.2	1 545.0	11 175.4	10 542.1	633.4	5.7	10 553.7	11 155.7
3rd quarter ...	12 535.5	8 094.9	1 040.9	273.4	2 173.6	1 943.3	990.7	1 505.8	11 029.7	10 572.2	457.5	4.1	10 466.9	10 899.2
4th quarter	12 386.0	8 062.8	1 001.3	299.8	2 079.8	1 930.8	988.6	1 444.6	10 941.4	10 283.5	657.8	6.0	10 481.8	10 969.2
2009														
1st quarter	12 061.8	7 762.4	944.2	310.8	1 965.9	2 039.8	961.3	1 202.8	10 858.9	10 195.1	663.9	6.1	10 104.6	10 948.5
2nd quarter ...	12 117.7	7 790.5	944.6	325.0	1 846.2	2 177.6	966.3	1 132.5	10 985.2	10 205.4	779.8	7.1	9 977.4	11 026.4
3rd quarter ...	12 066.8	7 774.0	976.9	344.4	1 756.6	2 178.3	963.4	1 133.8	10 933.0	10 322.6	610.4	5.6	9 863.5	10 905.4
4th quarter	12 132.9	7 821.0	1 026.3	354.6	1 703.2	2 194.4	966.6	1 139.9	10 993.0	10 377.4	615.6	5.6	9 846.3	10 891.0
2010														
1st quarter	12 234.8	7 801.7	1 017.6	380.5	1 706.0	2 301.1	972.0	1 193.4	11 041.5	10 459.1	582.4	5.3	9 808.3	10 902.0
2nd quarter ...	12 413.4	7 947.1	1 024.7	397.3	1 719.7	2 308.6	984.0	1 215.7	11 197.6	10 543.3	654.4	5.8	9 965.9	11 043.8
3rd quarter ...	12 543.9	8 019.1	1 029.2	408.3	1 739.4	2 336.2	988.4	1 257.2	11 286.7	10 634.5	652.1	5.8	10 037.8	11 098.8
4th quarter	12 716.4	8 077.9	1 059.3	425.0	1 793.5	2 352.9	992.0	1 290.7	11 425.7	10 794.6	631.1	5.5	10 137.2	11 176.2
2011														
1st quarter	13 077.6	8 209.7	1 103.2	460.1	1 854.2	2 364.0	913.6	1 425.4	11 652.2	10 923.8	728.4	6.3	10 401.7	11 312.9
2nd quarter ...	13 194.8	8 248.9	1 125.2	478.0	1 897.2	2 361.8	916.3	1 443.1	11 751.7	11 052.3	699.3	6.0	10 412.2	11 295.2
3rd quarter ...	13 347.3	8 332.0	1 161.8	491.6	1 932.2	2 353.8	924.1	1 470.7	11 876.6	11 158.0	718.6	6.1	10 510.8	11 355.1
4th quarter	13 398.4	8 285.4	1 184.5	511.6	1 971.9	2 362.3	917.2	1 473.5	11 924.9	11 230.7	694.2	5.8	10 515.2	11 362.0
2012														
1st quarter	13 662.4	8 504.0	1 213.6	517.0	2 026.0	2 343.4	941.6	1 472.4	12 190.0	11 362.0	828.0	6.8	10 722.7	11 547.8
2nd quarter ...	13 814.1	8 550.0	1 240.2	523.0	2 081.4	2 364.4	944.9	1 492.8	12 321.3	11 415.6	905.7	7.4	10 813.5	11 636.7
3rd quarter ...	13 867.1	8 587.6	1 245.8	527.3	2 086.0	2 368.5	948.0	1 511.7	12 355.4	11 476.9	878.5	7.1	10 824.2	11 630.4
4th quarter	14 316.9	8 798.0	1 266.0	534.0	2 301.6	2 389.1	971.8	1 568.7	12 748.1	11 573.6	1 174.6	9.2	11 168.1	11 936.1
2013														
1st quarter	13 891.3	8 696.7	1 288.9	547.9	2 040.3	2 406.0	1 088.5	1 641.1	12 250.3	11 683.3	567.0	4.6	10 717.4	11 431.2
2nd quarter ...	14 025.2	8 820.4	1 279.7	556.5	2 057.7	2 415.9	1 105.0	1 680.8	12 344.4	11 734.7	609.7	4.9	10 821.3	11 506.5
3rd quarter ...	14 136.3	8 875.7	1 287.5	569.7	2 076.9	2 438.3	1 111.8	1 673.2	12 463.1	11 830.4	632.7	5.1	10 859.1	11 569.3
4th quarter	14 220.7	8 965.9	1 284.3	579.4	2 066.8	2 446.4	1 122.0	1 696.0	12 524.7	11 974.4	550.3	4.4	10 891.6	11 585.6
2014														
1st quarter	14 433.5	9 103.7	1 304.8	591.0	2 102.7	2 476.0	1 144.5	1 736.0	12 697.5	12 060.3	637.2	5.0	11 017.0	11 698.8
2nd quarter ...	14 612.8	9 177.3	1 346.3	605.5	2 121.8	2 513.1	1 151.2	1 754.1	12 858.7	12 235.2	623.5	4.8	11 089.0	11 784.7
3rd quarter ...	14 774.8	9 289.9	1 357.8	618.4	2 115.0	2 556.5	1 162.9	1 792.0	12 982.7	12 377.0	605.7	4.7	11 164.6	11 863.1
4th quarter	14 955.7	9 424.9	1 377.9	628.4	2 130.6	2 571.0	1 177.2	1 838.8	13 116.8	12 502.5	614.3	4.7	11 329.0	11 998.7

Table 4-2. Personal Consumption Expenditures by Major Type of Product

(Billions of dollars, quarterly data are at seasonally adjusted rates.)

NIPA Table 2.3.5

Year and quarter	Personal consumption expenditures, total	Goods										
		Total goods	Durable goods					Nondurable goods				
			Durable goods, total	Motor vehicles and parts	Furnishings and household equipment	Recreational goods and vehicles	Other durable goods	Nondurable goods, total	Food and beverages off-premises	Clothing and footwear	Gasoline and other energy goods	Other nondurable goods
1950	192.2	116.8	32.4	13.7	11.8	4.1	2.9	84.4	41.4	18.9	8.9	15.2
1951	208.5	124.8	31.7	12.1	12.4	4.1	3.2	93.0	46.0	20.5	9.6	16.9
1952	219.5	128.8	31.2	11.4	12.2	4.3	3.4	97.5	48.4	21.2	10.2	17.8
1953	233.0	134.8	34.6	13.8	12.6	4.7	3.5	100.2	49.3	21.3	10.8	18.8
1954	239.9	135.8	33.7	12.7	12.5	4.9	3.6	102.1	50.6	21.4	11.3	18.8
1955	258.7	147.4	40.7	17.7	14.0	5.3	3.7	106.7	52.0	22.4	12.4	19.9
1956	271.6	152.2	40.2	15.7	14.8	5.7	4.0	112.0	54.2	23.4	13.3	21.1
1957	286.7	159.6	42.0	17.5	14.8	5.8	4.0	117.6	57.1	23.6	14.2	22.6
1958	296.0	161.6	39.5	15.0	14.6	5.9	4.1	122.0	59.8	23.9	14.7	23.6
1959	317.5	172.6	44.9	18.8	15.5	6.4	4.2	127.7	61.6	25.4	15.3	25.5
1960	331.6	177.0	45.6	19.6	15.4	6.4	4.3	131.4	62.6	25.9	15.8	27.1
1961	342.0	178.8	44.2	17.7	15.6	6.6	4.3	134.6	63.7	26.6	15.7	28.6
1962	363.1	189.0	49.5	21.4	16.4	6.9	4.7	139.5	64.7	27.9	16.3	30.7
1963	382.5	198.2	54.2	24.2	17.5	7.6	4.9	143.9	65.9	28.6	16.9	32.5
1964	411.2	212.3	59.6	25.8	19.5	8.8	5.5	152.7	69.5	31.1	17.7	34.5
1965	443.6	229.7	66.4	29.6	20.7	10.1	6.0	163.3	74.4	32.7	19.1	37.1
1966	480.6	249.6	71.7	29.9	22.6	12.3	6.9	177.9	80.6	35.8	20.7	40.8
1967	507.4	259.0	74.0	29.6	23.7	13.6	7.1	185.0	82.6	37.5	21.9	43.0
1968	557.4	284.6	84.8	35.4	26.1	15.3	8.0	199.8	88.8	41.3	23.2	46.5
1969	604.5	304.7	90.5	37.4	27.6	16.7	8.7	214.2	95.4	44.3	25.0	49.5
1970	647.7	318.8	90.0	34.5	28.2	17.9	9.4	228.8	103.5	45.5	26.3	53.6
1971	701.0	342.1	102.4	43.2	29.9	19.2	10.1	239.7	107.1	49.0	27.6	55.9
1972	769.4	373.8	116.4	49.4	33.5	22.6	11.0	257.4	114.5	53.5	29.4	60.0
1973	851.1	416.6	130.5	54.4	38.0	25.3	12.9	286.1	126.7	59.2	34.3	65.8
1974	932.0	451.5	130.2	48.2	40.9	26.6	14.5	321.4	143.0	62.4	43.8	72.1
1975	1 032.8	491.3	142.2	52.6	42.6	30.4	16.5	349.2	156.6	66.9	48.0	77.7
1976	1 150.2	546.3	168.6	68.2	47.2	34.2	19.1	377.7	167.3	72.2	53.0	85.2
1977	1 276.7	600.4	192.0	79.8	53.4	37.7	21.1	408.4	179.8	79.3	57.8	91.5
1978	1 426.2	663.6	213.3	89.2	59.0	41.7	23.5	450.2	196.1	89.3	61.5	103.3
1979	1 589.5	737.9	226.3	90.2	65.3	45.8	25.1	511.6	218.4	96.4	80.4	116.5
1980	1 754.6	799.8	226.4	84.4	67.8	46.5	27.6	573.4	239.2	103.0	101.9	129.3
1981	1 937.5	869.4	243.9	93.0	71.5	49.9	29.6	625.4	255.3	113.2	113.4	143.5
1982	2 073.9	899.3	253.0	100.0	71.8	51.3	29.9	646.3	267.1	116.7	108.4	154.0
1983	2 286.5	973.8	295.0	122.9	79.8	58.7	33.7	678.8	277.0	126.4	106.5	168.8
1984	2 498.2	1 063.7	342.2	147.2	88.8	67.8	38.3	721.5	291.1	137.6	108.2	184.6
1985	2 722.7	1 137.6	380.4	170.1	94.6	74.1	41.6	757.2	303.0	146.8	110.5	196.9
1986	2 898.4	1 195.6	421.4	187.5	103.5	83.0	47.5	774.2	316.4	157.2	91.2	209.4
1987	3 092.1	1 256.3	442.0	188.2	109.5	91.8	52.5	814.3	324.3	167.7	96.4	225.9
1988	3 346.9	1 337.3	475.1	202.2	115.2	99.9	57.8	862.3	342.8	178.2	99.9	241.4
1989	3 592.8	1 423.8	494.3	207.8	121.4	103.9	61.3	929.5	365.4	190.4	110.4	263.3
1990	3 825.6	1 491.3	497.1	205.1	120.9	105.6	65.5	994.2	391.2	195.2	124.2	283.6
1991	3 960.2	1 497.4	477.2	185.7	118.8	107.7	64.9	1 020.3	403.0	199.1	121.1	297.1
1992	4 215.7	1 563.3	508.1	204.8	124.3	111.0	68.0	1 055.2	404.5	211.2	125.0	314.5
1993	4 471.0	1 642.3	551.5	224.7	131.4	123.5	72.0	1 090.8	413.5	219.1	126.9	331.4
1994	4 741.0	1 746.6	607.2	249.8	140.5	140.3	76.5	1 139.4	432.1	227.4	129.2	350.6
1995	4 984.2	1 815.5	635.7	255.7	146.7	153.7	79.6	1 179.8	443.7	231.2	133.4	371.4
1996	5 268.1	1 917.7	676.3	273.5	153.5	164.9	84.3	1 241.4	461.9	239.5	144.7	395.2
1997	5 560.7	2 006.8	715.5	293.1	160.5	174.6	87.3	1 291.2	474.8	247.5	147.7	421.3
1998	5 903.0	2 108.7	779.3	320.2	173.6	191.4	94.2	1 329.4	487.4	257.8	132.4	451.8
1999	6 307.0	2 286.8	855.6	350.7	191.2	210.9	102.7	1 431.2	515.5	271.1	146.5	498.0
2000	6 792.4	2 452.9	912.6	363.2	208.1	230.9	110.4	1 540.3	540.6	280.8	184.5	534.4
2001	7 103.1	2 525.2	941.5	383.3	214.9	234.9	108.4	1 583.7	564.0	277.9	178.0	563.9
2002	7 384.1	2 598.6	985.4	401.3	225.9	244.8	113.4	1 613.2	575.1	278.8	167.9	591.4
2003	7 765.5	2 721.6	1 017.5	401.5	235.2	259.2	121.7	1 704.0	599.6	285.3	196.4	622.7
2004	8 260.0	2 900.3	1 079.8	409.3	254.3	284.1	132.1	1 820.4	632.6	297.5	232.7	657.6
2005	8 794.1	3 080.3	1 127.2	410.0	271.3	305.0	141.0	1 953.1	668.2	310.7	283.8	690.4
2006	9 304.0	3 235.8	1 156.1	395.0	283.6	324.1	153.5	2 079.7	700.3	320.2	319.7	739.6
2007	9 750.5	3 361.6	1 184.6	400.6	283.5	335.8	164.8	2 176.9	737.3	323.7	345.5	770.4
2008	10 013.6	3 375.7	1 102.3	339.6	268.7	329.3	164.6	2 273.4	772.9	319.5	389.1	791.9
2009	9 847.0	3 198.4	1 023.3	317.1	244.3	303.8	158.2	2 175.1	770.0	306.5	284.5	814.2
2010	10 202.2	3 362.8	1 070.7	342.0	250.4	312.7	165.6	2 292.1	788.9	320.6	333.4	849.2
2011	10 689.3	3 596.5	1 125.3	363.5	260.7	321.0	180.2	2 471.1	829.1	338.9	409.6	893.5
2012	11 050.6	3 739.1	1 191.9	395.8	271.4	336.6	188.1	2 547.2	848.8	354.3	416.9	927.3
2013	11 392.3	3 836.8	1 237.8	416.7	280.2	346.8	194.1	2 598.9	866.0	362.5	413.0	957.5
2014	11 865.9	3 948.4	1 280.2	440.2	287.9	354.6	197.5	2 668.2	886.5	368.9	401.1	1 011.7
2012												
1st quarter	10 956.2	3 714.4	1 178.8	387.7	272.4	332.9	185.8	2 535.6	845.0	353.3	414.3	923.1
2nd quarter	11 008.3	3 717.2	1 181.6	391.1	269.6	334.8	186.0	2 535.6	847.3	351.6	412.9	923.9
3rd quarter	11 073.6	3 744.7	1 194.2	397.2	270.7	337.9	188.4	2 550.6	848.9	352.2	418.1	927.4
4th quarter	11 164.3	3 780.0	1 212.9	407.0	272.8	340.9	192.2	2 567.1	854.0	356.1	422.3	934.7
2013												
1st quarter	11 271.8	3 827.7	1 235.4	417.3	277.7	346.8	193.7	2 592.3	863.5	362.4	421.3	945.1
2nd quarter	11 322.8	3 810.5	1 235.6	416.2	279.1	346.4	193.9	2 574.9	860.8	362.3	402.3	949.5
3rd quarter	11 417.7	3 844.0	1 237.5	415.2	281.8	347.3	193.1	2 606.5	867.6	362.4	414.8	961.7
4th quarter	11 556.9	3 864.8	1 242.8	417.9	282.2	346.9	195.7	2 622.0	872.1	362.9	413.5	973.5
2014												
1st quarter	11 640.3	3 874.7	1 243.1	421.6	281.5	344.8	195.2	2 631.6	876.7	361.4	413.1	980.4
2nd quarter	11 813.0	3 951.5	1 279.1	439.9	287.8	353.5	197.9	2 672.4	885.3	368.8	413.4	1 004.9
3rd quarter	11 949.1	3 987.4	1 295.1	447.7	290.2	359.1	198.2	2 692.2	890.3	371.2	406.6	1 024.0
4th quarter	12 061.4	3 980.1	1 303.5	451.6	292.3	361.1	198.6	2 676.6	893.8	374.0	371.4	1 037.4

Table 4-2. Personal Consumption Expenditures by Major Type of Product—*Continued*

(Billions of dollars, quarterly data are at seasonally adjusted rates.)   NIPA Table 2.3.5

| | Services | | | | | | | | | Nonprofit institutions serving households (NPISHs) | | |
| | | Household consumption expenditures for services | | | | | | | | | | |
Year and quarter	Services	Household services, total	Housing and utilities	Health care	Transportation services	Recreation services	Food services and accommodations	Financial services and insurance	Other services	Final consumption expenditures	Gross output	Less: receipts from sales of goods and services
1950	75.4	72.9	25.1	6.4	5.4	3.6	12.7	5.6	14.1	2.4	. . .	. . .
1951	83.7	81.1	28.1	6.9	6.0	3.8	15.0	6.3	15.1	2.6	. . .	. . .
1952	90.7	87.8	31.2	7.6	6.3	4.0	16.0	6.7	16.0	2.9	. . .	. . .
1953	98.2	95.2	34.5	8.4	6.8	4.2	16.5	7.8	17.1	3.0	. . .	. . .
1954	104.2	100.9	37.4	9.3	6.8	4.5	16.6	8.6	17.8	3.2	. . .	. . .
1955	111.3	107.9	40.0	9.9	7.1	4.8	17.0	9.6	19.4	3.4	. . .	. . .
1956	119.4	115.6	42.9	10.9	7.6	5.2	17.7	10.4	20.9	3.8	. . .	. . .
1957	127.1	123.1	45.9	12.0	8.0	5.2	18.5	11.1	22.4	4.0	. . .	. . .
1958	134.5	130.1	49.2	13.4	8.1	5.4	18.7	11.6	23.8	4.3	. . .	. . .
1959	144.9	140.0	52.8	14.8	8.7	5.9	19.7	12.5	25.5	4.9	13.9	9.0
1960	154.6	149.5	56.7	16.0	9.2	6.5	20.5	13.6	27.1	5.1	14.8	9.8
1961	163.2	157.9	60.3	17.1	9.6	6.9	21.0	14.8	28.3	5.2	15.8	10.5
1962	174.1	168.7	64.5	19.1	10.1	7.5	22.3	15.4	29.9	5.5	16.9	11.5
1963	184.3	178.6	68.2	21.0	10.6	7.9	23.3	15.9	31.6	5.8	18.3	12.6
1964	198.9	192.5	72.1	24.2	11.4	8.5	24.9	17.7	33.8	6.4	20.3	13.8
1965	213.9	206.9	76.6	26.0	12.1	9.0	27.2	19.4	36.6	7.0	22.1	15.1
1966	231.0	223.5	81.2	28.7	13.1	9.8	29.6	21.3	39.9	7.5	24.3	16.9
1967	248.4	240.4	86.3	31.9	14.3	10.5	31.0	22.8	43.6	8.0	27.0	18.9
1968	272.8	264.0	92.7	36.6	15.9	11.7	34.6	25.8	46.8	8.8	30.3	21.6
1969	299.8	290.4	101.0	42.1	18.0	12.9	37.5	28.5	50.5	9.4	34.0	24.6
1970	328.9	318.4	109.4	47.7	20.0	14.0	41.6	31.1	54.6	10.5	38.1	27.6
1971	358.9	347.2	120.0	53.7	22.4	15.1	43.8	34.1	58.1	11.7	42.8	31.1
1972	395.6	382.8	131.2	59.8	24.5	16.3	48.9	38.3	63.7	12.8	47.4	34.5
1973	434.5	420.8	143.5	67.2	26.1	18.3	54.8	41.5	69.3	13.8	51.8	38.1
1974	480.5	465.0	158.6	76.1	28.5	20.9	60.6	45.9	74.4	15.5	58.8	43.3
1975	541.4	524.4	176.5	89.0	32.0	23.7	68.8	54.0	80.3	17.0	67.2	50.2
1976	603.9	584.9	194.7	101.8	36.2	26.5	77.8	59.3	88.6	19.0	76.3	57.3
1977	676.3	655.7	217.8	115.7	41.4	29.6	85.7	67.8	97.7	20.6	85.2	64.5
1978	762.6	739.6	244.3	131.2	45.2	32.9	97.1	80.6	108.3	23.0	96.7	73.6
1979	851.6	825.4	273.4	148.8	50.7	36.7	110.9	87.6	117.2	26.1	109.4	83.2
1980	954.8	924.8	312.5	171.7	55.4	40.8	121.7	95.6	127.1	30.0	126.1	96.1
1981	1 068.1	1 034.0	352.1	201.9	59.8	47.1	133.9	102.0	137.2	34.1	145.7	111.5
1982	1 174.6	1 136.7	387.5	225.2	61.7	52.5	142.5	116.3	150.9	38.0	163.8	125.8
1983	1 312.7	1 272.0	421.2	253.1	68.9	59.4	153.6	145.9	169.9	40.8	179.2	138.5
1984	1 434.5	1 389.1	457.5	276.5	80.0	66.1	164.9	156.6	187.5	45.4	194.4	149.0
1985	1 585.1	1 537.2	500.6	302.2	90.1	74.0	174.3	188.1	207.9	47.9	209.3	161.4
1986	1 702.8	1 650.2	537.0	330.2	95.0	80.4	186.7	199.8	221.2	52.6	227.3	174.7
1987	1 835.8	1 780.1	571.6	366.0	103.1	87.3	204.4	205.3	242.4	55.7	246.9	191.2
1988	2 009.6	1 946.3	614.4	410.1	114.2	99.2	225.8	219.8	262.8	63.3	275.5	212.2
1989	2 169.0	2 101.0	655.2	451.2	121.8	110.7	242.6	238.4	281.1	68.0	301.2	233.2
1990	2 334.3	2 258.5	696.5	506.2	126.4	121.8	262.7	247.4	297.5	75.9	334.4	258.6
1991	2 462.7	2 382.6	735.2	555.8	123.7	127.2	273.4	266.8	300.5	80.1	362.9	282.8
1992	2 652.4	2 564.5	771.1	612.8	133.6	139.8	286.3	295.1	325.7	87.9	396.4	308.5
1993	2 828.7	2 738.6	814.9	648.8	146.1	153.4	298.4	332.6	344.4	90.1	418.7	328.7
1994	2 994.5	2 896.7	863.3	680.5	161.9	164.7	308.3	346.9	371.2	97.8	440.1	342.3
1995	3 168.6	3 066.3	913.7	719.9	177.9	181.1	316.1	366.4	391.2	102.3	458.5	356.2
1996	3 350.4	3 240.4	962.4	752.1	195.0	195.6	326.6	392.3	416.4	110.0	483.1	373.1
1997	3 554.0	3 448.4	1 009.8	790.9	214.3	208.3	343.4	429.2	452.3	105.6	502.6	397.0
1998	3 794.3	3 670.5	1 065.5	832.0	227.6	220.2	361.8	467.3	496.0	123.8	542.5	418.7
1999	4 020.3	3 882.0	1 123.1	863.6	244.1	238.1	380.3	509.1	523.7	138.2	576.3	438.1
2000	4 339.5	4 181.5	1 198.6	918.4	263.5	254.4	408.8	566.3	571.5	158.0	621.6	463.6
2001	4 577.9	4 398.8	1 287.5	996.6	264.7	262.3	419.7	552.8	615.3	179.1	676.4	497.4
2002	4 785.5	4 587.1	1 333.6	1 082.9	258.2	271.4	436.3	562.6	642.2	198.3	737.1	538.7
2003	5 044.0	4 838.5	1 394.1	1 154.6	265.5	289.2	461.9	588.5	684.7	205.5	774.6	569.1
2004	5 359.8	5 153.4	1 469.1	1 240.1	276.6	312.1	496.4	635.3	723.8	206.4	819.0	612.6
2005	5 713.8	5 503.6	1 583.6	1 322.3	289.4	328.9	530.6	689.6	759.1	210.3	868.5	658.2
2006	6 068.2	5 829.0	1 682.4	1 394.2	302.1	351.9	566.3	724.2	807.9	239.2	932.2	693.0
2007	6 388.9	6 140.2	1 758.2	1 481.8	312.2	375.8	595.6	768.5	848.0	248.8	983.1	734.4
2008	6 637.9	6 355.8	1 839.1	1 556.5	311.7	384.5	612.5	771.5	880.1	282.1	1 040.9	758.8
2009	6 648.5	6 372.5	1 881.0	1 627.4	289.7	376.0	600.3	719.0	879.2	276.0	1 072.6	796.5
2010	6 839.4	6 564.0	1 909.0	1 690.7	292.9	385.1	617.7	763.2	905.4	275.4	1 105.9	830.5
2011	7 092.8	6 817.8	1 959.9	1 764.7	308.1	400.6	649.5	795.8	939.3	275.0	1 139.6	864.6
2012	7 311.5	7 018.7	1 995.4	1 835.9	319.5	419.8	685.1	789.3	973.8	292.9	1 193.0	900.1
2013	7 555.5	7 251.6	2 057.4	1 880.7	333.9	434.7	710.2	837.7	997.0	303.9	1 233.2	929.3
2014	7 917.5	7 595.2	2 142.6	1 954.0	354.5	455.5	750.9	882.7	1 055.0	322.3	1 278.3	956.0
2012												
1st quarter	7 241.8	6 961.9	1 967.6	1 824.5	312.6	411.5	673.1	803.3	969.3	280.0	1 176.1	896.1
2nd quarter	7 291.1	6 997.6	1 993.0	1 828.8	320.6	418.4	681.9	785.5	969.5	293.5	1 185.8	892.3
3rd quarter	7 328.9	7 036.6	2 009.3	1 842.7	322.5	422.2	688.7	779.2	972.1	292.3	1 200.4	908.1
4th quarter	7 384.3	7 078.7	2 011.7	1 847.5	322.2	427.1	696.8	789.3	984.2	305.7	1 209.7	904.0
2013												
1st quarter	7 444.1	7 146.7	2 035.3	1 853.5	328.2	430.5	705.2	812.6	981.4	297.3	1 210.4	913.1
2nd quarter	7 512.3	7 211.1	2 051.6	1 870.8	331.3	427.6	704.2	833.3	992.4	301.2	1 228.2	927.1
3rd quarter	7 573.7	7 268.4	2 058.0	1 886.7	337.4	437.0	709.3	841.5	998.6	305.2	1 236.9	931.6
4th quarter	7 692.1	7 380.2	2 084.7	1 911.9	338.6	443.6	722.2	863.6	1 015.6	311.9	1 257.3	945.4
2014												
1st quarter	7 765.6	7 450.2	2 127.4	1 905.0	345.8	449.9	725.7	865.8	1 030.7	315.4	1 246.9	931.5
2nd quarter	7 861.5	7 542.0	2 134.5	1 938.7	350.9	450.8	744.5	876.9	1 045.7	319.5	1 269.4	949.9
3rd quarter	7 961.7	7 636.1	2 143.0	1 968.6	357.4	457.5	757.2	890.9	1 061.5	325.6	1 287.2	961.6
4th quarter	8 081.3	7 752.3	2 165.4	2 003.5	364.1	463.8	776.1	897.4	1 081.9	329.0	1 309.9	980.9

. . . = Not available.

Table 4-3. Chain-Type Quantity Indexes for Personal Consumption Expenditures by Major Type of Product

(Index numbers, 2009 = 100.)

NIPA Table 2.3.3

Year and quarter	Personal consumption expend-itures, total	Goods										
		Total goods	Durable goods					Nondurable goods				
			Durable goods, total	Motor vehicles and parts	Furnishings and household equipment	Recreational goods and vehicles	Other durable goods	Nondurable goods, total	Food and beverages off-premises	Clothing and footwear	Gasoline and other energy goods	Other nondurable goods
1955	16.6	17.7	8.0	20.6	12.6	0.8	8.4	26.3	41.3	14.3	44.2	15.6
1956	17.1	18.0	7.7	17.5	13.2	0.9	8.8	27.3	42.7	14.7	46.1	16.3
1957	17.5	18.3	7.8	18.3	12.9	0.9	8.9	27.8	43.7	14.6	47.3	16.9
1958	17.7	18.1	7.2	15.2	12.8	0.9	9.0	28.2	43.9	14.7	49.4	17.2
1959	18.7	19.2	8.0	18.1	13.6	1.0	9.2	29.4	45.7	15.5	50.6	18.2
1960	19.2	19.5	8.2	19.2	13.4	1.0	9.3	29.9	46.0	15.6	51.4	19.1
1961	19.6	19.7	7.9	17.3	13.5	1.0	9.5	30.5	46.7	15.9	51.1	20.1
1962	20.6	20.7	8.8	20.5	14.2	1.1	10.4	31.5	47.0	16.6	52.7	21.5
1963	21.4	21.5	9.6	23.1	15.2	1.2	10.8	32.2	47.4	16.9	54.5	22.5
1964	22.7	22.8	10.5	24.4	16.9	1.4	11.7	33.7	49.0	18.2	57.5	23.5
1965	24.1	24.4	11.8	28.2	18.0	1.6	12.9	35.4	51.4	19.0	60.2	24.9
1966	25.5	26.0	12.8	28.7	19.6	2.0	14.8	37.3	53.4	20.3	63.5	26.9
1967	26.3	26.5	13.0	28.0	20.0	2.2	14.9	38.1	54.7	20.4	65.1	27.7
1968	27.8	28.1	14.5	32.4	21.2	2.4	16.4	39.7	57.1	21.2	67.9	28.8
1969	28.8	29.0	15.0	33.5	21.7	2.5	17.0	40.8	58.6	21.6	70.8	29.6
1970	29.5	29.2	14.6	30.0	21.6	2.7	17.9	41.8	60.3	21.4	73.5	30.6
1971	30.6	30.4	16.1	35.9	22.6	2.8	18.7	42.5	61.0	22.3	76.1	30.7
1972	32.5	32.4	18.1	40.8	24.9	3.3	19.7	44.3	62.2	23.9	79.9	32.2
1973	34.1	34.1	20.0	44.8	27.6	3.6	22.4	45.5	61.1	25.6	84.5	34.4
1974	33.8	32.8	18.7	37.4	27.5	3.6	23.5	44.4	59.9	25.1	77.6	34.3
1975	34.6	33.1	18.7	37.2	26.0	3.9	24.9	44.8	61.0	25.7	79.5	33.2
1976	36.5	35.4	21.1	44.7	27.6	4.2	27.4	46.9	64.0	26.9	83.7	34.5
1977	38.0	36.9	22.9	49.4	30.2	4.5	28.9	48.0	64.9	28.4	85.2	35.1
1978	39.7	38.4	24.1	51.7	31.7	4.8	30.5	49.7	64.6	31.4	86.6	37.6
1979	40.7	39.0	24.0	48.6	33.0	5.1	30.1	51.0	65.5	33.2	84.1	39.8
1980	40.5	38.0	22.1	42.4	31.8	4.9	27.5	50.9	66.2	34.2	76.6	40.4
1981	41.1	38.5	22.3	43.3	31.2	5.0	28.0	51.6	66.0	36.4	75.7	41.4
1982	41.7	38.8	22.3	44.5	29.8	5.0	28.0	52.1	67.3	37.0	75.8	41.2
1983	44.1	41.2	25.5	53.0	32.3	5.8	30.5	53.8	69.0	39.5	77.4	42.3
1984	46.4	44.2	29.1	61.7	35.6	6.8	34.0	56.0	70.4	42.8	79.5	44.6
1985	48.9	46.5	32.0	69.7	37.5	7.6	36.5	57.7	72.4	44.7	81.1	45.8
1986	50.9	49.1	35.1	74.7	40.5	8.8	40.7	59.8	73.9	48.1	85.2	46.8
1987	52.6	50.0	35.8	71.7	42.3	9.8	42.2	60.8	73.4	49.8	86.8	48.5
1988	54.8	51.9	37.8	75.9	43.8	10.7	43.6	62.4	75.4	51.3	89.3	49.6
1989	56.4	53.2	38.6	75.7	46.0	11.2	44.1	64.1	76.3	54.0	90.7	51.3
1990	57.6	53.5	38.5	74.5	45.4	11.5	44.4	64.8	77.9	53.6	89.1	52.6
1991	57.7	52.4	36.4	65.6	44.3	11.9	42.4	64.6	77.8	53.7	88.4	52.3
1992	59.9	54.1	38.5	71.0	45.9	12.6	43.3	65.9	77.5	56.5	91.9	53.4
1993	62.0	56.3	41.4	75.0	48.2	14.5	45.5	67.6	78.1	58.9	94.2	55.3
1994	64.4	59.3	44.7	79.7	50.8	16.9	47.6	70.2	80.3	62.2	95.7	58.1
1995	66.3	61.1	46.4	78.4	53.1	19.3	48.7	71.9	80.7	64.8	97.5	60.5
1996	68.6	63.8	49.9	82.2	55.4	22.3	51.9	74.0	81.5	67.9	99.0	63.2
1997	71.2	66.9	54.0	87.8	58.0	25.8	54.5	76.2	82.2	70.2	101.0	66.6
1998	75.0	71.3	60.5	97.0	62.8	30.8	59.9	79.0	83.4	74.5	103.9	70.2
1999	79.0	76.9	68.2	105.9	70.1	37.2	67.0	83.0	86.8	79.3	106.3	74.4
2000	83.0	80.9	74.1	109.3	76.8	43.5	73.0	85.7	88.9	83.2	103.5	78.1
2001	85.1	83.4	78.0	114.9	80.8	47.5	71.4	87.2	90.1	84.0	103.4	80.6
2002	87.3	86.6	83.7	120.9	86.7	52.9	75.8	88.8	90.5	86.5	104.2	83.0
2003	90.1	90.8	89.7	124.4	92.8	59.8	82.9	91.9	92.6	90.8	104.3	87.2
2004	93.5	95.4	97.0	127.9	101.6	68.9	90.3	94.9	94.8	95.0	105.2	91.0
2005	96.8	99.3	102.3	126.2	108.4	78.2	96.9	98.0	98.4	100.1	104.7	94.1
2006	99.7	102.9	106.7	121.5	113.9	88.5	104.0	101.2	101.4	103.6	104.5	98.7
2007	102.0	105.7	111.6	123.9	114.8	98.4	108.9	103.0	102.8	105.7	104.3	101.3
2008	101.6	103.1	105.9	107.5	109.6	101.6	105.3	101.8	101.5	105.2	99.6	101.7
2009	100.0	100.0	100.0	100.0	100.0	100.0	100.0	100.0	100.0	100.0	100.0	100.0
2010	101.9	103.4	106.1	102.0	107.0	110.9	104.2	102.2	102.1	105.3	99.2	102.3
2011	104.2	106.7	112.5	105.3	113.2	121.9	110.0	104.0	103.3	109.4	96.4	106.0
2012	105.8	109.6	120.8	113.3	118.2	136.0	114.1	104.7	103.3	110.6	94.9	108.2
2013	107.6	113.0	127.8	118.5	124.5	148.1	118.0	106.7	104.3	112.1	96.6	111.3
2014	110.4	116.7	135.3	125.1	132.6	158.5	122.0	108.9	104.9	113.7	97.3	116.1
2012												
1st quarter	105.4	108.8	118.6	111.3	118.3	131.4	111.9	104.5	103.2	111.2	93.9	108.1
2nd quarter	105.6	109.1	119.4	111.9	117.1	134.3	112.8	104.6	103.3	109.5	95.9	107.9
3rd quarter	105.9	109.9	121.4	113.6	117.9	137.6	114.9	104.9	103.4	111.3	95.7	107.9
4th quarter	106.2	110.5	123.8	116.2	119.4	140.8	116.8	104.8	103.5	110.2	94.1	108.8
2013												
1st quarter	106.8	112.1	126.4	118.8	121.7	145.0	117.5	106.0	104.3	111.8	95.7	110.2
2nd quarter	107.2	112.5	127.1	118.5	123.0	147.1	117.4	106.2	103.8	112.5	96.4	110.5
3rd quarter	107.6	113.2	128.1	118.0	126.0	149.3	117.3	106.8	104.4	111.8	96.9	111.7
4th quarter	108.6	114.1	129.4	118.7	127.4	150.8	119.7	107.5	104.9	112.2	97.2	112.9
2014												
1st quarter	108.9	114.4	130.3	119.9	128.0	151.6	120.0	107.6	105.0	111.3	97.1	113.4
2nd quarter	109.9	116.2	134.6	124.9	132.2	156.5	122.0	108.5	105.0	113.3	96.6	115.5
3rd quarter	110.9	117.4	137.1	127.2	134.1	161.3	122.2	109.2	104.8	114.0	96.7	117.2
4th quarter	112.0	118.6	139.1	128.6	136.1	164.7	123.7	110.0	104.6	116.1	98.7	118.1

Table 4-3. Chain-Type Quantity Indexes for Personal Consumption Expenditures by Major Type of Product—*Continued*

(Index numbers, 2009 = 100.)

NIPA Table 2.3.3

| Year and quarter | Services | Household consumption expenditures for services | | | | | | | | Nonprofit institutions serving households (NPISHs) | | |
		Household services, total	Housing and utilities	Health care	Transportation services	Recreation services	Food services and accommodations	Financial services and insurance	Other services	Final consumption expenditures	Gross output	Less: receipts from sales of goods and services
1955	15.1	16.1	16.6	11.2	20.9	9.9	27.4	10.3	19.9	2.5	. . .	. . .
1956	15.8	16.8	17.5	11.9	21.4	10.4	28.2	10.9	20.7	2.7	. . .	. . .
1957	16.4	17.4	18.4	12.6	21.8	10.0	28.6	11.2	21.5	2.8	. . .	. . .
1958	16.9	18.0	19.3	13.6	21.5	10.0	28.1	11.5	22.2	2.9	. . .	. . .
1959	17.7	18.8	20.4	14.6	22.4	10.7	28.7	11.8	23.1	3.2	13.2	20.1
1960	18.4	19.5	21.5	14.8	23.1	11.3	29.0	12.2	23.9	3.6	13.7	20.1
1961	19.1	20.2	22.6	15.4	23.4	11.7	29.1	12.9	24.6	3.7	14.3	21.2
1962	20.0	21.2	23.9	16.8	24.2	12.3	30.2	12.9	25.6	3.8	15.1	22.6
1963	20.9	22.1	25.0	17.9	25.3	12.8	30.9	13.3	26.5	3.9	15.9	24.1
1964	22.1	23.4	26.2	20.0	26.7	13.3	32.5	14.3	27.7	4.3	17.2	25.6
1965	23.3	24.7	27.6	20.9	28.0	13.8	34.8	15.2	29.3	4.6	18.2	27.2
1966	24.5	25.9	28.9	22.0	29.7	14.7	36.5	15.7	31.0	4.7	19.4	29.4
1967	25.5	27.0	30.2	23.1	31.2	15.2	36.2	16.5	32.9	4.9	20.6	31.4
1968	26.8	28.4	31.7	24.8	33.2	16.1	38.4	17.4	33.8	5.2	22.0	33.7
1969	28.0	29.7	33.4	26.7	35.5	17.1	39.2	17.6	34.8	5.2	23.1	36.0
1970	29.1	30.8	34.7	28.1	36.7	17.7	40.6	18.3	35.9	5.6	24.3	37.7
1971	30.1	31.9	36.2	30.1	38.3	18.3	40.6	18.9	36.0	5.9	26.0	40.6
1972	31.9	33.7	38.1	32.2	40.4	19.3	43.7	20.0	37.6	6.2	27.5	43.0
1973	33.4	35.4	39.9	34.5	41.1	20.9	45.8	21.2	38.7	6.2	28.3	44.5
1974	34.0	36.1	41.8	35.7	41.4	22.3	45.4	21.7	37.4	6.1	28.6	45.6
1975	35.3	37.5	43.1	37.5	41.9	23.5	47.3	23.8	37.7	6.2	29.7	47.9
1976	36.8	39.1	44.4	39.2	44.0	25.1	50.2	25.1	39.2	6.6	31.3	50.3
1977	38.3	40.7	45.6	41.1	47.1	26.7	51.5	26.6	41.1	6.7	32.5	52.6
1978	40.1	42.6	47.8	43.0	48.2	28.0	53.7	28.0	43.3	7.0	34.3	55.6
1979	41.3	43.9	49.5	44.4	49.7	29.3	55.4	28.8	43.6	7.2	35.3	57.1
1980	42.0	44.6	51.2	45.7	46.8	30.3	55.4	29.2	43.4	7.6	36.4	58.4
1981	42.7	45.2	51.9	47.9	45.0	32.9	55.9	29.0	43.2	8.2	37.9	60.1
1982	43.6	45.9	52.3	48.0	44.0	34.5	56.3	31.2	44.1	9.7	39.5	60.5
1983	45.8	48.2	53.4	49.5	47.4	37.4	58.1	35.7	47.0	11.2	41.0	60.8
1984	47.6	49.8	55.2	50.3	52.9	39.9	59.8	36.1	49.3	13.0	42.4	60.7
1985	50.1	52.4	57.4	51.8	58.5	42.8	60.6	40.0	52.7	14.1	43.9	62.1
1986	51.7	54.0	58.8	53.4	61.0	44.8	62.3	41.8	53.3	16.0	46.1	63.6
1987	54.1	56.3	60.4	55.6	63.5	46.8	65.6	44.2	57.1	17.3	47.9	65.5
1988	56.5	58.7	62.5	57.8	67.2	51.3	69.5	45.1	59.4	19.8	50.5	67.3
1989	58.3	60.3	64.0	58.5	68.7	54.5	71.4	47.6	61.2	22.8	52.3	67.6
1990	60.0	61.8	65.2	60.4	68.6	56.8	73.9	48.7	62.3	27.8	55.5	68.8
1991	61.0	62.6	66.6	61.6	65.3	56.4	74.0	52.8	60.0	31.7	57.5	69.4
1992	63.5	64.8	68.0	63.5	68.7	60.1	75.9	56.5	62.4	38.3	60.6	70.4
1993	65.4	66.7	69.8	63.8	72.5	63.9	77.5	60.5	63.8	41.4	62.1	71.1
1994	67.5	68.6	72.1	64.3	79.4	67.2	78.7	61.9	66.2	45.1	63.5	71.4
1995	69.5	70.6	74.3	65.6	85.4	72.3	78.9	64.0	67.6	47.2	64.3	71.6
1996	71.5	72.6	76.0	67.0	92.4	75.6	79.3	66.3	70.0	49.9	66.0	72.8
1997	73.8	75.2	77.7	69.0	99.4	78.0	81.0	69.7	73.9	46.0	66.9	75.9
1998	77.2	78.5	80.1	71.3	103.7	80.4	83.1	75.9	79.4	50.5	70.1	78.5
1999	80.2	81.5	82.4	72.4	109.6	84.3	85.2	83.3	81.9	54.4	72.5	80.2
2000	84.2	85.5	85.1	74.9	114.9	86.7	89.1	91.7	87.7	58.9	75.3	82.0
2001	86.2	87.3	87.4	78.6	114.1	86.5	88.9	89.8	91.5	63.8	78.9	85.0
2002	87.8	88.6	87.9	83.3	110.7	87.0	90.2	89.3	92.0	70.3	83.5	88.7
2003	89.7	90.4	89.1	85.6	111.5	90.0	93.5	89.4	94.6	74.7	85.3	89.2
2004	92.6	93.4	91.3	88.6	114.4	94.6	97.3	93.0	96.8	76.2	87.5	91.8
2005	95.6	96.5	95.1	91.6	115.5	97.0	100.8	97.9	97.9	76.1	89.7	94.9
2006	98.2	98.7	96.9	93.7	115.8	100.4	104.1	100.2	100.8	85.7	93.1	95.9
2007	100.1	100.7	97.9	96.1	117.0	104.3	105.4	103.3	102.9	88.0	95.3	98.0
2008	100.9	101.0	98.9	98.2	110.9	103.5	104.3	102.6	102.6	99.1	98.4	98.1
2009	100.0	100.0	100.0	100.0	100.0	100.0	100.0	100.0	100.0	100.0	100.0	100.0
2010	101.2	101.2	101.2	101.3	99.1	101.3	101.5	102.1	100.6	100.8	101.3	101.4
2011	103.1	103.2	102.5	103.9	101.5	103.6	104.2	103.9	102.5	99.7	102.3	103.1
2012	103.9	103.8	102.6	106.1	103.3	105.7	106.9	98.3	104.1	106.6	105.3	104.8
2013	104.9	104.8	103.1	107.2	106.6	107.6	108.5	99.3	104.4	108.6	106.5	105.9
2014	107.5	107.3	104.3	110.1	111.8	110.7	111.8	100.5	108.5	110.8	108.0	107.2
2012												
1st quarter	103.8	103.8	101.9	106.2	101.5	104.5	106.0	101.9	104.2	101.8	104.5	105.4
2nd quarter	103.9	103.8	102.8	105.9	103.6	105.7	106.5	98.4	103.7	106.8	104.8	104.2
3rd quarter	103.9	103.8	103.1	106.2	104.2	105.9	107.1	96.4	103.8	107.1	105.8	105.4
4th quarter	104.1	103.8	102.5	106.2	103.8	106.7	107.8	96.3	104.5	110.9	105.9	104.4
2013												
1st quarter	104.3	104.1	103.1	105.9	105.1	107.1	108.6	98.2	103.4	108.1	105.4	104.5
2nd quarter	104.6	104.5	103.1	106.9	106.3	106.3	107.7	99.3	104.1	107.3	106.4	106.1
3rd quarter	105.0	104.8	102.8	107.5	107.4	108.0	108.0	99.3	104.5	108.5	106.7	106.1
4th quarter	105.9	105.7	103.4	108.4	107.4	109.0	109.7	100.4	105.5	110.6	107.8	106.9
2014												
1st quarter	106.3	106.1	104.5	107.8	109.6	109.8	109.5	99.9	106.6	110.1	106.2	105.0
2nd quarter	106.9	106.8	104.2	109.3	110.7	109.6	111.3	100.1	107.7	110.5	107.5	106.5
3rd quarter	107.8	107.6	103.9	110.7	112.6	110.9	112.4	100.9	109.0	111.7	108.5	107.5
4th quarter	108.9	108.8	104.4	112.6	114.4	112.4	114.1	101.2	110.8	110.9	109.9	109.7

. . . = Not available.

Table 4-4. Chain-Type Price Indexes for Personal Consumption Expenditures by Major Type of Product

(Index numbers, 2009 =1000.)

NIPA Table 2.3.4

Year and quarter	Personal consumption expenditures, total	Total goods	Goods									
			Durable goods					Nondurable goods				
			Durable goods, total	Motor vehicles and parts	Furnishings and household equipment	Recreational goods and vehicles	Other durable goods	Nondurable goods, total	Food and beverages off-premises	Clothing and footwear	Gasoline and other energy goods	Other nondurable goods
1955	15.8	26.1	49.8	27.1	45.6	208.8	28.2	18.6	16.4	51.0	9.8	15.7
1956	16.1	26.5	51.0	28.3	46.0	211.1	28.5	18.9	16.5	52.0	10.1	16.0
1957	16.6	27.3	52.9	30.1	46.8	218.6	28.6	19.4	17.0	52.7	10.6	16.5
1958	17.0	28.0	53.8	31.2	46.7	224.6	28.7	19.9	17.7	53.0	10.5	16.9
1959	17.3	28.1	54.7	32.8	46.7	218.1	28.8	19.9	17.5	53.4	10.6	17.1
1960	17.5	28.3	54.5	32.2	47.1	219.6	28.9	20.2	17.7	54.1	10.8	17.4
1961	17.7	28.4	54.6	32.4	47.3	218.4	28.8	20.3	17.7	54.5	10.8	17.5
1962	17.9	28.6	54.8	32.9	47.2	216.0	28.7	20.4	17.9	54.6	10.9	17.5
1963	18.1	28.8	55.0	33.2	47.3	215.6	28.9	20.6	18.1	55.1	10.9	17.8
1964	18.4	29.1	55.3	33.4	47.3	213.0	29.6	20.9	18.4	55.6	10.8	18.0
1965	18.7	29.4	54.8	33.1	47.0	210.0	29.4	21.2	18.8	56.1	11.2	18.3
1966	19.2	30.1	54.7	32.9	47.4	207.7	29.4	21.9	19.6	57.6	11.4	18.6
1967	19.6	30.6	55.6	33.4	48.5	209.0	30.1	22.3	19.6	60.0	11.8	19.1
1968	20.4	31.7	57.4	34.5	50.4	213.1	30.8	23.1	20.2	63.4	12.0	19.8
1969	21.3	32.9	59.0	35.2	52.2	218.0	32.3	24.1	21.1	66.8	12.4	20.6
1970	22.3	34.2	60.3	36.3	53.3	218.3	33.2	25.2	22.3	69.3	12.6	21.5
1971	23.3	35.2	62.4	38.0	54.3	226.0	34.1	25.9	22.8	71.8	12.8	22.3
1972	24.1	36.1	63.0	38.1	55.0	229.3	35.2	26.7	23.9	73.1	12.9	22.9
1973	25.4	38.2	64.0	38.3	56.3	232.8	36.3	28.9	26.9	75.5	14.3	23.5
1974	28.0	43.0	68.2	40.7	60.9	243.1	39.1	33.3	31.0	81.1	19.9	25.8
1975	30.3	46.5	74.3	44.7	67.0	259.2	42.1	35.8	33.3	84.8	21.2	28.8
1976	32.0	48.3	78.3	48.1	69.9	268.1	44.1	37.0	34.0	87.5	22.3	30.3
1977	34.1	50.9	81.8	50.9	72.4	275.8	46.1	39.1	36.0	91.2	23.9	32.0
1978	36.5	54.0	86.4	54.4	76.1	285.7	48.6	41.6	39.4	92.9	24.9	33.8
1979	39.7	59.1	92.2	58.5	80.8	298.5	52.7	46.1	43.3	94.8	33.6	36.0
1980	44.0	65.7	100.2	62.9	87.4	315.0	63.4	51.8	46.9	98.2	46.7	39.3
1981	47.9	70.6	106.8	67.7	93.9	329.2	66.9	55.8	50.3	101.5	52.7	42.6
1982	50.6	72.6	111.0	71.0	98.7	336.8	67.6	57.0	51.6	103.0	50.3	45.9
1983	52.7	73.9	113.3	73.2	101.0	332.7	69.7	58.0	52.2	104.4	48.3	49.1
1984	54.7	75.3	114.9	75.3	102.2	328.0	71.2	59.2	53.7	104.9	47.8	50.9
1985	56.7	76.5	116.2	77.0	103.3	322.3	72.0	60.3	54.3	107.2	47.9	52.9
1986	57.9	76.1	117.4	79.1	104.4	312.0	73.7	59.5	55.6	106.7	37.6	55.0
1987	59.7	78.6	120.8	82.8	106.1	308.1	78.7	61.6	57.4	109.8	39.0	57.2
1988	62.0	80.6	122.8	84.1	107.6	306.1	83.9	63.5	59.1	113.3	39.3	59.7
1989	64.6	83.7	125.0	86.5	107.9	305.3	87.8	66.7	62.2	115.0	42.8	63.0
1990	67.4	87.2	126.3	86.8	109.0	302.8	93.3	70.5	65.2	118.7	49.0	66.2
1991	69.7	89.3	128.1	89.3	109.6	299.0	96.7	72.6	67.3	121.0	48.2	69.7
1992	71.5	90.4	129.0	90.9	110.9	289.8	99.3	73.6	67.8	121.9	47.8	72.4
1993	73.3	91.2	130.3	94.5	111.5	279.4	100.1	74.2	68.7	121.3	47.3	73.6
1994	74.8	92.1	132.8	98.9	113.2	273.6	101.7	74.6	69.9	119.2	47.5	74.1
1995	76.4	92.9	133.8	102.8	113.1	262.1	103.3	75.4	71.4	116.4	48.1	75.4
1996	78.0	94.0	132.5	104.9	113.4	243.5	102.7	77.1	73.6	115.0	51.4	76.8
1997	79.3	93.9	129.6	105.3	113.2	223.1	101.3	77.9	75.0	115.1	51.4	77.6
1998	79.9	92.4	125.9	104.1	113.1	204.3	99.4	77.3	75.9	113.0	44.8	79.1
1999	81.1	92.9	122.5	104.5	111.7	186.5	96.9	79.2	77.2	111.5	48.5	82.2
2000	83.1	94.8	120.3	104.8	110.8	174.8	95.7	82.7	79.0	110.1	62.7	84.0
2001	84.7	94.7	118.0	105.3	108.9	162.9	96.0	83.5	81.3	108.0	60.5	85.9
2002	85.9	93.8	115.0	104.7	106.7	152.4	94.6	83.5	82.5	105.1	56.6	87.5
2003	87.6	93.7	110.9	101.8	103.7	142.7	92.8	85.3	84.1	102.5	66.2	87.8
2004	89.7	95.0	108.8	100.9	102.4	135.7	92.5	88.2	86.7	102.2	77.8	88.8
2005	92.3	97.0	107.7	102.5	102.4	128.4	91.9	91.6	88.2	101.3	95.2	90.1
2006	94.7	98.3	105.9	102.5	101.9	120.6	93.3	94.4	89.7	100.9	107.5	92.1
2007	97.1	99.4	103.8	102.0	101.1	112.3	95.7	97.2	93.2	99.9	116.4	93.4
2008	100.1	102.4	101.8	99.7	100.4	106.7	98.9	102.7	98.9	99.1	137.3	95.6
2009	100.0	100.0	100.0	100.0	100.0	100.0	100.0	100.0	100.0	100.0	100.0	100.0
2010	101.7	101.6	98.6	105.7	95.8	92.9	100.4	103.1	100.3	99.3	118.1	102.0
2011	104.1	105.4	97.7	108.9	94.2	86.7	103.6	109.2	104.3	101.1	149.3	103.5
2012	106.1	106.7	96.4	110.2	94.0	81.5	104.2	111.8	106.7	104.6	154.4	105.3
2013	107.6	106.2	94.7	110.9	92.1	77.1	104.0	112.0	107.8	105.5	150.3	105.7
2014	109.1	105.8	92.5	111.0	88.9	73.6	102.4	112.7	109.8	105.9	144.9	107.1
2012												
1st quarter	105.6	106.7	97.1	109.8	94.2	83.4	105.0	111.5	106.3	103.6	155.1	104.9
2nd quarter	105.9	106.5	96.7	110.2	94.2	82.0	104.3	111.4	106.6	104.8	151.3	105.2
3rd quarter	106.2	106.6	96.1	110.2	94.0	80.8	103.7	111.8	106.7	104.4	153.5	105.6
4th quarter	106.8	107.0	95.7	110.5	93.5	79.6	104.0	112.6	107.2	105.4	157.7	105.6
2013												
1st quarter	107.2	106.7	95.5	110.8	93.3	78.7	104.2	112.4	107.6	105.8	154.8	105.4
2nd quarter	107.3	105.9	95.0	110.7	92.8	77.5	104.4	111.4	107.7	105.1	146.7	105.5
3rd quarter	107.7	106.2	94.4	111.0	91.5	76.6	104.1	112.2	107.9	105.8	150.4	105.8
4th quarter	108.1	105.9	93.8	111.1	90.7	75.7	103.4	112.1	108.0	105.6	149.5	105.9
2014												
1st quarter	108.5	105.9	93.2	110.9	90.0	74.8	102.8	112.4	108.4	105.9	149.5	106.2
2nd quarter	109.1	106.3	92.9	111.1	89.1	74.3	102.6	113.2	109.5	106.2	150.3	106.8
3rd quarter	109.4	106.2	92.3	111.0	88.6	73.2	102.5	113.3	110.3	106.2	147.7	107.3
4th quarter	109.3	104.9	91.6	110.8	87.9	72.1	101.5	111.8	110.9	105.1	132.2	107.9

Table 4-4. Chain-Type Price Indexes for Personal Consumption Expenditures by Major Type of Product—*Continued*

(Index numbers, 2009 =1000.)

NIPA Table 2.3.4

Year and quarter	Services	Household consumption expenditures for services								Nonprofit institutions serving households (NPISHs)		
		Household services, total	Housing and utilities	Health care	Transportation services	Recreation services	Food services and accommodations	Financial services and insurance	Other services	Final consumption expenditures	Gross output	Less: receipts from sales of goods and services
1955	11.1	10.6	12.8	5.4	11.8	13.1	10.3	13.2	10.9	48.3	. . .	. . .
1956	11.4	10.8	13.0	5.6	12.2	13.5	10.4	13.6	11.3	50.5	. . .	. . .
1957	11.7	11.1	13.3	5.8	12.7	14.0	10.8	14.0	11.7	52.8	. . .	. . .
1958	12.0	11.4	13.5	6.1	13.1	14.5	11.1	14.3	12.0	54.2	. . .	. . .
1959	12.3	11.7	13.7	6.2	13.4	14.9	11.5	15.1	12.3	55.2	9.8	5.7
1960	12.6	12.0	14.0	6.7	13.7	15.4	11.8	15.7	12.7	51.4	10.1	6.1
1961	12.9	12.3	14.2	6.8	14.1	15.8	12.0	16.3	12.8	52.0	10.3	6.2
1962	13.1	12.5	14.3	7.0	14.4	16.2	12.3	16.9	13.0	52.7	10.5	6.4
1963	13.3	12.7	14.5	7.2	14.5	16.6	12.6	17.0	13.3	53.6	10.7	6.5
1964	13.6	12.9	14.6	7.4	14.7	17.0	12.8	17.7	13.6	53.8	11.0	6.8
1965	13.8	13.2	14.8	7.7	14.9	17.4	13.0	18.1	14.0	55.3	11.3	7.0
1966	14.2	13.5	15.0	8.0	15.2	17.8	13.5	19.2	14.4	57.3	11.7	7.2
1967	14.7	14.0	15.2	8.5	15.8	18.5	14.3	19.7	14.8	59.2	12.2	7.6
1968	15.3	14.6	15.6	9.0	16.5	19.4	15.0	21.1	15.5	61.4	12.9	8.0
1969	16.1	15.4	16.1	9.7	17.5	20.3	15.9	23.0	16.2	65.3	13.7	8.6
1970	17.0	16.2	16.8	10.4	18.9	21.2	17.1	24.2	17.0	68.1	14.6	9.2
1971	17.9	17.1	17.6	11.0	20.2	22.1	18.0	25.6	18.0	72.0	15.3	9.6
1972	18.7	17.8	18.3	11.4	21.0	22.7	18.7	27.2	19.0	74.9	16.1	10.1
1973	19.6	18.7	19.1	12.0	21.9	23.5	19.9	27.8	20.1	79.8	17.1	10.7
1974	21.3	20.2	20.2	13.1	23.8	25.1	22.2	30.1	22.2	91.3	19.1	11.9
1975	23.1	22.0	21.8	14.6	26.4	27.0	24.2	32.3	23.8	99.7	21.1	13.2
1976	24.7	23.5	23.3	16.0	28.4	28.3	25.8	33.6	25.3	104.9	22.7	14.3
1977	26.6	25.3	25.4	17.3	30.3	29.7	27.7	36.2	26.6	112.0	24.4	15.4
1978	28.6	27.3	27.2	18.8	32.3	31.5	30.1	41.0	28.0	119.4	26.3	16.6
1979	31.0	29.5	29.4	20.6	35.2	33.5	33.4	43.2	30.1	131.1	28.9	18.3
1980	34.2	32.6	32.5	23.1	40.9	36.1	36.6	46.5	32.8	143.3	32.3	20.6
1981	37.7	36.0	36.0	25.9	45.8	38.4	39.9	50.0	36.1	150.4	35.9	23.3
1982	40.6	38.9	39.4	28.8	48.4	40.5	42.2	52.9	39.0	142.5	38.7	26.1
1983	43.2	41.5	41.9	31.5	50.2	42.2	44.0	58.0	41.2	131.8	40.8	28.6
1984	45.4	43.8	44.0	33.8	52.2	44.1	46.0	61.7	43.3	126.1	42.7	30.8
1985	47.7	46.1	46.4	35.9	53.2	46.0	47.9	66.9	44.8	123.3	44.5	32.6
1986	49.6	48.1	48.6	38.0	53.8	47.7	49.9	67.9	47.2	119.3	46.0	34.5
1987	51.1	49.6	50.3	40.4	56.0	49.6	51.9	64.7	48.3	117.0	48.0	36.7
1988	53.5	52.1	52.3	43.6	58.7	51.5	54.2	67.7	50.4	115.6	50.9	39.6
1989	56.0	54.6	54.4	47.4	61.2	54.0	56.6	69.7	52.2	108.1	53.7	43.3
1990	58.5	57.3	56.8	51.5	63.6	57.0	59.2	70.7	54.3	99.0	56.2	47.2
1991	60.7	59.8	58.7	55.4	65.3	60.0	61.6	70.3	57.0	91.5	58.8	51.1
1992	62.8	62.1	60.3	59.3	67.2	61.8	62.9	72.6	59.4	83.2	61.0	55.0
1993	65.0	64.5	62.0	62.5	69.5	63.8	64.1	76.5	61.4	78.7	62.8	58.0
1994	66.8	66.3	63.6	65.0	70.4	65.2	65.2	77.9	63.7	78.6	64.6	60.2
1995	68.6	68.2	65.4	67.4	71.9	66.6	66.8	79.6	65.8	78.5	66.5	62.4
1996	70.5	70.0	67.3	69.0	72.8	68.8	68.6	82.4	67.7	79.9	68.3	64.3
1997	72.4	72.0	69.1	70.4	74.4	71.0	70.6	85.6	69.6	83.3	70.0	65.7
1998	73.9	73.3	70.8	71.7	75.8	72.8	72.5	85.7	71.0	88.9	72.1	67.0
1999	75.4	74.8	72.4	73.3	76.9	75.1	74.4	85.0	72.8	92.1	74.1	68.6
2000	77.5	76.8	74.9	75.4	79.2	78.0	76.5	85.9	74.2	97.2	77.0	70.9
2001	79.9	79.1	78.4	77.9	80.1	80.6	78.6	85.6	76.5	101.7	80.0	73.5
2002	82.0	81.2	80.6	79.9	80.5	82.9	80.5	87.7	79.4	102.2	82.3	76.2
2003	84.5	84.0	83.2	82.9	82.2	85.5	82.2	91.5	82.4	99.6	84.7	80.1
2004	87.1	86.6	85.5	86.0	83.4	87.7	85.0	95.0	85.1	98.1	87.3	83.8
2005	89.9	89.5	88.6	88.7	86.5	90.2	87.7	97.9	88.2	100.2	90.3	87.1
2006	93.0	92.6	92.3	91.4	90.0	93.2	90.6	100.6	91.2	101.1	93.3	90.7
2007	96.0	95.7	95.5	94.8	92.1	95.9	94.2	103.5	93.7	102.4	96.2	94.0
2008	98.9	98.8	98.9	97.4	97.0	98.8	97.8	104.6	97.5	103.1	98.6	97.1
2009	100.0	100.0	100.0	100.0	100.0	100.0	100.0	100.0	100.0	100.0	100.0	100.0
2010	101.7	101.8	100.2	102.5	102.0	101.1	101.3	104.0	102.4	98.9	101.8	102.8
2011	103.5	103.7	101.7	104.4	104.8	102.8	103.9	106.5	104.2	99.9	103.9	105.2
2012	105.8	106.1	103.4	106.3	106.8	105.6	106.8	111.7	106.4	99.5	105.7	107.8
2013	108.3	108.6	106.1	107.8	108.1	107.4	109.0	117.3	108.7	101.4	107.9	110.2
2014	110.8	111.0	109.2	109.1	109.5	109.5	111.9	122.1	110.6	105.4	110.3	112.0
2012												
1st quarter	105.0	105.2	102.7	105.6	106.4	104.8	105.8	109.6	105.8	99.6	104.9	106.7
2nd quarter	105.6	105.8	103.1	106.1	106.9	105.3	106.6	111.0	106.4	99.6	105.5	107.5
3rd quarter	106.1	106.4	103.6	106.6	106.8	106.0	107.2	112.3	106.5	98.9	105.8	108.2
4th quarter	106.7	107.0	104.4	106.9	107.1	106.5	107.6	114.0	107.1	99.9	106.5	108.7
2013												
1st quarter	107.4	107.7	105.0	107.6	107.8	106.9	108.2	115.1	108.0	99.7	107.1	109.6
2nd quarter	108.0	108.3	105.8	107.5	107.5	107.0	108.9	116.7	108.5	101.7	107.7	109.7
3rd quarter	108.5	108.8	106.5	107.9	108.4	107.7	109.4	117.9	108.7	101.9	108.1	110.2
4th quarter	109.2	109.5	107.2	108.4	108.8	108.3	109.6	119.6	109.5	102.1	108.8	111.0
2014												
1st quarter	109.9	110.2	108.2	108.6	108.9	109.0	110.5	120.5	110.0	103.8	109.5	111.4
2nd quarter	110.6	110.8	108.9	109.0	109.5	109.4	111.5	121.8	110.5	104.8	110.1	111.9
3rd quarter	111.1	111.4	109.6	109.3	109.6	109.7	112.3	122.8	110.8	105.6	110.6	112.3
4th quarter	111.6	111.8	110.3	109.3	109.9	109.7	113.4	123.4	111.1	107.5	111.1	112.3

. . . = Not available.

Figure 4-2: Personal Consumption Expenditures by Type of Expenditure, 1948 and 2014

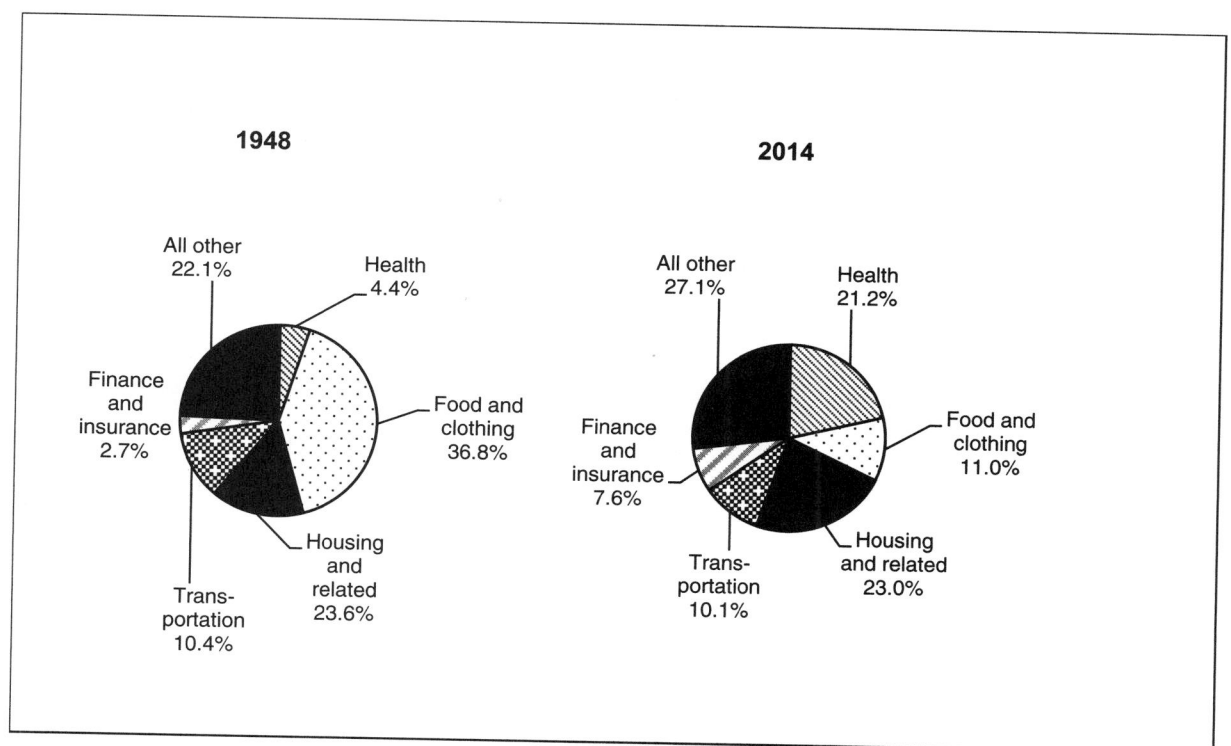

- Figure 4-2 compares the composition of household consumer spending (excluding the net spending of nonprofit institutions) in 1948 and 2014.

- Household spending on health in 2014 made up 21.2 percent of all household consumption spending—nearly five times the percentage in 1948. It is important to recognize that household consumption spending, as presented in these data, includes (in health spending and in the total) medical care payments made by government and private insurance on behalf of individuals as well as out-of-pocket consumer payments. (Table 4-5)

- In 2014, a much smaller share was required for food and clothing than in 1948, as seen in Figure 4-2. The shares of housing-related spending and transportation were similar in the two years. The share of finance and insurance spending nearly tripled, and households also spent a larger share on the remaining category, here labeled "all other," which includes communication, recreation, education, food services, accommodations, and other miscellaneous goods and services. (Table 4-5)

Table 4-5. Household Consumption Expenditures by Function

(Billions of dollars.)

Year	Household consumption expenditures, total	Food and beverages off-premises	Clothing, footwear, and related services	Housing, utilities, and fuels	Furnishings, household equipment, and maintenance	Health	Transportation	Communication	Recreation	Education	Food services and accommodations	Financial services and insurance	Other goods and services	Foreign travel and expenditures, net
1939	66.2	15.2	7.7	12.3	5.5	2.8	6.3	0.7	3.6	0.6	4.1	2.3	5.0	0.2
1940	70.2	15.9	8.1	12.8	6.0	3.0	7.0	0.7	3.9	0.6	4.4	2.4	5.3	0.1
1941	80.0	18.2	9.5	13.7	7.1	3.2	8.3	0.8	4.5	0.6	5.3	2.5	6.0	0.1
1942	87.7	21.6	11.8	14.8	7.4	3.6	5.4	1.0	4.9	0.7	6.9	2.6	6.8	0.2
1943	98.4	24.3	14.4	15.5	7.4	4.0	5.4	1.2	5.3	0.8	9.1	2.8	8.0	0.3
1944	107.0	26.0	15.7	16.2	8.0	4.5	5.7	1.3	5.8	0.9	10.9	3.0	8.5	0.6
1945	118.2	28.2	17.6	16.9	8.9	4.8	6.6	1.4	6.5	0.9	12.7	3.2	9.3	1.2
1946	142.3	34.9	19.7	18.8	12.7	5.9	12.1	1.6	9.0	1.0	12.7	3.8	10.3	-0.1
1947	159.9	40.2	20.4	21.2	15.5	6.6	15.4	1.7	9.8	1.2	12.5	4.2	11.1	0.0
1948	172.7	41.8	21.8	23.9	16.8	7.6	18.0	1.9	10.3	1.3	12.6	4.7	11.7	0.3
1949	176.1	40.4	21.1	25.6	16.3	7.9	21.2	2.1	10.6	1.4	12.4	4.9	11.8	0.6
1950	189.8	41.4	21.4	28.4	18.7	8.5	24.6	2.3	11.7	1.5	12.7	5.6	12.2	0.7
1951	205.9	46.0	23.1	31.6	19.7	9.3	24.2	2.6	12.3	1.6	15.0	6.3	13.3	0.9
1952	216.6	48.4	23.9	34.6	19.3	10.1	24.4	2.9	13.0	1.7	16.0	6.7	14.3	1.1
1953	230.0	49.3	24.2	37.9	20.0	11.0	28.0	3.2	13.8	1.8	16.5	7.8	15.0	1.5
1954	236.7	50.6	24.3	40.9	19.9	11.9	27.4	3.3	14.3	1.9	16.6	8.6	15.4	1.5
1955	255.3	52.0	25.4	43.8	22.3	12.8	33.4	3.6	15.4	2.1	17.0	9.6	16.3	1.6
1956	267.8	54.2	26.5	46.8	23.6	14.1	32.7	3.9	16.4	2.4	17.7	10.4	17.5	1.7
1957	282.7	57.1	26.8	50.0	23.9	15.5	35.7	4.3	16.8	2.6	18.5	11.1	18.8	1.7
1958	291.7	59.8	27.1	53.3	24.1	17.1	33.7	4.5	17.3	2.9	18.7	11.6	19.9	1.9
1959	312.6	61.6	28.6	56.9	25.6	18.8	38.8	4.8	18.8	3.1	19.7	12.5	21.4	2.0
1960	326.5	62.6	29.3	60.5	26.2	20.4	40.8	5.2	19.7	3.4	20.5	13.6	22.4	2.1
1961	336.7	63.7	29.9	64.0	26.8	21.8	39.3	5.6	20.5	3.6	21.0	14.8	23.7	2.0
1962	357.6	64.7	31.3	68.2	28.3	24.3	44.1	5.9	22.1	4.0	22.3	15.4	24.9	2.3
1963	376.7	65.9	32.1	72.2	29.8	26.4	47.8	6.4	23.9	4.3	23.3	15.9	26.2	2.5
1964	404.8	69.5	34.7	76.2	32.7	29.8	50.7	6.9	26.3	4.8	24.9	17.7	27.8	2.6
1965	436.6	74.4	36.5	81.0	34.7	32.0	56.5	7.5	28.9	5.5	27.2	19.4	30.2	2.9
1966	473.1	80.6	39.8	85.9	37.8	35.0	59.0	8.1	33.4	6.2	29.6	21.3	33.3	3.1
1967	499.4	82.6	41.7	91.1	39.7	38.4	61.0	8.9	35.8	6.9	31.0	22.8	35.8	3.8
1968	548.7	88.8	45.6	97.4	43.2	43.8	69.8	9.7	39.9	7.7	34.6	25.8	38.6	3.7
1969	595.0	95.4	48.8	105.5	45.4	50.0	75.9	10.7	43.7	8.7	37.5	28.5	41.0	4.0
1970	637.2	103.5	49.9	113.8	46.6	56.8	76.5	11.6	47.0	9.9	41.6	31.1	44.3	4.5
1971	689.3	107.1	53.4	124.5	48.8	63.4	88.7	12.8	50.1	10.9	43.8	34.1	47.0	4.8
1972	756.6	114.5	58.0	136.2	53.5	70.4	98.3	14.4	56.2	11.7	48.9	38.3	51.0	5.2
1973	837.4	126.7	63.7	149.7	59.9	78.7	108.6	16.1	63.0	13.0	54.8	41.5	56.9	4.7
1974	916.5	143.0	66.9	166.3	64.6	88.7	112.8	17.7	68.9	14.2	60.6	45.9	62.2	4.7
1975	1 015.7	156.6	71.4	184.8	67.8	102.7	124.4	20.0	77.1	15.9	68.8	54.0	67.8	4.4
1976	1 131.2	167.3	76.9	204.6	75.0	116.8	147.4	22.4	86.2	17.4	77.8	59.3	76.3	3.8
1977	1 256.0	179.8	84.3	228.7	84.0	131.6	168.1	24.3	94.9	18.8	85.7	67.8	83.8	4.3
1978	1 403.2	196.1	94.6	255.6	93.6	149.4	184.5	27.0	106.3	20.9	97.1	80.6	93.2	4.3
1979	1 563.4	218.4	101.9	287.5	104.3	169.9	207.1	29.4	118.9	22.9	110.9	87.6	100.4	4.1
1980	1 724.6	239.2	108.8	327.7	110.7	195.5	226.5	31.8	127.4	25.4	121.7	95.6	110.7	3.5
1981	1 903.4	255.3	119.1	367.6	118.3	228.9	250.7	36.0	141.6	28.3	133.9	102.0	121.2	0.4
1982	2 035.9	267.1	122.7	401.7	121.0	254.9	255.9	41.1	151.4	31.0	142.5	116.3	127.8	2.5
1983	2 245.8	277.0	132.9	434.6	132.3	287.1	284.9	44.8	169.3	34.3	153.6	145.9	143.4	5.4
1984	2 452.8	291.1	144.7	471.1	147.1	315.2	321.8	48.4	190.0	37.7	164.9	156.6	157.7	6.6
1985	2 674.8	303.0	154.3	513.9	156.0	345.3	357.4	53.1	207.2	41.2	174.3	188.1	173.3	7.7
1986	2 845.8	316.4	165.1	548.1	168.7	378.4	362.6	56.9	225.4	44.5	186.7	199.8	190.0	3.3
1987	3 036.4	324.3	176.4	582.6	176.9	419.9	376.6	60.0	247.0	48.8	204.4	205.3	208.2	6.1
1988	3 283.6	342.8	188.1	625.9	186.6	470.7	404.8	63.1	273.4	54.4	225.8	219.8	225.4	2.8
1989	3 524.8	365.4	201.2	666.9	197.5	519.0	428.3	67.3	295.7	60.6	242.6	238.4	245.7	-3.7
1990	3 749.8	391.2	206.5	709.3	200.6	583.7	442.9	70.1	314.7	66.0	262.7	247.4	262.3	-7.7
1991	3 880.0	403.0	210.1	747.5	199.1	638.4	418.3	73.9	326.3	70.6	273.4	266.8	268.0	-15.2
1992	4 127.7	404.5	223.0	783.3	209.4	700.4	451.3	81.1	346.8	76.4	286.3	295.1	290.1	-20.0
1993	4 380.9	413.5	231.1	827.3	221.9	741.7	485.3	85.8	378.4	81.1	298.4	332.6	304.5	-20.7
1994	4 643.3	432.1	240.1	876.1	238.6	779.9	528.2	93.3	414.0	86.4	308.3	346.9	316.9	-17.4
1995	4 881.9	443.7	244.7	926.7	251.7	826.0	554.1	98.9	449.8	92.3	316.1	366.4	332.7	-21.3
1996	5 158.0	461.9	253.5	976.7	263.7	868.3	598.9	108.3	481.5	99.6	326.6	392.3	350.8	-24.2
1997	5 455.1	474.8	262.0	1 023.1	277.3	919.9	641.8	120.1	509.5	107.1	343.4	429.2	368.4	-21.5
1998	5 779.2	487.4	273.1	1 077.0	297.1	979.7	668.6	129.5	544.3	115.2	361.8	467.3	393.7	-15.6
1999	6 168.8	515.5	287.2	1 135.5	320.2	1 033.3	729.0	142.3	589.9	123.9	380.3	509.1	429.4	-27.0
2000	6 634.4	540.6	297.5	1 214.5	343.4	1 109.6	795.4	158.3	633.7	134.3	408.8	566.3	458.5	-26.4
2001	6 924.0	564.0	294.6	1 303.0	352.4	1 209.4	810.5	164.9	647.0	143.6	419.7	552.8	477.9	-15.8
2002	7 185.7	575.1	295.2	1 347.9	365.3	1 317.1	813.1	168.9	669.3	149.5	436.3	562.6	496.8	-11.4
2003	7 560.0	599.6	301.5	1 411.6	380.4	1 411.3	846.0	174.4	704.3	159.5	461.9	588.5	526.5	-5.3
2004	8 053.6	632.6	313.5	1 488.4	407.1	1 516.2	899.3	181.1	758.7	169.0	496.4	635.3	559.1	-3.1
2005	8 583.8	668.2	326.6	1 606.0	431.2	1 614.0	960.8	187.0	804.6	180.5	530.6	689.6	589.5	-4.7
2006	9 064.8	700.3	336.3	1 706.1	449.9	1 717.3	992.9	201.2	854.1	193.1	566.3	724.2	624.5	-1.5
2007	9 501.7	737.3	339.7	1 783.8	453.7	1 826.8	1 032.7	216.4	893.8	206.0	595.6	768.5	657.6	-10.4
2008	9 731.5	772.9	335.4	1 869.9	442.0	1 914.2	1 009.7	230.7	899.6	218.4	612.5	771.5	673.0	-18.1
2009	9 571.0	770.0	321.6	1 905.3	409.8	2 000.9	867.0	230.6	861.8	229.1	600.3	719.0	672.7	-17.0
2010	9 926.8	788.9	335.8	1 935.1	417.3	2 080.4	942.1	239.6	888.3	244.9	617.7	763.2	700.6	-27.3
2011	10 414.3	829.1	354.6	1 989.0	435.2	2 176.9	1 052.0	253.7	922.8	256.3	649.5	795.8	733.1	-33.7
2012	10 757.8	848.8	370.1	2 021.8	452.4	2 266.2	1 105.7	264.6	968.2	262.5	685.1	789.3	754.9	-31.8
2013	11 088.4	866.0	378.6	2 084.8	467.0	2 332.4	1 136.1	271.0	1 001.4	268.9	710.2	837.7	773.9	-39.8
2014	11 543.6	886.5	385.7	2 170.9	481.6	2 446.9	1 167.5	287.2	1 040.7	277.0	750.9	882.7	799.3	-33.4

Table 4-6. Personal Saving: Households and Nonprofit Institutions Serving Household (NPISHs)

(Billions of dollars, except as noted.)

NIPA Table 2.9

Year	Personal saving as a percentage of disposable personal income (percent)	Households				Nonprofit Institutions Serving Households (NPISHs)			
		Disposable income	Less: outlays	Equals: household saving		Income	Less: gross output	Equals: Nonprofit institution saving	Nonprofit institution saving as a percentage of nonprofit income and receipts from sales
				Billions of dollars	Percent of income				
2009	6.1	10 940.0	10 175.0	765.0	7.0	276.1	370.4	-94.3	-8.8
2010	5.6	11 248.6	10 534.7	714.0	6.3	299.4	379.1	-79.8	-7.1
2011	5.7	11 792.0	11 041.0	751.1	6.4	301.1	383.9	-82.9	-7.1
2012	5.6	12 253.0	11 484.2	768.8	6.3	318.2	399.6	-81.4	-6.7

NOTES AND DEFINITIONS, CHAPTER 4

SOURCE: U.S. DEPARTMENT OF COMMERCE, BUREAU OF ECONOMIC ANALYSIS (BEA)

All personal income and personal consumption expenditure series are from the National Income and Product Accounts (NIPAs), released July 30, 2015. All quarterly series are shown at seasonally adjusted annual rates. Current and constant dollar values are in billions of dollars. Indexes of price and quantity are based on the average for the year 2009, which equals 100.

The 2013 NIPA comprehensive revision included a major definitional revision: accrual accounting for defined benefit pension programs. Last year this caused upward revisions to personal income receipts on assets for 1929–2012 and upward revisions to the supplements component of employee compensation for 1929–1975, 1989–2002, and 2004 forward.

Tables 4-1 through 4-4 cover all income and spending by the personal sector, which includes nonprofit institutions serving households (NPISHs). In a new feature introduced in the 2009 comprehensive revision of the NIPAs, Tables 4-2, 4-3, and 4-4 show the services component of personal consumption expenditures broken down into separate aggregates for "household consumption expenditures for services" and "final consumption expenditures" by NPISHs.

The last two tables give further details of the separate accounts for households and NPISHs that are only available annually. Table 4-5 shows a more detailed functional breakdown of household consumption expenditures, not including NPISHs. Table 4-6 shows income, spending, and saving data estimated separately for households and NPISHs but data is only available to 2012.

In several cases, the notes and definitions below will refer to *imputations* or *imputed values*. See the notes and definitions to Chapter 1 for an explanation of imputation and the role it plays in national and personal income measurement.

Tables 4-1 through 4-4

Sources and disposition of personal income; Personal consumption expenditures by major type of product

Definitions

Personal income is the income received by persons residing in the United States from participation in production, from government and business transfer payments, and from government interest, which is treated similarly to a transfer payment rather than as income from participation in production. *Persons* denotes the total for individuals, *nonprofit institutions that primarily serve households (NPISHs)*, private noninsured

welfare funds, and private trust funds. Personal income, outlays, and saving excluding NPISHs are referred to as *household* income, outlays, and saving. All proprietors' income is treated as received by individuals. Life insurance carriers and private noninsured pension funds are not counted as persons, but their saving is credited to persons.

Income from the sale of illegal goods and services is excluded by definition from national and personal income, and the value of purchases of illegal goods and services is not included in personal consumption expenditures.

Personal income is the sum of compensation received by employees, proprietors' income with inventory valuation and capital consumption adjustments (IVA and CCAdj), rental income of persons with capital consumption adjustment, personal receipts on assets, and personal current transfer receipts, less contributions for social insurance.

Personal income differs from national income in that it includes current transfer payments and interest received by persons, regardless of source, while it excludes the following national income components: employee and employer contributions for social insurance; business transfer payments, interest payments, and other payments on assets other than to persons; taxes on production and imports less subsidies; the current surplus of government enterprises; and undistributed corporate profits with IVA and CCAdj. The relationships of GDP, gross and net national product, national income, and personal income are displayed in Table 1-11.

Compensation of employees is the sum of wages and salaries and supplements to wages and salaries, as defined in the *national* income account (see Table 1-13 and the notes and definitions to Chapter 1).

As in *national* income, the *compensation of employees* component of personal income refers to compensation received by residents of the United States, including compensation from the rest of the world, but excludes compensation from domestic industries to workers residing in the rest of the world.

Wages and salaries consists of the monetary remuneration of employees, including wages and salaries as conventionally defined; the compensation of corporate officers; corporate directors' fees paid to directors who are also employees of the corporation; the value of employee exercise of "nonqualified stock options"; commissions, tips, and bonuses; voluntary employee contributions to certain deferred-compensation plans, such as 401(k) plans; and receipts in kind that represent income. This category also now includes judicial fees to jurors and witnesses, compensation of prison inmates, and marriage fees to justices of the peace, which earlier were classified as "other labor income". As of the 2013 revision, wages and salaries are now measured on an accrual basis, that is to say when earned rather than when paid, consistent with the treatment in the gross domestic income and national income tables.

Supplements to wages and salaries consists of employer contributions to employee pension and insurance funds and to government social insurance funds. In a substantial change introduced in the 2013 revision, defined benefit pension plan transactions are now recorded on an accrual basis instead of a cash transactions basis: employees are now credited with defined pension benefits, based on actuarial estimates of pension costs, at the time they earn them. (This was already the case with defined contribution plans.)

The following two categories, *proprietors' income* and *rental income,* are both measured net of depreciation of the capital (structures, equipment, and intellectual property products) involved. BEA calculates normal depreciation, based on the estimated life of the capital, and subtracts it from the estimated value of receipts to yield net income.

Proprietors' income with inventory valuation and capital consumption adjustments is the current production income (including income-in-kind) of sole proprietors and partnerships and of tax exempt cooperatives. The imputed net rental income of owner occupants of farm dwellings is included. Dividends and monetary interest received by proprietors of nonfinancial business and rental incomes received by persons not primarily engaged in the real estate business are excluded. These incomes are included in personal income receipts on assets and rental income of persons, respectively. Fees paid to outside directors of corporations are included. The two valuation adjustments are designed to obtain income measures that exclude any element of capital gains: inventory withdrawals are valued at replacement cost, rather than historical cost, and charges for depreciation are on an economically consistent accounting basis and are valued at replacement cost.

Rental income of persons with capital consumption adjustment consists of the net current production income of persons from the rental of real property (other than the incomes of persons primarily engaged in the real estate business), the imputed net rental income of owner occupants of nonfarm dwellings, and the royalties received by persons from patents, copyrights, and rights to natural resources. The capital consumption adjustment converts charges for depreciation to an economically consistent accounting basis valued at replacement cost. Rental income is net of interest and other expenses, and hence is affected by changing indebtedness and interest payments on owner-occupied and other housing.

Personal income receipts on assets consists of personal interest income and personal dividend income.

Personal interest income is the interest income (monetary and imputed) of persons from all sources, including interest paid by government to government employee retirement plans as well as government interest paid directly to persons.

Personal dividend income is the dividend income of persons from all sources, excluding capital gains distributions. It equals net dividends paid by corporations (dividends paid by corporations minus dividends received by corporations) less a small amount of corporate dividends received by general government. Dividends received by government employee retirement systems are included in personal dividend income.

Personal current transfer receipts is income payments to persons for which no current services are performed. It consists of government social benefits to persons and net receipts from business.

Government social benefits to persons consists of benefits from the following categories of programs:

Social Security and Medicare, consisting of federal old-age, survivors, disability, and health insurance benefits distributed from the Social Security and Medicare trust funds;

Medicaid, the federal-state means-tested program covering medical expenses for lower-income children and adults as well as nursing care expenses; *Unemployment insurance*; *Veterans' benefits; Other government benefits to persons*, which includes pension benefit guaranty; workers' compensation; military medical insurance; temporary disability insurance; food stamps; Black Lung benefits; supplemental security income; family assistance, which consists of aid to families with dependent children and (beginning in 1996) assistance programs operating under the Personal Responsibility and Work Opportunity Reconciliation Act of 1996; educational assistance; and the earned income credit. Government payments to nonprofit institutions, other than for work under research and development contracts, also are included. Payments from government employee retirement plans are not included.

Note that the value of Medicare and Medicaid spending, though in practice it is usually paid directly from the government to the health care provider, is treated as if it were cash income to the consumer which is then expended in personal consumption expenditures; this value is not treated in the national accounts as a government purchase of medical services but as a government benefit paid to persons, which then finances personal consumption spending.

Contributions for government social insurance, domestic, which is subtracted to arrive at personal income, includes payments by U.S. employers, employees, self-employed, and other individuals who participate in the following programs: old-age, survivors, and disability insurance (Social Security); hospital insurance and supplementary medical insurance (Medicare); unemployment insurance; railroad retirement; veterans' life insurance; and temporary disability insurance. Contributions to government employee retirement plans are not included in this item.

In the 2009 comprehensive revision, most transactions between the U.S. government and economic agents in Guam, the U.S. Virgin Islands, American Samoa, Puerto Rico, and the Northern Mariana Islands are treated as government transactions with the rest of the world. Since the NIPAs only cover the 50 states and the District of Columbia, the *domestic* contributions to government social insurance funds are the only ones that need to be subtracted from NIPA payroll data to calculate personal income. The social insurance receipts of governments, shown in Chapter 6, will be somewhat larger than this personal income entry because they will include contributions from residents of those territories and commonwealths.

Personal current taxes is tax payments (net of refunds) by persons residing in the United States that are not chargeable to business expenses, including taxes on income, on realized net capital gains, and on personal property. As of the 1999 revisions, estate and gift taxes are classified as capital transfers and are not included in personal current taxes.

Disposable personal income is personal income minus personal current taxes. It is the income from current production that is available to persons for spending or saving. However, it is not the cash flow available, since it excludes realized capital gains. Disposable personal income in chained (2009) dollars represents the inflation-adjusted value of disposable personal income, using the implicit price deflator for personal consumption expenditures.

Personal income excluding current transfer receipts, also shown in chained (2009) dollars using the implicit price deflator for personal consumption expenditures, is an important business cycle indicator, to which particular attention is paid because it is calculated monthly as well as quarterly and annually, and thus can help establish monthly cycle turning point dates. As a pre-income-tax measure which excludes transfer payments, it is a better measure of income generated by the economy than alternative monthly income indicators such as total or disposable personal income, which are more oriented toward purchasing power.

Personal outlays is the sum of *personal consumption expenditures* (defined below), *personal interest payments,* and *personal current transfer payments.*

Personal interest payments is non-mortgage interest paid by households. As noted above in the definition of rental income, mortgage interest has been subtracted from gross rental or imputed rental receipts of persons to yield a net rental income estimate; hence, it is not included as an interest outlay in this category.

Personal current transfer payments to government includes donations, fees, and fines paid to federal, state, and local governments.

Personal current transfer payments to the rest of the world (net) are personal remittances in cash and in kind to the rest of the world less such remittances from the rest of the world.

Personal saving is derived by subtracting personal outlays from disposable personal income. It is the current net saving of individuals (including proprietors), nonprofit institutions that primarily serve individuals, life insurance carriers, retirement funds (including those of government employees), private noninsured welfare funds, and private trust funds. Conceptually, personal saving may also be viewed as the sum of the net acquisition of financial assets and the change in physical assets less the sum of net borrowing and consumption of fixed capital. In either case, it is defined to exclude both realized and unrealized capital gains.

Note that in the context of national income accounting, the term just defined is *saving,* not "savings." *Saving* refers to a <u>flow</u> of income during a particular time span (such as a year or a quarter) that is not consumed. It is therefore available to finance a commensurate <u>flow</u> of investment during that time span. Strictly defined, "savings" denotes an accumulated <u>stock</u> of monetary funds—possibly the cumulative effects of successive periods of *saving*—available to the owner in asset form, such as in a bank savings account.

Personal consumption expenditures (PCE) are goods and services purchased by persons residing in the United States. Persons are defined as individuals and nonprofit institutions that primarily serve individuals. PCE mostly consists of purchases of new goods and services by individuals from business, including purchases financed by insurance (such as both private and government medical insurance). In addition, PCE includes purchases of new goods and services by nonprofit institutions, net purchases of used goods by individuals and nonprofit institutions, and purchases abroad of goods and services by U.S. residents traveling or working in foreign countries. PCE also includes purchases for certain goods and services provided by the government, primarily tuition payments for higher education, charges for medical care, and charges for water and sanitary services. Finally, PCE includes imputed purchases that keep PCE invariant to changes in the way that certain activities are carried out. For example, to take account of the value of the services provided by owner-occupied housing, PCE includes an imputation equal to what (estimated) rent homeowners would pay if they rented their houses from themselves. (See the discussion of imputation in the notes and definitions to Chapter 1.) Actual purchases of residential structures by individuals are classified as gross private domestic investment.

In the 2009 comprehensive revision, the classification system used for breakdowns of PCE was revised, and new calculations were introduced separating the consumption spending of the household sector proper from that of nonprofit institutions serving households.

Goods is the sum of *Durable* and *Nondurable goods.*

The PCE category *Durable goods* is subdivided into *Motor vehicles and parts, Furnishings and household equipment* (which includes appliances), *Recreational goods and vehicles* (which includes video, audio, photographic, and information processing equipment and media), and *Other durable goods.*

Nondurable goods encompasses *Food and beverages off-premises, Clothing and footwear, Gasoline and other energy goods,* and *Other nondurable goods.* This food and beverages category no longer includes meals and beverages purchased for consumption on the premises, which are now included in services, since they have a high service component and since their prices are much more stable than those of off-premises food and beverages.

Services, total is subdivided into *Household services* and *Final consumption expenditures of nonprofit institutions serving households (NPISHs).* The latter is the difference between the *gross output* of NPISHs and the amounts that they receive from sales of goods and services to households—for example, payments for services of a nonprofit hospital. Such sales of goods and services appear in the appropriate category of household expenditures—for example, *Health* in the case of the hospital services.

The components of *Household services* are *Housing and utilities, Health care, Transportation services, Recreation services, Food services and accommodations* (which includes meals and beverages purchased for consumption on premises, as well as payments for hotels and similar accommodations), *Financial services and insurance,* and *Other services.*

These are the categories used in the quarterly data presented in Tables 4-2, 4-3, and 4-4. This classification system is not particularly helpful with respect to the objective of spending. For example, the *Health care* component of services does not include drugs and medicines, which are included instead in nondurable goods. For a more precise classification of consumption spending by objective, see Table 4-5, Household Consumption Expenditures by Function, described in more detail below. This classification by type of expenditure is only available on an annual basis, and later than the principal quarterly NIPA data.

Data availability

Monthly data on personal income and spending are made available in a BEA press release, usually distributed the first business day following the monthly release of the latest quarterly national income and product account (NIPA) estimates. Monthly and quarterly data are subsequently published each month in the BEA's Survey of Current Business. Current and historical data are available on the BEA Web site at <http://

www.bea.gov>, and may also be obtained from the STAT-USA subscription Web site at <http://www.stat-usa.gov>.

References

References can be found in the notes and definitions to Chapter 1. A discussion of monthly estimates of personal income and its disposition appears in the November 1979 edition of the *Survey of Current Business.* Additional and more recent information can be found in the articles listed in the notes and definitions for Chapter 1.

Table 4-5

Household consumption expenditures by function

SOURCE: BUREAU OF ECONOMIC ANALYSIS (BEA)

In this table, also derived from the NIPAs, annual estimates of the current-dollar value of PCE by households—excluding the "final" consumption expenditures of nonprofit institutions serving households (NPISHs); see definition above—are presented by function.

Definitions

Food and beverages includes food and beverages (including alcoholic beverages) purchased for home consumption and food produced and consumed on farms.

Clothing, footwear, and related services includes purchases, rental, cleaning, and repair of clothing and footwear.

Housing, utilities, and fuels includes rents paid for rental housing, imputed rent of owner-occupied dwellings, and purchase of fuels and utility services.

Furnishings, household equipment, and routine household maintenance includes furniture, floor coverings, household textiles, appliances, tableware etc., tools, and other supplies and services.

Health includes drugs, other medical products and equipment, and outpatient, hospital, and nursing home services.

Transportation includes the purchase and operation of motor vehicles and public transportation services.

Communication includes telephone equipment, postal and delivery services, telecommunication services, and Internet access.

Recreation includes video and audio equipment, computers, and related services; sports vehicles and other sports goods and services; memberships and admissions; magazines, newspapers, books, and stationery; pets and related goods and services;

photo goods and services; tour services; and legal gambling. (As noted earlier, purchases of goods and services that are illegal and the incomes from such purchases are outside the scope of the national income and product accounts.)

Education includes educational services and books.

Food services and accommodations includes meals and beverages purchased for consumption on the premises, food furnished to employees, and hotel and other accommodations including housing at schools.

Financial services and insurance consists of financial services and life, household, medical care, motor vehicle, and other insurance.

Other goods and services includes personal goods (such as cosmetics, jewelry, and luggage) and services, social services and religious activities, professional and other services, and tobacco.

Foreign travel and expenditures, net consists of foreign travel spending and other expenditures abroad by U.S. residents minus expenditures in the United States by nonresidents. A negative figure indicates that foreigners spent more here than U.S. residents spent abroad. Positive values for this foreign travel category, indicating that U.S. residents spent more abroad than foreigners spent here, appear in the 1980s when the dollar was strong against other major currencies. (The international value of the dollar is shown in Table 13-8.) Negative values in subsequent years have resulted in part from the weakening of the dollar, which discouraged U.S. residents' travel abroad and encouraged tourism by foreigners in the United States. The negative sign does not indicate a drain on GDP—these effects of a weaker dollar are in fact positive for real GDP—but rather reflects the fact that the goods and services purchased by foreigners in the United States must be subtracted from the total consumer purchases recorded in the other columns of this table in order to be added to other exports and classified in the category of exports rather than in the consumption spending of U.S. residents.

Data availability and revisions

Data are updated once a year, after the general midyear revision of the NIPAs, and are available on the BEA Web site at <http://www.bea.gov>.

Table 4-6

Personal Saving: Households and Nonprofit Institutions Serving Households

SOURCE: BUREAU OF ECONOMIC ANALYSIS (BEA)

As noted above, the "personal" sector includes not only households but also "nonprofit institutions serving households" (NPISHs). This category comprises all nonprofit institutions except those that are considered to be serving government and business, such as chambers of commerce and trade associations. Those institutions are included in the business sector instead.

For annual (not quarterly) data beginning with 1992, BEA now compiles and makes available tables showing personal income and its disposition for households and NPISHs separately. Each major type of income and expenditure is estimated separately for the two groups. Household receipts from NPISHs, purchases from NPISHs, and contributions to NPISHs are identified separately instead of being netted out as they are in the quarterly accounts. Selected aggregates for households and NPISHs are shown in Table 4-6.

Data Availability and References

These data and the data on income and outlays for the household and nonprofit sectors on which they are based usually become available about two months after the release of the midyear revision of the NIPAs. They are published in Table 2.9 in the NIPA tables on the BEA Web site at <http://www.bea.gov>. An article from the April 2003 *Survey,* "Income and Outlays of Households and of Nonprofit Institutions Serving Households," can also be found on the BEA Web site.

CHAPTER 5: SAVING AND INVESTMENT

**Figure 5-1: National Saving, Investment, and Borrowing, 1950–2014
(percent of gross national income)**

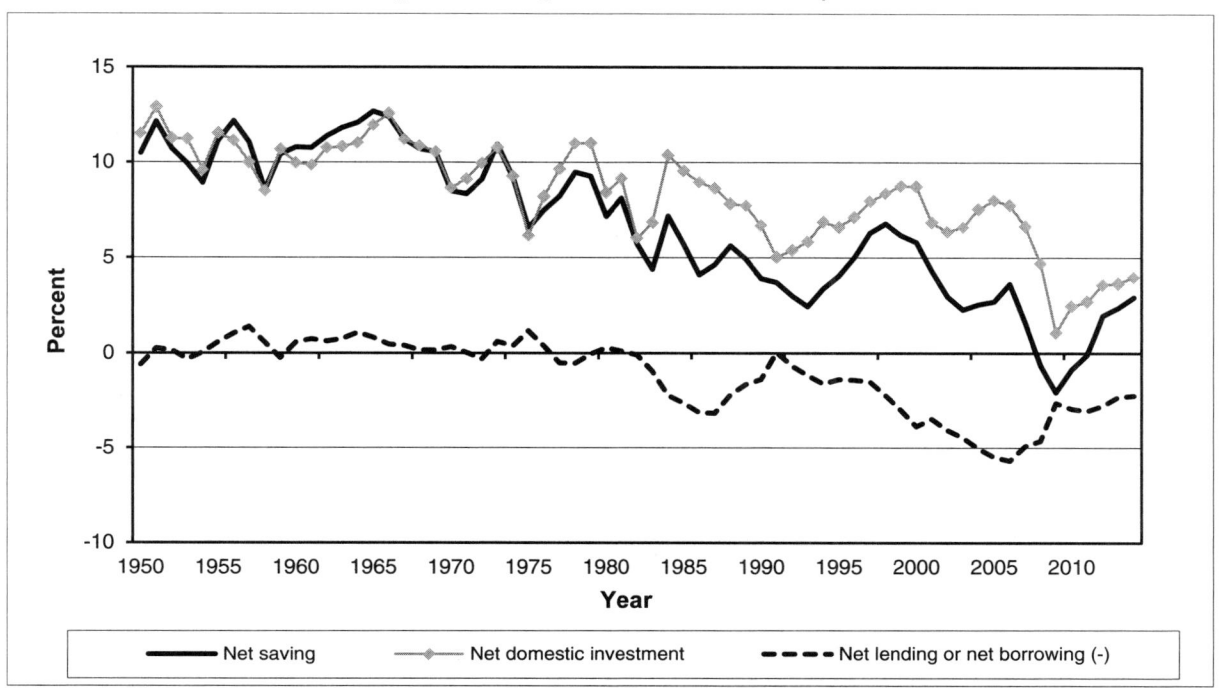

- Net national saving—the middle line in Figure 5-1—averaged 4.9 percent of gross national income (GNI) in the years 1984 through 2000, which was already lower than the mostly double-digit rates seen in the 1950s and 1960s. Net saving is gross saving by U.S. persons, businesses, and governments, <u>less</u> the consumption of fixed capital. Thus, it represents saving available for investment over and above the replacement of the existing capital stock. (Tables 5-1A and B)

- In the years 2001–2007 the national saving rate fell even more, averaging 2.9 percent. Record net borrowing from the rest of the world was required to finance net investment that far exceeded domestic net saving. (Table 5-1A)

- In the recession that began at the end of 2007, national saving fell into negative territory for the first time since the depression years 1931 through 1934. Government deficits soared as the Great Recession cut deeply into tax revenues and called forth both automatic and discretionary anti-recession spending. But unlike in the Great Depression, net investment remained positive. (Tables 5-1A and B)

- In 2014, the national saving rate had recovered to a positive 2.9 percent, as the federal deficit continued to decline. (Table 5-1A)

- The net investment rate also recovered and remained above the saving rate, so overseas borrowing of 2.3 percent of GNI was required to finance it. (Table 5-1A)

Table 5-1A. Saving and Investment: Recent Data

(Billions of dollars, except as noted; quarterly data are at seasonally adjusted annual rates.)   **NIPA Tables 1.7.5, 5.1**

Year and quarter	Gross saving												
		Net saving						Consumption of fixed capital					
			Private			Government			Private			Government	
	Total	Total	Total	Personal saving	Domestic corporate business	Federal	State and local	Total	Total	Domestic business	House-holds and institutions	Federal	State and local
1955	96.4	47.5	45.9	28.2	17.6	-0.6	2.2	48.9	35.0	28.9	6.1	10.7	3.2
1956	109.6	55.4	51.1	34.7	16.4	1.4	3.0	54.1	38.8	32.2	6.6	11.7	3.6
1957	111.8	52.9	52.9	36.9	16.0	-2.6	2.6	58.9	42.3	35.2	7.1	12.7	3.9
1958	103.8	41.3	52.2	38.9	13.3	-12.0	1.1	62.4	44.9	37.5	7.4	13.4	4.1
1959	120.1	54.7	56.4	37.1	19.2	-3.9	2.2	65.4	46.8	39.0	7.8	14.3	4.4
1960	127.0	59.1	56.4	37.8	18.5	0.2	2.6	67.9	48.2	40.0	8.2	15.1	4.5
1961	131.7	61.1	63.5	44.4	19.2	-4.7	2.2	70.6	49.8	41.3	8.5	16.0	4.8
1962	143.5	69.4	71.3	46.4	24.9	-5.3	3.4	74.1	51.8	42.9	8.8	17.1	5.2
1963	154.2	76.2	74.6	46.7	27.9	-2.1	3.7	78.0	54.2	44.9	9.3	18.3	5.5
1964	166.0	83.6	86.2	54.8	31.4	-6.9	4.3	82.4	57.3	47.4	9.9	19.2	5.9
1965	182.9	94.9	96.3	58.3	38.0	-5.5	4.1	88.0	61.6	50.9	10.7	20.0	6.4
1966	196.4	101.1	102.9	61.4	41.6	-7.0	5.2	95.3	67.2	55.6	11.5	21.0	7.1
1967	200.4	96.9	111.7	72.2	39.5	-19.5	4.7	103.5	73.3	60.9	12.4	22.4	7.8
1968	214.5	101.2	110.7	72.1	38.6	-13.7	4.3	113.3	80.6	67.0	13.6	24.1	8.6
1969	233.1	108.2	109.2	75.0	34.2	-5.1	4.1	124.9	89.4	74.2	15.2	25.8	9.7
1970	228.2	91.4	123.2	96.1	27.2	-34.8	3.0	136.8	98.3	81.8	16.5	27.6	10.9
1971	246.2	97.3	147.5	110.1	37.5	-50.8	0.6	148.9	107.6	89.4	18.2	29.0	12.2
1972	277.7	116.8	157.2	109.2	48.0	-48.9	8.4	160.9	117.5	97.2	20.3	30.1	13.3
1973	335.3	157.2	185.3	131.8	53.5	-37.7	9.6	178.1	131.5	108.2	23.3	31.7	14.9
1974	349.3	143.1	181.4	141.7	39.7	-40.6	2.3	206.2	153.2	126.1	27.0	34.7	18.3
1975	348.2	110.7	213.3	159.0	54.3	-97.0	-5.6	237.5	178.8	147.9	30.9	37.8	21.0
1976	399.5	140.3	217.3	147.3	70.0	-79.9	2.8	259.2	196.5	162.2	34.3	40.6	22.1
1977	459.6	171.3	234.7	148.2	86.6	-71.9	8.4	288.3	221.1	181.5	39.6	43.7	23.5
1978	548.2	223.1	269.5	166.6	102.9	-59.8	13.4	325.1	252.1	205.5	46.6	47.5	25.5
1979	613.8	242.7	279.0	177.5	101.4	-44.5	8.2	371.1	290.7	236.4	54.4	51.8	28.6
1980	630.6	204.6	285.5	213.2	72.3	-86.3	5.4	426.0	335.0	272.8	62.2	57.9	33.1
1981	745.2	260.2	341.9	252.5	89.4	-85.8	4.1	485.0	381.9	313.5	68.5	65.3	37.8
1982	727.9	193.6	363.3	277.7	85.6	-164.6	-5.1	534.3	420.4	347.5	72.9	72.7	41.3
1983	719.5	158.9	362.7	247.0	115.7	-205.0	1.3	560.5	438.8	362.8	76.0	79.0	42.8
1984	884.5	290.2	461.6	312.1	149.5	-192.3	20.9	594.3	463.5	382.7	80.9	86.4	44.4
1985	884.0	247.3	422.7	265.1	157.5	-195.6	20.3	636.7	496.4	410.3	86.2	93.3	46.9
1986	867.8	185.7	377.9	269.4	108.5	-212.7	20.4	682.2	531.6	438.1	93.4	100.3	50.3
1987	952.2	224.2	375.3	252.1	123.2	-163.2	12.1	728.0	566.3	464.5	101.8	107.5	54.1
1988	1 080.1	297.7	438.1	294.8	143.3	-157.3	17.0	782.4	608.3	498.4	109.9	116.3	57.8
1989	1 113.6	277.5	426.7	316.5	110.2	-156.6	7.4	836.1	650.1	531.8	118.2	124.2	61.9
1990	1 117.6	230.7	438.1	335.4	102.7	-200.9	-6.5	886.8	689.0	563.9	125.1	131.1	66.7
1991	1 157.9	226.8	498.1	365.9	132.2	-246.2	-25.1	931.1	722.4	591.8	130.6	137.9	70.9
1992	1 152.6	192.9	563.1	426.0	137.1	-332.7	-37.5	959.7	744.2	607.9	136.3	141.4	74.1
1993	1 167.9	164.3	513.3	367.6	145.6	-311.8	-37.2	1 003.6	780.0	634.2	145.7	145.3	78.3
1994	1 299.1	243.6	524.2	331.4	192.8	-253.7	-27.0	1 055.6	824.3	669.0	155.3	148.3	82.9
1995	1 429.5	306.8	579.2	352.9	226.2	-240.4	-31.5	1 122.8	882.6	717.8	164.8	151.9	88.3
1996	1 581.3	405.3	596.3	345.2	251.1	-178.5	-12.5	1 176.0	931.0	758.4	172.7	152.4	92.6
1997	1 783.6	543.6	633.1	352.2	280.9	-91.2	1.7	1 240.0	990.1	807.9	182.1	153.0	96.9
1998	1 932.4	622.1	604.0	405.3	198.7	2.7	15.4	1 310.3	1 054.9	860.4	194.5	153.6	101.8
1999	2 003.6	602.7	526.8	303.3	223.5	66.6	9.2	1 400.9	1 135.9	925.0	210.9	156.8	108.1
2000	2 119.8	605.5	439.1	307.7	131.4	156.5	9.9	1 514.2	1 236.6	1 006.5	230.1	161.5	116.2
2001	2 068.5	464.5	515.3	335.2	180.2	14.5	-65.3	1 604.0	1 317.7	1 067.5	250.2	163.3	123.0
2002	1 990.6	328.5	719.9	405.3	314.7	-270.5	-120.9	1 662.1	1 368.0	1 101.4	266.6	165.0	129.0
2003	1 991.1	263.9	788.2	409.6	378.6	-402.9	-121.4	1 727.2	1 422.4	1 131.6	290.8	170.3	134.5
2004	2 146.7	315.0	822.6	409.4	413.2	-399.2	-108.4	1 831.7	1 509.3	1 185.9	323.4	178.6	143.8
2005	2 338.6	356.6	727.9	243.1	484.8	-304.7	-66.6	1 982.0	1 635.3	1 273.2	362.1	189.4	157.3
2006	2 648.1	512.1	778.5	331.4	447.1	-227.0	-39.4	2 136.0	1 765.0	1 368.8	396.2	200.7	170.3
2007	2 500.3	236.0	574.4	309.8	264.6	-265.7	-72.7	2 264.4	1 865.0	1 451.2	413.7	212.8	186.6
2008	2 268.4	-95.0	704.1	536.7	167.3	-634.0	-165.1	2 363.4	1 936.9	1 522.3	414.6	226.3	200.2
2009	2 067.6	-300.8	1 219.9	667.4	552.9	-1 248.8	-271.9	2 368.4	1 925.7	1 522.4	403.3	234.5	208.2
2010	2 251.6	-130.0	1 436.0	630.0	811.9	-1 328.7	-237.3	2 381.6	1 923.5	1 523.0	400.5	245.3	212.7
2011	2 434.6	-16.1	1 444.0	710.1	733.9	-1 244.1	-215.9	2 450.6	1 971.1	1 572.8	398.2	257.4	222.2
2012	2 861.2	327.0	1 637.9	946.7	691.2	-1 090.1	-220.8	2 534.2	2 038.0	1 633.4	404.6	264.3	231.9
2013	3 039.2	406.3	1 234.4	589.9	644.5	-640.9	-187.1	2 632.8	2 126.6	1 699.4	427.2	267.7	238.5
2014	3 266.8	520.1	1 319.2	620.2	699.0	-631.5	-167.7	2 746.7	2 229.9	1 775.2	454.8	270.7	246.1
2012													
1st quarter	2 791.1	289.8	1 621.6	828.0	793.6	-1 107.1	-224.7	2 501.2	2 010.2	1 610.9	399.4	262.2	228.8
2nd quarter	2 830.4	306.0	1 638.4	905.7	732.7	-1 102.0	-230.4	2 524.4	2 029.1	1 627.2	401.9	264.0	231.3
3rd quarter	2 850.5	304.0	1 605.9	878.5	727.3	-1 079.5	-222.3	2 546.5	2 047.9	1 641.6	406.3	265.4	233.2
4th quarter	2 973.0	408.3	1 685.6	1 174.6	511.0	-1 071.6	-205.6	2 564.7	2 064.7	1 653.9	410.8	265.8	234.3
2013													
1st quarter	2 913.9	324.2	1 295.3	567.0	728.3	-790.6	-180.4	2 589.7	2 087.6	1 670.4	417.2	266.4	235.7
2nd quarter	3 049.1	430.7	1 128.7	609.7	519.0	-525.9	-172.0	2 618.3	2 113.4	1 690.2	423.1	267.5	237.5
3rd quarter	3 069.1	423.5	1 329.1	632.7	696.5	-707.7	-198.0	2 645.7	2 138.4	1 708.3	430.1	268.0	239.4
4th quarter	3 124.6	447.0	1 184.5	550.3	634.2	-539.6	-197.9	2 677.6	2 167.1	1 728.7	438.4	269.0	241.5
2014													
1st quarter	3 107.2	398.9	1 207.4	637.2	570.2	-619.2	-189.3	2 708.3	2 195.2	1 747.2	448.0	269.6	243.5
2nd quarter	3 252.0	519.3	1 309.5	623.5	686.0	-630.0	-160.3	2 732.8	2 217.3	1 766.4	450.9	270.2	245.3
3rd quarter	3 340.2	578.7	1 394.8	605.7	789.1	-650.1	-166.0	2 761.5	2 243.1	1 785.7	457.4	271.2	247.2
4th quarter	3 367.6	583.4	1 365.3	614.3	751.0	-626.7	-155.2	2 784.2	2 264.0	1 801.3	462.8	271.9	248.3

Table 5-1A. Saving and Investment: Recent Data—*Continued*

(Billions of dollars, except as noted; quarterly data are at seasonally adjusted annual rates.)

NIPA Tables 1.7.5, 5.1

| Year and quarter | Gross domestic investment, capital account transactions, and net lending, NIPAs | | | | | | Statistical discrepancy | Net domestic investment | Gross national income | Gross saving as a percent of gross national income | Net saving as a percent of gross national income |
| | Total | Gross domestic investment | | | Capital account transactions, net | Net lending or net borrowing (-), NIPAs | | | | | |
		Total	Private	Government							
1955	98.5	98.1	73.8	24.4	. . .	2.5	2.1	49.2	426.5	22.6	11.1
1956	107.5	104.8	77.7	27.1	. . .	4.7	-2.1	50.7	455.0	24.1	12.2
1957	111.5	106.7	76.5	30.2	. . .	6.6	-0.4	47.8	478.3	23.4	11.1
1958	104.4	103.6	70.9	32.6	. . .	2.7	0.6	41.1	484.1	21.4	8.5
1959	120.2	121.5	85.7	35.9	. . .	-1.3	0.1	56.1	525.1	22.9	10.4
1960	125.6	122.5	86.5	36.0	. . .	3.2	-1.4	54.6	547.8	23.2	10.8
1961	130.7	126.5	86.6	39.9	. . .	4.2	-1.0	55.9	567.8	23.2	10.8
1962	143.4	139.6	97.0	42.6	. . .	3.8	-0.1	65.5	609.3	23.5	11.4
1963	152.7	147.7	103.3	44.4	. . .	4.9	-1.5	69.7	644.6	23.9	11.8
1964	166.0	158.5	112.2	46.4	. . .	7.5	0.0	76.2	690.7	24.0	12.1
1965	183.7	177.5	129.6	47.9	. . .	6.2	0.8	89.5	748.2	24.4	12.7
1966	201.6	197.8	144.2	53.6	. . .	3.8	5.1	102.5	815.0	24.1	12.4
1967	203.8	200.4	142.7	57.7	. . .	3.5	3.4	96.8	863.7	23.2	11.2
1968	217.7	216.2	156.9	59.2	. . .	1.5	3.2	102.8	945.4	22.7	10.7
1969	234.7	233.1	173.6	59.5	0.0	1.6	1.6	108.2	1 024.4	22.8	10.6
1970	233.6	229.8	170.1	59.8	0.0	3.7	5.3	93.1	1 076.9	21.2	8.5
1971	255.6	255.3	196.8	58.5	0.0	0.3	9.5	106.5	1 165.9	21.1	8.3
1972	284.8	288.8	228.1	60.7	0.0	-4.1	7.1	127.9	1 283.9	21.6	9.1
1973	341.4	332.6	266.9	65.6	0.0	8.8	6.1	154.5	1 435.1	23.4	11.0
1974	356.7	350.7	274.5	76.2	0.0	5.9	7.4	144.5	1 556.9	22.4	9.2
1975	361.5	341.7	257.3	84.4	0.1	19.8	13.2	104.1	1 688.7	20.6	6.6
1976	420.0	412.9	323.2	89.6	0.1	7.0	20.5	153.7	1 874.0	21.3	7.5
1977	478.9	489.8	396.6	93.2	0.1	-11.0	19.3	201.4	2 087.0	22.0	8.2
1978	571.3	583.9	478.4	105.6	0.1	-12.7	23.2	258.9	2 355.0	23.3	9.5
1979	658.6	659.8	539.7	120.1	0.1	-1.3	44.8	288.6	2 619.3	23.4	9.3
1980	674.6	666.1	530.1	136.0	0.1	8.4	43.9	240.0	2 852.8	22.1	7.2
1981	782.0	778.6	631.2	147.3	0.1	3.3	36.7	293.5	3 207.2	23.2	8.1
1982	734.7	738.0	581.0	156.9	0.1	-3.4	6.8	203.7	3 374.7	21.6	5.7
1983	773.6	808.7	637.5	171.2	0.1	-35.2	54.2	248.1	3 621.1	19.9	4.4
1984	923.2	1 013.3	820.1	193.2	0.1	-90.2	38.7	418.9	4 038.3	21.9	7.2
1985	935.2	1 049.5	829.6	219.9	0.1	-114.4	51.3	412.9	4 320.8	20.5	5.7
1986	944.6	1 087.2	849.1	238.1	0.1	-142.8	76.7	405.1	4 530.4	19.2	4.1
1987	992.7	1 146.8	892.2	254.6	0.1	-154.2	40.6	418.9	4 847.2	19.6	4.6
1988	1 079.6	1 195.4	937.0	258.4	0.1	-115.9	-0.5	413.0	5 275.8	20.5	5.6
1989	1 177.8	1 270.1	999.7	270.4	0.3	-92.7	64.2	434.0	5 618.3	19.8	4.9
1990	1 208.9	1 283.8	993.5	290.4	7.4	-82.3	91.4	397.0	5 922.9	18.9	3.9
1991	1 246.3	1 238.4	944.3	294.1	5.3	2.6	88.4	307.3	6 117.3	18.9	3.7
1992	1 263.6	1 309.1	1 013.0	296.1	-1.3	-44.3	110.9	349.4	6 459.5	17.8	3.0
1993	1 320.2	1 398.7	1 106.8	291.9	0.9	-79.4	152.3	395.1	6 758.4	17.3	2.4
1994	1 436.0	1 550.7	1 256.5	294.2	1.3	-116.0	136.8	495.1	7 195.8	18.1	3.4
1995	1 520.1	1 625.2	1 317.5	307.7	0.4	-105.5	90.6	502.4	7 602.3	18.8	4.0
1996	1 637.9	1 752.0	1 432.1	320.0	0.2	-114.3	56.6	576.0	8 075.4	19.6	5.0
1997	1 795.8	1 925.1	1 595.6	329.5	0.5	-129.8	12.3	685.2	8 620.3	20.7	6.3
1998	1 872.2	2 076.7	1 735.3	341.4	0.2	-204.7	-60.1	766.5	9 167.6	21.1	6.8
1999	1 966.1	2 252.7	1 884.2	368.5	4.5	-291.1	-37.5	851.8	9 725.3	20.6	6.2
2000	2 020.3	2 424.0	2 033.8	390.3	0.3	-404.1	-99.5	909.8	10 421.3	20.3	5.8
2001	1 953.5	2 342.3	1 928.6	413.6	-12.9	-375.8	-115.0	738.3	10 788.6	19.2	4.3
2002	1 917.8	2 368.6	1 925.0	443.6	0.5	-451.3	-72.8	706.5	11 098.9	17.9	3.0
2003	1 977.5	2 493.2	2 027.9	465.3	2.1	-517.8	-13.6	766.0	11 591.4	17.2	2.3
2004	2 138.1	2 765.1	2 276.7	488.5	-2.8	-624.2	-8.6	933.4	12 372.6	17.4	2.5
2005	2 303.1	3 040.8	2 527.1	513.6	-12.9	-724.8	-35.5	1 058.8	13 221.8	17.7	2.7
2006	2 430.8	3 233.0	2 680.6	552.3	2.1	-804.2	-217.3	1 097.0	14 140.8	18.7	3.6
2007	2 517.8	3 236.0	2 643.7	592.2	-0.1	-718.0	17.5	971.6	14 585.7	17.1	1.6
2008	2 367.8	3 059.4	2 424.8	634.6	-5.4	-686.2	99.4	696.1	14 791.2	15.3	-0.6
2009	2 143.2	2 525.1	1 878.1	647.0	0.6	-382.5	75.3	156.8	14 494.5	14.3	-2.1
2010	2 306.7	2 752.6	2 100.8	651.8	0.7	-446.6	49.2	371.0	15 121.1	14.9	-0.9
2011	2 396.2	2 877.8	2 239.9	637.9	1.6	-483.2	-38.3	427.1	15 802.9	15.4	-0.1
2012	2 658.0	3 126.1	2 511.7	614.4	-6.5	-461.7	-203.3	591.9	16 596.1	17.2	2.0
2013	2 861.5	3 257.3	2 665.0	592.3	0.8	-396.6	-177.6	624.5	17 091.2	17.8	2.4
2014	3 054.7	3 455.9	2 860.0	595.8	0.5	-401.6	-212.0	709.2	17 823.2	18.3	2.9
2012											
1st quarter	2 572.4	3 084.4	2 460.8	623.6	0.6	-512.6	-218.7	583.1	16 443.8	17.0	1.8
2nd quarter	2 662.0	3 157.6	2 534.8	622.8	1.4	-496.9	-168.3	633.2	16 521.6	17.1	1.9
3rd quarter	2 706.7	3 142.8	2 529.9	612.9	2.3	-438.4	-143.8	596.3	16 608.8	17.2	1.8
4th quarter	2 690.8	3 119.7	2 521.3	598.4	-30.3	-398.7	-282.2	555.0	16 810.2	17.7	2.4
2013											
1st quarter	2 728.4	3 169.6	2 578.3	591.4	0.6	-441.9	-185.5	580.0	16 847.3	17.3	1.9
2nd quarter	2 788.7	3 210.7	2 620.4	590.3	1.3	-423.3	-260.3	592.4	17 034.4	17.9	2.5
3rd quarter	2 914.1	3 306.2	2 711.5	594.7	1.0	-393.2	-155.1	660.5	17 146.5	17.9	2.5
4th quarter	3 015.0	3 342.6	2 749.9	592.8	0.4	-328.1	-109.6	665.0	17 336.5	18.0	2.6
2014											
1st quarter	2 931.9	3 334.7	2 751.1	583.5	0.6	-403.3	-175.3	626.3	17 418.4	17.8	2.3
2nd quarter	3 065.0	3 438.8	2 841.6	597.2	0.4	-374.2	-187.0	706.0	17 714.0	18.4	2.9
3rd quarter	3 116.2	3 508.9	2 910.2	598.7	0.4	-393.1	-224.0	747.4	18 018.0	18.5	3.2
4th quarter	3 105.8	3 541.1	2 937.2	603.9	0.4	-435.7	-261.8	756.9	18 142.4	18.6	3.2

. . . = Not available.

Table 5-1B. Saving and Investment: Historical Data

(Billions of dollars, except as noted; quarterly data are at seasonally adjusted annual rates.)　　　　　　　　　　　　　**NIPA Tables 1.7.5, 5.1**

Year and quarter	Gross saving								Gross domestic investment and net lending, NIPAs				Net domestic invest-ment	Gross national income	Net saving as a percent-age of gross national income
	Total	Net saving			Consumption of fixed capital				Gross domestic investment			Net lending or net borrow-ing (-), NIPAs			
		Private	Government		Total	Private	Government		Total	Private	Govern-ment				
			Federal	State and local			Federal	State and local							
1929	20.1	7.6	0.8	1.3	10.4	9.4	0.2	0.8	20.1	17.2	2.9	0.8	9.7	104.6	9.3
1930	15.8	4.5	0.0	1.1	10.2	9.2	0.2	0.8	14.7	11.4	3.3	0.7	4.5	93.3	6.0
1931	9.1	1.2	-2.3	0.8	9.5	8.6	0.2	0.7	9.6	6.5	3.1	0.2	0.1	77.2	-0.5
1932	4.0	-3.2	-1.6	0.5	8.3	7.5	0.2	0.7	4.1	1.8	2.3	0.2	-4.2	59.6	-7.3
1933	3.9	-3.1	-1.2	0.2	8.0	7.0	0.2	0.7	4.3	2.3	2.0	0.2	-3.7	57.0	-7.1
1934	7.0	0.1	-2.6	1.1	8.4	7.3	0.3	0.9	7.0	4.3	2.7	0.4	-1.4	66.7	-2.1
1935	10.4	3.2	-2.3	1.0	8.5	7.3	0.3	0.8	10.2	7.4	2.9	-0.1	1.8	74.8	2.6
1936	12.3	5.1	-3.6	2.1	8.8	7.5	0.3	0.9	13.6	9.4	4.2	-0.1	4.8	83.9	4.2
1937	17.1	5.8	-0.2	1.8	9.7	8.4	0.4	1.0	16.9	13.0	3.9	0.2	7.1	93.4	7.9
1938	12.7	2.8	-1.8	1.7	10.0	8.6	0.4	1.0	12.2	7.9	4.3	1.2	2.2	87.1	3.1
1939	14.6	5.3	-2.5	1.7	10.1	8.6	0.4	1.1	14.8	10.2	4.6	1.0	4.7	92.6	4.8
1940	19.5	8.3	-1.0	1.6	10.6	9.0	0.5	1.1	19.0	14.6	4.4	1.5	8.4	102.2	8.7
1941	31.1	16.9	0.6	1.6	12.1	10.0	0.9	1.2	30.2	19.4	10.8	1.3	18.1	129.5	14.7
1942	41.6	37.0	-11.4	1.1	14.9	11.2	2.2	1.4	40.7	11.8	29.0	-0.1	25.9	167.3	16.0
1943	47.0	45.0	-17.1	1.1	18.0	11.5	5.0	1.5	47.3	7.4	39.9	-2.1	29.3	205.3	14.1
1944	42.8	49.8	-29.5	1.1	21.4	12.0	7.9	1.5	47.3	9.2	38.1	-2.0	25.9	222.4	9.7
1945	32.6	40.3	-32.1	1.1	23.2	12.5	9.3	1.4	37.7	12.4	25.3	-1.3	14.5	224.6	4.2
1946	41.5	23.1	-8.2	0.8	25.8	14.2	10.0	1.6	37.8	33.1	4.7	4.9	12.1	227.2	6.9
1947	49.3	17.6	2.4	0.1	29.2	17.7	9.6	1.9	42.8	37.1	5.7	9.3	13.6	248.2	8.1
1948	61.5	29.2	0.9	0.1	31.4	20.8	8.4	2.1	58.8	50.3	8.5	2.4	27.4	276.5	10.9
1949	49.6	25.3	-8.5	0.5	32.3	22.6	7.6	2.2	50.4	39.1	11.3	0.9	18.1	272.4	6.3
1950	64.9	29.3	1.8	0.3	33.4	24.3	6.9	2.2	68.0	56.5	11.5	-1.8	34.6	300.4	10.5
1951	79.8	36.0	4.5	1.5	37.8	27.7	7.4	2.6	82.3	62.8	19.6	0.9	44.6	345.8	12.2
1952	79.9	39.5	-2.1	1.9	40.6	29.5	8.3	2.8	81.9	57.3	24.6	0.6	41.3	367.1	10.7
1953	82.0	40.4	-4.2	2.3	43.5	31.3	9.2	2.9	87.1	60.4	26.7	-1.3	43.6	387.9	9.9
1954	80.8	40.7	-8.0	2.0	46.0	33.0	10.1	3.0	83.5	58.1	25.4	0.2	37.5	390.4	8.9
1947															
1st quarter	47.5	16.8	2.8	0.1	27.7	16.3	9.7	1.8	40.8	35.9	5.0	9.4	13.1	241.3	8.2
2nd quarter	46.8	15.7	2.1	0.2	28.8	17.3	9.6	1.8	39.6	34.5	5.1	9.9	10.9	244.6	7.4
3rd quarter	48.9	19.8	-0.7	0.0	29.8	18.2	9.7	1.9	41.0	34.9	6.1	10.1	11.2	249.1	7.7
4th quarter	53.8	18.1	5.3	-0.1	30.5	19.1	9.4	2.0	49.8	43.2	6.6	7.8	19.3	257.7	9.0
1948															
1st quarter	59.0	23.6	5.0	-0.3	30.8	19.9	8.9	2.0	54.7	47.2	7.5	6.5	24.0	266.9	10.6
2nd quarter	62.7	29.0	2.5	0.1	31.2	20.6	8.5	2.1	58.6	50.3	8.3	4.5	27.4	275.5	11.5
3rd quarter	62.0	31.4	-1.1	0.0	31.7	21.2	8.3	2.2	61.3	52.5	8.8	4.3	29.6	280.8	10.8
4th quarter	62.4	32.7	-2.7	0.4	32.0	21.7	8.1	2.2	60.7	51.3	9.4	3.9	28.7	283.0	10.7
1949															
1st quarter	54.7	27.9	-6.0	0.6	32.3	22.1	8.0	2.2	53.4	43.1	10.2	5.9	21.1	275.9	8.1
2nd quarter	48.6	25.0	-9.2	0.4	32.3	22.4	7.7	2.2	47.5	36.2	11.3	5.8	15.2	272.4	6.0
3rd quarter	50.1	26.6	-9.5	0.6	32.3	22.8	7.4	2.2	51.5	39.5	11.9	4.7	19.1	272.5	6.5
4th quarter	44.8	21.6	-9.5	0.3	32.4	23.1	7.2	2.2	49.2	37.5	11.8	2.5	16.8	268.7	4.6
1950															
1st quarter	53.2	32.3	-11.6	0.0	32.5	23.4	7.0	2.1	57.4	46.7	10.7	1.7	25.0	279.1	7.4
2nd quarter	61.7	29.8	-0.6	-0.3	32.8	23.9	6.8	2.1	63.4	52.3	11.1	1.2	30.6	291.6	9.9
3rd quarter	67.1	23.1	9.6	0.8	33.6	24.6	6.8	2.2	70.4	58.6	11.7	-1.2	36.8	309.5	10.8
4th quarter	77.6	32.0	10.0	0.8	34.9	25.5	7.0	2.3	80.8	68.4	12.3	-0.6	45.9	321.3	13.3
1951															
1st quarter	74.3	23.7	12.7	1.7	36.3	26.6	7.2	2.5	79.5	64.6	14.9	-0.2	43.2	334.5	11.4
2nd quarter	82.5	38.6	5.0	1.5	37.4	27.5	7.3	2.6	85.6	67.4	18.2	1.6	48.2	342.9	13.2
3rd quarter	80.8	41.7	-0.6	1.3	38.3	28.2	7.4	2.7	83.1	62.0	21.1	3.4	44.8	349.2	12.2
4th quarter	81.6	40.1	0.7	1.6	39.1	28.7	7.7	2.7	81.2	57.1	24.1	3.8	42.1	356.4	11.9
1952															
1st quarter	82.0	39.5	1.2	1.8	39.6	29.0	7.9	2.7	82.2	58.1	24.1	3.3	42.7	358.5	11.8
2nd quarter	76.0	37.0	-2.4	1.3	40.2	29.3	8.1	2.8	77.3	53.0	24.3	1.6	37.1	361.1	9.9
3rd quarter	79.3	41.0	-4.8	2.1	41.0	29.7	8.4	2.9	82.1	57.2	24.8	-0.4	41.1	368.4	10.4
4th quarter	82.3	40.8	-2.5	2.3	41.7	30.2	8.7	2.8	86.0	60.7	25.3	-1.4	44.3	380.6	10.7
1953															
1st quarter	84.0	41.3	-1.5	1.7	42.5	30.7	8.9	2.9	88.2	61.7	26.5	-1.1	45.7	387.5	10.7
2nd quarter	84.2	41.5	-3.3	2.8	43.2	31.1	9.2	2.9	89.3	62.1	27.1	-1.7	46.0	391.1	10.5
3rd quarter	83.7	40.2	-2.6	2.3	43.8	31.6	9.3	2.9	88.4	61.4	27.0	-1.0	44.6	390.0	10.2
4th quarter	76.0	38.5	-9.3	2.4	44.4	32.0	9.5	2.9	82.4	56.4	25.9	-0.8	38.0	382.9	8.3
1954															
1st quarter	78.9	41.3	-9.8	2.4	45.0	32.4	9.8	2.8	82.1	55.7	26.4	-0.7	37.2	385.2	8.8
2nd quarter	79.3	39.8	-8.4	2.1	45.7	32.8	10.0	3.0	81.4	55.4	25.9	-0.2	35.7	386.2	8.7
3rd quarter	80.2	39.7	-7.6	1.8	46.3	33.2	10.2	3.0	83.7	59.0	24.7	-0.1	37.4	390.2	8.7
4th quarter	84.7	42.1	-6.3	1.9	47.0	33.5	10.4	3.0	86.6	62.1	24.5	0.7	39.7	399.8	9.4
1955															
1st quarter	89.9	43.7	-2.9	1.7	47.5	33.9	10.5	3.0	92.9	68.7	24.1	0.7	45.4	412.8	10.3
2nd quarter	95.4	45.8	-0.6	2.0	48.2	34.5	10.6	3.1	97.4	72.7	24.8	-0.6	49.2	422.9	11.2
3rd quarter	97.9	46.8	-0.7	2.5	49.3	35.3	10.8	3.2	99.0	74.7	24.3	0.3	49.7	431.4	11.2
4th quarter	102.3	47.2	1.9	2.6	50.6	36.2	11.0	3.3	103.2	78.9	24.3	-0.2	52.6	439.0	11.8
1956															
1st quarter	105.7	48.3	2.3	2.9	52.1	37.3	11.4	3.5	103.9	78.3	25.6	-0.1	51.7	444.2	12.1
2nd quarter	107.6	50.3	0.7	3.1	53.5	38.4	11.6	3.6	103.6	77.0	26.6	1.4	50.1	451.4	12.0
3rd quarter	111.6	52.6	1.2	3.1	54.8	39.3	11.8	3.7	106.0	78.3	27.7	2.1	51.2	457.5	12.4
4th quarter	113.4	53.1	1.4	2.9	56.0	40.2	12.0	3.8	105.8	77.1	28.6	4.0	49.8	466.9	12.3

Table 5-1B. Saving and Investment: Historical Data—*Continued*

(Billions of dollars, except as noted; quarterly data are at seasonally adjusted annual rates.)

NIPA Tables 1.7.5, 5.1

Year and quarter	Gross saving								Gross domestic investment and net lending, NIPAs				Net domestic invest-ment	Gross national income	Net saving as a percent-age of gross national income
	Total	Net saving			Consumption of fixed capital				Gross domestic investment			Net lending or net borrow-ing (-), NIPAs			
		Private	Government		Total	Private	Government		Total	Private	Govern-ment				
			Federal	State and local			Federal	State and local							
1957															
1st quarter	114.3	53.2	0.4	3.4	57.3	41.1	12.4	3.8	107.5	77.7	29.8	4.3	50.2	474.9	12.0
2nd quarter	114.3	54.6	-1.5	2.8	58.4	41.9	12.6	3.9	107.6	77.9	29.7	3.6	49.2	478.1	11.7
3rd quarter	114.2	53.8	-1.6	2.5	59.5	42.7	12.8	4.0	109.9	79.3	30.6	3.5	50.4	482.9	11.3
4th quarter	104.6	49.9	-7.7	1.9	60.4	43.4	13.1	4.0	101.9	71.0	30.8	2.9	41.4	477.3	9.2
1958															
1st quarter	100.7	48.8	-10.2	1.0	61.1	44.0	13.1	4.0	98.0	66.7	31.3	0.6	36.9	472.2	8.4
2nd quarter	97.3	49.5	-15.0	0.8	62.0	44.7	13.2	4.1	97.0	65.1	32.0	0.0	35.1	475.0	7.4
3rd quarter	104.9	53.6	-12.5	0.9	62.9	45.2	13.5	4.2	104.9	72.0	32.9	0.5	42.0	488.2	8.6
4th quarter	112.1	56.9	-10.6	1.9	63.8	45.7	13.8	4.2	114.3	80.0	34.3	-0.7	50.6	500.9	9.6
1959															
1st quarter	117.8	56.5	-4.5	1.4	64.5	46.2	14.0	4.3	119.4	83.2	36.2	-4.1	54.9	513.6	10.4
2nd quarter	124.9	59.6	-1.8	2.0	65.1	46.6	14.2	4.3	125.5	89.4	36.1	-4.7	60.4	528.3	11.3
3rd quarter	117.3	53.2	-4.2	2.6	65.8	47.0	14.4	4.4	119.7	83.6	36.1	-3.4	54.0	526.2	9.8
4th quarter	120.4	56.1	-4.9	2.8	66.4	47.4	14.6	4.4	121.5	86.5	34.9	-3.9	55.1	532.1	10.1
1960															
1st quarter	133.1	58.7	4.7	2.7	67.0	47.7	14.8	4.5	131.6	96.5	35.1	-1.2	64.6	546.0	12.1
2nd quarter	126.4	55.0	1.3	2.5	67.6	48.0	15.0	4.5	122.3	87.1	35.2	-0.5	54.7	547.3	10.8
3rd quarter	127.1	56.7	-0.4	2.5	68.2	48.4	15.2	4.6	123.2	86.4	36.8	0.5	55.0	549.4	10.7
4th quarter	121.5	55.0	-4.9	2.5	68.8	48.7	15.5	4.6	112.8	76.0	36.9	1.4	44.0	548.3	9.6
1961															
1st quarter	124.7	57.8	-4.7	2.1	69.5	49.1	15.7	4.7	118.0	78.4	39.6	1.8	48.5	550.9	10.0
2nd quarter	127.1	61.4	-6.4	1.9	70.2	49.5	15.9	4.8	122.6	84.1	38.5	0.6	52.4	561.3	10.1
3rd quarter	134.6	66.1	-4.9	2.4	70.9	50.0	16.1	4.8	130.8	90.9	39.9	0.3	59.8	571.8	11.1
4th quarter	140.3	68.8	-2.9	2.6	71.8	50.5	16.4	4.9	134.5	92.9	41.6	0.1	62.8	587.2	11.7
1962															
1st quarter	141.6	71.3	-5.4	3.0	72.7	51.0	16.7	5.0	140.0	98.1	42.0	-0.6	67.3	597.3	11.5
2nd quarter	142.1	71.0	-5.6	3.2	73.5	51.5	16.9	5.1	138.6	96.7	41.9	0.8	65.0	605.3	11.3
3rd quarter	144.5	71.0	-4.9	3.8	74.6	52.1	17.3	5.2	141.3	98.2	43.1	0.1	66.7	612.7	11.4
4th quarter	145.6	71.8	-5.5	3.7	75.6	52.6	17.7	5.3	138.4	95.0	43.5	-1.5	62.8	621.8	11.3
1963															
1st quarter	149.2	72.7	-3.4	3.4	76.5	53.2	17.9	5.4	142.9	99.7	43.3	-0.6	66.4	629.5	11.5
2nd quarter	153.9	73.9	-1.1	3.6	77.5	53.8	18.2	5.5	145.2	101.6	43.6	1.0	67.7	639.6	11.9
3rd quarter	154.7	73.8	-1.6	4.0	78.5	54.5	18.4	5.6	150.4	104.6	45.8	0.2	72.0	649.0	11.7
4th quarter	159.0	78.0	-2.3	3.8	79.5	55.2	18.7	5.7	152.3	107.2	45.1	1.3	72.8	660.2	12.0
1964															
1st quarter	161.9	82.4	-5.5	4.5	80.6	55.9	18.9	5.8	156.2	110.5	45.8	3.2	75.6	673.6	12.1
2nd quarter	163.0	87.2	-10.2	4.3	81.8	56.8	19.1	5.9	157.0	110.5	46.5	1.9	75.3	684.9	11.9
3rd quarter	166.4	85.7	-6.7	4.4	83.0	57.7	19.3	6.0	159.2	112.6	46.6	2.5	76.2	697.5	12.0
4th quarter	172.8	89.5	-5.1	4.1	84.2	58.7	19.5	6.1	161.7	115.0	46.7	2.6	77.5	706.9	12.5
1965															
1st quarter	180.7	92.2	-0.9	3.9	85.6	59.7	19.6	6.2	172.7	126.5	46.2	0.3	87.2	726.9	13.1
2nd quarter	182.7	93.5	-2.0	4.1	87.1	60.9	19.8	6.4	173.9	127.0	46.9	1.4	86.8	739.7	12.9
3rd quarter	183.2	99.8	-9.4	4.1	88.8	62.1	20.1	6.5	180.1	131.2	48.9	0.7	91.3	752.6	12.6
4th quarter	184.9	99.8	-9.6	4.2	90.5	63.5	20.3	6.7	183.2	133.8	49.5	1.1	92.8	773.7	12.2
1966															
1st quarter	194.3	100.9	-4.1	5.2	92.3	65.0	20.5	6.8	196.1	144.2	51.9	-0.3	103.8	795.8	12.8
2nd quarter	194.8	100.7	-5.6	5.4	94.3	66.4	20.9	7.0	195.4	143.5	51.9	-1.1	101.1	807.7	12.4
3rd quarter	195.3	101.5	-7.8	5.4	96.3	67.9	21.2	7.2	197.4	143.2	54.2	-2.2	101.1	821.0	12.1
4th quarter	201.3	108.6	-10.3	4.8	98.3	69.4	21.5	7.4	202.1	145.9	56.2	-1.3	103.8	835.5	12.3
1967															
1st quarter	197.6	111.3	-19.3	5.2	100.2	70.9	21.8	7.5	200.7	142.8	57.9	-0.8	100.5	843.8	11.5
2nd quarter	194.0	107.4	-20.5	4.7	102.3	72.5	22.2	7.7	194.0	137.5	56.6	-1.5	91.7	852.5	10.7
3rd quarter	201.8	111.8	-18.8	4.2	104.6	74.1	22.6	7.9	200.8	142.8	57.9	-2.5	96.2	870.2	11.2
4th quarter	208.4	116.1	-19.4	4.8	106.9	75.8	23.1	8.1	205.9	147.7	58.3	-2.8	99.0	888.4	11.4
1968															
1st quarter	207.2	110.5	-16.9	4.3	109.4	77.6	23.5	8.3	210.6	152.3	58.4	-4.2	101.2	911.9	10.7
2nd quarter	214.0	115.6	-18.6	5.1	111.9	79.5	23.9	8.5	218.5	158.9	59.5	-3.8	106.5	935.6	10.9
3rd quarter	215.4	106.9	-10.1	4.0	114.5	81.6	24.3	8.6	215.2	155.7	59.5	-4.8	100.7	957.3	10.5
4th quarter	221.4	109.6	-9.3	3.6	117.4	83.7	24.7	8.9	220.3	160.8	59.5	-5.5	102.9	976.7	10.6
1969															
1st quarter	229.9	103.6	2.2	3.7	120.5	86.1	25.2	9.2	233.9	172.4	61.5	-4.7	113.4	996.2	11.0
2nd quarter	231.1	105.3	-1.5	3.9	123.5	88.3	25.6	9.5	232.4	172.7	59.7	-5.5	109.0	1 015.6	10.6
3rd quarter	238.1	115.9	-8.6	4.6	126.3	90.6	26.0	9.8	237.5	177.6	59.9	-4.5	111.2	1 037.1	10.8
4th quarter	233.2	112.2	-12.5	4.3	129.2	92.8	26.4	10.1	228.6	171.6	57.0	-3.3	99.4	1 048.6	9.9
1970															
1st quarter	227.2	113.0	-22.2	4.3	132.2	94.9	26.9	10.4	227.1	168.1	59.0	-2.5	94.9	1 056.1	9.0
2nd quarter	229.8	123.5	-32.6	3.7	135.2	97.1	27.4	10.8	230.3	171.5	58.8	-1.4	95.1	1 071.0	8.8
3rd quarter	231.1	129.4	-39.5	3.0	138.3	99.4	27.8	11.1	234.1	173.9	60.2	-3.1	95.8	1 088.6	8.5
4th quarter	224.7	127.1	-44.7	0.9	141.4	101.7	28.2	11.5	227.8	166.8	61.1	-3.7	86.4	1 092.0	7.6
1971															
1st quarter	238.6	139.6	-45.5	0.0	144.6	104.1	28.6	11.8	247.5	189.5	58.0	-3.1	103.0	1 132.0	8.3
2nd quarter	243.2	147.6	-52.4	0.5	147.5	106.5	28.9	12.1	255.7	197.3	58.3	-7.9	108.1	1 154.8	8.3
3rd quarter	249.1	150.3	-51.7	0.2	150.3	108.8	29.1	12.3	261.2	202.1	59.2	-7.6	110.9	1 175.8	8.4
4th quarter	253.7	152.7	-53.7	1.7	153.1	111.1	29.3	12.7	256.9	198.4	58.5	-10.6	103.8	1 201.0	8.4

Table 5-1B. Saving and Investment: Historical Data—*Continued*

(Billions of dollars, except as noted; quarterly data are at seasonally adjusted annual rates.)   **NIPA Tables 1.7.5, 5.1**

Year and quarter	Gross saving									Gross domestic investment and net lending, NIPAs					Net domestic invest-ment	Gross national income	Net saving as a percent-age of gross national income
	Total	Net saving				Consumption of fixed capital				Gross domestic investment			Net lending or net borrow-ing (-), NIPAs				
		Private	Government			Total	Private	Government		Total	Private	Govern-ment					
			Federal	State and local				Federal	State and local								
1972																	
1st quarter	263.3	150.5	-45.7	2.4	156.1	113.4	29.8	12.9	273.0	213.0	60.0	-13.2	116.9	1 237.4	8.7		
2nd quarter	265.5	146.6	-51.4	11.2	159.0	116.0	29.9	13.1	287.8	226.8	61.0	-12.9	128.7	1 260.7	8.4		
3rd quarter	279.7	155.4	-40.7	2.6	162.4	118.8	30.2	13.4	292.2	233.1	59.1	-12.6	129.8	1 293.8	9.1		
4th quarter	302.2	176.4	-57.8	17.5	166.0	121.8	30.4	13.8	302.3	239.7	62.6	-11.8	136.3	1 343.7	10.1		
1973																	
1st quarter	316.3	173.6	-40.0	12.4	170.2	125.2	30.9	14.2	320.5	254.3	66.2	-8.5	150.3	1 384.9	10.5		
2nd quarter	324.5	180.4	-40.8	9.7	175.1	129.0	31.4	14.6	333.8	268.2	65.6	-6.3	158.7	1 414.5	10.6		
3rd quarter	338.9	186.4	-36.6	8.7	180.4	133.4	32.0	15.0	328.9	264.3	64.6	-1.4	148.5	1 448.3	10.9		
4th quarter	361.7	200.8	-33.4	7.7	186.6	138.3	32.6	15.6	347.1	280.9	66.2	1.0	160.5	1 492.6	11.7		
1974																	
1st quarter	355.9	192.2	-35.3	5.4	193.6	143.8	33.3	16.5	339.3	268.4	71.0	-0.6	145.7	1 511.8	10.7		
2nd quarter	346.1	178.5	-37.9	3.8	201.6	149.7	34.1	17.8	353.5	277.4	76.1	-13.8	151.9	1 540.5	9.4		
3rd quarter	346.1	169.1	-36.2	2.8	210.3	156.1	35.2	19.1	349.1	271.0	78.1	-15.0	138.8	1 575.3	8.6		
4th quarter	349.0	185.9	-53.3	-2.7	219.1	163.0	36.1	20.0	360.8	281.3	79.5	-9.0	141.7	1 600.2	8.1		
1975																	
1st quarter	330.0	185.0	-75.1	-7.5	227.7	170.3	36.8	20.6	327.4	244.3	83.1	6.4	99.7	1 615.7	6.3		
2nd quarter	329.6	233.0	-132.4	-5.9	235.0	176.6	37.5	20.8	322.5	243.3	79.2	9.7	87.5	1 653.8	5.7		
3rd quarter	360.3	213.5	-89.7	-4.6	241.1	182.0	38.1	21.1	350.6	265.2	85.4	5.3	109.5	1 718.1	6.9		
4th quarter	373.1	221.6	-90.7	-4.3	246.4	186.3	38.8	21.4	366.1	276.2	89.9	5.6	119.7	1 767.3	7.2		
1976																	
1st quarter	392.5	222.7	-80.8	-0.1	250.8	189.6	39.5	21.7	397.6	304.6	92.9	-2.7	146.8	1 822.1	7.8		
2nd quarter	399.4	218.0	-76.2	1.8	255.8	193.7	40.1	22.0	411.3	322.3	89.0	-7.7	155.5	1 852.7	7.8		
3rd quarter	402.5	217.9	-79.5	2.3	261.7	198.6	41.0	22.2	417.0	328.3	88.7	-14.8	155.3	1 890.7	7.4		
4th quarter	403.5	210.8	-83.0	7.2	268.5	204.2	41.9	22.4	425.6	337.6	87.9	-14.1	157.0	1 930.4	7.0		
1977																	
1st quarter	412.2	202.9	-72.2	5.3	276.2	210.7	42.6	22.9	451.8	360.3	91.5	-28.8	175.6	1 981.7	6.9		
2nd quarter	454.2	229.3	-66.3	7.2	284.1	217.5	43.4	23.3	483.9	389.7	94.2	-29.7	199.8	2 060.1	8.3		
3rd quarter	481.6	251.7	-73.1	10.8	292.2	224.5	44.0	23.7	507.8	414.1	93.6	-28.8	215.6	2 125.0	8.9		
4th quarter	490.3	255.0	-76.0	10.4	300.9	231.8	45.0	24.1	515.6	422.3	93.3	-37.8	214.7	2 181.2	8.7		
1978																	
1st quarter	502.9	259.2	-78.2	11.9	309.9	239.4	46.0	24.6	528.4	434.8	93.6	-47.2	218.5	2 230.3	8.7		
2nd quarter	541.4	262.5	-58.9	18.1	319.7	247.5	47.0	25.2	575.6	470.6	105.0	-31.7	255.9	2 334.0	9.5		
3rd quarter	561.2	273.7	-53.1	10.7	330.0	256.2	48.0	25.8	602.1	492.4	109.7	-32.4	272.1	2 390.3	9.7		
4th quarter	587.1	282.5	-49.2	13.1	340.7	265.4	48.8	26.4	629.7	515.8	113.9	-25.9	289.0	2 465.4	10.0		
1979																	
1st quarter	609.9	288.7	-39.6	8.7	352.2	275.2	49.8	27.2	635.6	525.8	109.8	-27.6	283.4	2 533.3	10.2		
2nd quarter	612.3	279.2	-39.2	7.8	364.5	285.3	51.0	28.1	656.3	539.3	117.0	-32.3	291.8	2 584.0	9.6		
3rd quarter	615.0	273.2	-44.8	9.3	377.3	295.8	52.4	29.1	671.0	545.6	125.4	-33.8	293.6	2 648.1	9.0		
4th quarter	618.0	274.8	-54.4	7.1	390.5	306.6	53.8	30.2	676.1	547.9	128.2	-39.2	285.6	2 711.7	8.4		
1980																	
1st quarter	615.9	268.4	-63.5	6.9	404.2	317.7	55.3	31.3	690.3	554.6	135.8	-48.8	286.1	2 770.8	7.6		
2nd quarter	604.6	271.6	-87.4	2.0	418.5	329.0	57.0	32.5	654.0	519.3	134.7	-26.1	235.6	2 776.5	6.7		
3rd quarter	622.0	284.9	-100.3	4.3	433.2	340.7	58.7	33.8	629.4	495.1	134.4	-6.4	196.2	2 858.8	6.6		
4th quarter	680.0	317.2	-93.7	8.4	448.2	352.5	60.6	35.0	690.4	551.5	138.9	-22.0	242.2	3 004.9	7.7		
1981																	
1st quarter	710.2	310.3	-71.8	8.4	463.3	364.7	62.4	36.3	765.8	619.4	146.4	-29.9	302.5	3 105.9	7.9		
2nd quarter	720.6	313.3	-75.6	4.6	478.3	376.4	64.4	37.4	755.2	609.8	145.4	-30.0	276.9	3 162.5	7.7		
3rd quarter	777.2	363.1	-82.6	4.3	492.4	387.8	66.2	38.4	798.0	652.3	145.7	-25.7	305.6	3 266.0	8.7		
4th quarter	773.0	380.8	-113.3	-0.7	506.2	398.8	68.1	39.3	795.3	643.4	151.9	-33.2	289.0	3 294.3	8.1		
1982																	
1st quarter	740.8	358.0	-133.2	-3.5	519.6	409.4	70.0	40.2	738.5	588.3	150.2	-35.5	219.0	3 311.5	6.7		
2nd quarter	764.6	377.0	-139.3	-4.1	531.1	418.0	72.0	41.0	750.2	593.6	156.6	-23.6	219.1	3 369.1	6.9		
3rd quarter	732.3	373.7	-175.8	-5.6	540.0	424.7	73.6	41.7	750.5	593.0	157.5	-49.2	210.5	3 398.0	5.7		
4th quarter	674.0	344.7	-210.2	-7.2	546.7	429.5	75.1	42.1	712.8	549.2	163.6	-51.5	166.1	3 420.4	3.7		
1983																	
1st quarter	693.5	359.9	-207.0	-10.8	551.3	432.3	76.6	42.4	730.1	565.5	164.5	-42.1	178.8	3 485.7	4.1		
2nd quarter	703.8	348.8	-200.8	-0.8	556.6	436.0	78.0	42.6	781.1	613.8	167.3	-64.5	224.5	3 570.9	4.1		
3rd quarter	706.8	354.6	-217.3	6.2	563.4	440.6	79.8	42.9	826.9	652.3	174.7	-85.9	263.5	3 657.9	3.9		
4th quarter	773.8	387.4	-194.9	10.4	570.9	446.2	81.5	43.2	896.7	718.5	178.2	-96.5	325.8	3 769.7	5.4		
1984																	
1st quarter	857.7	438.3	-179.8	19.1	580.0	452.6	83.8	43.6	974.7	790.9	183.8	-115.7	394.7	3 911.4	7.1		
2nd quarter	875.8	451.8	-189.0	23.7	589.3	459.5	85.6	44.2	1 008.7	818.9	189.8	-125.6	419.4	4 007.6	7.1		
3rd quarter	901.4	479.5	-195.4	18.3	599.0	467.0	87.3	44.7	1 032.9	838.9	194.1	-127.9	433.9	4 083.6	7.4		
4th quarter	903.4	476.9	-205.2	22.7	609.1	474.9	89.0	45.2	1 036.8	831.7	205.1	-136.8	427.7	4 150.9	7.1		
1985																	
1st quarter	893.1	418.2	-167.8	22.6	620.1	483.4	90.8	45.9	1 017.7	809.9	207.9	-115.2	397.6	4 227.5	6.5		
2nd quarter	890.7	455.2	-217.1	21.8	630.9	492.0	92.4	46.5	1 045.7	827.0	218.7	-139.2	414.8	4 286.3	6.1		
3rd quarter	868.9	403.3	-196.1	19.5	642.1	500.7	94.2	47.2	1 048.9	822.2	226.7	-143.9	406.8	4 358.3	5.2		
4th quarter	883.1	413.9	-201.5	17.1	653.5	509.6	95.9	48.0	1 085.8	859.5	226.2	-160.9	432.3	4 411.2	5.2		
1986																	
1st quarter	899.3	410.2	-201.5	25.6	665.0	518.6	97.6	48.8	1 092.0	863.5	228.6	-128.4	427.1	4 474.0	5.2		
2nd quarter	874.3	402.5	-224.2	19.4	676.6	527.4	99.4	49.8	1 089.9	855.2	234.7	-142.0	413.3	4 497.0	4.4		
3rd quarter	841.8	361.7	-229.9	22.3	687.8	536.0	101.1	50.7	1 082.1	835.8	246.3	-150.3	394.3	4 547.7	3.4		
4th quarter	855.8	337.2	-195.1	14.5	699.3	544.3	103.2	51.8	1 084.8	842.1	242.8	-150.4	385.5	4 602.7	3.4		

Table 5-1B. Saving and Investment: Historical Data—*Continued*

(Billions of dollars, except as noted; quarterly data are at seasonally adjusted annual rates.)

Year and quarter	Gross saving								Gross domestic investment and net lending, NIPAs				Net domestic invest-ment	Gross national income	Net saving as a percent-age of gross national income
	Total	Net saving			Consumption of fixed capital				Gross domestic investment			Net lending or net borrow-ing (-), NIPAs			
		Private	Government		Total	Private	Government		Total	Private	Govern-ment				
			Federal	State and local			Federal	State and local							
1987															
1st quarter	902.1	379.9	-194.7	7.1	709.8	552.3	104.8	52.7	1 118.6	871.2	247.4	-151.1	408.8	4 685.0	4.1
2nd quarter	929.0	329.8	-141.6	19.5	721.2	561.2	106.4	53.7	1 128.3	874.6	253.7	-154.5	407.1	4 794.7	4.3
3rd quarter	964.1	372.3	-153.3	11.5	733.7	570.7	108.4	54.6	1 135.5	876.5	259.0	-154.2	401.8	4 901.0	4.7
4th quarter	1 013.5	419.2	-163.1	10.2	747.1	581.0	110.6	55.4	1 204.9	946.5	258.4	-157.2	457.8	5 008.0	5.3
1988															
1st quarter	1 032.9	420.7	-163.8	14.4	761.6	592.1	113.1	56.4	1 162.1	908.6	253.5	-127.0	400.5	5 113.2	5.3
2nd quarter	1 072.7	439.5	-155.8	13.3	775.6	603.0	115.4	57.3	1 193.0	934.5	258.5	-110.1	417.4	5 220.1	5.7
3rd quarter	1 100.1	440.7	-151.2	21.2	789.4	613.8	117.4	58.3	1 200.7	942.0	258.7	-106.6	411.4	5 325.4	5.8
4th quarter	1 114.8	451.4	-158.6	19.0	803.0	624.4	119.4	59.2	1 225.6	962.8	262.8	-119.7	422.6	5 444.2	5.7
1989															
1st quarter	1 152.0	453.4	-136.3	18.5	816.4	634.9	121.4	60.2	1 268.8	1 005.4	263.4	-106.8	452.4	5 539.6	6.1
2nd quarter	1 109.8	424.7	-158.2	13.6	829.7	645.1	123.3	61.3	1 268.5	1 001.0	267.5	-93.7	438.8	5 585.0	5.0
3rd quarter	1 103.4	416.9	-163.5	7.2	842.8	655.2	125.1	62.4	1 271.5	996.5	275.0	-81.8	428.7	5 649.3	4.6
4th quarter	1 089.3	411.9	-168.5	-9.7	855.5	665.1	126.8	63.6	1 271.7	995.9	275.8	-88.5	416.2	5 699.3	4.1
1990															
1st quarter	1 107.5	432.1	-195.3	2.5	868.2	674.8	128.7	64.8	1 297.5	1 010.8	286.6	-90.9	429.2	5 820.5	4.1
2nd quarter	1 139.6	463.9	-201.7	-3.4	880.8	684.4	130.3	66.1	1 303.2	1 014.8	288.4	-73.0	422.4	5 915.5	4.4
3rd quarter	1 110.4	421.7	-196.7	-7.9	893.3	693.8	132.0	67.5	1 291.4	1 000.7	290.7	-82.5	398.1	5 958.0	3.6
4th quarter	1 112.8	434.7	-209.9	-17.0	905.0	703.0	133.6	68.5	1 243.2	947.6	295.7	-82.7	338.2	5 997.7	3.5
1991															
1st quarter	1 205.7	493.5	-184.1	-20.9	917.2	712.1	135.7	69.4	1 215.4	924.6	290.7	42.1	298.1	6 038.1	4.8
2nd quarter	1 148.4	489.7	-244.1	-25.0	927.8	719.9	137.4	70.5	1 221.7	926.6	295.1	14.2	293.9	6 084.1	3.6
3rd quarter	1 127.8	483.5	-269.3	-23.0	936.6	726.2	139.0	71.4	1 243.0	947.5	295.6	-29.0	306.4	6 141.3	3.1
4th quarter	1 149.8	525.7	-287.4	-31.4	942.9	731.2	139.6	72.1	1 273.7	978.8	294.9	-17.0	330.8	6 205.4	3.3
1992															
1st quarter	1 161.5	570.2	-324.7	-31.4	947.4	734.8	139.9	72.7	1 257.1	956.8	300.3	-22.0	309.7	6 339.8	3.4
2nd quarter	1 178.2	591.1	-331.4	-36.0	954.6	740.0	140.9	73.7	1 310.8	1 013.1	297.7	-39.8	356.2	6 431.2	3.5
3rd quarter	1 129.3	553.3	-343.9	-43.1	963.0	746.7	141.7	74.6	1 318.5	1 024.2	294.3	-46.8	355.5	6 479.2	2.6
4th quarter	1 141.6	537.8	-330.6	-39.5	973.9	755.1	143.2	75.6	1 350.2	1 058.0	292.2	-68.6	376.3	6 587.7	2.5
1993															
1st quarter	1 135.3	538.1	-340.6	-48.0	985.8	765.0	144.0	76.8	1 372.3	1 083.9	288.4	-59.2	386.6	6 605.7	2.3
2nd quarter	1 173.5	522.2	-306.0	-40.5	997.7	774.9	144.9	78.0	1 387.8	1 094.5	293.3	-73.9	390.1	6 720.4	2.6
3rd quarter	1 147.4	494.5	-317.2	-39.2	1 009.3	784.9	145.6	78.8	1 387.4	1 095.9	291.4	-77.0	378.1	6 777.8	2.0
4th quarter	1 215.3	498.3	-283.4	-21.2	1 021.6	795.0	146.7	79.8	1 447.3	1 153.0	294.3	-107.6	425.8	6 929.6	2.8
1994															
1st quarter	1 236.1	498.9	-266.5	-29.5	1 033.2	805.1	146.9	81.1	1 485.3	1 202.1	283.3	-92.2	452.2	7 007.3	2.9
2nd quarter	1 301.7	521.4	-236.8	-29.6	1 046.8	816.9	147.7	82.2	1 555.4	1 265.1	290.3	-111.9	508.7	7 148.2	3.6
3rd quarter	1 311.3	523.7	-254.6	-20.3	1 062.4	830.2	148.7	83.6	1 553.9	1 251.6	302.4	-121.9	491.5	7 252.6	3.4
4th quarter	1 347.5	552.8	-256.9	-28.4	1 079.9	845.1	150.0	84.9	1 607.9	1 307.2	300.7	-137.9	528.0	7 375.1	3.6
1995															
1st quarter	1 400.0	584.0	-254.1	-29.4	1 099.5	861.7	151.5	86.4	1 632.8	1 327.3	305.5	-118.6	533.3	7 461.6	4.0
2nd quarter	1 397.1	567.2	-241.8	-44.3	1 116.1	876.6	151.7	87.7	1 613.9	1 303.8	310.1	-118.3	497.8	7 540.2	3.7
3rd quarter	1 439.3	585.2	-245.2	-31.9	1 131.3	890.1	152.3	88.9	1 609.9	1 303.2	306.7	-101.0	478.6	7 654.6	4.0
4th quarter	1 481.7	580.3	-222.3	-20.5	1 144.3	902.0	152.2	90.1	1 644.1	1 335.6	308.4	-84.0	499.8	7 752.7	4.4
1996															
1st quarter	1 522.5	605.4	-223.1	-15.8	1 156.0	912.3	152.5	91.2	1 670.0	1 355.2	314.7	-102.2	514.0	7 885.8	4.6
2nd quarter	1 562.5	590.9	-179.9	-16.9	1 168.3	923.9	152.4	92.0	1 736.5	1 418.6	317.9	-108.6	568.1	8 025.9	4.9
3rd quarter	1 598.6	596.2	-169.6	-10.3	1 182.3	936.9	152.4	93.1	1 796.1	1 474.4	321.7	-132.8	613.8	8 120.9	5.1
4th quarter	1 641.7	592.6	-141.4	-6.8	1 197.4	951.1	152.2	94.1	1 805.5	1 480.0	325.5	-113.6	608.1	8 269.0	5.4
1997															
1st quarter	1 701.9	613.1	-120.7	-4.8	1 214.2	966.6	152.5	95.2	1 852.3	1 522.0	330.4	-131.4	638.1	8 406.7	5.8
2nd quarter	1 771.3	644.7	-102.5	-2.6	1 231.7	982.2	153.1	96.3	1 919.9	1 589.9	330.0	-101.7	688.2	8 535.9	6.3
3rd quarter	1 820.4	634.2	-68.7	6.5	1 248.5	997.9	153.3	97.3	1 956.6	1 625.3	331.3	-122.7	708.2	8 701.4	6.6
4th quarter	1 840.6	640.3	-72.8	7.7	1 265.5	1 013.6	153.1	98.7	1 971.8	1 645.3	326.5	-163.3	706.3	8 837.3	6.5
1998															
1st quarter	1 912.0	638.8	-22.6	13.9	1 281.9	1 029.5	152.7	99.7	2 036.9	1 712.3	324.6	-164.3	754.9	8 955.1	7.0
2nd quarter	1 917.5	615.2	-8.8	11.0	1 300.1	1 046.0	153.3	100.8	2 031.7	1 694.8	336.9	-195.4	731.5	9 099.2	6.8
3rd quarter	1 960.4	605.2	21.7	14.2	1 319.3	1 063.2	153.7	102.5	2 091.5	1 739.8	351.8	-224.1	772.2	9 249.5	6.9
4th quarter	1 939.6	556.9	20.6	22.5	1 339.7	1 081.0	154.6	104.0	2 146.8	1 794.4	352.4	-235.2	807.1	9 366.4	6.4
1999															
1st quarter	2 035.6	615.8	47.5	12.2	1 360.2	1 099.5	155.2	105.5	2 206.9	1 850.6	356.3	-241.2	846.7	9 538.8	7.1
2nd quarter	1 987.5	535.7	62.8	3.9	1 385.1	1 121.5	156.3	107.3	2 210.0	1 845.8	364.2	-273.7	824.9	9 635.2	6.3
3rd quarter	1 974.7	481.7	71.5	8.7	1 412.8	1 146.9	157.0	108.9	2 261.5	1 890.9	370.6	-306.6	848.7	9 756.3	5.8
4th quarter	2 016.5	474.2	84.8	12.1	1 445.4	1 175.8	158.6	111.0	2 332.2	1 949.4	382.8	-342.9	886.8	9 970.8	5.7
2000															
1st quarter	2 143.1	463.7	176.2	22.0	1 481.2	1 208.2	160.0	112.9	2 333.6	1 945.9	387.7	-376.5	852.5	10 247.4	6.5
2nd quarter	2 124.8	447.3	146.4	22.2	1 508.9	1 232.5	161.0	115.4	2 457.7	2 071.8	386.0	-386.4	948.8	10 365.2	5.9
3rd quarter	2 142.0	453.7	153.7	6.5	1 528.1	1 248.7	162.1	117.3	2 447.4	2 055.8	391.6	-424.0	919.2	10 505.0	5.8
4th quarter	2 069.1	391.7	149.8	-11.2	1 538.7	1 256.8	162.8	119.1	2 457.3	2 061.6	395.7	-429.4	918.6	10 567.4	5.0
2001															
1st quarter	2 143.9	467.8	130.0	-24.7	1 570.8	1 287.0	162.9	120.9	2 369.2	1 967.5	401.7	-419.2	798.4	10 742.3	5.3
2nd quarter	2 128.5	490.5	92.8	-53.5	1 598.7	1 313.2	163.3	122.3	2 388.7	1 967.0	421.7	-379.9	790.0	10 807.5	4.9
3rd quarter	2 046.6	637.4	-130.2	-76.5	1 616.0	1 328.9	163.4	123.6	2 344.0	1 937.3	406.7	-360.0	728.1	10 781.5	4.0
4th quarter	1 954.9	465.7	-34.7	-106.4	1 630.4	1 341.6	163.6	125.2	2 267.1	1 842.7	424.4	-344.2	636.7	10 823.2	3.0

Table 5-1B. Saving and Investment: Historical Data—*Continued*

(Billions of dollars, except as noted; quarterly data are at seasonally adjusted annual rates.)   **NIPA Tables 1.7.5, 5.1**

Year and quarter	Gross saving										Gross domestic investment and net lending, NIPAs					Net domestic invest-ment	Gross national income	Net saving as a percent-age of gross national income
	Total	Net saving				Consumption of fixed capital					Gross domestic investment			Net lending or net borrow-ing (-), NIPAs				
		Private	Government			Total	Private	Government			Total	Private	Govern-ment					
			Federal	State and local				Federal	State and local									
2002																		
1st quarter	2 010.1	715.2	-228.0	-117.3		1 640.2	1 349.3	164.1	126.8		2 344.4	1 910.0	434.4	-406.9		704.2	10 957.8	3.4
2nd quarter	1 993.4	730.7	-266.5	-123.3		1 652.5	1 359.6	164.5	128.4		2 365.0	1 925.6	439.4	-451.7		712.5	11 047.0	3.1
3rd quarter	1 964.0	687.7	-276.9	-116.1		1 669.3	1 374.1	165.4	129.8		2 375.8	1 927.9	448.0	-453.3		706.6	11 124.7	2.6
4th quarter	1 994.9	746.1	-310.6	-126.9		1 686.3	1 389.0	166.2	131.1		2 389.0	1 936.5	452.5	-493.1		702.7	11 266.1	2.7
2003																		
1st quarter	1 941.7	728.0	-333.4	-154.9		1 702.0	1 401.6	167.7	132.7		2 415.5	1 960.2	455.3	-533.4		713.6	11 339.2	2.1
2nd quarter	1 977.8	799.8	-401.8	-136.7		1 716.5	1 413.2	169.4	133.9		2 431.6	1 970.5	461.0	-519.2		715.1	11 494.5	2.3
3rd quarter	1 985.2	829.7	-472.5	-107.0		1 735.0	1 428.6	171.3	135.1		2 520.5	2 048.3	472.2	-516.5		785.5	11 668.0	2.1
4th quarter	2 059.9	795.3	-403.8	-87.0		1 755.4	1 446.0	173.0	136.4		2 605.2	2 132.8	472.4	-502.2		849.8	11 864.0	2.6
2004																		
1st quarter	2 068.5	841.5	-441.0	-115.2		1 783.3	1 470.1	175.0	138.1		2 630.4	2 155.2	475.3	-540.6		847.2	12 075.6	2.4
2nd quarter	2 144.0	855.6	-402.2	-122.6		1 813.2	1 494.4	177.4	141.3		2 747.1	2 259.5	487.6	-617.7		933.9	12 279.7	2.7
3rd quarter	2 213.2	849.4	-373.1	-109.1		1 846.1	1 520.7	179.7	145.8		2 805.7	2 311.3	494.4	-623.0		959.6	12 505.4	2.9
4th quarter	2 161.0	743.8	-380.5	-86.6		1 884.3	1 552.0	182.4	149.9		2 877.4	2 380.8	496.6	-715.6		993.1	12 630.0	2.2
2005																		
1st quarter	2 282.7	740.2	-312.9	-66.6		1 922.0	1 584.9	185.2	151.9		2 973.3	2 475.2	498.2	-686.5		1 051.3	12 903.7	2.8
2nd quarter	2 286.0	707.3	-310.0	-70.7		1 959.3	1 616.0	187.9	155.4		2 979.1	2 469.5	509.6	-705.8		1 019.8	13 077.9	2.5
3rd quarter	2 328.7	705.5	-307.9	-69.9		2 000.9	1 650.8	190.6	159.5		3 046.6	2 527.2	519.4	-674.3		1 045.7	13 325.3	2.5
4th quarter	2 456.8	758.7	-288.1	-59.3		2 045.5	1 689.5	193.7	162.4		3 163.9	2 636.5	527.4	-832.7		1 118.4	13 580.2	3.0
2006																		
1st quarter	2 668.7	855.5	-242.5	-26.5		2 082.2	1 721.4	196.6	164.2		3 233.9	2 699.7	534.3	-792.5		1 151.7	13 946.4	4.2
2nd quarter	2 641.6	788.2	-244.3	-21.3		2 119.1	1 751.1	199.4	168.6		3 250.7	2 697.0	553.7	-815.2		1 131.6	14 074.1	3.7
3rd quarter	2 630.2	761.1	-234.0	-49.7		2 152.8	1 779.0	202.0	171.8		3 240.2	2 684.4	555.8	-859.0		1 087.4	14 214.3	3.4
4th quarter	2 652.0	709.4	-187.3	-60.1		2 190.0	1 808.6	204.8	176.6		3 207.2	2 641.6	565.7	-750.2		1 017.2	14 328.3	3.2
2007																		
1st quarter	2 561.9	614.3	-213.8	-66.0		2 227.4	1 837.5	208.2	181.7		3 209.8	2 634.2	575.6	-799.5		982.3	14 453.2	2.3
2nd quarter	2 568.3	622.0	-251.9	-55.4		2 253.7	1 857.5	211.3	185.0		3 262.6	2 671.9	590.7	-756.3		1 009.0	14 576.5	2.2
3rd quarter	2 456.7	542.0	-286.9	-74.9		2 276.5	1 874.0	214.4	188.1		3 255.5	2 658.2	597.2	-686.0		979.0	14 604.5	1.2
4th quarter	2 414.3	519.1	-309.9	-94.6		2 299.8	1 891.0	217.3	191.6		3 215.9	2 610.6	605.3	-630.3		916.1	14 708.6	0.8
2008																		
1st quarter	2 359.9	558.4	-409.0	-117.3		2 327.7	1 911.7	221.2	194.9		3 138.4	2 527.0	611.4	-732.3		810.6	14 802.2	0.2
2nd quarter	2 278.7	827.0	-780.5	-120.9		2 353.0	1 930.3	224.8	197.9		3 126.0	2 493.3	632.8	-718.2		773.0	14 867.9	-0.5
3rd quarter	2 248.9	716.1	-663.6	-183.2		2 379.7	1 949.6	228.4	201.6		3 081.6	2 435.9	645.8	-684.6		701.9	14 920.9	-0.9
4th quarter	2 186.1	714.7	-682.8	-238.9		2 393.0	1 955.9	231.0	206.2		2 891.7	2 243.1	648.6	-609.8		498.7	14 573.8	-1.4
2009																		
1st quarter	2 104.8	1 026.4	-1 040.1	-267.1		2 385.6	1 944.4	232.7	208.5		2 614.9	1 972.1	642.7	-393.1		229.3	14 395.0	-2.0
2nd quarter	2 020.4	1 254.9	-1 334.7	-266.7		2 367.0	1 924.8	234.0	208.1		2 477.8	1 825.9	651.9	-361.4		110.8	14 368.9	-2.4
3rd quarter	1 990.2	1 261.6	-1 340.9	-285.6		2 355.2	1 912.6	234.8	207.7		2 437.8	1 786.4	651.4	-373.5		82.6	14 489.4	-2.5
4th quarter	2 154.9	1 337.0	-1 279.6	-268.3		2 365.8	1 920.7	236.6	208.4		2 570.1	1 928.0	642.1	-401.9		204.3	14 724.5	-1.4
2010																		
1st quarter	2 128.7	1 371.1	-1 351.9	-260.3		2 369.8	1 919.7	240.2	210.0		2 624.9	1 989.5	635.4	-435.8		255.1	14 826.8	-1.6
2nd quarter	2 194.5	1 420.9	-1 338.4	-262.9		2 374.9	1 918.9	244.1	211.9		2 748.0	2 092.7	655.3	-450.4		373.1	14 995.7	-1.2
3rd quarter	2 337.3	1 495.6	-1 319.2	-221.6		2 382.5	1 921.9	246.9	213.6		2 825.1	2 164.6	660.5	-475.8		442.6	15 251.3	-0.3
4th quarter	2 346.0	1 456.6	-1 305.3	-204.4		2 399.1	1 933.6	250.1	215.4		2 812.5	2 156.5	656.0	-424.4		413.4	15 410.7	-0.3
2011																		
1st quarter	2 318.2	1 350.3	-1 236.4	-215.1		2 419.4	1 947.8	253.9	217.7		2 761.1	2 123.5	637.7	-487.6		341.8	15 510.6	-0.7
2nd quarter	2 353.4	1 424.1	-1 313.2	-200.5		2 442.9	1 965.5	256.7	220.7		2 851.8	2 212.7	639.1	-509.0		408.9	15 698.8	-0.6
3rd quarter	2 479.7	1 475.2	-1 231.2	-226.9		2 462.6	1 979.8	258.9	223.8		2 865.7	2 228.2	637.5	-462.3		403.1	15 917.3	0.1
4th quarter	2 587.0	1 526.3	-1 195.8	-221.2		2 477.7	1 991.1	260.1	226.5		3 032.5	2 395.2	637.3	-473.6		554.7	16 084.9	0.7
2012																		
1st quarter	2 791.1	1 621.6	-1 107.1	-224.7		2 501.2	2 010.2	262.2	228.8		3 084.4	2 460.8	623.6	-512.6		583.1	16 443.8	1.8
2nd quarter	2 830.4	1 638.4	-1 102.0	-230.4		2 524.4	2 029.1	264.0	231.3		3 157.6	2 534.8	622.8	-496.9		633.2	16 521.6	1.9
3rd quarter	2 850.5	1 605.9	-1 079.5	-222.3		2 546.5	2 047.9	265.4	233.2		3 142.8	2 529.9	612.9	-438.4		596.3	16 608.8	1.8
4th quarter	2 973.0	1 685.6	-1 071.6	-205.6		2 564.7	2 064.7	265.8	234.3		3 119.7	2 521.3	598.4	-398.7		555.0	16 810.2	2.4
2013																		
1st quarter	2 913.9	1 295.3	-790.6	-180.4		2 589.7	2 087.6	266.4	235.7		3 169.6	2 578.3	591.4	-441.9		580.0	16 847.3	1.9
2nd quarter	3 049.1	1 128.7	-525.9	-172.0		2 618.3	2 113.4	267.5	237.5		3 210.7	2 620.4	590.3	-423.3		592.4	17 034.4	2.5
3rd quarter	3 069.1	1 329.1	-707.7	-198.0		2 645.7	2 138.4	268.0	239.4		3 306.2	2 711.5	594.7	-393.2		660.5	17 146.5	2.5
4th quarter	3 124.6	1 184.5	-539.6	-197.9		2 677.6	2 167.1	269.0	241.5		3 342.6	2 749.9	592.8	-328.1		665.0	17 336.5	2.6
2014																		
1st quarter	3 107.2	1 207.4	-619.2	-189.3		2 708.3	2 195.2	269.6	243.5		3 334.7	2 751.1	583.5	-403.3		626.3	17 418.4	2.3
2nd quarter	3 252.0	1 309.5	-630.0	-160.3		2 732.8	2 217.3	270.2	245.3		3 438.8	2 841.6	597.2	-374.2		706.0	17 714.0	2.9
3rd quarter	3 340.2	1 394.8	-650.1	-166.0		2 761.5	2 243.1	271.2	247.2		3 508.9	2 910.2	598.7	-393.1		747.4	18 018.0	3.2
4th quarter	3 367.6	1 365.3	-626.7	-155.2		2 784.2	2 264.0	271.9	248.3		3 541.1	2 937.2	603.9	-435.7		756.9	18 142.4	3.2

Table 5-2. Gross Private Fixed Investment by Type

(Billions of dollars, quarterly data are at seasonally adjusted annual rates.)

NIPA Table 5.3.5

Year and quarter	Total gross private fixed investment	Nonresidential											
		Total	Structures						Equipment				
			Total	Comm-ercial and health care	Manufac-turing	Power and communi-cation	Mining explor-ation, shafts, and wells	Other non-residential structures	Total	Information processing equipment			Industrial equipment
										Total	Computers and peripheral equipment	Other information processing	
1955	68.8	43.4	15.2	3.4	2.3	3.3	2.5	3.7	23.9	2.8	. . .	2.8	7.3
1956	73.7	49.7	18.2	4.2	3.2	4.1	2.7	4.0	26.3	3.4	. . .	3.4	8.8
1957	75.7	53.1	19.0	4.1	3.6	4.5	2.6	4.1	28.6	4.0	. . .	4.0	9.6
1958	71.3	48.5	17.6	4.2	2.4	4.4	2.4	4.2	24.9	3.6	. . .	3.6	8.2
1959	81.7	53.1	18.1	4.6	2.1	4.3	2.5	4.7	28.3	4.0	0.0	4.0	8.5
1960	83.2	56.4	19.6	4.8	2.9	4.4	2.3	5.2	29.7	4.7	0.2	4.6	9.4
1961	83.6	56.6	19.7	5.5	2.8	4.1	2.3	5.0	28.9	5.1	0.3	4.8	8.8
1962	90.9	61.2	20.8	6.2	2.8	4.1	2.5	5.2	32.1	5.5	0.3	5.1	9.3
1963	97.7	64.8	21.2	6.1	2.9	4.4	2.3	5.6	34.4	6.1	0.7	5.4	10.0
1964	107.3	72.2	23.7	6.8	3.6	4.8	2.4	6.2	38.7	6.8	0.9	5.9	11.4
1965	120.4	85.2	28.3	8.2	5.1	5.4	2.4	7.2	45.8	7.8	1.2	6.7	13.7
1966	130.6	97.2	31.3	8.3	6.6	6.3	2.5	7.8	53.0	9.7	1.7	8.0	16.2
1967	132.8	99.2	31.5	8.2	6.0	7.1	2.4	7.8	53.7	10.1	1.9	8.2	16.9
1968	147.9	107.7	33.6	9.4	6.0	8.3	2.4	7.8	58.5	10.6	1.9	8.7	17.3
1969	164.4	120.0	37.7	11.7	6.8	8.7	2.8	7.8	65.2	12.8	2.4	10.4	19.1
1970	168.0	124.6	40.3	12.5	7.0	10.2	2.8	7.8	66.4	14.3	2.7	11.6	20.3
1971	188.6	130.4	42.7	14.9	6.3	11.0	2.7	7.9	69.1	14.9	2.8	12.2	19.5
1972	219.0	146.6	47.2	17.6	5.9	12.1	3.1	8.6	78.9	16.7	3.5	13.2	21.4
1973	251.1	172.7	55.0	19.8	7.9	13.8	3.5	9.9	95.1	19.9	3.5	16.3	26.0
1974	260.5	191.1	61.2	20.6	10.0	15.1	5.2	10.3	104.3	23.1	3.9	19.2	30.7
1975	263.5	196.8	61.4	17.7	10.6	15.7	7.4	10.1	107.6	23.8	3.6	20.2	31.3
1976	306.1	219.3	65.9	18.1	10.1	18.2	8.6	11.0	121.2	27.5	4.4	23.1	34.1
1977	374.3	259.1	74.6	20.3	11.1	19.3	11.5	12.5	148.7	33.7	5.7	28.0	39.4
1978	452.6	314.6	93.6	25.3	16.2	21.4	15.4	15.2	180.6	42.3	7.6	34.8	47.7
1979	521.7	373.8	117.7	33.5	22.0	24.6	19.0	18.5	208.1	50.4	10.2	40.2	56.2
1980	536.4	406.9	136.2	41.0	20.5	27.3	27.4	20.0	216.4	58.9	12.5	46.4	60.7
1981	601.4	472.9	167.3	48.3	25.4	30.0	42.5	21.2	240.9	69.6	17.1	52.5	65.5
1982	595.9	485.1	177.6	55.8	26.1	29.6	44.8	21.3	234.9	74.2	18.9	55.3	62.7
1983	643.3	482.2	154.3	55.8	19.5	25.8	30.0	23.3	246.5	83.7	23.9	59.8	58.9
1984	754.7	564.3	177.4	70.6	20.9	26.5	31.3	28.1	291.9	101.2	31.6	69.6	68.1
1985	807.8	607.7	194.5	84.1	24.1	26.5	27.9	31.8	307.9	106.6	33.7	72.9	72.5
1986	842.6	607.8	176.5	80.9	21.0	28.3	15.7	30.7	317.7	111.1	33.4	77.7	75.4
1987	865.0	615.2	174.2	80.8	21.2	25.4	13.1	33.7	320.9	112.2	35.8	76.4	76.7
1988	918.5	662.3	182.8	86.3	23.2	25.0	15.7	32.5	346.8	120.8	38.0	82.8	84.2
1989	972.0	716.0	193.7	88.3	28.8	27.5	14.9	34.3	372.2	130.7	43.1	87.6	93.3
1990	978.9	739.2	202.9	87.5	33.6	26.3	17.9	37.6	371.9	129.6	38.6	90.9	92.1
1991	944.7	723.6	183.6	68.9	31.4	31.6	18.5	33.2	360.8	129.2	37.7	91.5	89.3
1992	996.7	741.9	172.6	64.5	29.0	33.9	14.2	31.0	381.7	142.1	44.0	98.1	93.0
1993	1 086.0	799.2	177.2	69.4	23.6	33.2	16.6	34.5	425.1	153.3	47.9	105.4	102.2
1994	1 192.7	868.9	186.8	75.4	28.9	31.2	16.4	34.9	476.4	167.0	52.4	114.6	113.6
1995	1 286.3	962.2	207.3	83.1	35.5	33.1	15.0	40.6	528.1	188.4	66.1	122.3	129.0
1996	1 401.3	1 043.2	224.6	91.5	38.2	29.2	16.8	48.9	565.3	204.7	72.8	131.9	136.5
1997	1 524.7	1 149.1	250.3	104.3	37.6	28.8	22.4	57.2	610.9	222.8	81.4	141.4	140.4
1998	1 671.6	1 252.8	275.1	116.0	40.5	34.2	22.3	62.2	660.0	240.1	87.9	152.2	147.4
1999	1 823.4	1 361.6	283.9	125.4	35.1	40.4	18.3	64.7	713.6	259.8	97.2	162.5	149.1
2000	1 979.2	1 493.8	318.1	139.3	37.6	48.1	23.7	69.4	766.1	293.8	103.2	190.6	162.9
2001	1 966.9	1 453.9	329.7	137.3	37.8	51.1	34.6	68.9	711.5	265.9	87.6	178.4	151.9
2002	1 906.5	1 348.9	282.9	119.4	22.7	51.0	30.2	59.5	659.6	236.7	79.7	157.0	141.7
2003	2 008.7	1 371.7	281.8	115.0	21.4	48.1	38.5	58.8	669.0	241.0	78.3	162.8	143.4
2004	2 212.8	1 463.1	301.8	125.3	23.2	43.1	47.3	62.9	719.2	253.1	81.5	171.6	144.2
2005	2 467.5	1 611.5	345.6	135.9	28.4	48.1	69.4	63.9	790.7	262.8	80.0	182.8	162.4
2006	2 613.7	1 776.3	415.6	156.3	32.3	55.8	96.0	75.1	856.1	282.3	86.4	195.9	181.6
2007	2 609.3	1 920.6	496.9	181.8	40.2	81.6	102.2	91.1	885.8	303.2	87.7	215.5	194.1
2008	2 456.8	1 941.0	552.4	181.8	52.8	95.6	117.0	105.2	825.1	291.2	83.8	207.5	192.9
2009	2 025.7	1 633.4	438.2	126.7	56.3	95.8	75.0	84.5	644.3	256.1	76.8	179.3	152.1
2010	2 039.3	1 658.2	362.0	92.0	39.8	83.8	86.2	60.3	731.8	276.7	81.3	195.4	152.9
2011	2 198.1	1 812.1	381.6	93.2	39.0	81.8	112.3	55.4	838.2	277.7	76.4	201.3	190.5
2012	2 449.9	2 007.7	448.0	103.7	45.8	102.4	134.1	62.0	937.9	288.6	79.7	208.9	211.4
2013	2 593.2	2 084.3	462.1	109.8	48.8	98.8	137.7	67.0	972.3	296.6	82.1	214.5	207.0
2014	2 782.9	2 233.7	507.0	127.5	56.1	106.3	144.4	72.8	1 036.7	308.0	79.3	228.7	223.8
2012													
1st quarter	2 395.3	1 971.5	439.7	100.8	43.5	101.3	135.1	59.0	920.4	292.1	82.4	209.7	207.4
2nd quarter	2 445.5	2 016.2	455.7	103.8	45.7	104.8	139.4	62.0	940.7	287.9	80.2	207.8	214.7
3rd quarter	2 455.9	2 011.7	452.8	105.7	46.5	103.5	133.7	63.4	935.4	282.4	74.9	207.6	209.2
4th quarter	2 502.9	2 031.2	443.8	104.6	47.6	99.8	128.3	63.4	955.2	292.0	81.4	210.6	214.4
2013													
1st quarter	2 541.8	2 052.1	438.2	107.1	47.5	85.9	133.7	64.0	969.1	297.9	83.4	214.5	211.2
2nd quarter	2 571.7	2 064.6	453.9	105.8	46.1	93.9	141.1	67.0	968.0	295.2	79.9	215.3	206.0
3rd quarter	2 606.0	2 085.9	474.4	109.6	50.8	103.6	142.0	68.4	959.3	298.8	81.7	217.0	206.7
4th quarter	2 653.5	2 134.5	481.8	116.7	50.9	111.9	133.8	68.4	992.8	294.6	83.4	211.2	204.0
2014													
1st quarter	2 708.4	2 181.9	504.9	117.9	51.5	127.3	139.3	68.9	1 003.5	298.1	77.5	220.6	215.8
2nd quarter	2 752.7	2 211.7	505.7	122.8	52.0	113.4	146.4	71.0	1 023.2	310.7	79.7	231.0	224.1
3rd quarter	2 821.8	2 267.0	505.4	129.9	56.9	99.4	146.0	73.1	1 065.3	304.7	80.4	224.3	229.2
4th quarter	2 848.7	2 274.1	512.0	139.3	63.9	85.0	145.7	78.2	1 055.0	318.4	79.6	238.8	226.1

. . . = Not available.

Table 5-2. Gross Private Fixed Investment by Type—*Continued*

(Billions of dollars, quarterly data are at seasonally adjusted annual rates.)   NIPA Table 5.3.5

Year and quarter	Nonresidential—*Continued*							Residential						
	Equipment—*Continued*		Intellectual property				Total	Total	Residential structures					Residential equipment
	Transportation equipment	Other nonresidential equipment	Total	Software [1]	Research and development [2]	Entertainment, literary, and artistic originals			Total	Permanent site			Other residential structures	
										Total	Single family	Multifamily		
1955	7.5	6.3	4.3	...	2.7	1.6	25.4	25.0	18.6	...	...	6.4	0.4
1956	7.4	6.7	5.2	...	3.6	1.7	24.0	23.5	16.5	...	...	7.0	0.5
1957	8.3	6.7	5.6	...	3.7	1.9	22.6	22.2	15.1	...	...	7.1	0.5
1958	6.1	6.9	6.0	...	4.0	2.0	22.8	22.3	15.4	13.1	2.3	6.9	0.5
1959	8.3	7.6	6.6	0.0	4.4	2.2	28.6	28.1	19.7	16.7	3.0	8.4	0.6
1960	8.5	7.1	7.1	0.1	4.9	2.2	26.9	26.3	17.5	14.9	2.6	8.8	0.5
1961	8.0	7.0	8.0	0.2	5.2	2.7	27.0	26.5	17.4	14.1	3.3	9.1	0.5
1962	9.8	7.5	8.4	0.2	5.6	2.6	29.6	29.1	19.9	15.1	4.8	9.2	0.5
1963	9.4	8.8	9.2	0.4	6.0	2.8	32.9	32.3	22.4	16.0	6.4	9.8	0.6
1964	10.6	9.9	9.8	0.5	6.5	2.8	35.1	34.5	24.1	17.6	6.4	10.4	0.6
1965	13.2	11.0	11.1	0.7	7.2	3.2	35.2	34.5	23.8	17.8	6.0	10.6	0.7
1966	14.5	12.7	12.8	1.0	8.1	3.7	33.4	32.7	21.8	16.6	5.2	10.9	0.7
1967	14.3	12.4	14.0	1.2	9.0	3.8	33.6	32.9	21.5	16.8	4.7	11.4	0.7
1968	17.6	13.0	15.6	1.3	9.9	4.3	40.2	39.3	26.7	19.5	7.2	12.6	0.9
1969	18.9	14.4	17.2	1.8	11.0	4.4	44.4	43.4	29.2	19.7	9.5	14.1	1.0
1970	16.2	15.6	17.9	2.3	11.5	4.1	43.4	42.3	27.1	17.5	9.5	15.2	1.1
1971	18.4	16.3	18.7	2.4	11.9	4.4	58.2	56.9	38.7	25.8	12.9	18.2	1.3
1972	21.8	19.0	20.6	2.8	12.9	4.9	72.4	70.9	50.1	32.8	17.2	20.8	1.5
1973	26.6	22.6	22.7	3.2	14.6	4.9	78.3	76.6	54.6	35.2	19.4	22.0	1.7
1974	26.3	24.3	25.5	3.9	16.4	5.2	69.5	67.6	43.4	29.7	13.7	24.2	1.9
1975	25.2	27.4	27.8	4.8	17.5	5.5	66.7	64.8	36.3	29.6	6.7	28.5	1.9
1976	30.0	29.6	32.2	5.2	19.6	7.4	86.6	84.6	50.8	43.9	6.9	33.9	2.1
1977	39.3	36.3	35.8	5.5	21.8	8.6	115.2	112.8	72.2	62.2	10.0	40.6	2.4
1978	47.3	43.2	40.4	6.3	24.9	9.1	138.0	135.3	85.6	72.8	12.8	49.7	2.7
1979	53.6	47.9	48.1	8.1	29.1	10.9	147.8	144.7	89.3	72.3	17.0	55.4	3.2
1980	48.4	48.3	54.4	9.8	34.2	10.3	129.5	126.1	69.6	52.9	16.7	56.5	3.4
1981	50.6	55.2	64.8	11.8	39.7	13.2	128.5	124.9	69.4	52.0	17.5	55.4	3.6
1982	46.8	51.2	72.7	14.0	44.8	13.9	110.8	107.2	57.0	41.5	15.5	50.2	3.7
1983	53.5	50.4	81.3	16.4	49.6	15.3	161.1	156.9	95.0	72.5	22.4	61.9	4.2
1984	64.4	58.1	95.1	20.4	56.9	17.8	190.4	185.6	114.6	86.4	28.2	71.0	4.7
1985	69.0	59.9	105.3	23.8	63.0	18.6	200.1	195.0	115.9	87.4	28.5	79.1	5.1
1986	70.5	60.7	113.5	25.6	66.5	21.4	234.8	229.3	135.2	104.1	31.0	94.1	5.5
1987	68.1	63.9	120.1	29.0	69.2	21.9	249.8	244.0	142.7	117.2	25.5	101.3	5.8
1988	72.9	69.0	132.7	34.2	75.5	23.0	256.2	250.1	142.4	120.1	22.3	107.7	6.1
1989	67.9	80.2	150.1	41.9	82.8	25.4	256.0	249.9	143.2	120.9	22.3	106.6	6.1
1990	70.0	80.2	164.4	47.6	89.3	27.5	239.7	233.7	132.1	112.9	19.3	101.5	6.0
1991	71.5	70.8	179.1	53.7	96.0	29.4	221.2	215.4	114.6	99.4	15.1	100.8	5.7
1992	74.7	72.0	187.7	57.9	98.6	31.2	254.7	248.8	135.1	122.0	13.1	113.8	5.9
1993	89.4	80.2	196.9	64.3	99.2	33.4	286.8	280.7	150.9	140.1	10.8	129.8	6.1
1994	107.7	88.1	205.7	68.3	101.3	36.1	323.8	317.6	176.4	162.3	14.1	141.2	6.2
1995	116.1	94.7	226.8	74.6	112.0	40.2	324.1	317.7	171.4	153.5	17.9	146.3	6.3
1996	123.2	101.0	253.3	85.5	123.6	44.3	358.1	351.7	191.1	170.8	20.3	160.6	6.3
1997	135.5	112.1	288.0	107.5	134.4	46.1	375.6	369.3	198.1	175.2	22.9	171.3	6.3
1998	147.1	125.4	317.7	126.0	143.3	48.3	418.8	412.1	224.0	199.4	24.6	188.2	6.7
1999	174.4	130.4	364.0	157.3	155.7	51.0	461.8	454.5	251.3	223.8	27.4	203.2	7.3
2000	170.8	138.6	409.5	184.5	169.5	55.6	485.4	477.7	265.0	236.8	28.3	212.7	7.7
2001	154.2	139.5	412.6	186.6	171.3	54.7	513.0	505.2	279.4	249.1	30.3	225.8	7.8
2002	141.6	139.6	406.4	183.0	165.7	57.6	557.6	549.6	298.8	265.9	33.0	250.7	8.0
2003	134.1	150.5	420.9	191.0	167.2	62.7	636.9	628.7	345.7	310.6	35.1	283.0	8.3
2004	159.2	162.7	442.1	205.1	173.0	64.1	749.7	740.7	417.5	377.6	39.9	323.2	9.0
2005	179.6	186.0	475.1	217.2	188.1	69.8	856.1	846.4	480.8	433.5	47.3	365.6	9.6
2006	194.3	198.0	504.6	228.9	204.5	71.2	837.4	827.4	468.8	416.0	52.8	358.6	10.0
2007	188.8	199.6	537.9	244.2	223.3	70.4	688.7	678.8	354.1	305.2	49.0	324.7	9.9
2008	146.2	194.9	563.4	258.5	237.7	67.2	515.9	506.5	230.1	185.8	44.3	276.4	9.3
2009	70.6	165.6	550.9	256.8	229.0	65.1	392.2	383.9	133.9	105.3	28.5	250.1	8.3
2010	127.5	174.7	564.3	252.0	240.2	72.2	381.1	372.7	127.3	112.6	14.7	245.5	8.3
2011	173.9	196.2	592.2	269.8	250.0	72.4	386.0	377.5	123.2	108.2	15.0	254.2	8.6
2012	213.1	224.8	621.7	284.3	263.0	74.5	442.2	433.4	154.5	132.0	22.5	278.9	8.9
2013	240.6	228.1	649.9	295.0	279.2	75.7	508.9	499.7	202.3	170.8	31.5	297.5	9.2
2014	272.4	232.6	690.0	313.0	298.3	78.6	549.2	539.9	235.4	193.6	41.8	304.5	9.3
2012													
1st quarter	206.5	214.4	611.4	280.3	257.2	74.0	423.8	414.9	137.8	119.3	18.5	277.1	8.9
2nd quarter	213.7	224.5	619.7	284.5	260.9	74.3	429.4	420.6	146.6	125.3	21.3	274.0	8.8
3rd quarter	212.1	231.6	623.6	283.9	265.0	74.7	444.1	435.3	158.7	135.0	23.7	276.6	8.8
4th quarter	220.2	228.6	632.3	288.5	268.8	75.0	471.7	462.7	175.0	148.5	26.5	287.7	9.0
2013													
1st quarter	225.3	234.8	644.8	295.3	274.3	75.2	489.6	480.4	189.7	161.0	28.6	290.8	9.2
2nd quarter	241.3	225.6	642.7	290.4	277.0	75.3	507.1	497.9	200.6	170.5	30.1	297.3	9.2
3rd quarter	237.9	215.9	652.2	295.8	280.7	75.8	520.0	510.8	206.4	174.6	31.8	304.4	9.2
4th quarter	257.9	236.2	660.0	298.7	284.7	76.5	519.0	509.8	212.4	177.0	35.4	297.4	9.2
2014													
1st quarter	256.6	233.0	673.6	304.6	291.4	77.5	526.4	517.3	222.1	185.3	36.8	295.2	9.2
2nd quarter	261.3	227.1	682.8	310.4	294.0	78.4	540.9	531.7	229.2	188.5	40.7	302.5	9.3
3rd quarter	287.6	243.8	696.3	317.7	299.5	79.0	554.8	545.6	236.2	192.8	43.5	309.3	9.3
4th quarter	283.9	226.5	707.2	319.4	308.1	79.6	574.6	565.3	254.2	207.9	46.3	311.1	9.3

[1]Excludes software "embedded," or bundled, in computers and other equipment. Includes software development expenditures.
[2]Excludes software development.
. . . = Not available.

Table 5-3. Real Gross Private Fixed Investment by Type

(Billions of chained [2009] dollars, quarterly data are at seasonally adjusted annual rates.)

NIPA Table 5.3.6

Year and quarter	Total gross private fixed investment	Nonresidential											
		Total	Structures						Equipment				
			Total	Commercial and health care	Manufacturing	Power and communication	Mining exploration, shafts, and wells	Other nonresidential structures	Total	Information processing equipment			Industrial equipment
										Total	Computers and peripheral equipment[1]	Other information processing	
1999	2 165.9	1 510.1	494.9	199.0	53.9	62.8	64.5	94.7	662.4	149.5	29.2	127.3	182.8
2000	2 316.2	1 647.7	533.5	212.3	55.6	72.5	80.5	97.5	726.9	180.4	35.4	153.2	198.5
2001	2 280.0	1 608.4	525.4	202.0	54.1	74.7	94.9	93.0	695.7	178.2	36.3	148.5	183.9
2002	2 201.1	1 498.0	432.5	171.1	31.6	72.9	69.4	78.6	658.0	169.9	38.0	135.0	171.6
2003	2 289.5	1 526.1	415.8	160.3	29.2	67.2	79.3	75.6	679.0	185.8	41.7	147.3	172.2
2004	2 443.9	1 605.4	414.1	164.2	30.1	56.1	84.2	76.7	731.2	204.5	46.8	160.7	169.1
2005	2 611.0	1 717.4	421.2	162.8	34.2	58.1	92.1	72.7	801.6	222.2	52.1	172.6	183.6
2006	2 662.5	1 839.6	451.5	172.6	36.5	61.7	99.5	79.7	870.8	250.9	64.3	187.5	199.1
2007	2 609.6	1 948.4	509.0	189.9	43.1	85.9	97.9	91.8	898.3	279.9	72.7	207.9	205.3
2008	2 432.6	1 934.4	540.2	182.8	53.8	94.5	105.0	103.4	836.1	281.0	77.1	204.2	195.5
2009	2 025.7	1 633.4	438.2	126.7	56.3	95.8	75.0	84.5	644.3	256.1	76.8	179.3	152.1
2010	2 056.2	1 673.8	366.3	95.2	40.8	80.4	87.8	62.0	746.7	281.4	84.7	196.8	151.3
2011	2 186.7	1 802.3	374.7	94.7	39.1	74.1	110.9	56.2	847.9	285.9	83.0	202.8	183.3
2012	2 400.4	1 964.1	423.1	102.8	44.9	89.7	123.8	61.5	939.2	303.1	88.4	214.5	199.8
2013	2 501.9	2 023.7	429.7	106.4	46.8	85.6	126.7	64.3	969.5	314.4	92.0	222.3	194.8
2014	2 633.8	2 148.3	464.6	120.3	52.0	90.9	135.0	66.9	1 026.2	326.4	89.0	236.8	208.9
2005													
1st quarter	2 558.8	1 681.9	423.1	164.0	34.8	57.2	90.9	74.5	774.2	214.3	48.8	168.6	179.4
2nd quarter	2 599.2	1 706.1	420.9	163.3	33.4	58.3	93.1	71.6	791.0	218.0	50.4	170.5	177.4
3rd quarter	2 640.4	1 737.4	418.6	161.1	34.0	57.9	92.9	71.6	817.9	226.2	52.7	176.2	185.0
4th quarter	2 645.5	1 744.3	422.3	162.8	34.6	59.1	91.5	73.0	823.4	230.3	56.6	175.2	192.6
2006													
1st quarter	2 700.7	1 808.7	437.8	166.5	34.4	60.7	99.5	75.2	866.5	246.3	60.3	187.8	190.8
2nd quarter	2 676.8	1 831.3	450.9	171.9	36.8	59.6	100.8	80.1	869.6	247.6	62.8	185.9	202.6
3rd quarter	2 649.6	1 853.1	458.9	176.7	38.5	61.8	99.6	80.9	871.9	255.1	67.0	188.4	201.2
4th quarter	2 622.8	1 865.2	458.4	175.4	36.1	64.7	98.1	82.6	875.2	254.7	67.2	187.9	201.7
2007													
1st quarter	2 618.2	1 897.2	474.8	183.8	37.3	72.6	97.7	82.4	886.1	270.6	71.1	200.0	197.7
2nd quarter	2 624.9	1 934.4	500.6	189.7	39.4	82.3	98.3	90.2	896.2	272.7	69.8	203.8	210.6
3rd quarter	2 609.0	1 964.4	524.0	192.8	46.2	90.6	98.6	95.5	900.9	279.5	72.6	207.7	211.7
4th quarter	2 586.3	1 997.6	536.8	193.2	49.7	98.2	96.9	98.9	910.0	296.7	77.5	220.0	201.2
2008													
1st quarter	2 539.1	1 998.1	539.0	191.3	50.0	100.2	96.5	101.0	899.4	294.6	81.1	213.8	201.0
2nd quarter	2 503.4	1 986.6	547.7	188.9	53.8	95.4	103.4	105.6	876.6	294.1	81.9	212.4	199.4
3rd quarter	2 424.1	1 933.0	543.7	183.3	55.1	90.0	108.7	105.7	831.6	281.2	76.3	205.2	195.6
4th quarter	2 263.8	1 820.1	530.3	167.8	56.3	92.2	111.4	101.4	736.8	254.1	68.9	185.4	186.0
2009													
1st quarter	2 089.3	1 688.3	490.5	146.2	61.5	93.8	96.7	92.0	653.9	245.6	69.9	175.8	161.0
2nd quarter	2 011.0	1 634.0	453.3	133.1	60.1	96.3	73.6	90.3	631.6	246.4	73.2	173.1	152.5
3rd quarter	2 008.4	1 613.1	422.6	120.1	55.1	100.9	63.9	82.6	639.9	261.4	77.5	183.9	148.5
4th quarter	1 994.1	1 598.4	386.5	107.4	48.5	92.0	65.7	73.1	651.9	270.9	86.5	184.5	146.3
2010													
1st quarter	1 997.9	1 615.0	359.7	99.7	46.2	72.7	76.5	65.0	697.7	276.0	87.6	188.5	143.0
2nd quarter	2 062.8	1 659.3	369.8	95.6	44.2	80.4	86.8	62.9	735.2	277.8	86.4	191.5	151.1
3rd quarter	2 060.8	1 692.8	364.4	93.1	38.8	78.3	93.1	60.9	766.2	282.5	83.0	199.5	152.8
4th quarter	2 103.1	1 728.1	371.2	92.4	34.1	90.0	94.7	59.0	787.8	289.5	81.6	207.7	158.3
2011													
1st quarter	2 098.4	1 724.1	343.0	89.5	33.1	67.9	99.6	53.2	810.6	279.8	76.9	202.5	171.8
2nd quarter	2 140.2	1 761.0	366.7	93.9	37.6	73.3	105.9	56.2	819.3	286.6	83.5	203.0	174.1
3rd quarter	2 227.5	1 840.8	388.2	97.1	42.0	77.7	114.5	56.9	871.0	288.9	86.7	202.2	188.2
4th quarter	2 280.6	1 883.1	400.9	98.2	43.8	77.3	123.6	58.3	890.8	288.2	84.7	203.4	198.9
2012													
1st quarter	2 360.4	1 938.1	419.5	100.7	42.8	89.4	126.8	59.1	924.4	304.6	91.0	213.6	197.0
2nd quarter	2 399.8	1 973.7	429.9	103.0	44.7	91.8	128.1	61.6	944.0	302.2	89.0	213.1	203.0
3rd quarter	2 400.4	1 963.4	425.5	104.3	45.5	90.4	122.3	62.7	936.0	297.3	83.1	213.8	197.5
4th quarter	2 441.0	1 981.4	417.5	103.2	46.6	87.1	118.1	62.5	952.6	308.2	90.7	217.4	201.7
2013													
1st quarter	2 470.6	2 000.7	411.0	105.1	46.2	74.8	123.5	62.5	967.4	315.3	93.2	222.1	198.5
2nd quarter	2 486.3	2 005.7	422.6	103.1	44.4	81.5	129.1	64.8	965.3	312.8	89.3	223.2	193.9
3rd quarter	2 509.5	2 023.1	440.4	105.9	48.5	89.6	130.7	65.5	956.0	317.0	91.6	225.2	194.7
4th quarter	2 541.0	2 065.5	444.7	111.7	47.9	96.5	123.6	64.6	989.3	312.5	93.7	218.8	192.0
2014													
1st quarter	2 578.3	2 106.9	464.6	112.1	48.2	109.7	129.2	64.2	997.9	316.2	87.2	228.5	202.2
2nd quarter	2 613.4	2 129.8	464.4	116.2	48.3	97.2	136.7	65.9	1 013.7	329.0	89.3	239.0	209.2
3rd quarter	2 663.5	2 176.3	462.3	122.3	52.6	84.7	136.8	66.9	1 053.1	322.8	90.1	232.2	213.5
4th quarter	2 679.7	2 180.0	467.1	130.5	58.9	72.0	137.3	70.7	1 040.0	337.6	89.3	247.5	210.8

[1]See notes and definitions.

Table 5-3. Real Gross Private Fixed Investment by Type—*Continued*

(Billions of chained [2009] dollars, quarterly data are at seasonally adjusted annual rates.)

NIPA Table 5.3.6

Year and quarter	Equipment—*Continued*		Intellectual property				Total	Residential structures		Permanent site			Other residential structures	Residential equipment
	Transportation equipment	Other nonresidential equipment	Total	Software [2]	Research and development [3]	Entertainment, literary, and artistic originals		Total	Total	Total	Single family	Multifamily		
1999	208.4	161.4	391.1	154.5	183.9	55.9	633.8	626.5	357.7	311.2	43.6	269.4	7.2
2000	204.1	170.5	426.1	175.9	193.0	59.3	637.9	630.1	360.6	314.6	42.8	270.1	7.6
2001	184.9	169.2	428.0	177.1	195.6	57.5	643.7	635.7	362.7	315.1	44.7	273.5	7.8
2002	167.2	167.9	425.9	176.9	190.5	60.3	682.7	674.5	377.3	327.3	47.1	297.2	8.0
2003	154.8	179.3	442.2	189.0	189.1	64.8	744.5	735.9	414.2	362.2	48.3	321.9	8.5
2004	176.5	192.4	464.9	207.9	191.0	65.8	818.9	809.2	462.2	405.7	52.0	347.6	9.5
2005	197.9	210.9	495.0	221.2	202.3	71.3	872.6	862.5	494.8	433.0	57.2	368.3	9.9
2006	212.6	219.6	517.5	230.3	215.0	72.1	806.6	796.3	451.6	390.7	57.6	345.2	10.1
2007	203.6	217.0	542.4	244.2	227.9	70.3	654.8	644.9	336.1	283.7	51.0	309.3	9.8
2008	156.9	206.5	558.8	256.2	235.5	67.1	497.7	488.4	223.1	178.2	44.9	265.6	9.3
2009	70.6	165.6	550.9	256.8	229.0	65.1	392.2	383.9	133.9	105.3	28.5	250.1	8.3
2010	136.9	179.8	561.3	254.2	234.4	72.7	382.4	373.6	128.5	114.4	14.3	245.1	8.8
2011	183.0	199.3	581.3	271.8	236.7	73.1	384.5	375.3	123.9	109.2	15.0	251.3	9.2
2012	218.9	221.7	603.8	286.6	242.9	74.8	436.5	427.1	153.8	132.1	21.9	273.4	9.4
2013	243.1	222.8	626.9	295.8	255.3	76.0	478.0	467.9	191.6	161.9	29.8	276.9	10.1
2014	271.8	224.8	659.5	315.0	266.8	78.2	486.4	475.8	209.1	170.9	38.6	267.4	10.6
2005													
1st quarter	189.7	203.7	487.0	216.6	200.6	69.7	856.4	846.4	483.4	423.4	55.4	363.6	9.7
2nd quarter	196.7	212.2	495.0	221.8	202.1	70.9	872.3	862.2	491.5	429.8	57.3	371.3	9.8
3rd quarter	206.9	213.0	499.9	223.1	204.9	71.8	881.9	871.8	498.0	435.4	58.2	374.4	9.8
4th quarter	198.4	214.9	498.0	223.3	201.6	72.9	879.9	869.6	506.2	443.5	58.1	364.0	10.1
2006													
1st quarter	219.6	221.9	503.8	225.7	205.2	72.6	871.7	861.1	504.4	441.8	58.0	357.4	10.3
2nd quarter	209.9	221.5	511.0	228.1	210.6	72.2	827.8	817.5	470.2	408.9	57.5	347.9	10.1
3rd quarter	209.0	217.2	522.9	231.7	219.6	71.7	781.6	771.4	433.7	374.2	56.6	338.1	10.0
4th quarter	211.8	217.7	532.1	235.9	224.7	71.7	745.2	735.2	398.0	337.8	58.3	337.6	9.8
2007													
1st quarter	212.8	213.2	537.0	241.5	224.7	70.8	711.2	701.1	371.9	313.7	56.6	329.7	9.9
2nd quarter	201.8	219.5	538.9	242.2	226.2	70.5	682.7	672.8	355.2	301.4	52.0	318.1	9.8
3rd quarter	199.2	217.9	541.1	244.7	225.9	70.5	639.2	629.4	328.0	277.7	48.8	301.8	9.7
4th quarter	200.5	217.4	552.4	248.3	234.7	69.4	586.1	576.4	289.4	241.8	46.7	287.5	9.7
2008													
1st quarter	198.5	211.1	561.2	256.0	236.6	68.6	540.0	530.5	255.7	209.4	46.0	275.2	9.5
2nd quarter	175.8	211.8	563.3	257.0	238.6	67.7	516.3	506.7	239.5	193.0	46.4	267.6	9.6
3rd quarter	147.7	210.6	558.2	257.7	234.2	66.3	490.9	481.7	213.5	168.2	45.3	268.4	9.2
4th quarter	105.5	192.7	552.5	254.2	232.7	65.6	443.6	434.9	183.9	142.2	41.8	251.0	8.6
2009													
1st quarter	68.6	178.8	543.6	252.8	226.2	64.6	401.0	392.6	147.0	109.5	37.6	245.6	8.4
2nd quarter	67.2	165.5	549.4	255.2	229.1	65.1	377.0	368.8	124.5	93.1	31.4	244.4	8.1
3rd quarter	70.0	159.9	550.9	257.7	228.4	64.7	395.4	387.1	132.1	106.8	25.3	255.0	8.3
4th quarter	76.5	158.2	559.8	261.4	232.3	66.1	395.7	387.2	131.9	112.0	20.0	255.3	8.4
2010													
1st quarter	109.7	170.7	557.6	256.0	232.7	68.9	383.0	374.4	131.3	115.7	15.8	243.1	8.6
2nd quarter	130.9	177.8	554.7	250.9	231.5	72.3	403.5	394.6	135.5	121.7	14.1	259.1	8.9
3rd quarter	152.0	182.2	563.0	253.3	235.6	74.0	368.1	359.3	126.0	112.6	13.7	233.3	8.8
4th quarter	155.1	188.3	570.0	256.7	237.8	75.4	375.1	366.2	121.2	107.7	13.8	245.0	8.9
2011													
1st quarter	168.1	194.4	571.9	262.2	236.5	73.2	374.4	365.4	121.6	108.2	13.6	243.7	9.1
2nd quarter	167.1	194.9	576.3	268.4	235.7	72.4	379.3	370.2	121.1	107.2	14.1	249.0	9.2
3rd quarter	188.5	209.0	583.5	275.2	235.9	72.8	386.8	377.5	124.9	109.5	15.6	252.6	9.3
4th quarter	208.5	199.0	593.3	281.2	238.6	74.0	397.6	388.2	128.1	111.8	16.5	260.1	9.4
2012													
1st quarter	213.9	213.4	596.1	282.3	239.6	74.7	422.5	413.1	138.7	120.6	18.3	274.4	9.4
2nd quarter	220.7	222.2	601.7	286.4	241.1	74.8	426.3	417.1	146.9	126.3	20.9	270.2	9.2
3rd quarter	217.6	227.4	603.7	286.4	243.1	74.7	437.3	427.9	157.4	134.5	23.0	270.7	9.3
4th quarter	223.5	223.8	613.8	291.5	247.7	75.1	459.8	450.2	172.3	147.0	25.5	278.2	9.5
2013													
1st quarter	228.5	230.1	625.3	296.7	253.5	75.5	469.9	460.0	183.5	156.3	27.4	276.9	9.9
2nd quarter	244.0	220.3	620.3	290.5	254.0	75.9	480.3	470.3	191.6	163.2	28.7	279.1	10.0
3rd quarter	239.6	210.7	628.3	296.2	256.4	75.9	486.0	475.8	195.2	165.4	30.1	281.1	10.2
4th quarter	260.4	230.0	633.7	299.9	257.4	76.6	475.9	465.7	195.9	162.9	33.2	270.3	10.2
2014													
1st quarter	258.5	226.3	645.7	305.8	262.8	77.3	472.6	462.3	200.5	166.5	34.2	262.5	10.3
2nd quarter	261.7	219.8	653.4	311.6	264.5	77.8	484.4	473.8	207.0	169.7	37.7	267.5	10.6
3rd quarter	286.5	235.4	663.8	319.1	267.1	78.3	488.5	477.8	208.4	168.8	40.1	270.1	10.7
4th quarter	280.4	217.9	675.0	323.4	272.8	79.2	500.2	489.3	220.7	178.6	42.6	269.4	10.9

[2]Excludes software "embedded," or bundled, in computers and other equipment.
[3]Excludes software development.

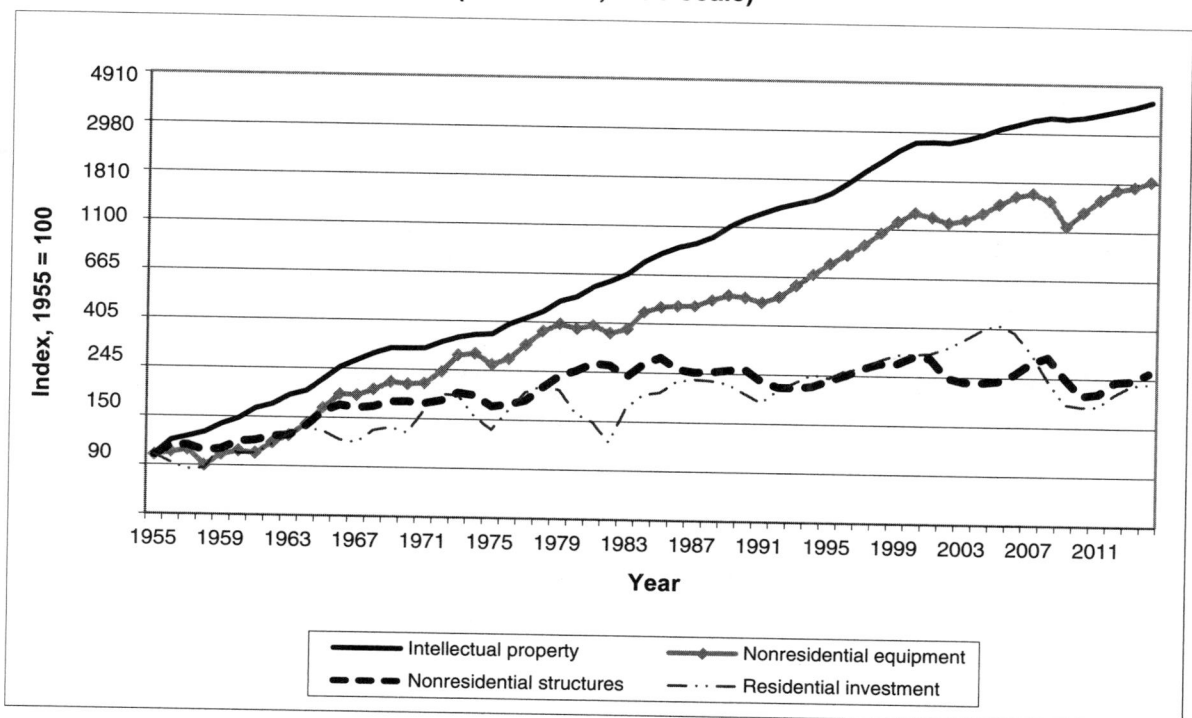

Figure 5-2: Real Private Fixed Investment by Major Type, 1955–2014
(1995 = 100, ratio scale)

- Between 1955 and 2006, which was the recent high point for total real (constant-dollar) investment, the quantity of real gross private fixed investment increased eightfold, with an average annual growth rate of 4.2 percent. Every major type of investment grew in real terms between those two years, but as Figure 5-2 indicates, by far the fastest-growing major category has been "intellectual property products." Computer software is the main driver of growth in this category, but it also includes research and development and "entertainment, literary, and artistic originals." (Table 5-4)

- Between 2006 and 2009, overall gross investment fell 24 percent in real terms—a collapse unprecedented in the postwar period. By 2014, gross investment nearly regained the 2006 level, only 1.1 percent below the all-time high of 131.4 (Table 5-4)

- Intellectual property investment barely hesitated in 2009 and went on to new record peaks in each following year. Equipment purchases regained their previous high in 2012 and went on to a new record in 2014. But in 2014, spending on both nonresidential and especially residential structures remained well below earlier levels. (Table 5-4)

Table 5-4. Chain-Type Quantity Indexes for Private Fixed Investment by Type

(Index numbers, 2009 = 100, quarterly data are seasonally adjusted.)   **NIPA Table 5.3.3**

Year and quarter	Total gross private fixed investment	Nonresidential											
		Total	Structures						Equipment				
			Total	Commercial and health care	Manufacturing	Power and communication	Mining exploration, shafts, and wells	Other nonresidential structures	Total	Information processing equipment			Industrial equipment
										Total	Computers and peripheral equipment[1]	Other information processing	
1955	16.4	10.4	40.7	29.5	42.7	29.9	84.6	43.9	8.7	0.2	...	2.8	37.0
1956	16.6	11.1	45.0	33.3	56.1	35.0	81.8	43.4	8.9	0.3	...	3.2	40.8
1957	16.5	11.3	45.0	31.6	59.5	36.3	77.2	43.4	9.1	0.3	...	3.7	41.3
1958	15.5	10.3	42.5	33.3	41.0	34.9	72.2	45.4	7.8	0.3	...	3.3	34.4
1959	17.6	11.1	43.5	36.1	36.6	33.5	74.1	50.2	8.7	0.3	0.0	3.6	35.0
1960	17.8	11.7	47.0	38.4	49.6	33.8	69.6	55.7	9.1	0.4	0.0	4.1	37.7
1961	17.9	11.8	47.6	43.8	48.5	31.6	70.9	54.4	8.9	0.4	0.0	4.4	35.7
1962	19.4	12.7	49.8	48.9	49.0	31.8	74.3	55.6	9.9	0.5	0.0	4.6	37.5
1963	20.9	13.5	50.4	47.3	49.2	34.0	69.8	58.8	10.7	0.5	0.0	4.8	40.5
1964	22.8	14.9	55.6	51.4	59.1	37.0	74.8	64.4	12.0	0.6	0.0	5.3	45.8
1965	25.2	17.4	64.5	60.3	81.7	40.9	73.8	72.5	14.2	0.7	0.0	6.0	54.0
1966	26.8	19.6	68.9	58.9	101.6	46.7	70.0	75.2	16.4	0.9	0.0	7.0	62.1
1967	26.5	19.5	67.2	56.6	89.4	51.1	66.9	73.6	16.2	1.0	0.0	7.0	62.4
1968	28.4	20.4	68.1	61.9	86.0	56.7	67.3	65.0	17.2	1.0	0.0	7.2	61.1
1969	30.0	21.8	71.8	71.5	90.5	56.7	70.1	64.5	18.6	1.2	0.0	8.4	65.2
1970	29.4	21.7	72.0	72.4	87.4	62.1	66.0	60.6	18.3	1.4	0.0	9.0	66.1
1971	31.4	21.6	70.8	79.1	72.1	62.6	61.1	56.8	18.4	1.4	0.0	9.1	60.7
1972	35.0	23.5	73.0	86.4	63.0	65.3	65.5	57.5	20.8	1.6	0.0	9.7	65.5
1973	38.0	26.6	79.0	90.3	78.1	69.4	69.9	61.9	24.6	2.0	0.0	11.7	77.4
1974	35.9	26.9	77.3	84.7	89.0	65.0	83.1	56.6	25.2	2.2	0.0	13.0	83.3
1975	32.4	24.4	69.2	66.0	85.3	59.9	97.1	49.9	22.5	2.2	0.0	12.5	70.7
1976	35.6	25.8	70.8	65.1	78.8	65.3	104.8	52.4	23.9	2.5	0.0	13.7	71.0
1977	40.4	28.6	73.7	68.5	80.9	64.3	118.3	55.3	27.6	3.1	0.1	16.4	75.3
1978	45.1	32.6	84.4	78.1	107.9	67.4	134.9	62.8	31.8	4.0	0.1	19.6	83.7
1979	47.7	35.8	95.1	93.1	132.6	70.0	143.7	69.0	34.4	4.9	0.2	22.0	89.7
1980	44.9	35.8	100.7	102.4	110.9	70.6	201.9	67.0	32.9	5.7	0.3	23.7	85.9
1981	46.1	38.0	108.7	110.8	125.9	72.4	234.7	64.9	34.1	6.6	0.4	25.0	84.5
1982	43.0	36.6	106.9	120.7	121.6	68.4	217.0	61.2	31.5	6.6	0.4	25.2	77.2
1983	46.2	36.5	95.4	117.1	87.9	58.8	179.6	64.6	33.0	7.7	0.6	26.5	71.1
1984	53.7	42.6	108.7	142.6	91.0	60.1	204.2	75.7	39.4	9.8	1.0	30.1	81.3
1985	56.6	45.4	116.4	164.6	101.8	59.4	182.0	83.3	41.5	10.7	1.2	31.1	85.1
1986	57.7	44.6	103.7	152.9	85.5	63.4	106.6	78.3	42.0	11.5	1.4	32.4	84.7
1987	58.0	44.6	100.7	147.4	83.3	56.4	104.2	82.9	42.1	12.0	1.8	31.1	82.6
1988	59.9	46.9	101.3	151.8	87.9	53.2	114.3	77.3	44.9	13.1	2.0	33.2	86.7
1989	61.8	49.5	103.3	149.8	105.4	55.3	103.4	78.9	47.3	14.4	2.5	34.7	92.8
1990	61.0	50.1	104.9	143.9	119.3	51.4	119.5	83.8	46.3	14.6	2.5	35.6	87.4
1991	57.8	48.1	93.2	111.8	109.9	61.1	116.8	72.7	44.2	14.9	2.7	35.4	81.8
1992	61.0	49.5	87.6	103.9	100.9	64.7	96.7	67.4	46.8	17.0	3.7	37.5	83.3
1993	65.7	53.2	87.3	108.1	79.3	61.7	112.4	72.7	52.8	19.4	4.7	40.4	90.4
1994	71.0	57.4	88.9	113.1	93.8	56.0	109.2	71.1	59.2	22.0	5.8	44.2	98.4
1995	75.4	63.0	94.6	119.8	110.6	57.1	92.7	79.6	66.4	26.5	8.8	47.5	108.0
1996	82.1	68.7	100.0	129.1	116.3	49.1	98.8	93.6	72.7	32.1	12.7	52.1	112.0
1997	89.1	76.1	107.3	142.6	111.1	47.4	116.2	106.2	80.8	38.7	18.4	56.6	114.5
1998	98.2	84.3	112.8	151.5	114.8	55.6	101.6	112.0	91.4	47.8	26.7	63.7	119.4
1999	106.9	92.4	112.9	157.0	95.8	65.6	86.0	112.1	102.8	58.4	38.0	71.0	120.2
2000	114.3	100.9	121.7	167.6	98.8	75.7	107.4	115.4	112.8	70.4	46.1	85.4	130.6
2001	112.6	98.5	119.9	159.4	96.0	78.0	126.6	110.1	108.0	69.6	47.2	82.8	120.9
2002	108.7	91.7	98.7	135.0	56.1	76.1	92.6	93.0	102.1	66.3	49.5	75.3	112.8
2003	113.0	93.4	94.9	126.5	51.9	70.1	105.8	89.5	105.4	72.5	54.4	82.2	113.3
2004	120.6	98.3	94.5	129.6	53.5	58.6	112.3	90.8	113.5	79.9	61.0	89.7	111.2
2005	128.9	105.1	96.1	128.5	60.8	60.7	122.9	86.0	124.4	86.8	67.9	96.3	120.7
2006	131.4	112.6	103.0	136.3	64.8	64.4	132.7	94.3	135.2	98.0	83.8	104.6	130.9
2007	128.8	119.3	116.2	149.9	76.6	89.7	130.6	108.6	139.4	109.3	94.7	115.9	135.0
2008	120.1	118.4	123.3	144.3	95.6	98.6	140.1	122.4	129.8	109.7	100.4	113.9	128.5
2009	100.0	100.0	100.0	100.0	100.0	100.0	100.0	100.0	100.0	100.0	100.0	100.0	100.0
2010	101.5	102.5	83.6	75.1	72.5	83.9	117.1	73.3	115.9	109.9	110.3	109.8	99.5
2011	107.9	110.3	85.5	74.7	69.5	77.3	147.9	66.5	131.6	111.6	108.1	113.1	120.5
2012	118.5	120.2	96.6	81.1	79.7	93.6	165.2	72.8	145.8	118.3	115.2	119.6	131.4
2013	123.5	123.9	98.1	84.0	83.1	89.4	169.0	76.2	150.5	122.8	119.8	124.0	128.1
2014	130.0	131.5	106.0	95.0	92.4	94.9	180.1	79.2	159.3	127.5	115.9	132.1	137.4
2012													
1st quarter	116.5	118.7	95.7	79.5	76.0	93.3	169.2	70.0	143.5	118.9	118.5	119.1	129.5
2nd quarter	118.5	120.8	98.1	81.3	79.4	95.8	170.8	72.9	146.5	118.0	115.9	118.8	133.5
3rd quarter	118.5	120.2	97.1	82.3	80.8	94.4	163.2	74.2	145.3	116.1	108.3	119.2	129.9
4th quarter	120.5	121.3	95.3	81.5	82.7	90.9	157.6	74.0	147.9	120.3	118.1	121.3	132.6
2013													
1st quarter	122.0	122.5	93.8	82.9	82.0	78.1	164.7	73.9	150.1	123.1	121.4	123.9	130.5
2nd quarter	122.7	122.8	96.4	81.4	78.9	85.1	172.2	76.7	149.8	122.1	116.3	124.5	127.5
3rd quarter	123.9	123.9	100.5	83.6	86.2	93.6	174.3	77.5	148.4	123.8	119.3	125.6	128.0
4th quarter	125.4	126.5	101.5	88.2	85.1	100.8	164.9	76.5	153.5	122.0	122.1	122.0	126.3
2014													
1st quarter	127.3	129.0	106.0	88.5	85.6	114.6	172.4	75.9	154.9	123.5	113.6	127.5	133.0
2nd quarter	129.0	130.4	106.0	91.7	85.9	101.5	182.4	77.9	157.3	128.5	116.3	133.3	137.6
3rd quarter	131.5	133.2	105.5	96.5	93.4	88.5	182.4	79.2	163.4	126.0	117.4	129.5	140.4
4th quarter	132.3	133.5	106.6	103.0	104.6	75.1	183.1	83.7	161.4	131.8	116.3	138.0	138.6

[1]See notes and definitions.
. . . = Not available.

Table 5-4. Chain-Type Quantity Indexes for Private Fixed Investment by Type—*Continued*

(Index numbers, 2009 = 100, quarterly data are seasonally adjusted.)   **NIPA Table 5.3.3**

Year and quarter	Nonresidential—Continued						Residential						
	Equipment—Continued		Intellectual property				Total	Residential structures					Residential equipment
								Total	Permanent site			Other residential structures	
	Transportation equipment	Other nonresidential equipment	Total	Software 2	Research and development 3	Entertainment, literary, and artistic originals			Total	Single family	Multifamily		
1955	54.1	26.3	2.9	...	6.2	17.1	53.1	55.0	123.1	...	...	20.2	8.9
1956	48.6	27.1	3.4	...	7.9	16.8	48.9	50.5	106.6	...	...	21.6	9.9
1957	52.0	25.7	3.5	...	8.0	18.0	46.0	47.4	96.9	...	...	21.9	9.9
1958	37.9	26.0	3.6	...	8.5	18.4	46.5	47.9	99.4	103.2	77.8	21.4	10.5
1959	50.2	28.0	4.0	0.0	9.2	20.3	58.1	60.0	126.6	131.3	100.0	25.8	12.1
1960	51.8	25.7	4.2	0.0	10.1	18.9	54.2	55.9	111.8	116.1	88.0	26.9	11.3
1961	48.9	25.4	4.7	0.0	10.7	22.8	54.4	56.1	111.2	110.0	110.9	27.5	11.4
1962	60.3	27.1	4.9	0.1	11.6	21.9	59.6	61.5	126.8	117.3	161.3	27.9	12.0
1963	58.4	31.5	5.4	0.1	12.5	23.5	66.6	68.8	143.9	125.3	216.5	30.1	13.4
1964	66.1	34.9	5.6	0.2	13.4	22.3	70.6	72.9	153.6	137.4	215.0	31.4	14.4
1965	82.8	38.8	6.3	0.2	15.0	24.8	68.8	70.8	146.9	134.3	193.3	31.6	16.1
1966	91.0	43.6	7.2	0.3	16.8	27.0	63.0	64.7	128.9	119.6	162.0	31.5	16.5
1967	88.0	41.2	7.7	0.4	18.5	26.8	61.4	63.0	122.8	117.2	140.7	31.9	16.9
1968	105.8	41.7	8.3	0.4	20.0	28.1	69.7	71.4	144.3	128.9	203.3	33.7	20.1
1969	110.0	44.5	8.8	0.6	21.3	26.5	71.9	73.5	148.5	122.3	252.9	34.7	22.9
1970	90.3	46.5	8.8	0.7	21.4	23.2	68.1	69.4	134.3	106.3	247.6	35.6	25.0
1971	97.5	46.3	8.8	0.7	21.4	22.9	86.2	88.2	181.0	147.6	315.1	40.3	28.0
1972	113.3	52.5	9.4	0.9	22.4	24.6	101.2	103.4	219.0	175.4	394.5	44.1	33.6
1973	136.2	61.3	9.9	1.0	23.9	23.6	100.6	102.5	218.0	171.6	405.6	43.2	37.8
1974	123.3	60.6	10.2	1.2	24.0	23.9	80.8	81.9	157.7	131.7	261.1	42.6	38.5
1975	106.2	56.1	10.2	1.4	23.6	23.1	71.1	71.9	120.7	120.2	116.5	46.0	35.8
1976	118.1	56.5	11.4	1.5	25.1	29.4	86.8	88.1	158.7	167.4	112.8	51.2	37.7
1977	143.6	63.6	12.1	1.5	26.4	32.8	104.6	106.4	204.8	215.1	149.6	55.5	41.3
1978	158.7	70.1	13.0	1.8	28.5	32.2	111.6	113.5	214.2	222.2	168.5	61.3	44.9
1979	165.6	71.4	14.5	2.3	30.6	37.0	107.4	108.9	200.4	196.9	205.8	61.4	49.2
1980	135.2	64.2	15.2	2.7	32.7	33.5	84.9	85.7	140.8	129.4	184.3	56.5	49.2
1981	131.5	65.9	16.9	3.1	34.8	40.5	77.9	78.4	129.9	117.8	177.2	51.3	49.2
1982	116.5	57.0	17.9	3.6	36.6	40.8	63.8	63.9	101.2	90.3	144.5	44.1	47.2
1983	131.2	55.0	19.3	4.3	38.6	43.0	90.6	91.4	165.4	156.8	197.8	52.8	52.7
1984	156.3	62.3	22.0	5.4	42.6	47.9	104.0	105.0	194.3	181.9	241.7	58.6	58.5
1985	162.4	62.8	23.9	6.4	46.3	47.7	106.4	107.2	191.8	180.4	235.5	63.1	63.1
1986	156.2	61.7	25.6	7.2	48.2	52.7	119.6	120.6	214.1	206.5	242.5	71.8	68.2
1987	148.5	63.4	26.6	8.2	49.1	51.8	121.9	123.0	217.0	223.1	191.3	73.7	71.0
1988	157.2	66.5	28.5	9.7	51.1	52.3	120.8	121.7	209.2	220.4	163.2	75.7	73.4
1989	141.8	74.2	31.8	12.5	54.4	54.7	116.9	117.7	204.0	214.0	162.8	72.4	73.8
1990	139.9	71.4	34.5	14.8	57.3	56.6	107.0	107.5	184.3	194.5	142.1	67.1	71.6
1991	136.0	61.0	36.7	16.7	59.9	57.2	97.5	97.8	158.6	170.5	109.5	65.3	68.8
1992	139.1	60.7	38.9	19.7	60.0	60.0	110.9	111.6	185.0	207.0	93.0	72.6	70.9
1993	165.8	66.5	40.6	22.0	59.7	63.3	120.0	120.9	197.5	226.7	75.0	80.0	72.3
1994	194.3	71.8	42.2	24.2	59.7	66.6	130.7	131.9	221.1	250.9	96.9	84.7	72.8
1995	209.0	75.7	45.3	26.6	62.7	72.1	126.3	127.3	206.5	227.8	120.1	85.1	73.8
1996	215.9	78.6	50.4	31.2	68.2	77.3	136.6	138.0	225.9	248.8	132.8	91.1	73.4
1997	231.5	86.2	57.0	40.4	72.1	79.6	139.9	141.4	227.1	248.0	143.1	95.5	72.8
1998	250.3	95.0	63.1	48.8	75.7	83.4	152.0	153.6	248.7	275.1	141.5	102.8	77.9
1999	295.3	97.5	71.0	60.2	80.3	85.9	161.6	163.2	267.2	295.4	152.7	107.7	86.1
2000	289.3	102.9	77.3	68.5	84.3	91.0	162.6	164.1	269.3	298.7	150.1	108.0	91.6
2001	262.1	102.2	77.7	69.0	85.4	88.2	164.1	165.6	270.9	299.1	156.6	109.4	93.3
2002	237.0	101.4	77.3	68.9	83.2	92.6	174.0	175.7	281.8	310.7	164.9	118.9	96.1
2003	219.4	108.3	80.3	73.6	82.6	99.6	189.8	191.7	309.4	343.8	169.2	128.7	102.0
2004	250.1	116.2	84.4	81.0	83.4	101.1	208.8	210.8	345.2	385.1	182.4	139.0	113.7
2005	280.5	127.4	89.8	86.1	88.3	109.5	222.5	224.7	369.6	411.1	200.6	147.3	118.7
2006	301.3	132.6	93.9	89.7	93.9	110.7	205.6	207.4	337.3	370.9	201.9	138.1	121.0
2007	288.5	131.0	98.4	95.1	99.5	108.0	166.9	168.0	251.1	269.3	178.8	123.7	117.5
2008	222.3	124.7	101.4	99.8	102.8	103.0	126.9	127.2	166.7	169.2	157.2	106.2	111.3
2009	100.0	100.0	100.0	100.0	100.0	100.0	100.0	100.0	100.0	100.0	100.0	100.0	100.0
2010	194.0	108.6	101.9	99.0	102.4	111.6	97.5	97.3	96.0	108.6	50.2	98.0	106.0
2011	259.4	120.4	105.5	105.8	103.3	112.3	98.0	97.8	92.6	103.6	52.4	100.5	111.0
2012	310.2	133.9	109.6	111.6	106.0	114.9	111.3	111.2	114.9	125.4	76.9	109.3	112.6
2013	344.6	134.5	113.8	115.2	111.5	116.6	121.9	121.9	143.1	153.7	104.6	110.7	120.9
2014	385.1	135.8	119.7	122.7	116.5	120.0	124.0	123.9	156.2	162.2	135.4	106.9	127.7
2012													
1st quarter	303.1	128.9	108.2	109.9	104.6	114.7	107.7	107.6	103.6	114.5	64.2	109.7	112.6
2nd quarter	312.8	134.2	109.2	111.5	105.3	114.8	108.7	108.6	109.8	119.9	73.1	108.1	111.2
3rd quarter	308.4	137.3	109.6	111.5	106.1	114.7	111.5	111.5	117.5	127.7	80.7	108.3	112.4
4th quarter	316.7	135.2	111.4	113.5	108.1	115.3	117.2	117.3	128.7	139.5	89.5	111.3	114.4
2013													
1st quarter	323.8	139.0	113.5	115.5	110.7	115.9	119.8	119.8	137.1	148.4	96.2	110.7	118.6
2nd quarter	345.8	133.0	112.6	113.1	110.9	116.6	122.5	122.5	143.1	154.9	100.5	111.6	119.9
3rd quarter	339.6	127.2	114.0	115.4	111.9	116.5	123.9	123.9	145.8	157.0	105.3	112.4	122.2
4th quarter	369.1	138.9	115.0	116.8	112.4	117.6	121.3	121.3	146.3	154.7	116.3	108.1	123.1
2014													
1st quarter	366.4	136.6	117.2	119.1	114.8	118.7	120.5	120.4	149.7	158.1	120.0	105.0	123.6
2nd quarter	370.8	132.7	118.6	121.3	115.5	119.4	123.5	123.4	154.6	161.1	132.0	107.0	127.7
3rd quarter	406.0	142.1	120.5	124.3	116.6	120.2	124.5	124.5	155.7	160.3	140.3	108.0	128.5
4th quarter	397.4	131.6	122.5	126.0	119.1	121.6	127.5	127.5	164.8	169.5	149.1	107.8	131.0

2Excludes software "embedded," or bundled, in computers and other equipment.
3Excludes software development.
. . . = Not available.

Table 5-5A. Current-Cost Net Stock of Fixed Assets: Recent Data

(Billions of dollars, year-end estimates.)

Year	Total	Private						Government							
		Total	Nonresidential				Resi-dential	Total	Nonresidential				Resi-dential	Federal	State and local
			Total	Equip-ment	Struc-tures	Intellec-tual property products			Total	Equip-ment	Struc-tures	Intellect-ual property products			
1950	871.9	655.2	335.4	98.8	223.7	12.8	319.9	216.7	210.4	39.1	163.5	7.7	6.4	107.5	109.2
1951	957.7	713.3	365.7	109.1	243.0	13.6	347.6	244.4	236.5	43.0	184.8	8.8	7.9	120.0	122.9
1952	1 012.5	751.3	385.8	114.9	256.3	14.6	365.6	261.2	253.8	49.4	194.7	9.6	7.4	127.0	130.2
1953	1 051.6	782.7	403.2	124.4	262.6	16.2	379.5	268.9	261.0	56.3	194.2	10.5	7.8	135.1	128.8
1954	1 099.4	814.7	414.5	128.2	268.6	17.7	400.2	284.8	274.3	62.9	199.7	11.6	10.5	138.7	134.5
1955	1 196.3	888.2	456.6	141.2	295.8	19.6	431.7	308.1	300.5	68.3	218.9	13.3	7.6	148.1	149.4
1956	1 301.0	957.9	505.0	158.6	324.4	22.1	452.9	343.1	334.2	72.4	245.9	15.9	8.9	159.1	169.4
1957	1 368.6	1 008.3	540.1	172.9	342.8	24.4	468.2	360.3	350.9	74.7	257.2	19.0	9.4	168.5	177.6
1958	1 414.8	1 033.4	550.9	178.0	346.4	26.4	482.6	381.4	371.2	76.2	272.9	22.1	10.2	172.6	189.7
1959	1 471.3	1 077.5	573.5	186.6	357.9	29.0	504.0	393.8	382.7	80.5	277.2	24.9	11.1	180.2	196.0
1960	1 521.4	1 110.5	586.4	192.7	362.6	31.2	524.0	410.9	399.2	83.5	287.6	28.1	11.7	185.4	205.5
1961	1 581.3	1 147.1	603.9	196.1	374.1	33.7	543.3	434.2	421.6	87.5	302.6	31.5	12.5	188.4	217.9
1962	1 653.5	1 189.9	626.3	203.7	386.8	35.9	563.5	463.6	450.2	94.5	320.4	35.3	13.4	194.7	233.3
1963	1 717.0	1 228.2	650.2	212.3	399.0	38.9	578.1	488.7	475.0	96.6	337.8	40.6	13.7	204.8	248.7
1964	1 829.9	1 313.4	688.9	224.9	422.1	41.9	624.6	516.5	501.9	98.7	356.9	46.3	14.6	215.4	265.4
1965	1 953.8	1 402.4	738.4	242.5	450.1	45.8	664.0	551.4	536.1	100.4	383.6	52.2	15.3	227.9	288.9
1966	2 119.4	1 521.6	803.8	270.0	483.3	50.5	717.7	597.8	581.4	104.1	418.2	59.1	16.4	249.5	319.2
1967	2 284.0	1 636.0	870.7	296.2	518.2	56.3	765.3	648.0	630.7	109.9	454.3	66.6	17.3	271.9	348.8
1968	2 510.4	1 804.2	957.4	326.5	568.1	62.8	846.8	706.2	686.8	113.8	498.0	75.1	19.4	302.1	387.3
1969	2 742.0	1 962.3	1 055.3	360.1	624.7	70.5	907.0	779.7	758.1	117.4	555.9	84.8	21.6	329.7	437.4
1970	2 988.6	2 120.4	1 161.1	394.7	688.8	77.5	959.3	868.3	845.2	123.0	627.6	94.6	23.0	354.3	499.0
1971	3 293.2	2 352.1	1 274.6	422.5	769.6	82.5	1 077.5	941.1	915.3	124.0	688.7	102.6	25.8	377.9	550.1
1972	3 619.0	2 593.3	1 385.1	455.1	841.3	88.7	1 208.1	1 025.7	996.8	126.4	759.6	110.8	28.9	409.5	603.3
1973	4 102.1	2 946.4	1 560.1	507.1	954.6	98.4	1 386.3	1 155.7	1 123.0	130.5	868.9	123.6	32.7	454.0	692.2
1974	4 876.0	3 467.8	1 893.4	625.5	1 156.0	111.9	1 574.4	1 408.1	1 371.6	143.7	1 089.2	138.7	36.6	525.7	876.5
1975	5 267.8	3 785.6	2 083.1	716.2	1 245.4	121.5	1 702.5	1 482.3	1 442.2	157.4	1 135.4	149.5	40.1	578.0	918.2
1976	5 738.0	4 168.4	2 279.9	792.5	1 354.4	132.9	1 888.6	1 569.5	1 524.8	170.9	1 193.3	160.6	44.7	635.5	959.4
1977	6 408.3	4 735.4	2 532.4	891.6	1 494.9	145.8	2 203.0	1 672.9	1 621.5	188.2	1 259.4	173.8	51.5	705.1	1 026.0
1978	7 241.3	5 412.2	2 869.9	1 018.0	1 688.7	163.2	2 542.3	1 829.1	1 769.6	200.6	1 378.7	190.3	59.5	795.1	1 129.3
1979	8 343.6	6 264.0	3 313.6	1 181.9	1 944.9	186.8	2 950.3	2 079.7	2 008.9	216.5	1 579.4	213.0	70.8	895.7	1 299.2
1980	9 494.9	7 117.3	3 799.9	1 369.9	2 216.2	213.8	3 317.4	2 377.6	2 299.9	241.7	1 817.7	240.5	77.7	990.9	1 508.0
1981	10 476.9	7 859.9	4 299.9	1 528.4	2 526.5	244.9	3 560.0	2 617.0	2 531.9	271.0	1 991.3	269.6	85.1	1 060.8	1 671.8
1982	11 065.2	8 296.6	4 588.8	1 619.9	2 694.8	274.1	3 707.8	2 768.6	2 678.4	294.0	2 091.3	293.1	90.2	1 102.4	1 764.8
1983	11 448.5	8 599.0	4 744.4	1 670.5	2 769.8	304.1	3 854.6	2 849.6	2 748.8	322.1	2 110.4	316.4	100.7	1 175.0	1 788.5
1984	12 081.7	9 111.9	5 040.7	1 758.8	2 943.4	338.5	4 071.2	2 969.8	2 865.3	343.2	2 182.1	340.1	104.4	1 269.6	1 850.4
1985	12 723.9	9 618.4	5 332.1	1 858.0	3 101.5	372.6	4 286.3	3 105.5	2 999.9	362.3	2 273.9	363.6	105.6	1 377.0	1 935.4
1986	13 524.6	10 230.1	5 603.4	1 964.7	3 232.2	406.4	4 626.7	3 294.6	3 185.0	388.6	2 412.1	384.3	109.5	1 522.3	2 063.4
1987	14 320.6	10 842.8	5 918.7	2 055.3	3 414.7	448.7	4 924.0	3 477.8	3 358.4	410.7	2 532.9	414.8	119.4	1 652.7	2 185.0
1988	15 201.4	11 535.3	6 310.7	2 178.0	3 641.4	491.3	5 224.6	3 666.1	3 531.1	442.2	2 642.1	446.7	135.0	1 800.3	2 289.8
1989	16 067.4	12 201.9	6 699.1	2 300.6	3 858.4	540.1	5 502.9	3 865.4	3 721.3	476.3	2 772.8	472.2	144.2	1 925.7	2 415.0
1990	16 828.8	12 772.0	7 070.0	2 423.7	4 055.0	591.4	5 702.0	4 056.8	3 907.9	514.1	2 897.4	496.4	148.9	2 039.1	2 541.3
1991	17 252.2	13 056.3	7 240.3	2 482.2	4 116.3	641.7	5 816.0	4 195.9	4 046.0	545.4	2 985.0	515.6	150.0	2 117.4	2 621.0
1992	17 978.9	13 607.2	7 485.7	2 544.4	4 253.0	688.3	6 121.5	4 371.7	4 212.9	571.1	3 110.0	531.8	158.8	2 193.4	2 738.9
1993	18 883.3	14 319.9	7 836.6	2 642.4	4 462.6	731.5	6 483.3	4 563.4	4 393.3	594.2	3 254.9	544.3	170.0	2 302.2	2 879.2
1994	20 010.7	15 198.9	8 269.5	2 785.0	4 701.0	783.6	6 929.4	4 811.8	4 630.4	622.2	3 445.5	562.6	181.5	2 424.1	3 060.5
1995	20 980.1	15 945.2	8 717.6	2 959.2	4 917.2	841.2	7 227.6	5 034.9	4 846.8	630.0	3 639.8	577.0	188.1	2 529.3	3 240.8
1996	21 976.9	16 758.6	9 143.6	3 104.0	5 139.3	900.2	7 615.0	5 218.3	5 021.9	629.7	3 808.0	584.1	196.4	2 627.9	3 394.8
1997	23 119.4	17 692.7	9 664.1	3 235.2	5 449.2	979.7	8 028.6	5 426.7	5 229.9	622.1	4 011.7	596.1	196.8	2 718.0	3 576.6
1998	24 411.0	18 761.2	10 213.0	3 384.7	5 762.9	1 065.4	8 548.2	5 649.9	5 443.0	626.3	4 206.6	610.1	206.8	2 833.8	3 766.5
1999	25 974.3	20 010.2	10 833.0	3 578.7	6 067.1	1 187.2	9 177.2	5 964.1	5 744.2	644.1	4 468.6	631.4	219.9	2 991.1	4 020.3
2000	27 695.3	21 397.7	11 588.0	3 805.5	6 471.4	1 311.1	9 809.7	6 297.7	6 066.0	645.5	4 767.3	653.2	231.7	3 201.8	4 309.9
2001	29 244.4	22 679.7	12 163.2	3 912.3	6 884.4	1 366.5	10 516.5	6 564.7	6 318.2	642.0	5 011.0	665.2	246.5	3 364.3	4 553.5
2002	30 682.8	23 824.8	12 603.0	3 968.7	7 220.0	1 414.3	11 221.9	6 857.9	6 597.8	655.1	5 257.3	685.4	260.1	3 527.5	4 798.5
2003	32 367.4	25 212.6	13 052.3	4 040.8	7 522.7	1 488.7	12 160.3	7 154.8	6 876.2	671.5	5 480.9	723.8	278.6	3 679.2	5 024.4
2004	35 681.5	27 741.6	14 158.6	4 257.2	8 343.9	1 557.5	13 583.1	7 939.9	7 633.8	701.6	6 170.2	762.0	306.1	3 899.5	5 662.8
2005	39 294.7	30 609.2	15 461.0	4 481.8	9 320.4	1 658.8	15 148.3	8 685.5	8 350.4	727.7	6 818.2	804.5	335.1	4 107.8	6 259.0
2006	42 506.5	32 918.8	16 729.9	4 784.0	10 187.1	1 758.8	16 188.9	9 587.8	9 238.9	763.4	7 632.9	842.6	348.9	4 300.5	7 008.0
2007	44 400.8	34 066.4	17 667.0	5 020.9	10 770.8	1 875.3	16 399.4	10 334.4	9 988.5	798.1	8 294.2	896.2	345.9	4 476.0	7 623.1
2008	45 856.4	34 833.9	18 748.7	5 267.6	11 511.8	1 969.3	16 085.2	11 022.5	10 686.6	852.6	8 897.2	936.8	335.9	4 578.6	8 193.3
2009	44 944.9	33 859.9	18 151.4	5 182.7	10 943.7	2 025.0	15 708.5	11 085.1	10 756.6	890.6	8 901.2	964.8	328.5	4 588.1	8 243.0
2010	45 859.5	34 344.5	18 561.6	5 268.0	11 188.6	2 105.0	15 782.9	11 515.0	11 182.9	926.3	9 228.0	1 028.5	332.1	4 586.7	8 557.5
2011	47 313.6	35 178.1	19 287.1	5 478.3	11 606.4	2 202.3	15 891.1	12 135.4	11 798.2	957.5	9 781.6	1 059.1	337.2	4 723.3	9 068.6
2012	48 711.9	36 191.4	19 874.2	5 656.5	11 896.3	2 321.4	16 317.1	12 520.6	12 172.5	971.7	10 118.3	1 082.4	348.1	4 840.1	9 388.3
2013	50 949.1	38 054.2	20 654.0	5 831.1	12 400.4	2 422.4	17 400.3	12 894.9	12 525.0	979.8	10 437.9	1 107.4	369.9	4 942.2	9 703.2

Table 5-5B. Current-Cost Net Stock of Fixed Assets: Historical Data

(Billions of dollars, year-end estimates.)

Year	Total	Private						Government							
		Total	Nonresidential				Resi-dential	Total	Nonresidential				Resi-dential	Federal	State and local
			Total	Equip-ment	Struc-tures	Intellect-ual property products			Total	Equip-ment	Struc-tures	Intellect-ual property products			
1925	260.9	222.9	126.5	31.1	93.5	1.9	96.4	38.1	38.1	2.9	35.1	0.1	0.0	9.2	28.9
1926	270.0	231.1	131.0	32.8	96.2	2.0	100.0	39.0	39.0	2.8	36.0	0.1	0.0	9.0	30.0
1927	276.2	236.4	133.7	33.5	98.1	2.1	102.7	39.8	39.8	2.8	36.9	0.1	0.0	8.7	31.1
1928	288.6	248.1	137.3	34.2	100.9	2.3	110.8	40.5	40.5	2.6	37.7	0.1	0.0	8.3	32.2
1929	291.9	251.2	136.6	34.3	99.9	2.5	114.6	40.7	40.7	2.4	38.1	0.2	0.0	7.9	32.8
1930	278.6	239.0	129.8	32.7	94.7	2.5	109.2	39.6	39.6	2.3	37.1	0.2	0.0	7.5	32.1
1931	241.2	205.1	115.9	29.7	83.7	2.5	89.2	36.1	36.1	2.3	33.6	0.2	0.0	7.0	29.2
1932	223.1	187.3	107.4	26.7	78.3	2.4	79.9	35.8	35.8	2.3	33.2	0.3	0.0	6.9	28.9
1933	238.1	196.1	109.0	26.4	80.2	2.4	87.2	41.9	41.9	2.3	39.2	0.4	0.0	7.8	28.9
1934	244.2	198.3	110.3	26.5	81.3	2.6	87.9	46.0	45.9	2.5	43.0	0.4	0.0	8.8	34.1
1935	248.0	199.2	110.0	25.9	81.3	2.8	89.2	48.8	48.8	2.7	45.6	0.4	0.0	10.0	37.1
1936	274.4	220.1	121.0	27.8	90.1	3.1	99.0	54.3	54.2	2.9	50.8	0.5	0.1	11.6	38.8
1937	288.8	231.4	126.2	29.9	92.8	3.4	105.2	57.4	57.2	3.1	53.6	0.5	0.2	12.8	42.7
1938	291.1	231.6	124.9	29.9	91.3	3.7	106.8	59.4	59.2	3.3	55.4	0.5	0.2	13.5	44.6
1939	297.1	235.3	125.2	30.5	90.7	4.0	110.1	61.8	61.5	3.5	57.5	0.6	0.3	14.2	45.9
1940	321.9	254.1	133.3	32.8	96.1	4.3	120.8	67.8	67.3	3.8	62.8	0.6	0.5	16.0	47.6
1941	367.1	282.4	150.6	37.6	107.8	5.1	131.8	84.6	83.6	7.2	75.5	0.9	1.0	24.5	51.8
1942	419.5	302.0	160.2	38.5	115.6	6.0	141.8	117.6	115.9	20.4	94.2	1.3	1.7	50.2	60.1
1943	467.3	316.7	163.0	38.9	117.2	6.8	153.7	150.6	148.1	44.8	101.0	2.2	2.6	82.1	67.4
1944	501.3	328.9	164.9	38.8	118.6	7.5	164.1	172.3	169.5	64.7	101.3	3.4	2.8	105.5	68.5
1945	543.9	352.6	179.8	44.2	127.6	8.1	172.8	191.3	188.3	74.7	109.3	4.3	3.0	121.8	66.9
1946	637.2	433.5	220.5	53.3	158.1	9.1	212.9	203.7	199.7	69.4	125.2	5.0	4.0	125.9	69.5
1947	734.2	516.1	265.2	65.5	189.1	10.6	250.9	218.1	212.5	60.6	146.4	5.5	5.6	124.9	77.8
1948	780.2	561.6	291.0	80.3	199.4	11.3	270.5	218.7	213.7	50.9	156.7	6.1	5.0	117.2	93.3
1949	785.9	580.6	296.2	84.6	199.9	11.7	284.4	205.4	200.2	43.0	150.4	6.8	5.2	108.4	101.5
															96.9

Table 5-6A. Chain-Type Quantity Indexes for Net Stock of Fixed Assets: Recent Data

(Index numbers, 2009 = 100.)

Year	Total	Private						Government							
		Total	Nonresidential				Resi-dential	Total	Nonresidential				Resi-dential	Federal	State and local
			Total	Equip-ment	Struc-tures	Intellect-ual property products			Total	Equip-ment	Struc-tures	Intellect-ual property products			
1950	17.8	16.9	15.4	9.3	24.2	3.6	18.9	20.9	21.0	24.6	23.1	4.9	17.1	34.0	15.1
1951	18.5	17.5	15.9	9.9	24.8	3.7	19.7	21.7	21.8	26.4	23.8	5.2	18.4	35.5	15.6
1952	19.2	18.1	16.4	10.3	25.4	3.9	20.4	22.9	23.0	29.6	24.7	5.6	19.9	38.0	16.2
1953	20.0	18.8	17.0	10.8	26.0	4.3	21.2	24.1	24.2	33.0	25.6	6.1	21.2	40.7	16.9
1954	20.7	19.4	17.5	11.2	26.7	4.6	22.0	25.2	25.3	34.8	26.7	6.7	21.8	42.4	17.7
1955	21.6	20.2	18.1	11.7	27.5	4.9	23.0	26.2	26.3	35.5	27.7	7.4	22.2	43.4	18.6
1956	22.4	21.0	18.8	12.2	28.4	5.3	23.8	27.2	27.3	35.9	28.8	8.6	22.8	44.5	19.5
1957	23.2	21.7	19.5	12.8	29.2	5.7	24.6	28.2	28.3	36.4	29.8	10.0	23.9	45.8	20.5
1958	23.9	22.3	20.0	12.9	29.9	6.1	25.4	29.4	29.5	37.0	31.1	11.3	25.9	47.1	21.6
1959	24.8	23.0	20.5	13.2	30.7	6.5	26.4	30.7	30.8	38.6	32.3	12.6	28.0	49.0	22.7
1960	25.6	23.7	21.1	13.6	31.5	6.9	27.3	32.0	32.0	39.7	33.5	14.0	29.6	50.6	23.8
1961	26.5	24.5	21.7	13.9	32.4	7.4	28.2	33.4	33.5	41.4	34.8	15.7	31.6	52.7	25.1
1962	27.5	25.3	22.4	14.4	33.3	7.8	29.2	35.0	35.0	43.2	36.1	17.5	33.8	54.9	26.3
1963	28.5	26.2	23.1	15.0	34.2	8.3	30.4	36.5	36.6	44.2	37.6	20.0	34.9	56.9	27.7
1964	29.7	27.3	24.0	15.7	35.3	8.8	31.6	38.1	38.1	44.9	39.1	22.7	36.1	58.8	29.1
1965	31.0	28.5	25.2	16.9	36.6	9.4	32.8	39.7	39.7	44.9	40.8	25.5	37.4	60.4	30.7
1966	32.4	29.7	26.7	18.3	38.1	10.2	33.8	41.4	41.5	45.5	42.5	28.7	38.8	62.3	32.4
1967	33.6	30.8	27.9	19.5	39.4	10.9	34.7	43.3	43.3	46.5	44.2	31.8	40.4	64.3	34.2
1968	35.0	32.1	29.2	20.7	40.7	11.7	35.8	45.0	45.0	46.5	46.0	34.8	42.0	65.6	36.1
1969	36.3	33.3	30.6	22.1	42.2	12.4	36.9	46.4	46.4	46.1	47.6	37.5	43.9	66.5	37.8
1970	37.4	34.5	31.9	23.2	43.6	13.0	37.9	47.6	47.6	45.5	48.9	39.4	46.0	66.9	39.3
1971	38.6	35.7	32.9	24.2	44.9	13.4	39.4	48.4	48.4	43.6	50.2	40.9	47.9	66.5	40.8
1972	39.9	37.2	34.2	25.4	46.3	13.9	41.1	49.3	49.2	42.0	51.3	42.4	49.5	66.3	42.1
1973	41.3	38.8	35.8	27.3	47.8	14.4	42.8	50.1	50.1	40.8	52.5	43.8	51.1	66.2	43.3
1974	42.5	40.1	37.2	29.0	49.1	14.9	43.9	51.0	51.0	40.6	53.6	44.7	52.5	66.3	44.6
1975	43.4	41.0	38.1	29.9	50.2	15.3	44.8	51.9	51.8	40.6	54.6	45.4	54.3	66.5	45.8
1976	44.5	42.1	39.2	31.0	51.3	15.9	46.0	52.8	52.7	40.8	55.6	46.4	55.7	66.9	46.9
1977	45.8	43.6	40.5	32.6	52.4	16.6	47.7	53.6	53.5	41.1	56.4	47.5	56.9	67.3	47.9
1978	47.4	45.3	42.2	34.6	53.8	17.5	49.5	54.6	54.5	41.4	57.5	48.9	58.0	67.9	49.0
1979	49.0	47.1	44.1	36.9	55.6	18.6	51.1	55.7	55.6	42.1	58.5	50.4	59.1	68.7	50.2
1980	50.4	48.5	45.8	38.5	57.5	19.6	52.1	56.8	56.7	43.1	59.6	51.9	60.4	69.6	51.4
1981	51.7	49.9	47.7	40.0	59.7	21.0	52.9	57.8	57.6	44.3	60.4	53.5	62.0	70.7	52.4
1982	52.7	50.9	49.1	40.8	61.7	22.3	53.3	58.7	58.5	45.8	61.1	55.1	63.4	72.0	53.1
1983	53.8	52.1	50.4	41.6	63.2	23.8	54.5	59.7	59.5	47.9	61.8	56.9	65.2	73.6	53.9
1984	55.4	53.8	52.3	43.3	65.3	25.7	55.9	61.0	60.8	50.8	62.6	59.0	66.6	75.5	54.9
1985	57.2	55.6	54.3	44.9	67.6	27.8	57.3	62.6	62.4	54.5	63.6	61.8	68.5	78.1	56.1
1986	58.9	57.3	56.0	46.2	69.4	29.8	59.1	64.3	64.1	58.7	64.7	64.5	70.4	80.8	57.4
1987	60.5	58.9	57.5	47.2	71.1	31.7	60.9	66.1	65.9	62.9	65.8	67.4	72.4	83.7	58.7
1988	62.1	60.6	59.1	48.4	72.8	33.6	62.5	67.7	67.5	66.1	67.0	69.7	74.2	85.6	60.1
1989	63.7	62.1	60.7	49.8	74.4	36.0	64.0	69.2	68.9	69.4	68.1	71.5	75.8	87.2	61.6
1990	65.2	63.6	62.3	50.7	76.2	38.4	65.3	70.8	70.6	72.8	69.4	73.1	77.6	88.8	63.2
1991	66.3	64.6	63.4	51.3	77.4	40.8	66.2	72.3	72.0	75.3	70.7	74.1	79.1	89.8	64.9
1992	67.4	65.7	64.4	52.0	78.2	43.2	67.4	73.6	73.4	77.3	72.1	74.7	80.8	90.6	66.5
1993	68.8	67.1	65.8	53.5	79.2	45.4	68.8	74.7	74.5	78.1	73.3	75.0	82.2	90.8	68.0
1994	70.2	68.7	67.3	55.6	80.0	47.4	70.5	75.7	75.4	78.3	74.6	75.2	83.4	90.6	69.5
1995	71.8	70.4	69.2	58.2	81.2	49.6	72.0	76.8	76.5	78.4	75.9	75.2	84.8	90.5	71.1
1996	73.7	72.5	71.5	61.2	82.6	52.6	73.8	78.0	77.7	78.5	77.5	75.3	86.3	90.7	72.7
1997	75.7	74.7	74.1	64.6	84.2	56.4	75.6	79.2	78.9	78.1	79.1	75.6	87.8	90.3	74.6
1998	78.0	77.3	77.1	68.6	85.9	60.5	77.7	80.4	80.1	78.2	80.6	76.1	89.1	90.0	76.5
1999	80.4	80.0	80.2	73.1	87.6	65.4	79.9	81.8	81.5	78.8	82.3	76.7	90.4	89.8	78.6
2000	83.0	82.9	83.7	77.9	89.6	70.4	82.1	83.3	83.0	79.1	84.1	77.6	91.5	89.5	80.9
2001	85.1	85.2	86.2	81.1	91.4	74.1	84.2	85.0	84.7	79.6	85.9	78.9	92.7	89.5	83.2
2002	87.1	87.2	87.8	83.1	92.4	76.8	86.6	86.9	86.6	80.9	88.0	80.8	94.0	90.1	85.6
2003	89.1	89.2	89.3	85.1	93.3	79.5	89.2	88.9	88.7	82.3	90.0	83.3	95.3	91.2	88.0
2004	91.3	91.4	90.9	87.7	94.0	82.5	92.1	90.9	90.7	84.3	91.9	86.2	96.4	92.5	90.3
2005	93.4	93.7	92.7	91.1	94.7	85.9	94.9	92.6	92.4	86.5	93.4	89.1	97.4	93.8	92.1
2006	95.8	96.2	95.0	95.2	95.8	89.6	97.6	94.4	94.3	89.4	95.1	92.0	97.8	95.1	94.2
2007	97.8	98.3	97.5	99.2	97.4	93.6	99.3	96.3	96.2	92.5	96.7	94.8	98.5	96.6	96.2
2008	99.4	99.8	99.6	101.4	99.2	97.4	99.9	98.2	98.1	96.6	98.4	97.5	99.2	98.3	98.1
2009	100.0	100.0	100.0	100.0	100.0	100.0	100.0	100.0	100.0	100.0	100.0	100.0	100.0	100.0	100.0
2010	100.7	100.3	100.6	100.5	100.2	102.7	100.0	101.7	101.7	103.2	101.5	102.4	101.6	101.9	101.7
2011	101.5	101.0	101.7	102.6	100.5	105.8	100.1	103.1	103.1	105.0	102.8	104.5	102.6	103.2	103.0
2012	102.4	101.9	103.2	105.2	101.2	109.0	100.3	104.1	104.1	106.3	103.6	106.2	102.9	104.0	104.1
2013	103.5	103.1	104.8	108.2	101.9	112.2	101.1	104.8	104.8	106.7	104.4	107.1	103.2	104.0	105.1

Table 5-6B. Chain-Type Quantity Indexes for Net Stock of Fixed Assets: Historical Data

(Index numbers, 2009 = 100.)

Year	Total	Private						Government							
		Total	Nonresidential				Resi-dential	Total	Nonresidential				Resi-dential	Federal	State and local
			Total	Equip-ment	Struc-tures	Intellect-ual property products			Total	Equip-ment	Struc-tures	Intellect-ual property products			
1925	10.4	12.0	11.2	5.4	19.9	0.8	13.2	5.8	6.0	2.1	8.6	0.10	0.00	4.3	6.7
1926	10.8	12.5	11.5	5.6	20.5	0.8	13.8	6.0	6.2	2.1	9.0	0.12	0.00	4.2	7.1
1927	11.2	12.9	11.8	5.7	21.2	0.9	14.3	6.3	6.5	2.1	9.4	0.13	0.00	4.1	7.5
1928	11.5	13.3	12.2	5.8	21.7	1.0	14.8	6.6	6.8	2.1	9.9	0.14	0.00	4.1	8.0
1929	11.9	13.6	12.6	6.0	22.4	1.1	15.0	7.1	7.3	2.2	10.6	0.15	0.03	4.1	8.7
1930	12.1	13.8	12.8	6.0	22.9	1.2	15.1	7.5	7.7	2.2	11.2	0.20	0.06	4.1	9.3
1931	12.2	13.8	12.7	5.8	23.0	1.2	15.1	7.9	8.1	2.2	11.9	0.26	0.08	4.2	9.9
1932	12.1	13.6	12.5	5.5	22.8	1.3	15.0	8.2	8.5	2.2	12.4	0.33	0.11	4.4	10.4
1933	12.0	13.4	12.2	5.2	22.6	1.3	14.9	8.5	8.7	2.2	12.8	0.39	0.13	4.7	10.6
1934	12.0	13.3	12.1	5.0	22.4	1.4	14.8	8.8	9.0	2.2	13.2	0.42	0.15	5.0	10.8
1935	12.0	13.2	12.0	5.0	22.2	1.5	14.8	9.1	9.4	2.4	13.7	0.45	0.23	5.6	11.1
1936	12.2	13.3	12.1	5.1	22.2	1.6	14.9	9.6	9.9	2.5	14.4	0.49	0.65	6.1	11.6
1937	12.4	13.4	12.2	5.3	22.2	1.8	15.0	10.1	10.3	2.6	15.1	0.52	1.22	6.5	12.0
1938	12.6	13.4	12.2	5.3	22.2	1.9	15.0	10.6	10.8	2.8	15.8	0.56	1.45	7.0	12.6
1939	12.8	13.5	12.3	5.3	22.2	2.0	15.2	11.1	11.4	2.9	16.6	0.60	1.88	7.3	13.2
1940	13.1	13.7	12.4	5.6	22.3	2.2	15.5	11.6	11.9	3.0	17.3	0.65	3.15	7.9	13.7
1941	13.6	14.0	12.7	5.8	22.4	2.4	15.7	13.0	13.2	5.6	18.5	0.88	5.71	11.5	14.0
1942	14.5	14.0	12.6	5.8	22.2	2.6	15.8	16.7	16.9	17.1	20.8	1.21	8.53	22.9	14.0
1943	15.4	13.9	12.5	5.6	22.0	2.6	15.7	21.1	21.4	39.4	21.7	1.76	12.13	37.6	13.9
1944	16.2	13.8	12.5	5.7	21.8	2.7	15.6	24.8	25.2	60.8	21.9	2.51	12.99	50.0	13.7
1945	16.6	13.9	12.7	6.0	21.8	2.8	15.5	26.1	26.5	68.1	22.0	3.12	13.19	54.6	13.6
1946	16.6	14.4	13.2	6.6	22.3	3.0	16.0	24.3	24.6	55.6	21.9	3.54	14.64	48.5	13.6
1947	16.7	15.0	13.8	7.4	22.7	3.2	16.6	22.6	22.9	44.0	21.9	3.82	15.09	42.8	13.8
1948	17.0	15.6	14.4	8.3	23.2	3.4	17.3	21.5	21.7	34.5	22.1	4.16	15.37	38.4	14.1
1949	17.3	16.2	14.8	8.8	23.7	3.5	18.0	21.1	21.3	29.5	22.6	4.51	16.30	36.2	14.5

Table 5-7. Capital Expenditures

(Millions of dollars, except totals are shown in billions.)

Capital expenditures	All companies												
	2001	2002	2003	2004	2005	2006	2007	2008	2009	2010	2011	2012	2013
TOTAL (billions)	1 109.0	997.9	975.0	1 042.1	1 144.8	1 309.9	1 354.7	1 374.2	1 090.7	1 105.7	1 243.0	1 424.2	1 488.2
Structures	363 748	358 484	344 641	368 707	401 653	488 701	525 273	562 381	449 545	428 713	471 779	570 489	577 948
New	335 538	321 191	305 291	324 680	365 938	448 861	480 839	522 999	422 780	394 517	442 745	534 696	544 997
Used	28 210	37 293	39 350	44 028	35 715	39 840	44 434	39 382	26 765	34 196	29 034	35 793	32 951
Equipment	745 256	639 410	630 373	673 353	743 130	821 238	829 455	811 779	641 149	676 989	771 177	853 661	910 252
New	706 617	598 668	579 414	628 591	701 247	777 059	790 407	765 279	606 576	639 214	730 033	800 519	856 739
Used	38 639	40 741	50 960	44 762	41 884	44 179	39 048	46 501	34 572	37 775	41 144	53 142	53 513
Not distributed as structures or equipment	0	0	0	0	0	0	0	0	0	0	0	0	0
CAPITALIZED COMPUTER SOFTWARE [1]	. . .	. . .	. . .	. . .	. . .	. . .	. . .	. . .	. . .	. . .	. . .	. . .	. . .
Prepackaged	. . .	. . .	. . .	. . .	. . .	. . .	. . .	. . .	. . .	. . .	. . .	. . .	. . .
Vendor-customized	. . .	. . .	. . .	. . .	. . .	. . .	. . .	. . .	. . .	. . .	. . .	. . .	. . .
Internally-developed	. . .	. . .	. . .	. . .	. . .	. . .	. . .	. . .	. . .	. . .	. . .	. . .	. . .
CAPITAL LEASE AND CAPITALIZED INTEREST EXPENSES [1]													
Capital leases	15 529	15 334	15 641	17 996	18 103	24 442	20 210	20 169	17 410	15 780	20 509	26 087	26 898
Capitalized interest	. . .	. . .	. . .	. . .	. . .	. . .	. . .	. . .	. . .	. . .	. . .	. . .	. . .

Capital expenditures	Companies with employees												
	2001	2002	2003	2004	2005	2006	2007	2008	2009	2010	2011	2012	2013
TOTAL (billions)	1 052.3	917.5	886.9	953.2	1 062.6	1 217.1	1 270.5	1 294.5	1 015.3	1 036.2	1 169.6	1 334.9	1 397.8
Structures	346 221	325 168	314 021	335 405	368 791	453 893	490 779	529 393	414 051	395 531	440 893	533 115	542 167
New	323 871	299 941	281 892	300 371	341 223	420 090	457 233	500 474	395 022	366 853	414 958	501 420	514 068
Used	22 349	25 227	32 128	35 034	27 568	33 802	33 546	28 919	19 030	28 678	25 935	31 695	28 099
Equipment	706 123	592 321	572 825	617 766	693 745	763 215	779 744	765 098	601 270	640 631	728 710	801 820	855 602
New	679 090	564 218	540 611	588 110	664 648	734 160	750 353	728 322	577 051	612 441	697 766	759 632	814 699
Used	27 033	28 103	32 214	29 656	29 096	29 055	29 391	36 776	24 219	28 190	30 944	42 189	40 903
Not distributed as structures or equipment	0	0	0	0	0	0	0	0	0	0	0	0	0
CAPITALIZED COMPUTER SOFTWARE [1]	. . .	. . .	49 869	49 868	49 149	58 522	63 116	72 241	. . .	63 780	71 068	87 474	90 003
Prepackaged	. . .	. . .	17 307	17 306	17 630	21 181	21 777	26 260	. . .	21 749	23 242	27 868	29 003
Vendor-customized	. . .	. . .	15 554	15 553	13 876	16 912	17 990	19 259	. . .	17 264	20 346	23 507	24 255
Internally-developed	. . .	. . .	17 008	17 008	17 643	20 433	23 350	26 723	. . .	24 768	27 480	36 099	36 745
CAPITAL LEASE AND CAPITALIZED INTEREST EXPENSES [1]													
Capital leases	15 500	15 092	15 137	17 526	17 640	23 923	19 432	19 422	. . .	15 212	20 145	25 301	26 196
Capitalized interest	11 969	. . .	. . .	. . .	. . .	. . .	. . .	. . .	. . .	. . .	. . .	. . .	. . .

Capital expenditures	Companies without employees												
	2001	2002	2003	2004	2005	2006	2007	2008	2009	2010	2011	2012	2013
TOTAL (billions)	56.7	80.4	88.2	88.9	82.2	92.8	84.2	79.7	75.4	69.5	73.4	89.2	90.4
Structures	17 527	33 316	30 621	33 302	32 862	34 809	34 494	32 988	35 493	33 182	30 886	37 374	35 780
New	11 667	21 250	23 399	24 309	24 715	28 771	23 606	22 525	27 758	27 664	27 787	33 276	30 929
Used	5 860	12 066	7 222	8 993	8 146	6 038	10 888	10 463	7 735	5 518	3 099	4 098	4 851
Equipment	39 133	47 088	57 549	55 587	49 386	58 023	49 711	46 681	39 878	36 357	42 467	51 840	54 650
New	27 528	34 450	38 803	40 481	36 598	42 899	40 054	36 957	29 525	26 773	32 267	40 887	42 040
Used	11 605	12 638	18 746	15 106	12 787	15 124	9 657	9 724	10 353	9 585	10 200	10 953	12 610
Not distributed as structures or equipment	0	0	0	0	0	0	0	0	0	0	0	0	0
CAPITALIZED COMPUTER SOFTWARE [1]	. . .	. . .	. . .	. . .	. . .	. . .	. . .	. . .	. . .	. . .	. . .	. . .	. . .
Prepackaged	. . .	. . .	. . .	. . .	. . .	. . .	. . .	. . .	. . .	. . .	. . .	. . .	. . .
Vendor-customized	. . .	. . .	. . .	. . .	. . .	. . .	. . .	. . .	. . .	. . .	. . .	. . .	. . .
Internally-developed	. . .	. . .	. . .	. . .	. . .	. . .	. . .	. . .	. . .	. . .	. . .	. . .	. . .
CAPITAL LEASE AND CAPITALIZED INTEREST EXPENSES [1]													
Capital leases	29	242	504	469	463	519	778	747	577	568	365	786	702
Capitalized interest	. . .	. . .	. . .	. . .	. . .	. . .	. . .	. . .	. . .	. . .	. . .	. . .	. . .

[1]Included in structures and equipment data shown above.

. . . = Not available.

Table 5-8. Capital Expenditures for Structures and Equipment for Companies with Employees by Major Industry Sector

(Millions of dollars.)

Year and type of expenditure	Total	Forestry, fishing, and agricultural services (113–115)	Mining (21)	Utilities (22)	Construction (23)	Manufacturing (31–33)			Wholesale trade (42)	Retail trade (44–45)	Transportation and warehousing (48–49)	Information (51)
						Total	Durable goods industries (321, 327, 33)	Nondurable goods industries (31, 322–326)				
1998												
Total expenditures	896 452	854	40 424	36 010	26 867	203 587	117 901	85 685	29 169	57 276	51 287	96 487
Structures, total	300 283	206	26 503	18 574	7 062	39 028	19 406	19 622	7 480	25 105	13 036	24 721
New	260 008	158	24 714	17 771	4 749	37 122	18 449	18 673	6 738	23 104	12 365	24 218
Used	40 275	49	1 789	804	2 313	1 906	957	949	742	2 001	671	503
Equipment, total	596 169	648	13 921	17 436	19 805	164 559	98 496	66 063	21 690	32 171	38 251	71 766
New	570 397	603	12 625	17 266	15 346	159 363	95 571	63 792	20 470	30 359	33 409	70 827
Used	25 773	46	1 296	170	4 458	5 196	2 925	2 271	1 220	1 812	4 842	939
1999												
Total expenditures	974 631	1 716	30 586	42 802	23 110	196 399	117 005	79 394	32 442	64 063	57 299	122 827
Structures, total	293 787	344	17 626	21 241	1 753	33 985	17 320	16 665	7 264	29 494	14 122	34 924
New	276 094	331	17 039	20 784	1 505	32 814	16 581	16 233	6 508	28 670	13 859	33 733
Used	17 693	13	587	457	248	1 171	739	432	756	824	263	1 191
Equipment, total	680 843	1 371	12 960	21 561	21 356	162 414	99 685	62 729	25 179	34 569	43 178	87 903
New	656 344	1 190	12 167	20 545	18 600	157 715	96 434	61 281	23 714	33 567	40 425	85 310
Used	24 499	182	793	1 016	2 756	4 699	3 251	1 448	1 465	1 002	2 752	2 593
2000												
Total expenditures	1 089 862	1 488	42 522	61 302	25 049	214 827	133 786	81 041	33 579	69 791	59 851	160 177
Structures, total	338 120	139	28 620	29 472	2 803	39 434	21 228	18 207	8 923	32 037	13 457	41 502
New	309 541	134	25 500	29 258	2 583	36 643	19 748	16 895	8 364	30 413	13 190	40 062
Used	28 579	5	3 120	214	220	2 791	1 480	1 312	559	1 624	267	1 440
Equipment, total	751 742	1 350	13 902	31 830	22 245	175 393	112 558	62 835	24 656	37 754	46 394	118 675
New	718 227	1 086	12 854	27 937	17 788	169 454	108 703	60 751	23 610	36 428	43 455	117 835
Used	33 515	264	1 048	3 893	4 458	5 939	3 856	2 083	1 046	1 326	2 938	841
2001												
Total expenditures	1 052 344	1 532	51 278	82 823	24 802	192 835	118 875	73 959	29 981	66 917	57 756	144 793
Structures, total	346 221	226	32 678	38 093	3 859	39 815	22 032	17 784	6 932	30 010	16 594	41 742
New	323 871	149	31 825	36 504	3 389	38 001	20 701	17 301	5 357	29 118	14 479	41 384
Used	22 349	77	853	1 588	470	1 814	1 331	483	1 575	892	2 116	358
Equipment, total	706 123	1 306	18 600	44 731	20 943	153 019	96 844	56 176	23 049	36 906	41 161	103 051
New	679 090	1 091	17 567	42 939	17 432	148 397	94 251	54 145	20 757	35 074	38 521	102 410
Used	27 033	215	1 033	1 792	3 511	4 623	2 592	2 030	2 292	1 833	2 640	641
2002												
Total expenditures	917 490	1 910	42 467	65 502	24 773	157 243	84 062	73 181	26 789	59 316	47 124	88 156
Structures, total	325 168	184	30 685	29 893	1 890	32 643	15 133	17 510	5 885	26 286	14 498	33 607
New	299 941	118	29 775	29 008	1 254	31 022	14 396	16 626	5 447	25 051	13 870	33 472
Used	25 227	66	910	886	456	1 622	737	885	438	1 234	628	135
Equipment, total	592 321	1 726	11 783	35 609	23 063	124 600	68 929	55 671	20 904	33 030	32 626	54 550
New	564 218	1 319	10 262	34 816	19 257	118 621	66 112	52 510	18 562	31 157	29 178	54 247
Used	28 103	407	1 520	793	3 806	5 978	2 817	3 161	2 342	1 873	3 447	303
2003												
Total expenditures	886 846	1 894	50 548	54 569	23 159	149 065	80 226	68 839	26 014	65 868	44 460	80 524
Structures, total	314 021	202	36 617	24 841	1 676	31 108	13 330	17 778	5 615	29 675	13 005	30 765
New	281 892	177	35 897	24 580	1 424	29 315	12 631	16 685	4 921	27 393	11 779	30 406
Used	32 128	25	720	261	251	1 793	700	1 093	694	2 282	1 226	358
Equipment, total	572 825	1 692	13 931	29 729	21 484	117 956	66 895	51 061	20 399	36 193	31 454	49 759
New	540 611	1 267	12 135	29 044	16 170	112 102	62 810	49 292	19 457	32 162	26 786	47 857
Used	32 214	425	1 796	685	5 313	5 855	4 086	1 769	942	4 031	4 668	1 902
2004												
Total expenditures	953 171	2 081	51 253	50 409	28 627	156 651	85 119	71 532	32 314	72 170	46 054	83 488
Structures, total	335 405	324	34 564	24 398	4 511	31 823	13 606	18 217	7 133	33 308	13 992	28 636
New	300 371	309	33 583	23 626	4 167	30 016	12 818	17 198	6 555	31 486	13 018	26 253
Used	35 034	15	982	772	345	1 807	788	1 019	578	1 822	975	2 384
Equipment, total	617 766	1 757	16 689	26 011	24 115	124 828	71 513	53 315	25 181	38 862	32 062	54 852
New	588 110	1 507	15 415	25 724	18 939	120 481	68 904	51 576	21 888	36 965	28 472	53 120
Used	29 656	250	1 274	286	5 176	4 347	2 609	1 738	3 293	1 897	3 590	1 732
2005												
Total expenditures	1 062 536	2 702	66 746	58 032	30 072	165 634	92 180	73 455	40 578	73 531	56 926	91 373
Structures, total	368 791	344	46 433	24 186	2 544	34 132	14 735	19 397	9 184	34 119	17 855	31 977
New	341 223	283	45 655	23 485	2 247	32 564	14 033	18 531	8 830	33 360	16 954	31 716
Used	27 568	61	777	701	297	1 569	703	866	355	759	901	262
Equipment, total	693 745	2 358	20 313	33 847	27 528	131 502	77 444	54 058	31 394	39 412	39 072	59 396
New	664 648	2 016	18 495	33 083	22 082	126 387	73 889	52 498	28 224	38 301	34 953	59 071
Used	29 096	341	1 818	764	5 446	5 115	3 555	1 560	3 169	1 111	4 119	325
2006												
Total expenditures	1 217 107	2 672	99 309	69 757	30 257	192 364	106 843	85 521	36 600	86 735	68 021	104 373
Structures, total	453 893	391	68 662	30 587	2 556	41 617	17 515	24 103	10 375	43 188	20 852	31 947
New	420 090	316	67 322	29 294	2 217	39 419	16 243	23 176	9 956	41 985	19 765	31 621
Used	33 802	75	1 340	1 293	338	2 198	1 272	926	419	1 203	1 087	326
Equipment, total	763 215	2 281	30 647	39 170	27 701	150 747	89 328	61 419	26 226	43 547	47 168	72 425
New	734 160	1 846	28 813	37 617	23 276	146 551	86 637	59 914	24 366	41 943	41 258	71 830
Used	29 055	435	1 833	1 553	4 425	4 196	2 692	1 504	1 860	1 604	5 911	595

Table 5-8. Capital Expenditures for Structures and Equipment for Companies with Employees by Major Industry Sector—*Continued*

(Millions of dollars.)

Year and type of expenditure	Finance and insurance (52)	Real estate and rental and leasing (53)	Professional, scientific, and technical services (54)	Manage-ment of companies and enterprises (55)	Adminis-trative and support and waste manage-ment (56)	Educational services (61)	Health care and social assistance (62)	Arts, entertain-ment, and recreation (71)	Accom-modation and food services (72)	Other services, except public admin-istration (81)	Structure and equipment expenditures serving multiple industries
1998											
Total expenditures	118 173	85 184	22 277	1 821	13 110	12 983	47 109	8 994	20 822	20 627	3 392
Structures, total	27 221	36 775	4 886	753	4 288	9 109	23 971	5 045	12 045	13 737	738
New	16 858	24 109	4 572	502	3 745	8 734	21 328	4 838	10 402	13 280	699
Used	10 362	12 666	314	251	543	374	2 643	206	1 643	457	39
Equipment, total	90 952	48 409	17 390	1 068	8 822	3 874	23 138	3 949	8 777	6 890	2 654
New	90 058	46 877	16 868	1 030	8 346	3 825	22 465	3 752	8 005	6 296	2 609
Used	894	1 532	522	38	476	49	672	197	772	594	46
1999											
Total expenditures	130 101	100 629	29 546	6 065	16 227	13 532	51 342	13 355	23 328	16 902	2 359
Structures, total	20 080	33 903	6 780	1 668	2 875	9 767	25 922	8 119	13 431	9 975	516
New	17 918	30 295	6 168	1 509	2 773	9 140	24 159	7 971	11 391	9 033	495
Used	2 162	3 608	613	159	102	627	1 763	148	2 040	941	21
Equipment, total	110 021	66 726	22 766	4 397	13 353	3 766	25 420	5 236	9 897	6 928	1 843
New	109 577	63 555	22 153	4 319	12 323	3 668	24 945	5 125	9 324	6 370	1 752
Used	444	3 171	613	78	1 029	97	475	111	573	558	91
2000											
Total expenditures	133 684	92 456	34 055	5 054	17 506	18 223	52 166	19 125	26 307	21 125	1 572
Structures, total	23 010	24 815	8 141	1 570	4 032	13 699	26 868	12 245	13 873	13 274	206
New	20 298	17 793	7 470	955	3 504	12 965	23 999	11 627	12 879	11 705	200
Used	2 712	7 022	671	615	528	735	2 869	618	993	1 569	6
Equipment, total	110 675	67 641	25 914	3 484	13 475	4 523	25 299	6 880	12 434	7 852	1 366
New	109 678	62 175	24 847	3 403	12 723	4 338	24 407	6 161	11 501	7 192	1 357
Used	997	5 466	1 067	81	752	186	892	719	933	659	10
2001											
Total expenditures	131 105	82 674	30 464	3 035	15 785	17 377	52 932	14 974	21 365	29 006	911
Structures, total	22 744	20 489	7 258	933	3 527	12 852	27 030	8 998	12 248	20 031	163
New	19 571	17 325	6 793	869	3 367	11 860	25 241	8 157	11 402	18 918	162
Used	3 173	3 164	465	64	160	991	1 789	841	846	1 112	0
Equipment, total	108 361	62 185	23 206	2 102	12 258	4 525	25 902	5 976	9 117	8 976	749
New	107 268	60 295	22 330	2 019	11 644	4 238	24 573	5 590	7 921	8 300	725
Used	1 093	1 891	876	83	613	287	1 329	386	1 196	676	24
2002											
Total expenditures	128 444	94 529	25 864	3 430	14 719	19 532	59 311	13 169	22 409	21 269	1 532
Structures, total	24 308	35 579	7 129	933	3 276	14 655	30 291	7 758	12 157	13 261	250
New	19 748	30 227	6 424	913	2 948	13 601	27 273	7 332	10 848	11 363	248
Used	4 739	5 352	706	21	328	1 055	3 018	425	1 309	1 899	2
Equipment, total	103 956	58 949	18 735	2 497	11 443	4 876	29 021	5 412	10 252	8 007	1 282
New	103 421	56 847	18 021	2 481	10 585	4 690	28 196	5 132	9 290	6 858	1 276
Used	535	2 102	714	16	857	186	825	280	962	1 149	6
2003											
Total expenditures	120 787	87 952	24 703	3 298	16 612	16 667	61 151	11 029	21 036	26 035	1 476
Structures, total	26 200	25 028	5 314	925	3 976	11 984	30 996	6 800	10 568	18 518	209
New	17 908	16 446	4 671	869	3 213	11 569	28 885	6 532	9 417	16 288	202
Used	8 292	8 583	643	56	763	415	2 111	268	1 151	2 230	7
Equipment, total	94 587	62 923	19 389	2 373	12 636	4 683	30 155	4 229	10 468	7 517	1 267
New	94 205	61 253	18 675	2 368	11 374	4 569	29 497	4 038	9 684	6 706	1 263
Used	383	1 671	714	5	1 262	114	658	192	783	811	4
2004											
Total expenditures	153 629	91 606	26 688	2 825	17 455	18 919	64 561	12 165	20 641	19 701	1 572
Structures, total	43 919	27 277	6 007	860	2 567	13 728	32 608	7 360	9 860	12 278	321
New	30 216	21 610	5 714	798	2 309	12 781	30 668	7 196	9 126	10 867	307
Used	13 703	5 667	293	62	259	947	1 939	164	734	1 411	13
Equipment, total	109 710	64 329	20 681	1 965	14 888	5 190	31 953	4 804	10 781	7 423	1 252
New	109 244	61 947	20 081	1 931	12 692	4 965	31 280	4 677	10 373	6 788	1 248
Used	466	2 382	600	34	2 196	225	673	128	408	635	3
2005											
Total expenditures	161 389	103 022	33 066	2 809	18 194	17 484	73 825	14 165	30 718	20 105	2 163
Structures, total	39 383	24 791	8 717	857	3 051	12 711	39 089	9 242	17 679	12 036	460
New	31 023	17 341	7 633	795	2 759	11 913	37 493	8 805	16 567	11 350	452
Used	8 360	7 450	1 084	62	292	798	1 597	436	1 112	686	8
Equipment, total	122 005	78 231	24 350	1 951	15 143	4 773	34 736	4 924	13 039	8 069	1 703
New	121 511	76 894	23 887	1 917	13 523	4 597	34 110	4 757	11 950	7 209	1 681
Used	494	1 337	463	34	1 620	176	626	166	1 089	861	22
2006											
Total expenditures	163 069	132 073	30 284	3 306	19 231	22 615	75 296	17 156	36 217	25 959	1 813
Structures, total	41 326	40 794	6 971	875	3 613	17 537	41 197	11 733	22 585	16 621	467
New	34 028	30 240	6 375	799	3 485	16 203	37 765	11 326	21 774	15 754	446
Used	7 298	10 554	596	76	128	1 334	3 433	406	811	866	21
Equipment, total	121 743	91 280	23 313	2 432	15 618	5 078	34 099	5 424	13 632	9 339	1 346
New	121 157	88 957	22 867	2 188	14 932	4 983	33 508	5 121	13 161	8 463	1 322
Used	586	2 323	446	244	686	95	591	303	472	875	24

Table 5-8. Capital Expenditures for Structures and Equipment for Companies with Employees by Major Industry Sector—Continued

(Millions of dollars.)

Year and type of expenditure	Total	Forestry, fishing, and agricultural services (113–115)	Mining (21)	Utilities (22)	Construction (23)	Manufacturing (31–33) Total	Durable goods industries (321, 327, 33)	Nondurable goods industries (31, 322–326)	Wholesale trade (42)	Retail trade (44–45)	Transportation and warehousing (48–49)	Information (51)
2007												
Total expenditures	1 270 522	2 149	120 681	85 354	36 692	197 298	107 664	89 633	30 776	82 511	67 351	106 084
Structures, total	490 779	469	85 242	40 178	3 529	42 458	17 879	24 579	7 526	41 527	23 712	29 081
New	457 233	320	83 206	37 647	2 704	41 247	17 431	23 816	7 091	40 471	22 808	28 304
Used	33 546	149	2 036	2 531	824	1 211	447	763	436	1 056	904	777
Equipment, total	779 744	1 681	35 440	45 176	33 164	154 840	89 786	65 054	23 250	40 983	43 639	77 003
New	750 353	1 368	33 095	44 107	27 325	150 333	87 020	63 313	21 690	39 668	39 238	76 143
Used	29 391	313	2 344	1 069	5 838	4 507	2 766	1 741	1 560	1 316	4 400	861
2008												
Total expenditures	1 294 491	2 337	149 272	98 668	40 838	213 117	103 022	110 095	32 370	73 234	79 617	103 327
Structures, total	529 393	421	109 683	43 515	11 129	49 346	18 896	30 450	8 387	36 147	30 078	27 376
New	500 474	417	105 064	41 746	10 525	48 184	18 168	30 015	7 958	35 342	29 214	27 080
Used	28 919	4	4 618	1 769	603	1 162	728	434	430	805	863	296
Equipment, total	765 098	1 917	39 590	55 154	29 709	163 771	84 125	79 645	23 982	37 087	49 539	75 951
New	728 322	1 610	35 928	53 486	22 404	158 104	80 690	77 414	22 554	36 328	41 877	75 342
Used	36 776	307	3 662	1 668	7 305	5 667	3 435	2 232	1 429	759	7 662	609
2009												
Total expenditures	1 015 322	2 168	100 564	103 024	19 751	155 153	76 039	79 114	25 252	58 428	55 702	88 373
Structures, total	414 051	460	72 255	45 973	4 556	35 735	13 054	22 680	5 485	28 205	22 088	21 764
New	395 022	453	69 942	45 168	4 215	34 537	12 273	22 264	5 131	27 220	21 128	21 410
Used	19 030	7	2 313	805	341	1 198	782	416	354	985	961	354
Equipment, total	601 270	1 708	28 308	57 051	15 195	119 418	62 985	56 434	19 767	30 223	33 614	66 609
New	577 051	1 428	26 790	54 848	11 815	115 470	60 699	54 772	18 512	29 063	30 182	65 879
Used	24 219	279	1 518	2 204	3 380	3 948	2 286	1 662	1 255	1 160	3 432	731
2010												
Total expenditures	1 036 153	3 255	115 749	94 462	17 856	160 798	86 570	74 227	31 075	65 252	58 952	97 150
Structures, total	396 398	679	85 221	43 896	2 633	31 166	14 099	17 068	6 879	29 169	23 401	21 771
New	367 759	671	82 147	42 853	2 361	30 069	13 492	16 576	5 709	27 608	22 622	20 696
Used	28 639	8	3 074	1 044	272	1 098	606	491	1 170	1 561	778	1 074
Equipment, total	639 755	2 576	30 528	50 566	15 223	129 631	72 472	57 160	24 196	36 084	35 551	75 379
New	611 573	1 979	28 820	48 675	11 377	125 911	70 692	55 219	21 756	34 457	29 912	74 657
Used	28 182	597	1 708	1 891	3 846	3 720	1 780	1 940	2 440	1 626	5 639	723
2011												
Total expenditures	1 169 604	3 063	165 693	98 047	21 778	192 441	110 151	82 290	35 745	68 131	72 722	100 057
Structures, total	440 893	529	124 508	46 729	2 867	36 339	17 394	18 946	7 988	27 332	29 026	20 152
New	414 958	518	120 421	45 882	2 590	34 737	16 655	18 081	7 512	26 419	28 148	19 734
Used	25 935	11	4 086	847	277	1 602	738	864	476	912	878	418
Equipment, total	728 710	2 534	41 185	51 319	18 910	156 102	92 758	63 344	27 757	40 799	43 696	79 905
New	697 766	2 050	39 373	48 843	13 895	151 094	89 389	61 705	26 699	39 575	37 612	79 686
Used	30 944	484	1 813	2 476	5 015	5 009	3 369	1 639	1 058	1 224	6 084	219
2012												
Total expenditures	1 334 421	3 149	196 653	124 958	23 555	203 119	113 299	89 820	40 852	77 567	81 792	106 537
Structures, total	533 042	496	150 653	70 940	1 975	43 080	20 181	22 900	9 367	33 443	32 397	23 263
New	501 764	452	146 020	69 578	1 821	41 765	19 563	22 202	8 324	30 978	31 393	22 844
Used	31 279	44	4 633	1 362	154	1 316	618	697	1 043	2 464	1 003	419
Equipment, total	801 378	2 653	46 000	54 017	21 580	160 039	93 118	66 921	31 485	44 124	49 395	83 274
New	759 355	2 266	43 985	50 358	16 446	153 572	89 830	63 742	29 297	42 466	42 663	82 762
Used	42 023	387	2 015	3 660	5 134	6 467	3 288	3 179	2 187	1 658	6 732	512
2013												
Total expenditures	1 397 769	2 992	198 060	111 680	27 618	219 767	121 141	98 626	38 310	77 492	93 397	123 057
Structures, total	542 167	493	148 178	58 079	2 586	46 434	20 315	26 119	9 975	33 973	37 644	33 054
New	514 068	475	144 654	56 381	2 144	43 937	19 544	24 393	9 494	33 249	36 453	32 558
Used	28 099	18	3 523	1 698	442	2 497	770	1 727	481	724	1 191	496
Equipment, total	855 602	2 499	49 882	53 602	25 032	173 333	100 827	72 506	28 335	43 519	55 754	90 002
New	814 699	2 128	47 481	50 277	20 655	167 860	97 843	70 017	27 189	42 410	48 755	89 598
Used	40 903	371	2 402	3 324	4 377	5 473	2 984	2 489	1 147	1 109	6 999	404

Table 5-8. Capital Expenditures for Structures and Equipment for Companies with Employees by Major Industry Sector—*Continued*

(Millions of dollars.)

Year and type of expenditure	Finance and insurance (52)	Real estate and rental and leasing (53)	Professional, scientific, and technical services (54)	Management of companies and enterprises (55)	Administrative and support and waste management (56)	Educational services (61)	Health care and social assistance (62)	Arts, entertainment, and recreation (71)	Accommodation and food services (72)	Other services, except public administration (81)	Structure and equipment expenditures serving multiple industries
2007											
Total expenditures	172 894	117 969	31 804	4 542	18 167	23 238	84 160	18 769	38 021	29 680	2 380
Structures, total	45 159	41 222	7 453	1 472	3 859	17 910	45 361	12 589	22 211	19 165	656
New	36 507	34 026	6 944	1 404	3 677	17 322	43 522	11 894	21 226	16 264	650
Used	8 652	7 196	509	69	182	588	1 839	695	984	2 901	6
Equipment, total	127 735	76 747	24 351	3 070	14 308	5 328	38 799	6 180	15 810	10 515	1 725
New	126 763	74 735	23 931	2 943	13 599	5 253	38 258	5 916	14 671	9 593	1 724
Used	972	2 012	420	127	709	75	541	264	1 139	922	1
2008											
Total expenditures	132 913	106 910	32 980	4 567	16 552	27 426	90 248	17 109	40 519	28 312	4 175
Structures, total	25 058	45 929	8 836	1 304	4 133	21 698	50 105	11 594	24 947	18 673	1 035
New	22 640	36 532	8 481	1 241	3 789	20 632	47 205	11 224	24 271	17 899	1 030
Used	2 418	9 397	355	63	344	1 065	2 900	370	675	775	6
Equipment, total	107 855	60 981	24 144	3 264	12 420	5 728	40 143	5 515	15 572	9 638	3 139
New	107 108	59 117	23 349	3 146	11 687	5 672	39 161	5 340	14 012	8 974	3 124
Used	747	1 864	794	117	733	56	981	175	1 560	664	15
2009											
Total expenditures	99 466	72 902	28 163	4 719	19 234	28 018	79 370	16 265	26 439	29 296	3 034
Structures, total	21 825	26 564	6 669	1 371	5 876	22 388	44 375	11 035	14 735	22 054	641
New	20 419	22 350	5 975	1 334	5 361	21 577	42 188	10 804	13 607	21 564	639
Used	1 406	4 214	694	36	515	810	2 187	231	1 128	490	2
Equipment, total	77 641	46 339	21 494	3 349	13 359	5 630	34 994	5 230	11 704	7 243	2 393
New	77 169	44 594	20 980	3 311	12 471	5 403	34 271	5 073	10 858	6 545	2 389
Used	473	1 745	514	38	888	227	723	157	846	698	4
2010											
Total expenditures	103 093	81 282	28 203	4 946	16 873	23 368	78 381	12 121	19 915	20 951	2 471
Structures, total	16 209	32 375	5 706	1 567	3 552	17 673	42 861	7 709	9 765	13 605	562
New	13 653	23 085	5 365	1 517	3 466	16 678	40 113	7 551	9 051	11 987	558
Used	2 556	9 290	341	50	86	995	2 748	158	714	1 618	4
Equipment, total	86 884	48 908	22 497	3 379	13 321	5 695	35 520	4 412	10 151	7 346	1 909
New	86 401	47 593	21 889	3 359	12 626	5 553	34 808	4 164	8 856	6 879	1 902
Used	483	1 315	608	20	695	142	713	248	1 294	467	7
2011											
Total expenditures	109 229	91 124	28 109	5 449	18 423	21 019	83 114	11 430	24 833	16 064	3 133
Structures, total	14 405	33 540	6 733	1 368	3 536	15 037	42 910	6 589	12 021	8 675	608
New	12 238	24 764	6 340	1 308	3 422	14 444	40 534	. . .	11 352	7 867	. . .
Used	2 167	8 776	393	60	114	593	2 376	. . .	669	807	. . .
Equipment, total	94 823	57 583	21 376	4 081	14 887	5 982	40 204	4 841	12 811	7 389	2 524
New	94 551	55 163	20 822	4 020	14 340	5 910	39 342	. . .	10 892	7 031	. . .
Used	272	2 420	554	61	546	72	862	. . .	1 920	358	. . .
2012											
Total expenditures	130 168	115 652	31 605	6 916	18 811	21 629	88 860	13 296	28 802	16 789	3 711
Structures, total	17 749	42 034	7 536	2 555	3 578	15 721	45 981	8 055	14 154	9 078	988
New	14 141	31 344	7 098	2 429	3 452	15 449	43 773	8 031	13 359	8 537	977
Used	3 608	10 690	438	126	126	272	2 208	24	794	541	12
Equipment, total	112 419	73 618	24 069	4 361	15 233	5 908	42 879	5 241	14 649	7 711	2 722
New	107 539	70 375	23 183	4 290	14 059	5 806	41 973	5 052	13 471	7 110	2 683
Used	4 880	3 243	886	71	1 174	102	905	189	1 178	601	40
2013											
Total expenditures	139 947	113 901	35 622	6 389	22 042	22 611	93 265	14 981	34 532	18 645	3 463
Structures, total	16 064	39 337	8 557	1 699	4 287	16 580	48 607	8 263	16 304	11 189	866
New	13 772	31 713	8 332	1 644	4 021	15 256	46 187	7 969	14 303	10 667	858
Used	2 292	7 624	225	55	266	1 324	2 420	294	2 000	521	8
Equipment, total	123 884	74 564	27 064	4 690	17 755	6 031	44 657	6 718	18 228	7 456	2 597
New	119 341	69 522	26 403	4 645	16 828	5 883	43 411	6 221	16 509	7 007	2 575
Used	4 542	5 042	661	45	927	148	1 246	497	1 719	449	22

. . . = Not available.

NOTES AND DEFINITIONS, CHAPTER 5

Tables 5-1 through 5-4
Gross Saving and Investment Accounts

SOURCE: U.S. DEPARTMENT OF COMMERCE, BUREAU OF ECONOMIC ANALYSIS (BEA)

All of the data for this chapter is from the July 30, 2015 National Income and Product Accounts (NIPA) publication. Explanation of NIPA data is described in the Notes and Definitions to Chapter 1. All quarterly series are shown at seasonally adjusted annual rates. Current and constant dollar values are in billions of dollars. Constant dollar values are in 2009 dollars. Indexes of quantity are based on the average for the year 2009, set to equal 100.

In 2013, a comprehensive revision of NIPA included a major expansion of the investment accounts. Expenditures for research and development are now recognized as fixed investment. Before 2013, they were treated as if they were costs of producing this year's output. R&D spending by business, government, and nonprofit institutions serving households (NPISHs) is now counted as fixed investment. It is depreciated (with the estimated depreciation added to capital consumption allowances), so that there can be either positive or negative net investment in R&D. A similar treatment is now given to expenditures by private enterprises for the creation of entertainment, literary, and artistic originals. Finally, an expanded set of ownership transfer costs for residential fixed assets is recognized as fixed investment.

Definitions: Table 5-1

Gross saving is saving before the deduction of allowances for the consumption of fixed capital. It represents the amount of saving available to finance gross investment. *Net saving* is gross saving minus allowances for fixed capital consumption. It represents the amount of saving available for financing expansion of the capital stock, and comprises net private saving (the sum of personal saving, undistributed corporate profits, and wage accruals less disbursements) and the net saving of federal, state, and local governments.

Personal saving is derived by subtracting personal outlays from disposable personal income. (See Chapter 4 for more information.) It is the current net saving of individuals (including proprietors of unincorporated businesses), nonprofit institutions that primarily serve individuals, life insurance carriers, retirement funds, private noninsured welfare funds, and private trust funds. Conceptually, personal saving may also be viewed as the sum for all persons (including institutions as previously defined) of the net acquisition of financial assets and the change in physical assets, less the sum of net borrowing and consumption of fixed capital. In either case, it is defined to exclude capital gains. That is, it excludes profits on the increase in the value of homes,

securities, and other property—whether realized or unrealized—and therefore includes the noncorporate inventory valuation adjustment and the capital consumption adjustment (IVA and CCAdj, respectively). (See notes and definitions to Chapter 1.)

The net saving of *Domestic corporate business* is corporate profits after tax less dividends plus the corporate IVA and corporate CCAdj. (See notes and definitions for Chapter 1.)

Government net saving was formerly called "current surplus or deficit (-) of general government." (See Chapter 6 for further detail from the government accounts.) Where current receipts of government exceed current expenditures, government has a current surplus (indicated by a positive value) and saving is made available to finance investment by government or other sectors—for example, by the repayment of debt, which can free up funds for private investment. Where current expenditures exceed current receipts, there is a government deficit (indicated by a negative value) and government must borrow, drawing on funds that would otherwise be available for private investment. In these accounts, current expenditures are defined to include a charge for the consumption of fixed capital.

Consumption of fixed capital is an accounting charge for the using-up of private and government fixed capital, including software, located in the United States. It is based on studies of prices of used equipment and structures in resale markets. As of the 2013 revision, it also includes estimated charges for the using-up of the research and development and other intellectual property capital now defined as investment spending.

For general government and nonprofit institutions that primarily serve individuals, consumption of fixed capital is recorded in government consumption expenditures and in personal consumption expenditures (PCE), respectively, and taken to be the value of the current services of the fixed capital assets owned and used by these entities and the estimated using-up of R&D and other intellectual property.

Private consumption of fixed capital consists of tax-return-based depreciation charges for corporations and nonfarm proprietorships and historical-cost depreciation (calculated by the Bureau of Economic Analysis [BEA] using a geometric pattern of price declines) for farm proprietorships, rental income of persons, and nonprofit institutions, minus the capital consumption adjustments. (In other words, in the NIPA treatment of saving, the amount of the CCAdj is taken out of book depreciation and added to income and profits—a reallocation from one form of gross saving to another.) It also includes the charges for the using-up of private R&D and other intellectual property, as described above.

Gross private domestic investment consists of gross private fixed investment and change in private inventories. (See the notes and definitions for Chapter 1.)

Gross government investment consists of federal, state, and local general government and government enterprise expenditures for fixed assets (structures, equipment, and intellectual property). Government inventory investment is included in government consumption expenditures. For further detail, see Chapter 6.

Capital account transactions, net are the net cash or in-kind transfers between the United States and the rest of the world that are linked to the acquisition or disposition of assets rather than the purchase or sale of currently-produced goods and services. When positive, it represents a net transfer from the United States to the rest of the world; when negative, it represents a net transfer to the United States from the rest of the world. This is a definitional category that was introduced in the 1999 revision of the NIPAs. Estimates are available only from 1982 forward. With the new treatment of disaster losses and disaster insurance introduced in the 2009 revision, this line will include disaster-related insurance payouts to the rest of the world less what is received from the rest of the world.

Net lending or net borrowing (-), NIPAs is equal to the international balance on current account as measured in the NIPAs (see Chapter 7) less capital account transactions, net. When positive, this represents net investment by the United States in the rest of the world; when negative, it represents net borrowing by the United States from the rest of the world. For data before 1982, net lending or net borrowing equals the NIPA balance on current account, because estimates of capital account transactions are not available.

By definition, gross national saving must equal the sum of gross domestic investment, capital account transactions, and net international lending (where net international borrowing appears as negative lending). In practice, due to differences in measurement, these two aggregates differ by the *statistical discrepancy* calculated in the product and income accounts. (See Chapter 1.) Gross saving is therefore equal to the sum of gross domestic investment, capital account transactions, and net international lending minus the statistical discrepancy. Where the statistical discrepancy is negative, it means that the sum of measured investment, capital transactions, and net international lending has fallen short of measured saving.

Net domestic investment is gross domestic investment minus consumption of fixed capital, calculated by the editors from the data shown in the table.

Gross national income is national income plus the consumption of fixed capital. (See Chapter 1 for further information.) This is a new concept introduced in the 2003 revision. It is conceptually equal to gross national product, but differs by the statistical discrepancy. Gross national income is an appropriate denominator for the national saving ratios. Saving was previously shown as a percentage of gross national product; in the revision, it is instead shown as a percentage of the income-side

equivalent of gross national product. Since saving is measured as a residual from income, it is appropriate to involve consistent measurements—and consistent imperfections in those measurements—in both the numerator and the denominator of the fraction.

Definitions: Tables 5-2 through 5-4

Gross private fixed investment comprises both nonresidential and residential fixed investment. It consists of purchases of fixed assets, which are commodities that will be used in a production process for more than one year, including replacements and additions to the capital stock, and intellectual property, including software, research and development, and entertainment, literary, and artistic originals. It is "gross" in the sense that it is measured before a deduction for consumption of fixed capital. It covers investment by private businesses and nonprofit institutions in the United States, regardless of whether the investment is owned by U.S. residents. It does not include purchases of the same types of equipment, structures, or intellectual property by government agencies, which are included in government gross investment. It also does not include investment by U.S. residents in other countries.

Gross nonresidential fixed investment consists of structures, equipment, and intellectual property that are not related to personal residences.

Nonresidential structures consists of new construction, brokers' commissions on sales of structures, and net purchases (purchases less sales) of used structures by private business and by nonprofit institutions from government agencies. New construction includes hotels, motels, and mining exploration, shafts, and wells.

Other nonresidential structures consists primarily of religious, educational, vocational, lodging, railroads, farm, and amusement and recreational structures, net purchases of used structures, and brokers' commissions on the sale of structures.

Nonresidential equipment consists of private business purchases—on capital account—of new machinery, equipment, and vehicles; dealers' margins on sales of used equipment; and net purchases (purchases less sales) of used equipment from government agencies, persons, and the rest of the world. (However, it does not include the personal-use portion of equipment purchased for both business and personal use. This is included in PCE.)

Computers have displayed phenomenal growth in numbers and power not easily represented by index numbers or constant-dollar estimates at the scale shown in these tables. Zero entries shown in the quantity indexes for early years actually represent very small quantities. Because of rapid growth in computing power and declines in its price, constant-dollar measures are deemed not meaningful and are not calculated by BEA.

Other information processing includes communication equipment, nonmedical instruments, medical equipment and instruments, photocopy and related equipment, and office and accounting equipment.

Other nonresidential equipment consists primarily of furniture and fixtures, agricultural machinery, construction machinery, mining and oilfield machinery, service industry machinery, and electrical equipment not elsewhere classified.

Intellectual property comprises information processing software, research and development, and entertainment, literary, and artistic originals.

Software excludes the value of software "embedded," or bundled, in computers and other equipment, which is instead included in the value of that equipment.

Research and development consists of expenditures for both purchased and own-account R&D by businesses, NPISHs, and general governments. Government R&D expenditures are treated as investment regardless of whether the R&D is protected or made freely available to the public. Investment is measured as the sum of production costs.

Entertainment, literary, and other artistic originals include theatrical movies, long-lived television programs, books, music, and other miscellaneous entertainment.

Residential private fixed investment consists of both *structures* and residential producers' durable *equipment*—that is, equipment owned by landlords and rented to tenants. Investment in *structures* consists of new units, improvements to existing units, manufactured homes, brokers' commissions and other ownership transfer costs on the sale of residential property, and net purchases (purchases less sales) of used structures from government agencies.

Other residential structures consists primarily of manufactured homes, improvements, dormitories, net purchases of used structures, and brokers' commissions on the sale of residential structures.

Real gross private investment (Table 5-3) and *chain-type quantity indexes for private fixed investment* (Table 5-4) are defined and explained in the notes and definitions to Chapter 1. The chained-dollar (2009) estimates in Table 5-3 are constructed by applying the changes in the chain-type quantity indexes, as shown in Table 5-4, to the 2009 current-dollar values. Thus, they do not contain any information about time trends that is not already present in the quantity indexes.

In Table 5-4, the user may wish to distinguish between the use of the "not available" symbol (…) and the publication of zero values (0.0). The "not available" values shown for computers and software mean that BEA has no separate estimates of

their values; they are included in total "information processing equipment and software." The zeroes indicate quantities so small relative to the 2009 base that they round to zero, but they do exist and are included in the higher-level aggregates.

As the quantity indexes are chain-weighted at the basic level of aggregation, chained constant-dollar components generally do not add to the chained constant-dollar totals. For this reason, BEA only makes available year-2009-dollar estimates back to 1999 (except for the very highest levels of aggregation of gross domestic product [GDP]), since the addition problem is less severe for years close to the base year. However, the addition problem is so severe for computers that BEA does not even publish recent year-2009-dollar values for this component. BEA notes that "The quantity index for computers can be used to accurately measure the real growth rate of this component. However, because computers exhibit rapid changes in prices relative to other prices in the economy, the chained-dollar estimates should not be used to measure the component's relative importance or its contribution to the growth rate of more aggregate series." (Footnote to BEA Table 5.3.6, *Survey of Current Business*, available on the BEA Web site at <http://www.bea.gov>.) Accurate estimates of these contributions are shown in BEA Table 5.3.2, which is published in the *Survey of Current Business* and can be found on the BEA Web site.

Data availability, revisions, and references

See the information on the NIPAs at the end of the notes and definitions to Chapter 1. All current and historical data are available on the BEA Web site at <http://www.bea.gov> or the STAT-USA subscription Web site at <http://www.stat-usa.gov>.

Tables 5-5 and 5-6

Current-Cost Net Stock of Fixed Assets; Chain-Type Quantity Indexes for Net Stock of Fixed Assets

SOURCE: U.S. DEPARTMENT OF COMMERCE, BUREAU OF ECONOMIC ANALYSIS (BEA)

The Bureau of Economic Analysis (BEA) calculates annual, end-of-year measurements, integrated with the national income and product accounts (NIPAs), of the level of the stock of fixed assets in the U.S. economy, or what is commonly called the "capital stock." (The fixed investment component of the GDP is a flow, or the increment of new capital goods into the capital stock.) Data on consumer stocks of durable goods are also included in the accounts, but are not shown here. Historical data are available back to 1901, with detailed estimates of net stocks, depreciation, and investment by type and by NAICS (North American Industry Classification System) industry. From this data system, *Business Statistics* presents time series data on the net stock of fixed assets valued in current dollars and also as constant-dollar quantity indexes.

The expanded definition of investment introduced in the 2013 comprehensive revision of the NIPAs, explained at the beginning of the Notes and Definitions to this chapter, was not incorporated in the fixed assets accounts until October 2013, so this edition of *Business Statistics* now publishes for the first time fixed assets data including the new NIPA categories.

Definitions and methods

The definitions of capital stock categories are now the same as the fixed investment categories listed earlier in these Notes and Definitions.

The values of fixed capital and depreciation typically reported by businesses are inadequate for economic analysis and are not typically used in these measures. In business reports, capital is generally valued at historical costs—each year's capital acquisition in the prices of the year acquired—and the totals thus represent a mixture of pricing bases. Reported depreciation is generally based on historical cost and on depreciation rates allowable by federal income tax law, rather than on a realistic rate of economic depreciation.

In these data, the *net stock of fixed assets* is measured by a perpetual inventory method. In other words, net stock at any given time is the cumulative value of past gross investment less the cumulative value of past depreciation (measured by "consumption of fixed capital," the component of the NIPAs that is subtracted from GDP in order to yield net domestic product) and also less damages from disasters and war losses that exceed normal depreciation (such as Hurricane Katrina and the terrorist attacks of September 11, 2001).

The initial calculations using this perpetual inventory method are performed in real terms for each type of asset. They are then aggregated to higher levels using an annual-weighted Fisher-type index. (See the definition of *real or chained-dollar estimates* in the notes and definitions for Chapter 1.) This provides the *chain-type quantity indexes* shown in Table 5-6. Growth rates in these indexes measure real growth in the capital stock.

The real values are then converted to a *current-cost* basis to yield the values shown in Table 5-5. They are converted by multiplying the real values by the appropriate price index for the period under consideration. A major use of the current-cost net stock figures is comparison with the value of output in that year; for example, the current-cost net stock of fixed assets for the total economy divided by the current-dollar value of GDP yields a capital-output ratio for the entire economy. Growth rates in current-cost values will reflect both the real growth measured by the quantity indexes and the increase in the value at current prices of the existing stock.

Data availability and references

The 2015 Capital Spending Report: U.S. Capital Spending Patterns, 2004–2013 was released July 9, 2015. Full historical data are available on the BEA Web site at <www.bea.gov> (select "Fixed Assets").

Tables 5-7 and 5-8
Annual Capital Expenditures

SOURCE: U.S. DEPARTMENT OF COMMERCE, CENSUS BUREAU

These data are from the Census Bureau's Annual Capital Expenditures Survey (ACES). The survey provides detailed information on capital investment in new and used structures and equipment by nonfarm businesses.

The survey is based on a stratified random sample of approximately 46,000 companies with employees and 30,000 non-employer businesses (businesses with an owner but no employees). For companies with employees, the Census Bureau reports data for 132 separate industry categories from the North American Industry Classification System (NAICS). Major exclusions are foreign operations of U.S. businesses, businesses in U.S. territories, government operations (including the U.S. Postal Service), agricultural production companies, and private households.

Table 5-8 shows these data for the major NAICS sectors. Total capital expenditures, with no industry detail, are reported for the nonemployer businesses and are shown in Table 5-7, where they can be compared with the totals for companies with employees. The 1999 ACES was the first to use NAICS, providing data for the years 1998 forward on that basis.

Definitions

Capital expenditures include all capitalized costs during the year for both new and used structures and equipment, including software, that were chargeable to fixed asset accounts for which depreciation or amortization accounts are ordinarily maintained. For projects lasting longer than one year, this definition includes gross additions to construction-in-progress accounts, even if the asset was not in use and not yet depreciated. For *capital leases*, the company using the asset (lessee) is asked to include the cost or present value of the leased assets in the year in which the lease was entered. Also included in capital expenditures are capitalized leasehold improvements and capitalized interest charges on loans used to finance capital projects.

Structures consist of the capitalized costs of buildings and other structures and all necessary expenditures to acquire, construct, and prepare the structures. The costs of any machinery and equipment that is integral to or built-in features of the structures are classified as structures. Also included are major additions and alterations to existing structures and capitalized repairs and improvements to buildings.

New structures include new buildings and other structures not previously owned, as well as buildings and other structures that have been previously owned but not used or occupied.

Used structures are buildings and other structures that have been previously owned and occupied.

Equipment includes machinery, furniture and fixtures, computers, and vehicles used in the production and distribution of goods and services. Expenditures for machinery and equipment that is housed in structures and can be removed or replaced without significantly altering the structure are classified as equipment.

New equipment consists of machinery and equipment purchased new, as well as equipment produced in the company for the company's own use.

Used equipment is secondhand machinery and equipment.

Capital leases consist of new assets acquired under capital lease arrangements entered into during the year. Capital leases are defined by the criteria in the Financial Accounting Standards (FASB) Number 13.

Capitalized computer software consists of costs of materials and services directly related to the development or acquisition of software; payroll and payroll-related costs for employees directly associated with software development; and interest cost incurred while developing the software. Capitalized computer software is defined by the criteria in Statement of Position 98-1, Accounting for the Costs of Computer Software Developed or Obtained for Internal Use.

Prepackaged software is purchased off-the-shelf through retailers or other mass-market outlets for internal use by the company and includes the cost of licensing fees and service/maintenance agreements.

Vendor-customized software is externally developed by vendors and customized for the company's use.

Internally-developed software is developed by the company's employees for internal use and includes loaded payroll (salaries, wages, benefits, and bonuses related to all software development activities).

Data availability and references

Current and historical data and references are available on the Census Bureau Web site at <http://www.census.gov/econ/aces>.

CHAPTER 6: GOVERNMENT

Section 6a: Federal Government in the National Income and Product Accounts

Figure 6-1: Federal Government Saving and Dis-saving, 1955–2014
(surplus+/ deficit−, as a percent of GDP)

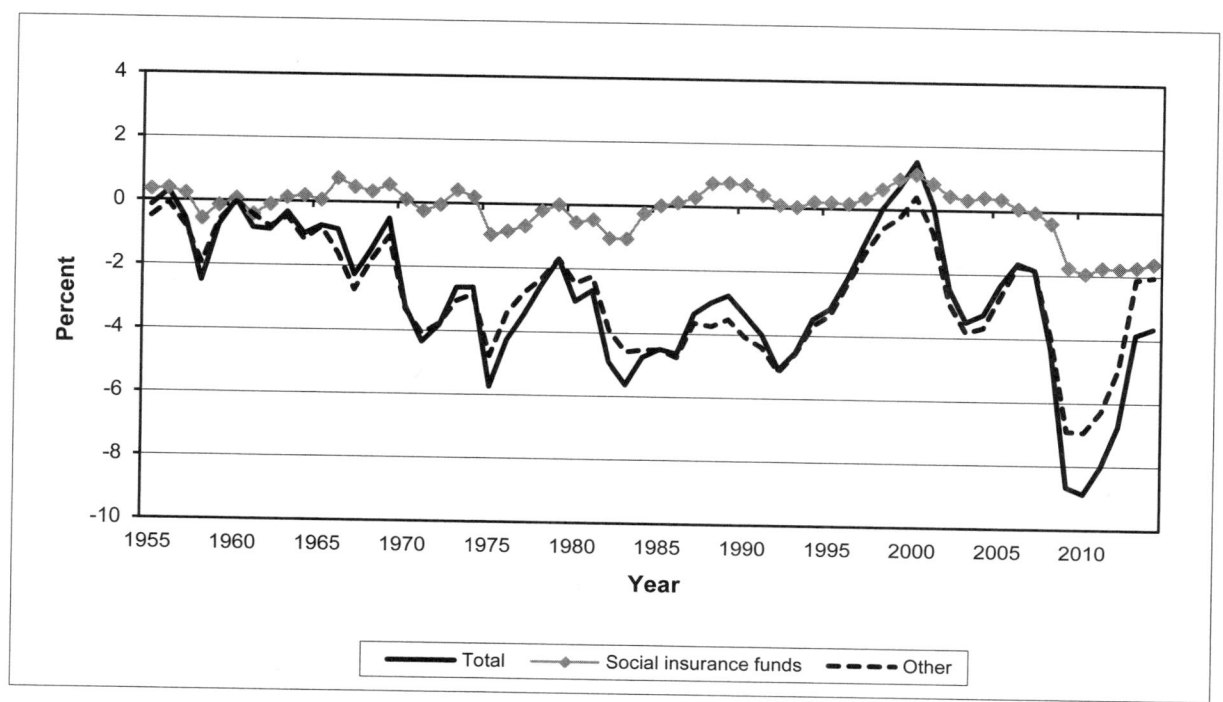

- In the recovery and economic expansion of the 2000s, the federal budget never got back to a surplus such as those achieved in 1999 and 2000. With the onset of the most severe recession of the postwar period beginning in December 2007, deficits grew rapidly, due both to the "automatic stabilizers"; such as unemployment insurance, built into the budget structure and to anti-recession programs such as bank bailouts. (Table 6-1)

- In calendar 2009, the NIPA budget deficit peaked at 9.8 percent of GDP, including $279.3 billion deficit in social insurance funds. This was not as great as World War II deficits but exceeded in scale the deficits of the 1930s. By 2014, the deficit shrank to half its peak size and was 3.7 percent of GDP, the smallest since 2007. (Tables 6-1, 1-1, and 6-14B)

- The main contributors to the rise in the deficit from 2007 to 2010 were increasing social benefits to persons, such as Social Security and unemployment insurance, and a drop in non-social-insurance tax receipts. Federal consumption spending and grants to state and local governments also rose. The deficit shrinkage from 2010 to 2014 was powered mainly by a resurgence in non-social-insurance tax receipts. (Table 6-1)

- The deficit in the social insurance funds failed to improve. The payroll-based taxes that fund Social Security and Medicare reflect the sluggishness in wage growth and do not benefit from increases in profits or higher-income compensation. (Table 6-1)

- Total federal government current expenditures have increased from 16.8 percent of gross domestic product (GDP) in 1955 to 24.4 percent in 2009, falling back somewhat to 21.1 percent in 2014. The composition of current expenditures changed significantly over the last 59 years. "Consumption" spending on defense and nondefense programs fell significantly, while social benefits to persons, such as Social Security and Medicare, increased substantially. (Tables 6-1, 1-1 and 6-3)

Table 6-1. Federal Government Current Receipts and Expenditures

(National income and product accounts, calendar years, billions of dollars, quarterly data are at seasonally adjusted annual rates.)

NIPA Table 3.2

				Current receipts										
		Current tax receipts							Contribu-tions for govern-ment social insurance	Income receipts on assets			Current transfer receipts	Current surplus of govern-ment enter-prises
Year and quarter	Total current receipts	Total tax receipts [1]	Personal current taxes	Taxes on production and imports		Taxes on corporate income		Taxes from the rest of the world		Interest receipts	Dividends	Rents and royalties		
				Excise taxes	Customs duties	Federal Reserve banks	Other corporate taxes							
1955	71.1	62.0	30.5	9.8	0.7	0.3	20.8	. . .	8.8	. . .	. . .	0.1	0.2	. . .
1956	75.8	65.8	33.9	10.2	0.7	0.4	20.5	. . .	9.6	. . .	. . .	0.1	0.3	. . .
1957	79.3	67.9	36.0	10.7	0.8	0.5	19.9	. . .	11.0	. . .	. . .	0.1	0.3	. . .
1958	76.1	64.6	35.5	10.4	0.8	0.5	17.4	. . .	11.0	. . .	. . .	0.1	0.3	. . .
1959	86.6	73.2	38.5	11.2	1.0	0.9	21.6	0.1	13.5	. . .	. . .	0.1	0.3	-0.5
1960	93.6	76.5	41.8	12.0	1.1	0.9	20.6	0.1	16.0	1.3	. . .	0.2	0.3	-0.7
1961	95.1	77.5	42.7	12.1	1.0	0.7	20.8	0.1	16.6	1.4	. . .	0.2	0.4	-0.9
1962	103.2	83.3	46.5	12.9	1.2	0.8	21.7	0.1	18.6	1.6	. . .	0.2	0.4	-0.9
1963	111.3	88.6	49.1	13.5	1.2	0.9	23.7	0.2	21.1	1.7	. . .	0.2	0.5	-0.7
1964	111.3	87.7	46.0	14.1	1.3	1.6	24.6	0.2	21.8	1.7	. . .	0.2	0.6	-0.8
1965	120.4	95.6	51.1	13.8	1.6	1.3	27.6	0.2	22.7	1.8	. . .	0.2	0.9	-0.9
1966	137.4	104.7	58.6	12.6	1.9	1.6	29.8	0.2	30.6	2.0	. . .	0.2	1.0	-1.2
1967	146.3	109.8	64.4	13.3	1.9	1.9	28.1	0.2	34.1	2.3	. . .	0.3	1.0	-1.3
1968	170.6	129.7	76.4	14.6	2.3	2.5	33.6	0.3	37.9	2.7	. . .	0.3	1.0	-1.0
1969	191.8	146.0	91.7	15.4	2.4	3.0	33.0	0.4	43.3	2.5	. . .	0.3	1.0	-1.3
1970	185.1	137.9	88.9	15.6	2.5	3.5	27.1	0.4	45.5	2.8	. . .	0.4	1.0	-2.5
1971	190.7	138.6	85.8	15.9	3.1	3.4	30.1	0.4	50.3	3.1	. . .	0.5	0.9	-2.8
1972	219.0	158.2	102.8	15.5	3.0	3.2	33.4	0.4	58.3	3.3	. . .	0.5	1.1	-2.4
1973	249.2	173.0	109.6	16.5	3.3	4.3	38.9	0.4	74.5	3.4	. . .	0.7	1.0	-3.4
1974	278.5	192.1	126.5	16.4	3.7	5.6	39.6	0.4	84.1	3.6	. . .	0.9	1.1	-3.3
1975	276.8	186.8	120.7	16.2	5.9	5.4	38.2	0.5	88.1	4.3	. . .	1.0	1.1	-4.4
1976	322.6	218.3	141.6	16.8	4.6	5.9	48.7	0.7	99.8	5.2	. . .	1.1	1.2	-2.9
1977	363.9	247.6	162.5	17.3	5.4	5.9	55.7	0.7	111.1	5.8	. . .	1.3	1.6	-3.4
1978	423.8	286.8	189.2	18.2	7.1	7.0	64.4	1.0	128.7	7.4	. . .	1.5	2.2	-2.9
1979	487.0	326.1	224.9	18.2	7.5	9.3	65.1	1.1	149.8	9.2	. . .	2.1	2.5	-2.7
1980	533.7	356.2	250.6	26.5	7.2	11.7	58.6	1.6	163.6	11.3	. . .	3.0	3.1	-3.6
1981	621.1	408.3	291.2	41.3	8.6	14.0	51.7	1.5	193.0	14.8	. . .	4.4	3.1	-2.6
1982	618.7	387.0	295.6	32.3	8.6	15.2	33.8	1.4	206.0	18.3	. . .	5.1	4.4	-2.1
1983	644.8	393.7	286.8	35.3	9.1	14.2	47.1	1.2	223.1	20.4	. . .	4.3	5.2	-1.9
1984	711.2	425.7	301.9	35.4	11.9	16.1	59.2	1.3	254.1	22.8	. . .	4.9	6.3	-2.7
1985	775.7	460.7	336.5	33.9	12.2	17.8	58.5	1.9	277.9	25.6	. . .	4.6	8.6	-1.6
1986	817.9	479.8	350.6	30.0	13.7	17.8	66.0	1.7	298.9	28.8	. . .	3.3	7.6	-0.6
1987	899.5	544.2	393.0	30.4	15.5	17.7	85.4	2.0	317.4	25.1	. . .	3.1	10.2	-0.5
1988	962.4	567.2	403.8	33.4	16.4	17.4	93.8	2.4	354.8	27.4	. . .	2.8	9.6	0.7
1989	1 042.5	622.8	453.1	32.3	17.5	21.6	95.6	2.7	378.0	25.9	. . .	3.0	11.8	1.1
1990	1 087.6	644.2	472.1	33.4	17.5	23.6	94.5	3.0	402.0	26.9	. . .	3.5	13.3	-2.3
1991	1 107.8	637.9	463.6	44.9	16.8	20.8	89.2	2.6	420.6	26.2	. . .	3.8	17.2	2.1
1992	1 154.4	662.2	477.5	45.0	18.3	16.8	102.0	2.6	444.0	22.2	. . .	3.5	18.4	4.1
1993	1 231.0	715.3	507.7	46.5	19.8	16.0	122.5	2.7	465.5	22.8	. . .	3.8	20.2	3.5
1994	1 329.3	783.9	545.1	57.5	21.4	20.5	136.3	3.1	496.2	20.0	. . .	3.6	21.6	4.0
1995	1 417.4	849.1	590.3	55.7	19.8	23.4	155.9	3.9	521.9	20.8	. . .	3.0	17.5	5.0
1996	1 536.3	937.0	668.4	53.6	19.2	20.1	170.5	5.2	545.4	22.5	. . .	4.1	22.7	4.5
1997	1 667.3	1 035.8	749.8	58.2	19.6	20.7	182.3	5.1	579.4	21.0	. . .	4.5	20.1	6.6
1998	1 789.8	1 121.8	831.2	61.1	19.6	26.6	177.7	5.7	617.4	17.3	. . .	4.2	21.5	7.6
1999	1 905.4	1 199.9	897.6	64.3	19.2	25.4	187.6	5.9	654.8	17.1	. . .	4.0	22.4	7.2
2000	2 068.2	1 313.9	999.8	66.1	21.1	25.3	194.1	7.3	698.6	19.3	. . .	6.3	24.8	5.3
2001	2 031.8	1 253.9	996.3	64.6	20.6	27.1	137.6	7.7	723.3	18.0	. . .	8.4	25.5	2.8
2002	1 870.6	1 077.7	832.8	66.9	19.9	24.5	126.0	7.6	739.4	15.3	. . .	6.5	24.9	6.9
2003	1 895.1	1 075.5	778.5	68.7	21.4	22.0	175.8	9.0	763.2	16.5	. . .	7.0	26.2	6.7
2004	2 027.4	1 158.7	803.2	72.0	23.3	18.1	232.2	10.0	808.9	16.6	0.1	8.7	29.6	4.9
2005	2 303.5	1 389.3	936.8	74.1	25.3	21.5	319.5	12.1	853.4	17.3	0.2	9.7	32.7	0.9
2006	2 537.7	1 563.4	1 054.6	72.6	26.7	29.1	366.0	14.6	905.7	18.8	0.3	9.9	37.9	1.8
2007	2 667.2	1 642.4	1 169.7	65.8	28.8	34.6	328.2	15.3	947.2	22.1	0.2	11.1	42.0	2.0
2008	2 579.5	1 520.7	1 174.3	64.7	29.2	31.7	202.0	18.8	974.4	19.5	0.6	13.8	49.7	0.8
2009	2 238.4	1 171.1	864.5	68.3	23.1	47.4	153.0	14.8	950.8	22.8	18.7	7.0	67.2	0.8
2010	2 443.3	1 352.7	941.6	68.2	28.6	79.3	219.4	15.7	970.9	29.5	17.0	8.0	68.1	-3.1
2011	2 574.1	1 553.8	1 129.1	76.7	31.9	75.4	224.0	16.7	904.0	27.7	18.8	9.9	67.1	-7.1
2012	2 699.1	1 661.1	1 164.7	81.7	33.5	88.4	274.7	18.2	938.1	21.3	21.1	10.2	56.1	-8.9
2013	3 141.3	1 825.0	1 300.6	90.4	35.4	79.6	299.6	19.3	1 093.4	22.8	131.3	9.1	71.1	-11.3
2014	3 265.2	1 974.4	1 396.9	100.5	37.3	96.9	321.0	21.7	1 145.2	23.4	40.7	10.6	80.6	-9.7
2012														
1st quarter	2 664.2	1 629.6	1 137.8	81.9	32.1	99.6	261.5	16.6	928.1	22.7	21.0	10.1	60.5	-7.8
2nd quarter	2 678.6	1 647.8	1 150.2	80.4	34.0	90.3	275.5	17.4	931.5	20.6	21.2	10.3	55.7	-8.5
3rd quarter	2 687.7	1 660.6	1 162.7	80.6	34.0	85.0	280.8	17.5	934.6	20.8	21.2	10.2	49.6	-9.1
4th quarter	2 765.8	1 706.6	1 208.3	83.7	33.8	78.8	280.9	21.1	958.4	21.1	21.1	10.3	58.6	-10.4
2013														
1st quarter	2 976.7	1 771.9	1 263.4	87.6	35.2	67.3	299.6	18.8	1 075.4	22.4	41.6	8.8	66.9	-10.2
2nd quarter	3 253.8	1 809.7	1 294.4	90.4	34.6	76.8	294.9	18.7	1 091.7	22.9	266.7	8.7	65.4	-11.3
3rd quarter	3 086.4	1 844.2	1 311.0	91.6	35.1	84.6	302.0	19.9	1 098.2	23.1	59.5	9.4	63.5	-11.4
4th quarter	3 248.2	1 874.0	1 333.6	92.1	36.8	89.9	301.9	19.7	1 108.2	22.9	157.4	9.5	88.5	-12.3
2014														
1st quarter	3 215.5	1 921.9	1 359.3	99.7	36.8	100.4	302.9	23.0	1 130.7	22.9	71.1	9.8	68.5	-9.5
2nd quarter	3 256.3	1 970.2	1 380.2	100.2	36.9	101.8	330.8	20.3	1 137.4	23.1	41.4	10.6	83.4	-9.9
3rd quarter	3 293.4	1 989.7	1 406.5	101.7	37.3	93.2	328.7	22.4	1 149.1	23.4	23.0	11.3	106.5	-9.6
4th quarter	3 295.7	2 015.6	1 441.7	100.4	38.4	92.2	321.7	21.2	1 163.5	24.3	27.5	10.7	63.8	-9.8

[1]Does not include "contributions for government social insurance" (the taxes that fund Social Security, Medicare, and unemployment insurance), which are shown separately in column 9.
. . . = Not available.

Table 6-1. Federal Government Current Receipts and Expenditures—*Continued*

(National income and product accounts, calendar years, billions of dollars, quarterly data are at seasonally adjusted annual rates.)

NIPA Table 3.2

Year and quarter	Total current expenditures	Consumption expenditures	Government social benefits — Benefits to persons	Government social benefits — Benefits to the rest of the world	Other current transfer payments — Grants-in-aid to state and local governments	Other current transfer payments — Payments to the rest of the world (net)	Interest payments — Total	Interest payments — To persons and business	Interest payments — To the rest of the world	Subsidies	Net federal government saving, NIPA (surplus + / deficit -) — Total	Net federal government saving — Social insurance funds	Net federal government saving — Other
1955	71.6	46.8	11.5	...	2.3	2.2	7.9	...	0.1	0.9	-0.6	1.5	-2.1
1956	74.4	47.4	12.3	...	2.4	2.0	8.8	...	0.2	1.5	1.4	1.7	-0.3
1957	81.9	50.9	14.5	...	2.8	1.9	9.9	...	0.2	1.9	-2.6	1.1	-3.7
1958	88.1	52.6	18.2	...	3.2	2.0	10.0	...	0.1	1.9	-12.0	-2.7	-9.4
1959	90.5	51.8	18.6	...	3.6	4.0	11.4	...	0.3	2.1	-3.9	-0.7	-3.2
1960	93.4	50.9	19.9	0.2	3.8	3.5	13.9	13.5	0.3	1.1	0.2	0.4	-0.2
1961	99.8	52.7	23.1	0.3	4.3	3.5	13.9	13.6	0.3	2.0	-4.7	-2.3	-2.4
1962	108.5	59.0	23.5	0.3	4.7	3.6	15.1	14.8	0.3	2.3	-5.3	-0.6	-4.8
1963	113.5	61.2	24.6	0.3	5.2	3.6	16.3	15.9	0.4	2.2	-2.1	0.8	-3.0
1964	118.2	63.1	25.2	0.3	6.0	3.4	17.5	17.0	0.5	2.7	-6.9	1.3	-8.1
1965	125.9	66.5	27.3	0.5	6.6	3.6	18.6	18.1	0.5	3.0	-5.5	0.4	-5.9
1966	144.3	76.5	29.9	0.5	9.4	4.0	20.3	19.7	0.5	3.9	-7.0	6.0	-13.0
1967	165.7	88.0	36.5	0.6	10.9	4.0	21.9	21.3	0.6	3.8	-19.5	4.1	-23.6
1968	184.3	96.8	41.9	0.6	11.8	4.5	24.6	23.9	0.7	4.1	-13.7	3.2	-16.9
1969	196.9	100.4	45.8	0.6	13.7	4.5	27.5	26.7	0.8	4.5	-5.1	5.7	-10.8
1970	219.9	102.3	55.6	0.7	18.3	4.8	33.3	32.4	0.9	4.8	-34.8	1.0	-35.7
1971	241.5	106.6	66.1	0.8	22.1	6.0	35.2	33.5	1.8	4.6	-50.8	-3.0	-47.8
1972	267.9	112.2	72.9	1.0	30.5	7.2	37.6	35.1	2.6	6.6	-48.9	-0.6	-48.2
1973	286.9	113.9	84.5	1.2	33.5	5.4	43.3	39.6	3.7	5.1	-37.7	5.9	-43.6
1974	319.1	122.5	103.1	1.3	34.9	6.0	48.0	43.9	4.0	3.2	-40.6	3.2	-43.9
1975	373.8	132.9	132.3	2.0	43.6	6.1	52.5	48.1	4.3	4.3	-97.0	-16.3	-80.7
1976	402.4	139.0	143.5	2.5	49.1	4.5	58.9	54.6	4.3	4.9	-79.9	-16.0	-63.8
1977	435.8	149.6	154.4	2.6	54.8	4.2	65.3	60.0	5.2	6.9	-71.9	-14.1	-57.8
1978	483.7	162.0	162.7	2.7	63.5	5.0	79.1	70.9	8.2	8.7	-59.8	-4.7	-55.1
1979	531.5	176.0	183.0	3.0	64.0	5.8	91.5	80.9	10.6	8.2	-44.5	0.0	-44.5
1980	619.9	202.1	220.3	3.5	69.7	7.3	107.5	95.7	11.9	9.4	-86.3	-15.8	-70.5
1981	706.9	231.3	250.7	4.3	69.4	6.7	133.4	117.2	16.3	11.1	-85.8	-14.3	-71.5
1982	783.3	255.7	281.9	4.1	66.3	8.1	152.7	134.7	18.0	14.6	-164.6	-34.4	-130.3
1983	849.8	277.9	303.6	3.6	67.9	8.9	167.0	148.9	18.1	20.9	-205.0	-37.9	-167.2
1984	903.5	292.0	309.7	3.7	72.3	11.2	193.8	173.7	20.2	20.7	-192.3	-9.4	-183.0
1985	971.3	316.8	325.9	4.0	76.2	13.8	213.7	191.6	22.2	21.0	-195.6	0.9	-196.5
1986	1 030.6	336.5	344.3	4.4	82.4	14.2	224.2	200.9	23.3	24.6	-212.7	5.7	-218.3
1987	1 062.7	347.8	357.2	4.3	78.4	12.7	232.3	208.2	24.1	30.0	-163.2	14.5	-177.6
1988	1 119.8	360.8	378.4	4.6	85.7	13.2	247.9	219.2	28.8	29.2	-157.3	39.1	-196.4
1989	1 199.1	380.2	411.7	5.1	91.8	13.5	269.7	235.1	34.5	27.1	-156.6	42.6	-199.3
1990	1 288.5	401.8	447.0	6.2	104.4	13.5	289.0	253.0	36.1	26.6	-200.9	42.4	-243.3
1991	1 354.0	423.9	494.0	6.3	124.0	-25.6	304.4	268.3	36.1	27.1	-246.2	24.7	-270.9
1992	1 487.0	430.2	551.8	6.2	141.7	20.6	306.9	272.6	34.3	29.7	-332.7	5.4	-338.0
1993	1 542.8	427.7	583.7	6.2	155.7	21.7	311.4	277.3	34.2	36.3	-311.8	2.8	-314.6
1994	1 583.0	427.3	609.0	6.8	166.8	19.9	320.8	284.5	36.4	32.2	-253.7	15.4	-269.0
1995	1 658.2	427.7	647.1	6.8	174.5	15.4	352.3	305.2	47.1	34.5	-240.8	15.6	-256.5
1996	1 714.8	428.4	682.1	7.6	181.5	20.4	360.0	303.2	56.8	34.9	-178.5	12.9	-191.4
1997	1 758.5	438.7	707.9	7.9	188.1	17.0	365.6	295.9	69.7	33.4	-91.2	28.9	-120.1
1998	1 787.0	436.4	722.1	8.2	200.8	18.0	365.6	293.5	72.1	35.9	2.7	58.3	-55.6
1999	1 838.8	455.6	739.9	8.5	219.2	18.7	352.2	285.4	66.7	44.8	66.6	92.5	-25.9
2000	1 911.7	475.1	773.4	8.7	233.1	22.4	353.7	289.3	64.4	45.3	156.5	114.3	42.2
2001	2 017.4	505.4	840.8	9.4	261.3	18.3	331.2	274.1	57.1	51.1	14.5	88.1	-73.7
2002	2 141.1	560.3	917.5	9.7	287.2	23.3	302.7	253.4	49.3	40.5	-270.5	49.7	-320.2
2003	2 297.9	628.5	967.5	10.1	321.7	28.6	292.6	245.2	47.4	49.0	-402.9	37.8	-440.7
2004	2 426.6	681.4	1 019.5	10.7	332.2	30.8	306.1	251.3	54.8	46.0	-399.2	51.2	-450.4
2005	2 608.2	723.4	1 084.4	11.2	343.4	40.9	344.4	276.4	68.0	60.5	-304.7	48.4	-353.2
2006	2 764.8	763.9	1 189.2	12.4	340.8	35.0	372.3	286.5	85.9	51.1	-227.0	11.8	-238.8
2007	2 932.8	798.4	1 264.2	13.3	359.0	42.3	408.2	309.2	99.0	47.5	-265.7	-4.1	-261.6
2008	3 213.5	879.8	1 464.6	15.5	371.0	45.0	388.0	290.9	97.1	49.6	-634.0	-54.9	-579.1
2009	3 487.2	933.7	1 616.2	16.0	458.1	52.7	353.6	264.8	88.8	56.9	-1 248.8	-253.1	-995.7
2010	3 772.0	1 003.9	1 757.9	16.5	505.3	53.5	380.6	288.0	92.6	54.3	-1 328.7	-290.9	-1 037.8
2011	3 818.3	1 006.1	1 779.9	17.1	472.5	57.6	425.7	328.2	97.5	59.5	-1 244.1	-271.0	-973.2
2012	3 789.1	1 007.8	1 783.6	18.0	444.0	55.3	422.9	327.0	95.9	57.6	-1 090.1	-289.1	-800.9
2013	3 782.2	961.3	1 823.2	18.8	450.1	53.9	416.1	319.5	96.5	58.9	-640.9	-288.4	-352.5
2014	3 896.7	955.3	1 877.3	19.5	494.8	52.3	440.1	346.2	93.9	57.4	-631.5	-279.3	-352.2
2012													
1st quarter	3 771.2	1 011.6	1 774.3	17.7	439.7	56.9	413.1	319.0	94.1	58.0	-1 107.1	-289.2	-817.9
2nd quarter	3 780.6	1 006.0	1 777.8	17.9	439.1	55.3	426.9	334.3	92.6	57.6	-1 102.0	-290.9	-811.1
3rd quarter	3 767.3	1 012.5	1 785.6	18.1	443.0	56.5	395.8	299.1	96.7	55.8	-1 079.5	-294.6	-785.0
4th quarter	3 837.4	1 001.2	1 796.7	18.2	454.1	52.6	455.7	355.6	100.2	58.9	-1 071.6	-281.8	-789.8
2013													
1st quarter	3 767.3	978.5	1 816.5	18.6	440.5	52.7	401.9	303.2	98.7	58.7	-790.6	-298.2	-492.4
2nd quarter	3 779.8	967.0	1 816.1	18.8	450.5	53.8	414.3	316.1	98.1	59.3	-525.9	-281.1	-244.8
3rd quarter	3 794.1	950.8	1 826.0	19.0	458.4	57.6	423.3	328.1	95.2	59.0	-707.7	-285.9	-421.7
4th quarter	3 787.7	948.7	1 834.0	19.0	451.1	51.4	424.9	330.7	94.2	58.6	-539.6	-288.6	-251.0
2014													
1st quarter	3 834.7	952.9	1 849.1	19.3	468.6	53.2	433.8	340.3	93.5	57.6	-619.2	-276.6	-342.6
2nd quarter	3 886.3	950.9	1 875.3	19.4	484.2	50.8	448.2	355.5	92.7	57.4	-630.0	-282.9	-347.1
3rd quarter	3 943.5	968.2	1 886.0	19.5	514.1	52.1	445.9	351.2	94.7	57.7	-650.1	-280.8	-369.3
4th quarter	3 922.4	949.1	1 898.8	19.6	512.5	53.2	432.3	337.7	94.6	57.0	-626.7	-277.1	-349.7

. . . = Not available.

Table 6-2. Federal Government Consumption Expenditures and Gross Investment

(National income and product accounts, calendar years, billions of dollars, quarterly data are at seasonally adjusted annual rates.)

NIPA Tables 3.9.5, 3.10.5

Year and quarter	Total	Federal government consumption expenditures and gross investment												
		Consumption expenditures					Gross investment						
								National defense			Nondefense		
		Total	Compensation of general government employees	Consumption of general government fixed capital	Intermediate goods and services purchased [1]	Less: Own-account investment and sales to other sectors	Total	Structures	Equipment	Intellectual property	Structures	Equipment	Intellectual property
1955	61.0	46.8	22.9	10.7	15.5	2.2	14.2	2.1	7.8	3.0	0.6	0.2	0.4
1956	63.1	47.4	23.5	11.6	14.1	1.8	15.8	2.1	7.8	4.1	0.9	0.2	0.6
1957	68.4	50.9	24.3	12.6	16.4	2.4	17.6	2.3	8.2	4.9	1.1	0.2	0.9
1958	71.5	52.6	25.3	13.3	16.5	2.6	18.9	2.6	8.5	5.2	1.4	0.2	1.1
1959	73.5	51.8	25.8	14.2	14.5	2.7	21.8	2.5	10.7	5.7	1.5	0.2	1.1
1960	72.8	50.9	26.6	15.0	12.0	2.7	21.9	2.2	10.1	5.9	1.7	0.3	1.7
1961	77.4	52.7	27.7	15.9	11.9	2.8	24.6	2.4	11.5	6.5	1.9	0.3	2.1
1962	85.5	59.0	29.5	17.0	15.6	3.1	26.5	2.0	12.5	6.7	2.1	0.3	2.9
1963	87.8	61.2	30.8	18.1	15.6	3.4	26.7	1.6	10.9	6.9	2.3	0.4	4.5
1964	90.2	63.1	33.0	19.0	14.9	3.8	27.1	1.3	10.1	6.9	2.5	0.6	5.7
1965	93.1	66.5	34.8	19.8	16.0	4.2	26.7	1.1	8.9	6.7	2.8	0.5	6.8
1966	106.5	76.5	39.8	20.8	20.6	4.7	30.1	1.3	10.4	7.0	2.8	0.6	7.9
1967	120.0	88.0	43.8	22.2	26.5	4.5	31.9	1.2	12.2	7.9	2.2	0.6	7.8
1968	127.9	96.8	48.3	23.8	29.3	4.6	31.1	1.2	10.8	7.9	2.1	0.5	8.6
1969	131.1	100.4	51.4	25.5	28.7	5.1	30.7	1.5	9.7	8.2	1.9	0.6	8.8
1970	132.7	102.3	55.2	27.2	25.3	5.4	30.5	1.3	9.5	8.1	2.1	0.7	8.8
1971	134.4	106.6	58.8	28.6	25.0	5.8	27.8	1.8	5.5	8.4	2.5	0.8	8.9
1972	141.5	112.2	62.6	29.6	26.9	6.9	29.3	1.8	5.3	9.2	2.7	1.1	9.2
1973	145.6	113.9	64.6	31.2	25.8	7.7	31.7	2.1	6.0	9.7	3.1	1.1	9.6
1974	158.1	122.5	67.8	34.0	29.2	8.6	35.7	2.2	8.2	10.0	3.4	1.5	10.4
1975	172.8	132.9	72.5	37.0	31.8	8.4	39.8	2.3	9.9	10.5	4.1	1.6	11.5
1976	183.8	139.0	76.5	39.8	31.3	8.5	44.7	2.1	12.1	11.3	4.6	1.8	12.7
1977	198.8	149.6	80.9	42.8	35.6	9.7	49.2	2.4	13.3	12.3	5.0	2.3	14.0
1978	216.7	162.0	87.1	46.4	39.3	10.8	54.7	2.5	14.3	13.3	6.1	2.7	15.9
1979	237.7	176.0	92.0	50.6	45.8	12.4	61.7	2.5	17.4	14.9	6.3	2.7	17.9
1980	272.4	202.1	100.8	56.6	58.4	13.6	70.3	3.2	19.8	17.2	7.1	3.2	19.8
1981	311.7	231.3	112.2	63.8	69.6	14.3	80.4	3.2	24.1	20.9	7.7	3.3	21.2
1982	345.6	255.7	122.0	71.0	77.6	14.9	90.0	4.0	29.1	25.2	6.8	3.9	21.1
1983	380.2	277.9	127.7	77.2	88.8	15.9	102.3	4.8	35.2	29.8	6.7	4.3	21.6
1984	407.6	292.0	136.5	84.6	88.3	17.4	115.6	4.9	41.1	35.0	7.0	4.7	22.8
1985	449.3	316.8	145.0	91.4	99.1	18.7	132.5	6.2	47.9	41.3	7.3	5.1	24.6
1986	478.4	336.5	149.1	98.2	108.8	19.6	141.9	6.8	52.7	43.9	8.0	4.8	25.7
1987	500.2	347.8	153.1	105.4	110.2	20.9	152.4	7.7	55.0	48.1	9.0	5.2	27.4
1988	508.8	360.8	161.9	114.0	107.4	22.5	148.0	7.4	49.6	48.5	6.8	6.1	29.6
1989	531.4	380.2	168.5	121.6	114.0	23.9	151.2	6.4	51.5	47.3	6.9	7.2	31.9
1990	560.0	401.8	176.0	128.3	123.1	25.6	158.2	6.1	54.6	46.6	8.0	8.1	34.8
1991	580.7	423.9	186.5	134.8	129.4	26.8	156.8	4.6	53.4	43.3	9.2	8.9	37.4
1992	586.6	430.2	189.6	138.1	129.4	26.9	156.4	5.2	50.7	41.3	10.3	10.0	38.9
1993	578.4	427.7	188.1	141.7	125.1	27.2	150.7	5.3	44.7	39.2	11.2	9.9	40.4
1994	572.7	427.3	186.1	144.5	126.1	29.3	145.4	5.8	41.9	38.1	10.2	7.5	41.9
1995	575.4	427.7	183.3	148.0	123.5	27.3	147.7	6.7	39.8	38.4	10.8	8.6	43.4
1996	578.2	428.4	182.2	148.3	125.5	27.6	149.8	6.3	39.9	38.9	11.3	9.7	43.8
1997	582.4	438.7	183.5	148.9	131.9	25.6	143.7	6.1	33.6	39.2	9.9	10.0	44.9
1998	584.1	436.4	185.8	149.2	128.1	26.6	147.7	5.8	34.0	39.4	10.8	10.2	47.5
1999	610.4	455.6	191.7	152.0	137.4	25.6	154.9	5.4	36.8	39.3	10.7	11.9	50.7
2000	632.4	475.1	202.4	156.3	144.6	28.2	157.4	5.4	37.8	40.2	8.4	10.8	54.8
2001	669.2	505.4	211.2	158.0	165.8	29.6	163.8	5.3	39.9	42.5	8.1	10.0	58.1
2002	740.6	560.3	236.4	159.8	195.6	31.5	180.3	6.1	45.6	47.0	10.0	12.0	59.6
2003	824.8	628.5	266.9	165.1	229.9	33.5	196.4	7.1	50.2	53.7	10.3	12.4	62.7
2004	892.4	681.4	284.2	173.3	258.5	34.6	211.0	6.9	56.7	59.8	9.6	13.4	64.6
2005	946.3	723.4	303.7	183.8	275.2	39.2	222.9	7.2	60.7	64.5	8.1	15.2	67.3
2006	1 002.0	763.9	314.8	194.8	294.4	40.0	238.0	7.8	66.8	67.5	9.4	17.4	69.2
2007	1 049.8	798.4	329.6	206.7	302.3	40.2	251.4	10.0	70.8	71.9	11.4	16.1	71.3
2008	1 155.6	879.8	350.2	220.1	352.3	42.8	275.8	13.7	83.8	73.8	11.4	17.6	75.5
2009	1 217.7	933.7	375.5	228.1	374.4	44.3	284.0	17.1	86.0	71.8	12.0	17.7	79.3
2010	1 303.9	1 003.9	404.8	238.8	406.6	46.3	300.0	16.7	90.3	72.6	16.0	19.1	85.3
2011	1 303.5	1 006.1	413.6	250.5	392.6	50.6	297.4	13.3	87.5	73.8	16.7	18.3	87.7
2012	1 292.5	1 007.8	411.6	257.2	385.9	47.0	284.7	8.1	85.2	70.6	14.5	18.8	87.5
2013	1 230.6	961.3	402.8	260.4	344.3	46.3	269.4	6.5	78.7	68.1	11.7	16.2	88.2
2014	1 219.9	955.3	406.5	263.4	332.1	46.7	264.6	5.3	75.4	67.8	12.2	17.2	86.7
2012													
1st quarter	1 300.5	1 011.6	414.5	255.1	389.1	47.2	288.9	9.6	86.1	72.2	15.0	19.0	87.1
2nd quarter	1 293.7	1 006.0	412.7	256.9	384.6	48.1	287.7	8.3	87.0	71.1	14.7	19.1	87.5
3rd quarter	1 297.0	1 012.5	410.8	258.3	389.7	46.3	284.4	7.0	86.9	70.0	14.0	19.0	87.5
4th quarter	1 278.9	1 001.2	408.6	258.6	380.0	46.0	277.7	7.6	80.6	69.3	14.2	18.0	88.0
2013													
1st quarter	1 250.4	978.5	406.2	259.2	359.6	46.5	271.9	6.8	78.9	68.8	11.9	16.8	88.6
2nd quarter	1 234.2	967.0	403.9	260.2	349.3	46.4	267.2	6.8	76.2	68.1	11.6	16.1	88.4
3rd quarter	1 220.4	950.8	397.9	260.7	338.6	46.4	269.6	6.7	79.2	67.9	11.7	15.8	88.3
4th quarter	1 217.6	948.7	403.3	261.7	329.8	46.1	268.8	5.7	80.3	67.6	11.5	16.0	87.7
2014													
1st quarter	1 214.8	952.9	405.6	262.3	330.7	45.6	261.8	5.6	73.2	67.7	11.9	16.5	87.0
2nd quarter	1 216.9	950.9	406.9	262.8	329.0	47.8	266.0	5.3	77.6	67.7	11.9	17.0	86.5
3rd quarter	1 233.1	968.2	407.4	263.8	343.3	46.3	264.9	5.3	76.0	67.9	11.9	17.2	86.7
4th quarter	1 214.7	949.1	406.2	264.5	325.3	46.9	265.6	5.0	74.8	68.0	13.1	18.2	86.6

[1]Includes general government intermediate inputs for goods and services sold to other sectors and for own-account investment.

Table 6-3. Federal Government Defense and Nondefense Consumption Expenditures by Type

(National income and product accounts, calendar years, billions of dollars, quarterly data are at seasonally adjusted annual rates.)

NIPA Table 3.10.5

Year and quarter	Defense consumption expenditures [1]						Nondefense consumption expenditures [1]					
	Total	Compensation of general government employees	Consumption of general government fixed capital	Intermediate goods and services purchased [2]			Total	Compensation of general government employees	Consumption of general government fixed capital	Intermediate goods and services purchased [2]		
				Durable goods	Nondurable goods	Services				Durable goods	Nondurable goods	Services
1955	39.4	19.3	9.8	6.0	1.7	3.9	7.4	3.7	0.8	0.0	2.4	1.5
1956	40.9	19.6	10.7	5.9	1.7	4.2	6.4	3.9	0.9	0.1	0.5	1.7
1957	44.6	20.1	11.7	6.7	2.0	5.6	6.3	4.2	0.9	0.1	0.3	1.8
1958	46.0	20.6	12.3	7.0	2.0	5.8	6.6	4.8	1.0	0.0	0.5	1.2
1959	42.0	20.7	13.0	5.0	1.8	3.2	9.8	5.1	1.1	0.1	2.4	2.1
1960	42.6	21.1	13.8	4.4	1.7	3.5	8.3	5.6	1.2	0.0	0.5	1.9
1961	44.2	21.7	14.5	3.6	2.2	4.0	8.5	6.1	1.4	0.1	-0.3	2.3
1962	48.6	22.9	15.4	4.6	2.8	4.7	10.4	6.5	1.6	0.1	1.1	2.4
1963	50.5	23.6	16.3	4.7	2.5	5.2	10.7	7.2	1.9	0.1	0.6	2.6
1964	51.4	25.2	16.7	4.0	2.8	4.7	11.7	7.8	2.3	0.1	0.3	3.0
1965	53.9	26.4	17.1	4.2	3.2	5.1	12.5	8.3	2.7	0.1	0.4	3.1
1966	63.8	30.8	17.5	6.2	4.7	7.0	12.7	9.0	3.3	0.1	-0.7	3.3
1967	73.7	34.2	18.4	6.2	7.3	9.7	14.3	9.7	3.8	0.1	0.1	3.1
1968	81.4	37.6	19.4	7.5	8.4	10.5	15.4	10.7	4.4	0.1	0.8	2.0
1969	82.6	40.0	20.3	6.5	7.6	10.5	17.8	11.5	5.1	0.1	1.4	2.6
1970	81.8	41.9	21.3	6.1	5.4	9.6	20.5	13.3	5.9	0.1	0.5	3.6
1971	82.3	43.4	21.9	4.6	4.4	10.6	24.3	15.5	6.7	0.1	0.9	4.4
1972	84.4	45.6	22.3	5.5	4.7	9.5	27.8	17.0	7.3	0.2	1.2	5.8
1973	84.3	46.1	23.0	5.3	4.3	9.3	29.6	18.4	8.2	0.2	1.0	5.8
1974	88.8	47.7	24.6	5.0	5.2	10.7	33.6	20.1	9.4	0.2	1.4	6.7
1975	94.3	50.2	26.3	5.8	5.1	10.9	38.6	22.3	10.7	0.3	2.1	7.6
1976	98.2	51.8	28.1	5.7	4.4	11.7	40.8	24.7	11.7	0.3	2.1	7.1
1977	104.9	53.9	30.0	7.6	4.5	12.7	44.7	27.0	12.8	0.4	2.5	7.8
1978	113.0	57.6	32.2	9.0	4.9	13.3	49.0	29.5	14.2	0.5	3.2	8.4
1979	122.9	60.9	34.5	10.8	6.2	14.9	53.0	31.1	16.1	0.6	3.3	10.0
1980	140.8	66.7	38.1	12.3	10.0	18.7	61.3	34.0	18.4	0.8	5.5	11.2
1981	162.9	76.3	42.8	15.7	11.8	22.0	68.4	35.9	21.0	0.8	8.7	10.5
1982	184.6	84.8	47.8	19.1	11.5	28.1	71.1	37.2	23.2	0.8	7.5	10.7
1983	199.6	89.3	52.5	24.6	11.3	28.9	78.3	38.4	24.7	0.8	10.1	13.1
1984	213.6	95.9	58.2	26.6	10.4	30.7	78.4	40.7	26.3	0.9	5.8	13.9
1985	230.5	102.4	63.7	29.0	9.9	34.7	86.2	42.6	27.7	0.9	8.9	15.7
1986	245.8	106.2	69.4	31.7	10.2	38.3	90.7	42.9	28.8	0.9	11.7	16.1
1987	259.2	109.5	75.3	33.6	10.2	40.9	88.6	43.6	30.1	1.0	6.2	18.3
1988	274.2	113.8	81.9	33.4	10.6	45.4	86.7	48.1	32.1	1.1	-0.8	17.7
1989	283.5	117.9	87.5	32.0	10.8	46.5	96.7	50.6	34.1	1.2	5.1	18.2
1990	295.4	121.2	92.2	31.6	11.0	51.8	106.4	54.8	36.1	1.4	5.0	22.2
1991	310.6	126.8	96.4	31.0	10.7	58.1	113.3	59.7	38.4	1.5	5.9	22.3
1992	307.5	126.8	98.1	28.4	9.4	57.6	122.7	62.8	40.1	1.6	6.5	25.9
1993	300.8	121.0	99.7	26.4	8.5	58.1	126.9	67.1	42.0	1.6	7.6	22.9
1994	294.5	117.4	100.8	22.9	7.6	60.3	132.8	68.7	43.7	1.5	6.1	27.7
1995	291.1	114.1	101.8	20.9	6.3	60.1	136.6	69.2	46.2	1.4	7.5	27.3
1996	291.5	112.0	100.6	20.8	7.6	62.9	136.9	70.2	47.7	1.5	6.6	26.0
1997	292.5	111.4	99.5	20.9	7.6	65.0	146.2	72.0	49.4	1.6	8.5	28.4
1998	288.5	110.8	98.2	20.9	7.0	63.0	148.0	75.1	51.0	1.5	9.4	26.2
1999	301.2	112.7	98.4	22.2	8.2	71.3	154.3	79.0	53.6	1.7	7.2	26.9
2000	308.3	116.9	99.4	22.1	10.4	71.8	166.8	85.5	56.9	1.8	9.3	29.0
2001	325.1	123.2	99.0	22.3	10.3	84.6	180.3	88.0	59.0	1.9	12.2	34.6
2002	358.1	139.4	99.0	23.2	11.5	101.1	202.2	97.0	60.8	2.2	12.7	44.8
2003	408.9	160.5	101.9	25.7	13.4	124.4	219.5	106.4	63.2	2.3	15.6	48.5
2004	446.8	172.2	107.3	28.8	17.1	138.8	234.6	112.1	66.0	2.5	17.2	54.0
2005	475.9	186.1	114.4	29.6	20.9	144.1	247.5	117.6	69.4	2.7	19.1	58.8
2006	500.3	192.9	121.8	33.0	22.3	151.6	263.6	121.9	73.0	3.0	20.2	64.3
2007	526.1	201.5	129.9	36.3	23.8	156.5	272.3	128.1	76.9	3.0	20.0	62.7
2008	582.8	214.4	139.1	42.9	30.5	179.1	297.0	135.9	81.0	3.3	23.7	72.9
2009	613.3	228.8	144.6	45.8	24.4	192.8	320.4	146.7	83.5	3.5	26.4	81.4
2010	653.2	245.0	151.1	47.0	26.8	206.8	350.7	159.7	87.7	3.9	28.4	93.7
2011	662.3	251.3	158.3	45.0	33.1	200.6	343.8	162.3	92.3	3.6	24.5	85.7
2012	653.9	248.7	161.7	45.3	31.9	192.2	353.9	163.0	95.5	3.7	24.0	88.8
2013	614.4	240.3	162.2	39.8	27.2	170.1	346.9	162.5	98.3	3.4	22.0	81.8
2014	599.8	239.7	162.3	37.1	24.3	161.1	355.5	166.8	101.0	3.5	22.0	84.1
2012												
1st quarter	658.6	251.0	160.8	45.5	34.0	193.6	353.0	163.5	94.4	3.7	23.8	88.6
2nd quarter	652.4	249.5	161.6	45.2	32.1	189.9	353.6	163.2	95.2	3.7	24.3	89.5
3rd quarter	657.6	248.3	162.3	45.8	30.8	196.0	354.9	162.5	96.0	3.7	24.0	89.4
4th quarter	647.1	245.9	162.1	44.7	30.7	189.2	354.1	162.7	96.5	3.6	24.0	87.7
2013												
1st quarter	629.3	243.3	162.0	39.7	30.2	179.5	349.2	162.9	97.1	3.5	22.9	83.8
2nd quarter	621.2	241.8	162.3	40.2	27.2	175.1	345.8	162.1	97.9	3.4	21.9	81.7
3rd quarter	605.4	235.4	162.1	40.2	26.9	166.0	345.4	162.5	98.6	3.3	21.7	80.4
4th quarter	601.7	240.8	162.3	39.1	24.8	159.9	347.0	162.5	99.4	3.4	21.5	81.3
2014												
1st quarter	600.3	240.3	162.3	37.3	23.7	161.6	352.6	165.2	100.1	3.5	22.0	82.6
2nd quarter	597.9	240.3	162.1	37.2	24.0	158.9	353.0	166.5	100.7	3.5	21.5	83.9
3rd quarter	610.4	239.8	162.4	35.5	25.6	171.6	357.8	167.6	101.4	3.6	22.5	84.5
4th quarter	590.4	238.1	162.5	38.3	23.8	152.2	358.6	168.0	102.0	3.6	22.1	85.3

[1] Excludes government sales to other sectors and government own-account investment (construction and software).
[2] Includes general government intermediate inputs for goods and services sold to other sectors and for own-account investment.

Table 6-4. National Defense Consumption Expenditures and Gross Investment: Selected Detail

(National income and product accounts, calendar years, billions of dollars, quarterly data are at seasonally adjusted annual rates.)

NIPA Table 3.11.5

Year and quarter	Defense consumption expenditures								Defense gross investment				
	Compensation of general government employees		Intermediate goods and services purchased [1]						Aircraft	Missiles	Ships	Software	Research and develop-ment
			Durable goods	Nondurable goods		Services							
	Military	Civilian	Aircraft	Petroleum products	Ammu-nition	Installation support	Weapons support	Personnel support					
1972	30.2	15.4	2.7	1.8	2.0	3.8	1.6	1.3	2.6	1.5	1.8	0.3	8.9
1973	30.3	15.8	2.4	1.7	1.7	3.8	1.5	1.4	2.3	1.5	1.6	0.3	9.4
1974	30.9	16.7	2.0	2.8	1.4	4.6	1.8	1.5	2.3	1.7	2.2	0.4	9.6
1975	32.0	18.2	2.1	2.9	1.1	4.8	1.7	1.6	3.6	1.3	2.2	0.5	10.0
1976	32.6	19.2	2.0	2.5	0.6	5.3	1.9	1.7	3.4	1.4	2.4	0.5	10.8
1977	33.7	20.2	3.3	2.4	0.8	5.8	1.9	1.9	3.7	1.2	3.1	0.6	11.7
1978	35.4	22.2	3.5	2.5	1.0	5.9	2.1	2.1	3.7	1.1	3.9	0.7	12.6
1979	37.4	23.5	4.8	3.6	1.2	6.6	2.7	2.1	4.8	1.8	4.3	0.8	14.0
1980	41.5	25.2	5.6	6.8	1.4	8.3	3.9	2.3	6.1	2.3	4.1	1.0	16.2
1981	48.8	27.6	7.8	7.7	1.6	9.6	4.8	2.9	7.5	2.8	5.1	1.3	19.6
1982	54.9	29.9	10.2	6.8	2.1	12.6	6.3	3.6	8.4	3.4	6.2	1.4	23.7
1983	57.8	31.5	13.6	6.4	2.5	12.4	7.0	3.9	10.1	4.6	7.1	1.7	28.1
1984	62.0	33.9	14.0	5.9	2.2	13.8	7.2	3.7	10.9	5.7	8.0	2.2	32.8
1985	66.2	36.1	15.4	5.8	1.3	15.1	8.4	5.0	13.4	6.6	9.0	2.7	38.6
1986	69.4	36.8	17.2	3.6	3.6	16.0	9.4	6.2	17.9	7.9	8.9	3.2	40.7
1987	72.2	37.3	18.2	3.9	2.8	17.7	9.2	6.8	17.6	8.7	8.8	3.6	44.5
1988	74.8	39.0	17.9	3.5	3.5	18.3	10.3	9.5	13.5	7.8	8.6	4.3	44.3
1989	76.5	41.4	16.4	4.2	3.1	18.0	10.5	10.2	12.2	8.8	10.0	4.8	42.5
1990	78.5	42.7	14.8	5.3	2.8	21.4	11.6	10.1	12.0	11.2	10.8	5.2	41.4
1991	82.4	44.4	13.6	4.7	2.7	22.9	10.0	9.5	9.2	10.8	10.2	5.4	37.9
1992	80.9	45.9	12.2	3.5	2.6	23.1	9.4	13.7	8.3	10.6	10.1	5.6	35.6
1993	75.1	45.9	10.7	3.2	2.5	25.2	8.8	14.7	9.3	7.9	8.7	5.4	33.7
1994	71.7	45.7	9.2	3.0	1.8	26.2	9.4	16.3	10.5	5.7	8.1	5.3	32.8
1995	69.5	44.6	8.9	2.8	1.2	25.2	9.5	17.0	9.0	4.7	8.0	5.3	33.1
1996	67.7	44.3	8.8	3.4	1.4	26.0	9.0	19.3	9.2	4.1	6.8	5.5	33.4
1997	67.8	43.6	9.4	2.9	1.7	25.1	10.5	21.3	5.8	2.9	6.1	5.6	33.6
1998	68.0	42.8	9.9	2.1	1.9	23.9	10.0	20.6	5.8	3.3	6.4	5.9	33.5
1999	69.8	42.9	10.5	2.6	1.9	25.0	11.3	26.0	7.0	2.9	6.8	5.9	33.3
2000	72.9	44.1	9.8	4.1	1.8	25.1	11.7	26.1	7.8	2.7	6.6	6.0	34.2
2001	78.4	44.8	9.8	4.2	2.1	27.4	14.8	32.4	8.5	3.3	7.2	5.8	36.7
2002	89.7	49.7	9.8	4.6	2.5	30.7	18.2	42.1	9.4	3.3	8.7	5.6	41.4
2003	107.4	53.1	11.3	5.3	2.6	35.7	22.5	49.5	9.4	3.5	9.5	5.4	48.2
2004	113.9	58.3	12.0	7.0	3.6	36.6	23.5	61.9	11.1	4.0	10.0	5.7	54.1
2005	123.3	62.7	10.7	10.1	4.0	35.8	26.1	66.3	13.5	4.0	9.8	5.9	58.5
2006	127.8	65.1	11.1	11.4	4.2	38.2	27.5	71.0	13.6	4.5	10.5	6.2	61.3
2007	133.2	68.3	11.5	12.2	4.1	38.2	28.6	70.0	12.9	4.3	10.3	6.5	65.4
2008	142.8	71.6	12.8	17.6	4.5	41.4	30.9	86.1	13.7	4.3	11.0	6.9	67.0
2009	152.0	76.8	14.7	10.5	4.2	44.1	32.6	93.6	13.5	5.1	11.1	6.8	65.0
2010	159.6	85.5	16.1	13.7	4.2	46.2	36.8	99.1	16.9	5.6	11.8	7.3	65.3
2011	160.6	90.7	18.0	19.2	4.3	44.2	35.0	96.8	20.7	5.1	11.7	7.7	66.2
2012	158.7	90.0	19.4	18.3	4.3	41.8	33.4	98.1	20.1	6.9	12.0	7.7	62.9
2013	152.8	87.5	17.9	14.1	3.5	37.4	26.9	90.8	21.7	6.5	12.5	7.7	60.4
2014	149.9	89.7	16.4	11.2	3.5	39.6	27.3	79.7	19.8	6.6	13.2	7.9	59.9
2008													
1st quarter	138.7	70.8	11.5	16.9	4.5	39.7	29.8	78.9	8.9	4.4	9.7	6.9	67.1
2nd quarter	141.5	71.5	12.4	20.1	4.1	39.2	27.5	80.6	14.6	4.7	11.0	6.9	67.2
3rd quarter	144.5	72.2	13.4	20.3	4.6	43.4	33.9	90.7	14.5	4.5	11.7	7.0	67.0
4th quarter	146.4	72.0	14.0	13.2	4.7	43.2	32.5	94.4	16.8	3.8	11.7	6.8	66.5
2009													
1st quarter	150.6	74.8	13.5	8.6	3.8	42.4	29.5	87.7	12.5	4.2	10.5	6.7	65.6
2nd quarter	152.0	74.6	14.3	9.0	4.3	43.8	32.1	94.4	15.2	4.7	10.9	6.8	65.0
3rd quarter	153.0	77.5	14.9	11.6	4.1	44.7	33.9	96.1	12.8	6.5	10.9	6.8	64.7
4th quarter	152.4	80.4	16.0	12.7	4.5	45.3	35.0	96.3	13.5	4.9	12.3	7.0	64.6
2010													
1st quarter	160.1	82.6	13.8	13.1	4.2	44.9	33.6	97.4	15.0	5.6	10.7	7.2	65.1
2nd quarter	160.1	84.4	15.4	14.0	4.5	46.0	36.2	98.6	17.0	5.7	11.3	7.2	65.2
3rd quarter	159.3	86.6	16.3	13.4	3.9	48.3	40.6	103.4	16.0	5.4	11.9	7.4	65.4
4th quarter	158.8	88.2	19.0	14.2	4.2	45.7	36.8	97.2	19.6	5.5	13.2	7.5	65.5
2011													
1st quarter	160.3	89.0	15.6	17.8	4.1	43.8	32.9	94.3	19.3	5.2	10.6	7.6	65.7
2nd quarter	160.7	90.0	17.6	19.5	4.1	45.2	36.5	100.9	21.1	5.7	11.5	7.7	65.9
3rd quarter	161.0	91.4	18.9	19.8	4.3	45.7	38.0	103.6	21.6	5.1	11.4	7.7	66.3
4th quarter	160.3	92.5	19.9	19.4	4.6	42.2	32.6	88.6	20.7	4.6	13.1	7.8	66.8
2012													
1st quarter	160.5	90.5	18.5	20.2	4.4	42.9	34.8	95.1	19.3	6.8	12.1	7.7	64.5
2nd quarter	159.4	90.1	18.6	18.4	4.4	41.9	33.7	94.9	20.2	7.0	12.2	7.8	63.3
3rd quarter	158.4	89.9	19.8	17.4	4.3	42.3	34.0	101.7	22.5	6.6	11.6	7.7	62.3
4th quarter	156.5	89.3	20.5	17.0	4.1	40.3	31.2	100.7	18.6	7.0	11.9	7.7	61.6
2013													
1st quarter	154.2	89.1	17.1	16.6	3.9	37.8	28.0	97.8	22.1	5.3	11.9	7.9	61.0
2nd quarter	153.2	88.6	17.7	13.8	3.7	37.3	27.1	95.5	18.7	6.5	12.4	7.7	60.5
3rd quarter	152.4	83.1	18.5	13.8	3.4	36.9	26.0	88.4	21.4	7.9	12.7	7.7	60.1
4th quarter	151.4	89.4	18.3	12.1	3.1	37.4	26.6	81.4	24.4	6.2	13.0	7.7	59.9
2014													
1st quarter	151.4	89.0	16.6	11.0	3.1	38.4	26.7	81.8	18.1	5.9	13.1	7.8	59.9
2nd quarter	150.9	89.5	16.5	11.2	3.2	39.2	27.1	77.9	21.9	6.4	13.4	7.9	59.9
3rd quarter	149.7	90.1	15.4	12.4	3.5	41.1	28.4	87.6	20.0	6.7	13.5	8.0	59.9
4th quarter	147.8	90.4	17.1	10.3	4.0	39.7	26.7	71.5	19.2	7.4	12.9	8.0	60.0

[1]Includes general government intermediate inputs for goods and services sold to other sectors and for own-account investment.

Table 6-5. Federal Government Output, Lending and Borrowing, and Net Investment

(National income and product accounts, calendar years, billions of dollars, quarterly data are at seasonally adjusted annual rates.)

NIPA Tables 3.2, 3.10.5

Year and quarter	Output						Net lending (net borrowing -)							Net investment
	Gross		Value added		Intermediate goods and services purchased [1]		Net saving, current (surplus +, deficit -)	Plus: capital transfer receipts	Minus			Plus: Consumption of fixed capital	Equals: Net lending (borrowing -)	
	Defense	Non-defense	Defense	Non-defense	Defense	Non-defense			Gross investment	Capital transfer payments	Net purchases of non-produced assets			
1960	44.4	9.2	34.8	6.8	9.6	2.4	0.2	1.8	21.9	2.6	0.5	15.1	-7.9	6.8
1961	46.0	9.6	36.2	7.4	9.8	2.1	-4.7	2.0	24.6	2.9	0.5	16.0	-14.7	8.6
1962	50.4	11.6	38.4	8.1	12.1	3.5	-5.3	2.1	26.5	3.1	0.6	17.1	-16.3	9.4
1963	52.3	12.3	39.9	9.1	12.4	3.2	-2.1	2.2	26.7	3.6	0.5	18.3	-16.3	8.4
1964	53.3	13.6	41.9	10.1	11.4	3.5	-6.9	2.6	27.1	4.1	0.6	19.2	-16.9	7.9
1965	55.9	14.7	43.5	11.1	12.4	3.6	-5.5	2.8	26.7	4.0	0.5	20.0	-13.9	6.7
1966	66.1	15.0	48.3	12.3	17.9	2.7	-7.0	3.0	30.1	4.4	0.6	21.0	-18.0	9.1
1967	75.7	16.8	52.5	13.5	23.2	3.3	-19.5	3.1	31.9	4.3	-0.2	22.4	-30.0	9.5
1968	83.4	18.0	57.0	15.1	26.4	2.9	-13.7	3.1	31.1	6.0	-0.9	24.1	-22.7	7.0
1969	84.9	20.7	60.3	16.6	24.6	4.1	-5.1	3.6	30.7	5.9	0.1	25.8	-12.5	4.9
1970	84.2	23.5	63.2	19.2	21.0	4.3	-34.8	3.7	30.5	5.3	-0.3	27.6	-38.9	2.9
1971	84.9	27.5	65.3	22.1	19.6	5.4	-50.8	4.6	27.8	5.9	-0.4	29.0	-50.5	-1.2
1972	87.6	31.5	67.9	24.4	19.7	7.2	-48.9	5.4	29.3	6.1	-0.7	30.1	-48.1	-0.8
1973	88.0	33.6	69.2	26.6	18.9	6.9	-37.7	5.1	31.7	6.0	-3.2	31.7	-35.3	0.0
1974	93.2	37.8	72.3	29.5	20.9	8.3	-40.6	4.8	35.7	7.9	-5.7	34.7	-39.1	1.0
1975	98.4	43.0	76.6	33.0	21.8	10.0	-97.0	4.9	39.8	9.7	-0.4	37.8	-103.4	2.0
1976	101.7	45.9	79.9	36.3	21.8	9.5	-79.9	5.6	44.7	10.6	-2.4	40.6	-86.6	4.1
1977	108.7	50.5	83.9	39.8	24.9	10.8	-71.9	7.2	49.2	11.2	-1.4	43.7	-80.0	5.5
1978	117.0	55.8	89.8	43.7	27.2	12.1	-59.8	5.2	54.7	12.0	-0.6	47.5	-73.2	7.2
1979	127.3	61.1	95.4	47.1	31.9	13.9	-44.5	5.5	61.7	14.5	-2.8	51.8	-60.7	9.9
1980	145.8	69.9	104.9	52.5	40.9	17.4	-86.3	6.5	70.3	16.7	-4.1	57.9	-104.8	12.4
1981	168.7	76.9	119.1	56.9	49.6	20.1	-85.8	6.9	80.4	15.7	-5.5	65.3	-104.3	15.1
1982	191.3	79.4	132.6	60.4	58.7	19.0	-164.6	7.5	90.0	14.7	-3.7	72.7	-185.4	17.3
1983	206.5	87.2	141.7	63.2	64.8	24.0	-205.0	5.8	102.3	15.6	-4.9	79.0	-233.2	23.3
1984	221.8	87.6	154.1	67.0	67.7	20.5	-192.3	6.0	115.6	17.8	-4.0	86.4	-229.4	29.2
1985	239.7	95.7	166.1	70.3	73.7	25.4	-195.6	6.4	132.5	19.6	-1.2	93.3	-246.8	39.2
1986	255.7	100.3	175.6	71.7	80.1	28.6	-212.7	7.0	141.9	20.1	-3.0	100.3	-264.3	41.6
1987	269.5	99.2	184.8	73.7	84.8	25.5	-163.2	7.2	152.4	19.1	-0.4	107.5	-219.5	44.9
1988	285.1	98.2	195.7	80.2	89.4	18.0	-157.3	7.6	148.0	19.8	-0.2	116.3	-201.0	31.7
1989	294.8	109.2	205.4	84.7	89.4	24.5	-156.6	8.9	151.2	20.2	-0.7	124.2	-194.3	27.0
1990	307.9	119.5	213.4	90.9	94.5	28.6	-200.9	11.6	158.2	28.2	-0.8	131.1	-243.8	27.1
1991	322.9	127.9	223.1	98.2	99.7	29.7	-246.2	11.0	156.8	26.5	0.1	137.9	-280.8	18.9
1992	320.2	136.9	224.8	102.9	95.4	34.0	-332.7	11.3	156.4	22.6	0.2	141.4	-359.1	15.0
1993	313.7	141.1	220.7	109.0	93.0	32.1	-311.8	12.9	150.7	24.3	0.2	145.3	-328.8	5.4
1994	309.0	147.7	218.2	112.5	90.8	35.3	-253.7	15.1	145.4	26.0	0.1	148.3	-261.7	-2.9
1995	303.3	151.6	215.9	115.4	87.4	36.2	-240.8	14.9	147.7	27.9	-7.9	151.9	-241.6	-4.2
1996	304.0	152.0	212.6	117.9	91.4	34.1	-178.5	17.5	149.8	28.4	-4.8	152.4	-182.0	-2.6
1997	304.3	159.9	210.9	121.4	93.5	38.5	-91.2	20.6	143.7	29.2	-8.8	153.0	-81.7	-9.3
1998	299.9	163.2	208.9	126.1	91.0	37.1	2.7	25.2	147.7	28.9	-6.0	153.6	10.9	-5.9
1999	312.7	168.4	211.0	132.7	101.7	35.7	66.6	28.8	154.9	36.6	-1.2	156.8	62.0	-1.9
2000	320.7	182.6	216.3	142.4	104.4	40.2	156.5	28.1	157.4	37.0	-0.6	161.5	152.3	-4.1
2001	339.4	195.6	222.2	147.0	117.2	48.7	14.5	28.0	163.8	42.5	-1.5	163.3	0.8	0.5
2002	374.2	217.6	238.3	157.8	135.8	59.8	-270.5	25.3	180.3	49.7	-0.3	165.0	-309.9	15.3
2003	426.0	235.9	262.5	169.6	163.6	66.3	-402.9	22.0	196.4	63.1	-0.9	170.3	-469.1	26.1
2004	464.2	251.8	279.5	178.1	184.7	73.8	-399.2	24.6	211.0	64.0	-0.8	178.6	-470.1	32.4
2005	495.1	267.5	300.5	187.0	194.6	80.5	-304.7	25.0	222.9	85.3	-2.0	189.4	-396.6	33.5
2006	521.6	282.4	314.7	194.9	206.9	87.5	-227.0	27.8	238.0	71.0	-14.4	200.7	-293.2	37.3
2007	548.0	290.6	331.4	204.9	216.6	85.7	-265.7	26.5	251.4	79.4	-3.3	212.8	-353.9	38.6
2008	605.9	316.7	353.4	216.9	252.4	99.9	-634.0	28.3	275.8	145.9	-20.4	226.3	-780.6	49.5
2009	636.5	341.5	373.5	230.2	263.1	111.3	-1 248.8	20.6	284.0	206.9	-8.9	234.5	-1 475.7	49.5
2010	676.8	373.4	396.1	247.5	280.6	126.0	-1 328.7	15.1	300.0	141.4	-1.0	245.3	-1 508.7	54.7
2011	688.3	368.4	409.6	254.5	278.7	113.9	-1 244.1	9.6	297.4	123.5	-0.9	257.4	-1 397.1	40.0
2012	679.7	375.0	410.4	258.5	269.4	116.5	-1 090.1	14.1	284.7	99.0	-2.0	264.3	-1 193.4	20.4
2013	639.7	367.9	402.5	260.7	237.2	107.2	-640.9	20.9	269.4	79.0	-2.4	267.7	-698.3	1.7
2014	624.4	377.5	402.0	267.9	222.4	109.7	-631.5	18.8	264.6	77.6	-2.7	270.7	-681.4	-6.1
2012														
1st quarter	684.8	373.9	411.8	257.8	273.0	116.1	-1 107.1	11.7	288.9	101.4	-1.4	262.2	-1 222.1	26.7
2nd quarter	678.3	375.9	411.1	258.4	267.2	117.5	-1 102.0	12.9	287.7	86.4	-1.3	264.0	-1 197.9	23.7
3rd quarter	683.2	375.6	410.6	258.6	272.6	117.1	-1 079.5	14.8	284.4	88.1	-1.4	265.4	-1 170.5	19.0
4th quarter	672.6	374.6	408.0	259.2	264.7	115.4	-1 071.6	17.0	277.7	120.3	-3.8	265.8	-1 183.1	11.9
2013														
1st quarter	654.7	370.2	405.3	260.0	249.4	110.2	-790.6	19.7	271.9	84.1	-1.9	266.4	-858.6	5.5
2nd quarter	646.5	366.9	404.1	260.0	242.4	106.9	-525.9	20.4	267.2	77.5	-2.9	267.5	-579.8	-0.3
3rd quarter	630.7	366.5	397.5	261.0	233.1	105.5	-707.7	22.1	269.6	81.0	-3.7	268.0	-764.5	1.6
4th quarter	626.8	368.0	403.1	261.9	223.7	106.1	-539.6	21.3	268.8	73.4	-1.3	269.0	-590.2	-0.2
2014														
1st quarter	625.2	373.4	402.6	265.3	222.6	108.1	-619.2	20.2	261.8	77.5	-1.2	269.6	-667.3	-7.8
2nd quarter	622.5	376.2	402.5	267.2	220.1	109.0	-630.0	19.1	266.0	78.7	-1.8	270.2	-683.5	-4.2
3rd quarter	634.9	379.5	402.2	269.0	232.7	110.6	-650.1	18.1	264.9	79.2	-6.5	271.2	-698.5	-6.3
4th quarter	615.0	381.0	400.7	270.0	214.3	111.0	-626.7	17.8	265.6	75.0	-1.3	271.9	-676.3	-6.3

[1] Includes general government intermediate inputs for goods and services sold to other sectors and for own-account investment.

Table 6-6. Chain-Type Quantity Indexes for Federal Government Defense and Nondefense Consumption Expenditures and Gross Investment

(Seasonally adjusted, 2009 = 100.)

NIPA Tables 3.9.3, 3.10.3

| Year and quarter | Defense consumption expenditures [1] | | | | | | Defense gross investment | Nondefense consumption expenditures [1] | | | | | | Non-defense gross investment |
| | Total | Compensation of general government employees | Consumption of general government fixed capital | Intermediate goods and services purchased [2] | | | | Total | Compensation of general government employees | Consumption of general government fixed capital | Intermediate goods and services purchased [2] | | | |
				Durable goods	Non-durable goods	Services					Durable goods	Non-durable goods excluding CCC inventory change	Services	
1960	57.5	121.2	45.2	36.9	61.5	17.5	41.2	21.3	50.1	6.9	2.0	5.5	15.6	13.9
1961	59.0	123.8	47.2	30.3	78.3	19.4	45.5	21.0	51.4	7.7	2.7	8.5	18.6	16.3
1962	64.0	129.1	49.5	37.4	102.6	22.2	46.7	24.9	54.1	8.6	3.3	12.7	18.5	20.1
1963	64.3	126.8	51.5	37.7	91.6	23.2	42.8	24.8	57.2	10.2	3.7	12.7	19.4	26.8
1964	63.0	126.8	52.8	31.9	104.3	19.1	40.1	25.8	58.6	12.1	4.7	12.9	22.0	32.2
1965	63.9	127.0	53.5	33.1	117.8	19.6	36.4	26.7	59.7	14.3	4.9	13.6	21.6	36.8
1966	72.6	139.9	54.1	48.2	168.0	25.1	40.4	25.9	62.1	17.0	5.2	13.7	22.3	41.2
1967	81.7	152.3	55.7	47.5	257.7	32.0	45.4	28.6	65.1	19.5	5.1	15.4	20.3	37.9
1968	85.4	154.3	57.1	55.1	295.9	33.2	41.4	28.9	66.6	22.0	3.4	10.2	12.5	38.6
1969	82.5	154.5	57.6	46.0	262.6	31.0	38.6	31.6	67.2	24.3	3.5	10.6	15.2	37.2
1970	75.8	143.3	57.3	41.2	182.8	28.7	35.3	32.9	68.1	26.3	4.0	13.4	20.8	35.8
1971	70.1	132.4	55.8	29.6	149.5	29.2	27.6	35.8	70.4	28.0	5.1	16.5	24.2	35.7
1972	65.7	122.4	54.0	36.8	152.3	24.6	24.8	39.0	72.4	29.5	8.1	20.1	31.8	36.9
1973	61.2	116.1	52.6	33.6	113.2	22.7	25.9	39.0	72.6	31.0	7.4	19.2	30.1	37.0
1974	59.5	114.4	51.5	29.1	97.8	23.8	27.8	41.6	76.2	32.3	8.0	20.3	31.2	37.2
1975	58.3	112.8	50.8	30.7	81.0	21.9	28.9	43.4	77.6	33.7	8.6	18.4	31.6	38.2
1976	57.0	110.6	50.6	27.8	65.0	21.9	30.7	43.3	81.4	35.1	9.0	18.3	26.5	40.5
1977	57.4	109.6	50.6	34.8	61.4	21.9	31.4	45.0	83.2	36.7	11.7	18.0	28.8	43.0
1978	57.8	110.4	50.7	38.3	62.2	21.0	31.7	46.7	85.4	38.7	13.3	26.6	29.6	47.5
1979	58.3	109.5	51.1	41.7	64.1	21.6	34.7	47.6	85.3	40.8	15.6	26.1	32.3	48.1
1980	60.0	110.1	51.9	44.0	70.1	24.0	37.3	50.8	87.6	42.9	17.5	25.4	33.0	49.3
1981	63.0	113.5	53.3	51.6	74.1	26.0	41.2	52.1	85.0	44.8	16.5	47.5	28.0	48.4
1982	66.5	116.1	55.4	56.8	73.8	31.3	46.5	51.1	83.4	46.3	15.1	35.5	26.5	44.8
1983	69.5	117.9	58.5	67.9	77.3	31.4	53.9	54.6	84.6	47.7	16.3	44.3	32.0	44.7
1984	71.3	119.6	62.6	69.0	73.1	32.7	61.0	52.9	84.7	49.0	17.6	46.2	32.9	46.1
1985	75.1	121.8	67.9	74.7	71.3	36.3	72.0	55.9	84.8	50.4	18.2	40.1	35.7	48.6
1986	79.1	122.3	73.9	80.2	90.4	38.8	79.8	57.8	83.6	51.9	17.9	34.2	35.5	49.9
1987	81.9	123.4	79.8	85.3	88.5	39.7	86.7	56.3	85.1	53.3	20.3	39.7	39.9	53.3
1988	83.8	121.9	84.7	87.9	85.8	42.0	81.2	53.1	87.2	54.9	21.5	39.5	37.6	52.6
1989	84.3	121.9	88.1	84.5	83.0	42.0	79.2	57.5	87.7	56.5	24.2	35.3	37.3	55.2
1990	84.7	121.1	90.6	81.5	74.1	44.3	79.1	61.6	92.1	58.3	27.7	37.5	44.2	59.4
1991	86.0	120.7	91.8	77.7	75.5	47.8	72.8	62.0	91.8	60.3	29.2	32.9	43.8	63.2
1992	82.4	113.7	91.9	69.9	69.8	46.5	68.9	65.6	93.5	62.1	31.8	40.9	49.4	67.0
1993	79.6	108.9	90.9	63.6	64.0	45.8	61.7	65.0	93.4	63.8	31.0	44.5	41.8	68.3
1994	76.1	103.3	89.1	54.5	58.3	46.3	57.8	65.6	90.8	65.3	29.2	37.4	49.2	65.1
1995	73.1	97.6	87.1	49.7	47.7	44.7	55.4	65.0	87.2	66.8	28.6	42.2	47.4	66.6
1996	71.8	93.5	85.2	49.3	52.7	45.8	55.0	63.7	84.8	68.6	32.5	36.4	44.7	68.5
1997	70.8	90.1	83.4	49.5	53.1	46.5	51.1	66.4	84.3	70.1	35.1	44.4	47.5	68.2
1998	68.9	87.2	81.6	49.9	54.8	44.2	51.2	66.0	85.3	72.1	35.1	48.3	43.5	72.0
1999	70.0	85.1	80.2	53.0	61.3	49.2	51.7	66.8	85.4	74.6	39.4	36.0	44.1	76.4
2000	69.0	84.4	79.0	52.5	64.3	48.1	52.3	69.5	88.1	77.2	43.5	40.9	46.2	75.4
2001	71.0	85.0	78.3	52.9	66.1	54.7	55.3	73.5	88.0	79.4	46.6	54.3	53.0	77.2
2002	74.8	87.2	78.1	55.0	75.5	63.6	62.5	79.0	89.7	81.6	57.2	59.5	67.0	82.6
2003	80.7	90.2	79.5	60.5	81.8	75.5	69.5	82.4	91.9	83.8	59.0	73.3	70.7	85.6
2004	84.8	91.9	81.9	66.9	93.0	81.6	76.1	84.4	91.1	85.9	65.2	81.9	76.3	86.4
2005	85.7	92.2	85.1	67.4	93.6	82.4	80.0	85.5	90.9	88.4	71.3	82.3	80.3	87.5
2006	86.6	90.8	88.5	73.4	91.5	83.8	84.5	88.2	90.9	91.3	79.9	80.1	85.0	91.4
2007	88.0	90.5	92.1	80.6	92.6	84.1	89.2	88.1	91.5	94.2	81.6	78.0	80.1	92.5
2008	94.0	93.9	96.1	94.2	95.6	93.1	97.9	93.6	94.9	97.1	92.6	88.1	90.0	95.8
2009	100.0	100.0	100.0	100.0	100.0	100.0	100.0	100.0	100.0	100.0	100.0	100.0	100.0	100.0
2010	103.7	103.2	103.1	102.5	96.4	105.4	101.4	105.9	104.3	102.8	110.6	105.6	111.9	108.2
2011	102.1	104.3	105.4	97.4	98.8	99.1	96.4	100.9	103.1	106.2	102.8	86.3	98.8	108.3
2012	99.7	102.2	106.2	97.2	94.4	93.7	89.5	103.1	103.6	109.0	104.2	82.0	100.7	105.5
2013	93.0	98.6	105.7	84.8	80.7	81.8	83.4	99.2	100.6	111.0	96.7	73.5	91.7	100.5
2014	89.5	96.6	104.4	78.7	72.8	76.2	80.0	99.6	100.5	112.3	100.3	73.6	92.8	98.9
2012														
1st quarter	100.6	103.2	106.1	97.6	99.5	94.8	91.8	103.1	103.9	108.1	103.9	81.1	100.9	106.2
2nd quarter	99.5	102.5	106.2	96.9	96.0	92.6	90.8	103.0	103.8	108.7	105.0	83.5	101.4	106.0
3rd quarter	100.2	102.0	106.2	98.3	92.4	95.4	89.3	103.3	103.3	109.3	104.7	81.9	101.3	105.0
4th quarter	98.4	101.2	106.1	96.0	89.6	91.8	86.1	103.0	103.4	109.9	103.4	81.4	99.3	104.8
2013														
1st quarter	95.6	100.4	106.0	84.9	87.3	86.7	84.5	101.2	103.2	110.4	99.1	76.9	94.3	102.1
2nd quarter	94.5	99.9	105.8	85.7	82.1	84.4	82.3	99.8	102.1	110.8	96.2	73.5	91.7	100.6
3rd quarter	91.8	97.1	105.6	85.7	79.8	79.6	83.6	99.1	101.4	111.2	95.4	72.5	90.0	100.0
4th quarter	90.2	97.1	105.2	83.1	73.5	76.5	83.0	96.8	95.6	111.6	96.4	71.1	90.9	99.1
2014														
1st quarter	90.0	97.6	104.8	79.3	69.5	76.9	79.0	99.6	100.7	111.9	98.0	72.3	91.8	98.8
2nd quarter	89.3	97.2	104.5	79.0	70.5	75.1	81.2	99.0	100.4	112.2	99.9	72.7	92.6	98.5
3rd quarter	90.7	96.3	104.2	75.3	75.5	80.9	80.3	99.8	100.4	112.5	101.0	74.8	92.7	98.5
4th quarter	87.9	95.3	104.0	81.1	75.8	71.9	79.5	100.0	100.4	112.8	102.1	74.4	94.0	100.0

[1]Excludes government sales to other sectors and government own-account investment (construction and software).
[2]Includes general government intermediate inputs for goods and services sold to other sectors and for own-account investment.

Table 6-7. Chain-Type Quantity Indexes for National Defense Consumption Expenditures and Gross Investment: Selected Detail

(Seasonally adjusted, 2009 = 100.)

NIPA Table 3.11.3

Year and quarter	Compensation of general government employees		Intermediate goods and services purchased [1]						Defense gross investment				
			Durable goods	Nondurable goods		Services			Aircraft	Missiles	Ships	Software	Research and development
	Military	Civilian	Aircraft	Petroleum products	Ammunition	Installation support	Weapons support	Personnel support					
1972	120.6	124.4	61.0	309.3	189.9	40.3	22.0	11.6	25.7	30.4	73.8	6.0	51.7
1973	113.8	119.3	51.0	195.8	148.1	37.3	20.3	10.9	22.6	31.8	62.2	7.2	51.4
1974	109.8	122.4	39.6	177.9	101.3	40.6	21.9	10.7	22.7	35.2	76.8	8.3	47.8
1975	107.4	122.4	36.5	149.7	70.5	39.7	18.6	9.9	34.3	25.7	68.7	9.7	46.0
1976	104.8	120.9	30.6	124.1	35.4	40.8	19.8	9.5	32.1	21.9	70.4	10.2	47.4
1977	103.9	119.8	46.7	105.6	48.4	40.5	18.8	9.7	33.5	17.1	82.2	10.5	48.8
1978	102.9	124.0	47.7	105.0	55.9	37.9	18.5	9.5	31.7	14.1	92.5	12.3	49.4
1979	101.3	124.6	59.4	106.8	62.1	39.8	22.4	8.4	39.7	28.4	95.2	14.7	51.3
1980	102.3	124.4	64.5	118.2	62.3	45.1	29.0	8.3	47.5	41.0	83.7	16.8	54.0
1981	105.6	127.9	83.1	116.1	70.4	48.9	31.9	9.3	54.9	47.6	95.4	20.0	60.0
1982	107.5	132.1	97.2	109.3	86.7	59.8	39.6	11.1	55.2	61.4	111.2	22.0	67.6
1983	109.4	133.7	118.3	117.0	101.7	56.6	41.6	12.2	62.7	77.8	123.6	25.5	76.7
1984	110.7	135.9	111.8	116.7	86.1	61.2	41.7	11.3	67.4	93.5	130.9	33.7	85.8
1985	112.3	139.6	120.1	118.7	51.3	65.3	47.4	14.7	92.0	106.6	143.9	41.1	98.8
1986	113.3	138.8	132.9	118.6	138.2	65.7	52.4	17.3	140.3	135.1	138.9	48.9	102.6
1987	114.7	139.2	142.3	121.8	104.9	69.9	50.6	17.6	161.0	153.7	135.1	54.6	110.4
1988	113.9	136.2	147.3	102.6	121.0	69.6	55.0	20.9	132.3	139.9	128.0	63.3	105.1
1989	113.3	137.5	138.9	112.6	101.2	67.8	53.9	21.3	121.0	160.2	142.1	72.5	97.8
1990	113.6	134.3	122.0	111.7	91.3	76.2	57.5	19.6	111.6	208.1	149.9	78.6	93.1
1991	115.0	130.1	109.2	110.3	86.1	80.7	47.2	17.4	80.3	209.2	134.5	80.8	82.6
1992	105.2	129.4	95.2	92.3	81.8	80.0	42.5	24.0	70.3	206.9	130.0	87.2	75.9
1993	99.8	125.8	82.5	88.7	81.2	86.3	38.3	25.0	75.7	150.2	109.7	83.2	70.5
1994	95.0	118.6	70.1	91.3	55.9	87.4	39.9	26.8	75.6	110.3	98.7	81.9	67.0
1995	90.1	111.6	66.8	82.9	35.8	81.1	39.5	26.9	61.1	92.9	92.9	80.4	64.8
1996	86.8	105.8	66.2	83.8	41.9	82.6	36.6	29.6	59.3	82.7	78.5	84.5	64.4
1997	84.5	100.3	70.8	75.2	51.5	79.4	41.6	32.0	41.2	61.2	69.6	86.9	63.3
1998	82.6	95.7	75.1	73.4	58.3	74.7	39.2	30.2	41.5	68.9	73.6	92.7	62.2
1999	81.1	92.3	79.3	81.2	59.3	76.9	43.7	36.9	43.2	62.4	78.0	92.4	60.7
2000	81.8	89.2	73.8	74.9	56.4	76.3	43.8	35.5	50.4	58.8	74.2	91.2	60.4
2001	83.5	87.7	72.8	87.6	64.4	81.0	54.4	42.5	58.9	73.8	81.3	86.4	64.6
2002	86.6	88.4	73.1	100.9	78.3	88.3	65.8	53.4	67.9	73.8	97.3	84.5	72.7
2003	91.3	88.2	82.4	97.9	81.1	98.2	79.7	60.9	68.3	76.0	104.7	82.6	83.2
2004	92.3	91.0	85.9	103.2	106.3	96.3	81.1	74.3	82.0	86.3	106.2	86.4	91.4
2005	91.8	93.1	75.8	100.5	110.6	90.1	87.6	77.8	102.8	83.7	101.2	89.5	96.6
2006	89.6	93.3	76.3	99.4	108.7	92.5	90.0	81.0	104.7	93.0	105.2	92.4	99.2
2007	88.9	93.8	79.2	98.4	101.8	89.0	91.7	77.2	99.8	88.6	98.3	96.4	103.1
2008	92.9	96.1	88.0	99.3	104.2	93.1	96.6	93.4	102.2	86.0	101.2	100.6	102.7
2009	100.0	100.0	100.0	100.0	100.0	100.0	100.0	100.0	100.0	100.0	100.0	100.0	100.0
2010	101.6	106.5	109.9	101.4	99.2	101.8	111.3	104.7	124.2	108.1	103.4	107.4	98.1
2011	101.2	110.3	122.2	104.6	95.3	93.1	103.2	100.5	148.2	95.5	97.7	112.5	96.4
2012	98.5	109.5	130.4	99.3	95.1	87.6	96.6	100.5	147.9	125.6	98.9	113.2	90.0
2013	96.1	103.7	119.8	77.7	77.1	77.0	76.8	91.7	163.1	118.3	102.8	112.7	85.7
2014	93.0	103.5	108.9	64.2	75.3	80.2	76.3	79.4	149.5	122.5	107.3	115.2	83.6
2008													
1st quarter	90.5	94.3	79.6	96.0	108.8	90.5	94.2	86.2	66.9	87.5	91.2	100.7	103.6
2nd quarter	91.2	95.7	85.4	101.1	95.2	87.9	86.4	87.6	108.9	92.8	101.2	101.3	103.1
3rd quarter	93.8	97.1	92.0	98.7	104.5	96.5	105.6	98.0	108.9	89.0	106.0	101.2	102.2
4th quarter	96.0	97.3	95.0	101.6	108.3	97.7	99.9	101.8	123.8	74.8	106.3	99.4	101.7
2009													
1st quarter	97.3	97.1	91.5	92.7	91.4	97.6	90.2	93.9	92.2	83.7	94.4	98.2	101.1
2nd quarter	99.7	98.5	97.3	97.5	102.6	100.2	98.5	100.9	112.4	93.0	97.5	98.9	100.4
3rd quarter	101.5	100.6	102.0	107.9	98.8	100.8	104.0	102.5	94.8	127.7	97.8	98.9	100.4
4th quarter	101.4	103.8	109.1	102.0	107.2	101.4	107.3	102.6	100.7	95.6	110.3	102.4	98.6
2010													
1st quarter	101.9	104.3	94.1	102.1	100.3	99.6	102.3	103.4	111.8	110.2	94.9	105.8	98.8
2nd quarter	101.9	105.3	104.7	104.1	105.2	101.3	109.8	104.3	126.4	111.9	98.8	105.5	98.1
3rd quarter	101.5	107.2	111.1	100.0	93.1	106.6	122.7	108.9	117.9	105.8	104.3	108.4	98.3
4th quarter	101.1	109.0	129.6	99.3	98.0	99.7	110.4	102.0	140.7	104.5	115.6	109.8	97.2
2011													
1st quarter	101.1	109.4	106.6	105.8	92.2	93.9	98.1	98.4	134.1	98.7	89.9	110.8	96.3
2nd quarter	101.3	109.7	119.5	100.1	91.2	94.5	107.9	104.8	151.7	104.9	96.9	112.1	96.0
3rd quarter	101.3	110.4	128.1	104.2	95.7	95.3	111.6	107.2	155.3	94.2	94.8	113.1	96.2
4th quarter	101.2	111.7	134.8	108.3	102.1	88.9	95.3	91.6	151.6	84.3	109.1	114.1	96.9
2012													
1st quarter	99.7	110.2	124.8	107.5	97.5	90.0	101.0	97.9	140.7	120.4	100.7	112.8	92.8
2nd quarter	98.8	109.6	125.3	101.8	97.2	87.6	97.6	97.4	146.9	129.7	101.0	113.8	90.6
3rd quarter	98.3	109.4	133.5	97.2	95.3	88.5	97.9	103.9	164.4	122.9	95.3	112.6	88.7
4th quarter	97.4	108.7	138.1	90.7	90.5	84.2	90.0	102.7	139.4	129.4	98.8	113.5	87.9
2013													
1st quarter	96.5	108.1	115.1	87.8	85.4	78.4	80.2	99.3	166.8	98.9	98.2	114.6	87.2
2nd quarter	96.4	106.8	118.5	79.4	80.1	77.0	77.4	96.7	141.9	117.7	102.3	111.5	86.0
3rd quarter	96.1	99.2	123.4	76.6	74.5	75.8	74.1	89.1	161.7	143.1	104.9	112.5	85.2
4th quarter	95.3	100.6	122.3	67.0	68.6	76.9	75.4	81.8	182.2	113.7	105.9	112.3	84.3
2014													
1st quarter	94.4	103.7	110.4	59.9	67.1	78.2	75.4	81.9	135.2	107.8	106.7	113.6	84.1
2nd quarter	93.8	103.7	109.8	61.2	70.0	79.1	75.9	77.7	164.5	119.1	108.5	114.3	83.8
3rd quarter	92.7	103.3	102.0	68.8	76.5	82.6	79.4	87.1	151.6	125.1	109.5	116.3	83.4
4th quarter	91.1	103.3	113.4	67.1	87.8	81.0	74.5	70.9	146.6	137.9	104.5	116.7	83.1

[1]Includes general government intermediate inputs for goods and services sold to other sectors and for own-account investment.

Section 6b: State and Local Government in the National Income and Product Accounts

**Figure 6-2: State and Local Government Current Receipts and Expenditures and Net Lending (Borrowing-)
1955–2013 (percent of GDP)**

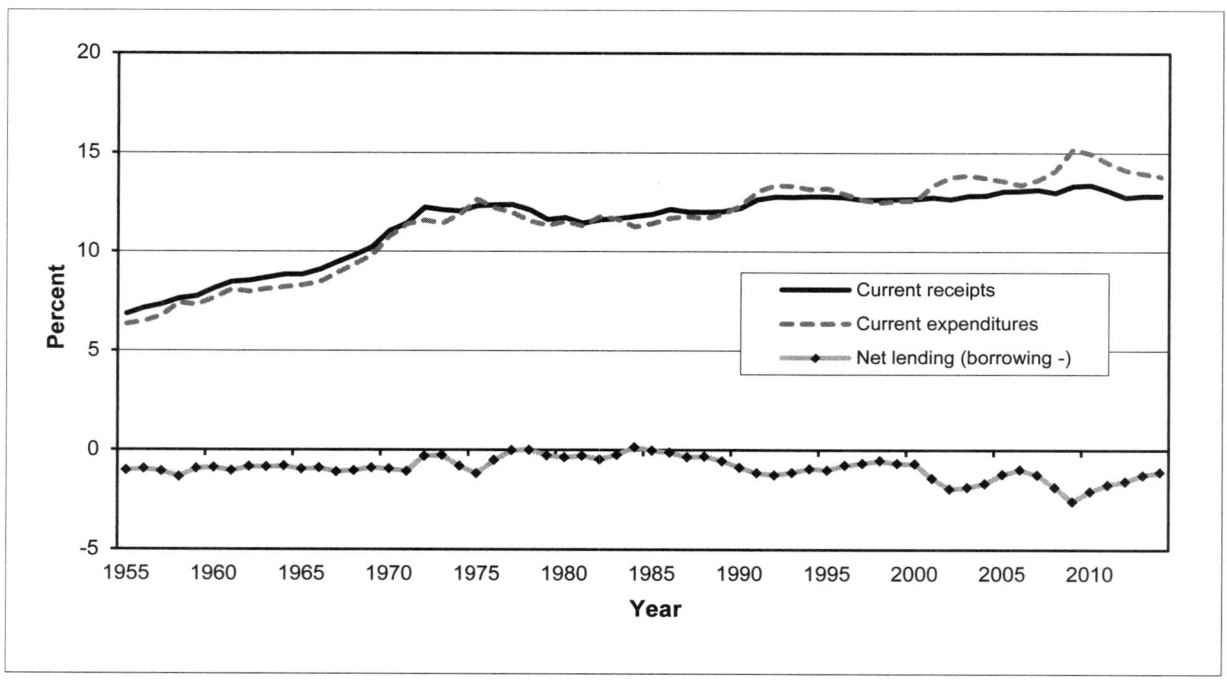

- Both current receipts and current spending of state and local governments have increased as a share of gross domestic product (GDP) over the postwar period, but the growth slowed markedly after the early 1970s. (Tables 6-8 and 1-1)

- State and local governments have consistently been net borrowers in capital markets, as can be seen by the negative values in Figure 6-2. Although they are usually constrained to balance their statutory budgets, they have consistently made net investments and been able to borrow for that purpose. In addition, as revealed by the accrual accounting adopted in the NIPA accounts last year, they have often incurred hidden deficits by failing to fund commitments for public employee retirement benefits. (Table 6-10)

- A larger gap between current expenditures and current receipts appeared during the slow-growth years 2001–2003, and a still-greater one during the Great Recession beginning in 2008. Generally, in both of those periods of rising deficits, receipts barely kept pace with the economy, while general ("consumption") expenditures, social benefits, and interest payments all fueled higher spending. (Table 6-8)

- After 2009, aggregate state and local spending and borrowing declined as the economy continued to struggle after the Great Recession. (Table 6-8)

Table 6-8. State and Local Government Current Receipts and Expenditures

(National income and product accounts, calendar years, billions of dollars, quarterly data are at seasonally adjusted annual rates.)

NIPA Table 3.3

Year and quarter	Total current receipts	Current receipts								Income receipts on assets		
		Current tax receipts						Taxes on corporate income	Contributions for government social insurance	Interest receipts	Dividends	Rents and royalties
		Total tax receipts	Personal current taxes		Taxes on production and imports							
			Income taxes	Other personal taxes	Sales taxes	Property taxes	Other taxes on prod. and imports					
1955	29.2	24.4	1.3	1.0	7.1	10.4	3.5	1.0	0.3	0.6	. . .	0.3
1956	32.2	27.0	1.6	1.1	8.0	11.5	3.8	1.0	0.4	0.7	. . .	0.3
1957	34.8	29.0	1.7	1.2	8.6	12.6	3.9	1.0	0.4	0.7	. . .	0.3
1958	36.8	30.6	1.8	1.2	10.0	13.8	2.8	1.0	0.4	0.8	. . .	0.4
1959	40.4	33.8	2.2	1.6	11.1	14.8	2.9	1.2	0.4	0.9	. . .	0.3
1960	44.2	37.0	2.5	1.7	12.2	16.2	3.1	1.2	0.5	1.0	. . .	0.3
1961	47.7	39.7	2.8	1.8	13.0	17.6	3.2	1.3	0.5	1.1	. . .	0.4
1962	51.6	42.8	3.2	1.8	14.0	19.0	3.3	1.5	0.5	1.1	. . .	0.4
1963	55.5	45.8	3.4	2.0	15.0	20.2	3.5	1.7	0.6	1.2	. . .	0.4
1964	60.6	49.8	4.0	2.1	16.5	21.7	3.7	1.8	0.7	1.5	. . .	0.4
1965	65.8	53.9	4.4	2.2	18.2	23.2	3.9	2.0	0.8	1.8	. . .	0.4
1966	74.1	58.8	5.4	2.4	20.0	24.5	4.3	2.2	0.8	2.1	. . .	0.5
1967	81.6	64.0	6.1	2.5	21.4	27.0	4.4	2.6	0.9	2.4	. . .	0.6
1968	92.5	73.4	7.8	2.7	25.1	29.9	4.6	3.3	0.9	2.8	. . .	0.7
1969	104.3	82.5	9.8	3.0	28.6	32.8	4.7	3.6	1.0	3.6	. . .	0.8
1970	118.9	91.3	10.9	3.3	31.6	36.7	5.0	3.7	1.1	4.3	. . .	0.8
1971	133.6	101.7	12.4	3.5	35.4	40.4	5.7	4.3	1.2	4.6	. . .	0.9
1972	156.9	115.6	17.2	3.7	39.8	43.2	6.4	5.3	1.3	4.9	. . .	1.0
1973	172.8	126.3	18.9	4.0	44.1	46.4	7.0	6.0	1.5	6.6	0.0	1.1
1974	186.4	136.0	20.4	4.2	48.2	49.0	7.7	6.7	1.7	8.9	0.0	1.3
1975	207.7	147.4	22.5	4.4	51.7	53.4	8.1	7.3	1.8	9.8	0.0	1.3
1976	231.9	165.7	26.3	4.8	57.8	58.2	9.0	9.6	2.2	9.0	0.0	1.3
1977	257.9	183.7	30.4	5.0	64.0	63.2	9.7	11.4	2.8	10.4	0.0	1.3
1978	285.3	198.2	35.0	5.5	71.0	63.7	10.9	12.1	3.4	13.3	0.1	1.3
1979	305.8	212.0	38.2	5.8	77.3	64.4	12.7	13.6	3.9	18.1	0.1	1.9
1980	335.3	230.0	42.6	6.3	82.9	68.8	15.0	14.5	3.6	23.1	0.1	3.1
1981	367.0	255.8	47.9	6.7	90.7	77.1	17.9	15.4	3.9	28.5	0.1	3.3
1982	388.1	273.2	51.9	7.3	96.2	85.3	18.5	14.0	4.0	33.1	0.2	3.5
1983	424.8	300.9	58.3	7.8	107.7	91.9	19.4	15.9	4.1	37.0	0.2	4.3
1984	475.6	337.3	67.5	8.6	121.0	99.7	21.8	18.8	4.7	42.6	0.2	4.9
1985	516.9	363.7	72.1	9.2	131.1	107.5	23.5	20.2	4.9	50.1	0.2	5.4
1986	556.8	389.5	77.4	9.8	139.9	116.2	23.7	22.7	6.0	52.6	0.2	6.2
1987	585.0	422.1	86.0	10.6	150.3	126.4	24.9	23.9	7.2	53.0	0.2	5.3
1988	629.9	452.8	90.6	11.5	162.4	136.5	25.7	26.0	8.4	56.6	0.2	4.4
1989	680.8	488.0	102.3	12.4	172.3	149.9	26.9	24.2	9.0	62.3	0.2	4.1
1990	729.6	519.1	109.6	13.0	184.3	161.5	28.3	22.5	10.0	64.1	0.2	4.2
1991	779.5	544.3	111.7	13.6	190.7	176.1	28.6	23.6	11.6	62.4	0.3	4.5
1992	835.6	579.8	120.4	14.9	204.3	184.7	31.1	24.4	13.1	58.8	0.5	4.8
1993	877.1	604.7	126.2	14.8	216.4	187.3	33.1	26.9	14.1	56.0	0.6	4.5
1994	934.1	644.2	132.2	15.7	231.4	199.4	35.5	30.0	14.5	58.2	0.8	4.5
1995	979.8	672.1	141.7	16.4	242.7	202.6	37.0	31.7	13.6	63.6	1.0	4.5
1996	1 032.6	709.6	152.3	16.3	256.2	212.4	39.4	33.0	12.5	67.7	1.4	4.6
1997	1 085.8	749.9	164.7	17.3	268.7	223.5	41.6	34.1	10.8	71.8	1.5	4.8
1998	1 148.7	794.9	183.0	18.2	283.9	231.0	43.9	34.9	10.4	75.0	1.6	4.6
1999	1 221.8	840.4	195.5	19.0	301.6	242.8	45.8	35.8	9.8	78.6	1.5	5.1
2000	1 303.1	893.2	217.4	19.4	316.8	254.7	49.8	35.2	10.8	86.3	1.4	6.3
2001	1 352.6	914.3	223.3	19.7	321.8	268.0	52.6	28.9	13.7	81.3	1.4	6.5
2002	1 388.4	928.5	201.3	20.5	331.1	289.3	55.4	30.9	15.8	70.5	1.6	6.6
2003	1 474.6	978.6	204.7	22.1	348.9	307.0	62.0	34.0	19.9	64.5	1.7	7.6
2004	1 575.1	1 057.8	223.6	23.8	371.1	326.2	71.5	41.7	24.7	66.4	2.0	8.5
2005	1 708.8	1 166.5	251.5	24.9	402.5	351.3	81.4	54.9	24.6	76.8	2.0	9.8
2006	1 810.9	1 254.5	276.2	26.3	431.8	375.0	85.9	59.2	21.5	94.7	2.1	10.4
2007	1 900.6	1 321.3	296.4	27.1	448.9	403.8	87.2	57.9	18.9	104.2	2.2	11.5
2008	1 909.1	1 328.9	307.0	26.5	444.8	413.8	89.4	47.4	18.7	91.0	2.6	12.1
2009	1 919.2	1 268.1	259.5	28.3	423.9	435.1	75.8	45.6	18.6	74.4	2.1	11.2
2010	1 998.5	1 305.6	267.1	30.5	446.0	435.0	79.4	47.7	18.1	69.1	2.3	11.2
2011	2 030.5	1 368.3	292.9	31.2	466.7	439.2	88.1	50.2	18.2	64.8	2.6	11.7
2012	2 057.2	1 416.1	314.3	32.4	482.8	442.2	92.0	52.5	18.0	59.8	3.3	12.3
2013	2 136.5	1 479.8	339.2	32.9	507.2	449.5	95.4	55.5	18.6	58.0	3.7	12.6
2014	2 225.0	1 517.5	349.9	33.4	524.9	455.6	95.4	58.3	18.9	58.7	3.8	13.2
2012												
1st quarter	2 033.6	1 400.5	302.5	32.2	481.3	441.0	92.8	50.8	18.0	61.6	3.0	12.1
2nd quarter	2 044.7	1 409.5	310.3	32.3	481.4	441.3	92.2	52.0	18.0	60.1	3.4	12.3
3rd quarter	2 056.1	1 414.7	316.7	32.3	480.3	442.3	89.6	53.4	18.0	59.0	3.4	12.3
4th quarter	2 094.2	1 439.5	327.7	32.7	488.0	444.1	93.3	53.7	18.2	58.4	3.5	12.4
2013												
1st quarter	2 123.1	1 478.7	344.9	32.7	504.0	446.6	95.3	55.3	18.4	58.0	3.7	12.4
2nd quarter	2 144.3	1 488.7	353.5	32.9	503.4	448.8	94.3	55.9	18.5	57.9	3.7	12.5
3rd quarter	2 138.0	1 473.4	329.1	33.1	509.4	450.6	96.5	54.8	18.7	58.0	3.8	12.6
4th quarter	2 140.5	1 478.4	329.5	32.9	512.2	452.2	95.6	56.0	18.8	58.2	3.7	12.8
2014												
1st quarter	2 167.7	1 494.1	343.8	33.0	513.5	453.4	92.7	57.8	18.9	58.3	3.7	12.9
2nd quarter	2 214.9	1 504.4	340.4	33.4	522.8	454.8	95.6	57.4	18.9	58.6	3.8	13.1
3rd quarter	2 252.3	1 526.9	351.9	33.7	528.7	456.3	97.8	58.7	18.9	58.9	3.8	13.2
4th quarter	2 265.1	1 544.6	363.5	33.6	534.6	457.8	95.7	59.4	18.8	59.2	3.9	13.4

. . . = Not available.

Table 6-8. State and Local Government Current Receipts and Expenditures—Continued

(National income and product accounts, calendar years, billions of dollars, quarterly data are at seasonally adjusted annual rates.)

NIPA Table 3.3

Year and quarter	Current receipts—Continued				Current surplus of government enterprises	Current expenditures					Net state and local government saving, NIPA (surplus + / deficit -)		
	Current transfer receipts												
	Total	Federal grants-in-aid	From business, net	From persons		Total	Consumption expenditures	Government social benefits to persons	Interest payments	Subsidies	Total	Social insurance funds	Other
1955	2.9	2.3	0.2	0.4	0.7	27.0	22.1	3.3	1.6	. . .	2.2	0.1	2.1
1956	3.0	2.4	0.2	0.4	0.8	29.2	24.0	3.3	1.9	. . .	3.0	0.1	2.9
1957	3.5	2.8	0.2	0.5	0.8	32.1	26.4	3.6	2.1	. . .	2.6	0.1	2.5
1958	4.0	3.2	0.2	0.5	0.8	35.7	29.4	4.0	2.3	. . .	1.1	0.0	1.1
1959	4.0	3.6	0.1	0.3	1.0	38.2	31.2	4.3	2.7	0.0	2.2	0.0	2.2
1960	4.3	3.8	0.2	0.3	1.2	41.6	34.1	4.6	3.0	0.0	2.6	0.0	2.5
1961	4.9	4.3	0.2	0.4	1.2	45.5	37.2	5.0	3.3	0.0	2.2	0.0	2.2
1962	5.5	4.7	0.2	0.5	1.3	48.2	39.3	5.3	3.5	0.0	3.4	0.0	3.4
1963	6.0	5.2	0.3	0.5	1.5	51.8	42.3	5.7	3.8	0.0	3.7	0.0	3.7
1964	6.8	6.0	0.3	0.5	1.5	56.3	46.0	6.2	4.1	0.0	4.3	0.0	4.3
1965	7.4	6.6	0.3	0.5	1.6	61.7	50.6	6.7	4.5	0.0	4.1	0.1	4.0
1966	10.4	9.4	0.3	0.7	1.5	68.9	56.4	7.6	4.9	0.0	5.2	0.1	5.1
1967	12.3	10.9	0.5	0.9	1.4	76.9	62.4	9.2	5.2	0.0	4.7	0.1	4.6
1968	13.3	11.8	0.5	1.0	1.3	88.2	70.7	11.4	6.0	0.0	4.3	0.1	4.1
1969	15.3	13.7	0.5	1.1	1.3	100.2	80.4	13.2	6.6	0.0	4.1	0.2	3.9
1970	20.1	18.3	0.6	1.2	1.3	115.9	92.1	16.1	7.7	0.0	3.0	0.2	2.8
1971	24.1	22.1	0.6	1.4	1.1	133.0	104.2	19.3	9.4	0.0	0.6	0.2	0.4
1972	32.8	30.5	0.7	1.7	1.2	148.5	115.4	22.0	11.1	0.1	8.4	0.3	8.2
1973	36.1	33.5	0.9	1.7	1.2	163.1	126.8	24.1	12.2	0.1	9.6	0.3	9.3
1974	37.9	34.9	1.1	2.0	0.6	184.1	144.5	25.3	14.2	0.1	2.3	0.4	1.9
1975	47.2	43.6	1.2	2.4	0.1	213.3	165.6	30.8	16.7	0.2	-5.6	0.5	-6.0
1976	53.3	49.1	1.4	2.9	0.2	229.1	177.2	34.1	17.6	0.2	2.8	0.6	2.2
1977	59.6	54.8	1.6	3.3	0.1	249.5	193.0	37.0	19.2	0.2	8.4	1.0	7.5
1978	69.0	63.5	1.9	3.7	0.0	271.9	209.9	40.8	21.0	0.2	13.4	1.5	12.0
1979	70.3	64.0	2.2	4.1	-0.5	297.6	229.4	44.3	23.5	0.3	8.2	1.8	6.4
1980	76.9	69.7	2.5	4.7	-1.4	329.9	252.8	51.2	25.6	0.4	5.4	1.3	4.1
1981	78.0	69.4	2.9	5.7	-2.6	362.9	276.1	57.1	29.3	0.4	4.1	1.3	2.8
1982	75.9	66.3	3.2	6.4	-1.7	393.2	297.4	61.2	34.2	0.5	-5.1	1.2	-6.3
1983	78.7	67.9	3.6	7.2	-0.4	423.6	316.7	66.9	39.5	0.4	1.3	1.2	0.1
1984	84.7	72.3	4.2	8.1	1.3	454.7	340.0	71.2	43.2	0.4	20.9	1.4	19.5
1985	89.8	76.2	4.4	9.2	2.9	496.7	371.8	77.3	47.3	0.3	20.3	1.3	18.9
1986	99.8	82.4	6.7	10.6	2.6	536.4	399.9	84.3	51.8	0.3	20.4	1.9	18.6
1987	94.4	78.4	4.9	11.2	2.7	572.9	428.3	90.7	53.5	0.3	12.1	2.2	9.9
1988	103.1	85.7	5.4	12.0	4.4	612.9	458.9	98.5	55.1	0.4	17.0	2.5	14.5
1989	111.6	91.8	6.4	13.4	5.6	673.4	501.3	109.3	62.3	0.4	7.4	2.3	5.1
1990	126.4	104.4	7.1	14.9	5.6	736.0	546.2	127.7	61.8	0.4	-6.5	2.0	-8.4
1991	150.7	124.0	7.9	18.7	5.7	804.6	580.1	156.5	67.6	0.4	-25.1	2.4	-27.5
1992	172.8	141.7	9.2	21.9	5.8	873.1	619.0	180.0	73.6	0.4	-37.5	3.1	-40.7
1993	189.8	155.7	10.5	23.5	7.3	914.3	646.5	195.2	72.2	0.4	-37.2	4.2	-41.4
1994	204.1	166.8	12.0	25.2	7.8	961.0	682.2	206.7	71.8	0.3	-27.0	4.6	-31.6
1995	214.4	174.5	13.5	26.5	10.6	1 011.4	716.8	217.6	76.6	0.3	-31.5	4.0	-35.6
1996	224.4	181.5	15.2	27.8	12.4	1 045.0	748.1	224.3	72.4	0.3	-12.5	2.8	-15.3
1997	236.1	188.1	17.7	30.3	10.9	1 084.1	785.9	227.6	70.2	0.4	1.7	1.2	0.5
1998	253.5	200.8	21.6	31.1	8.7	1 133.3	835.7	235.8	61.4	0.4	15.4	1.7	13.7
1999	277.4	219.2	24.0	34.2	9.0	1 212.6	902.0	252.3	57.8	0.4	9.2	1.7	7.5
2000	299.7	233.1	28.6	38.0	5.4	1 293.2	969.1	271.4	52.1	0.5	9.9	2.0	7.9
2001	333.1	261.3	29.8	42.0	2.4	1 417.9	1 039.7	305.1	65.4	7.7	-65.3	2.6	-67.9
2002	365.4	287.2	32.6	45.6	0.1	1 509.4	1 091.0	333.0	84.4	0.9	-120.9	1.4	-122.3
2003	405.0	321.7	33.8	49.5	-2.8	1 596.0	1 127.1	353.6	115.2	0.1	-121.4	3.2	-124.7
2004	422.4	332.2	36.5	53.7	-6.7	1 683.4	1 187.6	385.0	110.5	0.4	-108.4	7.3	-115.7
2005	436.4	343.4	36.5	56.5	-7.3	1 775.4	1 256.6	406.6	111.8	0.4	-66.6	7.2	-73.8
2006	438.9	340.8	38.8	59.3	-11.1	1 850.3	1 325.9	403.9	120.1	0.4	-39.4	4.6	-44.0
2007	460.9	359.0	40.5	61.4	-18.5	1 973.3	1 411.4	433.3	121.5	7.1	-72.7	2.7	-75.4
2008	477.8	371.0	43.6	63.3	-22.0	2 074.1	1 488.7	455.4	127.0	3.0	-165.1	1.7	-166.8
2009	566.1	458.1	44.0	64.0	-21.4	2 191.2	1 508.4	492.6	188.8	1.4	-271.9	2.2	-274.1
2010	612.0	505.3	43.4	63.2	-19.8	2 235.8	1 518.3	523.8	192.1	1.6	-237.3	3.2	-240.5
2011	582.1	472.5	44.2	65.4	-17.4	2 246.4	1 524.8	530.4	190.7	0.5	-215.9	4.4	-220.4
2012	558.0	444.0	44.0	70.1	-10.4	2 277.9	1 536.3	540.0	201.2	0.5	-220.8	4.2	-225.0
2013	571.2	450.1	49.6	71.5	-7.5	2 323.6	1 560.7	562.3	200.1	0.5	-187.1	4.1	-191.2
2014	621.5	494.8	48.7	72.8	-8.6	2 392.7	1 601.0	609.9	181.4	0.5	-167.7	4.2	-171.9
2012													
1st quarter	551.8	439.7	43.6	68.5	-13.5	2 258.3	1 536.4	523.4	198.1	0.5	-224.7	4.4	-229.1
2nd quarter	552.5	439.1	43.6	69.8	-10.9	2 275.2	1 530.8	543.4	200.5	0.5	-230.4	4.2	-234.7
3rd quarter	557.7	443.0	44.0	70.7	-9.1	2 278.4	1 534.2	541.5	202.4	0.5	-222.3	4.1	-226.4
4th quarter	570.1	454.1	44.8	71.2	-7.9	2 299.8	1 543.9	551.7	203.7	0.5	-205.6	4.0	-209.6
2013													
1st quarter	559.3	440.5	47.6	71.2	-7.5	2 303.5	1 549.9	548.7	204.4	0.5	-180.4	4.0	-184.4
2nd quarter	570.3	450.5	48.5	71.4	-7.4	2 316.3	1 554.0	558.7	203.0	0.5	-172.0	4.0	-176.0
3rd quarter	578.9	458.4	49.0	71.5	-7.4	2 336.1	1 565.2	571.0	199.4	0.5	-198.0	4.1	-202.1
4th quarter	576.4	451.1	53.5	71.8	-7.6	2 338.5	1 573.6	570.8	193.6	0.5	-197.9	4.1	-202.1
2014													
1st quarter	587.9	468.6	47.2	72.1	-8.1	2 357.0	1 585.8	585.1	185.7	0.5	-189.3	4.3	-193.6
2nd quarter	624.7	484.2	47.3	72.5	-8.5	2 375.2	1 598.2	595.8	180.8	0.5	-160.3	4.3	-164.5
3rd quarter	639.5	514.1	52.4	73.0	-8.8	2 418.4	1 610.5	628.4	178.9	0.5	-166.0	4.3	-170.3
4th quarter	634.0	512.5	47.8	73.7	-8.9	2 420.3	1 609.5	630.2	180.1	0.5	-155.2	4.1	-159.4

. . . = Not available.

Table 6-9. State and Local Government Consumption Expenditures and Gross Investment

(National income and product accounts, calendar years, billions of dollars, quarterly data are at seasonally adjusted annual rates.)

NIPA Tables 3.9.5, 3.10.5

Year and quarter	Total	State and local government consumption expenditures and gross investment											
		Consumption expenditures [1]								Gross investment			
		Total	Compensation of general government employees	Consumption of general government fixed capital	Intermediate goods and services purchased [2]	Less Own-account investment	Less Sales to other sectors Total [3]	Tuition and related educational charges	Health and hospital charges	Total	Structures	Equipment	Intellectual property
1960	48.2	34.1	26.4	3.6	8.9	0.9	3.9	0.4	1.0	14.1	12.7	1.2	0.2
1961	52.5	37.2	29.1	3.8	9.6	1.0	4.3	0.5	1.0	15.3	13.8	1.2	0.2
1962	55.4	39.3	31.2	4.1	10.1	1.1	4.9	0.6	1.3	16.1	14.5	1.3	0.2
1963	60.0	42.3	33.9	4.4	10.8	1.3	5.6	0.7	1.3	17.8	16.0	1.5	0.3
1964	65.3	46.0	37.0	4.7	11.9	1.3	6.3	0.8	1.5	19.3	17.2	1.7	0.3
1965	71.7	50.6	40.7	5.1	13.4	1.4	7.2	1.0	1.8	21.2	19.0	1.8	0.4
1966	79.8	56.4	45.5	5.7	14.9	1.5	8.2	1.2	2.1	23.5	21.0	2.0	0.4
1967	88.1	62.4	50.6	6.2	16.4	1.6	9.3	1.4	2.5	25.7	23.0	2.2	0.5
1968	98.8	70.7	57.6	6.9	18.6	1.8	10.7	1.6	3.1	28.1	25.2	2.3	0.6
1969	109.3	80.4	64.6	7.8	21.8	1.9	11.8	1.9	3.5	28.8	25.6	2.6	0.7
1970	121.4	92.1	73.2	8.8	25.3	2.1	13.1	2.4	3.8	29.3	25.8	2.8	0.8
1971	134.9	104.2	82.4	9.9	29.1	2.2	14.9	2.9	4.6	30.7	27.0	2.9	0.8
1972	146.7	115.4	91.7	10.7	32.0	2.3	16.7	3.2	5.6	31.3	27.1	3.3	0.9
1973	160.8	126.8	100.7	11.9	35.3	2.4	18.7	3.7	6.6	34.0	29.1	3.8	1.0
1974	185.0	144.5	110.5	14.7	42.6	2.8	20.5	4.0	7.4	40.5	34.7	4.6	1.2
1975	210.2	165.6	124.0	16.7	50.5	3.0	22.6	4.3	8.5	44.6	38.1	5.1	1.3
1976	222.1	177.2	133.3	17.4	55.0	3.0	25.6	4.7	9.9	44.9	38.1	5.3	1.5
1977	237.0	193.0	145.1	18.4	60.8	3.1	28.3	5.2	10.9	44.0	36.9	5.4	1.6
1978	260.7	209.9	158.9	19.9	66.6	3.5	32.0	5.8	12.7	50.8	42.8	6.1	1.9
1979	287.8	229.4	174.2	22.2	73.9	4.3	36.6	6.4	15.2	58.4	49.0	7.1	2.2
1980	318.5	252.8	191.6	25.7	81.6	4.9	41.2	7.2	17.3	65.7	55.1	8.1	2.6
1981	343.0	276.1	208.5	29.4	91.1	5.3	47.6	8.3	21.0	66.9	55.4	8.5	3.0
1982	364.4	297.4	224.8	32.1	100.0	5.7	53.8	9.4	24.5	67.0	54.2	9.4	3.4
1983	385.6	316.7	240.9	33.1	109.0	6.1	60.1	10.6	27.8	68.8	54.2	10.8	3.8
1984	417.5	340.0	259.2	34.1	118.4	7.0	64.7	11.7	29.4	77.6	60.5	12.7	4.4
1985	459.2	371.8	283.2	35.9	131.4	7.9	70.8	12.7	32.0	87.3	67.6	14.8	5.0
1986	496.1	399.9	305.8	38.6	141.7	8.8	77.4	13.8	34.8	96.2	74.2	16.4	5.6
1987	530.5	428.3	329.6	41.6	150.0	9.5	83.4	15.0	37.0	102.2	78.8	17.2	6.2
1988	569.3	458.9	356.3	44.5	159.8	10.4	91.2	16.6	40.3	110.4	84.8	18.6	7.0
1989	620.5	501.3	391.1	47.7	175.8	11.9	101.4	18.4	45.0	119.2	88.7	21.9	8.6
1990	678.3	546.2	428.7	51.6	190.5	13.1	111.6	20.3	50.0	132.2	98.5	23.9	9.7
1991	717.4	580.1	458.5	55.1	204.7	14.1	124.1	22.6	57.0	137.3	103.2	23.5	10.6
1992	758.8	619.0	495.3	57.6	218.9	14.4	138.4	25.4	65.3	139.7	104.2	24.0	11.4
1993	787.7	646.5	519.2	60.8	233.8	14.8	152.5	27.4	73.1	141.2	104.5	24.9	11.9
1994	831.1	682.2	545.5	64.3	251.3	15.4	163.5	29.3	78.8	148.8	108.7	28.1	12.0
1995	876.8	716.8	569.6	68.6	270.3	16.1	175.6	31.1	85.0	160.0	117.3	30.5	12.3
1996	918.2	748.1	591.4	72.0	285.5	16.8	184.0	32.9	86.6	170.2	126.8	30.5	12.8
1997	971.8	785.9	619.0	75.7	304.1	18.5	194.3	35.4	89.9	185.8	139.5	32.0	14.3
1998	1 029.4	835.7	652.5	79.8	326.4	19.3	203.7	37.9	93.4	193.7	143.6	34.7	15.5
1999	1 115.6	902.0	695.1	84.9	357.1	20.7	214.4	40.5	96.7	213.6	159.7	37.4	16.5
2000	1 202.0	969.1	740.4	91.4	391.9	22.8	231.8	43.6	104.0	232.9	176.0	38.8	18.1
2001	1 289.5	1 039.7	794.4	96.9	425.0	25.2	251.4	46.1	116.2	249.8	192.3	38.4	19.1
2002	1 354.3	1 091.0	836.4	101.4	444.0	26.1	264.6	49.3	120.7	263.3	205.8	38.0	19.4
2003	1 396.0	1 127.1	876.5	105.2	450.8	26.6	278.8	53.4	124.8	268.9	211.1	37.6	20.2
2004	1 465.0	1 187.6	926.3	111.6	472.2	27.8	294.7	56.7	130.9	277.5	219.1	37.2	21.2
2005	1 547.4	1 256.6	965.0	121.8	507.3	29.6	308.0	60.9	132.3	290.8	231.5	37.1	22.1
2006	1 640.2	1 325.9	1 011.1	131.7	542.2	31.6	327.5	65.7	141.3	314.3	251.2	39.1	24.0
2007	1 752.2	1 411.4	1 065.5	144.7	577.8	33.6	343.0	69.6	149.8	340.8	271.2	43.9	25.8
2008	1 847.6	1 488.7	1 117.7	155.5	606.6	35.8	355.2	73.8	157.6	358.8	285.3	45.7	27.8
2009	1 871.4	1 508.4	1 141.9	162.1	609.9	36.2	369.4	79.2	167.0	363.0	289.8	44.5	28.7
2010	1 870.2	1 518.3	1 167.4	164.9	610.0	35.2	388.8	85.2	175.3	351.9	280.5	41.8	29.5
2011	1 865.3	1 524.8	1 171.4	171.6	618.8	35.5	401.5	88.7	181.6	340.5	271.1	39.3	30.1
2012	1 866.1	1 536.3	1 180.9	178.9	622.2	35.2	410.5	91.3	186.0	329.7	259.8	38.9	31.0
2013	1 883.6	1 560.7	1 205.8	183.7	626.3	34.6	420.6	94.0	191.0	322.9	250.7	40.4	31.8
2014	1 932.3	1 601.0	1 238.9	189.3	638.2	35.2	430.1	96.3	196.0	331.3	256.8	41.7	32.7
2012													
1st quarter	1 871.0	1 536.4	1 177.5	176.6	625.2	35.5	407.4	90.4	184.8	334.6	265.6	38.4	30.6
2nd quarter	1 865.9	1 530.8	1 176.6	178.5	620.2	35.5	409.1	90.9	185.3	335.2	265.1	39.2	30.9
3rd quarter	1 862.6	1 534.2	1 180.5	179.9	620.4	35.2	411.4	91.6	186.3	328.5	258.5	39.0	31.0
4th quarter	1 864.6	1 543.9	1 189.0	180.6	623.0	34.6	414.0	92.3	187.5	320.7	250.2	39.1	31.3
2013													
1st quarter	1 869.4	1 549.9	1 194.9	181.6	625.5	34.5	417.6	93.3	189.4	319.5	248.6	39.1	31.8
2nd quarter	1 877.2	1 554.0	1 201.2	182.9	623.6	34.6	419.0	93.6	190.1	323.1	251.3	40.3	31.6
3rd quarter	1 890.3	1 565.2	1 209.5	184.3	627.3	34.7	421.2	94.2	191.4	325.1	252.4	40.9	31.9
4th quarter	1 897.5	1 573.6	1 217.5	186.0	629.0	34.5	424.4	95.0	193.0	323.9	250.5	41.4	32.0
2014													
1st quarter	1 907.5	1 585.8	1 223.9	187.5	635.8	34.4	427.0	95.6	194.4	321.7	248.4	41.0	32.3
2nd quarter	1 929.4	1 598.2	1 234.6	188.8	639.8	35.2	429.7	96.2	195.8	331.3	257.4	41.3	32.6
3rd quarter	1 944.3	1 610.5	1 244.8	190.1	642.4	35.4	431.4	96.6	196.6	333.8	259.1	41.8	32.9
4th quarter	1 947.8	1 609.5	1 252.2	190.7	634.7	35.7	432.4	96.8	197.0	338.3	262.5	42.9	33.0

[1]Excludes government sales to other sectors and government own-account investment (construction and software).
[2]Includes general government intermediate inputs for goods and services sold to other sectors and for own-account investment.
[3]Includes components not shown separately.

Table 6-10. State and Local Government Output, Lending and Borrowing, and Net Investment

(National income and product accounts, calendar years, billions of dollars, quarterly data are at seasonally adjusted annual rates.)

NIPA Tables 3.3, 3.10.5

Year and quarter	Output			Net lending (net borrowing -)								Net investment
	Gross	Value added	Intermediate goods and services purchased [1]	Net saving, current (surplus +, deficit -)	Plus: Capital transfer receipts	Minus			Plus: consumption of fixed capital	Equals: Net lending (borrowing -)	
						Gross investment	Capital transfer payments	Net purchases of nonproduced assets			
1955	25.1	19.1	6.0	2.2	1.0	10.1	...	0.6	3.2	-4.4	6.9
1956	27.2	21.3	5.9	3.0	1.1	11.4	...	0.7	3.6	-4.3	7.8
1957	30.0	23.6	6.4	2.6	1.6	12.7	...	0.7	3.9	-5.1	8.8
1958	33.4	25.9	7.5	1.1	2.7	13.7	...	0.8	4.1	-6.5	9.6
1959	35.8	27.4	8.3	2.2	3.5	14.1	...	0.8	4.4	-4.9	9.7
1960	38.9	30.0	8.9	2.6	3.0	14.1	...	0.9	4.5	-4.8	9.6
1961	42.6	32.9	9.6	2.2	3.3	15.3	...	1.0	4.8	-5.9	10.5
1962	45.4	35.3	10.1	3.4	3.5	16.1	...	1.1	5.2	-5.1	10.9
1963	49.1	38.3	10.8	3.7	4.1	17.8	...	1.2	5.5	-5.5	12.3
1964	53.6	41.7	11.9	4.3	4.7	19.3	...	1.3	5.9	-5.6	13.4
1965	59.2	45.8	13.4	4.1	4.7	21.2	...	1.3	6.4	-7.2	14.8
1966	66.1	51.2	14.9	5.2	5.1	23.5	...	1.4	7.1	-7.4	16.4
1967	73.3	56.9	16.4	4.7	5.1	25.7	...	1.4	7.8	-9.5	17.9
1968	83.2	64.5	18.6	4.3	6.8	28.1	...	1.4	8.6	-9.8	19.5
1969	94.2	72.4	21.8	4.1	6.8	28.8	...	1.0	9.7	-9.2	19.1
1970	107.3	82.0	25.3	3.0	6.2	29.3	...	1.1	10.9	-10.3	18.4
1971	121.4	92.2	29.1	0.6	7.0	30.7	...	1.6	12.2	-12.5	18.5
1972	134.4	102.4	32.0	8.4	7.3	31.3	...	1.7	13.3	-4.0	18.0
1973	147.9	112.6	35.3	9.6	7.3	34.0	...	1.7	14.9	-3.9	19.1
1974	167.8	125.2	42.6	2.3	9.2	40.5	...	1.9	18.3	-12.6	22.2
1975	191.2	140.7	50.5	-5.6	11.0	44.6	...	1.9	21.0	-20.1	23.6
1976	205.7	150.8	55.0	2.8	12.0	44.9	...	1.7	22.1	-9.7	22.8
1977	224.4	163.5	60.8	8.4	13.1	44.0	...	1.6	23.5	-0.5	20.5
1978	245.4	178.8	66.6	13.4	13.7	50.8	...	1.8	25.5	0.0	25.3
1979	270.3	196.4	73.9	8.2	16.2	58.4	...	2.0	28.6	-7.3	29.8
1980	298.9	217.3	81.6	5.4	18.6	65.7	...	2.2	33.1	-10.8	32.6
1981	329.0	237.8	91.1	4.1	17.8	66.9	...	2.2	37.8	-9.4	29.1
1982	356.9	256.9	100.0	-5.1	16.9	67.0	...	2.2	41.3	-16.1	25.7
1983	382.9	273.9	109.0	1.3	18.0	68.8	...	2.2	42.8	-9.0	26.0
1984	411.7	293.3	118.4	20.9	20.1	77.6	...	2.6	44.4	5.3	33.2
1985	450.5	319.1	131.4	20.3	22.0	87.3	...	3.1	46.9	-1.3	40.4
1986	486.1	344.4	141.7	20.4	23.0	96.2	...	3.7	50.3	-6.1	45.9
1987	521.3	371.2	150.0	12.1	22.3	102.2	...	4.2	54.1	-17.9	48.1
1988	560.5	400.8	159.8	17.0	23.1	110.4	...	4.3	57.8	-16.9	52.6
1989	614.6	438.8	175.8	7.4	23.4	119.2	0.0	4.9	61.9	-31.4	57.3
1990	670.8	480.3	190.5	-6.5	25.0	132.2	0.0	5.7	66.7	-52.7	65.5
1991	718.3	513.7	204.7	-25.1	25.8	137.3	0.0	5.8	70.9	-71.6	66.4
1992	771.9	553.0	218.9	-37.5	26.9	139.7	0.0	5.9	74.1	-82.0	65.6
1993	813.8	580.0	233.8	-37.2	28.2	141.2	0.0	5.9	78.3	-77.8	62.9
1994	861.1	609.9	251.3	-27.0	29.9	148.8	0.0	6.2	82.9	-69.1	65.9
1995	908.6	638.2	270.3	-31.5	32.4	160.0	0.0	6.6	88.3	-77.5	71.7
1996	948.9	663.4	285.5	-12.5	33.8	170.2	0.0	6.0	92.6	-62.2	77.6
1997	998.7	694.7	304.1	1.7	35.2	185.8	0.0	5.8	96.9	-57.9	88.9
1998	1 058.7	732.3	326.4	15.4	35.9	193.7	0.0	7.6	101.8	-48.3	91.9
1999	1 137.1	780.0	357.1	9.2	40.0	213.6	0.0	8.6	108.1	-64.8	105.5
2000	1 223.7	831.8	391.9	9.9	44.2	232.9	0.0	8.6	116.2	-71.2	116.7
2001	1 316.3	891.3	425.0	-65.3	51.7	249.8	0.0	10.1	123.0	-150.5	126.8
2002	1 381.8	937.8	444.0	-120.9	52.9	263.3	0.0	11.2	129.0	-213.5	134.3
2003	1 432.5	981.7	450.8	-121.4	52.0	268.9	0.0	11.4	134.5	-215.2	134.4
2004	1 510.1	1 037.9	472.2	-108.4	52.4	277.5	4.5	11.3	143.8	-205.4	133.7
2005	1 594.1	1 086.8	507.3	-66.6	56.8	290.8	6.4	10.0	157.3	-159.7	133.5
2006	1 685.0	1 142.8	542.2	-39.4	57.8	314.3	0.0	11.0	170.3	-136.6	144.0
2007	1 788.0	1 210.2	577.8	-72.7	59.3	340.8	0.0	13.6	186.6	-181.2	154.2
2008	1 879.7	1 273.2	606.6	-165.1	63.2	358.8	0.0	13.8	200.2	-274.3	158.6
2009	1 913.9	1 304.0	609.9	-271.9	67.7	363.0	0.0	12.3	208.2	-371.4	154.8
2010	1 942.3	1 332.3	610.0	-237.3	76.7	351.9	0.0	10.6	212.7	-310.3	139.2
2011	1 961.8	1 343.0	618.8	-215.9	73.8	340.5	0.0	9.2	222.2	-269.6	118.3
2012	1 982.0	1 359.8	622.2	-220.8	74.2	329.7	0.0	9.1	231.9	-253.6	97.8
2013	2 015.8	1 389.5	626.3	-187.1	71.4	322.9	0.0	9.6	238.5	-209.7	84.4
2014	2 066.3	1 428.1	638.2	-167.7	71.0	331.3	0.0	9.9	246.1	-191.8	85.2
2012											
1st quarter	1 979.3	1 354.1	625.2	-224.7	70.5	334.6	0.0	9.0	228.8	-268.9	105.8
2nd quarter	1 975.4	1 355.1	620.2	-230.4	72.1	335.2	0.0	9.1	231.3	-271.3	103.9
3rd quarter	1 980.8	1 360.3	620.4	-222.3	72.4	328.5	0.0	9.2	233.2	-254.4	95.3
4th quarter	1 992.5	1 369.5	623.0	-205.6	81.6	320.7	0.0	9.3	234.3	-219.8	86.4
2013											
1st quarter	2 002.0	1 376.5	625.5	-180.4	72.0	319.5	0.0	9.4	235.7	-201.6	83.8
2nd quarter	2 007.6	1 384.1	623.6	-172.0	68.8	323.1	0.0	9.5	237.5	-198.3	85.6
3rd quarter	2 021.1	1 393.8	627.3	-198.0	74.1	325.1	0.0	9.7	239.4	-219.3	85.7
4th quarter	2 032.5	1 403.6	629.0	-197.9	70.6	323.9	0.0	9.8	241.5	-219.5	82.4
2014											
1st quarter	2 047.2	1 411.4	635.8	-189.3	70.1	321.7	0.0	9.9	243.5	-207.4	78.2
2nd quarter	2 063.1	1 423.3	639.8	-160.3	71.9	331.3	0.0	9.9	245.3	-184.3	86.0
3rd quarter	2 077.3	1 434.9	642.4	-166.0	74.9	333.8	0.0	10.0	247.2	-187.7	86.6
4th quarter	2 077.6	1 442.9	634.7	-155.2	67.2	338.3	0.0	9.9	248.3	-188.0	90.0

[1] Includes general government intermediate inputs for goods and services sold to other sectors and for own-account investment.
. . . = Not available.

Table 6-11. Chain-Type Quantity Indexes for State and Local Government Consumption Expenditures and Gross Investment

(Seasonally adjusted, 2009 = 100.)

NIPA Tables 3.9.3, 3.10.3

Year and quarter	Total	Consumption expenditures [1]				Less				Gross investment			
		Total	Compensation of general government employees	Consumption of general government fixed capital	Intermediate goods and services purchased [2]	Own-account investment	Sales to other sectors Total [3]	Tuition and related educational charges	Health and hospital charges	Total	Structures	Equipment	Intellectual property
1960	25.6	24.3	32.6	14.5	10.5	20.3	13.8	14.0	10.6	29.2	44.0	5.4	2.4
1961	27.1	25.6	34.3	15.3	11.2	21.4	14.9	15.3	10.9	31.5	47.7	5.5	2.7
1962	27.9	26.3	35.5	16.1	11.7	23.0	16.6	17.3	12.7	32.7	49.2	5.9	3.0
1963	29.6	27.5	37.3	17.1	12.4	25.8	18.5	19.7	13.2	35.6	53.3	6.7	3.6
1964	31.6	29.3	39.5	18.2	13.6	26.1	20.4	23.1	14.2	38.2	56.8	7.6	4.0
1965	33.7	31.1	41.9	19.4	15.0	27.2	22.8	26.8	16.3	40.9	60.8	8.1	4.5
1966	35.8	33.0	44.3	20.6	16.2	29.0	24.9	30.4	18.6	43.6	64.7	8.8	5.2
1967	37.5	34.5	46.1	22.0	17.5	29.3	27.4	33.9	21.1	46.4	68.8	9.2	5.9
1968	39.8	36.8	48.8	23.3	19.3	30.9	29.9	38.1	24.6	48.5	71.9	9.6	6.3
1969	41.2	39.1	51.0	24.7	21.4	31.4	31.0	41.9	25.5	46.5	68.1	10.2	7.0
1970	42.4	41.5	53.3	25.9	23.6	32.2	32.3	48.8	25.9	43.7	63.1	10.6	7.7
1971	43.7	43.6	55.4	27.0	25.8	32.6	35.1	55.0	30.2	42.6	61.0	10.7	8.0
1972	44.7	45.2	57.3	28.0	27.4	32.3	37.6	58.4	34.6	41.2	58.0	12.0	8.4
1973	45.9	46.8	59.3	29.1	28.2	32.2	39.1	63.0	38.4	41.5	57.5	13.4	8.9
1974	47.6	48.9	61.5	30.1	29.5	33.8	39.0	62.8	39.6	41.9	57.4	14.6	9.2
1975	49.3	51.3	63.3	31.1	31.9	32.7	39.5	62.8	40.7	41.5	56.9	14.1	9.9
1976	49.7	52.0	64.1	32.1	32.9	30.6	41.8	64.9	43.2	40.9	55.9	13.8	10.5
1977	49.9	53.0	65.0	32.8	34.0	29.3	43.2	67.5	44.0	38.5	52.2	13.4	11.0
1978	51.6	54.1	66.5	33.6	35.0	31.6	45.4	71.2	47.1	41.9	57.1	14.0	12.2
1979	52.3	54.4	67.6	34.5	35.0	35.3	47.6	73.2	51.1	44.0	59.6	15.2	13.4
1980	52.2	54.2	68.5	35.4	33.7	36.8	48.4	75.7	51.5	44.3	59.3	16.1	14.2
1981	51.2	54.0	68.2	36.2	33.9	36.2	50.2	77.3	54.8	40.6	53.5	15.8	15.1
1982	51.2	54.8	68.6	36.9	35.4	36.8	51.5	77.2	56.4	38.2	49.1	16.6	16.2
1983	51.9	55.5	68.1	37.7	37.8	37.2	53.3	79.5	57.9	38.8	48.6	18.9	17.5
1984	53.9	56.7	68.3	38.7	39.8	40.5	53.4	79.3	56.5	43.4	53.9	22.1	19.4
1985	56.9	59.2	70.2	40.1	43.1	43.9	55.3	79.3	57.8	48.1	59.1	25.5	21.8
1986	59.8	61.9	72.2	41.8	46.7	48.0	57.3	79.9	59.3	51.5	62.8	28.0	24.2
1987	61.1	63.2	73.4	43.5	47.7	49.9	58.5	80.5	59.3	52.9	64.2	29.2	25.9
1988	63.4	65.4	75.8	45.3	49.2	52.3	59.7	82.9	59.4	55.7	67.0	31.1	28.8
1989	66.0	67.8	78.0	47.6	51.6	56.9	61.4	85.5	59.8	58.7	68.4	35.9	34.2
1990	68.7	70.0	80.1	50.2	53.3	59.7	62.6	87.4	60.5	63.3	73.5	38.6	38.0
1991	70.2	71.5	80.8	52.7	56.0	62.1	64.7	88.8	63.0	64.8	76.0	37.2	40.9
1992	71.6	73.1	82.0	55.0	58.7	61.5	67.6	90.4	66.7	65.6	76.3	38.0	44.4
1993	72.5	74.4	82.8	57.1	61.3	61.4	70.7	89.3	70.6	65.0	74.5	39.3	45.4
1994	74.5	76.4	84.1	59.2	64.7	62.2	73.1	89.4	73.4	66.9	75.1	44.2	45.9
1995	76.5	78.2	85.6	61.3	67.3	63.0	75.7	89.7	76.7	69.7	77.7	48.4	45.7
1996	78.3	79.7	86.7	63.6	69.1	64.7	77.1	90.0	76.4	72.9	81.6	49.7	48.0
1997	81.1	81.8	88.2	66.2	72.6	70.2	79.7	92.1	78.2	78.4	87.1	54.3	53.8
1998	84.3	85.1	89.8	69.3	78.3	72.1	82.1	94.6	80.5	80.7	86.9	61.8	58.9
1999	87.8	88.0	90.9	72.7	83.7	75.4	84.3	97.4	81.9	87.1	93.1	69.3	62.4
2000	90.3	89.9	92.6	76.1	87.0	79.8	88.5	100.8	85.9	92.0	98.2	73.2	66.7
2001	93.6	92.9	94.5	79.5	93.2	86.1	93.3	101.4	93.1	96.6	103.8	74.8	69.7
2002	96.3	95.4	96.2	82.5	96.8	88.0	95.2	101.4	93.5	100.1	108.1	76.3	71.2
2003	95.9	94.8	96.5	84.9	94.3	87.5	95.7	101.4	91.9	100.8	108.3	77.0	74.5
2004	95.8	94.9	96.6	87.4	94.3	88.4	96.6	98.2	92.2	99.6	106.3	76.9	78.0
2005	95.8	95.5	97.0	89.7	94.7	90.9	97.0	98.2	90.1	97.0	102.2	78.1	81.1
2006	96.7	96.2	97.6	92.1	96.2	94.6	99.1	99.2	92.6	98.7	102.3	84.9	87.0
2007	98.1	97.7	98.8	94.8	97.6	97.5	99.7	99.1	95.0	99.7	101.0	97.2	91.9
2008	98.5	97.9	99.9	97.6	95.2	99.9	98.9	98.9	97.1	100.6	100.7	102.1	96.9
2009	100.0	100.0	100.0	100.0	100.0	100.0	100.0	100.0	100.0	100.0	100.0	100.0	100.0
2010	97.3	97.4	99.0	101.9	96.2	95.7	102.2	102.3	102.2	96.7	96.4	94.7	102.1
2011	94.1	94.8	97.5	103.4	92.3	94.1	102.6	101.5	103.8	91.0	90.0	89.7	102.6
2012	92.3	94.0	96.7	104.6	90.9	91.4	102.2	99.7	103.9	85.3	83.1	87.9	104.3
2013	91.4	93.6	96.4	105.7	90.2	88.3	102.1	98.5	104.6	82.1	78.4	91.4	106.1
2014	92.0	94.2	96.8	106.7	90.7	88.2	102.3	97.3	106.0	82.4	78.4	93.5	107.9
2012													
1st quarter	93.0	94.3	96.9	104.2	91.6	92.8	102.4	100.2	104.3	87.4	85.9	87.0	103.5
2nd quarter	92.7	94.1	96.8	104.5	91.1	92.5	102.2	99.8	103.8	86.8	84.9	88.4	104.2
3rd quarter	92.2	93.9	96.7	104.7	90.7	91.2	102.1	99.5	103.7	84.6	82.3	87.8	104.3
4th quarter	91.6	93.7	96.5	105.0	90.3	89.3	102.0	99.1	103.9	82.5	79.5	88.3	105.3
2013													
1st quarter	91.3	93.5	96.3	105.3	90.2	88.6	102.0	98.9	104.1	81.9	78.5	88.6	106.5
2nd quarter	91.4	93.5	96.3	105.5	90.2	88.6	102.2	98.4	104.6	82.4	78.9	91.2	105.3
3rd quarter	91.4	93.5	96.4	105.8	90.1	88.4	102.1	98.3	104.9	82.4	78.7	92.5	106.1
4th quarter	91.4	93.7	96.5	106.1	90.2	87.6	102.2	98.2	105.0	81.6	77.6	93.2	106.4
2014													
1st quarter	91.4	93.9	96.6	106.3	90.4	86.9	102.3	97.8	105.5	80.6	76.4	92.2	106.9
2nd quarter	92.0	94.2	96.8	106.6	90.6	88.4	102.3	97.3	105.9	82.5	78.7	92.6	107.6
3rd quarter	92.1	94.3	96.9	106.8	90.8	88.6	102.4	97.4	106.1	82.7	78.8	93.4	108.3
4th quarter	92.4	94.5	97.1	107.1	90.9	89.0	102.4	96.6	106.5	83.7	79.6	95.8	108.8

[1]Excludes government sales to other sectors and government own-account investment (construction and software).
[2]Includes general government intermediate inputs for goods and services sold to other sectors and for own-account investment.
[3]Includes components not shown separately.

Table 6-12. State Government Current Receipts and Expenditures

(National income and product accounts, calendar years, billions of dollars.) NIPA Table 3.20

Year	Current receipts												
	Total [1]	Current tax receipts								Contribu-tions for govern-ment social insurance	Income receipts on assets		
		Total	Personal current taxes		Taxes on production and imports				Taxes on corporate income		Total [1]	Interest receipts	Rents and royalties
			Total [1]	Income taxes	Total	Sales taxes	Property taxes	Other					
1959	21.6	16.7	3.1	2.0	12.5	10.0	0.5	2.0	1.1	0.4	0.5	0.3	0.2
1960	23.3	18.1	3.4	2.3	13.5	10.8	0.5	2.2	1.2	0.5	0.5	0.4	0.2
1961	25.0	19.3	3.7	2.5	14.4	11.6	0.5	2.3	1.3	0.5	0.6	0.4	0.2
1962	27.1	21.0	4.0	2.8	15.4	12.6	0.6	2.3	1.5	0.5	0.6	0.4	0.2
1963	29.1	22.4	4.3	3.1	16.4	13.4	0.6	2.4	1.6	0.6	0.6	0.4	0.2
1964	31.8	24.5	4.9	3.6	17.7	14.5	0.6	2.6	1.8	0.7	0.7	0.4	0.2
1965	35.1	26.9	5.4	3.9	19.6	16.1	0.7	2.8	1.9	0.8	0.8	0.5	0.3
1966	41.5	30.2	6.4	4.8	21.7	18.0	0.7	3.0	2.2	0.8	0.9	0.6	0.3
1967	45.6	32.7	7.0	5.3	23.3	19.4	0.7	3.1	2.5	0.9	1.1	0.8	0.3
1968	53.8	38.6	8.8	6.9	26.7	22.8	0.8	3.2	3.1	0.9	1.7	1.4	0.3
1969	61.6	44.0	10.8	8.6	29.9	25.7	0.9	3.3	3.4	1.0	2.1	1.8	0.3
1970	69.1	48.1	12.0	9.6	32.7	28.2	0.9	3.6	3.5	1.1	2.5	2.2	0.3
1971	78.2	53.8	13.4	11.0	36.3	31.4	1.0	3.9	4.0	1.2	2.7	2.3	0.4
1972	95.0	63.5	17.9	15.2	40.7	35.2	1.1	4.4	5.0	1.3	2.9	2.5	0.4
1973	103.1	70.2	19.8	16.8	44.7	38.8	1.2	4.7	5.7	1.5	3.9	3.3	0.5
1974	112.1	75.9	21.1	18.0	48.4	42.0	1.1	5.3	6.3	1.7	5.0	4.4	0.6
1975	125.8	81.9	23.2	19.9	51.8	44.7	1.4	5.6	6.9	1.8	5.6	5.0	0.6
1976	141.7	93.8	27.0	23.4	57.7	49.9	1.5	6.3	9.1	2.2	5.3	4.7	0.6
1977	158.1	105.1	30.9	27.2	63.4	55.0	1.5	6.9	10.8	2.8	6.1	5.4	0.6
1978	177.2	117.4	35.6	31.6	70.3	60.8	1.9	7.6	11.5	3.4	7.4	6.7	0.6
1979	194.8	128.9	38.9	34.6	77.1	65.7	2.3	9.0	12.9	3.9	10.3	9.2	1.1
1980	216.0	140.9	43.7	39.1	83.4	70.0	2.6	10.8	13.7	3.6	13.4	11.2	2.0
1981	236.4	155.6	48.5	43.6	92.7	76.5	2.7	13.6	14.5	3.9	15.6	13.2	2.2
1982	244.7	162.3	52.3	47.0	97.0	80.3	2.8	13.9	13.1	4.0	17.5	15.3	2.1
1983	269.3	180.5	58.9	53.2	106.8	90.0	3.0	13.8	14.9	4.1	19.5	17.2	2.2
1984	303.7	205.4	68.2	61.9	119.7	100.9	3.4	15.5	17.4	4.7	22.4	19.8	2.5
1985	328.6	220.9	73.2	66.1	129.0	109.0	3.5	16.5	18.7	4.9	26.1	23.4	2.6
1986	354.0	234.0	78.3	70.7	134.9	115.8	3.6	15.6	20.7	6.0	27.5	24.6	2.7
1987	375.0	253.7	87.5	79.1	144.3	124.6	3.7	16.0	21.8	7.2	28.4	25.6	2.6
1988	403.1	269.4	90.4	81.5	155.2	135.1	3.8	16.3	23.8	8.4	30.8	28.0	2.7
1989	435.2	288.4	102.4	92.9	163.5	142.3	4.3	17.0	22.4	9.0	32.8	30.2	2.4
1990	469.2	305.6	109.6	99.6	175.4	152.5	4.6	18.3	20.5	10.0	33.9	31.4	2.3
1991	504.1	314.2	111.8	101.4	180.8	157.5	4.9	18.3	21.6	11.6	34.1	31.2	2.6
1992	551.4	338.8	120.6	109.0	195.9	169.7	6.1	20.1	22.2	13.1	33.6	30.4	2.7
1993	584.8	357.1	126.3	114.9	206.3	179.4	5.9	21.0	24.5	14.1	32.4	29.4	2.5
1994	621.6	380.4	132.1	120.2	220.8	191.7	7.0	22.1	27.5	14.5	33.9	30.6	2.5
1995	653.2	401.5	140.9	128.4	231.3	200.5	7.2	23.6	29.2	13.6	36.9	33.4	2.6
1996	686.2	425.9	150.9	138.6	245.0	211.8	8.2	25.0	29.9	12.5	39.4	35.3	2.7
1997	719.6	449.1	162.7	149.7	255.4	221.3	8.1	26.0	31.0	10.8	41.8	37.5	2.7
1998	764.1	480.7	180.4	166.8	268.8	233.3	8.5	27.0	31.6	10.4	43.3	39.2	2.4
1999	812.5	507.9	192.6	178.4	283.0	245.9	9.1	27.9	32.3	9.8	46.6	42.5	2.6
2000	867.7	540.1	213.5	199.2	294.8	255.5	7.8	31.6	31.7	10.8	49.3	44.3	3.6
2001	904.5	546.8	220.1	205.7	300.8	259.9	8.1	32.8	25.9	13.7	46.5	41.4	3.7
2002	917.8	533.7	199.1	184.3	309.6	268.0	7.7	33.9	25.0	15.8	42.4	37.2	3.7
2003	970.5	558.8	202.4	186.4	328.9	282.0	9.1	37.8	27.5	19.9	42.0	35.9	4.4
2004	1 048.7	606.4	220.3	203.4	352.3	300.5	8.3	43.5	33.8	24.7	44.4	37.4	5.1
2005	1 136.5	676.3	246.5	229.0	385.3	325.6	9.1	50.6	44.5	24.6	50.6	42.7	6.0
2006	1 193.9	728.1	271.0	252.5	409.1	346.6	9.7	52.7	48.0	21.5	59.2	50.7	6.5
2007	1 247.9	759.7	288.9	269.8	424.0	359.0	9.8	55.2	46.9	18.9	65.0	55.3	7.5
2008	1 264.0	763.6	299.8	280.9	425.4	354.3	9.7	61.3	38.4	18.7	60.1	49.6	7.9
2009	1 267.1	688.2	256.6	236.3	393.2	335.6	10.4	47.2	38.4	18.6	52.2	43.0	7.0
2010	1 336.1	720.0	264.7	242.2	415.5	354.7	10.7	50.1	39.8	18.1	51.3	42.4	6.6
2011	1 357.8	773.2	293.2	270.5	437.6	369.9	9.8	57.9	42.4	18.3	50.7	41.8	6.7
2012	1 372.3	804.9	313.8	290.4	448.3	379.2	9.7	59.3	42.9	17.5	50.1	40.8	6.9

[1]Includes components not shown separately.

Table 6-12. State Government Current Receipts and Expenditures—*Continued*

(National income and product accounts, calendar years, billions of dollars.)

Year	Current receipts—Continued Current transfer receipts					Current expenditures					Net state government saving, NIPA (surplus + / deficit -)		
	Total	Federal grants-in-aid	Local grants-in-aid	From business, net	From persons	Total[1]	Consumption expenditures	Government social benefits to persons	Grants-in-aid to local governments	Interest payments	Total	Social insurance funds	Other
1959	3.6	3.2	0.2	0.0	0.1	20.9	8.2	3.6	7.8	1.2	0.7	0.0	0.7
1960	3.7	3.3	0.2	0.0	0.1	22.9	8.9	3.8	8.8	1.3	0.4	0.0	0.4
1961	4.2	3.7	0.3	0.0	0.1	25.0	9.6	4.1	9.8	1.5	0.0	0.0	0.0
1962	4.6	4.1	0.3	0.1	0.2	27.0	10.2	4.4	10.8	1.6	0.1	0.0	0.1
1963	5.0	4.5	0.3	0.1	0.2	29.4	11.0	4.7	11.9	1.7	-0.3	0.0	-0.3
1964	5.5	4.9	0.3	0.1	0.2	31.9	11.8	5.1	13.0	1.8	-0.1	0.0	-0.1
1965	6.1	5.5	0.3	0.1	0.3	35.6	13.0	5.5	15.0	2.0	-0.4	0.1	-0.5
1966	8.9	8.2	0.4	0.1	0.3	40.7	14.6	6.4	17.4	2.2	0.8	0.1	0.6
1967	10.3	9.4	0.5	0.1	0.3	46.8	16.7	7.7	19.9	2.3	-1.2	0.1	-1.3
1968	11.8	10.7	0.6	0.1	0.3	54.6	19.2	9.5	23.0	2.7	-0.8	0.1	-1.0
1969	13.7	12.4	0.8	0.1	0.4	62.8	22.4	10.8	26.4	2.9	-1.2	0.2	-1.3
1970	16.6	15.2	0.9	0.1	0.4	72.8	25.8	12.9	30.4	3.4	-3.7	0.2	-3.9
1971	19.9	18.4	1.0	0.1	0.4	82.9	28.8	15.3	34.3	4.2	-4.7	0.2	-5.0
1972	26.4	24.6	1.1	0.2	0.5	92.9	31.5	17.5	38.5	5.0	2.2	0.3	1.9
1973	26.6	24.5	1.2	0.2	0.7	103.3	35.3	19.4	42.6	5.4	-0.1	0.3	-0.4
1974	28.6	26.3	1.3	0.2	0.8	116.5	42.1	19.9	47.3	6.4	-4.4	0.4	-4.8
1975	35.4	32.4	1.7	0.2	1.0	134.8	49.1	24.2	52.8	7.5	-9.0	0.5	-9.5
1976	39.1	35.4	2.3	0.3	1.2	145.6	52.8	26.9	57.0	7.7	-4.0	0.6	-4.6
1977	42.8	38.8	2.4	0.3	1.4	158.0	57.5	29.1	61.6	8.5	0.1	1.0	-0.9
1978	47.4	43.1	2.5	0.3	1.5	174.2	63.1	32.0	68.2	9.3	3.0	1.5	1.5
1979	50.1	45.9	2.2	0.4	1.6	193.8	70.0	35.4	76.3	10.3	1.0	1.8	-0.8
1980	56.5	52.1	2.3	0.4	1.7	217.8	78.8	41.3	84.6	11.1	-1.8	1.3	-3.2
1981	59.7	54.6	2.7	0.5	2.0	239.8	86.9	46.7	91.3	12.6	-3.4	1.3	-4.7
1982	58.7	52.7	3.1	0.6	2.3	257.0	93.7	51.0	95.3	14.6	-12.4	1.2	-13.6
1983	62.4	55.0	4.2	0.6	2.6	274.7	99.5	55.9	99.9	16.7	-5.5	1.2	-6.7
1984	67.7	59.0	5.0	0.8	3.0	297.5	106.9	59.8	109.8	17.9	6.2	1.4	4.8
1985	72.2	62.6	5.2	0.9	3.6	327.9	117.4	65.2	121.2	20.8	0.6	1.3	-0.7
1986	81.5	69.3	5.3	2.8	4.1	352.3	124.9	71.4	130.1	22.2	1.7	1.9	-0.1
1987	80.3	69.4	5.5	0.9	4.5	374.8	132.7	77.4	139.5	20.9	0.2	2.2	-2.0
1988	88.0	76.2	5.6	1.1	5.2	402.7	142.4	84.4	149.8	21.2	0.4	2.5	-2.1
1989	98.1	85.1	5.8	1.3	5.9	440.8	153.9	94.4	162.6	24.7	-5.6	2.3	-7.9
1990	112.4	97.6	6.2	1.6	6.9	480.7	167.2	111.0	173.1	23.8	-11.5	2.0	-13.4
1991	136.7	117.1	7.6	2.0	10.0	532.2	175.4	137.6	186.1	27.3	-28.1	2.4	-30.5
1992	158.0	134.3	9.0	2.6	12.1	580.8	183.9	159.5	201.0	30.4	-29.4	3.1	-32.6
1993	172.7	147.6	10.1	2.9	12.1	614.6	193.1	173.6	212.9	29.1	-29.8	4.2	-34.0
1994	183.7	156.9	11.0	3.4	12.4	649.8	204.5	184.4	226.2	28.4	-28.1	4.6	-32.8
1995	191.3	164.0	11.1	4.1	12.2	685.0	213.6	194.8	239.0	30.8	-31.8	4.0	-35.8
1996	197.9	168.9	12.0	5.0	12.0	708.1	219.7	202.5	250.3	27.9	-21.8	2.8	-24.7
1997	207.2	174.1	13.5	6.6	13.0	735.5	231.4	206.8	263.0	25.7	-15.9	1.2	-17.1
1998	219.3	182.9	13.3	9.8	13.2	774.0	248.3	214.6	282.4	19.8	-9.9	1.7	-11.6
1999	238.2	199.1	12.9	11.4	14.9	836.1	272.6	230.3	306.6	17.1	-23.6	1.7	-25.3
2000	258.8	212.6	14.0	15.0	17.2	896.0	292.8	248.4	331.0	13.5	-28.4	2.0	-30.3
2001	289.7	238.9	14.9	16.1	19.8	984.0	314.4	281.0	350.7	20.2	-79.5	2.6	-82.1
2002	317.7	263.5	15.5	17.2	21.5	1 037.5	320.3	307.2	367.5	31.5	-119.7	1.4	-121.1
2003	340.5	285.1	16.4	16.6	22.3	1 086.6	319.2	326.2	383.5	47.5	-116.1	3.2	-119.4
2004	363.4	303.4	17.6	17.7	24.6	1 139.7	327.1	355.8	401.6	44.5	-91.0	7.3	-98.3
2005	374.1	312.2	16.6	18.4	26.9	1 195.2	347.4	375.2	413.9	46.8	-58.7	7.2	-65.9
2006	375.4	314.2	15.6	18.2	28.0	1 239.7	361.2	371.3	441.7	52.3	-45.8	4.6	-50.5
2007	397.4	332.2	17.7	19.0	29.0	1 324.9	384.6	398.5	469.2	51.8	-77.0	2.7	-79.7
2008	415.6	346.6	17.7	21.1	30.7	1 383.9	407.7	418.6	486.1	54.1	-119.9	1.7	-121.6
2009	501.2	432.8	16.5	21.7	30.7	1 455.0	411.7	453.0	486.3	87.3	-187.9	2.2	-190.1
2010	539.5	473.3	16.6	20.1	30.1	1 487.1	411.2	481.5	488.8	88.4	-151.0	3.2	-154.2
2011	507.6	441.0	16.6	19.7	31.3	1 515.1	425.5	489.9	494.6	88.4	-157.2	4.2	-161.4
2012	491.2	424.0	16.8	18.8	32.4	1 579.2	459.7	501.9	502.8	97.8	-206.9	3.9	-210.9

[1]Includes components not shown separately.

Table 6-13. Local Government Current Receipts and Expenditures

(National income and product accounts, calendar years, billions of dollars.)   **NIPA Table 3.21**

Year	Total [1]	Current receipts											
		Current tax receipts							Taxes on corporate income	Contributions for government social insurance	Income receipts on assets		
		Total	Personal current taxes		Taxes on production and imports								
			Total [1]	Income taxes	Total	Sales taxes	Property taxes	Other			Total [1]	Interest receipts	Rents and royalties
1959	27.0	17.1	0.8	0.2	16.4	1.2	14.3	0.9	0.0	...	0.7	0.5	0.1
1960	30.0	18.8	0.8	0.3	18.0	1.3	15.7	0.9	0.0	...	0.8	0.7	0.1
1961	32.9	20.3	0.9	0.3	19.4	1.4	17.0	1.0	0.0	...	0.9	0.7	0.2
1962	35.6	21.8	1.0	0.3	20.8	1.5	18.4	1.0	0.0	...	1.0	0.8	0.2
1963	38.7	23.4	1.1	0.4	22.3	1.6	19.7	1.0	0.0	...	1.0	0.9	0.2
1964	42.3	25.3	1.2	0.5	24.1	1.9	21.1	1.1	0.0	...	1.3	1.1	0.2
1965	46.1	27.0	1.2	0.5	25.7	2.1	22.5	1.1	0.0	...	1.4	1.2	0.2
1966	50.5	28.5	1.4	0.6	27.1	2.0	23.8	1.3	0.0	...	1.7	1.4	0.3
1967	56.5	31.3	1.6	0.8	29.5	1.9	26.2	1.3	0.2	...	2.0	1.6	0.3
1968	62.6	34.8	1.7	0.9	32.8	2.3	29.1	1.4	0.3	...	1.7	1.4	0.4
1969	70.1	38.4	2.0	1.1	36.1	2.9	31.9	1.4	0.3	...	2.2	1.8	0.4
1970	81.4	43.2	2.3	1.3	40.6	3.5	35.7	1.5	0.2	...	2.6	2.2	0.5
1971	90.9	47.9	2.5	1.5	45.2	4.0	39.5	1.8	0.3	...	2.8	2.3	0.5
1972	101.9	52.0	3.0	2.0	48.8	4.6	42.2	2.0	0.3	...	3.0	2.4	0.6
1973	114.0	56.1	3.0	2.0	52.7	5.2	45.2	2.3	0.3	...	3.9	3.3	0.6
1974	123.8	60.2	3.4	2.3	56.4	6.1	47.9	2.4	0.3	...	5.2	4.5	0.7
1975	137.7	65.5	3.7	2.5	61.4	7.0	51.9	2.5	0.4	...	5.6	4.9	0.7
1976	150.8	71.9	4.1	2.8	67.3	7.9	56.7	2.7	0.5	...	5.1	4.4	0.7
1977	165.3	78.6	4.5	3.2	73.6	9.0	61.7	2.9	0.6	...	5.6	4.9	0.7
1978	180.5	80.8	4.9	3.4	75.3	10.2	61.8	3.3	0.6	...	7.2	6.5	0.7
1979	191.3	83.1	5.1	3.6	77.3	11.5	62.1	3.7	0.6	...	9.8	8.9	0.9
1980	208.3	89.1	5.1	3.5	83.3	12.8	66.2	4.2	0.7	...	12.9	11.8	1.1
1981	226.9	100.2	6.2	4.3	93.0	14.3	74.4	4.3	1.0	...	16.4	15.3	1.1
1982	244.4	110.8	6.9	4.9	103.0	15.9	82.5	4.6	1.0	...	19.2	17.8	1.4
1983	262.5	120.4	7.2	5.1	112.1	17.7	88.9	5.5	1.0	...	21.9	19.8	2.1
1984	289.9	131.9	7.8	5.6	122.7	20.1	96.3	6.3	1.4	...	25.2	22.8	2.4
1985	318.4	142.8	8.2	6.0	133.1	22.1	104.0	7.0	1.5	...	29.5	26.7	2.7
1986	342.5	155.6	8.9	6.8	144.7	24.1	112.6	8.1	2.0	...	31.4	27.9	3.5
1987	360.1	168.5	9.1	6.8	157.3	25.7	122.7	8.9	2.1	...	30.1	27.4	2.7
1988	387.9	183.3	11.7	9.1	169.4	27.2	132.7	9.4	2.3	...	30.4	28.6	1.7
1989	420.0	199.6	12.3	9.4	185.6	30.1	145.6	10.0	1.8	...	33.8	32.1	1.7
1990	446.2	213.6	12.9	10.0	198.7	31.8	157.0	9.9	2.0	...	34.5	32.7	1.8
1991	475.9	230.1	13.5	10.3	214.5	33.2	171.1	10.2	2.1	...	33.2	31.2	1.9
1992	501.1	241.0	14.7	11.4	224.2	34.6	178.6	11.0	2.1	...	30.4	28.4	2.0
1993	522.2	247.7	14.8	11.3	230.5	37.0	181.3	12.1	2.4	...	28.7	26.6	2.1
1994	556.9	263.8	15.9	12.0	245.4	39.7	192.4	13.3	2.5	...	29.6	27.6	2.0
1995	584.6	270.7	17.2	13.3	251.0	42.2	195.3	13.4	2.5	...	32.2	30.3	2.0
1996	617.4	283.7	17.8	13.7	262.9	44.4	204.2	14.4	3.1	...	34.3	32.4	2.0
1997	652.4	300.8	19.3	14.9	278.4	47.4	215.5	15.6	3.1	...	36.3	34.3	2.1
1998	690.4	314.2	20.9	16.2	290.0	50.6	222.5	16.9	3.4	...	38.0	35.8	2.2
1999	739.5	332.5	21.9	17.1	307.1	55.6	233.7	17.8	3.5	...	38.6	36.1	2.5
2000	791.8	353.1	23.2	18.1	326.5	61.3	246.9	18.3	3.5	...	44.6	42.0	2.7
2001	825.4	367.5	22.9	17.6	341.6	61.9	260.0	19.8	3.0	...	42.6	39.8	2.8
2002	865.1	394.8	22.7	17.1	366.2	63.1	281.6	21.5	5.9	...	36.2	33.2	2.9
2003	915.7	419.8	24.4	18.3	389.0	66.8	297.9	24.2	6.5	...	31.9	28.6	3.2
2004	957.8	451.5	27.1	20.3	416.4	70.5	317.9	28.0	7.9	...	32.4	29.0	3.4
2005	1 016.4	490.2	30.0	22.5	449.8	76.8	342.3	30.7	10.4	...	38.0	34.2	3.8
2006	1 089.2	526.4	31.5	23.6	483.6	85.2	365.3	33.1	11.3	...	48.0	44.0	3.9
2007	1 154.8	561.6	34.6	26.5	516.0	90.0	394.1	32.0	11.0	...	52.9	48.9	4.0
2008	1 164.4	565.3	33.8	26.1	522.6	90.4	404.0	28.1	9.0	...	45.6	41.4	4.2
2009	1 171.2	580.0	31.2	23.3	541.6	88.3	424.7	28.6	7.2	...	35.7	31.4	4.2
2010	1 184.5	585.7	33.0	25.0	544.9	91.2	424.4	29.3	7.8	...	31.3	26.7	4.6
2011	1 200.4	593.1	33.8	25.7	550.9	93.8	427.1	30.1	8.4	...	29.3	24.5	4.8
2012	1 204.4	600.3	35.1	26.9	556.7	95.7	430.3	30.7	8.5	...	28.4	23.4	5.0

[1]Includes components not shown separately.
. . . = Not available.

Table 6-13. Local Government Current Receipts and Expenditures—*Continued*

(National income and product accounts, calendar years, billions of dollars.)

NIPA Table 3.21

Year	Current receipts—*Continued*					Current expenditures					Net local government saving, NIPA (surplus + / deficit -)		
	Current transfer receipts												
	Total	Federal grants-in-aid	State grants-in-aid	From business, net	From persons	Total ¹	Consumption expenditures	Government social benefits to persons	Grants-in-aid to state governments	Interest payments	Total	Social insurance funds	Other
1959	8.4	0.4	7.8	0.1	0.1	25.5	23.0	0.7	0.2	1.5	1.5	...	1.5
1960	9.6	0.5	8.8	0.1	0.2	27.9	25.2	0.8	0.2	1.7	2.2	...	2.2
1961	10.8	0.6	9.8	0.2	0.3	30.7	27.7	0.9	0.3	1.8	2.2	...	2.2
1962	11.9	0.6	10.8	0.2	0.3	32.3	29.1	0.9	0.3	1.9	3.3	...	3.3
1963	13.1	0.8	11.9	0.2	0.3	34.7	31.3	1.0	0.3	2.1	4.0	...	4.0
1964	14.6	1.1	13.0	0.2	0.3	37.9	34.2	1.0	0.3	2.3	4.4	...	4.4
1965	16.6	1.1	15.0	0.3	0.3	41.6	37.6	1.1	0.3	2.5	4.5	...	4.5
1966	19.3	1.2	17.4	0.2	0.4	46.1	41.7	1.3	0.4	2.7	4.4	...	4.4
1967	22.4	1.5	19.9	0.4	0.6	50.6	45.6	1.6	0.5	2.9	5.9	...	5.9
1968	25.2	1.1	23.0	0.4	0.7	57.5	51.5	2.0	0.6	3.3	5.1	...	5.1
1969	28.8	1.3	26.4	0.4	0.7	64.9	58.1	2.4	0.8	3.6	5.3	...	5.3
1970	34.8	3.2	30.4	0.4	0.8	74.7	66.3	3.2	0.9	4.3	6.7	...	6.7
1971	39.5	3.8	34.3	0.5	0.9	85.6	75.4	4.0	1.0	5.2	5.3	...	5.3
1972	46.0	5.9	38.5	0.5	1.1	95.6	83.9	4.5	1.1	6.1	6.3	...	6.3
1973	53.2	8.9	42.6	0.7	1.0	104.3	91.5	4.7	1.2	6.8	9.8	...	9.8
1974	57.9	8.7	47.3	0.9	1.1	117.0	102.4	5.4	1.3	7.9	6.8	...	6.8
1975	66.4	11.2	52.8	1.0	1.4	134.3	116.5	6.6	1.7	9.2	3.5	...	3.5
1976	73.5	13.6	57.0	1.1	1.7	144.0	124.4	7.3	2.3	9.8	6.8	...	6.8
1977	80.9	16.0	61.6	1.3	1.9	156.9	135.5	8.0	2.4	10.7	8.4	...	8.4
1978	92.3	20.4	68.2	1.5	2.2	170.1	146.8	8.7	2.5	11.7	10.4	...	10.4
1979	98.8	18.1	76.3	1.8	2.6	184.0	159.4	8.9	2.2	13.2	7.2	...	7.2
1980	107.3	17.6	84.6	2.0	3.0	201.1	174.0	9.9	2.3	14.5	7.2	...	7.2
1981	112.2	14.8	91.3	2.4	3.7	219.4	189.2	10.4	2.7	16.7	7.5	...	7.5
1982	115.6	13.5	95.3	2.7	4.1	237.1	203.7	10.2	3.1	19.6	7.3	...	7.3
1983	120.4	13.0	99.9	3.0	4.5	255.8	217.2	11.0	4.2	22.8	6.7	...	6.7
1984	131.7	13.3	109.8	3.4	5.2	275.2	233.0	11.4	5.0	25.3	14.7	...	14.7
1985	144.0	13.6	121.2	3.5	5.7	298.8	254.4	12.1	5.2	26.4	19.6	...	19.6
1986	153.7	13.2	130.1	3.9	6.5	323.8	275.0	12.9	5.3	29.6	18.7	...	18.7
1987	159.2	9.0	139.5	4.0	6.7	348.3	295.6	13.4	5.5	32.6	11.9	...	11.9
1988	170.5	9.5	149.8	4.3	6.9	371.3	316.5	14.1	5.6	33.8	16.6	...	16.6
1989	181.9	6.8	162.6	5.1	7.5	407.0	347.4	15.0	5.8	37.6	13.0	...	13.0
1990	193.4	6.7	173.1	5.5	8.0	441.2	379.0	16.6	6.2	38.0	5.0	...	5.0
1991	207.7	7.0	186.1	5.9	8.7	472.9	404.7	18.9	7.6	40.3	3.0	...	3.0
1992	224.8	7.4	201.0	6.7	9.8	509.2	435.2	20.5	9.0	43.2	-8.1	...	-8.1
1993	240.0	8.1	212.9	7.7	11.4	529.6	453.4	21.6	10.1	43.1	-7.4	...	-7.4
1994	257.6	9.9	226.2	8.6	12.9	555.8	477.7	22.4	11.0	43.3	1.2	...	1.2
1995	273.2	10.5	239.0	9.4	14.3	584.3	503.2	22.9	11.1	45.8	0.3	...	0.3
1996	288.7	12.6	250.3	10.2	15.7	608.0	528.4	21.8	12.0	44.5	9.4	...	9.4
1997	305.4	14.0	263.0	11.1	17.3	634.8	554.5	20.8	13.5	44.5	17.6	...	17.6
1998	330.0	17.9	282.4	11.8	17.9	665.1	587.4	21.1	13.3	41.7	25.3	...	25.3
1999	358.7	20.1	306.6	12.7	19.3	706.6	629.4	22.1	12.9	40.7	32.9	...	32.9
2000	385.8	20.5	331.0	13.5	20.8	753.6	676.3	23.0	14.0	38.6	38.3	...	38.3
2001	409.1	22.4	350.7	13.7	22.3	811.2	725.4	24.0	14.9	45.3	14.2	...	14.2
2002	430.7	23.7	367.5	15.4	24.1	866.4	770.8	25.8	15.5	52.8	-1.2	...	-1.2
2003	464.4	36.6	383.5	17.2	27.1	921.0	808.0	27.3	16.4	67.7	-5.3	...	-5.3
2004	478.3	28.8	401.6	18.8	29.1	975.2	860.5	29.2	17.6	65.9	-17.4	...	-17.4
2005	492.8	31.1	413.9	18.1	29.6	1 024.3	909.2	31.4	16.6	65.0	-7.9	...	-7.9
2006	520.8	26.6	441.7	20.6	31.3	1 082.8	964.8	32.6	15.6	67.8	6.4	...	6.4
2007	550.4	26.8	469.2	21.5	32.5	1 150.6	1 026.8	34.8	17.7	69.7	4.3	...	4.3
2008	566.0	24.4	486.1	22.4	32.6	1 209.6	1 081.0	36.8	17.7	73.0	-45.2	...	-45.2
2009	567.7	25.3	486.3	22.3	33.3	1 255.2	1 096.7	39.6	16.5	101.4	-84.0	...	-84.0
2010	577.8	31.9	488.8	23.3	33.1	1 270.8	1 107.1	42.3	16.6	103.7	-86.3	...	-86.3
2011	585.4	31.4	494.6	24.4	33.9	1 256.2	1 092.0	42.1	16.6	104.5	-55.9	...	-55.9
2012	581.0	19.2	502.8	23.1	35.1	1 250.2	1 076.7	42.4	16.8	113.2	-45.8	...	-45.8

¹Includes components not shown separately.
. . . = Not available.

Section 6c: Federal Government Budget Accounts

Figure 6-3: Federal Debt as a Percent of GDP, 1940–2014

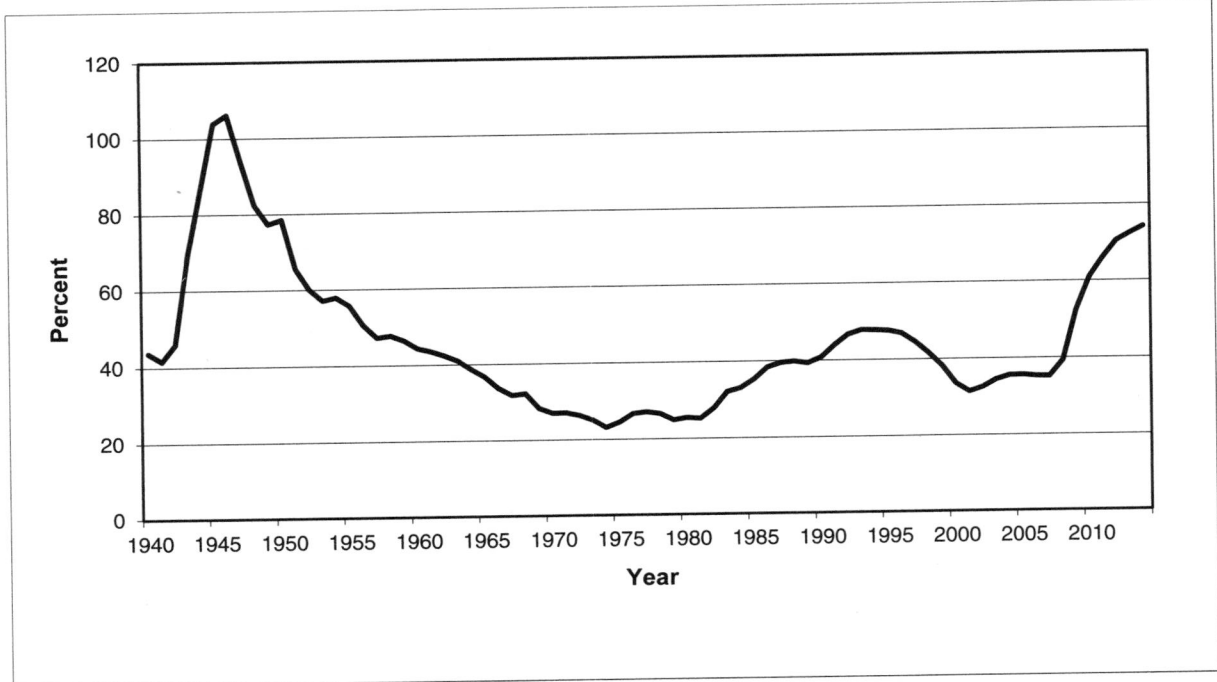

- The "debt held by the public" is generally thought to be a more significant measure of the burden of the federal debt on credit markets than the gross debt, because it nets out the intragovernmental debt of the Social Security and other U.S. government trust funds. The ratio of debt held by the public to GDP was reduced in the late 1990s, began to creep back upward after 2001, and then rose rapidly beginning in 2008, as the recession reduced revenues and increased spending, and taxes were reduced further. The spending increases were a result of both automatic stabilizer programs, such as unemployment insurance, and an unprecedented level of spending for stimulus and financial rescue programs. At the end of fiscal year 2014, the debt held by the public was 74.1 percent of GDP, the highest since 1950. (Tables 6-14 and 6-15)

- At the end of 2014, foreign residents—including central banks—held $6.0 trillion of Treasury debt, 47.5 percent of the $12.8 trillion total debt held by the public. (Table 6-15)

Table 6-14A. Federal Government Receipts and Outlays by Fiscal Year [1]

(Budget accounts, millions of dollars.)

Year	Total receipts, net	Total outlays, net	Budget surplus or deficit (-) Total	On-budget	Off-budget	Sources of financing, total — Borrowing from the public	Other financing	Individual income taxes	Corporate income taxes	Social insurance taxes and contributions — Employment taxes and contributions	Unemployment insurance	Other retirement contributions
1940	6 548	9 468	-2 920	-3 484	564	...	...	892	1 197	725	1 015	45
1941	8 712	13 653	-4 941	-5 594	653	5 451	-510	1 314	2 124	827	1 056	57
1942	14 634	35 137	-20 503	-21 333	830	19 530	973	3 263	4 719	1 064	1 299	89
1943	24 001	78 555	-54 554	-55 595	1 041	60 013	-5 459	6 505	9 557	1 338	1 477	229
1944	43 747	91 304	-47 557	-48 735	1 178	57 030	-9 473	19 705	14 838	1 557	1 644	272
1945	45 159	92 712	-47 553	-48 720	1 167	50 386	-2 833	18 372	15 988	1 592	1 568	291
1946	39 296	55 232	-15 936	-16 964	1 028	6 679	9 257	16 098	11 883	1 517	1 316	282
1947	38 514	34 496	4 018	2 861	1 157	-17 522	13 504	17 935	8 615	1 835	1 329	259
1948	41 560	29 764	11 796	10 548	1 248	-8 069	-3 727	19 315	9 678	2 168	1 343	239
1949	39 415	38 835	580	-684	1 263	-1 948	1 368	15 552	11 192	2 246	1 205	330
1950	39 443	42 562	-3 119	-4 702	1 583	4 701	-1 582	15 755	10 449	2 648	1 332	358
1951	51 616	45 514	6 102	4 259	1 843	-4 697	-1 405	21 616	14 101	3 688	1 609	377
1952	66 167	67 686	-1 519	-3 383	1 864	432	1 087	27 934	21 226	4 315	1 712	418
1953	69 608	76 101	-6 493	-8 259	1 766	3 625	2 868	29 816	21 238	4 722	1 675	423
1954	69 701	70 855	-1 154	-2 831	1 677	6 116	-4 962	29 542	21 101	5 192	1 561	455
1955	65 451	68 444	-2 993	-4 091	1 098	2 117	876	28 747	17 861	5 981	1 449	431
1956	74 587	70 640	3 947	2 494	1 452	-4 460	513	32 188	20 880	7 059	1 690	571
1957	79 990	76 578	3 412	2 639	773	-2 836	-576	35 620	21 167	7 405	1 950	642
1958	79 636	82 405	-2 769	-3 315	546	7 016	-4 247	34 724	20 074	8 624	1 933	682
1959	79 249	92 098	-12 849	-12 149	-700	8 365	4 484	36 719	17 309	8 821	2 131	770
1960	92 492	92 191	301	510	-209	2 139	-2 440	40 715	21 494	11 248	2 667	768
1961	94 388	97 723	-3 335	-3 766	431	1 517	1 818	41 338	20 954	12 679	2 903	857
1962	99 676	106 821	-7 146	-5 881	-1 265	9 653	-2 507	45 571	20 523	12 835	3 337	875
1963	106 560	111 316	-4 756	-3 966	-789	5 968	-1 212	47 588	21 579	14 746	4 112	946
1964	112 613	118 528	-5 915	-6 546	632	2 871	3 044	48 697	23 493	16 959	3 997	1 007
1965	116 817	118 228	-1 411	-1 605	194	3 929	-2 518	48 792	25 461	17 358	3 803	1 081
1966	130 835	134 532	-3 698	-3 068	-630	2 936	762	55 446	30 073	20 662	3 755	1 129
1967	148 822	157 464	-8 643	-12 620	3 978	2 912	5 731	61 526	33 971	27 823	3 575	1 221
1968	152 973	178 134	-25 161	-27 742	2 581	22 919	2 242	68 726	28 665	29 224	3 346	1 354
1969	186 882	183 640	3 242	-507	3 749	-11 437	8 195	87 249	36 678	34 236	3 328	1 451
1970	192 807	195 649	-2 842	-8 694	5 852	5 090	-2 248	90 412	32 829	39 133	3 464	1 765
1971	187 139	210 172	-23 033	-26 052	3 019	19 839	3 194	86 230	26 785	41 699	3 674	1 952
1972	207 309	230 681	-23 373	-26 068	2 695	19 340	4 033	94 737	32 166	46 120	4 357	2 097
1973	230 799	245 707	-14 908	-15 246	338	18 533	-3 625	103 246	36 153	54 876	6 051	2 187
1974	263 224	269 359	-6 135	-7 198	1 063	2 789	3 346	118 952	38 620	65 888	6 837	2 347
1975	279 090	332 332	-53 242	-54 148	906	51 001	2 241	122 386	40 621	75 199	6 771	2 565
1976	298 060	371 792	-73 732	-69 427	-4 306	82 704	-8 972	131 603	41 409	79 901	8 054	2 814
TQ	81 232	95 975	-14 744	-14 065	-679	18 105	-3 361	38 801	8 460	21 801	2 698	720
1977	355 559	409 218	-53 659	-49 933	-3 726	53 595	64	157 626	54 892	92 199	11 312	2 974
1978	399 561	458 746	-59 185	-55 416	-3 770	58 022	1 163	180 988	59 952	103 388	13 850	3 237
1979	463 302	504 028	-40 726	-39 633	-1 093	33 180	7 546	217 841	65 677	120 005	15 387	3 494
1980	517 112	590 941	-73 830	-73 141	-689	71 617	2 213	244 069	64 600	138 748	15 336	3 719
1981	599 272	678 241	-78 968	-73 859	-5 109	77 487	1 481	285 917	61 137	162 973	15 763	3 984
1982	617 766	745 743	-127 977	-120 593	-7 384	135 165	-7 188	297 744	49 207	180 686	16 600	4 212
1983	600 562	808 364	-207 802	-207 692	-110	212 693	-4 891	288 938	37 022	185 764	18 799	4 429
1984	666 438	851 805	-185 367	-185 269	-98	169 707	15 660	298 415	56 893	209 650	25 138	4 580
1985	734 037	946 344	-212 308	-221 529	9 222	200 285	12 023	334 531	61 331	234 646	25 758	4 759
1986	769 155	990 382	-221 227	-237 915	16 688	233 363	-12 136	348 959	63 143	255 062	24 098	4 742
1987	854 288	1 004 017	-149 730	-168 357	18 627	149 130	600	392 557	83 926	273 028	25 575	4 715
1988	909 238	1 064 416	-155 178	-192 265	37 087	161 863	-6 685	401 181	94 508	305 093	24 584	4 658
1989	991 105	1 143 744	-152 639	-205 393	52 754	139 100	13 539	445 690	103 291	332 859	22 011	4 546
1990	1 031 958	1 252 994	-221 036	-277 626	56 590	220 842	194	466 884	93 507	353 891	21 635	4 522
1991	1 054 988	1 324 226	-269 238	-321 435	52 198	277 441	-8 203	467 827	98 086	370 526	20 922	4 568
1992	1 091 208	1 381 529	-290 321	-340 408	50 087	310 738	-20 417	475 964	100 270	385 491	23 410	4 788
1993	1 154 335	1 409 386	-255 051	-300 398	45 347	248 659	6 392	509 680	117 520	396 939	26 556	4 805
1994	1 258 566	1 461 753	-203 186	-258 840	55 654	184 669	18 517	543 055	140 385	428 810	28 004	4 661
1995	1 351 790	1 515 742	-163 952	-226 367	62 415	171 313	-7 361	590 244	157 004	451 045	28 878	4 550
1996	1 453 053	1 560 484	-107 431	-174 019	66 588	129 695	-22 264	656 417	171 824	476 361	28 584	4 469
1997	1 579 232	1 601 116	-21 884	-103 248	81 364	38 271	-16 387	737 466	182 293	506 751	28 202	4 418
1998	1 721 728	1 652 458	69 270	-29 925	99 195	-51 245	-18 025	828 586	188 677	540 014	27 484	4 333
1999	1 827 452	1 701 842	125 610	1 920	123 690	-88 736	-36 874	879 480	184 680	580 888	26 480	4 473
2000	2 025 191	1 788 950	236 241	86 422	149 819	-222 559	-13 682	1 004 462	207 289	620 456	27 640	4 761
2001	1 991 082	1 862 846	128 236	-32 445	160 681	-90 189	-38 047	994 339	151 075	661 444	27 812	4 713
2002	1 853 136	2 010 894	-157 758	-317 417	159 659	220 812	-63 054	858 345	148 044	668 544	27 619	4 594
2003	1 782 314	2 159 899	-377 585	-538 418	160 833	373 016	4 569	793 699	131 778	674 981	33 366	4 631
2004	1 880 114	2 292 841	-412 727	-567 961	155 234	382 101	30 626	808 959	189 371	689 360	39 453	4 594
2005	2 153 611	2 471 957	-318 346	-493 611	175 265	296 668	21 678	927 222	278 282	747 664	42 002	4 459
2006	2 406 869	2 655 050	-248 181	-434 494	186 313	236 760	11 421	1 043 908	353 915	790 043	43 420	4 358
2007	2 567 985	2 728 686	-160 701	-342 153	181 452	206 157	-45 456	1 163 472	370 243	824 258	41 091	4 258
2008	2 523 991	2 982 544	-458 553	-641 848	183 295	767 921	-309 368	1 145 747	304 346	856 459	39 527	4 169
2009	2 104 989	3 517 677	-1 412 688	-1 549 681	136 993	1 741 657	-328 969	915 308	138 229	848 885	37 889	4 143
2010	2 162 706	3 457 079	-1 294 373	-1 371 378	77 005	1 474 175	-179 802	898 549	191 437	815 894	44 823	4 097
2011	2 303 466	3 603 059	-1 299 593	-1 366 775	67 182	1 109 305	190 288	1 091 473	181 085	758 516	56 241	4 035
2012	2 450 164	3 537 127	-1 086 963	-1 148 876	61 913	1 152 944	-65 981	1 132 206	242 289	774 927	66 647	3 740
2013	2 775 103	3 454 605	-679 502	-718 965	39 463	701 446	-21 944	1 316 405	273 506	887 445	56 811	3 564
2014	3 001 721	3 650 526	-648 805	-669 910	21 105	1 290 266	...	1 386 068	332 740	956 951	60 393	3 765

[1] Fiscal years through 1976 are from July 1 through June 30. Beginning with October 1976 (fiscal year 1977), fiscal years are from October 1 through September 30. The period from July 1 through September 30, 1976, is a separate fiscal period known as the transition quarter (TQ) and is not included in any fiscal year.
... = Not available.

Table 6-14A. Federal Government Receipts and Outlays by Fiscal Year [1]—*Continued*

(Budget accounts, millions of dollars.)

| Year | Receipts by source—*Continued* | | | | | Outlays by function | | | | | | |
	Excise taxes	Estate and gift taxes	Customs duties and fees	Federal reserve deposits	All other	National defense	International affairs	General science, space, and technology	Energy	Natural resources and environment	Agriculture	Commerce and housing credit
1940	1 977	353	331	. . .	14	1 660	51	0	88	997	369	550
1941	2 552	403	365	. . .	14	6 435	145	0	91	817	339	398
1942	3 399	420	369	. . .	11	25 658	968	4	156	819	344	1 521
1943	4 096	441	308	. . .	50	66 699	1 286	1	116	726	343	2 151
1944	4 759	507	417	. . .	48	79 143	1 449	48	65	642	1 275	624
1945	6 265	637	341	. . .	105	82 965	1 913	111	25	455	1 635	-2 630
1946	6 998	668	424	. . .	109	42 681	1 935	34	41	482	610	-1 857
1947	7 211	771	477	15	69	12 808	5 791	5	18	700	814	-923
1948	7 356	890	403	100	68	9 105	4 566	1	292	780	69	306
1949	7 502	780	367	187	54	13 150	6 052	48	341	1 080	1 924	800
1950	7 550	698	407	192	55	13 724	4 673	55	327	1 308	2 049	1 035
1951	8 648	708	609	189	72	23 566	3 647	51	383	1 310	-323	1 228
1952	8 852	818	533	278	81	46 089	2 691	49	474	1 233	176	1 278
1953	9 877	881	596	298	81	52 802	2 119	49	425	1 289	2 253	910
1954	9 945	934	542	341	88	49 266	1 596	46	432	1 007	1 817	-184
1955	9 131	924	585	251	90	42 729	2 223	74	325	940	3 514	92
1956	9 929	1 161	682	287	140	42 523	2 414	79	174	870	3 486	506
1957	10 534	1 365	735	434	139	45 430	3 147	122	240	1 098	2 288	1 424
1958	10 638	1 393	782	664	123	46 815	3 364	141	348	1 407	2 411	930
1959	10 578	1 333	925	491	171	49 015	3 144	294	382	1 632	4 509	1 933
1960	11 676	1 606	1 105	1 093	119	48 130	2 988	599	464	1 559	2 623	1 618
1961	11 860	1 896	982	788	130	49 601	3 184	1 042	510	1 779	2 641	1 203
1962	12 534	2 016	1 142	718	125	52 345	5 639	1 723	604	2 044	3 562	1 424
1963	13 194	2 167	1 205	828	194	53 400	5 308	3 051	530	2 251	4 384	62
1964	13 731	2 394	1 252	947	139	54 757	4 945	4 897	572	2 364	4 609	418
1965	14 570	2 716	1 442	1 372	222	50 620	5 273	5 823	699	2 531	3 954	1 157
1966	13 062	3 066	1 767	1 713	163	58 111	5 580	6 717	612	2 719	2 447	3 245
1967	13 719	2 978	1 901	1 805	302	71 417	5 566	6 233	782	2 869	2 990	3 979
1968	14 079	3 051	2 038	2 091	400	81 926	5 301	5 524	1 037	2 988	4 544	4 280
1969	15 222	3 491	2 319	2 662	247	82 497	4 600	5 020	1 010	2 900	5 826	-119
1970	15 705	3 644	2 430	3 266	158	81 692	4 330	4 511	997	3 065	5 166	2 112
1971	16 614	3 735	2 591	3 533	325	78 872	4 159	4 182	1 035	3 915	4 290	2 366
1972	15 477	5 436	3 287	3 252	380	79 174	4 781	4 175	1 296	4 241	5 227	2 222
1973	16 260	4 917	3 188	3 495	425	76 681	4 149	4 032	1 237	4 775	4 821	931
1974	16 844	5 035	3 334	4 845	523	79 347	5 710	3 980	1 303	5 697	2 194	4 705
1975	16 551	4 611	3 676	5 777	935	86 509	7 097	3 991	2 916	7 346	2 997	9 947
1976	16 963	5 216	4 074	5 451	2 576	89 619	6 433	4 373	4 204	8 184	3 109	7 619
TQ	4 473	1 455	1 212	1 500	111	22 269	2 458	1 162	1 129	2 524	972	931
1977	17 548	7 327	5 150	5 908	623	97 241	6 353	4 736	5 770	10 032	6 734	3 093
1978	18 376	5 285	6 573	6 641	778	10 449	7 482	4 926	7 991	10 983	11 301	6 254
1979	18 745	5 411	7 439	8 327	925	11 634	7 459	5 234	9 179	12 135	11 176	4 686
1980	24 329	6 389	7 174	11 767	981	13 399	12 714	5 831	10 156	13 858	8 774	9 390
1981	40 839	6 787	8 083	12 834	956	15 751	13 104	6 468	15 166	13 568	11 241	8 206
1982	36 311	7 991	8 854	15 186	975	18 530	12 300	7 199	13 527	12 998	15 866	6 256
1983	35 300	6 053	8 655	14 492	1 108	20 990	11 848	7 934	9 353	12 672	22 814	6 681
1984	37 361	6 010	11 370	15 684	1 328	22 741	15 869	8 311	7 073	12 586	13 526	6 959
1985	35 992	6 422	12 079	17 059	1 460	25 274	16 169	8 622	5 608	13 345	25 477	4 337
1986	32 919	6 958	13 327	18 374	1 574	27 337	14 146	8 962	4 690	13 628	31 368	5 058
1987	32 457	7 493	15 085	16 817	2 635	28 199	11 645	9 200	4 072	13 355	26 513	6 434
1988	35 227	7 594	16 198	17 163	3 031	29 036	10 466	10 820	2 296	14 601	17 137	19 163
1989	34 386	8 745	16 334	19 604	3 639	30 355	9 583	12 821	2 705	16 169	16 859	29 709
1990	35 345	11 500	16 707	24 319	3 647	29 932	13 758	14 426	3 341	17 055	11 804	67 599
1991	42 402	11 138	15 949	19 158	4 412	27 328	15 846	16 092	2 436	18 544	15 054	76 270
1992	45 569	11 143	17 359	22 920	4 293	29 834	16 090	16 389	4 499	20 001	15 087	10 918
1993	48 057	12 577	18 802	14 908	4 491	29 108	17 218	17 006	4 319	20 224	20 245	-2 185
1994	55 225	15 225	20 099	18 023	5 081	28 164	17 067	16 189	5 218	21 000	14 914	-4 228
1995	57 484	14 763	19 301	23 378	5 143	27 206	16 429	16 692	4 936	21 889	9 671	-1 780
1996	54 014	17 189	18 670	20 477	5 048	26 574	13 487	16 684	2 839	21 503	9 035	-1 047
1997	56 924	19 845	17 928	19 636	5 769	27 050	15 173	17 136	1 475	21 201	8 889	-1 464
1998	57 673	24 076	18 297	24 540	8 048	26 819	13 054	18 172	1 270	22 278	12 077	1 007
1999	70 414	27 782	18 336	25 917	9 010	27 476	15 239	18 084	911	23 943	22 879	2 641
2000	68 865	29 010	19 914	32 293	10 506	29 436	17 213	18 594	-761	25 003	36 458	3 207
2001	66 232	28 400	19 369	26 124	11 576	30 473	16 485	19 753	9	25 532	26 252	5 731
2002	66 989	26 507	18 602	23 683	10 206	34 845	22 315	20 734	475	29 426	21 965	-407
2003	67 524	21 959	19 862	21 878	12 636	40 473	21 199	20 831	-725	29 667	22 496	727
2004	69 855	24 831	21 083	19 652	12 956	45 581	26 870	23 029	-147	30 694	15 439	5 265
2005	73 094	24 764	23 379	19 297	13 448	495 294	34 565	23 597	440	27 983	26 565	7 566
2006	73 961	27 877	24 810	29 945	14 632	521 820	29 499	23 584	785	33 025	25 969	6 187
2007	65 069	26 044	26 010	32 043	15 497	551 258	28 482	24 407	-852	31 721	17 662	487
2008	67 334	28 844	27 568	33 598	16 399	616 066	28 857	26 773	631	31 820	18 387	27 870
2009	62 483	23 482	22 453	34 318	17 799	661 012	37 529	28 417	4 755	35 573	22 237	291 535
2010	66 909	18 885	25 298	75 845	20 969	693 485	45 195	30 100	11 618	43 667	21 356	-82 316
2011	72 381	7 399	29 519	82 546	20 271	705 554	45 685	29 466	12 174	45 473	20 662	-12 573
2012	79 061	13 973	30 307	81 957	25 057	677 852	47 189	29 060	14 858	41 631	17 791	40 823
2013	84 007	18 912	31 815	75 767	26 871	633 385	46 418	28 908	11 042	38 145	29 492	-83 199
2014	93 528	15 746	34 966	90 422	27 142	620 562	48 472	28 718	13 375	39 102	22 659	-82 283

[1] Fiscal years through 1976 are from July 1 through June 30. Beginning with October 1976 (fiscal year 1977), fiscal years are from October 1 through September 30. The period from July 1 through September 30, 1976, is a separate fiscal period known as the transition quarter (TQ) and is not included in any fiscal year.
. . . = Not available.

Table 6-14A. Federal Government Receipts and Outlays by Fiscal Year [1]—*Continued*

(Budget accounts, millions of dollars.)

Year	Outlays by function—*Continued*										
	Transportation	Community and regional development	Education, employment, and social services	Health	Medicare	Income security	Social Security	Veterans benefits and services	Administration of justice	General government	Net interest
1940	392	285	1 972	55	0	1 514	28	570	81	274	899
1941	353	123	1 592	60	0	1 855	91	560	92	306	943
1942	1 283	113	1 062	71	0	1 828	137	501	117	397	1 052
1943	3 220	219	375	92	0	1 739	177	276	154	673	1 529
1944	3 901	238	160	174	0	1 503	217	-126	192	900	2 219
1945	3 654	243	134	211	0	1 137	267	110	178	581	3 112
1946	1 970	200	85	201	0	2 384	358	2 465	176	825	4 111
1947	1 130	302	102	177	0	2 820	466	6 344	176	1 114	4 204
1948	787	78	191	162	0	2 499	558	6 457	170	1 045	4 341
1949	916	-33	178	197	0	3 174	657	6 599	184	824	4 523
1950	967	30	241	268	0	4 097	781	8 834	193	986	4 812
1951	956	47	235	323	0	3 352	1 565	5 526	218	1 097	4 665
1952	1 124	73	339	347	0	3 655	2 063	5 341	267	1 163	4 701
1953	1 264	117	441	336	0	3 823	2 717	4 519	243	1 209	5 156
1954	1 229	100	370	307	0	4 434	3 352	4 613	257	799	4 811
1955	1 246	129	445	291	0	5 071	4 427	4 675	256	651	4 850
1956	1 450	92	591	359	0	4 734	5 478	4 891	302	1 201	5 079
1957	1 662	135	590	479	0	5 427	6 661	5 005	303	1 360	5 354
1958	2 334	169	643	541	0	7 535	8 219	5 350	325	655	5 604
1959	3 655	211	789	685	0	8 239	9 737	5 443	356	926	5 762
1960	4 126	224	968	795	0	7 378	11 602	5 441	366	1 184	6 947
1961	3 987	275	1 063	913	0	9 683	12 474	5 705	400	1 354	6 716
1962	4 290	469	1 241	1 198	0	9 207	14 365	5 619	429	1 049	6 889
1963	4 596	574	1 458	1 451	0	9 311	15 788	5 514	465	1 230	7 740
1964	5 242	933	1 555	1 788	0	9 657	16 620	5 675	489	1 518	8 199
1965	5 763	1 114	2 140	1 791	0	9 469	17 460	5 716	536	1 499	8 591
1966	5 730	1 105	4 363	2 543	64	9 678	20 694	5 916	564	1 603	9 386
1967	5 936	1 108	6 453	3 351	2 748	10 261	21 725	6 735	618	1 719	10 268
1968	6 316	1 382	7 634	4 390	4 649	11 816	23 854	7 032	659	1 757	11 090
1969	6 526	1 552	7 548	5 162	5 695	13 076	27 298	7 631	766	1 939	12 699
1970	7 008	2 392	8 634	5 907	6 213	15 655	30 270	8 669	959	2 320	14 380
1971	8 052	2 917	9 849	6 843	6 622	22 946	35 872	9 768	1 307	2 442	14 841
1972	8 392	3 423	12 529	8 674	7 479	27 650	40 157	10 720	1 684	2 960	15 478
1973	9 066	4 605	12 745	9 356	8 052	28 276	49 090	12 003	2 174	9 774	17 349
1974	9 172	4 229	12 457	10 733	9 639	33 713	55 867	13 374	2 505	10 032	21 449
1975	10 918	4 322	16 022	12 930	12 875	50 176	64 658	16 584	3 028	10 374	23 244
1976	13 739	5 442	18 910	15 734	15 834	60 799	73 899	18 419	3 430	9 706	26 727
TQ	3 358	1 569	5 169	3 924	4 264	14 985	19 763	3 960	918	3 878	6 949
1977	14 829	7 021	21 104	17 302	19 345	61 060	85 061	18 022	3 701	12 791	29 901
1978	15 521	11 841	26 710	18 524	22 768	61 505	93 861	18 961	3 923	11 961	35 458
1979	18 079	10 480	30 223	20 494	26 495	66 376	10 407	19 914	4 286	12 241	42 633
1980	21 329	11 252	31 843	23 169	32 090	86 557	118 547	21 169	4 702	12 975	52 533
1981	23 379	10 568	33 152	26 866	39 149	100 290	139 584	22 973	4 908	11 373	68 766
1982	20 625	8 347	26 612	27 445	46 567	108 150	155 964	23 938	4 842	10 861	85 032
1983	21 334	7 564	26 197	28 641	52 588	123 030	170 724	24 824	5 246	11 181	89 808
1984	23 669	7 673	26 920	30 417	57 540	113 350	178 223	25 575	5 811	11 746	111 110
1985	25 838	7 676	28 592	33 541	65 822	128 970	188 623	26 251	6 426	11 515	129 478
1986	28 113	7 233	29 776	35 933	70 164	120 630	198 757	26 314	6 735	12 491	136 017
1987	26 222	5 049	28 921	39 964	75 120	124 080	207 352	26 729	7 715	7 487	138 612
1988	27 272	5 293	30 931	44 483	78 878	130 377	219 341	29 367	9 397	9 399	151 800
1989	27 608	5 362	35 328	48 380	84 964	137 426	232 542	30 003	9 644	9 316	169 862
1990	29 485	8 531	37 171	57 699	98 102	148 668	248 623	29 034	10 185	10 460	184 347
1991	31 099	6 810	41 235	71 168	104 488	172 460	269 015	31 275	12 486	11 566	194 448
1992	33 332	6 836	42 741	89 486	119 024	199 560	287 585	34 037	14 650	12 881	199 344
1993	35 004	9 146	47 380	99 401	130 552	209 960	304 580	35 642	14 650	12 943	198 713
1994	38 066	10 620	43 286	107 102	144 747	217 160	319 565	37 559	15 193	11 159	202 930
1995	39 350	10 746	51 027	115 390	159 855	223 790	335 846	37 862	15 516	13 799	232 113
1996	39 565	10 741	48 321	119 360	174 225	229 730	349 671	36 956	16 508	11 755	241 090
1997	40 767	11 049	48 975	123 830	190 016	235 030	365 251	39 283	17 898	12 547	243 980
1998	40 343	9 771	50 512	131 420	192 822	237 750	379 215	41 741	20 617	15 544	241 110
1999	42 532	11 865	50 605	141 040	190 447	242 470	390 037	43 155	23 359	15 363	229 755
2000	46 853	10 623	53 764	154 504	197 113	253 724	409 423	46 989	26 536	13 013	222 948
2001	54 447	11 773	57 094	172 234	217 384	269 770	432 958	45 098	28 499	14 358	206 167
2002	61 833	12 981	70 566	196 490	230 855	312 720	452 931	50 929	30 201	16 951	170 949
2003	67 069	18 850	82 587	219 541	249 433	334 632	474 680	56 984	35 061	17 094	153 073
2004	64 627	15 820	87 974	240 122	269 360	333 059	495 548	59 746	35 340	23 164	160 245
2005	67 894	26 262	97 555	250 548	298 638	345 847	523 305	70 120	45 576	22 338	183 986
2006	70 244	54 465	118 482	252 739	329 868	352 477	548 549	69 811	40 019	16 997	226 603
2007	72 905	29 567	91 656	266 382	375 407	365 975	586 153	72 818	41 016	18 177	237 109
2008	77 616	23 952	91 287	280 599	390 758	431 313	617 027	84 653	42 362	17 425	252 757
2009	84 289	27 676	79 749	334 335	430 093	533 224	682 963	95 429	48 097	20 323	186 902
2010	91 972	23 894	128 598	369 068	451 636	622 210	706 737	108 384	52 581	22 017	196 194
2011	92 966	23 883	101 233	372 504	485 653	597 352	730 811	127 189	54 383	23 014	229 962
2012	93 019	25 132	90 823	346 742	471 793	541 344	773 290	124 595	56 056	27 476	220 408
2013	91 673	32 336	72 808	358 315	497 826	536 511	813 551	138 938	56 277	28 036	220 885
2014	95 519	33 305	100 460	450 795	519 027	542 237	857 319	151 165	52 601	27 755	223 450
									53 102	22 407	

[1] Fiscal years through 1976 are from July 1 through June 30. Beginning with October 1976 (fiscal year 1977), fiscal years are from October 1 through September 30. The period from July 1 through September 30, 1976, is a separate fiscal period known as the transition quarter (TQ) and is not included in any fiscal year.
. . . = Not available.

Table 6-14B. The Federal Budget and GDP

(Billions of dollars; percent.)

Year	Fiscal year GDP	Billions of dollars						Percent of GDP					
		Receipts			Outlays		Total budget surplus or deficit	Receipts			Outlays		Total budget surplus or deficit
		Total	Individual income taxes	Corporate income taxes	Total	National defense		Total	Individual income taxes	Corporate income taxes	Total	National defense	
1929	. . .	3.9	. . .	. . .	3.1	. . .	0.7	. . .	. . .	. . .	. . .	. . .	. . .
1930	98.4	4.1	. . .	. . .	3.3	. . .	0.7	4.1	. . .	. . .	3.4	. . .	0.8
1931	84.8	3.1	. . .	. . .	3.6	. . .	-0.5	3.7	. . .	. . .	4.2	. . .	-0.5
1932	68.5	1.9	. . .	. . .	4.7	. . .	-2.7	2.8	. . .	. . .	6.8	. . .	-4.0
1933	58.3	2.0	. . .	. . .	4.6	. . .	-2.6	3.4	. . .	. . .	7.9	. . .	-4.5
1934	62.0	3.0	0.4	0.4	6.5	. . .	-3.6	4.8	0.7	0.6	10.6	. . .	-5.8
1935	70.5	3.6	0.5	0.5	6.4	. . .	-2.8	5.1	0.7	0.8	9.1	. . .	-4.0
1936	79.6	3.9	0.7	0.7	8.2	. . .	-4.3	4.9	0.8	0.9	10.3	. . .	-5.4
1937	88.9	5.4	1.1	1.0	7.6	. . .	-2.2	6.1	1.2	1.2	8.5	. . .	-2.5
1938	90.2	6.8	1.3	1.3	6.8	. . .	-0.1	7.5	1.4	1.4	7.6	. . .	-0.1
1939	90.4	6.3	1.0	1.1	9.1	. . .	-2.8	7.0	1.1	1.2	10.1	. . .	-3.1
1940	98.2	6.5	0.9	1.2	9.5	1.7	-2.9	6.7	0.9	1.2	9.6	1.7	-3.0
1941	116.2	8.7	1.3	2.1	13.7	6.4	-4.9	7.5	1.1	1.8	11.7	5.5	-4.3
1942	147.7	14.6	3.3	4.7	35.1	25.7	-20.5	9.9	2.2	3.2	23.8	17.4	-13.9
1943	184.6	24.0	6.5	9.6	78.6	66.7	-54.6	13.0	3.5	5.2	42.6	36.1	-29.6
1944	213.8	43.7	19.7	14.8	91.3	79.1	-47.6	20.5	9.2	6.9	42.7	37.0	-22.2
1945	226.4	45.2	18.4	16.0	92.7	83.0	-47.6	19.9	8.1	7.1	41.0	36.6	-21.0
1946	228.0	39.3	16.1	11.9	55.2	42.7	-15.9	17.2	7.1	5.2	24.2	18.7	-7.0
1947	238.9	38.5	17.9	8.6	34.5	12.8	4.0	16.1	7.5	3.6	14.4	5.4	1.7
1948	262.4	41.6	19.3	9.7	29.8	9.1	11.8	15.8	7.4	3.7	11.3	3.5	4.5
1949	276.8	39.4	15.6	11.2	38.8	13.2	0.6	14.2	5.6	4.0	14.0	4.8	0.2
1950	279.0	39.4	15.8	10.4	42.6	13.7	-3.1	14.1	5.6	3.7	15.3	4.9	-1.1
1951	327.4	51.6	21.6	14.1	45.5	23.6	6.1	15.8	6.6	4.3	13.9	7.2	1.9
1952	357.5	66.2	27.9	21.2	67.7	46.1	-1.5	18.5	7.8	5.9	18.9	12.9	-0.4
1953	382.5	69.6	29.8	21.2	76.1	52.8	-6.5	18.2	7.8	5.6	19.9	13.8	-1.7
1954	387.7	69.7	29.5	21.1	70.9	49.3	-1.2	18.0	7.6	5.4	18.3	12.7	-0.3
1955	407.0	65.5	28.7	17.9	68.4	42.7	-3.0	16.1	7.1	4.4	16.8	10.5	-0.7
1956	439.0	74.6	32.2	20.9	70.6	42.5	3.9	17.0	7.3	4.8	16.1	9.7	0.9
1957	464.2	80.0	35.6	21.2	76.6	45.4	3.4	17.2	7.7	4.6	16.5	9.8	0.7
1958	474.3	79.6	34.7	20.1	82.4	46.8	-2.8	16.8	7.3	4.2	17.4	9.9	-0.6
1959	505.6	79.2	36.7	17.3	92.1	49.0	-12.8	15.7	7.3	3.4	18.2	9.7	-2.5
1960	535.1	92.5	40.7	21.5	92.2	48.1	0.3	17.3	7.6	4.0	17.2	9.0	0.1
1961	547.6	94.4	41.3	21.0	97.7	49.6	-3.3	17.2	7.5	3.8	17.8	9.1	-0.6
1962	586.9	99.7	45.6	20.5	106.8	52.3	-7.1	17.0	7.8	3.5	18.2	8.9	-1.2
1963	619.3	106.6	47.6	21.6	111.3	53.4	-4.8	17.2	7.7	3.5	18.0	8.6	-0.8
1964	662.9	112.6	48.7	23.5	118.5	54.8	-5.9	17.0	7.3	3.5	17.9	8.3	-0.9
1965	710.7	116.8	48.8	25.5	118.2	50.6	-1.4	16.4	6.9	3.6	16.6	7.1	-0.2
1966	781.9	130.8	55.4	30.1	134.5	58.1	-3.7	16.7	7.1	3.8	17.2	7.4	-0.5
1967	838.2	148.8	61.5	34.0	157.5	71.4	-8.6	17.8	7.3	4.1	18.8	8.5	-1.0
1968	899.3	153.0	68.7	28.7	178.1	81.9	-25.2	17.0	7.6	3.2	19.8	9.1	-2.8
1969	982.3	186.9	87.2	36.7	183.6	82.5	3.2	19.0	8.9	3.7	18.7	8.4	0.3
1970	1 049.1	192.8	90.4	32.8	195.6	81.7	-2.8	18.4	8.6	3.1	18.6	7.8	-0.3
1971	1 119.3	187.1	86.2	26.8	210.2	78.9	-23.0	16.7	7.7	2.4	18.8	7.0	-2.1
1972	1 219.5	207.3	94.7	32.2	230.7	79.2	-23.4	17.0	7.8	2.6	18.9	6.5	-1.9
1973	1 356.0	230.8	103.2	36.2	245.7	76.7	-14.9	17.0	7.6	2.7	18.1	5.7	-1.1
1974	1 486.2	263.2	119.0	38.6	269.4	79.3	-6.1	17.7	8.0	2.6	18.1	5.3	-0.4
1975	1 610.6	279.1	122.4	40.6	332.3	86.5	-53.2	17.3	7.6	2.5	20.6	5.4	-3.3
1976	1 790.3	298.1	131.6	41.4	371.8	89.6	-73.7	16.6	7.4	2.3	20.8	5.0	-4.1
1977	2 028.4	355.6	157.6	54.9	409.2	97.2	-53.7	17.5	7.8	2.7	20.2	4.8	-2.6
1978	2 278.2	399.6	181.0	60.0	458.7	104.5	-59.2	17.5	7.9	2.6	20.1	4.6	-2.6
1979	2 570.0	463.3	217.8	65.7	504.0	116.3	-40.7	18.0	8.5	2.6	19.6	4.5	-1.6
1980	2 796.8	517.1	244.1	64.6	590.9	134.0	-73.8	18.5	8.7	2.3	21.1	4.8	-2.6
1981	3 138.4	599.3	285.9	61.1	678.2	157.5	-79.0	19.1	9.1	1.9	21.6	5.0	-2.5
1982	3 313.9	617.8	297.7	49.2	745.7	185.3	-128.0	18.6	9.0	1.5	22.5	5.6	-3.9
1983	3 541.1	600.6	288.9	37.0	808.4	209.9	-207.8	17.0	8.2	1.0	22.8	5.9	-5.9
1984	3 952.8	666.4	298.4	56.9	851.8	227.4	-185.4	16.9	7.5	1.4	21.5	5.8	-4.7
1985	4 270.4	734.0	334.5	61.3	946.3	252.7	-212.3	17.2	7.8	1.4	22.2	5.9	-5.0
1986	4 536.1	769.2	349.0	63.1	990.4	273.4	-221.2	17.0	7.7	1.4	21.8	6.0	-4.9
1987	4 781.9	854.3	392.6	83.9	1 004.0	282.0	-149.7	17.9	8.2	1.8	21.0	5.9	-3.1
1988	5 155.1	909.2	401.2	94.5	1 064.4	290.4	-155.2	17.6	7.8	1.8	20.6	5.6	-3.0
1989	5 570.0	991.1	445.7	103.3	1 143.7	303.6	-152.6	17.8	8.0	1.9	20.5	5.4	-2.7
1990	5 914.6	1 032.0	466.9	93.5	1 253.0	299.3	-221.0	17.4	7.9	1.6	21.2	5.1	-3.7
1991	6 110.0	1 055.0	467.8	98.1	1 324.2	273.3	-269.2	17.3	7.7	1.6	21.7	4.5	-4.4
1992	6 434.7	1 091.2	476.0	100.3	1 381.5	298.3	-290.3	17.0	7.4	1.6	21.5	4.6	-4.5
1993	6 794.9	1 154.3	509.7	117.5	1 409.4	291.1	-255.1	17.0	7.5	1.7	20.7	4.3	-3.8
1994	7 197.8	1 258.6	543.1	140.4	1 461.8	281.6	-203.2	17.5	7.5	2.0	20.3	3.9	-2.8

. . . = Not available.

Table 6-14B. The Federal Budget and GDP—*Continued*

(Billions of dollars; percent.)

Year	Fiscal year GDP	Billions of dollars						Percent of GDP					
		Receipts			Outlays		Total budget surplus or deficit	Receipts			Outlays		Total budget surplus or deficit
		Total	Individual income taxes	Corporate income taxes	Total	National defense		Total	Individual income taxes	Corporate income taxes	Total	National defense	
1995	7 583.3	1 351.8	590.2	157.0	1 515.7	272.1	-164.0	17.8	7.8	2.1	20.0	3.6	-2.2
1996	7 978.3	1 453.1	656.4	171.8	1 560.5	265.7	-107.4	18.2	8.2	2.2	19.6	3.3	-1.3
1997	8 483.2	1 579.2	737.5	182.3	1 601.1	270.5	-21.9	18.6	8.7	2.1	18.9	3.2	-0.3
1998	8 954.8	1 721.7	828.6	188.7	1 652.5	268.2	69.3	19.2	9.3	2.1	18.5	3.0	0.8
1999	9 514.0	1 827.5	879.5	184.7	1 701.8	274.8	125.6	19.2	9.2	1.9	17.9	2.9	1.3
2000	10 154.0	2 025.2	1 004.5	207.3	1 789.0	294.4	236.2	19.9	9.9	2.0	17.6	2.9	2.3
2001	10 568.4	1 991.1	994.3	151.1	1 862.8	304.7	128.2	18.8	9.4	1.4	17.6	2.9	1.2
2002	10 879.4	1 853.1	858.3	148.0	2 010.9	348.5	-157.8	17.0	7.9	1.4	18.5	3.2	-1.5
2003	11 334.0	1 782.3	793.7	131.8	2 159.9	404.7	-377.6	15.7	7.0	1.2	19.1	3.6	-3.3
2004	12 090.7	1 880.1	809.0	189.4	2 292.8	455.8	-412.7	15.6	6.7	1.6	19.0	3.8	-3.4
2005	12 890.5	2 153.6	927.2	278.3	2 472.0	495.3	-318.3	16.7	7.2	2.2	19.2	3.8	-2.5
2006	13 686.6	2 406.9	1 043.9	353.9	2 655.1	521.8	-248.2	17.6	7.6	2.6	19.4	3.8	-1.8
2007	14 324.9	2 568.0	1 163.5	370.2	2 728.7	551.3	-160.7	17.9	8.1	2.6	19.0	3.8	-1.1
2008	14 756.1	2 524.0	1 145.7	304.3	2 982.5	616.1	-458.6	17.1	7.8	2.1	20.2	4.2	-3.1
2009	14 413.6	2 105.0	915.3	138.2	3 517.7	661.0	-1 412.7	14.6	6.4	1.0	24.4	4.6	-9.8
2010	14 791.4	2 162.7	898.5	191.4	3 457.1	693.5	-1 294.4	14.6	6.1	1.3	23.4	4.7	-8.8
2011	15 387.1	2 303.5	1 091.5	181.1	3 603.1	705.6	-1 299.6	15.0	7.1	1.2	23.4	4.6	-8.4
2012	16 094.2	2 450.2	1 132.2	242.3	3 537.1	677.9	-1 087.0	15.2	7.0	1.5	22.0	4.2	-6.8
2013	16 618.6	2 775.1	1 316.4	273.5	3 454.6	633.4	-679.5	16.7	7.9	1.6	20.8	3.8	-4.1
2014	17 332.3	3 001.7	1 386.1	332.7	3 650.5	620.6	-648.8	17.3	8.0	1.9	21.1	3.6	3.7

Table 6-15. Federal Government Debt by Fiscal Year

(Billions of dollars, except as noted.)

| Year | Federal government debt held by the public at end of fiscal year | | Gross federal debt at end of fiscal year held by: | | | | | | |
| | Debt held by the public | Debt/GDP ratio (percent) | Total | Social Security funds [1] | Other U.S. government accounts | Federal Reserve System | Private investors | | |
							Total	Foreign residents	Domestic investors
1940	43	43.6	51	2	6	2	40	...	...
1941	48	41.5	58	2	7	2	46	...	...
1942	68	45.9	79	3	8	3	65	...	...
1943	128	69.2	143	4	11	7	121	...	...
1944	185	86.4	204	5	14	15	170	...	...
1945	235	103.9	260	7	18	22	213	...	...
1946	242	106.1	271	8	21	24	218	...	...
1947	224	93.9	257	9	24	22	202	...	...
1948	216	82.4	252	10	26	21	195	...	...
1949	214	77.4	253	11	27	19	195	...	...
1950	219	78.5	257	13	25	18	201	...	...
1951	214	65.5	255	15	26	23	191	...	...
1952	215	60.1	259	17	28	23	192	...	...
1953	218	57.1	266	18	29	25	194	...	...
1954	224	57.9	271	20	26	25	199	...	...
1955	227	55.7	274	21	27	24	203	...	...
1956	222	50.6	273	23	28	24	198	...	...
1957	219	47.2	272	23	30	23	196	...	...
1958	226	47.7	280	24	29	25	201	...	...
1959	235	46.4	287	23	30	26	209	...	...
1960	237	44.3	291	23	31	27	210	...	...
1961	238	43.5	293	23	31	27	211	...	...
1962	248	42.3	303	22	33	30	218	...	...
1963	254	41.0	310	21	35	32	222	...	...
1964	257	38.7	316	22	37	35	222	...	...
1965	261	36.7	322	22	39	39	222	12	210
1966	264	33.7	328	22	43	42	222	12	210
1967	267	31.8	340	26	48	47	220	11	209
1968	290	32.2	369	28	51	52	237	11	226
1969	278	28.3	366	32	56	54	224	10	214
1970	283	27.0	381	38	60	58	225	14	211
1971	303	27.1	408	41	64	66	238	32	206
1972	322	26.4	436	44	70	71	251	49	202
1973	341	25.1	466	44	81	75	266	59	207
1974	344	23.1	484	46	94	81	263	57	206
1975	395	24.5	542	48	99	85	310	66	244
1976	477	26.7	629	45	107	95	383	70	313
TQ	496	26.2	644	44	105	97	399	75	324
1977	549	27.1	706	40	118	105	444	96	348
1978	607	26.6	777	35	134	115	492	121	371
1979	640	24.9	829	33	156	116	525	120	405
1980	712	25.5	909	32	165	121	591	122	469
1981	789	25.2	995	27	178	124	665	131	534
1982	925	27.9	1 137	19	193	134	790	141	649
1983	1 137	32.1	1 372	32	202	156	982	160	822
1984	1 307	33.1	1 565	32	225	155	1 152	176	976
1985	1 507	35.3	1 817	40	270	170	1 337	223	1 114
1986	1 741	38.4	2 121	46	334	191	1 550	266	1 284
1987	1 890	39.5	2 346	65	391	212	1 678	280	1 398
1988	2 052	39.8	2 601	104	445	229	1 822	346	1 476
1989	2 191	39.3	2 868	157	520	220	1 971	395	1 576
1990	2 412	40.8	3 206	215	580	234	2 177	464	1 713
1991	2 689	44.0	3 598	268	641	259	2 430	506	1 924
1992	3 000	46.6	4 002	319	683	296	2 703	563	2 140
1993	3 248	47.8	4 351	366	737	326	2 923	619	2 304
1994	3 433	47.7	4 643	423	788	355	3 078	682	2 396
1995	3 604	47.5	4 921	483	833	374	3 230	820	2 410
1996	3 734	46.8	5 181	550	898	391	3 343	993	2 350
1997	3 772	44.5	5 369	631	966	425	3 348	1 231	2 117
1998	3 721	41.6	5 478	730	1 027	458	3 263	1 224	2 039
1999	3 632	38.2	5 606	855	1 118	497	3 136	1 281	1 855
2000	3 410	33.6	5 629	1 007	1 212	511	2 898	1 039	1 859
2001	3 320	31.4	5 770	1 170	1 280	534	2 785	1 006	1 779
2002	3 540	32.5	6 198	1 329	1 329	604	2 936	1 201	1 735
2003	3 913	34.5	6 760	1 485	1 362	656	3 257	1 454	1 803
2004	4 296	35.5	7 355	1 635	1 424	700	3 595	1 799	1 796
2005	4 592	35.6	7 905	1 809	1 504	736	3 856	1 930	1 926
2006	4 829	35.3	8 451	1 994	1 628	769	4 060	2 025	2 035
2007	5 035	35.2	8 951	2 181	1 735	780	4 255	2 235	2 020
2008	5 803	39.3	9 986	2 366	1 817	491	5 312	2 802	2 510
2009	7 545	52.3	11 876	2 504	1 827	769	6 776	3 571	3 205
2010	9 019	60.9	13 529	2 585	1 925	812	8 207	4 324	3 883
2011	10 128	65.9	14 764	2 653	1 982	1 665	8 464	4 912	3 551
2012	11 281	70.4	16 051	2 718	2 052	1 645	9 636	5 476	4 160
2013	11 983	72.3	16 719	2 756	1 981	2 072	9 910	5 653	4 258
2014	12 780	74.1	17 794	2 783	2 232	2 452	10 328	6 066	4 262

[1]Sum of old age and survivors insurance fund and disability insurance trust fund.
. . . = Not available.

Section 6d: Government Output and Employment

Figure 6-4: Government Employment, 1955–2014
(ratio scale)

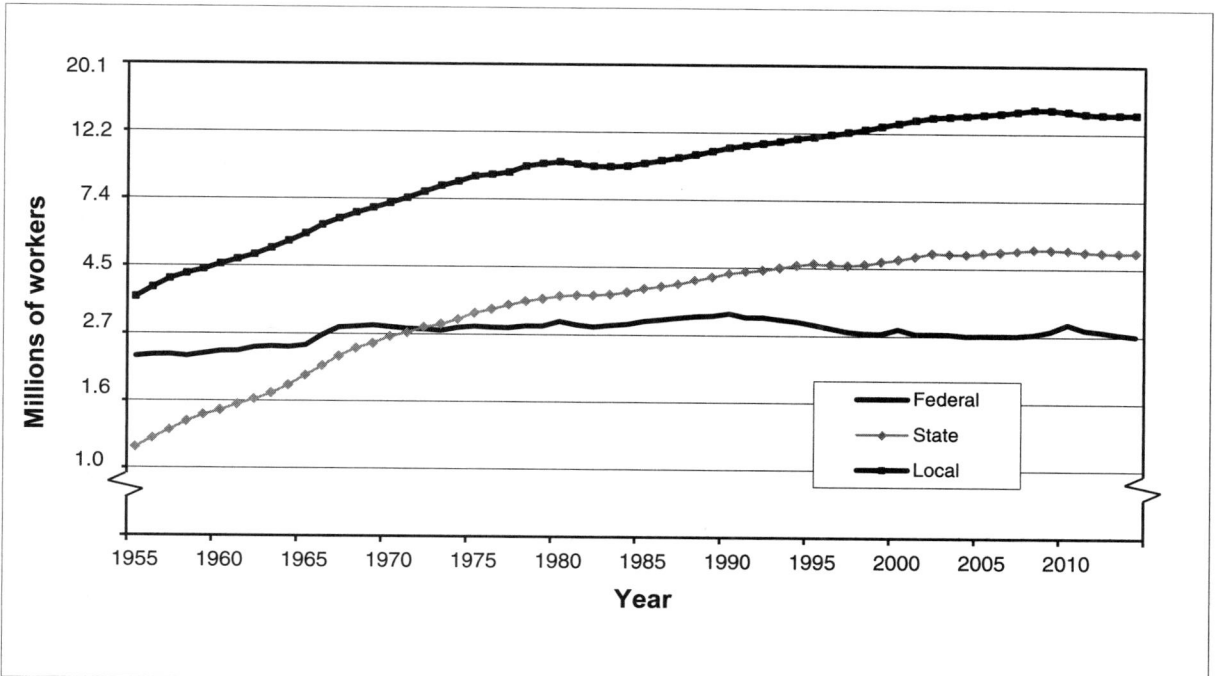

- Since 1955 to 2014, total reported employment of civilians by all levels of government has increased 211 percent—an annual rate of 1.9 percent per year—and government's proportion of total nonfarm payroll employment has risen from 13.8 percent to 15.7 percent. Federal employment rose 19 percent; state government employment rose 333 percent, with 54 percent of this increase due to education; and local government rose 295 percent, with 57 percent of this increase due to education. However budget cuts hit all levels of government employment. For example, the Defense Department lost 30 percent of its employees. (Tables 6-17 and 10-8B)

- Contracting and outsourcing of federal government spending can be seen in comparisons between government purchases and government value added. From 1955 to 2014, the volume (measured by the quantity index) of "intermediate" goods and services purchased for nondefense purposes rose 448 percent, compared with the 359 percent rise in real nondefense value added by government itself in such activities. (Real value added comprises the input of government employees and government-owned capital, valued in constant dollars). For defense, government value added rose 20 percent over that period, while purchases of goods and services rose 128 percent in real terms. (Table 6-16)

- A similar process has occurred at state and local governments, where real value added increased 330.3 percent while goods and services purchased rose 1,020 percent. (Table 6-16)

Table 6-16. Chain-Type Quantity Indexes for Government Output

(Seasonally adjusted, 2009 = 100.)

NIPA Table 3.10.3

Year and quarter	Federal government									State and local government		
	Gross output of general government			Value added			Intermediate goods and services purchased [1]			Gross output of general government	Value added	Intermediate goods and services purchased [1]
	Total	Defense	Nondefense	Total	Defense	Nondefense	Total	Defense	Nondefense			
1955	46.5	60.3	22.5	59.9	83.0	22.8	27.4	33.4	16.1	17.3	22.8	8.1
1956	44.8	59.7	18.8	59.7	82.4	23.3	24.4	32.9	9.7	18.0	24.3	7.8
1957	46.5	62.4	18.6	60.2	82.7	24.1	27.1	37.9	8.8	18.9	25.6	8.2
1958	46.0	61.8	18.0	59.2	80.7	25.0	27.0	38.8	7.0	20.5	27.2	9.4
1959	45.1	56.4	25.3	59.3	80.6	25.4	25.1	27.5	19.2	21.4	28.3	10.0
1960	44.0	56.8	21.6	61.0	82.1	27.4	21.0	26.7	10.4	22.5	29.8	10.5
1961	44.9	58.2	21.5	62.9	84.6	28.5	20.5	26.9	9.0	23.8	31.3	11.2
1962	49.4	63.0	25.5	66.0	88.4	30.4	26.4	32.6	14.5	24.6	32.5	11.7
1963	49.8	63.1	26.3	67.2	88.9	32.8	25.8	32.5	13.2	26.0	34.2	12.4
1964	49.6	62.1	27.5	68.5	89.8	34.7	23.7	29.0	13.5	27.8	36.2	13.6
1965	50.7	63.1	28.8	69.6	90.3	36.7	24.8	30.6	13.7	29.7	38.4	15.0
1966	56.0	71.7	28.4	74.4	96.4	39.4	30.5	42.1	9.8	31.6	40.7	16.2
1967	62.3	79.9	31.2	79.4	102.8	42.4	37.7	52.4	11.8	33.2	42.4	17.5
1968	64.6	83.4	31.5	81.4	104.6	44.6	40.3	57.9	9.8	35.5	45.0	19.3
1969	63.9	80.8	34.2	82.3	105.0	46.3	37.8	51.6	13.1	37.6	47.0	21.4
1970	60.2	74.4	35.2	79.7	99.8	47.8	32.9	43.7	13.4	39.8	49.1	23.6
1971	57.7	68.9	37.9	76.8	93.8	49.9	31.0	38.6	16.5	41.9	51.1	25.8
1972	56.7	65.2	41.4	73.9	88.0	51.7	32.4	37.5	21.8	43.7	52.9	27.4
1973	54.0	61.1	41.2	71.9	84.2	52.6	28.8	32.7	20.3	45.2	54.8	28.2
1974	54.0	59.7	43.7	72.0	82.8	55.1	28.6	31.2	22.5	46.9	56.8	29.5
1975	53.6	58.1	45.4	71.9	81.7	56.5	27.8	29.0	24.3	48.9	58.5	31.9
1976	52.6	56.5	45.5	72.1	80.5	59.2	25.3	27.0	21.0	49.8	59.3	32.9
1977	53.6	56.9	47.5	72.5	80.1	60.9	26.9	28.4	23.0	50.8	60.2	34.0
1978	54.6	57.3	49.6	73.6	80.5	63.1	27.8	28.8	24.7	52.1	61.6	35.0
1979	55.4	57.9	50.9	73.9	80.3	64.1	29.2	30.2	26.2	52.8	62.8	35.0
1980	57.5	59.6	53.6	75.2	81.0	66.4	32.0	32.9	29.1	52.8	63.6	33.7
1981	59.6	62.6	54.3	76.6	83.4	66.1	34.9	36.2	30.9	52.8	63.6	33.9
1982	61.5	66.1	53.0	78.1	85.8	66.2	37.1	40.7	28.0	53.8	64.0	35.4
1983	64.6	69.0	56.5	80.2	88.4	67.5	41.1	43.8	34.0	54.6	63.8	37.8
1984	65.4	71.0	54.9	82.4	91.5	68.3	40.1	44.5	29.3	55.7	64.2	39.8
1985	69.0	74.9	57.9	85.3	95.5	69.2	44.3	47.9	35.0	58.1	66.0	43.1
1986	72.3	78.9	59.9	87.5	98.9	69.3	48.9	52.5	39.4	60.7	68.0	46.7
1987	73.8	81.7	58.9	90.3	102.5	70.8	48.6	54.2	34.9	62.0	69.3	47.7
1988	74.1	83.6	56.2	92.1	104.3	72.7	47.0	56.2	25.6	64.0	71.7	49.2
1989	75.9	84.1	60.6	93.6	106.1	73.8	49.2	55.2	35.0	66.3	73.9	51.6
1990	77.6	84.7	64.4	95.4	107.0	77.0	50.7	55.3	39.7	68.4	76.1	53.3
1991	78.6	85.7	65.3	96.0	107.4	77.9	52.1	57.0	40.6	70.0	77.1	56.0
1992	77.4	82.3	68.3	94.4	103.9	79.6	51.4	53.8	45.6	71.8	78.4	58.7
1993	75.2	79.5	67.3	92.9	100.9	80.4	48.5	51.4	41.5	73.4	79.5	61.3
1994	73.5	76.5	68.0	90.3	97.2	79.8	48.0	49.4	44.7	75.5	80.9	64.7
1995	71.0	73.0	67.3	87.5	93.3	78.5	45.9	46.4	44.8	77.4	82.5	67.3
1996	69.7	71.8	65.9	85.4	90.2	78.1	45.7	47.4	41.8	78.9	83.8	69.1
1997	69.5	70.6	67.7	84.0	87.6	78.5	47.4	48.0	46.0	81.2	85.4	72.6
1998	68.4	68.6	68.0	83.1	85.2	79.9	45.9	46.5	44.2	84.3	87.2	78.3
1999	69.1	69.7	68.1	82.5	83.4	81.1	48.5	51.2	42.0	87.0	88.7	83.7
2000	69.6	68.9	71.0	83.0	82.5	83.8	49.1	50.6	45.7	89.4	90.5	87.0
2001	72.3	71.1	74.5	83.3	82.5	84.7	55.1	55.6	53.9	92.8	92.7	93.2
2002	76.6	75.0	79.5	84.8	83.6	86.6	63.8	63.3	65.0	95.3	94.5	96.8
2003	81.5	80.8	82.9	87.0	85.9	88.8	72.8	73.6	70.7	94.9	95.1	94.3
2004	84.7	84.7	84.8	88.4	87.9	89.1	79.0	80.2	76.1	95.1	95.5	94.3
2005	86.1	85.8	86.6	89.6	89.4	89.9	80.6	80.9	79.8	95.7	96.1	94.7
2006	87.5	87.0	88.5	90.3	89.9	91.1	83.0	82.8	83.4	96.7	96.9	96.2
2007	88.3	88.3	88.2	91.6	91.1	92.5	82.9	84.4	79.5	98.1	98.3	97.6
2008	94.0	94.3	93.6	95.1	94.8	95.7	92.3	93.6	89.4	98.2	99.6	95.2
2009	100.0	100.0	100.0	100.0	100.0	100.0	100.0	100.0	100.0	100.0	100.0	100.0
2010	104.3	103.5	105.8	103.4	103.2	103.8	105.8	104.0	110.1	98.3	99.3	96.2
2011	102.0	102.3	101.5	104.5	104.7	104.2	97.9	98.9	95.8	96.3	98.2	92.3
2012	100.8	99.9	102.5	104.4	103.7	105.5	95.0	94.4	96.2	95.5	97.7	90.9
2013	95.3	93.3	98.8	102.5	101.3	104.3	83.8	82.3	87.5	95.1	97.5	90.2
2014	93.2	89.8	99.3	101.6	99.6	104.7	79.9	76.3	88.3	95.7	98.1	90.7
2012												
1st quarter	101.4	100.8	102.4	104.7	104.3	105.4	96.0	95.9	96.2	95.8	97.8	91.6
2nd quarter	100.8	99.7	102.7	104.5	103.9	105.5	94.8	93.8	97.0	95.6	97.7	91.1
3rd quarter	101.1	100.3	102.6	104.3	103.6	105.4	95.9	95.6	96.6	95.4	97.7	90.7
4th quarter	99.9	98.6	102.2	104.1	103.1	105.7	93.2	92.3	95.0	95.2	97.5	90.3
2013												
1st quarter	97.5	95.9	100.7	103.8	102.6	105.7	87.6	86.6	90.2	95.1	97.4	90.2
2nd quarter	96.4	94.7	99.4	103.3	102.2	105.2	85.3	84.4	87.5	95.1	97.4	90.2
3rd quarter	94.4	92.1	98.7	102.1	100.4	104.9	82.3	80.7	86.0	95.1	97.5	90.1
4th quarter	92.6	90.6	96.4	100.6	100.2	101.3	80.0	77.3	86.4	95.2	97.6	90.2
2014												
1st quarter	93.4	90.4	99.0	102.0	100.4	104.6	79.8	76.5	87.5	95.4	97.8	90.4
2nd quarter	92.9	89.6	99.0	101.8	100.0	104.6	79.0	75.3	87.7	95.6	98.0	90.6
3rd quarter	94.0	91.0	99.4	101.4	99.4	104.7	82.2	79.5	88.6	95.7	98.1	90.8
4th quarter	92.3	88.3	99.8	101.0	98.6	104.8	78.6	73.9	89.5	95.9	98.3	90.9

[1] Includes general government intermediate inputs for goods and services sold to other sectors and for own-account investment.

Table 6-17. Government Employment

(Calendar years, payroll employment in thousands.)

Year and month	Total government employment	Federal			State			Local		
		Total	Department of Defense	Postal Service	Total	Education	State government hospitals	Total	Education	Local government hospitals
1950	6 120	2 023	533	516	. . .	. . .	. . .	. . .	. . .	. . .
1951	6 502	2 415	797	521	. . .	. . .	. . .	. . .	. . .	. . .
1952	6 727	2 539	868	542	. . .	. . .	. . .	. . .	. . .	. . .
1953	6 758	2 418	818	530	. . .	. . .	. . .	. . .	. . .	. . .
1954	6 858	2 295	744	533	. . .	. . .	. . .	. . .	. . .	. . .
1955	7 021	2 295	744	534	1 168	308	. . .	3 558	1 751	. . .
1956	7 386	2 318	749	539	1 249	334	. . .	3 819	1 884	. . .
1957	7 724	2 326	729	555	1 328	363	. . .	4 071	2 026	. . .
1958	7 946	2 298	695	567	1 415	389	. . .	4 232	2 115	. . .
1959	8 192	2 342	699	578	1 484	420	. . .	4 366	2 198	. . .
1960	8 464	2 381	681	591	1 536	448	. . .	4 547	2 314	. . .
1961	8 706	2 391	683	601	1 607	474	. . .	4 708	2 411	. . .
1962	9 004	2 455	697	601	1 669	511	. . .	4 881	2 522	. . .
1963	9 341	2 473	687	603	1 747	557	. . .	5 121	2 674	. . .
1964	9 711	2 463	676	604	1 856	609	. . .	5 392	2 839	. . .
1965	10 191	2 495	679	619	1 996	679	. . .	5 700	3 031	. . .
1966	10 910	2 690	741	686	2 141	775	. . .	6 080	3 297	. . .
1967	11 525	2 852	802	719	2 302	873	. . .	6 371	3 490	. . .
1968	11 972	2 871	801	729	2 442	958	. . .	6 660	3 649	. . .
1969	12 330	2 893	815	737	2 533	1 042	. . .	6 904	3 785	. . .
1970	12 687	2 865	756	741	2 664	1 104	. . .	7 158	3 912	. . .
1971	13 012	2 828	731	731	2 747	1 149	. . .	7 437	4 091	. . .
1972	13 465	2 815	720	703	2 859	1 188	459	7 790	4 262	467
1973	13 862	2 794	696	698	2 923	1 205	472	8 146	4 433	477
1974	14 303	2 858	698	710	3 039	1 267	483	8 407	4 584	483
1975	14 820	2 882	704	699	3 179	1 323	503	8 758	4 722	489
1976	15 001	2 863	693	676	3 273	1 371	518	8 865	4 786	492
1977	15 258	2 859	676	657	3 377	1 385	538	9 023	4 859	494
1978	15 812	2 893	661	660	3 474	1 367	541	9 446	4 958	535
1979	16 068	2 894	649	673	3 541	1 378	538	9 633	4 989	571
1980	16 375	3 000	645	673	3 610	1 398	530	9 765	5 090	604
1981	16 180	2 922	655	675	3 640	1 420	515	9 619	5 095	622
1982	15 982	2 884	690	684	3 640	1 433	494	9 458	5 049	635
1983	16 011	2 915	699	685	3 662	1 450	471	9 434	5 020	644
1984	16 159	2 943	716	706	3 734	1 488	459	9 482	5 076	623
1985	16 533	3 014	738	750	3 832	1 540	449	9 687	5 221	608
1986	16 838	3 044	736	792	3 893	1 561	438	9 901	5 358	601
1987	17 156	3 089	736	815	3 967	1 586	439	10 100	5 469	606
1988	17 540	3 124	719	835	4 076	1 621	446	10 339	5 590	619
1989	17 927	3 136	735	838	4 182	1 668	442	10 609	5 740	632
1990	18 415	3 196	722	825	4 305	1 730	426	10 914	5 902	646
1991	18 545	3 110	702	813	4 355	1 768	417	11 081	5 994	653
1992	18 787	3 111	702	800	4 408	1 799	419	11 267	6 076	665
1993	18 989	3 063	670	793	4 488	1 834	414	11 438	6 206	673
1994	19 275	3 018	657	821	4 576	1 882	407	11 682	6 329	673
1995	19 432	2 949	627	850	4 635	1 919	395	11 849	6 453	669
1996	19 539	2 877	597	867	4 606	1 911	376	12 056	6 592	648
1997	19 664	2 806	588	866	4 582	1 904	360	12 276	6 759	632
1998	19 909	2 772	550	881	4 612	1 922	346	12 525	6 921	630
1999	20 307	2 769	525	890	4 709	1 983	344	12 829	7 120	626
2000	20 790	2 865	510	880	4 786	2 031	343	13 139	7 294	622
2001	21 118	2 764	504	873	4 905	2 113	345	13 449	7 479	628
2002	21 513	2 766	499	842	5 029	2 243	349	13 718	7 654	642
2003	21 583	2 761	486	809	5 002	2 255	348	13 820	7 709	651
2004	21 621	2 730	473	782	4 982	2 238	348	13 909	7 765	656
2005	21 804	2 732	488	774	5 032	2 260	350	14 041	7 856	655
2006	21 974	2 732	493	770	5 075	2 293	357	14 167	7 913	647
2007	22 218	2 734	491	769	5 122	2 318	360	14 362	7 987	654
2008	22 509	2 762	496	747	5 177	2 354	361	14 571	8 084	659
2009	22 555	2 832	519	703	5 169	2 360	359	14 554	8 079	661
2010	22 490	2 977	545	659	5 137	2 373	354	14 376	8 013	650
2011	22 086	2 859	559	631	5 078	2 374	348	14 150	7 873	648
2012	21 920	2 820	552	611	5 055	2 389	349	14 045	7 778	647
2013	21 864	2 766	536	595	5 048	2 393	353	14 050	7 783	650
2014	21 863	2 729	522	593	5 060	2 409	347	14 074	7 791	644

. . . = Not available.

NOTES AND DEFINITIONS, CHAPTER 6

Tables 6-1 through 6-13 and 6-16
Federal, State, and Local Government in the National Income and Product Accounts

SOURCE: U.S. DEPARTMENT OF COMMERCE, BUREAU OF ECONOMIC ANALYSIS (BEA)

These data are from the national income and product accounts (NIPAs), as redefined in the 2013 comprehensive NIPA revision and updated in the 2015 annual revision. For general information about the NIPAs and the 2013 revision, see the notes and definitions for Chapter 1.

Changes in definitions made in the 2013 revision had significant effects on some components of the government accounts. Recognition of research and development spending, whether undertaken by private industry and organizations or by government, as fixed, depreciable capital investment increased the amount of investment and capital consumption charges. The change to accrual accounting for defined benefit plans, which increased personal income and saving by recognizing benefits of such plans when earned instead of when paid, generally increased employee compensation spending and government deficits. (An exception occurs in the Federal accounts in some years when the Federal government has made large cash contributions to its pension funds as "catch up" payments, which under the previous cash accounting was registered as personal income and compensation at the time instead of when accrued. In those years, the redefinition makes employee compensation smaller.)

The framework for the government accounts

In an earlier major revision in 2003, a new framework was introduced for government consumption expenditures—federal, state, and local—that explicitly recognizes the services produced by general government. Governments serve several functions in the economy. Three of these functions are recognized in the NIPAs: the production of nonmarket services; the consumption of these services, as the value of services provided to the general public is treated as government consumption expenditures; and the provision of transfer payments. These functions are financed through taxation, through contributions to social insurance funds, and by borrowing in the world's capital markets.

In this framework, the value of the government services produced and consumed (most of which are not sold in the market) is measured as the sum of the costs of the three major inputs: compensation of government employees, consumption of fixed capital (CFC), and intermediate goods and services purchased. The purchase from the private sector of goods and services by government, classified as final sales to government before the 2003 revision, was reclassified as intermediate purchases.

The value of government final purchases of consumption expenditures and gross investment, which constitutes the contribution of government demand to the gross domestic product (GDP), was not changed by this reclassification, since the previous definition of that contribution was the sum of compensation, CFC, and goods and services purchased. However, the distribution of GDP by type of product was changed—final sales of goods were reduced by the amount of goods purchased by government, and final sales of services were increased by the same amount.

In addition to this change in the conceptual framework, a number of the categories of government receipts and expenditures were redefined to make more precise distinctions. For example, items that used to be called "nontax payments" and included with taxes are now classified as transfer or fee payments and not included in taxes.

Finally, the concept previously known as "current surplus or deficit (-), national income and product accounts" was renamed "net government saving." This recognizes, in part, the role of government in the capital markets. When government runs a current surplus, net government saving is positive and funds are made available (for example, by retiring outstanding government debt) to finance investment—both private-sector capital spending and government investment. By the same token, when government runs a current deficit, or "dis-saves," it must borrow funds that would otherwise be available to finance investment.

However, this definition of net government saving does not give a complete picture of governments' role in capital markets, because it is based on current receipts and expenditures alone and does not include government investment activity.

In the NIPAs, the capital spending of all levels of government is treated the same way as the accounts treat private investment spending. A depreciation, or more precisely "consumption of fixed capital" (CFC), entry for existing capital is calculated, using estimated replacement costs and realistic depreciation rates. In the government accounts this CFC value is entered as one element of current expenditures and output. Capital spending is excluded from government current expenditures but appears in the account for "net lending or borrowing (-)."

The basic concept expressed in the net lending section of the NIPAs is that when CFC exceeds actual investment expenditures, governments have a positive net cash flow and can lend (or repay debt); if gross investment exceeds CFC, government must borrow to finance the difference, indicating negative net cash flow and requiring borrowing. (As will be seen below in the definitions, capital transfer and purchase accounts also enter into the calculation of net lending.)

The federal *budget* accounts (see Tables 6-14 and 6-15) do not draw a distinction between current and capital spending. The budget accounts of individual state and local governments typically separate capital from current spending and allow capital spending to be financed by borrowing—even when deficit financing of current spending is constitutionally forbidden. However, neither federal nor state and local government budget accounts typically show depreciation as a current expense in the way that is standard to private-sector accounting or in the way adopted in the NIPAs.

Notes on the data

Government receipts and expenditures data are derived from the U.S. government accounts and from Census Bureau censuses and surveys of the finances of state and local governments. However, BEA makes a number of adjustments to the data to convert them from fiscal year to calendar year and quarter bases and to agree with the concepts of national income accounting. Data are converted from the cash basis usually found in financial statements to the timing bases required for the NIPAs. In the NIPAs, receipts from businesses are generally on an accrual basis, purchases of goods and services are recorded when delivered, and receipts from and transfer payments to persons are on a cash basis. The federal receipts and expenditure data from the NIPAs in Table 6-1 therefore differ from the federal receipts and outlay data in Table 6-14. Among other differences, the latter are by fiscal year and are on a modified cash basis.

The NIPA data on government receipts and expenditures record transactions of governments (federal, state, and local) with other U.S. residents and foreigners. Each entry in the government receipts and expenditures account has a corresponding entry elsewhere in the NIPAs. Thus, for example, the sum of personal current taxes received by federal and state and local governments (Tables 6-1 and 6-8) is equal to personal current taxes paid, as shown in personal income (Table 4-1).

Definitions: general

In the 2003 revision of the NIPAs, several items appear separately that were previously treated as "negative expenditures" and netted against other items on the expenditures side. This grossing-up of the accounts raises both receipts and outlays and has no effect on net saving. Grossing-up has been applied to taxes from the rest of the world, interest receipts (back to 1960 for the federal government and back to 1946 for state and local governments), dividends, and subsidies and the current surplus of government enterprises (back to 1959).

Definitions: current receipts

Current tax receipts includes personal current taxes, taxes on production and imports, taxes on corporate income and (for the federal government only) taxes from the rest of the world. The category *total tax receipts* does not include *contributions for government social insurance,* which are the taxes levied to finance Social Security, unemployment insurance, and Medicare, and are included in *receipts* in the budget accounts (Table 6-14). Analysts using NIPA data to analyze tax burdens as they

are usually understood should add *contributions for government social insurance* to *tax receipts* for this purpose.

Personal current taxes is personal tax payments from residents of the United States that are not chargeable to business expense. Personal taxes consist of taxes on income, including on realized net capital gains, and on personal property. Personal contributions for social insurance are not included in this category. As of the 1999 revisions, estate and gift taxes are classified as capital transfers and are no longer included in personal current taxes. However, estate and gift taxes continue to be included in federal government receipts in Table 6-14.

Taxes on production and imports in the case of the federal government consists of *excise taxes* and *customs duties*. In the case of state and local governments, these taxes include *sales taxes*, *property taxes* (including residential real estate taxes), and *Other* taxes such as motor vehicle licenses, severance taxes, and special assessments. Before the 2003 revision, all of these taxes were components of "indirect business tax and nontax liabilities."

Taxes on corporate income covers federal, state, and local government taxes on all corporate income subject to taxes. This taxable income includes capital gains and other income excluded from NIPA profits. The taxes are measured on an accrual basis, net of applicable tax credits. Federal corporate income tax receipts in the NIPAs include, but show separately, receipts from *Federal Reserve Banks* that represent the return of the surplus earnings of the Federal Reserve system. (In the budget accounts in Table 6-14, these are classified not as corporate taxes but as the major component of "Miscellaneous receipts.")

Contributions for social insurance includes employer and personal contributions for Social Security, Medicare, unemployment insurance, and other government social insurance programs. As of the 1999 revisions, contributions to government employee retirement plans are no longer included in this category; these plans are now treated the same as private pension plans.

Income receipts on assets consists of *interest, dividends* and *rents and royalties.*

Interest receipts (1960 to the present for federal government; 1946 to the present for state and local governments) consists of monetary and imputed interest received on loans and investments. In the NIPAs, this no longer includes interest received by government employee retirement plans, which is now credited to personal income. However, such interest received is still deducted from interest paid in the budget accounts that are shown in Table 6-14. Before the indicated years, receipts are deducted from aggregate interest payments in the NIPAs. Hence, they are not shown as receipts, and net interest is presented on the expenditure side. In the federal budget accounts in Table 6-14, net interest (total interest expenditures minus interest receipts) is the interest "expenditure" concept used throughout the period covered.

Current transfer receipts includes receipts in categories other than those specified above from persons and business. In the case of state and local government accounts (Table 6-8), it also includes *federal grants-in-aid,* a component of federal expenditures. Receipts from *business* and *persons* were previously included with income taxes in "tax and nontax payments." They consist of federal deposit insurance premiums and other nontaxes (largely fines and regulatory and inspection fees), state and local fines and other nontaxes (largely donations and tobacco settlements), and net insurance settlements paid to governments as policyholders.

The *current surplus of government enterprises* is the current operating revenue and subsidies received from other levels of government by such enterprises less their current expenses. No deduction is made for depreciation charges or net interest paid. Before 1959, this category of receipts is treated as a deduction from subsidies. In the <u>federal</u> NIPA accounts before 1959, there is no entry shown for the current surplus on the receipts side, and on the expenditure side, there is an entry for subsidies, which is net of the current surplus. (Subsidies are usually a larger amount than the enterprise surplus in the federal accounts.) In the <u>state and local</u> NIPA accounts before 1959, there is an entry for the surplus on the receipts side, which is net of subsidies. (Subsidies are typically smaller than the enterprise surplus in state and local finance.)

Definitions: consumption expenditures, saving, and gross investment

Government consumption expenditures is expenditures by governments (federal or state and local) on services for current consumption. It includes *compensation of general government employees* (including employer contributions to government employee retirement plans, as of the 1999 revision); an allowance for *consumption of general government fixed capital (CFC),* including R&D and software (depreciation); and *intermediate goods and services purchased.* (See the general discussion above for an explanation.) The estimated value of *own-account investment*—investment goods, including R&D and software, produced by government resources and purchased inputs—is subtracted here, and added to *government gross investment. Sales to other sectors*—primarily tuition payments received from individuals for higher education and charges for medical care to individuals—are also deducted, since these are counted elsewhere in the accounts, as (for example) personal consumption expenditures for those categories.

Government social benefits consists of payments to individuals for which the individuals do not render current services. Examples are Social Security benefits, Medicare, Medicaid, unemployment benefits, and public assistance. Retirement payments to retired government employees from their pension plans are no longer included in this category.

Government social benefits to persons consists of payments to persons residing in the United States (with a corresponding entry of an equal amount in the personal income receipts accounts). Government social benefits to the *rest of the world* appear only in the federal government account, and are transfers, mainly retirement benefits, to former residents of the United States.

Other current transfer payments (federal account only) includes *grants-in-aid to state and local governments* and *grants to the rest of the world*—military and nonmilitary grants to foreign governments.

Federal grants-in-aid comprises net payments from federal to state and local governments that are made to help finance programs such as health (Medicaid), public assistance (the old Aid to Families with Dependent Children and the new Temporary Assistance for Needy Families), and education. Investment grants to state and local governments for highways, transit, air transportation, and water treatment plants are now classified as capital transfers and are no longer included in this category. However, such investment grants continue to be included as federal government outlays in Table 6-14.

Interest payments is monetary interest paid to U.S. and foreign persons and businesses and to foreign governments for public debt and other financial obligations. As noted above, from 1960 forward for the federal government and from 1946 forward for state and local governments, this represents gross total (not net) interest payments. Before those dates in the NIPAs, and throughout the federal budget accounts presented in Table 6-14, net instead of aggregate interest is shown; that is, gross total interest paid less interest received.

Subsidies are monetary grants paid by government to business, including to government enterprises at another level of government. Subsidies no longer include federal maritime construction subsidies, which are now classified as a capital transfer. For years prior to 1959, subsidies continue to be presented net of the *current surplus of government enterprises*, because detailed data to separate the series are not available for this period. See the entry for *current surplus of government enterprises*, described above, for explanation of the pre-1959 treatment of this item in the federal accounts in *Business Statistics*, which differs from the treatment in the state and local accounts.

Net saving, NIPA (surplus+/deficit-), is the sum of current receipts less the sum of current expenditures. This is shown separately for *social insurance funds* (which, in the case of the federal government, include Social Security and other trust funds) and *other* (all other government).

Gross government investment consists of general government and government enterprise expenditures for fixed assets—*structures, equipment,* and *intellectual property* (R&D and software). The expenditures include the compensation of government employees producing the assets and the purchase of goods and services as intermediate inputs to be incorporated in the assets. Government inventory investment is included in government consumption expenditures.

Capital consumption. Consumption of fixed capital (CFC; economic depreciation) is included in government consumption expenditures as a partial measure of the value of the services of general government fixed assets, including structures, equipment, R&D, and software.

Definitions: output, lending and borrowing, and net investment

In Tables 6-5 and 6-10, current-dollar values of gross output and value added of government are presented, as described in the general discussion above. *Gross output* of government is the sum of the *intermediate goods and services purchased* by government and the value added by government as a producing industry. *Value added* consists of compensation of general government employees and consumption of general government fixed capital. Since this depreciation allowance is the only entry on the product side of the accounts measuring the output associated with such capital, a zero <u>net</u> return on these assets is implicitly assumed.

Gross output minus own-account investment and sales to other sectors (see the previous description) yields *government consumption expenditures*, which represents the contribution of government consumption spending to final demands in GDP.

Net lending (net borrowing -) consists of current *net saving* as defined above, plus the *consumption of fixed capital* (CFC, from the current expenditure account), minus *gross investment*, plus *capital transfer receipts*, and minus *capital transfer payments* and *net purchases of non-produced assets.* (If this definition sounds somehow counter-intuitive, it should be remembered that "subtraction" in this context means "increasing the deficit [negative value] which must be financed.)

Capital transfer receipts and *payments* include grants between levels of government, or between government and the private sector, associated with acquisition or disposal of assets rather than with current consumption expenditures. Examples are federal grants to state and local government for highways, transit, air transportation, and water treatment plants; federal shipbuilding subsidies and other subsidies to businesses; and lump-sum payments to amortize the unfunded liability of the Uniformed Services Retiree Health Care Fund. Government capital transfer receipts include estate and gift taxes, which are no longer included in personal tax receipts. (Federal estate and gift taxes are shown in Table 6-14, where they are reported on a fiscal year basis, and are similar in order of magnitude to the calendar year values for federal capital transfer receipts in Table 6-5.)

Non-produced assets are land and radio spectrum. Unusually large negative entries for net purchases of non-produced assets

in some recent years result from the negative purchase–that is, the sale–of spectrum.

The values of *net investment* shown in these tables are calculated by the editor, as gross investment minus the consumption of fixed capital.

Definitions: chain-type quantity indexes

Chain-type quantity indexes represent changes over time in real values, removing the effects of inflation. Indexes for key categories in the government expenditure accounts, as well as for government gross output, value added, and intermediate goods and services purchased, use the chain formula described in the notes and definitions for Chapter 1 and are expressed as index numbers, with the average for the year 2009 equal to 100.

Data availability

The most recent data are published each month in the Survey of Current Business. Current and historical data may be obtained from the BEA Web site at <http://www.bea.gov> and the STAT-USA subscription Web site at <http://www.stat-usa.gov>.

References

See the references regarding the 2013 comprehensive revision of the NIPAs in the notes and definitions for Chapter 1. NIPA concepts and their differences from the budget estimates are discussed in "NIPA Estimates of the Federal Sector and the Federal Budget Estimates," *Survey of Current Business,* March 2007, p. 11.

For information about the classification of government expenditures into current consumption and gross investment, first undertaken in the 1996 comprehensive revisions, see the Survey of Current Business article, "Preview of the Comprehensive Revision of the National Income and Product Accounts: Recognition of Government Investment and Incorporation of a New Methodology for Calculating Depreciation" September 1995. Other sources of information about the NIPAs are listed in the notes and definitions for Chapter 1.

Tables 6-12 and 6-13 State Government Current Receipts and Expenditures; Local Government Current Receipts and Expenditures

SOURCE: BUREAU OF ECONOMIC ANALYSIS (BEA)

In the standard presentation of the state and local sector of the national income and product accounts (NIPAs) such as in Tables 6-8 through 6-11 above, state and local governments are combined. Annual measures for aggregate state governments and aggregate local governments are also available on the BEA Web site. These measures are shown in Tables 6-12 and 6-13. The definitions are the same as in the other NIPA tables described above.

The data shown here now reflect the 2013 comprehensive revision, affecting some concepts, that has been incorporated in the quarterly and annual data elsewhere in this chapter and this volume.

Two categories not shown in Table 6-8 appear in each table, detailing inter-governmental flows that are consolidated in Table 6-8. State government receipts include not only *federal grants-in-aid* but also *local grants-in-aid*, and state government expenditures include *grants-in-aid to local governments*. Local government receipts include not only *federal grants-in-aid* but also *state grants-in-aid*, and local government expenditures include *grants-in-aid to state governments*. To make room for these columns, the components *current surplus of government enterprises* and *subsidies* are not shown, though they are included in total current receipts and total current expenditures respectively.

These measures are described in "Receipts and Expenditures of State Governments and of Local Governments," *Survey of Current Business*, October 2005. Data back to 1959 are available on the BEA Web site at <http://www.bea.gov>.

Tables 6-14A and 6-14B

Federal Government Receipts and Outlays by Fiscal Year; The Federal Budget and GDP

SOURCE: U.S. OFFICE OF MANAGEMENT AND BUDGET

These data on federal government receipts and outlays are on a modified cash basis and are from the *Budget of the United States Government: Historical Tables*. The data are by federal fiscal years, which are defined as July 1 through June 30 through 1976 and October 1 through September 30 for 1977 and subsequent years. They are identified by the year of the final fiscal quarter—i.e., the year from July 1, 1975, through June 30, 1976, is identified as Fiscal 1976, and the year from October 1, 1976, through June 30, 1977, is identified as Fiscal Year 1977. The period July 1 through September 30, 1976, is a separate fiscal period known as the transition quarter (TQ) and is not included in any fiscal year.

There are numerous differences in both timing and definition between these estimates and the NIPA estimates in Tables 6-1 through 6-7. See the notes and definitions for those tables for the definitional differences that were introduced with the 1999 comprehensive revision of the NIPAs.

Definitions

The definitions for these tables are not affected by the 2013, 2003, or 1999 changes in the government sectors of the NIPAs.

Table references will be given indicating the source of each item in the *Historical Tables*; for example, "HT Table 1.1."

Receipts consist of gifts and of taxes or other compulsory payments to the government. Other types of payments to the government are netted against outlays. (HT Table 1.1)

Outlays occur when the federal government liquidates an obligation through a cash payment or when interest accrues on public debt issues. Beginning with the data for 1992, outlays include the subsidy cost of direct and guaranteed loans made. Before 1992, the costs and repayments associated with such loans are recorded on a cash basis. As noted previously, various types of nontax receipts are netted against cash outlays. These accounts do not distinguish between investment outlays and current consumption and do not include allowances for depreciation. (HT Table 1.1)

The *total budget surplus (deficit-)* is receipts minus outlays. It is sometimes presented, including in Table 6-14, as composed of two components, *on-budget and off-budget*. By law, two government programs that are included in the federal receipts and outlays totals are "off-budget"—old-age, survivors, and disability insurance (Social Security) and the Postal Service. The former accounts for nearly all of the off-budget activity. The *surplus (deficit-)* not accounted for by these two programs is the on-budget surplus or deficit. The *on-budget deficit* is based on an arbitrary distinction and is not customarily referred to as the *budget deficit*, a term reserved in customary use for the total deficit. (HT Table 1.1)

Sources of financing is the means by which the total deficit is financed or the surplus is distributed. By definition, sources of financing sum to the total deficit or surplus with the sign reversed. The principal source is *borrowing from the public*, shown as a positive number, that is, the increase in the debt held by the public. (This entry is calculated by the editors as the change in the debt held by the public as shown in HT Table 7.1.) When there is a budget surplus, as in fiscal years 1998 to 2001, this provides resources for debt reduction, which is indicated by a minus sign in this column. *Other financing* includes drawdown (or buildup, shown here with a minus sign) in Treasury cash balances, seigniorage on coins, direct and guaranteed loan account cash transactions, and miscellaneous other transactions. Large negative "other financing" in 2008 through 2010 resulted from direct loans and asset purchases under TARP and other emergency financial procedures; in other words, the government borrowed from the public to undertake these loans and asset purchases, but they are not included in budget expenditures or the budget deficit. *Other financing* is calculated by the editors, by reversing the sign of the surplus/deficit—so that the deficit becomes a positive number—and subtracting the value of borrowing from the public.

Some of the categories of *receipts by source* are self-explanatory. *Employment taxes and contributions* includes taxes for old-age, survivors, and disability insurance (Social Security), hospital insurance (Medicare), and railroad retirement funds. *Other retirement contributions* includes the employee share of payments for retirement pensions, mainly those for federal employees. *Excise taxes* includes federal taxes on alcohol, tobacco, telephone service, and transportation fuels, as well as taxes funding smaller programs such as black lung disability and vaccine injury compensation. *Miscellaneous receipts* includes deposits of earnings by the Federal Reserve system and all other receipts. (HT Tables 2.1, 2.4, and 2.5)

Outlays by function presents outlays according to the major purpose of the spending. Functional classifications cut across departmental and agency lines. Most categories of offsetting receipts are netted against cash outlays in the appropriate function, which explains how recorded outlays in *energy* and *commerce and housing credit* (which, as its name suggests, includes loan programs) can be negative. There is also a category of "undistributed offsetting receipts" (not shown), always with a negative sign, that includes proceeds from the sale or lease of assets and payments from federal agencies to federal retirement funds and to the Social Security and Medicare trust funds. Note that *Social Security* is recorded separately from other *income security* outlays, and *Medicare* separately from other *health* outlays. (HT Table 3.1) For further explanation, consult the *Budget of the United States Government.*

In order to provide authoritative comparisons of these budget values with the overall size of the economy, a special calculation of gross domestic product by fiscal year is supplied to the Office of Management and Budget by the BEA, and is shown in Table 6-14B. That table also displays selected budget aggregates in dollar values and as a percent of GDP. (HT Tables 1.2, 1.3, 2.3, and 3.1)

Data availability and references

Definitions, budget concepts, and historical data are from *Budget of the United States Government for Fiscal Year 2015: Historical Tables*, available on the Office of Management and Budget Web site at <http://www.whitehouse.gov/omb/Budget/historicals>

Similarly defined data for the latest month, the year-ago month, and the current and year-ago fiscal year to date are published in the *Monthly Treasury Statement* prepared by the Financial Management Service, U.S. Department of the Treasury. For those who need up-to-date budget information, this publication is available on the Financial Management Service Web site at <http://www.fms.treas.gov>. As these monthly figures are never revised to agree with the final annual data, they are not published in this volume.

Table 6-15

Federal Government Debt by Fiscal Year

SOURCE: U.S. OFFICE OF MANAGEMENT AND BUDGET

Debt outstanding at the end of each fiscal year is from the *Budget of the United States Government.* Most securities are

recorded at sales price plus amortized discount or less amortized premium.

Definitions

Federal government debt held by the public consists of all federal debt held outside the federal government accounts—by individuals, financial institutions (including the Federal Reserve Banks), and foreign individuals, businesses, and central banks. It does not include federal debt held by federal government trust funds such as the Social Security trust fund. The level and change of the ratio of this debt to the value of gross domestic product (GDP) provide proportional measures of the impact of federal borrowing on credit markets. (HT Table 7.1) This measure of debt held by the public is very similar in concept and scope to the total federal government credit market debt outstanding in the flow-of-funds accounts, shown in *Business Statistics* in Table 12-5; however, it is not identical, being priced somewhat differently, and is shown here in Chapter 6 on a fiscal year rather than calendar year basis.

Gross federal debt—total. This is the total debt owed by the U.S. Treasury. It includes a small amount of matured debt. (HT Table 7.1)

Debt held by Social Security funds is the sum of the end-year trust fund balances for old age and survivors insurance and disability insurance. The separate disability trust fund begins in 1957. (HT Table 13.1)

Debt held by other U.S. government accounts is calculated by the editors by subtracting the Social Security debt holdings from the total debt held by federal government accounts, which is shown in HT Table 7.1. It includes the balances in all the other trust funds, including the Medicare funds, federal employee retirement funds, and the highway trust fund.

Debt held by the Federal Reserve System is the total value of Treasury securities held by the 12 Federal Reserve Banks, which are acquired in open market operations that carry out monetary policy. (HT Table 7.1)

Debt held by private investors is calculated by subtracting the Federal Reserve debt from the total debt held by the public, and is shown as "Debt Held by the Public: Other" in HT Table 7.1.

Debt held by foreign residents is based on surveys by the Treasury Department. (Table 5-7, *Budget of the United States for Fiscal Year 2015: Analytical Perspectives.*)

Debt held by domestic investors is calculated by the editors by subtracting the foreign-held debt from the total debt held by private investors.

The "debt subject to statutory limitation," not shown here, is close to the gross federal debt in concept and size, but there are some relatively minor definitional differences specified by law. The debt limit can only be changed by an Act of Congress. For information about the debt subject to limit and other debt subjects, see the latest *Budget of the United States Government: Historical Statistics* and *Analytical Perspectives.*

Data availability and references

For the end-of-fiscal-year data, see *Historical Tables* and *Analytical Perspectives* in the *Budget of the United States Government*, which is available on the OMB Web site at <http://www.whitehouse.gov/omb/Budget>. In the *Analytical Perspectives,* debt analysis and data are included in the "Economic and Budget Analysis" section.

Recent quarterly data, measured on a somewhat different basis, are found in the *Treasury Bulletin* in the chapter on "Ownership of Federal Securities (OFS)," in Tables OFS-1 and OFS-2. The *Treasury Bulletin* can be accessed on the Internet at <http://www.fms.treas.gov/bulletin>. Holdings by Social Security funds are also available in the *Bulletin* in the chapter on "Federal Debt," Table FD-3. The Disability Fund is listed separately from the Old-Age and Survivors Fund.

Table 6-17

Government Employment

SOURCE: U.S. DEPARTMENT OF LABOR, BUREAU OF LABOR STATISTICS (SEE NOTES AND DEFINITIONS FOR TABLE 10-8).

Government payroll employment includes federal, state, and local activities such as legislative, executive, and judicial functions, as well as all government owned and government operated business enterprises, establishments, and institutions (arsenals, navy yards, hospitals, etc.), and government force account construction. The figures relate to civilian employment only. The Bureau of Labor Statistics (BLS) considers regular fulltime teachers (private and governmental) to be employed during the summer vacation period, regardless of whether they are specifically paid in those months.

Employment in federal government establishments reflects employee counts as of the pay period containing the 12th of the month. Federal government employment excludes employees of the Central Intelligence Agency and the National Security Agency.

CHAPTER 7: U.S. FOREIGN TRADE AND FINANCE

Section 7a: Foreign Transactions in the National Income and Product Accounts

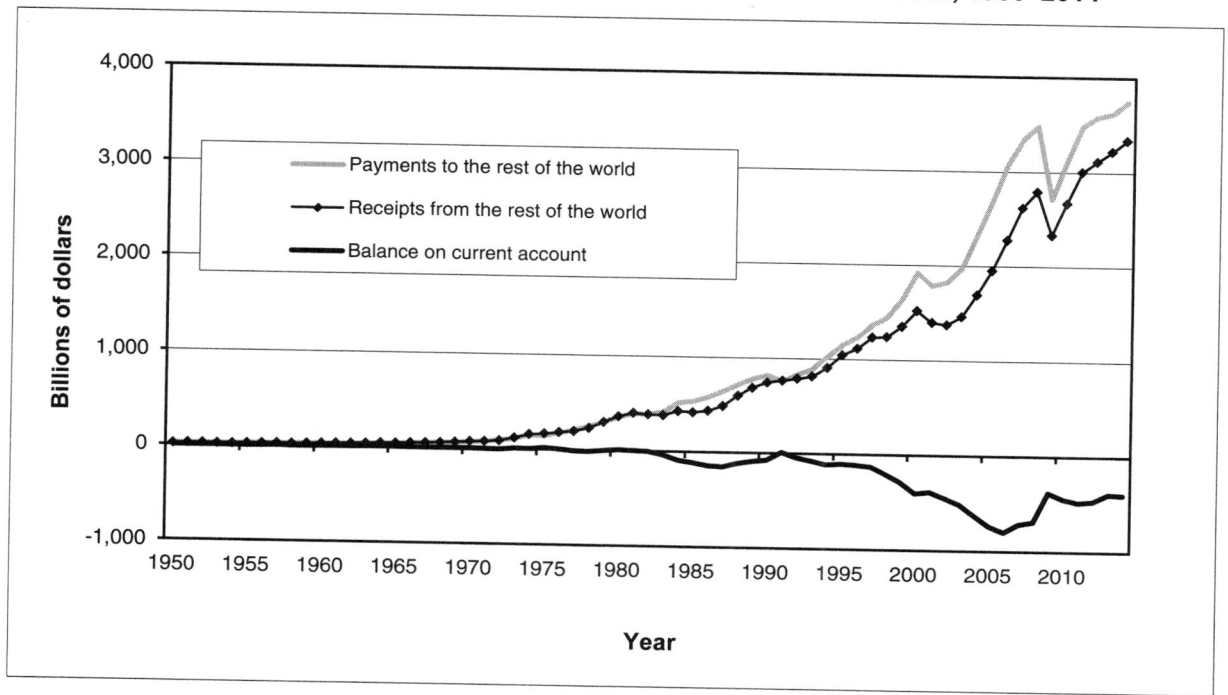

Figure 7-1: Receipts, Payments, and Balance on Current Account, 1950–2014

- Beginning in 1983, chronic current-account deficits in U.S. transactions with the rest of the world have emerged and increased, requiring increasing net capital inflows from abroad to finance them. The only current-account surplus since then occurred in 1991, when payments from other countries financed most of the cost of the first Gulf War. In 2006 the NIPA deficit reached a record $804 billion, 5.8 percent of GDP. Since 2006, the current account deficit has declined by half. (Tables 7-1 and 1-1A)

- U.S. current-account deficits typically diminish somewhat during recessions, as receipts hold up somewhat better than payments. The deficit diminished to $377 billion, 2.6 percent of GDP, in 2009, the recession's low point. The gap was $401 billion in 2014, 2.3 percent of GDP. (Tables 7-1 and 1-1A)

- Looking at quarterly data on the real volume of flows of goods and services in U.S. trade, the quantity index for exports of goods and services fell below 100 to 96.7 in the first quarter of 2009 but rebounded to 133.77, an increase of 38 percent in the fourth quarter of 2014. Imports of goods and services, also in real terms suffered the same trend as exports. In the second quarter of 2009 it decreased to 96.09 but rose to 130.47 in the fourth quarter of 2014, a 35.8 percent increase. (Table 7-2)

Table 7-1. Foreign Transactions in the National Income and Product Accounts

(Billions of dollars, quarterly data are at seasonally adjusted annual rates.)   **NIPA Table 4.1**

Year and quarter	Current receipts from the rest of the world					Current payments to the rest of the world						Balance on current account, NIPAs	Net lending or net borrowing (-), NIPAs
	Total	Exports of goods and services			Income receipts	Total	Imports of goods and services			Income payments	Current taxes and transfer payments, net		
		Goods 1		Services 1			Goods 1		Services 1				
		Durable	Nondurable				Durable	Nondurable					
1950	14.5	5.1	5.1	2.1	2.2	16.4	3.0	6.1	2.5	0.7	4.0	-1.8	-1.8
1951	19.9	6.6	7.6	2.9	2.8	19.0	3.8	7.4	3.4	0.9	3.5	0.9	0.9
1952	19.3	6.9	6.5	3.0	2.9	18.7	4.1	6.7	4.5	0.9	2.6	0.6	0.6
1953	18.2	6.9	5.5	2.9	2.8	19.5	4.1	6.9	5.0	0.9	2.5	-1.3	-1.3
1954	18.9	7.1	5.8	2.9	3.0	18.7	3.6	6.7	5.1	0.9	2.3	0.2	0.2
1955	21.2	8.2	6.2	3.3	3.5	20.8	4.5	7.1	5.7	1.1	2.6	0.4	0.4
1956	25.2	9.8	7.8	3.7	3.9	22.5	5.2	7.6	6.1	1.1	2.5	2.7	2.7
1957	28.3	10.9	8.6	4.5	4.3	23.6	5.3	8.0	6.7	1.2	2.4	4.7	4.7
1958	24.4	9.0	7.4	4.1	3.9	23.6	5.0	8.0	7.1	1.2	2.4	0.8	0.8
1959	27.0	8.9	7.5	6.3	4.3	28.3	6.6	8.7	7.0	1.5	4.4	-1.3	-1.3
1960	31.9	11.3	9.2	6.6	4.9	28.8	6.4	8.9	7.6	1.8	4.1	3.2	3.2
1961	32.9	11.5	9.4	6.7	5.3	28.7	6.0	9.0	7.6	1.8	4.2	4.2	4.2
1962	35.0	12.0	9.7	7.4	5.9	31.2	6.9	9.9	8.1	1.8	4.4	3.8	3.8
1963	37.6	12.7	10.7	7.7	6.5	32.7	7.4	10.3	8.4	2.1	4.5	4.9	4.9
1964	42.3	14.7	12.1	8.3	7.2	34.8	8.4	11.0	8.7	2.3	4.4	7.5	7.5
1965	45.0	15.8	12.1	9.2	7.9	38.9	10.4	11.8	9.3	2.6	4.7	6.2	6.2
1966	49.0	17.7	13.4	9.8	8.1	45.2	13.3	13.1	10.7	3.0	5.1	3.8	3.8
1967	52.1	18.6	13.9	10.9	8.7	48.7	14.5	13.2	12.2	3.3	5.5	3.5	3.5
1968	58.0	21.2	14.5	12.2	10.1	56.5	18.8	15.1	12.6	4.0	5.9	1.5	1.5
1969	63.7	23.9	14.8	13.2	11.8	62.1	20.8	16.1	13.7	5.7	5.9	1.6	1.6
1970	72.5	27.4	17.7	14.7	12.8	68.8	22.8	18.1	14.9	6.4	6.6	3.7	3.7
1971	77.0	27.9	18.3	16.8	14.0	76.7	26.6	19.9	15.8	6.4	7.9	0.3	0.3
1972	87.1	31.4	21.2	18.3	16.3	91.2	33.3	23.6	17.3	7.7	9.2	-4.0	-4.1
1973	118.8	42.3	33.5	19.5	23.5	109.9	40.8	31.0	19.3	10.9	7.9	8.9	8.8
1974	156.5	57.7	45.8	23.2	29.8	150.5	50.3	54.2	22.9	14.3	8.7	6.0	5.9
1975	166.7	65.2	47.3	26.2	28.0	146.9	45.6	53.4	23.7	15.0	9.1	19.8	19.8
1976	181.9	70.9	50.6	28.0	32.4	174.8	56.8	67.8	26.5	15.5	8.1	7.1	7.0
1977	196.6	74.4	54.0	30.9	37.2	207.5	69.2	83.4	29.8	16.9	8.1	-10.9	-11.0
1978	233.1	87.5	62.4	37.0	46.3	245.8	89.0	88.4	34.8	24.7	8.8	-12.6	-12.7
1979	298.5	109.6	77.6	42.9	68.3	299.6	100.4	112.3	39.9	36.4	10.6	-1.2	-1.3
1980	359.9	135.7	94.8	50.3	79.1	351.4	111.9	136.6	45.3	44.9	12.6	8.5	8.4
1981	397.3	143.2	102.0	60.0	92.0	393.9	126.0	141.8	49.9	59.1	17.0	3.4	3.3
1982	384.2	128.5	94.1	60.7	101.0	387.5	125.1	125.4	52.6	64.5	19.8	-3.3	-3.4
1983	378.9	123.8	90.3	62.9	101.9	413.9	147.3	125.4	56.0	64.8	20.5	-35.1	-35.2
1984	424.2	135.2	96.1	71.1	121.9	514.3	192.4	143.9	68.8	85.6	23.6	-90.1	-90.2
1985	415.9	139.9	87.6	75.7	112.7	530.2	204.2	139.1	73.9	87.3	25.7	-114.3	-114.4
1986	432.3	145.3	86.1	89.6	111.3	575.0	238.8	131.2	82.9	94.4	27.8	-142.7	-142.8
1987	487.2	166.9	98.6	98.4	123.3	641.3	264.2	150.6	93.9	105.8	26.8	-154.1	-154.2
1988	596.7	211.9	120.1	112.5	152.1	712.4	294.8	157.3	101.9	129.5	29.0	-115.7	-115.9
1989	682.0	242.5	132.2	129.5	177.7	774.3	310.3	174.5	106.2	152.9	30.4	-92.4	-92.7
1990	740.7	265.3	138.0	148.6	188.8	815.6	314.5	193.5	121.7	154.2	31.7	-74.9	-82.3
1991	763.3	285.6	144.6	164.8	168.4	755.4	315.5	185.2	122.8	136.8	-4.9	7.9	2.6
1992	785.1	304.2	151.1	177.7	152.1	830.7	346.7	198.2	122.9	121.0	41.9	-45.6	-44.3
1993	810.4	317.9	149.9	187.1	155.6	888.9	386.4	206.4	127.2	123.6	45.4	-78.5	-79.4
1994	905.5	353.8	164.6	202.6	184.5	1 020.2	454.0	222.8	136.6	160.7	46.1	-114.7	-116.0
1995	1 042.6	398.6	193.8	220.4	229.8	1 147.7	510.8	246.7	145.1	201.1	44.1	-105.1	-105.5
1996	1 114.0	426.4	202.4	238.8	246.4	1 228.1	533.4	274.1	156.5	214.6	49.5	-114.1	-114.3
1997	1 233.9	488.4	211.5	253.9	280.1	1 363.2	588.5	297.1	170.1	256.0	51.4	-129.3	-129.8
1998	1 239.8	492.4	200.2	260.4	286.8	1 444.3	637.7	293.0	184.9	268.5	60.0	-204.5	-204.7
1999	1 313.4	508.7	203.0	280.3	321.4	1 600.4	715.8	335.4	197.4	294.3	57.5	-287.0	-291.5
2000	1 479.5	573.4	223.9	299.6	382.7	1 883.8	822.9	428.6	221.2	345.7	65.4	-404.2	-404.6
2001	1 352.0	525.3	218.6	282.9	325.3	1 741.0	757.7	419.0	218.7	273.5	72.1	-389.0	-376.0
2002	1 318.3	492.8	220.4	289.3	315.8	1 769.2	774.2	425.1	229.6	267.2	73.0	-450.9	-451.4
2003	1 396.4	501.8	239.6	298.9	356.1	1 912.9	806.3	489.9	247.7	289.0	80.0	-516.6	-518.7
2004	1 633.0	565.7	268.7	347.1	451.4	2 259.4	936.5	575.0	289.1	362.3	96.4	-626.4	-623.7
2005	1 884.7	629.8	296.8	382.3	575.8	2 627.5	1 025.7	693.7	310.7	483.2	114.2	-742.9	-730.0
2006	2 200.6	715.0	334.6	426.7	724.2	3 004.6	1 131.2	768.5	347.6	656.6	100.7	-804.0	-806.1
2007	2 540.3	782.9	383.5	498.2	875.7	3 257.9	1 176.2	827.5	379.4	750.1	124.7	-717.6	-717.5
2008	2 698.9	829.2	469.6	543.1	856.9	3 385.0	1 163.0	986.4	415.6	684.9	135.1	-686.1	-680.7
2009	2 236.6	671.6	393.5	522.6	648.9	2 613.9	893.8	696.5	392.9	497.8	132.9	-377.3	-377.8
2010	2 572.4	801.4	478.2	572.7	720.0	3 020.3	1 106.9	842.9	415.2	514.1	141.2	-447.9	-448.6
2011	2 899.0	894.0	572.9	639.5	792.6	3 379.5	1 238.7	1 006.0	441.6	546.0	147.2	-480.5	-482.1
2012	2 988.0	940.9	586.2	667.0	793.8	3 470.2	1 328.7	977.4	456.4	566.5	141.3	-482.2	-475.7
2013	3 072.6	957.3	605.5	699.4	810.4	3 494.8	1 360.5	941.7	468.1	586.1	138.3	-422.2	-423.0
2014	2 341.9	994.9	623.1	723.9	854.3	3 742.5	1 450.1	938.4	483.4	591.2	177.9	-401.1	-401.6
2012													
1st quarter	3 082.4	943.7	567.4	658.4	809.7	3 594.4	1 327.9	1 003.4	452.9	558.5	251.6	-512.0	-512.6
2nd quarter	3 094.0	940.9	589.0	669.8	786.5	3 589.5	1 332.9	989.8	458.0	555.0	253.8	-495.6	-496.9
3rd quarter	3 132.5	938.3	599.3	671.7	804.9	3 568.6	1 325.3	959.3	459.9	567.8	256.3	-436.2	-438.4
4th quarter	3 146.7	936.5	588.6	688.8	805.0	3 575.7	1 327.9	956.7	461.3	574.4	255.5	-428.9	-398.7
2013													
1st quarter	3 160.7	940.0	589.9	696.7	805.2	3 602.0	1 341.0	953.3	461.4	584.1	262.1	-441.3	-441.9
2nd quarter	3 189.2	960.6	580.7	696.3	825.8	3 611.1	1 354.7	942.4	468.2	578.6	267.2	-422.0	-423.3
3rd quarter	3 229.6	953.4	607.4	703.5	833.2	3 621.8	1 366.1	940.2	470.5	569.3	275.7	-392.2	-393.2
4th quarter	3 305.1	971.3	640.4	712.8	840.5	3 632.7	1 379.4	930.3	479.0	571.2	272.8	-327.6	-328.1
2014													
1st quarter	3 281.7	967.1	618.4	716.0	840.0	3 684.4	1 393.0	964.6	473.3	581.2	272.4	-402.7	-403.3
2nd quarter	3 383.4	993.2	634.8	728.2	850.4	3 757.2	1 453.3	950.4	483.3	593.3	276.9	-373.8	-374.2
3rd quarter	3 361.1	1 010.4	631.5	718.7	869.7	3 753.7	1 460.6	932.1	482.5	597.8	280.7	-392.7	-393.1
4th quarter	3 339.1	1 008.8	607.8	732.9	857.0	3 774.4	1 493.5	906.5	494.6	592.3	287.5	-435.3	-435.7

1 Exports and imports of certain goods, primarily military equipment purchased and sold by the federal government, are included in services. Beginning with 1986, repairs and alterations of equipment are reclassified from goods to services.

Table 7-2. Chain-Type Quantity Indexes for Exports and Imports of Goods and Services

(Index numbers, 2009 = 100; quarterly indexes are seasonally adjusted.)

NIPA Table 4.2.3

Year and quarter	Exports of goods and services					Imports of goods and services				
	Total	Goods [1]			Services [1]	Total	Goods [1]			Services [1]
		Total	Durable	Nondurable			Total	Durable	Nondurable	
1970	11.78	11.31	8.61	19.00	13.35	12.79	11.29	6.68	22.57	20.40
1971	11.99	11.30	8.57	19.09	14.32	13.47	12.24	7.36	23.96	19.82
1972	12.92	12.52	9.47	21.26	14.26	14.99	13.90	8.46	26.76	20.66
1973	15.35	15.59	11.93	26.06	14.51	15.68	14.89	9.01	28.87	19.97
1974	16.57	16.92	13.82	26.04	15.30	15.33	14.47	9.04	27.07	19.94
1975	16.46	16.57	13.56	25.42	16.21	13.62	12.65	7.39	25.11	19.08
1976	17.18	17.42	13.81	27.95	16.38	16.29	15.51	9.05	30.81	20.40
1977	17.60	17.76	13.85	29.11	17.12	18.07	17.40	10.25	34.32	21.41
1978	19.45	19.60	15.35	31.97	19.04	19.63	18.96	11.84	35.44	22.94
1979	21.38	21.68	17.30	34.42	20.39	19.96	19.28	12.11	35.85	23.25
1980	23.68	24.34	19.35	38.86	21.24	18.63	17.85	12.21	30.86	22.74
1981	23.97	24.18	18.74	40.05	23.32	19.12	18.22	13.23	29.94	24.07
1982	22.14	22.14	16.39	39.04	22.30	18.88	17.76	13.38	28.19	25.35
1983	21.57	21.42	16.00	37.33	22.26	21.27	20.17	16.12	30.02	27.39
1984	23.33	22.94	17.60	38.50	24.88	26.44	25.06	21.45	34.19	34.26
1985	24.11	23.74	18.98	37.49	25.58	28.16	26.62	23.60	34.61	36.87
1986	25.96	25.02	20.12	39.12	29.25	30.56	29.35	25.79	38.69	37.28
1987	28.79	28.07	23.14	42.08	31.46	32.37	30.71	26.93	40.64	41.68
1988	33.46	33.06	28.48	45.93	35.21	33.64	31.96	28.05	42.19	43.09
1989	37.33	36.84	32.37	49.38	39.43	35.13	33.33	29.29	43.91	45.18
1990	40.62	39.99	35.86	51.61	43.19	36.38	34.30	30.07	45.39	48.13
1991	43.31	42.68	38.47	54.49	45.93	36.33	34.46	30.23	45.52	46.88
1992	46.31	45.89	41.55	58.09	48.40	38.88	37.71	33.40	49.00	45.61
1993	47.83	47.38	43.70	57.73	50.02	42.24	41.48	37.36	52.30	46.83
1994	52.06	51.93	48.93	60.40	53.52	47.27	47.02	43.53	56.18	49.32
1995	57.41	57.97	55.86	64.31	57.14	51.06	51.25	48.52	58.49	50.81
1996	62.10	63.13	62.31	66.63	60.73	55.50	56.06	53.72	62.40	53.46
1997	69.50	72.27	73.60	71.20	63.92	62.97	64.14	62.58	68.89	58.11
1998	71.13	73.85	75.94	71.07	65.69	70.33	71.74	70.83	75.19	64.43
1999	73.01	76.93	79.48	73.19	64.79	77.46	80.92	81.05	82.24	62.47
2000	79.26	84.71	89.22	76.73	67.80	87.55	91.52	93.35	89.65	70.35
2001	74.63	79.49	81.82	76.27	64.40	85.06	88.56	87.51	92.04	69.90
2002	73.34	76.78	77.23	77.69	66.15	88.18	91.88	91.22	94.66	72.18
2003	74.64	78.22	78.61	79.29	67.13	92.12	96.40	95.14	100.34	73.71
2004	81.91	84.92	87.25	82.18	75.66	102.63	107.16	108.45	107.06	83.08
2005	87.04	91.12	95.44	84.67	78.51	109.13	114.31	117.66	111.25	86.82
2006	94.90	99.71	105.72	90.26	84.86	116.03	121.07	128.13	113.09	94.30
2007	103.69	107.17	114.76	95.03	96.46	118.95	123.30	131.40	114.03	100.16
2008	109.64	113.75	120.63	102.73	101.08	115.91	118.71	126.32	109.99	103.91
2009	100.00	100.00	100.00	100.00	100.00	100.00	100.00	100.00	100.00	100.00
2010	111.90	114.38	116.85	110.31	106.77	112.72	114.87	122.54	105.64	103.79
2011	119.56	121.82	126.86	113.90	114.92	118.88	121.50	134.02	107.09	107.98
2012	123.45	126.27	132.70	116.37	117.62	121.65	124.07	143.54	102.82	111.65
2013	127.21	129.84	135.25	121.34	121.80	123.05	125.23	148.44	100.31	114.13
2014	131.04	135.48	127.24	138.21	123.01	127.52	130.57	151.22	89.24	119.37
2008										
1st quarter	109.46	113.77	120.75	102.60	100.46	119.08	122.62	131.94	112.04	103.79
2nd quarter	112.74	117.27	125.09	104.87	103.29	118.01	121.51	131.53	110.28	102.88
3rd quarter	111.24	116.54	124.46	103.95	100.14	115.62	118.46	127.30	108.45	103.54
4th quarter	105.13	107.41	112.24	99.49	100.44	110.91	112.25	114.50	109.20	105.43
2009										
1st quarter	96.70	96.48	97.53	94.76	97.13	100.18	100.24	97.07	104.27	99.93
2nd quarter	96.95	95.84	94.79	97.63	99.24	96.09	95.30	93.36	97.71	99.28
3rd quarter	100.35	100.54	100.00	101.42	99.98	99.69	99.67	100.57	98.46	99.76
4th quarter	105.99	107.15	107.68	106.19	103.64	104.04	104.78	108.99	99.56	101.03
2010										
1st quarter	107.58	110.20	110.91	108.97	102.21	106.75	108.12	112.58	102.57	101.10
2nd quarter	110.10	113.05	116.36	107.64	104.01	111.83	114.08	120.97	105.72	102.51
3rd quarter	113.21	115.48	118.44	110.61	108.54	115.77	118.24	126.79	107.98	105.52
4th quarter	116.68	118.80	121.70	114.02	112.32	116.52	119.04	129.81	106.30	106.03
2011										
1st quarter	117.29	119.62	123.39	113.51	112.50	117.41	120.59	131.76	107.48	104.02
2nd quarter	119.08	121.07	126.48	112.62	115.03	118.29	120.81	131.52	108.21	107.78
3rd quarter	120.33	122.10	127.93	113.05	116.78	119.25	121.48	135.00	106.13	110.06
4th quarter	121.54	124.51	129.63	116.43	115.37	120.58	123.11	137.80	106.56	110.05
2012										
1st quarter	122.35	125.07	133.26	112.69	116.73	121.29	123.87	143.32	102.70	110.49
2nd quarter	123.72	126.52	132.55	117.18	117.93	121.88	124.39	143.89	103.11	111.46
3rd quarter	124.33	127.22	132.63	118.74	118.37	122.07	124.58	143.57	103.79	111.65
4th quarter	124.19	125.99	132.10	116.53	120.52	120.91	123.21	143.57	101.09	111.41
2013										
1st quarter	124.49	126.12	132.42	116.39	121.18	121.15	123.54	145.17	100.20	111.24
2nd quarter	126.00	128.42	136.01	116.85	121.01	122.77	125.16	147.67	100.94	112.89
3rd quarter	127.29	129.99	135.17	121.82	121.72	123.51	125.97	149.87	100.39	113.32
4th quarter	130.64	134.58	137.52	129.55	122.50	123.83	126.19	151.26	99.46	114.07
2014										
1st quarter	128.40	131.30	136.72	122.78	122.42	124.68	127.64	152.71	100.87	112.33
2nd quarter	131.44	135.12	140.01	127.32	123.85	127.58	130.69	159.12	100.62	114.56
3rd quarter	132.01	137.09	142.48	128.56	121.58	127.33	130.42	159.89	99.33	114.38
4th quarter	133.77	138.42	142.76	131.45	124.19	130.47	133.54	164.41	101.01	117.64

[1] Exports and imports of certain goods, primarily military equipment purchased and sold by the federal government, are included in services. Beginning with 1986, repairs and alterations of equipment are reclassified from goods to services.

Table 7-3. Chain-Type Price Indexes for Exports and Imports of Goods and Services

(Index numbers, 2009 = 100; quarterly indexes are seasonally adjusted.)

NIPA Table 4.2.4

Year and quarter	Exports of goods and services					Imports of goods and services				
	Total	Goods [1]			Services [1]	Total	Goods [1]			Services [1]
		Total	Durable	Nondurable			Total	Durable	Nondurable	
1970	32.62	37.40	47.32	23.64	22.76	22.20	22.75	38.14	11.50	19.80
1971	33.81	38.40	48.42	24.40	24.23	23.57	23.92	40.46	11.95	21.59
1972	35.30	39.42	49.40	25.28	26.50	25.22	25.75	44.02	12.68	22.66
1973	39.94	45.62	52.77	32.66	27.82	29.60	30.35	50.68	15.44	26.22
1974	49.21	57.43	62.20	44.69	31.33	42.35	45.42	62.26	28.75	31.18
1975	54.23	63.74	71.64	47.24	33.49	45.87	49.22	69.09	30.51	33.71
1976	56.01	65.46	76.46	45.99	35.43	47.26	50.54	70.21	31.60	35.23
1977	58.29	67.89	79.98	47.13	37.42	51.42	55.17	75.56	34.91	37.73
1978	61.85	71.81	84.90	49.60	40.22	55.05	58.85	84.12	35.81	41.16
1979	69.29	81.11	94.35	57.33	43.52	64.46	69.39	92.78	45.00	46.48
1980	76.32	88.88	104.36	61.98	49.07	80.29	87.56	102.59	63.56	53.94
1981	81.97	95.19	113.77	64.74	53.35	84.61	92.44	106.64	67.99	56.29
1982	82.35	94.39	116.68	61.26	56.37	81.76	88.70	104.68	63.87	56.34
1983	82.68	93.83	115.18	61.47	58.61	78.70	85.00	102.25	59.94	55.41
1984	83.44	94.67	114.37	63.43	59.22	78.02	84.41	100.38	60.41	54.46
1985	80.97	89.96	109.75	59.40	61.35	75.45	81.09	96.81	57.72	54.39
1986	79.60	86.84	107.56	55.94	63.45	75.45	79.27	103.61	48.69	60.28
1987	81.38	88.82	107.43	59.56	64.81	80.02	84.93	109.78	53.20	61.14
1988	85.55	94.30	110.80	66.48	66.25	83.85	88.97	117.59	53.54	64.12
1989	86.97	95.51	111.56	68.06	68.09	85.68	91.46	118.52	57.07	63.78
1990	87.46	94.67	110.16	67.95	71.31	88.14	93.14	117.05	61.23	68.56
1991	88.44	94.62	110.51	67.44	74.36	87.40	91.38	116.78	58.41	71.07
1992	88.00	93.15	109.01	66.11	76.11	87.47	90.88	116.15	58.09	73.06
1993	88.14	92.68	108.31	65.97	77.51	86.80	89.87	115.73	56.66	73.68
1994	89.16	93.73	107.65	69.26	78.45	87.62	90.52	116.72	56.93	75.13
1995	91.15	95.95	106.24	76.60	79.92	90.02	92.93	117.78	60.56	77.48
1996	89.94	93.51	101.88	77.21	81.50	88.45	90.58	111.11	63.05	79.41
1997	88.35	90.92	98.81	75.49	82.32	85.38	86.84	105.23	61.92	79.41
1998	86.26	88.05	96.55	71.58	82.15	80.78	81.59	100.75	55.95	77.85
1999	85.58	86.86	95.30	70.50	82.77	81.28	81.69	98.83	58.55	80.43
2000	87.16	88.37	95.68	74.15	84.54	84.82	85.99	98.63	68.64	80.01
2001	86.65	87.85	95.59	72.83	84.05	82.72	83.55	96.87	65.36	79.64
2002	86.09	87.21	95.00	72.10	83.70	81.71	82.09	94.96	64.48	80.97
2003	87.79	88.99	95.04	76.80	85.19	84.51	84.55	94.82	70.09	85.55
2004	90.85	92.25	96.54	83.09	87.79	88.47	88.70	96.62	77.12	88.58
2005	94.72	95.47	98.25	89.09	93.18	93.80	94.58	97.53	89.53	91.09
2006	97.98	98.83	100.70	94.20	96.22	97.66	98.67	98.78	97.56	93.83
2007	101.11	102.19	101.57	102.56	98.82	101.02	102.19	100.15	104.20	96.42
2008	105.81	107.20	102.35	116.17	102.81	111.59	113.85	103.01	128.76	101.81
2009	100.00	100.00	100.00	100.00	100.00	100.00	100.00	100.00	100.00	100.00
2010	104.26	105.03	102.11	110.17	102.64	105.80	106.74	101.07	114.55	101.82
2011	110.96	113.05	104.93	127.82	106.48	113.94	116.18	103.41	134.87	104.11
2012	111.94	113.55	105.57	128.03	108.50	114.50	116.87	103.56	136.47	104.05
2013	112.00	113.01	105.38	126.83	109.87	113.53	115.61	102.54	134.79	104.40
2014	112.25	112.12	115.24	131.57	112.61	113.57	115.02	117.59	151.28	107.25
2008										
1st quarter	104.47	105.76	101.82	112.80	101.75	108.92	111.09	101.26	124.40	99.59
2nd quarter	107.35	109.41	103.00	121.37	102.86	114.56	117.31	103.74	136.06	102.66
3rd quarter	108.98	110.96	103.65	124.79	104.66	117.70	120.82	104.54	143.52	104.10
4th quarter	102.44	102.69	100.92	105.74	101.98	105.17	106.19	102.49	111.04	100.89
2009										
1st quarter	99.01	98.56	99.41	96.98	99.96	96.38	95.72	99.79	90.63	99.08
2nd quarter	98.96	99.10	99.08	99.12	98.70	97.91	97.66	99.19	95.61	98.90
3rd quarter	100.24	100.36	100.10	100.88	99.96	101.33	101.59	100.06	103.41	100.28
4th quarter	101.79	101.98	101.41	103.02	101.38	104.39	105.02	100.96	110.35	101.74
2010										
1st quarter	102.68	103.03	101.45	105.78	101.96	105.93	106.95	100.98	115.10	101.56
2nd quarter	103.82	104.40	101.94	108.69	102.60	105.39	106.31	101.23	113.28	101.46
3rd quarter	104.06	104.77	101.98	109.64	102.59	104.74	105.51	100.71	112.08	101.48
4th quarter	106.49	107.93	103.10	116.56	103.41	107.14	108.17	101.37	117.75	102.76
2011										
1st quarter	109.20	111.16	104.03	124.05	105.01	111.49	113.29	102.52	128.92	103.60
2nd quarter	111.52	113.82	104.91	130.09	106.58	114.90	117.21	103.68	137.05	104.75
3rd quarter	112.16	114.40	105.59	130.49	107.35	114.83	117.18	104.00	136.47	104.46
4th quarter	110.95	112.81	105.17	126.67	106.97	114.55	117.04	103.44	137.05	103.62
2012										
1st quarter	111.69	113.44	105.44	127.97	107.93	115.76	118.35	103.67	140.27	104.33
2nd quarter	111.99	113.53	105.69	127.75	108.68	115.05	117.42	103.64	137.81	104.60
3rd quarter	111.92	113.48	105.34	128.28	108.58	113.37	115.31	103.29	132.69	104.84
4th quarter	112.29	113.66	105.56	128.38	109.37	114.51	116.59	103.48	135.86	105.38
2013										
1st quarter	112.64	113.88	105.68	128.80	110.02	114.70	116.78	103.35	136.59	105.57
2nd quarter	111.85	112.67	105.16	126.27	110.11	113.58	115.41	102.63	134.04	105.58
3rd quarter	112.03	112.72	105.02	126.67	110.60	113.36	115.12	101.97	134.47	105.68
4th quarter	112.06	112.43	105.16	125.58	111.33	113.55	115.09	102.02	134.29	106.88
2014										
1st quarter	112.88	113.36	105.32	127.94	111.90	114.47	116.13	102.06	137.29	107.24
2nd quarter	112.90	113.10	105.62	126.63	112.50	114.09	115.64	102.19	135.61	107.37
3rd quarter	112.62	112.43	105.59	124.75	113.11	113.85	115.34	102.20	134.73	107.36
4th quarter	110.61	109.62	105.21	117.42	112.92	111.85	112.99	101.64	128.83	107.02

[1] Exports and imports of certain goods, primarily military equipment purchased and sold by the federal government, are included in services. Beginning with 1986, repairs and alterations of equipment are reclassified from goods to services.

Table 7-4. Exports and Imports of Selected NIPA Types of Product

(Billions of dollars, quarterly data are at seasonally adjusted annual rates.)   **NIPA Table 4.2.5**

Year and quarter	Exports — Goods					Exports — Services		Imports — Goods						Imports — Services	
	Foods, feeds, and beverages	Industrial supplies and materials	Capital goods, except automotive	Automotive vehicles, engines, and parts	Consumer goods, except food and automotive	Travel	Other business services	Foods, feeds, and beverages	Industrial supplies and materials, except petroleum and products	Petroleum and products	Capital goods, except automotive	Automotive vehicles, engines, and parts	Consumer goods, except food and automotive	Travel	Other business services
1970	5.9	13.8	14.7	3.9	2.8	2.3	1.0	6.1	12.3	2.9	4.0	5.7	7.4	4.0	0.6
1971	6.1	12.6	15.4	4.7	2.9	2.5	1.3	6.4	13.5	3.7	4.3	7.6	8.4	4.4	0.7
1972	7.5	13.9	16.9	5.5	3.6	2.8	1.5	7.3	15.9	4.7	5.9	9.0	11.1	5.0	0.8
1973	15.2	19.7	22.0	7.0	4.8	3.4	1.7	9.1	19.2	8.4	8.3	10.7	12.9	5.5	0.9
1974	18.6	29.9	30.9	8.8	6.4	4.0	3.0	10.6	27.0	26.6	9.8	12.4	14.4	6.0	1.9
1975	19.2	29.3	36.6	10.8	6.6	4.7	3.7	9.6	23.6	27.0	10.2	12.1	13.2	6.4	2.3
1976	19.8	31.6	39.1	12.2	8.0	5.7	4.5	11.5	28.5	34.6	12.3	16.8	17.2	6.9	2.9
1977	19.7	33.2	39.8	13.5	8.9	6.2	4.9	14.0	33.4	45.0	14.0	19.4	21.8	7.5	3.2
1978	25.7	38.4	47.5	15.2	11.4	7.2	6.2	15.8	39.3	42.6	19.3	25.0	29.4	8.5	3.9
1979	30.5	53.3	60.2	17.9	14.0	8.4	7.3	18.0	45.0	60.4	24.6	26.6	31.3	9.4	4.6
1980	36.3	68.0	76.3	17.4	17.8	10.6	8.6	18.6	47.4	79.5	31.6	28.3	34.3	10.4	5.1
1981	38.8	65.7	84.2	19.7	17.7	15.6	10.5	18.6	52.0	78.4	37.1	31.0	38.4	11.8	6.0
1982	32.2	61.8	76.5	17.2	16.1	15.5	13.8	17.5	45.3	62.0	38.4	34.3	39.7	12.8	7.0
1983	32.1	57.1	71.7	18.5	14.9	14.8	14.1	18.8	51.1	55.1	43.7	43.0	47.3	13.6	6.8
1984	32.2	61.9	77.0	22.4	15.1	21.3	14.5	21.9	62.6	58.1	60.4	56.5	61.1	23.4	7.7
1985	24.6	59.4	79.3	24.9	14.6	22.4	14.8	21.8	59.2	51.4	61.3	64.9	66.3	25.1	8.8
1986	23.5	59.0	82.8	25.1	16.7	25.5	23.3	24.4	62.4	34.3	72.0	78.1	79.4	26.5	13.3
1987	25.2	67.4	92.7	27.6	20.3	29.0	24.2	24.8	66.1	42.9	85.1	85.2	88.8	29.9	16.7
1988	33.8	84.2	119.1	33.4	27.0	35.2	25.7	24.9	76.7	39.6	102.2	87.9	96.4	32.8	17.8
1989	36.3	95.4	136.9	35.1	35.9	43.0	30.3	24.9	78.8	50.9	112.3	87.4	103.6	34.2	19.2
1990	35.1	101.9	153.0	36.2	43.5	50.9	32.7	26.4	78.2	62.3	116.4	88.2	105.0	38.2	22.4
1991	35.7	106.2	166.6	39.9	46.6	56.7	39.9	26.2	75.7	51.7	121.1	85.5	107.7	36.2	25.9
1992	40.3	105.2	176.4	46.9	51.2	64.0	41.1	27.6	82.4	51.6	134.8	91.5	122.4	39.6	24.3
1993	40.5	102.9	182.7	51.6	54.5	67.9	43.5	27.9	88.7	51.5	153.2	102.1	133.7	41.9	26.6
1994	42.4	115.4	205.7	57.5	59.7	69.4	49.9	31.0	104.9	51.3	185.0	118.1	145.9	45.1	30.3
1995	50.8	141.0	234.4	61.4	64.2	74.9	53.6	33.2	119.6	56.0	222.1	123.7	159.7	46.4	33.7
1996	56.0	141.3	254.0	64.4	69.3	81.8	61.3	35.7	124.6	72.7	228.4	128.7	172.5	49.7	38.1
1997	52.0	153.0	295.8	73.4	77.0	86.2	71.2	39.7	134.7	71.8	253.6	139.4	195.2	53.8	41.4
1998	46.8	143.3	299.8	72.5	79.4	85.1	78.1	41.3	142.2	50.9	269.8	148.6	218.5	58.5	45.6
1999	46.0	145.7	311.2	75.3	80.9	92.3	79.6	44.1	149.8	72.1	296.1	178.2	243.7	59.6	56.2
2000	47.9	171.1	357.0	80.4	89.3	100.2	83.1	46.5	175.2	126.1	347.7	195.0	284.6	65.8	61.6
2001	49.4	159.5	321.7	75.4	88.3	86.7	87.9	47.2	167.4	109.4	299.2	188.7	287.1	60.7	66.9
2002	49.6	157.3	290.4	78.9	84.3	81.9	95.1	50.3	161.4	109.3	284.9	202.8	311.3	59.9	74.1
2003	55.0	173.3	293.7	80.6	89.9	80.3	102.1	56.5	177.4	140.4	297.6	209.2	338.4	61.9	79.6
2004	56.6	206.3	327.5	89.2	103.2	92.4	118.4	63.0	228.2	189.9	346.1	227.3	378.1	74.0	89.9
2005	59.0	236.8	358.4	98.4	115.2	101.5	128.5	69.1	267.9	263.2	382.8	238.7	412.7	80.0	95.8
2006	66.0	279.1	404.0	107.3	129.0	105.1	150.8	76.1	293.5	316.7	422.6	256.0	447.6	84.2	126.6
2007	84.3	316.3	433.0	121.3	145.9	119.0	183.9	83.0	297.9	346.7	449.1	258.5	479.8	89.2	149.3
2008	108.3	386.9	457.7	121.5	161.2	133.8	202.3	90.4	318.8	476.1	458.7	233.2	485.7	92.5	174.0
2009	93.9	293.5	391.5	81.7	149.3	119.9	210.9	82.9	196.7	267.7	374.1	159.2	429.9	81.4	178.5
2010	107.7	388.6	447.8	112.0	164.9	137.0	226.7	92.5	249.5	353.6	450.4	225.6	485.1	86.6	183.6
2011	126.2	485.3	494.2	133.0	174.7	150.9	249.4	108.3	292.8	462.1	513.4	255.2	515.9	89.7	197.3
2012	132.9	482.4	527.5	146.2	181.0	161.2	260.3	111.1	288.9	434.3	551.8	298.5	518.8	100.3	197.7
2013	136.2	492.1	534.6	152.6	188.4	173.1	273.3	116.0	291.1	387.6	557.8	309.6	533.9	104.7	202.3
2014	143.8	500.0	551.3	159.7	198.3	177.2	292.5	126.7	316.1	350.9	595.7	328.5	559.4	110.8	209.6
2009															
1st quarter	86.0	262.8	394.3	68.3	145.0	116.4	208.7	83.0	209.2	222.6	372.2	129.8	424.6	81.0	173.2
2nd quarter	95.6	272.4	377.3	68.0	144.2	116.8	207.6	82.1	174.9	239.8	352.0	129.2	419.4	78.0	178.1
3rd quarter	93.5	308.2	383.7	88.3	149.7	121.5	208.3	82.3	187.6	289.0	371.1	174.4	426.1	83.5	179.0
4th quarter	100.6	330.7	410.7	102.3	158.2	124.9	219.1	84.1	214.9	319.4	400.9	203.4	449.4	83.1	183.7
2010															
1st quarter	104.0	355.1	423.8	106.5	162.4	130.7	210.4	88.1	237.2	353.8	410.4	203.1	455.9	85.1	177.5
2nd quarter	96.8	385.5	443.1	111.0	159.6	133.9	216.9	91.6	251.2	355.1	442.0	225.5	479.5	85.8	180.9
3rd quarter	106.4	388.6	455.5	112.5	163.8	139.3	232.6	94.2	252.2	346.4	466.3	234.2	503.1	87.3	184.5
4th quarter	123.6	425.1	469.0	118.0	173.9	144.0	246.8	96.0	257.2	359.3	483.0	239.8	502.0	88.3	191.3
2011															
1st quarter	127.6	461.4	473.3	127.7	169.3	144.7	241.4	103.0	281.9	441.7	492.3	251.8	510.0	85.2	186.2
2nd quarter	127.6	489.8	493.5	128.9	175.4	153.6	248.7	108.8	297.3	480.8	508.1	232.5	519.4	91.1	200.0
3rd quarter	125.9	495.8	499.7	136.6	176.1	152.4	255.9	108.1	301.9	459.8	520.8	262.6	515.6	90.4	204.3
4th quarter	123.9	494.0	510.3	139.0	178.1	152.7	251.6	113.2	289.9	466.2	532.5	274.1	518.5	92.1	198.8
2012															
1st quarter	117.9	488.2	526.5	147.8	177.5	155.9	259.4	112.2	287.5	466.6	552.8	296.4	513.4	99.1	198.0
2nd quarter	132.4	490.8	525.0	148.1	180.8	161.6	262.1	109.9	287.9	446.6	556.9	296.9	517.9	100.0	200.1
3rd quarter	150.9	475.3	531.1	144.2	182.1	164.4	261.3	110.4	291.2	407.9	550.0	300.0	521.4	100.8	200.5
4th quarter	130.9	478.6	527.2	144.5	183.5	164.6	271.5	112.0	288.7	416.2	547.4	300.7	522.6	101.6	202.2
2013															
1st quarter	135.4	481.0	524.2	149.9	182.6	171.6	271.7	115.0	295.3	398.7	551.9	296.2	529.3	101.7	198.9
2nd quarter	124.5	478.7	538.8	153.8	193.4	170.1	272.9	116.5	291.0	381.3	550.2	307.3	533.6	103.9	204.0
3rd quarter	134.2	494.3	534.9	152.7	187.8	174.9	276.2	115.4	287.8	391.6	560.6	316.5	534.8	104.2	207.2
4th quarter	150.6	515.2	540.1	154.3	189.7	175.0	286.0	117.0	290.5	379.5	568.8	318.4	538.1	106.6	208.4
2014															
1st quarter	146.6	494.5	539.9	151.4	193.9	176.8	283.8	120.9	310.3	384.3	572.8	312.7	546.2	105.2	203.5
2nd quarter	145.7	508.6	549.2	159.6	199.4	179.7	293.3	129.2	315.5	358.7	594.7	331.8	561.0	111.6	206.3
3rd quarter	138.6	515.3	556.6	166.5	199.6	174.9	290.1	128.2	317.4	344.2	605.2	333.8	556.6	111.1	205.2
4th quarter	144.1	481.6	559.6	161.2	200.3	177.6	302.8	128.4	320.8	316.6	610.2	335.7	573.8	115.3	209.6

Table 7-5. Chain-Type Quantity Indexes for Exports and Imports of Selected NIPA Types of Product

(Index numbers, 2009 = 100; quarterly indexes are seasonally adjusted.)   **NIPA Table 4.2.3**

Year and quarter	Exports							Imports						
	Goods					Services		Goods					Services	
	Foods, feeds, and beverages	Industrial supplies and materials	Capital goods, except auto-motive	Auto-motive vehicles, engines, and parts	Consumer goods, except food and auto-motive	Travel	Other business services	Foods, feeds, and beverages	Petroleum and products	Capital goods, except auto-motive	Auto-motive vehicles, engines, and parts	Consumer goods, except food and auto-motive	Travel	Other business services
1970	25.60	24.03	4.38	23.93	6.21	12.22	1.67	30.90	25.80	0.88	21.91	6.43	22.46	1.05
1972	29.42	23.14	5.01	30.44	7.28	13.70	2.16	33.96	36.04	1.12	28.95	8.24	24.26	1.19
1973	38.08	28.47	6.36	35.75	8.88	15.74	2.35	34.83	51.20	1.38	29.88	8.46	22.89	1.34
1974	34.13	29.29	7.95	39.87	11.05	17.13	3.84	32.22	49.29	1.47	31.73	7.61	20.55	2.69
1975	36.10	25.63	8.07	41.98	10.18	18.52	4.45	28.50	48.47	1.40	25.18	5.90	19.82	3.04
1976	40.97	27.68	7.96	43.89	11.48	21.10	5.15	32.44	58.45	1.69	33.37	7.62	21.08	3.65
1977	40.93	27.91	7.83	44.21	12.42	21.14	5.31	32.11	70.32	1.81	35.35	9.20	21.72	3.82
1978	50.57	30.84	8.94	45.39	14.34	22.71	6.29	36.05	66.48	2.33	38.25	11.30	22.44	4.47
1979	53.65	35.32	10.73	45.68	15.08	24.35	7.01	37.01	67.25	2.85	36.99	11.39	21.89	5.06
1980	60.48	40.09	12.53	38.47	18.27	27.20	7.49	32.21	54.31	3.36	36.64	11.47	21.86	5.17
1981	61.74	37.39	12.58	38.03	17.52	36.19	8.60	33.51	47.59	3.96	35.46	12.56	23.83	5.79
1982	58.01	36.26	11.12	31.16	15.77	33.40	10.65	34.16	40.93	4.31	37.96	13.13	28.27	6.53
1983	55.45	34.50	10.72	32.24	14.42	29.67	10.35	37.08	40.50	5.21	46.46	15.80	32.02	6.06
1984	53.96	36.26	11.88	38.04	14.35	41.21	10.32	42.00	42.78	7.79	59.69	19.95	57.88	6.77
1985	46.69	36.47	13.05	41.40	13.92	41.25	10.16	43.82	40.17	8.78	66.89	21.77	63.86	7.56
1986	48.17	38.10	14.24	40.71	15.40	45.51	15.53	44.85	49.67	9.96	72.41	24.12	59.42	11.01
1987	51.56	39.05	16.44	43.89	18.12	49.37	15.54	45.97	51.88	11.38	74.30	24.90	70.34	12.62
1988	56.66	44.02	20.91	52.09	23.14	57.58	16.46	44.15	57.38	13.11	72.43	25.27	72.36	13.46
1989	58.94	48.95	24.25	53.55	29.67	68.03	19.20	45.14	62.05	14.83	70.59	26.45	74.63	15.75
1990	60.80	51.84	28.05	53.62	34.81	76.37	19.99	46.87	62.71	16.02	70.69	25.98	79.73	17.09
1991	61.96	55.36	30.70	57.51	36.07	79.96	23.50	44.75	62.48	17.23	65.91	26.43	72.41	19.07
1992	70.23	56.40	33.63	66.29	38.85	88.02	23.75	47.24	65.31	19.96	69.30	29.18	74.68	17.76
1993	69.88	54.90	35.83	72.27	40.82	92.10	24.84	47.80	71.54	23.28	76.15	31.60	78.39	18.82
1994	70.61	57.75	41.35	79.89	44.60	93.22	28.29	48.89	76.38	28.55	85.39	34.24	81.25	21.26
1995	78.00	62.30	49.27	84.20	47.27	99.07	29.86	50.12	75.00	35.15	86.87	36.93	82.13	23.40
1996	76.75	65.46	57.10	87.31	50.42	105.49	33.64	55.13	81.32	41.30	89.81	39.76	85.40	25.66
1997	77.23	71.17	69.99	98.83	55.61	108.51	38.70	60.71	84.69	51.83	97.07	45.55	92.82	27.50
1998	76.45	70.38	72.97	97.49	57.30	105.55	42.72	65.16	90.53	59.61	103.35	51.69	105.02	30.67
1999	78.68	72.60	77.01	100.56	58.58	111.46	35.12	71.99	97.29	68.42	123.08	58.05	105.16	29.27
2000	82.62	79.02	88.59	106.20	64.43	115.58	37.89	76.69	100.84	82.20	133.14	68.35	118.66	33.82
2001	84.84	75.82	79.80	99.25	63.92	98.98	41.80	80.13	103.81	72.86	128.78	69.46	110.29	38.06
2002	83.09	76.19	72.87	103.34	61.37	93.27	46.55	84.40	101.39	71.74	137.92	76.14	104.97	41.61
2003	84.53	78.33	74.59	104.81	65.04	89.00	50.88	90.90	108.16	75.94	141.51	82.95	99.92	45.37
2004	79.37	83.58	83.51	115.18	73.98	98.26	59.18	96.41	115.31	89.47	151.45	92.22	112.87	52.69
2005	83.67	85.65	91.13	125.49	81.69	93.93	63.45	99.77	117.63	99.63	157.13	99.74	115.17	57.56
2006	90.30	91.99	102.00	135.12	90.33	92.96	72.91	105.93	115.42	110.93	167.81	107.76	115.34	73.69
2007	98.17	96.91	110.29	151.02	100.00	101.36	88.16	107.24	112.68	118.39	167.81	113.97	112.91	87.56
2008	104.78	107.53	116.90	149.67	108.19	108.70	94.61	106.02	108.81	120.33	147.91	112.59	109.91	99.12
2009	100.00	100.00	100.00	100.00	100.00	100.00	100.00	100.00	100.00	100.00	100.00	100.00	100.00	100.00
2010	110.34	115.61	113.70	136.42	109.28	110.82	106.38	102.28	100.49	121.33	140.87	112.92	104.14	103.22
2011	109.98	123.16	124.45	159.27	114.24	116.11	114.39	104.21	98.59	138.00	154.42	118.04	104.96	110.88
2012	108.96	125.21	131.75	171.89	116.59	120.64	118.12	108.09	90.59	148.00	176.75	117.00	117.22	111.77
2013	111.32	130.31	132.65	178.46	122.68	128.40	121.53	112.30	84.10	151.08	183.85	120.64	120.36	115.80
2014	120.21	134.93	136.27	185.72	130.86	128.56	123.01	118.15	80.27	161.57	197.04	129.94	128.85	112.86
2009														
1st quarter	94.80	93.43	100.78	83.52	97.30	97.95	99.49	101.73	109.85	99.02	81.85	98.59	101.68	98.39
2nd quarter	99.25	95.69	96.90	83.34	97.24	98.77	99.93	100.18	98.57	94.26	81.62	97.61	96.07	100.79
3rd quarter	98.57	104.10	98.15	108.18	99.98	101.04	98.29	99.42	96.88	99.32	109.47	99.26	101.80	99.30
4th quarter	107.38	106.79	104.17	124.97	105.49	102.24	102.30	98.67	94.70	107.41	127.06	104.54	100.45	101.53
2010														
1st quarter	110.86	110.76	107.73	129.83	108.28	106.44	98.73	101.93	97.91	110.41	127.19	105.92	102.75	98.76
2nd quarter	103.50	115.45	112.60	135.45	106.12	108.91	101.44	103.06	102.67	119.19	141.30	111.23	103.88	101.43
3rd quarter	109.97	116.28	115.75	137.04	108.71	112.80	109.73	103.79	103.83	125.77	146.18	117.23	105.19	104.60
4th quarter	117.03	119.96	118.73	143.38	114.01	115.15	115.61	100.36	97.53	129.93	148.80	117.33	104.76	108.08
2011														
1st quarter	113.05	121.43	119.74	154.54	111.25	113.40	111.43	101.73	101.37	132.24	155.32	118.30	100.22	104.37
2nd quarter	110.50	121.84	124.31	155.03	114.79	118.29	113.52	102.65	99.19	136.34	140.19	119.37	105.70	112.07
3rd quarter	107.50	122.78	125.54	162.92	114.63	116.32	116.75	103.15	96.83	139.92	157.66	117.41	105.32	114.95
4th quarter	108.88	126.58	128.22	164.58	116.30	116.45	115.87	109.33	96.97	143.50	164.49	117.08	108.60	112.12
2012														
1st quarter	102.87	124.31	131.80	174.45	114.95	117.56	118.39	107.95	91.32	147.84	177.42	115.73	114.72	111.26
2nd quarter	111.86	126.47	131.11	173.86	116.50	121.26	118.68	106.00	91.57	149.19	176.24	116.69	116.39	112.07
3rd quarter	118.26	125.21	132.83	169.32	117.17	123.14	118.37	108.22	90.73	147.47	177.84	117.84	117.20	112.29
4th quarter	102.44	125.85	131.58	169.97	117.81	122.46	121.84	110.71	88.21	147.00	177.62	117.75	116.80	112.50
2013														
1st quarter	107.06	125.83	130.12	175.50	118.17	127.08	121.12	113.12	84.23	148.56	175.00	119.30	117.71	110.27
2nd quarter	100.62	127.82	134.11	180.06	126.03	126.40	120.80	113.20	84.99	148.90	182.75	120.35	120.38	113.16
3rd quarter	110.15	131.30	132.97	178.60	122.70	129.06	121.49	111.14	84.68	152.08	189.72	121.06	121.23	114.36
4th quarter	126.87	136.99	134.23	180.17	123.93	129.13	124.58	112.36	82.76	154.25	190.88	121.87	123.08	114.30
2014														
1st quarter	121.93	128.55	134.00	176.73	127.72	129.30	122.98	114.06	83.54	155.47	187.04	123.09	121.82	111.46
2nd quarter	116.52	135.34	135.63	185.64	131.57	130.02	127.23	121.09	79.29	161.25	198.16	126.14	128.87	113.27
3rd quarter	115.82	138.24	137.47	193.33	131.32	126.29	124.79	119.19	77.50	163.89	200.69	125.10	129.38	112.15
4th quarter	126.58	137.59	138.01	187.18	132.84	128.63	130.22	118.27	80.74	165.66	202.28	129.46	135.34	114.57

Section 7b: U.S. International Transactions Accounts

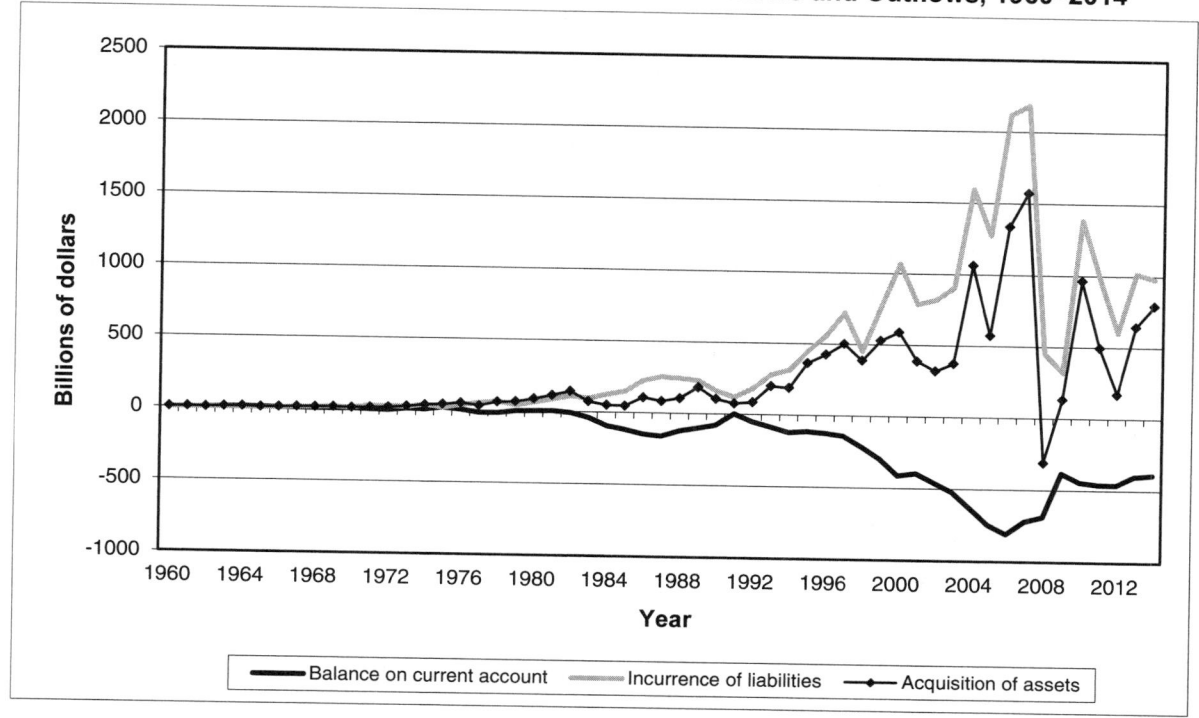

Figure 7-2: Balance on Current Account and Financial Inflows and Outflows, 1960–2014

- The U.S. current-account international balance is also recorded in the International Transactions Accounts (ITAs). The definitional differences between this balance and the balance in the NIPAs are minor, and the trends in the two measures are similar. The ITAs measure the current account surplus or deficit (commonly known as the "balance of payments") and directly measure the financial flows required to finance it. (Table 7-6A and 7-6B)

- Figure 7-2 above shows the current-account balance since 1960, culminating in a $390 billion deficit in 2014, and the corresponding estimated financial flows. U.S. acquisition of financial assets abroad contributed a further outflow, amounting to $792 billion, in 2014. Financing the sum of these was borrowing ("incurrence of liabilities") estimated at $977 billion. The net of the estimated financial flows does not exactly equal the current-account balance because of capital transactions, derivatives, and the ITA statistical discrepancy. (Table 7-6A)

- Large quarterly and annual variations in 2008 and subsequent years in many types of financial flows, including those involving official assets, are evidence of an extreme amount of international financial turbulence and official intervention. (Table 7-6A and 7-6B)

- Through the early 1980s, the United States was still a net creditor with respect to the rest of the world, meaning that the value of the stock of U.S.-owned assets abroad exceeded the value of U.S. liabilities to the rest of the world. Since then, persistent borrowing to finance current-account deficits has cumulated, resulting in a growing net debtor status, with the value of U.S. liabilities exceeding the value of its assets by more than $7.0 trillion as of the end of 2014. (Table 7-8)

Table 7-6A. U.S. International Transactions: Recent Data

(Millions of dollars, seasonally adjusted.)

	Current account — Exports of goods and services and income receipts (credits)											Secondary income (current transfer) receipts
		Exports of goods and services			Primary income receipts							
Year and quarter	Total goods and services and income receipts	Total goods and services exports	Goods exports	Services exports	Total primary income receipts	Investment income receipts					Compensation of employees receipts	
						Total investment income receipts	Direct investment income receipts	Portfolio investment income receipts	Other investment income receipts	Reserve asset income receipts		
1960	30 555	25 939	19 650	6 289	4 616	4 616	...	...	...	...	...	...
1961	31 403	26 403	20 108	6 295	5 000	5 000	...	...	...	...	...	...
1962	33 340	27 722	20 781	6 941	5 618	5 618	...	...	...	...	...	...
1963	35 776	29 620	22 272	7 348	6 156	6 156	...	...	...	...	...	...
1964	40 164	33 340	25 501	7 839	6 824	6 824	...	...	...	...	...	...
1965	42 722	35 285	26 461	8 824	7 437	7 437	...	...	...	...	...	...
1966	46 454	38 926	29 310	9 616	7 528	7 528	...	...	...	...	...	...
1967	49 354	41 333	30 666	10 667	8 021	8 021	...	...	...	...	...	...
1968	54 912	45 544	33 626	11 918	9 368	9 368	...	...	...	...	...	...
1969	60 133	49 220	36 414	12 806	10 913	10 913	...	...	...	...	...	...
1970	68 388	56 640	42 469	14 171	11 748	11 748	...	...	...	...	...	...
1971	72 383	59 677	43 319	16 358	12 706	12 706	...	...	...	...	...	...
1972	81 987	67 223	49 381	17 842	14 764	14 764	...	...	...	...	...	...
1973	113 051	91 242	71 410	19 832	21 809	21 809	...	...	...	...	...	...
1974	148 484	120 897	98 306	22 591	27 587	27 587	...	...	...	...	...	...
1975	157 936	132 585	107 088	25 497	25 351	25 351	...	...	...	...	...	...
1976	172 090	142 716	114 745	27 971	29 374	29 374	...	...	...	...	...	...
1977	184 657	152 302	120 816	31 486	32 355	32 355	...	...	...	...	...	...
1978	220 515	178 428	142 075	36 353	42 087	42 087	...	...	...	...	...	...
1979	287 967	224 132	184 439	39 693	63 835	63 835	...	...	...	...	...	...
1980	344 440	271 835	224 250	47 585	72 605	72 605	...	...	...	...	...	...
1981	380 928	294 399	237 044	57 355	86 529	86 529	...	...	...	...	...	...
1982	371 757	275 235	211 157	64 078	96 522	96 522	...	...	...	...	...	...
1983	362 137	266 106	201 799	64 307	96 031	96 031	...	...	...	...	...	...
1984	406 733	291 094	219 926	71 168	115 639	115 639	...	...	...	...	...	...
1985	394 117	289 071	215 915	73 156	105 046	105 046	...	...	...	...	...	...
1986	412 832	310 034	223 344	86 690	102 798	101 890	...	...	...	...	908	...
1987	462 472	348 869	250 208	98 661	113 603	112 609	...	...	...	...	994	...
1988	572 816	431 150	320 230	110 920	141 666	140 671	...	...	...	...	995	...
1989	653 387	487 003	359 916	127 087	166 384	165 367	...	...	...	...	1 017	...
1990	712 128	535 234	387 401	147 833	176 894	175 722	...	...	...	...	1 172	...
1991	733 670	578 343	414 083	164 260	155 327	154 037	...	...	...	...	1 290	...
1992	755 964	616 882	439 631	177 251	139 082	137 286	...	...	...	...	1 796	...
1993	784 469	642 863	456 943	185 920	141 606	139 786	...	...	...	...	1 820	...
1994	872 701	703 254	502 859	200 395	169 447	167 504	...	...	...	...	1 943	...
1995	1 008 048	794 387	575 204	219 183	213 661	211 482	...	...	...	...	2 179	...
1996	1 081 132	851 602	612 113	239 489	229 530	227 349	...	...	...	...	2 181	...
1997	1 195 810	934 453	678 366	256 087	261 357	259 087	...	...	...	...	2 270	...
1998	1 199 418	933 174	670 416	262 758	266 244	263 807	...	...	...	...	2 437	...
1999	1 304 557	969 867	698 524	271 343	300 300	296 054	136 502	72 171	86 145	1 236	4 246	34 390
2000	1 471 532	1 075 321	784 940	290 381	358 822	354 427	158 182	78 401	116 573	1 270	4 395	37 390
2001	1 345 165	1 005 654	731 331	274 323	298 203	293 691	134 437	73 914	84 029	1 311	4 512	41 308
2002	1 318 790	978 706	698 036	280 670	287 505	282 936	150 395	81 923	49 568	1 050	4 570	52 580
2003	1 409 053	1 020 418	730 446	289 972	326 698	322 026	190 704	90 652	39 587	1 083	4 671	61 938
2004	1 642 291	1 161 549	823 584	337 966	420 590	415 856	255 405	108 647	50 637	1 165	4 734	60 152
2005	1 895 983	1 286 022	913 016	373 006	543 982	539 186	301 184	129 691	107 126	1 185	4 796	65 980
2006	2 222 124	1 457 642	1 040 905	416 738	693 089	688 020	333 235	166 146	187 414	1 226	5 069	71 393
2007	2 569 492	1 653 548	1 165 151	488 396	844 033	838 814	380 844	221 610	234 910	1 449	5 219	71 912
2008	2 751 949	1 841 612	1 308 795	532 817	823 707	818 342	423 365	241 329	152 076	1 572	5 364	86 630
2009	2 285 922	1 583 053	1 070 331	512 722	614 379	608 639	370 301	184 417	53 140	781	5 740	88 491
2010	2 630 799	1 853 606	1 290 273	563 333	684 915	678 984	447 773	194 852	35 660	699	5 931	92 278
2011	2 987 571	2 127 021	1 499 240	627 781	759 727	753 622	477 415	237 343	38 018	846	6 105	100 822
2012	3 085 260	2 216 540	1 561 689	654 850	762 885	756 531	460 329	260 081	35 648	474	6 354	105 835
2013	3 178 744	2 280 194	1 592 784	687 410	780 120	773 425	466 706	275 704	30 637	377	6 695	118 429
2014	3 306 574	2 343 205	1 632 639	710 565	823 353	816 445	476 617	308 205	31 321	301	6 909	140 016
2011												
1st quarter	719 078	511 743	360 151	151 592	182 773	181 249	118 012	53 915	9 103	219	1 523	24 562
2nd quarter	745 539	530 519	373 260	157 259	189 491	187 964	119 612	58 495	9 632	225	1 527	25 529
3rd quarter	763 083	542 974	382 183	160 791	194 717	193 185	121 324	62 415	9 215	232	1 531	25 392
4th quarter	759 871	541 785	383 646	158 139	192 746	191 224	118 467	62 518	10 069	170	1 523	25 340
2012												
1st quarter	765 208	547 584	387 616	159 968	193 149	191 612	118 467	63 048	9 927	170	1 538	24 475
2nd quarter	768 069	554 179	391 764	162 415	188 807	187 244	112 351	65 889	8 878	125	1 563	25 083
3rd quarter	771 158	555 214	391 998	163 216	188 749	187 153	113 402	64 924	8 730	97	1 596	27 194
4th quarter	780 824	559 563	390 311	169 251	192 180	190 523	116 109	66 219	8 113	82	1 657	29 082
2013												
1st quarter	780 878	562 411	392 605	169 806	190 175	188 515	113 660	66 767	7 958	130	1 660	28 292
2nd quarter	786 909	565 335	394 988	170 347	193 497	191 826	115 441	68 496	7 786	103	1 671	28 078
3rd quarter	796 943	570 756	398 088	172 668	196 002	194 324	117 248	69 473	7 525	78	1 678	30 184
4th quarter	814 014	581 692	407 103	174 589	200 446	198 759	120 357	70 968	7 368	66	1 686	31 876
2014												
1st quarter	813 153	577 133	401 429	175 704	202 235	200 517	118 165	74 511	7 745	96	1 718	33 785
2nd quarter	835 686	587 873	409 152	178 721	204 850	203 125	118 170	76 908	7 973	74	1 725	42 962
3rd quarter	830 374	589 263	412 933	176 331	209 715	207 980	121 657	78 498	7 755	70	1 734	31 396
4th quarter	827 361	588 935	409 126	179 810	206 554	204 822	118 625	78 287	7 849	61	1 731	31 872

. . . = Not available.

Table 7-6A. U.S. International Transactions: Recent Data—*Continued*

(Millions of dollars, seasonally adjusted.)

Year and quarter	Total goods and services and income receipts	Imports of goods and services and income payments (debits)									
		Current account—*Continued*									
		Imports of goods and services			Primary income payments						Secondary income (current transfer) payments
		Total goods and services imports	Goods	Services	Total primary income payments	Investment income payments				Compensation of employees payments	
						Total investment income payments	Direct investment income payments	Portfolio investment income payments	Other investment income payments		
1960	27 732	22 433	14 758	7 675	1 238	1 238	...	...	...	...	4 061
1961	27 581	22 208	14 537	7 671	1 245	1 245	...	...	...	...	4 128
1962	29 953	24 352	16 260	8 092	1 324	1 324	...	...	...	...	4 277
1963	31 365	25 411	17 048	8 363	1 561	1 561	...	...	...	...	4 393
1964	33 342	27 319	18 700	8 619	1 783	1 783	...	...	...	...	4 240
1965	37 293	30 621	21 510	9 111	2 088	2 088	...	...	...	...	4 584
1966	43 425	35 987	25 493	10 494	2 482	2 482	...	...	...	...	4 956
1967	46 770	38 729	26 866	11 863	2 747	2 747	...	...	...	...	5 294
1968	54 299	45 292	32 991	12 301	3 378	3 378	...	...	...	...	5 629
1969	59 734	49 130	35 807	13 323	4 869	4 869	...	...	...	...	5 735
1970	66 055	54 385	39 866	14 519	5 514	5 514	...	...	...	...	6 156
1971	73 818	60 980	45 579	15 401	5 436	5 436	...	...	...	...	7 402
1972	87 780	72 664	55 797	16 867	6 572	6 572	...	...	...	...	8 544
1973	105 912	89 342	70 499	18 843	9 656	9 656	...	...	...	...	6 914
1974	146 521	125 189	103 811	21 378	12 084	12 084	...	...	...	...	9 248
1975	139 822	120 181	98 185	21 996	12 565	12 565	...	...	...	...	7 076
1976	167 796	148 798	124 228	24 570	13 312	13 312	...	...	...	...	5 686
1977	198 992	179 547	151 907	27 640	14 218	14 218	...	...	...	...	5 227
1978	235 659	208 191	176 002	32 189	21 680	21 680	...	...	...	...	5 788
1979	288 250	248 696	212 007	36 689	32 961	32 961	...	...	...	...	6 593
1980	342 124	291 242	249 750	41 492	42 533	42 533	...	...	...	...	8 349
1981	375 898	310 570	265 067	45 503	53 626	53 626	...	...	...	...	11 702
1982	377 296	299 392	247 642	51 750	61 359	61 359	...	...	...	...	16 545
1983	400 828	323 874	268 901	54 973	59 643	59 643	...	...	...	...	17 311
1984	501 074	400 166	332 418	67 748	80 574	80 574	...	...	...	...	20 334
1985	512 274	410 951	338 088	72 863	79 324	79 324	...	...	...	...	21 999
1986	560 007	448 572	368 425	80 147	87 304	84 626	...	...	...	2 678	24 131
1987	623 127	500 553	409 765	90 788	99 309	96 971	...	...	...	2 338	23 265
1988	693 969	545 714	447 189	98 525	122 981	121 134	...	...	...	1 847	25 274
1989	752 874	580 145	477 665	102 480	146 560	144 274	...	...	...	2 286	26 169
1990	791 097	616 098	498 438	117 660	148 345	144 881	...	...	...	3 464	26 654
1991	730 773	609 479	491 020	118 459	131 198	127 172	...	...	...	4 026	-9 904
1992	807 574	656 094	536 528	119 566	114 845	110 093	...	...	...	4 752	36 635
1993	869 272	713 174	589 394	123 780	116 287	111 155	...	...	...	5 132	39 811
1994	994 314	801 747	668 690	133 057	152 302	146 350	...	...	...	5 952	40 265
1995	1 121 616	890 771	749 374	141 397	192 771	186 508	...	...	...	6 263	38 074
1996	1 205 896	955 667	803 113	152 554	207 212	200 912	...	...	...	6 300	43 017
1997	1 336 538	1 042 726	876 794	165 932	248 750	242 084	...	...	...	6 666	45 062
1998	1 414 479	1 099 314	918 637	180 677	261 978	254 984	...	...	...	6 994	53 187
1999	1 600 087	1 228 485	1 035 592	192 893	288 366	276 957	58 313	145 305	73 339	11 410	83 236
2000	1 882 288	1 447 837	1 231 722	216 115	339 643	328 688	63 253	164 757	100 678	10 955	94 808
2001	1 740 493	1 367 165	1 153 701	213 465	268 474	256 761	18 555	162 458	75 748	11 713	104 853
2002	1 776 877	1 397 660	1 173 281	224 379	262 331	249 969	48 049	159 827	42 093	12 362	116 886
2003	1 930 395	1 514 308	1 272 089	242 219	283 938	271 030	78 037	163 525	29 467	12 908	132 150
2004	2 276 059	1 771 433	1 488 349	283 083	356 463	342 490	104 554	195 794	42 142	13 973	148 164
2005	2 641 418	2 000 267	1 695 820	304 448	476 349	460 441	127 979	238 558	93 904	15 909	164 801
2006	3 028 851	2 219 358	1 878 194	341 165	649 752	633 326	159 189	304 934	169 203	16 426	159 740
2007	3 288 135	2 358 922	1 986 347	372 575	743 429	727 707	136 261	381 788	209 658	15 722	185 784
2008	3 438 590	2 550 339	2 141 287	409 052	677 561	660 500	139 073	400 032	121 395	17 061	210 691
2009	2 666 714	1 966 827	1 580 025	386 801	490 794	476 376	112 610	332 495	31 271	14 418	209 093
2010	3 074 729	2 348 263	1 938 950	409 313	507 254	493 292	159 757	313 527	20 008	13 962	219 212
2011	3 446 914	2 675 646	2 239 886	435 761	538 766	524 582	178 862	324 944	20 776	14 184	232 502
2012	3 546 009	2 754 145	2 303 785	450 360	559 892	545 088	178 712	345 251	21 125	14 804	231 972
2013	3 578 998	2 756 586	2 294 453	462 134	580 466	564 897	175 830	372 738	21 125	14 804	231 972
2014	3 696 100	2 851 529	2 374 101	477 428	585 369	569 031	176 152	378 705	14 174	16 339	259 202
2011											
1st quarter	837 659	646 061	541 686	104 375	132 471	129 038	44 119	80 014	4 904	3 434	59 126
2nd quarter	866 146	669 398	559 978	109 421	138 272	134 753	48 817	80 778	5 158	3 519	58 476
3rd quarter	871 062	676 936	565 490	111 446	137 104	133 525	46 040	82 474	5 011	3 579	57 022
4th quarter	872 048	683 251	572 732	110 519	130 919	127 266	39 886	81 677	5 703	3 653	57 878
2012											
1st quarter	889 171	692 038	581 054	110 983	139 618	136 051	46 844	83 428	5 780	3 566	57 515
2nd quarter	886 944	692 215	580 003	112 212	137 316	133 518	42 636	85 441	5 441	3 798	57 412
3rd quarter	883 290	683 733	570 941	112 793	141 069	137 316	46 353	85 756	5 207	3 753	58 487
4th quarter	886 605	686 158	571 786	114 372	141 889	138 202	42 879	90 627	4 696	3 686	58 558
2013											
1st quarter	886 365	683 359	570 164	113 195	144 192	140 431	44 052	91 911	4 468	3 761	58 813
2nd quarter	893 055	687 134	572 071	115 063	145 990	142 053	44 894	93 019	4 140	3 937	59 931
3rd quarter	898 247	691 953	576 024	115 929	144 478	140 557	43 217	93 434	3 905	3 922	61 816
4th quarter	901 330	694 140	576 193	117 947	145 806	141 857	43 667	94 374	3 815	3 950	61 831
2014											
1st quarter	909 597	702 551	585 739	116 812	143 941	139 993	42 456	94 048	3 489	3 947	63 105
2nd quarter	927 725	716 585	597 265	119 320	146 915	142 815	45 765	93 380	3 670	4 100	64 225
3rd quarter	928 279	715 134	596 009	119 126	147 985	143 868	44 940	95 412	3 516	4 117	65 160
4th quarter	930 499	717 258	595 089	122 170	146 529	142 354	42 992	95 864	3 498	4 175	66 712

. . . = Not available.

Table 7-6A. U.S. International Transactions: Recent Data—Continued

(Millions of dollars, seasonally adjusted.)

Year and quarter	Capital account		Financial account							
			Net U.S. acquisition of financial assets excluding financial derivatives (net increase in assets/financial outflows+)							
				Direct investment assets			Portfolio investment assets			
	Capital transfer receipts and other credits	Capital transfer payments and other debits	Total net acquisition of assets	Total direct investment assets	Direct equity assets	Direct debt instruments assets	Total portfolio investment assets	Equity and investment fund shares assets	Short-term debt securities assets	Long-term debt securities assets
1960	. . .	. . .	4 099	2 940	. . .	. . .	. . .	. . .	. . .	. . .
1961	. . .	. . .	5 538	2 654	. . .	. . .	. . .	. . .	. . .	. . .
1962	. . .	. . .	4 174	2 851	. . .	. . .	. . .	. . .	. . .	. . .
1963	. . .	. . .	7 270	3 483	. . .	. . .	. . .	. . .	. . .	. . .
1964	. . .	. . .	9 560	3 759	. . .	. . .	. . .	. . .	. . .	. . .
1965	. . .	. . .	5 715	5 011	. . .	. . .	. . .	. . .	. . .	. . .
1966	. . .	. . .	7 321	5 419	. . .	. . .	. . .	. . .	. . .	. . .
1967	. . .	. . .	9 757	4 806	. . .	. . .	. . .	. . .	. . .	. . .
1968	. . .	. . .	10 977	5 294	. . .	. . .	. . .	. . .	. . .	. . .
1969	. . .	. . .	11 584	5 960	. . .	. . .	. . .	. . .	. . .	. . .
1970	. . .	. . .	9 336	7 590	. . .	. . .	. . .	. . .	. . .	. . .
1971	. . .	. . .	12 474	7 618	. . .	. . .	. . .	. . .	. . .	. . .
1972	. . .	. . .	14 497	7 747	. . .	. . .	. . .	. . .	. . .	. . .
1973	. . .	. . .	22 874	11 353	. . .	. . .	. . .	. . .	. . .	. . .
1974	. . .	. . .	34 745	9 052	. . .	. . .	. . .	. . .	. . .	. . .
1975	. . .	. . .	39 703	14 244	. . .	. . .	. . .	. . .	. . .	. . .
1976	. . .	. . .	51 269	11 949	. . .	. . .	. . .	. . .	. . .	. . .
1977	. . .	. . .	34 785	11 891	. . .	. . .	. . .	. . .	. . .	. . .
1978	. . .	. . .	61 130	16 057	. . .	. . .	. . .	. . .	. . .	. . .
1979	. . .	. . .	66 053	25 223	. . .	. . .	. . .	. . .	. . .	. . .
1980	. . .	. . .	86 968	19 222	. . .	. . .	. . .	. . .	. . .	. . .
1981	. . .	. . .	114 147	9 624	. . .	. . .	. . .	. . .	. . .	. . .
1982	. . .	. . .	142 722	19 397	. . .	. . .	. . .	. . .	. . .	. . .
1983	. . .	. . .	74 690	20 844	. . .	. . .	. . .	. . .	. . .	. . .
1984	. . .	. . .	50 740	26 770	. . .	. . .	. . .	. . .	. . .	. . .
1985	. . .	. . .	47 064	21 241	. . .	. . .	. . .	. . .	. . .	. . .
1986	. . .	. . .	107 252	19 524	. . .	. . .	. . .	. . .	. . .	. . .
1987	. . .	. . .	84 058	39 795	. . .	. . .	. . .	. . .	. . .	. . .
1988	. . .	. . .	105 747	21 701	. . .	. . .	. . .	. . .	. . .	. . .
1989	0	207	182 908	50 973	. . .	. . .	. . .	. . .	. . .	. . .
1990	0	7 220	103 985	59 934	. . .	. . .	. . .	. . .	. . .	. . .
1991	0	5 130	75 753	49 253	. . .	. . .	. . .	. . .	. . .	. . .
1992	1 536	87	84 899	58 755	. . .	. . .	. . .	. . .	. . .	. . .
1993	5	719	199 399	82 799	. . .	. . .	. . .	. . .	. . .	. . .
1994	3	1 114	188 758	89 988	. . .	. . .	. . .	. . .	. . .	. . .
1995	259	481	363 555	110 041	. . .	. . .	. . .	. . .	. . .	. . .
1996	2	9	424 548	103 024	. . .	. . .	. . .	. . .	. . .	. . .
1997	15	271	502 024	121 352	. . .	. . .	. . .	. . .	. . .	. . .
1998	16	24	385 936	174 751	. . .	. . .	. . .	. . .	. . .	. . .
1999	36	4 212	527 407	248 279	163 178	85 101	141 007	114 311	18 771	7 925
2000	35	36	589 315	188 004	171 644	16 360	159 713	106 714	31 805	21 194
2001	13 228	30	387 067	146 800	130 725	16 076	106 919	109 119	16 275	-18 475
2002	52	193	319 742	179 556	127 976	51 579	79 532	16 954	30 964	31 614
2003	80	1 900	373 016	197 160	156 173	40 987	133 059	118 003	-12 910	27 967
2004	3 754	705	1 062 783	378 134	296 184	81 951	191 956	84 753	20 523	86 679
2005	15 462	2 346	572 317	61 925	51 621	10 304	267 290	186 684	18 822	61 784
2006	0	1 788	1 336 866	296 059	266 312	29 748	493 366	137 331	115 742	240 293
2007	494	110	1 572 509	532 939	431 378	101 561	380 807	147 782	15 190	217 835
2008	6 170	159	-309 468	351 724	360 130	-8 406	-284 269	-38 550	-82 645	-163 075
2009	0	140	132 204	313 726	262 058	51 669	375 883	63 696	136 127	176 059
2010	0	157	963 449	354 575	343 040	11 535	199 620	79 150	62 279	58 190
2011	0	1 186	496 320	440 405	401 533	38 872	85 365	6 950	-51 256	129 671
2012	7 668	764	171 418	375 537	319 024	56 513	239 773	103 254	-6 598	143 117
2013	0	412	644 763	408 243	352 106	56 137	489 877	275 244	45 373	169 260
2014	0	45	792 145	357 190	355 622	1 568	538 058	436 526	15 299	86 232
2011										
1st quarter	0	29	389 189	130 051	91 591	38 460	115 962	27 881	27 876	60 205
2nd quarter	0	854	-334	142 096	121 388	20 708	69 344	6 401	17 964	44 979
3rd quarter	0	300	81 134	67 344	84 865	-17 521	-43 647	2 052	-79 058	33 360
4th quarter	0	3	26 331	100 915	103 689	-2 774	-56 295	-29 384	-18 037	-8 873
2012										
1st quarter	0	53	-74 077	110 579	77 173	33 406	1 416	18 867	-17 380	-71
2nd quarter	0	241	-184 459	81 728	76 471	5 257	53 051	54 824	5 945	-7 719
3rd quarter	0	470	293 633	87 078	83 632	3 446	128 276	32 526	37 312	58 438
4th quarter	7 668	*	136 320	96 152	81 748	14 404	57 030	-2 963	-32 476	92 469
2013										
1st quarter	0	40	221 653	77 992	79 387	-1 395	157 860	67 295	22 289	68 276
2nd quarter	0	227	143 657	120 947	87 046	33 900	115 004	92 820	20 489	1 695
3rd quarter	0	146	83 999	105 008	99 586	5 422	61 121	19 686	17 508	23 927
4th quarter	0	*	195 454	104 296	86 087	18 210	155 892	95 443	-14 913	75 362
2014										
1st quarter	0	43	151 706	55 050	56 131	-1 081	98 981	82 823	16 158	-7 942
2nd quarter	0	2	239 149	90 293	85 576	4 716	195 068	90 670	104 399	45 519
3rd quarter	0	1	359 601	99 300	96 520	2 780	162 884	131 572	31 312	-2 587
4th quarter	0	*	41 690	112 547	117 395	-4 848	81 125	131 463	-50 338	-19 691

. . . = Not available.
* = Between zero and +/- $500,000.

Table 7-6A. U.S. International Transactions: Recent Data—*Continued*

(Millions of dollars, seasonally adjusted.)

Financial account—*Continued*

Net U.S. acquisition of financial assets excluding financial derivatives (net increase in assets/financial outflows +)—*Continued*

Year and quarter	Total other investment assets[1]	Currency and deposits assets	Loan assets	Trade credit and advances assets	Total reserve assets	Monetary gold	Special drawing rights assets	Reserve positions in the IMF	Total other reserve assets[2]	Currency and deposits reserve assets	Securities reserve assets
1960	2 641	...	...	...	...	...	...	...	-2 145	...	...
1961	2 729	...	...	...	...	...	...	...	-607	...	...
1962	1 889	...	...	...	...	...	...	...	-1 535	...	...
1963	3 060	...	...	...	...	...	...	...	-378	...	...
1964	5 294	...	...	...	...	...	...	...	-171	...	...
1965	1 170	...	...	...	...	...	...	...	-1 225	...	...
1966	1 752	...	...	...	...	...	...	...	-570	...	...
1967	3 696	...	...	...	...	...	...	...	-53	...	...
1968	3 244	...	...	...	...	...	...	...	870	...	...
1969	2 896	...	...	...	...	...	...	...	1 179	...	...
1970	3 151	...	...	...	...	...	...	...	-2 481	...	...
1971	6 092	...	...	...	...	...	...	...	-2 349	...	...
1972	6 127	...	...	...	...	...	...	...	4	...	...
1973	11 007	...	...	...	...	...	...	...	-158	...	...
1974	22 373	...	...	...	...	...	...	...	1 467	...	...
1975	18 363	...	...	...	...	...	...	...	849	...	...
1976	27 877	...	...	...	...	...	...	...	2 558	...	...
1977	17 060	...	...	...	...	...	...	...	375	...	...
1978	42 179	...	...	...	...	...	...	...	-732	...	...
1979	27 267	...	...	...	...	...	...	...	1 133	...	...
1980	53 550	...	...	...	...	...	...	...	8 154	...	...
1981	83 697	...	...	...	...	...	...	...	5 176	...	...
1982	105 965	...	...	...	...	...	...	...	4 965	...	...
1983	50 588	...	...	...	...	...	...	...	1 195	...	...
1984	17 340	...	...	...	...	...	...	...	3 132	...	...
1985	18 957	...	...	...	...	...	...	...	3 858	...	...
1986	79 057	...	...	...	...	...	...	...	-313	...	...
1987	45 508	...	...	...	...	...	...	...	-9 148	...	...
1988	75 544	...	...	...	...	...	...	...	3 913	...	...
1989	75 476	...	...	...	...	...	...	...	25 293	...	...
1990	11 336	...	...	...	...	...	...	...	2 158	...	...
1991	210	...	...	...	...	...	...	...	-5 763	...	...
1992	-20 639	...	...	...	...	...	...	...	-3 901	...	...
1993	-22 696	...	...	...	...	...	...	...	1 379	...	...
1994	50 028	...	...	...	...	...	...	...	-5 346	...	...
1995	100 266	...	...	...	...	...	...	...	9 742	...	...
1996	168 013	...	...	...	...	...	...	...	-6 668	...	...
1997	258 626	...	...	...	...	...	...	...	1 010	...	...
1998	72 216	...	...	...	...	...	...	...	6 783	...	...
1999	146 868	...	...	5 227	-8 747	0	-10	-5 484	-8 747	...	...
2000	241 308	...	...	680	290	0	722	-2 308	290	...	...
2001	128 437	...	...	-5 267	4 911	0	630	3 600	4 911	...	...
2002	56 973	...	...	-633	3 681	0	475	2 632	3 681	...	...
2003	44 321	51 302	-9 261	2 280	-1 524	0	-601	-1 494	-1 524	293	191
2004	495 498	240 360	256 244	-1 106	-2 806	0	398	-3 826	-2 806	242	298
2005	257 196	82 879	173 031	1 286	-14 094	0	-4 511	-10 200	-14 094	224	309
2006	549 814	154 026	392 255	3 534	-2 373	0	223	-3 331	-2 373	309	308
2007	658 641	375 146	272 812	10 683	122	0	154	-1 021	122	517	288
2008	-381 770	123 493	-501 550	-3 712	4 848	0	106	3 473	4 848	587	443
2009	-609 662	-394 461	-215 735	535	52 256	0	48 230	3 357	52 256	138	480
2010	407 420	150 249	251 128	6 043	1 835	0	31	1 293	1 835	55	439
2011	-45 327	-89 161	39 821	4 013	15 877	0	-1 752	18 079	15 877	110	-598
2012	-448 352	-515 933	66 892	689	4 460	0	37	4 032	4 460	24	365
2013	-250 260	-115 641	-137 978	9 805	-3 097	0	22	-3 438	-3 097	3	315
2014	-99 520	-147 354	54 595	-6 761	-3 583	0	23	-3 849	243	5	234
2011											
1st quarter	139 558	107 550	36 980	-4 972	3 619	0	-1 961	6 428	-848	17	-873
2nd quarter	-218 041	-208 168	-9 558	-315	6 267	0	159	5 974	134	28	93
3rd quarter	53 358	64 551	-19 675	8 482	4 079	0	27	3 909	143	33	99
4th quarter	-20 201	-53 094	32 073	819	1 912	0	23	1 768	121	32	82
2012											
1st quarter	-187 305	-200 297	15 694	-2 703	1 233	0	11	1 078	144	15	127
2nd quarter	-322 526	-320 600	-3 522	1 596	3 289	0	10	3 179	100	5	94
3rd quarter	77 446	25 150	52 476	-180	833	0	10	744	79	2	77
4th quarter	-15 967	-20 187	2 244	1 976	-895	0	6	-969	68	2	67
2013											
1st quarter	-15 074	-39 132	25 742	-1 684	875	0	5	755	115	1	115
2nd quarter	-92 105	-38 151	-57 810	3 855	-189	0	6	-287	92	1	91
3rd quarter	-81 129	-37 055	-44 021	-53	-1 001	0	5	-1 071	65	1	64
4th quarter	-61 952	-1 305	-61 889	1 242	-2 782	0	6	-2 835	47	1	45
2014											
1st quarter	24 101	-1 369	-43 231	49 346	-956	0	8	-1 040	76	-956	72
2nd quarter	58 879	-46 986	-5 194	-44 455	773	0	8	710	55	773	51
3rd quarter	33 899	98 306	32 190	67 876	-889	0	4	-951	59	-889	58
4th quarter	-30 647	-149 471	-131 119	-18 173	-2 511	0	3	-2 568	54	-2 511	53

[1]Includes insurance technical reserves, not shown separately.
[2]Includes financial derivatives and other claims, not shown seperately.
. . . = Not available.

Table 7-6A. U.S. International Transactions: Recent Data—*Continued*

(Millions of dollars, seasonally adjusted.)

	Financial account—*Continued*												
	Net U.S. incurrence of liabilities excluding financial derivatives (net increase in liabilities/financial inflow+)												
		Direct investment liabilities			Portfolio investment liabilities				Other investment liabilities				
Year and quarter	Total net incurrence of liabilities	Total direct investment liabilities	Direct equity liabilities	Direct debt instruments liabilities	Total portfolio liabilities	Equity and investment fund shares liabilities	Short-term debt securities liabilities	Long-term debt securities liabilities	Total other investment liabilities[1]	Currency and deposits liabilities	Loan liabilities	Trade credit and advances liabilities	Special drawing rights allocations
1960	2 294	315	...	...	573	...	...	...	1 406	...	...	...	...
1961	2 705	311	...	...	709	...	...	...	1 685	...	...	...	...
1962	1 912	346	...	...	1 478	...	...	...	88	...	...	...	...
1963	3 217	231	...	...	953	...	...	...	2 033	...	...	...	...
1964	3 643	322	...	...	201	...	...	...	3 120	...	...	...	...
1965	741	414	...	...	-630	...	...	...	957	...	...	...	...
1966	3 661	426	...	...	-977	...	...	...	4 212	...	...	...	...
1967	7 379	698	...	...	3 144	...	...	...	3 537	...	...	...	...
1968	9 928	808	...	...	3 780	...	...	...	5 340	...	...	...	...
1969	12 702	1 263	...	...	719	...	...	...	10 720	...	...	...	...
1970	7 226	1 464	...	...	11 710	...	...	...	-5 948	...	...	...	...
1971	23 687	368	...	...	28 835	...	...	...	-5 516	...	...	...	...
1972	22 171	948	...	...	13 123	...	...	...	8 100	...	...	...	...
1973	18 388	2 800	...	...	4 790	...	...	...	10 798	...	...	...	...
1974	35 228	4 761	...	...	5 500	...	...	...	24 967	...	...	...	...
1975	16 870	2 603	...	...	12 761	...	...	...	1 506	...	...	...	...
1976	37 840	4 347	...	...	16 165	...	...	...	17 328	...	...	...	...
1977	52 770	3 728	...	...	37 615	...	...	...	11 427	...	...	...	...
1978	66 275	7 896	...	...	30 083	...	...	...	28 296	...	...	...	...
1979	40 693	11 876	...	...	-13 502	...	...	...	42 319	...	...	...	...
1980	62 036	16 918	...	...	23 825	...	...	...	21 293	...	...	...	...
1981	85 684	25 196	...	...	17 509	...	...	...	42 979	...	...	...	...
1982	109 897	27 475	...	...	19 695	...	...	...	62 727	...	...	...	...
1983	95 715	18 688	...	...	18 382	...	...	...	58 645	...	...	...	...
1984	126 413	34 832	...	...	38 695	...	...	...	52 886	...	...	...	...
1985	146 544	22 057	...	...	68 004	...	...	...	56 483	...	...	...	...
1986	223 854	30 946	...	...	104 497	...	...	...	88 411	...	...	...	...
1987	251 863	63 232	...	...	79 631	...	...	...	109 000	...	...	...	...
1988	244 008	56 910	...	...	86 786	...	...	...	100 312	...	...	...	...
1989	230 302	75 801	...	...	74 852	...	...	...	79 649	...	...	...	...
1990	162 109	71 247	...	...	25 767	...	...	...	65 095	...	...	...	...
1991	119 586	34 535	...	...	72 562	...	...	...	12 489	...	...	...	...
1992	178 842	30 315	...	...	92 199	...	...	...	56 328	...	...	...	...
1993	278 607	50 211	...	...	174 387	...	...	...	54 009	...	...	...	...
1994	312 995	55 942	...	...	131 849	...	...	...	125 204	...	...	...	...
1995	446 393	69 067	...	...	254 431	...	...	...	122 895	...	...	...	...
1996	559 027	97 644	...	...	392 107	...	...	...	69 276	...	...	...	...
1997	720 999	122 150	...	...	311 105	...	...	...	287 744	...	...	...	...
1998	452 901	211 152	...	...	225 878	...	...	...	15 871	...	...	...	...
1999	765 555	312 789	225 690	87 099	278 697	112 289	-6 900	173 308	174 069	...	...	-4 526	0
2000	1 067 016	350 066	259 380	90 686	441 966	193 600	5 393	242 973	274 984	...	...	10 375	0
2001	787 321	171 472	107 051	64 420	431 492	121 464	3 149	306 879	184 357	...	...	5 156	0
2002	820 257	109 468	106 927	2 541	504 155	54 067	76 547	373 541	206 634	...	...	15 754	0
2003	905 899	111 346	107 707	3 638	550 163	33 981	31 099	485 083	244 390	30 846	214 539	-995	0
2004	1 595 116	207 878	142 434	65 444	867 340	61 786	99 851	705 703	519 899	131 503	386 418	1 979	0
2005	1 273 038	138 328	112 459	25 869	832 037	89 258	-45 310	788 088	302 673	-124 782	415 824	11 632	0
2006	2 116 304	294 289	184 143	110 146	1 126 735	145 481	22 756	958 498	695 280	224 386	465 221	5 673	0
2007	2 183 538	340 066	190 418	149 648	1 156 612	275 617	158 983	722 012	686 860	239 302	426 981	20 576	0
2008	454 051	332 734	294 861	37 874	523 683	126 804	287 226	109 652	-402 367	74 441	-483 554	6 746	0
2009	318 350	153 787	148 465	5 322	357 352	219 302	-124 007	262 056	-192 789	-74 225	-172 464	6 301	47 598
2010	1 386 345	259 345	203 148	56 197	820 434	178 952	-53 031	694 513	306 566	115 678	172 256	18 632	0
2011	977 073	257 411	185 051	72 361	311 626	123 357	-86 722	274 991	408 036	475 678	-84 789	17 147	0
2012	601 973	217 777	191 427	26 349	746 988	239 060	16 281	491 655	-362 799	-245 009	-129 409	11 619	0
2013	1 017 669	294 972	226 834	68 138	501 975	-85 407	46 718	529 632	231 753	172 286	47 606	11 861	0
2014	977 421	131 831	68 854	62 977	705 030	155 077	22 935	527 019	140 559	51 031	75 265	14 263	0
2011													
1st quarter	592 847	69 714	38 586	31 128	149 211	38 993	-33 158	143 377	373 921	150 002	222 517	1 403	0
2nd quarter	125 789	74 432	56 468	17 964	105 650	34 442	-14 924	86 133	-54 293	78 386	-135 202	2 523	0
3rd quarter	245 696	57 328	47 078	10 250	77 147	18 955	-23 362	81 554	111 221	222 985	-124 494	12 730	0
4th quarter	12 742	55 937	42 919	13 019	-20 383	30 967	-15 277	-36 072	-22 813	24 306	-47 609	490	0
2012													
1st quarter	183 933	40 210	33 557	6 653	249 732	64 095	-11 165	196 802	-106 008	-125 940	16 022	3 909	0
2nd quarter	-151 218	67 418	49 265	18 153	7 962	30 707	-12 196	-10 549	-226 598	-183 974	-44 776	2 153	0
3rd quarter	298 348	44 111	38 442	5 669	222 638	30 867	49 642	142 129	31 600	83 599	-58 505	6 506	0
4th quarter	270 910	66 038	70 164	-4 125	266 664	113 391	-10 000	163 274	-61 793	-18 694	-42 150	-949	0
2013													
1st quarter	285 407	44 526	39 788	4 739	155 583	-22 550	69 180	108 952	85 298	6 687	76 171	2 439	0
2nd quarter	224 716	82 156	61 980	20 175	-25 746	-32 706	-32 741	39 701	168 307	103 956	61 347	3 004	0
3rd quarter	165 707	71 130	55 579	15 551	207 881	61 828	-52 805	198 857	-113 303	-21 130	-94 906	2 733	0
4th quarter	341 838	97 161	69 487	27 673	153 226	-91 980	63 085	182 122	91 451	82 773	4 994	3 684	0
2014													
1st quarter	271 921	-105 425	-97 740	-7 685	242 627	99 113	13 573	129 941	134 719	-5 754	127 315	13 157	0
2nd quarter	283 271	78 405	58 756	19 649	88 549	15 070	-24 913	98 392	116 317	103 243	7 984	5 089	0
3rd quarter	364 518	106 473	59 437	47 036	240 879	75 555	-8 106	173 430	17 166	41 638	-19 894	-4 578	0
4th quarter	57 712	52 378	48 401	3 977	132 976	-34 660	42 380	125 256	-127 642	-88 097	-40 140	595	0

[1]Includes insurance technical resreves, not shown separately.
. . . = Not available.

Table 7-6A. U.S. International Transactions: Recent Data—*Continued*

(Millions of dollars, seasonally adjusted.)

Year and quarter	Financial account—Continued: Financial derivatives other than reserves, net	Statistical discrepancy: Total	Statistical discrepancy: Seasonal adjustment discrepancy	Balances — Current account: Total balance on current account	Balances on goods and services: Total balance on goods and services	Balance on goods	Balance on services	Balance on primary income	Balance on secondary income	Balance on capital account	Net lending (+) or net borrowing (-): Based on current and capital account transactions	Based on financial account transactions
1960	...	-1 019	0	2 825	3 508	4 892	-1 385	3 378	-4 061	0	2 825	1 805
1961	...	-989	0	3 821	4 194	5 571	-1 377	3 755	-4 128	0	3 821	2 833
1962	...	-1 123	0	3 387	3 371	4 521	-1 151	4 294	-4 277	0	3 387	2 262
1963	...	-361	0	4 414	4 210	5 224	-1 014	4 595	-4 393	0	4 414	4 053
1964	...	-907	0	6 823	6 022	6 801	-780	5 041	-4 240	0	6 823	5 917
1965	...	-457	0	5 430	4 664	4 951	-287	5 349	-4 584	0	5 430	4 974
1966	...	629	0	3 031	2 939	3 817	-878	5 046	-4 956	0	3 031	3 660
1967	...	-205	0	2 584	2 604	3 800	-1 196	5 274	-5 294	0	2 584	2 378
1968	...	438	0	611	250	635	-385	5 990	-5 629	0	611	1 049
1969	...	-1 517	0	399	90	607	-517	6 044	-5 735	0	399	-1 118
1970	...	-219	0	2 331	2 255	2 603	-348	6 234	-6 156	0	2 331	2 110
1971	...	-9 779	0	-1 433	-1 301	-2 260	959	7 270	-7 402	0	-1 433	-11 213
1972	...	-1 879	0	-5 796	-5 443	-6 416	973	8 192	-8 544	0	-5 796	-7 674
1973	...	-2 654	0	7 140	1 900	911	989	12 153	-6 914	0	7 140	4 486
1974	...	-2 444	0	1 961	-4 293	-5 505	1 212	15 503	-9 248	0	1 961	-483
1975	...	4 717	0	18 117	12 403	8 903	3 500	12 786	-7 076	0	18 117	22 833
1976	...	9 134	0	4 296	-6 082	-9 483	3 402	16 062	-5 686	0	4 296	13 429
1977	...	-3 651	0	-14 336	-27 247	-31 091	3 845	18 137	-5 227	0	-14 336	-17 985
1978	...	9 997	0	-15 143	-29 763	-33 927	4 164	20 407	-5 788	0	-15 143	-5 145
1979	...	25 647	0	-285	-24 566	-27 568	3 003	30 874	-6 593	0	-285	25 360
1980	...	22 614	0	2 318	-19 407	-25 500	6 093	30 072	-8 349	0	2 318	24 932
1981	...	23 433	0	5 029	-16 172	-28 023	11 851	32 903	-11 702	0	5 029	28 463
1982	...	38 362	0	-5 537	-24 156	-36 485	12 330	35 163	-16 545	0	-5 537	32 825
1983	...	17 666	0	-38 691	-57 767	-67 102	9 335	36 388	-17 311	0	-38 691	-21 025
1984	...	18 673	0	-94 344	-109 074	-112 492	3 418	35 065	-20 334	0	-94 344	-75 673
1985	...	18 677	0	-118 155	-121 879	-122 173	294	25 722	-21 999	0	-118 155	-99 480
1986	...	30 570	0	-147 176	-138 539	-145 081	6 543	15 494	-24 131	0	-147 176	-116 602
1987	...	-7 149	0	-160 655	-151 683	-159 557	7 874	14 294	-23 265	0	-160 655	-167 805
1988	...	-17 108	0	-121 153	-114 566	-126 959	12 394	18 685	-25 274	0	-121 153	-138 261
1989	...	52 299	0	-99 487	-93 142	-117 749	24 607	19 824	-26 169	-207	-99 694	-47 394
1990	...	28 066	0	-78 969	-80 865	-111 037	30 173	28 549	-26 654	-7 221	-86 190	-58 124
1991	...	-41 601	0	2 897	-31 136	-76 937	45 802	24 129	9 904	-5 129	-2 232	-43 833
1992	...	-43 776	0	-51 613	-39 212	-96 897	57 685	24 237	-36 635	1 449	-50 164	-93 943
1993	...	6 313	0	-84 805	-70 311	-132 451	62 141	25 319	-39 811	-714	-85 519	-79 208
1994	...	-1 514	0	-121 612	-98 493	-165 831	67 338	17 145	-40 265	-1 112	-122 724	-124 237
1995	...	30 951	0	-113 567	-96 384	-174 170	77 786	20 890	-38 074	-221	-113 788	-82 838
1996	...	-9 706	0	-124 764	-104 065	-191 000	86 935	22 318	-43 017	-8	-124 772	-134 479
1997	...	-77 995	0	-140 726	-108 273	-198 428	90 155	12 607	-45 062	-256	-140 982	-218 975
1998	...	148 106	0	-215 062	-166 140	-248 221	82 081	4 266	-53 187	-7	-215 069	-66 965
1999	...	61 558	0	-295 530	-258 617	-337 068	78 450	11 933	-48 846	-4 176	-299 706	-238 148
2000	...	-66 944	0	-410 756	-372 517	-446 783	74 266	19 178	-57 418	-1	-410 757	-477 701
2001	...	-18 124	0	-395 328	-361 511	-422 370	60 858	29 729	-63 545	13 198	-382 130	-400 254
2002	...	-42 287	0	-458 087	-418 955	-475 245	56 290	25 174	-64 307	-141	-458 228	-500 515
2003	...	-9 721	0	-521 342	-493 890	-541 643	47 754	42 760	-70 212	-1 821	-523 162	-532 883
2004	...	98 385	0	-633 768	-609 883	-664 766	54 882	64 127	-88 012	3 049	-630 719	-532 334
2005	...	31 597	0	-745 434	-714 245	-782 804	68 558	67 632	-98 822	13 116	-732 319	-700 721
2006	-29 710	-634	0	-806 726	-761 716	-837 289	75 573	43 337	-88 347	-1 788	-808 514	-809 148
2007	-6 222	101 008	0	-718 643	-705 375	-821 196	115 821	100 604	-113 872	384	-718 260	-617 251
2008	32 947	-49 941	0	-690 789	-708 726	-832 492	123 765	146 146	-124 061	6 010	-680 631	-730 572
2009	-44 816	149 970	0	-384 023	-383 774	-509 694	125 920	123 584	-120 602	-140	-380 932	-230 962
2010	-14 076	7 116	0	-441 961	-494 658	-648 678	154 020	177 661	-126 934	-157	-444 087	-436 972
2011	-35 006	-55 229	0	-460 354	-548 625	-740 646	192 020	220 961	-131 680	-1 186	-460 530	-515 759
2012	7 064	30 353	0	-449 670	-537 605	-742 095	204 490	202 993	-126 138	6 904	-453 845	-441 249
2013	2 248	30 008	0	-376 760	-476 392	-701 669	225 276	199 654	-123 515	-412	-400 666	-395 831
2014	-54 372	149 923	0	-389 526	-508 324	-741 462	233 138	237 984	-119 185	-45	-389 571	-239 648
2011												
1st quarter	-2 952	-88 000	14 214	-118 240	-134 319	-181 536	47 217	50 302	-34 564	-29	-118 610	-206 609
2nd quarter	-9 806	-14 467	-13 542	-121 031	-138 879	-186 717	47 838	51 219	-32 948	-854	-121 461	-135 929
3rd quarter	1 617	-54 665	-27 968	-108 409	-133 962	-183 307	49 345	57 613	-31 630	-300	-108 279	-162 945
4th quarter	-23 865	101 904	27 298	-112 675	-141 466	-189 086	47 620	61 827	-32 538	-3	-112 180	-10 276
2012												
1st quarter	7 339	-126 656	13 161	-121 536	-144 454	-193 439	48 984	53 532	-33 040		-124 015	-250 671
2nd quarter	-2 419	83 455	-15 445	-117 964	-138 036	-188 239	50 203	51 490	-32 329	-53	-119 115	-35 660
3rd quarter	5 129	113 016	-25 063	-105 427	-128 519	-178 943	50 424	47 680	-31 293	-241	-112 602	414
4th quarter	-2 985	-39 461	27 348	-104 742	-126 596	-181 475	54 879	50 291	-29 477	-470	-98 113	-137 574
2013												
1st quarter	-3 948	37 825	16 071	-102 719	-120 948	-177 560	56 611	45 983	-30 522	-40	-105 527	-67 702
2nd quarter	-3 302	22 011	-12 764	-97 615	-121 799	-177 083	55 284	47 507	-31 854	-227	-106 372	-84 362
3rd quarter	6 569	26 311	-22 871	-94 794	-121 197	-177 936	56 739	51 524	-31 632	-146	-101 450	-75 140
4th quarter	2 929	-56 138	19 564	-81 633	-112 448	-169 090	56 642	54 639	-29 508	*	-87 317	-143 455
2014												
1st quarter	6 147	-17 582	18 645	-96 443	-125 418	-184 310	58 892	58 294	-29 319	-43	-96 486	-114 068
2nd quarter	-4 513	43 406	-11 087	-92 039	-128 712	-188 113	59 401	57 935	-21 263	-2	-92 041	-48 635
3rd quarter	-24 269	68 720	-29 823	-97 905	-125 871	-183 076	57 205	61 730	-33 764	-1	-97 906	-29 186
4th quarter	-31 737	55 379	22 265	-103 138	-128 323	-185 963	57 640	60 025	-34 840	*	-103 138	-47 759

... = Not available.
* = Between zero and +/-$500,000

Table 7-6B. U.S. International Transactions: Historical Quarterly

(Millions of dollars, seasonally adjusted.)

Year and quarter	Total goods and services and income receipts	Exports of goods and services — Total goods and services exports	Goods exports	Services exports	Primary income receipts — Total primary income receipts	Total investment income receipts	Direct investment income receipts	Portfolio investment income receipts	Other investment income receipts	Reserve asset income receipts	Compensation of employees receipts	Secondary income (current transfer) receipts
2000												
1st quarter	353 685	259 157	188 500	70 657	85 194	84 095	38 599	19 586	25 593	318	1 099	9 333
2nd quarter	367 362	267 643	194 669	72 973	90 682	89 584	39 668	20 010	29 596	310	1 098	9 037
3rd quarter	373 453	275 192	201 805	73 387	88 834	87 736	37 938	19 499	29 983	316	1 098	9 426
4th quarter	377 034	273 329	199 965	73 364	94 112	93 012	41 978	19 307	31 401	326	1 100	9 593
2001												
1st quarter	362 566	268 966	196 777	72 189	83 800	82 673	35 582	19 247	27 462	383	1 127	9 800
2nd quarter	346 972	259 041	188 506	70 535	77 769	76 642	34 625	18 484	23 204	329	1 127	10 162
3rd quarter	325 106	243 986	175 954	68 032	70 691	69 562	32 249	17 779	19 217	317	1 129	10 428
4th quarter	310 523	233 660	170 094	63 566	65 944	64 814	31 981	18 404	14 147	282	1 130	10 919
2002												
1st quarter	317 160	237 401	168 795	68 607	67 918	66 779	35 080	19 215	12 222	262	1 140	11 840
2nd quarter	330 213	246 016	175 834	70 181	71 444	70 303	37 174	20 092	12 800	237	1 141	12 753
3rd quarter	338 319	249 202	178 451	70 751	75 471	74 327	39 713	21 656	12 678	280	1 144	13 646
4th quarter	333 101	246 085	174 956	71 129	72 676	71 531	38 432	20 961	11 867	271	1 145	14 340
2003												
1st quarter	337 839	247 468	177 549	69 919	76 297	75 134	42 908	22 306	9 613	307	1 164	14 074
2nd quarter	343 382	248 233	178 539	69 694	79 062	77 896	45 297	21 875	10 446	278	1 167	16 086
3rd quarter	353 826	255 843	182 340	73 503	81 975	80 805	47 712	23 102	9 737	254	1 169	16 008
4th quarter	374 001	268 873	192 018	76 855	89 359	88 187	54 785	23 370	9 787	245	1 172	15 770
2004												
1st quarter	393 020	280 458	198 160	82 298	97 696	96 513	61 265	25 462	9 499	287	1 183	14 866
2nd quarter	403 930	287 866	204 315	83 551	101 654	100 474	62 918	26 699	10 602	255	1 180	14 410
3rd quarter	413 288	291 660	207 629	84 031	107 020	105 835	64 547	27 609	13 395	285	1 184	14 609
4th quarter	432 053	301 565	213 480	88 086	114 220	113 033	66 676	28 877	17 142	338	1 187	16 268
2005												
1st quarter	457 649	311 731	219 595	92 135	126 709	125 512	73 077	31 156	20 973	305	1 197	19 209
2nd quarter	464 003	319 410	227 952	91 458	130 577	129 380	73 141	31 720	24 244	275	1 197	14 017
3rd quarter	476 236	321 561	228 416	93 145	138 300	137 100	75 602	32 467	28 729	302	1 200	16 375
4th quarter	498 094	333 321	237 053	96 268	148 394	147 193	79 364	34 348	33 179	302	1 201	16 378
2006												
1st quarter	525 635	348 984	249 672	99 312	157 652	156 392	79 449	36 773	39 897	274	1 259	18 999
2nd quarter	550 892	361 325	258 172	103 152	172 108	170 843	83 795	40 449	46 326	273	1 264	17 459
3rd quarter	560 339	365 686	262 364	103 322	178 404	177 134	84 203	43 154	49 436	341	1 270	16 249
4th quarter	585 258	381 648	270 696	110 952	184 925	183 651	85 788	45 770	51 755	338	1 275	18 685
2007												
1st quarter	599 916	391 610	276 803	114 807	192 957	191 660	87 357	49 395	54 547	361	1 297	15 349
2nd quarter	630 323	404 234	285 920	118 314	209 426	208 125	93 837	53 570	60 372	347	1 301	16 662
3rd quarter	658 173	419 325	295 651	123 674	219 999	218 692	97 526	58 726	62 075	364	1 308	18 848
4th quarter	681 081	438 378	306 777	131 601	221 651	220 337	102 124	59 919	57 917	377	1 313	21 052
2008												
1st quarter	691 838	454 689	323 714	130 975	218 387	217 051	110 051	62 413	44 139	448	1 336	18 763
2nd quarter	716 264	479 164	342 964	136 200	216 645	215 304	115 089	61 940	37 905	371	1 341	20 454
3rd quarter	713 731	481 623	347 210	134 413	210 713	209 367	110 630	60 156	38 091	491	1 346	21 394
4th quarter	630 118	426 136	294 907	131 229	177 963	176 621	87 595	56 821	31 943	263	1 341	26 018
2009												
1st quarter	552 102	378 634	254 211	124 423	150 426	149 005	81 622	48 899	18 246	237	1 421	23 042
2nd quarter	549 098	379 502	254 057	125 445	147 059	145 627	86 869	44 090	14 512	156	1 432	22 538
3rd quarter	574 553	398 428	270 281	128 147	155 049	153 606	97 135	45 390	10 851	231	1 443	21 076
4th quarter	610 170	426 489	291 783	134 707	161 845	160 401	104 675	46 038	9 532	157	1 444	21 835
2010												
1st quarter	624 806	438 333	304 463	133 870	165 373	163 897	108 450	46 725	8 498	223	1 476	21 100
2nd quarter	644 991	452 371	315 242	137 129	169 200	167 716	110 740	47 748	9 106	122	1 484	23 419
3rd quarter	662 831	468 345	325 220	143 125	171 337	169 851	111 924	48 667	9 077	182	1 486	23 149
4th quarter	698 170	494 555	345 348	149 208	179 006	177 521	116 659	51 712	8 979	172	1 484	24 609
2011												
1st quarter	719 078	511 743	360 151	151 592	182 773	181 249	118 012	53 915	9 103	219	1 523	24 562
2nd quarter	745 539	530 519	373 260	157 259	189 491	187 964	119 612	58 495	9 632	225	1 527	25 529
3rd quarter	763 083	542 974	382 183	160 791	194 717	193 185	121 324	62 415	9 215	232	1 531	25 392
4th quarter	759 871	541 785	383 646	158 139	192 746	191 224	118 467	62 518	10 069	170	1 523	25 340
2012												
1st quarter	765 208	547 584	387 616	159 968	193 149	191 612	118 467	63 048	9 927	170	1 538	24 475
2nd quarter	768 069	554 179	391 764	162 415	188 807	187 244	112 351	65 889	8 878	125	1 563	25 083
3rd quarter	771 158	555 214	391 998	163 216	188 749	187 153	113 402	64 924	8 730	97	1 596	27 194
4th quarter	780 824	559 563	390 311	169 251	192 180	190 523	116 109	66 219	8 113	82	1 657	29 082
2013												
1st quarter	780 878	562 411	392 605	169 806	190 175	188 515	113 660	66 767	7 958	130	1 660	28 292
2nd quarter	786 909	565 335	394 988	170 347	193 497	191 826	115 441	68 496	7 786	103	1 671	28 078
3rd quarter	796 943	570 756	398 088	172 668	196 002	194 324	117 248	69 473	7 525	78	1 678	30 184
4th quarter	814 014	581 692	407 103	174 589	200 446	198 759	120 357	70 968	7 368	66	1 686	31 876
2014												
1st quarter	813 153	577 133	401 429	175 704	202 235	200 517	118 165	74 511	7 745	96	1 718	33 785
2nd quarter	835 686	587 873	409 152	178 721	204 850	203 125	118 170	76 908	7 973	74	1 725	42 962
3rd quarter	830 374	589 263	412 933	176 331	209 715	207 980	121 657	78 498	7 755	70	1 734	31 396
4th quarter	827 361	588 935	409 126	179 810	206 554	204 822	118 625	78 287	7 849	61	1 731	31 872

Table 7-6B. U.S. International Transactions: Historical Quarterly—*Continued*

(Millions of dollars, seasonally adjusted.)

Year and quarter	Total goods and services and income receipts	Imports of goods and services: Total goods and services imports	Goods	Services	Total primary income payments	Total investment income payments	Direct investment income payments	Portfolio investment income payments	Other investment income payments	Compensation of employees payments	Secondary income (current transfer) payments
2000											
1st quarter	450 496	347 328	295 400	51 928	81 594	78 904	17 486	39 513	21 905	2 690	21 573
2nd quarter	466 127	357 221	303 489	53 733	86 514	83 762	17 440	41 434	24 889	2 751	22 392
3rd quarter	480 170	370 672	314 558	56 114	86 082	83 352	14 965	41 512	26 875	2 730	23 416
4th quarter	485 498	372 616	318 276	54 341	85 453	82 670	13 362	42 299	27 009	2 783	27 429
2001											
1st quarter	469 444	365 864	311 376	54 488	78 889	75 988	9 029	41 872	25 088	2 900	24 692
2nd quarter	443 104	346 841	292 071	54 770	70 804	67 912	5 608	41 800	20 503	2 892	25 459
3rd quarter	429 573	333 380	279 859	53 521	69 615	66 663	8 500	39 849	18 315	2 952	26 578
4th quarter	398 363	321 075	270 395	50 680	49 168	46 200	-4 580	38 937	11 843	2 968	28 120
2002											
1st quarter	421 151	329 867	274 921	54 946	60 966	57 907	8 886	39 029	9 992	3 059	30 318
2nd quarter	445 226	348 503	293 371	55 132	69 139	66 004	14 455	40 006	11 543	3 135	27 584
3rd quarter	453 188	355 116	299 455	55 660	69 630	66 607	15 321	40 531	10 754	3 023	28 443
4th quarter	457 310	364 175	305 534	58 641	62 595	59 449	9 385	40 260	9 804	3 146	30 540
2003											
1st quarter	472 826	370 927	312 769	58 158	69 728	66 500	18 645	40 102	7 753	3 229	32 171
2nd quarter	472 651	370 618	313 208	57 409	69 134	65 958	18 247	39 920	7 791	3 176	32 899
3rd quarter	484 200	378 715	316 504	62 211	72 119	68 887	20 418	41 475	6 994	3 232	33 366
4th quarter	500 721	394 048	329 607	64 441	72 958	69 686	20 728	42 028	6 930	3 272	33 715
2004											
1st quarter	530 605	415 616	347 597	68 019	76 716	73 333	21 996	43 880	7 457	3 383	38 274
2nd quarter	560 746	438 214	367 997	70 217	86 955	83 433	28 164	46 908	8 361	3 522	35 576
3rd quarter	572 832	447 757	376 563	71 194	89 606	86 149	26 120	48 629	11 399	3 458	35 469
4th quarter	611 878	469 846	396 192	73 654	103 186	99 575	28 274	56 377	14 925	3 610	38 846
2005											
1st quarter	627 457	477 364	403 172	74 192	107 251	103 357	30 522	54 982	17 852	3 894	42 841
2nd quarter	643 484	491 049	415 859	75 190	113 911	109 936	31 016	57 750	21 170	3 976	38 524
3rd quarter	662 563	502 936	426 218	76 718	118 945	114 926	28 663	60 826	25 437	4 019	40 681
4th quarter	707 913	528 917	450 570	78 347	136 242	132 222	37 778	64 999	29 445	4 020	42 755
2006											
1st quarter	723 694	541 090	458 054	83 036	144 842	140 792	35 970	69 043	35 779	4 050	37 762
2nd quarter	753 264	552 494	467 891	84 603	160 543	156 416	39 989	74 466	41 961	4 127	40 227
3rd quarter	776 402	564 969	480 544	84 425	170 207	166 124	43 418	78 208	44 498	4 083	41 226
4th quarter	775 491	560 805	471 705	89 100	174 161	169 994	39 812	83 216	46 966	4 166	40 525
2007											
1st quarter	799 009	569 542	479 603	89 939	181 944	178 100	39 676	88 701	49 723	3 844	47 523
2nd quarter	819 439	583 556	491 220	92 336	193 043	189 030	39 632	95 364	54 034	4 013	42 841
3rd quarter	829 126	594 038	499 623	94 415	189 166	185 285	32 398	97 775	55 112	3 881	45 922
4th quarter	840 562	611 787	515 902	95 885	179 276	175 293	24 555	99 948	50 789	3 984	49 499
2008											
1st quarter	873 469	640 240	540 391	99 850	179 716	175 246	37 384	99 561	38 301	4 470	53 512
2nd quarter	893 477	665 513	563 433	102 081	176 911	172 703	41 284	101 116	30 303	4 208	51 052
3rd quarter	890 064	671 072	566 834	104 238	166 672	162 508	31 226	101 394	29 887	4 164	52 320
4th quarter	781 582	573 513	470 629	102 883	154 261	150 042	29 178	97 960	22 904	4 219	53 808
2009											
1st quarter	648 884	473 405	377 709	95 696	125 107	121 293	18 325	91 869	11 099	3 814	50 372
2nd quarter	637 138	460 946	366 041	94 905	122 693	119 035	28 377	81 812	8 846	3 658	53 499
3rd quarter	667 930	496 976	400 231	96 745	117 126	113 612	27 967	79 425	6 221	3 514	53 829
4th quarter	712 764	535 501	436 044	99 456	125 868	122 436	37 941	79 389	5 106	3 433	51 395
2010											
1st quarter	733 779	556 287	456 924	99 363	121 588	118 249	35 332	78 336	4 582	3 339	55 903
2nd quarter	759 541	581 125	480 442	100 683	124 968	121 474	38 291	77 907	5 276	3 494	53 447
3rd quarter	781 206	597 721	494 007	103 715	128 508	124 908	42 088	77 587	5 234	3 600	54 977
4th quarter	800 204	613 130	507 578	105 552	132 190	128 660	44 046	79 697	4 917	3 529	54 884
2011											
1st quarter	837 659	646 061	541 686	104 375	132 471	129 038	44 119	80 014	4 904	3 434	59 126
2nd quarter	866 146	669 398	559 978	109 421	138 272	134 753	48 817	80 778	5 158	3 519	58 476
3rd quarter	871 062	676 936	565 490	111 446	137 104	133 525	46 040	82 474	5 011	3 579	57 022
4th quarter	872 048	683 251	572 732	110 519	130 919	127 266	39 886	81 677	5 703	3 653	57 878
2012											
1st quarter	889 171	692 038	581 054	110 983	139 618	136 051	46 844	83 428	5 780	3 566	57 515
2nd quarter	886 944	692 215	580 003	112 212	137 316	133 518	42 636	85 441	5 441	3 798	57 412
3rd quarter	883 290	683 733	570 941	112 793	141 069	137 316	46 353	85 756	5 207	3 753	58 487
4th quarter	886 605	686 158	571 786	114 372	141 889	138 202	42 879	90 627	4 696	3 686	58 558
2013											
1st quarter	886 365	683 359	570 164	113 195	144 192	140 431	44 052	91 911	4 468	3 761	58 813
2nd quarter	893 055	687 134	572 071	115 063	145 990	142 053	44 894	93 019	4 140	3 937	59 931
3rd quarter	898 247	691 953	576 024	115 929	144 478	140 557	43 217	93 434	3 905	3 922	61 816
4th quarter	901 330	694 140	576 193	117 947	145 806	141 857	43 667	94 374	3 815	3 950	61 384
2014											
1st quarter	909 597	702 551	585 739	116 812	143 941	139 993	42 456	94 048	3 489	3 947	63 105
2nd quarter	927 725	716 585	597 265	119 320	146 915	142 815	45 765	93 380	3 670	4 100	64 225
3rd quarter	928 279	715 134	596 009	119 126	147 985	143 868	44 940	95 412	3 516	4 117	65 160
4th quarter	930 499	717 258	595 089	122 170	146 529	142 354	42 992	95 864	3 498	4 175	66 712

Table 7-6B. U.S. International Transactions: Historical Quarterly—*Continued*

(Millions of dollars, seasonally adjusted.)

	Capital account		Financial account							
			Net U.S. acquisition of financial assets excluding financial derivatives (net increase in assets/financial outflows+)							
				Direct investment assets			Portfolio investment assets			
Year and quarter	Capital transfer receipts and other credits	Capital transfer payments and other debits	Total net acquisition of assets	Total direct investment assets	Direct equity assets	Direct debt instruments assets	Total portfolio investment assets	Equity and investment fund shares assets	Short-term debt securities assets	Long-term debt securities assets
2000										
1st quarter	7	7	223 945	51 273	44 581	6 692	41 619	18 791	9 077	13 751
2nd quarter	9	7	110 453	55 181	52 971	2 210	28 526	47 224	-9 645	-9 053
3rd quarter	10	20	81 470	36 241	32 244	3 997	46 849	16 579	14 486	15 784
4th quarter	9	3	173 449	45 311	41 850	3 461	42 719	24 120	17 887	712
2001										
1st quarter	9	8	208 168	27 355	30 761	-3 406	35 356	21 546	10 001	3 809
2nd quarter	8	5	94 853	34 934	30 062	4 872	44 656	55 707	-5 544	-5 507
3rd quarter	13 201	12	-32 394	44 791	38 412	6 379	-9 868	10 889	1 771	-22 528
4th quarter	11	4	116 439	39 719	31 488	8 231	36 775	20 977	10 047	5 751
2002										
1st quarter	12	5	89 344	52 658	39 543	13 115	14 587	-1 999	5 575	11 011
2nd quarter	13	15	158 367	54 818	26 636	28 182	42 115	19 007	21 380	1 728
3rd quarter	13	82	4 431	38 488	33 304	5 184	-9 506	-12 825	-4 622	7 941
4th quarter	14	91	67 602	33 594	28 497	5 097	32 336	12 771	8 631	10 934
2003										
1st quarter	18	100	91 398	31 741	32 586	-845	11 012	33 519	-20 656	-1 852
2nd quarter	19	1 271	162 163	51 249	36 244	15 005	42 216	18 705	9 437	14 073
3rd quarter	21	513	9 494	49 338	36 829	12 509	13 261	38 797	-15 010	-10 527
4th quarter	22	16	109 958	64 829	50 511	14 318	66 571	26 981	13 318	26 272
2004										
1st quarter	14	71	371 068	94 373	70 219	24 154	44 589	16 883	9 204	18 502
2nd quarter	15	15	181 437	86 313	67 917	18 396	53 688	40 251	5 605	7 831
3rd quarter	3 707	535	185 655	68 192	48 773	19 420	46 656	17 914	-4 567	33 309
4th quarter	17	85	324 622	129 255	109 275	19 980	47 023	9 705	10 281	27 038
2005										
1st quarter	19	2 179	129 547	59 175	57 489	1 685	60 613	46 089	1 499	13 024
2nd quarter	20	103	238 470	57 621	45 043	12 578	61 965	30 023	4 713	27 229
3rd quarter	15 401	40	207 876	-8 649	-22 309	13 660	58 471	51 420	-4 842	11 893
4th quarter	22	25	-3 576	-46 222	-28 603	-17 619	86 242	59 152	17 453	9 637
2006										
1st quarter	0	1 220	425 750	96 862	72 181	24 681	100 461	42 452	24 403	33 606
2nd quarter	0	487	244 758	55 963	43 652	12 311	109 822	21 858	26 206	61 758
3rd quarter	0	2	298 490	75 251	71 246	4 006	145 027	9 052	67 335	68 640
4th quarter	0	79	367 869	67 983	79 233	-11 250	138 056	63 969	-2 203	76 289
2007										
1st quarter	0	0	548 472	162 170	120 837	41 333	97 818	51 222	-21 214	67 810
2nd quarter	494	51	577 929	103 145	102 037	1 108	173 884	34 154	61 495	78 235
3rd quarter	0	57	214 487	101 921	79 745	22 176	131 122	64 311	13 834	52 977
4th quarter	0	2	231 621	165 703	128 759	36 944	-22 018	-1 906	-38 924	18 812
2008										
1st quarter	0	8	251 987	105 855	89 761	16 094	26 446	18 023	9 007	-583
2nd quarter	0	18	-162 285	110 839	90 634	20 205	-6 532	12 510	-7 559	-11 484
3rd quarter	6 170	126	-95 456	84 700	92 874	-8 174	-139 775	-23 639	-24 284	-91 853
4th quarter	0	7	-303 714	50 330	86 861	-36 531	-164 407	-45 444	-59 809	-59 155
2009										
1st quarter	0	20	-120 969	77 013	50 774	26 240	71 200	-640	28 244	43 596
2nd quarter	0	29	-26 790	87 319	53 244	34 075	138 043	35 252	34 830	67 960
3rd quarter	0	36	315 013	92 331	76 769	15 562	144 273	26 223	77 021	41 028
4th quarter	0	56	-35 051	57 063	81 271	-24 208	22 368	2 861	-3 969	23 475
2010										
1st quarter	0	3	254 955	98 741	114 335	-15 595	78 773	11 291	31 918	35 564
2nd quarter	0	2	161 680	69 595	82 187	-12 592	-1 863	22 259	-16 057	-8 064
3rd quarter	0	146	305 667	103 639	88 347	15 292	49 064	16 899	9 994	22 171
4th quarter	0	7	241 147	82 600	58 170	24 430	73 645	28 701	36 424	8 519
2011										
1st quarter	0	29	389 189	130 051	91 591	38 460	115 962	27 881	27 876	60 205
2nd quarter	0	854	-334	142 096	121 388	20 708	69 344	6 401	17 964	44 979
3rd quarter	0	300	81 134	67 344	84 865	-17 521	-43 647	2 052	-79 058	33 360
4th quarter	0	3	26 331	100 915	103 689	-2 774	-56 295	-29 384	-18 037	-8 873
2012										
1st quarter	0	53	-74 077	110 579	77 173	33 406	1 416	18 867	-17 380	-71
2nd quarter	0	241	-184 459	81 728	76 471	5 257	53 051	54 824	5 945	-7 719
3rd quarter	0	470	293 633	87 078	83 632	3 446	128 276	32 526	37 312	58 438
4th quarter	7 668	*	136 320	96 152	81 748	14 404	57 030	-2 963	-32 476	92 469
2013										
1st quarter	0	40	221 653	77 992	79 387	-1 395	157 860	67 295	22 289	68 276
2nd quarter	0	227	143 657	120 947	87 046	33 900	115 004	92 820	20 489	1 695
3rd quarter	0	146	83 999	105 008	99 586	5 422	61 121	19 686	17 508	23 927
4th quarter	0	*	195 454	104 296	86 087	18 210	155 892	95 443	-14 913	75 362
2014										
1st quarter	0	43	151 706	55 050	56 131	-1 081	98 981	82 823	16 158	-7 942
2nd quarter	0	2	239 149	90 293	85 576	4 716	195 068	90 670	104 399	45 519
3rd quarter	0	1	359 601	99 300	96 520	2 780	162 884	131 572	31 312	-2 587
4th quarter	0	*	41 690	112 547	117 395	-4 848	81 125	131 463	-50 338	-19 691

* = Between zero and +/- $500,000 .

Table 7-6B. U.S. International Transactions: Historical Quarterly—Continued

(Millions of dollars, seasonally adjusted.)

Year and quarter	Total other investment assets[1]	Currency and deposits assets	Loan assets	Trade credit and advances assets	Total reserve assets	Monetary gold	Special drawing rights assets	Reserve positions in the IMF	Total other reserve assets[2]	Currency and deposits reserve assets	Securities reserve assets
2000											
1st quarter	130 499	...	...	28	554	0	180	237	137	...	...
2nd quarter	28 766	...	...	-42	-2 020	0	180	-2 328	128	...	...
3rd quarter	-1 966	...	...	70	346	0	182	-1 300	1 464	...	...
4th quarter	84 009	...	...	624	1 410	0	180	1 083	147	...	...
2001											
1st quarter	145 647	...	...	-3 679	-190	0	189	-574	195	...	...
2nd quarter	13 920	...	...	2 127	1 343	0	156	1 015	172	...	...
3rd quarter	-70 876	...	...	-1 520	3 559	0	145	3 242	172	...	...
4th quarter	39 746	...	...	-2 195	199	0	140	-83	142	...	...
2002											
1st quarter	22 489	...	...	-1 488	-390	0	109	-652	153	...	...
2nd quarter	59 591	...	...	-1 562	1 843	0	107	1 607	129	...	...
3rd quarter	-25 967	...	...	-760	1 416	0	132	1 136	148	...	...
4th quarter	860	...	...	3 177	812	0	127	541	144	...	...
2003											
1st quarter	48 728	14 629	35 084	-986	-83	0	-897	644	170	80	66
2nd quarter	68 529	62 656	3 500	2 372	170	0	102	-86	154	79	52
3rd quarter	-53 715	-41 378	-11 305	-1 032	611	0	97	383	131	70	41
4th quarter	-19 221	15 394	-36 541	1 926	-2 221	0	97	-2 435	117	64	32
2004											
1st quarter	232 663	84 764	147 635	264	-557	0	100	-815	158	65	72
2nd quarter	42 558	41 318	519	721	-1 122	0	90	-1 345	133	59	54
3rd quarter	71 235	-365	74 283	-2 683	-429	0	98	-676	149	55	74
4th quarter	149 041	114 643	33 807	591	-697	0	110	-990	183	63	99
2005											
1st quarter	15 091	93 898	-78 615	-192	-5 331	0	-1 713	-3 763	145	60	64
2nd quarter	118 087	8 743	108 816	528	797	0	97	564	136	56	59
3rd quarter	162 818	31 213	133 148	-1 543	-4 765	0	-2 976	-1 951	162	55	87
4th quarter	-38 799	-50 974	9 681	2 493	-4 796	0	81	-5 050	174	54	100
2006											
1st quarter	228 939	151 125	75 714	2 099	-513	0	67	-729	149	60	66
2nd quarter	78 412	18 484	58 896	1 033	560	0	51	351	158	70	62
3rd quarter	79 218	-51 720	131 893	-955	-1 006	0	54	-1 275	215	83	101
4th quarter	163 245	36 137	125 751	1 357	-1 415	0	51	-1 678	212	96	79
2007											
1st quarter	288 412	127 453	160 213	746	72	0	43	-212	241	110	91
2nd quarter	300 926	105 985	189 735	5 205	-26	0	39	-294	229	125	60
3rd quarter	-18 611	5 831	-24 549	107	54	0	37	-230	247	135	64
4th quarter	87 914	135 876	-52 587	4 625	22	0	35	-285	272	147	73
2008											
1st quarter	119 409	-65 984	186 877	-1 484	276	0	29	-112	359	155	148
2nd quarter	-267 858	-74 301	-197 882	4 326	1 267	0	22	955	290	161	70
3rd quarter	-40 559	25 875	-64 059	-2 374	179	0	30	-256	405	167	165
4th quarter	-192 762	237 904	-426 485	-4 180	3 126	0	25	2 886	215	104	59
2009											
1st quarter	-270 164	-195 260	-77 750	2 846	982	0	15	754	213	45	142
2nd quarter	-255 783	-129 850	-122 709	-3 224	3 632	0	8	3 485	139	40	84
3rd quarter	29 388	-52 726	82 994	-881	49 021	0	47 720	1 098	203	34	164
4th quarter	-113 102	-16 625	-98 270	1 793	-1 379	0	487	-1 980	114	20	90
2010											
1st quarter	76 668	21 615	56 223	-1 171	773	0	7	581	185	14	168
2nd quarter	93 783	15 594	75 057	3 131	165	0	6	77	82	14	66
3rd quarter	151 867	58 505	93 881	-519	1 096	0	8	956	132	12	115
4th quarter	85 102	54 535	25 966	4 601	-200	0	10	-321	111	15	90
2011											
1st quarter	139 558	107 550	36 980	-4 972	3 619	0	-1 961	6 428	-848	17	-873
2nd quarter	-218 041	-208 168	-9 558	-315	6 267	0	159	5 974	134	28	93
3rd quarter	53 358	64 551	-19 675	8 482	4 079	0	27	3 909	143	33	99
4th quarter	-20 201	-53 094	32 073	819	1 912	0	23	1 768	121	32	82
2012											
1st quarter	-187 305	-200 297	15 694	-2 703	1 233	0	11	1 078	144	15	127
2nd quarter	-322 526	-320 600	-3 522	1 596	3 289	0	10	3 179	100	5	94
3rd quarter	77 446	25 150	52 476	-180	833	0	10	744	79	2	77
4th quarter	-15 967	-20 187	2 244	1 976	-895	0	6	-969	68	2	67
2013											
1st quarter	-15 074	-39 132	25 742	-1 684	875	0	5	755	115	1	115
2nd quarter	-92 105	-38 151	-57 810	3 855	-189	0	6	-287	92	1	91
3rd quarter	-81 129	-37 055	-44 021	-53	-1 001	0	5	-1 071	65	1	64
4th quarter	-61 952	-1 305	-61 889	1 242	-2 782	0	6	-2 835	47	1	45
2014											
1st quarter	24 101	-1 369	-43 231	49 346	-956	0	8	-1 040	76	-956	72
2nd quarter	58 879	-46 986	-5 194	-44 455	773	0	8	710	55	773	51
3rd quarter	33 899	98 306	32 190	67 876	-889	0	4	-951	59	-889	58
4th quarter	-30 647	-149 471	-131 119	-18 173	-2 511	0	3	-2 568	54	-2 511	53

[1]Includes insurance technical reserves, not shown separately.
[2]Includes financial derivatives and other claims, not shown seperately.
... = Not available.

Table 7-6B. U.S. International Transactions: Historical Quarterly—*Continued*

(Millions of dollars, seasonally adjusted.)

Year and quarter	Total net incurrence of liabilities	Direct investment liabilities			Portfolio investment liabilities				Other investment liabilities				Special drawing rights allocations
		Total direct investment liabilities	Direct equity liabilities	Direct debt instruments liabilities	Total portfolio liabilities	Equity and investment fund shares liabilities	Short-term debt securities liabilities	Long-term debt securities liabilities	Total other investment liabilities[1]	Currency and deposits liabilities	Loan liabilities	Trade credit and advances liabilities	
2000													
1st quarter	259 121	68 433	45 442	22 991	134 402	66 486	4 335	63 581	56 286	. . .	. . .	-348	0
2nd quarter	249 716	94 821	80 853	13 968	70 703	33 967	-16 162	52 898	84 192	. . .	. . .	1 082	0
3rd quarter	241 687	76 602	36 167	40 435	108 863	53 656	-10 271	65 478	56 222	. . .	. . .	2 321	0
4th quarter	316 494	110 212	96 920	13 292	127 998	39 491	27 491	61 016	78 284	. . .	. . .	7 320	0
2001													
1st quarter	322 741	51 119	29 649	21 470	121 347	39 931	-13 633	95 049	150 275	. . .	. . .	5 077	0
2nd quarter	215 018	67 489	48 443	19 046	97 661	34 674	-5 665	68 652	49 868	. . .	. . .	-660	0
3rd quarter	24 690	14 247	3 681	10 566	69 079	13 694	17 570	37 815	-58 636	. . .	. . .	3 423	0
4th quarter	224 872	38 617	25 279	13 338	143 405	33 165	4 877	105 363	42 850	. . .	. . .	-2 684	0
2002													
1st quarter	177 728	28 988	18 625	10 363	105 962	23 561	15 154	67 247	42 778	. . .	. . .	4 950	0
2nd quarter	249 980	25 849	30 662	-4 813	159 177	10 735	38 426	110 016	64 954	. . .	. . .	6 506	0
3rd quarter	165 658	19 252	28 773	-9 521	118 453	7 157	14 722	96 574	27 953	. . .	. . .	4 211	0
4th quarter	226 890	35 378	28 866	6 512	120 563	12 614	8 245	99 704	70 949	. . .	. . .	87	0
2003													
1st quarter	249 994	46 254	46 711	-457	98 883	-2 736	10 511	91 109	104 857	2 301	103 326	-769	0
2nd quarter	222 468	-723	-1 001	278	192 011	19 656	16 300	156 055	31 180	43 382	-10 319	-1 884	0
3rd quarter	137 917	7 167	16 487	-9 320	82 599	-4 760	-11 509	98 868	48 151	-42 634	91 901	-1 116	0
4th quarter	295 521	58 649	45 512	13 137	176 670	21 822	15 797	139 051	60 202	27 797	29 630	2 775	0
2004													
1st quarter	476 574	43 090	17 471	25 619	220 812	5 266	41 581	173 965	212 671	14 690	194 030	3 951	0
2nd quarter	342 567	43 594	41 148	2 446	223 468	8 562	5 802	209 104	75 505	17 638	58 631	-764	0
3rd quarter	290 343	50 308	34 518	15 789	162 890	982	24 547	137 362	77 145	35 721	41 605	-181	0
4th quarter	485 633	70 886	49 297	21 589	260 169	46 977	27 921	185 272	154 578	63 454	92 151	-1 027	0
2005													
1st quarter	234 558	39 247	36 487	2 760	185 008	19 272	-23 527	189 263	10 303	-74 180	81 122	3 361	0
2nd quarter	320 955	7 069	17 169	-10 100	160 648	12 282	-9 470	157 836	153 238	116 413	30 253	6 571	0
3rd quarter	428 918	41 530	18 534	22 997	215 051	31 743	-28 550	211 858	172 337	62 474	110 276	-412	0
4th quarter	288 608	50 481	40 269	10 212	271 331	25 961	16 238	229 132	-33 204	-229 490	194 173	2 112	0
2006													
1st quarter	583 709	82 419	48 634	33 784	246 292	64 241	-4 928	186 980	254 998	70 161	180 702	4 135	0
2nd quarter	428 454	86 414	46 414	39 999	264 826	23 008	34 501	207 318	77 215	42 382	30 675	4 157	0
3rd quarter	528 542	58 597	38 580	20 017	304 112	35 406	-10 951	279 656	165 833	-13 928	180 819	-1 058	0
4th quarter	575 599	66 859	50 515	16 345	311 505	22 826	4 134	284 545	197 234	125 771	73 025	-1 561	0
2007													
1st quarter	787 854	110 946	54 979	55 967	376 689	42 505	43 203	290 980	300 219	35 832	261 858	2 529	0
2nd quarter	732 101	79 920	53 374	26 546	393 364	104 760	-30 338	318 942	258 817	67 839	179 843	11 135	0
3rd quarter	294 397	110 805	68 654	42 151	73 339	20 534	60 335	-7 530	110 252	49 516	55 977	4 759	0
4th quarter	369 187	38 395	13 411	24 984	313 221	107 818	85 783	119 620	17 571	86 115	-70 697	2 153	0
2008													
1st quarter	469 902	102 201	71 215	30 986	234 853	69 376	55 597	109 881	132 848	-58 884	180 810	10 921	0
2nd quarter	-4 165	82 335	44 641	37 694	222 919	38 344	-1 713	186 288	-309 419	-82 602	-232 727	5 910	0
3rd quarter	90 107	80 728	72 147	8 581	25 970	11 297	75 421	-60 748	-16 590	16 253	-34 877	2 035	0
4th quarter	-101 793	67 471	106 858	-39 387	39 941	7 788	157 922	-125 769	-209 205	199 673	-396 759	-12 119	0
2009													
1st quarter	-114 662	1 786	7 758	-5 972	95 940	15 113	69 628	11 199	-212 388	-157 224	-53 540	-1 624	0
2nd quarter	-16 403	51 646	27 323	24 323	71 704	49 891	-30 798	52 612	-139 753	-109 843	-33 328	3 418	0
3rd quarter	341 399	60 730	41 250	19 480	72 049	85 700	-32 105	18 454	208 621	107 086	45 526	8 410	47 598
4th quarter	108 016	39 625	72 134	-32 509	117 659	68 599	-130 731	179 791	-49 268	85 756	-131 121	-3 903	0
2010													
1st quarter	315 593	40 376	30 030	10 346	187 308	65 165	-27 618	149 761	87 909	24 164	55 567	8 178	0
2nd quarter	184 104	34 099	31 115	2 984	131 528	34 570	5 822	91 136	18 477	22 112	-10 010	6 376	0
3rd quarter	553 513	102 800	76 185	26 615	328 881	40 716	24 538	263 628	121 832	37 366	84 797	-331	0
4th quarter	333 134	82 070	65 818	16 251	172 716	38 502	-55 774	189 988	78 348	32 036	41 903	4 409	0
2011													
1st quarter	592 847	69 714	38 586	31 128	149 211	38 993	-33 158	143 377	373 921	150 002	222 517	1 403	0
2nd quarter	125 789	74 432	56 468	17 964	105 650	34 442	-14 924	86 133	-54 293	78 386	-135 202	2 523	0
3rd quarter	245 696	57 328	47 078	10 250	77 147	18 955	-23 362	81 554	111 221	222 985	-124 494	12 730	0
4th quarter	12 742	55 937	42 919	13 019	-20 383	30 967	-15 277	-36 072	-22 813	24 306	-47 609	490	0
2012													
1st quarter	183 933	40 210	33 557	6 653	249 732	64 095	-11 165	196 802	-106 008	-125 940	16 022	3 909	0
2nd quarter	-151 218	67 418	49 265	18 153	7 962	30 707	-12 196	-10 549	-226 598	-183 974	-44 776	2 153	0
3rd quarter	298 348	44 111	38 442	5 669	222 638	30 867	49 642	142 129	31 600	83 599	-58 505	6 506	0
4th quarter	270 910	66 038	70 164	-4 125	266 664	113 391	-10 000	163 274	-61 793	-18 694	-42 150	-949	0
2013													
1st quarter	285 407	44 526	39 788	4 739	155 583	-22 550	69 180	108 952	85 298	6 687	76 171	2 439	0
2nd quarter	224 716	82 156	61 980	20 175	-25 746	-32 706	-32 741	39 701	168 307	103 956	61 347	3 004	0
3rd quarter	165 707	71 130	55 579	15 551	207 881	61 828	-52 805	198 857	-113 303	-21 130	-94 906	2 733	0
4th quarter	341 838	97 161	69 487	27 673	153 226	-91 980	63 085	182 122	91 451	82 773	4 994	3 684	0
2014													
1st quarter	271 921	-105 425	-97 740	-7 685	242 627	99 113	13 573	129 941	134 719	-5 754	127 315	13 157	0
2nd quarter	283 271	78 405	58 756	19 649	88 549	15 070	-24 913	98 392	116 317	103 243	7 984	5 089	0
3rd quarter	364 518	106 473	59 437	47 036	240 879	75 555	-8 106	173 430	17 166	41 638	-19 894	-4 578	0
4th quarter	57 712	52 378	48 401	3 977	132 976	-34 660	42 380	125 256	-127 642	-88 097	-40 140	595	0

[1]Includes financial derivatives and other claims, not shown seperately.
. . . = Not available.

Table 7-6B. U.S. International Transactions: Historical Quarterly—Continued

(Millions of dollars, seasonally adjusted.)

Year and quarter	Financial account—Continued. Financial derivatives other than reserves, net	Statistical discrepancy Total	Seasonal adjustment discrepancy	Balance on current account Total balance on current account	Balances on goods and services Total balance on goods and services	Balance on goods	Balance on services	Balance on primary income	Balance on secondary income	Balance on capital account	Net lending (+) or net borrowing (-) Based on current and capital account transactions	Based on financial account transactions
2000												
1st quarter	. . .	61 635	7 084	-96 811	-88 171	-106 900	18 729	3 600	-12 240	. . .	-96 811	-35 176
2nd quarter	. . .	-40 500	-733	-98 765	-89 579	-108 819	19 241	4 168	-13 355	2	-98 763	-139 263
3rd quarter	. . .	-53 490	-10 847	-106 717	-95 480	-112 753	17 273	2 752	-13 989	-10	-106 727	-160 217
4th quarter	. . .	-34 587	4 497	-108 464	-99 287	-118 310	19 023	8 659	-17 836	6	-108 458	-143 045
2001												
1st quarter	. . .	-7 694	6 711	-106 879	-96 898	-114 599	17 701	4 911	-14 892	. . .	-106 879	-114 573
2nd quarter	. . .	-24 036	-2 547	-96 133	-87 800	-103 565	15 764	6 965	-15 297	4	-96 129	-120 165
3rd quarter	. . .	34 195	-10 039	-104 468	-89 394	-103 905	14 511	1 076	-16 150	13 188	-91 279	-57 084
4th quarter	. . .	-20 599	5 866	-87 840	-87 415	-100 301	12 886	16 775	-17 201	6	-87 834	-108 433
2002												
1st quarter	. . .	15 601	10 097	-103 992	-92 466	-106 126	13 661	6 953	-18 479	7	-103 985	-88 384
2nd quarter	. . .	23 402	-2 395	-115 013	-102 488	-117 537	15 049	2 305	-14 831	-2	-115 015	-91 613
3rd quarter	. . .	-46 289	-14 507	-114 869	-105 913	-121 004	15 091	5 842	-14 797	-69	-114 938	-161 227
4th quarter	. . .	-35 002	6 804	-124 209	-118 090	-130 578	12 488	10 081	-16 200	-77	-124 286	-159 288
2003												
1st quarter	. . .	-23 528	8 593	-134 986	-123 459	-135 220	11 762	6 569	-18 097	-82	-135 068	-158 597
2nd quarter	. . .	70 216	-1 101	-129 269	-122 384	-134 670	12 285	9 928	-16 813	-1 252	-130 521	-60 305
3rd quarter	. . .	2 443	-13 166	-130 374	-122 872	-134 164	11 292	9 855	-17 358	-492	-130 866	-128 423
4th quarter	. . .	-58 849	5 678	-126 719	-125 175	-137 590	12 414	16 401	-17 945	5	-126 714	-185 563
2004												
1st quarter	. . .	32 137	7 506	-137 586	-135 158	-149 437	14 279	20 980	-23 408	-56	-137 642	-105 505
2nd quarter	. . .	-4 314	-1 661	-156 815	-150 348	-163 682	13 334	14 699	-21 166	. . .	-156 815	-161 130
3rd quarter	. . .	51 683	-17 132	-159 544	-156 097	-168 934	12 837	17 413	-20 860	3 173	-156 371	-104 688
4th quarter	. . .	18 882	11 289	-179 825	-168 281	-182 712	14 431	11 034	-22 578	-68	-179 893	-161 011
2005												
1st quarter	. . .	66 956	12 116	-169 807	-165 634	-183 577	17 943	19 458	-23 632	-2 160	-171 967	-105 011
2nd quarter	. . .	97 078	-711	-179 480	-171 639	-187 907	16 268	16 666	-24 507	-83	-179 563	-82 485
3rd quarter	. . .	-50 077	-22 777	-186 327	-181 376	-197 802	16 427	19 355	-24 306	15 362	-170 965	-221 042
4th quarter	. . .	-82 361	11 372	-209 820	-195 596	-213 518	17 922	12 153	-26 376	-3	-209 822	-292 184
2006												
1st quarter	-1 633	39 686	9 207	-198 058	-192 106	-208 382	16 276	12 810	-18 763	-1 220	-199 278	-159 592
2nd quarter	-14 090	5 072	-2 993	-202 372	-191 169	-209 719	18 550	11 565	-22 768	-487	-202 859	-197 787
3rd quarter	-15 134	-29 121	-19 887	-216 063	-199 284	-218 180	18 896	8 197	-24 976	-2	-216 065	-245 186
4th quarter	1 147	-16 271	13 673	-190 233	-179 157	-201 009	21 851	10 765	-21 840	-79	-190 312	-206 583
2007												
1st quarter	-14 795	-55 083	10 249	-199 093	-177 931	-202 800	24 868	11 013	-32 175	0	-199 093	-254 176
2nd quarter	1 007	35 509	-1 542	-189 117	-179 322	-205 300	25 978	16 384	-26 179	443	-188 674	-153 165
3rd quarter	-5 942	85 159	-24 306	-170 954	-174 713	-203 972	29 259	30 833	-27 074	-57	-171 011	-85 852
4th quarter	13 508	35 425	15 601	-159 481	-173 409	-209 124	35 716	42 374	-28 447	-2	-159 483	-124 058
2008												
1st quarter	7 966	-28 312	7 721	-181 630	-185 551	-216 677	31 126	38 670	-34 749	-8	-183 095	-209 950
2nd quarter	2 355	21 466	-5 107	-177 213	-186 349	-220 469	34 120	39 734	-30 598	-18	-178 261	-155 765
3rd quarter	4 886	-10 387	-30 220	-176 334	-189 449	-219 624	30 175	44 041	-30 926	6 043	-170 869	-180 677
4th quarter	17 740	-32 708	27 607	-151 465	-147 376	-175 722	28 346	23 701	-27 790	-7	-152 555	-184 180
2009												
1st quarter	-7 146	83 349	10 808	-96 782	-94 771	-123 499	28 728	25 319	-27 330	-20	-98 252	-13 453
2nd quarter	-7 561	70 120	-7 354	-88 040	-81 444	-111 984	30 540	24 366	-30 962	-29	-89 060	-17 948
3rd quarter	-10 645	56 382	-23 012	-93 378	-98 547	-129 950	31 403	37 922	-32 753	-36	-94 167	-37 032
4th quarter	-19 464	-59 880	19 560	-102 595	-109 012	-144 262	35 250	35 977	-29 560	-56	-102 686	-162 530
2010												
1st quarter	-16 152	32 185	12 928	-108 972	-117 954	-152 461	34 507	43 785	-34 803	-3	-108 215	-76 790
2nd quarter	-9 980	82 148	-11 474	-114 550	-128 754	-165 200	36 446	44 232	-30 028	-2	-114 038	-32 404
3rd quarter	11 893	-117 432	-21 882	-118 375	-129 376	-168 786	39 411	42 828	-31 828	-146	-117 990	-235 953
4th quarter	163	10 216	20 429	-102 033	-118 575	-162 230	43 656	46 816	-30 275	-7	-101 876	-91 825
2011												
1st quarter	-2 952	-88 000	14 214	-118 581	-134 319	-181 536	47 217	50 302	-34 564	-29	-118 268	-206 609
2nd quarter	-9 806	-14 467	-13 542	-120 608	-138 879	-186 717	47 838	51 219	-32 948	-854	-121 885	-135 929
3rd quarter	1 617	-54 665	-27 968	-107 979	-133 962	-183 307	49 345	57 613	-31 630	-300	-108 709	-162 945
4th quarter	-23 865	101 904	27 298	-112 177	-141 466	-189 086	47 620	61 827	-32 538	-3	-112 678	-10 276
2012												
1st quarter	7 339	-126 656	13 161	-123 962	-144 454	-193 439	48 984	53 532	-33 040	-53	-121 589	-259 562
2nd quarter	-2 419	83 455	-15 445	-118 875	-138 036	-188 239	50 203	51 490	-32 329	-241	-118 205	-39 823
3rd quarter	5 129	113 016	-25 063	-112 132	-128 519	-178 943	50 424	47 680	-31 293	-470	-105 897	-1 500
4th quarter	-2 985	-39 461	27 348	-105 781	-126 596	-181 475	54 879	50 291	-29 477	7 668	-97 074	-140 364
2013												
1st quarter	-3 948	37 825	16 071	-105 487	-120 948	-177 560	56 611	45 983	-30 522	-40	-102 758	-45 448
2nd quarter	-3 302	22 011	-12 764	-106 146	-121 799	-177 083	55 284	47 507	-31 854	-227	-97 841	-27 649
3rd quarter	6 569	26 311	-22 871	-101 305	-121 197	-177 936	56 739	51 524	-31 632	-146	-94 939	-136 247
4th quarter	2 929	-56 138	19 564	-87 317	-112 448	-169 090	56 642	54 639	-29 508	. . .	-81 633	-186 486
2014												
1st quarter	6 147	-17 582	18 645	-96 443	-125 418	-184 310	58 892	58 294	-29 319	-43	-96 486	-114 068
2nd quarter	-4 513	43 406	-11 087	-92 039	-128 712	-188 113	59 401	57 935	-21 263	-2	-92 041	-48 635
3rd quarter	-24 269	68 720	-29 823	-97 905	-125 871	-183 076	57 205	61 730	-33 764	-1	-97 906	-29 186
4th quarter	-31 737	55 379	22 265	-103 138	-128 323	-185 963	57 640	60 025	-34 840	. . .	-103 138	-47 759

. . . = Not available.
* = Less than $500,000 (+/-).

Table 7-7. Foreigners' Transactions in Long-Term Securities with U.S. Residents

(Billions of dollars, not seasonally adjusted.)

Year and month	Gross purchases from U.S. residents	Gross sales to U.S. residents	Transactions in U.S. domestic securities between foreigners and U.S. residents — Net purchases — Total	Private — Total	Private — Treasury bonds and notes	Private — Government agency bonds	Private — Corporate bonds	Private — Equities	Official — Total	Official — Treasury bonds and notes
1977	60.7	30.1	30.6	. . .	. . .	. . .	. . .	. . .	. . .	. . .
1978	60.5	51.1	9.4	3.6	1.0	0.6	0.3	1.7	5.8	3.7
1979	72.9	67.2	5.7	2.5	1.2	0.1	0.2	1.1	3.2	1.7
1980	106.9	91.1	15.8	6.6	1.0	0.4	0.9	4.3	9.2	3.9
1981	126.5	100.5	26.0	10.2	3.3	0.3	1.9	4.8	15.6	11.7
1982	159.5	136.8	22.7	9.2	2.8	0.3	2.5	3.6	13.5	14.6
1983	223.4	211.7	11.7	13.2	4.6	0.5	1.7	6.4	-1.5	0.8
1984	335.5	304.0	31.5	33.8	21.0	1.2	12.5	-0.9	-2.4	0.5
1985	667.2	588.9	78.3	71.9	21.1	4.6	41.4	4.8	6.3	8.1
1986	1 355.4	1 266.9	88.5	76.4	5.2	8.2	45.1	18.0	12.1	14.2
1987	1 692.1	1 623.0	69.1	37.5	-5.5	3.5	22.7	16.8	31.7	31.1
1988	1 827.9	1 753.1	74.8	49.4	22.2	5.4	21.3	0.4	25.4	26.6
1989	2 431.7	2 335.2	96.5	66.5	27.4	13.7	17.5	7.9	30.0	26.8
1990	2 111.2	2 092.4	18.8	-3.6	-5.3	5.6	9.8	-13.7	22.5	23.3
1991	2 382.1	2 324.0	58.1	54.3	18.7	8.9	16.5	10.1	3.8	1.2
1992	2 677.8	2 604.6	73.2	63.1	32.4	14.3	20.0	-3.7	10.1	6.9
1993	3 212.5	3 101.4	111.1	103.2	22.2	31.4	29.9	19.6	7.9	1.3
1994	3 351.1	3 210.7	140.4	94.9	37.0	15.6	38.0	4.3	45.4	41.8
1995	3 737.6	3 505.7	231.9	185.3	94.5	25.0	57.6	8.2	46.5	39.6
1996	4 667.6	4 297.4	370.2	278.1	146.4	36.7	82.2	12.7	92.1	85.8
1997	6 573.3	6 185.3	388.0	339.7	140.2	45.3	82.8	71.3	48.3	44.0
1998	7 633.5	7 355.7	277.8	270.8	44.9	50.5	121.7	53.7	6.9	4.1
1999	7 483.5	7 133.3	350.2	338.8	-0.1	71.9	158.8	108.2	11.4	-9.9
2000	8 684.1	8 226.3	457.8	420.1	-47.7	111.9	182.1	173.8	37.7	-6.3
2001	10 261.8	9 740.9	520.8	494.2	15.0	146.6	218.2	114.4	26.7	3.5
2002	13 022.9	12 475.4	547.6	508.3	112.8	166.6	176.7	52.2	39.3	7.1
2003	13 526.0	12 806.1	719.9	585.0	159.7	129.9	260.3	35.0	134.9	103.8
2004	15 178.9	14 262.4	916.5	680.9	150.9	205.7	298.0	26.2	235.6	201.1
2005	17 157.5	16 145.9	1 011.6	891.1	269.4	187.6	353.1	81.0	120.4	68.7
2006	21 077.1	19 933.9	1 143.2	946.6	125.9	193.8	482.2	144.6	196.6	69.6
2007	29 730.6	28 724.8	1 005.8	818.1	195.0	99.9	342.8	180.4	187.8	3.0
2008	30 724.9	30 310.0	414.9	311.9	238.7	-7.4	59.2	21.4	103.0	76.2
2009	20 479.7	19 840.9	638.9	511.0	377.0	31.4	-38.4	141.1	127.9	161.4
2010	25 017.0	24 108.7	908.3	776.1	531.6	146.2	-14.0	112.3	132.2	172.1
2011	27 818.8	27 325.5	493.4	322.6	288.4	57.6	-44.0	20.6	170.7	144.2
2012	24 593.4	23 959.2	634.1	408.2	206.6	134.2	-31.0	98.4	225.9	209.9
2013	27 557.8	27 475.5	82.3	3.5	51.3	-13.1	1.4	-36.1	78.8	-8.4
2014	2 322.3	2 301.5	16.3	14.2	10.0	3.6	1.5	-0.9	6.5	3.7
2012										
January	2 055.7	1 953.5	102.2	68.3	54.5	11.3	-0.8	3.3	34.0	33.1
February	2 194.6	2 172.1	22.5	2.1	-0.2	1.7	-7.8	8.4	20.4	13.3
March	2 222.9	2 200.3	22.6	-5.7	-16.5	9.2	-3.3	5.0	28.3	34.0
April	2 137.1	2 095.6	41.5	25.8	27.5	2.0	-3.7	0.0	15.7	19.2
May	2 333.1	2 249.1	83.9	51.5	52.7	4.4	-7.1	1.4	32.5	22.2
June	1 998.4	1 988.9	9.5	0.3	10.6	16.6	-20.8	-6.2	9.3	22.9
July	1 924.1	1 851.6	72.5	47.3	24.5	16.5	-1.1	7.3	25.3	31.9
August	2 051.1	1 968.2	82.9	52.8	19.7	16.3	11.3	5.5	30.1	19.0
September	1 989.4	1 967.1	22.4	7.3	-22.5	14.2	-8.6	24.2	15.1	2.2
October	2 095.3	2 061.7	33.6	27.4	6.7	15.0	3.4	2.4	6.2	7.1
November	1 818.1	1 753.4	64.7	64.7	28.1	8.0	6.0	22.6	0.1	-3.5
December	1 773.4	1 697.7	75.7	66.6	21.6	18.9	1.5	24.6	9.2	8.4
2013										
January	2 057.5	2 007.4	50.1	-12.6	-21.3	-1.0	4.9	4.8	62.7	53.1
February	2 313.0	2 302.4	10.6	12.9	9.1	-2.2	8.3	-2.2	-2.3	-6.8
March	2 242.0	2 243.9	-2.0	-6.6	5.9	-8.0	-8.5	4.1	4.6	-17.1
April	2 374.8	2 384.6	-9.8	-2.7	-15.0	6.8	-4.7	10.2	-7.1	-23.8
May	2 769.0	2 767.4	1.6	-42.2	-29.3	-9.3	6.2	-9.8	43.8	40.3
June	2 627.3	2 705.9	-78.6	-82.4	-40.1	-9.4	-7.1	-25.8	3.8	-0.7
July	2 350.7	2 313.6	37.1	32.1	40.6	2.4	-0.7	-10.2	5.0	-15.9
August	2 239.3	2 252.3	-13.0	-8.2	-4.5	8.7	1.4	-13.8	-4.8	-10.9
September	2 299.3	2 241.2	58.0	73.3	46.8	10.1	5.4	11.1	-15.3	-23.2
October	2 260.2	2 212.3	47.9	52.6	34.8	1.6	3.3	12.9	-4.7	-1.9
November	2 043.2	2 052.3	-9.1	-19.2	-10.3	-2.2	-1.4	-5.3	10.2	10.2
December	2 018.6	2 035.2	-16.6	0.3	29.6	-10.3	-5.9	-13.1	-16.9	-11.8
2014										
January	2 350.9	2 369.3	18.4	-1.9	12.1	-3.8	-4.9	-5.3	-16.5	-16.7
February	2 226.7	2 137.7	89.0	70.5	73.9	-0.9	-1.5	-0.8	18.5	16.6
March	2 541.4	2 529.1	12.4	6.0	17.8	-7.2	-8.2	5.5	6.4	12.1
April	2 444.9	2 454.9	-99.9	-28.0	-29.4	-2.4	2.8	-9.0	10.0	18.8
May	2 299.9	2 263.3	36.6	12.2	8.3	-1.6	-3.3	-9.0	1.1	19.7
June	2 237.7	2 256.1	-18.4	-44.6	-40.8	1.4	2.2	-9.0	26.3	20.0
July	1 972.3	1 976.3	-3.9	1.9	5.2	7.2	-8.5	-2.0	-5.8	-6.0
August	2 062.7	2 036.2	26.5	20.7	22.1	11.3	-8.6	4.4	14.6	3.6
September	2 399.1	2 304.8	94.2	79.7	44.2	11.7	19.4	6.3	-27.1	3.9
October	2 807.9	2 822.8	-15.0	-15.4	-3.1	2.2	18.7	25.5	6.0	-2.5
November	2 076.1	2 016.9	59.2	53.0	2.7	5.3	5.6	4.6	6.2	-7.5
December	2 448.2	2 451.2	-3.0	17.0	1.4	5.3	5.6	4.6	-19.9	-17.0

. . . = Not available.

Table 7-7. Foreigners' Transactions in Long-Term Securities with U.S. Residents—*Continued*

(Billions of dollars, not seasonally adjusted.)

Year and month	Transactions in U.S. domestic securities between foreigners and U.S. residents—Continued — Net purchases—Continued — Official—Continued — Government agency bonds	Corporate bonds	Equities	Transactions in foreign securities between foreigners and U.S. residents — Gross purchases from U.S. residents	Gross sales to U.S. residents	Net purchases [1] — Total	Bonds	Equities	Net long-term securities transactions	Other acquisitions of long-term securities, net	Net foreign acquisition of long-term securities
1977	. . .	. . .	. . .	10.3	15.8	-5.5	-5.1	-0.4	25.1	. . .	. . .
1978	0.7	0.7	0.7	14.8	18.5	-3.7	-4.2	0.5	5.7	. . .	. . .
1979	0.5	0.4	0.6	17.3	22.1	-4.8	-4.0	-0.8	0.9	0.1	1.0
1980	2.2	2.0	1.1	25.0	28.1	-3.1	-1.0	-2.1	12.7	-1.6	11.0
1981	1.3	1.6	1.0	26.9	32.6	-5.7	-5.5	-0.2	20.3	-5.2	15.0
1982	-0.7	-0.7	0.3	34.3	42.3	-8.0	-6.6	-0.2	14.7	-5.4	9.3
1983	-0.5	-0.8	-1.0	49.6	56.6	-7.0	-3.2	-3.8	4.7	-3.2	1.5
1984	0.0	-0.8	-2.1	70.8	75.9	-5.1	-3.9	-1.1	26.4	-1.5	24.9
1985	-0.3	-1.6	0.1	102.1	110.0	-7.9	-4.0	-3.9	70.4	-2.3	68.1
1986	-1.2	-1.6	0.7	216.1	221.7	-5.6	-3.7	-1.9	82.9	-2.3	80.8
1987	1.6	-0.4	-0.6	294.5	301.4	-6.9	-8.0	1.1	62.2	-1.0	61.3
1988	1.3	-0.1	-2.4	293.9	303.3	-9.4	-7.4	-2.0	65.4	0.2	65.6
1989	1.4	-0.2	2.0	344.6	363.2	-18.6	-5.5	-13.1	77.9	0.0	78.0
1990	0.7	-0.1	-1.4	437.7	468.9	-31.2	-21.9	-9.2	-12.4	3.9	-8.5
1991	1.3	0.4	0.9	450.9	497.7	-46.8	-14.8	-32.0	11.3	0.4	11.7
1992	3.9	0.8	-1.5	663.6	711.5	-47.9	-15.6	-32.3	25.3	-0.3	25.0
1993	4.0	0.6	2.0	991.4	1 134.5	-143.1	-80.4	-62.7	-32.0	1.1	-30.8
1994	6.1	0.0	-2.5	1 234.5	1 291.8	-57.3	-9.2	-48.1	83.1	0.5	83.5
1995	3.7	0.2	3.0	1 235.1	1 333.8	-98.7	-48.4	-50.3	133.2	0.4	133.6
1996	5.0	1.5	-0.2	1 564.4	1 675.0	-110.6	-51.4	-59.3	259.6	-0.5	259.1
1997	4.5	1.5	-1.7	2 207.7	2 296.8	-89.1	-48.1	-40.9	298.9	0.0	298.9
1998	6.3	0.2	-3.7	2 257.8	2 269.0	-11.2	-17.3	6.2	266.6	0.1	266.7
1999	20.4	1.5	-0.6	1 975.6	1 965.6	10.0	-5.7	15.6	360.2	0.0	360.2
2000	40.9	2.0	1.1	2 761.1	2 778.3	-17.1	-4.1	-13.1	440.7	-59.8	380.8
2001	17.4	3.8	2.0	2 557.8	2 577.4	-19.6	30.5	-50.1	501.2	-41.5	459.8
2002	28.6	5.6	-2.0	2 640.0	2 613.0	27.0	28.5	-1.5	574.6	-39.3	535.2
2003	25.9	5.4	-0.3	2 761.8	2 818.4	-56.5	32.0	-88.6	663.3	-138.9	524.5
2004	20.8	11.5	2.2	3 123.1	3 276.0	-152.8	-67.9	-85.0	763.6	-38.8	724.8
2005	31.6	19.1	1.0	3 700.0	3 872.4	-172.4	-45.1	-127.3	839.2	-143.0	696.2
2006	92.6	28.6	5.8	5 515.9	5 766.8	-250.9	-144.5	-106.5	892.3	-174.6	717.7
2007	119.1	50.6	15.1	8 189.1	8 418.3	-229.2	-133.9	-95.3	776.6	-235.2	541.4
2008	-31.3	34.7	23.4	7 714.9	7 640.7	74.2	53.9	20.2	489.1	-197.9	291.2
2009	-42.9	-2.3	11.7	5 121.4	5 308.3	-186.8	-127.5	-59.4	452.0	-205.1	246.9
2010	-38.2	0.8	-2.5	7 323.8	7 439.1	-115.3	-54.6	-60.6	793.0	-234.7	558.3
2011	23.3	-1.2	4.5	7 499.3	7 623.6	-124.3	-52.6	-71.7	369.0	-174.2	194.8
2012	-1.3	7.0	10.3	7 385.4	7 406.7	-21.2	19.9	-41.1	612.9	-237.2	375.7
2013	75.2	16.2	-4.1	8 155.9	8 375.6	-219.8	-45.6	-174.2	-137.5	-210.2	-347.6
2014	2.6	0.6	-0.4	762.1	759.9	2.2	11.0	-8.8	22.9	-7.0	15.9
2012											
January	-0.1	-0.2	1.1	592.3	582.3	9.9	14.4	-4.5	112.1	-17.1	95.0
February	7.4	0.7	-1.1	644.5	659.4	-14.9	-8.6	-6.3	7.6	-13.5	-6.0
March	-5.4	-0.8	0.4	719.4	705.3	14.0	17.3	-3.3	36.6	-18.0	18.6
April	-6.2	0.5	2.2	615.0	615.2	-0.2	3.2	-3.5	41.3	-19.1	22.2
May	8.5	0.7	1.1	639.5	632.9	6.6	16.2	-9.6	90.6	-17.4	73.2
June	-14.3	-2.8	3.5	601.4	595.8	5.7	11.7	-6.0	15.2	-17.8	-2.6
July	-8.0	0.6	0.8	557.7	549.5	8.1	8.9	-0.8	80.7	-19.1	61.6
August	9.4	1.6	0.1	520.9	510.0	10.9	13.4	-2.5	93.8	-17.9	75.9
September	9.8	2.7	0.4	621.5	636.3	-14.9	-21.7	6.8	7.5	-21.8	-14.2
October	-3.0	0.9	1.2	666.4	691.8	-25.4	-25.5	0.1	8.2	-14.8	-6.6
November	1.4	2.2	-0.1	627.6	637.6	-10.0	-3.2	-6.7	54.8	-39.4	15.4
December	-0.7	0.9	0.6	579.4	590.5	-11.1	-6.2	-4.9	64.6	-21.3	43.3
2013											
January	5.4	3.0	1.2	689.8	712.5	-22.7	-2.8	-19.9	27.4	-21.7	5.7
February	3.7	1.0	-0.3	624.1	649.2	-25.1	-6.1	-19.0	-14.5	-19.5	-34.0
March	16.7	1.9	3.2	683.5	711.2	-27.7	-0.8	-26.9	-29.7	-18.4	-48.0
April	16.0	-0.2	0.8	721.6	734.1	-12.5	4.7	-17.2	-22.3	-19.7	-42.0
May	-1.1	3.0	1.6	734.8	761.7	-26.8	-10.7	-16.1	-25.2	-19.4	-44.6
June	3.9	1.9	-1.4	678.5	667.2	11.3	14.9	-3.5	-67.3	-18.5	-85.8
July	20.1	0.0	0.7	677.7	693.4	-15.6	0.4	-16.0	21.5	-16.5	4.9
August	8.1	1.0	-3.1	615.2	616.5	-1.3	11.1	-12.4	-14.3	-15.3	-29.7
September	4.7	1.9	1.4	700.9	732.6	-31.7	-24.8	-6.8	26.4	-13.3	13.0
October	1.0	1.3	-5.1	751.5	770.7	-19.2	-6.5	-12.7	28.7	-11.6	17.1
November	1.7	0.8	-2.6	689.9	708.9	-19.0	-14.5	-4.4	-28.0	-11.2	-39.2
December	-5.1	0.5	-0.5	588.3	617.7	-29.4	-10.2	-19.3	-46.0	-24.9	-70.9
2014											
January	0.5	0.0	-0.4	774.0	751.8	22.2	33.5	-11.4	3.7	-9.7	-6.0
February	2.5	-0.5	0.0	691.2	691.9	-0.7	0.8	-1.5	88.3	-10.4	77.9
March	-1.4	1.0	-5.2	813.9	870.0	-56.1	1.4	-57.5	-43.7	53.2	9.5
April	0.3	-0.3	-0.9	778.9	807.1	-28.2	-0.2	-28.0	-38.2	-9.9	-48.2
May	3.7	1.2	-0.2	778.0	795.2	-17.2	-1.0	-16.2	19.4	-10.5	8.9
June	5.0	-0.3	1.5	809.8	810.8	-1.1	-13.9	12.8	-19.4	-11.1	-30.5
July	0.3	1.4	-1.5	703.1	717.8	-14.7	-6.1	-8.6	-18.6	-29.5	-48.1
August	-1.0	1.3	2.0	652.7	627.2	25.5	8.1	17.5	52.1	-17.2	34.9
September	9.3	1.3	0.0	853.0	786.9	66.1	40.1	26.0	160.4	-11.2	149.1
October	1.6	1.6	-0.2	856.9	843.3	13.6	27.6	-14.0	-1.4	-13.1	-14.5
November	14.6	-0.5	-0.3	680.1	705.8	-25.7	3.6	-29.3	33.5	-12.4	21.2
December	-4.0	0.9	0.3	753.3	711.1	42.2	37.9	4.3	39.2	-2.2	37.0

[1](-) indicates net U.S. acquisitions of foreign securities.
. . . = Not available.

Table 7-8. International Investment Position of the United States

(End of period, millions of dollars.)

Year	U.S. net international investment position			U.S. assets							
	Total	Total, excluding financial derivatives	Financial derivatives other than reserves, net	Total assets	Assets excluding financial derivatives	By functional category					
						Direct investment at market value	Portfolio investment			Gross positive fair value, financial derivatives other than reserves	Other investment
							Total[1]	Equity and investment fund shares	Long-term debt securities		
1980	296 862	296 862	...	839 083	839 083	297 349	78 028	18 930	43 524	...	292 294
1981	226 992	226 992	...	832 943	832 943	239 080	88 494	16 467	45 675	...	380 801
1982	238 366	238 366	...	1 030 358	1 030 358	295 981	104 809	17 442	56 604	...	486 123
1983	261 494	261 494	...	1 206 656	1 206 656	351 325	110 787	26 154	58 569	...	621 434
1984	140 140	140 140	...	1 214 478	1 214 478	357 920	112 609	25 994	62 810	...	638 909
1985	104 281	104 281	...	1 392 053	1 392 053	475 693	138 735	44 383	75 020	...	659 695
1986	109 232	109 232	...	1 679 716	1 679 716	615 138	182 167	72 399	85 724	...	742 536
1987	59 616	59 616	...	1 850 216	1 850 216	681 751	215 285	94 700	93 889	...	790 810
1988	21 479	21 479	...	2 098 851	2 098 851	782 947	305 186	128 662	104 187	...	866 539
1989	-33 713	-33 713	...	2 447 740	2 447 740	929 965	395 727	197 345	116 949	...	953 334
1990	-149 523	-149 523	...	2 415 654	2 415 654	853 331	425 538	197 596	144 717	...	962 121
1991	-243 314	-243 314	...	2 605 674	2 605 674	962 582	525 355	278 976	176 774	...	958 514
1992	-432 129	-432 129	...	2 611 230	2 611 230	943 364	586 206	314 266	200 817	...	934 225
1993	-121 772	-121 772	...	3 234 733	3 234 733	1 204 611	916 315	543 862	309 666	...	948 862
1994	-110 311	-110 311	...	3 434 637	3 434 637	1 234 084	990 838	626 762	310 391	...	1 046 321
1995	-277 567	-277 567	...	4 094 375	4 094 375	1 493 609	1 278 722	790 615	413 310	...	1 145 983
1996	-328 306	-328 306	...	4 791 796	4 791 796	1 749 299	1 573 208	1 006 135	481 411	...	1 308 550
1997	-788 225	-788 225	...	5 536 514	5 536 514	2 036 671	1 841 029	1 207 787	543 396	...	1 523 978
1998	-1 033 775	-1 033 775	...	6 368 620	6 368 620	2 469 095	2 149 431	1 474 983	594 400	...	1 604 088
1999	-1 002 268	-1 002 268	...	7 611 443	7 611 443	3 051 404	2 650 768	2 003 716	548 233	...	1 772 853
2000	-1 536 826	-1 536 826	...	7 641 748	7 641 748	2 934 570	2 556 158	1 852 842	572 692	...	2 022 620
2001	-2 295 050	-2 295 050	...	7 170 013	7 170 013	2 554 463	2 316 634	1 612 673	557 062	...	2 168 955
2002	-2 410 951	-2 410 951	...	7 065 177	7 065 177	2 283 141	2 276 589	1 373 980	716 249	...	2 346 845
2003	-2 293 013	-2 293 013	...	8 620 934	8 620 934	3 037 312	3 176 287	2 079 422	880 963	...	2 223 758
2004	-2 363 392	-2 363 392	...	10 589 003	10 589 003	3 746 863	3 828 305	2 560 418	1 003 420	...	2 824 244
2005	-1 857 865	-1 915 780	57 915	13 357 001	12 166 972	4 047 170	4 628 978	3 317 705	1 037 271	1 190 029	3 302 781
2006											
1st quarter	-1 656 271	-1 722 627	66 356	14 466 414	13 276 558	4 380 797	5 038 569	3 682 411	1 054 251	1 189 856	3 650 900
2nd quarter	-1 679 424	-1 747 363	67 939	14 805 682	13 509 632	4 410 235	5 121 916	3 673 580	1 114 349	1 296 050	3 760 430
3rd quarter	-2 006 413	-2 066 720	60 307	15 275 332	14 081 168	4 601 077	5 428 603	3 828 619	1 214 438	1 194 164	3 839 868
4th quarter	-1 808 474	-1 868 310	59 836	16 409 857	15 170 862	4 929 892	6 017 080	4 328 960	1 299 281	1 238 995	4 004 037
2007											
1st quarter	-1 654 830	-1 711 802	56 972	17 305 871	16 050 296	5 216 131	6 288 275	4 536 363	1 390 060	1 255 575	4 317 610
2nd quarter	-1 422 046	-1 478 860	56 814	18 840 267	17 293 555	5 583 502	6 852 231	4 958 299	1 465 702	1 546 712	4 632 953
3rd quarter	-1 232 107	-1 303 056	70 949	19 681 427	17 960 822	5 812 922	7 272 284	5 262 469	1 573 519	1 720 605	4 623 609
4th quarter	-1 279 493	-1 350 965	71 472	20 704 503	18 145 171	5 857 923	7 262 045	5 247 990	1 630 165	2 559 332	4 747 993
2008											
1st quarter	-1 849 701	-1 980 458	130 757	21 886 438	17 700 163	5 451 453	6 844 546	4 786 880	1 659 850	4 186 275	5 095 671
2nd quarter	-1 835 095	-1 945 457	110 362	21 013 398	17 374 981	5 365 469	6 669 792	4 701 709	1 573 348	3 638 417	5 032 141
3rd quarter	-3 309 696	-3 413 010	103 314	18 431 592	15 190 540	4 558 476	5 374 215	3 636 110	1 364 843	3 241 052	4 966 064
4th quarter	-3 995 303	-4 154 938	159 635	19 423 416	13 295 966	3 707 211	4 320 819	2 748 428	1 258 288	6 127 450	4 974 204
2009											
1st quarter	-3 856 708	-4 008 267	151 559	18 147 396	12 585 545	3 497 940	4 087 167	2 456 973	1 281 373	5 561 851	4 697 126
2nd quarter	-3 200 061	-3 361 609	161 548	17 932 161	13 877 711	4 113 456	4 984 745	3 162 209	1 444 856	4 054 450	4 464 995
3rd quarter	-2 670 164	-2 815 808	145 644	19 732 946	15 601 910	4 794 375	5 879 511	3 836 151	1 593 378	4 131 036	4 544 656
4th quarter	-2 627 626	-2 753 961	126 335	19 426 459	15 936 680	4 945 292	6 058 554	3 995 295	1 625 768	3 489 779	4 529 030
2010											
1st quarter	-2 769 546	-2 882 780	113 234	19 752 973	16 323 927	5 058 482	6 286 609	4 135 014	1 685 518	3 429 046	4 570 889
2nd quarter	-3 181 212	-3 280 424	99 212	19 796 742	15 486 430	4 540 945	5 840 898	3 734 612	1 678 247	4 310 312	4 666 038
3rd quarter	-2 746 809	-2 851 320	104 511	21 966 656	17 182 958	5 163 300	6 724 001	4 475 807	1 809 406	4 783 698	4 832 049
4th quarter	-2 511 788	-2 622 170	110 382	21 767 827	18 115 514	5 486 391	7 160 366	4 900 246	1 787 310	3 652 313	4 980 084
2011											
1st quarter	-2 638 599	-2 743 797	105 198	22 149 169	18 954 866	5 811 089	7 497 835	5 159 980	1 853 998	3 194 303	5 142 596
2nd quarter	-2 785 715	-2 883 910	98 195	22 447 716	18 974 492	5 855 672	7 644 691	5 204 875	1 929 578	3 473 224	4 945 067
3rd quarter	-4 133 952	-4 239 860	105 908	22 300 371	17 086 773	4 955 939	6 672 316	4 287 221	1 955 276	5 213 598	4 898 673
4th quarter	-4 454 997	-4 541 036	86 039	22 208 896	17 492 318	5 214 826	6 871 732	4 501 438	1 953 663	4 716 578	4 868 723
2012											
1st quarter	-4 581 557	-4 657 843	76 286	22 271 644	18 321 405	5 673 500	7 398 899	5 002 083	1 995 620	3 950 239	4 676 428
2nd quarter	-5 263 421	-5 331 010	67 589	21 511 319	17 355 499	5 383 077	7 077 986	4 666 919	2 002 304	4 155 820	4 337 816
3rd quarter	-5 005 381	-5 057 874	52 493	22 322 658	18 397 052	5 748 867	7 617 470	5 038 916	2 130 338	3 925 606	4 424 438
4th quarter	-4 578 245	-4 636 021	57 776	22 520 346	18 900 585	5 938 327	7 967 014	5 311 509	2 240 596	3 619 761	4 422 876
2013											
1st quarter	-5 110 866	-5 150 891	40 025	22 650 385	19 402 008	6 185 179	8 230 586	5 524 329	2 274 833	3 248 377	4 433 184
2nd quarter	-5 523 614	-5 582 966	59 352	21 904 000	19 078 933	6 146 656	8 146 302	5 508 752	2 185 715	2 825 067	4 339 768
3rd quarter	-4 994 895	-5 042 858	47 963	22 954 418	20 193 002	6 690 152	8 721 240	6 037 266	2 225 021	2 761 416	4 298 183
4th quarter	-5 382 996	-5 456 542	73 546	23 709 843	20 890 008	7 080 058	9 183 060	6 444 232	2 292 118	2 819 835	4 178 557
2014											
1st quarter	-5 483 360	-5 552 781	69 421	24 080 862	21 425 380	2 655 482	9 400 599	6 627 771	2 340 052	2 655 482	4 370 859
2nd quarter	-5 518 617	-5 551 951	33 334	24 987 306	22 280 432	2 706 874	9 997 286	7 061 208	2 456 927	2 706 874	4 324 592
3rd quarter	-6 204 917	-6 259 130	54 213	24 596 646	21 798 389	2 798 257	9 710 959	6 803 745	2 435 922	2 798 257	4 411 573
4th quarter	-7 019 699	-7 093 546	73 847	24 595 547	21 371 012	3 224 535	9 572 539	6 719 690	2 402 678	3 224 535	4 240 188

[1]Includes components not shown separately.
. . . = Not available.

Table 7-8. International Investment Position of the United States—*Continued*

(End of period, millions of dollars.)

Year	U.S. assets — Reserve assets — Total¹	U.S. assets — Reserve assets — Monetary gold	U.S. liabilities — Total	U.S. liabilities — Liabilities excluding financial derivatives	U.S. liabilities — Direct investment at market value	Portfolio investment — Total¹	Portfolio investment — Equity and investment fund shares	Long-term debt securities — Treasury bonds and notes	Long-term debt securities — Other long-term securities
1980	171 412	155 816	542 221	542 221	297 349	78 028	18 930	69 855	20 506
1981	124 568	105 644	605 951	605 951	239 080	88 494	16 467	80 195	24 057
1982	143 445	120 635	791 992	791 992	295 981	104 809	17 442	95 059	30 216
1983	123 110	100 484	945 162	945 162	351 325	110 787	26 154	94 894	29 243
1984	105 040	81 202	1 074 338	1 074 338	357 920	112 609	25 994	123 920	44 086
1985	117 930	85 834	1 287 772	1 287 772	475 693	138 735	44 383	157 259	92 584
1986	139 875	102 428	1 570 484	1 570 484	615 138	182 167	72 399	178 990	148 634
1987	162 370	127 648	1 790 600	1 790 600	681 751	215 285	94 700	194 558	174 566
1988	144 179	107 434	2 077 372	2 077 372	782 947	305 186	128 662	238 782	200 833
1989	168 714	105 164	2 481 453	2 481 453	929 965	395 727	197 345	332 642	239 440
1990	174 664	102 406	2 565 177	2 565 177	853 331	425 538	197 596	341 567	247 114
1991	159 223	92 561	2 848 988	2 848 988	962 582	525 355	278 976	365 555	282 589
1992	147 435	87 168	3 043 359	3 043 359	943 364	586 206	314 266	392 695	309 354
1993	164 945	102 556	3 356 505	3 356 505	1 204 611	916 315	543 862	417 812	367 466
1994	163 394	100 110	3 544 948	3 544 948	1 234 084	990 838	626 762	469 633	383 251
1995	176 061	101 279	4 371 942	4 371 942	1 493 609	1 278 722	790 615	619 592	482 290
1996	160 739	96 698	5 120 102	5 120 102	1 749 299	1 573 208	1 006 135	803 456	571 422
1997	134 836	75 929	6 324 739	6 324 739	2 036 671	1 841 029	1 207 787	959 973	661 376
1998	146 006	75 291	7 402 395	7 402 395	2 469 095	2 149 431	1 474 983	982 750	782 085
1999	136 418	75 950	8 613 711	8 613 711	3 051 404	2 650 768	2 003 716	872 690	913 177
2000	128 400	71 799	9 178 574	9 178 574	2 934 570	2 556 158	1 852 842	843 580	1 198 002
2001	129 961	72 328	9 465 063	9 465 063	2 554 463	2 316 634	1 612 673	876 971	1 485 952
2002	158 602	90 806	9 476 128	9 476 128	2 283 141	2 276 589	1 373 980	1 016 580	1 720 841
2003	183 577	108 866	10 913 947	10 913 947	3 037 312	3 176 287	2 079 422	1 222 605	1 953 987
2004	189 591	113 947	12 952 395	12 952 395	3 746 863	3 828 305	2 560 418	1 489 885	2 365 314
2005	188 043	134 175	15 214 866	14 082 752	4 047 170	4 628 978	3 317 705	1 719 663	2 725 265
2006									
1st quarter	206 293	152 221	16 122 685	14 999 185	3 387 219	7 602 527	2 454 992	1 711 099	2 846 467
2nd quarter	217 052	160 430	16 485 106	15 256 995	3 402 912	7 791 430	2 431 169	1 726 941	3 005 787
3rd quarter	211 620	156 703	17 281 746	16 147 889	3 571 141	8 342 232	2 599 784	1 811 861	3 313 960
4th quarter	219 853	165 267	18 218 331	17 039 172	3 752 602	8 843 523	2 791 893	1 872 847	3 557 374
2007									
1st quarter	228 280	173 047	18 960 701	17 762 098	3 859 621	9 271 729	2 848 797	1 942 381	3 811 943
2nd quarter	224 869	170 105	20 262 313	18 772 415	4 100 970	9 780 484	3 129 523	1 964 881	4 042 723
3rd quarter	252 007	194 294	20 913 533	19 263 877	4 239 248	10 033 110	3 222 228	1 986 163	4 115 575
4th quarter	277 211	218 025	21 983 996	19 496 136	4 134 239	10 326 974	3 231 651	2 073 744	4 221 532
2008									
1st quarter	308 493	244 109	23 736 139	19 680 621	3 917 702	10 368 656	3 011 024	2 200 862	4 297 351
2nd quarter	307 579	243 259	22 848 492	19 320 437	3 911 825	10 327 562	2 969 288	2 210 757	4 284 552
3rd quarter	291 785	231 296	21 741 288	18 603 550	3 712 136	9 878 568	2 731 517	2 329 086	3 880 435
4th quarter	293 732	227 439	23 418 718	17 450 903	3 091 240	9 475 873	2 132 433	2 494 964	3 748 688
2009									
1st quarter	303 312	239 664	22 004 103	16 593 811	2 839 930	9 168 152	1 904 734	2 559 225	3 534 874
2nd quarter	314 516	244 371	21 132 222	17 239 320	3 141 287	9 633 155	2 252 181	2 605 142	3 637 019
3rd quarter	383 368	260 388	22 403 110	18 417 718	3 497 706	10 251 103	2 688 029	2 723 242	3 732 227
4th quarter	403 804	284 380	22 054 085	18 690 641	3 618 630	10 463 234	2 917 681	2 920 160	3 647 956
2010									
1st quarter	407 947	291 702	22 522 519	19 206 707	3 769 042	10 810 833	3 137 639	3 135 897	3 597 062
2nd quarter	438 549	325 305	22 977 954	18 766 864	3 456 621	10 684 333	2 814 256	3 342 873	3 580 866
3rd quarter	463 609	341 779	24 713 465	20 034 278	3 789 895	11 527 670	3 169 658	3 661 688	3 725 011
4th quarter	488 673	367 537	24 279 615	20 737 684	4 099 097	11 869 262	3 545 769	3 748 544	3 655 679
2011									
1st quarter	503 346	376 297	24 787 768	21 698 663	4 283 086	12 215 888	3 793 751	3 875 948	3 659 899
2nd quarter	529 062	393 687	25 233 431	21 858 402	4 316 300	12 432 716	3 829 897	4 049 180	3 682 190
3rd quarter	559 845	423 628	26 434 323	21 326 633	3 907 462	12 212 692	3 366 482	4 339 272	3 660 084
4th quarter	537 037	400 355	26 663 893	22 033 354	4 199 225	12 647 243	3 841 901	4 356 681	3 617 936
2012									
1st quarter	572 578	434 742	26 853 201	22 979 248	4 553 282	13 323 328	4 355 167	4 510 887	3 640 438
2nd quarter	556 620	418 006	26 774 740	22 686 509	4 487 971	13 297 524	4 261 853	4 680 774	3 551 049
3rd quarter	606 277	464 422	27 328 039	23 454 926	4 690 702	13 814 030	4 508 584	4 793 665	3 657 579
4th quarter	572 368	433 434	27 098 591	23 536 606	4 670 942	13 978 875	4 545 371	4 909 828	3 678 933
2013									
1st quarter	553 058	417 941	27 761 250	24 552 898	5 018 930	14 569 596	5 000 428	5 001 076	3 653 589
2nd quarter	446 207	311 707	27 427 614	24 661 899	5 131 714	14 432 860	5 076 621	4 919 659	3 554 128
3rd quarter	483 426	346 878	27 949 313	25 235 860	5 342 443	14 882 136	5 376 543	5 009 541	3 666 475
4th quarter	448 333	314 975	29 092 840	26 346 551	5 790 551	15 503 192	5 821 487	5 108 856	3 680 194
2014									
1st quarter	470 884	337 791	29 564 222	26 978 161	5 683 630	15 938 103	6 051 072	5 260 807	3 721 651
2nd quarter	477 865	343 871	30 505 923	27 832 383	5 934 993	16 423 330	6 352 073	5 260 807	3 721 651
3rd quarter	443 987	318 113	30 801 563	28 057 519	6 023 492	16 570 603	6 450 520	5 260 807	3 721 651
4th quarter	434 251	315 368	31 615 246	28 464 558	6 228 795	16 917 146	6 665 202	5 260 807	3 721 651

¹Includes components not shown separately.

Section 7c: Exports and Imports

Figure 7-3: Foreign Trade Balances on Goods and Services, 1960–2014

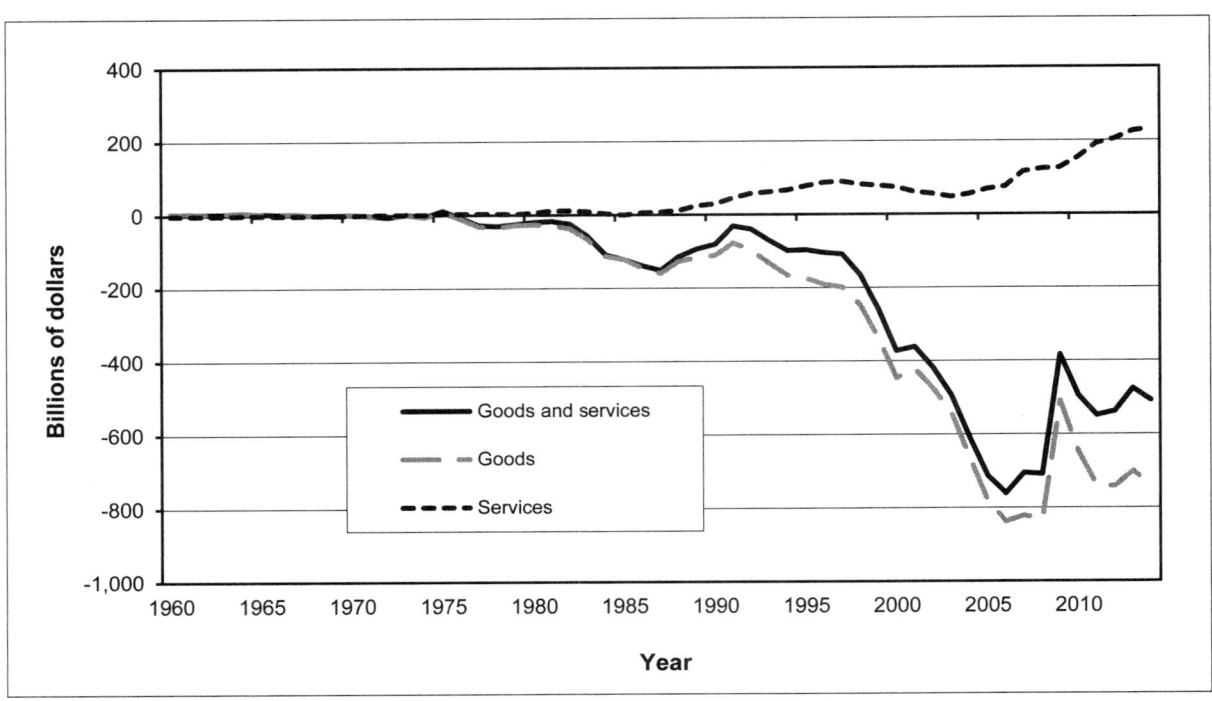

- U.S. imports of goods and services exceeded exports by a record $762 billion in 2006. This negative "trade balance" (to differentiate it from the more comprehensive "current account deficit" including income payments and receipts that is shown in earlier pages) diminished to $384 billion in 2009 but was back at $508 billion in 2014. (Table 7-9)

- Canada and Mexico are the principal trading partners of the United States, with relations governed by the North American Free Trade Agreement (NAFTA). In 2014, U.S. goods exports to those two countries brought in $553 billion, compared with $276 billion in exports to the European Union and $333 billion in exports to China, Japan, and the newly industrialized countries of Asia (the NICS—Hong Kong, South Korea, Singapore, and Taiwan). (Table 7-13)

- U.S. goods imports from Canada and Mexico in 2014 amounted to $637 billion, more than the $418 billion imported from the European Union but less than the $733 billion from China, Japan, and the Asian NICS. (Table 7-14)

- The value of imports from China, which grew by an average 23 percent <u>per year</u> from 2001 to 2006, slowed to a 7 percent annual rate of increase between 2006 and 2014. (Table 7-14)

- The persistent and growing U.S. surplus on services is in contrast with the goods deficit, though it offsets only about a third of it. Revised categories permit a more detailed look at the composition of the total services surplus, which was $233 billion in 2014. The largest component, $88 billion, was "Charges for the use of intellectual property" (formerly known as "royalties and license fees"). There was a $66 billion surplus on "travel for all purposes including education," which includes the spending of foreigners here for tourism and education. The U.S. runs a deficit on insurance services but a $68 billion surplus on financial services. (Tables 7-15A and 7-16A)

Table 7-9. U.S. Exports and Imports of Goods and Services

(Balance of payments basis; millions of dollars, seasonally adjusted.)

Year and month	Goods and services			Goods			Services		
	Exports	Imports	Balance	Exports	Imports	Balance	Exports	Imports	Balance
1970	56 640	54 386	2 254	42 469	39 866	2 603	14 171	14 520	-349
1971	59 677	60 979	-1 302	43 319	45 579	-2 260	16 358	15 400	958
1972	67 222	72 665	-5 443	49 381	55 797	-6 416	17 841	16 868	973
1973	91 242	89 342	1 900	71 410	70 499	911	19 832	18 843	989
1974	120 897	125 190	-4 293	98 306	103 811	-5 505	22 591	21 379	1 212
1975	132 585	120 181	12 404	107 088	98 185	8 903	25 497	21 996	3 501
1976	142 716	148 798	-6 082	114 745	124 228	-9 483	27 971	24 570	3 401
1977	152 301	179 547	-27 246	120 816	151 907	-31 091	31 485	27 640	3 845
1978	178 428	208 191	-29 763	142 075	176 002	-33 927	36 353	32 189	4 164
1979	224 131	248 696	-24 565	184 439	212 007	-27 568	39 692	36 689	3 003
1980	271 834	291 241	-19 407	224 250	249 750	-25 500	47 584	41 491	6 093
1981	294 398	310 570	-16 172	237 044	265 067	-28 023	57 354	45 503	11 851
1982	275 236	299 391	-24 156	211 157	247 642	-36 485	64 079	51 749	12 329
1983	266 106	323 874	-57 767	201 799	268 901	-67 102	64 307	54 973	9 335
1984	291 094	400 166	-109 072	219 926	332 418	-112 492	71 168	67 748	3 420
1985	289 070	410 950	-121 880	215 915	338 088	-122 173	73 155	72 862	294
1986	310 033	448 572	-138 538	223 344	368 425	-145 081	86 689	80 147	6 543
1987	348 869	500 552	-151 684	250 208	409 765	-159 557	98 661	90 787	7 874
1988	431 149	545 715	-114 566	320 230	447 189	-126 959	110 919	98 526	12 393
1989	487 003	580 144	-93 141	359 916	477 665	-117 749	127 087	102 479	24 607
1990	535 233	616 097	-80 864	387 401	498 438	-111 037	147 832	117 659	30 173
1991	578 344	609 479	-31 135	414 083	491 020	-76 937	164 261	118 459	45 802
1992	616 882	656 094	-39 212	439 631	536 528	-96 897	177 251	119 566	57 685
1993	642 863	713 174	-70 311	456 943	589 394	-132 451	185 920	123 780	62 141
1994	703 254	801 747	-98 493	502 859	668 690	-165 831	200 395	133 057	67 338
1995	794 387	890 771	-96 384	575 204	749 374	-174 170	219 183	141 397	77 786
1996	851 602	955 667	-104 065	612 113	803 113	-191 000	239 489	152 554	86 935
1997	934 453	1 042 726	-108 273	678 366	876 794	-198 428	256 087	165 932	90 155
1998	933 174	1 099 314	-166 140	670 416	918 637	-248 221	262 758	180 677	82 081
1999	969 867	1 228 485	-258 617	698 524	1 035 592	-337 068	271 343	192 893	78 450
2000	1 075 321	1 447 837	-372 517	784 940	1 231 722	-446 783	290 381	216 115	74 266
2001	1 005 654	1 367 165	-361 511	731 331	1 153 701	-422 370	274 323	213 465	60 858
2002	978 706	1 397 660	-418 955	698 036	1 173 281	-475 245	280 670	224 379	56 290
2003	1 020 418	1 514 308	-493 890	730 446	1 272 089	-541 643	289 972	242 219	47 754
2004	1 161 549	1 771 433	-609 883	823 584	1 488 349	-664 766	337 966	283 083	54 882
2005	1 286 022	2 000 267	-714 245	913 016	1 695 820	-782 804	373 006	304 448	68 558
2006	1 457 642	2 219 358	-761 716	1 040 905	1 878 194	-837 289	416 738	341 165	75 573
2007	1 653 548	2 358 922	-705 375	1 165 151	1 986 347	-821 196	488 396	372 575	115 821
2008	1 841 612	2 550 339	-708 726	1 308 795	2 141 287	-832 492	532 817	409 052	123 765
2009	1 583 053	1 966 827	-383 774	1 070 331	1 580 025	-509 694	512 722	386 801	125 920
2010	1 853 606	2 348 263	-494 658	1 290 273	1 938 950	-648 678	563 333	409 313	154 020
2011	2 127 021	2 675 646	-548 625	1 499 240	2 239 886	-740 646	627 781	435 761	192 020
2012	2 216 540	2 754 145	-537 605	1 561 689	2 303 785	-742 095	654 850	450 360	204 490
2013	2 280 194	2 756 586	-476 392	1 592 784	2 294 453	-701 669	687 410	462 134	225 276
2014	2 218 989	2 755 762	-508 324	1 632 639	2 374 101	-741 462	710 565	477 428	233 137
2012									
January	179 606	230 873	-51 266	127 140	194 068	-66 927	52 466	36 805	15 661
February	181 720	225 058	-43 338	128 281	188 119	-59 838	53 439	36 940	16 499
March	186 257	236 107	-49 850	132 195	198 868	-66 673	54 063	37 239	16 824
April	184 543	232 317	-47 773	130 545	194 920	-64 375	53 998	37 397	16 601
May	184 306	231 490	-47 184	130 100	194 028	-63 928	54 206	37 462	16 744
June	185 330	228 408	-43 078	131 119	191 055	-59 936	54 211	37 353	16 858
July	183 673	227 507	-43 834	130 026	189 965	-59 939	53 647	37 542	16 105
August	182 845	227 380	-44 536	128 309	189 720	-61 411	54 536	37 661	16 875
September	188 696	228 846	-40 150	133 663	191 256	-57 593	55 033	37 591	17 442
October	183 512	225 870	-42 358	127 682	187 845	-60 163	55 830	38 025	17 805
November	186 286	232 891	-46 604	129 697	194 585	-64 888	56 589	38 306	18 283
December	189 765	227 399	-37 634	132 932	189 357	-56 424	56 833	38 042	18 791
2013									
January	187 478	229 683	-42 205	130 653	191 846	-61 192	56 825	37 838	18 987
February	188 030	229 800	-41 770	131 420	192 107	-60 688	56 610	37 693	18 917
March	186 903	223 876	-36 973	130 532	186 211	-55 680	56 371	37 665	18 707
April	187 763	228 180	-40 417	131 326	190 084	-58 758	56 437	38 096	18 342
May	187 206	232 037	-44 831	130 319	193 671	-63 352	56 887	38 366	18 521
June	190 366	226 918	-36 552	133 343	188 316	-54 973	57 023	38 602	18 421
July	189 902	229 321	-39 419	132 830	190 851	-58 021	57 072	38 470	18 603
August	190 606	230 121	-39 515	132 829	191 356	-58 527	57 777	38 765	19 012
September	190 249	232 512	-42 263	132 430	193 817	-61 387	57 819	38 695	19 125
October	193 971	233 053	-39 083	136 141	193 884	-57 742	57 829	39 170	18 659
November	194 922	230 894	-35 972	136 752	191 517	-54 765	58 170	39 377	18 793
December	192 799	230 193	-37 393	134 210	190 792	-56 583	58 590	39 400	19 189
2014									
January	192 879	232 341	-39 462	133 738	193 706	-59 968	59 141	38 635	20 506
February	189 494	232 330	-42 836	131 768	193 060	-61 292	57 726	39 270	18 456
March	194 760	237 881	-43 121	135 923	198 973	-63 050	58 837	38 908	19 929
April	195 024	239 294	-44 270	135 556	199 877	-64 321	59 468	39 417	20 051
May	197 269	239 339	-42 070	137 314	199 405	-62 091	59 955	39 934	20 021
June	195 580	237 950	-42 370	136 282	197 982	-61 700	59 298	39 968	19 330
July	196 906	238 318	-41 412	138 406	198 584	-60 178	58 500	39 734	18 766
August	197 303	238 578	-41 275	138 155	198 979	-60 824	59 148	39 599	19 549
September	195 053	238 239	-43 186	136 371	198 446	-62 075	58 682	39 793	18 889
October	197 759	240 513	-42 754	138 107	200 024	-61 917	59 652	40 489	19 163
November	196 200	236 222	-40 022	136 474	195 805	-59 331	59 726	40 417	19 309
December	194 975	240 524	-45 549	134 544	199 260	-64 716	60 431	41 264	19 167

Table 7-10. U.S. Exports of Goods by End-Use and Advanced Technology Categories

(Census basis, except as noted; billions of dollars; seasonally adjusted, except as noted.)

Year and month	Total exports of goods			Principal end-use category							Advanced technology products [1]
	Total, balance of payments basis	Net adjustments	Total, Census basis	Foods, feeds, and beverages	Industrial supplies and materials		Capital goods, except automotive	Automotive vehicles, engines, and parts	Consumer goods, except automotive	Other goods	
					Total	Petroleum and products					
1980	224.25	3.55	220.70	36.28	72.09	3.57	76.28	17.44	17.75	. . .	. . .
1981	237.04	3.31	233.74	38.84	70.19	4.56	84.17	19.69	17.70	. . .	. . .
1982	211.16	-1.12	212.28	32.20	64.05	6.87	76.50	17.23	16.13	. . .	. . .
1983	201.80	0.09	201.71	32.09	58.94	5.59	71.66	18.46	14.93	. . .	. . .
1984	219.93	1.18	218.74	32.20	64.12	5.43	77.01	22.42	15.09	. . .	. . .
1985	215.92	3.29	212.62	24.57	61.16	5.71	79.32	24.95	14.59	. . .	. . .
1986	223.34	-3.13	226.47	23.52	64.72	4.43	82.82	25.10	16.73	. . .	. . .
1987	250.21	-3.70	253.90	25.23	70.05	4.63	92.71	27.58	20.31	. . .	. . .
1988	320.23	-3.11	323.34	33.77	90.02	4.48	119.10	33.40	26.98	. . .	. . .
1989	359.92	-3.08	363.00	36.34	98.36	6.46	136.94	35.05	36.01	. . .	. . .
1990	387.40	-5.57	392.97	35.18	105.55	8.36	153.07	36.07	43.60	20.73	. . .
1991	414.08	-7.77	421.85	35.79	109.69	8.40	166.72	39.72	46.65	23.66	. . .
1992	439.63	-8.54	448.17	40.34	109.59	7.62	176.50	46.71	51.31	24.39	. . .
1993	456.94	-7.92	464.86	40.59	111.89	7.49	182.85	51.35	54.56	23.89	. . .
1994	502.86	-9.77	512.63	41.96	121.55	6.97	205.82	57.31	59.86	26.50	. . .
1995	575.20	-9.54	584.74	50.47	146.37	8.10	234.46	61.26	64.31	28.72	. . .
1996	612.11	-12.96	625.08	55.53	147.98	9.63	253.99	64.24	70.11	33.85	. . .
1997	678.37	-10.82	689.18	51.51	158.32	10.42	295.87	73.30	77.96	33.51	. . .
1998	670.42	-11.72	682.14	46.40	148.31	8.08	299.87	72.39	80.29	35.44	. . .
1999	683.97	-11.83	695.80	45.98	147.52	8.62	310.79	75.26	80.92	35.32	. . .
2000	771.99	-9.92	781.92	47.87	172.62	12.01	356.93	80.36	89.38	34.77	227.39
2001	718.71	-10.39	729.10	49.41	160.10	10.64	321.71	75.44	88.33	34.11	199.63
2002	682.42	-10.68	693.10	49.62	156.81	10.34	290.44	78.94	84.36	32.94	178.57
2003	713.42	-11.36	724.77	55.03	173.04	12.69	293.67	80.63	89.91	32.49	180.21
2004	807.52	-11.26	818.78	56.57	203.96	17.08	331.56	89.21	103.08	34.40	201.42
2005	894.63	-11.35	905.98	58.96	233.05	22.66	363.32	98.41	115.29	36.96	216.06
2006	1 015.81	-10.16	1 025.97	66.00	276.00	31.57	404.00	107.30	129.10	43.60	252.71
2007	1 138.38	-9.82	1 148.20	84.30	316.40	37.76	433.00	121.30	146.00	47.30	264.88
2008	1 307.50	20.06	1 287.44	108.35	388.03	67.18	457.66	121.45	161.28	50.67	270.13
2009	1 069.73	13.69	1 056.04	93.91	296.51	49.18	391.24	81.72	149.46	43.22	244.71
2010	1 288.80	10.30	1 278.50	107.72	391.66	70.83	447.54	112.01	165.23	54.34	273.31
2011	1 495.85	15.56	1 480.29	126.25	501.08	113.71	493.96	133.04	175.30	52.89	287.72
2012	1 561.69	15.99	1 545.70	132.91	501.17	123.46	527.24	146.15	181.66	56.58	305.01
2013	1 592.78	13.19	1 579.59	136.18	509.31	137.56	534.21	152.56	189.09	58.25	319.79
2014	1 632.64	12.11	1 620.53	143.75	505.11	144.30	551.06	159.69	198.91	62.01	421.34
2012											
January	127.14	1.40	125.74	10.05	41.74	9.21	42.87	12.30	14.66	4.13	22.56
February	128.28	1.51	126.77	9.68	41.93	9.70	43.63	12.09	14.81	4.63	23.43
March	132.20	1.28	130.91	10.12	43.61	10.55	45.10	12.10	14.95	5.04	28.06
April	130.55	1.53	129.01	10.72	43.00	10.58	43.53	12.20	15.07	4.50	23.77
May	130.10	1.11	128.99	11.49	41.90	10.16	44.05	12.14	15.00	4.42	24.89
June	131.12	1.29	129.83	10.85	42.29	10.34	43.72	12.61	15.46	4.90	26.55
July	130.03	1.53	128.50	12.42	40.29	9.79	43.91	12.37	15.26	4.27	24.58
August	128.31	1.40	126.91	11.46	39.53	9.32	44.18	12.13	15.07	4.55	25.60
September	133.66	1.34	132.33	13.11	42.44	11.10	44.69	11.95	15.35	4.78	25.82
October	127.68	1.18	126.50	11.11	39.83	10.48	43.46	11.78	15.40	4.92	26.11
November	129.70	1.22	128.48	11.02	40.77	10.83	44.08	12.29	15.41	4.92	26.10
December	132.93	1.19	131.74	10.88	43.85	11.41	44.03	12.21	15.24	5.54	27.54
2013											
January	130.65	1.49	129.16	11.52	41.26	9.44	44.10	12.23	15.65	4.40	24.01
February	131.42	0.93	130.49	11.59	43.05	10.81	43.24	12.42	15.16	5.03	22.66
March	130.53	1.19	129.34	10.79	42.63	9.72	43.51	12.28	14.91	5.22	27.98
April	131.33	1.00	130.32	10.38	41.71	9.85	44.20	12.70	16.73	4.60	24.69
May	130.32	0.96	129.36	10.23	40.79	10.26	44.88	12.98	15.61	4.88	27.14
June	133.34	0.63	132.71	10.58	42.33	11.48	45.63	12.65	16.45	5.08	29.20
July	132.83	1.17	131.66	10.81	43.33	12.09	44.57	12.52	15.77	4.67	26.74
August	132.83	1.31	131.52	10.47	42.86	12.25	44.69	13.06	15.63	4.82	26.73
September	132.43	1.15	131.28	12.02	41.35	11.79	44.59	13.13	15.64	4.55	26.75
October	136.14	0.93	135.22	12.53	43.38	12.70	45.08	13.02	16.36	4.86	27.70
November	136.75	1.35	135.40	12.56	43.36	13.09	45.27	13.06	15.81	5.34	27.95
December	134.21	1.07	133.14	12.71	43.28	14.08	44.46	12.51	15.37	4.81	28.24
2014											
January	133.74	1.63	132.11	12.13	43.17	12.06	44.58	12.36	15.65	4.23	25.27
February	131.77	0.66	131.11	12.07	40.76	11.33	44.31	12.43	16.62	4.92	24.45
March	135.92	1.26	134.66	12.46	41.72	11.63	46.01	10.07	16.40	5.01	29.34
April	135.57	1.14	134.41	112.20	41.93	11.80	45.90	12.92	16.40	5.05	27.07
May	137.31	1.28	136.03	12.32	42.31	13.04	45.74	13.48	16.67	5.14	27.65
June	136.28	1.15	135.13	11.88	42.21	12.76	45.60	13.50	18.92	5.01	28.84
July	138.41	1.22	137.18	11.65	43.14	13.51	46.14	14.76	16.52	4.97	27.11
August	138.15	0.72	137.43	10.91	43.96	13.61	46.91	13.41	16.90	5.34	28.88
September	136.37	0.69	135.68	12.10	42.26	12.29	46.03	13.46	16.60	5.22	28.32
October	138.11	0.90	137.21	12.02	41.90	10.91	47.70	13.60	16.95	5.05	30.47
November	136.47	0.99	135.48	12.08	42.27	11.31	45.73	13.17	16.59	5.64	28.21
December	134.54	0.45	134.09	11.91	39.50	10.04	46.40	13.55	16.68	6.05	31.11

[1] Not seasonally adjusted.
. . . = Not available.

Table 7-11. U.S. Imports of Goods by End-Use and Advanced Technology Categories

(Census basis, except as noted; billions of dollars; seasonally adjusted, except as noted.)

Year and month	Total imports of goods			Principal end-use category							Advanced technology products [1]
	Total, balance of payments basis	Net adjustments	Total, Census basis	Foods, feeds, and beverages	Industrial supplies and materials		Capital goods, except automotive	Automotive vehicles, engines, and parts	Consumer goods, except automotive	Other goods	
					Total	Petroleum and products					
1980	249.75	4.23	245.52	18.55	124.96	...	30.72	28.13	34.22	...	...
1981	265.07	3.76	261.31	18.53	131.10	...	36.86	30.80	38.30	...	...
1982	247.64	3.70	243.94	17.47	107.82	...	38.22	34.26	39.66	...	...
1983	268.90	7.18	261.72	18.56	105.63	...	42.61	42.04	46.59	...	...
1984	332.42	1.91	330.51	21.92	122.72	...	60.15	56.77	61.19	...	...
1985	338.09	1.71	336.38	21.89	112.48	...	60.81	65.21	66.43	...	...
1986	368.43	2.75	365.67	24.40	101.37	...	71.86	78.25	79.43	...	...
1987	409.77	3.48	406.28	24.81	110.67	...	84.77	85.17	88.82	...	...
1988	447.19	5.26	441.93	24.93	118.06	...	101.79	87.95	96.42	...	...
1989	477.37	3.72	473.65	25.08	132.40	...	112.45	87.38	102.26	...	...
1990	498.34	2.36	495.98	26.65	143.41	62.16	116.04	87.69	105.29	16.09	...
1991	490.98	2.53	488.45	26.21	131.38	51.78	120.80	84.94	107.78	15.94	...
1992	536.46	3.80	532.66	27.61	138.64	51.60	134.25	91.79	122.66	17.71	...
1993	589.44	8.78	580.66	27.87	145.61	51.50	152.37	102.42	134.02	18.39	...
1994	668.59	5.33	663.26	27.87	145.61	51.28	152.37	102.42	134.02	18.39	...
1995	749.57	6.03	743.54	33.18	181.85	56.16	221.43	123.80	159.91	23.39	...
1996	803.33	8.04	796.77	35.74	204.43	72.75	228.07	128.95	172.00	26.11	...
1997	876.37	6.66	869.70	39.69	213.77	71.77	253.28	139.81	193.81	29.34	...
1998	917.18	5.28	911.90	41.24	200.14	50.90	269.56	149.05	216.52	35.39	...
1999	1 029.99	5.37	1 024.62	43.60	221.39	67.81	295.72	178.96	241.91	43.04	...
2000	1 224.42	6.40	1 218.02	45.98	298.98	120.28	347.03	195.88	281.83	48.33	222.08
2001	1 145.90	4.90	1 141.00	46.64	273.87	103.59	297.99	189.78	284.29	48.42	195.18
2002	1 164.72	3.35	1 161.37	49.69	267.69	103.51	283.32	203.74	307.84	49.08	195.15
2003	1 260.72	3.60	1 257.12	55.83	313.82	133.10	295.87	210.14	333.88	47.59	207.03
2004	1 477.09	7.39	1 469.70	62.14	412.83	180.46	343.49	228.20	372.94	50.11	238.28
2005	1 681.78	8.33	1 673.46	68.09	523.77	251.86	379.33	239.45	407.24	55.57	290.76
2006	1 861.38	7.44	1 853.94	74.94	601.99	302.43	418.26	256.63	442.64	59.49	290.76
2007	1 969.38	12.41	1 956.96	81.68	634.75	330.98	444.49	258.92	474.89	62.23	326.81
2008	2 137.61	33.97	2 103.64	89.00	779.48	453.28	453.74	231.24	481.64	68.54	331.18
2009	1 575.49	15.87	1 559.63	81.62	462.38	253.69	370.48	157.65	427.33	60.17	300.89
2010	1 938.95	25.09	1 913.86	91.75	603.10	336.11	449.39	225.10	483.23	61.30	354.25
2011	2 239.89	31.93	2 207.95	107.48	755.78	439.34	510.80	254.62	514.11	65.17	386.44
2012	2 303.79	27.48	2 276.30	110.27	730.66	415.17	548.71	297.79	516.93	71.95	396.23
2013	2 294.45	26.13	2 268.32	115.15	681.58	369.69	554.52	308.80	532.74	75.54	401.08
2014	2 374.10	26.42	2 347.68	125.76	666.75	334.01	591.11	327.65	557.78	78.63	421.34
2012											
January	194.07	2.52	191.55	9.52	64.28	38.51	44.75	24.46	42.77	5.77	29.36
February	188.12	2.28	185.84	8.98	61.57	35.52	44.78	24.17	40.36	5.97	29.23
March	198.87	2.40	196.47	9.16	64.98	38.48	47.46	24.84	43.82	6.21	35.08
April	194.92	2.26	192.66	9.22	64.71	38.50	45.82	24.21	42.88	5.83	30.48
May	194.03	2.27	191.76	9.11	61.27	35.03	46.84	24.87	43.54	6.14	33.72
June	191.06	2.29	188.77	9.04	59.76	33.54	46.02	25.13	42.64	6.18	33.40
July	189.97	2.24	187.73	9.12	57.93	31.50	45.90	25.65	43.14	5.99	33.02
August	189.72	2.28	187.44	9.14	59.02	32.79	45.38	25.15	42.71	6.05	32.32
September	191.26	2.28	188.97	9.29	59.82	32.93	45.48	24.18	44.19	6.02	32.93
October	187.85	2.33	185.52	8.93	59.21	34.04	45.54	24.61	41.26	5.99	36.06
November	194.59	2.21	192.38	9.40	60.89	33.79	45.28	25.54	45.14	6.14	37.82
December	189.36	2.15	187.21	9.37	57.23	30.54	45.48	24.97	44.48	5.68	32.80
2013											
January	191.85	2.11	189.74	9.27	60.34	33.45	45.94	24.05	44.04	6.11	31.28
February	192.11	2.34	189.77	9.59	58.51	31.96	46.19	24.66	44.91	5.91	27.90
March	186.21	2.13	184.08	9.52	56.99	30.59	44.65	24.58	41.91	6.44	31.59
April	190.08	2.12	187.96	9.60	56.73	30.59	45.48	25.22	44.31	6.62	32.52
May	193.67	2.02	191.65	9.84	57.46	31.26	45.70	26.10	45.50	7.07	34.13
June	188.32	2.04	186.28	9.60	55.18	29.41	46.01	25.60	43.72	6.19	32.93
July	190.85	2.17	188.68	9.58	56.51	31.08	45.63	26.08	44.47	6.42	34.43
August	191.36	2.23	189.13	9.63	56.56	30.94	46.75	26.12	43.83	6.25	32.51
September	193.82	2.12	191.70	9.61	57.22	31.42	46.90	26.78	45.02	6.17	35.06
October	193.88	2.19	191.70	9.79	57.23	31.28	46.88	26.24	45.06	6.50	37.32
November	191.52	2.27	189.24	9.61	54.41	28.84	47.40	27.06	45.01	5.76	37.28
December	190.79	2.39	188.40	9.53	54.45	28.88	47.00	26.32	44.99	6.12	34.14
2014											
January	193.71	2.31	191.40	9.72	57.53	30.55	47.54	25.67	45.02	5.91	30.22
February	193.06	2.41	190.65	9.69	57.44	30.39	46.94	25.91	44.68	5.97	27.40
March	198.97	2.42	196.55	10.56	58.17	30.35	47.74	26.40	46.46	7.23	33.21
April	199.88	2.22	197.66	10.66	57.28	29.66	48.57	26.99	47.09	7.07	35.11
May	199.40	2.15	197.25	10.60	55.49	28.23	49.59	28.99	46.78	6.50	35.24
June	197.98	2.21	195.77	10.78	55.52	27.56	49.46	27.46	46.01	6.54	35.84
July	198.58	2.14	196.44	10.73	55.67	28.23	49.30	28.54	45.49	6.70	34.21
August	198.98	2.11	196.87	10.50	55.67	27.27	50.73	27.48	46.03	6.46	33.30
September	198.45	2.13	196.32	10.64	54.62	26.46	50.06	27.19	47.18	6.62	38.62
October	200.02	2.10	197.93	10.82	54.76	26.32	50.56	28.00	47.30	6.49	39.46
November	195.80	2.12	193.69	10.47	51.03	23.68	50.40	27.52	47.93	6.32	39.66
December	199.26	2.11	197.15	10.58	53.55	25.30	50.22	28.19	47.81	6.80	39.04

[1]Not seasonally adjusted.
. . . = Not available.

Table 7-12. U.S. Exports and Imports of Goods by Principal End-Use Category in Constant Dollars

(Census basis; billions of 2009 chain-weighted dollars, except as noted; seasonally adjusted.)

Year and month	Exports							Imports						
	Total	Foods, feeds, and beverages	Industrial supplies and materials	Capital goods, except automotive	Auto-motive vehicles, engines, and parts	Consumer goods, except automotive	Other goods	Total	Foods, feeds, and beverages	Industrial supplies and materials	Capital goods, except automotive	Auto-motive vehicles, engines, and parts	Consumer goods, except automotive	Other goods
1986 [1]	227.20	22.30	57.30	75.80	21.70	. . .	. . .	365.40	24.40	101.30	71.80	78.20	79.40	. . .
1987 [1]	254.10	24.30	66.70	86.20	24.60	. . .	. . .	406.20	24.80	111.00	84.50	85.00	88.70	. . .
1988 [1]	322.40	32.30	85.10	109.20	29.30	. . .	. . .	441.00	24.80	118.30	101.40	87.70	95.90	. . .
1989 [1]	363.80	37.20	99.30	138.80	34.80	. . .	. . .	473.20	25.10	132.30	113.30	86.10	102.90	. . .
1990 [1]	393.60	35.10	104.40	152.70	37.40	39.22	18.70	495.30	26.60	146.20	116.40	87.30	105.70	14.46
1991 [1]	421.70	35.70	109.70	166.70	40.00	40.42	21.11	488.50	26.50	131.60	120.70	85.70	108.00	14.15
1992 [1]	448.20	40.30	109.10	175.90	47.00	43.60	21.71	532.70	27.60	138.60	134.30	91.80	122.70	15.46
1993 [1]	471.17	40.19	111.08	190.02	51.93	54.03	23.91	591.45	28.03	151.26	160.16	100.73	132.92	18.35
1994 [1]	522.29	40.43	114.17	225.76	56.54	58.97	26.41	675.05	29.52	168.80	199.56	112.13	144.22	20.82
1994	550.74	70.21	177.34	158.53	64.72	68.86	34.59	718.78	40.30	351.05	104.93	134.94	149.71	24.36
1995	607.14	77.48	189.34	184.12	68.50	72.85	35.52	780.92	41.33	361.34	126.52	137.25	161.15	25.72
1996	671.49	75.01	200.96	218.55	71.29	78.19	41.47	862.39	45.76	383.36	152.61	141.93	172.59	28.71
1997	761.13	74.80	217.46	267.75	80.44	85.87	41.19	982.15	50.15	409.79	191.10	153.44	196.50	32.48
1998	779.10	74.33	216.64	279.58	78.51	89.22	44.60	1 097.87	53.96	449.16	219.20	163.03	222.76	40.02
1999	804.15	76.88	218.21	294.71	81.30	89.85	44.57	1 230.04	58.93	456.33	251.42	194.72	250.12	48.84
2000	892.79	81.16	240.09	341.04	85.97	98.62	42.90	1 393.19	62.76	484.79	301.69	211.69	294.21	54.02
2001	837.60	83.31	229.28	307.59	80.38	97.52	42.14	1 347.00	65.19	482.40	266.29	205.19	299.06	54.53
2002	799.01	81.43	225.53	280.73	83.78	93.44	40.58	1 395.87	69.49	484.45	261.65	219.65	326.76	56.27
2003	822.70	82.79	235.44	288.75	85.14	98.54	39.09	1 472.99	75.91	503.93	279.49	225.32	354.90	53.72
2004	894.61	76.45	251.33	324.20	93.52	112.18	39.64	1 646.37	80.59	566.27	329.08	240.95	393.62	54.98
2005	957.75	79.97	258.79	353.83	102.09	123.61	40.79	1 762.48	83.57	595.14	365.98	250.33	425.74	58.94
2006	1 054.35	85.72	278.59	398.12	110.10	135.92	46.00	1 867.72	88.43	597.42	408.89	267.07	459.94	61.62
2007	1 138.01	91.11	297.50	428.78	123.19	149.94	47.50	1 904.34	89.18	579.33	435.52	264.43	485.82	65.33
2008	1 219.45	96.38	333.48	455.75	122.03	162.16	48.10	1 848.83	87.20	552.02	445.24	232.70	480.18	65.65
2009	1 056.04	93.91	296.51	391.24	81.72	149.46	43.22	1 559.63	81.62	462.38	370.48	157.65	427.33	60.17
2010	1 213.96	103.02	339.99	447.21	111.51	161.64	51.24	1 790.74	84.71	488.95	453.76	223.75	482.77	59.53
2011	1 307.42	101.01	370.11	494.78	130.44	168.23	45.82	1 900.89	87.25	497.19	514.57	246.10	505.47	60.39
2012	1 359.38	100.98	374.73	528.69	141.11	172.48	48.74	1 948.43	90.10	479.58	554.63	282.47	500.86	66.46
2013	1 398.20	101.08	392.16	533.12	146.53	181.39	50.47	1 969.16	93.18	463.65	566.34	293.82	517.09	70.25
2014	1 620.53	143.75	505.11	551.06	159.69	198.91	62.01	237.68	125.76	666.75	591.11	327.65	557.78	78.63
2011														
January	106.63	8.53	30.91	39.05	10.53	13.68	3.86	159.71	7.15	43.32	42.17	21.18	41.40	4.68
February	103.74	8.42	29.39	39.32	9.99	13.46	3.33	154.35	7.19	40.16	40.12	19.60	43.38	4.72
March	108.67	8.87	30.64	40.35	11.07	13.90	3.97	157.89	6.88	42.48	41.09	21.02	41.77	4.95
April	109.52	8.60	31.43	41.39	10.46	14.02	3.70	155.10	6.96	40.73	41.89	18.49	42.81	5.02
May	108.39	8.55	30.35	41.26	10.67	13.87	3.99	157.74	7.12	42.27	42.54	18.82	42.36	4.98
June	106.18	8.13	29.40	40.58	10.59	14.32	3.65	157.72	7.42	41.67	42.61	18.57	42.67	5.38
July	109.51	8.38	30.76	41.78	11.46	13.79	3.72	159.03	7.04	41.53	43.60	20.87	42.22	4.71
August	108.94	8.17	31.09	41.33	10.81	14.04	3.73	158.01	7.19	40.52	43.46	20.45	42.25	5.40
September	110.40	8.15	31.62	41.69	11.12	14.35	3.70	158.49	7.40	41.12	43.33	21.53	41.29	4.81
October	112.42	8.41	31.88	42.74	11.24	14.22	4.21	160.52	7.75	40.92	44.62	21.29	42.34	4.94
November	110.56	8.34	31.07	42.43	10.96	14.32	3.83	159.88	7.57	41.00	44.02	21.69	41.40	5.40
December	112.46	8.46	31.57	42.86	11.55	14.25	4.14	162.44	7.59	41.47	45.13	22.60	41.57	5.40
2012														
January	111.14	8.19	30.94	43.09	11.93	13.98	3.58	162.28	7.61	40.97	45.04	23.43	41.45	5.34
February	111.45	7.91	30.69	43.76	11.71	14.09	4.00	157.52	7.38	39.17	45.07	23.12	39.10	5.53
March	114.72	8.11	31.83	45.19	11.69	14.20	4.32	165.35	7.37	40.64	47.79	23.70	42.41	5.73
April	112.74	8.43	31.31	43.58	11.75	14.34	3.85	162.57	7.44	40.86	46.23	22.94	41.46	5.37
May	113.42	8.96	31.23	44.04	11.69	14.22	3.81	163.20	7.42	39.57	47.31	23.59	42.15	5.66
June	115.96	8.70	32.68	43.79	12.16	14.67	4.29	162.84	7.35	40.22	46.55	23.83	41.29	5.71
July	114.23	9.29	31.23	44.05	11.90	14.51	3.72	163.63	7.49	40.18	46.46	24.30	41.84	5.55
August	111.80	8.27	30.06	44.36	11.72	14.33	3.92	162.81	7.58	40.32	45.99	23.83	41.51	5.61
September	115.37	9.32	31.50	44.88	11.52	14.55	4.08	162.98	7.56	40.19	45.99	22.86	42.94	5.57
October	110.22	8.05	29.39	43.58	11.38	14.56	4.20	158.87	7.30	39.03	46.10	23.22	39.90	5.51
November	112.65	7.91	30.73	44.18	11.87	14.59	4.22	165.25	7.79	40.34	45.93	24.09	43.70	5.66
December	115.69	7.83	33.13	44.18	11.79	14.45	4.76	161.14	7.80	38.09	46.17	23.58	43.10	5.23
2013														
January	113.26	8.39	31.10	44.07	11.78	14.84	3.78	162.72	7.83	39.68	46.61	22.67	42.61	5.63
February	113.80	8.28	32.12	43.17	11.93	14.43	4.29	162.64	7.86	38.55	46.95	23.26	43.43	5.44
March	113.56	7.87	32.21	43.45	11.79	14.24	4.48	158.52	7.69	38.14	45.38	23.21	40.61	5.93
April	115.18	7.74	31.96	44.08	12.20	16.03	3.98	162.38	7.83	38.26	46.34	23.89	42.80	6.10
May	115.08	7.57	31.88	44.80	12.48	14.97	4.25	167.01	7.96	39.66	46.68	24.77	44.14	6.55
June	118.06	7.77	33.12	45.54	12.16	15.81	4.42	162.51	7.82	38.07	47.06	24.35	42.43	5.76
July	117.17	7.90	34.00	44.49	12.02	15.15	4.07	164.53	7.71	38.82	46.71	24.92	43.25	6.01
August	117.05	7.92	33.28	44.63	12.55	15.07	4.20	164.71	7.75	38.64	47.91	24.98	42.61	5.85
September	116.33	8.97	31.85	44.48	12.62	15.09	3.95	166.73	7.68	38.96	48.04	25.63	43.80	5.78
October	120.52	9.50	33.87	44.98	12.48	15.76	4.24	167.02	7.79	39.22	48.04	25.11	43.83	6.09
November	120.41	9.58	33.63	45.12	12.53	15.21	4.65	165.53	7.68	37.84	48.47	25.87	43.77	5.39
December	117.79	9.60	33.14	44.31	12.00	14.80	4.16	164.85	7.58	37.83	48.17	25.17	43.81	5.72
2014														
January	132.11	12.13	43.17	44.58	11.83	15.65	4.23	191.40	9.72	57.53	47.54	25.67	45.02	5.90
February	131.11	12.07	40.76	44.31	11.91	16.62	3.90	190.65	9.69	57.44	46.94	25.91	44.68	6.00
March	134.66	12.46	41.72	46.01	12.53	16.39	5.01	196.55	10.56	58.17	47.74	26.40	46.46	7.23
April	134.41	12.20	41.93	45.90	12.36	16.40	5.05	197.66	10.66	57.28	48.57	26.99	47.09	7.07
May	136.03	12.32	42.31	45.74	12.88	16.67	5.51	197.25	10.60	55.49	49.59	28.29	46.78	6.50
June	135.13	11.88	42.21	45.60	12.88	16.92	5.01	195.77	10.78	55.52	49.46	27.46	46.01	6.53
July	137.18	11.65	43.14	46.14	14.07	16.52	4.97	196.44	10.73	55.67	49.30	28.54	45.49	6.70
August	137.43	10.91	43.14	46.91	12.80	16.90	5.34	196.87	10.50	55.67	50.73	27.48	46.03	6.46
September	135.68	12.10	42.26	46.03	12.84	16.60	5.22	193.32	10.64	54.62	50.06	27.19	47.18	6.62
October	137.21	12.02	41.90	47.70	12.95	16.95	5.05	197.93	10.82	54.76	50.56	28.00	47.30	6.50
November	135.48	12.08	42.27	45.73	12.56	16.59	5.64	193.69	10.47	51.03	50.40	27.52	47.93	6.32
December	134.09	11.91	39.50	46.40	12.92	16.68	6.05	197.15	10.58	53.55	50.22	28.19	47.81	6.80

[1]Data on the 2009 chain-weighted dollar basis are only available from 1994 forward. To provide more historical range, values in 1992 dollars are shown for the years 1986–1994.
. . . = Not available.

Table 7-13. U.S. Exports of Goods by Selected Regions and Countries

(Census f.a.s. basis; millions of dollars, not seasonally adjusted.)

Year and month	Total, all countries	European Union, 15 countries	European Union	Euro area	Asian NICS	OPEC	Brazil	Canada	China	Japan	Mexico
1978	...	32 051	...	...	...	16 655	2 981	30 540	824	12 885	6 680
1979	...	42 582	...	...	...	15 051	3 442	37 599	1 724	17 581	9 847
1980	...	53 679	...	...	...	17 759	4 344	40 331	3 755	20 790	15 145
1981	...	52 363	...	...	...	21 533	3 798	44 602	3 603	21 823	17 789
1982	...	47 932	...	...	...	22 863	3 423	37 887	2 912	20 966	11 817
1983	201 708	44 311	...	...	...	16 905	2 557	43 345	2 173	21 894	9 082
1984	218 743	46 976	...	...	...	14 387	2 640	51 777	3 004	23 575	11 992
1985	212 621	48 994	...	...	16 918	12 478	3 140	47 251	3 856	22 631	13 635
1986	226 471	53 154	...	...	18 290	10 844	3 885	45 333	3 106	26 882	12 392
1987	254 122	60 575	...	...	23 547	11 057	4 040	59 814	3 497	28 249	14 582
1988	322 426	75 755	...	...	34 816	13 994	4 266	71 622	5 022	37 725	20 629
1989	363 812	86 331	...	...	38 429	13 196	4 804	78 809	5 755	44 494	24 982
1990	393 592	98 027	...	...	40 734	13 703	5 048	83 674	4 806	48 580	28 279
1991	421 730	103 123	...	...	45 628	19 054	6 148	85 150	6 278	48 125	33 277
1992	448 165	102 958	...	...	48 592	21 960	5 751	90 594	7 419	47 813	40 592
1993	465 090	96 973	...	...	52 501	19 500	6 058	100 444	8 763	47 892	41 581
1994	512 625	102 818	...	...	59 595	17 868	8 102	114 439	9 282	53 488	50 844
1995	584 740	123 671		...	74 234	19 533	11 439	127 226	11 754	64 343	46 292
1996	625 073	127 710		...	75 768	22 275	12 718	134 210	11 993	67 607	56 792
1997	689 180	140 773		...	78 225	25 525	15 915	151 767	12 862	65 549	71 389
1998	682 139	149 035		...	63 269	25 154	15 142	156 604	14 241	57 831	78 773
1999	695 797	151 814		...	70 989	20 166	13 203	166 600	13 111	57 466	86 909
2000	781 918	165 065	...	116 212	84 624	19 078	15 321	178 941	16 185	64 924	111 349
2001	729 101	158 768	...	112 903	71 981	20 052	15 879	163 424	19 182	57 452	101 297
2002	693 101	143 691	...	105 838	69 770	18 812	12 376	160 923	22 128	51 449	97 470
2003	724 771	151 731	...	113 132	71 601	17 279	11 211	169 924	28 368	52 004	97 412
2004	814 875	168 572	171 230	127 158	82 997	22 256	13 886	189 880	34 428	53 569	110 731
2005	901 082	...	185 166	137 497	86 003	31 641	15 372	211 899	41 192	54 681	120 248
2006	1 025 967	...	211 887	155 735	96 496	38 658	18 887	230 656	53 673	58 459	133 722
2007	1 148 199	...	244 166	180 232	105 751	48 485	24 172	248 888	62 937	61 160	135 918
2008	1 287 442	...	271 810	199 986	108 947	64 880	32 299	261 150	69 733	65 142	151 220
2009	1 056 043	...	220 599	162 002	90 380	49 857	26 095	204 658	69 497	51 134	128 892
2010	1 278 495	...	239 591	176 587	120 450	54 226	35 418	249 256	91 911	60 472	163 665
2011	1 482 508	...	269 069	196 310	137 075	64 809	43 019	281 292	104 122	65 800	198 289
2012	1 545 703	...	265 376	193 947	134 599	81 732	43 807	292 651	110 516	69 964	215 907
2013	1 579 593	...	262 151	198 078	140 201	84 679	44 119	301 610	121 736	65 206	226 079
2014	1 620 532	...	276 143	205 456	142 237	82 346	42 429	312 421	123 676	66 827	240 249
2012											
January	117 847	...	21 098	15 177	9 562	5 857	3 053	22 078	8 360	5 601	17 013
February	123 613	...	22 541	15 919	11 747	5 715	3 150	23 510	8 785	5 469	16 936
March	140 254	...	25 211	18 192	12 789	7 292	3 971	26 418	9 812	6 121	19 008
April	127 416	...	22 363	16 317	11 828	6 310	3 641	24 496	8 467	5 812	17 223
May	131 232	...	22 857	16 986	11 252	6 443	3 488	25 913	8 960	5 686	18 438
June	132 577	...	23 215	17 379	11 979	7 225	3 590	25 858	8 479	5 985	17 475
July	121 400	...	20 603	14 954	10 164	6 366	3 472	22 775	8 515	5 572	17 540
August	128 585	...	21 479	15 944	10 139	6 635	3 958	24 836	8 615	6 267	19 220
September	128 254	...	21 338	15 465	10 833	6 979	3 920	24 148	8 804	6 074	17 458
October	133 627	...	21 684	15 876	10 410	6 725	4 143	25 679	10 822	5 675	20 454
November	130 170	...	21 364	15 642	11 162	7 339	3 829	24 680	10 587	5 686	18 765
December	130 728	...	21 623	16 038	12 733	8 845	3 592	22 261	10 309	6 017	16 377
2013											
January	123 130	...	20 249	14 844	10 275	7 669	3 071	23 248	9 383	5 161	17 906
February	123 536	...	20 169	14 518	11 804	6 781	3 575	23 272	9 134	4 998	17 705
March	136 762	...	23 006	17 236	12 811	8 185	3 743	26 173	9 534	5 571	18 092
April	129 465	...	21 005	16 440	10 479	6 834	3 363	26 270	8 948	5 060	19 797
May	133 007	...	22 466	16 995	11 524	7 228	3 376	26 525	8 749	5 778	19 230
June	134 830	...	22 839	16 777	12 288	7 374	3 878	25 484	9 219	5 672	17 988
July	127 358	...	20 878	16 251	11 075	5 985	4 389	23 689	8 723	5 172	19 597
August	132 604	...	21 957	16 428	12 133	6 731	4 232	25 433	9 350	5 664	19 213
September	128 515	...	22 734	17 454	11 338	6 742	3 720	24 959	9 522	5 526	18 063
October	142 182	...	23 303	17 447	12 230	7 242	3 943	27 118	13 105	5 501	21 093
November	136 249	...	22 744	17 496	11 891	6 486	3 123	25 724	13 065	5 844	19 303
December	131 956	...	20 800	16 180	12 352	7 421	3 706	23 716	13 006	5 260	18 093
2014											
January	126 517	...	22 691	...	13 063	6 279	3 990	24 386	10 850	5 673	19 443
February	123 591	...	22 317	...	11 646	6 427	3 727	25 310	10 132	5 652	19 890
March	142 184	...	22 958	...	11 720	6 256	3 763	25 455	10 277	5 694	19 589
April	133 875	...	23 134	...	11 774	6 810	3 539	25 777	9 922	5 573	19 788
May	138 122	...	23 339	...	11 657	7 343	3 668	26 142	10 074	5 245	20 709
June	138 358	...	23 893	...	11 739	6 698	3 484	26 239	10 171	5 584	20 257
July	133 198	...	24 313	...	10 902	7 040	3 481	27 168	10 180	5 631	20 452
August	137 420	...	23 612	...	11 595	7 425	3 335	26 598	10 352	6 059	20 295
September	133 360	...	22 225	...	12 163	7 132	3 442	26 342	10 118	5 468	19 957
October	145 436	...	22 846	...	12 853	7 081	3 503	26 501	10 690	5 460	20 061
November	134 726	...	22 400	...	11 639	6 907	3 293	26 399	10 429	5 026	20 123
December	133 746	...	22 415	...	11 485	6 948	3 205	26 103	10 482	5 764	19 687

¹See notes and definitions for definitions of regions.

. . . = Not available.

Table 7-14. U.S. Imports of Goods by Selected Regions and Countries

(Census Customs basis; millions of dollars, not seasonally adjusted.)

Year and month	Total, all countries	Selected regions [1]					Selected countries				
		European Union, 15 countries	European Union	Euro area	Asian NICS	OPEC	Brazil	Canada	China	Japan	Mexico
1978	...	29 009	...	...	...	...	2 826	33 525	...	24 458	6 094
1979	...	33 295	...	...	...	...	3 118	38 046	...	26 248	8 800
1980	...	35 958	...	...	...	...	3 715	41 455	...	30 701	12 520
1981	...	41 624	...	...	...	...	4 475	46 414	...	37 612	13 765
1982	...	42 509	...	...	...	...	4 285	46 477	...	37 744	15 566
1983	261 723	43 892	...	...	...	...	4 946	52 130	...	41 183	16 776
1984	330 510	57 360	...	...	...	...	7 621	66 478	...	57 135	18 020
1985	336 383	67 822	...	...	39 066	22 801	7 526	69 006	3 862	68 783	19 132
1986	365 672	75 736	...	...	46 136	19 751	6 813	68 253	4 771	81 911	17 302
1987	406 241	81 188	...	...	57 663	23 952	7 865	71 085	6 294	84 575	20 271
1988	440 952	84 939	...	...	63 030	22 962	9 294	81 398	8 511	89 519	23 260
1989	473 211	85 153	...	...	62 774	30 611	8 410	87 953	11 990	93 553	27 162
1990	495 311	91 868	...	...	60 573	38 052	7 898	91 380	15 237	89 684	30 157
1991	488 453	86 481	...	...	59 276	32 644	6 717	91 064	18 969	91 511	31 130
1992	532 662	93 993	...	...	62 384	33 200	7 609	98 630	25 728	97 414	35 211
1993	580 656	97 941	...	...	64 572	31 739	7 479	111 216	31 540	107 246	39 918
1994	663 252	110 875	...	...	71 388	31 685	8 683	128 406	38 787	119 156	49 494
1995	743 545	131 871	...	...	82 008	35 606	8 833	144 370	45 543	123 479	62 100
1996	795 287	142 947	...	...	82 770	44 285	8 773	155 893	51 513	115 187	74 297
1997	869 703	157 528	...	...	86 164	44 025	9 625	167 234	62 558	121 663	85 938
1998	911 897	176 380	...	...	85 960	33 925	10 102	173 256	71 169	121 845	94 629
1999	1 024 616	195 227	...	...	95 103	41 977	11 314	198 711	81 788	130 864	109 721
2000	1 218 023	220 019	...	163 520	111 438	67 090	13 853	230 838	100 018	146 479	135 926
2001	1 140 998	220 057	...	166 373	93 202	59 754	14 466	216 268	102 278	126 473	131 338
2002	1 161 366	225 771	...	172 573	91 850	53 245	15 781	209 088	125 193	121 429	134 616
2003	1 257 121	244 826	...	187 204	92 818	68 344	17 910	221 595	152 436	118 037	138 060
2004	1 469 705	272 439	281 959	209 606	105 476	92 099	21 160	256 360	196 682	129 805	155 902
2005	1 673 454	298 879	309 628	228 881	102 609	127 169	24 436	290 384	243 470	138 004	170 109
2006	1 853 938	319 590	330 482	246 667	109 730	150 758	26 367	302 438	287 774	148 181	198 253
2007	1 956 961	...	354 409	266 074	111 260	165 651	25 644	317 057	321 443	145 463	210 714
2008	2 103 641	...	367 617	277 658	106 763	242 579	30 453	339 491	337 773	139 262	215 942
2009	1 559 625	...	281 801	212 557	86 854	111 602	20 070	226 248	296 374	95 804	176 654
2010	1 913 857	...	319 264	242 215	106 446	149 893	23 958	277 637	364 953	120 552	229 986
2011	2 207 954	...	368 464	285 023	121 592	191 470	31 737	315 325	399 371	128 928	262 874
2012	2 276 302	...	381 753	294 445	123 450	180 752	32 123	324 264	425 626	146 438	277 594
2013	2 268 321	...	387 591	302 058	123 854	152 690	27 634	332 553	440 448	138 573	280 529
2014	2 343 205	...	418 201	326 994	132 395	132 349	30 537	342 798	466 755	134 004	294 074
2012											
January	183 533	...	29 592	22 782	9 331	15 767	3 004	26 787	34 418	11 756	21 504
February	171 829	...	28 538	21 726	9 235	12 163	2 635	26 230	28 105	12 433	22 617
March	197 350	...	34 910	26 928	10 219	16 584	3 303	29 185	31 431	13 310	25 115
April	189 468	...	31 286	24 129	10 851	17 769	2 908	27 803	33 017	12 087	22 757
May	198 411	...	33 452	25 656	10 963	17 677	2 484	27 613	34 939	12 111	24 815
June	191 788	...	31 455	24 277	10 556	15 727	2 908	27 331	35 951	11 998	23 514
July	192 840	...	33 344	25 751	10 911	14 738	2 659	24 974	37 932	12 490	22 526
August	194 960	...	33 041	25 347	10 204	14 752	3 060	27 028	37 282	12 958	23 764
September	185 686	...	29 523	22 587	10 447	14 172	2 396	26 052	37 893	10 978	22 151
October	198 768	...	32 521	24 878	11 021	15 226	2 300	27 661	40 257	12 684	24 818
November	194 555	...	33 649	26 212	10 136	13 954	2 302	27 752	39 544	11 811	23 731
December	177 114	...	30 444	23 615	9 577	12 222	2 164	25 849	34 858	11 822	20 281
2013											
January	185 190	...	28 557	22 510	10 328	14 341	2 145	28 057	37 194	11 292	21 556
February	170 358	...	29 170	22 612	8 981	10 358	1 977	25 847	32 743	10 948	22 070
March	181 855	...	33 388	25 559	10 109	12 673	1 971	28 342	27 295	12 156	23 150
April	190 561	...	33 302	26 457	10 867	13 481	2 154	28 528	33 135	11 985	24 362
May	196 686	...	33 147	25 895	11 097	13 457	2 570	28 505	36 619	11 134	24 482
June	184 965	...	30 318	22 919	10 548	13 019	2 331	27 102	35 886	11 257	22 929
July	197 384	...	34 816	27 233	11 070	13 500	2 687	26 244	38 805	11 980	23 550
August	193 110	...	31 295	24 566	10 171	13 903	2 516	27 789	39 165	12 014	23 992
September	191 968	...	31 391	24 042	10 756	12 440	2 708	28 162	40 152	11 124	23 280
October	205 098	...	37 058	29 399	10 548	12 805	2 273	29 622	41 849	11 912	25 307
November	188 681	...	33 069	25 774	9 886	11 303	2 078	27 387	40 107	11 607	23 722
December	182 465	...	32 081	25 063	9 490	11 410	2 224	26 969	37 498	11 164	22 128
2014											
January	190 970	...	33 494	...	10 295	13 419	2 334	27 401	37 564	11 334	23 414
February	175 075	...	32 725	...	9 959	13 279	2 416	27 957	37 969	11 157	24 035
March	199 471	...	34 582	...	11 434	12 263	2 341	28 639	37 515	11 397	23 890
April	206 040	...	35 672	...	11 278	11 924	2 303	28 184	38 060	11 055	24 192
May	205 614	...	35 957	...	11 202	11 112	2 487	29 388	38 220	11 349	24 313
June	203 038	...	35 566	...	11 206	10 366	2 586	29 451	38 932	11 345	24 766
July	209 897	...	34 569	...	10 791	11 711	2 597	30 394	37 919	11 192	24 911
August	201 999	...	36 025	...	11 200	10 197	2 713	29 542	39 000	10 971	24 839
September	208 381	...	34 663	...	11 153	10 214	2 510	29 952	40 223	11 163	24 513
October	216 440	...	34 579	...	11 094	9 646	2 756	29 297	40 306	11 133	25 504
November	194 978	...	35 130	...	11 499	8 749	2 691	28 433	40 388	10 869	24 593
December	200 643	...	35 239	...	11 284	9 470	2 805	29 160	40 659	11 039	25 104

[1] See notes and definitions for definitions of regions.
. . . = Not available.

Table 7-15A. U.S. Exports of Services: Recent Data

(Balance of payments basis, millions of dollars, seasonally adjusted.)

Year and month	Total services	Maintenance and repair services, n.i.e.	Transport	Travel for all purposes including education	Insurance services	Financial services	Charges for the use of intellectual property n.i.e	Telecommunications, computer and information services	Other business services	Government goods and services, n.i.e.
1999	271 343	3 812	43 218	92 338	3 052	19 433	47 731	12 287	40 976	8 495
2000	290 381	4 686	45 758	100 187	3 631	22 117	51 808	12 215	40 497	9 481
2001	274 323	5 575	41 716	86 733	3 424	21 899	49 489	12 829	44 146	8 514
2002	280 670	5 769	41 912	81 869	4 415	24 496	53 859	12 451	47 996	7 903
2003	289 972	5 458	41 446	80 332	5 974	27 840	56 813	14 061	48 775	7 903
2004	337 966	5 342	47 723	92 387	7 314	36 389	67 094	14 962	54 398	9 274
2005	373 006	7 218	52 622	101 470	7 566	39 878	74 448	15 515	58 302	12 357
2006	416 738	7 673	57 462	105 140	9 445	47 882	83 549	17 184	68 619	15 989
2007	488 396	9 062	65 824	119 037	10 841	61 376	97 803	20 192	82 382	19 783
2008	532 817	10 019	74 973	133 761	13 403	63 027	102 125	23 119	92 738	21 879
2009	512 722	12 077	62 189	119 902	14 586	64 437	98 406	23 816	95 984	19 652
2010	563 333	13 860	71 656	137 010	14 397	72 348	107 521	25 038	101 029	21 324
2011	627 781	14 279	79 830	150 867	15 114	78 271	123 333	29 171	112 568	20 474
2012	654 850	15 115	83 592	161 249	16 534	76 605	125 492	32 103	119 892	24 348
2013	687 410	16 295	87 267	173 131	16 096	84 066	129 178	32 103	119 892	24 267
2014	710 565	22 389	90 031	177 241	17 417	87 290	130 362	33 409	123 447	24 522
2013								35 885	129 514	20 438
January	56 825	1 196	7 250	14 232	1 357	6 828	10 775	2 773	10 296	2 117
February	56 610	1 131	7 350	14 254	1 333	6 792	10 735	2 752	10 165	2 099
March	56 371	1 114	7 273	14 214	1 320	6 773	10 738	2 758	10 094	2 087
April	56 437	1 126	7 253	14 093	1 316	6 912	10 786	2 793	10 084	2 073
May	56 887	1 162	7 324	14 249	1 318	6 912	10 829	2 814	10 084	2 073
June	57 023	1 239	7 302	14 294	1 326	7 011	10 868	2 820	10 106	2 073
July	57 072	1 439	7 026	14 368	1 339	6 936	10 903	2 811	10 161	2 077
August	57 777	1 528	7 116	14 801	1 349	6 862	10 880	2 800	10 248	2 076
September	57 819	1 557	7 193	14 572	1 356	6 870	10 798	2 786	10 326	2 107
October	57 829	1 618	7 235	14 562	1 359	7 002	10 658	2 770	10 395	2 160
November	58 170	1 616	7 365	14 671	1 361	7 329	10 596	2 764	10 456	1 842
December	58 590	1 568	7 580	14 820	1 360	7 383	10 612	2 769	10 522	1 892
									10 593	1 919
2014										
January	59 141	1 646	7 533	15 232	1 408	7 060	10 806	2 924	10 562	1 970
February	57 726	1 632	7 118	14 232	1 388	6 924	10 882	2 923	10 645	1 983
March	58 837	1 726	7 431	14 726	1 405	7 088	10 940	2 960	10 652	1 910
April	59 468	1 810	7 473	14 919	1 458	7 478	10 982	3 035	10 582	1 731
May	59 955	1 883	7 674	15 158	1 483	7 520	10 976	3 070	10 549	1 643
June	59 298	1 898	7 427	14 852	1 481	7 458	10 923	3 065	10 554	1 638
July	58 500	1 869	7 421	14 418	1 452	7 184	10 822	3 019	10 597	1 717
August	59 148	1 911	7 695	14 869	1 441	7 043	10 769	2 988	10 706	1 725
September	58 682	1 890	7 505	14 435	1 447	7 124	10 764	2 973	10 880	1 664
October	59 652	1 985	7 510	14 673	1 471	7 559	10 805	2 974	11 120	1 554
November	59 726	2 041	7 457	14 837	1 487	7 336	10 836	2 975	11 287	1 469
December	60 431	2 097	7 787	14 889	1 495	7 515	10 858	2 978	11 380	1 433

n.i.e = Not included elsewhere.

Table 7-15B. U.S. Exports of Services: Historical

(Balance of payments basis, millions of dollars, seasonally adjusted.)

Year	Total	Travel	Passenger fares	Other transportation	Royalties and license fees	Other private services (financial, professional, etc.)	Transfers under U.S. military sales contracts [1]	U.S. government miscellaneous services
1960	6 290	919	175	1 607	837	570	2 030	153
1961	6 295	947	183	1 620	906	607	1 867	164
1962	6 941	957	191	1 764	1 056	585	2 193	195
1963	7 348	1 015	205	1 898	1 162	613	2 219	236
1964	7 840	1 207	241	2 076	1 314	651	2 086	265
1965	8 824	1 380	271	2 175	1 534	714	2 465	285
1966	9 616	1 590	317	2 333	1 516	814	2 721	326
1967	10 667	1 646	371	2 426	1 747	951	3 191	336
1968	11 917	1 775	411	2 548	1 867	1 024	3 939	353
1969	12 806	2 043	450	2 652	2 019	1 160	4 138	343
1970	14 171	2 331	544	3 125	2 331	1 294	4 214	332
1971	16 358	2 534	615	3 299	2 545	1 546	5 472	347
1972	17 841	2 817	699	3 579	2 770	1 764	5 856	357
1973	19 832	3 412	975	4 465	3 225	1 985	5 369	401
1974	22 591	4 032	1 104	5 697	3 821	2 321	5 197	419
1975	25 497	4 697	1 039	5 840	4 300	2 920	6 256	446
1976	27 971	5 742	1 229	6 747	4 353	3 584	5 826	489
1977	31 485	6 150	1 366	7 090	4 920	3 848	7 554	557
1978	36 353	7 183	1 603	8 136	5 885	4 717	8 209	620
1979	39 692	8 441	2 156	9 971	6 184	5 439	6 981	520
1980	47 584	10 588	2 591	11 618	7 085	6 276	9 029	398
1981	57 354	12 913	3 111	12 560	7 284	10 250	10 720	517
1982	64 079	12 393	3 174	12 317	5 603	17 444	12 572	576
1983	64 307	10 947	3 610	12 590	5 778	18 192	12 524	666
1984	71 168	17 177	4 067	13 809	6 177	19 255	9 969	714
1985	73 155	17 762	4 411	14 674	6 678	20 035	8 718	878
1986	86 689	20 385	5 582	15 438	8 113	28 027	8 549	595
1987	98 661	23 563	7 003	17 027	10 174	29 263	11 106	526
1988	110 919	29 434	8 976	19 311	12 139	31 111	9 284	664
1989	127 087	36 205	10 657	20 526	13 818	36 729	8 564	587
1990	147 832	43 007	15 298	22 042	16 634	40 251	9 932	668
1991	164 261	48 385	15 854	22 631	17 819	47 748	11 135	690
1992	177 252	54 742	16 618	21 531	20 841	50 292	12 387	841
1993	185 920	57 875	16 528	21 958	21 695	53 510	13 471	883
1994	200 395	58 417	16 997	23 754	26 712	60 841	12 787	887
1995	219 183	63 395	18 909	26 081	30 289	65 048	14 643	818
1996	239 489	69 809	20 422	26 074	32 470	73 340	16 446	928
1997	256 087	73 426	20 868	27 006	33 228	83 929	16 675	955
1998	262 758	71 325	20 098	25 604	35 626	91 774	17 405	926
1999	268 790	75 161	19 425	23 792	47 731	96 812	5 211	657

Note: The category "Royalties and license fees" is the earlier terminology for the category called "Charges for the use of intellectual property n.i.e" in the revised and updated data shown in Tables 7-15A/7-16A. Other categories differ in both title and content; see the Notes and Definitions.

[1]Contains goods that cannot be separately identified.

Table 7-16A. U.S. Imports of Services: Recent Data

(Balance of payments basis, millions of dollars, seasonally adjusted.)

Year and month	Total services	Maintenance and repair services, n.i.e.	Transport	Travel for all purposes including education	Insurance services	Financial services	Charges for the use of intellectual property n.i.e	Telecommunications, computer and information services	Other business services	Government goods and services, n.i.e.
1999	192 893	1 278	49 620	59 592	9 389	8 280	13 302	13 332	23 887	14 212
2000	216 115	2 569	57 606	65 787	11 284	10 936	16 606	12 397	24 414	14 516
2001	213 465	1 999	53 840	60 730	16 706	10 157	16 661	12 421	25 629	15 322
2002	224 379	2 217	51 491	59 942	21 927	8 963	19 493	11 721	29 274	19 353
2003	242 219	2 246	57 863	61 884	25 233	8 948	19 259	13 063	30 103	19 353
2004	283 083	2 395	69 158	74 024	29 089	11 156	23 691	14 210	33 065	26 296
2005	304 448	3 015	75 643	79 988	28 710	12 126	25 577	15 975	35 960	27 454
2006	341 165	4 583	77 962	84 206	39 382	14 733	25 038	19 776	48 130	27 353
2007	372 575	5 209	79 326	89 235	47 517	19 197	26 479	22 384	54 968	28 260
2008	409 052	5 742	83 988	92 545	58 913	17 218	29 623	24 655	67 488	28 880
2009	386 801	5 938	64 133	81 421	63 801	14 415	31 297	25 784	68 553	31 460
2010	409 313	6 909	74 628	86 623	61 478	15 502	32 551	29 015	70 646	31 960
2011	435 761	8 236	81 377	89 700	55 654	17 368	36 087	32 756	83 289	31 293
2012	450 360	7 970	85 029	100 317	53 203	16 975	39 502	32 156	87 347	27 861
2013	462 134	7 620	90 754	104 677	50 454	18 683	39 015	32 877	92 710	25 343
2014	477 428	7 468	94 219	110 787	50 096	19 503	42 124	33 314	96 752	24 163
2013										
January	37 838	627	7 459	8 510	4 223	1 479	3 406	2 597	7 397	2 139
February	37 693	614	7 602	8 518	4 149	1 433	3 321	2 601	7 340	2 115
March	37 665	628	7 396	8 636	4 135	1 466	3 275	2 647	7 370	2 111
April	38 096	644	7 453	8 676	4 180	1 523	3 270	2 737	7 487	2 126
May	38 366	659	7 497	8 658	4 226	1 560	3 246	2 787	7 598	2 134
June	38 602	657	7 527	8 768	4 274	1 537	3 204	2 798	7 702	2 135
July	38 470	667	7 459	8 657	4 323	1 524	3 143	2 769	7 799	2 129
August	38 765	668	7 543	8 827	4 323	1 513	3 130	2 759	7 882	2 120
September	38 695	658	7 519	8 662	4 274	1 588	3 165	2 767	7 953	2 108
October	39 170	603	7 685	8 886	4 176	1 674	3 249	2 793	8 010	2 094
November	39 377	596	7 866	8 862	4 106	1 702	3 297	2 808	8 062	2 077
December	39 400	598	7 748	9 018	4 066	1 682	3 308	2 814	8 110	2 056
2014										
January	38 635	568	7 623	8 706	4 154	1 574	3 277	2 783	7 933	2 018
February	39 270	587	7 642	8 742	4 107	1 510	3 987	2 781	7 903	2 010
March	38 908	607	7 827	8 860	4 119	1 562	3 232	2 777	7 912	2 012
April	39 417	627	7 783	9 127	4 189	1 602	3 336	2 770	7 958	2 025
May	39 934	627	7 877	9 396	4 222	1 638	3 411	2 768	7 959	2 035
June	39 968	623	7 756	9 377	4 217	1 673	3 589	2 774	7 917	2 043
July	39 734	625	7 725	9 320	4 174	1 663	3 562	2 785	7 831	2 048
August	39 599	606	7 783	9 246	4 157	1 652	3 491	2 789	7 833	2 041
September	39 793	623	7 869	9 200	4 165	1 688	3 518	2 785	7 924	2 021
October	40 489	636	7 992	9 567	4 198	1 680	3 550	2 773	8 103	1 990
November	40 417	657	7 947	9 455	4 206	1 628	3 576	2 766	8 216	1 967
December	41 264	681	8 395	9 792	4 188	1 634	3 595	2 763	8 262	1 953

n.i.e = Not included elsewhere.

Table 7-16B. U.S. Imports of Services: Historical

(Balance of payments basis, millions of dollars, seasonally adjusted.)

Year	Total	Travel	Passenger fares	Other transportation	Royalties and license fees	Other private services (financial, professional, etc.)	Direct defense expenditures [1]	U.S. government miscellaneous services
1960	7 674	1 750	513	1 402	74	593	3 087	254
1961	7 671	1 785	506	1 437	89	588	2 998	268
1962	8 092	1 939	567	1 558	100	528	3 105	296
1963	8 362	2 114	612	1 701	112	493	2 961	370
1964	8 619	2 211	642	1 817	127	527	2 880	415
1965	9 111	2 438	717	1 951	135	461	2 952	457
1966	10 494	2 657	753	2 161	140	506	3 764	513
1967	11 863	3 207	829	2 157	166	565	4 378	561
1968	12 302	3 030	885	2 367	186	668	4 535	631
1969	13 322	3 373	1 080	2 455	221	751	4 856	586
1970	14 520	3 980	1 215	2 843	224	827	4 855	576
1971	15 400	4 373	1 290	3 130	241	956	4 819	592
1972	16 868	5 042	1 596	3 520	294	1 043	4 784	589
1973	18 843	5 526	1 790	4 694	385	1 180	4 629	640
1974	21 379	5 980	2 095	5 942	346	1 262	5 032	722
1975	21 996	6 417	2 263	5 708	472	1 551	4 795	789
1976	24 570	6 856	2 568	6 852	482	2 006	4 895	911
1977	27 640	7 451	2 748	7 972	504	2 190	5 823	951
1978	32 189	8 475	2 896	9 124	671	2 573	7 352	1 099
1979	36 689	9 413	3 184	10 906	831	2 822	8 294	1 239
1980	41 491	10 397	3 607	11 790	724	2 909	10 851	1 214
1981	45 503	11 479	4 487	12 474	650	3 562	11 564	1 287
1982	51 749	12 394	4 772	11 710	795	8 159	12 460	1 460
1983	54 973	13 149	6 003	12 222	943	8 001	13 087	1 568
1984	67 748	22 913	5 735	14 843	1 168	9 040	12 516	1 534
1985	72 862	24 558	6 444	15 643	1 170	10 203	13 108	1 735
1986	80 147	25 913	6 505	17 766	1 401	13 146	13 730	1 686
1987	90 787	29 310	7 283	19 010	1 857	16 485	14 950	1 893
1988	98 526	32 114	7 729	20 891	2 601	17 667	15 604	1 921
1989	102 479	33 416	8 249	22 172	2 528	18 930	15 313	1 871
1990	117 659	37 349	10 531	24 966	3 135	22 229	17 531	1 919
1991	118 459	35 322	10 012	24 975	4 035	25 590	16 409	2 116
1992	119 566	38 552	10 603	23 767	5 161	25 386	13 835	2 263
1993	123 779	40 713	11 410	24 524	5 032	27 760	12 086	2 255
1994	133 057	43 782	13 062	26 019	5 852	31 565	10 217	2 560
1995	141 397	44 916	14 663	27 034	6 919	35 199	10 043	2 623
1996	152 554	48 078	15 809	27 403	7 837	39 679	11 061	2 687
1997	165 932	52 051	18 138	28 959	9 161	43 154	11 707	2 762
1998	180 677	56 483	19 971	30 363	11 235	47 591	12 185	2 849
1999	195 172	59 332	20 946	31 494	13 302	55 885	11 849	2 364

Note: The category "Royalties and license fees" is the earlier terminology for the category called "Charges for the use of intellectual property n.i.e" in the revised and updated data shown in Tables 7-15A/7-16A. Other categories differ in both title and content; see the Notes and Definitions.

[1]Contains goods that cannot be separately identified.

Table 7-17. U.S. Export and Import Price Indexes by End-Use Category

(2000 = 100, not seasonally adjusted.)

Year and month	Exports			Imports		
	All commodities	Agricultural	Nonagricultural	All commodities	Petroleum [1]	Nonpetroleum
1990	95.5	105.1	94.4	94.0	75.5	97.1
1991	96.3	103.4	95.4	94.2	67.3	98.7
1992	96.3	102.5	95.7	94.9	62.9	100.0
1993	96.9	104.4	96.2	94.6	57.7	100.6
1994	98.9	109.4	98.0	96.2	54.3	103.2
1995	103.9	119.0	102.5	100.6	59.8	107.2
1996	104.5	132.6	101.6	101.6	71.1	106.4
1997	103.1	120.6	101.3	99.1	66.0	104.1
1998	99.7	108.8	98.8	93.1	44.8	100.4
1999	98.4	101.1	98.2	93.9	60.1	99.0
2000	100.0	100.0	100.0	100.0	100.0	100.0
2001	99.2	101.2	99.0	96.5	82.8	98.5
2002	98.2	103.2	97.8	94.1	85.3	96.2
2003	99.7	112.3	98.8	96.9	103.2	97.3
2004	103.6	123.4	102.1	102.3	134.6	99.8
2005	106.9	121.0	105.9	110.0	185.1	102.5
2006	110.7	125.8	109.6	115.4	223.3	104.2
2007	116.1	150.9	113.6	120.2	249.1	107.0
2008	123.1	183.5	118.8	134.1	343.2	112.7
2009	117.4	160.0	114.3	118.6	219.9	108.0
2010	123.1	172.6	119.6	126.8	282.2	111.0
2011	133.0	211.0	127.5	140.6	385.1	115.9
2012	133.5	216.1	127.6	141.0	384.0	116.3
2013	133.0	219.7	126.7	139.5	374.2	115.6
2014	132.3	213.8	126.3	138.0	353.2	115.7
2011						
January	129.1	204.7	123.6	133.0	324.7	113.6
February	130.8	214.1	124.8	135.3	342.5	114.4
March	132.7	218.8	126.5	139.3	380.2	115.0
April	133.8	217.8	127.7	142.9	410.7	115.9
May	134.3	215.5	128.4	143.1	407.6	116.4
June	134.5	217.2	128.6	142.2	397.8	116.4
July	134.0	208.5	128.7	142.4	399.2	116.5
August	134.6	211.9	129.1	141.9	390.0	116.8
September	135.3	216.0	129.5	141.7	386.5	117.0
October	132.6	201.9	127.7	141.2	385.5	116.6
November	132.7	205.3	127.5	142.2	398.8	116.3
December	132.1	200.5	127.3	142.2	397.8	116.4
2012						
January	132.5	202.8	127.5	142.2	397.9	116.4
February	133.1	202.0	128.3	142.2	399.0	116.3
March	134.1	206.9	128.9	144.2	418.5	116.7
April	134.7	211.0	129.2	144.1	416.0	116.7
May	134.0	212.0	128.4	142.0	392.3	116.6
June	131.7	204.5	126.5	138.7	357.2	116.3
July	132.2	216.7	126.2	137.7	348.8	115.9
August	133.4	227.0	126.7	139.4	370.5	115.8
September	134.5	229.9	127.6	140.8	385.5	116.0
October	134.6	226.0	128.0	141.2	385.3	116.4
November	133.8	227.1	127.1	140.2	374.0	116.4
December	133.6	227.4	126.9	139.4	363.1	116.5
2013						
January	134.1	224.6	127.5	140.1	371.2	116.6
February	135.1	229.1	128.3	141.3	385.7	116.6
March	134.4	224.9	127.9	141.2	385.6	116.5
April	133.6	220.1	127.3	140.2	374.2	116.5
May	132.9	222.5	126.4	139.4	367.4	116.1
June	132.8	224.2	126.2	138.8	364.9	115.7
July	132.6	223.5	126.0	138.9	374.4	115.0
August	131.9	214.2	126.0	139.4	385.2	114.8
September	132.4	215.4	126.4	139.8	389.6	114.8
October	131.6	212.6	125.8	138.9	375.6	114.9
November	131.8	212.1	125.9	137.7	358.4	115.0
December	132.3	212.8	126.4	137.8	357.7	115.2
2014						
January	132.7	212.7	126.9	138.3	358.0	115.7
February	133.7	215.6	127.7	139.8	376.7	116.0
March	134.9	221.7	128.6	140.5	378.8	116.5
April	133.5	225.0	127.0	139.7	374.5	116.1
May	133.7	225.6	127.0	140.1	381.5	116.0
June	133.0	221.4	126.6	140.5	387.9	115.8
July	133.1	217.5	126.9	140.1	382.2	115.8
August	132.4	210.8	126.6	139.0	368.6	115.7
September	131.9	207.5	126.3	137.9	354.9	115.6
October	130.7	202.9	125.4	136.0	329.4	115.4
November	129.5	203.2	124.1	133.5	297.6	115.1
December	128.3	201.8	122.9	130.1	248.7	115.1

[1] Petroleum and petroleum products.

NOTES AND DEFINITIONS, CHAPTER 7

This chapter presents data from two different data systems on international flows of goods, services, income payments, and financial transactions as they affect the U.S. economy. Tables 7-1 through 7-5 present data on the value, quantities, and prices of foreign transactions in the national income and product accounts (NIPAs). Tables 7-6 through 7-8 show foreign transactions and investment positions in current-dollar values as depicted in the U.S. international transactions accounts (ITAs). Both sets of accounts are prepared by the Bureau of Economic Analysis (BEA) and draw on the same original source data. The Census Bureau source data for exports and imports of goods and services are presented in greater detail in Tables 7-9 through 7-16. Table 7-17 shows selected summary values for export and import price indexes compiled by the Bureau of Labor Statistics (BLS).

Due to a few differences in concept, scope, and definitions, the aggregate values of international transactions in the NIPAs (shown in Tables 7-1 and 7-4) are not exactly equal to the values for similar concepts in the ITAs or the Census values that serve as their sources, shown in Tables 7-6 through 7-16. The principal sources of differences are as follows:

- The NIPAs cover only the 50 states and the District of Columbia. The ITAs include the U.S. territories and Puerto Rico as part of the U.S. economy.

- Gold is treated differently.

- Services without payment by financial intermediaries except life insurance carriers (imputed interest) is treated differently.

A reconciliation of the two sets of international accounts is published from time to time in the *Survey of Current Business*.

The conventions of presentation no longer differ between the two sets of international accounts. In all the tables that follow, as in their source documents, values of imports of goods and services and of all other transactions that result in a payment to the rest of the world—income payments to foreigners, net transfers to foreigners, and net acquisition of assets from abroad—are presented normally as positive. Where a minus sign does appear, it means that the usual direction of flow is reversed—for example, in the columns of the financial account in Table 7-6 labeled as "Net U.S. acquisition of financial assets," a minus sign would indicate net sales of such assets.

Tables 7-1 and 7-4

Foreign Transactions in the National Income and Product Accounts

SOURCE: U.S. DEPARTMENT OF COMMERCE, BUREAU OF ECONOMIC ANALYSIS

See the notes and definitions to Chapter 1 for an overview of the national income and product accounts (NIPAs).

In the 2003 comprehensive revision, the NIPA foreign transactions account was split into two accounts—the current account and the capital account. (This change had already been made in the ITAs.) Most international transactions fall into the current account, but occasionally there are substantial flows in the capital account when major already-existing assets are transferred. An example of this is the U.S. government's transfer of the Panama Canal to the Republic of Panama in 1999.

Definitions

In accordance with the split between current and capital account, there are now two NIPA measures of the balance of international transactions.

The *balance on current account, national income and product accounts* is *current receipts from the rest of the world* minus *current payments to the rest of the world*. A negative value indicates that current payments exceed current receipts.

Net lending or net borrowing (-), national income and product accounts is equal to the balance on current account less capital account transactions with the rest of the world (net). Capital account transactions with the rest of the world (net) is not shown separately in Table 7-1 (for space reasons) but can be calculated from that table as the difference between net lending/borrowing and the current account balance. (A similar measure, a component of the ITAs, is shown explicitly in Table 7-6.) Capital account transactions with the rest of the world are cash or in-kind transfers linked to the acquisition or disposition of an existing, nonproduced, nonfinancial asset. In contrast, the current account is limited to flows associated with current production of goods and services.

Net lending or net borrowing provides an indirect measure of the net acquisition of foreign assets by U.S. residents less the net acquisition of U.S. assets by foreign residents. These asset flows are measured directly in the ITAs. See Table 7-6 and its notes and definitions for a more extensive discussion of the relationship between the balances on current and capital account and international asset flows.

Current receipts from the rest of the world is *exports of goods and services* plus *income receipts*.

Current payments to the rest of the world is *imports of goods and services* plus *income payments* plus *current taxes and transfer payments (net)*.

Exports and imports of goods and services. Goods, in general, are products that can be stored or inventoried. *Services*, in general, are products that cannot be stored and are consumed at the place and time of their purchase. Goods imports include expenditures abroad by U.S. residents, except for travel. Services include foreign travel by U.S. residents, expenditures in the United States by foreign travelers, and exports and imports of certain goods—primarily military equipment purchased and sold by the federal government. See the following paragraph for the definition of *travel.*

Table 7-4 shows values for selected components of total goods and services; the components shown will not add to the total because of omitted items. In the case of goods, a miscellaneous "other" category is not shown. In the case of services, only two components are shown in this table. One is *travel* (for all purposes including education), which does not include passenger fares but includes as exports spending by foreign tourists and students in the United States, and includes as imports all other spending abroad by tourists and students from the United States. The other component shown here is a category called *other business services*, which includes the professional and financial services (for example, computer services) that have accounted for a large part of the long-term growth in the service category. The remaining components of total services are transport (of both persons and goods), charges for the use of intellectual property not elsewhere classified, government goods and services not elsewhere classified, and a miscellaneous, smaller *other* category. They are shown separately in Tables 7-15 and 7-16.

Income receipts and payments. Income receipts—receipts from abroad of factor (labor or capital) income by U.S. residents— are analogous to exports and are combined with them to yield total *current receipts from the rest of the world. Income payments* by U.S. entities of factor income to entities abroad are analogous to imports.

Current taxes and transfer payments (net) consists of net payments between the United States and abroad that do not involve payment for the services of the labor or capital factors of production, purchase of currently-produced goods and services, or transfer of an existing asset. It includes net flows from persons, government, and business. The types of payments included are personal remittances from U.S. residents to the rest of the world, net of remittances from foreigners to U.S. residents; government grants; and transfer payments from businesses. Only the net payment to the rest of the world is shown. It usually appears in these accounts as a positive value, with transfers from the United States to abroad exceeding the reverse flow. An exception came in 1991, when U.S. allies in the Gulf War reimbursed the United States for the cost of the war, causing the only current-account surplus since 1981. This resulted in net payments to the United States from the rest of the world and appears as a negative entry in the net transfer payments column of the NIPA accounts.

Tables 7-2, 7-3 and 7-5

Chain-Type Quantity and Price Indexes for NIPA Foreign Transactions

These indexes represent the separation of the current-dollar values in Tables 7-1 and 7-4 into their real quantity and price trends components. (See the notes and definitions to Chapter 1 for a general explanation of chained-dollar estimates of real output and prices.) As those notes explain, quantity indexes are shown instead of constant-dollar estimates, because BEA no longer publishes its real output estimates before 1999 in any detail in the constant-dollar form. Therefore, quantity indexes are the only comprehensive source of information about longer-term trends in real volumes.

Table 7-6A and B

U.S. International Transactions: Recent Data

SOURCE: U.S. DEPARTMENT OF COMMERCE, BUREAU OF ECONOMIC ANALYSIS

The U.S. international transactions accounts (ITAs), or "balance of payments accounts," provide a comprehensive view of economic and financial transactions between the United States and foreign countries, measured in current dollars only—unlike the NIPAs, in which price and quantity trends are also estimated. Direct measurement of financial asset and liability flows further distinguishes this set of accounts from the NIPAs.

As was mentioned briefly in the introduction to these Notes and Definitions, the ITAs have been revised and updated, and in addition are now presented in an entirely different manner.

There is no change in the underlying concept: the U.S. balance on current account is still the sum of exports and income receipts, minus the sum of imports and income payments. When it is positive, it necessarily implies net acquisition of assets abroad, and when it is negative, it necessarily implies incurrence of liabilities abroad.

The old, pre-2014 system, which was shown in previous editions of *Business Statistics,* classified all current and financial transactions into debit and credit entries and presented all debits with a negative sign, so that the whole system in theory summed to zero. This method of presentation was not in agreement with other reporting systems, such as the NIPAs and the trade accounts published by the Census Bureau; and while it was internally consistent and logical, it was difficult to interpret and explain. The new system is more straightforward, much easier to explain, and brings the statistics into closer alignment with other statistical systems and international guidelines. Because the debit flows are now presented as normally positive values, balances must be defined as subtractions rather than algebraic sums, probably making them easier to grasp.

The data set now presents as positive values exports, imports, income receipts, income payments, transfers made, transfers received, acquisitions of assets, and incurrences of liabilities. Negative signs are only uses to specify negative income (losses), net sales of assets, net repayment of liabilities, and balances. Current-account and capital-account balances indicate the difference between underlying gross credit and debit flows (for example, exports less imports) and can be positive or negative. For the financial account, net borrowing is calculated as the difference between the net acquisition of financial assets excluding financial derivatives and the net incurrence of liabilities excluding financial derivatives, plus net transactions in financial derivatives.

Definitions

Exports and imports of goods and services. See Tables 7-9 through 7-16 for composition and definitions of goods and services.

Primary income payments and receipts comprise *investment income* and *compensation of employees.*

Investment income includes *direct investment income receipts* (income from direct international ownership of businesses), *portfolio investment income* (dividends and interest from international holdings of stocks and bonds), *other investment income receipts,* and in the case of the United States, *reserve asset income receipts* from official ownership of international reserve assets.

Secondary income includes foreign aid, remittances, U.S. government pensions, and other current international receipts and payments that are not compensation or investment income.

The *capital account* includes capital transfers and the acquisition and disposal of non-produced nonfinancial assets. The major type of *capital transfers* is debt forgiveness. As of the 2010 comprehensive revision, and beginning with the data for 1982, migrants' transfers—the net worth of individuals who immigrate or emigrate during a period—are excluded from the capital account, as they do not generate transactions between a resident and a nonresident. This change is in accordance with international guidelines. Migrants' investments in their country of origin will continue to be recorded in the international investment position accounts (shown in Table 7-8) when migration changes the status of these investments from domestic to international, but they will enter the position as "other changes in value." Non-produced nonfinancial assets include rights to natural resources, patents, copyrights, trademarks, franchises, and leases. In the July 2009 revision, insurance payments for extraordinary disaster losses such as those caused by major hurricanes and the 2001 terror attack were shifted to the capital account from the current unilateral transfers account.

The *financial account* comprises *net U.S. acquisition of financial assets excluding financial derivatives*, which when positive represent a financial outflow, or U.S. investment abroad; *net U.S. incurrence of liabilities excluding financial derivatives*, which when positive represents a financial inflow, or U.S. borrowing abroad; and *financial derivatives other than reserves, net.*

Financial assets include *direct investment assets,* which in turn comprise *direct equity assets* and *direct debt instruments assets; portfolio investment assets*, which in turn comprise *equity and investment fund shares assets, short-term debt securities assets,* and *long term debt securities assets; other investment assets,* which include *currency and deposits, loans, trade credit and advances,* and insurance technical reserves; and U.S. *reserve assets.* (For the definition of *direct investment,* see the Notes and Definitions for Table 7-8.)

Net U.S. incurrence of liabilities excluding financial derivatives, i.e. U.S. borrowing, is reported in categories comparable to those in the asset accounts.

Financial derivatives other than reserves are reported on a net basis.

The *total balance on current account,* the featured measure of U.S. transactions with the rest of the world, is the sum of the *balance on goods and services, balance on primary income,* and *balance on secondary income.* It is sometimes just referred to as the "balance of payments."

The *balance on goods* is the excess of exports of goods over imports of goods. A minus sign indicates an excess of imports over exports. A similar concept, which appears in monthly trade reports, is called the "merchandise trade balance."

The *balance on services* is the excess of service exports over service imports. A minus sign indicates an excess of imports over exports.

The *balance on goods and services* is the sum of the balance on goods and the balance on services. This concept is accurately described as the "balance of trade."

The *balance on capital account* is *capital transfer receipts and other credits* minus *capital transfer payments and other debits.*

By definition, the sum of the current and capital account balances should be the amount of *net lending (+) or net borrowing (-)* required, and it is shown at the end of Table 7-6A, in the column headed *Based on current and capital account transactions.* Also shown is the actual estimate of net lending or net borrowing *Based on financial account transactions,* which is *Total net acquisition of assets* minus *Total net incurrence of liabilities* plus *Financial derivatives other than reserves, net.* This sum is usually not equal to the sum of the current and capital accounts, which are measured from different sources. The difference between the two estimates of lending/borrowing is the *statistical discrepancy.* (Note that there is also a statistical discrepancy in the NIPAs, which also arises from measurement differences, but is not the same as the discrepancy in the ITAs.) In the quarterly accounts, a part of this discrepancy, the *seasonal adjustment discrepancy*, results from separate seasonal adjustments of the components of the accounts.

Data availability

Quarterly estimates are reported in a press release around the middle of the third month of each quarter, available on the BEA Web site at <http://www.bea.gov>. The data published here were released on June 18, 2015, and provide revised and restructured information in detail back to the first quarter of 1999. Data for earlier years have not been revised, but key aggregates and components for those years are presented in a format consistent with the new structure. Complete historical data are available on the BEA Web site at <http://www.bea.gov/>.

References

Articles in the March 2014 and June 2014 *Survey of Current Business* describe the 2014 restructuring and revision of the U.S. International Transactions Accounts (ITAs). The *SCB* is available on the BEA Web site. Further information is provided in "U.S. International Economic Accounts: Concepts and Methods," also available on the BEA website.

Table 7-7

Foreigners' Transactions in Long-Term Securities with U.S. Residents

SOURCE: U.S. DEPARTMENT OF THE TREASURY

Some of the transactions that go into the ITA financial account are collected monthly. Since December 2003, these transactions have been reported by the Treasury Department in a monthly press release. They are presented in Table 7-7.

These data cover transactions in long-term securities, measured at market value plus or minus commissions and fees, between foreigners and U.S. residents. They have more reporting gaps than the more comprehensive quarterly current account data in Table 7-6. These monthly data do not include direct investment, currency flows, changes in bank accounts, or transactions in short-term securities. They may be distorted by inappropriate reporting of repurchases and securities lending transactions. The data are more timely but less detailed than other information sources and are not reliable for country-by-country detail. They are based on a reporting panel of some 250 banks, securities dealers, and other enterprises with cross-border transactions of at least $50 million. This survey was designed to provide timely information for the balance of payments accounts, and its use for other applications—particularly those involving country detail—is less appropriate.

Definitions and notes on the data

U.S. residents includes any individual, corporation, or organization located in the United States (including branches, subsidiaries, and affiliates of foreign entities located in the United States) and any corporation incorporated in the United States, even if it has no physical presence in the country.

Gross purchases minus *gross sales* equals *net purchases*. Positive values for net purchases of U.S. securities by foreigners indicate capital inflows from foreigners to U.S. residents (and increased liabilities to foreigners on the part of the U.S. residents). Negative values for net purchases of foreign securities from U.S. residents indicate a capital outflow from U.S. residents to foreigners (and increased liabilities to U.S. residents on the part of foreigners). The algebraic sum of the two net purchases components gives *net long-term securities transactions*. When positive, this indicates that the net capital inflows on U.S. securities exceed the net U.S. acquisitions of foreign securities.

Other acquisitions of long-term securities, net consists of estimated foreign acquisitions of U.S. equity through stock swaps, plus the increase in nonmarketable treasury bonds and notes issued to official institutions and other residents of foreign countries, minus estimated unrecorded principal payments to foreigners on domestic corporate and agency asset-backed securities, minus estimated U.S. acquisitions of foreign equity through stock swaps.

Net foreign acquisition of long-term securities is the sum of *net long-term securities transactions* and *other acquisitions of long-term securities*.

Revisions

The monthly and annual data are revised frequently, when quarterly and annual benchmark data become available. The June release usually includes the final results from an annual survey of foreign holding of U.S. securities.

Data availability and references

Data for the latest month and recent historical data are published in a press release available around the middle of the second following month. The press release, supporting descriptions, references, and other relevant information concerning the Treasury International Capital System (TIC) can be found online at <http://www.treas.gov/tic>.

Table 7-8

International Investment Position of the United States

SOURCE: U.S. DEPARTMENT OF COMMERCE, BUREAU OF ECONOMIC ANALYSIS

The data presented in Tables 7-1 through 7-7 all represent <u>flows</u> of goods, services, and money over the designated time periods. Table 7-8, in contrast, is a measure of <u>stocks</u>, or total holdings of money and other claims. The data on the international investment position of the United States measure the extent to which the United States and its residents hold claims of ownership on foreigners or are creditors of foreigners; the extent to which foreigners, including foreign governments, hold claims of ownership on assets located in the United States or are creditors of

U.S. residents and entities; and the net difference between the two amounts. This difference measures the amount by which the United States is a net creditor of the rest of the world or a net debtor to the rest of the world. A position of net U.S. indebtedness is represented by a minus sign in the net international investment position.

These accounts were revised in June 2014 consistent with the 2014 comprehensive revision of the International Transaction Accounts (ITAs) described in the Notes and Definitions to Table 7-6, above. The principal difference from earlier presentations is that direct investment is now valued at market value. (Previously, the featured measure was based on estimates of current replacement costs.) Quarterly estimates of the position are now available for the first time.

Changes in the net investment position can arise in two principal ways.

The first way is through inflows or outflows of capital. A net inflow of capital increases U.S. indebtedness to foreigners, while a net outflow increases foreigners' indebtedness to the United States. A deficit in the U.S. international current account requires an equivalent inflow of foreign capital, while a surplus would require an equivalent outflow of U.S. capital; see the notes for Table 7-6 for further explanation.

The second way is through valuation adjustments, which are of several kinds: changes in market prices of assets; changes in exchange rates, which can cause revaluation of foreign-currency-denominated assets; and miscellaneous other adjustments due to changes in coverage, statistical discrepancies, and the like. Valuation adjustments are shown separately from financial flows in the *Survey of Current Business* articles accompanying each annual update (see below for reference). They were particularly sharp in 2008 and 2009, far exceeding the actual net volume of financial flows in both years.

For the years 2005 forward, assets and the net position include financial derivatives, which introduces a break in the series. The values for financial derivatives are shown separately so that the user can eliminate them from the calculation if desired.

Definitions: direct investment, current cost, and market value

Direct investment occurs when an individual or business in one country (the parent) obtains a lasting interest in, and a degree of influence over the management of, a business enterprise in another country (the affiliate). The U.S. data define this degree of interest to be ownership of at least 10 percent of the voting securities of an incorporated business enterprise or the equivalent interest in an unincorporated business enterprise.

When direct investment positions are valued at the historical costs carried on the books of the affiliated companies, much of

the investment will reflect the price levels of earlier time periods. Restating it at *market value* revalues the owners' equity portion of the direct investment positions using indexes of stock market prices. Stock price changes reflect changes not only in the value of tangible assets, but also in the value of intangible assets and in the outlook for a country or industry.

Definitions: net international investment position

U.S. net international investment position is defined as the value of *U.S. assets* minus the value of *U.S. liabilities.*

U.S. assets is the sum of *direct investment at market value, portfolio investment, gross positive fair value of financial derivatives other than reserves, other investment,* and *U.S. reserve assets.*

As a component of U.S. assets, the *financial derivatives* category is the sum of derivatives positions with a positive "fair value" to U.S. residents. The fair value of a derivatives contract is the amount for which the contract could be exchanged between willing parties. A derivatives contract between a U.S. and a foreign resident with a positive fair value represents the amount that the foreign resident would have to pay to the U.S. resident if the contract was terminated.

Reserve assets includes gold, valued at the current market price; special drawing rights; the U.S. reserve position in the International Monetary Fund; and official holdings of foreign currencies.

U.S. liabilities is the sum of foreign *direct investment* in the United States *at market value, portfolio investment, long-term debt securities, gross negative fair value of financial derivatives other than reserves,* and *other investment,* which includes *currency and deposits* and *loans.*

As a component of foreign-owned assets in the United States, the *financial derivatives* entry consists of derivatives positions with a negative "fair value" to U.S. residents. A contract with a negative fair value represents the amount that the U.S. resident would have to pay to the foreign resident if the contract was terminated.

Data availability

Data on the U.S. International Investment Position (IIP) are now released quarterly, around the end of the succeeding quarter. The estimates shown here reflect the annual revisions released June 30, 2015. All the data are available on the BEA Web site at <http://www.bea.gov>.

References

A detailed discussion of the IIP statistics and the comprehensive revision is scheduled for publication in the July 2014 issue of the *Survey of Current Business.* Also see the references for Table 7-6.

Tables 7-9 through 7-16

Exports and Imports of Goods and Services

SOURCES: U.S. DEPARTMENT OF COMMERCE, CENSUS BUREAU AND BUREAU OF ECONOMIC ANALYSIS

These tables present the source data used to build up the aggregate measures of goods and services flows shown in Tables 7-1 through 7-6. These data are compiled and published monthly, making trends evident before the publication of the quarterly aggregate estimates. They also provide more detail than the quarterly aggregates.

Monthly and annual data on exports and imports of *goods* are compiled by the Census Bureau from documents collected by the U.S. Customs Service. The Bureau of Economic Analysis (BEA) makes certain adjustments to these data (as described below) to place the estimates on a *balance of payments* basis— a basis consistent with the national and international accounts.

Data on exports and imports of *services* are prepared by BEA from a variety of sources. Monthly data on services are available from January 1992. Annual and quarterly data for earlier years are available as part of the international transactions accounts. Current data on goods and services are available each month in a joint Census Bureau-BEA press release.

In the case of some of the detailed breakdowns of exports and imports, such as by end-use categories, monthly data may not sum exactly to annual totals. This is due to later revisions, which are made only to annual data and are not allocated to monthly data. Also, the constant-dollar figures expressed in 2009 dollars are now calculated using chain weights. Therefore, the 2009-dollar detail will not add to the 2009-dollar totals.

In addition, monthly and annual data on exports and imports of goods for individual countries and various country groupings do not reflect subsequent revisions of annual total data. These country data are compiled by the Census Bureau for all countries, although this volume includes only a selection of the most significant countries and areas. The full set of data can be accessed on the Census Web site at <http://www.census.gov>.

Definitions: Goods

Goods: Census basis. The Census basis goods data are compiled from documents collected by the U.S. Customs Service. They reflect the movement of goods between foreign countries and the 50 states, the District of Columbia, Puerto Rico, the U.S. Virgin Islands, and U.S. Foreign Trade Zones. They include government and nongovernment shipments of goods, and exclude shipments between the United States and its territories and possessions; transactions with U.S. military, diplomatic, and consular installations abroad; U.S. goods returned to the United States by its armed forces; personal and household effects of travelers; and intransit shipments. The general import values reflect the total arrival of merchandise from foreign countries that immediately enters consumption channels, warehouses, or Foreign Trade Zones.

For *imports,* the value reported is the U.S. Customs Service appraised value of merchandise (generally, the price paid for merchandise for export to the United States). Import duties, freight, insurance, and other charges incurred in bringing merchandise to the United States are excluded.

Exports are valued at the f.a.s. (free alongside ship) value of merchandise at the U.S. port of export, based on the transaction price including inland freight, insurance, and other charges incurred in placing the merchandise alongside the carrier at the U.S. port of exportation.

Goods: balance of payments (BOP) basis. Goods on a Census basis are adjusted by BEA to goods on a BOP basis to bring the data in line with the concepts and definitions used to prepare the international and national accounts. In general, the adjustments include changes in ownership that occur without goods passing into or out of the customs territory of the United States. These adjustments are necessary to supplement coverage of the Census basis data, to eliminate duplication of transactions recorded elsewhere in the international accounts, and to value transactions according to a standard definition. With the June 4, 2013 release, improved BOP adjustments involving U.S. military transactions were introduced for data beginning with 1999.

The *export* adjustments include the following: (1) The deduction of *U.S. military sales contracts.* The Census Bureau has included these contracts in the goods data, but BEA includes them in the service category "Transfers Under U.S. Military Sales Contracts." BEA's source material for these contracts is more comprehensive but does not distinguish between goods and services. (2) The addition of *private gift parcels* mailed to foreigners by individuals through the U.S. Postal Service. Only commercial shipments are covered in Census goods exports. (3) The addition to *nonmonetary gold exports* of gold purchased by foreign official agencies from private dealers in the United States and held at the Federal Reserve Bank of New York. The Census data include only gold that leaves the customs territory. (4) *Smaller adjustments* includes deductions for repairs of goods, exposed motion picture film, and military grant aid, and additions for sales of fish in U.S. territorial waters, exports of electricity to Mexico, and vessels and oil rigs that change ownership without export documents being filed.

The *import* adjustments include the following: (1) On *inland freight in Canada,* the customs value for imports for certain Canadian goods is the point of origin in Canada. BEA makes an addition for the inland freight charges of transporting these Canadian goods to the U.S. border. (2) An addition is made to *nonmonetary gold imports* for gold sold by foreign official agencies to private purchasers out of stock held at the Federal Reserve Bank of New York. The Census Bureau data include only gold that enters the customs territory. (3) A deduction is made for *imports by U.S. military agencies.* The Census Bureau has included these contracts in the goods data, but BEA includes them in the service category "Direct Defense Expenditures." BEA's source material is more comprehensive but does not distinguish between goods and services. (4) *Smaller adjustments* includes deductions for repairs of goods and for exposed motion picture film and additions for imported electricity from Mexico, conversion of vessels for commercial use, and repairs to U.S. vessels abroad.

Definitions: Services

These statistics are estimates of service transactions between foreign countries and the 50 states, the District of Columbia, Puerto Rico, the U.S. Virgin Islands, and other U.S. territories and possessions. Transactions with U.S. military, diplomatic, and consular installations abroad are excluded because they are considered to be part of the U.S. economy.

In the 2014 comprehensive revision of the ITAs, new categories have been introduced in the services reports, beginning with January 1999. The 9 new categories, shown in Tables 7-15A and 7-16A, are as follows:

Maintenance and repair services n.i.e. (not included elsewhere) were previously included in "other private services."

Transport includes the previous categories of "passenger fares" and "other transportation."

Travel for all purposes including education is broader than the previous "travel" category and now includes business travel, expenditures by border, seasonal, and other short-term workers, and personal travel including that related to health and education. As before, it consists of expenditures for food, lodging, recreation, gifts, and other items incidental to a foreign visit but not the actual transportation expenses.

Insurance services and *financial services* were previously included in other private services.

Charges for the use of intellectual property n.i.e. was previously named "royalties and license fees."

Telecommunications, computer, and information services and *other business services* were previously included in "other private services."

Government goods and services n.i.e. replaces the government categories in the previous system.

Earlier services definitions

In Tables 7-15B and 7-16B, showing data before 1999, services are classified in the broad categories described below. For six of these categories, the definitions are the same for imports and exports. For the seventh, the export category is "Transfers under U.S. Military Sales Contracts," while for imports, the category is "Direct Defense Expenditures."

Travel includes purchases of services and goods by U.S. travelers abroad and by foreign visitors to the United States. A traveler is defined as a person who stays for a period of less than one year in a country where the person is not a resident. Included are expenditures for food, lodging, recreation, gifts, and other items incidental to a foreign visit. Not included are the international costs of the travel itself, which are covered in *passenger fares* (see below).

Passenger fares consists of fares paid by residents of one country to residents in other countries. Receipts consist of fares received by U.S. carriers from foreign residents for travel between the United States and foreign countries and between two foreign points. Payments consist of fares paid by U.S. residents to foreign carriers for travel between the United States and foreign countries.

Other transportation includes charges for the transportation of goods by ocean, air, waterway, pipeline, and rail carriers to and from the United States. Included are freight charges, operating expenses that transportation companies incur in foreign ports, and payments for vessel charter and aircraft and freight car rentals.

Royalties and license fees consists of transactions with foreign residents involving intangible assets and proprietary rights, such as the use of patents, techniques, processes, formulas, designs, knowhow, trademarks, copyrights, franchises, and manufacturing rights. The term *royalties* generally refers to payments for the utilization of copyrights or trademarks, and the term *license fees* generally refers to payments for the use of patents or industrial processes.

Other private services includes transactions with "affiliated" foreigners for which no identification by type is available and transactions with unaffiliated foreigners.

The term "affiliated" refers to a direct investment relationship, which exists when a U.S. person has ownership or control (directly or indirectly) of 10 percent or more of a foreign business enterprise, or when a foreign person has a similar interest in a U.S. enterprise.

Transactions with "unaffiliated" foreigners in this "other private services" category consist of education services, financial services, insurance services, telecommunications services, and business, professional, and technical services. Included in the last group are advertising services; computer and data processing services; database and other information services; research, development, and testing services; management, consulting, and public relations services; legal services; construction, engineering, architectural, and mining services; industrial engineering services; installation, maintenance, and repair of equipment; and other services, including medical services and film and tape rental.

The insurance component of "other private services" was measured before the July 2003 revision as premiums less actual losses paid or recovered. Furthermore, catastrophic losses were entered immediately when the loss occurred, rather than when the insurance claim was actually paid out. This led to sharp swings for any month in which catastrophic losses occurred, such as Hurricane Katrina in August 2005 or the September 11, 2001, terror attacks. In the accounts as revised in July 2003 and presented here, insurance services are now measured as premiums less "normal" losses. Normal losses consist of a measure of expected regularly occurring losses based on six years of past experience <u>plus</u> an additional allowance for catastrophic loss. Catastrophic losses, when they occur, are added in equal increments to the estimate of regularly occurring losses over the 20 years following the occurrence. As adoption of this methodology introduces a difference between actual and normal losses, an amount equal to the difference is entered in the international accounts as a capital account transaction.

Transfers under U.S. military sales contracts (exports only) includes exports in which U.S. government military agencies participate. This category has included both goods, such as equipment, and services, such as repair services and training, that could not be separately identified. In the 2010 and 2013 annual revisions, more precise breakdowns between goods and services in this category were introduced and incorporated as revised estimates of services and of the BOP goods adjustment, beginning with the data for 2007. Transfers of goods and services under U.S. military grant programs are included.

Direct defense expenditures (imports only) consists of expenditures incurred by U.S. military agencies abroad, including expenditures by U.S. personnel, payments of wages to foreign residents, construction expenditures, payments for foreign contractual services, and procurement of foreign goods. Improved breakdowns between goods and services are now incorporated beginning with statistics for 1999.

U.S. government miscellaneous services includes transactions of U.S. government nonmilitary agencies with foreign residents. Most of these transactions involve the provision of services to, or purchases of services from, foreigners. Transfers of some goods are also included.

Services estimates are based on quarterly, annual, and benchmark surveys and partial information generated from monthly reports. Service transactions are estimated at market prices. Estimates are seasonally adjusted when statistically significant seasonal patterns are present.

Definitions: Area groupings

The Census trade statistics for groups of countries present "groups as they were at the time of reporting", which means that as multinational organizations such as the European Union expand, the statistics for trade with that group include the added country only beginning with the year it entered the group. The European Union was expanded from 15 to 28 nations as of July 1, 2013, and data for that year are available for both the new and the old group; to provide historical perspective, they are both shown here, along with the historical data back to 1974 for the original group.

The *European Union* now includes 28 countries: Austria, Belgium, Bulgaria, Croatia, Cyprus, Czech Republic, Denmark, Estonia, Finland, France, Germany, Greece, Hungary, Ireland, Italy, Latvia, Lithuania, Luxembourg, Malta, Netherlands, Poland, Portugal, Romania, Slovakia, Slovenia, Spain, Sweden, and the United Kingdom. The last country to join was Croatia in July 2013.

The *Asian Newly Industrialized Countries (NICS)* includes Hong Kong SAR, South Korea, Singapore, and Taiwan. This group was initially called the *Four Asian Tigers.*

The twelve *Organization of Petroleum Exporting Countries (OPEC)* currently consists of Algeria, Angola, Ecuador, Iran, Iraq, Kuwait, Libya, Nigeria, Qatar, Saudi Arabia, the United Arab Emirates, and Venezuela. Ecuador Indonesia is no longer a member as of January 2009.

Notes on the data

U.S./Canada data exchange and substitution. The data for U.S. exports to Canada are derived from import data compiled by Canada. The use of Canada's import data to produce U.S. export data requires several alignments in order to compare the two series.

- *Coverage*: Canadian imports are based on country of origin. U.S. goods shipped from a third country are included, but U.S. exports exclude these foreign shipments. U.S. export coverage also excludes certain Canadian postal shipments.

- *Valuation*: Canadian imports are valued at their point of origin in the United States. However, U.S. exports are valued at the port of exit in the United States and include inland freight charges, making the U.S. export value slightly larger. Canada requires inland freight to be reported.

- *Reexports*: U.S. exports include re-exports of foreign goods. Again, the aggregate U.S. export figure is slightly larger.

- *Exchange Rate*: Average monthly exchange rates are applied to convert the published data to U.S. currency.

End-use categories and seasonal adjustment of trade in goods. Goods are initially classified under the Harmonized System, which describes and measures the characteristics of goods traded. Combining trade into approximately 140 export and 140 import enduse categories makes it possible to examine goods according to their principal uses. These categories are used as the basis for computing the seasonal and working-day adjusted data. Adjusted data are then summed to the six end-use aggregates for publication.

The seasonal adjustment procedure is based on a model that estimates the monthly movements as percentages above or below the general level of each end-use commodity series (unlike other methods that redistribute the actual series values over the calendar year). Imports of petroleum and petroleum products are adjusted for the length of the month.

Data availability

Data are released monthly in a joint Census Bureau-BEA press release (FT-900), which is published about six weeks after the end of the month to which the data pertain. The release and historical data are available on the Census Bureau Web site at <http://www.census.gov/foreigntrade/www/>.

Revisions

Data for recent years are normally revised annually. In some cases, revisions to annual totals are not distributed to monthly data; therefore, monthly data may not sum to the revised total shown. Data on trade in services may be subject to extensive revision as part of BEA's annual revision of the international transactions accounts (ITAs), usually released in July.

References

See the references for Table 7-6.

Table 7-17

Export and Import Price Indexes

SOURCE: U.S. DEPARTMENT OF LABOR, BUREAU OF LABOR STATISTICS

The International Price Program of the Bureau of Labor Statistics (BLS) collects price data for nonmilitary goods traded between the United States and the rest of the world and for selected transportation services in international markets. BLS aggregates the goods price data into export and import price indexes. Summary values of these price indexes for goods are presented in *Business Statistics*. For product and locality detail on international prices for both goods and services, see the *Handbook of U.S. Labor Statistics,* also published by Bernan Press.

Definitions

The *export* price index provides a measure of price change for all goods sold by U.S. residents (businesses and individuals located within the geographic boundaries of the United States, whether or not owned by U.S. citizens) to foreign buyers.

The *import* price index provides a measure of price change for goods purchased from other countries by U.S. residents.

Notes on the data

Published index series use a base year of 2000 = 100 whenever possible.

The product universe for both the import and export indexes includes raw materials, agricultural products, and manufactures. Price data are primarily collected by mail questionnaire, and directly from the exporter or importer in all but a few cases.

To the greatest extent possible, the data refer to prices at the U.S. border for exports and at either the foreign border or the U.S. border for imports. For nearly all products, the prices refer to transactions completed during the first week of the month and represent the actual price for which the product was bought or sold, including discounts, allowances, and rebates.

For the export price indexes, the preferred pricing basis is f.a.s. (free alongside ship) U.S. port of exportation. Where necessary, adjustments are made to reported prices to place them on this basis. An attempt is made to collect two prices for imports: f.o.b. (free on board) at the port of exportation and c.i.f. (cost, insurance, and freight) at the U.S. port of importation. Adjustments are made to account for changes in product characteristics in order to obtain a pure measure of price change.

The indexes are weighted indexes of the Laspeyres type. (See "General Notes" at the beginning of this volume for further explanation.) The values assigned to each weight category are based on trade value figures compiled by the Census Bureau. They are reweighted annually, with a two-year lag (as concurrent value data are not available) in revisions.

The merchandise price indexes are published using three different classification systems: the Harmonized System, the Bureau of Economic Analysis End-Use System, and the Standard International Trade Classification (SITC) system. The aggregate indexes shown here are from the End-Use System.

Data availability

Indexes are published monthly in a press release and a more detailed report. Indexes are published for detailed product categories, as well as for all commodities. Aggregate import indexes by country or region of origin also are available, as are indexes for selected categories of internationally traded services. Additional information is available from the Division of International Prices in the Bureau of Labor Statistics. Complete historical data are available on the BLS Web site at <http://www.bls.gov>.

References

The indexes are described in "BLS to Produce Monthly Indexes of Export and Import Prices," *Monthly Labor Review* (December 1988), and Chapter 15, "International Price Indexes," *BLS Handbook of Methods* Bulletin 2490 (April 1997).

CHAPTER 8: PRICES

Figure 8-1: Inflation Indicators, 1946–2014

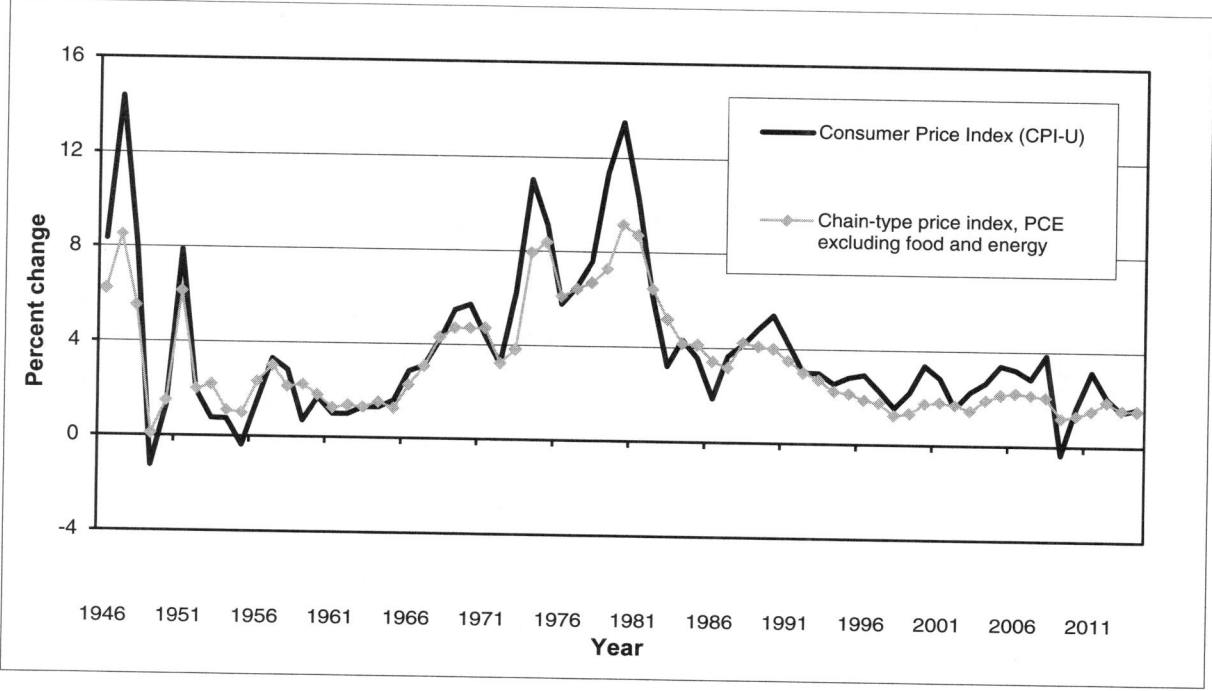

- Figure 8-1 shows annual rates of change in the Consumer Price Index for All Urban Consumers (CPI-U), the most widely used measure of the general price level. It also shows changes in the chain-type price index for personal consumption expenditures (PCE) excluding food and energy, which provides one widely used measure of the "core" or underlying rate of inflation. (Tables 8-1, 8-4, and 1-6)

- Sharp swings in energy prices caused the all-items CPI to drop 0.4 percent in 2009—the first year-to-year deflation registered since 1955—and swing back up to 3.2 percent inflation in 2011. Inflation measured by CPI-U dropped back to 1.6 percent in 2014. (Table 8-4)

- The core PCE inflation rate strips out volatile food and energy prices, in order to try to isolate the "underlying" rate of inflation, and is based on a concept slightly different from the CPI (see Notes and definitions for details). It shows a deceleration of inflation from 2.2 percent in 2005–2007 to an average of 1.4 percent in 2009 through 2014. (Table 8-4)

- From 1965 to 2014, commodity (goods) prices in the CPI-U rose at an average rate of 3.5 percent per year, but services prices increased at an average annual rate of 5.0 percent. (Table 8-1A)

- The Producer Price Index (PPI) measures prices at the point of production, rather than at the consumer level. For most of its history, the PPI has measured goods only. The Finished Goods PPI rose at a 3.7 percent annual rate from 1965 to 2014, very similar to the rate for commodities alone in the CPI. The PPI for "unprocessed nonfood materials less energy," also known (in the old goods-only system) as "crude nonfood materials less energy") is a sensitive leading indicator, not of aggregate prices, but of general business conditions. (Tables 8-1A and B)

- A broader system of PPIs including services and construction as well as goods was introduced in 2014, featuring a more detailed representation by stages of production as well. These new measures only go back to November 2009—not enough time yet to determine what kind of signals about future inflation they will contain. (Tables 8-5 and 8-6)

Table 8-1A. Summary Consumer and Producer Price Indexes: Recent Data

(Seasonally adjusted.)

Year and month	Urban wage earners and clerical workers (CPI-W), all items	Consumer Price Index, 1982–1984 = 100 — All urban consumers (CPI-U) — All items	Food	Energy	All items less food and energy	Commodities	Services	Producer Price Indexes for goods, 1982 = 100 — Finished goods — Total	Less food and energy	Processed goods for intermediate demand — Total	Processed materials less food and energy	Unprocessed goods for intermediate demand — Total	Unprocessed nonfood materials less energy
1965	31.7	31.5	32.2	22.9	32.7	35.2	26.6	34.1	. . .	31.2	. . .	31.1	. . .
1966	32.6	32.4	33.8	23.3	33.5	36.1	27.6	35.2	. . .	32.0	. . .	33.1	. . .
1967	33.6	33.4	34.1	23.8	34.7	36.8	28.8	35.6	. . .	32.2	. . .	31.3	. . .
1968	35.0	34.8	35.3	24.2	36.3	38.1	30.3	36.6	. . .	33.0	. . .	31.8	. . .
1969	36.9	36.7	37.1	24.8	38.4	39.9	32.4	38.0	. . .	34.1	. . .	33.9	. . .
1970	39.0	38.8	39.2	25.5	40.8	41.7	35.0	39.3	. . .	35.4	. . .	35.2	. . .
1971	40.7	40.5	40.4	26.5	42.7	43.2	37.0	40.5	. . .	36.8	. . .	36.0	. . .
1972	42.1	41.8	42.1	27.2	44.0	44.5	38.4	41.8	. . .	38.2	. . .	39.9	. . .
1973	44.7	44.4	48.2	29.4	45.6	47.8	40.1	45.6	48.1	42.4	44.3	54.5	70.8
1974	49.6	49.3	55.1	38.1	49.4	53.5	43.8	52.6	53.6	52.5	54.0	61.4	83.3
1975	54.1	53.8	59.8	42.1	53.9	58.2	48.0	58.2	59.7	58.0	60.2	61.6	69.3
1976	57.2	56.9	61.6	45.1	57.4	60.7	52.0	60.8	63.1	60.9	63.8	63.4	80.2
1977	60.9	60.6	65.5	49.4	61.0	64.2	56.0	64.7	66.9	64.9	67.6	65.5	79.8
1978	65.6	65.2	72.0	52.5	65.5	68.8	60.8	69.8	71.9	69.5	72.5	73.4	87.8
1979	73.1	72.6	79.9	65.7	71.9	76.6	67.5	77.6	78.3	78.4	80.7	85.9	106.2
1980	82.9	82.4	86.8	86.0	80.8	86.0	77.9	88.0	87.1	90.3	90.3	95.3	113.1
1981	91.4	90.9	93.6	97.7	89.2	93.2	88.1	96.1	94.6	98.6	97.7	103.0	111.7
1982	96.9	96.5	97.4	99.2	95.8	97.0	96.0	100.0	100.0	100.0	100.0	100.0	100.0
1983	99.8	99.6	99.4	99.9	99.6	99.8	99.4	101.6	103.0	100.6	101.6	101.3	105.3
1984	103.3	103.9	103.2	100.9	104.6	103.2	104.6	103.7	105.5	103.1	104.7	103.5	111.7
1985	106.9	107.6	105.6	101.6	109.1	105.4	109.9	104.7	108.1	102.7	105.2	95.8	104.9
1986	108.6	109.6	109.0	88.2	113.5	104.4	115.4	103.2	110.6	99.1	104.9	87.7	103.1
1987	112.5	113.6	113.5	88.6	118.2	107.7	120.2	105.4	113.3	101.5	107.8	93.7	115.7
1988	117.0	118.3	118.2	89.3	123.4	111.5	125.7	108.0	117.0	107.1	115.2	96.0	133.0
1989	122.6	124.0	125.1	94.3	129.0	116.7	131.9	113.6	122.1	112.0	120.2	103.1	137.9
1990	129.0	130.7	132.4	102.1	135.5	122.8	139.2	119.2	126.6	114.5	120.9	108.9	136.3
1991	134.3	136.2	136.3	102.5	142.1	126.6	146.3	121.7	131.1	114.4	121.4	101.2	128.2
1992	138.2	140.3	137.9	103.0	147.3	129.1	152.0	123.2	134.2	114.7	122.0	100.4	128.4
1993	142.1	144.5	140.9	104.2	152.2	131.5	157.9	124.7	135.8	116.2	123.8	102.4	140.2
1994	145.6	148.2	144.3	104.6	156.5	133.8	163.1	125.5	137.1	118.5	127.1	101.8	156.2
1995	149.8	152.4	148.4	105.2	161.2	136.4	168.7	127.9	140.0	124.9	135.2	102.7	173.6
1996	154.1	156.9	153.3	110.1	165.6	139.9	174.1	131.3	142.0	125.7	134.0	113.8	155.8
1997	157.6	160.5	157.3	111.5	169.5	141.8	179.4	131.8	142.4	125.6	134.2	111.1	156.5
1998	159.7	163.0	160.7	102.9	173.4	141.9	184.2	130.7	143.7	123.0	133.5	96.8	142.1
1999	163.2	166.6	164.1	106.6	177.0	144.4	188.8	133.0	146.1	123.2	133.1	98.2	135.2
2000	168.9	172.2	167.8	124.6	181.3	149.2	195.3	138.0	148.0	129.2	136.6	120.6	145.2
2001	173.5	177.1	173.1	129.3	186.1	150.7	203.4	140.7	150.0	129.7	136.4	121.0	130.7
2002	175.9	179.9	176.2	121.7	190.5	149.7	209.8	138.9	150.2	127.8	135.8	108.1	135.7
2003	179.8	184.0	180.0	136.5	193.2	151.2	216.5	143.3	150.5	133.7	138.5	135.3	152.5
2004	184.5	188.9	186.2	151.4	196.6	154.7	222.8	148.5	152.7	142.6	146.5	159.0	193.0
2005	191.0	195.3	190.7	177.1	200.9	160.2	230.1	155.7	156.4	154.0	154.6	182.2	202.4
2006	197.1	201.6	195.2	196.9	205.9	164.0	238.9	160.4	158.7	164.0	163.8	184.8	244.5
2007	202.8	207.3	202.9	207.7	210.7	167.5	246.8	166.6	161.7	170.7	168.4	207.1	282.6
2008	211.1	215.3	214.1	236.7	215.6	174.8	255.5	177.1	167.2	188.3	180.9	251.8	324.4
2009	209.6	214.5	218.0	193.1	219.2	169.7	259.2	172.5	171.5	172.5	173.4	175.2	248.4
2010	214.0	218.1	219.6	211.4	221.3	174.6	261.3	179.8	173.6	183.4	180.8	212.2	329.1
2011	221.6	224.9	227.8	243.9	225.0	183.9	265.8	190.5	177.8	199.8	192.0	249.4	390.4
2012	226.2	229.6	233.8	246.1	229.8	187.6	271.4	194.2	182.4	200.7	192.6	241.3	369.6
2013	229.3	233.0	237.0	244.4	233.8	187.7	277.9	196.6	185.1	200.8	193.8	246.6	351.2
2014	232.8	236.7	242.7	243.6	237.9	187.9	285.1	200.4	188.6	202.1	195.4	249.4	345.9
2013													
January	227.8	231.4	236.0	242.6	232.2	187.5	275.1	196.0	183.9	201.4	193.6	249.5	365.2
February	229.4	232.8	236.1	253.8	232.6	189.6	275.7	197.1	184.2	203.2	194.7	246.9	363.0
March	228.7	232.2	236.3	246.0	232.8	188.1	276.1	196.1	184.5	201.3	194.5	247.4	365.5
April	227.9	231.7	236.7	238.8	232.9	186.6	276.4	194.7	184.7	199.9	194.0	247.3	355.8
May	228.3	232.0	236.4	240.5	233.1	186.6	277.1	196.1	184.9	200.3	193.7	250.1	349.8
June	229.0	232.6	236.8	243.2	233.5	187.3	277.6	196.4	185.1	200.5	193.7	248.2	346.6
July	229.4	233.0	237.1	244.0	233.9	187.5	278.1	196.4	185.3	200.6	193.4	251.0	346.4
August	229.8	233.4	237.4	245.0	234.3	187.8	278.7	197.0	185.4	200.7	193.6	246.8	345.6
September	230.1	233.8	237.6	245.9	234.6	187.9	279.3	197.4	185.4	200.6	193.6	242.9	342.4
October	230.2	233.9	237.8	244.8	234.9	187.7	279.8	197.1	185.4	199.9	193.5	238.5	343.7
November	230.3	234.0	238.1	242.4	235.3	187.3	280.4	197.1	185.8	200.8	193.7	243.6	348.2
December	231.0	234.7	238.2	246.5	235.6	188.2	280.9	198.2	186.6	200.8	193.7	243.6	348.2
2014													
January	231.4	235.1	238.5	248.3	236.0	188.1	281.8	199.3	187.5	202.3	194.5	248.2	354.9
February	231.6	235.4	239.4	247.2	236.2	188.0	282.4	199.5	187.7	202.8	195.2	259.8	351.1
March	232.0	235.8	240.4	247.3	236.6	187.8	283.4	200.0	187.7	202.9	194.9	260.8	349.3
April	232.5	236.2	241.2	247.0	237.1	188.4	283.7	200.8	187.9	202.9	195.3	263.6	354.1
May	233.1	237.0	242.2	248.9	237.7	188.8	284.8	201.1	188.3	203.1	195.2	260.7	353.2
June	233.6	237.3	242.4	250.2	238.0	189.1	285.3	201.9	188.6	203.4	195.3	257.9	347.4
July	233.7	237.6	243.2	249.8	238.2	189.1	285.7	201.8	188.8	203.6	196.0	253.4	348.4
August	233.5	237.4	243.8	245.6	238.3	188.5	285.9	201.5	189.0	203.4	196.4	245.6	345.5
September	233.7	237.6	244.7	243.8	238.7	188.5	286.3	201.3	189.3	203.0	196.3	245.9	345.8
October	233.7	237.8	245.1	240.9	239.1	188.2	286.9	200.8	189.5	201.0	195.7	237.7	337.1
November	232.6	237.1	245.6	230.9	239.3	186.3	287.4	199.2	189.6	198.9	194.8	234.7	331.8
December	231.5	236.3	246.2	220.1	239.4	184.0	288.0	196.9	190.0	196.2	194.3	223.8	330.5

. . . = Not available.

Table 8-1B. Summary Consumer and Producer Price Indexes: Historical Data, 1947 to Date

(Seasonally adjusted.)

Year and month	Urban wage earners and clerical workers (CPI-W), all items	Consumer Price Index, 1982–1984 = 100 — All urban consumers (CPI-U)						Producer Price Index for goods, 1982 = 100 — Finished goods		Processed goods for intermediate demand		Unprocessed goods for intermediate demand	
		All items	Food	Energy	All items less food and energy	Commod-ities	Services	Total	Less food and energy	Total	Processed materials less foods and energy	Total	Unprocessed nonfood materials less energy
1946	19.6	19.5	19.8	. . .	. . .	22.9	14.1	. . .	. . .	. . .	. . .	31.7	. . .
1947	22.5	22.3	24.1	. . .	. . .	27.6	14.7	26.4	. . .	23.3	. . .	34.7	. . .
1948	24.2	24.1	26.1	. . .	. . .	29.6	15.6	28.5	. . .	25.2	. . .	30.1	. . .
1949	24.0	23.8	25.0	. . .	. . .	28.8	16.4	27.7	. . .	24.2	. . .		. . .
1950	24.2	24.1	25.4	. . .	. . .	29.0	16.9	28.2	. . .	25.3	. . .	32.7	. . .
1951	26.1	26.0	28.2	. . .	. . .	31.6	17.8	30.8	. . .	28.4	. . .	37.6	. . .
1952	26.7	26.5	28.7	. . .	. . .	32.0	18.6	30.6	. . .	27.5	. . .	34.5	. . .
1953	26.9	26.7	28.3	. . .	. . .	31.9	19.4	30.3	. . .	27.7	. . .	31.9	. . .
1954	27.0	26.9	28.2	. . .	. . .	31.6	20.0	30.4	. . .	27.9	. . .	31.6	. . .
1955	26.9	26.8	27.8	. . .	. . .	31.3	20.4	30.5	. . .	28.4	. . .	30.4	. . .
1956	27.3	27.2	28.0	. . .	. . .	31.6	20.9	31.3	. . .	29.6	. . .	30.6	. . .
1957	28.3	28.1	28.9	21.5	28.9	32.6	21.8	32.5	. . .	30.3	. . .	31.2	. . .
1958	29.1	28.9	30.2	21.5	29.6	33.3	22.6	33.2	. . .	30.4	. . .	31.9	. . .
1959	29.3	29.1	29.7	21.9	30.2	33.3	23.3	33.1	. . .	30.8	. . .	31.1	. . .
1960	29.8	29.6	30.0	22.4	30.6	33.6	24.1	33.4	. . .	30.8	. . .	30.4	. . .
1961	30.1	29.9	30.4	22.5	31.0	33.8	24.5	33.4	. . .	30.6	. . .	30.2	. . .
1962	30.4	30.2	30.6	22.6	31.4	34.1	25.0	33.5	. . .	30.6	. . .	30.5	. . .
1963	30.8	30.6	31.1	22.6	31.8	34.4	25.5	33.4	. . .	30.7	. . .	29.9	. . .
1964	31.2	31.0	31.5	22.5	32.3	34.8	26.0	33.5	. . .	30.8	. . .	29.6	. . .
1947													
January	21.6	21.5	22.8	. . .	. . .	. . .	. . .	. . .	. . .	. . .	. . .	. . .	. . .
February	21.7	21.6	23.1	. . .	. . .	. . .	. . .	. . .	. . .	. . .	. . .	. . .	. . .
March	22.1	22.0	23.8	. . .	. . .	. . .	. . .	. . .	. . .	. . .	. . .	. . .	. . .
April	22.1	22.0	23.5	. . .	. . .	. . .	. . .	26.0	. . .	23.1	. . .	30.7	. . .
May	22.1	22.0	23.4	. . .	. . .	. . .	. . .	26.1	. . .	23.0	. . .	30.4	. . .
June	22.2	22.1	23.5	. . .	. . .	. . .	. . .	26.2	. . .	23.2	. . .	30.6	. . .
July	22.4	22.2	23.8	. . .	. . .	. . .	. . .	26.2	. . .	23.2	. . .	31.0	. . .
August	22.5	22.4	24.1	. . .	. . .	. . .	. . .	26.3	. . .	23.3	. . .	31.6	. . .
September	23.0	22.8	24.8	. . .	. . .	. . .	. . .	26.7	. . .	23.7	. . .	32.4	. . .
October	23.0	22.9	24.9	. . .	. . .	. . .	. . .	26.8	. . .	24.0	. . .	33.7	. . .
November	23.2	23.1	25.2	. . .	. . .	. . .	. . .	27.1	. . .	24.3	. . .	33.9	. . .
December	23.5	23.4	25.7	. . .	. . .	. . .	. . .	27.7	. . .	24.5	. . .	35.3	. . .
1948													
January	23.8	23.7	26.1	. . .	. . .	. . .	. . .	28.1	. . .	25.0	. . .	36.2	. . .
February	23.8	23.7	25.9	. . .	. . .	. . .	. . .	27.9	. . .	24.7	. . .	34.4	. . .
March	23.6	23.5	25.3	. . .	. . .	. . .	. . .	28.0	. . .	24.8	. . .	33.5	. . .
April	24.0	23.8	26.0	. . .	. . .	. . .	. . .	28.1	. . .	25.1	. . .	34.2	. . .
May	24.1	24.0	26.3	. . .	. . .	. . .	. . .	28.4	. . .	25.1	. . .	35.3	. . .
June	24.3	24.2	26.5	. . .	. . .	. . .	. . .	28.6	. . .	25.4	. . .	36.2	. . .
July	24.5	24.4	26.7	. . .	. . .	. . .	. . .	28.8	. . .	25.4	. . .	36.1	. . .
August	24.6	24.4	26.5	. . .	. . .	. . .	. . .	28.9	. . .	25.5	. . .	35.5	. . .
September	24.5	24.4	26.3	. . .	. . .	. . .	. . .	28.8	. . .	25.5	. . .	34.9	. . .
October	24.4	24.3	26.1	. . .	. . .	. . .	. . .	28.7	. . .	25.5	. . .	33.8	. . .
November	24.3	24.2	25.7	. . .	. . .	. . .	. . .	28.5	. . .	25.4	. . .	33.5	. . .
December	24.2	24.1	25.5	. . .	. . .	. . .	. . .	28.5	. . .	25.2	. . .	33.0	. . .
1949													
January	24.2	24.0	25.4	. . .	. . .	. . .	. . .	28.3	. . .	25.2	. . .	32.0	. . .
February	24.1	23.9	25.3	. . .	. . .	. . .	. . .	28.0	. . .	24.8	. . .	30.9	. . .
March	24.0	23.9	25.3	. . .	. . .	. . .	. . .	28.0	. . .	24.7	. . .	30.8	. . .
April	24.1	23.9	25.3	. . .	. . .	. . .	. . .	27.9	. . .	24.5	. . .	30.2	. . .
May	24.0	23.9	25.2	. . .	. . .	. . .	. . .	27.8	. . .	24.3	. . .	30.1	. . .
June	24.1	23.9	25.3	. . .	. . .	. . .	. . .	27.7	. . .	24.1	. . .	29.7	. . .
July	23.8	23.7	24.8	. . .	. . .	. . .	. . .	27.5	. . .	24.1	. . .	29.2	. . .
August	23.8	23.7	24.8	. . .	. . .	. . .	. . .	27.4	. . .	23.9	. . .	29.2	. . .
September	23.9	23.8	25.0	. . .	. . .	. . .	. . .	27.4	. . .	23.9	. . .	29.5	. . .
October	23.8	23.7	24.8	. . .	. . .	. . .	. . .	27.3	. . .	23.8	. . .	29.5	. . .
November	23.8	23.7	24.8	. . .	. . .	. . .	. . .	27.2	. . .	23.7	. . .	29.6	. . .
December	23.8	23.6	24.5	. . .	. . .	. . .	. . .	27.2	. . .	23.8	. . .	29.6	. . .
1950													
January	23.6	23.5	24.3	. . .	. . .	. . .	. . .	27.2	. . .	23.8	. . .	29.6	. . .
February	23.7	23.6	24.7	. . .	. . .	. . .	. . .	27.2	. . .	23.9	. . .	30.5	. . .
March	23.8	23.6	24.6	. . .	. . .	. . .	. . .	27.3	. . .	24.1	. . .	30.3	. . .
April	23.8	23.7	24.6	. . .	. . .	. . .	. . .	27.3	. . .	24.2	. . .	30.5	. . .
May	23.9	23.8	24.8	. . .	. . .	. . .	. . .	27.5	. . .	24.6	. . .	31.6	. . .
June	24.0	23.9	25.1	. . .	. . .	. . .	. . .	27.6	. . .	24.7	. . .	32.1	. . .
July	24.2	24.1	25.6	. . .	. . .	. . .	. . .	28.0	. . .	25.3	. . .	33.3	. . .
August	24.3	24.2	25.8	. . .	. . .	. . .	. . .	28.6	. . .	25.6	. . .	34.0	. . .
September	24.5	24.3	25.8	. . .	. . .	. . .	. . .	28.9	. . .	26.2	. . .	34.5	. . .
October	24.6	24.5	26.0	. . .	. . .	. . .	. . .	29.0	. . .	26.7	. . .	34.5	. . .
November	24.7	24.6	26.1	. . .	. . .	. . .	. . .	29.4	. . .	26.9	. . .	35.4	. . .
December	25.1	25.0	26.9	. . .	. . .	. . .	. . .	30.0	. . .	27.8	. . .	36.7	. . .

. . . = Not available.

Table 8-1B. Summary Consumer and Producer Price Indexes: Historical Data, 1947 to Date—*Continued*

(Seasonally adjusted.)

Year and month	Consumer Price Index, 1982–1984 = 100							Producer Price Index for goods, 1982 = 100					
	Urban wage earners and clerical workers (CPI-W), all items	All urban consumers (CPI-U)						Finished goods		Processed goods for intermediate demand		Unprocessed goods for intermediate demand	
		All items	Food	Energy	All items less food and energy	Commodities	Services	Total	Less food and energy	Total	Processed materials less foods and energy	Total	Unprocessed nonfood materials less energy
1951													
January	25.5	25.4	27.6	. . .	. . .	. . .	. . .	30.5	. . .	28.5	. . .	38.2	. . .
February	26.0	25.8	28.5	. . .	. . .	. . .	. . .	30.8	. . .	28.7	. . .	39.6	. . .
March	26.0	25.9	28.4	. . .	. . .	. . .	. . .	30.9	. . .	28.8	. . .	39.1	. . .
April	26.1	25.9	28.2	. . .	. . .	. . .	. . .	30.9	. . .	28.8	. . .	39.1	. . .
May	26.1	26.0	28.3	. . .	. . .	. . .	. . .	31.1	. . .	28.8	. . .	38.4	. . .
June	26.1	25.9	28.0	. . .	. . .	. . .	. . .	31.0	. . .	28.7	. . .	38.1	. . .
July	26.1	25.9	27.9	. . .	. . .	. . .	. . .	30.8	. . .	28.4	. . .	36.8	. . .
August	26.0	25.9	27.8	. . .	. . .	. . .	. . .	30.7	. . .	28.0	. . .	36.2	. . .
September	26.2	26.0	27.9	. . .	. . .	. . .	. . .	30.6	. . .	28.0	. . .	35.9	. . .
October	26.3	26.2	28.4	. . .	. . .	. . .	. . .	30.8	. . .	27.9	. . .	36.7	. . .
November	26.5	26.3	28.6	. . .	. . .	. . .	. . .	30.9	. . .	27.9	. . .	36.4	. . .
December	26.6	26.5	28.9	. . .	. . .	. . .	. . .	30.9	. . .	27.8	. . .	36.6	. . .
1952													
January	26.6	26.5	28.9	. . .	. . .	. . .	. . .	30.8	. . .	27.8	. . .	35.8	. . .
February	26.6	26.4	28.6	. . .	. . .	. . .	. . .	30.7	. . .	27.7	. . .	35.5	. . .
March	26.5	26.4	28.5	. . .	. . .	. . .	. . .	30.9	. . .	27.6	. . .	35.0	. . .
April	26.6	26.5	28.7	. . .	. . .	. . .	. . .	30.7	. . .	27.5	. . .	34.9	. . .
May	26.6	26.5	28.7	. . .	. . .	. . .	. . .	30.7	. . .	27.5	. . .	34.8	. . .
June	26.7	26.5	28.6	. . .	. . .	. . .	. . .	30.7	. . .	27.6	. . .	34.6	. . .
July	26.8	26.7	28.9	. . .	. . .	. . .	. . .	30.8	. . .	27.5	. . .	34.6	. . .
August	26.8	26.7	28.9	. . .	. . .	. . .	. . .	30.7	. . .	27.6	. . .	34.7	. . .
September	26.8	26.6	28.7	. . .	. . .	. . .	. . .	30.6	. . .	27.6	. . .	33.8	. . .
October	26.8	26.7	28.8	. . .	. . .	. . .	. . .	30.5	. . .	27.5	. . .	33.8	. . .
November	26.8	26.7	28.8	. . .	. . .	. . .	. . .	30.4	. . .	27.4	. . .	33.7	. . .
December	26.9	26.7	28.6	. . .	. . .	. . .	. . .	30.2	. . .	27.3	. . .	32.9	. . .
1953													
January	26.8	26.6	28.4	. . .	. . .	. . .	. . .	30.3	. . .	27.4	. . .	32.5	. . .
February	26.7	26.6	28.3	. . .	. . .	. . .	. . .	30.2	. . .	27.4	. . .	32.4	. . .
March	26.8	26.6	28.3	. . .	. . .	. . .	. . .	30.3	. . .	27.5	. . .	32.4	. . .
April	26.8	26.7	28.1	. . .	. . .	. . .	. . .	30.2	. . .	27.5	. . .	31.6	. . .
May	26.9	26.7	28.2	. . .	. . .	. . .	. . .	30.3	. . .	27.6	. . .	31.8	. . .
June	26.9	26.8	28.4	. . .	. . .	. . .	. . .	30.4	. . .	27.7	. . .	31.4	. . .
July	26.9	26.8	28.2	. . .	. . .	. . .	. . .	30.5	. . .	28.0	. . .	32.3	. . .
August	27.0	26.9	28.3	. . .	. . .	. . .	. . .	30.4	. . .	27.9	. . .	31.8	. . .
September	27.0	26.9	28.4	. . .	. . .	. . .	. . .	30.4	. . .	27.9	. . .	32.0	. . .
October	27.1	27.0	28.4	. . .	. . .	. . .	. . .	30.4	. . .	27.9	. . .	31.4	. . .
November	27.0	26.9	28.1	. . .	. . .	. . .	. . .	30.3	. . .	27.8	. . .	31.2	. . .
December	27.0	26.9	28.3	. . .	. . .	. . .	. . .	30.4	. . .	27.8	. . .	31.7	. . .
1954													
January	27.1	26.9	28.5	. . .	. . .	. . .	. . .	30.5	. . .	27.9	. . .	32.0	. . .
February	27.1	27.0	28.5	. . .	. . .	. . .	. . .	30.4	. . .	27.9	. . .	32.0	. . .
March	27.1	26.9	28.4	. . .	. . .	. . .	. . .	30.4	. . .	27.9	. . .	32.1	. . .
April	27.0	26.9	28.4	. . .	. . .	. . .	. . .	30.6	. . .	27.9	. . .	32.2	. . .
May	27.1	26.9	28.4	. . .	. . .	. . .	. . .	30.6	. . .	27.9	. . .	32.1	. . .
June	27.1	26.9	28.4	. . .	. . .	. . .	. . .	30.4	. . .	27.8	. . .	31.5	. . .
July	27.0	26.9	28.4	. . .	. . .	. . .	. . .	30.5	. . .	27.9	. . .	31.4	. . .
August	27.0	26.9	28.3	. . .	. . .	. . .	. . .	30.4	. . .	27.9	. . .	31.3	. . .
September	27.0	26.8	28.0	. . .	. . .	. . .	. . .	30.3	. . .	27.8	. . .	31.5	. . .
October	26.9	26.7	27.9	. . .	. . .	. . .	. . .	30.2	. . .	27.8	. . .	31.2	. . .
November	26.9	26.8	27.9	. . .	. . .	. . .	. . .	30.3	. . .	27.9	. . .	31.4	. . .
December	26.9	26.8	27.8	. . .	. . .	. . .	. . .	30.3	. . .	27.9	. . .	30.8	. . .
1955													
January	26.9	26.8	27.8	. . .	. . .	. . .	. . .	30.4	. . .	27.9	. . .	31.1	. . .
February	27.0	26.8	28.0	. . .	. . .	. . .	. . .	30.5	. . .	28.0	. . .	31.0	. . .
March	26.9	26.8	28.0	. . .	. . .	. . .	. . .	30.3	. . .	28.0	. . .	30.7	. . .
April	26.9	26.8	28.0	. . .	. . .	. . .	. . .	30.4	. . .	28.1	. . .	31.0	. . .
May	26.9	26.8	27.9	. . .	. . .	. . .	. . .	30.4	. . .	28.1	. . .	30.2	. . .
June	26.9	26.7	27.7	. . .	. . .	. . .	. . .	30.5	. . .	28.2	. . .	30.7	. . .
July	26.9	26.8	27.7	. . .	. . .	. . .	. . .	30.4	. . .	28.4	. . .	30.4	. . .
August	26.9	26.7	27.6	. . .	. . .	. . .	. . .	30.4	. . .	28.5	. . .	30.1	. . .
September	27.0	26.9	27.8	. . .	. . .	. . .	. . .	30.5	. . .	28.8	. . .	30.4	. . .
October	27.0	26.8	27.7	. . .	. . .	. . .	. . .	30.6	. . .	28.9	. . .	30.4	. . .
November	27.0	26.9	27.6	. . .	. . .	. . .	. . .	30.6	. . .	28.9	. . .	29.4	. . .
December	27.0	26.9	27.6	. . .	. . .	. . .	. . .	30.7	. . .	29.0	. . .	29.5	. . .
1956													
January	27.0	26.8	27.5	. . .	. . .	31.2	20.7	30.7	. . .	29.1	. . .	29.4	. . .
February	27.0	26.9	27.5	. . .	. . .	31.1	20.7	30.8	. . .	29.2	. . .	29.9	. . .
March	27.1	26.9	27.5	. . .	. . .	31.2	20.7	30.9	. . .	29.4	. . .	29.8	. . .
April	27.1	26.9	27.6	. . .	. . .	31.3	20.8	31.0	. . .	29.5	. . .	30.3	. . .
May	27.2	27.0	27.8	. . .	. . .	31.4	20.8	31.2	. . .	29.6	. . .	30.7	. . .
June	27.3	27.2	28.1	. . .	. . .	31.5	20.9	31.4	. . .	29.6	. . .	30.5	. . .
July	27.4	27.3	28.4	. . .	. . .	31.8	20.9	31.3	. . .	29.4	. . .	30.5	. . .
August	27.5	27.3	28.2	. . .	. . .	31.7	21.0	31.4	. . .	29.7	. . .	31.0	. . .
September	27.5	27.4	28.2	. . .	. . .	31.8	21.1	31.6	. . .	29.8	. . .	31.0	. . .
October	27.7	27.5	28.3	. . .	. . .	32.0	21.1	31.8	. . .	30.0	. . .	31.0	. . .
November	27.7	27.5	28.4	. . .	. . .	32.0	21.2	31.9	. . .	30.0	. . .	31.1	. . .
December	27.8	27.6	28.5	. . .	. . .	32.1	21.3	31.9	. . .	30.1	. . .	31.7	. . .

. . . = Not available.

Table 8-1B. Summary Consumer and Producer Price Indexes: Historical Data, 1947 to Date—*Continued*

(Seasonally adjusted.)

Year and month	Consumer Price Index, 1982–1984 = 100							Producer Price Index for goods, 1982 = 100					
	Urban wage earners and clerical workers (CPI-W), all items	All urban consumers (CPI-U)						Finished goods		Processed goods for intermediate demand		Unprocessed goods for intermediate demand	
		All items	Food	Energy	All items less food and energy	Commod-ities	Services	Total	Less food and energy	Total	Processed materials less foods and energy	Total	Unproces-sed nonfood materials less energy
1957													
January	27.8	27.7	28.4	21.3	28.5	32.1	21.4	32.1	...	30.3	...	31.3	...
February	28.0	27.8	28.7	21.4	28.6	32.3	21.4	32.2	...	30.3	...	31.0	...
March	28.0	27.9	28.6	21.5	28.7	32.3	21.6	32.1	...	30.3	...	30.9	...
April	28.1	27.9	28.6	21.6	28.8	32.4	21.6	32.3	...	30.2	...	30.8	...
May	28.2	28.0	28.7	21.6	28.8	32.4	21.7	32.3	...	30.2	...	30.7	...
June	28.3	28.1	28.9	21.6	28.9	32.5	21.8	32.5	...	30.3	...	31.5	...
July	28.4	28.2	29.1	21.5	29.0	32.6	21.8	32.6	...	30.3	...	32.0	...
August	28.4	28.3	29.4	21.4	29.0	32.8	21.9	32.6	...	30.4	...	32.0	...
September	28.5	28.3	29.2	21.4	29.1	32.8	22.0	32.6	...	30.4	...	31.2	...
October	28.5	28.3	29.2	21.4	29.2	32.7	22.1	32.7	...	30.3	...	31.0	...
November	28.6	28.4	29.2	21.5	29.3	32.8	22.2	32.9	...	30.4	...	31.1	...
December	28.6	28.5	29.2	21.5	29.3	32.9	22.2	33.0	...	30.4	...	31.5	...
1958													
January	28.8	28.6	29.8	21.6	29.3	33.1	22.3	33.2	...	30.4	...	31.4	...
February	28.9	28.7	29.9	21.3	29.4	33.2	22.4	33.2	...	30.3	...	31.9	...
March	29.0	28.9	30.5	21.4	29.5	33.4	22.4	33.4	...	30.3	...	32.3	...
April	29.1	28.9	30.6	21.4	29.5	33.5	22.5	33.2	...	30.2	...	31.8	...
May	29.1	28.9	30.5	21.5	29.5	33.5	22.6	33.2	...	30.3	...	32.4	...
June	29.1	28.9	30.3	21.5	29.6	33.4	22.6	33.3	...	30.3	...	32.0	...
July	29.1	28.9	30.2	21.6	29.6	33.3	22.7	33.2	...	30.3	...	32.1	...
August	29.1	28.9	30.1	21.7	29.6	33.3	22.7	33.2	...	30.4	...	31.9	...
September	29.1	28.9	30.0	21.7	29.7	33.3	22.8	33.2	...	30.4	...	31.6	...
October	29.1	28.9	30.0	21.7	29.7	33.2	22.8	33.2	...	30.4	...	31.9	...
November	29.1	29.0	30.0	21.4	29.8	33.3	22.8	33.2	...	30.5	...	32.1	...
December	29.1	29.0	29.9	21.4	29.9	33.3	22.8	33.1	...	30.6	...	31.6	...
1959													
January	29.2	29.0	30.0	21.4	29.9	33.3	22.9	33.1	...	30.6	...	31.6	...
February	29.2	29.0	29.8	21.6	29.9	33.3	23.0	33.2	...	30.7	...	31.4	...
March	29.1	29.0	29.7	21.7	30.0	33.2	23.0	33.2	...	30.7	...	31.5	...
April	29.1	29.0	29.5	21.8	30.0	33.2	23.1	33.2	...	30.7	...	31.7	...
May	29.2	29.0	29.5	21.8	30.1	33.3	23.2	33.3	...	30.9	...	31.5	...
June	29.3	29.1	29.7	21.9	30.2	33.3	23.2	33.2	...	30.9	...	31.3	...
July	29.3	29.2	29.6	21.8	30.2	33.3	23.3	33.1	...	30.8	...	31.0	...
August	29.3	29.2	29.6	21.9	30.2	33.3	23.4	33.0	...	30.8	...	30.7	...
September	29.4	29.3	29.7	21.9	30.3	33.5	23.5	33.4	...	30.8	...	30.9	...
October	29.5	29.4	29.7	22.2	30.4	33.5	23.6	33.1	...	30.8	...	30.7	...
November	29.5	29.4	29.7	22.2	30.4	33.5	23.6	33.0	...	30.9	...	30.5	...
December	29.6	29.4	29.6	22.3	30.5	33.5	23.7	33.0	...	30.9	...	30.3	...
1960													
January	29.5	29.4	29.6	22.3	30.5	33.5	23.7	33.1	...	30.8	...	30.4	...
February	29.6	29.4	29.5	22.2	30.6	33.4	23.8	33.1	...	30.9	...	30.4	...
March	29.6	29.4	29.6	22.3	30.6	33.5	23.9	33.4	...	30.9	...	30.7	...
April	29.7	29.5	30.0	22.4	30.6	33.6	23.9	33.4	...	30.8	...	30.8	...
May	29.7	29.6	30.0	22.3	30.6	33.6	24.0	33.4	...	30.8	...	30.8	...
June	29.8	29.6	30.0	22.4	30.7	33.6	24.0	33.4	...	30.9	...	30.4	...
July	29.7	29.6	29.9	22.5	30.6	33.5	24.1	33.5	...	30.8	...	30.4	...
August	29.8	29.6	30.0	22.5	30.6	33.6	24.1	33.4	...	30.8	...	29.8	...
September	29.8	29.6	30.1	22.6	30.6	33.6	24.2	33.4	...	30.8	...	30.0	...
October	29.9	29.8	30.3	22.5	30.8	33.7	24.2	33.7	...	30.8	...	30.2	...
November	30.0	29.8	30.5	22.7	30.8	33.8	24.3	33.7	...	30.7	...	30.2	...
December	30.0	29.8	30.5	22.6	30.7	33.9	24.3	33.6	...	30.7	...	30.3	...
1961													
January	30.0	29.8	30.5	22.7	30.8	33.8	24.4	33.6	...	30.6	...	30.4	...
February	30.0	29.8	30.5	22.6	30.8	33.8	24.4	33.7	...	30.7	...	30.5	...
March	30.0	29.8	30.5	22.6	30.9	33.8	24.4	33.6	...	30.8	...	30.3	...
April	30.0	29.8	30.4	22.2	30.9	33.8	24.5	33.4	...	30.7	...	30.2	...
May	30.0	29.8	30.3	22.4	30.9	33.8	24.5	33.3	...	30.6	...	29.9	...
June	30.0	29.8	30.2	22.5	31.0	33.8	24.5	33.3	...	30.5	...	29.5	...
July	30.1	29.9	30.3	22.5	31.0	33.9	24.5	33.3	...	30.5	...	29.7	...
August	30.1	29.9	30.3	22.5	31.1	33.9	24.6	33.4	...	30.5	...	30.5	...
September	30.2	30.0	30.3	22.6	31.1	33.9	24.6	33.3	...	30.5	...	30.3	...
October	30.2	30.0	30.3	22.4	31.1	33.9	24.7	33.3	...	30.4	...	30.3	...
November	30.2	30.0	30.3	22.5	31.2	33.8	24.7	33.4	...	30.5	...	30.2	...
December	30.2	30.0	30.3	22.4	31.2	33.9	24.8	33.4	...	30.6	...	30.6	...
1962													
January	30.2	30.0	30.4	22.4	31.2	33.9	24.8	33.5	...	30.5	...	30.6	...
February	30.3	30.1	30.5	22.6	31.2	34.0	24.8	33.6	...	30.6	...	30.5	...
March	30.4	30.2	30.6	22.4	31.3	34.0	24.9	33.5	...	30.6	...	30.5	...
April	30.4	30.2	30.7	22.7	31.3	34.1	24.9	33.5	...	30.6	...	30.1	...
May	30.4	30.2	30.6	22.7	31.4	34.1	25.0	33.4	...	30.6	...	30.1	...
June	30.4	30.2	30.5	22.5	31.4	34.1	25.0	33.4	...	30.6	...	29.9	...
July	30.4	30.2	30.4	22.3	31.4	34.0	25.1	33.4	...	30.6	...	30.2	...
August	30.5	30.3	30.6	22.4	31.5	34.1	25.1	33.5	...	30.6	...	30.5	...
September	30.6	30.4	30.9	22.8	31.5	34.3	25.1	33.8	...	30.6	...	31.2	...
October	30.6	30.4	30.8	22.7	31.5	34.2	25.1	33.6	...	30.6	...	30.8	...
November	30.6	30.4	30.9	22.7	31.5	34.3	25.2	33.6	...	30.5	...	31.0	...
December	30.6	30.4	30.7	22.8	31.6	34.2	25.2	33.5	...	30.5	...	30.6	...

. . . = Not available.

Table 8-1B. Summary Consumer and Producer Price Indexes: Historical Data, 1947 to Date—*Continued*

(Seasonally adjusted.)

| | Consumer Price Index, 1982–1984 = 100 | | | | | | | Producer Price Index for goods, 1982 = 100 | | | | | |
| Year and month | Urban wage earners and clerical workers (CPI-W), all items | All urban consumers (CPI-U) | | | | | | Finished goods | | Processed goods for intermediate demand | | Unprocessed goods for intermediate demand | |
		All items	Food	Energy	All items less food and energy	Commodities	Services	Total	Less food and energy	Total	Processed materials less foods and energy	Total	Unprocessed nonfood materials less energy
1963													
January	30.6	30.4	31.0	22.8	31.5	34.3	25.3	33.4	. . .	30.5	. . .	30.3	. . .
February	30.7	30.5	31.1	22.7	31.6	34.3	25.3	33.4	. . .	30.5	. . .	30.0	. . .
March	30.7	30.5	31.0	22.7	31.7	34.3	25.3	33.3	. . .	30.5	. . .	29.6	. . .
April	30.7	30.5	30.9	22.6	31.7	34.3	25.4	33.3	. . .	30.5	. . .	29.8	. . .
May	30.7	30.5	30.9	22.6	31.7	34.3	25.4	33.4	. . .	30.7	. . .	29.6	. . .
June	30.8	30.6	31.0	22.5	31.8	34.4	25.5	33.5	. . .	30.7	. . .	29.9	. . .
July	30.9	30.7	31.2	22.7	31.8	34.5	25.5	33.4	. . .	30.7	. . .	30.0	. . .
August	30.9	30.8	31.2	22.6	31.9	34.6	25.6	33.4	. . .	30.7	. . .	29.9	. . .
September	30.9	30.7	31.1	22.5	31.9	34.5	25.6	33.4	. . .	30.7	. . .	29.8	. . .
October	30.9	30.8	31.0	22.7	32.0	34.5	25.6	33.5	. . .	30.8	. . .	29.9	. . .
November	31.0	30.8	31.2	22.6	32.0	34.6	25.7	33.5	. . .	30.8	. . .	30.2	. . .
December	31.1	30.9	31.3	22.6	32.1	34.7	25.8	33.4	. . .	30.8	. . .	29.4	. . .
1964													
January	31.1	30.9	31.4	22.8	32.2	34.7	25.8	33.5	. . .	30.8	. . .	29.8	. . .
February	31.1	30.9	31.4	22.2	32.2	34.7	25.8	33.5	. . .	30.8	. . .	29.4	. . .
March	31.1	30.9	31.4	22.6	32.2	34.7	25.8	33.4	. . .	30.8	. . .	29.5	. . .
April	31.1	31.0	31.4	22.5	32.2	34.7	25.9	33.5	. . .	30.8	. . .	29.5	. . .
May	31.2	31.0	31.4	22.5	32.2	34.7	25.9	33.5	. . .	30.7	. . .	29.4	. . .
June	31.2	31.0	31.4	22.6	32.3	34.7	26.0	33.5	. . .	30.6	. . .	29.0	. . .
July	31.2	31.0	31.5	22.5	32.3	34.7	26.0	33.5	. . .	30.7	. . .	29.2	. . .
August	31.2	31.1	31.4	22.6	32.3	34.7	26.0	33.6	. . .	30.6	. . .	29.4	. . .
September	31.3	31.1	31.6	22.5	32.3	34.8	26.0	33.6	. . .	30.7	. . .	30.1	. . .
October	31.3	31.1	31.6	22.5	32.4	34.8	26.1	33.6	. . .	30.8	. . .	29.8	. . .
November	31.4	31.2	31.7	22.5	32.5	34.9	26.2	33.6	. . .	30.8	. . .	29.9	. . .
December	31.4	31.3	31.7	22.6	32.5	35.0	26.2	33.6	. . .	30.9	. . .	29.8	. . .
1965													
January	31.5	31.3	31.6	22.8	32.6	35.0	26.3	33.6	. . .	30.9	. . .	29.5	. . .
February	31.5	31.3	31.5	22.7	32.6	34.9	26.4	33.7	. . .	30.9	. . .	29.9	. . .
March	31.5	31.3	31.7	22.6	32.6	35.0	26.4	33.7	. . .	31.0	. . .	30.0	. . .
April	31.6	31.4	31.8	22.9	32.7	35.0	26.5	34.0	. . .	31.1	. . .	30.4	. . .
May	31.7	31.5	32.1	23.0	32.7	35.1	26.5	34.1	. . .	31.1	. . .	30.8	. . .
June	31.8	31.6	32.6	23.1	32.7	35.3	26.5	34.2	. . .	31.2	. . .	31.6	. . .
July	31.8	31.6	32.5	23.0	32.7	35.3	26.6	34.1	. . .	31.2	. . .	31.2	. . .
August	31.7	31.6	32.4	23.0	32.7	35.2	26.6	34.2	. . .	31.3	. . .	31.5	. . .
September	31.8	31.6	32.3	23.1	32.8	35.2	26.7	34.3	. . .	31.3	. . .	31.4	. . .
October	31.8	31.7	32.5	23.0	32.8	35.3	26.8	34.4	. . .	31.3	. . .	31.8	. . .
November	31.9	31.8	32.6	23.1	32.9	35.4	26.9	34.5	. . .	31.4	. . .	32.1	. . .
December	32.0	31.9	32.8	23.1	33.0	35.5	26.9	34.7	. . .	31.4	. . .	32.7	. . .
1966													
January	32.1	31.9	33.0	23.1	33.0	35.6	27.0	34.7	. . .	31.4	. . .	33.1	. . .
February	32.3	32.1	33.5	23.2	33.1	35.8	27.0	35.0	. . .	31.6	. . .	33.7	. . .
March	32.4	32.2	33.8	23.2	33.1	35.9	27.1	35.0	. . .	31.7	. . .	33.5	. . .
April	32.5	32.3	33.8	23.2	33.3	36.0	27.3	35.1	. . .	31.8	. . .	33.3	. . .
May	32.5	32.4	33.7	23.2	33.4	36.0	27.4	35.1	. . .	32.0	. . .	33.0	. . .
June	32.6	32.4	33.7	23.3	33.5	36.0	27.5	34.9	. . .	32.0	. . .	33.0	. . .
July	32.6	32.5	33.5	23.4	33.6	36.1	27.7	35.1	. . .	32.2	. . .	33.4	. . .
August	32.8	32.7	34.0	23.3	33.7	36.2	27.7	35.4	. . .	32.3	. . .	33.5	. . .
September	32.9	32.8	34.1	23.4	33.8	36.4	27.9	35.6	. . .	32.2	. . .	33.4	. . .
October	33.0	32.9	34.2	23.4	34.0	36.4	28.0	35.5	. . .	32.1	. . .	32.9	. . .
November	33.1	32.9	34.1	23.5	34.0	36.4	28.2	35.5	. . .	32.2	. . .	32.3	. . .
December	33.1	32.9	34.0	23.5	34.1	36.4	28.2	35.4	. . .	32.2	. . .	32.1	. . .
1967													
January	33.1	32.9	33.9	23.6	34.2	36.4	28.3	35.4	. . .	32.2	. . .	32.2	. . .
February	33.2	33.0	33.8	23.7	34.2	36.4	28.4	35.3	. . .	32.1	. . .	31.5	. . .
March	33.2	33.0	33.8	23.6	34.3	36.4	28.5	35.3	. . .	32.1	. . .	31.1	. . .
April	33.3	33.1	33.7	23.9	34.4	36.4	28.6	35.3	. . .	32.1	. . .	30.7	. . .
May	33.3	33.1	33.7	23.9	34.5	36.5	28.6	35.4	. . .	32.1	. . .	31.1	. . .
June	33.5	33.3	34.0	23.8	34.6	36.6	28.8	35.7	. . .	32.2	. . .	31.4	. . .
July	33.6	33.4	34.1	23.8	34.7	36.8	28.8	35.7	. . .	32.2	. . .	31.3	. . .
August	33.7	33.5	34.3	23.9	34.9	37.0	28.9	35.8	. . .	32.2	. . .	31.3	. . .
September	33.8	33.6	34.3	24.0	35.0	37.0	29.0	35.8	. . .	32.3	. . .	31.2	. . .
October	33.9	33.7	34.4	23.9	35.1	37.1	29.2	35.9	. . .	32.3	. . .	31.3	. . .
November	34.0	33.9	34.5	24.0	35.2	37.2	29.2	35.9	. . .	32.4	. . .	31.1	. . .
December	34.1	34.0	34.6	23.9	35.4	37.4	29.4	36.0	. . .	32.6	. . .	31.5	. . .
1968													
January	34.3	34.1	34.6	24.0	35.5	37.5	29.5	36.1	. . .	32.6	. . .	31.4	. . .
February	34.4	34.2	34.8	24.1	35.7	37.6	29.6	36.2	. . .	32.7	. . .	31.5	. . .
March	34.5	34.3	34.9	24.1	35.8	37.7	29.8	36.3	. . .	32.8	. . .	31.6	. . .
April	34.6	34.4	35.0	24.0	35.9	37.8	29.9	36.5	. . .	32.8	. . .	31.7	. . .
May	34.7	34.5	35.1	24.1	36.0	37.8	30.0	36.5	. . .	32.8	. . .	31.5	. . .
June	34.9	34.7	35.2	24.2	36.2	38.0	30.2	36.6	. . .	32.9	. . .	31.3	. . .
July	35.0	34.9	35.3	24.2	36.4	38.1	30.4	36.7	. . .	33.0	. . .	31.6	. . .
August	35.2	35.0	35.4	24.3	36.5	38.3	30.6	36.8	. . .	33.0	. . .	31.7	. . .
September	35.3	35.1	35.6	24.3	36.7	38.4	30.7	37.0	. . .	33.1	. . .	31.9	. . .
October	35.5	35.3	35.9	24.3	36.9	38.6	30.9	37.0	. . .	33.2	. . .	32.1	. . .
November	35.6	35.4	35.9	24.4	37.1	38.7	31.0	37.1	. . .	33.2	. . .	32.8	. . .
December	35.8	35.6	36.0	24.3	37.2	38.8	31.2	37.1	. . .	33.4	. . .	32.4	. . .

. . . = Not available.

Table 8-1B. Summary Consumer and Producer Price Indexes: Historical Data, 1947 to Date—*Continued*

(Seasonally adjusted.)

Year and month	Urban wage earners and clerical workers (CPI-W), all items	All items	Food	Energy	All items less food and energy	Commodities	Services	Finished goods Total	Finished goods Less food and energy	Processed goods for intermediate demand Total	Processed materials less foods and energy	Unprocessed goods for intermediate demand Total	Unprocessed nonfood materials less energy
1969													
January	35.9	35.7	36.1	24.4	37.3	38.9	31.4	37.2	...	33.6	...	32.6	...
February	36.0	35.8	36.1	24.4	37.6	39.0	31.5	37.2	...	33.7	...	32.3	...
March	36.3	36.1	36.2	24.7	37.8	39.3	31.8	37.4	...	33.9	...	32.7	...
April	36.5	36.3	36.4	24.9	38.1	39.4	32.0	37.6	...	33.8	...	33.1	...
May	36.6	36.4	36.6	24.8	38.1	39.5	32.2	37.8	...	33.9	...	34.0	...
June	36.8	36.6	37.0	25.0	38.3	39.8	32.3	38.0	...	34.0	...	34.5	...
July	37.0	36.8	37.3	24.9	38.5	39.9	32.5	38.1	...	34.0	...	34.1	...
August	37.1	36.9	37.5	24.9	38.7	40.1	32.7	38.2	...	34.2	...	34.4	...
September	37.3	37.1	37.7	25.0	38.9	40.2	33.0	38.3	...	34.2	...	34.4	...
October	37.5	37.3	37.8	25.0	39.1	40.4	33.1	38.5	...	34.4	...	34.8	...
November	37.7	37.5	38.2	25.0	39.2	40.6	33.3	38.8	...	34.6	...	35.2	...
December	37.9	37.7	38.6	25.1	39.4	40.8	33.5	38.9	...	34.7	...	35.1	...
1970													
January	38.1	37.9	38.7	25.1	39.6	41.0	33.8	39.1	...	35.0	...	35.1	...
February	38.3	38.1	38.9	25.1	39.8	41.2	34.0	39.0	...	35.0	...	35.2	...
March	38.5	38.3	38.9	25.0	40.1	41.2	34.4	39.1	...	34.9	...	35.6	...
April	38.7	38.5	39.0	25.5	40.4	41.4	34.6	39.1	...	35.1	...	35.5	...
May	38.8	38.6	39.2	25.4	40.5	41.5	34.8	39.1	...	35.2	...	35.0	...
June	39.0	38.8	39.2	25.3	40.8	41.6	35.0	39.2	...	35.3	...	35.0	...
July	39.1	38.9	39.2	25.5	40.9	41.7	35.2	39.2	...	35.5	...	35.1	...
August	39.2	39.0	39.2	25.4	41.1	41.8	35.4	39.2	...	35.5	...	34.7	...
September	39.4	39.2	39.4	25.6	41.3	42.0	35.6	39.6	...	35.6	...	35.5	...
October	39.6	39.4	39.5	25.9	41.5	42.2	35.8	39.6	...	35.8	...	35.5	...
November	39.8	39.6	39.5	26.0	41.8	42.3	36.0	39.8	...	35.9	...	35.1	...
December	40.0	39.8	39.5	26.2	42.0	42.5	36.2	39.8	...	35.9	...	34.5	...
1971													
January	40.1	39.9	39.4	26.3	42.1	42.5	36.4	39.9	...	36.0	...	34.8	...
February	40.2	39.9	39.5	26.2	42.2	42.6	36.5	40.1	...	36.1	...	35.9	...
March	40.2	40.0	39.8	26.2	42.2	42.7	36.5	40.2	...	36.3	...	35.4	...
April	40.4	40.1	40.1	26.1	42.4	42.9	36.6	40.3	...	36.3	...	36.0	...
May	40.5	40.3	40.3	26.2	42.6	43.1	36.7	40.5	...	36.5	...	36.0	...
June	40.7	40.5	40.5	26.3	42.8	43.2	37.0	40.6	...	36.7	...	36.2	...
July	40.9	40.6	40.6	26.3	42.9	43.3	37.1	40.4	...	36.9	...	35.9	...
August	41.0	40.7	40.6	26.8	43.0	43.4	37.3	40.7	...	37.2	...	35.8	...
September	41.0	40.8	40.6	26.9	43.0	43.4	37.4	40.7	...	37.2	...	35.7	...
October	41.1	40.9	40.7	27.0	43.1	43.5	37.5	40.7	...	37.1	...	36.4	...
November	41.2	41.0	40.9	26.9	43.2	43.5	37.6	40.8	...	37.2	...	37.0	...
December	41.4	41.1	41.3	27.0	43.3	43.8	37.7	41.1	...	37.4	...	37.2	...
1972													
January	41.5	41.2	41.1	27.0	43.5	43.8	37.9	41.0	...	37.5	...	37.8	...
February	41.6	41.4	41.7	26.8	43.6	44.0	38.0	41.3	...	37.7	...	38.1	...
March	41.7	41.4	41.6	26.9	43.6	44.0	38.1	41.3	...	37.8	...	38.1	...
April	41.7	41.5	41.6	26.9	43.8	44.1	38.2	41.3	...	37.9	...	38.7	...
May	41.8	41.6	41.7	27.0	43.9	44.2	38.3	41.5	...	38.0	...	39.3	...
June	41.9	41.7	41.9	27.0	44.0	44.3	38.4	41.7	...	38.0	...	39.4	...
July	42.1	41.8	42.1	27.1	44.1	44.5	38.5	41.8	...	38.1	...	40.0	...
August	42.2	41.9	42.2	27.3	44.3	44.5	38.6	42.0	...	38.2	...	40.3	...
September	42.3	42.1	42.5	27.6	44.3	44.8	38.7	42.2	...	38.5	...	40.5	...
October	42.5	42.2	42.8	27.7	44.4	44.9	38.8	42.0	...	38.7	...	40.9	...
November	42.6	42.4	43.0	27.9	44.4	45.1	38.9	42.3	...	39.0	...	42.0	...
December	42.8	42.5	43.2	27.8	44.6	45.2	39.0	42.7	...	39.6	...	43.8	...
1973													
January	43.0	42.7	44.0	27.9	44.6	45.5	39.1	43.0	...	39.8	...	45.0	...
February	43.2	43.0	44.6	28.2	44.8	45.9	39.2	43.5	...	40.4	...	47.1	...
March	43.6	43.4	45.8	28.3	45.0	46.4	39.4	44.4	...	41.1	...	49.3	...
April	43.9	43.7	46.5	28.6	45.1	46.8	39.5	44.7	...	41.3	...	50.1	...
May	44.2	43.9	47.1	28.8	45.3	47.2	39.6	45.0	...	42.2	...	52.5	...
June	44.4	44.2	47.6	29.2	45.4	47.5	39.8	45.5	...	43.0	...	55.0	...
July	44.5	44.2	47.7	29.2	45.5	47.5	39.9	45.4	...	42.3	...	52.5	...
August	45.3	45.0	50.5	29.4	45.7	48.7	40.2	47.0	...	43.5	...	64.1	...
September	45.4	45.2	50.4	29.4	46.0	48.7	40.5	46.9	...	43.0	...	60.9	...
October	45.8	45.6	50.7	30.3	46.3	49.0	41.0	46.8	...	43.4	...	58.5	...
November	46.2	45.9	51.4	31.5	46.5	49.5	41.3	47.2	...	43.8	...	59.0	...
December	46.5	46.3	51.9	32.5	46.7	49.9	41.5	47.6	...	44.8	...	59.1	...
1974													
January	47.0	46.8	52.5	34.1	46.9	50.5	41.8	48.8	49.7	45.9	47.5	63.3	86.3
February	47.6	47.3	53.6	35.4	47.2	51.3	42.0	49.7	50.0	46.8	48.1	64.3	86.5
March	48.1	47.8	54.2	36.9	47.6	51.9	42.4	50.2	50.5	48.1	49.5	62.3	88.3
April	48.3	48.1	54.1	37.6	47.9	52.1	42.6	50.7	51.1	49.0	50.9	60.6	89.7
May	48.8	48.6	54.5	38.3	48.5	52.7	43.1	51.3	52.2	50.6	52.5	58.3	83.8
June	49.2	49.0	54.5	38.6	49.0	53.1	43.5	51.3	53.1	51.5	53.7	55.4	82.9
July	49.6	49.3	54.3	38.9	49.5	53.3	44.0	52.7	54.0	53.4	55.2	59.8	84.2
August	50.2	49.9	55.1	39.2	50.2	54.1	44.5	53.7	55.0	55.8	57.0	62.9	85.5
September	50.9	50.6	56.2	39.3	50.7	54.8	45.0	54.3	55.7	55.9	57.6	60.9	82.5
October	51.3	51.0	56.8	39.2	51.2	55.3	45.4	55.3	56.7	57.2	58.2	63.2	80.6
November	51.8	51.5	57.5	39.4	51.6	55.8	45.8	56.4	57.4	57.8	58.8	64.2	77.6
December	52.2	51.9	58.2	39.6	52.0	56.3	46.2	56.4	57.9	57.8	59.1	61.5	71.6

. . . = Not available.

Table 8-1B. Summary Consumer and Producer Price Indexes: Historical Data, 1947 to Date—*Continued*

(Seasonally adjusted.)

Year and month	Urban wage earners and clerical workers (CPI-W), all items	Consumer Price Index, 1982–1984 = 100						Producer Price Index for goods, 1982 = 100					
		All urban consumers (CPI-U)						Finished goods		Processed goods for intermediate demand		Unprocessed goods for intermediate demand	
		All items	Food	Energy	All items less food and energy	Commodities	Services	Total	Less food and energy	Total	Processed materials less foods and energy	Total	Unprocessed nonfood materials less energy
1975													
January	52.6	52.3	58.4	40.0	52.3	56.7	46.5	56.7	58.3	58.0	59.6	59.6	69.8
February	52.9	52.6	58.5	40.3	52.8	56.9	46.9	56.6	58.7	57.8	59.8	57.9	69.2
March	53.1	52.8	58.4	40.6	53.0	57.1	47.0	56.6	59.0	57.4	59.7	57.1	68.2
April	53.3	53.0	58.3	41.0	53.3	57.2	47.3	57.1	59.2	57.5	59.7	59.5	67.7
May	53.4	53.1	58.6	41.3	53.5	57.5	47.5	57.4	59.3	57.3	59.7	61.2	68.8
June	53.8	53.5	59.2	41.7	53.8	57.9	47.8	57.9	59.5	57.3	59.8	61.5	66.5
July	54.3	54.0	60.3	42.5	54.0	58.6	48.0	58.4	59.8	57.5	59.9	62.4	66.5
August	54.5	54.2	60.3	42.8	54.2	58.7	48.3	58.9	59.9	58.0	60.1	63.0	67.7
September	54.9	54.6	60.7	43.2	54.5	59.0	48.7	59.3	60.2	58.2	60.3	64.5	71.2
October	55.2	54.9	61.3	43.5	54.8	59.4	49.0	59.8	60.6	58.8	61.0	65.1	71.5
November	55.6	55.3	61.7	43.9	55.2	59.7	49.6	60.0	61.0	59.0	61.4	64.4	71.9
December	55.9	55.6	62.1	44.1	55.5	59.9	49.9	60.1	61.4	59.2	61.8	64.0	73.1
1976													
January	56.2	55.8	61.9	44.5	55.9	60.0	50.5	60.0	61.7	59.4	62.1	63.0	72.4
February	56.2	55.9	61.3	44.4	56.2	59.9	50.8	59.9	61.9	59.6	62.3	62.1	73.8
March	56.3	56.0	60.9	44.1	56.5	59.8	51.1	60.0	62.2	59.8	62.6	61.5	74.5
April	56.5	56.1	60.9	43.9	56.7	59.9	51.3	60.3	62.3	60.0	62.8	63.9	78.1
May	56.7	56.4	61.1	44.1	57.0	60.2	51.4	60.4	62.4	60.3	63.2	63.6	80.6
June	57.0	56.7	61.3	44.4	57.2	60.4	51.7	60.5	62.8	60.8	63.6	65.2	82.8
July	57.3	57.0	61.6	44.8	57.6	60.7	52.1	60.7	63.1	61.1	63.9	64.8	87.3
August	57.6	57.3	61.8	45.2	57.9	61.0	52.4	60.9	63.5	61.3	64.3	63.6	84.1
September	57.9	57.6	62.1	45.7	58.2	61.3	52.8	61.1	63.9	61.9	64.7	63.4	84.4
October	58.2	57.9	62.4	46.1	58.5	61.6	53.1	61.4	64.1	62.0	65.0	63.0	82.2
November	58.4	58.1	62.3	46.8	58.7	61.7	53.4	61.9	64.6	62.4	65.3	63.4	81.8
December	58.7	58.4	62.5	47.5	58.9	62.0	53.7	62.4	64.9	62.8	65.6	64.5	81.1
1977													
January	59.1	58.7	62.7	48.1	59.3	62.3	54.1	62.5	65.1	63.0	65.8	64.3	78.7
February	59.6	59.3	63.9	48.1	59.7	63.0	54.4	63.2	65.4	63.3	65.9	65.7	79.7
March	59.9	59.6	64.2	48.4	60.0	63.2	54.8	63.7	65.7	63.9	66.4	66.6	81.5
April	60.3	60.0	65.0	48.6	60.3	63.7	55.2	64.0	65.9	64.4	66.7	68.3	82.1
May	60.6	60.2	65.3	48.9	60.6	63.9	55.4	64.4	66.1	64.9	67.1	67.6	82.5
June	60.9	60.5	65.7	48.9	61.0	64.2	55.8	64.6	66.5	64.9	67.4	65.5	79.7
July	61.2	60.8	65.9	49.1	61.2	64.4	56.3	64.8	66.8	65.1	67.9	64.7	78.8
August	61.4	61.1	66.2	49.5	61.5	64.6	56.6	65.2	67.3	65.4	68.2	63.9	79.2
September	61.7	61.3	66.4	49.8	61.8	64.8	56.9	65.5	67.8	65.7	68.7	63.7	79.2
October	61.9	61.6	66.6	50.5	62.0	65.0	57.2	65.9	68.2	65.8	68.8	64.0	78.5
November	62.3	62.0	67.1	51.3	62.3	65.5	57.6	66.4	68.8	66.3	69.1	65.4	78.4
December	62.6	62.3	67.4	51.6	62.7	65.7	57.9	66.7	69.0	66.6	69.4	66.4	80.1
1978													
January	63.0	62.7	67.9	51.1	63.1	66.1	58.3	67.0	69.2	66.9	69.8	67.3	80.3
February	63.3	63.0	68.6	50.6	63.4	66.4	58.7	67.5	69.5	67.4	70.3	68.4	80.6
March	63.8	63.4	69.5	51.0	63.8	66.8	59.1	67.8	69.9	67.8	70.6	69.8	80.3
April	64.2	63.9	70.6	51.4	64.3	67.4	59.6	68.6	70.6	68.1	71.1	72.1	82.2
May	64.8	64.5	71.6	51.7	64.7	68.0	60.0	69.1	71.1	68.7	71.6	72.8	84.6
June	65.3	65.0	72.7	51.9	65.2	68.6	60.5	69.7	71.7	69.2	72.2	74.6	87.4
July	65.8	65.5	73.0	52.1	65.6	69.1	61.0	70.3	72.3	69.4	72.5	74.2	89.6
August	66.2	65.9	73.3	52.6	66.1	69.4	61.5	70.4	72.8	69.9	73.2	73.7	90.4
September	66.7	66.5	73.6	53.2	66.7	70.0	62.1	71.1	73.5	70.5	73.7	75.1	92.3
October	67.4	67.1	74.2	54.1	67.2	70.6	62.6	71.4	73.4	71.3	74.5	77.0	94.7
November	67.8	67.5	74.7	54.9	67.6	71.1	63.1	72.0	74.1	71.9	75.2	77.4	96.3
December	68.3	67.9	75.1	55.9	68.0	71.6	63.3	72.8	74.7	72.4	75.6	78.0	96.8
1979													
January	68.8	68.5	76.4	55.8	68.5	72.2	63.8	73.7	75.3	73.1	76.3	80.1	96.4
February	69.6	69.2	77.7	55.9	69.2	72.9	64.4	74.4	75.9	73.7	77.0	82.1	99.6
March	70.3	69.9	78.4	57.4	69.8	73.8	64.9	75.0	76.4	74.6	77.8	83.8	104.2
April	71.1	70.6	79.0	59.5	70.3	74.7	65.5	75.8	77.0	75.7	78.9	84.4	105.1
May	71.9	71.4	79.7	62.0	70.8	75.6	66.2	76.2	77.4	76.6	79.6	84.7	106.7
June	72.7	72.2	80.0	64.7	71.3	76.4	66.8	76.6	78.0	77.5	80.1	85.6	111.6
July	73.5	73.0	80.5	67.3	71.9	77.2	67.6	77.4	78.5	78.7	81.1	86.5	109.4
August	74.2	73.7	80.4	69.7	72.7	77.9	68.5	78.2	78.8	79.8	81.8	85.5	106.4
September	75.0	74.4	80.9	71.9	73.3	78.6	69.2	79.5	79.7	81.1	82.7	87.9	106.5
October	75.7	75.2	81.5	73.5	74.0	79.3	70.1	80.4	80.4	82.4	83.9	88.8	108.9
November	76.5	76.0	82.0	74.8	74.8	80.0	71.1	81.4	81.0	83.2	84.5	90.0	111.3
December	77.3	76.9	82.8	76.8	75.7	80.8	72.0	82.2	81.7	84.0	85.2	91.2	111.3
1980													
January	78.5	78.0	83.3	79.1	76.7	82.0	73.1	83.4	83.3	86.0	87.2	90.9	112.6
February	79.4	79.0	83.4	81.9	77.5	82.8	74.1	84.6	84.2	87.6	88.2	92.6	115.3
March	80.6	80.1	84.1	84.5	78.6	83.9	75.4	85.5	84.7	88.2	88.6	90.8	111.7
April	81.4	80.9	84.7	85.4	79.5	84.4	76.6	86.2	85.5	88.5	88.8	88.3	109.9
May	82.2	81.7	85.2	86.4	80.1	84.9	77.6	86.6	85.7	89.0	89.1	89.5	107.2
June	83.0	82.5	85.7	86.5	81.0	85.3	79.0	87.3	86.6	89.8	89.8	90.1	106.1
July	83.1	82.6	86.6	86.7	80.8	85.9	78.5	88.7	87.7	90.5	90.3	94.6	109.6
August	83.7	83.2	88.0	87.2	81.3	86.9	78.5	89.7	88.4	91.5	91.1	99.0	112.4
September	84.4	83.9	89.1	87.5	82.1	87.8	79.0	90.1	88.8	91.9	91.4	100.4	116.2
October	85.3	84.7	89.8	88.0	83.0	88.5	80.0	90.8	89.6	92.8	92.1	102.2	118.2
November	86.2	85.6	90.8	88.8	83.9	89.2	81.1	91.4	90.1	93.5	92.6	103.5	119.8
December	87.0	86.4	91.3	90.7	84.9	89.7	82.2	91.8	90.4	94.4	93.7	102.7	119.3

Table 8-1B. Summary Consumer and Producer Price Indexes: Historical Data, 1947 to Date—*Continued*

(Seasonally adjusted.)

Year and month	Urban wage earners and clerical workers (CPI-W), all items	Consumer Price Index, 1982–1984 = 100 — All urban consumers (CPI-U) All items	Food	Energy	All items less food and energy	Commodities	Services	Producer Price Index for goods, 1982 = 100 — Finished goods Total	Less food and energy	Processed goods for intermediate demand Total	Processed materials less foods and energy	Unprocessed goods for intermediate demand Total	Unprocessed nonfood materials less energy
1981													
January	87.7	87.2	91.6	92.1	85.4	90.4	83.0	92.8	91.4	95.6	94.7	103.4	113.3
February	88.6	88.0	92.1	95.2	85.9	91.4	83.7	93.6	92.0	96.1	94.9	104.2	106.2
March	89.1	88.6	92.6	97.4	86.4	91.9	84.4	94.7	92.6	97.1	95.6	103.8	108.9
April	89.6	89.1	92.8	97.6	87.0	92.0	85.3	95.7	93.5	98.3	96.6	104.2	111.9
May	90.2	89.7	92.8	97.9	87.8	92.4	86.4	96.0	94.0	98.7	97.1	103.8	113.7
June	90.9	90.5	93.2	97.3	88.6	92.9	87.5	96.5	94.6	99.0	97.7	104.9	115.5
July	92.0	91.5	93.9	97.3	89.8	93.6	88.9	96.7	94.8	99.2	98.4	105.0	116.4
August	92.7	92.2	94.4	97.8	90.7	94.0	89.9	96.8	95.3	99.7	98.9	104.0	115.5
September	93.5	93.1	94.8	98.6	91.8	94.6	91.2	97.2	95.9	99.7	99.3	102.7	112.6
October	93.8	93.4	95.0	99.2	92.1	94.7	91.7	97.6	96.5	99.8	99.5	101.2	110.8
November	94.2	93.8	95.1	100.5	92.5	94.9	92.5	97.9	97.0	99.9	99.7	99.7	107.5
December	94.5	94.1	95.3	101.5	93.0	95.1	93.0	98.3	97.6	100.0	99.8	98.8	106.0
1982													
January	94.8	94.4	95.6	100.6	93.3	95.2	93.5	98.9	98.1	100.4	99.9	99.7	101.2
February	95.1	94.7	96.3	98.0	93.8	95.4	93.9	98.8	98.1	100.3	100.0	100.0	100.7
March	95.0	94.7	96.2	96.6	93.9	95.3	94.0	98.8	98.7	99.9	99.9	99.7	100.0
April	95.3	95.0	96.4	94.2	94.7	95.1	94.9	99.0	99.0	99.7	99.8	100.2	101.1
May	96.1	95.9	97.2	95.7	95.4	96.0	95.7	99.0	99.4	99.7	100.1	101.9	102.2
June	97.3	97.0	98.1	98.4	96.1	97.4	96.5	99.8	99.9	99.8	100.0	101.8	101.0
July	97.8	97.5	98.2	99.3	96.7	97.9	97.0	100.2	100.1	100.0	99.8	100.7	101.4
August	98.1	97.7	98.0	99.8	97.1	97.9	97.6	100.6	100.6	99.9	99.7	99.8	100.0
September	98.1	97.7	98.2	100.3	97.2	97.8	97.6	100.7	100.8	100.0	100.2	99.2	98.9
October	98.5	98.1	98.2	101.7	97.5	98.2	97.9	101.0	101.3	99.9	100.2	98.7	97.7
November	98.4	98.0	98.2	102.5	97.3	98.3	97.7	101.4	101.6	100.1	100.2	99.2	96.3
December	98.1	97.7	98.2	102.8	97.2	98.3	96.9	101.8	102.2	100.1	100.3	98.8	95.9
1983													
January	98.2	97.9	98.1	99.6	97.6	98.3	97.5	101.0	101.8	99.8	100.3	98.8	97.3
February	98.2	98.0	98.2	97.7	98.0	98.1	97.9	101.1	102.2	100.0	100.8	100.0	99.8
March	98.5	98.1	98.8	96.8	98.2	98.2	98.1	101.0	102.5	99.7	100.8	100.5	102.2
April	99.1	98.8	99.2	98.9	98.6	98.9	98.7	101.1	102.4	99.5	100.9	101.2	102.1
May	99.5	99.2	99.5	100.4	98.9	99.5	98.9	101.4	102.6	99.8	101.0	100.9	104.3
June	99.7	99.4	99.6	100.6	99.2	99.8	99.2	101.6	102.8	100.2	101.3	100.5	104.8
July	100.0	99.8	99.6	100.9	99.8	100.2	99.6	101.6	103.1	100.5	101.8	99.5	106.2
August	100.5	100.1	99.7	101.2	100.1	100.5	99.8	101.9	103.5	100.9	102.0	102.2	108.4
September	100.7	100.4	100.0	101.0	100.5	100.7	100.2	102.2	103.5	101.6	102.3	103.3	109.0
October	101.0	100.8	100.3	100.8	101.0	101.0	100.7	102.2	103.6	101.7	102.5	103.2	109.1
November	101.2	101.1	100.3	100.5	101.5	101.1	101.3	102.0	103.8	101.8	102.8	102.3	109.9
December	101.3	101.4	100.6	100.0	101.8	101.2	101.6	102.3	104.1	101.9	103.1	103.5	111.2
1984													
January	101.8	102.1	102.0	100.2	102.5	101.9	102.1	103.0	104.5	102.1	103.4	104.6	111.5
February	102.0	102.6	102.7	101.4	102.8	102.4	102.6	103.4	104.7	102.5	103.8	103.8	113.8
March	102.0	102.9	102.9	101.4	103.2	102.6	103.0	103.8	105.2	103.0	104.4	105.7	114.8
April	102.2	103.3	102.9	101.7	103.7	102.9	103.5	103.9	105.3	103.2	104.5	105.2	115.1
May	102.5	103.5	102.7	101.6	104.1	103.0	103.9	103.8	105.3	103.4	104.6	104.5	115.7
June	102.7	103.7	103.1	100.8	104.5	103.1	104.2	103.8	105.5	103.6	104.8	103.3	114.1
July	103.2	104.1	103.3	100.5	105.0	103.2	104.9	104.0	105.7	103.4	104.9	104.0	112.0
August	104.1	104.4	103.9	100.1	105.4	103.4	105.4	103.8	105.9	103.2	105.1	103.3	109.6
September	104.5	104.7	103.8	100.6	105.8	103.6	105.9	103.8	106.2	103.1	105.0	102.8	110.5
October	104.7	105.1	104.0	101.1	106.2	103.9	106.3	103.6	105.9	103.2	105.1	101.5	108.5
November	104.8	105.3	104.1	100.8	106.4	103.9	106.7	104.0	106.2	103.2	105.3	101.9	107.7
December	104.9	105.5	104.5	100.1	106.8	103.9	107.1	104.0	106.3	103.2	105.3	101.4	107.3
1985													
January	105.2	105.7	104.7	100.3	107.1	104.1	107.4	104.0	106.9	103.1	105.3	99.9	107.4
February	105.7	106.3	105.2	100.3	107.7	104.7	107.9	104.1	107.3	102.8	105.3	99.4	107.2
March	106.1	106.8	105.5	101.3	108.1	105.1	108.4	104.1	107.6	102.7	105.2	97.6	107.0
April	106.4	107.0	105.4	102.3	108.4	105.4	108.7	104.6	107.6	102.9	105.2	96.7	107.4
May	106.6	107.2	105.2	102.2	108.8	105.2	109.4	104.9	107.8	103.2	105.3	95.8	105.3
June	106.9	107.5	105.5	102.2	109.1	105.3	109.8	104.6	108.2	102.6	105.5	95.2	103.6
July	107.0	107.7	105.5	102.2	109.4	105.3	110.3	104.7	108.4	102.3	105.3	94.9	104.3
August	107.1	107.9	105.6	101.2	109.8	105.2	110.7	104.5	108.5	102.3	105.3	92.9	103.6
September	107.3	108.1	105.8	101.2	110.0	105.4	111.0	103.8	107.9	102.2	105.2	91.8	103.3
October	107.7	108.5	105.8	101.2	110.5	105.6	111.5	104.9	108.9	102.3	105.1	94.1	103.7
November	108.2	109.0	106.5	101.8	111.1	106.1	112.1	105.5	109.1	102.5	105.1	95.7	103.0
December	108.7	109.5	107.3	102.4	111.4	106.6	112.5	106.0	109.1	102.9	105.1	95.5	102.4
1986													
January	109.1	109.9	107.5	102.6	111.9	106.9	113.1	105.5	109.3	102.4	105.0	94.2	103.6
February	108.8	109.7	107.3	99.5	112.2	106.0	113.5	104.1	109.5	101.2	104.9	90.5	103.5
March	108.1	109.1	107.5	92.6	112.5	104.5	114.1	102.8	109.6	99.9	105.0	88.2	103.8
April	107.7	108.7	107.7	87.2	112.9	103.3	114.6	102.3	110.1	98.9	104.7	85.6	103.9
May	107.8	109.0	108.2	87.2	113.1	103.5	114.8	102.8	110.2	98.7	104.6	86.5	104.1
June	108.3	109.4	108.3	88.8	113.4	103.8	115.5	103.1	110.5	98.6	104.7	86.2	104.7
July	108.3	109.5	109.1	85.6	113.8	103.7	115.7	102.3	110.7	98.0	104.8	86.4	105.3
August	108.4	109.6	110.1	83.6	114.2	103.6	116.1	102.7	110.8	98.0	104.9	86.7	99.7
September	108.8	110.0	110.2	84.4	114.6	104.0	116.5	102.9	110.7	98.5	105.1	86.6	100.3
October	108.9	110.2	110.5	82.8	115.0	104.0	116.9	103.5	111.8	98.3	105.1	87.4	102.0
November	109.2	110.4	111.1	82.1	115.3	104.2	117.2	103.4	112.0	98.3	105.2	87.6	102.8
December	109.5	110.8	111.4	82.5	115.6	104.5	117.5	103.6	112.1	98.5	105.3	86.9	104.1

Table 8-1B. Summary Consumer and Producer Price Indexes: Historical Data, 1947 to Date—*Continued*

(Seasonally adjusted.)

| Year and month | Urban wage earners and clerical workers (CPI-W), all items | Consumer Price Index, 1982–1984 = 100 — All urban consumers (CPI-U) | | | | | | Producer Price Index for goods, 1982 = 100 — Finished goods | | Processed goods for intermediate demand | | Unprocessed goods for intermediate demand | |
		All items	Food	Energy	All items less food and energy	Commod-ities	Services	Total	Less food and energy	Total	Processed materials less foods and energy	Total	Unproces-sed nonfood materials less energy
1987													
January	110.2	111.4	111.8	85.4	115.9	105.5	117.9	104.1	112.5	99.0	105.6	89.3	105.4
February	110.7	111.8	112.2	87.4	116.2	106.1	118.3	104.4	112.3	99.8	105.9	90.2	106.2
March	111.1	112.2	112.4	87.6	116.6	106.5	118.6	104.5	112.4	99.9	106.2	90.5	106.5
April	111.6	112.7	112.6	87.6	117.3	106.9	119.2	105.1	112.9	100.3	106.5	92.5	107.5
May	111.9	113.0	113.2	87.1	117.7	107.2	119.6	105.2	113.0	100.8	107.0	93.8	110.0
June	112.4	113.5	113.9	88.5	117.9	107.7	120.0	105.5	113.1	101.4	107.5	94.5	113.2
July	112.7	113.8	113.7	89.2	118.3	108.0	120.3	105.7	113.3	101.9	107.9	95.6	115.9
August	113.2	114.3	113.9	90.5	118.7	108.5	120.9	105.9	113.6	102.4	108.3	96.5	119.1
September	113.6	114.7	114.3	90.3	119.2	108.8	121.4	106.2	113.9	102.6	108.9	96.0	122.8
October	113.9	115.0	114.5	89.6	119.8	109.0	121.8	106.0	114.0	103.1	109.6	95.8	126.6
November	114.2	115.4	114.5	90.0	120.1	109.3	122.2	106.0	114.2	103.5	110.1	95.1	127.5
December	114.4	115.6	115.1	89.5	120.4	109.3	122.6	105.8	114.3	103.8	110.7	94.9	127.9
1988													
January	114.7	116.0	115.6	88.8	120.9	109.5	123.0	106.4	115.0	104.1	111.8	94.2	129.4
February	114.9	116.2	115.6	88.7	121.2	109.5	123.5	106.3	115.3	104.4	112.2	95.2	131.7
March	115.2	116.5	115.8	88.4	121.7	109.8	123.9	106.6	115.6	104.8	112.8	94.1	133.0
April	115.8	117.2	116.4	88.8	122.3	110.5	124.4	107.0	115.9	105.5	113.6	95.4	132.1
May	116.2	117.5	116.9	88.5	122.7	110.7	124.8	107.2	116.2	106.2	114.3	95.8	130.7
June	116.6	118.0	117.6	88.9	123.2	111.2	125.4	107.5	116.6	107.4	114.9	97.0	131.1
July	117.3	118.5	118.8	89.4	123.6	111.9	125.8	108.4	117.2	108.3	115.8	96.7	133.2
August	117.7	119.0	119.4	90.1	124.0	112.2	126.4	108.8	117.7	108.5	116.3	97.0	134.3
September	118.2	119.5	120.1	89.8	124.7	112.8	126.9	109.0	118.1	108.7	116.8	97.0	133.3
October	118.6	119.9	120.3	89.8	125.2	113.0	127.5	109.2	118.4	108.6	117.3	96.6	133.6
November	118.9	120.3	120.5	89.8	125.6	113.3	127.9	109.6	118.7	108.8	118.0	95.2	136.0
December	119.3	120.7	121.1	89.6	126.0	113.5	128.4	110.0	119.2	109.4	118.6	98.1	137.6
1989													
January	119.9	121.2	121.6	90.3	126.5	114.1	128.9	111.1	119.9	110.8	119.5	102.0	140.6
February	120.3	121.6	122.5	90.8	126.9	114.5	129.4	111.9	120.5	111.3	119.9	101.7	140.3
March	120.9	122.2	123.2	91.8	127.4	115.1	130.0	112.3	120.7	111.9	120.2	102.9	140.6
April	121.9	123.1	123.9	96.6	127.8	116.5	130.5	113.1	120.8	112.5	120.5	104.1	140.3
May	122.5	123.7	124.7	97.4	128.3	117.1	131.1	114.0	121.6	112.6	120.6	104.5	139.8
June	122.8	124.1	125.1	96.9	128.8	117.2	131.6	114.0	122.2	112.5	120.6	103.2	137.9
July	123.2	124.5	125.6	96.7	129.2	117.3	132.3	113.8	122.1	112.2	120.3	103.5	135.9
August	123.2	124.5	125.9	94.9	129.5	117.0	132.8	113.4	122.7	111.8	120.2	101.2	136.8
September	123.4	124.8	126.3	93.8	129.9	117.2	133.1	114.0	123.1	112.1	120.2	102.5	137.5
October	123.9	125.4	126.8	94.4	130.6	117.8	133.7	114.6	123.5	112.2	120.3	102.7	137.9
November	124.4	125.9	127.4	93.9	131.1	118.1	134.3	114.8	123.9	112.0	120.0	103.5	134.9
December	124.9	126.3	127.8	94.2	131.6	118.4	134.9	115.5	124.2	112.2	119.8	105.1	132.8
1990													
January	126.1	127.5	129.7	98.9	132.1	120.2	135.4	117.7	124.5	113.7	120.0	106.7	132.7
February	126.6	128.0	130.8	98.2	132.7	120.7	136.0	117.6	124.9	112.8	119.9	106.8	131.6
March	127.0	128.6	131.0	97.6	133.5	120.9	136.8	117.5	125.3	112.9	120.2	105.1	133.9
April	127.3	128.9	130.8	97.5	134.0	121.0	137.4	117.4	125.5	113.1	120.5	102.7	137.0
May	127.5	129.1	131.1	96.7	134.4	121.0	137.9	117.5	126.0	113.1	120.6	103.1	138.0
June	128.2	129.9	132.1	97.3	135.1	121.6	138.8	117.6	126.4	112.9	120.4	100.6	137.3
July	128.8	130.5	132.8	97.1	135.8	122.0	139.6	117.9	126.6	112.8	120.6	101.0	138.0
August	129.9	131.6	133.2	101.6	136.6	123.2	140.6	119.2	127.1	114.0	120.8	110.5	140.1
September	130.9	132.5	133.6	106.5	137.1	124.5	141.1	120.7	127.7	115.8	121.5	115.8	139.9
October	131.7	133.4	134.1	110.8	137.6	125.8	141.6	121.9	128.0	117.4	122.1	125.8	138.4
November	132.1	133.7	134.5	111.2	138.0	126.0	142.2	122.6	128.4	117.7	122.3	117.8	135.7
December	132.5	134.2	134.6	111.0	138.6	126.3	142.7	122.0	128.6	116.9	122.1	110.8	133.8
1991													
January	132.9	134.7	135.0	108.5	139.5	126.3	143.7	122.6	129.5	116.9	122.4	113.3	134.2
February	132.9	134.8	135.1	104.5	140.2	125.9	144.4	121.8	129.8	115.9	122.1	104.1	133.7
March	133.0	134.8	135.3	101.9	140.5	125.5	144.7	121.3	130.1	114.7	121.7	100.5	131.8
April	133.3	135.1	136.1	101.2	140.9	126.0	144.9	121.3	130.4	114.2	121.5	100.2	131.7
May	133.8	135.6	136.6	102.1	141.3	126.4	145.4	121.6	130.6	114.1	121.3	100.9	130.4
June	134.1	136.0	137.4	101.1	141.8	126.7	145.9	121.4	130.7	113.9	121.3	99.2	126.1
July	134.3	136.2	136.7	100.7	142.3	126.6	146.5	121.1	131.0	113.6	121.1	99.4	125.4
August	134.6	136.6	136.2	101.1	142.9	126.8	146.9	121.3	131.3	113.8	121.0	99.1	125.8
September	135.0	137.0	136.4	101.5	143.4	127.0	147.6	121.5	131.8	114.0	121.0	98.4	125.7
October	135.2	137.2	136.2	101.6	143.7	127.0	148.0	121.9	132.3	114.0	121.1	100.8	125.4
November	135.8	137.8	136.7	102.4	144.2	127.6	148.5	122.4	132.5	114.1	121.1	100.7	124.4
December	136.2	138.2	137.0	103.1	144.7	127.9	149.2	122.3	132.6	114.0	121.1	98.2	123.4
1992													
January	136.2	138.3	136.6	101.5	145.1	127.6	149.6	122.0	133.0	113.4	121.0	97.2	123.4
February	136.5	138.6	137.1	101.2	145.4	127.8	149.9	122.3	133.1	113.8	121.3	98.6	125.2
March	136.9	139.1	137.6	101.2	145.9	128.2	150.4	122.4	133.4	113.9	121.5	97.1	127.7
April	137.2	139.4	137.5	101.4	146.3	128.3	150.9	122.5	133.8	114.1	121.7	98.1	128.4
May	137.5	139.7	137.2	102.0	146.8	128.6	151.3	122.9	134.3	114.5	121.8	100.3	129.1
June	138.0	140.1	137.6	103.3	147.1	129.1	151.7	123.4	134.1	115.1	122.0	101.6	128.8
July	138.4	140.5	137.4	103.7	147.6	129.3	152.2	123.3	134.3	115.2	122.1	101.6	129.6
August	138.7	140.8	138.4	103.5	147.9	129.6	152.6	123.4	134.3	115.1	122.3	100.7	130.4
September	139.0	141.1	138.9	103.6	148.1	129.9	152.9	123.7	134.6	115.3	122.4	102.8	130.4
October	139.5	141.7	138.9	104.3	148.8	130.2	153.7	124.2	134.9	115.3	122.4	102.8	128.9
November	139.8	142.1	138.7	105.1	149.2	130.3	154.3	124.1	135.1	115.1	122.4	102.5	128.2
December	140.1	142.3	138.8	105.3	149.6	130.5	154.7	124.2	135.2	115.1	122.5	101.3	130.5

Table 8-1B. Summary Consumer and Producer Price Indexes: Historical Data, 1947 to Date—Continued

(Seasonally adjusted.)

Year and month	Urban wage earners and clerical workers (CPI-W), all items	Consumer Price Index, 1982–1984 = 100						Producer Price Index for goods, 1982 = 100					
		All urban consumers (CPI-U)						Finished goods		Processed goods for intermediate demand		Unprocessed goods for intermediate demand	
		All items	Food	Energy	All items less food and energy	Commodities	Services	Total	Less food and energy	Total	Processed materials less foods and energy	Total	Unprocessed nonfood materials less energy
1993													
January	140.5	142.8	139.1	105.0	150.1	130.7	155.3	124.4	135.6	115.4	122.9	101.7	135.0
February	140.8	143.1	139.6	104.3	150.6	131.1	155.6	124.7	135.9	115.9	123.5	101.2	136.8
March	141.0	143.3	139.6	104.9	150.8	131.1	156.0	125.0	136.1	116.3	123.8	101.7	137.0
April	141.4	143.8	140.0	104.9	151.4	131.4	156.7	125.7	136.5	116.6	124.0	103.2	138.4
May	141.8	144.2	141.0	104.3	151.8	131.6	157.3	125.7	136.6	116.3	123.7	105.6	140.3
June	142.0	144.3	140.6	103.9	152.1	131.3	157.8	125.2	136.4	116.3	123.7	103.8	140.3
July	142.1	144.5	140.6	103.4	152.3	131.3	158.1	125.1	136.6	116.3	123.7	101.6	142.1
August	142.4	144.8	141.1	103.4	152.8	131.6	158.6	123.9	134.9	116.2	123.9	100.8	140.4
September	142.5	145.0	141.4	103.0	152.9	131.3	159.0	124.1	134.9	116.3	124.0	101.2	140.7
October	143.2	145.6	142.0	105.3	153.4	132.2	159.4	124.2	135.0	116.4	124.0	103.7	142.6
November	143.4	146.0	142.3	104.4	153.9	132.4	159.9	124.4	135.3	116.5	124.3	103.0	144.1
December	143.7	146.3	142.8	103.7	154.3	132.4	160.5	124.4	135.7	116.2	124.5	101.7	145.3
1994													
January	143.8	146.3	142.9	102.8	154.5	132.3	160.8	124.8	136.3	116.5	124.7	103.8	148.3
February	144.0	146.7	142.7	104.1	154.8	132.4	161.4	125.0	136.3	116.9	124.9	102.1	151.0
March	144.3	147.1	142.7	104.3	155.3	132.5	162.0	125.1	136.4	117.1	125.1	103.8	151.5
April	144.5	147.2	143.0	103.7	155.5	132.6	162.2	125.1	136.6	117.1	125.3	103.8	150.7
May	144.8	147.5	143.3	102.8	155.9	132.9	162.4	125.1	137.0	117.2	125.6	102.2	149.7
June	145.3	147.9	143.8	103.1	156.4	133.5	162.8	125.2	137.2	117.8	126.3	102.7	151.2
July	145.9	148.4	144.6	104.5	156.7	134.1	163.1	125.7	137.3	118.3	126.7	101.7	155.5
August	146.5	149.0	145.1	106.7	157.1	134.7	163.8	126.2	137.6	119.1	127.4	101.6	158.8
September	146.8	149.3	145.3	106.1	157.5	134.8	164.1	125.9	137.7	119.6	128.4	99.7	160.5
October	146.9	149.4	145.3	105.7	157.8	134.8	164.5	125.5	137.4	120.1	129.3	98.6	161.3
November	147.3	149.8	145.6	106.1	158.2	135.0	165.0	126.1	137.6	121.0	130.3	99.8	166.6
December	147.6	150.1	146.8	105.9	158.3	135.4	165.2	126.6	137.9	121.5	131.0	101.1	169.9
1995													
January	148.0	150.5	146.7	105.7	159.0	135.4	166.0	126.9	138.4	122.8	132.6	102.1	174.5
February	148.4	150.9	147.3	105.8	159.4	135.6	166.5	127.2	138.7	123.7	133.7	102.9	176.5
March	148.6	151.2	147.1	105.5	159.9	135.6	167.1	127.4	139.0	124.3	134.3	102.3	177.8
April	149.2	151.8	148.1	105.6	160.4	136.2	167.7	127.7	139.3	125.0	135.2	103.7	180.2
May	149.5	152.1	148.2	105.8	160.7	136.4	168.1	127.8	139.7	125.2	135.5	102.4	179.6
June	149.8	152.4	148.3	106.7	161.1	136.6	168.5	127.8	139.8	125.5	135.7	103.0	179.5
July	149.9	152.6	148.5	105.8	161.4	136.6	168.9	128.0	140.2	125.6	136.1	101.6	176.4
August	150.2	152.9	148.6	105.6	161.8	136.8	169.3	127.9	140.2	125.6	136.1	99.7	173.4
September	150.4	153.1	149.1	104.1	162.2	136.8	169.7	128.1	140.2	125.5	136.2	102.0	170.9
October	150.8	153.5	149.5	104.4	162.7	137.1	170.3	128.4	141.0	125.4	135.8	101.9	166.6
November	150.9	153.7	149.6	103.4	163.0	137.0	170.7	128.7	141.3	125.2	135.5	104.1	163.6
December	151.3	153.9	149.9	104.4	163.1	137.3	170.9	129.3	141.5	125.4	135.2	106.5	162.3
1996													
January	152.0	154.7	150.4	106.9	163.7	138.2	171.5	129.7	141.5	125.5	134.8	109.8	162.6
February	152.3	155.0	150.8	107.1	164.0	138.3	172.0	129.7	141.6	125.0	134.4	111.6	162.1
March	152.9	155.5	151.4	108.3	164.4	139.0	172.4	130.5	141.6	125.3	134.1	109.8	158.2
April	153.4	156.1	152.0	111.2	164.6	139.6	172.8	130.9	141.6	125.7	133.8	114.2	156.7
May	153.8	156.4	151.9	112.0	165.0	139.7	173.4	130.9	142.0	126.2	134.0	114.6	157.6
June	154.0	156.7	152.9	110.3	165.4	139.8	173.8	131.3	142.2	125.8	133.9	112.2	154.6
July	154.3	157.0	153.4	110.1	165.7	139.8	174.4	131.2	142.2	125.5	133.6	114.6	152.2
August	154.5	157.2	153.9	109.7	166.0	139.8	174.9	131.6	142.3	125.6	133.6	115.3	152.5
September	154.9	157.7	154.6	109.8	166.5	140.3	175.4	131.7	142.2	126.1	134.0	112.7	153.5
October	155.4	158.2	155.5	110.5	166.8	140.8	175.8	132.4	142.3	126.0	133.7	111.9	153.3
November	155.9	158.7	156.1	111.8	167.2	141.4	176.3	132.5	142.1	125.8	133.7	115.7	153.0
December	156.3	159.1	156.3	113.9	167.4	141.7	176.7	132.9	142.3	126.4	133.9	122.5	153.6
1997													
January	156.6	159.4	155.9	115.2	167.8	141.8	177.3	133.0	142.5	126.6	134.1	127.5	156.2
February	156.9	159.7	156.5	115.0	168.1	142.1	177.6	132.7	142.4	126.5	134.1	116.6	157.6
March	156.9	159.8	156.6	113.0	168.4	141.8	178.0	132.6	142.6	126.1	134.2	107.5	158.7
April	157.0	159.9	156.5	111.0	168.9	141.6	178.4	131.8	142.6	125.6	134.1	107.8	155.8
May	157.0	159.9	156.6	108.8	169.2	141.4	178.7	131.5	142.4	125.4	134.2	109.1	157.0
June	157.3	160.2	156.9	110.0	169.4	141.5	179.2	131.3	142.4	125.4	134.2	106.2	156.9
July	157.4	160.4	157.2	109.1	169.7	141.4	179.7	130.9	142.2	125.1	134.2	106.2	155.7
August	157.8	160.8	157.7	110.9	169.8	141.9	179.9	131.4	142.3	125.3	134.3	106.8	156.8
September	158.2	161.2	158.0	112.4	170.2	142.2	180.4	131.6	142.6	125.5	134.3	108.4	155.8
October	158.4	161.5	158.3	111.8	170.6	142.2	180.9	131.9	142.6	125.4	134.3	113.4	156.7
November	158.6	161.7	158.6	111.4	170.8	142.1	181.4	131.6	142.4	125.6	134.4	115.8	156.5
December	158.6	161.8	158.7	109.8	171.2	142.1	181.7	131.4	142.3	125.4	134.4	108.8	154.2
1998													
January	158.8	162.0	159.5	107.5	171.6	142.0	182.1	130.7	142.4	124.6	134.3	102.8	150.4
February	158.7	162.0	159.4	105.1	171.9	141.8	182.3	130.6	142.6	124.2	134.2	100.8	150.1
March	158.7	162.0	159.7	103.3	172.2	141.4	182.8	130.5	143.3	123.7	134.1	99.5	148.7
April	158.8	162.2	159.7	102.4	172.5	141.3	183.3	130.7	143.4	123.6	134.0	100.6	147.3
May	159.3	162.6	160.3	103.2	172.9	141.7	183.7	130.5	143.5	123.5	133.9	99.6	146.2
June	159.5	162.8	160.2	103.6	173.2	141.8	184.0	130.4	143.5	123.1	133.6	97.1	145.9
July	159.8	163.2	160.6	103.3	173.5	142.1	184.3	130.7	143.8	123.0	133.5	97.4	143.4
August	160.0	163.4	161.0	102.1	174.0	142.2	184.7	130.4	143.8	122.7	133.4	93.6	139.4
September	160.1	163.5	161.1	101.3	174.2	142.0	185.1	130.4	144.0	122.3	133.1	91.4	137.6
October	160.5	163.9	162.0	101.5	174.4	142.3	185.5	130.9	144.2	122.2	132.7	93.9	134.0
November	160.7	164.1	162.2	101.1	174.8	142.2	186.0	130.8	144.3	122.0	132.5	93.6	131.6
December	161.1	164.4	162.4	100.1	175.4	142.5	186.4	131.3	145.8	121.3	132.2	90.2	129.4

Table 8-1B. Summary Consumer and Producer Price Indexes: Historical Data, 1947 to Date—*Continued*

(Seasonally adjusted.)

Year and month	Urban wage earners and clerical workers (CPI-W), all items	Consumer Price Index, 1982–1984 = 100						Producer Price Index for goods, 1982 = 100					
		All urban consumers (CPI-U)						Finished goods		Processed goods for intermediate demand		Unprocessed goods for intermediate demand	
		All items	Food	Energy	All items less food and energy	Commod-ities	Services	Total	Less food and energy	Total	Processed materials less foods and energy	Total	Unproces-sed nonfood materials less energy
1999													
January	161.4	164.7	163.0	99.7	175.6	142.8	186.6	131.7	145.6	121.2	132.0	91.0	128.7
February	161.3	164.7	163.3	99.2	175.6	142.4	186.9	131.2	145.7	120.8	131.8	89.0	130.5
March	161.4	164.8	163.3	100.4	175.7	142.4	187.4	131.5	145.7	121.1	131.9	89.6	129.6
April	162.4	165.9	163.5	105.5	176.3	144.0	187.9	132.1	145.7	121.9	132.0	91.3	128.7
May	162.6	166.0	163.8	104.9	176.5	143.9	188.1	132.3	145.7	122.2	132.4	96.8	130.5
June	162.6	166.0	163.7	104.5	176.6	143.8	188.3	132.4	145.8	122.6	132.8	97.0	131.6
July	163.3	166.7	163.9	106.7	177.1	144.5	188.9	132.7	145.8	123.4	133.3	97.3	133.6
August	163.8	167.1	164.2	109.5	177.3	145.0	189.3	133.5	145.7	124.1	133.6	102.4	136.3
September	164.6	167.8	164.6	111.8	177.8	145.9	189.8	134.5	146.5	124.6	133.9	106.4	138.8
October	164.9	168.1	165.0	112.0	178.1	146.1	190.2	134.4	146.9	124.9	134.3	103.8	142.5
November	165.1	168.4	165.3	111.5	178.4	145.9	190.9	134.9	146.9	125.4	134.5	109.7	144.4
December	165.6	168.8	165.5	113.8	178.7	146.5	191.2	135.2	147.0	125.8	134.7	104.4	147.6
2000													
January	166.0	169.3	165.6	115.0	179.3	146.7	192.0	135.2	146.8	126.4	135.1	106.8	150.5
February	166.7	170.0	166.2	118.8	179.4	147.6	192.5	136.6	147.3	127.5	135.5	111.0	151.3
March	167.8	171.0	166.5	124.3	180.0	149.1	193.1	137.3	147.4	128.4	136.0	113.2	150.5
April	167.6	170.9	166.7	120.9	180.3	148.5	193.5	136.9	147.4	128.3	136.5	111.3	148.8
May	167.9	171.2	167.3	120.0	180.7	148.5	194.0	137.0	147.8	128.2	136.6	115.1	147.8
June	169.0	172.2	167.4	126.8	181.1	149.6	194.9	138.1	147.8	129.3	136.9	124.8	145.1
July	169.5	172.7	168.3	127.3	181.5	149.8	195.7	138.2	148.1	129.6	137.1	122.1	142.8
August	169.3	172.7	168.7	123.8	181.9	149.2	196.3	137.9	148.2	129.3	136.9	117.6	141.2
September	170.3	173.6	168.9	129.2	182.3	150.4	196.9	139.0	148.6	130.3	137.0	125.6	142.9
October	170.5	173.9	169.0	129.6	182.6	150.1	197.7	139.5	148.5	130.7	137.1	130.2	142.1
November	170.8	174.2	169.2	129.2	183.1	150.3	198.1	140.2	148.7	130.7	136.9	129.1	139.6
December	171.2	174.6	170.0	130.1	183.3	150.4	198.8	140.5	148.9	131.3	136.9	141.1	139.5
2001													
January	172.2	175.6	170.3	135.0	183.9	150.6	200.6	141.7	149.5	132.1	137.1	165.6	138.7
February	172.5	176.0	171.2	134.1	184.4	150.8	201.2	141.9	149.2	131.8	137.3	141.7	136.5
March	172.6	176.1	171.7	131.7	184.7	150.5	201.6	141.2	149.5	131.0	137.4	132.4	135.0
April	173.0	176.4	172.1	132.3	185.1	150.9	202.0	142.0	149.8	130.9	137.3	133.0	131.3
May	174.0	177.3	172.4	138.4	185.3	151.9	202.7	142.3	150.1	131.1	137.3	130.5	130.9
June	174.2	177.7	173.1	136.9	186.0	151.9	203.5	141.8	150.2	130.9	137.1	119.9	129.7
July	173.8	177.4	173.6	129.6	186.4	150.9	203.8	140.1	150.5	129.4	136.4	113.3	130.6
August	173.8	177.4	174.0	127.3	186.7	150.4	204.4	140.7	150.5	129.1	135.9	112.3	128.4
September	174.7	178.1	174.2	130.9	187.1	151.6	204.5	141.3	150.7	129.3	135.9	107.2	128.8
October	173.9	177.6	174.8	122.9	187.4	150.3	204.8	139.0	149.8	127.6	135.4	97.4	126.5
November	173.7	177.5	174.9	116.9	188.1	149.2	205.6	138.5	150.2	127.0	135.1	102.7	126.2
December	173.4	177.4	174.7	113.9	188.4	148.3	206.1	138.0	150.4	126.1	134.8	95.5	125.7
2002													
January	173.7	177.7	175.3	114.2	188.7	148.3	206.8	137.7	150.0	125.7	134.7	99.8	126.2
February	173.9	178.0	175.7	113.5	189.1	148.3	207.5	138.0	150.1	125.5	134.6	98.4	127.5
March	174.5	178.5	176.1	117.6	189.2	149.0	207.9	138.8	150.0	126.4	135.0	103.8	128.1
April	175.4	179.3	176.4	121.5	189.7	150.0	208.5	138.7	150.3	127.2	135.3	108.1	130.8
May	175.5	179.5	175.8	121.9	190.0	149.7	209.0	138.4	150.2	127.1	135.3	109.0	134.2
June	175.7	179.6	175.9	121.6	190.2	149.7	209.3	138.8	150.5	127.3	135.6	105.1	138.2
July	176.1	180.0	176.1	122.4	190.5	149.9	209.9	138.6	150.0	127.7	136.0	106.5	140.8
August	176.6	180.5	176.1	123.1	191.1	150.2	210.6	138.7	149.9	128.0	136.2	108.3	140.0
September	176.8	180.8	176.5	123.7	191.3	150.2	211.1	139.2	150.3	128.9	136.5	110.8	140.2
October	177.2	181.2	176.4	126.9	191.5	150.5	211.7	140.0	150.5	129.8	136.7	112.6	140.0
November	177.5	181.5	176.9	126.7	191.9	150.5	212.4	140.0	150.3	129.9	136.8	116.6	141.0
December	177.7	181.8	177.1	127.1	192.1	150.3	213.0	139.7	149.5	130.0	136.7	118.9	141.3
2003													
January	178.6	182.6	177.1	133.5	192.4	151.3	213.7	141.1	149.8	131.4	137.2	128.0	143.3
February	179.7	183.6	178.1	140.8	192.5	152.7	214.2	142.7	149.9	133.8	138.1	134.3	148.1
March	180.1	183.9	178.4	143.9	192.5	152.6	215.0	144.0	150.7	136.3	138.6	152.2	147.5
April	179.2	183.2	178.5	136.5	192.5	151.1	215.1	142.2	149.9	133.1	138.3	128.2	145.9
May	178.7	182.9	178.8	129.4	192.9	149.4	216.0	141.9	150.1	132.4	138.4	129.9	146.0
June	178.9	183.1	179.7	129.8	193.0	149.7	216.2	142.7	150.1	133.1	138.4	135.5	145.7
July	179.4	183.7	179.8	132.2	193.4	150.3	216.8	142.8	150.3	133.3	138.2	131.9	148.5
August	180.3	184.5	180.5	137.8	193.6	151.4	217.2	143.7	150.5	133.9	138.4	130.8	152.1
September	180.9	185.1	180.9	142.9	193.7	152.1	217.8	144.0	150.4	133.8	138.8	134.4	156.2
October	180.6	184.9	181.6	137.8	194.0	151.1	218.4	144.8	151.1	134.2	139.1	138.2	160.2
November	180.6	185.0	182.6	136.9	194.0	151.1	218.6	144.6	151.0	134.2	139.3	137.9	165.6
December	181.0	185.5	183.5	138.8	194.2	151.6	219.0	145.1	151.0	135.0	139.6	142.4	171.0
2004													
January	181.9	186.3	183.4	143.9	194.6	152.5	219.7	145.9	151.4	136.6	140.5	148.7	179.7
February	182.4	186.7	183.9	145.8	194.9	153.1	220.1	145.8	151.3	137.8	141.8	150.8	190.0
March	182.7	187.1	184.2	145.1	195.5	153.3	220.8	146.2	151.8	138.4	142.9	153.2	195.0
April	182.8	187.4	184.6	143.4	195.9	153.0	221.4	147.2	151.9	140.1	144.6	156.2	187.1
May	183.8	188.2	186.1	147.6	196.2	154.2	221.9	148.4	152.3	141.7	145.7	160.6	177.6
June	184.4	188.9	186.4	151.5	196.6	154.9	222.7	148.4	152.8	142.2	146.2	161.5	176.3
July	184.6	189.1	186.8	151.1	196.8	154.6	223.2	148.2	152.5	142.9	146.9	161.3	195.7
August	184.7	189.2	187.0	151.5	196.9	154.4	223.7	148.6	152.9	144.4	148.4	161.7	201.6
September	185.3	189.8	186.9	152.9	197.5	154.9	224.2	148.8	153.2	144.8	149.6	154.0	198.3
October	186.4	190.8	187.8	158.6	197.9	156.7	224.6	151.2	153.7	146.6	150.2	161.0	204.6
November	187.4	191.7	188.4	163.8	198.3	157.8	225.4	152.1	154.1	147.9	150.7	172.7	208.9
December	187.4	191.7	188.4	162.3	198.6	157.4	225.8	151.4	154.5	147.7	151.3	167.2	206.0

Table 8-1B. Summary Consumer and Producer Price Indexes: Historical Data, 1947 to Date—*Continued*

(Seasonally adjusted.)

Year and month	Urban wage earners and clerical workers (CPI-W), all items	Consumer Price Index, 1982–1984 = 100 — All urban consumers (CPI-U)						Producer Price Index for goods, 1982 = 100 — Finished goods		Processed goods for intermediate demand		Unprocessed goods for intermediate demand	
		All items	Food	Energy	All items less food and energy	Commodities	Services	Total	Less food and energy	Total	Processed materials less foods and energy	Total	Unprocessed nonfood materials less energy
2005													
January	187.2	191.6	188.7	157.2	199.0	156.8	226.2	151.9	155.4	148.5	152.4	164.2	203.7
February	188.0	192.4	188.6	161.8	199.4	157.5	226.9	152.7	155.3	149.5	153.2	162.9	200.2
March	188.6	193.1	189.1	163.5	200.1	157.9	228.0	153.7	155.6	150.7	153.8	170.5	199.6
April	189.3	193.7	190.4	166.7	200.2	158.6	228.5	154.2	156.0	151.3	153.9	175.0	203.5
May	189.1	193.6	190.6	163.3	200.5	158.1	228.9	153.9	156.4	150.6	153.5	169.1	196.6
June	189.3	193.7	190.5	163.7	200.6	158.0	229.1	153.9	156.2	151.1	153.3	165.5	188.9
July	190.6	194.9	190.9	172.8	200.9	159.6	229.9	155.0	156.8	152.3	153.5	174.4	190.5
August	192.0	196.1	191.1	183.5	201.1	161.5	230.4	156.3	156.9	153.2	153.4	181.5	200.9
September	195.1	198.8	191.5	208.2	201.3	166.0	231.4	158.8	157.1	157.2	155.0	200.3	211.3
October	195.2	199.1	192.0	205.9	202.0	164.8	233.1	160.5	156.8	162.3	157.2	212.7	207.7
November	193.7	198.1	192.6	191.0	202.5	161.8	234.2	158.7	156.8	160.3	157.9	209.9	214.0
December	193.7	198.1	192.9	187.6	202.8	161.5	234.4	159.6	156.8	160.2	158.5	202.0	216.7
2006													
January	195.1	199.3	193.6	196.6	203.2	162.9	235.5	160.5	157.5	162.4	159.9	203.2	216.7
February	195.0	199.4	193.7	194.1	203.6	162.5	235.9	158.7	158.0	161.6	160.4	186.6	224.0
March	195.3	199.7	194.0	192.0	204.3	162.6	236.5	159.3	158.4	161.5	161.1	179.6	227.1
April	196.4	200.7	193.8	198.5	204.8	164.1	237.1	160.6	158.5	163.0	162.0	182.9	238.2
May	197.0	201.3	194.1	199.8	205.4	164.6	237.8	160.6	158.9	164.4	163.7	184.4	259.1
June	197.4	201.8	194.7	199.8	205.9	164.8	238.5	161.4	159.0	165.2	164.7	178.5	255.3
July	198.6	202.9	195.2	207.9	206.3	166.4	239.2	161.0	158.1	165.5	165.6	180.5	259.5
August	199.5	203.8	195.7	211.9	206.8	167.2	239.9	162.1	158.7	166.5	166.3	187.0	251.7
September	198.3	202.8	196.3	198.1	207.2	164.6	240.7	160.2	159.2	164.7	166.2	182.7	255.2
October	197.1	201.9	196.9	184.1	207.6	162.5	241.0	158.7	158.5	163.0	166.2	168.6	249.7
November	197.2	202.0	197.0	184.1	207.8	162.0	241.7	160.0	159.9	163.8	165.5	189.4	249.8
December	198.4	203.1	197.1	192.7	208.1	163.4	242.4	161.1	160.0	164.7	165.6	195.4	253.7
2007													
January	198.6	203.4	198.4	190.3	208.6	163.3	243.2	160.9	160.2	164.1	165.6	184.9	257.2
February	199.4	204.2	199.7	192.3	209.1	164.1	244.1	162.7	160.9	165.3	165.6	201.6	265.9
March	200.7	205.3	200.4	200.2	209.4	165.6	244.7	164.1	160.9	166.7	166.3	203.6	282.7
April	201.3	205.9	201.0	203.3	209.7	166.2	245.3	165.3	161.0	168.3	167.7	204.0	285.1
May	202.3	206.8	201.7	208.6	210.1	167.3	245.9	166.0	161.4	169.7	168.6	204.8	280.3
June	202.7	207.2	202.6	209.8	210.4	167.5	246.6	166.1	161.7	170.4	169.0	205.9	280.7
July	203.0	207.6	203.2	209.6	210.8	167.8	247.1	167.2	162.1	171.8	169.6	203.7	283.0
August	203.0	207.7	204.0	206.4	211.1	167.5	247.5	166.0	162.3	170.1	168.9	198.6	284.2
September	204.0	208.5	205.0	210.7	211.6	168.5	248.2	167.6	162.3	171.4	169.0	203.2	290.8
October	204.7	209.2	205.7	212.4	212.1	169.0	249.1	169.3	162.9	172.7	169.7	214.4	295.0
November	206.5	210.8	206.5	223.8	212.7	171.5	249.8	172.4	163.4	176.7	171.0	229.5	293.4
December	207.1	211.4	206.9	225.6	213.2	172.0	250.5	171.7	163.4	176.9	171.2	235.6	294.7
2008													
January	207.9	212.2	208.1	226.8	213.8	172.7	251.3	173.3	164.1	179.2	172.7	243.3	309.4
February	208.4	212.6	208.9	229.7	213.9	173.0	251.8	173.9	164.8	180.8	173.8	253.3	319.5
March	209.2	213.4	209.3	233.3	214.4	173.7	252.9	175.4	165.1	184.6	175.9	264.2	329.6
April	209.8	214.0	211.1	234.8	214.6	174.1	253.6	175.9	165.8	186.4	178.3	272.8	362.2
May	211.1	215.2	212.0	243.9	214.9	175.5	254.7	178.4	166.3	191.1	181.1	287.3	368.9
June	213.7	217.5	213.3	262.1	215.4	178.8	255.8	181.2	166.6	195.3	183.7	294.2	372.2
July	215.5	219.1	215.4	271.1	216.0	180.7	257.1	183.4	167.4	200.6	187.4	303.4	384.8
August	215.0	218.7	216.5	262.6	216.4	179.6	257.6	182.0	168.1	198.1	188.6	270.3	373.5
September	215.1	218.9	217.8	260.1	216.7	179.8	257.6	182.7	168.9	198.0	188.8	255.2	338.4
October	212.7	217.0	218.7	238.1	216.8	175.8	257.7	178.3	170.5	189.4	184.9	215.9	278.6
November	207.9	213.1	219.1	195.2	216.9	168.0	257.8	172.9	170.4	179.7	180.4	187.3	226.9
December	205.9	211.4	219.1	176.6	216.9	164.5	258.0	169.7	170.8	172.3	176.2	176.7	223.0
2009													
January	206.5	212.0	219.2	178.8	217.3	165.3	258.4	170.8	170.8	172.4	174.8	173.1	226.0
February	207.4	212.8	219.0	184.9	217.8	166.8	258.7	170.6	170.9	170.9	173.5	163.4	224.5
March	207.1	212.6	218.5	178.8	218.3	166.2	258.7	169.1	171.2	168.3	172.7	160.1	221.3
April	207.4	212.7	218.2	177.1	218.7	166.5	258.7	170.0	171.3	168.4	171.8	162.4	222.1
May	207.8	213.0	217.8	179.7	218.9	167.2	258.6	170.3	171.2	169.4	171.4	167.5	232.2
June	209.9	214.7	217.8	196.9	219.2	170.7	258.7	173.5	171.8	171.7	171.8	175.0	240.5
July	210.0	214.7	217.4	195.6	219.3	170.5	258.7	171.5	171.4	171.1	172.2	168.0	246.6
August	210.9	215.5	217.4	201.5	219.5	171.3	259.3	173.9	171.8	173.8	173.2	176.1	263.8
September	211.3	215.9	217.3	202.8	219.9	171.9	259.6	173.5	171.6	174.3	174.2	174.1	268.8
October	211.9	216.5	217.5	204.6	220.5	172.7	260.0	174.3	171.5	175.0	174.5	186.9	273.8
November	212.7	217.1	217.6	210.3	220.6	173.8	260.2	176.6	172.1	176.9	174.9	195.3	274.4
December	213.0	217.3	217.9	210.3	220.8	174.2	260.3	177.1	172.1	177.8	175.9	200.8	288.3
2010													
January	213.4	217.5	218.5	212.8	220.6	174.9	259.8	178.9	172.5	180.8	177.0	214.0	305.2
February	213.3	217.3	218.6	209.6	220.7	174.3	260.0	177.7	172.6	180.4	178.4	208.8	306.1
March	213.3	217.4	219.0	209.3	220.8	174.1	260.3	178.9	172.9	181.3	179.6	212.1	322.3
April	213.2	217.4	219.2	209.2	220.8	173.9	260.7	178.9	172.9	182.8	181.4	210.6	332.9
May	212.9	217.3	219.3	206.6	221.0	173.4	260.9	178.9	173.4	183.4	181.8	206.2	328.1
June	212.9	217.2	219.3	203.8	221.2	172.9	261.2	178.3	173.6	182.4	180.9	201.5	315.4
July	213.5	217.6	219.2	206.9	221.4	173.4	261.5	178.5	173.7	181.9	180.2	207.1	312.8
August	213.9	217.9	219.5	208.8	221.5	173.8	261.7	179.4	173.9	182.8	180.5	211.4	324.5
September	214.3	218.3	220.2	209.8	221.7	174.4	261.9	180.1	174.3	183.5	180.9	209.7	335.1
October	215.1	219.0	220.5	216.7	221.8	175.7	262.1	181.6	174.3	185.8	182.0	216.9	346.1
November	215.5	219.6	220.9	219.5	222.1	176.5	262.4	182.4	174.3	187.3	183.1	219.5	355.5
December	216.9	220.5	221.2	227.1	222.3	177.9	262.7	183.9	174.6	189.3	184.1	229.7	367.6

Table 8-1B. Summary Consumer and Producer Price Indexes: Historical Data, 1947 to Date—*Continued*

(Seasonally adjusted.)

| | | Consumer Price Index, 1982–1984 = 100 | | | | | | Producer Price Index for goods, 1982 = 100 | | | | | |
| | Urban wage earners and clerical workers (CPI-W), all items | All urban consumers (CPI-U) | | | | | | Finished goods | | Processed goods for intermediate demand | | Unprocessed goods for intermediate demand | |
Year and month		All items	Food	Energy	All items less food and energy	Commod-ities	Services	Total	Less food and energy	Total	Processed materials less foods and energy	Total	Unproces-sed nonfood materials less energy
2011													
January	217.4	221.1	222.5	229.2	222.7	178.9	263.1	185.4	175.3	192.0	186.5	237.3	382.6
February	218.1	221.9	223.6	232.4	223.2	179.9	263.7	187.3	175.7	194.7	188.7	243.3	391.7
March	218.4	223.0	225.3	240.1	223.4	181.8	264.1	188.6	176.3	197.5	190.1	247.5	385.5
April	220.7	224.1	226.1	247.1	223.8	183.4	264.5	190.2	176.8	200.1	192.4	260.3	396.0
May	221.7	224.9	226.9	250.6	224.3	184.5	265.0	191.2	177.1	202.0	193.5	253.1	391.3
June	221.7	224.8	227.4	245.4	224.8	184.1	265.3	190.6	177.5	202.3	193.8	253.9	396.6
July	222.3	225.4	228.4	246.4	225.2	184.6	265.9	191.3	178.3	203.3	194.3	255.3	400.4
August	222.9	226.1	229.5	247.1	225.8	185.3	266.6	191.1	178.5	201.8	194.1	250.7	402.6
September	223.5	226.7	230.6	249.8	226.1	186.0	267.1	192.7	179.0	202.7	194.2	251.4	401.9
October	223.5	226.8	230.9	247.5	226.5	185.9	267.5	192.4	179.4	200.8	193.0	244.4	383.8
November	223.9	227.2	231.1	247.1	226.9	186.1	267.9	192.8	179.6	200.9	192.2	250.8	376.2
December	223.8	227.1	231.6	243.0	227.3	185.6	268.4	192.6	180.0	200.1	191.1	244.9	375.6
2012													
January	224.3	227.8	232.3	244.2	227.8	186.3	268.9	193.2	180.7	200.2	191.8	247.8	384.3
February	224.9	228.3	232.3	248.4	228.0	187.3	269.0	193.7	181.0	200.8	193.2	245.8	383.6
March	225.5	228.9	232.8	250.1	228.5	188.0	269.5	193.9	181.4	203.1	194.5	247.7	386.0
April	225.9	229.2	233.2	249.0	228.9	188.1	270.1	193.5	181.7	201.9	194.8	240.6	380.2
May	225.5	228.8	233.2	241.9	229.3	186.9	270.5	192.7	181.9	200.6	194.2	232.7	372.7
June	225.3	228.6	233.6	236.1	229.8	185.9	271.1	192.1	182.2	198.9	192.1	224.4	355.5
July	225.2	228.6	233.7	233.6	230.0	185.5	271.4	192.4	183.0	198.1	191.4	231.3	353.7
August	226.6	229.9	234.1	245.5	230.2	187.6	272.0	194.7	183.2	199.9	191.3	242.3	361.7
September	227.9	231.1	234.3	254.5	230.6	189.3	272.6	196.6	183.2	202.0	192.0	245.1	365.6
October	228.5	231.7	234.8	257.4	231.0	190.0	273.2	196.9	183.2	202.4	192.1	244.3	359.2
November	227.7	231.2	235.3	248.2	231.3	188.3	273.9	195.5	183.5	200.6	192.0	246.2	364.1
December	227.6	231.2	235.7	244.8	231.6	187.6	274.4	195.3	183.6	200.7	192.3	248.6	369.5
2013													
January	227.7	231.4	236.0	242.6	232.2	187.5	275.1	196.0	183.9	201.4	193.6	249.5	365.2
February	229.2	232.8	236.1	253.8	232.6	189.6	275.7	197.1	184.2	203.2	194.7	246.9	363.0
March	228.5	232.2	236.3	246.0	232.8	188.1	276.1	196.1	184.5	201.3	194.5	247.4	365.5
April	228.0	231.7	236.7	238.8	232.9	186.6	276.4	194.7	184.7	199.9	194.0	247.3	355.8
May	229.4	232.0	236.4	240.5	233.1	186.6	277.1	196.1	184.9	200.3	193.7	250.1	349.8
June	229.3	232.6	236.8	243.2	233.5	187.3	277.6	196.4	185.1	200.5	193.7	248.2	346.6
July	229.7	233.0	237.1	244.0	233.9	187.5	278.1	196.4	185.3	200.6	193.4	251.0	346.4
August	229.8	233.4	237.4	245.0	234.3	187.8	278.7	197.0	185.4	200.7	193.6	246.8	345.6
September	230.1	233.8	237.6	245.9	234.6	187.9	279.3	197.0	185.4	200.7	193.6	246.5	342.4
October	230.1	233.9	237.8	244.8	234.9	187.7	279.8	197.4	185.4	200.6	193.6	242.9	340.8
November	230.3	234.0	238.1	242.4	235.3	187.3	280.4	197.1	185.8	199.9	193.5	238.5	343.7
December	230.9	234.7	238.2	246.5	235.6	188.2	280.9	198.2	186.6	200.8	193.7	243.6	348.2
2014													
January	231.4	235.1	238.5	248.3	236.0	188.1	281.8	199.3	187.5	202.3	194.5	248.2	354.9
February	231.6	235.4	239.4	247.2	236.2	188.0	282.4	199.5	187.7	202.8	195.2	259.8	351.1
March	232.0	235.8	240.4	247.3	236.6	187.8	283.4	200.0	187.7	202.9	194.9	260.8	349.3
April	232.5	236.2	241.2	247.0	237.1	188.4	283.7	200.8	187.9	202.9	195.3	263.6	354.1
May	233.1	237.0	242.2	248.9	237.7	188.8	284.8	201.1	188.3	203.1	195.2	260.7	353.2
June	233.6	237.3	242.4	250.2	238.0	189.1	285.3	201.9	188.6	203.4	195.3	257.9	347.4
July	233.7	237.6	243.2	249.8	238.2	189.1	285.7	201.8	188.8	203.6	196.0	253.4	348.4
August	233.5	237.4	243.8	245.6	238.3	188.5	285.9	201.5	189.0	203.4	196.4	245.6	345.5
September	233.7	237.6	244.7	243.8	238.7	188.5	286.3	201.3	189.3	203.0	196.3	245.9	345.8
October	233.7	237.8	245.1	240.9	239.1	188.2	286.9	200.8	189.5	201.0	195.7	237.7	337.1
November	232.6	237.1	245.6	230.9	239.3	186.3	287.4	199.2	189.6	198.9	194.8	234.7	331.8
December	231.5	236.3	246.2	220.1	239.4	184.0	288.0	196.9	190.0	196.2	194.3	223.8	330.5

Table 8-1C. Consumer and Producer Price Indexes: Historical Data, 1913–1949

(Not seasonally adjusted.)

Year and month	Consumer price indexes, 1982–1984 =100				Producer Price Indexes for goods, 1982 = 100			
	All urban consumers (CPI-U)		Urban wage earners and clerical workers (CPI-W)		All commodities		Farm products	Industrial commodities
	Index	Percent change	Index	Percent change	Index	Percent change		
1913	9.9	. . .	10.0	. . .	12.0	. . .	18.0	11.9
1914	10.0	1.0	10.1	1.0	11.8	-1.7	17.9	11.3
1915	10.1	1.0	10.2	1.0	12.0	1.7	18.0	11.6
1916	10.9	7.9	11.0	7.8	14.7	22.5	21.3	15.0
1917	12.8	17.4	12.9	17.3	20.2	37.4	32.6	19.5
1918	15.1	18.0	15.1	17.1	22.6	11.9	37.4	21.1
1919	17.3	14.6	17.4	15.2	23.9	5.8	39.8	22.0
1920	20.0	15.6	20.1	15.5	26.6	11.3	38.0	27.4
1921	17.9	-10.5	18.0	-10.4	16.8	-36.8	22.3	17.8
1922	16.8	-6.1	16.9	-6.1	16.7	-0.6	23.7	17.4
1923	17.1	1.8	17.2	1.8	17.3	3.6	24.9	17.8
1924	17.1	0.0	17.2	0.0	16.9	-2.3	25.2	17.0
1925	17.5	2.3	17.6	2.3	17.8	5.3	27.7	17.5
1926	17.7	1.1	17.8	1.1	17.2	-3.4	25.3	17.0
1927	17.4	-1.7	17.5	-1.7	16.5	-4.1	25.1	16.0
1928	17.1	-1.7	17.2	-1.7	16.7	1.2	26.7	15.8
1929	17.1	0.0	17.2	0.0	16.4	-1.8	26.4	15.6
1930	16.7	-2.3	16.8	-2.3	14.9	-9.1	22.4	14.5
1931	15.2	-9.0	15.3	-8.9	12.6	-15.4	16.4	12.8
1932	13.7	-9.9	13.7	-10.5	11.2	-11.1	12.2	11.9
1933	13.0	-5.1	13.0	-5.1	11.4	1.8	13.0	12.1
1934	13.4	3.1	13.5	3.8	12.9	13.2	16.5	13.3
1935	13.7	2.2	13.8	2.2	13.8	7.0	19.8	13.3
1936	13.9	1.5	13.9	0.7	13.9	0.7	20.4	13.5
1937	14.4	3.6	14.4	3.6	14.9	7.2	21.8	14.5
1938	14.1	-2.1	14.2	-1.4	13.5	-9.4	17.3	13.9
1939	13.9	-1.4	14.0	-1.4	13.3	-1.5	16.5	13.9
1940	14.0	0.7	14.1	0.7	13.5	1.5	17.1	14.1
1941	14.7	5.0	14.8	5.0	15.1	11.9	20.8	15.1
1942	16.3	10.9	16.4	10.8	17.0	12.6	26.7	16.2
1943	17.3	6.1	17.4	6.1	17.8	4.7	30.9	16.5
1944	17.6	1.7	17.7	1.7	17.9	0.6	31.2	16.7
1945	18.0	2.3	18.1	2.3	18.2	1.7	32.4	17.0
1946	19.5	8.3	19.6	8.3	20.8	14.3	37.5	18.6
1947	22.3	14.4	22.5	14.8	25.6	23.1	45.1	22.7
1948	24.1	8.1	24.2	7.6	27.7	8.2	48.5	24.6
1949	23.8	-1.2	24.0	-0.8	26.3	-5.1	41.9	24.1
1913								
January	9.8	. . .	9.9	. . .	12.1	. . .	17.6	12.3
February	9.8	0.0	9.8	-1.0	12.0	-0.8	17.5	12.2
March	9.8	0.0	9.8	0.0	12.0	0.0	17.6	12.1
April	9.8	0.0	9.9	1.0	12.0	0.0	17.5	12.0
May	9.7	-1.0	9.8	-1.0	11.9	-0.8	17.4	11.9
June	9.8	1.0	9.8	0.0	11.9	0.0	17.6	11.8
July	9.9	1.0	9.9	1.0	12.0	0.8	18.1	11.8
August	9.9	0.0	10.0	1.0	12.0	0.0	18.2	11.7
September	10.0	1.0	10.0	0.0	12.2	1.7	18.8	11.8
October	10.0	0.0	10.1	1.0	12.2	0.0	18.8	11.8
November	10.1	1.0	10.1	0.0	12.1	-0.8	18.9	11.7
December	10.0	-1.0	10.1	0.0	11.9	-1.7	18.5	11.6
1914								
January	10.0	0.0	10.1	0.0	11.8	-0.8	18.4	11.5
February	9.9	-1.0	10.0	-1.0	11.8	0.0	18.3	11.5
March	9.9	0.0	10.0	0.0	11.7	-0.8	18.2	11.5
April	9.8	-1.0	9.9	-1.0	11.7	0.0	18.0	11.5
May	9.9	1.0	9.9	0.0	11.6	-0.9	18.0	11.4
June	9.9	0.0	10.0	1.0	11.6	0.0	18.1	11.3
July	10.0	1.0	10.1	1.0	11.6	0.0	18.0	11.2
August	10.2	2.0	10.2	1.0	12.0	3.4	18.3	11.2
September	10.2	0.0	10.3	1.0	12.1	0.8	17.9	11.3
October	10.1	-1.0	10.2	-1.0	11.7	-3.3	17.2	11.0
November	10.2	1.0	10.2	0.0	11.7	0.0	17.6	11.0
December	10.1	-1.0	10.2	0.0	11.6	-0.9	17.4	11.0
1915								
January	10.1	0.0	10.2	0.0	11.8	1.7	18.1	11.1
February	10.0	-1.0	10.1	-1.0	11.8	0.0	18.4	11.0
March	9.9	-1.0	10.0	-1.0	11.8	0.0	17.9	11.0
April	10.0	1.0	10.1	1.0	11.8	0.0	18.2	11.1
May	10.1	1.0	10.1	0.0	11.9	0.8	18.2	11.2
June	10.1	0.0	10.2	1.0	11.8	-0.8	17.7	11.4
July	10.1	0.0	10.2	0.0	11.9	0.8	18.1	11.5
August	10.1	0.0	10.2	0.0	11.8	-0.8	17.9	11.5
September	10.1	0.0	10.2	0.0	11.8	0.0	17.5	11.7
October	10.2	1.0	10.3	1.0	12.1	2.5	18.1	11.9
November	10.3	1.0	10.4	1.0	12.3	1.7	18.0	12.3
December	10.3	0.0	10.4	0.0	12.8	4.1	18.4	12.9

. . . = Not available.

Table 8-1C. Consumer and Producer Price Indexes: Historical Data, 1913–1949—*Continued*

(Not seasonally adjusted.)

| Year and month | Consumer price indexes, 1982–1984 =100 | | | | Producer Price Indexes for goods, 1982 = 100 | | | |
| | All urban consumers (CPI-U) | | Urban wage earners and clerical workers (CPI-W) | | All commodities | | Farm products | Industrial commodities |
	Index	Percent change	Index	Percent change	Index	Percent change		
1916								
January	10.4	1.0	10.5	1.0	13.3	3.9	19.4	13.6
February	10.4	0.0	10.5	0.0	13.5	1.5	19.4	14.0
March	10.5	1.0	10.6	1.0	13.9	3.0	19.4	14.4
April	10.6	1.0	10.7	0.9	14.1	1.4	19.6	14.6
May	10.7	0.9	10.7	0.0	14.2	0.7	19.8	14.7
June	10.8	0.9	10.9	1.9	14.3	0.7	19.7	14.8
July	10.8	0.0	10.9	0.0	14.4	0.7	20.3	14.6
August	10.9	0.9	11.0	0.9	14.7	2.1	21.7	14.6
September	11.1	1.8	11.2	1.8	15.0	2.0	22.6	14.8
October	11.3	1.8	11.3	0.9	15.7	4.7	23.7	15.5
November	11.5	1.8	11.5	1.8	16.8	7.0	25.3	16.8
December	11.6	0.9	11.6	0.9	17.1	1.8	25.0	17.7
1917								
January	11.7	0.9	11.8	1.7	17.6	2.9	26.2	18.3
February	12.0	2.6	12.0	1.7	18.0	2.3	27.2	18.6
March	12.0	0.0	12.1	0.8	18.5	2.8	28.6	18.8
April	12.6	5.0	12.6	4.1	19.7	6.5	31.6	19.0
May	12.8	1.6	12.9	2.4	20.8	5.6	33.6	19.8
June	13.0	1.6	13.0	0.8	21.0	1.0	33.8	20.4
July	12.8	-1.5	12.9	-0.8	21.2	1.0	34.0	20.7
August	13.0	1.6	13.1	1.6	21.5	1.4	34.6	20.7
September	13.3	2.3	13.3	1.5	21.3	-0.9	34.3	20.1
October	13.5	1.5	13.6	2.3	21.1	-0.9	35.2	19.1
November	13.5	0.0	13.6	0.0	21.2	0.5	36.0	19.2
December	13.7	1.5	13.8	1.5	21.2	0.0	35.6	19.5
1918								
January	14.0	2.2	14.0	1.4	21.6	1.9	37.0	19.9
February	14.1	0.7	14.2	1.4	21.1	-2.3	37.1	19.0
March	14.0	-0.7	14.1	-0.7	21.8	3.3	37.3	20.2
April	14.2	1.4	14.3	1.4	22.1	1.4	36.6	20.7
May	14.5	2.1	14.5	1.4	22.1	0.0	35.4	21.0
June	14.7	1.4	14.8	2.1	22.2	0.5	35.4	21.3
July	15.1	2.7	15.2	2.7	22.7	2.3	37.0	21.5
August	15.4	2.0	15.4	1.3	23.2	2.2	38.6	21.7
September	15.7	1.9	15.8	2.6	23.7	2.2	39.6	22.1
October	16.0	1.9	16.1	1.9	23.5	-0.8	38.2	22.1
November	16.3	1.9	16.3	1.2	23.5	0.0	38.0	22.1
December	16.5	1.2	16.6	1.8	23.5	0.0	38.1	21.8
1919								
January	16.5	0.0	16.6	0.0	23.2	-1.3	38.9	21.1
February	16.2	-1.8	16.2	-2.4	22.4	-3.4	37.5	20.6
March	16.4	1.2	16.5	1.9	22.6	0.9	38.5	20.1
April	16.7	1.8	16.8	1.8	22.9	1.3	40.0	20.0
May	16.9	1.2	17.0	1.2	23.3	1.7	40.9	20.2
June	16.9	0.0	17.0	0.0	23.4	0.4	39.6	21.1
July	17.4	3.0	17.5	2.9	24.3	3.8	41.5	22.1
August	17.7	1.7	17.8	1.7	24.9	2.5	41.3	23.1
September	17.8	0.6	17.9	0.6	24.3	-2.4	38.7	23.2
October	18.1	1.7	18.2	1.7	24.4	0.4	38.5	23.5
November	18.5	2.2	18.6	2.2	24.9	2.0	40.3	23.8
December	18.9	2.2	19.0	2.2	26.0	4.4	41.8	24.7
1920								
January	19.3	2.1	19.4	2.1	27.2	4.6	43.0	26.1
February	19.5	1.0	19.6	1.0	27.1	-0.4	41.2	27.1
March	19.7	1.0	19.8	1.0	27.3	0.7	41.5	27.7
April	20.3	3.0	20.4	3.0	28.5	4.4	42.5	28.7
May	20.6	1.5	20.7	1.5	28.8	1.1	42.8	29.0
June	20.9	1.5	21.0	1.4	28.7	-0.3	42.3	29.0
July	20.8	-0.5	20.9	-0.5	28.6	-0.3	40.5	29.5
August	20.3	-2.4	20.4	-2.4	27.8	-2.8	37.8	29.7
September	20.0	-1.5	20.1	-1.5	26.8	-3.6	36.4	28.5
October	19.9	-0.5	20.0	-0.5	24.9	-7.1	32.2	26.9
November	19.8	-0.5	19.9	-0.5	23.0	-7.6	30.0	24.5
December	19.4	-2.0	19.5	-2.0	20.8	-9.6	26.4	22.7
1921								
January	19.0	-2.1	19.1	-2.1	19.6	-5.8	25.6	21.1
February	18.4	-3.2	18.5	-3.1	18.1	-7.7	23.4	19.4
March	18.3	-0.5	18.4	-0.5	17.7	-2.2	22.7	18.7
April	18.1	-1.1	18.2	-1.1	17.0	-4.0	20.9	18.4
May	17.7	-2.2	17.8	-2.2	16.6	-2.4	21.0	17.9
June	17.6	-0.6	17.7	-0.6	16.1	-3.0	20.3	17.4
July	17.7	0.6	17.8	0.6	16.1	0.0	21.8	16.9
August	17.7	0.0	17.8	0.0	16.1	0.0	22.5	16.5
September	17.5	-1.1	17.6	-1.1	16.1	0.0	22.7	16.5
October	17.5	0.0	17.6	0.0	16.2	0.6	22.7	17.0
November	17.4	-0.6	17.5	-0.6	16.2	0.0	22.1	17.3
December	17.3	-0.6	17.4	-0.6	16.0	-1.2	22.2	17.0

Table 8-1C. Consumer and Producer Price Indexes: Historical Data, 1913–1949—*Continued*

(Not seasonally adjusted.)

Year and month	Consumer price indexes, 1982–1984 =100				Producer Price Indexes for goods, 1982 = 100			
	All urban consumers (CPI-U)		Urban wage earners and clerical workers (CPI-W)		All commodities		Farm products	Industrial commodities
	Index	Percent change	Index	Percent change	Index	Percent change		
1922								
January	16.9	-2.3	17.0	-2.3	15.7	-1.9	22.2	16.7
February	16.9	0.0	17.0	0.0	16.0	1.9	24.0	16.6
March	16.7	-1.2	16.8	-1.2	16.0	0.0	23.6	16.5
April	16.7	0.0	16.8	0.0	16.1	0.6	23.4	16.6
May	16.7	0.0	16.8	0.0	16.6	3.1	23.8	17.4
June	16.7	0.0	16.8	0.0	16.6	0.0	23.4	17.4
July	16.8	0.6	16.9	0.6	17.1	3.0	24.1	18.1
August	16.6	-1.2	16.7	-1.2	17.0	-0.6	23.0	18.2
September	16.6	0.0	16.7	0.0	17.1	0.6	23.3	18.2
October	16.7	0.6	16.8	0.6	17.2	0.6	23.8	17.9
November	16.8	0.6	16.9	0.6	17.3	0.6	24.7	17.7
December	16.9	0.6	17.0	0.6	17.3	0.0	25.0	17.7
1923								
January	16.8	-0.6	16.9	-0.6	17.6	1.7	25.1	18.2
February	16.8	0.0	16.9	0.0	17.8	1.1	25.3	18.6
March	16.8	0.0	16.9	0.0	18.0	1.1	25.3	18.8
April	16.9	0.6	17.0	0.6	17.9	-0.6	24.8	18.7
May	16.9	0.0	17.0	0.0	17.5	-2.2	24.4	18.3
June	17.0	0.6	17.1	0.6	17.3	-1.1	24.2	17.9
July	17.2	1.2	17.3	1.2	17.0	-1.7	23.7	17.6
August	17.1	-0.6	17.2	-0.6	16.9	-0.6	24.2	17.4
September	17.2	0.6	17.3	0.6	17.2	1.8	25.3	17.3
October	17.3	0.6	17.4	0.6	17.1	-0.6	25.4	17.1
November	17.3	0.0	17.4	0.0	17.0	-0.6	25.7	16.9
December	17.3	0.0	17.4	0.0	16.9	-0.6	25.5	16.9
1924								
January	17.3	0.0	17.4	0.0	17.2	1.8	25.6	17.4
February	17.2	-0.6	17.3	-0.6	17.2	0.0	25.0	17.6
March	17.1	-0.6	17.2	-0.6	17.0	-1.2	24.2	17.5
April	17.0	-0.6	17.1	-0.6	16.7	-1.8	24.6	17.3
May	17.0	0.0	17.1	0.0	16.5	-1.2	24.0	17.0
June	17.0	0.0	17.1	0.0	16.4	-0.6	23.8	16.7
July	17.1	0.6	17.2	0.6	16.5	0.6	24.9	16.6
August	17.0	-0.6	17.1	-0.6	16.7	1.2	25.7	16.6
September	17.1	0.6	17.2	0.6	16.7	0.0	25.3	16.6
October	17.2	0.6	17.3	0.6	16.9	1.2	26.0	16.6
November	17.2	0.0	17.3	0.0	17.1	1.2	26.2	16.8
December	17.3	0.6	17.4	0.6	17.5	2.3	27.3	17.1
1925								
January	17.3	0.0	17.4	0.0	17.7	1.1	28.7	17.3
February	17.2	-0.6	17.3	-0.6	17.9	1.1	28.4	17.7
March	17.3	0.6	17.4	0.6	17.9	0.0	28.5	17.5
April	17.2	-0.6	17.3	-0.6	17.5	-2.2	27.1	17.2
May	17.3	0.6	17.4	0.6	17.5	0.0	27.1	17.3
June	17.5	1.2	17.6	1.1	17.7	1.1	27.6	17.5
July	17.7	1.1	17.8	1.1	18.0	1.7	28.3	17.6
August	17.7	0.0	17.8	0.0	17.9	-0.6	28.1	17.4
September	17.7	0.0	17.8	0.0	17.8	-0.6	27.7	17.4
October	17.7	0.0	17.8	0.0	17.8	0.0	27.0	17.5
November	18.0	1.7	18.1	1.7	18.0	1.1	27.3	17.6
December	17.9	-0.6	18.0	-0.6	17.8	-1.1	26.6	17.6
1926								
January	17.9	0.0	18.0	0.0	17.8	0.0	27.1	17.5
February	17.9	0.0	18.0	0.0	17.6	-1.1	26.5	17.3
March	17.8	-0.6	17.9	-0.6	17.3	-1.7	25.7	17.1
April	17.9	0.6	18.0	0.6	17.3	0.0	26.0	17.0
May	17.8	-0.6	17.9	-0.6	17.3	0.0	25.8	17.0
June	17.7	-0.6	17.8	-0.6	17.3	0.0	25.5	17.0
July	17.5	-1.1	17.6	-1.1	17.1	-1.2	24.9	16.9
August	17.4	-0.6	17.5	-0.6	17.1	0.0	24.6	16.9
September	17.5	0.6	17.6	0.6	17.2	0.6	25.1	16.9
October	17.6	0.6	17.7	0.6	17.1	-0.6	24.7	16.9
November	17.7	0.6	17.8	0.6	17.0	-0.6	23.9	16.9
December	17.7	0.0	17.8	0.0	16.9	-0.6	24.0	16.7
1927								
January	17.5	-1.1	17.6	-1.1	16.4	-3.0	24.3	16.4
February	17.4	-0.6	17.5	-0.6	16.6	1.2	24.1	16.3
March	17.3	-0.6	17.4	-0.6	16.5	-0.6	23.8	16.1
April	17.3	0.0	17.4	0.0	16.3	-1.2	23.8	15.9
May	17.4	0.6	17.5	0.6	16.2	-0.6	24.3	15.9
June	17.6	1.1	17.7	1.1	16.2	0.0	24.3	15.9
July	17.3	-1.7	17.4	-1.7	16.2	0.0	24.6	15.9
August	17.2	-0.6	17.3	-0.6	16.4	1.2	25.8	15.9
September	17.3	0.6	17.4	0.6	16.6	1.2	26.7	16.0
October	17.4	0.6	17.5	0.6	16.7	0.6	26.5	15.9
November	17.3	-0.6	17.4	-0.6	16.6	-0.6	26.3	15.8
December	17.3	0.0	17.4	0.0	16.6	0.0	26.3	15.9

Table 8-1C. Consumer and Producer Price Indexes: Historical Data, 1913–1949—*Continued*

(Not seasonally adjusted.)

Year and month	Consumer price indexes, 1982–1984 =100				Producer Price Indexes for goods, 1982 = 100			
	All urban consumers (CPI-U)		Urban wage earners and clerical workers (CPI-W)		All commodities		Farm products	Industrial commodities
	Index	Percent change	Index	Percent change	Index	Percent change		
1928								
January	17.3	0.0	17.4	0.0	16.6	0.0	26.8	15.8
February	17.1	-1.2	17.2	-1.1	16.5	-0.6	26.4	15.8
March	17.1	0.0	17.2	0.0	16.5	0.0	26.1	15.8
April	17.1	0.0	17.2	0.0	16.7	1.2	27.1	15.8
May	17.2	0.6	17.3	0.6	16.8	0.6	27.7	15.8
June	17.1	-0.6	17.2	-0.6	16.7	-0.6	26.9	15.8
July	17.1	0.0	17.2	0.0	16.8	0.6	27.4	15.8
August	17.1	0.0	17.2	0.0	16.8	0.0	27.0	15.8
September	17.3	1.2	17.4	1.2	17.0	1.2	27.5	15.8
October	17.2	-0.6	17.3	-0.6	16.7	-1.8	26.1	15.8
November	17.2	0.0	17.3	0.0	16.5	-1.2	25.7	15.8
December	17.1	-0.6	17.2	-0.6	16.5	0.0	26.2	15.8
1929								
January	17.1	0.0	17.2	0.0	16.5	0.0	26.7	15.7
February	17.1	0.0	17.2	0.0	16.4	-0.6	26.6	15.6
March	17.0	-0.6	17.1	-0.6	16.6	1.2	27.1	15.7
April	16.9	-0.6	17.0	-0.6	16.5	-0.6	26.5	15.6
May	17.0	0.6	17.1	0.6	16.3	-1.2	25.8	15.6
June	17.1	0.6	17.2	0.6	16.4	0.6	26.1	15.6
July	17.3	1.2	17.4	1.2	16.6	1.2	27.1	15.6
August	17.3	0.0	17.4	0.0	16.6	0.0	27.1	15.5
September	17.3	0.0	17.4	0.0	16.6	0.0	26.9	15.6
October	17.3	0.0	17.4	0.0	16.4	-1.2	26.2	15.6
November	17.3	0.0	17.4	0.0	16.1	-1.8	25.5	15.5
December	17.2	-0.6	17.3	-0.6	16.1	0.0	25.7	15.4
1930								
January	17.1	-0.6	17.2	-0.6	15.9	-1.2	25.5	15.2
February	17.0	-0.6	17.1	-0.6	15.7	-1.3	24.7	15.1
March	16.9	-0.6	17.0	-0.6	15.5	-1.3	23.9	15.0
April	17.0	0.6	17.1	0.6	15.5	0.0	24.2	15.0
May	16.9	-0.6	17.0	-0.6	15.3	-1.3	23.5	14.9
June	16.8	-0.6	16.9	-0.6	15.0	-2.0	22.5	14.6
July	16.6	-1.2	16.7	-1.2	14.5	-3.3	21.0	14.4
August	16.5	-0.6	16.6	-0.6	14.5	0.0	21.4	14.2
September	16.6	0.6	16.7	0.6	14.5	0.0	21.5	14.2
October	16.5	-0.6	16.6	-0.6	14.3	-1.4	20.8	14.0
November	16.4	-0.6	16.5	-0.6	14.0	-2.1	20.0	13.8
December	16.1	-1.8	16.2	-1.8	13.7	-2.1	19.0	13.6
1931								
January	15.9	-1.2	16.0	-1.2	13.5	-1.5	18.4	13.4
February	15.7	-1.3	15.7	-1.9	13.2	-2.2	17.7	13.3
March	15.6	-0.6	15.6	-0.6	13.1	-0.8	17.8	13.1
April	15.5	-0.6	15.5	-0.6	12.9	-1.5	17.7	12.9
May	15.3	-1.3	15.4	-0.6	12.6	-2.3	16.9	12.8
June	15.1	-1.3	15.2	-1.3	12.4	-1.6	16.5	12.6
July	15.1	0.0	15.2	0.0	12.4	0.0	16.4	12.6
August	15.1	0.0	15.1	-0.7	12.4	0.0	16.1	12.6
September	15.0	-0.7	15.1	0.0	12.3	-0.8	15.3	12.6
October	14.9	-0.7	15.0	-0.7	12.1	-1.6	14.8	12.4
November	14.7	-1.3	14.8	-1.3	12.1	0.0	14.8	12.5
December	14.6	-0.7	14.7	-0.7	11.8	-2.5	14.1	12.3
1932								
January	14.3	-2.1	14.4	-2.0	11.6	-1.7	13.3	12.2
February	14.1	-1.4	14.2	-1.4	11.4	-1.7	12.8	12.1
March	14.0	-0.7	14.1	-0.7	11.4	0.0	12.7	12.0
April	13.9	-0.7	14.0	-0.7	11.3	-0.9	12.4	12.0
May	13.7	-1.4	13.8	-1.4	11.1	-1.8	11.8	11.9
June	13.6	-0.7	13.7	-0.7	11.0	-0.9	11.6	11.9
July	13.6	0.0	13.7	0.0	11.1	0.9	12.1	11.8
August	13.5	-0.7	13.5	-1.5	11.2	0.9	12.4	11.9
September	13.4	-0.7	13.5	0.0	11.3	0.9	12.4	11.9
October	13.3	-0.7	13.4	-0.7	11.1	-1.8	11.8	11.9
November	13.2	-0.8	13.3	-0.7	11.0	-0.9	11.8	11.9
December	13.1	-0.8	13.2	-0.8	10.8	-1.8	11.1	11.7
1933								
January	12.9	-1.5	13.0	-1.5	10.5	-2.8	10.8	11.4
February	12.7	-1.6	12.8	-1.5	10.3	-1.9	10.3	11.2
March	12.6	-0.8	12.7	-0.8	10.4	1.0	10.8	11.2
April	12.6	0.0	12.6	-0.8	10.4	0.0	11.2	11.1
May	12.6	0.0	12.7	0.8	10.8	3.8	12.7	11.3
June	12.7	0.8	12.8	0.8	11.2	3.7	13.4	11.7
July	13.1	3.1	13.2	3.1	11.9	6.3	15.2	12.3
August	13.2	0.8	13.3	0.8	12.0	0.8	14.6	12.6
September	13.2	0.0	13.3	0.0	12.2	1.7	14.4	13.0
October	13.2	0.0	13.3	0.0	12.3	0.8	14.1	13.1
November	13.2	0.0	13.3	0.0	12.3	0.0	14.3	13.1
December	13.2	0.0	13.2	-0.8	12.2	-0.8	14.0	13.2

Table 8-1C. Consumer and Producer Price Indexes: Historical Data, 1913–1949—*Continued*

(Not seasonally adjusted.)

Year and month	Consumer price indexes, 1982–1984 =100				Producer Price Indexes for goods, 1982 = 100			
	All urban consumers (CPI-U)		Urban wage earners and clerical workers (CPI-W)		All commodities		Farm products	Industrial commodities
	Index	Percent change	Index	Percent change	Index	Percent change		
1934								
January	13.2	0.0	13.3	0.8	12.4	1.6	14.8	13.3
February	13.3	0.8	13.4	0.8	12.7	2.4	15.5	13.4
March	13.3	0.0	13.4	0.0	12.7	0.0	15.5	13.4
April	13.3	0.0	13.4	0.0	12.7	0.0	15.1	13.4
May	13.3	0.0	13.4	0.0	12.7	0.0	15.1	13.4
June	13.4	0.8	13.4	0.0	12.9	1.6	16.0	13.3
July	13.4	0.0	13.4	0.0	12.9	0.0	16.3	13.3
August	13.4	0.0	13.5	0.7	13.2	2.3	17.6	13.3
September	13.6	1.5	13.7	1.5	13.4	1.5	18.5	13.3
October	13.5	-0.7	13.6	-0.7	13.2	-1.5	17.8	13.3
November	13.5	0.0	13.5	-0.7	13.2	0.0	17.8	13.3
December	13.4	-0.7	13.5	0.0	13.3	0.8	18.2	13.3
1935								
January	13.6	1.5	13.7	1.5	13.6	2.3	19.6	13.2
February	13.7	0.7	13.8	0.7	13.7	0.7	20.0	13.2
March	13.7	0.0	13.8	0.0	13.7	0.0	19.7	13.2
April	13.8	0.7	13.9	0.7	13.8	0.7	20.3	13.1
May	13.8	0.0	13.8	-0.7	13.8	0.0	20.3	13.2
June	13.7	-0.7	13.8	0.0	13.8	0.0	19.8	13.3
July	13.7	0.0	13.7	-0.7	13.7	-0.7	19.5	13.3
August	13.7	0.0	13.7	0.0	13.9	1.5	20.0	13.3
September	13.7	0.0	13.8	0.7	13.9	0.0	20.1	13.2
October	13.7	0.0	13.8	0.0	13.9	0.0	19.7	13.3
November	13.8	0.7	13.9	0.7	13.9	0.0	19.6	13.4
December	13.8	0.0	13.9	0.0	14.0	0.7	19.8	13.4
1936								
January	13.8	0.0	13.9	0.0	13.9	-0.7	19.7	13.4
February	13.8	0.0	13.8	-0.7	13.9	0.0	20.1	13.4
March	13.7	-0.7	13.8	0.0	13.7	-1.4	19.3	13.4
April	13.7	0.0	13.8	0.0	13.7	0.0	19.4	13.4
May	13.7	0.0	13.8	0.0	13.5	-1.5	19.0	13.4
June	13.8	0.7	13.9	0.7	13.7	1.5	19.7	13.4
July	13.9	0.7	14.0	0.7	13.9	1.5	20.5	13.5
August	14.0	0.7	14.1	0.7	14.0	0.7	21.2	13.5
September	14.0	0.0	14.1	0.0	14.0	0.0	21.2	13.5
October	14.0	0.0	14.1	0.0	14.0	0.0	21.2	13.6
November	14.0	0.0	14.1	0.0	14.2	1.4	21.5	13.8
December	14.0	0.0	14.1	0.0	14.5	2.1	22.4	14.0
1937								
January	14.1	0.7	14.2	0.7	14.8	2.1	23.1	14.2
February	14.1	0.0	14.2	0.0	14.9	0.7	23.1	14.3
March	14.2	0.7	14.3	0.7	15.1	1.3	23.8	14.5
April	14.3	0.7	14.4	0.7	15.2	0.7	23.3	14.7
May	14.4	0.7	14.4	0.0	15.1	-0.7	22.7	14.7
June	14.4	0.0	14.5	0.7	15.0	-0.7	22.3	14.6
July	14.5	0.7	14.5	0.0	15.2	1.3	22.6	14.7
August	14.5	0.0	14.6	0.7	15.1	-0.7	21.8	14.6
September	14.6	0.7	14.7	0.7	15.1	0.0	21.7	14.6
October	14.6	0.0	14.6	-0.7	14.7	-2.6	20.3	14.5
November	14.5	-0.7	14.5	-0.7	14.4	-2.0	19.1	14.3
December	14.4	-0.7	14.5	0.0	14.1	-2.1	18.4	14.2
1938								
January	14.2	-1.4	14.3	-1.4	14.0	-0.7	18.1	14.2
February	14.1	-0.7	14.2	-0.7	13.8	-1.4	17.6	14.1
March	14.1	0.0	14.2	0.0	13.7	-0.7	17.7	14.1
April	14.2	0.7	14.2	0.0	13.5	-1.5	17.2	14.0
May	14.1	-0.7	14.2	0.0	13.5	0.0	17.0	13.9
June	14.1	0.0	14.2	0.0	13.5	0.0	17.3	13.8
July	14.1	0.0	14.2	0.0	13.6	0.7	17.5	13.9
August	14.1	0.0	14.2	0.0	13.4	-1.5	17.0	13.9
September	14.1	0.0	14.2	0.0	13.5	0.7	17.2	13.9
October	14.0	-0.7	14.1	-0.7	13.4	-0.7	16.8	13.8
November	14.0	0.0	14.1	0.0	13.4	0.0	17.1	13.7
December	14.0	0.0	14.1	0.0	13.3	-0.7	17.0	13.6
1939								
January	14.0	0.0	14.0	-0.7	13.3	0.0	17.0	13.6
February	13.9	-0.7	14.0	0.0	13.3	0.0	16.9	13.6
March	13.9	0.0	13.9	-0.7	13.2	-0.8	16.6	13.7
April	13.8	-0.7	13.9	0.0	13.1	-0.8	16.1	13.7
May	13.8	0.0	13.9	0.0	13.1	0.0	16.1	13.7
June	13.8	0.0	13.9	0.0	13.0	-0.8	15.7	13.6
July	13.8	0.0	13.9	0.0	13.0	0.0	15.8	13.6
August	13.8	0.0	13.9	0.0	12.9	-0.8	15.4	13.6
September	14.1	2.2	14.2	2.2	13.6	5.4	17.3	14.0
October	14.0	-0.7	14.1	-0.7	13.7	0.7	16.9	14.2
November	14.0	0.0	14.1	0.0	13.6	-0.7	17.0	14.3
December	14.0	0.0	14.0	-0.7	13.7	0.7	17.1	14.3

Table 8-1C. Consumer and Producer Price Indexes: Historical Data, 1913–1949—*Continued*

(Not seasonally adjusted.)

Year and month	Consumer price indexes, 1982–1984 =100				Producer Price Indexes for goods, 1982 = 100			
	All urban consumers (CPI-U)		Urban wage earners and clerical workers (CPI-W)		All commodities		Farm products	Industrial commodities
	Index	Percent change	Index	Percent change	Index	Percent change		
1940								
January	13.9	-0.7	14.0	0.0	13.7	0.0	17.4	14.3
February	14.0	0.7	14.1	0.7	13.6	-0.7	17.3	14.2
March	14.0	0.0	14.1	0.0	13.5	-0.7	17.1	14.1
April	14.0	0.0	14.1	0.0	13.5	0.0	17.5	14.0
May	14.0	0.0	14.1	0.0	13.5	0.0	17.1	14.0
June	14.1	0.7	14.1	0.0	13.4	-0.7	16.7	14.0
July	14.0	-0.7	14.1	0.0	13.4	0.0	16.8	14.0
August	14.0	0.0	14.1	0.0	13.4	0.0	16.5	14.0
September	14.0	0.0	14.1	0.0	13.4	0.0	16.7	14.0
October	14.0	0.0	14.1	0.0	13.6	1.5	16.8	14.2
November	14.0	0.0	14.1	0.0	13.7	0.7	17.2	14.3
December	14.1	0.7	14.2	0.7	13.8	0.7	17.6	14.3
1941								
January	14.1	0.0	14.2	0.0	13.9	0.7	18.1	14.3
February	14.1	0.0	14.2	0.0	13.9	0.0	17.7	14.3
March	14.2	0.7	14.2	0.0	14.0	0.7	18.1	14.4
April	14.3	0.7	14.4	1.4	14.4	2.9	18.8	14.6
May	14.4	0.7	14.5	0.7	14.6	1.4	19.3	14.9
June	14.7	2.1	14.7	1.4	15.0	2.7	20.7	15.1
July	14.7	0.0	14.8	0.7	15.3	2.0	21.7	15.2
August	14.9	1.4	14.9	0.7	15.6	2.0	22.1	15.5
September	15.1	1.3	15.2	2.0	15.8	1.3	23.0	15.6
October	15.3	1.3	15.4	1.3	15.9	0.6	22.7	15.9
November	15.4	0.7	15.5	0.6	15.9	0.0	22.9	15.9
December	15.5	0.6	15.5	0.0	16.2	1.9	23.9	15.9
1942								
January	15.7	1.3	15.7	1.3	16.5	1.9	25.5	16.1
February	15.8	0.6	15.9	1.3	16.7	1.2	25.6	16.1
March	16.0	1.3	16.1	1.3	16.8	0.6	26.0	16.2
April	16.1	0.6	16.2	0.6	17.0	1.2	26.4	16.2
May	16.3	1.2	16.3	0.6	17.0	0.0	26.3	16.3
June	16.3	0.0	16.4	0.6	17.0	0.0	26.3	16.3
July	16.4	0.6	16.5	0.6	17.0	0.0	26.6	16.3
August	16.5	0.6	16.6	0.6	17.1	0.6	26.8	16.2
September	16.5	0.0	16.6	0.0	17.2	0.6	27.2	16.2
October	16.7	1.2	16.8	1.2	17.2	0.0	27.5	16.2
November	16.8	0.6	16.9	0.6	17.3	0.6	27.9	16.3
December	16.9	0.6	17.0	0.6	17.4	0.6	28.7	16.3
1943								
January	16.9	0.0	17.0	0.0	17.5	0.6	29.5	16.4
February	16.9	0.0	17.0	0.0	17.7	1.1	30.0	16.4
March	17.2	1.8	17.3	1.8	17.8	0.6	31.0	16.4
April	17.4	1.2	17.5	1.2	17.9	0.6	31.2	16.5
May	17.5	0.6	17.6	0.6	17.9	0.0	31.7	16.5
June	17.5	0.0	17.6	0.0	17.9	0.0	31.9	16.5
July	17.4	-0.6	17.5	-0.6	17.8	-0.6	31.5	16.5
August	17.3	-0.6	17.4	-0.6	17.8	0.0	31.2	16.5
September	17.4	0.6	17.5	0.6	17.8	0.0	31.0	16.5
October	17.4	0.0	17.5	0.0	17.8	0.0	30.9	16.5
November	17.4	0.0	17.5	0.0	17.7	-0.6	30.6	16.6
December	17.4	0.0	17.5	0.0	17.8	0.6	30.7	16.6
1944								
January	17.4	0.0	17.5	0.0	17.8	0.0	30.7	16.6
February	17.4	0.0	17.5	0.0	17.8	0.0	30.9	16.7
March	17.4	0.0	17.5	0.0	17.9	0.6	31.2	16.7
April	17.5	0.6	17.6	0.6	17.9	0.0	31.1	16.7
May	17.5	0.0	17.6	0.0	17.9	0.0	31.0	16.7
June	17.6	0.6	17.7	0.6	18.0	0.6	31.5	16.7
July	17.7	0.6	17.8	0.6	17.9	-0.6	31.3	16.7
August	17.7	0.0	17.8	0.0	17.9	0.0	30.9	16.8
September	17.7	0.0	17.8	0.0	17.9	0.0	31.0	16.8
October	17.7	0.0	17.8	0.0	17.9	0.0	31.2	16.8
November	17.7	0.0	17.8	0.0	18.0	0.6	31.4	16.8
December	17.8	0.6	17.9	0.6	18.0	0.0	31.6	16.8
1945								
January	17.8	0.0	17.9	0.0	18.1	0.6	31.9	16.8
February	17.8	0.0	17.9	0.0	18.1	0.0	32.1	16.9
March	17.8	0.0	17.9	0.0	18.1	0.0	32.1	16.9
April	17.8	0.0	17.9	0.0	18.2	0.6	32.5	16.9
May	17.9	0.6	18.0	0.6	18.3	0.5	32.8	16.9
June	18.1	1.1	18.2	1.1	18.3	0.0	32.9	16.9
July	18.1	0.0	18.2	0.0	18.3	0.0	32.5	17.0
August	18.1	0.0	18.2	0.0	18.2	-0.5	32.0	17.0
September	18.1	0.0	18.2	0.0	18.1	-0.5	31.4	17.0
October	18.1	0.0	18.2	0.0	18.2	0.6	32.1	17.0
November	18.1	0.0	18.2	0.0	18.4	1.1	33.1	17.0
December	18.2	0.6	18.3	0.5	18.4	0.0	33.2	17.1

Table 8-1C. Consumer and Producer Price Indexes: Historical Data, 1913–1949—*Continued*

(Not seasonally adjusted.)

| Year and month | Consumer price indexes, 1982–1984 =100 | | | | Producer Price Indexes for goods, 1982 = 100 | | | |
| | All urban consumers (CPI-U) | | Urban wage earners and clerical workers (CPI-W) | | All commodities | | Farm products | Industrial commodities |
	Index	Percent change	Index	Percent change	Index	Percent change		
1946								
January	18.2	0.0	18.3	0.0	18.4	0.0	32.7	17.1
February	18.1	-0.5	18.2	-0.5	18.5	0.5	33.0	17.2
March	18.3	1.1	18.4	1.1	18.8	1.6	33.6	17.4
April	18.4	0.5	18.5	0.5	19.0	1.1	34.1	17.5
May	18.5	0.5	18.6	0.5	19.1	0.5	34.7	17.7
June	18.7	1.1	18.8	1.1	19.4	1.6	35.4	18.0
July	19.8	5.9	19.9	5.9	21.5	10.8	39.6	18.6
August	20.2	2.0	20.3	2.0	22.2	3.3	40.6	19.0
September	20.4	1.0	20.5	1.0	21.4	-3.6	39.0	19.1
October	20.8	2.0	20.9	2.0	23.1	7.9	41.7	19.7
November	21.3	2.4	21.5	2.9	24.1	4.3	42.8	20.6
December	21.5	0.9	21.6	0.5	24.3	0.8	42.4	21.2
1947								
January	21.5	0.0	21.6	0.0	24.5	0.8	41.6	21.8
February	21.5	0.0	21.6	0.0	24.7	0.8	42.6	22.0
March	21.9	1.9	22.1	2.3	25.3	2.4	45.5	22.3
April	21.9	0.0	22.1	0.0	25.1	-0.8	44.0	22.4
May	21.9	0.0	22.0	-0.5	25.0	-0.4	43.6	22.3
June	22.0	0.5	22.2	0.9	25.0	0.0	43.8	22.4
July	22.2	0.9	22.4	0.9	25.3	1.2	44.3	22.5
August	22.5	1.4	22.6	0.9	25.6	1.2	44.8	22.8
September	23.0	2.2	23.1	2.2	26.1	2.0	46.6	23.1
October	23.0	0.0	23.1	0.0	26.4	1.1	47.4	23.3
November	23.1	0.4	23.3	0.9	26.7	1.1	47.7	23.6
December	23.4	1.3	23.6	1.3	27.2	1.9	50.1	23.9
1948								
January	23.7	1.3	23.8	0.8	27.7	1.8	51.2	24.3
February	23.5	-0.8	23.6	-0.8	27.2	-1.8	47.7	24.1
March	23.4	-0.4	23.6	0.0	27.2	0.0	47.6	24.1
April	23.8	1.7	23.9	1.3	27.4	0.7	48.3	24.3
May	23.9	0.4	24.1	0.8	27.5	0.4	49.4	24.3
June	24.1	0.8	24.2	0.4	27.7	0.7	50.4	24.4
July	24.4	1.2	24.5	1.2	28.0	1.1	50.2	24.6
August	24.5	0.4	24.6	0.4	28.2	0.7	49.6	24.9
September	24.5	0.0	24.6	0.0	28.1	-0.4	48.8	25.0
October	24.4	-0.4	24.5	-0.4	27.8	-1.1	46.9	25.0
November	24.2	-0.8	24.4	-0.4	27.8	0.0	46.3	25.1
December	24.1	-0.4	24.2	-0.8	27.6	-0.7	45.2	25.1
1949								
January	24.0	-0.4	24.2	0.0	27.3	-1.1	43.8	24.9
February	23.8	-0.8	23.9	-1.2	26.8	-1.8	42.0	24.7
March	23.8	0.0	24.0	0.4	26.8	0.0	42.7	24.6
April	23.9	0.4	24.0	0.0	26.5	-1.1	42.7	24.3
May	23.8	-0.4	24.0	0.0	26.3	-0.8	42.7	24.0
June	23.9	0.4	24.0	0.0	26.0	-1.1	41.8	23.8
July	23.7	-0.8	23.8	-0.8	26.0	0.0	41.7	23.7
August	23.8	0.4	23.9	0.4	26.0	0.0	41.7	23.8
September	23.9	0.4	24.0	0.4	26.1	0.4	41.8	23.8
October	23.7	-0.8	23.9	-0.4	26.0	-0.4	41.0	23.8
November	23.8	0.4	23.9	0.0	26.0	0.0	40.9	23.8
December	23.6	-0.8	23.8	-0.4	25.9	-0.4	40.3	23.8

Figure 8-2: Consumer Prices: All Items, Medical Care, and Apparel, 1970–2014
(ratio scale)

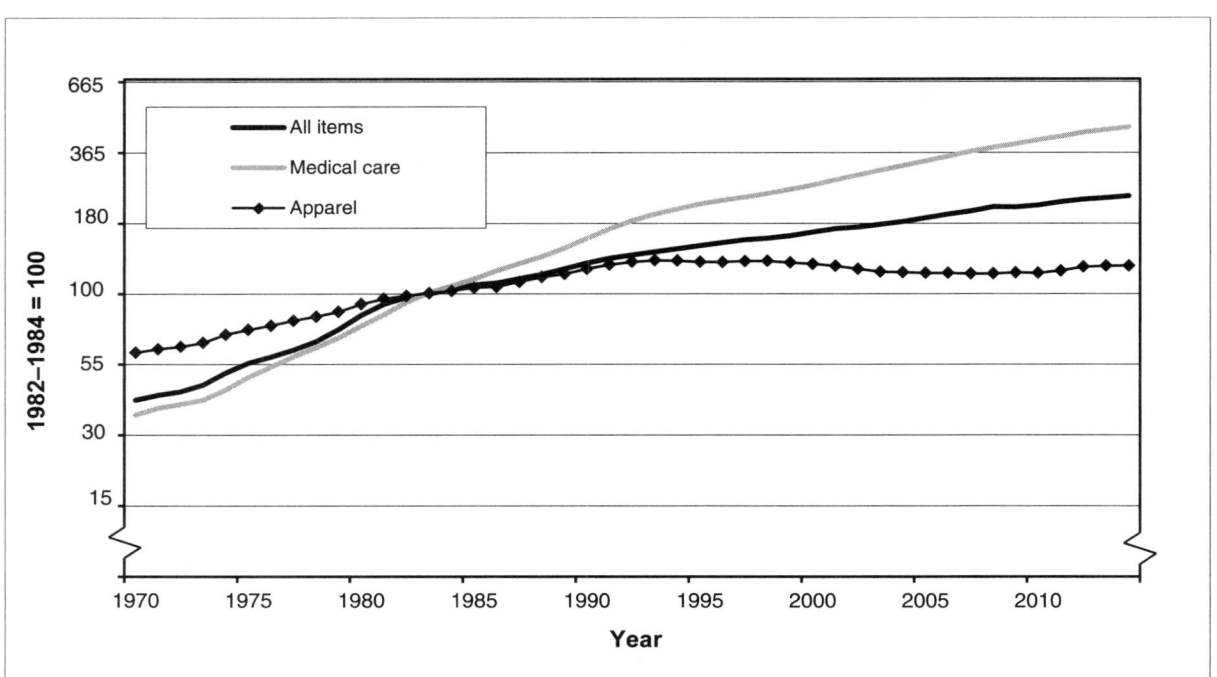

- Figure 8-2 charts two components of the Consumer Price Index for All Urban Consumers (CPI-U) along with the all-items total. Since all three indexes have the base years 1982–1984, they converge around 100 in those years. However, over the entire postwar period, the trends of the two components are very different. (Table 8-2)

- Apparel has been one of the areas most subject to international competition, and the apparel index shows far less growth than the overall average of prices.

- Medical care, on the other hand, has little price competition from producers in other countries. It is often paid for by third-party insurers, both government and private, rather than directly by consumers. Furthermore, it is characterized by trend growth in demand, due to rising income and expectations and to technological progress. All of these economic factors cause medical care prices to rise faster than the general price level.

- Medical care has arguably been overstated in the CPI due to the difficulties of making quality adjustments. Quality adjustments in the indexes have been much improved in recent years, although such improvements are not retroactively introduced into the official CPIs. But even since 1997, when a major improvement was introduced into the hospital cost component of the CPI, measured medical care prices have increased at a 3.8 percent annual rate, while the total CPI rose at a 2.4 percent average annual rate. (Table 8-2)

Table 8-2. Consumer Price Indexes and Purchasing Power of the Dollar

(1982–1984 = 100, seasonally adjusted, except as noted.)

Year and month	CPI-U, All items: Not seasonally adjusted	CPI-U, All items: Seasonally adjusted — Index	CPI-U, All items: Seasonally adjusted — Percent change from previous period	CPI-U, Food and beverages: Total	Total food	Food at home: Total	Food at home: Cereals and bakery products	Food at home: Meats, poultry, fish, and eggs	Food at home: Dairy and related products[1]	Food at home: Fruits and vegetables	Food at home: Non-alcoholic beverages	Food at home: Other food at home	Food away from home[1]	Alcoholic beverages
1970	38.8	38.8	5.7	40.1	39.2	39.9	37.1	44.6	44.7	37.8	27.1	32.9	37.5	52.1
1971	40.5	40.5	4.4	41.4	40.4	40.9	38.8	44.1	46.1	39.7	28.1	34.3	39.4	54.2
1972	41.8	41.8	3.2	43.1	42.1	42.7	39.0	48.0	46.8	41.6	28.0	34.6	41.0	55.4
1973	44.4	44.4	6.2	48.8	48.2	49.7	43.5	60.9	51.2	47.4	30.1	36.7	44.2	56.8
1974	49.3	49.3	11.0	55.5	55.1	57.1	56.5	62.2	60.7	55.2	35.9	47.8	49.8	61.1
1975	53.8	53.8	9.1	60.2	59.8	61.8	62.9	67.0	62.6	56.9	41.3	55.4	54.5	65.9
1976	56.9	56.9	5.8	62.1	61.6	63.1	61.5	68.0	67.7	58.4	49.4	56.4	58.2	68.1
1977	60.6	60.6	6.5	65.8	65.5	66.8	62.5	67.4	69.5	63.8	74.4	68.4	62.6	70.0
1978	65.2	65.2	7.6	72.2	72.0	73.8	68.1	77.6	74.2	70.9	78.7	73.6	68.3	74.1
1979	72.6	72.6	11.3	79.9	79.9	81.8	74.9	89.0	82.8	76.6	82.6	79.0	75.9	79.9
1980	82.4	82.4	13.5	86.7	86.8	88.4	83.9	92.0	90.9	82.1	91.4	88.4	83.4	86.4
1981	90.9	90.9	10.3	93.5	93.6	94.8	92.3	96.0	97.4	92.0	95.3	94.9	90.9	92.5
1982	96.5	96.5	6.2	97.3	97.4	98.1	96.5	96.5	99.6	97.4	94.9	95.3	95.8	96.7
1983	99.6	99.6	3.2	99.5	99.4	99.1	99.6	96.5	98.8	97.0	97.9	97.3	100.0	100.4
1984	103.9	103.9	4.3	103.2	103.2	102.8	103.9	101.3	101.3	105.7	102.3	103.1	104.2	103.0
1985	107.6	107.6	3.6	105.6	105.6	104.3	107.9	100.1	103.2	108.4	104.3	105.7	108.3	106.4
1986	109.6	109.6	1.9	109.1	109.0	107.3	110.9	104.5	103.3	109.4	110.4	109.4	112.5	111.1
1987	113.6	113.6	3.6	113.5	113.5	111.9	114.8	110.5	105.9	119.1	107.5	110.5	117.0	114.1
1988	118.3	118.3	4.1	118.2	118.2	116.6	122.1	114.3	108.4	128.1	107.5	113.1	121.8	118.6
1989	124.0	124.0	4.8	124.9	125.1	124.2	132.4	121.3	115.6	138.0	111.3	119.1	127.4	123.5
1990	130.7	130.7	5.4	132.1	132.4	132.3	140.0	130.0	126.5	149.0	113.5	123.4	133.4	129.3
1991	136.2	136.2	4.2	136.8	136.3	135.8	145.8	132.6	125.1	155.8	114.1	127.3	137.9	142.8
1992	140.3	140.3	3.0	138.7	137.9	136.8	151.5	130.9	128.5	155.4	114.3	128.8	140.7	147.3
1993	144.5	144.5	3.0	141.6	140.9	140.1	156.6	135.5	129.4	159.0	114.6	130.5	143.2	149.6
1994	148.2	148.2	2.6	144.9	144.3	144.1	163.0	137.2	131.7	165.0	123.2	135.6	145.7	151.5
1995	152.4	152.4	2.8	148.9	148.4	148.8	167.5	138.8	132.8	177.7	131.7	140.8	149.0	153.9
1996	156.9	156.9	3.0	153.7	153.3	154.3	174.0	144.8	142.1	183.9	128.6	142.9	152.7	158.5
1997	160.5	160.5	2.3	157.7	157.3	158.1	177.6	148.5	145.5	187.5	133.4	147.3	157.0	162.8
1998	163.0	163.0	1.6	161.1	160.7	161.1	181.1	147.3	150.8	198.2	133.0	150.8	161.1	165.7
1999	166.6	166.6	2.2	164.6	164.1	164.2	185.0	147.9	159.6	203.1	134.3	153.5	165.1	169.7
2000	172.2	172.2	3.4	168.4	167.8	167.9	188.3	154.5	160.7	204.6	137.8	155.6	169.0	174.7
2001	177.1	177.1	2.8	173.6	173.1	173.4	193.8	161.3	167.1	212.2	139.2	159.6	173.9	179.3
2002	179.9	179.9	1.6	176.8	176.2	175.6	198.0	162.1	168.1	220.9	139.8	160.8	178.3	183.6
2003	184.0	184.0	2.3	180.5	180.0	179.4	202.8	169.3	167.9	225.9	139.8	162.6	182.1	187.2
2004	188.9	188.9	2.7	186.6	186.2	186.2	206.0	181.7	180.2	232.7	140.4	164.9	187.5	192.1
2005	195.3	195.3	3.4	191.2	190.7	189.8	209.0	184.7	182.4	241.4	144.4	167.0	193.4	195.9
2006	201.6	201.6	3.2	195.7	195.2	193.1	212.8	186.6	181.4	252.9	147.4	169.6	199.4	200.7
2007	207.3	207.3	2.8	203.3	202.9	201.2	222.1	195.6	194.8	262.6	153.4	173.3	206.7	207.0
2008	215.3	215.3	3.8	214.2	214.1	214.1	244.9	204.7	210.4	278.9	160.0	184.2	215.8	214.5
2009	214.5	214.5	-0.4	218.2	218.0	215.1	252.6	203.8	197.0	272.9	163.0	191.2	223.3	220.8
2010	218.1	218.1	1.6	220.0	219.6	215.8	250.4	207.7	199.2	273.5	161.6	191.1	226.1	223.3
2011	224.9	224.9	3.2	227.9	227.8	226.2	260.3	223.2	212.7	284.7	166.8	197.4	231.4	226.7
2012	229.6	229.6	2.1	233.7	233.8	231.8	267.7	231.0	217.3	282.8	168.6	204.8	238.0	230.8
2013	233.0	233.0	1.5	237.0	237.0	233.9	270.4	236.0	217.6	290.0	166.9	204.8	243.1	234.6
2014	236.7	236.7	1.6	242.4	242.7	239.5	271.1	253.0	225.3	294.4	166.0	206.2	249.0	237.3
2013														
January	230.3	231.4	0.1	235.8	236.0	233.6	269.1	233.7	220.3	289.1	168.2	205.7	240.7	232.4
February	232.2	232.8	0.6	236.0	236.1	233.8	269.2	234.8	219.5	291.4	168.3	204.4	240.9	233.3
March	232.8	232.2	-0.2	236.2	236.3	233.7	269.7	234.8	218.1	290.6	168.1	205.1	241.4	233.7
April	232.5	231.7	-0.2	236.7	236.7	233.9	271.2	235.2	218.1	287.3	168.4	205.9	242.2	234.2
May	232.9	232.0	0.1	236.3	236.4	233.0	270.3	234.8	216.3	287.3	166.9	204.9	242.6	234.2
June	233.5	232.6	0.3	236.8	236.8	233.6	271.5	235.7	216.1	287.3	167.2	205.4	243.0	234.5
July	233.6	233.0	0.2	237.0	237.1	233.7	270.5	236.2	215.9	290.3	166.3	205.4	243.4	235.0
August	233.9	233.4	0.2	237.4	237.4	234.0	270.9	237.5	216.8	294.2	166.3	203.4	243.8	235.3
September	234.1	233.8	0.2	237.5	237.6	234.1	271.2	238.1	217.0	292.2	166.0	204.1	244.0	235.3
October	233.5	233.9	0.1	237.8	237.8	234.4	270.5	239.7	217.6	292.4	166.0	204.1	244.4	235.6
November	233.1	234.0	0.1	238.0	238.1	234.4	270.6	239.3	217.5	291.2	165.5	204.5	245.0	235.8
December	233.0	234.7	0.3	238.1	238.2	234.3	270.2	240.1	218.4	287.6	165.9	204.7	245.3	236.2
2014														
January	233.9	235.1	0.2	238.4	238.5	234.7	271.1	241.1	219.4	287.7	165.6	204.9	245.5	236.2
February	234.8	235.4	0.1	239.3	239.4	235.8	270.5	244.1	220.9	290.2	165.3	205.2	246.2	235.7
March	236.3	235.8	0.2	240.2	240.4	236.9	270.9	246.3	223.1	292.3	165.1	205.2	246.9	236.2
April	237.1	236.2	0.2	241.0	241.2	237.9	270.8	249.9	224.2	294.2	165.0	204.9	247.5	236.4
May	237.9	237.0	0.3	241.9	242.2	239.2	270.7	252.8	225.5	296.3	165.4	205.3	248.0	236.7
June	238.3	237.3	0.2	242.1	242.4	239.2	270.7	253.2	224.5	295.8	165.6	205.6	248.4	236.7
July	238.3	237.6	0.1	242.8	243.2	240.0	271.2	254.0	225.1	296.2	166.2	206.8	249.2	236.4
August	237.9	237.4	-0.1	243.5	243.8	240.8	271.6	258.3	226.4	294.6	166.1	206.6	249.8	237.9
September	238.0	237.6	0.1	244.3	244.7	241.6	271.0	260.7	227.6	294.7	166.4	207.5	250.6	238.1
October	237.4	237.8	0.1	244.8	245.1	242.1	271.5	260.0	228.8	298.0	166.9	206.9	251.1	238.4
November	236.2	237.1	-0.3	245.3	245.6	242.3	271.2	261.6	228.4	296.0	166.9	206.9	252.0	239.9
December	234.8	236.3	-0.3	245.9	246.2	242.9	271.6	262.0	229.9	296.9	167.0	207.8	252.6	239.2

[1]Not seasonally adjusted.

Table 8-2. Consumer Price Indexes and Purchasing Power of the Dollar—*Continued*

(1982–1984 = 100, seasonally adjusted, except as noted.)

Year and month	CPI-U, Housing												
	Total	Shelter						Fuels and utilities				Household furnishings and operations	
		Total	Rent of shelter [2]	Rent of primary residence	Lodging away from home [3]	Owners' equivalent rent of primary residence [2]	Tenants' and household insurance [1,3]	Total	Fuels		Water and sewer and trash collection services [3]	Total	Household operations [1,3]
									Fuel oil and other fuels	Energy services			
1970	36.4	35.5	...	46.5	...	...	...	29.1	17.0	25.4	...	46.8	...
1971	38.0	37.0	...	48.7	...	...	...	31.1	18.2	27.1	...	48.6	...
1972	39.4	38.7	...	50.4	...	...	...	32.5	18.3	28.5	...	49.7	...
1973	41.2	40.5	...	52.5	...	...	...	34.3	21.1	29.9	...	51.1	...
1974	45.8	44.4	...	55.2	...	...	...	40.7	33.2	34.5	...	56.8	...
1975	50.7	48.8	...	58.0	...	...	...	45.4	36.4	40.1	...	63.4	...
1976	53.8	51.5	...	61.1	...	...	...	49.4	38.8	44.7	...	67.3	...
1977	57.4	54.9	...	64.8	...	...	...	54.7	43.9	50.5	...	70.4	...
1978	62.4	60.5	...	69.3	...	...	...	58.5	46.2	55.0	...	74.7	...
1979	70.1	68.9	...	74.3	...	...	...	64.8	62.4	61.0	...	79.9	...
1980	81.1	81.0	...	80.9	...	...	...	75.4	86.1	71.4	...	86.3	...
1981	90.4	90.5	...	87.9	...	...	...	86.4	104.6	81.9	...	93.0	...
1982	96.9	96.9	...	94.6	...	...	...	94.9	103.4	93.2	...	98.0	...
1983	99.5	99.1	102.7	100.1	...	102.5	...	100.2	97.2	101.5	...	100.2	...
1984	103.6	104.0	107.7	105.3	...	107.3	...	104.8	99.4	105.4	...	101.9	...
1985	107.7	109.8	113.9	111.8	...	113.2	...	106.5	95.9	107.1	...	103.8	...
1986	110.9	115.8	120.2	118.3	...	119.4	...	104.1	77.6	105.7	...	105.2	...
1987	114.2	121.3	125.9	123.1	...	124.8	...	103.0	77.9	103.8	...	107.1	...
1988	118.5	127.1	132.0	127.8	...	131.1	...	104.4	78.1	104.6	...	109.4	...
1989	123.0	132.8	138.0	132.8	...	137.4	...	107.8	81.7	107.5	...	111.2	...
1990	128.5	140.0	145.5	138.4	...	144.8	...	111.6	99.3	109.3	...	113.3	...
1991	133.6	146.3	152.1	143.3	...	150.4	...	115.3	94.6	112.6	...	116.0	...
1992	137.5	151.2	157.3	146.9	...	155.5	...	117.8	90.7	114.8	...	118.0	...
1993	141.2	155.7	162.0	150.3	...	160.5	...	121.3	90.3	118.5	...	119.3	...
1994	144.8	160.5	167.0	154.0	...	165.8	...	122.8	88.8	119.2	...	121.0	...
1995	148.5	165.7	172.4	157.8	...	171.3	...	123.7	88.1	119.2	...	123.0	...
1996	152.8	171.0	178.0	162.0	...	176.8	...	127.5	99.2	122.1	...	124.7	...
1997	156.8	176.3	183.4	166.7	...	181.9	...	130.8	99.8	125.1	...	125.4	...
1998	160.4	182.1	189.6	172.1	109.0	187.8	99.8	128.5	90.0	121.2	101.6	126.6	101.5
1999	163.9	187.3	195.0	177.5	112.3	192.9	101.3	128.8	91.4	120.9	104.0	126.7	104.5
2000	169.6	193.4	201.3	183.9	117.5	198.7	103.7	137.9	129.7	128.0	106.5	128.2	110.5
2001	176.4	200.6	208.9	192.1	118.6	206.3	106.2	150.2	129.3	142.4	109.6	129.1	115.6
2002	180.3	208.1	216.7	199.7	118.3	214.7	108.7	143.6	115.5	134.4	113.0	128.3	119.0
2003	184.8	213.1	221.9	205.5	119.3	219.9	114.8	154.5	139.5	145.0	117.2	126.1	121.8
2004	189.5	218.8	227.9	211.0	125.9	224.9	116.2	161.9	160.5	150.6	124.0	125.5	125.0
2005	195.7	224.4	233.7	217.3	130.3	230.2	117.6	179.0	208.6	166.5	130.3	126.1	130.3
2006	203.2	232.1	241.9	225.1	136.0	238.2	116.5	194.7	234.9	182.1	136.8	127.0	136.6
2007	209.6	240.6	250.8	234.7	142.8	246.2	117.0	200.6	251.5	186.3	143.7	126.9	140.6
2008	216.3	246.7	257.2	243.3	143.7	252.4	118.8	220.0	334.4	202.2	152.1	127.8	147.5
2009	217.1	249.4	259.9	248.8	134.2	256.6	121.5	210.7	239.8	193.6	161.1	128.7	150.3
2010	216.3	248.4	258.8	249.4	133.7	256.6	125.7	214.2	275.1	192.9	170.9	125.5	150.3
2011	219.1	251.6	262.2	253.6	137.4	259.6	127.4	220.4	337.1	194.4	179.6	124.9	151.8
2012	222.7	257.1	267.8	260.4	140.5	264.8	131.3	219.0	335.9	189.7	189.3	125.7	155.2
2013	227.4	263.1	274.0	267.7	142.4	270.7	135.4	225.2	332.0	194.8	197.6	124.8	157.6
2014	233.2	270.5	281.8	276.2	148.5	277.8	141.9	234.6	338.9	203.4	204.9	123.1	161.6
2013													
January	225.1	260.2	271.1	264.2	142.0	267.8	133.9	222.0	338.1	191.6	194.5	125.4	156.4
February	225.6	260.7	271.7	264.9	142.2	268.3	135.5	223.1	346.1	192.4	195.0	125.4	156.7
March	225.8	261.2	272.1	265.6	142.1	268.7	135.4	222.4	341.6	191.6	195.7	125.1	157.0
April	226.3	261.6	272.6	266.0	142.6	269.2	134.0	223.9	330.5	193.7	196.3	125.0	156.4
May	226.9	262.2	273.2	266.8	143.2	269.8	134.5	225.5	321.6	196.0	196.9	125.1	156.5
June	227.3	262.8	273.7	267.4	143.3	270.4	134.9	225.6	318.8	195.9	197.5	125.1	157.3
July	227.5	263.2	274.1	267.9	143.7	270.8	135.8	225.5	320.8	195.6	198.1	124.7	157.5
August	227.9	263.9	274.8	268.8	143.0	271.4	135.1	225.3	325.6	195.1	198.2	124.6	158.2
September	228.4	264.4	275.4	269.4	142.7	272.0	135.5	226.7	330.7	196.2	198.9	124.6	158.5
October	228.7	264.7	275.9	269.9	139.0	272.6	135.9	227.3	331.0	196.7	199.7	124.3	158.9
November	229.2	265.5	276.6	270.4	143.0	273.2	136.5	227.6	334.2	196.8	200.2	124.0	159.1
December	229.7	266.2	277.4	271.2	142.7	274.0	137.3	228.0	345.3	196.6	200.7	123.8	159.2
2014													
January	230.6	266.9	278.0	271.9	144.3	274.5	138.2	232.0	368.7	200.2	201.1	123.8	159.2
February	231.2	267.5	278.7	272.4	144.9	275.0	138.8	234.3	394.4	201.7	201.6	123.4	158.5
March	232.1	268.2	279.4	273.3	146.5	275.7	140.2	237.4	365.9	206.4	202.3	123.3	158.7
April	231.9	268.8	280.1	274.1	146.9	276.3	140.1	233.0	346.1	201.7	203.0	123.3	160.2
May	232.7	269.7	280.8	275.0	149.7	276.9	141.8	235.0	339.1	204.4	203.4	123.1	160.6
June	233.0	270.2	281.4	275.8	147.6	277.5	141.6	234.9	332.3	204.3	204.0	123.2	161.7
July	233.6	270.9	282.1	276.7	148.2	278.2	142.8	235.5	332.2	204.7	205.0	123.1	162.3
August	233.9	271.5	282.7	277.4	149.2	278.7	143.2	235.1	330.4	204.1	205.6	122.9	162.9
September	234.3	272.2	283.5	278.2	149.9	279.4	143.6	234.5	327.2	203.3	206.5	122.8	162.8
October	234.8	272.8	284.2	278.9	151.0	280.0	143.5	234.4	319.8	203.2	207.6	123.3	164.2
November	235.1	273.5	284.8	279.8	151.4	280.6	143.7	234.0	313.3	202.6	208.7	122.9	164.1
December	235.5	274.0	285.4	280.4	152.1	281.1	145.0	235.1	297.8	204.2	209.8	122.6	163.7

[1]Not seasonally adjusted.
[2]December 1982 = 100.
[3]December 1997 = 100.
. . . = Not available.

Table 8-2. Consumer Price Indexes and Purchasing Power of the Dollar—*Continued*

(1982–1984 = 100, seasonally adjusted, except as noted.)

Year and month	CPI-U, Apparel					CPI-U, Transportation								
							Private transportation						Motor vehicle parts and equipment	Motor vehicle mainte-nance and repair [1]
								New and used motor vehicles			Motor fuel			
	Total	Men's and boys' apparel	Women's and girls' apparel	Infants' and toddlers' apparel	Footwear	Total	Total	Total [3]	New vehicles	Used cars and trucks	Total	Gasoline (all types)		
1970	59.2	62.2	71.8	39.2	56.8	37.5	37.5	. . .	53.1	31.2	27.9	27.9	. . .	36.6
1971	61.1	63.9	74.4	40.0	58.6	39.5	39.4	. . .	55.3	33.0	28.1	28.1	. . .	39.3
1972	62.3	64.7	76.2	41.1	60.3	39.9	39.7	. . .	54.8	33.1	28.4	28.4	. . .	41.1
1973	64.6	67.1	78.8	42.5	62.8	41.2	41.0	. . .	54.8	35.2	31.2	31.2	. . .	43.2
1974	69.4	72.4	83.5	54.2	66.6	45.8	46.2	. . .	58.0	36.7	42.2	42.2	. . .	47.6
1975	72.5	75.5	85.5	64.5	69.6	50.1	50.6	. . .	63.0	43.8	45.1	45.1	. . .	53.7
1976	75.2	78.1	87.9	68.0	72.3	55.1	55.6	. . .	67.0	50.3	47.0	47.0	. . .	57.6
1977	78.6	81.7	90.6	74.6	75.7	59.0	59.7	. . .	70.5	54.7	49.7	49.7	. . .	61.9
1978	81.4	83.5	92.4	77.4	79.0	61.7	62.5	. . .	75.9	55.8	51.8	51.8	77.6	67.0
1979	84.9	85.4	94.0	79.0	85.3	70.5	71.7	. . .	81.9	60.2	70.1	70.2	85.1	73.7
1980	90.9	89.4	96.0	85.5	91.8	83.1	84.2	. . .	88.5	62.3	97.4	97.5	95.3	81.5
1981	95.3	94.2	97.5	92.9	96.7	93.2	93.8	. . .	93.9	76.9	108.5	108.5	101.0	89.2
1982	97.8	97.6	98.5	96.3	99.1	97.0	97.1	. . .	97.5	88.8	102.8	102.8	103.6	96.0
1983	100.2	100.3	100.2	101.1	99.8	99.3	99.3	. . .	99.9	98.7	99.4	99.4	100.7	100.3
1984	102.1	102.1	101.3	102.6	101.1	103.7	103.6	. . .	102.6	112.5	97.9	97.8	95.6	103.8
1985	105.0	105.0	104.9	107.2	102.3	106.4	106.2	. . .	106.1	113.7	98.7	98.6	95.9	106.8
1986	105.9	106.2	104.0	111.8	101.9	102.3	101.2	. . .	110.6	108.8	77.1	77.0	95.4	110.3
1987	110.6	109.1	110.4	112.1	105.1	105.4	104.2	. . .	114.4	113.1	80.2	80.1	96.1	114.8
1988	115.4	113.4	114.9	116.4	109.9	108.7	107.6	. . .	116.5	118.0	80.9	80.8	97.9	119.7
1989	118.6	117.0	116.4	119.1	114.4	114.1	112.9	. . .	119.2	120.4	88.5	88.5	100.2	124.9
1990	124.1	120.4	122.6	125.8	117.4	120.5	118.8	. . .	121.4	117.6	101.2	101.0	100.9	130.1
1991	128.7	124.2	127.6	128.9	120.9	123.8	121.9	. . .	126.0	118.1	99.4	99.2	102.2	136.0
1992	131.9	126.5	130.4	129.3	125.0	126.5	124.6	. . .	129.2	123.2	99.0	99.0	103.1	141.3
1993	133.7	127.5	132.6	127.1	125.9	130.4	127.5	91.8	132.7	133.9	98.0	97.7	101.6	145.9
1994	133.4	126.4	130.9	128.1	126.0	134.3	131.4	95.5	137.6	141.7	98.5	98.2	101.4	150.2
1995	132.0	126.2	126.9	127.2	125.4	139.1	136.3	99.4	141.0	156.5	100.0	99.8	102.1	154.0
1996	131.7	127.7	124.7	129.7	126.6	143.0	140.0	101.0	143.7	157.0	106.3	105.9	102.2	158.4
1997	132.9	130.1	126.1	129.0	127.6	144.3	141.0	100.5	144.3	151.1	106.2	105.8	101.9	162.7
1998	133.0	131.8	126.0	126.1	128.0	141.6	137.9	100.1	143.4	150.6	92.2	91.6	101.1	167.1
1999	131.3	131.1	123.3	129.0	125.7	144.4	140.5	100.1	142.9	152.0	100.7	100.1	100.5	171.9
2000	129.6	129.7	121.5	130.6	123.8	153.3	149.1	100.8	142.8	155.8	129.3	128.6	101.5	177.3
2001	127.3	125.7	119.3	129.2	123.0	154.3	150.0	101.3	142.1	158.7	124.7	124.0	104.8	183.5
2002	124.0	121.7	115.8	126.4	121.4	152.9	148.8	99.2	140.0	152.0	116.6	116.0	106.9	190.2
2003	120.9	118.0	113.1	122.1	119.6	157.6	153.6	96.5	137.9	142.9	135.8	135.1	107.8	195.6
2004	120.4	117.5	113.0	118.5	119.3	163.1	159.4	94.2	137.1	133.3	160.4	159.7	108.7	200.2
2005	119.5	116.1	110.8	116.7	122.6	173.9	170.2	95.6	137.9	139.4	195.7	194.7	111.9	206.9
2006	119.5	114.1	110.7	116.5	123.5	180.9	177.0	95.6	137.6	140.0	221.0	219.9	117.3	215.6
2007	119.0	112.4	110.3	113.9	122.4	184.7	180.8	94.3	136.3	135.7	239.1	238.0	121.6	223.0
2008	118.9	113.0	107.5	113.8	124.2	195.5	191.0	93.3	134.2	134.0	279.7	277.5	128.7	233.9
2009	120.1	113.6	108.1	114.5	126.9	179.3	174.8	93.5	135.6	127.0	202.0	201.6	134.1	243.3
2010	119.5	111.9	107.1	114.2	128.0	193.4	188.7	97.1	138.0	143.1	239.2	238.6	137.0	248.0
2011	122.1	114.7	109.2	113.6	128.5	212.4	207.6	99.8	141.9	149.0	302.6	301.7	143.9	253.1
2012	126.3	119.5	113.0	119.7	131.8	217.3	212.8	100.6	144.2	150.3	312.7	311.5	148.6	257.6
2013	127.4	121.6	113.3	116.5	135.0	217.4	212.4	100.9	145.8	149.9	303.9	302.6	146.4	261.6
2014	127.5	120.6	114.4	117.6	135.5	215.9	211.0	100.8	146.3	149.1	292.4	290.9	144.8	266.0
2013														
January	128.0	121.7	114.1	118.8	135.3	216.8	211.6	100.9	145.7	149.2	303.0	301.6	147.9	259.8
February	128.1	121.2	114.4	119.9	135.8	222.3	217.5	100.9	145.3	150.0	325.8	324.8	147.7	260.2
March	127.0	120.4	113.0	117.1	135.1	218.8	213.6	100.9	145.4	150.3	310.2	308.9	147.9	260.2
April	126.8	121.8	112.1	115.1	135.4	214.3	209.2	100.9	145.6	150.0	292.9	291.4	147.2	260.3
May	126.9	122.0	111.7	116.7	135.5	214.7	209.6	100.7	145.6	149.3	294.8	293.6	146.8	261.1
June	127.1	121.9	111.8	116.5	136.5	216.3	211.3	100.8	145.9	149.1	300.8	299.7	146.4	261.4
July	127.8	121.3	113.9	115.9	135.5	217.2	212.2	100.7	146.0	148.7	302.7	301.5	146.1	262.2
August	127.7	121.9	114.0	115.5	135.1	217.7	212.9	100.7	146.0	148.9	305.2	304.0	145.7	262.5
September	127.4	121.3	113.9	115.2	134.5	218.1	213.2	101.0	146.1	149.6	305.5	304.2	145.4	263.0
October	126.9	122.1	112.7	115.1	134.0	217.7	212.7	101.2	146.0	150.6	302.7	301.4	145.2	263.1
November	127.1	121.4	113.3	116.2	133.9	216.7	211.5	101.3	145.9	151.4	297.4	296.1	145.1	262.9
December	128.1	122.0	115.3	116.9	133.5	218.7	213.8	101.3	145.9	151.8	305.6	304.4	145.7	263.1
2014														
January	127.8	121.3	115.4	116.5	132.9	218.2	213.4	101.1	145.8	151.4	304.7	303.3	145.4	263.7
February	127.4	121.5	114.4	116.6	133.4	217.1	212.3	101.0	145.8	151.0	299.7	298.3	145.2	264.5
March	127.6	121.2	114.7	117.7	133.9	216.3	211.4	101.0	145.8	150.4	296.0	294.4	145.1	264.1
April	127.6	121.0	114.8	118.1	133.9	217.9	213.0	101.0	146.1	150.1	301.4	299.6	145.3	264.5
May	127.8	121.0	115.3	118.1	134.3	218.8	213.5	100.9	146.3	149.5	302.8	301.1	145.0	265.0
June	128.2	121.2	115.6	117.7	134.8	219.5	214.1	100.6	145.9	149.3	306.0	304.4	144.6	265.7
July	128.3	121.7	114.8	117.8	136.5	218.9	214.0	100.8	146.3	149.1	304.7	303.0	144.7	266.3
August	127.8	120.1	114.6	117.6	136.5	216.8	212.2	100.8	146.5	149.1	296.4	294.8	144.9	266.1
September	127.9	120.6	114.3	117.7	137.4	216.2	211.6	100.8	146.6	149.0	293.6	292.1	144.5	267.3
October	127.6	119.7	114.3	117.9	137.4	215.2	210.3	100.8	146.8	148.1	287.6	286.2	144.4	268.1
November	126.7	119.4	113.1	117.5	136.8	210.3	205.2	100.5	146.7	146.7	266.9	265.5	144.1	268.4
December	125.6	118.5	111.3	117.5	137.3	204.4	199.2	100.3	146.7	145.5	242.5	241.0	144.7	268.6

[1]Not seasonally adjusted.
[3]December 1997 = 100.
. . . = Not available.

Table 8-2. Consumer Price Indexes and Purchasing Power of the Dollar—Continued

(1982–1984 = 100, seasonally adjusted, except as noted.)

Year and month	CPI-U, Transportation—Continued		CPI-U, Medical care					CPI-U, Recreation		CPI-U, Education and communication			
					Medical care services						Education		
	Public transportation	Transportation services	Medical care, total	Medical care commodities	Total	Professional services	Hospital and related services	Total [3]	Video and audio [3]	Total [3]	Total [3]	Educational books and supplies	Tuition, other school fees, and childcare
1970	35.2	40.2	34.0	46.5	32.3	37.0	...	...	...	...	...	38.8	...
1971	37.8	43.4	36.1	47.3	34.7	39.4	...	...	...	...	...	41.4	...
1972	39.3	44.4	37.3	47.4	35.9	40.8	...	...	...	...	...	44.2	...
1973	39.7	44.7	38.8	47.5	37.5	42.2	...	...	...	...	...	45.6	...
1974	40.6	46.3	42.4	49.2	41.4	45.8	...	...	...	...	...	47.2	...
1975	43.5	49.8	47.5	53.3	46.6	50.8	...	...	...	...	...	50.3	...
1976	47.8	56.9	52.0	56.5	51.3	55.5	...	...	...	...	...	53.7	...
1977	50.0	61.5	57.0	60.2	56.4	60.0	...	...	...	...	...	56.9	...
1978	51.5	64.4	61.8	64.4	61.2	64.5	55.1	...	...	...	...	61.6	59.8
1979	54.9	69.5	67.5	69.0	67.2	70.1	61.0	...	...	...	...	65.7	64.7
1980	69.0	79.2	74.9	75.4	74.8	77.9	69.2	...	...	...	...	71.4	71.2
1981	85.6	88.6	82.9	83.7	82.8	85.9	79.1	...	...	...	...	80.3	79.9
1982	94.9	96.1	92.5	92.3	92.6	93.2	90.3	...	...	...	...	91.0	90.5
1983	99.5	99.1	100.6	100.2	100.7	99.8	100.5	...	...	...	...	100.3	99.7
1984	105.7	104.8	106.8	107.5	106.7	107.0	109.2	...	...	...	...	108.7	109.8
1985	110.5	110.0	113.5	115.2	113.2	113.5	116.1	...	...	...	...	118.2	119.7
1986	117.0	116.3	122.0	122.8	121.9	120.8	123.1	...	...	...	...	128.1	129.6
1987	121.1	121.9	130.1	131.0	130.0	128.8	131.6	...	...	...	...	138.1	140.0
1988	123.3	128.0	138.6	139.9	138.3	137.5	143.9	...	...	...	...	148.1	151.0
1989	129.5	135.6	149.3	150.8	148.9	146.4	160.5	...	...	...	...	158.0	162.7
1990	142.6	144.2	162.8	163.4	162.7	156.1	178.0	...	...	...	...	171.3	175.7
1991	148.9	151.2	177.0	176.8	177.1	165.7	196.1	...	...	...	...	180.3	191.4
1992	151.4	155.7	190.1	188.1	190.5	175.8	214.0	...	...	...	...	190.3	208.5
1993	167.0	162.9	201.4	195.0	202.9	184.7	231.9	90.7	96.5	85.5	78.4	197.6	225.3
1994	172.0	168.6	211.0	200.7	213.4	192.5	245.6	92.7	95.4	88.8	83.3	205.5	239.8
1995	175.9	175.9	220.5	204.5	224.2	201.0	257.8	94.5	95.1	92.2	88.0	214.4	253.8
1996	181.9	180.5	228.2	210.4	232.4	208.3	269.5	97.4	96.6	95.3	92.7	226.9	267.1
1997	186.7	185.0	234.6	215.3	239.1	215.4	278.4	99.6	99.4	98.4	97.3	238.4	280.4
1998	190.3	187.9	242.1	221.8	246.8	222.2	287.5	101.1	101.1	100.3	102.1	250.8	294.2
1999	197.7	190.7	250.6	230.7	255.1	229.2	299.5	102.0	100.7	101.2	107.0	261.7	308.4
2000	209.6	196.1	260.8	238.1	266.0	237.7	317.3	103.3	101.0	102.5	112.5	279.9	324.0
2001	210.6	201.9	272.8	247.6	278.8	246.5	338.3	104.9	101.5	105.2	118.5	295.9	341.1
2002	207.4	209.1	285.6	256.4	292.9	253.9	367.8	106.2	102.8	107.9	126.0	317.6	362.1
2003	209.3	216.3	297.1	262.8	306.0	261.2	394.8	107.5	103.6	109.8	134.4	335.4	386.7
2004	209.1	220.6	310.1	269.3	321.3	271.5	417.9	108.6	104.2	111.6	143.7	351.0	414.3
2005	217.3	225.7	323.2	276.0	336.7	281.7	439.9	109.4	104.2	113.7	152.7	365.6	440.9
2006	226.6	230.8	336.2	285.9	350.6	289.3	468.1	110.9	104.6	116.8	162.1	388.9	468.1
2007	230.0	233.7	351.1	290.0	369.3	300.8	498.9	111.4	102.9	119.6	171.4	420.4	494.1
2008	250.5	244.1	364.1	296.0	384.9	311.0	534.0	113.3	102.6	123.6	181.3	450.2	522.1
2009	236.3	251.0	375.6	305.1	397.3	319.4	567.9	114.3	101.3	127.4	190.9	482.1	549.0
2010	251.4	259.8	388.4	314.7	411.2	328.2	607.7	113.3	99.1	129.9	199.3	505.6	573.2
2011	269.4	268.0	400.3	324.1	423.8	335.7	641.5	113.4	98.4	131.5	207.8	529.5	597.2
2012	271.4	272.9	414.9	333.6	440.3	342.0	672.1	114.7	99.4	133.8	216.3	562.6	621.0
2013	278.9	280.0	425.1	335.1	454.0	349.5	701.3	115.3	99.7	135.9	224.5	594.7	643.7
2014	276.4	285.3	435.3	343.4	464.8	355.2	733.8	115.5	99.8	137.5	231.9	615.4	664.8
2013													
January	281.5	278.7	421.1	334.5	448.5	346.1	688.2	115.0	99.4	135.2	221.5	583.3	635.3
February	279.8	278.8	421.8	333.7	450.0	346.9	692.1	115.3	99.7	135.5	221.9	584.9	636.4
March	282.7	279.4	422.9	334.2	451.2	347.8	694.6	115.2	99.7	135.7	222.5	589.1	638.0
April	277.9	278.3	422.9	334.2	451.3	348.6	692.2	115.1	99.5	135.4	223.2	591.0	639.8
May	278.1	278.5	422.4	332.9	451.1	348.4	693.1	115.3	99.6	135.6	223.7	593.8	641.2
June	277.6	278.7	424.1	334.0	453.0	349.5	696.5	115.2	99.6	135.7	224.4	596.0	643.3
July	277.5	280.6	424.8	334.5	453.7	350.0	697.6	115.3	99.6	135.7	224.9	600.0	644.5
August	275.9	280.3	427.2	335.8	456.6	350.1	709.9	115.3	99.7	135.9	225.3	590.0	646.3
September	277.1	280.9	428.4	336.3	458.1	350.8	713.9	115.3	99.7	136.1	225.4	595.8	646.2
October	279.0	281.7	428.7	337.8	457.9	351.3	712.6	115.4	99.9	136.4	226.4	600.7	648.9
November	280.9	282.1	428.7	337.9	457.8	351.7	711.8	115.7	100.1	136.6	227.2	604.0	651.2
December	278.4	282.0	428.7	335.4	458.8	352.4	713.9	115.3	99.8	136.9	227.9	607.2	653.2
2014													
January	275.0	282.1	430.0	337.3	459.9	352.6	718.3	115.5	99.9	137.1	228.1	597.8	654.4
February	275.2	282.7	431.4	339.5	461.0	352.8	722.5	115.6	99.9	137.0	229.0	603.7	656.7
March	275.9	283.2	432.1	338.7	462.3	353.3	727.1	115.5	100.1	137.1	229.7	602.8	658.9
April	277.9	284.5	433.2	339.5	463.5	353.9	730.8	115.8	100.2	137.4	230.5	608.1	660.9
May	285.6	286.8	434.5	341.4	464.5	355.0	733.2	115.7	100.2	137.5	231.2	610.7	662.8
June	287.0	287.3	435.1	343.3	464.6	354.8	733.9	115.8	100.2	137.8	232.3	611.9	666.2
July	277.4	285.7	435.8	344.4	465.1	354.9	735.7	115.7	99.9	137.9	232.3	614.9	666.1
August	272.1	284.8	436.0	344.4	465.4	355.7	736.9	115.3	99.4	137.9	232.7	620.6	666.9
September	271.8	285.0	436.9	346.0	466.0	355.9	738.6	115.4	99.5	137.9	232.9	623.4	667.2
October	273.5	286.6	437.7	346.6	466.8	356.5	740.4	115.6	100.0	137.6	234.1	627.1	670.6
November	273.4	287.0	439.4	348.5	468.5	358.0	742.7	115.4	99.5	137.5	234.7	628.9	672.5
December	270.4	286.9	441.4	351.5	470.0	358.4	746.3	115.3	100.0	137.4	235.4	634.7	674.1

[3]December 1997 = 100.
. . . = Not available.

Table 8-2. Consumer Price Indexes and Purchasing Power of the Dollar—*Continued*

(1982–1984 = 100, seasonally adjusted except as noted.)

Year and month	CPI-U, Education and communication—Continued: Communication, Information and information processing — Total 3	Total 3	Telephone services 1,3	Information technology, hardware, and services — Total 1,4	Personal computers and peripheral equipment 1,5	CPI-U, Other goods and services — Total	Tobacco and smoking products 1	Personal care — Total	Personal care products 1	Personal care services 1	CPI-W, All items, not seasonally adjusted	Purchasing power of the dollar, CPI-U, 1982–1984 = $1.00, not seasonally adjusted
1970	. . .	. . .	. . .	. . .	. . .	40.9	43.1	43.5	42.7	44.2	39.0	2.574
1971	. . .	. . .	. . .	. . .	. . .	42.9	44.9	44.9	44.0	45.7	40.7	2.466
1972	. . .	. . .	. . .	. . .	. . .	44.7	47.4	46.0	45.2	46.8	42.1	2.391
1973	. . .	. . .	. . .	. . .	. . .	46.4	48.7	48.1	46.4	49.7	44.7	2.251
1974	. . .	. . .	. . .	. . .	. . .	49.8	51.1	52.8	51.5	53.9	49.6	2.029
1975	. . .	. . .	. . .	. . .	. . .	53.9	54.7	57.9	58.0	57.7	54.1	1.859
1976	. . .	. . .	. . .	. . .	. . .	57.0	57.0	61.7	61.3	61.9	57.2	1.757
1977	. . .	. . .	. . .	. . .	. . .	60.4	59.8	65.7	64.7	66.4	60.9	1.649
1978	. . .	. . .	. . .	. . .	. . .	64.3	63.0	69.9	68.2	71.3	65.6	1.532
1979	. . .	. . .	. . .	. . .	. . .	68.9	66.8	75.2	72.9	77.2	73.1	1.380
1980	. . .	. . .	. . .	. . .	. . .	75.2	72.0	81.9	79.6	83.7	82.9	1.215
1981	. . .	. . .	. . .	. . .	. . .	82.6	77.8	89.1	87.8	90.2	91.4	1.098
1982	. . .	. . .	. . .	. . .	. . .	91.1	86.5	95.4	95.1	95.7	96.9	1.035
1983	. . .	. . .	. . .	. . .	. . .	101.1	103.4	100.3	100.7	100.0	99.8	1.003
1984	. . .	. . .	. . .	. . .	. . .	107.9	110.1	104.3	104.2	104.4	103.3	0.961
1985	. . .	. . .	. . .	. . .	. . .	114.5	116.7	108.3	107.6	108.9	106.9	0.928
1986	. . .	. . .	. . .	. . .	. . .	121.4	124.7	111.9	111.3	112.5	108.6	0.913
1987	. . .	. . .	. . .	. . .	. . .	128.5	133.6	115.1	113.9	116.2	112.5	0.880
1988	. . .	. . .	. . .	. . .	. . .	137.0	145.8	119.4	118.1	120.7	117.0	0.846
1989	. . .	. . .	. . .	96.3	. . .	147.7	164.4	125.0	123.2	126.8	122.6	0.807
1990	. . .	. . .	. . .	93.5	. . .	159.0	181.5	130.4	128.2	132.8	129.0	0.766
1991	. . .	. . .	. . .	88.6	. . .	171.6	202.7	134.9	132.8	137.0	134.3	0.734
1992	. . .	. . .	. . .	83.7	. . .	183.3	219.8	138.3	136.5	140.0	138.2	0.713
1993	96.7	97.7	. . .	78.8	. . .	192.9	228.4	141.5	139.0	144.0	142.1	0.692
1994	97.6	98.6	. . .	72.0	. . .	198.5	220.0	144.6	141.5	147.9	145.6	0.675
1995	98.8	98.7	. . .	63.8	. . .	206.9	225.7	147.1	143.1	151.5	149.8	0.656
1996	99.6	99.5	. . .	57.2	. . .	215.4	232.8	150.1	144.3	156.6	154.1	0.638
1997	100.3	100.4	. . .	50.1	. . .	224.8	243.7	152.7	144.2	162.4	157.6	0.623
1998	98.7	98.5	100.7	39.9	875.1	237.7	274.8	156.7	148.3	166.0	159.7	0.614
1999	96.0	95.5	100.1	30.5	598.7	258.3	355.8	161.1	151.8	171.4	163.2	0.600
2000	93.6	92.8	98.5	25.9	459.9	271.1	394.9	165.6	153.7	178.1	168.9	0.581
2001	93.3	92.3	99.3	21.3	330.1	282.6	425.2	170.5	155.1	184.3	173.5	0.565
2002	92.3	90.8	99.7	18.3	248.4	293.2	461.5	174.7	154.7	188.4	175.9	0.556
2003	89.7	87.8	98.3	16.1	196.9	298.7	469.0	178.0	153.5	193.2	179.8	0.544
2004	86.7	84.6	95.8	14.8	171.2	304.7	478.0	181.7	153.9	197.6	184.5	0.530
2005	84.7	82.6	94.9	13.6	143.2	313.4	502.8	185.6	154.4	203.9	191.0	0.512
2006	84.1	81.7	95.8	12.5	120.9	321.7	519.9	190.2	155.8	209.7	197.1	0.496
2007	83.4	80.7	98.2	10.6	108.4	333.3	554.2	195.6	158.3	216.6	202.8	0.482
2008	84.2	81.4	100.5	10.1	94.9	345.4	588.7	201.3	159.3	223.7	211.1	0.465
2009	85.0	81.9	102.4	9.7	82.3	368.6	730.3	204.6	162.6	227.6	209.6	0.466
2010	84.7	81.5	102.4	9.4	76.4	381.3	807.3	206.6	161.1	229.6	214.0	0.459
2011	83.3	80.0	101.2	9.0	68.9	387.2	834.8	208.6	160.5	230.8	221.6	0.445
2012	83.1	79.5	101.7	8.7	62.3	394.4	853.5	212.1	162.2	234.2	226.2	0.436
2013	82.6	78.9	101.6	8.5	56.8	401.0	876.8	215.0	161.8	238.8	229.3	0.429
2014	82.1	78.2	101.1	8.4	52.6	408.1	903.3	218.0	163.4	242.0	232.8	0.422
2013												
January	82.9	79.3	101.9	8.6	59.1	397.5	864.2	213.5	160.6	237.1	227.8	0.434
February	83.1	79.4	101.9	8.6	58.7	398.3	865.6	213.9	160.8	237.3	229.4	0.431
March	83.0	79.4	101.9	8.7	58.2	399.0	866.3	214.4	162.7	237.7	228.7	0.430
April	82.5	78.8	101.2	8.6	57.4	400.0	873.0	214.6	162.0	238.3	227.9	0.430
May	82.5	78.8	101.3	8.6	57.2	400.4	873.5	214.8	161.2	238.3	228.3	0.429
June	82.4	78.7	101.3	8.5	56.7	400.6	872.3	215.0	161.8	238.2	229.0	0.428
July	82.3	78.6	101.4	8.5	56.0	401.2	878.0	215.0	161.3	239.1	229.4	0.428
August	82.3	78.6	101.3	8.5	55.9	402.3	883.0	215.4	162.4	239.7	229.8	0.428
September	82.6	78.8	101.5	8.5	56.1	402.5	883.9	215.5	162.5	239.8	230.1	0.427
October	82.6	78.8	101.7	8.4	55.3	402.8	886.4	215.5	161.8	239.2	230.2	0.428
November	82.5	78.7	101.6	8.4	54.9	403.4	887.4	215.8	161.9	240.1	230.3	0.429
December	82.6	78.8	101.6	8.4	55.6	404.2	889.3	216.3	162.4	240.7	231.0	0.429
2014												
January	82.7	78.9	102.0	8.4	54.8	405.1	892.7	216.7	162.7	240.7	231.4	0.428
February	82.4	78.6	101.6	8.4	54.2	405.8	895.0	217.0	163.0	240.7	231.6	0.426
March	82.3	78.5	101.5	8.4	54.0	406.4	898.2	217.1	163.2	241.1	232.0	0.423
April	82.4	78.6	101.6	8.4	53.9	406.6	899.9	217.2	163.3	241.0	232.5	0.422
May	82.3	78.5	101.5	8.4	53.4	407.5	902.5	217.6	162.9	241.6	233.1	0.420
June	82.3	78.4	101.5	8.4	53.0	408.2	909.4	217.6	162.9	241.8	233.6	0.420
July	82.3	78.5	101.5	8.4	52.7	408.3	901.1	218.3	163.7	242.0	233.7	0.420
August	82.3	78.4	101.5	8.4	52.1	408.8	902.5	218.5	164.2	242.3	233.5	0.420
September	82.2	78.3	101.4	8.3	51.6	409.0	902.3	218.7	164.6	242.2	233.7	0.420
October	81.5	77.6	100.2	8.3	51.2	410.5	909.2	219.2	164.5	243.1	233.7	0.421
November	81.2	77.3	99.7	8.3	50.5	410.2	911.7	218.9	164.5	243.2	232.6	0.423
December	80.9	77.0	99.5	8.3	49.7	410.8	915.7	219.1	162.9	244.3	231.5	0.426

[1] Not seasonally adjusted.
[3] December 1997 = 100.
[4] December 1988 = 100.
[5] December 2007 = 100.
. . . = Not available.

Table 8-3. Alternative Measures of Total and Core Consumer Prices: Index Levels

(Various bases; monthly data seasonally adjusted, except as noted.)

Year and month	CPIs, all items						CPIs, all items less food and energy			Chain-type price indexes for personal consumption expenditures (PCE), 2009 = 100			
										PCE, total	PCE, market-based	Excluding food and energy	
	CPI-U, 1982–1984 = 100	CPI-W, 1982–1984 = 100	CPI-U-X1, 1982–1984 = 100	CPI-E, Dec. 1982 = 100, not seasonally adjusted	CPI-U-RS, Dec. 1977 = 100, not seasonally adjusted	C-CPI-U, Dec. 1999 = 100, not seasonally adjusted	CPI-U, 1982–1984 = 100	CPI-U-RS, Dec. 1977 = 100, not seasonally adjusted	C-CPI-U, Dec. 1999 = 100, not seasonally adjusted			PCE, total	PCE, market-based
1975	53.8	54.1	56.2	...	...	...	53.9	...	...	30.3	...	30.6	...
1976	56.9	57.2	59.4	...	...	...	57.4	...	...	32.0	...	32.4	...
1977	60.6	60.9	63.2	...	...	...	61.0	...	...	34.1	...	34.5	...
1978	65.2	65.6	67.5	...	104.4	...	65.5	103.6	...	36.5	...	36.8	...
1979	72.6	73.1	74.0	...	114.3	...	71.9	111.0	...	39.7	...	39.5	...
1980	82.4	82.9	82.3	...	127.1	...	80.8	120.9	...	44.0	...	43.1	...
1981	90.9	91.4	90.1	...	139.2	...	89.2	132.2	...	47.9	...	46.9	...
1982	96.5	96.9	95.6	...	147.6	...	95.8	142.4	...	50.6	...	49.9	...
1983	99.6	99.8	99.6	102.1	153.8	...	99.6	150.4	...	52.7	...	52.5	...
1984	103.9	103.3	103.9	106.5	160.2	...	104.6	157.9	...	54.7	...	54.6	...
1985	107.6	106.9	107.6	110.5	165.7	...	109.1	164.8	...	56.7	...	56.9	...
1986	109.6	108.6	109.6	113.3	168.7	...	113.5	171.4	...	57.9	...	58.9	...
1987	113.6	112.5	113.6	117.7	174.4	...	118.2	178.1	...	59.7	59.1	60.7	60.2
1988	118.3	117.0	118.3	122.7	180.8	...	123.4	185.2	...	62.0	61.4	63.3	62.8
1989	124.0	122.6	124.0	128.9	188.6	...	129.0	192.6	...	64.6	64.3	65.9	65.6
1990	130.7	129.0	130.7	136.6	197.9	...	135.5	201.4	...	67.4	67.4	68.5	68.6
1991	136.2	134.3	136.2	143.0	205.1	...	142.1	209.9	...	69.7	70.0	70.9	71.5
1992	140.3	138.2	140.3	147.6	210.3	...	147.3	216.4	...	71.5	72.0	73.0	73.9
1993	144.5	142.1	144.5	152.2	215.5	...	152.2	222.5	...	73.3	73.7	75.0	75.8
1994	148.2	145.6	148.2	156.6	220.0	...	156.5	227.7	...	74.8	75.2	76.7	77.4
1995	152.4	149.8	152.4	161.2	225.3	...	161.2	233.4	...	76.4	76.7	78.3	79.1
1996	156.9	154.1	156.9	166.1	231.4	...	165.6	239.1	...	78.0	78.2	79.8	80.3
1997	160.5	157.6	160.5	170.1	236.4	...	169.5	244.4	...	79.3	79.4	81.2	81.5
1998	163.0	159.7	163.0	173.2	239.6	...	173.4	249.7	...	79.9	79.8	82.2	82.4
1999	166.6	163.2	166.6	177.3	244.7	...	177.0	254.7	...	81.1	81.0	83.3	83.5
2000	172.2	168.9	172.2	183.5	253.0	102.0	181.3	261.0	101.4	83.1	82.9	84.7	84.7
2001	177.1	173.5	177.1	189.2	260.1	104.3	186.1	268.0	103.5	84.7	84.5	86.3	86.2
2002	179.9	175.9	179.9	192.7	264.3	105.6	190.5	274.1	105.4	85.9	85.4	87.8	87.5
2003	184.0	179.8	184.0	197.4	270.2	107.8	193.2	278.1	106.6	87.6	87.1	89.0	88.7
2004	188.9	184.5	188.9	203.3	277.5	110.5	196.6	283.1	108.4	89.7	89.1	90.8	90.3
2005	195.3	191.0	195.3	210.4	286.9	113.7	200.9	289.2	110.4	92.3	91.6	92.7	92.0
2006	201.6	197.1	201.6	217.3	296.2	117.0	205.9	296.4	112.9	94.7	94.1	94.8	94.0
2007	207.3	202.8	207.3	223.8	304.6	120.0	210.7	303.3	115.0	97.1	96.4	96.8	96.0
2008	215.3	211.1	215.3	232.4	316.3	124.4	215.6	310.3	117.3	100.1	99.6	98.8	98.1
2009	214.5	209.6	214.5	231.9	315.2	123.9	219.2	315.6	119.1	100.0	100.0	100.0	100.0
2010	218.1	214.0	218.1	235.0	320.3	125.6	221.3	318.6	120.0	101.7	101.5	101.3	101.0
2011	224.9	221.6	224.9	241.8	330.4	129.5	225.0	323.9	121.9	104.1	104.0	102.8	102.5
2012	229.6	226.2	229.6	246.7	337.3	132.0	229.8	330.7	124.3	106.1	105.9	104.7	104.3
2013	233.0	229.3	233.0	250.6	342.2	...	233.8	336.6	...	107.3	107.0	106.1	105.6
2014	236.7	232.8	236.7	255.2	347.8	...	237.9	342.4	...	108.8	108.3	107.6	106.9
2013													
January	231.4	227.8	231.4	247.9	338.3	132.1	232.2	333.4	125.1	106.7	106.5	105.5	105.1
February	232.8	229.4	232.8	249.6	341.1	133.2	232.6	334.6	125.5	107.1	106.9	105.6	105.2
March	232.2	228.7	232.2	250.2	342.0	133.6	232.8	335.5	125.9	107.0	106.8	105.7	105.3
April	231.7	227.9	231.7	250.1	341.6	[1]133.4	232.9	335.7	[1]126.0	106.9	106.6	105.7	105.2
May	232.0	228.3	232.0	250.5	342.2	133.6	233.1	336.1	126.0	107.0	106.7	105.9	105.3
June	232.6	229.0	232.6	251.2	343.0	133.9	233.5	336.3	126.1	107.3	107.0	106.0	105.5
July	233.0	229.4	233.0	251.3	343.2	133.9	233.9	336.5	126.2	107.4	107.2	106.1	105.6
August	233.4	229.8	233.4	251.6	343.6	134.1	234.3	337.2	126.4	107.5	107.2	106.3	105.7
September	233.8	230.1	233.8	251.8	344.0	134.3	234.6	338.0	126.7	107.6	107.3	106.4	105.8
October	233.9	230.2	233.9	251.3	343.1	133.9	234.9	338.5	126.8	107.7	107.3	106.5	105.9
November	234.0	230.3	234.0	250.9	342.4	133.6	235.3	338.6	126.9	107.8	107.4	106.6	106.0
December	234.7	231.0	234.7	251.0	342.4	133.5	235.6	338.3	126.7	107.9	107.6	106.7	106.1
2014													
January	235.1	231.4	235.1	252.1	343.6	134.1	236.0	338.8	126.9	108.0	107.7	106.8	106.2
February	235.4	231.6	235.4	253.1	344.9	134.6	236.2	339.8	127.3	108.1	107.7	106.9	106.2
March	235.8	232.0	235.8	254.5	347.1	135.4	236.6	341.0	127.7	108.3	107.9	107.1	106.4
April	236.2	232.5	236.2	255.2	348.3	135.9	237.1	341.9	128.0	108.5	108.1	107.3	106.6
May	237.0	233.1	237.0	256.1	349.5	[1]136.3	237.7	342.6	[1]128.3	108.8	108.3	107.5	106.7
June	237.3	233.6	237.3	256.7	350.1	[1]136.6	238.0	342.8	[1]128.3	109.0	108.6	107.6	106.9
July	237.6	233.7	237.6	256.7	350.0	[1]136.5	238.2	342.8	[1]128.3	109.1	108.7	107.7	107.0
August	237.4	233.5	237.4	256.3	349.4	[1]136.2	238.3	343.0	[1]128.4	109.1	108.6	107.8	107.1
September	237.6	233.7	237.6	256.5	349.7	[1]136.3	238.7	343.8	[1]128.7	109.2	108.7	107.9	107.2
October	237.8	233.7	237.8	256.1	348.8	[1]136.0	239.1	344.6	[1]129.0	109.2	108.7	108.1	107.3
November	237.1	232.6	237.1	255.1	346.9	[1]135.1	239.3	344.4	[1]128.8	109.0	108.4	108.1	107.3
December	236.3	231.5	236.3	254.1	345.0	[1]134.2	239.4	343.7	[1]128.6	108.8	108.2	108.1	107.3

[1]Interim values.
... = Not available.

Table 8-4. Alternative Measures of Total and Core Consumer Prices: Inflation Rates

(Percent changes from year earlier, except as noted; monthly data seasonally adjusted, except as noted.)

Year and month	CPIs, all items						CPIs, all items less food and energy			Chain-type price indexes for personal consumption expenditures (PCE), 2009 = 100			
	CPI-U, 1982–1984 = 100	CPI-W, 1982–1984 = 100	CPI-U-X1, 1982–1984 = 100	CPI-E, Dec. 1982 = 100, not seasonally adjusted	CPI-U-RS, Dec. 1977 = 100, not seasonally adjusted	C-CPI-U, Dec. 1999 = 100, not seasonally adjusted	CPI-U, 1982–1984 = 100	CPI-U-RS, Dec. 1977 = 100, not seasonally adjusted	C-CPI-U, Dec. 1999 = 100, not seasonally adjusted	PCE, total	PCE, market-based	Excluding food and energy PCE, total	Excluding food and energy PCE, market-based
1960	1.7	1.7	1.9	...	...	...	1.3	...	...	...	...	1.7	...
1961	1.0	1.0	0.9	...	...	...	1.3	...	...	...	...	1.3	...
1962	1.0	1.0	0.9	...	...	...	1.3	...	...	1.2	...	1.4	...
1963	1.3	1.3	1.5	...	...	...	1.3	...	...	1.0	...	1.3	...
1964	1.3	1.3	1.2	...	...	...	1.6	...	...	1.2	...	1.5	...
1965	1.6	1.6	1.5	...	...	...	1.2	...	...	1.2	...	1.3	...
1966	2.9	2.8	2.9	...	...	...	2.4	...	...	2.5	...	2.3	...
1967	3.1	3.1	3.1	...	...	...	3.6	...	...	2.5	...	3.1	...
1968	4.2	4.2	3.9	...	...	...	4.6	...	...	3.9	...	4.3	...
1969	5.5	5.4	4.5	...	...	...	5.8	...	...	4.5	...	4.7	...
1970	5.7	5.7	4.8	...	...	...	6.3	...	...	4.7	...	4.7	...
1971	4.4	4.4	4.4	...	...	...	4.7	...	...	4.3	...	4.7	...
1972	3.2	3.4	3.0	...	...	...	3.0	...	...	3.4	...	3.2	...
1973	6.2	6.2	6.3	...	...	...	3.6	...	...	5.4	...	3.8	...
1974	11.0	11.0	10.0	...	...	...	8.3	...	...	10.4	...	7.9	...
1975	9.1	9.1	8.3	...	...	...	9.1	...	...	8.4	...	8.4	...
1976	5.8	5.7	5.7	...	...	...	6.5	...	...	5.5	...	6.1	...
1977	6.5	6.5	6.4	...	...	...	6.3	...	...	6.5	...	6.4	...
1978	7.6	7.7	6.8	...	...	...	7.4	...	...	7.0	...	6.7	...
1979	11.3	11.4	9.6	...	9.5	...	9.8	7.1	...	8.9	...	7.3	...
1980	13.5	13.4	11.2	...	11.2	...	12.4	8.9	...	10.7	...	9.2	...
1981	10.3	10.3	9.5	...	9.5	...	10.4	9.3	...	8.9	...	8.7	...
1982	6.2	6.0	6.1	...	6.0	...	7.4	7.7	...	5.5	...	6.5	...
1983	3.2	3.0	4.2	...	4.2	...	4.0	5.6	...	4.3	...	5.2	...
1984	4.3	3.5	4.3	4.3	4.2	...	5.0	5.0	...	3.8	...	4.2	...
1985	3.6	3.5	3.6	3.8	3.4	...	4.3	4.4	...	3.5	...	4.1	...
1986	1.9	1.6	1.9	2.5	1.8	...	4.0	4.0	...	2.2	...	3.4	...
1987	3.6	3.6	3.6	3.9	3.4	...	4.1	3.9	...	3.0	...	3.2	...
1988	4.1	4.0	4.1	4.2	3.7	...	4.4	4.0	...	3.9	3.9	4.2	4.3
1989	4.8	4.8	4.8	5.0	4.3	...	4.5	4.0	...	4.3	4.6	4.1	4.4
1990	5.4	5.2	5.4	6.0	4.9	...	5.0	4.6	...	4.3	4.9	4.0	4.6
1991	4.2	4.1	4.2	4.7	3.6	...	4.9	4.2	...	3.3	3.8	3.5	4.2
1992	3.0	2.9	3.0	3.2	2.5	...	3.7	3.1	...	2.6	2.8	3.0	3.3
1993	3.0	2.8	3.0	3.2	2.5	...	3.3	2.8	...	2.5	2.4	2.7	2.6
1994	2.6	2.5	2.6	2.9	2.1	...	2.8	2.3	...	2.1	1.9	2.2	2.1
1995	2.8	2.9	2.8	2.9	2.4	...	3.0	2.5	...	2.1	2.0	2.1	2.1
1996	3.0	2.9	3.0	3.1	2.7	...	2.7	2.4	...	2.1	1.9	1.9	1.6
1997	2.3	2.3	2.3	2.4	2.2	...	2.4	2.2	...	1.7	1.5	1.7	1.5
1998	1.6	1.3	1.6	1.8	1.4	...	2.3	2.2	...	0.8	0.6	1.2	1.1
1999	2.2	2.2	2.2	2.3	2.1	...	2.1	2.0	...	1.5	1.4	1.3	1.2
2000	3.4	3.5	3.4	3.5	3.4	...	2.4	2.5	...	2.5	2.4	1.7	1.5
2001	2.8	2.7	2.8	3.1	2.8	2.3	2.6	2.7	2.1	1.9	1.9	1.8	1.8
2002	1.6	1.4	1.6	1.8	1.6	1.2	2.4	2.3	1.8	1.3	1.1	1.7	1.5
2003	2.3	2.2	2.3	2.5	2.2	2.1	1.4	1.5	1.1	2.0	1.9	1.5	1.4
2004	2.7	2.6	2.7	3.0	2.7	2.5	1.8	1.8	1.7	2.4	2.4	1.9	1.7
2005	3.4	3.5	3.4	3.5	3.4	2.9	2.2	2.2	1.8	2.9	2.8	2.2	2.0
2006	3.2	3.2	3.2	3.3	3.2	2.9	2.5	2.5	2.3	2.7	2.7	2.2	2.2
2007	2.8	2.9	2.8	3.0	2.8	2.5	2.3	2.3	1.8	2.5	2.5	2.2	2.0
2008	3.8	4.1	3.8	3.8	3.8	3.7	2.3	2.3	2.0	3.1	3.4	2.1	2.3
2009	-0.4	-0.7	-0.4	-0.2	-0.3	-0.5	1.7	1.7	1.5	-0.1	0.4	1.2	1.9
2010	1.6	2.1	1.6	1.4	1.6	1.4	1.0	1.0	0.7	1.7	1.5	1.3	1.0
2011	3.2	3.6	3.2	2.9	3.2	3.1	1.7	1.7	1.6	2.5	2.5	1.5	1.4
2012	2.1	2.1	2.1	2.1	2.1	1.9	2.1	2.1	2.0	1.8	1.8	1.8	1.8
2013	1.5	1.4	1.5	1.6	1.5	...	1.8	1.8	...	1.2	1.1	1.3	1.2
2014	1.6	1.5	1.6	1.8	1.6	...	1.7	1.7	...	1.3	1.2	1.4	1.2
Percent change, annual rate:													
1978–2014	3.6	3.6	3.5	...	3.4	...	3.6	3.4	...	3.1	...	3.0	...
1983–2014	2.8	2.8	2.8	3.0	2.7	...	2.8	2.7	...	2.4	...	2.3	...
2000–2014	2.3	2.3	2.3	2.4	2.3	...	2.0	2.0	...	1.9	1.9	1.7	1.7
2014													
January	1.6	1.6	1.6	1.7	1.6	[1]1.5	1.6	1.6	...	1.2	1.1	1.2	1.0
February	1.1	0.9	1.1	1.4	1.1	[1]1.0	1.6	1.6	...	1.0	0.7	1.2	1.0
March	1.5	1.4	1.5	1.7	1.5	[1]1.4	1.6	1.6	...	1.2	1.0	1.3	1.1
April	2.0	2.0	2.0	2.0	2.0	[1]1.8	1.8	1.8	...	1.5	1.4	1.4	1.3
May	2.1	2.1	2.1	2.3	2.1	[1]2.0	1.9	1.9	...	1.7	1.5	1.5	1.4
June	2.0	2.0	2.0	2.2	2.1	[1]2.0	1.9	1.9	...	1.6	1.5	1.5	1.3
July	2.0	1.9	2.0	2.1	2.0	[1]1.9	1.9	1.9	...	1.6	1.5	1.5	1.3
August	1.7	1.6	1.7	1.9	1.7	[1]1.6	1.7	1.7	...	1.5	1.3	1.5	1.3
September	1.6	1.5	1.6	1.9	1.7	[1]1.5	1.7	1.7	...	1.5	1.3	1.5	1.3
October	1.6	1.5	1.6	1.9	1.7	[1]1.5	1.8	1.8	...	1.4	1.2	1.5	1.3
November	1.3	1.0	1.3	1.7	1.3	[1]1.1	1.7	1.7	...	1.2	1.0	1.4	1.2
December	0.7	0.2	0.7	1.3	0.8	[1]0.5	1.6	1.6	...	0.8	0.6	1.3	1.2

[1] Interim values.
... = Not available.

Table 8-5. Producer Price Indexes for Goods and Services: Final Demand

(November 2009 =100, except as noted.)

Year and month	Final demand	Final demand goods						Final demand services				Final demand construction	Final demand less food and energy (April 2010 =100)
		Final demand goods	Final demand foods	Final demand energy goods	Final demand goods less food and energy			Final demand services	Final demand trade services	Final demand transportation and warehousing services	Final demand services less trade, transportation, and warehousing		
					Total	Finished goods less foods and energy (1982 =100)							
						Total	Private capital equipment						
NOT SEASONALLY ADJUSTED													
2010	101.8	102.8	103.7	107.2	101.4	173.6	157.3	101.3	101.7	103.2	100.9	100.3	. . .
2011	105.7	109.9	112.5	126.2	104.9	177.8	159.7	103.4	104.0	110.0	102.5	102.5	102.7
2012	107.7	111.7	115.9	126.3	106.8	182.4	162.8	105.4	106.7	114.2	103.9	105.5	104.7
2013	109.1	112.6	117.8	125.3	107.9	185.1	164.2	107.1	108.2	115.3	105.8	107.5	106.2
2014	110.9	114.1	121.6	124.2	109.5	188.6	166.5	109.0	110.2	117.7	107.5	110.6	108.1
2011													
January	103.4	106.2	108.2	114.9	103.3	175.8	158.4	101.9	101.2	106.1	101.8	101.0	101.2
February	104.2	107.6	112.2	117.4	103.8	176.1	158.7	102.3	102.3	107.2	101.8	101.0	101.6
March	105.2	109.0	111.5	125.4	104.0	176.4	158.8	103.1	104.2	109.5	101.9	101.0	102.2
April	105.9	110.5	112.4	131.1	104.5	176.9	159.2	103.3	104.1	110.2	102.2	101.8	102.5
May	106.1	111.1	111.3	134.9	104.7	176.9	159.2	103.3	104.5	110.8	102.0	101.8	102.5
June	106.0	110.7	112.4	130.6	104.9	177.2	159.5	103.5	104.2	110.8	102.3	101.8	102.7
July	106.3	111.1	112.7	131.1	105.3	177.9	159.7	103.6	103.7	111.2	102.7	102.9	102.9
August	106.4	110.7	113.9	127.6	105.4	178.1	159.7	104.1	105.0	111.2	102.9	103.0	103.3
September	106.6	111.2	114.7	129.1	105.5	178.3	159.8	104.1	105.4	110.3	102.8	102.9	103.3
October	106.3	110.4	113.2	124.8	105.9	179.8	161.2	104.0	104.7	110.9	102.9	104.3	103.4
November	106.4	110.4	114.2	124.7	105.7	179.9	161.3	104.1	104.6	111.1	103.1	104.4	103.4
December	106.0	109.8	113.4	122.2	105.7	180.1	161.4	103.8	104.0	111.3	102.9	104.3	103.2
2012													
January	106.6	110.5	113.7	123.3	106.3	181.3	162.1	104.3	104.3	112.3	103.5	105.0	103.7
February	107.1	111.1	113.6	125.8	106.5	181.5	162.3	104.8	105.8	113.2	103.5	105.0	104.2
March	107.7	112.1	114.4	130.0	106.7	181.6	162.3	105.2	106.8	114.5	103.4	105.2	104.5
April	108.0	112.3	114.5	130.9	106.8	181.7	162.5	105.5	106.9	115.0	103.8	105.6	104.7
May	107.8	111.6	114.3	127.2	106.8	181.7	162.4	105.6	107.6	114.7	103.6	105.6	104.8
June	107.4	110.8	114.9	123.0	106.5	181.8	162.5	105.5	107.1	114.9	103.7	105.6	104.7
July	107.4	111.0	116.1	122.5	106.7	182.6	162.8	105.3	106.4	114.2	103.8	105.6	104.6
August	107.7	112.3	117.4	128.3	106.8	182.7	162.8	105.1	105.4	114.6	104.0	105.7	104.5
September	108.2	113.1	118.0	132.5	106.7	182.5	162.5	105.5	106.3	113.5	104.2	105.6	104.7
October	108.3	112.7	117.5	129.3	107.1	183.7	163.7	105.9	107.4	114.6	104.2	105.8	105.1
November	108.2	111.6	118.3	122.5	107.1	183.8	163.7	106.2	108.2	114.3	104.3	105.8	105.3
December	108.0	111.3	118.0	120.6	107.2	183.8	163.5	106.1	108.0	114.3	104.3	105.8	105.3
2013													
January	108.3	111.9	118.4	121.9	107.6	184.5	163.8	106.2	107.2	114.9	104.8	106.4	105.5
February	108.8	112.8	117.3	127.2	107.9	184.7	163.9	106.5	107.4	115.0	105.1	106.4	105.7
March	109.1	112.9	118.6	126.2	107.9	184.7	163.8	106.9	108.3	116.0	105.3	106.4	106.1
April	109.0	112.4	117.0	125.1	107.9	184.7	163.9	107.0	108.6	115.0	105.4	106.8	106.1
May	108.8	112.8	118.3	126.3	107.8	184.7	163.9	106.5	107.0	114.4	105.4	106.9	105.7
June	109.2	112.9	118.6	126.8	107.8	184.7	163.8	107.0	107.8	115.7	105.7	106.9	106.1
July	109.5	113.0	118.7	126.9	107.9	184.9	163.8	107.4	108.6	116.0	105.9	107.4	106.4
August	109.5	113.1	118.0	128.3	107.8	184.9	163.7	107.4	108.3	116.2	106.1	107.5	106.4
September	109.4	112.9	117.6	127.7	107.7	184.6	163.9	107.4	108.6	114.4	106.1	107.7	106.4
October	109.7	112.5	117.3	124.3	108.2	185.9	165.2	108.0	109.5	115.3	106.4	109.0	106.9
November	109.4	112.0	117.2	121.1	108.2	186.1	165.4	107.8	109.1	114.6	106.5	109.1	106.8
December	109.3	112.2	117.0	121.7	108.6	186.8	165.6	107.5	107.6	116.6	106.4	109.2	106.6
2014													
January	109.7	113.1	117.6	123.2	109.3	188.1	166.2	107.6	107.4	116.1	106.9	109.8	107.0
February	110.1	113.5	118.1	124.7	109.4	188.2	166.3	108.2	108.7	115.8	107.1	109.9	107.4
March	110.8	114.3	120.0	127.9	109.2	187.9	166.1	108.8	109.9	117.4	107.4	110.0	107.8
April	111.0	115.2	123.0	129.8	109.4	187.9	166.1	108.7	109.4	118.1	107.3	110.3	107.7
May	111.1	115.0	122.6	129.4	109.3	188.0	166.1	108.8	110.2	118.1	107.2	110.3	107.9
June	111.2	115.4	123.1	130.7	109.4	188.2	166.1	108.8	109.3	119.0	107.4	110.4	107.8
July	111.6	115.3	123.0	129.9	109.6	188.4	166.2	109.5	111.1	119.0	107.6	110.8	108.4
August	111.6	115.0	122.5	128.9	109.5	188.4	166.1	109.5	110.5	119.3	108.0	110.9	108.4
September	111.1	114.6	122.2	127.0	109.5	188.4	166.1	109.1	109.8	117.4	107.8	110.9	108.1
October	111.4	113.6	122.4	119.6	110.0	188.9	167.5	110.0	112.6	117.4	107.8	111.4	108.9
November	110.8	112.5	122.3	113.9	109.8	189.9	167.4	110.7	111.6	117.2	107.9	111.4	108.6
December	110.3	110.9	122.1	105.6	109.8	190.0	167.2	109.8	111.9	117.5	107.9	111.6	108.7

. . . = Not available.

Table 8-5. Producer Price Indexes for Goods and Services: Final Demand—*Continued*

(November 2009 =100, except as noted.)

Year and month	Final demand	Final demand goods						Final demand services				Final demand con-struction	Final demand less food and energy (April 2010 =100)
		Final demand goods	Final demand foods	Final demand energy goods	Final demand goods less food and energy			Final demand services	Final demand trade services	Final demand transpor-tation and ware-housing services	Final demand services less trade, transpor-tation, and ware-housing		
					Total	Finished goods less foods and energy (1982 =100)							
						Total	Private capital equip-ment						
SEASONALLY ADJUSTED													
2011													
January	103.7	106.7	108.5	118.6	103.1	175.3	158.0	102.1	101.9	106.2	101.8	101.0	101.2
February	104.3	108.0	112.6	120.2	103.6	175.7	158.3	102.2	102.3	107.2	101.7	100.9	101.5
March	105.0	108.8	111.7	124.1	104.0	176.3	158.7	102.9	103.8	108.7	101.8	101.0	102.0
April	105.5	109.8	112.2	127.5	104.5	176.8	159.2	103.1	103.8	109.2	102.2	101.8	102.4
May	105.8	110.4	111.1	130.8	104.7	177.1	159.3	103.3	104.4	110.2	102.0	101.8	102.5
June	105.9	110.2	111.8	128.1	105.0	177.5	159.8	103.5	104.4	110.2	102.4	101.8	102.7
July	106.1	110.6	112.4	128.2	105.4	178.3	160.2	103.6	104.0	110.4	102.7	102.9	103.0
August	106.3	110.4	113.6	125.4	105.5	178.5	160.1	104.0	105.0	110.9	102.9	103.0	103.3
September	106.7	111.2	114.4	128.4	105.8	179.0	160.4	104.2	105.4	111.5	102.8	103.0	103.5
October	106.4	110.8	113.6	127.1	105.7	179.4	160.7	103.8	104.2	111.6	102.9	104.3	103.2
November	106.6	111.0	114.6	127.9	105.6	179.6	160.9	104.2	104.6	111.9	103.2	104.4	103.4
December	106.5	110.7	113.6	126.9	105.7	180.0	161.2	104.1	104.3	112.2	103.1	104.4	103.4
2012													
January	106.9	111.2	114.2	127.4	106.1	180.7	161.6	104.5	105.1	112.5	103.4	105.0	103.8
February	107.2	111.5	114.2	128.5	106.3	181.0	162.0	104.8	105.8	113.3	103.4	105.0	104.1
March	107.4	111.8	114.6	128.6	106.7	181.4	162.2	105.0	106.4	113.7	103.3	105.2	104.3
April	107.6	111.6	114.2	127.0	106.8	181.7	162.5	105.3	106.5	114.0	103.8	105.6	104.6
May	107.5	111.0	114.1	124.0	106.8	181.9	162.6	105.6	107.5	114.2	103.6	105.6	104.8
June	107.3	110.4	114.3	120.8	106.6	182.2	162.8	105.5	107.3	114.2	103.7	105.6	104.7
July	107.3	110.6	115.6	120.1	106.8	183.0	163.3	105.4	106.7	113.8	103.8	105.6	104.6
August	107.5	111.9	117.0	125.8	106.9	183.2	163.3	105.1	105.4	114.2	104.0	105.7	104.5
September	108.2	112.9	117.6	131.1	107.0	183.2	163.2	105.6	106.2	114.6	104.3	105.6	104.8
October	108.3	113.0	117.8	131.7	107.0	183.2	163.2	105.7	106.8	115.1	104.2	105.8	104.9
November	108.4	112.2	118.6	125.8	107.1	183.5	163.3	106.3	108.1	115.2	104.4	105.8	105.3
December	108.5	112.2	118.4	125.4	107.2	183.6	163.3	106.4	108.3	115.1	104.5	105.8	105.5
2013													
January	108.6	112.6	119.1	126.0	107.4	183.9	163.3	106.4	108.0	115.1	104.7	106.4	105.6
February	108.9	113.2	118.0	129.6	107.7	184.2	163.5	106.5	107.5	115.2	105.0	106.4	105.6
March	108.8	112.7	118.8	125.2	107.8	184.5	163.7	106.7	107.9	115.3	105.2	106.3	105.8
April	108.6	111.8	116.6	121.9	107.8	184.7	163.8	106.8	108.3	114.1	105.3	106.7	106.0
May	108.6	112.4	118.1	123.8	107.9	184.9	164.0	106.5	107.0	114.0	105.4	106.9	105.7
June	109.0	112.5	118.0	124.4	108.0	185.1	164.1	107.1	108.1	114.9	105.7	106.9	106.2
July	109.3	112.5	118.1	124.4	108.0	185.3	164.2	107.4	108.9	115.4	105.9	107.4	106.5
August	109.3	112.7	117.5	125.5	108.0	185.4	164.2	107.4	108.3	115.6	106.0	107.5	106.4
September	109.4	112.7	117.3	125.7	108.0	185.4	164.6	107.5	108.5	115.5	106.2	107.7	106.5
October	109.6	112.8	117.5	126.2	108.0	185.4	164.7	107.7	108.8	115.8	106.4	109.0	106.7
November	109.7	112.6	117.5	124.4	108.2	185.8	165.0	107.9	109.1	115.6	106.5	109.1	106.9
December	109.8	113.2	117.5	126.5	108.5	186.6	165.3	107.7	107.9	117.4	106.6	109.2	106.8
2014													
January	110.1	113.8	118.3	127.5	109.0	187.5	165.7	107.9	108.1	116.5	106.8	109.8	107.1
February	110.3	113.9	118.9	126.8	109.1	187.7	165.9	108.1	108.8	116.1	107.0	109.8	107.3
March	110.6	114.2	120.3	127.3	109.1	187.7	166.0	108.6	109.5	116.7	107.2	109.9	107.6
April	110.7	114.5	122.5	126.7	109.3	187.9	166.1	108.5	109.0	117.3	107.3	110.3	107.6
May	111.0	114.6	122.4	127.2	109.4	188.3	166.3	108.9	110.2	117.7	107.2	110.3	107.9
June	111.1	114.9	122.5	128.1	109.5	188.6	166.4	108.8	109.6	118.2	107.5	110.4	107.9
July	111.4	114.8	122.2	127.1	109.7	188.8	166.6	109.5	111.3	118.4	107.6	110.8	108.4
August	111.3	114.5	121.9	125.8	109.7	189.0	166.7	109.4	110.6	118.6	107.9	110.9	108.4
September	111.1	114.4	121.8	124.7	109.9	189.3	166.8	109.1	109.7	118.4	107.9	110.9	108.2
October	111.4	113.9	122.5	121.5	109.8	189.5	167.0	109.8	111.9	117.9	107.9	111.5	108.7
November	111.1	113.0	122.6	117.0	109.7	189.6	167.0	109.8	111.5	118.3	108.0	111.5	108.7
December	110.8	111.6	122.5	109.3	109.7	189.8	166.8	110.1	112.1	118.3	108.2	111.6	108.9

Table 8-6. Producer Price Indexes for Goods and Services: Intermediate Demand

(November 2009 = 100, except as noted.)

Year and month	Intermediate demand by commodity type						Intermediate demand by production flow (Prices of inputs to indicated stage of production)			
	Processed goods (1982=100)	Unprocessed goods (1982=100)	Services	Construction	Processed materials less foods and energy (1982=100)	Unprocessed nonfood materials less energy (1982=100)	Stage 4 intermediate demand	Stage 3 intermediate demand	Stage 2 intermediate demand	Stage 1 intermediate demand
NOT SEASONALLY ADJUSTED										
2010	183.4	212.2	101.1	101.1	180.8	329.1	102.0	104.2	103.5	106.2
2011	199.9	249.4	103.2	102.3	192.0	390.4	106.9	111.7	112.9	115.7
2012	200.7	241.4	105.3	103.8	192.6	369.6	108.6	112.7	110.7	114.7
2013	200.8	246.7	107.2	105.7	193.8	351.2	109.9	114.1	112.8	114.8
2014	201.9	249.3	108.9	108.0	195.2	345.7	111.2	116.9	112.2	116.1
2011										
January	190.6	235.9	102.1	101.6	186.5	381.1	104.1	107.3	108.9	111.1
February	193.7	242.8	102.3	101.8	188.7	391.6	104.9	109.3	109.8	112.8
March	197.6	248.2	102.6	101.9	190.2	387.8	106.0	110.8	112.0	114.7
April	201.0	261.3	103.3	101.7	192.6	399.1	107.1	112.4	116.2	116.4
May	203.2	255.5	103.5	102.2	193.8	393.8	107.6	112.7	115.6	117.8
June	203.3	256.9	103.6	102.4	193.9	399.6	107.8	113.3	114.9	118.1
July	204.1	256.9	103.6	102.5	194.4	401.0	108.0	113.3	115.5	118.8
August	202.8	251.2	103.8	102.7	194.2	402.2	107.9	113.3	112.6	118.2
September	203.2	251.1	103.7	102.8	194.2	401.4	107.9	112.8	113.6	118.0
October	200.2	242.8	103.6	102.9	192.9	381.2	107.1	111.7	111.6	115.4
November	199.9	248.5	103.5	102.9	192.0	373.5	107.2	111.8	113.1	113.6
December	198.5	242.0	103.4	102.9	190.9	372.7	106.9	111.3	111.1	113.1
2012										
January	198.8	246.0	104.4	103.7	191.7	383.3	107.5	111.9	111.7	113.9
February	200.0	245.2	104.6	103.7	193.2	383.5	107.9	112.3	111.4	114.6
March	203.3	248.7	104.6	103.8	194.6	387.6	108.5	113.2	112.3	116.7
April	203.0	242.0	104.9	103.8	195.0	382.7	108.6	112.8	111.2	116.6
May	201.5	234.9	105.1	103.9	194.5	374.4	108.5	112.5	109.2	115.6
June	199.7	227.1	104.9	103.9	192.3	357.7	108.2	112.2	106.7	113.6
July	198.8	233.0	105.2	103.9	191.4	354.2	108.3	111.8	108.3	113.2
August	200.7	242.7	105.2	103.9	191.2	361.4	108.9	112.6	110.7	114.1
September	202.7	244.9	105.5	103.9	191.9	365.2	109.4	113.2	111.7	115.0
October	201.8	242.3	106.3	103.9	192.0	356.4	109.4	113.5	111.8	114.5
November	199.5	244.0	106.8	103.9	191.8	361.6	109.1	113.3	111.7	114.0
December	199.2	245.4	106.4	103.9	192.1	366.7	108.9	113.0	111.6	114.2
2013										
January	200.0	247.3	106.8	104.9	193.5	364.2	109.4	113.5	112.3	114.2
February	202.5	246.1	106.7	105.3	194.7	363.0	109.8	114.3	112.5	115.4
March	201.5	248.7	106.9	105.7	194.6	367.1	109.7	114.1	112.6	115.3
April	200.8	249.2	107.4	105.6	194.2	358.3	109.9	114.3	113.4	114.6
May	201.0	252.5	106.9	105.6	193.9	351.3	109.8	114.5	113.3	114.5
June	201.3	251.3	107.2	105.6	193.8	349.0	110.0	114.6	113.4	114.9
July	201.3	252.9	107.2	105.6	193.4	347.0	110.1	114.0	114.4	115.3
August	201.6	247.2	107.4	105.8	193.6	345.7	110.3	114.1	113.6	115.7
September	201.5	246.2	107.4	106.1	193.5	342.0	110.2	114.0	113.8	115.3
October	200.1	241.2	107.6	106.1	193.4	338.7	110.1	113.8	112.0	114.4
November	198.8	236.7	107.8	106.1	193.3	341.7	109.8	113.7	110.3	114.0
December	199.3	240.7	107.5	106.0	193.5	346.1	109.8	113.6	111.4	114.4
2014										
January	200.9	246.0	108.0	107.0	194.4	354.2	110.3	115.1	112.3	116.1
February	202.1	258.6	108.2	107.2	195.2	351.3	110.5	115.9	116.5	116.4
March	203.0	262.0	108.7	107.3	195.0	350.7	111.2	117.5	115.3	116.6
April	203.8	265.4	108.5	107.6	195.5	356.3	111.4	118.0	115.4	116.6
May	203.8	263.0	108.5	107.6	195.4	354.4	111.4	117.7	115.1	116.5
June	204.3	260.5	108.6	107.8	195.4	349.1	111.6	117.7	115.0	117.1
July	204.5	255.3	109.2	108.1	196.0	348.7	111.9	118.1	113.9	118.2
August	204.4	245.9	109.2	108.2	196.4	345.6	111.9	117.6	112.0	118.2
September	203.8	245.6	109.0	108.4	196.2	345.4	111.8	117.8	111.3	117.4
October	200.5	236.2	109.5	108.7	195.5	335.2	111.3	117.0	108.5	115.5
November	197.7	232.9	109.4	108.9	194.6	329.9	110.8	116.3	107.0	113.2
December	194.2	219.7	109.4	108.9	193.4	327.9	110.3	113.8	104.3	111.6

Table 8-6. Producer Price Indexes for Goods and Services: Intermediate Demand—*Continued*

(November 2009 = 100, except as noted.)

Year and month	Intermediate demand by commodity type						Intermediate demand by production flow (Prices of inputs to indicated stage of production)			
	Processed goods (1982=100)	Unprocessed goods (1982=100)	Services	Construction	Processed materials less foods and energy (1982=100)	Unprocessed nonfood materials less energy (1982 =100)	Stage 4 intermediate demand	Stage 3 intermediate demand	Stage 2 intermediate demand	Stage 1 intermediate demand
SEASONALLY ADJUSTED										
2011										
January	192.0	237.3	102.1	101.5	186.6	382.6	104.5	107.8	109.2	112.1
February	194.7	243.3	102.2	101.6	188.8	391.7	105.2	109.5	110.0	113.4
March	197.5	247.5	102.5	101.7	190.2	385.5	105.9	110.5	112.0	114.6
April	200.1	260.3	103.2	101.7	192.4	396.0	106.7	112.0	116.0	116.1
May	202.0	253.1	103.4	102.1	193.6	391.3	107.2	112.0	115.3	117.1
June	202.3	253.9	103.5	102.3	193.8	396.6	107.4	112.7	114.6	117.2
July	203.2	255.3	103.6	102.5	194.3	400.4	107.7	112.9	115.3	117.8
August	201.8	250.7	103.8	102.7	194.2	402.6	107.6	113.0	112.6	117.3
September	202.7	251.4	103.8	102.9	194.2	401.9	107.7	112.8	113.5	117.5
October	200.9	244.4	103.6	103.0	193.0	383.8	107.3	112.1	111.7	115.8
November	201.0	250.8	103.6	103.1	192.3	376.2	107.6	112.4	113.3	114.6
December	200.1	244.9	103.7	103.3	191.1	375.6	107.5	112.3	111.5	114.4
2012										
January	200.2	247.8	104.4	103.6	191.9	384.3	107.9	112.5	112.0	114.7
February	200.8	245.8	104.6	103.5	193.2	383.6	108.1	112.5	111.6	115.1
March	203.1	247.7	104.5	103.6	194.6	386.0	108.4	112.8	112.3	116.7
April	201.9	240.6	104.8	103.7	194.8	380.2	108.3	112.3	111.0	116.3
May	200.6	232.7	104.9	103.8	194.2	372.7	108.2	111.9	108.9	115.2
June	198.9	224.4	104.8	103.8	192.1	355.5	108.0	111.7	106.4	112.8
July	198.1	231.3	105.1	103.9	191.4	353.7	108.1	111.6	108.1	112.4
August	199.9	242.3	105.2	104.0	191.3	361.7	108.6	112.4	110.6	113.4
September	202.0	245.2	105.6	104.0	192.0	365.6	109.3	113.2	111.6	114.5
October	202.4	244.3	106.3	104.1	192.1	359.2	109.6	113.8	112.0	114.8
November	200.6	246.3	106.9	104.1	192.0	364.1	109.4	113.8	111.9	114.9
December	200.7	248.7	106.7	104.4	192.3	369.5	109.4	113.9	112.0	115.2
2013										
January	201.4	249.6	106.8	104.7	193.6	365.2	109.8	114.2	112.7	115.0
February	203.3	247.0	106.7	105.1	194.7	363.0	110.0	114.5	112.7	115.8
March	201.3	247.5	106.8	105.5	194.5	365.5	109.7	113.8	112.6	115.3
April	199.9	247.3	107.3	105.5	194.0	355.8	109.6	113.8	113.2	114.4
May	200.3	250.2	106.8	105.5	193.7	349.8	109.5	113.9	113.1	114.2
June	200.5	248.3	107.1	105.6	193.7	346.6	109.7	114.1	113.0	114.2
July	200.6	251.0	107.1	105.6	193.4	346.4	109.8	113.7	114.2	114.4
August	200.7	246.9	107.4	105.9	193.6	345.6	110.0	113.9	113.5	114.9
September	200.7	246.5	107.5	106.1	193.6	342.4	110.0	113.9	113.6	114.7
October	200.6	242.9	107.6	106.3	193.6	340.8	110.2	114.1	112.1	114.7
November	199.9	238.5	107.9	106.3	193.5	343.7	110.1	114.2	110.5	114.9
December	200.8	243.6	107.7	106.5	193.7	348.2	110.3	114.5	111.8	115.4
2014										
January	202.3	248.3	108.1	106.8	194.5	354.9	110.7	115.8	112.7	116.9
February	202.8	259.8	108.2	106.9	195.2	351.1	110.7	116.1	116.7	116.9
March	202.9	260.8	108.6	107.1	194.9	349.3	111.2	117.2	115.3	116.6
April	202.9	263.6	108.4	107.3	195.3	354.1	111.1	117.4	115.2	116.4
May	203.1	260.7	108.4	107.5	195.2	353.2	111.2	117.2	114.9	116.2
June	203.4	257.9	108.5	107.8	195.3	347.4	111.3	117.1	114.7	116.3
July	203.6	253.4	109.2	108.1	196.0	348.4	111.6	117.7	113.7	117.3
August	203.4	245.7	109.2	108.3	196.4	345.5	111.6	117.4	111.9	117.3
September	203.0	245.9	109.1	108.4	196.3	345.8	111.5	117.7	111.2	116.8
October	201.0	237.7	109.5	108.9	195.7	337.1	111.5	117.3	108.6	115.8
November	198.9	234.7	109.5	109.3	194.8	331.8	111.2	116.9	107.2	114.1
December	195.4	222.4	109.7	109.3	193.6	329.8	110.8	114.7	104.7	112.5

Table 8-7. Producer Price Indexes by Major Commodity Groups

(1982 = 100.)

Year and month	All commodities	Farm products	Processed foods and feeds	Industrial commodities													
				Total	Textile products and apparel	Hides, leather, and related products	Fuels and related products and power	Chemicals and allied products	Rubber and plastics products	Lumber and wood products	Pulp, paper, and allied products	Metals and metal products	Machinery and equipment	Furniture and household durables	Non-metallic mineral products	Transportation equipment	Miscellaneous products
1950	27.3	44.0	33.2	25.0	50.2	32.9	12.6	30.4	35.6	31.4	25.7	22.0	22.6	40.9	23.5	. . .	28.6
1951	30.4	51.2	36.9	27.6	56.0	37.7	13.0	34.8	43.7	34.1	30.5	24.5	25.3	44.4	25.0	. . .	30.3
1952	29.6	48.4	36.4	26.9	50.5	30.5	13.0	33.0	39.6	33.2	29.7	24.5	25.3	43.5	25.0	. . .	30.2
1953	29.2	43.8	34.8	27.2	49.3	31.0	13.4	33.4	36.9	33.1	29.6	25.3	25.9	44.4	26.0	. . .	31.0
1954	29.3	43.2	35.4	27.2	48.2	29.5	13.2	33.8	37.5	32.5	29.6	25.5	26.3	44.9	26.6	. . .	31.3
1955	29.3	40.5	33.8	27.8	48.2	29.4	13.2	33.7	42.4	34.1	30.4	27.2	27.2	45.1	27.3	. . .	31.3
1956	30.3	40.0	33.8	29.1	48.2	31.2	13.6	33.9	43.0	34.6	32.4	29.6	29.3	46.3	28.5	. . .	31.7
1957	31.2	41.1	34.8	29.9	48.3	31.2	14.3	34.6	42.8	32.8	33.0	30.2	31.4	47.5	29.6	. . .	32.6
1958	31.6	42.9	36.5	30.0	47.4	31.6	13.7	34.9	42.8	32.5	33.4	30.0	32.1	47.9	29.9	. . .	33.3
1959	31.7	40.2	35.6	30.5	48.1	35.9	13.7	34.8	42.6	34.7	33.7	30.6	32.8	48.0	30.3	. . .	33.4
1960	31.7	40.1	35.6	30.5	48.6	34.6	13.9	34.8	42.7	33.5	34.0	30.6	33.0	47.8	30.4	. . .	33.6
1961	31.6	39.7	36.2	30.4	47.8	34.9	14.0	34.5	41.1	32.0	33.0	30.5	33.0	47.5	30.5	. . .	33.7
1962	31.7	40.4	36.5	30.4	48.2	35.3	14.0	33.9	39.9	32.2	33.4	30.2	33.0	47.2	30.5	. . .	33.9
1963	31.6	39.6	36.8	30.3	48.2	34.3	13.9	33.5	40.1	32.8	33.1	30.3	33.1	46.9	30.3	. . .	34.2
1964	31.6	39.0	36.7	30.5	48.5	34.4	13.5	33.6	39.6	33.5	33.0	31.1	33.3	47.1	30.4	. . .	34.4
1965	32.3	40.7	38.0	30.9	48.8	35.9	13.8	33.9	39.7	33.7	33.3	32.0	33.7	46.8	30.4	. . .	34.7
1966	33.3	43.7	40.2	31.5	48.9	39.4	14.1	34.0	40.5	35.2	34.2	32.8	34.7	47.4	30.7	. . .	35.3
1967	33.4	41.3	39.8	32.0	48.9	38.1	14.4	34.2	41.4	35.1	34.6	33.2	35.9	48.3	31.2	. . .	36.2
1968	34.2	42.3	40.6	32.8	50.7	39.3	14.3	34.1	42.8	39.8	35.0	34.0	37.0	49.7	32.4	. . .	37.0
1969	35.6	45.0	42.7	33.9	51.8	41.5	14.6	34.2	43.6	44.0	36.0	36.0	38.2	50.7	33.6	40.4	38.1
1970	36.9	45.8	44.6	35.2	52.4	42.0	15.3	35.0	44.9	39.9	37.5	38.7	40.0	51.9	35.3	41.9	39.8
1971	38.1	46.6	45.5	36.5	53.3	43.4	16.6	35.6	45.2	44.7	38.1	39.4	41.4	53.1	38.2	44.2	40.8
1972	39.8	51.6	48.0	37.8	55.5	50.0	17.1	35.6	45.3	50.7	39.3	40.9	42.3	53.8	39.4	45.5	41.5
1973	45.0	72.7	58.9	40.3	60.5	54.5	19.4	37.6	46.6	62.2	42.3	44.0	43.7	55.7	40.7	46.1	43.3
1974	53.5	77.4	68.0	49.2	68.0	55.2	30.1	50.2	56.4	64.5	52.5	57.0	50.0	61.8	47.8	50.3	48.1
1975	58.4	77.0	72.6	54.9	67.4	56.5	35.4	62.0	62.2	62.1	59.0	61.5	57.9	67.5	54.4	56.7	53.4
1976	61.1	78.8	70.8	58.4	72.4	63.9	38.3	64.0	66.0	72.2	62.1	65.0	61.3	70.3	58.2	60.5	55.6
1977	64.9	79.4	74.0	62.5	75.3	68.3	43.6	65.9	69.4	83.0	64.6	69.3	65.2	73.2	62.6	64.6	59.4
1978	69.9	87.7	80.6	67.0	78.1	76.1	46.5	68.0	72.4	96.9	67.7	75.3	70.3	77.5	69.6	69.5	66.7
1979	78.7	99.6	88.5	75.7	82.5	96.1	58.9	76.0	80.5	105.5	75.9	86.0	76.7	82.8	77.6	75.3	75.5
1980	89.8	102.9	95.9	88.0	89.7	94.7	82.8	89.0	90.1	101.5	86.3	95.0	86.0	90.7	88.4	82.9	93.6
1981	98.0	105.2	98.9	97.4	97.6	99.3	100.2	98.4	96.4	102.8	94.8	99.6	94.4	95.9	96.7	94.3	96.1
1982	100.0	100.0	100.0	100.0	100.0	100.0	100.0	100.0	100.0	100.0	100.0	100.0	100.0	100.0	100.0	100.0	100.0
1983	101.3	102.4	101.8	101.1	100.3	103.2	95.9	100.3	100.8	107.9	103.3	101.8	102.7	103.4	101.6	102.8	104.8
1984	103.7	105.5	105.4	103.3	102.7	109.0	94.8	102.9	102.3	108.0	110.3	104.8	105.1	105.7	105.4	105.2	107.0
1985	103.2	95.1	103.5	103.7	102.9	108.9	91.4	103.7	101.9	106.6	113.3	104.4	107.2	107.1	108.6	107.9	109.4
1986	100.2	92.9	105.4	100.0	103.2	113.0	69.8	102.6	101.9	107.2	116.1	103.2	108.8	108.2	110.0	110.5	111.6
1987	102.8	95.5	107.9	102.6	105.1	120.4	70.2	106.4	103.0	112.8	121.8	107.1	110.4	109.9	110.0	112.5	114.9
1988	106.9	104.9	112.7	106.3	109.2	131.4	66.7	116.3	109.3	118.9	130.4	118.7	113.2	113.1	111.2	114.3	120.2
1989	112.2	110.9	117.8	111.6	112.3	136.3	72.9	123.0	112.6	126.7	137.8	124.1	117.4	116.9	112.6	117.7	126.5
1990	116.3	112.2	121.9	115.8	115.0	141.7	82.3	123.6	113.6	129.7	141.2	122.9	120.7	119.2	114.7	121.5	134.2
1991	116.5	105.7	121.9	116.5	116.3	138.9	81.2	125.6	115.1	132.1	142.9	120.2	123.0	121.2	117.2	126.4	140.8
1992	117.2	103.6	122.1	117.4	117.8	140.4	80.4	125.9	115.1	146.6	147.3	123.2	119.2	123.4	117.3	130.4	145.3
1993	118.9	107.1	124.0	119.0	118.0	143.7	80.0	128.2	116.0	174.0	152.5	124.2	119.2	124.0	120.0	133.7	145.4
1994	120.4	106.3	125.5	120.7	118.3	148.5	77.8	132.1	117.6	180.0	152.5	124.8	125.1	126.1	124.2	137.2	141.9
1995	124.7	107.4	127.0	125.5	120.8	153.7	78.0	142.5	124.3	178.1	172.2	134.5	126.6	128.2	129.0	139.7	145.4
1996	127.7	122.4	133.3	127.3	122.4	150.5	85.8	142.1	123.8	176.1	168.7	131.0	126.5	130.4	131.0	141.7	147.7
1997	127.6	112.9	134.0	127.7	122.6	154.2	86.1	143.6	123.2	183.8	167.9	131.8	125.9	130.8	133.2	141.6	150.9
1998	124.4	104.6	131.6	124.8	122.9	148.0	75.3	143.9	122.6	179.1	171.7	127.8	124.9	131.3	135.4	141.2	156.0
1999	125.5	98.4	131.1	126.5	121.1	146.0	80.5	144.2	122.5	183.6	174.1	124.6	124.3	131.7	138.9	141.8	166.6
2000	132.7	99.5	133.1	134.8	121.4	151.5	103.5	151.0	125.5	178.2	183.7	128.1	124.0	132.6	142.5	143.8	170.8
2001	134.2	103.8	137.3	135.7	121.3	158.4	105.3	151.8	127.2	174.4	184.8	125.4	123.7	133.5	144.3	145.2	181.3
2002	131.1	99.0	136.2	132.4	119.9	157.6	93.2	151.9	126.8	173.3	185.9	125.9	122.9	133.9	146.2	144.6	182.4
2003	138.1	111.5	143.4	139.1	119.8	162.3	112.9	161.8	130.1	177.4	190.0	129.2	121.9	133.9	148.2	145.7	179.6
2004	146.7	123.3	151.2	147.6	121.0	164.5	126.9	174.4	133.8	195.6	195.7	149.6	122.1	135.1	153.2	148.6	183.2
2005	157.4	118.5	153.1	160.2	122.8	165.4	156.4	192.0	143.8	196.5	202.6	160.8	123.7	139.4	164.2	151.0	195.1
2006	164.7	117.0	153.8	168.8	124.5	168.4	166.7	205.8	153.8	194.4	209.8	181.6	127.3	144.7	179.9	152.6	205.6
2007	172.6	143.4	165.1	175.1	125.8	173.6	177.6	214.8	155.0	192.4	216.9	193.5	129.7	148.9	186.2	155.0	210.3
2008	189.6	161.3	180.5	192.3	128.9	173.1	214.6	245.5	165.9	191.3	226.8	213.0	131.3	153.1	197.1	158.6	216.6
2009	172.9	134.6	176.2	174.8	129.5	157.0	158.7	229.4	165.2	182.8	225.6	186.8	131.3	153.1	202.4	162.2	217.5
2010	184.7	151.0	182.3	187.0	131.7	181.4	185.8	246.6	170.7	192.7	236.9	207.6	131.1	153.2	201.8	163.4	221.5
2011	201.0	186.7	197.5	202.0	141.7	199.9	215.9	275.1	182.7	194.7	245.1	225.9	132.7	156.4	205.0	166.1	229.2
2012	202.2	192.5	205.2	202.1	142.2	202.3	212.1	276.6	186.9	201.6	244.2	219.9	134.2	160.6	211.0	169.8	235.6
2013	203.4	195.3	208.3	203.0	143.4	217.9	211.8	279.2	189.0	214.9	248.8	213.5	135.2	161.1	216.9	171.8	239.5
2014	205.3	197.4	216.5	204.1	145.5	229.1	209.8	280.9	190.2	224.2	250.5	215.0	136.2	163.2	223.7	174.1	243.0

. . . = Not available.

NOTES AND DEFINITIONS, CHAPTER 8

This chapter presents price indexes from two major price collection systems, both conducted by the U.S. Bureau of Labor Statistics. In 2014, the Producer Price Index system was expanded to include services and construction as well as goods. A new index for "Final Demand" for goods, services, and construction, with more than double the scope, is now presented alongside the familiar Finished Goods index. The expanded system is only available beginning in November 2009, and the historical Producer Price Indexes for goods—with data going back to 1913—are also maintained and carried forward. See the Notes and Definitions for Tables 8-5 through 8-7, below, for further information.

Tables 8-1 through 8-4
Consumer Price Indexes

SOURCES: U.S. DEPARTMENT OF LABOR, BUREAU OF LABOR STATISTICS (BLS) AND U.S. DEPARTMENT OF COMMERCE, BUREAU OF ECONOMIC ANALYSIS (BEA)

The Consumer Price Index (CPI), which is compiled by the Bureau of Labor Statistics (BLS), was originally conceived as a statistical measure of the average change in the cost to consumers of a market basket of goods and services purchased by urban wage earners and clerical workers. In 1978, its scope was broadened to also provide a measure of the change in the cost of the average market basket for <u>all</u> urban consumers. There was still a demand for a wage-earner index, so both versions have been calculated and published since then. The most commonly cited measure in this system is the Consumer Price Index for All Urban Consumers (CPI-U). The wage-earner alternative, used according to law for calculating cost of living adjustments in many government programs, including Social Security, and also used by choice of the contracting parties in wage agreements, is called the Consumer Price Index for Urban Wage Earners and Clerical Workers (CPI-W). Both are presented by the BLS back to 1913, and reproduced in *Business Statistics*; however, the <u>movements</u> (percent changes) in the two indexes before 1978 are identical and are based on the wage-earner market basket. (The pre-1978 <u>levels</u> of the two indexes differ because of differences between 1978 and the reference base period.)

These CPIs have typically been called "cost-of-living" indexes, even though the original fixed market basket concept does not correspond to economists' definition of a cost-of- living index, which is the cost of maintaining a constant standard of living or level of satisfaction. In recent years, the concept measured in practice in the CPI has developed into something intended to be closer to the theoretical definition of a cost-of-living index. In addition, a new variation of the CPI—the Chained Consumer Price Index for All Urban Consumers (C-CPI-U)—is intended to provide an even closer approximation.

The reference base for the total BLS Consumer Price Index and most of its components is currently 1982–1984 = 100. However, new products that have been introduced into the index since January 1982 are shown on later reference bases, as is the entire C-CPI-U.

Price indexes for personal consumption expenditures (PCE) are calculated and published by the Bureau of Economic Analysis (BEA) as a part of the national income and product accounts (NIPAs). (See Chapters 1 and 4 and their notes and definitions.) Monthly, quarterly, and annual values are all available. The reference base for these indexes is the average in the NIPA base year, 2009. These indexes differ in a number of other respects from the CPIs, and are often emphasized by the Federal Reserve in its analyses of the nation's economy. Four important NIPA aggregate price indexes are shown in Tables 8-3 and 8-4 for convenient comparison with the CPIs. See the definitions for those tables for more information.

The CPI-U and the CPI-W

The *CPI-U*, which is displayed in Tables 8-1 through 8-4 and also provides all of the component category sub-indexes shown in Table 8-2, uses the consumption patterns for all urban consumers, who currently comprise about 89 percent of the population.

A slightly different index that is widely used for adjusting wages and government benefits is the *CPI-W*, of which the all-items total is shown in each of Tables 8-1 through 8-4. It represents the buying habits of only urban wage earners and clerical workers, who currently comprise about 28 percent of the population. The weights are derived from the same Consumer Expenditure Surveys (CES) used for the CPI-U weights, and are changed on the same schedule. However, they include only consumers from the specified categories instead of all urban consumers.

Beginning with January 2012, the weights in both indexes are based on consumer expenditures in the 2009–2010 period. From January 2010 to December 2011, 2007–2008 weights were used; from January 2008 to December 2009, 2005–2006 weights; from January 2006 to December 2007, 2003–2004 weights; from January 2004 to December 2005, 2001–2002 weights; from January 2002 to December 2003, 1999–2000 weights; and from January 1998 to December 2001, 1993–1995 weights. The weights will continue to be updated at two-year intervals, with new weights introduced in the January indexes of each even-numbered year. Previously, new weights were introduced only at the time of a major revision, which translated into a lag of a decade or more.

Specifically, the CPI weights for 1964 through 1977 were derived from reported expenditures of a sample of wageearner and clericalworker families and individuals in 1960–1961 and adjusted for price changes between the survey dates and 1963. Weights for the 1978–1986 period were derived from a survey undertaken during the 1972–1974 period and adjusted for price change between the survey dates and December 1977. For 1987 through 1997, the spending patterns reflected in the CPI were derived from a survey undertaken during the 1982–1984 period. The reported expenditures were adjusted for price change between the survey dates and December 1986.

The CPI was overhauled and updated in the latest major revision, which took effect in January 1998. In addition, new products and improved methods are regularly introduced into the index, usually in January.

The latest change in methods was the introduction of a geometric mean formula for calculating many of the basic components of the index. Beginning with the index for January 1999, this formula is used for categories comprising approximately 61 percent of total consumer spending. The new formula allows for the possibility that some consumers may react to changing relative prices within a category by substituting items whose relative prices have declined for products whose relative prices have risen, while maintaining their overall level of satisfaction. The geometric mean formula is not used for a few categories in which consumer substitution in the short term is not feasible, currently housing rent and utilities.

The CPI-U was introduced in 1978. Before that time, only CPI-W data were available. The movements of the CPI-U before 1978 are therefore based on the changes in the CPI-W. However, the index levels are different because the two indexes differed in the 1982–1984 base period.

Because the official CPI-U and CPI-W are so widely used in "escalation"—the calculation of cost-of-living adjustments for wages and other private contracts, and for government payments and tax parameters—these price indexes are not retrospectively revised to incorporate new information and methods. (An exception is occasionally made for outright error, which happened in September 2000 and affected the data for January through August of that year.) Instead, the new information and methods of calculation are introduced in the current index and affect future index changes only. In Tables 8-3 and 8-4, PCE indexes, which are subject to routine revision, and special CPI indexes that have been retrospectively revised are presented. These indexes can be used by researchers to provide more consistent historical information.

Notes on the CPI data

The CPI is based on prices of food, clothing, shelter, fuel, utilities, transportation, medical care, and other goods and services that people buy for daytoday living. The quantity and quality of these priced items are kept essentially constant between revisions to ensure that only price changes will be measured. All taxes directly associated with the purchase and use of these items, such as sales and property taxes, are included in the index; the effects of income and payroll tax changes are not included.

Data are collected on about 80,000 individually defined goods and services from about 26,000 retail and service establishments and about 4,000 housing units in 87 urban areas across the country. These data are used to develop the U.S. city average.

Periodic major revisions of the indexes update the content and weights of the market basket of goods and services; update the statistical sample of urban areas, outlets, and unique items used in calculating the CPI; and improve the statistical methods used. In addition, retail outlets and items are resampled on a rotating 5-year basis. Adjustments for changing quality are made at times of major product changes, such as the annual auto model changeover. Other methodological changes are introduced from time to time.

The CES provides the weights—that is, the relative importance—used to combine the individual price changes into subtotals and totals. This survey is composed of two separate surveys: an interview survey and a diary survey, both of which are conducted by the Census Bureau for BLS. Each expenditure reported in the two surveys is classified into a series of detailed categories, which are then combined into expenditure classes and ultimately into major expenditure groups. CPI data as of 1998 are grouped into eight such categories: (1) food and beverages, (2) housing, (3) apparel, (4) transportation, (5) medical care, (6) recreation, (7) education and communication, and (8) other goods and services.

Seasonally adjusted national CPI indexes are published for selected series for which there is a significant seasonal pattern of price change. The factors currently in use were derived by the X13ARIMA-SEATS seasonal adjustment method. Some series with extreme or sharp movements are seasonally adjusted using Intervention Analysis Seasonal Adjustment. Seasonally adjusted indexes and seasonal factors for the preceding five years are updated annually based on data through the previous December. Due to these revisions, BLS advises against the use of seasonally adjusted data for escalation. Detailed descriptions of seasonal adjustment procedures are available upon request from BLS.

BLS estimates the "standard error"—the error due to collecting data from a sample instead of the universe—of the one-month percent change in the not-seasonally-adjusted U.S. all-items index in 2013 was 0.03 percentage point. This means that for the 2013 median 0.12 percent change in the All Items CPI-U, BLS is 95 percent confident that the actual percent change based on all retail prices would fall between 0.06 and 0.18 percent. Monthly percent changes in the seasonally adjusted indexes, in contrast, may be revised by 0.1 percentage point when reviewed at the end of the year, and occasionally by even more.

CPI Definitions

Definitions of the major CPI groupings were modified beginning with the data for January 1998. These modifications were carried back to 1993. The following definitions are the current definitions currently used for the CPI components.

The *food and beverage index* includes both food at home and food away from home (restaurant meals and other food bought and eaten away from home).

The *housing index* measures changes in rental costs and expenses connected with the acquisition and operation of a home. The CPIU, beginning with data for January 1983, and the CPIW, beginning with data for January 1985, reflect a change in the methodology used to compute the homeownership component. A rental equivalence measure replaced an asset-price approach, which included purchase prices and interest costs. The intent of the change was to separate shelter costs from the investment component of homeownership, so that the index would only reflect the cost of the shelter services provided by owner-occupied homes. In addition to measures of the cost of shelter, the housing category includes insurance, fuel, utilities, and household furnishings and operations.

The *apparel index* includes the purchase of apparel and footwear.

The *private transportation index* includes prices paid by urban consumers for such items as new and used automobiles and other vehicles, gasoline, motor oil, tires, repairs and maintenance, insurance, registration fees, driver's licenses, parking fees, and the like. Auto finance charges, like mortgage interest payments, are considered to be a cost of asset acquisition, not of current consumption. Therefore, they are no longer included in the CPI. City bus, streetcar, subway, taxicab, intercity bus, airplane, and railroad coach fares are some of the components of the *public transportation index*.

The *medical care index* includes prices for professional medical services, hospital and related services, prescription and non-prescription drugs, and other medical care commodities. The weight for the portion of health insurance premiums that is used to cover the costs of these medical goods and services is distributed among the items; the weight for the portion of health insurance costs attributable to administrative expenses and profits of insurance providers constitutes a separate health insurance item. Effective with the January 1997 data, the method of calculating the hospital cost component was changed from the pricing of individual commodities and services to a more comprehensive cost-of-treatment approach.

Recreation includes components formerly listed in housing, apparel, entertainment, and "other goods and services."

Education and communication is a new group including components formerly categorized in housing and "other goods and services," such as telephone services and computers.

Other goods and services now includes tobacco, personal care, and miscellaneous.

Table 8-2
Purchasing Power of the Dollar

SOURCE: U.S. DEPARTMENT OF LABOR, BUREAU OF LABOR STATISTICS (BLS)

The purchasing power of the dollar measures changes in the quantity of goods and services a dollar will buy at a particular date compared with a selected base date. It must be defined in terms of the following: (1) the specific commodities and services that are to be purchased with the dollar; (2) the market level (producer, retail, etc.) at which they are purchased; and (3) the dates for which the comparison is to be made. Thus, the purchasing power of the dollar for a selected period, compared with another period, may be measured in terms of a single commodity or a large group of commodities such as all goods and services purchased by consumers at retail.

The purchasing power of the dollar is computed by dividing the price index number for the base period by the price index number for the comparison date and expressing the result in dollars and cents. The base period is the period in which the price index equals 100; the average purchasing power in that base period—1982–1984 in the case of the measure shown here—is therefore $1.00.

Purchasing power estimates in terms of both the CPI-U and the CPI-W are calculated by BLS, based on indexes not adjusted for seasonal variation, and published in the CPI press release. The CPI-U version is shown here.

Alternative price measures in Tables 8-3 and 8-4

Table 8-3 shows the all-items CPI-U and CPI-W, along with a number of other indexes that various analysts of price trends have preferred as measures of the price level. Table 8-4 shows the inflation rates (percent changes in price levels) implied by each of the indexes in Table 8-3.

As food and energy prices are volatile and frequently determined by forces separate from monetary aggregate demand pressures, many analysts prefer an index of prices excluding those components. Indexes *excluding food and energy* are known as *core* indexes, and inflation rates calculated from them are known as *core inflation rates*.

The *CPI-U-X1* is a special experimental version of the CPI that researchers have used to provide a more historically consistent series. As explained above, the official CPI-U treated homeownership on an asset-price basis until January 1983. It then changed to a rental equivalence method. The CPI-U-X1 incorporates a rental equivalence approach to homeowners' costs for the years 1967–1982 as well. It is rebased to the December 1982 value of the CPI-U (1982–1984 = 100); thus, it is identical to the CPI-U in December 1982 and all subsequent periods, as can be seen in Table 8-3. For this reason, it is not updated or published in the CPI news release or on the BLS Web site. We continue to present it here because it provides the only available data before 1978 on changes in an improved and more consistent CPI.

The *CPI-E* is an experimental re-weighting of components of the CPI-U to represent price change for the goods and services purchased by Americans age 62 years and over, who accounted for 16.5 percent of the total number of urban consumer units in the 2001–2002 CES.

BLS does not consider the CPI-E to be an ideal measure of price change for older Americans. Because the sample is small, the sampling error in the weights is greater than the error in the all-urban index. The products and outlets sampled are those characteristic of the general urban population rather than older residents. In addition, senior discounts are not included in the prices collected. Such discounts are included—appropriately—in the weights, which are based on the expenditures reported by the older consumers' households. Therefore, such discounts are only a problem if they do not move proportionately to general prices.

The *CPI-U-RS* is a "research series" CPI that retroactively incorporates estimates of the effects of most of the methodological changes implemented since 1978, including the rental equivalence method, new or improved quality adjustments, and improvement of formulas to eliminate bias and allow for some consumer substitution within categories. This index is calculated from 1977 onward. Its reference base is December 1977 = 100. Thus, although it generally shows less <u>increase</u> than the official index, its current <u>levels</u> are considerably higher because the earlier reference base period had lower prices. Unlike the official CPIs and the CPI-U-X1, its historical values will be revised each time a significant change is made in the calculation of the current index. This index is not seasonally adjusted and is not included in the CPI news release. It is available on the BLS Web site, along with an explanation and background material. The CPI-U-RS is used by BLS in the calculation of historical trends in real compensation per hour in its Productivity and Costs system; see Table 9-3 and its notes and definitions. It is also now used by the Census Bureau to convert household incomes into constant dollars, as seen in Chapter 3. And it is used by the editor in some analytical calculations in this volume.

The *C-CPI-U* (Chained Consumer Price Index for All Urban Consumers) is a new, supplemental index that has been published in the monthly CPI news release since August 2002. It is available only from December 1999 to date and is calculated with the base December 1999 = 100; it is not seasonally adjusted. It is designed to be a still-closer approximation to a true cost-of-living index than the CPI-U and the CPI-W, in that it assumes that consumers substitute between as well as within categories

as relative prices change, in order to maintain a fixed basket of "consumer satisfaction."

The C-CPI-U is technically a "superlative" index, using a method known as the "Tornqvist formula" to incorporate the composition of consumer spending in the current period as well as in the earlier base period. (All of the other Consumer Price Indexes use a "Laspeyres" formula; see the General Notes at the beginning of this volume.) As it requires consumer expenditure data for the current as well as the earlier period, its final version can only be calculated after the expenditure data become available—about two years later—and is approximated in more recent periods by making more extensive use of the geometric mean formula (see above). With the release of January 2014 data, the indexes for 2012 were revised to their final form, and the initial indexes for 2013 were revised to "interim" levels, shown in Tables 8-3 and 8-4.

Personal consumption expenditure (PCE) chain-type price indexes are calculated by the Bureau of Economic Analysis (BEA) in the framework of the national income and product accounts (NIPAs). (See the notes and definitions for Chapters 1 and 4.) The scope of NIPA PCE is broader than the scope of the CPI. PCE includes the rural as well as the urban population and also covers the consumption spending of nonprofit entities. The CPI includes only consumer out-of-pocket cash spending, whereas PCE includes some imputed services and includes expenditures financed by government and private insurance, particularly in the medical care area. For this reason, there is a large difference between the relatively small weight of medical care spending in the CPI and the markedly greater percentage of PCE that is accounted for by total medical care spending. Housing, on the other hand, has a somewhat smaller weight in PCE while all non-housing components have a higher weight. The reason for this is that the CES—the survey on which the CPI weights are based—tends to report housing expenditures accurately and somewhat underestimate other spending. This suggests that the weight of housing relative to all other products may be overestimated in the CPI but measured more correctly in the PCE price index.

PCE chain-type indexes use the expenditure weights of both the earlier and the later period to determine the aggregate price change between the two periods. (See the notes and definitions for Chapter 1, as well as the General Notes on index number formulas.) Thus, they are subject to revision as improved data on the composition of consumption spending become available, and in this respect resemble the C-CPI-U.

For a large share of PCE, the price movements for basic individual spending categories are determined by CPI components. Hence, the differences between the rates of change in the aggregate CPI and PCE indexes are largely the result of the different weights, but also reflect some alternative methodologies and the previously mentioned differences in scope.

Market-based PCE indexes are based on household expenditures for which there are observable price measures. They exclude most implicit prices (for example, the services furnished without payment by financial intermediaries) and they exclude items not deflated by a detailed component of either the Consumer Price Index (CPI) or the Producer Price Index (PPI). This means that the price observations that make up these new aggregate measures are all based on observed market transactions, making them "market-based price indexes." The imputed rent for owner-occupied housing is included in the market-based price index, since it is based on observed rentals of comparable homes. Household insurance premiums are also included in the market-based index, since they are deflated by the CPI for tenants' and household insurance. Excluded are services furnished without payment by financial intermediaries, most insurance purchases, expenses of NPISHs (nonprofit institutions serving households), legal gambling (illegal gambling is excluded from all measures), margins on used light motor vehicles, and expenditures by U.S. residents working and traveling abroad. Also excluded are medical, hospitalization, and income loss insurance; expense of handling life insurance; motor vehicle insurance; and workers' compensation.

The *inflation rates* shown in Table 8-4 are percent changes in the price indexes introduced in Table 8-3. For annual indexes, the rate is the percent change from the previous year. For monthly indexes, the rate is the percent change from the same month a year earlier. To give an indication of the longer-run implications of these different price indicators, comparisons of compound annual inflation rates, calculated by the editor, are also shown for the 1978–2013, 1983–2013, and 2000–2013 periods, using the growth rate formula presented in the article at the beginning of this volume.

Data availability and references

The CPI-U, CPI-W, and C-CPI-U are initially issued in a press release two to three weeks after the end of the month for which the data were collected. This release and detailed and complete current and historical data on the CPI and its variants and components, along with extensive documentation, are available on the BLS Web site at <http://www.bls.gov/cpi>. Seasonal factors and seasonally adjusted indexes are revised once a year with the issuance of the January index.

Information available on the BLS Web site includes "Common Misconceptions about the Consumer Price Index: Questions and Answers;" another fact sheet on frequently asked questions; a fact sheet on seasonal adjustment; Chapter 17 of the *BLS Handbook of Methods*, entitled "The Consumer Price Index"; a section entitled "Note on Chained Consumer Price Index for All Urban Consumers"; and a number of explanatory CPI fact sheets on specific subjects.

As previously indicated, the CPI-U-X1 is not currently published because its recent values are identical to the CPI-U. The CPI-E is

presented in articles in the CPI section of the BLS Web site, the most recent of which is "Experimental Consumer Price Index for Americans 62 Years of Age and Older, 1998–2005"; recent values are available by request from BLS. The CPI-U-RS is updated each month in a report entitled "CPI Research Series Using Current Methods" on the site. In both cases, the reports describe the indexes and provide references.

The monthly PCE indexes are included in the personal income report issued by BEA, which is published near the end of the following month. These indexes are revised month-by-month to reflect new information and annually to reflect the annual and quinquennial benchmarking of the NIPAs. The complete historical record can be found on the BEA Web site at <http://www.bea.gov> in the Personal Income and Outlays section of the NIPA tables, in tables entitled "Price Indexes for Personal Consumption Expenditures by Major Type of Product."

Two special editions of the *Monthly Labor Review* were devoted to CPI issues. The December 1996 issue describes the subsequently implemented 1997 and 1998 revisions in a series of articles, and the December 1993 issue, entitled *The Anatomy of Price Change*, includes the following articles: "The Consumer Price Index: Underlying Concepts and Caveats"; "Basic Components of the CPI: Estimation of Price Changes"; "The Commodity Substitution Effect in CPI Data, 1982–1991"; and "Quality Adjustment of Price Indexes."

The new formula for calculating basic components is described in "Incorporating a Geometric Mean Formula into the CPI," *Monthly Labor Review* (October 1998). For a detailed discussion of the treatment of homeownership, see "Changing the Homeownership Component of the Consumer Price Index to Rental Equivalence," *CPI Detailed Report* (January 1983).

For a comprehensive professional review of CPI concepts and methodology, see Charles Schultze and Christopher Mackie, ed., *At What Price? Conceptualizing and Measuring Cost-of-Living and Price Indexes* (Washington, DC: National Academy Press, 2001). Earlier references include: "Using Survey Data to Assess Bias in the Consumer Price Index," *Monthly Labor Review* (April 1998); Joel Popkin, "Improving the CPI: The Record and Suggested Next Steps," *Business Economics*, Vol. XXXII, No. 3 (July 1997), pages 42–47; *Measurement Issues in the Consumer Price Index* (Bureau of Labor Statistics, U.S. Department of Labor, June 1997); *Toward a More Accurate Measure of the Cost of Living* (Final Report to the Senate Finance Committee from the Advisory Commission to Study the Consumer Price Index, December 4, 1996)—also known as the "Boskin Commission" report; and *Government Price Statistics* (U.S. Congress Joint Economic Committee, 87th Congress, 1st Session, January 24, 1961)—also known as the "Stigler Committee" report.

For an explanation of the differences between the CPI-U and the PCE index, see Clinton P. McCully, Brian C. Moyer, and

Kenneth J. Stewart, "Comparing the Consumer Price Index and the Personal Consumption Expenditures Price Index," *Survey of Current Business,* November 2007, pp. 26-33.

Tables 8-1 and 8-5 through 8-7
Producer Price Indexes

SOURCE: U.S. DEPARTMENT OF LABOR, BUREAU OF LABOR STATISTICS (BLS)

The Bureau of Labor Statistics first compiled and published a "Wholesale Price Index," measuring prices of various goods from the perspective of the seller, in 1902; it covered the years 1890–1901. Over the years this index was broadened and refined. In a major revamping in 1978, it was structured into an input-output format, differentiated between stages of processing, and renamed the Producer Price Index. The index for "Finished Goods," from the stage-of-processing system, became the featured "headline" number. Still, this index only covered goods.

New FD-ID system (Tables 8-5 and 8-6)

Over subsequent years the Bureau instituted collection of an increasing number of prices for services as well. All prices are collected within an industry input-output structure, with one of the most important purposes being to measure real output quantities by deflating industry outputs and inputs. In the new aggregation system introduced in February 2014, prices for goods, services, and construction have been integrated into a set of Final Demand-Intermediate Demand (FD-ID) indexes, organized by class of buyer, degree of fabrication, and stage of production. Its principal components are calculated beginning in November 2009 with that month as the reference base (i.e. November 2009 = 100). Components of the previous goods PPI system continue to be calculated on the base 1982 = 100 as well.

In the new FD-ID system, all products, including services and construction, are referred to as "commodities." In the old PPI system and in the CPI system, the term "commodities" refers to goods only; note, for example, how the CPI components are aggregated into summary measures of "commodities" [goods] and services, displaying different trends and behaviors. Unless and until these terminologies are reconciled, users need to be mindful of which system they are operating in.

More that 100,000 producer price quotations are collected each month; more than 10,000 indexes for individual products and groups of products are released each month. The prices are organized into three sets of PPIs: the FD-ID indexes; commodity indexes; and indexes for the net output of industries and their products.

Final demand. The final demand portion of the FD-ID structure measures price change for commodities sold for personal consumption, capital investment, government, and export. *Final demand trade services* measures changes in margins received by wholesalers and retailers. The other main components are *final demand goods, final demand transportation and warehousing services, other final demand services,* and *final demand construction.* The total index for final demand is now featured by BLS in its press release as its "headline number," replacing the previously featured Finished Goods index.

Intermediate demand. This portion of the system tracks price changes for goods, services, and construction products sold to businesses as inputs to production and not as capital investment. There are two parallel treatments.

The first treatment organizes intermediate demand commodities by type, including the distinction between *processed goods* and *unprocessed goods,* which is carried over from the older PPI goods system.

The second system organizes intermediate demand commodities into production stages, with the explicit goal of developing a forward-flow model of production and price change. For each production stage, the intermediate demand index measures the prices of <u>inputs</u> to the included industries. Many commodities, for example energy products, are sold to both final demand and various intermediate stages of production; their weight is allocated proportionately to all the consuming stages of production and their price movements are proportionately represented in each stage.

Industries assigned to *Stage 4* primarily produce final demand commodities. The intermediate demand index for Stage 4 measures inputs to those industries, such as motor vehicle parts, beef and veal, and long distance motor carrying.

Industries assigned to *Stage 3* produce the output sold to Stage 4, and therefore include motor vehicle parts and slaughtering. Examples of inputs to Stage 3 included in their intermediate demand index include slaughter steers and heifers, industrial electric power, steel plates, and temporary help services.

Industries assigned to *Stage 2* include petroleum refining, electricity, and insurance agencies. The goods and services that they purchase and that are included in their intermediate demand index include crude oil and business loans.

Industries assigned to *Stage 1* include oil and gas extraction, paper mills, and advertising services. Inputs to those industries include electric power and solid waste collection. According to BLS, "It should be noted that all inputs purchased by stage 1 industries are by definition produced either within stage 1 or by later stages of processing, leaving stage 1 less useful for price transmission analysis."

Commodity indexes

Aggregation by *commodity* organizes the price measures by similarity of product or end use, disregarding industry of origin. For the original Wholesale Price Index (goods only), this was the principal means of aggregation; in Table 8-1C, producer price indexes are shown for *farm products, industrial commodities*, and *"all commodities"* back to the year 1913. Table 8-7 shows 16 goods commodity groups from 1950 to date. Whatever their imperfections, these measures provide the longest historical perspective for producer prices.

The major goods commodity groups—particularly the totals for all commodities and industrial commodities—came under criticism in the energy price crisis of the early 1970s, for aggregating successive stages of processing of the same product (e.g. crude oil) and thus exaggerating price trends. As a result, the stage-of-processing grouping was introduced in 1978, and the finished goods components, in total and minus food and energy, became the headline Producer Price Indexes.

Stage of processing indexes

In the PPI for goods as reconstructed in 1978 and shown in Table 8-1B, the three major indexes are: (1) *finished goods*, or goods that will not undergo further processing and are ready for sale to the ultimate user (such as automobiles, meats, apparel, and machine tools, and also unprocessed foods such as eggs and fresh vegetables, that are ready for the consumer); (2) *processed goods for intermediate demand* (formerly *intermediate materials, supplies, and components*), or goods that have been processed but require further processing before they become finished goods (such as steel mill products, cotton yarns, lumber, and flour), as well as physically complete goods that are purchased by business firms as inputs for their operations (such as diesel fuel and paper boxes); and (3) *unprocessed goods for intermediate demand (*formerly *crude materials for further processing)*, or goods entering the market for the first time that have not been manufactured or fabricated and are not sold directly to consumers (such as ores, scrap metals, crude petroleum, raw cotton, and livestock).

Notes on the data

The probability sample used for calculating the PPI provides more than 100,000 price quotations per month. To the greatest extent possible, prices used in calculating the PPI represent prices received by domestic producers in the first important commercial transaction for each commodity. These indexes attempt to measure only price changes (changes in receipts per unit of measurement not influenced by changes in quality, quantity sold, terms of sale, or level of distribution). Transaction prices are sought instead of list or book prices. Price data are collected monthly via Internet, mail, and fax. Prices are obtained directly from producing companies on a voluntary and confidential basis. Prices are generally reported for the Tuesday of the week containing the 13th day of the month. Samples are updated regularly.

The BLS revises the PPI weighting structure when data from economic censuses become available. Beginning with data for January 2012, the weights used to construct the PPI reflect 2007 shipments values as measured by the 2007 Economic Censuses. Data for January 2007 through December 2011 used 2002 values; 2002 through 2006, 1997 shipments values; 1996 through 2001, 1992 values; 1992 through 1995, 1987 values; 1987 through 1991, 1982 values; 1976 through 1986, 1972 values; and 1967 through 1975, 1963 values.

Price indexes are available in unadjusted form and are also adjusted for seasonal variation using the X-12-ARIMA method. Since January 1988, BLS has also used X-12-ARIMA Intervention Analysis Seasonal Adjustment for a small number of series to remove unusual values that might distort seasonal patterns before calculating the seasonal adjustment factors. Seasonal factors for the PPI are revised annually to take into account the most recent 12 months of data. Seasonally adjusted data for the previous 5 years are subject to these annual revisions.

The newer FD-ID indexes are only available beginning in November 2009. Hence, they only regard, so far, the recovery and expansion phase of a particularly severe business cycle; the editor suggests that up to now, both seasonal adjustments and broader inferences about relative price behavior are necessarily based on a short and possibly unrepresentative time period. Partly for that reason, we present both unadjusted and seasonally adjusted indexes in Tables 8-5 and 8-6.

Data availability and references

The indexes are initially issued in a press release two to three weeks after the end of the month for which the data were collected. Data are subsequently published in greater detail in a monthly BLS publication, *PPI Detailed Report*. Each month, data for the fourth previous month (both unadjusted and seasonally adjusted) are revised to reflect late reports and corrections.

The press release, the *PPI Detailed Report*, detailed and complete current and historical data, and extensive documentation are available at <http://www.bls.gov/ppi>. The items available on this Web site include Chapter 14 of the *BLS Handbook of Methods*, "Producer Price Indexes"; a selection of *Monthly Labor Review* articles on the PPI; and fact sheets on a number of issues and index components.

CHAPTER 9: EMPLOYMENT COSTS, PRODUCTIVITY, AND PROFITS

Section 9a: Employment Cost Indexes

Figure 9-1: Changes in Wages and Salaries and in Benefit Costs, Private Nonfarm Industry, 1980–2014

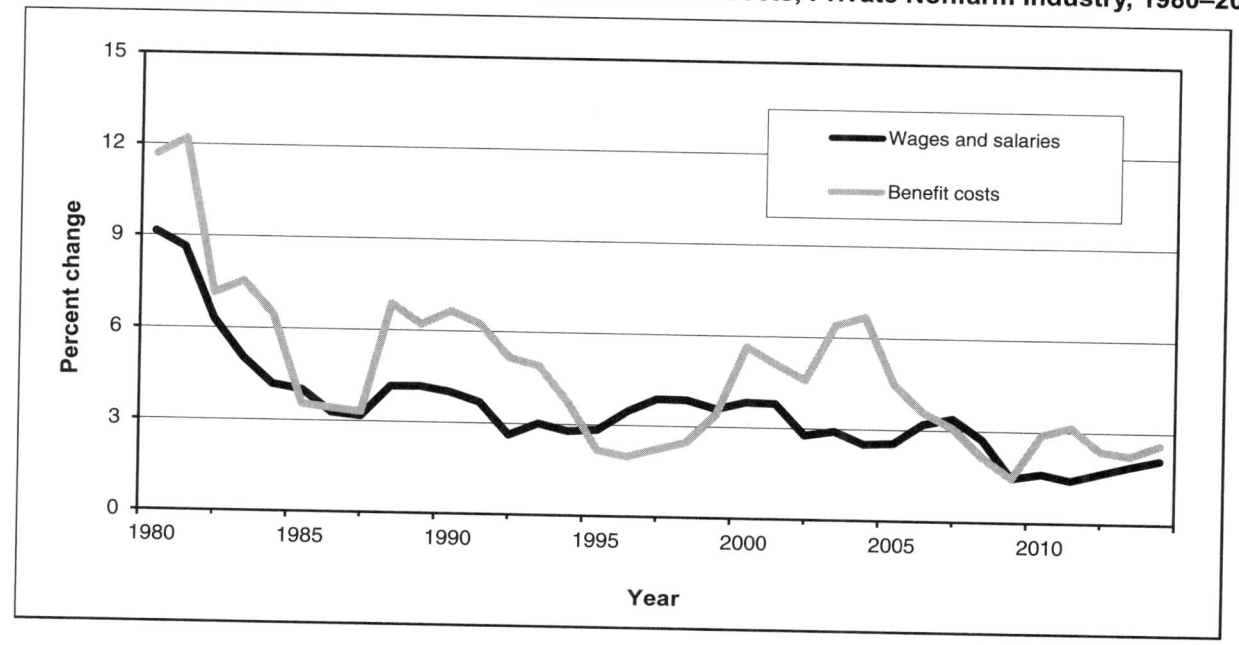

- The Employment Cost Index measures average increases in the dollar value of hourly compensation for nonfarm wage and salary workers, holding the composition of employment constant so as to reflect only the aggregate of changes affecting individual defined jobs. (The analogy is to the Consumer Price Index, which holds the market basket constant in any individual time period so as to reflect only an aggregate of price changes affecting individual defined products.) This makes the ECI the most accurate indicator of changes in price for a typical unit of labor.

- Between the last two business cycle peaks, from 2000 to 2007, average compensation for private industry workers rose at a 3.5 percent annual rate. Compensation includes wages, salaries, and benefits, but not stock options. The chain price index for personal consumption expenditures (PCE) rose at a 2.2 percent rate, implying an average real compensation increase of 1.3 percent per year. (Tables 9-1, 9-2, and 8-3)

- From 2007 to 2014, compensation rose at a 2.1 percent rate while PCE prices rose at a 2.15 percent pace, implying that real compensation per hour fell .05 percent per year. (Tables 9-1, 9-2, and 8-3)

- It is often claimed that worker productivity pays off in real worker compensation, but these gains in real compensation were, in both periods, significantly lower than the gains in nonfarm business productivity shown in a following table—a 2.9 percent rate from 2000 to 2007 and 1.3 percent from 2007 to 2014. (Table 9-3A)

- The ECI reports separately the rates of increase for wages and salaries and for benefits such as health insurance, as shown in Figure 9-1. (Tables 9-1 and 9-2)

Table 9-1. Employment Cost Indexes, NAICS Basis

(December 2005 [not seasonally adjusted] = 100; annual values are for December, not seasonally adjusted; quarterly values, seasonally adjusted, except as noted.)

Year and month	All civilian workers [1]	State and local government workers	All private industry workers	Management, professional, and related	Sales and office	Natural resources, construction, and maintenance	Production, transportation, and material moving	Service occupations	Goods-producing industries Total	Manufacturing	Service-providing	Union [2]	Non-union [2]
TOTAL COMPENSATION													
2002	90.0	89.7	90.0	89.7	89.8	89.7	90.3	92.0	89.0	88.7	90.4	88.2	90.3
2003	93.5	92.8	93.6	93.8	93.1	93.3	93.6	95.0	92.6	92.4	94.0	92.3	93.9
2004	97.0	96.1	97.2	97.1	96.8	97.1	97.8	97.7	96.9	96.9	97.3	97.3	97.2
2005	100.0	100.0	100.0	100.0	100.0	100.0	100.0	100.0	100.0	100.0	100.0	100.0	100.0
2006	103.3	104.1	103.2	103.5	102.9	103.6	102.3	103.1	102.5	101.8	103.4	103.0	103.2
2007	106.7	108.4	106.3	106.8	106.1	106.7	104.5	107.0	105.0	103.8	106.7	105.1	106.5
2008	109.5	111.6	108.9	109.9	107.9	109.6	106.9	109.8	107.5	105.9	109.4	108.0	109.1
2009	111.0	114.2	110.2	110.7	109.2	111.2	108.9	111.8	108.6	107.0	110.8	111.1	110.1
2010	113.2	116.2	112.5	113.0	111.6	113.3	111.5	113.5	111.1	110.0	113.0	114.8	112.1
2011	115.5	117.7	115.0	115.4	114.2	115.8	114.2	115.4	113.8	113.1	115.3	117.9	114.5
2012	117.7	119.9	117.1	117.7	116.3	117.8	116.0	117.4	115.6	114.9	117.6	120.5	116.6
2013	120.0	122.2	119.4	120.2	119.0	120.1	118.0	119.0	117.7	117.0	120.0	122.6	119.0
2014	122.7	124.7	122.2	123.0	121.9	123.2	120.6	121.1	120.3	119.8	122.8	126.7	121.5
2003													
March	91.2	90.4	91.4	91.5	90.9	91.0	91.6	93.0	90.6	90.6	91.7	89.5	91.8
June	92.0	91.3	92.2	92.2	91.7	92.0	92.4	93.5	91.4	91.3	92.4	90.7	92.5
September	92.9	92.0	93.2	93.2	92.8	92.8	93.2	94.4	92.1	92.0	93.5	91.6	93.5
December	93.6	92.7	93.8	94.1	93.4	93.7	93.7	95.1	92.8	92.6	94.1	92.3	93.9
2004													
March	94.6	93.5	94.9	94.7	94.5	95.0	95.4	95.9	94.5	94.6	95.0	94.5	95.0
June	95.5	94.4	95.8	95.5	95.5	95.9	96.5	96.7	95.4	95.6	96.0	95.9	95.9
September	96.4	95.1	96.7	96.4	96.5	96.4	97.4	97.2	96.4	96.7	96.8	96.7	96.7
December	97.1	95.9	97.3	97.4	97.0	97.3	97.9	97.8	97.1	97.1	97.4	97.3	97.2
2005													
March	98.0	97.0	98.2	98.4	97.9	98.0	98.5	98.4	98.0	98.2	98.3	97.9	98.3
June	98.6	97.8	98.8	99.0	98.4	98.7	99.0	99.0	98.9	99.0	98.8	98.8	98.9
September	99.3	98.7	99.5	99.6	99.2	99.4	99.6	99.6	99.7	99.7	99.4	99.6	99.5
December	100.1	99.8	100.2	100.3	100.1	100.2	100.1	100.1	100.2	100.2	100.2	100.0	100.0
2006													
March	100.7	100.5	100.8	101.0	100.6	100.9	100.4	100.8	100.3	99.9	100.9	100.5	100.9
June	101.6	101.5	101.6	101.8	101.5	102.0	101.0	101.5	101.2	100.9	101.8	101.8	101.7
September	102.6	102.8	102.5	102.9	102.2	102.9	101.7	102.2	101.9	101.4	102.7	102.4	102.6
December	103.4	103.9	103.3	103.8	103.0	103.7	102.4	103.2	102.7	102.0	103.5	103.0	103.2
2007													
March	104.2	105.1	103.9	104.5	103.8	104.1	102.5	104.4	102.9	101.9	104.3	102.7	104.2
June	105.1	106.2	104.8	105.5	104.5	104.9	103.3	105.2	103.8	102.8	105.2	103.9	105.1
September	105.9	107.2	105.6	106.3	105.2	105.8	103.9	106.3	104.4	103.2	106.0	104.4	105.9
December	106.8	108.3	106.5	107.1	106.2	106.8	104.7	107.2	105.2	104.0	106.9	105.1	106.5
2008													
March	107.6	109.0	107.2	108.0	106.8	107.7	105.5	107.8	106.0	104.6	107.6	105.9	107.5
June	108.3	109.8	108.0	108.8	107.4	108.2	106.0	108.7	106.7	105.0	108.4	106.7	108.3
September	109.1	110.9	108.6	109.6	107.8	108.9	106.5	109.4	107.2	105.6	109.1	107.4	108.9
December	109.6	111.6	109.1	110.2	108.0	109.7	107.0	109.9	107.7	106.1	109.5	108.0	109.1
2009													
March	109.9	112.4	109.3	110.2	108.1	109.9	107.7	110.6	107.9	106.4	109.8	109.1	109.4
June	110.2	113.2	109.5	110.4	108.2	110.3	108.1	111.0	108.1	106.6	110.0	109.8	109.6
September	110.7	113.5	109.9	110.6	108.8	110.7	108.6	111.6	108.3	106.8	110.5	110.5	109.9
December	111.1	114.1	110.4	111.0	109.3	111.3	109.0	112.0	108.8	107.3	110.9	111.1	110.1
2010													
March	111.8	114.5	111.1	111.7	109.9	112.3	109.9	112.3	109.7	108.4	111.5	112.8	110.9
June	112.3	115.1	111.6	112.1	110.6	112.6	110.4	112.6	110.2	109.0	112.1	113.7	111.4
September	112.8	115.5	112.1	112.7	111.1	112.9	111.2	113.3	110.9	109.9	112.5	114.6	111.8
December	113.3	116.1	112.6	113.3	111.7	113.4	111.6	113.6	111.2	110.2	113.1	114.8	112.1
2011													
March	114.0	116.6	113.3	114.0	112.2	113.9	112.2	114.5	112.0	111.3	113.8	115.6	113.0
June	114.7	117.0	114.2	114.7	113.2	114.8	113.5	114.7	113.2	112.6	114.5	117.1	113.8
September	115.1	117.3	114.6	115.1	113.7	115.4	113.7	115.0	113.3	112.8	115.0	117.4	114.2
December	115.6	117.7	115.1	115.7	114.2	115.9	114.3	115.5	113.9	113.3	115.5	117.9	114.5
2012													
March	116.2	118.3	115.7	116.4	115.1	116.4	114.5	116.0	114.1	113.4	116.3	119.3	115.3
June	116.8	118.9	116.3	116.9	115.7	116.9	115.0	116.4	114.6	113.9	116.9	120.2	116.0
September	117.3	119.5	116.8	117.3	116.2	117.5	115.6	116.9	115.3	114.6	117.3	120.5	116.3
December	117.8	119.9	117.2	118.0	116.4	118.0	116.1	117.4	115.7	115.1	117.7	120.5	116.6
2013													
March	118.4	120.5	117.9	118.5	117.4	118.7	116.7	117.8	116.4	115.6	118.4	121.5	117.3
June	119.0	121.0	118.5	119.2	117.8	119.0	117.1	118.3	116.9	116.2	119.0	122.1	118.0
September	119.5	121.4	119.0	119.9	118.3	119.7	117.5	118.4	117.4	116.7	119.5	122.5	118.5
December	120.1	122.2	119.6	120.4	119.1	120.3	118.1	119.0	117.8	117.2	120.1	122.6	119.0
2014													
March	120.5	122.8	119.9	120.8	119.5	120.9	118.9	119.1	118.5	118.0	120.4	123.5	119.4
June	121.4	123.4	120.9	121.8	120.3	122.0	119.5	119.5	119.1	118.6	121.5	125.0	120.4
September	122.2	124.0	121.7	122.6	121.1	122.6	120.2	120.5	119.8	119.3	122.3	125.8	121.1
December	122.8	124.8	122.3	123.2	121.9	123.4	120.7	121.1	120.4	120.0	122.9	126.7	121.5

[1] Excludes farm workers, private household workers, and federal government employees.
[2] Not seasonally adjusted.

Table 9-1. Employment Cost Indexes, NAICS Basis—*Continued*

(December 2005 [not seasonally adjusted] = 100; annual values are for December, not seasonally adjusted; quarterly values, seasonally adjusted, except as noted.)

Year and month	All civilian workers [1]	State and local government workers	All private industry workers	Management, professional, and related	Sales and office	Natural resources, construction, and maintenance	Production, transportation, and material moving	Service occupations	Goods-producing industries Total	Goods-producing industries Manufacturing	Service-providing	Union [2]	Non-union [2]
WAGES AND SALARIES													
2002	92.4	93.0	92.2	91.7	91.7	92.6	93.3	93.9	92.6	92.8	92.1	92.7	92.1
2003	95.1	95.0	95.1	95.3	94.3	95.2	95.4	96.1	94.9	95.1	95.2	94.8	95.2
2004	97.5	97.0	97.6	97.8	97.2	97.5	97.8	97.9	97.2	97.4	97.7	98.0	97.7
2005	100.0	100.0	100.0	100.0	100.0	100.0	100.0	100.0	100.0	100.0	100.0	100.0	100.0
2006	103.2	103.5	103.2	103.6	103.0	103.4	102.4	102.9	102.9	102.3	103.3	102.2	103.4
2007	106.7	107.1	106.6	107.2	106.2	107.1	105.0	107.1	106.0	104.9	106.8	104.9	107.0
2008	109.6	110.4	109.4	110.5	108.0	110.5	107.8	110.1	109.0	107.7	109.6	108.3	109.7
2009	111.2	112.5	110.8	111.5	109.4	112.0	109.6	112.3	110.0	108.9	111.1	111.6	111.0
2010	113.0	113.8	112.8	113.7	111.5	113.3	111.3	113.5	111.6	110.7	113.1	114.2	113.0
2011	114.6	114.9	114.6	115.5	113.6	115.4	112.8	115.1	113.5	112.7	114.9	116.3	114.8
2012	116.5	116.2	116.6	117.7	115.8	116.7	115.1	116.8	115.4	114.8	117.0	119.1	116.8
2013	118.7	117.5	119.0	120.2	118.4	118.8	116.8	118.3	117.6	117.2	119.4	121.8	119.2
2014	121.2	119.4	121.6	122.8	121.3	121.4	117.2	119.9	120.1	119.8	122.1	125.6	121.7
2003													
March	93.3	93.5	93.3	93.3	92.5	93.4	94.1	. . .	93.3	93.8	93.2	93.0	93.3
June	93.9	94.1	93.8	93.9	93.2	94.0	94.6	. . .	94.0	94.4	93.8	93.8	94.0
September	94.6	94.4	94.7	94.8	94.1	94.6	95.1	. . .	94.5	94.8	94.7	94.4	94.9
December	95.1	94.9	95.2	95.4	94.5	95.3	95.4	. . .	95.0	95.3	95.2	94.9	95.1
2004													
March	95.7	95.5	95.7	95.9	95.2	95.9	96.0	. . .	95.6	95.7	95.8	95.6	95.8
June	96.3	96.0	96.4	96.4	96.0	96.5	96.7	. . .	96.2	96.4	96.5	96.4	96.5
September	97.0	96.3	97.2	97.2	97.0	97.0	97.6	. . .	97.2	97.4	97.2	97.1	97.3
December	97.5	96.9	97.7	98.0	97.3	97.6	97.9	. . .	97.4	97.6	97.8	97.6	97.6
2005													
March	98.2	97.7	98.3	98.6	98.0	98.0	98.4	. . .	97.9	98.2	98.4	97.9	98.3
June	98.7	98.3	98.8	99.1	98.4	98.6	98.9	. . .	98.6	98.8	98.9	98.7	98.9
September	99.3	98.8	99.4	99.5	99.2	99.3	99.5	. . .	99.4	99.6	99.4	99.5	99.5
December	100.1	99.8	100.1	100.2	100.1	100.1	100.1	. . .	100.2	100.2	100.1	100.0	100.0
2006													
March	100.7	100.4	100.8	101.0	100.6	100.8	100.6	100.6	100.7	100.2	100.8	100.3	100.8
June	101.5	101.2	101.6	101.9	101.5	101.8	101.1	101.3	101.7	101.6	101.6	101.2	101.8
September	102.5	102.4	102.5	102.9	102.2	102.7	101.7	101.9	102.2	101.8	102.6	101.7	102.7
December	103.3	103.4	103.3	103.8	103.0	103.4	102.5	103.0	103.0	102.5	103.4	102.3	103.3
2007													
March	104.3	104.2	104.3	104.9	104.0	104.3	103.2	104.6	103.9	103.2	104.4	102.8	104.5
June	105.1	105.0	105.1	105.7	104.7	105.1	103.8	105.4	104.6	103.8	105.2	103.7	105.3
September	105.9	106.0	105.9	106.6	105.2	106.1	104.4	106.4	105.4	104.4	106.1	104.4	106.2
December	106.8	107.0	106.7	107.4	106.2	107.1	105.0	107.2	106.1	105.1	106.9	104.7	106.9
2008													
March	107.6	107.8	107.6	104.9	106.9	108.2	106.0	107.8	107.1	105.9	107.7	105.5	107.9
June	108.5	108.6	108.4	105.7	106.9	108.9	106.8	108.9	107.9	106.7	108.6	106.7	108.7
September	109.2	109.7	109.0	106.6	107.9	109.7	107.4	109.6	108.5	107.3	109.2	107.4	109.4
December	109.7	110.3	109.5	107.4	108.0	110.5	107.9	110.2	109.1	107.9	109.7	108.1	109.6
2009													
March	110.0	111.0	109.8	110.9	108.1	110.7	108.3	110.9	109.2	108.0	110.0	108.8	110.0
June	110.4	111.7	110.1	111.1	108.2	111.1	108.8	111.3	109.4	108.3	110.2	109.6	110.2
September	110.8	111.9	110.5	111.3	108.9	111.5	109.3	111.7	109.7	108.6	110.7	110.2	110.6
December	111.2	112.4	111.0	111.8	109.5	112.1	112.0	112.4	110.2	109.1	111.2	110.2	110.6
2010													
March	111.7	112.8	111.4	112.3	109.8	112.6	109.9	112.5	110.5	109.3	111.7	111.5	111.4
June	112.1	113.2	111.9	112.8	110.5	112.8	110.3	112.8	110.9	109.9	111.7	111.5	111.9
September	112.5	113.3	112.3	113.4	110.8	113.0	111.0	113.2	111.4	110.5	112.6	112.1	111.9
December	113.0	113.8	112.9	113.9	111.5	113.3	111.3	113.5	111.7	110.9	113.2	112.7	112.4
2011													
March	113.4	114.1	113.2	114.4	111.8	113.8	111.6	114.2	112.2	111.4	113.6	113.6	113.2
June	113.9	114.4	113.7	114.7	112.5	114.5	112.0	114.3	112.7	111.9	114.1	114.0	113.8
September	114.3	114.5	114.2	115.3	113.1	115.0	112.4	114.6	113.1	112.5	114.6	114.6	114.3
December	114.7	114.8	114.7	115.7	113.7	115.4	112.9	115.1	113.6	113.0	115.0	114.9	114.6
2012													
March	115.3	115.2	115.3	116.3	114.6	115.7	113.7	115.4	114.0	113.5	115.7	115.6	115.2
June	115.8	115.6	115.8	116.8	115.0	116.0	114.1	115.8	114.4	113.9	116.2	116.2	115.9
September	116.2	115.8	116.3	117.2	115.7	116.4	114.6	116.2	115.0	114.5	116.7	116.9	116.3
December	116.6	116.1	116.7	117.8	115.8	116.7	115.2	116.8	115.5	115.0	117.1	117.4	116.5
2013													
March	117.2	116.4	117.4	118.5	116.7	117.3	115.8	117.2	116.1	115.6	117.7	118.4	117.2
June	117.7	116.7	118.0	119.2	117.2	117.7	116.2	117.6	116.7	116.3	118.4	119.0	117.9
September	118.1	116.9	118.4	119.8	117.7	118.4	116.6	117.6	117.3	116.8	118.8	119.6	118.4
December	118.8	117.4	119.1	120.4	118.4	118.8	117.3	118.3	117.7	117.4	119.5	119.8	118.9
2014													
March	119.1	117.8	119.4	120.7	118.8	119.4	118.0	118.5	118.2	118.0	119.7	120.5	119.2
June	119.9	118.3	120.3	121.5	119.5	120.1	118.8	119.0	118.9	118.8	120.6	121.2	120.2
September	120.6	118.9	121.1	122.4	120.3	120.7	119.5	120.1	119.5	119.3	121.5	122.1	121.0
December	121.3	119.4	121.7	122.9	121.3	121.4	120.0	120.7	120.2	120.0	122.1	123.1	121.5

[1]Excludes farm workers, private household workers, and federal government employees.
[2]Not seasonally adjusted.
. . . = Not available.

Table 9-1. Employment Cost Indexes, NAICS Basis—*Continued*

(December 2005 [not seasonally adjusted] = 100; annual values are for December, not seasonally adjusted; quarterly values, seasonally adjusted, except as noted.)

Year and month	All civilian workers [1]	State and local government workers	Private industry workers										Union [2]	Non-union [2]
			All private industry workers	By occupational group					By industry				
				Management, professional, and related	Sales and office	Natural resources, construction, and maintenance	Production, transportation, and material moving	Service occupations	Goods-producing industries		Service-providing		
									Total	Manufacturing			
TOTAL BENEFITS													
2002	84.3	83.0	84.7	84.7	84.7	84.1	84.5	86.5	82.3	81.3	85.8	81.2	85.5
2003	89.7	88.2	90.2	90.1	90.0	89.8	90.2	91.7	88.2	87.3	91.0	88.1	90.6
2004	95.7	94.1	96.2	95.4	95.8	96.4	97.7	97.0	96.3	96.0	96.1	96.8	96.0
2005	100.0	100.0	100.0	100.0	100.0	100.0	100.0	100.0	100.0	100.0	100.0	100.0	100.0
2006	103.6	105.2	103.1	103.4	102.9	104.0	102.0	103.6	101.7	100.8	103.7	104.2	102.9
2007	106.8	111.0	105.6	106.0	106.0	105.9	103.7	106.7	103.2	101.7	106.6	105.8	105.6
2008	109.1	114.2	107.7	108.5	107.8	107.7	105.1	108.8	104.7	102.5	108.9	107.8	107.6
2009	110.7	117.7	108.7	108.8	108.7	109.5	107.4	110.5	105.8	103.6	109.9	111.4	108.2
2010	113.9	121.1	111.9	111.2	111.8	113.2	112.0	113.5	110.1	108.8	112.6	117.9	110.6
2011	117.5	123.6	115.9	115.2	115.5	116.8	117.0	116.4	114.4	113.9	116.4	122.8	114.4
2012	120.3	127.8	118.2	117.9	117.6	120.2	118.0	119.2	116.0	115.0	119.1	125.6	116.7
2013	123.0	132.0	120.5	120.2	120.5	122.9	119.5	121.0	118.0	116.6	121.5	127.3	119.1
2014	126.2	135.8	123.5	123.4	123.4	127.1	122.1	122.2	120.7	119.8	124.6	132.6	121.7
2003													
March	86.3	84.1	87.0	87.1	86.6	86.0	86.7	88.5	85.2	84.7	87.7	83.9	87.8
June	87.5	85.4	88.1	88.0	88.0	87.6	88.1	89.4	86.5	85.7	88.8	85.7	88.8
September	88.9	86.9	89.4	89.5	89.3	88.7	89.4	90.8	87.5	86.8	90.2	87.2	89.9
December	90.0	88.0	90.5	90.7	90.4	90.3	90.4	92.0	88.4	87.5	91.4	88.1	90.6
2004													
March	92.1	89.5	92.9	91.9	92.5	92.9	94.4	94.3	92.4	92.7	93.0	92.8	93.0
June	93.7	91.1	94.4	93.4	94.2	94.5	96.0	95.9	93.8	94.1	94.6	95.0	94.5
September	94.8	92.5	95.4	94.5	95.2	95.4	97.1	96.7	95.0	95.4	95.5	96.0	95.2
December	95.9	93.9	96.5	95.9	96.1	96.9	98.0	97.3	96.5	96.1	96.5	96.8	96.0
2005													
March	97.5	95.6	98.0	97.9	97.5	98.0	98.7	98.0	98.3	98.2	97.9	98.0	98.2
June	98.4	96.8	98.8	98.8	98.4	98.9	99.2	98.8	99.5	99.4	98.6	98.9	99.0
September	99.4	98.4	99.7	99.8	99.3	99.7	99.9	99.5	100.3	100.1	99.4	99.8	99.6
December	100.2	99.9	100.3	100.4	100.2	100.4	100.1	100.3	100.2	100.1	100.3	100.0	100.0
2006													
March	100.8	100.8	100.8	101.0	100.7	101.1	100.0	101.3	99.4	98.6	101.3	100.8	101.0
June	101.7	102.0	101.6	101.7	101.5	102.4	100.8	102.1	100.3	99.6	102.2	102.7	101.5
September	102.7	103.5	102.5	102.8	102.1	103.4	101.6	103.0	101.3	100.7	103.0	103.4	102.3
December	103.7	105.1	103.4	103.8	103.0	104.4	102.3	103.9	102.0	101.1	104.0	104.2	102.9
2007													
March	104.0	107.1	103.1	103.5	103.3	103.5	101.1	104.0	100.9	99.4	104.0	102.4	103.4
June	105.2	108.7	104.2	104.8	104.2	104.5	102.3	105.0	102.1	100.8	105.1	104.1	104.3
September	106.0	109.7	105.0	105.5	105.2	105.2	102.7	106.0	102.4	100.9	106.0	104.3	105.1
December	107.0	110.9	105.9	106.4	106.1	106.3	103.9	107.0	103.4	101.9	106.9	105.8	105.6
2008													
March	107.5	111.4	106.4	107.1	106.5	106.6	104.4	107.4	104.0	102.2	107.4	106.6	106.5
June	108.1	112.4	106.9	107.8	106.9	106.7	104.4	108.3	104.3	102.0	108.0	106.6	107.1
September	108.8	113.3	107.5	108.5	107.6	107.4	104.8	108.7	104.6	102.4	108.7	107.2	107.6
December	109.3	114.1	107.9	109.0	108.0	108.0	105.3	109.2	105.0	102.8	109.1	107.8	107.6
2009													
March	109.6	115.3	108.1	108.5	108.0	108.3	106.4	109.5	105.4	103.4	109.2	109.5	107.9
June	109.9	116.2	108.2	108.7	108.0	108.5	106.7	109.8	105.5	103.4	109.3	110.3	108.0
September	110.4	116.8	108.6	108.9	108.6	109.1	107.1	110.4	105.6	103.4	109.9	110.9	108.2
December	110.9	117.7	109.1	109.2	108.9	109.8	107.5	110.9	106.2	104.0	110.2	111.4	108.2
2010													
March	112.0	118.1	110.3	110.0	110.1	111.6	109.9	111.5	108.4	106.6	111.1	114.8	109.5
June	112.7	119.1	110.9	110.3	110.9	112.1	110.7	112.3	108.9	107.4	111.7	116.2	110.0
September	113.5	120.2	111.6	110.9	111.6	112.8	111.7	113.3	110.0	108.7	112.3	117.6	110.4
December	114.1	121.2	112.1	111.7	112.1	113.5	112.2	113.8	110.2	108.9	112.9	117.9	110.6
2011													
March	115.4	122.0	113.6	113.2	113.3	114.2	113.5	115.3	111.7	111.0	114.3	119.0	112.6
June	116.8	122.5	115.2	114.6	114.9	115.6	116.4	116.0	114.1	113.9	115.7	122.3	113.9
September	117.1	123.1	115.4	114.7	115.3	116.1	116.3	116.0	113.8	113.4	116.0	122.0	114.0
December	117.7	123.7	116.1	115.7	115.8	117.1	117.1	116.7	114.6	114.0	116.7	122.8	114.4
2012													
March	118.5	124.7	116.8	116.6	116.6	117.9	116.1	117.8	114.2	113.2	117.8	122.9	115.6
September	119.3	125.8	117.5	117.1	117.4	118.8	117.0	118.2	114.9	113.9	118.5	124.3	116.2
December	119.9	127.1	118.0	117.6	117.4	119.8	117.6	118.8	115.7	114.7	118.9	125.5	116.4
December	120.5	128.0	118.5	118.4	117.9	120.6	118.1	119.4	116.1	115.1	119.4	125.6	116.7
2013													
March	121.3	129.1	119.1	118.5	119.0	121.6	118.7	119.8	117.0	115.7	120.0	126.6	117.7
June	121.9	129.9	119.7	119.2	119.4	121.9	119.0	120.3	117.3	116.1	120.6	127.3	118.3
September	122.6	130.9	120.3	120.1	120.1	122.6	119.1	120.8	117.6	116.4	121.4	127.1	118.9
December	123.2	132.1	120.7	120.7	120.8	123.3	119.6	121.2	118.1	116.7	121.8	127.3	119.1
2014													
March	123.8	133.0	121.3	121.0	121.2	124.0	120.5	120.9	119.2	118.1	122.2	128.5	119.9
June	125.1	134.2	122.6	122.3	122.6	125.9	120.9	121.1	119.4	118.2	123.8	131.3	120.9
September	125.7	134.8	123.2	123.0	123.0	126.6	121.6	121.7	120.3	119.3	124.4	131.9	121.4
December	126.4	136.0	123.8	123.8	123.7	127.6	122.2	122.3	120.8	119.9	125.0	132.6	121.7

[1] Excludes farm workers, private household workers, and federal government employees.
[2] Not seasonally adjusted.

Table 9-2. Employment Cost Indexes, SIC Basis

(Not seasonally adjusted, December 2005 = 100; annual values are for December.)

Year	All civilian workers [1,2]	State and local government workers [2]	All private industry workers [2]	Private industry workers excluding sales occupations	Production and nonsupervisory occupations	White-collar occupations	Blue-collar occupations	Service occupations [2]	Goods-producing Total [2]	Construction [2]	Manufacturing [2]	Service-providing Total [2]	Transportation and utilities	Wholesale trade	Retail trade	Finance, insurance, and real estate [2]	Services
TOTAL COMPENSATION																	
1979	...	...	32.8	32.5	...	31.2	35.0	33.9	33.7	...	33.1	32.0	...	...	...	...	...
1980	...	...	35.9	35.9	...	34.2	38.5	37.1	37.0	...	36.4	35.1	...	...	...	...	...
1981	39.0	36.8	39.5	39.4	40.1	37.6	42.2	40.5	40.7	...	40.0	38.6	...	...	...	...	...
1982	41.5	39.4	42.0	42.0	42.8	40.1	44.7	43.9	43.2	...	42.4	41.1	...	...	...	...	...
1983	43.9	41.8	44.4	44.4	45.2	42.7	47.0	46.3	45.3	...	44.6	43.8	...	...	...	...	...
1984	46.2	44.6	46.6	46.7	47.3	44.8	49.0	49.4	47.4	...	46.9	46.0	...	...	...	...	...
1985	48.2	47.1	48.4	48.3	49.1	47.0	50.5	50.9	49.0	50.8	48.4	48.1	50.6	...	52.4	44.7	46.1
1986	49.9	49.6	49.9	49.9	50.5	48.6	51.9	52.4	50.5	52.3	50.0	49.6	51.8	48.5	53.5	46.1	48.1
1987	51.7	51.8	51.6	51.7	52.2	50.4	53.5	53.7	52.1	54.2	51.5	51.4	53.3	50.4	54.8	47.0	50.5
1988	54.2	54.7	54.1	54.1	54.8	52.9	55.9	56.5	54.4	56.5	53.8	54.0	54.9	52.5	58.0	50.0	53.5
1989	56.9	58.1	56.7	56.5	57.6	55.7	58.2	59.0	56.7	59.0	56.3	56.8	56.9	57.1	59.9	52.7	56.4
1990	59.7	61.5	59.3	59.3	60.1	58.4	60.7	61.8	59.4	60.9	59.1	59.4	59.1	58.2	62.5	54.9	59.9
1991	62.3	63.7	61.9	62.0	62.7	61.0	63.4	64.7	62.1	63.3	61.9	61.9	61.7	60.7	65.2	57.2	62.5
1992	64.4	66.0	64.1	64.2	64.9	63.1	65.6	66.7	64.5	65.6	64.3	63.9	63.9	62.5	66.9	57.9	65.2
1993	66.7	67.9	66.4	66.6	67.3	65.4	68.1	68.8	67.0	67.1	66.9	66.2	66.1	64.4	68.9	60.5	67.5
1994	68.7	69.9	68.5	68.6	69.2	67.5	70.0	70.8	69.0	69.6	69.0	68.1	68.7	66.4	70.8	61.8	69.4
1995	70.6	72.0	70.2	70.4	71.0	69.4	71.7	72.1	70.7	71.1	70.8	70.0	71.2	69.4	72.3	64.0	70.9
1996	72.6	73.9	72.4	72.4	73.1	71.7	73.6	74.2	72.7	72.9	72.9	72.3	73.4	71.5	75.1	65.5	73.1
1997	75.0	75.6	74.9	74.9	75.4	74.4	75.5	77.2	74.5	74.8	74.6	75.1	75.5	73.8	77.7	69.9	75.9
1998	77.6	77.8	77.5	77.2	78.1	77.3	77.6	79.4	76.5	77.4	76.6	78.0	78.4	78.0	80.0	74.1	78.2
1999	80.2	80.5	80.2	80.0	80.4	79.9	80.2	82.1	79.1	79.9	79.2	80.6	80.1	81.1	83.0	77.1	80.9
2000	83.6	82.9	83.6	83.6	84.0	83.6	83.6	85.3	82.6	84.6	82.3	84.2	83.5	84.4	86.4	81.0	84.5
2001	87.0	86.4	87.1	87.0	87.4	87.1	86.7	89.1	85.7	88.2	85.3	87.8	87.5	87.2	90.3	83.9	88.3
2002	90.0	89.9	90.0	89.9	90.2	89.9	89.8	92.0	88.9	91.0	88.5	90.5	91.0	91.1	91.9	87.6	90.7
2003	93.5	92.9	93.6	93.6	93.6	93.6	93.4	94.9	92.4	94.1	92.2	94.2	94.0	94.0	94.9	94.1	94.0
2004	96.9	96.1	97.1	97.2	97.2	96.9	97.5	97.7	96.8	96.4	96.7	97.3	97.6	96.5	97.1	96.7	97.5
2005	100.0	100.0	100.0	100.0	100.0	100.0	100.0	100.0	100.0	100.0	100.0	100.0	100.0	100.0	100.0	100.0	100.0
WAGES AND SALARIES																	
1979	...	...	36.1	36.1	36.8	34.1	39.4	37.9	38.2	41.4	37.5	34.9	39.1	33.7	39.7	32.8	31.7
1980	...	...	39.4	39.3	40.3	37.1	43.1	41.0	41.8	45.0	41.0	38.0	43.5	37.1	42.5	35.2	34.5
1981	42.3	40.1	42.8	42.9	43.9	40.4	46.8	44.4	45.4	49.0	44.5	41.4	47.1	40.0	45.6	38.8	38.1
1982	45.0	42.7	45.5	45.6	46.7	43.1	49.4	48.2	48.0	51.5	47.0	44.2	50.5	42.5	47.5	41.3	41.2
1983	47.3	45.0	47.8	47.9	48.9	45.7	51.3	50.4	49.9	53.0	49.0	46.7	53.0	45.1	49.5	44.3	43.9
1984	49.4	47.7	49.8	50.1	50.8	47.6	53.1	53.5	51.8	53.7	51.2	48.7	54.8	47.6	52.0	43.9	46.7
1985	51.5	50.3	51.8	51.9	52.9	50.0	55.0	54.8	53.6	55.3	53.0	51.0	56.9	49.7	54.5	47.9	48.4
1986	53.3	53.0	53.5	53.6	54.3	51.7	56.4	56.2	55.3	56.7	54.8	52.5	57.9	51.5	55.7	49.2	50.3
1987	55.2	55.2	55.2	55.5	56.0	53.6	58.1	57.6	57.1	58.6	56.6	54.3	59.1	53.6	57.2	49.8	53.0
1988	57.5	57.9	57.5	57.5	58.4	56.1	59.9	60.1	58.9	60.7	58.3	56.9	60.6	55.6	60.1	52.9	55.6
1989	60.1	61.0	59.9	59.8	61.0	58.7	62.0	62.3	61.2	62.8	60.6	59.5	62.2	60.7	62.0	55.7	58.3
1990	62.6	64.2	62.3	62.4	63.2	61.2	64.2	64.8	63.4	64.1	63.1	61.8	64.3	61.2	64.2	57.6	61.6
1991	64.9	66.4	64.6	64.7	65.4	63.5	66.4	67.4	65.8	66.0	65.6	64.1	66.6	63.6	66.6	59.6	63.8
1992	66.6	68.4	66.3	66.5	67.2	65.2	68.1	68.8	67.6	67.3	67.6	65.7	68.7	65.5	68.2	59.5	66.0
1993	68.7	70.2	68.3	68.5	69.2	67.4	70.0	70.3	69.6	68.6	69.7	67.8	70.9	67.1	70.2	62.1	68.0
1994	70.6	72.4	70.2	70.5	71.1	69.3	72.0	72.4	71.7	70.8	71.8	69.6	73.5	69.1	71.9	62.8	70.0
1995	72.7	74.7	72.2	72.5	73.0	71.3	74.1	74.0	73.7	72.5	73.9	71.7	76.0	72.4	73.6	65.1	71.7
1996	75.1	76.8	74.7	74.9	75.5	73.8	76.3	76.6	76.0	74.6	76.3	74.2	78.1	74.7	76.8	67.2	74.2
1997	77.9	78.9	77.6	77.7	78.3	77.0	78.8	79.9	78.3	77.1	78.6	77.4	80.7	77.0	79.7	71.8	77.5
1998	80.8	81.3	80.6	80.4	81.4	80.3	81.3	82.4	81.1	79.9	81.3	80.5	83.0	81.5	82.2	76.9	80.1
1999	83.6	84.2	83.5	83.4	83.8	83.1	84.0	85.1	83.8	82.5	84.1	83.4	84.8	84.5	85.2	79.8	83.0
2000	86.7	87.0	86.7	86.7	87.1	86.4	87.1	88.3	87.1	86.9	87.1	86.6	87.5	87.4	88.6	83.4	86.3
2001	90.0	90.2	90.0	90.0	90.4	89.6	90.5	91.8	90.2	90.4	90.2	89.9	91.7	89.3	91.9	85.8	90.0
2002	92.6	93.1	92.4	92.5	92.6	92.0	93.0	94.1	92.9	92.8	93.0	92.3	94.7	92.8	93.2	89.4	92.0
2003	95.2	95.0	95.2	95.4	95.1	95.2	95.2	96.2	95.1	95.1	95.2	95.3	96.2	95.3	95.5	95.9	94.8
2004	97.5	97.0	97.5	97.8	97.5	97.5	97.6	97.9	97.4	97.0	97.5	97.7	98.6	96.6	97.2	97.7	97.8
2005	100.0	100.0	100.0	100.0	100.0	100.0	100.0	100.0	100.0	100.0	100.0	100.0	100.0	100.0	100.0	100.0	100.0

[1]Excludes farm workers, private household workers, and federal government employees.
[2]Roughly continuous and comparable with new NAICS-based series. See notes and definitions for more information.
. . . = Not available.

Table 9-2. Employment Cost Indexes, SIC Basis—*Continued*

(Not seasonally adjusted, December 2005 = 100; annual values are for December.)

Year	All civilian workers [1,2]	State and local government workers [2]	Private industry workers		By occupational group				By industry division								
									Goods-producing industries			Service-providing industries					
			All private industry workers [2]	Private industry workers excluding sales occupations	Production and nonsupervisory occupations	White-collar occupations	Blue-collar occupations	Service occupations [2]	Total [2]	Construction [2]	Manufacturing [2]	Total [2]	Transportation and utilities	Wholesale trade	Retail trade	Finance, insurance, and real estate [2]	Services

TOTAL BENEFITS

1979	...	...	25.7	...	...	24.7	27.4	...	26.0	...	25.8	25.4	...	...	...	...	...
1980	...	...	28.7	...	...	27.7	30.4	...	28.8	...	28.5	28.6	...	...	...	...	...
1981	31.8	...	32.2	...	...	31.1	34.0	...	32.4	...	32.1	31.9	...	...	...	...	...
1982	34.2	...	34.5	...	...	33.3	36.5	...	34.8	...	34.4	34.1	...	...	...	...	...
1983	36.8	...	37.1	...	...	35.8	39.1	...	37.2	...	36.9	36.8	...	...	...	...	...
1984	39.3	...	39.5	...	...	38.3	41.4	...	39.6	...	39.3	39.4	...	...	...	...	...
1985	40.8	...	40.9	...	...	40.0	42.5	41.2	40.8	...	40.4	40.9	...	...	...	...	...
1986	42.4	...	42.3	...	...	41.4	43.8	42.9	42.0	...	41.6	42.5	...	...	...	...	...
1987	44.0	...	43.7	...	...	42.9	45.3	43.9	43.2	...	42.7	44.2	...	...	...	...	...
1988	47.0	...	46.7	...	...	45.6	48.6	47.4	46.3	...	46.0	47.1	...	...	...	...	...
1989	50.1	52.2	49.6	...	...	48.6	51.2	50.5	48.8	...	48.7	50.2	...	...	...	...	...
1990	53.5	55.8	52.9	...	...	52.0	54.4	53.8	52.3	...	52.1	53.4	...	...	...	...	...
1991	56.5	58.0	56.2	...	...	55.2	57.8	57.7	55.5	...	55.2	56.7	...	...	...	...	...
1992	59.5	61.1	59.1	...	...	57.8	61.0	61.0	58.7	...	58.3	59.4	...	...	...	...	...
1993	62.2	62.9	62.0	...	...	60.5	64.4	64.4	62.0	...	61.8	62.0	...	...	...	...	...
1994	64.4	64.6	64.3	...	...	63.2	66.2	66.0	64.1	...	63.9	64.4	...	...	...	...	...
1995	65.8	66.3	65.7	...	...	64.8	67.2	66.6	65.2	...	65.0	66.0	...	...	...	...	...
1996	67.1	67.8	67.0	...	...	66.2	68.4	67.3	66.4	...	66.5	67.3	...	...	...	...	...
1997	68.5	68.6	68.5	...	...	68.0	69.4	69.6	67.3	...	67.4	69.2	...	...	...	...	...
1998	70.3	70.7	70.2	...	...	69.9	70.7	70.9	68.1	...	67.9	71.4	...	...	...	...	...
1999	72.6	72.7	72.6	...	...	72.3	73.0	73.4	70.5	...	70.3	73.8	...	...	...	...	...
2000	76.2	74.4	76.7	...	...	76.5	76.9	76.6	74.3	...	73.6	78.1	...	...	...	...	...
2001	80.2	78.5	80.6	...	...	81.1	79.5	81.3	77.3	...	76.3	82.5	...	...	...	...	...
2002	84.2	83.3	84.4	...	...	84.6	83.8	85.7	81.3	...	80.4	86.1	...	...	...	...	...
2003	89.5	88.4	89.8	...	...	89.7	89.8	91.3	87.4	...	86.7	91.2	...	...	...	...	...
2004	95.7	94.3	96.0	...	...	95.3	97.3	97.1	95.7	...	95.3	96.2	...	...	...	...	...
2005	100.0	100.0	100.0	...	...	100.0	100.0	100.0	100.0	...	100.0	100.0	...	...	...	...	...

[1]Excludes farm workers, private household workers, and federal government employees.
[2]Roughly continuous and comparable with new NAICS-based series. See notes and definitions for more information.
. . . = Not available.

Section 9b: Productivity and Related Data

Figure 9-2: Change in Labor Productivity, Nonfarm Business, 1948–2014

- As Figure 9-2 demonstrates, the rate of change in U.S. nonfarm labor productivity has often been quite variable from year to year. Up through the 1980s, productivity tended to decline (growth rates were less than zero) in recession years but rebound sharply in recovery. One explanation of this was that firms expected that declines in demand would be temporary, and therefore held on to their experienced workers in order to be prepared for the recovery. (Table 9-3A and B)

- In the 1990s and 2000s, productivity growth rates were still variable, but output per hour no longer declined even in a severe recession. This suggests a somewhat greater tendency to regard negative demand trends as lasting. (Table 9-3A)

- On average, measuring between cyclically high growth years, nonfarm productivity grew at a 2.8 percent annual rate from 1948 to 1973. Productivity growth slowed between 1973 and 1989, averaging just 1.4 percent. From 1989 to 2014, however, productivity growth came partway back, to an average of 2.8 percent per year. (Table 9-3A and B)

- Real hourly compensation—measured differently in this data set, including stock options and affected by changes in the composition of employment—shows the same lag behind productivity in the 21st century as did the ECI: it rises at a 1.1 percent rate from 2000 to 2007, versus 2.6 percent for productivity; and it is unchanged—no growth in pay at all—from 2007 to 2014, versus a 1.5 percent per year gain for productivity. This lag mainly reflects an unprecedented decline to unprecedented levels in the labor share of the total value of sector output. The labor share index was essentially trendless from 1950 to 2000—in fact, it was identical in those two years. But it fell 6 percent over the completed 2000–2007 cycle and has dropped another 5.8 percent since then. (Table 9-3A)

Table 9-3A. Productivity and Related Data: Recent Data

(2009 = 100, seasonally adjusted.)

Year and quarter	Output per hour of all persons	Output	Hours of all persons	Employ- ment	Average weekly hours	Unit labor costs	Compen- sation per hour	Real hourly compen- sation	Labor share	Unit nonlabor payments	Implicit price deflator	Current dollar output	Compen- sation	Nonlabor payments	Output per job
1950	24.8	14.0	56.4	48.2	117.0	18.2	4.5	36.8	108.5	14.8	16.8	2.4	2.6	2.1	29.1
1951	25.6	14.9	58.3	49.5	117.7	19.4	5.0	37.3	107.1	16.3	18.1	2.7	2.9	2.4	30.1
1952	26.4	15.4	58.4	49.7	117.4	20.0	5.3	38.9	109.1	16.0	18.3	2.8	3.1	2.5	31.0
1953	27.4	16.2	59.1	50.4	117.2	20.5	5.6	41.1	111.0	15.6	18.4	3.0	3.3	2.5	32.1
1954	28.0	16.0	57.1	49.2	116.1	20.7	5.8	42.1	111.5	15.6	18.5	3.0	3.3	2.5	32.5
1955	29.2	17.3	59.3	50.6	117.0	20.3	5.9	43.3	108.3	16.6	18.8	3.2	3.5	2.9	34.1
1956	29.2	17.6	60.2	51.7	116.4	21.6	6.3	45.5	111.4	16.3	19.4	3.4	3.8	2.9	34.0
1957	30.2	17.9	59.3	51.6	115.0	22.3	6.7	46.9	111.5	16.8	20.0	3.6	4.0	3.0	34.7
1958	31.0	17.6	56.6	49.6	114.2	22.6	7.0	47.6	111.1	17.2	20.4	3.6	4.0	3.0	35.4
1959	32.2	19.0	59.0	51.1	115.4	22.7	7.3	49.2	110.5	17.6	20.6	3.9	4.3	3.3	37.1
1960	32.7	19.3	59.1	51.4	114.9	23.3	7.6	50.4	111.9	17.4	20.8	4.0	4.5	3.4	37.6
1961	33.9	19.7	58.2	50.9	114.4	23.3	7.9	51.8	111.3	17.7	21.0	4.1	4.6	3.5	38.8
1962	35.5	21.0	59.3	51.5	115.0	23.3	8.3	53.6	110.0	18.2	21.2	4.4	4.9	3.8	40.8
1963	36.8	22.0	59.7	51.8	115.2	23.2	8.6	54.7	109.0	18.6	21.3	4.7	5.1	4.1	42.4
1964	38.1	23.4	61.4	52.8	116.3	23.3	8.9	56.1	108.3	19.1	21.5	5.0	5.5	4.5	44.3
1965	39.5	25.0	63.5	54.3	116.9	23.3	9.2	57.2	106.7	19.8	21.9	5.5	5.8	5.0	46.1
1966	41.1	26.7	65.1	55.9	116.5	23.9	9.8	59.4	106.8	20.3	22.4	6.0	6.4	5.4	47.8
1967	42.0	27.3	64.9	56.7	114.6	24.7	10.4	60.9	107.4	20.6	23.0	6.3	6.7	5.6	48.2
1968	43.5	28.7	65.9	57.8	114.1	25.7	11.2	63.0	107.7	21.4	23.9	6.9	7.4	6.1	49.6
1969	43.7	29.6	67.6	59.6	113.4	27.4	12.0	63.9	109.6	21.7	25.0	7.4	8.1	6.4	49.6
1970	44.6	29.5	66.3	59.4	111.5	28.9	12.9	65.0	110.8	22.2	26.1	7.7	8.5	6.5	49.7
1971	46.4	30.7	66.1	59.5	111.0	29.4	13.7	66.0	108.3	24.0	27.2	8.3	9.0	7.4	51.5
1972	47.9	32.7	68.1	61.3	111.2	30.3	14.5	68.0	107.7	25.1	28.1	9.2	9.9	8.2	53.3
1973	49.3	34.9	70.7	63.9	110.7	31.7	15.7	69.1	107.3	26.6	29.6	10.3	11.1	9.3	54.6
1974	48.5	34.4	70.9	64.9	109.2	35.3	17.1	68.0	108.7	28.6	32.5	11.2	12.1	9.8	53.0
1975	50.2	34.0	67.8	63.0	107.7	37.8	19.0	69.0	106.0	32.7	35.6	12.1	12.9	11.1	54.1
1976	51.9	36.3	70.1	64.9	107.9	39.5	20.5	70.4	105.2	34.8	37.5	13.6	14.3	12.6	56.0
1977	52.8	38.4	72.8	67.7	107.4	41.9	22.1	71.4	105.4	36.8	39.7	15.3	16.1	14.1	56.7
1978	53.4	40.8	76.5	71.5	107.0	44.9	24.0	72.4	105.6	39.2	42.5	17.4	18.3	16.0	57.2
1979	53.4	42.3	79.1	74.2	106.5	49.2	26.3	72.5	106.7	41.8	46.1	19.5	20.8	17.7	56.9
1980	53.4	41.9	78.4	74.4	105.3	54.5	29.1	72.2	108.6	44.2	50.2	21.0	22.8	18.5	56.2
1981	54.6	43.1	78.9	75.2	105.0	58.4	31.9	72.2	106.5	49.9	54.8	23.6	25.2	21.5	57.3
1982	54.2	41.8	77.1	73.9	104.3	63.1	34.2	73.1	108.8	50.9	58.0	24.2	26.4	21.3	56.5
1983	56.2	44.1	78.5	74.6	105.2	63.6	35.8	73.3	106.1	55.0	60.0	26.5	28.1	24.2	59.1
1984	57.7	48.0	83.1	78.3	106.0	64.7	37.3	73.5	104.7	57.7	61.7	29.6	31.0	27.7	61.2
1985	59.0	50.2	85.0	80.3	105.9	66.5	39.2	74.6	104.7	59.8	63.5	31.9	33.3	29.8	62.5
1986	60.7	52.0	85.7	81.6	105.0	68.3	41.4	77.4	106.1	58.9	64.3	33.5	35.5	30.6	63.7
1987	61.0	53.9	88.2	83.8	105.3	70.5	43.0	77.7	107.4	58.9	65.6	35.3	38.0	31.7	64.2
1988	62.0	56.2	90.7	86.4	104.9	73.1	45.3	79.0	108.0	60.2	67.7	38.0	41.1	33.8	65.0
1989	62.7	58.3	93.1	88.3	105.4	74.5	46.7	78.0	106.1	64.2	70.2	40.9	43.4	37.4	66.1
1990	64.1	59.3	92.5	88.8	104.1	77.6	49.7	79.1	107.0	65.4	72.5	43.0	46.0	38.8	66.7
1991	65.2	58.9	90.3	87.5	103.3	79.9	52.1	80.1	107.2	67.1	74.5	43.9	47.1	39.6	67.4
1992	68.1	61.4	90.1	87.0	103.6	81.0	55.2	82.7	107.0	68.4	75.7	46.5	49.8	42.0	70.6
1993	68.2	63.2	92.6	88.8	104.2	82.1	56.0	81.9	106.0	71.1	77.5	49.0	51.9	44.9	71.1
1994	68.8	66.2	96.3	91.9	104.8	82.2	56.6	81.0	104.3	74.2	78.9	52.2	54.5	49.1	72.1
1995	69.0	68.3	99.0	94.5	104.8	83.5	57.7	80.7	104.1	75.7	80.2	54.8	57.1	51.7	72.3
1996	71.1	71.5	100.6	96.5	104.2	84.5	60.1	81.8	103.7	77.3	81.5	58.3	60.4	55.3	74.1
1997	72.4	75.3	103.9	99.2	104.8	85.9	62.3	83.0	103.9	78.1	82.7	62.3	64.7	58.8	75.9
1998	74.7	79.2	106.0	101.2	104.7	88.3	65.9	86.7	106.2	75.9	83.1	65.8	69.9	60.1	78.2
1999	77.3	83.6	108.1	102.9	105.1	89.1	68.8	88.7	106.4	76.3	83.7	70.0	74.4	63.8	81.2
2000	79.9	87.3	109.3	104.6	104.4	92.4	73.9	92.0	108.4	75.3	85.3	74.5	80.7	65.8	83.4
2001	82.1	87.9	107.0	103.9	103.0	94.1	77.3	93.6	108.4	76.7	86.8	76.3	82.7	67.4	84.6
2002	85.6	89.5	104.5	101.6	102.8	92.2	79.0	94.2	105.5	80.7	87.4	78.2	82.5	72.2	88.0
2003	88.9	92.3	103.8	101.4	102.3	92.1	82.0	95.6	104.0	83.7	88.6	81.8	85.1	77.3	91.0
2004	91.8	96.5	105.1	102.8	102.3	93.4	85.8	97.4	103.1	86.8	90.7	87.5	90.1	83.7	93.9
2005	93.7	100.1	106.8	104.7	102.1	94.8	88.8	97.6	101.4	91.6	93.5	93.6	94.9	91.8	95.7
2006	94.6	103.3	109.1	106.7	102.3	97.6	92.3	98.3	101.6	93.9	96.0	99.2	100.8	97.0	96.8
2007	96.0	105.5	109.8	107.6	102.1	100.4	96.4	99.8	102.2	95.2	98.2	103.6	105.9	100.5	98.1
2008	96.8	104.2	107.7	106.0	101.5	102.2	99.0	98.6	102.5	96.3	99.8	104.0	106.6	100.4	98.3
2009	100.0	100.0	100.0	100.0	100.0	100.0	100.0	100.0	100.0	100.0	100.0	100.0	100.0	100.0	100.0
2010	103.3	103.2	99.9	98.8	101.1	98.6	101.9	100.2	97.5	104.7	101.1	104.4	101.8	108.0	104.4
2011	103.4	105.3	101.9	100.4	101.6	100.7	104.1	99.3	97.4	107.0	103.3	108.9	106.1	112.7	105.0
2012	104.3	108.6	104.1	102.3	101.8	102.6	107.0	100.0	97.5	108.9	105.2	114.3	111.4	118.3	106.1
2013	105.5	111.6	105.8	104.0	101.6	102.8	108.4	100.8	96.3	112.2	106.7	119.1	114.7	125.2	107.2
2014	106.0	114.8	108.3	106.3	101.9	104.8	111.0	100.6	96.9	112.8	108.1	124.1	120.3	129.5	108.0
2012															
1st quarter	103.8	107.7	103.7	101.7	102.0	102.2	106.1	99.7	97.8	107.6	104.5	112.5	110.1	116.0	105.9
2nd quarter	104.4	108.3	103.8	102.1	101.7	101.9	106.4	99.7	97.0	109.3	105.0	113.8	110.4	118.5	106.1
3rd quarter	104.7	109.2	104.2	102.5	101.7	101.6	106.4	99.3	96.2	111.1	105.6	115.2	110.9	121.3	106.5
4th quarter	104.2	109.1	104.8	102.9	101.8	104.7	109.1	101.2	98.9	107.5	105.9	115.6	114.3	117.3	106.0
2013															
1st quarter	104.7	110.0	105.1	103.3	101.8	102.7	107.5	99.3	96.6	111.2	106.3	116.9	113.0	122.4	106.5
2nd quarter	105.0	110.6	105.4	103.7	101.6	103.5	108.6	100.4	97.1	110.7	106.5	117.8	114.4	122.5	106.6
3rd quarter	105.8	112.2	106.0	104.4	101.6	102.7	108.6	99.9	96.0	112.9	106.9	120.0	115.2	126.7	107.5
4th quarter	106.6	113.5	106.5	104.8	101.6	102.3	109.0	99.9	95.4	114.0	107.2	121.6	116.1	129.4	108.3
2014															
1st quarter	105.1	112.5	107.0	105.3	101.6	105.3	110.8	101.0	98.0	110.6	107.5	121.0	118.5	124.4	106.8
2nd quarter	105.9	114.1	107.7	105.9	101.8	104.3	110.5	100.1	96.4	113.5	108.2	123.4	119.0	129.5	107.8
3rd quarter	106.8	115.9	108.5	106.5	101.9	104.0	111.0	100.3	95.9	114.7	108.5	125.7	120.5	132.9	108.8
4th quarter	106.2	116.7	109.9	107.6	102.1	105.4	111.9	101.3	97.3	112.4	108.3	126.4	123.0	131.2	108.4

Table 9-3A. Productivity and Related Data: Recent Data—*Continued*

(2009 = 100, seasonally adjusted.)

Year and quarter	Nonfarm business sector														
	Output per hour of all persons	Output	Hours of all persons	Employ-ment	Average weekly hours	Unit labor costs	Compen-sation per hour	Real hourly compen-sation	Labor share	Unit nonlabor payments	Implicit price deflator	Current dollar output	Compen-sation	Nonlabor payments	Output per job
1950	28.1	13.7	48.9	41.2	118.6	17.3	4.9	39.6	108.3	14.2	16.0	2.2	2.4	1.9	33.4
1951	28.8	14.8	51.2	43.0	118.9	18.4	5.3	39.9	107.7	15.2	17.1	2.5	2.7	2.2	34.3
1952	29.4	15.2	51.7	43.6	118.7	19.0	5.6	41.3	109.2	15.2	17.4	2.6	2.9	2.3	34.9
1953	30.1	16.0	53.0	44.9	118.2	19.6	5.9	43.3	110.4	15.2	17.8	2.8	3.1	2.4	35.6
1954	30.7	15.7	51.2	43.7	117.3	19.8	6.1	44.3	110.8	15.2	17.9	2.8	3.1	2.4	36.0
1955	32.0	17.1	53.3	45.0	118.5	19.7	6.3	46.1	108.2	16.2	18.2	3.1	3.4	2.8	37.9
1956	31.8	17.4	54.6	46.3	118.0	21.0	6.7	48.2	111.5	15.8	18.9	3.3	3.7	2.8	37.6
1957	32.7	17.7	54.3	46.5	116.7	21.7	7.1	49.4	111.4	16.4	19.5	3.5	3.8	2.9	38.1
1958	33.4	17.4	52.0	44.9	115.9	22.1	7.4	49.9	111.6	16.6	19.8	3.4	3.8	2.9	38.7
1959	34.6	18.8	54.4	46.5	117.1	22.1	7.7	51.5	110.2	17.2	20.1	3.8	4.2	3.2	40.5
1960	35.0	19.2	54.8	47.0	116.5	22.8	8.0	52.8	112.3	16.8	20.3	3.9	4.4	3.2	40.8
1961	36.1	19.6	54.2	46.6	116.1	22.8	8.2	54.0	111.5	17.2	20.5	4.0	4.5	3.4	42.0
1962	37.8	20.9	55.4	47.5	116.5	22.7	8.6	55.6	109.9	17.8	20.7	4.3	4.7	3.7	44.0
1963	39.1	21.9	56.0	48.0	116.5	22.7	8.9	56.8	109.1	18.2	20.8	4.6	5.0	4.0	45.5
1964	40.2	23.3	58.0	49.2	117.9	22.8	9.2	57.8	107.9	18.7	21.1	4.9	5.3	4.4	47.4
1965	41.5	25.0	60.3	51.0	118.3	22.8	9.5	58.8	106.7	19.4	21.4	5.3	5.7	4.8	49.1
1966	43.0	26.8	62.4	53.0	117.8	23.3	10.0	60.5	106.6	19.8	21.8	5.9	6.2	5.3	50.6
1967	43.8	27.3	62.4	53.8	115.8	24.2	10.6	62.1	107.4	20.2	22.5	6.2	6.6	5.5	50.7
1968	45.3	28.8	63.5	55.1	115.1	25.1	11.4	64.1	107.4	21.0	23.4	6.7	7.2	6.0	52.2
1969	45.4	29.7	65.3	57.1	114.3	26.8	12.2	65.0	109.7	21.1	24.4	7.2	7.9	6.3	51.9
1970	46.1	29.6	64.3	57.1	112.5	28.3	13.0	65.7	110.7	21.7	25.5	7.6	8.4	6.4	51.8
1971	47.9	30.7	64.1	57.3	111.9	28.9	13.8	66.8	108.4	23.5	26.6	8.2	8.9	7.2	53.6
1972	49.5	32.8	66.2	59.0	112.1	29.7	14.7	68.9	108.3	24.3	27.4	9.0	9.7	8.0	55.5
1973	51.0	35.2	68.9	61.7	111.7	31.0	15.8	69.8	109.2	24.8	28.4	10.0	10.9	8.7	57.0
1974	50.2	34.6	69.0	62.7	110.1	34.5	17.3	68.8	110.1	27.0	31.4	10.9	12.0	9.3	55.3
1975	51.6	34.1	66.0	60.8	108.5	37.2	19.2	69.7	107.0	31.3	34.7	11.8	12.6	10.7	56.0
1976	53.3	36.5	68.4	62.9	108.7	38.7	20.6	71.0	105.7	33.7	36.6	13.4	14.1	12.3	58.0
1977	54.2	38.6	71.1	65.8	108.0	41.2	22.3	72.2	105.8	35.8	38.9	15.0	15.9	13.8	58.6
1978	55.0	41.1	74.8	69.5	107.7	44.1	24.2	73.2	106.3	37.8	41.5	17.1	18.1	15.6	59.2
1979	54.8	42.5	77.5	72.4	107.0	48.5	26.6	73.3	107.7	40.2	45.0	19.1	20.6	17.1	58.7
1980	54.8	42.1	76.8	72.6	105.8	53.7	29.4	73.0	109.0	43.1	49.3	20.7	22.6	18.1	58.0
1981	55.7	43.1	77.4	73.4	105.4	58.0	32.3	73.1	107.4	48.4	54.0	23.2	25.0	20.8	58.6
1982	55.1	41.7	75.7	72.3	104.7	62.8	34.6	73.9	109.5	49.8	57.4	23.9	26.2	20.8	57.7
1983	57.5	44.4	77.2	73.0	105.7	62.9	36.2	74.1	106.1	54.2	59.2	26.3	27.9	24.0	60.8
1984	58.8	48.1	81.9	76.9	106.4	64.2	37.7	74.2	105.4	56.3	60.9	29.3	30.9	27.1	62.6
1985	59.7	50.2	84.0	79.1	106.2	66.3	39.6	75.3	105.3	58.3	62.9	31.6	33.2	29.3	63.4
1986	61.5	52.1	84.7	80.5	105.2	68.0	41.8	78.2	106.6	58.0	63.8	33.2	35.4	30.2	64.7
1987	61.8	54.0	87.2	82.8	105.4	70.2	43.4	78.5	107.9	57.9	65.1	35.1	37.9	31.2	65.2
1988	62.8	56.4	89.8	85.4	105.1	72.6	45.7	79.6	108.3	59.3	67.1	37.8	41.0	33.4	66.1
1989	63.4	58.5	92.2	87.3	105.6	74.1	47.0	78.5	106.6	63.1	69.5	40.6	43.3	36.9	67.0
1990	64.7	59.4	91.8	88.0	104.4	77.2	49.9	79.5	107.5	64.4	71.8	42.7	45.8	38.2	67.5
1991	65.9	59.0	89.6	86.5	103.6	79.6	52.4	80.5	107.5	66.3	74.1	43.7	47.0	39.2	68.2
1992	68.7	61.4	89.4	86.1	103.9	80.9	55.6	83.3	107.4	67.5	75.3	46.2	49.7	41.4	71.4
1993	68.8	63.3	92.1	88.1	104.5	81.8	56.2	82.3	106.1	70.4	77.0	48.8	51.8	44.6	71.9
1994	69.4	66.3	95.4	91.0	104.9	82.0	56.9	81.6	104.5	73.5	78.5	52.0	54.3	48.7	72.8
1995	69.9	68.6	98.1	93.6	104.8	83.0	58.1	81.2	104.0	75.3	79.8	54.7	56.9	51.6	73.3
1996	71.8	71.7	99.8	95.8	104.2	84.2	60.4	82.3	104.0	76.4	80.9	58.0	60.3	54.7	74.8
1997	73.0	75.4	103.3	98.5	104.9	85.7	62.5	83.4	104.1	77.5	82.3	62.1	64.6	58.5	76.6
1998	75.2	79.4	105.6	100.7	104.8	88.0	66.2	87.0	106.3	75.5	82.8	65.7	69.9	60.0	78.8
1999	77.7	83.8	107.9	102.6	105.2	88.8	68.9	88.8	106.2	76.3	83.6	70.0	74.4	63.9	81.7
2000	80.2	87.5	109.0	104.4	104.5	92.3	74.0	92.3	108.3	75.3	85.2	74.5	80.7	65.8	83.8
2001	82.4	88.1	106.9	103.8	103.0	93.8	77.3	93.6	108.3	76.6	86.6	76.3	82.6	67.5	84.9
2002	86.0	89.7	104.3	101.4	102.8	91.9	79.0	94.3	105.3	80.9	87.3	78.3	82.4	72.5	88.4
2003	89.1	92.5	103.7	101.4	102.3	92.0	82.0	95.7	104.0	83.5	88.5	81.8	85.1	77.2	91.2
2004	91.9	96.6	105.1	102.7	102.3	93.3	85.7	97.4	103.3	86.2	90.3	87.2	90.1	83.3	94.0
2005	93.8	100.2	106.9	104.6	102.1	94.7	88.8	97.6	101.4	91.5	93.4	93.6	94.9	91.7	95.8
2006	94.7	103.4	109.3	106.7	102.4	97.5	92.3	98.3	101.6	93.9	96.0	99.3	100.9	97.1	96.9
2007	96.2	105.8	110.0	107.7	102.2	100.1	96.3	99.7	102.2	94.9	97.9	103.6	105.9	100.4	98.3
2008	96.9	104.4	107.8	106.1	101.6	102.1	98.9	98.6	102.6	95.8	99.4	103.9	106.6	100.0	98.5
2009	100.0	100.0	100.0	100.0	100.0	100.0	100.0	100.0	100.0	100.0	100.0	100.0	100.0	100.0	100.0
2010	103.3	103.2	99.9	98.8	101.1	98.7	102.0	100.3	97.7	104.2	101.0	104.2	101.8	107.5	104.5
2011	103.5	105.5	101.9	100.3	101.6	100.7	104.2	99.4	98.0	105.7	102.8	108.4	106.2	111.5	105.1
2012	104.5	108.9	104.2	102.3	101.8	101.8	107.1	100.0	97.9	107.8	104.7	113.9	111.5	117.3	106.4
2013	105.4	111.7	105.9	104.2	101.7	102.7	108.2	99.7	96.8	110.9	106.1	118.5	114.7	123.8	107.2
2014	106.2	115.1	108.4	106.4	101.9	104.6	111.0	100.6	97.2	111.7	107.6	123.8	120.3	128.5	108.2
2012															
1st quarter	104.0	107.9	103.7	101.7	102.0	102.1	106.3	99.9	98.3	106.5	103.9	112.2	110.2	114.9	106.1
2nd quarter	104.6	108.5	103.8	102.0	101.7	101.8	106.5	99.8	97.4	108.3	104.5	113.4	110.5	117.5	106.4
3rd quarter	105.0	109.5	104.3	102.5	101.7	101.4	106.5	99.4	96.6	110.0	105.0	115.0	111.0	120.5	106.8
4th quarter	104.4	109.5	104.9	103.0	101.9	104.4	109.1	101.1	99.2	106.3	105.2	115.3	114.4	116.5	106.4
2013															
1st quarter	104.6	110.2	105.3	103.4	101.8	102.5	107.2	99.1	97.2	109.6	105.5	116.2	113.0	120.7	106.5
2nd quarter	104.8	110.7	105.6	104.0	101.6	103.4	108.3	100.2	97.6	109.4	105.9	117.2	114.4	121.1	106.5
3rd quarter	105.7	112.2	106.2	104.5	101.6	102.6	108.5	99.7	96.5	111.6	106.4	119.4	115.2	125.3	107.4
4th quarter	106.5	113.5	106.6	104.9	101.6	102.3	108.9	99.8	95.8	113.0	106.7	121.2	116.1	128.3	108.2
2014															
1st quarter	105.2	112.9	107.2	105.4	101.7	105.1	110.6	100.8	98.3	109.5	106.9	120.7	118.6	123.6	107.0
2nd quarter	106.0	114.4	107.9	106.0	101.8	104.1	110.3	100.0	96.9	112.2	107.5	122.9	119.1	128.3	107.9
3rd quarter	107.0	116.1	108.5	106.5	101.9	103.9	111.1	100.4	96.2	113.7	107.9	125.3	120.6	132.0	109.0
4th quarter	106.4	116.9	109.8	107.6	102.1	105.3	112.0	101.4	97.6	111.5	107.9	126.1	123.1	130.3	108.7

Table 9-3A. Productivity and Related Data: Recent Data—*Continued*

(2009 = 100, seasonally adjusted.)

Year and quarter	\[Nonfinancial corporations\] Output per hour of all persons	Output	Hours of all persons	Compensation per hour	Real hourly compensation	Unit costs: Total	Unit costs: Labor costs	Unit costs: Nonlabor costs	Unit profits	Implicit price deflator	\[Manufacturing\] Output per hour of all persons	Output	Hours of all persons	Compensation per hour	Real hourly compensation	Unit labor costs
1950	28.5	11.7	41.0	5.6	45.8	17.2	19.8	12.0	37.9	19.3	...	...	...	...	...	...
1951	28.2	12.3	43.6	6.2	46.3	18.7	21.8	12.6	40.7	21.0	...	...	...	...	...	...
1952	28.9	12.8	44.3	6.5	48.1	19.4	22.5	13.1	36.6	21.2	...	...	...	...	...	...
1953	30.1	13.7	45.7	6.9	50.4	19.6	22.8	13.1	34.4	21.1	...	...	...	...	...	...
1954	31.4	13.6	43.3	7.1	51.7	19.6	22.6	13.4	33.5	21.0	...	...	...	...	...	...
1955	33.3	15.2	45.8	7.4	53.8	19.1	22.1	13.0	39.1	21.2	...	...	...	...	...	...
1956	33.5	15.8	47.1	7.8	56.4	20.2	23.4	13.9	36.6	21.9	...	...	...	...	...	...
1957	34.2	16.0	46.7	8.3	57.8	21.2	24.3	15.0	35.2	22.6	...	...	...	...	...	...
1958	34.9	15.4	44.0	8.6	58.4	21.9	24.7	16.4	31.9	23.0	...	...	...	...	...	...
1959	36.6	17.1	46.7	9.0	60.2	21.5	24.4	15.8	37.1	23.2	...	...	...	...	...	...
1960	37.3	17.7	47.4	9.3	61.5	22.0	25.0	16.2	34.2	23.3	...	...	...	...	...	...
1961	38.5	18.1	47.0	9.6	62.9	22.1	24.9	16.5	34.2	23.4	...	...	...	...	...	...
1962	40.2	19.6	48.8	10.0	64.7	22.0	24.8	16.3	36.8	23.5	...	...	...	...	...	...
1963	41.7	20.8	50.0	10.3	65.8	21.8	24.7	16.2	39.0	23.6	...	...	...	...	...	...
1964	42.3	22.3	52.7	10.5	66.2	21.9	24.8	16.2	40.3	23.8	...	...	...	...	...	...
1965	43.4	24.2	55.7	10.8	67.0	21.9	24.8	16.1	43.5	24.2	...	...	...	...	...	...
1966	44.3	26.0	58.6	11.4	68.8	22.5	25.7	16.2	43.5	24.7	...	...	...	...	...	...
1967	45.1	26.7	59.2	12.0	70.5	23.5	26.7	17.2	40.7	25.3	...	...	...	...	...	...
1968	46.7	28.4	60.9	12.9	72.6	24.5	27.6	18.3	40.8	26.2	...	...	...	...	...	...
1969	46.8	29.6	63.2	13.8	73.5	26.2	29.5	19.8	36.9	27.3	...	...	...	...	...	...
1970	47.1	29.3	62.3	14.7	74.2	28.3	31.2	22.3	30.3	28.5	...	...	...	...	...	...
1971	49.0	30.5	62.2	15.6	75.3	29.0	31.8	23.4	34.4	29.6	...	...	...	...	...	...
1972	50.0	32.8	65.6	16.4	76.8	29.7	32.8	23.4	37.5	30.5	...	...	...	...	...	...
1973	50.5	34.8	68.9	17.6	77.5	31.5	34.8	24.7	39.0	32.2	...	...	...	...	...	...
1974	49.5	34.2	69.2	19.2	76.2	35.3	38.8	28.4	35.6	35.3	...	...	...	...	...	...
1975	51.4	33.8	65.7	21.2	77.1	38.3	41.2	32.5	43.0	38.8	...	...	...	...	...	...
1976	53.1	36.5	68.7	22.8	78.4	39.3	42.9	32.2	50.7	40.5	...	...	...	...	...	...
1977	54.5	39.2	71.9	24.6	79.5	41.2	45.1	33.4	55.1	42.7	...	...	...	...	...	...
1978	55.2	41.8	75.6	26.8	81.0	44.0	48.6	34.9	58.6	45.5	...	...	...	...	...	...
1979	54.8	43.1	78.6	29.3	80.8	48.2	53.5	37.7	56.2	49.1	...	...	...	...	...	...
1980	54.7	42.7	78.1	32.3	80.1	54.1	59.1	44.3	50.8	53.8	...	...	...	...	...	...
1981	56.1	44.4	79.2	35.2	79.7	58.6	62.8	50.3	59.6	58.7	...	...	...	...	...	...
1982	56.3	43.4	77.1	37.5	80.2	63.0	66.6	55.8	55.6	62.2	...	...	...	...	...	...
1983	58.3	45.6	78.2	39.1	80.1	63.4	67.1	56.1	64.4	63.5	...	...	...	...	...	...
1984	59.6	49.6	83.2	40.8	80.3	64.2	68.4	55.8	75.5	65.4	...	...	...	...	...	...
1985	61.0	51.9	85.1	42.8	81.5	65.8	70.2	57.1	72.7	66.5	...	...	...	...	...	...
1986	62.4	53.3	85.4	45.2	84.5	68.3	72.5	60.1	60.2	67.5	48.2	74.1	148.8	44.4	80.3	92.1
1987	63.7	56.1	88.1	46.8	84.6	69.2	73.5	60.6	64.4	68.7	49.3	76.8	153.3	46.2	80.5	93.6
1988	65.5	59.5	90.8	49.1	85.7	70.6	75.0	61.7	68.9	70.4	50.0	76.7	154.2	47.7	79.8	95.4
1989	64.8	60.7	93.6	50.5	84.5	73.7	78.0	65.2	62.9	72.6	51.2	76.2	150.4	50.1	79.8	97.8
1990	65.5	61.6	94.0	53.0	84.4	76.7	81.0	68.2	59.3	74.9	52.6	76.6	144.1	52.8	81.2	100.5
1991	67.1	61.2	91.3	55.5	85.3	78.8	82.7	71.1	60.8	76.9	54.4	79.2	143.3	55.6	83.3	102.2
1992	68.8	63.1	91.7	58.4	87.5	79.8	84.8	69.7	63.0	78.0	55.7	82.0	145.2	56.3	82.4	101.2
1993	68.9	64.7	93.9	59.2	86.5	80.5	85.9	69.7	73.1	79.7	57.6	88.4	148.7	57.2	82.0	99.4
1994	70.1	68.6	97.9	59.9	85.9	80.3	85.5	70.0	87.4	81.1	60.3	91.1	149.6	58.3	81.6	96.6
1995	70.9	71.9	101.4	60.9	85.2	80.6	85.8	70.3	92.5	81.9	62.5	95.4	149.4	60.1	81.8	96.0
1996	73.8	76.2	103.2	63.2	86.1	80.2	85.7	69.5	99.2	82.2	66.1	104.1	152.0	62.1	82.9	94.0
1997	75.8	81.2	107.1	65.3	87.1	80.5	86.2	69.1	101.7	82.7	70.1	108.0	151.7	65.2	85.8	93.0
1998	78.4	85.9	109.5	69.1	90.9	81.8	88.1	69.3	90.5	82.7	73.7	113.3	150.6	68.2	87.8	92.5
1999	80.8	90.5	112.0	72.3	93.1	83.2	89.4	70.7	84.1	83.2	...	...	...	...	...	...
2000	84.2	95.5	113.4	77.6	96.6	85.8	92.1	73.2	70.0	84.2	77.7	108.3	138.9	73.3	91.3	94.4
2001	84.7	93.5	110.3	79.5	96.3	88.7	93.8	78.4	56.9	85.3	79.6	108.3	136.1	76.8	93.0	91.0
2002	88.1	94.3	107.0	81.0	96.6	87.6	91.9	79.0	69.2	85.7	85.7	111.2	129.2	79.5	94.8	90.8
2003	91.6	96.3	105.2	83.6	97.6	86.9	91.3	78.1	84.4	86.6	90.5	111.8	122.9	82.2	95.9	91.9
2004	94.8	100.6	106.2	86.6	98.4	86.8	91.4	77.6	102.7	88.5	92.7	114.8	122.2	85.2	96.8	91.5
2005	96.6	104.0	107.7	89.3	98.1	88.7	92.5	81.1	116.7	91.6	96.6	117.6	120.8	88.4	97.1	91.5
2006	98.4	108.0	109.8	92.0	97.9	90.1	93.5	83.2	130.9	94.4	97.0	118.0	121.7	90.6	96.4	93.3
2007	98.9	109.0	110.2	95.5	98.8	93.9	96.6	88.6	116.8	96.3	100.3	120.8	119.6	94.2	97.4	93.9
2008	99.3	107.6	108.4	98.3	98.0	97.5	99.0	94.3	105.3	98.3	100.3	107.7	114.9	96.7	96.4	96.4
2009	100.0	100.0	100.0	100.0	100.0	100.0	100.0	100.0	100.0	100.0	100.0	101.4	100.0	100.0	100.0	100.0
2010	105.3	105.5	100.2	101.5	99.9	96.5	96.4	96.8	129.7	100.0	106.2	107.8	101.5	103.0	99.6	95.3
2011	105.1	108.2	102.9	103.7	98.9	98.6	98.6	98.6	133.7	102.3	107.0	110.4	103.1	104.8	98.3	97.0
2012	107.1	112.9	105.3	106.6	99.7	99.0	99.5	97.9	144.3	103.7	108.1	113.6	105.2	104.8	97.1	95.6
2013	107.4	115.5	107.5	108.1	99.5	99.7	100.6	98.0	146.4	104.6	110.2	117.2	106.9	107.9	97.8	95.9
2014	108.0	119.3	110.5	110.2	99.8	100.5	102.0	97.4	145.6	105.2	112.6	122.5	106.9	108.2	98.6	96.2
2012																
1st quarter	107.0	112.3	104.9	106.1	99.7	98.7	99.1	97.8	141.1	103.1	107.7	112.0	104.0	104.7	98.4	97.2
2nd quarter	107.5	113.0	105.1	106.2	99.6	98.4	98.8	97.8	146.2	103.4	107.9	112.7	104.4	104.7	98.2	97.1
3rd quarter	106.5	112.3	105.4	106.2	99.1	99.2	99.7	98.3	144.1	103.9	108.0	113.0	104.6	104.3	97.4	96.6
4th quarter	107.5	113.9	105.9	108.1	100.3	99.6	100.6	97.5	145.7	104.4	108.7	113.6	104.6	105.5	97.9	97.1
2013																
1st quarter	107.1	114.3	106.8	107.6	99.4	99.7	100.5	98.2	145.0	104.4	109.3	115.0	105.2	104.7	96.8	95.8
2nd quarter	108.0	115.6	107.1	108.3	100.1	99.4	100.3	97.5	148.0	104.5	110.4	115.9	105.0	105.6	97.1	95.6
3rd quarter	107.4	115.7	107.7	108.1	99.4	99.8	100.7	98.1	147.0	104.8	110.4	115.9	105.0	105.6	96.8	95.6
4th quarter	107.3	116.3	108.4	108.3	99.2	100.0	100.9	98.2	145.5	104.8	110.6	117.2	106.0	105.6	96.8	95.5
2014																
1st quarter	107.0	116.5	108.9	109.9	100.2	101.4	102.8	98.8	134.6	104.9	111.3	117.7	105.7	107.8	98.2	96.8
2nd quarter	107.5	118.4	110.1	109.5	99.2	100.3	101.9	97.3	148.2	105.3	112.4	119.8	106.6	107.3	97.2	95.5
3rd quarter	108.2	120.0	110.9	110.2	99.5	100.3	101.8	97.3	150.0	105.5	113.3	121.2	107.0	107.8	97.4	95.2
4th quarter	109.1	122.1	111.9	111.0	100.5	99.9	101.7	96.4	149.4	105.1	113.3	122.5	108.2	108.9	98.6	96.2

. . . = Not available.

Table 9-3B. Productivity and Related Data: Historical Data

(2009 = 100, seasonally adjusted.)

Year and quarter	Business sector								Nonfarm business sector							
	Output per hour of all persons	Output	Hours of all persons	Compensation per hour	Real compensation per hour	Unit labor costs	Unit nonlabor payments	Implicit price deflator	Output per hour of all persons	Output	Hours of all persons	Compensation per hour	Real compensation per hour	Unit labor costs	Unit nonlabor payments	Implicit price deflator
1947	21.5	12.3	57.1	3.8	33.7	17.9	12.9	15.8	24.9	12.1	48.5	4.1	36.1	16.5	12.2	14.7
1948	22.5	12.9	57.5	4.2	33.9	18.6	14.3	16.8	25.6	12.6	49.2	4.5	36.3	17.5	13.2	15.7
1949	23.0	12.8	55.7	4.2	34.8	18.4	14.1	16.6	26.4	12.5	47.3	4.6	37.8	17.5	13.6	15.8
1947																
1st quarter	21.5	12.2	56.8	3.7	33.4	17.2	12.7	15.3	24.6	11.9	48.3	4.0	35.7	16.1	11.7	14.3
2nd quarter	21.6	12.2	56.7	3.8	33.8	17.6	12.6	15.5	25.2	12.2	48.3	4.1	36.0	16.1	12.2	14.5
3rd quarter	21.4	12.2	57.2	3.9	33.6	18.1	12.9	15.9	24.4	11.8	48.4	4.2	36.3	17.1	12.4	15.1
4th quarter	21.7	12.5	57.6	4.0	33.9	18.5	13.4	16.4	25.5	12.4	48.9	4.3	36.1	16.8	12.6	15.1
1948																
1st quarter	22.2	12.7	57.3	4.1	33.6	18.3	13.9	16.5	25.6	12.6	49.2	4.4	36.2	17.1	12.8	15.3
2nd quarter	22.6	13.0	57.3	4.1	33.5	18.2	14.5	16.6	25.5	12.5	49.2	4.4	36.1	17.4	13.0	15.6
3rd quarter	22.5	13.0	57.9	4.2	33.8	18.7	14.4	16.9	25.5	12.6	49.5	4.5	36.3	17.7	13.3	15.9
4th quarter	22.6	13.0	57.5	4.3	34.8	19.0	14.1	17.0	25.6	12.6	49.1	4.6	37.0	17.8	13.7	16.1
1949																
1st quarter	22.5	12.8	56.7	4.2	34.5	18.7	14.2	16.8	25.9	12.5	48.2	4.6	37.5	17.8	13.5	16.0
2nd quarter	22.6	12.7	56.2	4.2	34.2	18.5	14.0	16.6	26.2	12.4	47.4	4.6	37.7	17.6	13.4	15.8
3rd quarter	23.3	12.9	55.3	4.2	35.0	18.2	14.2	16.5	26.8	12.6	46.9	4.6	38.1	17.2	13.8	15.8
4th quarter	23.4	12.7	54.6	4.3	35.4	18.3	13.9	16.5	26.6	12.5	46.8	4.6	38.0	17.3	13.6	15.7
1950																
1st quarter	24.4	13.4	54.7	4.4	36.7	18.1	14.1	16.4	27.6	13.0	47.1	4.7	39.1	17.1	13.9	15.8
2nd quarter	24.7	13.8	55.9	4.5	36.9	18.2	14.2	16.5	27.9	13.5	48.3	4.8	39.7	17.3	13.8	15.9
3rd quarter	25.1	14.4	57.4	4.6	36.8	18.2	15.1	16.9	28.5	14.2	49.8	4.9	39.7	17.3	14.3	16.0
4th quarter	25.2	14.5	57.7	4.6	36.8	18.4	15.7	17.3	28.5	14.3	50.3	5.0	39.9	17.7	14.5	16.4
1951																
1st quarter	25.2	14.7	58.3	4.8	36.6	19.1	16.3	17.9	28.6	14.6	51.1	5.2	39.3	18.1	15.1	16.8
2nd quarter	25.3	14.8	58.6	4.9	37.3	19.5	16.0	18.1	28.5	14.7	51.5	5.3	39.8	18.5	15.0	17.0
3rd quarter	26.0	15.1	57.9	5.0	37.8	19.3	16.4	18.1	29.1	14.9	51.0	5.3	40.2	18.3	15.5	17.1
4th quarter	25.9	15.1	58.1	5.1	37.8	19.6	16.4	18.3	29.2	14.9	51.0	5.4	40.4	18.6	15.4	17.3
1952																
1st quarter	26.0	15.2	58.4	5.1	37.9	19.6	16.2	18.2	29.3	15.1	51.4	5.5	40.7	18.7	15.3	17.3
2nd quarter	26.3	15.2	57.8	5.2	38.5	19.8	15.9	18.2	29.3	15.0	51.1	5.5	40.9	18.9	15.1	17.3
3rd quarter	26.4	15.3	58.0	5.3	38.9	20.1	16.0	18.4	29.2	15.0	51.5	5.6	41.1	19.2	15.1	17.5
4th quarter	26.8	15.9	59.4	5.4	39.7	20.3	15.8	18.4	29.8	15.7	52.9	5.7	42.1	19.3	15.3	17.6
1953																
1st quarter	27.2	16.2	59.7	5.5	40.6	20.3	15.7	18.4	30.0	16.0	53.4	5.8	42.7	19.4	15.2	17.6
2nd quarter	27.4	16.4	59.6	5.6	40.8	20.3	15.7	18.4	30.1	16.1	53.5	5.9	43.0	19.5	15.3	17.7
3rd quarter	27.4	16.2	59.1	5.7	41.2	20.6	15.5	18.5	30.2	16.0	53.0	5.9	43.3	19.6	15.2	17.8
4th quarter	27.4	15.9	58.1	5.7	41.1	20.7	15.5	18.5	30.1	15.7	52.2	6.0	43.6	19.9	14.9	17.8
1954																
1st quarter	27.4	15.8	57.7	5.7	41.3	20.8	15.4	18.6	30.2	15.5	51.5	6.0	43.9	20.0	14.9	17.9
2nd quarter	27.7	15.8	56.9	5.8	42.0	20.8	15.3	18.5	30.4	15.5	51.1	6.1	44.0	19.9	15.1	17.9
3rd quarter	28.2	16.0	56.7	5.8	42.2	20.5	15.7	18.5	30.9	15.7	50.9	6.1	44.5	19.7	15.3	17.9
4th quarter	28.6	16.3	57.1	5.9	42.9	20.5	15.8	18.5	31.3	16.1	51.5	6.2	45.1	19.7	15.6	18.0
1955																
1st quarter	29.0	16.9	58.2	5.8	42.7	20.1	16.6	18.6	31.9	16.7	52.3	6.2	45.3	19.4	16.1	18.1
2nd quarter	29.3	17.2	58.8	5.9	43.2	20.2	16.5	18.7	32.0	17.0	53.0	6.3	45.8	19.6	16.1	18.1
3rd quarter	29.2	17.5	59.7	5.9	43.5	20.3	16.7	18.8	32.1	17.2	53.6	6.4	46.5	19.8	16.2	18.3
4th quarter	29.1	17.5	60.4	6.0	43.7	20.6	16.7	19.0	32.0	17.4	54.2	6.4	46.8	20.1	16.2	18.5
1956																
1st quarter	29.0	17.4	60.2	6.2	44.8	21.3	16.3	19.2	31.6	17.3	54.6	6.5	47.5	20.6	15.9	18.6
2nd quarter	29.1	17.6	60.4	6.3	45.4	21.6	16.1	19.3	31.8	17.4	54.7	6.7	48.1	20.9	15.7	18.8
3rd quarter	29.1	17.5	60.1	6.3	45.4	21.8	16.4	19.5	31.8	17.3	54.5	6.8	48.4	21.2	15.8	19.0
4th quarter	29.7	17.8	60.0	6.5	46.1	21.8	16.5	19.6	32.1	17.6	54.8	6.9	48.8	21.4	15.9	19.1
1957																
1st quarter	29.9	17.9	59.9	6.6	46.6	22.1	16.7	19.9	32.5	17.8	54.8	7.0	49.1	21.4	16.4	19.3
2nd quarter	29.9	17.8	59.6	6.7	46.7	22.3	16.7	20.0	32.4	17.7	54.7	7.0	49.1	21.7	16.2	19.4
3rd quarter	30.2	18.0	59.5	6.7	46.7	22.3	17.0	20.1	32.8	17.9	54.4	7.1	49.4	21.7	16.5	19.5
4th quarter	30.6	17.8	58.2	6.9	47.3	22.5	16.7	20.1	32.9	17.6	53.3	7.2	49.8	21.9	16.3	19.6
1958																
1st quarter	30.3	17.2	56.6	6.9	47.1	22.8	16.8	20.3	32.5	16.9	52.1	7.2	49.2	22.3	16.1	19.7
2nd quarter	30.8	17.3	56.1	6.9	46.9	22.5	17.1	20.3	33.1	17.0	51.3	7.3	49.3	22.0	16.4	19.7
3rd quarter	31.3	17.7	56.5	7.1	48.2	22.7	17.2	20.4	33.7	17.5	52.0	7.5	50.5	22.1	16.5	19.8
4th quarter	31.7	18.2	57.4	7.1	48.3	22.5	17.7	20.5	34.3	18.1	52.7	7.5	50.6	21.8	17.1	19.9
1959																
1st quarter	32.0	18.6	58.3	7.2	48.9	22.7	17.5	20.5	34.3	18.5	53.8	7.6	51.1	22.0	17.1	20.0
2nd quarter	32.1	19.1	59.6	7.2	48.8	22.5	17.7	20.5	34.7	19.0	54.8	7.6	51.4	22.0	17.3	20.0
3rd quarter	32.2	19.0	59.1	7.3	49.1	22.7	17.6	20.6	34.7	18.9	54.6	7.7	51.4	22.1	17.3	20.1
4th quarter	32.3	19.1	59.0	7.4	49.5	23.0	17.5	20.7	34.6	18.9	54.6	7.7	51.6	22.4	17.1	20.2
1960																
1st quarter	33.2	19.6	58.9	7.6	50.8	23.0	17.7	20.7	35.4	19.5	55.0	7.9	52.7	22.3	17.3	20.2
2nd quarter	32.6	19.4	59.5	7.6	50.2	23.3	17.3	20.8	34.9	19.2	55.1	8.0	52.7	22.8	16.7	20.3
3rd quarter	32.7	19.4	59.4	7.6	50.2	23.2	17.5	20.8	35.0	19.2	54.8	8.0	53.0	22.9	16.8	20.3
4th quarter	32.4	19.0	58.7	7.7	50.3	23.6	17.0	20.9	34.6	18.8	54.2	8.0	52.9	23.3	16.4	20.4

Table 9-3B. Productivity and Related Data: Historical Data—*Continued*

(2009 = 100, seasonally adjusted.)

Year and quarter	Business sector								Nonfarm business sector							
	Output per hour of all persons	Output	Hours of all persons	Compensation per hour	Real compensation per hour	Unit labor costs	Unit nonlabor payments	Implicit price deflator	Output per hour of all persons	Output	Hours of all persons	Compensation per hour	Real compensation per hour	Unit labor costs	Unit nonlabor payments	Implicit price deflator
1961																
1st quarter	32.8	19.1	58.4	7.7	50.7	23.6	17.2	20.9	35.0	18.9	53.9	8.1	53.2	23.2	16.6	20.4
2nd quarter	33.9	19.6	57.7	7.9	51.8	23.3	17.6	20.9	36.1	19.4	53.8	8.2	54.0	22.8	17.2	20.5
3rd quarter	34.3	19.9	58.1	8.0	52.0	23.2	17.9	21.0	36.5	19.8	54.1	8.3	54.2	22.7	17.4	20.5
4th quarter	34.6	20.3	58.7	8.1	52.5	23.2	18.0	21.0	36.9	20.2	54.8	8.4	54.5	22.6	17.5	20.5
1962																
1st quarter	35.0	20.7	59.3	8.1	52.8	23.2	18.2	21.1	37.5	20.6	55.0	8.5	55.1	22.6	17.7	20.6
2nd quarter	35.2	21.0	59.6	8.2	53.3	23.4	18.1	21.2	37.4	20.8	55.7	8.5	55.3	22.8	17.7	20.7
3rd quarter	35.7	21.2	59.3	8.3	53.5	23.2	18.3	21.2	37.9	21.1	55.6	8.6	55.5	22.7	17.9	20.7
4th quarter	36.0	21.2	58.9	8.4	54.1	23.3	18.2	21.2	38.3	21.1	55.2	8.7	55.9	22.7	17.8	20.7
1963																
1st quarter	36.2	21.5	59.3	8.4	54.2	23.3	18.4	21.2	38.4	21.3	55.5	8.8	56.3	22.8	17.9	20.8
2nd quarter	36.5	21.8	59.7	8.5	54.3	23.2	18.5	21.3	38.8	21.7	55.9	8.8	56.5	22.7	18.1	20.8
3rd quarter	37.3	22.3	59.7	8.6	54.8	23.1	18.8	21.3	39.6	22.2	56.0	8.9	56.7	22.5	18.4	20.8
4th quarter	37.4	22.4	60.0	8.7	55.2	23.3	18.8	21.4	39.6	22.4	56.5	9.0	57.2	22.7	18.3	20.9
1964																
1st quarter	37.8	23.0	60.7	8.8	55.4	23.1	19.1	21.5	39.9	23.0	57.5	9.0	56.9	22.5	18.8	21.0
2nd quarter	38.0	23.2	61.3	8.8	55.7	23.2	19.1	21.5	40.2	23.2	57.8	9.1	57.5	22.6	18.8	21.0
3rd quarter	38.3	23.6	61.6	8.9	56.3	23.3	19.1	21.6	40.5	23.6	58.1	9.2	58.1	22.7	18.9	21.1
4th quarter	38.1	23.6	62.0	9.0	56.5	23.6	18.9	21.7	40.2	23.6	58.7	9.3	58.2	23.1	18.5	21.2
1965																
1st quarter	38.8	24.4	62.7	9.1	56.8	23.4	19.4	21.8	40.8	24.3	59.6	9.3	58.3	22.9	19.0	21.3
2nd quarter	38.8	24.7	63.6	9.1	56.8	23.5	19.5	21.8	41.0	24.7	60.2	9.4	58.3	22.9	19.1	21.3
3rd quarter	39.8	25.2	63.5	9.3	57.3	23.3	20.0	21.9	41.7	25.2	60.4	9.5	58.8	22.7	19.5	21.4
4th quarter	40.4	25.9	64.1	9.4	57.7	23.2	20.4	22.0	42.5	25.9	60.9	9.6	59.3	22.7	19.8	21.5
1966																
1st quarter	41.1	26.6	64.8	9.6	58.5	23.3	20.5	22.1	43.1	26.6	61.8	9.8	59.8	22.7	19.9	21.5
2nd quarter	40.9	26.7	65.2	9.8	59.0	23.8	20.1	22.3	42.8	26.7	62.4	9.9	60.2	23.2	19.7	21.8
3rd quarter	41.0	26.8	65.3	9.9	59.4	24.2	20.2	22.5	42.9	26.9	62.7	10.1	60.5	23.5	19.7	21.9
4th quarter	41.3	26.9	65.2	10.1	59.9	24.4	20.4	22.7	43.2	27.0	62.5	10.2	60.8	23.7	20.1	22.2
1967																
1st quarter	41.7	27.2	65.2	10.2	60.3	24.4	20.6	22.8	43.5	27.2	62.5	10.4	61.5	23.8	20.2	22.3
2nd quarter	42.1	27.1	64.5	10.3	61.0	24.6	20.5	22.9	43.7	27.1	62.1	10.5	62.1	24.1	20.0	22.4
3rd quarter	42.1	27.3	64.9	10.5	61.1	24.8	20.6	23.1	43.9	27.3	62.3	10.7	62.3	24.3	20.2	22.6
4th quarter	42.2	27.5	65.2	10.6	61.1	25.1	20.8	23.3	44.1	27.6	62.6	10.8	62.5	24.6	20.4	22.8
1968																
1st quarter	43.2	28.2	65.3	10.9	62.3	25.2	21.2	23.5	45.0	28.2	62.7	11.1	63.6	24.7	20.8	23.0
2nd quarter	43.6	28.7	65.8	11.1	62.8	25.4	21.5	23.8	45.5	28.8	63.3	11.3	64.0	24.8	21.2	23.3
3rd quarter	43.6	28.9	66.1	11.3	63.1	25.9	21.3	24.0	45.5	29.0	63.7	11.5	64.2	25.2	20.9	23.5
4th quarter	43.6	29.0	66.5	11.5	63.6	26.4	21.4	24.3	45.4	29.1	64.1	11.7	64.6	25.8	21.0	23.8
1969																
1st quarter	43.7	29.5	67.5	11.6	63.1	26.5	21.9	24.6	45.7	29.6	64.7	11.9	64.7	25.9	21.4	24.1
2nd quarter	43.7	29.5	67.6	11.9	63.7	27.2	21.7	24.9	45.4	29.6	65.3	12.1	64.7	26.6	21.2	24.3
3rd quarter	43.8	29.7	67.8	12.1	64.2	27.7	21.6	25.1	45.4	29.8	65.6	12.3	65.0	27.0	21.1	24.6
4th quarter	43.7	29.5	67.5	12.4	64.6	28.3	21.4	25.4	45.2	29.6	65.4	12.5	65.3	27.7	20.8	24.8
1970																
1st quarter	43.9	29.5	67.1	12.6	64.8	28.7	21.4	25.7	45.3	29.5	65.2	12.7	65.4	28.1	20.9	25.1
2nd quarter	44.4	29.5	66.5	12.8	64.7	28.8	22.2	26.0	46.0	29.6	64.3	12.9	65.5	28.1	21.7	25.5
3rd quarter	45.2	29.8	66.0	13.0	65.1	28.8	22.5	26.2	46.7	29.9	64.0	13.2	65.9	28.2	22.0	25.6
4th quarter	44.9	29.4	65.4	13.2	65.0	29.3	22.6	26.5	46.3	29.4	63.5	13.3	65.6	28.7	22.2	26.0
1971																
1st quarter	46.2	30.3	65.7	13.4	65.7	29.0	23.7	26.8	47.7	30.4	63.8	13.6	66.4	28.4	23.1	26.2
2nd quarter	46.2	30.6	66.1	13.6	65.8	29.3	24.0	27.1	47.8	30.6	64.0	13.8	66.8	28.8	23.5	26.5
3rd quarter	46.8	30.8	65.9	13.8	66.3	29.5	24.4	27.3	48.2	30.9	64.0	13.9	67.0	28.9	23.8	26.8
4th quarter	46.4	30.9	66.6	13.9	66.3	29.9	24.1	27.5	47.9	31.0	64.7	14.0	67.0	29.3	23.5	26.9
1972																
1st quarter	46.9	31.6	67.5	14.2	67.4	30.4	24.2	27.8	48.5	31.8	65.5	14.4	68.2	29.7	23.8	27.2
2nd quarter	48.0	32.6	67.8	14.4	67.7	30.0	25.1	27.9	49.5	32.7	66.0	14.6	68.6	29.4	24.4	27.3
3rd quarter	48.1	32.9	68.3	14.6	67.9	30.2	25.4	28.2	49.8	33.0	66.3	14.8	69.0	29.7	24.5	27.5
4th quarter	48.6	33.5	69.0	14.9	68.6	30.5	25.7	28.5	50.2	33.6	67.0	15.1	69.5	30.0	24.4	27.7
1973																
1st quarter	49.5	34.6	69.9	15.3	69.5	30.8	25.9	28.8	51.3	34.9	68.0	15.5	70.3	30.1	24.7	27.8
2nd quarter	49.7	35.1	70.6	15.5	69.0	31.2	26.5	29.2	51.4	35.3	68.7	15.7	69.8	30.5	24.9	28.1
3rd quarter	49.0	34.8	71.0	15.8	68.9	32.2	26.5	29.8	50.9	35.2	69.2	15.9	69.6	31.3	24.6	28.5
4th quarter	49.2	35.1	71.5	16.1	68.5	32.7	27.4	30.5	50.6	35.2	69.6	16.3	69.3	32.2	25.0	29.2
1974																
1st quarter	48.5	34.6	71.4	16.4	67.7	33.8	27.5	31.1	50.4	34.9	69.3	16.6	68.8	33.0	25.5	29.8
2nd quarter	48.7	34.7	71.3	16.9	68.0	34.7	28.1	31.9	50.3	34.9	69.4	17.1	68.8	33.9	26.8	30.9
3rd quarter	48.2	34.2	70.9	17.4	68.3	36.1	28.6	33.0	49.8	34.4	69.2	17.6	68.9	35.3	27.1	31.9
4th quarter	48.6	34.0	69.9	17.9	67.9	36.7	30.2	34.0	50.2	34.2	68.0	18.1	68.7	36.0	28.5	32.9
1975																
1st quarter	49.3	33.3	67.6	18.4	68.6	37.4	31.2	34.8	50.6	33.4	65.9	18.6	69.3	36.8	30.0	33.9
2nd quarter	50.1	33.6	67.1	18.8	69.2	37.6	32.1	35.3	51.5	33.6	65.3	19.0	69.9	36.9	31.0	34.4
3rd quarter	50.6	34.3	67.8	19.1	68.8	37.7	33.5	35.9	52.0	34.3	65.9	19.3	69.7	37.2	32.0	35.0
4th quarter	50.8	34.9	68.7	19.5	68.9	38.3	33.9	36.5	52.1	34.9	67.0	19.7	69.6	37.7	32.4	35.5

Table 9-3B. Productivity and Related Data: Historical Data—*Continued*

(2009 = 100, seasonally adjusted.)

Year and quarter	Business sector								Nonfarm business sector							
	Output per hour of all persons	Output	Hours of all persons	Compensation per hour	Real compensation per hour	Unit labor costs	Unit nonlabor payments	Implicit price deflator	Output per hour of all persons	Output	Hours of all persons	Compensation per hour	Real compensation per hour	Unit labor costs	Unit nonlabor payments	Implicit price deflator
1976																
1st quarter	51.5	35.9	69.7	19.9	69.6	38.6	34.3	36.8	52.9	36.0	68.1	20.0	70.1	37.9	33.1	35.9
2nd quarter	51.8	36.2	69.9	20.2	70.2	39.0	34.6	37.2	53.4	36.4	68.2	20.4	70.8	38.2	33.6	36.3
3rd quarter	51.9	36.4	70.2	20.6	70.4	39.7	34.8	37.7	53.5	36.6	68.4	20.8	71.2	39.0	33.8	36.8
4th quarter	52.2	36.8	70.4	21.1	71.1	40.4	35.4	38.3	53.6	36.9	68.8	21.3	71.6	39.7	34.4	
1977																
1st quarter	52.5	37.3	71.1	21.5	71.1	41.0	36.1	38.9	54.0	37.5	69.5	21.7	71.7	40.2	35.0	38.0
2nd quarter	52.6	38.2	72.7	21.9	71.0	41.6	36.5	39.4	54.2	38.4	70.9	22.1	71.9	40.8	35.6	38.6
3rd quarter	53.3	39.0	73.2	22.3	71.5	41.9	37.0	39.9	54.7	39.2	71.6	22.6	72.3	41.2	36.3	39.1
4th quarter	52.7	39.0	74.0	22.7	71.7	43.1	37.4	40.7	54.0	39.1	72.3	22.9	72.5	42.5	36.2	39.8
1978																
1st quarter	52.5	39.1	74.4	23.4	72.9	44.6	37.0	41.4	54.1	39.3	72.7	23.7	73.8	43.9	35.7	40.5
2nd quarter	53.5	40.9	76.5	23.7	72.1	44.2	39.1	42.1	55.1	41.2	74.8	24.0	73.0	43.5	37.7	41.1
3rd quarter	53.7	41.4	77.1	24.1	71.9	44.8	39.9	42.8	55.1	41.6	75.4	24.3	72.8	44.2	38.5	41.8
4th quarter	53.8	42.0	77.9	24.6	72.2	45.8	40.8	43.7	55.5	42.3	76.3	24.9	73.0	44.9	39.4	42.6
1979																
1st quarter	53.5	42.0	78.5	25.4	72.8	47.4	40.4	44.5	55.0	42.3	76.9	25.7	73.5	46.7	38.7	43.3
2nd quarter	53.4	42.1	78.7	26.0	72.5	48.6	41.7	45.7	54.8	42.3	77.2	26.2	73.2	47.8	40.1	44.6
3rd quarter	53.4	42.4	79.4	26.6	72.3	49.7	42.4	46.7	54.8	42.6	77.8	26.8	73.0	49.0	40.8	45.6
4th quarter	53.3	42.5	79.6	27.2	72.2	51.0	42.7	47.5	54.7	42.7	78.0	27.5	73.0	50.3	41.1	46.5
1980																
1st quarter	53.7	42.6	79.3	28.0	72.1	52.2	43.4	48.5	55.0	42.8	77.8	28.3	72.8	51.5	42.2	47.6
2nd quarter	53.1	41.4	77.9	28.8	72.2	54.2	43.3	49.6	54.4	41.6	76.4	29.0	72.9	53.4	42.8	49.0
3rd quarter	53.1	41.2	77.6	29.4	72.2	55.4	44.2	50.7	54.6	41.5	76.1	29.8	72.9	54.5	43.1	49.7
4th quarter	53.7	42.2	78.6	30.2	72.3	56.3	46.1	52.0	55.2	42.5	77.0	30.6	73.2	55.4	44.4	50.8
1981																
1st quarter	54.8	43.3	79.1	31.0	72.1	56.6	48.9	53.3	56.1	43.5	77.5	31.4	73.1	55.9	47.4	52.4
2nd quarter	54.3	42.9	78.9	31.6	72.2	58.1	49.2	54.4	55.4	42.9	77.5	31.9	73.0	57.6	47.6	53.4
3rd quarter	55.0	43.4	79.0	32.2	72.2	58.6	50.9	55.3	55.9	43.3	77.5	32.6	73.1	58.4	49.2	54.6
4th quarter	54.3	42.7	78.7	32.7	72.1	60.3	50.6	56.3	55.2	42.6	77.2	33.1	73.0	60.0	49.4	55.6
1982																
1st quarter	53.9	41.7	77.4	33.6	73.1	62.3	49.6	57.0	54.8	41.6	75.9	34.0	73.9	62.0	48.5	56.4
2nd quarter	54.1	42.0	77.6	33.9	73.1	62.7	50.6	57.7	54.9	41.9	76.2	34.3	73.8	62.4	49.6	57.1
3rd quarter	54.1	41.7	77.1	34.4	72.9	63.6	51.3	58.4	55.0	41.6	75.7	34.8	73.7	63.3	50.1	57.8
4th quarter	54.6	41.7	76.4	34.9	73.1	63.9	52.1	58.9	55.5	41.6	75.0	35.3	73.9	63.6	51.0	58.4
1983																
1st quarter	55.2	42.4	76.8	35.3	73.3	63.9	53.1	59.4	56.3	42.5	75.4	35.7	74.3	63.4	51.9	58.6
2nd quarter	56.2	43.6	77.6	35.6	73.3	63.4	54.5	59.7	57.6	43.9	76.3	36.1	74.2	62.6	53.5	58.8
3rd quarter	56.4	44.6	79.1	35.8	72.9	63.5	55.8	60.3	58.0	45.1	77.8	36.3	73.9	62.5	55.4	59.5
4th quarter	56.9	45.7	80.4	36.3	73.2	63.8	56.3	60.6	58.3	46.2	79.2	36.7	74.0	62.9	55.7	59.9
1984																
1st quarter	57.2	46.9	82.0	36.7	73.1	64.2	56.8	61.1	58.4	47.1	80.7	37.1	73.9	63.6	55.4	60.2
2nd quarter	57.7	47.9	83.0	37.1	73.1	64.3	57.8	61.6	58.7	48.1	81.8	37.5	73.9	63.8	56.4	60.7
3rd quarter	58.0	48.4	83.4	37.6	73.6	64.8	58.0	62.0	59.0	48.5	82.2	38.0	74.4	64.4	56.7	61.2
4th quarter	58.1	48.7	83.9	37.9	73.6	65.3	58.2	62.3	59.0	48.8	82.7	38.3	74.3	64.9	56.9	61.5
1985																
1st quarter	58.3	49.3	84.5	38.4	73.9	65.9	59.0	63.0	59.1	49.3	83.4	38.8	74.6	65.6	57.8	62.4
2nd quarter	58.6	49.8	85.0	38.8	74.0	66.3	59.3	63.4	59.3	49.8	83.9	39.2	74.7	66.0	58.2	62.8
3rd quarter	59.5	50.6	85.1	39.5	74.7	66.3	59.9	63.6	60.1	50.6	84.2	39.8	75.3	66.2	59.1	63.2
4th quarter	59.7	51.0	85.4	40.2	75.5	67.3	59.1	63.9	60.3	51.0	84.6	40.5	76.0	67.1	58.1	63.4
1986																
1st quarter	60.3	51.5	85.4	40.7	76.1	67.6	59.3	64.1	61.0	51.6	84.5	41.1	76.7	67.3	58.6	63.7
2nd quarter	60.7	51.7	85.2	41.2	77.3	67.9	59.2	64.2	61.5	51.8	84.3	41.6	78.0	67.6	58.4	63.7
3rd quarter	61.0	52.3	85.7	41.7	77.7	68.3	59.0	64.4	61.8	52.3	84.7	42.1	78.5	68.1	57.9	63.8
4th quarter	60.9	52.5	86.3	42.2	78.3	69.4	58.1	64.6	61.7	52.6	85.3	42.6	79.0	69.1	57.0	64.1
1987																
1st quarter	60.6	52.9	87.3	42.4	77.8	70.0	58.1	65.0	61.4	53.0	86.3	42.8	78.5	69.8	57.1	64.5
2nd quarter	61.0	53.6	87.9	42.7	77.5	70.1	58.8	65.4	61.8	53.7	86.8	43.1	78.3	69.8	57.9	64.9
3rd quarter	61.1	54.0	88.4	43.2	77.6	70.7	59.1	65.9	61.8	54.1	87.4	43.6	78.3	70.5	58.2	65.4
4th quarter	61.5	55.0	89.3	43.7	77.9	71.1	59.4	66.2	62.3	55.1	88.4	44.1	78.6	70.8	58.5	65.6
1988																
1st quarter	61.8	55.2	89.4	44.5	78.8	72.1	59.3	66.7	62.6	55.3	88.4	44.9	79.5	71.8	58.2	66.1
2nd quarter	61.8	56.0	90.6	45.1	78.9	72.9	59.5	67.3	62.7	56.3	89.7	45.4	79.5	72.4	58.6	66.7
3rd quarter	62.0	56.3	90.8	45.6	79.1	73.6	60.5	68.1	62.9	56.6	89.9	46.0	79.6	73.1	59.5	67.4
4th quarter	62.2	57.1	91.8	45.9	78.8	73.9	61.3	68.6	63.2	57.4	90.9	46.3	79.5	73.3	60.7	68.1
1989																
1st quarter	62.3	57.7	92.7	46.1	78.4	74.1	62.7	69.3	63.1	57.9	91.8	46.5	79.0	73.7	61.4	68.6
2nd quarter	62.6	58.2	93.0	46.4	77.6	74.1	64.4	70.0	63.3	58.4	92.2	46.7	78.1	73.7	63.3	69.4
3rd quarter	62.9	58.6	93.3	46.7	77.7	74.4	65.0	70.4	63.6	58.8	92.4	47.1	78.2	74.0	64.1	69.8
4th quarter	62.9	58.7	93.3	47.4	78.1	75.3	64.6	70.8	63.7	58.8	92.4	47.7	78.6	75.0	63.5	70.2
1990																
1st quarter	63.6	59.4	93.4	48.5	78.6	76.2	65.2	71.6	64.2	59.5	92.6	48.7	79.0	75.8	64.0	70.9
2nd quarter	64.2	59.6	92.8	49.5	79.6	77.1	65.4	72.2	64.8	59.7	92.1	49.7	79.9	76.7	64.3	71.6
3rd quarter	64.6	59.5	92.1	50.2	79.4	77.8	65.8	72.8	65.1	59.6	91.5	50.4	79.7	77.5	64.7	72.2
4th quarter	64.0	58.7	91.8	50.6	78.8	79.1	65.2	73.3	64.5	58.8	91.1	50.8	79.1	78.8	64.4	72.8

Table 9-3B. Productivity and Related Data: Historical Data—*Continued*

(2009 = 100, seasonally adjusted.)

Year and quarter	Business sector								Nonfarm business sector							
	Output per hour of all persons	Output	Hours of all persons	Compensation per hour	Real compensation per hour	Unit labor costs	Unit nonlabor payments	Implicit price deflator	Output per hour of all persons	Output	Hours of all persons	Compensation per hour	Real compensation per hour	Unit labor costs	Unit nonlabor payments	Implicit price deflator
1991																
1st quarter	64.1	58.3	90.8	51.0	78.9	79.4	66.2	73.9	64.7	58.3	90.1	51.2	79.3	79.1	65.5	73.4
2nd quarter	65.2	58.8	90.3	51.9	80.0	79.6	67.0	74.3	65.8	58.9	89.6	52.2	80.4	79.3	66.1	73.8
3rd quarter	65.6	59.2	90.2	52.5	80.4	80.0	67.7	74.8	66.3	59.3	89.5	52.8	80.9	79.7	67.0	74.4
4th quarter	66.0	59.4	90.0	53.1	80.8	80.5	67.6	75.1	66.6	59.5	89.4	53.4	81.3	80.2	66.7	74.6
1992																
1st quarter	67.4	60.3	89.5	54.5	82.4	80.9	67.3	75.2	67.9	60.3	88.9	54.8	82.9	80.7	66.4	74.7
2nd quarter	67.9	61.1	90.0	54.9	82.5	80.8	68.1	75.5	68.4	61.1	89.3	55.3	83.1	80.8	67.1	75.1
3rd quarter	68.5	61.8	90.2	55.5	82.9	81.1	68.6	75.9	69.0	61.7	89.5	55.9	83.5	81.0	67.6	75.4
4th quarter	68.8	62.5	90.8	55.9	82.9	81.2	69.6	76.4	69.4	62.5	90.1	56.3	83.4	81.1	68.8	75.9
1993																
1st quarter	68.3	62.5	91.4	55.5	81.8	81.2	70.6	76.8	68.9	62.6	90.9	55.8	82.2	80.9	70.1	76.4
2nd quarter	68.0	62.9	92.4	56.0	82.0	82.3	70.3	77.3	68.5	63.0	91.9	56.2	82.3	82.0	69.6	76.8
3rd quarter	68.0	63.2	92.9	56.1	81.7	82.4	71.2	77.7	68.7	63.4	92.4	56.3	82.0	81.9	70.7	77.3
4th quarter	68.6	64.2	93.7	56.5	81.9	82.4	72.0	78.1	69.1	64.4	93.2	56.8	82.2	82.2	71.2	77.6
1994																
1st quarter	68.9	65.0	94.4	56.2	81.2	81.6	73.7	78.3	69.5	65.0	93.5	56.5	81.7	81.4	72.9	77.8
2nd quarter	68.8	66.1	96.0	56.6	81.3	82.2	73.6	78.6	69.5	66.1	95.1	57.0	81.9	82.0	72.9	78.2
3rd quarter	68.4	66.5	97.1	56.6	80.6	82.6	74.0	79.0	69.0	66.5	96.3	56.9	81.2	82.5	73.5	78.7
4th quarter	69.0	67.4	97.7	56.8	80.7	82.4	75.2	79.4	69.7	67.5	96.8	57.3	81.3	82.1	74.7	79.0
1995																
1st quarter	68.7	67.6	98.4	57.1	80.5	83.1	75.1	79.7	69.6	67.8	97.5	57.5	81.1	82.6	74.9	79.4
2nd quarter	68.9	67.8	98.5	57.4	80.3	83.4	75.5	80.1	69.8	68.1	97.5	57.8	81.0	82.8	75.4	79.7
3rd quarter	68.9	68.6	99.5	57.8	80.5	83.8	75.7	80.4	69.8	68.9	98.6	58.2	81.0	83.3	75.4	80.0
4th quarter	69.6	69.2	99.5	58.4	81.0	83.9	76.2	80.7	70.4	69.5	98.7	58.8	81.5	83.5	75.6	80.2
1996																
1st quarter	70.2	69.8	99.4	59.2	81.5	84.3	76.5	81.0	71.0	70.0	98.5	59.6	82.1	84.0	75.5	80.5
2nd quarter	71.2	71.2	100.1	59.9	81.7	84.2	77.6	81.4	71.9	71.4	99.3	60.3	82.3	83.9	76.4	80.8
3rd quarter	71.5	72.0	100.8	60.5	82.1	84.6	77.3	81.6	72.2	72.2	100.1	60.8	82.5	84.2	76.6	81.0
4th quarter	71.5	73.0	102.0	60.7	81.8	84.9	77.8	81.9	72.2	73.1	101.4	61.0	82.2	84.6	77.0	81.4
1997																
1st quarter	71.3	73.6	103.1	61.2	82.0	85.8	77.6	82.4	72.0	73.7	102.4	61.6	82.5	85.6	76.7	81.9
2nd quarter	72.2	74.9	103.7	61.7	82.5	85.4	78.5	82.5	72.8	75.0	103.1	62.1	83.0	85.2	78.0	82.2
3rd quarter	72.9	76.0	104.3	62.4	83.0	85.6	78.9	82.8	73.4	76.1	103.7	62.7	83.4	85.4	78.3	82.4
4th quarter	73.3	76.7	104.7	63.6	84.2	86.8	77.6	83.0	73.7	76.8	104.2	63.8	84.4	86.6	77.2	82.6
1998																
1st quarter	73.7	77.5	105.2	64.7	85.6	87.8	76.3	83.0	74.2	77.7	104.8	64.9	85.8	87.5	75.8	82.7
2nd quarter	74.1	78.4	105.8	65.6	86.4	88.5	75.5	83.0	74.7	78.6	105.2	65.8	86.7	88.1	75.2	82.7
3rd quarter	75.2	79.6	105.9	66.6	87.3	88.6	75.7	83.2	75.7	79.8	105.4	66.8	87.7	88.3	75.4	82.9
4th quarter	75.7	81.2	107.3	66.9	87.4	88.3	76.2	83.2	76.2	81.4	106.9	67.1	87.6	88.0	75.7	82.9
1999																
1st quarter	76.5	82.0	107.1	68.1	88.6	89.0	75.9	83.5	76.9	82.2	106.9	68.2	88.7	88.6	75.5	83.2
2nd quarter	76.7	82.7	107.9	68.2	88.2	89.0	76.0	83.6	77.0	82.9	107.7	68.3	88.3	88.7	76.0	83.4
3rd quarter	77.3	83.9	108.6	68.8	88.2	89.0	76.6	83.8	77.7	84.2	108.4	68.9	88.3	88.7	76.6	83.7
4th quarter	78.5	85.6	109.0	70.1	89.3	89.3	76.8	84.1	79.0	85.9	108.7	70.3	89.5	89.1	76.9	84.0
2000																
1st quarter	78.3	85.8	109.5	72.7	91.7	92.8	73.2	84.6	78.7	85.9	109.2	73.0	92.0	92.7	73.1	84.5
2nd quarter	80.0	87.7	109.5	73.0	91.4	91.2	76.5	85.1	80.4	87.8	109.3	73.2	91.6	91.1	76.4	85.0
3rd quarter	80.1	87.7	109.5	74.5	92.4	93.0	75.1	85.5	80.4	87.8	109.3	74.7	92.6	92.9	75.1	85.5
4th quarter	81.0	88.2	108.9	75.0	92.4	92.6	76.6	85.9	81.2	88.3	108.8	75.1	92.5	92.5	76.5	85.8
2001																
1st quarter	80.7	87.7	108.7	76.9	93.7	95.2	74.0	86.3	80.9	87.9	108.6	76.9	93.8	95.0	73.9	86.2
2nd quarter	82.0	88.2	107.6	77.1	93.4	94.1	76.8	86.9	82.3	88.5	107.5	77.1	93.4	93.7	76.8	86.7
3rd quarter	82.4	87.7	106.4	77.2	93.3	93.7	77.5	86.9	82.7	88.0	106.4	77.2	93.3	93.3	77.4	86.7
4th quarter	83.5	87.9	105.3	77.8	94.1	93.2	78.3	87.0	83.7	88.1	105.1	77.9	94.2	93.0	78.4	86.9
2002																
1st quarter	85.1	88.9	104.4	78.2	94.2	91.9	80.2	87.0	85.6	89.2	104.2	78.3	94.3	91.4	80.3	86.8
2nd quarter	85.4	89.3	104.7	78.9	94.3	92.4	80.0	87.2	85.7	89.6	104.5	79.0	94.4	92.2	80.4	87.2
3rd quarter	86.1	89.8	104.3	79.3	94.3	92.1	81.2	87.5	86.4	90.0	104.2	79.4	94.4	91.9	81.3	87.5
4th quarter	86.0	89.8	104.4	79.5	93.9	92.5	81.5	87.9	86.2	89.9	104.3	79.6	94.0	92.3	81.6	87.8
2003																
1st quarter	86.9	90.2	103.9	80.0	93.6	92.1	82.9	88.2	87.1	90.3	103.7	80.1	93.7	91.9	82.9	88.2
2nd quarter	88.3	91.3	103.4	81.6	95.6	92.4	82.8	88.4	88.3	91.3	103.4	81.5	95.5	92.3	82.7	88.3
3rd quarter	89.9	93.3	103.7	82.6	96.1	91.8	84.5	88.8	90.2	93.4	103.6	82.7	96.2	91.7	84.3	88.6
4th quarter	90.6	94.5	104.3	83.7	97.0	92.3	84.6	89.1	91.0	94.8	104.1	83.8	97.1	92.0	84.1	88.7
2004																
1st quarter	91.0	95.1	104.6	83.7	96.1	92.0	86.6	89.7	91.0	95.2	104.6	83.7	96.1	91.9	85.8	89.4
2nd quarter	91.6	95.9	104.7	85.3	97.2	93.1	86.8	90.4	91.9	96.2	104.6	85.3	97.3	92.8	85.9	89.9
3rd quarter	92.0	96.9	105.4	86.7	98.2	94.3	86.1	90.9	92.2	97.1	105.3	86.8	98.3	94.1	85.6	90.6
4th quarter	92.6	97.9	105.7	87.3	97.9	94.3	87.8	91.6	92.5	97.9	105.9	87.1	97.7	94.2	87.3	91.3
2005																
1st quarter	93.5	99.1	106.0	87.9	98.1	94.0	90.0	92.3	93.5	99.2	106.1	87.8	97.9	93.9	89.8	92.2
2nd quarter	93.2	99.6	106.9	88.2	97.7	94.6	90.8	93.0	93.4	99.7	106.7	88.3	97.8	94.5	90.6	92.9
3rd quarter	94.0	100.6	107.0	89.3	97.5	95.0	92.4	93.9	94.1	100.7	107.0	89.4	97.5	95.0	92.3	93.8
4th quarter	94.2	101.3	107.5	90.0	97.3	95.6	93.3	94.6	94.2	101.4	107.7	89.9	97.3	95.5	93.2	94.6

Table 9-3B. Productivity and Related Data: Historical Data—*Continued*

(2009 = 100, seasonally adjusted.)

Year and quarter	Business sector								Nonfarm business sector							
	Output per hour of all persons	Output	Hours of all persons	Compensation per hour	Real compensation per hour	Unit labor costs	Unit nonlabor payments	Implicit price deflator	Output per hour of all persons	Output	Hours of all persons	Compensation per hour	Real compensation per hour	Unit labor costs	Unit nonlabor payments	Implicit price deflator
2006																
1st quarter	94.8	102.8	108.4	91.9	98.9	97.0	92.7	95.2	94.7	102.9	108.6	91.8	98.8	96.9	92.6	95.1
2nd quarter	94.7	103.1	108.8	91.9	97.9	97.0	94.4	95.9	94.7	103.1	108.9	91.9	97.9	97.0	94.4	95.9
3rd quarter	94.2	103.1	109.5	92.0	97.1	97.6	94.9	96.5	94.7	103.3	109.6	92.0	97.1	97.6	94.9	96.5
4th quarter	94.8	104.2	109.9	93.6	99.2	98.7	93.8	96.6	95.0	104.4	109.9	93.6	99.3	98.6	93.6	96.5
2007																
1st quarter	94.8	104.3	109.9	95.8	100.6	101.1	92.8	97.6	95.1	104.5	109.9	95.9	100.7	100.9	92.5	97.4
2nd quarter	95.6	105.3	110.1	96.1	99.8	100.5	95.0	98.2	95.7	105.6	110.3	95.9	99.6	100.2	94.7	97.9
3rd quarter	96.7	106.1	109.7	96.5	99.6	99.8	96.6	98.4	96.8	106.5	110.0	96.2	99.3	99.4	96.3	98.1
4th quarter	97.0	106.3	109.6	97.3	99.2	100.3	96.5	98.8	97.2	106.7	109.7	97.2	99.1	100.0	96.0	98.4
2008																
1st quarter	96.1	105.1	109.3	98.2	99.1	102.2	94.9	99.1	96.2	105.3	109.4	98.2	99.0	102.0	94.2	98.7
2nd quarter	97.1	105.6	108.7	98.4	97.9	101.3	97.1	99.6	97.2	105.8	108.9	98.3	97.8	101.1	96.5	99.2
3rd quarter	97.3	104.7	107.6	99.2	97.3	101.9	97.9	100.3	97.4	105.0	107.7	99.1	97.2	101.7	97.4	99.9
4th quarter	96.8	101.6	105.0	100.2	100.5	103.5	95.3	100.1	96.8	101.7	105.0	100.2	100.5	103.5	95.0	100.0
2009																
1st quarter	97.5	99.7	102.3	97.7	98.7	100.2	100.4	100.3	97.6	99.8	102.3	97.7	98.7	100.1	100.5	100.3
2nd quarter	99.4	99.4	100.1	100.1	100.6	100.7	98.7	99.9	99.5	99.5	100.0	100.1	100.6	100.7	98.8	99.9
3rd quarter	101.0	99.8	98.8	100.8	100.5	99.9	99.7	99.8	100.9	99.7	98.8	100.8	100.6	100.7	98.8	99.9
4th quarter	102.2	101.0	98.8	101.4	100.3	99.2	101.2	100.1	102.1	101.0	98.9	101.4	100.3	99.3	100.9	100.0
2010																
1st quarter	102.6	101.5	98.9	100.7	99.4	98.1	103.8	100.5	102.7	101.5	98.9	100.7	99.4	98.1	103.6	100.4
2nd quarter	103.0	102.8	99.7	101.8	100.5	98.8	103.7	100.9	103.0	102.7	99.7	101.9	100.6	98.9	103.4	100.8
3rd quarter	103.6	103.8	100.2	102.3	100.7	98.7	104.8	101.3	103.6	103.8	100.2	102.4	100.8	98.8	104.4	101.2
4th quarter	103.9	104.7	100.7	102.7	100.3	98.8	106.2	101.9	104.0	104.7	100.7	102.8	100.4	98.9	105.5	101.6
2011																
1st quarter	103.1	104.1	101.0	104.5	100.9	101.4	103.7	102.3	103.1	104.1	100.9	104.7	101.1	101.5	102.4	101.9
2nd quarter	103.4	105.1	101.6	104.0	99.4	100.6	106.6	103.1	103.5	105.2	101.7	104.1	99.5	100.6	105.3	102.6
3rd quarter	103.1	105.3	102.2	104.6	99.2	101.4	107.2	103.8	103.3	105.5	102.2	104.7	99.4	101.4	105.7	103.2
4th quarter	103.9	106.9	102.9	103.3	97.6	99.4	110.5	104.0	104.0	107.0	102.9	103.4	97.7	99.4	109.3	103.5
2012																
1st quarter	103.8	107.7	103.7	106.1	99.7	102.2	107.6	104.5	104.0	107.9	103.7	106.3	99.9	102.1	106.5	103.9
2nd quarter	104.4	108.3	103.8	106.4	99.7	101.9	109.3	105.0	104.6	108.5	103.8	106.5	99.8	101.8	108.3	104.5
3rd quarter	104.7	109.2	104.2	106.4	99.3	101.6	111.1	105.6	105.0	109.5	104.3	106.5	99.4	101.4	110.0	105.0
4th quarter	104.2	109.1	104.8	109.1	101.2	104.7	107.5	105.9	104.4	109.5	104.9	109.1	101.1	104.4	106.3	105.2
2013																
1st quarter	104.7	110.0	105.1	107.5	99.3	102.7	111.2	106.3	104.6	110.2	105.3	107.2	99.1	102.5	109.6	105.5
2nd quarter	105.0	110.6	105.4	108.6	100.4	103.5	110.7	106.5	104.8	110.7	105.6	108.3	100.2	103.4	109.4	105.9
3rd quarter	105.8	112.2	106.0	108.6	99.9	102.7	112.9	106.9	105.7	112.2	106.2	108.5	99.7	102.6	111.6	106.4
4th quarter	106.6	113.5	106.5	109.0	99.9	102.3	114.0	107.2	106.5	113.5	106.6	108.9	99.8	102.3	113.0	106.7
2014																
1st quarter	105.1	112.5	107.0	110.8	101.0	105.3	110.6	107.5	105.2	112.9	107.2	110.6	100.8	105.1	109.5	106.9
2nd quarter	105.9	114.1	107.7	110.5	100.1	104.3	113.5	108.2	106.0	114.4	107.9	110.3	100.0	104.1	112.2	107.5
3rd quarter	106.8	115.9	108.5	111.0	100.3	104.0	114.7	108.5	107.0	116.1	108.5	111.1	100.4	103.9	113.7	107.9
4th quarter	106.2	116.7	109.9	111.9	101.3	105.4	112.4	108.3	106.4	116.9	109.8	112.0	101.4	105.3	111.5	107.9

Section 9c: Returns and Profits by Industry

Figure 9-3: Rates of Return, Nonfinancial Industry Groups, 1998–2014

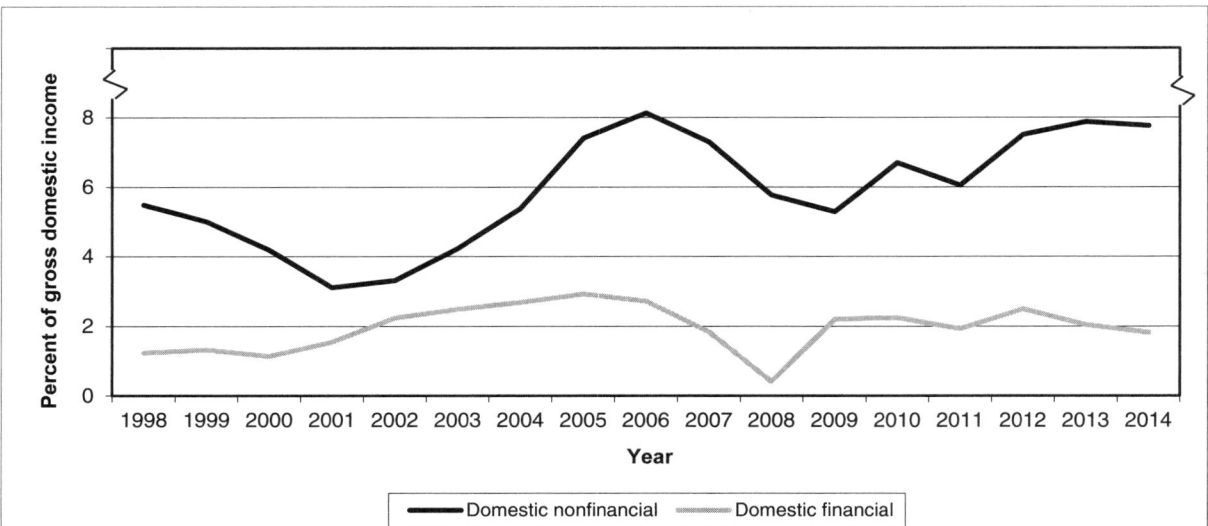

- In Chapter 1, Table 1-16 and Figure 1-4, the rising share of capital income (net operating surplus) in the total value of economic output was demonstrated. Chapter 9 presents further information on the return on capital and on its corporate profits component by industry.

- Rates of return on physical capital in domestic nonfinancial industry groups are shown in Table 9-4. The rate of return is the net operating surplus—the sum of corporate profits, net interest, transfer payments, and proprietors' income—as a percentage of the value of the net stock of physical capital plus inventories. These are presented for the first time using a new, more detailed industrial classification, which highlights the variation among industries—when measured as the return on the value of the industry's "produced assets." Measured this way, the construction industry shows a huge profit rate because it leases, not owns, most of its productive assets. There are no rates of return calculated for financial industries, which presumably would present even greater difficulty in identifying and measuring the capital base. (Table 9-4)

- Figure 9-3 charts domestic corporate profits, a major portion of the total return to capital, as a percent of gross domestic income. The profits are from Table 9-5 (not including the Federal Reserve Banks) and the denominator is GDI as shown in Table 1-16. They tend to follow the business cycle up and down, but both financial and nonfinancial profits show an underlying upward trend over the last 15 years. In 2014, a year when the unemployment rate was 6.2 percent, nonfinancial profits were 7.4 percent of income, compared with 5.5 percent of income in 1998 when unemployment was a much lower 4.5 percent. Financial profits were 2.6 percent in 2014, compared with 1.2 percent in 1998. (Tables 9-5 and 1-16)

Table 9-4. Rates of Return and Related Data for Major Nonfinancial Industry Groups

Year	Nonfinancial corporations	Nonfinancial industries							
		Total	Mining	Utilities	Construction	Durable-goods manufacturing	Nondurable-goods manufacturing	Wholesale trade	Retail trade
NET OPERATING SURPLUS BEFORE TAX (Billions of dollars)									
1998	738.7	1 369.9	-9.4	47.5	104.8	141.1	182.1	109.2	121.2
1999	751.9	1 452.2	-4.4	58.4	114.4	127.1	203.4	109.5	118.8
2000	723.9	1 432.4	17.3	52.6	126.4	125.8	200.0	116.4	115.8
2001	656.3	1 424.0	21.9	56.0	133.3	59.0	215.5	106.9	118.5
2002	719.3	1 533.2	7.9	41.7	137.3	85.9	212.5	105.2	123.7
2003	815.0	1 730.2	27.9	47.0	159.5	120.2	233.2	119.1	133.7
2004	964.1	1 959.7	42.0	55.4	195.8	137.3	271.1	143.6	130.8
2005	1 118.7	2 141.7	72.4	47.5	229.7	164.2	293.5	163.3	139.6
2006	1 269.3	2 233.3	85.0	63.4	236.9	176.5	337.2	179.8	138.5
2007	1 225.8	2 325.5	105.5	58.2	232.5	176.9	347.2	198.0	117.0
2008	1 172.2	2 350.8	163.8	53.4	175.6	139.5	329.8	210.2	103.7
2009	1 073.5	2 193.8	82.8	62.6	165.6	93.3	368.5	199.9	127.2
2010	1 352.5	2 486.5	117.3	74.0	156.9	170.4	379.6	228.1	140.0
2011	1 419.1	2 582.9	161.4	70.7	158.2	178.7	397.9	225.4	135.9
2012	1 561.3	2 686.0	153.2	60.6	177.7	194.8	418.7	248.0	153.5
2013	1 592.6	2 832.6	172.5	67.6	187.1	211.5	407.5	258.8	163.2
2014	1 614.2	. . .	. . .	. . .	. . .	. . .	. . .	. . .	. . .
PRODUCED ASSETS, AVERAGE OF YEAR-END VALUES (Billions of dollars)									
1998	8 104.7	10 563.7	545.8	972.5	152.4	1 416.8	1 083.5	626.4	914.8
1999	8 540.0	11 192.1	539.5	1 004.6	170.4	1 485.3	1 137.3	664.3	983.1
2000	9 084.1	11 956.3	585.6	1 062.8	183.3	1 559.1	1 184.9	704.3	1 056.2
2001	9 545.0	12 414.9	663.5	1 117.3	190.2	1 578.3	1 195.8	687.1	1 086.5
2002	9 858.0	12 862.9	736.5	1 160.2	199.9	1 579.3	1 230.7	699.3	1 151.2
2003	10 177.3	13 337.0	790.5	1 210.4	205.9	1 584.1	1 269.1	721.8	1 211.5
2004	10 769.0	14 480.2	944.2	1 341.5	227.6	1 652.1	1 348.5	789.6	1 338.1
2005	11 701.4	15 822.3	1 239.4	1 433.4	251.1	1 740.7	1 442.4	876.1	1 434.6
2006	12 683.6	17 099.6	1 438.4	1 532.1	274.9	1 831.1	1 522.8	953.6	1 538.4
2007	13 539.3	18 122.6	1 521.2	1 653.1	288.0	1 924.0	1 660.3	1 018.7	1 619.3
2008	14 265.3	19 052.1	1 608.4	1 810.1	300.2	2 011.3	1 714.4	1 048.9	1 667.9
2009	14 351.3	18 400.8	1 421.3	1 776.0	275.2	1 941.4	1 730.4	988.1	1 571.9
2010	14 349.7	19 019.4	1 505.6	1 896.9	265.3	1 981.6	1 806.9	1 056.3	1 602.2
2011	14 943.3	19 866.0	1 566.9	2 033.7	267.2	2 066.8	1 897.8	1 131.6	1 659.0
2012	15 499.5	20 506.6	1 643.9	2 117.0	275.3	2 122.1	1 946.3	1 189.9	1 715.1
2013	16 009.1	21 285.9	1 779.1	2 165.0	286.9	2 183.0	1 995.9	1 232.6	1 777.2
2014	16 794.1	. . .	. . .	. . .	. . .	. . .	. . .	. . .	. . .
RATES OF RETURN BEFORE TAX (Percent)									
1998	9.1	13.3	-1.7	4.9	72.7	10.2	17.1	17.8	13.7
1999	8.8	13.3	-0.8	5.9	70.9	8.8	18.3	17.0	12.5
2000	8.0	12.4	3.1	5.1	71.5	8.3	17.2	17.0	11.4
2001	6.9	11.7	3.5	5.1	71.4	3.8	18.1	15.4	11.1
2002	7.3	12.1	1.1	3.7	70.4	5.4	17.5	15.2	11.1
2003	8.0	13.2	3.7	4.0	78.6	7.6	18.7	16.8	11.3
2004	9.0	14.1	4.8	4.3	90.3	8.5	20.7	19.0	10.3
2005	9.6	14.1	6.6	3.4	96.0	9.7	21.0	19.6	10.1
2006	10.0	13.6	6.3	4.3	90.1	9.9	22.7	19.6	9.3
2007	9.1	13.2	7.1	3.7	82.6	9.4	21.8	20.1	7.4
2008	8.2	12.6	10.5	3.1	59.7	7.1	19.5	20.3	6.3
2009	7.5	11.7	5.5	3.5	57.6	4.7	21.4	19.6	7.9
2010	9.4	13.3	8.0	4.0	58.1	8.7	21.5	22.3	8.8
2011	9.5	13.3	10.5	3.6	59.4	8.8	21.5	20.6	8.3
2012	10.1	13.3	9.5	2.9	65.5	9.3	21.8	21.4	9.1
2013	9.9	13.6	10.1	3.2	66.6	9.8	20.7	21.4	9.3
2014	9.6	. . .	. . .	. . .	. . .	. . .	. . .	. . .	. . .
NET OPERATING SURPLUS BEFORE TAX AS A SHARE OF NET VALUE ADDED (Percent)									
1998	17.4	24.8	-24.6	38.9	28.9	20.0	36.9	20.7	20.1
1999	16.8	24.7	-10.5	42.2	28.8	17.6	38.9	20.1	19.0
2000	15.2	23.0	25.8	38.4	28.8	16.6	37.7	20.0	17.6
2001	14.0	22.7	28.9	40.2	28.7	8.9	39.6	18.7	17.7
2002	15.2	23.8	13.5	31.0	29.2	13.0	39.6	18.4	17.9
2003	16.6	25.5	33.9	33.4	31.8	17.4	41.5	19.8	18.4
2004	18.3	26.8	40.7	35.9	34.9	18.8	44.9	21.9	17.5
2005	19.9	27.6	50.0	31.8	36.8	21.2	46.3	23.1	17.7
2006	21.1	27.0	49.7	36.3	35.6	21.7	49.4	23.7	17.1
2007	19.9	27.0	52.3	33.1	34.2	21.3	49.6	24.7	14.5
2008	19.0	26.8	58.6	31.0	28.5	17.9	48.0	25.7	13.2
2009	18.6	26.4	46.7	34.1	30.6	14.1	51.5	26.2	16.5
2010	22.0	28.6	53.3	37.5	30.8	22.9	51.7	28.2	17.5
2011	22.0	28.5	57.4	35.5	30.8	22.8	52.5	26.6	16.6
2012	22.8	28.3	54.0	32.1	32.1	23.6	53.1	27.6	17.9
2013	22.6	28.7	56.3	34.1	32.0	24.8	52.1	27.9	18.3
2014	22.0	. . .	. . .	. . .	. . .	. . .	. . .	. . .	. . .

. . . = Not available.

Table 9-5. Corporate Profits with Inventory Valuation Adjustment by Industry Group, NAICS Basis

(Billions of dollars, quarterly data are at seasonally adjusted annual rates.)   **NIPA Table 6.16D**

Year and quarter	Total	Domestic industries												
		Financial			Nonfinancial									
		Total	Federal Reserve banks	Other financial	Total	Utilities	Manufacturing							
							Total	Durable goods						
								Fabricated metal products	Machinery	Computer and electronic products	Electrical equipment, appliances, and components	Motor vehicles, bodies and trailers, and parts	Other durable goods
1998	743.8	641.1	25.6	113.3	502.1	33.3	193.5	16.8	16.1	19.8	8.8	16.9	35.6
1999	762.2	640.2	26.7	127.9	485.6	34.4	184.5	16.4	12.7	6.6	10.2	13.8	37.4
2000	730.3	584.1	31.2	118.5	434.4	24.3	175.6	15.6	9.4	20.5	6.9	4.0	25.8
2001	698.7	528.3	28.9	166.1	333.3	22.5	75.1	9.2	2.2	-29.1	1.1	-6.8	14.0
2002	795.1	636.3	23.5	247.2	365.6	11.1	75.1	8.7	3.2	-24.3	-2.1	-3.0	20.6
2003	959.9	793.3	20.1	286.5	486.7	13.5	125.3	8.6	3.2	-6.3	1.5	7.9	17.8
2004	1 215.2	1 010.1	20.0	329.4	660.7	20.5	182.7	12.3	8.5	1.2	-0.2	-5.0	33.8
2005	1 621.2	1 382.1	26.6	383.1	972.4	30.8	277.7	18.2	18.0	15.7	-1.8	0.3	56.8
2006	1 815.7	1 559.6	33.8	381.3	1 144.4	55.1	349.7	18.4	23.2	29.0	10.7	-5.3	68.0
2007	1 708.9	1 355.5	36.0	265.5	1 054.0	49.5	321.9	21.0	25.0	24.7	-1.5	-15.7	65.2
2008	1 345.5	938.8	35.1	60.4	843.4	30.1	240.6	16.5	18.8	26.1	4.4	-39.6	38.1
2009	1 479.2	1 122.0	47.3	315.5	759.2	23.8	171.4	11.7	9.4	26.4	8.9	-54.3	32.3
2010	1 799.7	1 404.5	71.6	334.8	998.2	30.3	287.6	15.3	17.4	46.9	10.2	-9.7	48.0
2011	1 738.5	1 316.6	75.9	300.0	940.7	9.8	298.1	16.1	24.3	32.7	4.8	-0.3	54.8
2012	2 126.6	1 724.8	71.7	417.2	1 235.9	12.9	404.2	23.8	32.5	45.7	11.8	22.1	68.2
2013	2 238.7	1 835.6	79.6	453.9	1 302.1	20.9	402.4	23.3	33.2	43.7	13.1	22.7	70.2
2014	1 603.8	1 197.0	72.4	300.9	823.7	-2.9	261.1	14.6	20.6	31.7	6.0	-7.3	45.0
2013													
1st quarter	2 127.5	1 736.0	70.2	358.4	1 307.4	19.0	407.6	24.4	29.4	49.4	12.8	19.4	70.2
2nd quarter	2 172.5	1 761.1	73.5	342.9	1 344.6	33.1	418.7	24.1	34.8	50.4	12.0	21.8	69.7
3rd quarter	2 167.5	1 741.0	82.0	337.9	1 321.2	30.5	420.2	22.1	34.6	52.3	15.9	24.5	73.9
4th quarter	2 192.0	1 762.2	92.6	337.0	1 332.4	23.1	459.0	21.7	36.3	52.4	15.2	22.4	65.6
2014													
1st quarter	2 054.4	1 639.9	97.3	282.5	1 260.1	38.9	380.4	22.0	30.3	48.0	16.0	19.1	66.6
2nd quarter	2 203.7	1 795.0	104.6	337.0	1 353.3	32.0	454.7	23.4	33.3	49.8	16.5	24.7	70.9
3rd quarter	2 295.0	1 867.9	106.8	340.5	1 420.7	23.1	458.0	25.7	33.0	52.8	16.6	25.5	80.4
4th quarter	2 266.3	1 843.6	104.8	320.1	1 418.7	16.9	466.1	24.1	30.7	60.0	15.9	30.0	77.6

Year and quarter	Domestic industries—Continued										Rest of the world, net
	Nonfinancial—Continued										
	Manufacturing—Continued										
	Nondurable goods					Wholesale trade	Retail trade	Transportation and warehousing	Information	Other nonfinancial	
	Total	Food and beverage and tobacco products	Petroleum and coal products	Chemical products	Other nondurable goods						
1998	79.4	21.9	4.3	33.4	19.8	57.3	62.5	12.8	33.1	109.7	102.8
1999	87.5	31.7	2.4	31.8	21.7	55.6	59.5	7.2	20.8	123.5	122.0
2000	93.3	25.8	25.9	25.1	16.6	59.5	51.3	9.5	-11.9	126.1	146.2
2001	84.5	28.5	27.5	22.0	6.6	51.1	71.3	-0.7	-26.4	140.2	170.4
2002	72.0	26.9	3.8	29.9	11.4	55.8	83.7	-6.0	-3.1	149.0	158.8
2003	92.6	25.9	26.0	32.2	8.5	59.3	90.5	4.8	16.3	177.1	166.6
2004	132.1	26.8	50.1	39.2	16.0	74.7	93.2	12.0	52.7	224.9	205.0
2005	170.5	29.5	79.9	41.2	19.9	96.2	121.7	27.7	91.3	327.2	239.1
2006	205.7	35.0	73.5	70.0	27.1	105.9	132.5	41.2	107.0	353.1	256.2
2007	203.0	31.7	78.7	69.3	23.3	103.2	119.0	23.9	108.4	328.2	353.4
2008	176.3	31.0	89.9	50.1	5.4	90.6	80.3	28.8	92.2	280.8	406.7
2009	137.0	46.4	13.7	58.6	18.2	89.3	108.7	22.4	81.2	262.3	357.2
2010	159.5	46.1	24.8	64.7	23.9	102.4	118.6	44.7	95.1	319.5	395.2
2011	165.6	40.6	45.8	58.2	20.9	94.4	114.3	30.4	83.8	309.9	421.9
2012	200.1	45.5	54.3	68.9	31.4	136.6	157.2	51.9	101.1	372.0	401.8
2013	196.1	54.2	42.9	66.3	32.8	154.5	171.2	62.6	108.3	382.2	403.1
2014	150.6	41.1	29.7	57.3	22.4	71.7	108.1	26.8	84.1	274.8	406.8
2013											
1st quarter	202.1	47.1	50.1	72.2	32.7	151.2	158.3	53.8	121.4	398.0	391.5
2nd quarter	205.8	50.9	44.7	76.8	33.5	147.7	167.5	51.4	131.1	395.2	411.4
3rd quarter	197.0	61.6	33.0	67.8	34.4	144.6	163.8	51.3	125.4	385.5	426.5
4th quarter	245.3	58.9	65.7	82.4	38.4	138.5	148.0	55.6	139.8	368.4	429.9
2014											
1st quarter	178.4	41.2	44.1	65.7	27.4	125.7	142.5	58.5	131.0	383.3	414.5
2nd quarter	236.0	54.6	58.6	87.7	35.0	134.5	154.7	70.0	131.1	376.4	408.6
3rd quarter	224.0	61.4	53.8	72.1	36.8	170.1	157.7	72.2	123.2	416.3	427.1
4th quarter	227.7	63.5	57.3	74.7	32.2	160.5	178.8	60.6	120.0	414.9	422.7

NOTES AND DEFINITIONS, CHAPTER 9

General note on data on compensation per hour

This chapter includes two data series with similar names—the Employment Cost Index for total compensation and the index of compensation per hour—that often display different behavior. Both are compiled and published by the Bureau of Labor Statistics (BLS), but the definitions, sources, and methods of compilation are different. Users should be aware of these differences and of the consequent differences in the appropriate uses and interpretations for each of the two series.

The *Employment Cost Index (ECI)* (Tables 9-1 and 9-2) measures changes in hourly compensation for "all civilian workers", which is not quite as broad as it sounds, as it excludes federal government workers, farm workers, and private household workers. Indexes are also published for subgroups including state and local workers, "all private industry" (again excluding farm and private household workers), and a number of industry and occupational subgroups.

The ECI is calculated and published separately for *total compensation* and for the two components of hourly compensation, *wages and salaries* and the employer cost of employee *benefits*. It is constructed by analogy with the Consumer Price Index (CPI); that is, it holds the composition of employment constant in order to isolate hourly compensation trends that take place for individual occupations, which are then aggregated, using fixed relative importance weights. The ECI is based on a sample survey and may be revised from time to time, due to updated classification, weighting, and seasonal adjustments. However, it is not subject to major benchmark revision of the underlying wage, salary, and benefit rate observations. By design, it excludes any representation of employee stock options. As it is based on a sample survey, the ECI is measured "from the bottom up," aggregating from individual employers' reports to higher levels. The ECI is frequently and appropriately used as the best available measure of the general trend of wages and of the extent of inflationary pressure exerted on prices by labor costs.

The *compensation per hour* component of the report on "Productivity and Costs" (Table 9-3) is calculated and published for total compensation in total business, nonfarm business, nonfinancial corporations, and manufacturing. The nonfarm business category is similar in scope to the "all private industry" category in the ECI. The measures in Table 9-3, however, are compiled "from the top down," starting with aggregate estimates of compensation and hours, then dividing the former by the latter. Compensation per hour is affected by changes in the composition of employment. If the composition of employment shifts toward a larger proportion of higher-paid employees and/ or industries, compensation per hour will rise even if there is no increase in hourly compensation for any individual worker.

In addition, *compensation per hour* includes the value of exercised stock options as expensed by companies. Also included are other transitory payments, many of which may be of little relevance to the typical worker or to ongoing production costs. These values are not reported immediately. Instead, they are incorporated when later, more comprehensive reports are received. This process can lead to dramatic revisions in compensation per hour and in the unit labor costs index, which is based on compensation. For example, the fourth-quarter 2004 increase in compensation per hour in nonfarm business was initially reported at an annual rate of 3.1 percent. Four months later, the reported rate for the same time period was 10.2 percent. The rate of increase from a year earlier was revised from 3.6 to 5.9 percent. According to then-Federal Reserve Chairman Alan Greenspan, in testimony before the Joint Economic Committee on June 9, 2005, this reflected "a large but apparently transitory surge in bonuses and the proceeds of stock option exercises," not a potentially inflationary acceleration in the rate of labor compensation increase. More recently, it was reported in August 2009 that "first-quarter unit labor costs were revised to negative 2.7% from positive 3%." (*Wall Street Journal,* August 12, 2009, p. A2.)

These characteristics suggest that *compensation per hour* should not be considered a reliable or appropriate indicator of wage or compensation trends for typical workers. It is useful in conjunction with the productivity series, because aggregate productivity is subject to the same composition shifts—higher-productivity industries also tend to have higher-paid employees. Hence, the measure of *unit labor costs* (derived by dividing compensation per hour by output per hour in this system) is not distorted when the composition of output shifts toward higher-productivity industries. The shift affects the numerator and denominator of the ratio similarly. However, both compensation and unit labor costs can still be distorted by transitory payments, such as those discussed above.

There are other, probably less important differences between the two measures. Compensation per hour refers to the entire quarter, while the ECI is observed in the terminal month of each quarter. Tips and other forms of compensation not provided by employers are included in hourly compensation but not in the ECI. The ECI excludes persons working for token wages, business owners and others who set their own wage, and family workers who do not earn a market wage; all of these workers are included in the productivity and cost accounts. Hourly compensation excludes employees of nonprofit institutions serving individuals—about 10 percent of private workers (mostly in education and medical care) who are within the scope of the ECI. Hourly compensation measures include an estimate for the unincorporated self-employed, who are assumed to earn the same hourly compensation as other employees in the sector. Implicitly, unpaid family workers also are included in the hourly compensation measures with the assumption that their hourly compensation is zero. Both of these groups are also excluded from the ECI.

Tables 9-1 and 9-2

Employment Cost Indexes

SOURCE: U.S. DEPARTMENT OF LABOR, BUREAU OF LABOR STATISTICS (BLS)

The Employment Cost Index (ECI) is a quarterly measure of the change in the cost of labor, independent of the influence of employment shifts among occupations and industries. It uses a fixed market basket of labor—similar in concept to the Consumer Price Index's fixed market basket of goods and services—to measure changes over time in employer costs of employing labor. Data are quarterly in all cases and are reported for the final month of each quarter. These measures are expressed as indexes, with the not-seasonally-adjusted value for December 2005 set at 100.

Care should be used in comparing the ECI with other data sets. The "all private industry" category in the ECI excludes farm and household workers (it is sometimes, and more precisely, called "private nonfarm industry"), and the "all civilian workers" category excludes federal government, farm, and household workers.

The data for 1979 through 2005, which are presented in Table 9-2 and are the official ECI measures for that time period, were based on the 1987 Standard Industrial Classification (SIC) and 1990 Occupational Classification System (OCS).

Currently the ECI is compiled based on the 2012 North American Industry Classification System (NAICS) and the 2000 Standard Occupational Classification Manual (SOC). These data, along with comparable data for 2001 through 2005, are shown in Table 9-1.

For certain broad categories shown in this volume—indicated by footnote 2 in Table 9-2—the old SIC categories are roughly comparable and continuous with the data for 2006 and subsequent years. (However, they differ slightly on overlap dates, and should be "linked" if a continuous time series is desired; see the article at the beginning of this volume.) Many of the new industry and occupational categories are not continuous with the old series shown here, and some of the old categories are not being continued because BLS finds them obsolete and no longer meaningful.

Definitions

Total compensation comprises wages, salaries, and the employer's costs for employee benefits. Excluded from wages and salaries and employee benefits are the value of stock option exercises and items such as payment-in-kind, free room and board, and tips.

Wages and salaries consists of straight-time earnings per hour before payroll deductions, including production bonuses,

incentive earnings, commissions, and cost-of-living adjustments. These wage rates exclude premium pay for overtime and for work on weekends and holidays, shift differentials, and nonproduction bonuses such as lump-sum payments provided in lieu of wage increases. According to BLS, wages and salaries are about 70 percent of total compensation.

Benefits includes the cost to employers for paid leave—vacations, holidays, sick leave, and other leave; for supplemental pay—premium pay for work in addition to the regular work schedule (such as overtime, weekends, and holidays), shift differentials, and nonproduction bonuses (such as referral bonuses and lump-sum payments provided in lieu of wage increases); for insurance benefits—life, health, short-term disability, and long-term disability; for retirement and savings benefits—defined benefit and defined contribution plans; and for legally required benefits—Social Security, Medicare, federal and state unemployment insurance, and workers' compensation. Severance pay and supplemental unemployment benefit (SUB) plans are included in the data through December 2005 but were dropped beginning with the March 2006 data. The combined cost of these two benefits accounted for less than one-tenth of one percent of compensation, and according to BLS, dropping these benefits has had virtually no impact on the index. According to BLS, benefit costs are about 30 percent of total compensation.

Civilian workers are private industry workers, as defined below, and workers in state and local government. Federal workers are not included.

Private industry workers are paid workers in private industry excluding farms and private households. To be included in the ECI, employees in occupations must receive cash payments from the establishment for services performed and the establishment must pay the employer's portion of Medicare taxes on that individual's wages. Major exclusions from the survey are the self-employed, individuals who set their own pay (for example, proprietors, owners, major stockholders, and partners in unincorporated firms), volunteers, unpaid workers, family members being paid token wages, individuals receiving long-term disability compensation, and U.S. citizens working overseas.

Private industry workers excluding incentive paid occupations is a new category introduced in the 2006 revision to eliminate the quarter-to-quarter variability related to the way workers (for example, salespersons working on commission) are paid. (The category *private industry workers excluding sales occupations* was intended to serve a similar purpose in the previous SIC-based classification system, but was much less accurate in separately identifying workers with highly variable compensation.)

Goods-producing industries include mining, construction, and manufacturing.

Service-providing industries include the following NAICS industries: wholesale trade; retail trade; transportation and warehousing; utilities; information; finance and insurance; real estate and rental and leasing; professional, scientific, and technical services; management of companies and enterprises; administrative and support and waste management and remediation services; education services; health care and social assistance; arts, entertainment, and recreation; accommodation and food services; and other services, except public administration.

Notes on the data

Employee benefit costs are calculated as cents per hour worked.

The December 2014 data were collected from probability samples of approximately 37,700 occupational observations in about 8,700 sample establishments in private industry, and approximately 9,000 occupations within about 1,500 establishments in state and local governments. The private industry sample is rotated over approximately five years. The state and local government sample is replaced less frequently; the latest sample was introduced in September 2007.

Currently, the sample establishments are classified in industry categories based on the NAICS. Within an establishment, specific job categories are selected and classified into approximately 800 occupational classifications according to the SOC. Similar procedures were followed under the previous classification systems. Data are collected each quarter for the pay periods including the 12th day of March, June, September, and December.

Aggregate indexes are calculated using fixed employment weights. Beginning with December 2013, estimates are based on 2012 employment weight, using Occupational Employment counts. From March 2006 through November 2013, ECI weights were based on fixed employment counts for 2002 from the BLS Occupational Employment Statistics survey. Employment data from the 2012 Survey were introduced in December 2013. ECI measures were based on 1990 employment counts from March 1995 through December 2005 and 1980 census employment counts from June 1986 through December 1994. Prior to June 1986, they were based on 1970 census employment counts.

Use of fixed weights ensures that changes in the indexes reflect only changes in hourly compensation, not employment shifts among industries or occupations with different levels of wages and compensation. This feature distinguishes the ECI from other compensation series such as average hourly earnings (see Chapter 10 and its notes and definitions) and the compensation per hour component of the productivity series (see Table 9-3 and its notes and definitions, and the general note above), each of which is affected by such employment shifts.

Data availability

Data for wages and salaries for the private nonfarm economy are available beginning with the data for 1975; data for compensation begin with the 1980 data. The series for state and local government and for the civilian nonfarm economy begin with the 1981 data. All series are available on the BLS Web site at <http://www.bls.gov>.

Wage and salary change and compensation cost change data also are available by major occupational and industry groups, as well as by region and collective bargaining status. Information on wage and salary change is available from 1975 to the present for most of these series. Compensation cost change data are available from 1980 to the present for most series. For 10 occupational and industry series, benefit cost change data are available from the early 1980s to the present. For state and local governments and the civilian economy (state and local governments plus private industry), wage and salary change and compensation cost change data are available for major occupational and industry series. BLS provides data for all these series from June 1981 to the present.

Updates are available about four weeks after the end of the reference quarter. Reference quarters end in March, June, September, and December. Seasonal adjustment factors and seasonally adjusted indexes are released in late April.

References

Explanatory notes, including references, are included in a Technical Note in each quarter's ECI news release, and can be found on the BLS Web site, in the PDF version of the release.

More detailed information on the ECI is available from Chapter 8, "National compensation measures," (www.bls.gov/opub/hom/pdf/homch8.pdf) from the BLS Handbook of Methods, and several articles published in the Monthly Labor Review and Compensation and Working Conditions. The articles and other descriptive pieces are available at www.bls.gov/ect/#publications, by calling (202) 691-6199, or sending e-mail to NCSinfo@bls.gov.

Table 9-3A and 9-3B

Productivity and Related Data

The indexes of productivity and costs for the entire postwar period, 1947 through 2014, have been revised to reflect the 2013 and 2014 comprehensive revisions of the National Income and Product Accounts (NIPAs).

Productivity measures relate real physical output to real input. They encompass a family of measures that includes single-factor input measures, such as output per unit of labor input or output per unit of capital input, as well as measures of multifactor productivity—that is, output per unit of combined labor and capital inputs. The indexes published in this book are indexes of labor productivity expressed in terms of output per hour of labor input. (A larger group of BLS productivity measures can be found in Bernan Press's *Handbook of U.S. Labor Statistics*.) All data are presented as indexes with a base of 2009 = 100.

Definitions

Current dollar output is the current-dollar value of the goods and services produced in the specified sector. *Output* is the constant-dollar value of the same goods and services, derived as current-dollar output divided by the sector *implicit price deflator.* All these data are derived from components of the NIPAs; see Notes on the data below, and for general information on the NIPAs, see the Notes and Definitions to Chapter 1.

Output per hour of all persons (labor productivity) is the value of goods and services in constant dollars produced per hour of labor input. By definition, nonfinancial corporations include no self-employed persons. Productivity in this sector is expressed as *output per hour of all employees. Output per person* is output divided by the index for employment instead of by the index for hours of all persons.

Compensation is the total value of the wages and salaries of employees, plus employers' contributions for social insurance and private benefit plans, plus wages, salaries, and supplementary payments for the self-employed. *Compensation per hour* is compensation divided by *hours of all persons.* Included in compensation is the value of exercised stock options that companies report as a charge against earnings. Stock option values are reported with a delay; consequently, recent values are estimated based on extrapolation. They are revised to actual values when the data become available; sometimes the revisions are very large. The labor compensation of proprietors cannot be explicitly identified and must be estimated. This is done by assuming that proprietors have the same hourly compensation as employees in the same sector. The quarterly labor productivity and cost measures do not contain estimates of compensation for unpaid family workers.

Real compensation per hour is compensation per hour deflated by the Consumer Price Index Research Series (CPI-U-RS) for the period 1978 through 2013. (For current quarters, before the CPI-U-RS becomes available, changes in the CPI-U are used.) Changes in the Consumer Price Index for Urban Wage Earners and Clerical Workers (CPI-W) are used for data before 1978, as there was no CPI-U (or CPIU-RS) for that period. See the Notes and Definitions to Chapter 8 for explanation of the CPI-U, the CPI-W, and the CPI-U-RS.

Unit labor costs are the current-dollar labor costs expended in the production of a unit of output. They are derived by dividing compensation by output.

Unit nonlabor payments include profits, depreciation, interest, rental income of persons, and indirect taxes per unit of output.

They are computed by subtracting current-dollar compensation of all persons from current-dollar value of output, providing the data for the index of total *nonlabor payments,* which is then divided by output.

Unit nonlabor costs are available for nonfinancial corporations only. They contain all the components of unit nonlabor payments except unit profits (and rental income of persons, which is zero by definition for nonfinancial corporations).

Unit profits, the other component of unit nonlabor payments, are also only available for nonfinancial corporations.

Hours of all persons (labor input) consists of the total hours at work (*employment* multiplied by *average weekly hours*) of payroll workers, self-employed persons, and unpaid family workers. For the nonfinancial corporations data, there are no self-employed persons; the data represent *employee hours.*

Labor share is the total dollar amount of labor compensation divided by the total current-dollar value of output.

Notes on the data

Output for the business sector is equal to constant-dollar gross domestic product minus: the rental value of owner-occupied dwellings, the output of nonprofit institutions, the output of paid employees of private households, and general government output. The measures are derived from national income and product account (NIPA) data supplied by the U.S. Department of Commerce's Bureau of Economic Analysis (BEA). For manufacturing, BLS produces annual estimates of sectoral output. Quarterly manufacturing output indexes derived from the Federal Reserve Board of Governors' monthly indexes of industrial production (see Chapter 2) are adjusted to these annual measures by the BLS, and are also used to project the quarterly values in the current period. The business sector accounted for 76 percent of the value of GDP in 2013; nonfarm business, for 74 percent.

Nonfinancial corporate output consists of business output minus unincorporated businesses and those corporations classified as offices of bank holding companies, offices ofother holding companies, or offices in the finance and insurance sector. Nonfinancial corporations accounted for approximately 49 percent of the value of GDP in 2013. Unit profits and unit nonlabor costs can be calculated separately for this sector and are shown in this table.

Compensation and hours data are developed from BLS and BEA data. The primary source for hours and employment is BLS's Current Employment Statistics (CES) program (see the notes and definitions for Chapter 10). Other data sources are the Current Population Survey (CPS) and the National Compensation Survey (NCS). Weekly paid hours are adjusted to hours at work using the NCS. For paid employees, hours at work differ from hours paid, in that they exclude paid vacation and holidays, paid sick leave, and other paid personal or administrative leave.

Although the labor productivity measures relate output to labor input, they do not measure the contribution of labor or any other specific factor of production. Instead, they reflect the joint effect of many influences, including changes in technology; capital investment; level of output; utilization of capacity, energy, and materials; the organization of production; managerial skill; and the characteristics and efforts of the work force.

Revisions

Data for recent years are revised frequently to take account of revisions in the output and labor input measures that underlie the estimates. Customarily, all revisions to source data are reflected in the release following the source data revision. Data in this volume were released August 8, 2014, and reflect the midyear 2014 revisions to the NIPAs and all revisions in labor input and compensation available up to that release date, including the annual benchmark revision of the CES and updated seasonal factors.

Data availability

Series are available quarterly and annually. Quarterly measures are based entirely on seasonally adjusted data. For some detailed manufacturing series (not shown here), only annual averages are available. Productivity indexes are published early in the second and third months of each quarter, reflecting new data for preceding quarters. Complete historical data are available on the BLS Web site at <http://www.bls.gov>.

BLS also publishes productivity estimates for a number of individual industries. A release entitled "Productivity and Costs by Industry" is available on the BLS Web site at <http://www.bls.gov>.

References

Further information is available in the Technical Notes and footnotes on the most current monthly release, available on the Web site, and from the following sources: Chapter 10, "Productivity Measures: Business Sector and Major Subsectors," *BLS Handbook of Methods*—Bulletin 2490 (April 1997) and the following *Monthly Labor Review* articles: "Alternative Measures of Supervisory Employee Hours and Productivity Growth" (April 2004); "Possible Measurement Bias in Aggregate Productivity Growth" (February 1999); "Improvements to the Quarterly Productivity Measures" (October 1995); "Hours of Work: A New Base for BLS Productivity Statistics" (February 1990); and "New Sector Definitions for Productivity Series" (October 1976).

Table 9-4

Rates of Return and Related Data for Major Nonfinancial Industry Groups

SOURCE: U.S. DEPARTMENT OF COMMERCE, BUREAU OF ECONOMIC ANALYSIS

This table presents data on the net operating surplus and rate of return for five major nonfinancial industry groups from 1997 through 2012, based on the NAICS. The industry groups include both corporations and proprietors. Therefore, their data differ from the data for nonfinancial corporations alone, which are available through 2013 and shown for comparison purposes in the first column of this table. (Nonfinancial corporation rates of return and related data can also be found in Table 1-16.)

Definitions

Net operating surplus for the nonfinancial industries includes corporate profits, net interest, business current transfer payments, and proprietors' income (mainly the income of unincorporated self-employed workers).

Produced assets is the average of the end-year values for the current and previous year of the net stock of capital plus inventories, valued at current cost.

Rate of return is net operating surplus as a percent of the average value of produced assets at the beginning and end of the year.

Share of net value added is the net operating surplus as a percent of total value added in the industry. Value added is the portion of total national gross domestic product (GDP) produced in the industry and includes the net operating surplus, compensation of employees, taxes on production and imports less subsidies, and consumption of fixed capital.

Data availability, revisions, and references

These data were presented for the first time and described in "Returns for Domestic Nonfinancial Business," *Survey of Current Business,* May 2007, pp. 6-10. The data were most recently revised and updated in the June 2014 *Survey of Current Business.*

Table 9-5

Corporate Profits with Inventory Valuation Adjustment by Industry Group

SOURCE: U.S. DEPARTMENT OF COMMERCE, BUREAU OF ECONOMIC ANALYSIS

These profits measures are derived from the NIPAs and classified according to the NAICS. See the notes and definitions to Chapter 1 for definitions, data availability, and references. Note that this industry breakdown of profits incorporates the inventory valuation adjustment (IVA), which eliminates any capital gain element in profits arising from changes in the prices at which inventories are valued, but does <u>not</u> incorporate the capital consumption adjustment (CCAdj), which adjusts historical costs of fixed capital to replacement costs and uses actual rather than tax-based service lives. This is because the CCAdj is calculated by BEA at an aggregate level, whereas the IVA is calculated at an industry level.

CHAPTER 10: EMPLOYMENT, HOURS, AND EARNINGS

Section 10a: Labor Force, Employment, and Unemployment

Figure 10-1: Labor Force Participation Rate and Employment/Population Ratio, 1948–2014

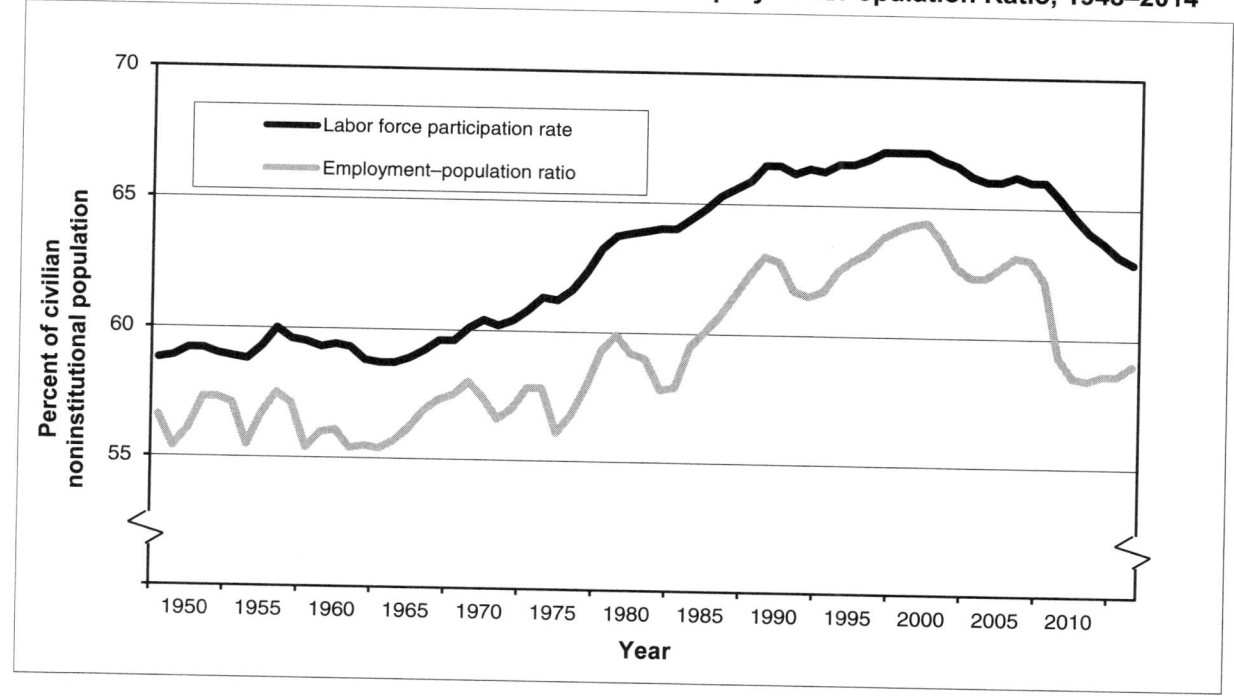

- From a high point in January 2008 to a low in December 2009, 8.1 million Americans lost jobs, based on total civilian employment smoothed for population adjustments. (Table 10-6) The employment/population ratio, charted in Figure 10-1 above, registered the steepest plunge of the postwar period. (Tables 10-1A and B) However, this 5.5 percent employment decline during 2008 and 2009 was nowhere near the length and scale of job loss in the Great Depression, when jobs dropped 22 percent from 1929 to 1932. (Table 10-21)

- By July 2015—the latest month available as this was written—there were 10.8 million more persons employed than at the December 2009 low, using the December 2009 figure in Table 10-6, which is based on population controls consistent with the current estimates. The employment/population ratio, which got as low as 58.2 percent in some months in 2010 and 2011 and remained at 58.6 percent from 2012 to 2014, rose to 59.3 in July 2015. (Tables 10-1A and B,10-6, and recent data)

- Beginning in 2001, the number of people who either had jobs or were unemployed and looking for a job began to decline relative to the size of the total working-age population. This drop in labor force participation, unprecedented in the period since 1948 during which these data have been collected, accelerated in 2009 through 2011—even as the recovery was beginning—and continued throughout 2014. (Tables 10-1A and B and recent data)

Table 10-1A. Summary Labor Force, Employment, and Unemployment: Recent Data

(Thousands of persons, percent, seasonally adjusted, except as noted.)

Year and month	Civilian noninsti-tutional population [1]	Civilian labor force		Employment, thousands of persons						Employ-ment-popul-ation ratio, percent	Unemployment		
		Thous-ands of persons	Participa-tion rate (percent)	Total	By age and sex			By industry			Thousands of persons		Rate (percent)
					Men, 20 years and over	Women, 20 years and over	Both sexes, 16 to 19 years	Agri-cultural	Nonagri-cultural		Total	Unem-ployed 15 weeks and over	
1965	126 513	74 455	58.9	71 088	43 422	22 630	5 037	4 361	66 726	56.2	3 366	755	4.5
1966	128 058	75 770	59.2	72 895	43 668	23 510	5 721	3 979	68 915	56.9	2 875	526	3.8
1967	129 874	77 347	59.6	74 372	44 294	24 397	5 681	3 844	70 527	57.3	2 975	448	3.8
1968	132 028	78 737	59.6	75 920	44 859	25 281	5 780	3 817	72 103	57.5	2 817	412	3.6
1969	134 335	80 734	60.1	77 902	45 388	26 397	6 117	3 606	74 296	58.0	2 832	375	3.5
1970	137 085	82 771	60.4	78 678	45 581	26 952	6 144	3 463	75 215	57.4	4 093	663	4.9
1971	140 216	84 382	60.2	79 367	45 912	27 246	6 209	3 394	75 972	56.6	5 016	1 187	5.9
1972	144 126	87 034	60.4	82 153	47 130	28 276	6 746	3 484	78 669	57.0	4 882	1 167	5.6
1973	147 096	89 429	60.8	85 064	48 310	29 484	7 271	3 470	81 594	57.8	4 365	826	4.9
1974	150 120	91 949	61.3	86 794	48 922	30 424	7 448	3 515	83 279	57.8	5 156	955	5.6
1975	153 153	93 775	61.2	85 846	48 018	30 726	7 103	3 408	82 438	56.1	7 929	2 505	8.5
1976	156 150	96 158	61.6	88 752	49 190	32 226	7 336	3 331	85 421	56.8	7 406	2 366	7.7
1977	159 033	99 009	62.3	92 017	50 555	33 775	7 688	3 283	88 734	57.9	6 991	1 942	7.1
1978	161 910	102 251	63.2	96 048	52 143	35 836	8 070	3 387	92 661	59.3	6 202	1 414	6.1
1979	164 863	104 962	63.7	98 824	53 308	37 434	8 083	3 347	95 477	59.9	6 137	1 241	5.8
1980	167 745	106 940	63.8	99 303	53 101	38 492	7 710	3 364	95 938	59.2	7 637	1 871	7.1
1981	170 130	108 670	63.9	100 397	53 582	39 590	7 225	3 368	97 030	59.0	8 273	2 285	7.6
1982	172 271	110 204	64.0	99 526	52 891	40 086	6 549	3 401	96 125	57.8	10 678	3 485	9.7
1983	174 215	111 550	64.0	100 834	53 487	41 004	6 342	3 383	97 450	57.9	10 717	4 210	9.6
1984	176 383	113 544	64.4	105 005	55 769	42 793	6 444	3 321	101 685	59.5	8 539	2 737	7.5
1985	178 206	115 461	64.8	107 150	56 562	44 154	6 434	3 179	103 971	60.1	8 312	2 305	7.2
1986	180 587	117 834	65.3	109 597	57 569	45 556	6 472	3 163	106 434	60.7	8 237	2 232	7.0
1987	182 753	119 865	65.6	112 440	58 726	47 074	6 641	3 208	109 232	61.5	7 425	1 983	6.2
1988	184 613	121 669	65.9	114 968	59 781	48 383	6 805	3 169	111 800	62.3	6 701	1 610	5.5
1989	186 393	123 869	66.5	117 342	60 837	49 745	6 750	3 199	114 142	63.0	6 528	1 375	5.3
1990	189 164	125 840	66.5	118 793	61 678	50 535	6 610	3 223	115 570	62.8	7 047	1 525	5.6
1991	190 925	126 346	66.2	117 718	61 178	50 634	5 906	3 269	114 449	61.7	8 628	2 357	6.8
1992	192 805	128 105	66.4	118 492	61 496	51 328	5 669	3 247	115 245	61.5	9 613	3 408	7.5
1993	194 838	129 200	66.3	120 259	62 355	52 099	6 035	3 115	117 144	61.7	8 940	3 094	6.9
1994	196 814	131 056	66.6	123 060	63 294	53 606	6 162	3 409	119 651	62.5	7 996	2 860	6.1
1995	198 584	132 304	66.6	124 900	64 085	54 396	6 419	3 440	121 460	62.9	7 404	2 363	5.6
1996	200 591	133 943	66.8	126 708	64 897	55 311	6 500	3 443	123 264	63.2	7 236	2 316	5.4
1997	203 133	136 297	67.1	129 558	66 284	56 613	6 661	3 399	126 159	63.8	6 739	2 062	4.9
1998	205 220	137 673	67.1	131 463	67 135	57 278	7 051	3 378	128 085	64.1	6 210	1 637	4.5
1999	207 753	139 368	67.1	133 488	67 761	58 555	7 172	3 281	130 207	64.3	5 880	1 480	4.2
2000	212 577	142 583	67.1	136 891	69 634	60 067	7 190	2 464	134 427	64.4	5 692	1 318	4.0
2001	215 092	143 734	66.8	136 933	69 776	60 417	6 740	2 299	134 635	63.7	6 801	1 752	4.7
2002	217 570	144 863	66.6	136 485	69 734	60 420	6 332	2 311	134 174	62.7	8 378	2 904	5.8
2003	221 168	146 510	66.2	137 736	70 415	61 402	5 919	2 275	135 461	62.3	8 774	3 378	6.0
2004	223 357	147 401	66.0	139 252	71 572	61 773	5 907	2 232	137 020	62.3	8 149	3 072	5.5
2005	226 082	149 320	66.0	141 730	73 050	62 702	5 978	2 197	139 532	62.7	7 591	2 619	5.1
2006	228 815	151 428	66.2	144 427	74 431	63 834	6 163	2 206	142 221	63.1	7 001	2 266	4.6
2007	231 867	153 124	66.0	146 047	75 337	64 799	5 911	2 095	143 952	63.0	7 078	2 303	4.6
2008	233 788	154 287	66.0	145 362	74 750	65 039	5 573	2 168	143 194	62.2	8 924	3 188	5.8
2009	235 801	154 142	65.4	139 877	71 341	63 699	4 837	2 103	137 775	59.3	14 265	7 272	9.3
2010	237 830	153 889	64.7	139 064	71 230	63 456	4 378	2 206	136 858	58.5	14 825	8 786	9.6
2011	239 618	153 617	64.1	139 869	72 182	63 360	4 327	2 254	137 615	58.4	13 747	8 077	8.9
2012	243 284	154 975	63.7	142 469	73 403	64 640	4 426	2 186	140 283	58.6	12 506	6 996	8.1
2013	245 679	155 389	63.2	143 929	74 176	65 295	4 458	2 130	141 799	58.6	11 460	6 117	7.4
2014	247 947	155 922	62.9	146 305	75 471	66 287	4 548	2 237	144 068	59.0	9 617	4 714	6.2
2013													
January	244 663	155 699	63.6	143 384	74 084	64 790	4 510	2 057	141 234	58.6	12 315	6 573	7.9
February	244 828	155 511	63.5	143 464	74 183	64 911	4 370	2 070	141 393	58.6	12 047	6 485	7.7
March	244 995	155 099	63.3	143 393	74 190	64 838	4 365	2 020	141 350	58.5	11 706	6 355	7.5
April	245 175	155 359	63.4	143 676	74 161	65 148	4 368	2 048	141 604	58.6	11 683	6 329	7.5
May	245 363	155 609	63.4	143 919	74 137	65 323	4 459	2 081	141 860	58.7	11 690	6 287	7.5
June	245 552	155 822	63.5	144 075	74 265	65 340	4 470	2 091	142 021	58.7	11 747	6 218	7.5
July	245 756	155 693	63.4	144 285	74 301	65 514	4 470	2 171	142 081	58.7	11 408	6 031	7.3
August	245 959	155 435	63.2	144 179	74 015	65 743	4 421	2 205	141 918	58.6	11 256	5 973	7.2
September	246 168	155 473	63.2	144 270	74 151	65 539	4 580	2 208	142 058	58.6	11 203	5 927	7.2
October	246 381	154 625	62.8	143 485	73 808	65 229	4 448	2 208	141 449	58.2	11 140	5 824	7.2
November	246 567	155 284	63.0	144 443	74 373	65 547	4 523	2 139	142 317	58.6	10 841	5 786	7.0
December	246 745	154 937	62.8	144 586	74 467	65 617	4 502	2 229	142 337	58.6	10 351	5 530	6.7
2014													
January	230 244	149 943	65.1	140 818	74 905	65 913	4 388	1 999	141 527	58.1	10 280	5 392	6.6
February	230 421	150 207	65.2	140 989	74 820	66 168	4 312	1 973	142 160	58.3	10 387	5 657	6.7
March	230 600	150 488	65.3	141 293	75 284	66 009	4 504	2 008	143 082	58.7	10 384	5 708	6.6
April	230 787	149 878	64.9	141 239	75 163	66 076	4 485	2 048	143 718	58.9	9 696	5 139	6.2
May	230 978	150 006	64.9	141 323	75 159	66 164	4 545	2 101	144 297	59.1	9 761	4 898	6.3
June	231 178	150 059	64.9	141 771	75 504	66 267	4 476	2 288	144 815	59.4	9 453	4 448	6.1
July	231 394	150 396	65.0	141 881	75 631	66 250	4 520	2 403	144 862	59.4	9 648	4 452	6.2
August	231 607	150 441	65.0	141 956	75 668	66 289	4 495	2 472	144 175	59.1	9 568	4 321	6.1
September	231 831	150 200	64.8	142 081	75 889	66 192	4 527	2 482	144 459	59.1	9 237	4 242	5.9
October	232 049	150 377	64.8	142 488	75 928	66 560	4 772	2 517	145 419	59.5	8 983	4 251	5.7
November	232 243	150 627	64.9	142 569	75 675	66 894	4 762	2 332	145 335	59.3	9 071	4 144	5.8
December	232 432	150 383	64.7	142 658	76 026	66 632	4 784	2 220	144 970	59.1	8 688	3 922	5.6

[1]Not seasonally adjusted.

Table 10-1B. Summary Labor Force, Employment, and Unemployment: Historical

(Thousands of persons, percent, seasonally adjusted, except as noted.)

Year and month	Civilian noninsti-tutional population [1]	Civilian labor force Thousands of persons	Civilian labor force Participation rate (percent)	Employment Total	By age and sex Men, 20 years and over	By age and sex Women, 20 years and over	By age and sex Both sexes, 16 to 19 years	By industry Agricultural	By industry Nonagricultural	Employment-population ratio, percent	Unemployment Total	Unemployment Unemployed 15 weeks and over	Rate (percent) [2]
14 Years and Over													
1929	. . .	49 180	. . .	47 630	. . .	. . .	. . .	10 450	37 180	. . .	1 550	. . .	3.2
1930	. . .	49 820	. . .	45 480	. . .	. . .	. . .	10 340	35 140	. . .	4 340	. . .	8.7
1931	. . .	50 420	. . .	42 400	. . .	. . .	. . .	10 290	32 110	. . .	8 020	. . .	15.9 (15.3)
1932	. . .	51 000	. . .	38 940	. . .	. . .	. . .	10 170	28 770	. . .	12 060	. . .	23.6 (22.5)
1933	. . .	51 590	. . .	38 760	. . .	. . .	. . .	10 090	28 670	. . .	12 830	. . .	24.9 (20.6)
1934	. . .	52 230	. . .	40 890	. . .	. . .	. . .	9 900	30 990	. . .	11 340	. . .	21.7 (16.0)
1935	. . .	52 870	. . .	42 260	. . .	. . .	. . .	10 110	32 150	. . .	10 610	. . .	20.1 (14.2)
1936	. . .	53 440	. . .	44 410	. . .	. . .	. . .	10 000	34 410	. . .	9 030	. . .	16.9 (9.9)
1937	. . .	54 000	. . .	46 300	. . .	. . .	. . .	9 820	36 480	. . .	7 700	. . .	14.3 (9.1)
1938	. . .	54 610	. . .	44 220	. . .	. . .	. . .	9 690	34 530	. . .	10 390	. . .	19.0 (12.5)
1939	. . .	55 230	. . .	45 750	. . .	. . .	. . .	9 610	36 140	. . .	9 480	. . .	17.2 (11.3)
1940	99 840	55 640	55.7	47 520	. . .	. . .	. . .	9 540	37 980	47.6	8 120	. . .	14.6 (9.5)
1941	99 900	55 910	56.0	50 350	. . .	. . .	. . .	9 100	41 250	50.4	5 560	. . .	9.9 (6.0)
1942	98 640	56 410	57.2	53 750	. . .	. . .	. . .	9 250	44 500	54.5	2 660	. . .	4.7 (3.1)
1943	94 640	55 540	58.7	54 470	. . .	. . .	. . .	9 080	45 390	57.6	1 070	. . .	1.9 (1.8)
1944	93 220	54 630	58.6	53 960	. . .	. . .	. . .	8 950	45 010	57.9	670	. . .	1.2
1945	94 090	53 860	57.2	52 820	. . .	. . .	. . .	8 580	44 240	56.1	1 040	. . .	1.9
1946	103 070	57 520	55.8	55 250	. . .	. . .	. . .	8 320	46 930	53.6	2 270	. . .	3.9
1947	106 018	60 168	56.8	57 812	. . .	. . .	. . .	8 256	49 557	54.5	2 356	. . .	3.9
16 Years and Over													
1947	101 827	59 350	58.3	57 038	. . .	. . .	. . .	7 890	49 148	56.0	2 311	. . .	3.9
1948	103 068	60 621	58.8	58 343	39 382	14 936	4 026	7 629	50 714	56.6	2 276	309	3.8
1949	103 994	61 286	58.9	57 651	38 803	15 137	3 712	7 658	49 993	55.4	3 637	684	5.9
1950	104 995	62 208	59.2	58 918	39 394	15 824	3 703	7 160	51 758	56.1	3 288	782	5.3
1951	104 621	62 017	59.2	59 961	39 626	16 570	3 767	6 726	53 235	57.3	2 055	303	3.3
1952	105 231	62 138	59.0	60 250	39 578	16 958	3 719	6 500	53 749	57.3	1 883	232	3.0
1953	107 056	63 015	58.9	61 179	40 296	17 164	3 720	6 260	54 919	57.1	1 834	210	2.9
1954	108 321	63 643	58.8	60 109	39 634	17 000	3 475	6 205	53 904	55.5	3 532	812	5.5
1955	109 683	65 023	59.3	62 170	40 526	18 002	3 642	6 450	55 722	56.7	2 852	702	4.4
1956	110 954	66 552	60.0	63 799	41 216	18 767	3 818	6 283	57 514	57.5	2 750	533	4.1
1957	112 265	66 929	59.6	64 071	41 239	19 052	3 778	5 947	58 123	57.1	2 859	560	4.3
1958	113 727	67 639	59.5	63 036	40 411	19 043	3 582	5 586	57 450	55.4	4 602	1 452	6.8
1959	115 329	68 369	59.3	64 630	41 267	19 524	3 838	5 565	59 065	56.0	3 740	1 040	5.5
1960	117 245	69 628	59.4	65 778	41 543	20 105	4 129	5 458	60 318	56.1	3 852	957	5.5
1961	118 771	70 459	59.3	65 746	41 342	20 296	4 108	5 200	60 546	55.4	4 714	1 532	6.7
1962	120 153	70 614	58.8	66 702	41 815	20 693	4 195	4 944	61 759	55.5	3 911	1 119	5.5
1963	122 416	71 833	58.7	67 762	42 251	21 257	4 255	4 687	63 076	55.4	4 070	1 088	5.7
1964	124 485	73 091	58.7	69 305	42 886	21 903	4 516	4 523	64 782	55.7	3 786	973	5.2
1948													
January	102 603	60 095	58.6	58 061	39 386	14 556	4 119	8 077	49 984	56.6	2 034	311	3.4
February	102 698	60 524	58.9	58 196	39 480	14 621	4 095	7 696	50 500	56.7	2 328	283	3.8
March	102 771	60 070	58.5	57 671	39 098	14 481	4 092	7 333	50 338	56.1	2 399	292	4.0
April	102 831	60 677	59.0	58 291	39 157	15 001	4 133	7 557	50 734	56.7	2 386	324	3.9
May	102 923	59 972	58.3	57 854	39 139	14 712	4 003	7 141	50 713	56.2	2 118	329	3.5
June	102 992	60 957	59.2	58 743	39 392	15 213	4 138	7 591	51 152	57.0	2 214	322	3.6
July	103 216	61 181	59.3	58 968	39 607	15 348	4 013	7 602	51 366	57.1	2 213	295	3.6
August	103 240	60 806	58.9	58 456	39 510	14 994	3 952	7 562	50 894	56.6	2 350	332	3.9
September	103 291	60 815	58.9	58 513	39 324	15 207	3 982	7 865	50 648	56.6	2 302	298	3.8
October	103 361	60 646	58.7	58 387	39 522	14 956	3 909	7 626	50 761	56.5	2 259	324	3.7
November	103 424	60 702	58.7	58 417	39 459	15 054	3 904	7 624	50 793	56.5	2 285	282	3.8
December	103 468	61 169	59.1	58 740	39 539	15 137	4 064	7 984	50 756	56.8	2 429	305	4.0
1949													
January	103 529	60 771	58.7	58 175	39 233	14 991	3 951	7 790	50 385	56.2	2 596	315	4.3
February	103 559	61 057	59.0	58 208	39 117	15 117	3 974	8 022	50 186	56.2	2 849	374	4.7
March	103 665	61 073	58.9	58 043	39 015	15 069	3 959	8 008	50 035	56.0	3 030	414	5.0
April	103 739	61 007	58.8	57 747	38 993	14 978	3 776	7 911	49 836	55.7	3 260	483	5.3
May	103 845	61 259	59.0	57 552	38 701	15 066	3 785	8 067	49 485	55.4	3 707	602	6.1
June	103 930	60 948	58.6	57 172	38 632	15 003	3 537	7 802	49 370	55.0	3 776	705	6.2
July	104 042	61 301	58.9	57 190	38 405	15 244	3 541	8 021	49 169	55.0	4 111	848	6.7
August	104 121	61 590	59.2	57 397	38 610	15 181	3 606	7 604	49 793	55.1	4 193	917	6.8
September	104 219	61 633	59.1	57 584	38 744	15 129	3 711	7 297	50 287	55.3	4 049	973	6.6
October	104 338	62 185	59.6	57 269	38 394	15 260	3 615	6 814	50 455	54.9	4 916	1 000	7.9
November	104 421	62 005	59.4	58 009	38 860	15 422	3 727	7 497	50 512	55.6	3 996	1 056	6.4
December	104 524	61 908	59.2	57 845	38 908	15 300	3 637	7 379	50 466	55.3	4 063	961	6.6

[1]Not seasonally adjusted.
[2]In 1930 through 1943, the official BLS data count persons on work relief as unemployed. The unemployment rates for those years shown in parentheses count persons on work relief as employed, which is more consistent with the postwar practice. See notes and definitions.
. . . = Not available.

Table 10-1B. Summary Labor Force, Employment, and Unemployment: Historical—*Continued*

(Thousands of persons, percent, seasonally adjusted, except as noted.)

Year and month	Civilian noninsti- tutional popu- lation [1]	Civilian labor force		Employment, thousands of persons						Employ- ment- population ratio, percent	Unemployment		
		Thousands of persons	Participa- tion rate (percent)	Total	By age and sex			By industry			Thousands of persons		Rate (percent) [2]
					Men, 20 years and over	Women, 20 years and over	Both sexes, 16 to 19 years	Agri- cultural	Nonagri- cultural		Total	Unem- ployed 15 weeks and over	
1950													
January	104 619	61 661	58.9	57 635	38 780	15 255	3 600	7 065	50 570	55.1	4 026	947	6.5
February	104 737	61 687	58.9	57 751	38 818	15 339	3 594	7 057	50 694	55.1	3 936	947	6.4
March	104 844	61 604	58.8	57 728	38 851	15 366	3 511	7 116	50 612	55.1	3 876	912	6.3
April	104 943	62 158	59.2	58 583	39 100	15 831	3 652	7 264	51 319	55.8	3 575	920	5.8
May	105 014	62 083	59.1	58 649	39 416	15 628	3 605	7 277	51 372	55.8	3 434	890	5.5
June	105 104	62 419	59.4	59 052	39 476	15 953	3 623	7 285	51 767	56.2	3 367	868	5.4
July	105 194	62 121	59.1	59 001	39 517	15 793	3 691	7 126	51 875	56.1	3 120	769	5.0
August	105 282	62 596	59.5	59 797	39 879	16 124	3 794	7 248	52 549	56.8	2 799	633	4.5
September	105 269	62 349	59.2	59 575	39 865	15 902	3 808	6 992	52 583	56.6	2 774	648	4.4
October	105 096	62 428	59.4	59 803	39 737	16 175	3 891	7 371	52 432	56.9	2 625	545	4.2
November	104 979	62 286	59.3	59 697	39 668	16 195	3 834	7 163	52 534	56.9	2 589	507	4.2
December	104 872	62 068	59.2	59 429	39 536	16 149	3 744	6 760	52 669	56.7	2 639	482	4.3
1951													
January	104 844	61 941	59.1	59 636	39 595	16 279	3 762	6 828	52 808	56.9	2 305	438	3.7
February	104 604	61 778	59.1	59 661	39 695	16 257	3 709	6 738	52 923	57.0	2 117	386	3.4
March	104 629	62 526	59.8	60 401	40 013	16 557	3 831	6 858	53 543	57.7	2 125	355	3.4
April	104 541	61 808	59.1	59 889	39 804	16 426	3 659	6 722	53 167	57.3	1 919	294	3.1
May	104 491	62 044	59.4	60 188	39 752	16 581	3 855	6 752	53 436	57.6	1 856	269	3.0
June	104 488	61 615	59.0	59 620	39 538	16 368	3 714	6 529	53 091	57.1	1 995	258	3.2
July	104 504	62 106	59.4	60 156	39 483	16 898	3 775	6 601	53 555	57.6	1 950	260	3.1
August	104 536	61 927	59.2	59 994	39 508	16 665	3 821	6 790	53 204	57.4	1 933	249	3.1
September	104 588	61 780	59.1	59 713	39 416	16 504	3 793	6 558	53 155	57.1	2 067	223	3.3
October	104 690	62 204	59.4	60 010	39 555	16 674	3 781	6 636	53 374	57.3	2 194	269	3.5
November	104 740	62 014	59.2	59 836	39 504	16 669	3 663	6 699	53 137	57.1	2 178	316	3.5
December	104 810	62 457	59.6	60 497	39 691	16 946	3 860	7 065	53 432	57.7	1 960	269	3.1
1952													
January	104 862	62 432	59.5	60 460	39 714	17 001	3 745	7 148	53 312	57.7	1 972	282	3.2
February	104 868	62 419	59.5	60 462	39 772	16 935	3 755	7 020	53 442	57.7	1 957	248	3.1
March	104 860	61 721	58.9	59 908	39 580	16 627	3 701	6 468	53 440	57.1	1 813	234	2.9
April	104 906	61 720	58.8	59 909	39 542	16 659	3 708	6 525	53 384	57.1	1 811	242	2.9
May	104 996	62 058	59.1	60 195	39 588	16 844	3 763	6 334	53 861	57.3	1 863	219	3.0
June	105 118	62 103	59.1	60 219	39 558	16 837	3 824	6 529	53 690	57.3	1 884	210	3.0
July	105 246	61 962	58.9	59 971	39 496	16 778	3 697	6 334	53 637	57.0	1 991	194	3.2
August	105 346	61 877	58.7	59 790	39 289	16 867	3 634	6 174	53 616	56.8	2 087	211	3.4
September	105 436	62 457	59.2	60 521	39 386	17 477	3 658	6 537	53 984	57.4	1 936	249	3.1
October	105 591	61 971	58.7	60 132	39 451	17 032	3 649	6 363	53 769	56.9	1 839	230	3.0
November	105 706	62 491	59.1	60 748	39 549	17 450	3 749	6 509	54 239	57.5	1 743	216	2.8
December	105 812	62 621	59.2	60 954	40 011	17 181	3 762	6 361	54 593	57.6	1 667	238	2.7
1953													
January	106 594	63 439	59.5	61 600	40 256	17 482	3 862	6 642	54 958	57.8	1 839	268	2.9
February	106 678	63 520	59.5	61 884	40 546	17 321	4 017	6 463	55 421	58.0	1 636	208	2.6
March	106 744	63 657	59.6	62 010	40 648	17 397	3 965	6 420	55 590	58.1	1 647	213	2.6
April	106 826	63 167	59.1	61 444	40 346	17 242	3 856	6 362	55 082	57.5	1 723	180	2.7
May	106 910	62 615	58.6	61 019	40 323	16 983	3 713	5 937	55 082	57.1	1 596	176	2.5
June	106 978	63 063	58.9	61 456	40 358	17 301	3 797	6 361	55 095	57.4	1 607	213	2.5
July	107 034	63 057	58.9	61 397	40 378	17 341	3 678	6 267	55 130	57.4	1 660	168	2.6
August	107 132	62 816	58.6	61 151	40 352	17 108	3 691	6 319	54 832	57.1	1 665	177	2.7
September	107 253	62 727	58.5	60 906	40 192	17 063	3 651	6 198	54 708	56.8	1 821	178	2.9
October	107 383	62 867	58.5	60 893	40 155	17 236	3 502	6 096	54 797	56.7	1 974	190	3.1
November	107 504	62 949	58.6	60 738	40 163	16 974	3 601	6 345	54 393	56.5	2 211	259	3.5
December	107 623	62 795	58.3	59 977	39 885	16 599	3 493	5 929	54 048	55.7	2 818	309	4.5
1954													
January	107 763	63 101	58.6	60 024	39 834	16 574	3 616	6 073	53 951	55.7	3 077	372	4.9
February	107 880	63 994	59.3	60 663	39 899	17 162	3 602	6 590	54 073	56.2	3 331	532	5.2
March	107 987	63 793	59.1	60 186	39 497	17 022	3 667	6 395	53 791	55.7	3 607	765	5.7
April	108 080	63 934	59.2	60 185	39 613	17 015	3 557	6 142	54 043	55.7	3 749	774	5.9
May	108 184	63 675	58.9	59 908	39 467	16 975	3 466	6 210	53 698	55.4	3 767	879	5.9
June	108 267	63 343	58.5	59 792	39 476	16 894	3 422	6 162	53 630	55.2	3 551	880	5.6
July	108 344	63 302	58.4	59 643	39 467	16 777	3 399	6 222	53 421	55.0	3 659	932	5.8
August	108 440	63 707	58.7	59 853	39 582	16 868	3 403	6 087	53 766	55.2	3 854	1 002	6.0
September	108 546	64 209	59.2	60 282	39 702	17 133	3 447	6 453	53 829	55.5	3 927	1 017	6.1
October	108 668	63 936	58.8	60 270	39 618	17 209	3 443	6 242	54 028	55.5	3 666	1 009	5.7
November	108 798	63 759	58.6	60 357	39 745	17 213	3 399	5 934	54 423	55.5	3 402	975	5.3
December	108 892	63 312	58.1	60 116	39 763	17 121	3 232	5 848	54 268	55.2	3 196	827	5.0

[1]Not seasonally adjusted.
[2]In 1930 through 1943, the official BLS data count persons on work relief as unemployed. The unemployment rates for those years shown in parentheses count persons on work relief as employed, which is more consistent with the postwar practice. See notes and definitions.

Table 10-1B. Summary Labor Force, Employment, and Unemployment: Historical—*Continued*

(Thousands of persons, percent, seasonally adjusted, except as noted.)

Year and month	Civilian noninsti- tutional popu- lation [1]	Civilian labor force		Employment, thousands of persons						Employ- ment- population ratio, percent	Unemployment		
		Thousands of persons	Participa- tion rate (percent)	Total	By age and sex			By industry			Thousands of persons		Rate (percent) [2]
					Men, 20 years and over	Women, 20 years and over	Both sexes, 16 to 19 years	Agri- cultural	Nonagri- cultural		Total	Unem- ployed 15 weeks and over	
1955													
January	109 059	63 910	58.6	60 753	39 937	17 375	3 441	6 113	54 640	55.7	3 157	882	4.9
February	109 078	63 696	58.4	60 727	39 964	17 413	3 350	5 854	54 873	55.7	2 969	826	4.7
March	109 254	63 882	58.5	60 964	40 111	17 415	3 438	6 242	54 722	55.8	2 918	816	4.6
April	109 377	64 564	59.0	61 515	40 120	17 867	3 528	6 363	55 152	56.2	3 049	811	4.7
May	109 544	64 381	58.8	61 634	40 410	17 665	3 559	6 327	55 307	56.3	2 747	734	4.3
June	109 680	64 482	58.8	61 781	40 444	17 837	3 500	6 243	55 538	56.3	2 701	668	4.2
July	109 792	65 145	59.3	62 513	40 751	18 123	3 639	6 438	56 075	56.9	2 632	640	4.0
August	109 882	65 581	59.7	62 797	40 747	18 377	3 673	6 575	56 222	57.1	2 784	535	4.2
September	109 977	65 628	59.7	62 950	40 920	18 285	3 745	6 819	56 131	57.2	2 678	558	4.1
October	110 085	65 821	59.8	62 991	40 858	18 327	3 806	6 728	56 263	57.2	2 830	572	4.3
November	110 177	66 037	59.9	63 257	40 936	18 422	3 899	6 655	56 602	57.4	2 780	564	4.2
December	110 296	66 445	60.2	63 684	41 063	18 630	3 991	6 653	57 031	57.7	2 761	581	4.2
1956													
January	110 390	66 419	60.2	63 753	41 203	18 691	3 859	6 590	57 163	57.8	2 666	561	4.0
February	110 478	66 124	59.9	63 518	41 175	18 582	3 761	6 457	57 061	57.5	2 606	545	3.9
March	110 582	66 175	59.8	63 411	41 199	18 496	3 716	6 221	57 190	57.3	2 764	521	4.2
April	110 650	66 264	59.9	63 614	41 289	18 629	3 696	6 460	57 154	57.5	2 650	476	4.0
May	110 810	66 722	60.2	63 861	41 166	18 844	3 851	6 375	57 486	57.6	2 861	506	4.3
June	110 903	66 702	60.1	63 820	41 196	18 748	3 876	6 335	57 485	57.5	2 882	516	4.3
July	111 019	66 752	60.1	63 800	41 216	18 718	3 866	6 320	57 480	57.5	2 952	523	4.4
August	111 099	66 673	60.0	63 972	41 265	18 864	3 843	6 280	57 692	57.6	2 701	543	4.1
September	111 222	66 714	60.0	64 079	41 221	19 019	3 839	6 375	57 704	57.6	2 635	577	3.9
October	111 335	66 546	59.8	63 975	41 261	18 928	3 786	6 137	57 838	57.5	2 571	530	3.9
November	111 432	66 657	59.8	63 796	41 208	18 846	3 742	5 997	57 799	57.3	2 861	575	4.3
December	111 526	66 700	59.8	63 910	41 192	18 859	3 859	5 806	58 104	57.3	2 790	567	4.2
1957													
January	111 626	66 428	59.5	63 632	41 168	18 740	3 724	5 790	57 842	57.0	2 796	509	4.2
February	111 711	66 879	59.9	64 257	41 341	19 115	3 801	6 125	58 132	57.5	2 622	530	3.9
March	111 824	66 913	59.8	64 404	41 500	19 066	3 838	5 963	58 441	57.6	2 509	514	3.7
April	111 933	66 647	59.5	64 047	41 345	18 937	3 765	5 836	58 211	57.2	2 600	516	3.9
May	112 031	66 695	59.5	63 985	41 334	18 897	3 754	5 999	57 986	57.1	2 710	538	4.1
June	112 172	67 052	59.8	64 196	41 411	18 973	3 812	6 002	58 194	57.2	2 856	526	4.3
July	112 317	67 336	60.0	64 540	41 472	19 262	3 806	6 401	58 139	57.5	2 796	535	4.2
August	112 421	66 706	59.3	63 959	41 243	19 020	3 696	5 898	58 061	56.9	2 747	542	4.1
September	112 554	67 064	59.6	64 121	41 213	19 116	3 792	5 728	58 393	57.0	2 943	559	4.4
October	112 710	67 066	59.5	64 046	41 069	19 160	3 817	5 875	58 171	56.8	3 020	650	4.5
November	112 874	67 123	59.5	63 669	40 853	19 082	3 734	5 686	57 983	56.4	3 454	674	5.1
December	113 013	67 398	59.6	63 922	40 884	19 285	3 753	6 037	57 885	56.6	3 476	731	5.2
1958													
January	113 138	67 095	59.3	63 220	40 617	19 035	3 568	5 831	57 389	55.9	3 875	879	5.8
February	113 234	67 201	59.3	62 898	40 336	18 951	3 611	5 654	57 244	55.5	4 303	1 005	6.4
March	113 337	67 223	59.3	62 731	40 180	18 968	3 583	5 561	57 170	55.3	4 492	1 128	6.7
April	113 415	67 647	59.6	62 631	40 129	18 969	3 533	5 602	57 029	55.2	5 016	1 387	7.4
May	113 534	67 895	59.8	62 874	40 253	18 978	3 643	5 647	57 227	55.4	5 021	1 493	7.4
June	113 647	67 674	59.5	62 730	40 208	19 008	3 514	5 510	57 220	55.2	4 944	1 677	7.3
July	113 727	67 824	59.6	62 745	40 270	19 039	3 436	5 525	57 220	55.2	5 079	1 796	7.5
August	113 835	68 037	59.8	63 012	40 343	19 103	3 566	5 673	57 339	55.4	5 025	1 888	7.4
September	113 977	68 002	59.7	63 181	40 564	19 033	3 584	5 453	57 728	55.4	4 821	1 795	7.1
October	114 138	68 045	59.6	63 475	40 699	19 091	3 685	5 563	57 912	55.6	4 570	1 708	6.7
November	114 283	67 658	59.2	63 470	40 684	19 157	3 629	5 571	57 899	55.5	4 188	1 570	6.2
December	114 429	67 740	59.2	63 549	40 666	19 170	3 713	5 521	58 028	55.5	4 191	1 490	6.2
1959													
January	114 582	67 936	59.3	63 868	40 769	19 292	3 807	5 481	58 387	55.7	4 068	1 396	6.0
February	114 712	67 649	59.0	63 684	40 699	19 167	3 818	5 429	58 255	55.5	3 965	1 277	5.9
March	114 849	68 068	59.3	64 267	41 079	19 379	3 809	5 677	58 590	56.0	3 801	1 210	5.6
April	114 986	68 339	59.4	64 768	41 419	19 498	3 851	5 893	58 875	56.3	3 571	1 039	5.2
May	115 144	68 178	59.2	64 699	41 355	19 565	3 779	5 792	58 907	56.2	3 479	965	5.1
June	115 287	68 278	59.2	64 849	41 387	19 658	3 804	5 712	59 137	56.3	3 429	963	5.0
July	115 429	68 539	59.4	65 011	41 596	19 595	3 820	5 564	59 447	56.3	3 528	889	5.1
August	115 555	68 432	59.2	64 844	41 485	19 568	3 791	5 442	59 402	56.1	3 588	889	5.2
September	115 668	68 545	59.3	64 770	41 351	19 531	3 888	5 447	59 323	56.0	3 775	895	5.5
October	115 798	68 821	59.4	64 911	41 362	19 702	3 847	5 355	59 556	56.1	3 910	883	5.7
November	115 916	68 533	59.1	64 530	41 062	19 594	3 874	5 480	59 050	55.7	4 003	982	5.8
December	116 040	68 994	59.5	65 341	41 651	19 717	3 973	5 458	59 883	56.3	3 653	920	5.3

[1]Not seasonally adjusted.
[2]In 1930 through 1943, the official BLS data count persons on work relief as unemployed. The unemployment rates for those years shown in parentheses count persons on work relief as employed, which is more consistent with the postwar practice. See notes and definitions.

Table 10-1B. Summary Labor Force, Employment, and Unemployment: Historical—*Continued*

(Thousands of persons, percent, seasonally adjusted, except as noted.)

Year and month	Civilian noninstitutional population [1]	Civilian labor force		Employment, thousands of persons						Employment-population ratio, percent	Unemployment		
					By age and sex			By industry			Thousands of persons		
		Thousands of persons	Participation rate (percent)	Total	Men, 20 years and over	Women, 20 years and over	Both sexes, 16 to 19 years	Agricultural	Nonagricultural		Total	Unemployed 15 weeks and over	Rate (percent) [2]
1960													
January	116 594	68 962	59.1	65 347	41 637	19 686	4 024	5 458	59 889	56.0	3 615	915	5.2
February	116 702	68 949	59.1	65 620	41 729	19 765	4 126	5 443	60 177	56.2	3 329	841	4.8
March	116 827	68 399	58.5	64 673	41 320	19 388	3 965	4 959	59 714	55.4	3 726	959	5.4
April	116 910	69 579	59.5	65 959	41 641	20 110	4 208	5 471	60 488	56.4	3 620	896	5.2
May	117 033	69 626	59.5	66 057	41 668	20 186	4 203	5 359	60 698	56.4	3 569	797	5.1
June	117 167	69 934	59.7	66 168	41 553	20 290	4 325	5 416	60 752	56.5	3 766	854	5.4
July	117 281	69 745	59.5	65 909	41 490	20 257	4 162	5 542	60 367	56.2	3 836	921	5.5
August	117 431	69 841	59.5	65 895	41 503	20 316	4 076	5 520	60 375	56.1	3 946	927	5.6
September	117 521	70 151	59.7	66 267	41 604	20 493	4 170	5 755	60 512	56.4	3 884	982	5.5
October	117 643	69 884	59.4	65 632	41 464	20 076	4 092	5 436	60 196	55.8	4 252	1 189	6.1
November	117 829	70 439	59.8	66 109	41 543	20 384	4 182	5 513	60 596	56.1	4 330	1 223	6.1
December	118 001	70 395	59.7	65 778	41 416	20 332	4 030	5 622	60 156	55.7	4 617	1 142	6.6
1961													
January	118 155	70 447	59.6	65 776	41 363	20 325	4 088	5 422	60 354	55.7	4 671	1 328	6.6
February	118 250	70 420	59.6	65 588	41 177	20 392	4 019	5 472	60 116	55.5	4 832	1 416	6.9
March	118 358	70 703	59.7	65 850	41 273	20 459	4 118	5 406	60 444	55.6	4 853	1 463	6.9
April	118 503	70 267	59.3	65 374	41 206	20 145	4 023	5 037	60 337	55.2	4 893	1 598	7.0
May	118 638	70 452	59.4	65 449	41 139	20 261	4 049	5 099	60 350	55.2	5 003	1 686	7.1
June	118 767	70 878	59.7	65 993	41 349	20 446	4 198	5 220	60 773	55.6	4 885	1 651	6.9
July	118 889	70 536	59.3	65 608	41 245	20 252	4 111	5 153	60 455	55.2	4 928	1 830	7.0
August	119 006	70 534	59.3	65 852	41 362	20 279	4 211	5 366	60 486	55.3	4 682	1 649	6.6
September	119 107	70 217	59.0	65 541	41 400	20 112	4 029	5 021	60 520	55.0	4 676	1 531	6.7
October	119 202	70 492	59.1	65 919	41 509	20 338	4 072	5 203	60 716	55.3	4 573	1 481	6.5
November	119 153	70 376	59.1	66 081	41 556	20 330	4 195	5 090	60 991	55.5	4 295	1 388	6.1
December	119 214	70 077	58.8	65 900	41 534	20 287	4 079	4 992	60 908	55.3	4 177	1 361	6.0
1962													
January	119 300	70 189	58.8	66 108	41 547	20 501	4 060	5 094	61 014	55.4	4 081	1 235	5.8
February	119 360	70 409	59.0	66 538	41 745	20 693	4 100	5 289	61 249	55.7	3 871	1 244	5.5
March	119 476	70 414	58.9	66 493	41 696	20 567	4 230	5 157	61 336	55.7	3 921	1 162	5.6
April	119 702	70 278	58.7	66 372	41 647	20 567	4 158	5 009	61 363	55.4	3 906	1 122	5.6
May	119 813	70 551	58.9	66 688	41 847	20 558	4 283	4 964	61 724	55.7	3 863	1 134	5.5
June	119 943	70 514	58.8	66 670	41 761	20 547	4 362	4 943	61 727	55.6	3 844	1 079	5.5
July	120 128	70 302	58.5	66 483	41 671	20 592	4 220	4 840	61 643	55.3	3 819	1 049	5.4
August	120 323	70 981	59.0	66 968	41 900	20 841	4 227	4 866	62 102	55.7	4 013	1 081	5.7
September	120 653	71 153	59.0	67 192	42 020	20 982	4 190	4 867	62 325	55.7	3 961	1 096	5.6
October	120 856	70 917	58.7	67 114	42 086	20 856	4 172	4 816	62 298	55.5	3 803	1 022	5.4
November	121 045	70 871	58.5	66 847	41 985	20 794	4 068	4 831	62 016	55.2	4 024	1 051	5.7
December	121 236	70 854	58.4	66 947	41 934	20 831	4 182	4 647	62 300	55.2	3 907	1 068	5.5
1963													
January	121 463	71 146	58.6	67 072	41 938	20 933	4 201	4 882	62 190	55.2	4 074	1 122	5.7
February	121 633	71 262	58.6	67 024	41 876	21 046	4 102	4 652	62 372	55.1	4 238	1 137	5.9
March	121 824	71 423	58.6	67 351	42 047	21 162	4 142	4 696	62 655	55.3	4 072	1 087	5.7
April	121 986	71 697	58.8	67 642	42 131	21 281	4 230	4 670	62 972	55.5	4 055	1 071	5.7
May	122 162	71 832	58.8	67 615	42 145	21 225	4 245	4 729	62 886	55.3	4 217	1 157	5.9
June	122 352	71 626	58.5	67 649	42 268	21 185	4 196	4 642	63 007	55.3	3 977	1 067	5.6
July	122 521	71 956	58.7	67 905	42 427	21 268	4 210	4 694	63 211	55.4	4 051	1 070	5.6
August	122 667	71 786	58.5	67 908	42 400	21 185	4 323	4 604	63 304	55.4	3 878	1 114	5.4
September	122 821	72 131	58.7	68 174	42 500	21 317	4 357	4 650	63 524	55.5	3 957	1 069	5.5
October	123 014	72 281	58.8	68 294	42 437	21 456	4 401	4 702	63 592	55.5	3 987	1 071	5.5
November	123 192	72 418	58.8	68 267	42 415	21 553	4 299	4 694	63 573	55.4	4 151	1 054	5.7
December	123 360	72 188	58.5	68 213	42 427	21 481	4 305	4 629	63 584	55.3	3 975	1 007	5.5
1964													
January	123 560	72 356	58.6	68 327	42 510	21 462	4 355	4 603	63 724	55.3	4 029	1 057	5.6
February	123 707	72 683	58.8	68 751	42 579	21 652	4 520	4 563	64 188	55.6	3 932	1 015	5.4
March	123 857	72 713	58.7	68 763	42 600	21 685	4 478	4 366	64 397	55.5	3 950	1 039	5.4
April	124 019	73 274	59.1	69 356	42 885	22 110	4 361	4 414	64 942	55.9	3 918	934	5.3
May	124 204	73 395	59.1	69 631	43 025	22 103	4 503	4 603	65 028	56.1	3 764	975	5.1
June	124 386	73 032	58.7	69 218	42 760	21 995	4 463	4 556	64 662	55.6	3 814	1 047	5.2
July	124 567	73 007	58.6	69 399	42 998	21 846	4 555	4 591	64 808	55.7	3 608	1 002	4.9
August	124 731	73 118	58.6	69 463	42 963	22 002	4 498	4 573	64 890	55.7	3 655	934	5.0
September	124 920	73 290	58.7	69 578	43 009	21 863	4 706	4 619	64 959	55.7	3 712	917	5.1
October	125 108	73 308	58.6	69 582	43 023	21 984	4 575	4 550	65 032	55.6	3 726	903	5.1
November	125 291	73 286	58.5	69 735	43 171	21 954	4 610	4 496	65 239	55.7	3 551	922	4.8
December	125 468	73 465	58.6	69 814	43 109	22 136	4 569	4 322	65 492	55.6	3 651	873	5.0

[1]Not seasonally adjusted.
[2]In 1930 through 1943, the official BLS data count persons on work relief as unemployed. The unemployment rates for those years shown in parentheses count persons on work relief as employed, which is more consistent with the postwar practice. See notes and definitions.

Table 10-1B. Summary Labor Force, Employment, and Unemployment: Historical—*Continued*

(Thousands of persons, percent, seasonally adjusted, except as noted.)

Year and month	Civilian noninsti- tutional popu- lation [1]	Civilian labor force		Employment, thousands of persons						Employ- ment- population ratio, percent	Unemployment		
		Thousands of persons	Participa- tion rate (percent)	Total	By age and sex			By industry			Thousands of persons		Rate (percent) [2]
					Men, 20 years and over	Women, 20 years and over	Both sexes, 16 to 19 years	Agri- cultural	Nonagri- cultural		Total	Unem- ployed 15 weeks and over	
1965													
January	125 647	73 569	58.6	69 997	43 237	22 282	4 478	4 271	65 726	55.7	3 572	793	4.9
February	125 810	73 857	58.7	70 127	43 279	22 276	4 572	4 322	65 805	55.7	3 730	919	5.1
March	125 985	73 949	58.7	70 439	43 370	22 373	4 696	4 318	66 121	55.9	3 510	796	4.7
April	126 155	74 228	58.8	70 633	43 397	22 416	4 820	4 424	66 209	56.0	3 595	796	4.8
May	126 320	74 466	59.0	71 034	43 579	22 494	4 961	4 724	66 310	56.2	3 432	736	4.6
June	126 499	74 412	58.8	71 025	43 487	22 759	4 779	4 444	66 581	56.1	3 387	786	4.6
July	126 573	74 761	59.1	71 460	43 489	22 841	5 130	4 390	67 070	56.5	3 301	683	4.4
August	126 756	74 616	58.9	71 362	43 447	22 783	5 132	4 355	67 007	56.3	3 254	733	4.4
September	126 906	74 502	58.7	71 286	43 371	22 684	5 231	4 271	67 015	56.2	3 216	732	4.3
October	127 043	74 838	58.9	71 695	43 461	22 819	5 415	4 418	67 277	56.4	3 143	672	4.2
November	127 171	74 797	58.8	71 724	43 447	22 829	5 448	4 093	67 631	56.4	3 073	645	4.1
December	127 294	75 093	59.0	72 062	43 513	22 983	5 566	4 159	67 903	56.6	3 031	659	4.0
1966													
January	127 394	75 186	59.0	72 198	43 495	23 098	5 605	4 077	68 121	56.7	2 988	623	4.0
February	127 514	74 954	58.8	72 134	43 528	23 089	5 517	4 078	68 056	56.6	2 820	594	3.8
March	127 626	75 075	58.8	72 188	43 576	23 109	5 503	4 069	68 119	56.6	2 887	583	3.8
April	127 744	75 338	59.0	72 510	43 679	23 227	5 604	4 108	68 402	56.8	2 828	575	3.8
May	127 879	75 447	59.0	72 497	43 710	23 282	5 505	3 930	68 567	56.7	2 950	534	3.9
June	127 983	75 647	59.1	72 775	43 662	23 359	5 754	3 967	68 808	56.9	2 872	475	3.8
July	128 102	75 736	59.1	72 860	43 574	23 422	5 864	3 920	68 940	56.9	2 876	427	3.8
August	128 240	76 046	59.3	73 146	43 636	23 605	5 905	3 921	69 225	57.0	2 900	464	3.8
September	128 359	76 056	59.3	73 258	43 718	23 881	5 659	3 952	69 306	57.1	2 798	488	3.7
October	128 494	76 199	59.3	73 401	43 776	23 881	5 744	3 912	69 489	57.1	2 798	494	3.7
November	128 627	76 610	59.6	73 840	43 804	24 130	5 906	3 945	69 895	57.4	2 770	464	3.6
December	128 730	76 641	59.5	73 729	43 820	24 025	5 884	3 906	69 823	57.3	2 912	488	3.8
1967													
January	128 909	76 639	59.5	73 671	44 029	23 872	5 770	3 890	69 781	57.1	2 968	489	3.9
February	129 032	76 521	59.3	73 606	43 997	23 919	5 690	3 723	69 883	57.0	2 915	459	3.8
March	129 190	76 328	59.1	73 439	43 922	23 832	5 685	3 757	69 682	56.8	2 889	436	3.8
April	129 344	76 777	59.4	73 882	44 061	24 161	5 660	3 748	70 134	57.1	2 895	428	3.8
May	129 515	76 773	59.3	73 844	44 100	24 172	5 572	3 658	70 186	57.0	2 929	417	3.8
June	129 722	77 270	59.6	74 278	44 230	24 303	5 745	3 689	70 589	57.3	2 992	422	3.9
July	129 918	77 464	59.6	74 520	44 364	24 416	5 740	3 833	70 687	57.4	2 944	412	3.8
August	130 187	77 712	59.7	74 767	44 410	24 600	5 757	3 963	70 804	57.4	2 945	441	3.8
September	130 392	77 812	59.7	74 854	44 535	24 683	5 636	3 851	71 003	57.4	2 958	448	3.8
October	130 582	78 194	59.9	75 051	44 610	24 802	5 639	4 008	71 043	57.5	3 143	472	4.0
November	130 754	78 191	59.8	75 125	44 625	24 914	5 586	3 933	71 192	57.5	3 066	490	3.9
December	130 936	78 491	59.9	75 473	44 719	25 104	5 650	4 076	71 397	57.6	3 018	485	3.8
1968													
January	131 112	77 578	59.2	74 700	44 606	24 581	5 513	3 908	70 792	57.0	2 878	503	3.7
February	131 277	78 230	59.6	75 229	44 659	24 881	5 689	3 959	71 270	57.3	3 001	468	3.8
March	131 412	78 256	59.6	75 379	44 663	25 019	5 697	3 904	71 475	57.4	2 877	447	3.7
April	131 553	78 270	59.5	75 561	44 753	25 072	5 736	3 875	71 686	57.4	2 709	393	3.5
May	131 712	78 847	59.9	76 107	44 841	25 513	5 753	3 814	72 293	57.8	2 740	395	3.5
June	131 872	79 120	60.0	76 182	44 914	25 466	5 802	3 806	72 376	57.8	2 938	405	3.7
July	132 053	78 970	59.8	76 087	44 935	25 347	5 805	3 820	72 267	57.6	2 883	426	3.7
August	132 251	78 811	59.6	76 043	44 897	25 201	5 945	3 736	72 307	57.5	2 768	393	3.5
September	132 446	78 858	59.5	76 172	44 893	25 445	5 834	3 758	72 414	57.5	2 686	375	3.4
October	132 617	78 913	59.5	76 224	44 884	25 475	5 865	3 741	72 483	57.5	2 689	386	3.4
November	132 903	79 209	59.6	76 494	44 996	25 674	5 824	3 758	72 736	57.6	2 715	357	3.4
December	133 120	79 463	59.7	76 778	45 262	25 712	5 804	3 746	73 032	57.7	2 685	351	3.4
1969													
January	133 324	79 523	59.6	76 805	45 154	25 777	5 874	3 704	73 101	57.6	2 718	339	3.4
February	133 465	80 019	60.0	77 327	45 339	26 092	5 896	3 770	73 557	57.9	2 692	358	3.4
March	133 639	80 079	59.9	77 367	45 305	26 115	5 947	3 668	73 699	57.9	2 712	353	3.4
April	133 821	80 281	60.0	77 523	45 262	26 233	6 028	3 629	73 894	57.9	2 758	386	3.4
May	134 027	80 125	59.8	77 412	45 278	26 283	5 851	3 706	73 706	57.8	2 713	387	3.4
June	134 213	80 696	60.1	77 880	45 313	26 429	6 138	3 663	74 217	58.0	2 816	368	3.5
July	134 414	80 827	60.1	77 959	45 305	26 516	6 138	3 548	74 411	58.0	2 868	377	3.5
August	134 597	81 106	60.3	78 250	45 513	26 556	6 181	3 613	74 637	58.1	2 856	373	3.5
September	134 774	81 290	60.3	78 250	45 447	26 572	6 231	3 551	74 699	58.1	3 040	391	3.7
October	135 012	81 494	60.4	78 445	45 488	26 658	6 299	3 517	74 928	58.1	3 049	374	3.7
November	135 239	81 397	60.2	78 541	45 505	26 652	6 384	3 477	75 064	58.1	2 856	392	3.5
December	135 489	81 624	60.2	78 740	45 577	26 832	6 331	3 409	75 331	58.1	2 884	413	3.5

[1] Not seasonally adjusted.
[2] In 1930 through 1943, the official BLS data count persons on work relief as unemployed. The unemployment rates for those years shown in parentheses count persons on work relief as employed, which is more consistent with the postwar practice. See notes and definitions.

Table 10-1B. Summary Labor Force, Employment, and Unemployment: Historical—*Continued*

(Thousands of persons, percent, seasonally adjusted, except as noted.)

Year and month	Civilian noninsti-tutional popu-lation 1	Civilian labor force		Employment, thousands of persons						Employ-ment-population ratio, percent	Unemployment		
		Thousands of persons	Participa-tion rate (percent)	Total	By age and sex			By industry			Thousands of persons		Rate (percent) 2
					Men, 20 years and over	Women, 20 years and over	Both sexes, 16 to 19 years	Agri-cultural	Nonagri-cultural		Total	Unem-ployed 15 weeks and over	
1970													
January	135 713	81 981	60.4	78 780	45 654	26 908	6 218	3 422	75 358	58.0	3 201	431	3.9
February	135 957	82 151	60.4	78 698	45 627	26 828	6 243	3 439	75 259	57.9	3 453	470	4.2
March	136 179	82 498	60.6	78 863	45 668	26 933	6 262	3 499	75 364	57.9	3 635	534	4.4
April	136 416	82 727	60.6	78 930	45 679	27 114	6 137	3 568	75 362	57.9	3 797	602	4.6
May	136 686	82 483	60.3	78 564	45 666	26 739	6 159	3 547	75 017	57.5	3 919	591	4.8
June	136 928	82 484	60.2	78 413	45 554	26 904	5 955	3 555	74 858	57.3	4 071	657	4.9
July	137 196	82 901	60.4	78 726	45 516	27 083	6 127	3 517	75 209	57.4	4 175	662	5.0
August	137 455	82 880	60.3	78 624	45 495	27 011	6 118	3 418	75 206	57.2	4 256	705	5.1
September	137 717	82 954	60.2	78 498	45 535	26 784	6 179	3 451	75 047	57.0	4 456	788	5.4
October	137 988	83 276	60.4	78 685	45 508	27 058	6 119	3 337	75 348	57.0	4 591	771	5.5
November	138 264	83 548	60.4	78 650	45 540	27 020	6 090	3 372	75 278	56.9	4 898	871	5.9
December	138 529	83 670	60.4	78 594	45 466	27 038	6 090	3 380	75 214	56.7	5 076	1 102	6.1
1971													
January	138 795	83 850	60.4	78 864	45 527	27 173	6 164	3 393	75 471	56.8	4 986	1 113	5.9
February	139 021	83 603	60.1	78 700	45 455	27 040	6 205	3 288	75 412	56.6	4 903	1 068	5.9
March	139 285	83 575	60.0	78 588	45 520	26 967	6 101	3 356	75 232	56.4	4 987	1 098	6.0
April	139 566	83 946	60.1	78 987	45 789	26 984	6 214	3 574	75 413	56.6	4 959	1 149	5.9
May	139 826	84 135	60.2	79 139	45 917	27 056	6 166	3 449	75 690	56.6	4 996	1 173	5.9
June	140 090	83 706	59.8	78 757	45 879	27 013	5 865	3 334	75 423	56.2	4 949	1 167	5.9
July	140 343	84 340	60.1	79 305	46 000	27 054	6 251	3 386	75 919	56.5	5 035	1 251	6.0
August	140 596	84 673	60.2	79 539	46 041	27 171	6 327	3 395	76 144	56.6	5 134	1 261	6.1
September	140 869	84 731	60.1	79 689	46 090	27 390	6 209	3 367	76 322	56.6	5 042	1 239	6.0
October	141 146	84 872	60.1	79 918	46 132	27 538	6 248	3 405	76 513	56.6	4 954	1 268	5.8
November	141 393	85 458	60.4	80 297	46 209	27 721	6 367	3 410	76 887	56.8	5 161	1 277	6.0
December	141 666	85 625	60.4	80 471	46 280	27 791	6 400	3 371	77 100	56.8	5 154	1 283	6.0
1972													
January	142 736	85 978	60.2	80 959	46 471	27 956	6 532	3 366	77 593	56.7	5 019	1 257	5.8
February	143 017	86 036	60.2	81 108	46 600	28 016	6 492	3 358	77 750	56.7	4 928	1 292	5.7
March	143 263	86 611	60.5	81 573	46 821	28 126	6 626	3 438	78 135	56.9	5 038	1 232	5.8
April	143 483	86 614	60.4	81 655	46 863	28 114	6 678	3 382	78 273	56.9	4 959	1 203	5.7
May	143 760	86 809	60.4	81 887	46 950	28 184	6 753	3 412	78 475	57.0	4 922	1 168	5.7
June	144 033	87 006	60.4	82 083	47 147	28 175	6 761	3 402	78 681	57.0	4 923	1 141	5.7
July	144 285	87 143	60.4	82 230	47 244	28 225	6 761	3 461	78 769	57.0	4 913	1 154	5.6
August	144 522	87 517	60.6	82 578	47 321	28 382	6 875	3 603	78 975	57.1	4 939	1 156	5.6
September	144 761	87 392	60.4	82 543	47 394	28 417	6 732	3 568	78 975	57.0	4 849	1 131	5.5
October	144 988	87 491	60.3	82 616	47 354	28 438	6 824	3 634	78 982	57.0	4 875	1 123	5.6
November	145 211	87 592	60.3	82 990	47 529	28 567	6 894	3 517	79 473	57.2	4 602	1 040	5.3
December	145 446	87 943	60.5	83 400	47 747	28 698	6 955	3 596	79 804	57.3	4 543	1 006	5.2
1973													
January	145 720	87 487	60.0	83 161	47 701	28 596	6 864	3 456	79 705	57.1	4 326	947	4.9
February	145 943	88 364	60.5	83 912	47 884	28 995	7 033	3 415	80 497	57.5	4 452	894	5.0
March	146 230	88 846	60.8	84 452	48 117	29 110	7 225	3 469	80 983	57.8	4 394	889	4.9
April	146 459	89 018	60.8	84 559	48 098	29 304	7 157	3 407	81 152	57.7	4 459	809	5.0
May	146 719	88 977	60.6	84 648	48 068	29 432	7 148	3 376	81 272	57.7	4 329	816	4.9
June	146 981	89 548	60.9	85 185	48 244	29 505	7 436	3 509	81 676	58.0	4 363	779	4.9
July	147 233	89 604	60.9	85 299	48 452	29 592	7 255	3 540	81 759	57.9	4 305	756	4.8
August	147 471	89 509	60.7	85 204	48 353	29 578	7 273	3 425	81 779	57.8	4 305	788	4.8
September	147 731	89 838	60.8	85 488	48 408	29 710	7 370	3 342	82 146	57.9	4 350	785	4.8
October	147 980	90 131	60.9	85 987	48 631	29 885	7 471	3 424	82 563	58.1	4 144	793	4.6
November	148 219	90 716	61.2	86 320	48 764	30 071	7 485	3 593	82 727	58.2	4 396	832	4.8
December	148 479	90 890	61.2	86 401	48 902	29 991	7 508	3 658	82 743	58.2	4 489	767	4.9
1974													
January	148 753	91 199	61.3	86 555	49 107	29 893	7 555	3 756	82 799	58.2	4 644	799	5.1
February	148 982	91 485	61.4	86 754	49 057	30 146	7 551	3 824	82 930	58.2	4 731	829	5.2
March	149 225	91 453	61.3	86 819	48 986	30 293	7 540	3 726	83 093	58.2	4 634	849	5.1
April	149 478	91 287	61.1	86 669	48 853	30 376	7 440	3 582	83 087	58.0	4 618	889	5.1
May	149 750	91 596	61.2	86 891	49 039	30 424	7 428	3 529	83 362	58.0	4 705	880	5.1
June	150 012	91 868	61.2	86 941	48 946	30 512	7 483	3 386	83 555	58.0	4 927	926	5.4
July	150 248	92 212	61.4	87 149	48 883	30 869	7 397	3 436	83 713	58.0	5 063	924	5.5
August	150 493	92 059	61.2	87 037	48 950	30 662	7 425	3 429	83 608	57.8	5 022	960	5.5
September	150 753	92 488	61.4	87 051	48 978	30 569	7 504	3 460	83 591	57.7	5 437	1 021	5.9
October	151 009	92 518	61.3	86 995	48 959	30 570	7 466	3 431	83 564	57.6	5 523	1 072	6.0
November	151 256	92 766	61.3	86 626	48 833	30 424	7 369	3 405	83 221	57.3	6 140	1 128	6.6
December	151 494	92 780	61.2	86 144	48 458	30 431	7 255	3 361	82 783	56.9	6 636	1 326	7.2

1Not seasonally adjusted.
2In 1930 through 1943, the official BLS data count persons on work relief as unemployed. The unemployment rates for those years shown in parentheses count persons on work relief as employed, which is more consistent with the postwar practice. See notes and definitions.

Table 10-1B. Summary Labor Force, Employment, and Unemployment: Historical—*Continued*

(Thousands of persons, percent, seasonally adjusted, except as noted.)

Year and month	Civilian noninsti-tutional popu-lation 1	Civilian labor force Thousands of persons	Civilian labor force Participa-tion rate (percent)	Employment Total	By age and sex Men, 20 years and over	By age and sex Women, 20 years and over	By age and sex Both sexes, 16 to 19 years	By industry Agri-cultural	By industry Nonagri-cultural	Employ-ment-population ratio, percent	Unemployment Thousands of persons Total	Unemployment Unem-ployed 15 weeks and over	Rate (percent) 2
1975													
January	151 755	93 128	61.4	85 627	48 086	30 343	7 198	3 401	82 226	56.4	7 501	1 555	8.1
February	151 990	92 776	61.0	85 256	47 927	30 215	7 114	3 361	81 895	56.1	7 520	1 841	8.1
March	152 217	93 165	61.2	85 187	47 776	30 334	7 077	3 358	81 829	56.0	7 978	2 074	8.6
April	152 443	93 399	61.3	85 189	47 759	30 410	7 020	3 315	81 874	55.9	8 210	2 442	8.8
May	152 704	93 884	61.5	85 451	47 835	30 483	7 133	3 560	81 891	56.0	8 433	2 643	9.0
June	152 976	93 575	61.2	85 355	47 754	30 618	6 983	3 368	81 987	55.8	8 220	2 843	8.8
July	153 309	94 021	61.3	85 894	48 050	30 794	7 050	3 457	82 437	56.0	8 127	2 943	8.6
August	153 580	94 162	61.3	86 234	48 239	30 966	7 029	3 429	82 805	56.1	7 928	2 862	8.4
September	153 848	94 202	61.2	86 279	48 126	30 979	7 174	3 508	82 771	56.1	7 923	2 906	8.4
October	154 082	94 267	61.2	86 370	48 165	31 121	7 084	3 397	82 973	56.1	7 897	2 689	8.4
November	154 338	94 250	61.1	86 456	48 203	31 135	7 118	3 331	83 125	56.0	7 794	2 789	8.3
December	154 589	94 409	61.1	86 665	48 266	31 268	7 131	3 259	83 406	56.1	7 744	2 868	8.2
1976													
January	154 853	94 934	61.3	87 400	48 592	31 595	8 967	3 387	84 013	56.4	7 534	2 713	7.9
February	155 066	94 998	61.3	87 672	48 721	31 680	8 981	3 304	84 368	56.5	7 326	2 519	7.7
March	155 306	95 215	61.3	87 985	48 836	31 842	9 007	3 296	84 689	56.7	7 230	2 441	7.6
April	155 529	95 746	61.6	88 416	49 097	31 951	9 151	3 438	84 978	56.8	7 330	2 210	7.7
May	155 765	95 847	61.5	88 794	49 193	32 147	9 155	3 367	85 427	57.0	7 053	2 115	7.4
June	156 026	95 885	61.5	88 563	49 010	32 267	8 943	3 310	85 253	56.8	7 322	2 332	7.6
July	156 276	96 583	61.8	89 093	49 236	32 334	9 204	3 358	85 735	57.0	7 490	2 316	7.8
August	156 525	96 741	61.8	89 223	49 417	32 437	9 168	3 380	85 843	57.0	7 518	2 378	7.8
September	156 779	96 553	61.6	89 173	49 485	32 390	8 968	3 278	85 895	56.9	7 380	2 296	7.6
October	156 993	96 704	61.6	89 274	49 524	32 412	9 054	3 316	85 958	56.9	7 430	2 292	7.7
November	157 235	97 254	61.9	89 634	49 561	32 753	9 055	3 263	86 371	57.0	7 620	2 354	7.8
December	157 438	97 348	61.8	89 803	49 599	32 914	9 011	3 251	86 552	57.0	7 545	2 375	7.8
1977													
January	157 688	97 208	61.6	89 928	49 738	32 872	9 025	3 185	86 743	57.0	7 280	2 200	7.5
February	157 913	97 785	61.9	90 342	49 838	32 997	9 198	3 222	87 120	57.2	7 443	2 174	7.6
March	158 131	98 115	62.0	90 808	50 031	33 246	9 257	3 212	87 596	57.4	7 307	2 057	7.4
April	158 371	98 330	62.1	91 271	50 185	33 470	9 289	3 313	87 958	57.6	7 059	1 936	7.2
May	158 657	98 665	62.2	91 754	50 280	33 851	9 279	3 432	88 322	57.8	6 911	1 928	7.0
June	158 928	99 093	62.4	91 959	50 544	33 678	9 525	3 340	88 619	57.9	7 134	1 918	7.2
July	159 185	98 913	62.1	92 084	50 597	33 749	9 377	3 247	88 837	57.8	6 829	1 907	6.9
August	159 430	99 366	62.3	92 441	50 745	33 809	9 550	3 260	89 181	58.0	6 925	1 836	7.0
September	159 674	99 453	62.3	92 702	50 825	34 218	9 340	3 201	89 501	58.1	6 751	1 853	6.8
October	159 915	99 815	62.4	93 052	51 046	34 187	9 441	3 272	89 780	58.2	6 763	1 789	6.8
November	160 129	100 576	62.8	93 761	51 316	34 536	9 551	3 375	90 386	58.6	6 815	1 804	6.8
December	160 376	100 491	62.7	94 105	51 492	34 668	9 406	3 320	90 785	58.7	6 386	1 717	6.4
1978													
January	160 617	100 873	62.8	94 384	51 542	34 948	9 473	3 434	90 950	58.8	6 489	1 643	6.4
February	160 831	100 837	62.7	94 519	51 578	35 118	9 448	3 320	91 199	58.8	6 318	1 584	6.3
March	161 038	101 092	62.8	94 755	51 635	35 310	9 441	3 351	91 404	58.8	6 337	1 531	6.3
April	161 263	101 574	63.0	95 394	51 912	35 546	9 518	3 349	92 045	59.2	6 180	1 502	6.1
May	161 518	101 896	63.1	95 769	52 050	35 597	9 668	3 325	92 444	59.3	6 127	1 420	6.0
June	161 794	102 371	63.3	96 343	52 240	35 828	9 781	3 483	92 860	59.5	6 028	1 352	5.9
July	162 034	102 399	63.2	96 090	52 190	35 764	9 749	3 441	92 649	59.3	6 309	1 373	6.2
August	162 259	102 511	63.2	96 431	52 228	35 856	9 903	3 401	93 030	59.4	6 080	1 242	5.9
September	162 502	102 795	63.3	96 670	52 284	36 274	9 700	3 400	93 270	59.5	6 125	1 308	6.0
October	162 783	103 080	63.3	97 133	52 448	36 525	9 727	3 409	93 724	59.7	5 947	1 319	5.8
November	163 017	103 562	63.5	97 485	52 802	36 559	9 704	3 284	94 201	59.8	6 077	1 242	5.9
December	163 272	103 809	63.6	97 581	52 807	36 686	9 708	3 396	94 185	59.8	6 228	1 269	6.0
1979													
January	163 516	104 057	63.6	97 948	53 072	36 697	9 749	3 305	94 643	59.9	6 109	1 250	5.9
February	163 726	104 502	63.8	98 329	53 233	36 904	9 762	3 373	94 956	60.1	6 173	1 297	5.9
March	164 027	104 589	63.8	98 480	53 120	37 159	9 751	3 368	95 112	60.0	6 109	1 365	5.8
April	164 162	104 172	63.5	98 103	53 085	36 944	9 652	3 291	94 812	59.8	6 069	1 272	5.8
May	164 459	104 171	63.3	98 331	53 178	37 134	9 553	3 272	95 059	59.8	5 840	1 239	5.6
June	164 720	104 638	63.5	98 679	53 309	37 221	9 664	3 331	95 348	59.9	5 959	1 171	5.7
July	164 970	105 002	63.6	99 006	53 384	37 514	9 606	3 335	95 671	60.0	5 996	1 123	5.7
August	165 198	105 096	63.6	98 776	53 336	37 548	9 456	3 374	95 402	59.8	6 320	1 203	6.0
September	165 431	105 530	63.8	99 340	53 510	37 798	9 623	3 371	95 969	60.0	6 190	1 172	5.9
October	165 813	105 700	63.7	99 404	53 478	37 931	9 574	3 325	96 079	59.9	6 296	1 219	6.0
November	166 051	105 812	63.7	99 574	53 435	38 065	9 599	3 436	96 138	60.0	6 238	1 239	5.9
December	166 300	106 258	63.9	99 933	53 555	38 259	9 690	3 400	96 533	60.1	6 325	1 277	6.0

1Not seasonally adjusted.
2In 1930 through 1943, the official BLS data count persons on work relief as unemployed. The unemployment rates for those years shown in parentheses count persons on work relief as employed, which is more consistent with the postwar practice. See notes and definitions.

Table 10-1B. Summary Labor Force, Employment, and Unemployment: Historical—*Continued*

(Thousands of persons, percent, seasonally adjusted, except as noted.)

Year and month	Civilian noninsti-tutional popu-lation [1]	Civilian labor force		Employment, thousands of persons						Employ-ment-population ratio, percent	Unemployment		
					By age and sex			By industry			Thousands of persons		
		Thousands of persons	Participa-tion rate (percent)	Total	Men, 20 years and over	Women, 20 years and over	Both sexes, 16 to 19 years	Agri-cultural	Nonagri-cultural		Total	Unem-ployed 15 weeks and over	Rate (percent) [2]
1980													
January	166 544	106 562	64.0	99 879	53 501	38 367	9 590	3 316	96 563	60.0	6 683	1 353	6.3
February	166 759	106 697	64.0	99 995	53 686	38 389	9 501	3 397	96 598	60.0	6 702	1 358	6.3
March	166 984	106 442	63.7	99 713	53 353	38 406	9 500	3 418	96 295	59.7	6 729	1 457	6.3
April	167 197	106 591	63.8	99 233	53 035	38 427	9 272	3 326	95 907	59.4	7 358	1 694	6.9
May	167 407	106 929	63.9	98 945	52 915	38 335	9 457	3 382	95 563	59.1	7 984	1 740	7.5
June	167 643	106 780	63.7	98 682	52 712	38 312	9 438	3 296	95 386	58.9	8 098	1 760	7.6
July	167 932	107 159	63.8	98 796	52 733	38 374	9 499	3 319	95 477	58.8	8 363	1 995	7.8
August	168 103	107 105	63.7	98 824	52 815	38 511	9 247	3 234	95 590	58.8	8 281	2 162	7.7
September	168 297	107 098	63.6	99 077	52 866	38 595	9 289	3 443	95 634	58.9	8 021	2 309	7.5
October	168 503	107 405	63.7	99 317	53 094	38 620	9 319	3 372	95 945	58.9	8 088	2 306	7.5
November	168 695	107 568	63.8	99 545	53 210	38 795	9 246	3 396	96 149	59.0	8 023	2 329	7.5
December	168 883	107 352	63.6	99 634	53 333	38 737	9 175	3 492	96 142	59.0	7 718	2 406	7.2
1981													
January	169 104	108 026	63.9	99 955	53 392	39 042	9 300	3 429	96 526	59.1	8 071	2 389	7.5
February	169 280	108 242	63.9	100 191	53 445	39 280	9 257	3 345	96 846	59.2	8 051	2 344	7.4
March	169 453	108 553	64.1	100 571	53 662	39 464	9 212	3 365	97 206	59.4	7 982	2 276	7.4
April	169 641	108 925	64.2	101 056	53 886	39 628	9 289	3 529	97 527	59.6	7 869	2 231	7.2
May	169 829	109 222	64.3	101 048	53 879	39 759	9 160	3 369	97 679	59.5	8 174	2 221	7.5
June	170 042	108 396	63.7	100 298	53 576	39 682	8 780	3 334	96 964	59.0	8 098	2 250	7.5
July	170 246	108 556	63.8	100 693	53 814	39 683	8 839	3 296	97 397	59.1	7 863	2 166	7.2
August	170 399	108 725	63.8	100 689	53 718	39 723	8 931	3 379	97 310	59.1	8 036	2 241	7.4
September	170 593	108 294	63.5	100 064	53 625	39 342	8 835	3 361	96 703	58.7	8 230	2 261	7.6
October	170 809	109 024	63.8	100 378	53 482	39 843	8 851	3 412	96 966	58.8	8 646	2 303	7.9
November	170 996	109 236	63.9	100 207	53 335	39 908	8 852	3 415	96 792	58.6	9 029	2 345	8.3
December	171 166	108 912	63.6	99 645	53 149	39 708	8 602	3 227	96 418	58.2	9 267	2 374	8.5
1982													
January	171 335	109 089	63.7	99 692	53 103	39 821	8 676	3 393	96 299	58.2	9 397	2 409	8.6
February	171 489	109 467	63.8	99 762	53 172	39 859	8 697	3 375	96 387	58.2	9 705	2 758	8.9
March	171 667	109 567	63.8	99 672	53 054	39 936	8 550	3 372	96 300	58.1	9 895	2 965	9.0
April	171 844	109 820	63.9	99 576	53 081	39 848	8 605	3 351	96 225	57.9	10 244	3 086	9.3
May	172 026	110 451	64.2	100 116	53 234	40 121	8 753	3 434	96 682	58.2	10 335	3 276	9.4
June	172 190	110 081	63.9	99 543	52 933	40 219	8 293	3 331	96 212	57.8	10 538	3 451	9.6
July	172 364	110 342	64.0	99 493	52 896	40 228	8 380	3 402	96 091	57.7	10 849	3 555	9.8
August	172 511	110 514	64.1	99 633	52 797	40 336	8 514	3 408	96 225	57.8	10 881	3 696	9.8
September	172 690	110 721	64.1	99 504	52 760	40 275	8 469	3 385	96 119	57.6	11 217	3 889	10.1
October	172 881	110 744	64.1	99 215	52 624	40 105	8 499	3 489	95 726	57.4	11 529	4 185	10.4
November	173 058	111 050	64.2	99 112	52 537	40 111	8 520	3 510	95 602	57.3	11 938	4 485	10.8
December	173 199	111 083	64.1	99 032	52 497	40 164	8 397	3 414	95 618	57.2	12 051	4 662	10.8
1983													
January	173 354	110 695	63.9	99 161	52 487	40 268	8 335	3 439	95 722	57.2	11 534	4 668	10.4
February	173 505	110 634	63.8	99 089	52 453	40 336	8 159	3 382	95 707	57.1	11 545	4 641	10.4
March	173 656	110 587	63.7	99 179	52 615	40 368	8 098	3 360	95 819	57.1	11 408	4 612	10.3
April	173 794	110 828	63.8	99 560	52 814	40 542	8 094	3 341	96 219	57.3	11 268	4 370	10.2
May	173 953	110 796	63.7	99 642	52 922	40 538	8 006	3 328	96 314	57.3	11 154	4 538	10.1
June	174 125	111 879	64.3	100 633	53 515	40 695	8 448	3 462	97 171	57.8	11 246	4 470	10.1
July	174 306	111 756	64.1	101 208	53 835	41 041	8 207	3 481	97 727	58.1	10 548	4 329	9.4
August	174 440	112 231	64.3	101 608	53 837	41 314	8 379	3 502	98 106	58.2	10 623	4 070	9.5
September	174 602	112 298	64.3	102 016	53 983	41 650	8 147	3 347	98 669	58.4	10 282	3 854	9.2
October	174 779	111 926	64.0	102 039	54 146	41 597	8 010	3 303	98 736	58.4	9 887	3 648	8.8
November	174 951	112 228	64.1	102 729	54 499	41 788	8 075	3 291	99 438	58.7	9 499	3 535	8.5
December	175 121	112 327	64.1	102 996	54 662	41 852	8 089	3 332	99 664	58.8	9 331	3 379	8.3
1984													
January	175 533	112 209	63.9	103 201	54 975	41 812	7 965	3 293	99 908	58.8	9 008	3 254	8.0
February	175 679	112 615	64.1	103 824	55 213	42 196	7 958	3 353	100 471	59.1	8 791	2 991	7.8
March	175 824	112 713	64.1	103 967	55 281	42 328	7 926	3 233	100 734	59.1	8 746	2 881	7.8
April	175 969	113 098	64.3	104 336	55 373	42 512	7 988	3 291	101 045	59.3	8 762	2 858	7.7
May	176 123	113 649	64.5	105 193	55 661	43 071	7 944	3 343	101 850	59.7	8 456	2 884	7.4
June	176 284	113 817	64.6	105 591	55 996	42 944	8 131	3 383	102 208	59.9	8 226	2 612	7.2
July	176 440	113 972	64.6	105 435	55 921	42 979	8 045	3 344	102 091	59.8	8 537	2 638	7.5
August	176 583	113 682	64.4	105 163	55 930	42 885	7 809	3 286	101 877	59.6	8 519	2 604	7.5
September	176 763	113 857	64.4	105 490	56 095	42 967	7 951	3 393	102 097	59.7	8 367	2 538	7.3
October	176 956	114 019	64.4	105 638	56 183	43 052	7 862	3 194	102 444	59.7	8 381	2 526	7.4
November	177 135	114 170	64.5	105 972	56 274	43 244	7 844	3 394	102 578	59.8	8 198	2 438	7.2
December	177 306	114 581	64.6	106 223	56 313	43 472	7 933	3 385	102 838	59.9	8 358	2 401	7.3

[1] Not seasonally adjusted.
[2] In 1930 through 1943, the official BLS data count persons on work relief as unemployed. The unemployment rates for those years shown in parentheses count persons on work relief as employed, which is more consistent with the postwar practice. See notes and definitions.

Table 10-1B. Summary Labor Force, Employment, and Unemployment: Historical—*Continued*

(Thousands of persons, percent, seasonally adjusted, except as noted.)

Year and month	Civilian noninsti-tutional popu-lation [1]	Civilian labor force		Employment, thousands of persons						Employ-ment-population ratio, percent	Unemployment		
		Thousands of persons	Participa-tion rate (percent)	Total	By age and sex			By industry			Thousands of persons		Rate (percent) [2]
					Men, 20 years and over	Women, 20 years and over	Both sexes, 16 to 19 years	Agri-cultural	Nonagri-cultural		Total	Unem-ployed 15 weeks and over	
1985													
January	177 384	114 725	64.7	106 302	56 184	43 589	8 036	3 317	102 985	59.9	8 423	2 284	7.3
February	177 516	114 876	64.7	106 555	56 216	43 787	8 020	3 317	103 238	60.0	8 321	2 389	7.2
March	177 667	115 328	64.9	106 989	56 356	44 035	8 062	3 250	103 739	60.2	8 339	2 394	7.2
April	177 799	115 331	64.9	106 936	56 374	44 000	7 958	3 306	103 630	60.1	8 395	2 393	7.3
May	177 944	115 234	64.8	106 932	56 531	43 905	7 966	3 280	103 652	60.1	8 302	2 292	7.2
June	178 096	114 965	64.6	106 505	56 288	43 958	7 680	3 161	103 344	59.8	8 460	2 310	7.4
July	178 263	115 320	64.7	106 807	56 435	43 975	8 013	3 143	103 664	59.9	8 513	2 329	7.4
August	178 405	115 291	64.6	107 095	56 655	44 103	7 714	3 121	103 974	60.0	8 196	2 258	7.1
September	178 572	115 905	64.9	107 657	56 845	44 395	7 818	3 064	104 593	60.3	8 248	2 242	7.1
October	178 770	116 145	65.0	107 847	56 969	44 565	7 889	3 051	104 796	60.3	8 298	2 295	7.1
November	178 940	116 135	64.9	108 007	56 972	44 617	7 852	3 062	104 945	60.4	8 128	2 207	7.0
December	179 112	116 354	65.0	108 216	56 995	44 889	7 826	3 141	105 075	60.4	8 138	2 208	7.0
1986													
January	179 670	116 682	64.9	108 887	57 637	44 944	7 704	3 287	105 600	60.6	7 795	2 089	6.7
February	179 821	116 882	65.0	108 480	57 269	44 804	7 895	3 083	105 397	60.3	8 402	2 308	7.2
March	179 985	117 220	65.1	108 837	57 353	44 960	7 977	3 200	105 637	60.5	8 383	2 261	7.2
April	180 148	117 316	65.1	108 952	57 358	45 081	8 058	3 153	105 799	60.5	8 364	2 162	7.1
May	180 311	117 528	65.2	109 089	57 287	45 289	7 997	3 150	105 939	60.5	8 439	2 232	7.2
June	180 503	118 084	65.4	109 576	57 471	45 621	8 024	3 193	106 383	60.7	8 508	2 320	7.2
July	180 682	118 129	65.4	109 810	57 514	45 837	7 914	3 141	106 669	60.8	8 319	2 269	7.0
August	180 828	118 150	65.3	110 015	57 597	45 926	7 920	3 082	106 933	60.8	8 135	2 276	6.9
September	180 997	118 395	65.4	110 085	57 630	45 972	7 945	3 171	106 914	60.8	8 310	2 318	7.0
October	181 186	118 516	65.4	110 273	57 660	46 046	7 977	3 128	107 145	60.9	8 243	2 188	7.0
November	181 363	118 634	65.4	110 475	57 941	46 070	7 891	3 220	107 255	60.9	8 159	2 202	6.9
December	181 547	118 611	65.3	110 728	58 185	46 132	7 769	3 148	107 580	61.0	7 883	2 161	6.6
1987													
January	181 827	118 845	65.4	110 953	58 264	46 219	7 861	3 143	107 810	61.0	7 892	2 168	6.6
February	181 998	119 122	65.5	111 257	58 279	46 444	7 969	3 208	108 049	61.1	7 865	2 117	6.6
March	182 179	119 270	65.5	111 408	58 362	46 549	7 913	3 214	108 194	61.2	7 862	2 070	6.6
April	182 344	119 336	65.4	111 794	58 503	46 746	7 916	3 246	108 548	61.3	7 542	2 091	6.3
May	182 533	120 008	65.7	112 434	58 713	47 052	8 075	3 345	109 089	61.6	7 574	2 104	6.3
June	182 703	119 644	65.5	112 246	58 581	47 102	7 857	3 216	109 030	61.4	7 398	2 087	6.2
July	182 885	119 902	65.6	112 634	58 740	47 229	7 911	3 235	109 399	61.6	7 268	1 921	6.1
August	183 002	120 318	65.7	113 057	58 810	47 322	8 232	3 112	109 945	61.8	7 261	1 878	6.0
September	183 161	120 011	65.5	112 909	58 964	47 285	7 945	3 189	109 720	61.6	7 102	1 866	5.9
October	183 311	120 509	65.7	113 282	59 073	47 533	8 074	3 219	110 063	61.8	7 227	1 794	6.0
November	183 470	120 540	65.7	113 505	59 210	47 622	8 002	3 145	110 360	61.9	7 035	1 797	5.8
December	183 620	120 729	65.7	113 793	59 217	47 781	8 092	3 213	110 580	62.0	6 936	1 767	5.7
1988													
January	183 822	120 969	65.8	114 016	59 346	47 862	8 110	3 247	110 769	62.0	6 953	1 714	5.7
February	183 969	121 156	65.9	114 227	59 535	47 919	8 025	3 201	111 026	62.1	6 929	1 738	5.7
March	184 111	120 913	65.7	114 037	59 393	48 090	7 854	3 169	110 868	61.9	6 876	1 744	5.7
April	184 232	121 251	65.8	114 650	59 832	48 147	7 937	3 224	111 426	62.2	6 601	1 563	5.4
May	184 374	121 071	65.7	114 292	59 644	47 946	7 912	3 121	111 171	62.0	6 779	1 647	5.6
June	184 562	121 473	65.8	114 927	59 751	48 146	8 193	3 111	111 816	62.3	6 546	1 531	5.4
July	184 729	121 665	65.9	115 060	59 888	48 186	8 198	3 060	112 000	62.3	6 605	1 601	5.4
August	184 830	122 125	66.1	115 282	59 877	48 467	8 201	3 119	112 163	62.4	6 843	1 639	5.6
September	184 962	121 960	65.9	115 356	59 980	48 511	8 124	3 165	112 191	62.4	6 604	1 569	5.4
October	185 114	122 206	66.0	115 638	60 023	48 859	7 961	3 231	112 407	62.5	6 568	1 562	5.4
November	185 244	122 637	66.2	116 100	60 042	49 254	7 904	3 241	112 859	62.7	6 537	1 468	5.3
December	185 402	122 622	66.1	116 104	60 059	49 257	7 966	3 194	112 910	62.6	6 518	1 490	5.3
1989													
January	185 644	123 390	66.5	116 708	60 477	49 529	8 019	3 287	113 421	62.9	6 682	1 480	5.4
February	185 777	123 135	66.3	116 776	60 588	49 497	7 871	3 234	113 542	62.9	6 359	1 304	5.2
March	185 897	123 227	66.3	117 022	60 795	49 503	7 809	3 198	113 824	62.9	6 205	1 353	5.0
April	186 024	123 565	66.4	117 097	60 764	49 565	7 929	3 162	113 935	62.9	6 468	1 397	5.2
May	186 181	123 474	66.3	117 099	60 795	49 583	7 890	3 125	113 974	62.9	6 375	1 348	5.2
June	186 329	123 995	66.5	117 418	61 054	49 542	8 094	3 068	114 350	63.0	6 577	1 300	5.3
July	186 483	123 967	66.5	117 472	60 947	49 693	7 961	3 227	114 245	63.0	6 495	1 435	5.2
August	186 598	124 166	66.5	117 655	60 915	49 804	8 126	3 284	114 371	63.1	6 511	1 302	5.2
September	186 726	123 944	66.4	117 354	60 668	50 015	7 870	3 219	114 135	62.8	6 590	1 360	5.3
October	186 871	124 211	66.5	117 581	60 958	49 871	7 940	3 215	114 366	62.9	6 630	1 392	5.3
November	187 017	124 637	66.6	117 912	60 958	50 221	7 964	3 132	114 780	63.0	6 725	1 418	5.4
December	187 165	124 497	66.5	117 830	61 068	50 116	7 851	3 188	114 642	63.0	6 667	1 375	5.4

[1]Not seasonally adjusted.
[2]In 1930 through 1943, the official BLS data count persons on work relief as unemployed. The unemployment rates for those years shown in parentheses count persons on work relief as employed, which is more consistent with the postwar practice. See notes and definitions.

Table 10-1B. Summary Labor Force, Employment, and Unemployment: Historical—*Continued*

(Thousands of persons, percent, seasonally adjusted, except as noted.)

Year and month	Civilian noninstitutional population [1]	Civilian labor force — Thousands of persons	Civilian labor force — Participation rate (percent)	Employment — Total	By age and sex — Men, 20 years and over	By age and sex — Women, 20 years and over	By age and sex — Both sexes, 16 to 19 years	By industry — Agricultural	By industry — Nonagricultural	Employment-population ratio, percent	Unemployment — Total	Unemployment — Unemployed 15 weeks and over	Rate (percent) [2]
1990													
January	188 413	125 833	66.8	119 081	61 742	50 436	8 103	3 210	115 871	63.2	6 752	1 412	5.4
February	188 516	125 710	66.7	119 059	61 805	50 438	8 015	3 188	115 871	63.2	6 651	1 350	5.3
March	188 630	125 801	66.7	119 203	61 832	50 463	8 061	3 260	115 943	63.2	6 598	1 331	5.2
April	188 778	125 649	66.6	118 852	61 579	50 457	7 987	3 231	115 621	63.0	6 797	1 376	5.4
May	188 913	125 893	66.6	119 151	61 778	50 646	7 911	3 266	115 885	63.1	6 742	1 415	5.4
June	189 058	125 573	66.4	118 983	61 762	50 550	7 783	3 245	115 738	62.9	6 590	1 436	5.2
July	189 188	125 732	66.5	118 810	61 683	50 514	7 777	3 192	115 618	62.8	6 922	1 534	5.5
August	189 342	125 990	66.5	118 802	61 715	50 635	7 708	3 197	115 605	62.7	7 188	1 607	5.7
September	189 528	125 892	66.4	118 524	61 608	50 587	7 575	3 206	115 318	62.5	7 368	1 695	5.9
October	189 710	125 995	66.4	118 536	61 606	50 616	7 565	3 270	115 266	62.5	7 459	1 689	5.9
November	189 872	126 070	66.4	118 306	61 545	50 541	7 506	3 189	115 117	62.3	7 764	1 831	6.2
December	190 017	126 142	66.4	118 241	61 506	50 530	7 516	3 245	114 996	62.2	7 901	1 804	6.3
1991													
January	190 163	125 955	66.2	117 940	61 383	50 472	7 478	3 208	114 732	62.0	8 015	1 866	6.4
February	190 271	126 020	66.2	117 755	61 117	50 523	7 405	3 270	114 485	61.9	8 265	1 955	6.6
March	190 381	126 238	66.3	117 652	61 144	50 422	7 447	3 177	114 475	61.8	8 586	2 137	6.8
April	190 517	126 548	66.4	118 109	61 280	50 760	7 381	3 241	114 868	62.0	8 439	2 206	6.7
May	190 650	126 176	66.2	117 440	61 052	50 457	7 303	3 275	114 165	61.6	8 736	2 252	6.9
June	190 800	126 331	66.2	117 639	61 147	50 585	7 248	3 300	114 339	61.7	8 692	2 533	6.9
July	190 946	126 154	66.1	117 568	61 179	50 636	7 138	3 319	114 249	61.6	8 586	2 388	6.8
August	191 116	126 150	66.0	117 484	61 122	50 601	7 105	3 313	114 171	61.5	8 666	2 460	6.9
September	191 302	126 650	66.2	117 928	61 279	50 864	7 123	3 319	114 609	61.6	8 722	2 497	6.9
October	191 497	126 642	66.1	117 800	61 174	50 811	7 185	3 289	114 511	61.5	8 842	2 638	7.0
November	191 657	126 701	66.1	117 770	61 201	50 759	7 169	3 296	114 474	61.4	8 931	2 718	7.0
December	191 798	126 664	66.0	117 466	61 074	50 728	7 104	3 146	114 320	61.2	9 198	2 892	7.3
1992													
January	191 953	127 261	66.3	117 978	61 116	51 095	7 138	3 155	114 823	61.5	9 283	3 060	7.3
February	192 067	127 207	66.2	117 753	61 062	51 033	7 083	3 239	114 514	61.3	9 454	3 182	7.4
March	192 204	127 604	66.4	118 144	61 363	51 204	6 998	3 236	114 908	61.5	9 460	3 196	7.4
April	192 354	127 841	66.5	118 426	61 468	51 323	6 910	3 245	115 181	61.6	9 415	3 130	7.4
May	192 503	128 119	66.6	118 375	61 513	51 245	7 028	3 213	115 162	61.5	9 744	3 444	7.6
June	192 663	128 459	66.7	118 419	61 537	51 383	7 137	3 297	115 122	61.5	10 040	3 758	7.8
July	192 826	128 563	66.7	118 713	61 641	51 458	7 087	3 285	115 428	61.6	9 850	3 614	7.7
August	193 018	128 613	66.6	118 826	61 681	51 386	7 194	3 279	115 547	61.6	9 787	3 579	7.6
September	193 229	128 501	66.5	118 720	61 663	51 359	7 216	3 274	115 446	61.4	9 781	3 504	7.6
October	193 442	128 026	66.2	118 628	61 550	51 373	6 985	3 254	115 374	61.3	9 398	3 505	7.3
November	193 621	128 441	66.3	118 876	61 644	51 535	7 164	3 207	115 669	61.4	9 565	3 397	7.4
December	193 784	128 554	66.3	118 997	61 721	51 524	7 174	3 259	115 738	61.4	9 557	3 651	7.4
1993													
January	193 962	128 400	66.2	119 075	61 895	51 505	7 089	3 222	115 853	61.4	9 325	3 346	7.3
February	194 108	128 458	66.2	119 275	61 963	51 573	7 144	3 125	116 150	61.4	9 183	3 190	7.1
March	194 248	128 598	66.2	119 542	62 007	51 808	7 132	3 119	116 423	61.5	9 056	3 115	7.0
April	194 398	128 584	66.1	119 474	62 032	51 732	7 091	3 074	116 400	61.5	9 110	3 014	7.1
May	194 549	129 264	66.4	120 115	62 309	51 996	7 244	3 100	117 015	61.7	9 149	3 101	7.1
June	194 719	129 411	66.5	120 290	62 409	52 183	7 114	3 108	117 182	61.8	9 121	3 141	7.0
July	194 882	129 397	66.4	120 467	62 497	52 088	7 205	3 126	117 341	61.8	8 930	3 046	6.9
August	195 063	129 619	66.4	120 856	62 634	52 294	7 264	3 026	117 830	62.0	8 763	3 026	6.8
September	195 259	129 268	66.2	120 554	62 437	52 241	7 180	3 174	117 380	61.7	8 714	3 042	6.7
October	195 444	129 573	66.3	120 823	62 614	52 379	7 171	3 084	117 739	61.8	8 750	3 029	6.8
November	195 625	129 711	66.3	121 169	62 732	52 531	7 248	3 157	118 012	61.9	8 542	2 986	6.6
December	195 794	129 941	66.4	121 464	62 760	52 813	7 178	3 116	118 348	62.0	8 477	2 968	6.5
1994													
January	195 953	130 596	66.6	121 966	62 798	53 052	7 486	3 302	118 664	62.2	8 630	3 060	6.6
February	196 090	130 669	66.6	122 086	62 708	53 266	7 457	3 339	118 747	62.3	8 583	3 118	6.6
March	196 213	130 400	66.5	121 930	62 780	53 099	7 381	3 354	118 576	62.1	8 470	3 055	6.5
April	196 363	130 621	66.5	122 290	62 906	53 274	7 551	3 428	118 862	62.3	8 331	2 921	6.4
May	196 510	130 779	66.6	122 864	63 116	53 624	7 466	3 409	119 455	62.5	7 915	2 836	6.1
June	196 693	130 561	66.4	122 634	63 041	53 393	7 527	3 299	119 335	62.3	7 927	2 735	6.1
July	196 859	130 652	66.4	122 706	63 034	53 531	7 453	3 333	119 373	62.3	7 946	2 822	6.1
August	197 043	131 275	66.6	123 342	63 294	53 744	7 619	3 451	119 891	62.6	7 933	2 750	6.0
September	197 248	131 421	66.6	123 687	63 631	53 991	7 352	3 430	120 257	62.7	7 734	2 746	5.9
October	197 430	131 744	66.7	124 112	63 818	54 071	7 543	3 490	120 622	62.9	7 632	2 955	5.8
November	197 607	131 891	66.7	124 516	64 080	54 168	7 423	3 574	120 942	63.0	7 375	2 666	5.6
December	197 765	131 951	66.7	124 721	64 359	54 054	7 599	3 577	121 144	63.1	7 230	2 488	5.5

[1] Not seasonally adjusted.
[2] In 1930 through 1943, the official BLS data count persons on work relief as unemployed. The unemployment rates for those years shown in parentheses count persons on work relief as employed, which is more consistent with the postwar practice. See notes and definitions.

Table 10-1B. Summary Labor Force, Employment, and Unemployment: Historical—*Continued*

(Thousands of persons, percent, seasonally adjusted, except as noted.)

Year and month	Civilian noninsti-tutional popu-lation [1]	Civilian labor force		Employment, thousands of persons						Employ-ment-population ratio, percent	Unemployment		
					By age and sex			By industry			Thousands of persons		
		Thousands of persons	Participa-tion rate (percent)	Total	Men, 20 years and over	Women, 20 years and over	Both sexes, 16 to 19 years	Agri-cultural	Nonagri-cultural		Total	Unem-ployed 15 weeks and over	Rate (percent) [2]
1995													
January	197 753	132 038	66.8	124 663	64 185	54 087	7 650	3 519	121 144	63.0	7 375	2 396	5.6
February	197 886	132 115	66.8	124 928	64 378	54 226	7 659	3 620	121 308	63.1	7 187	2 345	5.4
March	198 007	132 108	66.7	124 955	64 321	54 141	7 742	3 634	121 321	63.1	7 153	2 287	5.4
April	198 148	132 590	66.9	124 945	64 165	54 366	7 774	3 566	121 379	63.1	7 645	2 473	5.8
May	198 286	131 851	66.5	124 421	63 829	54 272	7 664	3 349	121 072	62.7	7 430	2 577	5.6
June	198 452	131 949	66.5	124 522	63 992	54 020	7 850	3 461	121 061	62.7	7 427	2 266	5.6
July	198 615	132 343	66.6	124 816	63 962	54 476	7 798	3 379	121 437	62.8	7 527	2 311	5.7
August	198 801	132 336	66.6	124 852	63 875	54 434	7 910	3 374	121 478	62.8	7 484	2 391	5.7
September	199 005	132 611	66.6	125 133	64 179	54 507	7 825	3 285	121 848	62.9	7 478	2 306	5.6
October	199 192	132 716	66.6	125 388	64 272	54 692	7 774	3 438	121 950	62.9	7 328	2 272	5.5
November	199 355	132 614	66.5	125 188	63 931	54 850	7 765	3 338	121 850	62.8	7 426	2 339	5.6
December	199 508	132 511	66.4	125 088	64 041	54 674	7 768	3 352	121 736	62.7	7 423	2 331	5.6
1996													
January	199 634	132 616	66.4	125 125	64 180	54 580	7 733	3 483	121 642	62.7	7 491	2 371	5.6
February	199 772	132 952	66.6	125 639	64 398	54 844	7 688	3 547	122 092	62.9	7 313	2 307	5.5
March	199 921	133 180	66.6	125 862	64 506	54 994	7 673	3 489	122 373	63.0	7 318	2 454	5.5
April	200 101	133 409	66.7	125 994	64 481	55 067	7 774	3 406	122 588	63.0	7 415	2 455	5.6
May	200 278	133 667	66.7	126 244	64 683	55 034	7 841	3 473	122 771	63.0	7 423	2 403	5.6
June	200 459	133 697	66.7	126 602	64 940	55 177	7 739	3 424	123 178	63.2	7 095	2 355	5.3
July	200 641	134 284	66.9	126 947	65 068	55 362	7 859	3 433	123 514	63.3	7 337	2 297	5.5
August	200 847	134 054	66.7	127 172	65 216	55 525	7 731	3 395	123 777	63.3	6 882	2 267	5.1
September	201 060	134 515	66.9	127 536	65 169	55 669	7 935	3 448	124 088	63.4	6 979	2 220	5.2
October	201 273	134 921	67.0	127 890	65 460	55 750	7 980	3 463	124 427	63.5	7 031	2 268	5.2
November	201 463	135 007	67.0	127 771	65 320	55 896	7 875	3 356	124 415	63.4	7 236	2 159	5.4
December	201 636	135 113	67.0	127 860	65 435	55 849	7 883	3 445	124 415	63.4	7 253	2 124	5.4
1997													
January	202 285	135 456	67.0	128 298	65 679	56 024	7 930	3 449	124 849	63.4	7 158	2 162	5.3
February	202 388	135 400	66.9	128 298	65 758	55 955	7 948	3 353	124 945	63.4	7 102	2 140	5.2
March	202 513	135 891	67.1	128 891	65 974	56 270	7 951	3 419	125 472	63.6	7 000	2 110	5.2
April	202 674	136 016	67.1	129 143	66 092	56 347	7 974	3 462	125 681	63.7	6 873	2 176	5.1
May	202 832	136 119	67.1	129 464	66 328	56 446	7 964	3 437	126 027	63.8	6 655	2 121	4.9
June	203 000	136 211	67.1	129 412	66 308	56 573	7 849	3 409	126 003	63.7	6 799	2 085	5.0
July	203 166	136 477	67.2	129 822	66 422	56 785	7 975	3 422	126 400	63.9	6 655	2 119	4.9
August	203 364	136 618	67.2	130 010	66 508	56 852	7 922	3 359	126 651	63.9	6 608	2 004	4.8
September	203 570	136 675	67.1	130 019	66 483	56 931	7 873	3 392	126 627	63.9	6 656	2 074	4.9
October	203 767	136 633	67.1	130 179	66 511	56 982	7 876	3 312	126 867	63.9	6 454	1 950	4.7
November	203 941	136 961	67.2	130 653	66 765	57 039	8 042	3 386	127 267	64.1	6 308	1 817	4.6
December	204 098	137 155	67.2	130 679	66 643	57 219	7 923	3 405	127 274	64.0	6 476	1 901	4.7
1998													
January	204 238	137 095	67.1	130 726	66 750	56 941	8 171	3 299	127 389	64.0	6 368	1 833	4.6
February	204 400	137 112	67.1	130 807	66 856	56 992	8 137	3 284	127 522	64.0	6 306	1 809	4.6
March	204 546	137 236	67.1	130 814	66 721	57 080	8 235	3 146	127 650	64.0	6 422	1 772	4.7
April	204 731	137 150	67.0	131 209	67 151	57 074	8 071	3 334	127 852	64.1	5 941	1 476	4.3
May	204 899	137 372	67.0	131 325	67 164	57 155	8 228	3 360	127 959	64.1	6 047	1 490	4.4
June	205 085	137 455	67.0	131 244	67 054	57 156	8 268	3 380	127 874	64.0	6 212	1 613	4.5
July	205 270	137 588	67.0	131 329	67 119	57 192	8 221	3 455	127 913	64.0	6 259	1 577	4.5
August	205 479	137 570	67.0	131 390	66 985	57 332	8 289	3 509	127 970	63.9	6 179	1 626	4.5
September	205 699	138 286	67.2	131 986	67 254	57 520	8 489	3 500	128 399	64.2	6 300	1 688	4.6
October	205 919	138 279	67.2	131 999	67 433	57 529	8 347	3 593	128 389	64.1	6 280	1 582	4.5
November	206 104	138 381	67.1	132 280	67 591	57 638	8 269	3 375	128 897	64.2	6 100	1 590	4.4
December	206 270	138 634	67.2	132 602	67 548	57 840	8 340	3 246	129 320	64.3	6 032	1 559	4.4
1999													
January	206 719	139 003	67.2	133 027	67 679	58 256	8 367	3 233	129 802	64.4	5 976	1 490	4.3
February	206 873	138 967	67.2	132 856	67 498	58 129	8 399	3 246	129 647	64.2	6 111	1 551	4.4
March	207 036	138 730	67.0	132 947	67 660	58 132	8 343	3 238	129 656	64.2	5 783	1 472	4.2
April	207 236	138 959	67.1	132 955	67 542	58 260	8 334	3 336	129 615	64.2	6 004	1 480	4.3
May	207 427	139 107	67.1	133 311	67 539	58 440	8 454	3 335	129 937	64.3	5 796	1 505	4.2
June	207 632	139 329	67.1	133 378	67 700	58 641	8 175	3 386	129 982	64.2	5 951	1 624	4.3
July	207 828	139 439	67.1	133 414	67 731	58 490	8 306	3 346	130 146	64.2	6 025	1 513	4.3
August	208 038	139 430	67.0	133 591	67 768	58 707	8 208	3 234	130 366	64.2	5 838	1 455	4.2
September	208 265	139 622	67.0	133 707	67 882	58 735	8 323	3 173	130 434	64.2	5 915	1 449	4.2
October	208 483	139 771	67.0	133 993	67 840	58 921	8 394	3 229	130 758	64.3	5 778	1 438	4.1
November	208 666	140 025	67.1	134 309	68 094	59 018	8 358	3 343	130 989	64.4	5 716	1 378	4.1
December	208 832	140 177	67.1	134 523	68 217	59 056	8 370	3 260	131 257	64.4	5 653	1 375	4.0

[1] Not seasonally adjusted.
[2] In 1930 through 1943, the official BLS data count persons on work relief as unemployed. The unemployment rates for those years shown in parentheses count persons on work relief as employed, which is more consistent with the postwar practice. See notes and definitions.

Table 10-1B. Summary Labor Force, Employment, and Unemployment: Historical—*Continued*

(Thousands of persons, percent, seasonally adjusted, except as noted.)

Year and month	Civilian noninstitutional population [1]	Civilian labor force Thousands of persons	Civilian labor force Participation rate (percent)	Employment Total	By age and sex Men, 20 years and over	By age and sex Women, 20 years and over	By age and sex Both sexes, 16 to 19 years	By industry Agricultural	By industry Nonagricultural	Employment-population ratio, percent	Unemployment Total	Unemployment Unemployed 15 weeks and over	Rate (percent) [2]
2000													
January	211 410	142 267	67.3	136 559	69 419	59 842	8 360	2 613	133 863	64.6	5 708	1 380	4.0
February	211 576	142 456	67.3	136 598	69 505	59 887	8 359	2 731	133 912	64.6	5 858	1 300	4.1
March	211 772	142 434	67.3	136 701	69 482	59 977	8 355	2 579	134 022	64.6	5 733	1 312	4.0
April	212 018	142 751	67.3	137 270	69 519	60 358	8 458	2 505	134 806	64.7	5 481	1 261	3.8
May	212 242	142 388	67.1	136 630	69 399	59 951	8 344	2 480	134 144	64.4	5 758	1 325	4.0
June	212 466	142 591	67.1	136 940	69 629	60 027	8 308	2 445	134 528	64.5	5 651	1 242	4.0
July	212 677	142 278	66.9	136 531	69 525	60 011	8 078	2 408	134 196	64.2	5 747	1 343	4.0
August	212 916	142 514	66.9	136 662	69 823	59 719	8 280	2 433	134 311	64.2	5 853	1 394	4.1
September	213 163	142 518	66.9	136 893	69 700	60 083	8 176	2 384	134 489	64.2	5 625	1 290	3.9
October	213 405	142 622	66.8	137 088	69 762	60 238	8 124	2 319	134 808	64.2	5 534	1 337	3.9
November	213 540	142 962	66.9	137 322	69 910	60 269	8 211	2 330	134 921	64.3	5 639	1 315	3.9
December	213 736	143 248	67.0	137 614	69 939	60 503	8 258	2 389	135 194	64.4	5 634	1 329	3.9
2001													
January	213 888	143 800	67.2	137 778	70 064	60 609	8 243	2 360	135 304	64.4	6 023	1 372	4.2
February	214 110	143 701	67.1	137 612	69 959	60 615	8 154	2 370	135 291	64.3	6 089	1 491	4.2
March	214 305	143 924	67.2	137 783	69 881	60 902	8 120	2 350	135 372	64.3	6 141	1 521	4.3
April	214 525	143 569	66.9	137 299	69 916	60 523	7 970	2 336	135 036	64.0	6 271	1 499	4.4
May	214 732	143 318	66.7	137 092	69 865	60 509	7 760	2 353	134 735	63.8	6 226	1 502	4.3
June	214 950	143 357	66.7	136 873	69 690	60 371	7 942	2 082	134 755	63.7	6 484	1 532	4.5
July	215 180	143 654	66.8	137 071	69 808	60 480	7 929	2 295	134 858	63.7	6 583	1 653	4.6
August	215 420	143 284	66.5	136 241	69 585	60 301	7 531	2 305	133 944	63.2	7 042	1 861	4.9
September	215 665	143 989	66.8	136 846	69 933	60 265	7 836	2 322	134 558	63.5	7 142	1 950	5.0
October	215 903	144 086	66.7	136 392	69 621	60 168	7 858	2 327	134 098	63.2	7 694	2 082	5.3
November	216 117	144 240	66.7	136 238	69 444	60 174	7 873	2 203	133 955	63.0	8 003	2 318	5.5
December	216 315	144 305	66.7	136 047	69 551	60 095	7 712	2 293	133 751	62.9	8 258	2 444	5.7
2002													
January	216 506	143 883	66.5	135 701	69 308	60 032	7 619	2 385	133 233	62.7	8 182	2 578	5.7
February	216 663	144 653	66.8	136 438	69 534	60 479	7 650	2 397	134 127	63.0	8 215	2 608	5.7
March	216 823	144 481	66.6	136 177	69 480	60 190	7 802	2 368	133 816	62.8	8 304	2 719	5.7
April	217 006	144 725	66.7	136 126	69 574	60 204	7 621	2 371	133 833	62.7	8 599	2 852	5.9
May	217 198	144 938	66.7	136 539	69 981	60 226	7 588	2 260	134 278	62.9	8 399	2 967	5.8
June	217 407	144 808	66.6	136 415	69 769	60 297	7 617	2 161	134 135	62.7	8 393	3 023	5.8
July	217 630	144 803	66.5	136 413	69 806	60 290	7 591	2 324	134 107	62.7	8 390	2 966	5.8
August	217 866	145 009	66.6	136 705	69 937	60 560	7 477	2 127	134 593	62.7	8 304	2 887	5.7
September	218 107	145 552	66.7	137 302	70 207	60 679	7 667	2 285	135 102	63.0	8 251	2 971	5.7
October	218 340	145 314	66.6	137 008	69 948	60 663	7 537	2 471	134 580	62.7	8 307	3 042	5.7
November	218 548	145 041	66.4	136 521	69 615	60 697	7 487	2 261	134 171	62.5	8 520	3 062	5.9
December	218 741	145 066	66.3	136 426	69 620	60 667	7 385	2 352	134 071	62.4	8 640	3 271	6.0
2003													
January	219 897	145 937	66.4	137 417	69 919	61 406	7 358	2 337	135 045	62.5	8 520	3 166	5.8
February	220 114	146 100	66.4	137 482	70 262	61 159	7 322	2 234	135 306	62.5	8 618	3 161	5.9
March	220 317	146 022	66.3	137 434	70 243	61 317	7 143	2 263	135 232	62.4	8 588	3 161	5.9
April	220 540	146 474	66.4	137 633	70 311	61 374	7 223	2 150	135 561	62.4	8 842	3 348	6.0
May	220 768	146 500	66.4	137 544	70 215	61 393	7 228	2 183	135 370	62.3	8 957	3 318	6.1
June	221 014	147 056	66.5	137 790	70 159	61 747	7 268	2 185	135 419	62.3	9 266	3 552	6.3
July	221 252	146 485	66.2	137 474	70 190	61 437	7 150	2 187	135 242	62.1	9 011	3 633	6.2
August	221 507	146 445	66.1	137 549	70 227	61 442	7 035	2 313	135 200	62.1	8 896	3 557	6.1
September	221 779	146 530	66.1	137 609	70 631	61 119	7 112	2 349	135 355	62.0	8 921	3 486	6.1
October	222 039	146 716	66.1	137 984	70 685	61 451	7 060	2 479	135 571	62.1	8 732	3 451	6.0
November	222 279	147 000	66.1	138 424	70 935	61 494	7 112	2 373	136 003	62.3	8 576	3 420	5.8
December	222 509	146 729	65.9	138 411	71 170	61 396	6 978	2 243	136 145	62.2	8 317	3 366	5.7
2004													
January	222 161	146 842	66.1	138 472	71 318	61 183	7 194	2 196	136 228	62.3	8 370	3 364	5.7
February	222 357	146 709	66.0	138 542	71 122	61 514	7 077	2 210	136 362	62.3	8 167	3 248	5.6
March	222 550	146 944	66.0	138 453	71 155	61 534	6 930	2 180	136 302	62.2	8 491	3 314	5.8
April	222 757	146 850	65.9	138 680	71 121	61 647	7 093	2 241	136 474	62.3	8 170	2 971	5.6
May	222 967	147 065	66.0	138 852	71 180	61 762	7 126	2 300	136 556	62.3	8 212	3 103	5.6
June	223 196	147 460	66.1	139 174	71 562	61 793	7 007	2 237	136 748	62.4	8 286	3 130	5.6
July	223 422	147 692	66.1	139 556	71 780	61 884	7 166	2 222	137 354	62.5	8 136	2 918	5.5
August	223 677	147 564	66.0	139 573	71 808	61 836	7 123	2 333	137 230	62.4	7 990	2 846	5.4
September	223 941	147 415	65.8	139 487	71 744	61 859	7 056	2 251	137 323	62.3	7 927	2 910	5.4
October	224 192	147 793	65.9	139 732	71 860	61 942	7 180	2 216	137 598	62.3	8 061	3 041	5.5
November	224 422	148 162	66.0	140 231	72 110	62 088	7 216	2 206	137 978	62.5	7 932	2 960	5.4
December	224 640	148 059	65.9	140 125	72 058	62 136	7 202	2 171	137 947	62.4	7 934	2 927	5.4

[1]Not seasonally adjusted.
[2]In 1930 through 1943, the official BLS data count persons on work relief as unemployed. The unemployment rates for those years shown in parentheses count persons on work relief as employed, which is more consistent with the postwar practice. See notes and definitions.

Table 10-1B. Summary Labor Force, Employment, and Unemployment: Historical—*Continued*

(Thousands of persons, percent, seasonally adjusted, except as noted.)

Year and month	Civilian noninstitutional population [1]	Civilian labor force		Employment, thousands of persons						Employment-population ratio, percent	Unemployment		Rate (percent) [2]
		Thousands of persons	Participation rate (percent)	Total	Men, 20 years and over	Women, 20 years and over	Both sexes, 16 to 19 years	Agricultural	Nonagricultural		Thousands of persons Total	Unemployed 15 weeks and over	
2005													
January	224 837	148 029	65.8	140 245	72 063	62 260	7 071	2 112	138 111	62.4	7 784	2 851	5.3
February	225 041	148 364	65.9	140 385	72 299	62 253	7 073	2 129	138 267	62.4	7 980	2 896	5.4
March	225 236	148 391	65.9	140 654	72 478	62 222	7 185	2 180	138 462	62.4	7 737	2 817	5.2
April	225 441	148 926	66.1	141 254	72 860	62 483	7 190	2 248	138 992	62.7	7 672	2 678	5.2
May	225 670	149 261	66.1	141 609	73 133	62 557	7 201	2 225	139 379	62.8	7 651	2 683	5.1
June	225 911	149 238	66.1	141 714	73 223	62 516	7 140	2 302	139 276	62.7	7 524	2 405	5.0
July	226 153	149 432	66.1	142 026	73 337	62 691	7 150	2 308	139 789	62.8	7 406	2 449	5.0
August	226 421	149 779	66.2	142 434	73 513	62 844	7 240	2 183	140 277	62.9	7 345	2 569	4.9
September	226 693	149 954	66.1	142 401	73 333	63 035	7 141	2 181	140 276	62.8	7 553	2 537	5.0
October	226 959	150 001	66.1	142 548	73 445	63 127	7 124	2 191	140 435	62.8	7 453	2 492	5.0
November	227 204	150 065	66.0	142 499	73 341	63 127	7 265	2 174	140 299	62.7	7 566	2 486	5.0
December	227 425	150 030	66.0	142 752	73 467	63 209	7 139	2 094	140 635	62.8	7 279	2 429	4.9
2006													
January	227 553	150 214	66.0	143 150	73 892	63 151	7 197	2 164	140 933	62.9	7 064	2 270	4.7
February	227 763	150 641	66.1	143 457	73 972	63 304	7 298	2 178	141 254	63.0	7 184	2 546	4.8
March	227 975	150 813	66.2	143 741	74 228	63 353	7 342	2 153	141 604	63.1	7 072	2 373	4.7
April	228 199	150 881	66.1	143 761	74 204	63 413	7 198	2 249	141 388	63.0	7 120	2 353	4.7
May	228 428	151 069	66.1	144 089	74 229	63 656	7 215	2 194	141 859	63.1	6 980	2 303	4.6
June	228 671	151 354	66.2	144 353	74 261	63 866	7 393	2 256	142 019	63.1	7 001	2 127	4.6
July	228 912	151 377	66.1	144 202	74 011	64 030	7 324	2 278	142 066	63.0	7 175	2 289	4.7
August	229 167	151 716	66.2	144 625	74 384	64 139	7 266	2 240	142 440	63.1	7 091	2 293	4.7
September	229 420	151 662	66.1	144 815	74 866	63 922	7 196	2 182	142 661	63.1	6 847	2 231	4.5
October	229 675	152 041	66.2	145 314	74 833	64 298	7 289	2 183	143 222	63.3	6 727	2 062	4.4
November	229 905	152 406	66.3	145 534	74 962	64 328	7 331	2 164	143 350	63.3	6 872	2 159	4.5
December	230 108	152 732	66.4	145 970	75 232	64 518	7 287	2 233	143 716	63.4	6 762	2 083	4.4
2007													
January	230 650	153 144	66.4	146 028	75 238	64 621	7 240	2 214	143 785	63.3	7 116	2 156	4.6
February	230 834	152 983	66.3	146 057	75 239	64 750	7 133	2 295	143 741	63.3	6 927	2 211	4.5
March	231 034	153 051	66.2	146 320	75 386	64 928	7 061	2 178	144 153	63.3	6 731	2 255	4.4
April	231 253	152 435	65.9	145 586	75 342	64 366	6 985	2 069	143 385	63.0	6 850	2 281	4.5
May	231 480	152 670	66.0	145 903	75 386	64 724	6 888	2 081	143 773	63.0	6 766	2 231	4.4
June	231 713	153 041	66.0	146 063	75 327	64 788	7 109	1 946	144 112	63.0	6 979	2 281	4.6
July	231 958	153 054	66.0	145 905	75 247	64 766	6 953	2 016	144 041	62.9	7 149	2 364	4.7
August	232 211	152 749	65.8	145 682	75 195	64 838	6 714	1 863	143 865	62.7	7 067	2 333	4.6
September	232 461	153 414	66.0	146 244	75 273	65 086	7 001	2 095	144 148	62.9	7 170	2 355	4.7
October	232 715	153 183	65.8	145 946	75 146	64 842	7 039	2 121	143 926	62.7	7 237	2 300	4.7
November	232 939	153 835	66.0	146 595	75 683	64 985	7 071	2 148	144 413	62.9	7 240	2 366	4.7
December	233 156	153 918	66.0	146 273	75 510	64 910	7 032	2 219	144 018	62.7	7 645	2 501	5.0
2008													
January	232 616	154 063	66.2	146 378	75 551	65 058	7 015	2 205	144 168	62.9	7 685	2 540	5.0
February	232 809	153 653	66.0	146 156	75 450	65 021	6 820	2 190	143 943	62.8	7 497	2 446	4.9
March	232 995	153 908	66.1	146 086	75 294	65 074	6 813	2 172	143 871	62.7	7 822	2 491	5.1
April	233 198	153 769	65.9	146 132	75 182	65 107	6 947	2 115	143 874	62.7	7 637	2 687	5.0
May	233 405	154 303	66.1	145 908	74 953	65 137	7 182	2 113	143 737	62.5	8 395	2 780	5.4
June	233 627	154 313	66.1	145 737	74 975	65 169	6 925	2 127	143 629	62.4	8 575	2 913	5.6
July	233 864	154 469	66.1	145 532	74 950	65 103	6 909	2 134	143 519	62.2	8 937	3 114	5.8
August	234 107	154 641	66.1	145 203	74 658	65 008	6 801	2 148	143 086	62.0	9 438	3 420	6.1
September	234 360	154 570	66.0	145 076	74 456	65 078	6 850	2 231	142 796	61.9	9 494	3 626	6.1
October	234 612	154 876	66.0	144 802	74 263	65 103	6 793	2 199	142 689	61.7	10 074	3 990	6.5
November	234 828	154 639	65.9	144 100	73 943	64 885	6 612	2 207	141 962	61.4	10 538	3 923	6.8
December	235 035	154 655	65.8	143 369	73 311	64 813	6 601	2 209	141 139	61.0	11 286	4 547	7.3
2009													
January	234 739	154 210	65.7	142 152	72 724	64 209	5 218	2 147	140 029	60.6	12 058	4 764	7.8
February	234 913	154 538	65.8	141 640	72 260	64 195	5 185	2 130	139 493	60.3	12 898	5 455	8.3
March	235 086	154 133	65.6	140 707	71 629	64 027	5 051	2 031	138 664	59.9	13 426	5 886	8.7
April	235 271	154 509	65.7	140 656	71 599	64 021	5 036	2 146	138 437	59.8	13 853	6 385	9.0
May	235 452	154 747	65.7	140 248	71 410	63 807	5 031	2 145	138 036	59.6	14 499	7 022	9.4
June	235 655	154 716	65.7	140 009	71 326	63 747	4 937	2 165	137 841	59.4	14 707	7 837	9.5
July	235 870	154 502	65.5	139 901	71 273	63 761	4 867	2 126	137 819	59.3	14 601	7 839	9.5
August	236 087	154 307	65.4	139 492	71 111	63 633	4 749	2 088	137 371	59.1	14 814	7 828	9.6
September	236 322	153 827	65.1	138 818	70 844	63 324	4 649	2 033	136 734	58.7	15 009	8 402	9.8
October	236 550	153 784	65.0	138 432	70 713	63 275	4 445	2 039	136 483	58.5	15 352	8 648	10.0
November	236 743	153 878	65.0	138 659	70 774	63 242	4 463	2 098	136 640	58.6	15 219	8 755	9.9
December	236 924	153 111	64.6	138 013	70 479	63 086	4 449	2 087	135 904	58.3	15 098	8 835	9.9
2010													
January	236 832	153 404	64.8	138 451	70 506	63 515	4 430	2 131	136 390	58.5	14 953	8 903	9.7
February	236 998	153 720	64.9	138 599	70 601	63 505	4 493	2 307	136 333	58.5	15 121	8 933	9.8
March	237 159	153 964	64.9	138 752	70 876	63 378	4 498	2 211	136 588	58.5	15 212	9 096	9.9
April	237 329	154 642	65.2	139 309	71 356	63 416	4 537	2 288	136 966	58.7	15 333	9 133	9.9
May	237 499	154 106	64.9	139 247	71 378	63 436	4 433	2 197	136 998	58.6	14 858	8 892	9.6
June	237 690	153 631	64.6	139 148	71 353	63 555	4 240	2 140	136 975	58.5	14 483	8 898	9.4
July	237 890	153 706	64.6	139 179	71 457	63 415	4 307	2 172	136 934	58.5	14 527	8 704	9.5
August	238 099	154 087	64.7	139 427	71 607	63 420	4 400	2 163	137 187	58.6	14 660	8 405	9.5
September	238 322	153 971	64.6	139 393	71 592	63 533	4 268	2 161	137 209	58.5	14 578	8 444	9.5
October	238 530	153 631	64.4	139 111	71 432	63 382	4 297	2 338	136 891	58.3	14 520	8 617	9.5
November	238 715	154 127	64.6	139 030	71 140	63 494	4 396	2 191	136 872	58.2	15 097	8 697	9.8
December	238 889	153 639	64.3	139 266	71 470	63 493	4 302	2 186	137 072	58.3	14 373	8 549	9.4

[1]Not seasonally adjusted.
[2]In 1930 through 1943, the official BLS data count persons on work relief as unemployed. The unemployment rates for those years shown in parentheses count persons on work relief as employed, which is more consistent with the postwar practice. See notes and definitions.

Table 10-1B. Summary Labor Force, Employment, and Unemployment: Historical—*Continued*

(Thousands of persons, percent, seasonally adjusted, except as noted.)

Year and month	Civilian noninstitutional population [1]	Civilian labor force		Employment, thousands of persons						Employment-population ratio, percent	Unemployment		
		Thousands of persons	Participation rate (percent)	Total	By age and sex			By industry			Thousands of persons		Rate (percent) [2]
					Men, 20 years and over	Women, 20 years and over	Both sexes, 16 to 19 years	Agricultural	Nonagricultural		Total	Unemployed 15 weeks and over	
2011													
January	238 704	153 198	64.2	139 287	71 544	63 413	4 330	2 270	137 036	58.4	13 910	8 430	9.1
February	238 851	153 280	64.2	139 422	71 819	63 281	4 322	2 266	137 182	58.4	13 858	8 213	9.0
March	239 000	153 403	64.2	139 655	71 834	63 461	4 360	2 260	137 471	58.4	13 748	8 184	9.0
April	239 146	153 566	64.2	139 622	71 946	63 373	4 302	2 143	137 438	58.4	13 944	8 007	9.1
May	239 313	153 526	64.2	139 653	72 120	63 267	4 266	2 230	137 395	58.4	13 873	8 189	9.0
June	239 489	153 379	64.0	139 409	71 999	63 134	4 276	2 253	137 136	58.2	13 971	8 107	9.1
July	239 671	153 309	64.0	139 524	72 008	63 293	4 223	2 225	137 215	58.2	13 785	8 151	9.0
August	239 871	153 724	64.1	139 904	72 217	63 339	4 348	2 344	137 470	58.3	13 820	8 214	9.0
September	240 071	154 059	64.2	140 154	72 409	63 372	4 372	2 232	137 904	58.4	13 905	8 282	9.0
October	240 269	153 940	64.1	140 335	72 415	63 540	4 381	2 211	138 283	58.4	13 604	7 808	8.8
November	240 441	154 072	64.1	140 747	72 861	63 489	4 396	2 251	138 500	58.5	13 326	7 713	8.6
December	240 584	153 927	64.0	140 836	73 039	63 406	4 390	2 362	138 454	58.5	13 090	7 555	8.5
2012													
January	242 269	154 328	63.7	141 677	73 083	64 219	4 375	2 211	139 437	58.5	12 650	7 467	8.2
February	242 435	154 826	63.9	141 943	73 103	64 436	4 403	2 193	139 782	58.5	12 883	7 373	8.3
March	242 604	154 811	63.8	142 079	73 181	64 521	4 377	2 246	139 888	58.6	12 732	7 216	8.2
April	242 784	154 565	63.7	141 963	73 131	64 456	4 376	2 203	139 712	58.5	12 603	7 056	8.2
May	242 966	154 946	63.8	142 257	73 245	64 600	4 412	2 278	139 980	58.6	12 689	7 069	8.2
June	243 155	155 134	63.8	142 432	73 294	64 629	4 509	2 221	140 246	58.6	12 702	7 170	8.2
July	243 354	154 970	63.7	142 272	73 301	64 456	4 515	2 212	140 020	58.5	12 698	6 946	8.2
August	243 566	154 669	63.5	142 204	73 197	64 644	4 364	2 106	140 017	58.4	12 464	6 848	8.1
September	243 772	155 018	63.6	142 947	73 677	64 857	4 414	2 178	140 773	58.6	12 070	6 728	7.8
October	243 983	155 507	63.7	143 369	73 923	64 980	4 466	2 176	141 379	58.8	12 138	6 795	7.8
November	244 174	155 279	63.6	143 233	73 807	64 962	4 465	2 126	141 110	58.7	12 045	6 563	7.8
December	244 350	155 485	63.6	143 212	73 924	64 901	4 387	2 066	141 121	58.6	12 273	6 634	7.9
2013													
January	244 663	155 699	63.6	143 384	74 084	64 790	4 510	2 057	141 234	58.6	12 315	6 573	7.9
February	244 828	155 511	63.5	143 464	74 183	64 911	4 370	2 070	141 393	58.6	12 047	6 485	7.7
March	244 995	155 099	63.3	143 393	74 190	64 838	4 365	2 020	141 350	58.5	11 706	6 355	7.5
April	245 175	155 359	63.4	143 676	74 161	65 115	4 368	2 048	141 604	58.6	11 683	6 329	7.5
May	245 363	155 609	63.4	143 919	74 137	65 323	4 459	2 081	141 860	58.7	11 690	6 287	7.5
June	245 552	155 822	63.5	144 075	74 265	65 340	4 470	2 091	142 021	58.7	11 747	6 218	7.5
July	245 756	155 693	63.4	144 285	74 301	65 514	4 470	2 171	142 081	58.7	11 408	6 031	7.3
August	245 959	155 435	63.2	144 179	74 015	65 743	4 421	2 205	141 918	58.6	11 256	5 973	7.2
September	246 168	155 473	63.2	144 270	74 151	65 539	4 580	2 208	142 058	58.6	11 203	5 927	7.2
October	246 381	154 625	62.8	143 485	73 808	65 229	4 448	2 208	141 449	58.2	11 140	5 824	7.2
November	246 567	155 284	63.0	144 443	74 373	65 547	4 523	2 139	142 317	58.6	10 841	5 786	7.0
December	246 745	154 937	62.8	144 586	74 467	65 617	4 502	2 229	142 337	58.6	10 351	5 530	6.7
2014													
January	230 244	149 943	65.1	140 818	74 905	65 913	4 388	1 999	141 527	58.1	10 280	5 392	6.6
February	230 421	150 207	65.2	140 989	74 820	66 168	4 312	1 973	142 160	58.3	10 387	5 657	6.7
March	230 600	150 488	65.3	141 293	75 284	66 009	4 504	2 008	143 082	58.7	10 384	5 708	6.6
April	230 787	149 878	64.9	141 239	75 163	66 076	4 485	2 048	143 718	58.9	9 696	5 139	6.2
May	230 978	150 006	64.9	141 323	75 159	66 164	4 545	2 101	144 297	59.1	9 761	4 898	6.3
June	231 178	150 059	64.9	141 771	75 504	66 267	4 476	2 288	144 815	59.4	9 453	4 448	6.1
July	231 394	150 396	65.0	141 881	75 631	66 250	4 520	2 403	144 862	59.4	9 648	4 452	6.2
August	231 607	150 441	65.0	141 956	75 668	66 289	4 495	2 472	144 175	59.1	9 568	4 321	6.1
September	231 831	150 200	64.8	142 081	75 889	66 192	4 527	2 482	144 459	59.1	9 237	4 242	5.9
October	232 049	150 377	64.8	142 488	75 928	66 560	4 772	2 517	145 419	59.5	8 983	4 251	5.7
November	232 243	150 627	64.9	142 569	75 675	66 894	4 762	2 332	145 335	59.3	9 071	4 144	5.8
December	232 432	150 383	64.7	142 658	76 026	66 632	4 784	2 220	144 970	59.1	8 688	3 922	5.6

[1] Not seasonally adjusted.
[2] In 1930 through 1943, the official BLS data count persons on work relief as unemployed. The unemployment rates for those years shown in parentheses count persons on work relief as employed, which is more consistent with the postwar practice. See notes and definitions.

Table 10-2. Labor Force and Employment by Major Age and Sex Groups

(Thousands of persons, percent, seasonally adjusted.)

Year and month	Civilian labor force (thousands)			Participation rate (percent)			Employment (thousands)			Employment-population ratio, percent		
	Men, 20 years and over	Women, 20 years and over	Both sexes, 16 to 19 years	Men, 20 years and over	Women, 20 years and over	Both sexes, 16 to 19 years	Men, 20 years and over	Women, 20 years and over	Both sexes, 16 to 19 years	Men, 20 years and over	Women, 20 years and over	Both sexes, 16 to 19 years
1965	44 857	23 686	5 910	83.9	39.4	45.7	43 422	22 630	5 036	81.2	39.4	38.9
1966	44 788	24 431	6 558	83.6	40.1	48.2	43 668	23 510	5 721	81.5	40.1	42.1
1967	45 354	25 475	6 521	83.4	41.1	48.4	44 294	24 397	5 682	81.5	41.1	42.2
1968	45 852	26 266	6 619	83.1	41.6	48.3	44 859	25 281	5 781	81.3	41.6	42.2
1969	46 351	27 413	6 970	82.8	42.7	49.4	45 388	26 397	6 117	81.1	42.7	43.4
1970	47 220	28 301	7 249	82.6	43.3	49.9	45 581	26 952	6 144	79.7	43.3	42.3
1971	48 009	28 904	7 470	82.1	43.3	49.7	45 912	27 246	6 208	78.5	43.3	41.3
1972	49 079	29 901	8 054	81.6	43.7	51.9	47 130	28 276	6 746	78.4	43.7	43.5
1973	49 932	30 991	8 507	81.3	44.4	53.7	48 310	29 484	7 271	78.6	44.4	45.9
1974	50 879	32 201	8 871	81.0	45.3	54.8	48 922	30 424	7 448	77.9	45.3	46.0
1975	51 494	33 410	8 870	80.3	46.0	54.0	48 018	30 726	7 104	74.8	46.0	43.3
1976	52 288	34 814	9 056	79.8	47.0	54.5	49 190	32 226	7 336	75.1	47.0	44.2
1977	53 348	36 310	9 351	79.7	48.1	56.0	50 555	33 775	7 688	75.6	48.1	46.1
1978	54 471	38 128	9 652	79.8	49.6	57.8	52 143	35 836	8 070	76.4	49.6	48.3
1979	55 615	39 708	9 638	79.8	50.6	57.9	53 308	37 434	8 083	76.5	50.6	48.5
1980	56 455	41 106	9 378	79.4	51.3	56.7	53 101	38 492	7 710	74.6	51.3	46.6
1981	57 197	42 485	8 988	79.0	52.1	55.4	53 582	39 590	7 225	74.0	52.1	44.6
1982	57 980	43 699	8 526	78.7	52.7	54.1	52 891	40 086	6 549	71.8	52.7	41.5
1983	58 744	44 636	8 171	78.5	53.1	53.5	53 487	41 004	6 342	71.4	53.1	41.5
1984	59 701	45 900	7 943	78.3	53.7	53.9	55 769	42 793	6 444	73.2	53.7	43.7
1985	60 277	47 283	7 901	78.1	54.7	54.5	56 562	44 154	6 434	73.3	54.7	44.4
1986	61 320	48 589	7 926	78.1	55.5	54.7	57 569	45 556	6 472	73.3	55.5	44.6
1987	62 095	49 783	7 988	78.0	56.2	54.7	58 726	47 074	6 640	73.8	56.2	45.5
1988	62 768	50 870	8 031	77.9	56.8	55.3	59 781	48 383	6 805	74.2	56.8	46.8
1989	63 704	52 212	7 954	78.1	57.7	55.9	60 837	49 745	6 759	74.5	57.7	47.5
1990	64 916	53 131	7 792	78.2	58.0	53.7	61 678	50 535	6 581	74.3	58.0	45.3
1991	65 374	53 708	7 265	77.7	57.9	51.6	61 178	50 634	5 906	72.7	57.9	42.0
1992	66 213	54 796	7 096	77.7	58.5	51.3	61 496	51 328	5 669	72.1	58.5	41.0
1993	66 642	55 388	7 170	77.3	58.5	51.5	62 355	52 099	5 805	72.3	58.5	41.7
1994	66 921	56 655	7 481	76.8	59.3	52.7	63 294	53 606	6 161	72.6	59.3	43.4
1995	67 324	57 215	7 765	76.7	59.4	53.5	64 085	54 396	6 419	73.0	59.4	44.2
1996	68 044	58 094	7 806	76.8	59.9	52.3	64 897	55 311	6 500	73.2	59.9	43.5
1997	69 166	59 198	7 932	77.0	60.5	51.6	66 284	56 613	6 661	73.7	60.5	43.4
1998	69 715	59 702	8 256	76.8	60.4	52.8	67 135	57 278	7 051	73.9	60.4	45.1
1999	70 194	60 840	8 333	76.7	60.7	52.0	67 761	58 555	7 172	74.0	60.7	44.7
2000	72 010	62 301	8 271	76.7	60.6	52.0	69 634	60 067	7 189	74.2	60.6	45.2
2001	72 816	63 016	7 902	76.5	60.6	49.6	69 776	60 417	6 740	73.3	60.6	42.3
2002	73 630	63 648	7 585	76.3	60.5	47.4	69 734	60 420	6 332	72.3	60.5	39.6
2003	74 623	64 716	7 170	75.9	60.6	44.5	70 415	61 402	5 919	71.7	60.6	36.8
2004	75 364	64 923	7 114	75.8	60.3	43.9	71 572	61 773	5 907	71.9	60.3	36.4
2005	76 443	65 714	7 164	75.8	60.4	43.7	73 050	62 702	5 978	72.4	60.4	36.5
2006	77 562	66 585	7 281	75.9	60.5	43.7	74 431	63 834	6 162	72.9	60.5	36.9
2007	78 596	67 516	7 012	75.9	60.6	41.3	75 337	64 799	5 911	72.8	60.6	34.8
2008	79 047	68 382	6 858	75.7	60.9	40.2	74 750	65 039	5 573	71.6	60.9	32.6
2009	78 897	68 856	6 390	74.8	60.8	37.5	71 341	63 699	4 837	67.6	60.8	28.4
2010	78 994	68 990	5 906	74.1	60.3	34.9	71 230	63 456	4 378	66.8	60.3	25.9
2011	79 080	68 810	5 727	73.4	59.8	34.1	72 182	63 360	4 327	67.0	59.8	25.8
2012	79 387	69 765	5 823	73.0	59.3	34.3	73 403	64 640	4 426	67.5	59.3	26.1
2013	79 744	69 860	5 785	72.5	58.8	34.5	74 176	65 295	4 458	67.4	58.8	26.6
2014	80 056	70 212	5 654	71.9	58.5	34.0	75 471	66 287	4 548	67.8	55.2	27.3
2013												
January	79 984	69 817	5 898	73.1	59.0	35.0	74 084	64 790	4 510	67.7	54.7	26.7
February	79 897	69 770	5 844	72.9	58.9	34.7	74 183	64 911	4 370	67.7	54.8	25.9
March	79 731	69 629	5 739	72.7	58.7	34.1	74 190	64 838	4 365	67.7	54.7	25.9
April	79 868	69 764	5 727	72.8	58.8	34.0	74 161	65 148	4 368	67.6	54.9	26.0
May	79 867	69 871	5 872	72.7	58.9	34.9	74 137	65 323	4 459	67.5	55.0	26.5
June	79 855	70 099	5 868	72.6	59.0	34.9	74 265	65 340	4 470	67.5	55.0	26.6
July	79 871	69 986	5 836	72.6	58.9	34.7	74 301	65 514	4 470	67.5	55.1	26.6
August	79 610	70 115	5 710	72.3	58.9	34.1	74 015	65 743	4 421	67.2	55.2	26.4
September	79 757	69 898	5 818	72.3	58.7	34.7	74 151	65 539	4 580	67.2	55.0	27.4
October	79 267	69 652	5 706	71.8	58.4	34.1	73 808	65 229	4 448	66.8	54.7	26.6
November	79 700	69 871	5 713	72.1	58.5	34.2	74 373	65 547	4 523	67.3	54.9	27.1
December	79 464	69 831	5 642	71.8	58.5	33.8	74 467	65 617	4 502	67.3	54.9	27.0
2014												
January	110 746	119 497	16 671	72.1	58.6	33.2	74 905	65 913	4 388	67.6	55.2	26.3
February	110 838	119 583	16 664	72.1	58.8	32.9	74 820	66 168	4 312	67.5	55.3	25.9
March	110 930	119 669	16 658	72.2	58.8	34.2	75 284	66 009	4 504	67.9	55.2	27.0
April	111 027	119 760	16 652	71.9	58.5	33.3	75 163	66 076	4 485	67.7	55.2	26.9
May	111 126	119 852	16 644	71.8	58.5	33.8	75 159	66 164	4 545	67.6	55.2	27.3
June	111 230	119 948	16 636	72.0	58.4	33.9	75 504	66 267	4 476	67.9	55.2	26.9
July	111 342	120 052	16 629	72.0	58.5	34.0	75 631	66 250	4 520	67.9	55.2	27.2
August	111 451	120 156	16 622	72.0	58.4	33.6	75 668	66 289	4 495	67.9	55.2	27.0
September	111 567	120 265	16 615	71.9	58.2	34.0	75 889	66 192	4 527	68.0	55.0	27.2
October	111 679	120 370	16 608	71.7	58.4	35.3	75 928	66 560	4 772	68.0	55.3	28.7
November	111 778	120 465	16 602	71.6	58.6	34.8	75 675	66 894	4 762	67.7	55.5	28.7
December	111 875	120 557	16 595	71.8	58.2	34.6	76 026	66 632	4 784	68.0	55.3	28.8

Table 10-3. Employment by Type of Job

(Thousands of persons, seasonally adjusted, except as noted.)

Year and month	Agricultural	By class of worker — Nonagricultural industries: Total	Wage and salary: Total	Government	Private households [1]	Other private industries	Self-employed (unincorporated)	Unpaid family workers [1]	Multiple jobholders: Total (thousands)	Percent of total employed	Employed part-time: Economic reasons	Non-economic reasons
1965	4 361	66 726	60 031	9 608	...	...	6 097	600	...	...	2 209	8 466
1966	3 979	68 915	62 362	10 323	...	...	5 991	564	...	...	1 960	8 112
1967	3 844	70 527	64 848	11 146	...	...	5 174	505	...	...	2 163	8 701
1968	3 817	72 103	66 519	11 590	...	...	5 102	485	...	...	1 970	9 075
1969	3 606	74 296	68 528	12 025	...	...	5 252	517	...	...	2 056	9 652
1970	3 463	75 215	69 491	12 431	...	...	5 221	502	...	...	2 446	9 999
1971	3 394	75 972	70 120	12 799	...	...	5 327	522	...	...	2 688	10 152
1972	3 484	78 669	72 785	13 393	...	...	5 365	519	...	...	2 648	10 612
1973	3 470	81 594	75 580	13 655	...	...	5 474	540	...	...	2 554	10 972
1974	3 515	83 279	77 094	14 124	...	...	5 697	489	...	...	2 988	11 153
1975	3 408	82 438	76 249	14 675	...	...	5 705	483	...	...	3 804	11 228
1976	3 331	85 421	79 175	15 132	...	...	5 783	464	...	...	3 607	11 607
1977	3 283	88 734	82 121	15 361	...	...	6 114	498	...	...	3 608	12 120
1978	3 387	92 661	85 753	15 525	...	...	6 429	479	...	...	3 516	12 650
1979	3 347	95 477	88 222	15 635	...	...	6 791	463	...	...	3 577	12 893
1980	3 364	95 938	88 525	15 912	...	...	7 000	413	...	...	4 321	13 067
1981	3 368	97 030	89 543	15 689	...	...	7 097	390	...	...	4 768	13 025
1982	3 401	96 125	88 462	15 516	...	...	7 262	401	...	...	6 170	12 953
1983	3 383	97 450	89 500	15 537	...	...	7 575	376	...	...	6 266	12 911
1984	3 321	101 685	93 565	15 770	...	...	7 785	335	...	...	5 744	13 169
1985	3 179	103 971	95 871	16 031	...	...	7 811	289	...	...	5 590	13 489
1986	3 163	106 434	98 299	16 342	...	...	7 881	255	...	...	5 588	13 935
1987	3 208	109 232	100 771	16 800	...	...	8 201	260	...	...	5 401	14 395
1988	3 169	111 800	103 021	17 114	...	...	8 519	260	...	...	5 206	14 963
1989	3 199	114 142	105 259	17 469	...	...	8 605	279	...	...	4 894	15 393
1990	3 223	115 570	106 598	17 769	...	...	8 719	253	...	...	5 204	15 341
1991	3 269	114 449	105 373	17 934	...	...	8 851	226	...	...	6 161	15 172
1992	3 247	115 245	106 437	18 136	...	...	8 575	233	...	...	6 520	14 918
1993	3 115	117 144	107 966	18 579	...	...	8 959	218	7 260	5.9	6 481	15 240
1994	3 409	119 651	110 517	18 293	...	...	9 003	131	7 693	6.2	4 625	17 638
1995	3 440	121 460	112 448	18 362	...	...	8 902	110	7 832	6.2	4 473	17 734
1996	3 443	123 264	114 171	18 217	...	...	8 971	122	7 955	6.1	4 315	17 770
1997	3 399	126 159	116 983	18 131	...	...	9 056	120	7 926	6.0	4 068	18 149
1998	3 378	128 085	119 019	18 383	...	...	8 962	103	7 802	5.8	3 665	18 530
1999	3 281	130 207	121 323	18 903	...	...	8 790	95	7 604	5.6	3 357	18 758
2000	2 464	134 427	125 114	19 248	718	105 148	9 205	108	7 357	5.4	3 227	18 814
2001	2 299	134 635	125 407	19 335	694	105 378	9 121	107	7 291	5.3	3 715	18 790
2002	2 311	134 174	125 156	19 636	757	104 764	8 923	95	7 315	5.3	4 213	18 843
2003	2 275	135 461	126 015	19 634	764	105 616	9 344	101	7 315	5.3	4 701	19 014
2004	2 232	137 020	127 463	19 983	779	106 701	9 467	90	7 473	5.4	4 567	19 380
2005	2 197	139 532	129 931	20 357	812	108 761	9 509	93	7 546	5.3	4 350	19 491
2006	2 206	142 221	132 449	20 337	803	111 309	9 685	87	7 576	5.2	4 162	19 591
2007	2 095	143 952	134 283	21 003	813	112 467	9 557	112	7 655	5.2	4 401	19 756
2008	2 168	143 194	133 882	21 258	805	111 819	9 219	93	7 620	5.2	5 875	19 343
2009	2 103	137 775	128 713	21 178	783	106 752	8 995	66	7 271	5.2	8 913	18 710
2010	2 206	136 858	127 914	21 003	667	106 244	8 860	84	6 878	4.9	8 874	18 251
2011	2 254	137 615	128 934	20 536	722	107 676	8 603	78	6 880	4.9	8 560	18 334
2012	2 186	140 283	131 452	20 360	738	110 355	8 749	81	6 943	4.9	8 122	18 806
2013	2 130	141 799	133 111	20 247	723	112 141	8 619	70	7 002	4.9	7 935	18 903
2014	2 517	144 982	133 402	20 135	820	115 267	8 602	64	7 146	4.9	7 109	19 148
2013												
January	2 057	141 234	132 468	20 635	799	110 986	8 728	78	6 902	4.8	7 983	18 556
February	2 070	141 393	132 689	20 489	676	111 432	8 680	76	7 268	5.1	7 991	18 925
March	2 020	141 350	132 744	20 585	659	111 494	8 412	113	7 085	4.9	7 663	18 784
April	2 048	141 604	132 861	20 319	617	111 911	8 651	77	6 982	4.9	7 929	18 921
May	2 081	141 860	133 166	20 342	663	112 221	8 601	65	6 952	4.8	7 917	18 957
June	2 091	142 021	133 245	20 166	702	112 456	8 654	71	7 044	4.9	8 194	19 032
July	2 171	142 081	133 220	20 006	704	112 465	8 850	62	7 036	4.9	8 180	19 099
August	2 205	141 918	133 247	20 373	680	112 252	8 646	74	7 048	4.9	7 898	19 305
September	2 208	142 058	133 323	20 172	694	112 454	8 614	44	7 007	4.9	7 914	18 919
October	2 208	141 449	132 859	19 706	796	112 370	8 528	57	6 948	4.8	8 016	18 755
November	2 139	142 317	133 694	20 086	849	112 760	8 547	62	6 880	4.8	7 723	18 858
December	2 229	142 337	133 858	20 063	837	112 918	8 506	57	6 877	4.8	7 771	18 731
2014												
January	2 171	143 010	134 376	20 387	806	113 191	755	27	6 685	4.7	7 274	19 317
February	2 148	143 196	134 482	20 255	822	113 388	765	16	7 163	5.0	7 204	19 085
March	2 155	143 560	134 791	20 415	861	113 536	744	16	7 143	4.9	7 449	19 275
April	2 167	143 566	134 918	20 316	868	113 742	768	10	7 162	4.9	7 460	18 915
May	2 054	143 843	135 334	20 050	867	114 481	741	22	7 305	5.0	7 268	19 149
June	2 165	144 078	135 610	20 288	859	114 464	737	25	6 960	4.7	7 496	19 844
July	2 161	144 192	135 725	20 350	889	114 481	708	28	6 787	4.6	7 433	19 650
August	2 265	144 111	135 641	20 027	789	114 787	732	18	6 819	4.7	7 223	19 538
September	2 377	144 254	135 452	19 751	747	114 968	783	23	7 100	4.8	7 058	19 579
October	2 402	144 982	136 016	19 885	773	115 281	784	28	7 773	5.3	7 012	19 793
November	2 392	144 939	136 093	19 956	791	115 361	749	16	7 549	5.1	6 851	19 971
December	2 358	145 101	136 415	19 956	771	115 676	815	30	7 308	5.0	6 790	19 730

[1] Not seasonally adjusted.
. . . = Not available.

Figure 10-2: Unemployment Rate, 1948–2014

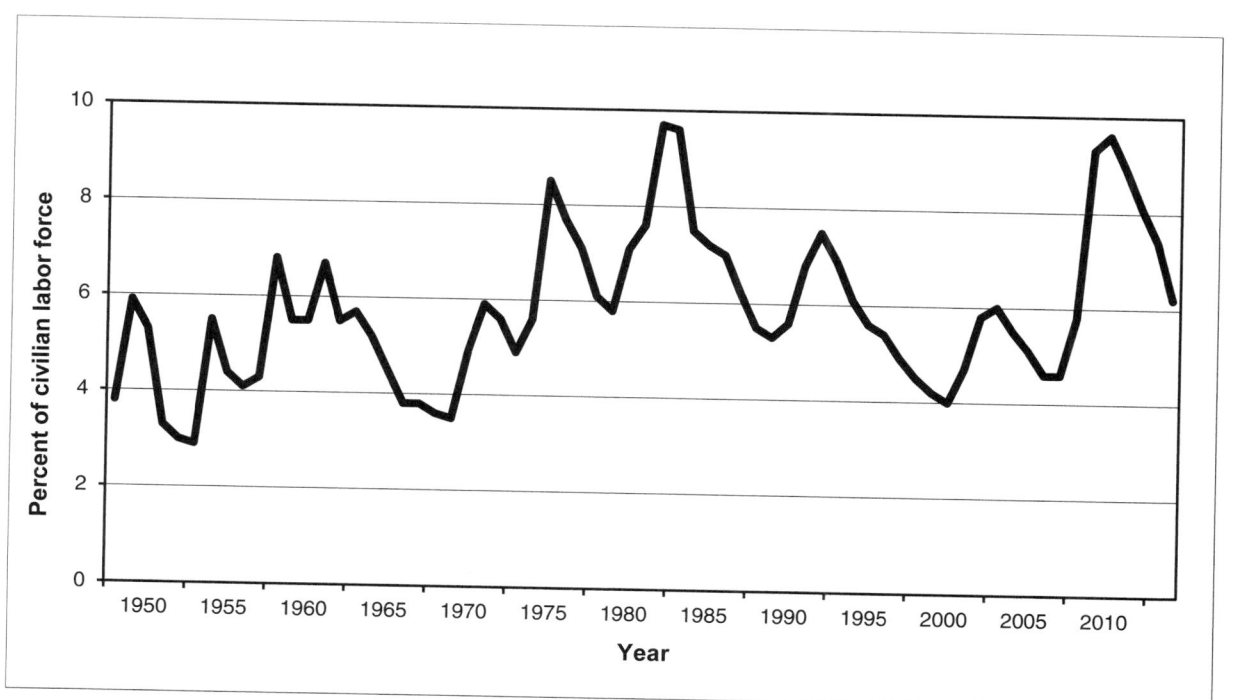

- The unemployment rate peaked at 10.0 percent in October 2009 (lagging, as it usually does, the business cycle trough, which was in June 2009). This was not quite as high as the postwar record of 10.8 percent, set in November and December 1982. Yet the employment losses of 2008–2009 were proportionately greater than the 2 percent drop in 1981–1982. The discrepancy is in labor force behavior. Recently, workers responded to job losses by dropping out of the labor force; in 1982, in contrast, labor force participation rates actually increased slightly. (Tables 10-1A and B)

- Unemployment hovered near 10 percent through early 2010, but has declined significantly since then to 5.3 percent in July 2015, reflecting continued employment growth with little or no labor force expansion. (Tables 10-1A and B and recent data)

- In December 2014, the median unemployed worker had been out of work 17.0 weeks, but duration then declined rapidly to 11.3 weeks in July 2015. Still, this was in excess of the 10.1 weeks of the recession years 1983 and 2003. Median duration is more representative of the typical job-seeker than "average duration," which is distorted by the presence of a few extremely long-term unemployed and recently by a technical statistical problem. Even by this better measure, the rise in long-term unemployment has been large—and even understates the problem, since it does not include discouraged workers. (Table 10-5)

- Adding discouraged workers, workers marginally attached to the labor force, and persons on involuntary part time to get a comprehensive measure of the work gap, BLS calculates the "U-6" rate of combined unemployment and underutilization, which rose from 8.3 percent in the high-employment year 2007 to 16.7 percent in 2010. U-6 has since declined to 10.4 percent in July 2015. (Table 10-5 and recent data)

Table 10-4. Unemployment by Demographic Group

(Unemployment in thousands of persons and as a percent of the civilian labor force in group, seasonally adjusted, except as noted.)

Year and month	Unemployment (thousands of persons)				Unemployment rate (percent)								
						By age and sex			By race				
	Total	Men, 20 years and over	Women, 20 years and over	Both sexes, 16 to 19 years	All civilian workers	Men, 20 years and over	Women, 20 years and over	Both sexes, 16 to 19 years	White	Black and other	Black or African American	Asian [1]	Hispanic or Latino ethnicity
1970	4 093	1 638	1 349	1 106	4.9	3.5	4.8	15.3	4.5	8.2	...	...	...
1971	5 016	2 097	1 658	1 262	5.9	4.4	5.7	16.9	5.4	9.9	...	...	...
1972	4 882	1 948	1 625	1 308	5.6	4.0	5.4	16.2	5.1	10.0	10.4	...	...
1973	4 365	1 624	1 507	1 235	4.9	3.3	4.9	14.5	4.3	9.0	9.4	...	7.5
1974	5 156	1 957	1 777	1 422	5.6	3.8	5.5	16.0	5.0	9.9	10.5	...	8.1
1975	7 929	3 476	2 684	1 767	8.5	6.8	8.0	19.9	7.8	13.8	14.8	...	12.2
1976	7 406	3 098	2 588	1 719	7.7	5.9	7.4	19.0	7.0	13.1	14.0	...	11.5
1977	6 991	2 794	2 535	1 663	7.1	5.2	7.0	17.8	6.2	13.1	14.0	...	10.1
1978	6 202	2 328	2 292	1 583	6.1	4.3	6.0	16.4	5.2	11.9	12.8	...	9.1
1979	6 137	2 308	2 276	1 555	5.8	4.2	5.7	16.1	5.1	11.3	12.3	...	8.3
1980	7 637	3 353	2 615	1 669	7.1	5.9	6.4	17.8	6.3	13.1	14.3	...	10.1
1981	8 273	3 615	2 895	1 763	7.6	6.3	6.8	19.6	6.7	14.2	15.6	...	10.4
1982	10 678	5 089	3 613	1 977	9.7	8.8	8.3	23.2	8.6	17.3	18.9	...	13.8
1983	10 717	5 257	3 632	1 829	9.6	8.9	8.1	22.4	8.4	17.8	19.5	...	13.7
1984	8 539	3 932	3 107	1 499	7.5	6.6	6.8	18.9	6.5	14.4	15.9	...	10.7
1985	8 312	3 715	3 129	1 468	7.2	6.2	6.6	18.6	6.2	13.7	15.1	...	10.5
1986	8 237	3 751	3 032	1 454	7.0	6.1	6.2	18.3	6.0	13.1	14.5	...	10.6
1987	7 425	3 369	2 709	1 347	6.2	5.4	5.4	16.9	5.3	11.6	13.0	...	8.8
1988	6 701	2 987	2 487	1 226	5.5	4.8	4.9	15.3	4.7	10.4	11.7	...	8.2
1989	6 528	2 867	2 467	1 194	5.3	4.5	4.7	15.0	4.5	10.0	11.4	...	8.0
1990	7 047	3 239	2 596	1 212	5.6	5.0	4.9	15.5	4.8	10.1	11.4	...	8.2
1991	8 628	4 195	3 074	1 359	6.8	6.4	5.7	18.7	6.1	11.1	12.5	...	10.0
1992	9 613	4 717	3 469	1 427	7.5	7.1	6.3	20.1	6.6	12.7	14.2	...	11.6
1993	8 940	4 287	3 288	1 365	6.9	6.4	5.9	19.0	6.1	11.7	13.0	...	10.8
1994	7 996	3 627	3 049	1 320	6.1	5.4	5.4	17.6	5.3	10.5	11.5	...	9.9
1995	7 404	3 239	2 819	1 346	5.6	4.8	4.9	17.3	4.9	9.6	10.4	...	9.3
1996	7 236	3 146	2 783	1 306	5.4	4.6	4.8	16.7	4.7	9.3	10.5	...	8.9
1997	6 739	2 882	2 585	1 271	4.9	4.2	4.4	16.0	4.2	8.8	10.0	...	7.7
1998	6 210	2 580	2 424	1 205	4.5	3.7	4.1	14.6	3.9	7.8	8.9	...	7.2
1999	5 880	2 433	2 285	1 162	4.2	3.5	3.8	13.9	3.7	7.0	8.0	...	6.4
2000	5 692	2 376	2 235	1 081	4.0	3.3	3.6	13.1	3.5	6.7	7.6	3.6	5.7
2001	6 801	3 040	2 599	1 162	4.7	4.2	4.1	14.7	4.2	7.7	8.6	4.5	6.6
2002	8 378	3 896	3 228	1 253	5.8	5.3	5.1	16.5	5.1	9.2	10.2	5.9	7.5
2003	8 774	4 209	3 314	1 251	6.0	5.6	5.1	17.5	5.2	...	10.8	6.0	7.7
2004	8 149	3 791	3 150	1 208	5.5	5.0	4.9	17.0	4.8	...	10.4	4.4	7.0
2005	7 591	3 392	3 013	1 186	5.1	4.4	4.6	16.6	4.4	...	10.0	4.0	6.0
2006	7 001	3 131	2 751	1 119	4.6	4.0	4.1	15.4	4.0	...	8.9	3.0	5.2
2007	7 078	3 259	2 718	1 101	4.6	4.1	4.0	15.7	4.1	...	8.3	3.2	5.6
2008	8 924	4 297	3 342	1 285	5.8	5.4	4.9	18.7	5.2	...	10.1	4.0	7.6
2009	14 265	7 555	5 157	1 552	9.3	9.6	7.5	24.3	8.5	...	14.8	7.3	12.1
2010	14 825	7 763	5 534	1 528	9.6	9.8	8.0	25.9	8.7	...	16.0	7.5	12.5
2011	13 747	6 898	5 450	1 400	8.9	8.7	7.9	24.4	7.9	...	15.8	7.0	11.5
2012	12 506	5 984	5 125	1 397	8.1	7.5	7.3	24.0	7.2	...	13.8	5.9	10.3
2013	11 460	5 568	4 565	1 327	7.4	7.0	6.5	22.9	6.5	...	13.1	5.2	9.1
2014	9 617	4 585	3 926	1 106	6.2	5.7	5.6	19.6	5.3	...	11.3	5.0	7.4
2013													
January	12 497	6 007	5 075	1 416	8.0	7.5	7.3	23.9	7.1	...	13.7	6.4	9.7
February	11 967	5 627	4 864	1 476	7.7	7.0	7.0	25.2	6.8	...	13.9	6.0	9.6
March	11 653	5 485	4 784	1 384	7.5	6.9	6.9	24.1	6.7	...	13.1	5.0	9.3
April	11 735	5 698	4 654	1 383	7.6	7.1	6.7	24.1	6.7	...	13.1	5.3	9.2
May	11 671	5 701	4 554	1 416	7.5	7.1	6.5	24.2	6.7	...	13.4	4.5	9.0
June	11 736	5 596	4 780	1 360	7.5	7.0	6.8	23.3	6.6	...	13.8	4.7	9.0
July	11 357	5 556	4 448	1 352	7.3	7.0	6.4	23.2	6.5	...	12.4	5.4	9.3
August	11 241	5 605	4 341	1 294	7.2	7.0	6.2	22.5	6.4	...	13.0	5.2	9.2
September	11 251	5 664	4 358	1 229	7.2	7.1	6.2	21.1	6.3	...	13.1	5.4	9.0
October	11 161	5 505	4 398	1 259	7.2	6.9	6.3	22.2	6.3	...	13.0	5.3	9.0
November	10 814	5 314	4 308	1 192	7.0	6.7	6.2	20.9	6.1	...	12.4	5.2	8.7
December	10 376	5 018	4 208	1 150	6.7	6.3	6.0	20.4	6.0	...	11.8	4.1	8.4
2014													
January	10 280	4 994	5 064	1 416	6.6	6.3	5.9	20.8	5.7	...	12.1	4.8	8.3
February	10 387	5 064	4 155	1 476	6.7	6.3	5.9	21.3	5.8	...	12.0	5.9	8.1
March	10 384	4 841	4 354	1 384	6.6	6.0	6.2	20.9	5.7	...	12.2	5.4	7.9
April	9 696	4 674	3 964	1 383	6.2	5.9	5.7	19.1	5.3	...	11.4	5.9	7.5
May	9 761	4 677	4 006	1 416	6.3	5.9	5.7	19.2	5.4	...	11.4	5.6	7.7
June	9 453	4 552	3 736	1 360	6.1	5.7	5.3	20.7	5.3	...	10.7	4.8	7.6
July	9 648	4 543	3 972	1 352	6.2	5.7	5.7	20.0	5.3	...	11.4	4.2	7.6
August	9 568	4 543	3 942	1 294	6.1	5.7	5.6	19.4	5.3	...	11.6	4.6	7.4
September	9 237	4 273	3 845	1 229	5.9	5.3	5.5	19.8	5.1	...	11.0	4.5	7.0
October	8 983	4 094	3 794	1 259	5.7	5.1	5.4	18.7	4.9	...	10.9	5.0	6.8
November	9 071	4 354	3 705	1 192	5.8	5.4	5.2	17.5	4.9	...	11.0	4.7	6.6
December	8 688	4 245	3 479	1 150	5.6	5.3	5.0	16.8	4.8	...	10.4	4.2	6.5

[1]Not seasonally adjusted.
. . . = Not available.

Table 10-5. Unemployment Rates and Related Data

(Seasonally adjusted, except as noted.)

Year and month	Unemployment rates by marital status (percent of labor force in group)			Unemployment rates by reason for unemployment (percent of total civilian labor force in group.)					Duration of unemployment		Alternative measures of labor under-utilization (percent)		
	Married men, spouse present	Married women, spouse present	Women who maintain families[1]	Total	Job losers and persons who completed temporary jobs	Job leavers	Reentrants	New entrants	Average (mean) weeks unemployed	Median weeks unemployed	Including discouraged workers (U-4)	Including all marginally attached workers (U-5)	Including marginally attached and under-employed (U-6)
1970	2.6	4.9	5.4	4.9	2.2	0.7	1.5	0.6	8.6	4.9	. . .	. . .	. . .
1971	3.2	5.7	7.3	5.9	2.8	0.7	1.7	0.7	11.3	6.3	. . .	. . .	. . .
1972	2.8	5.4	7.2	5.6	2.4	0.7	1.7	0.8	12.0	6.2	. . .	. . .	. . .
1973	2.3	4.7	7.1	4.9	1.9	0.8	1.5	0.7	10.0	5.2	. . .	. . .	. . .
1974	2.7	5.3	7.0	5.6	2.4	0.8	1.6	0.7	9.8	5.2	. . .	. . .	. . .
1975	5.1	7.9	10.0	8.5	4.7	0.9	2.0	0.9	14.2	8.4	. . .	. . .	. . .
1976	4.2	7.1	10.1	7.7	3.8	0.9	2.0	0.9	15.8	8.2	. . .	. . .	. . .
1977	3.6	6.5	9.4	7.1	3.2	0.9	2.0	1.0	14.3	7.0	. . .	. . .	. . .
1978	2.8	5.5	8.5	6.1	2.5	0.9	1.8	0.9	11.9	5.9	. . .	. . .	. . .
1979	2.8	5.1	8.3	5.8	2.5	0.8	1.7	0.8	10.8	5.4	. . .	. . .	. . .
1980	4.2	5.8	9.2	7.1	3.7	0.8	1.8	0.8	11.9	6.5	. . .	. . .	. . .
1981	4.3	6.0	10.4	7.6	3.9	0.8	1.9	0.9	13.7	6.9	. . .	. . .	. . .
1982	6.5	7.4	11.7	9.7	5.7	0.8	2.2	1.1	15.6	8.7	. . .	. . .	. . .
1983	6.5	7.0	12.2	9.6	5.6	0.7	2.2	1.1	20.0	10.1	. . .	. . .	. . .
1984	4.6	5.7	10.3	7.5	3.9	0.7	1.9	1.0	18.2	7.9	. . .	. . .	. . .
1985	4.3	5.6	10.4	7.2	3.6	0.8	2.0	0.9	15.6	6.8	. . .	. . .	. . .
1986	4.4	5.2	9.8	7.0	3.4	0.9	1.8	0.9	15.0	6.9	. . .	. . .	. . .
1987	3.9	4.3	9.2	6.2	3.0	0.8	1.6	0.8	14.5	6.5	. . .	. . .	. . .
1988	3.3	3.9	8.1	5.5	2.5	0.8	1.5	0.7	13.5	5.9	. . .	. . .	. . .
1989	3.0	3.7	8.1	5.3	2.4	0.8	1.5	0.5	11.9	4.8	. . .	. . .	. . .
1990	3.4	3.8	8.3	5.6	2.7	0.8	1.5	0.5	12.0	5.3	. . .	. . .	. . .
1991	4.4	4.5	9.3	6.8	3.7	0.8	1.7	0.6	13.7	6.8	. . .	. . .	. . .
1992	5.1	5.0	10.0	7.5	4.2	0.8	1.8	0.7	17.7	8.7	. . .	. . .	. . .
1993	4.4	4.6	9.7	6.9	3.8	0.8	1.7	0.7	18.0	8.3	. . .	. . .	. . .
1994	3.7	4.1	8.9	6.1	2.9	0.6	2.1	0.5	18.8	9.2	6.5	7.4	10.9
1995	3.3	3.9	8.0	5.6	2.6	0.6	1.9	0.4	16.6	8.3	5.9	6.7	10.1
1996	3.0	3.6	8.2	5.4	2.5	0.6	1.9	0.4	16.7	8.3	5.7	6.5	9.7
1997	2.7	3.1	8.1	4.9	2.2	0.6	1.7	0.4	15.8	8.0	5.2	5.9	8.9
1998	2.4	2.9	7.2	4.5	2.1	0.5	1.5	0.4	14.5	6.7	4.7	5.4	8.0
1999	2.2	2.7	6.4	4.2	1.9	0.6	1.4	0.3	13.4	6.4	4.4	5.0	7.4
2000	2.0	2.7	5.9	4.0	1.8	0.5	1.4	0.3	12.6	5.9	4.2	4.8	7.0
2001	2.7	3.1	6.6	4.7	2.4	0.6	1.4	0.3	13.1	6.8	4.9	5.6	8.1
2002	3.6	3.7	8.0	5.8	3.2	0.6	1.6	0.4	16.6	9.1	6.0	6.7	9.6
2003	3.8	3.7	8.5	6.0	3.3	0.6	1.7	0.4	19.2	10.1	6.3	7.0	10.1
2004	3.1	3.5	8.0	5.5	2.8	0.6	1.6	0.5	19.6	9.8	5.8	6.5	9.6
2005	2.8	3.3	7.8	5.1	2.5	0.6	1.6	0.4	18.4	8.9	5.4	6.1	8.9
2006	2.4	2.9	7.1	4.6	2.2	0.5	1.5	0.4	16.8	8.3	4.9	5.5	8.2
2007	2.5	2.8	6.5	4.6	2.3	0.5	1.4	0.4	16.8	8.5	4.9	5.5	8.3
2008	3.4	3.6	8.0	5.8	3.1	0.6	1.6	0.5	17.9	9.4	6.1	6.8	10.5
2009	6.6	5.5	11.5	9.3	5.9	0.6	2.1	0.7	24.4	15.1	9.7	10.5	16.2
2010	6.8	5.9	12.3	9.6	6.0	0.6	2.3	0.8	33.0	21.4	10.3	11.1	16.7
2011	5.8	5.6	12.4	8.9	5.3	0.6	2.2	0.8	39.3	21.4	9.5	10.4	15.9
2012	4.9	5.3	11.4	8.1	4.4	0.6	2.2	0.8	39.4	19.3	8.6	9.5	14.7
2013	4.3	4.6	10.2	7.4	3.9	0.6	2.1	0.8	36.5	17.0	7.9	8.8	13.8
2014	3.4	3.8	6.6	6.2	3.1	0.5	1.8	0.7	33.7	14.0	6.6	7.5	12.0
2013													
January	4.6	5.2	11.3	8.0	4.3	0.6	2.3	0.8	35.5	16.2	8.5	9.4	14.5
February	4.5	4.8	11.0	7.7	4.1	0.6	2.1	0.8	36.7	17.5	8.2	9.2	14.3
March	4.2	4.7	10.7	7.5	4.0	0.6	2.0	0.8	36.9	17.7	8.0	8.9	13.8
April	4.4	4.5	10.3	7.6	4.1	0.6	2.1	0.8	36.5	17.1	8.0	8.9	14.0
May	4.4	4.4	9.9	7.5	3.9	0.6	2.1	0.8	36.9	17.0	8.0	8.8	13.8
June	4.3	4.7	10.7	7.5	3.9	0.7	2.1	0.8	35.9	16.6	8.1	9.0	14.2
July	4.3	4.5	10.5	7.3	3.8	0.6	2.1	0.8	37.1	16.3	7.9	8.7	13.8
August	4.3	4.2	11.0	7.2	3.8	0.6	2.0	0.8	37.4	16.8	7.7	8.6	13.6
September	4.4	4.4	8.8	7.2	3.8	0.6	2.0	0.8	37.2	16.5	7.7	8.6	13.6
October	4.5	4.6	9.5	7.2	4.0	0.6	2.0	0.8	35.5	16.1	7.7	8.6	13.7
November	4.2	4.4	9.7	7.0	3.7	0.6	2.0	0.7	36.8	17.0	7.4	8.2	13.1
December	3.9	4.4	8.7	6.7	3.5	0.6	2.0	0.8	36.8	17.0	7.2	8.1	13.1
2014													
January	3.8	3.9	9.1	6.6	3.4	0.5	1.9	0.8	35.3	15.9	7.1	8.1	12.7
February	3.8	4.2	9.1	6.7	3.5	0.5	1.9	0.8	36.9	16.2	7.1	8.0	12.6
March	3.7	4.2	9.0	6.6	3.5	0.5	1.9	0.7	35.2	15.9	7.1	7.9	12.6
April	3.5	3.9	8.5	6.2	3.3	0.5	1.7	0.7	34.8	15.6	6.7	7.5	12.3
May	3.3	4.0	8.4	6.3	3.2	0.6	1.8	0.7	34.3	14.5	6.7	7.5	12.1
June	3.4	3.8	8.1	6.1	3.1	0.5	1.7	0.7	33.3	13.2	6.5	7.3	12.0
July	3.3	3.9	9.1	6.2	3.1	0.5	1.8	0.7	32.5	13.5	6.6	7.5	12.2
August	3.2	3.7	9.3	6.1	3.1	0.5	1.8	0.7	31.9	13.3	6.6	7.4	12.0
September	2.9	3.6	8.3	5.9	2.9	0.5	1.8	0.7	31.8	13.3	6.3	7.3	11.7
October	3.0	3.5	8.7	5.7	2.8	0.5	1.8	0.7	32.9	13.5	6.2	7.1	11.5
November	3.2	3.4	8.2	5.8	2.9	0.5	1.8	0.7	33.0	12.8	6.2	7.1	11.4
December	3.0	3.2	7.8	5.6	2.8	0.5	1.7	0.6	32.8	12.6	6.0	6.9	11.2

[1]Not seasonally adjusted.
. . . = Not available.

Table 10-6. Labor Force and Employment Estimates Smoothed for Population Adjustments (Unofficial)

(Thousands of persons, seasonally adjusted.)

Year	January	February	March	April	May	June	July	August	September	October	November	December
CIVILIAN LABOR FORCE												
1990	125 845	125 734	125 837	125 697	125 953	125 645	125 816	126 087	126 001	126 116	126 203	126 287
1991	126 112	126 189	126 420	126 742	126 382	126 549	126 384	126 392	126 905	126 909	126 981	126 956
1992	127 566	127 524	127 934	128 184	128 475	128 829	128 945	129 008	128 908	128 444	128 872	128 998
1993	128 856	128 926	129 079	129 077	129 772	129 932	129 931	130 166	129 826	130 145	130 296	130 539
1994	131 210	131 296	131 038	131 272	131 444	131 237	131 341	131 980	132 139	132 477	132 637	132 710
1995	132 811	132 901	132 906	133 404	132 673	132 784	133 193	133 199	133 489	133 607	133 517	133 426
1996	133 545	133 896	134 138	134 381	134 654	134 697	135 302	135 083	135 560	135 982	136 082	136 202
1997	136 560	136 517	137 025	137 164	137 281	137 387	137 668	137 824	137 894	137 865	138 209	138 418
1998	138 370	138 401	138 539	138 465	138 703	138 800	138 947	138 942	139 679	139 685	139 801	140 070
1999	140 456	140 433	140 207	140 452	140 615	140 852	140 977	140 981	141 189	141 353	141 623	141 790
2000	142 260	142 443	142 414	142 724	142 355	142 551	142 232	142 461	142 458	142 556	142 889	143 168
2001	143 713	143 607	143 823	143 462	143 204	143 237	143 527	143 150	143 848	143 938	144 085	144 143
2002	143 715	144 477	144 299	144 536	144 742	144 605	144 593	144 792	145 327	145 083	144 803	144 822
2003	145 054	145 193	145 091	145 517	145 519	146 047	145 456	145 392	145 453	145 614	145 871	145 579
2004	146 111	145 963	146 182	146 074	146 273	146 651	146 867	146 724	146 561	146 922	147 274	147 156
2005	147 161	147 480	147 493	148 010	148 329	148 292	148 470	148 800	148 960	148 992	149 041	148 992
2006	149 292	149 704	149 862	149 917	150 091	150 361	150 371	150 695	150 629	150 993	151 342	151 653
2007	151 885	151 711	151 764	151 138	151 356	151 709	151 708	151 390	152 035	151 791	152 422	152 490
2008	153 260	152 844	153 090	152 943	153 466	153 468	153 614	153 777	153 698	153 994	153 750	153 758
2009	153 759	154 082	153 674	154 044	154 277	154 242	154 025	153 826	153 344	153 297	153 386	152 618
2010	153 161	153 478	153 724	154 402	153 869	153 396	153 473	153 855	153 741	153 403	153 900	153 414
2011	153 485	153 572	153 701	153 870	153 835	153 694	153 629	154 051	154 392	154 278	154 416	154 276
2012	154 422	154 924	154 913	154 671	155 056	155 248	155 087	154 790	155 143	155 636	155 412	155 622
2013	156 059	155 635	155 271	155 653	155 820	156 026	155 903	155 806	155 832	154 903	155 600	155 348
2014	155 771	155 979	156 478	155 722	155 937	156 014	156 369	156 345	156 177	156 582	156 747	156 479
CIVILIAN EMPLOYMENT, TOTAL												
1990	119 093	119 082	119 238	118 898	119 209	119 052	118 891	118 894	118 628	118 651	118 432	118 379
1991	118 089	117 915	117 823	118 293	117 634	117 845	117 785	117 712	118 169	118 052	118 033	117 740
1992	118 265	118 050	118 454	118 748	118 709	118 764	119 071	119 195	119 101	119 020	119 280	119 413
1993	119 503	119 715	119 995	119 938	120 594	120 781	120 970	121 373	121 081	121 363	121 722	122 031
1994	122 547	122 679	122 534	122 908	123 497	123 277	123 362	124 013	124 372	124 811	125 230	125 448
1995	125 402	125 681	125 720	125 722	125 207	125 321	125 629	125 677	125 972	126 241	126 052	125 963
1996	126 013	126 542	126 779	126 924	127 189	127 562	127 922	128 161	128 540	128 909	128 801	128 904
1997	129 358	129 370	129 981	130 247	130 584	130 544	130 970	131 172	131 194	131 368	131 859	131 898
1998	131 958	132 053	132 072	132 484	132 614	132 545	132 643	132 718	133 333	133 359	133 655	133 994
1999	134 436	134 276	134 381	134 402	134 775	134 855	134 905	135 097	135 227	135 529	135 862	136 092
2000	136 552	136 585	136 681	137 243	136 597	136 900	136 485	136 609	136 833	137 022	137 249	137 534
2001	137 691	137 519	137 683	137 193	136 979	136 754	136 945	136 109	136 707	136 246	136 086	135 889
2002	135 536	136 266	135 998	135 941	136 347	136 216	136 207	136 492	137 082	136 781	136 289	136 187
2003	136 580	136 622	136 552	136 727	136 616	136 838	136 501	136 553	136 590	136 940	137 354	137 318
2004	137 771	137 827	137 724	137 935	138 092	138 398	138 763	138 766	138 666	138 895	139 377	139 257
2005	139 407	139 533	139 786	140 369	140 708	140 798	141 094	141 486	141 439	141 571	141 508	141 746
2006	142 251	142 544	142 814	142 821	143 135	143 385	143 222	143 630	143 806	144 289	144 495	144 915
2007	144 807	144 821	145 068	144 326	144 626	144 770	144 599	144 364	144 907	144 597	145 226	144 892
2008	145 583	145 354	145 276	145 314	145 083	144 905	144 693	144 358	144 223	143 943	143 237	142 502
2009	141 691	141 176	140 242	140 187	139 776	139 534	139 422	139 010	138 334	137 946	138 168	137 520
2010	138 202	138 351	138 505	139 062	139 002	138 904	138 937	139 186	139 153	138 873	138 793	139 030
2011	139 529	139 669	139 908	139 880	139 916	139 676	139 796	140 182	140 437	140 624	141 042	141 136
2012	141 764	142 034	142 174	142 061	142 359	142 537	142 381	142 316	143 063	143 489	143 357	143 339
2013	143 539	143 646	143 597	143 894	144 125	144 266	144 522	144 541	144 556	143 716	144 761	144 948
2014	145 467	145 568	146 069	146 002	146 152	146 537	146 696	146 752	146 914	147 573	147 650	147 767

Table 10-7. Insured Unemployment

(Averages of weekly data; thousands of persons, except as noted.)

Year and month	State programs, seasonally adjusted			Federal programs, not seasonally adjusted				
	Initial claims	Insured unemployment	Insured unemployment rate (percent) [1]	Initial claims		Persons claiming benefits		
				Federal employees	Newly discharged veterans	Federal employees	Newly discharged veterans	Extended benefits
1976	383	2 978	4.5	. . .	. . .	. . .	. . .	. . .
1977	374	2 644	3.9	. . .	. . .	. . .	. . .	. . .
1978	341	2 337	3.3	. . .	. . .	. . .	. . .	. . .
1979	383	2 428	3.0	. . .	. . .	. . .	. . .	. . .
1980	488	3 365	3.9	. . .	. . .	. . .	. . .	. . .
1981	451	3 032	3.5	. . .	. . .	. . .	. . .	. . .
1982	586	4 094	4.7	. . .	. . .	. . .	. . .	. . .
1983	441	3 337	3.9	. . .	. . .	. . .	. . .	. . .
1984	374	2 452	2.8	. . .	. . .	. . .	. . .	. . .
1985	392	2 584	2.9	. . .	. . .	. . .	. . .	. . .
1986	378	2 632	2.8	2.13	2.52	20.70	17.46	23.87
1987	325	2 273	2.4	2.19	2.57	21.22	17.66	8.89
1988	309	2 075	2.1	2.32	2.74	23.00	18.12	1.17
1989	330	2 174	2.1	2.14	2.31	22.14	15.13	0.61
1990	385	2 539	2.4	2.45	2.54	24.12	18.45	2.45
1991	447	3 338	3.2	2.55	2.93	30.52	22.70	32.09
1992	409	3 208	3.1	2.75	4.95	32.07	60.60	4.59
1993	344	2 768	2.6	2.55	3.94	32.10	54.43	8.56
1994	340	2 667	2.5	2.54	3.02	32.15	37.50	30.33
1995	359	2 590	2.4	4.57	2.51	32.24	29.64	14.22
1996	352	2 552	2.3	7.33	2.13	29.16	24.23	5.32
1997	322	2 300	2.0	2.01	1.75	23.57	19.56	5.39
1998	317	2 213	1.9	1.64	1.41	19.47	15.63	6.59
1999	298	2 186	1.8	1.48	1.18	16.83	14.21	2.86
2000	299	2 112	1.7	1.73	1.05	18.76	12.54	0.58
2001	406	3 016	2.4	1.47	1.15	18.44	14.04	0.57
2002	404	3 570	2.8	1.46	1.22	17.61	16.15	11.10
2003	402	3 532	2.8	1.56	1.46	18.18	19.78	22.35
2004	342	2 930	2.3	1.50	1.89	18.10	26.93	3.03
2005	331	2 660	2.1	1.46	2.03	16.88	27.59	1.11
2006	312	2 456	1.9	1.34	1.96	15.47	26.32	1.22
2007	321	2 548	1.9	1.30	1.68	14.90	22.80	0.00
2008	418	3 337	2.5	1.26	1.63	14.53	22.16	3.43
2009	574	5 808	4.4	1.63	2.05	20.06	30.44	388.98
2010	459	4 544	3.6	2.72	2.55	28.32	39.22	571.43
2011	409	3 744	3.0	2.20	2.56	31.18	39.14	633.42
2012	374	3 319	2.6	1.48	2.56	20.42	39.72	179.91
2013	343	2 978	2.3	4.01	2.26	21.73	34.82	0.46
2014	308	2 590	2.2	1.33	1.82	16.33	26.02	0.79
2012								
January	381	3 475	2.8	2.07	2.74	30.47	42.84	498.94
February	366	3 418	2.7	1.34	2.54	28.02	41.96	471.98
March	365	3 358	2.7	1.20	2.47	23.88	41.33	436.39
April	380	3 315	2.6	1.22	2.39	19.63	40.14	355.66
May	372	3 312	2.6	1.26	2.49	16.38	38.61	250.37
June	379	3 314	2.6	1.42	2.56	16.29	38.19	60.58
July	369	3 295	2.6	1.49	2.50	17.63	39.38	15.23
August	373	3 308	2.6	1.23	2.60	17.39	38.69	3.89
September	381	3 298	2.6	1.26	2.64	16.88	38.14	19.36
October	364	2 889	2.5	1.87	2.94	18.13	39.08	36.02
November	403	2 837	2.6	1.72	2.42	19.40	39.33	38.14
December	363	2 879	2.5	1.73	2.51	21.67	39.45	18.59
2013								
January	359	3 169	2.5	1.84	2.60	22.72	40.24	0.89
February	354	3 110	2.4	1.36	2.42	21.85	39.22	0.60
March	350	3 069	2.4	1.15	2.34	19.99	38.18	0.52
April	344	3 031	2.3	1.47	2.15	18.53	37.04	0.39
May	345	2 983	2.3	1.32	2.12	17.47	35.47	0.41
June	345	2 979	2.3	1.50	2.22	17.20	33.95	0.39
July	342	3 005	2.3	2.11	2.22	20.54	35.07	1.24
August	333	2 940	2.3	1.39	2.26	20.35	33.07	0.29
September	315	2 891	2.2	1.13	2.12	19.63	32.41	0.25
October	353	2 889	2.2	33.54	2.78	43.02	31.85	0.25
November	331	2 837	2.2	1.96	2.05	20.05	31.24	0.19
December	352	2 879	2.2	1.79	1.89	21.78	30.76	0.20
2014								
January	329	2 907	2.2	1.75	2.08	22.94	31.37	0.67
February	337	2 891	2.2	1.20	1.87	21.27	29.40	0.78
March	324	2 809	2.1	1.05	1.85	18.30	27.60	0.56
April	321	2 713	2.1	1.11	1.63	15.00	25.90	1.38
May	313	2 640	2.0	1.00	1.60	12.48	24.70	0.88
June	314	2 584	2.0	1.23	1.79	11.73	23.61	1.81
July	300	2 534	1.9	1.73	1.81	14.30	24.00	2.45
August	302	2 517	1.9	1.17	1.98	14.81	24.21	0.69
September	296	2 434	1.9	1.21	1.87	15.92	24.62	0.05
October	284	2 388	1.8	1.60	2.16	15.90	25.30	0.12
November	293	2 390	1.8	1.49	1.59	16.67	27.11	0.07
December	288	2 391	1.8	1.45	1.60	17.70	24.94	0.05

[1] Insured unemployed as a percent of employment covered by state programs.
. . . = Not available.

Section 10b: Payroll Employment, Hours, and Earnings

Figure 10-3: Total Nonfarm Payroll Employment, 1946–2014

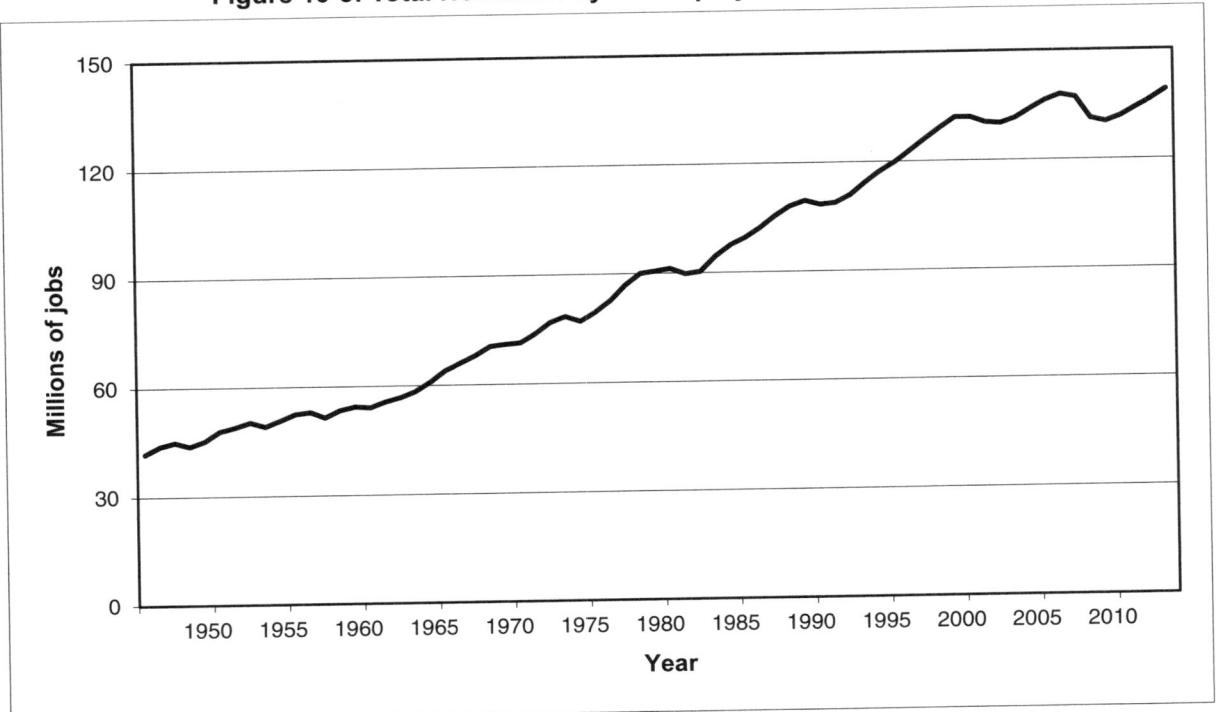

- Nonfarm payroll employment peaked in January 2008 and plunged 6.3 percent, a postwar record, between then and its lowest point in February 2010. The total number of jobs lost by this measure was 8.7 million. (Table 10-9)

- Data for July 2015 indicate a nonfarm payroll job gain of 10.8 million since the February 2010 low, comparable to the recent gains in the household survey featured in the previous section. Differences in concepts and measurement practice between these two employment surveys are discussed in the Notes and Definitions to this chapter. (Table 10-9 and recent data)

- Based on annual average data, payroll employment grew by 5.9 million jobs between the 2000 and 2007 business cycle high points, an average growth rate of 0.6 percent per year during the latest completed cycle. The previous business cycle lasted 10 years between high points, from 1990 to 2000. During that period, 22.5 million jobs were added to U.S. nonfarm payrolls, for an annual average growth rate of 1.9 percent per year. (Table 10-8B)

- The diffusion index indicates the percentage of private industries in which employment is higher than six months earlier. Diffusion indexes measure the extent to which expansion or contraction have spread throughout the economy; indexes below 50 percent indicate recession. This index reached a low of 12.2 percent in April 2009—lower than the lowest points reached in any of the previous four recessions (1980, 1981–1982, 1990–1991, and 2001), and thus indicating the most widespread and pervasive decline in 30 years or more. Gains have been widespread during the recovery, with 74 percent of industries showing increases in early 2012. However by July 2015, the data reveals a slippage to 64.4. (Tables 10-8A and recent data)

Table 10-8A. Nonfarm Payroll Employment by NAICS Supersector: Recent Data

(Thousands; seasonally adjusted, except as noted.)

Year and month	Total	Private							Service-providing				
		Total	Goods-producing						Total	Private			
			Total	Mining and logging	Construc-tion	Manufacturing				Total	Trade, transportation, and utilities		
						Total	Durable	Nondurable			Total	Wholesale trade	Retail trade
2005	134 005	112 201	22 190	628	7 336	14 227	8 956	5 271	111 814	90 010	25 959	5 764	15 280
2006	136 398	114 424	22 530	684	7 691	14 155	8 981	5 174	113 867	91 894	26 276	5 905	15 353
2007	137 936	115 718	22 233	724	7 630	13 879	8 808	5 071	115 703	93 485	26 630	6 015	15 520
2008	137 170	114 661	21 335	767	7 162	13 406	8 463	4 943	115 835	93 326	26 293	5 943	15 283
2009	131 233	108 678	18 558	694	6 016	11 847	7 284	4 564	112 675	90 121	24 906	5 587	14 522
2010	130 275	107 785	17 751	705	5 518	11 528	7 064	4 464	112 524	90 034	24 636	5 452	14 440
2011	131 842	109 756	18 047	788	5 533	11 726	7 273	4 453	113 795	91 708	25 065	5 543	14 668
2012	134 104	112 184	18 420	848	5 646	11 927	7 470	4 457	115 683	93 763	25 476	5 667	14 841
2013	136 368	114 504	18 700	868	5 827	12 006	7 543	4 463	117 668	95 804	25 870	5 747	15 077
2014	139 047	117 180	19 223	896	6 138	12 188	7 685	4 503	119 820	97 957	26 384	5 826	15 364
2010													
January	129 705	107 225	17 716	667	5 587	11 462	6 992	4 470	111 989	89 509	24 539	5 452	14 381
February	129 655	107 187	17 635	674	5 508	11 453	6 983	4 470	112 020	89 552	24 541	5 446	14 394
March	129 811	107 300	17 676	682	5 536	11 458	7 000	4 458	112 135	89 624	24 576	5 445	14 420
April	130 062	107 492	17 735	687	5 555	11 493	7 028	4 465	112 327	89 757	24 576	5 443	14 414
May	130 578	107 586	17 747	696	5 524	11 527	7 054	4 473	112 831	89 839	24 603	5 440	14 437
June	130 456	107 696	17 756	701	5 512	11 543	7 070	4 473	112 700	89 940	24 624	5 444	14 436
July	130 395	107 816	17 781	708	5 502	11 571	7 100	4 471	112 614	90 035	24 660	5 447	14 454
August	130 353	107 933	17 792	717	5 525	11 550	7 087	4 463	112 561	90 141	24 650	5 447	14 451
September	130 296	108 040	17 783	723	5 503	11 557	7 099	4 458	112 513	90 257	24 691	5 453	14 472
October	130 537	108 239	17 795	731	5 507	11 557	7 106	4 451	112 742	90 444	24 741	5 463	14 500
November	130 674	108 388	17 822	737	5 504	11 581	7 120	4 461	112 852	90 566	24 736	5 469	14 481
December	130 745	108 482	17 788	734	5 462	11 592	7 132	4 460	112 957	90 694	24 758	5 476	14 484
2011													
January	130 815	108 554	17 788	736	5 432	11 620	7 166	4 454	113 027	90 766	24 810	5 480	14 538
February	130 983	108 777	17 855	738	5 464	11 653	7 191	4 462	113 128	90 922	24 887	5 497	14 555
March	131 195	109 008	17 904	754	5 475	11 675	7 213	4 462	113 291	91 104	24 905	5 513	14 567
April	131 517	109 328	17 967	767	5 496	11 704	7 237	4 467	113 550	91 361	24 993	5 524	14 632
May	131 619	109 494	18 008	777	5 520	11 711	7 255	4 456	113 611	91 486	25 025	5 533	14 643
June	131 836	109 680	18 036	789	5 524	11 723	7 273	4 450	113 800	91 644	25 083	5 542	14 679
July	131 942	109 899	18 106	800	5 551	11 755	7 300	4 455	113 836	91 793	25 127	5 546	14 714
August	132 064	110 024	18 122	806	5 553	11 763	7 302	4 461	113 942	91 902	25 136	5 555	14 710
September	132 285	110 292	18 171	815	5 590	11 766	7 311	4 455	114 114	92 121	25 168	5 558	14 736
October	132 468	110 469	18 177	820	5 584	11 773	7 328	4 445	114 291	92 292	25 197	5 576	14 738
November	132 632	110 660	18 181	825	5 585	11 771	7 332	4 439	114 451	92 479	25 233	5 584	14 757
December	132 828	110 882	18 236	832	5 606	11 798	7 363	4 435	114 592	92 646	25 265	5 605	14 762
2012													
January	133 188	111 246	18 304	840	5 627	11 837	7 395	4 442	114 884	92 942	25 355	5 621	14 818
February	133 414	111 474	18 327	846	5 622	11 859	7 419	4 440	115 087	93 147	25 368	5 632	14 803
March	133 657	111 720	18 377	849	5 627	11 901	7 447	4 454	115 280	93 343	25 396	5 642	14 808
April	133 753	111 822	18 396	850	5 630	11 916	7 460	4 456	115 357	93 426	25 417	5 656	14 833
May	133 863	111 953	18 394	853	5 613	11 928	7 470	4 458	115 469	93 559	25 457	5 666	14 827
June	133 951	112 028	18 411	852	5 620	11 939	7 480	4 459	115 540	93 617	25 447	5 673	14 814
July	134 111	112 200	18 465	851	5 635	11 979	7 518	4 461	115 646	93 735	25 451	5 680	14 802
August	134 261	112 336	18 452	849	5 647	11 956	7 492	4 464	115 809	93 884	25 470	5 683	14 802
September	134 422	112 495	18 436	846	5 648	11 942	7 477	4 465	115 986	94 059	25 495	5 673	14 834
October	134 647	112 750	18 452	839	5 666	11 947	7 481	4 466	116 195	94 298	25 545	5 688	14 861
November	134 850	112 961	18 484	846	5 687	11 951	7 493	4 458	116 366	94 477	25 618	5 693	14 915
December	135 064	113 176	18 536	851	5 720	11 965	7 505	4 460	116 528	94 640	25 638	5 698	14 917
2013													
January	135 261	113 395	18 579	854	5 743	11 982	7 514	4 468	116 682	94 816	25 691	5 714	14 944
February	135 541	113 658	18 651	858	5 789	12 004	7 527	4 477	116 890	95 007	25 691	5 716	14 953
March	135 682	113 822	18 680	860	5 813	12 007	7 533	4 474	117 002	95 142	25 683	5 718	14 944
April	135 885	114 010	18 669	857	5 811	12 001	7 533	4 468	117 216	95 341	25 718	5 724	14 967
May	136 084	114 232	18 671	861	5 816	11 994	7 531	4 463	117 413	95 561	25 760	5 732	15 002
June	136 285	114 433	18 684	864	5 829	11 991	7 532	4 459	117 601	95 749	25 811	5 737	15 040
July	136 434	114 603	18 679	867	5 830	11 982	7 526	4 456	117 755	95 924	25 862	5 749	15 089
August	136 636	114 783	18 696	870	5 836	11 990	7 540	4 450	117 940	96 087	25 911	5 760	15 118
September	136 800	114 936	18 718	876	5 849	11 993	7 549	4 444	118 082	96 218	25 973	5 771	15 146
October	137 037	115 183	18 756	881	5 864	12 011	7 562	4 449	118 281	96 427	26 017	5 769	15 187
November	137 311	115 455	18 824	882	5 896	12 046	7 581	4 465	118 487	96 631	26 090	5 786	15 210
December	137 395	115 541	18 811	882	5 876	12 053	7 581	4 472	118 584	96 730	26 156	5 797	15 262
2014													
January	137 642	115 831	18 984	876	6 006	12 102	7 597	4 505	118 658	96 847	26 155	5 779	15 257
February	137 830	116 006	19 031	877	6 032	12 122	7 614	4 508	118 799	96 975	26 141	5 788	15 238
March	138 055	116 229	19 073	880	6 062	12 131	7 628	4 503	118 982	97 156	26 190	5 793	15 265
April	138 385	116 542	19 131	886	6 103	12 142	7 640	4 502	119 254	97 411	26 260	5 808	15 308
May	138 621	116 780	19 156	888	6 114	12 154	7 659	4 495	119 465	97 624	26 297	5 814	15 318
June	138 907	117 052	19 190	892	6 121	12 177	7 678	4 499	119 717	97 862	26 362	5 827	15 357
July	139 156	117 295	19 243	900	6 152	12 191	7 693	4 498	119 913	98 052	26 413	5 834	15 382
August	139 369	117 504	19 277	903	6 169	12 205	7 709	4 496	120 092	98 227	26 467	5 839	15 379
September	139 619	117 739	19 315	910	6 191	12 214	7 719	4 495	120 304	98 424	26 467	5 844	15 410
October	139 840	117 957	19 349	911	6 201	12 237	7 740	4 497	120 491	98 608	26 517	5 853	15 436
November	140 263	118 371	19 425	912	6 231	12 282	7 768	4 514	120 838	98 946	26 615	5 861	15 498
December	140 592	118 690	19 489	913	6 275	12 301	7 782	4 519	121 103	99 201	26 669	5 876	15 497

Table 10-8A. Nonfarm Payroll Employment by NAICS Supersector: Recent Data—*Continued*

(Thousands; seasonally adjusted, except as noted.)

							Service-providing—*Continued*							Diffusion index, 6-month span, private nonfarm [2]
	Private—*Continued*						Government							
Year and month								Federal		State		Local		
	Information	Financial activities	Profes-sional and business services	Education and health services	Leisure and hospitality	Other services	Total	Total	Depart-ment of Defense [1]	Total	Education	Total	Education	
2005	3 061	8 197	16 954	17 630	12 816	5 395	21 804	2 732	488	5 032	2 260	14 041	7 856	62.9
2006	3 038	8 367	17 566	18 099	13 110	5 438	21 974	2 732	493	5 075	2 293	14 167	7 913	59.3
2007	3 032	8 348	17 942	18 613	13 427	5 494	22 218	2 734	491	5 122	2 318	14 362	7 987	56.4
2008	2 984	8 206	17 735	19 156	13 436	5 515	22 509	2 762	496	5 177	2 354	14 571	8 084	26.9
2009	2 804	7 838	16 579	19 550	13 077	5 367	22 555	2 832	519	5 169	2 360	14 554	8 079	18.9
2010	2 707	7 695	16 728	19 889	13 049	5 331	22 490	2 977	545	5 137	2 373	14 376	8 013	61.6
2011	2 674	7 697	17 332	20 228	13 353	5 360	22 086	2 859	559	5 078	2 374	14 150	7 873	72.0
2012	2 676	7 784	17 932	20 698	13 768	5 430	21 920	2 820	552	5 055	2 389	14 045	7 778	62.3
2013	2 685	7 880	18 560	21 102	14 242	5 464	21 864	2 766	536	5 048	2 393	14 050	7 783	65.0
2014	2 740	7 979	19 096	21 475	14 710	5 537	21 863	2 724	522	5 060	2 409	14 074	7 791	74.0
2010														
January	2 743	7 732	16 514	19 728	12 931	5 322	22 480	2 860	534	5 141	2 357	14 479	8 064	27.7
February	2 733	7 725	16 551	19 753	12 933	5 316	22 468	2 871	536	5 147	2 366	14 450	8 052	27.7
March	2 718	7 707	16 540	19 808	12 947	5 328	22 511	2 922	538	5 140	2 359	14 449	8 053	35.6
April	2 715	7 708	16 616	19 825	12 981	5 336	22 570	2 986	540	5 136	2 363	14 448	8 056	43.9
May	2 710	7 699	16 644	19 846	13 007	5 330	22 992	3 415	542	5 135	2 370	14 442	8 059	49.6
June	2 700	7 691	16 704	19 876	13 031	5 314	22 760	3 193	545	5 139	2 374	14 428	8 068	56.4
July	2 700	7 681	16 719	19 896	13 053	5 326	22 579	3 054	547	5 138	2 376	14 387	8 032	57.6
August	2 702	7 678	16 765	19 936	13 087	5 323	22 420	2 945	549	5 130	2 371	14 345	7 997	60.6
September	2 700	7 681	16 789	19 931	13 132	5 333	22 256	2 869	550	5 126	2 371	14 261	7 925	61.6
October	2 696	7 684	16 852	19 988	13 125	5 358	22 298	2 866	552	5 139	2 385	14 293	7 966	61.4
November	2 689	7 680	16 953	20 032	13 130	5 346	22 286	2 866	554	5 139	2 389	14 281	7 961	61.2
December	2 684	7 684	17 031	20 041	13 159	5 337	22 263	2 870	556	5 135	2 393	14 258	7 949	65.5
2011														
January	2 684	7 679	17 059	20 058	13 149	5 327	22 261	2 874	558	5 141	2 404	14 246	7 942	64.4
February	2 671	7 675	17 103	20 074	13 196	5 336	22 206	2 875	558	5 107	2 379	14 224	7 924	63.4
March	2 670	7 679	17 186	20 086	13 247	5 331	22 187	2 876	560	5 096	2 378	14 215	7 921	66.7
April	2 675	7 678	17 236	20 150	13 286	5 343	22 189	2 872	559	5 091	2 375	14 226	7 939	65.7
May	2 677	7 699	17 287	20 161	13 290	5 347	22 125	2 872	559	5 082	2 371	14 171	7 895	67.2
June	2 685	7 689	17 292	20 204	13 338	5 353	22 156	2 859	558	5 079	2 373	14 218	7 953	70.3
July	2 676	7 693	17 320	20 247	13 372	5 358	22 043	2 860	558	5 058	2 379	14 125	7 859	73.3
August	2 632	7 702	17 379	20 283	13 396	5 374	22 040	2 852	558	5 080	2 386	14 108	7 842	69.5
September	2 679	7 699	17 445	20 332	13 416	5 382	21 993	2 846	559	5 079	2 378	14 068	7 802	72.0
October	2 680	7 710	17 496	20 364	13 463	5 382	21 999	2 849	561	5 055	2 369	14 095	7 831	68.0
November	2 674	7 723	17 542	20 401	13 514	5 392	21 972	2 843	560	5 048	2 365	14 081	7 817	68.4
December	2 683	7 733	17 610	20 410	13 542	5 403	21 946	2 839	559	5 041	2 358	14 066	7 800	67.8
2012														
January	2 673	7 733	17 694	20 479	13 594	5 414	21 942	2 833	557	5 048	2 373	14 061	7 793	72.2
February	2 673	7 741	17 752	20 563	13 638	5 412	21 940	2 827	555	5 049	2 376	14 064	7 796	74.1
March	2 675	7 765	17 790	20 593	13 703	5 421	21 937	2 826	553	5 053	2 379	14 058	7 788	73.9
April	2 677	7 766	17 835	20 613	13 700	5 418	21 931	2 826	554	5 058	2 383	14 047	7 781	74.2
May	2 680	7 778	17 864	20 656	13 705	5 419	21 910	2 825	554	5 049	2 379	14 036	7 770	75.2
June	2 675	7 781	17 912	20 666	13 711	5 425	21 923	2 824	553	5 056	2 387	14 043	7 772	70.8
July	2 679	7 781	17 964	20 689	13 739	5 432	21 911	2 814	552	5 053	2 388	14 044	7 774	64.8
August	2 680	7 789	17 998	20 706	13 810	5 431	21 925	2 819	551	5 058	2 397	14 048	7 781	64.4
September	2 673	7 803	18 014	20 765	13 868	5 441	21 927	2 819	550	5 074	2 411	14 034	7 772	62.3
October	2 672	7 812	18 078	20 858	13 889	5 444	21 897	2 821	550	5 052	2 395	14 024	7 762	61.7
November	2 681	7 816	18 132	20 862	13 921	5 447	21 889	2 816	547	5 052	2 395	14 021	7 760	63.4
December	2 674	7 827	18 165	20 904	13 981	5 451	21 888	2 814	547	5 050	2 393	14 024	7 763	67.6
2013														
January	2 673	7 835	18 210	20 921	14 028	5 458	21 866	2 809	547	5 034	2 371	14 023	7 763	65.5
February	2 692	7 847	18 295	20 948	14 078	5 456	21 883	2 810	547	5 049	2 392	14 024	7 764	70.1
March	2 694	7 853	18 362	20 989	14 112	5 449	21 860	2 789	545	5 056	2 400	14 015	7 764	71.0
April	2 688	7 863	18 434	21 040	14 145	5 453	21 875	2 791	543	5 053	2 400	14 031	7 768	70.1
May	2 686	7 872	18 511	21 069	14 198	5 465	21 852	2 768	540	5 047	2 394	14 037	7 769	69.7
June	2 685	7 885	18 570	21 084	14 249	5 465	21 852	2 767	537	5 034	2 383	14 051	7 770	66.9
July	2 697	7 901	18 621	21 108	14 272	5 463	21 831	2 756	534	5 025	2 372	14 050	7 779	65.3
August	2 669	7 897	18 663	21 172	14 306	5 469	21 853	2 749	532	5 039	2 386	14 065	7 795	62.7
September	2 682	7 896	18 700	21 181	14 315	5 471	21 864	2 744	531	5 051	2 397	14 069	7 798	65.0
October	2 688	7 903	18 753	21 212	14 380	5 474	21 854	2 732	527	5 057	2 400	14 065	7 794	64.4
November	2 689	7 899	18 826	21 237	14 417	5 473	21 856	2 739	527	5 060	2 405	14 057	7 781	67.4
December	2 674	7 901	18 842	21 242	14 435	5 480	21 854	2 736	525	5 064	2 410	14 054	7 773	66.9
2014														
January	2 724	7 918	18 771	21 249	14 494	5 536	21 811	2 731	525	5 053	5 053	14 027	2 402	73.4
February	2 720	7 931	18 840	21 279	14 526	5 538	21 824	2 730	525	5 061	5 061	14 033	2 408	74.3
March	2 723	7 933	18 879	21 314	14 565	5 552	21 826	2 727	524	5 057	5 057	14 042	2 406	75.9
April	2 728	7 942	18 951	21 353	14 610	5 567	21 843	2 726	523	5 060	5 060	14 057	2 409	77.2
May	2 723	7 951	19 005	21 409	14 667	5 572	21 841	2 726	522	5 054	5 054	14 061	2 401	76.4
June	2 735	7 968	19 079	21 452	14 698	5 568	21 855	2 726	521	5 057	5 057	14 072	2 405	72.6
July	2 740	7 984	19 124	21 497	14 721	5 573	21 861	2 724	521	5 051	5 051	14 086	2 397	76.0
August	2 753	7 997	19 180	21 539	14 746	5 585	21 865	2 727	521	5 042	5 042	14 096	2 392	74.1
September	2 757	8 007	19 231	21 585	14 795	5 582	21 880	2 725	521	5 062	5 062	14 093	2 412	74.0
October	2 754	8 014	19 271	21 613	14 850	5 589	21 883	2 720	519	5 067	5 067	14 096	2 415	74.0
November	2 761	8 042	19 367	21 664	14 892	5 605	21 892	2 729	520	5 072	5 072	14 091	2 424	78.1
December	2 767	8 049	19 439	21 718	14 948	5 611	21 902	2 732	520	5 079	5 079	14 091	2 430	79.3

[1]Not seasonally adjusted.
[2]See notes and definitions for explanation. September value used to represent year.

Table 10-8B. Nonfarm Payroll Employment by NAICS Supersector: Historical Annual

(Thousands.)

Year	Total	Private								Service-providing				
		Total	Goods-producing							Total	Private			
			Total	Mining and logging	Construc-tion	Manufacturing					Total	Trade, transportation, and utilities		
						Total	Durable	Nondurable				Total	Wholesale trade	Retail trade
1939	30 645	26 606	11 511	856	1 205	9 450	4 654	4 796		19 134	15 094	6 739	1 508	3 158
1940	32 407	28 156	12 378	927	1 352	10 099	5 261	4 839		20 029	15 778	7 043	1 571	3 324
1941	36 600	31 874	14 940	967	1 852	12 121	6 778	5 343		21 660	16 934	7 550	1 679	3 552
1942	40 213	34 621	17 275	1 010	2 234	14 030	8 502	5 528		22 938	17 347	7 607	1 635	3 522
1943	42 574	36 353	18 738	958	1 627	16 153	10 583	5 570		23 837	17 615	7 628	1 566	3 479
1944	42 006	35 819	17 981	926	1 152	15 903	10 372	5 531		24 026	17 839	7 805	1 585	3 516
1945	40 510	34 428	16 308	864	1 190	14 255	8 732	5 523		24 203	18 121	8 048	1 672	3 624
1946	41 759	36 054	16 122	885	1 724	13 513	7 535	5 978		25 637	19 932	8 945	1 962	4 118
1947	43 945	38 379	17 314	976	2 051	14 287	8 079	6 208		26 631	21 064	9 452	2 116	4 393
1948	44 954	39 213	17 579	1 014	2 241	14 324	8 028	6 296		27 376	21 634	9 716	2 230	4 524
1949	43 843	37 893	16 464	948	2 236	13 281	7 240	6 041		27 379	21 430	9 579	2 227	4 520
1950	45 287	39 167	17 343	924	2 405	14 013	7 809	6 204		27 945	21 824	9 694	2 255	4 580
1951	47 930	41 427	18 703	956	2 678	15 070	8 738	6 332		29 227	22 725	10 089	2 335	4 758
1952	48 909	42 182	18 928	928	2 709	15 291	8 979	6 312		29 981	23 254	10 302	2 408	4 880
1953	50 310	43 552	19 733	902	2 700	16 131	9 690	6 441		30 577	23 820	10 504	2 444	5 012
1954	49 093	42 235	18 515	825	2 688	15 002	8 773	6 229		30 578	23 720	10 357	2 454	4 999
1955	50 744	43 722	19 234	828	2 881	15 524	9 161	6 363		31 510	24 489	10 612	2 505	5 158
1956	52 473	45 087	19 799	859	3 082	15 858	9 435	6 424		32 674	25 288	10 921	2 583	5 315
1957	52 959	45 235	19 669	864	3 007	15 798	9 452	6 346		33 290	25 566	10 942	2 593	5 328
1958	51 426	43 480	18 319	801	2 862	14 656	8 480	6 176		33 107	25 161	10 656	2 551	5 267
1959	53 374	45 182	19 163	789	3 050	15 325	8 988	6 337		34 211	26 018	10 960	2 638	5 453
1960	54 296	45 832	19 182	771	2 973	15 438	9 071	6 367		35 114	26 650	11 147	2 690	5 589
1961	54 105	45 399	18 647	728	2 908	15 011	8 711	6 300		35 458	26 752	11 040	2 681	5 560
1962	55 659	46 655	19 203	709	2 997	15 498	9 099	6 399		36 455	27 451	11 215	2 737	5 672
1963	56 764	47 423	19 385	694	3 060	15 631	9 226	6 405		37 379	28 038	11 367	2 780	5 781
1964	58 391	48 680	19 733	697	3 148	15 888	9 414	6 474		38 658	28 947	11 677	2 856	5 977
1965	60 874	50 683	20 595	694	3 284	16 617	9 973	6 644		40 279	30 089	12 139	2 967	6 262
1966	64 020	53 110	21 740	690	3 371	17 680	10 803	6 878		42 280	31 370	12 611	3 080	6 530
1967	65 931	54 406	21 882	679	3 305	17 897	10 952	6 945		44 049	32 524	12 950	3 158	6 711
1968	68 023	56 050	22 292	671	3 410	18 211	11 137	7 074		45 731	33 759	13 334	3 236	6 977
1969	70 512	58 181	22 893	683	3 637	18 573	11 396	7 177		47 619	35 288	13 853	3 344	7 295
1970	71 006	58 318	22 179	677	3 654	17 848	10 762	7 086		48 827	36 139	14 144	3 418	7 463
1971	71 335	58 323	21 602	658	3 770	17 174	10 229	6 944		49 734	36 721	14 318	3 424	7 657
1972	73 798	60 333	22 299	672	3 957	17 669	10 630	7 039		51 499	38 034	14 788	3 547	8 038
1973	76 912	63 050	23 450	693	4 167	18 589	11 414	7 176		53 462	39 600	15 349	3 688	8 371
1974	78 389	64 086	23 364	755	4 095	18 514	11 432	7 082		55 025	40 721	15 693	3 823	8 536
1975	77 069	62 250	21 318	802	3 608	16 909	10 266	6 643		55 751	40 932	15 606	3 810	8 600
1976	79 502	64 501	22 025	832	3 662	17 531	10 640	6 891		57 477	42 476	16 128	3 920	8 966
1977	82 593	67 334	22 972	865	3 940	18 167	11 132	7 035		59 620	44 362	16 765	4 055	9 359
1978	86 826	71 014	24 156	902	4 322	18 932	11 770	7 162		62 670	46 858	17 658	4 280	9 879
1979	89 933	73 865	24 997	1 008	4 562	19 426	12 220	7 206		64 936	48 869	18 303	4 485	10 180
1980	90 533	74 158	24 263	1 077	4 454	18 733	11 679	7 054		66 270	49 895	18 413	4 557	10 244
1981	91 297	75 117	24 118	1 180	4 304	18 634	11 611	7 023		67 179	50 999	18 604	4 634	10 364
1982	89 689	73 706	22 550	1 163	4 024	17 363	10 610	6 753		67 138	51 156	18 457	4 575	10 372
1983	90 295	74 284	22 110	997	4 065	17 048	10 326	6 722		68 186	52 174	18 668	4 559	10 635
1984	94 548	78 389	23 435	1 014	4 501	17 920	11 050	6 870		71 113	54 954	19 653	4 788	11 223
1985	97 532	81 000	23 585	974	4 793	17 819	11 034	6 784		73 947	57 415	20 379	4 915	11 733
1986	99 500	82 661	23 318	829	4 937	17 552	10 795	6 757		76 182	59 343	20 795	4 935	12 078
1987	102 116	84 960	23 470	771	5 090	17 609	10 767	6 842		78 647	61 490	21 302	5 003	12 419
1988	105 378	87 838	23 909	770	5 233	17 906	10 969	6 938		81 469	63 929	21 974	5 153	12 808
1989	108 051	90 124	24 045	750	5 309	17 985	11 004	6 981		84 006	66 079	22 510	5 284	13 108
1990	109 527	91 112	23 723	765	5 263	17 695	10 737	6 958		85 804	67 389	22 666	5 268	13 182
1991	108 427	89 881	22 588	739	4 780	17 068	10 220	6 848		85 839	67 293	22 281	5 185	12 896
1992	108 802	90 015	22 095	689	4 608	16 799	9 946	6 853		86 707	67 921	22 125	5 110	12 828
1993	110 935	91 946	22 219	666	4 779	16 774	9 901	6 872		88 716	69 727	22 378	5 093	13 021
1994	114 398	95 124	22 774	659	5 095	17 020	10 132	6 889		91 624	72 350	23 128	5 247	13 491
1995	117 407	97 975	23 156	641	5 274	17 241	10 373	6 868		94 251	74 819	23 834	5 433	13 897
1996	119 836	100 297	23 409	637	5 536	17 237	10 486	6 751		96 427	76 888	24 239	5 522	14 143
1997	122 951	103 287	23 886	654	5 813	17 419	10 705	6 714		99 065	79 401	24 700	5 664	14 389
1998	126 157	106 248	24 354	645	6 149	17 560	10 911	6 649		101 803	81 894	25 186	5 795	14 609
1999	129 240	108 933	24 465	598	6 545	17 322	10 831	6 491		104 775	84 468	25 771	5 893	14 970
2000	132 019	111 230	24 649	599	6 787	17 263	10 877	6 386		107 370	86 581	26 225	5 933	15 280
2001	132 074	110 956	23 873	606	6 826	16 441	10 336	6 105		108 201	87 083	25 983	5 773	15 239
2002	130 628	109 115	22 557	583	6 716	15 259	9 485	5 774		108 071	86 558	25 497	5 652	15 025
2003	130 318	108 735	21 816	572	6 735	14 509	8 964	5 546		108 501	86 918	25 287	5 608	14 917
2004	131 749	110 128	21 882	591	6 976	14 315	8 925	5 390		109 866	88 246	25 533	5 663	15 058
2005	134 005	112 201	22 190	628	7 336	14 227	8 956	5 271		111 814	90 010	25 959	5 764	15 280
2006	136 398	114 424	22 530	684	7 691	14 155	8 981	5 174		113 867	91 894	26 276	5 905	15 353
2007	137 936	115 718	22 233	724	7 630	13 879	8 808	5 071		115 703	93 485	26 630	6 015	15 520
2008	137 170	114 661	21 335	767	7 162	13 406	8 463	4 943		115 835	93 326	26 293	5 943	15 283
2009	131 233	108 678	18 558	694	6 016	11 847	7 284	4 564		112 675	90 121	24 906	5 587	14 522
2010	130 275	107 785	17 751	705	5 518	11 528	7 064	4 464		112 524	90 034	24 636	5 452	14 440
2011	131 842	109 756	18 047	788	5 533	11 726	7 273	4 453		113 795	91 708	25 065	5 543	14 668
2012	134 104	112 184	18 420	848	5 646	11 927	7 470	4 457		115 683	93 763	25 476	5 667	14 841
2013	136 368	114 504	18 700	868	5 827	12 006	7 543	4 463		117 668	95 804	25 870	5 747	15 077
2014	139 047	117 180	19 223	896	6 138	12 188	7 685	4 503		119 820	97 957	26 384	5 826	15 364

Table 10-8B. Nonfarm Payroll Employment by NAICS Supersector: Historical Annual—*Continued*

(Thousands.)

Year			Service-providing—*Continued*											Diffusion index, 6-month span, private nonfarm [2]
	Private—*Continued*						Government							
								Federal		State		Local		
	Information	Financial activities	Profes-sional and business services	Education and health services	Leisure and hospitality	Other services	Total	Total	Depart-ment of Defense [1]	Total	Education	Total	Education	
1939	1 141	1 386	1 976	1 405	1 896	553	4 040	950	133	. . .	. . .	. . .	. . .	. . .
1940	1 196	1 424	2 073	1 470	1 995	578	4 251	1 045	182	. . .	. . .	. . .	. . .	. . .
1941	1 342	1 466	2 265	1 566	2 130	616	4 726	1 406	375	. . .	. . .	. . .	. . .	. . .
1942	1 470	1 455	2 410	1 632	2 133	641	5 592	2 322	920	. . .	. . .	. . .	. . .	. . .
1943	1 605	1 431	2 518	1 660	2 122	652	6 222	3 047	1 361	. . .	. . .	. . .	. . .	. . .
1944	1 635	1 414	2 523	1 667	2 142	654	6 187	3 071	1 352	. . .	. . .	. . .	. . .	. . .
1945	1 581	1 435	2 495	1 698	2 200	664	6 082	2 945	1 234	. . .	. . .	. . .	. . .	. . .
1946	1 594	1 619	2 666	1 885	2 485	737	5 705	2 365	746	. . .	. . .	. . .	. . .	. . .
1947	1 658	1 674	2 828	2 015	2 650	788	5 567	1 985	499	. . .	. . .	. . .	. . .	. . .
1948	1 669	1 742	2 893	2 077	2 726	812	5 742	1 954	511	. . .	. . .	. . .	. . .	. . .
1949	1 583	1 768	2 853	2 097	2 729	820	5 950	2 001	531	. . .	. . .	. . .	. . .	. . .
1950	1 625	1 825	2 928	2 144	2 769	839	6 120	2 023	533	. . .	. . .	. . .	. . .	. . .
1951	1 718	1 890	3 061	2 221	2 877	870	6 502	2 415	797	. . .	. . .	. . .	. . .	. . .
1952	1 736	1 964	3 128	2 281	2 950	894	6 727	2 539	868	. . .	. . .	. . .	. . .	. . .
1953	1 785	2 036	3 215	2 335	3 030	916	6 758	2 418	818	. . .	. . .	. . .	. . .	. . .
1954	1 693	2 118	3 197	2 385	3 034	936	6 858	2 295	744	. . .	. . .	. . .	. . .	. . .
1955	1 735	2 212	3 320	2 491	3 140	978	7 021	2 295	744	1 168	308	3 558	1 751	. . .
1956	1 778	2 299	3 437	2 593	3 242	1 018	7 386	2 318	749	1 249	334	3 819	1 884	. . .
1957	1 780	2 348	3 504	2 676	3 267	1 050	7 724	2 326	729	1 328	363	4 071	2 026	. . .
1958	1 674	2 386	3 449	2 695	3 243	1 058	7 946	2 298	695	1 415	389	4 232	2 115	. . .
1959	1 718	2 454	3 591	2 822	3 365	1 107	8 192	2 342	699	1 484	420	4 366	2 198	. . .
1960	1 728	2 532	3 694	2 937	3 460	1 152	8 464	2 381	681	1 536	448	4 547	2 314	. . .
1961	1 693	2 590	3 744	3 030	3 468	1 188	8 706	2 391	683	1 607	474	4 708	2 411	. . .
1962	1 723	2 656	3 885	3 172	3 557	1 243	9 004	2 455	697	1 669	511	4 881	2 522	. . .
1963	1 735	2 731	3 990	3 288	3 639	1 288	9 341	2 473	687	1 747	557	5 121	2 674	. . .
1964	1 766	2 811	4 137	3 438	3 772	1 346	9 711	2 463	676	1 856	609	5 392	2 839	. . .
1965	1 824	2 878	4 306	3 587	3 951	1 404	10 191	2 495	679	1 996	679	5 700	3 031	. . .
1966	1 908	2 961	4 517	3 770	4 127	1 475	10 910	2 690	741	2 141	775	6 080	3 297	. . .
1967	1 955	3 087	4 720	3 986	4 269	1 558	11 525	2 852	802	2 302	873	6 371	3 490	. . .
1968	1 991	3 234	4 918	4 191	4 453	1 638	11 972	2 871	801	2 442	958	6 660	3 649	. . .
1969	2 048	3 404	5 156	4 428	4 670	1 731	12 330	2 893	815	2 533	1 042	6 904	3 785	. . .
1970	2 041	3 532	5 267	4 577	4 789	1 789	12 687	2 865	756	2 664	1 104	7 158	3 912	. . .
1971	2 009	3 651	5 328	4 675	4 914	1 827	13 012	2 828	731	2 747	1 149	7 437	4 091	. . .
1972	2 056	3 784	5 523	4 863	5 121	1 900	13 465	2 815	720	2 859	1 188	7 790	4 262	. . .
1973	2 135	3 920	5 774	5 092	5 341	1 990	13 862	2 794	696	2 923	1 205	8 146	4 433	. . .
1974	2 160	4 023	5 974	5 322	5 471	2 078	14 303	2 858	698	3 039	1 267	8 407	4 584	. . .
1975	2 061	4 047	6 034	5 497	5 544	2 144	14 820	2 882	704	3 179	1 323	8 758	4 722	. . .
1976	2 111	4 155	6 287	5 756	5 794	2 244	15 001	2 863	693	3 273	1 371	8 865	4 786	. . .
1977	2 185	4 348	6 587	6 052	6 065	2 359	15 258	2 859	676	3 377	1 385	9 023	4 859	77.5
1978	2 287	4 599	6 972	6 427	6 411	2 505	15 812	2 893	661	3 474	1 367	9 446	4 958	75.6
1979	2 375	4 843	7 312	6 768	6 631	2 637	16 068	2 894	649	3 541	1 378	9 633	4 989	57.7
1980	2 361	5 025	7 544	7 077	6 721	2 755	16 375	3 000	645	3 610	1 398	9 765	5 090	61.2
1981	2 382	5 163	7 782	7 364	6 840	2 865	16 180	2 922	655	3 640	1 420	9 619	5 095	39.0
1982	2 317	5 209	7 848	7 526	6 874	2 924	15 982	2 884	690	3 640	1 433	9 458	5 049	34.8
1983	2 253	5 334	8 039	7 781	7 078	3 021	16 011	2 915	699	3 662	1 450	9 434	5 020	78.2
1984	2 398	5 553	8 464	8 211	7 489	3 186	16 159	2 943	716	3 734	1 488	9 482	5 076	64.9
1985	2 437	5 815	8 871	8 679	7 869	3 366	16 533	3 014	738	3 832	1 540	9 687	5 221	59.5
1986	2 445	6 128	9 211	9 086	8 156	3 523	16 838	3 044	736	3 893	1 561	9 901	5 358	62.4
1987	2 507	6 385	9 608	9 543	8 446	3 699	17 156	3 089	736	3 967	1 586	10 100	5 469	73.5
1988	2 585	6 500	10 090	10 096	8 778	3 907	17 540	3 124	719	4 076	1 621	10 339	5 590	66.3
1989	2 622	6 562	10 555	10 652	9 062	4 116	17 927	3 136	735	4 182	1 668	10 609	5 740	54.6
1990	2 688	6 614	10 848	11 024	9 288	4 261	18 415	3 196	722	4 305	1 730	10 914	5 902	36.7
1991	2 677	6 561	10 714	11 556	9 256	4 249	18 545	3 110	702	4 355	1 768	11 081	5 994	43.9
1992	2 641	6 559	10 970	11 948	9 437	4 240	18 787	3 111	702	4 408	1 799	11 267	6 076	62.9
1993	2 668	6 742	11 495	12 362	9 732	4 350	18 989	3 063	670	4 488	1 834	11 438	6 206	72.0
1994	2 738	6 910	12 174	12 872	10 100	4 428	19 275	3 018	657	4 576	1 882	11 682	6 329	80.5
1995	2 843	6 866	12 844	13 360	10 501	4 572	19 432	2 949	627	4 635	1 919	11 849	6 453	69.1
1996	2 940	7 018	13 462	13 761	10 777	4 690	19 539	2 877	597	4 606	1 911	12 056	6 592	77.8
1997	3 084	7 255	14 335	14 185	11 018	4 825	19 664	2 806	588	4 582	1 904	12 276	6 759	79.9
1998	3 218	7 565	15 147	14 570	11 232	4 976	19 909	2 772	550	4 612	1 922	12 525	6 921	69.3
1999	3 419	7 753	15 957	14 939	11 543	5 087	20 307	2 769	525	4 709	1 983	12 829	7 120	69.3
2000	3 630	7 783	16 666	15 247	11 862	5 168	20 790	2 865	510	4 786	2 031	13 139	7 294	58.1
2001	3 629	7 900	16 476	15 801	12 036	5 258	21 118	2 764	504	4 905	2 113	13 449	7 479	31.8
2002	3 395	7 956	15 976	16 377	11 986	5 372	21 513	2 766	499	5 029	2 243	13 718	7 654	37.3
2003	3 188	8 078	15 987	16 805	12 173	5 401	21 583	2 761	486	5 002	2 255	13 820	7 709	39.6
2004	3 118	8 105	16 394	17 192	12 493	5 409	21 621	2 730	473	4 982	2 238	13 909	7 765	59.7
2005	3 061	8 197	16 954	17 630	12 816	5 395	21 804	2 732	488	5 032	2 260	14 041	7 856	62.9
2006	3 038	8 367	17 566	18 099	13 110	5 438	21 974	2 732	493	5 075	2 293	14 167	7 913	59.3
2007	3 032	8 348	17 942	18 613	13 427	5 494	22 218	2 734	491	5 122	2 318	14 362	7 987	56.4
2008	2 984	8 206	17 735	19 156	13 436	5 515	22 509	2 762	496	5 177	2 354	14 571	8 084	26.9
2009	2 804	7 838	16 579	19 550	13 077	5 367	22 555	2 832	519	5 169	2 360	14 554	8 079	18.9
2010	2 707	7 695	16 728	19 889	13 049	5 331	22 490	2 977	545	5 137	2 373	14 376	8 013	61.6
2011	2 674	7 697	17 332	20 228	13 353	5 360	22 086	2 859	559	5 078	2 374	14 150	7 873	72.0
2012	2 676	7 784	17 932	20 698	13 768	5 430	21 920	2 820	552	5 055	2 389	14 045	7 778	62.3
2013	2 685	7 880	18 560	21 102	14 242	5 464	21 864	2 766	536	5 048	2 393	14 050	7 783	65.0
2014	2 740	7 979	19 096	21 475	14 710	5 537	21 863	2 724	522	5 060	2 409	14 074	7 791	74.0

[1]Not seasonally adjusted.
[2]See notes and definitions for explanation. September value used to represent year.
. . . = Not available.

Table 10-9. Employment, Hours, and Earnings, Total Nonfarm and Manufacturing, Historical Annual and Monthly

(Wage and salary workers on nonfarm payrolls, seasonally adjusted.)

| Year and month | All wage and salary workers (thousands) | | | | | Production and nonsupervisory workers on private payrolls | | | | | | | |
	Total	Private Total	Goods-producing Total	Manufacturing	Service-providing	Number (thousands) Total private	Number Manufacturing	Average hours per week Total private	Average hours Manufacturing	Average hourly earnings Total private	Average hourly Manufacturing	Average weekly earnings Total private	Average weekly Manufacturing
1939	30 645	26 606	11 511	9 450	19 134	...	8 163	...	37.7	...	0.49	...	18.47
1940	32 407	28 156	12 378	10 099	20 029	...	8 737	...	38.2	...	0.53	...	20.25
1941	36 600	31 874	14 940	12 121	21 660	...	10 641	...	40.7	...	0.61	...	24.83
1942	40 213	34 621	17 275	14 030	22 938	...	12 447	...	43.2	...	0.74	...	31.97
1943	42 574	36 353	18 738	16 153	23 837	...	14 407	...	45.1	...	0.86	...	38.79
1944	42 006	35 819	17 981	15 903	24 026	...	14 031	...	45.4	...	0.91	...	41.31
1945	40 510	34 428	16 308	14 255	24 203	...	12 445	...	43.6	...	0.90	...	39.24
1946	41 759	36 054	16 122	13 513	25 637	...	11 781	...	40.4	...	0.95	...	38.38
1947	43 945	38 379	17 314	14 287	26 631	...	12 453	...	40.5	...	1.10	...	44.55
1948	44 954	39 213	17 579	14 324	27 376	...	12 383	...	40.1	...	1.20	...	48.12
1949	43 843	37 893	16 464	13 281	27 379	...	11 355	...	39.2	...	1.25	...	49.00
1950	45 287	39 167	17 343	14 013	27 945	...	12 032	...	40.6	...	1.32	...	53.59
1951	47 930	41 427	18 703	15 070	29 227	...	12 808	...	40.7	...	1.45	...	59.02
1952	48 909	42 182	18 928	15 291	29 981	...	12 797	...	40.8	...	1.53	...	62.42
1953	50 310	43 552	19 733	16 131	30 577	...	13 437	...	40.6	...	1.63	...	66.18
1954	49 093	42 235	18 515	15 002	30 578	...	12 300	...	39.7	...	1.66	...	65.90
1955	50 744	43 722	19 234	15 524	31 510	...	12 735	...	40.8	...	1.74	...	70.99
1956	52 473	45 087	19 799	15 858	32 674	...	12 869	...	40.5	...	1.84	...	74.52
1957	52 959	45 235	19 669	15 798	33 290	...	12 640	...	39.9	...	1.93	...	77.01
1958	51 426	43 480	18 319	14 656	33 107	...	11 532	...	39.2	...	1.99	...	78.01
1959	53 374	45 182	19 163	15 325	34 211	...	12 089	...	40.3	...	2.08	...	83.82
1960	54 296	45 832	19 182	15 438	35 114	...	12 074	...	39.8	...	2.15	...	85.57
1961	54 105	45 399	18 647	15 011	35 458	...	11 612	...	39.9	...	2.20	...	87.78
1962	55 659	46 655	19 203	15 498	36 455	...	11 986	...	40.5	...	2.27	...	91.94
1963	56 764	47 423	19 385	15 631	37 379	...	12 051	...	40.6	...	2.34	...	95.00
1964	58 391	48 680	19 733	15 888	38 658	40 575	12 298	38.5	40.8	2.53	2.41	97.41	98.33
1946													
January	39 832	34 047	15 031	12 719	24 801	...	10 990	...	40.9	...	0.86	...	35.17
February	39 251	33 473	14 308	11 922	24 943	...	10 292	...	40.4	...	0.85	...	34.34
March	40 193	34 435	15 017	12 545	25 176	...	10 989	...	40.6	...	0.89	...	36.13
April	40 909	35 148	15 439	13 200	25 470	...	11 616	...	40.4	...	0.92	...	37.17
May	41 349	35 617	15 875	13 389	25 474	...	11 758	...	39.8	...	0.93	...	37.01
June	41 733	36 053	16 206	13 598	25 527	...	11 905	...	40.0	...	0.94	...	37.60
July	42 153	36 471	16 461	13 771	25 692	...	12 065	...	40.2	...	0.96	...	38.59
August	42 643	36 962	16 728	13 981	25 915	...	12 241	...	40.6	...	0.98	...	39.79
September	42 909	37 240	16 912	14 135	25 997	...	12 311	...	40.4	...	0.99	...	40.00
October	43 094	37 430	17 002	14 182	26 092	...	12 302	...	40.4	...	1.00	...	40.40
November	43 397	37 758	17 157	14 310	26 240	...	12 421	...	40.3	...	1.02	...	41.11
December	43 379	37 751	17 164	14 301	26 215	...	12 419	...	40.5	...	1.02	...	41.31
1947													
January	43 539	37 920	17 213	14 328	26 326	...	12 445	...	40.5	...	1.03	...	41.72
February	43 563	37 957	17 200	14 278	26 363	...	12 487	...	40.4	...	1.04	...	42.02
March	43 606	38 018	17 196	14 259	26 410	...	12 518	...	40.3	...	1.06	...	42.72
April	43 492	37 934	17 178	14 240	26 314	...	12 531	...	40.5	...	1.06	...	42.93
May	43 638	38 087	17 176	14 189	26 462	...	12 449	...	40.4	...	1.08	...	43.63
June	43 808	38 284	17 253	14 200	26 555	...	12 389	...	40.4	...	1.10	...	44.44
July	43 743	38 219	17 106	14 076	26 637	...	12 265	...	40.4	...	1.10	...	44.44
August	43 959	38 440	17 280	14 200	26 679	...	12 370	...	40.0	...	1.11	...	44.40
September	44 201	38 662	17 398	14 315	26 803	...	12 430	...	40.5	...	1.11	...	44.96
October	44 415	38 849	17 499	14 393	26 916	...	12 464	...	40.5	...	1.13	...	45.77
November	44 487	38 902	17 517	14 414	26 970	...	12 494	...	40.5	...	1.14	...	46.17
December	44 579	38 974	17 563	14 428	27 016	...	12 526	...	40.8	...	1.16	...	47.33
1948													
January	44 682	39 058	17 625	14 438	27 057	...	12 520	...	40.5	...	1.16	...	46.98
February	44 537	38 922	17 447	14 339	27 090	...	12 437	...	40.2	...	1.16	...	46.63
March	44 681	39 058	17 544	14 364	27 137	...	12 489	...	40.4	...	1.16	...	46.86
April	44 370	38 727	17 302	14 183	27 068	...	12 304	...	40.1	...	1.17	...	46.92
May	44 795	39 114	17 508	14 235	27 287	...	12 344	...	40.2	...	1.18	...	47.44
June	45 033	39 297	17 633	14 318	27 400	...	12 402	...	40.3	...	1.19	...	47.96
July	45 160	39 386	17 649	14 359	27 511	...	12 417	...	40.2	...	1.21	...	48.64
August	45 176	39 385	17 655	14 353	27 521	...	12 397	...	40.2	...	1.23	...	49.45
September	45 295	39 490	17 741	14 441	27 554	...	12 450	...	40.1	...	1.24	...	49.72
October	45 251	39 422	17 683	14 390	27 568	...	12 364	...	39.8	...	1.25	...	49.75
November	45 194	39 325	17 599	14 292	27 595	...	12 302	...	39.8	...	1.26	...	50.15
December	45 029	39 141	17 417	14 086	27 612	...	12 127	...	39.6	...	1.26	...	49.90
1949													
January	44 671	38 777	17 170	13 867	27 501	...	11 905	...	39.4	...	1.26	...	49.64
February	44 500	38 607	17 019	13 734	27 481	...	11 792	...	39.4	...	1.26	...	49.64
March	44 238	38 323	16 848	13 581	27 390	...	11 654	...	39.1	...	1.26	...	49.27
April	44 230	38 282	16 685	13 439	27 545	...	11 517	...	38.8	...	1.25	...	48.50
May	43 982	38 020	16 492	13 269	27 490	...	11 352	...	38.9	...	1.25	...	48.63
June	43 739	37 783	16 351	13 178	27 388	...	11 266	...	39.0	...	1.26	...	49.14
July	43 529	37 567	16 222	13 067	27 307	...	11 168	...	39.2	...	1.26	...	49.39
August	43 622	37 637	16 327	13 158	27 295	...	11 251	...	39.2	...	1.25	...	49.00
September	43 784	37 794	16 403	13 225	27 381	...	11 284	...	39.4	...	1.25	...	49.25
October	42 950	36 980	15 739	12 891	27 211	...	10 940	...	39.6	...	1.24	...	49.10
November	43 245	37 295	16 040	12 882	27 205	...	10 964	...	39.1	...	1.24	...	48.48
December	43 517	37 565	16 217	13 062	27 300	...	11 173	...	39.4	...	1.25	...	49.25

. . . = Not available.

Table 10-9. Employment, Hours, and Earnings, Total Nonfarm and Manufacturing, Historical Annual and Monthly—*Continued*

(Wage and salary workers on nonfarm payrolls, seasonally adjusted.)

Year and month	All wage and salary workers (thousands)					Production and nonsupervisory workers on private payrolls							
	Total	Private			Service-providing	Number (thousands)		Average hours per week		Average hourly earnings, dollars		Average weekly earnings, dollars	
		Total	Goods-producing			Total private	Manufac-turing	Total private	Manufac-turing	Total private	Manufac-turing	Total private	Manufac-turing
			Total	Manufac-turing									
1950													
January	43 528	37 594	16 255	13 161	27 273	. . .	11 258	. . .	39.6	. . .	1.27	. . .	50.29
February	43 298	37 372	16 035	13 169	27 263	. . .	11 262	. . .	39.7	. . .	1.26	. . .	50.02
March	43 952	37 874	16 482	13 290	27 470	. . .	11 362	. . .	39.7	. . .	1.28	. . .	50.82
April	44 376	38 282	16 718	13 471	27 658	. . .	11 528	. . .	40.3	. . .	1.29	. . .	51.99
May	44 718	38 675	17 080	13 780	27 638	. . .	11 855	. . .	40.3	. . .	1.30	. . .	52.39
June	45 084	39 062	17 288	13 923	27 796	. . .	11 979	. . .	40.6	. . .	1.30	. . .	52.78
July	45 454	39 364	17 464	14 072	27 990	. . .	12 107	. . .	40.9	. . .	1.31	. . .	53.58
August	46 188	40 001	17 917	14 461	28 271	. . .	12 476	. . .	41.3	. . .	1.33	. . .	54.93
September	46 442	40 214	18 040	14 561	28 402	. . .	12 519	. . .	40.8	. . .	1.33	. . .	54.26
October	46 712	40 463	18 249	14 737	28 463	. . .	12 659	. . .	41.1	. . .	1.36	. . .	55.90
November	46 778	40 516	18 288	14 762	28 490	. . .	12 682	. . .	41.0	. . .	1.37	. . .	56.17
December	46 855	40 541	18 283	14 782	28 572	. . .	12 710	. . .	40.9	. . .	1.39	. . .	56.85
1951													
January	47 288	40 936	18 518	14 950	28 770	. . .	12 816	. . .	41.0	. . .	1.40	. . .	57.40
February	47 577	41 195	18 666	15 076	28 911	. . .	12 929	. . .	40.9	. . .	1.41	. . .	57.67
March	47 871	41 461	18 754	15 125	29 117	. . .	12 936	. . .	41.0	. . .	1.42	. . .	58.22
April	47 856	41 405	18 810	15 166	29 046	. . .	12 960	. . .	41.0	. . .	1.43	. . .	58.63
May	47 953	41 536	18 829	15 164	29 124	. . .	12 941	. . .	41.0	. . .	1.44	. . .	59.04
June	48 068	41 569	18 826	15 176	29 242	. . .	12 934	. . .	40.9	. . .	1.45	. . .	59.31
July	48 062	41 524	18 747	15 110	29 315	. . .	12 848	. . .	40.6	. . .	1.45	. . .	58.87
August	48 009	41 490	18 709	15 061	29 300	. . .	12 772	. . .	40.4	. . .	1.46	. . .	58.98
September	47 955	41 403	18 622	14 996	29 333	. . .	12 659	. . .	40.4	. . .	1.46	. . .	58.98
October	48 009	41 432	18 630	14 973	29 379	. . .	12 615	. . .	40.3	. . .	1.47	. . .	59.24
November	48 148	41 522	18 617	14 999	29 531	. . .	12 628	. . .	40.4	. . .	1.48	. . .	59.79
December	48 309	41 621	18 698	15 045	29 611	. . .	12 667	. . .	40.7	. . .	1.49	. . .	60.64
1952													
January	48 298	41 709	18 719	15 067	29 579	. . .	12 675	. . .	40.8	. . .	1.49	. . .	60.79
February	48 522	41 872	18 813	15 105	29 709	. . .	12 689	. . .	40.8	. . .	1.49	. . .	60.79
March	48 504	41 842	18 775	15 127	29 729	. . .	12 695	. . .	40.6	. . .	1.51	. . .	61.31
April	48 616	41 954	18 806	15 162	29 810	. . .	12 713	. . .	40.3	. . .	1.51	. . .	60.85
May	48 645	41 951	18 784	15 143	29 861	. . .	12 676	. . .	40.5	. . .	1.51	. . .	61.16
June	48 286	41 574	18 419	14 828	29 867	. . .	12 353	. . .	40.6	. . .	1.51	. . .	61.31
July	48 144	41 407	18 268	14 707	29 876	. . .	12 233	. . .	40.2	. . .	1.50	. . .	60.30
August	48 923	42 205	18 928	15 279	29 995	. . .	12 764	. . .	40.7	. . .	1.53	. . .	62.27
September	49 319	42 585	19 206	15 553	30 113	. . .	13 007	. . .	41.1	. . .	1.55	. . .	63.71
October	49 598	42 782	19 312	15 690	30 286	. . .	13 122	. . .	41.2	. . .	1.56	. . .	64.27
November	49 816	43 015	19 473	15 843	30 343	. . .	13 262	. . .	41.2	. . .	1.58	. . .	65.10
December	50 164	43 229	19 610	15 973	30 554	. . .	13 375	. . .	41.2	. . .	1.58	. . .	65.10
1953													
January	50 145	43 351	19 721	16 067	30 424	. . .	13 447	. . .	41.1	. . .	1.59	. . .	65.35
February	50 339	43 542	19 841	16 158	30 498	. . .	13 529	. . .	41.0	. . .	1.61	. . .	66.01
March	50 475	43 691	19 909	16 270	30 566	. . .	13 620	. . .	41.2	. . .	1.61	. . .	66.33
April	50 432	43 662	19 908	16 293	30 524	. . .	13 629	. . .	40.9	. . .	1.62	. . .	66.26
May	50 491	43 774	19 930	16 341	30 561	. . .	13 645	. . .	41.0	. . .	1.62	. . .	66.42
June	50 522	43 788	19 909	16 343	30 613	. . .	13 636	. . .	40.9	. . .	1.63	. . .	66.67
July	50 536	43 813	19 910	16 353	30 626	. . .	13 653	. . .	40.7	. . .	1.64	. . .	66.75
August	50 487	43 733	19 834	16 278	30 653	. . .	13 564	. . .	40.7	. . .	1.64	. . .	66.75
September	50 365	43 616	19 726	16 151	30 639	. . .	13 419	. . .	40.1	. . .	1.65	. . .	66.17
October	50 242	43 478	19 578	15 981	30 664	. . .	13 244	. . .	40.1	. . .	1.65	. . .	66.17
November	49 907	43 158	19 315	15 728	30 592	. . .	12 990	. . .	40.0	. . .	1.65	. . .	66.00
December	49 702	42 959	19 173	15 581	30 529	. . .	12 847	. . .	39.7	. . .	1.65	. . .	65.51
1954													
January	49 468	42 708	18 963	15 440	30 505	. . .	12 706	. . .	39.5	. . .	1.65	. . .	65.18
February	49 382	42 599	18 880	15 307	30 502	. . .	12 593	. . .	39.7	. . .	1.65	. . .	65.51
March	49 158	42 362	18 748	15 197	30 410	. . .	12 493	. . .	39.6	. . .	1.65	. . .	65.34
April	49 178	42 372	18 602	15 065	30 576	. . .	12 361	. . .	39.7	. . .	1.65	. . .	65.51
May	48 965	42 136	18 476	14 974	30 489	. . .	12 282	. . .	39.7	. . .	1.67	. . .	66.30
June	48 896	42 050	18 400	14 910	30 496	. . .	12 220	. . .	39.7	. . .	1.67	. . .	66.30
July	48 835	41 967	18 280	14 799	30 555	. . .	12 121	. . .	39.7	. . .	1.66	. . .	65.90
August	48 825	41 933	18 251	14 772	30 574	. . .	12 089	. . .	39.8	. . .	1.66	. . .	66.07
September	48 882	41 988	18 261	14 805	30 621	. . .	12 104	. . .	39.9	. . .	1.66	. . .	66.23
October	48 944	42 044	18 321	14 841	30 623	. . .	12 142	. . .	39.7	. . .	1.67	. . .	66.30
November	49 178	42 214	18 438	14 913	30 740	. . .	12 206	. . .	40.1	. . .	1.68	. . .	67.37
December	49 331	42 374	18 508	14 967	30 823	. . .	12 254	. . .	40.1	. . .	1.68	. . .	67.37
1955													
January	49 497	42 544	18 609	15 034	30 888	. . .	12 309	. . .	40.4	. . .	1.69	. . .	68.28
February	49 644	42 721	18 726	15 138	30 918	. . .	12 408	. . .	40.6	. . .	1.70	. . .	69.02
March	49 963	43 025	18 910	15 258	31 053	. . .	12 524	. . .	40.7	. . .	1.71	. . .	69.60
April	50 247	43 288	19 067	15 375	31 180	. . .	12 626	. . .	40.8	. . .	1.71	. . .	69.77
May	50 512	43 521	19 223	15 493	31 289	. . .	12 731	. . .	41.1	. . .	1.73	. . .	71.10
June	50 790	43 770	19 331	15 585	31 459	. . .	12 810	. . .	40.8	. . .	1.73	. . .	70.58
July	50 985	43 936	19 376	15 614	31 609	. . .	12 818	. . .	40.7	. . .	1.75	. . .	71.23
August	51 111	44 088	19 432	15 679	31 679	. . .	12 866	. . .	40.7	. . .	1.76	. . .	71.63
September	51 262	44 195	19 427	15 668	31 835	. . .	12 830	. . .	40.7	. . .	1.77	. . .	72.04
October	51 431	44 313	19 482	15 740	31 949	. . .	12 896	. . .	41.0	. . .	1.77	. . .	72.57
November	51 592	44 509	19 554	15 813	32 038	. . .	12 967	. . .	41.1	. . .	1.78	. . .	73.16
December	51 805	44 673	19 608	15 859	32 197	. . .	13 009	. . .	40.9	. . .	1.78	. . .	72.80

. . . = Not available.

Table 10-9. Employment, Hours, and Earnings, Total Nonfarm and Manufacturing, Historical Annual and Monthly—*Continued*

(Wage and salary workers on nonfarm payrolls, seasonally adjusted.)

Year and month	All wage and salary workers (thousands)					Production and nonsupervisory workers on private payrolls								
	Total	Private			Service-providing	Number (thousands)		Average hours per week		Average hourly earnings, dollars		Average weekly earnings, dollars	
		Total	Goods-producing			Total private	Manufac-turing	Total private	Manufac-turing	Total private	Manufac-turing	Total private	Manufac-turing
			Total	Manufac-turing									
1956													
January	51 975	44 808	19 665	15 882	32 310	. . .	13 011	. . .	40.8	. . .	1.78	. . .	72.62
February	52 167	44 955	19 731	15 889	32 436	. . .	12 986	. . .	40.7	. . .	1.79	. . .	72.85
March	52 295	45 043	19 691	15 829	32 604	. . .	12 905	. . .	40.6	. . .	1.80	. . .	73.08
April	52 375	45 099	19 811	15 909	32 564	. . .	12 970	. . .	40.5	. . .	1.82	. . .	73.71
May	52 506	45 139	19 825	15 893	32 681	. . .	12 925	. . .	40.4	. . .	1.83	. . .	73.93
June	52 584	45 217	19 905	15 835	32 679	. . .	12 836	. . .	40.3	. . .	1.83	. . .	73.75
July	51 954	44 549	19 390	15 468	32 564	. . .	12 435	. . .	40.3	. . .	1.82	. . .	73.35
August	52 630	45 179	19 922	15 893	32 708	. . .	12 860	. . .	40.3	. . .	1.85	. . .	74.56
September	52 601	45 120	19 860	15 863	32 741	. . .	12 822	. . .	40.5	. . .	1.87	. . .	75.74
October	52 781	45 262	19 918	15 937	32 863	. . .	12 908	. . .	40.6	. . .	1.88	. . .	76.33
November	52 822	45 269	19 886	15 916	32 936	. . .	12 864	. . .	40.4	. . .	1.88	. . .	75.95
December	52 930	45 346	19 926	15 957	33 004	. . .	12 882	. . .	40.6	. . .	1.91	. . .	77.55
1957													
January	52 888	45 268	19 833	15 970	33 055	. . .	12 881	. . .	40.4	. . .	1.90	. . .	76.76
February	53 097	45 451	19 933	15 998	33 164	. . .	12 885	. . .	40.5	. . .	1.91	. . .	77.36
March	53 157	45 485	19 936	15 994	33 221	. . .	12 855	. . .	40.4	. . .	1.92	. . .	77.57
April	53 238	45 537	19 887	15 970	33 351	. . .	12 811	. . .	40.0	. . .	1.91	. . .	76.40
May	53 149	45 436	19 834	15 931	33 315	. . .	12 762	. . .	40.0	. . .	1.92	. . .	76.80
June	53 066	45 364	19 777	15 873	33 289	. . .	12 697	. . .	40.0	. . .	1.92	. . .	76.80
July	53 123	45 369	19 735	15 854	33 388	. . .	12 669	. . .	40.0	. . .	1.93	. . .	77.20
August	53 126	45 369	19 728	15 867	33 398	. . .	12 673	. . .	40.0	. . .	1.94	. . .	77.60
September	52 932	45 183	19 545	15 710	33 387	. . .	12 528	. . .	39.7	. . .	1.95	. . .	77.42
October	52 765	44 997	19 421	15 599	33 344	. . .	12 437	. . .	39.4	. . .	1.96	. . .	77.22
November	52 559	44 790	19 260	15 466	33 299	. . .	12 301	. . .	39.2	. . .	1.96	. . .	76.83
December	52 385	44 539	19 111	15 332	33 274	. . .	12 170	. . .	39.1	. . .	1.95	. . .	76.25
1958													
January	52 077	44 256	18 902	15 130	33 175	. . .	11 969	. . .	38.9	. . .	1.95	. . .	75.86
February	51 576	43 744	18 529	14 908	33 047	. . .	11 757	. . .	38.7	. . .	1.95	. . .	75.47
March	51 300	43 452	18 335	14 670	32 965	. . .	11 532	. . .	38.8	. . .	1.96	. . .	76.05
April	51 027	43 159	18 120	14 506	32 907	. . .	11 373	. . .	38.9	. . .	1.96	. . .	76.24
May	50 913	43 019	18 008	14 414	32 905	. . .	11 294	. . .	38.9	. . .	1.97	. . .	76.63
June	50 912	42 986	17 984	14 408	32 928	. . .	11 300	. . .	39.1	. . .	1.98	. . .	77.42
July	51 037	43 065	18 038	14 450	32 999	. . .	11 349	. . .	39.3	. . .	1.98	. . .	77.81
August	51 231	43 219	18 147	14 524	33 084	. . .	11 412	. . .	39.5	. . .	2.01	. . .	79.40
September	51 506	43 490	18 331	14 658	33 175	. . .	11 556	. . .	39.5	. . .	2.00	. . .	79.00
October	51 486	43 455	18 218	14 503	33 268	. . .	11 394	. . .	39.6	. . .	2.00	. . .	79.20
November	51 944	43 916	18 610	14 827	33 334	. . .	11 702	. . .	39.9	. . .	2.03	. . .	81.00
December	52 088	43 988	18 592	14 877	33 496	. . .	11 743	. . .	39.9	. . .	2.04	. . .	81.40
1959													
January	52 480	44 375	18 796	14 998	33 684	. . .	11 849	. . .	40.2	. . .	2.04	. . .	82.01
February	52 687	44 571	18 890	15 115	33 797	. . .	11 950	. . .	40.3	. . .	2.05	. . .	82.62
March	53 016	44 884	19 069	15 259	33 947	. . .	12 078	. . .	40.4	. . .	2.07	. . .	83.63
April	53 320	45 178	19 269	15 385	34 051	. . .	12 185	. . .	40.5	. . .	2.08	. . .	84.24
May	53 549	45 396	19 378	15 487	34 171	. . .	12 277	. . .	40.7	. . .	2.08	. . .	84.66
June	53 679	45 536	19 462	15 554	34 217	. . .	12 330	. . .	40.6	. . .	2.09	. . .	84.85
July	53 803	45 630	19 529	15 623	34 274	. . .	12 366	. . .	40.3	. . .	2.09	. . .	84.23
August	53 334	45 153	19 049	15 202	34 285	. . .	11 936	. . .	40.4	. . .	2.07	. . .	83.63
September	53 429	45 190	19 052	15 254	34 377	. . .	11 984	. . .	40.4	. . .	2.08	. . .	84.03
October	53 359	45 094	18 925	15 158	34 434	. . .	11 864	. . .	40.1	. . .	2.07	. . .	83.01
November	53 635	45 351	19 108	15 300	34 527	. . .	11 991	. . .	39.9	. . .	2.07	. . .	82.59
December	54 175	45 807	19 425	15 573	34 750	. . .	12 254	. . .	40.3	. . .	2.11	. . .	85.03
1960													
January	54 274	45 967	19 491	15 687	34 783	. . .	12 362	. . .	40.6	. . .	2.13	. . .	86.48
February	54 513	46 187	19 605	15 765	34 908	. . .	12 434	. . .	40.3	. . .	2.14	. . .	86.24
March	54 458	45 933	19 373	15 707	35 085	. . .	12 362	. . .	40.0	. . .	2.14	. . .	85.60
April	54 812	46 278	19 446	15 654	35 366	. . .	12 299	. . .	40.0	. . .	2.14	. . .	85.60
May	54 473	46 041	19 374	15 575	35 099	. . .	12 218	. . .	40.1	. . .	2.14	. . .	85.81
June	54 347	45 915	19 240	15 466	35 107	. . .	12 102	. . .	39.9	. . .	2.14	. . .	85.39
July	54 304	45 862	19 170	15 413	35 134	. . .	12 047	. . .	39.9	. . .	2.14	. . .	85.39
August	54 271	45 799	19 105	15 360	35 166	. . .	11 986	. . .	39.7	. . .	2.15	. . .	85.36
September	54 228	45 734	19 057	15 330	35 171	. . .	11 956	. . .	39.4	. . .	2.16	. . .	85.10
October	54 144	45 642	18 952	15 231	35 192	. . .	11 846	. . .	39.7	. . .	2.16	. . .	85.75
November	53 962	45 446	18 799	15 112	35 163	. . .	11 726	. . .	39.3	. . .	2.15	. . .	84.50
December	53 744	45 147	18 548	14 947	35 196	. . .	11 556	. . .	38.4	. . .	2.16	. . .	82.94
1961													
January	53 683	45 119	18 508	14 863	35 175	. . .	11 473	. . .	39.3	. . .	2.16	. . .	84.89
February	53 556	44 969	18 418	14 801	35 138	. . .	11 414	. . .	39.4	. . .	2.16	. . .	85.10
March	53 662	45 051	18 438	14 802	35 224	. . .	11 410	. . .	39.5	. . .	2.16	. . .	85.32
April	53 626	44 997	18 432	14 825	35 194	. . .	11 444	. . .	39.5	. . .	2.18	. . .	86.11
May	53 785	45 121	18 523	14 932	35 262	. . .	11 544	. . .	39.7	. . .	2.19	. . .	86.94
June	53 977	45 289	18 618	14 981	35 359	. . .	11 593	. . .	40.0	. . .	2.20	. . .	88.00
July	54 123	45 399	18 640	15 029	35 483	. . .	11 639	. . .	40.0	. . .	2.21	. . .	88.40
August	54 298	45 534	18 725	15 093	35 573	. . .	11 701	. . .	40.1	. . .	2.22	. . .	89.02
September	54 388	45 592	18 730	15 080	35 658	. . .	11 679	. . .	39.5	. . .	2.20	. . .	86.90
October	54 522	45 717	18 805	15 143	35 717	. . .	11 731	. . .	40.3	. . .	2.23	. . .	89.87
November	54 743	45 931	18 927	15 259	35 816	. . .	11 842	. . .	40.7	. . .	2.23	. . .	90.76
December	54 871	46 035	18 981	15 309	35 890	. . .	11 872	. . .	40.4	. . .	2.24	. . .	90.50

. . . = Not available.

Table 10-9. Employment, Hours, and Earnings, Total Nonfarm and Manufacturing, Historical Annual and Monthly—*Continued*

(Wage and salary workers on nonfarm payrolls, seasonally adjusted.)

Year and month	All wage and salary workers (thousands)					Production and nonsupervisory workers on private payrolls							
	Total	Private			Service-providing	Number (thousands)		Average hours per week		Average hourly earnings, dollars		Average weekly earnings, dollars	
		Total	Goods-producing			Total private	Manufac-turing	Total private	Manufac-turing	Total private	Manufac-turing	Total private	Manufac-turing
			Total	Manufac-turing									
1962													
January	54 891	46 040	18 936	15 322	35 955	. . .	11 865	. . .	40.0	. . .	2.25	. . .	90.00
February	55 187	46 309	19 109	15 411	36 078	. . .	11 950	. . .	40.4	. . .	2.26	. . .	91.30
March	55 276	46 375	19 109	15 451	36 167	. . .	11 970	. . .	40.6	. . .	2.26	. . .	91.76
April	55 602	46 680	19 258	15 524	36 344	. . .	12 034	. . .	40.6	. . .	2.26	. . .	91.76
May	55 627	46 669	19 253	15 513	36 374	. . .	12 011	. . .	40.6	. . .	2.27	. . .	92.16
June	55 644	46 644	19 186	15 518	36 458	. . .	12 006	. . .	40.5	. . .	2.26	. . .	91.53
July	55 746	46 720	19 248	15 522	36 498	. . .	12 004	. . .	40.5	. . .	2.27	. . .	91.94
August	55 838	46 775	19 251	15 517	36 587	. . .	11 990	. . .	40.5	. . .	2.28	. . .	92.34
September	55 977	46 888	19 305	15 568	36 672	. . .	12 033	. . .	40.5	. . .	2.28	. . .	92.34
October	56 041	46 927	19 301	15 569	36 740	. . .	12 034	. . .	40.3	. . .	2.29	. . .	92.29
November	56 056	46 911	19 260	15 530	36 796	. . .	11 977	. . .	40.5	. . .	2.29	. . .	92.75
December	56 028	46 902	19 219	15 520	36 809	. . .	11 961	. . .	40.3	. . .	2.29	. . .	92.29
1963													
January	56 116	46 912	19 257	15 545	36 859	. . .	11 974	. . .	40.5	. . .	2.30	. . .	93.15
February	56 230	46 999	19 228	15 542	37 002	. . .	11 965	. . .	40.5	. . .	2.31	. . .	93.56
March	56 322	47 077	19 233	15 564	37 089	. . .	11 990	. . .	40.5	. . .	2.32	. . .	93.96
April	56 580	47 316	19 343	15 602	37 237	. . .	12 029	. . .	40.5	. . .	2.32	. . .	93.96
May	56 616	47 328	19 399	15 641	37 217	. . .	12 066	. . .	40.5	. . .	2.33	. . .	94.37
June	56 658	47 356	19 371	15 624	37 287	. . .	12 050	. . .	40.7	. . .	2.34	. . .	95.24
July	56 794	47 460	19 423	15 646	37 371	. . .	12 080	. . .	40.6	. . .	2.35	. . .	95.41
August	56 910	47 542	19 437	15 644	37 473	. . .	12 060	. . .	40.6	. . .	2.34	. . .	95.00
September	57 077	47 660	19 483	15 674	37 594	. . .	12 088	. . .	40.6	. . .	2.36	. . .	95.82
October	57 284	47 805	19 517	15 714	37 767	. . .	12 131	. . .	40.7	. . .	2.36	. . .	96.05
November	57 255	47 771	19 456	15 675	37 799	. . .	12 072	. . .	40.7	. . .	2.37	. . .	96.46
December	57 360	47 863	19 493	15 712	37 867	. . .	12 108	. . .	40.6	. . .	2.38	. . .	96.63
1964													
January	57 487	47 925	19 406	15 715	38 081	39 913	12 132	38.2	40.1	2.50	2.38	95.50	95.44
February	57 751	48 170	19 570	15 742	38 181	40 123	12 165	38.5	40.7	2.50	2.38	96.25	96.87
March	57 898	48 287	19 587	15 770	38 311	40 171	12 190	38.5	40.6	2.50	2.38	96.25	96.63
April	57 922	48 278	19 593	15 785	38 329	40 209	12 211	38.6	40.7	2.52	2.40	97.27	97.68
May	58 089	48 419	19 630	15 812	38 459	40 332	12 231	38.6	40.8	2.52	2.40	97.27	97.92
June	58 221	48 552	19 682	15 839	38 539	40 448	12 255	38.6	40.8	2.53	2.41	97.66	98.33
July	58 413	48 736	19 740	15 887	38 673	40 624	12 309	38.5	40.8	2.53	2.41	97.41	98.33
August	58 619	48 887	19 810	15 948	38 809	40 771	12 354	38.5	40.9	2.55	2.42	98.18	98.98
September	58 903	49 117	19 943	16 073	38 960	41 026	12 479	38.5	40.9	2.55	2.44	98.18	99.80
October	58 794	48 949	19 723	15 821	39 071	40 828	12 224	38.5	40.7	2.55	2.40	98.18	97.68
November	59 217	49 338	20 026	16 096	39 191	41 157	12 477	38.6	41.0	2.56	2.42	98.82	99.22
December	59 421	49 524	20 111	16 176	39 310	41 307	12 551	38.7	41.2	2.58	2.44	99.85	100.53
1965													
January	59 583	49 646	20 173	16 245	39 410	41 453	12 603	38.7	41.3	2.58	2.45	99.85	101.19
February	59 800	49 826	20 216	16 291	39 584	41 583	12 644	38.7	41.3	2.59	2.46	100.23	101.60
March	60 003	49 993	20 292	16 353	39 711	41 674	12 701	38.7	41.3	2.60	2.47	100.62	102.01
April	60 259	50 208	20 317	16 418	39 942	41 885	12 752	38.7	41.2	2.60	2.47	100.62	101.76
May	60 492	50 398	20 444	16 477	40 048	42 044	12 792	38.8	41.3	2.62	2.49	101.66	102.84
June	60 690	50 562	20 522	16 554	40 168	42 183	12 854	38.6	41.2	2.62	2.49	101.13	102.59
July	60 963	50 762	20 611	16 669	40 352	42 364	12 962	38.6	41.2	2.63	2.49	101.52	102.59
August	61 228	50 957	20 726	16 732	40 502	42 537	12 994	38.5	41.1	2.64	2.50	101.64	102.75
September	61 490	51 152	20 808	16 802	40 682	42 726	13 046	38.6	41.1	2.65	2.51	102.29	103.16
October	61 718	51 340	20 895	16 864	40 823	42 871	13 100	38.5	41.2	2.66	2.52	102.41	103.82
November	61 997	51 561	21 021	16 962	40 976	43 045	13 175	38.6	41.3	2.67	2.52	103.06	104.08
December	62 321	51 822	21 151	17 051	41 170	43 270	13 243	38.6	41.3	2.68	2.53	103.45	104.49
1966													
January	62 528	51 987	21 214	17 143	41 314	43 401	13 301	38.6	41.5	2.68	2.54	103.45	105.41
February	62 796	52 185	21 315	17 288	41 481	43 552	13 426	38.7	41.7	2.69	2.56	104.10	106.75
March	63 192	52 500	21 515	17 400	41 677	43 801	13 508	38.7	41.6	2.70	2.56	104.49	106.50
April	63 436	52 677	21 568	17 517	41 868	43 959	13 598	38.7	41.8	2.71	2.58	104.88	107.84
May	63 711	52 890	21 675	17 625	42 036	44 138	13 678	38.5	41.5	2.72	2.58	104.72	107.07
June	64 110	53 208	21 846	17 733	42 264	44 390	13 753	38.5	41.4	2.72	2.58	104.72	106.81
July	64 301	53 327	21 872	17 760	42 429	44 484	13 758	38.4	41.2	2.74	2.60	105.22	107.12
August	64 507	53 501	21 972	17 882	42 535	44 596	13 843	38.4	41.4	2.75	2.61	105.60	108.05
September	64 644	53 581	21 948	17 886	42 696	44 659	13 841	38.3	41.2	2.76	2.63	105.71	108.36
October	64 854	53 727	21 991	17 956	42 863	44 789	13 906	38.4	41.3	2.77	2.64	106.37	109.03
November	65 019	53 816	21 988	17 981	43 031	44 834	13 918	38.3	41.2	2.78	2.65	106.47	109.18
December	65 200	53 944	22 008	17 998	43 192	44 916	13 906	38.2	40.9	2.78	2.64	106.20	107.98
1967													
January	65 407	54 092	22 057	18 033	43 350	45 051	13 925	38.3	41.1	2.79	2.65	106.86	108.92
February	65 428	54 075	21 987	17 978	43 441	44 967	13 853	37.9	40.4	2.81	2.67	106.50	107.87
March	65 530	54 133	21 919	17 940	43 611	44 991	13 797	37.9	40.5	2.81	2.67	106.50	108.14
April	65 467	54 032	21 842	17 878	43 625	44 871	13 712	37.8	40.4	2.82	2.68	106.60	108.27
May	65 619	54 145	21 779	17 832	43 840	44 961	13 664	37.8	40.4	2.83	2.69	106.97	108.68
June	65 750	54 216	21 761	17 812	43 989	45 004	13 632	37.8	40.4	2.84	2.69	107.35	108.68
July	65 887	54 343	21 772	17 784	44 115	45 105	13 602	37.8	40.5	2.86	2.71	108.11	109.76
August	66 142	54 552	21 887	17 905	44 255	45 267	13 681	37.8	40.6	2.87	2.73	108.49	110.84
September	66 164	54 541	21 775	17 794	44 389	45 236	13 559	37.8	40.6	2.88	2.73	108.86	110.84
October	66 225	54 583	21 779	17 800	44 446	45 278	13 587	37.8	40.6	2.89	2.74	109.24	111.24
November	66 703	55 008	21 996	17 985	44 707	45 701	13 777	37.9	40.6	2.91	2.75	110.29	111.65
December	66 900	55 165	22 037	18 025	44 863	45 800	13 782	37.7	40.7	2.92	2.77	110.08	112.74

. . . = Not available.

Table 10-9. Employment, Hours, and Earnings, Total Nonfarm and Manufacturing, Historical Annual and Monthly—Continued

(Wage and salary workers on nonfarm payrolls, seasonally adjusted.)

Year and month	All wage and salary workers (thousands)					Production and nonsupervisory workers on private payrolls							
	Total	Private			Service-providing	Number (thousands)		Average hours per week		Average hourly earnings, dollars		Average weekly earnings, dollars	
		Total	Goods-producing			Total private	Manufac-turing	Total private	Manufac-turing	Total private	Manufac-turing	Total private	Manufac-turing
			Total	Manufac-turing									
1968													
January	66 805	55 011	21 917	18 040	44 888	45 655	13 798	37.6	40.4	2.94	2.81	110.54	113.52
February	67 215	55 396	22 117	18 054	45 098	45 980	13 793	37.8	40.8	2.95	2.82	111.51	115.06
March	67 295	55 453	22 119	18 067	45 176	46 041	13 803	37.7	40.8	2.97	2.84	111.97	115.87
April	67 555	55 677	22 207	18 131	45 348	46 239	13 858	37.6	40.3	2.98	2.85	112.05	114.86
May	67 653	55 748	22 255	18 190	45 398	46 267	13 900	37.7	40.9	3.00	2.87	113.10	117.38
June	67 904	55 917	22 264	18 228	45 640	46 402	13 921	37.8	40.9	3.01	2.88	113.78	117.79
July	68 125	56 107	22 329	18 265	45 796	46 563	13 953	37.7	40.8	3.03	2.89	114.23	117.91
August	68 328	56 286	22 350	18 254	45 978	46 670	13 903	37.7	40.7	3.03	2.89	114.23	117.62
September	68 487	56 420	22 390	18 252	46 097	46 792	13 914	37.7	40.9	3.06	2.92	115.36	119.43
October	68 720	56 619	22 419	18 293	46 301	46 990	13 974	37.7	41.0	3.07	2.94	115.74	120.54
November	68 985	56 878	22 512	18 346	46 473	47 244	14 028	37.5	40.9	3.09	2.96	115.88	121.06
December	69 246	57 101	22 617	18 410	46 629	47 385	14 044	37.5	40.7	3.11	2.97	116.63	120.88
1969													
January	69 438	57 229	22 644	18 432	46 794	47 529	14 086	37.7	40.8	3.12	2.99	117.62	121.99
February	69 700	57 476	22 755	18 502	46 945	47 696	14 134	37.5	40.4	3.14	3.00	117.75	121.20
March	69 905	57 676	22 813	18 558	47 092	47 852	14 169	37.6	40.8	3.15	3.01	118.44	122.81
April	70 072	57 827	22 815	18 554	47 257	47 959	14 144	37.7	41.0	3.17	3.03	119.51	124.23
May	70 328	58 044	22 899	18 588	47 429	48 122	14 161	37.6	40.7	3.19	3.04	119.94	123.73
June	70 636	58 277	22 981	18 640	47 655	48 329	14 206	37.5	40.7	3.20	3.05	120.00	124.14
July	70 729	58 389	22 990	18 642	47 739	48 435	14 194	37.5	40.6	3.22	3.08	120.75	125.05
August	71 006	58 633	23 111	18 767	47 895	48 616	14 287	37.5	40.6	3.24	3.10	121.50	125.86
September	70 917	58 538	22 988	18 620	47 929	48 524	14 159	37.5	40.6	3.26	3.12	122.25	126.67
October	71 120	58 690	22 976	18 613	48 144	48 669	14 174	37.5	40.6	3.26	3.12	122.67	126.77
November	71 087	58 639	22 840	18 467	48 247	48 589	14 035	37.4	40.5	3.28	3.13	123.38	127.17
December	71 240	58 763	22 884	18 485	48 356	48 638	14 013	37.5	40.6	3.30	3.15	123.75	127.89
1970													
January	71 176	58 680	22 726	18 424	48 450	48 564	13 964	37.3	40.4	3.31	3.16	123.46	127.66
February	71 304	58 786	22 747	18 361	48 557	48 600	13 897	37.3	40.2	3.33	3.17	124.21	127.43
March	71 452	58 849	22 738	18 360	48 714	48 690	13 917	37.2	40.1	3.35	3.19	124.62	127.92
April	71 348	58 643	22 552	18 207	48 796	48 480	13 785	37.0	39.8	3.36	3.19	124.32	126.96
May	71 123	58 455	22 336	18 029	48 787	48 287	13 616	37.0	39.8	3.38	3.22	125.06	128.16
June	71 029	58 362	22 241	17 930	48 788	48 225	13 554	36.9	39.8	3.39	3.24	125.09	128.95
July	71 053	58 356	22 195	17 877	48 858	48 243	13 527	37.0	40.0	3.41	3.25	126.17	130.00
August	70 933	58 222	22 105	17 779	48 828	48 088	13 449	37.0	39.8	3.43	3.26	126.91	129.75
September	70 948	58 207	21 988	17 692	48 960	48 101	13 401	36.8	39.6	3.45	3.29	126.96	130.28
October	70 519	57 726	21 477	17 173	49 042	47 619	12 905	36.8	39.5	3.46	3.26	127.33	128.77
November	70 409	57 579	21 345	17 024	49 064	47 466	12 781	36.7	39.5	3.47	3.26	127.35	128.77
December	70 790	57 945	21 673	17 309	49 117	47 778	13 062	36.8	39.5	3.50	3.32	128.80	131.14
1971													
January	70 866	57 988	21 594	17 280	49 272	47 859	13 069	36.8	39.9	3.52	3.36	129.54	134.06
February	70 806	57 929	21 514	17 216	49 292	47 779	13 033	36.7	39.7	3.54	3.39	129.92	134.58
March	70 859	57 951	21 491	17 154	49 368	47 819	12 984	36.7	39.8	3.56	3.39	130.65	134.92
April	71 037	58 092	21 552	17 149	49 485	47 966	12 993	36.8	39.9	3.57	3.41	131.38	136.06
May	71 247	58 277	21 645	17 225	49 602	48 153	13 081	36.7	40.0	3.60	3.43	132.12	137.20
June	71 253	58 245	21 568	17 139	49 685	48 108	13 012	36.8	39.9	3.62	3.45	133.22	137.66
July	71 315	58 304	21 564	17 126	49 751	48 169	13 001	36.7	40.0	3.63	3.46	133.22	138.40
August	71 370	58 329	21 570	17 115	49 800	48 164	12 993	36.7	39.8	3.66	3.48	134.32	138.50
September	71 617	58 549	21 650	17 154	49 967	48 363	13 038	36.7	39.7	3.67	3.48	134.69	138.16
October	71 642	58 527	21 604	17 126	50 038	48 305	13 027	36.8	39.9	3.68	3.50	135.42	139.65
November	71 846	58 698	21 684	17 166	50 162	48 441	13 064	36.9	40.0	3.69	3.49	136.16	139.60
December	72 108	58 918	21 741	17 202	50 367	48 613	13 078	36.9	40.2	3.73	3.55	137.64	142.71
1972													
January	72 445	59 179	21 865	17 283	50 580	49 035	13 173	36.9	40.2	3.80	3.57	140.22	143.51
February	72 652	59 354	21 915	17 361	50 737	49 143	13 235	36.9	40.4	3.82	3.61	140.96	145.84
March	72 945	59 616	22 036	17 447	50 909	49 437	13 316	36.9	40.4	3.84	3.63	141.70	146.65
April	73 163	59 805	22 099	17 508	51 064	49 562	13 373	36.9	40.5	3.86	3.65	142.43	147.83
May	73 467	60 051	22 222	17 602	51 245	49 745	13 451	36.8	40.5	3.87	3.67	142.42	148.64
June	73 760	60 355	22 282	17 641	51 478	49 995	13 475	36.9	40.6	3.88	3.68	143.17	149.41
July	73 708	60 226	22 162	17 556	51 546	49 844	13 387	36.8	40.5	3.90	3.69	143.52	149.45
August	74 138	60 608	22 400	17 741	51 738	50 155	13 562	36.8	40.6	3.92	3.73	144.26	151.44
September	74 263	60 688	22 456	17 774	51 807	50 226	13 572	36.9	40.6	3.94	3.75	145.39	152.25
October	74 673	61 067	22 613	17 893	52 060	50 552	13 681	37.0	40.7	3.97	3.78	146.89	153.85
November	74 967	61 324	22 688	18 005	52 279	50 789	13 783	36.9	40.7	3.98	3.79	146.86	154.25
December	75 270	61 586	22 772	18 158	52 498	51 054	13 902	36.8	40.6	4.01	3.83	147.57	155.50
1973													
January	75 621	61 931	22 955	18 276	52 666	51 349	14 006	36.8	40.4	4.03	3.86	148.30	155.94
February	76 017	62 306	23 160	18 410	52 857	51 685	14 127	36.9	40.9	4.04	3.87	149.08	158.28
March	76 285	62 540	23 262	18 493	53 023	51 901	14 181	37.0	40.9	4.06	3.88	150.22	158.69
April	76 455	62 678	23 316	18 530	53 139	51 983	14 192	36.9	40.8	4.08	3.91	150.55	159.53
May	76 646	62 829	23 382	18 564	53 264	52 082	14 217	36.9	40.7	4.10	3.93	151.29	159.95
June	76 887	63 015	23 485	18 606	53 402	52 233	14 253	36.9	40.7	4.12	3.95	152.03	160.77
July	76 911	63 046	23 522	18 598	53 389	52 240	14 232	36.9	40.7	4.15	3.98	153.14	161.99
August	77 166	63 262	23 559	18 629	53 607	52 394	14 251	36.9	40.6	4.16	4.00	153.50	162.40
September	77 276	63 384	23 548	18 609	53 728	52 410	14 213	36.8	40.7	4.19	4.03	154.19	164.02
October	77 606	63 629	23 641	18 702	53 965	52 655	14 289	36.7	40.6	4.21	4.05	154.51	164.43
November	77 912	63 877	23 719	18 773	54 193	52 845	14 342	36.9	40.6	4.23	4.07	156.09	165.24
December	78 035	63 965	23 779	18 820	54 256	52 954	14 386	36.7	40.6	4.25	4.09	155.98	166.05

Table 10-9. Employment, Hours, and Earnings, Total Nonfarm and Manufacturing, Historical Annual and Monthly—Continued

(Wage and salary workers on nonfarm payrolls, seasonally adjusted.)

Year and month	All wage and salary workers (thousands)					Production and nonsupervisory workers on private payrolls							
	Total	Private			Service-providing	Number (thousands)		Average hours per week		Average hourly earnings, dollars		Average weekly earnings, dollars	
		Total	Goods-producing			Total private	Manufacturing	Total private	Manufacturing	Total private	Manufacturing	Total private	Manufacturing
			Total	Manufacturing									
1974													
January	78 104	64 014	23 709	18 788	54 395	52 896	14 340	36.6	40.5	4.26	4.10	155.92	166.05
February	78 254	64 119	23 718	18 727	54 536	52 970	14 269	36.6	40.4	4.29	4.13	157.01	166.85
March	78 296	64 144	23 687	18 700	54 609	52 951	14 223	36.6	40.4	4.31	4.15	157.75	167.66
April	78 382	64 191	23 670	18 702	54 712	53 006	14 225	36.4	39.5	4.34	4.16	157.98	164.32
May	78 547	64 326	23 635	18 688	54 912	53 094	14 199	36.5	40.3	4.39	4.25	160.24	171.28
June	78 602	64 363	23 591	18 690	55 011	53 106	14 197	36.5	40.2	4.43	4.30	161.70	172.86
July	78 635	64 347	23 462	18 656	55 173	53 046	14 152	36.5	40.1	4.45	4.33	162.43	173.63
August	78 619	64 291	23 396	18 570	55 223	53 026	14 089	36.5	40.2	4.49	4.38	163.89	176.08
September	78 611	64 189	23 274	18 492	55 337	52 915	14 025	36.4	40.0	4.53	4.42	164.89	176.80
October	78 629	64 145	23 118	18 364	55 511	52 835	13 884	36.3	40.0	4.56	4.48	165.53	179.20
November	78 261	63 729	22 773	18 077	55 488	52 411	13 607	36.1	39.5	4.57	4.49	164.98	177.36
December	77 657	63 098	22 303	17 693	55 354	51 856	13 259	36.1	39.3	4.61	4.52	166.42	177.64
1975													
January	77 297	62 673	21 974	17 344	55 323	51 438	12 933	36.1	39.2	4.61	4.54	166.42	177.97
February	76 919	62 172	21 512	17 004	55 407	50 934	12 622	35.9	38.9	4.63	4.58	166.22	178.16
March	76 649	61 895	21 274	16 853	55 375	50 665	12 483	35.7	38.8	4.66	4.63	166.36	179.64
April	76 461	61 666	21 109	16 759	55 352	50 442	12 407	35.8	39.0	4.66	4.63	166.83	180.57
May	76 623	61 796	21 097	16 746	55 526	50 557	12 406	35.9	39.0	4.68	4.65	168.01	181.35
June	76 520	61 736	21 018	16 690	55 502	50 537	12 371	35.9	39.2	4.72	4.68	169.45	183.46
July	76 769	61 908	20 981	16 678	55 788	50 729	12 374	35.9	39.4	4.73	4.71	169.81	185.57
August	77 155	62 285	21 176	16 824	55 979	51 070	12 538	36.1	39.7	4.77	4.75	172.20	188.58
September	77 230	62 406	21 284	16 904	55 946	51 182	12 617	36.1	39.8	4.79	4.78	172.92	190.24
October	77 535	62 635	21 384	16 984	56 151	51 375	12 687	36.1	39.9	4.81	4.80	173.64	191.52
November	77 680	62 777	21 442	17 025	56 238	51 456	12 700	36.1	39.9	4.85	4.83	175.09	192.72
December	78 018	63 072	21 602	17 140	56 416	51 759	12 811	36.2	40.2	4.87	4.86	176.29	195.37
1976													
January	78 506	63 537	21 799	17 287	56 707	52 182	12 945	36.3	40.3	4.90	4.90	177.87	197.47
February	78 817	63 836	21 893	17 384	56 924	52 430	13 030	36.3	40.4	4.94	4.94	179.32	199.58
March	79 049	64 062	21 980	17 470	57 069	52 615	13 092	36.0	40.2	4.96	4.98	178.56	200.20
April	79 292	64 307	22 050	17 541	57 242	52 812	13 160	36.0	39.6	4.98	4.98	179.28	197.21
May	79 311	64 340	21 988	17 513	57 323	52 802	13 130	36.1	40.3	5.02	5.04	181.22	203.11
June	79 376	64 413	21 982	17 521	57 394	52 830	13 121	36.1	40.2	5.04	5.07	181.94	203.81
July	79 547	64 554	21 988	17 524	57 559	52 975	13 124	36.1	40.3	5.07	5.11	183.03	205.93
August	79 704	64 697	22 038	17 596	57 666	53 072	13 195	36.0	40.2	5.12	5.16	184.32	207.43
September	79 892	64 921	22 142	17 665	57 750	53 268	13 253	36.0	40.2	5.15	5.20	185.40	209.04
October	79 905	64 877	22 037	17 548	57 868	53 164	13 109	35.9	40.0	5.17	5.19	185.60	207.60
November	80 237	65 164	22 207	17 682	58 030	53 362	13 199	35.9	40.1	5.21	5.25	187.04	210.53
December	80 448	65 373	22 261	17 719	58 187	53 542	13 230	35.9	39.9	5.23	5.29	187.76	211.07
1977													
January	80 692	65 636	22 320	17 803	58 372	53 755	13 305	35.6	39.4	5.26	5.35	187.26	210.79
February	80 988	65 932	22 478	17 843	58 510	54 016	13 331	36.0	40.2	5.30	5.36	190.80	215.47
March	81 391	66 341	22 672	17 941	58 719	54 389	13 424	35.9	40.3	5.33	5.40	191.35	217.62
April	81 729	66 654	22 807	18 024	58 922	54 672	13 490	36.0	40.4	5.37	5.45	193.32	220.18
May	82 089	66 957	22 919	18 107	59 170	54 940	13 567	36.0	40.5	5.40	5.49	194.40	222.35
June	82 488	67 281	23 046	18 192	59 442	55 194	13 622	36.0	40.5	5.43	5.54	195.48	224.37
July	82 836	67 537	23 106	18 259	59 730	55 396	13 670	35.9	40.4	5.46	5.58	196.01	225.43
August	83 074	67 746	23 124	18 276	59 950	55 543	13 679	35.9	40.4	5.48	5.61	196.73	226.64
September	83 532	68 129	23 244	18 334	60 288	55 858	13 714	35.9	40.4	5.51	5.65	197.81	228.26
October	83 794	68 331	23 279	18 356	60 515	56 003	13 722	36.0	40.6	5.56	5.69	200.16	231.01
November	84 173	68 658	23 371	18 419	60 802	56 281	13 771	35.9	40.5	5.59	5.72	200.68	231.66
December	84 408	68 870	23 371	18 531	61 037	56 465	13 861	35.8	40.4	5.61	5.75	200.84	232.30
1978													
January	84 595	68 984	23 374	18 593	61 221	56 547	13 917	35.3	39.5	5.66	5.83	199.80	230.29
February	84 948	69 277	23 453	18 639	61 495	56 768	13 950	35.6	39.9	5.69	5.86	202.56	233.81
March	85 461	69 730	23 649	18 699	61 812	57 176	13 992	35.8	40.5	5.73	5.88	205.13	238.14
April	86 163	70 366	24 008	18 772	62 155	57 711	14 037	35.8	40.4	5.79	5.93	207.28	239.57
May	86 509	70 675	24 082	18 848	62 427	57 941	14 096	35.8	40.4	5.82	5.96	208.36	240.78
June	86 951	71 099	24 238	18 919	62 713	58 262	14 129	35.9	40.6	5.87	6.01	210.73	244.01
July	87 205	71 304	24 300	18 951	62 905	58 422	14 152	35.9	40.6	5.90	6.06	211.81	246.04
August	87 481	71 590	24 374	19 006	63 107	58 626	14 187	35.8	40.5	5.93	6.09	212.29	246.65
September	87 618	71 799	24 444	19 068	63 174	58 819	14 241	35.8	40.5	5.97	6.15	213.73	249.08
October	87 954	72 096	24 548	19 142	63 406	59 017	14 291	35.8	40.5	6.03	6.20	215.87	251.10
November	88 391	72 497	24 678	19 257	63 713	59 377	14 388	35.7	40.6	6.06	6.26	216.34	254.16
December	88 673	72 762	24 758	19 334	63 915	59 599	14 459	35.7	40.5	6.10	6.31	217.77	255.56
1979													
January	88 810	72 873	24 740	19 388	64 070	59 659	14 497	35.6	40.4	6.14	6.36	218.58	256.94
February	89 054	73 107	24 784	19 409	64 270	59 840	14 501	35.7	40.5	6.18	6.40	220.63	259.20
March	89 480	73 524	24 998	19 453	64 482	60 216	14 526	35.8	40.6	6.22	6.45	222.68	261.87
April	89 418	73 441	24 958	19 450	64 460	60 069	14 515	35.3	39.3	6.22	6.43	219.57	252.70
May	89 791	73 801	25 071	19 509	64 720	60 369	14 551	35.6	40.2	6.28	6.52	223.57	262.10
June	90 109	74 064	25 161	19 553	64 948	60 583	14 566	35.6	40.2	6.32	6.56	224.99	263.71
July	90 215	74 065	25 163	19 531	65 052	60 559	14 536	35.6	40.2	6.36	6.59	226.42	264.92
August	90 297	74 068	25 059	19 406	65 238	60 517	14 397	35.6	40.1	6.40	6.63	227.84	265.86
September	90 325	74 197	25 088	19 442	65 237	60 631	14 440	35.6	40.1	6.45	6.67	229.62	267.47
October	90 482	74 346	25 038	19 390	65 444	60 748	14 384	35.6	40.2	6.47	6.71	230.33	269.74
November	90 576	74 403	24 947	19 299	65 629	60 781	14 295	35.6	40.1	6.51	6.74	231.76	270.27
December	90 673	74 493	24 970	19 301	65 703	60 863	14 300	35.5	40.1	6.57	6.80	233.24	272.68

Table 10-9. Employment, Hours, and Earnings, Total Nonfarm and Manufacturing, Historical Annual and Monthly—*Continued*

(Wage and salary workers on nonfarm payrolls, seasonally adjusted.)

Year and month	All wage and salary workers (thousands)					Production and nonsupervisory workers on private payrolls							
		Private			Service-providing	Number (thousands)		Average hours per week		Average hourly earnings, dollars		Average weekly earnings, dollars	
	Total	Total	Goods-producing Total	Goods-producing Manufacturing		Total private	Manufacturing	Total private	Manufacturing	Total private	Manufacturing	Total private	Manufacturing
1980													
January	90 802	74 601	24 949	19 282	65 853	60 899	14 241	35.4	40.0	6.57	6.82	232.58	272.80
February	90 882	74 656	24 874	19 219	66 008	60 966	14 170	35.4	40.1	6.63	6.88	234.70	275.89
March	90 994	74 698	24 818	19 217	66 176	60 990	14 165	35.3	39.9	6.70	6.95	236.51	277.31
April	90 850	74 267	24 507	18 973	66 343	60 544	13 914	35.2	39.8	6.72	6.97	236.54	277.41
May	90 419	73 965	24 234	18 726	66 185	60 198	13 632	35.1	39.3	6.76	7.02	237.28	275.89
June	90 099	73 658	23 968	18 490	66 131	59 895	13 405	35.0	39.2	6.82	7.10	238.70	278.32
July	89 837	73 419	23 698	18 276	66 139	59 698	13 227	34.9	39.1	6.86	7.16	239.41	279.96
August	90 097	73 687	23 860	18 414	66 237	59 913	13 349	35.1	39.5	6.91	7.24	242.54	285.98
September	90 210	73 880	23 931	18 445	66 279	60 079	13 396	35.1	39.6	6.95	7.30	243.95	289.08
October	90 491	74 105	24 012	18 506	66 479	60 244	13 437	35.2	39.8	7.02	7.38	247.10	293.72
November	90 748	74 357	24 123	18 601	66 625	60 455	13 528	35.3	39.9	7.09	7.47	250.28	298.05
December	90 943	74 570	24 182	18 640	66 761	60 611	13 550	35.3	40.1	7.13	7.52	251.69	301.55
1981													
January	91 037	74 677	24 152	18 639	66 885	60 715	13 545	35.4	40.1	7.19	7.58	254.53	303.96
February	91 105	74 759	24 118	18 613	66 987	60 742	13 518	35.2	39.8	7.23	7.62	254.50	303.28
March	91 210	74 918	24 203	18 647	67 007	60 881	13 550	35.3	40.0	7.29	7.68	257.34	307.20
April	91 283	75 023	24 151	18 711	67 132	60 979	13 594	35.3	40.1	7.33	7.76	258.75	311.18
May	91 293	75 095	24 148	18 766	67 145	60 981	13 633	35.3	40.2	7.37	7.81	260.16	313.96
June	91 490	75 331	24 290	18 789	67 200	61 141	13 632	35.2	40.0	7.42	7.85	261.18	314.00
July	91 602	75 427	24 302	18 785	67 300	61 228	13 629	35.2	39.9	7.46	7.89	262.59	314.81
August	91 566	75 456	24 258	18 748	67 308	61 223	13 573	35.2	40.0	7.53	7.97	265.06	318.80
September	91 479	75 448	24 210	18 712	67 269	61 241	13 565	35.0	39.6	7.57	8.03	264.95	317.99
October	91 380	75 311	24 051	18 566	67 329	61 074	13 399	35.1	39.6	7.59	8.06	266.41	319.18
November	91 171	75 093	23 875	18 409	67 296	60 825	13 235	35.1	39.4	7.64	8.08	268.16	318.35
December	90 893	74 820	23 656	18 223	67 237	60 520	13 033	34.9	39.2	7.64	8.09	266.64	317.13
1982													
January	90 567	74 526	23 362	18 047	67 205	60 218	12 874	34.1	37.3	7.72	8.26	263.25	308.10
February	90 562	74 551	23 361	17 981	67 201	60 285	12 831	35.1	39.6	7.73	8.21	271.32	325.12
March	90 432	74 408	23 214	17 857	67 218	60 150	12 727	34.9	39.1	7.76	8.24	270.82	322.18
April	90 152	74 142	22 996	17 683	67 156	59 877	12 566	34.8	39.1	7.77	8.28	270.40	323.75
May	90 107	74 104	22 884	17 588	67 223	59 851	12 506	34.8	39.1	7.83	8.33	272.48	325.70
June	89 864	73 848	22 643	17 430	67 221	59 599	12 365	34.8	39.2	7.85	8.37	273.18	328.10
July	89 522	73 632	22 434	17 278	67 088	59 422	12 261	34.8	39.2	7.89	8.40	274.57	329.28
August	89 364	73 434	22 268	17 160	67 096	59 213	12 153	34.7	39.0	7.94	8.43	275.52	328.77
September	89 183	73 260	22 146	17 004	67 037	59 078	12 104	34.8	39.0	7.94	8.45	276.31	329.55
October	88 906	72 950	21 879	16 853	67 027	58 761	11 880	34.6	38.9	7.96	8.44	275.42	328.32
November	88 783	72 806	21 736	16 722	67 047	58 625	11 766	34.6	39.0	7.98	8.46	276.11	329.94
December	88 769	72 788	21 688	16 690	67 081	58 599	11 746	34.7	39.0	8.02	8.49	278.29	331.11
1983													
January	88 993	72 970	21 757	16 705	67 236	58 828	11 783	34.8	39.3	8.06	8.52	280.49	334.84
February	88 918	72 914	21 676	16 706	67 242	58 803	11 794	34.5	39.3	8.10	8.59	279.45	337.59
March	89 090	73 085	21 649	16 711	67 441	58 971	11 817	34.7	39.6	8.10	8.59	281.07	340.16
April	89 366	73 376	21 729	16 794	67 637	59 214	11 894	34.8	39.7	8.13	8.61	282.92	341.82
May	89 643	73 638	21 829	16 885	67 814	59 458	11 987	34.9	40.0	8.17	8.64	285.13	345.60
June	90 022	74 002	21 949	16 960	68 073	59 819	12 054	34.9	40.1	8.19	8.66	285.83	347.27
July	90 440	74 429	22 103	17 059	68 337	60 203	12 155	34.9	40.3	8.23	8.71	287.23	351.01
August	90 132	74 116	22 207	17 118	67 925	59 834	12 200	34.9	40.3	8.20	8.71	286.18	351.01
September	91 247	75 205	22 381	17 255	68 866	60 859	12 318	35.0	40.6	8.26	8.76	289.10	355.66
October	91 518	75 532	22 546	17 367	68 972	61 108	12 408	35.2	40.6	8.31	8.80	292.51	357.28
November	91 871	75 874	22 698	17 479	69 173	61 392	12 503	35.1	40.6	8.32	8.84	292.03	358.90
December	92 227	76 219	22 803	17 551	69 424	61 680	12 553	35.1	40.5	8.33	8.87	292.38	359.24
1984													
January	92 673	76 663	22 942	17 630	69 731	61 925	12 617	35.1	40.6	8.38	8.91	294.14	361.75
February	93 154	77 129	23 146	17 728	70 008	62 342	12 703	35.3	41.1	8.37	8.92	295.46	366.61
March	93 429	77 399	23 209	17 806	70 220	62 531	12 768	35.1	40.7	8.41	8.96	295.19	364.67
April	93 792	77 717	23 305	17 872	70 487	62 817	12 814	35.2	40.8	8.45	8.98	297.44	366.38
May	94 100	77 997	23 389	17 916	70 711	63 029	12 840	35.1	40.7	8.44	8.99	296.24	365.89
June	94 479	78 352	23 497	17 967	70 982	63 313	12 871	35.1	40.6	8.48	9.03	297.65	366.62
July	94 792	78 620	23 571	18 013	71 221	63 532	12 901	35.1	40.6	8.52	9.05	299.05	367.43
August	95 034	78 810	23 608	18 034	71 426	63 670	12 906	35.0	40.5	8.52	9.09	298.20	368.15
September	95 344	79 089	23 617	18 019	71 727	63 889	12 880	35.1	40.5	8.56	9.12	300.46	369.36
October	95 630	79 356	23 626	18 024	72 004	64 100	12 868	34.9	40.5	8.55	9.15	298.40	370.58
November	95 979	79 668	23 639	18 016	72 340	64 343	12 846	35.0	40.4	8.57	9.19	299.95	371.28
December	96 107	79 825	23 673	18 023	72 434	64 460	12 848	35.1	40.5	8.61	9.22	302.21	373.41
1985													
January	96 373	80 037	23 672	18 009	72 701	64 678	12 833	34.9	40.3	8.61	9.27	300.49	373.58
February	96 497	80 148	23 621	17 966	72 876	64 775	12 784	34.8	40.1	8.64	9.29	300.67	372.53
March	96 843	80 448	23 661	17 939	73 182	65 026	12 758	34.9	40.4	8.67	9.32	302.58	376.53
April	97 039	80 609	23 644	17 886	73 395	65 133	12 701	34.9	40.5	8.69	9.35	303.28	378.68
May	97 313	80 839	23 632	17 855	73 681	65 328	12 673	34.9	40.4	8.70	9.37	303.63	378.55
June	97 459	80 961	23 592	17 819	73 867	65 403	12 635	34.9	40.5	8.74	9.39	305.03	380.30
July	97 649	81 029	23 549	17 776	74 100	65 450	12 596	34.8	40.4	8.74	9.42	304.15	380.57
August	97 842	81 223	23 546	17 756	74 296	65 633	12 593	34.8	40.6	8.77	9.43	305.20	382.86
September	98 045	81 407	23 528	17 718	74 517	65 769	12 556	34.8	40.6	8.80	9.44	306.24	383.26
October	98 233	81 579	23 529	17 708	74 704	65 939	12 556	34.8	40.7	8.79	9.46	305.89	385.02
November	98 442	81 768	23 520	17 697	74 922	66 089	12 545	34.8	40.7	8.82	9.49	306.94	386.24
December	98 609	81 915	23 518	17 693	75 091	66 219	12 550	34.9	40.9	8.87	9.55	309.56	390.60

Table 10-9. Employment, Hours, and Earnings, Total Nonfarm and Manufacturing, Historical Annual and Monthly—Continued

(Wage and salary workers on nonfarm payrolls, seasonally adjusted.)

Year and month	All wage and salary workers (thousands)					Production and nonsupervisory workers on private payrolls							
	Total	Private			Service-providing	Number (thousands)		Average hours per week		Average hourly earnings, dollars		Average weekly earnings, dollars	
		Total	Goods-producing			Total private	Manufac-turing	Total private	Manufac-turing	Total private	Manufac-turing	Total private	Manufac-turing
			Total	Manufac-turing									
1986													
January	98 734	82 019	23 530	17 686	75 204	66 316	12 546	35.0	40.7	8.85	9.53	309.75	387.87
February	98 841	82 082	23 485	17 663	75 356	66 387	12 530	34.8	40.7	8.88	9.56	309.02	389.09
March	98 935	82 180	23 428	17 624	75 507	66 425	12 498	34.8	40.7	8.89	9.58	309.37	389.91
April	99 122	82 357	23 427	17 616	75 695	66 554	12 495	34.7	40.5	8.89	9.56	308.48	387.18
May	99 249	82 459	23 349	17 593	75 900	66 635	12 474	34.8	40.7	8.90	9.59	309.72	390.31
June	99 155	82 376	23 263	17 530	75 892	66 558	12 424	34.7	40.7	8.91	9.58	309.18	389.91
July	99 473	82 694	23 235	17 497	76 238	66 829	12 389	34.6	40.6	8.92	9.60	308.63	389.76
August	99 587	82 787	23 225	17 489	76 362	66 927	12 399	34.7	40.7	8.94	9.61	310.22	391.13
September	99 934	83 024	23 216	17 498	76 718	67 133	12 411	34.6	40.7	8.94	9.60	309.32	390.72
October	100 120	83 151	23 208	17 477	76 912	67 230	12 396	34.6	40.6	8.96	9.62	310.02	390.57
November	100 306	83 301	23 204	17 472	77 102	67 368	12 407	34.7	40.7	9.00	9.64	312.30	392.35
December	100 511	83 490	23 237	17 478	77 274	67 517	12 425	34.6	40.8	9.01	9.66	311.75	394.13
1987													
January	100 683	83 638	23 232	17 465	77 451	67 638	12 405	34.7	40.8	9.02	9.67	312.99	394.54
February	100 915	83 879	23 296	17 499	77 619	67 869	12 438	34.9	41.2	9.05	9.69	315.85	399.23
March	101 164	84 100	23 307	17 507	77 857	68 015	12 446	34.7	41.0	9.07	9.71	314.73	398.11
April	101 502	84 393	23 342	17 525	78 160	68 261	12 465	34.7	40.8	9.08	9.71	315.08	396.17
May	101 728	84 616	23 390	17 542	78 338	68 467	12 481	34.8	41.0	9.11	9.73	317.03	398.93
June	101 900	84 776	23 390	17 537	78 510	68 579	12 482	34.7	40.9	9.11	9.74	316.12	398.37
July	102 247	85 087	23 455	17 593	78 792	68 819	12 521	34.7	41.0	9.12	9.74	316.46	399.34
August	102 418	85 246	23 506	17 630	78 912	68 941	12 560	34.9	40.9	9.18	9.80	320.38	400.82
September	102 646	85 511	23 566	17 691	79 080	69 164	12 614	34.7	40.8	9.19	9.85	318.89	401.88
October	103 138	85 869	23 655	17 729	79 483	69 442	12 637	34.8	41.1	9.22	9.84	320.86	404.42
November	103 370	86 071	23 711	17 775	79 659	69 621	12 678	34.8	41.0	9.27	9.87	322.60	404.67
December	103 664	86 317	23 772	17 809	79 892	69 852	12 707	34.6	41.0	9.28	9.89	321.09	405.49
1988													
January	103 758	86 393	23 668	17 790	80 090	69 859	12 684	34.6	41.1	9.29	9.91	321.43	407.30
February	104 211	86 822	23 769	17 823	80 442	70 255	12 706	34.7	41.1	9.29	9.92	322.36	407.71
March	104 487	87 040	23 824	17 844	80 663	70 397	12 712	34.5	40.9	9.31	9.94	321.20	406.55
April	104 732	87 280	23 880	17 874	80 852	70 604	12 733	34.6	41.0	9.36	9.99	323.86	409.59
May	104 961	87 480	23 896	17 892	81 065	70 749	12 747	34.6	41.0	9.41	10.02	325.59	410.82
June	105 324	87 809	23 951	17 916	81 373	71 031	12 767	34.6	41.1	9.42	10.04	325.93	412.64
July	105 546	88 052	23 966	17 926	81 580	71 235	12 774	34.7	41.1	9.45	10.05	327.92	413.06
August	105 670	88 126	23 926	17 891	81 744	71 287	12 752	34.5	40.9	9.46	10.07	326.37	411.86
September	106 009	88 375	23 942	17 914	82 067	71 487	12 764	34.5	41.0	9.51	10.12	328.10	414.92
October	106 277	88 607	23 987	17 966	82 290	71 680	12 812	34.7	41.1	9.56	10.16	331.73	417.58
November	106 616	88 870	24 030	18 003	82 586	71 902	12 851	34.5	41.1	9.58	10.19	330.51	418.81
December	106 906	89 170	24 054	18 025	82 852	72 175	12 864	34.6	40.9	9.60	10.20	332.16	417.18
1989													
January	107 168	89 394	24 097	18 057	83 071	72 393	12 882	34.7	41.1	9.65	10.23	334.86	420.45
February	107 426	89 614	24 080	18 055	83 346	72 577	12 880	34.5	41.2	9.68	10.26	333.96	422.71
March	107 619	89 797	24 069	18 060	83 550	72 695	12 878	34.5	41.1	9.70	10.29	334.65	422.92
April	107 792	89 952	24 100	18 055	83 692	72 819	12 867	34.6	41.1	9.75	10.28	337.35	422.51
May	107 910	90 034	24 089	18 040	83 821	72 889	12 852	34.4	41.0	9.73	10.30	334.71	422.30
June	108 026	90 114	24 052	18 013	83 974	72 941	12 822	34.4	40.9	9.77	10.33	336.09	422.50
July	108 066	90 161	24 027	17 980	84 039	72 972	12 790	34.5	40.9	9.82	10.36	338.79	423.72
August	108 115	90 126	24 048	17 964	84 067	72 940	12 790	34.5	40.9	9.83	10.39	339.14	424.95
September	108 365	90 338	24 000	17 922	84 365	73 114	12 745	34.4	40.8	9.87	10.41	339.53	424.73
October	108 476	90 443	23 997	17 895	84 479	73 211	12 723	34.6	40.8	9.93	10.43	343.58	425.54
November	108 753	90 696	24 009	17 886	84 744	73 427	12 713	34.4	40.7	9.93	10.44	341.59	424.91
December	108 849	90 774	23 949	17 881	84 900	73 504	12 705	34.3	40.5	9.98	10.49	342.31	424.85
1990													
January	109 183	91 032	23 981	17 796	85 202	73 738	12 738	34.5	40.5	10.02	10.52	345.69	426.06
February	109 432	91 255	24 071	17 893	85 361	73 935	12 848	34.4	40.6	10.07	10.64	346.41	431.98
March	109 647	91 353	24 023	17 868	85 624	73 995	12 821	34.4	40.7	10.11	10.70	347.78	435.49
April	109 688	91 311	23 967	17 846	85 721	73 961	12 804	34.3	40.5	10.12	10.68	347.46	432.54
May	109 838	91 239	23 887	17 796	85 951	73 873	12 755	34.3	40.6	10.16	10.74	348.49	436.04
June	109 863	91 307	23 850	17 777	86 013	73 867	12 739	34.4	40.7	10.20	10.78	351.22	438.75
July	109 833	91 273	23 745	17 703	86 088	73 807	12 673	34.2	40.6	10.22	10.80	349.52	438.48
August	109 613	91 156	23 648	17 649	85 965	73 744	12 624	34.2	40.5	10.24	10.81	350.21	437.81
September	109 525	91 088	23 571	17 609	85 954	73 636	12 596	34.2	40.5	10.28	10.86	351.58	439.83
October	109 366	90 923	23 473	17 577	85 893	73 504	12 577	34.1	40.4	10.30	10.92	351.23	441.17
November	109 216	90 766	23 283	17 428	85 933	73 351	12 439	34.2	40.2	10.32	10.89	352.94	437.78
December	109 160	90 692	23 203	17 395	85 957	73 285	12 415	34.2	40.3	10.35	10.93	353.97	440.48
1991													
January	109 039	90 565	23 060	17 329	85 979	73 143	12 351	34.1	40.2	10.38	10.98	353.96	441.40
February	108 735	90 253	22 900	17 211	85 835	72 855	12 242	34.1	40.1	10.39	10.97	354.30	439.90
March	108 577	90 089	22 779	17 140	85 798	72 704	12 191	34.0	40.0	10.41	11.00	353.94	440.00
April	108 367	89 882	22 688	17 094	85 679	72 535	12 157	34.0	40.1	10.46	11.05	355.64	443.11
May	108 240	89 742	22 617	17 069	85 623	72 438	12 148	34.0	40.1	10.49	11.09	356.66	444.71
June	108 338	89 777	22 571	17 044	85 767	72 459	12 135	34.1	40.5	10.51	11.13	358.73	450.77
July	108 302	89 704	22 507	17 015	85 795	72 427	12 130	34.1	40.6	10.54	11.17	359.41	452.39
August	108 308	89 741	22 493	17 025	85 815	72 484	12 153	34.1	40.6	10.56	11.18	360.10	453.91
September	108 340	89 797	22 466	17 010	85 874	72 501	12 140	34.1	40.6	10.58	11.22	360.78	455.53
October	108 356	89 763	22 418	16 999	85 938	72 476	12 138	34.2	40.6	10.59	11.25	362.18	456.75
November	108 299	89 672	22 316	16 961	85 983	72 405	12 102	34.1	40.7	10.61	11.26	361.80	458.28
December	108 324	89 683	22 274	16 916	86 050	72 448	12 075	34.1	40.7	10.64	11.27	362.82	458.69

Table 10-9. Employment, Hours, and Earnings, Total Nonfarm and Manufacturing, Historical Annual and Monthly—Continued

(Wage and salary workers on nonfarm payrolls, seasonally adjusted.)

Year and month	All wage and salary workers (thousands)					Production and nonsupervisory workers on private payrolls							
	Total	Private			Service-providing	Number (thousands)		Average hours per week		Average hourly earnings, dollars		Average weekly earnings, dollars	
		Total	Goods-producing			Total private	Manufac-turing	Total private	Manufac-turing	Total private	Manufac-turing	Total private	Manufac-turing
			Total	Manufac-turing									
1992													
January	108 378	89 690	22 214	16 840	86 164	72 490	12 013	34.1	40.6	10.65	11.24	363.17	456.34
February	108 313	89 624	22 141	16 828	86 172	72 467	12 015	34.1	40.7	10.67	11.30	363.85	459.91
March	108 368	89 653	22 127	16 805	86 241	72 484	12 006	34.1	40.7	10.70	11.32	364.87	460.72
April	108 527	89 788	22 132	16 831	86 395	72 637	12 029	34.3	41.0	10.72	11.36	367.70	464.62
May	108 654	89 901	22 135	16 835	86 519	72 752	12 046	34.3	40.9	10.74	11.39	368.38	465.85
June	108 721	89 959	22 097	16 826	86 624	72 788	12 042	34.2	40.8	10.77	11.41	368.33	465.53
July	108 790	89 973	22 075	16 820	86 715	72 809	12 049	34.2	40.8	10.79	11.43	369.02	466.34
August	108 930	90 047	22 045	16 783	86 885	72 886	12 020	34.2	40.8	10.82	11.46	370.04	467.57
September	108 966	90 137	22 020	16 761	86 946	72 988	12 002	34.3	40.7	10.82	11.45	371.13	466.02
October	109 145	90 317	22 028	16 750	87 117	73 143	11 999	34.2	40.8	10.85	11.47	371.41	467.98
November	109 284	90 443	22 042	16 758	87 242	73 294	12 012	34.2	40.9	10.87	11.49	371.75	469.94
December	109 494	90 616	22 075	16 768	87 419	73 478	12 031	34.2	40.9	10.89	11.51	372.78	470.76
1993													
January	109 805	90 904	22 133	16 791	87 672	73 754	12 060	34.3	41.1	10.93	11.55	375.24	474.71
February	110 047	91 145	22 188	16 805	87 859	74 011	12 072	34.3	41.1	10.94	11.57	375.59	475.53
March	109 998	91 091	22 142	16 795	87 856	73 928	12 074	34.1	40.8	10.99	11.59	374.76	472.87
April	110 306	91 368	22 131	16 772	88 175	74 153	12 056	34.4	41.5	10.99	11.64	378.40	483.06
May	110 573	91 622	22 189	16 766	88 384	74 410	12 056	34.3	41.1	11.02	11.66	377.99	479.23
June	110 754	91 785	22 165	16 742	88 589	74 511	12 039	34.3	40.9	11.03	11.67	378.67	477.30
July	111 053	91 993	22 184	16 740	88 869	74 706	12 043	34.4	41.1	11.05	11.69	380.46	480.46
August	111 212	92 184	22 203	16 741	89 009	74 881	12 050	34.3	41.1	11.08	11.72	380.04	481.69
September	111 451	92 410	22 252	16 769	89 199	75 072	12 080	34.4	41.3	11.10	11.76	381.84	485.69
October	111 737	92 695	22 306	16 778	89 431	75 318	12 092	34.4	41.3	11.13	11.79	382.87	486.93
November	111 999	92 931	22 347	16 800	89 652	75 537	12 119	34.4	41.3	11.15	11.83	383.56	488.58
December	112 311	93 202	22 413	16 815	89 898	75 762	12 140	34.4	41.4	11.18	11.88	384.59	491.83
1994													
January	112 583	93 436	22 465	16 855	90 118	75 967	12 181	34.4	41.4	11.21	11.89	385.62	492.25
February	112 783	93 633	22 451	16 862	90 332	76 174	12 198	34.2	40.9	11.25	11.97	384.75	489.57
March	113 248	94 058	22 550	16 897	90 698	76 536	12 234	34.5	41.7	11.25	11.95	388.13	498.32
April	113 597	94 374	22 641	16 933	90 956	76 833	12 276	34.5	41.8	11.27	11.96	388.82	498.73
May	113 931	94 667	22 704	16 962	91 227	77 112	12 304	34.5	41.8	11.29	11.98	389.85	500.76
June	114 247	94 973	22 764	17 010	91 483	77 363	12 351	34.5	41.8	11.31	12.01	390.54	502.02
July	114 624	95 323	22 806	17 025	91 818	77 658	12 367	34.6	41.8	11.34	12.02	392.36	502.44
August	114 902	95 596	22 876	17 081	92 026	77 901	12 428	34.5	41.7	11.36	12.05	391.92	502.49
September	115 253	95 916	22 947	17 114	92 306	78 166	12 459	34.5	41.6	11.39	12.09	392.96	502.94
October	115 468	96 124	22 975	17 145	92 493	78 349	12 489	34.5	41.8	11.42	12.11	394.34	506.20
November	115 887	96 520	23 050	17 186	92 837	78 697	12 529	34.5	41.7	11.45	12.15	395.03	507.87
December	116 162	96 774	23 095	17 217	93 067	78 942	12 558	34.5	41.8	11.47	12.17	396.06	508.71
1995													
January	116 487	97 090	23 146	17 261	93 341	79 181	12 593	34.5	41.8	11.49	12.19	396.41	509.54
February	116 691	97 284	23 103	17 265	93 588	79 338	12 602	34.4	41.7	11.52	12.24	396.63	510.41
March	116 913	97 486	23 151	17 263	93 762	79 518	12 600	34.3	41.5	11.55	12.25	396.17	508.38
April	117 075	97 641	23 174	17 278	93 901	79 651	12 608	34.3	41.1	11.56	12.25	396.85	503.48
May	117 059	97 641	23 120	17 259	93 939	79 673	12 590	34.2	41.2	11.60	12.28	396.72	505.94
June	117 294	97 849	23 137	17 247	94 157	79 842	12 574	34.3	41.2	11.63	12.31	398.91	507.17
July	117 395	97 958	23 118	17 217	94 277	79 909	12 538	34.3	41.1	11.67	12.38	400.28	508.82
August	117 644	98 215	23 164	17 240	94 480	80 159	12 566	34.3	41.2	11.69	12.39	401.31	510.47
September	117 885	98 455	23 207	17 246	94 678	80 356	12 567	34.3	41.2	11.73	12.41	402.34	511.29
October	118 041	98 577	23 207	17 217	94 834	80 477	12 535	34.3	41.2	11.75	12.43	403.37	512.12
November	118 189	98 726	23 200	17 209	94 989	80 551	12 515	34.3	41.3	11.78	12.45	404.05	514.19
December	118 321	98 855	23 208	17 230	95 113	80 702	12 551	34.2	40.9	11.81	12.49	403.90	510.84
1996													
January	118 303	98 853	23 196	17 208	95 107	80 627	12 517	33.8	39.7	11.87	12.60	401.21	500.22
February	118 735	99 250	23 281	17 230	95 454	81 019	12 533	34.3	41.3	11.87	12.55	407.14	518.32
March	119 001	99 469	23 276	17 193	95 725	81 197	12 488	34.3	41.1	11.89	12.50	407.83	513.75
April	119 165	99 650	23 316	17 204	95 849	81 364	12 505	34.2	41.1	11.96	12.69	409.03	521.56
May	119 485	99 956	23 357	17 221	96 128	81 625	12 518	34.3	41.4	11.97	12.71	410.91	526.19
June	119 774	100 246	23 399	17 226	96 375	81 838	12 522	34.4	41.5	12.03	12.76	414.18	529.54
July	120 029	100 482	23 417	17 222	96 612	82 037	12 517	34.3	41.4	12.06	12.79	413.66	529.51
August	120 202	100 698	23 479	17 255	96 723	82 234	12 546	34.4	41.5	12.09	12.83	416.24	532.45
September	120 427	100 860	23 497	17 252	96 930	82 358	12 544	34.4	41.6	12.14	12.85	417.62	534.56
October	120 677	101 123	23 546	17 268	97 131	82 606	12 559	34.4	41.4	12.16	12.83	418.30	531.16
November	120 976	101 411	23 585	17 278	97 391	82 791	12 560	34.4	41.5	12.21	12.88	420.02	534.52
December	121 146	101 575	23 598	17 284	97 548	82 960	12 571	34.4	41.7	12.25	12.95	421.40	540.02
1997													
January	121 382	101 789	23 619	17 298	97 763	83 106	12 579	34.3	41.4	12.29	12.99	421.89	537.79
February	121 684	102 086	23 686	17 316	97 998	83 387	12 592	34.4	41.6	12.32	13.00	423.81	540.80
March	122 000	102 392	23 739	17 340	98 261	83 617	12 613	34.5	41.8	12.37	13.04	426.77	545.07
April	122 293	102 690	23 766	17 350	98 527	83 868	12 618	34.6	41.8	12.39	13.03	428.69	544.65
May	122 551	102 950	23 809	17 362	98 742	84 093	12 633	34.6	41.7	12.43	13.07	430.08	545.02
June	122 818	103 158	23 834	17 387	98 984	84 232	12 647	34.3	41.5	12.46	13.09	427.72	543.24
July	123 131	103 445	23 862	17 389	99 269	84 480	12 645	34.5	41.6	12.50	13.09	431.25	544.54
August	123 092	103 475	23 952	17 452	99 140	84 427	12 699	34.6	41.7	12.57	13.17	434.92	549.19
September	123 604	103 925	23 996	17 465	99 608	84 822	12 711	34.6	41.7	12.60	13.17	436.31	549.19
October	123 945	104 207	24 053	17 513	99 892	85 032	12 746	34.6	41.8	12.67	13.29	438.38	555.52
November	124 251	104 490	24 112	17 556	100 139	85 226	12 777	34.5	41.8	12.72	13.32	440.11	556.78
December	124 554	104 788	24 184	17 588	100 370	85 459	12 800	34.6	41.9	12.75	13.35	441.50	559.37

Table 10-9. Employment, Hours, and Earnings, Total Nonfarm and Manufacturing, Historical Annual and Monthly—Continued

(Wage and salary workers on nonfarm payrolls, seasonally adjusted.)

Year and month	All wage and salary workers (thousands)					Production and nonsupervisory workers on private payrolls							
	Total	Private			Service-providing	Number (thousands)		Average hours per week		Average hourly earnings, dollars		Average weekly earnings, dollars	
		Total	Goods-producing			Total private	Manufac-turing	Total private	Manufac-turing	Total private	Manufac-turing	Total private	Manufac-turing
			Total	Manufac-turing									
1998													
January	124 830	105 060	24 262	17 619	100 568	85 621	12 818	34.6	41.9	12.79	13.35	442.88	559.37
February	125 026	105 240	24 283	17 627	100 743	85 790	12 828	34.5	41.7	12.84	13.39	444.61	558.36
March	125 177	105 385	24 264	17 637	100 913	85 820	12 822	34.5	41.6	12.88	13.43	444.71	558.69
April	125 456	105 640	24 340	17 637	101 116	86 040	12 814	34.4	41.3	12.92	13.40	444.79	553.42
May	125 862	105 987	24 361	17 624	101 501	86 320	12 790	34.5	41.5	12.97	13.45	448.76	558.18
June	126 080	106 201	24 387	17 608	101 693	86 470	12 769	34.4	41.4	12.99	13.43	447.20	556.00
July	126 204	106 274	24 238	17 422	101 966	86 488	12 558	34.5	41.4	13.01	13.34	448.85	552.28
August	126 551	106 592	24 420	17 563	102 131	86 774	12 702	34.5	41.4	13.08	13.46	451.61	557.24
September	126 775	106 790	24 420	17 558	102 355	86 935	12 715	34.4	41.3	13.11	13.52	451.33	558.38
October	126 971	106 970	24 405	17 511	102 566	87 085	12 673	34.5	41.4	13.15	13.53	453.68	560.14
November	127 254	107 210	24 394	17 465	102 860	87 251	12 634	34.4	41.4	13.17	13.54	453.39	560.56
December	127 601	107 522	24 454	17 449	103 147	87 517	12 625	34.5	41.5	13.22	13.56	456.09	562.74
1999													
January	127 726	107 642	24 401	17 427	103 325	87 577	12 605	34.4	41.3	13.27	13.59	456.83	561.27
February	128 137	107 993	24 434	17 395	103 703	87 891	12 575	34.4	41.3	13.30	13.63	457.52	564.28
March	128 244	108 076	24 378	17 368	103 866	87 954	12 562	34.3	41.3	13.33	13.69	457.56	565.40
April	128 619	108 382	24 424	17 343	104 195	88 183	12 540	34.4	41.4	13.38	13.73	460.62	567.05
May	128 831	108 602	24 445	17 333	104 386	88 368	12 534	34.3	41.4	13.43	13.80	460.65	571.32
June	129 092	108 820	24 434	17 295	104 658	88 543	12 503	34.4	41.3	13.47	13.86	463.71	572.42
July	129 411	109 072	24 474	17 308	104 937	88 751	12 525	34.4	41.4	13.52	13.92	465.09	576.29
August	129 578	109 203	24 468	17 288	105 110	88 862	12 502	34.4	41.5	13.54	13.93	466.12	578.10
September	129 791	109 387	24 485	17 281	105 306	89 003	12 495	34.3	41.5	13.61	13.99	467.17	580.59
October	130 192	109 735	24 506	17 273	105 686	89 307	12 484	34.4	41.4	13.64	13.99	469.22	579.19
November	130 483	109 987	24 561	17 282	105 922	89 526	12 488	34.4	41.4	13.66	14.01	469.90	580.01
December	130 778	110 238	24 582	17 280	106 196	89 745	12 490	34.4	41.4	13.70	14.06	471.62	582.08
2000													
January	131 008	110 437	24 627	17 283	106 381	89 897	12 491	34.4	41.5	13.75	14.13	473.34	586.40
February	131 138	110 539	24 608	17 284	106 530	89 977	12 481	34.4	41.5	13.80	14.15	474.72	587.23
March	131 606	110 873	24 705	17 302	106 901	90 244	12 490	34.4	41.4	13.84	14.18	476.44	587.05
April	131 893	111 091	24 688	17 298	107 205	90 468	12 477	34.4	41.6	13.90	14.23	478.50	591.97
May	132 119	110 972	24 647	17 279	107 472	90 375	12 464	34.3	41.3	13.94	14.23	478.14	587.70
June	132 074	111 187	24 674	17 298	107 400	90 544	12 468	34.3	41.3	13.98	14.30	479.86	590.59
July	132 251	111 384	24 717	17 322	107 534	90 674	12 474	34.3	41.5	14.03	14.32	481.23	594.28
August	132 237	111 400	24 684	17 288	107 553	90 698	12 431	34.2	41.0	14.07	14.36	481.19	588.76
September	132 371	111 636	24 642	17 230	107 729	90 847	12 382	34.3	41.1	14.13	14.40	484.66	591.84
October	132 357	111 614	24 639	17 218	107 718	90 835	12 357	34.3	41.1	14.18	14.49	486.37	595.54
November	132 582	111 822	24 624	17 203	107 958	90 966	12 336	34.2	41.1	14.24	14.52	487.01	596.77
December	132 724	111 920	24 576	17 182	108 148	91 015	12 307	34.0	40.4	14.29	14.50	485.86	585.80
2001													
January	132 694	111 859	24 531	17 102	108 163	90 965	12 229	34.2	40.6	14.29	14.48	489.06	587.89
February	132 766	111 860	24 473	17 027	108 293	90 923	12 155	34.0	40.5	14.37	14.55	490.02	589.28
March	132 741	111 796	24 408	16 937	108 333	90 876	12 085	34.1	40.5	14.42	14.58	492.06	590.49
April	132 460	111 468	24 254	16 802	108 206	90 640	11 982	34.0	40.5	14.45	14.64	491.64	592.92
May	132 422	111 393	24 119	16 661	108 303	90 565	11 859	34.0	40.4	14.50	14.69	493.00	593.48
June	132 293	111 156	23 967	16 517	108 326	90 369	11 739	34.0	40.3	14.55	14.74	494.70	594.02
July	132 178	110 993	23 836	16 381	108 342	90 253	11 632	34.0	40.6	14.55	14.82	495.04	601.69
August	132 020	110 802	23 668	16 233	108 352	90 100	11 495	33.9	40.3	14.60	14.85	494.94	598.46
September	131 778	110 536	23 537	16 117	108 241	89 837	11 400	33.8	40.2	14.64	14.89	495.17	598.58
October	131 454	110 179	23 379	15 973	108 075	89 552	11 286	33.7	40.1	14.66	14.90	494.38	597.49
November	131 160	109 834	23 210	15 826	107 950	89 232	11 175	33.8	40.1	14.72	14.96	497.87	599.90
December	130 989	109 634	23 095	15 712	107 894	89 142	11 081	33.9	40.2	14.75	15.01	500.36	603.40
2002													
January	130 847	109 470	22 959	15 585	107 888	89 083	10 993	33.8	40.1	14.76	15.05	499.23	603.51
February	130 714	109 324	22 875	15 514	107 839	89 048	10 951	33.8	40.3	14.78	15.11	499.90	608.93
March	130 695	109 264	22 786	15 443	107 909	89 006	10 901	33.9	40.6	14.82	15.15	502.74	615.09
April	130 615	109 172	22 689	15 392	107 926	88 851	10 859	33.9	40.6	14.84	15.17	503.08	615.90
May	130 607	109 093	22 604	15 337	108 003	88 711	10 824	33.9	40.6	14.88	15.24	504.77	618.74
June	130 664	109 115	22 579	15 299	108 085	88 636	10 797	34.0	40.7	14.94	15.27	506.81	621.49
July	130 579	109 035	22 521	15 256	108 058	88 487	10 764	33.8	40.4	14.98	15.29	506.66	617.72
August	130 564	108 975	22 450	15 172	108 114	88 414	10 697	33.9	40.5	15.02	15.34	509.52	621.27
September	130 504	108 958	22 398	15 120	108 106	88 395	10 668	33.9	40.5	15.07	15.38	511.21	622.89
October	130 629	109 070	22 326	15 061	108 303	88 469	10 631	33.8	40.3	15.12	15.46	511.39	623.04
November	130 639	109 058	22 283	14 993	108 356	88 432	10 583	33.8	40.4	15.15	15.48	512.41	625.39
December	130 481	108 893	22 189	14 912	108 292	88 246	10 523	33.8	40.5	15.21	15.53	514.44	628.97
2003													
January	130 575	108 949	22 149	14 869	108 426	88 294	10 484	33.8	40.3	15.22	15.59	514.77	628.28
February	130 422	108 798	22 024	14 782	108 398	88 148	10 416	33.7	40.3	15.29	15.63	515.61	629.89
March	130 212	108 602	21 946	14 722	108 266	87 860	10 357	33.8	40.4	15.29	15.64	517.14	631.86
April	130 167	108 572	21 864	14 609	108 303	87 815	10 256	33.6	40.1	15.27	15.62	513.74	626.36
May	130 156	108 589	21 831	14 556	108 325	87 775	10 218	33.7	40.2	15.33	15.69	516.96	630.74
June	130 166	108 560	21 788	14 493	108 378	87 764	10 165	33.7	40.3	15.36	15.72	517.97	633.52
July	130 189	108 556	21 707	14 401	108 482	87 740	10 093	33.6	40.1	15.40	15.76	517.78	631.98
August	130 148	108 592	21 707	14 377	108 441	87 806	10 084	33.7	40.2	15.42	15.79	519.99	634.76
September	130 250	108 746	21 700	14 347	108 550	87 924	10 059	33.6	40.5	15.42	15.84	518.45	641.52
October	130 446	108 888	21 691	14 334	108 755	88 022	10 054	33.7	40.6	15.43	15.82	520.33	642.29
November	130 462	108 927	21 687	14 315	108 775	88 061	10 039	33.8	40.9	15.47	15.89	523.22	649.90
December	130 586	109 040	21 703	14 300	108 883	88 130	10 031	33.6	40.7	15.47	15.91	520.13	647.54

Table 10-9. Employment, Hours, and Earnings, Total Nonfarm and Manufacturing, Historical Annual and Monthly—*Continued*

(Wage and salary workers on nonfarm payrolls, seasonally adjusted.)

Year and month	All wage and salary workers (thousands)					Production and nonsupervisory workers on private payrolls							
	Total	Private			Service-providing	Number (thousands)		Average hours per week		Average hourly earnings, dollars		Average weekly earnings, dollars	
		Total	Goods-producing			Total private	Manufacturing	Total private	Manufacturing	Total private	Manufacturing	Total private	Manufacturing
			Total	Manufacturing									
2004													
January	130 747	109 209	21 716	14 291	109 031	88 236	10 027	33.7	40.9	15.50	15.94	522.69	651.95
February	130 791	109 241	21 692	14 278	109 099	88 250	10 012	33.8	41.0	15.54	15.98	525.59	655.18
March	131 123	109 535	21 758	14 287	109 365	88 506	10 025	33.7	40.9	15.56	16.01	524.71	654.81
April	131 372	109 758	21 803	14 316	109 569	88 752	10 060	33.7	40.7	15.59	16.06	525.72	653.64
May	131 679	110 065	21 881	14 342	109 798	89 062	10 091	33.8	41.0	15.64	16.07	528.97	660.48
June	131 753	110 152	21 885	14 332	109 868	89 200	10 087	33.6	40.7	15.67	16.11	526.85	655.68
July	131 785	110 179	21 899	14 329	109 886	89 304	10 095	33.7	40.8	15.70	16.14	529.43	658.51
August	131 917	110 291	21 943	14 344	109 974	89 440	10 115	33.8	40.8	15.74	16.20	532.35	660.96
September	132 079	110 444	21 956	14 330	110 123	89 625	10 104	33.8	40.8	15.78	16.30	533.70	665.04
October	132 425	110 769	22 004	14 332	110 421	89 940	10 103	33.8	40.6	15.81	16.27	535.05	660.56
November	132 490	110 798	21 998	14 308	110 492	89 973	10 078	33.7	40.5	15.84	16.30	534.15	660.15
December	132 619	110 926	22 006	14 288	110 613	90 116	10 063	33.7	40.6	15.87	16.34	536.74	663.40
2005													
January	132 753	111 018	21 959	14 258	110 794	90 228	10 045	33.7	40.6	15.91	16.38	536.50	665.03
February	132 992	111 248	22 037	14 274	110 955	90 456	10 052	33.8	40.6	15.93	16.43	538.77	667.06
March	133 126	111 386	22 066	14 269	111 060	90 633	10 056	33.7	40.4	15.97	16.44	538.53	664.18
April	133 489	111 735	22 136	14 250	111 353	90 972	10 048	33.8	40.4	16.01	16.46	541.48	664.98
May	133 664	111 883	22 171	14 255	111 493	91 098	10 061	33.7	40.4	16.04	16.53	540.89	667.81
June	133 909	112 146	22 186	14 228	111 723	91 350	10 047	33.7	40.4	16.08	16.54	542.23	668.22
July	134 282	112 425	22 204	14 225	112 078	91 587	10 039	33.7	40.5	16.15	16.58	544.93	671.49
August	134 478	112 615	22 227	14 202	112 251	91 773	10 043	33.7	40.5	16.17	16.63	545.27	673.52
September	134 545	112 700	22 226	14 175	112 319	91 866	10 046	33.8	40.7	16.19	16.59	547.90	675.21
October	134 629	112 800	22 292	14 192	112 337	91 967	10 073	33.8	41.0	16.29	16.69	550.94	685.96
November	134 966	113 107	22 357	14 187	112 609	92 318	10 093	33.8	40.9	16.31	16.67	551.62	681.80
December	135 125	113 246	22 377	14 194	112 748	92 471	10 112	33.7	40.8	16.36	16.67	551.67	680.14
2006													
January	135 402	113 555	22 468	14 211	112 934	92 825	10 153	33.9	41.0	16.42	16.69	557.32	684.29
February	135 717	113 839	22 536	14 210	113 181	93 092	10 164	33.8	41.0	16.48	16.69	557.36	684.29
March	135 997	114 094	22 572	14 214	113 425	93 389	10 174	33.8	41.1	16.54	16.71	559.39	686.78
April	136 179	114 260	22 631	14 226	113 548	93 568	10 190	33.9	41.3	16.64	16.75	564.44	691.78
May	136 202	114 276	22 596	14 202	113 606	93 631	10 179	33.8	41.1	16.65	16.77	563.11	689.25
June	136 279	114 357	22 597	14 212	113 682	93 695	10 190	33.9	41.2	16.72	16.79	567.49	691.75
July	136 486	114 513	22 590	14 188	113 896	93 836	10 177	33.9	41.4	16.78	16.80	569.52	695.52
August	136 670	114 659	22 571	14 158	114 099	93 978	10 158	33.9	41.2	16.83	16.83	570.88	693.40
September	136 827	114 745	22 537	14 125	114 290	94 019	10 120	33.8	41.0	16.87	16.83	570.54	691.71
October	136 829	114 761	22 455	14 074	114 374	94 039	10 071	33.9	41.1	16.94	16.90	574.61	696.28
November	137 039	114 956	22 408	14 041	114 631	94 269	10 047	33.8	41.0	16.98	16.91	574.26	693.31
December	137 210	115 122	22 404	14 014	114 806	94 447	10 041	33.9	41.1	17.05	16.97	578.33	695.77
2007													
January	137 448	115 353	22 439	14 008	115 009	94 676	10 036	33.8	41.0	17.09	17.02	577.98	697.82
February	137 536	115 405	22 334	13 997	115 202	94 706	10 035	33.7	40.9	17.16	17.06	578.63	699.46
March	137 724	115 575	22 391	13 970	115 333	94 917	10 011	33.9	41.3	17.22	17.10	584.44	706.23
April	137 802	115 627	22 350	13 945	115 452	95 003	10 006	33.9	41.3	17.28	17.21	586.47	710.77
May	137 946	115 753	22 322	13 928	115 624	95 152	10 007	33.8	41.1	17.34	17.23	586.43	709.88
June	138 017	115 810	22 322	13 910	115 695	95 265	9 996	33.9	41.3	17.41	17.28	590.88	715.39
July	137 984	115 813	22 277	13 889	115 707	95 350	9 990	33.8	41.3	17.46	17.29	590.82	714.08
August	137 908	115 742	22 166	13 829	115 802	95 304	9 944	33.8	41.3	17.51	17.35	592.18	716.56
September	138 053	115 774	22 093	13 790	115 960	95 381	9 933	33.8	41.3	17.57	17.37	594.20	717.38
October	138 135	115 838	22 055	13 763	116 080	95 486	9 911	33.8	41.2	17.58	17.35	594.54	714.82
November	138 253	115 919	22 015	13 757	116 238	95 589	9 920	33.8	41.3	17.64	17.43	596.91	719.86
December	138 350	115 974	21 976	13 746	116 374	95 672	9 924	33.8	41.1	17.70	17.44	598.60	716.78
2008													
January	138 365	115 977	21 947	13 725	116 418	95 688	9 914	33.7	41.1	17.75	17.50	598.51	719.25
February	138 279	115 862	21 898	13 697	116 381	95 592	9 888	33.7	41.2	17.80	17.57	602.32	723.88
March	138 199	115 756	21 820	13 659	116 379	95 539	9 866	33.8	41.3	17.87	17.63	604.68	728.12
April	137 985	115 535	21 680	13 598	116 305	95 359	9 810	33.7	41.1	17.92	17.62	606.37	724.18
May	137 803	115 320	21 599	13 564	116 204	95 192	9 779	33.7	41.1	17.98	17.69	606.60	727.06
June	137 631	115 114	21 483	13 504	116 148	95 008	9 721	33.7	41.0	18.04	17.75	608.62	729.53
July	137 421	114 853	21 360	13 430	116 061	94 805	9 655	33.6	41.0	18.11	17.80	609.17	729.80
August	137 162	114 595	21 250	13 358	115 912	94 569	9 586	33.7	40.9	18.18	17.80	613.34	728.02
September	136 710	114 173	21 101	13 275	115 609	94 222	9 504	33.6	40.5	18.21	17.83	612.53	722.12
October	136 236	113 687	20 897	13 149	115 339	93 822	9 384	33.5	40.5	18.27	17.91	614.21	725.36
November	135 471	112 911	20 625	13 036	114 846	93 119	9 290	33.4	40.2	18.32	17.95	612.56	719.80
December	134 774	112 218	20 323	12 851	114 451	92 532	9 137	33.3	39.8	18.38	18.00	612.72	716.40
2009													
January	133 976	111 397	19 888	12 560	114 088	91 792	8 889	33.3	39.7	18.41	18.01	613.72	715.00
February	133 275	110 699	19 576	12 381	113 699	91 235	8 741	33.2	39.6	18.45	18.08	613.20	715.97
March	132 449	109 889	19 226	12 207	113 223	90 546	8 592	33.1	39.3	18.50	18.13	613.01	712.51
April	131 765	109 088	18 893	12 029	112 872	89 846	8 453	33.1	39.6	18.51	18.17	613.67	717.32
May	131 411	108 794	18 655	11 862	112 756	89 635	8 311	33.1	39.3	18.53	18.13	614.01	712.51
June	130 944	108 368	18 422	11 726	112 522	89 262	8 203	33.0	39.6	18.57	18.18	613.14	719.93
July	130 617	108 096	18 276	11 666	112 341	89 055	8 172	33.1	39.9	18.60	18.28	616.65	730.17
August	130 401	107 864	18 150	11 625	112 251	88 869	8 148	33.1	40.0	18.66	18.33	618.31	733.60
September	130 174	107 723	18 042	11 590	112 132	88 757	8 133	33.1	40.0	18.71	18.43	619.96	736.80
October	129 976	107 452	17 917	11 540	112 059	88 525	8 100	33.0	40.2	18.75	18.39	619.41	738.88
November	129 970	107 437	17 871	11 511	112 099	88 538	8 079	33.2	40.5	18.81	18.42	624.82	745.61
December	129 687	107 205	17 794	11 477	111 893	88 401	8 050	33.2	40.6	18.84	18.41	626.15	747.85

Table 10-9. Employment, Hours, and Earnings, Total Nonfarm and Manufacturing, Historical Annual and Monthly—Continued

(Wage and salary workers on nonfarm payrolls, seasonally adjusted.)

Year and month	All wage and salary workers (thousands)					Production and nonsupervisory workers on private payrolls							
	Total	Private			Service-providing	Number (thousands)		Average hours per week		Average hourly earnings, dollars		Average weekly earnings, dollars	
		Total	Goods-producing			Total private	Manufacturing	Total private	Manufacturing	Total private	Manufacturing	Total private	Manufacturing
			Total	Manufacturing									
2010													
January	129 705	107 225	17 716	11 462	111 989	88 410	8 040	33.3	40.8	18.89	18.43	629.04	751.94
February	129 655	107 187	17 635	11 453	112 020	88 365	8 032	33.1	40.4	18.91	18.46	625.92	745.78
March	129 811	107 300	17 676	11 458	112 135	88 501	8 030	33.3	41.0	18.92	18.47	630.04	757.27
April	130 062	107 492	17 735	11 493	112 327	88 646	8 053	33.4	41.2	18.96	18.51	633.26	762.61
May	130 578	107 586	17 747	11 527	112 831	88 704	8 080	33.4	41.4	19.01	18.59	634.93	769.63
June	130 456	107 696	17 756	11 543	112 700	88 816	8 101	33.4	41.0	19.03	18.58	635.60	761.78
July	130 395	107 816	17 781	11 571	112 614	88 895	8 115	33.4	41.2	19.06	18.62	636.60	767.14
August	130 353	107 933	17 792	11 550	112 561	88 971	8 093	33.5	41.2	19.11	18.65	640.19	768.38
September	130 296	108 040	17 783	11 557	112 513	89 060	8 092	33.5	41.3	19.13	18.72	640.86	773.14
October	130 537	108 239	17 795	11 557	112 742	89 240	8 090	33.5	41.3	19.22	18.72	643.87	773.14
November	130 674	108 388	17 822	11 581	112 852	89 356	8 101	33.5	41.3	19.22	18.76	643.87	774.79
December	130 745	108 482	17 788	11 592	112 957	89 464	8 110	33.5	41.3	19.22	18.78	643.87	775.61
2011													
January	130 815	108 554	17 788	11 620	113 027	89 487	8 133	33.4	41.0	19.31	18.89	644.95	774.49
February	130 983	108 777	17 855	11 653	113 128	89 657	8 160	33.5	41.3	19.31	18.90	646.89	780.57
March	131 195	109 008	17 904	11 675	113 291	89 901	8 186	33.6	41.4	19.32	18.90	649.15	782.46
April	131 517	109 328	17 967	11 704	113 550	90 166	8 213	33.6	41.4	19.36	18.91	650.50	782.87
May	131 619	109 494	18 008	11 711	113 611	90 295	8 218	33.6	41.5	19.41	18.93	652.18	785.60
June	131 836	109 680	18 036	11 723	113 800	90 461	8 224	33.6	41.3	19.42	18.91	652.51	780.98
July	131 942	109 899	18 106	11 755	113 836	90 652	8 251	33.7	41.4	19.49	18.94	656.81	784.12
August	132 064	110 024	18 122	11 763	113 942	90 751	8 256	33.6	41.4	19.49	18.90	654.86	782.46
September	132 285	110 292	18 171	11 766	114 114	90 997	8 261	33.6	41.4	19.51	18.91	655.54	782.87
October	132 468	110 469	18 177	11 773	114 291	91 151	8 269	33.7	41.6	19.55	18.99	658.84	789.98
November	132 632	110 660	18 181	11 771	114 451	91 341	8 267	33.7	41.5	19.57	18.96	659.51	786.84
December	132 828	110 882	18 236	11 798	114 592	91 564	8 293	33.7	41.6	19.57	18.99	659.51	789.98
2012													
January	133 188	111 246	18 304	11 837	114 884	91 909	8 323	33.8	41.8	19.58	19.02	661.80	795.04
February	133 414	111 474	18 327	11 859	115 087	92 152	8 352	33.7	41.8	19.60	19.01	660.52	794.62
March	133 657	111 720	18 377	11 901	115 280	92 344	8 392	33.7	41.6	19.65	19.02	662.21	791.23
April	133 753	111 822	18 396	11 916	115 357	92 444	8 400	33.7	41.6	19.70	19.09	663.89	794.14
May	133 863	111 953	18 394	11 928	115 469	92 531	8 412	33.6	41.5	19.69	19.02	661.58	789.33
June	133 951	112 028	18 411	11 939	115 540	92 579	8 414	33.7	41.6	19.72	19.08	664.56	793.73
July	134 111	112 200	18 465	11 979	115 646	92 721	8 453	33.7	41.7	19.76	19.11	665.91	796.89
August	134 261	112 336	18 452	11 956	115 809	92 847	8 426	33.6	41.5	19.75	19.06	663.60	790.99
September	134 422	112 495	18 436	11 942	115 986	92 995	8 406	33.6	41.5	19.78	19.07	664.61	791.41
October	134 647	112 750	18 452	11 947	116 195	93 220	8 411	33.6	41.5	19.80	19.10	665.28	792.65
November	134 850	112 961	18 484	11 951	116 366	93 371	8 414	33.7	41.6	19.85	19.15	668.95	796.64
December	135 064	113 176	18 536	11 965	116 528	93 543	8 416	33.7	41.7	19.89	19.14	670.29	798.14
2013													
January	135 261	113 395	18 579	11 982	116 682	93 686	8 423	33.6	41.6	19.95	19.15	670.32	796.64
February	135 541	113 658	18 651	12 004	116 890	93 903	8 429	33.8	41.9	20.00	19.22	676.00	805.32
March	135 682	113 822	18 680	12 007	117 002	94 016	8 420	33.8	41.9	20.02	19.22	676.68	805.32
April	135 885	114 010	18 669	12 001	117 216	94 175	8 414	33.7	41.8	20.04	19.21	675.35	802.98
May	136 084	114 232	18 671	11 994	117 413	94 352	8 397	33.7	41.8	20.06	19.25	676.02	804.65
June	136 285	114 433	18 684	11 991	117 601	94 505	8 391	33.7	41.9	20.12	19.28	678.04	807.83
July	136 434	114 603	18 679	11 982	117 755	94 660	8 383	33.5	41.7	20.15	19.27	675.03	803.56
August	136 636	114 783	18 696	11 990	117 940	94 815	8 390	33.7	41.9	20.17	19.33	679.73	809.93
September	136 800	114 936	18 718	11 993	118 082	94 932	8 394	33.6	41.9	20.21	19.35	679.06	810.77
October	137 037	115 183	18 756	12 011	118 281	95 172	8 410	33.6	41.9	20.25	19.37	680.40	811.60
November	137 311	115 455	18 824	12 046	118 487	95 397	8 442	33.7	42.0	20.30	19.42	684.11	815.64
December	137 395	115 541	18 811	12 053	118 584	95 471	8 444	33.5	41.9	20.35	19.45	681.73	814.96
2014													
January	137 642	115 831	18 984	12 102	117 060	95 644	8 486	33.5	41.6	20.40	19.44	683.40	808.70
February	137 830	116 006	19 031	12 122	117 766	95 860	8 512	33.5	41.6	20.48	19.48	686.08	810.37
March	138 055	116 229	19 073	12 131	118 539	96 056	8 524	33.7	42.0	20.50	19.52	690.85	819.84
April	138 385	116 542	19 131	12 142	119 454	96 322	8 534	33.7	41.9	20.52	19.49	691.52	816.63
May	138 621	116 780	19 156	12 154	120 122	96 516	8 539	33.7	42.2	20.55	19.53	692.54	824.17
June	138 907	117 052	19 190	12 177	120 426	96 772	8 561	33.7	42.1	20.59	19.55	693.88	823.06
July	139 156	117 295	19 243	12 191	119 238	96 953	8 573	33.7	42.0	20.63	19.59	695.23	822.78
August	139 369	117 504	19 277	12 205	119 551	97 118	8 588	33.7	42.0	20.68	19.63	696.92	824.46
September	139 619	117 739	19 315	12 214	120 289	97 266	8 588	33.7	42.1	20.68	19.62	696.92	826.00
October	139 840	117 957	19 349	12 237	121 362	97 388	8 601	33.7	42.1	20.72	19.65	698.26	827.27
November	140 263	118 371	19 425	12 282	121 933	97 671	8 640	33.8	42.2	20.77	19.64	702.03	828.81
December	140 592	118 690	19 489	12 301	122 095	97 923	8 663	33.8	42.1	20.72	19.62	700.34	826.00

Figure 10-4: Average Weekly Hours of All Employees, 2010–2014

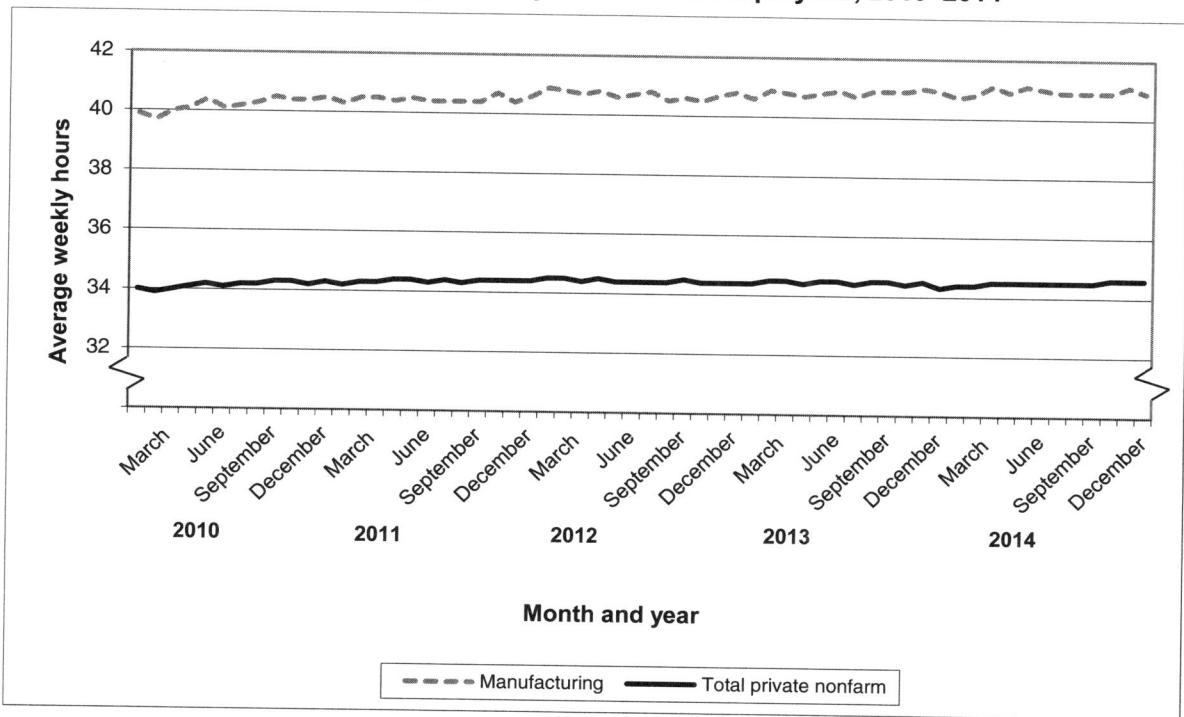

- The payroll survey now includes hours and earnings data for all nonfarm jobs, as well as the hours and earnings for production and nonsupervisory worker jobs that have been collected for many years. The newer, more comprehensive series are available beginning with March 2006. The new monthly data on the workweek for all nonfarm jobs and for manufacturing are shown in Figure 10-4. (Table 10-10)

- Firms experiencing increases in demand are likely to meet that demand, at first, by having their existing employees work longer hours. If the demand increase is sustained, they become more likely to hire more people. This is the basis for the long-time reputation of the workweek as a leading indicator for employment. As Figure 10-4 demonstrates, the all-employee workweek at manufacturing—the most cyclical sector—has been trending upward, though irregularly, since a low point of 38.5 hours in May 2009. The workweek for all private nonfarm industry reached a low point of 33.8 hours in 2009. It has increased little since then and appeared stuck at around 34.6 hours through July 2015. (Table 10-10 and recent data)

- It is important to note that the "average" all-employee workweek of about 34 1/2 hours reported in the payroll survey is not necessarily an accurate representation of how many hours per week a typical American worker works. This is because it is based on a count of jobs, as reported by employers. Suppose a full-time worker takes a second, "moonlighting" part-time job, newly created in another industry. This reduces the average workweek reported by the payroll survey, even though the individual is working longer hours than before. If a new labor force entrant takes a half-time job, it reduces the average workweek even if no other workers are working less. For measures of the workweek as reported by persons in the Current Population Survey, see Table 10-19, Figure 10-5, and the discussions of each.

Table 10-10. Average Weekly Hours of All Employees on Private Nonfarm Payrolls by NAICS Supersector

(Hours per week, seasonally adjusted.)

Year and month	Total private	Mining and logging	Construc-tion	Manufacturing		Trade, transportation, and utilities			Informa-tion	Financial activities	Profes-sional and business services	Education and health services	Leisure and hospitality	Other services
				Average weekly hours	Overtime hours	Total	Wholesale trade	Retail trade						
2007	34.6	44.0	38.0	40.0	3.3	34.5	38.1	31.7	36.1	36.6	35.4	33.5	26.1	32.9
2008	34.4	43.7	37.8	39.8	3.0	34.4	38.4	31.4	36.5	36.5	35.2	33.6	25.9	32.9
2009	33.9	42.1	37.1	39.0	2.3	34.1	37.9	31.3	36.5	36.6	35.0	32.9	25.6	31.6
2010	34.1	43.4	37.8	40.2	3.0	34.2	38.1	31.3	36.5	36.9	35.4	32.7	25.7	31.6
2011	34.4	44.5	38.3	40.5	3.2	34.6	38.6	31.6	36.6	37.3	35.7	32.7	25.9	31.7
2012	34.5	44.0	38.7	40.7	3.3	34.6	38.7	31.7	36.6	37.4	36.0	32.8	26.1	31.6
2013	34.4	43.9	39.0	40.8	3.4	34.5	38.7	31.4	36.7	37.1	36.1	32.7	26.0	31.7
2014	34.5	34.5	39.0	41.0	3.5	34.5	38.9	31.3	36.8	37.3	36.3	32.7	26.2	31.8
2010														
January	34.0	43.0	37.3	39.9	2.8	34.1	37.8	31.3	36.6	36.8	35.4	32.8	25.6	31.9
February	33.9	43.0	36.4	39.7	2.7	34.0	37.8	31.2	36.5	36.8	35.1	32.8	25.7	31.6
March	34.0	43.3	37.3	40.0	2.9	34.0	37.9	31.2	36.5	36.9	35.4	32.7	25.7	31.5
April	34.1	43.7	38.0	40.1	2.9	34.2	38.0	31.3	36.6	36.9	35.3	32.8	25.8	31.6
May	34.2	43.9	37.6	40.4	3.1	34.2	38.1	31.3	36.5	37.0	35.4	32.8	25.8	31.7
June	34.1	43.2	37.7	40.1	3.0	34.2	38.1	31.3	36.6	37.2	35.2	32.7	25.7	31.6
July	34.2	43.8	37.7	40.2	3.0	34.3	38.2	31.4	36.6	37.0	35.5	32.7	25.8	31.7
August	34.2	43.9	37.9	40.3	3.1	34.4	38.2	31.5	36.7	37.0	35.4	32.7	25.8	31.7
September	34.3	43.4	38.2	40.5	3.2	34.4	38.3	31.4	36.6	37.1	35.6	32.8	25.9	31.9
October	34.3	43.6	38.2	40.4	3.2	34.5	38.4	31.5	36.8	37.1	35.7	32.8	25.9	31.7
November	34.2	42.9	38.2	40.4	3.2	34.4	38.4	31.4	36.6	37.1	35.6	32.7	25.9	31.7
December	34.3	44.1	38.0	40.5	3.2	34.6	38.4	31.6	36.5	37.2	35.6	32.7	25.8	31.7
2011														
January	34.2	44.6	37.6	40.3	3.2	34.4	38.5	31.4	36.5	37.0	35.6	32.7	25.8	31.7
February	34.3	44.1	37.7	40.5	3.2	34.5	38.5	31.4	36.6	37.1	35.7	32.7	25.9	31.7
March	34.3	44.4	37.9	40.5	3.2	34.6	38.6	31.5	36.7	37.1	35.6	32.8	25.8	31.7
April	34.4	44.6	38.1	40.4	3.1	34.7	38.6	31.7	36.7	37.2	35.7	32.9	26.0	31.8
May	34.4	44.8	38.4	40.5	3.1	34.5	38.6	31.5	36.6	37.2	35.7	32.8	25.8	31.8
June	34.3	44.5	38.4	40.4	3.1	34.6	38.7	31.5	36.6	37.3	35.7	32.8	25.8	31.8
July	34.4	44.2	38.5	40.4	3.1	34.6	38.7	31.6	36.7	37.4	35.8	32.9	26.0	31.8
August	34.3	44.1	38.2	40.4	3.2	34.5	38.6	31.5	36.4	37.2	35.7	32.7	25.9	31.6
September	34.4	44.5	38.4	40.4	3.2	34.7	38.9	31.7	36.7	37.5	35.8	32.8	26.0	31.7
October	34.4	45.4	38.3	40.7	3.3	34.6	38.8	31.7	36.8	37.5	35.8	32.7	26.1	31.7
November	34.4	43.9	38.3	40.4	3.3	34.6	38.9	31.7	36.8	37.4	35.8	32.7	26.1	31.7
December	34.4	44.6	38.5	40.6	3.3	34.7	38.8	31.8	36.7	37.3	35.8	32.7	26.1	31.7
2012														
January	34.5	45.5	38.6	40.9	3.4	34.7	38.8	31.8	36.8	37.3	35.8	32.7	26.2	31.7
February	34.5	44.7	38.7	40.8	3.3	34.7	38.8	31.9	36.8	37.3	35.9	32.8	26.0	31.7
March	34.4	44.1	38.6	40.7	3.3	34.6	38.7	31.8	36.7	37.3	35.8	32.8	26.1	31.7
April	34.5	44.1	38.8	40.8	3.3	34.6	38.7	31.7	36.6	37.2	35.9	32.8	26.1	31.7
May	34.4	43.6	38.5	40.6	3.3	34.5	38.6	31.6	36.6	37.0	35.9	32.8	26.1	31.6
June	34.4	43.9	38.6	40.7	3.2	34.5	38.6	31.6	36.6	37.1	35.9	32.8	26.1	31.6
July	34.4	44.0	38.5	40.8	3.2	34.5	38.5	31.5	36.5	37.1	36.0	32.8	26.0	31.6
August	34.4	43.5	38.6	40.5	3.2	34.5	38.6	31.5	36.4	37.2	36.0	32.8	26.0	31.5
September	34.5	43.3	38.9	40.6	3.2	34.6	38.9	31.6	36.5	37.3	36.1	32.8	26.0	31.6
October	34.4	43.4	38.8	40.5	3.2	34.5	38.5	31.5	36.3	37.2	35.8	32.8	26.0	31.6
November	34.4	43.2	39.0	40.7	3.3	34.6	38.5	31.6	36.4	37.3	36.0	32.7	26.0	31.5
December	34.4	43.5	39.2	40.8	3.3	34.5	38.6	31.5	36.6	37.2	36.0	32.7	26.1	31.6
2013														
January	34.4	42.7	38.9	40.6	3.3	34.4	38.5	31.4	36.4	37.0	36.0	32.7	26.1	31.6
February	34.5	43.4	39.2	40.9	3.3	34.6	38.7	31.6	36.4	37.2	36.1	32.8	26.1	31.7
March	34.5	43.3	39.1	40.8	3.4	34.7	38.8	31.7	36.5	37.2	36.1	32.8	26.2	31.9
April	34.4	43.2	39.0	40.7	3.4	34.5	38.5	31.4	36.6	37.2	36.0	32.7	26.1	31.8
May	34.5	43.8	39.2	40.8	3.3	34.6	38.8	31.6	36.7	37.2	36.1	32.8	26.0	31.9
June	34.5	44.2	39.0	40.9	3.4	34.5	38.8	31.4	37.0	37.3	36.1	32.8	26.0	31.8
July	34.4	44.0	38.9	40.7	3.2	34.6	38.7	31.5	36.8	37.0	36.0	32.7	25.9	31.7
August	34.5	44.1	39.1	40.9	3.4	34.6	38.9	31.5	36.8	37.3	36.1	32.7	26.0	31.8
September	34.5	44.3	39.2	40.9	3.4	34.6	38.8	31.4	36.8	37.1	36.1	32.7	26.0	31.7
October	34.4	44.1	38.8	40.9	3.4	34.5	38.9	31.3	36.8	37.1	36.0	32.7	25.9	31.7
November	34.5	44.6	39.2	41.0	3.4	34.4	38.9	31.2	36.8	37.2	36.2	32.7	26.0	31.7
December	34.3	44.8	38.7	40.9	3.5	34.4	38.6	31.3	36.9	37.0	36.0	32.6	25.7	31.6
2014														
January	34.4	44.1	38.6	40.7	3.5	34.4	38.8	31.1	36.6	37.1	36.1	32.7	26.1	31.7
February	34.4	45.1	38.5	40.8	3.4	34.3	38.7	31.1	36.8	37.2	36.1	32.7	26.1	31.7
March	34.5	45.7	39.1	41.1	3.5	34.4	38.9	31.2	36.9	37.3	36.3	32.7	26.2	31.8
April	34.5	44.6	39.1	40.9	3.5	34.5	38.8	31.4	36.8	37.1	36.2	32.7	26.2	31.8
May	34.5	44.5	39.0	41.1	3.5	34.5	38.9	31.3	36.8	37.3	36.3	32.7	26.1	31.8
June	34.5	44.9	39.1	41.0	3.5	34.4	38.9	31.2	36.6	37.2	36.2	32.7	26.1	31.7
July	34.5	44.5	39.2	40.9	3.5	34.5	38.9	31.3	36.7	37.2	36.2	32.7	26.2	31.7
August	34.5	44.9	39.2	40.9	3.4	34.5	38.9	31.3	36.6	37.2	36.2	32.8	26.2	31.8
September	34.5	44.5	39.0	40.9	3.5	34.5	38.9	31.3	36.7	37.3	36.2	32.8	26.2	31.8
October	34.6	45.0	39.1	40.9	3.4	34.6	38.9	31.4	36.7	37.4	36.3	32.8	26.2	31.8
November	34.6	44.9	39.0	41.1	3.5	34.6	38.9	31.4	36.7	37.3	36.3	32.8	26.2	31.8
December	34.6	44.9	39.2	40.9	3.6	34.6	38.9	31.4	36.3	37.4	36.3	32.7	26.3	31.8

Table 10-11. Indexes of Aggregate Weekly Hours of All Employees on Private Nonfarm Payrolls by NAICS Supersector

(2007 =100, seasonally adjusted.)

Year and month	Total private	Mining and logging	Construc-tion	Manu-facturing	Trade, transportation, and utilities			Information	Financial activities	Profes-sional and business services	Education and health services	Leisure and hospitality	Other services
					Total	Wholesale trade	Retail trade						
2007	100.0	100.0	100.0	100.0	100.0	100.0	100.0	100.0	100.0	100.0	100.0	100.0	100.0
2008	98.7	105.2	93.3	96.0	98.5	99.6	97.6	99.6	98.2	98.2	103.4	99.1	100.4
2009	92.1	91.9	77.0	83.1	92.5	92.4	92.2	93.5	94.0	91.4	103.3	95.4	94.1
2010	91.9	96.1	71.9	83.4	91.7	90.6	91.9	90.3	93.0	93.1	104.4	95.9	93.4
2011	94.3	110.2	73.1	85.4	94.2	93.4	94.1	89.4	93.9	97.4	106.3	98.7	94.2
2012	96.7	117.1	75.4	87.4	95.9	95.8	95.4	89.6	95.2	101.6	109.0	102.6	95.2
2013	98.6	119.8	78.3	88.2	97.1	97.1	96.2	89.9	95.8	105.3	110.8	105.7	96.1
2014	101.2	126.3	82.5	89.8	99.1	98.9	97.8	92.0	97.4	108.9	112.8	109.9	98.2
2010													
January	91.1	90.1	71.8	82.3	91.0	89.9	91.4	91.7	93.2	91.9	103.9	94.5	94.1
February	90.8	91.1	69.1	81.8	90.7	89.8	91.2	91.1	93.1	91.4	104.0	94.8	93.1
March	91.2	92.8	71.2	82.5	90.9	90.0	91.4	90.6	93.1	92.1	104.0	94.9	93.0
April	91.6	94.3	72.8	82.9	91.4	90.2	91.6	90.8	93.2	92.3	104.4	95.6	93.4
May	92.0	96.0	71.6	83.8	91.5	90.4	91.8	90.3	93.3	92.7	104.5	95.8	93.6
June	91.8	95.2	71.6	83.3	91.6	90.5	91.8	90.2	93.7	92.5	104.3	95.6	93.0
July	92.2	97.4	71.5	83.7	92.0	90.8	92.2	90.2	93.1	93.3	104.4	96.1	93.5
August	92.3	98.9	72.2	83.7	92.2	90.8	92.5	90.6	93.0	93.3	104.6	96.3	93.5
September	92.6	98.6	72.5	84.2	92.4	91.1	92.3	90.2	93.3	94.0	104.9	97.0	94.3
October	92.8	100.2	72.5	84.0	92.8	91.5	92.8	90.6	93.4	94.6	105.2	97.0	94.1
November	92.7	99.3	72.5	84.2	92.5	91.6	92.4	89.9	93.3	94.9	105.1	97.0	93.9
December	93.0	101.7	71.5	84.5	93.2	91.7	93.0	89.5	93.6	95.4	105.2	96.9	93.7
2011													
January	92.8	103.1	70.4	84.2	92.8	92.0	92.7	89.5	93.1	95.5	105.3	96.8	93.6
February	93.3	102.3	71.0	84.9	93.3	92.3	92.8	89.3	93.3	96.0	105.4	97.5	93.7
March	93.5	105.2	71.5	85.1	93.7	92.9	93.2	89.5	93.3	96.2	105.7	97.5	93.6
April	94.0	107.5	72.2	85.1	94.3	93.0	94.2	89.7	93.5	96.8	106.4	98.6	94.1
May	94.2	109.4	73.1	85.3	93.9	93.2	93.7	89.5	93.8	97.1	106.1	97.8	94.2
June	94.0	110.3	73.1	85.2	94.4	93.6	93.9	89.7	93.9	97.1	106.4	98.2	94.3
July	94.5	111.1	73.7	85.4	94.6	93.7	94.4	89.7	94.2	97.5	106.9	99.2	94.4
August	94.3	111.7	73.1	85.5	94.3	93.6	94.1	87.5	93.8	97.6	106.4	99.0	94.1
September	94.8	114.0	74.0	85.5	95.0	94.3	94.9	89.8	94.6	98.2	107.0	99.5	94.5
October	95.0	117.0	73.7	86.2	94.8	94.4	94.9	90.1	94.7	98.5	106.9	100.3	94.5
November	95.2	113.8	73.7	85.6	95.0	94.8	95.0	89.9	94.6	98.8	107.1	100.6	94.7
December	95.4	116.6	74.4	86.2	95.3	94.9	95.4	89.9	94.5	99.2	107.1	100.8	94.9
2012													
January	95.9	120.1	74.9	87.1	95.7	95.1	95.7	89.8	94.5	99.6	107.5	101.6	95.1
February	96.1	118.8	75.0	87.0	95.7	95.3	95.9	89.8	94.6	100.2	108.2	101.2	95.1
March	96.1	117.7	74.9	87.1	95.6	95.3	95.7	89.7	94.9	100.2	108.4	102.0	95.2
April	96.4	117.8	75.3	87.5	95.6	95.5	95.5	89.5	94.6	100.7	108.5	102.0	95.2
May	96.3	116.9	74.5	87.1	95.5	95.4	95.2	89.6	94.3	100.9	108.7	102.1	94.9
June	96.3	117.5	74.8	87.4	95.5	95.5	95.1	89.4	94.5	101.1	108.8	102.1	95.0
July	96.5	117.7	74.8	87.9	95.5	95.4	94.7	89.3	94.5	101.7	108.9	101.9	95.1
August	96.6	116.1	75.1	87.1	95.6	95.7	94.7	89.1	94.9	101.9	109.0	102.4	94.8
September	97.0	115.1	75.7	87.2	95.9	96.3	95.2	89.1	95.3	102.3	109.3	102.9	95.3
October	97.0	114.4	75.8	87.0	95.8	95.6	95.1	88.6	95.2	101.8	109.8	103.0	95.3
November	97.1	114.8	76.5	87.5	96.4	95.6	95.7	89.1	95.5	102.7	109.5	103.3	95.1
December	97.3	116.3	77.3	87.8	96.2	96.0	95.4	89.4	95.4	102.9	109.7	104.1	95.4
2013													
January	97.5	114.6	77.0	87.5	96.1	96.0	95.3	88.9	94.9	103.1	109.8	104.5	95.6
February	98.0	117.0	78.2	88.3	96.7	96.5	96.0	89.5	95.6	103.9	110.3	104.8	95.8
March	98.2	117.0	78.3	88.1	96.9	96.8	96.2	89.8	95.7	104.3	110.5	105.5	96.3
April	98.0	116.3	78.1	87.9	96.5	96.2	95.5	89.8	95.8	104.4	110.4	105.3	96.1
May	98.5	118.5	78.6	88.0	96.9	97.0	96.3	90.0	95.9	105.1	110.9	105.3	96.6
June	98.7	120.0	78.4	88.2	96.8	97.1	95.9	90.7	96.3	105.4	111.0	105.7	96.3
July	98.6	119.9	78.2	87.7	97.3	97.1	96.5	90.6	95.7	105.4	110.8	105.5	96.0
August	99.0	120.6	78.7	88.2	97.5	97.8	96.7	89.7	96.5	106.0	111.1	106.1	96.4
September	99.1	121.9	79.0	88.2	97.7	97.7	96.6	90.1	95.9	106.2	111.2	106.2	96.1
October	99.1	122.1	78.4	88.4	97.6	97.9	96.6	90.3	96.0	106.2	111.3	106.3	96.1
November	99.6	123.6	79.7	88.9	97.6	98.2	96.4	90.4	96.2	107.2	111.5	107.0	96.1
December	99.1	124.2	78.4	88.7	97.9	97.6	97.0	90.1	95.7	106.7	111.1	105.9	95.9
2014													
January	99.6	121.4	79.9	88.6	97.9	97.8	96.4	91.1	96.2	106.6	111.5	107.9	97.2
February	99.8	124.3	80.1	89.0	97.5	97.7	96.3	91.4	96.6	107.0	111.7	108.2	97.3
March	100.2	126.4	81.7	89.7	98.0	98.3	96.7	91.8	96.9	107.8	111.9	108.9	97.8
April	100.5	124.2	82.3	89.3	98.5	98.3	97.6	91.7	96.5	107.9	112.1	108.9	97.8
May	100.7	124.2	82.2	89.9	98.7	98.7	97.4	91.5	97.1	108.5	112.4	109.2	98.1
June	101.0	125.9	82.5	89.8	98.6	98.9	97.3	91.4	97.1	108.6	112.6	109.2	98.2
July	101.2	125.8	83.1	89.7	99.1	99.0	97.8	91.8	97.3	108.9	112.8	109.5	97.8
August	101.3	127.4	83.4	89.8	99.2	99.1	97.8	92.0	97.4	109.2	113.4	110.0	97.9
September	101.5	127.2	83.2	89.9	99.3	99.2	98.0	92.4	97.8	109.5	113.6	110.2	98.4
October	102.0	128.8	83.6	90.0	99.3	99.3	98.5	92.3	98.2	110.0	113.8	110.6	98.4
November	102.4	128.7	83.8	90.8	100.2	99.5	98.8	92.5	98.2	110.6	114.0	111.0	98.5
December	102.7	128.8	84.8	90.5	100.4	99.7	98.8	91.7	98.6	111.0	114.0	111.3	98.8

Table 10-12. Average Hourly Earnings of All Employees on Private Nonfarm Payrolls by NAICS Supersector

(Dollars, seasonally adjusted.)

Year and month	Total private	Mining and logging	Construction	Manufacturing	Trade, transportation, and utilities			Information	Financial activities	Professional and business services	Education and health services	Leisure and hospitality	Other services
					Total	Wholesale trade	Retail trade						
2007	20.95	24.91	23.02	21.50	18.58	23.96	15.13	28.09	25.64	24.68	21.23	12.39	17.62
2008	21.60	26.20	23.96	22.16	18.93	24.37	15.21	28.66	26.18	25.82	21.99	12.77	18.17
2009	22.19	27.29	24.83	23.04	19.32	25.41	15.39	29.40	26.53	27.03	22.27	12.97	19.54
2010	22.57	27.39	25.19	23.31	19.65	26.13	15.56	30.53	27.21	27.24	22.81	13.08	20.16
2011	23.04	28.10	25.41	23.69	20.04	26.38	15.86	31.59	27.91	27.76	23.47	13.23	20.50
2012	23.50	28.76	25.73	23.92	20.50	26.89	16.30	31.83	29.26	28.13	24.05	13.37	20.85
2013	23.96	29.73	26.12	24.35	20.97	27.64	16.62	32.90	30.15	28.52	24.44	13.50	21.40
2014	24.47	30.78	26.69	24.81	21.39	28.09	17.00	34.01	30.76	29.28	24.74	13.91	21.98
2010													
January	22.42	27.02	25.11	23.17	19.59	26.18	15.50	29.84	26.98	27.14	22.44	13.13	20.06
February	22.45	27.08	25.22	23.22	19.58	26.16	15.48	30.16	27.00	27.22	22.49	13.11	20.09
March	22.47	27.08	25.18	23.18	19.62	26.15	15.55	30.18	27.07	27.16	22.57	13.09	20.10
April	22.50	27.16	25.10	23.22	19.64	26.11	15.62	30.12	27.18	27.17	22.71	13.07	20.09
May	22.54	27.39	25.16	23.32	19.61	26.12	15.50	30.32	27.21	27.23	22.76	13.09	20.10
June	22.54	27.40	25.13	23.23	19.61	26.10	15.53	30.42	27.18	27.26	22.77	13.07	20.17
July	22.60	27.58	25.18	23.36	19.65	26.11	15.57	30.52	27.36	27.29	22.85	13.09	20.10
August	22.64	27.61	25.18	23.44	19.64	26.03	15.56	30.72	27.33	27.38	22.94	13.10	20.12
September	22.68	27.78	25.20	23.44	19.71	26.21	15.58	30.99	27.36	27.40	22.96	13.09	20.16
October	22.74	27.60	25.31	23.47	19.78	26.27	15.66	31.16	27.42	27.44	23.03	13.09	20.26
November	22.74	27.73	25.32	23.41	19.78	26.19	15.67	31.29	27.41	27.40	23.07	13.09	20.38
December	22.77	27.64	25.35	23.50	19.80	26.24	15.67	31.09	27.55	27.32	23.17	13.11	20.35
2011													
January	22.86	27.94	25.47	23.63	19.86	26.29	15.72	31.45	27.54	27.49	23.19	13.18	20.38
February	22.86	28.01	25.41	23.50	19.89	26.27	15.74	31.54	27.61	27.54	23.20	13.18	20.38
March	22.88	28.08	25.34	23.55	19.89	26.19	15.74	31.80	27.68	27.52	23.27	13.18	20.32
April	22.93	28.26	25.38	23.61	19.95	26.27	15.80	31.69	27.68	27.61	23.34	13.22	20.37
May	23.00	28.20	25.36	23.71	19.99	26.29	15.83	31.60	27.72	27.65	23.47	13.26	20.43
June	23.02	27.89	25.36	23.69	20.03	26.38	15.82	31.51	27.81	27.75	23.44	13.23	20.48
July	23.11	27.82	25.36	23.76	20.12	26.44	15.99	31.53	27.86	27.96	23.59	13.21	20.53
August	23.08	28.03	25.47	23.70	20.07	26.45	15.84	31.67	27.94	27.85	23.54	13.21	20.56
September	23.12	28.07	25.50	23.75	20.05	26.40	15.80	31.42	28.10	27.88	23.62	13.27	20.55
October	23.22	28.16	25.49	23.89	20.18	26.55	15.95	31.75	28.29	27.96	23.69	13.29	20.57
November	23.20	28.28	25.45	23.74	20.22	26.52	16.05	31.67	28.34	27.96	23.67	13.31	20.61
December	23.22	28.44	25.49	23.85	20.22	26.52	16.03	31.72	28.35	27.90	23.71	13.33	20.65
2012													
January	23.25	28.04	25.50	23.87	20.20	26.50	16.02	31.61	28.59	27.84	23.88	13.33	20.60
February	23.30	28.55	25.54	23.84	20.23	26.53	16.07	31.63	28.73	27.91	23.95	13.33	20.62
March	23.37	28.69	25.67	23.88	20.30	26.66	16.10	31.63	28.92	28.00	24.02	13.35	20.69
April	23.40	28.79	25.66	23.92	20.35	26.69	16.14	31.74	29.07	27.97	23.98	13.36	20.73
May	23.41	28.57	25.71	23.83	20.41	26.74	16.21	31.79	29.14	28.04	23.95	13.34	20.75
June	23.47	28.83	25.72	23.92	20.50	26.79	16.34	31.81	29.10	28.07	24.04	13.39	20.78
July	23.52	28.90	25.74	23.95	20.54	26.85	16.35	31.90	29.18	28.14	24.06	13.40	20.85
August	23.51	28.70	25.75	23.90	20.54	26.91	16.34	31.59	29.29	28.08	24.08	13.38	20.92
September	23.58	28.90	25.86	23.95	20.60	26.96	16.42	31.77	29.43	28.20	24.14	13.39	20.97
October	23.56	28.56	25.83	23.92	20.60	27.05	16.43	31.76	29.52	28.16	24.10	13.37	20.98
November	23.64	28.80	25.89	23.99	20.65	27.20	16.38	31.92	29.66	28.25	24.21	13.38	20.99
December	23.71	29.17	25.93	24.05	20.72	27.36	16.47	32.26	29.77	28.34	24.25	13.38	21.08
2013													
January	23.75	29.03	25.97	24.03	20.79	27.31	16.54	32.43	29.92	28.41	24.26	13.38	21.14
February	23.79	28.81	26.00	24.13	20.77	27.30	16.54	32.47	29.97	28.40	24.39	13.39	21.19
March	23.81	29.09	25.99	24.15	20.86	27.51	16.59	32.62	29.92	28.46	24.31	13.43	21.19
April	23.86	29.12	26.04	24.18	20.92	27.60	16.61	32.82	30.00	28.48	24.35	13.43	21.24
May	23.89	29.50	26.05	24.26	20.92	27.59	16.59	32.67	30.01	28.48	24.37	13.45	21.30
June	23.98	29.87	26.13	24.39	20.99	27.73	16.63	32.94	30.19	28.52	24.46	13.47	21.38
July	23.97	29.48	26.17	24.36	20.99	27.71	16.63	32.78	30.28	28.50	24.44	13.50	21.40
August	24.03	29.88	26.18	24.42	21.05	27.71	16.70	32.83	30.31	28.57	24.53	13.53	21.45
September	24.06	30.02	26.17	24.49	21.08	27.83	16.67	33.13	30.30	28.58	24.53	13.55	21.54
October	24.09	30.26	26.19	24.50	21.12	27.82	16.71	33.19	30.31	28.60	24.54	13.57	21.61
November	24.15	30.50	26.23	24.58	21.17	27.96	16.71	33.43	30.32	28.73	24.57	13.59	21.65
December	24.17	30.59	26.35	24.60	21.11	27.87	16.66	33.43	30.37	28.78	24.55	13.65	21.72
2014													
January	24.22	30.56	26.38	24.64	21.21	27.94	16.78	33.43	30.40	28.95	24.57	13.68	21.79
February	24.30	30.74	26.55	24.70	21.27	27.93	16.85	33.42	30.48	29.04	24.57	13.79	21.77
March	24.34	30.74	26.49	24.73	21.32	28.00	16.89	33.70	30.62	29.09	24.61	13.74	21.77
April	24.34	30.65	26.57	24.68	21.35	28.07	16.94	33.88	30.56	29.11	24.60	13.77	21.84
May	24.40	30.85	26.61	24.72	21.39	28.07	16.98	33.87	30.59	29.21	24.66	13.82	21.87
June	24.46	30.97	26.70	24.82	21.39	28.03	17.01	34.00	30.76	29.26	24.68	13.90	21.95
July	24.47	30.80	26.69	24.83	21.38	28.00	17.03	34.10	30.75	29.30	24.70	13.93	21.99
August	24.55	30.90	26.73	24.90	21.47	28.21	17.08	34.16	30.85	29.39	24.78	13.99	22.05
September	24.55	30.90	26.81	24.85	21.44	28.08	17.08	34.33	30.91	29.39	24.77	14.03	22.08
October	24.59	30.92	26.85	24.93	21.46	28.10	17.12	34.15	30.91	29.42	24.83	14.11	22.11
November	24.68	30.81	26.91	24.96	21.53	28.24	17.18	34.38	31.09	29.53	24.99	14.11	22.18
December	24.62	30.70	26.81	24.87	21.49	28.19	17.12	34.35	31.05	29.48	24.90	14.10	22.17

Table 10-13. Average Weekly Earnings of All Employees on Private Nonfarm Payrolls by NAICS Supersector

(Dollars, seasonally adjusted.)

Year and month	Total private	Mining and logging	Construction	Manu-facturing	Trade, transportation, and utilities			Information	Financial activities	Profes-sional and business services	Education and health services	Leisure and hospitality	Other services
					Total	Wholesale trade	Retail trade						
2007	724.33	1 094.81	875.06	861.19	641.51	913.03	479.81	1 014.35	937.69	874.68	710.62	323.54	578.84
2008	743.93	1 144.63	905.68	882.19	651.96	936.17	478.00	1 047.50	956.67	909.23	739.33	330.32	597.13
2009	752.13	1 150.12	922.54	898.44	659.78	963.44	481.18	1 073.27	971.73	947.10	733.12	331.64	618.18
2010	769.97	1 189.32	952.78	937.34	672.58	994.71	487.66	1 114.65	1 004.14	963.57	745.88	336.83	637.65
2011	791.55	1 250.91	973.85	958.84	692.51	1 019.05	500.75	1 156.56	1 039.70	991.87	768.79	342.67	649.87
2012	810.46	1 263.98	997.01	974.15	709.33	1 041.41	515.81	1 166.45	1 093.00	1 013.76	789.16	349.12	659.49
2013	825.05	1 306.59	1 018.26	994.42	723.49	1 070.34	522.12	1 206.64	1 119.77	1 029.13	799.66	350.89	679.08
2014	845.06	1 380.80	1 040.75	1 016.42	738.34	1 092.30	532.49	1 250.30	1 146.48	1 061.92	809.58	364.19	698.71
2010													
January	762.28	1 161.86	936.60	924.48	668.02	989.60	485.15	1 092.14	992.86	960.76	736.03	336.13	639.91
February	761.06	1 164.44	918.01	921.83	665.72	988.85	482.98	1 100.84	993.60	955.42	737.67	336.93	634.84
March	763.98	1 172.56	939.21	927.20	667.08	991.09	485.16	1 101.57	998.88	961.46	738.04	336.41	633.15
April	767.25	1 186.89	953.80	931.12	671.69	992.18	488.91	1 102.39	1 002.94	959.10	744.89	337.21	634.84
May	770.87	1 202.42	946.02	942.13	670.66	995.17	485.15	1 106.68	1 006.77	963.94	746.53	337.72	637.17
June	768.61	1 183.68	947.40	931.52	670.66	994.41	486.09	1 113.37	1 011.10	959.55	744.58	335.90	637.37
July	772.92	1 208.00	949.29	939.07	674.00	997.40	488.90	1 117.03	1 012.32	968.80	747.20	337.72	637.17
August	774.29	1 212.08	954.32	944.63	675.62	994.35	490.14	1 127.42	1 011.21	969.25	750.14	337.98	637.80
September	777.92	1 205.65	962.64	949.32	678.02	1 003.84	489.21	1 134.23	1 015.06	975.44	753.09	339.03	643.10
October	779.98	1 203.36	966.84	948.19	682.41	1 008.77	493.29	1 146.69	1 017.28	979.61	755.38	339.03	642.24
November	777.71	1 189.62	967.22	945.76	680.43	1 005.70	492.04	1 145.21	1 016.91	975.44	754.39	339.03	646.05
December	781.01	1 218.92	963.30	951.75	685.08	1 007.62	495.17	1 134.79	1 024.86	972.59	757.66	338.24	645.10
2011													
January	781.81	1 246.12	957.67	952.29	683.18	1 012.17	493.61	1 147.93	1 018.98	978.64	758.31	340.04	646.05
February	784.10	1 235.24	957.96	951.75	686.21	1 011.40	494.24	1 154.36	1 024.33	983.18	758.64	341.36	646.05
March	784.78	1 246.75	960.39	953.78	688.19	1 010.93	495.81	1 167.06	1 026.93	979.71	763.26	340.04	644.14
April	788.79	1 260.40	966.98	953.84	692.27	1 014.02	500.86	1 163.02	1 029.70	985.68	767.89	343.72	647.77
May	791.20	1 263.36	973.82	960.26	689.66	1 014.79	498.65	1 156.56	1 031.18	987.11	769.82	342.11	649.67
June	789.59	1 241.11	973.82	957.08	693.04	1 020.91	498.33	1 153.27	1 037.31	990.68	768.83	341.33	651.26
July	794.98	1 229.64	976.36	959.90	696.15	1 023.23	505.28	1 157.15	1 041.96	1 000.97	776.11	343.46	652.85
August	791.64	1 236.12	972.95	957.48	692.42	1 020.97	498.96	1 152.79	1 039.37	994.25	769.76	342.14	649.70
September	795.33	1 249.12	979.20	959.50	695.74	1 026.96	500.86	1 153.11	1 053.75	998.10	774.74	345.02	651.44
October	798.77	1 278.46	976.27	972.32	698.23	1 030.14	505.62	1 168.40	1 060.88	1 000.97	774.66	346.87	652.07
November	798.08	1 241.49	974.74	959.10	699.61	1 031.63	508.79	1 165.46	1 059.92	1 000.97	774.01	347.39	653.34
December	798.77	1 268.42	981.37	968.31	701.63	1 028.98	509.75	1 164.12	1 057.46	998.82	775.32	347.91	654.61
2012													
January	802.13	1 275.82	984.30	976.28	700.94	1 028.20	509.44	1 163.25	1 066.41	996.67	780.88	349.25	653.02
February	803.85	1 276.19	988.40	972.67	701.98	1 029.36	512.63	1 163.98	1 071.63	1 001.97	785.56	346.58	653.65
March	803.93	1 265.23	990.86	971.92	702.38	1 031.74	511.98	1 160.82	1 078.72	1 002.40	787.86	348.44	655.87
April	807.30	1 269.64	995.61	975.94	704.11	1 032.90	511.64	1 161.68	1 081.40	1 004.12	786.54	348.70	657.14
May	805.30	1 245.65	989.84	967.50	704.15	1 032.16	512.24	1 163.51	1 078.18	1 006.64	785.56	348.17	655.70
June	807.37	1 265.64	992.79	973.54	707.25	1 034.09	516.34	1 164.25	1 079.61	1 007.71	788.51	349.48	656.65
July	809.09	1 271.60	990.99	977.16	708.63	1 033.73	515.03	1 164.35	1 082.58	1 013.04	789.17	348.40	658.86
August	808.74	1 248.45	993.95	967.95	708.63	1 038.73	514.71	1 149.88	1 089.59	1 010.88	789.82	347.88	658.98
September	813.51	1 251.37	1 005.95	972.37	712.76	1 048.74	518.87	1 159.61	1 097.74	1 018.02	791.79	348.14	662.65
October	810.46	1 239.50	1 002.20	968.76	710.70	1 041.43	517.55	1 152.89	1 098.14	1 008.13	790.48	347.62	662.97
November	813.22	1 244.16	1 009.71	976.39	714.49	1 047.20	517.61	1 161.89	1 106.32	1 017.00	791.67	347.88	661.19
December	815.62	1 268.90	1 016.46	981.24	714.84	1 056.10	518.81	1 180.72	1 107.44	1 020.24	792.98	349.22	666.13
2013													
January	817.00	1 239.58	1 010.23	975.62	715.18	1 051.44	519.36	1 180.45	1 107.04	1 022.76	793.30	349.22	668.02
February	820.76	1 250.35	1 019.20	986.92	718.64	1 056.51	522.66	1 181.91	1 114.88	1 025.24	799.99	349.48	671.72
March	821.45	1 259.60	1 016.21	985.32	723.84	1 067.39	525.90	1 190.63	1 113.02	1 027.41	797.37	351.87	675.96
April	820.78	1 257.98	1 015.56	984.13	721.74	1 062.60	521.55	1 201.21	1 116.00	1 025.28	796.25	350.52	675.43
May	824.21	1 292.10	1 021.16	989.81	723.83	1 070.49	524.24	1 198.99	1 116.37	1 028.13	799.34	349.70	679.47
June	827.31	1 320.25	1 019.07	997.55	724.16	1 075.92	522.18	1 218.78	1 126.09	1 029.57	802.29	350.22	679.88
July	824.57	1 297.12	1 018.01	991.45	726.25	1 072.38	523.85	1 206.30	1 120.36	1 026.00	799.19	349.65	678.38
August	829.04	1 317.71	1 023.64	998.78	728.33	1 077.92	526.05	1 208.14	1 130.56	1 031.38	802.13	351.78	682.11
September	830.07	1 329.89	1 025.86	1 001.64	729.37	1 079.80	523.44	1 219.18	1 124.13	1 031.74	802.13	352.30	682.82
October	828.70	1 334.47	1 016.17	1 002.05	728.64	1 082.60	523.02	1 221.39	1 124.50	1 029.60	802.46	351.46	685.04
November	833.18	1 360.30	1 028.22	1 007.78	728.25	1 087.64	521.35	1 230.22	1 127.90	1 040.03	803.44	353.34	686.31
December	829.03	1 370.43	1 019.75	1 006.14	726.18	1 075.78	521.46	1 233.57	1 123.69	1 036.08	800.33	350.81	686.35
2014													
January	833.17	1 347.70	1 018.27	1 002.85	729.62	1 084.07	521.86	1 223.54	1 127.84	1 045.10	803.44	357.05	690.74
February	835.92	1 386.37	1 022.18	1 007.76	729.56	1 080.89	524.04	1 229.86	1 133.86	1 048.34	803.44	359.92	690.11
March	839.73	1 404.82	1 035.76	1 016.40	733.41	1 089.20	526.97	1 243.53	1 142.13	1 055.97	804.75	359.99	692.29
April	839.73	1 366.99	1 038.89	1 009.41	736.58	1 089.12	531.92	1 246.78	1 133.78	1 053.78	804.42	360.77	694.51
May	841.80	1 372.83	1 037.79	1 015.99	737.96	1 091.92	531.47	1 246.42	1 141.01	1 060.32	806.38	360.70	695.47
June	843.87	1 390.55	1 043.97	1 017.62	735.82	1 090.37	530.71	1 244.40	1 144.27	1 059.21	807.04	362.79	695.82
July	844.22	1 370.60	1 046.25	1 015.55	737.61	1 089.20	533.04	1 251.47	1 143.90	1 060.66	807.69	364.97	697.08
August	846.98	1 387.41	1 047.82	1 018.41	740.72	1 097.37	534.60	1 250.26	1 147.62	1 063.92	812.78	366.54	701.19
September	846.98	1 375.05	1 045.59	1 016.37	739.68	1 092.31	534.60	1 259.91	1 152.94	1 063.92	812.46	367.59	702.14
October	850.81	1 391.40	1 049.84	1 019.64	742.52	1 093.09	537.57	1 253.31	1 156.03	1 067.95	814.42	367.59	702.14
November	853.93	1 383.37	1 049.49	1 025.86	744.94	1 098.54	539.45	1 261.75	1 159.66	1 071.94	819.67	369.68	703.10
December	851.85	1 378.43	1 050.95	1 017.18	743.55	1 096.59	537.57	1 246.91	1 161.27	1 070.12	814.23	370.83	705.01

Table 10-14. Production and Nonsupervisory Workers on Private Nonfarm Payrolls by NAICS Supersector

(Thousands, seasonally adjusted.)

Year and month	Total private	Mining and logging	Construction	Manufacturing	Trade, transportation, and utilities			Information	Financial activities	Professional and business services	Education and health services	Leisure and hospitality	Other services
					Total	Wholesale trade	Retail trade						
1965	42 302	523	2 906	12 905	10 702	. . .	. . .	1 268	2 434	3 515	3 443	3 443	1 161
1966	44 292	517	2 977	13 703	11 095	. . .	. . .	1 334	2 492	3 715	3 623	3 607	1 230
1967	45 185	501	2 903	13 714	11 369	. . .	. . .	1 365	2 585	3 890	3 818	3 734	1 306
1968	46 519	491	2 986	13 908	11 688	. . .	. . .	1 394	2 700	4 067	4 008	3 898	1 379
1969	48 246	501	3 177	14 147	12 152	. . .	. . .	1 438	2 841	4 252	4 196	4 089	1 452
1970	48 180	496	3 158	13 490	12 388	. . .	. . .	1 422	2 922	4 321	4 305	4 185	1 494
1971	48 151	474	3 238	13 034	12 502	. . .	. . .	1 392	2 978	4 354	4 372	4 286	1 521
1972	49 971	494	3 425	13 497	12 954	2 920	7 257	1 437	3 066	4 518	4 531	4 467	1 583
1973	52 235	502	3 576	14 227	13 437	3 041	7 551	1 504	3 164	4 748	4 747	4 664	1 666
1974	52 846	550	3 469	14 040	13 700	3 148	7 673	1 516	3 217	4 907	4 941	4 766	1 740
1975	51 010	581	2 990	12 576	13 578	3 121	7 714	1 416	3 227	4 939	5 088	4 821	1 795
1976	52 916	606	2 999	13 127	14 038	3 212	8 048	1 459	3 300	5 153	5 309	5 046	1 880
1977	55 207	636	3 209	13 591	14 579	3 323	8 396	1 514	3 452	5 404	5 561	5 284	1 978
1978	58 188	658	3 544	14 150	15 329	3 509	8 861	1 586	3 645	5 717	5 874	5 588	2 099
1979	60 404	737	3 760	14 458	15 843	3 667	9 113	1 650	3 825	5 993	6 158	5 772	2 209
1980	60 377	785	3 623	13 667	15 907	3 708	9 158	1 626	3 957	6 197	6 447	5 850	2 318
1981	60 967	861	3 469	13 492	16 004	3 753	9 238	1 633	4 052	6 396	6 700	5 944	2 414
1982	59 475	834	3 208	12 315	15 821	3 662	9 254	1 564	4 055	6 421	6 822	5 976	2 458
1983	60 018	698	3 240	12 121	15 999	3 639	9 494	1 502	4 128	6 581	7 045	6 161	2 542
1984	63 333	714	3 614	12 821	16 797	3 821	9 964	1 631	4 289	6 918	7 385	6 491	2 672
1985	65 456	686	3 868	12 648	17 427	3 935	10 399	1 660	4 476	7 258	7 789	6 817	2 827
1986	66 825	577	3 984	12 449	17 769	3 941	10 704	1 663	4 698	7 532	8 130	7 066	2 957
1987	68 725	541	4 088	12 537	18 196	3 989	10 986	1 717	4 861	7 859	8 513	7 310	3 104
1988	71 059	545	4 199	12 765	18 771	4 132	11 306	1 775	4 894	8 256	8 985	7 587	3 280
1989	72 960	526	4 257	12 805	19 230	4 235	11 565	1 807	4 931	8 648	9 465	7 833	3 459
1990	73 721	538	4 115	12 669	19 032	4 198	11 308	1 866	4 973	8 889	9 784	8 299	3 555
1991	72 567	515	3 674	12 164	18 640	4 122	11 008	1 871	4 914	8 748	10 257	8 247	3 539
1992	72 854	478	3 546	12 020	18 506	4 071	10 931	1 871	4 924	8 971	10 607	8 406	3 526
1993	74 671	462	3 704	12 070	18 752	4 072	11 104	1 896	5 084	9 451	10 961	8 667	3 623
1994	77 478	461	3 973	12 361	19 392	4 196	11 502	1 928	5 220	10 078	11 397	8 979	3 689
1995	79 943	458	4 113	12 567	19 984	4 361	11 841	2 007	5 199	10 645	11 829	9 330	3 812
1996	81 888	461	4 325	12 532	20 325	4 423	12 057	2 096	5 322	11 161	12 195	9 565	3 907
1997	84 313	479	4 546	12 673	20 698	4 523	12 274	2 181	5 482	11 896	12 566	9 780	4 013
1998	86 516	473	4 807	12 729	21 059	4 605	12 440	2 217	5 692	12 566	12 903	9 947	4 124
1999	88 647	438	5 105	12 524	21 576	4 673	12 772	2 351	5 818	13 184	13 217	10 216	4 219
2000	90 543	446	5 295	12 428	21 965	4 686	13 040	2 502	5 819	13 790	13 487	10 516	4 296
2001	90 202	457	5 332	11 677	21 709	4 555	12 952	2 531	5 888	13 588	13 986	10 662	4 373
2002	88 645	436	5 196	10 768	21 337	4 474	12 774	2 398	5 964	13 049	14 471	10 576	4 449
2003	87 938	420	5 123	10 189	21 078	4 396	12 655	2 347	6 052	12 911	14 726	10 666	4 426
2004	89 212	440	5 309	10 072	21 319	4 444	12 788	2 371	6 052	13 287	14 984	10 955	4 425
2005	91 401	473	5 611	10 060	21 830	4 584	13 030	2 386	6 127	13 854	15 359	11 263	4 438
2006	93 727	519	5 903	10 137	22 166	4 724	13 110	2 399	6 312	14 446	15 783	11 568	4 494
2007	95 203	547	5 883	9 975	22 546	4 851	13 317	2 403	6 365	14 784	16 261	11 861	4 578
2008	94 610	574	5 521	9 629	22 337	4 822	13 134	2 388	6 320	14 585	16 777	11 873	4 606
2009	89 556	510	4 567	8 322	21 116	4 506	12 472	2 240	6 066	13 520	17 166	11 560	4 488
2010	88 875	525	4 172	8 077	20 874	4 378	12 425	2 170	5 942	13 699	17 452	11 507	4 458
2011	90 537	594	4 184	8 228	21 234	4 443	12 647	2 148	5 900	14 251	17 736	11 772	4 491
2012	92 715	641	4 246	8 400	21 617	4 562	12 793	2 164	5 986	14 802	18 165	12 154	4 558
2013	94 580	639	4 401	8 412	21 882	4 632	12 921	2 178	6 064	15 351	18 519	12 579	4 642
2014	96 794	658	4 631	8 568	22 281	4 707	13 113	2 221	6 157	15 795	18 859	12 981	4 642
2013													
January	93 686	631	4 337	8 423	21 755	4 603	12 832	2 164	6 028	15 041	18 362	12 379	4 566
February	93 903	635	4 372	8 429	21 759	4 606	12 841	2 177	6 033	15 123	18 389	12 429	4 557
March	94 016	635	4 392	8 420	21 740	4 607	12 823	2 180	6 033	15 178	18 421	12 468	4 549
April	94 175	632	4 391	8 414	21 762	4 609	12 839	2 178	6 056	15 229	18 462	12 495	4 556
May	94 352	632	4 392	8 397	21 792	4 619	12 861	2 180	6 059	15 304	18 488	12 548	4 560
June	94 505	632	4 400	8 391	21 826	4 624	12 893	2 175	6 067	15 359	18 503	12 589	4 563
July	94 660	637	4 397	8 383	21 874	4 635	12 934	2 196	6 083	15 400	18 526	12 605	4 559
August	94 815	638	4 401	8 390	21 914	4 642	12 958	2 175	6 084	15 447	18 575	12 630	4 561
September	94 932	644	4 418	8 394	21 968	4 654	12 976	2 178	6 078	15 474	18 591	12 626	4 561
October	95 172	649	4 436	8 410	21 998	4 654	13 005	2 181	6 082	15 532	18 611	12 708	4 565
November	95 397	648	4 466	8 442	22 051	4 671	13 008	2 177	6 082	15 590	18 646	12 734	4 561
December	95 471	649	4 444	8 444	22 109	4 676	13 056	2 165	6 087	15 611	18 649	12 746	4 567
2014													
January	95 644	644	4 545	8 486	22 094	4 664	13 036	2 208	6 096	15 524	18 651	12 784	4 612
February	95 860	645	4 564	8 512	22 108	4 674	13 040	2 203	6 114	15 602	18 688	12 813	4 611
March	96 056	648	4 582	8 524	22 142	4 676	13 056	2 207	6 115	15 641	18 719	12 850	4 628
April	96 322	653	4 620	8 534	22 199	4 699	13 080	2 212	6 129	15 687	18 751	12 897	4 640
May	96 516	653	4 615	8 539	22 225	4 702	13 088	2 205	6 137	15 735	18 804	12 959	4 644
June	96 772	654	4 621	8 561	22 287	4 716	13 120	2 217	6 156	15 796	18 848	12 993	4 639
July	96 953	658	4 647	8 573	22 316	4 716	13 132	2 222	6 171	15 832	18 888	13 004	4 642
August	97 118	661	4 655	8 588	22 332	4 723	13 129	2 239	6 177	15 870	18 925	13 021	4 650
September	97 266	666	4 672	8 588	22 341	4 722	13 138	2 236	6 189	15 916	18 963	13 052	4 643
October	97 388	669	4 673	8 601	22 374	4 728	13 157	2 234	6 186	15 935	18 982	13 098	4 636
November	97 671	669	4 682	8 640	22 437	4 729	13 192	2 240	6 204	15 996	19 018	13 120	4 665
December	97 923	669	4 719	8 663	22 478	4 741	13 187	2 245	6 213	16 025	19 069	13 172	4 670

. . . = Not available.

Table 10-15. Average Weekly Hours of Production and Nonsupervisory Workers on Private Nonfarm Payrolls by NAICS Supersector

(Hours per week, seasonally adjusted.)

Year and month	Total private	Mining and logging	Construction	Manufacturing		Trade, transportation, and utilities			Information	Financial activities	Professional and business services	Education and health services	Leisure and hospitality	Other services
				Average weekly hours	Overtime hours	Total	Wholesale trade	Retail trade						
1965	38.6	43.7	37.9	41.2	3.6	39.6	. . .	. . .	38.3	37.1	37.3	35.2	32.5	36.1
1966	38.5	44.1	38.1	41.4	3.9	39.1	. . .	. . .	38.3	37.2	37.0	34.9	31.9	35.8
1967	37.9	43.9	38.1	40.6	3.3	38.5	. . .	. . .	37.6	36.9	36.6	34.5	31.3	35.4
1968	37.7	44.0	37.8	40.7	3.6	38.2	. . .	. . .	37.6	36.8	36.3	34.1	30.8	35.0
1969	37.5	44.3	38.4	40.6	3.6	37.9	. . .	. . .	37.6	36.9	36.3	34.1	30.4	35.0
1970	37.0	43.9	37.8	39.8	2.9	37.6	. . .	. . .	37.2	36.6	35.9	33.8	30.0	34.7
1971	36.7	43.7	37.6	39.9	2.9	37.4	. . .	. . .	37.0	36.4	35.5	33.3	29.9	34.2
1972	36.9	44.1	37.0	40.6	3.4	37.4	39.8	35.1	37.3	36.4	35.5	33.3	29.7	34.2
1973	36.9	43.8	37.2	40.7	3.8	37.2	39.6	34.8	37.3	36.4	35.5	33.3	29.4	34.1
1974	36.4	43.7	37.1	40.0	3.2	36.8	39.2	34.3	37.0	36.3	35.3	33.1	29.1	33.9
1975	36.0	43.7	36.9	39.5	2.6	36.4	39.1	34.0	36.6	36.2	35.1	33.0	28.8	33.8
1976	36.1	44.2	37.3	40.1	3.1	36.3	39.1	33.8	36.7	36.2	34.9	32.7	28.5	33.6
1977	35.9	44.7	37.0	40.3	3.4	36.0	39.2	33.3	36.8	36.2	34.7	32.5	28.1	33.4
1978	35.8	44.9	37.3	40.4	3.6	35.6	39.2	32.7	36.8	36.1	34.6	32.3	27.7	33.2
1979	35.6	44.7	37.5	40.2	3.3	35.4	39.2	32.4	36.6	35.9	34.4	32.2	27.4	33.0
1980	35.2	44.9	37.5	39.6	2.8	35.0	38.8	31.9	36.4	36.0	34.3	32.1	27.0	33.0
1981	35.2	45.1	37.4	39.8	2.8	35.0	38.9	31.9	36.3	36.0	34.3	32.1	26.9	33.0
1982	34.7	44.1	37.2	38.9	2.3	34.6	38.7	31.7	35.8	36.0	34.2	32.1	26.8	33.0
1983	34.9	43.9	37.6	40.1	2.9	34.6	38.8	31.6	36.2	35.9	34.4	32.1	26.8	33.0
1984	35.1	44.6	38.2	40.6	3.4	34.7	38.9	31.6	36.6	36.2	34.3	32.0	26.7	32.9
1985	34.9	44.6	38.2	40.5	3.3	34.4	38.8	31.2	36.5	36.1	34.2	31.9	26.4	32.8
1986	34.7	43.6	37.9	40.7	3.4	34.1	38.7	31.0	36.4	36.1	34.3	32.0	26.2	32.9
1987	34.7	43.5	38.2	40.9	3.7	34.1	38.5	31.0	36.5	36.0	34.3	32.0	26.3	32.8
1988	34.6	43.3	38.2	41.0	3.8	33.8	38.5	30.9	36.1	35.6	34.2	32.0	26.3	32.9
1989	34.5	44.1	38.3	40.9	3.8	33.8	38.4	30.7	36.1	35.6	34.2	32.0	26.1	32.9
1990	34.3	45.0	38.3	40.5	3.9	33.7	38.4	30.6	35.8	35.5	34.2	31.9	26.0	32.8
1991	34.1	45.3	38.1	40.4	3.8	33.6	38.4	30.4	35.6	35.4	34.0	31.9	25.6	32.7
1992	34.2	44.6	38.0	40.7	4.0	33.8	38.5	30.7	35.8	35.6	34.0	32.0	25.7	32.6
1993	34.3	44.9	38.4	41.1	4.4	34.1	38.5	30.7	36.0	35.5	34.0	32.0	25.9	32.6
1994	34.5	45.3	38.8	41.7	5.0	34.3	38.8	30.9	36.0	35.5	34.1	32.0	26.0	32.7
1995	34.3	45.3	38.8	41.3	4.7	34.1	38.6	30.8	36.0	35.5	34.0	32.0	25.9	32.6
1996	34.3	46.0	38.9	41.3	4.8	34.1	38.6	30.7	36.3	35.5	34.1	31.9	25.9	32.5
1997	34.5	46.2	38.9	41.7	5.1	34.3	38.8	30.9	36.3	35.8	34.3	32.2	26.1	32.7
1998	34.5	44.9	38.8	41.4	4.9	34.2	38.6	30.9	36.6	36.0	34.3	32.2	26.2	32.6
1999	34.3	44.2	39.0	41.4	4.9	33.9	38.6	30.8	36.7	35.8	34.4	32.1	26.1	32.5
2000	34.3	44.4	39.2	41.3	4.7	33.8	38.8	30.7	36.8	35.9	34.5	32.2	26.1	32.5
2001	34.0	44.6	38.7	40.3	4.0	33.5	38.4	30.7	36.9	35.8	34.2	32.3	25.8	32.3
2002	33.9	43.2	38.4	40.5	4.2	33.6	38.0	30.9	36.5	35.6	34.2	32.4	25.8	32.1
2003	33.7	43.6	38.4	40.4	4.2	33.6	37.9	30.9	36.2	35.6	34.1	32.3	25.6	31.4
2004	33.7	44.5	38.3	40.8	4.6	33.5	37.8	30.7	36.3	35.6	34.2	32.4	25.7	31.0
2005	33.8	45.6	38.6	40.7	4.6	33.4	37.7	30.6	36.5	36.0	34.2	32.6	25.7	30.9
2006	33.9	45.6	39.0	41.1	4.4	33.4	38.0	30.5	36.6	35.8	34.6	32.5	25.7	30.9
2007	33.8	45.9	39.0	41.2	4.2	33.3	38.2	30.2	36.5	35.9	34.8	32.6	25.5	30.9
2008	33.6	45.1	38.5	40.8	3.7	33.2	38.2	30.0	36.7	35.9	34.8	32.4	25.2	30.8
2009	33.1	43.2	37.6	39.8	2.9	32.9	37.6	29.9	36.6	36.1	34.7	32.2	24.8	30.5
2010	33.4	44.6	38.4	41.1	3.8	33.3	37.9	30.2	36.3	36.2	35.1	32.1	24.8	30.7
2011	33.6	46.7	39.0	41.4	4.1	33.7	38.5	30.5	36.2	36.4	35.2	32.2	24.8	30.8
2012	33.7	46.6	39.3	41.7	4.2	33.8	38.7	30.6	36.0	36.8	35.3	32.3	25.0	30.7
2013	33.7	45.9	39.6	41.8	4.3	33.7	38.7	30.2	35.9	36.7	35.3	32.1	25.0	30.7
2014	33.7	47.4	39.6	42.0	4.5	33.6	38.6	30.0	35.9	36.8	35.6	32.0	25.1	30.7
2013														
January	33.6	44.5	39.3	41.6	4.3	33.5	38.6	30.0	35.8	36.6	35.3	32.2	25.0	30.6
February	33.8	45.6	39.6	41.9	4.3	33.8	38.8	30.3	35.8	36.7	35.4	32.3	25.0	30.8
March	33.8	45.7	39.7	41.9	4.4	33.9	38.8	30.4	35.9	36.7	35.4	32.3	25.0	30.8
April	33.7	45.5	39.6	41.8	4.3	33.6	38.6	30.1	35.9	36.7	35.4	32.3	25.0	30.8
May	33.7	46.1	39.9	41.8	4.3	33.9	38.9	30.4	36.0	36.7	35.3	32.2	25.0	30.8
June	33.7	45.8	39.6	41.9	4.3	33.7	38.7	30.2	36.1	36.8	35.3	32.1	25.0	30.7
July	33.5	45.9	39.5	41.7	4.3	33.5	38.6	30.0	35.9	36.5	35.2	31.9	24.8	30.6
August	33.7	46.1	39.7	41.9	4.3	33.8	38.8	30.4	35.9	36.7	35.3	32.0	25.0	30.7
September	33.6	46.1	39.7	41.9	4.3	33.6	38.6	30.1	36.0	36.8	35.3	32.0	25.0	30.7
October	33.6	45.3	39.5	41.9	4.4	33.6	38.6	30.1	35.9	36.6	35.3	32.0	25.0	30.7
November	33.7	46.1	39.7	42.0	4.5	33.6	38.8	30.0	35.9	36.7	35.3	32.0	25.0	30.6
December	33.5	46.9	39.0	41.9	4.5	33.5	38.6	30.0	36.1	36.6	35.2	32.1	24.8	30.8
2014														
January	33.5	46.4	38.5	41.6	4.4	33.5	38.5	29.8	35.8	36.6	35.4	31.9	25.0	30.7
February	33.5	47.5	38.6	41.6	4.3	33.3	38.5	29.7	36.0	36.6	35.4	31.9	25.1	30.6
March	33.7	47.9	39.6	42.0	4.5	33.5	38.7	29.9	35.9	36.8	35.5	31.9	25.2	30.8
April	33.7	47.1	39.8	41.9	4.4	33.6	38.6	30.1	35.9	36.6	35.5	32.0	25.2	30.7
May	33.7	47.0	39.7	42.2	4.6	33.6	38.7	29.9	35.9	36.7	35.6	32.0	25.2	30.8
June	33.7	47.4	39.7	42.1	4.5	33.6	38.6	30.0	35.9	36.7	35.4	31.9	25.1	30.7
July	33.7	47.4	39.9	42.0	4.4	33.5	38.6	29.9	35.8	36.7	35.6	31.9	25.0	30.7
August	33.7	47.7	39.8	42.0	4.4	33.6	38.6	30.0	35.9	36.7	35.6	32.0	25.2	30.7
September	33.7	47.1	39.7	42.1	4.5	33.6	38.6	30.0	35.8	36.7	35.6	32.0	25.1	30.7
October	33.7	47.6	39.6	42.1	4.4	33.6	38.5	30.0	36.1	36.8	35.6	32.0	25.1	30.7
November	33.8	47.6	39.7	42.2	4.6	33.7	38.6	30.1	36.0	36.8	35.7	32.0	25.1	30.7
December	33.8	47.6	39.9	42.1	4.6	33.9	38.6	30.3	35.8	36.8	35.7	32.0	25.2	30.8

. . . = Not available.

Table 10-16. Indexes of Aggregate Weekly Hours of Production and Nonsupervisory Workers on Private Nonfarm Payrolls by NAICS Supersector

(2002 = 100, seasonally adjusted.)

Year and month	Total private	Mining and logging	Construc-tion	Manu-facturing	Trade, transportation, and utilities			Information	Financial activities	Profes-sional and business services	Education and health services	Leisure and hospitality	Other services
					Total	Wholesale trade	Retail trade						
1965	54.4	121.6	55.2	122.1	59.0	. . .	. . .	55.5	42.6	29.4	25.9	41.0	29.4
1966	56.8	121.1	56.8	130.2	60.5	. . .	. . .	58.3	43.6	30.8	27.0	42.2	30.9
1967	57.0	117.0	55.4	127.8	61.1	. . .	. . .	58.6	44.9	31.9	28.1	42.9	32.4
1968	58.4	114.9	56.5	130.1	62.2	. . .	. . .	59.9	46.8	33.1	29.2	44.0	33.9
1969	60.4	118.1	61.0	131.9	64.3	. . .	. . .	61.8	49.4	34.6	30.5	45.6	35.6
1970	59.4	115.7	59.8	123.3	64.9	. . .	. . .	60.4	50.3	34.7	31.0	46.1	36.3
1971	59.0	109.9	61.0	119.3	65.1	. . .	. . .	58.7	51.1	34.7	31.1	46.9	36.5
1972	61.4	115.6	63.4	125.7	67.5	68.4	64.4	61.1	52.5	36.0	32.2	48.5	37.9
1973	64.2	117.0	66.7	132.9	69.6	71.0	66.4	64.1	54.2	37.8	33.7	50.3	39.9
1974	64.2	127.7	64.5	129.0	70.2	72.7	66.7	64.0	54.9	38.8	34.9	50.8	41.4
1975	61.1	134.9	55.2	113.9	68.9	71.8	66.4	59.1	55.0	38.9	35.8	50.9	42.6
1976	63.6	142.4	56.0	120.8	70.9	73.9	68.8	61.2	56.2	40.3	37.1	52.8	44.3
1977	66.1	151.1	59.4	125.8	73.1	76.7	70.7	63.5	58.8	42.1	38.6	54.4	46.3
1978	69.3	156.9	66.2	131.3	76.1	81.0	73.4	66.6	62.0	44.3	40.5	56.6	48.8
1979	71.6	175.2	70.6	133.3	78.3	84.6	74.7	69.0	64.7	46.3	42.3	57.9	51.2
1980	70.8	187.2	68.0	124.4	77.6	84.8	74.0	67.5	67.0	47.7	44.1	57.8	53.6
1981	71.4	206.2	64.9	123.1	78.0	86.0	74.5	67.7	68.6	49.2	45.9	58.7	55.8
1982	68.8	195.5	59.7	109.9	76.4	83.4	74.2	64.0	68.6	49.2	46.7	58.7	56.8
1983	69.8	162.8	61.0	111.6	77.2	83.3	76.0	62.1	69.8	50.7	48.3	60.4	58.9
1984	74.1	169.3	69.1	119.6	81.2	87.5	79.8	68.0	73.0	53.2	50.5	63.6	61.7
1985	76.0	162.7	73.9	117.5	83.5	89.9	82.2	69.1	76.1	55.6	53.1	66.0	65.0
1986	77.3	133.5	75.5	116.3	84.5	89.8	83.9	69.1	79.9	57.8	55.4	67.9	68.1
1987	79.5	125.2	78.1	117.8	86.5	90.5	86.3	71.5	82.3	60.3	58.1	70.5	71.5
1988	81.9	125.6	80.4	120.3	88.6	93.6	88.5	73.1	82.0	63.3	61.4	73.0	75.6
1989	83.9	123.2	81.7	120.3	90.5	95.9	90.0	74.4	82.6	66.3	64.7	74.9	79.7
1990	84.2	128.6	78.8	117.7	89.5	94.9	87.5	76.2	83.1	68.1	66.7	78.9	81.8
1991	82.4	123.8	70.1	112.8	87.4	93.3	84.8	76.1	82.0	66.7	69.8	77.3	81.1
1992	83.0	113.3	67.5	112.4	87.3	92.4	85.1	76.5	82.4	68.4	72.5	79.2	80.6
1993	85.3	110.3	71.3	113.9	89.1	92.4	86.3	78.0	84.9	71.9	74.9	82.1	82.8
1994	89.1	111.0	77.3	118.3	92.7	95.8	89.8	79.2	87.2	77.0	77.9	85.5	84.5
1995	91.5	110.3	79.9	119.0	95.1	99.2	92.3	82.5	86.9	81.2	80.8	88.5	87.0
1996	93.6	112.7	84.3	118.8	96.6	100.7	93.7	86.9	89.1	85.2	83.0	90.7	89.1
1997	97.0	117.6	88.6	121.4	98.9	103.4	95.9	90.4	92.3	91.5	86.4	93.4	91.9
1998	99.4	112.8	93.4	121.0	100.3	104.8	97.2	92.6	96.4	96.7	88.7	95.5	94.3
1999	101.5	102.9	99.7	119.0	101.9	106.2	99.5	98.5	98.1	101.7	90.6	97.8	96.2
2000	103.5	105.1	104.0	117.8	103.5	107.0	101.3	105.0	98.4	106.6	92.7	100.5	97.8
2001	102.1	108.3	103.2	108.1	101.5	102.9	100.5	106.7	99.3	104.0	96.5	100.6	99.0
2002	100.0	100.0	100.0	100.0	100.0	100.0	100.0	100.0	100.0	100.0	100.0	100.0	100.0
2003	98.7	97.4	98.4	94.5	98.6	98.0	98.9	97.0	101.3	98.7	101.6	100.0	97.4
2004	100.2	104.0	101.7	94.3	99.6	98.8	99.4	98.2	101.4	101.8	103.7	103.0	96.1
2005	102.8	114.7	108.3	93.9	101.6	101.8	100.8	99.4	103.7	106.3	106.8	106.2	96.2
2006	105.8	125.8	115.4	95.6	103.3	105.7	101.1	100.2	106.3	112.1	109.4	108.8	97.4
2007	107.3	133.5	114.7	94.4	104.8	109.2	101.8	100.1	107.6	115.3	113.0	110.8	99.3
2008	106.0	137.6	106.5	90.2	103.3	108.6	99.8	100.0	106.8	113.9	116.2	109.7	99.5
2009	98.8	117.2	85.9	76.1	96.8	99.9	94.3	93.5	103.1	105.2	117.9	105.1	96.0
2010	98.9	124.5	80.2	76.2	96.8	97.7	95.0	90.0	101.3	107.6	119.4	104.6	96.0
2011	101.4	147.4	81.7	78.3	99.7	100.7	97.7	88.9	101.2	112.4	122.0	106.9	96.8
2012	104.2	158.7	83.6	80.3	101.8	104.0	98.9	88.9	103.7	117.2	125.1	111.3	97.7
2013	106.1	155.7	87.2	80.8	102.7	105.6	98.7	89.3	104.6	121.6	126.8	115.1	98.2
2014	108.8	165.5	91.8	82.7	104.4	107.1	99.6	99.0	106.5	126.0	128.7	119.4	100.0
2013													
January	104.9	149.2	85.3	80.4	101.6	104.6	97.4	88.4	103.9	119.0	126.2	113.4	98.0
February	105.8	153.9	86.7	81.1	102.5	105.2	98.5	89.0	104.2	120.0	126.8	113.8	98.4
March	105.9	154.2	87.3	81.0	102.7	105.3	98.7	89.3	104.2	120.4	127.0	114.2	98.3
April	105.8	152.8	87.1	80.7	101.9	104.8	97.8	89.2	104.6	120.5	126.9	114.4	98.4
May	106.0	154.8	87.7	80.6	103.0	105.8	99.0	89.6	104.7	121.1	127.1	114.9	98.5
June	106.1	153.8	87.2	80.7	102.5	105.4	98.6	89.6	105.1	121.5	126.8	115.3	98.2
July	105.7	155.4	87.0	80.2	102.2	105.4	98.2	90.0	104.5	121.5	126.1	114.5	97.8
August	106.5	156.3	87.5	80.7	103.3	106.1	99.7	89.1	105.1	122.2	126.9	115.7	98.2
September	106.3	157.8	87.8	80.7	102.9	105.8	98.9	89.5	105.3	122.4	127.0	115.6	98.2
October	106.6	156.2	87.7	80.9	103.0	105.8	99.1	89.4	104.8	122.9	127.1	116.4	98.0
November	107.1	158.7	88.8	81.4	103.3	106.7	98.8	89.2	105.1	124.0	127.8	116.6	98.5
December	106.6	161.7	86.8	81.2	103.3	106.3	99.1	89.2	104.9	123.2	127.0	115.8	98.0
2014													
January	106.8	158.8	87.6	81.0	103.2	105.8	98.3	90.2	105.0	123.2	127.0	117.1	99.3
February	107.0	162.8	88.2	81.3	102.6	106.0	98.0	90.5	105.3	123.8	127.2	117.8	99.0
March	107.9	164.9	90.9	82.2	103.4	106.6	98.8	90.4	105.9	124.4	127.5	118.6	100.0
April	108.2	163.4	92.1	82.1	104.0	106.8	99.7	90.6	105.6	124.8	128.1	119.0	99.9
May	108.4	163.1	91.7	82.7	104.1	107.2	99.1	90.3	106.0	125.5	128.4	119.6	100.3
June	108.7	164.7	91.9	82.7	104.4	107.2	99.6	90.8	106.4	125.3	128.3	119.5	99.9
July	108.9	165.7	92.8	82.7	104.2	107.2	99.4	90.8	106.6	126.3	128.6	119.1	99.9
August	109.1	167.6	92.8	82.8	104.6	107.4	99.7	91.7	106.7	126.6	129.3	120.2	100.1
September	109.2	166.7	92.9	83.0	104.6	107.3	99.8	91.4	106.9	127.0	129.5	120.0	100.0
October	109.4	169.2	92.7	83.1	104.8	107.2	99.9	92.0	107.2	127.1	129.6	120.4	99.8
November	110.0	169.2	93.1	83.7	105.4	107.5	100.5	92.0	107.5	128.0	129.9	120.6	100.4
December	110.3	169.2	94.3	83.7	106.2	107.8	101.1	91.7	107.6	128.2	130.2	121.6	100.9

. . . = Not available.

Table 10-17. Average Hourly Earnings of Production and Nonsupervisory Workers on Private Nonfarm Payrolls by NAICS Supersector

(Dollars, seasonally adjusted.)

Year and month	Total private	Mining and logging	Construction	Manufacturing	Trade, transportation, and utilities — Total	Wholesale trade	Retail trade	Information	Financial activities	Professional and business services	Education and health services	Leisure and hospitality	Other services
1965	2.63	2.87	3.23	2.49	2.94	. . .	. . .	4.47	2.38	3.28	2.12	1.17	1.25
1966	2.73	3.00	3.41	2.60	3.04	. . .	. . .	4.56	2.47	3.39	2.23	1.26	1.37
1967	2.85	3.14	3.63	2.71	3.15	. . .	. . .	4.68	2.58	3.51	2.36	1.37	1.49
1968	3.02	3.30	3.92	2.89	3.32	. . .	. . .	4.85	2.75	3.65	2.49	1.53	1.62
1969	3.22	3.54	4.30	3.07	3.48	. . .	. . .	5.05	2.92	3.84	2.68	1.69	1.81
1970	3.40	3.77	4.74	3.24	3.65	. . .	. . .	5.25	3.07	4.04	2.88	1.82	2.01
1971	3.63	3.99	5.17	3.45	3.86	. . .	. . .	5.53	3.23	4.26	3.11	1.95	2.24
1972	3.90	4.28	5.55	3.70	4.23	4.58	3.52	5.87	3.37	4.50	3.33	2.08	2.46
1973	4.14	4.59	5.89	3.97	4.46	4.80	3.69	6.17	3.55	4.72	3.54	2.20	2.67
1974	4.43	5.09	6.29	4.31	4.74	5.11	3.92	6.52	3.80	5.01	3.82	2.40	2.95
1975	4.73	5.68	6.78	4.71	5.01	5.45	4.14	6.92	4.08	5.29	4.09	2.58	3.21
1976	5.06	6.19	7.17	5.10	5.31	5.75	4.36	7.37	4.30	5.60	4.39	2.78	3.51
1977	5.44	6.70	7.56	5.55	5.67	6.12	4.65	7.84	4.58	5.95	4.72	3.03	3.84
1978	5.88	7.44	8.11	6.05	6.11	6.61	5.00	8.34	4.93	6.32	5.07	3.33	4.19
1979	6.34	8.20	8.71	6.57	6.56	7.12	5.34	8.86	5.31	6.71	5.44	3.63	4.56
1980	6.85	8.97	9.37	7.15	7.04	7.68	5.71	9.47	5.82	7.22	5.93	3.98	5.05
1981	7.44	9.89	10.24	7.87	7.55	8.28	6.09	10.21	6.34	7.80	6.49	4.36	5.61
1982	7.87	10.64	11.04	8.36	7.91	8.81	6.34	10.76	6.82	8.30	7.00	4.63	6.11
1983	8.20	11.14	11.36	8.70	8.23	9.27	6.60	11.18	7.32	8.70	7.39	4.89	6.51
1984	8.49	11.54	11.56	9.05	8.45	9.61	6.73	11.50	7.65	8.98	7.66	4.99	6.79
1985	8.74	11.87	11.75	9.40	8.60	9.88	6.83	11.81	7.97	9.28	7.97	5.10	7.10
1986	8.93	12.14	11.92	9.60	8.74	10.07	6.93	12.08	8.37	9.55	8.24	5.20	7.38
1987	9.14	12.17	12.15	9.77	8.92	10.32	7.02	12.36	8.73	9.85	8.56	5.30	7.69
1988	9.44	12.45	12.52	10.05	9.15	10.71	7.23	12.63	9.07	10.22	8.95	5.50	8.08
1989	9.80	12.90	12.98	10.35	9.46	11.12	7.46	12.99	9.54	10.69	9.45	5.76	8.58
1990	10.20	13.40	13.42	10.78	9.83	11.58	7.71	13.40	9.98	11.14	9.98	6.02	9.08
1991	10.51	13.82	13.65	11.13	10.08	11.95	7.89	13.90	10.43	11.50	10.48	6.22	9.39
1992	10.77	14.09	13.81	11.40	10.30	12.21	8.12	14.29	10.86	11.78	10.85	6.36	9.66
1993	11.05	14.12	14.04	11.70	10.55	12.57	8.36	14.86	11.38	11.96	11.19	6.48	9.90
1994	11.34	14.41	14.38	12.04	10.80	12.93	8.61	15.32	11.84	12.15	11.48	6.62	10.18
1995	11.65	14.78	14.73	12.34	11.10	13.34	8.85	15.68	12.31	12.53	11.78	6.79	10.51
1996	12.04	15.09	15.11	12.75	11.46	13.80	9.21	16.30	12.75	13.00	12.15	6.99	10.85
1997	12.51	15.57	15.67	13.14	11.90	14.41	9.59	17.14	13.28	13.57	12.53	7.32	11.29
1998	13.01	16.20	16.23	13.45	12.40	15.07	10.05	17.67	14.00	14.27	12.96	7.67	11.79
1999	13.49	16.33	16.80	13.85	12.82	15.62	10.45	18.40	14.55	14.85	13.40	7.96	12.26
2000	14.02	16.55	17.48	14.32	13.31	16.28	10.87	19.07	15.04	15.52	13.91	8.32	12.73
2001	14.54	17.00	18.00	14.76	13.70	16.77	11.29	19.80	15.65	16.33	14.59	8.57	13.27
2002	14.97	17.19	18.52	15.29	14.02	16.98	11.67	20.20	16.25	16.80	15.16	8.81	13.72
2003	15.37	17.56	18.95	15.74	14.34	17.36	11.90	21.01	17.21	17.21	15.57	9.00	13.84
2004	15.69	18.07	19.23	16.14	14.58	17.65	12.08	21.40	17.58	17.48	16.08	9.15	13.98
2005	16.12	18.72	19.46	16.56	14.92	18.16	12.36	22.06	17.98	18.08	16.63	9.38	14.34
2006	16.75	19.90	20.02	16.81	15.39	18.91	12.57	22.23	18.83	19.13	17.30	9.75	14.77
2007	17.42	20.97	20.95	17.26	15.78	19.59	12.75	23.96	19.67	20.15	18.01	10.41	15.42
2008	18.07	22.50	21.87	17.75	16.16	20.13	12.87	24.78	20.32	21.18	18.75	10.84	16.09
2009	18.61	23.29	22.66	18.24	16.48	20.84	13.01	25.45	20.90	22.35	19.35	11.12	16.59
2010	19.05	23.82	23.22	18.61	16.82	21.54	13.25	25.87	21.55	22.78	19.98	11.31	17.06
2011	19.44	24.50	23.65	18.93	17.15	21.97	13.51	26.62	21.93	23.12	20.63	11.45	17.32
2012	19.74	25.79	23.97	19.08	17.43	22.24	13.82	27.04	22.82	23.29	20.94	11.62	17.59
2013	20.13	26.81	24.22	19.30	17.75	22.63	14.02	27.99	23.87	23.69	21.30	11.78	18.00
2014	19.58	24.84	23.71	19.02	17.28	22.10	13.69	26.77	22.38	23.10	20.86	11.56	17.41
2013													
January	19.60	25.52	23.78	19.01	17.30	22.04	13.73	26.70	22.46	23.09	20.87	11.55	17.47
February	19.65	25.62	23.91	19.02	17.37	22.15	13.78	26.82	22.49	23.21	20.88	11.60	17.49
March	19.70	25.93	23.87	19.09	17.40	22.17	13.78	26.88	22.58	23.24	20.91	11.62	17.50
April	19.69	25.66	23.91	19.02	17.41	22.13	13.83	26.84	22.67	23.22	20.90	11.62	17.55
May	19.72	25.84	23.92	19.08	17.48	22.22	13.88	26.88	22.71	23.20	20.92	11.63	17.57
June	19.76	26.08	23.99	19.11	17.47	22.21	13.83	27.12	22.80	23.23	20.92	11.64	17.62
July	19.75	25.83	24.01	19.06	17.42	22.20	13.81	27.09	22.85	23.26	20.94	11.64	17.64
August	19.78	25.76	24.05	19.07	17.44	22.24	13.82	27.26	22.98	23.34	20.98	11.64	17.65
September	19.80	25.92	24.06	19.10	17.45	22.24	13.85	27.17	23.08	23.33	20.98	11.66	17.68
October	19.85	26.13	24.07	19.15	17.50	22.39	13.84	27.30	23.20	23.40	20.98	11.66	17.68
November	19.89	26.25	24.12	19.14	17.50	22.41	13.87	27.54	23.34	23.49	21.02	11.66	17.70
December	19.95	26.27	24.17	19.15	17.57	22.34	13.91	27.85	23.43	23.59	21.06	11.67	17.75
											21.09	11.65	17.78
2014													
January	20.00	26.34	24.17	19.22	17.59	22.38	13.93	27.85	23.52	23.60	21.20	11.71	17.88
February	20.02	26.40	24.20	19.22	17.62	22.45	13.98	27.84	23.62	23.62	21.16	11.74	17.83
March	20.04	26.63	24.24	19.21	17.63	22.47	13.94	27.94	23.71	23.61	21.19	11.72	17.89
April	20.06	27.08	24.24	19.25	17.65	22.58	13.91	27.76	23.78	23.64	21.22	11.75	17.89
May	20.12	27.08	24.23	19.28	17.73	22.64	14.01	28.00	23.89	23.69	21.27	11.76	17.96
June	20.15	26.69	24.24	19.27	17.76	22.64	14.02	27.84	23.97	23.72	21.30	11.78	17.98
July	20.17	26.81	24.17	19.33	17.79	22.66	14.04	28.01	24.02	23.74	21.34	11.82	18.05
August	20.21	27.02	24.14	19.35	17.86	22.73	14.10	28.05	24.06	23.74	21.38	11.83	18.12
September	20.25	27.12	24.22	19.37	17.88	22.77	14.10	28.09	24.15	23.80	21.42	11.86	18.18
October	20.30	27.08	24.24	19.42	17.97	22.93	14.16	28.23	24.17	23.84	21.46	11.83	18.23
November	20.35	26.87	24.35	19.45	17.94	22.84	14.14	28.35	24.24	23.93	21.52	11.92	18.27
December	. . .	. . .	. . .	. . .	. . .	. . .	. . .	. . .	. . .	. . .	. . .	. . .	. . .

. . . = Not available.

Table 10-18. Average Weekly Earnings of Production and Nonsupervisory Workers on Private Nonfarm Payrolls by NAICS Supersector

(Dollars, seasonally adjusted.)

Year and month	Total private	Mining and logging	Construction	Manu-facturing	Trade, transportation, and utilities			Information	Financial activities	Professional and business services	Education and health services	Leisure and hospitality	Other services
					Total	Wholesale trade	Retail trade						
1965	101.51	125.48	122.35	102.69	116.36	. . .	. . .	171.24	88.50	122.30	74.84	38.06	45.30
1966	105.23	132.50	130.11	107.47	118.78	. . .	. . .	174.52	91.83	125.53	78.04	40.34	48.94
1967	108.07	137.76	138.55	109.85	121.57	. . .	. . .	176.09	95.35	128.34	81.34	43.06	52.69
1968	113.82	145.26	148.22	117.73	126.69	. . .	. . .	182.65	101.18	132.47	85.02	47.07	56.81
1969	120.70	157.11	164.88	124.74	132.13	. . .	. . .	190.18	107.91	139.37	91.46	51.29	63.44
1970	125.79	165.82	179.11	128.84	137.15	. . .	. . .	195.24	112.32	144.76	97.23	54.57	69.67
1971	133.22	174.18	194.70	137.59	144.11	. . .	. . .	204.50	117.60	151.51	103.57	58.39	76.58
1972	143.87	188.76	205.04	150.23	158.09	181.98	123.57	218.72	122.86	159.88	111.12	61.78	84.14
1973	152.59	201.43	219.32	161.59	165.61	190.33	128.16	230.48	129.32	167.40	117.85	64.92	91.06
1974	161.61	222.24	233.24	172.37	174.18	200.53	134.39	241.07	137.71	176.47	126.50	69.90	99.98
1975	170.29	248.38	249.70	185.69	182.61	212.85	140.99	253.21	147.75	185.81	134.83	74.49	108.67
1976	182.65	273.69	267.00	204.41	192.62	224.66	147.21	270.80	155.54	195.61	143.47	79.47	117.85
1977	195.58	299.46	279.61	224.01	203.87	239.57	154.51	288.29	165.47	206.78	153.38	85.20	128.12
1978	210.29	334.27	302.27	244.49	217.53	258.75	163.74	306.71	177.96	218.42	163.48	92.16	138.74
1979	225.69	366.58	326.55	263.99	232.36	278.74	173.18	324.51	190.72	231.16	174.80	99.47	150.47
1980	241.07	402.51	351.49	283.35	246.60	298.24	182.25	344.38	209.21	247.64	190.16	107.52	166.32
1981	261.53	446.10	382.75	312.74	263.93	322.08	193.97	370.36	228.21	267.46	208.06	117.49	184.77
1982	273.10	469.10	410.39	325.07	274.09	340.84	200.74	385.82	245.16	284.11	224.53	124.14	201.49
1983	286.43	488.89	427.00	348.89	284.76	359.98	208.81	404.89	262.83	298.74	237.40	130.82	214.87
1984	298.26	514.77	441.28	367.77	292.99	373.78	212.82	420.45	276.50	308.24	245.16	133.49	223.33
1985	304.62	529.62	448.35	380.60	295.81	383.22	213.38	430.86	287.66	317.41	254.19	134.71	232.81
1986	309.78	529.20	451.22	390.46	298.07	389.73	214.52	439.84	302.32	327.30	263.41	136.34	242.33
1987	317.39	529.72	463.78	400.00	304.10	397.39	218.05	450.77	314.01	337.57	273.49	139.45	252.58
1988	326.48	539.63	478.74	412.62	309.58	411.71	223.67	455.59	322.87	349.89	286.57	144.51	265.83
1989	338.34	568.55	497.43	423.58	319.40	427.40	229.14	468.77	339.46	365.93	302.70	150.29	282.09
1990	349.63	602.43	513.43	436.13	331.55	444.48	235.56	479.50	354.60	380.61	318.87	156.32	297.88
1991	358.46	625.46	520.41	449.83	339.10	459.17	240.13	495.14	369.57	391.06	334.07	159.20	306.75
1992	368.20	628.94	525.13	464.43	348.60	470.41	249.66	511.95	386.31	400.64	347.70	163.70	315.08
1993	378.89	634.77	539.81	480.89	359.51	484.46	256.89	535.19	403.68	406.20	358.44	167.54	322.69
1994	391.17	653.13	558.53	501.95	370.38	501.14	265.74	551.21	420.18	414.16	367.50	172.27	332.44
1995	400.04	670.40	571.57	509.26	378.79	515.14	272.63	564.92	437.26	426.54	376.94	175.74	342.36
1996	413.25	695.04	588.48	526.55	390.67	533.36	282.74	592.45	453.05	442.81	387.50	181.02	352.68
1997	431.86	720.07	609.48	548.26	407.63	559.39	295.94	622.37	475.03	465.51	403.63	190.66	368.63
1998	448.59	727.19	629.75	557.12	423.33	582.21	310.33	646.52	503.94	490.13	417.58	200.82	384.25
1999	463.15	721.77	655.11	573.29	434.31	602.77	321.71	675.47	520.74	510.99	429.98	208.05	398.77
2000	480.99	734.88	685.78	591.01	449.96	631.24	333.41	700.92	540.39	535.07	447.82	217.20	413.30
2001	493.74	757.96	695.86	595.19	459.53	643.45	346.16	731.18	560.46	557.84	471.36	220.73	428.64
2002	506.60	741.97	711.82	618.62	471.27	644.38	360.84	737.94	578.94	574.60	490.73	227.31	439.87
2003	517.82	765.94	727.00	636.03	481.14	657.29	367.18	760.84	611.82	587.02	503.27	230.49	434.41
2004	528.89	804.01	735.55	658.52	488.51	666.79	371.13	776.72	625.53	597.54	521.24	234.86	433.04
2005	544.05	853.87	750.37	673.30	498.46	685.00	377.58	805.11	646.48	618.71	541.78	241.36	443.40
2006	567.39	907.95	781.59	690.88	514.37	718.50	383.12	850.64	673.63	662.27	561.59	250.34	456.50
2007	589.27	962.63	816.23	711.53	525.91	748.94	385.00	874.45	706.52	700.82	586.41	265.54	477.06
2008	607.53	1 014.69	842.61	724.46	536.11	769.62	386.21	908.78	729.64	737.90	608.58	273.39	495.57
2009	616.01	1 006.67	851.76	726.12	541.88	784.49	388.57	931.08	754.90	775.81	622.73	275.95	506.26
2010	636.25	1 063.11	891.83	765.15	559.63	816.50	400.07	939.85	780.19	798.54	640.60	280.87	523.70
2011	653.19	1 144.64	921.84	784.29	577.71	845.44	412.09	964.85	798.68	813.37	665.05	283.82	532.63
2012	665.82	1 201.69	942.14	794.63	588.86	860.70	422.10	973.52	840.04	822.58	675.85	290.54	539.46
2013	677.67	1 230.00	958.67	807.51	597.51	875.82	423.00	1 005.49	875.22	837.27	683.48	294.34	553.12
2014	694.89	1 271.15	977.05	822.24	613.95	897.74	431.64	1 029.73	908.43	864.12	692.41	303.83	568.90
2013													
January	670.32	1 169.02	949.88	796.64	588.60	862.32	417.30	997.03	857.54	832.73	679.10	291.25	544.07
February	676.00	1 201.10	957.13	805.32	594.54	868.34	422.08	997.03	863.18	835.44	684.76	292.75	550.70
March	676.68	1 206.48	960.74	805.32	597.32	871.06	424.99	999.46	866.85	836.15	683.47	293.50	549.16
April	675.35	1 211.67	959.90	802.98	592.37	867.34	419.59	1 003.05	870.16	833.43	682.32	293.00	551.01
May	676.02	1 248.39	966.78	804.65	598.34	878.36	422.86	999.39	872.73	834.49	683.28	293.75	551.01
June	678.04	1 240.26	959.51	807.83	597.50	876.17	423.10	1 010.80	879.15	836.26	682.77	294.00	551.37
July	675.03	1 225.07	957.48	803.56	594.96	873.90	420.60	999.46	874.91	834.94	679.47	292.14	550.19
August	679.73	1 235.94	959.55	809.93	601.30	879.21	426.82	1 005.56	881.53	838.02	682.88	295.50	554.14
September	679.06	1 245.62	958.36	810.77	600.10	877.38	424.41	1 009.80	885.41	838.02	684.16	295.75	556.28
October	680.40	1 228.54	956.69	811.60	600.77	878.92	424.41	1 008.43	883.89	840.14	685.44	296.50	556.31
November	684.11	1 248.39	962.33	815.64	603.79	889.68	424.80	1 013.46	887.04	846.32	688.87	295.75	561.48
December	681.73	1 260.20	949.65	814.96	600.99	881.62	424.20	1 023.44	887.18	842.34	686.49	295.62	559.06
2014													
January	683.40	1 243.52	939.40	808.70	604.01	885.12	423.16	1 018.51	889.01	853.14	686.81	297.00	562.73
February	686.08	1 268.73	947.63	810.37	603.40	888.97	423.23	1 031.76	893.77	856.33	687.13	299.95	562.73
March	690.85	1 268.87	970.60	819.84	608.36	894.36	426.97	1 025.66	904.54	859.10	686.81	301.39	565.49
April	691.52	1 249.56	979.48	816.63	612.53	897.06	431.63	1 026.38	898.16	859.81	689.28	301.64	565.49
May	692.54	1 261.01	978.61	824.17	613.20	895.91	429.96	1 027.46	902.82	862.94	690.56	303.16	567.03
June	693.88	1 272.22	979.00	823.06	613.54	895.13	432.00	1 029.97	905.02	859.87	689.36	302.71	567.03
July	695.23	1 278.85	984.33	822.78	612.38	895.13	431.76	1 036.77	906.86	865.08	689.36	302.75	569.18
August	696.92	1 288.85	982.26	824.46	616.90	901.31	434.40	1 031.77	912.36	866.86	693.44	305.93	570.41
September	696.92	1 277.35	982.97	826.00	615.89	897.84	434.10	1 022.81	912.36	866.15	694.72	306.47	570.71
October	698.26	1 290.91	982.48	827.27	617.57	897.82	435.30	1 030.29	915.95	866.86	696.96	307.73	571.33
November	702.03	1 291.39	985.75	828.81	621.77	905.94	437.96	1 028.52	921.10	870.01	698.56	307.73	574.40
December	700.34	1 267.59	988.72	826.00	622.40	899.77	437.23	1 018.87	920.00	868.22	698.56	309.71	576.27

. . . = Not available.

Section 10c: Other Significant Labor Market Data

Figure 10-5: Average Hours Worked, Per Employed Person, 1948–2015

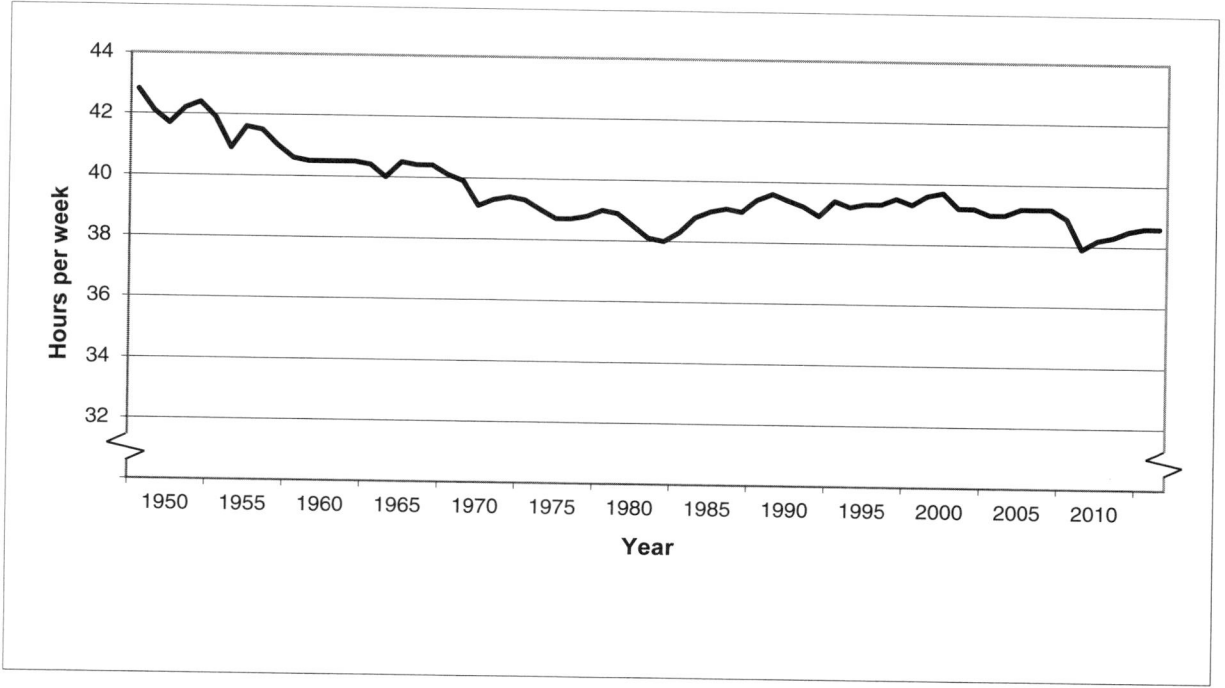

- This section of *Business Statistics* includes indicators of hours and earnings from the Current Population Statistics (household) survey that are, for some purposes, more appropriate than similarly-named indicators produced by the payroll survey and shown in the previous section. It also includes annual employment data from the Bureau of Economic Analysis, produced as part of the National Income and Product Accounts (NIPAS), that provide a consistent historical record of U.S. employment from 1929 through 2000.

- Figure 10-5 above shows annual averages of hours worked per week reported by all persons in the household survey employed in nonagricultural industries. Along with the recession dips expected in any measure of the average workweek, it displays a clear downward trend through the early 1970s, but no trend since then. The recession low in 2009 was actually slightly higher than the recession low in 1982. The 2000 peak is equal to the 1969 level. (Table 10-19)

- For comparison, average weekly hours for nonfarm production and nonsupervisory workers are also graphed in Figure 10-5. These are the workweeks reported by employers in the Current Employment Statistics (payroll) survey and they pertain to jobs, not to workers. (Table 10-15) This CES measure of "hours per job" represents many of the same workers as those in the "hours per employed person" measure shown in the graph, and was selected for the graph because it has the longest available history. But it is increasingly pulled downward by the increasing prevalence of part-time jobs. It is not a good indicator of either the level or the trend of the amount of work being done each week by the typical American worker. (Table 10-19)

- A look at some of the other categories in Table 10-19 confirms the absence of any significant downtrend in the workers' workweek in recent years. Note, for example, that men reported working an average of 41.7 hours at the pre-recession peak in 2007—just 18 minutes lower than the 1979 peak of 42.0—while women actually reported working 1 1/2 hours longer—36.1 hours in 2007 against 34.5 hours in 1979. (Table 10-19)

Table 10-19. Hours at Work, Current Population Survey

(Hours per week.)

Year and month	Hours per person, all industries				Hours per person, nonagricultural industries		
	Total	Men	Women	Persons who usually work full-time	All workers		Wage and salary workers
					Total	Usually work full-time	
1948	42.8	. . .	. . .	. . .	41.6	. . .	. . .
1949	42.1	. . .	. . .	. . .	40.9	. . .	. . .
1950	41.7	. . .	. . .	. . .	40.7	. . .	. . .
1951	42.2	. . .	. . .	. . .	41.3	. . .	. . .
1952	42.4	. . .	. . .	. . .	41.6	. . .	. . .
1953	41.9	. . .	. . .	. . .	41.1	. . .	. . .
1954	40.9	. . .	. . .	. . .	40.0	. . .	. . .
1955	41.6	. . .	. . .	. . .	40.9	. . .	. . .
1956	41.5	43.8	36.5	. . .	40.9	. . .	. . .
1957	41.0	43.4	36.1	. . .	40.5	. . .	. . .
1958	40.6	42.9	35.8	. . .	40.1	. . .	. . .
1959	40.5	42.8	35.6	. . .	40.0	. . .	. . .
1960	40.5	43.0	35.4	. . .	40.0	. . .	. . .
1961	40.5	43.0	35.3	. . .	40.1	. . .	. . .
1962	40.5	43.2	35.2	. . .	40.1	. . .	. . .
1963	40.4	43.2	35.1	. . .	40.1	. . .	. . .
1964	40.0	42.8	34.7	. . .	39.7	. . .	. . .
1965	40.5	43.3	35.1	. . .	40.2	. . .	. . .
1966	40.4	43.2	35.2	. . .	40.1	. . .	. . .
1967	40.4	43.3	35.2	. . .	40.0	. . .	. . .
1968	40.1	43.0	34.9	. . .	39.7	. . .	. . .
1969	39.9	42.9	34.9	. . .	39.5	. . .	. . .
1970	39.1	42.0	34.2	. . .	38.7	. . .	. . .
1971	39.3	42.2	34.3	. . .	38.9	. . .	. . .
1972	39.4	42.3	34.5	. . .	39.0	. . .	. . .
1973	39.3	42.4	34.4	. . .	39.0	. . .	. . .
1974	39.0	42.0	34.3	. . .	38.7	. . .	. . .
1975	38.7	41.6	34.1	. . .	38.4	. . .	. . .
1976	38.7	41.7	34.1	. . .	38.4	. . .	38.1
1977	38.8	41.9	34.2	. . .	38.5	. . .	38.3
1978	39.0	42.1	34.5	. . .	38.7	. . .	38.4
1979	38.9	42.0	34.5	. . .	38.6	. . .	38.4
1980	38.5	41.5	34.5	. . .	38.3	. . .	38.1
1981	38.1	41.1	34.1	. . .	37.9	. . .	37.7
1982	38.0	40.9	34.1	. . .	37.7	. . .	37.6
1983	38.3	41.2	34.5	. . .	38.1	. . .	37.9
1984	38.8	41.8	34.9	. . .	38.6	. . .	38.4
1985	39.0	42.0	35.2	. . .	38.9	. . .	38.7
1986	39.1	42.1	35.4	. . .	38.9	. . .	38.8
1987	39.0	42.0	35.3	. . .	38.8	. . .	38.7
1988	39.4	42.4	35.7	. . .	39.3	. . .	39.1
1989	39.6	42.6	35.8	. . .	39.4	. . .	39.3
1990	39.4	42.3	35.8	. . .	39.3	. . .	39.2
1991	39.2	42.0	35.8	. . .	39.1	. . .	39.0
1992	38.9	41.7	35.6	. . .	38.8	. . .	38.7
1993	39.4	42.2	36.0	. . .	39.3	. . .	39.2
1994	39.2	42.2	35.5	43.4	39.1	43.3	39.1
1995	39.3	42.3	35.6	43.4	39.2	43.2	39.2
1996	39.3	42.3	35.7	43.3	39.2	43.2	39.2
1997	39.5	42.4	36.0	43.4	39.4	43.3	39.4
1998	39.3	42.2	35.8	43.2	39.2	43.1	39.2
1999	39.6	42.4	36.2	43.4	39.5	43.3	39.5
2000	39.7	42.5	36.4	43.4	39.6	43.3	39.6
2001	39.2	41.9	36.1	42.9	39.2	42.8	39.2
2002	39.2	41.8	36.0	42.9	39.1	42.8	39.1
2003	39.0	41.7	35.9	42.9	39.0	42.7	39.0
2004	39.0	41.7	35.9	42.9	39.0	42.8	39.0
2005	39.2	41.8	36.1	42.9	39.1	42.8	39.1
2006	39.2	41.8	36.2	42.9	39.2	42.8	39.2
2007	39.2	41.7	36.1	42.8	39.1	42.7	39.2
2008	38.9	41.3	36.1	42.6	38.8	42.5	39.0
2009	37.9	40.2	35.3	41.9	37.8	41.8	38.0
2010	38.2	40.5	35.5	42.2	38.1	42.2	38.3
2011	38.3	40.6	35.6	42.4	38.2	42.3	38.4
2012	38.5	40.8	35.8	42.5	38.4	42.4	38.6
2013	38.6	40.9	36.0	42.6	38.5	42.5	38.7
2014	38.6	40.9	35.9	42.5	38.6	42.5	38.7

. . . = Not available.

Figure 10-6: Real Median Weekly Earnings

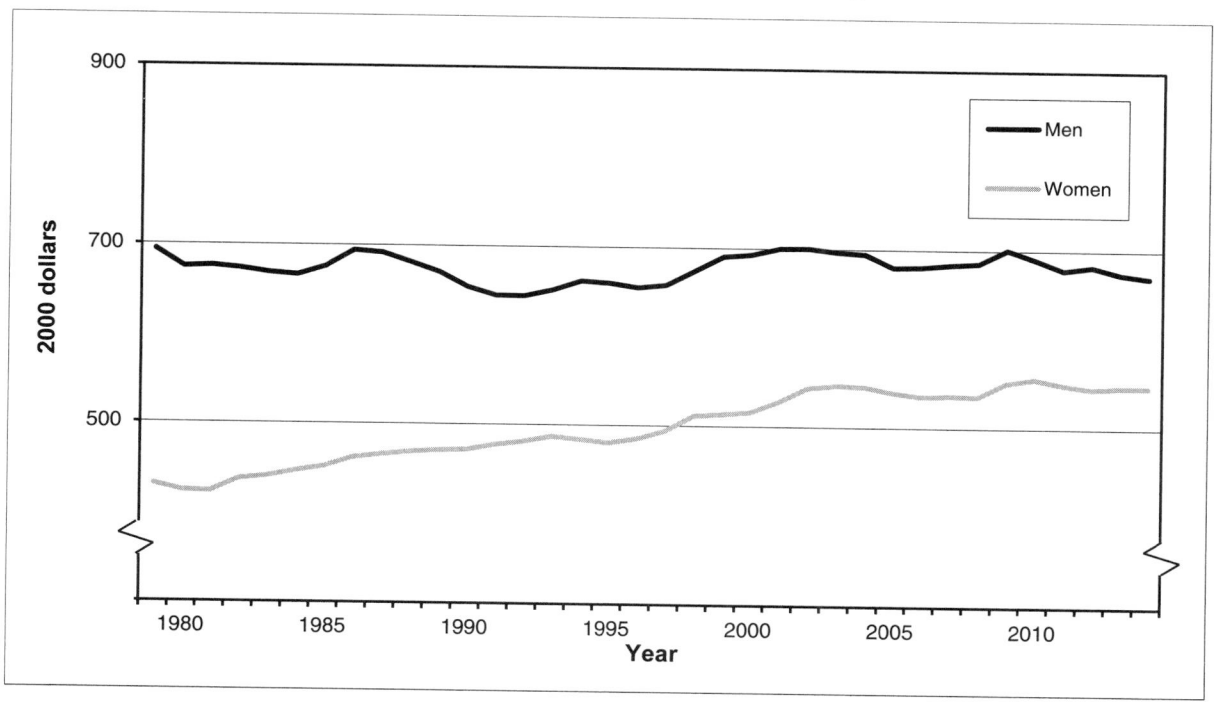

- "Median usual weekly earnings of full-time wage and salary workers," as shown in Table 10-20, are derived quarterly from the Current Population Survey, not from the payroll survey that provides the weekly earnings shown in Tables 10-9, 10-13, and 10-18. That is, they are collected from individual households in the CPS sample, providing better approximations of the paychecks of typical breadwinners than the payroll data on average weekly earnings (AWE). (See the Notes and Definitions to this chapter.)

- Focusing on workers 25 and over, women's earnings were moving closer to men's over most of the period covered in this survey, rising from 62.1 percent in 1979 to 78.5 percent in 2007, the latest high-employment year. Since then the ratio gained even further—to 81.6 percent in 2014—as men experienced real income losses. (Table 10-20)

- As Figure 10-6 shows, typical full-time workers age 25 and over of both sexes lost ground in real terms in many recent years. The median man's real earnings in 2014 was $670 while the median was $693 in 2000, and the median woman's only up at a 0.4 percent annual rate. (Table 10-20) In contrast, worker productivity (business output per worker hour) growth over that 14-year period was 2.2 percent per year. (Table 9-3A)

- Taking a longer look at the entire period shown here, men's real earnings have been essentially stagnant for the entire 35 years, while women's have increased 0.7 percent per year. For both sexes these earnings fall short of what might have been expected from the 2.0 percent rate of increase in worker productivity over those 35 years. (Tables 10-20 and 9-3A)

Table 10-20. Median Usual Weekly Earnings of Full-Time Wage and Salary Workers

(Current dollars, except as noted; not seasonally adjusted.)

Year and quarter	Total, 16 years and over	Sex and age								Race and ethnicity			
		Men, 16 years and over				Women, 16 years and over				White	Black or African American	Asian	Hispanic or Latino ethnicity
		Total	16 to 24 years	25 years and over		Total	16 to 24 years	25 years and over					
				Current dollars	2000 dollars [1]			Current dollars	2000 dollars [1]				
1979	241	292	196	314	694	182	154	195	431	248	199	. . .	194
1980	262	313	208	339	675	201	167	213	424	269	212	. . .	209
1981	284	340	218	372	676	219	180	233	423	291	235	. . .	223
1982	302	364	225	393	673	239	192	255	437	310	245	. . .	240
1983	313	379	223	407	669	252	198	268	440	320	261	. . .	250
1984	326	392	231	422	666	265	203	283	447	336	269	. . .	259
1985	344	407	241	443	676	277	211	296	452	356	277	. . .	270
1986	359	419	246	463	694	291	219	308	462	371	291	. . .	277
1987	374	434	257	477	692	303	227	321	465	384	301	. . .	285
1988	385	449	262	487	681	315	235	335	469	395	314	. . .	290
1989	399	468	271	500	670	328	246	351	471	409	319	. . .	298
1990	412	481	282	512	654	346	254	369	471	424	329	. . .	304
1991	426	493	285	523	645	366	266	387	477	442	348	. . .	312
1992	440	501	284	536	645	380	267	400	481	458	357	. . .	321
1993	459	510	288	555	651	393	273	415	487	475	369	. . .	331
1994	467	522	294	576	662	399	276	421	484	484	371	. . .	324
1995	479	538	303	588	660	406	275	428	480	494	383	. . .	329
1996	490	557	307	599	655	418	284	444	485	506	387	. . .	339
1997	503	579	317	615	658	431	292	462	494	519	400	. . .	351
1998	523	598	334	639	674	456	305	485	512	545	426	. . .	370
1999	549	618	356	668	690	473	324	497	514	573	445	. . .	385
2000	576	641	375	693	693	493	344	516	516	590	474	615	399
2001	596	670	391	720	700	512	353	543	528	610	491	639	417
2002	608	679	391	732	701	529	367	568	544	623	498	658	424
2003	620	695	398	744	697	552	371	584	547	636	514	693	440
2004	638	713	400	762	695	573	375	599	546	657	525	708	456
2005	651	722	409	771	680	585	381	612	540	672	520	753	471
2006	671	743	418	797	681	600	395	627	536	690	554	784	486
2007	695	766	443	823	684	614	409	646	537	716	569	830	503
2008	722	798	461	857	685	638	420	670	536	742	589	861	529
2009	739	819	458	873	701	657	424	687	552	757	601	880	541
2010	747	824	443	874	690	669	422	704	556	765	611	855	535
2011	756	832	455	886	678	684	421	718	550	775	615	866	549
2012	768	854	468	910	683	691	416	727	545	792	621	920	568
2013	776	860	479	912	674	706	423	740	547	802	629	942	578
2014	791	871	493	922	670	719	451	752	547	816	639	953	594
2007													
1st quarter	693	759	451	811	686	615	414	646	546	714	561	798	502
2nd quarter	690	763	436	819	679	607	404	635	527	713	562	827	503
3rd quarter	695	767	430	831	687	616	398	654	541	713	578	842	502
4th quarter	700	774	459	831	682	618	421	649	533	722	574	856	507
2008													
1st quarter	719	790	466	848	688	637	419	666	541	742	582	842	520
2nd quarter	719	800	469	862	685	634	415	668	531	738	591	855	537
3rd quarter	720	796	446	857	673	631	406	666	523	739	589	854	529
4th quarter	728	807	462	859	694	650	449	679	549	748	593	889	535
2009													
1st quarter	738	823	461	879	714	649	448	679	552	758	577	869	545
2nd quarter	734	815	450	872	701	652	413	679	546	754	592	909	547
3rd quarter	738	812	448	870	695	657	415	691	552	753	607	877	527
4th quarter	748	825	476	871	694	670	436	700	558	763	629	877	547
2010													
1st quarter	754	844	473	887	704	665	422	698	554	772	610	859	554
2nd quarter	740	810	442	861	680	672	417	704	556	756	607	873	529
3rd quarter	740	813	424	869	686	662	419	702	554	759	611	854	522
4th quarter	752	830	449	878	691	679	436	709	558	772	614	828	539
2011													
1st quarter	755	829	470	880	684	683	426	716	556	774	604	831	549
2nd quarter	753	825	446	884	698	689	417	720	569	770	623	872	565
3rd quarter	753	827	440	888	701	673	422	713	563	772	616	869	545
4th quarter	764	843	466	893	703	688	420	724	570	786	621	880	537
2012													
1st quarter	769	848	469	904	683	697	421	731	552	793	635	918	567
2nd quarter	771	865	460	918	688	689	409	727	545	792	637	930	576
3rd quarter	758	828	459	891	666	685	414	725	542	780	606	915	556
4th quarter	775	875	480	926	705	692	422	725	552	802	615	910	571
2013													
1st quarter	773	867	487	914	679	704	419	735	546	802	622	951	575
2nd quarter	776	860	479	913	675	707	422	743	549	799	634	973	572
3rd quarter	771	847	452	904	666	698	414	737	543	794	630	922	587
4th quarter	786	869	492	915	676	713	449	746	551	813	632	916	576
2014													
1st quarter	796	872	480	925	678	722	434	754	552	819	646	955	618
2nd quarter	780	857	481	914	662	716	449	750	543	802	649	954	609
3rd quarter	790	870	498	920	655	715	448	750	542	816	638	945	622
4th quarter	799	882	508	929	677	724	469	756	551	823	621	959	627

[1]Converted to 2000 dollars by the editor using CPI-U-RS. See notes and definitions.
. . . = Not available.

Table 10-21. Employment by SIC Industry, Historical Annual

(Full-time and part-time employees, thousands.)

NIPA Table 6.4A, B, and C

Year	Total employ- ment	Total domestic	Total private industries	Agriculture, forestry, and fisheries	Mining	Construc- tion	Manufacturing Total manu- facturing	Durable goods	Nondur- able goods	Transpor- tation and public utilities	Wholesale trade	Retail trade	Finance, insurance, and real estate	Services
1942 SIC														
1929	37 699	37 699	34 088	3 556	993	1 484	10 428	5 238	5 190	3 989	1 757	4 684	1 520	5 677
1930	35 590	35 590	31 811	3 337	932	1 366	9 309	4 457	4 852	3 742	1 693	4 469	1 491	5 472
1931	32 724	32 723	28 590	3 252	813	1 198	7 895	3 497	4 398	3 282	1 530	4 148	1 423	5 049
1932	29 445	29 444	25 071	3 028	672	907	6 678	2 724	3 954	2 826	1 380	3 688	1 358	4 534
1933	30 940	30 939	25 038	2 995	693	703	7 204	2 893	4 311	2 684	1 377	3 699	1 309	4 374
1934	34 238	34 237	27 417	2 986	822	806	8 364	3 587	4 777	2 774	1 492	4 075	1 332	4 766
1935	35 577	35 576	28 426	3 013	840	866	8 904	3 941	4 963	2 808	1 507	4 200	1 352	4 936
1936	38 599	38 598	30 548	3 106	897	1 104	9 645	4 460	5 185	2 973	1 612	4 543	1 401	5 267
1937	39 701	39 700	32 508	3 083	955	1 082	10 591	5 130	5 461	3 140	1 770	4 904	1 445	5 538
1938	38 322	38 321	30 124	2 949	859	1 055	9 131	4 085	5 046	2 837	1 767	4 780	1 436	5 310
1939	39 633	39 632	31 612	2 859	832	1 219	9 967	4 609	5 358	2 943	1 833	4 992	1 470	5 497
1940	41 437	41 435	33 518	2 809	927	1 285	10 882	5 367	5 515	3 064	1 899	5 321	1 518	5 813
1941	45 785	45 782	37 210	2 779	975	1 774	13 137	6 999	6 138	3 311	2 014	5 754	1 559	5 907
1942	50 219	50 214	39 728	2 692	985	2 131	15 284	8 846	6 438	3 458	1 916	5 623	1 531	6 108
1943	55 995	56 016	40 723	2 563	917	1 566	17 402	10 924	6 478	3 652	1 808	5 570	1 475	5 770
1944	57 221	57 276	39 749	2 372	879	1 110	17 050	10 722	6 328	3 822	1 828	5 529	1 447	5 712
1945	55 548	55 614	38 183	2 259	829	1 135	15 186	8 933	6 253	3 926	1 927	5 717	1 477	5 727
1946	49 643	49 690	40 379	2 343	871	1 739	14 493	7 742	6 751	4 113	2 286	6 769	1 692	6 073
1947	49 936	49 941	42 458	2 427	933	2 062	15 205	8 330	6 875	4 173	2 480	7 061	1 744	6 373
1948	51 332	51 325	43 431	2 498	981	2 278	15 276	8 309	6 967	4 212	2 573	7 223	1 811	6 579
1972 SIC														
1948	51 332	51 325	43 431	2 505	993	2 324	15 521	8 343	7 178	4 212	2 731	6 585	1 776	6 784
1949	50 358	50 373	41 857	2 418	923	2 212	14 429	7 508	6 921	4 026	2 653	6 552	1 805	6 839
1950	52 424	52 428	43 626	2 499	926	2 448	15 241	8 121	7 120	4 064	2 670	6 727	1 883	7 168
1951	56 415	56 470	46 112	2 418	939	2 727	16 453	9 144	7 309	4 267	2 817	7 123	1 970	7 398
1952	57 702	57 770	46 668	2 338	916	2 763	16 752	9 466	7 286	4 279	2 870	7 270	2 044	7 436
1953	58 918	58 996	47 873	2 277	876	2 743	17 587	10 144	7 443	4 326	2 901	7 403	2 125	7 635
1954	57 387	57 514	46 400	2 301	798	2 729	16 395	9 194	7 201	4 120	2 875	7 336	2 199	7 647
1955	59 080	59 218	48 036	2 233	804	2 879	16 965	9 617	7 348	4 182	2 930	7 547	2 302	8 194
1956	60 845	60 987	49 573	2 141	843	3 025	17 327	9 894	7 433	4 290	3 054	7 812	2 406	8 675
1957	61 308	61 441	49 732	2 114	840	2 945	17 245	9 894	7 351	4 276	3 078	7 881	2 459	8 894
1958	59 839	59 967	48 211	2 153	749	2 865	15 919	8 839	7 080	4 011	3 066	7 785	2 513	9 150
1959	61 587	61 721	49 781	2 133	717	3 001	16 656	9 385	7 271	4 015	3 129	8 046	2 578	9 506
1960	62 680	62 823	50 548	2 097	699	2 969	16 779	9 453	7 326	4 024	3 205	8 305	2 660	9 810
1961	62 881	63 006	50 374	2 121	666	2 946	16 333	9 075	7 258	3 920	3 218	8 276	2 719	10 175
1962	64 573	64 664	51 672	2 075	649	3 024	16 901	9 514	7 387	3 920	3 268	8 508	2 781	10 546
1963	65 619	65 691	52 444	2 043	632	3 112	17 028	9 631	7 397	3 919	3 314	8 737	2 857	10 802
1964	67 275	67 338	53 655	1 879	628	3 234	17 330	9 856	7 474	3 972	3 394	9 068	2 939	11 211
1965	69 692	69 713	55 598	1 775	634	3 382	18 120	10 445	7 675	4 050	3 518	9 466	3 047	11 606
1966	73 516	73 531	58 209	1 662	631	3 485	19 319	11 359	7 960	4 192	3 667	9 937	3 136	12 180
1967	75 442	75 457	59 288	1 568	614	3 441	19 544	11 507	8 037	4 289	3 759	10 234	3 245	12 594
1968	77 602	77 618	60 948	1 545	610	3 570	19 898	11 700	8 198	4 352	3 851	10 638	3 412	13 072
1969	79 850	79 872	62 877	1 530	624	3 738	20 306	11 982	8 324	4 472	3 981	11 115	3 564	13 547
1970	79 750	79 770	62 702	1 545	628	3 676	19 442	11 270	8 172	4 525	4 061	11 362	3 696	13 767
1971	79 554	79 573	62 529	1 535	615	3 735	18 611	10 636	7 975	4 488	4 087	11 615	3 777	14 066
1972	81 583	81 604	64 568	1 551	625	3 927	19 080	11 010	8 070	4 538	4 206	11 982	3 917	14 742
1973	85 202	85 226	67 939	1 637	639	4 217	20 139	11 884	8 255	4 689	4 422	12 589	4 138	15 469
1974	86 573	86 594	68 947	1 738	699	4 151	20 121	11 964	8 157	4 746	4 540	12 847	4 270	15 835
1975	85 044	85 069	67 069	1 711	753	3 675	18 379	10 724	7 655	4 581	4 465	12 977	4 319	16 209
1976	87 402	87 427	69 430	1 815	782	3 728	19 082	11 123	7 959	4 600	4 609	13 550	4 443	16 801
1977	90 421	90 444	72 275	1 760	827	4 006	19 801	11 665	8 136	4 734	4 781	14 195	4 641	17 530
1978	94 777	94 805	76 313	1 763	876	4 443	20 668	12 372	8 296	4 955	5 056	15 031	4 947	18 573
1979	98 017	98 039	79 137	1 816	948	4 710	21 182	12 848	8 334	5 167	5 295	15 461	5 198	19 359
1980	98 370	98 394	79 121	1 865	1 032	4 493	20 433	12 270	8 163	5 178	5 346	15 487	5 362	19 924
1981	99 225	99 287	80 139	1 844	1 151	4 338	20 328	12 194	8 134	5 219	5 466	15 659	5 488	20 646
1982	97 305	97 369	78 220	1 718	1 138	4 013	18 923	11 122	7 800	5 131	5 350	15 471	5 528	20 949
1983	98 041	98 111	78 939	1 835	964	4 070	18 527	10 784	7 742	5 027	5 323	15 916	5 667	21 610
1984	102 458	102 531	83 103	1 747	980	4 527	19 473	11 560	7 913	5 192	5 614	16 908	5 894	22 768
1985	104 987	105 059	85 264	1 632	935	4 809	19 348	11 552	7 795	5 269	5 757	17 654	6 132	23 728
1986	106 873	106 940	86 770	1 611	784	4 960	19 035	11 269	7 766	5 283	5 799	18 188	6 435	24 675
1987	109 754	109 820	89 270	1 671	727	5 069	19 091	11 222	7 869	5 412	5 916	18 788	6 707	25 887
1987 SIC														
1987	109 754	109 820	89 270	1 671	727	5 069	19 091	11 193	7 898	5 412	5 937	18 767	6 719	25 875
1988	112 864	112 939	92 033	1 765	729	5 212	19 450	11 437	8 012	5 553	6 085	19 345	6 806	27 089
1989	115 501	115 584	94 300	1 723	704	5 269	19 482	11 445	8 046	5 659	6 319	19 843	6 846	28 456
1990	116 964	117 046	95 233	1 740	721	5 226	19 173	11 153	8 020	5 811	6 251	19 912	6 876	29 522
1991	115 525	115 607	93 763	1 735	700	4 794	18 507	10 618	7 889	5 785	6 097	19 604	6 835	29 705
1992	115 968	116 046	94 151	1 694	644	4 635	18 148	10 310	7 837	5 748	6 090	19 710	6 761	30 721
1993	117 604	118 030	96 106	1 724	617	4 790	18 141	10 268	7 874	5 861	6 018	20 110	6 851	31 993
1994	120 379	120 858	98 853	1 761	608	5 121	18 388	10 485	7 902	6 049	6 197	20 811	6 993	32 924
1995	123 236	123 713	101 636	1 819	590	5 304	18 548	10 698	7 849	6 177	6 437	21 498	6 899	34 365
1996	125 461	125 901	103 832	1 841	583	5 579	18 529	10 815	7 714	6 298	6 522	21 869	7 011	35 601
1997	128 316	128 788	106 698	1 919	599	5 859	18 706	11 030	7 676	6 470	6 711	22 240	7 212	36 983
1998	131 563	132 031	109 709	1 961	591	6 178	18 849	11 231	7 618	6 680	6 876	22 595	7 491	38 488
1999	134 350	134 864	112 253	2 055	537	6 570	18 605	11 141	7 465	6 895	6 951	23 140	7 649	39 850
2000	137 228	137 691	114 597	2 068	537	6 870	18 500	11 142	7 358	7 089	7 058	23 643	7 674	41 157

Table 10-21. Employment by SIC Industry, Historical Annual—*Continued*

(Full-time and part-time employees, thousands.)

NIPA Table 6.4A, B, and C

Year	Total govern-ment		Federal government						State and local government						Rest of the world
		Total federal	General government				Govern-ment enterprises	Total state and local	General government				Govern-ment enterprises	
			General gov't total	Civilian [1]	Military	Work relief			General gov't total	Education	Other [1]	Work relief		
1942 SIC															
1929	3 611	981	644	267	377	. . .	337	2 630	2 509	1 067	1 442	. . .	121	0
1930	3 779	1 034	695	310	385	. . .	339	2 745	2 618	1 095	1 503	20	127	0
1931	4 133	1 019	683	296	387	. . .	336	3 114	2 984	1 105	1 580	299	130	1
1932	4 373	1 006	673	290	383	. . .	333	3 367	3 249	1 093	1 564	592	118	1
1933	5 901	1 470	1 135	294	370	471	335	4 431	4 317	1 069	1 524	1 724	114	1
1934	6 820	2 227	1 868	357	371	1 140	359	4 593	4 473	1 069	1 570	1 834	120	1
1935	7 150	2 209	1 835	449	396	990	374	4 941	4 815	1 097	1 621	2 097	126	1
1936	8 050	4 993	4 612	521	438	3 653	381	3 057	2 922	1 118	1 713	91	135	1
1937	7 192	4 085	3 698	517	474	2 707	387	3 107	2 967	1 149	1 762	56	140	1
1938	8 197	4 987	4 583	507	504	3 572	404	3 210	3 070	1 180	1 871	19	140	1
1939	8 020	4 754	4 342	560	566	3 216	412	3 266	3 123	1 207	1 877	39	143	1
1940	7 917	4 652	4 227	642	793	2 792	425	3 265	3 104	1 194	1 872	38	161	2
1941	8 572	5 281	4 829	944	1 693	2 192	452	3 291	3 119	1 256	1 846	17	172	3
1942	10 486	7 252	6 765	1 702	4 154	909	487	3 234	3 063	1 264	1 794	5	171	5
1943	15 293	12 155	11 611	2 497	9 029	85	544	3 138	2 965	1 256	1 709	. . .	173	-21
1944	17 527	14 405	13 885	2 520	11 365	. . .	520	3 122	2 956	1 256	1 700	. . .	166	-55
1945	17 431	14 258	13 722	2 420	11 302	. . .	536	3 173	3 007	1 273	1 734	. . .	166	-66
1946	9 311	5 902	5 294	1 822	3 472	. . .	608	3 409	3 236	1 347	1 889	. . .	173	-47
1947	7 483	3 808	3 268	1 436	1 832	. . .	540	3 675	3 481	1 445	2 036	. . .	194	-5
1948	7 894	4 007	3 437	1 428	2 009	. . .	570	3 887	3 657	1 504	2 153	. . .	230	7
1972 SIC															
1948	7 894	4 007	3 437	1 428	2 009	. . .	570	3 887	3 657	1 504	2 153	. . .	230	7
1949	8 516	4 462	3 857	1 448	2 409	. . .	605	4 054	3 815	1 581	2 234	. . .	239	-15
1950	8 802	4 603	4 016	1 468	2 548	. . .	587	4 199	3 947	1 636	2 311	. . .	252	-4
1951	10 358	6 131	5 519	1 817	3 702	. . .	612	4 227	3 967	1 684	2 283	. . .	260	-55
1952	11 102	6 737	6 081	1 910	4 171	. . .	656	4 365	4 067	1 762	2 305	. . .	298	-68
1953	11 123	6 611	5 976	1 823	4 153	. . .	635	4 512	4 209	1 851	2 358	. . .	303	-78
1954	11 114	6 394	5 759	1 702	4 057	. . .	635	4 720	4 415	1 946	2 469	. . .	305	-127
1955	11 182	6 234	5 601	1 711	3 890	. . .	633	4 948	4 637	2 076	2 561	. . .	311	-138
1956	11 414	6 202	5 563	1 738	3 825	. . .	639	5 212	4 900	2 199	2 701	. . .	312	-142
1957	11 709	6 277	5 618	1 734	3 884	. . .	659	5 432	5 117	2 310	2 807	. . .	315	-133
1958	11 756	6 044	5 373	1 691	3 682	. . .	671	5 712	5 375	2 430	2 945	. . .	337	-128
1959	11 940	6 030	5 349	1 721	3 628	. . .	681	5 910	5 516	2 559	2 957	. . .	394	-134
1960	12 275	6 090	5 390	1 770	3 620	. . .	700	6 185	5 777	2 732	3 045	. . .	408	-143
1961	12 632	6 200	5 481	1 772	3 709	. . .	719	6 432	6 022	2 863	3 159	. . .	410	-125
1962	12 992	6 349	5 618	1 833	3 785	. . .	731	6 643	6 228	3 012	3 216	. . .	415	-91
1963	13 247	6 302	5 568	1 852	3 716	. . .	734	6 945	6 521	3 214	3 307	. . .	424	-72
1964	13 683	6 382	5 641	1 838	3 803	. . .	741	7 301	6 861	3 431	3 430	. . .	440	-63
1965	14 115	6 387	5 625	1 856	3 769	. . .	762	7 728	7 276	3 705	3 571	. . .	452	-21
1966	15 322	7 057	6 222	1 978	4 244	. . .	835	8 265	7 800	4 049	3 751	. . .	465	-15
1967	16 169	7 497	6 623	2 100	4 523	. . .	874	8 672	8 199	4 321	3 878	. . .	473	-15
1968	16 670	7 551	6 669	2 112	4 557	. . .	882	9 119	8 625	4 582	4 043	. . .	494	-16
1969	16 995	7 492	6 599	2 083	4 516	. . .	893	9 503	8 991	4 828	4 163	. . .	512	-22
1970	17 068	7 129	6 217	2 042	4 175	. . .	912	9 939	9 404	5 060	4 344	. . .	535	-20
1971	17 044	6 717	5 807	2 002	3 805	. . .	910	10 327	9 778	5 298	4 480	. . .	549	-19
1972	17 036	6 308	5 427	2 017	3 410	. . .	881	10 728	10 164	5 467	4 697	. . .	564	-21
1973	17 287	6 174	5 293	2 001	3 292	. . .	881	11 113	10 524	5 641	4 883	. . .	589	-24
1974	17 647	6 146	5 251	2 049	3 202	. . .	895	11 501	10 879	5 858	5 021	. . .	622	-21
1975	18 000	6 060	5 183	2 075	3 108	. . .	877	11 940	11 280	6 052	5 228	. . .	660	-25
1976	17 997	5 934	5 080	2 085	2 995	. . .	854	12 063	11 400	6 124	5 276	. . .	663	-25
1977	18 169	5 871	5 027	2 090	2 937	. . .	844	12 298	11 638	6 251	5 387	. . .	660	-23
1978	18 492	5 881	5 031	2 117	2 914	. . .	850	12 611	11 922	6 292	5 630	. . .	689	-28
1979	18 902	5 881	5 016	2 126	2 890	. . .	865	13 021	12 289	6 361	5 928	. . .	732	-22
1980	19 273	6 010	5 140	2 221	2 919	. . .	870	13 263	12 506	6 481	6 025	. . .	757	-24
1981	19 148	6 006	5 133	2 131	3 002	. . .	873	13 142	12 389	6 466	5 923	. . .	753	-62
1982	19 149	6 084	5 207	2 113	3 094	. . .	877	13 065	12 307	6 421	5 886	. . .	758	-64
1983	19 172	6 095	5 246	2 117	3 129	. . .	849	13 077	12 315	6 478	5 837	. . .	762	-70
1984	19 428	6 196	5 316	2 143	3 173	. . .	880	13 232	12 459	6 581	5 878	. . .	773	-73
1985	19 795	6 311	5 401	2 180	3 221	. . .	910	13 484	12 692	6 759	5 933	. . .	792	-72
1986	20 170	6 384	5 427	2 164	3 263	. . .	957	13 786	12 981	6 940	6 041	. . .	805	-67
1987	20 550	6 475	5 493	2 190	3 303	. . .	982	14 075	13 258	6 992	6 266	. . .	817	-66
1987 SIC															
1987	20 550	6 475	5 493	2 190	3 303	. . .	982	14 075	13 258	6 992	6 266	. . .	817	-66
1988	20 906	6 470	5 465	2 192	3 273	. . .	1 005	14 436	13 608	7 257	6 351	. . .	828	-75
1989	21 284	6 483	5 471	2 207	3 264	. . .	1 012	14 801	13 955	7 458	6 497	. . .	846	-83
1990	21 813	6 532	5 520	2 315	3 205	. . .	1 012	15 281	14 403	7 670	6 733	. . .	878	-82
1991	21 844	6 349	5 356	2 211	3 145	. . .	993	15 495	14 605	7 787	6 818	. . .	890	-82
1992	21 895	6 177	5 211	2 231	2 980	. . .	966	15 718	14 863	7 887	6 976	. . .	855	-78
1993	21 924	5 929	4 976	2 176	2 800	. . .	953	15 995	15 126	8 070	7 056	. . .	869	-426
1994	22 005	5 719	4 749	2 101	2 648	. . .	970	16 286	15 380	8 227	7 153	. . .	906	-479
1995	22 077	5 556	4 571	2 027	2 544	. . .	985	16 521	15 593	8 392	7 201	. . .	928	-477
1996	22 069	5 386	4 398	1 952	2 446	. . .	988	16 683	15 754	8 526	7 228	. . .	929	-440
1997	22 090	5 266	4 276	1 900	2 376	. . .	990	16 824	15 890	8 740	7 150	. . .	934	-472
1998	22 322	5 191	4 200	1 878	2 322	. . .	991	17 131	16 191	8 932	7 259	. . .	940	-468
1999	22 611	5 136	4 146	1 855	2 291	. . .	990	17 475	16 530	9 152	7 378	. . .	945	-514
2000	23 094	5 235	4 260	1 976	2 284	. . .	975	17 859	16 904	9 389	7 515	. . .	955	-463

[1]Excluding work relief 1930–1943.
. . . = Not available.

NOTES AND DEFINITIONS, CHAPTER 10

General Note on Monthly Employment Data

This chapter presents data from two different data sets that measure employment monthly. Both are compiled and published by the Bureau of Labor Statistics (BLS), but each set has different characteristics. Users should be aware of these dissimilarities and the consequent differences in the appropriate uses and interpretations of data from the two systems.

One set of monthly employment estimates comes from the Current Population Survey (CPS), a large sample survey of approximately 60,000 U.S. households. The numbers in the sample are expanded to match the latest estimates of the total U.S. population. These are the most comprehensive estimates in their scope—that is, in the universe that they are designed to measure. These estimates represent all civilian workers, including the following groups that are excluded by definition from the other set of estimates: all farm workers; household workers (domestic servants); nonagricultural, nonincorporated self-employed workers; and nonagricultural unpaid family workers.

However, official CPS data are characterized by periodic discontinuities, which occur when new benchmarks for Census measures of the total population are introduced. These updates take place in a single month—usually January—and the official data for previous months are typically <u>not</u> modified to provide a smooth transition. Therefore, shorter-term comparisons (for a year or two or for a business cycle phase) will be misleading if such a discontinuity is included in the period. A recent example will illustrate. Beginning with January 2010, the estimates for civilian noninstitutional population, civilian labor force, and employment were all adjusted downward by about 250,000 persons. The reported seasonally adjusted change in employment from December 2009 to January 2010 was an increase of 541,000. If there had been no population control adjustment, the increase in employment would have been 784,000. Such discontinuities occur throughout the history of the series.

For users who would like to examine monthly CPS data in which these discontinuities have been smoothed, BLS now provides unofficial smoothed estimates of total labor force and total employment from January 1990 through December 2012 on its Web site, <http://www.bls.gov>. These two series are shown in Table 10-6.

The CPS is a count of persons employed, rather than a count of jobs. A person is counted as employed in this data set only once, no matter how many jobs he or she may hold. The CPS count is limited to persons 16 years of age and over.

The second set of employment estimates—the payroll survey—comes from a very large sample survey of about 143,000 business and government employers at approximately 557,000 worksites, the Current Employment Statistics (CES) survey. It is benchmarked annually to a survey of all employers. Benchmark data are introduced with a smooth adjustment back to the previous benchmark, thus preserving the continuity of the series and making it more appropriate for measurement of employment change over a year or two, a business cycle, or other short- to medium-length periods. This sample is much larger than the CPS sample, including about one-third of all nonfarm payroll employees, and consequently the threshold of statistical significance for changes is lower. The minimum size of the over-the-month change required to be statistically significant is about 90,000 jobs in the payroll survey, versus about 400,000 persons in the household survey.

Over recent years, benchmark revisions to payroll survey employment have ranged in magnitude from an upward revision of 0.6 percent, in 2006, to the March 2009 benchmark, which reduced the seasonally adjusted level of payroll employment in that month by 902,000 persons, or 0.7 percent. The most recent revision increased the level of employment in March 2013 by 347,000, or 0.3 percent. In absolute terms (that is, disregarding the sign), revisions have ranged from 0.1 to 0.7 percentage points over the latest 12 years and averaged 0.3 percentage points. Within that range, relatively large upward revisions have been seen for strong economies, and relatively large downward revisions for weak ones.

The scope of the CES survey is smaller than that of the CPS survey, as it is limited to wage and salary workers on nonfarm payrolls. There is also a significant definitional difference, because the CES survey is a count of jobs. Thus, a person with more than one nonfarm wage or salary job is counted as employed in each job. In addition, workers are not classified by age; as a result, there may be some workers younger than 16 years old in the job count.

Persons with a job but not at work (absent due to bad weather, work stoppages, personal reasons, and the like) are included in the household survey. However, they are excluded from the payroll survey if on leave without pay for the entire payroll period.

In addition to the differences in definitions and scope between the two series, there are also differences in sample design, collection methodology, and the sampling variability inherent in the surveys.

The payroll survey provides the most reliable and detailed information on employment by industry (for example, the data shown in Table 15-1). In addition, it provides data on weekly hours per job and hourly and weekly earnings per job.

The CPS employment estimates provide information not collected in the CES on employment by demographic characteristics, such as age, race, and Hispanic ethnicity; by education levels; and by occupation. A few of these tabulations are shown in *Business Statistics*. Many more breakdowns, in richer detail, can be found in the *Handbook of U.S. Labor Statistics*, also published by Bernan Press.

The differences between the two employment measurement systems are discussed in an article on the BLS Web site, "Employment from the BLS household and payroll surveys: summary of recent trends," which is updated monthly along with the release of the monthly data, and can be found under "Publications" on the CPS homepage at http://www.bls.gov. This article also includes references to further relevant studies.

Additional annual employment data

In addition to the CPS and CES monthly and annual data series, a third set of historical, annual-only estimates of employment is presented at the end of this chapter. These estimates of "full-time and part-time employees" by industry are compiled by the U.S. Department of Commerce, Bureau of Economic Analysis, as part of the National Income and Product Accounts (NIPAs). These estimates provide the most comprehensive and consistent employment estimates for the years before 1948.

Further detail on the historical and other characteristics of all of these employment series is presented below in the notes associated with specific data tables.

Tables 10-1 through 10-5

Labor Force, Employment, and Unemployment

SOURCE: U.S. DEPARTMENT OF LABOR, BUREAU OF LABOR STATISTICS (BLS)

Labor force, employment, and unemployment data are derived from the Current Population Survey (CPS), a sample survey of households conducted each month by the Census Bureau for the Bureau of Labor Statistics (BLS). The data pertain to the U.S. civilian noninstitutional population age 16 years and over.

Due to changes in questionnaire design and survey methodology, data for 1994 and subsequent years are not fully comparable with data for 1993 and earlier years. Additionally, discontinuities in the reported number of persons in the population, and consequently in the estimated numbers of employed and unemployed persons and the number of persons in the labor force, are introduced whenever periodic updates are made to U.S. population estimates.

For example, population controls based on Census 2000 were introduced beginning with the data for January 2000. These data are therefore not comparable with data for December 1999 and earlier. Data for 1990 through 1999 incorporate 1990 census–based population controls and are not comparable with the preceding years. An additional large population adjustment was introduced in January 2004, making the data from that time

forward not comparable with data for December 2003 and earlier; further adjustments have been made in each subsequent January and other discontinuities have been introduced in various earlier years, usually with January data. See "Notes on the Data," below, for information on adjustments in other years, including the incorporation of the 2010 Census count beginning in January 2012.

For the most part, these population adjustments distort comparisons involving the <u>numbers of persons</u> in the population, labor force, and employment. They generally have negligible effects on the <u>percentages</u> that comprise the most important features of the CPS: the unemployment rates, the labor force participation rates, and the employment-population ratios.

BLS now makes available unofficial smoothed data for the total number of persons in the civilian labor force and the number of persons employed for 1990 through 2012, which introduce the population adjustments gradually within the period shown. These data are shown in Table 10-6.

Beginning with the data for January 2000, data classified by industry and occupation use the North American Industry Classification System (NAICS) and the 2000 Standard Occupational Classification System. This creates breaks in the time series between December 1999 and January 2000 for occupational and industry data at all levels of aggregation. Since the recent history is so short, most CPS industry and occupation data have been dropped from *Business Statistics* in favor of other important and economically meaningful data for which a longer consistent history can be supplied. However, detailed employment data by occupation and industry can be found in Bernan Press's *Handbook of U.S. Labor Statistics*.

Pre-1948 data

The Census Bureau began the survey of households that provides labor force data in 1942, and the Census of Population supplied data for 1940. For the years before that, annual data for labor force, employment, and unemployment are retrospective estimates. The 1929–1947 estimates were made by BLS.

From 1929 to 1947, the data collected pertained to persons 14 years of age and over. From 1947 to the present the survey pertains to persons 16 years of age and over. Table 10-1C shows summary data for both age definitions in the overlap year, 1947. In that year, the unemployment rates are the same (3.9 percent) for both age definitions. However, the labor force participation rate and the employment/population ratio are higher when the 14- and 15-year-olds are excluded. Naturally, the raw numbers for population, labor force, and employment are smaller when the 14- and 15-year-olds are excluded.

The 1940 Census and the BLS data for 1931 through 1942 did not treat government work relief employment as employment; persons engaged in such work were counted as unemployed. In the labor force survey used today, anyone who worked for pay or profit is counted as employed (see the definitions below). Therefore, today's survey would count work relief as employment and not unemployment, and the BLS figures for the period before 1942 are not consistent with today's unemployment rates. Michael Darby calculated an alternative unemployment rate in which such workers are counted as employed, and this rate is shown in parentheses in Table 10-1C. Work relief employment is included in the BEA total employment figures in Table 10-21.

Race and ethnic origin

Data for two broad racial categories were made available beginning in 1954: *White* and *Black and other.* The latter included Asians and all other "nonwhite" races, and was discontinued after 2002. Data for *Blacks* only are available beginning with 1972; this category is now called *Black or African American.* Data for *Asians* are shown beginning with 2000. Persons in the remaining race categories—American Indian or Alaska Native, Native Hawaiian or Other Pacific Islanders, and persons who selected more than one race category when that became possible, beginning in 2003 (see below)—are included in the estimates of total employment and unemployment, but are not shown separately because their numbers are too small to yield quality estimates.

Hispanic or Latino ethnicity, previously labeled *Hispanic origin*, is not a racial category and is established in a survey question separate from the question about race. Persons of Hispanic or Latino ethnicity may be of any race.

In January 2003, changes that affected classification by race and Hispanic ethnicity were introduced. These changes caused discontinuities in race and ethnic group data between December 2002 and January 2003.

Individuals in the sample are now asked whether they are of Hispanic ethnicity <u>before</u> being asked about their race. Prior to 2003, individuals were asked their ethnic origin <u>after</u> they were asked about their race. Furthermore, respondents are now asked directly if they are Spanish, Hispanic, or Latino. Previously, they were identified based on their or their ancestors' country of origin.

Individuals in the sample are now allowed to choose more than one race category. Before 2003, they were required to select a single primary race. This change had no impact on the size of the overall civilian noninstitutional population and labor force. It did reduce the population and labor force levels of Whites and Blacks beginning in January 2003, as individuals who reported more than one race are now excluded from those groups.

BLS has estimated, based on a special survey, that these changes reduced the population and labor force levels for Whites by

about 950,000 and 730,000 persons, respectively, and for Blacks by about 320,000 and 240,000 persons, respectively, while having little or no impact on either of their unemployment rates. The changes did not affect the size of the Hispanic population or labor force, but they did cause an increase of about half a percentage point in the Hispanic unemployment rate.

Definitions

The employment status of the civilian population is surveyed each month with respect to a specific week in mid-month—not for the entire month. This is known as the "reference week." For a precise definition and explanation of the reference week, see Notes on the Data, which follows these definitions.

The *civilian noninstitutional population* comprises all civilians 16 years of age and over who are not inmates of penal or mental institutions, sanitariums, or homes for the aged, infirm, or needy.

Civilian employment includes those civilians who (1) worked for pay or profit at any time during the Sunday-through-Saturday week that includes the 12th day of the month (the reference week), or who worked for 15 hours or more as an unpaid worker in a family-operated enterprise; or (2) were temporarily absent from regular jobs because of vacation, illness, industrial dispute, bad weather, or similar reasons. Each employed person is counted only once; those who hold more than one job are counted as being in the job at which they worked the greatest number of hours during the reference week.

Unemployed persons are all civilians who were not employed (according to the above definition) during the reference week, but who were available for work—except for temporary illness—and who had made specific efforts to find employment sometime during the previous four weeks. Persons who did not look for work because they were on layoff are also counted as unemployed.

The *civilian labor force* comprises all civilians classified as employed or unemployed.

Civilians 16 years of age and over in the noninstitutional population who are not classified as employed or unemployed are defined as *not in the labor force*. This group includes those engaged in own-home housework; in school; unable to work because of longterm illness, retirement, or age; seasonal workers for whom the reference week fell in an "off" season (if not qualifying as unemployed by looking for a job); persons who became discouraged and gave up the search for work; and the voluntarily idle. Also included are those doing only incidental work (less than 15 hours) in a family-operated business during the reference week.

The civilian *labor force participation rate* represents the percentage of the civilian noninstitutional population (age 16 years and over) that is in the civilian labor force.

The *employment-population ratio* represents the percentage of the civilian noninstitutional population (age 16 years and over) that is employed. This is traditionally called a "ratio," although it is also traditionally expressed as a percent and therefore would be more appropriately called a "rate," as is the case with the labor force participation rate.

Employment is shown by *class of worker*, including a breakdown of total employment into *agricultural* and *nonagricultural* industries. Employment in *nonagricultural industries* includes *wage and salary workers*, the *self-employed*, and *unpaid family workers*.

Wage and salary workers receive wages, salaries, commissions, tips, and/or pay-in-kind. This category includes owners of self-owned incorporated businesses.

Self-employed workers are those who work for profit or for fees in their own business, profession, trade, or farm. This category includes only the unincorporated; a person whose business is incorporated is considered to be a wage and salary worker since he or she is a paid employee of a corporation, even if he or she is the corporation's president and sole employee. These categories are now labeled "Self-employed workers, unincorporated" to clarify this definition.

Wage and salary employment comprises *government* and *private industry* wage and salary workers. Domestic workers and other employees of *private households*, who are not included in the payroll employment series, are shown separately from *all other private industries*. The series for *government* and *other private industries* wage and salary workers are the closest in scope to similar categories in the payroll employment series.

Multiple jobholders are employed persons who, during the reference week, either had two or more jobs as a wage and salary worker, were self-employed and also held a wage and salary job, or worked as an unpaid family worker and also held a wage and salary job. This category does not include self-employed persons with multiple businesses or persons with multiple jobs as unpaid family workers. For purposes of industry and occupational classification, multiple jobholders are counted as being in the job at which they worked the greatest number of hours during the reference week.

Employed and at work part time does not include employed persons who were absent from their jobs during the entire reference week for reasons such as vacation, illness, or industrial dispute.

At work part time for economic reasons ("involuntary" part time) refers to individuals who worked 1 to 34 hours during the reference week because of slack work, unfavorable business conditions, an inability to find full-time work, or seasonal declines in demand. To be included in this category, workers must also indicate that they want and are available for full-time work.

At work part time for noneconomic reasons ("voluntary" part time) refers to persons who usually work part time and were at work for 1 to 34 hours during the reference week for reasons such as illness, other medical limitations, family obligations, education, retirement, Social Security limits on earnings, or working in an industry where the workweek is less than 35 hours. It also includes respondents who gave an economic reason but were not available for, or did not want, full-time work. At work part time for noneconomic reasons excludes persons who usually work full time, but who worked only 1 to 34 hours during the reference week for reasons such as holidays, illnesses, and bad weather.

The *long-term unemployed* are persons currently unemployed (searching or on layoff) who have been unemployed for 15 consecutive weeks or longer. If a person ceases to look for work for two weeks or more, or becomes temporarily employed, the continuity of longterm unemployment is broken. If he or she starts searching for work or is laid off again, the monthly CPS will record the length of his or her unemployment from the time the search recommenced or since the latest layoff.

The civilian *unemployment rate* is the number of unemployed as a percentage of the civilian labor force. The unemployment rates for groups within the civilian population (such as males age 20 years and over) are the number of unemployed in a group as a percent of that group's labor force.

Unemployment rates by reason provides a breakdown of the total unemployment rate. Each unemployed person is classified into one of four groups.

Job losers and persons who completed temporary jobs includes persons on temporary layoff, permanent job losers, and persons who completed temporary jobs and began looking for work after those jobs ended. These three categories are shown separately without seasonal adjustment in the BLS's "Employment Situation" news release and on its Web site. They are combined, under the title shown here, for the purpose of seasonal adjustment. This is the category of unemployment that responds most strongly to the business cycle.

Job leavers terminated their employment voluntarily and immediately began looking for work.

Reentrants are persons who previously worked, but were out of the labor force prior to beginning their current job search.

New entrants are persons searching for a first job who have never worked.

Each of these categories is expressed as a proportion of the entire civilian labor force, so that the sum of the four rates equals the unemployment rate for all civilian workers, except for possible discrepancies due to rounding or separate seasonal adjustment.

Median and average weeks unemployed are summary measures of the length of time that persons classified as unemployed have been looking for work. For persons on layoff, the duration represents the number of full weeks of the layoff. The *average (mean)* number of weeks is computed by aggregating all the weeks of unemployment experienced by all unemployed persons during their current spell of unemployment and dividing by the number of unemployed. The average can be distorted by what is called "top coding" because the length of unemployment is reported in ranges, including a top range of "over __ weeks", rather than exact numbers. See the paragraph below for further explanation. The *median* number of weeks unemployed is the number of weeks of unemployment experienced by the person at the midpoint of the distribution of all unemployed persons, as ranked by duration of unemployment, and is not distorted by top coding. Like medians in other economic time series, it is likely to be a better measure of typical experience.

Beginning with the data for January 2011 and phasing in through April 2011, respondents could report unemployment durations of up to 5 years; before that time, the "top code" was up to 2 years. This change causes a sharp increase in January 2011 and continued rises through April for *average weeks unemployed*. It did not affect total unemployment, total long-term unemployment, or the *median weeks unemployed*. Comparisons of the average weeks statistics on the old and new basis are available on the BLS Web site.

Alternative measures of labor underutilization are calculated by BLS and published in the monthly Employment Situation release. They measure alternative concepts of unused working capacity, and are numbered "U-1" through "U-6" in order of increasing breadth of the definition of underutilization.

"U-1" is persons unemployed 15 weeks or longer, as a percent of the civilian labor force. It is not shown in *Business Statistics*.

"U-2" is job losers and persons who completed temporary jobs, as a percent of the civilian labor force; it is shown in *Business Statistics* in the fifth column of Table 10-5.

"U-3" is the official rate, described above and shown in the final columns of Tables 10-1, the fifth column of Table 10-4, and the fourth column of Table 10-5.

"U-4" through "U-6" are shown in the last three columns of Table 10-5. They are based on additional labor force status questions, now included in the CPS survey, that were introduced beginning in 1994. U-4 and U-5 are increasingly broader rates of unemployment, while U-6 can be described as an "unemployment and underemployment rate."

"U-4" adds discouraged workers to unemployment and the labor force. Discouraged workers are persons not in the officially defined labor force who have given a job-market-related reason for not looking currently for a job—for example, they have not looked for a job because they believed that no jobs were available.

"U-5" adds both discouraged workers and all other "marginally attached" workers to unemployment and the labor force. "Marginally attached" workers are all persons who currently are neither working nor looking for work but indicate that they want and are available for a job and have looked for work some time in the recent past.

"U-6" adds persons employed part time for economic reasons, as shown in Table 10-3, to the number of persons counted as unemployed in "U-5", with the same labor force definition as in "U-5." This statistic, which measures a combination of unemployment and underemployment, is often cited in media reports on the employment situation.

For more information, see "BLS introduced new range of alternative unemployment measures" in the October 1995 issue of the *Monthly Labor Review.*

Notes on the data

The CPS data are collected by trained interviewers from about 60,000 sample households selected to represent the U.S. civilian noninstitutional population. The sample size was about 60,000 households from mid-1989 to mid-1995, but was reduced for budgetary reasons in two stages to about 50,000 households, beginning in January 1996. This sample size was maintained from 1996 through 2000. The sample size was increased back to 60,000 households, beginning with the data for July 2001, as part of a plan to meet the requirements of the State Children's Health Insurance Program legislation. The CPS provides data for other data series in addition to the BLS employment status data, such as household income and poverty (see Chapter 3) and health insurance.

The employment status data are based on the activity or status reported for the calendar week, Sunday through Saturday, that includes the 12th day of the month (the reference week). This specification is chosen so as to avoid weeks that contain major holidays. Households are interviewed in the week following the reference week. Sample households are phased in and out of the sample on a rotating basis. Consequently, three-fourths of the sample is the same for any two consecutive months. One-half of the sample is the same as the sample in the same month a year earlier.

Data relating to 1994 and subsequent years are not strictly comparable with data for 1993 and earlier years because of the major 1994 redesign of the survey questionnaire and collection methodology. The redesign included new and revised questions for the classification of individuals as employed or unemployed, the collection of new data on multiple jobholding, a change in the definition of discouraged workers, and the implementation of a more completely automated data collection.

The 1994 redesign of the CPS was the most extensive since 1967. However, there are many other significant periods of year-to-year noncomparability in the labor force data. These typically result from the introduction of new decennial census data into the CPS estimation procedures, expansions of the sample, or other improvements made to increase the reliability of the estimates. Each change introduces a new discontinuity, usually between December of the previous year and January of the newly altered year. The discontinuities are usually minor or negligible with respect to figures expressed as nationwide percentages (such as the unemployment rate or the labor force participation rate), but can be significant with respect to levels (such as labor force and employment in thousands of persons). A list of the dates of the major discontinuities follows, with BLS estimates of their quantitative impact on the national totals. (There are likely to be larger impacts on population subgroups.) The discontinuities occur in January unless otherwise indicated. Note that some of the changes caused adjustments that were carried back to an earlier year.

- 1953: 1950 census data introduced. Labor force and employment were raised by about 350,000.

- 1960: Alaska and Hawaii included. The labor force was increased by about 300,000, mainly in nonagricultural employment.

- 1962: 1960 census data introduced. Labor force and employment were reduced by about 200,000.

- 1972: 1970 census data introduced. Labor force and employment were raised by about 300,000.

- March 1973: Further 1970 census data were introduced, reducing White labor force and employment by about 150,000 and raising Black and other labor force and employment by approximately 210,000.

- July 1975: Adjustment for Vietnamese refugee inflow, raising total and Black and other population by 76,000.

- 1978: Sample expansion and revised estimation procedures increased labor force and employment by about 250,000.

- 1982: Change in estimation procedures introduced. To avoid major breaks, many series were reestimated back to 1970. This did not smooth the breaks occurring between 1972 and 1979.

- 1986, with revisions carried back to 1980: Adjustment for better estimates of immigration, raising labor force by nearly 400,000 and employment by 350,000, mainly among Hispanics.

- 1994: 1990 census data introduced and carried back to 1990, when employment was increased by about 880,000 and the unemployment rate was raised by about 0.1 percentage point.

- 1997: New estimates of immigration and emigration, raising labor force and employment by about 300,000, again mainly among Hispanics.

- 1998: New population estimates and estimation procedures, reducing labor force and employment by around 250,000.

- 1999: New information on immigration, raising labor force and employment by around 60,000, but lowering Hispanic employment by about 200,000.

- 2000: Census 2000 data introduced, using the 2002 NAICS and the 2000 Standard Occupational Classification System. The labor force was increased by about 1.6 million in January 2000, growing to around 2.5 million by December 2002.

- 2003: Further population estimates introduced (based on an annual population update and therefore not carried back to 2000), raising the labor force by 614,000.

- 2004: Population controls updated to reflect revised migration estimates, reducing labor force and employment by around 400,000, mostly among Hispanics.

- 2005: Updated migration and vital statistics data decreased labor force and employment by around 45,000.

- 2006: Updated migration and vital statistics data decreased labor force and employment by about 125,000.

- 2007: Updated migration and vital statistics data increased labor force and employment by about 150,000.

- 2008: Updated migration and vital statistics data decreased labor force by 637,000 and employment by 598,000.

- 2009: Updated migration adjustments, new vital statistics data, and methodological changes decreased labor force by 449,000 and employment by 407,000.

- 2010: Updated information on migration, vital statistics, and other data and methodological changes decreased labor force by 249,000 and employment by 243,000.

- 2011: Updated estimates reduced the labor force by 504,000, employment by 472,000, and unemployment by 32,000; raised the number of persons not in the labor force by 157,000; and had no effect on the unemployment rate.

- 2012: Reflecting the 2010 Census, the civilian noninstitutional population was increased by 1,510,000; the civilian labor force by 258,000; employment by 216,000; and unemployment by 42,000. BLS states, "Although the total unemployment rate was unaffected, the labor force participation rate and the employment-population ratio were each reduced by 0.3 percentage point. This was because the population increase was primarily among persons 55 and older and, to a lesser degree, persons 16 to 24 years of age. Both these age groups have lower levels of labor force participation than the general population."

- 2013: Updated population estimates increased the population by 138,000, the labor force by 136,000, and employment by 127,000. The rates and ratios were not affected.

- 2014: the smallest population control adjustment on record increased labor force by 24,000 and employment by 22,000, with no effect on rates or ratios.

For further information on these changes, see "Publications and Other Documentation" at http://www.bls.gov/cps.

The monthly labor force, employment, and unemployment data are seasonally adjusted by the X-12-ARIMA method. All seasonally adjusted civilian labor force and unemployment rate statistics, as well as major employment and unemployment estimates, are computed by aggregating independently adjusted series. For example, the seasonally adjusted level of total unemployment is the sum of the seasonally adjusted levels of unemployment for the four age/sex groups (men and women age 16 to 19 years, and men and women age 20 years and over). Seasonally adjusted employment is the sum of the seasonally adjusted levels of employment for the same four groups. The seasonally adjusted civilian labor force is the sum of all eight components. Finally, the seasonally adjusted civilian worker unemployment rate is calculated by taking total seasonally adjusted unemployment as a percent of the total seasonally adjusted civilian labor force.

To minimize subsequent revisions, BLS uses a concurrent technique that estimates factors for the latest month using the most recent data. Then, seasonal adjustment factors are fully revised at the end of each year to reflect recent experience. The revisions also affect the preceding four years. An article describing the seasonal adjustment methodology for the household survey data is available at http://www.bls.gov/cps/cpsrs2010.pdf.

Breakdowns other than the basic age/sex classification described above—such as the employment data by class of worker in Table 10-3—will not necessarily add to totals because of independent seasonal adjustment.

Data availability

Data for each month are usually released on the first Friday of the following month in the "Employment Situation" press release, which also includes data from the establishment survey (Tables 10-8 through 10-18 and Chapter 15). (The release date actually is determined by the timing of the survey week.) The press release and data are available on the BLS Web site at <http://www.bls.gov>. The *Monthly Labor Review*, also available online at the BLS Web site, features frequent articles analyzing developments in the labor force, employment, and unemployment.

Monthly and annual data on the current basis are available beginning with 1948. Historical unadjusted data are published in *Labor Force Statistics Derived from the Current Population Survey* (BLS Bulletin 2307). Historical seasonally adjusted data are available from BLS upon request. Complete historical data are available on the BLS Web site at <http://www.bls.gov/cps>.

Seasonal adjustment factors are revised each year for the five previous years, with the release of December data in early January. New population controls are introduced with the release of January data in early February.

BLS annual data for 1940 through 1947 are published on their Web site at <http://www.bls.gov>. The data for 1929 through 1939 were published in *Employment and Earnings,* May 1972, and in U.S. Commerce Department, Bureau of Economic Analysis, *Long-Term Economic Growth, 1860–1970,* June 1973, p. 163. The Lebergott estimates are also found in the latter volume.

The Darby alternative unemployment rate is found in Michael Darby, "Three-and-a-Half Million U.S. Employees Have Been Mislaid," *Journal of Political Economy,* February 1976, v. 84, no. 1. It is also displayed and discussed in Robert A. Margo, "Employment and Unemployment in the 1930s," *Journal of Economic Perspectives,* v. 7, no. 2, Spring 1993.

References

Comprehensive descriptive material can be found at <http://www.bls.gov/cps> under the "Publications and Other Documentation" section. Historical background on the CPS, as well as a description of the 1994 redesign, can be found in three articles from the September 1993 edition of *Monthly Labor Review*: "Why Is It Necessary to Change?"; "Redesigning the Questionnaire"; and "Evaluating Changes in the Estimates." The redesign is also described in the February 1994 issue of *Employment and Earnings.* See also Chapter 1, "Labor Force Data Derived from the Current Population Survey," *BLS Handbook of Methods*, Bulletin 2490 (April 1997).

Table 10-6

Labor Force and Employment Estimates Smoothed for Population Adjustments

SOURCE: U.S. DEPARTMENT OF LABOR, BUREAU OF LABOR STATISTICS

This table presents seasonally adjusted monthly estimates of total civilian labor force and total civilian employment in which discontinuities caused by the introduction of new population controls in the official series—as described above—have been smoothed (see box above). The method of smoothing is described in Marisa L. Di Natale, "Creating Comparability in CPS Employment Series," on the BLS Web site at <http://www.bls.gov/cps/cpscomp.pdf>. BLS notes that these series do not match the official estimates in BLS publications, which are also the data shown in all other tables in this volume.

Because the January 2014 population control adjustment was negligible in size (see above), no smoothing of the 2013 data was required. Hence, Table 10-6 was calculated only through the end of 2012, which can be considered continuous with the official data for 2013 and 2014.

Table 10-7

Insured Unemployment

SOURCE: U.S. DEPARTMENT OF LABOR, EMPLOYMENT AND TRAINING ADMINISTRATION

Definitions

State programs of unemployment insurance cover operations of regular programs under state unemployment insurance laws. In 1976, the law was amended to extend coverage to include virtually all state and local government employees, as well as many agricultural and domestic workers. (This took effect on January 1, 1978.) Benefits under state programs are financed by taxes levied by the states on employers.

Federal programs are those directly financed by the federal government. They include unemployment benefits for *federal employees* (Unemployment Compensation for Federal Employees, or UCFE), *newly discharged veterans* (Unemployment Compensation for Ex-Service Members, or UCX), *railroad retirement,* and *extended benefits,* which are sometimes enacted by Congress in times of widespread or protracted unemployment.

UCX pays benefits, based on service, to veterans who were on active duty and honorably separated. In the case of both UCFE and UCX, state laws determine the benefit amounts, number of weeks benefits can be paid, and other eligibility conditions.

An *initial claim* is the first claim in a benefit year filed by a worker after losing his or her job, or the first claim filed at the beginning of a subsequent period of unemployment in the same benefit year. The initial claim establishes the starting date for any insured unemployment that may result if the claimant is unemployed for one week or longer. Transitional claims (filed by claimants as they start a new benefit year in a continuing spell of unemployment) are excluded; therefore, these data more closely represent instances of new unemployment and are widely followed as a leading indicator of job market conditions.

Insured unemployment and *persons claiming benefits* both describe the average number of persons receiving benefits in the indicated month or year.

The *insured unemployment rate* for state programs is the level of insured unemployment as a percentage of employment covered by state programs.

Monthly averages in this book are averages, calculated by the editor, of the weekly data published by the Employment and Training Administration. Annual data are averages of the monthly data.

Data availability

Data are published in weekly press releases from the Employment and Training Administration. These releases are available on their Web site at <http://www.doleta.gov> under "Labor Market Data," as are historical data, under the category "UI/ Program Statistics."

Tables 10-8, 10-9, 10-14, 15-1, and 15-2

Nonfarm Payroll Employment

SOURCE: U.S. DEPARTMENT OF LABOR, BUREAU OF LABOR STATISTICS (BLS)

These nonfarm employment data, as well as the hours and earnings data in Tables 10-9 through 10-13, 10-15 through 10-18, and 15-3 through 15-6, are compiled from payroll records. Information is reported monthly on a voluntary basis to BLS and its cooperating state agencies by a large sample of establishments, representing all industries except farming. These data, formally known as the Current Employment Statistics (CES) survey, are often referred to as the "establishment data" or the "payroll data." They are also known as the BLS-790 survey.

The survey, originally based on a stratified quota sample, has been replaced on a phased-in basis by a stratified probability sample. The new sampling procedure went into effect for wholesale trade in June 2000; for mining, construction, and manufacturing in June 2001; and for retail trade, transportation and public utilities, and finance, insurance, and real estate in June 2002. The phase-in was completed in June 2003, upon its extension to the service industries. The phase-in schedule was slightly different for the state and area series.

The sample has always been very large. Currently, it includes approximately 145,000 businesses and government agencies covering about 557,000 individual worksites, which account for about one-third of total benchmark employment of payroll workers. The sample is drawn from a sampling frame of over 8 million unemployment insurance tax accounts.

Data are classified according to the North American Industry Classification System. BLS has reconstructed historical time series to conform with NAICS, to ensure that all published series have a NAICS-based history extending back to at least January 1990. NAICS-based history extends back to January 1939 for total nonfarm and other high-level aggregates. For more detailed series, the starting date for NAICS data varies depending on the extent of the definitional changes between the old Standard Industrial Classification (SIC) and NAICS.

Definitions

An *establishment* is an economic unit, such as a factory, store, or professional office, that produces goods or services at a single location and is engaged in one type of economic activity.

Employment comprises all persons who received pay (including holiday and sick pay) for any part of the payroll period that includes the 12th day of the month. The definition of the payroll period for each reporting respondent is that used by the employer; it could be weekly, biweekly, monthly, or other. Included are all fulltime and parttime workers in nonfarm establishments, including salaried officers of corporations. Persons holding more than one job are counted in each establishment that reports them. Not covered are proprietors, the selfemployed, unpaid volunteer and family workers, farm workers, domestic workers in households, and military personnel. Employees of the Central Intelligence Agency, the Defense Intelligence Agency, the National Geospatial-Intelligence Agency, and the National Security Agency are not included.

Persons on an establishment payroll who are on paid sick leave (when pay is received directly from the employer), on paid holiday or vacation, or who work during a portion of the pay period despite being unemployed or on strike during the rest of the period, are counted as employed. Not counted as employed are persons who are laid off, on leave without pay, on strike for the entire period, or hired but not paid during the period.

Intermittent workers are counted if they performed any service during the month. BLS considers regular fulltime teachers (private and government) to be employed during the summer vacation period, regardless of whether they are specifically paid during those months.

The *government* division includes federal, state, and local activities such as legislative, executive, and judicial functions, as well as the U.S. Postal Service and all governmentowned and governmentoperated business enterprises, establishments, and institutions (arsenals, navy yards, hospitals, state-owned utilities, etc.), and government force account construction. However, as indicated earlier, members of the armed forces and employees of certain national-security-related agencies are not included.

The monthly *diffusion index of employment change*, currently based on 271 private nonfarm NAICS industries, represents the percentage of those industries in which the seasonally adjusted level of employment in that month was higher than six months earlier, plus one-half of the percentage of industries with unchanged employment. Therefore, the diffusion index reported for September represents the change from March to September. *Business Statistics* uses the September value to represent the year as a whole, since it spans the year's mid-point. Diffusion indexes measure the dispersion of economic gains and losses, with values below 50 percent associated with recessions. The current NAICS-based series begins with January 1991. For October 1976 through December 1990, an earlier series is available based on 347 SIC industries (there are more industries using the older classification system because in SIC manufacturing industries were represented in greater detail). September values from this series are used here to represent the years 1977 through 1990.

Production and nonsupervisory workers include all *production and related workers* in mining and manufacturing; *construction workers* in construction; and *nonsupervisory workers* in transportation, communication, electric, gas, and sanitary services; wholesale and retail trade; finance, insurance, and real estate; and services. These groups account for about four-fifths of the total employment on private nonagricultural payrolls. Previously, this category was called "production or nonsupervisory workers." The definitions have not changed.

Production and related workers include working supervisors and all nonsupervisory workers (including group leaders and trainees) engaged in fabricating, processing, assembling, inspecting, receiving, storing, handling, packing, warehousing, shipping, trucking, hauling, maintenance, repair, janitorial, guard services, product development, auxiliary production for plant's own use (such as a power plant), record keeping, and other services closely associated with these production operations.

Construction workers include the following employees in the construction division of the NAICS: working supervisors, qualified craft workers, mechanics, apprentices, laborers, and the like, who are engaged in new work, alterations, demolition, repair, maintenance, and other tasks, whether working at the site of construction or working in shops or yards at jobs (such as precutting and preassembling) ordinarily performed by members of the construction trades.

Nonsupervisory employees include employees (not above the working supervisory level) such as office and clerical workers, repairers, salespersons, operators, drivers, physicians, lawyers, accountants, nurses, social workers, research aides, teachers, drafters, photographers, beauticians, musicians, restaurant workers, custodial workers, attendants, line installers and repairers, laborers, janitors, guards, and other employees at similar occupational levels whose services are closely associated with those of the employees listed.

Notes on the data

Benchmark adjustments. The establishment survey data are adjusted annually to comprehensive counts of employment, called "benchmarks." Benchmark information on employment by industry is compiled by state agencies from reports of establishments covered under state unemployment insurance laws; these form an annual compilation of administrative data known as the ES-202. These tabulations cover about 97 percent of all employees on nonfarm payrolls. Benchmark data for the residual are obtained from alternate sources, primarily from Railroad Retirement Board records and the Census Bureau's *County Business Patterns.* The latest benchmark adjustment, which is incorporated into the data in this volume, increased the employment level in the benchmark month March 2013 by 347,000 jobs, which was 0.3 percent.

The estimates for the benchmark month are compared with new benchmark levels for each industry. If revisions are necessary, the monthly series of estimates between benchmark periods are adjusted by graduated amounts between the new benchmark and the preceding one ("wedged back"), and the new benchmark level for each industry is then carried forward month by month based on the sample.

More specifically, the month-to-month changes for each estimation cell are based on changes in a matched sample for that cell, plus an estimate of net business births and deaths. The matched sample for each pair of months consists of establishments that have reported data for both months (which automatically excludes establishments that have gone out of business by the second month). Since new businesses are not immediately incorporated into the sample, a model-based estimate of net business births and deaths in that estimating cell is added. The birth/death adjustment factors are re-estimated quarterly based on the Quarterly Census of Employment and Wages.

Not-seasonally-adjusted data for all months since the last benchmark date are subject to revision.

Beginning in 1959, the data include Alaska and Hawaii. This inclusion resulted in an increase of 212,000 (0.4 percent) in total nonfarm employment for the March 1959 benchmark month.

Seasonal adjustment. The seasonal movements that recur periodically—such as warm and cold weather, holidays, and vacations—are generally the largest single component of monthtomonth changes in employment. After adjusting the data to remove such seasonal variation, basic trends become more evident. BLS uses X-12-ARIMA software to produce seasonal factors and perform concurrent seasonal adjustment, using the most recent 10 years of data. New factors are developed each month adding the most current data.

For most series, a special procedure called REGARIMA (regression with autocorrelated errors) is used before calculating the seasonal factors; this adjusts for the length of the interval (which can be either four or five weeks) between the survey weeks. REGARIMA has also been used to isolate extreme weather effects that distort the measurement of seasonal patterns in the construction industry, and to identify variations in local government employment due to the presence or absence of election poll workers.

Seasonal adjustment factors are directly applied to the component levels. Seasonally adjusted totals for employment series are then obtained by aggregating the seasonally adjusted components directly, while hours and earnings series represent weighted averages of the seasonally adjusted component series. Seasonally adjusted data are not published for a small number of series characterized by small seasonal components relative to their trend and/or irregular components. However, these series are used in aggregating to broader seasonally adjusted levels.

Revisions of the seasonally adjusted data, usually for the most recent five-year period, are made once a year coincident with the benchmark revisions. This means that these revisions typically extend back farther than the benchmark revisions.

Data availability

Employment data by industry division are available beginning with 1919. Data for each month usually are released on the first Friday of the following month in a press release that also contains data from the household survey (Tables 10-1 through 10-5). (The release date actually is determined by the timing of the survey week.) The *Monthly Labor Review* frequently contains articles analyzing developments in the labor force, employment, and unemployment. The *Monthly Labor Review,* press releases, and complete historical data are available on the BLS Web site at <http://www.bls.gov>.

Benchmark revisions and revised seasonally adjusted data for recent years are made each year with the release of January data in early February. Before 2004, the benchmark revisions were not made until June; the acceleration is due to earlier availability of the benchmark UI (ES-202) data.

References

References can be found at <http://www.bls.gov/ces> under the headings "Special Notices," "Benchmark Information," and "Technical Notes." Extensive changes incorporated in June 2003 are described in "Recent Changes in the National Current Employment Statistics Survey," *Monthly Labor Review,* June 2003. The latest benchmark revision is discussed in an article available on the Website. See also Chapter 2, "Employment, Hours, and Earnings from the Establishment Survey," *BLS Handbook of Methods,* Bulletin 2490 (April 1997).

Tables 10-9 through 10-11, 10-15, 10-16, 15-3, and 15-6

Average Hours Per Week; Aggregate Employee Hours

SOURCE: U.S. DEPARTMENT OF LABOR, BUREAU OF LABOR STATISTICS (BLS)

See the notes and definitions to Tables 10-8 and related tables, above, for an overall description of the "establishment" or "payroll" survey that is the source of hours data.

Hours and earnings have been reported for production and non-supervisory workers, as defined above, since the inception of the CES. Beginning with data for March 2006, such data have also been collected for all payroll employees. With sufficient history for calculation of seasonal adjustment factors, BLS began publishing all-employee hours and earnings in February 2010, and these new data are presented in *Business Statistics* Tables 10-10 through 10-13.

Definitions

Average weekly hours represents the average hours paid per worker during the pay period that includes the 12th of the month. Included are hours paid for holidays and vacations, as well as those paid for sick leave when pay is received directly from the firm.

Average weekly hours are different from standard or scheduled hours. Factors such as unpaid absenteeism, labor turnover, part-time work, and work stoppages can cause average weekly hours to be lower than scheduled hours of work for an establishment.

An important characteristic of these data is that average weekly hours pertain to jobs, not to persons; thus, a person with half-time jobs in two different establishments is represented in this series as two jobs that have 20-hour workweeks, not as one person with a 40-hour workweek.

Overtime hours represent the portion of average weekly hours worked in excess of regular hours, for which overtime premiums were paid. Weekend and holiday hours are included only if overtime premiums were paid. Hours for which only shift differential, hazard, incentive, or other similar types of premiums were paid are excluded.

Aggregate hours provide measures of changes over time in labor input to the industry, in index-number form. The indexes are obtained by multiplying seasonally adjusted employment by seasonally adjusted average weekly hours, dividing the resulting series by their monthly averages for a base period, and multiplying the results by 100, so that the annual average for the base period equals 100. For total private, goods-producing, service-providing, and major industry divisions, the indexes are obtained by summing the seasonally adjusted aggregate weekly employee hours for the component industries, dividing by the monthly average for the base period, and multiplying by 100. For the series covering production and nonsupervisory workers, the base period is 2002; for the all-employee series, the base period is 2007.

Notes on the data

Benchmark adjustments. Independent benchmarks are not available for the hours and earnings series. However, at the time of the annual adjustment of the employment series to new benchmarks, the levels of hours and earnings may be affected by the revised employment weights (which are used in computing the industry averages for hours and earnings), as well as by the changes in seasonal adjustment factors introduced with the benchmark revision.

Method of computing industry series. "Average weekly hours" for individual industries are computed by dividing worker hours (reported by establishments classified in each industry) by the number of workers reported for the same establishments. Estimates for divisions and major industry groups are averages (weighted by employment) of the figures for component industries.

Seasonal adjustment. Hours and earnings series are seasonally adjusted by applying factors directly to the corresponding unadjusted series. Data for some industries are not seasonally adjusted because the seasonal component is small relative to the trendcycle and/or irregular components. Consequently, they cannot be separated with sufficient precision.

Special adjustments are made to average weekly hours to account for the presence or absence of religious holidays in the April survey reference period and the occasional occurrence of Labor Day in the September reference period. In addition, REGARIMA modeling is used prior to seasonal adjustment to correct for reporting and processing errors associated with the number of weekdays in a month (rather than to correct for the 4- and 5-week effect, which is less significant for hours than it is for employment). This is of particular importance for average weekly hours in the service-providing industries other than retail trade. For this reason, BLS advises that calculations of over-the-year changes (for example, the change for the current month from a year earlier) should use seasonally adjusted data, since the actual not-seasonally-adjusted monthly data may be distorted.

Data availability

See data availability for Tables 10-8 and related, above.

References

See references for Tables 10-8 and related, above.

Tables 10-9, 10-12, 10-13, 10-17, 10-18, 15-4, and 15-5

Hourly and Weekly Earnings

SOURCE: U.S. DEPARTMENT OF LABOR, BUREAU OF LABOR STATISTICS (BLS)

See the notes and definitions to Tables 10-8 and related for an overall description of the "establishment" or "payroll" survey that is the source of these earnings data.

Hours and earnings have been reported for production and non-supervisory workers, as defined above, since the inception of the CES. Beginning with data for March 2006, such data have also been collected for all payroll employees. With sufficient history for calculation of seasonal adjustment factors, BLS began publishing all-employee hours and earnings in February 2010, and these data are presented in new *Business Statistics* Tables 10-10 through 10-13.

Definitions

Earnings are the payments that workers receive during the survey period (before deductions for taxes and other items), including premium pay for overtime or late-shift work but excluding irregular bonuses and other special payments. After being previously excluded, tips were asked to be reported beginning in September 2005. This made little difference in most industries, and BLS asserts that many respondents had already been including tips. In two industries, full-service restaurants and cafeterias, there was a substantial difference, and the historical earnings data for those industries have been reconstructed to reflect the new higher level of earnings.

Notes on the data

The hours and earnings series are based on reports of gross payroll and corresponding paid hours for full and part time workers who received pay for any part of the pay period that included the 12th of the month.

Total payrolls are before deductions, such as for the employee share of old-age and unemployment insurance, group insurance, withholding taxes, bonds, and union dues. The payroll figures also include pay for overtime, holidays, vacations, and sick leave (paid directly by the employer for the period reported). Excluded from the payroll figures are fringe benefits (health and other types of insurance and contributions to retirement, paid by the employer, and the employer share of payroll taxes), bonuses (unless earned and paid regularly each pay period), other pay not earned in the pay period reported (retroactive pay), and the value of free rent, fuel, meals, or other payment-in-kind.

Average hourly earnings data reflect not only changes in basic hourly and incentive wage rates, but also such variable factors as premium pay for overtime and late shift work and changes in output of workers paid on an incentive basis. Shifts in the volume of employment between relatively high paid and low paid work also affect the general average of hourly earnings.

Averages of hourly earnings should not be confused with wage rates, which represent the rates stipulated for a given unit of work or time, while earnings refer to the actual return to the worker for a stated period of time. The earnings series do not represent total labor cost to the employer because of the inclusion of tips and the exclusion of irregular bonuses, retroactive items, the cost of employer-provided benefits, and payroll taxes paid by employers.

Average weekly earnings are not the amounts available to workers for spending, since they do not reflect deductions such as income taxes and Social Security taxes. It is also important to understand that average weekly earnings represent earnings per job, not per worker (since a worker may have more than one job) and not per family (since a family may have more than one worker). A person with two half-time jobs will be reflected as two earners with low weekly earnings rather than as one person with the total earnings from his or her two jobs.

Method of computing industry series. Average hourly earnings are obtained by dividing the reported total worker payroll by total worker hours. Estimates for both hours and hourly earnings for nonfarm divisions and major industry groups are employment-weighted averages of the figures for component industries.

Average weekly earnings are computed by multiplying average hourly earnings by average weekly hours. In addition to the factors mentioned above, which exert varying influences upon average hourly earnings, average weekly earnings are affected by changes in the length of the workweek, part time work, work stoppages, labor turnover, and absenteeism. Persistent long term uptrends in the proportion of part time workers in retail trade and many of the service industries have reduced average workweeks (as measured here), and have similarly affected the average weekly earnings series.

Benchmark adjustments. Independent benchmarks are not available for the hours and earnings series. At the time of the annual adjustment of the employment series to new benchmarks, the levels of hours and earnings may be affected by the revised employment weights (which are used in computing the industry averages for hours and earnings), as well as by the changes in seasonal adjustment factors that were also introduced with the benchmark revision.

Seasonal adjustment. Hours and earnings series are seasonally adjusted by applying factors directly to the corresponding unadjusted series; seasonally adjusted average weekly earnings are the product of seasonally adjusted hourly earnings and weekly hours.

REGARIMA modeling is used to correct for reporting and processing errors associated with variations in the number of weekdays in a month (rather than for the 4- and 5-week effect, which is less significant for earnings than for employment). This is of particular importance for average hourly earnings in wholesale trade, financial activities, professional and business services, and other services. For this reason, BLS advises that calculations of over-the-year changes, for example the change for the current month from a year earlier, should use seasonally adjusted data, since the actual not seasonally adjusted monthly data may be distorted.

Data availability

See data availability for Tables 10-8 and related, above.

References

See references for Tables 10-8 and related, above.

Table 10-19

Hours at Work, Current Population Survey

This table presents annual average measures of hours worked per week reported by workers in the Current Population Survey, in response to questions asking for the hours worked in the survey week by each worker in the household on all his or her jobs combined. These measures are not published in regular BLS reports but are available on request. *Business Statistics* obtained these numbers from BLS staff and presents them here in annual average form.

Do CPS respondents overestimate the number of hours they work? One study made that claim, but a careful re-examination of the data by Harley Frazis and Jay Stewart in the June 2014 *Monthly Labor Review* indicates that respondents slightly underreport the hours that they actually worked during the reference week. (On the other hand, the authors also note that the reference week overestimates the average for the entire month because of the absence of holidays.) (*Monthly Labor Review* is available online at www.bls.gov.) In any event, the CPS data give a more accurate picture of trends in the workweeks of typical American workers than does the establishment (CES) survey.

Table 10-20

Median Usual Weekly Earnings of Full-Time Wage and Salary Workers
SOURCE: U.S. DEPARTMENT OF LABOR, BUREAU OF LABOR STATISTICS

These data are from the Current Population Survey, which was described in the notes to Tables 10-1 through 10-6. Because they are earnings per worker, not per job, and are limited to

full-time workers, the data are not distorted by the increasing proportion of part-time workers, as the CES earnings data are.

Definitions

Full-time wage and salary workers are those workers reported as "employed" in the CPS who receive wages, salaries, commissions, tips, pay in kind, or piece rates, and usually work 35 hours or more per week at their sole or principal job. Both private-sector and public-sector employees are included. All self-employed persons are excluded (even those whose businesses are incorporated). The number of full-time wage and salary workers was 103.7 million, seasonally adjusted, in the fourth quarter of 2012; these workers made up 72 percent of total civilian employment.

Usual weekly earnings are earnings before taxes and other deductions and include any overtime pay, commissions, or tips usually received. In the case of multiple jobholders they refer to the main job. The wording of the question was changed in January 1994 to better deal with persons who found it easier to report earnings on other than a weekly basis. Such reports are then converted to the weekly equivalent. According to BLS, "the term 'usual' is as perceived by the respondent. If the respondent asks for a definition of usual, interviewers are instructed to define the term as more than half the weeks worked during the past 4 or 5 months."

The *median* is the amount that divides a given earnings distribution into two equal groups, one having earnings above the median and the other having earnings below the median.

2000 dollars. For men 25 and older and women 25 and older, median usual weekly earnings are shown on both a current-dollar and a constant-dollar basis. The editor has converted the current-dollar figures to 2000 dollars using the CPI-U-RS, which is shown and described in Chapter 8. The CPI-U-RS was chosen because it is the deflator used by the Census Bureau to convert household income and earnings to constant dollars and by the Bureau of Labor Statistics to convert compensation per hour to constant dollars. It corrects historical values of the CPI to be consistent with current CPI methodology.

Race and ethnicity. See the notes to Tables 10-1 through 10-6 for the definitions of these categories.

Data availability

These data become available about 3 weeks after the end of each quarter in the "Usual Weekly Earnings of Wage and Salary Workers" press release, available on the BLS Web site at <http://www.bls.gov/cps>. Recent data are available at that location. Also available are greater detail by demographic and age groups, by occupation, by union status, and by education; distributional data, by deciles and quartiles; and earnings for part-time workers. Also available are earnings in 1982 dollars using the CPI-U. (In the opinion of the editor, these give a less accurate depiction of longer-term trends, which is why *Business Statistics* provides the CPI-U-RS data explained above.) Historical data are available upon request from BLS by telephone at (202) 691-6378.

Table 10-21

Full-Time and Part-Time Employees by SIC Industry, Historical Annual

These estimates, which are made only annually for the full year, are found in Tables 6-4 of the National Income and Product Accounts (NIPAs). They are like the payroll series in counting the number of jobs rather than the number of persons employed. However, they are broader than the payroll series in that they include private household employment (domestic service) in the "service" industry category. They exclude most of the agricultural employment reported in the CPS, but include members of the armed forces and all other government employment including work-relief agencies such as the Works Progress Administration and the Civilian Conservation Corps; these categories are shown separately in Table 10-21. This treatment is consistent with the rest of the NIPAs, in which GDP includes, as output, the work done by relief workers, and the buildings they constructed are included in investment and capital stock. The industry estimates are based on various versions of the Standard Industrial Classification system that were in effect at the time of compilation.

CHAPTER 11: ENERGY

Figure 11-1: Energy Consumption and Prices, 1950–2014

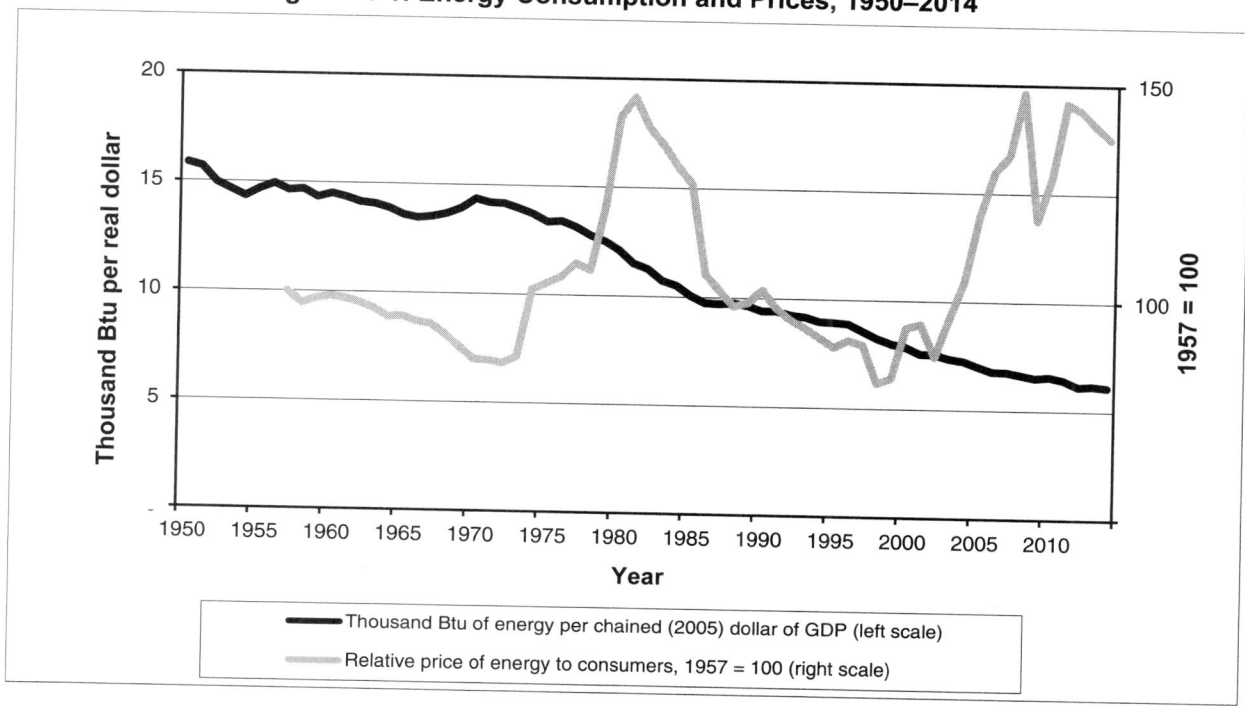

- The downward trend in energy use per dollar of real GDP, which can also be described as an increase in the energy efficiency of national production, may seem surprising in light of long-term trend increases in motor vehicle use, air conditioning, air travel, and other consumer uses of energy. Evidently, these increases are more than offset by factors such as the rising share of services and high-tech goods in GDP; the declining relative importance of energy-intensive materials production processes such as primary metals production; and the movement of population and economic activity to warmer states, which cuts more energy in heating costs than it increases on air-conditioning. Also, upswings in relative energy prices—measured as the ratio of the CPI for energy to the total CPI—appear to have been associated with somewhat faster declines in the energy/GDP trend. (Figure 11-1, from Tables 8-1 and 11-2)

- Net imports supplied 12.6 percent of total energy supply (production plus net imports) in 2014, down dramatically from a high of 30.3 percent in 2005, and marked the lowest energy dependence since 1972. From 2005 to 2014, energy imports dropped 33 percent, while domestic production was up 18 percent: a decrease in coal production over the period was more than offset by substantial increases in other energy sources (Table 11-1)

- Nuclear power, almost nonexistent in 1965, supplied 9.6 percent of total U.S. energy production in 2014. Renewable energy sources, which provided 6.7 percent in 1965, accounted for 11.1 percent in 2014. The remaining 79.3 percent in 2014 was accounted for by domestic fossil fuel production, compared with 93.2 percent in 1965. (Table 11-1)

- After reaching a high of $99.75 per barrel for crude oil in 2008, the price plummeted 37.8 percent in 2009, right in the middle of the Great Recession. Prices rebounded through 2013. However, prices declined again in 2014, dropping 5.2 percent. (Table 11-3)

Table 11-1. Energy Supply and Consumption

(Quadrillion Btu.)

Year and month	Imports	Exports	Production, by source								Consumption, by end-use sector			
				Fossil fuels					Nuclear electric power	Renew-able energy, total	Total	Residential and commercial	Industrial	Transport-ation
			Total	Total	Coal	Natural gas	Crude oil	Natural gas plant liquids						
1965	5.892	1.829	50.674	47.235	13.055	15.775	16.521	1.883	0.043	3.396	54.015	16.485	25.098	12.432
1966	6.146	1.829	53.532	50.035	13.468	17.011	17.561	1.996	0.064	3.432	57.014	17.493	26.422	13.100
1967	6.159	2.115	56.376	52.597	13.825	17.943	18.651	2.177	0.088	3.690	58.905	18.538	26.614	13.752
1968	6.905	1.998	58.220	54.306	13.609	19.068	19.308	2.321	0.142	3.773	62.415	19.665	27.883	14.866
1969	7.676	2.126	60.534	56.286	13.863	20.446	19.556	2.420	0.154	4.095	65.614	21.002	29.105	15.507
1970	8.342	2.632	63.495	59.186	14.607	21.666	20.401	2.512	0.239	4.070	67.838	22.112	29.628	16.098
1971	9.535	2.151	62.717	58.042	13.186	22.280	20.033	2.544	0.413	4.262	69.283	22.967	29.586	16.730
1972	11.387	2.118	63.904	58.938	14.092	22.208	20.041	2.598	0.584	4.382	72.688	24.040	30.930	17.717
1973	14.613	2.033	63.563	58.241	13.992	22.187	19.493	2.569	0.910	4.411	75.684	24.440	32.623	18.613
1974	14.304	2.203	62.345	56.331	14.074	21.210	18.575	2.471	1.272	4.742	73.962	24.048	31.787	18.120
1975	14.032	2.323	61.320	54.733	14.989	19.640	17.729	2.374	1.900	4.687	71.965	24.306	29.413	18.245
1976	16.760	2.172	61.561	54.723	15.654	19.480	17.262	2.327	2.111	4.727	75.975	25.474	31.393	19.101
1977	19.948	2.052	62.012	55.101	15.755	19.565	17.454	2.327	2.702	4.209	77.961	25.869	32.263	19.822
1978	19.106	1.920	63.104	55.074	14.910	19.485	18.434	2.245	3.024	5.005	79.950	26.644	32.688	20.617
1979	19.460	2.855	65.904	58.006	17.540	20.076	18.104	2.286	2.776	5.123	80.859	26.461	33.925	20.472
1980	15.796	3.695	67.175	59.008	18.598	19.908	18.249	2.254	2.739	5.428	78.067	26.332	32.039	19.697
1981	13.719	4.307	66.951	58.529	18.377	19.699	18.146	2.307	3.008	5.414	76.106	25.877	30.712	19.514
1982	11.861	4.608	66.569	57.458	18.639	18.319	18.309	2.191	3.131	5.980	73.099	26.391	27.614	19.089
1983	11.752	3.693	64.114	54.416	17.247	16.593	18.392	2.184	3.203	6.496	72.971	26.363	27.428	19.177
1984	12.471	3.786	68.840	58.849	19.719	18.008	18.848	2.274	3.553	6.438	76.632	27.403	29.570	19.656
1985	11.781	4.196	67.698	57.539	19.325	16.980	18.992	2.241	4.076	6.084	76.392	27.493	28.816	20.088
1986	14.151	4.021	67.066	56.575	19.509	16.541	18.376	2.149	4.380	6.111	76.647	27.581	28.274	20.789
1987	15.398	3.812	67.542	57.167	20.141	17.136	17.675	2.215	4.754	5.622	79.054	28.209	29.379	21.469
1988	17.296	4.366	68.919	57.875	20.738	17.599	17.279	2.260	5.587	5.457	82.709	29.711	30.677	22.318
1989	18.766	4.661	69.320	57.483	21.360	17.847	16.117	2.158	5.602	6.235	84.786	30.979	31.320	22.478
1990	18.817	4.752	70.705	58.560	22.488	18.326	15.571	2.175	6.104	6.041	84.485	30.265	31.810	22.420
1991	18.335	5.141	70.362	57.872	21.636	18.229	15.701	2.306	6.422	6.069	84.438	30.920	31.399	22.118
1992	19.372	4.937	69.956	57.655	21.694	18.375	15.223	2.363	6.479	5.821	85.783	30.797	32.571	22.415
1993	21.218	4.227	68.315	55.822	20.336	18.584	14.494	2.408	6.410	6.083	87.366	32.037	32.628	22.712
1994	22.307	4.035	70.726	58.044	22.202	19.348	14.103	2.391	6.694	5.988	89.088	32.209	33.520	23.365
1995	22.180	4.496	71.174	57.540	22.130	19.082	13.887	2.442	7.075	6.558	91.032	33.208	33.970	23.851
1996	23.633	4.613	72.486	58.387	22.790	19.344	13.723	2.530	7.087	7.012	94.022	34.675	34.903	24.439
1997	25.119	4.493	72.472	58.857	23.310	19.394	13.658	2.495	6.597	7.018	94.602	34.645	35.199	24.751
1998	26.473	4.237	72.876	59.314	24.045	19.613	13.235	2.420	7.068	6.494	95.019	34.921	34.841	25.260
1999	27.152	3.669	71.742	57.614	23.295	19.341	12.451	2.528	7.610	6.517	96.650	35.932	34.763	25.949
2000	28.865	3.962	71.332	57.366	22.735	19.662	12.358	2.611	7.862	6.104	98.819	37.599	34.662	26.555
2001	30.052	3.731	71.735	58.541	23.547	20.166	12.282	2.547	8.029	5.164	96.172	37.177	32.719	26.282
2002	29.331	3.608	70.713	56.834	22.732	19.382	12.160	2.559	8.145	5.734	97.647	38.135	32.661	26.846
2003	31.007	4.013	69.938	56.033	22.094	19.633	11.960	2.346	7.960	5.946	97.921	38.469	32.553	26.900
2004	33.492	4.351	70.232	55.942	22.852	19.074	11.550	2.466	8.223	6.067	100.090	38.741	33.515	27.843
2005	34.659	4.462	69.431	55.044	23.185	18.556	10.969	2.334	8.161	6.226	100.190	39.472	32.441	28.280
2006	34.649	4.727	70.746	55.938	23.790	19.022	10.771	2.356	8.215	6.594	99.492	38.386	32.390	28.717
2007	34.679	5.338	71.415	56.436	23.493	19.786	10.748	2.409	8.459	6.520	101.020	39.783	32.385	28.859
2008	32.970	6.949	73.220	57.587	23.851	20.703	10.613	2.419	8.426	7.206	98.906	40.086	31.333	27.486
2009	29.690	6.920	72.658	56.662	21.624	21.139	11.325	2.574	8.355	7.641	94.138	38.986	28.464	26.687
2010	29.866	8.176	74.777	58.230	22.038	21.806	11.605	2.781	8.434	8.112	97.480	39.891	30.523	27.059
2011	28.748	10.373	77.972	60.548	22.221	23.406	11.950	2.970	8.269	9.155	96.902	39.370	30.812	26.712
2012	27.068	11.267	79.199	62.324	20.677	24.610	13.791	3.246	8.062	8.813	94.487	37.357	30.908	26.219
2013	24.626	11.787	81.894	64.319	20.001	24.991	15.795	3.532	8.244	9.330	97.255	39.164	31.310	26.782
2014	23.313	12.321	87.154	69.169	20.287	26.516	18.339	4.028	8.329	9.656	98.459	40.011	31.308	27.142
2012														
January	2.165	0.885	6.856	5.315	1.681	2.084	1.277	0.274	0.746	0.795	8.988	4.142	2.699	2.148
February	1.805	0.854	6.234	4.884	1.576	1.891	1.157	0.259	0.642	0.708	8.017	3.618	2.445	1.955
March	2.027	1.020	6.813	5.384	1.720	2.086	1.291	0.286	0.658	0.772	8.382	3.567	2.579	2.237
April	2.055	0.905	6.615	5.202	1.600	2.037	1.284	0.280	0.593	0.820	7.519	2.852	2.483	2.188
May	2.137	0.995	6.923	5.407	1.692	2.107	1.314	0.294	0.657	0.860	7.617	2.708	2.621	2.289
June	2.039	0.958	6.738	5.221	1.646	2.030	1.262	0.283	0.694	0.823	7.719	2.924	2.549	2.244
July	2.168	1.014	7.064	5.514	1.718	2.152	1.342	0.301	0.737	0.813	8.268	3.259	2.644	2.359
August	2.157	1.017	7.126	5.640	1.831	2.148	1.349	0.313	0.745	0.741	8.166	3.173	2.625	2.364
September	2.065	0.955	6.792	5.408	1.681	2.071	1.345	0.311	0.688	0.697	7.637	2.845	2.570	2.220
October	2.017	1.062	6.891	5.490	1.635	2.151	1.385	0.319	0.660	0.741	7.723	2.758	2.655	2.312
November	1.925	0.983	6.869	5.428	1.635	2.113	1.374	0.306	0.679	0.762	8.137	3.216	2.696	2.228
December	2.066	1.139	6.972	5.427	1.586	2.119	1.415	0.306	0.745	0.800	9.082	4.102	2.742	2.237
2013														
January	2.061	1.030	7.186	5.598	1.686	2.167	1.440	0.305	0.763	0.825	9.581	4.664	2.766	2.148
February	1.806	0.914	6.437	5.076	1.530	1.947	1.319	0.280	0.655	0.707	8.455	3.968	2.469	2.017
March	1.983	1.068	7.255	5.750	1.766	2.181	1.481	0.322	0.652	0.853	8.555	3.709	2.608	2.239
April	1.956	0.977	7.068	5.619	1.684	2.122	1.486	0.326	0.589	0.860	7.556	2.792	2.529	2.239
May	1.987	1.005	7.319	5.801	1.699	2.222	1.548	0.332	0.658	0.860	7.659	2.771	2.584	2.305
June	1.833	1.022	7.184	5.615	1.606	2.160	1.509	0.340	0.712	0.857	7.791	2.975	2.548	2.267
July	2.001	1.067	7.462	5.889	1.712	2.258	1.565	0.353	0.752	0.822	8.227	3.196	2.645	2.382
August	1.981	1.076	7.492	5.995	1.771	2.287	1.580	0.356	0.743	0.754	8.210	3.168	2.658	2.380
September	1.894	0.968	7.228	5.812	1.695	2.218	1.550	0.349	0.706	0.710	7.636	2.868	2.558	2.210
October	1.905	1.013	7.444	6.028	1.732	2.306	1.630	0.361	0.652	0.764	7.776	2.775	2.638	2.369
November	1.883	1.030	7.325	5.831	1.657	2.260	1.571	0.343	0.681	0.813	8.194	3.329	2.630	2.236
December	2.023	1.151	7.754	6.156	1.749	2.387	1.659	0.360	0.767	0.832	8.820	3.797	2.674	2.350

Table 11-2. Energy Consumption Per Dollar of Real Gross Domestic Product

Year	Primary energy consumption (quadrillion Btu)			Gross domestic product (billions of chained [2009] dollars)	Energy consumption per real dollar of GDP (thousand Btu per chained [2005] dollar)		
	Total	Petroleum and natural gas	Other energy		Total	Petroleum and natural gas	Other energy
1950	34.616	19.284	15.332	2 184.0	15.85	8.83	7.02
1951	36.974	21.477	15.497	2 360.0	15.67	9.10	6.57
1952	36.748	22.505	14.243	2 456.1	14.96	9.16	5.80
1953	37.664	23.462	14.202	2 571.4	14.65	9.12	5.52
1954	36.639	24.169	12.470	2 556.9	14.33	9.45	4.88
1955	40.208	26.253	13.955	2 739.0	14.68	9.58	5.09
1956	41.754	27.551	14.203	2 797.4	14.93	9.85	5.08
1957	41.787	28.122	13.665	2 856.3	14.63	9.85	4.78
1958	41.645	29.190	12.455	2 835.3	14.69	10.30	4.39
1959	43.466	31.040	12.426	3 031.0	14.34	10.24	4.10
1960	45.086	32.305	12.782	3 108.7	14.50	10.39	4.11
1961	45.738	33.143	12.595	3 188.1	14.35	10.40	3.95
1962	47.826	34.780	13.047	3 383.1	14.14	10.28	3.86
1963	49.644	36.104	13.540	3 530.4	14.06	10.23	3.84
1964	51.815	37.589	14.226	3 734.0	13.88	10.07	3.81
1965	54.015	39.014	15.001	3 976.7	13.58	9.81	3.77
1966	57.014	41.396	15.618	4 238.9	13.45	9.77	3.68
1967	58.905	43.228	15.676	4 355.2	13.53	9.93	3.60
1968	62.415	46.189	16.225	4 569.0	13.66	10.11	3.55
1969	65.614	49.016	16.598	4 712.5	13.92	10.40	3.52
1970	67.838	51.315	16.523	4 722.0	14.37	10.87	3.50
1971	69.283	53.030	16.253	4 877.6	14.20	10.87	3.33
1972	72.688	55.645	17.043	5 134.3	14.16	10.84	3.32
1973	75.684	57.350	18.334	5 424.1	13.95	10.57	3.38
1974	73.962	55.186	18.776	5 396.0	13.71	10.23	3.48
1975	71.965	52.680	19.284	5 385.4	13.36	9.78	3.58
1976	75.975	55.523	20.452	5 675.4	13.39	9.78	3.60
1977	77.961	57.054	20.907	5 937.0	13.13	9.61	3.52
1978	79.950	57.963	21.987	6 267.2	12.76	9.25	3.51
1979	80.859	57.788	23.070	6 466.2	12.50	8.94	3.57
1980	78.067	54.440	23.627	6 450.4	12.10	8.44	3.66
1981	76.106	51.680	24.426	6 617.7	11.50	7.81	3.69
1982	73.099	48.588	24.511	6 491.3	11.26	7.49	3.78
1983	72.971	47.273	25.698	6 792.0	10.74	6.96	3.78
1984	76.632	49.447	27.185	7 285.0	10.52	6.79	3.73
1985	76.392	48.628	27.764	7 593.8	10.06	6.40	3.66
1986	76.647	48.790	27.857	7 860.5	9.75	6.21	3.54
1987	79.054	50.504	28.551	8 132.6	9.72	6.21	3.51
1988	82.709	52.671	30.038	8 474.5	9.76	6.22	3.54
1989	84.786	53.811	30.975	8 786.4	9.65	6.12	3.53
1990	84.485	53.155	31.330	8 955.0	9.43	5.94	3.50
1991	84.438	52.879	31.559	8 948.4	9.44	5.91	3.53
1992	85.783	54.239	31.544	9 266.6	9.26	5.85	3.40
1993	87.366	54.916	32.450	9 521.0	9.18	5.77	3.41
1994	89.088	56.286	32.803	9 905.4	8.99	5.68	3.31
1995	91.032	57.112	33.920	10 174.8	8.95	5.61	3.33
1996	94.022	58.760	35.262	10 561.0	8.90	5.56	3.34
1997	94.602	59.381	35.221	11 034.9	8.57	5.38	3.19
1998	95.019	59.648	35.372	11 525.9	8.24	5.18	3.07
1999	96.650	60.745	35.905	12 065.9	8.01	5.03	2.98
2000	98.819	62.090	36.729	12 559.7	7.87	4.94	2.92
2001	96.172	60.962	35.210	12 682.2	7.58	4.81	2.78
2002	97.647	61.736	35.911	12 908.8	7.56	4.78	2.78
2003	97.921	61.620	36.301	13 271.1	7.38	4.64	2.74
2004	100.094	63.150	36.944	13 773.5	7.27	4.58	2.68
2005	100.193	62.868	37.325	14 234.2	7.04	4.42	2.62
2006	99.492	62.062	37.430	14 613.8	6.81	4.25	2.56
2007	101.027	63.154	37.873	14 873.7	6.79	4.25	2.55
2008	98.906	60.750	38.156	14 830.4	6.67	4.10	2.57
2009	94.138	58.375	35.763	14 418.7	6.53	4.05	2.48
2010	97.480	60.064	37.416	14 783.8	6.59	4.06	2.53
2011	96.902	59.778	37.124	15 020.6	6.45	3.98	2.47
2012	94.487	60.105	34.382	15 369.2	6.15	3.91	2.24
2013	97.255	61.432	35.823	15 710.3	6.19	3.91	2.28
2014	98.459	62.375	36.084	16 085.6	6.12	3.88	2.24

Table 11-3. Petroleum and Petroleum Products—Prices, Imports, Domestic Production, and Stocks

(Not seasonally adjusted.)

Year and month	Crude oil futures price (dollars per barrel)		Imports				Supply (thousands of barrels per day)					Stocks (end of period, millions of barrels)		
			Total energy-related petroleum products (thousands of barrels)	Crude petroleum			Petroleum and products			Domestic production		Crude oil and petroleum products	Crude petroleum	
	Current dollars	2009 dollars		Thousands of barrels		Unit price (dollars per barrel)	Exports	Imports	Net imports	Crude oil	Natural gas plant liquids		Non-SPR	Strategic petroleum reserve
				Total	Average per day									
1983	30.66	58.15	. . .	1 293 819	3 545	30.00	739	5 051	4 312	8 688	1 559	1 454	344	379
1984	29.44	53.80	. . .	1 319 683	3 616	28.00	722	5 437	4 715	8 879	1 630	1 556	345	451
1985	27.89	49.22	. . .	1 260 856	3 454	26.00	781	5 067	4 286	8 971	1 609	1 519	321	493
1986	15.05	26.00	. . .	1 634 567	4 478	14.00	785	6 224	5 439	8 680	1 551	1 593	331	512
1987	19.15	32.10	. . .	1 744 977	4 781	17.00	764	6 678	5 914	8 349	1 595	1 607	349	541
1988	15.96	25.75	. . .	1 887 860	5 172	14.00	815	7 402	6 587	8 140	1 625	1 597	330	560
1989	19.58	30.29	. . .	2 146 552	5 881	16.00	859	8 061	7 202	7 613	1 546	1 581	341	580
1990	24.50	36.33	. . .	2 216 604	6 073	20.00	857	8 018	7 161	7 355	1 559	1 621	323	586
1991	21.50	30.87	2 828 953	2 146 064	5 880	17.00	1 001	7 627	6 626	7 417	1 659	1 617	325	569
1992	20.58	28.79	2 947 582	2 294 570	6 269	17.00	950	7 888	6 938	7 171	1 697	1 592	318	575
1993	18.48	25.22	3 257 008	2 543 374	6 968	15.00	1 003	8 620	7 618	6 847	1 736	1 647	335	587
1994	17.19	22.98	3 416 045	2 704 196	7 409	14.00	942	8 996	8 054	6 662	1 727	1 653	337	592
1995	18.40	24.10	3 361 882	2 767 312	7 582	16.00	949	8 835	7 886	6 560	1 762	1 563	303	592
1996	22.03	28.25	3 622 385	2 893 647	7 906	19.00	981	9 478	8 498	6 465	1 830	1 507	284	566
1997	20.61	25.98	3 802 574	3 069 430	8 409	18.00	1 003	10 162	9 158	6 452	1 817	1 560	305	563
1998	14.40	18.01	4 088 027	3 242 711	8 884	11.00	945	10 708	9 764	6 252	1 759	1 647	324	571
1999	19.30	23.80	4 081 181	3 228 092	8 844	16.00	940	10 852	9 912	5 881	1 850	1 493	284	567
2000	30.26	36.40	4 314 825	3 399 239	9 288	26.00	1 040	11 459	10 419	5 822	1 911	1 468	286	541
2001	25.95	30.63	4 475 026	3 471 067	9 510	21.00	971	11 871	10 900	5 801	1 868	1 586	312	550
2002	26.15	30.45	4 337 075	3 418 022	9 364	23.00	984	11 530	10 546	5 744	1 880	1 548	278	599
2003	30.99	35.39	4 654 638	3 676 005	10 071	27.00	1 027	12 264	11 238	5 649	1 719	1 568	269	638
2004	41.47	46.23	4 917 591	3 820 979	10 440	34.00	1 048	13 145	12 097	5 441	1 809	1 645	286	676
2005	56.70	61.46	5 004 339	3 754 671	10 287	47.00	1 165	13 714	12 549	5 181	1 717	1 698	324	685
2006	66.25	69.94	4 880 734	3 734 226	10 231	58.00	1 317	13 707	12 390	5 088	1 739	1 720	312	689
2007	72.41	74.57	4 807 811	3 690 568	10 111	64.00	1 433	13 468	12 036	5 077	1 783	1 665	286	697
2008	99.75	99.69	4 613 444	3 590 628	9 810	95.00	1 802	12 915	11 114	5 000	1 784	1 737	326	702
2009	62.09	62.09	4 266 007	3 314 787	9 082	57.00	2 024	11 691	9 667	5 350	1 910	1 776	325	727
2010	79.61	78.31	4 279 611	3 377 077	9 252	75.00	2 353	11 793	9 441	5 482	2 074	1 794	333	727
2011	95.11	91.38	4 164 117	3 321 918	9 101	100.00	2 986	11 436	8 450	5 645	2 216	1 750	331	696
2012	94.15	88.81	3 847 545	3 097 407	8 463	101.00	3 205	10 598	7 393	6 497	2 408	1 808	365	695
2013	98.05	91.46	3 549 945	2 813 770	7 709	97.00	3 621	9 859	6 237	7 465	2 606	1 761	357	696
2014	93.00	84.28	3 381 460	2 700 939	7 400	91.00	4 180	9 221	5 041	8 711	2 964	1 856	394	691
2014														
January	94.86	85.96	311 751	256 978	8 290	90.00	4 021	9 264	5 243	8 022	2 639	1 743	364	696
February	100.68	91.26	265 030	213 020	7 608	92.00	3 611	9 151	5 540	8 135	2 684	1 743	373	696
March	100.51	91.08	288 733	224 035	7 227	94.00	3 858	9 240	5 382	8 257	2 793	1 753	384	696
April	102.04	92.44	297 360	238 970	7 966	95.00	3 966	9 584	5 618	8 567	2 919	1 780	393	693
May	101.80	92.25	279 486	212 984	6 870	96.00	4 121	9 380	5 260	8 630	2 880	1 809	394	691
June	105.15	95.34	267 210	213 931	7 131	96.00	4 156	8 815	4 659	8 692	3 044	1 814	384	691
July	102.39	92.80	294 060	238 738	7 701	98.00	4 479	9 472	4 994	8 731	3 061	1 818	369	691
August	96.08	87.07	271 568	215 817	6 962	96.00	4 533	9 309	4 776	8 831	3 087	1 822	361	691
September	93.03	85.21	275 602	226 035	7 535	93.00	3 962	9 152	5 190	8 947	3 125	1 835	361	691
October	84.34	76.43	279 105	224 102	7 229	88.00	4 112	8 905	4 793	9 129	3 126	1 830	382	691
November	75.81	68.70	239 996	190 351	6 345	83.00	4 370	8 967	4 598	9 155	3 073	1 842	388	691
December	59.29	53.73	311 559	245 977	7 935	74.00	4 906	9 387	4 481	9 394	3 121	1 856	394	691

. . . = Not available.

NOTES AND DEFINITIONS, CHAPTER 11

Tables 11-1 and 11-2
Energy Supply and Consumption

SOURCES: U.S. DEPARTMENT OF ENERGY, ENERGY INFORMATION ADMINISTRATION; U.S. DEPARTMENT OF COMMERCE, BUREAU OF ECONOMIC ANALYSIS

Definitions

The *British thermal unit (Btu)* is a measure used to combine data for different energy sources into a consistent aggregate. It is the amount of energy required to raise the temperature of 1 pound of water 1 degree Fahrenheit when the water is near a temperature of 39.2 degrees Fahrenheit. To illustrate one of the factors used to convert volumes to Btu, conventional motor gasoline has a heat content of 5.253 million Btu per barrel. For further information, see the Energy Information Administration's *Monthly Energy Review*, Appendix A.

Production: Crude oil includes lease condensates.

Renewable energy, total includes conventional hydroelectric power, geothermal, solar thermal and photovoltaic, wind, and biomass. Hydroelectric power includes conventional electrical utility and industrial generation. Biomass includes wood, waste, and alcohol fuels (ethanol blended into motor gasoline).

The sum of domestic energy *production* and net imports of energy (*imports* minus *exports*) does not exactly equal domestic energy *consumption*. The difference is attributed to inventory changes; losses and gains in conversion, transportation, and distribution; the addition of blending compounds; shipments of anthracite to U.S. armed forces in Europe; and adjustments to account for discrepancies between reporting systems.

Consumption by end-use sector is based on total, not net, consumption—that is, each sector's consumption includes its electricity purchases as well as its own energy production. Electric utilities are not treated as a separate end-use sector. However, they are counted as primary producers in the production accounts, which measure only primary production. As a result, total national supply and consumption are in rough balance, though components may not add to exact totals, not only because of the miscellaneous adjustments described above, but also because of different sector-specific conversion factors.

References and notes on the data

All of these data are published each month in Tables 1.1, 1.2, 1.7, and 2.1 in the *Monthly Energy Review*. Annual data before 1973 are published in the *Annual Energy Review*. These two publications are no longer published in printed form but are available, along with all current and historical data, on the EIA Web site at <http://www.eia.doe.gov>.

The real gross domestic product (GDP) data used to calculate energy consumption per dollar of real GDP are from the Bureau of Economic Analysis; see Table 1-2 and the applicable notes and definitions in this volume of *Business Statistics*. The GDP numbers shown in this table reflect the comprehensive revision of July 2013, which increased the overall level of GDP by including as investment research, development, and creation of intellectual property. This changed the average level of the energy-to-GDP ratio but had little effect on its downward trend. The GDP estimate shown here also reflects subsequent revisions and updates made through June 2014.

Table 11-3 Petroleum and Petroleum Products—Prices, Imports, Domestic Production, and Stocks

SOURCES: FUTURES PRICES—U.S. DEPARTMENT OF ENERGY, ENERGY INFORMATION ADMINISTRATION (EIA), AND U.S. DEPARTMENT OF COMMERCE, BUREAU OF ECONOMIC ANALYSIS; IMPORTS—U.S. DEPARTMENT OF COMMERCE, CENSUS BUREAU (SEE NOTES AND DEFINITIONS FOR TABLES 7-9 THROUGH 7-14); SUPPLY (NET IMPORTS AND DOMESTIC PRODUCTION) AND STOCKS—EIA.

Definitions and notes on the data

The *crude oil futures price* in *current dollars per barrel* is the price for next-month delivery in Cushing, Oklahoma (a pipeline hub), of light, sweet crude oil, as determined by trading on the New York Mercantile Exchange (NYMEX). Official daily closing prices are reported each day at 2:30 p.m., and are tabulated weekly in Table 13 of *EIA's Weekly Petroleum Status Report*. The monthly averages shown in this volume are the average prices for the nearest future from each trading day of the month. For example, for most days in January, the futures contract priced will be for February; for the last few days in January, the February contract will have expired and the March contract will be quoted. The annual averages are averages of the monthly averages.

The *crude oil futures price* in *2009 dollars* is calculated by the editors, by dividing each month's current-dollar price by that month's chain price index for total personal consumption expenditures (PCE), with the price index average for the year 2009 set at 1.0000. The PCE chain price index is compiled by the Bureau of Economic Analysis (BEA). It is described in the notes and definitions for Chapter 1 and is also presented in Chapter 8, Table 8-2, and discussed in its notes and definitions.

The import data in Columns 3 through 6 of this table are those published as Exhibit 17, "Imports of Energy-related Petroleum Products, including Crude Petroleum," in the monthly Census-BEA foreign trade press release, FT900. *Total energy-related petroleum products* includes the following Standard International Trade Classification (SITC) commodity groupings: crude oil, petroleum preparations, and liquefied propane and butane gas.

The data in Columns 7 through 11, on exports, imports, and net imports (imports minus exports) of petroleum and products and domestic production of crude oil and natural gas plant liquids (all expressed as thousands of barrels per day), and in Columns 12 through 14, depicting stocks of crude oil in millions of barrels, are derived from the Department of Energy's weekly petroleum supply reporting system. They are published in EIA's *Monthly Energy Review*, Tables 3.1 and 3.4, which can be reached by searching the Web site. Stock totals are as of the end of the period. Geographic coverage includes the 50 states and the District of Columbia.

Data availability

Data on futures prices, petroleum supply and stocks are available from the EIA Web site at <http://www.eia.doe.gov>, under the categories "Publications and Reports/Monthly Energy Review" and "Petroleum/Weekly Petroleum Status Report." The *Monthly Energy Review* is no longer published in printed form.

The import data are available in the FT900 report from the Census Bureau at www.census.gov. See the notes and definitions for Tables 7-9 through 7-14 for further information.

CHAPTER 12: MONEY, INTEREST, ASSETS, LIABILITIES, AND ASSET PRICES

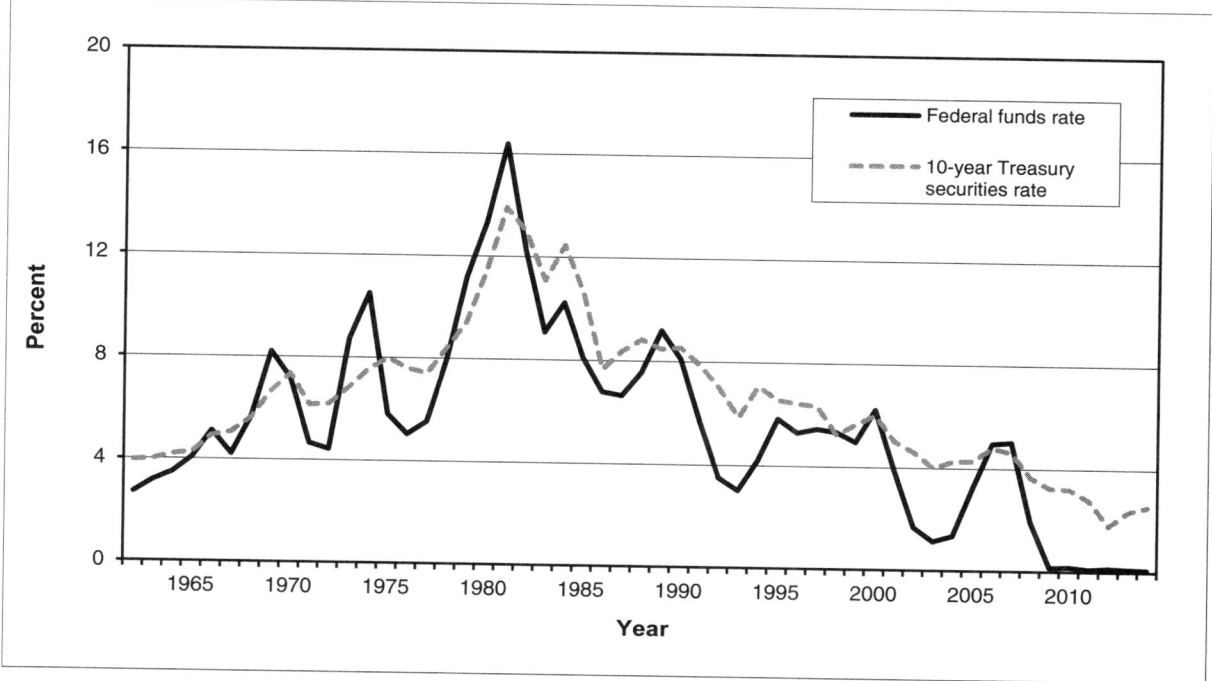

Figure 12-1: Federal Funds Rate and 10-Year Treasury Securities Rate, 1962–2014

- As the recession deepened, the Federal Reserve brought short-term interest rates lower than at any time since the Great Depression, World War II, and its aftermath. The federal funds rate—shown in Figure 12-1—has been held under 0.2 percent, and the "real" fed funds and other short-term interest rates (subtracting out current underlying inflation rates) have been negative since early 2008. (Tables 12-9A and B)

- Longer-term rates have also fallen. The nominal rate on Treasury 10-year securities, the ultimate in safe longer-term investments, is also shown in Figure 12-1. It reached a low point of 1.53 percent in July 2012 and has risen to 2.90 at the end of 2013. However the rate declined almost 24 percent between December 2013 and December 2014. Despite the huge volume of federal borrowing (see Tables 6-1, 6-14 and 12-5), this interest rate was still lower than at any time since 1955. (Tables 12-9A and B)

- The rate spread between Aaa-rated and Baa-rated corporate bonds, representing a market evaluation of risk, was more than 3 percentage points (300 "basis points") in December 2008. This exceeded the previous record postwar spreads seen in 1982. At the end of 2014, the spread was only 0.69 percentage point. (Table 12-9A and B)

- Looking at the easing in quantitative terms, the Federal Reserve added $1.3 trillion to its balance sheet during 2008 and another $1.8 trillion by the end of 2013. In October 2014, the Federal Reserve Board stopped buying bonds. Over the six years of the quantitative easing program, the Fed bought $4.5 trillion. The size of the monetary base has grown at a 28.5 percent annual rate over the 6 years since December 2007. (Table 12-3) But with financial institutions reluctant to lend and thereby create deposits, the money supply grew more tamely; M1 grew at an 11.7 percent annual rate over those years, while M2, the aggregate most closely associated with the dollar value of GDP and hence with economic activity and inflationary pressure, only increased at a 6.7 percent rate. (Table 12-1)

Table 12-1A. Money Stock Measures and Components of M1: Recent Data

(Billions of dollars, monthly data are averages of daily figures, annual data are for December.)

Year and month	Not seasonally adjusted		Seasonally adjusted					Other checkable deposits		
	M1	M2	M1	M2	Currency	Traveler's checks	Demand deposits	At commercial banks	At thrift institutions	Total
1960	144.5	315.3	140.7	312.4	28.7	0.3	111.6	0.0	0.0	0.0
1961	149.2	338.5	145.2	335.5	29.3	0.4	115.5	0.0	0.0	0.0
1962	151.9	365.8	147.8	362.7	30.3	0.4	117.1	0.0	0.0	0.0
1963	157.5	396.4	153.3	393.2	32.2	0.4	120.6	0.0	0.1	0.0
1964	164.9	428.3	160.3	424.7	33.9	0.5	125.8	0.0	0.1	0.0
1965	172.6	463.1	167.8	459.2	36.0	0.5	131.3	0.0	0.1	0.0
1966	176.9	483.7	172.0	480.2	38.0	0.6	133.4	0.0	0.1	0.0
1967	188.4	528.0	183.3	524.8	40.0	0.6	142.5	0.0	0.1	0.0
1968	202.8	569.7	197.4	566.8	43.0	0.7	153.6	0.0	0.1	0.0
1969	209.3	590.1	203.9	587.9	45.7	0.8	157.3	0.0	0.1	0.0
1970	220.1	627.8	214.4	626.5	48.6	0.9	164.7	0.0	0.1	0.0
1971	234.5	711.2	228.3	710.3	52.0	1.0	175.1	0.0	0.2	0.0
1972	256.1	803.1	249.2	802.3	56.2	1.2	191.6	0.0	0.2	0.0
1973	270.2	856.5	262.9	855.5	60.8	1.4	200.3	0.0	0.3	0.0
1974	281.8	903.5	274.2	902.1	67.0	1.7	205.1	0.2	0.4	0.2
1975	295.3	1 017.8	287.1	1 016.2	72.8	2.1	211.3	0.4	0.5	0.4
1976	314.5	1 153.5	306.2	1 152.0	79.5	2.6	221.5	1.3	1.4	1.3
1977	340.0	1 273.0	330.9	1 270.3	87.4	2.9	236.4	1.8	2.3	1.8
1978	367.9	1 370.8	357.3	1 366.0	96.0	3.3	249.5	5.3	3.1	5.3
1979	393.2	1 479.0	381.8	1 473.7	104.8	3.5	256.6	12.7	4.2	12.7
1980	419.5	1 604.8	408.5	1 599.8	115.3	3.9	261.2	20.8	7.3	20.8
1981	447.0	1 760.3	436.7	1 755.5	122.5	4.1	231.4	63.0	15.6	63.0
1982	485.8	1 914.3	474.8	1 906.4	132.5	4.1	234.1	80.5	23.6	80.5
1983	533.3	2 134.3	521.4	2 123.8	146.2	4.7	238.5	97.3	34.8	97.3
1984	564.6	2 318.8	551.6	2 306.8	156.1	5.0	243.4	104.7	42.4	104.7
1985	633.3	2 504.6	619.8	2 492.6	167.7	5.6	266.9	124.7	54.9	124.7
1986	739.8	2 741.9	724.7	2 729.2	180.4	6.1	302.9	161.0	74.2	161.0
1987	765.4	2 840.8	750.2	2 828.8	196.7	6.6	287.7	178.2	81.0	178.2
1988	803.1	3 003.0	786.7	2 990.6	212.0	7.0	287.1	192.5	88.1	192.5
1989	810.6	3 167.5	792.9	3 154.4	222.3	6.9	278.6	197.4	87.7	197.4
1990	842.7	3 286.0	824.7	3 272.7	246.5	7.7	276.8	208.7	85.0	208.7
1991	915.6	3 385.8	897.0	3 371.6	267.1	7.7	289.6	241.6	90.9	241.6
1992	1 045.6	3 439.7	1 024.9	3 423.1	292.1	8.2	340.0	280.8	103.8	280.8
1993	1 153.3	3 493.0	1 129.6	3 472.4	321.6	8.0	385.4	302.6	112.0	302.6
1994	1 174.5	3 506.4	1 150.7	3 485.0	354.5	8.6	383.6	297.4	106.6	297.4
1995	1 152.7	3 650.5	1 127.5	3 626.7	372.8	9.0	389.0	249.0	107.6	249.0
1996	1 105.8	3 826.1	1 081.3	3 804.9	394.6	8.8	402.1	172.1	103.6	172.1
1997	1 097.5	4 039.6	1 072.3	4 017.4	425.3	8.4	393.5	148.4	96.7	148.4
1998	1 121.2	4 381.0	1 095.0	4 356.6	460.4	8.5	376.3	143.9	105.9	143.9
1999	1 148.2	4 643.6	1 122.2	4 617.0	517.9	8.6	352.5	139.7	103.6	139.7
2000	1 111.7	4 931.3	1 087.8	4 903.7	531.3	8.3	309.6	133.2	105.5	133.2
2001	1 208.5	5 436.6	1 182.3	5 405.7	581.2	8.0	335.2	142.2	115.7	142.2
2002	1 245.5	5 772.5	1 219.2	5 740.4	626.2	7.8	305.9	154.3	125.0	154.3
2003	1 332.2	6 066.9	1 305.2	6 035.2	662.5	7.7	325.1	175.3	134.6	175.3
2004	1 401.2	6 417.5	1 375.5	6 388.4	697.8	7.6	342.3	187.0	140.8	187.0
2005	1 396.9	6 679.3	1 374.8	6 654.1	724.6	7.2	324.3	180.8	138.0	180.8
2006	1 387.3	7 070.1	1 368.3	7 046.0	750.2	6.7	305.6	176.8	128.9	176.8
2007	1 394.4	7 478.0	1 376.6	7 452.4	760.6	6.3	303.4	173.0	133.3	173.0
2008	1 631.9	8 207.5	1 607.1	8 177.0	816.2	5.5	473.3	178.8	133.3	178.8
2009	1 723.8	8 520.7	1 698.4	8 482.4	863.7	5.1	448.2	231.2	150.2	231.2
2010	1 870.8	8 831.4	1 841.8	8 782.9	918.8	4.7	519.3	235.8	163.2	235.8
2011	2 207.5	9 699.5	2 168.2	9 635.9	1 001.5	4.3	751.8	233.2	177.5	233.2
2012	2 505.4	10 499.5	2 457.7	10 423.6	1 090.5	3.8	920.5	244.6	198.3	244.6
2013	2 711.7	11 068.1	2 654.5	10 984.9	1 160.3	3.5	1 021.7	256.8	212.1	256.8
2014	2 976.7	11 719.9	2 910.4	11 630.5	1 252.2	2.9	1 165.9	267.2	222.0	267.2
2013										
January	2 477.8	10 474.7	2 467.6	10 452.7	1 097.2	3.8	919.0	249.0	198.6	249.0
February	2 451.9	10 448.1	2 470.4	10 449.4	1 099.9	3.8	920.1	246.8	199.8	246.8
March	2 493.0	10 594.4	2 474.8	10 519.8	1 104.3	3.8	920.1	243.2	203.6	243.2
April	2 538.3	10 622.9	2 511.0	10 553.4	1 109.4	3.7	945.7	250.2	202.1	250.2
May	2 514.9	10 545.7	2 522.0	10 587.2	1 116.3	3.7	949.5	249.4	203.1	249.4
June	2 519.6	10 610.0	2 517.9	10 639.9	1 122.7	3.7	940.4	246.7	204.4	246.7
July	2 538.9	10 644.7	2 545.6	10 700.7	1 130.5	3.6	952.0	252.0	207.4	252.0
August	2 531.7	10 694.2	2 557.3	10 754.5	1 137.6	3.6	958.5	249.8	207.8	249.8
September	2 549.0	10 763.9	2 578.8	10 809.4	1 145.4	3.6	964.6	255.6	209.6	255.6
October	2 614.7	10 897.3	2 620.2	10 920.4	1 152.2	3.6	998.0	255.6	210.9	255.6
November	2 601.5	10 941.3	2 622.2	10 929.8	1 154.8	3.5	996.5	255.0	212.4	255.0
December	2 711.7	11 068.1	2 654.5	10 984.9	1 160.3	3.5	1 021.7	256.8	212.1	256.8
2014										
January	2 694.3	11 061.9	2 683.2	11 037.5	1 165.7	3.5	1 041.9	258.3	213.9	258.3
February	2 698.5	11 113.3	2 718.6	11 118.5	1 171.7	3.4	1 067.5	259.6	216.4	259.6
March	2 765.5	11 238.3	2 745.0	11 161.3	1 190.1	3.4	1 074.1	260.1	217.3	260.1
April	2 801.9	11 291.8	2 771.4	11 217.4	1 198.4	3.3	1 092.6	260.9	216.1	260.9
May	2 774.5	11 234.5	2 784.6	11 282.6	1 204.7	3.3	1 098.4	260.4	217.7	260.4
June	2 817.0	11 296.0	2 813.0	11 330.7	1 211.4	3.3	1 114.1	265.5	218.8	265.5
July	2 834.2	11 351.2	2 839.5	11 405.8	1 217.5	3.2	1 133.2	265.7	219.8	265.7
August	2 782.9	11 383.5	2 816.0	11 443.6	1 223.3	3.2	1 105.4	265.1	219.0	265.1
September	2 827.3	11 433.8	2 856.9	11 481.5	1 228.0	3.1	1 145.0	262.7	218.1	262.7
October	2 855.1	11 498.6	2 862.5	11 521.8	1 232.7	3.0	1 144.7	261.6	220.4	261.6
November	2 849.1	11 574.6	2 876.5	11 564.8	1 242.0	3.0	1 148.3	261.5	221.7	261.5
December	2 976.7	11 719.9	2 910.4	11 630.5	1 252.2	2.9	1 165.9	267.2	222.0	267.2

Table 12-1B. Money Stock, Historical: 1892–1946

(Not seasonally adjusted, millions of dollars.)

Classification	1892	1893	1894	1895	1896	1897	1898	1899	1900	1901	1902
June 30											
Currency outside banks	1 015	1 081	972	971	974	1 013	1 150	1 181	1 331	1 395	1 431
Demand deposits adjusted	2 880	2 766	2 807	2 960	2 839	2 871	3 432	4 162	4 420	5 204	5 719
M1	3 895	3 847	3 779	3 931	3 813	3 884	4 582	5 343	5 751	6 599	7 150
Time deposits	1 929	2 007	1 994	2 088	2 220	2 305	2 397	2 617	3 015	3 315	3 565
M2	5 824	5 854	5 773	6 019	6 033	6 189	6 979	7 960	8 766	9 914	10 715
December 31											
Currency outside banks	. . .	. . .	. . .	. . .	. . .	. . .	. . .	. . .	. . .	. . .	. . .
Demand deposits adjusted	. . .	. . .	. . .	. . .	. . .	. . .	. . .	. . .	. . .	. . .	. . .
M1	. . .	. . .	. . .	. . .	. . .	. . .	. . .	. . .	. . .	. . .	. . .
Time deposits	. . .	. . .	. . .	. . .	. . .	. . .	. . .	. . .	. . .	. . .	. . .
M2	. . .	. . .	. . .	. . .	. . .	. . .	. . .	. . .	. . .	. . .	. . .

Classification	1903	1904	1905	1906	1907	1908	1909	1910	1911	1912	1913
June 30											
Currency outside banks	1 543	1 562	1 629	1 759	1 700	1 711	1 691	1 725	1 709	1 762	1 858
Demand deposits adjusted	5 962	6 256	7 069	7 504	7 872	7 384	7 768	8 254	8 668	9 156	9 140
M1	7 505	7 818	8 698	9 263	9 572	9 095	9 459	9 979	10 377	10 918	10 998
Time deposits	3 800	4 045	4 464	4 769	5 350	5 493	6 265	6 944	7 337	7 889	8 356
M2	11 305	11 863	13 162	14 032	14 922	14 588	15 724	16 923	17 714	18 807	19 354
December 31											
Currency outside banks	. . .	. . .	. . .	. . .	. . .	. . .	. . .	. . .	. . .	. . .	. . .
Demand deposits adjusted	. . .	. . .	. . .	. . .	. . .	. . .	. . .	. . .	. . .	. . .	. . .
M1	. . .	. . .	. . .	. . .	. . .	. . .	. . .	. . .	. . .	. . .	. . .
Time deposits	. . .	. . .	. . .	. . .	. . .	. . .	. . .	. . .	. . .	. . .	. . .
M2	. . .	. . .	. . .	. . .	. . .	. . .	. . .	. . .	. . .	. . .	. . .

Classification	1914	1915	1916	1917	1918	1919	1920	1921	1922	1923	1924
June 30											
Currency outside banks	1 533	1 575	1 876	2 276	3 298	3 593	4 105	3 677	3 346	3 739	3 650
Demand deposits adjusted	10 082	9 828	11 973	13 501	14 843	17 624	19 616	17 113	18 045	18 958	19 412
M1	11 615	11 403	13 849	15 777	18 141	21 217	23 721	20 790	21 391	22 697	23 062
Time deposits	8 350	9 231	10 313	11 543	11 717	13 423	15 834	16 583	17 437	19 722	21 259
M2	19 965	20 634	24 162	27 320	29 858	34 640	39 555	37 373	48 828	42 419	44 321
December 31											
Currency outside banks	. . .	. . .	. . .	. . .	. . .	. . .	. . .	. . .	. . .	3 726	3 696
Demand deposits adjusted	. . .	. . .	. . .	. . .	. . .	. . .	. . .	. . .	. . .	19 144	20 898
M1	. . .	. . .	. . .	. . .	. . .	. . .	. . .	. . .	. . .	22 870	24 594
Time deposits	. . .	. . .	. . .	. . .	. . .	. . .	. . .	. . .	. . .	20 379	22 232
M2	. . .	. . .	. . .	. . .	. . .	. . .	. . .	. . .	. . .	43 249	46 826

. . . = Not available.

Table 12-1C. Money Stock, Historical: January 1947–January 1959

(Averages of daily figures; seasonally adjusted, billions of dollars.)

Year and month	Money stock (M1)			Time deposits adjusted	M2 (M1 plus time deposits)
	Total	Currency component	Demand deposit component		
1947					
January	109.5	26.7	82.8	33.3	142.8
February	109.7	26.7	83.0	33.5	143.2
March	110.3	26.7	83.7	33.6	143.9
April	111.1	26.6	84.5	33.7	144.8
May	111.7	26.6	85.1	33.8	145.5
June	112.1	26.6	85.5	33.9	146.0
July	112.2	26.5	85.7	34.0	146.2
August	112.6	26.5	86.1	34.4	147.0
September	113.0	26.7	86.3	34.7	147.7
October	112.9	26.5	86.4	35.0	147.9
November	113.3	26.5	86.8	35.2	148.5
December	113.1	26.4	86.7	35.4	148.5
1948					
January	113.4	26.4	87.0	35.5	148.9
February	113.2	26.3	86.8	35.7	148.9
March	112.6	26.2	86.4	35.7	148.3
April	112.3	26.1	86.3	35.7	148.0
May	112.1	26.0	86.0	35.7	147.8
June	112.0	26.0	86.0	35.8	147.8
July	112.2	26.0	86.2	35.8	148.0
August	112.3	26.0	86.2	35.9	148.2
September	112.2	26.0	86.2	35.9	148.1
October	112.1	26.0	86.1	35.9	148.0
November	111.8	26.0	85.9	36.0	147.8
December	111.5	25.8	85.8	36.0	147.5
1949					
January	111.2	25.7	85.5	36.1	147.3
February	111.2	25.7	85.5	36.1	147.3
March	111.2	25.7	85.6	36.1	147.3
April	113.3	25.7	85.6	36.2	149.5
May	111.5	25.7	85.8	36.3	147.8
June	111.3	25.6	85.7	36.4	147.7
July	111.2	25.5	85.7	36.4	147.6
August	111.0	25.5	85.6	36.4	147.4
September	110.9	25.3	85.6	36.4	147.3
October	110.9	25.3	85.6	36.4	147.3
November	111.0	25.2	85.8	36.4	147.4
December	111.2	25.1	86.0	36.4	147.6
1950					
January	111.5	25.1	86.4	36.4	147.9
February	112.1	25.1	86.9	36.6	148.7
March	112.5	25.2	87.3	36.6	149.1
April	113.2	25.3	88.0	36.7	149.9
May	113.7	25.2	88.5	36.9	150.6
June	114.1	25.1	89.0	36.9	151.0
July	114.6	25.0	89.6	36.8	151.4
August	115.0	24.9	90.1	36.7	151.7
September	115.2	24.9	90.3	36.6	151.8
October	115.7	24.9	90.8	36.5	152.2
November	115.9	24.9	90.9	36.6	152.5
December	116.2	25.0	91.2	36.7	152.9
1951					
January	116.7	25.0	91.7	36.7	153.4
February	117.1	25.1	92.0	36.6	153.7
March	117.6	25.2	92.4	36.6	154.2
April	117.8	25.2	92.6	36.7	154.5
May	118.2	25.3	92.8	36.8	155.0
June	118.6	25.4	93.2	36.9	155.5
July	119.1	25.6	93.4	37.2	156.3
August	119.6	25.7	93.8	37.4	157.0
September	120.4	25.8	94.5	37.7	158.1
October	121.0	26.0	95.1	37.8	158.8
November	122.0	26.0	96.0	38.0	160.0
December	122.7	26.1	96.5	38.2	160.9
1952					
January	123.1	26.2	96.9	38.4	161.5
February	123.6	26.3	97.3	38.7	162.3
March	123.8	26.4	97.5	38.9	162.7
April	124.1	26.4	97.6	39.1	163.2
May	124.5	26.5	98.0	39.3	163.8
June	125.0	26.7	98.4	39.5	164.5
July	125.3	26.7	98.6	39.7	165.0
August	125.7	26.8	98.9	40.0	165.7
September	126.4	26.9	99.4	40.3	166.7
October	126.7	27.0	99.7	40.5	167.2
November	127.1	27.2	99.9	40.9	168.0
December	127.4	27.3	100.1	41.1	168.5

Table 12-1C. Money Stock, Historical: January 1947–January 1959—*Continued*

(Averages of daily figures; seasonally adjusted, billions of dollars.)

Year and month	Money stock (M1)			Time deposits adjusted	M2 (M1 plus time deposits)
	Total	Currency component	Demand deposit component		
1953					
January	127.3	27.4	99.9	41.4	168.7
February	127.4	27.5	99.9	41.6	169.0
March	128.0	27.6	100.4	41.9	169.9
April	128.3	27.7	100.7	42.1	170.4
May	128.5	27.7	100.7	42.4	170.9
June	128.5	27.7	100.7	42.6	171.1
July	128.6	27.8	100.8	42.9	171.5
August	128.7	27.8	100.9	43.2	171.9
September	128.6	27.8	100.8	43.5	172.1
October	128.7	27.8	100.9	43.9	172.6
November	128.7	27.8	100.9	44.2	172.9
December	128.8	27.7	101.1	44.5	173.3
1954					
January	129.0	27.7	101.3	44.8	173.8
February	129.1	27.7	101.5	45.2	174.3
March	129.2	27.6	101.6	45.6	174.8
April	128.6	27.6	101.0	46.1	174.7
May	129.7	27.6	102.1	46.5	176.2
June	129.9	27.5	102.3	46.8	176.7
July	130.3	27.5	102.8	47.3	177.6
August	130.7	27.5	103.2	47.8	178.5
September	130.9	27.4	103.5	47.9	178.8
October	131.5	27.4	104.1	48.1	179.6
November	132.1	27.4	104.7	48.2	180.3
December	132.3	27.4	104.9	48.3	180.6
1955					
January	133.0	27.4	105.6	48.5	181.5
February	133.9	27.5	106.4	48.7	182.6
March	133.6	27.5	106.0	48.8	182.4
April	133.9	27.5	106.3	49.0	182.9
May	134.6	27.6	107.0	49.0	183.6
June	134.4	27.6	106.8	49.2	183.6
July	134.8	27.7	107.2	49.3	184.1
August	134.8	27.7	107.0	49.3	184.1
September	135.0	27.7	107.3	49.6	184.6
October	135.2	27.8	107.4	49.7	184.9
November	134.9	27.8	107.1	49.9	184.8
December	135.2	27.8	107.4	50.0	185.2
1956					
January	135.5	27.9	107.7	49.9	185.4
February	135.5	27.9	107.7	49.9	185.4
March	135.7	27.9	107.8	50.1	185.8
April	136.0	27.9	108.1	50.3	186.3
May	135.8	27.9	107.9	50.4	186.2
June	136.0	27.9	108.1	50.7	186.7
July	136.0	28.0	108.0	50.9	186.9
August	135.7	28.0	107.8	51.2	186.9
September	136.2	28.0	108.2	51.5	187.7
October	136.3	28.0	108.2	51.6	187.9
November	136.6	28.1	108.4	51.8	188.4
December	136.9	28.2	108.7	51.9	188.8
1957					
January	136.9	28.2	108.6	52.6	189.5
February	136.8	28.2	108.6	53.1	189.9
March	136.9	28.2	108.7	53.7	190.6
April	136.9	28.2	108.7	54.0	190.9
May	137.0	28.2	108.8	54.5	191.5
June	136.9	28.3	108.6	54.8	191.7
July	137.0	28.3	108.7	55.3	192.3
August	137.1	28.3	108.8	55.7	192.8
September	136.8	28.3	108.4	56.1	192.9
October	136.5	28.3	108.2	56.6	193.1
November	136.3	28.3	108.0	57.0	193.3
December	135.9	28.3	107.6	57.4	193.3
1958					
January	135.5	28.3	107.2	57.6	193.1
February	136.2	28.2	107.9	59.2	195.4
March	136.5	28.2	108.3	60.5	197.0
April	137.0	28.2	108.7	61.5	198.5
May	137.5	28.3	109.2	62.3	199.8
June	138.4	28.3	110.1	63.2	201.6
July	138.4	28.4	110.0	64.0	202.4
August	139.1	28.4	110.7	64.6	203.7
September	139.5	28.5	111.1	64.8	204.3
October	140.1	28.5	111.6	64.9	205.0
November	140.9	28.5	112.4	65.2	206.1
December	141.1	28.6	112.6	65.4	206.5
1959					
January	142.2	28.7	113.5	66.3	208.5

Table 12-2. Components of Non-M1 M2

(Billions of dollars, seasonally adjusted; monthly data are averages of daily figures, annual data are for December.)

Year and month	Savings deposits			Small-denomination time deposits			Retail money funds	Total non-M1 M2
	At commercial banks	At thrift institutions	Total	At commercial banks	At thrift institutions	Total		
1960	58.3	100.8	159.1	9.7	2.8	12.5	. . .	171.7
1961	64.2	111.3	175.5	11.1	3.7	14.8	. . .	190.3
1962	71.3	123.4	194.8	15.5	4.6	20.1	. . .	214.9
1963	76.8	137.6	214.4	19.9	5.7	25.5	. . .	240.0
1964	82.9	152.4	235.2	22.4	6.8	29.2	. . .	264.4
1965	92.4	164.5	256.9	26.7	7.8	34.5	. . .	291.3
1966	89.9	163.3	253.1	38.7	16.3	55.0	. . .	308.1
1967	94.1	169.6	263.7	50.7	27.1	77.8	. . .	341.5
1968	96.1	172.8	268.9	63.5	37.1	100.5	. . .	369.4
1969	93.8	169.8	263.7	71.6	48.8	120.4	. . .	384.0
1970	98.6	162.3	261.0	79.3	71.9	151.2	. . .	412.1
1971	112.8	179.4	292.2	94.7	95.1	189.7	. . .	481.9
1972	124.8	196.6	321.4	108.2	123.5	231.6	. . .	553.0
1973	128.0	198.7	326.8	116.8	149.0	265.8	0.1	592.6
1974	136.8	201.8	338.6	123.1	164.8	287.9	1.4	627.9
1975	161.2	227.6	388.9	142.3	195.5	337.9	2.4	729.1
1976	201.8	251.4	453.2	155.5	235.2	390.7	1.8	845.8
1977	218.8	273.4	492.2	167.5	278.0	445.5	1.8	939.4
1978	216.5	265.4	481.9	185.1	335.8	521.0	5.8	1 008.7
1979	195.0	228.8	423.8	235.5	398.7	634.3	33.9	1 092.0
1980	185.7	214.5	400.3	286.2	442.3	728.5	62.5	1 191.3
1981	159.0	184.9	343.9	347.7	475.4	823.1	151.7	1 318.8
1982	190.1	210.0	400.1	379.9	471.0	850.9	180.5	1 431.5
1983	363.2	321.7	684.9	350.9	433.1	784.1	133.4	1 602.4
1984	389.3	315.4	704.7	387.9	500.9	888.8	161.7	1 755.2
1985	456.6	358.6	815.3	386.4	499.3	885.7	171.8	1 872.8
1986	533.5	407.4	940.9	369.4	489.0	858.4	205.3	2 004.5
1987	534.8	402.6	937.4	391.7	529.3	921.0	220.2	2 078.6
1988	542.4	383.9	926.4	451.2	585.9	1 037.1	240.4	2 203.9
1989	541.1	352.6	893.7	533.8	617.6	1 151.3	316.5	2 361.5
1990	581.3	341.6	922.9	610.7	562.6	1 173.3	351.8	2 448.0
1991	664.8	379.6	1 044.5	602.2	463.1	1 065.3	364.9	2 474.7
1992	754.2	433.1	1 187.2	508.1	359.7	867.7	343.2	2 398.2
1993	785.3	434.0	1 219.3	467.9	313.5	781.4	342.1	2 342.8
1994	752.8	398.5	1 151.3	503.6	313.9	817.5	365.6	2 334.3
1995	774.8	361.0	1 135.9	575.8	356.5	932.3	431.0	2 499.2
1996	906.0	368.7	1 274.8	594.2	353.7	947.9	500.9	2 723.6
1997	1 022.5	378.7	1 401.2	625.5	342.2	967.6	576.3	2 945.1
1998	1 187.4	416.1	1 603.6	626.4	324.9	951.3	706.7	3 261.6
1999	1 288.9	451.2	1 740.2	636.9	318.3	955.2	799.5	3 494.9
2000	1 426.1	454.5	1 880.6	700.8	345.3	1 046.0	889.2	3 815.9
2001	1 741.1	571.5	2 312.6	636.0	338.5	974.6	936.2	4 223.4
2002	2 058.5	713.3	2 771.9	591.3	303.5	894.7	854.6	4 521.2
2003	2 335.4	824.0	3 159.5	541.9	276.2	818.1	752.5	4 730.0
2004	2 631.4	875.7	3 507.1	551.9	276.5	828.4	677.3	5 012.9
2005	2 774.6	828.9	3 603.4	646.7	347.0	993.7	682.0	5 279.2
2006	2 911.8	783.7	3 695.5	780.7	425.4	1 206.0	776.2	5 677.7
2007	3 042.1	827.5	3 869.6	858.8	417.2	1 276.0	930.2	6 075.8
2008	3 322.1	769.3	4 091.4	1 078.8	378.8	1 457.6	1 020.9	6 569.9
2009	3 979.2	836.4	4 815.5	868.3	319.6	1 187.8	780.6	6 784.0
2010	4 410.0	923.6	5 333.7	661.7	270.8	932.5	675.0	6 941.2
2011	5 034.2	999.0	6 033.3	542.7	228.7	771.4	663.0	7 467.6
2012	5 727.0	959.0	6 686.0	460.4	176.7	637.2	642.7	7 965.9
2013	6 108.0	1 023.8	7 131.8	415.2	144.0	559.2	639.4	8 330.4
2014	6 502.6	1 081.8	7 584.4	378.4	131.5	509.9	625.9	8 720.2
2013								
January	5 725.0	975.6	6 700.6	453.9	175.7	629.5	655.0	7 985.1
February	5 730.8	985.5	6 716.3	447.8	173.1	621.0	641.8	7 979.0
March	5 788.8	995.0	6 783.9	449.8	169.2	619.0	642.1	8 045.0
April	5 791.1	998.6	6 789.7	446.6	166.0	612.6	640.1	8 042.3
May	5 818.5	1 010.3	6 828.8	440.3	162.5	602.8	633.6	8 065.2
June	5 872.2	1 014.7	6 887.0	430.3	158.9	589.2	645.8	8 122.0
July	5 908.6	1 013.8	6 922.4	424.9	153.3	578.2	654.5	8 155.1
August	5 963.4	1 014.5	6 977.9	423.1	148.2	571.4	647.9	8 197.2
September	5 997.8	1 017.5	7 015.4	418.4	147.1	565.4	649.7	8 230.6
October	6 062.8	1 026.1	7 088.9	416.1	146.9	563.0	648.2	8 300.2
November	6 085.0	1 022.1	7 107.1	413.8	145.0	558.8	641.6	8 307.5
December	6 108.0	1 023.8	7 131.8	415.2	144.0	559.2	639.4	8 330.4
2014								
January	6 134.7	1 030.3	7 165.0	408.7	143.1	551.8	637.5	8 354.3
February	6 174.8	1 038.5	7 213.2	407.0	141.8	548.8	637.9	8 399.9
March	6 191.6	1 045.0	7 236.6	405.6	139.4	545.0	634.8	8 416.3
April	6 218.8	1 050.3	7 269.1	402.1	138.9	541.0	636.0	8 446.1
May	6 257.9	1 065.4	7 323.3	401.1	137.6	538.8	636.0	8 498.0
June	6 282.8	1 068.0	7 350.9	399.1	137.0	536.1	630.7	8 517.7
July	6 337.5	1 067.3	7 404.8	398.3	136.6	534.8	626.8	8 566.4
August	6 394.7	1 073.5	7 468.2	395.4	135.3	530.6	628.9	8 627.6
September	6 397.7	1 075.1	7 472.8	391.7	134.4	526.1	625.6	8 624.5
October	6 431.4	1 077.5	7 508.9	387.2	133.5	520.7	629.7	8 659.3
November	6 469.1	1 076.2	7 545.3	382.2	132.7	514.9	628.1	8 688.3
December	6 502.6	1 081.8	7 584.4	378.4	131.5	509.9	625.9	8 720.2

. . . = Not available.

Table 12-3. Aggregate Reserves, Monetary Base, and FR Balance Sheet

(Millions of dollars; through May 2013, total, nonborrowed, and required reserves and monetary base adjusted for seasonality and changes in reserve requirements; annual data are for December.)

| Year and month | Reserves | | | | | Monetary base | Federal Reserve balance sheet: total assets |
	Total	Nonborrowed	Nonborrowed plus extended credit 1	Required	Excess reserves		
1965	12 316	11 872	11 872	11 892	423	49 620	. . .
1966	12 223	11 690	11 690	11 884	339	51 565	. . .
1967	13 180	12 952	12 952	12 805	375	54 579	. . .
1968	13 767	13 021	13 021	13 341	426	58 357	. . .
1969	14 168	13 049	13 049	13 882	286	61 569	. . .
1970	14 558	14 225	14 225	14 309	249	65 013	. . .
1971	15 230	15 104	15 104	15 049	182	69 108	. . .
1972	16 645	15 595	15 595	16 361	284	75 167	. . .
1973	17 021	15 723	15 723	16 717	304	81 073	. . .
1974	17 550	16 823	16 970	17 292	258	87 535	. . .
1975	17 822	17 692	17 704	17 556	266	93 887	. . .
1976	18 388	18 335	18 335	18 115	274	101 515	. . .
1977	18 990	18 420	18 420	18 800	190	110 324	. . .
1978	19 753	18 885	18 885	19 521	232	120 445	. . .
1979	20 720	19 248	19 248	20 279	442	131 143	. . .
1980	22 015	20 325	20 328	21 501	514	142 004	. . .
1981	22 443	21 807	21 956	22 124	319	149 021	. . .
1982	23 600	22 966	23 152	23 100	500	160 127	. . .
1983	25 367	24 593	24 595	24 806	561	175 467	. . .
1984	26 913	23 727	26 331	26 078	835	187 253	. . .
1985	31 569	30 251	30 749	30 505	1 064	203 556	. . .
1986	38 841	38 014	38 317	37 667	1 174	223 417	. . .
1987	38 913	38 136	38 618	37 893	1 020	239 830	. . .
1988	40 454	38 738	39 982	39 392	1 062	256 897	. . .
1989	40 487	40 222	40 241	39 545	942	267 761	. . .
1990	41 767	41 441	41 463	40 101	1 665	293 339	. . .
1991	45 516	45 324	45 325	44 526	990	317 523	. . .
1992	54 422	54 298	54 298	53 267	1 155	350 885	. . .
1993	60 567	60 485	60 484	59 497	1 070	386 720	. . .
1994	59 466	59 257	59 257	58 295	1 171	418 474	. . .
1995	56 484	56 226	56 226	55 193	1 291	434 645	. . .
1996	50 185	50 030	50 030	48 766	1 419	451 935	. . .
1997	46 876	46 551	46 551	45 189	1 687	479 798	. . .
1998	45 174	45 058	45 053	43 662	1 513	513 821	. . .
1999	42 149	41 829	41 787	40 855	1 295	593 383	. . .
2000	38 685	38 475	38 465	37 359	1 326	584 928	. . .
2001	41 384	41 317	41 338	39 740	1 643	635 575	. . .
2002	40 275	40 195	40 207	38 267	2 008	681 486	. . .
2003	42 542	42 496	. . .	41 495	1 047	720 115	. . .
2004	46 425	46 362	. . .	44 517	1 908	759 085	. . .
2005	44 963	44 795	. . .	43 063	1 900	787 369	. . .
2006	43 124	42 933	. . .	41 261	1 863	812 367	. . .
2007	43 133	27 702	. . .	41 348	1 785	824 809	. . .
2008	820 187	166 621	. . .	52 868	767 318	1 654 974	890 662
2009	1 138 682	968 755	. . .	63 483	1 075 199	2 019 228	2 239 457
2010	1 077 359	1 031 871	. . .	70 723	1 006 636	2 011 078	2 234 067
2011	1 597 100	1 587 574	. . .	94 894	1 502 206	2 612 081	2 420 570
2012	1 569 017	1 568 221	. . .	110 266	1 458 751	2 672 578	2 926 095
							2 907 300
2012							
January	1 614 301	1 605 687	. . .	94 850	1 519 451	2 638 114	2 919 545
February	1 657 931	1 649 998	. . .	97 811	1 560 121	2 690 184	2 925 722
March	1 607 819	1 600 490	. . .	98 226	1 509 593	2 648 070	2 878 137
April	1 584 770	1 577 905	. . .	98 593	1 486 176	2 631 478	2 866 561
May	1 556 689	1 550 503	. . .	99 230	1 457 460	2 609 131	2 842 654
June	1 557 175	1 551 961	. . .	99 699	1 457 475	2 615 664	2 863 547
July	1 584 049	1 579 791	. . .	101 000	1 483 049	2 649 396	2 846 757
August	1 582 288	1 579 017	. . .	104 538	1 477 750	2 654 458	2 812 806
September	1 515 888	1 513 923	. . .	106 447	1 409 441	2 597 251	2 804 457
October	1 525 145	1 523 679	. . .	106 870	1 418 275	2 615 620	2 823 137
November	1 546 809	1 545 758	. . .	111 505	1 435 304	2 643 297	2 851 362
December	1 569 017	1 568 221	. . .	110 266	1 458 751	2 672 578	2 907 300
2013							
January	1 630 872	1 630 307	. . .	111 413	1 519 460	2 740 902	3 008 704
February	1 731 409	1 730 944	. . .	114 621	1 616 788	2 843 658	3 090 600
March	1 813 069	1 812 675	. . .	114 915	1 698 154	2 929 464	3 202 256
April	1 882 385	1 881 984	. . .	113 551	1 768 834	3 004 480	3 318 649
May	1 980 436	1 980 025	. . .	117 090	1 863 346	3 109 893	3 385 128
BREAK IN SERIES: FOLLOWING DATA NOT SEASONALLY ADJUSTED. SEE NOTES AND DEFINITIONS							
May	1 930 723	1 981 574	. . .	67 375	1 863 348	3 116 932	3 385 128
June	2 010 604	2 062 555	. . .	63 667	1 946 937	3 201 472	3 478 672
July	2 094 225	2 147 346	. . .	63 296	2 030 929	3 290 898	3 571 797
August	2 199 056	2 252 314	. . .	65 189	2 133 867	3 398 930	3 644 456
September	2 281 080	2 333 577	. . .	67 208	2 213 872	3 486 917	3 734 018
October	2 374 958	2 427 559	. . .	66 713	2 308 245	3 589 503	3 843 396
November	2 463 012	2 516 872	. . .	70 483	2 392 529	3 684 554	3 925 876
December	2 485 248	2 540 848	. . .	69 029	2 416 219	3 717 466	4 032 575

1Extended credit program discontinued January 9, 2003. See notes and definitions for more information.
. . . = Not available.

Table 12-4A. Commercial Banks: Bank Credit and Selected Liabilities: Recent Data

(All commercial banks in the United States, billions of dollars, seasonally adjusted, annual data are for December.)

Year and month	Total	Securities in bank credit			Loans and leases in bank credit					
		Total	U.S. Treasury and agency securities	Other securities	Total	Commercial and industrial	Real estate			
							Total	Revolving home equity	Closed-end residential	Commercial
1960	197.9	78.3	63.1	15.2	114.6	42.1	28.1	. . .	. . .	. . .
1961	214.0	86.8	69.4	17.4	121.9	43.8	29.5	. . .	. . .	. . .
1962	232.8	90.8	69.9	20.9	136.2	47.4	33.3	. . .	. . .	. . .
1963	252.9	91.4	66.8	24.6	155.1	52.2	38.1	. . .	. . .	. . .
1964	273.3	93.7	66.2	27.4	172.6	58.3	42.5	. . .	. . .	. . .
1965	301.3	95.1	63.9	31.2	198.4	69.2	47.8	. . .	. . .	. . .
1966	320.4	96.8	61.5	35.4	215.0	79.0	52.5	. . .	. . .	. . .
1967	353.2	111.1	71.5	39.6	233.1	86.1	56.8	. . .	. . .	. . .
1968	393.0	121.6	74.8	46.8	261.0	96.2	63.3	. . .	. . .	. . .
1969	403.0	112.1	65.1	46.9	279.5	106.6	68.4	. . .	. . .	. . .
1970	437.4	129.3	74.5	54.8	295.8	111.4	71.3	. . .	. . .	. . .
1971	490.6	147.3	81.5	65.8	329.6	117.8	80.0	. . .	. . .	. . .
1972	563.7	159.7	86.9	72.8	388.1	133.1	96.9	. . .	. . .	. . .
1973	645.1	166.9	90.1	76.8	460.1	161.2	117.0	. . .	. . .	. . .
1974	710.0	172.1	88.2	83.9	518.5	191.3	129.8	. . .	. . .	. . .
1975	740.5	204.9	118.1	86.8	515.9	183.4	134.1	. . .	. . .	. . .
1976	801.5	226.7	137.5	89.1	553.3	185.2	148.5	. . .	. . .	. . .
1977	888.9	234.3	137.5	96.8	629.2	204.7	175.1	. . .	. . .	. . .
1978	1 009.1	240.2	138.4	101.9	735.9	237.2	210.5	. . .	. . .	. . .
1979	1 128.8	257.8	146.1	111.7	829.8	279.7	241.7	. . .	. . .	. . .
1980	1 228.3	293.4	171.5	121.9	893.0	312.0	262.3	. . .	. . .	. . .
1981	1 309.5	306.8	179.8	127.0	958.3	350.3	283.6	. . .	. . .	. . .
1982	1 409.7	333.8	202.4	131.4	1 028.8	392.0	299.7	. . .	. . .	. . .
1983	1 561.8	398.1	260.4	137.8	1 109.5	413.9	330.4	. . .	. . .	. . .
1984	1 728.5	401.1	260.0	141.1	1 266.3	473.4	376.2	. . .	. . .	. . .
1985	1 891.7	439.5	263.2	176.3	1 443.5	498.9	422.9	. . .	. . .	. . .
1986	2 085.9	497.9	309.2	188.7	1 578.7	539.2	490.8	. . .	. . .	. . .
1987	2 233.3	525.2	335.3	189.9	1 699.9	565.1	585.7	30.6	. . .	. . .
1988	2 407.1	549.5	359.8	189.7	1 849.6	604.6	663.0	41.2	. . .	. . .
1989	2 572.0	571.3	401.1	170.2	1 992.2	637.5	759.9	51.5	. . .	. . .
1990	2 711.0	620.1	460.3	159.8	2 082.5	641.5	841.7	63.4	. . .	. . .
1991	2 815.6	726.7	563.1	163.6	2 080.7	618.3	868.5	71.9	. . .	. . .
1992	2 916.1	825.6	665.9	159.7	2 082.8	596.5	887.7	75.0	. . .	. . .
1993	3 067.6	894.0	729.6	164.4	2 164.6	583.5	928.6	74.2	. . .	. . .
1994	3 243.0	891.5	721.3	170.2	2 341.3	643.6	987.6	76.1	. . .	. . .
1995	3 472.9	894.1	702.9	191.2	2 565.0	714.9	1 061.9	79.8	. . .	. . .
1996	3 655.9	894.8	699.9	194.9	2 744.1	778.5	1 122.2	85.8	. . .	. . .
1997	3 984.2	986.6	751.1	235.6	2 973.9	845.3	1 220.3	98.8	. . .	. . .
1998	4 399.9	1 096.4	795.1	301.3	3 271.0	938.8	1 311.2	97.2	. . .	. . .
1999	4 662.3	1 144.6	811.7	332.9	3 482.6	1 001.0	1 460.7	101.2	. . .	. . .
2000	5 063.7	1 174.7	789.1	385.6	3 849.7	1 085.2	1 639.9	128.0	. . .	. . .
2001	5 237.4	1 301.5	858.2	443.3	3 903.1	1 021.8	1 759.9	153.8	. . .	. . .
2002	5 668.3	1 486.9	1 027.6	459.3	4 155.3	957.8	2 013.0	212.4	. . .	. . .
2003	6 021.9	1 619.9	1 113.2	506.7	4 384.0	883.6	2 211.2	278.7	. . .	. . .
2004	6 605.4	1 744.2	1 171.7	572.6	4 849.4	906.4	2 556.5	395.3	1 081.4	1 079.8
2005	7 324.9	1 855.5	1 159.3	696.3	5 460.1	1 036.1	2 928.9	443.5	1 215.3	1 270.1
2006	8 119.5	1 991.5	1 219.0	772.5	6 117.1	1 182.6	3 373.6	468.3	1 445.9	1 459.3
2007	8 927.0	2 104.8	1 137.5	967.3	6 799.7	1 417.7	3 600.2	484.8	1 528.2	1 587.3
2008	9 386.7	2 097.8	1 254.1	843.7	7 255.7	1 558.8	3 819.6	588.2	1 502.8	1 728.5
2009	9 025.7	2 329.7	1 450.9	878.7	6 666.2	1 265.2	3 776.8	603.1	1 532.7	1 641.0
2010	9 240.5	2 429.9	1 642.5	787.4	6 762.0	1 192.4	3 613.5	581.9	1 531.0	1 500.6
2011	9 459.1	2 495.4	1 701.9	793.4	6 907.0	1 303.8	3 495.0	549.5	1 526.9	1 418.6
2012	10 017.2	2 735.6	1 876.1	859.5	7 224.3	1 475.8	3 550.8	515.2	1 606.9	1 428.7
2013	10 148.6	2 714.5	1 804.6	909.9	7 382.8	1 577.0	3 532.3	473.7	1 559.3	1 499.3
2014	10 905.8	2 924.9	2 040.0	884.9	7 930.2	1 776.5	3 638.9	458.0	1 575.0	1 606.0
2013										
January	10 004.9	2 732.0	1 866.3	865.7	7 256.2	1 485.8	3 560.2	511.3	1 615.5	1 433.4
February	9 990.5	2 725.1	1 857.3	867.8	7 271.4	1 492.4	3 554.0	508.6	1 613.3	1 432.1
March	9 977.0	2 720.6	1 848.5	872.0	7 271.1	1 500.6	3 547.1	505.1	1 610.5	1 431.5
April	10 034.4	2 753.5	1 868.5	885.0	7 295.1	1 509.1	3 551.4	499.6	1 614.6	1 437.2
May	10 026.8	2 744.9	1 850.7	894.2	7 294.8	1 512.7	3 544.2	494.6	1 605.6	1 444.0
June	10 021.1	2 729.4	1 839.7	889.7	7 306.4	1 525.1	3 543.8	491.5	1 604.2	1 448.1
July	9 991.3	2 704.2	1 812.6	891.6	7 319.3	1 535.0	3 538.2	488.3	1 594.6	1 455.3
August	9 991.7	2 692.9	1 794.1	898.8	7 312.4	1 535.7	3 528.0	486.2	1 578.0	1 463.7
September	10 018.5	2 679.0	1 784.0	895.1	7 333.2	1 541.4	3 527.3	483.3	1 572.2	1 471.8
October	10 050.1	2 685.9	1 786.1	899.8	7 356.2	1 554.3	3 525.8	480.3	1 563.7	1 481.8
November	10 086.9	2 701.0	1 797.2	903.7	7 370.2	1 563.3	3 530.2	476.4	1 560.8	1 493.0
December	10 148.6	2 714.5	1 804.6	909.9	7 382.8	1 577.0	3 532.3	473.7	1 559.3	1 499.3
2014										
January	10 145.0	2 726.0	1 816.2	909.7	7 405.3	1 587.0	3 535.3	471.2	1 557.5	1 506.6
February	10 202.8	2 741.2	1 828.0	913.1	7 467.6	1 622.7	3 545.2	469.1	1 559.5	1 516.6
March	10 276.1	2 760.9	1 844.2	916.7	7 527.4	1 638.8	3 558.0	469.0	1 567.1	1 521.9
April	10 338.0	2 772.6	1 858.9	913.7	7 573.0	1 655.2	3 571.2	467.8	1 570.1	1 533.4
May	10 408.0	2 794.5	1 884.2	910.2	7 620.0	1 667.5	3 580.6	466.5	1 572.2	1 542.0
June	10 479.8	2 812.2	1 898.9	913.3	7 674.3	1 680.1	3 598.0	465.4	1 580.9	1 551.6
July	10 537.0	2 838.0	1 925.8	912.3	7 729.0	1 700.2	3 607.9	464.2	1 581.5	1 562.2
August	10 597.1	2 840.2	1 938.4	901.8	7 775.0	1 718.0	3 617.5	462.3	1 583.2	1 572.0
September	10 661.6	2 858.7	1 971.8	886.9	7 801.9	1 729.5	3 621.1	460.8	1 580.5	1 579.7
October	10 698.6	2 866.2	1 988.5	877.7	7 833.2	1 737.0	3 624.0	460.3	1 575.6	1 588.1
November	10 783.2	2 879.1	1 999.5	879.6	7 890.8	1 757.0	3 628.5	459.4	1 572.9	1 596.2
December	10 905.8	2 924.9	2 040.0	884.9	7 930.2	1 776.5	3 638.9	458.0	1 575.0	1 606.0

. . . = Not available.

Table 12-4A. Commercial Banks: Bank Credit and Selected Liabilities: Recent Data—*Continued*

(All commercial banks in the United States, billions of dollars, seasonally adjusted, annual data are for December.)

Year and month	Bank credit				Deposits	Selected liabilities		
	Loans and leases in bank credit					Borrowings		
	Consumer loans			Other loans and leases		Total	From banks in the United States	From others
	Total	Credit cards and other revolving plans	Other consumer loans					
1960	22.0	...	...	22.4	...	...	...	...
1961	23.1	...	...	25.5	...	...	...	...
1962	25.3	...	...	30.2	...	...	...	...
1963	28.7	...	...	36.2	...	...	...	...
1964	33.3	...	...	38.5	...	...	...	...
1965	38.0	...	...	43.4	...	...	...	...
1966	40.1	...	...	43.4	...	...	...	...
1967	43.1	...	...	46.9	...	...	...	...
1968	48.5	...	...	53.0	...	...	...	...
1969	52.5	...	...	52.0	...	...	...	...
1970	54.5	...	...	58.6	...	...	...	...
1971	61.2	...	...	70.6	...	...	...	...
1972	71.3	...	...	86.8	...	...	...	...
1973	82.2	...	...	99.7	663.7	14.9	...	...
1974	85.3	...	...	112.2	731.4	19.5	...	...
1975	87.3	...	...	111.1	768.0	20.5		
1976	97.2	...	...	122.3	825.9	22.4		
1977	116.0	...	...	133.5	910.9	29.0	...	...
1978	136.8	...	...	151.3	1 004.0	53.3	...	...
1979	153.2	...	...	155.1	1 072.7	176.0	...	...
1980	148.2	...	...	170.5	1 185.1	211.5	...	...
1981	149.6	...	...	174.8	1 248.2	254.8	...	...
1982	152.9	...	...	184.2	1 365.5	280.6	...	...
1983	170.9	...	...	194.3	1 479.1	280.8	...	...
1984	205.3	...	...	211.3	1 612.4	315.2	...	...
1985	291.1	...	...	230.6	1 761.5	347.3	...	...
1986	314.7	...	...	234.0	1 924.5	391.4	...	...
1987	326.9	...	...	222.3	1 985.6	408.8	...	...
1988	355.3	...	...	227.0	2 115.7	457.9	...	...
1989	374.0	...	...	220.8	2 241.6	515.5	...	...
1990	376.0	...	...	223.3	2 339.0	526.1	...	...
1991	363.1	...	...	230.8	2 466.2	465.9	...	...
1992	354.1	...	...	244.5	2 497.4	467.8	...	...
1993	385.6	...	...	266.9	2 533.3	498.6	...	...
1994	443.3	...	...	266.7	2 532.6	584.7	...	...
1995	483.6	...	...	304.6	2 651.7	646.1	...	...
1996	508.8	...	...	334.6	2 834.3	683.7	301.2	382.5
1997	502.5	...	...	405.7	3 080.0	810.6	303.4	507.2
1998	497.8	...	...	523.2	3 293.8	945.5	317.1	628.4
1999	506.3	...	...	514.6	3 474.5	1 078.4	344.0	734.4
2000	555.6	228.3	327.3	569.0	3 724.2	1 171.2	377.6	793.5
2001	574.7	242.3	332.4	546.7	4 079.1	1 168.8	407.1	761.6
2002	611.9	255.9	356.0	572.6	4 351.6	1 318.3	423.9	894.4
2003	666.1	282.4	383.8	623.1	4 627.7	1 365.7	393.1	972.6
2004	692.9	298.3	394.5	693.7	5 155.0	1 479.7	399.6	1 080.2
2005	704.5	304.6	400.0	790.6	5 595.0	1 639.6	372.5	1 267.1
2006	738.6	314.0	424.6	822.4	6 098.3	1 870.8	408.2	1 462.6
2007	799.2	342.2	456.9	982.7	6 670.5	2 134.5	477.5	1 657.0
2008	876.2	385.1	491.1	1 001.1	7 212.8	2 458.7	383.0	2 075.7
2009	836.0	336.4	499.6	788.1	7 685.6	1 901.6	261.3	1 640.3
2010	1 113.9	604.4	509.5	842.3	7 864.7	1 886.5	229.1	1 657.4
2011	1 091.2	596.9	494.3	1 017.1	8 423.3	1 611.6	132.3	1 479.3
2012	1 115.6	602.4	513.2	1 082.0	9 244.1	1 543.6	151.5	1 392.1
2013	1 141.6	594.4	547.3	1 131.8	9 788.2	1 534.2	132.9	1 401.3
2014	1 199.1	618.9	580.2	1 315.7	10 445.5	1 776.6	112.1	1 664.5
2013								
January	1 118.8	603.2	515.7	1 091.4	9 248.7	1 565.4	156.9	1 408.5
February	1 122.5	604.4	518.1	1 102.5	9 258.7	1 569.6	155.0	1 414.6
March	1 125.8	605.5	520.3	1 097.5	9 329.6	1 552.4	153.5	1 398.9
April	1 129.6	606.6	522.9	1 104.9	9 363.9	1 531.1	149.9	1 381.2
May	1 133.1	607.3	525.9	1 104.8	9 392.6	1 539.4	142.9	1 396.5
June	1 137.9	608.9	528.9	1 099.8	9 433.9	1 527.5	141.7	1 385.8
July	1 137.8	606.6	531.3	1 108.3	9 498.9	1 516.5	138.7	1 377.9
August	1 140.7	606.2	534.5	1 108.0	9 546.3	1 515.8	135.8	1 380.0
September	1 143.7	606.5	537.2	1 120.7	9 599.6	1 519.6	135.6	1 384.0
October	1 148.4	608.0	540.4	1 127.7	9 689.4	1 530.0	134.9	1 395.1
November	1 143.6	599.6	544.0	1 133.1	9 717.8	1 542.4	134.9	1 407.5
December	1 141.6	594.4	547.3	1 131.8	9 788.2	1 534.2	132.9	1 401.3
2014								
January	1 144.3	594.7	549.6	1 138.7	9 852.7	1 553.4	137.4	1 416.0
February	1 147.9	596.3	551.7	1 151.8	9 917.2	1 559.1	140.3	1 418.8
March	1 151.3	595.8	555.5	1 179.3	9 991.2	1 596.2	146.1	1 450.1
April	1 158.7	599.3	559.4	1 187.9	10 077.4	1 620.5	139.2	1 481.3
May	1 164.8	601.8	563.0	1 207.0	10 144.1	1 646.2	139.7	1 506.5
June	1 171.1	603.9	567.1	1 225.2	10 175.3	1 697.1	139.0	1 558.1
July	1 179.4	607.1	572.3	1 241.4	10 238.7	1 723.8	149.2	1 574.7
August	1 183.1	609.1	574.0	1 256.4	10 252.0	1 727.6	133.3	1 594.4
September	1 188.1	611.7	576.5	1 263.1	10 334.7	1 744.7	129.4	1 615.3
October	1 192.6	613.9	578.7	1 279.6	10 296.2	1 767.1	125.5	1 641.6
November	1 197.8	616.5	581.2	1 307.6	10 378.3	1 770.2	117.9	1 652.3
December	1 199.1	618.9	580.2	1 315.7	10 445.5	1 776.6	112.1	1 664.5

. . . = Not available.

Figure 12-2: Debt Ratios, 1955–2014

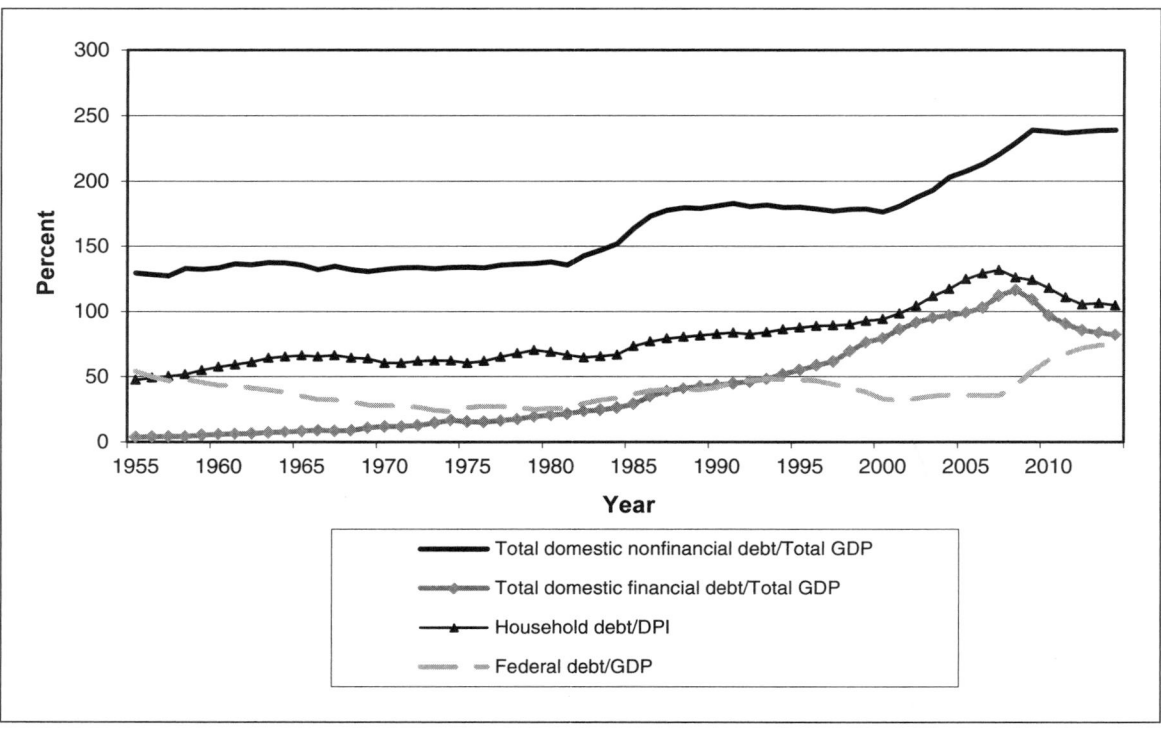

- Unsustainable debt growth was the source of the credit crisis and economic decline in 2007–2009. Traditionally, analysts have focused on the debt of nonfinancial sectors. Among the major nonfinancial divisions of the economy, the most striking expansion in debt relative to income occurred in the household sector. Household debt in 1984 was no higher, relative to disposable personal income, than it had been in 1964—but then it began a rapid and uninterrupted expansion. In 2002, debt rose above 100 percent of annual income, and it reached 132 percent at the end of 2007. After that, debt edged down and the ratio declined until 2013, when household debt rose, but less than income; the 2014 ratio, at 105.1 percent, was still higher than anything seen before 2003. (Table 12-5)

- During the expansion period, financial sector debt—much of it reflecting the securitization of nonfinancial sector debt, especially mortgages, in other words debt built upon other debt—grew somewhat more rapidly than nonfinancial sector debt. Between 1985 and 2007, financial sector debt rose from 29 percent to 112 percent of GDP, while total nonfinancial sector debt only grew from 164 to 226 percent.

- Up through 2003, the debt of federal government-related financial entities—government-sponsored enterprises (GSEs) such as "Fannie Mae" and "Freddie Mac" and mortgage pools backed by federal agencies and GSEs—and the debt of private financial sectors both rose rapidly. From 2003 to 2007, growth slowed in the government portion but accelerated in the private segment. After 2008, total private financial debt dropped dramatically and total financial debt fell to 82 percent of GDP at the end of 2014. (Tables 1-1 and 12-5)

- Debt of the federal government itself—that is, Treasury securities issued to fund budget deficits—contributed little, on balance, to the rising trend of aggregate debt—until the recession struck in 2008, revenues fell, and spending rose because of both recession-sensitive programs like unemployment insurance and new moves to stabilize credit markets and the economy. (Tables 12-5, 6-1 and 6-15)

Table 12-5. Credit Market Debt Outstanding, by Borrower and Lender

(Billions of dollars, except as noted; end of period; not seasonally adjusted.)

Year and quarter	Total	Domestic financial sectors			Domestic nonfinancial sectors										
					Total		Federal government			Households		Nonfinancial business		
		Total	Federal govern-ment-related	Private	Billions of dollars	Percent of GDP	Total	Treasury securities	Budget agency securities and mortgages	Billions of dollars	Percent of DPI	Total	Corporate	
													Total	Percent of sector value added
1955	582.2	15.1	3.2	11.9	550.7	129.2	230.0	228.4	1.6	138.5	47.5	136.1	101.2	45.7
1956	611.7	17.8	4.0	13.8	576.7	128.1	224.1	222.8	1.4	153.3	49.2	148.9	111.0	46.8
1957	642.9	20.7	5.1	15.5	603.7	127.1	221.9	220.1	1.7	165.8	50.3	161.0	120.6	48.7
1958	681.8	20.8	5.2	15.6	640.5	132.9	231.1	229.0	1.6	176.6	51.8	172.1	128.0	52.8
1959	739.0	27.4	7.5	20.0	690.1	132.1	238.0	236.2	0.9	198.5	55.0	186.9	136.6	50.3
1960	780.5	32.3	8.1	24.2	725.0	133.4	236.0	234.0	0.7	216.2	57.4	200.6	145.6	51.5
1961	829.0	34.7	8.9	25.8	768.9	136.5	243.2	240.7	1.0	233.2	59.2	214.7	153.0	52.7
1962	888.6	39.3	10.5	28.8	821.8	135.8	250.0	246.8	1.5	255.2	61.1	232.8	163.5	51.6
1963	954.5	46.4	12.0	34.3	877.4	137.4	253.8	250.7	1.4	282.1	64.4	252.2	174.2	51.6
1964	1 028.8	52.7	12.7	40.0	941.2	137.2	259.9	255.9	2.2	311.5	65.4	274.2	187.9	51.6
1965	1 107.2	61.4	15.1	46.4	1 008.4	135.6	261.5	257.0	2.7	339.9	66.2	303.8	208.2	52.0
1966	1 187.7	72.3	20.3	52.0	1 075.8	132.0	265.1	259.3	4.0	362.4	65.4	338.2	232.9	52.9
1967	1 275.9	73.2	20.4	52.8	1 159.5	134.6	278.1	268.2	8.2	393.2	66.3	370.9	255.2	55.1
1968	1 373.6	83.5	24.4	59.1	1 244.1	132.0	290.6	277.6	11.3	414.7	64.4	412.7	286.1	56.0
1969	1 491.5	111.0	33.8	77.2	1 331.3	130.5	287.4	276.8	9.0	444.8	63.9	460.8	318.9	57.5
1970	1 601.1	127.3	43.6	83.7	1 421.7	132.1	299.5	289.9	8.1	460.0	60.4	511.9	363.4	63.4
1971	1 750.4	137.8	49.5	88.2	1 556.1	133.2	324.4	315.9	7.0	501.5	60.4	563.4	392.2	63.5
1972	1 934.6	161.3	57.9	103.3	1 712.2	133.5	339.4	330.1	7.9	557.8	62.0	634.4	431.8	63.0
1973	2 171.4	207.9	77.9	130.0	1 896.2	132.7	346.3	336.7	8.4	627.5	62.4	727.6	497.4	64.7
1974	2 408.8	257.6	98.6	159.0	2 069.8	133.6	358.2	348.8	8.2	683.1	62.2	820.3	553.1	66.6
1975	2 617.0	261.3	108.9	152.4	2 260.4	133.8	443.9	434.9	7.9	736.9	60.4	860.3	572.7	63.7
1976	2 904.9	285.5	123.1	162.3	2 503.7	133.3	513.1	503.7	8.3	821.4	62.0	931.4	614.3	60.5
1977	3 292.8	339.1	145.5	193.6	2 825.1	135.4	569.4	560.9	7.6	949.4	65.2	1 050.1	690.3	60.2
1978	3 779.9	412.7	182.6	230.1	3 209.3	136.2	621.9	614.9	6.2	1 107.6	67.9	1 184.3	766.1	58.7
1979	4 282.5	508.9	231.8	277.1	3 596.5	136.6	657.7	652.1	4.9	1 272.8	70.3	1 343.8	851.8	58.7
1980	4 730.0	584.7	276.6	308.1	3 943.2	137.8	735.0	730.0	4.4	1 389.1	68.8	1 474.7	919.6	58.4
1981	5 267.8	689.2	324.0	365.2	4 349.2	135.4	820.5	815.9	4.1	1 498.2	66.6	1 658.5	1 038.7	58.1
1982	5 780.2	785.5	388.9	396.6	4 770.6	142.6	981.8	978.1	3.4	1 567.5	64.6	1 807.6	1 129.9	60.9
1983	6 462.5	890.1	456.6	433.5	5 344.2	146.9	1 167.0	1 163.4	3.3	1 719.8	65.7	1 996.2	1 247.2	62.8
1984	7 421.3	1 054.9	531.2	523.7	6 138.2	151.9	1 364.2	1 360.8	3.2	1 939.8	66.8	2 320.6	1 458.0	65.5
1985	8 705.7	1 259.0	631.7	627.2	7 111.8	163.6	1 589.9	1 586.6	3.2	2 272.0	73.3	2 572.0	1 638.9	69.2
1986	9 896.1	1 596.6	810.3	786.3	7 953.5	173.3	1 805.9	1 802.2	3.6	2 529.5	76.9	2 866.0	1 865.8	75.7
1987	10 913.7	1 899.7	977.6	922.1	8 656.8	177.8	1 949.8	1 944.6	5.1	2 747.1	79.3	3 117.4	2 059.2	77.9
1988	11 982.3	2 149.5	1 098.4	1 051.2	9 439.6	179.7	2 104.9	2 082.3	22.6	3 036.3	80.5	3 405.5	2 263.5	78.7
1989	12 933.0	2 402.8	1 247.8	1 155.0	10 141.0	179.2	2 251.2	2 227.0	24.2	3 305.1	81.6	3 644.3	2 454.1	81.2
1990	13 837.1	2 613.8	1 418.4	1 195.4	10 827.2	181.1	2 498.1	2 465.8	32.4	3 567.8	82.7	3 773.8	2 583.3	81.7
1991	14 469.4	2 766.8	1 564.2	1 202.6	11 296.4	183.0	2 776.4	2 757.8	18.6	3 755.0	83.7	3 686.4	2 524.4	78.1
1992	15 258.7	3 018.9	1 720.4	1 298.5	11 813.9	180.7	3 080.3	3 061.6	18.8	3 959.4	82.5	3 679.1	2 543.6	75.3
1993	16 333.8	3 317.2	1 885.7	1 431.5	12 496.1	181.7	3 336.5	3 309.9	26.6	4 201.3	84.0	3 805.2	2 690.4	76.1
1994	17 431.5	3 789.7	2 173.4	1 616.3	13 141.4	179.8	3 492.3	3 465.6	26.7	4 525.0	86.3	4 016.5	2 887.2	75.7
1995	18 654.8	4 226.3	2 377.7	1 848.5	13 797.9	180.0	3 636.7	3 608.5	28.2	4 844.5	87.6	4 269.8	3 095.2	76.6
1996	19 949.7	4 749.5	2 609.2	2 140.3	14 479.4	178.8	3 781.7	3 755.1	26.6	5 182.3	88.9	4 489.1	3 244.1	75.5
1997	21 340.6	5 299.7	2 822.8	2 476.9	15 239.2	177.0	3 804.8	3 778.3	26.5	5 489.2	89.3	4 868.3	3 521.3	76.4
1998	23 392.4	6 326.2	3 294.4	3 031.8	16 223.8	178.5	3 752.2	3 723.7	28.5	5 901.4	89.9	5 426.5	3 900.4	80.0
1999	25 445.8	7 376.5	3 887.7	3 488.8	17 265.4	178.7	3 681.0	3 652.7	28.3	6 375.3	92.7	6 028.2	4 308.3	83.3
2000	27 157.5	8 168.4	4 319.7	3 848.7	18 121.5	176.2	3 385.1	3 357.8	27.3	6 959.5	94.0	6 579.0	4 666.7	84.6
2001	29 217.3	9 156.8	4 962.3	4 194.5	19 211.1	180.9	3 379.5	3 352.7	26.8	7 625.7	98.4	6 902.6	4 826.8	88.2
2002	31 574.1	10 038.3	5 509.0	4 529.3	20 580.1	187.5	3 637.0	3 609.8	27.3	8 437.7	104.2	7 057.4	4 829.8	87.2
2003	34 324.6	10 945.2	5 944.5	5 000.7	22 222.8	193.1	4 033.1	4 008.2	24.9	9 472.5	111.6	7 148.8	4 847.3	84.7
2004	38 129.3	11 898.8	6 060.3	5 838.5	24 945.3	203.2	4 395.0	4 370.7	24.3	10 544.3	117.1	7 557.8	5 001.6	81.9
2005	41 488.1	12 958.0	6 140.7	6 817.3	27 179.5	207.6	4 701.9	4 678.0	23.8	11 721.3	124.7	8 166.5	5 268.5	80.7
2006	45 432.6	14 261.5	6 468.9	7 792.5	29 513.2	213.0	4 885.3	4 861.7	23.5	12 946.2	129.0	8 991.0	5 677.5	81.2
2007	50 106.0	16 205.5	7 374.6	8 831.9	31 902.8	220.4	5 122.3	5 099.2	23.1	13 831.4	131.6	10 111.7	6 336.5	88.0
2008	52 464.4	17 104.6	8 143.4	8 961.3	33 755.4	229.3	6 361.5	6 338.2	23.3	13 850.8	126.0	10 687.7	6 593.7	90.9
2009	52 191.2	15 715.6	8 083.3	7 632.3	34 469.7	239.1	7 805.4	7 781.9	23.5	13 559.6	123.9	10 136.3	6 150.9	89.7
2010	52 331.8	14 455.7	7 574.0	6 881.7	35 618.2	238.0	9 385.6	9 361.5	24.2	13 230.6	117.7	9 964.0	6 013.1	83.1
2011	53 272.4	14 036.3	7 552.1	6 484.2	36 751.2	236.8	10 453.6	10 428.3	25.3	13 057.8	110.6	10 254.6	6 308.0	83.1
2012	55 040.9	13 802.4	7 529.7	6 272.6	38 411.2	237.8	11 593.7	11 568.9	24.9	13 055.1	105.3	10 782.3	6 714.1	83.8
2013	56 677.2	13 949.2	7 769.7	6 179.5	39 762.4	238.6	12 352.8	12 328.3	24.5	13 170.4	106.3	11 298.0	7 115.3	85.6
2014	58 783.9	14 201.8	7 920.2	6 281.5	41 438.7	238.9	13 019.9	12 995.6	24.4	13 512.1	104.6	11 979.1	7 579.2	87.7
2012														
1st quarter	53 645.7	13 929.2	7 508.5	6 420.6	37 186.0	232.8	10 851.9	10 827.4	24.4	13 009.8	106.7	10 337.9	6 365.1	80.3
2nd quarter	53 859.6	13 755.3	7 517.2	6 238.2	37 534.7	232.8	11 050.1	11 025.6	24.5	13 053.7	105.9	10 437.6	6 431.7	80.5
3rd quarter	54 458.7	13 850.1	7 519.5	6 330.5	37 867.5	233.3	11 279.9	11 255.5	24.4	13 000.3	105.2	10 602.1	6 565.7	82.2
4th quarter	55 040.9	13 802.4	7 529.7	6 272.6	38 411.2	235.7	11 593.7	11 568.9	24.9	13 055.1	102.4	10 782.3	6 714.1	82.4
2013														
1st quarter	55 424.4	13 752.4	7 566.2	6 186.2	38 782.8	235.9	11 930.1	11 905.5	24.6	12 999.9	106.1	10 857.9	6 793.6	82.8
2nd quarter	55 541.8	13 763.0	7 635.8	6 127.2	38 937.8	235.6	11 912.9	11 887.9	25.0	13 027.7	105.5	11 010.9	6 908.9	83.0
3rd quarter	55 932.6	13 764.5	7 688.5	6 076.0	39 260.7	234.7	11 981.9	11 956.8	25.1	13 136.8	105.4	11 188.9	7 050.3	84.6
4th quarter	56 677.2	13 949.2	7 769.7	6 179.5	39 762.4	234.5	12 352.8	12 328.3	24.5	13 170.4	105.2	11 298.0	7 115.3	84.7
2014														
1st quarter	57 085.8	13 856.4	7 697.1	6 159.3	40 183.6	236.6	12 614.8	12 590.8	24.0	13 175.1	103.8	11 462.0	7 263.4	86.0
2nd quarter	57 558.8	13 946.8	7 750.6	6 196.2	40 392.6	233.9	12 568.4	12 544.4	24.0	13 286.6	103.3	11 603.2	7 345.6	85.6
3rd quarter	58 072.0	14 051.9	7 809.8	6 242.1	40 836.3	233.1	12 779.4	12 755.6	23.9	13 398.1	103.2	11 750.6	7 448.9	85.3
4th quarter	58 783.9	14 201.8	7 920.2	6 281.5	41 438.7	235.2	13 019.9	12 995.6	24.4	13 512.1	103.0	11 979.1	7 579.2	86.1

Table 12-5. Credit Market Debt Outstanding, by Borrower and Lender—Continued

(Billions of dollars, except as noted; end of period; not seasonally adjusted.)

| Year and quarter | Credit market debt outstanding owed by: —Continued | | | Credit market assets held by: | | | | | | | | | |
| | Domestic nonfinancial sectors —Continued | | Foreign credit market debt held in United States | | Selected government-related sectors | | | | | | | Selected domestic financial sectors | |
	Nonfinancial business —Continued Noncorporate	State and local governments		Total	Total	Federal government	Government-sponsored enterprises	Federally related mortgage pools	State and local governments	State and local retirement funds	Federal government retirement funds	Total, selected sectors	Monetary authority
1955	34.8	46.1	16.4	582.2	51.3	21.0	5.0	0.1	14.7	10.5	0.0	368.0	24.4
1956	37.9	50.4	17.3	611.7	55.4	21.6	6.0	0.1	15.9	11.7	0.0	389.5	24.7
1957	40.4	55.0	18.5	642.9	58.9	22.2	7.3	0.2	15.9	13.3	0.0	410.0	23.8
1958	44.2	60.7	20.5	681.8	62.6	23.6	7.7	0.2	16.1	15.0	0.0	443.6	26.3
1959	50.2	66.7	21.4	739.0	70.1	25.7	9.9	0.2	17.5	16.8	0.0	471.0	26.7
1960	55.0	72.2	23.2	780.5	76.0	26.7	11.1	0.2	19.1	18.9	0.0	502.5	27.0
1961	61.7	77.8	25.4	829.0	82.0	28.4	12.1	0.3	20.1	21.1	0.0	541.1	28.8
1962	69.3	83.8	27.5	888.6	89.4	30.3	13.7	0.4	21.7	23.2	0.0	587.2	30.5
1963	78.0	89.2	30.8	954.5	96.6	31.9	15.3	0.5	23.3	25.6	0.0	638.8	33.7
1964	86.3	95.6	34.9	1 028.8	104.6	34.6	16.0	0.6	25.0	28.3	0.0	695.9	36.6
1965	95.6	103.2	37.4	1 107.2	115.5	37.6	18.3	0.9	27.5	31.3	0.0	758.7	40.6
1966	105.3	110.0	39.5	1 187.7	129.9	42.8	23.3	1.3	27.5	34.9	0.0	804.3	43.7
1967	115.6	117.4	43.3	1 275.9	138.5	47.3	23.3	2.0	27.6	38.3	0.0	876.8	49.1
1968	126.6	126.1	46.0	1 373.6	154.4	52.2	26.5	2.5	31.4	41.6	0.0	942.4	53.0
1969	141.9	138.3	49.2	1 491.5	175.6	55.4	35.1	3.2	36.4	45.5	0.0	993.8	57.2
1970	148.6	150.3	52.0	1 601.1	191.5	58.2	43.9	4.8	35.1	49.6	0.0	1 066.0	62.2
1971	171.2	166.7	56.6	1 750.4	201.1	60.3	45.0	9.5	33.4	52.9	0.0	1 176.2	69.6
1972	202.6	180.7	61.1	1 934.6	223.0	62.1	49.0	14.4	40.1	57.4	0.0	1 318.7	71.2
1973	230.1	194.8	67.4	2 171.4	260.1	64.8	64.4	18.0	49.8	63.1	0.0	1 478.8	80.5
1974	267.2	208.2	81.3	2 408.8	304.7	72.2	85.3	21.5	56.4	69.4	0.0	1 606.8	85.3
1975	287.6	219.4	95.4	2 617.0	346.0	85.6	89.8	28.5	63.8	78.3	0.0	1 737.1	93.5
1976	317.1	237.8	115.8	2 904.9	398.7	93.8	94.5	40.7	82.0	87.7	0.0	1 926.4	100.3
1977	359.8	256.2	128.6	3 292.8	471.6	103.6	101.4	56.8	110.6	99.2	0.0	2 178.2	108.9
1978	418.2	295.6	157.9	3 779.9	582.3	120.3	128.1	70.4	147.5	116.0	0.0	2 455.9	117.4
1979	492.0	322.2	177.2	4 282.5	696.1	141.5	158.1	94.8	175.2	126.6	0.0	2 752.4	124.5
1980	555.1	344.4	202.1	4 730.0	804.6	165.6	184.5	114.0	193.4	147.2	0.0	2 998.1	128.0
1981	619.8	372.1	229.4	5 267.8	931.1	189.8	217.7	129.0	225.6	169.0	0.0	3 289.7	136.9
1982	677.7	413.8	224.1	5 780.2	1 059.1	206.0	233.7	178.5	250.1	190.7	0.0	3 559.3	144.5
1983	749.0	461.1	228.2	6 462.5	1 177.3	214.8	236.4	244.8	282.4	198.8	0.0	3 963.5	159.2
1984	862.6	513.6	228.1	7 421.3	1 339.0	231.9	265.9	289.0	319.0	233.2	0.0	4 525.0	167.6
1985	933.0	677.9	335.0	8 705.7	1 617.5	250.7	291.0	367.9	455.6	252.4	0.0	5 115.4	186.0
1986	1 000.2	752.1	346.1	9 896.1	1 919.9	257.4	307.6	531.6	525.8	297.5	0.0	5 793.2	205.5
1987	1 058.2	842.6	357.2	10 913.7	2 156.5	242.3	330.9	669.4	583.6	329.2	1.1	6 305.5	226.5
1988	1 141.9	893.0	393.1	11 982.3	2 298.8	216.8	364.2	745.3	618.6	351.2	2.7	6 820.4	241.2
1989	1 190.2	940.4	389.2	12 933.0	2 489.8	208.8	359.9	869.5	664.1	382.6	4.9	7 227.6	233.3
1990	1 190.5	987.4	396.2	13 837.1	2 751.4	242.6	373.9	1 019.9	703.4	403.9	7.6	7 560.4	241.4
1991	1 162.0	1 078.6	406.2	14 469.4	2 962.8	250.4	388.9	1 156.5	750.6	406.2	10.2	7 785.5	272.5
1992	1 135.5	1 095.1	425.8	15 258.7	3 177.5	238.5	458.1	1 272.0	752.3	443.3	13.3	8 143.5	300.4
1993	1 114.9	1 153.0	520.6	16 333.8	3 402.3	227.0	546.7	1 356.8	784.9	470.5	16.5	8 755.4	336.7
1994	1 129.3	1 107.5	500.4	17 431.5	3 592.6	221.5	667.9	1 472.4	729.9	480.9	20.0	9 217.6	368.2
1995	1 174.6	1 046.7	630.7	18 654.8	3 695.8	197.0	762.8	1 570.7	638.6	512.1	14.6	9 875.0	380.8
1996	1 245.1	1 026.2	720.9	19 949.7	3 919.7	201.1	833.8	1 711.7	604.8	542.2	26.0	10 415.0	393.1
1997	1 347.0	1 076.9	801.7	21 340.6	4 210.6	212.5	934.2	1 826.3	605.0	604.7	27.9	11 209.2	431.4
1998	1 526.0	1 143.8	842.4	23 392.4	4 905.1	218.3	1 251.5	2 019.0	714.6	671.0	30.7	12 385.3	452.5
1999	1 719.8	1 181.0	803.9	25 445.8	5 659.2	255.7	1 538.8	2 293.5	816.5	721.3	33.3	13 532.3	478.1
2000	1 912.3	1 197.9	867.6	27 157.5	6 227.6	262.6	1 794.4	2 493.2	887.3	754.7	35.4	14 422.1	511.8
2001	2 075.7	1 303.4	849.4	29 217.3	6 928.1	266.4	2 099.1	2 831.8	981.2	704.6	44.9	15 540.8	551.7
2002	2 227.6	1 447.9	955.7	31 574.1	7 538.6	274.4	2 323.1	3 158.6	1 067.4	656.9	58.1	16 818.1	629.4
2003	2 301.5	1 568.4	1 156.6	34 324.6	8 013.9	272.0	2 564.1	3 343.3	1 094.7	674.7	65.1	18 210.8	666.7
2004	2 556.2	2 448.2	1 285.2	38 129.3	8 246.6	274.3	2 613.0	3 384.0	1 206.1	699.1	70.1	19 827.4	717.8
2005	2 898.0	2 589.8	1 350.5	41 488.1	8 556.3	271.2	2 543.9	3 548.5	1 376.4	738.1	78.2	21 736.2	744.2
2006	3 313.4	2 690.8	1 657.9	45 432.6	9 149.5	294.3	2 590.5	3 841.1	1 504.8	831.8	86.9	23 786.1	778.9
2007	3 775.1	2 837.5	1 996.6	50 106.0	10 230.7	301.1	2 829.5	4 464.4	1 660.3	875.8	99.5	25 516.0	740.6
2008	4 094.0	2 855.4	1 604.6	52 464.4	10 935.8	394.5	3 037.5	4 961.4	1 562.9	856.0	123.5	26 343.7	986.0
2009	3 985.4	2 968.4	2 005.9	52 191.2	11 212.7	703.7	2 699.7	5 376.7	1 528.8	773.0	130.9	25 988.9	1 987.7
2010	3 950.9	3 038.0	2 257.9	52 331.8	10 799.9	791.8	6 333.1	1 139.5	1 598.4	795.3	141.8	25 567.5	2 259.2
2011	3 946.6	2 985.3	2 484.9	53 272.4	10 750.2	810.1	6 133.4	1 304.8	1 531.9	802.7	167.3	26 411.6	2 635.6
2012	4 068.2	2 980.0	2 827.4	55 040.9	10 814.8	915.1	5 914.8	1 437.0	1 559.2	806.0	182.7	27 412.0	2 670.0
2013	4 182.8	2 941.1	2 965.7	56 677.2	11 154.1	1 039.2	5 956.4	1 569.4	1 511.5	885.5	192.1	29 034.5	3 756.3
2014	4 399.9	2 927.5	3 143.5	58 783.9	11 527.2	1 154.4	6 014.4	1 644.7	1 584.0	920.6	209.0	30 663.0	4 236.9
2012													
1st quarter	3 972.8	2 986.3	2 530.6	53 645.7	10 746.2	825.3	6 095.8	1 329.9	1 518.2	810.2	166.9	26 558.4	2 613.4
2nd quarter	4 005.9	2 993.3	2 569.6	53 859.6	10 766.8	854.5	6 014.0	1 377.3	1 541.6	806.6	172.8	26 694.7	2 610.9
3rd quarter	4 036.4	2 985.3	2 741.1	54 458.7	10 787.4	896.7	5 950.1	1 408.0	1 553.8	800.9	178.0	26 921.3	2 565.1
4th quarter	4 068.2	2 980.0	2 827.4	55 040.9	10 814.8	915.1	5 914.8	1 437.0	1 559.2	806.0	182.7	27 412.0	2 670.1
2013													
1st quarter	4 064.3	2 994.9	2 889.2	55 424.4	10 889.1	962.0	5 899.5	1 462.7	1 569.2	816.5	179.2	27 804.4	2 939.8
2nd quarter	4 101.9	2 986.4	2 841.0	55 541.8	10 990.2	979.0	5 932.8	1 498.1	1 563.9	848.2	168.1	28 077.4	3 214.2
3rd quarter	4 138.6	2 953.1	2 907.4	55 932.6	10 975.1	1 020.8	5 954.6	1 540.8	1 522.0	864.2	72.8	28 455.8	3 475.1
4th quarter	4 182.8	2 941.1	2 965.7	56 677.2	11 154.1	1 039.2	5 956.4	1 569.4	1 511.5	885.5	192.1	29 034.5	3 756.3
2014													
1st quarter	4 198.6	2 931.8	3 045.9	57 085.8	11 196.3	1 082.5	5 924.2	1 585.8	1 520.2	890.1	193.6	29 312.8	3 970.1
2nd quarter	4 257.6	2 934.4	3 219.5	57 558.8	11 296.1	1 099.1	5 945.4	1 600.0	1 556.7	899.0	196.0	29 701.1	4 108.2
3rd quarter	4 301.6	2 908.3	3 183.8	58 072.0	11 402.2	1 139.6	5 968.1	1 623.6	1 549.9	919.8	201.1	30 134.0	4 188.2
4th quarter	4 399.9	2 927.5	3 143.5	58 783.9	11 527.2	1 154.4	6 014.4	1 644.7	1 584.0	920.6	209.0	30 663.0	4 236.9

Table 12-5. Credit Market Debt Outstanding, by Borrower and Lender—*Continued*

(Billions of dollars, except as noted; end of period; not seasonally adjusted.)

Year and quarter	Credit market assets held by:—*Continued*											
	Selected domestic financial sectors—*Continued*									House-holds	Foreign holdings in United States	All other financial and non-financial sectors
	U.S. chartered depository institutions	Credit unions	Life insurance companies	Property-casualty insurance companies	Private pension funds	Money market mutual funds	Mutual funds	Asset-backed security issuers	Finance companies			
1955	220.7	2.0	80.5	11.5	11.2	0.0	0.8	0.0	17.0	117.7	6.7	38.6
1956	233.2	2.4	85.6	11.9	12.7	0.0	1.1	0.0	18.0	124.9	7.3	34.5
1957	245.4	2.9	90.5	12.6	14.5	0.0	1.2	0.0	19.3	132.0	7.5	34.6
1958	268.7	3.1	95.5	13.4	16.2	0.0	1.5	0.0	19.0	132.7	7.5	35.4
1959	283.4	3.8	100.5	14.6	17.9	0.0	1.8	0.0	22.4	142.8	11.7	43.3
1960	302.2	4.5	105.6	15.5	19.7	0.0	2.0	0.0	25.9	151.0	12.6	38.5
1961	329.4	4.9	110.9	16.5	21.2	0.0	2.4	0.0	27.0	154.9	13.1	37.9
1962	361.6	5.6	116.9	18.0	22.9	0.0	2.6	0.0	29.2	158.3	14.8	38.9
1963	395.5	6.3	123.3	18.7	24.8	0.0	2.8	0.0	33.7	159.9	15.9	43.3
1964	434.1	7.2	130.3	19.5	27.2	0.0	3.2	0.0	37.9	166.2	16.9	45.1
1965	475.9	8.2	137.8	20.6	29.1	0.0	3.9	0.0	42.7	170.1	17.4	45.5
1966	501.3	9.4	145.9	22.0	31.9	0.0	5.1	0.0	44.9	190.1	17.3	46.1
1967	558.1	10.2	153.3	23.5	32.8	0.0	4.3	0.0	45.5	195.3	20.0	45.4
1968	603.0	11.7	160.7	25.4	33.8	0.0	4.1	0.0	50.6	203.6	22.6	50.6
1969	629.2	13.8	167.6	27.0	34.6	0.0	5.1	0.0	59.2	241.5	23.2	57.5
1970	679.3	15.2	174.6	30.9	36.6	0.0	5.7	0.0	61.5	242.5	35.0	66.1
1971	763.9	17.2	182.8	34.6	35.0	0.0	5.5	0.0	67.6	233.3	62.8	77.0
1972	872.6	20.1	192.5	38.3	40.5	0.0	6.0	0.0	77.5	230.0	73.2	89.7
1973	985.3	23.7	204.8	41.8	46.8	0.0	6.6	0.0	89.4	254.8	74.7	103.0
1974	1 072.4	26.4	217.7	46.4	55.6	0.8	7.4	0.0	94.8	299.6	79.8	117.8
1975	1 147.7	31.7	234.6	53.7	71.2	1.5	8.0	0.0	95.0	320.7	88.3	124.8
1976	1 268.4	38.4	258.3	66.2	77.8	2.1	8.4	0.0	106.6	331.8	98.9	149.1
1977	1 423.2	45.6	285.8	83.7	88.2	1.9	12.3	0.0	128.6	358.8	135.1	149.1
1978	1 596.7	52.0	318.9	100.2	98.7	5.1	12.5	0.0	154.2	409.0	161.5	171.2
1979	1 764.9	53.8	352.0	113.7	120.8	24.9	14.5	0.0	183.4	494.9	149.5	189.6
1980	1 902.1	53.0	385.1	123.5	151.4	42.0	17.1	0.0	195.8	529.6	169.8	228.0
1981	2 021.1	55.0	419.8	132.0	178.6	107.5	20.2	0.0	218.6	562.2	197.0	287.9
1982	2 137.4	57.3	463.2	139.6	225.4	137.6	25.4	0.0	228.9	627.9	240.0	294.0
1983	2 394.3	69.4	513.8	147.6	267.5	119.7	34.9	3.0	254.0	708.5	263.3	349.9
1984	2 694.1	85.0	570.1	162.0	305.8	164.1	53.9	19.8	302.5	803.1	342.6	411.7
1985	2 967.5	98.4	646.6	191.8	328.9	178.2	129.9	34.8	353.2	953.5	419.9	599.4
1986	3 217.3	113.9	734.5	234.6	333.2	213.1	259.9	71.4	409.9	988.2	536.4	658.3
1987	3 435.5	131.3	823.1	274.6	346.8	215.0	291.1	113.2	448.3	1 162.2	586.5	703.0
1988	3 657.7	148.9	927.2	306.0	368.6	225.5	304.5	147.6	493.3	1 404.9	688.6	769.5
1989	3 695.5	156.0	1 028.3	335.6	419.7	293.7	327.2	201.1	537.3	1 498.4	815.8	901.4
1990	3 644.8	166.6	1 134.5	364.2	462.4	371.3	360.1	250.3	564.8	1 749.0	881.7	894.8
1991	3 516.3	179.4	1 218.9	394.1	488.1	403.9	440.2	299.5	572.5	1 812.1	909.6	999.3
1992	3 509.0	197.1	1 304.4	410.6	514.2	408.6	566.4	357.9	575.0	1 879.1	983.1	1 075.5
1993	3 635.5	218.7	1 415.5	443.3	550.0	429.0	725.9	437.8	563.1	1 989.1	1 095.0	1 092.0
1994	3 786.5	246.8	1 487.5	465.6	589.4	459.0	718.8	501.0	595.1	2 388.6	1 162.8	1 070.0
1995	3 961.2	263.0	1 587.5	493.1	606.1	545.5	771.3	612.0	654.6	2 388.7	1 464.8	1 230.5
1996	4 099.9	288.5	1 657.0	514.2	598.4	634.3	820.2	712.2	697.1	2 520.5	1 795.6	1 298.9
1997	4 370.4	305.3	1 751.1	538.2	642.5	721.9	901.1	826.5	720.8	2 451.4	2 035.6	1 433.8
1998	4 707.5	324.2	1 828.0	548.9	633.5	970.8	1 028.4	1 078.8	812.8	2 475.7	2 202.0	1 424.3
1999	5 109.3	351.7	1 886.0	536.5	737.4	1 156.4	1 076.8	1 253.3	946.6	2 588.9	2 196.8	1 468.5
2000	5 493.4	379.7	1 943.9	534.3	614.5	1 325.8	1 103.1	1 413.6	1 101.9	2 465.8	2 451.9	1 590.2
2001	5 725.3	421.2	2 071.5	536.6	577.3	1 594.3	1 229.5	1 662.6	1 170.7	2 254.3	2 850.7	1 643.5
2002	6 144.5	465.4	2 300.3	584.7	570.5	1 564.8	1 368.1	1 897.9	1 292.5	2 244.3	3 323.6	1 649.5
2003	6 655.2	516.6	2 478.8	660.5	642.5	1 491.0	1 505.1	2 125.7	1 468.7	2 405.9	3 797.4	1 896.6
2004	7 323.4	556.6	2 643.9	746.5	642.0	1 346.3	1 619.8	2 555.6	1 675.9	3 283.6	4 580.9	2 190.8
2005	8 016.2	592.5	2 753.9	819.3	686.4	1 348.6	1 743.8	3 290.7	1 740.6	3 460.7	5 142.7	2 592.3
2006	8 633.9	622.6	2 786.4	864.1	741.7	1 570.2	1 928.7	4 050.5	1 809.1	3 466.7	6 154.2	2 876.0
2007	9 209.3	657.9	2 871.2	869.3	772.8	1 962.0	2 196.7	4 401.8	1 834.3	3 996.6	7 270.7	3 092.0
2008	9 459.7	701.1	2 882.8	853.4	765.8	2 689.9	2 229.2	4 006.3	1 769.4	4 466.0	7 481.9	3 237.0
2009	9 117.4	734.6	3 022.6	886.7	775.4	2 070.0	2 616.3	3 228.6	1 549.7	4 835.3	7 662.4	2 491.9
2010	9 356.2	758.6	3 174.2	890.6	895.9	1 673.4	2 969.9	2 184.1	1 405.4	4 915.1	8 413.9	2 635.5
2011	9 489.9	796.2	3 299.6	926.8	969.5	1 663.6	3 329.3	1 941.5	1 359.6	4 395.5	8 944.8	2 770.4
2012	9 866.3	842.3	3 373.9	927.8	1 116.2	1 580.9	3 981.3	1 728.3	1 324.9	4 208.9	9 508.7	3 096.5
2013	10 101.0	891.8	3 451.3	958.7	1 166.8	1 611.7	4 345.2	1 446.2	1 305.4	3 856.9	9 732.4	2 899.3
2014	10 762.9	951.7	3 551.0	974.5	1 199.9	1 490.8	4 822.1	1 354.3	1 318.9	3 314.5	10 328.2	2 951.0
2012												
1st quarter	9 498.9	814.6	3 330.7	922.2	1 006.5	1 600.7	3 540.0	1 884.5	1 346.9	4 322.8	9 085.8	2 932.5
2nd quarter	9 606.1	829.1	3 306.8	919.7	1 043.3	1 528.4	3 699.5	1 820.8	1 330.1	4 335.1	9 143.9	2 919.1
3rd quarter	9 705.9	837.8	3 349.8	921.0	1 080.5	1 520.2	3 851.6	1 761.6	1 327.5	4 298.6	9 404.4	3 047.3
4th quarter	9 866.3	842.3	3 373.9	927.8	1 116.2	1 580.9	3 981.3	1 728.3	1 324.9	4 208.9	9 508.7	3 096.5
2013												
1st quarter	9 833.4	855.1	3 384.5	933.4	1 123.4	1 562.4	4 184.5	1 676.3	1 311.6	4 057.0	9 637.8	3 036.1
2nd quarter	9 896.3	874.1	3 406.3	936.7	1 146.3	1 550.5	4 242.8	1 499.7	1 310.6	3 971.1	9 426.0	3 077.1
3rd quarter	9 925.3	886.7	3 424.4	943.5	1 156.9	1 572.4	4 287.7	1 472.6	1 311.2	3 883.8	9 564.6	3 053.3
4th quarter	10 101.0	891.8	3 451.3	958.7	1 166.8	1 611.7	4 345.2	1 446.2	1 305.4	3 856.9	9 732.4	2 899.3
2014												
1st quarter	10 167.7	903.8	3 477.1	955.0	1 164.8	1 521.0	4 462.9	1 396.5	1 293.8	3 666.5	9 967.4	2 942.9
2nd quarter	10 378.4	926.3	3 511.5	958.7	1 184.5	1 387.3	4 583.4	1 367.7	1 295.1	3 502.7	10 108.9	2 950.0
3rd quarter	10 527.8	945.2	3 536.5	969.2	1 195.9	1 419.6	4 692.3	1 363.0	1 296.4	3 419.0	10 183.0	2 933.8
4th quarter	10 762.9	951.7	3 551.0	974.5	1 199.9	1 490.8	4 822.1	1 354.3	1 318.9	3 314.5	10 328.2	2 951.0

Figure 12-3: Ratios of Household Debt Service and Financial Obligations to Disposable Personal Income, 1980–2014

- The finances of America's households—debts, assets, and the relationships between them—played a key role in the bubble and subsequent collapse of the 2000s. Some relevant indicators are presented in Table 12-6 and displayed in Figure 12-3 above.

- The most comprehensive is the ratio of household credit market debt outstanding to the value of all consumer assets, financial assets such as bank accounts and securities as well as real estate. As can be seen in Figure 12-3, this ratio rose to a new high in 2002, stayed there through 2006 as asset values kept pace with debt increases, and then soared still further through 2008, as debt stayed high while real estate values plunged. The reduction in this ratio since 2008 results from modest reductions in debt, rebuilding of financial assets, and some recovery in real estate prices from, 2012 to the present. (Tables 12-5, 12-6, and 12-11)

- One reason that the rise in the debt/asset ratio in the early 2000s was not taken as a warning sign by many analysts can be seen in the financial obligations ratio, which is the ratio of household payments for debt service, rent, property taxes, homeowners' insurance, and auto lease payments to disposable personal income. This held at modest levels in the early 2000s even while the debt ratio rose, because of lower interest rates. (Tables 12-6 and 12-11)

- The credit card charge-off and delinquency rates reported by banks show a delayed response to developments in the household ratios, as they represent the point at which the households' problems become the banks' problems. (Table 16-6)

- Focusing more narrowly on home mortgages, that form of debt as a percent of the value of home real estate has increased from a range of 30 to 35 percent that prevailed from 1960 through about 1987 to 64 percent in the years 2008 through 2011, before falling back to 48 percent at the end of 2014. In other words, homeowners as a group still now have only 49 percent equity in their homes, compared with the nearly 70 percent that they had as recently as 1982. (Table 12-7)

Table 12-6. Household Assets, Liabilities, Net Worth, Financial Obligations, and Delinquency Rates

(Billions of dollars, except as noted; end of period; not seasonally adjusted, except as noted.)

Year and quarter	Financial assets of the household sector [1]												
	Total [2]	Checkable deposits and currency	Time and savings deposits	Money market fund shares	Treasury securities	Agency- and GSE-backed securities	Municipal securities	Corporate and foreign bonds	Mortgages	Corporate equities	Mutual fund shares	Security credit	Life insurance reserves
1955	1 149.5	70.0	105.8	0.0	68.8	0.6	19.2	5.0	22.7	248.2	7.8	0.9	69.3
1956	1 231.0	71.9	115.2	0.0	70.2	1.0	21.9	6.1	24.3	271.0	9.0	0.9	72.7
1957	1 267.2	71.0	127.2	0.0	71.5	1.5	23.9	7.2	26.3	244.5	8.7	0.9	75.5
1958	1 406.8	73.7	141.3	0.0	68.6	0.8	24.6	7.9	28.9	322.3	13.2	1.2	78.5
1959	1 490.2	75.6	152.5	0.0	71.6	2.3	28.4	8.2	30.8	357.3	15.8	-0.4	82.0
1960	1 552.5	77.6	164.5	0.0	72.2	1.0	31.0	10.6	33.6	359.8	17.0	0.0	85.2
1961	1 706.2	77.0	182.8	0.0	71.9	0.6	32.5	10.8	36.8	443.2	22.9	-0.7	88.6
1962	1 753.7	77.2	208.8	0.0	73.7	0.2	32.1	10.2	39.0	431.2	20.9	-0.9	92.4
1963	1 862.0	82.1	234.9	0.0	72.9	0.0	32.1	10.1	40.5	469.9	24.8	-1.1	96.6
1964	2 027.3	84.9	261.0	0.0	73.6	0.2	34.9	10.3	42.1	544.1	28.4	-0.8	101.1
1965	2 207.7	91.6	288.5	0.0	74.8	1.1	36.5	9.0	42.6	616.1	34.4	-0.3	105.9
1966	2 255.4	93.5	307.1	0.0	79.1	5.9	41.2	11.1	44.6	548.3	33.9	-0.1	110.6
1967	2 520.8	103.8	342.3	0.0	79.0	6.3	38.2	15.1	46.6	682.1	43.0	2.2	115.5
1968	2 810.9	112.7	372.5	0.0	81.7	6.1	36.5	18.0	49.1	815.3	49.5	4.9	120.3
1969	2 797.2	110.9	381.3	0.0	93.2	11.3	47.2	22.0	49.2	667.4	45.6	2.7	125.4
1970	2 936.2	118.6	423.5	0.0	83.0	15.9	47.1	29.7	50.1	650.2	44.5	3.6	130.7
1971	3 260.3	132.1	491.0	0.0	74.2	14.6	46.0	37.4	47.3	743.7	53.0	3.6	137.1
1972	3 703.3	144.4	564.2	0.0	77.4	8.9	47.7	38.5	48.3	921.4	56.4	2.7	143.9
1973	3 752.3	152.5	624.9	0.0	88.5	8.3	55.1	41.5	47.2	693.9	43.7	3.6	151.3
1974	3 800.3	157.4	681.0	2.4	96.3	13.7	62.2	54.4	50.6	445.0	31.8	3.4	158.4
1975	4 272.7	158.7	762.2	3.7	111.8	7.6	66.8	64.3	50.5	584.6	38.7	4.7	168.6
1976	4 760.5	169.2	853.6	3.4	102.7	11.7	72.9	74.8	52.8	731.2	41.4	7.4	177.8
1977	5 081.4	184.2	955.1	3.2	104.5	8.4	78.8	80.1	55.4	631.0	40.4	5.3	187.8
1978	5 636.6	200.7	1 048.4	8.9	110.3	9.9	104.2	76.0	62.4	640.1	41.1	11.1	199.4
1979	6 400.4	220.5	1 116.0	39.5	155.9	12.5	123.6	75.3	71.6	767.9	44.8	14.4	210.3
1980	7 316.0	238.0	1 237.4	64.4	173.9	18.6	130.1	67.5	87.3	1 010.5	52.1	22.2	220.6
1981	7 787.0	284.4	1 305.3	154.6	168.8	14.2	160.3	75.5	101.4	905.2	52.6	18.4	230.1
1982	8 389.5	303.9	1 431.2	186.7	185.1	13.4	201.1	68.7	110.9	966.3	65.1	23.3	238.0
1983	9 151.7	313.6	1 633.5	149.9	230.7	14.5	246.6	61.6	111.3	1 088.6	98.0	22.6	246.7
1984	9 733.7	327.0	1 853.3	193.0	277.7	27.7	290.4	38.6	103.0	1 010.9	117.5	27.9	252.8
1985	10 855.2	344.8	2 094.7	196.3	282.2	23.4	395.1	80.1	116.2	1 229.5	213.8	49.8	264.3
1986	12 045.0	461.9	2 213.2	235.1	270.9	23.3	410.9	114.4	112.6	1 494.0	378.7	59.0	282.6
1987	12 814.4	460.9	2 352.4	256.0	308.2	32.1	516.6	129.7	120.2	1 462.6	424.5	41.1	309.5
1988	14 063.5	460.5	2 538.4	273.0	393.5	51.8	586.0	157.6	122.5	1 756.7	439.1	45.1	335.7
1989	15 404.7	462.2	2 624.0	351.1	394.9	74.8	613.3	196.1	131.4	2 147.5	513.0	55.3	365.3
1990	15 951.8	450.8	2 673.9	389.4	503.8	117.3	647.7	245.1	141.4	1 961.4	511.5	64.9	391.7
1991	17 376.4	505.0	2 591.8	407.7	535.3	115.5	701.8	257.9	143.1	2 759.2	645.0	95.5	418.6
1992	18 291.3	616.4	2 364.7	365.5	627.1	114.4	672.2	275.6	137.1	3 094.2	799.4	85.5	447.7
1993	19 617.4	667.5	2 242.0	363.5	672.9	58.3	640.8	422.3	129.7	3 437.0	1 098.0	112.3	484.8
1994	20 410.2	636.4	2 217.5	373.1	870.9	187.4	594.1	545.7	120.8	3 294.2	1 096.6	115.7	520.3
1995	22 778.3	586.5	2 345.4	472.4	836.7	216.3	533.4	616.9	113.6	4 434.2	1 253.0	145.4	566.2
1996	24 380.7	544.8	2 486.9	500.9	888.5	332.6	493.0	624.5	106.1	4 712.2	1 561.9	189.9	610.6
1997	27 476.0	503.9	2 623.0	571.2	797.1	390.3	497.6	590.1	99.0	6 114.2	1 873.1	219.8	665.0
1998	30 647.9	528.7	2 706.3	667.4	732.1	441.5	498.4	628.7	94.7	7 468.7	2 253.2	292.3	718.3
1999	34 910.1	508.9	2 807.9	769.5	809.5	540.5	526.9	524.5	102.0	9 720.0	2 763.7	349.7	783.9
2000	34 263.7	405.4	3 071.5	937.3	578.3	587.9	531.5	564.9	104.0	8 097.1	2 585.4	460.7	819.1
2001	33 675.1	480.1	3 354.6	1 101.0	433.9	385.0	587.9	647.5	109.2	6 788.3	2 499.2	502.1	880.0
2002	32 381.0	464.1	3 657.9	1 068.4	269.9	241.5	671.5	859.3	117.2	5 123.7	2 122.2	441.9	920.9
2003	36 929.6	458.0	4 015.7	954.5	416.9	376.7	687.2	722.5	122.2	6 714.0	2 790.6	521.1	1 013.2
2004	41 948.9	399.8	4 483.2	898.3	472.7	443.7	1 522.9	622.1	132.6	7 406.7	3 287.1	635.2	1 060.4
2005	45 475.4	285.9	4 965.0	942.7	425.7	587.4	1 600.6	599.1	140.8	8 026.1	3 521.2	623.4	1 082.6
2006	50 298.7	239.7	5 484.1	1 106.5	325.4	612.7	1 635.6	563.7	123.6	10 126.6	4 074.4	700.6	1 055.2
2007	52 967.4	153.3	5 973.6	1 345.7	202.4	873.3	1 673.5	924.2	110.7	9 912.3	4 591.5	917.0	1 077.2
2008	45 996.8	295.2	6 234.6	1 580.4	183.9	1 056.3	1 720.8	1 262.9	111.8	5 760.7	3 259.4	737.4	1 050.2
2009	48 618.0	396.1	6 326.0	1 312.9	853.3	356.4	1 827.9	1 548.5	110.9	7 255.8	4 100.4	701.7	1 109.5
2010	52 888.2	423.7	6 450.8	1 129.2	1 122.6	334.2	1 871.4	1 361.1	100.1	8 696.2	4 605.0	725.2	1 137.5
2011	54 071.3	728.8	6 820.0	1 109.9	717.0	299.3	1 805.7	1 355.3	100.9	8 498.4	4 622.5	726.1	1 199.3
2012	58 417.9	892.1	7 187.1	1 110.2	943.1	176.8	1 661.2	1 235.4	87.1	9 676.3	5 630.4	757.0	1 186.4
2013	65 352.0	1 013.6	7 398.4	1 135.7	956.6	141.1	1 605.9	976.9	76.2	12 501.8	7 023.0	815.5	1 233.0
2014	68 314.7	1 127.5	7 867.4	1 102.1	696.7	41.3	1 540.0	874.9	68.8	13 360.7	7 695.3	869.0	1 282.8
2012													
1st quarter	55 992.0	747.9	6 925.1	1 052.2	831.4	228.0	1 779.7	1 268.3	97.5	9 171.1	5 184.3	723.6	1 199.7
2nd quarter	55 796.9	768.6	6 996.1	1 024.2	866.9	226.7	1 778.4	1 256.1	93.7	8 844.9	5 156.8	742.9	1 172.9
3rd quarter	57 510.5	765.6	7 027.2	1 045.4	885.5	186.1	1 718.5	1 308.4	90.4	9 553.7	5 454.6	751.5	1 180.8
4th quarter	58 417.9	892.1	7 187.1	1 110.2	943.1	176.8	1 661.2	1 235.4	87.1	9 676.3	5 630.4	757.0	1 186.4
2013													
1st quarter	60 471.4	930.8	7 245.4	1 059.8	970.8	130.5	1 665.5	1 101.4	84.4	10 646.7	6 102.0	743.6	1 195.1
2nd quarter	61 321.0	904.2	7 253.9	1 052.3	1 021.2	146.7	1 657.8	960.3	81.4	10 937.4	6 240.4	794.0	1 201.8
3rd quarter	63 200.0	890.1	7 338.5	1 094.5	994.8	134.4	1 630.3	943.5	78.7	11 675.8	6 641.8	791.5	1 218.5
4th quarter	65 352.0	1 013.6	7 398.4	1 135.7	956.6	141.1	1 605.9	976.9	76.2	12 501.8	7 023.0	815.5	1 233.0
2014													
1st quarter	66 007.7	1 059.9	7 550.0	1 099.2	900.4	55.6	1 602.4	932.9	74.5	12 580.0	7 292.8	866.2	1 242.6
2nd quarter	67 288.6	1 078.2	7 573.4	1 069.5	721.1	60.8	1 600.7	952.4	72.5	13 307.1	7 579.3	866.6	1 256.7
3rd quarter	67 006.9	1 060.6	7 695.8	1 087.7	704.9	43.8	1 552.7	953.1	70.5	12 777.4	7 553.1	892.5	1 263.3
4th quarter	68 314.7	1 127.5	7 867.4	1 102.1	696.7	41.3	1 540.0	874.9	68.8	13 360.7	7 695.3	869.0	1 282.8

[1] Includes nonprofit organizations.
[2] Includes components not shown separately.

Table 12-6. Household Assets, Liabilities, Net Worth, Financial Obligations, and Delinquency Rates
—Continued

(Billions of dollars, except as noted; end of period; not seasonally adjusted, except as noted.)

Year and quarter	Financial assets of the household sector [1] —Continued		Nonfinancial assets of the household sector		Debt as a percent of total assets [1]	Total liabilities [1]	Net worth [1]	Ratios to disposable personal income (percent, seasonally adjusted)				Consumer credit card accounts held at banks (percent, seasonally adjusted)	
	Pension entitlements	Equity in non-corporate business	Total [1]	House-hold real estate [3]				Financial obligations ratio	Debt service ratios			Delin-quency rate	Charge-off rate
									Total	Mortgage	Consumer		
1955	173.8	343.8	565.5	367.4	8.1	144.4	1 570.5	...	...	...	...	...	...
1956	192.0	360.8	608.1	394.3	8.3	159.6	1 679.5	...	...	...	...	...	...
1957	221.3	373.2	643.8	417.2	8.7	172.1	1 738.9	...	...	...	...	...	...
1958	243.3	387.3	670.3	438.4	8.5	184.1	1 893.0	...	...	...	...	...	...
1959	262.2	388.6	706.0	463.6	9.0	206.7	1 989.6	...	...	...	...	...	...
1960	284.5	398.6	737.6	486.9	9.4	224.6	2 065.5	...	...	...	...	...	...
1961	306.7	415.8	769.6	511.1	9.4	242.9	2 232.9	...	...	...	...	...	...
1962	317.3	432.9	803.6	533.2	10.0	265.0	2 292.2	...	...	...	...	...	...
1963	340.3	438.5	839.2	553.2	10.4	294.0	2 407.1	...	...	...	...	...	...
1964	367.1	458.2	884.1	579.8	10.7	323.4	2 588.0	...	...	...	...	...	...
1965	397.9	485.0	930.9	605.6	10.8	352.8	2 785.8	...	...	...	...	...	...
1966	433.6	518.5	1 006.0	649.0	11.1	376.0	2 885.3	...	...	...	...	...	...
1967	471.8	543.2	1 074.4	685.7	10.9	410.9	3 184.4	...	...	...	...	...	...
1968	520.1	588.3	1 200.8	768.2	10.3	436.1	3 575.5	...	...	...	...	...	...
1969	573.5	623.3	1 308.6	832.4	10.8	463.8	3 642.0	...	...	...	...	...	...
1970	639.5	654.6	1 390.7	874.5	10.6	478.7	3 848.1	...	...	...	...	...	...
1971	714.6	720.9	1 517.9	957.2	10.5	524.1	4 254.1	...	...	...	...	...	...
1972	804.2	802.1	1 714.2	1 098.6	10.3	585.4	4 832.1	...	...	...	...	...	...
1973	852.6	938.1	1 943.2	1 251.4	11.0	652.0	5 043.4	...	...	...	...	...	...
1974	930.2	1 051.0	2 064.4	1 261.1	11.6	707.8	5 156.9	...	...	...	...	...	...
1975	1 037.1	1 149.6	2 286.5	1 413.7	11.2	763.8	5 795.4	...	...	...	...	...	...
1976	1 115.3	1 279.5	2 543.1	1 590.0	11.2	853.0	6 450.6	...	...	...	...	...	...
1977	1 215.0	1 443.3	2 947.3	1 886.8	11.8	984.3	7 044.4	...	...	...	...	...	...
1978	1 338.4	1 675.0	3 408.0	2 210.9	12.2	1 147.0	7 897.6	...	...	...	...	...	...
1979	1 475.7	1 944.2	3 962.0	2 603.3	12.3	1 314.6	9 047.8	...	...	...	...	...	...
1980	1 674.4	2 187.4	4 451.2	2 943.2	11.8	1 440.6	10 326.6	15.1	10.3	4.5	5.7	...	...
1981	1 841.7	2 345.1	4 916.6	3 293.0	11.8	1 550.7	11 153.1	15.4	10.4	4.8	5.6	...	...
1982	2 062.2	2 386.4	5 148.1	3 447.4	11.6	1 624.4	11 913.3	15.5	10.4	4.9	5.5	...	...
1983	2 325.8	2 445.0	5 410.9	3 606.0	11.8	1 788.2	12 774.4	15.5	10.5	4.9	5.6	...	...
1984	2 583.4	2 442.6	6 067.5	4 126.5	12.3	2 007.9	13 793.2	16.0	10.9	5.1	5.9	...	...
1985	2 847.1	2 506.9	6 784.2	4 699.0	12.9	2 362.2	15 277.2	17.1	11.8	5.5	6.3	...	2.98
1986	3 130.2	2 625.7	7 422.6	5 149.5	13.0	2 627.4	16 840.2	17.6	12.1	5.7	6.4	...	3.42
1987	3 400.4	2 739.2	8 042.6	5 598.6	13.2	2 835.2	18 021.8	17.3	11.8	5.7	6.1	...	3.26
1988	3 701.0	2 881.7	8 764.2	6 117.9	13.3	3 136.6	19 691.0	16.9	11.6	5.7	5.9	...	3.22
1989	4 141.8	3 000.5	9 464.6	6 641.1	13.3	3 421.5	21 447.9	17.0	11.8	6.0	5.8	...	3.26
1990	4 435.3	3 056.6	9 732.6	6 796.5	13.9	3 689.9	21 994.5	17.0	11.6	6.2	5.4	...	3.83
1991	4 847.0	3 015.5	9 946.6	6 968.9	13.7	3 902.0	23 421.0	16.5	11.2	6.1	5.0	5.30	4.65
1992	5 342.8	2 997.5	10 274.1	7 260.4	13.9	4 110.7	24 454.7	15.8	10.5	5.8	4.7	4.69	4.54
1993	5 774.4	3 137.0	10 645.8	7 515.2	13.9	4 381.8	25 881.5	15.7	10.4	5.6	4.8	3.90	3.34
1994	6 096.0	3 342.2	11 092.2	7 790.3	14.4	4 710.1	26 792.4	16.0	10.7	5.6	5.1	3.27	3.07
1995	6 717.6	3 517.3	11 497.7	8 055.5	14.1	5 041.7	29 234.3	16.6	11.3	5.6	5.6	3.93	3.94
1996	7 242.2	3 636.3	11 985.2	8 428.3	14.3	5 404.2	30 961.7	16.7	11.4	5.6	5.8	4.59	4.65
1997	8 047.2	4 018.5	12 688.2	8 854.7	13.7	5 757.0	34 407.2	16.6	11.3	5.6	5.7	4.79	5.40
1998	8 880.6	4 258.1	13 778.8	9 693.6	13.3	6 198.2	38 228.5	16.4	11.2	5.5	5.8	4.70	5.16
1999	9 712.2	4 492.3	14 963.5	10 641.2	12.8	6 753.5	43 120.0	16.7	11.6	5.6	6.0	4.51	4.46
2000	10 020.3	4 974.0	16 924.7	12 213.4	13.6	7 348.9	43 839.4	17.1	12.1	5.7	6.4	4.59	4.49
2001	10 197.3	5 171.6	18 458.7	13 568.9	14.6	7 974.0	44 159.8	17.7	12.6	5.9	6.7	4.75	6.20
2002	10 342.4	5 500.4	20 045.5	14 864.6	16.1	8 757.9	43 668.6	17.3	12.4	5.9	6.5	4.94	5.39
2003	11 417.2	6 085.3	21 915.4	16 478.5	16.1	9 832.7	49 012.3	16.9	12.2	5.8	6.4	4.53	5.87
2004	12 571.1	7 307.9	25 008.8	18 996.4	15.7	11 004.1	55 953.6	16.8	12.2	6.0	6.2	4.12	4.57
2005	13 471.3	8 423.9	28 540.5	22 038.9	15.8	12 162.4	61 853.5	17.3	12.6	6.5	6.1	3.59	6.01
2006	14 483.7	8 845.3	29 462.1	22 509.3	16.2	13 461.1	66 299.7	17.6	12.9	6.9	5.9	3.98	3.69
2007	15 267.2	8 933.1	28 149.7	20 665.4	17.1	14 395.3	66 721.8	18.1	13.2	7.2	6.0	4.59	4.34
2008	14 288.6	7 488.1	24 774.6	17 439.2	19.6	14 279.3	56 492.1	17.8	12.7	6.9	5.8	5.60	6.52
2009	15 458.1	6 258.6	23 715.2	16 989.0	18.7	14 062.8	58 270.4	17.0	11.9	6.5	5.4	6.29	10.43
2010	17 035.7	6 894.2	23 351.7	16 408.7	17.4	13 782.3	62 457.6	16.1	11.0	6.0	5.0	4.12	7.92
2011	17 447.7	7 587.0	23 378.2	16 091.8	16.9	13 570.9	63 878.6	15.7	10.4	5.4	5.0	3.25	4.70
2012	18 460.8	8 386.5	25 084.0	17 520.7	15.6	13 637.8	69 864.2	15.0	9.8	5.0	4.9	2.71	3.90
2013	19 893.7	9 502.9	27 702.2	19 654.9	14.2	13 792.5	79 261.7	15.4	10.0	4.8	5.2	2.39	3.40
2014	20 783.7	9 924.7	29 150.2	20 693.8	13.9	14 168.9	83 296.0	15.3	9.9	4.6	5.3	2.16	3.03
2012													
1st quarter	18 042.0	7 697.7	23 679.8	16 345.8	16.3	13 009.8	66 117.0	15.4	10.2	5.3	4.9	3.07	4.26
2nd quarter	17 969.8	7 870.8	24 120.3	16 732.5	16.3	13 053.7	66 339.0	15.4	10.1	5.2	4.9	2.92	3.91
3rd quarter	18 333.2	8 185.9	24 596.9	17 097.0	15.8	13 000.3	68 556.5	15.4	10.1	5.2	5.0	2.81	3.88
4th quarter	18 460.8	8 386.5	25 084.0	17 520.7	15.6	13 055.1	69 864.2	15.0	9.8	5.0	4.9	2.71	3.90
2013													
1st quarter	18 938.0	8 621.9	25 735.8	18 071.4	15.1	12 999.9	72 619.2	15.5	10.1	5.0	5.1	2.64	3.73
2nd quarter	19 092.5	8 929.8	26 502.9	18 689.0	14.8	13 027.7	74 211.5	15.4	10.0	4.9	5.1	2.53	3.44
3rd quarter	19 448.2	9 259.5	27 160.2	19 200.4	14.5	13 136.8	76 628.0	15.4	10.0	4.9	5.1	2.45	3.34
4th quarter	19 893.7	9 502.9	27 702.2	19 654.9	14.2	13 170.4	79 261.7	15.4	10.0	4.8	5.2	2.39	3.40
2014													
1st quarter	20 093.4	9 578.5	28 100.3	20 012.3	14.0	13 175.1	80 327.4	15.3	10.0	4.8	5.2	2.31	3.28
2nd quarter	20 402.1	9 668.0	28 384.8	20 163.9	13.9	13 286.6	81 724.3	15.3	9.9	4.7	5.2	2.25	3.28
3rd quarter	20 476.3	9 791.8	28 718.6	20 379.3	14.0	13 398.1	81 650.2	15.3	9.9	4.7	5.3	2.21	3.04
4th quarter	20 783.7	9 924.7	29 150.2	20 693.8	13.9	13 512.1	83 296.0	15.3	9.9	4.6	5.3	2.20	3.03

[1]Includes nonprofit organizations.
[3]Excludes nonprofit organizations.
. . . = Not available.

Table 12-7. Mortgage Debt Outstanding

(Billions of dollars, except as noted; end of period; not seasonally adjusted.)

Year and quarter	Total	By type of property					By type of holder						
		Home		Multi-family residences	Commercial	Farm	U.S.-chartered depository institutions	Life insurance companies	Federal and related agencies	Mortgage pools or trusts [1]			Other
		Billions of dollars	Percent of value of real estate							Total	Federally related agencies	ABS issuers	
1950	73	45	19	9	12	6	35	16	3	0	0	0	19
1951	83	52	19	11	13	7	40	19	3	0	0	0	20
1952	92	58	20	11	14	7	45	21	4	0	0	0	21
1953	101	66	21	12	16	8	51	23	5	0	0	0	22
1954	114	75	22	13	17	8	59	26	5	0	0	0	24
1955	130	88	24	13	19	9	69	29	5	0	0	0	26
1956	144	99	25	14	22	10	77	33	6	0	0	0	28
1957	157	107	26	15	24	10	83	35	7	0	0	0	30
1958	172	117	27	17	27	11	93	37	8	0	0	0	34
1959	191	130	28	19	30	12	105	39	10	0	0	0	37
1960	208	141	29	21	33	13	115	42	11	0	0	0	41
1961	229	154	30	24	37	14	127	44	12	0	0	0	46
1962	252	168	32	27	42	15	143	47	12	0	0	0	50
1963	279	185	33	30	47	17	164	51	11	1	1	0	53
1964	307	202	35	35	51	19	183	55	12	1	1	0	56
1965	335	219	36	38	56	21	202	60	13	1	1	0	59
1966	359	233	36	41	61	23	214	65	16	1	1	0	62
1967	382	246	36	45	66	25	228	68	19	2	2	0	65
1968	411	263	34	48	73	27	247	70	23	3	3	0	70
1969	440	279	33	53	79	29	264	72	28	3	3	0	73
1970	469	292	33	60	87	30	278	74	34	5	5	0	79
1971	518	318	33	70	97	32	313	75	37	10	10	0	83
1972	590	357	33	83	114	35	366	77	40	14	14	0	92
1973	667	400	32	93	134	40	418	81	47	18	18	0	102
1974	728	435	35	100	148	45	451	86	61	21	21	0	109
1975	786	474	34	101	161	50	485	89	73	29	29	0	110
1976	871	535	34	106	174	55	547	92	76	41	41	0	115
1977	999	628	33	114	193	64	637	97	84	57	57	0	125
1978	1 151	738	33	125	215	73	730	106	100	70	70	0	144
1979	1 317	856	33	135	239	87	808	118	121	95	95	0	175
1980	1 458	958	33	143	260	97	853	131	143	114	114	0	217
1981	1 580	1 030	31	142	300	107	890	138	160	129	129	0	262
1982	1 661	1 070	31	146	334	111	871	142	177	179	179	0	293
1983	1 851	1 186	33	161	389	114	950	151	188	245	245	0	316
1984	2 092	1 322	32	186	472	112	1 084	157	202	300	289	11	350
1985	2 369	1 527	32	206	542	94	1 189	172	213	392	368	25	402
1986	2 656	1 730	34	239	602	84	1 279	194	202	549	532	18	431
1987	2 957	1 928	34	258	694	76	1 403	212	189	701	669	31	452
1988	3 274	2 163	35	275	766	71	1 540	233	192	786	745	40	523
1989	3 527	2 370	36	287	801	69	1 609	254	198	922	870	53	543
1990	3 782	2 607	38	287	820	68	1 601	268	239	1 086	1 020	66	588
1991	3 933	2 775	40	284	806	67	1 527	260	266	1 270	1 156	113	610
1992	4 044	2 942	41	271	763	68	1 471	242	286	1 440	1 272	168	605
1993	4 175	3 101	41	268	738	68	1 494	224	326	1 561	1 357	204	570
1994	4 339	3 278	42	268	723	70	1 560	216	316	1 697	1 472	224	551
1995	4 525	3 446	43	274	734	72	1 642	213	308	1 812	1 571	241	550
1996	4 806	3 682	44	286	763	74	1 731	208	294	1 989	1 712	277	583
1997	5 119	3 917	44	298	826	79	1 840	207	285	2 167	1 826	340	621
1998	5 604	4 273	44	332	916	83	1 948	214	292	2 487	1 826	340	621
1999	6 211	4 698	44	373	1 052	87	2 133	231	320	2 832	2 294	539	694
2000	6 769	5 122	42	402	1 160	85	2 350	236	340	3 097	2 493	604	746
2001	7 478	5 675	42	444	1 270	89	2 511	243	372	3 558	2 832	726	794
2002	8 380	6 431	43	483	1 370	95	2 799	250	432	3 997	3 159	838	901
2003	9 391	7 255	44	556	1 497	83	3 084	261	694	4 356	3 343	1 012	997
2004	10 667	8 292	44	606	1 672	96	3 605	273	703	4 842	3 384	1 458	1 243
2005	12 110	9 421	43	669	1 916	105	4 055	285	665	5 704	3 548	2 156	1 400
2006	13 527	10 501	47	711	2 208	108	4 416	304	687	6 628	3 841	2 787	1 492
2007	14 624	11 241	54	797	2 474	113	4 659	326	725	7 436	4 464	2 972	1 478
2008	14 717	11 154	64	848	2 580	135	4 615	342	801	7 582	4 961	2 620	1 377
2009	14 427	10 939	64	855	2 487	146	4 372	326	816	7 627	5 377	2 250	1 286
2010	13 795	10 447	64	852	2 342	154	4 195	317	5 128	3 062	1 139	1 922	1 094
2011	13 483	10 201	63	856	2 259	167	4 050	332	5 034	3 008	1 305	1 703	1 059
2012	13 267	9 976	57	889	2 229	173	4 029	344	4 935	2 930	1 437	1 493	1 029
2013	13 279	9 885	50	926	2 290	178	3 983	363	4 993	2 792	1 569	1 222	1 147
2014	13 454	9 887	48	999	2 386	183	4 091	385	4 988	2 765	1 645	1 120	1 226
2012													
1st quarter	13 405	10 137	62	859	2 240	169	4 013	337	5 034	2 974	1 330	1 644	1 047
2nd quarter	13 337	10 076	60	866	2 224	170	4 016	341	4 982	2 963	1 377	1 585	1 035
3rd quarter	13 289	10 027	59	876	2 214	172	4 014	344	4 957	2 941	1 408	1 533	1 033
4th quarter	13 267	9 976	57	889	2 229	173	4 029	344	4 935	2 930	1 437	1 493	1 029
2013													
1st quarter	13 210	9 923	55	893	2 220	174	3 990	345	4 938	2 918	1 463	1 455	1 020
2nd quarter	13 215	9 900	53	903	2 236	176	3 983	349	4 949	2 781	1 498	1 283	1 153
3rd quarter	13 261	9 913	52	914	2 257	177	3 975	357	4 986	2 791	1 541	1 250	1 151
4th quarter	13 279	9 885	50	926	2 290	178	3 983	363	4 993	2 792	1 569	1 222	1 147
2014													
1st quarter	13 265	9 853	49	936	2 296	179	3 991	365	4 977	2 755	1 586	1 169	1 176
2nd quarter	13 297	9 851	49	949	2 316	180	4 039	370	4 957	2 747	1 600	1 147	1 184
3rd quarter	13 361	9 869	48	968	2 343	182	4 058	376	4 972	2 757	1 624	1 133	1 197
4th quarter	13 454	9 887	48	999	2 386	183	4 091	385	4 988	2 765	1 645	1 120	1 226

[1]Outstanding principal balances of mortgage-backed securities issued or guaranteed by the holder indicated.

Table 12-8. Consumer Credit

(Outstanding at end of period, billions of dollars.)

Year and month	Seasonally adjusted			Not seasonally adjusted						
	Total	By major credit type		Total 1	By major holder					
		Revolving	Non-revolving		Depository institutions	Finance companies 2	Credit unions	Federal government 2	Nonfinancial businesses	Securitized pools 3
1960	60.0	...	60.0	61.2	28.9	15.4	3.4	0.0	13.5	0.0
1961	62.2	...	62.2	63.4	30.7	15.5	3.6	0.0	13.6	0.0
1962	68.1	...	68.1	69.3	33.6	17.3	4.1	0.0	14.3	0.0
1963	76.6	...	76.6	77.9	38.3	19.6	4.5	0.0	15.5	0.0
1964	86.0	...	86.0	87.4	43.4	21.6	5.4	0.0	16.8	0.0
1965	96.0	...	96.0	97.5	49.1	23.9	6.5	0.0	18.1	0.0
1966	101.8	...	101.8	103.4	52.2	24.8	7.5	0.0	19.0	0.0
1967	106.8	...	106.8	108.6	55.8	24.6	8.3	0.0	19.9	0.0
1968	117.4	2.0	115.4	119.3	62.7	26.1	9.7	0.0	20.8	0.0
1969	127.2	3.6	123.6	129.2	67.8	27.8	11.7	0.0	21.9	0.0
1970	131.6	5.0	126.6	133.7	70.1	27.6	13.0	0.0	23.0	0.0
1971	146.9	8.2	138.7	149.2	79.0	29.2	14.8	0.0	26.2	0.0
1972	166.2	9.4	156.8	168.8	92.1	31.9	17.0	0.0	27.8	0.0
1973	190.1	11.3	178.7	193.0	108.1	35.4	19.6	0.0	29.8	0.0
1974	198.9	13.2	185.7	201.9	112.1	36.1	21.9	0.0	31.8	0.0
1975	204.0	14.5	189.5	207.0	116.2	32.6	25.7	0.0	32.6	0.0
1976	225.7	16.5	209.2	229.0	128.9	33.7	31.2	0.0	35.2	0.0
1977	260.6	37.4	223.1	264.9	152.1	37.3	37.6	0.5	37.4	0.0
1978	306.1	45.7	260.4	311.3	179.6	44.4	45.2	0.9	41.2	0.0
1979	348.6	53.6	295.0	354.6	205.7	55.4	47.4	1.5	44.6	0.0
1980	351.9	55.0	297.0	358.0	202.9	62.2	44.1	2.6	46.2	0.0
1981	371.3	60.9	310.4	377.9	208.2	70.1	46.7	4.8	48.1	0.0
1982	389.8	66.3	323.5	396.7	217.5	75.3	48.8	6.4	48.7	0.0
1983	437.1	79.0	358.0	444.9	245.2	83.3	56.1	4.6	55.7	0.0
1984	517.3	100.4	416.9	526.6	303.1	89.9	67.9	5.6	60.2	0.0
1985	599.7	124.5	475.2	610.6	354.8	111.7	74.0	6.8	63.3	0.0
1986	654.8	141.1	513.7	666.4	383.1	134.0	77.1	8.2	64.0	0.0
1987	686.3	160.9	525.5	698.6	399.4	140.0	81.0	10.0	68.1	0.0
1988	731.9	184.6	547.3	745.2	427.6	144.7	88.3	13.2	71.4	0.0
1989	794.6	211.2	583.4	809.3	445.8	138.9	91.7	16.0	69.6	47.3
1990	808.2	238.6	569.6	824.4	431.6	133.4	91.6	19.2	71.9	76.7
1991	798.0	263.8	534.3	815.6	412.3	121.6	90.3	21.1	67.3	103.0
1992	806.1	278.4	527.7	824.8	400.3	118.1	91.7	24.2	70.3	120.3
1993	865.7	309.9	555.7	886.2	433.6	116.1	101.6	27.2	77.2	130.5
1994	997.3	365.6	631.7	1 021.2	497.2	134.4	119.6	37.2	86.6	146.1
1995	1 140.7	443.9	696.8	1 168.2	542.4	152.1	131.9	43.5	85.1	213.1
1996	1 253.4	507.5	745.9	1 273.9	572.2	154.9	144.1	51.4	77.7	273.5
1997	1 324.8	540.0	784.8	1 344.2	562.2	167.5	152.4	57.2	84.4	320.5
1998	1 421.0	581.4	839.6	1 441.3	564.4	183.3	155.4	64.9	79.3	393.9
1999	1 531.1	610.7	920.4	1 553.6	569.5	201.6	167.9	81.8	76.1	456.7
2000	1 717.0	682.6	1 034.3	1 741.3	615.8	234.4	184.4	96.7	81.5	528.4
2001	1 867.9	714.8	1 153.0	1 891.8	639.5	280.0	189.6	111.9	73.1	597.8
2002	1 972.1	750.9	1 221.2	1 997.0	671.3	307.5	195.7	117.3	74.8	630.4
2003	2 077.4	768.3	1 309.1	2 102.9	747.3	393.0	205.9	102.9	59.1	594.8
2004	2 192.2	799.6	1 392.7	2 220.1	795.6	492.3	215.4	86.1	59.2	571.5
2005	2 290.9	829.5	1 461.4	2 320.6	816.1	516.5	228.6	89.8	59.6	609.9
2006	2 461.3	924.0	1 537.3	2 461.3	836.7	531.9	236.1	108.7	48.5	617.2
2007	2 615.1	1 002.0	1 613.1	2 615.1	894.9	572.1	236.6	115.7	50.0	652.5
2008	2 650.0	1 004.4	1 645.7	2 650.0	965.0	554.3	236.2	135.1	47.5	610.2
2009	2 552.3	916.4	1 635.9	2 552.3	906.3	471.9	237.1	223.1	43.8	572.5
2010	2 646.9	839.5	1 807.4	2 646.9	1 185.5	705.0	226.5	356.2	45.0	50.3
2011	2 755.4	841.2	1 914.2	2 755.4	1 192.6	687.6	223.0	484.7	46.9	46.2
2012	2 922.9	845.9	2 077.0	2 922.9	1 218.6	679.8	243.6	616.8	48.4	50.0
2013	3 098.8	858.2	2 240.6	3 098.8	1 271.6	679.1	265.6	729.8	44.3	49.1
2014	3 317.2	890.0	2 427.2	3 317.2	1 343.1	684.1	302.8	840.9	43.0	49.8
2013										
January	2 938.2	848.6	2 089.6	2 938.0	1 206.2	676.2	246.4	645.9	48.2	50.3
February	2 957.7	850.4	2 107.3	2 929.8	1 194.6	671.9	248.2	653.5	47.6	49.8
March	2 966.2	848.1	2 118.2	2 923.5	1 191.2	671.3	245.5	659.5	42.2	50.0
April	2 978.7	849.4	2 129.3	2 935.2	1 199.3	670.2	248.2	663.5	42.3	48.7
May	2 995.0	852.6	2 142.5	2 953.6	1 208.8	673.5	248.9	669.3	42.5	48.1
June	3 006.7	851.4	2 155.3	2 966.5	1 211.5	674.6	253.1	674.6	42.7	48.2
July	3 021.4	852.2	2 169.2	2 980.2	1 217.2	675.5	255.9	679.1	42.7	48.5
August	3 037.9	853.8	2 184.1	3 018.6	1 231.1	676.7	259.2	700.7	43.2	47.1
September	3 055.3	854.6	2 200.7	3 037.0	1 231.4	678.5	261.9	713.5	43.2	48.5
October	3 073.2	857.2	2 215.9	3 049.4	1 237.2	679.4	263.2	718.5	43.3	48.1
November	3 083.6	856.3	2 227.3	3 062.6	1 245.5	677.8	263.8	724.4	43.6	47.8
December	3 098.8	858.2	2 240.6	3 098.8	1 271.6	679.1	265.6	729.8	44.3	49.1
2014										
January	3 114.1	859.7	2 254.3	3 114.1	1 259.3	674.9	267.9	759.2	44.0	49.8
February	3 129.5	859.7	2 269.8	3 102.1	1 248.4	669.7	267.9	766.9	43.4	47.3
March	3 147.3	860.9	2 286.4	3 105.0	1 246.5	669.9	269.2	770.9	43.1	47.3
April	3 174.0	870.9	2 303.1	3 130.6	1 263.2	670.8	274.2	775.8	43.1	45.9
May	3 193.3	873.2	2 320.1	3 152.3	1 274.3	671.5	279.3	780.5	43.3	46.2
June	3 211.8	875.8	2 336.0	3 171.9	1 284.2	671.7	283.5	786.0	43.3	46.3
July	3 233.3	880.4	2 352.8	3 192.3	1 294.7	673.4	287.7	790.0	43.3	46.8
August	3 249.4	881.4	2 367.9	3 230.2	1 305.6	675.8	292.8	810.8	43.6	45.9
September	3 267.5	883.4	2 384.0	3 249.0	1 305.4	676.6	293.3	825.9	43.5	49.1
October	3 283.8	884.6	2 399.2	3 260.2	1 309.0	675.5	298.0	830.7	43.5	48.8
November	3 300.3	885.9	2 414.4	3 279.2	1 318.9	677.2	301.0	836.2	42.4	49.3
December	3 317.2	890.0	2 427.2	3 317.2	1 343.1	684.1	302.8	840.9	43.0	49.8

1Includes nonprofit and educational institutions, not shown.
2Student Loan Marketing Association (Sallie Mae) included in federal government sector until end of 2004, and in finance companies since then.
3Outstanding balances of pools upon which securities have been issued; these balances are no longer carried on the balance sheets of the loan originators.
. . . = Not available.

Table 12-9A. Summary Interest Rates, Bond Yields, and Stock Prices: Recent Data

(Percent per annum, except as noted.)

Year and month	Federal funds interest rate	Federal Reserve discount rate[1]	U.S. Treasury bills, secondary market, 3-month	Inflation: percent change from year earlier in PCE chain-type price index excluding food and energy	Real 3-month Treasury bill rate	Commercial paper, 3-month[2]	Bank prime rate	Treasury 10-year nominal yields	Bond yields Domestic corporate (Moody's) Aaa	Bond yields Domestic corporate (Moody's) Baa	State and local bonds (Bond Buyer)	Standard and Poor's composite (500 stocks) Index, 1941-1943 = 10	Standard and Poor's composite (500 stocks) Dividend-price ratio	Standard and Poor's composite (500 stocks) Earnings-price ratio
1970	7.17	5.95	6.39	4.69	1.70	...	7.91	7.35	8.04	9.11	6.33	83.22	3.83	6.45
1971	4.67	4.88	4.33	4.71	-0.38	5.25	5.73	6.16	7.39	8.56	5.47	98.29	3.14	5.41
1972	4.44	4.50	4.06	3.23	0.83	4.66	5.25	6.21	7.21	8.16	5.26	109.20	2.84	5.50
1973	8.74	6.45	7.04	3.82	3.22	8.21	8.03	6.85	7.44	8.24	5.19	107.43	3.06	7.12
1974	10.51	7.83	7.85	7.92	-0.07	10.05	10.81	7.56	8.57	9.50	6.17	82.85	4.47	11.59
1975	5.82	6.25	5.79	8.38	-2.59	6.26	7.86	7.99	8.83	10.61	7.05	86.16	4.31	9.15
1976	5.05	5.50	4.98	6.08	-1.10	5.24	6.84	7.61	8.43	9.75	6.64	102.01	3.77	8.90
1977	5.54	5.46	5.26	6.42	-1.16	5.54	6.83	7.42	8.02	8.97	5.68	98.20	4.62	10.79
1978	7.94	7.46	7.18	6.69	0.49	7.93	9.06	8.41	8.73	9.49	6.02	96.02	5.28	12.03
1979	11.20	10.29	10.05	7.27	2.78	10.95	12.67	9.43	9.63	10.69	6.52	103.01	5.47	13.46
1980	13.35	11.77	11.39	9.15	2.24	12.61	15.26	11.43	11.94	13.67	8.59	118.78	5.26	12.66
1981	16.39	13.42	14.04	8.73	5.31	15.34	18.87	13.92	14.17	16.04	11.33	128.05	5.20	11.96
1982	12.24	11.01	10.60	6.45	4.15	11.90	14.85	13.01	13.79	16.11	11.66	119.71	5.81	11.60
1983	9.09	8.50	8.62	5.18	3.44	8.88	10.79	11.10	12.04	13.55	9.51	160.41	4.40	8.03
1984	10.23	8.80	9.54	4.15	5.39	10.12	12.04	12.46	12.71	14.19	10.10	160.46	4.64	10.02
1985	8.10	7.69	7.47	4.12	3.35	7.95	9.93	10.62	11.37	12.72	9.10	186.84	4.25	8.12
1986	6.80	6.32	5.97	3.43	2.54	6.49	8.33	7.67	9.02	10.39	7.32	236.34	3.49	6.09
1987	6.66	5.66	5.78	3.18	2.60	6.82	8.21	8.39	9.38	10.58	7.64	286.83	3.08	5.48
1988	7.57	6.20	6.67	4.23	2.44	7.66	9.32	8.85	9.71	10.83	7.68	265.79	3.64	8.01
1989	9.21	6.93	8.11	4.07	4.04	8.99	10.87	8.49	9.26	10.18	7.23	322.84	3.45	7.42
1990	8.10	6.98	7.50	3.98	3.52	8.06	10.01	8.55	9.32	10.36	7.27	334.59	3.61	6.47
1991	5.69	5.45	5.38	3.50	1.88	5.87	8.46	7.86	8.77	9.80	6.92	376.18	3.24	4.79
1992	3.52	3.25	3.43	3.01	0.42	3.75	6.25	7.01	8.14	8.98	6.44	415.74	2.99	4.22
1993	3.02	3.00	3.00	2.72	0.28	3.22	6.00	5.87	7.22	7.93	5.60	451.41	2.78	4.46
1994	4.21	3.60	4.25	2.23	2.02	4.66	7.15	7.09	7.97	8.63	6.18	460.42	2.82	5.83
1995	5.83	5.21	5.49	2.14	3.35	5.93	8.83	6.57	7.59	8.20	5.95	541.72	2.56	6.09
1996	5.30	5.02	5.01	1.89	3.12	5.41	8.27	6.44	7.37	8.05	5.76	670.50	2.19	5.24
1997	5.46	5.00	5.06	1.75	3.31	5.49	8.44	6.35	7.27	7.87	5.52	873.43	1.77	4.57
1998	5.35	4.92	4.78	1.24	3.54	5.34	8.35	5.26	6.53	7.22	5.09	1 085.50	1.49	3.46
1999	4.97	4.62	4.64	1.33	3.31	5.18	8.00	5.65	7.05	7.88	5.43	1 327.33	1.25	3.17
2000	6.24	5.73	5.82	1.75	4.07	6.31	9.23	6.03	7.62	8.37	5.71	1 427.22	1.15	3.63
2001	3.88	3.40	3.40	1.81	1.59	3.65	6.91	5.02	7.08	7.95	5.15	1 194.18	1.32	2.95
2002	1.67	1.17	1.61	1.70	-0.09	1.69	4.67	4.61	6.49	7.80	5.04	993.94	1.61	2.92
2003	1.13	...	1.01	1.48	-0.47	1.11	4.12	4.01	5.66	6.76	4.75	965.23	1.77	3.84
2004	1.35	2.34	1.37	1.91	-0.54	1.41	4.34	4.27	5.63	6.39	4.68	1 130.65	1.72	4.89
2005	3.22	4.19	3.15	2.16	0.99	3.42	6.19	4.29	5.23	6.06	4.40	1 207.06	1.83	5.36
2006	4.97	5.96	4.73	2.24	2.49	5.10	7.96	4.80	5.59	6.48	4.40	1 310.67	1.87	5.78
2007	5.02	5.86	4.36	2.16	2.20	4.92	8.05	4.63	5.56	6.48	4.40	1 476.66	1.86	5.29
2008	1.92	2.39	1.37	2.06	-0.69	2.13	5.09	3.66	5.63	7.44	4.86	1 220.89	2.37	3.54
2009	0.16	0.50	0.15	1.19	-1.04	0.26	3.25	3.26	5.31	7.29	4.62	946.73	2.40	1.86
2010	0.18	0.72	0.14	1.29	-1.15	0.24	3.25	3.22	4.94	6.04	4.29	1 139.31	1.98	6.04
2011	0.10	0.75	0.05	1.49	-1.44	0.17	3.25	2.78	4.64	5.66	4.51	1 268.89	2.05	6.77
2012	0.14	0.75	0.09	1.83	-1.74	0.19	3.25	1.80	3.67	4.94	3.73	1 379.56	2.24	6.20
2013	0.11	0.75	0.06	1.34	-1.28	0.11	3.25	2.35	4.23	5.10	4.27	1 643.51	2.14	5.57
2014	0.09	0.75	0.03	1.41	-1.38	0.10	3.25	2.54	4.16	4.85	4.23	1 930.67	2.04	5.25
2013														
January	0.14	0.75	0.07	1.52	-1.45	0.16	3.25	1.91	3.80	4.73	3.60	1 480.40	2.24	...
February	0.15	0.75	0.10	1.51	-1.41	0.17	3.25	1.98	3.90	4.85	3.72	1 512.31	2.21	...
March	0.14	0.75	0.09	1.42	-1.33	0.15	3.25	1.96	3.93	4.85	3.96	1 550.83	2.19	5.59
April	0.15	0.75	0.06	1.28	-1.22	0.12	3.25	1.76	3.73	4.59	3.92	1 570.70	2.16	...
May	0.11	0.75	0.04	1.26	-1.22	0.10	3.25	1.93	3.89	4.73	3.72	1 639.84	2.12	...
June	0.09	0.75	0.05	1.27	-1.22	0.10	3.25	2.30	4.27	5.19	4.27	1 618.77	2.18	5.66
July	0.09	0.75	0.04	1.28	-1.24	0.11	3.25	2.58	4.34	5.32	4.56	1 668.68	2.14	...
August	0.08	0.75	0.04	1.33	-1.29	0.09	3.25	2.74	4.54	5.42	4.82	1 670.09	2.15	...
September	0.08	0.75	0.02	1.35	-1.33	0.08	3.25	2.81	4.64	5.47	4.79	1 687.17	2.13	5.61
October	0.09	0.75	0.05	1.26	-1.21	0.11	3.25	2.62	4.53	5.31	4.56	1 720.03	2.10	...
November	0.08	0.75	0.07	1.31	-1.24	0.09	3.25	2.72	4.63	5.38	4.60	1 783.54	2.03	...
December	0.09	0.75	0.07	1.34	-1.27	0.09	3.25	2.90	4.62	5.38	4.73	1 807.78	2.04	5.42
2014														
January	0.07	0.75	0.04	1.24	-1.20	0.09	3.25	2.86	4.49	5.19	4.59	1 822.36	2.02	...
February	0.07	0.75	0.05	1.23	-1.18	0.10	3.25	2.71	4.45	5.10	4.44	1 817.03	2.07	...
March	0.08	0.75	0.05	1.26	-1.21	0.10	3.25	2.72	4.38	5.06	4.46	1 863.52	2.04	5.39
April	0.09	0.75	0.03	1.44	-1.41	0.10	3.25	2.71	4.24	4.90	4.35	1 864.26	2.06	...
May	0.09	0.75	0.03	1.52	-1.49	0.10	3.25	2.56	4.16	4.76	4.29	1 889.77	2.08	...
June	0.10	0.75	0.04	1.50	-1.46	0.10	3.25	2.60	4.25	4.80	4.35	1 947.09	2.04	5.26
July	0.09	0.75	0.03	1.49	-1.46	0.10	3.25	2.54	4.16	4.73	4.33	1 973.10	2.00	...
August	0.09	0.75	0.03	1.47	-1.44	0.11	3.25	2.42	4.08	4.69	4.23	1 961.53	2.04	...
September	0.09	0.75	0.02	1.48	-1.46	0.10	3.25	2.53	4.11	4.80	4.13	1 993.23	2.01	5.37
October	0.09	0.75	0.02	1.49	-1.47	0.10	3.25	2.30	3.92	4.69	3.96	1 937.27	2.08	...
November	0.09	0.75	0.02	1.42	-1.40	0.10	3.25	2.33	3.92	4.79	3.96	2 044.57	2.00	...
December	0.12	0.75	0.03	1.34	-1.31	0.13	3.25	2.21	3.79	4.74	3.70	2 054.27	2.01	4.97

[1]Federal Reserve Bank of New York. Through 2002, represents the rate for adjustment credit. Beginning in 2003, represents the rate for primary credit. See notes and definitions for more information.
[2]Prior to September 1997, this series represents both nonfinancial and financial commercial paper rates. Beginning September 1997, rates for financial companies only are shown. See notes and definitions for more information.
. . . = Not available.

Table 12-9B. Summary Interest Rates, Bond Yields, and Stock Prices: Historical Data

(Percent per annum, except as noted.)

Year and month	Federal funds interest rate	Federal Reserve discount rate[1]	U.S. Treasury bills, secondary market, 3-month	Inflation[2]	Real 3-month Treasury bill rate	Commercial paper, 3-month[3]	Bank prime rate	Treasury 10-year nominal yields	Bond yields Domestic corporate (Moody's) Aaa	Baa	State and local bonds (Bond Buyer)	Standard and Poor's composite (500 stocks) Index, 1941-1943 = 10	Dividend-price ratio	Earnings-price ratio
1919	...	...	...	14.57	...	5.37	...	4.73	5.49	7.25	4.46	8.78	...	...
1920	...	...	5.42	15.61	-10.19	7.50	...	5.32	6.12	8.20	4.98	7.98	...	...
1921	...	...	4.83	-10.50	15.33	6.62	...	5.09	5.97	8.35	5.09	6.86	...	...
1922	...	...	3.47	-6.15	9.62	4.52	...	4.30	5.10	7.08	4.23	8.41	...	...
1923	...	...	3.93	1.79	2.14	5.07	...	4.36	5.12	7.24	4.25	8.57	...	...
1924	...	...	2.77	0.00	2.77	3.98	...	4.06	5.00	6.83	4.20	9.05	...	...
1925	...	...	3.03	2.34	0.69	4.02	...	3.86	4.88	6.27	4.09	11.15	...	...
1926	...	...	3.23	1.14	2.09	4.34	...	3.68	4.73	5.87	4.08	12.59	4.94	9.19
1927	...	...	3.10	-1.69	4.79	4.11	...	3.34	4.57	5.48	3.98	15.34	4.76	6.29
1928	...	...	3.97	-1.72	5.69	4.85	...	3.33	4.55	5.48	4.05	19.95	3.98	5.67
1929	...	5.17	4.42	0.00	4.42	5.85	5.5–6	3.60	4.73	5.90	4.27	26.02	3.47	7.51
1930	...	3.04	2.23	-2.34	4.57	3.59	3.5–6	3.29	4.55	5.90	4.07	21.03	4.51	6.33
1931	...	2.11	1.40	-8.98	10.38	2.64	2.75–5	3.34	4.58	7.62	4.01	13.66	6.15	7.51
1932	...	2.82	0.88	-9.87	10.75	2.73	3.25–4	3.68	5.01	9.30	4.65	6.93	7.43	5.95
1933	...	2.56	0.52	-5.11	5.62	1.73	1.5–4	3.31	4.49	7.76	4.71	8.96	4.21	4.36
1934	...	1.54	0.28	3.08	-2.80	1.02	1.50	3.12	4.00	6.32	4.03	9.84	3.72	5.16
1935	...	1.50	0.17	2.24	-2.07	0.76	1.50	2.79	3.60	5.75	3.41	10.60	3.82	7.23
1936	...	1.50	0.17	1.46	-1.29	0.75	1.50	2.65	3.24	4.77	3.07	15.47	3.44	6.57
1937	...	1.33	0.28	3.60	-3.32	0.94	1.50	2.68	3.26	5.03	3.10	15.41	4.86	8.25
1938	...	1.00	0.07	-2.08	2.15	0.81	1.50	2.56	3.19	5.80	2.91	11.49	5.18	5.55
1939	...	1.00	0.05	-1.42	1.47	0.59	1.50	2.36	3.01	4.96	2.76	12.06	4.05	7.34
1940	...	1.00	0.04	0.72	-0.68	0.56	1.50	2.21	2.84	4.75	2.50	11.02	5.59	9.80
1941	...	1.00	0.13	5.00	-4.87	0.53	1.50	2.12	2.77	4.33	2.10	9.82	6.82	12.14
1942	...	1.00	0.34	10.88	-10.54	0.66	1.50	2.46	2.83	4.28	2.36	8.67	7.24	11.42
1943	...	1.00	0.38	6.13	-5.75	0.69	1.50	2.47	2.73	3.91	2.06	11.50	4.93	7.82
1944	...	1.00	0.38	1.73	-1.35	0.73	1.50	2.48	2.72	3.61	1.86	12.47	4.86	7.34
1945	...	1.00	0.38	2.27	-1.89	0.75	1.50	2.37	2.62	3.29	1.67	15.16	4.17	6.39
1946	...	1.00	0.38	8.33	-7.95	0.81	1.50	2.19	2.53	3.05	1.64	17.08	3.85	6.31
1947	...	1.00	0.61	14.36	-13.75	1.03	1.63	2.25	2.61	3.24	2.01	15.17	4.93	10.69
1948	...	1.34	1.05	8.07	-7.02	1.44	1.88	2.44	2.82	3.47	2.40	15.53	5.54	14.60
1949	...	1.50	1.10	-1.24	2.34	1.49	2.00	2.31	2.66	3.42	2.21	15.23	6.59	15.48
1950	...	1.59	1.22	1.26	-0.04	1.45	2.07	2.32	2.62	3.24	1.98	18.40	6.57	13.99
1951	...	1.75	1.55	7.88	-6.33	2.16	2.56	2.57	2.86	3.41	2.00	22.34	6.13	11.82
1952	...	1.75	1.77	1.92	-0.15	2.33	3.00	2.68	2.96	3.52	2.19	24.50	5.80	9.47
1953	...	1.99	1.94	0.75	1.19	2.52	3.17	2.94	3.20	3.73	2.74	24.73	5.80	10.26
1954	...	1.60	0.94	0.75	0.19	1.58	3.05	2.55	2.90	3.51	2.39	29.69	4.95	8.57
1955	1.79	1.89	1.72	-0.37	2.09	2.18	3.16	2.84	3.05	3.53	2.48	40.49	4.08	7.95
1956	2.73	2.77	2.62	1.49	1.13	3.31	3.77	3.08	3.36	3.88	2.76	46.62	4.09	7.55
1957	3.11	3.12	3.22	3.31	-0.09	3.81	4.20	3.47	3.89	4.71	3.28	44.38	4.35	7.89
1958	1.57	2.15	1.77	2.85	-1.08	2.46	3.83	3.43	3.79	4.73	3.16	46.24	3.97	6.23
1959	3.31	3.36	3.39	0.69	2.70	3.97	4.48	4.07	4.38	5.05	3.56	57.38	3.23	5.78
1960	3.21	3.53	2.87	1.79	1.08	3.85	4.82	4.01	4.41	5.19	3.52	55.85	3.47	5.90
1961	1.95	3.00	2.35	1.26	1.10	2.97	4.50	3.90	4.35	5.08	3.45	66.27	2.98	4.62
1962	2.71	3.00	2.77	1.36	1.40	3.26	4.50	3.95	4.33	5.02	3.15	62.38	3.37	5.82
1963	3.18	3.23	3.16	1.30	1.86	3.55	4.50	4.00	4.26	4.86	3.17	69.87	3.17	5.50
1964	3.50	3.55	3.55	1.53	2.02	3.97	4.50	4.19	4.41	4.83	3.21	81.37	3.01	5.32
1965	4.07	3.55	3.95	1.27	2.69	...	4.54	4.28	4.49	4.87	3.26	88.17	3.00	5.59
1966	5.11	4.04	4.86	2.26	2.60	...	5.63	4.93	5.13	5.67	3.81	85.26	3.40	6.63
1967	4.22	4.50	4.29	3.07	1.23	...	5.63	5.07	5.51	6.23	3.94	91.93	3.20	5.73
1968	5.66	4.19	5.34	4.29	1.05	...	6.31	5.64	6.18	6.94	4.45	98.70	3.07	5.67
1969	8.21	5.17	6.67	4.69	1.98	...	7.96	6.67	7.03	7.81	5.72	97.84	3.24	6.08
1945														
January	...	1.00	0.38	2.30	-1.92	...	1.50	...	2.69	3.46	...	13.49	...	...
February	...	1.00	0.38	2.30	-1.92	...	1.50	...	2.65	3.41	...	13.94	...	...
March	...	1.00	0.38	2.30	-1.92	...	1.50	...	2.62	3.38	...	13.93	...	...
April	...	1.00	0.38	1.71	-1.33	...	1.50	...	2.61	3.36	...	14.28	...	...
May	...	1.00	0.38	2.29	-1.91	...	1.50	...	2.62	3.32	...	14.82	...	...
June	...	1.00	0.38	2.84	-2.46	...	1.50	...	2.61	3.29	...	15.09	...	...
July	...	1.00	0.38	2.26	-1.88	...	1.50	...	2.60	3.26	...	14.78	...	...
August	...	1.00	0.38	2.26	-1.88	...	1.50	...	2.61	3.26	...	14.83	...	...
September	...	1.00	0.38	2.26	-1.88	...	1.50	...	2.62	3.24	...	15.84	...	...
October	...	1.00	0.38	2.26	-1.88	...	1.50	...	2.62	3.20	...	16.50	...	...
November	...	1.00	0.38	2.26	-1.88	...	1.50	...	2.62	3.15	...	17.04	...	...
December	...	1.00	0.38	2.25	-1.87	...	1.50	...	2.61	3.10	...	17.33	...	...
1946														
January	...	1.00	0.38	2.25	-1.87	...	1.50	...	2.54	3.01	...	18.02	...	...
February	...	1.00	0.38	1.69	-1.31	...	1.50	...	2.48	2.95	...	18.07	...	...
March	...	1.00	0.38	2.81	-2.43	...	1.50	...	2.47	2.94	...	17.53	...	...
April	...	1.00	0.38	3.37	-2.99	...	1.50	...	2.46	2.96	...	18.66	...	...
May	...	1.00	0.38	3.35	-2.97	...	1.50	...	2.51	3.02	...	18.70	...	...
June	...	1.00	0.38	3.31	-2.93	...	1.50	...	2.49	3.03	...	18.58	...	...
July	...	1.00	0.38	9.39	-9.01	...	1.50	...	2.48	3.03	...	18.05	...	...
August	...	1.00	0.38	11.60	-11.22	...	1.50	...	2.51	3.03	...	17.70	...	...
September	...	1.00	0.38	12.71	-12.33	...	1.50	...	2.58	3.10	...	15.09	...	...
October	...	1.00	0.38	14.92	-14.54	...	1.50	...	2.60	3.15	...	14.75	...	...
November	...	1.00	0.38	17.68	-17.30	...	1.50	...	2.59	3.17	...	14.69	...	...
December	...	1.00	0.38	18.13	-17.75	...	1.50	...	2.61	3.17	...	15.13	...	...

[1]Federal Reserve Bank of New York. Through 2002, represents the rate for adjustment credit. Beginning in 2003, represents the rate for primary credit. See notes and definitions for more information.
[2]Change from a year earlier. Beginning in 1960, PCE except food and energy; before then, CPI-U
[3]Beginning 1997, rates for nonfinancial companies only are shown.
. . . = Not available.

Table 12-9B. Summary Interest Rates, Bond Yields, and Stock Prices: Historical Data—*Continued*

(Percent per annum, except as noted.)

Year and month	Federal funds interest rate	Federal Reserve discount rate[1]	U.S. Treasury bills, secondary market, 3-month	Inflation[2]	Real 3-month Treasury bill rate	Commercial paper, 3-month[3]	Bank prime rate	Treasury 10-year nominal yields	Bond yields Domestic corporate (Moody's) Aaa	Baa	State and local bonds (Bond Buyer)	S&P composite Index, 1941-1943 = 10	Dividend-price ratio	Earnings-price ratio
1947														
January	...	1.00	0.38	18.13	-17.75	...	1.50	...	2.57	3.13	...	15.21	...	...
February	...	1.00	0.38	18.78	-18.40	...	1.50	...	2.55	3.12	...	15.80	...	...
March	...	1.00	0.38	19.67	-19.29	...	1.50	...	2.55	3.15	...	15.16	...	...
April	...	1.00	0.38	19.02	-18.64	...	1.50	...	2.53	3.16	...	14.60	...	...
May	...	1.00	0.38	18.38	-18.00	...	1.50	...	2.53	3.17	...	14.34	...	...
June	...	1.00	0.38	17.65	-17.27	...	1.50	...	2.55	3.21	...	14.84	...	...
July	...	1.00	0.66	12.12	-11.46	...	1.50	...	2.55	3.18	...	15.77	...	...
August	...	1.00	0.75	11.39	-10.64	...	1.50	...	2.56	3.17	...	15.46	...	...
September	...	1.00	0.80	12.75	-11.95	...	1.50	...	2.61	3.23	...	15.06	...	...
October	...	1.00	0.85	10.58	-9.73	...	1.50	...	2.70	3.35	...	15.45	...	...
November	...	1.00	0.92	8.45	-7.53	...	1.50	...	2.77	3.44	...	15.27	...	...
December	...	1.00	0.95	8.84	-7.89	...	1.75	...	2.86	3.52	...	15.03	...	...
1948														
January	...	1.25	0.97	10.23	-9.26	...	1.75	...	2.86	3.52	...	14.83	...	...
February	...	1.25	1.00	9.30	-8.30	...	1.75	...	2.85	3.53	...	14.10	...	...
March	...	1.25	1.00	6.85	-5.85	...	1.75	...	2.83	3.53	...	14.30	...	...
April	...	1.25	1.00	8.68	-7.68	...	1.75	...	2.78	3.47	...	15.40	...	...
May	...	1.25	1.00	9.13	-8.13	...	1.75	...	2.76	3.38	...	16.15	...	...
June	...	1.25	1.00	9.55	-8.55	...	1.75	...	2.76	3.34	...	16.82	...	...
July	...	1.25	1.00	9.91	-8.91	...	1.75	...	2.81	3.37	...	16.42	...	...
August	...	1.50	1.06	8.89	-7.83	...	2.00	...	2.84	3.44	...	15.94	...	...
September	...	1.50	1.09	6.52	-5.43	...	2.00	...	2.84	3.45	...	15.76	...	...
October	...	1.50	1.12	6.09	-4.97	...	2.00	...	2.84	3.50	...	16.19	...	...
November	...	1.50	1.14	4.76	-3.62	...	2.00	...	2.84	3.53	...	15.29	...	...
December	...	1.50	1.16	2.99	-1.83	...	2.00	...	2.79	3.53	...	15.19	...	...
1949														
January	...	1.50	1.17	1.27	-0.10	...	2.00	...	2.71	3.46	...	15.36	...	...
February	...	1.50	1.17	1.28	-0.11	...	2.00	...	2.71	3.45	...	14.77	...	...
March	...	1.50	1.17	1.71	-0.54	...	2.00	...	2.70	3.47	...	14.91	...	...
April	...	1.50	1.17	0.42	0.75	...	2.00	...	2.70	3.45	...	14.89	...	...
May	...	1.50	1.17	-0.42	1.59	...	2.00	...	2.71	3.45	...	14.78	...	...
June	...	1.50	1.17	-0.83	2.00	...	2.00	...	2.71	3.47	...	13.97	...	...
July	...	1.50	1.02	-2.87	3.89	...	2.00	...	2.67	3.46	...	14.76	...	...
August	...	1.50	1.04	-2.86	3.90	...	2.00	...	2.62	3.40	...	15.29	...	...
September	...	1.50	1.07	-2.45	3.52	...	2.00	...	2.60	3.37	...	15.49	...	...
October	...	1.50	1.05	-2.87	3.92	...	2.00	...	2.61	3.36	...	15.89	...	...
November	...	1.50	1.08	-1.65	2.73	...	2.00	...	2.60	3.35	...	16.11	...	...
December	...	1.50	1.10	-2.07	3.17	...	2.00	...	2.58	3.31	...	16.54	...	...
1950														
January	...	1.50	1.07	-2.08	3.15	...	2.00	...	2.57	3.24	...	16.88	...	...
February	...	1.50	1.12	-1.26	2.38	...	2.00	...	2.58	3.24	...	17.21	...	...
March	...	1.50	1.12	-0.84	1.96	...	2.00	...	2.58	3.24	...	17.35	...	...
April	...	1.50	1.15	-1.26	2.41	...	2.00	...	2.60	3.23	...	17.84	...	...
May	...	1.50	1.16	-0.42	1.58	...	2.00	...	2.61	3.25	...	18.44	...	...
June	...	1.50	1.15	-0.42	1.57	...	2.00	...	2.62	3.28	...	18.74	...	...
July	...	1.50	1.16	1.69	-0.53	...	2.00	...	2.65	3.32	...	17.38	...	...
August	...	1.59	1.20	2.10	-0.90	...	2.00	...	2.61	3.23	...	18.43	...	...
September	...	1.75	1.30	2.09	-0.79	...	2.08	...	2.64	3.21	...	19.08	...	...
October	...	1.75	1.31	3.80	-2.49	...	2.25	...	2.67	3.22	...	19.87	...	...
November	...	1.75	1.36	3.78	-2.42	...	2.25	...	2.67	3.22	...	19.83	...	...
December	...	1.75	1.34	5.93	-4.59	...	2.25	...	2.67	3.20	...	19.75	...	...
1951														
January	...	1.75	1.34	8.09	-6.75	...	2.44	...	2.66	3.17	...	21.21	...	...
February	...	1.75	1.36	9.36	-8.00	...	2.50	...	2.66	3.16	...	22.00	...	...
March	...	1.75	1.40	9.32	-7.92	...	2.50	...	2.78	3.23	...	21.63	...	...
April	...	1.75	1.47	9.32	-7.85	...	2.50	...	2.87	3.35	...	21.92	...	...
May	...	1.75	1.55	9.28	-7.73	...	2.50	...	2.89	3.40	...	21.93	...	...
June	...	1.75	1.45	8.82	-7.37	...	2.50	...	2.94	3.49	...	21.55	...	...
July	...	1.75	1.56	7.47	-5.91	...	2.50	...	2.94	3.53	...	21.93	...	...
August	...	1.75	1.62	6.58	-4.96	...	2.50	...	2.88	3.50	...	22.89	...	...
September	...	1.75	1.63	6.97	-5.34	...	2.50	...	2.84	3.46	...	23.48	...	...
October	...	1.75	1.54	6.50	-4.96	...	2.62	...	2.89	3.50	...	23.36	...	...
November	...	1.75	1.56	6.88	-5.32	...	2.75	...	2.96	3.56	...	22.71	...	...
December	...	1.75	1.73	6.00	-4.27	...	2.85	...	3.01	3.61	...	23.41	...	...
1952														
January	...	1.75	1.57	4.33	-2.76	...	3.00	...	2.98	3.59	...	24.19	...	...
February	...	1.75	1.54	2.33	-0.79	...	3.00	...	2.93	3.53	...	23.75	...	...
March	...	1.75	1.59	1.94	-0.35	...	3.00	...	2.96	3.51	...	23.81	...	...
April	...	1.75	1.57	2.33	-0.76	...	3.00	...	2.93	3.50	...	23.74	...	...
May	...	1.75	1.67	1.93	-0.26	...	3.00	...	2.93	3.49	...	23.73	...	...
June	...	1.75	1.70	2.32	-0.62	...	3.00	...	2.94	3.50	...	24.38	...	...
July	...	1.75	1.81	3.09	-1.28	...	3.00	...	2.95	3.50	...	25.08	...	...
August	...	1.75	1.83	3.09	-1.26	...	3.00	...	2.94	3.51	...	25.18	...	...
September	...	1.75	1.71	2.30	-0.59	...	3.00	...	2.95	3.52	...	24.78	...	...
October	...	1.75	1.74	1.91	-0.17	...	3.00	...	3.01	3.54	...	24.26	...	...
November	...	1.75	1.85	1.14	0.71	...	3.00	...	2.98	3.53	...	25.03	...	...
December	...	1.75	2.09	0.75	1.34	...	3.00	...	2.97	3.51	...	26.04	...	...

[1]Federal Reserve Bank of New York. Through 2002, represents the rate for adjustment credit. Beginning in 2003, represents the rate for primary credit. See notes and definitions for more information.
[2]Change from a year earlier. Beginning in 1960, PCE except food and energy; before then, CPI-U
[3]Beginning 1997, rates for nonfinancial companies only are shown.
... = Not available.

Table 12-9B. Summary Interest Rates, Bond Yields, and Stock Prices: Historical Data—*Continued*

(Percent per annum, except as noted.)

Year and month	Federal funds interest rate	Federal Reserve discount rate¹	U.S. Treasury bills, secondary market, 3-month	Inflation²	Real 3-month Treasury bill rate	Commercial paper, 3-month³	Bank prime rate	Treasury 10-year nominal yields	Domestic corporate (Moody's) Aaa	Domestic corporate (Moody's) Baa	State and local bonds (Bond Buyer)	Index, 1941-1943 = 10	Dividend-price ratio	Earnings-price ratio
1953														
January	...	1.88	1.96	4.33	-2.37	...	3.00	...	3.02	3.51	2.44	26.18	...	...
February	...	2.00	1.97	2.33	-0.36	...	3.00	...	3.07	3.53	2.59	25.86	...	...
March	...	2.00	2.01	1.94	0.07	...	3.00	...	3.12	3.57	2.65	25.99	...	...
April	...	2.00	2.19	2.33	-0.14	...	3.03	2.83	3.23	3.65	2.67	24.71	...	...
May	...	2.00	2.16	1.93	0.23	...	3.25	3.05	3.34	3.78	2.82	24.84	...	...
June	...	2.00	2.11	2.32	-0.21	...	3.25	3.11	3.40	3.86	3.03	23.95	...	...
July	...	2.00	2.04	3.09	-1.05	...	3.25	2.93	3.28	3.86	2.95	24.29	...	...
August	...	2.00	2.04	3.09	-1.05	...	3.25	2.95	3.24	3.85	2.90	24.39	...	...
September ...	...	2.00	1.79	2.30	-0.51	...	3.25	2.87	3.29	3.88	2.87	23.27	...	...
October	...	2.00	1.38	1.91	-0.53	...	3.25	2.66	3.16	3.82	2.71	23.97	...	...
November	...	2.00	1.44	1.14	0.30	...	3.25	2.68	3.11	3.75	2.60	24.50	...	...
December	...	2.00	1.60	0.75	0.85	...	3.25	2.59	3.13	3.74	2.59	24.83	...	...
1954														
January	...	2.00	1.18	1.13	0.05	...	3.25	2.48	3.06	3.71	2.50	25.46	...	...
February	...	1.79	0.97	1.51	-0.54	...	3.25	2.47	2.95	3.61	2.42	26.02	...	...
March	...	1.75	1.03	1.13	-0.10	...	3.13	2.37	2.86	3.51	2.39	26.57	...	...
April	...	1.63	0.97	0.75	0.22	...	3.00	2.29	2.85	3.47	2.47	27.63	...	...
May	...	1.50	0.76	0.75	0.01	...	3.00	2.37	2.88	3.47	2.49	28.73	...	...
June	...	1.50	0.64	0.37	0.27	...	3.00	2.38	2.90	3.49	2.47	28.96	...	...
July	0.80	1.50	0.72	0.37	0.35	...	3.00	2.30	2.89	3.50	2.32	30.13	...	...
August	1.22	1.50	0.92	0.00	0.92	...	3.00	2.36	2.87	3.49	2.26	30.73	...	...
September ...	1.06	1.50	1.01	-0.37	1.38	...	3.00	2.38	2.89	3.47	2.31	31.45	...	...
October	0.85	1.50	0.98	-0.74	1.72	...	3.00	2.43	2.87	3.46	2.34	32.18	...	...
November	0.83	1.50	0.93	-0.37	1.30	...	3.00	2.48	2.89	3.45	2.32	33.44	...	...
December	1.28	1.50	1.15	-0.74	1.89	...	3.00	2.51	2.90	3.45	2.36	34.97	...	...
1955														
January	1.39	1.50	1.22	-0.74	1.96	...	3.00	2.61	2.93	3.45	2.40	35.60	...	...
February	1.29	1.50	1.17	-0.74	1.91	...	3.00	2.65	2.93	3.47	2.43	36.79	...	...
March	1.35	1.50	1.28	-0.74	2.02	...	3.00	2.68	3.02	3.48	2.44	36.50	...	...
April	1.43	1.63	1.59	-0.37	1.96	...	3.00	2.75	3.01	3.49	2.41	37.76	...	...
May	1.43	1.75	1.45	-0.74	2.19	...	3.00	2.76	3.04	3.50	2.38	37.60	...	...
June	1.64	1.75	1.41	-0.74	2.15	...	3.00	2.78	3.05	3.51	2.41	39.78	...	...
July	1.68	1.75	1.60	-0.37	1.97	...	3.00	2.90	3.06	3.52	2.54	42.69	...	...
August	1.96	1.97	1.90	-0.37	2.27	...	3.23	2.97	3.11	3.56	2.60	42.43	...	...
September ...	2.18	2.18	2.07	0.37	1.70	...	3.25	2.97	3.13	3.59	2.58	44.34	...	...
October	2.24	2.25	2.23	0.37	1.86	...	3.40	2.88	3.10	3.59	2.51	42.11	...	...
November	2.35	2.36	2.24	0.37	1.87	...	3.50	2.89	3.10	3.58	2.45	44.95	...	...
December	2.48	2.50	2.54	0.37	2.17	...	3.50	2.96	3.15	3.62	2.57	45.37	...	...
1956														
January	2.45	2.50	2.41	0.37	2.04	...	3.50	2.90	3.11	3.60	2.50	44.15	...	...
February	2.50	2.50	2.32	0.37	1.95	...	3.50	2.84	3.08	3.58	2.44	44.43	...	...
March	2.50	2.50	2.25	0.37	1.88	...	3.50	2.96	3.10	3.60	2.57	47.49	...	...
April	2.62	2.65	2.60	0.75	1.85	...	3.65	3.18	3.24	3.68	2.70	48.05	...	...
May	2.75	2.75	2.61	1.12	1.49	...	3.75	3.07	3.28	3.73	2.68	46.54	...	...
June	2.71	2.75	2.49	1.87	0.62	...	3.75	3.00	3.26	3.76	2.54	46.27	...	...
July	2.75	2.75	2.31	2.24	0.07	...	3.75	3.11	3.28	3.80	2.65	48.78	...	...
August	2.73	2.81	2.60	1.87	0.73	...	3.84	3.33	3.43	3.93	2.80	48.49	...	...
September ...	2.95	3.00	2.84	1.86	0.98	...	4.00	3.38	3.56	4.07	2.93	46.84	...	...
October	2.96	3.00	2.90	2.23	0.67	...	4.00	3.34	3.59	4.17	2.95	46.24	...	...
November	2.88	3.00	2.99	2.23	0.76	...	4.00	3.49	3.69	4.24	3.16	45.76	...	...
December	2.94	3.00	3.21	2.99	0.22	...	4.00	3.59	3.75	4.37	3.22	46.44	...	...
1957														
January	2.84	3.00	3.11	2.99	0.12	...	4.00	3.46	3.77	4.49	3.18	45.43	...	...
February	3.00	3.00	3.10	3.36	-0.26	...	4.00	3.34	3.67	4.47	3.00	43.47	...	...
March	2.96	3.00	3.08	3.73	-0.65	...	4.00	3.41	3.66	4.43	3.09	44.03	...	...
April	3.00	3.00	3.07	3.72	-0.65	...	4.00	3.48	3.67	4.44	3.13	45.05	...	...
May	3.00	3.00	3.06	3.70	-0.64	...	4.00	3.60	3.74	4.52	3.27	46.78	...	...
June	3.00	3.00	3.29	3.31	-0.02	...	4.00	3.80	3.91	4.63	3.41	47.55	...	...
July	2.99	3.00	3.16	3.28	-0.12	...	4.00	3.93	3.99	4.73	3.39	48.51	...	...
August	3.24	3.15	3.37	3.66	-0.29	...	4.42	3.93	4.10	4.82	3.54	45.84	...	...
September ...	3.47	3.50	3.53	3.28	0.25	...	4.50	3.92	4.12	4.93	3.53	43.98	...	...
October	3.50	3.50	3.58	2.91	0.67	...	4.50	3.97	4.10	4.99	3.42	41.24	...	...
November	3.28	3.23	3.31	3.27	0.04	...	4.50	3.72	4.08	5.09	3.37	40.35	...	...
December	2.98	3.00	3.04	2.90	0.14	...	4.50	3.21	3.81	5.03	3.04	40.33	...	...
1958														
January	2.72	2.94	2.44	3.62	-1.18	...	4.34	3.09	3.60	4.83	2.91	41.12	...	...
February	1.67	2.75	1.53	3.25	-1.72	...	4.00	3.05	3.59	4.66	3.02	41.26	...	...
March	1.20	2.35	1.30	3.60	-2.30	...	4.00	2.98	3.63	4.68	3.06	42.11	...	...
April	1.26	2.03	1.13	3.58	-2.45	...	3.83	2.88	3.60	4.67	2.96	42.34	...	...
May	0.63	1.75	0.91	3.21	-2.30	...	3.50	2.92	3.57	4.62	2.92	43.70	...	...
June	0.93	1.75	0.83	2.85	-2.02	...	3.50	2.97	3.57	4.55	2.97	44.75	...	...
July	0.68	1.75	0.91	2.47	-1.56	...	3.50	3.20	3.67	4.53	3.09	45.98	...	...
August	1.53	1.75	1.69	2.12	-0.43	...	3.50	3.54	3.85	4.67	3.35	47.70	...	...
September ...	1.76	1.91	2.44	2.12	0.32	...	3.83	3.76	4.09	4.87	3.54	48.96	...	...
October	1.80	2.00	2.63	2.12	0.51	...	4.00	3.80	4.11	4.92	3.45	50.95	...	...
November	2.27	2.40	2.67	2.11	0.56	...	4.00	3.74	4.09	4.87	3.32	52.50	...	...
December	2.42	2.50	2.77	1.76	1.01	...	4.00	3.86	4.08	4.85	3.33	53.49	...	...

¹Federal Reserve Bank of New York. Through 2002, represents the rate for adjustment credit. Beginning in 2003, represents the rate for primary credit. See notes and definitions for more information.
²Change from a year earlier. Beginning in 1960, PCE except food and energy; before then, CPI-U
³Beginning 1997, rates for nonfinancial companies only are shown.
. . . = Not available.

Table 12-9B. Summary Interest Rates, Bond Yields, and Stock Prices: Historical Data—*Continued*

(Percent per annum, except as noted.)

Year and month	Federal funds interest rate	Federal Reserve discount rate¹	U.S. Treasury bills, secondary market, 3-month	Inflation²	Real 3-month Treasury bill rate	Commercial paper, 3-month³	Bank prime rate	Treasury 10-year nominal yields	Bond yields: Domestic corporate (Moody's) Aaa	Baa	State and local bonds (Bond Buyer)	S&P composite (500 stocks) Index, 1941-1943 = 10	Dividend-price ratio	Earnings-price ratio
1959														
January	2.48	2.50	2.82	1.40	1.42	...	4.00	4.02	4.12	4.87	3.42	55.62	...	...
February	2.43	2.50	2.70	1.05	1.65	...	4.00	3.96	4.14	4.89	3.36	54.77	...	...
March	2.80	2.92	2.80	0.35	2.45	...	4.00	3.99	4.13	4.85	3.30	56.15	...	...
April	2.96	3.00	2.95	0.35	2.60	...	4.00	4.12	4.23	4.86	3.39	57.10	...	...
May	2.90	3.05	2.84	0.35	2.49	...	4.23	4.31	4.37	4.96	3.57	57.96	...	...
June	3.39	3.50	3.21	0.69	2.52	...	4.50	4.34	4.46	5.04	3.71	57.46	...	...
July	3.47	3.50	3.20	0.69	2.51	...	4.50	4.40	4.47	5.08	3.71	59.74	...	...
August	3.50	3.50	3.38	1.04	2.34	...	4.50	4.43	4.43	5.09	3.58	59.40	...	...
September	3.76	3.83	4.04	1.38	2.66	...	5.00	4.68	4.52	5.18	3.78	57.05	...	...
October	3.98	4.00	4.05	1.73	2.32	...	5.00	4.53	4.57	5.28	3.62	57.00	...	...
November	4.00	4.00	4.15	1.38	2.77	...	5.00	4.53	4.56	5.26	3.55	57.23	...	...
December	3.99	4.00	4.49	1.73	2.76	...	5.00	4.69	4.58	5.28	3.70	59.06	...	...
1960														
January	3.99	4.00	4.35	2.02	2.33	...	5.00	4.72	4.61	5.34	3.72	58.03	...	...
February	3.97	4.00	3.96	2.14	1.82	...	5.00	4.49	4.56	5.34	3.60	55.78	...	...
March	3.84	4.00	3.31	2.05	1.26	...	5.00	4.25	4.49	5.25	3.57	55.02	...	...
April	3.92	4.00	3.23	1.99	1.24	...	5.00	4.28	4.45	5.20	3.56	55.73	...	...
May	3.85	4.00	3.29	2.04	1.25	...	5.00	4.35	4.46	5.28	3.60	55.22	...	...
June	3.32	3.65	2.46	1.81	0.65	...	5.00	4.15	4.45	5.26	3.55	57.26	...	...
July	3.23	3.50	2.30	1.76	0.54	...	5.00	3.90	4.41	5.22	3.50	55.84	...	...
August	2.98	3.18	2.30	1.75	0.55	...	4.85	3.80	4.28	5.08	3.33	56.51	...	...
September	2.60	3.00	2.48	1.57	0.91	...	4.50	3.80	4.25	5.01	3.42	54.81	...	...
October	2.47	3.00	2.30	1.45	0.85	...	4.50	3.89	4.30	5.11	3.53	53.73	...	...
November	2.44	3.00	2.37	1.54	0.83	...	4.50	3.93	4.31	5.08	3.40	55.47	...	...
December	1.98	3.00	2.25	1.36	0.89	...	4.50	3.84	4.35	5.10	3.40	56.80	...	...
1961														
January	1.45	3.00	2.24	1.34	0.90	...	4.50	3.84	4.32	5.10	3.39	59.72	...	...
February	2.54	3.00	2.42	1.26	1.16	...	4.50	3.78	4.27	5.07	3.31	62.17	...	...
March	2.02	3.00	2.39	1.28	1.11	...	4.50	3.74	4.22	5.02	3.45	64.12	...	...
April	1.49	3.00	2.29	1.24	1.05	...	4.50	3.78	4.25	5.01	3.48	65.83	...	...
May	1.98	3.00	2.29	1.21	1.08	...	4.50	3.71	4.27	5.01	3.43	66.50	...	...
June	1.73	3.00	2.33	1.29	1.04	...	4.50	3.88	4.33	5.03	3.52	65.62	...	...
July	1.17	3.00	2.24	1.27	0.97	...	4.50	3.92	4.41	5.09	3.51	65.44	...	...
August	2.00	3.00	2.39	1.23	1.16	...	4.50	4.04	4.45	5.11	3.52	67.79	...	...
September	1.88	3.00	2.28	1.35	0.93	...	4.50	3.98	4.45	5.12	3.53	67.26	...	...
October	2.26	3.00	2.30	1.32	0.98	...	4.50	3.92	4.42	5.13	3.42	67.26	...	...
November	2.61	3.00	2.48	1.07	1.41	...	4.50	3.94	4.39	5.11	3.41	68.00	...	...
December	2.33	3.00	2.60	1.19	1.41	...	4.50	4.06	4.42	5.10	3.47	71.08	...	...
1962														
January	2.15	3.00	2.72	1.30	1.42	...	4.50	4.08	4.42	5.08	3.34	69.07	...	...
February	2.37	3.00	2.73	1.37	1.36	...	4.50	4.04	4.42	5.07	3.21	70.22	...	...
March	2.85	3.00	2.72	1.56	1.16	...	4.50	3.93	4.39	5.04	3.14	70.29	...	...
April	2.78	3.00	2.73	1.44	1.29	...	4.50	3.84	4.33	5.02	3.06	68.05	...	...
May	2.36	3.00	2.69	1.45	1.24	...	4.50	3.87	4.28	5.00	3.11	62.99	...	...
June	2.68	3.00	2.73	1.49	1.24	...	4.50	3.91	4.28	5.02	3.25	55.63	...	...
July	2.71	3.00	2.92	1.40	1.52	...	4.50	4.01	4.34	5.05	3.27	56.97	...	...
August	2.93	3.00	2.82	1.30	1.52	...	4.50	3.98	4.35	5.06	3.23	58.52	...	...
September	2.90	3.00	2.78	1.29	1.49	...	4.50	3.98	4.32	5.03	3.11	58.00	...	...
October	2.90	3.00	2.74	1.25	1.49	...	4.50	3.93	4.28	4.99	3.02	56.17	...	...
November	2.94	3.00	2.83	1.29	1.54	...	4.50	3.92	4.25	4.96	3.04	60.04	...	...
December	2.93	3.00	2.87	1.23	1.64	...	4.50	3.86	4.24	4.92	3.07	62.64	...	...
1963														
January	2.92	3.00	2.91	1.31	1.60	...	4.50	3.83	4.21	4.91	3.10	65.06	...	...
February	3.00	3.00	2.92	1.25	1.67	...	4.50	3.92	4.19	4.89	3.15	65.92	...	...
March	2.98	3.00	2.89	1.07	1.82	...	4.50	3.93	4.19	4.88	3.05	65.67	...	...
April	2.90	3.00	2.90	1.16	1.74	...	4.50	3.97	4.21	4.87	3.10	68.76	...	...
May	3.00	3.00	2.93	1.20	1.73	...	4.50	3.93	4.22	4.85	3.11	70.14	...	...
June	2.99	3.00	2.99	1.18	1.81	...	4.50	3.99	4.23	4.84	3.21	70.11	...	...
July	3.02	3.24	3.18	1.19	1.99	...	4.50	4.02	4.26	4.84	3.22	69.07	...	...
August	3.49	3.50	3.32	1.27	2.05	...	4.50	4.00	4.29	4.83	3.13	70.98	...	...
September	3.48	3.50	3.38	1.26	2.12	...	4.50	4.08	4.31	4.84	3.20	72.85	...	...
October	3.50	3.50	3.45	1.50	1.95	...	4.50	4.11	4.32	4.83	3.20	73.03	...	...
November	3.48	3.50	3.52	1.52	2.00	...	4.50	4.12	4.33	4.84	3.30	72.62	...	...
December	3.38	3.50	3.52	1.64	1.88	...	4.50	4.13	4.35	4.85	3.27	74.17	...	...
1964														
January	3.48	3.50	3.52	1.59	1.93	...	4.50	4.17	4.39	4.83	3.22	76.45	...	...
February	3.48	3.50	3.53	1.68	1.85	...	4.50	4.15	4.36	4.83	3.14	77.39	...	...
March	3.43	3.50	3.54	1.72	1.82	...	4.50	4.22	4.38	4.83	3.28	78.80	...	...
April	3.47	3.50	3.47	1.71	1.76	...	4.50	4.23	4.40	4.85	3.28	79.94	...	...
May	3.50	3.50	3.48	1.62	1.86	...	4.50	4.20	4.41	4.85	3.20	80.72	...	...
June	3.50	3.50	3.48	1.53	1.95	...	4.50	4.17	4.41	4.85	3.20	80.24	...	...
July	3.42	3.50	3.46	1.54	1.92	...	4.50	4.19	4.40	4.83	3.18	83.22	...	...
August	3.50	3.50	3.50	1.59	1.91	...	4.50	4.19	4.41	4.82	3.19	82.00	...	...
September	3.45	3.50	3.53	1.46	2.07	...	4.50	4.20	4.42	4.82	3.23	83.41	...	...
October	3.36	3.50	3.57	1.28	2.29	...	4.50	4.19	4.42	4.81	3.25	84.85	...	...
November	3.52	3.62	3.64	1.33	2.31	...	4.50	4.15	4.43	4.81	3.18	85.44	...	...
December	3.85	4.00	3.84	1.33	2.51	...	4.50	4.18	4.44	4.81	3.13	83.96	...	...

¹Federal Reserve Bank of New York. Through 2002, represents the rate for adjustment credit. Beginning in 2003, represents the rate for primary credit. See notes and definitions for more information.
²Change from a year earlier. Beginning in 1960, PCE except food and energy; before then, CPI-U
³Beginning 1997, rates for nonfinancial companies only are shown.
. . . = Not available.

Table 12-9B. Summary Interest Rates, Bond Yields, and Stock Prices: Historical Data—*Continued*

(Percent per annum, except as noted.)

Year and month	Federal funds interest rate	Federal Reserve discount rate[1]	U.S. Treasury bills, secondary market, 3-month	Inflation[2]	Real 3-month Treasury bill rate	Commercial paper, 3-month [3]	Bank prime rate	Treasury 10-year nominal yields	Domestic corporate (Moody's) Aaa	Domestic corporate (Moody's) Baa	State and local bonds (Bond Buyer)	Index, 1941-1943 = 10	Dividend-price ratio	Earnings-price ratio
1965														
January	3.90	4.00	3.81	1.31	2.50	...	4.50	4.19	4.43	4.80	3.06	86.12	...	...
February	3.98	4.00	3.93	1.23	2.70	...	4.50	4.21	4.41	4.78	3.09	86.75	...	...
March	4.04	4.00	3.93	1.19	2.74	...	4.50	4.21	4.42	4.78	3.17	86.83	...	...
April	4.09	4.00	3.93	1.21	2.72	...	4.50	4.20	4.43	4.80	3.15	87.97	...	...
May	4.10	4.00	3.89	1.30	2.59	...	4.50	4.21	4.44	4.81	3.17	89.28	...	...
June	4.04	4.00	3.80	1.20	2.60	...	4.50	4.21	4.46	4.85	3.24	85.04	...	...
July	4.09	4.00	3.84	1.19	2.65	...	4.50	4.20	4.48	4.88	3.27	84.91	...	...
August	4.12	4.00	3.84	1.25	2.59	...	4.50	4.25	4.49	4.88	3.24	86.49	...	...
September	4.01	4.00	3.92	1.32	2.60	...	4.50	4.29	4.52	4.91	3.35	89.38	...	...
October	4.08	4.00	4.03	1.24	2.79	...	4.50	4.35	4.56	4.93	3.40	91.39	...	...
November	4.10	4.00	4.09	1.28	2.81	...	4.50	4.45	4.60	4.95	3.45	92.15	...	...
December	4.32	4.42	4.38	1.45	2.93	...	4.92	4.62	4.68	5.02	3.54	91.73	...	...
1966														
January	4.42	4.50	4.59	1.35	3.24	...	5.00	4.61	4.74	5.06	3.52	93.32	...	...
February	4.60	4.50	4.65	1.48	3.17	...	5.00	4.83	4.78	5.12	3.64	92.69	...	...
March	4.65	4.50	4.59	1.56	3.03	...	5.35	4.87	4.92	5.32	3.72	88.88	...	...
April	4.67	4.50	4.62	1.80	2.82	...	5.50	4.75	4.96	5.41	3.56	91.60	...	...
May	4.90	4.50	4.64	1.89	2.75	...	5.50	4.78	4.98	5.48	3.65	86.78	...	...
June	5.17	4.50	4.50	2.25	2.25	...	5.52	4.81	5.07	5.58	3.77	86.06	...	...
July	5.30	4.50	4.80	2.45	2.35	...	5.75	5.02	5.16	5.68	3.95	85.84	...	...
August	5.53	4.50	4.96	2.44	2.52	...	5.88	5.22	5.31	5.83	4.12	80.65	...	...
September	5.40	4.50	5.37	2.64	2.73	...	6.00	5.18	5.49	6.09	4.12	77.81	...	...
October	5.53	4.50	5.35	3.02	2.33	...	6.00	5.01	5.41	6.10	3.93	77.13	...	...
November	5.76	4.50	5.32	3.09	2.23	...	6.00	5.16	5.35	6.13	3.86	80.99	...	...
December	5.40	4.50	4.96	3.09	1.87	...	6.00	4.84	5.39	6.18	3.86	81.33	...	...
1967														
January	4.94	4.50	4.72	3.15	1.57	...	5.96	4.58	5.20	5.97	3.54	84.45	...	...
February	5.00	4.50	4.56	3.08	1.48	...	5.75	4.63	5.03	5.82	3.52	87.36	...	...
March	4.53	4.50	4.26	3.09	1.17	...	5.71	4.54	5.13	5.85	3.55	89.42	...	...
April	4.05	4.10	3.84	3.02	0.82	...	5.50	4.59	5.11	5.83	3.60	90.96	...	...
May	3.94	4.00	3.60	2.97	0.63	...	5.50	4.85	5.24	5.96	3.89	92.59	...	...
June	3.98	4.00	3.54	2.89	0.65	...	5.50	5.02	5.44	6.15	3.96	91.43	...	...
July	3.79	4.00	4.21	2.93	1.28	...	5.50	5.16	5.58	6.26	4.02	93.01	...	...
August	3.90	4.00	4.27	3.06	1.21	...	5.50	5.28	5.62	6.33	3.99	94.49	...	...
September	3.99	4.00	4.42	3.10	1.32	...	5.50	5.30	5.65	6.40	4.12	95.81	...	...
October	3.88	4.00	4.56	3.14	1.42	...	5.50	5.48	5.82	6.52	4.29	95.66	...	...
November	4.13	4.18	4.73	3.20	1.53	...	5.68	5.75	6.07	6.72	4.34	92.66	...	...
December	4.51	4.50	4.97	3.14	1.83	...	6.00	5.70	6.19	6.93	4.43	95.30	...	...
1968														
January	4.60	4.50	5.00	3.49	1.51	...	6.00	5.53	6.17	6.84	4.29	95.04	...	...
February	4.71	4.50	4.98	3.75	1.23	...	6.00	5.56	6.10	6.80	4.31	90.75	...	...
March	5.05	4.66	5.17	4.01	1.16	...	6.00	5.74	6.11	6.85	4.54	89.09	...	...
April	5.76	5.20	5.38	4.10	1.28	...	6.20	5.64	6.21	6.97	4.34	95.67	...	...
May	6.11	5.50	5.66	4.26	1.40	...	6.50	5.87	6.27	7.03	4.54	97.87	...	...
June	6.07	5.50	5.52	4.40	1.12	...	6.50	5.72	6.28	7.07	4.49	100.53	...	...
July	6.02	5.50	5.31	4.40	0.91	...	6.50	5.50	6.24	6.98	4.33	100.30	...	...
August	6.03	5.48	5.09	4.49	0.60	...	6.50	5.42	6.02	6.82	4.21	98.11	...	...
September	5.78	5.25	5.19	4.55	0.64	...	6.45	5.46	5.97	6.79	4.38	101.34	...	...
October	5.91	5.25	5.35	4.59	0.76	...	6.25	5.58	6.09	6.84	4.49	103.76	...	...
November	5.82	5.25	5.45	4.65	0.80	...	6.25	5.70	6.19	7.01	4.60	105.40	...	...
December	6.02	5.36	5.96	4.71	1.25	...	6.60	6.03	6.45	7.23	4.82	106.48	...	...
1969														
January	6.30	5.50	6.14	4.67	1.47	...	6.95	6.04	6.59	7.32	4.85	102.04	...	...
February	6.61	5.50	6.12	4.58	1.54	...	7.00	6.19	6.66	7.30	4.98	101.46	...	...
March	6.79	5.50	6.02	4.66	1.36	...	7.24	6.30	6.85	7.51	5.26	99.30	...	...
April	7.41	5.95	6.11	4.68	1.43	...	7.50	6.17	6.89	7.54	5.19	101.26	...	...
May	8.67	6.00	6.04	4.71	1.33	...	7.50	6.32	6.79	7.52	5.33	104.62	...	...
June	8.90	6.00	6.44	4.66	1.78	...	8.23	6.57	6.98	7.70	5.75	99.14	...	...
July	8.61	6.00	7.00	4.80	2.20	...	8.50	6.72	7.08	7.84	5.75	94.71	...	...
August	9.19	6.00	6.98	4.69	2.29	...	8.50	6.69	6.97	7.86	6.00	94.18	...	...
September	9.15	6.00	7.09	4.69	2.40	...	8.50	7.16	7.14	8.05	6.26	94.51	...	...
October	9.00	6.00	7.00	4.71	2.29	...	8.50	7.10	7.33	8.22	6.09	95.52	...	...
November	8.85	6.00	7.24	4.72	2.52	...	8.50	7.14	7.35	8.25	6.30	96.21	...	...
December	8.97	6.00	7.82	4.78	3.04	...	8.50	7.65	7.72	8.65	6.82	91.11	...	...
1970														
January	8.98	6.00	7.87	4.72	3.15	...	8.50	7.79	7.91	8.86	6.63	90.31	...	...
February	8.98	6.00	7.13	4.76	2.37	...	8.50	7.24	7.93	8.78	6.22	87.16	...	...
March	7.76	6.00	6.63	4.66	1.97	...	8.39	7.07	7.84	8.63	6.05	88.65	...	...
April	8.10	6.00	6.51	4.67	1.84	...	8.00	7.39	7.83	8.70	6.65	85.95	...	...
May	7.94	6.00	6.84	4.61	2.23	...	8.00	7.91	8.11	8.98	7.00	76.06	...	...
June	7.60	6.00	6.68	4.63	2.05	...	8.00	7.84	8.48	9.25	6.93	75.59	...	...
July	7.21	6.00	6.45	4.54	1.91	...	8.00	7.46	8.44	9.40	6.42	75.72	...	...
August	6.61	6.00	6.41	4.61	1.80	...	8.00	7.53	8.13	9.44	6.17	77.92	...	...
September	6.29	6.00	6.12	4.62	1.50	...	7.83	7.39	8.09	9.39	6.31	82.58	...	...
October	6.20	6.00	5.91	4.69	1.22	...	7.50	7.33	8.03	9.33	6.37	84.37	...	...
November	5.60	5.85	5.28	4.82	0.46	...	7.28	6.84	8.05	9.38	5.71	84.28	...	...
December	4.90	5.52	4.87	4.96	-0.09	...	6.92	6.39	7.64	9.12	5.47	90.05	...	...

[1]Federal Reserve Bank of New York. Through 2002, represents the rate for adjustment credit. Beginning in 2003, represents the rate for primary credit. See notes and definitions for more information.
[2]Change from a year earlier. Beginning in 1960, PCE except food and energy; before then, CPI-U
[3]Beginning 1997, rates for nonfinancial companies only are shown.
. . . = Not available.

Table 12-9B. Summary Interest Rates, Bond Yields, and Stock Prices: Historical Data—*Continued*

(Percent per annum, except as noted.)

Year and month	Federal funds interest rate	Federal Reserve discount rate[1]	U.S. Treasury bills, secondary market, 3-month	Inflation[2]	Real 3-month Treasury bill rate	Commer-cial paper, 3-month [3]	Bank prime rate	Treasury 10-year nominal yields	Domestic corporate (Moody's) Aaa	Domestic corporate (Moody's) Baa	State and local bonds (Bond Buyer)	Index, 1941-1943 = 10	Dividend-price ratio	Earnings-price ratio
1971														
January	4.14	5.23	4.44	5.03	-0.59	. . .	6.29	6.24	7.36	8.74	5.35	93.49	. . .	. . .
February	3.72	4.91	3.70	5.03	-1.33	. . .	5.88	6.11	7.08	8.39	5.23	97.11	. . .	. . .
March	3.71	4.75	3.38	4.97	-1.59	. . .	5.44	5.70	7.21	8.46	5.17	99.60	. . .	. . .
April	4.15	4.75	3.86	4.95	-1.09	4.57	5.28	5.83	7.25	8.45	5.37	103.04	. . .	. . .
May	4.63	4.75	4.14	5.04	-0.90	5.06	5.46	6.39	7.53	8.62	5.90	101.64	. . .	. . .
June	4.91	4.75	4.75	5.07	-0.32	5.38	5.50	6.52	7.64	8.75	5.95	99.72	. . .	. . .
July	5.31	4.88	5.40	5.07	0.33	5.75	5.91	6.73	7.64	8.76	6.06	99.00	. . .	. . .
August	5.56	5.00	4.94	4.86	0.08	5.74	6.00	6.58	7.59	8.76	5.82	97.24	. . .	. . .
September ...	5.55	5.00	4.69	4.60	0.09	5.69	6.00	6.14	7.44	8.59	5.37	99.40	. . .	. . .
October	5.20	5.00	4.46	4.25	0.21	5.42	5.90	5.93	7.39	8.48	5.06	97.29	. . .	. . .
November	4.91	4.90	4.22	3.95	0.27	4.84	5.53	5.81	7.26	8.38	5.20	92.78	. . .	. . .
December	4.14	4.63	4.01	3.75	0.26	4.66	5.49	5.93	7.25	8.38	5.21	99.17	. . .	. . .
1972														
January	3.50	4.50	3.38	3.79	-0.41	4.03	5.18	5.95	7.19	8.23	5.12	103.30	. . .	. . .
February	3.29	4.50	3.20	3.68	-0.48	3.81	4.75	6.08	7.27	8.23	5.28	105.24	. . .	. . .
March	3.83	4.50	3.73	3.55	0.18	4.10	4.75	6.07	7.24	8.24	5.31	107.69	. . .	. . .
April	4.17	4.50	3.71	3.40	0.31	4.55	4.97	6.19	7.30	8.24	5.43	108.81	. . .	. . .
May	4.27	4.50	3.69	3.19	0.50	4.45	5.00	6.13	7.30	8.23	5.30	107.65	. . .	. . .
June	4.46	4.50	3.91	2.99	0.92	4.60	5.04	6.11	7.23	8.20	5.33	108.01	. . .	. . .
July	4.55	4.50	3.98	2.90	1.08	4.83	5.25	6.11	7.21	8.23	5.41	107.21	. . .	. . .
August	4.80	4.50	4.02	2.97	1.05	4.75	5.27	6.21	7.19	8.19	5.30	111.01	. . .	. . .
September ...	4.87	4.50	4.66	3.14	1.52	5.07	5.50	6.55	7.22	8.09	5.36	109.39	. . .	. . .
October	5.04	4.50	4.74	3.04	1.70	5.21	5.73	6.48	7.21	8.06	5.18	109.56	. . .	. . .
November	5.06	4.50	4.78	3.08	1.70	5.18	5.75	6.28	7.12	7.99	5.02	115.05	. . .	. . .
December	5.33	4.50	5.07	3.06	2.01	5.40	5.79	6.36	7.08	7.93	5.05	117.50	. . .	. . .
1973														
January	5.94	4.77	5.41	2.69	2.72	5.77	6.00	6.46	7.15	7.90	5.05	118.42	. . .	. . .
February	6.58	5.05	5.60	2.74	2.86	6.17	6.02	6.64	7.22	7.97	5.13	114.16	. . .	. . .
March	7.09	5.50	6.09	2.95	3.14	6.76	6.30	6.71	7.29	8.03	5.29	112.42	. . .	. . .
April	7.12	5.50	6.26	3.31	2.95	7.13	6.61	6.67	7.26	8.09	5.15	110.27	. . .	. . .
May	7.84	5.90	6.36	3.47	2.89	7.26	7.01	6.85	7.29	8.06	5.15	107.22	. . .	. . .
June	8.49	6.33	7.19	3.71	3.48	8.00	7.49	6.90	7.37	8.13	5.17	104.75	. . .	. . .
July	10.40	6.98	8.01	3.85	4.16	9.26	8.30	7.13	7.45	8.24	5.40	105.83	. . .	. . .
August	10.50	7.29	8.67	4.11	4.56	10.26	9.23	7.40	7.68	8.53	5.48	103.80	. . .	. . .
September ...	10.78	7.50	8.29	4.29	4.00	10.31	9.86	7.09	7.63	8.63	5.10	105.61	. . .	. . .
October	10.01	7.50	7.22	4.64	2.58	9.14	9.94	6.79	7.60	8.41	5.05	109.84	. . .	. . .
November	10.03	7.50	7.83	4.87	2.96	9.11	9.75	6.73	7.67	8.42	5.18	102.03	. . .	. . .
December	9.95	7.50	7.45	5.13	2.32	9.28	9.75	6.74	7.68	8.48	5.12	94.78	. . .	. . .
1974														
January	9.65	7.50	7.77	5.57	2.20	8.86	9.73	6.99	7.83	8.48	5.22	96.11	. . .	. . .
February	8.97	7.50	7.12	5.92	1.20	8.00	9.21	6.96	7.85	8.53	5.20	93.45	. . .	. . .
March	9.35	7.50	7.96	6.30	1.66	8.64	8.85	7.21	8.01	8.62	5.40	97.44	. . .	. . .
April	10.51	7.60	8.33	6.49	1.84	9.92	10.02	7.51	8.25	8.87	5.73	92.46	. . .	. . .
May	11.31	8.00	8.23	7.09	1.14	10.82	11.25	7.58	8.37	9.05	6.02	89.67	. . .	. . .
June	11.93	8.00	7.90	7.73	0.17	11.18	11.54	7.54	8.47	9.27	6.13	89.79	. . .	. . .
July	12.92	8.00	7.55	8.22	-0.67	11.93	11.97	7.81	8.72	9.48	6.68	82.82	. . .	. . .
August	12.01	8.00	8.96	8.76	0.20	11.79	12.00	8.04	9.00	9.77	6.71	76.03	. . .	. . .
September ...	11.34	8.00	8.06	9.19	-1.13	11.36	12.00	8.04	9.24	10.18	6.76	68.12	. . .	. . .
October	10.06	8.00	7.46	9.61	-2.15	9.55	11.68	7.90	9.27	10.48	6.57	69.44	. . .	. . .
November	9.45	8.00	7.47	9.88	-2.41	8.95	10.83	7.68	8.89	10.60	6.61	71.74	. . .	. . .
December	8.53	7.81	7.15	10.05	-2.90	9.18	10.50	7.43	8.89	10.63	7.05	67.07	. . .	. . .
1975														
January	7.13	7.40	6.26	10.16	-3.90	7.39	10.05	7.50	8.83	10.81	6.82	72.56	. . .	. . .
February	6.24	6.82	5.50	10.23	-4.73	6.36	8.96	7.39	8.62	10.65	6.39	80.10	. . .	. . .
March	5.54	6.40	5.49	9.96	-4.47	6.06	7.93	7.73	8.67	10.48	6.73	83.78	. . .	. . .
April	5.49	6.25	5.61	9.68	-4.07	6.11	7.50	8.23	8.95	10.58	6.95	84.72	. . .	. . .
May	5.22	6.12	5.23	9.09	-3.86	5.70	7.40	8.06	8.90	10.69	6.97	90.10	. . .	. . .
June	5.55	6.00	5.34	8.51	-3.17	5.67	7.07	7.86	8.77	10.62	6.94	92.40	. . .	. . .
July	6.10	6.00	6.13	8.22	-2.09	6.32	7.15	8.06	8.84	10.55	7.07	92.49	. . .	. . .
August	6.14	6.00	6.44	7.56	-1.12	6.59	7.66	8.40	8.95	10.59	7.17	85.71	. . .	. . .
September ...	6.24	6.00	6.42	7.18	-0.76	6.79	7.88	8.43	8.95	10.61	7.44	84.67	. . .	. . .
October	5.82	6.00	5.96	6.88	-0.92	6.35	7.96	8.14	8.86	10.62	7.39	88.57	. . .	. . .
November	5.22	6.00	5.48	6.80	-1.32	5.78	7.53	8.05	8.78	10.56	7.43	90.07	. . .	. . .
December	5.20	6.00	5.44	6.69	-1.25	5.88	7.26	8.00	8.79	10.56	7.31	88.70	. . .	. . .
1976														
January	4.87	5.79	4.87	6.62	-1.75	5.16	7.00	7.74	8.60	10.41	7.07	96.86	. . .	. . .
February	4.77	5.50	4.88	6.29	-1.41	5.13	6.75	7.79	8.55	10.24	6.94	100.64	. . .	. . .
March	4.84	5.50	5.00	6.08	-1.08	5.25	6.75	7.73	8.52	10.12	6.91	101.08	. . .	. . .
April	4.82	5.50	4.86	5.98	-1.12	5.09	6.75	7.56	8.40	9.94	6.60	101.93	. . .	. . .
May	5.29	5.50	5.20	6.03	-0.83	5.44	6.75	7.90	8.58	9.86	6.87	101.16	. . .	. . .
June	5.48	5.50	5.41	5.94	-0.53	5.83	7.20	7.86	8.62	9.89	6.87	101.77	. . .	. . .
July	5.31	5.50	5.23	5.86	-0.63	5.54	7.25	7.83	8.56	9.82	6.79	104.20	. . .	. . .
August	5.29	5.50	5.14	6.11	-0.97	5.36	7.01	7.77	8.45	9.64	6.61	103.29	. . .	. . .
September ...	5.25	5.50	5.08	6.15	-1.07	5.33	7.00	7.59	8.38	9.40	6.51	105.45	. . .	. . .
October	5.02	5.50	4.92	6.14	-1.22	5.10	6.77	7.41	8.32	9.29	6.30	101.89	. . .	. . .
November	4.95	5.43	4.75	5.92	-1.17	4.98	6.50	7.29	8.25	9.23	6.29	101.19	. . .	. . .
December	4.65	5.25	4.35	5.85	-1.50	4.66	6.35	6.87	7.98	9.12	5.94	104.66	. . .	. . .

[1]Federal Reserve Bank of New York. Through 2002, represents the rate for adjustment credit. Beginning in 2003, represents the rate for primary credit. See notes and definitions for more information.
[2]Change from a year earlier. Beginning in 1960, PCE except food and energy; before then, CPI-U
[3]Beginning 1997, rates for nonfinancial companies only are shown.
. . . = Not available.

Table 12-9B. Summary Interest Rates, Bond Yields, and Stock Prices: Historical Data—Continued

(Percent per annum, except as noted.)

Year and month	Federal funds interest rate	Federal Reserve discount rate[1]	U.S. Treasury bills, secondary market, 3-month	Inflation[2]	Real 3-month Treasury bill rate	Commercial paper, 3-month[3]	Bank prime rate	Treasury 10-year nominal yields	Bond yields: Domestic corporate (Moody's) Aaa	Baa	State and local bonds (Bond Buyer)	Index, 1941-1943 = 10	Dividend-price ratio	Earnings-price ratio
1977														
January	4.61	5.25	4.62	5.94	-1.32	4.72	6.25	7.21	7.96	9.08	5.87	103.81	...	...
February	4.68	5.25	4.67	6.16	-1.49	4.76	6.25	7.39	8.04	9.12	5.88	100.96	...	...
March	4.69	5.25	4.60	6.26	-1.66	4.75	6.25	7.46	8.10	9.12	5.89	100.57	...	...
April	4.73	5.25	4.54	6.37	-1.83	4.75	6.25	7.37	8.04	9.07	5.72	99.05	...	...
May	5.35	5.25	4.96	6.42	-1.46	5.26	6.41	7.46	8.05	9.01	5.75	98.76	...	...
June	5.39	5.25	5.02	6.62	-1.60	5.42	6.75	7.28	7.95	8.91	5.62	99.29	...	...
July	5.42	5.25	5.19	6.70	-1.51	5.39	6.75	7.33	7.94	8.87	5.63	100.18	...	...
August	5.90	5.27	5.49	6.61	-1.12	5.76	6.83	7.40	7.98	8.82	5.62	97.75	...	...
September	6.14	5.75	5.81	6.44	-0.63	6.10	7.13	7.34	7.92	8.80	5.51	96.23	...	...
October	6.47	5.80	6.16	6.44	-0.28	6.51	7.52	7.52	8.04	8.89	5.64	93.74	...	...
November	6.51	6.00	6.10	6.51	-0.41	6.54	7.75	7.58	8.08	8.95	5.49	94.28	...	...
December	6.56	6.00	6.07	6.51	-0.44	6.61	7.75	7.69	8.19	8.99	5.57	93.82	...	...
1978														
January	6.70	6.37	6.44	6.52	-0.08	6.75	7.93	7.96	8.41	9.17	5.71	90.25	...	...
February	6.78	6.50	6.45	6.29	0.16	6.76	8.00	8.03	8.47	9.20	5.62	88.98	...	...
March	6.79	6.50	6.29	6.42	-0.13	6.75	8.00	8.04	8.47	9.22	5.61	88.82	...	...
April	6.89	6.50	6.29	6.58	-0.29	6.82	8.00	8.15	8.56	9.32	5.79	92.71	...	...
May	7.36	6.84	6.41	6.66	-0.25	7.06	8.27	8.35	8.69	9.49	6.03	97.41	...	...
June	7.60	7.00	6.73	6.63	0.10	7.59	8.63	8.46	8.76	9.60	6.22	97.66	...	...
July	7.81	7.23	7.01	6.59	0.42	7.85	9.00	8.64	8.88	9.60	6.28	97.19	...	...
August	8.04	7.43	7.08	6.64	0.44	7.83	9.01	8.41	8.69	9.48	6.12	103.92	...	...
September	8.45	7.83	7.85	6.80	1.05	8.39	9.41	8.42	8.69	9.42	6.09	103.86	...	...
October	8.96	8.26	7.99	7.06	0.93	8.98	9.94	8.64	8.89	9.59	6.13	100.58	...	...
November	9.76	9.50	8.64	7.08	1.56	10.14	10.94	8.81	9.03	9.83	6.19	94.71	...	...
December	10.03	9.50	9.08	6.93	2.15	10.37	11.55	9.01	9.16	9.94	6.50	96.11	...	...
1979														
January	10.07	9.50	9.35	6.81	2.54	10.25	11.75	9.10	9.25	10.13	6.46	99.71	...	...
February	10.06	9.50	9.32	6.74	2.58	9.95	11.75	9.10	9.26	10.08	6.31	98.23	...	...
March	10.09	9.50	9.48	6.77	2.71	9.90	11.75	9.12	9.37	10.26	6.33	100.11	...	...
April	10.01	9.50	9.46	7.06	2.40	9.85	11.75	9.18	9.38	10.33	6.28	102.07	...	...
May	10.24	9.50	9.61	7.35	2.26	9.95	11.75	9.25	9.50	10.47	6.25	99.73	...	...
June	10.29	9.50	9.06	7.35	1.71	9.76	11.65	8.91	9.29	10.38	6.12	101.73	...	...
July	10.47	9.69	9.24	7.25	1.99	9.87	11.54	8.95	9.20	10.29	6.13	102.71	...	...
August	10.94	10.24	9.52	7.38	2.14	10.42	11.91	9.03	9.23	10.35	6.20	107.36	...	...
September	11.43	10.70	10.26	7.49	2.77	11.63	12.90	9.33	9.44	10.54	6.52	108.60	...	...
October	13.77	11.77	11.70	7.48	4.22	13.23	14.39	10.30	10.13	11.40	7.08	104.47	...	...
November	13.18	12.00	11.79	7.59	4.20	13.57	15.55	10.65	10.76	11.99	7.30	103.66	...	...
December	13.78	12.00	12.04	7.94	4.10	13.24	15.30	10.39	10.74	12.06	7.22	107.78	...	...
1980														
January	13.82	12.00	12.00	8.21	3.79	13.04	15.25	10.80	11.09	12.42	7.35	110.87	...	...
February	14.13	12.52	12.86	8.93	3.93	13.78	15.63	12.41	12.38	13.57	8.16	115.34	...	...
March	17.19	13.00	15.20	9.31	5.89	16.81	18.31	12.75	12.96	14.45	9.16	104.69	...	...
April	17.61	13.00	13.20	8.87	4.33	15.78	19.77	11.47	12.04	14.19	8.63	102.97	...	...
May	10.98	12.94	8.58	8.80	-0.22	9.49	16.57	10.18	10.99	13.17	7.59	107.69	...	...
June	9.47	11.40	7.07	8.91	-1.84	8.27	12.63	9.78	10.58	12.71	7.63	114.55	...	...
July	9.03	10.87	8.06	9.13	-1.07	8.41	11.48	10.25	11.07	12.65	8.13	119.83	...	...
August	9.61	10.00	9.13	9.20	-0.07	9.57	11.12	11.10	11.64	13.15	8.67	123.50	...	...
September	10.87	10.17	10.27	9.48	0.79	10.97	12.23	11.51	12.02	13.70	8.94	126.51	...	...
October	12.81	11.00	11.62	9.58	2.04	12.52	13.79	11.75	12.31	14.23	9.11	130.22	...	...
November	15.85	11.47	13.73	9.74	3.99	15.18	16.06	12.68	12.97	14.64	9.56	135.65	...	...
December	18.90	12.87	15.49	9.62	5.87	18.07	20.35	12.84	13.21	15.14	10.20	133.48	...	...
1981														
January	19.08	13.00	15.02	9.74	5.28	16.58	20.16	12.57	12.81	15.03	9.66	132.97	...	...
February	15.93	13.00	14.79	9.46	5.33	15.49	19.43	13.19	13.35	15.37	10.09	128.40	...	...
March	14.70	13.00	13.36	9.06	4.30	13.94	18.05	13.12	13.33	15.34	10.16	133.19	...	...
April	15.72	13.00	13.69	9.18	4.51	14.56	17.15	13.68	13.88	15.56	10.62	134.43	...	...
May	18.52	13.87	16.30	9.05	7.25	17.56	19.61	14.10	14.32	15.95	10.77	131.73	...	...
June	19.10	14.00	14.73	8.87	5.86	16.32	20.03	13.47	13.75	15.80	10.67	132.28	...	...
July	19.04	14.00	14.95	8.77	6.18	17.00	20.39	14.28	14.38	16.17	11.14	129.13	...	...
August	17.82	14.00	15.51	8.71	6.80	17.23	20.50	14.94	14.89	16.34	12.26	129.63	...	...
September	15.87	14.00	14.70	8.40	6.30	16.09	20.08	15.32	15.49	16.92	12.92	118.27	...	...
October	15.08	14.00	13.54	8.15	5.39	14.85	18.45	15.15	15.40	17.11	12.83	119.80	...	...
November	13.31	13.03	10.86	7.93	2.93	12.16	16.84	13.39	14.22	16.39	11.89	122.92	...	...
December	12.37	12.10	10.85	7.67	3.18	12.12	15.75	13.72	14.23	16.55	12.91	123.79	...	...
1982														
January	13.22	12.00	12.28	7.39	4.89	13.09	15.75	14.59	15.18	17.10	13.28	117.28	...	...
February	14.78	12.00	13.48	7.02	6.46	14.53	16.56	14.43	15.27	17.18	12.97	114.50	...	...
March	14.68	12.00	12.68	6.89	5.79	13.80	16.50	13.86	14.58	16.82	12.82	110.84	...	...
April	14.94	12.00	12.70	6.64	6.06	14.06	16.50	13.87	14.46	16.78	12.58	116.31	...	...
May	14.45	12.00	12.09	6.49	5.60	13.42	16.50	13.62	14.26	16.64	11.95	116.35	...	...
June	14.15	12.00	12.47	6.49	5.98	13.96	16.50	14.30	14.81	16.92	12.44	109.70	...	...
July	12.59	11.81	11.35	6.54	4.81	12.94	16.26	13.95	14.61	16.80	12.28	109.38	...	...
August	10.12	10.68	8.68	6.32	2.36	10.15	14.39	13.06	13.71	16.32	11.23	109.65	...	...
September	10.31	10.00	7.92	6.03	1.89	10.36	13.50	12.34	12.94	15.63	10.66	122.43	...	...
October	9.71	9.68	7.71	6.07	1.64	9.20	12.52	10.91	12.12	14.73	9.68	132.66	...	...
November	9.20	9.35	8.07	5.86	2.21	8.69	11.85	10.55	11.68	14.30	10.06	138.10	...	...
December	8.95	8.73	7.94	5.82	2.12	8.51	11.50	10.54	11.83	14.14	9.96	139.37	...	...

[1]Federal Reserve Bank of New York. Through 2002, represents the rate for adjustment credit. Beginning in 2003, represents the rate for primary credit. See notes and definitions for more information.
[2]Change from a year earlier. Beginning in 1960, PCE except food and energy; before then, CPI-U
[3]Beginning 1997, rates for nonfinancial companies only are shown.
. . . = Not available.

Table 12-9B. Summary Interest Rates, Bond Yields, and Stock Prices: Historical Data—*Continued*

(Percent per annum, except as noted.)

Year and month	Federal funds interest rate	Federal Reserve discount rate[1]	U.S. Treasury bills, secondary market, 3-month	Inflation[2]	Real 3-month Treasury bill rate	Commercial paper, 3-month[3]	Bank prime rate	Treasury 10-year nominal yields	Bond yields Domestic corporate (Moody's) Aaa	Bond yields Domestic corporate (Moody's) Baa	State and local bonds (Bond Buyer)	S&P composite (500 stocks) Index, 1941-1943 = 10	Dividend-price ratio	Earnings-price ratio
1983														
January	8.68	8.50	7.86	5.93	1.93	8.17	11.16	10.46	11.79	13.94	9.50	144.27	...	...
February	8.51	8.50	8.11	5.93	2.18	8.34	10.98	10.72	12.01	13.95	9.58	146.80	...	...
March	8.77	8.50	8.35	5.62	2.73	8.52	10.50	10.51	11.73	13.61	9.20	151.88	...	...
April	8.80	8.50	8.21	5.53	2.68	8.53	10.50	10.40	11.51	13.29	9.04	157.71	...	...
May	8.63	8.50	8.19	5.11	3.08	8.33	10.50	10.38	11.46	13.09	9.11	164.10	...	...
June	8.98	8.50	8.79	5.08	3.71	9.00	10.50	10.85	11.74	13.37	9.52	166.39	...	...
July	9.37	8.50	9.08	5.11	3.97	9.25	10.50	11.38	12.15	13.39	9.53	166.96	...	...
August	9.56	8.50	9.34	5.17	4.17	9.54	10.89	11.85	12.51	13.64	9.72	162.42	...	...
September	9.45	8.50	9.00	5.20	3.80	9.24	11.00	11.65	12.37	13.55	9.58	167.16	...	...
October	9.48	8.50	8.64	4.73	3.91	8.99	11.00	11.54	12.25	13.46	9.66	167.65	...	...
November	9.34	8.50	8.76	4.57	4.19	9.10	11.00	11.69	12.41	13.61	9.74	165.23	...	...
December	9.47	8.50	9.00	4.31	4.69	9.53	11.00	11.83	12.57	13.75	9.89	164.36	...	...
1984														
January	9.56	8.50	8.90	3.91	4.99	9.20	11.00	11.67	12.20	13.65	9.63	166.39	...	...
February	9.59	8.50	9.09	4.17	4.92	9.32	11.00	11.84	12.08	13.59	9.64	157.25	...	...
March	9.91	8.50	9.52	4.43	5.09	9.83	11.21	12.32	12.57	13.99	9.94	157.44	...	...
April	10.29	8.87	9.69	4.60	5.09	10.18	11.93	12.63	12.81	14.31	9.96	157.60	...	...
May	10.32	9.00	9.83	4.69	5.14	10.65	12.39	13.41	13.28	14.74	10.49	156.55	...	...
June	11.06	9.00	9.87	4.45	5.42	10.98	12.60	13.56	13.55	15.05	10.67	153.12	...	...
July	11.23	9.00	10.12	4.20	5.92	11.19	13.00	13.36	13.44	15.15	10.42	151.08	...	...
August	11.64	9.00	10.47	4.00	6.47	11.18	13.00	12.72	12.87	14.63	9.99	164.42	...	...
September	11.30	9.00	10.37	3.74	6.63	11.04	12.97	12.52	12.66	14.35	10.10	166.11	...	...
October	9.99	9.00	9.74	3.79	5.95	10.12	12.58	12.16	12.63	13.94	10.25	164.82	...	...
November	9.43	8.83	8.61	3.78	4.83	9.03	11.77	11.57	12.29	13.48	10.17	166.27	...	...
December	8.38	8.37	8.06	4.11	3.95	8.44	11.06	11.50	12.13	13.40	9.95	164.48	...	...
1985														
January	8.35	8.00	7.76	4.35	3.41	8.03	10.61	11.38	12.08	13.26	9.51	171.61	...	...
February	8.50	8.00	8.27	4.26	4.01	8.54	10.50	11.51	12.13	13.23	9.65	180.88	...	...
March	8.58	8.00	8.52	4.24	4.28	8.90	10.50	11.86	12.56	13.69	9.77	179.42	...	...
April	8.27	8.00	7.95	3.89	4.06	8.37	10.50	11.43	12.23	13.51	9.42	180.62	...	...
May	7.97	7.81	7.48	4.02	3.46	7.83	10.31	10.85	11.72	13.15	9.01	184.90	...	...
June	7.53	7.50	6.95	4.12	2.83	7.35	9.78	10.16	10.94	12.40	8.69	188.89	...	...
July	7.88	7.50	7.08	3.98	3.10	7.56	9.50	10.31	10.97	12.43	8.81	192.54	...	...
August	7.90	7.50	7.14	4.15	2.99	7.72	9.50	10.33	11.05	12.50	9.08	188.31	...	...
September	7.92	7.50	7.10	4.20	2.90	7.83	9.50	10.37	11.07	12.48	9.27	184.06	...	...
October	7.99	7.50	7.16	4.12	3.04	7.80	9.50	10.24	11.02	12.36	9.08	186.18	...	...
November	8.05	7.50	7.24	4.14	3.10	7.77	9.50	9.78	10.55	11.99	8.54	197.45	...	...
December	8.27	7.50	7.10	4.02	3.08	7.75	9.50	9.26	10.16	11.58	8.42	207.26	...	...
1986														
January	8.14	7.50	7.07	4.00	3.07	7.71	9.50	9.19	10.05	11.44	8.08	208.19	...	...
February	7.86	7.50	7.06	3.72	3.34	7.63	9.50	8.70	9.67	11.11	7.44	219.37	...	...
March	7.48	7.10	6.56	3.65	2.91	7.20	9.10	7.78	9.00	10.50	7.08	232.33	...	...
April	6.99	6.83	6.06	3.69	2.37	6.60	8.83	7.30	8.79	10.19	7.19	237.98	...	...
May	6.85	6.50	6.15	3.49	2.66	6.62	8.50	7.71	9.09	10.29	7.54	238.46	...	...
June	6.92	6.50	6.21	3.44	2.77	6.71	8.50	7.80	9.13	10.34	7.87	245.30	...	...
July	6.56	6.16	5.83	3.31	2.52	6.33	8.16	7.30	8.88	10.16	7.51	240.18	...	...
August	6.17	5.82	5.53	3.01	2.52	5.92	7.90	7.17	8.72	10.18	7.21	245.00	...	...
September	5.89	5.50	5.21	3.13	2.08	5.68	7.50	7.45	8.89	10.20	7.11	238.27	...	...
October	5.85	5.50	5.18	3.32	1.86	5.68	7.50	7.43	8.86	10.24	7.08	237.36	...	...
November	6.04	5.50	5.35	3.29	2.06	5.76	7.50	7.25	8.68	10.07	6.84	245.09	...	...
December	6.91	5.50	5.53	3.14	2.39	6.10	7.50	7.11	8.49	9.97	6.87	248.61	...	...
1987														
January	6.43	5.50	5.43	2.81	2.62	5.84	7.50	7.08	8.36	9.72	6.66	264.51	...	...
February	6.10	5.50	5.59	2.76	2.83	6.05	7.50	7.25	8.38	9.65	6.61	280.93	...	...
March	6.13	5.50	5.59	2.76	2.83	6.16	7.50	7.25	8.36	9.61	6.65	292.47	...	...
April	6.37	5.50	5.64	3.01	2.63	6.45	7.75	8.02	8.85	10.04	7.55	289.32	...	...
May	6.85	5.50	5.66	3.12	2.54	6.93	8.14	8.61	9.33	10.51	8.00	289.12	...	...
June	6.73	5.50	5.67	3.10	2.57	6.92	8.25	8.40	9.32	10.52	7.79	301.38	...	...
July	6.58	5.50	5.69	3.18	2.51	6.65	8.25	8.45	9.42	10.61	7.72	310.09	...	...
August	6.73	5.50	6.04	3.32	2.72	6.71	8.25	8.76	9.67	10.80	7.82	329.36	...	...
September	7.22	5.95	6.40	3.40	3.00	7.37	8.70	9.42	10.18	11.31	8.26	318.66	...	...
October	7.29	6.00	6.13	3.51	2.62	7.89	9.07	9.52	10.52	11.62	8.70	280.16	...	...
November	6.69	6.00	5.69	3.51	2.18	7.17	8.78	8.86	10.01	11.23	7.95	245.01	...	...
December	6.77	6.00	5.77	3.59	2.18	7.61	8.75	8.99	10.11	11.29	7.96	240.96	...	...
1988														
January	6.83	6.00	5.81	3.84	1.97	6.87	8.75	8.67	9.88	11.07	7.69	250.48	...	...
February	6.58	6.00	5.66	3.83	1.83	6.58	8.51	8.21	9.40	10.62	7.49	258.13	...	...
March	6.58	6.00	5.70	3.96	1.74	6.62	8.50	8.37	9.39	10.57	7.74	265.74	...	...
April	6.87	6.00	5.91	4.04	1.87	6.86	8.50	8.72	9.67	10.90	7.81	262.61	...	...
May	7.09	6.00	6.26	4.11	2.15	7.19	8.84	9.09	9.90	11.04	7.91	256.12	...	...
June	7.51	6.00	6.46	4.27	2.19	7.49	9.00	8.92	9.86	11.00	7.78	270.68	...	...
July	7.75	6.00	6.73	4.43	2.30	7.82	9.29	9.06	9.96	11.11	7.76	269.05	...	...
August	8.01	6.37	7.06	4.34	2.72	8.26	9.84	9.26	10.11	11.21	7.79	263.73	...	...
September	8.19	6.50	7.24	4.48	2.76	8.17	10.00	8.98	9.82	10.90	7.66	267.97	...	...
October	8.30	6.50	7.35	4.42	2.93	8.24	10.00	8.80	9.51	10.41	7.46	277.40	...	...
November	8.35	6.50	7.76	4.48	3.28	8.66	10.05	8.96	9.45	10.48	7.46	271.02	...	...
December	8.76	6.50	8.07	4.59	3.48	9.11	10.50	9.11	9.57	10.65	7.61	276.51	...	...

[1]Federal Reserve Bank of New York. Through 2002, represents the rate for adjustment credit. Beginning in 2003, represents the rate for primary credit. See notes and definitions for more information.
[2]Change from a year earlier. Beginning in 1960, PCE except food and energy; before then, CPI-U
[3]Beginning 1997, rates for nonfinancial companies only are shown.
. . . = Not available.

Table 12-9B. Summary Interest Rates, Bond Yields, and Stock Prices: Historical Data—*Continued*

(Percent per annum, except as noted.)

Year and month	Federal funds interest rate	Federal Reserve discount rate[1]	U.S. Treasury bills, secondary market, 3-month	Inflation[2]	Real 3-month Treasury bill rate	Commercial paper, 3-month[3]	Bank prime rate	Treasury 10-year nominal yields	Bond yields Domestic corporate (Moody's) Aaa	Bond yields Domestic corporate (Moody's) Baa	State and local bonds (Bond Buyer)	Standard and Poor's composite (500 stocks) Index, 1941-1943 = 10	Standard and Poor's composite (500 stocks) Dividend-price ratio	Standard and Poor's composite (500 stocks) Earnings-price ratio
1989														
January	9.12	6.50	8.27	4.62	3.65	9.04	10.50	9.09	9.62	10.65	7.35	285.41	...	...
February	9.36	6.59	8.53	4.67	3.86	9.37	10.93	9.17	9.64	10.61	7.44	294.01	...	...
March	9.85	7.00	8.82	4.52	4.30	9.95	11.50	9.36	9.80	10.67	7.59	292.71	...	...
April	9.84	7.00	8.65	4.36	4.29	9.81	11.50	9.18	9.79	10.61	7.49	302.25	...	...
May	9.81	7.00	8.43	4.31	4.12	9.47	11.50	8.86	9.57	10.46	7.25	313.93	...	...
June	9.53	7.00	8.15	4.14	4.01	9.11	11.07	8.28	9.10	10.03	7.02	323.73		
July	9.24	7.00	7.88	3.97	3.91	8.68	10.98	8.02	8.93	9.87	6.96	331.93	...	...
August	8.99	7.00	7.90	3.86	4.04	8.57	10.50	8.11	8.96	9.88	7.06	346.61	...	...
September	9.02	7.00	7.75	3.65	4.10	8.70	10.50	8.19	9.01	9.91	7.26	347.33	...	...
October	8.84	7.00	7.64	3.64	4.00	8.53	10.50	8.01	8.92	9.81	7.22	347.40	...	...
November	8.55	7.00	7.69	3.63	4.06	8.35	10.50	7.87	8.89	9.81	7.14	340.22	...	...
December	8.45	7.00	7.63	3.60	4.03	8.29	10.50	7.84	8.86	9.82	6.98	348.57		
1990														
January	8.23	7.00	7.64	3.47	4.17	8.10	10.11	8.21	8.99	9.94	7.10	339.97	...	...
February	8.24	7.00	7.74	3.71	4.03	8.14	10.00	8.47	9.22	10.14	7.22	330.45	...	...
March	8.28	7.00	7.90	3.90	4.00	8.28	10.00	8.59	9.37	10.21	7.29	338.47	...	...
April	8.26	7.00	7.77	3.87	3.90	8.30	10.00	8.79	9.46	10.30	7.39	338.18	...	...
May	8.18	7.00	7.74	3.87	3.87	8.25	10.00	8.76	9.47	10.41	7.35	350.25	...	...
June	8.29	7.00	7.73	4.00	3.73	8.14	10.00	8.48	9.26	10.22	7.24	360.39		
July	8.15	7.00	7.62	3.99	3.63	7.99	10.00	8.47	9.24	10.20	7.19	360.03	...	...
August	8.13	7.00	7.45	4.29	3.16	7.88	10.00	8.75	9.41	10.41	7.32	330.75	...	...
September	8.20	7.00	7.36	4.31	3.05	7.96	10.00	8.89	9.56	10.64	7.43	315.41	...	...
October	8.11	7.00	7.17	4.27	2.90	7.98	10.00	8.72	9.53	10.74	7.49	307.12	...	...
November	7.81	7.00	7.06	4.12	2.94	7.91	10.00	8.39	9.30	10.62	7.18	315.29	...	...
December	7.31	6.79	6.74	3.96	2.78	7.80	10.00	8.08	9.05	10.43	7.09	328.75		
1991														
January	6.91	6.50	6.22	4.08	2.14	7.10	9.52	8.09	9.04	10.45	7.08	325.49	...	...
February	6.25	6.00	5.94	3.85	2.09	6.49	9.05	7.85	8.83	10.07	6.91	362.26	...	...
March	6.12	6.00	5.91	3.57	2.34	6.41	9.00	8.11	8.93	10.09	7.10	372.28	...	...
April	5.91	5.98	5.65	3.46	2.19	6.07	9.00	8.04	8.86	9.94	7.02	379.68	...	...
May	5.78	5.50	5.46	3.57	1.89	5.92	8.50	8.07	8.86	9.86	6.95	377.99	...	...
June	5.90	5.50	5.57	3.39	2.18	6.11	8.50	8.28	9.01	9.96	7.13	378.29		
July	5.82	5.50	5.58	3.46	2.12	6.05	8.50	8.27	9.00	9.89	7.05	380.23	...	...
August	5.66	5.50	5.33	3.31	2.02	5.72	8.50	7.90	8.75	9.65	6.90	389.40	...	...
September	5.45	5.20	5.22	3.35	1.87	5.57	8.20	7.65	8.61	9.51	6.80	387.20	...	...
October	5.21	5.00	4.99	3.23	1.76	5.35	8.00	7.53	8.55	9.49	6.68	386.88	...	...
November	4.81	4.58	4.56	3.30	1.26	4.98	7.58	7.42	8.48	9.45	6.73	385.92	...	...
December	4.43	4.11	4.07	3.42	0.65	4.61	7.21	7.09	8.31	9.26	6.69	388.51		
1992														
January	4.03	3.50	3.80	3.19	0.61	4.07	6.50	7.03	8.20	9.13	6.54	416.08	...	...
February	4.06	3.50	3.84	3.20	0.64	4.11	6.50	7.34	8.29	9.23	6.74	412.56	...	...
March	3.98	3.50	4.04	3.25	0.79	4.30	6.50	7.54	8.35	9.25	6.76	407.36	...	...
April	3.73	3.50	3.75	3.39	0.36	4.04	6.50	7.48	8.33	9.21	6.67	407.41	...	...
May	3.82	3.50	3.63	3.13	0.50	3.88	6.50	7.39	8.28	9.13	6.57	414.81	...	...
June	3.76	3.50	3.66	2.98	0.68	3.92	6.50	7.26	8.22	9.05	6.49	408.27		
July	3.25	3.02	3.21	3.06	0.15	3.44	6.02	6.84	8.07	8.84	6.13	415.05	...	...
August	3.30	3.00	3.13	2.87	0.26	3.38	6.00	6.59	7.95	8.65	6.16	417.93	...	...
September	3.22	3.00	2.91	2.63	0.28	3.24	6.00	6.42	7.92	8.62	6.25	418.48	...	...
October	3.10	3.00	2.86	2.81	0.05	3.33	6.00	6.59	7.99	8.84	6.41	412.50	...	...
November	3.09	3.00	3.13	2.85	0.28	3.66	6.00	6.87	8.10	8.96	6.36	422.84	...	...
December	2.92	3.00	3.22	2.79	0.43	3.67	6.00	6.77	7.98	8.81	6.22	435.64		
1993														
January	3.02	3.00	3.00	2.82	0.18	3.25	6.00	6.60	7.91	8.67	6.16	435.23	...	...
February	3.03	3.00	2.93	2.74	0.19	3.18	6.00	6.26	7.71	8.39	5.87	441.70	...	...
March	3.07	3.00	2.95	2.70	0.25	3.17	6.00	5.98	7.58	8.15	5.64	450.16	...	...
April	2.96	3.00	2.87	2.67	0.20	3.14	6.00	5.97	7.46	8.14	5.76	443.08	...	...
May	3.00	3.00	2.96	2.87	0.09	3.14	6.00	6.04	7.43	8.21	5.73	445.25	...	...
June	3.04	3.00	3.07	2.89	0.18	3.25	6.00	5.96	7.33	8.07	5.63	448.06		
July	3.06	3.00	3.04	2.72	0.32	3.20	6.00	5.81	7.17	7.93	5.57	447.29	...	...
August	3.03	3.00	3.02	2.82	0.20	3.18	6.00	5.68	6.85	7.60	5.45	454.13	...	...
September	3.09	3.00	2.95	2.81	0.14	3.16	6.00	5.36	6.66	7.34	5.29	459.24	...	...
October	2.99	3.00	3.02	2.57	0.45	3.26	6.00	5.33	6.67	7.31	5.25	463.90	...	...
November	3.02	3.00	3.10	2.61	0.49	3.40	6.00	5.72	6.93	7.66	5.47	462.89	...	...
December	2.96	3.00	3.06	2.46	0.60	3.36	6.00	5.77	6.93	7.69	5.35	465.95		
1994														
January	3.05	3.00	2.98	2.24	0.74	3.19	6.00	5.75	6.92	7.65	5.31	472.99	...	...
February	3.25	3.00	3.25	2.27	0.98	3.49	6.00	5.97	7.08	7.76	5.40	471.58	...	...
March	3.34	3.00	3.50	2.40	1.10	3.85	6.06	6.48	7.48	8.13	5.91	463.81	...	...
April	3.56	3.00	3.68	2.25	1.43	4.05	6.45	6.97	7.88	8.52	6.23	447.23	...	...
May	4.01	3.24	4.14	2.13	2.01	4.57	6.99	7.18	7.99	8.62	6.19	450.90	...	...
June	4.25	3.50	4.14	2.25	1.89	4.57	7.25	7.10	7.97	8.65	6.11	454.83		
July	4.26	3.50	4.33	2.26	2.07	4.75	7.25	7.30	8.11	8.80	6.23	451.40	...	...
August	4.47	3.76	4.48	2.17	2.31	4.84	7.51	7.24	8.07	8.74	6.21	464.24	...	...
September	4.73	4.00	4.62	2.17	2.45	5.02	7.75	7.46	8.34	8.98	6.28	466.96	...	...
October	4.76	4.00	4.95	2.25	2.70	5.51	7.75	7.74	8.57	9.20	6.52	463.81	...	...
November	5.29	4.40	5.29	2.18	3.11	5.81	8.15	7.96	8.68	9.32	6.97	461.01	...	...
December	5.45	4.75	5.60	2.17	3.43	6.26	8.50	7.81	8.46	9.10	6.80	455.19	...	...

[1]Federal Reserve Bank of New York. Through 2002, represents the rate for adjustment credit. Beginning in 2003, represents the rate for primary credit. See notes and definitions for more information.
[2]Change from a year earlier. Beginning in 1960, PCE except food and energy; before then, CPI-U
[3]Beginning in 1997, rates for nonfinancial companies only are shown.
. . . = Not available.

Table 12-9B. Summary Interest Rates, Bond Yields, and Stock Prices: Historical Data—*Continued*

(Percent per annum, except as noted.)

Year and month	Federal funds interest rate	Federal Reserve discount rate[1]	U.S. Treasury bills, secondary market, 3-month	Inflation[2]	Real 3-month Treasury bill rate	Commercial paper, 3-month[3]	Bank prime rate	Treasury 10-year nominal yields	Bond yields — Domestic corporate (Moody's) Aaa	Bond yields — Domestic corporate (Moody's) Baa	State and local bonds (Bond Buyer)	S&P composite — Index, 1941-1943 = 10	S&P composite — Dividend-price ratio	S&P composite — Earnings-price ratio
1995														
January	5.53	4.75	5.71	2.34	3.37	6.22	8.50	7.78	8.46	9.08	6.53	465.25	. . .	. . .
February	5.92	5.25	5.77	2.28	3.49	6.15	9.00	7.47	8.26	8.85	6.22	481.92	. . .	. . .
March	5.98	5.25	5.73	2.17	3.56	6.15	9.00	7.20	8.12	8.70	6.10	493.15	. . .	. . .
April	6.05	5.25	5.65	2.25	3.40	6.12	9.00	7.06	8.03	8.60	6.02	507.91	. . .	. . .
May	6.01	5.25	5.67	2.19	3.48	6.06	9.00	6.63	7.65	8.20	5.95	523.81	. . .	. . .
June	6.00	5.25	5.47	2.05	3.42	5.94	9.00	6.17	7.30	7.90	5.84	539.35	. . .	. . .
July	5.85	5.25	5.42	1.99	3.43	5.79	8.80	6.28	7.41	8.04	5.92	557.37	. . .	. . .
August	5.74	5.25	5.40	2.13	3.27	5.82	8.75	6.49	7.57	8.19	6.06	559.11	. . .	. . .
September	5.80	5.25	5.28	2.11	3.17	5.74	8.75	6.20	7.32	7.93	5.91	578.77	. . .	. . .
October	5.76	5.25	5.28	2.11	3.17	5.82	8.75	6.04	7.12	7.75	5.80	582.92	. . .	. . .
November	5.80	5.25	5.36	1.99	3.37	5.74	8.75	5.93	7.02	7.68	5.64	595.53	. . .	. . .
December	5.60	5.25	5.14	2.10	3.04	5.64	8.65	5.71	6.82	7.49	5.45	614.57	. . .	. . .
1996														
January	5.56	5.24	5.00	1.98	3.02	5.40	8.50	5.65	6.81	7.47	5.43	614.42	. . .	. . .
February	5.22	5.00	4.83	1.95	2.88	5.15	8.25	5.81	6.99	7.63	5.43	649.54	. . .	. . .
March	5.31	5.00	4.96	1.94	3.02	5.31	8.25	6.27	7.35	8.03	5.79	647.07	. . .	. . .
April	5.22	5.00	4.95	1.84	3.11	5.39	8.25	6.51	7.50	8.19	5.94	647.17	. . .	. . .
May	5.24	5.00	5.02	1.85	3.17	5.39	8.25	6.74	7.62	8.30	5.98	661.23	. . .	. . .
June	5.27	5.00	5.09	1.85	3.24	5.49	8.25	6.91	7.71	8.40	6.02	668.50	. . .	. . .
July	5.40	5.00	5.15	1.88	3.27	5.53	8.25	6.87	7.65	8.35	5.92	644.07	. . .	. . .
August	5.22	5.00	5.05	1.73	3.32	5.42	8.25	6.64	7.46	8.18	5.76	662.68	. . .	. . .
September	5.30	5.00	5.09	1.90	3.19	5.52	8.25	6.83	7.66	8.35	5.87	674.88	. . .	. . .
October	5.24	5.00	4.99	1.89	3.10	5.43	8.25	6.53	7.39	8.07	5.72	701.45	. . .	. . .
November	5.31	5.00	5.03	1.96	3.07	5.41	8.25	6.20	7.10	7.79	5.59	735.67	. . .	. . .
December	5.29	5.00	4.91	1.85	3.06	5.51	8.25	6.30	7.20	7.89	5.64	743.25	. . .	. . .
1997														
January	5.25	5.00	5.03	1.84	3.19	5.30	8.25	6.58	7.42	8.09	5.72	766.22	. . .	. . .
February	5.19	5.00	5.01	1.92	3.09	5.27	8.25	6.42	7.31	7.94	5.63	798.39	. . .	. . .
March	5.39	5.00	5.14	1.92	3.22	5.39	8.30	6.69	7.55	8.18	5.76	792.16	. . .	. . .
April	5.51	5.00	5.16	1.98	3.18	5.57	8.50	6.89	7.73	8.34	5.88	763.93	. . .	. . .
May	5.50	5.00	5.05	1.89	3.16	5.57	8.50	6.71	7.58	8.20	5.70	833.09	. . .	. . .
June	5.56	5.00	4.93	1.96	2.97	5.54	8.50	6.49	7.41	8.02	5.53	876.29	. . .	. . .
July	5.52	5.00	5.05	1.83	3.22	5.49	8.50	6.22	7.14	7.75	5.35	925.29	. . .	. . .
August	5.54	5.00	5.14	1.70	3.44	5.48	8.50	6.30	7.22	7.82	5.41	927.74	. . .	. . .
September	5.54	5.00	4.95	1.59	3.36	5.48	8.50	6.21	7.15	7.70	5.39	937.02	. . .	. . .
October	5.50	5.00	4.97	1.51	3.46	5.51	8.50	6.03	7.00	7.57	5.38	951.16	. . .	. . .
November	5.52	5.00	5.14	1.41	3.73	5.60	8.50	5.88	6.87	7.42	5.33	938.92	. . .	. . .
December	5.50	5.00	5.16	1.44	3.72	5.67	8.50	5.81	6.76	7.32	5.19	962.37	. . .	. . .
1998														
January	5.56	5.00	5.04	1.47	3.57	5.42	8.50	5.54	6.61	7.19	5.06	963.36	. . .	. . .
February	5.51	5.00	5.09	1.34	3.75	5.42	8.50	5.57	6.67	7.25	5.10	1 023.74	. . .	. . .
March	5.49	5.00	5.03	1.20	3.83	5.46	8.50	5.65	6.72	7.32	5.21	1 076.83	. . .	. . .
April	5.45	5.00	4.95	1.20	3.75	5.46	8.50	5.64	6.69	7.33	5.23	1 112.20	. . .	. . .
May	5.49	5.00	5.00	1.22	3.78	5.48	8.50	5.65	6.69	7.30	5.20	1 108.42	. . .	. . .
June	5.56	5.00	4.98	0.95	4.03	5.48	8.50	5.50	6.53	7.13	5.12	1 108.39	. . .	. . .
July	5.54	5.00	4.96	1.16	3.80	5.48	8.50	5.46	6.55	7.15	5.14	1 156.58	. . .	. . .
August	5.55	5.00	4.90	1.40	3.50	5.48	8.50	5.34	6.52	7.14	5.10	1 074.63	. . .	. . .
September	5.51	5.00	4.61	1.18	3.43	5.31	8.49	4.81	6.40	7.09	4.99	1 020.64	. . .	. . .
October	5.07	4.86	3.96	1.22	2.74	5.04	8.12	4.53	6.37	7.18	4.93	1 032.47	. . .	. . .
November	4.83	4.63	4.41	1.19	3.22	5.06	7.89	4.83	6.41	7.34	5.03	1 144.43	. . .	. . .
December	4.68	4.50	4.39	1.31	3.08	5.00	7.75	4.65	6.22	7.23	4.98	1 190.05	. . .	. . .
1999														
January	4.63	4.50	4.34	1.36	2.98	4.77	7.75	4.72	6.24	7.29	5.01	1 248.77	. . .	. . .
February	4.76	4.50	4.44	1.29	3.15	4.79	7.75	5.00	6.40	7.39	5.03	1 246.58	. . .	. . .
March	4.81	4.50	4.44	1.21	3.23	4.81	7.75	5.23	6.62	7.53	5.10	1 281.66	. . .	. . .
April	4.74	4.50	4.29	1.26	3.03	4.79	7.75	5.18	6.64	7.48	5.08	1 334.76	. . .	. . .
May	4.74	4.50	4.50	1.23	3.27	4.81	7.75	5.54	6.93	7.72	5.18	1 332.07	. . .	. . .
June	4.76	4.50	4.57	1.39	3.18	4.98	7.75	5.90	7.23	8.02	5.37	1 322.55	. . .	. . .
July	4.99	4.50	4.55	1.29	3.26	5.11	8.00	5.79	7.19	7.95	5.36	1 380.99	. . .	. . .
August	5.07	4.56	4.72	1.15	3.57	5.25	8.06	5.94	7.40	8.15	5.58	1 327.49	. . .	. . .
September	5.22	4.75	4.68	1.43	3.25	5.32	8.25	5.92	7.39	8.20	5.69	1 318.17	. . .	. . .
October	5.20	4.75	4.86	1.40	3.46	5.88	8.25	6.11	7.55	8.38	5.92	1 300.01	. . .	. . .
November	5.42	4.86	5.07	1.48	3.59	5.81	8.37	6.03	7.36	8.15	5.86	1 391.00	. . .	. . .
December	5.30	5.00	5.20	1.44	3.76	5.87	8.50	6.28	7.55	8.19	5.95	1 428.68	. . .	. . .
2000														
January	5.45	5.00	5.32	1.51	3.81	5.74	8.50	6.66	7.78	8.33	6.08	1 425.59	. . .	. . .
February	5.73	5.24	5.55	1.66	3.89	5.87	8.73	6.52	7.68	8.29	6.00	1 388.87	. . .	. . .
March	5.85	5.34	5.69	1.84	3.85	6.00	8.83	6.26	7.68	8.37	5.83	1 442.21	. . .	. . .
April	6.02	5.50	5.66	1.66	4.00	6.11	9.00	5.99	7.64	8.40	5.75	1 461.36	. . .	. . .
May	6.27	5.71	5.79	1.69	4.10	6.54	9.24	6.44	7.99	8.90	6.00	1 418.48	. . .	. . .
June	6.53	6.00	5.69	1.71	3.98	6.57	9.50	6.10	7.67	8.48	5.80	1 461.96	. . .	. . .
July	6.54	6.00	5.96	1.75	4.21	6.52	9.50	6.05	7.65	8.35	5.63	1 473.00	. . .	. . .
August	6.50	6.00	6.09	1.83	4.26	6.49	9.50	5.83	7.55	8.26	5.51	1 485.46	. . .	. . .
September	6.52	6.00	6.00	1.82	4.18	6.47	9.50	5.80	7.62	8.35	5.56	1 468.05	. . .	. . .
October	6.51	6.00	6.11	1.80	4.31	6.51	9.50	5.74	7.55	8.34	5.59	1 468.05	. . .	. . .
November	6.51	6.00	6.17	1.88	4.29	6.50	9.50	5.72	7.45	8.28	5.54	1 375.04	. . .	. . .
December	6.40	6.00	5.77	1.80	3.97	6.34	9.50	5.24	7.21	8.02	5.22	1 330.93	. . .	. . .

[1]Federal Reserve Bank of New York. Through 2002, represents the rate for adjustment credit. Beginning in 2003, represents the rate for primary credit. See notes and definitions for more information.
[2]Change from a year earlier. Beginning in 1960, PCE except food and energy; before then, CPI-U
[3]Beginning 1997, rates for nonfinancial companies only are shown.
. . . = Not available.

Table 12-9B. Summary Interest Rates, Bond Yields, and Stock Prices: Historical Data—*Continued*

(Percent per annum, except as noted.)

Year and month	Federal funds interest rate	Federal Reserve discount rate[1]	U.S. Treasury bills, secondary market, 3-month	Inflation[2]	Real 3-month Treasury bill rate	Commercial paper, 3-month[3]	Bank prime rate	Treasury 10-year nominal yields	Domestic corporate (Moody's) Aaa	Domestic corporate (Moody's) Baa	State and local bonds (Bond Buyer)	Index, 1941-1943 = 10	Dividend-price ratio	Earnings-price ratio
2001														
January	5.98	5.52	5.15	1.87	3.28	5.49	9.05	5.16	7.15	7.93	5.10	1 335.63	. . .	. . .
February	5.49	5.00	4.88	1.88	3.00	5.14	8.50	5.10	7.10	7.87	5.18	1 305.75	. . .	. . .
March	5.31	4.81	4.42	1.77	2.65	4.78	8.32	4.89	6.98	7.84	5.13	1 185.85	. . .	. . .
April	4.80	4.28	3.87	1.89	1.98	4.44	7.80	5.14	7.20	8.07	5.27	1 189.84	. . .	. . .
May	4.21	3.73	3.62	1.82	1.80	3.93	7.24	5.39	7.29	8.07	5.29	1 270.37	. . .	. . .
June	3.97	3.47	3.49	2.00	1.49	3.67	6.98	5.28	7.18	7.97	5.20	1 238.71	. . .	. . .
July	3.77	3.25	3.51	2.04	1.47	3.59	6.75	5.24	7.13	7.97	5.20	1 204.45	. . .	. . .
August	3.65	3.16	3.36	1.98	1.38	3.42	6.67	4.97	7.02	7.85	5.03	1 178.50	. . .	. . .
September ...	3.07	2.77	2.64	1.17	1.47	2.81	6.28	4.73	7.17	8.03	5.09	1 044.64	. . .	. . .
October	2.49	2.02	2.16	1.76	0.40	2.28	5.53	4.57	7.03	7.91	5.05	1 076.59	. . .	. . .
November	2.09	1.58	1.87	1.79	0.08	1.97	5.10	4.65	6.97	7.81	5.04	1 129.68	. . .	. . .
December	1.82	1.33	1.69	1.74	-0.05	1.78	4.84	5.09	6.77	8.05	5.25	1 144.93	. . .	. . .
2002														
January	1.73	1.25	1.65	1.44	0.21	1.70	4.75	5.04	6.55	7.87	5.16	1 140.21	. . .	. . .
February	1.74	1.25	1.73	1.48	0.25	1.79	4.75	4.91	6.51	7.89	5.11	1 100.67	. . .	. . .
March	1.73	1.25	1.79	1.51	0.28	1.86	4.75	5.28	6.81	8.11	5.29	1 153.79	. . .	. . .
April	1.75	1.25	1.72	1.64	0.08	1.81	4.75	5.21	6.76	8.03	5.22	1 112.03	. . .	. . .
May	1.75	1.25	1.73	1.74	-0.01	1.78	4.75	5.16	6.75	8.09	5.19	1 079.27	. . .	. . .
June	1.75	1.25	1.70	1.66	0.04	1.76	4.75	4.93	6.63	7.95	5.09	1 014.05	. . .	. . .
July	1.73	1.25	1.68	1.59	0.09	1.75	4.75	4.65	6.53	7.90	5.02	903.59	. . .	. . .
August	1.74	1.25	1.62	1.72	-0.10	1.70	4.75	4.26	6.37	7.58	4.95	912.55	. . .	. . .
September ...	1.75	1.25	1.63	2.44	-0.81	1.72	4.75	3.87	6.15	7.40	4.74	867.81	. . .	. . .
October	1.75	1.25	1.58	1.80	-0.22	1.70	4.75	3.94	6.32	7.73	4.88	854.63	. . .	. . .
November	1.34	0.83	1.23	1.70	-0.47	1.36	4.35	4.05	6.31	7.62	4.95	909.93	. . .	. . .
December	1.24	0.75	1.19	1.75	-0.56	1.31	4.25	4.03	6.21	7.45	4.85	899.18	. . .	. . .
2003														
January	1.24	. . .	1.17	1.74	-0.57	1.26	4.25	4.05	6.17	7.35	4.90	895.84	. . .	. . .
February	1.26	2.25	1.17	1.68	-0.51	1.26	4.25	3.90	5.95	7.06	4.81	837.62	. . .	. . .
March	1.25	2.25	1.13	1.70	-0.57	1.19	4.25	3.81	5.89	6.95	4.76	846.62	. . .	. . .
April	1.26	2.25	1.13	1.51	-0.38	1.20	4.25	3.96	5.74	6.85	4.74	890.03	. . .	. . .
May	1.26	2.25	1.07	1.52	-0.45	1.19	4.25	3.57	5.22	6.38	4.41	935.96	. . .	. . .
June	1.22	2.20	0.92	1.42	-0.50	1.01	4.22	3.33	4.97	6.19	4.33	988.00	. . .	. . .
July	1.01	2.00	0.90	1.45	-0.55	1.01	4.00	3.98	5.49	6.62	4.74	992.54	. . .	. . .
August	1.03	2.00	0.95	1.35	-0.40	1.04	4.00	4.45	5.88	7.01	5.10	989.53	. . .	. . .
September ...	1.01	2.00	0.94	1.30	-0.36	1.04	4.00	4.27	5.72	6.79	4.92	1 019.44	. . .	. . .
October	1.01	2.00	0.92	1.34	-0.42	1.05	4.00	4.29	5.70	6.73	4.89	1 038.73	. . .	. . .
November	1.00	2.00	0.93	1.36	-0.43	1.06	4.00	4.30	5.65	6.66	4.73	1 049.90	. . .	. . .
December	0.98	2.00	0.90	1.41	-0.51	1.05	4.00	4.27	5.62	6.60	4.65	1 080.64	. . .	. . .
2004														
January	1.00	2.00	0.88	1.61	-0.73	1.01	4.00	4.15	5.54	6.44	4.61	1 132.52	. . .	. . .
February	1.01	2.00	0.93	1.68	-0.75	1.01	4.00	4.08	5.50	6.27	4.55	1 143.36	. . .	. . .
March	1.00	2.00	0.94	1.72	-0.78	1.00	4.00	3.83	5.33	6.11	4.41	1 123.98	. . .	. . .
April	1.00	2.00	0.94	1.86	-0.92	1.05	4.00	4.35	5.73	6.46	4.82	1 133.08	. . .	. . .
May	1.00	2.00	1.02	1.87	-0.85	1.07	4.00	4.72	6.04	6.75	5.07	1 102.78	. . .	. . .
June	1.03	2.01	1.27	2.02	-0.75	1.34	4.01	4.73	6.01	6.78	5.05	1 132.76	. . .	. . .
July	1.26	2.25	1.33	1.95	-0.62	1.50	4.25	4.50	5.82	6.62	4.87	1 105.85	. . .	. . .
August	1.43	2.43	1.48	1.94	-0.46	1.62	4.43	4.28	5.65	6.46	4.70	1 088.94	. . .	. . .
September ...	1.61	2.58	1.65	2.02	-0.37	1.75	4.58	4.13	5.46	6.27	4.56	1 117.66	. . .	. . .
October	1.76	2.75	1.76	2.06	-0.30	1.95	4.75	4.10	5.47	6.21	4.49	1 118.07	. . .	. . .
November	1.93	2.93	2.07	2.10	-0.03	2.18	4.93	4.19	5.52	6.20	4.52	1 168.94	. . .	. . .
December	2.16	3.15	2.19	2.12	0.07	2.34	5.15	4.23	5.47	6.15	4.48	1 199.21	. . .	. . .
2005														
January	2.28	3.25	2.33	2.18	0.15	2.53	5.25	4.22	5.36	6.02	4.41	1 181.41	. . .	. . .
February	2.50	3.49	2.54	2.17	0.37	. . .	5.49	4.17	5.20	5.82	4.35	1 199.63	. . .	. . .
March	2.63	3.58	2.74	2.23	0.51	2.82	5.58	4.50	5.40	6.06	4.57	1 194.90	. . .	. . .
April	2.79	3.75	2.78	2.10	0.68	2.97	5.75	4.34	5.33	6.05	4.46	1 164.42	. . .	. . .
May	3.00	3.98	2.84	2.19	0.65	3.09	5.98	4.14	5.15	6.01	4.31	1 178.28	. . .	. . .
June	3.04	4.01	2.97	2.05	0.92	3.27	6.01	4.00	4.96	5.86	4.23	1 202.26	. . .	. . .
July	3.26	4.25	3.22	2.04	1.18	3.47	6.25	4.18	5.06	5.95	4.31	1 222.24	. . .	. . .
August	3.50	4.44	3.44	2.06	1.38	3.64	6.44	4.26	5.09	5.96	4.32	1 224.27	. . .	. . .
September ...	3.62	4.59	3.42	2.11	1.31	3.72	6.59	4.20	5.13	6.03	4.29	1 225.91	. . .	. . .
October	3.78	4.75	3.71	2.21	1.50	4.01	6.75	4.46	5.35	6.30	4.49	1 191.96	. . .	. . .
November	4.00	5.00	3.88	2.29	1.59	4.23	7.00	4.54	5.42	6.39	4.57	1 237.37	. . .	. . .
December	4.16	5.15	3.89	2.28	1.61	. . .	7.15	4.47	5.37	6.32	4.46	1 262.07	. . .	. . .
2006														
January	4.29	5.26	4.24	2.15	2.09	. . .	7.26	4.42	5.29	6.24	4.37	1 278.72	. . .	. . .
February	4.49	5.50	4.43	2.12	2.31	4.55	7.50	4.57	5.35	6.27	4.41	1 276.65	. . .	. . .
March	4.59	5.53	4.51	2.11	2.40	4.76	7.53	4.72	5.53	6.41	4.44	1 293.74	. . .	. . .
April	4.79	5.75	4.60	2.24	2.36	4.87	7.75	4.99	5.84	6.68	4.58	1 302.18	. . .	. . .
May	4.94	5.93	4.72	2.20	2.52	5.01	7.93	5.11	5.95	6.75	4.59	1 290.00	. . .	. . .
June	4.99	6.02	4.79	2.37	2.42	5.29	8.02	5.11	5.89	6.78	4.60	1 253.12	. . .	. . .
July	5.24	6.25	4.95	2.34	2.61	. . .	8.25	5.09	5.85	6.76	4.61	1 260.24	. . .	. . .
August	5.25	6.25	4.96	2.45	2.51	5.21	8.25	4.88	5.68	6.59	4.39	1 287.15	. . .	. . .
September ...	5.25	6.25	4.81	2.39	2.42	5.21	8.25	4.72	5.51	6.43	4.27	1 317.81	. . .	. . .
October	5.25	6.25	4.92	2.27	2.65	5.19	8.25	4.73	5.51	6.42	4.30	1 363.38	. . .	. . .
November	5.25	6.25	4.94	2.07	2.87	5.17	8.25	4.60	5.33	6.20	4.14	1 388.63	. . .	. . .
December	5.24	6.25	4.85	2.13	2.72	5.19	8.25	4.56	5.32	6.22	4.11	1 416.42	. . .	. . .

[1]Federal Reserve Bank of New York. Through 2002, represents the rate for adjustment credit. Beginning in 2003, represents the rate for primary credit. See notes and definitions for more information.
[2]Change from a year earlier. Beginning in 1960, PCE except food and energy; before then, CPI-U
[3]Beginning 1997, rates for nonfinancial companies only are shown.
. . . = Not available.

Table 12-9B. Summary Interest Rates, Bond Yields, and Stock Prices: Historical Data—*Continued*

(Percent per annum, except as noted.)

Year and month	Federal funds interest rate	Federal Reserve discount rate[1]	U.S. Treasury bills, secondary market, 3-month	Inflation[2]	Real 3-month Treasury bill rate	Commercial paper, 3-month[3]	Bank prime rate	Treasury 10-year nominal yields	Bond yields: Domestic corporate (Moody's) Aaa	Baa	State and local bonds (Bond Buyer)	S&P composite Index, 1941-1943 = 10	Dividend-price ratio	Earnings-price ratio
2007														
January	5.25	6.25	4.98	2.35	2.63	5.17	8.25	4.76	5.40	6.34	4.23	1 424.16	1.81	...
February	5.26	6.25	5.03	2.45	2.58	5.18	8.25	4.72	5.39	6.28	4.22	1 444.79	1.82	
March	5.26	6.25	4.94	2.29	2.65	5.20	8.25	4.56	5.30	6.27	4.15	1 406.95	1.89	5.85
April	5.25	6.25	4.87	2.13	2.74	5.20	8.25	4.69	5.47	6.39	4.26	1 463.65	1.84	
May	5.25	6.25	4.73	2.03	2.70	5.19	8.25	4.75	5.47	6.39	4.31	1 511.14	1.81	...
June	5.25	6.25	4.61	1.95	2.66	5.23	8.25	5.10	5.79	6.70	4.60	1 514.49	1.81	5.65
July	5.26	6.25	4.82	1.98	2.84	5.22	8.25	5.00	5.73	6.65	4.56	1 520.70	1.80	
August	5.02	6.01	4.20	1.94	2.26	5.25	8.25	4.67	5.79	6.65	4.64	1 454.62	1.92	...
September	4.94	5.53	3.89	2.04	1.85	4.92	8.03	4.52	5.74	6.59	4.51	1 497.12	1.88	5.15
October	4.76	5.24	3.90	2.14	1.76	4.63	7.74	4.53	5.66	6.48	4.39	1 539.66	1.84	
November	4.49	5.00	3.27	2.27	1.00	4.42	7.50	4.15	5.44	6.40	4.46	1 463.39	1.95	...
December	4.24	4.83	3.00	2.32	0.68	4.23	7.33	4.10	5.49	6.65	4.42	1 479.23	1.93	4.51
2008														
January	3.94	4.48	2.75	2.14	0.61	3.25	6.98	3.74	5.33	6.54	4.27	1 378.76	2.06	...
February	2.98	3.50	2.12	2.02	0.10	2.72	6.00	3.74	5.53	6.82	4.64	1 354.87	2.10	
March	2.61	3.04	1.26	2.16	-0.90	2.35	5.66	3.51	5.51	6.89	4.93	1 316.94	2.17	4.57
April	2.28	2.49	1.29	2.19	-0.90	1.99	5.24	3.68	5.55	6.97	4.70	1 370.47	2.09	
May	1.98	2.25	1.73	2.28	-0.55	2.00	5.00	3.88	5.57	6.93	4.58	1 403.22	2.07	...
June	2.00	2.25	1.86	2.32	-0.46	2.21	5.00	4.10	5.68	7.07	4.69	1 341.25	2.15	4.01
July	2.01	2.25	1.63	2.31	-0.68	2.18	5.00	4.01	5.67	7.16	4.68	1 257.33	2.27	
August	2.00	2.25	1.72	2.26	-0.54	2.08	5.00	3.89	5.64	7.15	4.69	1 281.47	2.23	...
September	1.81	2.25	1.13	2.11	-0.98	2.13	5.00	3.69	5.65	7.31	4.86	1 217.01	2.36	3.94
October	0.97	1.81	0.67	1.85	-1.18	2.07	4.56	3.81	6.28	8.88	5.50	968.80	2.83	
November	0.39	1.25	0.19	1.69	-1.50	1.45	4.00	3.53	6.12	9.21	5.23	883.04	3.11	...
December	0.16	0.86	0.03	1.41	-1.38	0.97	3.61	2.42	5.05	8.43	5.56	877.56	3.00	1.65
2009														
January	0.15	0.50	0.13	1.23	-1.10	0.31	3.25	2.52	5.05	8.14	5.07	865.58	3.01	...
February	0.22	0.50	0.30	1.21	-0.91	0.48	3.25	2.87	5.27	8.08	4.90	805.23	3.07	
March	0.18	0.50	0.21	1.11	-0.90	0.37	3.25	2.82	5.50	8.42	4.99	757.13	2.92	0.86
April	0.15	0.50	0.16	1.25	-1.09	0.28	3.25	2.93	5.39	8.39	4.78	848.15	2.60	
May	0.18	0.50	0.18	1.16	-0.98	0.23	3.25	3.29	5.54	8.06	4.56	902.41	2.41	...
June	0.21	0.50	0.18	1.10	-0.92	0.26	3.25	3.72	5.61	7.50	4.81	926.12	2.35	0.82
July	0.16	0.50	0.18	0.97	-0.79	0.28	3.25	3.56	5.41	7.09	4.72	935.82	2.31	
August	0.16	0.50	0.17	0.97	-0.80	0.24	3.25	3.59	5.26	6.58	4.60	1 009.72	2.12	...
September	0.15	0.50	0.12	1.03	-0.91	0.19	3.25	3.40	5.13	6.31	4.24	1 044.55	2.06	1.19
October	0.12	0.50	0.07	1.33	-1.26	0.19	3.25	3.39	5.15	6.29	4.20	1 067.66	2.02	
November	0.12	0.50	0.05	1.42	-1.37	0.15	3.25	3.40	5.19	6.32	4.37	1 088.07	1.99	...
December	0.12	0.50	0.05	1.49	-1.44	0.16	3.25	3.59	5.26	6.37	4.21	1 110.38	1.95	4.57
2010														
January	0.11	0.50	0.06	1.56	-1.50	0.13	3.25	3.73	5.26	6.25	4.33	1 123.58	1.92	...
February	0.13	0.59	0.11	1.54	-1.43	0.15	3.25	3.69	5.35	6.34	4.36	1 089.16	2.00	
March	0.16	0.75	0.15	1.56	-1.41	0.20	3.25	3.73	5.27	6.27	4.36	1 152.05	1.90	5.21
April	0.20	0.75	0.16	1.33	-1.17	0.23	3.25	3.85	5.29	6.25	4.41	1 197.32	1.84	
May	0.20	0.75	0.16	1.35	-1.19	0.28	3.25	3.42	4.96	6.05	4.29	1 125.06	1.98	...
June	0.18	0.75	0.12	1.32	-1.20	0.32	3.25	3.20	4.88	6.23	4.36	1 083.36	2.09	6.51
July	0.18	0.75	0.16	1.36	-1.20	0.27	3.25	3.01	4.72	6.01	4.32	1 079.80	2.10	
August	0.19	0.75	0.16	1.33	-1.17	0.25	3.25	2.70	4.49	5.66	4.03	1 087.28	2.10	...
September	0.19	0.75	0.15	1.20	-1.05	0.24	3.25	2.65	4.53	5.66	3.87	1 122.08	2.06	6.30
October	0.19	0.75	0.13	0.98	-0.85	0.23	3.25	2.54	4.68	5.72	3.87	1 171.58	1.97	
November	0.19	0.75	0.14	0.99	-0.85	0.23	3.25	2.76	4.87	5.92	4.40	1 198.89	1.94	...
December	0.18	0.75	0.14	0.95	-0.81	0.23	3.25	3.29	5.02	6.10	4.92	1 241.53	1.90	6.15
2011														
January	0.17	0.75	0.15	1.00	-0.85	0.24	3.25	3.39	5.04	6.09	5.28	1 282.62	1.84	...
February	0.16	0.75	0.13	1.07	-0.94	0.23	3.25	3.58	5.22	6.15	5.15	1 321.12	1.80	
March	0.14	0.75	0.10	1.05	-0.95	0.23	3.25	3.41	5.13	6.03	4.92	1 304.49	1.90	6.13
April	0.10	0.75	0.06	1.23	-1.17	0.20	3.25	3.46	5.16	6.02	4.99	1 331.51	1.92	
May	0.09	0.75	0.04	1.35	-1.31	0.16	3.25	3.17	4.96	5.78	4.59	1 338.31	1.95	...
June	0.09	0.75	0.04	1.40	-1.36	0.15	3.25	3.00	4.99	5.75	4.51	1 287.29	2.04	6.35
July	0.07	0.75	0.04	1.50	-1.46	0.14	3.25	3.00	4.93	5.76	4.52	1 325.18	1.99	
August	0.10	0.75	0.02	1.62	-1.60	0.16	3.25	2.30	4.37	5.36	4.02	1 185.31	2.20	...
September	0.08	0.75	0.01	1.65	-1.64	0.14	3.25	1.98	4.09	5.27	4.01	1 173.88	2.25	7.69
October	0.07	0.75	0.02	1.71	-1.69	0.15	3.25	2.15	3.98	5.37	4.13	1 207.22	2.28	
November	0.08	0.75	0.01	1.77	-1.76	0.14	3.25	2.01	3.87	5.14	4.05	1 226.41	2.22	...
December	0.07	0.75	0.01	1.89	-1.88	0.14	3.25	1.98	3.93	5.25	3.95	1 243.32	2.24	6.91
2012														
January	0.08	0.75	0.03	2.01	-1.98	0.14	3.25	1.97	3.85	5.23	3.68	1 300.58	2.17	...
February	0.10	0.75	0.09	1.99	-1.90	0.17	3.25	1.97	3.85	5.14	3.66	1 352.49	2.11	
March	0.13	0.75	0.08	2.04	-1.96	0.18	3.25	2.17	3.99	5.23	3.91	1 389.24	2.09	6.29
April	0.14	0.75	0.08	1.96	-1.88	0.20	3.25	2.05	3.96	5.19	3.95	1 386.43	2.20	
May	0.16	0.75	0.09	1.86	-1.77	0.19	3.25	1.80	3.80	5.07	3.77	1 341.27	2.31	...
June	0.16	0.75	0.09	1.92	-1.83	0.21	3.25	1.62	3.64	5.02	3.94	1 323.48	2.38	6.45
July	0.16	0.75	0.10	1.86	-1.76	0.22	3.25	1.53	3.40	4.87	3.78	1 359.78	2.33	
August	0.13	0.75	0.10	1.70	-1.60	0.20	3.25	1.68	3.48	4.91	3.74	1 403.44	2.26	...
September	0.14	0.75	0.11	1.71	-1.60	0.20	3.25	1.72	3.49	4.84	3.73	1 443.42	2.21	6.00
October	0.16	0.75	0.10	1.76	-1.66	0.19	3.25	1.75	3.47	4.58	3.65	1 437.82	2.24	
November	0.16	0.75	0.09	1.67	-1.58	0.20	3.25	1.65	3.50	4.51	3.46	1 394.51	2.33	...
December	0.16	0.75	0.07	1.60	-1.53	0.20	3.25	1.72	3.65	4.63	3.48	1 422.29	2.28	6.07

[1]Federal Reserve Bank of New York. Through 2002, represents the rate for adjustment credit. Beginning in 2003, represents the rate for primary credit. See notes and definitions for more information.
[2]Change from a year earlier. Beginning in 1960, PCE except food and energy; before then, CPI-U
[3]Beginning 1997, rates for nonfinancial companies only are shown.
. . . = Not available.

Table 12-10. Selected Interest Rates

(Percent per annum; interest rates are nominal [not adjusted for inflation], except as noted.)

Year and month	Eurodollar deposits, 1-month	U.S. Treasury bills, secondary market, 6-month	CDs (secondary market) 3-month	Interest rate swaps		U.S. Treasury securities, constant maturities							
						Nominal yields					Inflation-indexed yields		
				1-year	30-year	1-year	5-year	10-year	20-year	30-year	5-year	20-year	Long-term average
1960	. . .	3.20	. . .	. . .	. . .	. . .	. . .	. . .	. . .	. . .	. . .	. . .	. . .
1961	. . .	2.59	. . .	. . .	. . .	3.10	3.70	3.95	. . .	. . .	. . .	. . .	. . .
1962	. . .	2.90	. . .	. . .	. . .	3.36	3.83	4.00	. . .	. . .	. . .	. . .	. . .
1963	. . .	3.26	. . .	. . .	. . .	3.85	4.07	4.19	. . .	. . .	. . .	. . .	. . .
1964	. . .	3.68	3.92	. . .	. . .				. . .	. . .	. . .	. . .	. . .
1965	. . .	4.05	4.36	. . .	. . .	4.15	4.25	4.28	. . .	. . .	. . .	. . .	. . .
1966	. . .	5.06	5.45	. . .	. . .	5.20	5.11	4.93	. . .	. . .	. . .	. . .	. . .
1967	. . .	4.61	4.99	. . .	. . .	4.88	5.10	5.07	. . .	. . .	. . .	. . .	. . .
1968	. . .	5.47	5.82	. . .	. . .	5.69	5.70	5.64	. . .	. . .	. . .	. . .	. . .
1969	. . .	6.86	7.23	. . .	. . .	7.12	6.93	6.67	. . .	. . .	. . .	. . .	. . .
1970	. . .	6.51	7.55	. . .	. . .	6.90	7.38	7.35	. . .	. . .	. . .	. . .	. . .
1971	6.40	4.52	5.00	. . .	. . .	4.89	5.99	6.16	. . .	. . .	. . .	. . .	. . .
1972	5.00	4.47	4.66	. . .	. . .	4.95	5.98	6.21	. . .	. . .	. . .	. . .	. . .
1973	9.19	7.20	9.30	. . .	. . .	7.32	6.87	6.85	. . .	. . .	. . .	. . .	. . .
1974	10.79	7.95	10.29	. . .	. . .	8.20	7.82	7.56	. . .	. . .	. . .	. . .	. . .
1975	6.35	6.10	6.44	. . .	. . .	6.78	7.78	7.99	. . .	. . .	. . .	. . .	. . .
1976	5.26	5.26	5.27	. . .	. . .	5.88	7.18	7.61	. . .	. . .	. . .	. . .	. . .
1977	5.75	5.52	5.63	. . .	. . .	6.08	6.99	7.42	. . .	7.75	. . .	. . .	. . .
1978	8.33	7.58	8.21	. . .	. . .	8.34	8.32	8.41	. . .	8.49	. . .	. . .	. . .
1979	11.66	10.04	11.20	. . .	. . .	10.65	9.51	9.43	. . .	9.28	. . .	. . .	. . .
1980	13.77	11.32	13.02	. . .	. . .	12.00	11.45	11.43	. . .	11.27	. . .	. . .	. . .
1981	16.72	13.81	15.93	. . .	. . .	14.80	14.25	13.92	. . .	13.45	. . .	. . .	. . .
1982	12.74	11.06	12.27	. . .	. . .	12.27	13.01	13.01	. . .	12.76	. . .	. . .	. . .
1983	9.38	8.74	9.07	. . .	. . .	9.58	10.79	11.10	. . .	11.18	. . .	. . .	. . .
1984	10.45	9.78	10.39	. . .	. . .	10.91	12.26	12.46	. . .	12.41	. . .	. . .	. . .
1985	8.12	7.65	8.04	. . .	. . .	8.42	10.12	10.62	. . .	10.79	. . .	. . .	. . .
1986	6.78	6.02	6.51	. . .	. . .	6.45	7.30	7.67	. . .	7.78	. . .	. . .	. . .
1987	6.88	6.03	6.87	. . .	. . .	6.77	7.94	8.39	. . .	8.59	. . .	. . .	. . .
1988	7.69	6.91	7.73	. . .	. . .	7.65	8.48	8.85	. . .	8.96	. . .	. . .	. . .
1989	9.16	8.03	9.09	. . .	. . .	8.53	8.50	8.49	. . .	8.45	. . .	. . .	. . .
1990	8.15	7.46	8.15	. . .	. . .	7.89	8.37	8.55	. . .	8.61	. . .	. . .	. . .
1991	5.81	5.44	5.83	. . .	. . .	5.86	7.37	7.86	. . .	8.14	. . .	. . .	. . .
1992	3.62	3.54	3.68	. . .	. . .	3.89	6.19	7.01	. . .	7.67	. . .	. . .	. . .
1993	3.07	3.12	3.17	. . .	. . .	3.43	5.14	5.87	6.29	6.59	. . .	. . .	. . .
1994	4.34	4.64	4.63	. . .	. . .	5.32	6.69	7.09	7.49	7.37	. . .	. . .	. . .
1995	5.86	5.56	5.92	. . .	. . .	5.94	6.38	6.57	6.95	6.88	. . .	. . .	. . .
1996	5.32	5.08	5.39	. . .	. . .	5.52	6.18	6.44	6.83	6.71	. . .	. . .	. . .
1997	5.52	5.18	5.62	. . .	. . .	5.63	6.22	6.35	6.69	6.61	. . .	. . .	. . .
1998	5.45	4.83	5.47	. . .	. . .	5.05	5.15	5.26	5.72	5.58	. . .	. . .	. . .
1999	5.15	4.75	5.33	. . .	. . .	5.08	5.55	5.65	6.20	5.87	. . .	. . .	. . .
2000	6.33	5.90	6.46	6.73	6.93	6.11	6.16	6.03	6.23	5.94	. . .	. . .	. . .
2001	3.81	3.34	3.71	3.87	6.20	3.49	4.56	5.02	5.63	5.49	. . .	. . .	. . .
2002	1.71	1.68	1.73	2.21	5.80	2.00	3.82	4.61	5.43	5.43	1.27	. . .	2.54
2003	1.14	1.05	1.15	1.36	5.24	1.24	2.97	4.01	4.96	. . .	1.04	2.14	2.21
2004	1.43	1.58	1.57	2.13	5.38	1.89	3.43	4.27	5.04	. . .	1.50	1.97	1.94
2005	3.33	3.39	3.51	4.04	5.03	3.62	4.05	4.29	4.64	. . .	1.50	1.97	1.94
2006	5.09	4.81	5.16	5.33	5.44	4.94	4.75	4.80	5.00	4.91	2.28	2.31	2.27
2007	5.28	4.44	5.27	5.09	5.45	4.53	4.43	4.63	4.91	4.84	2.15	2.36	2.34
2008	3.03	1.62	2.97	2.75	4.57	1.83	2.80	3.66	4.36	4.28	1.30	2.18	2.20
2009	0.61	0.28	0.55	0.90	3.87	0.47	2.20	3.26	4.11	4.08	1.06	2.21	2.24
2010	0.34	0.20	0.31	0.55	4.00	0.32	1.93	3.22	4.03	4.25	0.26	1.73	1.72
2011	0.30	0.10	0.30	0.48	3.65	0.18	1.52	2.78	3.62	3.91	-0.41	1.19	1.19
2012	0.31	0.13	0.28	0.45	2.66	0.17	0.76	1.80	2.54	2.92	-1.19	0.22	0.17
2013	0.22	0.09	0.21	0.32	3.37	0.13	1.17	2.35	3.12	3.45	-0.76	0.75	0.66
2014	0.18	0.06	. . .	0.31	3.32	0.12	1.64	2.54	3.07	3.34	-0.09	0.86	0.85
2013													
January	0.24	0.11	0.23	0.33	2.89	0.15	0.81	1.91	2.68	3.08	-1.39	0.20	0.03
February	0.24	0.12	0.22	0.33	3.01	0.16	0.85	1.98	2.78	3.17	-1.39	0.19	0.10
March	0.23	0.11	0.21	0.33	3.03	0.15	0.82	1.96	2.78	3.16	-1.43	0.19	0.13
April	0.23	0.09	0.20	0.32	2.85	0.12	0.71	1.76	2.55	2.93	-1.38	0.07	-0.01
May	0.22	0.08	0.20	0.31	3.03	0.12	0.84	1.93	2.73	3.11	-1.14	0.35	0.26
June	0.22	0.09	0.19	0.35	3.31	0.14	1.20	2.30	3.07	3.40	-0.59	0.98	0.83
July	0.22	0.07	. . .	0.35	3.59	0.12	1.40	2.58	3.31	3.61	-0.45	1.09	0.99
August	0.22	0.07	. . .	0.34	3.74	0.13	1.52	2.74	3.49	3.76	-0.33	1.16	1.08
September	0.22	0.04	. . .	0.33	3.78	0.12	1.60	2.81	3.53	3.79	-0.17	1.22	1.16
October	0.22	0.08	. . .	0.31	3.64	0.12	1.37	2.62	3.38	3.68	-0.41	1.05	0.99
November	0.21	0.10	. . .	0.28	3.72	0.12	1.37	2.72	3.50	3.80	-0.38	1.20	1.12
December	0.20	0.10	. . .	0.29	3.81	0.13	1.58	2.90	3.63	3.89	-0.09	1.32	1.27
2014													
January	0.19	0.07	. . .	0.30	3.76	0.12	1.65	2.86	3.52	3.77	-0.09	1.17	1.11
February	0.19	0.08	. . .	0.27	3.65	0.12	1.52	2.71	3.38	3.66	-0.26	1.12	1.04
March	0.19	0.08	. . .	0.28	3.60	0.13	1.64	2.72	3.35	3.62	-0.14	1.05	1.03
April	0.19	0.05	. . .	0.26	3.51	0.11	1.70	2.71	3.27	3.52	-0.11	0.98	0.96
May	0.19	0.05	. . .	0.26	3.36	0.10	1.59	2.56	3.12	3.39	-0.34	0.82	0.79
June	0.17	0.06	. . .	0.28	3.39	0.10	1.68	2.60	3.15	3.42	-0.29	0.84	0.81
July	0.17	0.06	. . .	0.31	3.30	0.11	1.70	2.54	3.07	3.33	-0.27	0.72	0.70
August	0.17	0.05	. . .	0.32	3.18	0.11	1.63	2.42	2.94	3.20	-0.21	0.64	0.63
September	0.17	0.04	. . .	0.36	3.24	0.11	1.77	2.53	3.01	3.26	0.10	0.81	0.83
October	0.17	0.05	. . .	0.32	3.03	0.10	1.55	2.30	2.77	3.04	0.06	0.74	0.75
November	0.17	0.07	. . .	0.34	3.02	0.13	1.62	2.33	2.76	3.04	0.14	0.77	0.78
December	0.18	0.11	. . .	0.41	2.80	0.21	1.64	2.21	2.55	2.83	0.37	0.73	0.74

. . . = Not available.

Figure 12-4: S&P Stock Price Index and FHFA House Price Index, 1976–2014

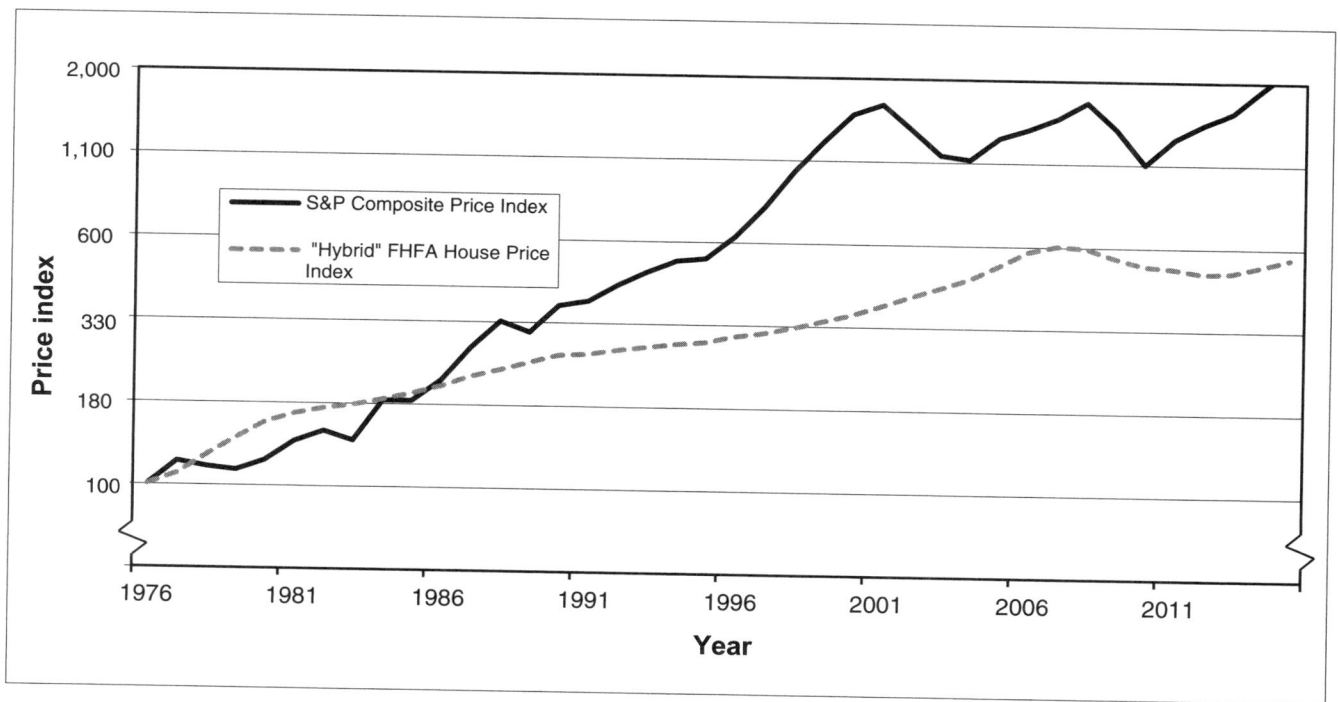

- The rise in prices of existing homes sold, as measured by the Federal Housing Finance Agency (FHFA) Purchase-Only House Price Index, ended in 2006, after annual rates of appreciation of 10 percent in 2004 and 2005. From the end of 2006 through the end of 2011, these prices declined 19 percent; they have recovered 13 percent in the three years since. (A different, privately compiled index, the Standard & Poor's Case-Shiller Home Price Index, is the measure most frequently quoted in the press. See the Notes and Definitions for a discussion of the characteristics of these different indexes.) (Table 12-11)

- For a longer perspective on house prices we have linked the Purchase-Only Index to a similar "House Price Index" for homes purchased and refinanced. This provides a price trend line extending back to 1975, with that year set at 100; this "Hybrid" FHFA House Price Index is shown in Figure 12-4. (Table 12-11)

- The long-terms gains in national average housing prices as estimated here have been no match for those in the prices of common stocks, as measured by the S&P 500-stock index, averaged for the year and also rebased to 1975=100. Over the last 38 years, house prices rose at an average 4.6 percent annual rate, while the index of stock prices, though more volatile than home prices, rose at an 8.1 percent rate. (These price increase calculations do not take account of tax considerations, stock dividends, or the value of shelter provided by the owner-occupied home. Past history is no guarantee of future results.) (Table 12-11)

Table 12-11. Selected Stock and Housing Market Data

Year and month	Stock price indexes			Interest rate on fixed-rate first mortgages	FHFA House Price Indexes			
					House Price Index (purchases and refinance)		Purchase-Only Index	
	Dow Jones industrials (30 stocks)	Standard and Poor's composite (500 stocks) (1941–1943 = 10)	Nasdaq composite (Feb. 5, 1971 = 100)		Level at end of period (1980:I = 100)	Appreciation from same quarter one year earlier (percent)	Level at end of period (1991:I = 100)	Appreciation from same quarter one year earlier (percent)
1960	618.04	55.85	...	...	...	...	...	...
1961	691.55	66.27	...	...	...	...	...	...
1962	639.76	62.38	...	...	...	...	...	...
1963	714.81	69.87	...	...	...	...	...	...
1964	834.05	81.37	...	...	...	...	...	...
1965	910.88	88.17	...	...	...	...	...	...
1966	873.60	85.26	...	...	...	...	...	...
1967	879.12	91.93	...	...	...	...	...	...
1968	906.00	98.70	...	...	...	...	...	...
1969	876.72	97.84	...	...	...	...	...	...
1970	753.19	83.22	...	...	...	...	...	...
1971	884.76	98.29	107.44	...	...	...	...	...
1972	950.71	109.20	128.52	7.38	...	...	...	...
1973	923.88	107.43	109.90	8.04	...	...	...	...
1974	759.37	82.85	76.29	9.19	...	...	...	...
1975	802.49	86.16	77.20	9.04	62.27	...	...	...
1976	974.92	102.01	89.90	8.86	67.44	8.30	...	...
1977	894.63	98.20	98.71	8.84	77.17	14.43	...	...
1978	820.23	96.02	117.53	9.63	87.50	13.39	...	...
1979	844.40	103.01	136.57	11.19	98.32	12.37	...	...
1980	891.41	118.78	168.61	13.77	104.81	6.60	...	...
1981	932.92	128.05	203.18	16.63	109.15	4.14	...	...
1982	884.36	119.71	188.97	16.08	112.19	2.79	...	...
1983	1 190.34	160.41	285.43	13.23	117.00	4.29	...	...
1984	1 178.48	160.46	248.88	13.87	122.46	4.67	...	...
1985	1 328.23	186.84	290.19	12.42	129.43	5.69	...	...
1986	1 792.76	236.34	366.96	10.18	138.80	7.24	...	...
1987	2 275.99	286.83	402.57	10.20	146.28	5.39	...	...
1988	2 060.82	265.79	374.43	10.34	154.54	5.65	...	...
1989	2 508.91	322.84	437.81	10.32	163.16	5.58	...	...
1990	2 678.94	334.59	409.17	10.13	165.11	1.20	101.46	...
1991	2 929.33	376.18	491.69	9.25	170.27	3.13	104.25	2.75
1992	3 284.29	415.74	599.26	8.40	174.38	2.41	107.09	2.72
1993	3 522.06	451.41	715.16	7.33	178.99	2.64	110.17	2.88
1994	3 793.77	460.42	751.65	8.35	181.82	1.58	113.10	2.66
1995	4 493.76	541.72	925.19	7.95	190.11	4.56	116.26	2.79
1996	5 742.89	670.50	1 164.96	7.80	194.94	2.54	120.11	3.31
1997	7 441.15	873.43	1 469.49	7.60	203.56	4.42	126.94	5.69
1998	8 625.52	1 085.50	1 794.91	6.94	213.88	5.07	134.84	6.22
1999	10 464.88	1 327.33	2 728.15	7.43	224.43	4.93	144.26	6.99
2000	10 734.90	1 427.22	3 783.67	8.06	240.31	7.08	153.99	6.74
2001	10 189.13	1 194.18	2 035.00	6.97	257.39	7.11	165.81	7.68
2002	9 226.43	993.94	1 539.73	6.54	274.65	6.71	178.82	7.85
2003	8 993.59	965.23	1 647.17	5.82	293.75	6.95	196.98	10.16
2004	10 317.39	1 130.65	1 986.53	5.84	323.99	10.29	217.06	10.19
2005	10 547.67	1 207.06	2 099.03	5.86	360.29	11.20	223.61	3.02
2006	11 408.67	1 310.67	2 265.17	6.41	376.72	4.56	218.06	-2.48
2007	13 169.98	1 476.66	2 577.12	6.34	372.71	-1.06	196.33	-9.97
2008	11 252.61	1 220.89	2 162.46	6.04	346.73	-6.97	191.79	-2.31
2009	8 876.15	946.73	1 841.03	5.04	328.71	-5.20	183.99	-4.07
2010	10 662.80	1 139.31	2 347.70	4.69	322.75	-1.81	179.79	-2.28
2011	11 966.36	1 268.89	2 680.42	4.46	312.55	-3.16	189.27	5.27
2012	12 967.08	1 379.56	2 965.77	3.66	314.80	0.72	203.58	7.56
2013	14 999.67	1 642.51	3 537.69	3.98	330.29	4.92	213.75	5.00
2014	16 773.99	1 930.67	4 374.31	4.17	348.77	5.60	213.75	5.00
2013								
January	13 615.32	1 480.40	3 125.91	3.41	...	...	...	...
February	13 967.33	1 512.31	3 169.21	3.53	316.46	2.31	191.56	6.93
March	14 418.26	1 550.83	3 236.17	3.57	...	...	...	...
April	14 675.91	1 570.70	3 251.35	3.45	...	...	...	...
May	15 172.18	1 639.84	3 440.38	3.54	321.58	4.32	200.31	7.38
June	15 035.75	1 618.77	3 416.74	4.07	...	...	...	...
July	15 390.21	1 668.68	3 559.71	4.37	...	...	...	...
August	15 195.35	1 670.09	3 639.93	4.46	326.98	4.72	204.21	8.16
September	15 269.84	1 687.17	3 731.26	4.49	...	...	...	...
October	15 289.29	1 720.03	3 848.20	4.19	...	...	...	...
November	15 870.83	1 783.54	3 957.53	4.26	330.29	4.92	203.58	7.56
December	16 095.77	1 807.78	4 075.88	4.46	...	...	...	...
2014								
January	16 243.72	1 822.36	4 154.36	4.43	...	...	...	...
February	15 958.44	1 817.03	4 199.45	4.30	333.38	5.35	204.62	6.82
March	16 308.63	1 863.52	4 276.36	4.34	...	...	...	...
April	16 399.50	1 864.26	4 119.31	4.34	...	...	...	...
May	16 567.25	1 889.77	4 135.37	4.19	340.73	5.95	211.54	5.61
June	16 843.75	1 947.09	4 332.74	4.16	...	...	...	...
July	16 988.26	1 973.10	4 434.13	4.13	...	...	...	...
August	16 775.15	1 961.53	4 464.83	4.12	345.88	5.78	213.90	4.75
September	17 098.13	1 993.23	4 551.58	4.16	...	...	...	...
October	16 701.87	1 937.27	4 403.23	4.04	...	...	...	...
November	17 648.98	2 044.57	4 687.70	4.00	348.77	5.60	213.75	5.00
December	17 754.24	2 054.27	4 732.70	3.86	...	...	...	...

. . . = Not available.

NOTES AND DEFINITIONS, CHAPTER 12

Most of the data in this chapter are found on the Federal Reserve Board Web site, <http://www.federalreserve.gov>. Current releases and most historical data are found at that site by selecting Economic Research & Data/Statistical Releases and Historical Data and then selecting the appropriate report. This is the location for all data not otherwise specified.

Historical data not found online are taken from two printed volumes of statistical data that were published by the Board of Governors of the Federal Reserve System: Banking and Monetary Statistics, 1943, and Banking and Monetary Statistics, 1941–1970, 1976. These will be referred to as B&MS 1943 and B&MS 1976.

Tables 12-1 and 12-2

Money Stock Measures and Components

SOURCE: BOARD OF GOVERNORS OF THE FEDERAL RESERVE SYSTEM

Estimates of two monetary aggregates (M1 and M2) and the components of these measures are published weekly. The monthly data are averages of daily figures. In addition, these measures are revised in subsequent releases.

The Federal Reserve Board ceased publication of the M3 aggregate on March 23, 2006. Weekly publication was also discontinued for the following components of M3: large-denomination time deposits, repurchase agreements (RPs), and Eurodollars. The Board continues to publish institutional money market mutual funds as a memorandum item in this release. Measures of large-denomination time deposits continue to be published in the Financial Accounts (Z.1 release) and in the H.8 release weekly for commercial banks.

The Board stated that "M3 does not appear to convey any additional information about economic activity that is not already embodied in M2 and has not played a role in the monetary policy process for many years. Consequently, the Board judged that the costs of collecting the underlying data and publishing M3 outweigh the benefits." ("Discontinuance of M3," H.6, Money Stock Measures [November 10, 2005, revised March 9, 2006]. [Accessed November 6, 2006.]

Definitions

M1 consists of (1) currency, (2) traveler's checks of nonbank issuers, (3) demand deposits, and (4) other checkable deposits.

M2 consists of M1 plus savings deposits (including money market deposit accounts), smalldenomination time deposits, and balances in retail money market mutual funds.

Currency consists of currency outside the U.S. Treasury, the Federal Reserve Banks, and the vaults of depository institutions.

Traveler's checks is the outstanding amount of U.S. dollar-denominated traveler's checks of nonbank issuers. Traveler's checks issued by depository institutions are included in demand deposits.

Demand deposits consists of demand deposits at domestically chartered commercial banks, U.S. branches and agencies of foreign banks, and Edge Act corporations (excluding those amounts held by depository institutions, the U.S. government, and foreign banks and official institutions) less cash items in the process of collection and Federal Reserve float. A "demand deposit" is a deposit that the depositor has a right to withdraw at any time without prior notice to the depository institution—most commonly, a checking account. "Federal Reserve float" is Federal Reserve credit that appears on the books of the depository institution of both the check writer and the check receiver while a check is being processed. This amount and cash items in the process of collection are subtracted to avoid double counting of deposits, so that they will not be counted both at the bank in which the check is deposited and at the bank on which the check is drawn.

Other checkable deposits at commercial banks consists of negotiable order of withdrawal (NOW) and automatic transfer service (ATS) balances at domestically chartered commercial banks, U.S. branches and agencies of foreign banks, and Edge Act corporations.

Other checkable deposits at thrift institutions consists of NOW and ATS balances at thrift institutions, credit union share draft balances, and demand deposits at thrift institutions.

Savings deposits includes money market deposit accounts and other savings deposits at *commercial banks* and *thrift institutions*.

Small time deposits are deposits issued at *commercial banks* and *thrift institutions* in amounts less than $100,000. All Individual Retirement Account (IRA) and Keogh account balances at commercial banks and thrift institutions are subtracted from small time deposits.

Retail money funds exclude IRA and Keogh account balances at money market mutual funds.

Institutional money funds are included in the money stock report for informational purposes. They are not part of M1 or M2.

Notes on the data

Seasonal adjustment. Seasonally adjusted M1 is calculated by summing currency, traveler's checks, demand deposits, and other checkable deposits (each seasonally adjusted separately). Seasonally adjusted M2 is computed by adjusting each of its nonM1 components and then adding this result to seasonally adjusted M1.

Revisions. Money stock measures are revised frequently and have a benchmark and seasonal factor review in the middle of the year; this review typically extends back a number of years. The monetary aggregates were redefined in major revisions introduced in 1980.

Historical: January 1947–January 1959. These data are not currently maintained online and are found in *B&MS* 1976. They are not continuous with the current data series; for that reason the values for January 1959 are shown so that users can link to the current data. The *demand deposit component* includes demand deposits held in commercial banks by individuals, partnerships, and corporations both domestic and foreign, and demand deposits held by nonbank financial institutions and foreign banks. Note that this includes demand deposit liabilities to foreign governments, central banks, and international institutions—said to be "relatively small" in the source document. *Time deposits adjusted* is time and savings deposits at commercial banks, other than large negotiable certificates of deposit (CDs), and excluding all deposits due to the U.S. government and domestic commercial banks. The editor has added this to the *Money stock (M1)* to approximate *M2*, which is not shown as such in the source document, over this period.

Historical: 1892–1946. These data are from *B&MS* 1943 and *B&MS* 1976. They pertain only to the last day of June and, after 1922, the last day of December, the "call dates" on which banks reported to the federal government. For more data and analysis concerning monetary developments in this period, including monthly money supply estimates, see Milton Friedman and Anna Jacobson Schwartz, *A Monetary History of the United States, 1867–1960,* Princeton, Princeton University Press, 1963. In Table 12-1B, *Demand deposits adjusted* refers to the elimination of interbank and U.S. government deposits and cash items in process of collection, not to seasonal adjustment, which is not applicable to call report data because they are only reported once or twice a year. The editor has retitled as *M1* the "Total" money stock shown in the source document, and has added time deposits to it in order to approximate *M2*, which is not shown in the source document.

Data availability

Estimates are released weekly in Federal Reserve Statistical Release H.6, "Money Stock Measures." Current and historical data are available on the Federal Reserve Web site.

References

Board of Governors of the Federal Reserve System, *The Federal Reserve System: Purposes and Functions,* available online at <http://www.federalreserve.gov> in the category "About the Fed/Features," includes a chapter discussing monetary policy and the monetary aggregates and a glossary of terms as an appendix.

An explanation of the 1980 redefinition of the monetary aggregates is found in the *Federal Reserve Bulletin* for February 1980.

Tables 12-3 and 12-1D

Aggregate Reserves, Monetary Base, and FR Balance Sheet

SOURCE: BOARD OF GOVERNORS OF THE FEDERAL RESERVE SYSTEM

New reporting basis, May 2013

In July 2013 the Federal Reserve Board issued a substantially revised format for reporting reserves of depository institutions and the monetary base. The revisions were made in response to the substantial growth in reserves undertaken beginning in 2008 to mitigate the effects of the financial crisis, and to recent changes in the administration of bank reserves. The concepts and procedures incorporated in the data through May 2013 in this volume and described below will not apply to the data that the Fed will be showing in the H.3 release going forward, which are shown in Table 12-3 for May through December 2013. Seasonally adjusted data—no longer relevant in a situation of vastly expanded reserves—are no longer published. Several new aggregates and interest rates are published to "give the public insight into how depository institutions collectively manage their reserves within the current framework for the implementation of monetary policy."

The new format enables calculations of concepts similar to "excess reserves," and a new simplified monetary base is nearly identical with the historical time series of that name; both are without seasonal adjustment, and are shown in Table 12-3.

Definitions for the data from May 2013 forward:

Values are shown in millions of dollars. Monthly data are prorated averages of biweekly averages.

Reserves, total equals total reserve balances maintained plus vault cash used to satisfy required reserves.

Nonborrowed reserves equals total reserves less total borrowings from the Federal Reserve.

Required reserves. Under the new reserve determination system, this is a data series now reported in the H.3 which represents the midpoint of a penalty-free band.

Excess reserves. This is no longer officially reported by the Federal Reserve because it "no longer aligns with the remuneration structure," and is no longer helpful in determining how depository institutions collectively manage their reserves; see "simplification of reserves administration", via links from

"Frequently asked questions", in the H.3 portion of the Fed website. Excess reserves is calculated by the editors as total reserves minus required reserves.

Monetary base is defined as total balances maintained plus currency in circulation.

The series *Federal Reserve balance sheet: total assets* was introduced in the 14th edition of *Business Statistics*. It demonstrates the extent to which the Federal Reserve has, beginning in 2007, undertaken "quantitative easing"—direct purchases of financial assets—in addition to conventional easing, which has consisted of reducing short-term interest rates to near zero and supporting that rate level with purchases and sales of short-term securities on the open market. The balance sheet data are accessed on a different part of the Federal Reserve Web site—"Monetary Policy" instead of "Economic Research and Data"—which features an extensive explanation and discussion of the meaning and importance of this indicator. The balance sheet is reported in millions of dollars for each Wednesday, and is shown here with the last Wednesday of the month representing the month and the last Wednesday of December representing the year. These values are not adjusted for seasonal variation.

Federal Reserve balance sheet: total assets is total assets from the Consolidated Statement of Condition of All Federal Reserve Banks, which is reported each Wednesday. The last Wednesday of the month is used to represent the month, and the last Wednesday in December is used to represent the year. Currently, the principal components of total assets are Treasury, federal agency, and mortgage-backed securities. Other types of assets representing Federal Reserve credit extension, some of which have varied during the course of the crisis, have been repurchase agreements; term auction credit; portfolio holdings of various limited liability companies (LLCs) set up to manage assets taken over from other institutions; liquidity swaps with foreign central banks; and other loans, including traditional loans to member commercial banks made at the discount rate (see the definitions for Table 12-9). Total assets are equal to the sum of Federal Reserve liabilities and capital. The principal components of liabilities are Federal Reserve notes and the deposits of member banks representing their reserves.

For further information, see "Aggregate Reserves of Depository Institutions and the Monetary Base - H.3" at <www.federalreserve.gov> under Economic Research & Data/Statistical Releases and Historical Data.

Definitions for data for May 2013 and earlier

The data on reserves and the monetary base presented here are in millions of dollars, seasonally adjusted (with one exception), and adjusted for changes in reserve requirements ("break-adjusted") in order to provide a consistent gauge of the effect of Federal Reserve open-market operations. Break adjustment is required because an observed increase in reserves will not represent an easing in monetary conditions if it is simply equal to the increase in reserves required by the Federal Reserve. Therefore, the mandated increases and decreases are deducted to provide the break-adjusted series. Monthly data are averages of daily figures. Annual data are for December.

Total reserves consists of reserve balances with the Federal Reserve Banks plus vault cash used to satisfy reserve requirements. Seasonally adjusted, break-adjusted total reserves equal seasonally adjusted, break-adjusted required reserves plus unadjusted excess reserves.

Seasonally adjusted, break-adjusted *nonborrowed reserves* equal seasonally adjusted, break-adjusted total reserves less unadjusted total borrowings of depository institutions from the Federal Reserve.

Extended credit consisted of borrowing at the discount window under the terms and conditions established for the extended credit program to help depository institutions deal with sustained liquidity pressures. Since there was not the same need to repay such borrowing promptly as there was with traditional short-term adjustment credit, the money market impact of extended credit was similar to that of nonborrowed reserves. The extended credit program was significant in the 1980s but used infrequently in subsequent years. It ended with the 2002 revision of the discount window program, effective January 9, 2003. See the explanation of the discount rate in the notes and definitions for Table 12-9A.

To adjust *required reserves* for discontinuities due to regulatory changes in reserve requirements, a multiplicative procedure is used to estimate what required reserves would have been in past periods, had current reserve requirements been in effect. Break-adjusted required reserves include required reserves against transactions deposits and personal time and savings deposits (but not reservable nondeposit liabilities).

Excess reserves, not seasonally adjusted equals unadjusted total reserves less unadjusted required reserves.

The seasonally adjusted, break-adjusted *monetary base* consists of (1) seasonally adjusted, break-adjusted total reserves; plus (2) the seasonally adjusted currency component of the money stock; plus (3) the seasonally adjusted, break-adjusted difference between current vault cash and the amount applied to satisfy current reserve requirements for all quarterly reporters on the "Report of Transaction Accounts, Other Deposits and Vault Cash" and for all weekly reporters whose vault cash exceeds their required reserves.

Federal Reserve balance sheet: total assets is as defined above—it has not been changed by the new reserve calculating and reporting system.

Data availability

Reserve and monetary base data are released weekly in Federal Reserve Release H.3, "Aggregate Reserves of Depository Institutions and the Monetary Base." Current and historical data are available on the Federal Reserve Web site.

The Federal Reserve balance sheet appears each week in the H.4.1 release, Factors Affecting Reserve Balances, released each Thursday at 4:30 p.m., and available on the Federal Reserve Web site under Economic Research and Data/Statistical Releases and Historical Data. However, to obtain the full historical data for total assets, the user must go to Monetary policy/Credit and liquidity programs and the balance sheet/Recent balance sheet trends/Total assets/View as table/All/Copy data. Other explanatory material, including a monthly report on changes in these programs, is available at the Monetary policy location.

Table 12-4A

Commercial Banks: Bank Credit and Selected Liabilities

SOURCE: BOARD OF GOVERNORS OF THE FEDERAL RESERVE SYSTEM

Definitions and notes on the data

This table presents selected balance sheet items (not a complete balance sheet with total assets and liabilities) for all commercial banks in the United States. This category covers the following types of institutions in the 50 states and the District of Columbia: domestically chartered commercial banks that report weekly (large domestic), other domestically chartered commercial banks (small domestic), branches and agencies of foreign banks, and Edge Act and Agreement corporations (foreign related institutions). International Banking Facilities are excluded.

Data are collected weekly for Wednesday values, and monthly data are pro rata averages of Wednesday values. Annual data represent December figures.

Data are complete for large domestic banks. Data for other institutions are estimated on the basis of weekly samples and end-of-quarter condition reports. Data are adjusted for breaks caused by the reclassifications of assets and liabilities.

Data before 1988 are based on previous versions of this survey—the G.7 release, "Loans and Securities at Commercial Banks," and the G.10 release, "Major Nondeposit Funds of Commercial Banks."

Most of the categories of credit and liabilities are self-explanatory.

U.S. Treasury and agency securities includes liabilities of the U.S. Treasury, liabilities of U.S. government agencies, and liabilities of U.S. government-sponsored enterprises.

Loans and leases in bank credit excludes various forms of credit extended to other commercial banks in the United States.

Security loans, previously shown as a separate category under "Loans and leases in bank credit", are now included in *"Other loans and leases."*

Allowances for loan and lease losses, interbank loans, cash assets, trading assets including derivatives, and other assets are not components of bank credit and are omitted from Table 12-4. Interbank loans include loans made to commercial banks, reverse RPs with commercial banks, and federal funds sold to commercial banks.

Selected liabilities show *deposits* and *borrowings.* Other components of total liabilities, "trading liabilities" and "other liabilities," are omitted.

Revisions

Data are revised annually around midyear to reflect new benchmark information and revised seasonal factors.

Data availability

Federal Reserve Statistical Release H.8, "Assets and Liabilities of Commercial Banks in the United States," is issued each Friday around 4:30 p.m. (EST). Current and historical data are available on the Federal Reserve Web site.

Table 12-5

Credit Market Debt Outstanding, by Borrower and Lender

SOURCE: BOARD OF GOVERNORS OF THE FEDERAL RESERVE SYSTEM

"The Financial Accounts of the United States," an expanded version of what was known before 2013 as the "Flow of Funds Accounts," are compiled quarterly by the Federal Reserve Board. They supplement the national income and product accounts (NIPAs) by providing a comprehensive and detailed accounting of financial transactions and a balance sheet for each financial and nonfinancial sector of the economy. Table 12-5 is taken from these accounts. It shows the *credit market debt outstanding owed* by the major sectors in the economy, and it shows the major lending sectors in the credit markets under *credit market assets held.* One purpose of these statistics is to show the comparative growth of the various lending sectors.

Aggregates of these data can include multiple layers of financial intermediation, such as banks making advances to finance companies that subsequently lend to households. Adding bank data to finance company data involves duplication of such debt. In macroeconomic analysis, the most widely used flow of funds measure is the total debt of domestic nonfinancial sectors. By eliminating the financial sectors, this measure has little duplication due to financial intermediation. The Federal Reserve uses this along with the monetary aggregates as an indicator of monetary conditions.

Definitions and notes on the data

Quarterly data on debt outstanding are shown on an end-of-period basis, not adjusted for seasonal variation or for "breaks" or discontinuities in the series. Due to these discontinuities, caution should be used in interpreting changes in debt levels. Break-adjusted values of changes, representing best estimates of actual fund flows, can be found in the quarterly flow of funds report, along with a suggested method for calculating percentage changes.

The data on credit market debt exclude corporate equities and mutual fund shares. However, these values of these instruments held by households and nonprofits appear as assets in the household sector accounts in Table 12-6.

Data for the current and several preceding years are revised each year to reflect revisions in source data, including the NIPAs; the revisions are issued about a month after the release of the annual NIPA revisions.

Sectors owing debt

Domestic financial sectors

Federal government-related sectors include government-sponsored enterprises (GSEs) such as Fannie Mae (originally the Federal National Mortgage Association), Freddie Mac (originally the Federal Home Loan Mortgage Corporation), and Ginnie Mae (originally the Government National Mortgage Association); agency and GSE-backed mortgage pools; and the monetary authority (Federal Reserve). However, the Federal Reserve usually owes no credit market debt.

The *private* sector includes a broad category introduced recently into the Flow of Funds accounts, "U.S.-chartered depository institutions", which replaces and comprises two earlier categories, commercial banks and bank holding companies and savings institutions; it also includes credit unions, life insurance companies, asset-backed securities (ABS) issuers, brokers and dealers, finance and mortgage companies, REITs (real estate investment trusts), and funding corporations.

Domestic nonfinancial sectors

Federal government consists of all federal government agencies and funds included in the unified budget. However, the District of Columbia government is included in the state and local sector.

Treasury securities as shown here excludes securities issued by the Treasury but held by agencies within the U.S. government (e.g., in the Social Security trust funds). In this respect, it corresponds to the "Federal debt" shown in Table 6-15, except that the latter table uses a fiscal-year basis rather than a calendar-year basis. Federal government debt as shown here is smaller than the official total public debt and the "debt subject to limit." Both of those include the securities held by U.S. government agencies. The value shown here is considered to be a more accurate measure of the effect of government borrowing in relation to the economy and credit markets than those obtained from the larger aggregates.

Budget agency securities and mortgages are those issued by government-owned corporations and agencies, such as the Export-Import Bank, that issue securities individually. There are no mortgages currently included in the debt of agencies.

Households also includes personal trusts, nonprofit organizations, and domestic hedge funds.

Nonfinancial noncorporate business now includes noncorporate farm business, formerly shown separately.

State and local governments represent operating funds only. State and local government retirement funds are included in the financial sector.

Foreign credit market debt held in the United States shows the foreign credit market debt owed to U.S. residents. This debt is included along with the debt of domestic financial and nonfinancial sectors in total credit market debt outstanding.

Percentage measures

Table 12-5 includes three measures of relative debt burdens, calculated by the editor.

Domestic nonfinancial debt as a percent of GDP is the total debt owed by domestic nonfinancial sectors as a percent of the current-dollar value of total Gross Domestic Product. (Table 1-1)

Household debt as a percent of DPI is the value of debt owed by households as a percent of the current-dollar value of disposable personal income. (Table 4-1)

Corporate nonfinancial business debt as a percent of sector value added is the total debt owed by domestic corporate nonfinancial business as a percent of the current-dollar gross value added of domestic corporate nonfinancial business. (Table 1-15)

For the annual ratios, debt outstanding at the end of the year is taken as a percent of the product or income data for the full preceding year. For the quarterly ratios, the debt outstanding at the end of the quarter is taken as a percent of the annual rate of the product or income flow for that quarter. This means that the end-year ratios will almost inevitably be higher than the corresponding end-quarter ratios and should therefore not be compared with them.

Credit market assets held by sector

Selected government-related sectors

This grouping includes two nonfinancial and four financial sectors. The nonfinancial sectors are the *federal government*, as reflected in the U.S. Budget accounts, and the operations of *state and local governments,* including the District of Columbia. *State and local employee retirement funds* and *federal government retirement funds* are shown separately and considered to be financial sectors. The other two government-related financial sectors are *government-sponsored enterprises (GSEs)* and *federally related mortgage pools.*

Government-sponsored enterprises (GSEs) are financial institutions that provide credit to housing, agriculture, and other specific areas of the economy, such as Federal Home Loan Banks, Fannie Mae, and Freddie Mac (see above for explanation of the latter two terms).

Federally related mortgage pools are entities established for bookkeeping purposes that record the issuance of pooled securities representing an interest in mortgages backed by federal agencies and GSEs. Rather than being composed of a group of institutions, the sector is made up of a set of contractual arrangements in regard to pooled mortgages.

Selected domestic financial sectors

The former categories "commercial banks" and "savings institutions" are now combined in the category *U.S.-chartered depository institutions.* The *monetary authority* (the Federal Reserve) has been put in this group because it is sometimes included in banking sector totals. Other important financial sectors are *credit unions, life insurance companies, property-casualty insurance companies,* and *private pension funds.* Additional private financial sectors are *money market mutual funds,* which issue shares and invest in short-term liquid assets; *mutual funds,* whose investments are not restricted to the short-term area; *asset-backed security (ABS) issuers,* which issue debt obligations that are backed by pooled assets, a financial procedure similar to that of federally related mortgage pools; and *finance companies,* which provide credit to businesses and individuals.

Private domestic nonfinancial sectors

Households were the dominant private domestic nonfinancial lenders in earlier years, but lending by domestic households has now been surpassed by *foreign holdings* of assets representing claims on U.S. entities.

A number of lending sectors of smaller importance are included in the category *"All other financial and nonfinancial."* One of those is nonfinancial business, a sector that is important on the borrowing side but not on the lending side. The financial sectors included in this total are closed-end funds, exchange-traded funds, real estate investment trusts (REITs), brokers and dealers, and funding corporations.

Data availability

Debt estimates are released quarterly, about nine weeks following the end of the quarter. The data can be found in Federal Reserve Statistical Release Z.1, "Financial Accounts of the United States," available on the Federal Reserve Web site. The data in Table 12-5 are found in the Summary section in Tables L.1 and L.2 of that release. Current and historical data are also available on the same Federal Reserve Web site.

References

A *Guide to the Flow of Funds (Financial) Accounts* can be ordered; ordering information is available on the Federal Reserve Web site along with the Z.1 release. Individual table descriptions can be accessed at the same location. The *Federal Reserve Bulletin* for July 2001 includes an article entitled "The U.S. Flow of Funds Accounts and Their Uses." To access *Bulletin* articles on the Federal Reserve Web site, select Economic Research & Data/ Federal Reserve Bulletin and select the year.

Table 12-6

Household Assets, Liabilities, Net Worth, Financial Obligations, and Delinquency Rates

SOURCE: BOARD OF GOVERNORS OF THE FEDERAL RESERVE SYSTEM

The quarterly data on household sector assets, liabilities, and net worth are also obtained from the Federal Reserve Board's Financial Accounts, which are described above. These data appear in Table B.100 of the Z.1 statistical release, also cited above.

The Federal Reserve has discontinued its earlier subset of financial obligations ratios that attempted to measure burdens separately for homeowners and renters. Those measures "are being eliminated because of challenges inherent in measuring them accurately," according to the announcement on the Fed website on December 9, 2013. Each ratio now presented is an aggregate of all designated payments by all households, whether owners or renters, to total disposable income for all households, as will be described more fully below in the definitions.

Definitions and notes on the data

Quarterly data on holdings of *financial assets* are shown on an end-of-period basis, not adjusted for seasonal variations. Data for the current and preceding years are revised annually to reflect revisions in source data.

It is important to note that for most categories in this reporting system, the values for the household sector are calculated as residuals. That is, starting with a known total (such as total Treasury securities outstanding), the amounts in that category reported or estimated to be held by other sectors are subtracted and the remainder is assigned to the household sector. This means that any error in estimating one of the other sectors causes an equal and opposite error in the household sector.

It should also be noted that the Financial Accounts "household" balance sheet includes nonprofit organizations, personal trusts, farm households, and domestic hedge funds, the last of which may account for the astonishing drop in "household" holdings of checkable deposits and currency in 2007 and the equally astonishing rise in 2011. Household sector assets exclude holdings by unincorporated businesses.

The table shows total household ownership of *checkable deposits and currency, time and savings deposits, money market fund shares, Treasury securities* (which now include the value of U. S. savings bonds), *agency- and GSE-backed securities, municipal securities, corporate and foreign bonds, mortgages, corporate equities* (at market value), *mutual fund shares* (with equities at market value and other assets at book value), *security credit, life insurance reserves, pension entitlements,* and *equity in noncorporate business.* Note that the reserves of life insurance companies, though held by institutions, are counted here as assets of the household sector. *Pension entitlements* includes the value of pension entitlements of private industry, federal, state, and local government employees, excluding Social Security. Bank personal trusts were formerly included as a type of household financial asset. However, in a recent revision of the flow of funds accounts, the various assets in these trusts were instead included in the appropriate categories, such as bonds, equities, and so forth. Included in total *financial assets,* but not shown separately, are foreign deposits, open market paper, and claims on insurance companies, such as unearned premium reserves of other insurance companies and health insurance reserves of life insurance companies.

Nonfinancial assets complete the asset side of the household balance sheet. Nonfinancial assets comprise equipment and software owned by nonprofit organizations, real estate, and consumer durable goods. *Household real estate* includes farm homes, mobile homes, second homes not rented, vacant homes for sale, vacant land, and owner-occupied housing. It is valued at market value, while equipment, software, and consumer durables are valued at replacement (current) cost.

Debt as a percent of total assets is calculated by the editor as household credit market debt outstanding, from Table 12-5, as a percent of the total of nonfinancial and financial assets in this table. It covers both households and nonprofit organizations, as defined above.

Total liabilities consists of household credit market debt, as shown in Table 12-5, plus security credit borrowing, trade payables of nonprofit organizations, and deferred and unpaid life insurance premiums.

Net worth is the sum of the value of financial and nonfinancial assets minus total liabilities.

The *household debt-service* and *financial obligations ratios* are estimated on a quarterly basis by the Federal Reserve based on aggregate data. They are seasonally adjusted, unlike almost all of the other data in Table 12-6. Fourth-quarter values are shown to represent the calendar year. The denominator for all of the ratios is total disposable personal income (DPI) from the NIPAs. (See Chapter 4.)

Debt service payments are the minimum required monthly payments of principal and interest on mortgage debt (including home equity loans), revolving credit (credit card debt), and auto, student, mobile home, recreational vehicle, marine, and personal loans. It is subdivided into mortgage debt, which includes home equity loans, and consumer debt, which includes the other categories listed.

Financial obligations include, in addition to debt service, rental payments on primary residences, property taxes, homeowners' insurance, and automobile lease payments.

The debt service ratios must be carefully interpreted. Most misleading and most likely to be misinterpreted: Because the denominator is total income, the *mortgage debt "ratio"* is well below the typical share of any homeowner's income claimed by mortgage payments: it is the share of everybody's personal income accounted for by homeowners' mortgage payments. Only the *financial obligations ratio* has a consistent match of obligated persons with the persons receiving income (all of them, in both cases).

Delinquency and *charge-off rates of credit card accounts held at banks* are compiled from the quarterly FFIEC (Federal Financial Institutions Examination Council).

Consolidated Reports of Condition and Income (FFIEC 031 through 034) and pertain to all insured U.S.-chartered commercial banks. The *delinquency rate* concerns loans past due 30 days or more and still accruing interest as well as those in nonaccrual status, measured as a percentage of end-of-period loans. The *charge-off rate* is the value of net charge-offs (loans removed from the books and charged against loss reserves, minus recoveries) as a percentage of average loans outstanding over the quarter, annualized.

Data availability

Household balance sheet estimates are released quarterly, about nine weeks following the end of a quarter, in the Federal Reserve Statistical Release Z.1, "Financial Accounts of the United States." Further information on data availability is given in the notes to Table 12-5, a table which is also derived from these accounts.

For information and data about the financial obligations and debt service ratios, see "Household Debt Service and Financial Obligations Ratios on the Federal Reserve website <www.federalreserve.gov> under the category of Economic Research and Data/Statistical Releases and Historical Data.

Delinquency and charge-off rates of credit card accounts held at banks are also available on the Federal Reserve Web site, listed under "Charge-off and Delinquency Rates on Loans and Leases at Commercial Banks." Rates are posted approximately 60 days after the end of the quarter.

Table 12-7

Mortgage Debt Outstanding

SOURCE: BOARD OF GOVERNORS OF THE FEDERAL RESERVE SYSTEM

These data are also published in the Federal Reserve's Statistical Release Z.1, "Financial Accounts of the United States," Table L.217. They are based on reports from various government and private organizations.

Definitions and notes on the data

By type of property

Home mortgages includes home equity loans; these are also shown separately elsewhere in this Federal Reserve statistical report.

Multifamily residences refers to mortgages on structures of five or more units.

By type of holder

Federal and related agencies shows mortgages held directly by the federal government and GSEs (see notes and definitions for Table 12-5 above).

Mortgage pools or trusts show mortgages that were refinanced by their holders through the issuance of mortgage-backed securities. They are shown in two columns: refinancings by *federally related agencies*—mainly the GSEs Fannie Mae, Freddie Mac, and Ginnie Mae (see above)—and refinancings by private

conduits (these are referred to as *ABS issuers* in these accounts, which stands for issuers of asset-backed securities).

Other holders encompasses a variety of groups, including finance companies, individuals, state and local governments, credit unions, and others.

Home mortgage debt as a percentage of the value of real estate is calculated by the editor, using total home mortgage debt, as shown in this table, as a percentage of the value of household real estate, which is shown in Table 12-6.

Data availability

Mortgage debt data are compiled quarterly about nine weeks following the end of the quarter in Federal Reserve Statistical Release Z.1, "Financial Accounts of the United States." The release and current and historical data are available on the Federal Reserve Web site.

Table 12-8

Consumer Credit

SOURCE: BOARD OF GOVERNORS OF THE FEDERAL RESERVE SYSTEM

The consumer credit series cover most short and intermediateterm credit extended to individuals through regular business channels, excluding loans secured by real estate (such as first and second mortgages and home equity credit). In October 2003, the scope of this survey was expanded to incorporate student loans extended by the federal government and by SLM Holding Corporation (SLM), the parent company of Sallie Mae (Student Loan Marketing Association). The historical data have been revised back to 1977 to reflect this inclusion.

The failure to include home equity credit is an important limitation of this data set. The household debt series presented in Table 12-5 are more comprehensive, comprising both mortgage and consumer debt.

Consumer credit is categorized by major types of credit and by major holders.

Definitions and notes on the data

The major types of consumer credit are *revolving* and *nonrevolving*.

Revolving credit includes credit arising from purchases on credit card plans of retail stores and banks, cash advances and check credit plans of banks, and some overdraft credit arrangements.

Nonrevolving credit includes automobile loans, mobile home loans, and all other loans not included in revolving credit, such as loans for education, boats, trailers, or vacations. These loans may be secured or unsecured.

Debt secured by real estate (including first liens, junior liens, and home equity loans) is excluded. Credit extended to governmental agencies and nonprofit or charitable organizations, as well as credit extended to business or to individuals exclusively for business purposes, is excluded.

Categories of *holders* include *U.S.-chartered depository institutions* (comprising commercial banks and savings institutions), *finance companies, credit unions, federal government, nonprofit and educational institutions, nonfinancial businesses*, and *pools of securitized assets*. The Student Loan Marketing Association (Sallie Mae) is included in "Federal government" until the end of 2004, at which time it became fully privatized. Beginning with the end of 2004, Sallie Mae is included in "Finance companies." Retailers and gasoline companies are included in the nonfinancial businesses category.

Federal government includes student loans originated by the Department of Education under the Federal Direct Loan Program and the Perkins Loan Program, as well as Federal Family Education Loan Program loans that the government purchased under the Ensuring Continued Access to Student Loans Act.

Nonprofit and educational institutions includes student loans originated under the Federal Family Education Loan Program and held by educational institutions and nonprofit organizations that are affiliated with state governments.

Pools of securitized assets comprises the outstanding balances of pools upon which securities have been issued; these balances are no longer carried on the balance sheets of the loan originators.

The consumer credit series are benchmarked to comprehensive data that periodically become available. Current monthly estimates are brought forward from the latest benchmarks in accordance with weighted changes indicated by sample data. Classifications are made on a "holder" basis. Thus, installment paper sold by retail outlets is included in the figures for the banks and finance companies that purchased the paper.

The amount of outstanding credit represents the sum of the balances in the installment receivable accounts of financial institutions and retail outlets at the end of each month.

The estimates of the amount of credit outstanding include any finance and insurance charges included as part of the installment contract. Unearned income on loans is included in some cases when lenders cannot separate the components.

The seasonally-adjusted data are adjusted for differences in the number of trading days and for seasonal influences.

Data availability

Current data are available monthly in the Federal Reserve Statistical Release G.19, "Consumer Credit," available along with all current and historical data on the Federal Reserve Web site. In the autumn of each year there is a revision of several years of past data reflecting benchmarking and seasonal factor review.

Tables 12-9, 12-10 and 12-11

Interest Rates, Bond Yields, Stock Prices, and Housing Market Data

SOURCES: BOARD OF GOVERNORS OF THE FEDERAL RESERVE SYSTEM; BUREAU OF ECONOMIC ANALYSIS; MOODY'S INVESTORS SERVICE; THE BOND BUYER; DOW JONES, INC.; STANDARD AND POOR'S CORPORATION; NEW YORK STOCK EXCHANGE; FEDERAL HOUSING FINANCE AGENCY (FHFA), PREVIOUSLY OFHEO (OFFICE OF FEDERAL HOUSING ENTERPRISE OVERSIGHT)

Definitions and notes on the data

Interest rates and bond yields are percents per year and are averages of business day figures, except as noted. With a few exceptions, they are nominal rates or yields not adjusted for inflation.

The daily effective *federal funds rate*—a principal marker for Federal Reserve monetary policy—is a weighted average of rates on trades through New York brokers. Monthly figures include each calendar day in the month. Annualized figures use a 360-day year.

The *Federal Reserve discount rate* is the rate for discount window borrowing at the Federal Reserve Bank of New York. Monthly figures include each calendar day in the month. Annualized figures use a 360-day year. Before 1945, annual averages calculated by editor.

Beginning in January 2003, the rules governing the discount window programs were revised. "Adjustment credit," which had been extended at a below-market rate (as can be seen in the average discount rates from 1978 through 2002 shown in Table 12-9, which are below the federal funds rate), was replaced by a new type of credit called "primary credit." Primary credit is available for very short terms as a backup source of liquidity to depository institutions in generally sound financial condition, as judged by the lending Federal Reserve Bank. Primary credit is extended at a rate above the federal funds rate, eliminating the incentive for institutions to exploit the spread of money market rates over the discount rate.

Through December 2002, Table 12-9 displays the adjustment credit rate. Beginning in February 2003, the new primary credit rate is shown. The rule change, and the change in discount rates shown, did not entail a change in the stance of monetary policy at that time; the overall stance of monetary policy was consistently measured by the level of the federal funds rate.

The *U.S. Treasury bills, 3-month rate* and the *U.S. Treasury bills, 6-month rate* are the yields on these securities based on their prices as traded in the secondary market. The rates are quoted on a discount basis. Annualized figures use a 360-day year. Early data are taken from *B&MS* 1943 and 1976. From 1934 to 1944, the 3-month rate is based on dealers' quotations. From 1931 through 1933, it is the average rate on new issues. For 1920 through 1930, it is the rate on 3- to 6-month Treasury notes and certificates.

The *inflation* column shown here, calculated by the editor, is the rate of change in the PCE chain-type price index, excluding food and energy, beginning in 1960. For monthly entries, it is the change from the same month a year earlier. This price index is calculated by the Bureau of Economic Analysis (BEA) and shown in Table 8-3. This inflation rate is shown along with other rates in Table 8-4; see the notes and definitions for that table. Before 1960, the inflation rates shown are the similarly-defined rates of change in the CPI-U.

The *real 3-month Treasury bill rate* is calculated by the editor by subtracting the inflation estimate from the nominal interest rate. Note that subtraction means changing the sign and adding; hence negative inflation (that is, price decline or deflation), as experienced in the 1930s, contributes to large positive real interest rates.

Commercial paper, 3-month rates are interpolated from data on certain commercial paper trades settled by the Depository Trust Company. This company is a clearinghouse and custodian for nearly all domestic commercial paper activity. The trades, which are on a discount basis, represent sales of commercial paper by dealers or direct issuers. Annualized figures use a 360-day year. From 1971 through September 1997, the series represented both nonfinancial and financial commercial paper. Since September 1997, rates have been reported separately for nonfinancial and financial companies; only rates for nonfinancial companies are shown here. This introduces a slight discontinuity in this series between August and September 1997. Before 1971, the prevailing rate in New York City for 4- to 6-month commercial paper; hence, this series is also discontinuous between December 1970 and January 1971, and is obtained from *B&MS* 1943 and 1976.

The *bank prime rate* is one of several base rates used by banks to price shortterm business loans. It is the rate posted by a majority of the top 25 (by amount of assets in domestic offices) insured U.S.-chartered commercial banks. Monthly figures include each calendar day in the month. Annualized figures use a 360-day year. Before 1949, the data are not on the Federal Reserve Web site but have been reproduced from *B&MS* 1976. In that volume, the prime rate is described as "the rate that banks charge their most creditworthy business customers on short-term loans", as posted by the largest banks. The same source goes on to write, "A nationally publicized and uniform prime rate did not emerge until the depression of the 1930s. The rate in that period—1 ½ percent—represented a floor below which banks were said to regard lending as unprofitable. The date shown [for the beginning of a changed rate] is that on

which the new rate was put into effect by the first bank to make the change. The table shows a range of rates for 1929–1933 because no information is available to indicate when the rate changed in that period." For further information, the source document cites "The Prime Rate," *Monthly Review,* Federal Reserve Bank of New York, April and May 1962, pp. 54-59 and 70-73, respectively.

U.S. Treasury securities, constant maturities. The rates shown for 1-year, 5-year, 10-year, 20-year, and 30-year securities are yields on actively traded issues adjusted to constant maturities. Yields on Treasury securities at "constant maturity" are interpolated by the Treasury Department from the daily yield curve. This curve, which relates the yield on a security to its time to maturity, is based on the closing market bid yields on actively traded Treasury securities in the overthecounter market. These market yields are calculated from composites of quotations reported by U.S. Government securities dealers to the Federal Reserve Bank of New York. The constant maturity yield values are read from the yield curve at fixed maturities. For example, this method provides a yield for a 10 year maturity, even if no outstanding security has exactly 10 years remaining to maturity. The 30-year series was discontinued as of February 2002, because the Treasury Department was no longer issuing such bonds at that time. However, issuance of 30-year bonds was resumed in 2005 as an additional means of financing rising deficits, and the 30-year interest rate series resumes in 2006. The current 20-year series begins with 1993 and is not comparable with an earlier 20-year series. For further information, see the historical data series on the Federal Reserve Web site.

Before 1962, the *Treasury 10-year* is not available on the constant-maturity basis. The entries in that column are from *B&MS* 1943 and 1976 where they are labeled "United States government bonds (long-term)." Before 1941, they represent yields on bonds that were partly tax-exempt. In 1941, the yield for the partly tax-exempt series was 1.95 percent—comparable with the entries for previous years—while the entry comparable with subsequent years was 2.12 percent.

Domestic corporate bond yields, Aaa and Baa. The rates shown are for general obligation bonds based on Thursday figures, and are provided by Moody's Investors Service and republished by the Federal Reserve. The Aaa rates through December 6, 2001 are averages of Aaa utility and Aaa industrial bond rates. As of December 7, 2001, these rates are averages of Aaa industrial bonds only.

The *state and local bond yields* are the Bond Buyer index as republished by the Federal Reserve. The index is based on 20 state and local government general obligation bonds of mixed quality maturing in 20 years or less. Quotes are as of the Thursday of each week. These rates have typically in the past been lower than those on U.S. Treasury or private long-term bonds because the interest on them is exempt from U.S. income taxes, but some recent data display different patterns because of changing assessments of credit risks relative to Treasury securities. Before 1953, the source is Standard and Poor's yields on high-grade municipal bonds as republished in *B&MS* 1943 and 1976.

Stock price indexes and yields. The *Dow Jones industrial* average is an average price of 30 stocks compiled by Dow Jones, Inc. The *Standard and Poor's composite* is an index of the prices of 500 stocks that are weighted by the volume of shares outstanding, accounting for about 90 percent of New York Stock Exchange value, with a base of 1941–1943 = 10, compiled by Standard and Poor's Corporation. (Before February 1957, these data are based on a conversion of an earlier 90-stock index, and are obtained from *B&MS* 1943 and 1976.) The *dividend-price ratio* is compiled by Standard and Poor's, covering the 500 stocks in the S&P index. It represents aggregate cash dividends (based on the latest known annual rate) divided by aggregate market value based on Wednesday closing prices. The *earnings/price ratio* measures earnings (after taxes) for four quarters, ending with the indicated quarter, as a ratio to stock prices for the last day of that quarter. Monthly data are averages of weekly figures; annual data are averages of monthly or quarterly figures. The *Nasdaq composite index* is an average price of over 5,000 stocks traded on the Nasdaq exchange.

The *Eurodollar deposits* rate shown is the bid rate at about 9:30 a.m. (EST) for 1-month Eurodollar deposits. Annualized figures use a 360-day year.

CDs (secondary market), 3-month rates are averages of dealer offering rates on nationally traded certificates of deposit. Annualized figures use a 360-day year.

Interest rate swaps. An interest rate swap is a type of financial market derivative in which two parties, known as "counterparties," exchange two streams of cash flows. The rates shown here are the results of transactions in which streams of fixed-rate interest flows are exchanged for streams of floating-rate interest flows. The rates shown are the fixed interest rates which are exchanged for floating-rate flows paying the three-month LIBOR (London Interbank Offered Rate, a rate at which highly-rated banks can borrow short-term). They are International Swaps and Derivatives Association (ISDA ®) mid-market par swap rates, collected at 11 a.m. EST by Garban Intercapital plc and published on Reuters Page ISDAFIX ®1. ISDAFIX is a registered service mark of ISDA. Reprinted by the Federal Reserve from Reuters Limited.

Inflation-indexed yields. In recent years, the Treasury Department has issued Treasury Inflation-Protected Securities (TIPS), which are marketable long-term bonds whose redemption value is increased by the change in the CPI-U from the date of purchase. (See notes and definitions to Chapter 8.) The purchaser of these bonds, unlike with ordinary securities, is guaranteed that the real value of his or her principal will remain intact. He or she need not make his or her own estimate of future inflation in

order to make a rational bid. Therefore, the observed purchase price represents a real rate of interest that purchasers and sellers are mutually willing to accept. Inflation-indexed yields are shown here for 5 and 20 years (adjusted to constant maturities by the Treasury) and for the long-term average, which is the unweighted average of the bid yields for all TIPS with remaining terms to maturity over 10 years.

The *fixed-rate first mortgage* rates are primary market contract interest rates on commitments for fixedrate conventional 30-year first mortgages. The rates are obtained by the Federal Reserve from the Federal Home Loan Mortgage Corporation (FHLMC, or Freddie Mac).

FHFA (formerly OFHEO) House Price Indexes. The value of single-family owner-occupied houses was an increasingly important element in the latest household wealth and credit expansion and subsequent collapse. The Federal Housing Finance Agency (FHFA), a government agency charged with regulation of the government-sponsored mortgage finance institutions Fannie Mae and Freddie Mac and the 12 Federal Home Loan Banks, uses data from those institutions to compile quarterly House Price Indexes of the value of existing single-family homes. Not included are condominiums, cooperatives, multi-unit properties, and planned unit developments. These indexes were developed by the predecessor agency, the Office of Federal Housing Enterprise Oversight (OFHEO), and have been published since the fourth quarter of 1995.

The data come from all properties for which a conventional, "conforming" mortgage has been purchased or guaranteed by Fannie Mae or Freddie Mac since January 1975. (Conventional mortgages are those not insured or guaranteed by the FHA, VA, or other federal government entities. A conforming mortgage is one no larger than the maximum that the insuring institution will insure. The limit has increased over time and has been $417,000 since the beginning of 2006. Loan limits for mortgages originated in the latter half of 2007 through Dec. 31, 2008, were raised to as much as $729,750 in high-cost areas in the continental United States. Legislation generally extended those limits for 2009-originated mortgages, and the limits for 2010 originations were further extended for certain places.) Every new mortgage transaction that can be matched against a previous transaction for that property yields a rate of price change over the period between the two transactions, which enters into the calculation of the index. This data set is very large, with about 32 million repeat transactions over the 32-year span. The index is computed using a modified version of the Case-Shiller geometric weighted repeat-sales procedure.

Due to the size of this data set, indexes so defined can be calculated, and are published, not only for the United States as a whole but also for regions, states, metropolitan statistical areas (MSAs) and metropolitan divisions (subdivisions of MSAs). Obviously, the national average price trend shown here is not representative of price behavior in some "hot" local markets.

In addition, FHFA now publishes Purchase-Only Indexes for the house purchase subgroup of new mortgage transactions, excluding refinancing transactions. Nation-wide, this index is based on 4.7 million transactions over the latest 16 years. While this is still a very large statistical base, it is subject to somewhat greater revision and is less reliable for smaller geographical areas.

The FHFA price indexes are subject to revision for preceding quarters and years, because each new transaction, when reported, affects the rate of price change for all periods since the last time that the property involved in the new transaction changed hands or was refinanced. Indeed, these indexes originally indicated that prices peaked in 2007, but more recent data show a 2006 peak.

Seasonally adjusted data are also available for the purchase-only indexes. Seasonal price patterns appear to have some significance, especially for regional indexes. The seasonally adjusted indexes are not shown here because the year-over-change, calculated from not-seasonally-adjusted data, is the main focus of attention.

The FHFA indexes do not come from a random sample of house prices, and users need to consider possible sources of bias. Expensive houses are under-represented in general because the transactions are limited to conforming mortgages. This is important if the price trends for expensive houses are different.

It has also been suspected that prices of houses that are refinanced may behave differently from the prices of houses sold. However, data for the period since 1991 in which both series are available provide little support for this view. Between the end of 1991 and the peak at the end of 2006, the total House Price Index rose 121 percent, identical with the Purchase-Only Index. Since then the total index has declined 12 percent and the prices of purchased homes, 9 percent.

In addition to these government-supplied measures, new privately-developed house price indexes—not available for publication in *Business Statistics*—are now receiving regular media attention, and even provide the basis for a futures contract trading on the Chicago Mercantile Exchange. Standard & Poor's now issues S&P/Case-Shiller® Home Price Indexes each month. They cover resales only for houses at all price ranges, based on information obtained from county assessor and recorder offices. They are value-weighted, meaning that price trends for more expensive homes have greater influence on changes in the index. (The FHFA index weights price trends equally for all properties.) S&P/Case-Shiller data are only collected for 20 major metropolitan statistical areas. Series description and data can be found at <http://www.homeprice.standardandpoors.com>.

Data availability and references

Interest rates and bond yields are published weekly in the Federal Reserve's H.15 release, "Selected Interest Rates"; the release and current and historical data are available on the Federal Reserve Web site and in *B&MS* 1943 and 1976. The starting dates for individual interest rate series vary; some date back to 1911, and many begin in the 1950s and 1960s.

Stock market data are published monthly in *Economic Indicators,* and until 2014 annually in *Economic Report of the President,* both available online at <http://www.gpo.gov>. Some historical interest rate data that are not available on the Federal Reserve Web site were also taken from past *Economic Reports of the President.*

The FHFA house price indexes for the United States as a whole, regions, states, and metropolitan and sub-metropolitan groups are published every 3 months, approximately 2 months after the end of the previous quarter. The release and supporting data and explanatory material are available at <http://www.fhfa.gov>.

The OFHEO (now FHFA) and other price indexes for houses are discussed and compared in Jordan Rappaport, "Comparing Aggregate Housing Price Measures," *Business Economics,* October 2007, pp. 55-65.

CHAPTER 13: INTERNATIONAL COMPARISONS

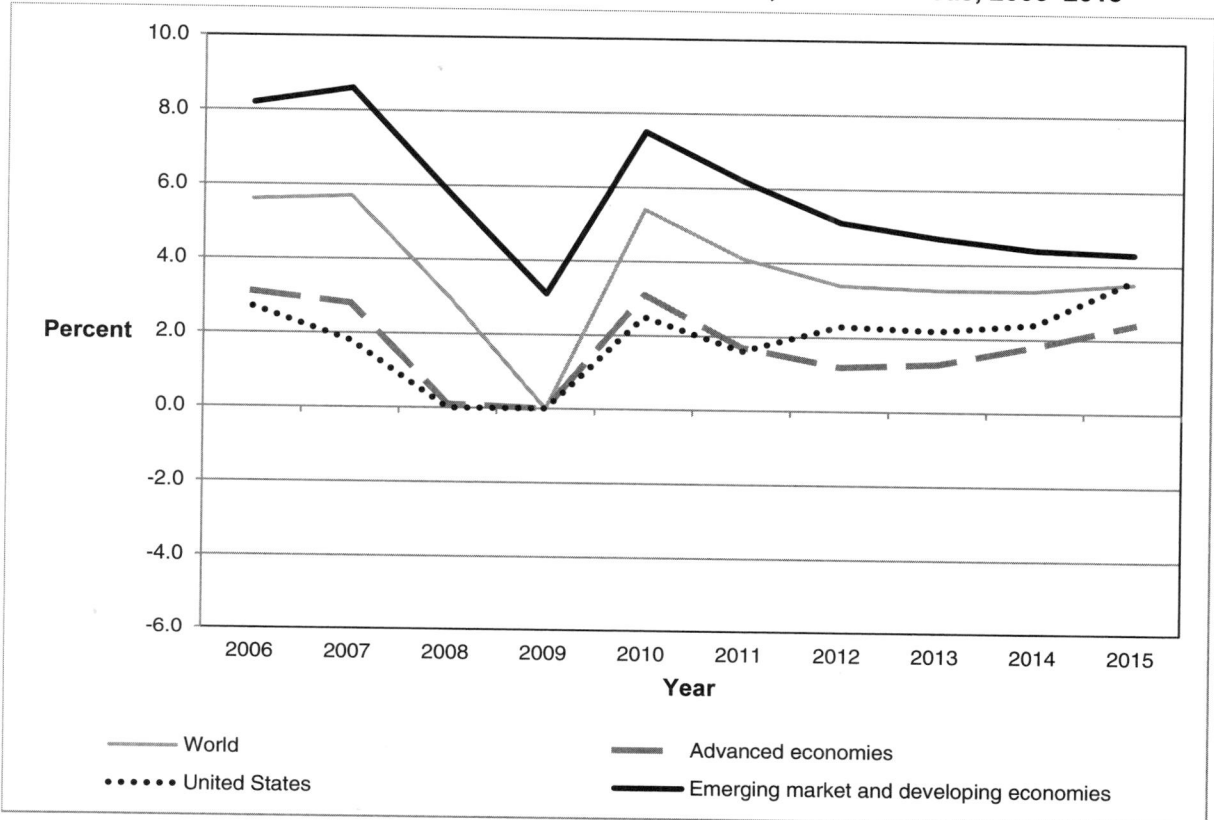

Figure 13-1: Growth Rates in Real Domestic Product, Selected Areas, 2006–2015

- The United States economy shrank 2.8 percent in 2008 but grew 2.8 percent in 2013. The International Monetary Fund (IMF) estimated that the U.S. economy would grow 2.4 percent in 2014. A robust recovery is estimated for 2015 at 3.6 percent (Table 13-1). Some economies survived the global down turn and actually experienced GDP growth. China, for example, grew 9.2 percent in 2009. However this was a slower rate than 2007. Russia suffered the largest contraction in its economy. The Russian GDP fell 7.8 percent. Italy, an original member of the European Union, experienced a decline of 5.5 percent.

- Listed in Table 13-2 are five 'major' currencies, the euro, the British pound, the Canadian dollar, the Japanese yen, and the Swiss franc. These are all major industrial countries whose currencies are freely traded on world markets. All of these measures are defined as the foreign currency price of the U.S dollar.

- Another currency listed is the Chinese yuan, which is not freely traded. China is able to control the international values of their currencies (through, for example, direct capital controls) and keep their currencies from appreciating relative to the dollar to maintain their competitiveness in the U.S. market.

Table 13-1. International Comparisons: Growth Rates in Real Gross Domestic Product

(Percent change at annual rate.)

Area and country	1996–2005 annual average	2006	2007	2008	2009	2010	2011	2012	2013	2014 [1]	2015 [1]
World	3.9	5.6	5.7	3.0	0.0	5.4	4.1	3.4	3.3	3.3	3.5
Advanced economies	2.8	3.1	2.8	0.1	-3.4	3.1	1.7	1.2	1.3	1.8	2.4
Of which:											
United States	3.4	2.7	1.8	-0.3	-2.8	2.5	1.6	2.3	2.2	2.4	3.6
Euro area [2]	2.1	3.3	3.0	0.4	-4.5	1.9	1.6	-0.7	-0.5	0.8	1.2
Germany	1.2	3.9	3.4	0.8	-5.1	3.9	3.4	0.9	0.2	1.5	1.3
France	2.3	2.4	2.4	0.2	-2.9	2.0	2.1	0.3	0.3	0.4	0.9
Italy	1.4	2.2	1.7	-1.2	-5.5	1.7	0.4	-2.4	-1.9	-0.4	0.4
Spain	3.7	4.1	3.5	0.9	-3.8	-0.2	0.1	-1.6	-1.2	1.4	2.0
Japan	1.0	1.7	2.2	-1.0	-5.5	4.7	-0.5	1.5	1.6	0.1	0.6
United Kingdom	3.4	2.8	3.4	-0.8	-5.2	1.7	1.1	0.3	1.7	2.6	2.7
Canada	3.3	2.6	2.0	1.2	-2.7	3.4	2.5	1.7	2.0	2.4	2.3
Other advanced economies	3.8	4.8	5.1	1.8	-1.0	5.9	3.3	2.0	2.2	2.8	3.0
Emerging and developing economies	5.2	8.2	8.6	5.8	3.1	7.5	6.2	5.1	4.7	4.4	4.3
Regional groups:											
Commonwealth of Independent States [3]	4.2	8.9	9.0	5.4	-6.2	5.0	4.8	3.4	2.2	0.9	-1.4
Russia	3.8	8.2	8.5	5.2	-7.8	4.5	4.3	3.4	1.3	0.6	-3.0
Excluding Russia	5.1	11.0	10.3	5.6	-2.3	6.1	6.1	3.6	4.3	1.5	2.4
Emerging and Developing Asia	6.9	10.1	11.2	7.1	7.5	9.5	7.7	6.7	6.6	6.5	6.4
China	9.2	12.7	14.2	9.6	9.2	10.4	9.3	7.7	7.8	7.4	6.8
India [4]	6.4	9.3	9.8	3.9	8.5	10.3	6.6	4.7	5.0	5.8	6.3
ASEAN-5 [5]	3.6	5.5	6.2	4.9	2.1	6.9	4.7	6.2	5.2	4.5	5.2
Emerging and Developing Europe	4.0	6.4	5.3	3.2	-3.6	4.7	5.5	1.4	2.8	2.7	2.9
Latin America and the Caribbean	2.9	5.7	5.8	3.9	-1.3	6.0	4.5	2.9	2.8	1.2	1.3
Brazil	2.4	4.0	6.1	5.2	-0.3	7.5	2.7	1.0	2.5	0.1	0.3
Mexico	3.4	5.0	3.1	1.4	-4.7	5.1	4.0	4.0	1.4	2.1	3.2
Middle East, North Africa, Afghanistan, and Pakistan	4.9	6.7	5.8	5.2	2.3	5.3	4.4	4.8	2.2	2.8	3.3
Saudi Arabia	3.3	5.6	6.0	8.4	1.8	7.4	8.6	5.8	2.7	3.6	2.8
Sub-Saharan Africa	5.4	7.0	7.9	6.3	4.1	6.9	5.1	4.4	5.2	4.8	4.9
Nigeria	9.6	8.8	9.6	8.6	9.6	10.6	4.9	4.3	5.4	6.1	4.8
South Africa	3.3	5.6	5.5	3.6	-1.5	3.1	3.6	2.5	2.2	1.4	2.1

[1]All figures are forecasts as published by the International Monetary Fund.
[2]In 2015, Euro area consists of: Austria, Belgium, Cyprus, Estonia, Finland, France, Germany, Greece, Ireland, Italy, Latvia, Luxembourg, Malta, Netherlands, Portugal, Slovak Republic, Slovenia, and Spain.
[3]Includes Georgia and Turkmenistan, which are not members of the Commonwealth of Independent States but are included for reasons of geography and similarity in economic structure.
[4]Data and forecasts are presented on a fiscal year basis and output growth is based on GDP at market prices.
[5]Consists of Indonesia, Malaysia, Philippines, Thailand, and Vietnam.

Table 13-2. Foreign Exchange Rates

(Not seasonally adjusted.)

Year and month	Foreign currency per U.S. dollar						
	Canadian dollar	Chinese yuan	European currency unit	German mark	Japanese yen	Switzerland franc	British pound
1971	1.0099	. . .	. . .	3.4673	348.05	4.1158	0.4091
1972	0.9908	. . .	. . .	3.1889	303.11	3.8181	0.3995
1973	1.0002	. . .	. . .	2.6719	271.40	3.1698	0.4077
1974	0.9781	. . .	. . .	2.5873	291.94	2.9791	0.4273
1975	1.0173	. . .	. . .	2.4614	296.77	2.5834	0.4501
1976	0.9861	. . .	. . .	2.5184	296.48	2.5003	0.5541
1977	1.0635	. . .	. . .	2.3225	268.38	2.4038	0.5731
1978	1.1408	. . .	. . .	2.0089	210.46	1.7899	0.5213
1979	1.1716	. . .	. . .	1.8331	219.21	1.6635	0.4712
1980	1.1694	. . .	. . .	1.8183	226.58	1.6776	0.4302
1981	1.1989	1.7090	. . .	2.2606	220.45	1.9647	0.4940
1982	1.2339	1.8973	. . .	2.4281	249.05	2.0318	0.5721
1983	1.2326	1.9809	. . .	2.5545	237.45	2.1004	0.6597
1984	1.2952	2.3346	. . .	2.8483	237.59	2.3517	0.7481
1985	1.3659	2.9446	. . .	2.9443	238.47	2.4576	0.7708
1986	1.3898	3.4610	. . .	2.1711	168.50	1.7988	0.6813
1987	1.3262	3.7314	. . .	1.7976	144.62	1.4916	0.6098
1988	1.2309	3.7314	. . .	1.7561	128.14	1.4633	0.5614
1989	1.1841	3.7690	. . .	1.8792	137.99	1.6354	0.6104
1990	1.1670	4.7955	. . .	1.6159	144.82	1.3898	0.5605
1991	1.1460	5.3348	. . .	1.6585	134.51	1.4338	0.5658
1992	1.2088	5.5266	. . .	1.5624	126.75	1.4069	0.5662
1993	1.2902	5.7767	. . .	1.6537	111.23	1.4780	0.6660
1994	1.3659	8.6401	. . .	1.6219	102.20	1.3668	0.6528
1995	1.3727	8.3709	. . .	1.4331	94.11	1.1822	0.6335
1996	1.3637	8.3387	. . .	1.5049	108.80	1.2364	0.6407
1997	1.3849	8.3193	. . .	1.7339	121.09	1.4508	0.6106
1998	1.4836	8.3006	. . .	1.7593	130.82	1.4497	0.6034
1999	1.4858	8.2783	0.9375	1.8359	113.71	1.5027	0.6184
2000	1.4855	8.2784	1.0830	. . .	107.82	1.6899	0.6598
2001	1.5490	8.2770	1.1167	. . .	121.52	1.6880	0.6946
2002	1.5706	8.2771	1.0579	. . .	125.27	1.5571	0.6656
2003	1.4012	8.2772	0.8836	. . .	115.92	1.3452	0.6117
2004	1.3016	8.2768	0.8039	. . .	108.16	1.2428	0.5456
2005	1.2115	8.1940	0.8034	. . .	110.14	1.2462	0.5493
2006	1.1344	7.9720	0.7962	. . .	116.35	1.2535	0.5425
2007	1.0742	7.6059	0.7294	. . .	117.77	1.1999	0.4995
2008	1.0668	6.9482	0.6801	. . .	103.38	1.0829	0.5392
2009	1.1414	6.8307	0.7177	. . .	93.60	1.0861	0.6389
2010	1.0301	6.7690	0.7532	. . .	87.75	1.0426	0.6466
2011	0.9890	6.4633	0.7184	. . .	79.71	0.8876	0.6236
2012	0.9994	6.3085	0.7774	. . .	79.81	0.9374	0.6307
2013	1.0300	6.1480	0.7527	. . .	97.56	0.9266	0.6391
2014	1.1043	6.1620	0.7520	. . .	105.74	0.9147	0.6066
2013							
January	0.9921	6.2215	0.7517	. . .	89.06	0.9234	0.6264
February	1.0098	6.2323	0.7492	. . .	93.00	0.9212	0.6462
March	1.0244	6.2154	0.7720	. . .	94.77	0.9466	0.6631
April	1.0187	6.1861	0.7678	. . .	97.76	0.9366	0.6531
May	1.0196	6.1416	0.7702	. . .	100.92	0.9557	0.6537
June	1.0314	6.1342	0.7577	. . .	97.24	0.9331	0.6455
July	1.0402	6.1343	0.7641	. . .	99.67	0.9449	0.6588
August	1.0407	6.1213	0.7511	. . .	97.81	0.9261	0.6450
September	1.0342	6.1198	0.7483	. . .	99.21	0.9231	0.6295
October	1.0363	6.1032	0.7328	. . .	97.77	0.9025	0.6212
November	1.0486	6.0929	0.7412	. . .	100.07	0.9129	0.6211
December	1.0639	6.0738	0.7295	. . .	103.46	0.8933	0.6104
2014							
January	1.0940	6.0509	0.7343	. . .	103.76	0.9038	0.6072
February	1.1054	6.0816	0.7318	. . .	102.13	0.8937	0.6039
March	1.1107	6.1729	0.7232	. . .	102.34	0.8805	0.6015
April	1.0992	6.2246	0.7241	. . .	102.46	0.8828	0.5971
May	1.0894	6.2380	0.7279	. . .	101.77	0.8883	0.5938
June	1.0830	6.2306	0.7356	. . .	102.06	0.8958	0.5914
July	1.0739	6.1984	0.7389	. . .	101.74	0.8978	0.5860
August	1.0926	6.1541	0.7510	. . .	102.94	0.9098	0.5988
September	1.1011	6.1382	0.7759	. . .	107.43	0.9370	0.6139
October	1.1212	6.1251	0.7888	. . .	108.03	0.9528	0.6221
November	1.1325	6.1249	0.8017	. . .	116.30	0.9642	0.6341
December	1.1532	6.1886	0.8111	. . .	119.32	0.9753	0.6392

. . . = Not available.

NOTES AND DEFINITIONS, CHAPTER 13

Table 13-1

International Comparisons: Growth Rates in Real Gross Domestic Product

SOURCE: ECONOMIC REPORT OF THE PRESIDENT, ANNUAL REPORT OF THE COUNCIL OF ECONOMIC ADVISERS, FEBRUARY 2015

Table 13-1 is reprinted from the February 2015 *Annual Report of the U.S. Council of Economic Advisers*, where it appears as Table B-4. It is based on data from the Department of Commerce's Bureau of Economic Analysis (BEA) and the International Monetary Fund. The report is found at <www.whitehouse.gov/administration/eop/cea/economic-report-of-the-President>.

Table 13-2
Foreign Exchange Rates

SOURCE: BOARD OF GOVERNORS OF THE FEDERAL RESERVE SYSTEM

Definitions and notes on the data

This table shows measures of the U.S. dollar relative to the currencies of some important individual countries and also relative to average values for major groups of countries. In *Business Statistics*, all of these measures are defined as the foreign currency price of the U.S. dollar. When the measure is relatively high, the dollar is relatively strong—but less competitive (in the sense of price competition)—and the other currency or group of currencies named in the measure is relatively weak and more competitive.

For consistency, this definition is used in *Business Statistics* even in the case of currencies that are commonly quoted in the financial press and elsewhere as dollars per foreign currency unit instead of foreign currency units per dollar. Notably, this is the case for the euro and for the British pound. Where *Business Statistics* shows the average 2014 value of the dollar as 0.7520 euros, the more usual statement—and the one found on the Federal Reserve release used as a source for this information—is that in 2010, the euro was worth on average $1.3297. (The value shown in the table is 1 divided by 1.3261, with slight rounding differences.) Where *Business Statistics* shows the 2014 value of the dollar as 0.6066 British pounds, the more usual statement is that the pound was worth $1.6484. The Canadian dollar is also sometimes quoted relative to the U.S. dollar, rather than as shown here.

The definition of the dollar's value used in *Business Statistics* is the most useful for economic analysis from the U.S. point of view and for foreign tourists in the United States. For American tourists overseas, it is easier to use the inverse of this measure, the value of the other currency; for example, the traveler in Paris can more easily translate prices into dollars by multiplying by the dollar value of the euro than by dividing by the euro value of the dollar.

The foreign exchange rates shown are averages of the daily noon buying rates for cable transfers in New York City certified for customs purposes by the Federal Reserve Bank of New York.

The introduction of the euro in January 1999 as the common currency for 11 European countries—Austria, Belgium, Finland, France, Germany, Ireland, Italy, Luxembourg, Netherlands, Portugal, and Spain—marked a major change in the international currency system, and the use of the euro subsequently spread to eight more countries. Greece entered the European Monetary Union (EMU) in January 2001 and Slovenia entered in January 2007. Cyprus and Malta joined in January 2008 and the Slovak Republic in January 2009. The Baltic countries of Estonia, Latvia and Lithuania converted to the euro in 2011, 2014 and 2015 respectively. The euro is also the national currency in Monaco, the Vatican City and San Marino, and is the de facto currency in Andorra, Kosovo, and Montenegro. The values of the currencies of these countries no longer fluctuate relative to each other, but the value of the euro still fluctuates relative to the dollar and to currencies for countries outside the EMU. The currency and coins of the individual countries continued to circulate from 1999 through the end of 2001, but in January 2002, new euro currency and coins were introduced, replacing the currency and coins of the individual countries. Once a country has entered the monetary union, its values relative to the <u>dollar</u> will continue to fluctuate—but only due to fluctuations in the value of the euro relative to the dollar.

There is no fully satisfactory historical equivalent to the euro. For comparisons over time, the Federal Reserve Board uses a "restated German mark," derived simply by dividing each historical value of the mark by the euro conversion factor, 1.95583. The G-10 dollar index described below includes five of the currencies that later merged into the euro, but also includes the currencies of Canada, Japan, the United Kingdom, Switzerland, and Sweden.

Data availability and references

Current press releases, historical data, and information on weights and methods for exchange rates and exchange rate indexes are available on the Federal Reserve Web site at <http://www.federalreserve.gov/>; go to "Economic Research and Data", then "Statistical Releases and Historical Data," and select the G.5 release. The dollar value indexes are described in the article "Indexes of the Foreign Exchange Value of the Dollar," *Federal Reserve Bulletin* (Winter 2005), also available on the Federal Reserve Web site.

Additional information on exchange rates can be found on the Federal Reserve Bank of St. Louis Web site at <http://www.stls.frb.org/fred/data/exchange.html>.

PART B

INDUSTRY PROFILES

CHAPTER 14: PRODUCT AND INCOME BY INDUSTRY

Figure 14-1: Growth Rates, Industry Groups and Selected Industries, 2005–2014

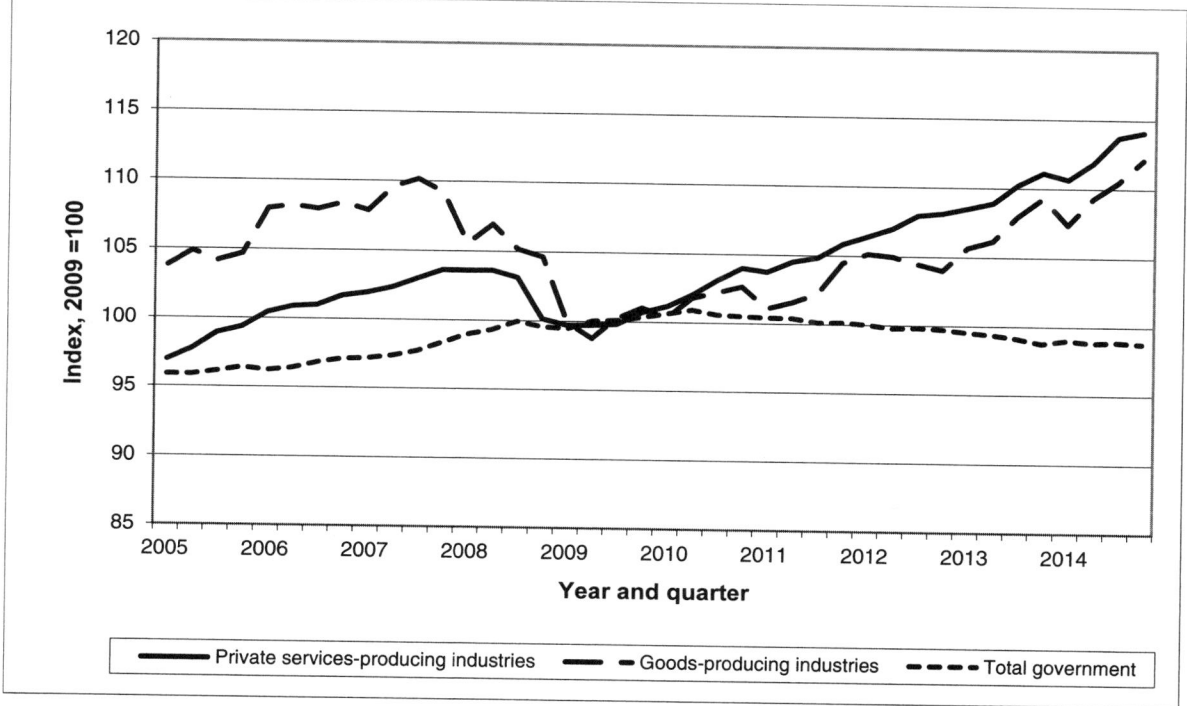

- BEA now publishes quarterly measures of GDP by industrial origin, in both current-dollar and real (quantity) terms. Industry output, sometimes referred to as "gross product originating in the industry," is here termed "value added". Figure 14-1 shows quantity indexes for real value added in the three major industry groupings of GDP. (Tables 14-1A and 14-2A show 22 component industries as well.) The quantity indexes, as well as the price indexes, all have, for statistical convenience, a base year of 2009, which happens to be the low point of the 2007–2009 Great Recession.

- Private services-producing industries, which accounted for two-thirds of total GDP in 2014, display less cyclical swing and more real growth than the goods sector, which was 20 percent of the total. Government production—the other 13 percent of total GDP—was comparatively stable, but this is an incomplete measurement of the counter-cyclical impact of government, as it does not include the effects of changes in tax receipts and payments. (Tables 14-1A and 14-2A)

- Table 14-3 can be used to assess the share of each industry group in total gross domestic factor income and the shares paid to employees and accruing to land and capital in each industry. For these purposes factor income is a better measure than the BEA definition of value added because value added includes, but factor income excludes, taxes on production and imports.

- In private goods-producing industries in 2013, employee compensation was 46.1 percent of gross factor income. (Table 14-3)

Table 14-1. Gross Domestic Product (Value Added) by Industry

(Billions of dollars.)

| Year | Total gross domestic product | Private industries | | | | | Manufacturing | | | | | | | |
		Total	Agriculture, forestry, fishing, and hunting	Mining	Utilities	Construc-tion	Durable goods	Nondurable goods	Wholesale trade	Retail trade	Transpor-tation and ware-housing	Information	Finance and insurance	Real estate and rental and leasing
1997	8 608.5	7 459.4	108.8	95.1	172.1	340.7	827.3	562.7	530.2	588.4	256.1	395.7	578.6	1 044.5
1998	9 089.2	7 894.0	99.9	81.4	163.9	380.5	852.7	582.4	565.5	635.8	278.2	435.5	639.8	1 083.2
1999	9 660.6	8 403.2	92.8	84.3	180.1	418.4	876.9	616.8	585.9	661.7	288.3	486.1	679.5	1 173.5
2000	10 284.8	8 956.0	98.5	110.5	180.2	462.3	927.0	628.4	625.0	695.6	305.6	472.2	750.4	1 241.9
2001	10 621.8	9 223.5	100.0	125.2	184.0	488.0	835.1	643.4	617.9	713.5	307.8	501.2	817.5	1 339.2
2002	10 977.5	9 499.5	95.8	113.4	180.1	494.9	834.7	638.0	617.2	738.3	305.3	549.5	835.2	1 411.2
2003	11 510.7	9 951.0	116.1	140.1	187.1	527.1	865.9	665.2	647.1	775.8	320.9	564.0	866.8	1 464.9
2004	12 274.9	10 628.0	142.7	167.6	202.7	587.5	908.5	710.7	703.5	802.7	351.1	620.8	890.3	1 534.0
2005	13 093.7	11 366.3	128.6	226.6	201.4	654.1	959.5	744.7	759.4	848.8	375.1	641.6	991.8	1 649.2
2006	13 855.9	12 045.4	128.3	273.4	230.0	698.2	1 005.4	798.9	815.7	878.1	407.6	649.0	1 048.8	1 721.9
2007	14 477.6	12 572.4	142.0	314.0	235.1	715.0	1 030.0	824.3	860.8	877.6	409.6	702.4	1 040.5	1 836.6
2008	14 718.6	12 716.2	154.5	401.5	237.5	653.0	994.4	819.7	877.8	856.1	422.4	730.5	907.2	1 897.3
2009	14 418.7	12 353.0	137.7	290.3	250.8	577.3	874.3	852.4	822.8	842.1	398.8	705.3	969.3	1 904.8
2010	14 964.4	12 826.5	160.2	331.7	267.0	541.6	956.6	874.0	868.5	868.8	425.1	730.2	1 005.8	1 945.7
2011	15 517.9	13 348.4	197.2	398.6	272.0	546.6	1 003.8	903.5	907.3	891.7	446.9	728.4	1 038.0	2 014.4
2012	16 163.2	13 972.0	195.3	406.7	264.6	586.7	1 054.3	940.3	965.7	932.6	464.1	741.6	1 125.8	2 092.4
2013	16 768.1	14 556.4	226.6	439.4	276.7	619.9	1 088.5	940.0	998.5	971.4	481.4	779.2	1 206.9	2 174.8
2014	17 418.9	15 175.3	210.2	461.3	291.3	652.7	1 135.9	954.8	1 037.7	1 014.0	506.2	808.0	1 261.3	2 265.8
2006														
1st quarter	13 648.9	11 867.8	123.3	268.2	223.4	700.1	1 005.5	783.6	796.9	875.6	399.4	630.7	1 046.6	1 676.2
2nd quarter ...	13 799.8	12 000.5	126.9	273.1	229.9	700.3	1 005.5	803.5	811.9	878.1	407.0	649.4	1 040.7	1 699.7
3rd quarter ...	13 908.5	12 088.1	130.2	277.5	235.2	693.0	995.6	810.0	822.4	879.7	409.4	662.1	1 045.0	1 732.7
4th quarter	14 066.4	12 225.4	133.1	274.8	231.4	699.6	1 014.9	798.3	831.5	878.9	414.5	653.8	1 063.1	1 778.9
2007														
1st quarter	14 233.2	12 356.9	140.7	280.9	232.2	713.7	1 010.2	795.2	850.4	876.1	403.6	669.0	1 082.9	1 797.3
2nd quarter ...	14 422.3	12 528.8	136.7	313.9	237.0	721.6	1 030.0	834.0	861.2	878.8	411.1	691.9	1 055.7	1 812.9
3rd quarter ...	14 569.7	12 654.4	139.0	319.2	239.2	719.5	1 046.7	825.3	862.5	878.8	407.1	716.9	1 037.4	1 848.8
4th quarter	14 685.3	12 749.5	151.6	342.0	231.9	705.1	1 033.2	842.7	869.3	876.7	416.5	731.7	986.1	1 887.3
2008														
1st quarter	14 668.4	12 698.2	165.1	362.9	222.1	670.5	1 009.2	805.3	870.6	850.8	413.0	726.1	1 010.8	1 886.4
2nd quarter ...	14 813.0	12 822.4	158.6	436.9	237.4	655.7	1 006.4	826.1	882.4	858.5	418.4	744.0	953.1	1 895.5
3rd quarter ...	14 843.0	12 827.9	149.5	443.4	246.4	645.3	998.7	846.2	887.0	863.7	423.7	743.8	889.7	1 897.3
4th quarter	14 549.9	12 516.2	144.9	362.6	244.1	640.4	963.5	801.1	871.3	851.5	434.4	708.0	775.3	1 909.9
2009														
1st quarter	14 383.9	12 337.3	130.3	301.5	256.5	606.3	891.7	819.4	828.8	837.1	405.6	703.1	909.7	1 914.6
2nd quarter ...	14 340.4	12 277.7	132.2	275.9	246.3	580.8	861.7	837.8	811.8	837.7	393.1	699.7	980.6	1 902.4
3rd quarter ...	14 384.1	12 312.7	138.0	280.0	243.9	570.5	858.9	865.8	814.0	836.3	393.4	698.6	990.2	1 903.8
4th quarter	14 566.5	12 484.3	150.1	304.0	256.4	551.5	884.9	886.8	836.7	857.4	403.2	719.9	996.5	1 898.4
2010														
1st quarter	14 681.1	12 568.1	149.3	329.6	267.4	533.3	903.0	881.2	844.4	854.6	407.1	714.7	995.7	1 919.3
2nd quarter ...	14 888.6	12 747.0	156.3	319.5	263.2	543.3	947.3	866.9	861.5	871.7	420.5	721.8	1 008.0	1 942.6
3rd quarter ...	15 057.7	12 911.6	164.0	326.6	267.8	544.8	980.7	867.6	884.3	871.8	433.4	742.5	996.2	1 948.0
4th quarter	15 230.2	13 079.4	171.2	351.3	269.6	545.1	995.4	880.2	883.6	877.1	439.5	741.7	1 023.4	1 973.0
2011														
1st quarter	15 238.4	13 080.0	197.9	368.1	260.6	528.7	990.7	874.0	886.4	878.7	439.8	724.5	1 029.3	1 961.2
2nd quarter ...	15 460.9	13 289.1	192.3	402.3	273.7	542.6	991.0	908.0	904.6	885.1	445.7	731.5	1 020.1	2 003.1
3rd quarter ...	15 587.1	13 410.9	200.4	402.6	274.0	552.8	1 000.6	913.8	906.7	893.8	446.2	726.3	1 047.0	2 024.5
4th quarter	15 785.3	13 613.7	198.3	421.5	279.9	562.4	1 033.1	918.0	931.4	909.2	455.8	731.4	1 055.7	2 068.8
2012														
1st quarter	15 956.5	13 769.0	197.4	415.7	257.2	578.2	1 041.5	935.7	953.6	924.4	459.2	735.7	1 059.3	2 061.0
2nd quarter ...	16 094.7	13 907.6	196.9	397.4	265.4	584.0	1 056.6	938.4	959.7	928.5	466.0	751.4	1 116.8	2 080.0
3rd quarter ...	16 268.9	14 077.8	191.7	401.3	268.6	588.8	1 061.7	959.6	975.6	937.4	466.9	751.3	1 147.7	2 113.6
4th quarter	16 332.5	14 133.4	195.1	412.4	267.1	595.6	1 057.3	927.4	973.8	940.0	464.4	727.9	1 179.3	2 115.0
2013														
1st quarter	16 502.4	14 297.3	235.1	416.0	274.2	603.4	1 070.4	940.9	981.3	957.9	474.2	762.5	1 168.2	2 138.8
2nd quarter ...	16 619.2	14 408.7	226.2	434.4	276.8	612.6	1 076.2	920.6	984.8	960.7	475.0	770.8	1 200.4	2 149.4
3rd quarter ...	16 872.3	14 661.7	229.6	460.0	275.4	626.6	1 095.0	928.7	1 008.4	977.6	480.8	779.1	1 220.6	2 193.9
4th quarter	17 078.3	14 857.9	215.7	447.3	280.3	637.1	1 112.4	969.6	1 019.5	989.3	495.7	804.3	1 238.5	2 217.1
2014														
1st quarter	17 044.0	14 813.6	200.6	459.9	293.8	634.7	1 103.8	941.6	1 012.9	984.8	492.4	796.7	1 209.2	2 219.5
2nd quarter ...	17 328.2	15 089.0	222.5	474.3	288.0	643.7	1 127.0	958.1	1 033.0	1 009.6	501.2	802.6	1 240.5	2 248.3
3rd quarter ...	17 599.8	15 352.3	208.9	476.1	289.5	659.8	1 152.0	963.4	1 044.2	1 022.2	513.0	813.1	1 308.8	2 285.3
4th quarter	17 703.7	15 446.3	209.0	435.1	294.1	672.7	1 160.7	956.2	1 060.6	1 039.4	518.2	819.5	1 286.5	2 310.0

Table 14-1. Gross Domestic Product (Value Added) by Industry—*Continued*

(Billions of dollars.)

Year	Professional, scientific, and technical services	Management of companies and enterprises	Administrative and waste management services	Educational services	Health care and social assistance	Arts, entertainment, and recreation	Accommodation and food services	Other services except government	Total government	Federal	State and local	Private goods-producing industries	Private services-producing industries	Information-communications-technology-producing industries[1]
1997	503.3	126.7	215.5	71.8	509.4	80.4	221.3	230.8	1 149.1	389.4	759.7	1 934.7	5 524.7	507.6
1998	546.8	141.0	231.6	74.5	531.2	82.8	238.5	248.8	1 195.2	394.6	800.6	1 996.9	5 897.1	540.5
1999	600.2	150.3	252.5	80.4	561.4	90.4	262.9	260.9	1 257.5	404.6	852.8	2 089.2	6 314.0	571.6
2000	656.0	173.2	281.9	86.1	595.4	99.0	286.8	279.9	1 328.8	421.9	906.9	2 226.7	6 729.3	624.0
2001	691.6	174.4	295.5	91.7	642.0	96.6	292.7	266.5	1 398.3	429.3	969.0	2 191.7	7 031.9	605.2
2002	718.2	176.6	300.7	98.6	692.7	103.8	309.4	285.9	1 478.0	460.8	1 017.2	2 176.8	7 322.7	623.1
2003	739.5	187.5	321.3	106.5	738.0	111.1	321.1	284.9	1 559.7	496.2	1 063.5	2 314.4	7 636.6	659.3
2004	787.4	206.7	346.5	116.7	788.8	118.0	343.5	298.5	1 646.9	523.7	1 123.3	2 516.9	8 111.0	713.9
2005	842.8	219.3	380.5	121.0	828.9	122.3	359.0	311.7	1 727.4	550.4	1 177.1	2 713.5	8 652.8	762.4
2006	903.7	238.5	399.4	129.9	883.0	130.3	379.7	325.7	1 810.4	575.2	1 235.2	2 904.2	9 141.2	800.3
2007	967.3	259.5	430.4	138.7	925.9	137.6	394.5	330.5	1 905.2	602.4	1 302.9	3 025.3	9 547.1	851.7
2008	1 053.3	261.5	438.2	149.3	996.0	140.1	394.9	330.8	2 002.4	633.3	1 369.2	3 023.1	9 693.1	884.0
2009	1 000.4	247.1	413.6	163.0	1 051.0	138.8	383.5	329.5	2 065.8	664.0	1 401.8	2 732.0	9 621.0	852.4
2010	1 022.0	268.2	439.5	169.3	1 079.2	144.4	396.2	332.4	2 137.9	701.1	1 436.7	2 864.1	9 962.4	876.3
2011	1 074.1	281.0	457.5	175.5	1 111.6	147.5	413.9	338.9	2 169.5	716.3	1 453.2	3 049.8	10 298.6	894.1
2012	1 127.0	306.2	484.2	181.2	1 152.3	155.9	439.5	355.7	2 191.2	717.6	1 473.6	3 183.2	10 788.7	919.1
2013	1 154.8	323.2	503.8	184.6	1 195.8	163.6	458.1	369.3	2 211.6	704.3	1 507.3	3 314.4	11 242.0	. . .
2014	1 220.8	345.0	532.5	191.1	1 244.3	174.6	482.5	385.3	2 243.6	704.8	1 538.8	3 415.0	11 760.3	. . .
2006														
1st quarter	889.0	233.3	395.8	127.2	867.7	128.4	375.2	321.7	1 781.1	571.5	1 209.6	2 880.7	8 987.1	. . .
2nd quarter	896.6	237.7	396.4	129.2	880.3	129.9	378.4	325.9	1 799.3	573.9	1 225.4	2 909.3	9 091.2	. . .
3rd quarter	905.7	238.1	398.5	130.7	885.9	130.0	379.9	326.5	1 820.4	576.4	1 243.9	2 906.3	9 181.9	. . .
4th quarter	923.6	244.8	406.8	132.6	898.1	132.8	385.3	328.8	1 841.0	579.0	1 261.9	2 920.6	9 304.8	. . .
2007														
1st quarter	935.1	257.2	414.9	135.5	905.7	135.7	390.0	330.5	1 876.3	594.0	1 282.3	2 940.7	9 416.2	. . .
2nd quarter	947.3	257.9	425.4	137.1	917.1	136.8	392.2	330.0	1 893.6	600.0	1 293.6	3 036.1	9 492.6	. . .
3rd quarter	978.9	260.4	436.5	139.5	932.3	138.7	396.2	331.3	1 915.3	606.7	1 308.6	3 049.8	9 604.6	. . .
4th quarter	1 008.0	262.7	444.5	142.5	948.5	139.3	399.5	330.3	1 935.8	608.7	1 327.1	3 074.7	9 674.8	. . .
2008														
1st quarter	1 028.9	259.1	438.9	144.9	970.4	138.8	395.2	329.2	1 970.2	622.9	1 347.3	3 013.1	9 685.1	. . .
2nd quarter	1 052.3	260.9	438.9	147.3	985.8	139.5	395.7	329.2	1 990.5	630.2	1 360.3	3 083.6	9 738.8	. . .
3rd quarter	1 068.7	263.6	439.1	151.1	1 003.1	140.1	396.5	330.8	2 015.1	637.8	1 377.4	3 083.1	9 744.7	. . .
4th quarter	1 063.6	262.5	436.0	153.9	1 024.8	142.1	392.2	334.1	2 033.8	642.1	1 391.6	2 912.5	9 603.7	. . .
2009														
1st quarter	1 025.0	239.6	418.5	161.1	1 035.6	139.2	383.2	330.4	2 046.7	655.6	1 391.1	2 749.1	9 588.1	. . .
2nd quarter	999.6	245.5	411.0	162.6	1 047.7	137.9	382.5	329.7	2 062.7	662.4	1 400.3	2 688.5	9 589.3	. . .
3rd quarter	991.0	250.8	409.0	163.4	1 053.9	139.3	383.6	328.4	2 071.5	666.5	1 405.0	2 713.1	9 599.6	. . .
4th quarter	985.8	252.7	416.0	164.9	1 066.0	138.9	384.5	329.6	2 082.2	671.4	1 410.8	2 777.4	9 706.9	. . .
2010														
1st quarter	997.8	260.1	427.2	166.8	1 061.2	141.3	387.3	326.6	2 113.0	690.8	1 422.2	2 796.5	9 771.6	. . .
2nd quarter	1 010.9	264.3	436.2	168.8	1 074.6	144.1	394.6	330.9	2 141.6	704.1	1 437.5	2 833.3	9 913.7	. . .
3rd quarter	1 032.4	269.8	444.0	170.3	1 087.1	145.1	399.9	335.4	2 146.1	703.7	1 442.3	2 883.7	10 027.9	. . .
4th quarter	1 046.9	278.7	450.6	171.1	1 093.9	147.4	403.1	336.8	2 150.8	705.9	1 444.9	2 943.1	10 136.3	. . .
2011														
1st quarter	1 053.0	281.2	450.4	173.7	1 095.7	146.1	405.4	334.6	2 158.3	711.6	1 446.8	2 959.5	10 120.5	. . .
2nd quarter	1 072.3	281.6	455.3	174.9	1 108.3	147.5	412.0	337.4	2 171.8	716.0	1 455.8	3 036.2	10 252.9	. . .
3rd quarter	1 082.1	279.7	460.5	176.6	1 117.5	149.9	416.0	340.1	2 176.2	718.4	1 457.8	3 070.1	10 340.9	. . .
4th quarter	1 088.9	281.7	463.8	176.7	1 124.8	146.5	422.3	343.4	2 171.7	719.2	1 452.4	3 133.3	10 480.3	. . .
2012														
1st quarter	1 113.9	299.9	478.7	180.2	1 140.6	152.8	434.3	349.8	2 187.5	721.8	1 465.7	3 168.5	10 600.6	. . .
2nd quarter	1 119.6	296.5	480.5	180.7	1 143.9	154.5	437.2	353.5	2 187.1	719.7	1 467.4	3 173.4	10 734.2	. . .
3rd quarter	1 126.0	306.8	487.8	181.5	1 155.0	156.8	440.7	358.6	2 191.1	716.8	1 474.3	3 203.3	10 874.5	. . .
4th quarter	1 148.5	321.6	489.9	182.7	1 169.7	159.4	445.6	360.8	2 199.0	712.3	1 486.8	3 187.8	10 945.6	. . .
2013														
1st quarter	1 126.8	315.8	491.6	181.7	1 185.2	158.6	450.6	364.2	2 205.1	709.2	1 496.0	3 265.8	11 031.5	. . .
2nd quarter	1 144.6	321.8	498.5	183.7	1 189.7	162.0	453.9	366.8	2 210.4	705.8	1 504.6	3 269.9	11 138.8	. . .
3rd quarter	1 168.6	327.0	508.8	185.5	1 199.7	164.9	460.9	370.6	2 210.6	698.8	1 511.9	3 339.8	11 321.9	. . .
4th quarter	1 179.2	328.0	516.2	187.4	1 208.5	168.8	467.1	375.7	2 220.4	703.5	1 516.9	3 382.2	11 475.7	. . .
2014														
1st quarter	1 188.2	335.2	517.9	188.5	1 218.2	170.5	467.9	377.5	2 230.3	705.1	1 525.2	3 340.6	11 473.1	. . .
2nd quarter	1 210.9	344.0	530.2	189.1	1 235.6	172.6	477.5	380.1	2 239.2	704.8	1 534.4	3 425.7	11 663.3	. . .
3rd quarter	1 232.0	347.1	537.0	192.5	1 252.7	176.9	488.3	389.5	2 247.5	703.9	1 543.6	3 460.1	11 892.2	. . .
4th quarter	1 252.3	353.6	544.8	194.2	1 270.6	178.4	496.3	394.0	2 257.4	705.5	1 551.9	3 433.6	12 012.7	. . .

[1]Consists of computer and electronic products manufacturing; publishing, including software; information and data processing services; and computer systems design and related services.
. . . = Not available.

Table 14-2. Chain-Type Quantity Indexes for Value Added by Industry

(New Series, 2009 = 100.)

Year	Total gross domestic product	Private industries												
							Manufacturing							
		Total	Agriculture, forestry, fishing, and hunting	Mining	Utilities	Construction	Durable goods	Nondurable goods	Wholesale trade	Retail trade	Transportation and warehousing	Information	Finance and insurance	Real estate and rental and leasing
1997	76.5	76.3	66.1	81.5	106.4	119.0	71.5	92.5	75.4	79.8	89.6	53.0	60.1	74.2
1998	79.9	79.9	63.6	85.6	101.5	123.9	77.4	92.5	81.7	87.3	92.9	58.0	67.0	75.0
1999	83.7	84.1	66.9	81.8	118.8	128.4	82.8	95.5	84.8	90.2	93.7	64.5	73.5	78.9
2000	87.1	87.6	76.8	72.6	121.2	133.2	92.2	94.7	90.0	92.9	95.3	63.1	80.8	80.8
2001	88.0	88.5	72.9	84.9	102.7	130.8	86.3	94.0	91.7	95.6	88.9	66.6	89.0	84.2
2002	89.5	90.0	75.7	83.4	104.7	126.7	88.0	93.8	92.0	99.2	86.1	73.1	89.4	85.7
2003	92.0	92.5	83.0	74.4	101.7	129.0	93.9	96.6	97.5	104.8	89.6	75.1	90.0	86.9
2004	95.5	96.2	88.2	73.7	106.6	133.5	100.0	102.7	102.8	106.3	98.4	83.4	89.8	89.2
2005	98.7	99.7	92.4	73.3	99.9	133.9	106.4	99.8	108.1	109.8	103.9	88.0	97.8	93.8
2006	101.4	102.6	96.2	81.2	105.3	130.5	113.8	102.3	112.2	110.4	110.3	90.1	102.0	95.4
2007	103.2	104.2	83.0	86.6	106.6	125.6	118.6	104.2	116.0	107.4	108.9	98.9	99.3	99.7
2008	102.9	103.3	88.6	87.6	107.5	114.7	117.3	99.0	114.7	102.9	108.8	103.8	86.4	101.4
2009	100.0	100.0	100.0	100.0	100.0	100.0	100.0	100.0	100.0	100.0	100.0	100.0	100.0	100.0
2010	102.5	102.4	101.9	93.9	109.4	95.6	111.6	99.0	103.1	102.4	105.7	104.2	99.9	102.7
2011	104.2	104.2	97.3	99.9	110.8	95.0	118.7	93.1	105.2	103.0	109.4	104.4	100.9	105.5
2012	106.6	106.7	94.0	110.1	111.3	98.9	122.5	91.3	108.6	104.7	109.7	106.1	105.2	107.5
2013	109.0	109.1	105.4	114.6	112.4	100.7	124.6	92.2	110.3	107.2	110.5	110.8	110.0	109.2
2014	111.6	112.0	97.7	122.9	112.3	100.1	127.7	96.1	113.1	110.5	112.0	114.6	111.9	110.9
2006														
1st quarter ..	100.9	102.2	92.5	80.2	100.5	134.7	113.2	100.5	111.8	111.2	109.8	87.0	102.2	94.2
2nd quarter	101.2	102.6	104.3	78.7	107.5	132.3	113.3	101.5	111.9	111.5	111.9	89.2	101.1	94.5
3rd quarter ..	101.3	102.6	97.2	80.5	108.4	129.5	113.2	103.1	112.2	108.6	110.5	92.3	102.1	95.2
4th quarter ..	102.1	103.2	90.6	85.3	104.9	125.7	115.3	104.1	112.9	110.3	109.1	92.0	102.7	97.5
2007														
1st quarter ..	102.1	103.3	87.1	86.3	104.0	125.6	115.1	102.6	113.3	108.6	106.1	94.3	104.0	98.1
2nd quarter	102.9	104.0	83.7	89.3	107.9	127.6	117.9	103.5	116.1	106.3	110.0	97.1	101.8	98.7
3rd quarter ..	103.6	104.6	79.0	86.7	106.7	126.2	120.9	105.4	116.6	107.1	107.2	100.8	98.9	100.2
4th quarter ..	104.0	104.9	82.2	83.9	107.9	123.0	120.7	105.3	118.0	107.4	112.5	103.4	92.7	101.7
2008														
1st quarter ..	103.3	104.0	90.2	80.5	107.2	117.7	119.3	97.7	117.4	105.0	111.6	103.1	94.7	101.3
2nd quarter	103.8	104.4	86.1	79.5	113.3	116.5	119.7	104.9	116.9	104.0	110.2	105.7	89.3	101.6
3rd quarter ..	103.3	103.6	83.7	84.9	112.7	115.5	118.6	97.8	114.8	102.8	110.2	106.1	85.1	101.2
4th quarter ..	101.1	101.2	94.5	105.2	96.8	109.2	111.4	95.8	109.6	99.8	103.2	100.3	76.4	101.3
2009														
1st quarter ..	99.7	99.8	95.4	110.0	95.5	101.3	101.3	94.7	102.1	99.7	97.0	98.8	94.0	100.8
2nd quarter	99.6	99.5	95.7	99.6	97.8	99.9	98.2	98.7	98.5	99.5	99.7	98.9	101.4	99.7
3rd quarter ..	99.9	99.9	107.0	96.6	100.6	101.3	98.6	101.6	98.1	99.4	100.6	99.3	103.1	99.7
4th quarter ..	100.9	100.8	101.9	93.8	106.1	97.5	102.0	105.0	101.3	101.4	102.6	102.9	101.5	99.8
2010														
1st quarter ..	101.3	101.0	98.6	92.3	111.7	94.5	105.0	102.9	100.3	101.0	102.7	102.3	100.7	101.2
2nd quarter	102.3	102.0	104.6	93.5	107.8	96.4	110.0	99.8	102.3	101.8	103.4	103.0	100.2	102.6
3rd quarter ..	103.0	102.9	104.2	93.7	108.9	95.7	114.3	97.4	105.0	103.5	107.0	106.3	98.2	102.9
4th quarter ..	103.6	103.7	100.0	96.2	109.2	95.5	117.3	95.9	104.9	103.2	109.5	105.3	100.6	104.2
2011														
1st quarter ..	103.2	103.2	100.9	94.7	105.0	93.1	117.1	93.2	105.0	103.1	108.9	103.5	101.6	103.4
2nd quarter	104.0	103.9	94.2	97.0	111.5	95.1	117.5	93.7	104.1	102.6	110.0	104.3	99.6	105.3
3rd quarter ..	104.2	104.2	94.7	101.1	110.7	95.6	118.6	92.4	103.7	102.9	108.8	105.0	101.0	105.8
4th quarter ..	105.4	105.5	99.5	106.9	116.0	96.4	121.6	93.0	108.3	103.4	110.0	104.7	101.3	107.5
2012														
1st quarter ..	105.9	106.1	97.7	106.3	108.9	98.6	121.9	94.0	107.7	105.1	111.1	105.6	100.4	106.6
2nd quarter	106.4	106.5	97.9	108.9	112.3	98.4	122.8	91.9	109.0	102.7	109.6	107.5	105.1	107.1
3rd quarter ..	107.0	107.1	91.9	111.5	113.0	98.6	122.7	90.6	109.5	106.2	109.3	107.5	106.5	108.3
4th quarter ..	107.0	107.2	88.7	113.6	111.2	99.9	122.6	88.6	108.3	104.8	108.9	104.0	108.7	107.8
2013														
1st quarter ..	107.8	107.9	100.5	111.2	113.1	100.0	123.4	91.1	108.9	107.3	110.4	108.3	108.0	108.4
2nd quarter	108.2	108.3	103.4	113.6	112.1	100.4	123.5	90.7	109.3	106.2	109.3	109.0	110.2	108.4
3rd quarter ..	109.4	109.7	109.1	115.5	112.1	101.6	125.1	92.2	111.4	107.5	110.0	111.4	110.5	109.8
4th quarter ..	110.4	110.7	108.5	118.1	112.3	101.0	126.2	94.9	111.6	107.8	112.2	114.6	111.4	110.2
2014														
1st quarter ..	109.8	109.9	93.7	115.8	106.7	98.9	124.8	95.5	110.5	108.9	111.4	112.8	108.5	110.0
2nd quarter	111.0	111.3	96.9	119.0	111.0	99.9	127.2	96.7	112.2	110.9	111.4	113.7	110.1	110.2
3rd quarter ..	112.4	113.0	98.7	125.9	115.8	100.4	129.4	95.1	114.2	111.2	113.2	115.5	115.6	111.4
4th quarter ..	113.0	113.6	101.7	130.7	115.6	101.1	129.5	97.3	115.5	111.0	112.1	116.3	113.3	111.9

Table 14-2. Chain-Type Quantity Indexes for Value Added by Industry—*Continued*

(New Series, 2009 = 100.)

Year	Professional, scientific, and technical services	Management of companies and enterprises	Administrative and waste management services	Educational services	Health care and social assistance	Arts, entertainment, and recreation	Accommodation and food services	Other services except government	Total government	Federal	State and local	Private goods-producing industries	Private services-producing industries	Information-communications-technology-producing industries[1]
						Private industries—*Continued*				Government				
1997	70.7	101.1	67.4	73.0	71.4	86.3	88.0	114.4	87.0	88.2	86.4	84.1	74.0	31.1
1998	74.4	104.5	69.7	71.9	72.2	86.2	90.8	118.9	88.0	88.0	88.0	87.7	77.6	37.0
1999	78.2	105.0	73.7	74.0	74.1	89.2	96.3	119.8	89.1	87.5	89.9	91.8	81.8	42.8
2000	81.8	110.4	79.4	76.4	75.9	93.2	102.2	122.4	90.8	88.5	92.0	96.6	85.0	50.7
2001	84.1	113.6	80.9	79.0	77.8	87.8	99.8	110.3	91.6	87.4	93.7	94.1	86.8	53.1
2002	86.2	112.8	81.1	80.3	81.2	92.0	101.7	113.3	93.3	89.1	95.4	94.2	88.8	56.8
2003	86.8	116.6	87.0	83.9	83.8	95.6	104.5	109.8	94.4	90.8	96.2	97.5	91.1	62.5
2004	90.0	110.9	91.1	88.1	87.0	99.0	109.6	111.5	95.3	92.5	96.6	102.6	94.3	70.6
2005	92.7	111.7	99.4	87.8	88.8	99.3	110.0	111.9	96.1	93.2	97.5	104.4	98.3	78.9
2006	96.0	112.7	101.7	89.9	92.4	102.3	112.2	112.3	96.7	93.7	98.1	108.1	101.0	86.2
2007	99.0	109.8	106.2	91.8	93.1	103.9	111.8	109.5	97.7	94.5	99.2	109.2	102.7	95.4
2008	106.5	109.2	107.0	95.4	98.2	103.5	108.2	105.4	99.5	97.1	100.6	105.6	102.6	102.3
2009	100.0	100.0	100.0	100.0	100.0	100.0	100.0	100.0	100.0	100.0	100.0	100.0	100.0	100.0
2010	100.9	107.7	107.1	101.1	100.4	104.4	103.4	98.3	100.7	102.5	99.8	101.8	102.6	104.6
2011	104.6	112.4	111.1	101.9	102.2	106.5	108.1	97.9	100.3	102.7	99.1	102.3	104.7	108.3
2012	108.0	121.5	116.4	101.7	103.9	109.3	110.3	99.9	99.8	102.2	98.7	104.6	107.4	112.2
2013	108.7	127.1	119.4	100.2	106.4	113.1	111.9	100.6	99.2	99.1	99.2	107.3	109.7	117.2
2014	113.3	139.2	123.9	100.6	109.3	118.0	114.4	102.3	98.9	97.8	99.4	109.8	112.6	...
2006														
1st quarter	95.8	113.3	101.6	89.2	91.9	102.3	112.8	113.0	96.2	93.2	97.7	108.0	100.4	...
2nd quarter	95.7	114.5	101.5	89.8	92.5	102.9	112.1	112.8	96.4	93.4	97.9	108.2	100.9	...
3rd quarter	95.9	111.9	101.7	90.2	92.3	101.5	111.5	112.1	96.8	94.1	98.2	107.9	101.0	...
4th quarter	96.5	111.3	101.8	90.3	92.7	102.7	112.3	111.5	97.1	94.2	98.5	108.4	101.7	...
2007														
1st quarter	96.8	112.3	102.7	90.8	92.2	103.4	112.9	110.7	97.2	94.2	98.6	107.9	101.9	...
2nd quarter	97.0	109.3	105.3	91.4	92.5	103.0	112.1	109.9	97.4	94.0	99.0	109.6	102.4	...
3rd quarter	99.8	108.8	107.9	92.3	93.2	104.9	110.5	109.2	97.7	94.8	99.1	110.2	103.0	...
4th quarter	102.5	108.9	108.9	92.9	94.4	104.4	111.6	108.3	98.4	95.1	99.9	109.2	103.6	...
2008														
1st quarter	104.4	107.6	107.1	93.6	96.3	103.6	109.9	106.7	99.0	95.9	100.5	105.5	103.6	...
2nd quarter	106.7	109.6	107.8	94.7	97.6	103.5	109.6	105.6	99.3	96.6	100.6	106.9	103.6	...
3rd quarter	108.1	110.7	107.9	96.7	99.0	103.2	108.1	105.1	99.9	97.7	101.0	105.2	103.1	...
4th quarter	107.0	109.2	105.1	96.8	100.0	103.8	105.2	104.4	99.6	98.2	100.2	104.6	100.2	...
2009														
1st quarter	102.9	97.5	100.8	100.3	99.8	100.4	101.2	101.7	99.5	98.6	99.9	99.9	99.7	...
2nd quarter	100.0	99.0	99.3	99.8	100.1	100.2	99.8	100.6	100.1	100.0	100.1	98.8	99.7	...
3rd quarter	99.0	101.4	99.2	99.7	99.8	99.5	99.0	99.1	100.1	100.4	100.0	100.3	99.8	...
4th quarter	98.0	102.1	100.7	100.2	100.4	99.9	100.0	98.6	100.4	100.9	100.1	101.0	100.7	...
2010														
1st quarter	99.1	104.5	104.8	100.7	99.6	102.5	101.2	97.3	100.6	101.8	100.1	100.4	101.2	...
2nd quarter	100.0	106.6	106.4	101.2	100.3	103.8	102.9	98.0	100.9	103.0	100.0	101.8	102.0	...
3rd quarter	101.8	108.0	107.9	101.1	100.8	104.2	104.0	99.0	100.6	102.5	99.7	102.2	103.1	...
4th quarter	102.8	111.4	109.2	101.5	101.2	107.0	105.4	99.0	100.5	102.6	99.5	102.7	104.0	...
2011														
1st quarter	102.9	112.4	109.3	102.5	101.3	105.6	106.6	97.9	100.4	102.7	99.4	101.1	103.8	...
2nd quarter	104.8	113.4	110.8	102.4	102.1	106.5	108.4	97.9	100.4	102.8	99.3	101.6	104.5	...
3rd quarter	105.1	111.3	111.8	101.9	102.5	108.4	108.9	97.9	100.1	102.6	99.0	102.2	104.8	...
4th quarter	105.5	112.3	112.2	100.9	102.7	105.4	108.7	98.0	100.1	102.7	98.9	104.5	105.8	...
2012														
1st quarter	107.4	119.5	115.7	102.1	103.6	108.2	110.4	99.2	100.0	102.8	98.7	105.2	106.4	...
2nd quarter	107.5	118.6	115.6	101.6	103.2	108.7	109.8	99.4	99.8	102.4	98.5	105.0	107.0	...
3rd quarter	107.5	120.8	116.9	101.6	103.8	109.2	109.9	100.4	99.8	102.1	98.7	104.5	107.9	...
4th quarter	109.4	127.0	117.4	101.4	104.9	111.0	111.2	100.4	99.7	101.6	98.8	104.0	108.1	...
2013														
1st quarter	106.7	121.9	117.1	99.8	106.1	110.6	112.0	100.2	99.5	100.7	99.0	105.7	108.5	...
2nd quarter	107.8	124.8	118.5	100.1	106.1	112.7	111.2	100.1	99.4	99.9	99.2	106.1	108.9	...
3rd quarter	109.8	129.8	120.4	100.5	106.6	113.4	111.5	100.5	99.1	98.6	99.4	107.9	110.2	...
4th quarter	110.6	131.9	121.9	100.4	106.9	115.7	112.9	101.4	98.8	97.3	99.5	109.3	111.1	...
2014														
1st quarter	110.9	134.2	121.6	100.5	107.8	116.0	112.9	101.4	99.0	98.6	99.2	107.4	110.7	...
2nd quarter	112.5	138.8	123.7	99.7	108.8	116.8	113.8	101.3	98.8	97.9	99.3	109.3	111.9	...
3rd quarter	113.9	141.7	124.7	101.1	109.8	118.8	115.0	103.1	98.9	97.5	99.5	110.5	113.7	...
4th quarter	115.7	142.2	125.7	101.0	110.8	120.3	115.8	103.5	98.8	97.4	99.4	112.1	114.1	...

[1]Consists of computer and electronic products manufacturing; publishing, including software; information and data processing services; and computer systems design and related services.
. . . = Not available.

Table 14-3. Gross Domestic Factor Income by Industry

(Billions of current dollars.)

NAICS industry	2001	2002	2003	2004	2005	2006	2007	2008	2009	2010	2011	2012	2013
Gross domestic factor income, total	9 952.9	10 256.3	10 751.7	11 457.4	12 220.1	12 915.4	13 497.7	13 729.3	13 451.0	13 963.1	14 475.4	15 089.1	15 665.7
Compensation of employees	6 053.8	6 149.7	6 372.7	6 748.8	7 097.9	7 513.7	7 908.8	8 090.0	7 795.7	7 969.5	8 277.1	8 614.9	8 853.6
Gross operating surplus	3 899.1	4 106.6	4 379.0	4 708.6	5 122.2	5 401.7	5 588.9	5 639.3	5 655.3	5 993.6	6 198.3	6 474.2	6 812.1
Private industries	8 542.0	8 763.6	9 176.5	9 793.9	10 475.7	11 087.5	11 573.8	11 706.5	11 362.7	11 804.5	12 283.2	12 875.5	13 429.7
Compensation of employees	4 934.3	4 958.1	5 106.2	5 405.9	5 693.8	6 047.5	6 367.8	6 472.5	6 129.5	6 246.0	6 540.0	6 871.9	7 094.3
Gross operating surplus	3 607.7	3 805.5	4 070.3	4 388.0	4 781.9	5 040.0	5 206.0	5 234.0	5 233.2	5 558.5	5 743.2	6 003.6	6 335.4
Agriculture, forestry, fishing, and hunting	114.6	100.9	124.2	147.6	143.1	134.8	144.5	156.7	140.1	162.5	197.2	195.0	226.5
Compensation of employees	31.4	31.7	31.7	35.0	34.7	38.0	41.5	42.2	42.2	41.4	41.0	47.4	50.6
Gross operating surplus	83.2	69.2	92.5	112.6	108.4	96.8	103.0	114.5	97.9	121.1	156.2	147.6	175.9
Mining	109.9	98.3	122.8	147.8	201.2	244.3	280.4	358.7	260.6	298.2	358.9	366.1	398.1
Compensation of employees	38.6	35.7	37.1	41.5	47.1	57.0	62.7	72.8	64.7	69.1	80.3	90.1	92.8
Gross operating surplus	71.3	62.6	85.7	106.3	154.1	187.3	217.7	285.9	195.9	229.1	278.6	276.0	305.3
Utilities	154.7	142.2	146.4	159.7	155.3	179.4	180.5	184.8	196.6	211.2	214.8	206.9	218.3
Compensation of employees	53.9	54.7	52.9	55.6	56.1	60.9	63.1	66.3	66.8	67.6	71.2	70.1	72.6
Gross operating surplus	100.8	87.5	93.5	104.1	99.2	118.5	117.4	118.5	129.8	143.6	143.6	136.8	145.7
Construction	1 431.4	1 423.3	1 480.1	1 566.5	1 648.4	1 746.5	1 794.1	1 748.1	1 648.9	1 752.1	1 825.9	1 912.2	1 943.8
Compensation of employees	881.9	846.9	847.4	874.0	895.8	924.7	944.4	932.6	836.0	847.9	883.4	918.1	932.5
Gross operating surplus	549.5	576.4	632.7	692.5	752.6	821.8	849.7	815.5	812.9	904.2	942.5	994.1	1 011.3
Durable goods manufacturing	816.9	815.9	846.4	888.5	938.3	983.4	1 006.6	969.3	848.1	931.5	978.4	1 028.0	1 059.8
Compensation of employees	582.8	553.2	550.0	573.4	590.5	615.6	628.2	616.2	540.1	547.0	579.7	604.7	613.1
Gross operating surplus	234.1	262.7	296.4	315.1	347.8	367.8	378.4	353.1	308.0	384.5	398.7	423.3	446.7
Nondurable goods manufacturing	614.6	607.5	633.8	678.0	710.1	763.1	787.5	778.8	800.8	820.6	847.6	884.1	884.0
Compensation of employees	299.1	293.8	297.5	300.6	305.3	309.1	316.2	316.4	295.9	300.9	303.8	313.3	319.4
Gross operating surplus	315.5	313.7	336.3	377.4	404.8	454.0	471.3	462.4	504.9	519.7	543.8	570.8	564.6
Wholesale trade	482.0	479.1	501.9	548.9	595.4	641.4	685.5	705.0	664.2	699.0	723.3	771.5	797.2
Compensation of employees	330.2	329.0	337.0	357.1	379.3	404.7	429.2	435.5	405.3	412.5	436.7	457.6	467.6
Gross operating surplus	151.8	150.1	164.9	191.8	216.1	236.7	256.3	269.5	258.9	286.5	286.6	313.9	329.6
Retail trade	578.3	598.5	628.3	645.1	678.0	696.8	693.3	676.9	674.2	690.3	705.2	741.0	770.9
Compensation of employees	416.7	428.4	444.7	459.2	477.5	492.3	506.1	500.5	474.5	479.5	496.6	511.7	529.2
Gross operating surplus	161.6	170.1	183.6	185.9	200.5	204.5	187.2	176.4	199.7	210.8	208.6	229.3	241.7
Transportation and warehousing	295.3	286.8	304.4	330.8	352.5	385.3	384.9	398.3	375.5	402.5	420.7	438.4	453.7
Compensation of employees	208.0	206.2	209.6	221.9	231.5	241.1	255.8	255.5	241.3	245.7	260.0	274.8	282.7
Gross operating surplus	87.3	80.6	94.8	108.9	121.0	144.2	129.1	142.8	134.2	156.8	160.7	163.6	171.0
Information	461.7	509.4	523.3	578.9	597.9	605.3	659.2	686.5	662.0	686.6	683.8	696.6	733.2
Compensation of employees	247.2	228.4	230.4	237.9	241.4	248.8	260.4	257.8	251.6	248.6	260.2	271.4	286.1
Gross operating surplus	214.5	281.0	292.9	341.0	356.5	356.5	398.8	428.7	410.4	438.0	423.6	425.2	447.1
Finance and insurance	788.5	804.4	833.0	853.2	952.1	1 007.1	996.0	860.9	921.2	957.7	988.0	1 074.9	1 154.7
Compensation of employees	445.6	444.0	460.5	498.5	535.4	579.8	618.2	612.9	549.0	574.3	606.8	631.1	642.3
Gross operating surplus	342.9	360.4	372.5	354.7	416.7	427.3	377.8	248.0	372.2	383.4	381.2	443.8	512.4
Real estate and rental and leasing	1 199.1	1 259.3	1 304.8	1 363.8	1 471.4	1 527.3	1 633.2	1 686.5	1 684.1	1 725.2	1 791.8	1 867.3	1 948.9
Compensation of employees	81.2	86.0	87.4	94.9	101.4	107.9	111.8	109.9	103.4	103.7	106.8	114.6	119.4
Gross operating surplus	1 117.9	1 173.3	1 217.4	1 268.9	1 370.0	1 419.4	1 521.4	1 576.6	1 580.7	1 621.5	1 685.0	1 752.7	1 829.5
Professional, scientific, and technical services	673.5	698.3	716.3	760.3	809.1	870.6	936.1	1 026.2	977.0	998.0	1 047.9	1 098.3	1 123.9
Compensation of employees	477.2	468.3	477.0	505.6	552.5	606.5	653.9	692.2	668.9	682.4	727.2	777.0	800.6
Gross operating surplus	196.3	230.0	239.3	254.7	256.6	264.1	282.2	334.0	308.1	315.6	320.7	321.3	323.3
Management of companies and enterprises	422.6	449.0	451.4	477.0	506.9	544.1	576.4	627.8	595.6	615.1	638.0	664.7	683.6
Compensation of employees	284.1	284.0	289.6	307.4	339.5	375.1	403.4	429.5	411.6	417.2	442.3	468.5	485.9
Gross operating surplus	138.5	165.0	161.8	169.6	167.4	169.0	173.0	198.3	184.0	197.9	195.7	196.2	197.7
Administrative and waste management services	289.4	294.2	314.4	339.0	372.6	390.9	421.3	429.3	404.7	430.2	447.7	473.9	493.1
Compensation of employees	224.0	227.8	235.4	253.0	274.6	292.4	310.0	313.9	289.2	306.6	322.3	342.8	355.9
Gross operating surplus	65.4	66.4	79.0	86.0	98.0	98.5	111.3	115.4	115.5	123.6	125.4	131.1	137.2
Educational services	87.7	94.2	101.7	111.5	115.2	123.6	132.0	142.4	155.4	161.6	167.5	173.2	176.4
Compensation of employees	79.6	88.7	94.2	101.9	105.5	112.8	120.7	129.1	139.5	145.2	152.4	159.8	162.3
Gross operating surplus	8.1	5.5	7.5	9.6	9.7	10.8	11.3	13.3	15.9	16.4	15.1	13.4	14.1
Health care and social assistance	627.0	676.3	720.1	769.4	807.2	859.6	900.6	972.3	1 026.0	1 054.1	1 090.0	1 128.1	1 171.9
Compensation of employees	524.9	565.9	606.4	650.2	687.5	733.3	775.1	824.6	863.0	889.2	923.0	957.5	992.8
Gross operating surplus	102.1	110.4	113.7	119.2	119.7	126.3	125.5	147.7	163.0	164.9	167.0	170.6	179.1
Arts, entertainment, and recreation	343.6	365.8	381.5	407.2	421.9	445.5	461.7	463.6	452.3	467.0	488.6	519.6	543.3
Compensation of employees	241.1	250.0	262.9	280.2	291.4	306.5	324.7	332.9	321.5	328.0	344.4	366.9	380.3
Gross operating surplus	102.5	115.8	118.6	127.0	130.5	139.0	137.0	130.7	130.8	139.0	144.2	152.7	163.0
Accommodation and food services	255.9	271.5	280.4	300.2	311.5	328.2	339.3	338.8	328.5	338.4	357.1	380.4	396.7
Compensation of employees	183.1	188.6	198.7	213.0	222.8	233.4	247.7	252.3	242.9	248.5	262.7	280.7	291.1
Gross operating surplus	72.8	82.9	81.7	87.2	88.7	94.8	91.6	86.5	85.6	89.9	94.4	99.7	105.6
Other services, except government	254.1	272.9	271.4	284.1	296.2	309.0	313.2	313.3	311.8	314.7	320.5	336.9	350.1
Compensation of employees	177.3	189.0	196.3	206.1	209.5	219.0	231.1	240.0	235.9	232.7	240.6	252.2	261.1
Gross operating surplus	76.8	83.9	75.1	78.0	86.7	90.0	82.1	73.3	75.9	82.0	79.9	84.7	89.0
Government	1 410.8	1 492.6	1 575.2	1 663.5	1 744.4	1 827.9	1 923.9	2 022.8	2 088.3	2 158.7	2 192.2	2 213.7	2 236.1
Compensation of employees	1 119.4	1 191.6	1 266.5	1 342.9	1 404.1	1 466.2	1 541.0	1 617.5	1 666.2	1 723.5	1 737.1	1 743.0	1 759.3
Gross operating surplus	291.4	301.0	308.7	320.6	340.3	361.7	382.9	405.3	422.1	435.2	455.1	470.7	476.8
Addenda:													
Private goods-producing industries	2 138.6	2 111.6	2 248.1	2 442.7	2 639.5	2 815.9	2 926.1	2 908.8	2 619.7	2 747.3	2 921.4	3 052.3	3 180.5
Compensation of employees	1 277.3	1 241.4	1 251.9	1 308.4	1 365.1	1 441.1	1 488.3	1 480.9	1 312.1	1 303.2	1 353.7	1 423.8	1 466.3
Gross operating surplus	861.3	870.2	996.2	1 134.3	1 274.4	1 374.8	1 437.8	1 427.9	1 307.6	1 444.1	1 567.7	1 628.5	1 714.2
Private services-producing industries	6 403.5	6 652.0	6 928.4	7 351.2	7 836.3	8 271.5	8 647.6	8 797.7	8 743.0	9 057.2	9 361.7	9 823.1	10 249.1
Compensation of employees	3 657.1	3 716.7	3 854.3	4 097.5	4 328.7	4 606.3	4 879.5	4 991.6	4 817.4	4 942.8	5 186.3	5 448.1	5 628.0
Gross operating surplus	2 746.4	2 935.3	3 074.1	3 253.7	3 507.6	3 665.2	3 768.1	3 806.1	3 925.6	4 114.4	4 175.4	4 375.0	4 621.1
Information-communications-technology-producing industries [1]	562.8	580.4	616.2	669.7	716.2	753.8	805.4	839.4	808.8	832.3	848.5	872.9	915.2
Compensation of employees	384.3	345.2	342.4	356.5	373.5	398.7	419.7	422.5	408.2	414.4	442.2	469.9	489.2
Gross operating surplus	178.5	235.2	273.8	313.2	342.7	355.1	385.7	416.9	400.6	417.9	406.3	403.0	426.0

[1]Consists of computer and electronic products manufacturing; publishing, including software; information and data processing services; and computer systems design and related services.

NOTES AND DEFINITIONS, CHAPTER 14

Tables 14-1 through 14-3
Gross Domestic Product (Value Added)
and Gross Factor Income by Industry

SOURCE: U.S. DEPARTMENT OF COMMERCE, BUREAU OF ECONOMIC ANALYSIS (BEA)

In the introduction to the notes and definitions for Chapter 1, it was observed that gross domestic product (GDP), while primarily measured as the sum of final demands for goods and services, is also the sum of the values created by each industry in the economy. In this chapter, selected data are presented from the industry accounts in the national income and product accounts (NIPAs). The industry accounts measure the contribution of each major industry to GDP.

New in the 20th edition of *Business Statistics* are quarterly estimates of current- and constant-dollar GDP by industry. These measures have been computed starting with the first quarter of 2005 and extending through a preliminary estimate for the first quarter of 2015; they are displayed for 2005–2014 in Tables 14-1A and 14-2A. They provide a complete accounting of the industrial origin of GDP, and measure the output of major industries on a more up-to-date basis than the annual measures previously available—within 120 days after the end of the reference quarter.

In recent years, estimates of GDP by industry have been prepared using a methodology integrated with annual input-output accounts in order to produce estimates of gross industry output, industry input, and the difference between the two—industry value added—with greater consistency and timeliness than was previously possible. The current integrated industry accounts also include a wealth of related information too extensive for inclusion here, such as quantity and price indexes for gross output and intermediate inputs, cost per unit of real value added allocated to the three components of value added, and components of domestic supply (domestic output, imports, exports, and inventory change).

The most precise estimates of GDP by NAICS industry begin with 1997, but the annual series were extended back to 1947, using approximations of current methods in earlier years when the source data were less comprehensive and were initially compiled on the older SIC classifications. Table 14-1B presents this "old series" current-dollar GDP for NAICS industry groups from 1947 through 2009; Table 14-2B presents "old series" indexes of real value added for each industry group.

The new figures for 1997 forward, unlike the "old series" data from last year's edition, reflect the conceptual and data changes made in the 2013 comprehensive revision of the NIPAs.

In Table 14-3, the editor presents a measure derived from the components of current-dollar value added as published by BEA. This measure, "gross domestic factor income," enables users to obtain a clearer picture of the quantitative impact of each industry on the economy's factors of production and of the shares of capital and labor in each industry.

The 2004 revision incorporated a change in terminology. An industry's contribution to total GDP, formerly referred to as "gross product originating" (GPO) or "gross product by industry," is now called "value added." This is consistent with the use of the term "value added" in most economic writing. However, it should not be confused with a concept known as "Census value added," which is used in U.S. censuses and surveys of manufactures. Census value added is calculated at the individual establishment level and, for that reason, does not exclude purchased business services. This means that census value added, while still an important gauge of relative importance, is not a true measure of economic value added.

Definitions and notes on the data

An industry's *gross domestic product (value added)*, formerly *GPO*, is equal to the market value of its gross output (which consists of the value, including taxes, of sales or receipts and other operating income plus the value of inventory change) minus the value of its intermediate inputs (energy, raw materials, semifinished goods, and services that are purchased from domestic industries or from foreign sources).

In concept, this is also equal to the sum of *compensation of employees, taxes on production and imports less subsidies,* and *gross operating surplus.* (See Chapter 1 and its notes and definitions for more information.)

The GDP data from 1997 forward are not comparable with the "old series" data for earlier years presented in Tables 14-1B and 14-2B, the major reason being that they do not reflect the conceptual revisions introduced in the comprehensive 2013 revision of the NIPAs (see the Notes and Definitions to Chapter 1). In particular, the new data include, while the old data exclude, the capitalized values of research and development, intellectual property, and all real estate transfer costs. This does not change labor compensation values—the associated workers were always included, it was just that their costs were taken to be written off in the first year. But it does increase across the board the non-labor share of the total value of output, by the amount of capital consumption and net investment. This is seen in labor compensation shares derived from Table 14-3, compared with those that would have been calculated on the old basis last year.

Compensation of employees consists of wage and salary accruals and supplements to wages and salaries. This approximates the labor share of production, subject to the note below about proprietors' income.

Taxes on production and imports less subsidies. Although this is shown in BEA source data as a single net line item, it represents two separate components.

Taxes on production and imports are included in the market value of the goods and services sold to final consumers and therefore in the consumer valuation of those goods. Since they are not part of the payments to the labor and capital inputs in the producing industries, they must be <u>added</u> to the sum of the returns to those inputs in order to account for the total value to consumers. Taxes that fall into this classification include property taxes, sales and excise taxes, and Customs duties.

BEA allocates these taxes to the industry level at which they are assessed by law. Most sales taxes are considered by BEA to be part of the value added by retail trade. Some sales taxes, most fuel taxes, and all customs duties are allocated by BEA to wholesale trade. Residential real property taxes, including those on owner-occupied dwellings, are allocated by BEA to the real estate industry.

Subsidies to business by government are included in the labor and/or capital payments made by that industry. Since they are payments to the industry in addition to the market values paid by consumers, they are *subtracted* from the values of the labor and capital inputs to make them consistent with the market values as defined in value added. The role of subsidies is obvious in the source data for the agricultural sector, where the net "taxes on production and imports less subsidies" has a negative sign: farm subsidies more than offset this industry's taxes on production and imports, which mainly consist of property taxes, since sales, excise, and import taxes are not levied on farms.

For private sector businesses, *gross operating surplus* consists of business income (corporate profits before tax, proprietors' income, and rental income of persons), net interest and miscellaneous payments, business current transfer payments (net), and capital consumption allowances. For government, households, and institutions, it consists of consumption of fixed capital and (for government) government enterprises' current surplus. This approximates the share of the value of production ascribable to capital and land as measured in the NIPAs accounts; however, as BEA notes, "an unknown portion [of proprietors' income] reflects the labor contribution of proprietors." (*Survey of Current Business*, June 2004, p. 27, footnote 7.) Another aspect to be noted is that gross operating surplus includes the return to owner-occupied housing in the real estate sector. Because there is in the NIPAs no employee compensation attributed to owner-occupied housing, the capital share in that industry as measured by gross operating surplus is very large.

Quantity indexes for value added. Measures of the constant-dollar change in each industry's gross output minus its intermediate input use are calculated by BEA, using a Fisher index-number formula which incorporates weights from two adjacent years. The changes for successive years are chained together in indexes, with the value for the year 2009 set at 100. The indexes are multiplied by 2009 current-dollar value added to provide estimates of value added in "chained 2009 dollars," but because the actual weights used change from year to year, components in chained 2009 dollars typically do not add up to total GDP in 2009 dollars—and do not contain any information not already summarized in the indexes. For that reason, only the indexes are published here.

Gross domestic factor income (not a category published as such in the NIPAs) is calculated by the editor as the sum of "compensation of employees" and "gross operating surplus," which the same as value added minus "taxes on production and imports less subsidies." The effect of this procedure is to take out the specified taxes, and to leave in the subsidies embedded in the employee compensation and gross operating surplus components. The editor believes that this provides a valuable alternative basis for assessing the importance of different industries in the economy, by measuring the value paid for by its labor and capital inputs, and for calculating the shares of labor and capital in each industry's output. The components shown in this table are found on the BEA website in a table entitled "Components of Value Added by Industry."

The editor's reasoning is based on the facts that more than half of these taxes are sales, excise, and import taxes, and the assignment of these taxes to industries is economically arbitrary. BEA assigns them to the industry with the legal liability to pay, not to the entity bearing the major incidence of the tax. Yet economists have demonstrated that most of the burdens of sales and excise taxes and import duties are not borne by the factors in the legally liable industry; instead, they are passed on to consumers. In addition, because the wholesale and retail trade industries are classified as "services-producing," BEA's allocation of those taxes has a very peculiar result: taxes on goods are represented as paid by "service" industries. The process adopted instead by the editor in Table 14-3, which excludes these taxes and focuses on "gross domestic factor income," has the effect (for example) of keeping the wholesale trade industry from appearing to be both larger and more heavily taxed than it really is.

Private goods-producing industries consists of agriculture, forestry, fishing, and hunting; mining; construction; and manufacturing.

Private services-producing industries consists of utilities; wholesale trade; retail trade; transportation and warehousing; information; finance, insurance, real estate, rental, and leasing; professional and business services; educational services, health care, and social assistance; arts, entertainment, recreation, accommodation, and food services; and other services, except government.

Information-communications-technology-producing industries is a category that cuts across the goods and services framework, consisting of computer and electronic products manufacturing; publishing industries (which includes software) from the information sector; information and data processing services; and computer systems design and related services.

Data Availability and References

The comprehensive revision of the industry accounts from 1997 forward and the new quarterly statistics are described in "Industry Economic Accounts: Results of the Comprehensive

Revision, Revised Statistics for 1997–2012" (*Survey of Current Business,* February 2014); "New Quarterly Statistics Detail Industries' Economic Performance," BEA news release, April 25, 2014; and "Prototype Quarterly Statistics on U.S. GDP by Industry, 2007–2011," June 2012, a "BEA Briefing." All are available on the BEA website, http://www.bea.gov. To access the historical data at <http://www.bea.gov>, click on "Annual Industry Accounts" and click on "Interactive Tables" under "Gross Domestic Product (GDP) by Industry."

"Old basis" annual GDP by industry data shown here were recalculated back to 1947 consistent with the 2009 comprehensive revision of the NIPAs. They were most recently presented and described in "Annual Industry Statistics: Revised Statistics for 2009–2011," *Survey of Current Business*, December 2012.

CHAPTER 15: EMPLOYMENT, HOURS, AND EARNINGS BY NAICS INDUSTRY

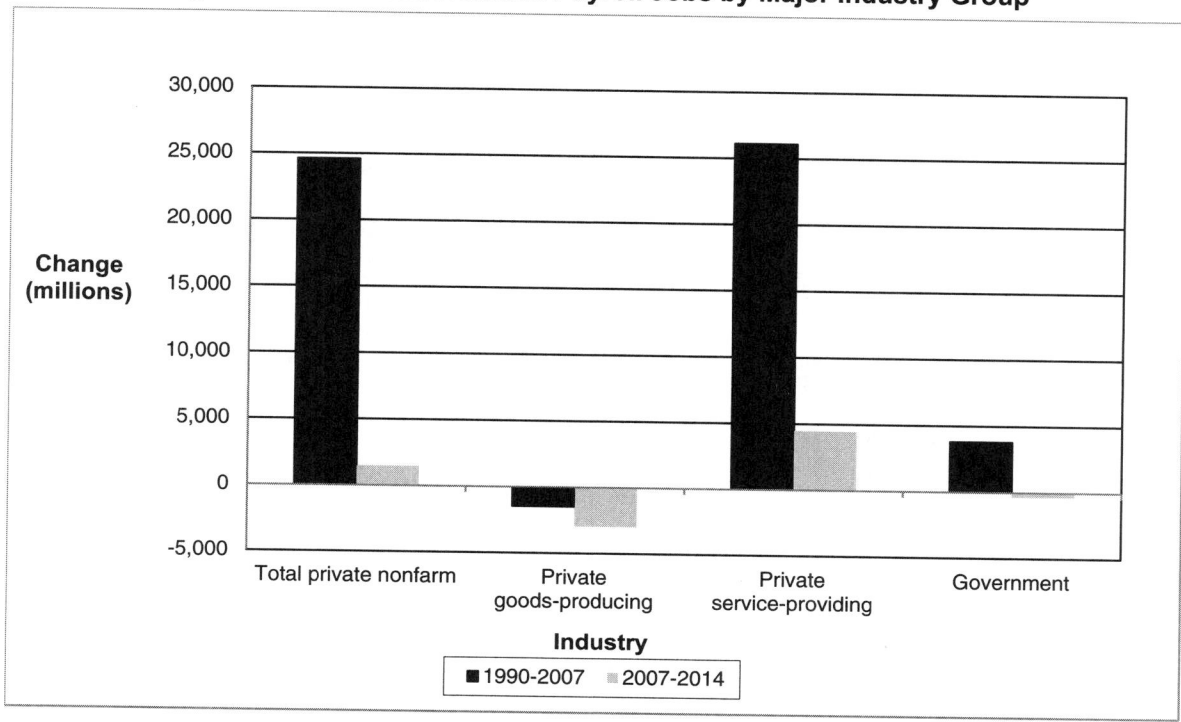

Figure 15-1: Net New Nonfarm Payroll Jobs by Major Industry Group

- From 1990 to the year of the business cycle peak in 2007, U.S. nonfarm employers added a net total of 28.4 million jobs, based on the annual averages displayed in this chapter. In comparison, private employers added 1.1 million jobs between 2007 and 2014.

- Employment began to decline in February 2008 and didn't begin to increase until March 2010, nine months after the recession's end, which the National Bureau of Economic Research Business Cycle Dating Committee places at June 2009. (Preliminary monthly data indicate that the previous peak was finally reached in May 2014.) (Table 10-9, Table 15-1, and recent data)

- Employment in 2014 finally exceeded 2007 employment. From 2007 to 2014, employment increased from 137.9 million to 139 million, an increase of 0.8%.

- The U.S. economy continues to shed goods-producing and government jobs. For example, construction jobs declined 1,492,000 between 2007 and 2014. On the other hand, private service-providing industries added 4,472,000 jobs between 2007 and 2014, up 4.8%. Knowledge-based employment, such as in Internet publishing and computer systems design companies, continues to grow. (Table 15-1)

- The average workweek for production and nonsupervisory workers is up since 2009 in most industries and industry groups. Goods-producing workers averaged 41.5 hours per week while servicing-providers work 32.4 hours. (Table 15-3)

- Average hourly earnings for production and nonsupervisory workers in 2014 ranged from a low of $12.09 in the leisure and hospitality sector to nearly $35.4 in petroleum and coal products manufacturing. (Table 15-4)

Table 15-1. Nonfarm Employment by Sector and Industry

(Wage and salary workers on nonfarm payrolls, thousands.)

Industry	1990	1991	1992	1993	1994	1995	1996	1997	1998	1999	2000
TOTAL NONFARM	109 527	108 427	108 802	110 935	114 398	117 407	119 836	122 951	126 157	129 240	132 019
Total Private	91 112	89 881	90 015	91 946	95 124	97 975	100 297	103 287	106 248	108 933	111 230
Goods-Producing	23 723	22 588	22 095	22 219	22 774	23 156	23 409	23 886	24 354	24 465	24 649
Mining and logging	765	739	689	666	659	641	637	654	645	598	599
Logging	84.6	78.7	78.7	81.0	82.0	82.5	80.7	82.1	80.0	80.8	79.0
Mining	680.1	660.5	609.8	584.9	576.5	558.1	556.4	571.3	564.7	517.4	520.2
Oil and gas extraction	190.2	191.0	182.2	170.9	162.4	151.7	146.9	144.1	140.8	131.2	124.9
Mining, except oil and gas [1]	302.2	285.1	271.8	250.9	255.2	252.4	249.4	249.5	243.1	234.5	224.8
Coal mining	136.0	125.6	117.5	100.2	103.5	96.7	90.5	89.4	85.3	78.6	72.2
Support activities for mining	187.6	184.5	155.7	163.1	158.8	154.0	160.1	177.7	180.8	151.7	170.6
Construction	5 263	4 780	4 608	4 779	5 095	5 274	5 536	5 813	6 149	6 545	6 787
Construction of buildings	1 413.0	1 252.9	1 187.3	1 227.4	1 300.8	1 325.4	1 380.2	1 435.4	1 508.8	1 586.3	1 632.5
Heavy and civil engineering	813.0	759.1	734.2	738.4	761.7	774.7	800.1	824.9	865.3	908.7	937.0
Specialty trade contractors	3 037.3	2 768.4	2 686.0	2 813.6	3 032.5	3 174.1	3 355.1	3 552.6	3 775.1	4 049.6	4 217.0
Manufacturing	17 695	17 068	16 799	16 774	17 020	17 241	17 237	17 419	17 560	17 322	17 263
Durable goods	10 737	10 220	9 946	9 901	10 132	10 373	10 486	10 705	10 911	10 831	10 877
Wood products	543.0	500.7	504.1	526.4	562.9	576.1	585.2	597.8	611.6	622.7	615.4
Nonmetallic mineral products	528.4	494.7	487.3	491.1	505.3	513.1	517.3	525.7	535.3	540.8	554.2
Primary metals	688.6	656.1	630.3	618.4	630.4	641.7	639.3	638.8	641.5	625.0	621.8
Fabricated metal products	1 610.0	1 541.3	1 497.2	1 509.5	1 565.3	1 623.4	1 647.5	1 695.8	1 739.5	1 728.4	1 752.6
Machinery	1 409.8	1 347.9	1 311.2	1 330.9	1 381.4	1 442.3	1 468.9	1 495.9	1 514.1	1 468.3	1 457.0
Computer and electronic products [1]	1 902.5	1 809.3	1 707.3	1 655.9	1 651.1	1 688.4	1 746.6	1 803.3	1 830.9	1 780.5	1 820.0
Computer and peripheral equipment	367.4	348.6	328.5	305.7	297.7	295.6	304.6	316.7	322.1	310.1	301.9
Communications equipment	223.0	212.5	202.0	202.6	210.0	224.3	228.9	235.0	237.4	228.7	238.6
Semiconductors and electronic components	574.0	546.6	519.4	519.4	535.4	571.0	606.6	639.8	649.8	630.5	676.3
Electronic instruments	634.8	598.0	556.2	525.3	501.4	490.5	497.8	502.8	509.2	498.3	487.7
Electrical equipment and appliances	633.1	597.7	579.4	575.8	588.5	592.8	591.0	586.3	591.6	588.0	590.9
Transportation equipment [1]	2 134.5	2 029.3	1 978.1	1 915.0	1 937.4	1 978.5	1 975.1	2 027.6	2 078.4	2 088.6	2 057.1
Motor vehicles and parts	1 054.2	1 017.6	1 047.0	1 077.8	1 168.5	1 241.5	1 240.3	1 253.9	1 271.5	1 312.5	1 313.6
Furniture and related products	601.7	561.5	563.2	575.7	600.4	607.0	604.2	615.5	641.6	665.2	680.1
Miscellaneous manufacturing	685.7	681.8	687.7	702.5	709.0	709.7	710.7	718.2	726.8	724.0	728.0
Nondurable goods [1]	6 958	6 848	6 853	6 872	6 889	6 868	6 751	6 714	6 649	6 491	6 386
Food manufacturing	1 507.3	1 515.2	1 518.3	1 534.6	1 539.2	1 560.0	1 562.0	1 557.9	1 554.9	1 549.8	1 553.1
Textile mills	491.8	479.9	479.0	478.7	477.6	468.5	443.2	436.2	424.5	397.1	378.2
Textile product mills	235.6	225.1	228.0	232.6	242.9	242.1	237.1	236.4	234.7	232.4	229.6
Apparel	902.8	876.9	879.3	857.3	831.9	791.1	722.3	680.8	621.4	540.5	483.5
Paper and paper products	647.2	638.5	639.6	639.7	639.4	639.5	631.4	630.6	624.9	615.6	604.7
Printing and related support activities	808.5	792.3	780.3	785.2	802.3	817.3	815.8	821.1	827.9	814.6	806.8
Petroleum and coal products	152.8	154.8	152.3	146.2	144.0	140.4	137.3	136.0	134.5	127.8	123.2
Chemicals	1 035.7	1 024.1	1 028.9	1 024.9	1 004.7	987.9	984.5	986.8	992.6	982.5	980.4
Plastics and rubber products	824.8	802.1	817.9	847.8	888.1	913.7	918.7	932.7	941.4	947.0	950.9
Service-Providing	85 804	85 839	86 707	88 716	91 624	94 251	96 427	99 065	101 803	104 775	107 370
Private Service-Providing	67 389	67 293	67 921	69 727	72 350	74 819	76 888	79 401	81 894	84 468	86 581
Trade, transportation, and utilities	22 666	22 281	22 125	22 378	23 128	23 834	24 239	24 700	25 186	25 771	26 225
Wholesale trade	5 268.4	5 185.3	5 109.7	5 093.2	5 247.3	5 433.1	5 522.0	5 663.9	5 795.2	5 892.5	5 933.2
Durable goods	2 833.7	2 766.6	2 698.8	2 687.0	2 786.0	2 908.8	2 977.8	3 071.9	3 162.4	3 219.6	3 250.7
Nondurable goods	1 900.2	1 891.3	1 891.5	1 888.3	1 927.0	1 969.3	1 977.5	2 007.9	2 032.7	2 061.1	2 064.8
Electronic markets, agents, and brokers	534.5	527.4	519.4	517.9	534.4	555.0	566.7	584.1	600.1	611.8	617.7
Retail trade	13 182.3	12 896.4	12 827.9	13 020.5	13 490.8	13 896.7	14 142.5	14 388.9	14 609.3	14 970.1	15 279.8
Motor vehicle and parts dealers [1]	1 494.4	1 435.1	1 428.1	1 475.3	1 564.7	1 627.1	1 685.6	1 723.4	1 740.9	1 796.6	1 846.9
Automobile dealers	983	938	935	970	1 032	1 072	1 113	1 134	1 142	1 180	1 216
Furniture and home furnishings stores	431.5	412.8	410.3	418.6	441.6	461.2	474.2	484.7	499.1	524.4	543.5
Electronics and appliance stores	450.7	449.4	446.3	459.4	495.7	534.7	555.5	575.2	590.6	623.8	647.3
Building material and garden supply stores	890.9	863.0	872.1	891.9	946.2	981.8	1 007.2	1 043.1	1 062.3	1 101.0	1 142.1
Food and beverage stores	2 778.8	2 767.9	2 743.9	2 774.8	2 825.0	2 879.8	2 927.8	2 956.9	2 965.7	2 984.5	2 993.0
Health and personal care stores	792.0	788.5	780.2	778.6	797.0	811.9	826.4	853.3	876.0	898.2	927.6
Gasoline stations	910.2	889.3	876.4	881.2	902.3	922.3	946.4	956.2	961.3	943.5	935.7
Clothing and clothing accessories stores	1 313.0	1 275.8	1 249.1	1 259.9	1 261.7	1 246.3	1 220.6	1 235.9	1 268.6	1 306.6	1 321.6
Sporting goods, hobby, book, and music stores	463.6	459.5	466.2	472.8	498.9	519.8	528.8	545.1	555.1	582.7	602.7
General merchandise stores [1]	2 499.8	2 416.7	2 414.2	2 450.2	2 541.0	2 635.4	2 657.3	2 686.5	2 686.5	2 751.8	2 819.8
Department stores	1 493.9	1 440.8	1 445.2	1 486.8	1 560.4	1 629.8	1 645.0	1 653.5	1 679.2	1 709.2	1 755.0
Miscellaneous store retailers	738.2	734.7	736.8	752.9	795.7	841.1	874.3	913.2	950.3	985.5	1 007.1
Nonstore retailers	419.2	403.7	404.5	404.9	421.2	435.4	438.5	444.5	453.0	471.6	492.4

[1] Includes other industries, not shown separately.

Table 15-1. Nonfarm Employment by Sector and Industry—*Continued*

(Wage and salary workers on nonfarm payrolls, thousands.)

Industry	2001	2002	2003	2004	2005	2006	2007	2008	2009	2010	2011	2012	2013	2014
TOTAL NONFARM	132 074	130 628	130 318	131 749	134 005	136 398	137 936	137 170	131 233	130 275	131 842	134 104	136 393	139 042
Total Private	110 956	109 115	108 735	110 128	112 201	114 424	115 718	114 661	108 678	107 785	109 756	112 184	114 541	117 180
Goods-Producing	23 873	22 557	21 816	21 882	22 190	22 530	22 233	21 335	18 558	17 751	18 047	18 420	18 738	19 223
Mining and logging	606	583	572	591	628	684	724	767	694	705	788	848	863	896
Logging	73.5	70.4	69.4	67.6	65.2	64.4	60.1	56.6	50.4	49.7	48.7	50.8	51.8	52.5
Mining	532.5	512.2	502.7	523.0	562.2	619.7	663.8	709.8	643.3	654.8	739.2	797.2	811.0	843.8
Oil and gas extraction	123.7	121.9	120.2	123.4	125.7	134.5	146.2	160.5	159.8	158.7	172.0	187.4	193.5	197.9
Mining, except oil and gas [1]	218.7	210.6	202.7	205.1	212.8	220.3	223.4	226.0	208.3	204.5	218.4	218.7	209.6	207.4
Coal mining	74.3	74.4	70.0	70.6	73.9	78.0	77.2	81.2	81.5	80.8	87.3	84.7	78.1	74.1
Support activities for mining	190.1	179.8	179.8	194.6	223.7	264.9	294.3	323.4	275.2	291.6	348.8	391.1	407.9	438.5
Construction	6 826	6 716	6 735	6 976	7 336	7 691	7 630	7 162	6 016	5 518	5 533	5 646	5 856	6 138
Construction of buildings	1 588.9	1 574.8	1 575.8	1 630.0	1 711.9	1 804.9	1 774.2	1 641.7	1 357.2	1 229.7	1 222.1	1 240.2	1 285.9	1 356.7
Heavy and civil engineering	953.0	930.6	903.1	907.4	951.2	985.1	1 005.4	964.5	851.3	825.1	836.8	868.3	885.0	914.7
Specialty trade contractors	4 283.9	4 210.4	4 255.7	4 438.6	4 673.1	4 901.1	4 850.2	4 555.8	3 807.9	3 463.4	3 474.4	3 537.1	3 684.4	3 866.8
Manufacturing	16 441	15 259	14 509	14 315	14 227	14 155	13 879	13 406	11 847	11 528	11 726	11 927	12 020	12 188
Durable goods	10 336	9 485	8 964	8 925	8 956	8 981	8 808	8 463	7 284	7 064	7 273	7 470	7 548	7 685
Wood products	576.3	557.0	539.5	551.6	561.0	560.6	517.1	457.7	360.2	342.1	337.1	339.1	353.2	371.7
Nonmetallic mineral products	544.5	516.0	494.2	505.5	505.3	509.6	500.5	465.0	394.3	370.9	366.6	365.3	373.4	385.9
Primary metals	570.9	509.4	477.4	466.8	466.0	464.0	455.8	442.0	362.1	362.3	388.3	402.0	395.3	400.5
Fabricated metal products	1 676.4	1 548.5	1 478.9	1 497.1	1 522.0	1 553.1	1 562.8	1 527.5	1 311.6	1 281.7	1 347.3	1 409.8	1 432.3	1 455.1
Machinery	1 370.6	1 231.8	1 151.6	1 145.2	1 165.5	1 183.2	1 187.1	1 187.6	1 028.6	996.1	1 055.8	1 098.5	1 104.5	1 128.7
Computer and electronic products [1]	1 748.8	1 507.2	1 355.2	1 322.8	1 316.4	1 307.5	1 272.5	1 244.2	1 136.9	1 094.6	1 103.5	1 089.0	1 065.6	1 050.2
Computer and peripheral equipment	286.2	250.0	224.0	210.0	205.1	196.2	186.2	183.2	166.4	157.6	157.4	157.4	157.5	162.8
Communications equipment	225.4	179.0	149.2	143.0	141.4	136.2	128.1	127.3	120.5	117.4	115.3	108.2	101.1	93.5
Semiconductors and electronic components	645.4	524.5	461.1	454.1	452.0	457.9	447.5	431.8	378.1	369.4	383.4	383.1	374.9	367.8
Electronic instruments	483.6	456.8	435.4	436.9	441.0	444.5	443.2	441.0	421.6	406.4	404.2	399.7	393.7	388.3
Electrical equipment and appliances	556.9	496.5	459.6	445.1	433.5	432.7	429.4	424.3	373.6	359.5	366.1	373.2	374.1	374.5
Transportation equipment [1]	1 939.1	1 830.0	1 775.1	1 766.7	1 772.3	1 768.9	1 711.9	1 608.0	1 347.9	1 333.1	1 381.5	1 461.1	1 508.8	1 562.6
Motor vehicles and parts	1 212.9	1 151.2	1 125.3	1 112.8	1 096.7	1 070.0	994.2	875.5	664.1	678.5	717.7	777.3	824.8	876.8
Furniture and related products	642.9	604.7	573.7	574.1	566.3	558.3	529.4	478.0	384.3	357.2	353.1	351.4	359.9	373.1
Miscellaneous manufacturing	709.5	683.3	658.3	650.6	647.2	643.7	641.7	628.9	584.4	566.8	573.7	580.1	580.5	582.7
Nondurable goods [1]	6 105	5 774	5 546	5 390	5 271	5 174	5 071	4 943	4 564	4 464	4 453	4 457	4 472	4 503
Food manufacturing	1 551.2	1 525.7	1 517.5	1 493.7	1 477.6	1 479.4	1 484.1	1 480.9	1 456.4	1 450.6	1 458.8	1 468.8	1 473.7	1 480.5
Textile mills	332.9	290.9	261.3	236.9	217.6	195.0	169.7	151.2	124.4	119.0	120.1	118.7	117.2	117.5
Textile product mills	217.0	204.2	187.7	183.2	176.4	166.7	157.7	147.2	125.7	119.0	117.6	116.3	114.4	114.6
Apparel	415.2	350.0	303.9	278.0	250.5	232.4	214.6	199.0	167.5	156.6	151.7	148.0	144.7	140.3
Paper and paper products	577.6	546.6	516.2	495.5	484.2	470.5	458.2	444.9	407.0	394.7	387.4	379.8	378.0	371.4
Printing and related support activities	768.3	706.6	680.4	662.6	646.3	634.4	622.0	594.1	521.9	487.6	471.8	461.8	452.0	452.7
Petroleum and coal products	121.1	118.1	114.3	111.7	112.1	113.2	114.5	117.4	115.3	113.9	111.8	112.1	110.4	110.7
Chemicals	959.0	927.5	906.1	887.0	872.1	865.9	860.9	847.1	804.1	786.5	783.6	783.3	792.7	803.9
Plastics and rubber products	896.2	846.8	814.3	804.7	802.3	785.5	757.2	729.4	624.9	624.8	635.2	645.1	659.2	674.7
Service-Providing	108 201	108 071	108 501	109 866	111 814	113 867	115 703	115 835	112 675	112 524	113 795	115 683	117 655	119 820
Private Service-Providing	87 083	86 558	86 918	88 246	90 010	91 894	93 485	93 326	90 121	90 034	91 708	93 763	95 803	97 957
Trade, transportation, and utilities	25 983	25 497	25 287	25 533	25 959	26 276	26 630	26 293	24 906	24 636	25 065	25 476	25 862	26 384
Wholesale trade	5 772.7	5 652.3	5 607.5	5 662.9	5 764.4	5 904.5	6 015.2	5 942.7	5 586.6	5 452.1	5 543.1	5 666.6	5 732.9	5 826.0
Durable goods	3 130.4	3 007.9	2 940.6	2 950.5	2 999.2	3 074.8	3 121.5	3 052.0	2 809.9	2 713.5	2 765.2	2 832.3	2 864.2	2 909.8
Nondurable goods	2 031.3	2 015.0	2 004.6	2 010.0	2 022.4	2 041.3	2 062.2	2 047.7	1 966.1	1 928.1	1 939.0	1 965.3	1 984.5	2 018.0
Electronic markets, agents, and brokers	611.1	629.4	662.2	702.4	742.8	788.5	831.5	842.9	810.7	810.5	839.0	869.1	884.3	898.2
Retail trade	15 238.6	15 025.1	14 917.3	15 058.2	15 279.6	15 353.3	15 520.0	15 283.0	14 522.3	14 440.4	14 667.8	14 840.8	15 078.8	15 364.3
Motor vehicle and parts dealers [1]	1 854.6	1 879.4	1 882.9	1 902.3	1 918.6	1 909.7	1 908.3	1 831.2	1 637.5	1 629.2	1 691.2	1 737.0	1 793.1	1 861.4
Automobile dealers	1 225	1 253	1 254	1 257	1 261	1 247	1 242	1 177	1 018	1 012	1 057	1 096	1 138	1 185
Furniture and home furnishings stores	541.2	538.7	547.3	563.4	576.1	586.9	574.6	531.1	449.2	437.9	438.9	439.4	445.8	454.6
Electronics and appliance stores	632.6	594.8	573.9	571.5	585.0	580.5	582.5	569.6	515.7	522.3	527.4	507.4	496.7	491.2
Building material and garden supply stores	1 151.8	1 176.5	1 185.0	1 227.1	1 276.1	1 324.1	1 309.3	1 248.0	1 155.6	1 131.8	1 145.7	1 174.2	1 207.7	1 234.8
Food and beverage stores	2 950.5	2 881.6	2 838.4	2 821.6	2 817.8	2 821.1	2 843.6	2 862.0	2 830.0	2 808.2	2 822.8	2 861.3	2 929.7	2 993.9
Health and personal care stores	951.5	938.8	938.1	941.1	953.7	961.1	993.1	1 002.8	986.0	980.5	980.9	997.9	1 015.8	1 021.0
Gasoline stations	925.3	895.9	882.0	875.6	871.1	864.1	861.5	842.4	825.5	819.3	831.0	843.5	866.3	881.0
Clothing and clothing accessories stores	1 321.1	1 312.5	1 304.5	1 364.3	1 414.6	1 450.9	1 500.0	1 468.0	1 363.9	1 352.5	1 360.9	1 391.4	1 390.9	1 378.6
Sporting goods, hobby, book, and music stores	601.1	591.8	584.7	585.9	597.9	606.0	623.3	621.9	589.2	579.1	577.9	582.2	602.5	612.9
General merchandise stores [1]	2 842.2	2 812.0	2 822.4	2 863.1	2 934.3	2 935.0	3 020.6	3 025.6	2 966.2	2 997.7	3 085.2	3 065.4	3 060.4	3 113.6
Department stores	1 768.3	1 684.0	1 620.6	1 605.3	1 595.1	1 557.2	1 591.5	1 540.5	1 472.9	1 501.6	1 538.6	1 454.9	1 348.3	1 349.5
Miscellaneous store retailers	993.3	959.5	930.7	913.5	899.9	881.0	865.4	842.5	782.4	761.5	772.4	794.0	802.5	817.8
Nonstore retailers	473.5	443.7	427.3	428.8	434.6	432.8	437.9	438.0	421.1	420.6	433.5	447.1	467.4	503.5

[1]Includes other industries, not shown separately.

Table 15-1. Nonfarm Employment by Sector and Industry—*Continued*

(Wage and salary workers on nonfarm payrolls, thousands.)

Industry	1990	1991	1992	1993	1994	1995	1996	1997	1998	1999	2000
Transportation and warehousing	3 475.6	3 462.8	3 461.8	3 553.8	3 701.0	3 837.8	3 935.3	4 026.5	4 168.0	4 300.3	4 410.3
Air transportation	529.2	525.4	519.6	516.6	511.2	510.9	525.7	542.0	562.7	586.3	614.4
Rail transportation	271.8	255.6	248.1	242.2	234.6	232.5	225.2	221.0	225.0	228.8	231.7
Water transportation	56.8	57.4	56.7	52.8	52.3	50.8	51.0	50.7	50.5	51.7	56.0
Truck transportation	1 122.4	1 104.6	1 107.4	1 154.8	1 206.2	1 249.1	1 282.4	1 308.2	1 354.4	1 391.5	1 405.8
Transit and ground passenger transportation	274.2	283.9	287.9	299.9	316.6	327.9	339.1	349.6	362.7	371.0	372.1
Pipeline transportation	59.8	60.7	60.1	58.7	57.0	53.6	51.4	49.7	48.1	46.9	46.0
Scenic and sightseeing transportation	15.7	16.5	17.7	19.3	21.3	22.0	23.2	24.5	25.4	26.1	27.5
Support activities for transportation	364.1	376.6	369.9	381.8	404.7	430.4	445.8	473.4	496.8	518.1	537.4
Couriers and messengers	375.0	378.9	388.8	414.3	466.2	516.8	539.9	546.0	568.2	585.9	605.0
Warehousing and storage	406.6	403.2	405.6	413.4	431.0	443.8	451.8	461.5	474.2	494.1	514.4
Utilities	740.0	736.1	726.0	710.7	689.3	666.2	639.6	620.9	613.4	608.5	601.3
Information	2 688	2 677	2 641	2 668	2 738	2 843	2 940	3 084	3 218	3 419	3 630
Publishing industries, except Internet	870.6	863.4	854.2	873.1	891.0	910.7	927.2	955.5	982.3	1 004.8	1 035.0
Motion picture and sound recording industries	254.6	258.9	254.3	259.6	278.4	311.1	334.7	353.0	369.5	384.4	382.6
Broadcasting, except Internet	283.8	281.2	279.7	284.0	290.1	298.1	309.1	313.0	321.2	329.4	343.5
Telecommunications	1 008.5	999.9	972.9	969.5	989.5	1 009.3	1 038.1	1 108.0	1 167.4	1 270.8	1 396.6
Data processing, hosting, and related services	211.4	212.8	219.6	223.4	226.9	242.6	252.0	268.4	282.8	307.1	315.7
Other information services [1]	59.3	61.2	60.5	58.1	62.5	71.8	79.0	85.5	95.3	121.9	157.1
Internet publishing and broadcasting	29.4	28.3	28.2	28.7	29.7	33.7	39.6	45.4	53.9	78.1	110.8
Financial activities	6 614	6 561	6 559	6 742	6 910	6 866	7 018	7 255	7 565	7 753	7 783
Finance and insurance	4 976	4 938	4 931	5 065	5 175	5 108	5 201	5 379	5 632	5 770	5 773
Monetary authorities–central bank	24.0	24.2	23.7	23.4	23.4	23.0	22.8	22.1	21.7	22.6	22.8
Credit intermediation and related activities [1]	2 424.8	2 352.4	2 317.3	2 360.7	2 375.7	2 314.4	2 368.2	2 433.6	2 531.9	2 591.0	2 547.8
Depository credit intermediation [1]	1 908.5	1 830.7	1 769.0	1 760.5	1 736.7	1 700.2	1 691.4	1 696.6	1 708.9	1 709.7	1 681.2
Commercial banking	1 361.8	1 333.7	1 302.8	1 308.7	1 297.4	1 281.7	1 275.1	1 277.9	1 286.0	1 281.2	1 250.5
Securities, commodity contracts, investments, and funds and trusts	488.7	486.8	508.0	541.5	588.6	597.4	625.7	674.5	734.5	782.2	851.1
Insurance carriers and related activities	2 038.9	2 074.5	2 081.9	2 139.6	2 187.7	2 172.7	2 183.9	2 248.8	2 343.7	2 374.5	2 351.1
Real estate and rental and leasing	1 637.1	1 623.0	1 627.7	1 676.3	1 734.2	1 758.1	1 817.1	1 875.9	1 933.7	1 982.5	2 010.6
Real estate	1 109.0	1 109.8	1 116.7	1 148.6	1 185.9	1 181.7	1 208.6	1 243.8	1 277.7	1 302.6	1 316.0
Rental and leasing services	514.2	499.4	496.4	511.0	529.9	557.4	587.7	609.5	630.8	653.1	666.8
Lessors of nonfinancial intangible assets	13.9	13.9	14.6	16.7	18.4	19.0	20.8	22.6	25.3	26.8	27.8
Professional and business services	10 848	10 714	10 970	11 495	12 174	12 844	13 462	14 335	15 147	15 957	16 666
Professional and technical services [1]	4 538.2	4 509.2	4 575.6	4 689.1	4 823.3	5 078.4	5 312.7	5 628.8	5 992.3	6 345.4	6 701.7
Legal services	943.6	946.0	949.8	963.9	965.6	959.2	968.4	987.5	1 021.1	1 051.4	1 065.7
Accounting and bookkeeping services	664.1	655.4	657.8	654.2	670.1	706.3	729.8	761.2	802.0	837.6	866.4
Architectural and engineering services	941.5	906.2	901.8	922.7	952.0	997.1	1 024.5	1 063.4	1 114.8	1 168.1	1 237.9
Computer systems design and related services	409.7	419.9	444.9	484.8	531.4	611.2	701.4	826.7	974.9	1 132.9	1 254.3
Management and technical consulting services	305.1	314.3	340.2	366.2	396.5	451.8	492.7	541.7	590.4	619.0	672.7
Management of companies and enterprises	1 667.4	1 638.1	1 623.4	1 640.1	1 665.9	1 685.8	1 702.7	1 729.7	1 756.1	1 773.8	1 796.0
Administrative and waste services	4 642.8	4 566.6	4 770.5	5 165.6	5 684.4	6 079.7	6 446.5	6 976.6	7 398.0	7 837.5	8 168.3
Administrative and support services [1]	4 413.3	4 334.3	4 533.8	4 917.0	5 423.7	5 806.4	6 164.5	6 686.0	7 098.7	7 527.0	7 855.4
Employment services [1]	1 512.1	1 466.0	1 610.4	1 884.3	2 246.8	2 448.1	2 625.3	2 953.9	3 245.8	3 581.6	3 849.3
Temporary help services	1 155.8	1 123.3	1 212.5	1 388.8	1 632.2	1 743.8	1 849.0	2 059.7	2 245.2	2 469.6	2 635.6
Business support services	504.6	503.3	524.5	549.0	574.4	629.8	678.3	733.9	772.2	780.5	786.7
Services to buildings and dwellings	1 174.6	1 150.9	1 159.7	1 197.9	1 267.2	1 302.4	1 361.5	1 424.1	1 460.0	1 534.7	1 570.5
Waste management and remediation services	229.4	232.4	236.7	248.6	260.7	273.3	282.0	290.5	299.3	310.5	312.9

[1]Includes other industries, not shown separately.

Table 15-1. Nonfarm Employment by Sector and Industry—*Continued*

(Wage and salary workers on nonfarm payrolls, thousands.)

Industry	2001	2002	2003	2004	2005	2006	2007	2008	2009	2010	2011	2012	2013	2014
Transportation and warehousing	4 372.0	4 223.6	4 185.4	4 248.6	4 360.9	4 469.6	4 540.9	4 508.3	4 236.4	4 190.7	4 301.6	4 415.8	4 498.0	4 640.4
Air transportation	615.3	563.5	528.3	514.5	500.8	487.0	491.8	490.7	462.8	458.3	456.9	459.2	444.3	442.1
Rail transportation	226.7	217.8	217.7	225.7	227.8	227.5	233.7	231.0	218.2	216.4	228.1	230.6	231.2	235.3
Water transportation	54.0	52.6	54.5	56.4	60.6	62.7	65.5	67.1	63.4	62.3	61.3	63.9	65.3	67.2
Truck transportation	1 386.8	1 339.3	1 325.6	1 351.7	1 397.6	1 435.8	1 439.2	1 389.0	1 268.2	1 250.4	1 300.5	1 349.4	1 382.1	1 415.8
Transit and ground passenger transportation	374.8	380.8	382.2	384.9	389.2	399.3	412.1	423.3	421.7	429.7	439.9	440.3	448.5	465.4
Pipeline transportation	45.4	41.7	40.2	38.4	37.8	38.7	39.9	41.7	42.6	42.3	42.9	43.6	44.5	47.0
Scenic and sightseeing transportation	29.1	25.6	26.6	27.2	28.8	27.5	28.6	28.0	27.6	27.3	27.5	28.0	29.1	30.6
Support activities for transportation	539.2	524.7	520.3	535.1	552.2	570.6	584.2	592.0	548.5	542.5	562.2	579.9	598.3	625.2
Couriers and messengers	587.0	560.9	561.7	556.6	571.4	582.4	580.7	573.4	546.3	528.1	529.2	534.1	543.9	574.1
Warehousing and storage	513.8	516.7	528.3	558.1	594.7	638.1	665.2	672.1	637.1	633.4	653.1	686.9	710.9	737.6
Utilities	599.4	596.2	577.0	563.8	554.0	548.5	553.4	558.9	560.0	552.8	552.6	552.8	551.9	552.9
Information	3 629	3 395	3 188	3 118	3 061	3 038	3 032	2 984	2 804	2 707	2 674	2 676	2 706	2 740
Publishing industries, except Internet	1 020.7	964.1	924.8	909.1	904.1	902.4	901.2	880.4	796.4	759.0	748.6	739.5	732.7	724.8
Motion picture and sound recording industries	376.8	387.9	376.2	385.0	377.5	375.7	380.6	371.3	357.6	370.2	362.1	362.3	370.5	376.2
Broadcasting, except Internet	344.6	334.1	324.3	325.0	327.7	328.3	325.2	318.7	300.5	290.3	283.2	285.1	283.7	285.7
Telecommunications	1 423.9	1 280.9	1 166.8	1 115.1	1 071.3	1 047.6	1 030.6	1 019.4	965.7	902.9	873.6	856.8	853.2	855.8
Data processing, hosting, and related services	316.8	303.9	280.0	267.1	262.5	263.2	267.8	260.3	248.5	243.0	245.8	254.9	269.6	279.4
Other information services [1]	146.5	123.6	115.9	116.9	117.7	120.8	126.3	133.5	135.0	141.7	160.0	177.2	196.2	217.8
Internet publishing and broadcasting	100.4	76.3	67.2	66.1	67.2	69.1	72.9	80.6	83.3	92.0	109.6	125.2	142.3	161.9
Financial activities	7 900	7 956	8 078	8 105	8 197	8 367	8 348	8 206	7 838	7 695	7 697	7 784	7 886	7 979
Finance and insurance	5 862	5 922	6 020	6 019	6 063	6 194	6 179	6 076	5 844	5 761	5 769	5 828	5 886	5 933
Monetary authorities–central bank	23.0	23.4	22.6	21.8	20.8	21.2	21.6	22.4	21.0	20.0	18.3	17.5	18.0	18.4
Credit intermediation and related activities [1]	2 597.7	2 686.0	2 792.4	2 817.0	2 869.0	2 924.9	2 866.3	2 732.7	2 590.2	2 550.0	2 554.1	2 583.3	2 614.1	2 566.5
Depository credit intermediation [1]	1 701.2	1 733.0	1 748.5	1 751.5	1 769.2	1 802.0	1 823.5	1 815.2	1 753.8	1 728.8	1 735.1	1 738.7	1 733.6	1 708.0
Commercial banking	1 258.4	1 278.1	1 280.1	1 280.8	1 296.0	1 322.9	1 351.4	1 357.5	1 316.9	1 305.9	1 314.5	1 320.6	1 313.9	1 293.5
Securities, commodity contracts, investments, and funds and trusts	879.0	836.4	803.9	813.1	834.2	868.9	899.6	916.2	862.1	850.4	860.1	859.3	865.0	881.3
Insurance carriers and related activities	2 362.3	2 376.4	2 401.5	2 367.5	2 338.9	2 379.1	2 391.6	2 405.1	2 370.6	2 340.6	2 336.4	2 368.3	2 388.9	2 467.0
Real estate and rental and leasing	2 038.4	2 033.3	2 057.5	2 085.5	2 133.5	2 172.5	2 169.1	2 129.6	1 994.0	1 933.8	1 927.4	1 955.2	2 000.2	2 046.2
Real estate	1 343.4	1 356.6	1 387.1	1 418.7	1 460.8	1 499.0	1 500.4	1 485.0	1 420.2	1 395.7	1 400.8	1 420.0	1 458.7	1 487.4
Rental and leasing services	666.3	649.1	643.1	641.1	645.8	645.5	640.3	616.9	547.3	513.5	502.2	511.0	517.7	535.3
Lessors of nonfinancial intangible assets	28.7	27.6	27.3	25.7	26.9	28.1	28.4	27.7	26.5	24.6	24.4	24.2	23.7	23.6
Professional and business services	16 476	15 976	15 987	16 394	16 954	17 566	17 942	17 735	16 579	16 728	17 332	17 932	18 515	19 096
Professional and technical services [1]	6 871.1	6 648.8	6 602.7	6 747.1	7 024.6	7 356.7	7 659.5	7 799.4	7 508.5	7 441.3	7 666.2	7 892.3	8 120.9	8 347.5
Legal services	1 091.3	1 115.3	1 142.1	1 163.1	1 168.0	1 173.2	1 175.4	1 161.5	1 124.9	1 114.2	1 115.7	1 124.0	1 128.5	1 119.9
Accounting and bookkeeping services	872.2	837.3	815.3	805.9	849.3	889.0	935.9	951.0	914.2	886.5	898.9	908.9	931.5	958.4
Architectural and engineering services	1 274.7	1 246.1	1 226.9	1 258.2	1 310.9	1 385.7	1 432.2	1 439.4	1 324.7	1 275.4	1 293.5	1 322.5	1 345.6	1 380.3
Computer systems design and related services	1 297.8	1 152.8	1 116.6	1 148.6	1 195.2	1 284.6	1 372.1	1 439.6	1 422.6	1 449.0	1 535.9	1 621.6	1 702.3	1 777.7
Management and technical consulting services	715.1	707.7	718.0	763.0	824.2	886.4	952.7	1 002.0	994.9	999.4	1 065.2	1 118.1	1 180.3	1 244.4
Management of companies and enterprises	1 779.0	1 705.4	1 687.2	1 724.4	1 758.9	1 810.9	1 866.4	1 904.5	1 866.9	1 872.3	1 933.6	2 023.3	2 102.9	2 169.4
Administrative and waste services	7 826.0	7 621.9	7 696.8	7 922.9	8 170.2	8 398.3	8 416.3	8 031.5	7 203.3	7 414.0	7 731.9	8 016.2	8 290.8	8 579.2
Administrative and support services [1]	7 508.7	7 303.6	7 374.7	7 594.4	7 832.5	8 050.2	8 061.3	7 674.7	6 851.6	7 056.7	7 366.7	7 644.3	7 913.3	8 193.6
Employment services [1]	3 468.2	3 273.2	3 326.4	3 455.5	3 606.9	3 680.9	3 545.9	3 133.0	2 480.8	2 722.5	2 942.1	3 134.1	3 268.5	3 420.9
Temporary help services	2 337.7	2 193.7	2 224.2	2 387.2	2 549.4	2 637.4	2 597.4	2 348.4	1 823.3	2 093.6	2 313.0	2 495.3	2 616.8	2 767.1
Business support services	779.7	756.6	749.7	757.8	766.4	792.9	817.4	832.3	820.0	808.6	814.5	828.5	856.1	883.7
Services to buildings and dwellings	1 606.2	1 606.1	1 636.1	1 693.7	1 737.5	1 801.4	1 849.5	1 839.8	1 753.3	1 745.0	1 788.6	1 830.0	1 884.7	1 940.3
Waste management and remediation services	317.3	318.3	322.1	328.6	337.6	348.1	355.0	356.8	351.7	357.3	365.3	371.9	377.5	385.6

[1]Includes other industries, not shown separately.

Table 15-1. Nonfarm Employment by Sector and Industry—*Continued*

(Wage and salary workers on nonfarm payrolls, thousands.)

Industry	1990	1991	1992	1993	1994	1995	1996	1997	1998	1999	2000
Education and health services	11 024	11 556	11 948	12 362	12 872	13 360	13 761	14 185	14 570	14 939	15 247
Educational services	1 688.0	1 736.6	1 713.1	1 755.4	1 894.9	2 010.2	2 077.6	2 155.0	2 232.9	2 320.4	2 390.4
Health care and social assistance	9 336.0	9 819.0	10 235.2	10 606.9	10 976.8	11 349.1	11 683.8	12 029.5	12 336.9	12 618.3	12 856.6
Health care	8 211.0	8 618.0	8 955.0	9 254.0	9 530.0	9 809.0	10 093.0	10 358.0	10 541.0	10 691.0	10 858.0
Ambulatory health care services [1]	2 842.0	3 028.4	3 199.9	3 385.5	3 578.8	3 767.5	3 939.9	4 093.0	4 161.2	4 226.6	4 320.3
Offices of physicians	1 278.0	1 345.2	1 401.1	1 442.0	1 480.9	1 540.4	1 603.8	1 660.5	1 723.6	1 786.6	1 839.9
Outpatient care centers	261.0	271.4	286.5	303.1	314.5	328.8	340.2	352.1	363.3	375.4	386.4
Home health care services	288.0	340.7	393.4	463.8	553.2	621.8	667.2	702.8	659.5	629.6	633.3
Hospitals	3 513.0	3 617.3	3 711.4	3 740.0	3 724.0	3 733.7	3 772.8	3 821.6	3 892.4	3 935.5	3 954.3
Nursing and residential care facilities [1]	1 856.0	1 972.0	2 043.5	2 128.1	2 227.0	2 307.7	2 379.9	2 443.4	2 487.3	2 528.8	2 583.2
Nursing care facilities	1 170.0	1 240.2	1 273.4	1 319.3	1 377.1	1 413.0	1 448.4	1 474.6	1 489.3	1 501.0	1 513.6
Social assistance [1]	1 125.0	1 201.3	1 280.4	1 353.3	1 447.0	1 540.2	1 591.2	1 671.5	1 796.0	1 927.5	1 998.8
Child day care services	388.0	413.2	446.5	468.9	510.0	557.1	559.2	570.4	615.1	673.7	695.8
Leisure and hospitality	9 288	9 256	9 437	9 732	10 100	10 501	10 777	11 018	11 232	11 543	11 862
Arts, entertainment, and recreation	1 132.0	1 177.0	1 236.3	1 301.9	1 375.6	1 459.4	1 522.1	1 599.9	1 645.2	1 709.1	1 787.9
Performing arts and spectator sports	273.0	283.0	289.5	286.8	296.1	307.7	328.6	349.6	350.0	361.1	381.8
Museums, historical sites, zoos, and parks	68.0	71.0	75.0	78.3	81.8	83.9	88.9	93.8	97.4	103.1	110.4
Amusements, gambling, and recreation	791.0	823.0	871.8	936.8	997.7	1 067.8	1 104.5	1 156.5	1 197.9	1 244.9	1 295.7
Accommodation and food services	8 156.0	8 079.0	8 200.5	8 430.4	8 724.1	9 041.6	9 254.3	9 417.9	9 586.2	9 833.7	10 073.5
Accommodation	1 616.0	1 574.0	1 561.5	1 580.5	1 615.3	1 652.5	1 698.9	1 729.5	1 773.5	1 831.7	1 884.4
Food services and drinking places	6 540.0	6 505.0	6 639.0	6 849.9	7 108.7	7 389.1	7 555.4	7 688.5	7 812.7	8 002.0	8 189.1
Other services	4 261	4 249	4 240	4 350	4 428	4 572	4 690	4 825	4 976	5 087	5 168
Repair and maintenance	1 009.0	960.0	964.0	998.0	1 023.5	1 078.9	1 135.5	1 169.3	1 189.2	1 222.0	1 241.5
Personal and laundry services	1 120.0	1 109.0	1 098.9	1 116.0	1 120.3	1 143.9	1 165.7	1 180.4	1 205.6	1 220.3	1 242.9
Membership associations and organizations	2 132.0	2 180.0	2 177.1	2 236.4	2 284.5	2 348.9	2 389.1	2 474.9	2 581.3	2 644.4	2 683.3
Government	18 415	18 545	18 787	18 989	19 275	19 432	19 539	19 664	19 909	20 307	20 790
Federal	3 196	3 110	3 111	3 063	3 018	2 949	2 877	2 806	2 772	2 769	2 865
Federal, except U.S. Postal Service	2 371.0	2 296.0	2 310.7	2 269.4	2 197.2	2 098.8	2 009.8	1 940.2	1 891.3	1 879.5	1 984.8
U.S. Postal Service	825.1	813.0	800.0	793.2	820.6	849.9	867.2	866.0	880.5	889.7	879.7
State government	4 305.0	4 355.0	4 408.0	4 488.0	4 576.0	4 635.0	4 606.0	4 582.0	4 612.0	4 709.0	4 786.0
Federal, except U.S. Postal Service	1 729.9	1 767.6	1 798.6	1 834.1	1 881.9	1 919.0	1 910.7	1 904.0	1 922.2	1 983.2	2 030.6
State government, excluding education	2 574.6	2 587.3	2 609.7	2 653.8	2 693.6	2 715.5	2 695.1	2 677.9	2 690.2	2 725.6	2 755.9
Local government	10 914.0	11 081.0	11 267.0	11 438.0	11 682.0	11 849.0	12 056.0	12 276.0	12 525.0	12 829.0	13 139.0
Local government education	5 902.1	5 994.1	6 075.9	6 206.3	6 329.4	6 453.1	6 592.3	6 758.5	6 920.9	7 120.4	7 293.9
Local government, excluding education	5 012.4	5 086.9	5 191.6	5 231.9	5 352.2	5 396.0	5 464.1	5 516.9	5 603.9	5 708.6	5 844.6

[1]Includes other industries, not shown separately.

Table 15-1. Nonfarm Employment by Sector and Industry—*Continued*

(Wage and salary workers on nonfarm payrolls, thousands.)

Industry	2001	2002	2003	2004	2005	2006	2007	2008	2009	2010	2011	2012	2013	2014
Education and health services	15 801	16 377	16 805	17 192	17 630	18 099	18 613	19 156	19 550	19 889	20 228	20 698	21 097	21 475
Educational services	2 510.6	2 642.8	2 695.1	2 762.5	2 835.8	2 900.9	2 941.4	3 039.7	3 090.4	3 155.1	3 249.6	3 341.1	3 354.4	3 417.4
Health care and social assistance	13 289.9	13 733.9	14 109.9	14 429.7	14 793.8	15 198.2	15 671.1	16 116.5	16 459.8	16 733.9	16 978.6	17 356.8	17 743.1	18 057.4
Health care	11 188.0	11 536.0	11 817.0	12 055.0	12 314.0	12 602.0	12 947.0	13 290.0	13 543.0	13 777.0	14 026.0	14 282.0	14 492.0	14 690.1
Ambulatory health care services [1]	4 461.5	4 633.2	4 786.4	4 952.3	5 113.5	5 285.8	5 473.5	5 646.6	5 793.4	5 974.7	6 136.2	6 306.5	6 476.5	6 644.8
Offices of physicians	1 911.2	1 967.8	2 002.5	2 047.8	2 093.5	2 147.8	2 201.6	2 252.6	2 279.1	2 312.7	2 344.1	2 390.2	2 429.2	2 470.2
Outpatient care centers	399.7	413.0	426.8	450.5	473.2	492.6	512.0	533.3	557.5	599.9	620.8	648.6	679.9	711.1
Home health care services	638.6	679.8	732.6	776.6	821.0	865.6	913.8	961.4	1 027.1	1 084.6	1 140.3	1 185.0	1 230.3	1 262.2
Hospitals	4 050.9	4 159.6	4 244.6	4 284.7	4 345.4	4 423.4	4 515.0	4 627.3	4 667.4	4 678.5	4 721.7	4 779.0	4 785.8	4 784.3
Nursing and residential care facilities [1]	2 675.8	2 743.3	2 786.2	2 818.4	2 855.0	2 892.5	2 958.3	3 016.1	3 082.2	3 123.7	3 168.1	3 196.2	3 229.2	3 261.1
Nursing care facilities	1 546.8	1 573.2	1 579.8	1 576.9	1 577.4	1 581.4	1 602.6	1 618.7	1 644.9	1 657.1	1 669.6	1 662.8	1 653.8	1 651.9
Social assistance [1]	2 101.8	2 197.9	2 292.8	2 374.4	2 479.9	2 596.4	2 724.4	2 826.6	2 916.8	2 957.0	2 952.7	3 075.2	3 251.6	3 367.3
Child day care services	714.6	744.1	755.3	764.7	789.7	818.3	850.4	859.4	852.8	848.0	849.4	851.3	843.3	853.2
Leisure and hospitality	12 036	11 986	12 173	12 493	12 816	13 110	13 427	13 436	13 077	13 049	13 353	13 768	14 254	14 710
Arts, entertainment, and recreation	1 824.4	1 782.6	1 812.9	1 849.6	1 892.3	1 928.5	1 969.2	1 970.1	1 915.5	1 913.3	1 919.1	1 968.6	2 029.7	2 103.4
Performing arts and spectator sports	382.3	363.7	371.7	367.5	376.3	398.5	405.0	405.7	396.8	406.2	394.2	402.4	419.2	447.9
Museums, historical sites, zoos, and parks	115.0	114.0	114.7	118.3	120.7	123.8	130.3	131.6	129.4	127.7	132.7	136.1	140.3	145.3
Amusements, gambling, and recreation	1 327.1	1 305.0	1 326.5	1 363.8	1 395.3	1 406.3	1 433.9	1 432.8	1 389.2	1 379.4	1 392.2	1 430.1	1 470.2	1 510.3
Accommodation and food services	10 211.3	10 203.2	10 359.8	10 643.2	10 923.0	11 181.1	11 457.4	11 466.3	11 161.9	11 135.4	11 433.6	11 799.7	12 224.2	12 606.3
Accommodation	1 852.2	1 778.6	1 775.4	1 789.5	1 818.6	1 832.1	1 866.9	1 868.7	1 763.0	1 759.6	1 800.5	1 825.1	1 864.9	1 889.3
Food services and drinking places	8 359.1	8 424.6	8 584.4	8 853.7	9 104.4	9 349.0	9 590.4	9 597.5	9 398.9	9 375.8	9 633.1	9 974.6	10 359.2	10 717.0
Other services	5 258	5 372	5 401	5 409	5 395	5 438	5 494	5 515	5 367	5 331	5 360	5 430	5 483	5 573
Repair and maintenance	1 256.5	1 246.9	1 233.6	1 228.8	1 236.0	1 248.5	1 253.4	1 227.0	1 150.4	1 138.8	1 168.7	1 194.0	1 216.6	1 240.3
Personal and laundry services	1 255.0	1 257.2	1 263.5	1 272.9	1 276.6	1 288.4	1 309.7	1 322.6	1 280.6	1 265.3	1 288.6	1 313.6	1 341.7	1 368.7
Membership associations and organizations	2 746.4	2 867.8	2 903.6	2 907.5	2 882.2	2 901.2	2 931.1	2 965.7	2 936.0	2 926.4	2 903.0	2 922.4	2 924.6	2 964.2
Government	21 118	21 513	21 583	21 621	21 804	21 974	22 218	22 509	22 555	22 490	22 086	21 920	21 853	21 863
Federal	2 764	2 766	2 761	2 730	2 732	2 732	2 734	2 762	2 832	2 977	2 859	2 820	2 769	2 729
Federal, except U.S. Postal Service	1 891.0	1 923.8	1 952.4	1 947.5	1 957.3	1 962.6	1 964.7	2 014.4	2 128.5	2 318.1	2 227.6	2 209.2	2 174.5	2 135.4
U.S. Postal Service	873.0	842.4	808.6	782.1	774.2	769.7	769.1	747.4	703.4	658.5	630.9	611.2	594.9	593.0
State government	4 905.0	5 029.0	5 002.0	4 982.0	5 032.0	5 075.0	5 122.0	5 177.0	5 169.0	5 137.0	5 078.0	5 055.0	5 046.0	5 060.0
Federal, except U.S. Postal Service	2 112.9	2 242.8	2 254.7	2 238.1	2 259.9	2 292.5	2 317.5	2 354.4	2 360.2	2 373.1	2 374.0	2 388.5	2 393.3	2 409.2
State government, excluding education	2 791.8	2 786.3	2 747.6	2 743.9	2 771.6	2 782.0	2 804.3	2 822.5	2 808.8	2 764.1	2 703.7	2 666.4	2 652.8	2 651.2
Local government	13 449.0	13 718.0	13 820.0	13 909.0	14 041.0	14 167.0	14 362.0	14 571.0	14 554.0	14 376.0	14 150.0	14 045.0	14 037.0	14 074.0
Local government education	7 479.3	7 654.4	7 709.4	7 765.2	7 856.1	7 913.0	7 986.8	8 083.9	8 078.8	8 013.4	7 872.5	7 777.9	7 776.7	7 791.2
Local government, excluding education	5 970.0	6 063.2	6 110.2	6 144.1	6 184.6	6 253.8	6 375.5	6 486.5	6 474.9	6 362.9	6 277.7	6 266.8	6 260.1	6 282.5

[1]Includes other industries, not shown separately.

Table 15-2. Production and Nonsupervisory Workers on Private Nonfarm Payrolls by Industry

(Wage and salary workers on nonfarm payrolls, thousands.)

Industry	1990	1991	1992	1993	1994	1995	1996	1997	1998	1999	2000
Total Private	73 721	72 567	72 854	74 671	77 478	79 943	81 888	84 313	86 516	88 647	90 543
Goods-Producing	17 322	16 352	16 044	16 236	16 795	17 137	17 318	17 698	18 008	18 067	18 169
Mining and logging	538	515	478	462	461	458	461	479	473	438	446
Construction	4 115	3 674	3 546	3 704	3 973	4 113	4 325	4 546	4 807	5 105	5 295
Manufacturing	12 669	12 164	12 020	12 070	12 361	12 567	12 532	12 673	12 729	12 524	12 428
Durable goods	7 397	7 001	6 853	6 880	7 134	7 352	7 426	7 599	7 721	7 651	7 659
Wood products	451.5	414.3	418.6	438.5	470.4	479.3	486.6	498.3	509.6	516.2	507.4
Nonmetallic mineral products	413.2	384.1	378.4	380.7	392.3	399.7	404.8	412.5	420.6	426.0	439.5
Primary metals	525.1	496.9	478.7	473.0	487.4	500.3	500.3	501.6	505.3	491.9	490.0
Fabricated metal products	1 190.1	1 131.6	1 101.0	1 116.9	1 172.0	1 223.0	1 241.6	1 285.3	1 319.6	1 304.9	1 325.8
Machinery	938.9	884.9	857.7	875.5	922.5	969.9	984.5	1 006.9	1 016.1	978.4	961.4
Computer and electronic products	980.2	925.6	876.3	856.0	864.0	890.3	915.3	951.1	964.7	932.9	949.3
Electrical equipment and appliances	465.2	435.6	425.0	422.0	434.7	438.4	433.9	427.7	431.8	433.2	433.1
Transportation equipment [1]	1 473.4	1 406.4	1 388.6	1 367.0	1 415.6	1 472.2	1 481.0	1 521.9	1 530.2	1 526.5	1 497.8
Motor vehicles and parts	869.5	840.1	868.0	896.0	978.4	1 048.9	1 052.4	1 062.4	1 050.2	1 075.8	1 073.0
Furniture and related products	475.2	440.1	442.9	454.0	475.7	480.0	477.9	489.8	512.2	532.4	544.4
Miscellaneous manufacturing	484.2	481.2	486.0	495.1	499.0	499.1	500.1	503.4	511.0	508.9	509.8
Nondurable goods [1]	5 272	5 163	5 167	5 191	5 227	5 214	5 106	5 075	5 008	4 872	4 769
Food manufacturing	1 165.0	1 174.2	1 182.0	1 195.3	1 200.4	1 221.0	1 227.7	1 227.7	1 227.6	1 228.7	1 227.9
Textile mills	417.9	407.2	406.0	403.9	403.3	393.2	371.7	367.1	357.2	333.7	315.2
Textile product mills	194.9	185.0	187.4	191.0	199.0	197.9	192.5	192.6	189.7	186.8	183.4
Apparel	805.2	781.0	785.3	764.0	740.1	697.9	631.1	593.7	534.0	458.3	403.8
Paper and paper products	493.2	488.4	489.9	490.9	492.8	493.8	487.5	488.7	484.1	474.0	467.5
Printing and related support activities	597.6	581.7	573.6	579.7	591.4	599.1	594.0	597.0	598.4	585.1	575.7
Petroleum and coal products	97.5	97.4	96.8	93.0	90.9	88.8	87.2	87.8	87.1	84.6	83.1
Chemicals	620.3	599.7	586.2	590.1	595.6	598.4	595.1	593.3	600.6	595.2	587.7
Plastics and rubber products	646.7	623.9	638.9	663.8	698.5	718.7	720.3	731.7	739.3	746.0	752.6
Private Service-Providing	56 399	56 215	56 810	58 436	60 683	62 806	64 570	66 615	68 508	70 580	72 374
Trade, transportation, and utilities	19 032	18 640	18 506	18 752	19 392	19 984	20 325	20 698	21 059	21 576	21 965
Wholesale trade	4 198	4 122	4 071	4 072	4 196	4 361	4 423	4 523	4 605	4 673	4 686
Retail trade	11 308	11 008	10 931	11 104	11 502	11 841	12 057	12 274	12 440	12 772	13 040
Transportation and warehousing	2 940.8	2 928.0	2 934.0	3 019.4	3 152.8	3 260.2	3 339.3	3 406.8	3 521.6	3 641.9	3 753.2
Utilities	584.9	581.5	569.5	556.5	540.9	521.8	505.5	493.8	492.2	489.2	485.1
Information	1 866.0	1 871.0	1 871.0	1 896.0	1 928.0	2 007.0	2 096.0	2 181.0	2 217.0	2 351.0	2 502.0
Financial activities	4 973.0	4 914.0	4 924.0	5 084.0	5 220.0	5 199.0	5 322.0	5 482.0	5 692.0	5 818.0	5 819.0
Professional and business services	8 889	8 748	8 971	9 451	10 078	10 645	11 161	11 896	12 566	13 184	13 790
Education and health services	9 784	10 257	10 607	10 961	11 397	11 829	12 195	12 566	12 903	13 217	13 487
Leisure and hospitality	8 299	8 247	8 406	8 667	8 979	9 330	9 565	9 780	9 947	10 216	10 516
Other services	3 555	3 539	3 526	3 623	3 689	3 812	3 907	4 013	4 124	4 219	4 296

[1]Includes other industries, not shown separately.

Table 15-2. Production and Nonsupervisory Workers on Private Nonfarm Payrolls by Industry
—Continued

(Wage and salary workers on nonfarm payrolls, thousands.)

Industry	2001	2002	2003	2004	2005	2006	2007	2008	2009	2010	2011	2012	2013	2014
Total Private	90 202	88 645	87 938	89 212	91 401	93 727	95 203	94 610	89 556	88 875	90 537	92 715	94 601	96 794
Goods-Producing	17 466	16 400	15 732	15 821	16 145	16 559	16 405	15 724	13 399	12 774	13 005	13 287	13 481	13 858
Mining and logging	457	436	420	440	473	519	547	574	510	525	594	641	636	658
Construction	5 332	5 196	5 123	5 309	5 611	5 903	5 883	5 521	4 567	4 172	4 184	4 246	4 423	4 631
Manufacturing	11 677	10 768	10 189	10 072	10 060	10 137	9 975	9 629	8 322	8 077	8 228	8 400	8 422	8 568
Durable goods	7 164	6 530	6 152	6 140	6 220	6 355	6 250	5 975	4 990	4 829	4 986	5 152	5 185	5 291
Wood products	470.0	450.3	434.4	445.4	454.4	451.2	407.0	357.5	277.8	269.0	268.7	271.8	283.0	298.0
Nonmetallic mineral products	427.1	398.8	374.7	387.8	387.0	391.2	383.6	363.4	302.7	283.5	277.6	273.4	274.7	281.7
Primary metals	446.9	396.2	370.3	363.7	362.7	362.6	357.5	347.7	272.5	275.3	301.2	316.7	305.9	311.4
Fabricated metal products	1 253.5	1 147.0	1 092.5	1 108.6	1 129.3	1 161.8	1 170.9	1 142.9	960.5	935.3	993.6	1 050.0	1 063.0	1 071.7
Machinery	890.7	786.9	732.3	729.7	748.9	769.8	774.0	771.7	641.0	615.9	662.3	699.8	699.1	716.9
Computer and electronic products	875.8	744.1	672.7	655.8	700.1	755.6	743.8	730.0	654.3	629.3	630.0	627.9	609.9	590.2
Electrical equipment and appliances	402.2	351.9	319.5	307.2	300.1	302.9	305.2	305.3	266.1	251.1	247.8	249.1	244.8	246.3
Transportation equipment [1]	1 398.7	1 310.2	1 269.3	1 265.2	1 276.8	1 303.7	1 274.5	1 177.2	948.1	937.0	972.0	1 024.3	1 053.2	1 106.8
Motor vehicles and parts	986.8	931.0	906.3	902.9	893.7	872.7	804.2	695.5	510.0	524.9	556.2	597.6	642.4	693.9
Furniture and related products	509.2	475.1	444.5	443.3	435.7	432.8	409.0	364.2	284.3	263.0	260.0	258.9	265.6	278.0
Miscellaneous manufacturing	489.8	469.2	442.1	432.2	424.4	423.4	424.6	415.6	382.2	370.2	372.8	379.8	385.9	390.1
Nondurable goods [1]	4 513	4 238	4 037	3 932	3 841	3 782	3 725	3 653	3 332	3 248	3 241	3 248	3 237	3 277
Food manufacturing	1 221.3	1 202.3	1 192.5	1 177.8	1 170.0	1 172.2	1 183.5	1 183.9	1 161.1	1 152.2	1 158.0	1 169.0	1 169.3	1 173.1
Textile mills	275.8	242.2	216.9	193.9	174.2	157.8	137.3	122.0	98.6	95.9	98.2	96.4	92.5	91.5
Textile product mills	173.7	162.0	148.3	147.1	143.0	134.9	123.2	115.3	97.7	91.7	89.2	84.8	83.0	85.4
Apparel	341.4	286.0	241.5	218.6	192.7	182.0	173.4	163.3	132.3	120.4	111.6	108.6	106.0	103.6
Paper and paper products	446.3	421.4	392.7	373.7	365.2	357.4	350.5	343.7	313.0	302.2	295.3	287.6	279.3	275.4
Printing and related support activities	544.4	492.6	471.2	459.5	447.3	446.6	442.6	424.5	369.3	341.7	327.1	315.7	309.9	310.9
Petroleum and coal products	80.9	78.0	74.4	76.7	75.4	72.2	72.6	77.1	69.7	69.5	69.8	72.4	69.9	71.1
Chemicals	562.2	531.9	524.9	520.2	510.0	507.7	504.4	512.5	478.7	473.8	479.8	490.8	490.4	497.4
Plastics and rubber products	704.4	661.9	633.4	625.6	620.4	607.6	592.3	571.5	476.5	472.0	481.7	486.9	496.6	517.9
Private Service-Providing	72 736	72 245	72 206	73 392	75 257	77 168	78 798	78 886	76 157	76 101	77 532	79 428	81 120	82 937
Trade, transportation, and utilities	21 709	21 337	21 078	21 319	21 830	22 166	22 546	22 337	21 116	20 874	21 234	21 617	21 875	22 281
Wholesale trade	4 555	4 474	4 396	4 444	4 584	4 724	4 851	4 822	4 506	4 378	4 443	4 562	4 621	4 706
Retail trade	12 952	12 774	12 655	12 788	13 030	13 110	13 317	13 134	12 472	12 425	12 647	12 793	12 923	13 113
Transportation and warehousing	3 718.2	3 611.3	3 563.1	3 637.1	3 774.0	3 889.1	3 934.6	3 930.7	3 688.1	3 627.1	3 703.4	3 820.0	3 885.8	4 014.1
Utilities	482.8	478.4	463.7	449.9	443.0	442.6	443.5	450.4	451.0	443.5	440.8	441.0	445.4	446.7
Information	2 531.0	2 398.0	2 347.0	2 371.0	2 386.0	2 399.0	2 403.0	2 388.0	2 240.0	2 170.0	2 148.0	2 164.0	2 194.0	2 221.0
Financial activities	5 888.0	5 964.0	6 052.0	6 052.0	6 127.0	6 312.0	6 365.0	6 320.0	6 066.0	5 942.0	5 900.0	5 986.0	6 068.0	6 157.0
Professional and business services	13 588	13 049	12 911	13 287	13 854	14 446	14 784	14 585	13 520	13 699	14 251	14 802	15 305	15 795
Education and health services	13 986	14 471	14 726	14 984	15 359	15 783	16 261	16 777	17 166	17 452	17 736	18 165	18 516	18 859
Leisure and hospitality	10 662	10 576	10 666	10 955	11 263	11 568	11 861	11 873	11 560	11 507	11 772	12 154	12 589	12 981
Other services	4 373	4 449	4 426	4 425	4 438	4 494	4 578	4 606	4 488	4 458	4 491	4 541	4 573	4 642

[1]Includes other industries, not shown separately.

Table 15-3. Average Weekly Hours of Production and Nonsupervisory Workers on Private Nonfarm Payrolls by Industry

(Hours.)

Industry	1990	1991	1992	1993	1994	1995	1996	1997	1998	1999	2000	2001
Total Private	34.3	34.1	34.2	34.3	34.5	34.3	34.3	34.5	34.5	34.3	34.3	34.0
Goods-Producing	40.1	40.1	40.2	40.6	41.1	40.8	40.8	41.1	40.8	40.8	40.7	39.9
Mining and logging	45.0	45.3	44.6	44.9	45.3	45.3	46.0	46.2	44.9	44.2	44.4	44.6
Construction	38.3	38.1	38.0	38.4	38.8	38.8	38.9	38.9	38.8	39.0	39.2	38.7
Manufacturing	40.5	40.4	40.7	41.1	41.7	41.3	41.3	41.7	41.4	41.4	41.3	40.3
Overtime hours	3.9	3.8	4.0	4.4	5.0	4.7	4.8	5.1	4.8	4.9	4.7	4.0
Durable goods	41.1	40.9	41.3	41.9	42.6	42.1	42.1	42.6	42.1	41.9	41.8	40.6
Overtime hours	3.9	3.7	3.9	4.5	5.3	5.0	5.0	5.4	5.0	5.0	4.8	3.9
Wood products	40.4	40.2	40.9	41.2	41.7	41.0	41.2	41.4	41.4	41.3	41.0	40.2
Nonmetallic mineral products	40.9	40.5	41.0	41.5	42.2	41.8	42.0	41.9	42.2	42.1	41.6	41.6
Primary metals	42.1	41.5	42.4	43.1	44.1	43.4	43.6	44.3	43.5	43.8	44.2	42.4
Fabricated metal products	41.0	40.8	41.2	41.6	42.3	41.9	41.9	42.3	41.9	41.7	41.9	40.7
Machinery	42.1	41.9	42.4	43.2	43.9	43.5	43.3	44.0	43.1	42.3	42.3	40.9
Computer and electronic products	41.3	40.9	41.4	41.7	42.2	42.2	41.9	42.5	41.9	41.5	41.4	39.8
Electrical equipment and appliances	41.2	41.4	41.8	42.4	43.0	41.9	42.1	42.1	41.8	41.8	41.6	39.8
Transportation equipment [1]	42.0	41.9	41.9	43.0	44.3	43.7	43.8	44.2	43.3	43.6	43.3	41.9
Motor vehicles and parts	41.4	41.5	41.6	43.3	44.8	43.8	43.8	43.9	42.6	43.8	43.4	41.6
Furniture and related products	38.0	37.8	38.6	39.0	39.3	38.5	38.2	39.1	39.4	39.3	39.2	38.3
Miscellaneous manufacturing	39.0	39.2	39.3	39.2	39.4	39.2	39.1	39.7	39.2	39.3	39.0	38.8
Nondurable goods [1]	39.6	39.7	40.0	40.1	40.5	40.1	40.1	40.5	40.5	40.5	40.3	39.9
Overtime hours	3.8	4.0	4.2	4.3	4.6	4.3	4.4	4.6	4.6	4.6	4.5	4.1
Food manufacturing	39.3	39.2	39.2	39.3	39.8	39.6	39.5	39.8	40.1	40.2	40.1	39.6
Textile mills	40.2	40.7	41.3	41.6	41.9	40.9	40.8	41.6	41.0	41.0	41.4	40.0
Textile product mills	38.5	38.6	38.7	39.2	39.4	38.6	38.8	39.2	39.2	39.1	38.7	38.4
Apparel	34.7	35.4	35.6	35.6	35.7	35.3	35.2	35.6	35.5	35.4	35.7	36.0
Paper and paper products	43.6	43.6	43.8	43.8	44.2	43.4	43.5	43.9	43.6	43.6	42.8	42.1
Printing and related support activities	38.7	38.6	39.0	39.2	39.6	39.1	39.1	39.5	39.3	39.1	39.2	38.7
Petroleum and coal products	44.4	43.9	43.6	44.0	44.3	43.7	43.7	43.1	43.6	42.6	42.7	43.8
Chemicals	42.8	43.1	43.3	43.2	43.4	43.4	43.3	43.4	43.2	42.8	42.2	41.9
Plastics and rubber products	40.6	40.5	41.2	41.4	41.8	41.1	41.0	41.4	41.3	41.3	40.8	40.0
Private Service-Providing	32.5	32.4	32.5	32.5	32.7	32.6	32.6	32.8	32.8	32.7	32.7	32.5
Trade, transportation, and utilities	33.7	33.6	33.8	34.1	34.3	34.1	34.1	34.3	34.2	33.9	33.8	33.5
Wholesale trade	38.4	38.4	38.5	38.5	38.8	38.6	38.6	38.8	38.6	38.6	38.8	38.4
Retail trade	30.6	30.4	30.7	30.7	30.9	30.8	30.7	30.9	30.9	30.8	30.7	30.7
Transportation and warehousing	37.7	37.3	37.4	38.9	39.5	38.9	39.1	39.4	38.7	37.6	37.4	36.7
Utilities	41.6	41.5	41.7	42.1	42.3	42.3	42.0	42.0	42.0	42.0	42.0	41.4
Information	35.8	35.6	35.8	36.0	36.0	36.0	36.3	36.3	36.6	36.7	36.8	36.9
Financial activities	35.5	35.4	35.6	35.5	35.5	35.5	35.5	35.8	36.0	35.8	35.9	35.8
Professional and business services	34.2	34.0	34.0	34.0	34.1	34.0	34.1	34.3	34.3	34.4	34.5	34.2
Education and health services	31.9	31.9	32.0	32.0	32.0	32.0	31.9	32.2	32.2	32.1	32.2	32.3
Leisure and hospitality	26.0	25.6	25.7	25.9	26.0	25.9	25.9	26.1	26.2	26.1	26.1	25.8
Other services	32.8	32.7	32.6	32.6	32.7	32.6	32.5	32.7	32.6	32.5	32.5	32.3

[1]Includes other industries, not shown separately.

Table 15-3. Average Weekly Hours of Production and Nonsupervisory Workers on Private Nonfarm Payrolls by Industry—Continued

(Hours.)

Industry	2002	2003	2004	2005	2006	2007	2008	2009	2010	2011	2012	2013	2014
Total Private	33.9	33.7	33.7	33.8	33.9	33.8	33.6	33.1	33.4	33.6	33.7	33.7	33.7
Goods-Producing	39.9	39.8	40.0	40.1	40.5	40.6	40.2	39.2	40.4	40.9	41.1	41.3	41.5
Mining and logging	43.2	43.6	44.5	45.6	45.6	45.9	45.1	43.2	44.6	46.7	46.6	45.9	47.4
Construction	38.4	38.4	38.3	38.6	39.0	39.0	38.5	37.6	38.4	39.0	39.3	39.6	39.6
Manufacturing	40.5	40.4	40.8	40.7	41.1	41.2	40.8	39.8	41.1	41.4	41.7	41.8	42.0
Overtime hours	4.2	4.2	4.6	4.6	4.4	4.2	3.7	2.9	3.8	4.1	4.2	4.3	4.5
Durable goods	40.8	40.8	41.3	41.1	41.4	41.5	41.1	39.8	41.4	41.9	42.0	42.2	42.5
Overtime hours	4.2	4.3	4.7	4.6	4.4	4.2	3.7	2.7	3.8	4.2	4.3	4.4	4.6
Wood products	39.9	40.4	40.7	40.0	39.8	39.4	38.6	37.4	39.1	39.7	41.1	42.7	42.0
Nonmetallic mineral products	42.0	42.2	42.4	42.2	43.0	42.3	42.1	40.8	41.7	42.3	42.2	42.5	43.3
Primary metals	42.4	42.3	43.1	43.1	43.6	42.9	42.2	40.7	43.7	44.6	43.8	43.8	44.2
Fabricated metal products	40.6	40.7	41.1	41.0	41.4	41.6	41.3	39.4	41.4	42.0	42.0	42.3	42.6
Machinery	40.5	40.8	42.0	42.1	42.4	42.6	42.3	40.1	42.1	43.1	42.8	42.9	43.0
Computer and electronic products	39.7	40.4	40.4	40.0	40.5	40.6	41.0	40.4	40.9	40.5	40.4	40.5	40.8
Electrical equipment and appliances	40.1	40.6	40.7	40.6	41.0	41.2	40.9	39.3	41.1	40.8	41.6	41.8	41.7
Transportation equipment [1]	42.5	41.9	42.5	42.4	42.7	42.8	41.9	41.2	42.9	43.2	43.8	43.6	43.6
Motor vehicles and parts	42.6	42.0	42.6	42.3	42.2	42.3	41.4	40.1	43.4	43.4	44.2	43.7	43.8
Furniture and related products	39.1	38.9	39.5	39.2	38.8	39.2	38.1	37.7	38.5	39.9	40.0	40.9	40.9
Miscellaneous manufacturing	38.7	38.4	38.5	38.7	38.7	38.9	38.9	38.5	38.7	38.9	39.2	40.1	40.2
Nondurable goods [1]	40.0	39.8	40.0	39.9	40.6	40.8	40.4	39.8	40.8	40.8	41.1	41.2	41.3
Overtime hours	4.2	4.1	4.4	4.4	4.4	4.2	3.7	3.3	3.8	4.0	4.1	4.3	4.3
Food manufacturing	39.6	39.3	39.3	39.0	40.1	40.7	40.5	40.0	40.7	40.2	40.6	40.8	40.8
Textile mills	40.6	39.1	40.1	40.3	40.6	40.3	38.7	37.7	41.2	41.7	42.6	41.5	41.5
Textile product mills	39.0	39.4	38.7	38.9	39.8	39.7	38.6	37.9	39.0	39.1	39.7	38.4	38.0
Apparel	36.7	35.6	36.1	35.8	36.5	37.2	36.4	36.0	36.6	38.2	37.1	38.1	38.5
Paper and paper products	41.8	41.5	42.1	42.5	42.9	43.1	42.9	41.8	42.9	42.9	42.9	43.1	43.6
Printing and related support activities	38.4	38.2	38.4	38.4	39.2	39.1	38.3	38.0	38.2	38.0	38.5	38.6	39.0
Petroleum and coal products	43.0	44.5	44.9	45.5	45.0	44.1	44.6	43.4	43.0	43.8	47.1	46.4	46.1
Chemicals	42.3	42.4	42.8	42.3	42.5	41.9	41.5	41.4	42.2	42.5	42.4	42.9	42.7
Plastics and rubber products	40.6	40.4	40.4	40.0	40.6	41.3	41.0	40.2	41.9	42.0	41.8	41.8	42.3
Private Service-Providing	32.5	32.4	32.3	32.4	32.4	32.4	32.3	32.1	32.2	32.4	32.5	32.4	32.4
Trade, transportation, and utilities	33.6	33.6	33.5	33.4	33.4	33.3	33.2	32.9	33.3	33.7	33.8	33.7	33.6
Wholesale trade	38.0	37.9	37.8	37.7	38.0	38.2	38.2	37.6	37.9	38.5	38.7	38.7	38.6
Retail trade	30.9	30.9	30.7	30.6	30.5	30.2	30.0	29.9	30.2	30.5	30.6	30.2	30.0
Transportation and warehousing	36.8	36.8	37.2	37.0	36.9	37.0	36.4	36.0	37.1	37.8	38.0	38.5	38.4
Utilities	40.9	41.1	40.9	41.1	41.4	42.4	42.7	42.0	42.0	42.1	41.1	41.7	42.3
Information	36.5	36.2	36.3	36.5	36.6	36.5	36.7	36.6	36.3	36.2	36.0	35.9	35.9
Financial activities	35.6	35.6	35.6	36.0	35.8	35.9	35.9	36.1	36.2	36.4	36.8	36.7	36.8
Professional and business services	34.2	34.1	34.2	34.2	34.6	34.8	34.8	34.7	35.1	35.2	35.3	35.4	35.6
Education and health services	32.4	32.3	32.4	32.6	32.5	32.6	32.4	32.2	32.1	32.2	32.3	32.1	32.0
Leisure and hospitality	25.8	25.6	25.7	25.7	25.7	25.5	25.2	24.8	24.8	24.8	25.0	25.0	25.1
Other services	32.1	31.4	31.0	30.9	30.9	30.9	30.8	30.5	30.7	30.8	30.7	30.8	30.7

[1]Includes other industries, not shown separately.

Table 15-4. Average Hourly Earnings of Production and Nonsupervisory Workers on Private Nonfarm Payrolls by Industry

(Dollars.)

Industry	1990	1991	1992	1993	1994	1995	1996	1997	1998	1999	2000
Total Private	10.20	10.51	10.77	11.05	11.34	11.65	12.04	12.51	13.01	13.49	14.02
Goods-Producing	11.46	11.76	11.99	12.28	12.63	12.96	13.38	13.82	14.23	14.71	15.27
Mining and logging	13.40	13.82	14.09	14.12	14.41	14.78	15.09	15.57	16.20	16.33	16.55
Construction	13.42	13.65	13.81	14.04	14.38	14.73	15.11	15.67	16.23	16.80	17.48
Manufacturing	10.78	11.13	11.40	11.70	12.04	12.34	12.75	13.14	13.45	13.85	14.32
Excluding overtime [1]	10.29	10.63	10.86	11.10	11.36	11.68	12.05	12.38	12.71	13.08	13.55
Durable goods	11.40	11.81	12.09	12.41	12.78	13.05	13.45	13.83	14.07	14.46	14.93
Wood products	8.82	9.02	9.24	9.40	9.66	9.92	10.24	10.52	10.85	11.18	11.63
Nonmetallic mineral products	11.11	11.34	11.57	11.83	12.11	12.39	12.80	13.17	13.59	13.97	14.53
Primary metals	12.97	13.37	13.72	14.08	14.47	14.75	15.12	15.39	15.66	16.00	16.64
Fabricated metal products	10.64	10.97	11.17	11.40	11.64	11.91	12.26	12.64	12.97	13.34	13.77
Machinery	11.73	12.12	12.40	12.72	12.94	13.13	13.49	13.94	14.23	14.77	15.21
Computer and electronic products	10.89	11.35	11.64	11.95	12.19	12.29	12.75	13.24	13.85	14.37	14.73
Electrical equipment and appliances	10.00	10.30	10.50	10.65	10.94	11.25	11.80	12.24	12.51	12.90	13.23
Transportation equipment [2]	14.44	15.12	15.59	16.21	16.93	17.21	17.66	17.99	17.91	18.24	18.89
Motor vehicles and parts	15.00	15.67	15.92	16.56	17.38	17.72	18.14	18.43	18.21	18.49	19.11
Furniture and related products	8.53	8.75	9.01	9.25	9.52	9.76	10.09	10.50	10.89	11.28	11.73
Miscellaneous manufacturing	8.87	9.15	9.43	9.64	9.90	10.23	10.59	10.89	11.18	11.55	11.93
Nondurable goods [2]	9.87	10.18	10.45	10.70	10.96	11.30	11.68	12.04	12.45	12.85	13.31
Food manufacturing	9.04	9.32	9.59	9.82	10.00	10.27	10.50	10.77	11.09	11.40	11.77
Textile mills	8.17	8.49	8.82	9.12	9.35	9.63	9.88	10.22	10.58	10.90	11.23
Textile product mills	7.37	7.60	7.85	8.10	8.29	8.60	8.95	9.30	9.61	10.04	10.31
Apparel	6.22	6.43	6.60	6.75	6.96	7.22	7.45	7.76	8.05	8.35	8.61
Paper and paper products	12.06	12.45	12.78	13.13	13.49	13.94	14.38	14.76	15.20	15.58	15.91
Printing and related support activities	11.11	11.32	11.53	11.67	11.89	12.08	12.41	12.78	13.20	13.67	14.09
Petroleum and coal products	17.00	17.90	18.83	19.43	19.96	20.24	20.18	21.10	21.75	22.22	22.80
Chemicals	12.85	13.30	13.70	13.97	14.33	14.86	15.37	15.78	16.23	16.40	17.09
Plastics and rubber products	9.76	10.07	10.35	10.56	10.66	10.86	11.17	11.48	11.79	12.25	12.70
Private Service-Providing	9.72	10.06	10.34	10.62	10.88	11.21	11.59	12.07	12.61	13.09	13.62
Trade, transportation, and utilities	9.83	10.08	10.30	10.55	10.80	11.10	11.46	11.90	12.40	12.82	13.31
Wholesale trade	11.58	11.95	12.21	12.57	12.93	13.34	13.80	14.41	15.07	15.62	16.28
Retail trade	7.71	7.89	8.12	8.36	8.61	8.85	9.21	9.59	10.05	10.45	10.87
Transportation and warehousing	12.50	12.61	12.77	12.71	12.84	13.18	13.45	13.78	14.12	14.56	15.05
Utilities	16.14	16.70	17.17	17.95	18.66	19.19	19.78	20.59	21.48	22.03	22.75
Information	13.40	13.90	14.29	14.86	15.32	15.68	16.30	17.14	17.67	18.40	19.07
Financial activities	9.98	10.43	10.86	11.38	11.84	12.31	12.75	13.28	14.00	14.55	15.04
Professional and business services	11.14	11.50	11.78	11.96	12.15	12.53	13.00	13.57	14.27	14.85	15.52
Education and health services	9.98	10.48	10.85	11.19	11.48	11.78	12.15	12.53	12.96	13.40	13.91
Leisure and hospitality	6.02	6.22	6.36	6.48	6.62	6.79	6.99	7.32	7.67	7.96	8.32
Other services	9.08	9.39	9.66	9.90	10.18	10.51	10.85	11.29	11.79	12.26	12.73

[1]Derived by assuming that overtime hours are paid at the rate of time and one-half.
[2]Includes other industries, not shown separately.

Table 15-4. Average Hourly Earnings of Production and Nonsupervisory Workers on Private Nonfarm Payrolls by Industry—*Continued*

(Dollars.)

Industry	2001	2002	2003	2004	2005	2006	2007	2008	2009	2010	2011	2012	2013	2014
Total Private	14.54	14.97	15.37	15.69	16.12	16.75	17.42	18.07	18.61	19.05	19.44	19.74	20.13	20.61
Goods-Producing	15.78	16.33	16.80	17.19	17.60	18.02	18.67	19.33	19.90	20.28	20.67	20.94	21.24	21.59
Mining and logging	17.00	17.19	17.56	18.07	18.72	19.90	20.97	22.50	23.29	23.82	24.50	25.79	26.80	26.85
Construction	18.00	18.52	18.95	19.23	19.46	20.02	20.95	21.87	22.66	23.22	23.65	23.97	24.22	24.67
Manufacturing	14.76	15.29	15.74	16.14	16.56	16.81	17.26	17.75	18.24	18.61	18.93	19.08	19.30	19.56
Excluding overtime [1]	14.06	14.54	14.96	15.29	15.68	15.96	16.43	16.97	17.59	17.78	18.03	18.16	18.34	18.57
Durable goods	15.38	16.02	16.45	16.82	17.33	17.68	18.20	18.71	19.36	19.80	20.11	20.18	20.35	20.66
Wood products	11.99	12.33	12.71	13.03	13.16	13.39	13.68	14.19	14.92	14.85	14.81	14.99	15.47	15.58
Nonmetallic mineral products	14.86	15.39	15.76	16.25	16.61	16.59	16.93	16.90	17.28	17.48	18.16	18.15	18.40	19.15
Primary metals	17.06	17.68	18.13	18.57	18.94	19.36	19.66	20.19	20.10	20.13	19.94	20.70	21.94	22.40
Fabricated metal products	14.19	14.68	15.01	15.31	15.80	16.17	16.53	16.99	17.48	17.94	18.13	18.26	18.35	18.68
Machinery	15.48	15.92	16.29	16.67	17.02	17.20	17.72	17.97	18.39	18.96	19.54	20.17	20.58	21.00
Computer and electronic products	15.42	16.20	16.68	17.27	18.39	18.94	19.94	21.04	21.87	22.78	23.32	23.34	23.41	23.36
Electrical equipment and appliances	13.78	13.98	14.36	14.90	15.24	15.53	15.93	15.78	16.27	16.87	17.96	18.03	18.04	18.28
Transportation equipment [2]	19.47	20.63	21.22	21.48	22.09	22.41	23.04	23.86	24.98	25.23	25.34	24.57	24.57	24.96
Motor vehicles and parts	19.66	21.09	21.68	21.71	22.26	22.14	22.00	22.21	21.86	22.02	21.93	21.27	21.08	21.42
Furniture and related products	12.14	12.62	12.99	13.16	13.45	13.80	14.32	14.54	15.04	15.06	15.24	15.46	15.59	15.67
Miscellaneous manufacturing	12.45	12.91	13.30	13.84	14.07	14.36	14.66	15.20	16.13	16.56	16.82	17.05	17.03	17.31
Nondurable goods [2]	13.75	14.15	14.63	15.05	15.26	15.33	15.67	16.15	16.56	16.80	17.06	17.29	17.57	17.74
Food manufacturing	12.18	12.55	12.80	12.98	13.04	13.13	13.55	14.00	14.39	14.41	14.63	15.02	15.44	15.55
Textile mills	11.40	11.73	11.99	12.13	12.38	12.55	13.00	13.58	13.71	13.56	13.79	13.51	13.90	14.15
Textile product mills	10.49	10.85	11.15	11.31	11.61	11.86	11.78	11.73	11.73	11.44	11.79	12.21	12.77	13.35
Apparel	8.83	9.11	9.58	9.77	10.26	10.65	11.05	11.40	11.37	11.43	11.96	12.89	13.21	13.51
Paper and paper products	16.38	16.85	17.33	17.91	17.99	18.01	18.44	18.89	19.29	20.04	20.28	20.42	20.32	20.35
Printing and related support activities	14.48	14.93	15.37	15.71	15.74	15.80	16.15	16.75	16.75	16.91	17.28	17.28	17.77	18.01
Petroleum and coal products	22.90	23.04	23.63	24.39	24.47	24.11	25.21	27.41	29.61	31.31	31.75	32.15	34.58	35.36
Chemicals	17.57	17.97	18.50	19.17	19.67	19.60	19.55	19.50	20.30	21.07	21.45	21.45	21.40	21.49
Plastics and rubber products	13.21	13.55	14.18	14.59	14.80	14.97	15.39	15.85	16.01	15.71	15.95	16.05	16.20	16.51
Private Service-Providing	14.18	14.58	14.98	15.28	15.73	16.41	17.09	17.75	18.34	18.79	19.18	19.49	19.90	20.40
Trade, transportation, and utilities	13.70	14.02	14.34	14.58	14.92	15.39	15.78	16.16	16.48	16.82	17.15	17.43	17.74	18.27
Wholesale trade	16.77	16.98	17.36	17.65	18.16	18.91	19.59	20.13	20.84	21.54	21.97	22.24	22.62	23.24
Retail trade	11.29	11.67	11.90	12.08	12.36	12.57	12.75	12.87	13.01	13.25	13.51	13.82	14.02	14.39
Transportation and warehousing	15.33	15.76	16.25	16.52	16.70	17.27	17.72	18.41	18.81	19.16	19.49	19.54	19.81	20.53
Utilities	23.58	23.96	24.77	25.61	26.68	27.40	27.88	28.83	29.48	30.04	30.82	31.61	32.27	32.88
Information	19.80	20.20	21.01	21.40	22.06	23.23	23.96	24.78	25.45	25.87	26.62	27.04	27.98	28.66
Financial activities	15.65	16.25	17.21	17.58	17.98	18.83	19.67	20.32	20.90	21.55	21.93	22.82	23.87	24.71
Professional and business services	16.33	16.80	17.21	17.48	18.08	19.13	20.15	21.18	22.35	22.78	23.12	23.29	23.72	24.28
Education and health services	14.59	15.16	15.57	16.08	16.63	17.30	18.01	18.75	19.35	19.98	20.63	20.94	21.29	21.65
Leisure and hospitality	8.57	8.81	9.00	9.15	9.38	9.75	10.41	10.84	11.12	11.31	11.45	11.62	11.78	12.09
Other services	13.27	13.72	13.84	13.98	14.34	14.77	15.42	16.09	16.59	17.06	17.32	17.59	18.00	18.52

[1]Derived by assuming that overtime hours are paid at the rate of time and one-half.
[2]Includes other industries, not shown separately.

Table 15-5. Average Weekly Earnings of Production and Nonsupervisory Workers on Private Nonfarm Payrolls by Industry

(Dollars.)

Industry	1990	1991	1992	1993	1994	1995	1996	1997	1998	1999	2000	2001
Total Private	349.63	358.46	368.20	378.89	391.17	400.04	413.25	431.86	448.59	463.15	480.99	493.74
Goods-Producing	459.52	471.32	482.58	498.79	519.58	528.51	546.41	568.43	580.99	599.99	621.86	629.91
Mining and logging	602.43	625.46	628.94	634.77	653.13	670.40	695.04	720.07	727.19	721.77	734.88	757.96
Construction	513.43	520.41	525.13	539.81	558.53	571.57	588.48	609.48	629.75	655.11	685.78	695.86
Manufacturing	436.13	449.83	464.43	480.89	501.95	509.26	526.55	548.26	557.12	573.29	591.01	595.19
Durable goods	468.43	483.24	499.56	519.89	544.63	549.45	566.53	589.06	591.80	606.55	624.38	624.54
Wood products	356.32	362.46	377.73	387.28	402.83	406.53	422.30	435.66	449.77	461.46	476.97	481.33
Nonmetallic mineral products	453.91	459.17	474.45	490.67	510.95	517.75	538.10	551.65	573.04	587.42	604.76	618.91
Primary metals	545.36	555.30	581.53	606.34	637.73	639.82	658.73	681.64	681.47	700.80	734.83	723.86
Fabricated metal products	436.09	447.94	459.67	474.21	492.07	498.58	513.47	534.38	543.24	555.86	576.71	576.71
Machinery	493.22	507.72	525.36	549.87	567.90	571.15	584.62	613.19	613.73	625.07	643.94	632.68
Computer and electronic products	450.06	464.31	482.05	498.95	514.98	518.19	534.39	562.68	579.85	596.37	609.97	613.18
Electrical equipment and appliances	412.42	426.81	439.04	451.44	470.24	471.72	496.69	515.77	522.54	538.98	550.48	548.03
Transportation equipment [1] ..	606.68	633.96	652.75	697.14	750.29	751.45	773.73	795.74	774.77	795.57	817.48	816.58
Motor vehicles and parts ...	621.68	650.36	662.82	717.68	779.29	776.41	794.09	808.28	775.56	809.31	828.73	818.68
Furniture and related products	324.37	330.64	348.07	360.81	373.90	375.18	385.82	410.48	428.67	443.68	459.95	464.87
Miscellaneous manufacturing	345.82	358.54	370.67	378.21	389.64	400.88	413.94	431.72	437.95	454.14	464.80	483.07
Nondurable goods [1]	390.65	404.25	417.95	429.15	443.85	452.77	467.91	487.04	504.02	520.02	536.85	548.30
Food manufacturing	355.80	364.90	375.69	386.07	398.53	406.75	414.74	428.58	444.72	458.73	472.09	481.81
Textile mills	328.11	345.48	364.45	379.74	391.64	394.17	403.08	425.53	434.15	447.38	464.51	456.64
Textile product mills	283.76	293.60	303.68	317.69	326.47	332.12	347.05	364.12	376.37	392.46	398.93	402.53
Apparel	215.89	227.82	235.13	239.88	248.51	254.91	261.99	276.01	286.17	295.62	307.51	317.63
Paper and paper products	525.58	542.08	559.98	575.60	595.85	604.66	625.38	647.64	662.27	679.05	681.38	689.76
Printing and related support activities	429.93	437.00	450.02	457.91	470.74	472.37	484.99	504.46	518.32	534.15	552.15	560.89
Petroleum and coal products	754.13	786.05	821.72	855.36	883.81	883.68	881.24	908.50	949.28	947.60	973.53	1 003.34
Chemicals	550.25	573.27	593.24	603.75	622.53	644.46	666.28	685.43	700.53	701.06	721.41	735.57
Plastics and rubber products	396.26	408.25	426.65	436.85	445.99	446.01	458.29	475.04	487.04	505.45	517.56	528.62
Private Service-Providing	315.95	325.82	335.95	345.65	355.60	364.80	377.37	395.57	413.65	427.98	445.74	461.02
Trade, transportation, and utilities	331.55	339.10	348.60	359.51	370.38	378.79	390.67	407.63	423.33	434.31	449.96	459.53
Wholesale trade	444.48	459.17	470.41	484.46	501.14	515.14	533.36	559.39	582.21	602.77	631.24	643.45
Retail trade	235.56	240.13	249.66	256.89	265.74	272.63	282.74	295.94	310.33	321.71	333.41	346.16
Transportation and warehousing	471.82	471.02	477.81	494.54	507.13	513.40	525.72	542.51	546.89	548.00	562.56	562.57
Utilities	670.80	693.61	716.65	756.50	790.13	811.72	831.24	865.02	902.44	924.40	955.09	977.25
Information	479.50	495.14	511.95	535.19	551.21	564.92	592.45	622.37	646.52	675.47	700.92	731.18
Financial activities	354.60	369.57	386.31	403.68	420.18	437.26	453.05	475.03	503.94	520.74	540.39	560.46
Professional and business services	380.61	391.06	400.64	406.20	414.16	426.54	442.81	465.51	490.13	510.99	535.07	557.84
Education and health services	318.87	334.07	347.70	358.44	367.50	376.94	387.50	403.63	417.58	429.98	447.82	471.36
Leisure and hospitality	156.32	159.20	163.70	167.54	172.27	175.74	181.02	190.66	200.82	208.05	217.20	220.73
Other services	297.88	306.75	315.08	322.69	332.44	342.36	352.68	368.63	384.25	398.77	413.30	428.64

[1]Includes other industries, not shown separately.

Table 15-5. Average Weekly Earnings of Production and Nonsupervisory Workers on Private Nonfarm Payrolls by Industry—*Continued*

(Dollars.)

Industry	2002	2003	2004	2005	2006	2007	2008	2009	2010	2011	2012	2013	2014
Total Private	506.60	517.82	528.89	544.05	567.39	589.27	607.53	616.01	636.25	653.19	665.82	677.67	694.89
Goods-Producing	651.61	669.13	688.03	705.31	730.16	757.50	776.66	779.68	818.96	844.89	861.39	877.09	895.09
Mining and logging	741.97	765.94	804.01	853.87	907.95	962.63	1 014.69	1 006.67	1 063.11	1 144.64	1 201.69	1 229.70	1 271.15
Construction	711.82	727.00	735.55	750.37	781.59	816.23	842.61	851.76	891.83	921.84	942.14	958.72	977.05
Manufacturing	618.62	636.03	658.49	673.30	690.88	711.53	724.46	726.12	765.15	784.29	794.63	807.37	822.24
Durable goods	652.84	671.35	694.06	712.85	732.00	754.61	767.99	771.39	819.02	841.89	848.35	859.69	877.36
Wood products	492.07	514.06	530.15	526.65	533.12	539.41	547.53	557.65	580.74	587.77	615.76	661.10	654.16
Nonmetallic mineral products	647.00	664.96	688.33	700.63	712.67	716.78	711.11	705.54	728.22	768.35	766.16	782.69	829.27
Primary metals	749.17	767.15	799.69	815.90	843.79	843.42	851.12	817.70	880.46	889.34	907.23	960.61	990.97
Fabricated metal products	596.45	610.44	628.80	647.24	668.94	687.16	701.57	689.22	742.61	762.17	767.68	775.50	795.78
Machinery	645.38	664.48	699.45	716.27	728.84	754.34	760.09	737.97	797.62	842.96	864.16	883.06	903.35
Computer and electronic products	642.77	674.69	697.97	735.59	766.75	809.10	861.58	883.02	932.26	943.88	944.02	948.79	952.82
Electrical equipment and appliances	560.33	583.27	607.00	618.88	637.04	656.46	645.60	639.34	693.49	732.16	749.91	753.07	762.95
Transportation equipment [1]	877.46	889.42	912.63	937.75	957.69	986.79	1 000.71	1 028.37	1 081.53	1 094.46	1 075.04	1 071.05	1 088.52
Motor vehicles and parts	898.54	910.02	924.72	940.64	934.41	930.51	920.57	876.45	956.36	952.12	940.00	920.56	939.02
Furniture and related products	493.95	505.26	519.61	527.49	535.90	561.08	553.90	566.75	579.66	608.00	617.74	628.36	641.43
Miscellaneous manufacturing	499.01	510.54	533.27	545.01	555.87	570.12	591.95	620.74	640.85	654.90	668.95	682.97	695.71
Nondurable goods [1]	566.72	582.61	602.56	609.04	622.00	639.99	652.22	658.54	685.07	696.03	710.13	723.57	733.45
Food manufacturing	497.25	502.92	509.55	508.55	526.02	551.21	566.88	575.40	586.52	588.19	609.69	629.70	634.75
Textile mills	476.52	469.33	486.68	498.47	509.39	524.40	525.00	516.86	559.13	574.61	575.75	577.18	586.45
Textile product mills	423.05	438.67	437.89	451.36	472.10	467.80	453.06	433.09	459.46	477.49	507.00	494.76	507.18
Apparel	334.24	340.73	352.04	366.93	389.05	411.57	415.10	408.86	418.28	456.97	478.33	503.01	520.57
Paper and paper products	705.20	719.55	754.17	764.15	772.57	795.58	809.57	806.19	858.65	870.53	877.14	874.85	888.31
Printing and related support activities	573.05	587.58	603.97	604.73	618.92	632.02	642.50	635.68	646.11	655.81	665.45	685.33	701.55
Petroleum and coal products	990.88	1 052.32	1 095.00	1 114.51	1 085.50	1 112.73	1 222.07	1 284.44	1 345.72	1 390.80	1 513.36	1 605.02	1 629.12
Chemicals	759.56	784.26	819.93	831.79	833.84	819.51	809.29	841.18	888.25	910.88	910.02	918.69	917.97
Plastics and rubber products	550.14	572.53	589.99	591.59	608.37	635.63	649.02	643.91	658.55	669.54	671.28	677.72	697.86
Private Service-Providing	473.87	484.76	494.08	509.31	532.27	554.29	573.57	587.64	605.23	621.13	633.25	645.00	661.64
Trade, transportation, and utilities	471.27	481.14	488.51	498.46	514.37	525.91	536.11	541.88	559.63	577.71	588.86	597.40	613.95
Wholesale trade	644.38	657.29	666.79	685.00	718.50	748.94	769.62	784.49	816.50	845.44	860.70	875.79	897.74
Retail trade	360.84	367.18	371.13	377.58	383.12	385.00	386.21	388.57	400.07	412.09	422.10	423.07	431.64
Transportation and warehousing	579.91	598.41	614.89	618.55	636.80	654.95	670.22	677.56	710.85	737.00	742.23	762.06	789.26
Utilities	979.26	1 017.44	1 048.01	1 095.91	1 135.57	1 182.65	1 230.65	1 239.34	1 262.89	1 296.92	1 298.23	1 344.70	1 389.61
Information	737.94	760.84	776.72	805.11	850.64	874.45	908.78	931.08	939.85	964.85	973.52	1 003.65	1 029.73
Financial activities	578.94	611.82	625.53	646.48	673.63	706.52	729.64	754.90	780.19	798.68	840.04	875.04	908.43
Professional and business services	574.60	587.02	597.54	618.71	662.27	700.82	737.90	775.81	798.54	813.37	822.58	838.67	864.12
Education and health services	490.73	503.27	521.24	541.78	561.59	586.41	608.58	622.73	640.60	665.05	675.85	683.27	692.41
Leisure and hospitality	227.31	230.49	234.86	241.36	250.34	265.54	273.39	275.95	280.87	283.82	290.54	294.31	303.83
Other services	439.87	434.41	433.04	443.40	456.50	477.06	495.57	506.26	523.70	532.63	539.46	553.77	568.90

[1]Includes other industries, not shown separately.

Table 15-6. Indexes of Aggregate Weekly Hours of Production and Nonsupervisory Workers on Private Nonfarm Payrolls by Industry

(2002 = 100.)

Industry	1990	1991	1992	1993	1994	1995	1996	1997	1998	1999	2000	2001
Total Private	84.2	82.4	83.0	85.3	89.1	91.5	93.6	97.0	99.4	101.5	103.5	102.1
Goods-Producing	106.1	100.1	98.7	100.8	105.6	106.8	108.1	111.2	112.3	112.6	113.1	106.5
Mining and logging	128.6	123.8	113.3	110.3	111.0	110.3	112.7	117.6	112.8	102.9	105.1	108.3
Construction	78.8	70.1	67.5	71.3	77.3	79.9	84.3	88.6	93.4	99.7	104.0	103.2
Manufacturing	117.7	112.8	112.4	113.9	118.3	119.0	118.8	121.4	121.0	119.0	117.8	108.1
Durable goods	114.2	107.6	106.4	108.3	114.2	116.4	117.5	121.6	122.0	120.6	120.4	109.3
Wood products	101.5	92.6	95.2	100.5	109.1	109.3	111.6	114.8	117.5	118.5	115.8	105.0
Nonmetallic mineral products	100.7	92.8	92.6	94.2	98.8	99.7	101.5	103.1	105.8	106.9	109.1	106.1
Primary metals	131.6	123.0	120.9	121.5	128.0	129.3	129.9	132.4	131.1	128.4	128.9	113.0
Fabricated metal products	104.7	99.1	97.3	99.7	106.3	109.9	111.6	116.6	118.6	116.7	119.1	109.3
Machinery	123.8	116.2	113.9	118.6	126.9	132.2	133.7	138.9	137.4	129.8	127.6	114.1
Computer and electronic products	137.2	128.2	122.9	121.1	123.6	127.1	130.0	136.8	136.7	131.1	133.1	117.9
Electrical equipment and appliances	136.0	127.9	125.9	126.8	132.4	130.3	129.4	127.7	127.8	128.3	127.7	113.4
Transportation equipment [1]	111.1	105.8	104.4	105.5	112.6	115.4	116.5	120.8	118.8	119.5	116.3	105.3
Motor vehicles and parts	90.9	87.9	91.1	97.9	110.6	115.9	116.1	117.5	112.8	118.7	117.3	103.6
Furniture and related products	97.1	89.4	92.0	95.3	100.5	99.2	98.3	102.9	108.4	112.6	114.7	104.8
Miscellaneous manufacturing	104.1	103.9	105.3	107.0	108.3	107.8	107.7	110.1	110.4	110.3	109.5	104.7
Nondurable goods [1]	123.0	120.8	121.7	122.7	124.7	123.1	120.5	120.9	119.4	116.1	113.3	106.0
Food manufacturing	96.2	96.5	97.2	98.6	100.4	101.6	101.8	102.6	103.3	103.7	103.4	101.4
Textile mills	170.4	168.4	170.3	170.8	171.6	163.5	154.1	155.2	148.9	139.1	132.4	112.2
Textile product mills	118.8	113.1	114.8	118.7	124.0	121.0	118.1	119.4	117.7	115.6	112.3	105.5
Apparel	266.5	263.6	266.6	259.0	252.1	234.8	211.6	201.3	180.9	154.6	137.5	117.1
Paper and paper products	121.9	120.6	121.7	122.0	123.5	121.5	120.2	121.6	119.6	117.2	113.5	106.6
Printing and related support activities	122.3	118.7	118.4	120.3	123.8	123.9	122.8	124.6	124.3	120.9	119.4	111.5
Petroleum and coal products	128.9	127.5	126.0	122.0	120.0	115.5	113.5	112.7	113.4	107.6	105.8	105.6
Chemicals	118.2	115.0	112.9	113.5	115.1	115.4	114.8	114.7	115.4	113.2	110.4	104.7
Plastics and rubber products	97.7	94.1	98.0	102.3	108.7	109.8	110.0	112.7	113.7	114.6	114.2	104.9
Private Service-Providing	78.1	77.5	78.6	81.0	84.5	87.1	89.5	93.0	95.7	98.3	100.9	100.8
Trade, transportation, and utilities	89.5	87.4	87.3	89.1	92.7	95.1	96.6	98.9	100.3	101.9	103.5	101.5
Wholesale trade	94.9	93.3	92.4	92.4	95.8	99.2	100.7	103.4	104.8	106.2	107.0	102.9
Retail trade	87.5	84.8	85.1	86.3	89.8	92.3	93.7	95.9	97.2	99.5	101.3	100.5
Transportation and warehousing	83.5	82.3	82.6	88.4	93.7	95.6	98.3	101.0	102.6	103.2	105.6	102.7
Utilities	124.3	123.5	121.6	119.9	117.1	112.9	108.6	106.1	105.7	105.0	104.1	102.3
Information	76.2	76.1	76.5	78.0	79.2	82.5	86.9	90.4	92.6	98.5	105.0	106.7
Financial activities	83.1	82.0	82.4	84.9	87.2	86.9	89.1	92.3	96.4	98.1	98.4	99.3
Professional and business services	68.1	66.7	68.4	71.9	77.0	81.2	85.2	91.5	96.7	101.7	106.6	104.0
Education and health services	66.7	69.8	72.5	74.9	77.9	80.8	83.0	86.4	88.7	90.6	92.7	96.5
Leisure and hospitality	78.9	77.3	79.2	82.1	85.5	88.5	90.7	93.4	95.5	97.8	100.5	100.6
Other services	81.8	81.1	80.6	82.8	84.5	87.0	89.1	91.9	94.3	96.2	97.8	99.0

[1] Includes other industries, not shown separately.

Table 15-6. Indexes of Aggregate Weekly Hours of Production and Nonsupervisory Workers on Private Nonfarm Payrolls by Industry—*Continued*

(2002 = 100.)

Industry	2002	2003	2004	2005	2006	2007	2008	2009	2010	2011	2012	2013	2014
Total Private	100.0	98.7	100.2	102.8	105.8	107.3	106.0	98.8	98.9	101.4	104.2	106.1	108.8
Goods-Producing	100.0	95.7	96.8	98.9	102.5	101.7	96.5	80.2	78.8	81.2	83.5	85.1	87.8
Mining and logging	100.0	97.4	104.0	114.7	125.8	133.5	137.6	117.2	124.5	147.4	158.7	155.0	165.5
Construction	100.0	98.4	101.7	108.3	115.4	114.7	106.5	85.9	80.2	81.7	83.6	87.7	91.8
Manufacturing	100.0	94.5	94.3	93.9	95.6	94.4	90.2	76.1	76.2	78.3	80.3	80.9	82.7
Durable goods	100.0	94.3	95.2	96.1	98.9	97.4	92.2	74.7	75.0	78.4	81.4	82.3	84.4
Wood products	100.0	97.8	100.8	101.2	99.9	89.3	76.7	57.8	58.5	59.3	62.1	67.3	69.6
Nonmetallic mineral products	100.0	94.3	98.0	97.4	100.3	96.9	91.2	73.8	70.5	70.1	68.9	69.7	72.8
Primary metals	100.0	93.4	93.3	93.1	94.2	91.4	87.4	66.1	71.7	80.1	82.7	79.8	82.1
Fabricated metal products	100.0	95.3	97.7	99.2	103.1	104.5	101.3	81.3	83.1	89.6	94.7	96.4	98.0
Machinery	100.0	93.6	96.0	98.8	102.2	103.3	102.3	80.6	81.2	89.6	94.0	94.0	96.7
Computer and electronic products	100.0	92.1	89.8	94.8	103.6	102.2	101.2	89.4	87.2	86.4	86.0	83.7	81.5
Electrical equipment and appliances	100.0	92.0	88.7	86.4	88.0	89.1	88.5	74.1	73.2	71.6	73.4	72.4	72.9
Transportation equipment [1]	100.0	95.5	96.5	97.3	100.0	98.0	88.6	70.1	72.1	75.3	80.4	82.4	86.6
Motor vehicles and parts	100.0	95.9	97.0	95.2	92.9	85.8	72.7	51.6	57.5	60.9	66.6	70.7	76.7
Furniture and related products	100.0	93.0	94.3	91.9	90.4	86.1	74.6	57.6	54.4	55.8	55.6	57.6	61.2
Miscellaneous manufacturing	100.0	93.6	91.8	90.6	90.4	91.0	89.2	81.1	79.0	80.0	82.2	85.3	86.4
Nondurable goods [1]	100.0	94.7	92.7	90.3	90.4	89.6	86.9	78.1	78.0	77.9	78.6	78.6	79.8
Food manufacturing	100.0	98.4	97.1	95.8	98.6	101.1	100.6	97.5	98.5	97.7	99.6	100.1	100.5
Textile mills	100.0	86.3	79.0	71.3	65.1	56.3	47.9	37.8	40.2	41.6	41.7	39.0	38.5
Textile product mills	100.0	92.4	90.2	88.0	85.0	77.5	70.5	58.5	56.5	55.2	53.3	50.5	51.3
Apparel	100.0	81.9	75.1	65.7	63.4	61.5	56.7	45.4	42.0	40.7	38.4	38.5	38.0
Paper and paper products	100.0	92.5	89.2	88.0	86.9	85.8	83.5	74.2	73.5	71.9	70.0	68.2	68.2
Printing and related support activities	100.0	95.3	93.4	90.9	92.5	91.6	86.1	74.1	69.0	65.6	64.3	63.2	64.1
Petroleum and coal products	100.0	98.7	102.6	102.4	96.9	95.6	102.4	90.2	89.1	91.2	101.6	96.8	97.6
Chemicals	100.0	99.0	99.0	95.9	96.1	94.1	94.6	88.3	88.9	90.6	92.6	93.6	94.5
Plastics and rubber products	100.0	95.2	94.2	92.3	91.9	91.1	87.1	71.3	73.6	75.3	75.8	77.3	81.5
Private Service-Providing	100.0	99.5	101.1	103.8	106.6	108.8	108.6	104.0	104.4	106.9	109.9	112.0	114.6
Trade, transportation, and utilities	100.0	98.6	99.6	101.6	103.3	104.8	103.3	96.8	96.8	99.7	101.8	102.7	104.4
Wholesale trade	100.0	98.0	98.8	101.8	105.7	109.2	108.6	99.9	97.7	100.7	104.0	105.3	107.1
Retail trade	100.0	98.9	99.4	100.8	101.1	101.8	99.8	94.3	95.0	97.7	98.9	98.7	99.6
Transportation and warehousing	100.0	98.8	101.9	105.2	107.9	109.4	107.7	100.0	101.3	105.4	109.2	112.5	116.2
Utilities	100.0	97.4	94.2	93.1	93.8	96.2	98.3	97.0	95.4	94.9	92.6	94.9	96.6
Information	100.0	97.0	98.2	99.4	100.2	100.1	100.0	93.5	90.0	88.9	88.9	89.8	91.1
Financial activities	100.0	101.3	101.4	103.7	106.3	107.6	106.8	103.1	101.3	101.2	103.7	104.7	106.5
Professional and business services	100.0	98.7	101.8	106.3	112.1	115.3	113.9	105.2	107.6	112.4	117.2	121.3	126.0
Education and health services	100.0	101.6	103.7	106.8	109.4	113.0	116.2	117.9	119.4	122.0	125.1	126.8	128.7
Leisure and hospitality	100.0	100.0	103.0	106.2	108.8	110.8	109.7	105.1	104.6	106.9	111.3	115.2	119.4
Other services	100.0	97.4	96.1	96.2	97.4	99.3	99.5	96.0	96.0	96.8	97.7	98.7	100.0

[1] Includes other industries, not shown separately.

NOTES AND DEFINITIONS, CHAPTER 15

Tables 15-1 through 15-6
Employment, Hours, and Earnings
by NAICS Industry

SOURCE: U.S. DEPARTMENT OF LABOR, BUREAU OF LABOR STATISTICS

See the notes and definitions for Tables 10-8 through 10-18 regarding definitions of *employment, production and non-supervisory workers, average weekly hours, overtime hours, average hourly earnings, average weekly earnings,* and the *indexes of aggregate weekly hours.* Availability and reference information is also provided in those notes and definitions.

CHAPTER 16: KEY SECTOR STATISTICS

Figure 16-1: Housing Starts, 1960–2014

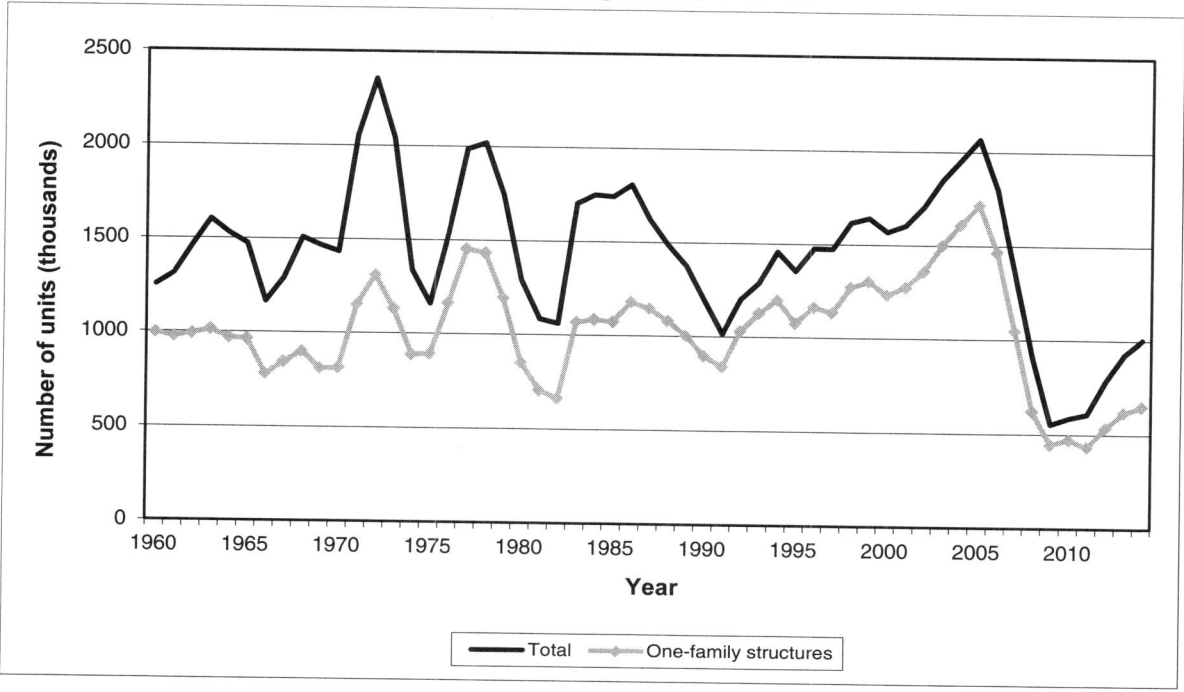

- The housing sector and associated financial excesses had the leading role in the boom and bust cycle of 2001–2009. In 2005, as shown in Figure 16-1, 2.1 million housing units were started, the highest since 1972. Of those, 1.7 million were one-family homes, an all-time record. By 2009, both total and single-family starts had plunged to the lowest levels of their 50-year history. With very modest recovery since then, starts remain at levels once viewed as recessionary. However in 2014, the housing starts nearly double to slightly more than 1,000,00. (Table 16-2)

- New orders for nondefense capital goods excluding aircraft and parts at U.S. manufacturing firms is a widely followed advance indicator for production of investment goods. The value of such orders fell 24 percent from 2007 to 2009, similar to their decline between 2000 and 2002. Their recovery since 2009 has been faster than it was in the 4 years following 2002, and the value of new orders in 2014 surpassed the peak in 2007. (Table 16-5)

- Sales of cars and light trucks fell to 10.4 million in 2009, down 6.5 million from their recent high in 2005; they recovered by 5.9 million from 2009 to 2014. (Table 16-7)

- Service industries were affected later and less by the Great Recession. They experienced revenue declines in late 2008 and early 2009 but then resumed growth. In the fourth quarter of 2014, information industry revenues were up 22 percent from the fourth quarter of 2008; professional, scientific, and technical services were up 14 percent; and administrative and support and waste management, which includes temporary help firms, were up 32 percent. Hospital revenues were up 37 percent. (Table 16-14)

- E-commerce grew from 0.6 percent of total retail sales at the end of 1999 to 6.6 percent (seasonally adjusted) at the end of 2014. (Table 16-9)

Table 16-1. New Construction Put in Place

(Billions of dollars, monthly data are at seasonally adjusted annual rates.)

Year and month	Total	Private											
		Total [1]	Residential	Office	Commercial		Health care	Educational	Amuse-ment and recreation	Transpor-tation	Commu-nication	Power	Manu-facturing
					Total [1]	Multi-retail							
1975	152.6	109.3	51.6	. . .	. . .	. . .	. . .	. . .	. . .	. . .	. . .	. . .	. . .
1976	172.1	128.2	68.3	. . .	. . .	. . .	. . .	. . .	. . .	. . .	. . .	. . .	. . .
1977	200.5	157.4	92.0	. . .	. . .	. . .	. . .	. . .	. . .	. . .	. . .	. . .	. . .
1978	239.9	189.7	109.8	. . .	. . .	. . .	. . .	. . .	. . .	. . .	. . .	. . .	. . .
1979	272.9	216.2	116.4	. . .	. . .	. . .	. . .	. . .	. . .	. . .	. . .	. . .	. . .
1980	273.9	210.3	100.4	. . .	. . .	. . .	. . .	. . .	. . .	. . .	. . .	. . .	. . .
1981	289.1	224.4	99.2	. . .	. . .	. . .	. . .	. . .	. . .	. . .	. . .	. . .	. . .
1982	279.3	216.3	84.7	. . .	. . .	. . .	. . .	. . .	. . .	. . .	. . .	. . .	. . .
1983	311.9	248.4	125.8	. . .	. . .	. . .	. . .	. . .	. . .	. . .	. . .	. . .	. . .
1984	370.2	300.0	155.0	. . .	. . .	. . .	. . .	. . .	. . .	. . .	. . .	. . .	. . .
1985	403.4	325.6	160.5	. . .	. . .	. . .	. . .	. . .	. . .	. . .	. . .	. . .	. . .
1986	433.5	348.9	190.7	. . .	. . .	. . .	. . .	. . .	. . .	. . .	. . .	. . .	. . .
1987	446.6	356.0	199.7	. . .	. . .	. . .	. . .	. . .	. . .	. . .	. . .	. . .	. . .
1988	462.0	367.3	204.5	. . .	. . .	. . .	. . .	. . .	. . .	. . .	. . .	. . .	. . .
1989	477.5	379.3	204.3	. . .	. . .	. . .	. . .	. . .	. . .	. . .	. . .	. . .	. . .
1990	476.8	369.3	191.1	. . .	. . .	. . .	. . .	. . .	. . .	. . .	. . .	. . .	. . .
1991	432.6	322.5	166.3	. . .	. . .	. . .	. . .	. . .	. . .	. . .	. . .	. . .	. . .
1992	463.7	347.8	199.4	. . .	. . .	. . .	. . .	. . .	. . .	. . .	. . .	. . .	. . .
1993	485.5	358.2	208.2	20.0	34.4	11.5	14.9	4.8	4.6	4.7	9.8	23.6	23.4
1994	531.9	401.5	241.0	20.4	39.6	12.2	15.4	5.0	5.1	4.7	10.1	21.0	28.8
1995	548.7	408.7	228.1	23.0	44.1	12.0	15.3	5.7	5.9	4.8	11.1	22.0	35.4
1996	599.7	453.0	257.5	26.5	49.4	13.3	15.4	7.0	7.0	5.8	11.8	17.4	38.1
1997	631.9	478.4	264.7	32.8	53.1	12.2	17.4	8.8	8.5	6.2	12.5	16.4	37.6
1998	688.5	533.7	296.3	40.4	55.7	13.3	17.7	9.8	8.6	7.3	12.5	21.7	40.5
1999	744.6	575.5	326.3	45.1	59.4	15.2	18.4	9.8	9.6	6.5	18.4	22.0	35.1
2000	802.8	621.4	346.1	52.4	64.1	14.9	19.5	11.7	8.8	6.9	18.8	29.3	37.6
2001	840.2	638.3	364.4	49.7	63.6	16.4	19.5	12.8	7.8	7.1	19.6	31.5	37.8
2002	847.9	634.4	402.0	44.3	62.5	15.6	27.1	73.9	17.3	25.8	18.5	36.8	22.9
2003	891.5	675.4	451.3	39.4	61.5	15.4	29.3	74.3	16.8	24.7	14.6	41.5	21.5
2004	991.4	771.2	538.4	42.4	67.1	18.8	32.2	74.3	16.7	25.1	15.5	35.6	23.4
2005	1 104.1	870.0	617.5	45.8	70.2	22.7	34.4	79.7	15.2	25.1	18.9	38.4	28.6
2006	1 167.2	911.8	619.8	54.2	76.7	29.1	38.5	84.9	19.0	28.0	22.2	42.2	32.7
2007	1 152.4	863.3	500.5	65.3	89.7	34.6	43.8	96.8	21.2	31.9	27.6	66.1	40.6
2008	1 068.4	759.7	350.3	55.5	82.7	32.0	38.4	18.6	10.5	9.9	26.3	69.2	53.6
2009	904.9	590.0	245.9	37.3	51.1	18.4	35.3	16.9	8.4	9.1	19.7	76.1	57.4
2010	806.0	502.1	238.8	24.4	37.2	12.5	29.6	13.4	6.5	9.9	17.7	66.1	40.6
2011	788.3	501.9	244.1	23.7	39.2	13.4	28.9	14.1	6.7	9.5	17.5	64.3	39.8
2012	861.2	581.9	280.6	27.4	44.3	14.9	31.4	16.6	6.2	10.9	16.0	86.4	46.8
2013	910.8	641.1	336.2	29.8	48.7	16.2	30.3	16.7	7.2	11.0	17.1	78.5	47.2
2014	960.6	686.6	349.0	36.9	55.4	18.6	28.9	16.5	7.7	11.9	15.9	88.8	55.0
2012													
January	823.6	541.9	249.4	25.6	41.6	14.7	31.2	16.2	6.2	10.3	16.7	87.0	43.7
February	825.8	542.4	251.2	26.3	41.4	14.8	31.6	16.1	5.9	9.7	16.2	86.0	43.9
March	834.8	554.6	257.1	27.0	42.8	15.5	31.2	16.4	5.9	10.2	15.7	88.1	45.2
April	842.9	564.8	263.1	26.2	44.1	16.1	32.3	16.5	6.1	10.8	16.0	88.6	45.7
May	861.9	578.0	271.7	26.3	44.4	16.1	32.3	16.6	6.1	10.8	15.6	92.2	47.0
June	873.1	584.2	278.0	26.6	44.4	15.4	32.4	16.7	5.9	10.9	15.9	91.4	47.1
July	864.7	583.3	274.7	27.8	44.7	15.1	32.1	17.3	6.3	10.9	16.3	90.6	47.1
August	868.2	588.5	284.7	27.9	44.7	15.0	32.2	16.6	6.6	10.9	15.4	87.0	46.9
September	876.1	602.5	295.0	28.9	45.7	14.6	30.6	16.7	6.3	11.3	16.6	88.0	48.0
October	883.9	608.6	303.1	29.2	46.1	14.0	30.1	16.8	6.6	11.7	15.6	84.4	48.6
November	879.5	606.6	306.3	28.0	44.7	13.9	29.7	16.3	6.3	11.4	16.0	84.5	47.7
December	882.6	616.0	312.5	28.6	44.3	13.2	30.7	17.0	6.1	10.9	15.7	84.5	49.0
2013													
January	869.2	605.3	316.5	28.3	45.6	14.2	31.9	16.7	5.9	10.7	15.8	70.5	47.1
February	879.6	609.6	320.8	27.5	47.9	14.3	31.5	16.8	5.8	10.5	15.7	68.4	47.2
March	871.9	611.0	322.6	28.2	46.9	14.2	30.2	16.5	6.3	10.8	16.7	67.9	47.4
April	885.0	614.4	324.4	27.1	46.5	14.2	30.1	16.5	6.7	11.1	16.8	72.0	45.7
May	896.6	626.5	330.0	28.1	48.2	15.1	30.5	17.9	7.2	11.2	16.5	73.3	45.1
June	900.3	627.6	331.3	28.4	47.4	15.4	29.4	16.7	7.3	11.4	17.6	74.7	45.9
July	906.6	632.7	331.5	29.5	48.0	16.0	30.2	17.0	7.4	11.7	17.2	75.7	46.6
August	915.3	644.4	339.2	29.9	47.9	16.3	29.8	16.6	8.2	11.1	17.7	76.4	49.0
September	924.2	657.8	346.5	31.4	49.6	17.2	30.2	16.4	8.0	10.9	18.0	81.7	46.3
October	939.9	665.5	347.3	32.0	51.3	18.6	30.7	17.3	8.1	10.8	16.9	85.0	46.7
November	952.5	683.9	354.5	33.1	53.3	19.6	30.4	16.0	8.0	11.1	18.6	90.1	48.7
December	961.2	695.4	364.0	33.7	53.1	19.4	29.4	16.4	7.6	10.9	17.4	93.1	51.0
2014													
January	954.6	694.1	364.1	33.6	50.3	18.2	29.0	16.1	7.1	10.9	16.1	95.6	52.3
February	947.1	686.2	357.3	33.3	50.9	18.4	28.7	15.9	7.0	11.1	17.5	95.4	49.8
March	947.3	682.3	358.1	33.5	51.3	18.0	28.4	16.0	6.8	11.3	17.7	94.1	46.3
April	960.3	689.0	360.8	35.8	51.9	17.5	28.4	16.6	7.4	11.6	16.0	90.8	49.6
May	972.8	696.4	357.0	36.5	52.6	18.3	29.0	16.4	7.2	12.5	16.2	94.3	54.5
June	957.1	684.3	350.6	36.1	53.9	18.3	29.1	16.7	7.8	11.9	15.4	89.7	53.7
July	960.0	682.8	348.9	36.1	54.9	18.8	28.6	16.4	7.3	11.8	15.2	90.4	53.5
August	961.1	684.4	346.2	37.3	56.0	18.9	28.6	16.7	7.2	11.4	15.7	88.5	56.0
September	966.4	692.1	346.4	39.5	58.6	19.1	29.0	16.8	8.0	11.4	15.5	87.4	57.9
October	980.4	694.9	347.9	39.9	59.1	18.8	28.9	16.6	8.4	11.6	15.2	85.3	59.7
November	974.3	697.9	346.9	39.3	60.1	18.9	29.5	16.8	8.3	13.5	15.3	84.7	60.6
December	984.5	704.5	349.6	40.1	61.0	19.0	29.5	16.2	9.1	13.2	15.7	83.5	63.7

[1]Includes categories not shown separately.
. . . = Not available.

Table 16-1. New Construction Put in Place—*Continued*

(Billions of dollars, monthly data are at seasonally adjusted annual rates.)

Year and month	Total	Public													Federal
		State and local													
		Total 1	Residential	Office	Health care	Educational	Public safety	Amusement and recreation	Transportation	Power	Highway and street	Sewage and waste disposal	Water supply		
1975	43.3	37.2	. . .	. . .	. . .	. . .	. . .	. . .	. . .	. . .	. . .	. . .	. . .		6.1
1976	44.0	37.2	. . .	. . .	. . .	. . .	. . .	. . .	. . .	. . .	. . .	. . .	. . .		6.8
1977	43.1	36.0	. . .	. . .	. . .	. . .	. . .	. . .	. . .	. . .	. . .	. . .	. . .		7.1
1978	50.1	42.0	. . .	. . .	. . .	. . .	. . .	. . .	. . .	. . .	. . .	. . .	. . .		8.1
1979	56.6	48.1	. . .	. . .	. . .	. . .	. . .	. . .	. . .	. . .	. . .	. . .	. . .		8.6
1980	63.6	54.0	. . .	. . .	. . .	. . .	. . .	. . .	. . .	. . .	. . .	. . .	. . .		9.6
1981	64.7	54.3	. . .	. . .	. . .	. . .	. . .	. . .	. . .	. . .	. . .	. . .	. . .		10.4
1982	63.1	53.1	. . .	. . .	. . .	. . .	. . .	. . .	. . .	. . .	. . .	. . .	. . .		10.0
1983	63.5	52.9	. . .	. . .	. . .	. . .	. . .	. . .	. . .	. . .	. . .	. . .	. . .		10.6
1984	70.2	59.0	. . .	. . .	. . .	. . .	. . .	. . .	. . .	. . .	. . .	. . .	. . .		11.2
1985	77.8	65.8	. . .	. . .	. . .	. . .	. . .	. . .	. . .	. . .	. . .	. . .	. . .		12.0
1986	84.6	72.2	. . .	. . .	. . .	. . .	. . .	. . .	. . .	. . .	. . .	. . .	. . .		12.4
1987	90.6	76.6	. . .	. . .	. . .	. . .	. . .	. . .	. . .	. . .	. . .	. . .	. . .		14.1
1988	94.7	82.5	. . .	. . .	. . .	. . .	. . .	. . .	. . .	. . .	. . .	. . .	. . .		12.3
1989	98.2	86.0	. . .	. . .	. . .	. . .	. . .	. . .	. . .	. . .	. . .	. . .	. . .		12.2
1990	107.5	95.4	. . .	. . .	. . .	. . .	. . .	. . .	. . .	. . .	. . .	. . .	. . .		12.1
1991	110.1	97.3	. . .	. . .	. . .	. . .	. . .	. . .	. . .	. . .	. . .	. . .	. . .		12.8
1992	115.8	101.5	. . .	. . .	. . .	. . .	. . .	. . .	. . .	. . .	. . .	. . .	. . .		14.4
1993	127.4	112.9	3.4	2.8	2.3	24.2	4.6	4.3	9.8	7.4	34.5	11.2	6.4		14.4
1994	130.4	116.0	4.2	3.0	2.4	25.3	4.5	4.7	9.2	5.1	37.3	12.0	6.4		14.4
1995	140.0	124.3	4.5	3.3	2.6	27.5	5.0	5.1	9.6	5.7	38.6	13.0	7.3		15.8
1996	146.7	131.4	3.7	3.6	2.8	31.0	5.5	5.0	10.4	4.8	40.6	13.6	7.7		15.3
1997	153.4	139.4	3.3	3.8	2.9	34.3	5.6	5.7	10.3	4.4	44.4	13.1	8.1		14.1
1998	154.8	140.5	3.2	3.7	2.3	35.1	6.1	6.2	10.5	2.8	45.4	13.2	8.9		14.3
1999	169.1	155.1	3.2	3.6	2.5	39.8	6.2	7.2	11.4	2.9	51.0	14.5	9.6		14.0
2000	181.3	167.2	3.0	4.5	2.8	46.8	5.9	7.6	13.0	5.5	51.6	14.0	9.5		14.2
2001	201.9	186.8	3.5	5.6	2.9	52.8	6.1	9.1	15.9	5.3	56.4	14.2	11.4		15.1
2002	213.4	196.9	3.8	6.3	3.5	59.5	6.0	9.2	17.3	3.8	56.7	15.3	11.7		16.6
2003	216.1	198.2	3.7	6.1	4.0	59.3	5.8	8.4	16.5	6.8	56.3	15.6	11.7		17.9
2004	220.2	201.8	4.1	6.0	5.0	59.7	5.5	7.8	16.4	7.0	57.4	17.1	12.0		18.3
2005	234.2	216.9	4.0	5.2	5.1	65.8	6.0	7.3	16.3	8.3	63.2	18.3	13.5		17.3
2006	255.4	237.8	4.3	5.6	5.6	69.8	6.6	9.4	17.7	7.8	71.0	21.5	14.3		17.6
2007	289.1	268.5	5.1	7.2	7.0	78.4	8.4	10.7	21.1	11.4	75.5	23.3	15.0		20.6
2008	308.7	285.0	4.9	8.5	7.0	84.5	9.7	10.9	23.2	11.0	80.4	24.1	16.0		23.7
2009	314.9	286.5	5.8	9.2	6.8	83.7	9.4	10.6	25.5	11.8	81.3	23.5	14.8		28.4
2010	304.0	272.8	7.6	8.3	6.2	71.9	7.6	9.7	26.5	10.8	81.3	24.6	14.4		31.1
2011	286.4	254.8	6.0	7.4	7.0	68.0	7.2	8.5	23.3	9.5	78.4	21.2	13.4		31.7
2012	279.3	252.4	4.7	6.1	7.0	65.6	7.6	8.9	24.8	9.8	79.7	20.9	12.7		26.9
2013	269.6	246.0	4.6	5.2	6.9	59.1	6.7	8.1	26.1	11.0	80.5	20.7	12.8		23.6
2014	273.9	251.1	4.2	5.4	6.4	59.9	6.2	8.7	27.7	10.8	83.3	21.5	12.3		22.9
2012															
January	281.7	253.8	5.3	7.0	6.9	68.2	7.9	9.0	22.9	9.0	76.9	22.8	13.7		27.9
February	283.4	255.8	4.8	6.5	7.0	66.6	7.9	9.2	23.8	9.2	80.8	22.4	13.3		27.6
March	280.2	251.4	4.5	6.5	7.1	67.2	7.8	9.1	22.5	8.5	79.0	21.9	12.8		28.8
April	278.1	251.0	4.7	6.4	7.0	65.5	7.7	8.8	22.2	8.6	81.3	21.5	13.0		27.1
May	284.0	256.0	4.5	6.2	7.2	64.8	7.8	9.4	24.2	10.0	83.9	21.2	12.8		27.6
June	288.9	261.5	4.7	6.0	7.0	68.2	7.9	9.2	26.0	10.1	84.9	20.5	12.5		27.4
July	281.3	255.0	4.5	5.8	7.1	68.4	7.9	9.0	25.4	9.3	81.0	19.9	12.2		26.3
August	279.7	252.9	4.7	6.0	7.0	64.6	7.8	8.3	25.1	10.4	81.2	20.5	12.4		26.8
September	273.6	248.2	4.6	5.8	6.9	64.5	7.2	9.1	25.3	10.5	76.5	20.4	12.5		25.3
October	275.3	248.0	4.7	5.7	7.0	62.9	7.5	8.6	26.8	11.2	76.1	20.3	12.5		27.2
November	273.0	246.8	4.7	5.7	7.0	62.2	7.1	8.3	26.1	11.1	76.6	20.8	12.6		26.2
December	266.6	240.5	4.4	5.4	7.1	62.3	7.1	8.2	25.9	9.0	73.9	20.0	13.2		26.1
2013															
January	264.0	239.4	4.2	5.3	6.5	60.4	6.5	8.5	25.5	9.7	75.6	19.4	13.5		24.6
February	270.0	246.0	4.2	5.2	6.8	62.0	7.1	8.0	25.9	11.0	77.7	20.4	13.2		24.0
March	260.9	237.0	4.8	4.8	6.8	58.6	6.9	8.1	25.5	10.6	74.1	19.4	13.0		23.8
April	270.6	246.4	4.9	5.0	7.3	58.6	6.9	7.9	27.3	10.5	79.7	20.7	13.1		24.2
May	270.1	245.8	4.9	4.9	7.3	58.7	7.1	7.5	25.9	11.0	80.2	21.0	13.3		24.3
June	272.7	248.7	4.8	5.4	7.7	61.6	6.6	7.7	25.8	11.5	81.5	19.5	12.5		24.0
July	274.0	250.0	5.1	5.2	7.4	61.0	5.9	7.6	26.5	11.5	81.6	20.9	13.0		24.0
August	270.9	247.9	5.1	5.1	7.5	58.6	6.4	8.4	25.5	10.3	82.6	21.9	12.5		22.9
September	266.3	243.9	4.5	5.0	7.1	56.0	6.9	8.2	26.6	10.7	80.7	21.6	12.6		22.4
October	274.4	250.5	4.6	5.5	7.3	58.5	6.9	8.6	27.7	10.8	81.6	21.7	13.1		23.9
November	268.6	245.6	4.4	5.3	6.8	58.3	6.7	8.3	25.8	11.8	80.8	20.0	12.9		23.0
December	265.7	242.3	4.1	5.4	6.2	56.1	6.1	8.4	26.1	12.2	81.8	20.5	11.4		23.4
2014															
January	260.6	238.2	3.5	5.3	6.4	56.2	6.4	7.8	26.1	11.0	81.2	19.0	11.5		22.4
February	260.9	237.4	3.8	5.7	6.2	56.9	6.2	7.7	26.5	11.1	80.3	18.7	10.7		23.5
March	265.0	241.8	3.7	5.9	6.0	58.0	6.1	7.7	27.4	10.6	82.3	18.9	11.5		23.1
April	271.3	247.8	3.8	5.5	6.1	59.9	6.4	8.1	27.4	10.7	82.9	20.1	12.2		23.5
May	276.5	255.4	3.8	5.4	6.2	61.7	6.7	9.3	28.0	11.7	84.6	20.6	12.6		21.1
June	272.9	249.8	4.3	5.3	6.5	61.2	6.1	8.7	27.1	11.3	78.6	23.2	12.3		23.1
July	277.2	254.5	4.4	5.3	6.6	61.7	6.0	9.1	27.6	11.0	82.9	22.2	12.5		22.7
August	276.7	254.3	4.4	5.2	6.8	60.8	6.2	9.0	27.5	11.1	83.5	22.1	12.4		22.3
September	274.3	253.5	4.6	5.2	6.6	60.7	6.1	8.9	28.1	9.9	83.0	21.8	13.0		20.8
October	285.6	260.5	4.1	5.6	6.5	61.3	6.5	8.8	29.4	11.0	87.0	22.1	12.8		25.0
November	276.4	252.9	4.5	5.1	6.2	58.8	6.0	9.0	28.6	8.3	86.4	22.6	12.6		23.5
December	280.0	256.1	4.7	5.4	5.9	60.1	5.9	9.0	27.9	11.6	83.5	24.4	13.0		23.9

1Includes categories not shown separately.
. . . = Not available.

Table 16-2. Housing Starts and Building Permits; New House Sales and Prices

Year and month	Housing starts and building permits									Shipments of manufactured homes (thousands, seasonally adjusted annual rate)	New house sales and prices		Median sales price (dollars)	Price index (2005 = 100)
	New private housing units (thousands)										Seasonally adjusted			
	Started (not seasonally adjusted)			Seasonally adjusted annual rate							Sold (thousands, annual rate)	For sale, end-of-period (thousands)		
				Started			Authorized by building permits							
	Total¹	One-family structures	Five units or more	Total¹	One-family structures	Five units or more	Total¹	One-family structures	Five units or more					
1975	1 160	892	204	1 160	892	204	939	675	200	213	549	316	39 300	22.1
1976	1 538	1 162	289	1 538	1 162	289	1 296	894	309	246	646	358	44 200	24.0
1977	1 987	1 451	414	1 987	1 451	414	1 690	1 126	443	266	819	408	48 800	27.0
1978	2 020	1 433	462	2 020	1 433	462	1 801	1 183	487	276	817	419	55 700	30.9
1979	1 745	1 194	429	1 745	1 194	429	1 552	982	445	277	709	402	62 900	35.3
1980	1 292	852	331	1 292	852	331	1 191	710	366	222	545	342	64 600	38.9
1981	1 084	705	288	1 084	705	288	986	564	319	241	436	278	68 900	42.0
1982	1 062	663	320	1 062	663	320	1 000	546	366	240	412	255	69 300	43.0
1983	1 703	1 068	522	1 703	1 068	522	1 605	901	570	296	623	304	75 300	43.9
1984	1 750	1 084	544	1 750	1 084	544	1 682	922	617	295	639	358	79 900	45.7
1985	1 742	1 072	576	1 742	1 072	576	1 733	957	657	284	688	350	84 300	46.2
1986	1 805	1 179	542	1 805	1 179	542	1 769	1 078	583	244	750	361	92 000	48.0
1987	1 621	1 146	409	1 621	1 146	409	1 535	1 024	421	233	671	370	104 500	50.6
1988	1 488	1 081	348	1 488	1 081	348	1 456	994	386	218	676	371	112 500	52.5
1989	1 376	1 003	318	1 376	1 003	318	1 338	932	340	198	650	366	120 000	54.6
1990	1 193	895	260	1 193	895	260	1 111	794	263	188	534	321	122 900	55.7
1991	1 014	840	138	1 014	840	138	949	754	152	171	509	284	120 000	56.4
1992	1 200	1 030	139	1 200	1 030	139	1 095	911	138	211	610	267	121 500	57.2
1993	1 288	1 126	133	1 288	1 126	133	1 199	987	160	254	666	295	126 500	59.4
1994	1 457	1 198	224	1 457	1 198	224	1 372	1 068	241	304	670	340	130 000	62.9
1995	1 354	1 076	244	1 354	1 076	244	1 333	997	272	340	667	374	133 900	64.3
1996	1 477	1 161	271	1 477	1 161	271	1 426	1 069	290	363	757	326	140 000	66.0
1997	1 474	1 134	296	1 474	1 134	296	1 441	1 062	310	354	804	287	146 000	67.5
1998	1 617	1 271	303	1 617	1 271	303	1 612	1 188	355	373	886	300	152 500	69.2
1999	1 641	1 302	307	1 641	1 302	307	1 664	1 247	351	348	880	315	161 000	72.8
2000	1 569	1 231	299	1 569	1 231	299	1 592	1 198	329	250	877	301	169 000	75.6
2001	1 603	1 273	293	1 603	1 273	293	1 637	1 236	335	193	908	310	175 200	77.9
2002	1 705	1 359	308	1 705	1 359	308	1 748	1 333	341	169	973	344	187 600	81.4
2003	1 848	1 499	315	1 848	1 499	315	1 889	1 461	346	131	1 086	377	195 000	86.0
2004	1 956	1 611	303	1 956	1 611	303	2 070	1 613	366	131	1 203	431	221 000	92.8
2005	2 068	1 716	311	2 068	1 716	311	2 155	1 682	389	147	1 283	515	240 900	100.0
2006	1 801	1 465	293	1 801	1 465	293	1 839	1 378	384	117	1 051	537	246 500	104.7
2007	1 355	1 046	277	1 355	1 046	277	1 398	980	359	96	776	496	247 900	104.9
2008	906	622	266	906	622	266	905	576	295	82	485	352	232 100	99.5
2009	554	445	97	554	445	97	583	441	121	50	375	232	216 700	95.1
2010	587	471	104	587	471	104	605	447	135	50	323	188	221 800	95.0
2011	609	431	167	609	431	167	624	418	184	52	306	150	227 200	94.3
2012	781	535	234	781	535	234	830	519	285	55	368	148	245 200	97.6
2013	925	618	294	925	618	294	991	621	341	60	429	186	268 900	104.7
2014	1 003	648	342	1 003	648	342	1 046	635	382	64	437	212	282 800	112.3
2012														
January	47	33	13	723	518	189	715	464	230	59	335	149	221 700	. . .
February	50	32	17	704	466	230	733	493	216	58	366	147	239 900	94.0
March	58	40	17	695	472	213	797	478	295	57	354	145	239 800	. . .
April	67	47	20	753	504	240	747	484	240	55	354	144	236 400	. . .
May	68	50	16	708	518	175	807	499	284	54	370	144	239 200	95.2
June	75	54	20	757	524	224	790	500	268	54	360	145	232 600	. . .
July	69	49	19	740	517	212	840	519	292	54	369	142	237 400	. . .
August	69	49	19	754	536	210	832	516	286	54	375	143	253 200	98.9
September	76	51	24	847	594	245	921	557	336	53	385	144	254 600	. . .
October	77	50	25	915	611	285	895	570	299	53	358	147	247 200	. . .
November	62	40	21	833	569	254	930	571	329	54	392	150	245 000	. . .
December	63	38	24	976	615	344	938	589	320	56	399	150	258 300	100.0
2013														
January	59	39	19	888	612	265	928	590	310	59	442	149	251 500	. . .
February	66	44	21	970	663	297	971	612	324	60	439	153	265 100	. . .
March	83	53	29	999	621	353	932	609	296	57	449	154	257 500	101.3
April	76	55	20	826	578	234	1 015	623	363	59	451	161	279 300	. . .
May	87	58	28	920	602	307	1 016	624	363	59	430	162	263 700	. . .
June	81	61	19	852	605	235	951	628	293	60	463	160	259 800	104.7
July	84	57	25	891	598	274	986	615	340	59	376	170	262 200	. . .
August	80	57	23	898	624	261	947	631	291	61	380	174	255 300	. . .
September	78	51	27	860	582	268	1 015	618	368	62	399	183	269 800	104.8
October	78	49	28	921	593	317	1 031	623	379	62	444	183	264 300	. . .
November	84	51	32	1 104	712	383	1 042	647	369	62	446	184	277 100	. . .
December	68	43	24	1 010	653	336	1 013	613	370	61	441	187	275 500	105.8
2014														
January	61	39	22	888	577	303	1 002	621	351	61	446	189	269 800	. . .
February	65	41	24	951	604	336	1 030	613	393	63	417	188	268 400	. . .
March	80	55	25	963	649	300	1 061	622	410	63	410	190	282 300	106.8
April	95	61	33	1 039	639	391	1 074	622	425	63	410	191	274 500	. . .
May	93	61	31	986	637	340	1 017	626	362	63	457	194	285 600	. . .
June	87	61	25	927	597	307	1 033	648	347	61	408	198	287 000	112.7
July	101	61	38	1 095	657	422	1 041	640	371	68	403	204	280 400	. . .
August	86	58	27	966	643	306	1 040	643	362	65	454	205	291 700	. . .
September	94	58	35	1 026	661	353	1 053	653	374	63	459	209	261 500	114.5
October	92	58	32	1 079	705	357	1 120	652	436	66	472	208	299 400	. . .
November	76	47	28	1 007	670	328	1 079	663	388	67	449	210	302 700	. . .
December	73	48	24	1 080	724	336	1 077	685	368	68	495	212	302 000	119.2

¹Includes structures with 2 to 4 units, not shown separately.
. . . = Not available.

Table 16-3. Manufacturers' Shipments

(Millions of dollars, seasonally adjusted.)

Year and month	Total	Total durable goods [1]	Total nondurable goods [1]	By topical categories								
				Construction materials and supplies	Information technology industries	Capital goods				Consumer goods		
						Total	Nondefense		Defense	Total	Durable	Nondurable
							Total	Excluding aircraft and parts				
1992	2 904 024	1 518 862	1 385 162	281 232	236 015	566 268	471 485	435 696	94 783	1 098 480	253 111	845 369
1993	3 020 497	1 604 544	1 415 953	303 391	241 680	580 859	493 875	463 753	86 984	1 127 629	274 813	852 816
1994	3 238 112	1 764 061	1 474 051	332 734	264 092	616 435	538 203	512 327	78 232	1 192 098	314 931	877 167
1995	3 479 677	1 902 815	1 576 862	353 198	291 885	666 167	590 578	565 729	75 589	1 256 611	324 036	932 575
1996	3 597 188	1 978 597	1 618 591	371 401	311 028	704 635	630 932	605 295	73 703	1 292 955	328 402	964 553
1997	3 834 699	2 147 384	1 687 315	399 880	349 846	779 232	702 971	665 074	76 261	1 358 516	360 193	998 323
1998	3 899 813	2 231 588	1 668 225	418 756	362 564	821 736	747 046	695 717	74 690	1 351 812	373 404	978 408
1999	4 031 887	2 326 736	1 705 151	434 138	374 384	839 754	768 799	713 042	70 955	1 424 828	412 646	1 012 182
2000	4 208 584	2 373 688	1 834 896	444 812	399 751	875 396	808 345	757 617	67 051	1 500 532	391 463	1 109 069
2001	3 970 499	2 174 406	1 796 093	424 517	353 237	801 999	728 495	678 288	73 504	1 480 495	367 522	1 112 973
2002	3 914 723	2 123 621	1 791 102	424 008	284 799	728 585	652 342	609 595	76 243	1 494 575	395 953	1 098 622
2003	4 015 388	2 142 589	1 872 799	429 183	274 829	719 602	634 273	600 616	85 329	1 584 329	418 821	1 165 508
2004	4 308 970	2 264 667	2 044 303	463 148	287 837	752 905	661 740	629 146	91 165	1 700 835	419 182	1 281 653
2005	4 742 077	2 424 844	2 317 233	509 865	295 447	821 906	730 368	686 939	91 538	1 895 119	422 555	1 472 564
2006	5 015 552	2 562 194	2 453 358	546 866	319 890	884 199	794 638	744 282	89 561	1 980 031	421 860	1 558 171
2007	5 319 457	2 687 028	2 632 429	560 208	322 846	936 404	836 426	768 662	99 978	2 106 081	421 822	1 684 259
2008	5 468 095	2 619 931	2 848 164	543 769	315 383	953 501	838 116	772 231	115 385	2 252 714	359 362	1 893 352
2009	4 419 501	2 062 631	2 356 870	426 353	264 405	815 857	692 374	636 669	123 483	1 846 487	271 838	1 574 649
2010	4 905 445	2 290 796	2 614 649	443 253	259 772	851 851	720 928	666 730	130 923	2 055 025	329 120	1 725 905
2011	5 481 372	2 493 364	2 988 008	470 668	261 097	916 551	795 403	731 244	121 148	2 367 362	351 762	2 015 600
2012	5 736 713	2 658 212	3 078 501	500 004	274 456	1 009 749	892 065	804 742	117 684	2 442 889	373 937	2 068 952
2013	5 846 768	2 707 110	3 139 658	523 243	271 170	1 007 639	891 417	798 513	116 222	2 509 014	402 102	2 106 912
2014	5 996 336	2 838 388	3 157 948	557 712	278 631	1 049 800	934 952	831 544	114 848	2 511 547	404 813	2 106 734
2011												
January	440 266	201 253	239 013	37 950	21 665	72 629	62 209	57 763	10 420	190 005	29 783	160 222
February	440 776	200 999	239 777	37 938	21 326	72 538	61 803	56 913	10 735	191 138	29 822	161 316
March	455 753	208 103	247 650	39 200	21 358	74 864	63 896	59 067	10 968	198 358	31 306	167 052
April	454 902	203 403	251 499	38 174	21 758	74 668	63 913	58 939	10 755	199 294	28 726	170 568
May	454 680	204 643	250 037	38 488	21 551	74 747	64 285	59 581	10 462	196 573	28 446	168 127
June	457 026	205 284	251 742	39 143	21 380	75 183	65 116	60 372	10 067	198 278	28 681	169 597
July	461 377	209 678	251 699	39 434	21 623	76 416	66 661	60 987	9 755	200 194	30 763	169 431
August	461 989	211 163	250 826	39 700	22 092	79 362	69 290	63 473	10 072	197 148	28 560	168 588
September	460 790	209 861	250 929	39 673	22 049	78 493	68 659	63 231	9 834	197 649	28 039	169 610
October	463 636	213 470	250 166	40 013	21 820	79 138	69 952	63 125	9 186	198 736	30 093	168 643
November	465 744	212 220	253 524	40 405	22 055	78 083	69 091	63 247	8 992	201 283	29 154	172 129
December	469 435	216 209	253 226	41 131	22 639	80 999	71 083	65 378	9 916	200 573	29 346	171 227
2012												
January	474 246	220 439	253 807	41 700	22 886	82 836	72 758	64 937	10 078	201 294	30 383	170 911
February	475 111	218 768	256 343	41 257	23 109	81 990	72 812	65 964	9 178	203 299	30 274	173 025
March	478 700	220 075	258 625	42 127	22 900	84 274	74 690	68 265	9 584	204 495	30 425	174 070
April	477 551	221 441	256 110	41 746	23 493	83 800	74 630	67 327	9 170	203 585	32 272	171 313
May	478 674	224 010	254 664	41 825	23 996	84 818	74 835	67 817	9 983	202 850	31 895	170 955
June	469 609	222 969	246 640	41 353	22 622	84 942	74 794	68 193	10 148	196 819	31 843	164 976
July	472 767	221 298	251 469	41 208	22 980	84 775	74 949	67 511	9 826	199 907	31 486	168 421
August	474 677	218 245	256 432	41 353	21 846	82 361	72 889	66 221	9 472	203 406	30 927	172 479
September	479 904	220 022	259 882	41 276	22 315	83 974	74 069	66 047	9 905	206 048	31 192	174 856
October	480 438	219 592	260 846	41 683	22 740	83 732	73 861	66 095	9 871	206 143	30 076	176 067
November	483 430	222 707	260 723	41 773	22 808	85 591	75 774	67 739	9 817	205 888	31 027	174 861
December	483 022	223 804	259 218	42 231	22 688	85 211	75 017	67 221	10 194	205 670	31 692	173 978
2013												
January	485 608	222 419	263 189	43 511	22 634	83 399	74 002	66 943	9 397	208 452	32 765	175 687
February	492 914	224 865	268 049	43 710	22 973	83 656	73 809	67 686	9 847	215 115	33 747	181 368
March	483 795	224 969	258 826	42 463	22 869	85 122	75 384	67 859	9 738	207 167	33 188	173 979
April	480 764	223 498	257 266	43 434	22 158	81 487	72 056	65 959	9 431	205 183	33 611	171 572
May	486 592	226 517	260 075	43 360	22 748	86 065	76 498	67 323	9 567	206 533	33 242	173 291
June	482 800	225 159	257 641	43 050	22 551	84 472	74 697	66 249	9 775	205 135	33 213	171 922
July	484 701	221 438	263 263	43 331	22 212	82 418	73 224	65 229	9 194	210 309	32 622	177 687
August	487 067	224 862	262 205	43 693	22 289	83 309	73 327	65 563	9 982	209 830	33 305	176 525
September	487 089	226 502	260 587	44 049	22 815	83 129	73 458	65 456	9 671	208 741	33 822	174 919
October	488 134	226 698	261 436	44 376	22 745	82 873	73 336	65 250	9 537	209 070	34 024	175 046
November	496 967	233 686	263 281	44 746	22 588	85 618	75 266	67 607	10 350	212 926	35 837	177 089
December	492 860	226 688	266 172	43 937	22 466	85 578	75 988	67 748	9 590	212 381	32 620	179 761
2014												
January	492 616	227 565	265 051	44 451	22 836	84 148	74 638	66 782	9 510	211 338	32 365	178 973
February	499 189	231 320	267 869	44 882	22 814	85 078	75 611	67 711	9 467	214 776	33 879	180 897
March	499 366	233 203	266 163	45 808	22 862	86 451	77 228	68 802	9 223	212 426	33 417	179 009
April	500 664	232 635	268 029	46 116	23 087	85 685	76 121	68 125	9 564	214 109	33 018	181 091
May	500 678	233 566	267 112	46 297	23 158	85 001	75 622	68 445	9 379	213 167	33 860	179 307
June	503 219	235 294	267 925	46 826	23 483	87 051	77 746	68 697	9 305	212 595	32 711	179 884
July	508 669	243 305	265 364	47 217	23 586	88 055	78 540	69 652	9 515	212 423	35 863	176 560
August	505 055	241 202	263 853	47 095	23 633	90 402	80 721	71 594	9 681	209 264	33 857	175 407
September	503 455	240 834	262 621	47 415	23 348	90 621	81 106	71 562	9 515	207 962	33 646	174 316
October	498 442	239 888	258 554	47 096	23 140	88 756	79 115	69 859	9 641	204 662	33 971	170 691
November	494 635	237 558	257 077	46 840	23 406	87 998	78 298	69 587	9 700	203 377	33 940	169 437
December	490 184	242 029	248 155	47 184	23 468	89 685	79 255	70 389	10 430	196 132	35 009	161 123

[1]Includes categories not shown separately.

Table 16-4. Manufacturers' Inventories

(Current cost basis, end of period; seasonally adjusted, millions of dollars.)

Year and month	Total	Total durable goods	Durables total by stage of fabrication			Total nondurable goods	Nondurables total by stage of fabrication		
			Materials and supplies	Work in process	Finished goods		Materials and supplies	Work in process	Finished goods
1992	378 609	237 854	69 621	104 132	64 101	140 755	53 149	23 383	64 223
1993	379 806	238 719	72 633	101 948	64 138	141 087	54 233	23 394	63 460
1994	399 934	253 095	78 482	106 521	68 092	146 839	57 113	24 444	65 282
1995	424 802	267 437	85 545	106 634	75 258	157 365	60 778	25 776	70 811
1996	430 366	272 428	86 265	110 527	75 636	157 938	59 157	26 485	72 296
1997	443 247	280 742	92 249	109 719	78 774	162 505	60 163	28 520	73 822
1998	448 398	290 105	93 393	114 959	81 753	158 293	58 171	27 038	73 084
1999	463 057	296 051	97 699	113 828	84 524	167 006	60 982	28 783	77 241
2000	480 823	306 067	105 841	110 938	89 288	174 756	61 473	30 077	83 206
2001	427 388	267 464	91 179	93 783	82 502	159 924	55 672	27 152	77 100
2002	422 679	260 265	88 376	92 333	79 556	162 414	56 526	27 938	77 950
2003	408 190	246 795	82 287	88 582	75 926	161 395	56 840	27 164	77 391
2004	440 738	264 905	92 158	90 885	81 862	175 833	61 747	30 053	84 033
2005	473 666	283 663	98 553	98 448	86 662	190 003	66 768	32 972	90 263
2006	522 437	317 440	111 713	106 290	99 437	204 997	70 297	37 150	97 550
2007	561 114	334 597	116 621	117 307	100 669	226 517	74 939	44 943	106 635
2008	541 421	330 120	117 635	111 660	100 825	211 301	71 995	41 211	98 095
2009	502 119	295 112	100 446	107 339	87 327	207 007	70 883	41 834	94 290
2010	550 333	321 953	106 684	123 698	91 571	228 380	75 266	45 546	107 568
2011	603 342	353 150	118 476	135 462	99 212	250 192	81 734	48 502	119 956
2012	626 018	366 644	124 343	139 850	102 451	259 374	84 008	51 161	124 205
2013	637 877	375 526	127 223	143 442	104 861	262 351	85 122	52 594	124 635
2014	652 927	398 295	134 399	154 939	108 957	254 632	84 068	49 139	121 425
2011									
January	557 003	325 747	108 038	125 133	92 576	231 256	76 010	45 567	109 679
February	563 016	328 993	108 561	126 046	94 386	234 023	77 943	45 607	110 473
March	570 631	334 766	109 870	129 442	95 454	235 865	78 520	45 561	111 784
April	581 684	338 431	111 863	130 606	95 962	243 253	79 714	47 900	115 639
May	587 555	342 977	113 120	132 891	96 966	244 578	80 113	47 524	116 941
June	590 416	344 695	113 991	133 302	97 402	245 721	79 987	48 113	117 621
July	593 290	347 523	114 704	134 494	98 325	245 767	79 389	47 620	118 758
August	595 437	349 962	115 575	135 136	99 251	245 475	80 436	46 478	118 561
September	593 685	349 584	115 950	134 144	99 490	244 101	79 389	46 322	118 390
October	599 936	351 234	116 637	134 895	99 702	248 702	81 876	47 514	119 312
November	602 615	352 827	117 205	135 944	99 678	249 788	81 720	47 964	120 104
December	603 342	353 150	118 476	135 462	99 212	250 192	81 734	48 502	119 956
2012									
January	606 769	355 097	119 690	136 219	99 188	251 672	82 138	49 472	120 062
February	609 108	355 874	119 737	136 755	99 382	253 234	82 336	49 812	121 086
March	611 139	358 170	121 470	136 942	99 758	252 969	83 030	49 476	120 463
April	612 500	358 956	121 799	137 062	100 095	253 544	84 658	48 360	120 526
May	612 684	360 767	121 869	137 484	101 414	251 917	83 728	49 002	119 187
June	613 366	361 572	122 192	138 026	101 354	251 794	84 010	49 008	118 776
July	615 201	363 534	122 686	139 009	101 839	251 667	84 299	48 165	119 203
August	618 844	365 453	122 962	140 045	102 446	253 391	84 370	48 914	120 107
September	622 703	365 610	123 970	139 542	102 098	257 093	84 782	50 965	121 346
October	623 514	366 872	124 241	139 439	103 192	256 642	84 226	50 590	121 826
November	624 058	367 345	124 156	139 930	103 259	256 713	83 617	51 077	122 019
December	626 018	366 644	124 343	139 850	102 451	259 374	84 008	51 161	124 205
2013									
January	628 764	367 463	124 545	140 449	102 469	261 301	84 865	51 331	125 105
February	629 626	368 277	124 896	141 386	101 995	261 349	83 907	52 306	125 136
March	630 705	367 454	124 543	141 597	101 314	263 251	84 590	52 628	126 033
April	631 822	368 588	124 210	142 935	101 443	263 234	83 671	53 801	125 762
May	629 795	367 623	124 633	141 612	101 378	262 172	83 756	52 758	125 658
June	629 505	368 253	124 028	142 188	102 037	261 252	82 429	52 512	126 311
July	631 435	369 078	124 367	142 657	102 054	262 357	83 125	52 902	126 330
August	632 951	369 132	125 632	141 282	102 218	263 819	84 576	52 912	126 331
September	634 318	371 568	125 760	142 744	103 064	262 750	84 122	52 780	125 848
October	635 017	372 415	126 042	142 964	103 409	262 602	84 385	52 454	125 763
November	634 622	373 172	126 292	142 692	104 188	261 450	84 473	52 146	124 831
December	637 877	375 526	127 223	143 442	104 861	262 351	85 122	52 594	124 635
2014									
January	639 912	377 096	128 524	143 882	104 690	262 816	85 509	52 932	124 375
February	644 348	380 421	129 911	144 854	105 656	263 927	85 609	54 064	124 254
March	646 376	382 224	130 340	145 609	106 275	264 152	85 152	54 720	124 280
April	648 424	382 412	130 315	145 745	106 352	266 012	85 908	55 302	124 802
May	653 504	385 849	131 665	147 644	106 540	267 655	86 701	55 811	125 143
June	654 262	387 540	132 336	148 940	106 264	266 722	86 168	55 479	125 075
July	653 974	389 252	133 334	149 324	106 594	264 722	85 737	54 958	124 027
August	654 356	390 907	133 396	150 495	107 016	263 449	85 066	55 107	123 276
September	655 456	392 885	132 557	151 824	108 504	262 571	85 213	54 343	123 015
October	655 571	394 605	132 967	153 162	108 476	260 966	85 122	52 713	123 131
November	656 070	396 418	133 420	154 242	108 756	259 652	84 921	51 537	123 194
December	652 927	398 295	134 399	154 939	108 957	254 632	84 068	49 139	121 425

Table 16-4. Manufacturers' Inventories—*Continued*

(Current cost basis, end of period; seasonally adjusted, millions of dollars.)

Year and month	Construction materials and supplies	Information technology industries	By topical categories						
			Capital goods				Consumer goods		
			Total	Nondefense		Defense	Total	Durable	Nondurable
				Total	Excluding aircraft and parts				
1992	36 730	40 177	120 501	97 319	78 883	23 182	103 310	20 805	82 505
1993	38 307	39 176	118 460	97 118	79 585	21 342	104 873	21 820	83 053
1994	40 879	41 538	123 368	103 320	85 717	20 048	109 536	23 948	85 588
1995	43 420	46 936	129 709	111 563	94 673	18 146	116 404	25 316	91 088
1996	44 124	43 556	132 746	115 211	93 441	17 535	116 351	24 752	91 599
1997	45 716	48 095	137 567	122 604	98 875	14 963	119 682	24 904	94 778
1998	46 498	45 321	145 034	127 085	97 338	17 949	117 344	24 890	92 454
1999	48 538	46 170	146 247	126 266	99 598	19 981	124 250	26 105	98 145
2000	50 516	52 712	149 005	131 652	110 119	17 353	130 846	27 298	103 548
2001	46 340	42 953	128 682	114 912	93 308	13 770	121 369	25 417	95 952
2002	46 593	38 977	122 402	107 985	88 478	14 417	124 688	25 704	98 984
2003	45 331	35 176	114 972	99 178	81 711	15 794	125 045	25 032	100 013
2004	51 193	33 107	117 730	99 031	83 780	18 699	133 985	26 276	107 709
2005	55 052	39 121	127 193	110 657	92 901	16 536	144 637	28 126	116 511
2006	60 892	39 869	139 502	122 512	101 843	16 990	153 328	27 764	125 564
2007	62 606	38 714	150 206	131 414	104 750	18 792	170 853	27 664	143 189
2008	61 802	37 426	150 572	134 102	107 185	16 470	154 154	24 456	129 698
2009	51 420	35 658	145 289	125 344	96 680	19 945	157 234	21 631	135 603
2010	53 947	36 280	159 888	139 146	102 491	20 742	172 848	22 583	150 265
2011	57 477	39 024	175 196	154 753	113 609	20 443	184 975	23 023	161 952
2012	59 874	39 849	184 085	163 581	118 033	20 504	191 651	24 605	167 046
2013	62 346	38 501	187 122	167 309	118 248	19 813	196 066	26 607	169 459
2014	65 277	39 099	198 021	177 264	121 296	20 757	189 765	28 302	161 463
2011									
January	54 329	36 500	162 052	141 192	103 701	20 860	173 761	22 792	150 969
February	54 699	36 978	163 275	142 481	104 986	20 794	175 778	22 998	152 780
March	55 278	37 835	167 131	145 491	106 749	21 640	177 124	22 840	154 284
April	55 937	38 405	168 667	147 252	108 004	21 415	183 106	22 877	160 229
May	56 571	38 793	170 985	149 198	109 491	21 787	182 900	22 909	159 991
June	56 570	39 039	171 828	150 586	110 285	21 242	182 691	22 870	159 821
July	56 730	39 309	173 053	151 829	111 041	21 224	181 970	23 135	158 835
August	57 055	39 545	174 232	152 962	111 986	21 270	180 908	23 151	157 757
September	57 161	39 513	173 289	152 586	112 156	20 703	178 925	23 300	155 625
October	57 285	39 609	174 714	153 909	113 397	20 805	182 642	23 171	159 471
November	57 554	39 587	175 604	154 737	114 050	20 867	184 237	22 986	161 251
December	57 477	39 024	175 196	154 753	113 609	20 443	184 975	23 023	161 952
2012									
January	57 364	39 394	176 869	156 394	115 353	20 475	186 056	23 007	163 049
February	57 455	39 568	177 676	157 232	115 957	20 444	187 379	22 829	164 550
March	57 524	39 834	178 920	158 899	116 758	20 021	186 999	23 066	163 933
April	57 844	39 971	179 593	159 249	117 235	20 344	187 258	23 136	164 122
May	58 046	39 658	180 712	160 175	117 494	20 537	185 618	23 381	162 237
June	58 632	39 151	181 059	160 660	117 201	20 399	185 784	23 572	162 212
July	58 901	39 234	182 625	161 876	118 027	20 749	185 544	23 650	161 894
August	59 028	39 315	184 220	163 266	118 373	20 954	187 590	23 881	163 709
September	59 371	39 477	184 097	163 644	118 283	20 453	190 633	23 843	166 790
October	59 572	39 649	184 372	164 164	118 466	20 208	190 267	24 193	166 074
November	59 590	39 821	185 154	164 427	118 465	20 727	189 968	24 334	165 634
December	59 874	39 849	184 085	163 581	118 033	20 504	191 651	24 605	167 046
2013									
January	59 935	40 324	185 842	165 143	118 586	20 699	192 589	24 158	168 431
February	60 040	40 180	186 775	165 715	118 245	21 060	192 124	24 237	167 887
March	60 323	39 651	186 113	165 584	118 088	20 529	193 246	24 052	169 194
April	60 570	39 497	186 840	166 153	117 740	20 687	193 152	24 310	168 842
May	60 491	39 576	185 670	165 125	117 546	20 545	192 904	24 398	168 506
June	60 386	39 744	185 937	164 975	117 228	20 962	191 313	24 358	166 955
July	60 469	39 398	185 655	164 883	117 180	20 772	192 834	24 501	168 333
August	60 660	38 625	184 866	165 211	116 973	19 655	194 568	25 024	169 544
September	60 773	38 622	186 088	165 818	117 441	20 270	194 187	25 650	168 537
October	61 206	38 237	186 268	166 243	117 572	20 025	195 034	26 002	169 032
November	61 760	38 322	185 921	166 394	117 495	19 527	195 294	26 309	168 985
December	62 346	38 501	187 122	167 309	118 248	19 813	196 066	26 607	169 459
2014									
January	62 588	38 380	187 471	167 769	117 920	19 702	197 389	27 297	170 092
February	62 677	38 432	189 568	169 157	118 758	20 411	198 172	27 689	170 483
March	62 951	38 570	190 342	169 755	118 980	20 587	198 299	27 901	170 398
April	63 118	38 572	190 535	170 236	119 318	20 299	199 722	27 458	172 264
May	63 365	38 694	192 655	172 440	119 882	20 215	200 240	27 272	172 968
June	63 609	38 407	193 193	172 421	119 755	20 772	200 589	27 633	172 956
July	63 689	38 846	194 459	173 913	120 281	20 546	198 728	27 822	170 906
August	63 892	39 102	194 889	174 221	120 656	20 668	197 343	27 853	169 490
September	63 987	38 933	195 946	175 479	121 249	20 467	196 791	28 024	168 767
October	64 323	38 956	196 865	176 198	121 326	20 667	194 760	27 997	166 763
November	64 657	39 046	197 580	176 754	121 179	20 826	193 375	28 067	165 308
December	65 277	39 099	198 021	177 264	121 296	20 757	189 765	28 302	161 463

Table 16-5. Manufacturers' New Orders

(Net, millions of dollars, seasonally adjusted.)

Year and month	Total ¹	Total durable goods ¹	Construction materials and supplies	Information technology industries	Capital goods Total	Nondefense Total	Excluding aircraft and parts	Defense	Consumer goods Total	Durable	Nondurable
1993	2 960 015	1 544 062	304 264	239 387	561 097	488 166	466 433	72 931	1 128 447	275 631	852 816
1994	3 199 686	1 725 635	335 962	265 010	616 252	542 094	523 461	74 158	1 192 584	315 417	877 167
1995	3 426 503	1 849 641	355 161	297 605	680 857	612 132	576 769	68 725	1 256 721	324 146	932 575
1996	3 567 384	1 948 793	373 536	310 074	737 268	648 797	607 174	88 471	1 293 537	328 984	964 553
1997	3 779 835	2 092 520	403 860	352 700	792 859	728 362	676 119	64 497	1 360 010	361 687	998 323
1998	3 808 143	2 139 918	419 330	365 723	809 727	745 600	698 279	64 127	1 352 708	374 300	978 408
1999	3 957 242	2 252 091	435 034	389 160	840 603	772 703	728 089	67 900	1 425 617	413 435	1 012 182
2000	4 161 472	2 326 576	446 792	409 500	910 933	831 335	767 754	79 598	1 501 810	392 741	1 109 069
2001	3 868 777	2 072 684	420 801	336 864	775 311	691 538	656 852	83 773	1 477 160	364 187	1 112 973
2002	3 823 055	2 031 953	423 553	273 765	698 796	622 311	589 005	76 485	1 494 103	395 481	1 098 622
2003	3 975 783	2 102 984	431 555	282 264	737 046	636 813	608 126	100 233	1 585 018	419 510	1 165 508
2004	4 289 012	2 244 709	468 732	293 798	787 786	688 858	643 983	98 928	1 701 561	419 908	1 281 653
2005	4 764 183	2 446 950	516 776	300 312	896 819	814 404	703 722	82 415	1 894 051	421 487	1 472 564
2006	5 089 794	2 636 436	549 452	332 577	992 687	889 523	775 093	103 164	1 979 172	421 001	1 558 171
2007	5 397 349	2 764 920	564 702	324 188	1 061 765	957 801	786 606	103 964	2 105 788	421 529	1 684 259
2008	5 447 024	2 598 860	543 166	314 938	1 005 055	877 605	779 253	127 450	2 251 439	358 087	1 893 352
2009	4 191 231	1 834 361	413 369	257 372	684 230	580 291	600 735	103 939	1 846 066	271 417	1 574 649
2010	4 875 763	2 261 114	450 316	262 051	877 852	739 870	676 132	137 982	2 054 671	328 766	1 725 905
2011	5 480 862	2 492 854	470 367	272 451	984 813	851 297	753 704	133 516	2 367 555	351 955	2 015 600
2012	5 738 185	2 659 684	499 670	281 177	1 070 608	946 647	814 780	123 961	2 443 229	374 277	2 068 952
2013	5 851 851	2 712 193	524 101	257 415	1 067 698	971 710	804 157	95 988	2 509 552	402 640	2 106 912
2014	6 055 007	2 897 059	563 804	290 161	1 150 776	1 037 179	856 385	113 597	2 512 223	405 489	2 106 734
2011											
January	443 169	204 156	38 785	22 716	80 280	64 735	59 194	15 545	189 964	29 742	160 222
February	433 249	193 472	38 353	23 100	72 795	62 510	57 841	10 285	191 302	29 986	161 316
March	458 253	210 603	39 212	21 566	83 098	70 573	60 980	12 525	198 425	31 373	167 052
April	451 744	200 245	38 271	21 516	78 423	65 796	60 643	12 627	199 295	28 727	170 568
May	455 835	205 798	38 396	22 348	81 935	69 563	62 596	12 372	196 424	28 297	168 127
June	450 696	198 954	39 013	22 385	77 124	66 676	61 973	10 448	198 270	28 673	169 597
July	460 422	208 723	39 196	22 358	80 939	70 149	63 812	10 790	200 231	30 800	169 431
August	466 005	215 179	39 050	23 437	89 392	77 986	64 129	11 406	197 000	28 412	168 588
September	458 583	207 654	39 497	23 493	82 225	71 186	65 346	11 039	197 608	27 998	169 610
October	458 264	208 098	39 526	23 395	80 466	71 116	66 336	9 350	198 817	30 174	168 643
November	470 289	216 765	40 682	22 998	86 351	76 685	64 466	9 666	201 462	29 333	172 129
December	479 396	226 170	41 001	23 477	92 630	85 067	68 184	7 563	200 604	29 377	171 227
2012											
January	480 042	226 235	41 952	24 025	95 526	86 150	68 171	9 376	201 273	30 362	170 911
February	481 363	225 020	41 783	24 448	92 796	83 882	69 707	8 914	203 387	30 362	173 025
March	481 143	222 518	42 332	23 959	89 094	79 091	70 869	10 003	204 418	30 348	174 070
April	477 415	221 305	41 969	24 869	86 395	78 372	69 275	8 023	203 611	32 298	171 313
May	473 266	218 602	42 257	24 600	85 583	76 758	69 596	8 825	202 892	31 937	170 955
June	468 270	221 630	41 873	22 537	89 259	76 669	67 899	12 590	196 807	31 831	164 976
July	479 285	227 816	42 060	23 596	97 276	84 878	66 629	12 398	199 911	31 490	168 421
August	460 119	203 687	40 449	22 212	74 267	67 154	65 089	7 113	203 442	30 963	172 479
September	476 243	216 361	41 412	21 924	85 294	76 286	64 467	9 008	206 119	31 263	174 856
October	481 712	220 866	41 989	22 994	89 782	81 181	67 139	8 601	206 271	30 204	176 067
November	480 070	219 347	41 761	22 997	83 107	74 740	67 813	8 367	206 025	31 164	174 861
December	488 940	229 722	39 302	22 678	99 097	78 849	66 451	20 248	205 532	31 554	173 978
2013											
January	482 501	219 312	42 993	21 599	85 495	78 299	70 597	7 196	208 459	32 772	175 687
February	498 494	230 445	43 959	21 321	92 397	83 992	66 503	8 405	215 190	33 822	181 368
March	470 914	212 088	42 374	20 101	78 726	73 523	66 128	5 203	207 096	33 117	173 979
April	478 528	221 262	42 988	21 939	84 158	77 450	67 460	6 708	205 223	33 651	171 572
May	490 414	230 339	43 624	22 585	93 257	84 533	68 246	8 724	206 602	33 311	173 291
June	497 601	239 960	43 026	22 066	103 058	92 354	68 273	10 704	205 256	33 334	171 922
July	481 545	218 282	43 476	21 302	84 518	76 061	66 250	8 457	210 387	32 700	177 687
August	481 969	219 764	43 883	20 652	82 904	74 839	66 123	8 065	209 997	33 472	176 525
September	489 578	228 991	44 171	21 953	90 514	81 034	66 145	9 480	208 658	33 739	174 919
October	486 171	224 735	44 572	21 581	84 874	77 081	64 135	7 793	209 062	34 016	175 046
November	500 668	237 387	44 935	21 738	95 087	86 748	68 129	8 339	213 059	35 970	177 089
December	494 659	228 487	44 561	20 982	91 047	84 350	67 321	6 697	212 401	32 640	179 761
2014											
January	491 214	226 163	45 090	23 732	88 508	80 531	70 441	7 977	211 275	32 302	178 973
February	500 673	232 804	45 531	23 310	86 394	78 026	69 762	8 368	214 611	33 714	180 897
March	504 510	238 347	46 177	23 961	93 334	83 085	71 545	10 249	212 472	33 463	179 009
April	509 166	241 137	46 800	24 597	99 127	81 933	70 144	17 194	214 243	33 152	181 091
May	501 954	234 842	47 258	23 655	89 343	80 546	69 224	8 797	213 230	33 923	179 307
June	510 052	242 127	47 516	24 726	94 879	84 621	73 227	10 258	212 830	32 946	179 884
July	565 232	299 868	47 473	24 261	147 832	139 590	72 360	8 242	212 280	35 720	176 560
August	505 642	241 789	47 771	25 044	95 682	87 448	73 653	8 234	209 315	33 908	175 407
September	500 812	238 191	47 492	24 428	91 370	83 139	73 990	8 231	208 121	33 805	174 316
October	496 308	237 754	48 156	24 186	89 940	80 128	69 793	9 812	204 725	34 034	170 691
November	493 017	235 940	47 374	24 465	90 594	81 725	70 600	8 869	203 389	33 952	169 437
December	474 894	226 739	46 818	24 124	81 156	73 440	71 217	7 716	196 384	35 261	161 123

¹Includes categories not shown separately.

Table 16-6. Manufacturers' Unfilled Orders, Durable Goods Industries

(End of period, millions of dollars, seasonally adjusted.)

Year and month	Total [1]	Transportation equipment		Construction materials and supplies	Information technology industries	By topical categories				Consumer durable goods
		Nondefense aircraft and parts	Defense aircraft and parts			Capital goods				
						Total	Nondefense		Defense	
							Total	Excluding aircraft and parts		
1992	450 897	127 509	49 494	20 897	80 289	319 065	179 580	92 503	139 485	3 792
1993	425 607	110 927	46 545	21 760	77 976	299 265	173 881	95 287	125 384	4 611
1994	434 899	101 157	44 651	25 090	79 071	299 296	178 007	106 779	121 289	5 121
1995	447 510	109 506	42 360	27 155	84 919	313 963	199 613	118 006	114 350	5 282
1996	489 147	130 580	45 203	29 436	84 227	346 596	217 605	120 276	128 991	5 821
1997	513 267	143 178	40 819	33 592	87 678	360 566	243 364	132 031	117 202	7 333
1998	496 229	137 223	37 688	34 264	90 853	348 249	241 435	134 291	106 814	8 261
1999	505 473	126 252	35 596	35 254	105 702	349 273	245 393	149 472	103 880	9 033
2000	549 298	138 155	42 409	37 395	115 502	384 610	268 107	159 631	116 503	10 355
2001	509 726	124 729	52 001	33 564	98 744	357 396	230 415	137 415	126 981	6 948
2002	479 749	114 657	58 013	33 133	88 057	328 117	200 752	117 171	127 365	6 521
2003	506 510	110 015	64 372	35 565	95 575	345 524	203 239	124 709	142 285	7 232
2004	558 720	123 397	57 545	41 324	101 275	379 888	229 962	139 536	149 926	8 111
2005	654 688	188 951	55 284	48 401	106 325	453 568	312 789	156 584	140 779	7 181
2006	798 211	266 359	59 855	50 905	118 936	561 017	406 447	187 545	154 570	6 407
2007	947 045	378 032	63 212	55 362	119 910	684 854	526 090	205 502	158 764	6 044
2008	996 124	418 384	72 555	54 699	119 682	737 457	566 071	213 031	171 386	4 588
2009	825 118	343 872	61 743	41 384	112 478	606 694	454 976	176 349	151 718	4 141
2010	869 235	350 914	62 136	48 634	114 696	633 038	474 267	186 229	158 771	3 698
2011	950 208	391 060	65 321	48 367	126 169	701 576	530 351	209 653	171 225	3 871
2012	1 021 440	446 864	76 484	47 974	132 625	760 748	583 283	219 421	177 465	4 155
2013	1 087 229	526 341	69 571	48 876	119 396	819 657	662 500	225 859	157 157	4 703
2014	1 210 631	613 126	68 308	55 105	131 064	918 885	762 711	250 610	156 174	5 347
2011										
January	879 054	352 909	63 595	49 469	115 747	640 689	476 793	187 660	163 896	3 657
February	878 793	353 094	63 364	49 884	117 521	640 946	477 500	188 588	163 446	3 821
March	888 100	358 084	63 942	49 896	117 729	649 180	484 177	190 501	165 003	3 888
April	891 800	359 230	64 436	49 993	117 487	652 935	486 060	192 205	166 875	3 889
May	900 391	362 070	65 846	49 901	118 284	660 123	491 338	195 220	168 785	3 740
June	900 877	362 643	65 326	49 771	119 289	662 064	492 898	196 821	169 166	3 732
July	906 528	364 275	65 060	49 533	120 024	666 587	496 386	199 646	170 201	3 769
August	917 517	372 896	66 671	48 883	121 369	676 617	505 082	200 302	171 535	3 621
September	922 052	373 236	65 630	48 707	122 813	680 349	507 609	202 417	172 740	3 580
October	923 556	371 746	65 325	48 220	124 388	681 677	508 773	205 628	172 904	3 661
November	934 895	378 685	65 976	48 497	125 331	689 945	516 367	206 847	173 578	3 840
December	950 208	391 060	65 321	48 367	126 169	701 576	530 351	209 653	171 225	3 871
2012										
January	962 324	401 176	65 644	48 619	127 308	714 266	543 743	212 887	170 523	3 850
February	974 907	409 436	66 519	49 145	128 647	725 072	554 813	216 630	170 259	3 938
March	981 946	412 561	68 604	49 350	129 706	729 892	559 214	219 234	170 678	3 861
April	987 525	415 335	69 001	49 573	131 082	732 487	562 956	221 182	169 531	3 887
May	988 459	416 962	68 890	50 005	131 686	733 252	564 879	222 961	168 373	3 929
June	993 558	420 114	69 186	50 525	131 601	737 569	566 754	222 667	170 815	3 917
July	1 006 890	431 555	69 679	51 377	132 217	750 070	576 683	221 785	173 387	3 921
August	997 617	427 768	69 884	50 473	132 583	741 976	570 948	220 653	171 028	3 957
September	1 000 029	432 421	71 219	50 609	132 192	743 296	573 165	219 073	170 131	4 028
October	1 007 878	438 957	72 385	50 915	132 446	749 346	580 485	220 117	168 861	4 156
November	1 009 778	441 021	73 668	50 903	132 635	746 862	579 451	220 191	167 411	4 293
December	1 021 440	446 864	76 484	47 974	132 625	760 748	583 283	219 421	177 465	4 155
2013										
January	1 023 578	448 242	76 583	47 456	131 590	762 844	587 580	223 075	175 264	4 162
February	1 034 203	459 770	74 681	47 705	129 938	771 585	597 763	221 892	173 822	4 237
March	1 026 822	459 819	72 723	47 616	127 170	765 189	595 902	220 161	169 287	4 166
April	1 029 668	464 043	72 255	47 170	126 951	767 860	601 296	221 662	166 564	4 206
May	1 038 621	471 785	71 636	47 434	126 788	775 052	609 331	222 585	165 721	4 275
June	1 058 743	489 874	71 456	47 410	126 303	793 638	626 988	224 609	166 650	4 396
July	1 060 390	490 465	72 154	47 555	125 393	795 738	629 825	225 630	165 913	4 474
August	1 060 196	492 096	71 840	47 745	123 756	795 333	631 337	226 190	163 996	4 641
September	1 067 915	500 068	72 416	47 867	122 894	802 718	638 913	226 879	163 805	4 558
October	1 070 930	505 561	71 597	48 063	121 730	804 719	642 658	225 764	162 061	4 550
November	1 080 034	517 068	69 924	48 252	120 880	814 188	654 138	226 286	160 050	4 683
December	1 087 229	526 341	69 571	48 876	119 396	819 657	662 500	225 859	157 157	4 703
2014										
January	1 091 532	528 701	68 850	49 515	120 292	824 017	668 393	229 518	155 624	4 640
February	1 098 532	533 854	69 170	50 164	120 788	825 333	670 808	231 569	154 525	4 475
March	1 109 361	538 470	68 810	50 533	121 887	832 216	676 665	234 312	155 551	4 521
April	1 123 491	542 281	68 574	51 217	123 397	845 658	682 477	236 331	163 181	4 655
May	1 130 082	546 048	68 898	52 178	123 894	850 000	687 401	237 110	162 599	4 718
June	1 142 235	549 801	70 536	52 868	125 137	857 828	694 276	241 640	163 552	4 953
July	1 204 617	610 698	70 125	53 124	125 812	917 605	755 326	244 348	162 279	4 810
August	1 210 827	615 707	69 661	53 800	127 223	922 885	762 053	246 407	160 832	4 861
September	1 213 630	616 904	68 259	53 877	128 303	923 634	764 086	248 835	159 548	5 020
October	1 216 967	618 417	68 866	54 937	129 349	924 818	765 099	248 769	159 719	5 083
November	1 220 658	620 604	69 126	55 471	130 408	927 414	768 526	249 782	158 888	5 095
December	1 210 631	613 126	68 308	55 105	131 064	918 885	762 711	250 610	156 174	5 347

[1] Includes categories not shown separately.

Table 16-7. Motor Vehicle Sales and Inventories

(Units.)

Year and month	Retail sales of new passenger cars						Retail inventories of new domestic passenger cars (thousands of units, end of period)		
	Thousands of units, not seasonally adjusted			Millions of units, seasonally adjusted annual rate			Not seasonally adjusted	Seasonally adjusted	Inventory to sales ratio
	Total	Domestic	Foreign	Total	Domestic	Foreign			
1975	8 537.9	6 950.9	1 586.9	8.538	6.951	1.587	1 419.0	1 468.0	2.200
1976	9 994.0	8 492.0	1 502.0	9.994	8.492	1.502	1 465.0	1 494.0	1.900
1977	11 046.0	8 971.2	2 074.8	11.046	8.971	2.075	1 731.0	1 743.0	2.300
1978	11 164.0	9 163.9	2 000.1	11.164	9.164	2.000	1 729.0	1 731.0	2.300
1979	10 558.8	8 230.1	2 328.7	10.559	8.230	2.329	1 691.0	1 667.0	2.400
1980	8 981.8	6 581.4	2 400.4	8.982	6.581	2.401	1 448.0	1 440.0	2.600
1981	8 534.3	6 208.8	2 325.5	8.535	6.209	2.326	1 471.0	1 495.0	3.600
1982	7 979.4	5 758.2	2 221.2	7.979	5.758	2.221	1 126.0	1 127.0	2.200
1983	9 178.6	6 793.0	2 385.6	9.179	6.793	2.386	1 352.0	1 350.0	2.000
1984	10 390.2	7 951.7	2 438.5	10.391	7.952	2.439	1 415.0	1 411.0	2.100
1985	10 978.4	8 204.7	2 773.7	10.979	8.205	2.774	1 630.0	1 619.0	2.500
1986	10 418.3	8 215.0	3 190.7	11.406	8.215	3.191	1 499.0	1 515.0	2.000
1987	10 170.9	7 080.9	3 090.0	10.171	7.081	3.090	1 680.0	1 716.0	2.800
1988	10 545.6	7 539.4	3 006.2	10.545	7.539	3.006	1 601.0	1 601.0	2.300
1989	9 776.8	7 078.1	2 698.7	9.777	7.078	2.699	1 669.0	1 687.0	3.100
1990	9 300.2	6 896.9	2 403.3	9.300	6.897	2.403	1 408.0	1 418.0	2.600
1991	8 175.0	6 136.9	2 038.1	8.175	6.137	2.038	1 283.0	1 296.0	2.600
1992	8 214.4	6 276.6	1 937.8	8.215	6.277	1.938	1 276.0	1 288.0	2.300
1993	8 517.7	6 734.0	1 783.7	8.518	6.734	1.784	1 364.9	1 377.3	2.359
1994	8 990.4	7 255.2	1 735.2	8.990	7.255	1.735	1 436.6	1 445.3	2.319
1995	8 620.4	7 114.1	1 506.3	8.620	7.114	1.506	1 618.5	1 629.8	2.565
1996	8 478.6	7 206.3	1 272.3	8.478	7.206	1.272	1 363.4	1 367.0	2.381
1997	8 217.7	6 862.3	1 355.4	8.218	6.862	1.356	1 329.9	1 339.6	2.267
1998	8 084.9	6 705.1	1 379.8	8.085	6.705	1.380	1 324.4	1 309.4	2.125
1999	8 637.7	6 918.8	1 718.9	8.638	6.919	1.719	1 367.6	1 346.5	2.268
2000	8 777.7	6 761.6	2 016.1	8.778	6.762	2.016	1 377.0	1 334.9	2.685
2001	8 352.1	6 254.4	2 097.7	8.352	6.254	2.098	955.7	919.8	2.135
2002	8 042.1	5 816.5	2 225.6	8.043	5.817	2.226	1 132.0	1 170.1	2.410
2003	7 555.6	5 472.6	2 083.0	7.556	5.473	2.083	1 115.8	1 162.1	2.570
2004	7 482.5	5 333.6	2 148.9	7.482	5.333	2.149	1 034.2	1 077.7	2.264
2005	7 660.4	5 473.6	2 186.8	7.661	5.474	2.187	930.6	965.9	2.185
2006	7 761.3	5 416.7	2 344.6	7.762	5.417	2.345	1 031.7	1 048.8	2.370
2007	7 562.1	5 197.1	2 365.0	7.562	5.197	2.365	906.8	917.1	2.114
2008	6 769.2	4 491.0	2 278.2	6.769	4.491	2.278	1 144.2	1 160.7	3.930
2009	5 401.5	3 558.4	1 843.1	5.401	3.558	1.843	686.4	702.1	2.070
2010	5 635.7	3 791.5	1 844.2	5.636	3.792	1.844	759.1	762.3	2.299
2011	6 089.7	4 142.8	1 946.9	6.090	4.143	1.947	813.0	777.5	2.158
2012	7 244.4	5 119.1	2 125.3	7.245	5.119	2.125	1 069.5	1 037.6	2.277
2013	7 585.3	5 432.7	2 152.6	7.586	5.434	2.153	1 259.3	1 216.9	2.763
2014	7 687.6	5 589.4	2 098.2	7.688	5.589	2.098	1 249.4	1 211.8	2.500
2012									
January	457.7	320.6	137.1	6.958	4.843	2.115	886.6	835.1	2.069
February	600.0	426.2	173.8	7.516	5.206	2.310	902.9	826.0	1.904
March	747.3	527.4	219.9	7.293	5.096	2.197	876.2	828.9	1.952
April	619.5	436.7	182.8	7.283	5.075	2.208	857.9	851.5	2.013
May	672.7	486.4	186.2	6.975	4.943	2.032	840.3	885.2	2.149
June	645.2	463.1	182.0	7.035	4.998	2.037	858.8	908.7	2.182
July	569.6	395.4	174.2	6.978	4.946	2.032	822.7	1 001.3	2.430
August	634.0	453.2	180.9	7.109	5.132	1.977	845.4	1 005.6	2.352
September	585.1	411.9	173.2	7.350	5.205	2.145	888.0	1 009.4	2.327
October	530.2	369.1	161.1	7.263	5.128	2.135	1 025.5	1 008.6	2.360
November	550.9	382.0	169.0	7.577	5.390	2.187	1 112.3	1 023.6	2.279
December	632.2	447.2	185.1	7.597	5.468	2.129	1 069.5	1 037.6	2.277
2013									
January	523.2	383.9	139.3	7.649	5.578	2.071	1 131.1	1 048.1	2.255
February	601.1	443.3	157.9	7.648	5.509	2.139	1 144.1	1 050.1	2.288
March	739.2	544.0	195.2	7.458	5.429	2.029	1 123.1	1 077.1	2.381
April	639.0	466.6	172.4	7.317	5.275	2.042	1 129.6	1 102.8	2.509
May	708.1	517.2	190.9	7.440	5.329	2.111	1 109.8	1 135.5	2.557
June	689.3	501.9	187.5	7.678	5.521	2.157	1 109.9	1 159.3	2.520
July	639.6	448.5	191.1	7.690	5.504	2.186	982.2	1 116.7	2.435
August	733.3	516.1	217.2	7.757	5.511	2.246	986.3	1 137.0	2.476
September	553.2	386.8	166.4	7.573	5.337	2.236	1 064.3	1 161.9	2.613
October	563.8	397.9	165.8	7.464	5.339	2.125	1 217.0	1 184.6	2.663
November	581.5	403.4	178.2	7.841	5.587	2.254	1 301.3	1 188.9	2.553
December	614.0	423.2	190.8	7.519	5.286	2.233	1 259.3	1 216.9	2.763
2014									
January	476.8	341.1	135.7	7.092	5.048	2.044	1 322.5	1 227.4	2.918
February	563.9	411.4	152.5	7.132	5.085	2.046	1 366.6	1 263.5	2.981
March	740.9	533.8	207.0	7.575	5.385	2.190	1 329.5	1 260.6	2.809
April	657.3	470.8	186.5	7.351	5.195	2.156	1 287.3	1 247.1	2.881
May	773.7	563.6	210.2	7.875	5.618	2.257	1 201.0	1 235.3	2.639
June	684.2	498.9	185.3	8.072	5.813	2.258	1 196.6	1 231.4	2.542
July	670.4	479.3	191.1	7.780	5.674	2.107	1 135.4	1 299.0	2.747
August	747.2	551.7	195.5	8.221	6.121	2.100	1 075.9	1 263.1	2.476
September	563.0	412.0	151.0	7.500	5.500	2.000	1 131.5	1 253.4	2.713
October	577.4	427.4	150.0	7.700	5.800	1.900	1 234.4	1 224.3	2.535
November	576.7	426.3	150.4	7.900	6.000	1.900	1 288.5	1 223.4	2.455
December	656.0	473.1	182.8	7.900	5.800	2.100	1 249.4	1 211.8	2.500

Table 16-7. Motor Vehicle Sales and Inventories—*Continued*

(Units.)

Year and month	Retail sales of new trucks and buses								Unit sales of cars and light trucks (millions of units, seasonally adjusted annual rate)		
	Thousands of units, not seasonally adjusted				Millions of units, seasonally adjusted annual rate						
	Total	0–14,000 pounds		14,001 pounds and over	Total	0–14,000 pounds		14,001 pounds and over	Total	Domestic	Foreign
		Domestic	Foreign			Domestic	Foreign				
1975	. . .	2 052.6	. . .	298.3	2.353	2.055	. . .	0.298	. . .	9.006	. . .
1976	3 300.5	2 738.3	237.5	324.7	3.296	2.733	0.239	0.324	12.966	11.225	1.741
1977	3 813.0	3 112.8	323.1	377.1	3.818	3.116	0.324	0.378	14.486	12.087	2.399
1978	4 256.8	3 481.1	335.9	439.8	4.249	3.469	0.340	0.440	14.973	12.633	2.340
1979	3 589.7	2 730.2	469.4	390.1	3.599	2.740	0.469	0.390	13.768	10.970	2.798
1980	2 487.4	1 731.1	484.6	271.7	2.482	1.731	0.480	0.271	11.193	8.312	2.881
1981	2 255.6	1 581.7	447.6	226.3	2.255	1.585	0.444	0.226	10.564	7.794	2.770
1982	2 562.8	1 967.5	410.4	184.9	2.569	1.971	0.413	0.185	10.363	7.729	2.634
1983	3 117.3	2 465.2	463.3	188.8	3.130	2.480	0.461	0.189	12.120	9.273	2.847
1984	4 093.1	3 207.2	607.7	278.2	4.086	3.199	0.609	0.278	14.199	11.151	3.048
1985	4 741.7	3 618.4	828.3	295.0	4.760	3.634	0.831	0.295	15.444	11.839	3.605
1986	4 912.1	3 671.4	967.2	273.5	4.918	3.676	0.969	0.273	16.051	11.891	4.160
1987	4 991.5	3 792.0	912.2	287.3	4.978	3.783	0.907	0.288	14.861	10.864	3.997
1988	5 231.9	4 199.7	697.9	334.3	5.225	4.194	0.697	0.334	15.436	11.733	3.703
1989	5 055.9	4 113.6	630.3	312.0	5.065	4.123	0.629	0.313	14.529	11.201	3.328
1990	4 837.0	3 956.8	602.7	277.5	4.840	3.960	0.602	0.278	13.862	10.857	3.005
1991	4 355.4	3 605.6	528.8	221.0	4.361	3.612	0.528	0.221	12.315	9.749	2.566
1992	4 892.2	4 247.0	395.9	249.3	4.893	4.247	0.398	0.248	12.860	10.524	2.336
1993	5 667.8	5 000.5	364.5	302.8	5.658	4.991	0.365	0.302	13.874	11.725	2.149
1994	6 407.3	5 658.2	396.3	352.8	6.408	5.659	0.395	0.354	15.044	12.914	2.130
1995	6 496.4	5 705.9	402.1	388.4	6.498	5.706	0.402	0.390	14.728	12.820	1.908
1996	6 977.6	6 179.8	438.7	359.1	6.976	6.180	0.439	0.357	15.097	13.386	1.711
1997	7 280.4	6 324.7	579.5	376.2	7.280	6.325	0.579	0.376	15.122	13.187	1.935
1998	7 882.4	6 802.0	656.1	424.3	7.883	6.802	0.656	0.425	15.543	13.507	2.036
1999	8 777.3	7 480.7	775.3	521.3	8.777	7.481	0.775	0.521	16.894	14.400	2.494
2000	9 033.0	7 719.7	852.3	461.9	9.033	7.720	0.852	0.461	17.350	14.482	2.868
2001	9 120.4	7 789.0	981.3	350.1	9.120	7.789	0.981	0.350	17.122	14.043	3.079
2002	9 096.5	7 707.8	1 066.3	322.4	9.096	7.708	1.066	0.322	16.817	13.525	3.292
2003	9 411.9	7 856.3	1 227.2	328.4	9.411	7.856	1.227	0.328	16.639	13.329	3.310
2004	9 815.8	8 138.0	1 246.2	431.6	9.813	8.138	1.246	0.429	16.866	13.471	3.395
2005	9 784.4	8 072.4	1 215.5	496.5	9.784	8.072	1.215	0.497	16.948	13.546	3.402
2006	9 287.0	7 396.0	1 346.6	544.4	9.288	7.396	1.347	0.545	16.505	12.813	3.692
2007	8 897.9	7 138.7	1 388.1	371.1	8.900	7.139	1.388	0.373	16.089	12.336	3.753
2008	15 408.6	5 329.2	9 780.9	298.5	6.724	5.329	1.097	0.298	13.195	9.820	3.375
2009	5 200.5	4 116.5	884.2	199.8	5.200	4.117	0.884	0.199	10.402	7.675	2.727
2010	6 136.6	5 020.3	898.7	217.6	6.137	5.021	0.899	0.218	11.555	8.812	2.743
2011	6 951.2	5 662.6	982.5	306.1	6.950	5.663	0.983	0.305	12.735	9.805	2.929
2012	7 544.1	6 137.5	1 060.8	345.8	7.527	6.120	1.061	0.346	14.425	11.239	3.186
2013	8 297.9	6 707.1	1 239.1	351.7	8.287	6.700	1.236	0.351	15.522	12.134	3.388
2014	9 154.4	7 387.7	1 360.0	406.7	9.131	7.371	1.354	0.405	16.413	12.961	3.453
2012											
January	477.0	378.2	74.3	24.5	7.324	5.921	1.061	0.342	13.940	10.764	3.176
February	572.7	463.8	82.0	26.9	7.288	5.881	1.051	0.356	14.448	11.087	3.361
March	684.6	548.0	104.8	31.8	7.246	5.835	1.057	0.354	14.185	10.931	3.254
April	590.1	479.1	82.6	28.4	7.399	5.951	1.094	0.354	14.328	11.026	3.302
May	689.3	562.2	95.3	31.8	7.457	6.007	1.089	0.361	14.071	10.950	3.121
June	666.5	545.3	90.9	30.3	7.527	6.120	1.061	0.346	14.216	11.118	3.098
July	608.9	493.7	86.3	28.9	7.482	6.079	1.045	0.358	14.102	11.025	3.077
August	676.5	555.7	90.5	30.3	7.529	6.184	0.986	0.359	14.279	11.316	2.963
September	625.4	512.7	86.2	26.5	7.750	6.324	1.082	0.344	14.756	11.529	3.227
October	586.4	482.5	75.1	28.8	7.457	6.168	0.977	0.312	.14.408	11.296	3.112
November	614.9	499.2	90.0	25.7	7.880	6.443	1.107	0.330	15.127	11.833	3.294
December	751.8	617.1	102.8	31.9	7.983	6.526	1.119	0.338	15.242	11.994	3.248
2013											
January	542.1	438.1	79.1	24.9	7.978	6.556	1.085	0.337	15.290	12.134	3.156
February	613.6	501.2	87.6	24.8	8.089	6.597	1.149	0.343	15.394	12.106	3.288
March	736.3	599.1	111.5	25.7	8.191	6.720	1.170	0.301	15.348	12.149	3.199
April	673.0	551.4	91.1	30.5	8.258	6.731	1.169	0.358	15.217	12.006	3.211
May	760.8	623.0	107.6	30.2	8.325	6.756	1.226	0.343	15.422	12.085	3.337
June	740.0	602.6	106.5	30.9	8.470	6.811	1.290	0.369	15.779	12.332	3.447
July	699.7	559.8	110.0	29.9	8.354	6.704	1.298	0.352	15.692	12.208	3.484
August	793.1	640.5	123.8	28.8	8.464	6.852	1.264	0.348	15.873	12.363	3.510
September	609.0	487.9	92.5	28.6	8.131	6.500	1.271	0.360	15.344	11.837	3.507
October	670.6	533.0	103.8	33.8	8.183	6.519	1.296	0.368	15.279	11.858	3.421
November	684.4	547.4	109.3	27.7	8.713	7.025	1.323	0.365	16.189	12.612	3.577
December	775.3	623.1	116.3	35.9	8.293	6.634	1.287	0.372	15.440	11.920	3.520
2014											
January	557.2	444.5	86.4	26.3	8.464	6.917	1.187	0.360	15.196	11.964	3.231
February	650.7	523.4	100.8	26.5	8.568	6.883	1.318	0.367	15.333	11.968	3.364
March	822.3	656.0	134.3	32.0	9.222	7.391	1.458	0.374	16.424	12.775	3.648
April	759.2	617.8	106.1	35.3	9.032	7.289	1.329	0.414	15.969	12.484	3.485
May	860.9	706.4	121.3	33.2	9.179	7.457	1.336	0.385	16.669	13.075	3.594
June	764.6	622.2	108.6	33.8	9.167	7.386	1.389	0.392	16.847	13.199	3.648
July	794.1	638.3	119.9	36.0	9.046	7.267	1.354	0.424	16.402	12.941	3.461
August	866.2	692.6	138.3	35.3	9.665	7.745	1.473	0.446	17.439	13.866	3.573
September	712.5	566.6	108.8	37.1	9.262	7.377	1.441	0.444	16.334	12.920	3.415
October	734.8	588.8	106.6	39.3	9.048	7.294	1.325	0.429	16.345	13.089	3.255
November	747.6	609.4	108.2	30.0	9.604	7.835	1.356	0.413	17.094	13.814	3.279
December	884.3	721.6	120.6	42.1	9.318	7.616	1.286	0.415	16.800	13.433	3.367

. . . = Not available.

Table 16-8. Retail and Food Services Sales

(All retail establishments and food services; millions of dollars; not seasonally adjusted.)

Year and month	Retail and food services, total [1]	Retail (NAICS industry categories) GAFO (department store type goods), total [2]	Motor vehicles and parts	Furniture and home furnishings	Electronics and appliances	Building materials and garden	Food and beverages	Health and personal care	Gasoline	Clothing and accessories	General merchandise	Nonstore retailers	Food services and drinking places
1992	2 014 102	533 388	418 393	52 336	42 631	130 989	370 513	89 699	156 324	120 103	247 876	78 501	202 865
1993	2 153 095	570 782	472 916	55 456	48 614	140 964	374 516	92 589	162 376	124 749	265 996	85 811	215 467
1994	2 330 235	616 347	541 141	60 416	57 266	157 228	384 340	96 359	171 222	129 083	285 190	96 280	225 000
1995	2 450 628	650 040	579 715	63 470	64 770	164 561	390 386	101 632	181 113	131 333	300 498	103 516	233 012
1996	2 603 794	682 613	627 507	67 707	68 363	176 683	401 073	109 554	194 425	136 581	315 305	117 761	242 245
1997	2 726 131	713 387	653 817	72 715	70 061	191 063	409 373	118 670	199 700	140 293	331 363	126 190	257 364
1998	2 852 956	757 936	688 415	77 412	74 527	202 423	416 525	129 582	191 727	149 151	351 081	133 904	271 194
1999	3 086 990	815 665	764 204	84 294	78 977	218 290	433 699	142 697	212 524	159 751	380 179	151 797	283 900
2000	3 287 537	862 739	796 210	91 170	82 206	228 994	444 764	155 233	249 816	167 674	404 228	180 453	304 261
2001	3 378 906	882 700	815 579	91 484	80 240	239 379	462 429	166 532	251 383	167 287	427 468	180 563	316 638
2002	3 459 077	912 707	818 811	94 438	83 740	248 539	464 856	179 983	250 619	172 304	446 520	189 279	330 525
2003	3 612 457	946 114	841 588	96 736	86 442	263 463	474 385	275 187	178 694	178 694	468 771	206 359	349 726
2004	3 846 605	1 003 891	866 372	103 757	93 896	295 274	490 380	324 006	324 006	190 253	497 382	228 977	373 557
2005	4 085 746	1 059 599	888 307	109 120	100 461	320 802	508 484	378 923	378 923	200 969	528 385	255 579	396 463
2006	4 294 359	1 110 155	899 997	112 795	105 477	334 130	525 232	421 976	421 976	213 189	554 256	284 343	422 786
2007	4 439 733	1 143 426	910 139	111 144	106 599	320 854	547 837	451 822	451 822	221 205	578 582	308 767	444 551
2008	4 392 750	1 136 469	785 953	98 799	105 402	301 911	569 598	503 739	503 739	215 446	595 202	319 223	456 442
2009	4 066 822	1 088 369	671 915	84 894	95 533	261 772	569 084	391 479	391 479	204 192	589 228	311 230	452 370
2010	4 288 339	1 114 590	743 167	85 408	97 642	260 737	581 546	448 693	448 693	212 847	604 210	340 902	467 476
2011	4 601 788	1 155 854	814 588	87 652	100 287	269 711	610 307	532 412	532 412	227 984	625 371	376 058	495 798
2012	4 831 131	1 192 197	887 990	91 552	102 644	281 869	629 880	555 407	555 407	238 773	643 039	406 420	524 894
2013	5 011 740	1 213 518	961 981	94 879	103 744	302 150	643 520	551 576	551 576	244 548	653 093	432 759	542 718
2014	5 208 443	1 236 878	1 033 910	98 232	106 081	318 690	662 853	536 802	536 802	248 848	667 475	458 088	576 154
2012													
January	355 332	83 427	62 266	6 886	7 687	18 008	49 905	22 863	41 332	14 317	45 683	32 515	39 706
February	372 782	91 233	70 552	7 192	8 122	18 530	48 920	22 740	42 150	17 869	49 683	31 750	41 005
March	414 545	98 786	81 433	7 811	8 385	24 194	52 623	23 987	48 326	20 100	53 167	33 163	45 727
April	393 289	91 767	73 695	6 894	7 128	26 028	50 922	22 748	47 610	18 560	50 655	30 547	43 834
May	418 940	97 879	79 995	7 705	7 883	29 419	54 046	23 515	49 157	19 905	53 149	32 429	45 566
June	401 295	95 577	76 096	7 394	7 916	25 809	52 806	22 170	46 462	18 661	52 333	30 516	44 975
July	396 336	93 560	75 353	7 560	8 102	23 954	52 992	22 305	46 655	18 191	50 785	30 379	44 575
August	418 268	101 692	80 856	8 065	8 385	24 203	53 588	23 128	50 210	20 657	53 737	33 036	45 000
September	386 068	91 956	71 403	7 427	7 744	22 350	51 295	21 517	47 240	18 353	49 383	30 965	43 082
October	399 904	93 953	72 359	7 234	7 595	24 678	52 437	22 992	49 049	18 811	51 456	34 108	43 619
November	411 618	109 593	69 744	8 220	10 336	23 524	53 145	22 479	44 522	21 948	59 091	39 774	42 496
December	462 754	142 774	74 238	9 164	13 361	21 172	57 201	25 355	42 694	31 401	73 917	47 238	45 309
2013													
January	376 460	86 349	69 354	7 223	8 107	19 319	51 951	23 520	41 832	15 161	46 677	36 707	41 787
February	374 901	89 323	73 073	6 997	8 197	18 692	48 898	21 971	42 258	17 378	48 570	33 403	41 470
March	422 763	100 641	83 674	7 753	8 242	23 190	54 597	23 788	47 725	19 186	50 040	34 186	45 506
April	409 414	92 307	81 555	7 167	7 353	28 893	50 613	23 104	46 756	19 088	54 869	34 219	47 429
May	438 038	100 644	86 770	7 879	7 904	32 849	55 561	23 853	49 088	20 771	53 270	31 756	45 379
June	415 748	96 826	82 695	7 582	7 886	27 918	53 486	22 426	48 331	18 933	53 270	31 756	45 379
July	423 397	96 621	86 202	7 984	8 089	27 655	54 721	23 389	49 616	19 130	52 042	33 155	45 417
August	436 029	104 842	88 914	8 457	8 438	26 298	55 333	23 692	49 298	21 520	55 326	34 174	46 828
September	397 059	92 967	75 834	7 831	7 909	24 484	51 832	23 084	45 767	18 122	50 000	32 869	43 592
October	416 487	98 030	79 229	8 018	8 124	26 313	53 765	24 440	46 155	19 844	53 018	35 368	46 007
November	424 166	112 518	75 914	8 812	10 442	24 053	54 683	23 510	42 016	22 410	60 519	39 666	45 238
December	477 278	142 450	78 767	9 176	13 053	22 486	58 080	26 984	42 734	31 521	74 020	52 087	46 542
2014													
January	383 459	85 984	71 011	7 132	7 954	19 955	53 828	24 385	42 164	15 070	47 375	37 601	42 905
February	380 246	89 228	75 690	7 172	7 910	19 041	49 656	22 997	40 152	17 427	48 933	34 788	42 875
March	432 827	99 124	91 420	8 028	8 447	24 422	53 925	24 863	45 742	19 968	53 990	37 433	49 399
April	431 335	96 818	88 955	7 705	7 512	30 564	53 697	24 658	46 630	20 217	52 801	35 719	47 713
May	458 705	103 651	94 358	8 293	8 066	33 889	57 208	25 398	49 803	21 451	56 914	35 554	51 072
June	433 388	97 307	87 810	7 762	7 998	30 506	54 678	24 669	48 322	18 829	53 888	34 869	47 863
July	443 153	99 088	92 458	8 262	8 259	29 078	56 680	25 053	49 438	19 700	53 669	35 467	48 659
August	450 365	107 249	93 793	8 591	8 519	26 852	56 553	25 107	48 302	21 855	57 071	35 388	50 098
September	420 516	95 340	84 687	8 203	8 509	26 617	53 633	25 077	45 062	18 564	50 691	36 007	47 090
October	437 277	100 820	85 699	8 254	8 400	27 808	56 122	25 971	44 942	20 117	54 645	38 170	50 161
November	437 196	115 295	80 156	8 767	10 857	25 345	56 263	24 518	39 730	23 300	62 077	41 538	47 615
December	499 976	146 974	87 873	10 063	13 650	24 613	60 610	29 448	36 515	32 350	75 421	55 554	50 704

[1] Includes store categories not shown separately.
[2] Includes furniture, home furnishings, electronics, appliances, clothing, sporting goods, hobby, book, music, general merchandise, office supplies, stationery, and gifts.

Table 16-8. Retail and Food Services Sales—*Continued*

(All retail establishments and food services; millions of dollars; seasonally adjusted.)

Year and month	Total	Retail and food services										
			Retail (NAICS industry categories)									
		Total	GAFO (department store type goods) [2]	Motor vehicles and parts	Furniture and home furnishings	Electronics and appliances	Building materials and garden	Food and beverages			Health and personal care	Gasoline
								Total [1]	Groceries	Beer, wine, and liquor		
1992	2 014 096	1 811 231	533 388	418 393	52 336	42 631	130 989	370 513	337 370	21 687	89 699	156 324
1993	2 153 090	1 937 623	570 782	472 916	55 456	48 614	140 964	374 516	341 318	21 538	92 589	162 376
1994	2 330 231	2 105 231	616 347	541 141	60 416	57 266	157 228	384 340	350 523	22 101	96 359	171 222
1995	2 450 625	2 217 613	650 040	579 715	63 470	64 770	164 561	390 386	356 409	22 007	101 632	181 113
1996	2 603 791	2 361 546	682 613	627 507	67 707	68 363	176 683	401 073	365 547	23 157	109 554	194 425
1997	2 726 129	2 468 765	713 387	653 817	72 715	70 061	191 063	409 373	372 570	24 081	118 670	199 700
1998	2 852 955	2 581 761	757 936	688 415	77 412	74 527	202 423	416 525	378 188	25 382	129 582	191 727
1999	3 086 988	2 803 088	815 665	764 204	84 294	78 977	218 290	433 699	394 250	26 476	142 697	212 524
2000	3 287 536	2 983 275	862 739	796 210	91 170	82 206	228 994	444 764	402 515	28 507	155 233	249 816
2001	3 378 905	3 062 267	882 700	815 579	91 484	80 240	239 379	462 429	418 127	29 621	166 532	251 383
2002	3 459 077	3 128 552	912 707	818 811	94 438	83 740	248 539	464 856	419 813	29 894	179 983	250 619
2003	3 612 457	3 262 731	946 114	841 588	96 736	86 442	263 463	474 385	427 987	30 469	192 426	275 187
2004	3 846 605	3 473 048	1 003 891	866 372	103 757	93 896	295 274	490 380	441 136	32 189	199 290	324 006
2005	4 085 746	3 689 283	1 059 599	888 307	109 120	100 461	320 802	508 484	457 667	33 567	210 085	378 923
2006	4 294 359	3 871 573	1 110 155	899 997	112 795	105 477	334 130	525 232	471 699	36 016	223 336	421 976
2007	4 439 733	3 995 182	1 143 426	910 139	111 144	106 599	320 854	547 837	491 360	38 128	237 164	451 822
2008	4 392 750	3 936 308	1 136 469	785 953	98 799	105 402	301 911	569 598	511 376	39 599	246 800	503 739
2009	4 066 822	3 614 452	1 088 369	671 915	84 894	95 533	261 772	569 084	510 359	40 443	253 278	391 479
2010	4 288 339	3 820 863	1 114 590	743 167	85 408	97 642	260 737	581 546	521 252	41 707	261 204	448 693
2011	4 601 788	3 291 402	1 155 854	814 588	87 652	100 287	269 711	610 307	548 336	42 812	272 707	532 412
2012	4 831 131	4 306 237	1 192 197	887 990	91 552	102 644	281 869	629 880	564 877	44 911	275 799	555 407
2013	5 011 740	4 469 022	1 213 518	961 981	94 879	103 744	302 150	643 520	576 421	46 624	283 761	551 576
2014	5 208 443	4 632 289	1 236 878	1 033 910	98 232	106 081	318 690	662 853	591 622	48 650	302 144	536 802
2012												
January	395 431	352 598	98 582	71 512	7 702	8 402	20 314	51 730	46 392	3 689	22 955	45 570
February	400 305	357 278	99 483	72 978	7 659	8 411	20 465	51 728	46 400	3 688	23 133	46 990
March	402 206	359 189	99 905	73 015	7 628	8 592	21 052	52 080	46 706	3 721	23 131	47 239
April	400 070	356 541	98 574	72 943	7 559	8 431	20 036	52 345	46 931	3 753	23 141	46 768
May	399 694	356 256	99 006	73 430	7 651	8 553	19 701	52 377	46 930	3 770	23 077	45 898
June	395 977	352 397	98 830	72 667	7 553	8 507	19 594	52 306	46 912	3 739	22 553	43 873
July	398 079	354 292	99 124	73 050	7 667	8 650	19 603	52 516	47 137	3 698	22 971	43 603
August	402 296	358 479	98 975	73 841	7 594	8 512	19 977	52 398	47 073	3 660	22 944	46 491
September	406 937	362 886	99 261	76 154	7 586	8 491	20 233	52 778	47 362	3 723	22 697	47 193
October	405 808	362 014	98 878	74 584	7 404	8 346	20 347	53 071	47 611	3 763	22 719	48 087
November	407 798	363 393	99 109	75 667	7 590	8 633	20 668	52 893	47 407	3 798	22 891	46 915
December	410 441	365 669	100 241	77 468	7 880	8 724	20 895	52 890	47 365	3 835	23 092	45 858
2013												
January	412 657	367 676	101 071	77 437	7 851	8 729	21 050	52 987	47 482	3 823	23 264	46 020
February	417 357	372 573	100 949	78 703	7 774	8 813	21 369	53 558	47 943	3 852	23 274	48 797
March	414 578	369 575	100 898	77 653	7 738	8 594	21 094	53 528	47 982	3 847	23 253	47 299
April	413 359	368 614	100 659	78 230	7 673	8 631	21 793	52 978	47 497	3 816	23 314	45 929
May	415 500	370 671	100 934	79 472	7 786	8 576	21 878	53 519	47 981	3 885	23 340	45 663
June	417 471	372 894	101 330	81 512	7 964	8 654	21 609	53 542	48 021	3 851	23 312	46 117
July	419 158	374 280	101 612	81 243	7 936	8 605	21 840	53 777	48 170	3 914	23 649	46 026
August	417 795	372 768	100 985	81 027	7 956	8 626	21 878	53 721	48 081	3 919	23 668	45 436
September	418 877	373 610	101 409	80 623	8 040	8 603	21 915	54 007	48 366	3 935	24 046	45 359
October	420 065	374 196	102 159	81 468	8 132	8 772	21 809	53 921	48 299	3 917	24 198	44 767
November	421 473	374 691	101 393	82 681	8 144	8 591	21 812	53 769	48 125	3 921	24 138	44 461
December	423 643	377 425	100 961	81 935	7 856	8 531	21 800	54 696	48 957	3 952	24 244	46 000
2014												
January	418 777	373 036	99 974	79 624	7 710	8 534	21 938	54 466	48 676	3 977	24 096	46 385
February	423 950	377 599	101 294	81 907	8 013	8 571	21 991	54 343	48 575	3 972	24 413	46 634
March	430 181	383 134	102 375	85 055	8 109	8 896	22 179	54 573	48 766	3 984	24 617	45 834
April	432 263	384 976	103 131	85 591	8 206	8 837	22 467	54 707	48 874	4 005	24 757	46 168
May	434 241	386 644	103 016	86 323	8 195	8 792	22 776	54 779	48 931	4 002	25 047	46 328
June	435 371	387 651	103 093	86 053	8 179	8 837	23 052	55 381	49 368	4 131	25 380	45 846
July	436 183	388 196	103 463	86 678	8 172	8 821	23 022	55 297	49 335	4 074	25 357	45 523
August	438 710	390 353	104 064	88 285	8 269	8 860	23 126	55 505	49 527	4 072	25 515	44 766
September	437 311	388 462	103 610	87 376	8 236	9 044	23 113	55 714	49 725	4 090	25 589	44 222
October	439 189	389 672	103 892	88 249	8 312	8 975	23 170	55 848	49 834	4 100	25 587	43 297
November	441 444	391 741	104 528	89 752	8 318	8 974	23 476	56 030	49 978	4 104	25 700	42 447
December	437 590	387 188	103 885	88 912	8 435	8 828	23 342	56 322	50 201	4 131	25 900	39 095

[1] Includes store categories not shown separately.
[2] Includes furniture, home furnishings, electronics, appliances, clothing, sporting goods, hobby, book, music, general merchandise, office supplies, stationery, and gifts.

Table 16-9. Quarterly U.S. Retail Sales: Total and E-Commerce

Year and quarter	Retail sales (millions of dollars)		E-commerce as a percent of total sales	Percent change from prior quarter		Percent change from same quarter a year ago	
	Total	E-commerce		Total sales	E-commerce sales	Total sales	E-commerce sales
NOT SEASONALLY ADJUSTED							
2013							
1st quarter	1 043 344	57 953	5.6	-8.7	-20.6	2.7	13.0
2nd quarter	1 124 886	59 825	5.3	7.8	3.2	4.2	15.1
3rd quarter	1 120 648	60 788	5.4	-0.4	1.6	4.9	14.2
4rd quarter	1 180 144	82 103	7.0	5.3	35.1	3.3	12.5
2014							
1st quarter	1 061 353	65 517	6.2	-10.1	-20.2	1.7	13.1
2nd quarter	1 176 780	68 858	5.9	10.9	5.1	4.6	15.1
3rd quarter	1 168 187	70 351	6.0	-0.7	2.2	4.2	15.7
4rd quarter	1 225 969	93 530	7.6	4.9	32.9	3.9	13.9
SEASONALLY ADJUSTED							
2001							
1st quarter	755 812	8 225	1.1	0.5	5.8	2.1	41.5
2nd quarter	764 041	8 357	1.1	1.1	1.6	3.2	28.6
3rd quarter	757 441	8 282	1.1	-0.9	-0.9	1.5	12.8
4th quarter	784 987	9 309	1.2	3.6	12.4	4.4	19.8
2002							
1st quarter	771 113	10 003	1.3	-1.8	7.5	2.0	21.6
2nd quarter	778 751	10 753	1.4	1.0	7.5	1.9	28.7
3rd quarter	788 436	11 486	1.5	1.2	6.8	4.1	38.7
4th quarter	791 372	12 245	1.5	0.4	6.6	0.8	31.5
2003							
1st quarter	798 317	12 807	1.6	0.9	4.6	3.5	28.0
2nd quarter	805 019	13 793	1.7	0.8	7.7	3.4	28.3
3rd quarter	827 707	14 800	1.8	2.8	7.3	5.0	28.9
4th quarter	830 668	15 603	1.9	0.4	5.4	5.0	27.4
2004							
1st quarter	846 082	16 739	2.0	1.9	7.3	6.0	30.7
2nd quarter	855 367	17 528	2.0	1.1	4.7	6.3	27.1
3rd quarter	868 427	18 504	2.1	1.5	5.6	4.9	25.0
4th quarter	890 999	19 669	2.2	2.6	6.3	7.3	26.1
2005							
1st quarter	897 672	20 845	2.3	0.7	6.0	6.1	24.5
2nd quarter	917 453	22 246	2.4	2.2	6.7	7.3	26.9
3rd quarter	934 050	23 667	2.5	1.8	6.4	7.6	27.9
4rd quarter	937 423	24 424	2.6	0.4	3.2	5.2	24.2
2006							
1st quarter	964 110	26 516	2.8	2.8	8.6	7.4	27.2
2nd quarter	966 847	27 413	2.8	0.3	3.4	5.4	23.2
3rd quarter	972 980	28 799	3.0	0.6	5.1	4.2	21.7
4rd quarter	973 714	30 287	3.1	0.1	5.2	3.9	24.0
2007							
1st quarter	985 634	31 868	3.2	1.2	5.2	2.2	20.2
2nd quarter	994 309	33 530	3.4	0.9	5.2	2.8	22.3
3rd quarter	1 002 875	34 718	3.5	0.9	3.5	3.1	20.6
4rd quarter	1 014 302	36 089	3.6	1.1	3.9	4.2	19.2
2008							
1st quarter	1 006 302	36 217	3.6	-0.8	0.4	2.1	13.6
2nd quarter	1 012 316	36 515	3.6	0.6	0.8	1.8	8.9
3rd quarter	999 031	36 063	3.6	-1.3	-1.2	-0.4	3.9
4rd quarter	911 072	33 342	3.7	-8.8	-7.5	-10.2	-7.6
2009							
1st quarter	889 355	34 276	3.9	-2.4	2.8	-11.6	-5.4
2nd quarter	892 150	35 241	4.0	0.3	2.8	-11.9	-3.5
3rd quarter	913 681	37 191	4.1	2.4	5.5	-8.5	3.1
4rd quarter	919 653	38 382	4.2	0.7	3.2	0.9	15.1
2010							
1st quarter	934 189	39 417	4.2	1.6	2.7	5.0	15.0
2nd quarter	949 479	41 252	4.3	1.6	4.7	6.4	17.1
3rd quarter	953 563	43 340	4.5	0.4	5.1	4.4	16.5
4rd quarter	982 186	45 326	4.6	3.0	4.6	6.8	18.1
2011							
1st quarter	1 005 638	47 005	4.7	2.4	3.7	7.6	19.3
2nd quarter	1 021 514	48 644	4.8	1.6	3.5	7.6	17.9
3rd quarter	1 029 979	49 885	4.8	0.8	2.6	8.0	15.1
4rd quarter	1 048 068	53 089	5.1	1.8	6.4	6.7	17.1
2012							
1st quarter	1 069 065	54 643	5.1	2.0	2.9	6.3	16.2
2nd quarter	1 065 194	55 730	5.2	-0.4	2.0	4.3	14.6
3rd quarter	1 075 657	57 776	5.4	1.0	3.7	4.4	15.8
4rd quarter	1 091 076	60 403	5.5	1.4	4.5	4.1	13.8
2013							
1st quarter	1 109 824	61 911	5.6	1.7	2.5	3.8	13.3
2nd quarter	1 112 179	64 014	5.8	0.2	3.4	4.4	14.9
3rd quarter	1 120 658	65 906	5.9	0.8	3.0	4.2	14.1
4rd quarter	1 126 312	68 026	6.0	0.5	3.2	3.2	12.6
2014							
1st quarter	1 133 058	70 102	6.2	0.6	3.1	2.1	13.2
2nd quarter	1 160 023	73 586	6.3	2.4	5.0	4.3	15.0
3rd quarter	1 167 011	76 172	6.5	0.6	3.5	4.1	15.6
4rd quarter	1 168 601	77 558	6.6	0.1	1.8	3.8	14.0

Table 16-10. Retail Inventories

(All retail stores; end of period, millions of dollars.)

Year and month	Not seasonally adjusted			Seasonally adjusted								
	Total	Excluding motor vehicles and parts	Motor vehicles and parts	Total	Excluding motor vehicles and parts	Motor vehicles and parts	Furniture, home furnishings, electronics, and appliances	Building materials and garden	Food and beverages	Clothing and accessories	General merchandise	
											Total	Department stores [1]
1992	256 167	184 701	71 466	260 277	191 119	69 158	16 183	21 099	27 408	27 390	49 306	37 878
1993	274 072	196 419	77 653	278 445	203 311	75 134	18 113	22 621	27 498	28 080	53 283	40 458
1994	299 812	211 223	88 589	304 519	218 757	85 762	20 397	24 857	28 112	29 518	56 581	41 908
1995	317 304	220 921	96 383	322 216	228 842	93 374	21 817	26 337	28 718	29 298	59 530	43 455
1996	328 160	227 888	100 272	333 255	236 015	97 240	22 253	27 447	29 658	29 778	60 591	44 124
1997	338 790	234 270	104 520	343 825	242 518	101 307	22 109	28 897	29 891	31 079	60 715	44 309
1998	351 255	245 400	105 855	356 518	253 888	102 630	22 665	30 921	30 837	32 308	61 542	43 438
1999	378 813	259 879	118 934	384 078	268 567	115 511	24 096	33 005	32 635	33 735	64 297	43 835
2000	400 394	268 982	131 412	405 931	277 829	128 102	25 622	34 269	32 108	36 753	64 929	42 667
2001	387 859	266 370	121 489	393 638	274 796	118 842	24 497	34 235	33 165	35 627	64 790	40 464
2002	409 314	271 757	137 557	415 137	280 240	134 897	25 853	36 086	32 907	37 401	66 006	38 750
2003	425 748	277 471	148 277	431 199	285 668	145 531	27 152	37 398	32 504	38 503	66 655	36 823
2004	454 848	297 561	157 287	460 284	305 890	154 394	30 043	41 593	33 437	41 417	70 969	37 230
2005	465 877	310 236	155 641	471 658	318 816	152 842	30 526	45 082	33 790	43 035	74 194	38 048
2006	480 521	324 028	156 493	486 439	332 848	153 591	30 753	47 034	34 706	47 338	75 625	37 173
2007	494 651	334 596	160 055	500 625	343 366	157 259	31 273	49 110	36 485	47 489	75 868	36 487
2008	471 795	323 452	148 343	477 449	331 482	145 967	27 699	46 550	37 300	46 077	72 912	33 232
2009	424 004	308 749	115 255	429 453	315 820	113 633	25 640	42 732	37 316	40 919	69 747	30 995
2010	449 572	320 626	128 946	455 051	327 847	127 204	27 282	43 013	38 699	42 039	73 394	31 082
2011	465 303	330 962	330 962	470 989	338 496	132 493	26 304	43 602	40 249	44 380	76 633	31 314
2012	499 610	340 531	159 079	505 169	348 535	156 634	27 307	45 047	41 199	46 563	77 662	29 842
2013	537 746	357 105	180 641	543 511	365 888	177 623	27 092	48 112	42 777	49 691	80 624	30 000
2014	552 803	364 838	187 965	558 321	373 869	184 452	27 283	49 883	44 372	51 107	81 014	28 653
2011												
January	446 349	318 271	128 078	455 612	328 862	126 750	27 122	43 433	38 959	42 204	73 177	31 113
February	446 156	318 852	127 304	453 034	328 267	124 767	26 692	43 473	38 945	42 492	72 964	31 039
March	458 924	328 249	130 675	460 066	332 824	127 242	27 063	43 827	39 187	42 848	74 872	31 464
April	460 355	329 434	130 921	460 492	333 159	127 333	26 986	43 863	39 461	42 978	74 598	31 320
May	456 982	328 208	128 774	461 709	333 888	127 821	26 716	43 834	39 465	43 396	74 740	31 320
June	455 272	327 780	127 492	462 458	334 873	127 585	26 794	43 883	39 584	43 370	75 133	31 264
July	449 223	327 191	122 032	460 841	333 951	126 890	26 719	43 753	39 773	43 412	74 784	31 209
August	456 371	333 105	123 266	465 781	336 547	129 234	26 751	43 805	40 001	44 064	75 589	31 392
September	469 268	344 767	124 501	466 662	336 870	129 792	26 431	44 014	40 082	44 379	75 708	31 397
October	491 021	360 916	130 105	466 952	336 968	129 984	26 421	44 035	40 070	44 745	75 763	31 347
November	500 244	365 459	134 785	470 268	338 535	131 733	26 347	44 041	40 181	44 840	76 179	31 338
December	465 303	330 962	134 341	470 989	338 496	132 493	26 304	43 602	40 249	44 380	76 633	31 314
2012												
January	465 347	328 157	137 190	474 053	338 530	135 523	26 472	44 072	40 291	44 588	76 396	30 828
February	471 628	330 846	140 782	478 040	339 896	138 144	26 533	44 364	40 607	44 616	76 634	30 613
March	480 443	336 192	144 251	481 679	340 675	141 004	26 704	44 301	41 036	44 821	76 123	30 086
April	484 751	337 158	147 593	484 930	341 056	143 874	26 821	44 624	40 610	44 613	76 327	30 389
May	485 503	338 081	147 422	490 133	343 683	146 450	27 115	44 947	40 653	45 047	77 070	30 402
June	485 197	336 657	148 540	492 891	344 089	148 802	27 233	44 924	40 830	45 878	76 629	30 279
July	484 355	338 338	146 017	497 317	345 324	151 993	27 142	45 133	40 911	46 286	76 728	30 144
August	489 830	343 003	146 827	500 526	346 529	153 997	27 091	45 314	40 928	46 448	77 099	30 044
September	502 315	353 703	148 612	500 486	345 803	154 683	26 993	45 306	41 102	46 326	75 989	29 130
October	527 575	371 894	155 681	502 781	347 638	155 143	27 248	45 431	40 927	46 256	77 330	29 770
November	534 552	374 812	159 740	503 860	347 969	155 891	27 389	45 218	41 109	46 425	76 968	29 581
December	499 610	340 531	159 079	505 169	348 535	156 634	27 307	45 047	41 199	46 563	77 662	29 842
2013												
January	505 366	343 186	162 180	513 306	353 458	159 848	27 361	45 976	41 496	47 054	79 483	30 013
February	509 364	345 841	163 523	515 300	354 494	160 806	28 023	46 097	41 754	47 329	79 028	30 099
March	511 574	347 853	163 721	512 699	352 155	160 544	27 046	46 187	41 639	47 049	78 594	29 922
April	515 617	350 306	165 311	515 938	354 405	161 533	26 750	46 433	41 940	47 849	79 134	30 101
May	514 078	349 530	164 548	518 938	355 319	163 619	26 576	46 667	42 306	47 747	79 088	29 995
June	511 890	347 694	164 196	520 148	355 658	164 490	26 223	46 842	42 354	47 754	79 069	29 959
July	509 514	350 492	159 022	523 102	357 644	165 458	26 234	47 036	42 440	48 079	79 516	30 028
August	513 716	355 531	158 185	525 138	359 172	165 966	26 271	47 350	42 401	48 419	79 388	29 895
September	531 634	369 027	162 607	529 716	360 842	168 874	26 591	47 590	42 403	48 671	79 909	29 952
October	560 263	386 727	173 536	534 223	361 604	172 619	26 691	47 678	42 623	48 694	80 299	30 020
November	572 289	392 310	179 979	540 313	364 722	175 591	26 700	48 151	42 921	49 183	80 730	29 984
December	537 746	357 105	180 641	543 511	365 888	177 623	27 092	48 112	42 777	49 691	80 624	30 000
2014												
January	538 162	357 560	180 602	545 599	367 784	177 815	26 436	48 408	42 517	50 084	81 442	30 242
February	539 507	359 892	179 615	545 216	368 312	176 904	27 347	48 416	42 855	49 770	80 959	29 938
March	543 937	364 750	179 187	545 113	368 960	176 153	26 888	48 605	43 187	49 814	81 447	29 898
April	546 859	364 620	182 239	546 956	368 884	178 072	27 088	48 596	43 593	49 621	80 934	29 496
May	542 588	362 828	179 760	547 944	369 023	178 921	27 168	48 321	43 494	49 898	80 865	29 388
June	541 715	361 723	179 992	550 434	370 118	180 316	27 412	48 540	43 473	49 896	81 073	29 324
July	541 777	364 157	177 620	556 180	371 465	184 715	27 391	48 811	43 690	49 993	81 342	29 163
August	542 044	367 703	174 341	554 795	371 615	183 180	27 590	48 964	43 860	49 740	81 309	29 175
September	558 223	380 666	177 557	556 747	372 293	184 454	27 167	49 478	43 991	50 086	81 500	29 179
October	584 553	399 056	185 497	557 744	373 391	184 353	26 810	49 896	44 191	50 445	81 127	29 141
November	587 320	400 903	186 417	554 624	372 922	181 702	27 076	49 753	44 119	50 487	80 887	29 038
December	552 803	364 838	187 965	558 321	373 869	184 452	27 283	49 883	44 372	51 107	81 014	28 653

[1] Excluding leased departments.

Table 16-11. Merchant Wholesalers—Sales and Inventories

(Millions of dollars.)

Year and month	Not seasonally adjusted						Seasonally adjusted					
	Sales			Inventories (current cost, end of period)			Sales			Inventories (current cost, end of period)		
	Total	Durable goods establishments	Nondurable goods establishments	Total	Durable goods establishments	Nondurable goods establishments	Total	Durable goods establishments	Nondurable goods establishments	Total	Durable goods establishments	Nondurable goods establishments
1992	1 767 130	861 182	905 948	197 793	121 809	75 984	1 767 130	861 182	905 948	196 914	123 435	73 479
1993	1 848 215	939 945	908 270	205 815	127 094	78 721	1 848 215	939 945	908 270	204 842	128 851	75 991
1994	1 974 899	1 037 638	937 261	222 826	139 941	82 885	1 974 899	1 037 638	937 261	221 978	141 975	80 003
1995	2 158 980	1 141 701	1 017 279	239 275	151 709	87 566	2 158 980	1 141 701	1 017 279	238 392	154 089	84 303
1996	2 284 343	1 190 342	1 094 001	241 396	154 207	87 189	2 284 343	1 190 342	1 094 001	241 058	156 683	84 375
1997	2 377 845	1 256 384	1 121 461	258 900	165 371	93 529	2 377 845	1 256 384	1 121 461	258 454	168 089	90 365
1998	2 427 120	1 306 545	1 120 575	272 575	175 994	96 581	2 427 120	1 306 545	1 120 575	272 297	178 918	93 379
1999	2 599 159	1 406 371	1 192 788	290 382	187 738	102 644	2 599 159	1 406 371	1 192 788	290 182	190 899	99 283
2000	2 814 554	1 486 673	1 327 881	309 710	198 525	111 185	2 814 554	1 486 673	1 327 881	309 191	201 797	107 394
2001	2 785 152	1 422 195	1 362 957	298 577	182 521	116 056	2 785 152	1 422 195	1 362 957	297 536	185 517	112 019
2002	2 835 528	1 421 503	1 414 025	302 715	182 150	120 565	2 835 528	1 421 503	1 414 025	301 281	185 048	116 233
2003	2 978 290	1 466 158	1 512 132	310 115	186 435	123 680	2 978 290	1 466 158	1 512 132	308 305	189 372	118 933
2004	3 330 007	1 689 588	1 640 419	341 641	213 590	128 051	3 330 007	1 689 588	1 640 419	340 281	216 684	123 597
2005	3 638 497	1 830 347	1 808 150	369 358	232 996	136 362	3 638 497	1 830 347	1 808 150	368 070	236 213	131 857
2006	3 941 258	2 005 139	1 936 119	400 223	256 290	143 933	3 941 258	2 005 139	1 936 119	398 969	259 671	139 298
2007	4 223 473	2 101 969	2 121 504	426 117	262 469	163 648	4 223 473	2 101 969	2 121 504	424 318	265 909	158 409
2008	4 519 236	2 123 985	2 395 251	444 430	278 750	165 680	4 519 236	2 123 985	2 395 251	443 905	282 469	161 436
2009	3 816 811	1 739 701	2 077 110	395 981	231 180	164 801	3 816 811	1 739 701	2 077 110	394 417	234 604	159 813
2010	4 318 429	1 990 944	2 327 485	439 681	253 405	186 276	4 318 429	1 990 944	2 327 485	437 273	257 356	179 917
2011	4 862 565	2 220 613	2 641 952	482 620	281 565	201 055	4 862 565	2 220 613	2 641 952	480 931	286 079	194 852
2012	5 165 158	2 379 057	2 786 101	514 640	305 220	209 420	5 165 158	2 379 057	2 786 101	512 794	310 227	202 567
2013	5 322 612	2 452 714	2 869 898	535 863	320 952	214 911	5 322 612	2 452 714	2 869 898	534 519	326 336	208 183
2014	5 551 108	2 588 460	2 962 648	571 604	346 351	225 253	5 551 108	2 588 460	2 962 648	570 198	352 162	218 036
2011												
January	360 800	159 201	201 599	446 385	257 277	189 108	393 940	178 635	215 305	440 966	258 876	182 090
February	349 670	155 184	194 486	451 026	260 871	190 155	389 742	176 019	213 723	445 455	261 152	184 303
March	430 050	195 570	234 480	454 667	261 023	193 644	400 193	180 858	219 335	450 232	262 504	187 728
April	403 523	178 476	225 047	453 290	263 066	190 224	404 310	181 119	223 191	452 820	263 271	189 549
May	411 273	178 696	232 577	457 144	268 326	188 818	400 813	178 800	222 013	462 068	268 908	193 160
June	422 518	193 144	229 374	460 453	272 908	187 545	404 114	181 626	222 488	467 098	272 789	194 309
July	391 994	179 729	212 265	465 645	277 652	187 993	407 392	188 764	218 628	470 091	275 406	194 685
August	432 106	202 580	229 526	463 330	278 779	184 551	411 917	191 476	220 441	471 741	278 447	193 294
September	417 668	197 852	219 816	465 775	281 601	184 174	411 298	189 283	222 015	468 121	279 776	188 345
October	417 360	194 353	223 007	477 922	285 450	192 472	415 221	191 331	223 890	472 957	282 282	190 675
November	410 580	189 108	221 472	477 384	283 874	193 510	411 822	189 581	222 241	474 190	282 933	191 257
December	415 023	196 720	218 303	482 620	281 565	201 055	419 135	195 824	223 311	480 931	286 079	194 852
2012												
January	399 348	181 524	217 824	486 707	286 378	200 329	423 849	196 815	227 034	481 869	288 017	193 852
February	400 017	182 778	217 239	493 250	290 201	203 049	427 857	198 841	229 016	487 895	290 436	197 459
March	449 647	208 082	241 565	494 535	291 585	202 950	429 309	198 020	231 289	489 295	293 112	196 183
April	434 231	193 316	240 915	494 255	296 462	197 793	435 096	196 801	238 295	492 715	296 357	196 358
May	452 608	204 251	248 357	489 784	298 229	191 555	428 442	198 265	230 177	494 122	298 721	195 401
June	430 002	202 578	227 424	488 911	300 650	188 261	422 064	196 036	226 028	496 466	300 513	195 953
July	418 011	192 814	225 197	495 241	305 124	190 117	422 721	196 380	226 341	501 259	302 688	198 571
August	445 542	208 199	237 343	492 730	302 421	190 309	426 339	196 564	229 775	502 967	302 275	200 692
September	417 231	194 632	222 599	504 179	306 533	197 646	436 445	198 845	237 600	509 663	304 747	204 916
October	457 590	213 036	244 554	515 091	311 466	203 625	429 564	196 708	232 856	508 609	308 402	200 207
November	437 822	202 638	235 184	517 153	310 393	206 760	437 698	201 961	235 737	512 371	309 644	202 727
December	423 109	195 209	227 900	514 640	305 220	209 420	438 647	200 768	237 879	512 794	310 227	202 567
2013												
January	424 634	192 761	231 873	522 942	311 255	211 687	439 252	203 216	236 036	517 541	313 012	204 529
February	397 681	178 754	218 927	520 619	312 802	207 817	442 886	202 698	240 188	515 337	313 091	202 246
March	441 652	204 607	237 045	521 917	313 177	208 740	434 514	201 652	232 862	515 871	314 491	201 380
April	446 982	205 837	241 145	519 914	316 701	203 213	434 305	202 372	231 933	517 195	316 162	201 033
May	465 280	208 289	256 991	510 103	313 453	196 650	441 216	202 686	238 530	514 341	313 774	200 567
June	436 324	203 748	232 576	507 947	314 237	193 710	441 424	203 633	237 791	515 210	314 241	200 969
July	445 907	202 658	243 249	511 645	318 914	192 731	439 055	200 936	238 119	515 917	316 259	199 658
August	451 232	209 581	241 651	511 612	318 773	192 839	443 024	203 292	239 732	519 728	318 634	201 094
September	437 727	209 079	228 648	519 227	320 934	198 293	444 956	207 019	237 937	522 990	319 107	203 883
October	479 505	225 076	254 429	534 309	323 287	211 022	449 757	207 299	242 458	528 399	320 409	207 990
November	440 498	201 736	238 762	536 666	322 417	214 249	453 110	207 312	245 798	531 826	321 877	209 949
December	455 190	210 588	244 602	535 863	320 952	214 911	455 866	208 893	246 973	534 519	326 336	208 183
2014												
January	431 276	195 034	236 242	543 190	326 211	216 979	448 019	206 530	241 489	538 410	327 999	210 411
February	404 220	181 862	222 358	546 469	330 666	215 803	451 007	206 960	244 047	541 020	330 580	210 440
March	463 657	212 404	251 253	553 305	332 001	221 304	460 125	210 600	249 525	546 613	333 065	213 548
April	474 044	215 009	259 035	555 616	336 787	218 829	463 651	212 708	250 943	552 130	335 806	216 324
May	478 615	213 676	264 939	549 816	338 977	210 839	465 860	213 770	252 090	554 387	339 168	215 219
June	473 802	223 560	250 242	548 349	341 422	206 927	466 321	216 676	249 645	556 193	341 315	214 878
July	476 250	219 081	257 169	551 970	345 197	206 773	468 699	217 092	251 607	556 636	342 300	214 336
August	462 251	217 800	244 451	551 585	345 235	206 350	466 534	218 206	248 328	560 382	345 108	215 274
September	474 909	229 501	245 408	557 582	349 734	207 848	466 414	219 137	247 277	561 836	347 953	213 883
October	497 111	239 309	257 802	571 003	350 619	220 384	466 173	220 588	245 585	565 118	348 039	217 079
November	440 086	208 689	231 397	574 837	351 465	223 372	465 997	221 336	244 661	569 479	351 179	218 300
December	474 887	232 535	242 352	571 604	346 351	225 253	461 666	224 119	237 547	570 198	352 162	218 036

. . . = Not available.

Table 16-12. Manufacturing and Trade Sales and Inventories

Year and month	Sales, billions of dollars					Inventories, billions of dollars, end of period, seasonally adjusted				Ratios, inventories to sales, seasonally adjusted [1]			
	Not seasonally adjusted, total	Seasonally adjusted				Total	Manufac-turing	Retail trade	Merchant wholesalers	Total	Manufac-turing	Retail trade	Merchant wholesalers
		Total	Manufac-turing	Retail trade	Merchant wholesalers								
1993	6 806.3	6 804.0	3 019.8	1 936.4	1 847.8	863.1	379.8	278.4	204.8	1.50	1.50	1.68	1.30
1994	7 318.2	7 321.7	3 241.5	2 103.3	1 976.9	926.4	399.9	304.5	222.0	1.46	1.44	1.66	1.29
1995	7 856.3	7 865.3	3 481.4	2 220.3	2 163.7	985.4	424.8	322.2	238.4	1.48	1.44	1.72	1.29
1996	8 243.1	8 217.6	3 586.0	2 355.6	2 276.0	1 004.7	430.4	333.3	241.1	1.45	1.44	1.67	1.27
1997	8 681.3	8 683.8	3 836.0	2 470.8	2 377.1	1 045.7	443.4	343.8	258.5	1.42	1.37	1.64	1.26
1998	8 908.7	8 906.6	3 897.6	2 582.6	2 426.3	1 077.5	448.6	356.5	272.3	1.43	1.37	1.64	1.26
1999	9 434.1	9 431.0	4 032.6	2 801.4	2 597.0	1 137.6	463.3	384.1	290.2	1.40	1.35	1.62	1.32
2000	10 006.4	9 998.7	4 202.1	2 979.3	2 817.3	1 196.1	481.0	405.9	309.2	1.41	1.35	1.59	1.29
2001	9 817.9	9 819.6	3 971.5	3 062.3	2 785.8	1 118.7	427.5	393.6	297.5	1.42	1.38	1.58	1.32
2002	9 878.8	9 881.1	3 916.9	3 129.7	2 834.5	1 139.2	422.7	415.1	301.3	1.36	1.29	1.55	1.26
2003	10 256.4	10 255.3	4 016.3	3 261.7	2 977.4	1 147.6	408.1	431.2	308.3	1.34	1.25	1.56	1.22
2004	11 112.0	11 069.5	4 293.3	3 460.9	3 315.4	1 241.2	440.7	460.3	340.3	1.30	1.19	1.56	1.17
2005	12 069.9	12 072.3	4 741.9	3 686.6	3 643.8	1 313.3	473.5	471.7	368.1	1.27	1.17	1.51	1.17
2006	12 828.4	12 840.6	5 016.4	3 877.7	3 946.6	1 407.6	522.2	486.4	399.0	1.28	1.20	1.49	1.17
2007	13 538.1	13 538.7	5 320.6	3 997.1	4 221.0	1 485.9	561.0	500.6	424.3	1.28	1.22	1.49	1.17
2008	13 923.6	13 876.9	5 446.8	3 928.7	4 501.4	1 462.5	541.1	477.4	443.9	1.31	1.26	1.52	1.19
2009	11 850.8	11 854.9	4 423.4	3 614.8	3 816.7	1 325.7	501.9	429.5	394.4	1.38	1.39	1.47	1.28
2010	13 044.7	13 041.3	4 908.3	3 819.4	4 313.6	1 443.6	551.3	455.1	437.3	1.27	1.28	1.39	1.14
2011	14 467.2	14 479.4	5 504.4	4 105.2	4 869.9	1 559.6	607.7	471.0	480.9	1.26	1.29	1.35	1.14
2012	15 204.7	15 184.0	5 725.0	4 301.0	5 158.0	1 640.5	622.5	505.2	512.8	1.27	1.29	1.38	1.16
2013	15 626.8	15 627.8	5 839.5	4 469.0	5 319.4	1 714.8	636.8	543.5	534.5	1.29	1.29	1.41	1.18
2014	16 155.5	16 148.1	5 970.9	4 628.7	5 548.5	1 781.5	652.9	558.3	570.2	1.31	1.31	1.43	1.20
2010													
January	950.4	1 044.6	394.6	309.1	340.9	1 327.8	503.4	429.8	394.6	1.27	1.28	1.39	1.16
February	947.8	1 047.8	392.9	308.8	346.1	1 334.9	508.0	431.1	395.7	1.27	1.29	1.40	1.14
March	1 120.8	1 067.3	400.5	316.2	350.6	1 343.6	511.2	434.7	397.8	1.26	1.28	1.37	1.13
April	1 089.8	1 079.6	405.1	318.1	356.4	1 350.0	515.0	436.2	398.8	1.25	1.27	1.37	1.12
May	1 086.0	1 073.9	402.4	316.0	355.5	1 351.8	514.8	436.3	400.6	1.26	1.28	1.38	1.13
June	1 120.1	1 072.4	402.1	315.4	354.9	1 363.6	519.4	441.3	403.0	1.27	1.29	1.40	1.14
July	1 075.7	1 084.0	409.1	315.7	359.2	1 374.9	522.5	444.6	407.8	1.27	1.28	1.41	1.14
August	1 117.5	1 090.9	411.9	317.5	361.5	1 386.3	525.2	448.4	412.7	1.27	1.28	1.41	1.14
September	1 108.4	1 099.5	415.9	320.3	363.3	1 403.1	531.0	453.0	419.2	1.28	1.28	1.41	1.15
October	1 114.3	1 114.0	417.3	324.9	371.7	1 417.2	537.2	452.2	427.8	1.27	1.29	1.39	1.15
November	1 116.5	1 126.1	423.6	327.3	375.3	1 426.7	543.3	452.9	430.5	1.27	1.28	1.38	1.15
December	1 197.5	1 141.2	433.0	330.0	378.2	1 443.6	551.3	455.1	437.3	1.26	1.27	1.38	1.16
2011													
January	1 062.4	1 167.7	441.0	332.8	393.9	1 455.0	558.4	455.6	441.0	1.25	1.27	1.37	1.12
February	1 057.6	1 166.0	441.6	334.7	389.7	1 463.1	564.6	453.0	445.5	1.25	1.28	1.35	1.14
March	1 261.0	1 195.9	457.5	338.2	400.2	1 483.0	572.7	460.1	450.2	1.24	1.25	1.36	1.13
April	1 199.1	1 200.2	455.9	340.0	404.3	1 497.7	584.3	460.5	452.8	1.25	1.28	1.35	1.12
May	1 227.4	1 196.2	455.8	339.7	400.8	1 514.7	590.9	461.7	462.1	1.27	1.30	1.36	1.15
June	1 255.1	1 205.2	459.2	341.9	404.1	1 523.8	594.2	462.5	467.1	1.26	1.29	1.35	1.16
July	1 179.5	1 212.6	462.7	342.6	407.4	1 528.2	597.3	460.8	470.1	1.26	1.29	1.35	1.15
August	1 269.8	1 219.2	465.2	342.1	411.9	1 537.1	599.6	465.8	471.7	1.26	1.29	1.36	1.15
September	1 230.2	1 219.9	463.3	345.3	411.3	1 533.0	598.2	466.7	468.1	1.26	1.29	1.35	1.14
October	1 225.2	1 228.8	465.0	348.6	415.2	1 544.5	604.6	467.0	473.0	1.26	1.30	1.34	1.14
November	1 217.0	1 228.4	466.8	349.7	411.8	1 551.9	607.5	470.3	474.2	1.26	1.30	1.34	1.15
December	1 282.7	1 239.1	470.3	349.7	419.1	1 559.6	607.7	471.0	480.9	1.26	1.29	1.35	1.15
2012													
January	1 151.3	1 250.6	474.1	352.6	423.8	1 566.6	610.7	474.1	481.9	1.25	1.29	1.34	1.14
February	1 187.7	1 259.4	474.3	357.3	427.9	1 578.2	612.2	478.0	487.9	1.25	1.29	1.34	1.14
March	1 322.1	1 266.0	477.5	359.2	429.3	1 584.6	613.6	481.7	489.3	1.25	1.28	1.34	1.14
April	1 259.6	1 267.9	476.3	356.5	435.1	1 592.6	615.0	484.9	492.7	1.26	1.29	1.36	1.13
May	1 320.9	1 262.5	477.8	356.3	428.4	1 599.3	615.0	490.1	494.1	1.27	1.29	1.38	1.15
June	1 276.2	1 242.5	468.0	352.4	422.1	1 604.2	614.9	492.9	496.5	1.29	1.31	1.40	1.18
July	1 228.2	1 250.9	473.9	354.3	422.7	1 615.0	616.5	497.3	501.3	1.29	1.30	1.40	1.19
August	1 316.1	1 260.3	475.5	358.5	426.3	1 622.7	619.2	500.5	503.0	1.29	1.30	1.40	1.18
September	1 247.2	1 280.4	481.1	362.9	436.4	1 632.7	622.6	500.5	509.7	1.28	1.29	1.38	1.17
October	1 311.0	1 272.9	481.3	362.0	429.6	1 633.7	622.3	502.8	508.6	1.28	1.29	1.39	1.18
November	1 277.2	1 283.3	482.2	363.4	437.7	1 638.6	622.3	503.9	512.4	1.28	1.29	1.39	1.17
December	1 307.1	1 287.3	483.0	365.7	438.6	1 640.5	622.5	505.2	512.8	1.27	1.29	1.38	1.17
2013													
January	1 210.2	1 290.9	484.0	367.7	439.3	1 655.7	624.8	513.3	517.5	1.28	1.29	1.40	1.18
February	1 185.7	1 305.3	489.8	372.6	442.9	1 655.8	625.1	515.3	515.3	1.27	1.28	1.38	1.16
March	1 319.7	1 286.0	481.9	369.6	434.5	1 654.9	626.3	512.7	515.9	1.29	1.30	1.39	1.19
April	1 294.0	1 281.9	479.0	368.6	434.3	1 661.3	628.1	515.9	517.2	1.30	1.31	1.40	1.19
May	1 358.7	1 296.2	484.3	370.7	441.2	1 660.9	627.6	518.9	514.3	1.28	1.30	1.40	1.17
June	1 304.8	1 296.0	481.7	372.9	441.4	1 663.8	628.4	520.1	515.2	1.28	1.30	1.39	1.17
July	1 299.1	1 299.8	486.5	374.3	439.1	1 668.5	629.5	523.1	515.9	1.28	1.29	1.40	1.18
August	1 344.8	1 303.8	488.0	372.8	443.0	1 675.5	630.6	525.1	519.7	1.29	1.29	1.41	1.17
September	1 290.6	1 306.7	488.1	373.6	445.0	1 685.6	632.9	529.7	523.0	1.29	1.30	1.42	1.18
October	1 355.7	1 312.7	488.7	374.2	449.8	1 695.8	633.2	534.2	528.4	1.29	1.30	1.43	1.17
November	1 297.5	1 322.6	494.8	374.7	453.1	1 705.7	633.6	540.3	531.8	1.29	1.28	1.44	1.17
December	1 366.0	1 326.0	492.7	377.4	455.9	1 714.8	636.8	543.5	534.5	1.29	1.29	1.44	1.17
2014													
January	1 228.3	1 310.4	489.4	373.0	448.0	1 722.0	638.0	545.6	538.4	1.31	1.30	1.46	1.20
February	1 201.1	1 322.8	494.2	377.7	451.0	1 728.6	642.4	545.2	541.0	1.31	1.30	1.44	1.20
March	1 364.6	1 338.4	496.0	382.4	460.1	1 735.2	643.4	545.2	546.6	1.30	1.30	1.43	1.19
April	1 360.0	1 345.4	497.9	385.7	461.7	1 745.6	646.5	547.0	552.2	1.30	1.30	1.42	1.20
May	1 397.1	1 349.8	497.3	386.6	465.9	1 754.3	651.9	547.9	554.4	1.30	1.31	1.42	1.19
June	1 381.6	1 355.3	501.3	387.7	466.3	1 759.6	653.0	550.4	556.2	1.30	1.30	1.42	1.19
July	1 368.6	1 365.0	508.1	388.2	468.7	1 765.9	653.1	556.2	556.6	1.29	1.29	1.43	1.19
August	1 376.4	1 359.6	502.7	390.4	466.5	1 768.8	653.6	554.8	560.4	1.30	1.30	1.42	1.20
September	1 369.5	1 357.9	503.0	388.5	466.4	1 773.7	655.1	556.7	561.8	1.31	1.30	1.43	1.20
October	1 400.9	1 354.3	498.5	389.7	466.2	1 778.4	655.6	557.7	565.1	1.31	1.32	1.43	1.21
November	1 300.3	1 351.3	493.5	391.7	466.0	1 780.0	655.9	554.6	569.5	1.32	1.33	1.42	1.22
December	1 407.1	1 337.8	489.0	387.2	461.7	1 781.5	652.9	558.3	570.2	1.33	1.34	1.44	1.24

[1]Annual data are averages of monthly ratios.

Table 16-13. Real Manufacturing and Trade Sales and Inventories

(Billions of chained [2009] dollars, ratios; seasonally adjusted; annual sales figures are averages of seasonally adjusted monthly data.)

NIPA Tables 1BU, 2BU, 3BU

Year and month	Sales, monthly average				Inventories, end of period				Ratios, end-of-period inventories to monthly average sales			
	Total	Manufac-turing	Retail trade	Merchant wholesalers	Total	Manufac-turing	Retail trade	Merchant wholesalers	Total	Manufac-turing	Retail trade	Merchant wholesalers
1997	853.3	400.7	238.2	227.4	1 218.9	545.0	370.4	310.6	1.43	1.36	1.56	1.37
1998	894.4	413.8	252.2	243.2	1 278.7	564.8	386.6	334.6	1.43	1.37	1.53	1.38
1999	944.1	427.0	270.6	262.8	1 345.4	582.8	414.1	354.8	1.43	1.37	1.53	1.35
2000	971.9	432.1	280.7	276.5	1 395.1	591.6	435.9	373.0	1.44	1.37	1.55	1.35
2001	959.2	408.2	288.0	278.3	1 345.5	562.3	424.6	363.1	1.40	1.38	1.47	1.31
2002	988.0	406.0	296.1	286.6	1 375.7	561.2	452.3	364.2	1.39	1.38	1.53	1.27
2003	1 006.0	406.8	307.5	292.5	1 390.1	552.3	471.4	366.6	1.38	1.36	1.53	1.25
2004	1 042.7	415.3	319.9	309.8	1 444.4	558.7	496.6	388.6	1.39	1.35	1.55	1.25
2005	1 087.1	434.0	332.0	324.8	1 493.6	581.6	501.8	410.4	1.37	1.34	1.51	1.26
2006	1 116.4	439.4	342.8	338.2	1 540.1	600.6	511.5	428.3	1.38	1.37	1.49	1.27
2007	1 139.0	450.1	347.5	346.4	1 574.3	618.1	518.1	438.2	1.38	1.37	1.49	1.27
2008	1 093.9	426.4	332.7	338.7	1 532.3	600.3	487.9	444.1	1.40	1.41	1.47	1.31
2009	991.5	368.8	314.4	308.3	1 410.3	574.0	438.2	398.0	1.42	1.56	1.39	1.29
2010	1 035.1	388.2	324.9	323.6	1 471.4	596.1	456.6	418.6	1.42	1.54	1.41	1.29
2011	1 069.1	402.5	335.1	334.2	1 504.7	617.3	455.5	431.1	1.41	1.53	1.36	1.29
2012	1 100.8	412.0	346.7	346.1	1 557.2	627.9	481.1	447.8	1.42	1.52	1.39	1.29
2013	1 139.2	419.5	362.8	362.1	1 614.6	635.3	509.5	470.0	1.42	1.51	1.40	1.30
2014	1 179.2	426.4	378.0	381.6	1 673.8	650.1	520.7	502.9	1.42	1.53	1.38	1.32
2010												
January	1 001.2	380.0	314.9	306.7	1 409.1	574.1	438.5	396.4	1.41	1.51	1.39	1.29
February	1 008.4	380.3	315.1	313.0	1 412.5	576.4	439.3	396.7	1.40	1.52	1.39	1.27
March	1 020.2	384.0	322.7	314.4	1 415.8	576.5	441.3	398.0	1.39	1.50	1.37	1.27
April	1 027.8	384.5	325.3	319.5	1 418.0	576.3	443.8	398.0	1.38	1.50	1.36	1.25
May	1 026.5	380.6	324.1	323.1	1 418.5	574.4	444.6	399.5	1.38	1.51	1.37	1.24
June	1 034.5	382.5	324.2	329.6	1 426.9	577.7	448.1	401.1	1.38	1.51	1.38	1.22
July	1 045.4	391.0	324.2	332.8	1 436.1	580.3	450.4	405.4	1.37	1.48	1.39	1.22
August	1 047.3	391.7	325.8	331.8	1 444.9	582.4	453.2	409.4	1.38	1.49	1.39	1.23
September	1 048.3	395.0	327.6	327.9	1 456.3	586.6	456.5	413.3	1.39	1.49	1.39	1.26
October	1 049.7	391.9	330.9	329.2	1 465.4	589.8	455.5	420.0	1.40	1.51	1.38	1.28
November	1 055.1	395.2	332.2	329.9	1 464.8	592.5	455.1	417.3	1.39	1.50	1.37	1.27
December	1 056.5	401.4	331.9	325.6	1 471.4	596.1	456.6	418.6	1.39	1.49	1.38	1.29
2011												
January	1 068.3	404.2	333.3	333.3	1 472.4	598.1	456.3	417.9	1.38	1.48	1.37	1.25
February	1 053.9	399.1	333.6	323.3	1 470.3	598.7	453.7	417.7	1.40	1.50	1.36	1.29
March	1 067.4	405.0	334.2	331.1	1 477.6	600.7	458.1	418.7	1.38	1.48	1.37	1.27
April	1 059.2	397.6	333.4	330.3	1 483.4	606.9	457.8	418.3	1.40	1.53	1.37	1.27
May	1 054.6	394.2	331.4	331.1	1 490.4	609.4	456.4	424.1	1.41	1.55	1.38	1.28
June	1 066.2	398.4	333.7	336.5	1 491.9	610.0	455.0	426.2	1.40	1.53	1.36	1.27
July	1 069.1	400.1	334.1	337.4	1 492.4	610.7	453.5	427.5	1.40	1.53	1.36	1.27
August	1 076.8	404.7	333.1	341.8	1 495.8	611.3	455.5	428.4	1.39	1.51	1.37	1.25
September	1 069.9	401.7	335.2	336.2	1 488.5	609.4	454.7	424.0	1.39	1.52	1.36	1.26
October	1 081.8	406.2	339.5	339.7	1 497.0	614.9	453.9	427.5	1.38	1.51	1.34	1.26
November	1 076.9	407.2	340.1	333.1	1 501.9	617.6	456.3	427.4	1.40	1.52	1.34	1.28
December	1 084.8	411.8	339.9	337.1	1 504.7	617.3	455.5	431.1	1.39	1.50	1.34	1.28
2012												
January	1 089.2	412.8	341.8	338.6	1 509.1	619.8	457.7	430.9	1.39	1.50	1.34	1.27
February	1 092.5	410.9	345.1	340.7	1 516.2	620.4	461.1	434.0	1.39	1.51	1.34	1.27
March	1 091.7	408.9	345.3	341.6	1 518.0	620.5	463.1	433.9	1.39	1.52	1.34	1.27
April	1 095.2	407.3	343.9	347.9	1 522.9	621.5	465.1	435.9	1.39	1.53	1.35	1.25
May	1 101.4	411.2	345.0	349.1	1 528.4	622.0	469.1	436.9	1.39	1.51	1.36	1.25
June	1 094.4	406.8	342.6	348.8	1 533.6	623.3	471.3	438.7	1.40	1.53	1.38	1.26
July	1 102.1	413.3	345.1	347.7	1 544.3	625.5	475.6	442.9	1.40	1.51	1.38	1.27
August	1 099.1	410.5	347.5	345.3	1 549.4	628.1	477.8	443.3	1.41	1.53	1.38	1.28
September	1 105.0	411.7	349.6	347.8	1 553.4	630.3	476.8	445.8	1.41	1.53	1.36	1.28
October	1 099.6	412.2	348.7	342.5	1 553.3	628.8	478.5	445.7	1.41	1.53	1.37	1.30
November	1 117.0	418.2	352.1	351.3	1 555.9	628.3	478.6	448.6	1.39	1.50	1.36	1.28
December	1 122.0	420.3	354.1	352.4	1 557.2	627.9	481.1	447.8	1.39	1.49	1.36	1.27
2013												
January	1 123.0	419.7	357.0	351.3	1 568.4	628.7	487.2	452.4	1.40	1.50	1.37	1.29
February	1 125.6	419.3	358.6	352.5	1 568.0	627.8	488.9	451.3	1.39	1.50	1.36	1.28
March	1 118.0	414.2	357.2	351.2	1 568.2	628.1	487.0	453.0	1.40	1.52	1.36	1.29
April	1 122.6	412.5	359.6	355.8	1 574.6	629.6	489.6	455.3	1.40	1.53	1.36	1.28
May	1 138.0	417.6	362.4	363.3	1 574.9	629.2	492.1	453.6	1.38	1.51	1.36	1.25
June	1 135.9	415.4	363.1	362.6	1 576.4	629.8	493.1	453.5	1.39	1.52	1.36	1.25
July	1 138.9	419.4	364.2	360.6	1 580.4	630.5	495.9	454.2	1.39	1.50	1.36	1.26
August	1 141.3	419.5	364.4	362.8	1 585.7	631.3	496.4	458.0	1.39	1.51	1.36	1.26
September	1 145.5	420.3	364.2	366.2	1 594.0	632.9	500.5	460.7	1.39	1.51	1.37	1.26
October	1 152.6	421.6	366.8	369.8	1 603.1	633.1	503.7	466.3	1.39	1.50	1.37	1.26
November	1 166.2	428.9	368.4	375.0	1 610.2	633.2	507.9	469.2	1.38	1.48	1.38	1.25
December	1 163.2	426.0	368.0	374.4	1 614.6	635.3	509.5	470.0	1.39	1.49	1.39	1.26
2014												
January	1 148.5	421.7	364.7	366.9	1 619.1	635.6	510.7	473.1	1.41	1.51	1.40	1.29
February	1 155.1	423.7	368.0	368.9	1 624.5	638.5	511.1	475.1	1.41	1.51	1.39	1.29
March	1 167.5	423.7	374.3	375.9	1 627.7	638.2	510.5	479.0	1.39	1.51	1.36	1.27
April	1 170.8	422.8	376.1	378.6	1 634.4	639.7	512.4	482.4	1.40	1.51	1.36	1.27
May	1 174.5	423.2	376.9	381.4	1 640.5	643.9	513.2	483.4	1.40	1.52	1.36	1.27
June	1 179.0	426.6	377.1	381.9	1 643.9	645.1	514.2	484.5	1.39	1.51	1.36	1.27
July	1 187.5	431.7	377.9	384.9	1 650.5	645.7	519.1	485.8	1.39	1.50	1.37	1.26
August	1 184.8	427.1	381.6	383.3	1 653.9	646.6	517.7	489.6	1.40	1.51	1.36	1.28
September	1 188.2	428.5	381.2	385.6	1 658.2	648.0	517.9	492.3	1.40	1.51	1.36	1.28
October	1 192.7	428.3	382.8	388.9	1 663.5	648.8	518.8	495.9	1.40	1.52	1.36	1.28
November	1 197.7	428.3	387.9	389.1	1 668.9	650.4	517.8	500.7	1.39	1.52	1.34	1.29
December	1 204.6	431.4	387.3	393.4	1 673.8	650.1	520.7	502.9	1.39	1.51	1.34	1.28

Table 16-14. Selected Services—Quarterly Estimated Revenue for Employer Firms

(Millions of dollars.)

2007 NAICS code	Kind of business	2009				2010			
		1st quarter	2nd quarter	3rd quarter	4th quarter	1st quarter	2nd quarter	3rd quarter	4th quarter
SEASONALLY ADJUSTED									
51	**Information**	267 295	267 672	268 727	271 149	273 020	275 596	279 697	281 694
5112	Software publishers	33 507	34 272	34 751	36 159	35 270	36 170	36 893	37 018
512	Motion picture and sound recording industries	22 679	22 577	22 438	22 668	23 745	23 583	23 959	23 831
54	**Professional, Scientific, and Technical Services**	315 525	311 905	312 245	312 472	319 838	320 622	327 187	330 817
5411	Legal services	59 165	59 430	59 765	59 037	60 258	59 081	60 459	60 431
5412	Accounting, tax preparation, bookkeeping, and payroll services	29 182	29 860	29 660	29 379	30 119	29 045	28 548	28 075
56 pt	**Administrative and Support and Waste Management and Remediation Services**	150 950	148 029	149 568	153 411	155 553	160 190	161 987	164 765
5613	Employment services	47 091	46 121	47 834	49 312	49 969	52 977	54 065	55 677
5615	Travel arrangement and reservation services	8 586	8 214	8 426	8 667	8 883	9 361	9 378	9 358
562	Waste management and remediation services	17 846	17 598	18 238	19 199	19 466	20 872	20 955	20 575
622	**Hospitals**	191 140	196 338	199 002	200 550	198 481	204 134	208 066	211 835
NOT SEASONALLY ADJUSTED									
51	**Information**	261 949	266 869	265 502	280 639	267 560	274 769	276 061	291 835
511	Publishing industries (except Internet)	62 649	65 110	64 981	71 454	62 352	65 419	66 138	71 809
51111	Newspaper publishers	8 780	9 230	8 979	9 369	8 252	8 709	8 594	9 140
51112	Periodical publishers	9 684	9 598	9 468	10 349	9 343	9 375	9 657	10 020
5111 pt	Book, directory and mailing list, and other publishers	11 717	12 216	14 007	11 816	10 757	11 310	13 429	11 707
5112	Software publishers	32 468	34 066	32 527	39 920	34 000	36 025	34 458	40 942
512	Motion picture and sound recording industries	22 089	22 261	21 226	24 822	23 128	23 182	22 713	26 095
515	Broadcasting (except Internet)	23 687	24 580	24 246	26 421	25 840	26 949	25 714	29 017
5151	Radio and television broadcasting	11 251	11 815	11 303	13 134	12 870	12 584	12 222	14 676
5152	Cable and other subscription programming	12 436	12 765	12 943	13 287	12 970	14 365	13 492	14 341
517	Telecommunications [1]	. . .	. . .	. . .	. . .	. . .	. . .	. . .	. . .
5171	Wired telecommunications carriers	. . .	. . .	. . .	. . .	. . .	. . .	. . .	. . .
5172	Wireless telecommunications carriers (except satellite)	45 504	46 006	46 861	47 314	47 668	48 068	49 696	50 094
54	**Professional, Scientific, and Technical Services** [1]	311 739	313 776	307 874	318 409	316 000	322 546	323 261	336 772
5411	Legal services	54 846	58 895	59 227	64 232	55 980	58 549	60 096	65 688
5412	Accounting, tax preparation, bookkeeping, and payroll services	34 814	31 592	25 478	26 147	35 932	30 584	24 808	24 818
5413	Architectural, engineering, and related services	61 135	59 264	58 160	56 401	53 253	55 496	57 707	59 743
5415	Computer systems design and related services	63 162	64 734	64 458	68 112	68 669	69 021	71 153	74 947
5416	Management, scientific, and technical consulting services	33 206	33 441	34 417	34 661	34 811	37 305	36 846	37 377
5417	Scientific research and development services	24 843	25 797	26 921	28 195	27 897	28 751	30 562	30 163
5418	Advertising and related services	20 319	19 966	20 019	22 214	20 710	22 000	21 939	24 195
56	**Administrative and Support and Waste Management and Remediation Services** [1]	146 978	149 394	151 271	154 224	151 588	161 386	163 949	165 758
561	Administrative and support services	129 917	131 409	132 522	135 217	132 940	140 013	142 323	145 471
5613	Employment services	46 338	45 660	47 690	50 742	49 269	52 235	53 849	57 514
5615	Travel arrangement and reservation services	8 320	8 740	8 561	8 242	8 599	9 951	9 566	8 881
562	Waste management and remediation services	17 061	17 985	18 749	19 007	18 648	21 373	21 626	20 287
622	**Hospitals**	193 243	197 320	197 211	199 347	200 466	205 155	206 193	210 776
623	**Nursing and Residential Care Facilities**	44 609	46 135	46 332	46 840	46 955	47 924	47 703	49 453

. . . = Not available.

[1] Includes components not shown separately.

Table 16-14. Selected Services—Quarterly Estimated Revenue for Employer Firms—*Continued*

(Millions of dollars.)

2007 NAICS code	Kind of business	2011				2012			
		1st quarter	2nd quarter	3rd quarter	4th quarter	1st quarter	2nd quarter	3rd quarter	4th quarter
SEASONALLY ADJUSTED									
51	**Information**	283 152	290 029	293 163	293 961	297 649	300 670	302 161	308 382
5112	Software publishers	37 915	38 994	40 203	40 068	39 896	40 103	39 880	41 333
512	Motion picture and sound recording industries	21 914	24 083	25 125	24 578	24 305	24 878	24 563	26 085
54	**Professional, Scientific, and Technical Services**	334 772	340 833	344 880	349 142	358 889	357 570	353 178	354 613
5411	Legal services	61 632	62 459	62 066	61 572	65 320	63 047	61 068	62 306
5412	Accounting, tax preparation, bookkeeping, and payroll services	29 316	30 180	30 971	31 372	32 176	32 821	33 122	33 111
56 pt	**Administrative and Support and Waste Management and Remediation Services**	167 073	170 489	173 069	171 952	175 795	176 375	181 870	182 661
5613	Employment services	57 470	58 711	59 679	58 244	59 852	61 384	64 791	65 598
5615	Travel arrangement and reservation services	9 225	9 776	9 959	10 332	10 235	10 211	10 440	10 040
562	Waste management and remediation services	20 937	20 611	21 446	20 837	21 252	21 133	20 971	20 966
622	**Hospitals**	212 648	216 431	214 205	221 404	227 080	227 450	230 702	230 201
NOT SEASONALLY ADJUSTED									
51	**Information**	277 489	289 159	288 766	305 132	291 696	299 467	297 326	320 717
511	Publishing industries (except Internet)	64 405	68 261	68 724	74 464	66 251	68 945	67 194	75 492
51111	Newspaper publishers	7 999	8 451	8 094	8 624	7 688	8 080	7 798	8 682
51112	Periodical publishers	9 299	9 556	9 800	10 251	9 596	9 843	9 528	10 320
5111 pt	Book, directory and mailing list, and other publishers	10 671	11 338	13 240	11 314	10 587	10 959	12 540	10 982
5112	Software publishers	36 436	38 916	37 590	44 275	38 380	40 063	37 328	45 508
512	Motion picture and sound recording industries	21 344	23 601	23 869	26 937	23 673	24 331	23 384	28 589
515	Broadcasting (except Internet)	27 249	28 721	27 205	29 820	28 928	30 092	29 852	32 124
5151	Radio and television broadcasting	12 991	13 043	12 268	14 375	13 546	13 699	14 216	15 367
5152	Cable and other subscription programming	14 258	15 678	14 937	15 445	15 382	16 393	15 636	16 757
517	Telecommunications [1]	. . .	. . .	. . .	. . .	. . .	. . .	138 610	143 288
5171	Wired telecommunications carriers	. . .	. . .	. . .	. . .	. . .	. . .	76 344	78 206
5172	Wireless telecommunications carriers (except satellite)	51 060	51 916	52 486	53 654	53 380	53 670	54 421	57 042
54	**Professional, Scientific, and Technical Services** [1]	330 420	342 878	341 086	355 427	353 865	360 073	349 293	361 351
5411	Legal services	57 133	61 834	61 569	67 545	60 160	62 290	60 396	69 160
5412	Accounting, tax preparation, bookkeeping, and payroll services	35 033	31 659	27 100	27 639	38 450	34 331	29 114	29 204
5413	Architectural, engineering, and related services	57 103	59 901	60 538	59 193	56 398	59 802	59 107	56 224
5415	Computer systems design and related services	73 138	74 828	76 012	81 467	80 922	81 376	80 273	83 934
5416	Management, scientific, and technical consulting services	36 773	38 926	38 904	40 235	39 169	42 678	39 850	40 985
5417	Scientific research and development services	30 627	32 685	33 040	32 778	34 154	33 730	34 513	33 333
5418	Advertising and related services	21 081	22 262	23 254	25 824	23 709	24 528	24 944	27 024
56	**Administrative and Support and Waste Management and Remediation Services** [1]	162 952	171 561	175 026	173 168	171 387	177 380	183 672	184 438
561	Administrative and support services	142 936	150 394	152 851	152 664	151 113	155 655	161 967	163 807
5613	Employment services	56 780	57 654	59 202	60 516	59 253	60 034	63 949	68 550
5615	Travel arrangement and reservation services	8 939	10 372	10 188	9 774	9 938	10 803	10 722	9 458
562	Waste management and remediation services	20 016	21 167	22 175	20 504	20 274	21 725	21 705	20 631
622	**Hospitals**	214 562	217 513	212 063	220 961	228 442	228 587	228 164	230 661
623	**Nursing and Residential Care Facilities**	49 181	50 227	50 362	50 306	50 968	51 391	51 685	51 921

. . . = Not available.
[1] Includes components not shown separately.

Table 16-14. Selected Services—Quarterly Estimated Revenue for Employer Firms—*Continued*

(Millions of dollars.)

2007 NAICS code	Kind of business	2013				2014			
		1st quarter	2nd quarter	3rd quarter	4th quarter	1st quarter	2nd quarter	3rd quarter	4th quarter
SEASONALLY ADJUSTED									
51	**Information**	306 848	308 775	314 473	319 732	324 586	326 869	329 470	334 030
5112	Software publishers	44 139	41 287	42 900	43 997	44 871	46 607	47 317	47 086
512	Motion picture and sound recording industries	24 036	24 739	26 700	27 844	28 097	26 773	26 988	25 774
54	**Professional, Scientific, and Technical Services**	355 611	361 980	365 859	369 251	366 957	374 592	384 402	387 085
5411	Legal services	58 596	62 935	63 211	64 004	61 187	62 394	64 835	63 431
5412	Accounting, tax preparation, bookkeeping, and payroll services	33 188	33 888	34 805	35 951	36 533	37 270	38 588	39 595
56 pt	**Administrative and Support and Waste Management and Remediation Services**	177 341	185 587	188 341	193 280	199 929	201 992	203 172	209 395
5613	Employment services	61 259	65 347	67 210	71 248	74 751	73 560	73 667	77 618
5615	Travel arrangement and reservation services	10 916	10 573	10 572	10 539	10 871	10 871	11 144	11 514
562	Waste management and remediation services	20 996	21 382	21 650	22 012	21 817	22 416	22 313	22 620
622	**Hospitals**	233 357	235 672	236 400	241 738	240 645	246 146	249 697	255 511
NOT SEASONALLY ADJUSTED									
51	**Information**	301 018	307 540	309 127	332 841	318 419	325 235	323 540	348 059
511	Publishing industries (except Internet)	68 699	70 133	70 361	78 041	69 650	75 100	73 181	80 957
51111	Newspaper publishers	7 280	7 861	7 486	8 226	7 124	7 330	7 234	7 872
51112	Periodical publishers	8 950	9 909	9 995	10 234	8 988	9 539	9 424	9 783
5111 pt	Book, directory and mailing list, and other publishers	9 875	11 159	12 640	11 316	10 103	11 764	12 092	11 743
5112	Software publishers	42 594	41 204	40 240	48 265	43 435	46 467	44 431	51 559
512	Motion picture and sound recording industries	23 435	24 195	25 392	30 489	27 451	26 211	25 612	28 197
515	Broadcasting (except Internet)	29 826	31 619	30 359	33 507	32 864	33 237	32 515	36 084
5151	Radio and television broadcasting	13 733	14 068	13 436	15 716	15 202	14 568	14 560	17 215
5152	Cable and other subscription programming	16 093	17 551	16 923	17 791	17 662	18 669	17 955	18 869
517	Telecommunications [1]	139 061	141 553	142 486	146 074	144 581	146 340	147 504	153 804
5171	Wired telecommunications carriers	76 645	77 725	77 141	78 657	77 952	79 019	78 821	80 038
5172	Wireless telecommunications carriers (except satellite)	54 470	55 606	56 893	59 034	58 103	58 527	59 525	64 177
54	**Professional, Scientific, and Technical Services** [1]	350 277	364 514	362 200	376 636	360 719	377 214	380 558	395 214
5411	Legal services	53 440	62 054	62 769	71 493	55 191	61 396	64 835	70 852
5412	Accounting, tax preparation, bookkeeping, and payroll services	39 593	35 379	30 698	31 781	43 474	38 835	34 073	35 081
5413	Architectural, engineering, and related services	55 288	57 452	59 481	56 362	51 533	57 059	58 242	57 828
5415	Computer systems design and related services	82 808	82 157	83 170	84 633	83 233	82 709	86 094	88 623
5416	Management, scientific, and technical consulting services	39 850	43 427	43 274	45 623	44 825	48 001	47 837	50 718
5417	Scientific research and development services	33 327	35 763	35 766	37 543	34 747	37 104	37 888	38 924
5418	Advertising and related services	25 199	26 157	25 488	26 861	25 919	28 207	27 791	29 218
56	**Administrative and Support and Waste Management and Remediation Services** [1]	173 106	186 565	189 930	195 594	195 287	202 883	204 425	212 168
561	Administrative and support services	153 118	164 542	167 544	173 912	174 561	179 772	181 376	189 842
5613	Employment services	60 830	63 779	66 000	74 882	74 377	71 647	71 973	81 887
5615	Travel arrangement and reservation services	10 643	11 154	10 857	9 907	10 654	11 458	11 434	10 800
562	Waste management and remediation services	19 988	22 023	22 386	21 682	20 726	23 111	23 049	22 326
622	**Hospitals**	234 290	236 850	233 563	242 947	241 126	247 377	246 451	257 300
623	**Nursing and Residential Care Facilities**	51 835	52 234	52 557	54 270	53 354	54 188	55 344	57 008

[1]Includes components not shown separately.

NOTES AND DEFINITIONS, CHAPTER 16

Table 16-1
Construction Put in Place

SOURCE: U.S. DEPARTMENT OF COMMERCE, CENSUS BUREAU

The Census Bureau's estimates of the value of new construction put in place are intended to provide monthly estimates of the total dollar value of construction work done in the United States.

Definitions and notes on the data

The estimates cover all construction work done each month on new private residential and nonresidential buildings and structures, public construction, and improvements to existing buildings and structures. Included are the cost of labor, materials, and equipment rental; cost of architectural and engineering work; overhead costs assigned to the project; interest and taxes paid during construction; and contractor's profits.

The total value put in place for a given period is the sum of the value of work done on all projects underway during this period, regardless of when work on each individual project was started or when payment was made to the contractors. For some categories, estimates are derived by distributing the total construction cost of the project by means of historic construction progress patterns. Published estimates represent payments made during a period for some categories.

The statistics on the value of construction put in place result from direct measurement and indirect estimation. A series results from direct measurement when it is based on reports of the actual value of construction progress or construction expenditures obtained in a complete census or a sample survey. All other series are developed by indirect estimation using related construction statistics. On an annual basis, estimates for series directly measured monthly, quarterly, or annually accounted for about 71 percent of total construction in 1998 (private multi-family residential, private residential improvements, private nonresidential buildings, farm nonresidential construction, public utility construction, all other private construction, and virtually all of public construction). On a monthly basis, directly measured data are available for about 55 percent of the value in place estimates.

Beginning in 1993, the Construction Expenditures Branch of the Census Bureau's Manufacturing and Construction Division began collecting these data using a new classification system, which bases project types on their end usage instead of on building/nonbuilding types. Data collection on this system for federal construction began in January 2002.

With the changes in project classifications, data presented in these tables for 1993 to date are not directly comparable with data for previous years, except at aggregate levels. For that reason, *Business Statistics* shows earlier historical data only at these aggregate levels. Although some categories, such as lodging, office, education, and religion, have the same names as categories in previously published data, there have been changes within the classifications that make these values non-comparable. For example, private medical office buildings were classified as "office" buildings previously, but are categorized as "health care" under the new classification.

The seasonally adjusted data are obtained by removing normal seasonal movement from the unadjusted data to bring out underlying trends and business cycles, which is accomplished by using the Census X-12-ARIMA method. Seasonal adjustment accounts for month-to-month variations resulting from normal or average changes in any phenomena affecting the data, such as weather conditions, the differing lengths of months, and the varying number of holidays, weekdays, and weekends within each month. It does not adjust for abnormal conditions within each month or for year-to-year variations in weather. The seasonally adjusted annual rate is the seasonally adjusted monthly rate multiplied by 12.

Residential consists of new houses, town houses, apartments, and condominiums for sale or rent; these dwellings are built by the owner or for the owner on contract. It includes improvements inside and outside residential structures, such as remodeling, additions, major replacements, and additions of swimming pools and garages. Manufactured housing, houseboats, and maintenance and repair work are not included.

Office includes general office buildings, administration buildings, professional buildings, and financial institution buildings. Office buildings at manufacturing sites are classified as *manufacturing,* but office buildings owned by manufacturing companies but not at such a site are included in the *office* category. In the state and local government category, *office* includes capitols, city halls, courthouses, and similar buildings.

Commercial includes buildings and structures used by the retail, wholesale, farm, and selected service industries. One of the subgroups of this category is *multi-retail,* which consists of department and variety stores, shopping centers and malls, and warehouse-type retail stores.

Health care includes hospitals, medical buildings, nursing homes, adult day-care centers, and similar institutions.

Educational includes schools at all levels, higher education facilities, trade schools, libraries, museums, and similar institutions.

Amusement and recreation includes theme and amusement parks, sports structures not located at educational institutions, fitness centers and health clubs, neighborhood centers, camps, movie theaters, and similar establishments.

Transportation includes airport facilities; rail facilities, track, and bridges; bus, rail, maritime, and air terminals; and docks, marinas, and similar structures.

Communication includes telephone, television, and radio distribution and maintenance structures.

Power includes electricity production and distribution and gas and crude oil transmission, storage, and distribution.

Manufacturing includes all buildings and structures at manufacturing sites but not the installation of production machinery or special-purpose equipment.

Included in *total private construction*, but not shown separately in these pages, are lodging facilities (hotels and motels), religious structures, and private public safety, sewage and waste disposal, water supply, highway and street, and conservation and development spending.

Included in *total state and local construction,* but not shown separately in these pages, are state and local construction of commercial buildings, conservation and development (dams, levees, jetties, and dredging), lodging, religious facilities, and communication structures.

Public safety includes correctional facilities, police and sheriffs' stations, fire stations, and similar establishments.

Highway and street includes pavement, lighting, retaining walls, bridges, tunnels, toll facilities, and maintenance and rest facilities.

Sewage and waste disposal includes sewage systems, solid waste disposal, and recycling.

Water supply includes water supply, transmission, and storage facilities.

Among the data sources for construction expenditures are the Census Bureau's Survey of Construction, Building Permits Survey, Consumer Expenditure Survey (conducted for the Bureau of Labor Statistics), Annual Capital Expenditures Survey, and Construction Progress Reporting Survey; also included are data from the F.W. Dodge Division of the McGraw-Hill Information Systems Company, the U.S. Department of Agriculture, and utility regulatory agencies.

Data availability

Each month's "Construction Spending" press release is released on the last workday of the following month. The release, more detailed data, and a discussion of methodologies can be found on the Census Bureau's Web site at <http://www.census.gov/constructionspending>. Current data at this site may reflect benchmarking since Table 16-1 was compiled.

Table 16-2 Housing Starts and Building Permits; New House Sales and Prices

SOURCES: U.S. DEPARTMENT OF COMMERCE, CENSUS BUREAU

These data are mainly found in two major Census Bureau reports, "New Residential Construction" and "New Residential Sales." They cover new housing units intended for occupancy and maintained by the occupants, excluding hotels, motels, and group residential structures. Manufactured home units are reported in a separate survey.

Definitions

A *housing unit* is a house, an apartment, or a group of rooms or single room intended for occupancy as separate living quarters. Occupants must live separately from other individuals in the building and have direct access to the housing unit from the outside of the building or through a common hall. Each apartment unit in an apartment building is counted as one housing unit. As of January 2000, a previous requirement for residents to have the capability to eat separately has been eliminated. (Based on the old definition, some senior housing projects were excluded from the multifamily housing statistics because individual units did not have their own eating facilities.) Housing starts exclude group quarters such as dormitories or rooming houses, transient accommodations such as motels, and manufactured homes. Publicly owned housing units are excluded, but units in structures built by private developers with subsidies or for sale to local public housing authorities are both classified as private housing.

The *start* of construction of a privately owned housing unit is when excavation begins for the footings or foundation of a building primarily intended as a housekeeping residential structure and designed for nontransient occupancy. All housing units in a multifamily building are defined as being started when excavation for the building begins.

One-family structures includes fully detached, semi-detached, row houses, and townhouses. In the case of attached units, each must be separated from the adjacent unit by a ground-to-roof wall to be classified as a one-unit structure and must not share facilities such as heating or water supply. Units built one on top of another and those built side-by-side without a ground-to-roof wall and/or with common facilities are classified by the number of units in the structure.

Apartment buildings are defined as buildings containing *five units or more*. The type of ownership is not the criterion—a condominium apartment building is not classified as one-family structures but as a multifamily structure.

A *manufactured* home is a moveable dwelling, 8 feet or more wide and 40 feet or more long, designed to be towed on its own chassis with transportation gear integral to the unit when it leaves the factory, and without need of a permanent foundation. Multiwides and expandable manufactured homes are included. Excluded are travel trailers, motor homes, and modular housing. The shipments figures are based on reports submitted by manufacturers on the number of homes actually shipped during the survey month. Shipments to dealers may not necessarily be placed for residential use in the same month as they are shipped. The number of manufactured "homes" used for nonresidential purposes (for example, those used for offices) is not known.

Units authorized by building permits represents the approximately 97 percent of housing in permit-requiring areas.

The *start* occurs when excavation begins for the footing or foundation. Starts are estimated for all areas, regardless of whether permits are required.

New house *sales* are reported only for new single-family residential structures. The sales transaction must intend to include both house and land. Excluded are houses built for rent, houses built by the owner, and houses built by a contractor on the owner's land. A sale is reported when a deposit is taken or a sales agreement is signed; this can occur prior to a permit being issued.

Once the sale is reported, the sold housing unit drops out of the survey. Consequently the Census Bureau does not find out if the sales contract is cancelled or if the house is ever resold. As a result, if conditions are worsening and cancellations are high, sales are temporarily overestimated. When conditions improve and the cancelled sales materialize as actual sales, the Census sales estimates are then underestimated because the case did not re-enter the survey. In the long run, cancellations do not cause the survey to overestimate or underestimate sales; but in the short run, cancellations and ultimate resales are not reflected in this survey, and fluctuations can appear less severe than in reality.

A house is *for sale* when a permit to build has been issued (or work begun in non-permit areas) and a sales contract has not been signed nor a deposit accepted.

The *sales price* used in this survey is the price agreed upon between the purchaser and the seller at the time the first sales contract is signed or deposit made. It includes the price of the improved lot. The *median sales price* is the sales price of the house that falls on the middle point of a distribution by price of the total number of houses sold. Half of the houses sold have a price lower than the median; half have a price higher than the median. Changes in the *sales price* data reflect changes in the

distribution of houses by region, size, and the like, as well as changes in the prices of houses with identical characteristics.

The *price index* measures the change in price of a new single-family house of constant physical characteristics, using the characteristics of houses built in 2005. Characteristics held constant include floor area, whether inside or outside a metropolitan area, number of bedrooms, number of bathrooms, number of fireplaces, type of parking facility, type of foundation, presence of a deck, construction method, exterior wall material, type of heating, and presence of air-conditioning. The indexes are calculated separately for attached and detached houses and combined with base period weights. The price measured includes the value of the lot.

See the notes and definitions to Table 12-11 for a discussion of the characteristics of other price indexes for single-family houses.

Notes on the data

Monthly permit authorizations are based on data collected by a mail survey from a sample of about 9,000 permit-issuing places, selected from and representing a universe of 20,000 such places in the United States. The remaining places are surveyed annually. Data for 1994 through 2003 represented 19,000 places; data for 1984 through 1993 represented 17,000 places; data for 1978 through 1983 represented 16,000 places; data for 1972 through 1977 represented 14,000 places; data for 1967 through 1971 represented 13,000 places; data for 1963 through 1966 represented 12,000 places; and data for 1959 through 1962 represented 10,000 places.

Housing starts and sales data are obtained from the Survey of Construction, for which Census Bureau field representatives sample both permit-issuing and non-permit-issuing places.

Effective with the January 2005 data release, the Survey of Construction implemented a new sample of building permit offices, replacing a previous sample selected in 1985. As a result, writes the Census Bureau, "Data users should uses caution when analyzing year over year changes in housing prices and characteristics between 2004 and 2005." In the newer sample, land may be more abundant, lot sizes larger, and sales prices lower.

For 2004, the permit data were compiled for both the new 20,000 place universe and the old 19,000 place universe. Ratios of the new estimates to the old were calculated by state for total housing units, structures by number of units, and valuation. For the United States as a whole, the new estimate was 100.9 percent of the old estimate.

Effective with the data for April 2001, the Census Bureau made changes to the methodology used for new house sales, including discontinuing an adjustment for construction in areas in which building permits are required without a permit being issued. It was believed that such unauthorized construction has virtually ceased. The upward adjustment was not phased out but dropped completely in revised estimates as of January 1999. The total effect of these changes was to lower the number of sales by about 2.9 percent relative to those published for earlier years.

The data used in the price index are collected in the Survey of Construction, through monthly interviews with the builders or owners. The size of the sample is currently about 20,000 observations per year.

Data availability and references

Housing starts and building permit data have been collected monthly by the Bureau of the Census since 1959.

The monthly report for "New Residential Construction" (permits, starts, and completions) is issued in the middle of the following month. The monthly report and associated descriptions and historical data can be found at <http://www.census.gov/construction/nrc>.

The monthly report for "New Residential Sales" (sales, houses for sale, and prices) is issued toward the end of the following month. The monthly report and associated descriptions and historical data can be found at <http://www.census.gov/construction/nrs>.

The manufactured housing data (not seasonally adjusted) and background information can be found at <http://www.manufacturedhousing.org/statistics>. Data with and without seasonal adjustment can be found at <http://www.census.gov/construction/mhs>.

Data and background on the price index for new one-family houses can be found at <http://www.census/gov>, in the alphabetical index under the category "Construction price indexes."

Tables 16-3 through 16-6
Manufacturers' Shipments, Inventories, and Orders

SOURCE: U.S. DEPARTMENT OF COMMERCE, CENSUS BUREAU

These data are from the Census Bureau's monthly M3 survey, a sample-based survey that provides measures of changes in the value of domestic manufacturing activity and indications of future production commitments. The sample is not a probability sample. It includes approximately 4,300 reporting units, including companies with $500 million or more in annual shipments and a selection of smaller companies. Currently, reported monthly data represent approximately 60 percent of shipments at the total manufacturing level.

One important technology industry, semiconductors, is represented in the shipments and inventories data in this report but not in new or unfilled orders. This affects the new and unfilled orders totals for computers and electronic products, durable goods industries, and total manufacturing. Based on shipments data, semiconductors accounted for about 15 percent of computers and electronic products, 3 percent of durable goods industries, and 1.5 percent of total manufacturing. Since semiconductors are intermediate materials and components rather than finished final products, the absence of these data does not distort new and unfilled orders data for important final demand categories, such as capital goods and information technology.

Definitions and notes on the data

Shipments. The value of shipments data represent net selling values, f.o.b. (free on board) plant, after discounts and allowances and excluding freight charges and excise taxes. For multi-establishment companies, the M3 reports are typically company- or division-level reports that encompass groups of plants or products. The data reported are usually net sales and receipts from customers and do not include the value of inter-plant transfers. The reported sales are used to calculate month-to-month changes that bring forward the estimates for the entire industry (that is, estimates of the statistical "universe") that have been developed from the Annual Survey of Manufactures (ASM). The value of products made elsewhere under contract from materials owned by the plant is also included in shipments, along with receipts for contract work performed for others, resales, miscellaneous activities such as the sale of scrap and refuse, and installation and repair work performed by employees of the plant.

Inventories. Inventories in the M3 survey are collected on a current cost or pre-LIFO (last in, first out) basis. As different inventory valuation methods are reflected in the reported data, the estimates differ slightly from replacement cost estimates. Companies using the LIFO method for valuing inventories report their pre-LIFO value; the adjustment to their base-period prices is excluded. In the ASM, inventories are collected according to this same definition.

Inventory data are requested from respondents by three stages of fabrication: finished goods, work in process, and raw materials and supplies. Response to the stage of fabrication inquiries is lower than for total inventories; not all companies keep their monthly data at this level of detail. It should be noted that a product considered to be a finished good in one industry, such as steel mill shapes, may be reported as a raw material in another industry, such as stamping plants. For some purposes, this difference in definitions is an advantage. When a factory accumulates inventory that it considers to be raw materials, it can be expected that that accumulation is intentional. But when a factory—whether a materials-making or a final-product producer—has a buildup of finished goods inventories, it may indicate involuntary accumulation as a result of sales falling short of expectations. Hence, the two types of accumulation can have different economic interpretations, even if they represent identical types of goods.

Like total inventories, stage of fabrication inventories are benchmarked to the ASM data. Stage of fabrication data are benchmarked at the major group level, as opposed to the level of total inventories, which is benchmarked at the individual industry level.

New orders (durable goods), as reported in the monthly survey, are net of order cancellations and include orders received and filled during the month as well as orders received for future delivery. They also include the value of contract changes that increase or decrease the value of the unfilled orders to which they relate. Orders are defined to include those supported by binding legal documents such as signed contracts, letters of award, or letters of intent, although this definition may not be strictly applicable in some industries.

New orders (nondurable goods) are equal to shipments, as order backlogs are not reported for these industries.

Unfilled orders (durable goods) includes new orders (as defined above) that have not been reflected as shipments. Generally, unfilled orders at the end of the reporting period are equal to unfilled orders at the beginning of the period plus net new orders received less net shipments.

Series are adjusted for seasonal variation and variation in the number of trading days in the month using the X-12-ARIMA version of the Census Bureau's seasonal adjustment program.

Benchmarking and revisions

The data shown in the volume have been benchmarked to the 2007 Economic Census and to ASMs through 2011. In each benchmark revision, new and unfilled orders are adjusted to be consistent with the benchmarked shipments and inventory data, seasonal adjustment factors are revised and updated, and other corrections are made.

Data availability and references

Data have been collected monthly since 1958.

The "Advance Report on Durable Goods Manufacturers' Shipments, Inventories and Orders" is available as a press release about 18 working days after the end of each month. It includes seasonally adjusted and not seasonally adjusted estimates of shipments, new orders, unfilled orders, and inventories for durable goods industries.

The monthly "Manufacturers' Shipments, Inventories, and Orders" report is released on the 23rd working day after the end of the month. Content includes revisions to the advance durable goods data, estimates for nondurable goods industries, tabulations by market category, and ratios of shipments to inventories and to unfilled orders. Revisions may affect selected data for the two previous months.

Press releases, historical data, descriptions of the survey, and documentation are available on the Census Bureau Web site at <http://www.census.gov>, under the category "Manufacturing" in the alphabetic listing there.

Table 16-7

Motor Vehicle Sales and Inventories

SOURCE: U.S. DEPARTMENT OF COMMERCE, BUREAU OF ECONOMIC ANALYSIS

Retail sales and *inventories of cars, trucks, and buses*. These estimates are prepared by the Bureau of Economic Analysis (BEA), based on data from the American Automobile Manufacturers Association, Ward's Automotive Reports, and other sources. Seasonal adjustments are recalculated annually. Data are available on the BEA Web site at <http://www.bea.gov> as a part of the national income and product accounts data set; they are found under the "Supplemental Estimates" heading. They are also available on the STAT-USA subscription Web site at <http://www.stat-usa.gov>.

Tables 16-8 and 16-10

Retail and Food Services Sales; Retail Inventories

SOURCE: U.S. DEPARTMENT OF COMMERCE, CENSUS BUREAU

Every month, the Census Bureau prepares estimates of retail sales and inventories by kind of business, based on a mail-out/mail-back survey of about 12,000 retail businesses with paid employees.

Retail sales and inventories are now compiled using the new NAICS classification system, which replaced the old SIC system. Historical data have been restated on the NAICS basis back to January 1992. In NAICS, Eating and drinking places and Mobile food services have been reclassified out of retail trade and into sector 72, Accommodation and food services, which also includes Hotels. The retail sales survey still collects and publishes sales data for Food services and drinking places. It no longer includes them in the Retail total, but they are included in a new Retail and food services total.

Subtotals of durable and nondurable goods are no longer published. They were always imprecise for retail sales, since general merchandise stores (including department stores) were included in nondurable goods, yet obviously sold substantial quantities of durable goods.

Definitions

Sales is the value of merchandise sold for cash or credit at retail or wholesale. Services that are incidental to the sale of merchandise, and excise taxes that are paid by the manufacturer or wholesaler and passed along to the retailer, are also included. Sales are net, after deductions for refunds and merchandise returns. They exclude sales taxes collected directly from customers and paid directly to a local, state, or federal tax agency. The sales estimates include only sales by establishments primarily engaged in retail trade, and are not intended to measure the total sales for a given commodity or merchandise line.

Inventories is the value of stocks of goods held for sale through retail stores, valued at cost, as of the last day of the report period. Stocks may be held either at the store or at warehouses that maintain supplies primarily intended for distribution to retail stores within the organization.

Leased departments consists of the operations of one company conducted within the establishment of another company, such as jewelry counters or optical centers within department stores. The values for sales and inventories at department stores in Tables 16-9 and 16-10 exclude sales of leased departments.

GAFO (department store type goods) is a special aggregate grouping of sales at general merchandise stores and at other stores that sell merchandise normally sold in department stores—clothing and accessories, furniture and home furnishings, electronics, appliances, sporting goods, hobby, book, music, office supplies, stationery, and gifts.

Notes on the data

The data published here have been benchmarked to the 2007, 2002, 1997, and 1992 Economic Censuses and the Annual Retail Trade Surveys for 2012 and previous years. Each year, the monthly series are benchmarked to the latest annual survey and new factors are incorporated to adjust for seasonal, trading-day, and holiday variations, using the Census Bureau's X-12-ARIMA program.

The survey sample is stratified by kind of business and estimated sales. All firms with sales above applicable size cutoffs are included. Firms are selected randomly from the remaining strata. The sample used for the end-of-month inventory estimates is a sub-sample of the monthly sales sample, about one-third of the size of the whole sample.

New samples, designed to produce NAICS estimates, were introduced with the 1999 Annual Retail Trade Survey and the March 2001 Monthly Retail Trade Survey. On November 30, 2006, another new sample was introduced, affecting the data for September 2006 and the following months. The sample is updated quarterly to take account of business births and deaths.

Data availability and references

An "Advance Monthly Retail Sales" report is released about nine working days after the close of the reference month, based on responses from a sub-sample of the complete retail sample.

The revised and more complete monthly "Retail Trade, Sales, and Inventories" reports are released six weeks after the close of the reference month. They contain preliminary figures for the current month and final figures for the prior 12 months. Statistics include retail sales, inventories, and ratios of inventories to sales. Data are both seasonally adjusted and unadjusted.

The "Annual Benchmark Report for Retail Trade" is released each spring. It includes updated seasonal adjustment factors; revised and benchmarked monthly estimates of sales and inventories; monthly data for the most recent 10 or more years; detailed annual estimates and ratios for the United States by kind of business; and comparable prior-year statistics and year-to-year changes.

All data are available on the Census Bureau Web site at <http://www.census.gov/retail>.

Table 16-9

Quarterly Retail Sales:
Total and E-Commerce

SOURCE: U.S. DEPARTMENT OF COMMERCE, CENSUS BUREAU

Beginning with the fourth quarter of 1999, the Census Bureau has conducted a quarterly survey of retail e-commerce sales from the Monthly Retail Trade Survey sample. (The monthly survey does not report electronic shopping separately; it is combined with mail order.) E-commerce sales are the sales of goods and services in which an order is placed by the buyer or the price and terms of sale are negotiated over the Internet or an extranet, Electronic Data Interchange (EDI) network, electronic mail, or other online system. Payment may or may not be made online. The quarterly release is issued around the 20th of February, May, August, and November, and is available along with full historical data on the Census Bureau Web site at <http://www.census.gov>. It can be located under the heading "Retail" in the alphabetical Web site index, under "E" for "Economic data and information."

These estimates reflect the NAICS definition of retail sales, which excludes food service. Online travel services, financial brokers and dealers, and ticket sales agencies are not classified as retail and are not included in these estimates; they are, however, included in the annual survey of selected services.

Table 16-11

Merchant Wholesalers—Sales and Inventories

SOURCE: U.S. DEPARTMENT OF COMMERCE, CENSUS BUREAU

These data are based on a monthly mail-out/mail-back sample survey conducted by the Census Bureau. The sample consists of about 4,900 establishments, with a response rate of about 60 percent; missing reports are imputed based on reports of similar reporters.

These data are now based on the new NAICS classification system, which replaced the old SIC system. Historical data have been restated on the NAICS basis back to January 1992.

Classification changes in NAICS

NAICS shifts a significant number of businesses from the Wholesale to the Retail sector. An important new criterion for classification concerns whether or not the establishment is intended to solicit walk-in traffic. If it is, and if it uses mass-media advertising, it is now classified as Retail, even if it also serves business and institutional clients.

Definitions

Merchant wholesalers includes merchant wholesalers that take title of the goods they sell, as well as jobbers, industrial distributors, exporters, and importers. The survey does not cover marketing sales offices and branches of manufacturing, refining, and mining firms, nor does it include NAICS 4251: Wholesale Electronic Markets and Agents and Brokers.

Notes on the data

Inventories are valued using methods other than LIFO (last in, first out) in order to better reflect the current costs of goods held as inventory.

A survey has been conducted monthly since 1946. New samples are drawn every 5 years, most recently in 2009. The samples are updated every quarter to add new businesses and to drop companies that are no longer active.

Data availability and references

"Monthly Wholesale Trade, Sales and Inventories" reports are released six weeks after the close of the reference month. They contain preliminary current-month figures and final figures for the previous month. Statistics include sales, inventories, and stock/sale ratios, along with standard errors. Data are both seasonally adjusted and unadjusted.

The "Annual Benchmark Report for Wholesale Trade" is released each spring. It contains estimated annual sales, monthly and year-end inventories, inventory/sales ratios, purchases, gross margins, and gross margin/sales ratios by kind of business. Annual estimates are benchmarked to annual surveys and the most recent census of wholesale trade. Monthly sales and inventories estimates are revised consistent with the annual data, seasonal adjustment factors are updated, and revised data for both seasonally adjusted and unadjusted values are published.

Data and documentation are available on the Census Bureau Web site at <http://www.census.gov>, under "Economic Indicators" and in the alphabetic index under "E" for economic data.

Tables 16-12 and 16-13

Manufacturing and Trade Sales and Inventories

SOURCES: U.S. DEPARTMENT OF COMMERCE, CENSUS BUREAU (CURRENT-DOLLAR SERIES) AND U.S. DEPARTMENT OF COMMERCE, BUREAU OF ECONOMIC ANALYSIS (BEA; CONSTANT-DOLLAR SERIES)

The current-dollar data on which these tables are based bring together summary data from the separate series on manufacturers' shipments, inventories, and orders; merchant wholesalers' sales and inventories; and retail sales and inventories, all of which are included in this chapter. Generally, current-dollar inventories are collected on a current cost (or pre-LIFO [last in, first out]) basis. See the notes and definitions for Tables 16-3, 16-4, 16-8 16-10, and 16-11 for further information about these data.

Based on these current-dollar values and relevant price data, BEA makes estimates of real sales, inventories, and inventory-sales ratios. Note, however, that annual figures for sales are shown as annual <u>totals</u> in Table 16-12 but as <u>averages</u> of the monthly data in Table 16-13, reflecting the practices of the respective source agencies. Also note that constant-dollar detail may not add to constant-dollar totals because of the chain-weighting formula; see the discussion of chain-weighted measures in the notes and definitions for Chapter 1. The constant-dollar estimates shown in this volume of *Business Statistics* are stated in 2009 dollars.

Inventory values are as of the end of the month or year. In Table 16-13, annual values for monthly current-dollar inventory-sales ratios are averages of seasonally adjusted monthly ratios. However, for the real ratios in Table 16-14, annual figures for inventory-sales ratios are calculated by BEA as year-end (December) inventories divided by the monthly average of sales for the entire year; this means that the annual ratios will not be equivalent to averages of month ratios. In all cases, the ratios in these two tables (like those in Table 1-8) represent the number of months' sales on hand as inventory at the end of the reporting period.

Data availability

Sales, inventories, and inventory-sales ratios for manufacturers, merchant wholesalers, and retailers are published monthly by the Census Bureau in a press release entitled "Manufacturing and Trade Inventories and Sales." Recent and historical data are available on the Census Bureau Web site at <http://www.census.gov/mtis/www/mtis.html>. They can also be found by going to the general Census website, <http://www.census.gov>, going to the alphabetical index, finding "Economic Data and Information" under "E" and then finding "Manufacturing and trade" under "Manufacturing" or "Sales."

Sales and inventories in constant dollars are available on the BEA Web site at <http://www.bea.gov>. To locate these data on that site, click on "National Economic Accounts." Scroll down to "Supplemental Estimates," click "Underlying Detail Tables," and then click on "List of Underlying Detail Tables." For the most recent data, if there is more than one table with the same title, select the last table listed.

Table 16-14

Selected Services, Quarterly: Estimated Revenue for Employer Firms

SOURCE: U.S. DEPARTMENT OF COMMERCE, CENSUS BUREAU

Census data on quarterly revenue for selected service industries are based on information collected from a probability sample that has been expanded over recent years to approximately 19,000 employer firms (firms with employees), chosen from the sample for the larger Service Annual Survey and expanded to represent totals—for employer firms only—for the selected industries. The sample is updated quarterly to account for business births, deaths, and other changes. Industries are defined according to the 2007 NAICS.

The scope of the survey and the size of the sample have increased several times since the inception of this survey in 2004. More industries are now available than are shown here in Table 16-15, which focuses on industries with a longer statistical history.

Definitions and notes on the data

These data are collected in current dollars only. See the Producer Price Indexes in Chapter 8 for indicators of price trends in various sectors.

Both taxable and tax-exempt firms are covered unless otherwise specified.

Generally, government enterprises are not within the scope (that is, the industries it is designed to cover) of the survey. *Utilities* excludes government-owned utilities and *Transportation and warehousing* excludes the U.S. Postal Service.

Private industries that are not within the scope of the survey are NAICS 482, rail transportation; 525, funds, trusts, and other financial vehicles; 51112, offices of notaries; 6111, 6112, and 6113, elementary, secondary, and post-secondary schools; 8131, religious organizations; 81393 (labor unions and similar), 81394 (political organizations, and 814 (private households).

Totals shown for sectors and subsectors may include data for kinds of business that are in the scope of the survey but are not shown separately in the detail beneath.

Data for selected industry groups are adjusted for seasonal variation using the Census Bureau's X-13 ARIMA-SEATS program.

Data availability and references

The quarterly release "U.S. Government Estimates of Quarterly Revenue for Selected Services" is available on the Census Web site at <http://www.census.gov/>, as "Quarterly Services Survey" listed under Q in the alphabetic index; historical, technical, and background information, including sampling errors, is also available there.

The revised and updated data through the fourth quarter of 2013 shown in this volume, benchmarked to Service Annual Surveys through 2012, were released on March 12, 2014.

INDEX